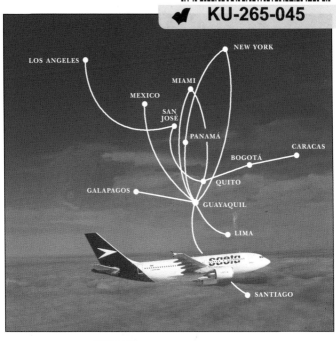

FLY SAETA...

THE AIRLINE OF ECUADOR, TO IMPORTANT DESTINATIONS IN NORTH AND SOUTH AMERICA.

Fly with SAETA to important cities in North and South America such as New York, Los Angeles, Miami, Panamá, Caracas, Bogotá, Lima, Santiago and San José, enjoying the Premier Service that only SAETA offers you.

SAETA also takes you to the most beautiful cities in Ecuador: Guayaquil, Quito and Cuenca; as well as Galapagos, "The Enchanted Islands".

GUAYAQUIL: (5934) 200277 - 205115 • QUITO: (5932) 254510 - 564969
• USA/CANADA TOLL FREE 1-800-82 SAETA.

If you're looking for the best Latin American coverage read this.

If you want to make sure you take in the spectacular contrasts of Latin America, you want to make sure you fly out with Iberia or Viasa.

Together, Iberia (the international airline of Spain) and Viasa (the international airline of Venezuela) link Europe to a range of destinations that's not only proved impossible to beat – it's never been matched.

The Iberia Group brings you closer to the sun-drenched beaches of the Caribbean, the glacial beauty of Tierra del Fuego and the distinctive colonial architecture of cities like Lima, by serving an incredible 26 locations.

In fact, Iberia has continued to expand and strengthen its links since establishing the first air connection between Europe and Latin America over 50 years ago.

ARUBA
ASUNCION
BOGOTA
BUENOS AIRES
CANCUN
CARACAS
CARTAGENA
GUATEMALA
HAVANA
LIMA
MANAGUA
MEXICO
MIAMI
MONTEVIDEO
PANAMA
PORLAMAR
PUNTA CANA
QUITO
RIO DE JANEIRO
SAN JOSE
SAN JUAN
SAN PEDRO SULA
SANTO DOMINGO
SAN SALVADOR
SANTIAGO DE CHILE
SÃO PAULO

In addition Viasa now offers the greatest choice of flights from Caracas to the whole of Latin America. So with Iberia and Viasa all your needs are covered.

What's more, by flying with Iberia or Viasa, you are guaranteed comfort and style. Whether you choose the exceptional value of the established 'Latin American Saver' fares in Economy Class or decide to treat yourself to the

luxury of First or Business Class, the Iberia Group gives you the best choice and the best value fares.

So if you're looking for the best Latin American coverage, you don't have to read between the lines, simply contact your local travel agent and ask about the Iberia Group, or call Iberia today on

0171-830 0011

1996

SOUTH AMERICAN HANDBOOK

SEVENTY SECOND EDITION

Editor *Ben Box*
Cartographer *Sebastian Ballard*

For my part, I travel not to go anywhere, but to go;
I travel for travel's sake … But the great affair is to
move; to feel the needs and hitches of life a little
more nearly; to get down off the feather bed of
civilisation, and to find the globe granite underfoot
and strewn with cutting flints.
Robert Louis Stevenson

2

TRADE & TRAVEL *Handbooks*

Trade & Travel Publications Ltd
6 Riverside Court, Lower Bristol Road, Bath BA2 3DZ, England
Telephone 01225 469141   Fax 01225 469461
Email 100660.1250@compuserve.com

©Trade & Travel Publications Ltd., September 1995

ISBN 0 900751 60 6   ISSN 0309-4529

CIP DATA: A catalogue record for this book is available from the British Library

In North America, published and distributed by

PASSPORT BOOKS
a division of *NTC Publishing Group*

4255 West Touhy Avenue, Lincolnwood (Chicago), Illinois 60646-1975, USA
Telephone 708-679-5500   Fax 708-679-2494   Email NTCPUB2@AOL.COM

ISBN 0-8442-8881-0

Library of Congress Catalog Card Number 95-69407

Passport Books and colophon are registered trademarks of NTC Publishing Group

IMPORTANT: While every endeavour is made to ensure that the facts printed in this book are correct at the time of going to press, travellers are cautioned to obtain authoritative advice from consulates, airlines, etc, concerning current travel and visa requirements and conditions before embarking. The publishers cannot accept legal responsibility for errors, however caused, that are printed in this book.

MAPS – Publisher's note: a number of frontiers in the area covered by this Handbook are disputed and the subject of territorial claims by various countries in the region. Neither the coloured nor the black and white maps in this book are intended to have any political significance or purport to show authenticated international boundaries.

Cover illustration by Suzanne Evans

Printed and bound in Great Britain by Clays Ltd., Bungay, Suffolk

CONTENTS

4

PREFACE

In *The Creature in the Map*, his book on Sir Walter Ralegh and other seekers of gold in what is now Venezuela, Charles Nicholl writes, "Where was El Dorado?

"The first and sensible answer is, nowhere...There have been remarkable discoveries in Latin America this century...There are probably others waiting to be found, but El Dorado will not be among them...In another sense, of course, El Dorado certainly did exist...as an idea in people's minds, as a destination for their journeys...". Ralegh's chart marked El Dorado as a city on the shores of a Lake Manoa. Even though modern day maps show no such lake or city, the place names and historical allusions provoke a sense of mystery. Anyone travelling in Latin America today will know of Kevin Healey's incomparable maps. It was therefore with great sadness at the news of his death that work began on this edition. Although so very different in approach from 16th-century charts, Kevin's dedication to accuracy provides his greatest legacy in that his maps also have the power to inspire adventure.

A failure to map areas where riches are thought to lie led partly to the recurrence of war between Ecuador and Peru over their disputed border in the Cordillera del Cóndor. The historical reasons behind the dispute are well-documented; the motives for the latest outbreak of fighting are less clear-cut than the international desire for its conclusion and the economic aftermath (especially in Ecuador). The effect on tourism was shortlived. The number of visitors to Ecuador remains high and in Peru tourism continues to rally after the doldrums of recent years.

The editor visited Ecuador and the Galápagos Islands in September/October 1994 (thanks are given at the end of the Ecuador chapter). He formed his own ideas about places visited for the first time, or revisited, but these impressions may well differ from those of our correspondents and of the tourists who so generously write to us. A consequence of Ecuador being so popular is that many travellers generate many opinions. More than ever over the past year it has been remarkable how many opposing views of the same places have been received. It is worth bearing in mind that besides "one man's meat" being "another man's poison", the quality of service may change between high and low season.

Readers familiar with the *Handbook* will notice that the **Information for Visitors** sections are now in two columns. This is the start of a process to make the book conform to the style of the other *Handbooks* in the Trade and Travel series. Hotel price categories have been narrowed at the upper end of the range to account for price rises in some countries and for the opening of more luxury hotels. The lower price categories remain unchanged. Some readers suggest that we omit the higher-priced establishments because "no one uses that part of the hotel list". This is not the case, even though the most visible part of the readership is probably that which stays in the cheaper places. The *Handbook's* comprehensiveness aims now, as it has done for many years, to "cater particularly for the requirements of the budget traveller, while at the same time paying due regard to the interests of the better-off" (1978 Preface).

Special thanks for their work on this edition go to our regular subeditors Cherry Austin, Sarah Cameron, John Hale, Charlie Nurse, Peter Pollard and the new members of the team, Alan Murphy (widely-travelled in South America, who subedited Argentina and helped with the final stages of editing) and Amanda Purves (who has lived in Venezuela and updated that chapter). Peter Pollard travelled to Colombia in 1995. Richard Robinson did a lot of research for the Venezuela chapter in late 1994. We are most grateful to our correspondents in the region, who are thanked at the end of the relevant chapters, and also to John Lewis for his annual reports from the business centres of the region. Finally we should like to thank Jo Morgan, Ann Griffiths and Claudia Golding for their tireless work in transferring all the material to disk.

The Editor

THE EDITOR

Ben Box

A doctorate in medieval Spanish and Portugese studies provided very few job prospects for Ben Box, but a fascination for all things Latin. While studying for his degree, Ben travelled extensively in Spain and Portugal. He turned his attention to contemporary Iberian and Latin American affairs in 1980, beginning a career as a freelance writer at that time. He contributed regularly to national newspapers and learned tomes, and after increasing involvement with the *South American Handbook*, became its editor in 1989. Although he has travelled from the US/Mexico border to southern Chile (not all in one go) and in the Caribbean, Ben recognises that there are always more places to explore. He also edits the *Mexico and Central American Handbook* and jointly edits the *Caribbean Islands Handbook* with Sarah Cameron. To seek diversion from a household immersed in Latin America, he plays village cricket in summer and cycles the lanes of Suffolk.

HOW TO USE THIS HANDBOOK

The South American Handbook is the most complete and up-to-date package of information for independent travellers on the sub-continent of South America (from the Darién Gap to Tierra del Fuego) currently in print. Its text is updated every year for the new edition which is published on 1 September. The text is based on the Editors' travels, contributions from national tourist authorities, notes from correspondents living in the countries we cover, detailed material and maps which Handbook users send us, and the extensive sources of information on Latin America available in London and elsewhere.

Editorial Logic Users of the Handbook will find that we employ a logical system of arrangement, which we believe is the most useful for travellers. The capital city is (with one exception, dictated by geography—Chile) the first place covered in detail. The territory is then divided into subsections which are numbered on the country contents and map as well as in the text. In the subsections, towns appear in sequence along a route, which falls within the natural geography of the region. The routes cover the most interesting places to visit and do not necessarily constitute the shortest possible distance from A to B. Details are also given of any interesting excursions or other sights that are off the route. Travellers can therefore plan their own itineraries according to the time available, and their own special interests.

Cross Referencing and Indexing There is a complete index at the end of the book. Personalities as well as place names and sites of interest are now included. The key used is as follows: Archaeological site ▲; Beach or Marine Resort ♠; Colonial City ✤; Festival, religious or otherwise ☆; Historical site ✲; Inland Resort ☀; Market, or traditional shopping ✿; National Park, Natural Feature, recommended Zoological or Botanical Garden ◆; People ❑.

To make it easier for Readers to find their way around the text, we have a comprehensive system of cross-references. For ease of use, the "see page" entry has been highlighted in heavier type. On the page referred to, you will find the entry again emphasised in some form of heavier type.

Maps The South American Handbook maps within the text are undergoing a programme of updating, improvement and expansion. Three types are used:

A Country Maps These appear at the start of each country chapter and show main access routes (not necessarily major roads in all cases), main towns, and divisions of the country as described in the text. These divisions are numbered on the map, in the country's contents list and at the text divisions in the chapter. The numbers are not recommendations as to which parts of the country are most interesting to visit, they are only for easy identification.

B Regional Maps The subsections of the country listed in the country contents has, where appropriate, its own regional map. These give extra information on a more detailed scale and show the main physical features, towns, means of communication and points of interest.

C City and Town Maps Generally these are detailed maps of town centres, showing means of access to bus and railway stations and airports. The main points of interest are indicated by means of a numbered key.

MAP SYMBOLS

International Border	`— · —`	Capital Cities	□
State / Province Border	`— — —`	Cities / Towns	o
Main Roads (National Highways)	`15`	Bus Stations	**B**
Other Roads	`——`	Hospitals	**H**
Jeepable Roads, Tracks, Trails, Paths, Ferries	`- - - -`	Post Office	**PO**
Railways, Station	`—■—`	Tourist Office	**ⓘ**
Contours (approx)	`〰`	Key Numbers	**27**
Mountains	Ⱶ	Airport	✕
Rivers	*Río Torola*	Church	✝
Waterfall	F	Camp site	⛺
Bridges	⤨	Refuge	⌂
Built Up Areas	▬	Lodge with facilities	⌂
Lakes, Dams, Reservoirs	◣	Wild Life Parks, Biological Reserves, Bird Sanctuaries	◆
Sand Banks, Beaches	▨	Archaeological Sites	▲
National Parks, Gardens, Stadiums	▨	Text Subdivisions	◆◆◆◆◆
Fortified Walls	▲ ▲ ▲		SAH 0

Introduction and Hints This first section in the book gives information and hints that apply generally to all the countries we cover on:

- ❏ travel to and in Latin America
- ❏ money
- ❏ law enforcement
- ❏ security
- ❏ responsible tourism
- ❏ travelling with children
- ❏ camping
- ❏ language
- ❏ photography
- ❏ surface transport
- ❏ hitchhiking
- ❏ motoring and motorcycling
- ❏ hiking and trekking
- ❏ river boats
- ❏ cycling

Health Information This major section by Dr David Snashall of St Thomas's Hospital Medical School, London, gives details of the health risks common in South America, and the sensible precautions travellers should take to combat them.

Country Sections Information is set out country by country in a constant sequence as follows:

- ❏ List of contents
- ❏ Description of physical geography

  history   people
  economy   present form of government
  music and dance

- ❏ Survey of Cities, Towns and places of interest

  things to do   things worth seeing
  where to stay   eating out
  services for visitors

❏ Information for visitors

documentation	how to get there
food	health precautions
the best time for visiting	clothing
currency regulations	other essential information

All those readers who have written with valuable updating material are listed with thanks at the end of each chapter.

Note The aim of the **Music and Dance** sections (specially written for us by Nigel Gallop) has been to give an overview of the traditional and popular music and dances of each country. Considerations of space and the desire to avoid a tedious inventory has meant that by no means every song style, dance or instrument has been noted. As to the performers mentioned, the choice has also been selective, giving preference to those who have achieved local fame over those who, for commercial or political reasons, have based themselves in Europe or North America and are probably already familiar to the overseas visitor. Readers may also notice that space has not been devoted to the forest indians, who are nevertheless present in most of the countries covered and whose music and dancing tends to exist only in its isolated cosmos, rarely relating to, or connecting with, national or regional musical cultures. Also not discussed, at present, is the classical music of the region.

Hotels and Restaurants In large cities, lists of hotels and restaurants include only those establishments for which positive recommendations have been received. In smaller towns, these lists contain both the favourable recommendations and others. In general, restaurants are grouped by neighbourhood and by type of cuisine.

Prices Our hotel price ranges, for double rooms with taxes and service charges but without meals unless stated, are as follows:

L1	Over US$200	**L2**	US$151-200	**L3**	US$101-150
A1	US$81-100	**A2**	US$61-80	**A3**	US$46-60
B	US$31-45	**C**	US$21-30	**D**	US$12-20
E	US$7-11	**F**	US$4-6	**G**	Up to US$3

Other abbreviations used in the book (apart from pp = per person; a/c = air conditioned; rm = room(s) in a hotel; flr = floor; rec = recommended; T = telephone; TCs = travellers' cheques; s/n = "sin número", no street number) should be self-explanatory.

We are grateful to those travellers, listed below, who have sent us important information for the "Introduction and Hints" section which follows: Mrs Carol Baillie (Grand Cayman, Cayman Islands), Dave Blackburn (Luton, UK) and Emily Smith (North Carolina, USA), Tim Burford (Linton, UK), Mark Davies and Tiffany Story (Amersham, UK and Santa Barbara, USA), Dr J Rudolf Dietrich (Basle, Switzerland), Gerd Dörner (Darmstadt, Germany), Patrick Ganahl (Wolfhausen, Switzerland), Michael Gonin (Canberra, Australia), Marten H Jacobsen and Brit R Lauritsen (Denmark), Sonja Jovanovic and Andrew Thompson (London, UK) a helpful letter, Kay Leissner (Gottingen, Germany), Gilles Lalonde (Quebec, Canada) a detailed account, M Leufgens and M Jollands (Alsdorf, Germany), Richard Leuwin (Antigua, Guatemala), Peter Koenen (Bocholt,Germany) and Scott Mattoon (San Francisco, USA), Marie-Helene Boone and Ulrich Nanz (Stuttgart, Germany), Jonathan Paisner (London, UK), Jerry Peek (Sepastopol, USA), Paul Schneider (Venice, USA), The Schweers (somewhere in Colombia), Ludwig Seitz (Dossenheim, Germany), Ron and Dorothy Thyer (Blackburn, Australia), and Ollo Wiemann (Trier, Germany).

WILL YOU HELP US?

We do all we can to get our facts right in the **SOUTH AMERICAN HANDBOOK**. Each section is thoroughly revised each year, but the territory is vast and our eyes cannot be everywhere. If you have enjoyed a tour, trek, train trip, beach, museum or any other activity and would like to share it, please write with all the details. We are always pleased to hear about any restaurants, bars or hotels you have enjoyed. When writing, please give the year on the cover of your *Handbook* and the page number referred to. In return we will send you details of our special guidebook offer.

Thank you very much indeed for your help.

TRADE & TRAVEL
Handbooks

Write to The Editor, *South American Handbook*, Trade & Travel, 6 Riverside Court, Lower Bristol Road, Bath BA2 3DZ. England
Fax 01225 469461   Email 100660.1250@compuserve.com

INTRODUCTION AND HINTS

AIR TRAVEL TO AND WITHIN LATIN AMERICA

Travel to and in South America All the main airlines plying to each country are given in the "Information for Visitors" sections. Airlines will only allow a certain weight of luggage without a surcharge; this is normally 30 kg for first class and 20 kg for business and economy classes, but these limits are often not strictly enforced when it is known that the plane is not going to be full. If you have special baggage requirements, check with an agency for the anomalies which exist on different weight allowances one way, for example. Passengers seeking a larger baggage allowance can route via USA, but with certain exceptions, the fares are slightly higher using this route. On the other hand, weight limits for internal flights are often lower; best to enquire beforehand.

Paul Davies, of Journey Latin America, has told us:
1 It is no longer generally cheaper to fly from London rather than a point in Europe to Latin American destinations; fares vary from airline to airline, destination to destination and according to time of year. Check with an agency for the best deal for when you wish to travel.

2 Most airlines offer discounted fares of one sort or another on scheduled flights. These are not offered by the airlines direct to the public, but through agencies who specialize in this type of fare*. The very busy seasons are 7 Dec–15 Jan and 10 July–10 Sept. If you intend travelling during those times, book as far ahead as possible.

3 Other fares fall into three groups, and are all on scheduled services:
A Excursion (return) fares with restricted validity eg 5-90 days. Carriers are introducing flexibility into these tickets, permitting a change of dates on payment of a fee.
B Yearly fares: these may be bought on a one-way or return basis. Some airlines require a specified return date, changeable upon payment of a fee. To leave the return completely open is possible for an extra fee. You must, fix the route (some of the cheapest flexible fares now have 6 months validity).

*In London, these include Journey Latin America, 16 Devonshire Road, Chiswick, London W4 2HD (T 0181-747 3108); Trailfinders, 48 Earl's Court Road, London W8 6EJ (T 0171-938 3366); South American Experience, 47 Causton Street, Pimlico, London SW1P 4AT (T 0171-976 5511); Last Frontiers, Swan House, High Street, Long Crendon, Buckinghamshire, HP18 9AF (T 01844 208405); Passage to South America, 41 North End Road, West Kensington, London W14 8SZ (T 0171-602 9889); STA Travel, Priory House, 6 Wrights Lane, London W8 6TA (T 0171-938 4711), Cox & Kings Travel, St James Court, 45 Buckingham Gate, London (T 0171-873 5001). (Ed.)

C Student (or Under 26) fares. (Do not assume that student tickets are the cheapest; though they are often very flexible, they are usually more expensive than A or B above). Some airlines are flexible on the age limit, others strict. One way and returns available, or "Open Jaws" (see below). NB There is less availability in the busy seasons (see above).

4 For people intending to travel a linear route and return from a different point from that which they entered, there are "Open Jaws" fares, which are available on student, yearly, or excursion fares.

5 Many of these fares require a change of plane at an intermediate point, and a stopover may be permitted, or even obligatory, depending on schedules. Simply because a flight stops at a given airport does not mean you can break your journey there—the airline must have traffic rights to pick up or set down passengers between points A and B before it will be permitted. This is where dealing with a specialized agency (like Journey Latin America!) will really pay dividends. There are dozens of agencies that offer the simple returns to Rio or Lima at roughly the same (discounted) fare. On multi-stop itineraries, the specialized agencies can often save clients hundreds of pounds.

6 Although it's a little more complicated, it's possible to sell tickets in London for travel originating in Latin America at substantially cheaper fares than those available locally. This is useful for the traveller who doesn't know where he will end up, or who plans to travel for more than a year. Because of high local taxes (see paragraph 7) a one-way ticket from Latin America is more expensive than a one-way in the other direction, so it's always best to buy a return. Taxes are calculated as a percentage of the full IATA fare; on a discounted fare the tax can therefore make up as much as 30-50% of the price.

7 Certain Latin American countries impose local tax on flights originating there. Among these are Ecuador, Peru, Bolivia, Uruguay, Colombia and Mexico. This often applies if you happen to have bought a ticket, say, London—Rio—Santiago—Lima—Los Angeles and then on to Australia.

8 There are several cheap French charters to Colombia, Ecuador, Peru, Bolivia and the southern countries, but no-one in the UK sells them.

Travellers starting their journey in continental Europe may try: Uniclam-Voyages, 63 rue Monsieur-le Prince, 75006 Paris for charters. The Swiss company, Balair (owned by Swissair) has regular charter flights to South America (every second week to Recife and Rio). For cheap flights in Switzerland, Globetrotter Travel Service, Renweg, 8001 Zürich, has been recommended. Also try Nouvelles Frontières, Paris, T (1) 41-41-58-58; Hajo Siewer Jet Tours, Martinstr 39, 57462 Olpe, Germany, T (02761) 924120. The German magazine *Reisefieber* is useful.

9 If you buy discounted air tickets *always* check the reservation with the airline concerned to make sure the flight still exists. Also remember the IATA airlines' schedules change in March and October each year, so if you're going to be away a long time it's best to leave return flight coupons open.

In addition, check whether you are entitled to any refund or re-issued ticket if you lose, or have stolen, a discounted air ticket. Some airlines require the repurchase of a ticket before you can apply for a refund, which will not be given until after the validity of the original ticket has expired. The Iberia group, for example, operates this costly system.

10 Note that some South American carriers change departure times of short-haul or domestic flights at short notice and, in some instances, schedules shown in the computers of transatlantic carriers differ from those actually flown by smaller, local carriers. If you book, and reconfirm, both your transatlantic and onward sectors through your transatlantic carrier you may find that your travel plans have been based on out of date information. The surest solution is to reconfirm your outward flight in an office of the onward carrier itself.

AeroPerú operates Sudameripass, a 45-day return ticket which is one of the cheapest ways of flying around the continent. If starting a journey in Miami, Mexico City or Cancún, it costs US$1,099 for up to 6 coupons on AeroPerú's network; if starting in Buenos Aires or Los Angeles it costs US$1,299. Extra coupons can be bought for US$100 each. There are seasonal permutations. Check with JLA for up-to-date details. Also worth noting here are Varig's Stopover Programme, which offers special rates for accommodation and transfers for Varig passengers throughout Latin America, and the Mercosur Airpass. The latter applies to Brazil, Argentina, Uruguay and Paraguay, using 9 local carriers, available to any passenger with a return ticket to a Mercosur country. It must be bought in conjunction with an international flight; minimum stay is 10 days, maximum 30, at least 2 countries must be visited. Maximum number of coupons is eight. Fares are calculated on a mileage basis and range from US$225 to US$870.

Miami is a good place for connections between South and Central America and Europe. Non-US citizens should note that it is very difficult to check air tickets purchased outside the USA through an agent in Miami and that it is unlikely that you will be allowed by US Immigration to enter the USA without an onward ticket already in your possession. Continental Airlines' hub, Houston, is another good place for connections.

Beware buying tickets from the general sales agents in Europe of minor Latin American airlines. They are sometimes incorrectly made out and therefore impossible to transfer or cash in. If you buy internal airline tickets in Latin American countries you may find cash refunds difficult to get if you change your plans: better to change your ticket for a different one. On the other hand you can save money by buying tickets in a country with a black exchange market, for local currency, for flights on its national airline. Overbooking by Latin American airlines is very common (largely due to repeated block bookings by travel agents, which everyone knows will not be used), so always reconfirm the next stage of your flight within 72 hrs of your intended departure. And it does no harm to reconfirm yet again in the last 24 hrs, just to show them you mean it, and turn up for the flight in good time (at least 2 hrs before departure).

We advise people who travel the cheap way in Latin America to pay for all transport as they go along, and not in advance. This advice does not apply to people on a tight schedule: paying as you go along may save money, but it is likely to waste your time somewhat. The one exception to this general principle is in transatlantic flights; here money is saved by booking as far as possible in one operation. International air tickets are very expensive if purchased in Latin America. If buying airline tickets routed through the USA, check that US taxes are included in the price.

The national airlines of Argentina, Bolivia, Brazil, Chile, Colombia, Peru and Venezuela operate airpass schemes within those countries at a set price. See the respective country sections.

The Amerbuspass covers the whole of Latin America, from Mexico City to Ushuaia, and entitles the holder to 15-20% discounts on tickets with participating operators; bookable in all Latin American capitals, Europe, Asia, Africa, Oceania, it is valid for 9,999 miles, up to 180 days. Unlimited stopovers, travel with either a confirmed or open itinerary. Contact TISA Internacional, B Irigoyen 1370, Oficina 25/26, 1138 Buenos Aires, Argentina, T 27-6591/631-1108, F 953-5508, or Av Larrazabal 493, Buenos Aires, PO Box 40 Suc 1 (B), 1401 Buenos Aires.

Travel to the USA Until July 1988 all foreigners (except Canadians) needed visas to enter the USA. Despite subsequent relaxations of visa requirements for British air travellers with round-trip tickets to the USA, it is advisable to have a visa to allow entry by land, or on airlines from South and Central America which are not "participating carriers" on the Visa Waiver scheme. If you are thinking of travelling via the USA, or of visiting the USA after Latin America, you are strongly advised to get your visa from a US Consulate in your own country, not while travelling.

The US Department of Agriculture places restrictions on agricultural items brought to the United States from foreign countires as well as those brought to the mainland from Hawaii, Puerto Rico, and the US Virgin Islands. Prohibited items can harbour foreign animal and plant pests and diseases that could seriously damage America's crops, livestock, pets and the environment.

Because of this threat, travellers are required to list on the Customs' declaration form any meats, fruits, vegetables, plants, animals, and plant and animal products they are bringing into the country. The declaration must list all agricultural items carried in baggage, hand luggage and in vehicles coming across the border.

USDA inspectors will confiscate illegal items for destruction. Travellers who fail to declare items can be fined up to US$100 on the spot, and their exit from the airport will be delayed. Some items are permitted. Call 301-436-5908 for a copy of the helpful pamphlet, "Travelers Tips". The best advice is to check before purchasing an agricultural item and trying to bring it back to the United States.

Shipping Voyages on passenger-carrying cargo vessels between South America and Europe, the USA, or elsewhere, are listed here: the Blue Star line sails from Tilbury to Hamburg, Bremen, Antwerp, thence to Montevideo via the Brazilian ports of Salvador, Santos and Rio de Janeiro, returning via Rio Grande, Santos, Salvador and Recife, and Rotterdam. 12 passengers are carried; fare to Montevideo, £1,610, round trip £3,010 pp. The Grimaldi Line sails from Tilbury to Brazil (Vitória, Rio, Santos, Paranaguá), via Hamburg, Amsterdam and Antwerp, round trip about 42 days, £2,400-3,900, also from Genoa to Paranaguá, Santos and Rio for £840-1,105 (T Genoa 010-55091, London 0171-930 5683, Rio 021-253 6599). The Dobson Line has services from the UK to Caribbean, Central and South American ports; itineraries change frequently and usually calls in port are quite long, fare is about £50 pp per day, incl meals.

Various German companies sail to the E coast of South America: either Tilbury, Hamburg, Bremen, Antwerp to Salvador, Santos and Recife, returning to Rotterdam and Tilbury (£3,000-3,300 round trip); or Felixstowe, Bremen, Hamburg, Rotterdam, Antwerp, Le Havre, Rio de Janeiro (21 days, £1,800-1,950), Santos, Buenos Aires (25 days, £2,200-2,350), Rio Grande, Santos, Felixstowe. Flensburger Befrachtungskontor UC Hansen of Germany has a 50-day round trip Antwerp, Manaus, Itacoatiara, Belém, Rouen/Honfleur, Bremen, costing £3,000. Fyffes has regular sailings Portsmouth-Suriname, 6 passengers on a banana boat, 35-38 day round trip, £1,980 pp.

From the USA, Ivaran Lines serve East Coast USA, Brazilian ports, Montevideo and Buenos Aires; the *Americana* container ship carries 80 passengers in luxury accommodation (New Orleans, Houston, Puerto Cabello, La Guaira, Rio, Santos, Buenos Aires, Montevideo, Rio Grande do Sul, Itajaí, Paranaguá, Santos, Salvador, Fortaleza, Bridgetown, San Juan, Veracruz, Tampico, New Orleans, £6,645-11,340 pp round trip, fares depend on season, one-way N or S possible). Ivaran also have the *San Antonio*, carrying 12 passengers on the route Port Elizabeth (New Jersey), Baltimore, Norfolk, Savannah, Miami, Puerto Cabello, La Guaira, Rio, Santos, Buenos Aires, Montevideo, Rio Grande do Sul, Itajaí, Santos, Rio (possibly Salvador and Fortaleza), Port Elizabeth; 44-day round trip £4,085-4,825 pp, one-way subject to availability. Lykes Line sail from Miami/New Orleans to Cartagena, then through the Panama Canal to Guayaquil, Callao and Valparaíso (a round trip costs US$3,300-3,500 pp). Egon Oldendorff carries passengers on its USA or Canada/South America routes.

From Europe and USA to the west coast of South America: the Mediterranean Shipping Company has vessels from Felixstowe, Antwerp, Hamburg, Bremerhaven and Le Havre to the US ports of New York, Charleston, Miami and Houston (among others). From these four ports, the same company sails to Guayaquil, Callao, Arica and Valparaíso. Transatlantic fares range from £850 (Felixstowe or Le Havre-New York) to £1,370 (Antwerp-Houston); US-South America fares range from £590 (Guayaquil-New York) to £2,020 (New York-Arica). A round trip from the USA to South America, embarking and disembarking at the same port costs £2,930 (Europe-USA round trip £2,080). Passengers buying round trips are given preference; one-way tickets are practically impossible to come by in the autumn and winter months, but can be bought in summer.

Our thanks are due to John Alton of Strand Cruise and Travel Centre, Charing Cross Shopping Concourse, The Strand, London WC2N 4HZ, T 0171-836 6363, F 0171-497 0078, for the above information. Enquiries regarding passages should be made through agencies in your own country, or through Strand Cruise and Travel Centre. In the USA, contact Freighter World Cruises, 180 South Lake Ave, Pasadena, CA 91101, T (818) 449-3106, or Travltips Cruise and Freighter Travel Association, 163-07 Depot Road, PO Box 188, Flushing, NY 11358, T (800) 872-8584. Do not try to get a passage on a non-passenger carrying cargo ship to South America from a European port; it is not possible.

Details on shipping cars are given in **Motoring**, below, and in the relevant country sections.

Note Some countries in Latin America officially require travellers who enter their territory to have an onward or return ticket. (Look under "Information for Visitors" sections for the countries you intend to visit.) In 1994-95 this regulation was rarely enforced by any country. (It does not apply to travellers with their own vehicles.) In lieu of an onward ticket out of the country you are entering, any ticket out of another Latin American country (or a ticket home) may suffice, or proof that you have sufficient funds to buy a ticket (a credit card will do).

DOCUMENTATION AND SECURITY

Passports Remember that Latin Americans, especially officials, are very document-minded. You should always carry your passport in a safe place about your person, or if not going far, leave it in the hotel safe. If staying in a country for several weeks, it is worth while registering at your Embassy or Consulate. Then, if your passport is stolen, the process of replacing it is simplified and speeded up. Keeping photocopies of essential documents, including your flight ticket, and some additional passport-sized photographs, is recommended

Remember that it is your responsibility to ensure that your passport is stamped in and out when you cross frontiers. The absence of entry and exit stamps can cause serious difficulties: seek out the proper migration offices if the stamping process is not carried out as you cross. Also, do not lose your entry card; replacing one causes a lot of trouble, and possibly expense. Citizens of countries which oblige visitors to have a visa (eg France) can expect more delays and problems at border crossings.

If planning to study in Latin America for a long period, make every effort to get a student visa in advance.

Identity and Membership Cards Membership cards of British, European and US motoring organizations have been found useful for discounts off hotel charges, car rentals, maps, towing charges, etc. Student cards must carry a photograph if they are to be of any use in Latin America for discounts. (If you describe yourself as a student on your tourist card you may be able to get discounts, even if you haven't a student card). Business people should carry a good supply of visiting cards, which are essential for good business relations in Latin America. Identity, membership or business cards in Spanish or Portuguese (or a translation) and an official letter of introduction in Spanish or Portuguese are also useful.

If you are in full-time education you will be entitled to an International Student Identity Card, which is distributed by student travel offices and travel agencies in 77 countries. The ISIC gives you special prices on all forms of transport (air, sea, rail etc), and access to a variety of other concessions and services. If you need to find the location of your nearest ISIC office contact: The ISIC Association, Box 9048, 1000 Copenhagen, Denmark T (+45) 33 93 93 03.

Money is best carried in US dollar travellers' cheques (denominations of US$50 and US$100 are preferable, though one does need a few of US$20) or cash. Sterling and other currencies are not recommended. Travellers' cheques are convenient but they attract thieves (though refunds can of course be arranged) and you will find that they are more difficult than dollar bills to change in small towns. Though the risk of loss is greater, many travellers take part of their funds in US dollar notes; better rates and lower commissions can usually be obtained for them. In many countries, US dollar notes are only accepted if they are in excellent condition (ie no writing, stamps, rips or other blemish; take brand new notes if you can). Low-value US dollar bills should be carried for changing into local currency if arriving in a country when banks or *casas de cambio* are closed (US$5 or US$10 bills). They are very useful for shopping: exchange shops (*casas de cambio*) tend to give better exchange rates than hotels or banks. The better hotels will normally change travellers' cheques for their guests (often at a rather poor rate), but if you're travelling on the cheap it is essential to keep in funds; watch weekends and public holidays carefully and never run out of local currency. Take plenty of local currency, in small denominations, when making trips into the interior. Spread your money around your person: less chance of thieves finding it all. Don't leave cash in your shoe, it may become too damaged to exchange or use.

We recommend in general the use of American Express, Visa or Thomas Cook US$ travellers' cheques, but should point out that less commission is often charged on Citibank or Bank of America cheques, if they are cashed at Latin American branches of those banks. These cheques are always accepted by banks, even though they may not be as well known outside banks as those of American Express, Visa or Thomas Cook. It is a good idea to take two kinds of cheque: if large numbers of one kind have recently been forged or stolen, making people suspicious, it is unlikely to have happened simultaneously with the other kind. Several banks charge a high fixed commission for changing travellers' cheques—sometimes as much as US$5-10 a cheque—because they don't really want to be bothered. Exchange houses (*casas de cambio*) are usually much better for this service. Some establishments may ask to see the customer's record of purchase before accepting travellers' cheques.

Most of the countries described in this book have freedom of exchange between US dollars and the local currency. A few have a parallel rate of exchange which is not always better than the official rate. Local conditions are described in the relevant chapters. Changing money on the street: if possible, do not do so alone. If unsure of the currency of the country you are about to enter, check rates with more than one changer at the border, or ask locals or departing travellers.

An increasingly popular and easy way of obtaining funds while travelling is with a credit card via an automatic telling machine (ATM). The Visa and Mastercard/

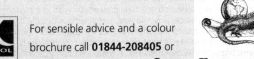

Plus/Cirrus networks are widespread. We give outlets' names in the text, but check before leaving home, as variations occur. Frequently, the rates of exchange on ATM withdrawals are the best available. It is also straightforward to obtain a cash advance against a credit card and, in the text, we give the names of banks that do this.

For purchases, credit cards of the Visa and Mastercard (Eurocard, Access) groups are useful, and American Express (Amex), Carte Blanche and Diners Club can be used. Conceal them very carefully (*not* under the insole of a shoe, however: that may render them unusable!), and make sure you know the correct procedure if they are lost or stolen. Credit card transactions are normally at an officially recognized rate of exchange (sometimes, if there are several, the least favourable one); you may find it much cheaper to pay cash and get the parallel rate. Many establishments in Latin America charge a fee of about 5% on credit card transactions (irrespective of any taxes); although forbidden by credit card company rules there is not a lot you can do about this, except get the charge itemized on the receipt and complain to the card company. For credit card security, insist that imprints are made in your presence and that any imprints incorrectly completed should be torn into tiny pieces. Also destroy the carbon papers after the form is completed (signatures can be copied from them).

NB In many countries, one can get at least US$500 in Amex travellers' cheques on the American Express card (US$1,000 on the gold card). One can also obtain cash at American Express via personal cheques, eg Eurocheque. If you are having additional sums of money sent out during a tour of Latin America, try to have it sent to one of the countries where you can easily exchange dollar travellers' cheques for dollars cash; see under the individual countries below for the current situation. Remember that a transfer of funds, even by telex, can take several days, and charges can be high; a recommended method is, before leaving, to find out which local bank is correspondent to your bank at home, then when you need funds, telex your own bank and ask them to telex the money to the local bank (confirming by air mail). It is possible to obtain money within hours by this method.

Whenever you leave a country, sell any local currency before leaving, because the further away you get, the less the value of a country's money. **Note** If departing by air, do not leave yourself too little money to pay the airport departure tax, which is never waived.

Americans should know that if they run out of funds they can usually expect no help from the US Embassy or Consul other than a referral to some welfare organization. Find out before you go precisely what services and assistance your embassy or consulate can provide if you find yourself in difficulties.

Law Enforcement Whereas in Europe and North America we are accustomed to law enforcement on a systematic basis, in general, enforcement in Latin America is achieved by periodic campaigns. The most typical is a round-up of criminals in the cities just before Christmas. In December, therefore, you may well be asked for identification at any time, and if you cannot produce it, you will be jailed. At first sight, on arrival, it may seem that you can flout the law with impunity, because everybody else is obviously doing so. If a visitor is jailed his friends should take him food every day. This is especially important for people on a diet, such as diabetics. It must also be borne in mind that in the event of a vehicle accident in which anyone is injured, all drivers involved are automatically detained until blame has been established, and this does not usually take less than 2 weeks.

Never offer a bribe unless you are fully conversant with the customs of the country. (In Chile, for instance, it would land you in serious trouble if you tried to bribe a *carabinero*.) Wait until the official makes the suggestion, or offer money in some form which is apparently not bribery, eg "In our country we have a system of on-the-spot fines (*multas de inmediato*). Is there a similar system here?" Do not assume that an official who accepts a bribe is prepared to do anything else that is illegal. You bribe him to persuade him to do his job, or to persuade him not to do it, or to do it more quickly, or more slowly. You do not bribe him to do something which is against the law. The mere suggestion would make him very upset. If an official suggests that a bribe must be paid before you can proceed on your way, be patient (assuming you have the time) and he may relent.

Security Generally speaking, most places in Latin America are no more dangerous than any major city in Europe or North America. In provincial towns, main places of interest, on day time buses and in ordinary restaurants the visitor should be quite safe. Nevertheless, in large cities particularly, crime exists, most of which is opportunistic. If you are aware of the dangers, act confidently and use your common sense you will lessen many of the risks. The following tips, all endorsed by travellers, are meant to forewarn, but not alarm, you. Keep all documents secure; hide your main cash supply in different places or under your clothes: extra pockets sewn inside shirts and trousers, pockets closed with a zip or safety pin, moneybelts (best worn below the waist rather than outside or at it or around the neck), neck or leg pouches, a thin chain for attaching a purse to your bag or under your clothes and elasticated support bandages for keeping money and cheques above the elbow or below the knee have been repeatedly recommended (the last by John Hatt in *The Tropical Traveller*). Keep cameras in bags (preferably with a chain or wire in the strap to defeat the slasher) or briefcases; take spare spectacles (eyeglasses); don't wear wrist-watches or jewellery. If you wear a shoulder-bag in a market, carry it in front of you. Backpacks are vulnerable to slashers: a good idea is to cover the pack with a sack (a plastic one will also keep out rain and dust) with maybe a layer of wire netting between, or make an inner frame of chicken wire. Use a pack which is lockable at its base.

Ignore mustard smearers and paint or shampoo sprayers, and strangers' remarks like "what's that on your shoulder?" or "have you seen that dirt on your shoe?" Furthermore, don't bend over to pick up money or other items in the street. These are all ruses intended to distract your attention and make you easy for an accomplice to steal from. If someone follows you when you're in the street, let him catch up with you and "give him the eye". While you should take local advice about being out at night, do not assume that daytime is safer than nighttime. If walking after dark, walk in the road, not on the pavement/sidewalk.

Be wary of "plainclothes policemen", insist on seeing identification and on going to the police station by main roads. Do not hand over your identification (or money—which he should not need to see anyway) until you are at the station. On no account take them directly back to your lodgings. Be even more suspicious if he seeks confirmation of his status from a passer-by. If someone tries to bribe you, insist on a receipt. If attacked, remember your assailants may well be armed, and try not to resist.

It is best, if you can trust your hotel, to leave any valuables you don't need in safe-deposit there, when sightseeing locally. Always keep an inventory of what you have deposited. If you don't trust the hotel, lock everything in your pack and secure that in your room (some people take eyelet-screws for padlocking cupboards or drawers). If you lose valuables, always report to the police and note details of the report—for insurance purposes.

When you have all your luggage with you at a bus or railway station, be especially careful: don't get into arguments with any locals if you can help it, and lock all the items together with a chain or cable if you are waiting for some time. Take a taxi between airport/bus station/railway station and hotel, if you can possibly afford it. Keep your bags with you in the taxi and pay only when you and your luggage are safely out of the vehicle. Make sure the taxi has inner door handles, in case a quick exit is needed. Avoid night buses; never arrive at night; and watch your belongings whether they are stowed inside or outside the cabin (roof top luggage racks create extra problems, which are sometimes unavoidable—make sure your bag is waterproof). Major bus lines often issue a luggage ticket when bags are stored in the bus' hold, generally a safe system. When getting on a bus, keep your ticket handy; someone sitting in your seat may be a distraction for an accomplice to rob you while you are sorting out the problem. Finally, never accept food, drink, sweets or cigarettes from unknown fellow-travellers on buses or trains. They may be drugged, and you would wake up hours later without your belongings. In this connection, never accept a bar drink from an opened bottle (unless you can see that that bottle is in general use): always have it uncapped in front of you.

For specific local problems, see under the individual countries in the text.

Drugs Users of drugs, even of soft ones, without medical prescription should be particularly careful, as some countries impose heavy penalties— up to 10 years' imprisonment—for even the simple possession of such substances. In this connection, the planting of drugs on travellers, by traffickers or the police, is not unknown. If offered drugs on the street, make no response at all and keep walking. Note that people who roll their own cigarettes are often suspected of carrying drugs and subjected to intensive searches. Advisable to stick to commercial brands of cigarettes—but better still not to smoke at all.

ACCOMMODATION

Hotels For about US$10, a cheap but not bad hotel room can be found in most countries, although in some of the Andean countries you may not have to pay that much. For the indigent, it is a good idea to ask for a boarding house—*casa de huéspedes, hospedaje, pensión, casa familial* or *residencial*, according to country; they are normally to be found in abundance near bus and railway stations and markets. Good value hotels can also be found near truckers' stops/service stations; they are usually secure. There are often great seasonal variations in hotel prices in resorts. Note that in the text "with bath" usually means "with shower and toilet", not "with bath tub". Remember, cheaper hotels don't always supply soap, towels and toilet paper; in colder (higher) regions they may not supply enough blankets, so take your own or a sleeping bag. Useful tips: book even cheap hotels in advance by registered mail, if you receive no reply don't worry; ask the car rental agency employees at the airport for advice when you arrive, as long as they are not busy they may have better value recommendations than airport tourist offices; always ask for the best room. To avoid price hikes for gringos, ask if there is a cheaper room.

Experiment in International Living Ltd, "Otesaga", West Malvern Road, Malvern, Worcestershire, WR14 4EN, T 01684-562577, F 562212, or Ubierstrasse 30, 5300 Bonn 2, T 0228-95-7220, F 0228-35-8282, can arrange stays with families from 1 to 4 weeks in Chile, Ecuador and Brazil; EIL has offices in 38 countries. This has been recommended as an excellent way to meet people and learn the language.

Note The electric showers used in innumerable hotels should be checked for obvious flaws in the wiring; try not to touch the rose while it is producing hot water.

Youth Hostels Organizations affiliated to the Youth Hostels movement exist in Argentina, Brazil, Colombia, Chile, Peru and Uruguay. There is an associate organization in Ecuador. Further information in the country sections and from the IYHA.

Meals In all countries except Brazil and Chile (where cold meats, cheese, eggs, fruit etc generally figure) breakfast usually means coffee or tea with rolls and butter, and anything more is charged extra. In Colombia and Ecuador breakfast usually means eggs, a roll, fruit juice and a mug of milk with coffee; say "breakfast without eggs" if you do not want that much. There is a paragraph on each nation's food under "Information for Visitors". Vegetarians should be able to list all the foods they cannot eat; saying "Soy vegetariano/a" (I'm a vegetarian) or "no como carne" (I don't eat meat) is often not enough. Most restaurants serve a daily special meal, usually at lunchtime, which is cheap and good. Other than that you can expect to pay between US$10-15 on breakfast and dinner per day.

Camping There is a growing network of organized campsites, to which reference is made in the text immediately below hotel lists, under each town. If there is no organized site in town, a football pitch or gravel pit might serve. Obey the following rules for "wild" camping: (1) arrive in daylight and pitch your tent as it gets dark; (2) ask permission to camp from the parish priest, or the fire chief, or the police, or a farmer regarding his own property; (3) never ask a group of people— especially young people; (4) never camp on a beach (because of sandflies and thieves). If you can't get information from anyone, camp in a spot where you can't be seen from the nearest inhabited place, or road, and make sure no one saw you go there. In Argentina and Brazil, it is common to camp at gas/petrol stations. As Béatrice Völkle of Gampelen, Switzerland, adds, camping wild may be preferable to those organized sites which are treated as discotheques, with only the afternoon reserved for sleeping.

If taking a cooker, the most frequent recommendation is a multifuel stove (eg MSR International, Coleman Peak 1), which will burn unleaded petrol or, if that is not available, kerosene, *benzina blanca*, etc. Alcohol-burning stoves are simple, reliable, but slow and you have to carry a lot of fuel: for a methylated spirit-burning stove, the following fuels apply, *alcohol desnaturalizado, alcohol metílico, alcohol puro (de caña)* or *alcohol para quemar*. Ask for 95%, but 70% will suffice. In all countries fuel can usually be found in chemists/pharmacies. Gas cylinders and bottles are usually exchangeable, but if not can be recharged; specify whether you use butane or propane. Gas canisters are not always available. The Camping Clube do Brasil gives 50% discounts to holders of international campers' cards.

Toilets Many hotels, restaurants and bars have inadequate water supplies. **Almost without exception used toilet paper should not be flushed down the pan, but placed in the receptacle provided.** This applies even in quite expensive hotels. Failing to observe this custom will block the pan or drain, a considerable health risk. It is quite common for people to stand on the toilet seat (facing the wall—easier to balance), as they do in Asia. If you are concerned about the hygiene of the facility, put paper on the seat.

Cockroaches These are ubiquitous and unpleasant, but not dangerous. Take some insecticide powder if staying in cheap hotels; Baygon (Bayer) has been recommended. Stuff toilet paper in any holes in walls that you may suspect of being parts of cockroach runs.

ETIQUETTE AND LANGUAGE

Travellers' Appearance There is a natural prejudice in all countries against travellers who ignore personal hygiene and have a generally dirty and unkempt appearance. Most Latin Americans, if they can afford it, devote great care to their clothes and appearance; it is appreciated if visitors do likewise. How you dress is mostly how people will judge you. Buying clothing locally can help you to look less like a tourist. The general prejudice previously reported against backpacks has virtually disappeared, unless carried by those whom officials identify as "hippies". One tip we have received; young people of informal dress and life-style may find it advantageous to procure a letter from someone in an official position testifying to their good character, on official-looking notepaper.

Some countries have laws or prejudices against the wearing by civilians of army-surplus clothing. Men wearing earrings are liable to be ridiculed in more "macho" communities (eg parts of Argentina). A medium weight shawl with some wool content is recommended for women: it can double as pillow, light blanket, bathrobe or sunscreen as required. For men, a smart jacket can be very useful.

Courtesy Remember that politeness—even a little ceremoniousness—is much appreciated. In this connection professional or business cards are useful. Men should always remove any headgear and say "con permiso" ("com licença" in Brazil) when entering offices, and be prepared to shake hands (this is much commoner in Latin America than in Europe or North America); always say "Buenos días" (until midday) or "Buenas tardes" ("Bom dia" or "Boa tarde" in Brazil) and wait for a reply before proceeding further; in a word, don't rush them! Always remember that the traveller from abroad has enjoyed greater advantages in life than most Latin American minor officials, and should be friendly and courteous in consequence. Never be impatient; do not criticize situations in public: the officials may know more English than you think and they can certainly interpret gestures and facial expressions. Be judicious about discussing politics with strangers. Politeness can be a liability, however, in some situations; most Latin Americans are disorderly queuers. In commercial transactions (buying a meal, goods in a shop, etc) politeness should be accompanied by firmness, and always ask the price first.

Politeness should also be extended to street traders; saying "No, gracias" with a smile is better than an arrogant dismissal. Whether you give money to beggars is a personal matter, but your decision should be influenced by whether a person is begging out of need or trying to cash in on the tourist trail. In the former case, local people giving may provide an indication. Giving money to children is a separate issue, upon which most agree: don't do it. There are occasions where giving food in a restaurant may be appropriate, but first inform yourself of local practice.

Moira Chubb, from New Zealand, suggests that if you are a guest and are offered food that arouses your suspicions, the only courteous way out is to feign an allergy or a stomach ailment. If worried about the purity of ice for drinks, ask for a beer.

Language Without some knowledge of Spanish you can become very frustrated and feel helpless in many situations. English, or any other language, is absolutely useless off the beaten track. Some initial study, to get you up to a basic Spanish vocabulary of 500 words or so, and a pocket dictionary and phrase-book, are most strongly recommended: your pleasure will be doubled if you can talk to the locals. Not all the locals speak Spanish, of course; apart from Brazil's Portuguese, you will find that some Indians in the more remote highland parts of Bolivia and Peru, and lowland Indians in Amazonia, speak only their indigenous languages, though there will usually be at least one person in each village who can speak Spanish (or Portuguese).

The basic Spanish of Hispanic America is that of south-western Spain, with soft "c's" and "z's" pronounced as "s", and not as "th" as in the other parts of Spain. Castilian Spanish is readily understood, but is not appreciated when spoken by non-Spaniards; try and learn the basic Latin American pronunciation. There are several regional variations in pronunciation, particularly in the River Plate countries, which are noted in the Argentine section "Information for Visitors". Differences in vocabulary also exist, both between peninsular Spanish and Latin American Spanish, and between the usages of the different countries.

If you are going to Brazil, you should learn some Portuguese. Spanish is not adequate: you may be understood but you will probably not be able to understand the answers. Language classes are available at low cost in a number of centres in South America, for instance Quito. See the text for details, under **Language Courses**.

INTERNAL SURFACE TRANSPORT

Before you start, remember that distances are great and journeys by land are long: plan accordingly and do not try to do too much in the time available.

Surface Transport   The continent has a growing road system for motor traffic, with frequent bus services. The buses are often comfortable; Brazil, Chile and Venezuela are the best; Colombia is quite good, Ecuador not far behind; Bolivia has good and bad; Peruvian buses are generally poor because of economic problems and the difficulties of Andean terrain. In mountainous country, however, do not expect buses to get to their destination, after long journeys, anywhere near on time. Do not turn up for a bus at the last minute; if it is full it may depart early. Tall travellers are advised to take aisle rather than window seats on long journeys as this allows more leg room. When the journey takes more than 3 or 4 hrs, meal stops at country inns or bars, good and bad, are the rule. Usually, no announcement is made on the duration of a stop: follow the driver, if he eats, eat. See what the locals are eating—and buy likewise, or make sure you're stocked up well on food and drink at the start. For drinks, stick to bottled water or soft drinks or coffee (black). The food sold by vendors at bus stops may be all right: watch if locals are buying, though unpeeled fruit is of course reliable. (See above on **Security** in buses.)

In most countries trains are slower than buses. They do tend, however, to provide finer scenery, and you can normally see much more wildlife than from the road—it is less disturbed by one or two trains a day than by the more frequent road traffic. Moreover, so many buses now show video films that you can't see the countryside because the curtains are drawn. Complaining to the conductor that you cannot see the beautiful landscape may persuade him to give you his seat at the front.

Hitchhiking   This custom is quite common in Latin America; travellers report varying degrees of success in virtually all countries. Neatness of appearance certainly helps. See in the **Information for Visitors** sections for local conditions. If trying to hitchhike away from main roads and in sparsely-populated areas, allow plenty of time.

Joanna Codrington writes: Hitchhiking in Latin America is reasonably safe and straightforward for males and couples, provided one speaks some Spanish/Portuguese. In Peru and Bolivia there is little private transport and trucks charge about $2/3$ the equivalent fare. But elsewhere cars and trucks will carry you free of charge, and will generally treat you as their guests. It is a most enjoyable mode of transport—a good way to meet the local people, to improve one's languages and to learn about the country. Truck drivers in particular are often well versed in things of interest one is passing, eg crops and industries.

Here are a few general hints: in remoter parts, make enquiries first about the volume of traffic on the road. On long journeys, set out at crack of dawn, which is when trucks usually leave. They tend to go longer distances than cars. Some trucking companies do not allow drivers to take hitchhikers.

Motoring   Binka and Robin le Breton write: *Preparing the Car*   What kind of motoring you do will depend on what kind of car you set out with. Four-wheel drive is not necessary, but it does give you greater flexibility in mountain and jungle territory, although you may not get far in Amazonas, where roads are frequently impassable. In Patagonia, main roads are gravel rather than paved: perfectly passable without four-wheel drive, just rough and dusty. Consider fitting wire guards for headlamps, and for windscreens too, if you don't mind peering out through a grill like a caged chimpanzee. Wherever you travel you should expect from time to time to find roads that are badly maintained, damaged or closed during the wet season, and delays because of floods, landslides and huge potholes. Don't plan your schedules too tightly.

Diesel cars are much cheaper to run than petrol ones, and the fuel is easily available; in Venezuela you may have to look hard for it outside Caracas. Most towns can supply a mechanic of sorts, and probably parts for Bosch fuel injection equipment. Watch the mechanics like a hawk, since there's always a brisk market in spares, and some of yours may be highly desirable. That apart, they enjoy a challenge, and can fix most things, eventually.

For prolonged motoring over 3000 metres, you may need to fit high altitude jets on your carburettors. Some fuel injection engines need adjusting too, and ignition settings may have to be changed: check the manufacturer's recommendations. The electronic ignition and fuel metering systems on modern emission controlled cars are allergic to humidity, heat and dust, and cannot be repaired by bush mechanics. Standard European and Japanese cars run on fuel with a higher octane rating than is commonly available in North, South or Central America, and in Brazil petrol (gasolina) is in fact gasohol, with a 12% admixture of alcohol. A high compression fuel injection engine will not like this. Unleaded fuel is available in Chile, Colombia and Ecuador, and to a small extent in Argentina. The most easily maintained petrol engined cars, then, are the types manufactured in Latin American countries, ie pre-emission control models such as the VW Kombi with carburettors and conventional (non-electronic) ignition, or the old type Toyota Landcruisers common in Central America. Older model American cars, especially Ford or GM pickups, are easily maintained, but high fuel consumption offsets this advantage. (Note that Colombia does not have a network for spares and repairs of VW, while Ecuador, Venezuela and Brazil do. Argentina is very expensive for maintenance of any make of car.)

Preparing the car for the journey is largely a matter of common sense: obviously any part that is not in first class condition should be replaced. It's well worth installing extra heavy-duty shock-absorbers (such as Spax or Koni) before starting out, because a long trip on rough roads in a heavily laden car will give heavy wear. Fit tubes on "tubeless" tyres, since air plugs for tubeless tyres are hard to find, and if you bend the rim on a pothole, the tyre will not hold air. Take spare tubes, and an extra spare tyre. Also take spare plugs, fan-belts, radiator hoses and headlamp bulbs; even though local equivalents can easily be found in cities, it is wise to take spares for those occasions late at night or in remote areas when you might need them. You can also change the fanbelt after a stretch of long, hot driving to prevent wear (eg after 15,000 km/10,000 miles). If your vehicle has more than one fanbelt, always replace them all at the same time (make sure you have the necessary tools if doing it yourself). If your car has sophisticated electrics, spare "black boxes" for the ignition and fuel injection are advisable, plus a spare voltage regulator or the appropriate diodes for the alternator, and elements for the fuel, air and oil filters if these are not a common type. (Some drivers take a spare alternator of the correct amperage, especially if the regulator is incorporated into the alternator.) Dirty fuel is a frequent problem, so be prepared to change filters more often than you would at home: in a diesel car you will need to check the sediment bowl often, too. An extra in-line fuel filter is a good idea if feasible (metal canister type preferable to plastic), and for travel on dusty roads an oil bath air filter is best for a diesel car. It is wise to carry a spade, jumper cables, tow rope and an air pump. Fit tow hooks to both sides of the vehicle frame. A 12 volt neon light for camping and repairs will be invaluable. Spare fuel containers should be steel and not plastic, and a siphon pipe is essential for those places where fuel is sold out of the drum. Take a 10 litre water container for self and vehicle. Note that in some areas gas stations are few and far between. Fill up when you see one: the next one may be out of fuel. Some countries have periodic fuel conservation strategies which means you can't get any after a certain hour in the evening, and often not at weekends either.

Apart from the mechanical aspects, spare no ingenuity in making your car secure. Your model should be the Brink's armoured van: anything less secure can be broken into by the determined and skilled thief. Use heavy chain and padlocks to chain doors shut, fit security catches on windows, remove interior window winders (so that a hand reaching in from a forced vent cannot open the window). All these will help, but none is foolproof. Anything on the outside—wing mirrors, spot lamps, motifs etc—is likely to be stolen too. So are wheels if not secured by locking nuts. Try never to leave the car unattended except in a locked garage or guarded parking space. Remove all belongings and leave the empty glove compartment open when the car is unattended. Also lock the clutch or accelerator to the steering wheel with a heavy, obvious chain or lock. Street children will generally protect your car fiercely in exchange for a tip. Be sure to note down key numbers and carry spares of the most important ones (but don't keep all spares inside the vehicle).

Documents　A *carnet de passage* is no longer necessary in any country (but please see **Additional notes** below). Land entry procedures for all countries—with the exception of Colombia—are simple, though time-consuming, as the car has to be checked by customs, police and agriculture officials. All you need is the registration document in the name of the driver, or, in the case of a car registered in someone else's name, a notarized letter of authorization. Most countries give a limited period of stay, but allow an extension if requested in advance. Of course, do be very careful to keep **all** the papers you are given when you enter, to produce when you leave. Bringing a car in by sea or air is much more complicated and expensive: generally you will have to hire an agent to clear it through customs, expensive and slow. Insurance for the vehicle against accident, damage or theft is best arranged in the country of origin, but it is getting increasingly difficult to find agencies who offer this service. In Latin American countries it is very expensive to insure against accident and theft, especially as you should take into account the value of the car increased by duties calculated in real (ie non devaluing) terms. If the car is stolen or written off you will be required to pay very high import duty on its value. A few countries insist on compulsory third party insurance, to be bought at the border: in other countries it's technically required, but not checked up on (Venezuela seems to be the only country where it is easy to obtain—Ed). Get the legally required minimum cover, not expensive, as soon as you can, because if you should be involved in an accident and are uninsured, your car could be confiscated. If anyone is hurt, do not pick them up (you may become liable). Seek assistance from the nearest police station or hospital if you are able to do so. You may find yourself facing a hostile crowd, even if you are not to blame.

Journey's End　When you finally reach your destination, what happens to the car? Shipping it back is one alternative. From Brazil, Grimaldi line to Genoa is the cheapest: there are also frequent sailings from Montevideo and Buenos Aires to most other destinations. The other alternative is to sell the car. Until now, this has been virtually impossible except in Paraguay, but the economic liberalization in Argentina, Chile and Brazil makes it legal—if not simple—to import cars into those

countries. Probably safer not to count on it though, unless you have the sort of car in great demand, like a Mercedes saloon. You can sell anything in Paraguay if you have the time. Legalizing the permanent import of a temporarily imported car costs about 30% of its street value. If you leave it to the buyer to "take care of" obtaining the correct documentation, you should not expect to receive a very favourable price. Dealers are adept at taking advantage of the fact that they can wait, and you cannot, so be prepared for "on—off—on again" dealing.

Car Hire The main international car hire companies operate in all countries, but they do tend to be very expensive, reflecting the high costs and accident rates. Hotels and tourist agencies will tell you where to find cheaper rates, but you will need to check that you have such basics as spare wheel, toolkit and functioning lights etc. You'll probably have more fun if you drive yourself, although it's always possible to hire a car with driver. If you plan to do a lot of driving and will have time at the end to dispose of it, investigate the possibility of buying a second hand car locally: since hiring is so expensive it may well work out cheaper and will probably do you just as well.

Car Hire Insurance Check exactly what the hirer's insurance policy covers. In many cases it will only protect you against minor bumps and scrapes, not major accidents, nor "natural" damage (eg flooding). Ask if extra cover is available. Also find out, if using a credit card, whether the card automatically includes insurance. Beware of being billed for scratches which were on the vehicle before you hired it.

Additional notes on motoring A great deal of conflicting information surrounds what documents are required in addition to the vehicle's registration. According to the RAC in the UK there are three recognized documents for taking a vehicle into South America: a *carnet de passages* issued by the Fedération Internationale de l'Automobile (FIA – Paris), a *carnet de passages* issued by the Alliance Internationale de Tourisme (AIT-Geneva), and the *Libreta de Pasos por Aduana* issued by the Federación Interamericana de Touring y Automóvil Clubs (FITAC). The following list gives official requirements, with comments about actual practice: **Argentina** requires a written undertaking that the car will be exported after a given period, either of the *carnets*, or the *libreta* (in practice, nothing is asked for beyond the title document, except at remote border crossings which may demand a *libreta*); **Bolivia**, *libreta* only; **Brazil**, a written undertaking only (nothing asked for); **Chile**, either *carnet*, or the *libreta* (in practice nothing asked for), insurance is obligatory; **Colombia**, either *carnet* or, according to a law of 31.12.1992, you have to purchase a bond on entry to the value of 10% of your vehicle (in practice, early 1995, nothing asked for), insurance is necessary; **Ecuador**, until 1995 either *carnet*, or the *libreta* was essential, but latest reports indicate that neither is now required (ask at an embassy in advance); **Paraguay**, either *carnet*, or the *libreta*; **Peru**, either *carnet*, the *libreta* and, for caravans and trailers, an inventory (the consulate in London says that a *libreta* is necessary, but if you cannot obtain one a written declaration that the car will leave Peru, authorized at a Peruvian consulate before leaving your home country, will do instead, in addition a traveller reports that *Formulario 015*, which can be requested at the border, entitles visitors to bring a vehicle into Peru duty free for 3 months, it is not extendable, it is free, but our correspondent was charged US$35 anyway); **Uruguay**, the *libreta* or the FIA *carnet* only (in practice nothing asked for); **Venezuela**, either *carnet* or the *libreta* (the consulate in London says a *Certificado de uso por turismo* must be completed at a Venezuelan embassy before arrival, no other documents required; in the USA the vehicle's title document must be legalized by a Venezuelan consul, US$100, this, plus title and a letter of intent from your shipper's agent must be taken to US customs at least 2 days before sailing, no *libreta* or *carnet* needed). In view of this confusion, contact the automobile clubs of the countries you intend to drive in and get their advice. In general, in 1994, motorists in South America seemed to fare better with a *carnet de passages* than without it.

The *libreta*, a 10-page book of three-part passes for customs, should be available from any South American automobile club member of FITAC; cost seems to be US$200, half refundable. The *carnet de passages* is issued only in the country where the vehicle is registered (in the UK it costs £65 for 25 pages, £55 for 10 pages, valid 12 months, either bank indemnity or insurance indemnity, half of the premium refundable value of the vehicle and countries to be visited required), available from the RAC or the AA. In the USA the AAA seems not to issue the *carnet*, although the HQ in Washington DC may give advice. It is available from the Canadian Automobile Association (1775 Courtwood Crescent, Ottawa, K2C 3JZ, T 613-226-7631, F 613-225-7383) for Canadian and US citizens, cost in late 1994 C$450; full details obtainable from the CAA. For this information thanks go to Paul Gowen, RAC Touring Information

Manager, Binka Le Breton, Mark Simril (who wrote to us and whose experiences were reported in *South American Explorer* No 30, November 1991), and other motorists.

While a normal car will reach most places of interest, high ground clearance is useful for badly surfaced or unsurfaced roads and for fording rivers: 4-wheel drive is recommended for mountain terrain and unmade roads off the beaten track.

If you want to buy a second-hand car, check for corrosion if making the deal in a coastal city and always check, if not change, the full set of tyres.

Shipping a vehicle From Europe or the USA you can either go to Panama and take the new *Crucero Express* ferry from Colón to Cartagena (Colombia), or shop around for the best value sailing to whichever port best suits your travelling plans. Try Boyd Steamship Corporation (T Balboa 636311), Buenaventura or Guayaquil; Sudamericana de Vapores (T Cristóbal 293844), Buenaventura; Central American Lines (T Colón 412880, Panama City 361036), Cartagena; Vencaribe (T Cristóbal 450461, Panama City 521258) or Cía Transatlántica España (T 696300) for Venezuela. Alternatively you can ship a vehicle from Europe to Brazil, Uruguay or Argentina. Vehicles can also be shipped from the USA. You have to get a special exemption in order to be allowed to be carried to Colombia in a non Colombian vessel, which takes time to obtain. Anything left inside the car while it is being shipped will be stolen. As long as your vehicle is not over 2.28m high, it can go in a container, but permission must be obtained for any belongings to remain in the car, and separate insurance for effects purchased. If the car is going ro-ro (drive on), it should be empty of all belongings, unless they are thoroughly secured.

A book containing much practical information on South American motoring conditions and requirements, as well as being a travelogue, is *Driving to Heaven*, by Derek Stansfield (available from the author, Ropley, Broad Oak, Sturminster Newton, Dorset DT10 2HG, T/F 01258-472534, £8.85 plus postage, if outside the UK).

Motorcycling The following advice was received from Ashley Rawlings of Bath (England): People are generally very amicable to motorcyclists and you can make many friends by returning friendship to those who show an interest in you.

The Machine should be off road capable: my choice would be the BMW R80/100/GS for its rugged and simple design and reliable shaft drive, but a Kawasaki KLR 650s, Honda Transalp/Dominator, or the ubiquitous Yamaha XT600 Tenere would also be suitable. Buying a bike in the States and driving down works out cheaper than buying one in the UK. A road bike can go most places an off road bike can go at the cost of greater effort.

Preparations: Many roads in Latin America are rough. Fit heavy duty front fork springs and the best quality rebuildable shock absorber you can afford (Ohlins, White Power). Fit lockable luggage such as Krausers (reinforce luggage frames) or make some detachable aluminium panniers. Fit a tank bag and tank panniers for better weight distribution. A large capacity fuel tank (Acerbis), +300 mile/480 km range is essential if going off the beaten track. A washable air filter is a good idea (K&N), also fuel filters, fueltap rubber seals and smaller jets for high altitude Andean motoring. A good set of trails-type tyres as well as a high mudguard are useful. Get to know the bike before you go, ask the dealers in your country what goes wrong with it and arrange a link whereby you can get parts flown out to you. If riding a chain driven bike, a fully enclosed chaincase is useful. A hefty bash plate/sump guard is invaluable.

Spares: Reduce service intervals by half if driving in severe conditions. A spare rear tyre is useful but you can buy modern tyres in most capital cities. Take oil filters, fork and shock seals, tubes, a good manual, spare cables (taped into position), a plug cap and spare plug lead. A spare electronic ignition is a good idea, try and buy a second hand one and make arrangements to have parts sent out to you. A first class tool kit is a must and if riding a bike with a chain then a spare set of sprockets and an 'o' ring chain should be carried. Spare brake and clutch levers should also be taken as these break easily in a fall. Parts are few and far between, but mechanics are skilled at making do and can usually repair things. Castrol oil can be bought everywhere and relied upon.

Take a puncture repair kit and tyre levers. Find out about any weak spots on the bike and improve them. Get the book for international dealer coverage from your manufacturer, but don't rely on it. They frequently have few or no parts for modern, large machinery.

Clothes and Equipment: A tough waterproof jacket, comfortable strong boots, gloves and a helmet with which you can use glass goggles (Halycon) which will not scratch and wear out like a plastic visor. The best quality tent and camping gear that you can afford and a petrol stove which runs on bike fuel is helpful.

Security: Not a problem in most countries. Try not to leave a fully laden bike on its own. An Abus D or chain will keep the bike secure. A cheap alarm gives you peace of mind if you leave the bike outside a hotel at night. Most hotels will allow you to bring the bike inside. Look for hotels that have a courtyard or more secure parking and never leave luggage on the bike overnight or whilst unattended.

Documents: Passport, International Driving Licence, bike registration document are necessary. The *carnet de passages* seems only to be absolutely necessary for Ecuador (Customs may allow you through in transit for a limited period), but in 1994 riders fared much better with a *carnet de passages* than without it. Get your licence endorsed by police in Bolivia.

Shipping: Bikes may be sent from Panama to Colombia by cargo flight (eg CAC). This costs approx US$150 for a 200kg bike (1994 price). You must drain the fuel, oil and battery acid, or remove the battery, but it is easier to disconnect and seal the overflow tube. Tape cardboard over fragile bits and insist on loading the bike yourself. The Darién Gap is impossible unless you carry the bike. See the Colombia chapter for the *Crucero Express* which carries motorbikes between Panama and Colombia.

Border Crossings Do not try to cross borders on a Sunday or a holiday anywhere as you are charged double the rate in Central America and a charge is levied on the usually free borders in South America. I found South American customs and immigration inspectors mostly to be friendly, polite and efficient. Central America, however, was a different story and it was sometimes very difficult to find out exactly what was being paid for. If in doubt ask to see the boss and/or the rule book.

Cycling Hallam Murray writes: Since the early 1980s, bicycle technology has improved in leaps and bounds. With the advent of Kevlar tyres and puncture-resistant inner tubes it is now theoretically possible to cycle from Alaska to Tierra del Fuego without so much as a single puncture. For the traveller with a zest for adventure and a limited budget there is unlikely to be a finer way to explore. At first glance a bicycle may not appear to be the most obvious vehicle for a major journey, but given ample time and reasonable energy it most certainly is the best. It can be ridden, carried by almost every form of transport from an aeroplane to a canoe, and can even be lifted across one's shoulders over short distances. On my most recent journey from Lake Titicaca to Tierra del Fuego—largely on unpaved roads, many of which would have defeated even the most robust car or truck—I was often envied by travellers using more orthodox transport, for I was able to travel at my own pace, to explore more remote regions and to meet people who are not normally in contact with tourists.

Choosing a Bicycle: The choice of bicycle depends on the type and length of expedition being undertaken and on the terrain and road surfaces likely to be encountered. Unless you are planning a journey almost exclusively on paved roads—when a high quality touring bike such as a Dawes Super Galaxy would probably suffice—I would strongly recommend a mountain bike. The good quality ones (and the cast iron rule is **never** to skimp on quality) are incredibly tough and rugged, with low gear ratios for difficult terrain, wide tyres with plenty of tread for good road-holding, cantilever brakes, and a low centre of gravity for improved stability. Expect to pay upwards of US$800 for such a machine. Although touring bikes, and to a lesser extent mountain bikes, and spares are available in the larger Latin American cities, remember that in the developing world most indigenous manufactured goods are shoddy and rarely last. In some countries, such as Mexico, Chile and Uruguay, imported components can be found but they tend to be extremely expensive. (Shimano parts are generally the easiest to find.) Buy everything you possibly can before you leave home.

Bicycle Equipment: A small but comprehensive tool kit (to include chain rivet and crank removers, a spoke key and possibly a block remover), a spare tyre and inner tubes, a puncture repair kit with plenty of extra patches and glue, a set of brake blocks, brake and gear cables and all types of nuts and bolts, at least 12 spokes (best taped to the chain stay), a light oil for the chain, tube of waterproof grease, a pump secured by a pump lock, a Blackburn parking block (my choice for the most invaluable accessory and they are cheap and virtually weightless), a cyclometer, a loud bell, and a secure lock and chain. *Richard's Bicycle Book* makes useful reading for even the most mechanically minded.

Luggage and equipment: Strong and waterproof front and back panniers are a must. When packed these are likely to be heavy and should be carried on the strongest racks available. Poor quality racks have ruined many a journey for they take incredible strain on unpaved roads. A top bag cum rucksack (eg Carradice) makes a good addition for use on and off the bike. I used a Cannondale front bag for my maps, camera, compass, altimeter, notebook and small tape-recorder. My total luggage weighed 27 kg—on the high side, but I never felt seriously overweight. (Other panniers rec are Ortlieb – front and back – which is waterpoof and almost "sandproof", and Karimoor.) "Gaffa" tape is excellent for protecting vulnerable parts of panniers and for carrying out all manner of repairs. My most vital equipment included a light and waterproof tent, a 3 season sleeping bag, an Optimus petrol stove (the best I have ever used for it is light and efficient and petrol can be found almost everywhere; also rec is the MSR XGK II multi-fuel stove – Andrew Dobbie, Swansea), a plastic survival bag for storing luggage at night when camping, 4 elastic straps, 4 one-litre water bottles, Swiss Army knife, torch, candle, comprehensive medical kit, money belts, a hat and sunglasses to protect against hours of ferocious tropical sun and small presents such as postcards of home, balloons and plastic badges. A rubber mouse can do wonders for making contact with children in isolated villages.

All equipment and clothes should be packed in plastic bags to give extra protection against dust and rain. (Also protect all documents, etc carried close to the body from sweat.) Always take the minimum clothing. It's better to buy extra items en route when you find you need them. Naturally the choice will depend on whether you are planning a journey through tropical lowlands, deserts, high mountains or a combination, and whether rain is to be expected. Generally it is best to carry several layers of thin light clothes than fewer heavy, bulky ones. Always keep one set of dry clothes, including long trousers, to put on at the end of the day. I would not have parted with my incredibly light, strong, waterproof and wind resistant goretex jacket and overtrousers. I could have sold them 100 times over and in Bolivia was even offered a young mule in exchange! I took two pairs of training shoes and found these to be ideal for both cycling and walking.

Useful Tips: Wind, not hills is the enemy of the cyclist. Try to make the best use of the times of day when there is little; mornings tend to be best but there is no steadfast rule. In parts of Patagonia there can be gusting winds of 80 kph around the clock at some times of year, whereas in other areas there can be none. Take care to avoid dehydration, by drinking regularly. In hot, dry areas with limited supplies of water, be sure to carry an ample supply. For food I carried the staples (sugar, salt, dried milk, tea, coffee, porridge oats, raisins, dried soups, etc) and supplemented these with whatever local foods I could find in the markets. Give your bicycle a thorough daily check for loose nuts or bolts or bearings. See that all parts run smoothly. A good chain should last 2,000 miles, 3,200 km or more but be sure to keep it as clean as possible—an old toothbrush is good for this—and to oil it lightly from time to time. Always camp out of sight of a road. Remember that thieves are attracted to towns and cities, so when sight-seeing, try to leave your bicycle with someone such as a café owner or a priest. Country people tend to be more honest and are usually friendly and very inquisitive. However, don't take unnecessary risks; always see that your bicycle is secure (most hotels will allow bikes to be kept in rooms). In more remote regions dogs can be vicious; carry a stick or some small stones to frighten them off. Traffic on main roads can be a nightmare; it is usually far more rewarding to keep to the smaller roads or to paths if they exist. Most towns have a bicycle shop of some description, but it is best to do your own repairs and adjustments whenever possible. In an emergency it is amazing how one can improvise with wire, string, dental floss, nuts and bolts, odd pieces of tin or "Gaffa" tape!

The Expedition Advisory Centre, administered by the Royal Geographical Society, 1, Kensington Gore, London SW7 2AR has published a useful monograph entitled *Bicycle Expeditions*, by Paul Vickers. Published in March 1990, it is available direct from the Centre, price £6.50 (postage extra if outside the UK). (In the UK there is also the Cyclist's Touring Club, CTC, Cotterell House, 69 Meadrow, Godalming, Surrey, GU7 3HS, T 0483-417217, for touring, and technical information.)

Most cyclists agree that the main danger comes from other traffic. A rearview mirror has been frequently recommended to forewarn you of vehicles which are too close behind. You also need to watch out for oncoming, overtaking vehicles, unstable loads on trucks, protruding loads etc. Make yourself conspicuous by wearing bright clothing and a helmet.

Ryan Flegal of Los Angeles, California, says that, instead of taking your own expensive bicycle from home with the attendant need for specialized tools and high risks of loss, one can buy a bike in Latin America. "Affix a sturdy rear rack, improvise securing luggage to the bicycle, and go. Carry only a patch kit and wrench to remove the wheel, and rely on the many bike mechanics in the area to do the rest". A steel frame is more durable when heavily laden and can be welded if damaged, unlike aluminium. If undertaking your own maintenance, make sure you know how to do it, and research what tyres you will need, before you go.

River Transport Geoffrey Dempsey has sent us the following note, with particular reference to Amazonia:

Because expanding air services have captured the lucrative end of the passenger market, passenger services on the rivers are in decline. Worst hit have been the upper reaches; rivers like the Ucayali in Peru, but the trend is apparent throughout the region. The situation has been aggravated for the casual traveller by a new generation of purpose-built tugs (all engine-room and bridge) that can handle up to a dozen freight barges but have no passenger accommodation. In Peru passenger boats must now supplement incomes by carrying cargo, and this lengthens their journey cycle. In the face of long delays, travellers might consider shorter "legs" involving more frequent changes of boat; though the more local the service, the slower and more uncomfortable it will be.

Hammocks, mosquito nets (not always good quality), plastic containers for water storage, kettles and cooking utensils can be purchased in any sizeable riverside town, as well as tinned food such as sardines, meat loaf, frankfurters, ham and fruit. Fresh bread, cake, eggs, fruit—papayas, bananas, pineapples, oranges etc—are available in most villages. Cabin bunks are provided with thin mattresses but these are often foul. Replacements can be bought locally but rolls of plastic foam that can be cut to size are also available and much cheaper. Eye-screws for securing washing lines and mosquito nets are useful, and tall passengers who are not taking a hammock and who may find insufficient headroom on some boats should consider a camp-chair. The writer yearned for a cushion.

HM Wams (Amsterdam) endorses the recommendation of taking hammock, mosquito net and food, adding that in Venezuelan Amazonas hitching rides on boats is possible if you camp at the harbour or police post where all boats must register. Take any boat going in your direction as long as it reaches the next police post. See the special section on the Brazilian Amazon, **p 539**.

Travelling with Children

Travelling with Children We are grateful to Tim and Arlene Frost, of New Zealand, for the following notes and to Linda and Lawrence Foster, of Wembley, Hallam and Carole Murray, of London, SW11, and Tim Butler and Valerie Fraser, of Lima, for additional suggestions:

People contemplating overland travel in South America with children should remember that a lot of time can be spent waiting for buses, trains, and especially for aeroplanes. On bus journeys, if the children are good at amusing themselves, or can readily sleep while travelling, the problems can be considerably lessened. If your child is of an early reading age, take reading material with you as it is difficult, and expensive to find. A bag of, say 30 pieces, of Duplo or Lego can keep young children occupied for hours. Travel on trains, while not as fast or at times as comfortable as buses, allows more scope for moving about. Some trains provide tables between seats, so that games can be played. Beware of doors left open for ventilation especially if air-conditioning is not working.

Food can be a problem if the children are not adaptable. It is easier to take biscuits, drinks, bread etc with you on longer trips than to rely on meal stops where the food may not be to taste. Avocados are safe, easy to eat and nutritious; they can be fed to babies as young as 6 months and most older children like them. A small immersion heater and jug for making hot drinks is invaluable, but remember that electric current varies. Try and get a dual-voltage one (110v and 220v).

Fares: On all long-distance buses you pay for each seat, and there are no half-fares if the children occupy a seat each. For shorter trips it is cheaper, if less comfortable, to seat small children on your knee. Often there are spare seats which children can occupy after tickets have been collected. In city and local excursion buses, small children generally do not pay a fare, but are not entitled to a seat when paying customers are standing. On sightseeing tours you should *always* bargain for a family rate—often children can go free. (In trains, reductions for children are general, but not universal.)

All civil airlines charge half for children under 12, but some military services don't have half-fares, or have younger age limits. Children's fares on Lloyd Aéreo Boliviano are considerably more than half, and there is only a 7kg baggage allowance. (LAB also checks children's ages on passports.) Note that a child travelling free on a long excursion is not always covered by the operator's travel insurance; it is adviseable to pay a small premium to arrange cover.

Hotels: In all hotels, try to negotiate family rates. If charges are per person, always insist that two children will occupy one bed only, therefore counting as one tariff. If rates are per bed, the same applies. In either case you can almost always get a reduced rate at cheaper hotels. Occasionally when travelling with a child you will be refused a room in a hotel that is "unsuitable". On river boat trips, unless you have very large hammocks, it may be more comfortable and cost effective to hire a 2-berth cabin for 2 adults and a child. (In restaurants, you can normally buy children's helpings, or divide one full-size helping between two children.)

Travel with children can bring you into closer contact with Latin American families and, generally, presents no special problems—in fact the path is often smoother for family groups. Officials tend to be more amenable where children are concerned and they are pleased if your child knows a little Spanish or Portuguese. Moreover, even thieves and pickpockets seem to have some of the traditional respect for families, and may leave you alone because of it!

Hiking and Trekking

Hiking and Trekking Hilary Bradt, the well-known trekker, author and publisher, writes: A network of paths and tracks covers much of South America and is in constant use by the local people. In countries with a large Indian population—Ecuador, Peru and Bolivia, for instance—you can walk just about anywhere, but in the more European countries, such as Venezuela, Chile and Argentina, you must usually limit yourself to the many excellent national parks with hiking trails. Most South American countries have an Instituto Geográfico Militar which sells topographical maps, scale 1:100,000 or 1:50,000. The physical features shown on these are usually accurate; the trails and place names less so. National Parks offices also sell maps.

Hiking and backpacking should not be approached casually. Even if you only plan to be out a couple of hours you should have comfortable, safe footwear (which can cope with the wet—Ed) and a daypack to carry your sweater and waterproof (which must be more than showerproof). At high altitudes the difference in temperature between sun and shade is remarkable. The longer trips mentioned in this book require basic backpacking equipment. Essential items are: backpack with frame, sleeping bag, closed cell foam mat for insulation, stove, tent or tarpaulin, dried food (not tins), water bottle, compass. Some but not all of these things are available locally.

When planning treks in the Andes you should be aware of the effects and dangers of acute mountain sickness, and cerebral and pulmonary oedema (see Health Information, **p 36**). These can be avoided by spending a few days acclimatizing to the altitude before starting your walk, and by climbing slowly. Otherwise there are fewer dangers than in most cities. Hikers have little to fear from the animal kingdom apart from insects (although it's best to avoid actually stepping on a snake), and robbery and assault are very rare. You are much more of a threat to the environment than vice versa. Leave no evidence of your passing; don't litter and don't give gratuitous presents of sweets or money to rural villagers. Respect their system of reciprocity; if they give you hospitality or food, then is the time to reciprocate with presents.

For trekking in mountain areas, where the weather can deteriorate rapidly (eg in Torres del Paine), trekkers should consider taking the following equipment (list supplied by Andrew Dobbie of Swansea, who adds that it "is in no way finite"): **Clothing:** warm hat (wool or man-made fibre), thermal underwear, T-shirts/shirts, trousers (quick-drying and preferably windproof, never jeans), warm (wool or fleece) jumper/jacket (preferably two), gloves, waterproof jacket and over trousers (preferably Gore-Tex), shorts, walking boots and socks, change of footwear or flip-flops. **Camping Gear:** tent (capable of withstanding high winds), sleeping mat (closed cell - Karrimat - or inflatable - Thermarest), sleeping bag (3-season minimum rating), sleeping bag liner, stove and spare parts, fuel, matches and lighter, cooking and eating utensils, pan scrubber, survival bag. **Food:** very much personal preference but at least two days more supplies than you plan to use; tea, coffee, sugar, dried milk; porridge, dried fruit, honey; soup, pasta, rice, soya (TVP); fresh fruit and vegetables; bread, cheese, crackers; biscuits, chocolate; salt, pepper, other herbs and spices, cooking oil. **Miscellaneous:** map and compass, torch and spare batteries, pen and notebook, Swiss army knife, sunglasses, sun cream, lip salve and insect repellent, first aid kit, water bottle, toiletries and towel.

Maps and Guide Books Those from the Institutos Geográficos Militares in the capitals (see above) are often the only good maps available in Latin America. It is therefore wise to get as many as possible in your home country before leaving, especially if travelling by land. A recommended series of general maps is that published by International Travel Map Productions (ITM), World Wide Books and Maps, 736A Granville Street, Vancouver BC, V6Z 1G3, Canada, compiled with historical notes, by the late Kevin Healey. Available are South America South, North East and North West (1:4,000,000), Amazon Basin (1:4,000,000), Ecuador (1:1,000,000), The Galapagos Islands (1:500,000), Easter Island (1:30,000), Argentina (1:4,000,000), Central America (1:1,800,000), Panama (1:800,000), Guatemala and El Salvador (1: 500,000), Costa Rica (1:500,000), Belize (1:350,000), Mexico (1:3,300,000), Mexico City (1:10,000), Mexico South (1:1,000,000), the Yucatán (1:1,000,000) and Baja California (1:1,000,000). Details of Bradt Publications' Backpacking Guide Series, other titles and imported maps and guides are mentioned in our country "Information for Visitors" sections.

A very useful book, highly recommended, aimed specifically at the budget traveller is *The Tropical Traveller*, by John Hatt (Penguin Books, 3rd edition, 1993).

The South American Explorers' Club is at Avenida Portugal 146 (Casilla 3714), Lima, Peru (T 425-0142), 1254 Toledo, Apartado 21-431, Eloy Alfaro, Quito, Ecuador (T 566-076), and 126 Indian Creek Road, Ithaca, NY 14850, USA T (607) 277-0488. (For further details see under Lima and Quito.) The South American Explorers Club is represented in the UK by Bradt Publications.

The Latin American Travel Advisor is a quarterly news bulletin with up-to-date detailed and reliable information on countries throughout South and Central America. The publication focuses on public safety, health, weather and natural phenomena, travel costs, the economy and politics. It includes maps, tables, and charts comparing different countries and analyzing trends. Every issue has a feature article, a detailed column about each country and a 2-page summary called *The Continent at a Glance*. Available by mail or fax. For a free sample copy contact PO Box 17-17-908, Quito, Ecuador, F 593-2-562-566, E-Mail rku@pi.pro.ec.on Internet.

Literature This Handbook does not at present have space to contain sections on Latin American literature. Interested readers are recommended to see Jason Wilson, *Traveller's Literary Companion, South and Central America* (Brighton, UK: In Print, 1993), which has extracts from works by Latin American writers and by non-Latin Americans about the various countries and has very useful bibliographies.

GENERAL ADVICE

Responsible Tourism Mark Eckstein of David Bellamy Associates writes:
Much has been written about the adverse impacts of tourism on the environment and local communities. It is usually assumed that this only applies to the more excessive end of the travel industry such as the Spanish Costas and Bali. However it now seems that travellers can have an impact at almost any density and this is especially true in areas "off the beaten track" where local people may not be used to western conventions and lifestyles, and natural environments may be very sensitive.

Of course, tourism can have a beneficial impact and this is something to which every traveller can contribute. Many National Parks are part funded by receipts from people who travel to see exotic plants and animals, the Galápagos (Ecuador) and Manu (Peru) National Parks are good examples of such sites. Similarly, travellers can promote patronage and protection of valuable archaeological sites and heritages through their interest and entrance fees.

However, where visitor pressure is high and/or poorly regulated, damage can occur. It is also unfortunately true that many of the most popular destinations are in ecologically sensitive areas easily disturbed by extra human pressures. This is particularly significant because the desire to visit sites and communities that are off the beaten track is a driving force for many travellers. Eventually the very features that tourists travel so far to see may become degraded and so we seek out new sites, discarding the old, and leaving someone else to deal with the plight of local communities and the damaged environment.

Fortunately, there are signs of a new awareness of the responsibilities that the travel industry and its clients need to endorse. For example, some tour operators fund local conservation projects and travellers are now more aware of the impact they may have on host cultures and environments. We can all contribute to the success of what is variously described as responsible, green or alternative tourism. All that is required is a little forethought and consideration.

It would be impossible to identify all the possible impacts that might need to be addressed by travellers, but it is worthwhile noting the major areas in which we can all take a more responsible attitude in the countries we visit. These include, changes to natural ecosystems (air, water, land, ecology and wildlife), cultural values (beliefs and behaviour) and the built environment (sites of antiquity and archaeological significance). At an individual level, travellers can reduce their impact if greater consideration is given to their activities. Canoe trips up the headwaters of obscure rivers make for great stories, but how do local communities cope with the sudden invasive interest in their lives? Will the availability of easy tourist money and gauche behaviour affect them for the worse, possibly diluting and trivialising the significance of culture and customs? Similarly, have the environmental implications of increased visitor pressure been considered? Where does the fresh fish that feeds the trip come from? Hand caught by line is fine, but is dynamite fishing really necessary, given the scale of damage and waste that results?

Some of these impacts are caused by factors beyond the direct control of travellers, such as the management and operation of a hotel chain. However, even here it is possible to voice concern about damaging activities and an increasing number of hotels and travel operators are taking "green concerns" seriously, even if it is only to protect their share of the market.

Environmental Legislation Legislation is increasingly being enacted to control damage to the environment, and in some cases this can have a bearing on travellers. The establishment of National Parks may involve rules and guidelines for visitors and these should always be followed. In addition there may be local or national laws controlling behaviour and use of natural resources (especially wildlife) that are being increasingly enforced. If in doubt, ask. Finally, international legislation, principally the Convention on International Trade in Endangered Species of Wild Fauna and Flora (CITES), may affect travellers.

CITES aims to control the trade in live specimens of endangered plants and animals and also "recognizable parts or derivatives" of protected species. Sale of Black Coral, Turtle shells, protected Orchids and other wildlife is strictly controlled by signatories of the convention. The full list of protected wildlife varies, so if you feel the need to purchase souvenirs and trinkets derived from wildlife, it would be prudent to check whether they are protected. Every country included in this Handbook is a signatory of CITES. In addition, most European countries, the USA and Canada are all signatories. Importation of CITES protected species into these countries can lead to heavy fines, confiscation of goods and even imprisonment. Information on the status of legislation and protective measures can be obtained from Traffic International, UK office T (01223) 277427.

Green Travel Companies and Information The increasing awareness of the environmental impact of travel and tourism has led to a range of advice and information services as well as spawning specialist travel companies who claim to provide "responsible travel" for clients. This is an expanding field and the veracity of claims needs to be substantiated in some cases. The following organizations and publications can provide useful information for those with an interest in pursuing responsible travel opportunities.

Organizations Green Flag International Aims to work with travel industry and conservation bodies to improve environments at travel destinations and also to promote conservation programmes at resort destinations. Provides a travellers' guide for "green" tourism as well as advice on destinations, T (UK—01223) 890250. **Tourism Concern** Aims to promote a greater understanding of the impact of tourism on host communities and environments; Southlands College, Wimbledon Parkside, London SW19 5NN, T (UK—0181) 944-0464). **Centre for Responsible Tourism** CRT coordinates a North American network and advises on N American sources of information on responsible tourism. CRT, 2 Kensington Rd, San Anselmo, California USA. **Centre for the Advancement of Responsive Travel** CART has a range of publications available as well as information on alternative holiday destinations. T (UK—01732) 352757.

Publications *The Good Tourist* by Katie Wood and Syd House (1991) published by Mandarin Paperbacks; addresses issues surrounding environmental impacts of tourism, suggests ways in which damage can be minimised, suggests a range of environmentally sensitive holidays and projects.

Souvenirs Remember that these can almost invariably be bought more cheaply away from the capital, though the choice may be less wide. Bargaining seems to be the general rule in most countries' street markets, but don't make a fool of yourself by bargaining over what, to you, is a small amount of money.

If British travellers have no space in their luggage, they might like to remember Tumi, the Latin American Craft Centre, who specialize in Mexican and Andean products and who produce cultural and educational videos for schools: at 23/2A Chalk Farm Road, London NW1 8AG (F 0171-485 4152), 8/9 New Bond Street Place, Bath BA1 1BH (T 01225 462367, F 01225 444870), 1/2 Little Clarendon St, Oxford OX1 2HJ (T/F 01865-512307), 82 Park St, Bristol BS1 5LA (T/F 0117 929 0391). Tumi (Music) Ltd specializes in different rhythms of Latin America. See *Arts and Crafts of South America*, by Lucy Davies and Mo Fini, published by Tumi (1994), for a fine introduction to the subject. In Edinburgh there is a Mexican shop called Azteca. There are similar shops in the USA; one good one is on the ground floor of Citicorp Center, Lexington Avenue and 53rd Street, New York.

Mail Postal services in most countries are not very efficient, and pilfering is frequent. All mail, especially packages, should be registered. Some travellers recommend that mail should be sent to one's Embassy (or, if a cardholder, American Express agent) rather than to the Poste Restante/General Delivery (*Lista de Correos*) department of a country's Post Office. Some Embassies and post offices, however, do not keep mail for more than a month. If there seems to be no mail at the Lista under the initial letter of your surname, ask them to look under the initial of your forename or your middle name. Remember that there is no W in Spanish; look under V, or ask. For the smallest risk of misunderstanding, use title, initial and surname only. (If you're a British male, and all else fails, ask them to look under "E" for "Esquire"!—Geoffrey van Dulken.) If having items sent to you by courier (eg DHL), do not use poste restante, but an address such as a hotel: a signature is required on receipt.

Phones US travellers should know about AT&T's "USA Direct", by which you can connect with an AT & T operator without going through a local one. It is much cheaper than operator-assisted calls and is widely available. Sprint and MCI are also available; details given under individual countries. Other countries have similar systems, eg UK, Canada; obtain details before leaving home.

Communicating by fax is a convenient way of sending messages home. Many places with public fax machines (post offices, telephone companies or shops) will receive messages as well as send. Fax machines are often switched off; you may have to phone to confirm receipt.

World Band Radio Richard Robinson writes: South America has more local and community radio stations than practically anywhere else in the world; a shortwave (world band) radio offers a practical means to brush up on the language, sample popular culture and absorb some of the richly varied regional music. International broadcasters such as the BBC World Service, the Voice of America and the Quito-based Evangelical station, HCJB, keep the traveller abreast of news and events, in both English and Spanish.

Compact or miniature portables are recommended, with digital tuning and a full range of shortwave bands, as well as FM, long and medium wave. Detailed advice on radio models (£150 for a decent one) and wavelengths can be found in the annual publication, *Passport to World Bank Radio* (Box 300, Penn's Park, PA 18943, USA). Details of local stations is listed in *World TV and Radio Handbook* (WRTH), PO Box 9027, 1006 AA Amsterdam, The Netherlands, US$19.95. Both of these, free wavelength guides and selected radio sets are available from the BBC World Service Bookshop, Bush House Arcade, Bush House, Strand, London WC2B 4PH, UK, T 071-2557 2576.

Photography Always ask permission before photographing people. The price of film varies from country to country, being cheapest in Chile (in the Iquique and Punta Arenas Tax Free Zones) and Paraguay (always check the expiry date). Cheap film can also be bought in the USA. Pre-paid Kodak slide film cannot be developed in South America; it is also very hard to find. Kodachrome is almost impossible to buy. Fuji film is usually harder to find than Kodak. Some travellers (but not all) have advised against mailing exposed films home; either take them with you, or have them developed, but not printed, once you have checked the laboratory's quality. Note that postal authorities may use less sensitive equipment for X-ray screening than the airports do. Modern controlled X-ray machines are supposed to be safe even when a slow film passes through it dozens of times, but it is worth trying to avoid X-ray as the doses are cumulative. Many airport officials will allow film to be passed outside X-ray arches; they may also hand-check a suitcase with a large quantity of film if asked politely.

Dan Buck and Anne Meadows write: A note on developing film in South America. Black and white is a problem. Often it is shoddily machine-processed and the negatives are ruined. Ask the store if you can see an example of their laboratory's work and if they hand-develop.

Jeremy Till and Sarah Wigglesworth suggest that exposed film can be protected in humid areas by putting it in a balloon and tying a knot. Similarly keeping your camera in a plastic bag may reduce the effects of humidity.

Travelling Alone   Many points of security, dress and language have been covered already. These additional hints have mainly been supplied by women, but most apply to any single traveller. When you set out, err on the side of caution until your instincts have adjusted to the customs of a new culture. If, as a single woman, you can befriend a local woman, you will learn much more about the country you are visiting. Unless actively avoiding foreigners like yourself, don't go too far from the beaten track; there is a very definite "gringo trail" which you can join, or follow, if seeking company. This can be helpful when looking for safe accommodation, especially if arriving after dark (which is best avoided). Remember that for a single woman a taxi at night can be as dangerous as wandering around on her own. At borders dress as smartly as possible. Travelling by train is a good way to meet locals, but buses are much easier for a person alone; on major routes your seat is often reserved and your luggage can usually be locked in the hold. It is easier for men to take the friendliness of locals at face value; women may be subject to much unwanted attention. To help minimize this, do not wear suggestive clothing and, advises Alex Rossi of Jawa Timur, Indonesia, do not flirt. By wearing a wedding ring, carrying a photograph of your "husband" and "children", and saying that your "husband" is close at hand, you may dissuade an aspiring suitor. If politeness fails, do not feel bad about showing offence and departing. When accepting a social invitation, make sure that someone knows the address and the time you left. Ask if you can bring a friend (even if you do not intend to do so). A good rule is always to act with confidence, as though you know where you are going, even if you do not. Someone who looks lost is more likely to attract unwanted attention. Do not disclose to strangers where you are staying. (Much of this information was supplied by Alex Rossi, and by Deirdre Mortell of Carrigaline, Co Cork).

Final Hints   Everybody has his/her own list. In addition to items already suggested above, those most often mentioned include air cushions for slatted seats, inflatable travel pillow for neck support, strong shoes (and remember that footwear over $9^1/_2$ English size, or 42 European size, is difficult to obtain in Latin America except Argentina and Brazil); a small first-aid kit and handbook, fully waterproof top clothing, waterproof treatment for leather footwear, wax earplugs (which are almost impossible to find outside large cities) and airline-type eye mask to help you sleep in noisy and poorly curtained hotel rooms, sandals (rubber-thong Japanese-type or other), a polyethylene sheet 2 x 1 metres to cover possibly infested beds and shelter your luggage, polyethylene bags of varying sizes (up to heavy duty rubbish bag size) with ties, a toilet bag you can tie round your waist, if you use an electric shaver, take a rechargeable type, a sheet sleeping-bag and pillow-case or separate pillow-case—in some countries they are not changed often in cheap hotels, a $1^1/_2$-2m piece of 100% cotton can be used as a towel, a bedsheet, beach towel, makeshift curtain and wrap; a mosquito net (or a hammock with a fitted net), a straw hat which can be rolled or flattened and reconstituted after 15 mins soaking in water, a clothes line, a nailbrush (useful for scrubbing dirt off clothes as well as off oneself), a vacuum flask, a water bottle, a small dual-voltage immersion heater, a small dual-voltage (or battery-driven) electric fan, tea bags, a light nylon waterproof shopping bag, a universal bath- and basin-plug of the flanged type that will fit any waste-pipe (or improvise one from a sheet of thick rubber), string, velcro, electrical insulating tape, large penknife preferably with tin and bottle openers, scissors and corkscrew—the famous Swiss Army range has been repeatedly recommended (for knife sharpening, go to a butcher's shop), collapsible drinking beaker, electric motor-cycle alarm for luggage protection, a flour sack and roll of wire mesh for ditto, alarm clock or watch, candle, torch (flashlight)—especially one that will clip on to a pocket or belt, pocket mirror, small transistor radio earphones, pocket dictionary, pocket calculator, an adaptor and flex to enable you to take power from an electric-light socket (the Edison screw type is the most commonly used), a padlock (combination lock is best) for the doors of the cheapest and most casual hotels (or for tent zip if camping), spare chain-lengths and padlock for securing luggage to bed or bus/train seat. Remember not to throw away spent batteries containing mercury or cadmium; take them home to be disposed of, or recycled properly.

Useful medicaments are given at the end of the "Health Information" section (**p 47**); to these might be added some lip salve with sun protection, and pre-moistened wipes (such as "Wet Ones"). Always carry toilet paper. Natural fabric sticking plasters, as well as being long-lasting, are much appreciated as gifts. Dental floss can be used for backpack repairs, in addition to its original purpose. **Never** carry firearms. Their possession could land you in serious trouble.

A note on **contact lens wearers**: most countries have a wide selection of products for the care of lenses, so you don't need to take kilos of lotions. Lens solution can be difficult to find in Peru and Bolivia and outside major cities. Ask for it in a chemist/pharmacy, rather than an optician's.

Be careful when asking directions. Women probably know more about the neighbourhood; men about more distant locations. Policemen are often helpful. However, many Latin Americans will give you the wrong answer rather than admit they do not know; this may be partly because they fear losing face, but is also because they like to please. You are more likely to get reliable information if you carefully refrain from asking leading questions.

Lastly, a good principle is to take half the clothes (trousers with plenty of pockets are very useful), and twice the money, that you think you will need.

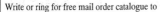

Are you **suffering** from

Wanderlust ?

then subscribe to the
magazine that guarantees
no cure !

Wanderlust is for people
who have a real *passion*
for travel. Its in-depth
features cover destinations
near and far, along with a
wide range of articles on
everything from health
advice to book & product
reviews. 76 pages,
full-colour throughout.

Whether you're seeking new frontiers, or alternative sides
to familiar places, *Wanderlust* gives you the information &
inspiration to keep your feet permanently itchy.

SO BE WARNED!

HEALTH INFORMATION

The following information has been compiled for us by Dr David Snashall, who is presently Senior Lecturer in Occupational Health at the United Medical Schools of Guys and St Thomas' Hospitals in London and Chief Medical Advisor of the British Foreign and Commonwealth Office. He has travelled extensively in Central and South America, worked in Peru and in East Africa and keeps in close touch with developments in preventative and tropical medicine. We incorporate also some welcome observations on the text by Dr C J Schofield, editor of Parasitology Today.

THE TRAVELLER to Latin America is inevitably exposed to health risks not encountered in Britain or the USA, especially if he/she spends time in the tropical regions. Epidemic diseases have been largely brought under control by vaccination programmes and public sanitation but, in rural areas, the latter is rudimentary and the chances of contracting infections of various sorts are much higher than at home.

There are English-speaking doctors in most major cities. If you fall ill the best plan may be to attend the out-patient department of a local hospital or contact your Embassy representative for the name of a reputable doctor. (We give the names of hospitals and some recommended doctors in the main city sections.— Ed.) Medical practices vary from those at home but remember they have particular experience in dealing with locally-occurring diseases.

Self-medication is undesirable except for minor complaints but may be forced on you by circumstances. Whatever the circumstances, be wary of medicines prescribed for you by pharmacists; many are poorly trained and unscrupulous enough to sell you potentially dangerous drugs or old stock they want to get rid of. The large number of pharmacies throughout Latin America is a considerable surprise to most people, as is the range of medicines you can purchase over the counter. There is a tendency towards over-prescription of drug mixtures and in general this should be resisted. Many drugs are manufactured under licence from American or European companies so the trade names may be familiar to you. This means that you do not need to carry a whole chest of medicines, but remember that the shelf-life of some items, especially vaccines and antibiotics, is markedly reduced in tropical conditions. Buy your supplies at the better outlets where they have refrigerators, even though it is more expensive. Check the expiry date of all preparations you buy.

Immigration officials sometimes confiscate scheduled drugs (Lomotil is an example) if they are not accompanied by a doctor's prescription.

With the following precautions and advice, you should keep as healthy as usual. Make local enquiries about health risks if you are apprehensive and take the general advice of European or North American families who have lived or are living in the country.

Before you go take out medical insurance. You should have a dental check-up, obtain a spare glasses prescription, a spare oral contraceptive prescription, and if you suffer from a chronic illness (such as diabetes, high blood pressure, ear or sinus troubles, cardiopulmonary disease or a nervous disorder) arrange for a check-up with your doctor, who can at the same time provide you with a letter explaining the details of your disability, if possible in English and Spanish (or Portuguese for Brazil). Check current practice in malaria prophylaxis (prevention).

Inoculations Smallpox vaccination is no longer required anywhere in the world. A major outbreak of cholera occurred, unusually, in Peru in 1990-91 and most other Latin American countries were affected subsequently. The epidemic continues, spread by travellers and fuelled by insanitary living conditions, untreated sewage and polluted water supplies. A vaccine against cholera is available but is not very effective and is not recognized as necessary for international travel by the World Health Organization. Nevertheless some immigration officials are demanding it in Latin America, so this should be borne in mind. Cholera is largely a water borne disease, either in drinking water, or via food which has been washed in contaminated water, or seafood which has been living in such water. The usual food hygiene precautions should protect the traveller from cholera; if they don't, the treatment is rapid rehydration with water and salts and sometimes the use of antibiotics.

The following vaccinations are recommended:

Yellow fever: this is a live vaccine not to be given to children under 9 months of age or persons allergic to eggs. Immunity lasts 10 years. An international certificate of yellow fever vaccination will be given and should be kept because it is sometimes asked for.

Typhoid (monovalent): one dose followed by a booster in a month's time. Immunity from this course lasts 2 to 3 years. An oral preparation is now available and a newer, more expensive vaccination against typhoid, Typhim Vi, less likely to cause post-injection symptoms.

Poliomyelitis: this is a live vaccine generally given orally and a full course consists of three doses with a booster in tropical regions every 3 to 5 years.

Tetanus: one dose should be given with a booster (vital) at 6 weeks and another at 6 months, and 10-yearly boosters thereafter are recommended.

Children should, in addition, be properly protected against diphtheria, and against pertussis (whooping cough), measles and HIB, which tend to be more

serious infections than at home. Measles, mumps and rubella vaccine is now widely available but those teenage girls who have not had rubella (German measles) should be tested and vaccinated. Consult your doctor for advice on tuberculosis inoculation: the disease is still widespread.

Infectious Hepatitis (jaundice) is endemic throughout Latin America and seems to be frequently caught by travellers. The main symptoms are pains in the stomach, lack of appetite, lassitude, and the typical yellow colour of the skin. Medically speaking there are two different types, the less serious but more common is hepatitis A, for which the best protection is the careful preparation of food, the avoidance of contaminated drinking water and scrupulous attention to toilet hygiene. Human normal immunoglobulin (gamma globulin) confers considerable protection against the disease and is particularly useful in epidemics; it should be obtained from a reputable source and is certainly useful for travellers who intend to live rough: they should have a shot before leaving and have it repeated every 6 months. The dose of gamma globulin depends on the concentration of the particular preparation used, so the manufacturer's advice should be taken. A smaller dose than usual can be given if exposure is for one or 2 months only. At last a vaccine is now in production and generally available against hepatitis A. Trials have shown it to be safe and effective. It is more expensive than gamma globulin, but the protection is better and lasts longer. Three doses over 6 months would appear to give immunity lasting up to 10 years; then boosters would be required. Havrix monodose is now available, and Junior Havrix.

The other, more serious, version is hepatitis B which is acquired usually by injections with unclean needles, blood transfusions, as a sexually transmitted disease and possibly by insect bites. This disease can be effectively prevented by a specific vaccination requiring three shots over 6 months before travelling but this is quite expensive. If you have had jaundice in the past it would be worthwhile having a blood test to see if you are immune to either of the two types because this might avoid the necessity for vaccination or gamma globulin.

Other vaccinations might be considered in the case of epidemics, eg meningitis. There is an effective vaccination against **rabies** which should be considered by all travellers, especially those going to remote areas and if there is a particular occupational risk, ie zoologists or veterinarians.

AIDS in South America is increasing in its prevalence, as in most countries, but is not wholly confined to the well known high risk sections of the population, ie homosexual men, intravenous drug abusers, prostitutes and children of infected mothers. Heterosexual transmission is now the dominant mode and so the main risk to travellers is from casual sex. The same precautions should be taken as when encountering any sexually transmitted disease. The AIDS virus (HIV) can be passed via unsterilized needles which have been previously used to inject an HIV positive patient, but the risk of this is very small indeed. It would however be sensible to check that needles have been properly sterilised or disposable needles used. If you wish to take your own disposable needles, be prepared to explain what they are for. The risk of receiving a blood transfusion with blood infected with the HIV virus is greater than from dirty needles because of the amount of fluid exchanged. Supplies of blood for transfusion should now be screened for HIV in all reputable hospitals so again the risk must be very small indeed. Catching the AIDS virus does not usually produce an illness in itself; the only way to be sure if you feel you have been put at risk is to have a blood test for HIV antibodies on your return to a place where there are reliable laboratory facilities. The test does not become positive for many weeks. Presently the higher risks are probably in Brazil and the West Indies.

Common Problems, some of which will almost certainly be encountered, are:

Heat and Cold Full acclimatization to high temperatures takes about 2 weeks and during this period it is normal to feel relatively apathetic, especially if the relative humidity is high. Drink plenty of water (up to 15 litres a day are required when working physically hard in the tropics), use salt on your food and avoid extreme exertion. Tepid showers are more cooling than hot or cold ones. Large hats do not cool you down, but do prevent sunburn. Remember that, especially in the highlands, there can be a large and sudden drop in temperature between sun and shade and between night and day, so dress accordingly. Warm jackets and woollens are essential after dark at high altitude.

Altitude   Acute mountain sickness or *soroche* can strike from about 3,000 metres upwards. It is more likely to affect those who ascend rapidly (eg by plane) and those who over-exert themselves. Teenagers are particularly prone. Past experience is not always a good guide: the author, having spent years in Peru travelling constantly between sea level and very high altitude, never suffered the slightest symptoms, then was severely affected climbing Kilimanjaro in Tanzania.

On reaching heights above 3,000 metres, heart pounding and shortness of breath, especially on exertion, are almost universal and a normal response to the lack of oxygen in the air. *Soroche* takes a few hours or days to come on and presents with headache, lassitude, dizziness, loss of appetite, nausea and vomiting. Insomnia is common and often associated with a suffocating feeling when lying in bed. Keen observers may note their breathing tends to wax and wane at night and their face tends to be puffy in the mornings—this is all part of the syndrome. The treatment is rest, pain killers (preferably not aspirin-based) for the headache and anti-sickness pills for vomiting. Oxygen may help at very high altitudes. Various local panaceas ("Coramina glucosada", "Effortil", "Micoren") have their advocates and *mate (or te) de coca* (an infusion of coca leaves, widely available) certainly alleviates some of the symptoms.

On arrival at places over 3,000 metres, a few hours' rest in a chair and avoidance of alcohol, cigarettes and heavy food will go a long way towards preventing *soroche*. Should the symptoms be severe and prolonged it is best to descend to lower altitude and re-ascend slowly or in stages. If this is impossible because of shortage of time or if the likelihood of acute mountain sickness is high then the drug Acetazolamide (Diamox) can be used as a preventative and continued during the ascent. There is good evidence of the value of this drug in the prevention of *soroche* but some people do experience funny side effects. The usual dose is 500 mg of the slow-release preparation each night, starting the night before ascending above 3,000 metres. (Detailed information is available from the Mountain Medicine Centre, c/o Dr Charles Clarke, Dept of Neurological Sciences, St Bartholomew's Hospital, 38 Little Britain, London EC1A 7BE—Ed.)

Other problems experienced at high altitude are sunburn, excessively dry air causing skin cracking, sore eyes (it may be wise to leave your contact lenses out) and stuffy noses. It is unwise to ascend to high altitude if you are pregnant, especially in the first 3 months, or if you have any history of heart, lung or blood disease, including sickle-cell.

There is a further, albeit rare, hazard due to rapid ascent to high altitude called acute pulmonary oedema. The condition can affect mountaineers; but also occurs in Andean natives returning from a period at the coast. The condition comes on quite rapidly with breathlessness, noisy breathing, cough, blueness of the lips and frothing at the mouth. Anybody developing this must be brought down as soon as possible, given oxygen and taken to hospital.

Rapid descent from high places will aggravate sinus and middle ear infections, and make bad teeth ache painfully. The same problems are sometimes experienced during descent at the end of a flight.

Despite these various hazards (mostly preventable) of high-altitude travel, many people find the environment healthier and more invigorating than at sea-level.

Intestinal Upsets Practically nobody escapes this one, so be prepared for it. Most of the time it is due to the insanitary preparation of food. Don't eat uncooked fish or vegetables, fruit with the skin on (always peel your fruit yourself), food that is exposed to flies, or salads. Tap water is rarely safe outside the major cities, especially in the rainy season, and stream water is often contaminated by communities living surprisingly high in the mountains. Filtered or bottled (make sure it is opened in your presence—Ed) water is usually available and safe. If your hotel has a central hot-water supply, this is safe to drink after cooling. Ice for drinks should be made from boiled water but rarely is, so stand your glass on the ice cubes rather than putting them in the drink. Dirty water should first be strained through a filter bag (available from camping shops) and then boiled or treated. Water in general can be rendered safe in the following ways: boil for 5 mins at sea level, longer at higher altitudes; or add 3 drops of household bleach (but not modern treated bleaches) to 1 pint of water and leave for 15 mins; or add 1 drop of tincture of iodine to 1 pint of water and leave for 3 mins. Commercial water-sterilizing tablets are available, for instance Sterotabs from Boots, England. (Also recommended are compact water filters, for instance Travel Well, Pre Mac (Kent) Ltd, Tunbridge Wells, or the Swiss-made Katadyn.)

Fresh, unpasteurized milk is a source of food poisoning germs, tuberculosis and brucellosis. This applies equally to ice-cream, yoghurt and cheese made from unpasteurized milk. Fresh milk can be rendered safe by heating it to 62°C for 30 mins followed by rapid cooling, or by boiling it. Matured or processed cheeses are safer than fresh varieties. Heat-treated (UHT), pasteurized or sterilized milk is becoming more available. Fruit juice should be pure, not diluted with water.

Diarrhoea – Diagnosis and treatment Diarrhoea is usually caused by eating food which is contaminated by food poisoning germs. Drinking water is rarely the culprit. Seawater or river water is more likely to be contaminated by sewage and so swimming in such dilute effluent can also be a cause. Infection with various organisms can give rise to diarrhoea, eg viruses, bacteria (eg Escherichia coli, probably the most common cause), protozoa (amoeba), salmonella and cholera. The diarrhoea may come on suddenly or rather slowly. It may or may nor be accompanied by vomiting or by severe abdominal pain and the passage of blood or mucus when it is called dysentery. How do you know which type you have and how to treat it?

If you can time the onset of the diarrhoea to the minute (acute) then it is probably due to a virus or a bacterium and/or the onset of dysentery. The treatment, in addition to rehydration is Ciprofloxacin 500 mgs every 12 hrs. The drug is now widely available as are various similar ones.

If the diarrhoea comes on slowly or intermittently (sub-acute) then it is more likely to be protozoal, ie caused by an amoeba or giardia and antibiotics will have little effect. These cases are best treated by a doctor, as is any outbreak of diarrhoea continuing for more than 3 days. Sometimes blood is passed in sub-acute amoebic dysentery and for this you should certainly seek medical help. If this is not available then the best treatment is probably Tinidazole (Fasigyn) 1 tablet 4 times a day for 3 days. If there are severe stomach cramps, the following drugs may help but are not very useful in the management of acute diarrhoea: Loperamide (Imodium, Arret) and Diphenoxylate with Atropine (Lomotil). They should not be given to children.

Any kind of diarrhoea whether or not accompanied by vomiting responds well to the replacement of water and salts taken as frequent small sips of some kind of rehydration solution. There are preparatory preparations consisting of sachets of powder which you dissolve in boiled water, or you can make you own by adding half a teaspoonful of salt (3.5 grams) and 4 tablespoonfuls of sugar (40 grams) to a litre of boiled water.

Thus the lynchpins of treatment for diarrhoea are rest, fluid and salt replacement, antibiotics such as Ciprofloxacin for the bacterial types and special diagnostic tests and medical treatment for the amoeba and giardia infections. Salmonella infections and cholera can be devastating diseases and it would be wise to get to a hospital as soon as possible if these were suspected. Fasting, peculiar diets and the consumption of large quantities of yoghurt have not been found useful in calming travellers diarrhoea or in rehabilitating inflamed bowels. Oral rehydration has on the other hand, especially in children, been a lifesaving technique and it should always be practised whatever other treatment you use. As there is some evidence that alcohol and milk might prolong diarrhoea they should probably be avoided during and immediately after an attack. Diarrhoea occurring day after day for long periods of time (chronic diarrhoea) is notoriously resistant to amateur attempts at treatment and again warrants proper diagnostic tests (most towns with reasonable-sized hospitals have laboratories for stool samples). There are ways of preventing travellers diarrhoea for short periods of time by taking antibiotics, but this is not a foolproof technique and should not be used other than in exceptional circumstances. Doxycycline is possibly the best drug. Some preventatives such as Enterovioform can have serious side effects if taken for long periods.

Paradoxically, constipation is also common, probably induced by dietary change, inadequate fluid intake in hot places and long bus journeys. Simple laxatives are useful in the short term (the Editor recommends Senokot) and bulky foods such as maize, beans and plenty of fruit are also useful.

Insects These can be a great nuisance, especially in the tropics, and some, of course, are carriers of serious diseases. The best way of keeping them away at night is to sleep off the ground with a mosquito net and to burn mosquito coils containing pyrethrum. The best way to use insecticide aerosol sprays is to spray the room thoroughly in all areas and then shut the door for a while, re-entering when the smell has dispersed. Tablets of insecticide are also available which, when placed on a heated mat plugged into a wall socket, fill the room with insecticide fumes in the same way. The best repellents contain di-ethyl-meta-toluamide (DET) or di-methyl phthalate—sold as "Deet", "Six-Twelve Plus", "Off", "Boots' Liquid Insect Repellent", "Autan", "Flypel". Liquid is best for arms and face (care around eyes) and aerosol spray for clothes and ankles to deter chiggers, mites and ticks. Liquid DEET suspended in water can be used to impregnate cotton clothes and mosquito nets.

If you are bitten, itching may be relieved by baking-soda baths, anti-histamine tablets (care with alcohol or driving), corticosteroid creams (great care—never use if any hint of sepsis) or by judicious scratching. Calamine lotion and cream have limited effectiveness and antihistamine creams (eg Antihisan, May & Baker) have a tendency to cause skin allergies and are, therefore, not generally recommended.

Bites which become infected (commonly in the tropics) should be treated with a local antiseptic or antibiotic cream, such as Cetrimide BP (Savlon) as should infected scratches.

Skin infestations with body lice (crabs) and scabies are, unfortunately, easy to pick up. Use gamma benzene hexachloride for lice and benzene benzoate solution for scabies. Crotamiton cream (Eurax, Geigy) alleviates itching and also kills a number of skin parasites. Malathion lotion 5% (Prioderm) kills lice effectively, but do not use the toxic agricultural insecticide Malathion.

Ticks attach themselves usually to the lower part of the body often after walking in areas where cattle have grazed. They take a while to attach themselves strongly but do swell up as they suck your blood. The important thing is to remove them gently so that they do not inject any disease into your body and if the head part of the tick is left inside the skin it may cause a nasty allergic reaction some days later, and become infected. Don't use petrol, vaseline, lighted cigarettes etc, to remove the tick but, with a pair of tweezers, remove the beast gently by gripping it at the attached (head) end and rock it out very much the way that a tooth is extracted.

Certain tropical flies which lay their eggs under the skin of sheep and cattle also occasionally do the same thing to humans with the unpleasant result that a maggot grows under the skin and this presents as a boil or pimple. The best way of removing these is to cover the boil with oil, vaseline or nail varnish so as to stop the maggot breathing, then to squeeze it out gently the next day.

Malaria in South America is theoretically confined to coastal and jungle zones but is now on the increase again. Mosquitoes do not thrive above 2,500 metres so you are safe at altitude. There are different varieties of malaria, some resistant to the normal drugs. Make local enquiries if you intend to visit possibly infected zones and use one of the following prophylactic regimes. Start taking the tablets a few days before exposure and continue to take them for 6 weeks after leaving the malarial zone. Remember to give the drugs to babies and children also. Opinion varies on the precise drugs and dosage to be used for protection; all the drugs may have some side effects, and it is important to balance the risk of catching the disease against the albeit rare side effects. The increasing complexity of the subject as the malarial parasite becomes immune to the new generation of drugs has made concentration on the physical prevention of being bitten by mosquitoes more important, ie the use of long-sleeved shirts/blouses and long trousers, repellents and nets. Clothes are now available impregnated with the insecticide Permethrin or Deltamethrin, or it is possible to impregnate the clothes yourself. Wide meshed nets impregnated with Permethrin are also becoming available, are lighter to carry and less claustrophobic to sleep in.

Prophylactic regimes:
Proguanil (Paludrine Zeneca 100 mg, 2 tablets daily) or Chloroquine (Avloclor; Zeneca, Malarivon; Wallace MFG; Nivaquine, May & Baker; Resochin, Bayer; Aralen 300 mg base (2 tablets) weekly).
   Where there is a high risk of Chloroquine-resistant falciparum malaria, take Chloroquine plus Proguanil in the above-mentioned doses.
   Some authorities are recommending alternative drugs for prophylaxis, eg Mefloquine, Doxycycline. Before going to a malarial area, seek expert advice since changes worldwide in the subject are so rapid.

You can catch malaria even when sticking to the above rules, although it is unlikely. If you do develop symptoms (high fever, shivering, headache, sometimes diarrhoea) seek medical advice immediately. If this is not possible, and there is a great likelihood of malaria, the *treatment* is:

Normal types: Chloroquine, a single dose of 4 tablets (600 mg) followed by 2 tablets (300 mg) in 6 hrs and 300 mg each day following.
Falciparum type or type in doubt: take local advice: a combination of quinine and Fansidar or Halofantrine.

If Falciparum type malaria is definitely diagnosed, it is wise to get to a good hospital as the treatment can be complex and the illness very serious.
   Pregnant women are particularly prone to malaria and should stick to Proguanil as a prophylactic. Chloroquine may cause eye damage if taken over a very long period. The safety of Fansidar has been questioned and, at the time of writing, it is not recommended for prophylaxis.

Chagas' Disease (South American Trypanosomiasis) is a chronic disease, very rarely caught by travellers, but very difficult to treat. It is transmitted by the simultaneous biting and excreting of the Reduvid bug (Triatoma or Rhodnius), also known as the *vinchuca*, or *barbeiro*. Somewhat resembling a small cockroach (coloured black and red, or black and yellow), this nocturnal "kissing bug" lives in poor adobe houses with dirt floors often frequented by oppossums. If you cannot avoid such accommodation, sleep off the floor with a candle lit, use a mosquito net, keep as much of your skin covered as possible and wash any bites thoroughly with soap and water, or a disinfectant.

Sunburn The burning power of the tropical sun, especially at high altitude, is phenomenal. Always wear a wide-brimmed hat and use some form of suncream lotion on untanned skin. Normal temperate-zone suntan lotions (protection factor up to 7) are not much good; you need to use the types designed specifically for the tropics, or for mountaineers or skiers, with protection factors up to 15. These are often not available in South America; a reasonable substitute is zinc oxide ointment. Glare from the sun can cause conjunctivitis, so wear sunglasses. especially on tropical beaches, where high protection-factor sunscreen cream should also be used.

Snakebite If you are unlucky enough to be bitten by a venomous snake, spider, scorpion or sea creature, try (within limits) to catch the animal for identification. The reactions to be expected are: fright, swelling, pain and bruising around the bite, soreness of the regional lymph glands, nausea, vomiting and fever. If any of the following symptoms supervene, get the victim to a doctor without delay: numbness and tingling of the face, muscular spasms, convulsion, shortness of breath and haemorrhage. The tiny coral snake, with red, black and white bands, is the most dangerous, but is very timid.

Commercial snakebite and scorpion kits are available, but only useful for the specific type of snake or scorpion for which they are designed. The serum has to be given intravenously so is not much good unless you have had some practice at making injections into veins. If the bite is on a limb, immobilize the limb and apply a tight bandage between the bite and the body, releasing it for 90 seconds every 15 mins. Reassurance of the bitten person is very important because death from snakebite is very rare. Do not slash the bite area and try to suck out the poison because this sort of heroism does more harm than good. Hospitals usually hold stocks of snake bite serum. Best precaution: don't walk in snake territory with bare feet or sandals—wear proper shoes or boots.

Spiders and Scorpions These may be found in the more basic hotels in the Andean countries. If bitten by *Latrodectus* or *Loxosceles* spiders, or stung by scorpions, rest and take plenty of fluids, and call a doctor. Precaution: keep beds away from the walls, and look inside shoes in morning.

Other Afflictions Remember that **rabies** is endemic throughout Latin America so avoid dogs that are behaving strangely, and cover your toes at night to foil the vampire bats, which also carry the disease. If you are bitten by a domestic or wild animal, don't leave things to chance. Scrub the wound with soap and water and/or disinfectant, try to have the animal captured (within limits) or at least determine its ownership where possible and seek medical assistance at once. The course of treatment depends on whether you have already been satisfactorily vaccinated against rabies. If you have (and this is worthwhile if you are spending lengths of time in developing countries) then some further doses of vaccine are all that is required. Human diploid cell vaccine is the best, but expensive: other, older kinds of vaccine such as that derived from duck embryos may be the only types available. These are effective, much cheaper and interchangeable generally with the human derived types. If not already vaccinated then anti-rabies serum (immunoglobulin) may be required in addition. It is wise to finish the course of treatment whether the animal survives or not.

Dengue fever has made its appearance in southern Mexico and the lower-lying parts of Central America; also in Brazil. No treatment: you must just avoid mosquito bites.

Typhus can still occur, carried by ticks. There is usually a reaction at the site of the bite and a fever: seek medical advice.

Intestinal worms are common, and the more serious ones such as **hookworm** can be contracted from walking barefoot on infested earth or beaches. Various other tropical diseases can be caught in jungle areas, usually transmitted by biting insects; they are often related to African diseases and were probably introduced by the slave trade from Africa. **Onchocerciasis** (river-blindness), carried by blackflies, is found in parts of Mexico and Venezuela. Cutaneous **leishmaniasis** (Espundia) is carried by sandflies and causes a sore that won't heal; wearing long trousers and long-sleeved shirts in infectious areas helps to avoid the fly. Epidemics of meningitis occur from time to time. Be careful about swimming in piranha- (or caribe-) infested rivers. It is a good idea not to swim naked: the candiru fish can follow urine currents and become lodged in body orifices; swimwear offers some protection.

Dangerous animals Apart from mosquitoes, the most dangerous animals are men, be they bandits or behind steering wheels. Think carefully about violent confrontations and wear a seatbelt, if you are lucky enough to have one available to you.

Prickly heat, a very common, intensely itchy rash, is avoided by frequent washing and by wearing loose clothing. Cured by allowing skin to dry off through use of powder, and spending 2 nights in an air-conditioned hotel! **Athlete's foot** and other fungal skin infections are best treated with Tinaderm or Canestan.

Psychological disorders First time exposure to countries where sections of the population live in extreme poverty or squalor and may even be starving can cause odd psychological reactions in visitors. So can the exceptional curiosity extended to visitors, especially women. Simply be prepared for this and try not to over-react.

When you return home Remember to take your anti-malarial tablets for 6 weeks. If you have had attacks of diarrhoea, it is worth having a stool specimen tested in case you have picked up amoebic dysentery. If you have been living rough, a blood test may be worthwhile to detect worms and other parasites. If you have been exposed to bilharzia by swimming in lakes, etc, check by means of a blood test when you get home, but leave it for 6 weeks because the test is slow to become positive. Report any untoward symptoms to your doctor and tell the doctor exactly where you have been and, if you know, what is the likelihood of diseases to which you were exposed.

Basic supplies The following items you may find useful to take with you from home: sunglasses (if you use clip-on sunglasses, take a spare pair – Ed), ear plugs, suntan cream, insect repellent, flea powder, mosquito net, coils or tablets, tampons, condoms, contraceptives, water sterilizing tablets, anti-malaria tablets, anti-infective ointment, dusting powder for feet, travel sickness pills, antacid tablets, anti-diarrhoea tablets, sachets of rehydration salts and a first aid kit.

Health packs containing sterile syringes, needles, gloves, etc, are available for travellers from various sources (eg Schiphol airport, Amsterdam); one such is made by Safa of Liverpool, UK. Emergency dental kits are available at leading retail outlets and dentists, made by Dental Save, 144 High St, Nailsea, Avon, BS19 1AP, UK, T 01275-810291, F 01275-858112, also available from Fiona Mahon Associates, PO Box 204, Hayes, Middx, UB4 9HN, UK, T 0181-842 3141, F 0181-845 7370.

Further information on health risks abroad, vaccinations, etc, may be available from a local travel clinic. If you wish to take specific drugs with you such as antibiotics, these are best prescribed by your own doctor. Beware, however, that not all doctors can be experts on the health problems of tropical countries. More detailed or more up-to-date information than local doctors can provide are available from various sources.

In the UK there are hospital departments specializing in tropical diseases in London, Liverpool, Birmingham and Glasgow and the Malaria Reference Laboratory at the London School of Hygiene and Tropical Medicine provides free advice about malaria, T 0891-600-350. In the USA the local public health services can give such information and information is available centrally from the Centres for Disease Control in Atlanta, T (404) 332 4559.

There are in addition computerized databases which can be accessed for a specific destination, up to the minute information. In the UK there is MASTA (Medical Advisory Service to Travellers Abroad), T 0171-631 4408, Tx 895 3474, F 0171-436 5389 and Travax (Glasgow, T 0141-946 7120, extension 247).

Further information on medical problems overseas can be obtained from the book by Richard Dawood (Editor) – Travellers Health, How to Stay Healthy Abroad, Oxford University Press, 1992, £7.99. We strongly recommend this revised and updated edition, especially to the intrepid traveller heading for the more out of the way places. General advice is also available in the UK in "Health Advice for Travellers" published jointly by the Department of Health and the Central Office of Information available free from your UK Travel Agent.

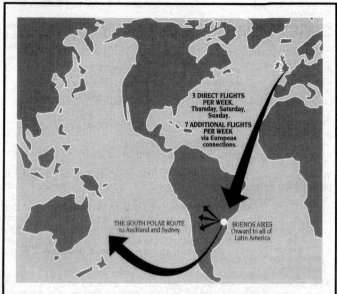

ARGENTINA

INTRODUCTION

ARGENTINA is the second largest country in area in South America, equivalent to 29% of that of Europe. It stretches 3,460 km from N to S and 1,580 km from E to W. Apart from the estuary of the Río de la Plata its coast line is 2,575 km long. Its W frontier runs along the crest of the high Andes, a formidable barrier between it and Chile. Its neighbours to the N are Bolivia and Paraguay and (in the NE) Brazil. To the E is Uruguay. Its far S limit is the Beagle Channel. The area figures exclude the sector of Antarctica claimed by Argentina.

Argentina is enormously varied both in its types of land and its climates. Geographers usually recognize four main physical areas: the Andes, the North and Mesopotamia, the Pampas, and Patagonia.

The first division, the Andes, includes the whole length of the Cordilleras, low and deeply glaciated in the Patagonian S, high and dry in the prolongation into NW Argentina of the Bolivian Altiplano, the high plateau. S of this is the very

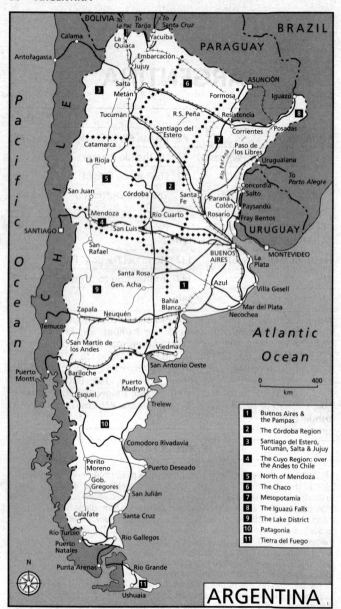

1 Buenos Aires & the Pampas
2 The Córdoba Region
3 Santiago del Estero, Tucumán, Salta & Jujuy
4 The Cuyo Region: over the Andes to Chile
5 North of Mendoza
6 The Chaco
7 Mesopotamia
8 The Iguazú Falls
9 The Lake District
10 Patagonia
11 Tierra del Fuego

ARGENTINA

parched desert and mountain region S of Tucumán and W of Córdoba. The oases strung along the eastern foot of the Andes—Jujuy, Salta, Tucumán, Catamarca, La Rioja, San Juan, Mendoza and the small town of San Rafael—were the first places to be colonized by the Spaniards.

The second division, the North and Mesopotamia, contains the vast forested plains of the Chaco, and the floodplain and gently rolling land known as the Argentine Mesopotamia lying between the rivers Paraná and Uruguay. The Province of Misiones in the NE is actually on the great Paraná plateau. These plains cover 582,750 sq km.

The third division, the pampa, takes up the heart of the land. These vast, rich plains lie S of the Chaco, E of the Andes, W of the Atlantic and the Río Paraná and N of the Río Colorado. The eastern part, which receives more rain, is usually called the Humid Pampa, and the western part the Dry Pampa. The Pampas stretch for hundreds of km in almost unrelieved flatness, covering some 650,000 sq km.

The final division is Patagonia, the area S of the Río Colorado—a land of arid, wind-swept plateaux cut across by ravines. In the deep S the wind is wilder and more continuous. There is no real summer, but to compensate for this the winters are rarely severe. Patagonia has about 780,000 sq km.

Three-quarters of Argentina's territory cannot be cultivated without irrigation but only 400,000 ha are artificially watered.

Climate ranges from sub-tropical in the N to cold temperate in Tierra del Fuego, but is temperate and quite healthy in the densely populated central zone. From mid-Dec to the end of Feb Buenos Aires can be oppressively hot and humid, with temperatures ranging from 27°C (80°F) to 35°C (95°F) and an average humidity of 70%. Beware of the high pollen count in the pollinating season if you have allergy problems. The winter months of Jun, Jul and Aug are best for a business visit, though spring weather in Buenos Aires is often very pleasant indeed. The skiing season in Bariloche ends by Aug 30. Corrientes and Misiones provinces are wet in Aug and especially Sep.

History When, in the early 16th century, the first Europeans came to Argentina, the native Indians had already halted the Inca drive S from Peru through Bolivia into N Argentina. The Spaniard Juan de Solís landed on the shores of the Plata estuary in 1516, but he was killed and the expedition failed. Magellan touched at the estuary four years later, but turned S to make his way into the Pacific. In 1527 both Sebastian Cabot and his rival Diego García sailed into the estuary and up the Paraná and the Paraguay. They formed a small settlement, Sancti Spiritus, at the junction of the Caraña and Coronda rivers near their confluence with the Paraná, but it was wiped out by the Indians about two years later and Cabot and García returned to Spain. Eight years later, in 1535, Pedro de Mendoza, with a large force well supplied with equipment and horses, founded a settlement at Buenos Aires. The natives soon made it too difficult for him; the settlement was abandoned and Mendoza returned home, but not before sending Juan de Ayolas with a small force up the Paraná. Ayolas set off for Peru, already conquered by Pizarro, leaving Irala in charge. It is not known for certain what happened to Ayolas, but in 1537 Irala and his men settled at Asunción, in Paraguay, where the natives were friendly. There were no further expeditions from Spain to colonize what is now called Argentina, and it was not until 1573 that the settlement at Asunción sent forces S to establish Santa Fe and not until 11 June 1580 that Juan de Garay refounded the settlement at Buenos Aires. It was only under his successor, Hernando Arias de Saavedra (1592-1614), that the new colony became secure.

In the meantime there had been successful expeditions into Argentina both from Peru and Chile—the first, from Peru, as early as 1543. These expeditions led, in the latter half of the 16th century, to the foundation at the eastern foot of the Andes of the oldest towns in Argentina: Santiago del Estero, Tucumán, Córdoba,

Salta, La Rioja and Jujuy by Spaniards from Peru following the old Inca road, and San Juan, Mendoza, and San Luis by those from Chile, across the Andes. Peru was given the viceroyalty over all the Spanish possessions in South America in 1543.

For 270 years after its foundation Buenos Aires was of little importance. Spanish stress was upon Lima, and Lima did not send its treasures home by way of Buenos Aires but through Panama and the Caribbean. Buenos Aires was not allowed by Spain to take part in any overseas trade until 1778; its population then was only 24,203. It was merely a military outpost for Spain to confront the Portuguese outpost at Colonia, across the estuary, and lived, in the main, by smuggling. Even when in 1776 the Viceroyalty of Río de la Plata was formed, it made little difference to Buenos Aires as a capital, for its control of the *cabildos* (town councils) in distant towns was very tenuous. When the British, following Spain's alliance with Napoleon, attacked Buenos Aires in 1806 and again in 1807 before being repulsed by local levies, there was no inkling of its future potential. But the defeat of these attacks, known as the Reconquista, had one important result: a great increase in the confidence of the *porteños* (the name given to those born in Buenos Aires) to deal with all comers, including the mother-country, whose restrictions were increasingly unpopular. On 25 May 1810, the *cabildo* of Buenos Aires deposed the viceroy and announced that it was governing henceforth on behalf of King Ferdinand VII, then a captive of Napoleon. Six years later, when Buenos Aires was threatened by invasion from Peru and blockaded by a Spanish fleet in the River Plate, a national congress held at Tucumán declared independence on 9 July 1816. The declaration was given reality by the genius and devotion of José de San Martín, who boldly marched an Argentine army across the Andes to free Chile, and (with the help of Lord Cochrane, commander of the Chilean Navy), embarked his forces for Peru, where he captured Lima, the first step in the liberation of Peru.

When San Martín returned home, it was to find the country rent by conflict between the central government and the provinces. Disillusioned, he retired to France. The internal conflict was to last a long time. On the one hand stood the Unitarist party, bent on central control; on the other the Federalist party, insisting on local autonomy. The latter had for members the great *caudillos*, the large landowners backed by the *gauchos*, suspicious of the cities. One of their leaders, Juan Manuel de Rosas, took control of the country in 1829. During his second term as Governor of Buenos Aires he asked for and was given extraordinary powers. The result was a 17-year reign of terror. His rule was an international scandal, and when he began a blockade of Asunción in 1845, Britain and France promptly countered with a three-year blockade of Buenos Aires. But in 1851 Justo José de Urquiza, Governor of Entre Ríos, one of his old henchmen, organized a triple *entente* of Brazil, Uruguay, and the Argentine opposition to overthrow him. He was defeated in 1852 at Caseros, a few km from Buenos Aires, and fled to England, where he farmed quietly for 25 years, dying at Southampton.

Rosas had started his career as a Federalist; once in power he was a Unitarist. His downfall meant the triumph of federalism. In 1853 a federal system was finally incorporated in the constitution, but the old quarrel had not been solved. In 1859, when the constitution was ratified, the capital moved to Paraná, the province of Buenos Aires seceded, and Buenos Aires, under Bartolomé Mitre, was defeated by the federal forces under Urquiza. Two years later Buenos Aires again fought the country, and this time it won. Once again it became the seat of the federal government, with Bartolomé Mitre as its first constitutional president. (It was during his term that the Triple Alliance of Argentina, Brazil, and Uruguay defeated Francisco Solano López of Paraguay.) There was another political flare-up of the old quarrel in 1880, ending in the humiliation of Buenos Aires, which then ceased to be the capital of its province; a new provincial capital was founded at La Plata, 56 km to the SE. At that time a young colonel, Julio A Roca, was finally subduing all the Indian tribes of the pampas and the South. This was an event which was to make possible the final supremacy of Buenos Aires over all rivals.

Politically Argentina was a constitutional republic with a very restricted suffrage up to the passage in 1912 of the Sáenz Peña law, which established universal manhood suffrage. From 1916 to 1930 the Unión Cívica Radical (founded in 1890) held power, under the leadership of Hipólito Yrigoyen and Marcelo T de Alvear, but lost it to the military uprising of 1930. Though seriously affected by the world depression of the 1930s, Argentina's rich soil and educated population had made it one of the ten wealthiest countries in the world, but this wealth was most unevenly distributed, and the political methods followed by the conservatives and their military associates in the 1930s denied the middle and working classes any effective share in their own country's wealth and government. In 1943 came another military coup, which had a distinctly fascist tinge; in 1946 emerged, as President, Gen Juan Domingo Perón, who based his power on an alliance between the army and labour; his contacts with labour were greatly assisted by his charismatic wife Eva (since commemorated in the rock-opera "Evita") and the living conditions of the workers were greatly improved—but at the expense of the economic state of the country. By the time a military coup unseated Perón in 1955 serious harm had been done; ever since, Argentina has been a politically divided society and has been struggling to recover its lost economic health.

An uneasy alternation of three military and two constitutional regimes followed between 1955 and 1973. Perón lived in exile in Madrid and his supporters were excluded from power by the armed forces. The military seized power in 1966 but were discredited by a deteriorating economy and the emergence of several guerrilla groups in a climate of tension and violence. Gen Perón again became President in Oct 1973, but died on 1 July 1974, leaving the Presidency to his widow, Vice-President María Estela Martínez de Perón. A chaotic political situation, of which a high level of violence (including guerrilla warfare) was a regrettable feature, followed his death; by Mar 1976 conditions in the country, both of violence and of economic crisis, had deteriorated to the point when the military felt again obliged to intervene. Sra de Perón was deposed from the Presidency by a military junta, led by Gen Jorge Videla, and guerrilla warfare and the other features of dissidence were repressed with great brutality: about 9,000 people (according to official statistics; human rights organizations believe the total at least doubles this) disappeared without trace during the so-called 'dirty war'. General Videla was appointed President in 1978 by the military leaders, for a three-year term. His nominated successor, Gen Roberto Viola took over as President for three years in Mar, 1981 but was replaced by Gen Leopoldo Galtieri in Dec 1981. The latter was in turn replaced in Jun 1982 by Gen (ret) Reynaldo Bignone.

Confidence in the military ebbed when their economic policies began to go sour in 1980. In 1982-83 pressure for a democratic restoration grew apace particularly after the South Atlantic conflict with Great Britain in 1982. General elections on 30 October 1983 were won by the Unión Cívica Radical (UCR), with Dr Raúl Alfonsín, its candidate, elected as president. During 1985 Generals Videla, Viola and Galtieri were sentenced to long terms of imprisonment for their parts in the 'dirty war', which caused friction between the Government and the armed forces. President Alfonsín's popularity gradually waned as his Government failed to solve economic problems. When Alfonsín was defeated by Dr Carlos Saúl Menem of the Partido Justicialista (Peronists) in May 1989, Alfonsín stepped down early because of economic instability. Strained relations between the Peronist Government and the military led to several rebellions, which Pres Menem attempted to appease by pardoning the imprisoned generals. His popularity among civilians declined, but in 1991-92 the Economy Minister, Domingo Cavallo, succeeded in restoring confidence in the economy and the Government as a whole. After triumphing in Oct 1993 congressional elections at the expense of the UCR, the Peronists themselves lost some ground in April 1994 elections to a constituent assembly. The party to gain most was Frente Grande, a broad coalition of left wing groups and disaffected Peronists, who captured the votes, especially in Buenos Aires, of those dissatisfied with conventional politics. Among the causes of the lost confidence were unrestrained corruption and a pact in Dec 1993 between Menem and Alfonsín pledging UCR support for constitutional changes which included re-election of the president for a second term of 4 years.

By the 1995 elections, the majority of the electorate favoured stability over constitutional concerns and returned Pres Menem, without recourse to a second ballot. The Peronists also increased their majority in congress. Menem's chief priority was to reduce unemployment, although this would be difficult given the government's insistence that the provinces restructure their finances and reduce inefficiencies. Despite the country's overall economic improvement, most provinces have not enjoyed prosperity. In early 1995, a series of revelations by army personnel concerning the disappearance of thousands of Argentines in the 1970s and 1980s reopened the wounds of the "dirty war", despite official attempts to suppress discussion of the subject.

The Transformation of the Pampas The pampas, the economic heart of the country, extend fanwise from Buenos Aires for a distance of between 550 and 650 km. Apart from three groups of *sierras* or low hills near Córdoba, Tandil and Bahía Blanca, the surface seems an endless flat monotony, relieved occasionally, in the SW, by sand dunes. There are few rivers. Drinking water is pumped to the surface from a depth of from 30 to 150m by the windpumps which are such a prominent feature of the landscape. There are no trees other than those that have been planted, except in the *monte* of the W. But there is, in most years, ample rainfall. It is greatest at Rosario, where it is about 1,020 mm, and evenly distributed throughout the year. The further S from Rosario, the less the rain. At Buenos Aires it is about 940 mm; it drops to 535 at Bahía Blanca, and is only 400 along the boundary of the Humid Pampa. The further from Rosario, too, the more the rainfall is concentrated during the summer. Over the whole of the pampa the summers are hot, the winters mild, but there is a large climatic difference between various regions: at Rosario the growing season between frosts is about 300 days; at Bahía Blanca it falls to 145 days.

When the Spanish arrived in Argentina the pampas were an area of tall coarse grasses. The cattle and horses they brought with them were soon to roam wild and in time transformed the Indian's way of life. The only part of the pampa occupied by the settlers was the so-called Rim, between the Río Salado, S of the capital, and the Paraná-Plata rivers. Here, in large *estancias*, cattle, horses and mules in great herds roamed the open range. There was a line of forts along the Río Salado: a not very effective protection against marauding Indians. The Spaniards had also brought European grasses with them; these soon supplanted the coarse native grasses, and formed a green carpet surface which stopped abruptly at the Río Salado.

The *estancia* owners and their dependent *gauchos* were in no sense an agricultural people, but towards the end of the 18th century, tenants—to the great contempt of both *estanciero* and *gaucho*—began to plant wheat in the valleys along the Paraná-Plata shore. The fall of Rosas in 1852, and the constitution of 1853, made it possible for Argentina to take a leap forward, but it must be remembered that its civilized population at that time was only 1,200,000.

The rapidly rising population of Europe during the latter half of the 19th century and the consequent demand for cheap food was the spur that impelled Argentina (as it did the United States and Canada) to occupy its grasslands and take to agriculture. This was made possible by the new techniques already developed: agricultural machinery, barbed wire, well-drilling machines and windpumps, roads and railways, and ocean-going steamships. Roads were, and are, a difficulty in the pampa; the soil lacks gravel or stones to surface the roads, and dirt roads become a quagmire in wet weather and a fume of dust in the dry. Railways, on the other hand, were simple and cheap to build. The system grew as need arose and capital (mostly from Britain) became available. The lines in the pampa radiate out fanwise (with intricate inter-communication) from the ports of Buenos Aires, Rosario, Santa Fe and Bahía Blanca. Argentina, unlike most other countries, had extensive railways before a road system was built.

The occupation of the pampa was finally achieved by a war against the Indians in 1878-83 which virtually exterminated them. Many of the officers were given gifts of land of more than 40,000 ha each. The pampa had passed into private hands on the old traditional pattern of large estates.

Cattle products—hides, tallow, and salt beef—had been the mainstay of Argentine overseas trade during the whole of the colonial period. In the early 19th century wool challenged the supremacy of cattle. The occupation of the grasslands did not, at first, alter the complexion of the foreign trade; it merely increased its volume. In 1877, however, the first ship with refrigeration chambers made it possible to send frozen beef to England, but the meat of the scrub cattle was too strong for English taste. As a result, pedigree bulls were imported from England and the upgrading of the herds began. The same process was applied to sheep. But the improved herds could only flourish where there were no ticks—prevalent in the N—and throve best where forage crops were available. Argentina adopted as its main forage crop alfalfa (lucerne), a plant like clover which proved extremely suitable on the pampa. It has since been supplemented with barley, oats, rye, maize, sorghum and oilseeds.

A striking thing about the Pampas is the bird life. Flamingoes rise in a pink and white cloud, heron egrets gleam white against the blue sky, pink spoonbills dig in the mud and rheas stalk in the distance. Most fascinating are the oven birds, the *horneros*, which build oven-shaped nests six times as big as themselves on the top of telegraph and fence posts.

The transformation of the pampa has had two profound effects. Because its newly-created riches flowed out and its needs flowed in mainly through Buenos Aires, that port grew from comparative insignificance into one of the great cities in the world. Also, the transformation of the Humid Pampa led, through immigration, to a vast predominance of the European strain. The first immigrants settled NW of Santa Fe in 1856. Between 1857 and 1930 total immigration was over six million, almost all from Europe. The process has continued; Italians have been by far the most numerous, followed by Spaniards, and then, far behind, groups of other Europeans and Latin Americans. British and North Americans normally came as stockbreeders, technicians and business executives.

The Argentine People In the Federal Capital and Province of Buenos Aires, where almost 40% of the population lives, the people are almost exclusively of European origin. In the far northern provinces, colonized from neighbouring countries, at least half the people are *mestizos* though they form about 15% of the population of the whole country. It is estimated that 12.8% are foreign born and generally of European origin, though there are also important communities of Syrians, Lebanese, Armenians, Japanese and, most recently, Koreans.

Not surprisingly, the traditional image of the Argentine is that of the *gaucho*; *gauchismo* has been a powerful influence in literature, sociology and folklore, and is celebrated each year in the week before the 'Day of Tradition', 10 Nov.

In the highlands of the NW, in the Chaco, Misiones and in the SW, there are still some indigenous groups. The exact total of the Indian population is unknown; estimates vary from 100,000 to 300,000. As was noted above, the pampas Indians were virtually exterminated in the 19th century; the Indians of Tierra del Fuego are extinct. Surviving peoples include the Wichi and others in Salta and Jujuy provinces (see p 108), various Chaco Indians (see p 147) and tribes related to the Mapuche and Tehuelche nations in the SW. A number of organizations represent indigenous interests, but any legislation, under federal law, has to be enacted separately by each province.

The Economy Argentina is one of the more highly developed countries of the region and is potentially one of the richest farming countries in the world. The importance of agriculture and livestock production is shown by the fact that this sector still provides over 50% of export earnings with sales of cereals, oilseeds, meat and processed foodstuffs. Although Argentina has lost its dominant position as an exporter of cereals and beef, it has great resources in relation to its population. Per capita income is therefore relatively high. Agriculture accounts for 6% of gdp. There has been a shift from livestock to crop production since the 1960s in line with changes in relative prices and the introduction of new technology which has sharply increased crop yields. Cereals account for a substantial proportion of crop production although the area sown to oilseeds has risen steeply, now exceeding that of wheat, and producing about 15 million tonnes of soyabeans and sunflower seed a year. Livestock, faced with stiff competition abroad from other exporting countries, has declined in importance. The cattle stock fell from around 57 million head in the late 1970s to 50m in 1993.

The manufacturing sector has developed behind high import protection barriers; it accounts for 22% of gdp and benefits from increased agricultural activity, so that natural resource-based and labour-intensive industries such as food processing, textiles and clothing are reasonably dynamic. Food processing and beverages account for a quarter of manufacturing output and a fifth of industrial employment. Investment in manufacturing remained low in the 1980s and early 1990s, first because of hyperinflation depressing domestic demand, then during the recession that followed the introduction of Menem's market reforms. In 1994, many companies restructured in readiness for the full implementation of the Mercosur common market in 1995 and to cope with the elimination of government support. The financial crisis that hit Argentina as a result of Mexico's late-1994 economic crisis led to reduced expectations for manufacturers through 1995. A shortage of credit, lower domestic demand and the knock-on effect of Brazil's economic problems all heralded weaker performance.

Energy development has been a priority with emphasis on hydro and nuclear power sources to reduce dependence upon thermal power. Argentina is virtually self-sufficient in oil; production in 1993 was 210 million barrels. There is an exportable surplus of natural gas and petroleum derivatives. The country's hydroelectric potential lies on the rivers Paraná and Uruguay in the N and on the network of rivers in Río Negro and Neuquén provinces. In 1992 hydroelectricity accounted for 34.8% of power generation, fossil fuels 52.6%, with nuclear power plants supplying the balance. Hydroelectricity's share was set to grow substantially after 1993 with Yacyretá, on the Paraná, and Piedra del Aguila, in the Andes, coming on stream. This would also reduce the incidence of power cuts.

Extremely high rates of inflation were recorded in the 1980s through a combination of large fiscal deficits, monetary expansion and a high velocity of circulation. These were difficult to contain because of structural imbalances in the economy caused by inadequate levels of investment and inefficiencies and corruption in both the public and private sectors. The Government introduced several stabilization programmes, the first of which was the Austral Plan, named after the new currency, but none was successful. The economic crisis deepened as management of public finances deteriorated, leading to hyperinflation and a sharp contraction in output and investment as confidence was eroded and the economy became increasingly dollarized. The Government which took office in July 1989, attempted to curb hyperinflation through a wide range of measures. Structural economic reform initially brought further recession, unemployment and declining living standards. After 1993, however, investment began to recover. Inflation fell from 171.7% in 1991 to 10.6% in 1993 and 3.9% in 1994, while gdp growth in excess of 6% was recorded in both 1993 and 1994 (8.9% in 1991, 8.7% in 1992). Much of the increase in economic growth and confidence was attributed to a currency convertibility law, which required the domestic currency to be fully backed by US dollars, so that monetary expansion was limited by the growth in international reserves. The government insisted that the convertibility law would not be modified in the wake of the Mexican financial crisis of Dec 1994. Despite capital flight of about US$8.5bn which caused severe problems in the banking system, high levels of domestic debt, rising unemployment to 12% of the workforce and the threat of recession, devaluation of the peso was ruled out. Instead, austerity measures were introduced and substantial aid was sought from multilateral institutions to help restructure the financial sector.

The external debt rose sharply in the 1980s to US$65bn in 1991, making Argentina the third largest debtor in the region. Debt rescheduling agreements negotiated with commercial bank creditors, new loans and IMF financing facilities, and World Bank loans all collapsed as the Government failed to implement fully its policy commitments. By the early 1990s, Argentina was seriously in arrears to commercial banks although arrears to multilateral agencies had been cleared. The Government sought to reduce its commercial bank commitments by cancelling debt through privatization. Despite an early failure of the sale of Aerolíneas Argentinas in 1992, the government pressed ahead with the sale of state companies. The largest, Yacimientos Petrolíferos Fiscales (YPF, the state oil company), was privatized in 1993. In 1992 the Government started negotiations to restructure its commercial bank debt by securitizing it into bonds, following the Mexican model of debt or debt service reduction. A successful conclusion was

Argentina : fact file

Geographic

Land area	2,780,400 sq km
forested	21.6%
pastures	51.9%
cultivated	9.9%

Demographic

Population (1994)	33,880,000
annual growth rate (1989-94)	1.3%
urban	86.9%
rural	13.1%
density	12.2 per sq km
Religious affiliation	
Roman Catholic	91.6%
Birth rate per 1,000 (1994)	19.6
	(world av 26.0)

Education and Health

Life expectancy at birth,	
male	68 years
female	74 years
Infant mortality rate	
per 1,000 live births (1992)	34.0
Physicians (1988)	1 per 326 persons
Hospital beds	1 per 205 persons
Calorie intake as %	
of FAO requirement	131%
Population age 25 and over	
with no formal schooling	5.7%
Literate males (over 15)	95.5%
Literate females (over 15)	95.1%

Economic

GNP (1993)	US$244,091mn
GNP per capita	US$7,290
Public external debt (1992)	
	US$46,835mn
Tourism receipts (1992)	US$3,090mn
Inflation (annual av 1990-93)	30.3%
Radio	1 per 1.6 persons
Television	1 per 4.7 persons
Telephone	1 per 7.0 persons

Employment

Population economically active (1990)	
	12,305,346
Unemployment rate (1989)	7.3%
% of labour force in	
agriculture	12.0
mining	0.5
manufacturing	19.9
construction	10.1
Military forces	69,800

Source *Encyclopaedia Britannica*

reached in April 1993, signalling Argentina's reentry into the international financial community.

Government The country's official name is República Argentina (RA), the Argentine Republic. The form of government has traditionally been a representative, republican federal system. Of the two legislative houses, the Senate has 46 seats, and the Chamber of Deputies 254. By the 1853 Constitution (amended in 1880) the country is divided into a Federal Capital (the city of Buenos Aires) and 23 Provinces. Each Province has its own Governor, Senate and Chamber of Deputies. The municipal government of the Federal Capital is exercised by a Mayor who is directly elected. The Constitution grants the city autonomous rule.

Communications Argentina has only four good seaports: Buenos Aires, La Plata, Rosario and Bahía Blanca. Necochea/Quequén is also a good port, but the swell can sometimes prevent ships entering or sailing for days. The two great rivers flowing southward into the Plata, the Paraná and the Uruguay, are not very reliable shipping routes. The Colorado and the Negro rivers in northern Patagonia are navigable by small vessels only. Internal air services are highly developed.

Most of Argentina is served by about 214,613 km of road, but only 28% are paved and a further 17% improved. The 34,183 km (1987) of railway line, owned mostly by British companies until they were taken over by the State in 1948, used to carry less than 10% of passengers and freight, until privatization in the early 1990s caused an even greater reduction in rail's share of national transportation.

Music and Dance Buenos Aires contains a third of the country's population and its music is the Tango. Indeed to the outside world there is no other Argentine music. Although also sung and played, the Tango was born as a dance just before the turn of the 20th century. The exact moment of the birth was not recorded by any contemporary observer and continues to be a matter of debate, though the roots can be traced. The name "Tango" predates the dance and was given to the carnivals (and dances) of the black inhabitants of the Río de la Plata in the early l9th century. Elements of the black tradition were taken over by whites, as the black population declined into insignificance. However, the name "Tango Americano" was also given to the Habanera (a Cuban descendent of the English Country Dance) which became the rage in Spain and bounced back into the Río de la Plata in the middle of the 19th centry, not only as a fashionable dance, together with the polka, mazurka, waltz and cuadrille, but also as a song form in the very popular "Zarzuelas", or Spanish operettas. However the Habanera led not a double, but a triple life, by also infiltrating the lowest levels of society directly from Cuba via sailors who arrived in the ports of Montevideo and Buenos Aires. Here it encountered the Milonga, originally a Gaucho song style, but by 1880 a dance, especially popular with the so-called "Compadritos" and "Orilleros", who frequented the port area and its brothels, whence the Argentine Tango emerged around the turn of the century to dazzle the populace with its brilliant, personalized footwork, which could not be accomplished without the partners staying glued together. As a dance it became the rage and, as the infant recording industry grew by leaps and bounds, it also became popular as a song and an instrumental genre, with the original violins and flutes being eclipsed by the *bandoneón* button accordion, then being imported from Germany. In 1911 the new dance took Paris by storm and returned triumphant to Buenos Aires. It achieved both respectability and notoriety, becoming a global phenomenon after the First World War. The golden voice of the renowned Carlos Gardel soon gave a wholly new dimension to the music of the Tango until his death in 1935. After losing some popularity in Argentina, it came to the forefront again in the 1940s (1920-50 is considered the real golden age). Its resurgence was assisted by Perón's decree that 50% of all music played on the radio must be Argentine, only to suffer a second, much more serious decline in the face of rock music over the past two decades. To see the Tango and Milonga danced in Buenos Aires today, you need to visit one of the clubs or *confiterías* where it is specially featured, see Buenos Aires **Nightclubs and Folklore.** Apart from Carlos Gardel, other great names connected with the Tango are Francisco Canaro (Uruguayan), Osvaldo Pugliese and Astor Piazzolla, who has modernized it by fusion with jazz styles (*nuevo tango*). Whilst the majority of Argentine young people will agree that the Tango represents the soul of Buenos Aires, don't expect them to dance it or listen to it. They are more likely to be interested in the country's indigenous rock music.

If the Tango represents the soul of Buenos Aires, this is not the case in the rest of the country. The provinces have a very rich and attractive heritage of folk dances, mainly for couples, with arms held out and fingers clicked or handkerchiefs waved, with the "Paso Valseado" as the basic step. Descended from the Zamacueca, and therefore a cousin of the Chilean Cueca and Peruvian Marinera, is the slow and stately Zamba, where the handkerchief is used to greatest effect. Equally popular throughout most of the country are the faster Gato, Chacarera and Escondido. These were the dances of the Gaucho and their rhythm evokes that of a cantering horse. Guitar and the *bombo* drum provide the accompaniment. Particularly spectacular is the Malambo, where the Gaucho shows off his dextrous footwork, the spurs of his boots adding a steely note to the rhythm.

Different regions of the country have their own specialities. The music of Cuyo in the W is sentimental and very similar to that of neighbouring Chile, with its Cuecas for dance and Tonadas for song. The NW on the other hand is Andean, with its musical culture closer to that of Bolivia, particularly on the Puna, where the Indians play the *quena* and *charango* and sound mournful notes on the great long *erke*. Here the dances are Bailecitos and Carnavalitos, while the songs are Vidalitas and the extraordinary high pitched Bagualas, the very essence of primeval pain. In the NE provinces of Corrientes and Misiones, the music shares cultural similarities with Paraguay. The Polca and Galopa are danced and the local Chamamé is sung, to the accordion or the harp, the style being sentimental. Santiago del Estero is the heartland of the Chacarera and the lyrics are often part Spanish and part Quichua, a local dialect of the Andean Quechua language. Down in the Province of Buenos Aires you are more likely to hear the Gauchos singing their Milongas, Estilos and Cifras and challenging each other to a Payada or rhymed duel. Argentina experienced a great folk revival in the 50's and 60's and some of the most celebrated groups are still drawing enthusiastic audiences today. These groups include Los Chalchaleros and Los Fronterizos, the perennial virtuoso singer and guitarist, Eduardo Falú and, more recently, León Gieco from Santa Fe.

BUENOS AIRES AND THE PAMPAS (1)

Apart from the capital itself, with its museums, theatres, public buildings, parks and shopping, this region contains the Tigre Delta (waterways, lunch spots) and Atlantic coastal resorts. Of these the most famous is Mar del Plata.

The Río de la Plata, or River Plate, on which Buenos Aires lies, is not a river but an estuary or great basin, 160 km long and from 37 to 90 km wide, into which flow the Ríos Paraná and Uruguay and their tributaries. It is muddy and shallow and the passage of ocean vessels is only made possible by continuous dredging. The tides are of little importance, for there is only a 1.2m rise and fall at spring tides. The depth of water is determined by the direction of the wind and the flow of the Paraná and Uruguay rivers.

Buenos Aires, the capital, spreads over some 200 sq km (together with Gran

BUENOS AIRES

Railway Stations:
T1. Retiro
T2. Lacroze
T3. Once
T4. Constitución
T5. Buenos Aires

Buenos Aires, the area is 4,326 sq km). The population of the Federal Capital itself is about 2.92 million, but the population of greater Buenos Aires (including the suburbs in the province of Buenos Aires) is 10.87 million.

NB Extreme humidity and unusual pollen conditions may affect asthma sufferers.

Buenos Aires has been virtually rebuilt since the beginning of this century and very few of the old buildings are left. In the centre, which has maintained the original lay-out since its foundation, the streets are often very narrow and are mostly one-way. Its original name, "Santa María del Buen Ayre" was a recognition of the good winds which brought sailors across the ocean.

The heart of the city, now as in colonial days, is the Plaza de Mayo, with the historic Cabildo, the Town Hall, where the movement for independence from Spain was first planned; the pink Casa Rosada (Presidential Palace); the Municipalidad (City Hall); and the Cathedral, where San Martín, the father of Argentine independence, is buried. (For a note on the Mothers of the Plaza de Mayo, **see p 66**). Within a few blocks are the fashionable church of Nuestra Señora de la Merced and the main banks and business houses.

Running W from the Plaza, the Avenida de Mayo leads 1½ km to the Congress building in the Plaza del Congreso. Halfway it crosses the wide Avenida Nueve de Julio. A tall obelisk commemorating the 400th anniversary of the city's founding stands in the Plaza de la República. The Av Nueve de Julio itself, one of the widest in the world, consists of three carriageways separated by wide grass borders. In the N the Av Nueve de Julio meets the Avenida del Libertador, the principal way out of the city to the N and W.

North of the Plaza de Mayo is the shopping, theatre and commercial area. The city's traditional shopping centre, Calle Florida (with excellent newsstands), is in this district. This is the popular down-town meeting place, particularly in the late afternoon; it is reserved for pedestrians only and the buskers in the 500 block are worth visiting. Another shopping street is Avenida Santa Fe, which crosses Florida at the Plaza San Martín; it has become so touristy and as expensive as Florida. Avenida Corrientes is the entertainment centre, a street of theatres, restaurants, cafés and night life. Close by, in Calle Lavalle (part reserved to pedestrians) and in nearby streets, there are numerous cinemas and many good and reasonable restaurants.

East of the Plaza de Mayo, behind the Casa Rosada, a broad avenue, Paseo Colón, runs S towards San Telmo and the picturesque old port district known as the Boca, where the Riachuelo flows into the Plata. The Boca is reached by bus 152 from Av LN Alem, or bus 29 from Plaza de Mayo, in the centre, US$0.50. For a tour of the Boca, start at Plaza Vuelta de Rocha, near Av Pedro de Mendoza and Dr Del Valle Iberlucea, then walk up Caminito, the little pedestrian street used as a theatre and an art market. Visit the Museo de Bellas Artes de la Boca (**see p 64**). The Boca, mostly Italian, has its own distinctive life and parts of it are becoming touristy, but the area, with the adjacent industrial and meat-packing suburb of Avellaneda across the high Avellaneda bridge, is generally dirty and run down, and assaults occasionally take place.

One of the few places which still have late colonial and Rosista buildings is the *barrio* of San Telmo, S of Plaza de Mayo, centred on Plaza Dorrego along the slope which marks the old beach of the Río de la Plata. It is a recognized artistic centre, with plenty of cafés and a pleasant atmosphere; and there is a regular Sat and Sun morning antiques market at the Plaza Dorrego (**see p 75**). The 29 bus connects the Boca with San Telmo, and passes the end of Calle Florida, the shopping street. East of San Telmo on the far side of the docks, the spacious Av Costanera runs along the Plata estuary. A stretch of marshland (claimed from the river by a system similar to the one used in the construction of the Dutch polders) forms the interesting **Costanera Sur Wildlife Reserve**, which has many *coypu* (large rodents) and many types of birds, including the rare black-headed duck and the curve-billed reed hunter. The entrance is at Av Tristán Achabal Rodríguez 1550 (reached by buses 4 and 2); it opens daily from 0700-2000 (free, guided tours available), but much can be seen from the road before then (binoculars useful). There are three trails ranging from 2 km to 6 km long. In summer it is very hot with little shade. For details, contact Fundación Vida Silvestre, Defensa 245, 6 piso, 1075 Buenos Aires, T 331-4864/343-3778.

The theatre retains its hold on the people of Buenos Aires. About 20 commercial theatres play the year round. Recommended is the Teatro Liceo. There are many amateur theatres. You are advised to book as early as possible for a seat at a concert, ballet, or opera.

NB Street numeration: numbers start from the dock side rising from E to W, but N/S streets are numbered from Av Rivadavia, 1 block N of Av de Mayo rising in both directions. Calle Juan D Perón used to be called Cangallo and MT de Alvear is still referred to by its old name, Charcas.

Principal Public Buildings

Casa de Gobierno on the E side of the Plaza de Mayo, and called the Casa Rosada because it is pink, contains the offices of the President of the Republic. (The Foreign Minister's offices are at the Palacio de San Martín, Plaza San Martín). The Casa Rosada is notable for its statuary, the rich furnishing of its halls and for its libraries, but it is not at present possible to visit the interior. The Museo de los Presidentes is on the lower floors (see under **Museums**). A tunnel connects the Casa Rosada with the port (Perón used this to escape in 1955).

The **Cabildo** on the W side of the same Plaza, the old town hall, was put up in 1711 but has been rebuilt several times. Its original structure, fittings and furniture were replaced in 1940 and it was declared a national monument. See under **Museums**.

Old Congress Hall on the S of the Square, built 1863, is a National Monument. It has been encircled and built over by a palatial bank building. Open Thur, 1500-1700, free.

Palacio del Congreso (Congress Hall) to the SW at the far end of Avenida de Mayo, of great size and in Greco-Roman architecture, is the seat of the legislature. It contains the Senate and the Chamber of Deputies. There is limited accommodation for the public at the sittings. It is open from 1700 onwards. Queue in front of desk assigned for minor parties, there they take your passport and give you a ticket for your seat and a pink slip to reclaim your passport. You may stay as long as you wish, but must remain seated. A guided tour (in English) can be taken on Mon, Tues and Fri at 1100 and 1700 when Congress is not sitting. Behind the building is a large white statue of Columbus. This is a quiet area, beware of robbery.

Teatro Colón, one of the world's great opera houses, overlooks Avenida 9 de Julio, with its main entrance on Libertad, between Tucumán and Viamonte. The Colón's interior is resplendent with red plush and gilt; the stage is huge, and salons, dressing rooms and banquet halls are equally sumptuous. Open daily to visitors (not Sun), opening hours vary according to time of year, guided tours Mon-Fri 0900-1600, Sat 0900-1200, in Spanish, French and English, US$5 (children US$2), from entrance at Viamonte 1180, rec. Closed Jan-Feb, check times in advance, T 382-0554. Tickets, sold several days before performance, on the Calle Tucumán side of the theatre. The season runs from Apr to early Dec, and there are concert performances most days. The cheapest seat is US$6 (available even on the same day), and there are free performances most days (Tues-Fri) at 1730 in the Salón Dorado—check programme in the visitors' entrance.

The **Bolsa de Comercio**, built in 1916, a handsome building, contains a stock exchange (entrance 25 de Mayo y Sarmiento), and a grain exchange (entrance at the corner of Av Corrientes and Bouchard, opposite Luna Park).

Churches

All historic churches are open 1630-1900; some at 0900-1100 also.

The **Cathedral**, Rivadavia 437, on the N of Plaza de Mayo is flanked by the former residence of the Archbishop. On this site was built the first church in Buenos Aires, which after reconstruction in 1677 collapsed in 1753 and the rebuilding was not completed until 1823. The eighteenth century towers were never rebuilt, so that the architectural proportions have suffered. A frieze upon the Greek façade represents Joseph and his brethren. The tomb (1878) of the Liberator, General José de San Martín, is imposing.

The **Church of San Ignacio de Loyola**, at Calles Alsina and Bolívar 225, founded in 1710, is the oldest Colonial building in Buenos Aires. It has two lofty towers. The **San Francisco**, Calles Alsina and Defensa, controlled by the Franciscan Order, was inaugurated in 1754 and given a new façade in 1808.

La Merced, Calles Juan D Perón and Reconquista 207, was founded 1604 and rebuilt 1732. One of the altars has a wooden figure of Nuestro Señor, carved during the 18th century by an Indian in Misiones. It has one of the best organs in the country, and one of the few fine carillons of bells in Buenos Aires.

Santo Domingo, on Defensa and Av Belgrano, was founded in 1756. During the British attack on Buenos Aires in 1806 some of Whitelocke's soldiers took refuge in the church. The local forces bombarded it (some of the hits can still be seen on one of the towers); the British capitulated and their regimental colours were preserved in the church. Adjoining is the Salón Belgraniano (with relics of General Belgrano and much colonial furniture). There are summer evening concerts in the church; check times.

El Pilar, Junín 1904, is a jewel of colonial architecture dating from 1732, in a delightful setting of public gardens. A fine wooden image of San Pedro de Alcántara, attributed to the famous 17th century Spanish sculptor Alonso Cano, is preserved in a side chapel on the left. The clock in the steeple is the oldest in the city, made by the Englishman Thomas Windmills, c 1740.

Next to it is the **Cemetery of the Recoleta**, entrance at Junín 1822 near Museo de Bellas Artes (see below). It is one of the sights of Buenos Aires (open 0700-1800). Evita Perón is buried there; her tomb is now marked besides the inscription, Familia Duarte—wardens will point out the grave. "A Doric portico gives on to the main, paved, cypress-lined avenue of a little city of the dead. At the end of the avenue there is a great bronze statue of the resurrected Saviour; on either side, hard up against each other, like houses in a street, there are the family vaults of the Argentine patricians. Every possible style of architecture is represented." G S Fraser, in *News from Latin America*. Bus 110 along Esmeralda, to Recoleta, then 10 mins walk or 8 blocks from Pueyrredón Subte station. On Sun there is a good craft market near the entrance. A cultural centre alongside the Recoleta cemetery specializes in contemporary local art with many free exhibitions by young artists. Another well known cemetery is that of La Chacarita, reached

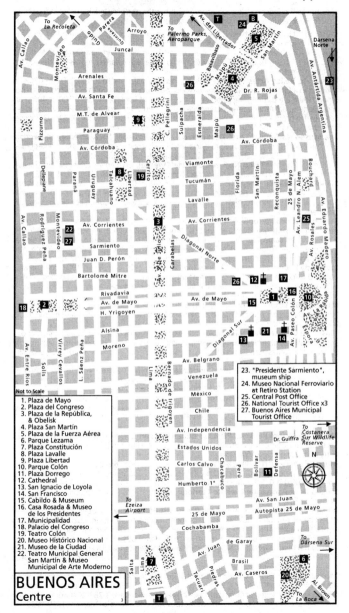

23. "Presidente Sarmiento",
    museum ship
24. Museo Nacional Ferroviario
    at Retiro Station
25. Central Post Office
26. National Tourist Office x3
27. Buenos Aires Municipal
    Tourist Office

Not to Scale

1. Plaza de Mayo
2. Plaza del Congreso
3. Plaza de la República,
   & Obelisk
4. Plaza San Martín
5. Plaza de la Fuerza Aérea
6. Parque Lezama
7. Plaza Constitución
8. Plaza Lavalle
9. Plaza Libertad
10. Parque Colón
11. Plaza Dorrego
12. Cathedral
13. San Ignacio de Loyola
14. San Francisco
15. Cabildo & Museum
16. Casa Rosada & Museo
    de los Presidentes
17. Municipalidad
18. Palacio del Congreso
19. Teatro Colón
20. Museo Histórico Nacional
21. Museo de la Ciudad
22. Teatro Municipal General
    San Martín & Museo
    Municipal de Arte Moderno

BUENOS AIRES
Centre

by Subte to the Federico Lacroze station, which has the much-visited, lovingly-tended tombs of Juan Perón and Carlos Gardel, the tango singer.

Museums, Libraries, Art Exhibitions Note: State museums and parks are free on Wed. Check opening hours with Tourist Office.

Museo de Gobierno (basement of Casa Rosada), Hipólito Yrigoyen 218 (open Wed-Thur 0900-1400, Fri, Sun 1400-1800). Historical memorabilia, particularly of former Presidents, 19th century tunnels.

Museo de Bellas Artes (National Gallery), Avenida del Libertador 1473, T 803-0802. In addition to a fine collection of European works, particularly strong in the 19th century French school, there are paintings representing the conquest of Mexico, executed 300 or 400 years ago, many good Argentine works incl new 19th and 20th century exhibits, and wooden carvings from the Argentine hinterland. Open Tues-Sun 1330-1930, Sat 0930-1930 (closes Jan-Feb). Entrance US$1 (Thur free), ISIC holders free. Warmly rec.

The Museo Nacional de Arte Decorativo is at Av Libertador 1902, collecions of painting, furniture, porcelain, crystal, sculpture; classical music concerts Wed and Thur, closed Tues, otherwise 1500-1900, T 802-6606, US$1, half-price to ISIC holders, closed Jan. The building is shared with the **Museo Nacional de Arte Oriental**; permanent exhibition of Chinese, Japanese, Hindu and Islamic art; open Wed-Mon, 1500-1900 (closed Jan), T 801-5988.

Biblioteca Nacional (The National Library), founded in 1810. About 500,000 volumes and 10,000 manuscripts, now housed in futuristic new building at Av del Libertador 1600 y Agüero 2502, T 806-6155, where only a fraction of the stock is available. Cultural events and festivals held here.

Museo Histórico Nacional, Defensa 1600, in San Telmo. Trophies and mementoes of historical events, divided into halls depicting stages of Argentine history. Here are San Martín's uniforms, a replica of his sabre, and the original furniture and door of the house in which he died at Boulogne. Open Thur-Sun 1400-1800. Entrance US$1; discount for ISIC and Youth card holders. For guided tours in English, French or Portuguese, T 27-4767/26-4588. Closed Jan-Feb.

Museo de la Ciudad, Alsina 412, open Mon-Fri, 1100-1900, Sun, 1500-1900, open all year, US$0.50 (Wed free), T 331-9855. Permanent exhibition covering social history and popular culture, special exhibitions on daily life in Buenos Aires changed every two months, and a reference library open to the public.

Museo y Biblioteca Mitre, San Martín 336, preserves intact the household of President Bartolomé Mitre; has coin and map collection and historical archives. Open Tues-Fri 1300-1800, US$1, T 394-8670.

Museo de Ciencias Naturales at Avenida Angel Gallardo 478, facing Parque Centenario. It houses palaeontological, zoological, mineralogical, botanical, archaeological and marine sections. Meteorites from Campo del Cielo on display. Open all year, daily, 1400-1900, US$0.20. Library, Mon-Fri, 1100-1700; T 982-5243.

Museo de la Dirección Nacional del Antártico, Angel Gallardo 470, in the Museo de Ciencias Naturales, Tues, Thur and Sun, 1400-1800. Specimens of flora, fauna and fossils and a library of taped birdsong, T 44-7327.

Museo Municipal de Arte Moderno, San Juan 350, with a salon at Avenida Corrientes 1530, 9th floor: international exhibitions and a permanent collection of 20th century art; open Mon-Fri 1000-2000, Sat and Sun 1200-2000, US$1.50 (US$1 at the salon, Wed free), T 374-9426.

Museo Municipal de Artes Plásticas Eduardo Sivori, Junín 1930 (in Cultural Centre, La Recoleta) and Corrientes 1530 8th floor, emphasis on 19th and 20th century Argentine art, entry US$1, open daily 1600-2000.

Museo de Bellas Artes de la Boca, Pedro de Mendoza 1835, Boca, has many works on local life, contemporary Argentine painting, also sculptures and figureheads rescued from ships. Tues-Fri 0900-1700, Sat-Sun 0900-1200, 1400-1800, T 21-1080, entrance free.

Museo de la Asociación Evaristo Carriego, Honduras 3784, tango museum of the writer, open Mon-Fri 1300-2000.

Museo de Motivos Populares Argentinos José Hernández, Av Libertador 2373, widest collection of Argentine flokloric art, with rooms dedicated to Indian, colonial and Gaucho artefacts; handicraft sale and library. Open Tues-Fri 1300-1700, Sat and Sun 1500-1900. T 802-7294 for guided visits in English or French. Entrance US$0.50 (closed in Feb).

Museo del Instituto Nacional Sanmartiniano, Gral Ramón Castilla and Av A M de Aguado; Mon-Fri 0900-1200 and 1400-1700; Sat, Sun 1400-1700. Replica of San Martín's house in exile in Boulogne-sur-Mer.

Museo de Arte Español Enrique Larreta, Juramento 2291, in Belgrano (entrance on Av Rafael Obligado). Sat-Sun 1500-1945; Mon-Fri 0900-1300, 1500-1945. Closed Thur and Jan. The home of the writer Larreta, with paintings and religious art; T 783-2640 for guided tour in language other than Spanish. Also **Biblioteca Alfonso El Sabio**, Mon-Fri, 1300-1930.

Museo del Cabildo y la Revolución de Mayo, Bolívar 65, is the old Cabildo building, converted into a museum in 1940. It contains paintings, documents, furniture, arms, medals, maps, recording the May 1810 revolution, and memorabilia of the 1806 British attack; also Jesuit art. Entry US$1 (retired persons free). Open Tues-Fri 1230-1900, Sun 1500-1900. T 334-1782 for English tours. Library, Mon-Fri, 1100-1900.

Museo de Arte Hispanoamericano Isaac Fernández Blanco, Suipacha 1422. Contains a most interesting and valuable collection of colonial art, especially silver, plus watercolours by Carlos Pellegrini, in a beautiful colonial mansion. Open Tues-Sun, 1500-1800, admission US$1. Thur free; closed Jan. For guided visits in English or French T 393-6318; guided tours in Spanish Sat, Sun 1530 and 1730.

Museo y Biblioteca Ricardo Rojas, Charcas 2837 (Tues-Fri 1400-1800). The famous writer Rojas lived in this beautiful colonial house for several decades. It contains his library, souvenirs of his travels, and many intriguing literary and historical curios.

Museo Numismático del Banco Central, San Martín 275, 2nd floor, fascinating, well kept, Mon-Fri 1000-1600, free, overlooks central foyer, ask guard for directions. Not to be confused with **Museo Numismático e Histórico del Banco Nacional**, B Mitre 326, 1st floor, coins and notes, furniture and historical documents, Mon-Fri 1000-1600, T 342-4041, ext 607.

"Presidente Sarmiento", Costanera Norte y Viamonte, next to Yacht Club, a sailing ship used as a naval training ship until 1961; now a museum. Open Sat-Sun 1400-1830, open all year, US$2.

Bank of London and South America (now Lloyds Bank, BLSA), Bartolomé Mitre and Reconquista, has a miniature museum on its fifth floor. Open during banking hours; the building, designed by SEPRA (Santiago Sánchez Elia, Federico Peralta Ramos, and Alfredo Agostini) and completed in 1963 is worth seeing. Next door is the **Banco de Córdoba**, designed by the brilliant Córdoba architect Miguel Angel Roca, completed in the early 1970s.

Museo Nacional de Aeronáutica, Av Costanera Rafael Obligado 4550, next to Jorge Newbery airport. Many civil and military aircraft, plus displays of navigational material, documents, equipment. Thur, Sat, Sun, holidays 1400-1900 (summer hours vary), T 773-0665.

Museo Nacional Ferroviario, Av Libertador 405, behind Retiro station. Mon-Fri, 0900-1800, Sat 0900-1200, free, T 325-5353. Archives 1100-1800. For railway fans, locomotives, machinery, documents of the Argentine system's history. Building in very poor condition.

Museo del Teatro Colón, Tucumán 1161. Mon-Fri 1000-1800. Documents and objects related to the theatre since 1908. T 35-5414/5/6, closed in summer.

Museo Histórico Saavedra (also known as the Museo Histórico de la Ciudad de Buenos Aires, not to be confused with Museo de la Ciudad), Crisólogo Larralde (Republiquetas) 6309. Tues-Sun, 1400-1800. City history from the eighteenth century, furniture, arms, documents, jewellery, coins and religious art; daily guided tours. T 572-0746. Free on Wed; closed Feb.

Museo de la Policía Federal San Martín 353, 7th and 8th floors, worth visiting. Interesting but extremely gruesome forensic section (for strong stomachs only, no one under 15 admitted),T 394-6857, Tues-Fri 1400-1800, US$1.

Museo Penitenciario Argentino Antonio Ballue, Humberto I 378, entrance US$1. Museum of the penal system, T 361-5803; Tues-Fri 1000-1200, 1400-1700, Sun 1000-1200, 1300-1700.

Museo del Teatro Nacional Cervantes, Córdoba 1199.

Museo Internacional de Caricatura y Humorismo, Lima 1037, open Mon, Tues, Thur, Fri, 1700-2000, Sat 1200-1700, originals of cartoons and caricatures of 20th century, but small international section, admission US$0.05.

Museo de Armas, Santa Fe 750. All kinds of weaponry related to Argentine history, incl the Malvinas conflict, plus Oriental weapons, T 312-9774, Wed-Fri 1500-1900, closed 15 Dec-14 Mar, US$1.

Museo de Telecomunicaciones in a magnificent building on the Costanera Sur, Av de los Italianos 851, T 312-5405 (used to belong to Cervecería Munich), Fri, Sat, Sun 1400-1800.

Jewish Museum, Libertad 773, religious objects relating to Jewish presence in Argentina, Tues-Thur 1600-1900.

Museo Histórico Sarmiento Cuba 2079, Belgrano, the National Congress and presidential offices in 1880; documents and personal effects of Sarmiento; library of his work, Wed-Fri 1430-1900, Sat, Sun, holidays 1500-1900, T 783-7555.

Museo Etnográfico J B Ambrosetti, Moreno 350, anthropological and ethnographic collections from around the world, incl Bolivian and Mapuche silverwork, US$1, Tues-Fri 1400-1600, Sat-Sun 1400-1900, T 342-4970.

Parks and Squares

Parque Lezama, Calles Defensa and Brasil, originally one of the most beautiful in the city, has been somewhat vandalized. There is a hippy fair at weekends and the park is very lively on Sun. It has an imposing statue of Pedro de Mendoza, the founder of the original city in 1535. The tradition is that the first founding took place on this spot. The Museo Histórico Nacional (**see above p 64**) is in the park.

The **Palermo Parks**, officially known as the Parque Tres de Febrero, with their magnificent avenues are the city's Bois de Boulogne. They are famous for their rose garden, Andalusian Patio, Japanese garden (admission US$2) with fish to feed and the Hipódromo Argentino, the Palermo race course, with seats for 45,000 (Sun, 1500, entry: US$3, senior citizens free). Opposite the parks are the Botanical and Zoological Gardens (the Zoo and Japanese Garden are closed on Mon). Nearby are the Municipal Golf Club, Buenos Aires Lawn Tennis Club, riding clubs and polo field, and the popular Club de Gimnasia y Esgrima (Athletic and Fencing Club). The **Planetarium** (just off Belisario Roldán, in the Park), is open Fri, Sat and Sun only (1930), entry US$2.50. At the entrance are several large meteorites from Campo del Cielo (**see p 148**). Reached by Subte line D. The **Show Grounds** of the Argentine Rural Society, next to Palermo Park, entrance on Plaza Italia, stage the Annual Livestock Exhibition in July, known as Exposición Rural.

The **Municipal Botanical Gardens**, Santa Fe 3951, entrance from Plaza Italia (take Subte, line D), contain characteristic specimens of the world's vegetation. The trees proper to the several provinces of Argentina are brought together in one section. The Gardens, closed at night, contain the Museo del Jardín Botánico, whose collection of Argentine flora is open daily 1000-1800, T 71-2951. The Gardens are full of stray cats, fed regularly by local residents. The **Zoo**, opp the Botanical Gardens, has been privatized and is open Tues-Fri 0930-1830, Sat-Sun 0930-1900, guided visits available, US$4 entry for adults, children under 13 free.

Plazas The most interesting is the Plaza de Mayo, containing so many public buildings, where the **Mothers of the Plaza de Mayo** march in remembrance of their children who disappeared during the crisis of the 1970s (their address is H Yrigoyen 1442). The Mothers still march anti-clockwise round the central monument every Thur at 1530, with photos of their "disappeared" loved-ones pinned to their chests. Others are the Plaza San Martín, with a monument to San Martín in the centre and, at the N end, a monument to those who fell in the South Atlantic conflict of 1982; the former Plaza Británica, now known as the Plaza de la Fuerza Aérea, with the clock tower presented by British and Anglo-Argentine residents, "a florid Victorian sentinel, royal crest upon its bosom" (frequently vandalized); in Plaza Canadá (in front of the Retiro Station) is a Pacific Northwest Indian totem pole, donated by the Canadian government; the Plaza Lavalle, which has secondhand bookstalls at the Calle Lavalle end; the Plaza del Congreso, the largest in the city, with a waterfall, floodlit at 2145; Plaza Francia, between Centro Cultural Recoleta and Museo de Bellas Artes, "hippy" fair on Sat and Sun, pleasant trees. There is also the great Plaza de la República, with a 67-metre obelisk at the junction between the Diagonal Norte, Av 9 de Julio and Avenida Corrientes.

Warning Buenos Aires is mostly a safe city, but street crime has risen since 1988, especially in the tourist season. Be particularly careful when boarding buses and near the Retiro train station. Beware of bagsnatching gangs in parks, markets and in the Subte, especially on Sun: they are not violent, but particularly skilful. See also **Security, p 223**, on mustard-spraying. If your passport is stolen, remember to get a new "entrada" stamp at the Dirección Nacional de Migraciones. Also changing money on the street is fraught with difficulties and can be dangerous: stick to the *cambios*.

Hotels All hotels, guest houses, inns and camping sites are graded by the number of beds available, and the services supplied. The Dirección de Turismo fixes maximum and minimum rates for 1, 2 and 3-star hotels, guest houses and inns, but there have been complaints that at 3 stars and below the ratings do not provide very useful guidance. Four and five-star hotels are free to apply any rate they wish. Hotels in the upper ranges can often be booked more cheaply through Buenos Aires Travel Agencies.

5-star hotels in our **L1-2** range are: *Caesar Park*, Posadas 1232, T 814 5146, covered pool, solarium; *Park Hyatt*, Cerrito 1433, T 326-1234, F 326-3032, new; *Libertador*, Av Córdoba y Maipú, T 322-2095, *Plaza*, Florida 1005, T 318-3000, good restaurant; *Alvear Palace*, Av Alvear 1891, T 804-4031/4041, an older-style hotel, near Recoleta, with roof garden, shopping gallery, elegant, good; *Sheraton*, San Martín 1225, T 311 6330, good buffet breakfast; *Claridge*, Tucumán 535, T 322-7700, highly rec, but not its restaurant; *Panamericano/Holiday Inn Crowne Plaza*, Carlos Pellegrini 525, T 393 6017; **L2** *Bauen*, Callao 360, T 476 1600.

4-star are *Etoile*, Presidente Roberto Ortiz 1835 in Recoleta, T 804 8603, outstanding location, rooftop pool, rooms with kitchenette, rec. **L3** *Bisonte Palace*, MT de Alvear y Suipacha, T 328-6621, very good, welcoming and **L3** *Gran King*, Lavalle 560, T 393

4012/4052, helpful, English spoken; **A2** *Torre*, Olleros 4186, T 552 6126; **L3** *Cambremon*, Suipacha 30, T 345-0118, F 345-4552, interior rooms very good, but front rooms noisy; **L2** *Regente Palace*, Suipacha 964, T 328 6628, very good, central, helpful, English spoken, buffet breakfast, sports facilities, will store luggage; **L2** *Crillón*, Santa Fe 796, T 312 8181; **A1** *Carsson*, Viamonte 650, T 322-3601, F 392 3551, good location, comfortable, friendly, quiet except rooms on street (ending in 17); **A1** *Los Dos Chinos*, Brasil 780, T 300 2021; **A1** *Bristol*, Cerrito 286, T 382-3228, F 382-3384, good breakfast; **L3** *Camino Real*, Maipú 572, T 322-3162, pleasant, clean, central; *Liberty*, Corrientes 632, T 325 0261, with breakfast, English spoken, luggage stored, clean, various sized rooms; **A2** *City*, Bolívar 160, T 342 6481, clean, rec; *Italia Romanelli*, Reconquista 647, T 312-6361, comfortable, rec; **L3** *Gran Hotel Buenos Aires*, MT de Alvear 767, T 312-3001, rundown but clean.

Other hotels: **A3** *Waldorf*, Paraguay 450, T 312-2079, clean, comfortable and plush, rooms of varying standards, garage, a/c, rec; **A2** *Gran Orly*, Paraguay 474, T/F 312-5344, good location, old fashioned, helpful, good lunches, English spoken, has some rooms for 4, will hold mail for guests, arranges tours and taxis; **L3** *Principado*, Paraguay 481, central, helpful, friendly; **L3** *Bisonte*, Paraguay 1207, T 394 8041, a/c, TV, bar, modern, central, good value; **A1** *Savoy*, Av Callao 181, T 372-5972, friendly and helpful; **A2** *Victory*, Maipú 880, T 314-0655, clean, a/c, modern, heating, TV, comfortable, front rooms noisy, luggage storage unreliable; **A3** *Plaza Roma*, Lavalle 110, breakfast incl, rec; **B** *Central Argentino*, Av del Libertador 174, T 312-6742, secure, clean, near Retiro stations, rec; **A1** *Embajador*, Pellegrini 1181, T 393 9485, good; **A3** *Goya*, Suipacha 748, T 322 9269, with bath, a/c, quiet, clean, nr Buquebus; **A2** *Eibar*, Florida 328, T 325 0969, breakfast incl, quiet, friendly, helpful, dingy, rundown.

A3 *San Antonio*, Paraguay 372, T 312 5381, with bath, nice atmosphere, garden, clean, rec; **A3** *Regidor*, Tucumán 451, T 393 9615, a/c, clean, breakfast incl, rec; **L3** *Lafayette*, Reconquista 546, T 393 9081; **B** *Central Córdoba*, San Martín 1021, T 312-8524, very central, clean, helpful, quiet, good value, will arrange transport to Ezeiza airport, US$35; **A3** *Promenade*, MT de Alvear 444, T 312-5681, 3-star, no charge for credit cards, breakfast extra, helpful, stores luggage, rec; **A2** *Regís*, Lavalle 813, T 327-2613, good value, nice atmosphere, quiet at back; **A2** *Sarmiento Palace*, Sarmiento 1953, T 953 3404, clean, comfortable, English spoken, rec; **B** *Orleans*, Callao 680, clean, small rooms, safe and friendly; **A3** *Gran Hotel de la Paix*, Rivadavia 1187, T 383 7140, old but good, clean, large rooms; *Majestic*, Libertad 121, T 351-949, Subte Lima, colonial, very clean, good value, breakfast incl, street facing rooms noisy; **A3** *Gran Hotel Hispano*, Av de Mayo 861, T 342-3472, spacious, clean, pleasant patio, stores luggage; **A3** *Astoria*, Av de Mayo 916, friendly, very clean; **C** *Marbella*, Av Corrientes 3193, T 887118, modernized, clean, friendly, quiet, breakfast pricey, fans, English spoken, highly rec, no credit cards; **A3** *Mundial*, Av de Mayo 1298, T 383 0011, with bath, clean, comfortable; **A2** *Orense*, Mitre 1359, good service, cooking facilities, basic, rec; **A2** *Deauville*, Talcahuano 1253, T 811 5732, a/c, restaurant and bar, garage, rec; **A3** *Super*, Gallo 1637, nr Av Santa Fe (Subte D, Agüero), T 824 1021, out of centre, a/c, pleasant.

B *Tres Sargentos*, Tres Sargentos 345, T 312 6081, clean, secure, modernized in 1994-95, new bathrooms, good value; **D** *Micki*, Talcahuano 362, T 371-2376, clean, no a/c, basic, good value; *Sportsman*, Rivadavia 1426, near Plaza Congreso, T 381-8021/2, clean, old fashioned, cheaper without bath, rec (10% discount for ISIC and youth card holders); **B** *Chile*, Av de Mayo 1297, T 383-7877, clean, friendly, noisy; **C** *La Argentina*, Av de Mayo 860, with bath, clean, friendly, central, very noisy; *Maipú*, Maipú 735, popular, hot water, clean, friendly, basic, stores luggage, laundry facilities, T 322-5142, rec; **B** *Uruguay*, Tacuarí 83, T 334 2788, central, clean, friendly, good value, rec; **A3** *Ayacucho Palace*, Ayacucho 1408, T 806 0611, 10 mins from centre bus 10, T 806 0611, 2 star, better value than central hotels, rec; **C** *Hispano Argentino*, Catamarca 167, T 975 543, some rooms with bath, clean, quiet, convenient; **A2** *Ecuador*, Adolfo Alsina 2820, nr Plaza Once, T 956-0533, rec; **C** *Gran Vía*, Sarmiento 1450, T 371-5763, with bath, clean, friendly; **B** *Aguirre*, Aguirre 1041, T 773-5027, clean, safe. **B** *Versalles*, Arenales 1394, T 811-5214, W of Av 9 de Julio, friendly, basic, clean, shower, no breakfast, fine staircase and mirrors; **C** *Central*, Alsina 1693, with bath.

   C range: *Frossard*, Tucumán 686, T 322-1811, inexpensive, hot showers, but not quiet (10% discount to ISIC members); *O'Rei*, Lavalle 733, T 393-7186, basic, central, gloomy, unfriendly, popular; *Bahía*, H Yrigoyen 3062, hot showers, pleasant, clean, safe, central but noisy (10% discount to ISIC members), rec; *Sarmiento*, Sarmiento 1162, T 350305, clean, central, popular, back rooms quieter, good value; *Vila Seca*, Av de Mayo 776, T 340-952, basic, friendly; *Petit Mitre*, B Mitre 4315, T 981-7768, offers 10% discount to ISIC and youth card holders; *Ceballos Palace*, Virrey Ceballos 261, 2 blocks from Congreso, T 372 7636, with bath, safe (next to police HQ). *Bolívar*, in Bolívar (San Telmo), with bath, clean; *Mediterráneo*, Rodríguez Peña 149, T 476 2852, with bath, basic, central, helpful, safe, stores luggage, limited cooking facilities, fridge, some rooms are dark, rec; *Plaza*, Rivadavia 1691, friendly, T 40-9747, many cheap hotels on Calle 25 de Mayo, none under US$15, all dirty.

   Youth Hostel, Brasil 675 near Constitución station (Subte C from bus terminal, last stop), T 362-9133, E pp with YHA card (ISIC card accepted), incl breakfast, sheets provided, hot water 24 hrs, clean, basic, rec, no cooking facilities, cheap meals, doors closed 1200-1800 and from 0200, single women not admitted. Women should be aware that they could attract unwelcome attention near Constitución station as prostitutes operate there. New **Youth Hostel** *Del Aguila*, Espinosa 1628, E pp, hot water, cooking and laundry facilities, T 581-6663 (buses 24, 105, 106, 109, 146), rec.

   Apartments   Contracts are usually for at least one year and owners will demand a guarantor or a deposit covering at least 6 months rent (security or cash). One agent is Sr Aguilar, Florida 520, 3°-314, T 322-4074. An agency which arranges sharing apartments (often with senior citizens), is Martha Baleiron, Esmeralda 1066, 5°"F", T 311 9944. US$50 fee if an apartment is found, US$10 if not. All agencies should provide contracts which should be read carefully. To rent flats on a daily basis try *Edificios Esmeralda*, Marcelo T de Alvear 842, T 311-3929, cleaning incl. Facilities for up to 6 persons; also *Edificio Suipacha*, Suipacha 1235, T/F 322-6685, US$120 per day. Also *Aspen Apartment Hotel*, Esmeralda 933, T 313-9011, US$136 per day; *Edificio Lemonde*, San Martín 839, T 313-2032, rec, though apartments overlooking road are noisy; *Residencial Trianon*, Callao 1869, T 812-3335, US$75-85 per day.

   NB   All the rates quoted are subject to alteration. It should be noted that for the most part they are the basic or minimum rates. Room tax is 15% and is not always incl in the price. Check when booking into a hotel whether breakfast is incl or not. Air conditioning is a must in high summer, but be prepared for frequent power cuts. Many of the cheaper hotels in the central area give large reductions on the daily rate for long stays. Hotels with red-green lights or marked *Albergue Transitorio* are hotels for homeless lovers (for stays of 1½-2 hrs).

   Camping   About 15 km out at Lomas de Zamora, US$3 pp per night, incl swimming pool, take bus 141 from Plaza Italia to Puente La Noria then No 540 to Villa Albertini which passes the entrance; information on all sites is available from the Automóvil Club Argentino and from the national tourist information office, which has a free booklet, *1ra Guía Argentina de*

Campamentos.
Good camping equipment and fuel from Fugate (no sign), Gascón 238 (off Rivadavia 4100 block), T 982-0203, also repairs equipment. Outside Mountain Equipment, Donado 4660, T 541-2084, and Acampar, H Yrigoyen 2835, T 783-0209. Munor, H Yrigoyen 283, Martínez, and Panamericana y Paraná, Martínez (Shopping Unicenter, 3rd level). Good camping stores also at Guatemala 5908 and 5451. Camping gas available at Mitre 111, Todo Gas, Paraná 550, and El Pescador, Paraguay y Libertad. Every kind of battery (incl for Petzl climbing lamps) at Callao 373. Cacique Camping manufacture camping equipment and clothing; their two shops: Arenales 1435, Barrio Norte, and San Lorenzo 4220, Munro, Provincia Buenos Aires, T 762 0261, F 756 1392 also sell the *South American Handbook*.

Restaurants "The Buenos Aires Herald" publishes a handy *Guide to Good Eating in Buenos Aires* (with a guide to local wines) by Dereck Foster. There is also *El Libro de los Restaurantes de Buenos Aires*, published annually, describing the city's major restaurants. Eating out in Buenos Aires is very good but is getting more expensive, especially in the posher places which charge in dollars. In 1995 good restaurants were charging US$30 and up pp; more modest places were charging US$20-25 pp. **NB** In many mid to upper range restaurants, lunch is far cheaper than dinner. Lunch or dinner in a normal restaurant cost US$7-12 (cutlet, salad, $1/4$ of table wine, dessert); a portion at a *comidas para llevar* (take away) place cost US$2.50-3.50. Many cheaper restaurants are *tenedor libre*, eat as much as you like for a fixed price.

The following list, for reasons of space, not quality, gives only those restaurants easily accessible for people staying in the city centre. In the banking district, between Av Corrientes and Plaza de Mayo: *Clark's*, Sarmiento 645, in old English outfitter's shop (also at Junín 1777), well cooked food, very expensive, busy, fish and lamb specialities (set lunch very good value); *Bolsa de Comercio*, 25 de Mayo 359, downstairs at the Stock Exchange, good but expensive; *London Grill*, Reconquista 455, British, busy, famous for roast beef and turkey curries; *El Pulpo*, Tucumán 400, seafood, great variety, big portions; *Sabot*, 25 de Mayo 756, good business lunches; *Brizzi*, Lavalle 445, business lunches, good and worth the price; *Blab*, Florida 325, sole, veal, pork specialities; *La Pipeta*, San Martín 498, serving for 30 years, closed Sun; *La Estancia*, Lavalle 941, popular with business people, excellent grills and service, expensive (US$30-40); *La Casona del Nonno*, Lavalle 827, popular, *parrilla* and pasta; *ABC*, Lavalle 545, traditional, good value if a bit dull; *El Palacio de la Papa Frita*, Lavalle 735 and 954, Corrientes 1612, 10% discount for ISIC and youth card holders; *Emporio de las Papas Fritas*, Maipú 431, good *parrillas*, good value; *La Rural*, Suipacha 453, rec for *parrillada* and *bife de lomo* but expensive, English-speaking head waiter is excellent; *Pizzería Roma*, Lavalle 800, cheap and good quality, delicious spicy *empanadas* and *ñoquis*, good breakfasts; *Los Inmortales*, Lavalle 746, specializes in pizza, also good. There are other locations; some serve *à la carte* dishes which are plentiful, and are open from 1500-2000 when most other restaurants are closed. *El Figón de Bonilla*, rustic style, L N Alem 673, good, another branch at Junín 1721; *Los Troncos*, Suipacha 732, good grills, expensive; *Catalinas*, Reconquista 875, seafood (very expensive though). A few blocks from this district: *El Aljibe*, at Sheraton, smoked salmon, tournedos Rossini, baby beef; *Dolli*, Av del Libertador 312, nr Retiro, very good food, fairly expensive; *La Chacra*, Córdoba 941 between Suipacha and 9 de Julio, expensive but good; *Bice*, Av Dávila 192, mostly Italian, good, about US$50 pp.

Walking up Avenida Quintana, you reach La Recoleta cemetery; on the corner is *La Biela* (see **Tea Rooms**, etc, below) and, opp, *Café de la Paix*. Turning left, towards Av Las Heras: *Gato Dumas*, Junín 1745, expensive but has good fixed price menus; *La Bianca*, Junín 1769, very good value for BsAs, lunch US$16 pp; *Harper's*, Junín 1773; *Hippopotamus*, Junín 1787, dinner expensive, good value executive lunch; *Munich Recoleta*, Junín 1871, good steaks, pleasant atmosphere, US$20 pp, no credit cards. On Roberto M Ortiz, No 1805, good pasta, lamb and fish but expensive; *Don Juan*, No 1827; *La Tasca de Germán*, No 1863, highly rec, European. Nearby, 2 blocks from Recoleta towards Av Callao, *Au Bec Fin*, Vicente López 1827, reservations needed, open 2000-0200 daily. In the San Telmo area: *El Sabor Escondido*, Cochabamba 435, good and reasonably priced; *Calle de Angeles*, Chile 318, nice setting in an old, covered street, high standards; *El Comité*, Carlos Calvo 375, good, but very dear; *El Repecho de San Telmo*, Carlos Calvo 242, excellent, expensive, reserve in advance (T 362-5473). For ice cream, *Sumo*, Independencia y Piedras. The Costanera along the river front is lined with little eating places: *El Rancho Inn* is best, try also *Happening* and *Los Años Locos*, good beef, *parrilla*, cold buffet. *Bulls and Bears*, Av R Obligado (Costanera Norte) s/n y J Salguero, very good grill, take colectivo 33 from Retiro or on LN Alem, or take taxi; in same area, but more elegant and more expensive is *Clo Clo*, La Pampa y Costanera, reservation required. Typical *parrilla* at *Rodizio*, Costanera Norte, opp Coconor, far end of Aeroparque, self-service and waiter service, other branches, eg Av Callao y Juncal, good value, popular.

Near the Teatro Colón: *Tomo Uno*, Carlos Pellegrini 521 (*Hotel Panamericano*), expensive, trout, mignon, shrimp, home-made pasta, closed Sun; *Posta del Gaucho*, Pellegrini 625, accepts Visa; *Edelweiss*, Libertad 432, tuna steaks, pasta, grill, expensive and famous; *La Emiliana*, Av Corrientes 1443, excellent, rec. By Congreso: *La Cabaña*, Entre Ríos 436, old tavern style, excellent food, pricey (US$40); *Quorum*, Combate de los Pozos 61, behind Congress, popular with politicians.

Typical Boca restaurants on Necochea, but check the hygiene. There are several others in the same street. They all serve antipasto, pasta and chicken; no point in looking for beef here. All bands are loud. The seafood restaurant *La Barca*, on river bank near Avellaneda bridge, rec; also rec for seafood and good value, *Viejo Puente*, Almirante Brown 1499. *El Pescadito*, P de Mendoza 1483, rec for pasta and seafood.

Other recommendations: *Pippo*, Montevideo 341, large pasta house, good simple food, very popular, also at Paraná 356; *Chiquilín*, Montevideo 321, pasta and meat, good value; *Nazarenas*, Reconquista 1132, good for beef, expensive, rec; *El Ceibal*, Av Las Heras 2379, inexpensive, very good *empanadas*; *Ostramar*, Santa Fe 3495 y Julián Alvarez (Subte station Ortiz, then walk back towards town), good quality fish; *El Salmón II*, Reconquista 1014, large portions of good food, not cheap.

Other Italian: *Broccolino*, Esmeralda 776, excellent, very popular, try *pechuguitas*; *Mama Liberata*, Maipù 642, excellent. 3 famous *pizzerías* in the centre are on Corrientes: *Banchero*, No 1298; *Las Cuartetas*, No 838, and *Los Inmortales*, No 1369, same chain as above. *Il Gatto*, Corrientes 959, popular and reasonably priced; *El Cuartito*, Talcahuano 937, excellent pizzas.

Swedish food at *Swedish Club*, Tacuarí 147, open to non-members. Hungarian: *Budapest*, 25 de Mayo 690, cheap. British: *The Alexandria*, San Martín 774, curries, fish and seafood, nice bar.

Vegetarian: *Granix*, Florida 126 and 467 *tenedor libre* US$8, bland but filling, lunchtime Mon-Fri. *Ever Green* is a chain of *tenedor libre* vegetarian restaurants, branches: Paraná 746, Tucumán 666, Sarmiento 1728 and Cabildo 2979; *Yin Yang*, Paraguay 858, excellent (health-food shop too, lunch only, closed Sun); *La Esquina de las Flores*, Córdoba 1599, excellent value, also good health-food shop; *Los Angeles*, Uruguay 707, US$5 for salad bar, main meal and dessert, rec; *La Huerta*, Paraguay 445, T 311-0470, macrobiotic, rec; *La Huerta II*, Lavalle 895, 2nd floor, *tenedor libre*, US$7, reasonable.

Oriental: *Chung Kiu*, Paraguay 725, Chinese, *tenedor libre*, US$6 with one drink; *La Cantina China*, Maipú 976, one of the oldest; *Nuevo Oriental*, Maipú near Lavalle, Chinese *tenedor libre*, US$6, good choice; another *tenedor libre* Chinese place on Av San Martín 1 block from Av 1B Justo, wide variety, US$6, good value; *Tsuru*, ground floor of *Sheraton*, authentic Japanese, small, rec.

Pumper-nic is a chain of rather pricey fast food restaurants. 2 *McDonalds* in the centre, one on Florida, one on Lavalle. *The Embers*, Callao 1111, fast food, 10% discount for ISIC and youth card holders. Try also restaurants in Supercoop stores at Sarmiento 1431, Lavalle 2530, Piedras y Rivadavia and Rivadavia 5708.

Cheap meals at *Los Teatros*, Talcahuano 354, good (live music 2300-0100, open 24 hrs). *Pizzalandia*, on Brasil (near Youth Hostel) serves cheap *empanadas*, *salteñas* and pizzas. Good snacks all day and night at Retiro and Constitución railway termini. For cheap snacks the markets are rec, eg El Retiro market on the 900 block of Av Libertador. *Tío Ivan*, Florida 142 Boston Gallery, cheap sandwich bar, 10% discount for ISIC and youth card holders; good sandwich bar at Lavalle 1610. Stalls of the Cooperadora de Acción Social offer cheap snacks, and can be found in several public areas, eg near the Recoleta. The snack bars in underground stations are also cheap. *DeliCity* bakeries, several branches, very fresh pastries, sweets, breads, authentic American donuts.

For restaurants with shows, see **Night Clubs and Folklore** below.

Tea Rooms, Cafés and Bars   *Richmond*, Florida 458 between Lavalle and Corrientes, genteel (chess played between 1200-2400); well-known are the *Confitería Suiza*, Tucumán 753, and the *Florida Garden* at Florida and Paraguay. *Confitería Ideal*, Suipacha 334, old, faded, good service, cakes and snacks, rec. Many on Av Libertador in the Palermo area. *Café Querandí*, Venezuela y Chacabuco, popular with intellectuals and students, good atmosphere, well known for its Gin Fizz. *Café Piazza*, Rivadavia 1400 block, excellent coffee, pretty setting. The more bohemian side of the city's intellectual life is centred on Avenida Corrientes, between Cerrito and Callao, where there are many bars and coffee shops, such as *La Paz* (open very late, Corrientes 1599, T 46-5542, 10% discount for ISIC and youth card members). *Pub Bar Bar O*, Tres Sargentos 415, good music and prices, gives similar discount. *El Molino*, Rivadavia and Callao, popular with politicians, nr Congress, Belle Epoque décor, frequent art sales, good value. *Café 1234*, Santa Fe 1234, good and reasonable. *Clásica y Moderna*, Callao y Paraguay, bookshop at back, expensive but very popular, open 24 hrs. Excellent ice-cream at *Freddo*, Av Santa Fe y Callao, or Ayacucho y Quintana. Next door (Quintana y Recoleta) is café *La Biela*, restaurant and *whiskería*, one of the places to be, elegant. Similarly popular, *Café Victoria*,

Roberto M Ortiz 1865, whiskería/sandwichería, typical of the Recoleta area. On Lavalle there are *whiskerías* and *cervecerías* where one can have either coffee or exotic drinks. *Barila*, Santa Fe 2375, has excellent confectionery. *Café Tortoni*, Av de Mayo 825-9, delicious cakes, coffee, a haunt of artists, very elegant, over 100 years old, interesting *peña* evenings of poetry and music. On Sat at 2315, it becomes a 'Catedral del Jazz', with Fenix Jazz Band, US$1 entrance. *Café El Verdi*, Paraguay 406, also has live music. *Babilonia*, Guardia Vieja 3360, popular, shows, bar, music, young, rocker crowd and intellectuals; *Parakultural New Border*, Chacabuco 1072, mostly avant-garde theatre, popular; *Die Schule*, Alsina 1760, hard rock bar with avant-garde theatre. A "bohemian, bizarre" bar is *El Dorado*, H Yrigoyen 971; gay bar, *Café de Abril*, Aráoz 2300 block. Good bars in San Telmo around Plaza Dorrego, eg *El Balcón de la Plaza*, and on Humberto I. Watch whisky prices in bars: much higher than in restaurants. Most cafés serve tea or coffee plus *facturas*, or pastries, for breakfast, US$2.50-3. Bakery shops sell 10 *facturas* for US$2.

Airline Offices Aerolíneas Argentinas (AR), Calle Perú 2; reservations and enquiries, T 393-5122, reservations 362-5008/6008. **Austral Líneas Aéreas**, Corrientes 485, T 49-9011/325-0505. **Líneas Aéreas del Estado** (LADE), Calle Perú 714, T 361-0278/0853, erratic schedules, uninformed office. **Líneas Aéreas Privadas Argentinas** (LAPA), Av Santa Fe 1970, T 812-3322 (reservations), or Aeroparque Puente Aéreo section, T 772-9920, cheapest fares to main tourist centres. **AeroPerú**, Santa Fe 840, T 311-6079. **Varig**, Florida 630, T 329-9201. **Lan Chile**, Paraguay 609 Piso 1, T 311-5334, 312-8161 for reconfirmations. See **Introduction and Hints**, or Brazil chapter for Mercosur Airpass.

Banks and Exchange Most banks charge very high commission especially on cheques (as much as US$10). Banks open Mon-Fri 1000-1500, be prepared for long delays. US dollar bills are often scanned electronically for forgeries, while cheques are sometimes very difficult to change and you may be asked for proof of purchase. American Express cheques are less of a problem than Thomas Cook. Practices are constantly changing. **Lloyds Bank** (BLSA) Ltd, corner of Reconquista and Bartolomé Mitre, Visa cash advances provided in both US dollars and pesos. It has 10 other branches in the city, and others in Greater Buenos Aires. **Royal Bank of Canada**, corner of Florida and JD Perón; branch at Av Callao 291. **Citibank**, B Mitre 502, changes only Citicorps TCs, no commission; branch at Florida 746. **First National Bank of Boston**, Florida 99. **Bank of America**, JD Perón y San Martín changes Bank of America TCs am only, into US$ at very high commission; branch at Paraguay 901 doesn't take American Express or Thomas Cook cheques. **Banco Tornquist**, Mitre 531, Crédit Lyonnais agents, advance cash on visa card. **Banco Holandés**, Florida 361. **Deutsche Bank**, B Mitre 401, changes Thomas Cook cheques, both give cash advances. **Banco Roberts**, 25 de Mayo 258, changes Thomas Cook without commission. Thomas Cook rep, **Fullers**, Esmeralda 1000 y MT de Alvear. **American Express** offices are at the corner of Arenales 707 y Maipú, by Plaza San Martín, T 312-0900, where you can apply for a card, get financial services and change Amex TCs (1000-1500 only, no commission into US$ or local cash). **Client Mail** in same building, Mon-Fri 0900-1800, Sat 0900-1300. **Mastercard**, Hipólito Yrigoyen 878 (US$500 limit for cash advance), or **Deutsche Bank**, Mitre 401; Mastercard ATMs (look for Link-Mastercard/Cirrus) at several locations, mostly Banco Nacional del Lavoro.

There are many *casas de cambio*, some of which deal in TCs; most are concentrated around San Martín and Corrientes (*Cambio Topaz*, No 1394-1400, recently rec, also **Casa Piano**, San Martín 345-347, changes TCs into pesos or US$ cash for 2-3% commission, *Cambios Trade Travel*, San Martín 967, 3% commission on TCs, and *Exprinter*, Suipacha 1107); open from Mon-Fri 1000-1600, Sat closed. Many *cambios* will exchange US$ TCs for US$ cash at commissions varying from 1.25 to 3%. If all *cambios* closed, try Mercadería de Remate de Aduana, Florida 8, or Eves, Tucumán 702, open until 1800 (but count your change). On Sat, Sun and holidays, cash may be exchanged in the *cambio* in some of the large supermarkets (eg *Carrefour*, Paseo Alcorta Shopping Center, open daily 1000-2200). There is no service charge on notes, only on cheques. Major credit cards usually accepted but surcharges were common in 1993/4. General Master Card office at Hipólito Yrigoyen 878, open 0930-1800, T 331-1022/2502/2549; another branch at Florida 274 (open 1000-1730). Visa, Corrientes 1437, 2nd floor, T 954-3333/2000, for stolen cards. Other South American currencies can only be exchanged in *casas de cambio*.

Cultural and Trade Associations Argentine Association of English Culture, Suipacha 1333 (library for members only); **British Chamber of Commerce**, Av Corrientes 457; **British Council**, MT de Alvear 590, Piso 4, T 311-9814/7519, F 311-7747 (open 1000-1200, 1430-1630). **Goethe Institut**, Av Corrientes 311, German library (open 1300-1900 exc Wed, and 1000-1400 first Sat of month) and newspapers, free German films shown, cultural programmes, German language courses; in the same building, upstairs, is the German Club, Corrientes 327. **Alliance Française**, Córdoba 946. **USA Chamber of Commerce**, Diagonal

Norte 567; **US Information Library** (Biblioteca Lincoln), Florida 935, reference and lending library, free, no identification needed, but take passport to become a member, on first five days of each month only, fixed address needed (closed Sat, Sun). **St Andrew's Society**, Perú 352.

Clubs American Club, Viamonte 1133, facing Teatro Colón, temporary membership available; **American Women's Club**, Av Córdoba 632, 11 piso. **English Club**, 25 de Mayo 586, T 311-9121, open for lunch only; temporary membership available to British business visitors. The American and English Clubs have reciprocal arrangements with many clubs in USA and UK. **Swedish Club**, Tacuarí 147. **Organización Hebrea Argentina Macabi**, Tucumán 3135, T 962-0947, social and sporting club for conservative Jews.

Embassies and Consulates All open Mon-Fri unless stated otherwise. **Bolivian Consulate**, Belgrano 1670, 2nd floor, T 381-0539, open 0900-1400, visa while you wait. **Brazilian Consulate**, Carlos Pellegrini 1363, 5th floor, open Mon-Fri, 0930-1400, visa takes 1 day, T 394-5260/5264. **Paraguayan Consulate**, Las Heras 2545, 0900-1400, T 322-6536. **Peruvian Consulate**, San Martín 691, 6th floor, T 311-7582, 0900-1400, visa US\$5, takes 1 day. **Uruguayan Consulate**, Ayacucho 1616, open 1000-1800, T 821-6031, visa takes up to 1 week. **Chilean Consulate**, Tagle 2762, T 394-6582, Mon-Thur 0930-1330, 1530-1830, Fri 0915-1430. **Ecuadorean Embassy**, Quintana 585, 9th and 19th floors, T 804-6408.

US Embassy and Consulate General, Cerviño 4320, T 777-4533/7007, 0900-1730, consulate, visas 0800-1100, calls between 1500 and 1700 (US Embassy Residence, Av Libertador 3502). **Australian Embassy**, Av Santa Fe 846 (Swissair Building), T 312-6841, Mon-Thur 0830-1230, 1330-1730, Fri 0830-1315. **Canadian Embassy**, Tagle 2828, T 312-9081. **South African Embassy**, Marcelo T de Alvear 590, 7 piso, T 311-8991/7, Mon-Thur 0900-1300, 1400-1630, Fri 0900-1330. **Israeli Embassy**, Av de Mayo 701, piso 9, T 342-6653. **Japanese Embassy**, Paseo Colón 275, 9 y 11 piso, T 343-2561, 0900-1300, 1430-1800.

Austrian Embassy, French 3671, T 802-1400, 0900-1200. **Belgian Embassy**, Defensa 113-8, T 331-0066/69, 0800-1300. **British Embassy**, Luis Agote 2412/52 (near corner Pueyrredón & Guido), T 803-7070, open 0915-1215, 1415-1615. **Danish Embassy**, L N Alem 1074, 9 piso, T 312-6901/6935, 0900-1230, 1500-1730. **Finnish Embassy**, Av Santa Fe 846, 5 piso, T 312-0600/70, Mon-Thur 0830-1700, Fri 0830-1200. **French Embassy**, Av Santa Fe 846, 3 piso, T 312-2425, 0900-1200. **German Embassy**, Villanueva 1055, Belgrano, T 771-5054/9, 0900-1200. **Greek Embassy**, R S Peña 547, 4 piso, T 342-4958, 1000-1300. **Irish Embassy**, Suipacha 1380, 2 piso, T 325-8588, 1000-1230. **Italian Embassy**, Billinghurst 2577, consulate at MT de Alvear 1149, T 325-6132, 0900-1300. **Netherlands Embassy**, Edificio Buenos Aires, Av de Mayo 701, 19° piso, T 334-4000, 0900-1200, 1300-1530. **Norwegian Embassy**, Esmeralda 909, 3 piso B, T 312-2204, 0900-1430. **Spanish Embassy**, Mariscal Ramón Castilla 2720, esq Av del Libertador 2075, T 811-0078, 0900-1330, 1500-1730. **Swedish Embassy**, Corrientes 330, 3 piso, T 311-3088/9, T 1000-1200. **Swiss Embassy**, Av Santa Fe 846, 12 piso, T 311-6491, open 0900-1200.

Night Clubs and Folklore Tango: *El Caminito de San Telmo*, Balcarce, good show costing US\$25 incl two drinks, best atmosphere at weekends; nearby are *Casablanca*, Balcarce 668, T 331-4621, excellent show, costing US\$40 pp incl drinks, and *La Ventana*, Balcarce 425, Mon-Sat shows at 2230, T 331-3648/334-1314, very touristy but very good show, US\$50 for show, dinner and unlimited wine, through an agency, 10% discount for ISIC and youth card holders, from Asatej office (see **Useful Addresses** below). Tango shows also at *Bar Sur*, Estados Unidos 299, and *Antigua Tasca de Cuchilleros*, Carlos Calvo 319, T 362-3811/28, pleasant surroundings, show US\$20, show and dinner, US\$32, both in San Telmo. Good show also at *La Veda*, Florida 1, reasonable meal with wine and other drinks. *Viejo Buzón*, Corrientes y Rodríguez Peña, good tango, no dinner but plenty of dancing, locals and tourists; *Café Mozart*, Esmeralda 754, tango, jazz, theatre, no dinner; *La Casa de Aníbal Troilo*, Carlos Calvo 2540, good singers and bands, for tourists; *Tango Danza*, José María Moreno 351, Fri, Sat, Sun, from 2200; *Salón La Argentina*, Rodríguez Peña 361, Thur-Sun, 2200, more modern-style tango. *Michelangelo*, Balcarce 433, T 334-4321, impressive setting, concert café in an old converted monastery, various types of music incl tango and folklore, Tues-Sun. The best affordable tango bars are in the Boca, but it is increasingly difficult to find authentic tango for locals; most are tourist-oriented. Four rec places are *Café Homero*, J A Cabrera 4946, Palermo, *Tarquino*, Brasil y Perú, *Italia Unita*, JD Perón 2535 and *Tortoni* (see below). Authentic tango at Cochabamba 444, pay US\$5 when leaving, young crowd, rec; lessons also available. *La Cumparsita*, Chile 302, T 361-6880, authentic tango, US\$50 for 2 incl wine; *Mesón Español*, Rodríguez Peña 369, T 35-0516, good folk music show and good food; *Galería Tango Argentino*, Boedo 722 y Independencia, T 93-1829/7527, Wed-Sat, less touristy than others, dinner (usually), show and dancing, has dancers and tango lessons (Mon-Fri, 1800-2100), well-known bands. *Paladium*, San Martín 954, tango/bolero dance hall; *Volver*, Corrientes 837, Mon-Fri, 1800-2100. Andean music at *Ollantaytambo*, Estados Unidos 541. Tango lessons at *Champagne Tango*, Rio de Janeiro 387, Tues, Fri, Sun.

Recommended night club/discos incl *Hippopotamus*, Junín 1787, Recoleta, French restaurant (lunch and dinner), fashionable night club; *Le Club*, small and exclusive, Quintana 111; *Cemento*, Estados Unidos 700 block, disco with live shows, usually hard rock and heavy metal, popular with younger crowd, as are *La City*, Alvarez Thomas y El Cano, and *Halley*, Corrientes 2020, heavy metal and hard rock. Also rec: *Mama Baker*, Santa Fe 2800; *Cinema*, Av Córdoba 4633, inside a former cinema; *El Dorado*, Hipólito Yrigoyen y 9 de Julio, interesting, different; *El Nacional*, Reconquista 915, in tunnels formerly used for smuggling; *El Angel*, Corrientes 1768 y Callao; *Club Coco Bahiano*, Carlos Calvo y Balcarce, live Brazilian music, crowded and friendly, open Fri and Sat till 0700, entry incl one drink US$9, rec. *Cachaça Tropical*, on Brasil (1 block from Plaza Constitución), big disco with Latin American music, good meeting place. *Roxy*, Rivadavia 1900 block, rock and roll, reggae, rec; *New York City*, Alvarez Thomas 1391, T 552-4141, young and middle-aged clientele, popular, chic, well-established. On the Costanera: *El Cielo*, on riverside, techno music popular with politicians, models, actors, etc; *Caix*, mega-disco with panoramic view of the river, young, trendy. *Age of Communication*, M T de Alvear 400 block, for the beautiful, young and rich. Gay discos: *Bunker*, Anchorena 1170, Thur-Sun; *Experiment*, C Pellegrini 1085, open nightly; *Enigma*, Esmeralda y Paraguay, also for heterosexuals. Some discos serve breakfast for additional charge at entry. Generally it is not worth going to discos before 0230 at weekends. Dress is usually smart.

Bars and restaurants in San Telmo district, with live music (usually beginning 2330-2400): *Players*, Humberto I 528 (piano bar); *Samovar de Rasputin*, Almte Brown, edge of Parque Lezama, good blues, dinner and/or show. Cover charges between US$5 and US$20, or more.

Jazz: *El Subsuelo*, JD Perón 1372, good bands featured; *Oliverio*, Paraná 328, excellent live jazz features the great Fats Fernández, Fri-Sat 2330 and 0100; *Café Tortoni*, Av de Mayo 829, T 342-4328, traditional jazz downstairs, Fri-Sun 2315, Fri tango concert 2130, rec, entry US$6; *Clásica y Moderna* Callao 893, expensive but classy, jazz usually on Wed night, no shows weekends.

Bailantas are music and dance halls where they play popular styles which for years have been despised as "low class". They are now fashionable among the upper classes. A popular place is *Fantástico*, Rivadavia 3400 block; also *Terremoto Bailable*, Paraguay y Thames; *Metropolis*, Santa Fe al Plaza Italia. For salsa: *El Club*, Yerbal 1572, friendly, for all ages, not trendy, all welcome; *La Salsera*, Yatay 961, highly regarded salsa place.

Cultural Events The Luna Park stadium holds pop/jazz concerts, ballet and musicals, at Bouchard 465, nr Correo Central, T 311-5100, free parking at Corrientes 161. Check "Musimundo" record shop on Santa Fe or Florida for latest information on rock concerts. Tickets to see big names can be very reasonable. Teatro Alvear, Corrientes 1659, T 46-9470, has free concerts Fri at 1300, usually Orquesta de Tango de BsAs. Tango Week, leading up to National Tango Day (11 Dec), has free events all over the city; details posted around the city and at tourist offices. Teatro Municipal General San Martín, Av Corrientes 1530, organizes many cultural activities of which quite a few are free of charge, incl concerts Sat and Sun evenings; the theatre's Sala Leopoldo Lugones shows international classic films, Sat-Sun, US$2. Free concerts at ProMusica music shop, Florida 638; schedule in window. Centro Cultural General San Martín, Sarmiento 1551, and the Centro Cultural de Recoleta, Junín 1930, next to the Recoleta cemetery have many free activities. Free lunchtime seasonal concerts on the lower ground floor of the Galeria Pacífico on Florida. Also worth a visit for the architecture and murals. Theatre ticket agency, La Cartelera, Lavalle 828. Look for details in main newspapers and weekly paper *La Maga*, US$3 from news stands. **NB** From mid-Dec to end-Feb most theatres and concert halls are closed.

Cinemas The selection of films is as good as anywhere else in the world and details are listed daily in all main newspapers. Films are shown uncensored. Tickets best booked early afternoon to ensure good seats (average price US$7 in 1995). Tickets obtainable, sometimes cheaper, from ticket agencies (*carteleras*), such as *Vea Más*, Paseo La Plaza, Corrientes 1600, local 19 (the cheapest), *Cartelera*, Lavalle 742, T 322 9263, *Teatro Lorange*, Corrientes 1372, T 372-7386, and *Cartelera Baires*, Corrientes 1372, local 25. Some cinemas offer 50% discounts on Wed. Almost all foreign films are shown with subtitles. Many cinemas on Lavalle, around Av Santa Fe and Callao and in Belgrano (Av Cabildo and environs). Film club at *Faro Gandhi*, Montevideo 453 on Fri and Sat evenings, showing old, foreign and "art" films, US$1.50, open to non-members. Free films at Asociación Bancaria, Sarmiento 337/341, T 313-9306/ 312-5011/17, once a month (Wed); old films at Cine en la Cinemateca Argentina, Sarmiento 2255, T 952-2170 (half price of other cinemas, plus 20% discount for ISIC holders), and at Sarmiento 2150, T 48-2170. ISIC holders also entitled to discounts at Cine IFT Sala 1, Boulogne Sur Mer 549

(50%). On Sat nights many central cinemas have *trasnoches*, late shows starting at 0100.

Urgent Medical Service (day and night) (Casualty ward: *Sala de guardia*) T 34-4001/4. *British Hospital*, Perdriel 74, T 23-1081, US$14 a visit; cheap dental treatment at Av Caseros y Perdriel 76. *German Hospital*, Pueyrredón 1658, between C Berutti and C Juncal, T 821-7661. Both maintain first-aid centres (*centros asistenciales*) as do the other main hospitals. *Children's Hospital* (Ricardo Gutiérrez), Bustamante 1399, T 86-5500. *Centro Gallego*, Belgrano 2199, T 47-3061. *Hospital Juan A Fernández*, Cerviño y Bulnes, good, medical attention. If affected by pollen, asthma sufferers can receive excellent treatment at the *University Hospital de Clínicas José de San Martín*, Córdoba 2351, T 821-6041, US$6 per treatment.

Innoculations *Centro Médico Rivadavia*, S de Bustamante 2531, Mon-Fri, 0730-1900 (bus 38, 59, 60 or 102 from Plaza Constitución), or *Guardia de Sanidad del Puerto*, Mon and Thur, 0800-1200, at Av Ing Huergo 690, T 334-1875, free, bus 20 or 22 from Retiro, no appointment required (typhus, cholera, Mon-Fri 0800-1200; yellow fever, Tues-Thur 1400-1600, but no hepatitis; take syringe and needle, particularly for insulin and TB). Buy the vaccines in *Laboratorio Biol*, Uriburu 159, or in larger chemists. *Hospital Rivadavia*, Calles Las Heras y Tagle, for polio inoculation. Free. Any hospital with an infectology department will do hepatitis A.

Language Schools *Verbum Language School*, Lavalle 357, 3°C2, T/F 393-8228, frequently rec, accommodation and social events offered. *Instituto de Lengua Española para Extranjeros*, Lavalle 1619, 7th C and 3rd E, T 375-0730, F 864-4942, US$15 per hour, rec by individuals and organizations alike. *Bromley Institute*, Paraná 641, 1A, T 40-4113, courses in Spanish, Portuguese, French, English, high standards, well-regarded, rec. Free Spanish classes at *Escuela Presidente Roca*, Libertad 581, T 35-2488, Mon-Fri, 1945-2145 (basic level only). Spanish classes also at *Instituto del Sur*, Av Callao 433, 9 S, T/F 49-8421, individual lessons, cheap; *Estudio Buenos Aires*, San Martín 881, 4° piso, T 312-8936, owner also lets out rooms; *Link Educational Services*, Arenales 2565, piso 5° B, T 825-3017. *Universidad de Buenos Aires*, 25 de Mayo, offers cheap, coherent courses. *AmeriSpan Unlimited* has an affiliated school; contact PO Box 40513, Philadelphia, PA 19106, USA, T 800-879-6640 or, outside N America 215-985-4522, F 215-985-4524, E-mail info@amerispan.com. For other schools teaching Spanish, and for private tutors look in *Buenos Aires Herald* in the classified ads. Enquire also at Asatej (see **Useful Addresses**).

Schools which teach English to Argentines include: International House, Pacheco de Melo 2555, British-owned and -run; Berlitz, Av de Mayo 847 (low rates of pay); Santiago del Estero 324; American Teachers, Viamonte y Florida, T 393-3331. There are many others; vacancies are advertised in the *Buenos Aires Herald*. Before being allowed to teach, you must offically have a work permit (difficult to obtain) but schools may offer casual employment without one (particularly to people searching for longer-term employment); if unsure of your papers, ask at Migraciones (address below). There are many "coordinadoras", usually women, who do not have an institute but run English "schools" out of their homes by hiring native English-speakers and sending them out on jobs. Pay varies between 10 and 25 pesos, depending on where you teach and on negotiation; the pay is usually better than in a fixed institute. Adverts occasionally appear in the *Herald*, but most contacts are by word of mouth.

Laundries *Tintorería Constitución*, Av Santiago del Estero 1572 (suits only). Many dry cleaners and many launderettes, eg Marcelo T de Alvear 861, in centre; Junín 15 y Rivadavia, Mon-Sat 0800-2100; Junín 529 y Lavalle; Rivadavia 1340; *Laverap*, Paraguay 888 y Suipacha, Córdoba 466, Local 6, T 312-5460, US$6.50 per load (10% discount to ISIC and youth card holders, also at Brasil y Bolívar and Rodríguez Peña 100-200), Arenales 894, Solís nr A Alsina (cheaper). The laundry at Brasil 554 costs US$2.50 per load, more for valet service. *Marva*, Juan D Perón 2000 y Ayacucho.

Libraries Harrods (2nd floor) on Florida. See also Biblioteca Nacional, under **Museums**, and **Cultural and Trade Associations**.

General Post Office (Correo Central – now privatized, Correos Argentinos, improved service), corner of Sarmiento and LN Alem, Mon-Fri, 0800-2000. *Poste Restante* on 1st floor (US$2.25 per letter), poor reports; very limited service on Sat (closes 1400). Fax service US$5 per minute. Philatelic section open Mon-Fri 1000-1800. Centro Postal Internacional, for all parcels over 1 kg for mailing abroad, at Av Antártida Argentina, near Retiro station, open 1100 to 1700. Check both Correo Central and Centro Postal Internacional for *poste restante* (US$1.15 to collect letters).

Telecommunications The State company Entel has now been privatized and the city is split into two telephone zones, owned by Telecom and Telefónica Argentina. Av Corrientes 705 (open 24 hrs) for international phone calls, fax, public telex in basement; alternatively in Central Post Office (more expensive), also telex. Other offices at San Martín 322, on Santa Fe 1841, on Agüero/Las Heras, and at Lavalle 613. *Fichas* or *cospeles* (tokens) for calls in the city from public telephone boxes cost US$0.25, obtained at newspaper stalls, cigarette *kioskos* and Telecom or Telefónica Argentina offices. Many phones now use phone cards costing 5 and 10 pesos (break off the corner tab before using); the cards of the two companies are interchangeable. (Payphones in Telecom and Telefónica Argentina offices reportedly use 5 cent coins.) International telephone calls from hotels may incur a 40%-50% commission in addition to government tax of about the same amount. For more details see **Postage and Telephone Rates** in Information for Visitors.

NB Since privatization, many phone prefixes in the city have been changed: 34 became 342, 30 - 343, 37 - 383, 38 - 381, 59 - 581, 45 - 476 or 372 depending on location, and 47 - 951. Further changes are likely and will be indicated on the first pages of the phone directory, or dial 110 to ask the operator.

Places of Worship The **Holy Cross**, Calle Estados Unidos 3150, established by the Passionists. **St John's Cathedral** (Anglican), 25 de Mayo 282 (services, Sun 0900 in English, 1030 in Spanish), was built half at the expense of the British Government and dedicated in 1831. **St Paul's, St Peter's, St Michael and All Angels** and **St Saviour's** are Anglican places of worship in the suburbs. **St Andrew's**, Calle Belgrano 579, is one of the 8 Scottish Presbyterian churches. The **American Church**, Corrientes 718, is Methodist, built in 1863; service at 1100. **First Methodist** (American) Church, Av Santa Fe 839, Acassuso.

German Evangelical Church, Esmeralda 162. **Swedish Church**, Azopardo 1422. The **Armenian Cathedral** of St Gregory the Illuminator at the Armenian Centre, and the **Russian Orthodox Cathedral** of The Holy Trinity (Parque Lezama) are interesting.

Synagogues The most important in Buenos Aires are the Congregación Israelita en la República Argentina, Libertad 705 (also has a small museum), and, the oldest, the Templo Israelita at Paso 423 (called the Paso Temple), traditional and conservative. An important orthodox temple is the Comunidad Israelita Ortodoxa, the seat of the rabbis of Argentina, Ecuador 530, T 862-2701. The Comunidad Betel, Av Elcano 3424, and the B'nai Tikvah, Vidal 2049, are for reformed worshippers. Congregación Emanu-El (reformed sect), Tronador 1455, take bus 140 from Av Córdoba to Alvarez Thomas block 1600, then turn right into Tronador.

Shopping Most shops close lunchtime on Sat. Visit the branches of *H Stern*, for fine jewellery at the Sheraton and Plaza Hotels, and at the International Airport. *Kelly's*, Paraguay 431, has a very large selection of reasonably-priced Argentine handicrafts in wool, leather, wood, etc. Excellent leatherwork at *LYK*, Paraguay y Maipú. *Artesanías Argentinas* (*ARAR*), at Montevideo 1386, T 812-2650, a non-profitmaking organization selling handicrafts (clothing, weaving, basketware, wooden goods etc) all with certificate of origin, expensive. *Campanera Dalla Fontana*, Reconquista 735, leather factory which is fast, efficient and reasonably priced for made-to-measure clothes. Good quality leather clothes factory at Boyacá 2030, T 582 6909 to arrange time with English speaking owner. *Aida*, Florida 670, can make a leather jacket to measure in 48 hours. *Creaciones Vartán*, Calle 97, No 2622, San Andrés (Colectivo 363), T 753-6660, good quality leather. *El Guasquero*, Av Santa Fe 3117, traditionally made leather goods. *Galería del Caminante*, Florida 844, has a variety of good shops with leather goods, arts and crafts, souvenirs, etc. Apart from shops on Florida and Santa Fe (especially between 1000 and 2000 blocks), Av Corrientes has many shops for men's clothes between 600 and 1000 blocks, and the shops on Arenales N of Av Santa Fe, and on Av Alvear on the way to Recoleta, have been rec. Av Cabildo in Belgrano district can be reached by 152 bus from Retiro for good shopping between 1600 and 2800 blocks. Many boutiques and places for casual clothes in Martínez suburb. *Pasaje de Defensa* is a beautifully restored colonial house containing small shops, on Defensa 791 in the San Telmo area. Calle Defensa is good for antique shops. There is a shopping mall, **Patio Bullrich**, between Av del Libertador y Posadas, at Montevideo, entrances on Posadas and Av del Libertador (No 750); boutiques are very expensive, but leather goods are of high quality. A new mall, very smart and expensive, is **Alto Palermo**, at Coronel Díaz y Santa Fe. **La Plaza Shopping Centre**, at Corrientes 1600, has a few restaurants and an open-air theatre. **Paseo Alcorta**, Av Alcorta y Salguero, 4 levels, cinemas, supermarket, stores, many cheap restaurants (take colectivo 130 from Correo Central); **Galerías Pacífico**, on Florida, between Córdoba and Viamonte, where the Bellas Artes museum used to be, is now a beautiful shopping mall with many exclusive shops and fast food restaurants in basement. Also good set-price restaurant on 2nd floor and concerts on lower-ground floor (see Cultural Events, p 73). **Galerías Broadway**, Florida 575, for cheap electronic goods, CDs, tapes. In the **Munro district** on Av Mitre either side of Calle Ugarte (buses, 130, 314, 41 from Av del Libertador, 50 mins) are cheap and varied fashion clothes incl jeans, fake designer labels, some secondhand. For cheap clothes and electrical goods try Mercadería de Remate de Aduana, Florida 8 (downtown).

Markets Sunday markets for souvenirs, antiques, etc: **Plaza Dorrego (San Telmo)** with food, dancers, buskers, Sun 0900-1700, on Humberto I and Defensa (entertaining, not cheap, an interesting array of "antiques"). **Feria Hippie**, in Recoleta, near cemetery, big craft and jewellery market, Sat and Sun, good street atmosphere, expensive. Also **Feria de Las Artes** (Fri, 1400-1700) on Defensa y Alsina. Sat craft, jewellery, etc market, at **Plaza Belgrano**, nr Belgrano station on Juramento, between Cuba y Obligado, 1000-2000. Handicraft markets at weekends at Parque Lezama and Plaza Italia, which also has a used book market Fri and Sat, a few stalls have English books, some stay open throughout the week. Another secondhand book market is at Plaza Lavalle in front of Tribunales, a few English titles (ask around), weekdays only. At **Parque Rivadavia**, Rivadavia 4900, around the *ombú* tree, records, books, magazines, stamps and coins, Sun 0900-1300, **Plazoleta Primera Junta**, Rivadavia and Centenera, books and magazines, Sat 1200-2000, Sun 1000-2000. **Parque Patricios**, Av Caseros entre Monteagudo y Pepiri, 1000-2000, antiques, books, art and stamps. **Plazoleta Santa Fe**, Santa Fe and Uriarte (Palermo) old books and magazines, same times as Primera Junta, and again, plastic arts in the **Caminito**, Vuelta de Rocha (Boca), 1000-1800. Sat market in **Plaza Centenario**, Díaz Vélez y L Marechal, 1000-2100 local crafts, good, cheap hand-made clothes. **Auction sales**: some bargains at weekday pm auctions, Edificio de Ventas, Banco de la Ciudad de Buenos Aires, Esmeralda 660. Souvenirs can be found in area around San Martín and Paraguay (not markets). Interesting market of gaucho items at Mataderos (unsafe area), bus 126 from Plaza de Mayo, 50 mins (Sun); closed in the summer.

Bookshops Many along Av Corrientes, W of Av 9 de Julio, though most have no foreign language sections. Try *Yenny* (No 571) for new English classics and *Fausto* (No 1316 and 1243) for second-hand selection. *ABC*, Av Córdoba 685 (limited selection of second-hand and best selection of new English books, good selection of German books) and Av del Libertador 13777 in Martínez suburb. *Joyce, Proust y Cía*, Tucumán 1545, 1st floor, T 40-3977, paperbacks in English, Portuguese, French, Italian, classics, language texts, etc, good prices. *Librería Rodríguez*, Sarmiento 835, good selection of English books and magazines, has another branch on Florida, 300 block; French bookshop at Calle Rivadavia 743; *Librería Goethe*, Lavalle 528, good selection of English and German books. Italian books at *Librería Leonardo*, Av Córdoba 335, also (with newspapers and magazines) *La Viscontea*, Libertad 1067. *Liberarte* has a good selection of alternative books and magazines in Spanish, international videos to rent, CDs, especially jazz and blues, concerts and shows in hall downstairs. Secondhand/exchange inside shopping arcade under Av 9 de Julio at the Obelisco, but poor stock. Also in the plaza behind the main post office (Corrientes 50). *Asatej Bookshop*, Florida 835, 1° of 104, T 312-8476, sells this *Handbook* "at the best price". Good bookshop at Florida 340, *El Ateneo* (basement, good selection of English books), *Kel Ediciones*, Talcahuano 1063, and Laprida 2488 in Florida suburb, also maintain a good stock of English books and sells *South American Handbook*. Prices at *Harrods* on Florida are lower than most. *LOLA*, Viamonte 976, 20D, T 476 0518, specializes in Latin American Natural History books. For used and rare books: *Fernández Blanco*, Tucumán 712; *Casa Figueroa*, Esmeralda 970; and *L'Amateur*, Esmeralda 882. Second-hand English language books from *British and American Benevolent Society*, Catamarca 45 (take train to Acassuso), and from *Entrelibros*, Av Cabildo 2280 and Santa Fe 2450, local 7.

Foreign newspapers at news stands on Florida, and at kiosk at Av Corrientes y Maipú.

Every Apr the Feria del Libro is held at the Centro De Exposiciones, F Alcorta y Pueyrredón, Recoleta; exhibitions, shows and books for sale in all languages.

Camera Repairs and Film Developing Film developing to international standards. There are many Kodak labs around Talcahuano. Fotospeed, Av Santa Fe 4838 (20% discount to SAHB owners!) for quality 2-hour service. For developing slides Esmeralda 444, fast service, and Kinefot, Talcahuano 244. 1-hr developing service is hard to find outside Buenos Aires. Camera repairs: several good shops on Talcahuano 100-400 blocks. Try also Casa Schwarz, Perú 989, international brands; Golden Lab, Lavalle 630, good prices for film; Horacio Calvo, Riobamba 183, all brands and variety of rare accessories, rec; fast service at Tacuarí 75; for Olympus cameras, Rodolfo Jablanca, Corrientes 2589. German spoken at Gerardo Föhse, Florida 890, fast, friendly.

Sports Association and rugby football are both played to a very high standard. Soccer fans should not miss a visit to see Boca Juniors ; matches Sun 1500-1800 (depending on time of year), Wed evenings, entry US$10 (stadium open weekdays for visits). Soccer season Sep-May/Jun, with a break at Christmas; rugby season Apr-Oct/Nov. Ice-hockey is becoming popular. Cricket is played at 4 clubs in Greater Buenos Aires between Nov and Mar. Polo: the high handicap season is Oct to Dec, but it is played all year round (low season Apr-Jun). Argentina has the top polo teams; a visit to the national finals at Palermo in Nov or Dec is rec. Horse racing at Palermo and San Isidro, a large, modern race course 25 mins from the city centre by train or road, is popular throughout the year. Riding school at Palermo, US$5 an hour.

The Tigre Boat Club, founded in 1888, is open to British or American visitors for a small fee and a limited period. The leading golf clubs are the Hurlingham, Ranelagh, Ituzaingó, Lomas, San Andrés, San Isidro, Sáenz Peña, Olivos, Jockey, Campos Argentinos and Hindú Country Club; visitors wishing to play should bring handicap certificate and make telephone booking. Weekend play possible only with a member. Good hotels may be able to make special arrangements. Municipal golf course in Palermo, open to anyone at any time. Tennis, squash and paddle tennis are popular: there are 5 squash clubs. The Argentine Tennis Open is in Nov; ATP tour. There are many private clubs. For aerobics try the San Martín Club, San Martín 645, T 311-9191, or the Gimnasio Olímpico Cancillería, Esmeralda 1042, no membership required.

Motor racing: Formula 1 championship is no longer held in Argentina, but efforts are being made to restore it. There are lots of rallies, stock racing and Formula 3 competitions, mostly from Mar to mid-Dec.

Gambling Weekly lotteries. Football pools, known as *Prode*.

Chess Club Argentino de Ajedrez, Paraguay 1858, open daily, arrive after 2000; special tournament every Sat, 1800. High standards.

Tours A good way of seeing Buenos Aires and its surroundings is by BAT, Buenos Aires Tur, Lavalle 1444, T 40-2304, almost hourly departures, or Autobuses Sudamericanos (TISA), information and booking office at Bernardo de Irigoyen 1370, 1st floor, Offices 25 and 26, T 27-6591, F 26-7933, or Av Larrazábal 493, T 642 7028 (Liniers). Prices range from US$13 to US$65. Also run buses to all major South American cities. At same address is Transporte Aero Costa Atlántica (TACA), passenger charter services to Mar del Plata, Villa Gesell, Pinamar and Santa Teresita, T 26-7795. For reservations in advance for sightseeing or other tours, with a 20% courtesy discount to *South American Handbook* readers, write to Casilla de Correo No 40, Sucursal 1(B), 1401 Buenos Aires. A 3-hour city tour of Buenos Aires in English and Spanish is run by City Tours, US$12, rec, as is Eurotur (T 312-6170), in English. Some tours incl dinner and a tango show, or a gaucho *fiesta* at a ranch, eg at *Santa Susana Estancia* (excellent food and dancing, although the gaucho part is somewhat showy). Bookable through most travel agents, US$50-65.

Travel Agents Among those rec are **Exprinter**, Suipacha 1107, T 312-2519, and San Martín 170, T 331-3050, Galería Güemes (especially their 5-day, 3-night tour to Iguazú and San Ignacio Miní); **American Express**, Arenales y Maipú; **Furlong**, Perón 338, T 318-3200, Thomas Cook representatives; **ATI**, Esmeralda 561, very efficient and helpful, with branches in Brazil; **Turismo Feeling** ("don't be put off by the name") L Alem 762, T 311-9422, excellent and reliable horseback and skiing trips; **Astra Travel**, Tucumán 358, 5th floor, English spoken by director, efficient; **Versailles**, Callao 257, 13th floor N, helpful, friendly; **Turismo Flyer**, Reconquista 621, 8° piso, T 313-8224, F 312-1330, English, Dutch and German spoken, accepts credit cards, rec. **Germania**, Lavalle 414, T 393-1265/0035, excellent service (English not spoken), especially for tours to the N, branch in Salta. **Lihue Expeditions**, Maipú 926, T 311-9610, helpful with all arrangements, especially wildlife tours and *estancia* visits. **Círculos Mágicos**, Uruguay 864, 3rd floor, T 815-2803, books visits to *estancias* at competitive rates. **Eves Turismo**, Tucumán 702, T 393-6151, helpful and efficient, rec for flights; **City Service**, Florida 890, T 312-8416/9; **Travel Up**, Maipú 474, 4° piso, T 326-4648; **Folgar**, Esmeralda 961, 3° piso E, T 311-6937. **Ruta 40**, P O Box 5210, 1000 Buenos Aires, T 782-7427, F 783-5557, jointly run by Federico Kirbus, the traveller and author (see **Tourist Information** in **Information for Visitors**). English is widely spoken.

Tourist Information National office at Santa Fe 883 with maps and literature covering the whole country. Open 1000-1700, Mon-Fri; T 312-2232, 312-5550. Has a guide to campsites throughout Argentina. Other offices at Aeroparque, T 773-9891/05 and at Ezeiza, T 480-0224/0011.

There are also helpful *Casas de Turismo* for most provinces (open Mon-Fri usually, 1000-1800, depending on office, check): **Buenos Aires**, Av Callao 237, T 40-7045; others on Callao are **Córdoba** (332, T 49-4277, F 476-2725), **Chaco** (322, T 476-0961, F 49-3777), **La Rioja** (745, T 326-1140, F 812-1339), **Mendoza** (445, T 40-7301, F 49-8296). Others: **Río Negro**, Tucumán 1920, T 40-7066, F 476-2126; **Chubut**, Paraguay 876, T 311-0428, F 313-7757; **Entre Ríos**, Suipacha 844, T 313-9327, F 312-5985; **Formosa**, H Irigoyen 1429, T 381-7048, F 381-2037; **Mar del Plata**, Santa Fe 1175; **Jujuy**, Santa Fe 967, 6th floor, T 393-6096; **Misiones**, Santa Fe 989, T 322-0677, F 393-1615; **Neuquén**, JD Perón 687, T/F 326-6812; **Salta**, Diagonal Norte (Roque Sáenz Peña) 933, T 326-1314; **Santa Cruz**, 25 de Mayo 377, 1st floor, T 343-3653, F 342-1667; **Catamarca**, Córdoba 2080, T 46-6893, F 46-6892; **Corrientes**, San Martín 333, 4th floor, T 394-7432, F 394-2808; **La Pampa**, Suipacha 346, T/F 326-0511; **San Juan**, Sarmiento 1251, T 382-5580, F 382-4729; **San Luis**, Azcuénaga 1083, T/F 822-0426; **Santa Fe**, Montevideo 373, 2nd floor, T 40-1825, F 40-4610; **Santiago**

del Estero, Florida 274, T 326-2720, F 326-5915; **Tucumán**, Mitre 836, 1st floor, T 345-2495, F 345-4924; **Tierra del Fuego**, Av Santa Fe 919, T/F 322-8855; **Patagonia**, Av de Mayo 801, T 342-0101; **Villa Gesell**, B Mitre 1702, T 46-5098, F 46-5199; **Bariloche** hotel, flat and bungalow service in Galería at Florida 520, room 116 (cheapest places not listed). Calafate bookings for *Refugio and Autocamping Lago Viedma*, excursions with Transporte Ruta 3 and lake excursions with Empresa Paraíso de Navegación booked from Turismo Argos, Maipú 812, 13th floor C, T 392-5460. (For bookings for *Hotel La Loma*, Calafate and further information on the area contact Paula Escabo, Av Callao 433, piso 8° P, T 371-9123.) For tourist information on Patagonia and bookings for cheap accommodation and youth hostels, contact Asatej, see **Useful Addresses** below.

Municipalidad de Buenos Aires, Sarmiento 1551, 5th floor open Mon-Fri 0930-1730, has an excellent free booklet about the city centre and maps. Further offices at Aeroparque (Aerolíneas Argentinas), Mon-Fri, 0830-2000 and Sat 0900-1900, and Ezeiza/Pistarini Airport, Mon-Fri 0830-2200; kiosks at Florida y Diagonal Norte and Florida y Córdoba, open at 0830-2030 Mon-Fri and 0900-1900 Sat, also small information stand on 2nd floor of Galerías Pacífico.

On Fri, the youth section of *Clarín (Sí)* lists free entertainments; *Página 12* has a youth supplement on Thur called *NO*, the paper lists current events in *Pasen y Vean* section on Fri; also the weekly *La Maga* and Sun tourism section of *La Nación*. *Where in Buenos Aires*, a tourist guide in English, published monthly, is available free in hotels, travel agencies, tourist kiosks on Florida, and in some news stands. The *Buenos Aires Times* is a bilingual monthly newspaper covering tourist topics, available in some hotels. A good guide to bus and subway routes is *Guía Peuser*; there is one for the city and one covering Greater Buenos Aires. A similar guide and map is "Lumi": both are available at news stands. Also handy is Auto Mapa's pocket-size "Plano guía" of the Federal Capital, available at news stands, US$8, or from sales office at Santa Fe 3117; Auto Mapa also publishes an increasing number of regional maps, Michelin-style, high quality. Country-wide maps at Instituto Geográfico Militar, Cabildo 301 (see **Maps** in Information for Visitors).

Useful Addresses Youth Hostel Association—information for all South America, Talcahuano 214, piso 3, T 45-1001 (post code: 1013 Buenos Aires). Buenos Aires hostels at Brasil 675, Nicasio Oroño 1593 and Espinosa 1628. **NB** A YHA card in Argentina costs US$20, ISIC cards also sold: Secretariat open Mon-Fri 1300-2000. (There are very few hostels near Route 3, the main road S from Buenos Aires.) **Asatej**, Argentine Youth and Student Travel Association, information for all South America, noticeboard useful for single travellers, booking for hotels and travel, the *Sleep Cheap Guide* lists economical accommodation in Argentina, Bolivia, Chile, Brazil, Uruguay and Peru (though limited), ISIC cards sold, English and French spoken, very helpful but limited travel information, Florida 835, piso 3, oficina 315, T 311-6953, F 311-6840, also Student Flight Centre at oficina 319 B, be prepared for a long wait and take US$ cash. **YMCA** (Central), Reconquista 439. **YWCA**, Tucumán 844. **Salvation Army**, Rivadavia 3255. **Municipalidad**, Av de Mayo 525, facing Plaza de Mayo. **Central Police Station**, Moreno 1550, T 38-8041 (emergency, T 101 from any phone, free). **Migraciones** (Immigration), Antártida Argentina 1365 (visas extended mornings only), T 312-3288/7985/8661, from 1230-1700. **Comisión Nacional de Museos y Monumentos y Lugares Históricos**, Av de Mayo 556; professional archaeology institute.

Local Bus services (*colectivos*) cover a very wide radius, and are clean, frequent, efficient and very fast (hang on tight). The basic fare is US$0.50; US$0.90 to the suburbs. Have coins ready for ticket machine as drivers no longer sell tickets. **NB** The number of the bus is not sufficient indication of destination, as each number has a variety of routes, but bus stops display routes of buses stopping there and little plaques are displayed in the driver's window. "Lumi" guide to all routes is available at news stands, US$7.50.

Tram A green and white old-fashioned street car operates on Sat and holidays 1600-1930 and Sun 1000-1300, 1600-1930 (not Easter Sun), free, along the streets of Caballito district. Operated by Asociación de los Amigos del Tranvía, T 476-0476.

Underground Railways ("Subte") Five lines link the outer parts of the City to the centre. "A" line runs under Calle Rivadavia, from Plaza de Mayo up to Primera Junta. "B" line from central Post Office, Avenida L N Alem, under Av Corrientes to Federico Lacroze railway station. "C" line links Plaza Constitución with the Retiro railway station, and provides connections with all the other lines. "D" line runs from Catedral, under the Diagonal Norte, Córdoba, Santa Fe and Palermo to Ministro Carranza (5300 block of Av Santa Fe; from Palermo to the end of the line is single track, running a shuttle service). Note that on Line "D" Canning station has become Scalabrini Ortiz; 9 de Julio station interconnects with Diagonal Norte ("D" and "C") and Carlos Pellegrini ("B"). "E" line runs from Bolívar (nr Plaza de Mayo) through San Juan to Avs Directorio and José María Moreno. The fare is US$0.45, the same for any direct trip or combination between lines; tokens (*fichas*) must be bought at booking offices (*boleterias*); buy a few in advance to save time. System operates 0530-2215, but some lines close before 2200. Line A, the oldest was built in 1913, the oldest underground in South America. Some trains date from the early part of the century too. The oldest and nicest station is Station Perú. Some stations on lines C and D have some very fine tile-work. Backpacks and luggage allowed. Beware bag-and jewellery-snatchers and pickpockets, particularly when doors are about to close. The tourist office gives out a map, which can also be bought on station platforms together with a booklet giving bus schedules.

Taxis are painted yellow and black, and carry *Taxi* flags. Fares are shown in pesos. The meter starts at 0.96 when the flag goes down; make sure it isn't running when you get in. A charge is sometimes made for each piece of hand baggage (ask first). Tips not usual. Beware of overcharging especially by remise (private clubs) and late at night. Remise service leaves from Constitución station, T 27-8111. Four common taxi driver tricks are 1) to take you on a longer than necessary ride; 2) to switch low-denomination notes for higher ones proffered by the passenger (don't back down, demand to go to the police station); 3) to grab the passenger's baggage and prevent him/her from leaving the taxi (scream for help); 4) to quote "old" prices for new, eg "quince" (15) for 1.50 pesos, "veinte y seis" (26) for 2.60 pesos, etc. If possible, keep your luggage with you. Worst places are the 2 airports and Retiro; make sure you know roughly what the fare should be before the journey. (As examples, from Aeroparque to: Ezeiza 32 pesos, Congreso 7 pesos, Plaza de Mayo 6 pesos, Retiro 5 pesos, La Boca 9 pesos.) Fares double for journeys outside city limits (General Paz circular highway). Alberto Pommerenck, T 654 5988, offers reasonable ½ day hire, knows suburban leather factories well, good driver.

Car Hire Cars for hire, expensive, can be got through hotel reception clerks. There is a 20% tax on car hire. It is difficult to hire cars during holiday periods, best to book from abroad. Use of Avis Car Credit card with central billing in one's home country is possible. See also **Information for Visitors**. Driving in Buenos Aires is no problem, provided you have eyes in the back of your head and good nerves. **Avis**, Cerrito 1527, T 326-5542; **A1 International**, San Luis 3138, T 963-3489/961-6666; **Hertz**, Ricardo Rojas 451, T 312-1317. There are several national rental agencies, eg **ALV**, Av Alvear 1883, T 805-4403; **Ricciard Libertador**, Av Libertador 2337/45, T 799-8514; **Localiza**, Paraguay 1122, T 375-1611.

Motoring Associations See p 227 for details of service. Parking, safely, at El Balneario within the old port, but ask the military post for permission first.

Airports Most international flights use Ezeiza airport (officially referred to as Ministro Pistarini), 35 km from the centre by a good divided lane highway, which links with the General Paz circular highway round the city. The airport has a duty free shop (expensive, for arrivals and departures), exchange facilities (US$5 fixed commission, but no commission for US$ cash), post office (open 0800-2000) and its hotel, the *Internacional*, is closed for renovation (no other hotels nearby). There is a *Devolución IVA* desk (return of VAT) for purchases such as leather goods. Airport information, T 480-0217. Reports of pilfering from luggage; to discourage this have your bags sealed after inspection at special counter by Your Packet International SA, US$5-10 per piece. Free hotel booking service at Tourist Information desk – helpful, with list of competitively-priced hotels.

  Manuel Tienda León runs a comfortable bus service between Ezeiza and the company offices at Santa Fe 790, next to *Hotel Crillon* (T/F 315-0489, F 311-3722, or airport T/F 480-0597/0374—24 hrs), every 20 mins until 1700, every 30 mins 1700-2200, US$14, return US$25, allow 50 mins for journey; at Ezeiza their stand is in Arrivals, if you have a hotel reservation, a minibus will drop you off at any hotel in the centre. Alternatively, if in a group of 2 or more, call Mary Maxwell, T 801 0546 (Spanish only) – competitive and efficient service to and from the airport. Best to call her in advance. Both airport ("rojos") and city ("amarillos") **taxis** are allowed to operate from Ezeiza; they have separate departure points: "rojos" in front of the central hall, "amarillos" 50 m to the left of the "Espígón Internacional". Fixed-price **remise taxis** can be booked from the Manuel Tienda León counter at Ezeiza, US$49 (incl US$2 toll) payable in advance. The taxi fare of US$30, however long the journey, is fixed by government; in reality drivers charge US$45 or more, or illegally use the meter (bargaining possible, essential when going from city to airport). Avoid unmarked cars at Ezeiza no matter how attractive the fare may sound; drivers are adept at separating you far from more money than you can possibly owe them. Always ask to see the taxi driver's licence; if you think you have been cheated, T 343-5001 to complain. If you take an "amarillo", the Policía Aeronáutica on duty notes down the car's licence and time of departure. Local electric trains go to Ezeiza suburb from the Constitución station. The train, marked "Ezeiza" costs US$0.80, and takes 40 mins. 1 block from the Ezeiza station, colectivo No 502 goes to the airport, US$0.60, and takes 20 mins.

No 86 **buses** (white and blue, marked "Fournier") also run to the centre from outside the airport terminal to the right, (*servicio diferencial* takes 1½ hrs, US$5, *servicio común* 2¼ hrs, US$1) between 0500 and 2400, US$3.50. To travel to Ezeiza, catch the bus in Plaza de Mayo or, preferably, at Av de Mayo y Perú—make sure it has "Aeropuerto" sign in the window as many 86s stop short of Ezeiza. Only one bag is normally allowed and passengers with backpacks may be charged double fare. A display in immigration in the terminal shows choices and prices of all ways into the city.

All internal flights, services to Punta del Este and Montevideo and flights from Latin American countries with an intermediate stop in Argentina are handled by Jorge Newbery Airport, usually known as Aeroparque, 4 km N of the centre near the New Port, T 771-2071. Duty free facilities as at Ezeiza. Tourist information, and luggage deposit, US$5 per piece. Exchange, Banco de la Nación (open until 2100, rates as in town). Manuel Tienda León bus also serves Aeroparque (see above for downtown address). Remise taxis for the centre cost US$10-15 depending on destination, reliable. Avoid unofficial taxis which can demand up to US$40. AR and Austral offer minibus services to Aeroparque every 20 mins, US$5. Local bus 45 runs from outside the airport to the Retiro metro and railway station, then follows Av L N Alem and Paseo Colón to La Boca (if going to airport take a 33 signed to Aeroparque, not all go there); *colectivos* 56 and 160 also go to Aeroparque; US$0.50. None is advisable with bulky luggage.

Manuel Tienda León operates buses between Ezeiza and Jorge Newbery airports, stopping in city centre, US$15. AR offer free transfers between Ezeiza and Aeroparque to passengers whose incoming and connecting flights are both on AR: ask at AR desk for a voucher.

Aerolíneas Argentinas and Austral offer daily flights to the main cities, for details see text under intended destination; **see also p 226** for the Visit Argentina fare. If travelling in the S, book ahead if possible with LADE, whose flights are cheaper than buses in most cases.

Passenger Boats The *Buenos Aires Herald* (English-language daily) notes all shipping movements. Flota Fluvial del Estado (Corrientes 489, T 311-0728) organizes cruises from Buenos Aires, Dársena Sur (dock T 361-4161/0346); up the Paraná river. South Coast, down to Punta Arenas and intermediate Patagonian ports, served by the Imp & Exp de la Patagonia and Elma (state shipping line). Very irregular sailings. For connections with Uruguay, **see p 81**.

Railways On 10 March 1994, the government withdrew its funding for Ferrocarriles Argentinos, handing responsibility for all services to the provinces through which the lines run. Few provinces accepted the responsibility, because of lack of resources. Most trains have therefore been suspended. Those that were operating in May 1995 are given below, but note that this can change at any moment.

There are 4 main terminals: **Retiro**: Services in operation: Mitre line to Córdoba, suspended Mar 1994; Tucumán, Mon and Fri, returning Thur and Sun, 14 hrs, US$50 pullman, US$40 1st, US$35 tourist (service being run by Tucumán provincial government). The terminal has a left-luggage facility, US$1.50 per bag per day.

Constitución: Ferrocarril Nacional Roca (Southern)—T 304-0021. Bariloche (via Bahía Blanca), Wed and Sun 0740 (but very unreliable service and future uncertain in early 1995), US$65 pullman, US$60 1st, US$44 tourist; San Antonio Oeste; US$30, 22 hrs; Mar del Plata 7 times daily from 0100-1830, US$30 pullman, US$19 1st, US$14 tourist; continues to Miramar. Necochea, Mon, Wed, Fri 2100 (daily in summer), returns Tues, Thur, Sun, US$20.50 pullman, US$16 1st class, US$14 2nd. The Automóvil Club Argentino provides car transporters for its members (see **ACA** in **Information for Visitors**).

Federico Lacroze: Ferrocarril Nacional Urquiza (North-Eastern)—T 55-5214. No services except the Tren Histórico. Every Sun a Scottish 1888 Neilson steam engine pulls old wooden carriages, either to Capilla del Señor with lunch or a folkloric show at an *estancia* (dep 1000, return 1900), or to Zárate across the Zárate-Brazo Largo bridges over the Paraná river (dep 0900). Prices from US$25-65, T 799-4263/856-5917/46-4186.

Once: Ferrocarril Nacional Sarmiento (Western)—T 87-0041/2/3, for services in the province of Buenos Aires.

NB The railways maintain an information centre and booking office at Maipú 88, but it is largely inactive. For Ferrocarriles Argentinos T 331-3280. There is a money-back scheme if the ticket is changed, ranging from 90% of the fare if within 96 hrs of purchase to 40% within 24 hrs of your trip.

Buses The long-distance bus station, Estación Terminal de Omnibus, is behind Retiro, on Av Ramos Mejía and Antártida Argentina (Subte C); T for information 311-6073/6088. All long distance buses leave from here. All offices are on the E side on the ground floor. There are too many bus companies to list them all, but at the information desk on the 2nd floor you can get information and prices of all the companies. The passage between the bus station and Retiro is packed with market stalls and is narrow (beware pickpockets), as are the turnstile exits from the platforms, all designed to inconvenience those with luggage (although, as one correspondent points out, this also slows down anyone trying to make a speedy escape with someone else's belongings). There are two left-luggage offices (US$5 per piece), open 0600-2300. Some bus companies charge extra for luggage (illegally). Fares may vary according to time of year and advance booking is advisable Dec-Mar. Some companies may give discounts, such as 20% to YHA or student-card holders and foreign, as well as Argentine teachers and university lecturers. Travellers have reported getting discounts without showing evidence of status, so it's always worth asking. For further details of bus services and fares, look under proposed destinations. There is a bank at the bus station. There are cinemas, cafés, shops, toilets and news stands, all overpriced. (Further modifications to improve comfort, including a special section for international travellers, were due to be completed by May 1995.) TISA is the agent for Amerbuspass, see above under **Tours** and in **Introduction and Hints, Travel To and In South America**.

Hitchhiking For Pinamar, Mar del Plata and nearby resorts, take bus for La Plata to Alpargatas *rotonda* roundabout. For points further S, take bus 96 to Ruta 3—the Patagonia road. Best to hitch from a service station where trucks stop. The police control point at Km 43 (S) is reported to be friendly and will help to find a lift for you. For Mendoza try truck drivers at the wine warehouses near Palermo station (take Subte to Puerto Pacífico, at Buenos Aires al Pacífico train station, at viaduct crossing Av Santa Fe/Av Cabildo; turn left into Av Juan B Justo for the warehouses).

Travel into Neighbouring Countries

By Road
Four branches of the Inter-American Highway run from Buenos Aires to the borders of Chile, Bolivia, Paraguay and Brazil. The roads are paved except when otherwise stated.

To Chile via Río Cuarto, Mercedes, San Luis, and Mendoza, Total: 1,310 km paved throughout. (Direct buses to Santiago, 23 hrs, US$70-75, eg Ahumada, El Rápido Internacional and others, 1,459 km; US$70-75 to Valparaíso or Viña del Mar, TAC, Fénix Pullman Norte.) There are also road connections between Catamarca and Copiapó, Bariloche and Osorno and Puerto Montt, and between Salta and Antofagasta.

To Bolivia via Rosario, Villa María, Córdoba, Santiago del Estero, Tucumán, and Jujuy. Total: 1,994 km. There is no direct bus service from Buenos Aires to La Paz but through connections can be booked (Sudamericanos, T 27-6591, goes via La Quiaca–Villazón, US$135, 48 hrs; Atahualpa, T 315-0601, goes via La Quiaca, US$95, or Pocitos, US$91, daily, then a new ticket to La Paz must be bought). If you wish to go part of the way by rail, train/bus combinations are possible via Tucumán.

To Paraguay via Rosario, Santa Fe, Resistencia, Clorinda and Asunción (via toll bridge). Total: 1,370 km. Buses take 20-22 hours, with 11 companies (all close to each other at the Retiro bus terminal). You have choice between *diferencial* (with business class seating, food, drinks, luxury service, US$95) and *común* (without food, but has a/c, toilet, US$60). Also 5 companies to Ciudad del Este, US$45; Caaguazú goes to Villarrica, and Expreso Río Paraná and La Encarnaceña go to Encarnación, US$46. Tickets can be bought up to 30 days in advance.
    Those who wish to drive to Paraguay via Misiones to visit San Ignacio Miní or the Iguazú Falls can take the direct route to Posadas and Iguazú (Route 12), crossing the Río Paraná by the Zárate-Brazo Largo bridges. Alternatively cross the river by the tunnel between Santa Fe and Paraná, or by the bridge between Resistencia and Corrientes and join Route 12. From Posadas cross the river to Encarnación by the bridge and take a good 370-km road to Asunción (see Paraguayan chapter).

To Brazil To the Iguazú Falls, follow route 12 via Posadas (see above under **To Paraguay**). An alternative route to the Brazilian frontier at Paso de los Libres is via the Zárate-Brazo Largo bridges over the Río Paraná, then following Route 14 via Colón and Concordia. Total: 668 km. Direct buses to Brazil via Paso de los Libres by Pluma (T 313-3901): São Paulo, 40 hrs US$145, Rio de Janeiro, 45 hrs, US$163; Porto Alegre, US$71; Curitiba, 38 hrs, US$128; Florianópolis, 32 hrs, US$115. To Rio, changing buses at Posadas and Foz do Iguaçu is almost half price, 50 hrs. A third route across the Río de la Plata and through Uruguay is a bit cheaper, not as long and offers a variety of transport and journey breaks. Tickets from Buen Viaje, Av Córdoba 415 (31-2953) or Pluma, Av Córdoba 461 (311-4871 or 311-5986).

To Uruguay Direct road connections by means of two bridges over the Río Uruguay between Puerto Colón and Paysandú and between Puerto Unzué and Fray Bentos (much slower than the air or sea routes given below). "*Bus de la carrera*" (office 65-67 Retiro, T 313-3695) links Montevideo and Buenos Aires, 8½ hrs, US$25. Departure from each city at 1000, 2200 and 2230 via Zárate-Gualeguaychú-Puerto Unzué-Fray Bentos-Mercedes.

To Peru Ormeño (T 313-2259) and El Rápido Internacional (T 393-5057) have a direct service Buenos Aires-Lima, from Retiro bus station, 3½ days, all meals incl, one night spent in Coquimbo, Chile (if you need a visa for Chile, get one before travelling), the route is: Mendoza, Coquimbo, Arica, Tacna, Nazca, Ica, Lima. El Rápido Internacional, from Buenos Aires bus terminal, ticket office 89, US$160.

Air, River and Railway Services

Brazil Daily air services to São Paulo, Rio de Janeiro and other Brazilian cities. No rail connections. Shipping service between Buenos Aires and Brazilian ports by various transatlantic lines. See *Buenos Aires Herald*, English-language daily.

Chile There are no passenger-train service across the Andes between Mendoza and Santiago, but the train service between Salta and Antofagasta is open again. Bus services are available on both these routes.

Foreign and national lines fly daily between Buenos Aires and Santiago, 1½-2 hrs.

Bolivia As of Mar 1993 there were no passenger rail services from Argentina to connect with the Bolivian lines from La Quiaca to La Paz and Pocitos to Santa Cruz de la Sierra. There are air services to La Paz and Santa Cruz de la Sierra by AR and LAB.

Paraguay There are no Argentine trains to the Paraguayan border. There are daily air services to Asunción by AR. See also Posadas, p 160. Occasional river boats to Asunción in May to Oct, 11 days, bed and private bath, food and nightly entertainment, US$400, reported good. Details from Tamul, Lavalle 388, T 393-2306/1533.

Uruguay Tickets heavily booked Dec-Mar, especially at weekends. **NB** No money changing facilities in Tigre, and poor elsewhere. Beware of overcharging by taxis from the harbour to the centre of Buenos Aires. Note: US$6 port tax is charged on all services to Colonia/Carmelo, US$10 on direct services to Montevideo (no tax payable for journeys from Uruguay to Argentina). Do not buy Uruguayan bus tickets in BsAs; wait till you get to Colonia.

Boat connections: 1) From Tigre to Carmelo, boats are operated by 2 companies, Cacciola at 0800 and 1730, 3 hrs, and Delta Nave, Mon-Sat 0830 and 1630, Sun 0830 and 2400, 3 hrs, both services US$11 to Carmelo, US$13 (Delta Nave) and US$18.50 (Cacciola) to Montevideo; tickets at Lavalle 623 and Florida 520, BsAs (T 322-9374/0026) or Estación Fluvial, *local* 13, Tigre. It is advisable to book in advance; connecting bus from Carmelo to Montevideo.

2) Direct to Montevideo, Buquebus, Córdoba 867, T 313-4444/5500, "Avión de Buquebus" 4 times a day, 0730, 1130, 1530, 1930 (Sun 0730, 1530 and 1930), 3 hrs (summer schedule), US$37 one way, vehicles US$90-100, bus connection to Punta del Este.

3) From Dársena Sur to Colonia, services by Ferrytur, Av Córdoba 699, T 394-8412 (port: Dársena Sur, Ribera Este, T 361-4161) at 0800 and 1600 (Mon-Fri), 0830 (Sat), US$18 (plus US$6 seaport tax), US$25 incl bus to Montevideo, 3 hrs to Colonia, total of 6 to Montevideo. Free bus will pick you up 1 hr before departure on Florida y Córdoba. Buquebus' ferry service BsAs to Colonia, plus bus to Montevideo, costs US$29 one way, 4 times a day. Uruguayan immigration officer on ferries. Ferrytur run a catamaran service BsAs-Colonia, with connecting bus to Montevideo, 45 mins, US$27, US$34 incl bus to Montevideo, cars US$70. Sailings may be cancelled in bad weather.

4) Puente Fluvial runs hydrofoils (*alíscafos*) to Colonia 3 times a day (winter) or 4 times a day (summer), 1 hr, US$27 one way, US$34 incl bus to Montevideo, US$42 to Punta del Este. There are also sailings La Plata-Colonia once a day on Fri, Sat and Sun. All tickets from Puente Fluvial, Córdoba 787, T 314 2473/2672/0969, or at dock at Madero y Córdoba, T 311 1346/6160; reconfirm seat in Montevideo.

Several airlines fly from Jorge Newbery Airport (Aeroparque, Puente Aéreo section) to Colonia 12 mins, US$30. Buy tickets directly at the LAPA or AUSA counters shortly before departure (except at weekends when flights are fully booked). Continue by bus to Montevideo (or special car connecting with Lapa flight, US$3-4 to Montevideo). Also from Jorge Newbery, shuttle service to Montevideo, known as Puente Aéreo and run by AR and Pluna, daily 0730 and 0910, 40 mins. Book at Jorge Newbery Airport or T 393-5122/773-0440. Punta del Este, 5 flights daily 15 Dec-1 Mar with AR, 40 mins, or Pluna (out of season, Fri only).

Suburbs of Buenos Aires

Avellaneda, a separate municipality of over 650,000 people, is one of the most important industrial centres in the country; the handling of hides, wool and animal produce is concentrated here. It is 5 km from Plaza Constitución station, on the other side of the Riachuelo river from Boca.

Quilmes (BsAs), with one of the world's largest breweries, an important industrial centre, was given that name because the Quilmes Indians were forcibly moved there in 1665 from the famous Inca site in Tucumán Province (**see p 108**)

The naturalist and writer WH Hudson (1841-1922) was born at Florencio Varela, near Quilmes, about 32 km from Buenos Aires. His birthplace is now a national monument. Hudson's *The Naturalist in La Plata*, reedited by Dover, is very useful on Argentine fauna.

Olivos, on the River Plate coast, 20 minutes by the Bartolomé Mitre Railway or 40 mins by Bus No 60, is a favourite residential district. The presidential residence is there, many foreign residents. Population, about 160,000. (A rec restaurant here is *Grinzing*, Córdoba 2864, European specialities, historical objects in house, garden with swimming pool.)

From Olivos station, walk up Calle Corrientes with its neocolonial architecture and old, shady trees. Taking Corrientes to the river you reach the Puerto de Olivos, mainly used for construction materials, but there are a marina (private yacht club) and several *parrilladas* (popular). On Sat and Sun a catamaran sails to Tigre, 2 hrs, rec trip past riverside mansions, sailing boats and windsurfers.

Martínez, nearby, is an attractive residential area overloooking the Río de la Plata, with an interesting shopping area. Sailing and windsurfing are well represented and river launches and other craft may be hired. At the Panamericana intersection with Edison and Paraná is the giant Unicenter shopping mall and supermarket.

San Isidro, just beyond Olivos, a resort for golf, yachting, swimming, and athletics, is one of the most attractive suburbs on the coast. Fashionable nightlife here, especially along the river bank. There is a magnificent turf racecourse, an attractive central plaza ("hippy" fair at weekends) and fine colonial buildings with a historical museum. Pop: 80,000.

Tigre (pop 40,000) on the delta of the Paraná, is about 29 km (45 minutes) by train from Buenos Aires, US$1.50 one way, every 10 mins during peak hours, otherwise every 15 or 20 mins. Take the 'C' line train from platform 1 or 2 at Retiro station (FC Mitre) to Bartolomé Mitre and change to Tren de la Costa. It can also be reached by bus 60 bajo, which takes a little longer; the 60 alto bus takes a faster road but is less interesting for sightseeing. Regattas are held in Nov and Mar on the Río Luján. There are numerous "recreos" and restaurants on the river front, but sleeping accommodation is not good. There is an excellent fruit market at nearby Canal San Fernando on Sun; craft market is tacky. Inland from Tigre are innumerable canals and rivulets, holiday homes, clubs (some beautiful buildings – the Italian club is in Venetian style) and a profitable fruit growing centre. The fishing is excellent and there is peace on the waterways, apart from motor-boats at week-ends. Regular launch services, each company with its own routes, for all parts of the Delta, including taxi launches—watch prices for these!—leave from wharf opposite railway station. Be warned that if you leave just before lunch the launch crew may stop along the way for a 1-1½ hr lunch break! Another journey through the Delta, with its lush tropical vegetation (even in winter) is fascinating. The option is a 1½-hr ride by catamaran (US$10); they dock on the other side of the bridge from the railway station and leave at 1330 and 1600 Mon-Fri, and hourly from 1300 on Sat and Sun; longer trips (4½ hrs) to the open Río de la Plata estuary are available. The snacks and refreshments on board are expensive: if you sit on the open deck you can eat your own food. Do not confuse the tourist catamarans with the *lanchas* which run regular passenger services between islands and are much cheaper (4 hr trip incl lunch stop, US$3). In the delta is *El Tropezón*, an old inn on Paraná de las Palmas island (the boat crews know it); C pp incl meals, formerly a haunt of Hemingway, now frequented by affluent *porteños*, highly rec despite the mosquitoes. Also rec, *Atelier*, *l'Marangatú* and *Fondeadero*. Delta **Youth Hostel** at Río Luján y Abra Vieja, Canal de San Fernando (take bus 170 from the square outside train station to the river. The YH is on an island. There is no ferry, ring bell on landing stage and wait, or ask a passing boat to take you across (or call Hostel manager who may pick you up), F pp, clean, hot showers, table tennis, volleyball, canoes; ask at Talcahuano 214, Buenos Aires. Bring all food in advance, there are basic cooking facilities. *Restaurant Sagitaria*, near railway station, good, cheap. Direct ferry to Carmelo, Uruguay (**see p 82**) from opposite railway station. A new rail line is being built out to the delta, 'Tren de la Costa'. Starts from new terminal on Av Maipú. Due to open Sep 1995.

The Museo Naval, Liniers 1264, T 749-6161, is worth a visit (open Mon-Fri 0800-1230, Sat and Sun 1400-1800). It contains models old and new, navigation instruments, flags and banners, and paintings of naval battles. There are also relics of the 1982 South Atlantic war on display outside. The Museo de la Reconquista, Liniers 818, T 749-0900, Wed-Sun 1500-1900, celebrates the reconquest of Buenos Aires from the British in 1806-07.

Martín García island (Juan Díaz de Solís' landfall in 1516) in the Río de la Plata, 45 km N of Buenos Aires, used to be a military base. Now it is an ecological/historical centre and an ideal excursion from the capital, with many trails through the thick cane brakes, trees and rocky outcrops – interesting birds and flowers. Some of the old buildings have a colonial air. Boat trips leave from Tigre at 0800, returning 1600, 3 hr journey. Reservations can be made through Cacciola, Florida 520, 1° piso, Of 113, T 394-4115, who also handle bookings for the inn and restaurant on the island. Excursion costs US$42 with *asado* lunch, US$25 without. For bungalow rental T (0315) 24546.

Other Towns in the Pampas

66 km W of the capital by Sarmiento railway from Once station (1-1½ hours) or by bus from Once station (1 hr) is **Luján** (pop 30,000), a place of pilgrimage for all devout Catholics in Argentina. An image of the Virgin was being taken from church to church in the area in 1630 by ox cart. At a certain spot the cart got stuck, in spite of strenuous efforts by men and oxen to move it. This was taken as a sign that the Virgin willed she should stay there. A chapel was built for the image, and around it grew Luján. The chapel has long since been superseded by an impressive neo-Gothic basilica and the Virgin now stands on the High Altar. 8 May is her day. Each arch of the church is dedicated to an Argentine province, and two of the transepts to Uruguay and Paraguay. Very heavy traffic at weekends.

Museo Colonial e Histórico (The Colonial and Historical Museum), in the old Cabildo building, is one of the most interesting museums in the country. Exhibits illustrate its historical and political development. Open Wed-Sat 1200-1800. No cameras allowed, and nowhere to store them. General Beresford, the commander of the British troops which seized Buenos Aires in 1806, was a prisoner here, and so, in later days, were Generals Mitre, Paz, and Belgrano. There are also museums devoted to transport and to religious ex-votos. The Río Luján is picturesque at this point, a favourite spot for picnic parties.

Hotel *La Paz*, 9 de Julio 1054, T 24034; several others. There are numerous **restaurants**: an excellent one is *L'Eau Vive* on the road to Buenos Aires at Constitución 2112; it is run by nuns, pleasant surroundings.

There are dozens of small, prosperous towns scattered throughout the vast area of the pampas. They serve as clearing centres for the cattle and grain and supply the rural population, which is much denser in the Humid Pampa than elsewhere in rural Argentina. Only the larger towns and resorts are dealt with here.

La Plata (pop 545,000), on the Río de la Plata 56 km SE of Buenos Aires was founded in 1882 as capital of Buenos Aires province after the city of Buenos Aires had become federal capital. Its port is accessible to ships of the largest tonnage. Its major industrial interest is the YPF petroleum refinery; a 72-km pipeline runs to the South Dock at Buenos Aires. Its Museo de Historia Natural is one of the best in Argentina and has several unique exhibits. A motorway is being built to link La Plata with Buenos Aires, via Riachuelo, Avellaneda, Berazategui, Gonnet and Tolosa.

Points of Interest The Museum at La Plata is famous for its collection of extinct animals. Its treasures are largely ethnological and include human skulls, mummies, and prehistoric implements. There are zoological, botanical, geological, mineralogical, palaeontological and archaeological sections, guided tours in Spanish. Highly rec, open daily, 1000-1900, US$3, closed in Jan and on public holidays (T 21-8217). Well laid-out Zoological Gardens; fine racecourse and Observatory. The Museum, Zoological Gardens, and Observatory are all in the public park; park entrance at Calle 1 y 53 (take bus to Plaza Moreno, US$0.50). The Muncipalidad and Cathedral ("a magnificent building with a classical Gothic interior") are in the Plaza Moreno. W of the city is the República de los Niños, an interesting children's village with scaled-down public buildings, built under the first Perón administration; take a green microbus 273 or a red and black 518 to República de los Niños from Plaza San Martín. To the NE are the Islas del Río Santiago, the Yacht Club, Arsenal and Naval Academy. At Punta Lara, an Argentine holiday resort nearby, there is a small, interesting nature reserve, slide show and tour, open to public Sat-Sun, 1000-1300 and 1400-1800.

Local Holiday Foundation of the City, 19 Nov.

Hotels A3 *San Marco*, Calle 54 No 523, T 40456/40923, good; *Corregidor*, Calle 26

BUENOS AIRES
& THE PAMPAS

between Av 53 and 54, 4-star, expensive; **D** *Roga*, Calle 54 No 334, close to museum; **D** *Plaza*, Calle 44 y 2, with bath; **D** *Roca*, Calle 1 y 42, with bath.

Restaurants Restaurants rarely open before 2100. *El Fogón*, Av 1, Calle 49; *Ianno*, rec, Calle 46 y 10; *Don Quijote*, Plaza Paso, good value, best in town, can get very crowded; Chinese "tenedor libre" at *Guinga*, Plaza Paso; *La Linterne*, Calle 60 y Av 1, upmarket, good value; *El Chaparral*, good *parrillada*, Calle 60 y Calle 117. Several reasonable restaurants around the bus station (which is in the red light area, though quite safe even at night). Recommended bar, with steak sandwiches, *El Modelo*, Calle 52 and 4. Best *empanadas* at *La Madrileña*, a hole-in-the-wall on Calle 60 between 5 and 6. Best bakery is *El Globo*, Calle 43 y 5.

Entertainments Tango and tropical music at *El Viejo Almacén*, on Diagonal 74, Calle 2. There are free concerts during the summer in the Bosque amphitheatre.

Tourist Office In the old white theatre on the main plaza, also at bus terminal. Turismo San Martín, Calle 51 between 7 and 8, rec.

Buses To Buenos Aires, 1½ hrs, US$3.20, about every half hour, Río de la Plata company (from Retiro in Buenos Aires day and night; from Plaza Constitución, daytime, and Once). **Train** from Constitución station, US$13 1st class, US$17 pullman.

On the coast 400 km S of Buenos Aires, lies Mar del Plata, the most celebrated Argentine seaside resort. The road and rail routes S to it are through Chascomús and Dolores. *Chascomús* (pop 22,200), 126 km from Buenos Aires, is on a wide plain on the shores of Lago Chascomús, which covers 3,000 ha and swells greatly in size during the rains. Its slightly brackish water is an important breeding place for *pejerrey* fish; amateur fishing competitions are held in the winter season. There is a *gaucho* museum, and also a Regatta Club, bathing beaches and 4 campsites including Monte Brown, on the far side of the lake (all nicely located, but poor facilities).

Dolores, 204 km (3½ hrs by bus) from Buenos Aires, has a district population of 30,000; it was founded in 1818, destroyed by Indians three years later, and rebuilt.

It is a grain and cattle farming centre, little changed since the 1940s. The Museo y Parque Libres del Sur, commemorating the revolt of the district against Rosas in the early 19C, is interesting and well displayed. *Hotel Plaza*, very pleasant.

San Clemente del Tuyú, 107 km E of Dolores, is the nearest Atlantic coastal resort to Buenos Aires. A family resort with little nightlife, it is cheaper than the more fashionable resorts further S. Frequent buses from Mar del Plata, with Empresa Costamar, first at 0700, US$11, 5 hrs. To Buenos Aires with several companies, US$15-20. 9 km away at **Punta Rasa**, there are an old lighthouse and a nature reserve owned by the Fundación Vida Silvestre, with interesting birdlife. (**Hotels** many along the promenade, incl **C** *Aquario*, Calle 15, clean, friendly, incl breakfast; **D** *Splendid*, on main shopping street; *Residencial-Restaurante Cueva*, Calle 4 y Calle 1, not very clean, poor service, but cheap beer; **D** *Residencial Bahía*, Calle 4, entre 1 y 15, breakfast incl, good; several campsites. *Restaurante Yo y Vos*, Calle 4 y Calle 17, large and cheap portions, friendly, good. US dollars can be changed at the Banco de la Provincia de Buenos Aires, Calle 1 y Calle 4, but TCs are not accepted anywhere in town.) 3 km from the centre, near the harbour, is *Mundo Marino*, the largest oceanarium in South America (T 0252-21071), with amusements and shows as well as whales, penguins, etc; open daily from 1000, closes 1530 May-Sep, 1630 Mar-Apr, Oct-Dec, 1800 Jan-Feb. Micro bus 500 goes there.

Pinamar, 89 km S of San Clemente, a resort with a casino, is eclipsing Mar del Plata. The water-skiing is good. Fish, including conger eel (*congrio*) may be bought on the beach from local fishermen. Tourist office, friendly and helpful, is in the main square.

Accommodation Many, from *Arenas*, Av Bunge 700, T 82444, 4 star, to *Berlín*, Rivadavia 326, T 82320, 1 star. All hotels fully booked throughout Jan-Mar (as much as two years in advance!). Houses and apartments can be rented from Dec-Mar: 2-room flats about US$800/month, up to US$5,000 for a mansion. In Mar rates are halved. **Youth Hostel** Nuestras Malvinas y Sarmiento, T 82908, and *Moby Dick* campsite at Ostende, T 86045. Many other campsites close to town.

Villa Gesell (pop 8,700), 22 km further S, is a modern resort with a chocolate factory, fine beaches and over 100 hotels, which has become very popular although less crowded than Mar del Plata. Tourist office at bus terminal. Direct bus service to Buenos Aires (US$29) by Empresas Antón and Río de la Plata (book in advance at weekends).

Hotels *Terrazas Club*, 4 star, suite accommodation, Av 2 between Calles 104 and 105, T 6 2181; *Colón*, 2 star, 3 blocks from beach at Av 4, Calle 104, T 62310, private bath, restaurant; **C** *Hostería Gran Chalet*, Paseo 105 No 447 y Av 4-5, T 62913, clean, rec; **D** *Bero*, Av 4 y Calle 141, T 66077, opposite bus terminal. Many others of all classes within 800m of sea. Many apartments for rent (rates as Pinamar). **Youth Hostel** *Albergue Camping El Coyote*, Alameda 212 y 306, Barrio Norte, T 68448.

Camping Sites Many, a few open all year round.

Air Flights with AR and LAPA, the latter for half the normal tariff.

Mar del Plata, the greatest Argentine resort, built at the turn of the century, is 130 km further S and 400 km from the capital. The normal population is 407,000, but during the summer about two million visitors stay there; there are all classes of apartment blocks, boarding houses and lodgings. It is necessary to book in advance between late Dec and mid-Mar (when the night-life continues all night). For the rest of the year the town is fairly quiet and good value. The city is famous for its casino: the upper floor is open to the public, US$5. Small but pleasant natural history museum in Plaza España off Playa La Perla. Interesting municipal art museum at Villa Ortiz Basualdo, Av Colón 1189. Centro Cultural Victoria Ocampo, Villa Victoria, Matheu 1851 (house prefabricated in England, early 20th century), where the famous author spent her summers until her death in late 1970s.

There are fine squares, especially Plaza San Martín, and eight km of beaches, including fashionable Playa Grande, with its private clubs and the summer estates of wealthy *porteños*; Playa Bristol, where the casino is; and Playa La Perla, with moderately priced hotels. At Punta Iglesia there is a large rock carving of Florentino Ameghino, the palaeontologist who collected most of the fossils in the museum at La Plata. The wooded municipally-owned Parque Camet is 8 km to the N. It has polo grounds and playing fields. For those who do not care for surf bathing, there are salt-water pools. Fishing is good all along the coast and *pejerrey, corvina* and *merluza* (hake) abound; you can charter a private launch for shark fishing.

The port can be reached by bus, 15 mins from bus terminal. There are a large fishing fleet, excursion boats, seafood restaurants and a huge sealion colony (walk along Escollera Sur-Southern breakwater). **Museo de Hombre del Puerto – Cleto Ciocchini**, Fri-Sun 1600-2000, US$1, at Padre J Dutto 383, shows the history of the port and its first Sicilian fishermen.

Visits can be paid to the rocky promontory of Cabo Corrientes to watch the breakers; to Punta Mogotes lighthouse (open Thur 1330-1700); to the Gruta de Lourdes, and the Bosque Peralta Ramos.

Local Holidays 10 Feb (Foundation of City); 10 Nov (Day of Tradition); 22 Nov (St Cecilia).
Mar del Plata is known for its hand-finished sweaters.

Hotels Four-star (category **L2-A1**) incl *Provincial*, 500 rooms, Blvd Marítimo 2500, T 24081/9; *Dos Reyes*, Av Colón 2129, T 28694; *Hermitage*, Blvd Peralta Ramos 2657, T 519081, 150 rooms; *Sasso*, M de Hoz 3545, T 840031 and *Gran Dora*, Buenos Aires 1841, T 25002/6. **L3-A3** *Astor*, Entre Ríos 1649, T 23051/4, small, no credit cards, 3 mins from beach. Among the 3-star hotels (category **A2-A3**) are *Benedetti*, Av Colón 2198, rec, T 30031/2; *Gran Continental*, Córdoba 1929, T 23027; *Presidente*, Corrientes 1516, T 28810. There are scores of other good hotels at reasonable rates eg **B** *O Sole Mío*, Av Independencia 1277, T 26685, half board, Italian run, highly rec; **C** *Boedo*, Almirante Brown 1771 (T 24695), with bath, hot water, clean, good value, near beaches (open Jan-Feb only); **C** *Europa*, Arenales 2735, 2 blocks from bus station (reductions in low season), clean, quiet, hot water; **D** *Hospedaje Paraná*, Lamadrid 2749, near bus terminal, with bath; **D** *Monterrey*, Lamadrid 2627, clean, good; **D** *Niza*, Santiago del Estero 1843 (E out of season), bath, clean, safe, friendly, rec; **D** *Peley*, on Alberdi near bus station, clean, comfortable, open all year, rec, good value restaurant. During summer months it is essential to book in advance. In the off-season, bargain everywhere. **Youth Hostel**, Tucumán 2728, T 27927, E pp, friendly, clean, only a small discount for YHA card holders. Many hotels and restaurants close when the summer is over; worth looking round the bus-station area out of season for lodging (eg *Little Hotel*) and food.
There are many houses and apartments for rent, built for retired people.

Camping *Pinar de la Serena* and other sites, reasonable prices. Several on the road S.

Restaurants *Hostería del Caballito Blanco*, Av Rivadavia 2534, excellent, German decor. *Cantina Capri*, Belgrano 2161 (near Casino), not cheap but excellent value; *La Paella*, Entre Ríos 2025, good; *La Caracola*, Martínez de Hoz y 12 de Octubre, seafood, good but dear; *Tía Teresa*, San Luis, near Colón, fresh pasta dishes, good value; *Lo de Terri*, Gascón y San Luis, *parrilla*, good *chorizo* and *vacio*; *Raviolandia*, Colón y Las Heras, good, cheap, try the seafood with rice. Vegetarian: *El Jardín*, San Martín 2463, *tenedor libre*, and *La Huerta*, San Martín 2300. Many *tenedor libre* restaurants of all kinds along San Martín. *Los Inmortales*, Corrientes 1662, good, moderately priced. Good value meals at *La Nueva Glorieta*, Alberti 1821, and *El Nuevo Hispano*, Alberti 1933. Best seafood, and cheapest, at Centro Comercial del Puerto (eg *Puerto Gallego*).

Banks and Exchange Lloyds Bank (BLSA) Ltd, Av Luro 3101. Open 1000-1600. Exchange houses on San Martín and surroundings. *Jonestur*, San Martín 2574, will collect on personal US bank cheques in 15 working days, at 2½% fee. Amex, Colón 2605, does not cash TCs.

Casino Open Dec to end-Apr, 1600-0330; 1600-0400 on Sat. Winter opening, May-Dec, Mon-Fri 1500-0230; weekends 1500-0300. Entrance US$5.

Cultural Events Reduced price tickets are often available from *Cartelera Baires*, Santa Fe 1844, local 33 or from *Galería de los Teatros*, Santa Fe 1751. **La Cultura** (formerly Sociedad de Cultura Inglesa), San Luis 2498, friendly, extensive library.

Post Office Av Luro 2460. **Telecommunications** Av Luro y Santiago del Estero.

Tourist Office Blvd Marítimo, Peralta Ramos 2267, T 41325, nr Casino, open 0800-1900, good information, incl bus routes to all sites of interest.

Immigration Office, Chile y Alberti, open in the morning, allow 2-3 weeks for renewing visas.

Air Services Camet airport, 10 km from town. Many flights daily to and from Buenos Aires with Austral, Lapa and AR. *Remise* taxi from airport to town, mini bus US$3.50.

Trains leave Buenos Aires from Constitución, 10 minutes from the centre by any bus marked

"Constitución". Trains (a/c) take at least 5¼ hrs. See under Buenos Aires, **Railways**. Book very early for Dec-Mar trips. Mar del Plata station is at Av Luro 4599, about 13 blocks from centre.

Buses Bus station at corner of Alberti y Las Heras, convenient. Companies from Retiro terminal in **Buenos Aires**: 6 hrs, US$26, Micromar (T BsAs 313-3173), Costera Criolla (T BsAs 313-3580, also has *coche cama* in evening), Empresa Argentina, Chevallier (T BsAs 313-3297). Bus to and from **Miramar** hourly day and night, 45 mins US$4. El Cóndor and Rápido Argentino to **La Plata**, day and night, US$20. La Estrella goes to **San Martín de los Andes**, US$56, and **Bariloche**, US$60 (none direct; change at Bahía Blanca or Tres Arroyos). To **Bahía Blanca**, only Pampa, 6 daily, US$25, 5½ hrs. To **San Clemente del Tuyú**, with Empresa Costamar, frequent service daily, first at 0700, US$11, 5 hrs. To **Puerto Madryn** and **Trelew**, Wed and Sat night. For hitchhiking S, take a colectivo to the monument to El Gaucho.

Outside the city the country is undulating. To the N (34 km) is a lagoon—the Mar Chiquita—joined to the sea by a narrow channel. There is good fishing, yachting, boating and bathing here. Picturesque spots reached from the road inland to Balcarce are (19 km) **Laguna de los Padres** (a **reserva provincial**), and Sierra de los Padres and (32 km beyond) the Laguna La Brava, at the foot of the Balcarce hills.

In these hills, 68 km W of Mar del Plata, is the town of *Balcarce* (pop 28,800), a centre for hill visits to La Brava, above Ruca-Lauquén, and the Cinco Cerros, five hills most strangely shaped. Balcarce is the birthplace of the great racing driver **Juan Fangio**; it has a racing circuit and a motor museum with all Fangio's racing cars and trophies (Calles 17 y 18, open 1100-1800, US$5, rec). Frequent buses from Mar del Plata; excellent *parrilladas* on the outskirts.

Hotel C *Balcarce*, Calle 17, T 22055, good.

Beyond Balcarce Route 226 runs 103 km NW to *Tandil*, at the northern end of the Sierra de Tandil, a ridge of hills which run W from the sea into the pampa for 250 km. Tandil is 390 km by road from Buenos Aires (US$15, 6 hrs) via Azul, 300 km direct. The air is splendidly clear and refreshing, and the Holy Week festivities are outstanding. There is a beautiful lake in the city. Excursions to the Sierra La Aurora. Population: 125,000.

Hotels C *Plaza*, General Pinto 438, T 27160, 3 star, very friendly, clean, comfortable and quiet. **D** *Kaiku*, Mitre 902, T 23114, basic; **D** *Turista*, 14 de Julio 60, T22626, 1 star. *Libertador*, Mitre 545, T 22127, central, good value. Others near railway station. Rec restaurant is *El Estribo*, San Martín 759, friendly, good atmosphere.

From Mar del Plata, along the rocky sea-front to the SW, there is a road (53 km) to *Miramar* (pop 17,500). Like Mar del Plata, this is a resort, but the cliffs backing the beach are higher, the surrounding hills more picturesque, and it is a good deal cheaper. There is a fine golf course at *Hotel Golf Roca* and a casino. Immediately S of the city limits is an extensive forest park on the beach, the **Vivero Dunícola**, whose vegetation stays green and blooming throughout the year, despite winter night-time temperatures below freezing. Fourteen km by road to the S, among dunes and black rocks, is Mar del Sur (*Atlantic Hotel*) with good fishing in a lagoon and bathing on the beach.

Hotels Dozens of hotels and apartments. **C** *Santa Eulalia I*, Calle 26 No 851, T 20808, friendly but run down; **C** *Villa Cruz*, Calle 19, No 864, friendly, clean, near the beach; *Gran*, Calle 29, No 586 esq 12, T 20358, 2 star; *Palace*, Calle 23, No 774, T 20358, 3 star.

Camping El Durazno, 3 km from town, good facilities, shops, restaurant, F pp, take bus 501 marked "Playas". Many sites, reasonably priced.

Exchange None for TCs; must go to Mar del Plata. Try *Ibertur* and *Sastre* property offices.

Tourist Office on central plaza, maps available.

Transport *El Neptuno* train, daily at 1530 from Buenos Aires to Mar del Plata arriving at 2045, continues to Miramar, arriving 2150. **Bus** Buenos Aires-Miramar with Chevallier, Micromar and Costera Criolla (8 a day, US$31). Rápido del Sud from Mar del Plata stops at Calles 34 y 23.

About 110 km further SW along the coast is another famous seaside resort, *Necochea*, 500 km from Buenos Aires. It stands next to Mar del Plata in repute.

The surroundings are picturesque. Visits can be paid to the Paseo del Puente, Punta Negra, the Cascada (or waterfalls) 16 km up the Río Quequén Grande, Los Manantiales, and the Laguna de los Padres. Grain is exported from the port. Urban population: 52,000 including large Danish colony: there are a Danish club and consulate. About 100,000 tourists visit during the season, for the 24-km long beach is one of the best in the country. There is a municipal recreation complex, boasting a large modern casino, various sports facilities, including skating rink, swimming pool, bowling, a cinema and children's play area. The Parque Miguel Lillo (named after the Argentine botanist) faces the beach, comprising 400 ha of conifers, nature park, swan lake with paddle boats, an amphitheatre, museum and go-cart track. The casino is open in summer. Airport.

Hotels The Hotel Association is at Av 79 with Calle 4. Most hotels are in the downtown area from Calle 2 (parallel with beach) N between Av 71-91; there are at least a hundred within 700m of the beach. **C** *Doramar*, Calle 83, No 357, T 25815, family run, friendly, helpful; **D** *Hospedaje Solchaga*, Calle 62, No 2822, T 25584, clean, excellent; **E** *Hospedaje Bayo*, Calle 87, No 363, T 23334.

Camping Beach sites reported expensive in summer.

Restaurants *Rex*, Calle 62, "a trip to 1952 Paris"; *Mi Cantina*, excellent family restaurant. *Parrilla El Palenque*, Av 79 y 6; *Pizzería Kapotte*, Av 79 next beach, both rec.

Language School Instituto Argentino de Idiomas, Galería Monviso, local 8, Calles 62 y 63, rec.

Tourist Office At the bus terminal by the river at corner of Av 47 and Calle 582; also on beach front at Av 79.

Railway Buenos Aires-Necochea (station at Quequén), see under Buenos Aires **Railways**.

Bus Bus terminal at Av 47 y Calle 582, 4 km from the centre. Local bus to centre from outside the terminal. To/from Buenos Aires, US$44, La Estrella, El Cóndor and Costera Criolla. To Mar del Plata US$6, to Bahía Blanca $16.

About 3½ km across the mouth of the river from Necochea is **Quequén**, with an excellent beach, good bathing, and pleasant scenery. The channel to the port has to be dredged daily. **Hotels** *Costa Azul*, *Continental*, *Quequén*; campsites.

Over 320 km W from Necochea by paved road through the coastal area is the port of Bahía Blanca, which can be reached from Buenos Aires by rail (900 km), by air, or by a 688-km paved road (Route 3) through Las Flores (pop 20,200), Azul, Juárez and Tres Arroyos.

Azul, 264 km SW of Buenos Aires, is a cattle centre with an attractive plaza, a French Gothic-style Cathedral and an ethnographic museum. Population: about 45,000. A good stopping place if driving S from Buenos Aires. The river has been dammed to provide a water-sports centre.

Hotels C *Gran Hotel Azul*, Colón 626, T 22011, excellent cafeteria; **D** *Residencial Blue*, Av Mitre 983, T 22742, clean, friendly, near bus station; *Argentino*, Yrigoyen 378, T 25953; *Torino*, San Martín 1000, T 22749. Municipal campsite.

Tres Arroyos (pop 85,000), about 195 km from Bahía Blanca, is a cattle and wheat growing centre of 70,000 people. Many inhabitants are of Dutch origin; there are a Dutch consulate and a primary school named Holanda, supported by funds of the Argentine Dutch. There is also an important Danish colony, with school, club and consulate. A 68-km paved road runs S to the sea at the pleasant little resort of **Claromecó**, with a beautiful beach of dark sand backed by high dunes.

Hotels and Restaurants at Tres Arroyos incl *Parque*, Pellegrini 23, rec (restaurant) and *Andrea*, Istilart 228, good; *Tres Arroyos*, friendly, modest. *Restaurant Di Troppo*, near *Hotel Parque*, good. At **Claromecó D** *Comercio*, good restaurant, pleasant atmosphere; *Pablo Satini's Bar*, on main street, 5 mins from beach, F off season, OK, safe deposit.

Camping at Claromecó Good campsite *Dunamar*, hot showers, fire pits and laundering basins, US$1 a day; also ACA campsite.

Bus Buenos Aires-Claromecó with El Cóndor, US$40. Tres Arroyos-Claromecó twice daily off season, extra buses from mid-Dec in season. Pampa bus to Mar del Plata 0650, 4½ hrs. Modern, efficient bus terminal a few blocks from centre of Tres Arroyos.

Bahía Blanca, population 300,000, the most important centre S of Mar del Plata, stands at the head of a large bay at the mouth of the Río Naposta. The region has over a million people. Bahía Blanca consists of the city itself, built back from the river front, and five ports at various distances from the city strung along the N bank of the Naposta: Arroyo Pareja and the naval base of Puerto Belgrano at the mouth of the estuary; Puerto Ingeniero White, 23 km inland (reached by buses 500, 501, 504 from the plaza), Puerto Galván, 3½ km beyond, and Cuatreros, 8 km upstream. The Barrio Inglés (direction Ingeniero White) is where the foremen and technicians of the port and railway construction teams lived; Brickman St is a row of late Victorian semi-detached houses. Managers lived at nearby Harding Green. Bahía Blanca is also a rail, air and pipeline terminal for the Río Negro valley.

The city has some fine modern buildings and two parks. There is a modest Zoological Garden in Parque Independencia, on the outskirts.

Museums Museo Histórico, Alsina 425, incl interesting photos of early Bahía Blanca; **Museo del Puerto**, Torres y Carrega, Ingeniero White; **Museo de Bellas Artes**, Alsina 65.

To the E of Bahía Blanca is an enormous stretch of sandy beaches, developed for visitors (in the afternoon, it is usually windy). *Pehuén-Có*, 70 km away (hotel, C, quiet and clean), is an example of the beaches with camping places, well shaded by pine trees (beware of jellyfish when wind is in the S). Signs to it on the main road 24 km from Bahía Blanca. Another fine beach, with hotels and camping places is *Monte Hermoso*, 106 km, 2 hrs by bus (4 a day in summer, 2 in winter) E of Bahía Blanca. Good cheap meals, several restaurants. (Its hotels are open only Jan-Mar; several campsites – incl *Las Dunas*, 30 mins walk W along the beach, US$3 pp, a friendly spot run by an elderly German couple.)

Local Holidays Sep 24 (Our Lady of Mercy); Nov 10 (Day of Tradition).

Hotels **A1** *Austral*, Colón 159, T 20241, F 553737, restaurant; **A3** *Argos*, España 149, T/F 40001, 3-star; **B** *ACA Motel Villa Borden*, Av Sesquicentenario, entre Rutas 3 y 35, T 40151, F 21098; **B** *Belgrano*, Belgrano 44, T 20240/30498; **B** *City*, Chiclana 226, T 30178; **B** *Italia*, Brown 181, T 20121, simple, clean, restaurant; **B** *Muñiz*, O'Higgins 23, T 20021, friendly, central; **B** *Santa Rosa*, Sarmiento 373, T 20012/3; **C** *Barne*, Hipólito Yrigoyen 270, T 30864/30294; **C** *Bayón*, Chiclana 487, T 22504, friendly, clean, safe; **C** *Victoria*, Gral Paz 82, T 20522, basic, friendly, hot water, rec; **D** *Argentino* (restaurant), Chiclana 466, T 21824; **D** *Del Sur*, 19 de Mayo 75, T 22452, with restaurant, noisy with traffic; **D** *Residencial Roma*, Cerri 759, T 38500, opposite railway station, with private bath, cheaper without; **D/E** *Hospedaje Andrea*, Lavalle, rooms a/c, very friendly. Many other *residenciales* near railway station. **E** *Milano*, 11 de Abril y Estomba, also bar, mainly for "aged bachelors".

Camping Balneario Maldonado, 2 km from centre, next to petrochemical plant, US$0.30 pp; salt water swimming pool, US$0.80, bus 514 along Av Colón every hr but only when beach is open, ie when sunny and not in evening. ACA campsite at Lagoda de Lobos, not rec. Many others.

Restaurants *La Cigala*, Cerri 757, opp railway station, very good; *Il Vesuvio*, San Martín 337, good lunch, cheap; *La Casita de Miguel*, San Martín 510, cheap comedor, good food; *Da Sergio*, Gorriti 61, good food, large portions, very good value. *Café La Bahía*, Chiclana 548, good value, rec; *Bar/Comedor* Andrea, Mitre y Casanova, similar. A few good fish restaurants at the harbour, eg *El Royal*. Very good seafood and fish at Ingeniero White.

Banks and Exchange Lloyds Bank (BLSA), Calle Chiclana 102. **Citibank**, Colón 58. Open 0800-1400 Nov 15-Mar 31, 1000-1600 Apr 1-Nov 14. **Amex**, Fortur, Soler 38, T 26290, *poste restante*, English spoken. **Casas de Cambio** Pullman, Av San Martín 171, will change US$ cheques into US$ notes, 3% commission on TCs; good rates (closes 1600). **Viajes Bahía Blanca**, Drago 63, good rates. All *casas de cambio* closed at weekends.

Launderette *Laverap*, Estomba 293 and at Colón y Güemes.

Post Office Moreno 43. **Telephones**, O'Higgins 203.

Shopping Good gaucho shop on Soler, nr Fortur (see below), genuine articles.

Tourist Office In town hall on main plaza, Alsina 25, very helpful.

Airport Comandante Espora, 15 km from centre. Austral and Aerolíneas Argentinas flights to **Buenos Aires** daily (except Sun), 0900 and 1745. To **Comodoro Rivadavia**, **Río Gallegos** and **Río Grande**, daily except Sun (Austral).

Trains Station at Av Gral Cerri 780, T 21168. Buenos Aires-Bariloche train passes through; see Buenos Aires **Railways**. To **Cipolletti** (Río Negro, opp Neuquén), daily except Sat, 2130, a/c, bar, video, waitress service.

Buses Terminal is 2½ km from centre at Estados Unidos y Brown, connected by *micro* bus service; no hotels nearby. To **Trelew**, 3 per week, US$32, 734 km. **Río Gallegos** with Don Otto US$80; **Mar del Plata**, with Río Paraná, daily at 2230, US$25, 5½ hrs. **Río Colorado** US$8. To **Buenos Aires** frequent, 8-11 hrs, US$33-49 depending on service (eg Don Otto, T BsAs 313-3580; La Estrella/Cóndor). To **Neuquén**, 6 a day, 9 hrs, US$16, 580 km, one company only. To **Zapala** 3 times daily, a pullman service with food and drinks sold, 15 hrs, US$25 with Alto Valle. To **Viedma** 3 a day, 4 hrs.

Hitchhiking S or W from Bahía Blanca is possible but not too easy. Most southbound traffic takes Route 22 via Río Colorado. N to Buenos Aires on Route 3 is "virtually impossible".

From Bahía Blanca Route 3, a well-built paved highway runs S to Comodoro Rivadavia and Río Gallegos. Another major paved highway, Route 22, runs W to Neuquén and the Lake District. Several routes go North.

Some 100 km to the N is the **Sierra de la Ventana**, a favourite and recommended area for excursions from Bahía Blanca, and a **reserva provincial**, protecting the range's flora and fauna. The small town of **_Tornquist_**, 32 km N of Bahía Blanca by Route 33, with an attractive church on the central plaza (post and phone office open 0800-1800), is a good starting point (**C** *Gran Central Hotel*, seedy but friendly; campsite). The town of Pigue is also recommended as a good base. From Route 33 take Route 76 towards the town of Sierra de la Ventana. After 32 km is the entrance to the **Parque Provincial**, with massive ornate gates from the Tornquist family home. From here it's a 3-hr walk to the summit of Cerro La Ventana, which has fantastic views from the "window" in the summit ridge (camping at the base, free, basic facilities, canteen). 5 km further is the forestry station, with audio-visual display, trips to see wild deer, wild horses, guanacos, and on Fri and Sun trips at 0900 to 2 caves, one an Indian cemetery, the other with petroglyphs (US$0.70). Villa Ventana, 10 km further, is a wooden settlement with excellent teashop, *Casa de Heidi*, and wholefood available from *Jardín de Aylem*. Municipal campsite by river with all facilities. The town of **_Sierra de la Ventana_**, further E, is a good centre for exploring the hills, with hotels **B** *Provincial*, T 915025; **D** *Argentino*, La Perlita; **Youth Hostel** *Albergue Sierra de la Ventana* (sleeping bag necessary) and the excellent *Don Diego* campsite (hot water, open all year round); also **G** pp *Yapay*, Av San Martín near bus terminal, clean, quiet, rec. Excellent tourist information. Tres Picos, rising bare and barren from the rich farmlands to 1,070m, is only 6¼ km away. There is a 9-hole golf course, and good trout fishing in the Río Sauce Grande. All points can be easily reached by bus from Bahía Blanca or Tornquist.

193 km N of Bahía Blanca by road/rail through Saavedra is **_Carhué_** (pop 18,000). Behind the town hall there is a museum of the wars against the Indians. Tourist information at bus station. Five km away is Lago Epecuén, which covers over 40,000 ha and is over twenty times saltier than the sea. No fish can live in it. These waters are recommended for chronic rheumatism and skin diseases. There are many hotels and *residenciales* at the lake side and the area is a tourist resort. The ghost town of Villa Epecuén, 15 km away, drowned by the lake in 1985, can be visited (unpaved road).

Services *Hotel Shalom*, Belgrano 880, T 2503, C, "eccentric but clean", breakfast extra; restaurant at bus terminal is reasonable. Free camping in the beach area, no facilities. Rotary Club campsite, 2 km from Carhué.

About 38 km by road NE of Carhué, on the Roca Railway, is **_Guaminí_**, a pleasant summer hill resort of 3,500 inhabitants on the shore of Laguna del Monte, not as salty as Lago Epecuén; *pejerrey* fishing. (**Hotels** *La Aragonesa*, *Roma*; *Camping Municipal* on lake.) From Guaminí take routes 65 and 205 back to Buenos Aires, via **Lobos** (excellent ACA campsite at lake 10 km S of Lobos).

Santa Rosa (pop 55,000), capital of the Province of La Pampa, is 332 km NW of Bahía Blanca by road, and 619 km E of Buenos Aires by Route 5, via Chivilcoy (pop 47,500) and Pehuajó (pop 26,800).

Hotels A2 *Calfucura*, Av San Martín 695, T 23608, 4-star, no meals, but excellent steak restaurant round the corner; **C** *Hostería Río Atuel*, Luro 256, opposite bus terminal, T 22597, very good, rec; **D** *San Martín* Alsina 101, clean, restaurant, garage; **D** *Motel Calden*, Route 35, Km 330, T 24311, good restaurant attached, large rooms.

THE CORDOBA REGION (2)

Córdoba, the Republic's second city, has some historic, colonial buildings and is an important route centre, especially for road travel to the NW. The Sierras de Córdoba contain many pleasant, small resorts in the hills.

Córdoba and NW Argentina The pattern of the land in Northern Argentina, from the crest of the Andes in the W to the Río Paraguay in the E, consists of a high, dry Altiplano rising to a Puna cut into on its E face by rivers which flow into the Lowlands. This configuration of the land, similar to Bolivia, is carried S into all the NW provinces of Argentina as far S as Tucumán, but the altitudes in Argentina are not so great as in Bolivia, and the whole area not so large. The E-running rivers born on the Puna flow into the Chaco; their broad valleys, or *quebradas*, make access to the heights comparatively easy. Between the base of the Puna and the Chaco lie a series of front range hogback hills running roughly from N to S; the lowlands between them are known in Argentina as the *valles*. Tucumán is the S boundary of this kind of land. N of Tucumán crops can be grown without irrigation (though there is irrigation where the soil is absorbent) but S of Tucumán is droughty land, with long N-S ranges of low hills such as the Sierras de Córdoba, set in plains which have salt flats and swamps in the depressions.

Settlement and Economy The Puna is windswept, stony and treeless: the only growth is a low, blackish shrub (*tola*), and an occasional cactus. The first Spanish expedition from Bolivia entered Argentina in 1542. A little later a better and lower route was discovered—the main route used today—descending from La Quiaca to Jujuy through the Quebrada de Humahuaca, with rugged and colourful mountain ranges closing in on both sides. Along this new route the Spaniards pressed S and founded a group of towns in the NW: Santiago del Estero (the first) in 1551, Tucumán in 1565, Córdoba in 1573, Salta in 1582, La Rioja in 1591, and Jujuy in 1592. Mendoza (1561), San Juan (1562), and San Luis (1598) were all colonized by people who crossed the passes from Chile. All these colonies were hemmed in by the warlike tribes of the Pampas, and until the war of extermination in 1880 the route from Buenos Aires to Córdoba was often unsafe. The Indians raided frequently for cattle, which they drove S and over the Andes for sale in Chile.

During the whole of the colonial era the trade of the area, mostly in mules, was with Bolivia and Peru rather than with Buenos Aires. The mules were bred mainly in the plains between Rosario, Santa Fe, and Córdoba, and driven finally into Salta for the great fair in Feb and Mar.

Historically, Tucumán was always important, for the two river routes of the Salado and the Dulce across the dry belt forced the mule traffic to pass through Tucumán on the way to Salta. Tucumán still produces most of Argentina's sugar.

Tobacco is a major crop, and an important factor in the North West is the growth of tourism.

In nearly all the provincial towns everything shuts between 1200 and 1600 except restaurants, hotels and post offices. There is nothing to do or see, and we suggest that this is a good time for travelling, although in many places it is also the hottest time of day. (Panamericano and Atahuallpa/Balut buses have been recommended in the NW as clean and with a good service.)

From Buenos Aires to Córdoba

If hitchhiking, take the train from Retiro (San Martín line) to Pilar to reach the main Córdoba highway via Rosario. There are two main road routes: the shorter (713 km) via Rosario and the longer (835 km) via Río Cuarto. The latter goes through **San Antonio de Areco**, 113 km NW of Buenos Aires (bus, 2hrs, US$4, every hour). Here is the Museo Gauchesco Ricardo Güiraldes, on Camino Güiraldes and Aureliano, a typical *estancia* of the late 19th century with manor house, mill, tavern, open Wed-Sun, 1000-1200, 1500-1800 in summer; in winter 1000-1200 and 1400-1700. Check if it is open in Jan-Feb. Güiraldes was a writer who described *gaucho* life; his best-known book is *Don Segundo Sombra*. Visitors can also see over Cina-Cina, a working *estancia*, tour for US$20 includes visit, typical lunch and riding display, rec. Día de la Tradición is a *gaucho* festival with traditional parades, games, events on horseback, music and dance, celebrated in the week up to 10 Nov each year. Accommodation is hard to find at this time.

Many handicrafts are sold, mainly *gaucho* objects, ceramics, silver, leather, colonial furniture. The Argentine artist Gasparini has a museum-school where he sells his drawings of *gauchos* to tourists; Calle de los Martínez, between Bolívar and Rivadavia. There is also a natural history museum, Parque Metri, on Matheu and Hernández. Sub-Dirección de Turismo at Alsina and Lavalle, T 2101. **Services C** *Hotel San Carlos*, Zapiola y Zerbione, T 22401, clean and friendly, ask in advance for meals; **D** *Residencial Areco*, Segundo Sombra y Rivadavia, T 22166, good, comfortable, clean. Opposite Museo Gauchesco is *Hostería del Palomar*, typical barbecue; *Restaurant La Porteña* on the riverside, typical, very good. Camping near town centre; also **Auto-camping La Porteña**, 12 km from town on the Güiraldes *estancia*, good access roads.

Beyond Pergamino, 146 km, is **Venado Tuerto**, a pleasant town of 58,000 people with a fine Country Club at which race meetings and tournaments are held twice a year (several hotels incl **B** *Touring*, cool, quiet, rec). At **Río Cuarto**, 138,000 people, there is a golf club and a fine old municipal building with a lookout tower worth seeing. In Apr/May one of the country's biggest motor races (*carrera de autos*) is held here.

Hotels C *Gran*, Sobremonte 725, T 33401, 3-star; **D** *Alihué*, Sarsfield 58, good value, very friendly, big rooms. Near bus station on Calle Sobremonte 100-200 block are 3 cheap *residenciales*, *El Ciervo*, *Hospedaje El Bambi*, *Residencial Monge*, all **D**. Municipal campsite, *El Verano*.

Cafés, bars Many on Calle Sobremonte, particularly *Café Latino* and *Gibbons*.

Exchange *Lucero Viajes*, Constitución 564, T 33656, only place changing TCs, 3% commission. *Coin*, Calle Buenos Aires on main plaza will change sterling.

Buses Buenos Aires, US$34, frequent service. Bus to **Mendoza**, US$24; to **Córdoba** US$10; frequent departures to **Santiago**.

Córdoba is 225 km N of Río Cuarto across flatlands and rolling hills. About half-way between the two, the road runs on the retaining wall of the great Río Tercero dam; the artificial lake here is used for recreation. The town of Río Tercero (several hotels) has gained in importance with the development of groundnut plantations and a local military factory.

Villa María, on the Mitre Railway and at a vital crossroads on the main Buenos Aires-Córdoba road, where it meets the most convenient highway route linking central Chile with Paraguay, Uruguay and Brazil, is a prosperous agricultural town (population 68,000). **Hotels C** *City*, Buenos Aires 1184, T 20948; **D** *Alcázar*, Alvear y Ocampo, T 22445, near bus station, good value.

Córdoba, capital of Córdoba Province and Argentina's second city, has about 1.2 million inhabitants; it stands at an altitude of 440m. The district is well known for its countryside and the city for its buildings; it was founded as early as 1573. The site of the first university in the country, founded in 1613 by the Jesuits, it now has two universities. It is an important industrial centre, the home of Argentina's motor industry. In the heart of the city is Plaza San Martín with a statue of the Liberator. On the W side is the old Cabildo, for many years used as the police headquarters, now a historical museum (see below). Next to it stands the Cathedral, the oldest in Argentina, started in 1697 and finished 1787, see the remarkable cupola. One of the features of this part of the city is its old churches. Near Plaza San Martín at Independencia 122 is the 16th century Carmelite convent and chapel of Santa Teresa, which houses the Museo de Arte Religioso. The church of La Compañia, on Calles Obispo Trejos and Caseros, with a simple façade, dates from about 1650 and is a far better building than the Cathedral; its façade was rebuilt in the 20th century. The barrel vault and cupola of the Capilla Doméstica of this church, built entirely of Paraguayan cedar, are unique. The basilica of La Merced at 25 de Mayo 83, was built in the early 19th century, though its fine gilt wooden pulpit dates from the colonial period. On its exterior, overlooking Calle Rivadavia, are fine murals by local artist Armando Sica. There are some pleasant small 18th century churches with striking bell gables and undulating pediments. The neo-gothic church of the Sagrado Corazón (Sacred Heart), built in 1933, at Buenos Aires e Yrigoyen, is also worth a visit. The Casa del Virrey (Viceroy's House), one block E of the Plaza San Martín, is a fine colonial building housing the Museo Histórico Provincial. Further E, at Blvd JD Perón, is the magnificent Mitre railway station, dating from the late 19th century, with its beautiful tiled *confitería*.

Although Córdoba was once very picturesque, industrialisation and population growth have turned it into a busy modern city with a flourishing shopping centre.

Museums Museo Histórico, in the old Cabildo, Plaza San Martín, free guided tours 1100 and 1700, Tues, Wed and Fri; **Museo Histórico Provincial**, in the Casa del Virrey Marqués de Sobremonte, Rosario de Santa Fe 318; **Museo de Ciencias Naturales**, Av Yrigoyen 115, open Mon-Fri 0800-1900, Sat 0900-1200, good guided tours (in Spanish, entry free, "interesting skeletons of prehistoric glyptodonts"); **Museo de Mineralogía y Geología** of the Universidad Nacional de Córdoba, V Sarsfield 299, open Mon-Fri, 1400-1600; **Museo de Zoología**, same address, open Mon-Fri 0900-1200, Wed-Fri 1600-1800, many birds but poorly displayed with no labels; **Museo del Teatro y de la Música**, in the Teatro San Martín, V Sarsfield 365, open Mon-Fri 0900-1200; **Museo Provincial de Bellas Artes**, Plaza España, open Tues-Fri 0900-1300, 1500-2000; **Museo Municipal de Bellas Artes**, Gral Paz 33, open Tues-Fri 0930-1330, 1630-2030, Sat 1630-2030; **Museo Histórico de la Ciudad**, Entre Ríos 40; **Centro de Arte Contemporáneo**, Parque San Martín; **Museo de Meteorología Nacional**, San Luis 801, open Tues-Fri 0900-1300, 1400-1800, Sat 0830-1230—nearby in Calle Laprida is Argentina's main observatory, open Wed 2000-2200; **Museo de Arte Religioso**, in the convent of Santa Teresa, Independencia 122, Sat 1030-1230.

Local Holidays 6 Jul (Foundation of the City); 30 Sep (St Jerome), 7-10 Oct.

Hotels More expensive hotels, mainly in the centre: **L3** *Crillón*, Rivadavia 85, T 46093, faded glory, very friendly, good restaurant, comfortable; **A2** *Mediterráneo*, Av MT de Alvear 10 T 24-0086; **B** *Cañada*, Av MT de Alvear 580, T 37589, good, incl conference facilities with full technical back-up, a/c, private bath, TV and video, restaurant, laundry, transport; **B** *Sussex*, San Jerónimo 125, T 229071, comfortable, roomy, discounts for ACA members; **B** *Windsor*, Buenos Aires 214, T 224012, comfortable, very good; **B** *Royal*, Blvd JD Perón 180, T 45000; all these have garages. **B** *Del Sol*, Balcarce 144, T 33961, with bath, clean, fan, a/c extra, piped music, rec. More economical: **C** *Garden*, 25 de Mayo 35, central, clean, secure, highly rec.

Hotels between Plaza San Martín and bus terminal, most of them in the cheaper brackets: On Corrientes, **D** *Bristol*, No 64, T 36222, bathroom, a/c, telephone; **D** *Hospedaje Suiza* (No 569), near bus terminal, very friendly but not too clean; **D** *Hospedaje Camacho* (No 519),

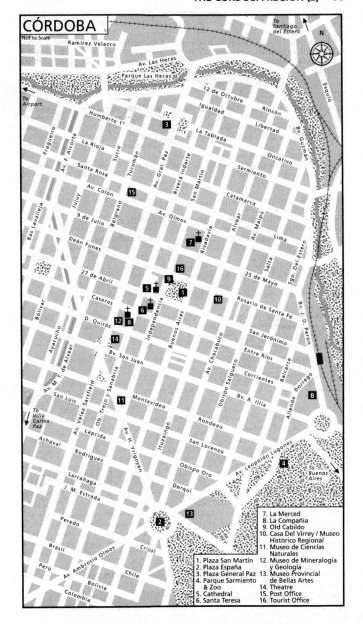

CÓRDOBA

Not to Scale

1. Plaza San Martín
2. Plaza España
3. Plaza General Paz
4. Parque Sarmiento & Zoo
5. Cathedral
6. Santa Teresa
7. La Merced
8. La Compañía
9. Old Cabildo
10. Casa Del Virrey / Museo Histórico Regional
11. Museo de Ciencias Naturales
12. Museo de Mineralogía y Geología
13. Museo Provincial de Bellas Artes
14. Theatre
15. Post Office
16. Tourist Office

clean, quiet, very friendly, rec; **D** *Residencial Mi Valle* (No 586), fan, shared bath, small, clean and nice, family-run, washing facilities, rec; **D** *Residencial Corrientes* (s/n) shared bath, not too clean, washing facilities, pleasant rooms. Plenty of hotels of all classes on San Jerónimo: **B** *Ritz* (No 495), T 45031, "clean but dilapidated"; **C** *Dallas* (No 339), T 46091, rec; **C** *Felipe II* (No 279), T 44752, in new part, D in old section, adequate; **D** *Corona* (No 574), T 228789, not incl breakfast, clean, comfortable, friendly. **C** *Roma Termini*, Entre Rios 687, close to bus terminal, spotless, welcoming; **D** *Florida*, Rosario de Santa Fe 459, T 26373, clean, friendly, rec, some rooms with a/c. On Balcarce: **C** *Mallorca*, No 73, T 39234, quite clean and near bus and railway stations, noisy; **D** *Residencial Plaza*, No 336, 150m from bus station, clean, friendly and quiet.

Near Alta Córdoba station (Belgrano railway): **B** *Yolanda* (opposite station), delightful rooms, friendly, excellent restaurant, highly rec; **C** *Las Colonias*, Cabrera 339; **D** *Italiano*, Cabrera 313; **D** *La Amistad*, Roque Sáenz Peña 1523, T 711943, basic, clean; **D** *Suguía*, Roque Sáenz Peña 1561; **E** *Hospedaje Bontempo*, Cabrera 177. The following offer 10% discount to ISIC card holders: *del Sol*, Balcarce 144 (see above), and on Blvd Pte Arturo Illia, *Damar*, No 518, *del Boulevard*, No 182, *Heydi*, No 615.

A2 *ACA Hotel Dr Cesar C Carman*, Av Sabattini (Ruta 9) y Bajada del Pucará, T 243565, A1 for non-members, very good.

Camping Municipal site, Gral San Martín, at the back of the Complejo Ferial (bus 31).

Restaurants There are numerous grills of all categories on the outskirts of the city, especially in the Cerro de las Rosas district, for meals out-of-doors when the weather is suitable. Many cheap restaurants along San Jerónimo incl *San Carlos*, No 431, good food and service. *Casino Español*, Rivadavia 63, good; *La Mamma*, Alcorta 270, excellent Italian, pricey; *Il Gatto*, Gral Paz y 9 de Julio, great pasta and pizzas, reasonably priced; *Romagnolo*, Av JD Perón y San Jerónimo, opposite the Mitre railway station, rec. *Betos*, San Juan 454, good *parrilla*, rec, pricey; *Fancy Café*, Andarte 317, good, cheap; *Firenze*, 25 de Mayo 220, busy, pleasant, traditional cafe. Excellent fruit juices (*licuados*) at *Kiosco Americano*, Tucumán 185 and at Gral Paz 242. Good *empanadas* at *La Vieja Esquina*, Belgrano y Caseros; *Empanadería La Alameda*, Obispo Trejo nr University, reasonable food, good student atmosphere, best 2200-2400. Icecream at branches of *Dolce Neve* throughout town; *Soppelsa's* ice cream is also highly rec, with several outlets.

Banks and Exchange Lloyds Bank (BLSA), Buenos Aires 23. Citibank, Rivadavia 104, poor rates. Banco Sudameris will buy Amex TCs at 1% commission. Banco Fegin for Mastercard. Banco de Galicia on Sucre for Amex cards. Amex, Simonelli Viajes, Av F Alcorta 50, T 26186. Many *cambios* on Rivadavia just off Plaza San Martín—shop around for best rate.

Cultural Institutes Asociación Argentina de Cultura Británica, Bv San Juan 137, good library, poor reading room. Open Mon-Fri 0900-1200, Mon, Wed, Fri 1600-1945, Tues, Thur 1500-1945. Goethe Institut, Bv Illia 356, open Tues-Fri 1700-2100.

Consulates Bolivia, Castro Barros 783, T 732827; Chile, Crisol 280, T 609622; Paraguay, 9 de Julio 573, T 226388; Peru, Poeta Lugones 212, T 603730. Austria, J Cortés 636, T 720450; Italy, Ayacucho 131, T 221020; Germany, A Olmos 501, T 692269; Spain, Bv Chacabuco 875, T 605013; Sweden, MT de Alvear 10, T 240094; Switzerland, Entre Ríos 185, L-10, T 226848; Belgium, F Posse 2533, T 813298; Finland, Chacabuco 716, T 605049.

Entertainment Discotheques Several on Av H Yrigoyen, expensive; late night rock music at *Música Pura*, Montevideo 100, Thur-Sat. Folk Music at *Pulpería El Viejo Rincón*, Dumesnil y Mendoza, excellent music till 0500.

Health English-speaking doctor, Ernesto J MacLoughlin, Centro Asistencial Privado de Enfermedades Renales, 9 de Julio 714, home Pérez del Viso 4316, T 814745. Dentist, Dra Olga Olmedo de Herrera, Fco J Muñiz 274, T 804378, her daughter speaks English and will translate.

Language Classes *Comisión de Intercambio Educativo*, San José de Calasanz 151, T 243606, offers classes mainly pre-arranged in Germany. (Contact Kommission für Bildungsaustausch, Wrangelstr 122, DW-2000 Hamburg 20.) *Interswop*, Mariano Fragueiro 2676, B Alta Córdoba, T/F 715442 (or Eppendorfer Weg 287, 20251 Hamburg, Germany, T/F 0049-40-484842) organizes stays abroad and language classes (about US$130/week, 25 hrs of classes) and accommodation at about US$10/day, also exchange programmes for any nationality (write to Hamburg address).

Laundry Chacabuco 32; *Laverap*, Paraná y Rondeau; *La Lavandería*, Avellaneda 182, local 4.

Post Office Parcel Service on the ground floor of the Correo Central, Av Colón 201, beside the customs office, up to 20 kg; wrapping service for small fee. **Telecommunications** Av Gen

Paz 36 and 27 de Abril 27.

Tourist Agencies *Carolina*, San Jerónimo 270, local 13/14, good value excursions but only run with minimum of 6 people; *El Delfín*, Gral Paz 250, local 140, 1° piso.

Tourist Office Dirección Provincial de Turismo, Tucumán 25. Municipal tourist information centre on San Martín at Rosario de Santa Fe 39. Information office also at bus station, has free maps; extensive information on accommodation and camping in the province, helpful. Tourist Office desk at airport often unmanned, but car-hire desks next to it are most helpful. A useful information booklet is the free monthly, *Plataforma 40*, put out by Nueva Estación Terminal de Omnibus de Córdoba (Netoc).

Club Andino, Deán Funes 2100, open Wed after 2100, closed Jan.

Local transport Municipal buses do not accept cash; you have to buy tokens (*cospeles*) or cards from kiosks, value US$0.55. Buses No 70, 71 and 73 run between the Mitre Station (and bus terminus) and the Belgrano station at Alto Córdoba.

Car Hire Avis at airport and Corrientes 452, T 227384. A1, Entre Ríos 70, T 224867. Localiza at airport and Castro Barros 1155, T 747747.

Air Pajas Blancas airport, 11 km from the city, is modern and has a good restaurant and a bank (open Mon-Fri 1000-1500). Taxi to airport, US$15. Airport bus leaves terminal opposite railway station; irregular schedule, 30 mins, US$1.50. Alternatively take local bus No 55 from Santa Rosa y Avellaneda (Plaza Colón), allow 1 hr. Several flights to **Buenos Aires** daily, about 1 hr (Austral offering 65% discount on nocturnal flights); to **Mendoza** daily, Austral; to **Tucumán** daily, Austral. To **San Juan**, also daily Austral; to **Salta** Mon AR, Tues-Sun Austral, who fly 5 days a week to **Jujuy**. AR once a week to **Santa Cruz**, Bolivia. Aerolíneas Argentinas, Av Colón 520, T 819676. Austral, Av Colón 678, T 810997. LAB, same location as Alitalia, Av 25 de Mayo 6625, 3rd floor. KLM, Av General Paz 159.

Railways See under Buenos Aires, **Railways** for existing services. A new tourist service, the Tren de las Sierras, runs from Rodríguez del Busto station (15 km out of town) to Capilla del Monte. Dep 0830, returns 1530, Tues, Thur, Fri, Sat, Sun, US$10 one way, incl taxi transfer from main bus terminal to Rodríguez del Busto.

Buses Excellent new bus station at Blvd Perón 300, with Tourist Office, many public telephones, shops incl food supermarket on 3rd floor, bank (does not change cheques), post office, police, restaurants, and showers in bathrooms (about 6 blocks from centre), crowded at weekends. To **Buenos Aires**, Ablo, Costera Criolla, Chevalier or Cacorba, 10 hours, US$39 *común*, US$55 *diferencial*: to **Salta** (US$41) and **Jujuy** (US$45), Panamericano, 4 daily, La Veloz del Norte twice, about 12 and 15 hours. To **Mendoza** (10 hours), 6 a day with TAC, frequent delays and breakdowns, 1 daily with Uspallata US$29; to **Tucumán**, US$25, 8 hrs, about 8 a day, Panamericano has more than other companies. To **Posadas** (Expreso Singer) Tues, Thur, Sat, 1730 arrive at Posadas at 1335; Thur and Sat bus continues to Iguazú arriving 1930 next day, no a/c. To **Santa Fe**, frequent, 5½ hrs, US$15. To **La Rioja** 3-4 a day with Cotil and El Cóndor, 6½ hrs; some go on to Catamarca. Córdoba-La Rioja-Aimogasta-**Tinogasta**- **Fiambalá** with El Cóndor, Tues, Thur, Fri; leaves Tinogasta 1140 arr Fiambalá 1240, returns from Fiambalá same day 1445, from Tinogasta at 1600 (**see also p 143**). La Calera bus leaves for **Belén** (Catamarca) on Mon, Wed, Fri, at 2100, arr Belén 1030; return journey, also via **Andalgalá**, Wed, Fri, Sun, dep 1600 arr Andalgalá 1735, dep 1750, arr Córdoba 0055. Cacorba, efficient a/c buses, serve **Villa Carlos Paz** (1 hr, frequent service, every 15 mins or so), **Cosquín** and **La Falda** in the Sierras of Córdoba.

To **Asunción** (Paraguay) direct with Brújula, four times a week, also with Cacorba 19 hrs, US$42. To **Montevideo** (Uruguay), dep 1700, Mon, Wed, Fri and Sun, with Encon, 15 hrs. To **Lima**, Peru, with Colta, dep Fri 2200, via Mendoza, 0700 San, arrives Lima Tues am, US$130. To **Pocitos** (Bolivian border) with Panamericano, Agustín Garzón 1229, San Vicente, Córdoba. In general, it is best to travel from Córdoba if you are going N, as at stations in between it may be hard to get a seat; a seat is only guaranteed if one pays US$1 extra.

The **Sierras of Córdoba**, rising in undulating hills from the pampas, their lower slopes often wooded, particularly in the S, attract each year a large number of visitors. The highest peak, Champaquí (2,975m) has a small lake about 2,550m up. The hills run, roughly, for 500 km from N to S; W of Córdoba they are 150 km wide. There are three ranges of them: the Sierra Grande, the longest, in the middle, with Sierra Chica to the E and Sierra de Guisapampa and its continuation, the Sierra de Pocho, to the W. A network of good roads gives pleasant contrasts of scenery, but there are few footpaths and trails for the walker. The region's climate is dry, sunny and exhilarating, especially in winter.

At the foot of the Sierra Chica are large dams to contain the waters of the Río Primero at Río Molinos (29 km from Córdoba, Route 5, good *pejerrey* and trout-fishing; bus to Villa Carlos Paz), San Roque, and Río Tercero. There are two other large dams in the hills, at Cruz del Eje and La Viña. They provide power and irrigation, and the lakes are in themselves attractive. The Government keeps them stocked with fish. Sailing is popular.

Information can be obtained at travel agencies, at the Dirección Provincial de Turismo or at Casa de Córdoba at Callao 332, Buenos Aires.

Note There are innumerable good hotels and *pensiones* in the Córdoba mountain region; names are therefore not always given. Many services in this area are closed out of season.

The Punilla Valley: *Villa Carlos Paz*, pop 46,000, is 36 km W of Córdoba (buses from Córdoba bus terminal every 15 mins in summer, 36 km, US$1.40; taxi from Córdoba airport, US$10.50; Buenos Aires-Villa Carlos Paz with Ablo, US$26—T BsAs 313-2995; also Cacorba, Chevallier, General Urquiza), on man-made Lago San Roque. It is the nearest resort to Córdoba and is therefore often crowded. Tours possible on amphibian buses which go as far as the two dams on the lake (US$10); launch trips also available. There is a pleasant 5 km walk to the dam from the outskirts of Villa Carlos Paz. At the Casa de Gaspar, Miguel Cané and El Redentor, roller-skating and optical illusions, Fri-Sun 1400-1900 out of season. A chair-lift runs up the slopes to a tearoom and night club overlooking the valley, between 0900 and 1900. Bus tours to areas such as Sierra Chica, for those who like snack bars, fun slides and gravity-defying houses.

Accommodation, Restaurants and Services Plenty of hotels, big and small, eg **B** *El Ciervo de Oro*, Hipólito Yrigoyen 995, T 22498, on the lake, rec; **D** *El Monte*, Caseros 45, T 22001, very good, rec. **D** *Mar del Plata*, friendly, rec; **D** *Villa Carlos Paz Parque*, Santa Fe 525, full board available, rec. Camping at ACA site and several others incl *Las Tolderías* and *Los Pinos*, rec, Curro Enrique y Lincoln (all open year). There are many campsites near the main road through the Punilla Valley, most open Dec-Apr only. Best buys: leather mats, bags, pottery. *Restaurant Carlos Paz* highly rec for food and setting. *Restaurant Pamilla Mingo*, Av Uruguay opp *Hotel Uruguay*, not cheap but good. **NB** Drinking water is not safe. Banco de Córdoba, Av San Martín, will change US$ cash only. Laundry at San Martín y Libertad. Post Office and telephone on Av Gral San Martín. **Tourist office** at bus station, very friendly.

A few km SW of Villa Carlos Paz is the small town at *Ycho Cruz*, by the San Antonio river (bus from Córdoba, with Emp Cotap, US$2; one hotel outside the centre, *Hostería Avenida*, E with bath, usually for air force personnel only, but open to the public if not busy, very clean and pleasant; also several campsites. The *Comedor Familiar* on the main street near the supermarket is rec, good and cheap). Continuing S from Ycho Cruz the road crosses the scenic Pampa de Achala, a huge desert plateau of grey granite, to the small village of El Condor (one bar and a service station, buses from Córdoba, US$5). 7 km N of El Condor is a wide trail leading to Quebrada de los Condoritos (6-7 km), with superb landscape and the chance of seeing condors in their easternmost habitat (thanks for this information to Ortelli Jiri Moreno, Como, Italy).

North of Villa Carlos Paz, on Route 38, a road branches W to Tanti from where local buses go to Los Gigantes, a paradise for climbers, 2-day treks possible. Club Andino has several *refugios*; details in Villa Carlos Paz.

From Villa Carlos Paz Route 38 runs N through the Punilla valley to the following string of resorts: *Cosquín*, 63 km from Córdoba, on the banks of the Río Cosquín, is known as the National Folklore Capital and is the site of the most important folklore festival, beginning last week in Jan. A new arena seating 10,000 spectators has been built and recent reports suggest the festival is becoming commercialized. Museo Camin Cosquín at Km 767, out of town, minerals and archaeology, rec. Bus Córdoba-Cosquín US$2.60, Empresa La Capillense; 1½ hrs, via Carlos Paz or with La Calera via the San Roque dam. Altitude, 720m; pop 16,000. Camping on S bank of river. Tourist office at San Martín 560, **D** *Hotel La Serrana*, P Ortiz 740, near bus station, friendly, good; likewise **D** *Hotel Italia*, across from bus station, rec; **E** pp *Residencial Cosquín*, Tucumán y Sabattini, clean; **E** *Hotel Petit*, Calle Sabattini, 2 blocks from bus station. Take a bus to the Pan de Azúcar hill from where there is a good view over the Punilla valley, at 0930, return 1630 or 2 hrs walk. Chairlift to top (all year round). 19 km N of Cosquín is *Valle Hermoso*, near La Falda (buses from Villa Carlos Paz). Altitude, 850m. Old restored chapel of San Antonio, a little gem. Riding, motoring. Youth hostel, address "Steinhaus", dirty, no heating, very cold, US$2 pp, pay extra for gas. Camping near river,

US$0.60 pp, all facilities, but not too clean.

La Falda (pop 30,000) 82 km from Córdoba, a good touring centre, friendly and peaceful. Bus from Córdoba 2 hrs, US$3. Altitude, 933m. Helpful tourist offices at bus station and in old railway station. Model railway museum at Las Murallas zoo at the end of Av 25 de Mayo. Nearby is the privately run Ambato Archaeological Museum; articles are well displayed, worth a visit, open Thur-Sun and public holidays 0900-2000, US$0.50 entrance. About 30 hotels in all categories, all full in Dec-Feb holiday season (eg **D** *Residencial Atena*, Rosario 329, clean, comfortable, rec), at other times a basic room with bath is in our E range. Houses for rent 1 Mar to 30 Nov on a monthly basis. *Restaurant El Bochín*, Av España 117, good, cheap. Jazz at old *Hotel Eden*; La Falda is visited mostly by the elderly; most hotels belong to pension funds. Tap water is not safe. Bancos de la Nación and de Suquía for exchange. Students of all nations welcome at Córdoba University holiday centre at Vaquerías, 2 km from La Falda. Travel agent Wella Viajes, Av Edén 412, loc 12, T 0548-21380, offers 15% discount to ISIC and youth card holders for trekking, climbing, etc to Cerro Champaquí. Camping near small river. (Bus from Buenos Aires, Cacorba, Cita, US$40.)

Excursions to Quebrada Chica, Cascada del Molino. Extensive hiking in surrounding hills. To La Candelaria, 53 km W along unpaved roads where there is a Jesuit *estancia* and chapel dating from 1693. From La Falda 3½ km N by Route 38 is **Huerta Grande**, at 971m, a bathing resort with good fishing and medicinal waters. Round trip excursion to *Cascadas de Olaén*. Take the road to Valle Hermoso S 10 km towards Cosquín, then follow dirt road about 12½ km to the crossing marked "Cascadas de Olaén"; from here walk 4½ km to the falls: quite spectacular canyon—the water splashes into a small lake full of little fish. Return to the dirt road and 2½ km to a monolith and another dirt road, which leads to La Falda. See the Pampa de Olaén, where there are many quartz mines.

Bus to Asunción, Cacorba, US$69. Connections to Rosario, Mendoza, Catamarca, Santiago del Estero, Tucumán, Salta and Jujuy.

La Cumbre, 12 km N of La Falda. Bus from Córdoba US$4, 2½ hrs. Altitude 1,141m. Trout streams with good fishing from Nov to Apr. Fiesta de la Cerveza Montañesa in Feb, first 3 weeks, beer, meat, hunting and fishing. Swimming, golf, tennis and hang gliding. Has an airport. **C** *Hotel Lima*, swimming pool, quiet, clean. Charming small inn, *Victoria*; *La Cumbre Inn*, large and commercial, good views; **D** *Residencial Peti*, good, friendly. Good restaurants.

Cruz Chica, 2 ½ km N of La Cumbre, altitude, 1,067m, has very English houses and gardens in pine woods. Most attractive. Good English boys' school.

Los Cocos, 8 km N of La Cumbre, is a delightful, extremely popular mountain resort with 3 first rate hotels and many holiday houses. **D** *Hostería Zanier*, full board B, rec. *Blair House*, English-style pub, rec. Hang-gliding nearby at Cuchi Corral.

Capilla del Monte, in the heart of the Sierras, 106 km from Córdoba (bus 3 hrs, US$5.20, from BsAs, General Urquiza, US$35; **C** *Hospedaje Italiano*, clean, showers, opposite bus station; municipal campsite on the way to Cerro Uritorco, G pp, rec, and also 9½ km from Capilla del Monte) . Altitude, 914m. Medicinal waters (good baths at La Toma), rocks and waterfalls and wide views; El Zapato rock is "graffiti–ridden", better are Los Mogotes, 3 km from town, reached through Paseo del Indio. Excursions in the hills, particularly to Cerro Uritorco (1,950m) and to Los Alazanes dam; good path on Uritorco, walk takes 2½ hrs. Permission to walk obtainable from a house beyond crossing (US$3). Many free walks after crossing bridge at La Toma, rec. You can walk on to the direct dirt road to San Marcos Sierra (22 km W); many parakeets and small farmhouses. Along the way you will also get views down to the *Cruz del Eje* dam (**B** *Hotel Posta de las Carretas*, Ruta 38 y R Moyano, T 0549-2517, good, service station and restaurants at the crossroads; camping possible at foot of dam, or stay at friendly, family-run **D** *Hotel España* in village, some private baths; rowboats for rent on dam's lake, where there is good fishing. Cruz del Eje (pop 23,100) is one of two towns with its own "micro-climate" (the other is Merlo in San Luis Province) and own honey production—try that made from carob (*algarrobo*) blossom (1 kg about US$2). Excellent trout fishing at Tío Mayo, an hour from Capilla del Monte by car.

A road runs **North from Córdoba** to *Ascochinga* via pleasant little townships such as Villa Allende, Río Ceballos, Salsipuedes and La Granja. At El Manzano, 40 km N of Córdoba, a road branches W to *Candonga*, altitude 810m. The historic church, now a National Monument, was built in 1730 as an oratory of the Jesuit Estancia of Santa Gertrudis. The arch protrudes to form a porch covering the entrance. 14 km N of Ascochinga is *Santa Catalina*, originally a Jesuit mission founded in 1622 and the most elaborate Jesuit establishment in the hills around Córdoba (no bus from Ascochinga, but 2 a day from Jesús María). (See the church begun in 1754, workshops and stone conduits; the families who now occupy the place as a summer home will show you round.)

Services In Ascochinga: **C** *Hostería El Cortijo*, full board only, good value, with bath, small swimming pool and river outside, horses for rent, US$1/hr; 5 km walk to Tres Cascadas falls and *balneario*. During winter, open weekends only. Campsite open all year. In **Río Ceballos**: **E** *Albergue La Gloria*, affiliated to IYHA, warmly rec; 5 campsites. Several campsites also at **Salsipuedes**.

From Ascochinga a road runs E for 20 km to **Jesús María** 51 km N of Córdoba on Route 9. Altitude, 533m (several hotels). Good 18th century Jesuit church and the remains of its once famous winery; in the cloister is an excellent Museo Jesuítico, said to be one of the best on the continent (Mon-Fri 0800-1200 and 1400-1900, Sat and Sun 1600-2000). Each Jan there is a gaucho and folklore festival, lasting 10 nights from 2nd week; very popular. Good trout, *dorado*, and carp fishing in winter. Direct bus from Córdoba, US$2, 1½ hrs. Some 4 km N of Jesús María is **Sinsacate**, with an interesting church. There is also a fine colonial posting inn, now a museum, with long, deep verandah and chapel attached. Route 9, the main road to Santiago del Estero, runs N. Another 132 km to **Villa de María**, the birthplace of Leopoldo Lugones, a poet of country life. His house is a museum. (**D** *Hotel City*, good.)

At Rayo Cortado, 22 km S of Villa de María, a turning leads W to **Cerro Colorado**, 160 km N of Córdoba, the former home of the Argentine folklore singer and composer Atahualpa Yupanqui. His house, now a museum can be visited, US$2 – ask in the village for the curator. There are more than 30,000 rock paintings by the Comechingones Indians in the nearby Cerro Colorado archaeological park and a small archaeological museum (US$1 entry, includes guide in English or Spanish). There is cheap accommodation (eg with Sosa family) and camping. You can stay with Don Elvio, who runs the *pulpería* near the archaeological station. Buses: from Córdoba, Tues, Wed, Thur, Sun, to Santiago del Estero, get off at Santa Elena, hitch from there (11 km); from Jesús María, daily 1610.

Southwest of Córdoba a scenic road climbs from Villa Carlos Paz through the Sierra Grande to another chain of resorts, Mina Clavero, Villa Dolores and Yacanto. **Mina Clavero** is 140 km from Córdoba by bus, 6 a day, 4 hrs, beautiful ride through grand lake and hill scenery, and curious palm trees. Three rivers, popular for swimming, pass through the town centre. Altitude, 915m. (**D** *Hospedaje El Clavero*, San Martín 1405, many others; Restaurant: *Rincón Suizo*, Calle Champaquí 1200, T 0544-70447, good pastries.) A good centre for exploring the high *sierra*. No money exchange available. There is a nice church and a most interesting museum, dedicated by a French archaeologist, 13 km S from Mina Clavero and about 5 km from the village of Nono, entrance US$3, called "Rocsen" open 0900 till sunset, with furniture, minerals, instruments, animals, etc.

Villa Dolores, 187 km from Córdoba (bus takes 5 hrs), 48 km SW of Mina Clavero. Altitude, 529m; pop 21,000. The road from Córdoba crosses the two mountain ranges to reach finally the Pampa de Achala (see p 98). (Hotels **E** *Hospedaje Cáceres*, Brizuela 390; **E** *Residencial Champaquí*, Erdman 162. **Camping** nearest site is Piedra Pintada, 15 min-bus-ride away, pleasant village well situated for walks into mountains.) Bus to San Luis 5¼ hrs.

Champaquí, 2,884m, the highest peak in the Sierras lies E of Villa Dolores. It can be reached from San Javier, 19 km SE of Villa Dolores. For summit, follow path to Capilla La Constancia, set in river valley with pine and nut trees, 2-3 hrs. Take water from here, then cross the river (path), keep left through a pinewood up to a mountain range and follow it up to the top of a huge plateau. Good path, about 4-5 hrs, and then you reach a square enclosure, whence you keep left. Follow stone mounds about 2 hrs until you see the higher of two peaks, which is Champaquí. Lovely views, descent to La Constancia 4 hrs. An alternative route is from Villa de las Rosas, 12 km E of Villa Dolores (several hotels). Neither route should be attempted in misty weather. A good base is *Vai Kunta*, 5885 Villa de las Rosas, run by Rolf Graf (Swiss), rooms for rent, good food, guiding service. Take any Córdoba-Villa Dolores bus to Villa de las Rosas; at bus station look for the *pizzería* where taxis to Los Nolles can be arranged. From Los Nolles it's a 2-hr walk to the house.

2 km S of San Javier, at the foot of Champaquí, in a region of woods and waterfalls is **Yacanto**. Reached by road from Villa Dolores. Curative waters.

A road **South from Córdoba** runs to Alta Gracia and to the Río Tercero dam. **Alta Gracia** (alt 580m; pop 39,000) is 29 km SW of Córdoba beside Lago Tajamar. (Bus ³⁄₄ hr, every 15 mins, US$0.75.) Interesting colonial church, finished about 1762,

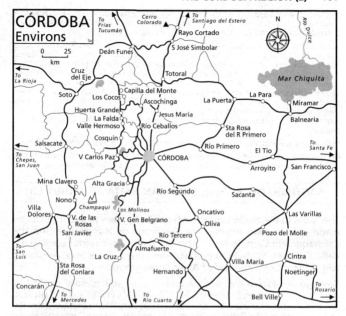

CÓRDOBA Environs

open am and after 1700, and buildings housing Museo del Virrey Liniers, on the Estancia de Alta Gracia, founded in 1588 and taken over by the Jesuits in 1643, open Tues-Fri 0900-1300, 1500-1830, Sat, Sun 0930-1230, 1530-1830, US$1 (all day in summer). There is also the Museo Manuel de Falla on Pellegrini Final, closed Mon, entry US$0.30, where the Spanish composer spent his last years. Take the local bus to La Paysanita or La Serranita for a quiet environment (but no cheap accommodation). Beautiful views from the Gruta de la Virgen de Lourdes, 3 km W of town.

Services *Hostería Reina*, Urquiza 129, good. Two camp sites, one scruffy, the other better and free in winter, which is by golf course. A few reasonably priced restaurants in town centre. Tourist office inside clock tower by Lago Tajamar. Casino.

To the Bosque Alegre and Observatory it is 24 km NW, open Thur 1600-1800, Sun 1000-1200 and 1600- 1800. Good views over Córdoba, Alta Gracia and the Sierra Grande. To the Río Tercero dam (site of a nuclear power staton) is 79 km further S; on the lake is a workers' holiday colony and an ACA *Unidad Turística*.

Villa General Belgrano, 58 km S of Alta Gracia is a completely German town founded by the surviving interned seamen from the *Graf Spee*, some of whom still live in the town. It is a pleasant resort and a good centre for excursions in the surrounding mountains. Beer festival in Oct. If walking between here and La Cumbrecita, lodge with Siegfried at *Alta Vista*, E, friendly. **Accommodation B** *Hotel Bremen*, Route 5 y Cerro Negro, T 6133, restaurant, sports facilities; **D** *Allgauer Hütten*, clean, friendly, quiet. There are two *Youth Hostels*, one at Estancia Alta Vista, 14 km from the town, and one, *El Rincón*, D, in beautiful surroundings, cooking facilities, highly rec, in the town (reservations—Patricia Mampsey, Casilla 64, T 6323); both offer discounts to ISIC and youth card holders (25% and 20% respectively). Buses to **Córdoba**, 2 hrs, US$4, 8 a day; to **Mendoza**, US$28; to **Buenos Aires**, Colta (T BsAs 313-0590), 1 a day, US$35.

La Cumbrecita is a German village 30 km W of Villa General Belgrano, reached from General

Belgrano by taxi (US$33, 1-1½ hrs) or by bus, Sun only. Good walking and riding. **Hotels**: **B** *Cascadas*, with pool, tennis etc; **B** *Panorama*, higher up hill (T 98406); three others (B) and **C** *Residencial Casa Rosita*. *Youth Hostel* at Villa Alpina, 17 km from the town.

Some 200 km NE of Córdoba the Río Dulce, flowing in places through salt flats, runs into the shallow **Mar Chiquita** on the S margin of the Chaco and about 320 km SE of Santiago del Estero. People who live in the valley of the Río Dulce are so used to the taste of its water that they often add a pinch of salt to the water they drink when away from home. Mar Chiquita, which is now growing rapidly, is naturally salty, and the water is warm. No river drains it, though two other rivers flow into it from the Sierras de Córdoba in the flood season. There are several islands in the lake. On its S shore is the small town of **Miramar**, which is being gradually overwhelmed by the expanding Mar Chiquita. The area is a very popular resort during the summer months; its salt waters are used in the treatment of rheumatic ailments and skin diseases.

Hotels *Savoy*, cheap, very friendly. **Camping** Autocamping Lilly, Bahía de los Sanavirones.

NB This Mar Chiquita and its town, Miramar, must not be confused with the other Mar Chiquita to the N of Mar del Plata and the seaside resort of Miramar, S of Mar del Plata.

SANTIAGO DEL ESTERO, TUCUMAN, SALTA AND JUJUY (3)

The route to the major tourist centre of Salta, from where trips can be made into Andean regions, the Quebrada de Humahuaca and the Calchaquí and Cachi valleys. There are prehispanic ruins near Tafí del Valle, Quilmes, Santa Rosa de Tastil and others. This is also a region in which there are a number of Amerindian groups.

Santiago del Estero, the oldest Argentine town, was founded in 1553 by conquistadores pushing S from Peru. It is 395 km N of Córdoba and 159 km SE of Tucumán. Population 201,000. On the main square, Plaza Libertad, stand the Municipalidad and the Cathedral (the fifth on the site). The fine Casa de Gobierno is on Plaza San Martín, 3 blocks away. In the convent of Santo Domingo, Urquiza y 25 de Mayo, is a "Holy Shroud", one of two copies of the "Turin Shroud", thought until recently to have covered the body of Christ. This copy was given by Philip II to his "beloved colonies of America". On Plaza Lugones is the pleasant old church of San Francisco, the oldest surviving church in the city, founded in 1565. At the back of the church is the cell of San Francisco Solano, patron saint of Tucumán, who stayed in Santiago in 1593. Beyond the church is the pleasant Parque Aguirre. Several public buildings, including the Casa de Gobierno, were severely burned and damaged in a popular upheaval in 1993 because of low incomes. Airport (Austral flights to Buenos Aires 5 times a week).

Museums Museo Arqueológico, Avellaneda 353, containing a large collection of Indian pottery and artefacts from the Chaco, brought together by Emil and Duncan Wagner, open Mon-Fri, 0800-1300, 1400-1900, Sat, 0900-1200, free; Museo Histórico, Urquiza 354, open Mon-Fri, 0830-1230, 1530-1830, Sat 0900-1200; Museo de Bellas Artes, Independencia between 9 de Julio and Urquiza, open Mon-Fri, 0900-1300; Museo Andrés Chazarreta, Mitre 127, handicrafts.

Festival Carnival in Feb is to be avoided: virtually everything throwable gets thrown by everyone at everyone else.

Hotels B *Gran Hotel*, Avellaneda e Independencia, T 214400, 4-star; *Libertador*, Catamarca 47, T 215766, 3-star; **B** *Residencial Rodas*, Gallo 432, clean, safe, overpriced. **D** *Embajador*, Buenos Aires 60; **D** *Residencial Emausi*, Av Moreno 600 block, with bath, good value. Around the bus terminus are: **D** *Residencial Santa Fe*, Santa Fe 255; *Santa Rita*, Santa Fe 273, clean, basic.

Camping Las Casuarinas in the Parque Aguirre.

Restaurant *Restaurant Sociedad Española*, Independencia 236, popular, good value; *Centro de Viajantes*, Buenos Aires 37, good value lunches; *Mía Mamma*, 24 de Septiembre 16, on Plaza, good restaurant/salad bar, pricey.

Exchange Banco Francés, 9 de Julio y 24 de Septiembre; **Noroeste Cambio**, 24 de

NORTH-WEST ARGENTINA

Septiembre 220, good rates. Amex, El Quijote Paladea Turismo, Independencia 342, T 213207.

Tourist Office on Plaza Libertad, very helpful.

Buses to **Resistencia**, 3 a day, 9 hrs, US$25, run by El Rayo company, via Quimili and Roque Sáenz Peña (8 hrs); to **Córdoba**, 12 a day, 7 hrs, US$16; to **Tucumán** (via Río Hondo) US$7. To **Buenos Aires**, several daily, 12 hrs, US$37, Cacorba, La Unión and Atahualpa. Four a day to Salta, US$23, Panamericano, 5½ hrs, at 7 hrs.

Termas de Río Hondo, 65 km N of Santiago del Estero along the road to Tucumán, is a major spa town, population 25,000. The thermal waters are recommended for blood pressure and rheumatism; good to drink, too, and used for the local soda water. Swimming (free) in a public pool called La Olla near the bridge which crosses the Río Hondo (see **Camping** below). Tourist office at Pasaje Borges, s/n. Frequent buses from Santiago del Estero, 1 hr, US$2 and from Tucumán, 2 hrs, US$4; Chevallier, La Estrella and others from Buenos Aires US$38 (US$75 return). The huge Río Hondo dam on the Río Dulce is close by; it forms a lake of 33,000 ha, used for sailing and fishing.

Hotels There are over 170 hotels, but at national holiday periods, and especially in Aug, accommodation is hard to find, so book well in advance. *Grand Hotel Río Hondo*, Hipólito Yrigoyen 552, T 21185; *Los Pinos*, Maipú 201, T 21175, pleasant; **C** *Ambassador*, Libertad 184, T 21196; *Aranjuez*, Av Alberdi 280, T 21108.

Camping Municipal site, Irigoyen y Ruta 9, near river bank; *La Olla*, left bank of river; ACA 3 km from town; *El Mirador*, Ruta 9 y Urquiza.

Tucumán (properly San Miguel de Tucumán, pop 400,000), capital of its province, is the busiest and the most populous city in the N. It stands on a plain, at 450m, but to the W towers the Sierra de Aconquija. The city was founded by Spaniards coming S from Peru in 1565. There are still some colonial buildings left, and among rows of elaborately stuccoed, spacious, one-storey houses (many of them sadly dilapidated) rise three or four handsome churches with blue and white tiled domes, and the elaborate Italianate Post Office. Summer weather can be very hot and sticky.

Tucumán's main square is Plaza Independencia. On its W side is the ornate Palacio de Gobierno, next is the church of San Francisco, with a picturesque façade. On the S side is the Cathedral, with an old rustic cross, kept near the baptismal font, used when founding the city. There are some unusual modern paintings inside the cathedral.

To the S, on Calle Congreso, is the **Casa Histórica** (see also below) where, in 1816, the Congress of the United Provinces of Río de la Plata met to draft the country's Declaration of Independence. The simple room in which this took place survived the destruction of the original house in 1908 and has now been enclosed in a reconstructed colonial museum. A bas-relief on the museum walls shows the delegates proclaiming independence. Some distance to the W is Plaza Belgrano, with a statue to General Belgrano, who won a decisive battle against the royalists on this site in 1812. Two blocks E is the University, with a grand view from the *vivero*. In the grounds is a good zoo, the Reserva Biológica San Javier. Nightly (not Tues, except in Jul) at 2030, *son et lumière* programme at Casa Histórica, in garden, in Spanish only, adults US$2, children US$1, tickets from tourist office on Plaza Independencia, no seats.

In the large Nueve de Julio park (avoid at night) is the house of Bishop Colombres, who introduced sugar cane to Tucumán in the early 19th century. In the house is his first milling machine. The province of Tucumán is the centre of Argentine sugar production. There are several mills nearby: the easiest to visit is Ingenio Concepción, a modern plant on the outskirts of town, guided tours in Spanish during harvest period only (15 Jul-early Nov), Mon-Sat, 0930 and 1030, no booking required. Take Aconquija bus for Santo Cristo from outside bus terminus in 24 de Septiembre, US$0.40, pay on bus, 15 mins.

Museums Casa Histórica (see above), Calle Congreso, open Tues-Fri 0830-1330, Tues, and Thur, 1700-2000, Sat, Sun 1000-1300, US$0.40. **Museo de Antropología y Etnografía,** 25 de Mayo 265 in University building, fine collection, open Mon-Fri, 0800-1200, 1600-2000. **Museo Folklórico Provincial,** 24 de Septiembre 565, open Mon 1730-2030, Tues-Fri, 0900-1230, 1730-2030, Sat, Sun, 1800-2100, free. **Instituto Miguel Lillo,** San Lorenzo y Lillo (30 mins walk from bus station), associated with the natural sciences department of the University, has a small but well-presented museum containing sections on geology and biology with some stuffed animals and a dinosaur skeleton, open Mon-Fri, 0900-1200, 1500-1800. The Institute also possesses a fine specialist library (not open to the public) which incl an original edition of Von Humboldt's travels in South America. **Casa Padilla,** Plaza Independencia, houses a collection of international art and antiques in the home of a prominent Tucumán family. Near the Casa Histórica at Calle Congreso 56 is the **Museo Histórico de la Provincia** (Casa de Avellaneda) open Mon-Fri, 0900-1230, 1700-2000, Sat-Sun, 1700-2000, closed for reorganization (early 1995); **Museo Iramaín,** Entre Rios 27, a very interesting memorial to the sculptor, open Mon-Fri, 0900-1900. **Museo de Bellas Artes,** 9 de Julio 48, between 24 de Septiembre and Alvarez, open Tues-Fri, 0900-1300, 1630-2100, Sat-Sun, 0900-1200, 1730-2030.

Local Holiday 24 Sep (Battle of Tucumán). 29 Sep, San Miguel. Independence celebrations incl music and speeches at the Casa Histórica on 8 Jul, followed by *gauchos* bringing in the National Flag at midnight. Next day there are markets and music. Also Día de la Tradición, 10 Nov.

Hotels L3 *Grand Hotel de Tucumán,* Av Soldati 380, T 245000, large, new five-star hotel opposite the Parque Centenario 9 de Julio, efficient, outstanding food and service, swimming pool, tennis courts, discotheque; **A1** *Carlos V,* 25 de Mayo 330, T 215042/221972, central, good service, a/c, bar, restaurant, excellent pasta, rec; **A2** *Metropol,* 24 de Septiembre 524, T 311180, good service, worth it; **B** *Gran Hotel Corona,* 24 de Septiembre on corner of Plaza Independencia, good location and facilities, run down; **B** *ACA Motel Tucumán,* Av Salta 2080,

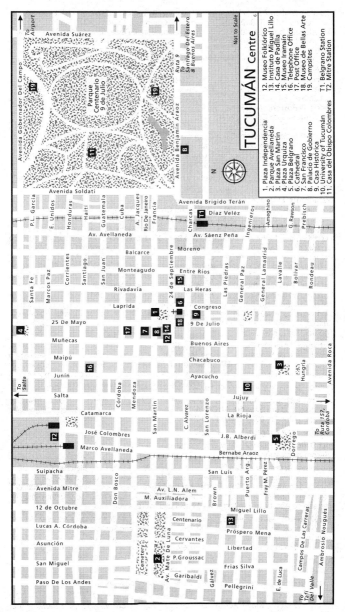

TUCUMÁN Centre

Not to Scale

1. Plaza Independencia
2. Parque Avellaneda
3. Plaza San Martín
4. Plaza Urquiza
5. Plaza Belgrano
6. Cathedral
7. San Francisco
8. Palacio de Gobierno
9. Casa Histórica
10. University of Tucumán
11. Casa del Obispo Colombres
12. Museo Folklórico
13. Instituto Miguel Lillo
14. Casa de Padilla
15. Museo Iramain
16. Telephone Office
17. Post Office
18. Museo de Bellas Arte
19. Campsites
T1. Belgrano Station
T2. Mitre Station

T 266037; **B** *Miami*, Junín 580, T 310265, garage; **B** *Premier*, with a/c, good, friendly, accepts Visa, Alvarez 510, T 310381. Also good: **C** *Congreso*, Congreso 74, T 216025, clean, old-fashioned but rec, with bath, plain, good location; **C** *Plaza*, San Martín 435, T 215502, built round a pretty central courtyard, basic but clean; **C** *Viena*, Santiago del Estero 1054, T 310313; **D** *Tucumán*, Catamarca 573, near Mitre station, clean, OK; **D** *La Vasca*, Mendoza 281, T 211288, with bath, clean, friendly, safe, rec; **D** *Casa de Huéspedes María Ruiz*, Rondeau 1824, clean, safe, rec.

There are hotels near the bus station, eg **B** *Colonial*, San Martín 35, 5 mins from bus station, modern, very clean, private bath, fan, laundry service, breakfast incl, rec; **B** *Mayoral*, 24 de Septiembre 364, T 228351, F 54-81-310080, 20% discount to *South American Handbook* readers; **D** *Boston*, Sáenz Peña, 77, nice courtyards, restaurant, but some rooms are very dirty; **D** *El Parque*, Sgto Gómez 22, across from bus station, fan, clean (though used as a brothel), friendly, safe; **D** *Florida*, 24 de Septiembre 610, T 221785, good value, clean, poorly-lit rooms, helpful; **D** *Independencia*, Balcarce, between San Martín and 24 de Septiembre, with fan, clean, quiet; **D** *Palace*, 24 de Septiembre 233, friendly, rec; **D** *Petit*, C Alvarez 765, T 213902, spacious, friendly, clean, quiet, with bath and breakfast incl, highly rec. Many cheap hotels in streets around General Belgrano station.

Camping Parque Nueve de Julio, 2 sites (US$0.25 per tent, US$0.25 pp). Two roadside camp sites 3 km E and NE of city centre.

Restaurants *El Duque*, San Lorenzo 464, very large, popular, good food, poor service. Good food, poor service in open air at *La Rural* and *Gran Grill* 38, Parque 9 de Julio; there are also several cafés in the park. *Ali Baba*, Junín 380, Arab specialities (Syrian owners), intimate, inexpensive, good, rec, closed lunchtime; *Adela*, 24 Septiembre 358, well prepared food, Arab specialities, good value; *La Leñita*, 25 de Mayo, 300 block, expensive, smart, good meat. *La Parrilla del Centro*, San Martín 381, excellent, reasonable prices; *Farolito Criollo*, Crisóstomo Alvarez 600, regional dishes, very cheap but dirty; *Pizzería La Esquina*, Mendoza y Laprida, good; *Las Gordas*, Plaza Independencia, pleasant, popular with locals, as is *La Plaza*, also on the square; *Las Brasas*, Maipú 740, good but not cheap. Good fast food at *Pic Nic*, San Juan 600 block and Ayacucho 500 block; *Augustus*, 24 Septiembre y Buenos Aires, good café; *Pastísima Rotisería*, Mendoza y Laprida and at San Martín 964, good cheap snacks, take out service; *La Vieja Casa*, Córdoba 680, good, inexpensive set lunch. Set lunches near bus station good value, for instance *Camboriú*, Av Brígido Terán, cheap, clean, and friendly. *Panadería Villecco*, Corrientes 751, good bread, also "integral". In this part of Argentina "black beer" (eg Salta Negra) is available.

Exchange American Express, Chacabuco 38, no longer changes cash or cheques. **Noroeste Cambios**, 24 de Septiembre 549 and San Martín 775, accepts cheques. **Dinar**, San Martín 645 and 742, accepts cash only, and **Maguitur**, San Martín 763, good rates for cash, accepts cheques (with high commission). (See note on provincial bonds used as currency, p 222.)

Casino Sarmiento y Maipú, open Fri, Sat, Sun, 2100-0230.

Cultural Institutes Alliance Française, Mendoza 255, free events in French. **Instituto Italiano di Cultura**, Salta 60; **ATICANA** (North American Centre) incl JF Kennedy Library, Salta 581, open Mon-Fri, 0800-1200, 1700-2100.

Laundry *Lava Expreso*, San Martín 929.

Post Office Córdoba y 25 de Mayo, open 0700-1300, 1600-2000 Mon-Fri, 0800-1300 Sat. **Telecommunications** Telecom, Maipú 360, open 24 hrs, best after 1900.

Shopping *Artesanía El Cardón*, Alvarez 427, excellent handicrafts; Mercado Artesanal, at the tourist office in Plaza Independencia, small, but nice selection of lace and leather work. *Librería San Martín* on 24 de Septiembre has English magazines. *Los Primos*, C Muñecas, secondhand books. All shops close 1200-1630. There is a lively fruit and vegetable market, Mercado de Abasto, at San Lorenzo and Miguel Lillo, worth a visit.

Travel Agents *Massini Viajes*, 24 de Septiembre 377, T 215616; *Viajes Ru-Mar*, Alvarez 566, organises day trips to Tafí del Valle, Quilmes etc, Sat, and Sun. *Delfín Turismo*, on 24 de Septiembre, very helpful, good excursions, operates in conjunction with Saltur of Salta. Excursions around the city are run by *Disney Tour*, San Lorenzo 435. Tours may be difficult to arrange out of peak season (eg Sep) owing to shortage of passengers.

Tourist Office in Plaza Independencia at 24 de Septiembre 484, helpful.

Taxis Meters may be rigged, arrange price in advance if possible.

Car Hire Avis, *Hotel del Sol*, Plaza Independencia; **Liprandi**, 24 de Septiembre 524, T 311210/212665; **Movil Renta**, San Lorenzo 370, T 218635/310550, F 310080 and at airport; Localiza, San Juan 959, T 311352.

Motorists should not park on the street overnight; pay US$5 for garage parking.

Car Repairs Rubén Boss, Av Aconquija 947, rec esp for Volkswagen.

Air Airport: Benjamín Matienzo, 15 km from town. Bus for each flight, US$1.50, starts from *Hotel Mayoral*, 24 de Septiembre 364. Taxi US$10. Daily flights to Buenos Aires with Aerolíneas Argentinas and Austral, and Lapa 3 times a week. Austral to Córdoba daily, Salta (also Lapa and Ladeco) and Jujuy. AR to Rio de Janeiro once a week.

Rail See under Buenos Aires, **Railways**, for schedules and fares.

N of Tucumán the Belgrano line runs via Rosario de la Frontera to Jujuy, and La Quiaca, on the Bolivian border, 644 km from Tucumán. No passenger service since Mar 1993.

Buses to Cafayate (8 hrs, US$17) via Tafí and Santa María (6 hrs) daily at 0600 and 1600. Direct bus in summer to Cafayate Tues, Thur, Sat, 6½ hrs, at 1000 (0600/0700 in winter), US$15. Direct to **Salta** (but not via Cafayate), 4½ hours, several daily, eg La Estrella, Veloz del Norte, US$18 (slow bus 5½ hrs). Plenty of buses to Jujuy, eg Veloz del Norte, 0900, 6 hrs. See note below on routes to Salta.

To **La Rioja**, 7 hrs, US$15. To **Catamarca**, 5 a day with Bosio, plus other lines. To **Santiago del Estero** (US$7), Paraná, Termas de Río Hondo, Orán, Resistencia, 11½ hrs, and Tinogasta. To **Buenos Aires**, Chevallier, La Estrella, Veloz del Norte, 16 hours, all with toilet, a/c, bar, video, 3 stops; book in advance; fares US$48-70.

For those who wish to travel direct from N Argentina to Central Chile, there are daily La Estrella buses (US$40) from Tucumán to **Mendoza**, leaving 1300, 1400 and 2000 (19 hours), via Catamarca, La Rioja, and San Juan. Bus to **Córdoba** 480 km, US$25, 7 hours, many companies (incl Sol and El Tucumano Panamericano). *La Veloz de Norte* serves free coffee, cake and soda. To **La Paz**, take bus to the frontier, then at Villazón, connect with train to Oruro and La Paz. New bus station is on Av Benjamín Araoz beside a huge shopping complex.

Excursions *Simoca*, 50 km S of Tucumán on Route 157, has an authentic Sat morning market, handicrafts and produce, Posta bus, several, 1½ hrs, US$2.50; essential to get there early. West of Tucumán in the Sierras de Aconquija are *Villa Nougués*, 36 km (one of the most interesting tours), the summer residence of the well-to-do Tucumanos (excellent hotel) and San Javier, 34 km (hotel), both reached by San Javier buses, 1200 and 1900. Aconquija park, with glorious trees, is at the foot of the mountains 14 km W of Tucumán. Bus at 1130 (the only one; returns immediately); tours from Terra, 9 de Julio 80. The Quebrada de Lules, the gorge of the Río Lules, is 20 km S of the city. *El Cadillal* dam, in the gorge of the Río Sali, 26 km N of Tucumán, supplies electricity and water for the city and permanent irrigation for 80,000 ha of parched land. There are restaurants, a good ACA campsite, good swimming, and a small archaeological museum at the dam. Reached by Sierras y Lagos buses every 1½ hrs approx, US$1.20, 45 mins, last buses back 1715 and 1945.

North from Tucumán From Tucumán there are 2 routes to Salta. The road via Santa María and Cafayate through the beautiful Quebrada de Cafayate (see p 108) is longer but much more interesting than the direct route via Rosario de la Frontera and Güemes. From Route 38 to Tafí del Valle on Route 307 is beautiful semi-tropical jungle with a white-water river. Beyond Tafí del Valle to Cafayate is largely gravel and the area is barren.

From Tucumán to Cafayate 46 km S of Tucumán Route 307 branches NW to *Tafí del Valle* about 3,000, 97 km from Tucumán, not to be confused with Tafí Viejo which is 10 km N of the city) known to archaeologists as a holy valley of the precolumbian Indian tribes. 10 km S of Tafí del Valle are Dique El Mollar, formerly La Angostura dam, and nearby the menhir park of *El Mollar*, with 129 standing stones (collected in the early years of this century from various sites) and good views (best to visit in am). Tours to El Mollar and Tafí are available from Travel Agencies in Tucumán, US$15 each for 4 people minimum. Daily bus from Tafí, 1215, 15 mins, US$1. Returns from El Mollar 1330. The Tucumán-Tafí bus stops nearby.

Tafí del Valle and El Mollar are often shrouded in fog because of the dam. Ten mins from Tafí is Capilla Jesuítica y Museo La Banda in the 16th century chapel of San Lorenzo (open 0900-1200, 1400-1800 daily, US$1).

Services B *Hostería ACA*, T 21027, comfortable, good value restaurant, garden; **D** *Colonial*,

T 21067, nr bus station, closed out of season, no singles, friendly, clean; **D** *Hotel Atep*, Los Menhires, nr bus station, E in winter, with bath, clean, friendly, rec; *Pensión*, opp *Colonial*, in billiard hall, ask in advance for hot water; **E** pp *hostal* run by Celia Correa, near church. Hotels and bungalows (C) at El Pinar del Ciervo, 1 km from the town at La Banda is **A+** *La Hacienda Le Pepe*, incl breakfast, English and French spoken, horses for rent. **Restaurants** *El Rancho de Félix*, rec; *El Portal de Tafí*, good, has video room (movies in summer only); *La Rueda*, at S entrance to village, inexpensive, rec; *Los Faroles*, pleasant cafe. **Camping** *Los Sauzales*, very clean, hot showers, rec. Autocamping (US$2 per tent, small cabins for rent, US$10). Try local cheese. For **Tours** throughout the NW from Tafí, contact Margarita and Bruno Widmer, T/F (0867) 21076.

Bus Tucumán-Tafí, with Aconquija, sit on left-hand side, travels through luxuriant gorge with sub-tropical vegetation, 4 a day, 3½ hrs, US$6. On this road at Km 27 there is a large statue of an Indian warrior known as El Indio, picnic area. To Cafayate 4 a day, 4 hrs, US$10. This is a magnificent ride through deep gorges, with giant cacti and bare mountains.

From Tafí the road runs 56 km NW over the 3,040m Infiernillo Pass and through attractive arid landscape to *Amaicha del Valle* (bus from Tucumán, US$7, 0600) which claims 360 sunny days a year, free municipal campsite, *Juan Bautista Alberdi*, 10 min out of town (blue gate) (**C** *Hostería Provincial*, T 21019, full board, showers not always hot, clean and friendly, rec; **E** *Pensión Albarracín*; **E** *Hostería Colonial*, with bath, friendly. **Restaurant** *Parrilla El Quipu*, 50 m from the centre). La Pachamama festival at end of pre-Lent Carnival; also see Sr Cruz' craft workshop.

From Amaicha the road is paved as far as the junction with Route 40 (15 km). A paved road also runs S from Amaicha 22 km to *Santa María*, pop 18,000.

Hotels B *Plaza*, on plaza, clean, small rm, slightly run down; **C** *Provincial de Turismo*, San Martín, friendly, rec, dining room, with bath; **D** *Residencial Alemán*, Quintana 144, small rooms but clean, friendly, quiet; **D** *Residencial Palacios*, Mitre 592, basic, hot water, clean, reasonable and friendly; **E** *Residencial Reinoso*, Av 1° de Mayo 649, good, 2 blocks from plaza, no sign, hot showers, clean, friendly. Municipal **campsite** at end of Sarmiento.

Restaurant *El Cardón*, Abel Acosta 158, cheap and good, regional dishes.

Buses To **Tucumán** 6 hrs, 0220, 0800, US$8.50. To **Cafayate**, 4 hrs, daily at 0700 exc Thur at 1030, US$10. Empresa Bosio goes to **Catamarca**, Sat; via Tucumán Sun at 1230, 9 hrs. Most start from Belgrano 271 on main Plaza; Empresa San Cayetano (600 block of Esquiú) to **Belén** 4 hrs, Mon, Wed, Fri at 0500.

Excursions to *Fuerte Quemado* (Indian ruins) 15 km N along Route 40, not as impressive as Quilmes (see below); Cerro Pintado, 8 km, coloured sandstone mountains; important ruins of Loma Rica, 18 km; Ampajango, 27 km S off Route 40, important indigenous finds.

   Quilmes (Tucumán)   37 km N, with splendid views from the fortifications and interesting cacti, has Inca ruins (dam, village and posting house—*tambo*), sleeping and camping facilities and a guide at the site from 0700 to 1730. Entry US$1.50. There is also a shop selling good indigenous crafts, particularly textiles. It is 5 km along a dirt road off the main Santa María-Cafayate road, and 16 km from Amaicha del Valle. There is also a provincial archaeological museum, plus good restaurant, bar, toilets, camping possibilities. For a day's visit take 0630 Aconquija bus from Cafayate to Santa María, alight at site and take returning bus which passes at 1100. Taxi from Cafayate US$60 return.

From Santa María Route 40 leads N to Cafayate (55 km, **see p 115** and S to Belén (176 km, **see p 143**).

North of Tucumán   Route 9 and the Belgrano railway run into the province of Salta. Both Salta and the neighbouring province of Jujuy are home to a number of Indian groups which are either historically indigenous to the area, or which migrated there from other Andean regions, the greater Amazon region, or the Guaraní-occupied territories to the E. The Mataco, Chorote, Chulupi and Toba have retained their own languages, but the Chiriguano language is spoken by the Chiriguano, the Tapiete and the Chane (who belong to the Arawak family of Indians, which originate in the very N of the sub-continent). (We are grateful to John Raspey for this information.) **NB** The best description of the most interesting places and events in NW Argentina is to be found in Federico Kirbus' *Guía de Aventuras y Turismo de la Argentina* (available at Librería La Rayuela, Buenos Aires 96, Salta and El Ateneo, Florida 340, basement, Buenos Aires).

145 km N of Tucumán is **Rosario de la Frontera**, a popular resort from Jun to Sep. Altitude: 769m. 8 km away are sulphur springs. Casino.

Hotels B pp *Termas*, Route 34, T 81004, full board, rambling place, good food but many rooms without private bath (6 km from bus station, taxi US$7). Baths US$1.50. About 1 km from *Hotel Termas* is *ACA motel*, T 81143. Across the road is man-made lake owned by Caza y Pesca Club—ask in your hotel for permission to fish. **D** *Real*, Güemes 185, basic, clean, not all doors close.

Buses To Tucumán, Güemes, Salta and Jujuy, frequent.

Excursions About 20 km N is the historical post house, Posta de **Yatasto**, with museum, 2 km E of the main road; campsite. To *El Naranjo* (19 km) a Jesuit colonial town; church contains images and carvings made by Indians.

About 80 km N of Rosario de la Frontera, at Lumbreras, a road branches off Route 9 and runs 80 km NE to the Parque Nacional **Finca El Rey**, a 44,160-hectare tropical forest and wildlife preserve set among 900-1,500m hills with clear streams (good fishing). It can also be reached from Salta, 196 km, US$50 pp round-trip excursions of at least 6 with agencies. There is a Park office in Salta, España 366, 3rd floor (helpful). Check here on timetable for Park truck. From Salta, take bus to Saravia, daily at 1630, 3 hours, US$4.20. Bus drops you at Paso de la Cruz, 38 km from park entrance and 50 km from the park headquarters. No public and little other traffic after this, but you may get a lift with local farm or roadbuilding vehicles. A truck leaves the Park HQ for the main road on Sun, Tues and Fri at 1600 to meet the bus going to Salta at 1825, but it rarely connects with the 1630 coming from Salta. Mosquitoes, ticks and chiggers thrive; take lotion. No accommodation while *Hostería El Rey* is closed (it is due to be transferred to private hands). Camping is free, there are several tent sites, but few facilities. Horseback riding. Landing strip for small planes. The access road is still poor and fords the river 9 times; passable for ordinary cars except in the wet season. Best time to visit is winter (drier).

From Güemes, 148 km N of Rosario de la Frontera, Route 9 runs W through the mountains for 43 km to **Salta**, at 1,190m, 370,000 people, on the Río Arias, in the Lerma valley, in a mountainous and strikingly beautiful district. Situated 1,600 km from Buenos Aires, Salta is now a great tourist and handicraft centre (prices are lower than in Tucumán or Buenos Aires) and the best starting place for tours of the NW. Capital of its province, it is a handsome city founded in 1582, with fine colonial buildings. Follow the ceramic pavement plaques, or get map from Tourist Office, for an interesting pedestrian tour. The Cathedral (open mornings and evenings), on the N side of the central Plaza 9 de Julio, was built 1858-1878; it contains the much venerated images of the Cristo del Milagro and of the Virgin Mary, the first sent from Spain in 1592, and has a rich interior mainly in red and gold, as well as a huge late baroque altar. The miracle was the sudden cessation of a terrifying series of earthquakes when the images were paraded through the streets on 15 September 1692. They still are, each Sep, when 80,000 people visit the town. On the opposite side of the Plaza is the Cabildo, built in 1783. The Convent of San Bernardo, at Caseros and Santa Fe, was built in colonial style in the mid-19th century; it has a famous wooden portal of 1762. Nuns are still living here so the inside of the convent is not open to visitors. San Francisco church, at Caseros and Córdoba, built in 1882, rises above the city centre skyline with its magnificent façade and red, yellow and grey coloured tower, said to be the tallest church tower in South America (open 0700-1200, 1730-2100, although the times are erratic).

E of the city centre is the Cerro San Bernardo (1,458m), accessible by modern cable car (*teleférico*), functions daily, 1600-2000, US$6 return, children US$3, from Parque San Martín, fine views. Near the *teleférico* station is a lake where rowing boats can be hired (US$3 for 20 mins). It takes about half an hour to walk back down the hill. Very beautifully set at the foot of the hill is an impressive statue by Víctor Cariño, 1931, to General Güemes, whose *gaucho* troops repelled seven powerful Spanish invasions from Bolivia between 1814 and 1821. Nearby, on Paseo Güemes, is the Museo Arqueológico, which contains many objects from Tastil (**see p 118**). A steep path (1,136 steps) behind the museum with Stations of the Cross leads to the top of the hill, where there is an old wooden cross, together with restaurant and artificial waterfalls.

Museums Museo Histórico del Norte, in the Cabildo Histórico, Caseros 549, colonial, historical and archaeological museum, guided tour in Spanish, rec, open Tues-Sat, 1000-1400, 1530-1930, Sun 1000-1400, US$1. **Museo de Bellas Artes**, Florida 20, open Mon-Sat 0900-1300, 1700-2100, Sun 0900-1200, US$0.60 (closed Jan). **Casa Uriburu**, Caseros 421, Tues-Sat, 1000-1400, 1530-1930, US$0.60, has relics of a distinguished *salteño* family. **Museo Folclórico Pajarito Velarde**, Pueyrredón 106. **Museo Antropológico**, behind the Güemes statue, open Tues-Fri 0830-1230, 1430-1830, Sat 1500-1830, Sun 1600-1830, US$1, interesting display. **Museo de Arte Popular y Artesanías Iberoamericanos**, Caseros 476, excellent display of contemporary Latin American handicrafts. **Museo de Ciencias Naturales**, in Parque San Martín, has a full display of over 150 regional stuffed birds and an interesting display of armadillos, rec, open Tues-Sun 1400-2000, US$0.25. **Museo de la Ciudad "Casa de Hernández"**, La Florida 97, Tues-Sat, 0900-1230, 1600-2030. Check opening times in summer at tourist office; many close then.

Festivals 15 Sep, Cristo del Milagro (see above); 24 Sep, commemorating the battles of Tucumán and Salta. On 16-17 Jun, folk music by youngsters in the evening and *gaucho* parade in the morning around the Güemes statue at the foot of Cerro San Bernardo. Salta celebrates Carnival with processions on the four weekends before Ash Wednesday at 2200 in Av Belgrano (seats optional at US$2-4); lots of shaving foam (*nieve*) in the early morning; also Mardi Gras (Shrove Tuesday) with a procession of decorated floats and of dancers with intricate masks of feathers and mirrors. It is the custom to squirt water at passers-by and *bombas de agua* (small balloons to be filled with water) are on sale for dropping from balconies on to unwary pedestrians below. Wear a light waterproof!

Hotels Salta is a favourite convention town. Some hotels close for a vacation during the Christmas season until Jan 10, so check. The last two weeks in Jul are often fully booked because of holidays. Accommodation is also very scarce around 10-16 Sep because of the celebrations of Cristo del Milagro. **A2 Salta**, Buenos Aires 1, in main plaza, T 211011, first class, cash discount, swimming pool, good restaurant on 3rd floor, room security inadequate; **A1 Portezuelo**, Av Del Turista 1, T 310104/5, F 310133, breakfast extra, some rooms a/c, English, German, French, Italian spoken, swimming pool, clean, helpful, good restaurant, rec, better than the ACA's **A2 Huaico**, Av Bolivia y P Costas, T 310571; **A2 California**, Alvarado 646, T 216266, one block from main plaza, singles are small, rec; **A2 Crillón**, near main plaza, Ituzaingó 30, T 220400, good rooms, noisy a/c, unhelpful, run down; **A3 Cristal**, Urquiza 616, T 222854, clean, a bit run down, helpful; **A2 Victoria Plaza**, Zuviría 16, T 211222, expensive but good restaurant, the foyer overlooking the plaza is one of the centres of *salteño* life; **B Cabildo**, Caseros 527, T 224589, pleasant, a bit run down. **B Colonial**, Zuviría 6, T 213057, with bath, a/c, rec, but 1st floor rooms noisy; **B Las Lajitas**, Pasaje Calesto Guana 336, T 234908, modern, clean, good value, ACA reduction, rec. On main plaza is **B Petit**, H Yrigoyen 225, T 213012, near bus terminus, pleasant, small, friendly, expensive breakfasts, rooms around courtyard with small swimming pool, a/c extra, French spoken; **B Regidor**, Buenos Aires 10, T 222070, English-speaking owner, avoid 1st floor, good value lunch, clean, comfortable, friendly.

   C Astur, Rivadavia 752, T 212107, with bath, rec; **C España**, España 319, T 217898, central but quiet, simple, rec; **C Florida**, Calle Florida y Urquiza 722, T 212133, with bath, very friendly, clean, will store luggage, rec; **C Italia**, Alberdi 231, T 214050, next to jazz club/casino, very clean and friendly, rec; **C Residencial Elena**, Buenos Aires 256, T 211529, clean, friendly and quiet, "charming", safe, try to get there early, even out of season; **C Residencial Balcarce**, Balcarce 460, T 218023, friendly, clean; **D Residencial San Jorge**, Esteco 244 y Ruiz de los Llanos 1164 (no sign), T 210443, with bath, parking, safe deposit, laundry and limited kitchen facilities, central heating, homely, guide for climbing, horse-trekking advice by proprietor, Sr. Dejean, also organizes local excursions by car, good value, very popular, highly rec; **C Residencial Centro**, Alvarado 630, T 211241, same owner as *Crisol*. **Residencial Provincial**, Santiago del Estero 555, friendly, hot water; **Residencial Viena**, Florida 184, small rooms, basic; **Residencial Crisol**, Ituzaingó 166, T 214462, hot water, clean, highly rec.

   E Casa de familia de María del Toffoli, Mendoza 915 (about 10 blocks from bus station), T 21-7383, nice atmosphere, comfortable, clean, roof terrace, cooking and laundry facilities, discount for ISIC and youth card holders, rec, rooms also at Nos 917 and 919, D, belonging to Sra Toffoli's sisters (reservations at No 917), cosy, highly rec. **E Hospedaje Doll**, Pasaje Ruiz de los Llanos 1360 (7 blocks from centre), with bath, friendly, safe, rec; **E Residencial Güemes**, Necochea y Balcarce, near railway station, basic, clean, private bath, laundry service. Many other cheap hotels near railway station (eg **E Internacional**, Ameghino 651, hot water, basic, with good cheap restaurant), but few near new bus station. **E Nápoli**, Mitre 1021, fairly near railway, basic, dirty, but café serves good coffee and bread, laundry, not rec. Private house, Pellegrini 408, E pp, not central but clean, peaceful, spacious patio. **Youth Hostel**

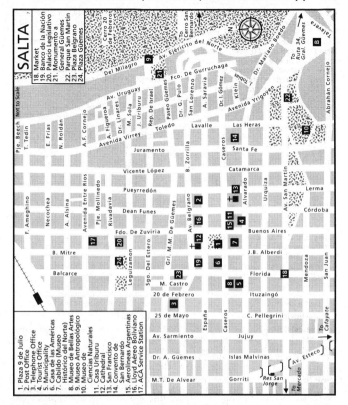

SALTA Not to Scale

Key:
1. Plaza 9 de Julio
2. Post Office
3. Telephone Office
4. Tourist Office
5. Municipality
6. Casa de las Américas
7. Cabildo (Museo Histórico del Norte)
8. Museo de Bellas Artes
9. Museo Antropológico
10. Museo de Ciencias Naturales
11. Casa Uriburu
12. Cathedral
13. San Francisco
14. Convento de San Bernardo
15. Aerolíneas Argentinas
16. Lloyd Aéreo Boliviano
17. ACA Service Station
18. Market
19. Banco de la Nación
20. Palacio Legislativo
21. Monumento a General Güemes
22. Parque San Martín
23. Plaza Belgrano
24. Plaza Güemes

Backpackers, Buenos Aires 930, T 087-233349, bus 12 from bus terminal or ½ hr walk, E pp in dormitories, laundry and kitchen facilities, stores luggage, information, bar, clean, hot showers, English, Greek and Hebrew spoken, friendly, frequently rec. *No me Olvides*, Av de los Pioneros, Km 0.800, F pp, shared rooms, cooking facilities, friendly, rec. **NB** Do not be tempted by touts at the bus station offering convenient accommodation.

Camping Casino Provincial municipal grounds, by river, 300 m artificial lake (popular Dec-Feb). Bus 13 to grounds. There is no signposting: leave the city heading S on Calle Jujuy, after 3 km you will see the Coca Cola plant on your left; turn left before the plant and then take the first road right. Charges US$3 per tent plus US$2 pp. Free hot showers available if there is gas (not often), safe, bathrooms run-down, disappointing. Also at *Motel Huaico*, Campo Castañares. *Municipal Campsite* at Campo Quijano, 30 km W of Salta, at the entrance to Quebrada del Toro gorge, hot showers, bungalows, plenty of room for pitching tents, rec, bus from Salta bus terminal. Camping shops: HR Maluf, San Martín y Buenos Aires, and one at La Rioja 995.

Restaurants *El Monumento*, Gurruchaga 20 (opp Güemes monument), good food, slow service, good atmosphere, reasonably priced; *Jockey Club*, Belgrano 366, good; *Maxims*, Mendoza y Florida, good; *La Castiza*, Alberdi 134, huge, little atmosphere, expensive; *Don José*, Urquiza 484, good, cheap, popular, asado de tira and grilled kid, warmly rec. *La Posta*, España 476, food and atmosphere both excellent, reasonable prices, highly rec; *El Viejo Jack*, Virrey Toledo 145, good meat dishes, "one of the best steaks in Argentina", huge portions, good value, repeatedly rec; *El Viejo Jack II*, Av Reyes Católicos 1465, gigantic servings of meat, reasonable prices, superb; *Mama Mía*, Las Heras y Virrey Toledo, cheap pasta; *Cantina*,

Caseros y 20 de Febrero, pizzas, steaks, good value; *Las Leñas*, Caseros 444, good beef, good value; *El Arriero*, Caseros 828, good steak and pasta; *9 de Julio*, Urquiza 1020, excellent lunch; *El Rescoldo*, Caseros 427, cheap lunches, rec; *Green Park*, Caseros 529, good snacks, and milk shakes; *El Mesón de Pepe*, Rivadavia 774, fish specialities, good but pricey. *La Posada*, Plaza 9 de Julio, good food and cheap for the location. Pleasant outdoor restaurants in Parque San Martín, at foot of Cerro San Bernardo. *Sociedad Española*, Balcarce 653, excellent cuisine; *JA*, Yrigoyen y San Martín, excellent kid; *Bar Copetín Le Mans*, in parque San Martín, lovely setting by artificial lake; *El Rincón del Artista*, San Martín 1240, cheap, lunch, closed evenings; *de Pablo*, Mitre 399, excellent set lunch; *Alvarez*, Buenos Aires y San Martín, cafeteria style, cheap and good. *Casa de Té*, Paseo Alberdi 422, chocolate and cakes; *Pub Yo Juan*, Balcarce 481, popular, live music at weekends; *Café del Paseo* at *Hotel Colonial*, Zuviría 6, open 24 hrs, superb breakfast. *Heladería Gianni*, España 486, ask for copa dell'Amore (expensive); excellent coffee served. *Cafe Río*, Mitre 40, good breakfasts for US$1.50; *Time*, Plaza 9 de Julio, good breakfasts, coffee and ice cream. Cheap restaurants near the railway and bus stations, which are also the cheapest places for breakfast. Many restaurants are lunch only, especially on San Martín near the Municipal Market. Cheapest food is from the numerous *superpanchito* stands (huge cheesedogs, US$0.50). Good supermarket, *Disco*, on Alberdi y Leguizamon.

Try local Cafayate wines, such as Michel Torino and Echart Privado, and typical Torrontés-grape wine. The local water also makes excellent beer.

Airline Offices Aerolíneas Argentinas, Caseros 475/485, T 310866; Lloyd Aéreo Boliviano, Buenos Aires 120, T217753 (will hold luggage and schedule a colectivo taxi); Austral, Caseros 475, T 310258.

Banks and Exchange Banks open 0730-1300. **Banco de la Nación**, Balcarce y España; **Banco Provincial de Salta**, España 526 on main square, changes TCs, 2.5% commission. **Banco de Galicia** does Visa cash advances without commission. **Banco Noroeste**, Caseros 600-700, Mastercard accepted. **Banco Roberts**, Mitre 143, good rates, changes cheques, 3% commission, rec. Amex, Chicoana Turismo, Av Belgrano y Zuviria 255, does not cash TCs. Many cambios on España: **Cambio Dinar**, Mitre 101 (Plaza 9 de Julio and España 609), changes Amex cheques (3% commission) and cash (poor rates), long queues. **Maguitur**, España 666, only cash; **Golden Life**, Mitre 95 (Plaza 9 de Julio), local 1, first floor, best rates for cash.

Cultural Institutes Alliance Française, Santa Fe 20, T 210827.

Consulates Bolivia, Los Almendros 161, T 223377, open Mon-Fri, 0900-1300 (unhelpful, better to go to Jujuy); Chile, Santiago del Estero, T 215757; Peru, 25 de Mayo 407, T 310201; Spain, Las Heras 1329, T 221420; Italy, Alvarado 1632, T 213881; France, Santa Fe 20, T 213336; Germany, Córdoba 202, T 216525, F 311772, consul Juan C Kühl, who also runs Kuehl travel agency and photo shop, helpful; Belgium, Pellegrini 835, T 233459

Music Folk music show and evening meal at Boliche Balderrama, San Martín 1126; Gauchos de Güemes, Uruguay 750; Casa Güemes, España 730. For something less touristy try Manolo, San Martín 1296 or El Monumento, O'Higgins 1050. Beware of bars which charge around US$7 pp for music, but which don't display charges.

Language School Academia de Idiomas del Norte, F Ameghino 426, T/F (087) 211985. Swiss run, branch also in Iquique, Chile.

Laundry Sol de Mayo, 25 de Mayo 755, service wash. Laverap, Santiago del Estero 363 (open Sun am) good, fast service, US$6 for one load; Marva, Juramento 315; La Baseta, Alvarado 1170.

Post Office Deán Funes 160, between España and Belgrano poste restante charges US$1.15 per letter. **Telephone** office at Av Belgrano 824, 24 hrs, international calls at Av Vicente López 146, 0800-1930.

Immigration Office Maipú 35, 0730-1230.

Shopping Mercado Municipal, corner of San Martín and Florida, for meat, fish, vegetables, empanadas, humitas and other produce and handicrafts, closed 1200-1700 and Sun. Mercado Artesanal on the outskirts of the city in the Casa El Alto Molino, a late 18th century mansion, at San Martín 2555, T 219195, Mon-Fri 0800-2000, Sat 0900-2000 (sometimes closes in summer) take bus 2, 3, or 7 from Av San Martín in centre and get off as bus crosses the railway line. Excellent range of goods but very expensive (eg poncho de Güemes for US$100 for the heaviest weight, down to US$30). Woodcarvings of birds etc from Tres Cerritas, Santiago del Estero 202. Tiwanaku, Caseros 424, good selection of local crafts. Centro de Comercialización de Artesanías, Catamarca 84, cheaper handicrafts than in tourist shops. For objets d'art and costume jewellery made of onyx, visit Onix Salta, Chile 1663. Feria del

Libro, Buenos Aires 83; *Librería Rayuela*, Buenos Aires 96, foreign-language books and magazines. Arts and handicrafts are often cheaper in surrounding villages.

Bicycles Shop at Pellegrini 824, Manresa, with imported equipment; helpful mechanic, S Fernández, Urquiza 1051.

Bathing Balneario Municipal, Virgilio Tedin 997, T 231140, on outskirts, reached by bus No 13 from Calle Ituzaingó, entry US$1. Bus fare US$0.50.

Travel Agencies *Saltur*, Caseros 525, T 212012, very efficient and rec for local tours, for instance to Cachi (no English-speaking guides). *Puna Expediciones*, Braquiquitos 399, T 212-797 (well qualified and experienced guide Luis H Aguilar can also be contacted through the *Residencial San Jorge*), organizes treks in remote areas, US$25 a day incl transport to trekking region, food, porters, highly rec. *Hernán Uriburu*, organizes trekking expeditions, Rivadavia 409, T 310603, expensive but highly professional. *Juan Kühl and Elke Schmitt*, Córdoba 202, at Urquiza, tours by light aeroplane, horseback, caravan, boat, German and English spoken, highly rec, also run photographic company. All agencies charge similar prices for tours: Salta city US$15; Quebrada del Toro US$18; Cachi US$45; Humahuaca US$50; San Antonio de las Cobres US$75; two-day tour to Cafayate, Angastaco, Molinos, Cachi, US$80. Out of season, tours often run only if there is sufficient demand; check carefully that tour will run on the day you want. Horse riding, even for the inexperienced, Sibylle and Hansruedi (Swiss), T (087) 921080, see **Excursions** below.

Tourist Office Provincial Tourist Office (Emsatur), Buenos Aires 93 (one block from main square). Open every day, except Sun, till 2100. Very helpful, gives free maps, also a self-guiding tour, Circuito Peatonal, to see important landmarks on foot. David speaks English. Municipal Tourist office, Buenos Aires 61, closed Sun, Jul, helpful, free maps. Both offices arrange accommodation in private houses in high season (Jul) and can arrange horse-riding, US$50 full day, US$30 half day incl horses, guide and meals, rec. Office at bus terminal, friendly, no maps.

Car Hire Avis, Alvarado 537, T 216344, rec; Rent A Car, Caseros 489 and 221; local companies reported to be cheaper: **ALE**, Caseros 753, T 223469; **López Fleming**, Gral Güemes 92, T 211381, new cars, cheap, friendly; **Ruiz Moreno**, Caseros 225, in *Hotel Salta*, good cars, helpful; **Renta Autos**, Caseros 400, also good. It may be cheaper and more convenient to hire a taxi for a fixed fee.

Airport AR to Santa Cruz (Bolivia) Mon 1520, and also LAB, US$203 return, dep Wed (which also flies to **Tarija** and **La Paz**), US$182 one-way, change at Santa Cruz). Ladeco flies daily **Santiago (Chile)-Antofagasta-Iquique-Salta**. AR, Austral and Lapa fly to **Bs As** (2 hrs, minimum) and **Córdoba**. Austral to **Bs As**, **Córdoba** and **Tucumán**. Lapa also fly to **Tucumán** and **Bs As**. Special, regular, bus service between airport and Aerolíneas Argentinas office on Caseros, 1 block from Plaza 9 de Julio, US$3; don't be fooled by taxi touts who tell you there is no bus for 3 hours! Taxi from airport to bus station US$7.

Railways As of Mar 1993, no rail services ran to Salta or N of Tucumán, except the Tren a Las Nubes (see below).

To Chile by rail: Argentine railways maintain a train service (freight only), from Salta to Socompa, where tourist cards are available and, with a lot of patience, you may get a train to Antofagasta (**see p 117** for description of line, tourist train to San Antonio de los Cobres, and goods train, and also for road taking similar route.) The surest direct routes Salta-Antofagasta are by air or bus.

Bus Services Bus terminal is 8 blocks E of the main plaza (T 214716 for information). There is a 24 hr Shell station behind bus terminal serving cheap snacks, friendly. To **Córdoba**, 4 a day, 12 hrs, US$41, with Expreso Panamericano (T 212460), luxury service with hostess, twice daily with Veloz del Norte. To **Bs As**, several daily, US$77, 19 hrs (Atahuallpa, La Estrella, incl snacks, dinner and breakfast in restaurant, comfortable, rec. 4 daily Veloz del Norte, US$84 with La Veloz del Norte, dep 1030. To **Puerto Iguazú**, via Tucumán, US$100. To **Mendoza** via Tucumán, several companies, daily, US$52, 20 hrs; the Andesmar Mon bus continues all the way to Río Gallegos, arriving Thur 1430, the other Andesmar services continue as far as Comodoro Rivadavia. To **Santiago del Estero**, 6 hrs, US$22. To **Tucumán**, 4 hrs, several firms (La Veloz del Norte rec, La Estrella), US$18. To **Embarcación** daily with Atahualpa at 0700, US$14.50. To **Jujuy**, Balut Hnos, or Atahualpa hourly between 0700 and 2300, "directo", US$7, 1¾ hrs along new road, 2¾ hrs along old road; to **La Rioja**, US$33; to **La Quiaca**, 11 hrs (see below). To **Belén**, Wed, US$26.

To **Cafayate**, US$10, 4 hrs, three a day, with El Indio at 0700, 1130 and 1800; to **Santa María**, El Indio, 6½ hrs, 0700. To **Cachi** (5 hrs, US$12), **Angastaco** (dep Thur 1300) and **Molinos** (7 hrs) Marcos Rueda daily (except Tues, Thur) at 1300, unreliable on Sun (sit on left). To **Rosario de la Frontera**, US$5, 2½ hrs, stewardess service, very pleasant trip. To **San**

Antonio de Los Cobres, 5½ hrs, El Quebradeño, Sun 1910, Mon, Tues, Sat 1530, Thur, Fri 1010, US$14. The Thur service runs up to the Tincalayu mining camp (arrives 2140), returning to Salta on Fri 1010, passing San Antonio at 1600. This bus is the only public transport going further into the puna than San Antonio.

To **Paraguay**: there is no direct bus from Salta to Asunción, but Salta provides the most reliable cheap land connection between Bolivia and Paraguay. Buses daily 1700, US$49 with La Veloz del Norte (20% reduction for students), Saenz Peña or Panamericano, 13 hrs to **Resistencia**, for crossing into Paraguay (take warm clothing for over-efficient a/c); for description of road, **see p 147**. Salta-**Formosa** with Atahualpa, which provides the quickest route to Asunción (change at Orán), operates only twice weekly because of the state of the road—Wed and Sun at 0630, 12 hrs, US$40. To **Chile**: Services to Calama, San Pedro de Atacama (both US$45), and Antofagasta are run by Géminis (behind bus terminal), Sat 1600 all year round, US$50, 20 hrs to Antofagasta, 14 hrs to Calama. Bus can be caught in San Antonio de los Cobres, book ahead and pay full fare. Atahualpa and Tramaca also have services to Calama (US$50), the latter offers meals and even a couple of rounds of Bingo! Book well in advance, may be difficult to get a reservation, so try at 1000 on day of departure for a cancellation. (Book tickets at Boletería Basio in terminal, T 313887.) Take warm clothes (at night ice sometimes forms on the insides of bus windows), a sheet to protect luggage against dust and food (NB Chilean customs will not allow fruit in). This route is usually closed for at least part of the winter and is liable to closure at other periods of the year.

Routes to Bolivia To La Quiaca, on Bolivian frontier, about 10 buses daily, Atahualpa (US$27), 11 hrs (via Jujuy, prolonged stop), can be very cold, dusty, not rec; best change to Panamericano in Jujuy. Buses also NE to Orán, 6 hrs, for connection with Tarija, Bolivia, which can involve taking overnight bus (Atahualpa, 7-10 hrs) to Aguas Blancas at 2200 (road now paved), arriving before dawn—cold—then crossing river in motor boats to Bermejo, Bolivia and the next bus out is often full. Spectacular 8 hr mountain ride alternative to the latter in open-air pick-up: hair-raising! Also to Yacuiba, via **Pocitos** (Bolivian frontier), for Santa Cruz, Bolivia. US$17 with Atahualpa to Pocitos, 7-10 hrs, very full, with passengers standing, can be uncomfortable, but road now paved. Customs at Pocitos not to be trusted—beware of theft; and overcharging for "excess baggage" (on bus), for which there is no official limit written up anywhere. (Hotel at Pocitos, **E** *Buen Gusto*, just tolerable.) Two trains Yacuiba-Santa Cruz per week. **See also p 126** on the route via Orán.

Excursions For routes to San Antonio de las Cobres incl the Tren a las Nubes, see below, **p 118**. Cabra Corral, one of the largest artificial lakes in Argentina, 81 km S of Salta via Coronel Moldes; water skiing, fishing, no hotels, just a camping site, restaurant and sailing club; the **B** *Hostería Cabra Corral*, T 231965, is 4 km from the lake, Route 68, half board, swimming pool, "delightful", rec. Paved road ends at the Presa General M Belgrano, impressive views of the bridge across the lake. 11 km NW of Salta is the wealthy neighbourhood of San Lorenzo (new restaurant in high tower, *El Castillo*, owned by John Johnston (US), good food and music, closed Mon, T 921052 for free taxi, 4-6 people); **A2** *Hostal Selva Montaña*, Calle Alfonsina Storní 2315, T 087 921184, luxurious, highly rec; camping and picnicking beside rocky stream and natural woodland. Sibylle Oeschger and Hansruedi Hintermann rent one rm (E pp) and offer horseriding tours, US$44 pp ½ day, incl dinner, or US$28 with coffee and biscuits, T 921080, they live at Villa San Lorenzo, 14 km from Salta (bus from terminal platform 15, hourly, ½ hr, US$1, get off 2 stops before the Quebrada). There is a frequent bus service to San Lorenzo, US$0.90 (about ½ hr). Bus stops in front of *Quebrada* restaurant (good food, friendly, quite expensive). Last bus back about 2330. To Jujuy and Humahuaca, day trip through many agencies, incl lunch. Ask the driver to return by the old Ruta 9, also called Camino de la Cornisa, a beautiful road, through jungle vegetation (huge trees and unexpected plants), a wonderful contrast to the desert all around. To Cuesta del Obispo and the Forgotten Valley, on return, with Saltur day trip, superb. To Cafayate (see below). The Finca El Rey National Park (**see p 109**) is about 200 km E of Salta, at junction of Chaco and pre-Andean regions.

At El Bordo, 45 km E of Salta, Sr de Arias offers luxury accommodation on his finca, L3 pp full board; excursions also arranged. Contact: *Finca El Bordo De Las Lanzas*, 4432 El Bordo, Salta, T 911788/310525.

A magnificent round trip of about 520 km can be taken going SW from Salta to Cafayate (well paved), then N through the Valles Calchaquíes and Cachi, and back E to Salta. (Most travel agencies in Salta offer the round trip, no student discounts, 12 hrs, includes a visit to a *bodega*.) The first part of this trip, S from Salta, goes through El Carril (30 km) where a road from Cachi intersects; continuing S for 25 km Coronel Moldes is reached. Here, a side road to the left goes to Embalse Cabra

Corral (see above). South of Coronel Moldes, Route 68 goes through the gorge of the Río de las Conchas (known as the **Quebrada de Cafayate**) with fascinating rock formations of differing colours, all signposted: Anfiteatro (a gorge), El Sapo, El Fraile, El Obelisco, Los Castillos. The road goes through wild and semi-arid landscapes with many wild birds, including ñandúes (rheas). The best place for lunch is at the *Hostería Talapampa* in Talapampa, approx 85 km S of Salta.

Cafayate (altitude 1,660m, population 8,432) is a clean, increasingly popular, little town, with low rainfall (none Mar-Oct), lying between two ranges of Andean foothills and surrounded by vineyards. A walk to La Cruz (3 hrs) takes you to a view of the Aconquija chain in the S to Nevado de Cachi in the N. Cafayate is much frequented by Argentine tourists and accommodation is hard to find at holiday periods (especially for a single person).

Cafayate is an important centre of wine production and home of several renowned *bodegas*. La Rosa owned by Michel Torino can be visited, Mon-Fri, 0800-1230, 1500-1830, weekends am only, no need to book, 30 min tours and tasting, reached by turning right 500m past the ACA *hostería*; Etchart, 2 kms on Ruta 40 to Tucumán, also has tours (T 21310/2), Mon-Fri 0800-1200, 1530-1830, weekends 0800-1200. La Banda, the oldest *bodega* in the valley (next to ACA *hostería*), is interesting because it is more primitive. The Museo de la Vid y el Vino in an old *bodega* is on Av Güemes, 2 blocks S of the plaza, US$0.50, very well laid out. Locally woven tapestries are interesting, and very expensive; visit the Calchaquí tapestry exhibition of Miguel Nanni on the main square. Also Platería of Jorge Barraco, Colón 147, for silver craft work. Oil paintings, woodcarving, metalwork and ceramics by Calixto Mamani can be seen in his art gallery at Rivadavia 452, or contact him at home at Rivadavia 254. Handicrafts in wood and silver by Oscar Hipaucha on main plaza. Pancho Silva and his family have a workshop at 25 de Mayo selling and displaying their own and locals' handicrafts. Souvenir prices are generally high. Local pottery in the Mercado Municipal de Artesanía on the main plaza.

Hotels B *Briones*, on main square, T 21270, clean and comfortable, with bath and hot water, accepts Amex card; **B** *Asembal*, Güemes y Almagro, T 21065, nice rooms with bath, good; **B** *Asturias*, Güemes 158, T 21328, rec; **C** *Hostería Cafayate* (ACA), T (0868) 21296, on N outskirts, modern, quiet (but cold), colonial-style, covered parking, unfriendly, good food, but restaurant may be closed; **C** *Gran Real*, Güemes 128, T 21016, pleasant, clean, rec; **D** *Colonial*, Almagro 134, charming patio; **D** *Confort*, Güemes 200 block, with bath, clean, comfortable. **D** *La Posta del Rey*, Güemes 415, T 21120, clean; **D** *Güemes*, Salta 13, one block off main plaza; **D** *Pensión Arroyo* (no sign), Niño 160, highly rec, friendly, clean; **D** *Hotel Tinkunaku*, Diego de Almagro 12, 1 block from plaza, with bath, clean, friendly; **D** *Vicano*, Toscana 273, clean, rec; *Residencial Familia Herrero*, cheap, clean. Accommodation in private houses is available. Municipal **campsite** Lorohuasi at S access to town, hot water, swimming pool, well maintained, bungalows for rent, D for 4 people; private campsite to N of town, opposite ACA *hostería*. Municipal campsite also at Animaña, 15 km N on Route 40.

Restaurants On the main plaza are *Cafayate*, simple, good regional dishes and nice atmosphere; *Confitería La Barra*, rec. *La Carreta de Don Olegario*, spotless but rather expensive; *El Gordo*, San Martín y Güemes, main plaza, excellent regional dishes, good local wines, friendly, reasonable prices, highly rec; *El Criollo*, Güemes 254, clean, pricey, rec; *La López Pereyra*, Güemes 375, good food, friendly. Several *comedores*, incl *Comedor Juli*, along Rivadavia (2 blocks N of Plaza), where the locals eat. Only the more expensive restaurants are open late. Try excellent *pan casero* (local bread).

Exchange 2 banks, incl Banco de la Nación, main plaza, for cash, TCs and credit cards.

Tourist Office Kiosk on the main plaza. Bike hire from Rentavel, Güemes 175. Horses can be hired from La Florida, Bodega Etchart Privado (2 km from Cafayate on road to Tucumán).

Bus Aconquija bus to **Tucumán** daily at 0630, 8 hours, US$17, also Sat 1500. Alternatively go to Santa María with 1100 El Indio bus, or 0630 Aconquija bus (2 hrs) over good dirt road, US$10, and then take bus to Tucumán. El Indio bus to and from **Salta** via the Quebrada de Cafayate, dep 0700, 1130 and 1800, 4 hrs, US$12.60 (worth travelling in daylight through beautiful views of yellow and red rock formations). To **Angastaco** (El Indio) 1100 daily except Sun, US$4, sit on the right, leaves Angastaco for the return journey at 0630.

One way of seeing the spectacular Quebrada de Cafayate (see above) is by taking the El Indio bus for Salta as far as Los Loros, Km 32. From here you can walk back (and catch a returning bus from Salta); alternatively hire a bike in Cafayate and take it on the early morning El Indio bus as far as Alemania (84 km) and then cycle back. **NB** The sun is very hot, take lots of water.

Continuing S from Cafayate, Route 40 goes to Santa María (**see p 108**), and SE to Tafí del Valle and Tucumán.

N of Cafayate Route 40 runs 160 km through the Valles Calchaquíes to Cachi. The road is mainly gravel and can be very difficult after rain, but the views, of the Andean-foothill desert country with its strange rock formations and unexpected colours, are fascinating. The population is largely Indian. Salta and the Valles Calchaquíes are the centre for US archaeologist John Hyslop's study of Inca roads in the Andes.

About 24 km N of Cafayate is **San Carlos** (altitude 1,710m), a small settlement destroyed four times by Indians. It has a pleasant white church completed 1854, a small archaeological museum, as well as a municipal campsite. **D** *Hostería*, T 218937. Artisans' shops and workshops, craft market near church: reasonable prices, limited variety.

Bus The El Indio bus on the Salta-Cafayate-Angastaco run arrives in San Carlos by noon and on the return journey at 0745.

N of San Carlos Ruta 40 enters the Calchaquí valley and climbs to **Angastaco**, 50 km from San Carlos, 2 km off the main road. The road passes through the spectacular **Quebrada de las Flechas**, remarkable for its formations and colours, 5-10 km S of Angastaco. This small town, expanding rapidly, is surrounded again by vineyards. You can sample the local Vino Patero, red or sweet white, in a house close to the river bridge; apparently *bodegas* can be visited, *vino patero* is supposed to be made by treading the grapes in the traditional manner. The Fiesta Patronal Virgen del Valle is held on the second weekend of Dec, with processions, folk music, dancing, many gauchos and rodeos.

Lodging and Transport D *Hostería*, T 222826, negotiable in low season, good, cheap and delicious meals on request, pool (empty), has its own small but informative archaeological museum. **F** pp *Residencial El Cardón*, good, clean, comfortable. Cheap restaurant (no sign) near the *hostería*. Buses: to Cachi and Salta, Fri, 1100 only; daily bus to San Carlos and Cafayate 0545 (Sat and holidays 0630). Taxi to Molinos US$15.

From the Angastaco turn-off it is 40 km on a winding road through beautiful and desolate rock formations to **Molinos**. The church, with its fine twin-domed bell-towers, built about 1720 and now covered in a yellowish paste to preserve it, contains the mummified body of the last Royalist governor of Salta, Don Nicolás Isasmendi Echalar. To protect it from visitors plucking its hair, this relic can no longer be viewed by the public. The priest is very knowledgeable about local history. A pleasant walk is down from the church, crossing a creek and then climbing a gentle hill, from which there are good views of Molinos and surrounding country.

Lodging and Transport A3 *Hostería Molinos*, T 214871, rec, new owner reported as unreliable with reservations, with breakfast, good meals, in Casa de Isasmendi, which also contains a small museum. Sra de Guaymas (known as "Sra Silvia") runs a restaurant and rents rooms, **E**, double only, basic, clean; there are other rooms to rent around the main square. Bus to Salta via Cachi, Thur, Fri, Sat, Mon at 0645, also Mon, Wed, Thur, Sat at 1315 with Marcos Rueda; 2 hrs to Cachi, US$4.50, 7 hrs to Salta. To Angastaco, Thur morning.

From Molinos it is 46 km to **Cachi** (Quechua for "salt"), a beautiful little town renowned for its weaving and other crafts; the natives claim people die only of old age, because the climate is very invigorating; altitude 2,280m. The church's floor, roof and confessional are made from the wood of the *cardón* cactus. The Museo Arqueológico (open Mon-Sat, 0800-1800, Sun, holidays 0900-1200) presents a small but interesting survey of pre-colonial Calchaquí culture, US$1.

Lodging and Transport B *ACA Hostería Cachi*, T 210001, on hill above the town, good, clean, pleasant; **E** *Albergue Municipal*, also has good municipal campsite with swimming pool and barbecue pits, on hill at S end of town. Restaurant in bus station is good, but avoid eating when buses arrive. **Buses** to Salta, 1400 daily (except Wed), also at 0900 Thur, Fri, Sat, Mon, 5 hrs, US$12; to Molinos 1200 daily; El Indio from Cafayate Thur am only, returning Thur pm.

At Cachi Adentro, 6 km W of Cachi, is the **C** *Hostal Samay Huasi*, a restored *hacienda*, pleasant and helpful owners, heating and hot water at all times; **A1** *Finca El Molino de Cachi Adentro*, a restored working mill, beautiful views, horse riding, rec, min stay 3 days, book in advance, T 8039339, F 4762065 (Bs As), T 213968, F 233122 (Salta); 3 buses a day from Cachi. Hire horses in the village, US$5 per hour. Fishing is also possible.

A trip to the Indian ruins at **Las Pailas**, 18 km W of Cachi, provides a fine 4 hrs walk (one way) in splendid surroundings. Take the 0730 or 1230 bus from Cachi to the school at Las Pailas, walking from there on a track towards the mountains. After 30 mins cross the river and ask at the house there for a guide to take you to the ruins. The ruins themselves are barely excavated and not especially impressive but the view is breathtaking, with huge cacti set against snow-topped Andean peaks. The walk back to Cachi is downhill; return bus to Cachi at 1900.

From Cachi, you follow Route 40 for 11 km N to Payogasta (new *Hostería*, clean), then turn right to Route 33. This road (gravel) climbs continuously up the Cuesta del Obispo passing a dead-straight stretch of 14 km known as La Recta del Tin-Tin with magnificent views of the **Los Cardones National Park** with the huge candelabra cacti, which grow up to 6m in height. (Elsewhere there are not many cacti left as they are used to make furniture.) It reaches the summit at Piedra de Molino (3,347m) after 43 km. Then it plunges down through the Quebrada de Escoipe. The road rejoins Route 68 at El Carril, from where it is 37 km. back to Salta.

N of Cachi Route 40 continues to **La Poma**, 54 km (altitude 3,015m) a beautiful hamlet (*hostería*, F, try bargaining). Marcos Rueda bus service from Salta, Tues, Thur and Sat, 1300 (via Cachi 1750), arrives La Poma 1945, departing next day 0645 and 1315. From La Poma the road runs N over the Paso Abra de Acay (4,900m—the highest pass in South America negotiable by car, often closed in summer by landslides) to San Antonio de los Cobres (see below). This road is in very poor condition (no buses). Don't go further than La Poma without finding out about road conditions. If you inform the Gendarmería Nacional, they will search for you if you don't arrive.

There is a 900 km long metre-gauge railway from Salta through the little town of **San Antonio de los Cobres** to Antofagasta, in N Chile (through trains only as far as Socompa, on the Chilean frontier). The Argentine section was engineered by Richard Maury, of Pennsylvania, who is commemorated by the station at Km 78 which bears his name. This remarkable project was built in stages between 1921 and 1948, by which time developments in road and air transport had already reduced its importance. No racks were used in its construction. The line includes 21 tunnels, 13 viaducts, 31 bridges, 2 loops and 2 zig-zags. From Salta the line climbs gently to Campo Quijano (Km 40, 1520m), where it enters the Quebrada del Toro, an impressive rock-strewn gorge. At El Alisal (Km 50) and Chorrillos (Km 66) there are zig-zags as the line climbs the side of the gorge before turning N into the valley of the Río Rosario near Puerto Tastil (Km 101, 2,675m), missing the archaeological areas around Santa Rosa de Tastil. At Km 122 and Km 129 the line goes into 360 degree loops before reaching Diego de Almagro (3,304m). At Abra Muñano (3,952m) the road to San Antonio can be seen zig-zagging its way up the end-wall of the Quebrada del Toro below. From Muñano (3,936m) the line drops slightly to San Antonio, Km 196.

San Antonio is a squat, ugly mining town on a bleak, high desert at 3,750m, pop: 2,200, only of interest if you want to visit the copper, zinc, lead and silver mines, truck from La Concordia company office, about 20 km. From the mine you can walk to La Polvorilla viaduct, 20 mins, vicuñas and condors en route. **A3** *Hostería de las Nubes*, edge of town on Salta road (T 087-909058, or Bs As 326-0126), modern, incl breakfast, spacious, rec; **F** *Hospedaje Belgrano*, painted blue, no heat, basic, expensive restaurant; **D** pp *Hospedaje Los Andes*, breakfast extra, very basic, but very friendly, both on main street. Accommodation may also be available in the school.

The spectacular viaduct at La Polvorilla is 21 km further at 4,190m, just beyond the branch line to the mines at La Concordia. The highest point on the line is reached at Abra Chorrillos (4,475m, Km 231). From here the line runs on another 335 km across a rocky barren plateau 3,500-4,300m above sea level before reaching Socompa (3,865m). The inhabitants of this area are Coya Indians who bear a far closer resemblance to their cousins in Bolivia then to the Salteño lowlanders. **NB** On all journeys on this line beware of *soroche* (altitude sickness): do not eat or drink to excess.

The *Tren a las Nubes* (Train to the Clouds) runs between Salta and La Polvorilla viaduct. The service operates every other Sat from Apr to Oct, weather permitting, and on additional days in the high season (Jul/Aug), depart 0700, return to Salta 2215, US$95, no discounts, credit cards not accepted (without meals, first class only, US$250 from Buenos Aires). The train is well-equipped with oxygen facilities and medical staff as well as a restaurant car and snack bar and explanations are available in English, Spanish, French and Italian. This service is operated privately and cannot be booked through Ferrocarriles Argentinos. Book in advance (especially in high season) through Movitren, Caseros 441, Salta, T 216394, F 311264, Operatur, Av Corrientes 534, 10th floor, Bs As, T 394-5399/4199/4668, or through any good travel agency. It can be very difficult get on the train from Salta as it is often booked up from Buenos Aires.

Freight trains still run on this line: a goods train to San Antonio with one passenger coach leaves Salta Wed only at 1015, 12 hrs, US$6.50, good cheap food available; return journey from San Antonio 1800. In practice this usually leaves several hours late so you see little on the journey. A goods train to Pocitos, beyond San Antonio, leaves Salta on Mon. On Wed a goods train with two passenger coaches leaves for Socompa at 1030, arriving at San Antonio 1530 and Socompa 1230 Thur, returning Fri 1600. Buy ticket 1 hr before departure, US$18.40 single, first class carriage has dining car (and heating if you're lucky) and is the same price. Long delays are common on this route and you may do the entire journey in the dark. Make friends with the guards by offering cigarettes and you may be able to sleep in their warm wagon.

Goods trains run from Socompa to Augusta Victoria and Baquedano (Chile) on Mon and Tues: officially the Chilean railway authorities do not permit passengers to travel on this line, but some travellers have managed to do so. There is also irregular service Socompa-Antofagasta. Chilean trains do not connect with trains from Salta and you may have to wait several days for a lift in a truck. There is no food or accommodation, but you may be able to sleep on the floor in the Chilean customs building.

Timetables for these services are meaningless—the line is single-track and goods trains are delayed for loading and unloading. Reliable information about departures from Salta can only be obtained from the Oficina de Trenes at the station (T 212641) and they will often not know until 2 hrs before departure. To secure seats get on the train while it is loading in the goods depot, about 400m down the line. Take plenty of food, water, camera film and warm clothing.

San Antonio can also be reached by Route 51 from Salta. This road is being upgraded as part of a new Brazil-Argentina-Chile route. From Campo Quijano it runs along the floor of the Quebrada del Toro (fords) before climbing the Abra Muñano in a long series of steep zig-zags. Buses to Salta, El Quebradeño, daily except Thur and Sat, 5½ hrs, US$14.

On a day trip from Salta by minibus, stop at Santa Rosa de *Tastil* to see Indian ruins and a small museum (US$0.50), rec. Alternatively, take the Empresa Quebradeño bus, Thur 1010 only, arriving 1600 at Tastil, which leaves you 4 hours at ruins (plenty of time) before catching the bus (1955) on its way back from San Antonio de los Cobres. A third alternative is to share a taxi. Basic accommodation next door to the museum, no electricity or heating, take food, water and candles. Try the *quesillo de cabra* (goat's cheese) from Estancia Las Cuevas. If hiking, take your own water, there is none in the mountains.

The road from San Antonio de los Cobres over the pass of Huaytiquina (4,200m) to San Pedro de Atacama is no longer in use. At its highest, this road is 4,560m, but it has been replaced by the less steep Sico Pass, which runs parallel to Huaytiquina. Fork left just before Catúa, cross the border at *Sico* (4,079m) and continue via Mina Laco and Socaire to Toconao (road very bad between these two points) where the road joins the Huaytiquina route. It is a very beautiful trip: you cross salt lakes with flamingoes and impressive desert. The road on the Argentine side is very good (although the section between Santa Rosa de Tastil and *Restaurancito Alfarcito* is very steep, not suitable for long vehicles). Gasoline is available in San Pedro and Calama. Because of snowfalls, this route may be closed 2-3 times a year, for 2 or 3 days each time. A car must be in very good condition to cope with the heights. Ask the *gendarmes* in San Antonio de los Cobres about road conditions, and complete exit formalities there; entry formalities must also be carried out at San Antonio (no facilities at border). **NB** Hitchhiking across the Andes from here is not recommended.

The direct road **from Salta to Jujuy**, Route 9 via La Caldera and El Carmen, is picturesque with its winding 92-km subtropical stretch, now paved, known as *la cornisa* (lush vegetation). Be careful as the road is very narrow and often wet. The longer road, via Güemes, is the better road for hitchhiking.

Jujuy (pronounced Hoo-hooey), formally San Salvador de Jujuy and often referred to by locals as San Salvador, is the capital of Jujuy province and stands at 1,260m, completely surrounded by wooded mountains. The city was founded first in 1561 and then in 1575, when it was destroyed by the Indians, and finally established in 1593. Population 230,000. In the eastern part of the city is the Plaza Belgrano, a fine square lined with orange trees. On the S side of the plaza stands the Casa de Gobierno, an elaborate French baroque-style palace (open Mon-Fri, 0800-1200, 1600-2000, but not always). On the W side is a colonial Cathedral with very fine 18th century images, pulpits, walls and paintings finished about 1746. It has been heavily restored, but in the nave is a superb wooden pulpit, carved by Indians and gilded, a colonial treasure without equal in Argentina. On Calle Lavalle you can see the doorway through which General Lavalle, the enemy of Rosas, was killed by a bullet in 1848, but the door is a copy; the original was taken to Buenos Aires. The Teatro Mitre (worth a visit) is at Alvear y Lamadrid. In the western part of the city are the Parque San Martín and an open space, La Tablada, where horses, mules and donkeys used to be assembled in caravans to be driven to the mines in Bolivia and Peru. See the Palacio de Tribunales near the river, one of the best modern buildings in Argentina. Streets are lined with bitter-orange trees. The scenery is varied and splendid, although the city itself has become a little shabby.

History The province of Jujuy bore the brunt of fighting during the Wars of Independence: between 1810 and 1822 the Spanish launched 11 invasions down the Quebrada de Humahuaca from Bolivia. In Aug 1812 Gen Belgrano, commanding the republican troops, ordered the city to be evacuated and destroyed before the advancing Spanish army. This event is marked on 23-24 Aug by festivities known as El Exodo Jujeño with gaucho processions and military parades. As a tribute to the city for obeying his orders, Belgrano donated a flag which is displayed in the Sala de la Bandera in the Casa de Gobierno.

Museums Museo Histórico Provincial, Lavalle 250, open daily 0830-1230, 1500-2000; **Museo de Paleontología y Mineralogía**, part of the University of Jujuy, Av Bolivia 2335, open Mon-Fri 0800-1300. **Museo de Bellas Artes**, Güemes 956, open Mon-Fri, 0800-1200, 1700-1900. **Police Museum**, in the Cabildo, open Mon-Fri 1000-1300, 1500-2100, Sat 1030-1230, 1830-2100, Sun 1830-2100; **Museo de la Iglesia San Francisco**, Belgrano y Lavalle, incl 17th century paintings from Cuzco and Chuquisaca. The **Estación Biológica de Fauna Silvestre**, Av Bolivia 2335, is open to the public on Sun (for private tours on other days, contact Dr Arturo A Canedi, T 25617-25845), very interesting.

Public Holidays 6 and 23-24 Aug (hotels fully booked). Festival on 6 Nov.

Hotels *Panorama*, Belgrano 1295, T 30183, 4-star, highly-regarded; **A2** *Augustus*, Belgrano 715, T 22668, 3 star, modern, comfortable but noisy. **A2** *Internacional*, Belgrano 501 (main square), T 22004; **A3** *Fenicia*, on riverside at 19 de Abril 427, T 28102, quiet. **B** *Avenida*, 19 de Abril 469, T 22678, on riverside, with good restaurant (C off season, cafeteria only); **B** *Hostería Posta de Lozano*, Route 9, Km 18, friendly, clean, good restaurant, pools with fresh mountain water, covered parking; **B** *Motel Huaico*, Route 9, just N of town, T 22274, good; **B** *Sumay*, Otero 232, T 22554, central, clean. **B** *Alto* **C** *La Viña*, Route 56, Km 5, T 26588, attractive, swimming pool, bus US$0.35 from town. **C** *Residencial Los Andes*, Siria 456, T 24315, clean, hot water, a bit prison-like. Across the street is **C** *Residencial San Carlos*, Siria 459, T 22286, modern, friendly, some rm a/c, others poorly ventilated, locked parking; **D** *Belgrano*, Belgrano 627, T 26459, old fashioned, hospitable, clean, walls thin so can be noisy, mixed reports but mostly rec; **D** *Chung King*, Alvear 627, T 28142, friendly, dark, very noisy, many mosquitoes, good restaurant. Near the bus terminal only **D** *San Antonio*, Lisandro de la Torre (opposite), modern, clean, quiet, highly rec. Several cheaper places near railway station: **E** *El Aguila*, Alvear 400, opp station, basic; **E** pp *Residencial Norte*, Alvear 446, without bath, basic, unfriendly; **E** *Residencial Río de Janeiro*, Av José de la Iglesia 1536, very basic, clean, close to bus station, bit run down.

Camping *Autocamping Municipal*, US$2.40 per tent, ask for a cheaper rate for one person. 14 km N of Jujuy on Humahuaca road, also *Autocamping*, 3 km N outside city at Huaico Chico, US$4 per tent, motel opposite. Buses 4 or 9 frequent. Hot showers (if you remind the staff), clothes washing facilities, very friendly.

Restaurants *El Cortijo*, Lavalle y San Martín, interesting salads, good vegetarian food, reasonably priced; *Restaurant Sociedad Española*, Belgrano y Pérez, elegant setting; *Bar La Royal* on Belgrano (near Lavalle), good but expensive; *Bar-Restaurant Sociedad Obrera*, Balcarce 357, for cheap food, but not attractive. *Chungking*, Alvear 627; *Restaurant Sirio Libanesa*, Lamadrid 568 (don't be put off by the uninviting entrance). *La Victoria*, Av El Exodo

642, away from centre, good; *Confitería Carena*, Belgrano 899, old-fashioned, good for breakfast; *La Ventana*, Belgrano 751, good cheap menu, good service, à-la-carte menu is expensive. *La Rueda*, Lavalle 320, good food and service, very popular, expensive; *Krysys*, Balcarce 272, excellent atmosphere but now expensive; *La Pizzería*, Alvear 921, warm welcome, pleasant atmosphere; *Ruta 9*, Costa Rica 968, Barrio Mariano Moreno (take taxi), good local food, Bolivian owners. Cheaper places behind bus terminus on Santiago del Estero and Alem. Very good ice cream at *Helados Xanthi*, Belgrano 515, made by Greek owner. *Opus-Café*, Belgrano 856, good coffee, music and atmosphere. Good bread and cake shop at Belgrano 619. Good sandwiches at *Rada Tilly*, 2 locations on Belgrano (one next to *Hotel Avenida*).

Banks and Exchange At banks; **Banco de la Provincia de Jujuy**, Lavalle, gives cash against Mastercard, no commission, also changes dollars; **Banco de Galicia**, US$10 commission on Amex TCs; **Horus**, Belgrano 722, good rates for cash, no cheques; **Dinar**, Belgrano 731, 4% commission on TCs. Travel agencies on Calle Belgrano also change cash and dollar TCs. Thomas Cook cheques cannot be changed. If desperate, ask the dueña of the *confitería* at bus station, rates not too unreasonable. (See note on provincial bonds used as currency, **p 222**).

Consulates Bolivia, Patricinio Argentino 641, T 23156, price of visa should be US$5, pay no more; **Spain**, R de Velasco 362, T 28193; **Italy**, Av Fascio 660, T 23199; **Paraguay**, Tacuarí 430, T 28178.

Laundry *Laverap*, Belgrano y Ramírez de Velazco.

Post Office at Independencia y Lamadrid, in Galería Impulso, Belgrano 775, and at bus terminal. **Telecom**, Senador Pérez 18 and Alvear, open 0700-0100.

Shopping Handicrafts are available at reasonable prices from vendors on Plaza Belgrano near the cathedral; *Regionales Lavalle*, Lavalle 268; *Centro de Arte y Artesanías*, Balcarce 427. *Librería Rayuela*, Belgrano 636; *Librería Belgrano*, Belgrano 602, English magazines and some books. *Farmacia Avenida*, Lavalle y Av 19 de Abril, 0800-2400.

Travel Agencies Many along Belgrano: *Alicia Viajes*, No 592, T 22541; *Giménez*, No 775, T 2924; *Turismo Lavalle*, No 340. All offer tours along the Quebrada de Humahuaca, 12 hrs, US$25. *Be Dor Turismo*, No 860 local 8, 10% for ISIC and youth card holders on local excursions.

Tourist Office Belgrano 690, T 28153, very helpful, open till 2000.
    For information on bird watching, contact Mario Daniel Cheronaza, Peatonal 38, No 848-830, Viviendas "El Arenal", Jujuy.

Migración, Belgrano 499.

Airport El Cadillal, 32 km SE, T 91505; Tea Turismo vans leave *Hotel Avenida* to meet arrivals, US$4.50. Service to **Buenos Aires** by Austral, 1 flight a day direct with bus connection to Tartagal (in the NE of the province) via San Pedro and Embarcación. Austral also flies to **Salta**, **Santiago del Estero**, **Tucumán** and **Córdoba**. Bus from airport to Jujuy takes 1 hr, US$4.

Train No passenger services as of Mar 1993.

Buses Terminus at Iguazú y Dorrego, 6 blocks S of centre. Young boys charge US$1 for loading luggage. To/from **Buenos Aires**, US$89, several daily with Balut Hnos (T Bs As 313-3175) and La Internacional. Via Tucumán to Córdoba, with Panamericano T 27281/27143 and La Veloz, daily, **Tucumán** 5 hrs, US$25, and **Córdoba**, 14 hrs US$45; to **Puerto Iguazú**, 2 a week, US$80, 30 hrs. To **Salta** hourly from 0700, 2¾ hours, US$11. To **La Quiaca**, 6½ hrs (many passport checks), Panamericano (best) and Atahuallpa, US$21.50. Road paved only as far as Humahuaca, reasonably comfortable, but very cold. To **Orán** daily at 1700; to **Humahuaca**, US$7, 3 hrs, sit on left side. To **Embarcación**, US$7 with Agencia Balut, via San Pedro and Libertador San Martín. Jujuy-**Purmamarca-Susques**, leaves Purmamarca at 1330 on Wed and Sat, returning Thur and Sun, crossing the Abra Potrerillos (4,164m) and the Salinas Grandes of Jujuy. To Tilcara 1½ hrs, US$4.
    To Chile: in 1991, the Jama pass was opened for traffic between Jujuy and Antofagasta, and is suitable for all traffic. Bus to **Calama**, via San Pedro de Atacama (15 hrs), Fri 1700, with Tramaca, US$39 incl cold dinner, breakfast, and bingo entertainment; to **Iquique** on Wed and Sat, Panamericano, US$25. Check weather conditions in advance.

Drivers should stock up with fuel here if taking the Purmamarca route to San Antonio de los Cobres.

19 km W of Jujuy is *Termas de Reyes*, where there are hot springs. This resort, with the *Gran Hotel Termas de Reyes* (B with breakfast, A3 half-board, A2 full board, refurbished, restaurant, friendly, T 0882-35500), is set among magnificent mountains 1 hr by bus from Jujuy

bus terminal or Av 19 de Abril, 6 times a day between 0630 and 1945, returning 0700-2040, US$1. US$3 to swim in the thermal pool at the hotel; municipal baths US$1, open daily 0800-1200 and 1400-1700 (Thur 1400-1700 only). It is possible to camp below the hotel free of charge. Cabins for rent beside river, F pp, shower and thermal bath.

North from Jujuy   Lovers of old churches will find Salta and Jujuy excellent centres. Franciscan and Dominican friars arrived in the area from Bolivia as early as 1550. The Jesuits followed about 1585. Along both the old Camino de los Incas (now non-existent) and the new route through the Quebrada de Iturbe the padres, in the course of two centuries, built simple but beautiful churches, of which about 20 survive. They are marked by crosses on the map on **p 103**. All of them can be visited by car from Salta or Jujuy, though some of the roads are very rough. A spare fuel can and water should be carried because service stations are far apart. (There are ACA stations at Jujuy, Humahuaca and La Quiaca, and YPF stations at Tilcara and Abra Pampa.)

One group, in the Puna de Atacama, on the old Camino de los Incas, can be reached by the road which runs W from Salta through the picturesque Quebrada del Toro to San Antonio de los Cobres (**see p 117**). The road S from San Antonio to Antofagasta de la Sierra (235 km) is pretty severe going. The road N to **Susques** (105 km) is comparatively comfortable, but runs through utter desert. There is poor lodging at Susques and an interesting 16th century chapel. Close to the Bolivian and Chilean frontier is El Toro, lovely ride through *altiplano*, past Laguna Turilari, mining territory, bizarre rock formations. Lodgings may be available in first-aid room, ask nurse, Don Juan Puca. From El Toro on to Coranzulí is very rough.

The second group can be reached from the road N from Jujuy to La Quiaca through the **Quebrada de Humahuaca**, which is itself beautiful, with a variety of rock colours and giant cacti in the higher, drier parts; Route 9, the Pan-American Highway through it has been paved as far as Iturbe. In the rainy season (Jan-Mar) this road is sometimes closed by flooding. After heavy rains ask the highway police before using minor roads.

Beyond Tumbaya, where there is a church originally built in 1796 and rebuilt in 1873, a road runs 5 km to **Purmamarca**, a very popular, picturesque village overlooked by a mountain: 7 colours can be distinguished in the rock strata (arrive before noon when sun is in the E); **E** pp *Ranchito del Rincón*, Sarmiento, new, clean, owners Yolanda and Zulma are friendly and helpful, highly rec; also 2 rm in shop, F pp, friendly, ask at the police station for the address, *comedor* on main square has good, cheap, local food. At the entrance to Purmamarca a right turn leads to a new gravel road, which leads through another *quebrada* over a 4,170-metre pass to the Salinas Grandes salt flats at about 3,500m on the Altiplano (fantastic views especially at sunset). In the winter months, on both sides of the road, three different ancient types of salt mining by hand can be seen. Look out for the spectacular rock formations on the road W from Purmamarca.

About 10 km N of the turn, on the Pan-American Highway, is **Maimará** (**D** *Pensión La Posta*, clean and friendly, the owners' son is a tourist guide and has helpful information, 5 km from Maimará). 3 km S of Maimará is a new folk museum called Posta de Hornillos in a recently restored colonial posting house, of which there used to be a chain from Buenos Aires to the Bolivian border (open, in theory, Wed-Mon 0900-1800, free).

22 km N of Purmamarca is **Tilcara**, where there is a reconstruction of a *pucará*, or Inca fortified village, set in botanical gardens containing only high altitude and Puna plants. Beautiful mountain views, rec. The Museo Arqueológico, attached to the University of Buenos Aires, contains a fine collection of precolumbian ceramics from the Andean regions of present day Argentina, Chile and Peru, open Tues-Sun 0900-1200, 1500-1800, highly rec, US$2, free entry Tues (admission incl botanical gardens and *pucará*, which is about 2 km from the museum). *Fiestas* on weekends in Jan. There are excellent craft stalls and shops around the main square, selling ponchos, sweaters and wooden items (dollars accepted). A rec art shop is near *Hotel El Antigal*.

Lodging and Food   **C** *Hotel de Turismo*, Belgrano 590, swimming pool, usually dry; **D** *El*

Antigal, pleasant, good restaurant, colonial style, stores luggage, rec; **E** *Residencial Edén*, dirty but one of cheapest; **E** *Hostería La Esperanza*, spacious rm, arranges walking tours; **E** *Residencial Frami*, near hospital. Private houses: **E** Peter Edmonds, Padilla 690, breakfast extra, guided tours; **E** Juan Brambati, San Martín s/n, comfortable, hot water, meals, highly rec, also does tours. Also at Radio Pirca, **E** pp, 3 blocks from plaza, use solar energy. Municipal campsite, dirty; *Camping El Jardín*, US$5, clean, hot showers. *Restaurant Pucará*, good value. *Café del Museo*, good coffee.

The churches of Huacalera, **Uquía**, and Humahuaca are on the main road. At **Huacalera** is the **C** *Hotel Monterrey*, friendly but run down. Two km S of Huacalera, a sundial 20m W of the road gives the exact latitude of the Tropic of Capricorn. At Uquía (church built 1691, with *cuzqueño* paintings), the walls of the naves are hung with 17th century paintings of winged angels in military dress: the so-called *ángeles arcabuceros*. Cactus-wood decoration is found in many local churches.

Both in Tilcara and Humahuaca there are displays of pictures of the Passion made entirely of flowers, leaves, grasses and seeds at Easter and a traditional procession on Holy Thursday night joined by thousands. No beef is sold during Holy Week in shops or restaurants. All along the Quebrada de Humahuaca the pre-Lent carnival celebrations are picturesque and colourful.

Humahuaca, altitude 2,940m, 129 km N of Jujuy (by bus 3 hrs, US$7), dates from 1594 but was almost entirely rebuilt in the mid 19th century. Population 4,000. Until the arrival of the railway in 1906, Humahuaca was an important trading centre. Today it is an attraction for coach trips from Salta and Jujuy; few tourists stay for more than a couple of hours, but it is an attractive and peaceful centre from which to explore the Quebrada de Humahuaca. The church, originally built in 1631, was completely rebuilt in 1873-80, it has a bell from 1641. A mechanical figure of San Francisco Solano blesses the town from the neo-colonial town hall at 1200. Overlooking the town is the massive Argentine National Independence Monument, built in 1924 and sited here because the valley was the scene of the heaviest fighting in the country during the Wars of Independence. There is a good Feria Artesanal on Av San Martín (on the far side of the railway line), but avoid the middle of the day when the coach parties arrive. Candelaria, Feb 2, is the town's main festival.

Museums Museo La Casa, Buenos Aires 296, next to the post office, open daily 1000-2000, US$3, guided tours in Spanish only, offers a fascinating insight into social customs in the mid-nineteenth century, rec; **Museo Ramoneda**, Salta y Santa Fe, private collection of contemporary art (hours unknown); **Museo Arqueológico Municipal**, at one side of Independence monument, Mon-Fri 0800-1200, 1400-1700, US$0.25; **Museo Nicasio Fernández Mar**, Buenos Aires, opposite *Hotel de Turismo*, memorial to the sculptor, open daily, free. **Museo Folklórico Regional**, Buenos Aires 435, run by Sixto Vásquez, US$10 incl guide.

Hotels D *Provincial de Turismo*, Buenos Aires 650, T 12, run down, swimming pool dry even in summer, poor service, modern building is sadly out of keeping with surroundings; **D** *Residencial Humahuaca*, Córdoba y Corrientes, one block N of bus station, some a/c, traditional, clean, friendly, rec. **D** *Residencial Colonial*, Entre Ríos 110, near bus terminus, T 21007, with bath, some windowless rooms, clean, laundry facilities. Youth Hostel, *Albergue Humahuaca*, Buenos Aires 435, clean, laundry and very limited cooking facilities, run down, cold, F pp, special price for ISIC and youth card holders.

Camping Across bridge by railway station, small charge incl use of facilities.

Restaurants Most restaurants open only during the day, difficult to find breakfast and the mediocre restaurant at the bus terminal is often the only place open in the evenings. *La Cacharpaya*, Jujuy 295, excellent, pricey; *Humahuaca Colonial*, Tucumán 22, good regional cooking, good value, but invaded by coach parties at midday; *El Rancho*, Belgrano s/n, just around the corner from market, lunches only, where the locals eat.

Exchange Bank. Try the handicraft shops on the main plaza, or the *Farmacia* at Córdoba 99; better rates at Youth Hostel, but best to change before you go. Credit cards are not accepted anywhere.

Tourist Office Kiosk in main plaza in high season. Sr Carlos Gómez Cardozo, Director of the Museo La Casa, is a mine of information on the area and may be able to arrange English-speaking guides at weekends.

Excursions To ***Coctaca***, 10 km NE, where there is an impressive and extensive series of pre-colonial agricultural terraces, covering 40 ha. To the mine at El Aguilar (see below), trucks leave Humahuaca early am.

20 km N of Humahuaca along Route 9, an unpaved road runs NE 8 km to Yrigoyen (railway station called Iturbe) and then over the 4,000m Abra del Cóndor before dropping steeply into the Quebrada de Iruya. ***Iruya***, 66 km from Humahuaca, is a beautiful walled village wedged on a hillside at 2,600m. It has a fine 17th century church and Rosario festival on first Sun in Oct. Accommodation at **F** pp *Albergue Belén*, very basic. The trips to Iruya offered by *pensiones* in Humahuaca, or even by people in the street, are overpriced. It is worthwhile staying in Iruya for a few days; it makes an extremely pleasant and friendly centre for horseback or walking trips (take sleeping bag). At Titiconte 4 km away, there are unrestored pre-Inca ruins (take guide). Puna Expediciones (**see Salta p 113**) runs a 7-day trek, Salta-Iruya-Nazareno-La Quiaca, walking between Iruya and Nazareno on small, remote paths where there are no tourists or motor vehicles, sleeping in local schoolhouses; rest of route is by truck.

Transport Daily bus service from Jujuy and Humahuaca to Yrigoyen by Panamericano, 1400 and 1900, 45 mins; in *Yrigoyen* (**F** *Pensión El Panamericano*, basic) you may be able to get a seat on a truck. Empresa Mendoza bus from Humahuaca, 0800, Wed and Sat 3 1/2 hrs journey, US$7 one way, waits 2-3 hrs in Iruya before returning; service varies according to time of year and is suspended in rainy season (esp Feb and Mar), one report says this journey can be dangerous as an overloaded bus follows a riverbed after the road ends, details from *Almacén Mendoza*, Salta y Belgrano, Humahuaca.

A pretty walk in Yrigoyen: "cross the bridge and go straight on until you reach a hairpin bend by some white rocks. A small path on the left of the bend follows a gorge to the top of the ridge. From here go straight ahead and turn right at the "crossroad" to a small ridge for panoramic views." (M Powell).

From Humahuaca to La Quiaca on the Bolivian border, Route 9 is unpaved and runs across the bleak and barren *puna*. At Tres Cruces, 62 km N of Humahuaca, a paved road runs S for 46 km to the mine at El Aguilar. ***Abra Pampa***, an important mining centre, population 4,000, is further N at Km 91 (**F** pp *Residencial El Norte*, Sarmiento 530, shared rm, clean, hot water, good food). From here an unpaved road leads NW to Laguna Pozuelos and on to the Rinconada gold mine. ***Laguna Pozuelos***, 3,650m, 50 km from Abra Pampa, is a flamingo reserve and natural monument. Bus daily at 1030 exc Sun via the mines at Pan de Azúcar and Rinconada, 4 hrs, US$3, dropping you at the park ranger station. If driving, the Laguna is 5 km from the road; walk last 800m to reach the edge of the lagoon. Temperatures can drop to -30°C in winter; if camping warm clothing, drinking water and food are essential. By car it is possible to drive N along the E side of the Laguna via Cienaguillas to reach La Quiaca. 15 km from Abra Pampa is the vicuña farm at Miraflores, the largest in Argentina. Information offered, photography permitted; colectivos go am Mon-Sat from Abra Pampa to the vicuña farm.

From a point 4 km N of Abra Pampa roads branch W to Cochinoca (25 km) and SW to ***Casabindo*** (62 km). "On 15 Aug at Casabindo, the local saint's day, the last and only *corrida de toros* in Argentina is held amidst a colourful popular celebration. The event is called "El Toreo de la Vincha"; in front of the church a bull defies onlookers to take a ribbon and medal which it carries. The Casabindo church itself is a magnificent building, being called "the cathedral of the Puna"." (Federico Kirbus).

Yavi, with the fine church of San Francisco, which has magnificent gold decoration and windows of onyx (1690), is 16 km E of La Quiaca, reached by a good, paved road; taxi available – US$25 return fare, including one hour wait. (Find the caretaker at her house and she will show you round the church, open Tues-Sun 0900-1200 and Tues-Fri 1500-1800.) Opposite this church is the house of the Marqués Campero y Tojo. Only a precarious road for trucks and pick-ups leads on to the two churches of Santa Victoria (a forlorn Indian village in a rain forest valley) and

Acoyte. At **Santa Catalina**, 67 km W of La Quiaca, along a poor road, there is also a 17th century church. (Bus from Jujuy to La Quiaca, 8 hrs, and Santa Catalina, 19 hrs, Mon and Fri.)

La Quiaca, 292 km from Jujuy at an altitude of 3,442m, is joined to its Bolivian neighbour, Villazón, by a concrete bridge. Warm clothing is essential all year round, but particularly in winter when temperatures can drop to -15°C. At the same time, care should be taken against sunburn during the day. On the third Sun in Oct the Manca Fiesta, or the festival of the pots, is held here, and the Colla Indians from Jujuy and the Bolivian *altiplano* come, carrying all sorts of pots; local food is eaten. Most commercial activity has moved to Villazón because everything is much cheaper in Bolivia.

Hotels C *Turismo*, Siria y San Martín, T 2243, rec, clean, modern, comfortable, hot water 1800-2400, heating from 2030-2400 in winter, restaurant; **D** *Cristal*, Sarmiento 543, T 2255, clean and comfortable, with café and bus office adjacent. **D** *Victoria*, opp railway station, clean, good hot showers; *Alojamiento Pequeño*, Av Bolívar 236, friendly, cheap, clean. **D** *La Frontera* hotel and restaurant, Belgrano y Siria, downhill from Atahuallpa bus stop, good; **E** *Residencial Independencia*, rec, near railway station and church, hot water but no room heating even in winter. *Restaurant Sirio-Libanesa*, near *Hotel Frontera*, good, cheap set meal.

Camping is possible near the control post on the outskirts of town; also at the ACA service station about 300 m from the border on the left (entering Argentina).

Exchange No facilities for changing cheques. There are several *cambios* in Villazón (open on Sun) which accept cash only and sell pesos as well as bolivianos. Rates are better in Villazón.

Medical There are a good hospital in La Quiaca and a doctor in Villazón. *Farmacia Nueva*, 1/2 block from Church, has remedies for *soroche* (mountain sickness).

Transport Difficult to obtain information in La Quiaca about buses leaving Villazón for points in Bolivia (see Bolivia, **South from La Paz** for Villazón), though Bolivian buses tend to be more reliable than Bolivian trains. New bus station in La Quiaca at Av España y Belgrano, 4 blocks from railway station; all bus companies have offices here, payment accepted in US$. 6-8 buses a day to **Salta** (US$27) via Humahuaca and Jujuy, US$22 with change of bus in Jujuy (5 hrs to Humahuaca, 6 hrs to Jujuy, 10 hrs to Salta). Panamericano has 5 buses a day to **Jujuy**, US$21.50, 6½ hrs. Some meal breaks, but take own food, as sometimes long delays. Buses may be stopped and searched for coca leaves. Bus to **Buenos Aires**, via Jujuy, US$89 incl meals, 28 hrs. As of Mar 1993, no passenger trains were running S of La Quiaca.

Entering Bolivia The frontier bridge is 10 blocks from bus terminal, 15 mins walk (taxi US$0.50).

Warning Those travellers who need a visa to enter Bolivia are advised to get it before arriving in La Quiaca because the consular staff there try to charge US$15 per visa; pleading may reduce the charge.

Motorists should visit the Servicio Nacional de Turismo to obtain the Hoja de Ruta, which all motorists must have. It is not restrictive in any practical sense; just a nuisance!

If leaving Argentina for a short stroll into Villazón, show your passport, but do not let it be stamped by Migración, otherwise you will have to wait 48 hrs before being allowed back into Argentina.

Entering Argentina Argentine immigration and customs are open 0800-2000 (signature needed from customs officer, who may be out for lunch); on Sat, Sun, and holidays there is a special fee of US$3 which may or may not be charged. Buses arriving outside these hours will have to wait, so check before travelling. You can cross the border at night, without luggage, and your passport will not be stamped. Formalities are usually very brief at the border but very thorough customs searches are made 100 km S of the border at Tres Cruces; be prepared for camera search.

NB Bolivian time is one hour earlier than Argentina. The Argentine frontier opens at 0800, the Bolivian at 0700.

North-East from Jujuy 63 km from Jujuy is **San Pedro de Jujuy**, a sugar town of 60,000 people. The Ingenio La Esperanza, on the outskirts, is a sugar-mill with hospital, housing and a recreation centre, formerly owned by the English Leach brothers. **C** *Hotel Alex 2*, R Leach 467, T 20269, private bath, fan, clean; *Alex I*, Tello 436, T 20299; **E** *Vélez Sarsfield*, V Sarsfield 154, T 20446; excellent restaurant at *Sociedad Sirio-Libanesa* on the plaza. Bus to Jujuy, US$2.50, 1½ hrs; to Embarcarción, Atahuallpa, US$6.50, 2½ hrs.

Libertador (formally Libertador General San Martín), another sugar town 50 km N of San Pedro, is a base for exploring the **Parque Nacional Calilegua**, an area of peaks and sub-tropical valleys, reached by dirt road from just N of the town. Camping site near the first ranger house, at Agua Negra. Drinking water from river nearby, and some cooking facilities and tables. The ranger, Angel Caradonna, and his wife, Mony, are very friendly and knowledgeable. Mony sells hand-painted T-shirts featuring the park's wildlife. There are over 200 species of bird here including the very rare black and chestnut eagle and the red-faced guan. There are 60 species of mammal including tapir, puma, deer and otters. 13 km further along the trail is the 2nd ranger house, at Mesada de las Colmenas (ask permission at the 1st ranger house to camp here). 10 km from here is the N boundary of the park, marked by an obelisk, and where the most interesting birds can be seen. An all-weather track leads from the village of San Francisco to Alto Calilegua (10 hrs walk), overlooked by the 2 highest peaks in the park – Cerro Amarillo (the tallest at 3720 m with Inca ruins at the top) and Cerro Hermoso. Condors and taruca deer may be seen. (Thanks for park information to Ortelli Jiri Moreno, Como, Italy.) The park entrance is 10 km along the dirt road (hitching from Libertador possible), which climbs through the park and beyond to Valle Grande (no accommodation, basic food supplies from shops), 90 km from Libertador. From here it is possible to walk to Humahuaca and Tilcara (allow at least 3 days; these walks are described in *Backpacking in Chile and Argentina* by Bradt Publications). Trucks run by Empresa Valle Grande, Libertad 780, leave Libertador, Tues, and Sat, 0730, 6 hrs if road conditions are good, very crowded, returning Sun and Thur 1000. Check with Sr Arcona (the driver, everyone knows him) who lives opposite the railway station, if the truck is going. Weather is unpredictable. Or contact Gustavo Lozano at Los Claveles 358, Barrio Jardín, T 21647, who will contact the ranger, Angel Caradonna to pick you up. Park headquarters are on San Lorenzo s/n, in Calilegua, 4 km from Libertador. T (0886) 22046.

Services at Libertador: **E** *Residencial Gloria*, Urquiza 270, clean, hot water; **E** *Ledesma*, Jujuy 473 just off plaza, friendly, large rooms but no keys, local radio station opposite so can be noisy; *Restaurant Sociedad Boliviana*, Victoria 711, where the locals eat. On Plaza San Martín, **Banco Roberts** changes dollars at a good rate. The tourist office in the bus station is unhelpful.

From Libertador, Route 34 runs NE 244 km, to the Bolivian frontier at Yacuiba (see **Eastern Bolivia** section), via Embarcación (Km 101) and Tartagal. **See p 114** for Pocitos border crossing.

Embarcación (pop 24,000) has several hotels (**D** *Punta Norte*, España 425, clean, a/c, friendly; Sr Sarmiento's Hotel; *Universal*, hot water), of which the cheaper are near the railway station. Restaurant of *Sociedad Sirio-Libanesa*, H Irigoyen and 9 de Julio, cheap and good. 2 km from Embarcación you can walk to the Loma Protestant mission for Mataes and Toba Indians, who sell unpainted pottery there. Buses go to Orán, 1 hr, US$1.70 on a paved road. Buses Embarcación-Pocitos (change at Tartagal, making sure your ticket is stamped with the next bus time or you won't be allowed on it); bus Buenos Aires-Pocitos US$91. Bus Embarcación-Salta US$14.50, 3 a day. Regular bus scheduled to run daily at 1300, 17 hrs, US$40, Atahuallpa, but frequently cancelled. Alternatively take bus to Pichanal, US$1.25, several, another bus to JV Gonzales, US$10, 1600, and change again for Resistencia, 2215. From here there are buses to Formosa and Clorinda.

Tartagal, 74 km N of Embarcación, pop 70,000, is an agricultural centre with a small museum featuring displays on animals of the Chaco and regional folk art. The director, Ramón Ramos, is very informative about the region. Animal masks and pottery are made by Indians nearby at Campo Durán. **Hotels**: *Argentino*, San Martín 54, T 21327, 3-star; *Espinillo*, San Martín 122, T 21007; *Residencial*

City, Alberdi 79, T 21558.

Another route to Bolivia is via *Orán*, 110 km N of Libertador on Route 50, an uninteresting place, pop 34,000. (**D** *Residencial Centro*, Pellegrini 332; **D** *Residencial Crillon*, 25 de Mayo 225, T 21101, dirty; **C** *Gran Hotel Orán*, Pellegrini 617, T 21214; **D** *Residencial Crisol*, López y Planes, hot water, friendly, rec.)

Buses, 6 daily to **Salta**, 7-10 hrs; direct bus to **Tucumán** at 2130, connecting for Mendoza bus which leaves at 1300. Bus to **Tartagal** daily at 0630 and 1800; to **Jujuy** at 1200 daily; to **Formosa**, US$28, 14 hrs, leaving Tues, Thur, Sat at 0930; to **Embarcación**, US$1.70. To **Resistencia**, Atahualpa buses every 2 hrs or so, 5 hrs, US$12.

There are frequent bus services to *Aguas Blancas* (45 mins, US$2, luggage checks on bus), on the frontier. There is nowhere to stay at Aguas Blancas nor anywhere to change money, but there are restaurants (*El Rinconcito de los Amigos*) and shops. The passport office is open from 0700 to 1200 and 1500 to 1900. Insist on getting an exit stamp. There is no exit tax. Buses run twice daily from Bermejo, across the river (ferry US$0.50), to Tarija (10 hrs).

If entering Argentina spend your remaining Bolivian money here, not accepted in Orán; buses to Orán every 45 mins to Güemes, 8 a day, US$10; through buses to Salta, Veloz del Norte and Atahuallpa, 3 daily each, US$17.50.

There is no direct bus from Orán to Asunción, Paraguay; take bus to Embarcación, from there bus to Formosa, then bus to Asunción.

THE CUYO REGION: OVER THE ANDES TO CHILE (4)

From the pampa to the heights of Aconcagua and the Uspallata Pass, en route to Santiago. Mendoza is a centre of wine making, fruit growing, winter sports (several ski resorts nearby) and climbing.

In the Cuyo region, in the W, there is little rain and nothing can be grown except under irrigation. On the irrigated lands grapes and fruit are possible, and alfalfa takes the place of the maize grown in the N. The two most important oases in this area of slight rainfall are Mendoza itself and San Rafael, 160 km to the S.

Of the 15 million hectares in Mendoza Province, only 2% are cultivated. Of the cultivated area 40% is given over to vines, 25% is under alfalfa grown for cattle, and the rest under olive groves and fruit trees. Petroleum is produced in the Province, and there are important uranium deposits.

NB No fresh fruit, vegetables or cold meats may be brought into the provinces of Mendoza, San Juan, Río Negro or Neuquén.

The Transandine Route Travelling from Buenos Aires westward across the pampa, one comes first to *Mercedes*, in Buenos Aires Province, a pleasant city with a population of 47,850. It has many fine buildings. (Not to be confused with Villa Mercedes in San Luis Province—see below.) Tourist Office on plaza, very friendly.

Hotels D *Loren* (no sign), Salta 228, friendly, clean, parking; **D** *Aragón*, ½ block from Plaza, friendly, hot water. **D** *Libertador*, opp bus station, good.

Junín, 256 km from Buenos Aires (Eva Perón was born near here) is close to lagoons from which fish are taken to the capital. Population, 63,700.

Accommodation A2 *Copahue*, Saavedra 80, T 23390, F 29041, faded, ACA discount; *Embajador*, Sáenz Peña y Pellegrini, T 21433. **Restaurant** *Paraje del Sauce*, Km 258 on Route 7, picturesque, good food but "don't stop there if you are in a rush". *El Quincho de Martín*, B de Miguel y Ruta 7, good.

At Rufino (pop 15,300), on Route 7, 452 km from Buenos Aires, is the rec **L3** *Hotel Astur*, Córdoba 81, C with ACA discount; also at **Laboulaye**, on Route 7, 517 km from Buenos Aires, there are several good and cheap hotels, eg *Victoria*, and **C** *Motel Ranquel Mapu*, Km 489, very good, but drinking water is a problem, bottled water supplied.

At *Villa Mercedes* (San Luis Province, pop 77,000), 693 km from Buenos Aires (where the old municipal market is now an arts and community centre), Route 8 runs NE to (122 km) Río Cuarto (pop 110,000). About 65 km beyond Villa Mercedes, the rolling hills of San Luis begin; beyond there are stretches of woodland.

Hotels ACA hotel **C** *San Martín*, Lavalle 435, T 22358, restaurant, garages, clean, friendly; the ACA restaurant at the service station on Route 7, outside town (just before junction with Route 8), is very good value. *Centro*, Junín 40, T 21212. Cheaper places on Mitre, eg: **D** *Residencial Cappola*, No 1134, clean, rec.

Air Airport: Villa Reynolds, 10 km from Villa Mercedes.

Bus Villa Mercedes—Buenos Aires US$28.

Merlo, some 150 km N of Villa Mercedes, is a small town on the western slopes of the Sierra de Comechingones. At 700 m above sea level it enjoys a fresher climate than the pampas in summer, and the area is being promoted for its rich wildlife, particularly birds. One hotel rec is the *Rincón del Este* (no price given), 5-6 km from the centre, and nearby are three camping sites. The tourist office is on the main plaza and the bus station 3 blocks away; frequent buses to and from **San Luis**, TAC to **Buenos Aires** at 1800.

Mac McCreadie from Villa Mercedes, recommends the following walks: Behind the *Hotel Rincón del Este* it is possible to climb the rocky watercourse above the *guardaparque's* cottage to a cross on a hill-top 1500 m above the plain. This is an energetic scramble and takes 1½-2 hrs, probably longer and tougher in the wet months. It is a further 500 m to the hill-crest at Cerro Linderos Alto over steep rocky ground. Two tracks exist. You have to select you route through spiny vegetation and over boulders. A sure footing and appropriate clothing will help. Stunning views W over the pampas towards the Sierras de San Luis and S towards peculiarly shaped hills near La Toma.

Lower down, again starting near the *guardaparque's* house, is a good walk of 3 to 4 hrs called El Circuito de Damiana Vega. This is less demanding but takes in the lushly wooded slopes along a 'ripio' (gravel road), negotiable by vehicles. The Circuito is named after a woman from the Comechingones indigenous people, who lives in a small house by the 'ripio'. In 1993 Damiana Vega was 110 years old, she welcomes visitors and likes to talk about the region.

8 km N of Merlo is *Piedra Blanca*, a small settlement in attractive surroundings, with several hotels. South of Merlo is a string of pretty villages along a scenic road running parallel to the main route (Ruta 148), S to Villa Mercedes, including Carpintería, Cortaderas, and Villa Larea.

San Luis, 98 km from Villa Mercedes, is the capital of the Province of San Luis. It stands at 765m at the S end of the Punta de los Venados hills. It was founded by Martín de Loyola, the governor of Chile, in 1596, and is still faintly colonial. The area is rich in minerals and an onyx quarry is worked. Visit the Centro Artesanal San Martín de Porras, run by the Dominican fathers, on 25 de Mayo, opp Palacio de Gobierno, where rugs are woven. Open 0700-1300 exc Sat and Sun. Population: 150,000. San Luis to Mendoza is 264 km.

A "Via Crucis" sculptured in white marble skirts the mountainside at Villa de la Quebrada, 35 km N. Beyond Salto Grande, Salto Colorado and the Gruta de la Virgen de las Flores is El Volcán (12 km; *balneario*, walks, picnics; *Hotel Andrea*) in whose neighbourhood is Cruz de Piedra dam (drives, fishing), and Carolina (placer gold mining, riding and fishing). Hotels and inns along the road.

Hotels Several on Av Pres Illia: *Quintana*, No 546, T/F 29548, best; **A2** *Aiello*, No 431, T 25644, F 25694, a/c, private bath, garages, rec. *Gran San Luis*, No 470, T 22881, pool, 50m from ACA; *Gran Hotel España*, No 300, T 25051; also *Novel*, Junín 748, all categories **B-C**. Others on Rivadavia, eg **B** *Gran Palace*, No 657, T 22059; *Intihuasi*, La Pampa 815 (behind Casa de Cultura), spotless, very friendly, TV, lounge, highly rec (price unknown). **D** *Rivadavia*, Estado de Israel 1470, T 22437, with bath, hot water, friendly, opp bus station; next door is *17 de Octubre*, which should be avoided, basic, dirty.

Camping Rio Volcán, 4 km from town.

Restaurants The majority close at weekends; hotel restaurants are closed Sun, *San Luis'* closes Sat too. *El Cantón de Neuchatel*, San Martín 745, opp Cathedral on main square, is open Sun, modest. *Michel*, Lafinur 1361, good food and service.

Exchange Very difficult to change TCs, try **Banco de Galicia**, Rivadavia y Belgrano, 1.5% commission.

Tourist Office Junín, opp Post Office, excellent.

Bus station at Viá España between San Martín y Rivadavia. **Train** Passenger services suspended.

16 km from San Luis is **L3** *Hotel Potrero de los Funes*, T (0652) 30125/20889, F 23898 or

BsAs 313-4886, F 312-3876 (25 de Mayo 516, piso 11), a luxury resort and casino on lake of the same name, which has its own microclimate (sports and watersports, lovely views but upkeep a little lacking). Route 146 runs N from San Luis towards Córdoba through Villa de la Quebrada, San Francisco del Monte de Oro, Luján and Villa Dolores. An alternative is to take Route 9 via Trapiche (*A2 Hostería Los Sauces*, bus from San Luis, US$4 return) to Carolina. A disused goldmine can be seen at Carolina, allegedly put out of action deliberately in the 1970s, in an attempt to force up the world price of gold. A statue of a gold miner overlooks the main street of what has become a ghost town. Near Carolina, at Gruta de Intihuasi, a natural arch forms a cave in which the mummified body of a child was found, estimated to be 8,500 years old. 4WD vehicles can drive up Tomolasta mountain (2,000m) to see typical San Luis landscapes. From this road the Cuesta Larga descends to San Francisco. At Luján a road heads W to meet the San Luis-San Juan road (Route 147) at La Tranca.

70 km NE of San Luis is *La Toma* (**D** *Hotel Gran Italia*, hot showers; *Residencial Days*, P Graciarena 158, private bath) the cheapest place to buy green onyx—about 20 shops. From here you can make an excursion to Cerros Rosario, interesting hills and rock scenery, 10 km NW; and San José del Morro, a group of mountains which were originally volcanoes (there is a model in the Museo de Ciencias in Buenos Aires). You will find a lot of rose-quartz.

Beyond San Luis Route 7 climbs to a height of 460m and descends and crosses the valley of the Río Desaguadero, which forms the provincial boundary with Mendoza. At **San Rafael** (273 km SW of San Luis, 242 m S of Mendoza), at the foot of the Andes, irrigation makes it possible to grow fruit in large quantities. 2 bodegas to visit, Suter and Bianchi (Monte Caseros y E Civit, rec). The town—there are some oil wells near—has a population of 72,200. There is a small but interesting natural history museum 6 km SE of town at Isla Río Diamante (Tues-Sun 0800-1200, 1500-1900, free; Iselin bus along Av JA Balloffet); zoo nearby. A road runs W over El Pehuenche pass to Talca (Chile). Bus to Mendoza, frequent, US$9. Bus to Neuquén, US$20.

Hotels C *Rex*, Yrigoyen 56, T 22177; **D** *Kalton*, Yrigoyen 120, T 22568/30047, excellent, clean, safe, good value; **E** *Martínez*, 30m from bus station, good, also cheap meals.

Campsites 2 sites (one of them ACA) at Isla Río Diamante, 6 km SE.

Tourist Office Av H Yrigoyen y Balloffet, very helpful. Ask for Aldo or Hector Seguín at España 437 for trekking and climbing information.

Above the town, up the Río Atuel valley, there is beautiful scenery in the **Valle Hermoso** up to the 3 dams of El Nihuil which provide irrigation water and hydroelectric power to Mendoza. There is fishing in the reservoir above the highest dam. In the Río Atuel canyon there are polychrome rocks in the spectacular gorge. 3 buses a day go to Valle Grande at the end of the canyon, US$3. Plenty of hotels and campsites, river rafting and horse riding. Good skiing at **Las Leñas**, 2,250m at the end of Valle Los Molles, a new resort with 33 pistes, three T-bars, three ski-lifts (US$35-45/day; equipment hire US$11-18). It claims to be the foremost ski resort in the S hemisphere. (Buses from Buenos Aires, 15 hrs, in skiing season only.) Three stonebuilt hotels: *Escorpio*, *Acuario* and *Gemini*, T for all 71100, and a disco, shop renting equipment and expensive restaurant. All the hotels are L2; for cheaper accommodation you have to stay in Los Molles (bus from San Rafael US$5.30, colectivo US$20; from Las Leñas US$0.70) where there is **B** *Hotel La Huenca*, a/c, clean. There is an airport in **Malargüe**, pop 8,600 (**B-C** *Hotel del Turismo*, San Martín 224, T 71042, quiet, rec; **C** *Hotel-Restaurant El Cisne*, Villegas 278, T 71350, clean, rec; *Portal del Valle*, T 71536, provides multilingual tour guides; several others) 70 km from Las Leñas, with flights to Buenos Aires. This area is developing as a tourist centre. Ask at the tourist office for information on Cavernas de Brujas and Pozos de Animas, both worth visiting.

Mendoza, at the foot of the Andes, 1,060 km from Buenos Aires, is linked to it by air, the San Martín railway and a paved road, which continues across the Andes to Chile. (No rail service now between Mendoza and Buenos Aires or Chile.)

Mendoza (756m) is an expanding and very pleasant city. Rainfall is slight, but irrigation has turned the area into an oasis of fruit trees and vineyards. The city was colonized from Chile in 1561 and named in honour of the then governor of Chile. It was from here that the Liberator José de San Martín set out to cross the Andes, to help in the liberation of Chile. Mendoza was completely destroyed by fire and earthquake in 1861, so today it is essentially a modern city of low dwellings (as a precaution against earthquakes), thickly planted with trees and gardens. The main street is Avenida San Martín, which runs S to N parallel to the San Martín railway line. Population of city 148,000, but with suburbs included, it is about 600,000.

See the Cerro de la Gloria, a hill above the great Parque San Martín on the W side of the city, crowned by an astonishing monument to San Martín. There is a great rectangular stone block with bas-reliefs depicting various episodes in the equipping of the Army of the Andes and the actual crossing. In front of the block, San Martín bestrides his charger. In the park at the foot of Cerro de la Gloria steep and twisting paths run to the Jardín Zoológico (US$1). Nearby in the park there are watercourses and a 1 km-long artificial lake, where regattas are held, and views of the Andes (when the amount of floating dust will allow) rising in a blue-black perpendicular wall, topped off in winter with dazzling snow, into a china-blue sky. The entrance to the Parque San Martín is ten blocks W of the Plaza Independencia, reached by bus 110 from the centre. An hourly bus ("Oro Negro") runs to the top of the Cerro de la Gloria from the E end of the park, on Av Libertad— it's a long walk (45 mins).

The best shopping centre is Avenida Las Heras, where there are good souvenir and handicraft shops; leather goods are cheaper here than in Buenos Aires. The municipal market is clean and well-stocked; worth a visit. Plaza Pellegrini (Av Alem y Av San Juan) is a beautiful small square where wedding photos are taken on Fri and Sat nights. The wine vintage festival, Fiesta de la Vendimia, is held in the amphitheatre of the Parque San Martín at the end of Mar. There is a wine museum (Av Peltier, at the Giol *bodega*—see below), with good guides and wine tasting, just behind the Palacio de Gobierno, opening hours from the tourist office. Outside Mendoza, about 40 km due E, there is a modern satellite town called San Martín. **NB** Official tours of the city are a waste of time and money; a large sign in Plaza Independencia shows a walking tour which takes about 2 hours. Beware theft in pedestrian areas.

Museums Museo Histórico San Martín, Av General San Martín 1846, seven blocks N of the Tourist Office, open Mon-Fri, 0900-1200, 1700-2000, US$1; Museo del Pasado Cuyano, Montevideo 544, beautifully furnished, has a collection on San Martín and history of Mendoza, open Mon-Fri 0930-1230, Tues and Thur, 1600-1730, but times vary, US$0.50; Museo de Historia Natural, in Parque San Martín, open Tues-Fri 0900-1200, 1600-2000, Sat, Sun 1600-2000; Museo de Ciencias Naturales y Antropológicas, Playas Serranes, Parque Gral San Martín, Tues-Fri 0900-1200, 1400-1800, Sat-Sun 1500-1900; Museo Municipal de Arte Moderno, underground (subsuelo) in Plaza Independencia, US$1.50, very small unless there is a special exhibition. The Acuario Municipal is underground at Buenos Aires e Ituzaingó, small but worth a visit, US$0.50, open Mon-Fri 1000-1200 and 1530-2000, Sat and Sun same times am. The Museo Arqueológico and the Museo de Ciencias Naturales are both in the Ciudad Universitaria—ask at Tourist Office for details. Worth seeing, also, are the ruins of the San Francisco church at Ituzaingó y Beltrán. Next to the ruins is a Museo del Area Fundicional, Alberdi y Videla Castillo, history of Mendoza, Tues-Sat 0800-1400, 1630-2230, Sun pm only, rec; in front of the museum are the ruins of the Jesuit church of San Francisco, part destroyed in the 1861 earthquake. Acuario Municipal, Buenos Aires e Ituzaingó; Serpentarium opposite (US$2).

Wine Wine *bodegas* (wine-making season Mar/Apr) and fruit preserving; visiting times available from Tourist Office. To the *Giol* winery, one of the world's biggest, take 150 or 151 bus marked "Maipú" (every hour, 0900-1230, 1500-1800), but check if winery is open before going, T 972090. The tour is rec in season (mid Mar to mid April). Also in Maipú district is *Peñaflor*, on Mitre, bus 17, good visit and generous tasting. *San Felipe* (Bodega La Rural), C Montecaseros, Coquimbito, Maipú, T 972013, a small bodega, is worth visiting, bus 170, tours 0900-1100, 1600-1800, tasting, Museo del Vino (fascinating), open Mon-Fri 0800-1100, 1500-1800. (In Maipú itself see the lovely square and eat at the *Club Social*, good simple food.) *Bodega de Arizu* is open 0900-1600, bus No 7 from city centre; many of the others also admit visitors, and offer you a glass after the visit. Try *Bodega Escorihuela* (bus 15 from centre Belgrano 1188, T 220215) if you are more interested in the information than the wine-tasting. The *Toso* bodega at JB Alberdi 808, T 380244, is small, old-fashioned, has excellent wines and an interesting, free guided tour, some tasting, highly rec. The *Orfila* bodega in San Martín, 40 km E, located in the house of the Liberator, also has a wine museum. Prices at the bodegas have roughly a 100% mark-up from supermarket prices. Recommended: Cruz del Sur from Bodega Arizu, Cuesta del Parral, Valroy-Borgoña, Valroy-Cabernet Sauvignon, Viejo Toro, Trapiche from Bodega Peñaflor, and Vino de Mesa de Arizu Tinto Seco. Many tourist agencies incl the bodegas in their half-day or day-long tours (US$4-8 but these visits are too short, with too few guides and little tasting—only of the cheaper wines, usually in plastic cups).

All Mendoza restaurants offer a tourist special of a bottle of wine for US$1.50.

Local Holidays 18 Jan (Crossing of the Andes); 25 Jul (St James); 8 Sep (Virgin of Carmen de Cuyo). Annual wine festival during the final week of Mar, when hotels fill up fast; book ahead! Prices rise at this time, and in Jul (the ski season) and Sep (the spring festival).

Hotels L3 *Aconcagua*, 4 star, comfortable, San Lorenzo 545, T 243321/243833, good but expensive restaurant, pool, disappointing tourist advice and bookings available. In our **A2-3** range: *Crillón*, Perú 1066, T 245525, small, clean but overpriced. *Plaza*, Chile 1124 on main plaza, T 233000, not too clean, but obliging; **A2** *Nutibara*, Bartolomé Mitre 867, T 245747/244658 (discounts for cash), central, colour TV, a/c, parking, no breakfast, modern swimming pool, rec; *Palace*, Las Heras 70, T 234200, a/c, bath, incl breakfast, central; *San Martín*, Espejo 435, T 380677, rec; *Vecchia Roma*, España 1619, T 231515 (next door to restaurant of same name), comfortable, safe. **B** *Balbi*, Las Heras 340, T 233500, small swimming pool, a/c but you must phone to have it turned on each time you return to your room, nice rooms; **B** *Argentino*, Espejo 455, Plaza Independencia, T 254000, good, breakfast incl (poor), quite comfortable. **B** *1 de Mayo*, Garibaldi 80, T 248820, highly rec, breakfast incl, 0800 checkout time; *Royal*, Las Heras 145, T 380522/380675, breakfast incl, friendly, clean, a/c, rec; *Center*, Alem 547, with bath, very clean; *Imperial*, Las Heras 84, T 284671, washing facilities, friendly, rec, may offer cheaper price.

In our price range **C**: *City*, Gen Paz 95, T 251343, clean, helpful; *Monterrey*, Gen Paz 360, good; *Gran Ritz*, Perú 1008, T 248506, clean, modern, good; *Vendimia*, Godoy Cruz 101, T 250675/233099, good; *Petit*, Perú 1459, T 232099, without breakfast, 1½ blocks from railway station, clean, friendly, rec; *Pacífico*, San Juan 1407, T 256286, modern, comfortable, clean; *Milena*, Pasaje Babilonia 17 (off San Juan nr Don Bosco), T 240284, 2 star, clean, nice atmosphere; *Messidor*, Alberdi 690, T 314013, reasonable, friendly, clean, comfortable, arranges tours; *Balcarce*, San Martín 1446, T 252579, clean, safe, very friendly, incl breakfast; *El Libertador*, España 247, T 290921, good; *Las Viñas*, Av Martínez de Rosas, clean.

The following are in our **D** range: *Galicia*, Av San Juan 881, near Av LM Alem, T 249619, very clean, hot water, use of kitchen, rec; *San Remo*, Godoy Cruz 477, T 234068, clean, quiet, central, stores luggage, secure parking, highly rec; *El Piño Azul* apartments, San Martín 2872 (T 304593); *Savoy*, Belgrano 1377, good, clean, some rooms without window, tours offered at 20% discount; *Mayo*, 25 de Mayo 1265, incl breakfast, good value. On Calle Juan B Justo: *Penitentes* (No 67), T 230208, with bath, a/c and heating, good, snack bar; *Ideal* (No 270, T 256842), transport to bus station. On Perú: *Zamora* (No 1156), T 257537, reasonable and friendly, converted house; *Residencial D'Amore* (No 1346), clean, no fans, good bathrooms, use of kitchen; *España* (No 1535), run down, basic, safe; *Dardex* (No 1735), 2 blocks from railway station, friendly. On General Paz: *Alcor* (No 86), T 380100/234800, central, good; *Gran Marta* (No 460), clean, but only cold showers, rec; *El Descanso* (No 464), basic; *Necochea*, Necochea 541, T 253501, pleasant, cheerful, English spoken; *Vigo*, Necochea 749, T 250208, good value, dark, good *comedor*; *Residencial Alberdi*, Alberdi 51, T 234110, family run, friendly, clean; *El Rosario*, Chile 1579, T 254765, good, clean, hot water, rec; *Quijote*, Av San Juan 1407, clean, friendly, restaurant; *Escorial*, San Luis 263, T 254777, very friendly and clean, rec. *Residencial Betty*, Güemes, cheap, good value. **E** *Gotelcas*, Juan B Justo 67, good, also acts as youth hostel.

Youth hostel Tirasso 2170, T 263300, E, take bus 20, "B Paraguayo", takes 20 mins, ask driver.

Camping In Parque General San Martín permitted, free, in cars, but not in tents. Three campsites at El Challao, 6 km W of the city centre, reached by colectivo No 11 leaving every hour, *Atsa*, friendly, swimming pool, good service, caters for families; noisy at weekends from disco. *Camping Suizo*, modern with pool, barbeques, hot showers, friendly, rec. *Saucelandia*, at Guaymallén, 9 km E of Mendoza. Mendoza is reportedly a good place to sell off camping equipment. White gas (*bencina blanca*) can be bought at Ferretería Alsina, Catamarca 37.

Restaurants *Trevi*, Las Heras 68, good food and service, rec. *Bárbaro*, San Martín 914, English spoken, speciality is roast kid, pricey but good. *Tristán Barraza*, Av Sarmiento 658 (*parrilla*), good. *Parrillada Arturito*, Chile 1515, good steak, popular with locals; *Montecatini*, Gral Paz 370, wide variety, good food, good value, rec; *Parrilla 14*, San Lorenzo

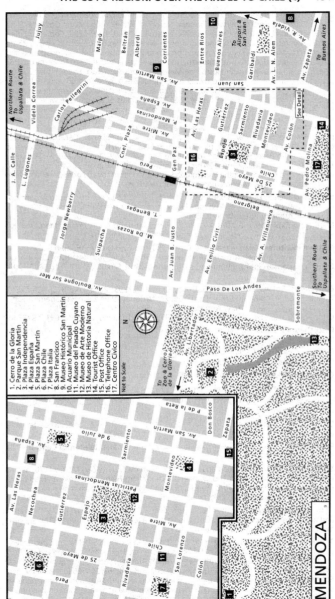

MENDOZA

1. Cerro de la Gloria
2. Parque San Martín
3. Plaza Independencia
4. Plaza España
5. Plaza San Martín
6. Plaza Chile
7. Plaza Italia
8. San Francisco
9. Museo Histórico San Martín
10. Acuario Municipal
11. Museo del Pasado Cuyano
12. Museo de Arte Moderno
13. Museo de Historia Natural
14. Tourist Office
15. Post Office
16. Telephone Office
17. Centro Cívico

Not to Scale

Northern Route To Uspallata a Chile

Southern Route To Uspallata & Chile

To Buenos Aires

To Airport & San Juan

To Zoo & Cerro de la Gloria

See Detail

65, good meat, rec; *Don Angelo*, Lavalle 150, cheap set meal; *Club Alemán*, Necochea 2261, Godoy Cruz, rec; *Club Sociedad Libanesa*, Necochea 538-42, good value; *Govinda*, Salta 1538, vegetarian, good and cheap set meal, open 1200-1600, 1900-2200; *Comedor Línea Verde*, Montecaseros 1177, vegetarian, *tenedor libre*; *El Dragón de Oro*, Chinese, 25 de Mayo 1553 (near Las Heras), very good; *Cervecería Zurich*, Las Heras 530, good food and service, cheap, rec. Ice cream at *Soppelso*, Las Heras y España and at Paseo Sarmiento, rec. *Sr Cheff*, restaurant/confitería at *Hotel 1 de Mayo*, Garibaldi 80. *Il Tucco*, Emilio Civit 556 (nr park gates), also same name and owner in centre at Paseo Sarmiento 68, excellent Italian restaurants, reasonable prices. Good value, and big "super pancho" sandwiches in many places, incl *Pizzería Seb*, Alem 431, only US$1.50 incl a glass of red or white wine; *Pizzería Mi Querencia*, Las Heras 519, very good pasta dishes. Huge sandwiches in *Belgrano*, on street of same name, crowded with locals, highly rec. Several places with cheap 3-course menus on San Juan, 1300 and 1400 blocks. *Aranjuez*, Lavalle y San Martín, nice cafe, good meeting place. *Mankie Snack Bar*, Las Heras y Mitre, excellent breakfasts; *Café de la Gente*, café/bookshop at Rivadavia 135, pleasant atmosphere. Several good snack bars (known as *carrito bars*): *Tío Paco*, Salta y Alem; *Torombola*, San Juan 1348; *Don Claudio*, Perú y Godoy; *El Gran Lomo*, Rivadavia 56, open 24 hrs, rec. There is a good, cheap café (excellent ice creams) next to the bus station, past the underground walkway. Out of town, *Lomo Loco*, a few km S on Luján road, locals' favourite *parrilla* but not cheap.

Banks and Exchange Lloyds Bank (BLSA), Gen Gutiérrez 72. Banco de Crédito Argentino, España 1168, cash advance on Visa card, high commission. American Express, Rivadavia 24, T 290374 Citibank Av San Martín 1099, gives US$ cash for cheques. Many *cambios* along San Martín, incl Exprinter, No 1198, best for cheques; Santiago No 1177, rec; Maguitur, No 1203. *Casas de cambio* open till 2000 Mon-Fri, and some open Sat, am.

Cultural Institutes Alianza Francesa, Chile 1754; Instituto Dante Alighieri (Italy), Espejo 638; Instituto Cultural Argentino-Norteamericano, Chile 985; Instituto Cuyano de Cultura Hispánica (Spain), Villanueva 389; Goethe Institut, Morón 265, Mon-Fri 0800-1200, 1600-2230.

Consulates Bolivia, Azopardo 276, Godoy Cruz, T 223893; Peru, Perú 8185, Carrodilla, T 390863; Chile, Av Emilio Civit, 296, T 255024; Uruguay, 9 de Julio 200. Spain, Agustín Alvarez 455, T 253947; Italy, Necochea 712, T 251886; France, Chile 1754, T 234614; Germany, Montevideo 127, 1° Piso D6, T 242539; Finland, Boulogne Sur Mer 631, T 973844.

Discothèques *Saudades*, Barraquero y San Martín; *Kalatraba*, Perú 1779; *El Diablo*, Ruta Internacional Vistalba Luján.

Cinema *Cine de Arte Eisenchlos*, 9 de Julio 500, Thur-Sun 2200. Free film shows at Salón Cultural Rivadavia, José V Zapata 349.

Casino 25 de Mayo 1123, daily 2100-0300.

There is a private **gynaecological clinic** at Gral Paz 445; helpful and relatively inexpensive.

Language Classes Sra Inés Perea de Bujaldon, Rioja 620, T 290429, teaches Spanish to German speakers, rec.

Coin-operated **laundromat**, Colón 543, also on Garibaldi near La Rioja, on Salta near San Luis, and at corner of San Juan and Rondeau. *Laverap*, Av Colón 547.

Post Office Av San Martín y Av Colón, unreliable *poste restante*. **Telefónica Central**, Chile 1574.

Shopping Leather goods good and cheap; try *Alain de France*, San Martín 1070, also at Andrade 147. Books (English and German selection) from *Historias* on Av San Martín and *Centro Internacional del Libro*, San Juan. English language magazines and *Buenos Aires Herald* usually available from kiosks on San Martín.

Mountain Climbing Information from Tourist Office. There is a three-day (Thur-Sat) climbing and trekking expedition via Godoy Cruz and Cacheuta to Cerro Penitentes (4,351m), sleeping in mountain refuge, food incl. See also p 135.

Travel Agencies Lots, especially in Las Heras, between Perú and San Martín. *Cuyo Travel*, Paseo Sarmiento 162, 10% discount for ISIC and youth card holders for trekking and climbing on Aconcagua. *Servicios Especiales Mendoza*, c/o Annette Schenker, Amigorena 65, 5500 Mendoza, F (061) 244721, 240131, or Radio, code 548, 242162/244505 (day or night, only Spanish spoken), run by Bernard Klapproth, guided tours around all Argentina, many languages spoken, waterskiing on El Carrizal lake, climbing Aconcagua and Andes, trekking and many other specialist programmes, access to Red Cross and Police, only company to cross Andes to Chile without papers. *Turismo Cóndor*, 25 de Mayo 1537, T 259341 (also at bus station), rec for tours in and around the city, and to El Cristo Redentor statue, good guides, Spanish only; *Mylatours*, Paseo Sarmiento 23, T 254516, rec. *Turismo Sepeán*, San Juan 1070, friendly and helpful, have branch in Santiago. *Turismo Cultural*, Rivadavia 211, T 242579, helpful. *Ibiza*, Espejo 217, T 258141, helpful and efficient. *Hunuc Huar Expediciones*, Av España 1340, 8 piso, oficina 7, and *Huera Pire*, Emilio Civit 320, specialize in assistance to climbers, especially on Aconcagua. *José Orviz*, Juan B Justo 550/536, T/F 256950/380085, guides, mules, transportation and hire of mountain trekking equipment.

Tourist Offices at airport, T 306484, helpful (frequently closed), at the bus terminal (helpful but limited English spoken), T 259709, at Municipalidad on Av España, at San Martín 1143 (evening city walks, US$1), at San Martín y Garibaldi, and at Mitre y Las Heras. They have a list of reasonable private lodgings and a hotel booking service (**C** range and upwards), and other literature incl lists of *bodegas* and an excellent free town and province map; the latter is also available at most kiosks. *Recreación*, leaflet lists all museums.

Car Hire Avis, Espejo 228; **Lis Car**, San Lorenzo 110, T 291416; **AS Rent-a-Car**, Garibaldi 186, T 248317; **Localiza**, at airport and Gutiérrez 453, T 254105. **Motorcycle repairs** César Armitrano, Rubén Zarate 138, 1600-2100, highly rec for assistance or a chat; he will let you work in his workshop.

Airport Plumerillo, 8 km from centre, reached by *remise* taxis (US$9, incl US$1 to enter airport grounds) and bus No 68 from the corner of San Juan and Alem which takes you close to the terminal (10 mins walk); make sure there is an "Aeropuerto" sign on the driver's window. Flying time from Buenos Aires: 1 hr 50 mins. AR flies 3 times a day (once on Sat); Austral twice a day (once on Sat), Lapa (not Sat). Austral offer a 65% discount on nocturnal flights. AR and Ladeco to **Santiago**, daily. Daily flight to **Córdoba** with Austral, AR fly to **San Juan** (Sun only). TAN flies to **Neuquén**. Aerolíneas Argentinas, Paseo Sarmiento 74, T 340170/100; Austral, Av San Martín 921, T 340088.

Buses Terminal on E side of Av Videla, 15 mins walk from centre. To **Bariloche**, Andesmar daily, TAC, 3 a week, US$70, on a mostly paved road, about 22 hrs, book well ahead; to **Córdoba**, TAC 5 daily, 9 hrs, US$29; to **San Rafael**, many daily, US$9; to **San Juan** at least every 2 hours, US$11, 2 hrs (several companies, incl TAC, El Cumbre and Villa del Sur y Media Agua). To **La Rioja** US$25, 10 hrs, 5 a day, 3 companies; similarly to **Catamarca**, 12 hrs, daily, US$20. 6 daily to **Tucumán**, US$40; to **Salta**, Andesmar daily (via Tucumán) at 1300 and 2130, 20 hrs, US$54 (plus 4 other companies). To **Puerto Iguazú** at 1930, Mon, Wed, Sat with Cotal, US$70, 38 hrs; alternatively take daily Villa Marta bus to Santa Fe and change for Iguazú bus, about 40 hrs incl waiting time. To **Comodoro Rivadavia**, daily with Andesmar, at 2000, US$100, 32 hrs incl 4 meal stops; the Tues and Sat departures continue to Río Gallegos, arriving 1450 Thur. To **Rosario**, US$40, 12 hrs. To **Buenos Aires** via Route 8, 2nd class US$54 (cheaper in winter), 1st class daily, US$60 (lines incl Chevallier, TAC Coop, Jocoli); luxury service daily at 1800 (Chevallier), US$76 incl meals; via Route 7 (Junín-Mercedes) at 2020, arrive 1205. Dull scenery, and very cold across the Pampas at night. 20% student discount on some routes (eg Comodoro Rivadavia). A US$1 tip is expected for removing luggage from buses.

International Buses For services to **Santiago** see p 137. To **La Serena**, Dec-Mar only. To **Lima**, El Rápido Mon, Wed, Sat 0900. To Montevideo, El Rápido, Tues.

Hitchhiking between Mendoza and Buenos Aires is quite easy. If hitching to San Juan, take bus No 6 to the airport near the highway. Hitching from Mendoza to Los Andes (Chile) is easy; go to the service station in Godoy Cruz suburb (also bus No 6), from where all trucks to Chile, Peru and elsewhere leave.

Excursions If driving in mountains remember to advance the spark by adjusting the distributor, or weaken the mixture in the carburettor, to avoid the car seizing up in the rarified air. Ask in agencies about river rafting, popular and fun. TAC and Uspallata buses run to the hot springs at *Cacheuta*, US$3.15 round trip, US$8 entry (indoor thermal baths for a variety of ailments, for residents only), 45 km to the SW (**L** *Hotel Termas*, T 259000/230422, full board; other hotels not rec, campsite). About 50 km N of Mendoza are the hot springs at Villavicencio, visited by many tourists. Pleasant walks in the area. The charming resort of *Potrerillos* is 13 km from Cacheuta, with ski slopes not far away and excellent birdwatching in summer. **A1** *Gran Hotel*, T 233000, with meals; ACA campsite. *Restaurant Armando* rec. In summer, you can hike 20 km from Potrerillos to Vallecito, a closed ski resort, taking two days. On the first you will see desert scenery, blooming cactus flowers, birds and an occasional goat or cow. The second you walk surrounded by peaks, a steep but not difficult climb to the San Antonio refuge, usually open with beds and meals. Two other popular resorts within a few km of the Mendoza are Barballón, to the NE, and Challao, to the NW. The small ski resort of Los Penitentes, 170 km away, can be reached by bus, 4 hrs (**see p 135**), equipment hire US$5 a day, lift ticket for a day US$9. The best skiing is at (2,250m) Valle de las Leñas, S of San Rafael in the Valle Hermoso (**see p 128**). Excursions also to the dam at El Nihuil, with artificial lake, and to the Río Atuel canyon, superb rock scenery (although the 16 hour round trip from Mendoza can be uncomfortable in hot weather, better to visit the canyon from San Rafael). On the road to Luján de Cuyo (buses go every 15 mins from near bus terminal) is an excellent fine arts museum dedicated to Argentine artists, surrounded by sculpture in gardens, admission US$1.50, open Tues-Fri 0930-1330, 1500-1900, Sat, Sun 1630-2030 (Museo Provincial de Bellas Artes Emiliano Guiñazu, **Casa de Fader**), worth visiting.

NB It is no longer possible to go from Mendoza to Santiago via the statue of El Cristo Redentor (Christ the Redeemer) at 3,854m. All buses and cars go through the tunnel to Chile, leaving the statue unseen above. To see the statue you must go on a 12 hr excursion from Mendoza (weekends early am, all travel agencies, highly rec) since the Chilean side of the frontier at the statue is closed. The excursion also includes Puente del Inca (see below).

Over the Andes to Chile

The route to Chile is sometimes blocked by snow in winter: if travelling by car in Jun-Sep enquire about road conditions from ACA in Mendoza (San Martín y Amigorena).

NB No visas into Chile are available at the border, so if you need one and haven't got it, you will be turned back. Tourist cards are given out on international buses.

There are 2 alternates of Route 7, which meet at **Uspallata**, the only settlement of any size between Mendoza and the Chilean frontier. The fully-paved S branch, via Cacheuta and Potrerillos, is wider and better than the N branch, which goes via Villavicencio with a stretch of one-way traffic just beyond the resort, where the road leads up spectacularly to the 3,050m high Cruz del Paramillo. This N branch is still unpaved. Near Uspallata are the ruins of Las Bóvedas, built by the Huarpe Indians under the Jesuits, and an Inca *tambería*; there is a small, interesting museum. They are just off the road which leads to Barreal and Calingasta (**see p 140**), unpaved for its first part and tricky when the snow melts and floods it in summer.

Hotels A2 *Valle Andino*, Ruta 7, T (0624) 20033, good rooms and restaurant, heating, pool, incl breakfast, ACA discount; **B** *Hotel Uspallata*, T 20003, dinner at 2100; payment for meals and drinks in cash, bowling alley, nice location, but hotel run down, service friendly, but vast herds of people get driven through it. **D** *Hostería Los Cóndores*, T 20002, clean, friendly.

Camping There is a run down ACA site at Uspallata, US$3 per head, full washing facilities, hot water.

The crossing of the Andes taken by San Martín is the old mountain trail the Spaniards named the Camino de los Andes. Beyond Uspallata is a vast, open, undulating plain, wild and bare. On all sides stand the grey, gaunt mountains. On the far side of this plain the valley narrows till Río Blanco is reached, and there the mountain torrents rush and froth into the river. At Punta de Vacas, look left up the Tupungato Valley at the majestic cone of **Tupungato**, one of the giants of the Andes, rising 6,550m. An equally majestic mass of pinnacled rocks, Los Penitentes, is passed on the left; they are about 7 km away. The climber to their base (an easy task from Puente del Inca with a guide) sees a remarkable sight. The higher rocks look like a church and the smaller, sharper rocks below give the impression of a number of cowled monks climbing upwards. Walking tours in the Tupungato area can be arranged by Quinche Romulo, Alte Brown, Tupungato, T 0622-88029.

Puente del Inca, 2,718m above sea level, 72 km W of Uspallata, is a sports resort set among mountains of great grandeur. Good views of Aconcagua can be had from above the village or by walking W along the old railway line. (**B-C** *Hostería Puente del Inca*, T 380480, less off-season, very pleasant atmosphere, but overpriced and poor service, more expensive if booked in Mendoza.) Camping possible next to the church, if your equipment can withstand the winds. 5 km from Puente del Inca on the road to Mendoza is a ski club, **E** *Cruz de Caña*, only open in season, friendly, with comfortable dormitories (**C** with 2 meals), and a good restaurant. The owner organizes trekking expeditions to Plaza de Mula; prices:

US$50 a day full board during expedition, and US$20 per mule.

The natural bridge after which Puente del Inca is named is one of the wonders of South America; it crosses the Río Mendoza at a height of 19m, has a span of 21m, and is 27m wide, and seems to have been formed by sulphur-bearing hot springs. Watch your footing on the steps; extremely slippery. There are hot thermal baths just under the bridge, a little dilapidated but a great place to soak. Puente del Inca is the best point for excursions into the higher Andean valleys or for a visit to the base of Aconcagua, which was first climbed by Zurbriggen of the Fitzgerald Expedition in 1897. Visits can be made on horseback from Puente del Inca to **Los Penitentes** (**A3-C** *Hotel Ayelén*, in middle of village, T 259990, price depends on room, clean, comfortable, pricey but the cheapest; **D** *La Taberna del Gringo*, Km 151, Villa Los Penitentes, rec, and others). Ski hire is US$35 a day; it may be cheaper to hire it in Mendoza. Lift pass is US$28 a day. Skiing is good with few people on slopes. A visit on foot to the green lake of Laguna de los Horcones is worthwhile (walk along road towards Chile, then after 1 km follow signs to mountain, excellent views of Aconcagua, especially am). Go by car (only with a well regulated engine) or bus or on horseback to the statue of El Cristo Redentor set above La Cumbre (or Uspallata) pass on the frontier at an altitude of 3,854m. It was erected jointly by Chile and Argentina in 1904 to celebrate King Edward VII's decision in the boundary dispute of 1902. It is, unfortunately, somewhat disappointing from the road, for it is completely dwarfed by the landscape. (The road from the tunnel to the statue is closed for the season after the first snowfall in Apr.)

Local bus (Expreso Uspallata) from Mendoza for Uspallata and Puente del Inca, US$8, 4 hrs, 0600 and 1000, returning from Puente del Inca 1200 and 1615; local buses also go on from Puente del Inca to Las Cuevas, Expreso Uspallata, US$12 return (**NB** take passport). Also note that buses from Mendoza through to Santiago de Chile do not stop here.

W of Puente del Inca, on the right, there is a good view of Aconcagua (6,959m), sharply silhouetted against the blue sky. In 1985, a complete Inca mummy was discovered at 5,300m on the mountain.

Best time for climbing **Aconcagua** (the highest peak in the Americas and a **national park**) is from end-Dec to Feb. For trekking or climbing it is first necessary to obtain a permit: 3-day trekking US$15, 5 days' trekking US$30. For climbing a 20-day permit is required. (Argentines US$40, foreigners US$80). Permits are sold only at Dirección de Recursos Naturales Renovables, address below. From Mendoza take a bus or colectivo to Puente del Inca. From here mules are available but cost US$25 per mule per day, with extra charges according to the weight of your pack (more economical to travel with a group); you have to pay for 3 days there and back (1 day rest) and for the muleteer and his wages (US$30 for more than 3 days). This only takes you to the base camp at Plaza de Mulas (4,200m), where there is now, nearby, the highest hotel in the world, *Refugio Plaza de Mulas* (see below), and a rescue patrol, crowded in summer. Also at 4,200m is Plaza de Francia, facing the south face, less crowded in summer. Plaza de Francia is about 25 km from Puente del Inca and can be reached in 2 stages via Confluencia (camping also available here, rec if pacing yourself). Of the huts above this height only La Libertad (Berlín) hut at about 6,000m is in serviceable condition. Both huts are small with no facilities. Take a tent able to withstand 100 mph + winds, and clothing and sleeping gear for temperatures below -20C. Allow at least one week for acclimatization at lower altitudes before attempting summit (4 days from Plaza de Mulas). Treks and climbs organized by Sr Fernando Grajales, the famous climber, in *Hostería Puente del Inca*, or at JF Moreno 898, 5500 Mendoza, Telex 55-154. Information also from Eduardo Enrique Esteban, Emilio Civit 320, Maipú, Mendoza, CP 5515, T/F (61) 973393 and Carlos and Amalia Cuesta, *Los Gateados*, nr Cementerio de los Andinistas, 1 km before Puente del Inca (Dec-Feb, or T Mendoza 391080/290410), rec for details on mules, trekking and climbing. Other guides can be found at the airport in Mendoza and further information from **Dirección de Recursos Naturales Renovables**, Parque Gral San Martín, Mendoza, T 252090 (see also under Mendoza: **Travel Agencies**).

Refugio Plaza de Mulas, US$140 pp full board, double rooms with bath, and dormitories for 10, US$30 pp without meals, good food, information, medical treatment, rec, also camping area. Altitude 4,370 m. In Mendoza you can book *refugio* reservations and programmes which incl trekking, climbing to the summit, with hotel accommodation or camping, prices from US$990 to US$1,890 for 10 days, T/F Mendoza 61-380383, Nueve de Julio 1126.

The Chilean frontier is beyond **Las Cuevas**, a neat, modern settlement being developed as a ski-ing resort (though there is no ski-lift as yet), but recently damaged by landslides and a fire. It is wise to take snow chains from Jun to Oct. Officially, driving without chains and a shovel is prohibited between Uspallata and the border, but this can be resolved in a friendly way with border police. Both ACA and Chilean Automobile Club sell, but do not rent, chains, but ask at YPF station in Uspallata about chain rental.

Hotel *Hostería Las Cuevas*, only one, poor food, no heating in annex. Food available at kiosk at Expreso Uspallata bus terminal point.

Beyond Las Cuevas, the road, completely paved, goes through the 4-km El Libertador-Las Cuevas toll road tunnel (US$2 for cars and VW buses). The old road over La Cumbre pass is now closed to through traffic; the famous statue of Christ

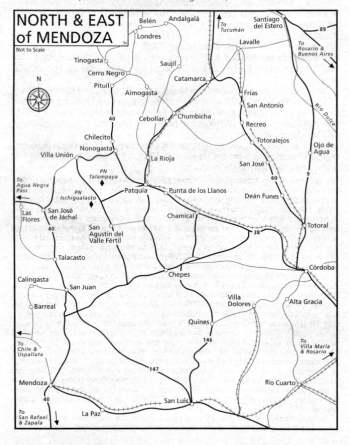

NORTH & EAST of MENDOZA

Not to Scale

can be visited only by excursion from Mendoza (see above).

Giuliano Sargenti of Quartino, Switzerland, recommends taking the 0600 bus from Mendoza to Las Cuevas (arrives 1030, or 1000 at Puente del Inca), walk 3 hrs to the Cristo Redentor, great views, then return to Las Cuevas in time for 1600 bus back to Puente del Inca or Mendoza.

Transport to Chile Turismo cars (Chi-Ar—some adverse reports—and Nevada) carrying up to 11 passengers (US$27, 5 hrs) and minibuses (5½-6 hrs) do the trip to **Santiago** daily. When booking, ensure that the car will pick you up and drop you at your hotel; have this written on your receipt, if not you will be dropped at the bus station. If travelling by bus from Mendoza to Santiago take a direct bus as it is not possible to walk across the border. Buses Mendoza to Santiago daily at 0600-1430; several companies, El Rápido, Tur Bus and TAC, rec; mixed reports on El Rápido and adverse reports on Chile Bus and Nevada Tours. Most buses are comfortable and fast (6½-8 hrs) and charge US$15-20, those with air-conditioning and hostess service (incl breakfast) charge more (US$25, TAC), worth it when crossing the border as waiting time can be a matter of several hours. Also 3 buses daily to Viña del Mar and 2 to Valparaíso, US$20-25. All companies in same part of Mendoza bus station: you can easily shop around. Children under 8 pay 60% of adult fare, but no seat; book at least one day ahead. If all seats booked try CATA, its service is reportedly less good than others thus it usually has some empty seats. Passport required, tourist cards given on bus. The ride is spectacular. Information at main bus station. If you want to return, buy an undated return ticket Santiago-Mendoza; it is cheaper. A taxi Mendoza-Santiago costs about US$90 for 4-5 people. For Chilean side, see Chile, **Santiago and the Heartland** (Section 3), To Buenos Aires across the Andes.

All Argentine entry and exit formalities are now dealt with at Punta de Vacas, 30 km E of Las Cuevas (entering Argentina by taxi, expect to be stopped and searched). A new customs post, Ingeniero Roque Carranza has been built near Laguna Los Horcones, nearer Las Cuevas. Car drivers can undertake all formalities in advance at Uspallata while refuelling. One can hitchhike, or possibly bargain with bus drivers for a seat, from Punta de Vacas to Santiago, but if one is dropped at the entrance to the tunnel in winter, one cannot walk through. Travellers report that customs men may help by asking motorists to take hitchhikers through to Chile. Chilean migration and customs check is W of the tunnel—searches for fruit, meat, vegetables, which may not be imported into Chile, in a new building with the bus parked inside. All luggage is X-rayed. Remove all camera film before boarding bus as hand-luggage isn't x-rayed. Customs at the frontier are closed 1200-1400. Members of ACA need only the *Libreta de Pasos por Aduana*, otherwise you need the *Documento de Exportación* to enter Chile. Good food at frontier hotel, and there is an excellent motel on the Chilean side about an hour down.

NORTH OF MENDOZA (5)

The oases of San Juan, La Rioja and Catamarca between the plains and the Andes. Interesting natural rock formations can be seen, especially Valle de la Luna and Puerta de Talampaya.

Of the three oases in the more arid zone N of Mendoza, San Juan is the most prosperous, wine and olives support La Rioja, but Catamarca is economically depressed. The first, 177 km from Mendoza by paved road, is

San Juan pop 122,000 at 650m, founded 1562 by Don Juan Jufré de Loaysa y Montese and capital of its namesake province. The city is proud of its sunny climate and clean, tree-lined streets. Nearly destroyed by a 1944 earthquake, the centre is well laid-out, with a modern cathedral. The birthplace of Domingo Sarmiento (President of the Republic, 1868-1874, also an important historian/educator) is a museum. The area is famous for its wine, "to be between San Juan and Mendoza" is an Argentine expression for having drunk too much. One of the country's largest wine producers, Bodegas Bragagnolo, on the outskirts of town at Route 40 y Av Benavídez, Chimbas, can be visited (bus 20 from terminal; guided tours daily 0830-1330, 1530-1930, not Sun). **Escuela de Fruticultura y Enología**, Sarmiento 196 (bus going W on Av San Martín), students show visitors round.

Museums Museo Casa de Sarmiento, Sarmiento y San Martín, open Tues-Sat 0830-1900;

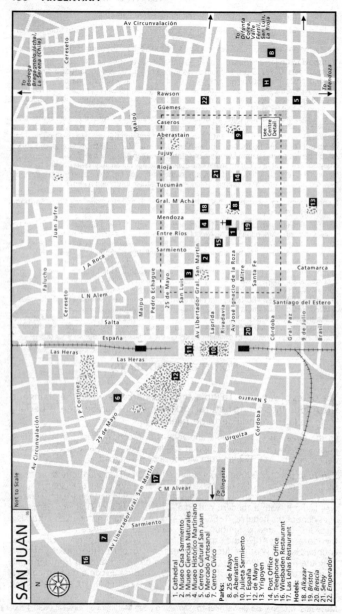

SAN JUAN

Not to Scale

Av Circunvalación

To Bodega Bragagnolo, Jáchal, La Serena (Chile)

Cereseto

Maipú

Juan Jufre

Falucho

J A Roca

L N Alem

Cereseto

Maipú

Pedro Echague

25 de Mayo

San Luis

Gral. Libertador San Martín

Laprida

Rivadavia

Av José Ignacio de la Roza

Mitre

Santa Fe

Córdoba

Gral. Paz

9 de Julio

Brasil

Rawson

Güemes

Caseros

Aberastain

Jujuy

Rioja

Tucumán

Gral. M Achá

Mendoza

Entre Ríos

Sarmiento

Salta

España

Las Heras

Las Heras

J P Cortinez

25 de Mayo

Av Circunvalación

Av Libertador Gral. San Martín

Sarmiento

C M Alvear

S Navarro

Córdoba

Urquiza

Catamarca

Santiago del Estero

To Difunta Correa, Valle Fertíl, San Luis, La Rioja

To Mendoza

To Calingasta

see Centre Detail

22 · **5** · **9** · **21** · **14** · **18** · **8** · **13** · **4** · **1** · **19** · **15** · **2** · **3** · **20** · **11** · **10** · **12** · **6** · **17** · **7** · **16** · **B** · **H**

1. Cathedral
2. Museo Casa Sarmiento
3. Museo Ciencias Naturales
4. Museo Histórico Martiniano
5. Centro Cultural San Juan
6. Mercado Artesanal
7. Centro Cívico

Parks:
8. 25 de Mayo
9. Aberastain
10. Julieta Sarmiento
11. España
12. de Mayo
13. Yrigoyen
14. Post Office
15. Telephone Office
16. Wiesbaden Restaurant
17. Las Leñas Restaurant

Hotels:
18. Alkazar
19. Bristol
20. Brescia
21. Selby
22. Emperador

SAN JUAN Centre

1. Cathedral
2. Museo Casa Sarmiento
3. Museo Ciencias Naturales
4. Museo Histórico Martiniano
5. Mercado Central
6. Teatro Sarmiento
7. Palacio Municipal
8. Parque 25 de Mayo
9. Parque Aberastain
10. Parque J M Paz
11. Parque Laprida
12. Tourist Office
13. Post Office
14. Telephone Office
15. Bolsa de Comercio
16. Cambio Cash
17. Cambio Santiago
18. Agencia Yafar
19. Agencia Agüero
20. Aerolíneas Argentinas
21. Sirio Libanés Restaurant
22. Soychú Restaurant
23. Club Español

Hotels:
24. *Alkazar*
25. *Nogaró*
26. *Bristol*
27. *Jardín Petit*
28. *Plaza*
29. *Selby*
30. *Lara*

Museo de Ciencias Naturales, Av San Martín y Catamarca, incl fossils from Ischigualasto Provincial Park (see below), open Mon-Sat, 0830-1230, 1630-2030, Sat 0900-1200, US$0.50; **Museo Histórico Sanmartiniano**, Laprida 96 Este, incl the restored cloisters and two cells of the Convent of Santo Domingo. San Martín slept in one of these cells on his way to lead the crossing of the Andes, closed Sun, US$0.40.

Hotels A1 *Alkazar*, Laprida 82 Este, T 214965, F 214977, incl breakfast, garage, new, good; **A2** *Hotel Nogaró*, de la Roza 132 Este, T 227501/5, pool, a/c, central, TV, in need of maintenance (1994), car park US$4 (ACA and US AAA discounts); **B** *Bristol*, Entre Rios 368 Sur, T 222629, a/c, hot water, clean, rec; **B** *Central*, Mitre 131 Este, T 223174, very clean and quiet, good beds, friendly owner; **B** *Jardín Petit*, 25 de Mayo 345 Este (ACA discount with cash), T 211825, hot water, pricey, parking lot next door US$5; **C** *Brescia*, España 336 Sur, near train station, T 225708; **C** *Plaza* Sarmiento 344 Sur, T 225179, friendly, noisy disco behind; **C** *Selby*, Rioja 183 Sur, T 224777. **B** *Embajador*, Rawson 25 Sur, T 225520, large rooms, clean, pleasant, café, good value; **C** *Residencial Hispano Americano*, Estados Unidos 381 Sur, T 221477, poor. Better cheaper hotels: **D** *Jessy-Mar*, Sarmiento 8 Norte, T 227195, small rooms, noisy; **D** *Residencial 12 de Diciembre*, Sarmiento 272 Norte, clean; **D** *Lara*, Sarmiento y Rivadavia, basic but clean, good value, rec. Several residenciales (**C**) along Av España, blocks 100-600 Sur.

Camping At Chimbas, 7 km N; 3 sites at Rivadavia, 8 km W.

Restaurants *Wiesbaden*, Circunvalación y San Martín, German-style, pleasant setting; *Soychú*, de la Roza 223 Oeste, excellent vegetarian food; *Club Sirio Libanés "El Polito"*, Entre Rios 33 Sur, pleasant decor, good food; *El Castillo de Oro*, de la Roza 199 Oeste, central, reasonable; *Comedor Central*, de la Roza 171 Este, not luxurious but good *locro* (stew) and *chivito* (goat). *Parrilla Bigotes*, Las Heras e Ignacio de la Roza, inexpensive "all you can eat" meat, chicken, salads. *Club Español*, Plaza 25 de Mayo, more expensive, large portions of mediocre food. Many *pizzerías*, *confiterías*, and sidewalk cafés, incl *Café Amadeus* and *Café del Aguila*. *Lomoteca San José*, San Martín 179, grills, inexpensive, late night music at weekends; *El Clavel de Oro*, Santa Fe y Entre Ríos, snacks, drinks; *Marilyn Bar*, San Martín y Mendoza, late night drinks. Eat under thatched shelters (*quinchos*) at *Las Leñas*, San Martín, 1600 Oeste.

Banks and Exchange Good rates at **Cambio Santiago**, Gral Acha 52, weekdays until 2000, Sat am. **Cambio Cash**, Tucumán 210 Sur; **Montemar**, Laprida 133 Sur; **Multicrédito**, Laprida y Mendoza; **Bolsa de Comercio**, Gral Acha 278 Sur.

Centro Cultural San Juan, Gral Paz 737 Este, concerts and other events.

Laundry *Marva*, San Luis y Av Rioja.

Shopping Mercado Artesanal at Av España y San Luis worth a visit.

Bicycle Repairs Ruedas Armado, San Martín y La Rioja, helpful.

Travel Agents *Yafar Turismo*, Caseros y Laprida, T 214476 (no tours); *Mario Agüero Turismo*, Gral Acha 17 Norte, T 220864, tours to Ischiqualasto subject to demand, US$50 pp plus US$3 National Park entry fee. *Dante Montes*, Santa Fe 56 Este. *Almen Tours*, San Martín 149 Este, T 211006. For mountain climbing contact Pablo Schlögl, 543 Haité Este, T 225132, rec as probably the most experienced mountaineer in Argentina.

Tourist Office, Sarmiento y San Martín, helpful, good brochures, open Mon-Sat, 0900-1330, 1430-2100, Sun 0900-1300; also at bus terminal. Arranges tours in summer only. Large-scale provincial maps available at bookshops. For information on Difunta Correa, consult Fundación Vallecito at Caucete. **ACA**, 9 de Julio 802 Este, useful information on routes, helpful. The **Diario de Cuyo** published a *Guía de Turismo* for San Juan province in Oct 1993 (similar to Chile's *Turistel* guides), very informative.

Car Hire **Parque Automotor**, España y San Martín, T 226018. Cash discount on request. Localiza, España 274 (Sur), T 229243.

Air Chacritas Airport, 14 km SE. From Buenos Aires with AR daily; AR once a week from Mendoza (Sun, 0855). Ladeco from Santiago 3 times a week; Mon, Wed, Sat Ladeco flies to/from La Serena, summer only (Dec-Feb).

Buses Terminal at Estados Unidos y Santa Fe, 9 blocks E of centre (buses 33 and 35 go through the centre). Long distance services to **La Rioja** (550 km, 9 hours, US$19), or go via Chepes, 0900 daily US$6, with connecting service from Chepes, Mon, Wed, Sun at 1600, 4 hrs, US$10, **Catamarca** (660 km over secondary roads, US$17, with connection to Salta, US$29), **Tucumán** (3 a day, 13 hrs, Libertador is cheapest), Córdoba, Santa Fe, Mar del Plata, Bahía Blanca and BsAs (Autotransporte San Juan, US$47). To **San Agustín** at 1800, US$11. Fifteen departures daily to and from **Mendoza** with TAC and El Cumbre, 2 hrs, US$11, try to sit in the shade (on W side in am, E in pm). Also service to provincial tourist destinations.

To Chile: only connection with **Santiago (Chile)** is via Mendoza; catch the TAC bus at 0600, arrives in Mendoza 0830 in time for bus to Santiago.

The Agua Negra pass (4,600m) has been reopened after having been closed in 1978. Cars can now cross the Andes over this spectacular high point, but it is only open Jan to early Apr; in winter it is closed by snow, in summer it may be closed by rain. No buses take this route. ACA, customs and immigration at Las Flores (see below) informs all the ACA stations in the country of road conditions. It takes approx 6 hrs from Las Flores in Argentina to Rivadavia in Chile (where the first service station can be found).

From San Juan Hitchhiking to La Rioja, take route 141 to Chepes (ACA *Hostería*), then N to Patquia; more traffic on provincial route 29, a well paved, but less interesting road than that via San Agustín or Jachal (see below).

Excursions To the Museo Arqueológico of the University of San Juan at La Laja, 20 km N, open Mon-Fri, 0900-1900, Sat, Sun, 1000-1300, US$2, which contains an outstanding collection of prehispanic indigenous artefacts, incl several well-preserved mummies. Inexpensive thermal baths nearby. Bus No 20 from San Juan, 2 a day, but you need to take the first (at 0830) to give time to return. To **Vallecito**, 64 km E, to the famous shrine to the **Difunta Correa**, an unofficial saint whose infant (according to legend) survived at her breast even after the mother's death from thirst in the desert. During Holy Week, up to 100,000 pilgrims visit the site, some crawling 100m on their knees. See the remarkable collection of personal items left in tribute, incl number plates from all over the world and even one policeman's detective school diploma! (*Residencial Difunta Correa*).

Along scenic provincial route 12 (open westbound mornings, eastbound afternoons), 135 km W of San Juan, lies **Calingasta**, in the valley of same name (annual cider festival in Apr). (**Hotels**: **C** *Calingasta*, T 22014, remodelled, swimming pool, full board available; **D** *La Capilla*, T 21033, incl breakfast, basic but very clean, family run and friendly, the family also sells the TAC bus tickets, and has the only public telephone in the village.) 40 km S on the road to Uspallata is **Barreal** (*Hotel Barreal*, T 0648-41000, good, also good value in restaurant;

Cabañas Doña Pipa, see below; also **E** *Hotel Jorge*, clean, very simple. *Posada San Eduardo*, small, quaint, few rooms with bath, open summer only; accommodation with Sr Patricio Sosa or Sr Cortez. *Restaurant Isidoro*, owned by local baker and sandyacht champion, reasonable, ask waiter for the day's recommendation; food also available at *Mama Rosa*). Tours of observatory at El Leoncito (at 2,348m), 26 km from Barreal (no public transport) can be arranged from San Juan. Bus El Triunfo San Juan-Barreal daily 0700, plus Mon, Wed, Fri, Sun at 2030 (return Mon, Wed, Fri, Sun 1330, 1600, Tues, Thur 1400, Sat 1600), 5 hrs, US$11. *Remise* service San Juan-Barreal, US$16 pp, T 211729, at Mendoza 416 Norte, San Juan, T 41023, Sr Pachá, *Restaurante Isidoro*, Barreal; leaves San Juan 0900, or 1000, leaves Barreal 1430. Omnibus Vitar from Mendoza (Las Heras 494, T 232876) Thur and Sat via Uspallata, continuing to Tamberías and Calingasta (return Fri and Sun); fare Barreal-Calingasta US$7. The road Uspallata-Barreal is bad (like a washboard on the gravel section in Mendoza province, broken pavement in San Juan province). Rafting trips can be arranged in Barreal, contact Sr Eduardo Conterno.

Sr Ramón Luis Ossa, physical education teacher at Barreal's high school, runs mule treks into the Andes, crossing the foothills in summer, from 10 to 21 days between Nov and April; he can be reached at *Cabañas Doña Pipa*, Mariano Moreno s/n, 5405 Barreal, Pcia San Juan, T (0648) 41004. The *cabañas* sleep 5, with bath, kitchen, sitting room, comfortable. We are grateful to Herbert Levi for a detailed account of Sr Ossa's treks (not printed for lack of space). In addition to the organizer's list of essentials, Sr Levi recommends the following on any Andean trip: metal drinking mugs, metal containers to prevent tubes of toothpaste etc emptying themselves in mule packs, long underpants to protect against chafing, woollen cap, insect repellent, sunburn cream, laxatives, soap, nylon groundsheet for sleeping bag (depending on weather), portable tent for privacy, and fishing gear for those who prefer catching their own meals (No 3 spoons best for Andean streams--permit required).

Climbing *Mercedario* (also El Ligua), 6,770m. No authorization is required, but it is advisable to inform the Gendarmería Nacional at Barreal. From Barreal go to Casas Amarillas on the Río Blanco, about 100 km on a gravel road. It may be possible to hire a Unimog 4 x 4 from the Gendarmería Nacional; guides (*baqueanos*) may also be hired, they can provide mules if necessary. The best time is mid-Dec to end-Feb; the types of terrain encountered are gravel, snow and rock. There is no rescue service. Nearby peaks incl Pico Polaco (6,050m), La Mesa (6,200m), Alma Negra (6,120m) and Ramada (6,410m). More information is available from Club Andino Mercedario, 9 de Julio 547 Este, 5400 San Juan, or Antonio Beorchia Nigris, director, Ciadam (Research Centre for Andean Archaeology), República del Líbano 2621, 5423 San Juan. **NB** Do not enter this region from Chile, it is illegal.

Route 40, the principal tourist route on the E Andean slope, heads N toward Cafayate and Salta, via San José de Jáchal. At Talacasto, 55 km from San Juan, route 436 branches toward Las Flores (Km 180) and the Chilean border at Agua Negra pass (4,600m—see under **Buses** above). Alternatively Route 141 runs directly N from Calingasta to Las Flores, a dirt road via Villa Nueva and Tocota, reported scenic but lonely.

At **Pismanta**, 5 km N of Las Flores, the **C** *Hotel Termas de Pismanta*, T 227501, has rooms for 120 guests, thermal baths between 38° and 44°C, a large swimming pool, medical attention, bowling, bingo occasionally, covered parking, well-maintained. Reservations in Buenos Aires (Maipú 331) and San Juan (San Martin y Sarmiento). From San Juan, two buses daily with TAC, four weekly with Empresa Iglesia, also from Mendoza. 22 km further N, in Rodeo, Ing Meglioli raises guanaco and vicuña, and sells local produce and crafts. From here, a scenic road, with several tunnels, follows the Río Jáchal 61 km E to **San José de Jáchal**, a wine and olive-growing center (pop 15,000), with many adobe buildings. Expreso Argentino bus from San Juan at 0730 arrives at 0940.

Services D *Plaza*, San Juan 545, T 20256; *San Martín*, Juan de Echegaray 387, T 20431; *El Chato Flores* restaurant, good. Camping.

From Jáchal, route 491 offers a scenic alternative to Villa Unión (see below), but buses now take new route 40 via Huaco. The undulating road, paved to the La Rioja border, crosses dozens of dry watercourses.

East of San Juan, one can make a loop via San Agustín del Valle Fértil and Villa Unión (La Rioja province). Turn off route 141 at Marayes (133 km), from which paved route 510 (poor) goes N 114 km to **San Agustín del Valle Fértil**. Pensiones

(*Andacollo*, *Los Olivos*; ask at bus station for family *Hospedaje Romero*, D) and private houses also provide lodging. There is a municipal swimming pool, and a lake with fishing. Tourist information on the plaza. Local weavers offer ponchos and blankets. Bus from San Juan US$9; San Juan-La Rioja bus stops in San Agustín about midnight, leaves at 0300, 4 hrs, US$9.50.

North of San Agustín, at a police checkpoint, 56 km by paved road, a side road goes NW for 17 km to the 62,000-ha *Ischigualasto* Provincial Park, also known as *Valle de la Luna* for its exotic desert landforms, entrance US$5. Here the skeletons of the oldest known dinosaurs have been found (230 million years). All private vehicles must be accompanied by rangers whose knowledge and interest vary greatly; fee US$2 pp. The circular tour, on an unpaved road, lasts 2-3 hours. Local bus from San Juan Mon and Fri to police checkpoint and on Sat afternoon, if demand is sufficient. Tours from San Juan, US$50 (not incl lunch); from San Agustín US$18 for a guide, ask at tourist office on plaza. Rec guide is Barros Lito, US$40 for full day tour of Valle and Talampaya in private car. Taxi to park US$55 (rec if there are 4-5 people).

Just beyond the police checkpoint, near Los Baldecitos, paved route 150 heads E to Patquia and then to La Rioja or Chilecito, while provincial route 26 heads N. 58 km N of the junction a paved road goes E to *Puerta de Talampaya* Provincial Park (open 0800-1630, entrance US$3), another collection of spectacular desert landforms (*Refugio* near the entrance, sleeping bag essential). Tours follow the dry bed of the Río Talampaya in four-wheel drive vehicles operated by park rangers (US$35 for 2-hr tour for 4-8 people, longer tours US$70 and US$110, rec). Herbert Levi writes "There are 6,000 year old petroglyphs with pictures depicting animals. The whole area is said to have been covered with water long ago; now there are two visible strata, the *tarjado* and the *talampaya*. After that one enters a canyon with "balconies", sheer overhanging walls. Coming out of the canyon there are rocks shaped like a cathedral, a bird, a castle, a chessboard, a monk, and three kings on a camel". Better to visit park in the morning and avoid strong winds in the afternoon. Tours, arranged through Dirección Provincial de Turismo in La Rioja, or Sr Furlin, park director, in Pagancillo, who can also arrange accommodation in the village (eg with Familia Flores, D pp, incl breakfast and dinner). Chilecito-San Juan buses pass Talampaya, drop off at Km 144. Patquia-Villa Unión buses pass Pagancillo.

From the park junction route 26 continues to *Villa Unión* (C *Hostería Provincial*, Dávila 61, T 7271, simple, rec; E *Hospedaje Paola*, main street opp police station, basic; next door is E *Hospedaje Changuito*, restaurant). Bus station behind plaza. Jeep excursions can be made to Ischigualasto and Talampaya, Laguna Verde and Laguna Veladero. The remains of a huge volcano crater, La Caldera del Inca, can also be visited from here. It spans 40 km across, between the peaks Pissis (6,882m) and Bonete (6,872m). The bottom of the crater is desert-like but with glaciers beneath the sand in parts, and with a lake frequented by flamingos and other birds. A fascinating area, but hard to reach. Ask for Werner Lorenz in the town for directions, or for organizing an expedition. The tourist office in Chilecito (below) may be able to help, or, in the same town, Jorge Llanos hires out vehicles.

From Villa Unión, partly paved route 40 crosses the Cuesta de Miranda, dropping through a deep narrow canyon in a series of hairpins. This beautiful canyon is not rec to drive through after rains, deep river crossings, even in 4WD. Ask about road conditions at the ACA service station in Villa Unión, or at the police checkpoint there. After 92 km, it intersects the paved Patquia-Chilecito road.

18 km N of the junction is *Chilecito*, La Rioja province's second town, pop 20,000. Founded in 1715, it has good views of Sierra de Famatina, especially from the top of El Portezuelo, an easy climb from the end of Calle El Maestro. At Los Sarmientos, 2 km N of town, is the Santa Clara church, dating from 1764. The region is famous for its wines, olives and walnuts.

Museums Samay Huasi, 3 km S of town, the house of Joaquín V González, founder of La Plata University, open 0800-1200 and 1500-1800, contains the Museo de Ciencias Naturales, Mineralogía y Arqueología, pleasant gardens, and good views of Chilecito, the Famatina ridge and connecting valley. Molino San Francisco y Museo de Chilecito, at J de Ocampo 63, has archaeological, historical and artistic exhibits, open Mon-Fri 0800-1300, 1400-1900.

Hotels B *ACA Chilecito*, Dr L Martínez y 8 de Julio, T 2201/2, good, clean, friendly, no credit cards, safe parking, pool, good restaurant; **C** *Riviera*, Castro Barros 133, rec, clean, hot showers; **D** *Belsavac*, 9 de Julio y Dávila, T 8277, good but paperthin walls; **D** *Wamatinag*,

Galeria Victoria, W side of Plaza Sarmiento, clean, pleasant, best value in town; **D** *Americano*, Libertad 68, T 8104, unfriendly; **D** *Bellia*, El Maestro y Libertad. The Tourist Office has a list of families offering accommodation, but not for singles.

Camping at Santa Florentina, 6 km NW of Chilecito and Las Talas, 2 km beyond.

Restaurants *El Gallo*, Perón e Illia, excellent; on Plaza Sarmiento are: *Chaplin*, best in town; *Robert Snak Bar*, light meals and drinks; *Vanesa*, good home-made ice-cream; *Toscanini*, Fátima y San Martín, good Italian food, inexpensive; *Ferrito*, Av Luna 661, pricey.

Tourist Office Libertad e Independencia, T 2688, very helpful.

Transport Líneas Aéreas Riojanas fly **La Rioja**-Chilecito, 20 min. Buses: to **San Juan**, Tues, Thur, Sat at 2200, arr 0705; to **Tinogasta** (Catamarca), Mon-Fri, direct at 0700 via route 11, returning same day at 0600; to Tinogasta Mon and Thur 0600, returning 1330 the same days; to **La Rioja**, 3 times daily with Cotil, to **Villa Unión** daily at 1345 with Cotil. Connections with **Catamarca** and **Córdoba** via La Rioja only.

Excursions La Mejicana mine via Santa Florentina road: a cable car system (built 1903) which brought ore 39 km to the railhead at Chilecito is now out of use, although it runs on some weekends between stations 1 and 3. For treks, and trips to see gold washers at Famatina or to Talampaya, ask for Carlos de Caro, or enquire at tourist office. To Famatina, a sleepy hamlet amid nut plantations, *hostería*, restaurants.

With construction of an excellent new road, route 40 now goes via Salicas, since the Cuesta de Zapata, N of Tinogasta, was closed after 1981 floods. 21 km N of Chilecito, the old road (now route 11) goes via Famatina to **Tinogasta**, a half-Indian former-copper mining town in an oasis of vineyards, olive groves, and poplars (pop 9,000).

Hotels B *Provincial de Turismo*, Romero y Gordillo, T 23911, clean but run down, restaurant; *Hostería Novel*, near airport.

Restaurants *Persegani*, Tristán Villafañe 373; *Rancho Huairapuca*, on Moreno.

Transport Buses: to **Tucumán**, Empresa Gutiérrez, Tues, Fri, Sun 1700, Mon, Tues, Fri, Sun 0615, Fri 0845, US$22; return Tues, Fri, Sun. To **Catamarca** 1700 and 0030 daily; to **La Rioja** 0930, El Cóndor, US$11. Services to **Chubut**, **Comodoro Rivadavia**, and **Caleta Olivia**, with Empresa Ortiz, reflect that this is the source region for labour in the Patagonian oilfields. To **Puerto Madryn** and **Comodoro Rivadavia**, Empresa Robledo, Tues and Fri at 1600. To **Copiapó**, Chile, in summer, an excursion bus crosses the San Francisco pass, Adbeca, T (0836) 30725, 3 day tour, US$220. For air services, see under Catamarca.

Mountaineering Tinogasta is the starting point for expeditions to the second highest mountain in South America. Most recent cartography has allowed for some corrections in altitude so that *Pissis* has been confirmed, at 6,882m, as higher than Ojos del Salado (6,879m). To get there take Route 60 which crosses Tinogasta in the direction of the San Francisco pass. Everyone has to register at the police station outside Fiambalá, take passport. Expeditions organized and horse riding with Omar Monuey, La Espiga de Oro, 25 de Mayo 436.

Fiambalá is 49 km N of Tinogasta. **C** *Hotel* with restaurant, and small, basic *pensión* (unsigned – ask), near which is a good restaurant. There is also a clean *hostería*. Drive or take a taxi from here to *aguaditas*, hot springs, US$1 entry, temperatures from 30°C to 54°C (make sure taxi fare includes wait and return). The entire province is rich in thermal mineral waters. There are vineyards in the valley. Empresa Gutiérrez daily at 1345 to Catamarca via Tinogasta (1500) and Cerro Negro junction (1610), connect with Coop Catamarca bus to Belén (from Catamarca), about 2 hrs by bad road. Also 0530 departure from Fiambalá. 4WD vehicles may be hired for approaching the Pissis-Ojos region; ask at the Intendencia. For transport into the *puna* ask for Sr Jonson Hugo Reynoso (check state of vehicles). 36 km beyond Fiambalá is Palo Blanco, in the *pre-puna* foothills.

From Chilecito, new route 40 goes to Pituil, where the paved section ends, and on to Salicas and Cerro Negro junction (59 km) with route 60, the Tinogasta-Aimogasta road. Turning left at Cerro Negro for 2 km, paved route 40 heads N to **Londres**, founded in 1558 and the second-oldest town in Argentina, named in honour of the marriage of Mary Tudor and Philip II. The town hall displays a glass coat-of-arms of the City of London and a copy of the marriage proposal. 15 km further (paved) is **Belén**, pop 8,800 (**B** *Hotel Samai*, Urquiza 349, clean, friendly, rec; **D** *Hotel Turismo*, cheap and good, with bath; *Hotel Provincial*, dilapidated. Good breakfast at bus terminal; *Restaurant Dalesio*, near YPF gas station, excellent and cheap; *El Amigazo*, behind church, good). The whole district is famous for weavings, ponchos, saddlebags and rugs. There are good views from the new statue of Virgin of Belén at the summit of the path beginning at Calle General Roca, and an interesting archaeological museum, Condor Huasi. Folklore festivals Oct and Christmas. Belén is encircled by mountains, except to the SE; lush vegetation along Río Belén. N of Belén Route 40 runs another 176 km, largely unpaved, to Santa María at Tucumán provincial border (**see p 108**), and on to Cafayate (**p 115**).

Transport Belén-Villavil (thermal springs – open Jan-April), incl side trip to Corral Quemado and end of line at Barranca Larga, 19 km N of Villavil, Tues, Thur, Sun at 0800, returns from Villavil at 1830. (Villavil may have to be abandoned, under threat of seismic collapse.) Sit on right-hand side for best views of impressive canyon and Río Bolsón reservoir. Belén-Santa María Tues 1330, Fri and Sun 2020; return Tues and Thur 0930, Sun 1945. Belén-Salta via Hualfín (mineral hot springs), Santa María, Cafayate Thur 0600.

From Cerro Negro it is 38 km SE to Aimogasta (national olive festival in May) and another 30 km to turnoff to Termas Santa Teresita. 15 km E on route 60 a good new road branches N to Saujil (60 km) and *Andalgalá* (130 km, pop 7,800), a beautiful town renowned for strong alcoholic drinks (*Hostería Provincial*, often full; *Residencial Galileo*; 3 bus lines to Catamarca). The road parallels the Salar de Pipanaco on the W and Sierra de Ambato on the E. At Minas Capillitas, rhodochrosite, Argentina's unofficial national stone is quarried; it can be bought at shops around the plaza in Andalgalá. Beyond Andalgalá, there is no public transport on the difficult but beautiful road to Santa María over the Cuesta de Capillitas, although trucks go weekdays to the mines just beyond the pass.

An alternative route to Salta is along Route 53 (43 on some maps), which branches W off Route 40 at a point 52 km N of Belén and runs via Antofagasta de la Sierra and San Antonio de los Cobres (petrol available—**see p 117**). This route is almost impassable in passenger cars after heavy rains, and requires enough fuel for 600 km at high altitudes on unmaintained roads (fill up at Hualfín, 10 km past turnoff to Route 53). Also, the stretch beyond the right turn at Puerto de Corral Quemado is very difficult (37 km of fords), to be avoided in summer rainy season. At Km 87 is Cerro Compo (3,125m), magnificent descent; at Km 99 the road turns right to Laguna Blanca, where there is a small vicuña farm (don't go straight at the junction). *Antofagasta de la Sierra* (260 km) can be reached by colectivo from Belén on Fri about 1000, arriving 2200, returning Mon 0700, or by hiring a pickup or hitching, or by plane, inquire at Dirección de Aeronáutica, Aerodromo de Choya (10 km from San Fernando del Valle de Catamarca), T 24750, bus L22 from airfield to centre (**C** *Pensión Darío*, blue door just off main square; *Almacén F Rodríguez*, Belgrano y Catamarca, serves meals, incl breakfast). No petrol station, but fuel obtainable from *intendencia*. Together with El Peñón and Laguna Blanca in the *puna*, and Villavil and La Hoyada in the *pre-puna*, this is the main township of NW Catamarca. La Hoyada can be reached from Santa María in the NE via provincial Route 118. There are lunar landscapes, with salt lakes, around Antofagasta, and many peaks over 5,000m. Deposits of marble, onyx, sulphur, mica, salts, borates, and gold are present. Wildlife in the sparsely populated region incl vicuña, guanaco, vizcacha, flamingoes, foxes and ostriches. **NB** Petrol/gasoline is rarely available in this region; remember that in the *puna* fuel consumption of carburettor engines is almost double that in the lowlands.

La Rioja, founded 1592, 106,000 people, is capital of its province, which is home of Argentine president Carlos Menem (he comes from Anillaco). Some colonial buildings survive, despite a major earthquake in 1894. The Convent of San Francisco, 25 de Mayo/Bazán y Bustos, contains the Niño Alcalde, a remarkable image of the infant Jesus as well as the cell (*celda*) in which San Francisco Solano lived and the orange tree, now dead, which he planted in 1592. To visit the tree when the church is closed, ring the bell at 25 de Mayo 218 next door. A visit may also be made to Los Padrecitos, 7 km from town, where a stone temple protects the remains of the 16th century adobe building where San Francisco converted the Indians of the Yacampis valley. The Convent of Santo Domingo, Luna y Lamadrid, is the oldest surviving temple in Argentina, dating from 1623. The Casa González, a brick "folly" in the form of a castle, is at Rivadavia 950.

La Rioja is known as "City of the Orange Trees," but there are also many specimens of the contorted, thorn-studded *palo borracho* tree, whose ripened avocado-like pods release large brown seeds in a kapok-like substance. It is also a common ornamental in Buenos Aires.

Museums Museo Folklórico, P Luna 811, Tues-Fri, 0900-1200, 1600-2000, Sat, Sun, 0900-1200, US$1.50; Museo Arqueológico Inca Huasi, Alberdi 650, owned by the Franciscan Order, contains a huge collection of fine Diaguita Indian ceramics, open Tues-Fri, 0800-1200, 1500-1900, US$1. Museo Histórico de la Provincia, Dávila 87, opening hours variable. Museo Municipal de Bellas Artes, Copiapó 253, works by local, national, and foreign artists.

NB Avoid arriving on Sat night as most things are shut on Sun.

Hotels Accommodation can be difficult to find, particularly in the lower price ranges. **A2** *Plaza*, San Nicolás y 9 de Julio, T 25215, rec but street noisy; *International Sussex*, Ortiz de Ocampo 1551, T 25413; *King's*, Quiroga 1070, T 25272; *Libertador*, Buenos Aires 253, T 27474, good value. *Talampaya*, Perón 951, T 24010; *Hotel de Turismo*, Perón y Quiroga, T 25240, offstreet parking, no breakfast; all **B**. **C** *Imperial*, Moreno 345, T 22478, clean, helpful; **C** *Residencial Petit*, Lagos 427, basic, friendly; **D** *Savoy*, Roque A Luna 14, T 26894, excellent value, hot shower. **D** *Pensión 9 de Julio*, Copiapó y Vélez Sarsfield, rec. Best of the *residenciales* is **D** *Sumaj Kanki*, Castro Barros y Lagos; **D** *Residencial Florida*, 8 de Diciembre 524, clean, basic, cheap. At Anillaco, on Highway 75 between La Rioja and Aimogasta, there is an *ACA Hostería*, T (0827) 794064, **E**, mixed reports. Tourist Office keeps a list of private lodgings, such as Sra Vera, Dávila 343.

Camping at Balneario Los Sauces, 13 km W.

Restaurants *Café Corredor*, San Martín y Pelagio Luna, good, cheap; *La Cantina de Juan*, Yrigoyen 190, excellent food, inexpensive; *Il Gatto*, Plaza 25 de Mayo, good pastas and salads; *Club Atlético Riojano*, Santa Fe between 9 de Julio and Buenos Aires, no atmosphere but cheap; good open air *churrasquería* next to *Hotel de Turismo*; *La Casona*, Rivadavia 449, very good and reasonably priced, rec; *Taberna Don Carlos*, Rivadavia 459, good fish and service; *Comedor Sociedad Española*, 9 de Julio 233, excellent pastas, inexpensive; *La Pomme*, Rivadavia y San Martín, open-air terrace, popular meeting place.

Banks and Exchange US$ cash changed at Banco de Galicia, Plaza 25 de Mayo (no commission on Visa cash advance), and Banco de Crédito, San Nicolás 476. Cheques difficult to change—try Banco de la Provincia, Bazán y Bustos, commission 8%. Better to change plenty before arriving (see note on provincial bonds used as currency, p 222).

Laundry *Laverap*, Av Perón 944.

Post Office Av Perón 258. **Telecommunications**, Perón 764.

Travel Agent *Zu Tours*, runs tours of Talampaya and Valle de la Luna, rec.

Tourist Office at Perón y Urquiza, T 28834.

Transport **By air**: Aerolíneas (T 27355) daily except Sun, at 0630, from Bs As; Líneas Aéreas Riojanas to Catamarca (0800 and 1330 weekdays), Chilecito.
   Buses: Terminal 7 blocks S of the Cathedral at Artigas y España. To Buenos Aires with General Urquiza, US$47, combination Ablo, via Córdoba. To Mendoza (US$25) and San Juan (US$19), night service with La Estrella or Libertador, with Andesmar, 1000, 8 hrs. To travel to San Juan by day (good scenery), take 0715 Cotil bus to Chepes (new bus station and ACA motel), then Cotil again next day to San Juan at 0900 or 20 de Junio bus at 1000 for San Juan or 1230 to San Luis. To Tinogasta, 0620, 2200, daily, US$11. To Tucumán (US$15), with Bosio and La Estrella. To Salta, Andesmar, 2100, arr 0700, US$33, video, sandwich, juice, coffee free, rec. Also provincial services.

Excursions To Ischigualasto and Talampaya (via Nonogasta, Cuesta de Miranda and Villa Unión, by private car with guide), costs US$190 for up to 5 people plus entrance fees, departs 0900. To Samay Huasi (see Chilecito, p 142). Fishing at El Portezuelo dam (see below). Swimming and fishing at Los Sauces dam, 15 km W; beyond Los Sauces is Sanagasta, El Cóndor buses, 45 mins, times vary. Good views of La Rioja from Cerro de la Cruz (1,680m), 12 km W, now a centre for hang-gliding, where condors and falcons may be sighted. Two hours to thermal springs at Santa Teresita.

A paved road runs to the third oasis, **Catamarca** (San Fernando del Valle de Catamarca), population 89,000, capital of its province, at 490m on the Río del Valle, between two S slopes of the Sierra de Aconquija, about 240 km S of Tucumán. Cattle, fruit, grapes and cotton are the main agricultural products, but it is also renowned for hand-woven ponchos and fruit preserves (try Casa Valdés, Sarmiento 586). Pilgrimages to the church of the Virgen del Valle. Therapeutic mineral springs. There are traces of Indian civilizations, including extensive agricultural terraces (now mostly abandoned), throughout the province. The *Zonda*, a strong dry mountain wind equivalent to the European *Föhn* or North American chinook or Santa Ana, can cause dramatic temperature increases. In Jul, regional handicrafts are sold at Festival del Poncho, a *feria* with four nights of music, mostly folklore of the NW.

Museums Instituto Cultural Esquiú, Sarmiento 450, incl important archaeological section, open Mon-Fri 0700-1300, 1430-2000, Sat, Sun, am only; **Museo Folklórico**, underground (subsuelo), Paseo Gral Navarro.

Hotels B *Ancasti*, Sarmiento 520, T 25001/4, restaurant; **C** *Inti Huasi*, República 297, T 24664; **D** *Colonial*, República 802, T 23502, no food, rec, clean, welcoming, good value; **D** *Delgado*, San Martín 788, basic, friendly; **D** *Suma Huasi*, Sarmiento 547, avoid TV lounge and rooms above it; *Centro*, Rosas y 9 de Julio, basic; **E** *Las Cumbres*, Plaza 25 de Agosto. Many *residenciales* around Avenida Güemes. Discounts to ACA members at *Ancasti, Inti Huasi*, and *Suma Huasi*. Provincial tourist office has a list of families who rent rooms.

Restaurants *Sociedad Española*, Urquiza 703; *La Cabaña*, Tucumán 1115, has folk dancing. *La Tinaja*, Sarmiento 500 block, excellent, pricey, live music, warmly rec; *Pizzería Maryeli*, Esquiú 521, basic (but good *empanadas*). *Sociedad Italiana*, M Moreno (off Paseo Gral Navarro), pastas, inexpensive; *Comedor Unión Obrera*, Sarmiento 857, good value, speciality *cabrito*; *Parrilla de Adrián*, Av Güemes block 500, good *asado*; *Montmartre*, Paseo Gral Navarro, good food, reasonably priced; *Marco Polo Bar*, Rivadavia 916, drinks, snacks. Many cheap restaurants along Av Güemes, bars and cafés along Rivadavia (pedestrian street).

Banks and Exchange Banco de Catamarca, Plaza 25 de Mayo, changes US$ cash but not cheques. Banco de Galicia changes cheques, US$10 commission.

Post Office San Martín 753, slow, open 0800-1300, 1600-2000. **Telephones**, Rivadavia 758, open 0700-2400, daily.

Shopping Catamarca specialities from: *Cuesta del Portezuelo*, Sarmiento 575; *Maica Regionales*, next to Aerolíneas Argentinas; and *Suma Regionales*, Sarmiento y Esquiú. Mercado Artesanal, Urquiza 945, wide range of handicrafts, open 0700-1300, 1400-2000, reached by infrequent colectivo 23 from centre.

Tourist Office Urquiza y Mota Botella, open 0800-2000, helpful. In small surrounding towns, go to municipal offices for information and maps.

Air Cooperativa de Transportes Catamarca, less dependable than Aerolíneas Riojanas, twice weekly Tinogasta to Belén. Officially departs Tinogasta 0810, but one is told to appear at municipal building at 0815 to be at plane at 0830. Route is circular: Catamarca-Tinogasta-Belén-Andalgalá-Catamarca, in small Piper or Cessna. AR offices on Sarmiento, next to *Hotel Suma Huasi*, T 24450/24460.

Buses Good bus information at bus terminal. To **Tucumán**, 4-5 daily with Bosio, 4½ hrs, US$10, several other companies; road paved, in good condition except for rough stretch at provincial border (Cuesta del Totoral has steep gradients, hairpins, potholes). To **BsAs**, US$50, 2nd class at 2200, 1st class at 1900, daily. To **Belén** via Cerro Negro with Coop Catamarca, returns from Belén daily 1300 (**see p 143**). Also Belén-Catamarca via Andalgalá; Coop Catamarca via Saujil, Poman, Chumbicha, Tues, Thur 1000, Fri, Sun 1300, about 8 hrs. Catamarca-El Rodeo-Las Juntas daily at 1300, returns from Las Juntas 1700. Five buses daily to **Córdoba**. To **Santiago del Estero**, 1630, US$12. There are several buses daily to Mendoza.

To **Copiapó**, Chile: weekly tourist buses, leaving Tinogasta on Fri to cross the San Francisco Pass, 3 days all incl, US$220 pp, run by AdBeCa, Catamarca, T 0833-30725/0836-2991, Dec to Feb only. Tours from Catamarca run to Chile.

Excursion To Dique Las Pirquitas, 3 hrs with local bus 1A from bus station. Bus stops at *Hostería de Turismo* (with restaurant) at Villa Pirquitas, about 45 min walk. Five morning buses from 0700, last returns at 2200. Opening hours Mon-Fri 1000-1900, Sat, Sun and holidays 0830-1900.

A road runs NE to **Lavalle** (towards Santiago del Estero). This 116 km run over the **Cuesta El Portezuelo** (1,980m), is scenic, but steep and difficult (to be paved, 1995). No bus service over Portezuelo to Lavalle, but a service to Frías, E, and also in Santiago del Estero province—No 9 and not No 18 (which crosses the Totoral), run by Coop de Transportes de Catamarca. Leaves 0500 Tues, Thur, Fri and Sat, arrives at Frías 1000, returns 1400, arrives in Catamarca 1900. From Frías travel to Lavalle.

Catamarca-Frías via Totoral, No 18 Mon, Wed, Fri, Sat 0500, arrives 1030, return 1330, arrives Catamarca 1900. No 14 via El Alto, longer trip, arrives Frías 1045. Catamarca-Lavalle via Totoral, same No 18, leaves Tues, Thur, and Sun 1100, arrives Lavalle 1510.

THE CHACO (6)

A sprawling alluvial lowland, rising gradually toward the W, covered by palm savanna and sometimes impenetrable thorn scrub; the birdlife is abundant and interesting.

Between the NW highlands already described and the Río Paraná to the E lies the Argentine Chaco, comprising the entire provinces of Formosa and Chaco, parts of Salta, Santiago del Estero and Santa Fe, and a tiny corner of the province of Córdoba. Its S limit is the Río Dulce valley, which forms a segment of the border between Santiago del Estero and Córdoba provinces. South America's highest temperatures, exceeding 45°C, have been recorded here, but winters are mild, with an occasional touch of frost in the S. Rain falls mostly in summer, decreasing from E to W. Numerous Indian peoples, who call themselves Wichi, inhabit the Chaco, including the Toba, Mataco, Mocoví, Pilagá, and some immigrant Mapuches from the S.

Communications Before the recent advent of modern highways, the Belgrano railway provided the only all-weather routes. There are two main N/S lines from Buenos Aires: the international route to La Paz and the line through Rosario and Santa Fe to Resistencia. Regular passenger rail services across the Chaco, N/S and from Resistencia to Metán have been suspended; determined train buffs may still be able to wangle a passage on a freight. Buses and planes provide the main means of transport.

Route 16, the main road across the Chaco runs NW from Resistencia to connect with Route 9, N of Metán and Rosario de la Frontera and provides the quickest route between Paraguay and NW Argentina. It is mostly paved and passes through **Pampa del Infierno** to the Santiago del Estero border. In Santiago province the road is good to Los Tigres, then less good to the Salta border. From this border to **Macapillo**, it is straight, well-paved. After Macapillo you can turn left, just before a railway crossing onto a dust road to Corral Quemado. At the T junction turn right and follow a dust road in reasonable condition for 50 km (50-60 kmph possible) to rejoin Route 16 at El Tunal. Turn left; the asphalt is good for a while then deteriorates to Route 9. Alternatively, after Macapillo, continue on Route 16 to **Joaquín V González**, around which the road is appalling and difficult after rain, then to Ceibalito, El Tunal and on to Route 9. At González, sidewalk **Restaurant Santa Cecilia** is good value. At Ceibalito, 18 km beyond González, an excellent lateral detour leaves Route 16 to connect with provincial Route 5 (passing Parque Nacional Finca El Rey, **see p 109**) and major N/S national Route 9 (at Lumbreras). This is a shorter, quicker route to Salta than via Rosario de la Frontera, but be sure to fill your tank in González, since there is no more petrol until General Güemes.

There are service stations at Roque Sáenz Peña, Pampa del Infierno (ACA *Hostería*), Pampa de los Guanacos (good hot, clean and free showers at the YPF station, and good value set dinner at the *comedor* next door), **Taco Pozo** (basic *hospedaje* ½ block from ACA station) and **El Quebrachal** (gaucho festival in late Nov), but during frequent power cuts they cannot pump fuel. In general, Chaco roads are poor, but provincial Route 94 from **Avia Terai** to General Pinedo, which continues as national Route 89 to Quimilí and Santiago del Estero, has an excellent paved surface. At the Avia Terai junction, it is easy to follow this route mistakenly rather than continue on Route 16 across the Chaco.

Tannin and cotton are the traditional great industries of the Chaco, although acreage planted to sunflowers has increased dramatically in recent years, along with maize and sorghum. The iron-hard *quebracho* (axe-breaker) tree, which grows only in the Argentine and Paraguayan Chaco, is the purest known source of tannin. The industry is struggling against competition from synthetic tannin and the huge mimosa plantations in South Africa. The more accessible eastern forests have nearly disappeared; deforestation of all species is proceeding rapidly in the N and W of the province, which produces charcoal for a military steel foundry in Jujuy. Small roadside factories also produce custom furniture.

Roque Sáenz Peña (population 75,000), 160 km NW of Resistencia on Route 16, offers almost no shade for relief from the overpowering summer heat. Its zoo, populated mostly with animals native to the region, is one of the country's best.

Hotels A2 *Gualok*, San Martín 1198, T 20521, incl use of thermal baths (also available to non-residents for a small charge); **B** *Augustus*, Belgrano 483, T 20068, a/c; **C** *Orel*, San Martín 130; *Residencial Asturias*, Belgrano 402, fair; *Residencial Sáenz Peña*, Subpalmira 464, T 20320, near bus station, cheap, clean, friendly.

Buses To **Buenos Aires**, daily 2000, US$40 (from Buenos Aires also daily 2000), La Estrella and La Internacional alternate days; to **Santiago del Estero** and **Tucumán**, Empresa El Rayo daily; to **Resistencia** (connection for Salta 1700 daily), 2 hrs, US$4.

Central Sáenz Peña has buses at 1100, 1530 and 2000 to the village of *Castelli* (tap water is suspect due to drought), about 100 km N, which has a large Toba Indian community and an *artesanía* shop (**E** *Hotel Guc*, basic). On route 16, 23 km E of Sáenz Peña, is Quitilipi, a Toba community with a free municipal campsite.

Between Resistencia and Sáenz Peña is **Parque Nacional Chaco**, an ecological island which preserves some of the last remaining eastern Chaco forest and savanna, and which is a good place to see the region's abundant bird life. The friendly park keeper will take you on a 1-2 hr walk, explaining about plants, animals and the region, rec. There are good free camping facilities, with cold showers, but the nearest supplies are in Capitán Solari, 6 km from the park entrance. From Resistencia, several buses go daily to Capitán Solari, but there is no public transport direct to the park. The rest of the Chaco is mostly cattle country, consisting of large estancias with low stocking rates.

Towns of the Chaco The most important ones—Resistencia and Formosa—are on the W bank of the Paraná and Paraguay and will be described, for convenience's sake, under Argentine Mesopotamia. Apart from Roque Sáenz Peña, the only other town of any importance is Santiago del Estero, on the W boundary of the Chaco.

Federico Kirbus tells us that on the border of Chaco and Santiago del Estero provinces is *Campo del Cielo*, a meteorite impact field about 15 km by 4 km where about 5,000 years ago a planetoid broke before landing into 30 main pieces. Some of the meteorites are on display in Buenos Aires (the Rivadavia Museum and the Planetarium), but the largest, "El Chaco" (33.4 tonnes), is on display at the Campo. Access from Route 89 (between Resistencia and Santiago del Estero) at Gancedo, where you travel 15 km S to Las Víboras (many buses).

MESOPOTAMIA (7)

This section begins at the Río de la Plata and ends at the magnificent Iguazú Falls on the Brazilian border. Two routes are followed, the Ríos Uruguay and Paraná, describing the river towns and beaches, and the Jesuit missions near Posadas (in particular San Ignacio Miní). Crossings to Uruguay and Paraguay are also given.

Between the Ríos Uruguay and Paraná lies Argentine Mesopotamia: the provinces of Entre Ríos, Corrientes, and Misiones. The distance between the rivers is 390 km in N Corrientes, but narrows to about 210 km in the latitude of Santa Fe. Mesopotamia was first colonized by Spaniards pushing S from Asunción to reoccupy Buenos Aires; Santa Fe was founded in 1573, Corrientes in 1588. From about 1880 there were Jewish agricultural settlements in Entre Ríos, promoted by Baron Hirsch for victims of pogroms in the Czarist empire (see "Los gauchos judíos" by Alberto Gerchunoff). Vestiges of these settlements remain at Domínguez (museum) and Basavilbaso, and across the river in Moiseville (Santa Fe).

Much of Entre Ríos and Corrientes is still pastoral, a land of large *estancias* raising cattle and sheep. Maize (a gamble in the N) is largely grown in southern Entre Ríos, which is also the most important producer of linseed, citrus fruit and poultry in Argentina. In Corrientes, along the banks of the Paraná between the cities of Corrientes and Posadas, rice and oranges are grown.

The province of Corrientes, in the N, is marshy and deeply-wooded, with low grass-covered hills rising from the marshes. The normal rainfall is about 2,000 mm, but the rains are not spread uniformly and drain off quickly through the sandy soil. Entre Ríos, to the S, has plains of rich pasture land not unlike those of Uruguay. Winters in Mesopotamia are mild; summers are hot with rain falling in short, sharp storms. Both Entre Ríos and Corrientes often suffer from summer drought.

Misiones Province, in the far NE, was first occupied by the Jesuit Fathers fleeing from the Brazilian Alto-Paraná region with their devoted Indian followers before the slave-hunting Bandeirantes. These missions and their history are described under Posadas (**see p 160**). Misiones is a hilly strip of land between the Uruguay and the Alto Paraná rivers, 80-100 km wide and about 400 km long; its capital is the river port of Posadas. Its boundary to the N is the river Iguazú, which here tumbles over the great Iguazú Falls. Misiones is on the Paraná Plateau; much of it is covered with forests of pine and cedar and broad-leaved trees, and the land, with its red soil, is reminiscent of Brazil. Here too the rainfall is heavy: twice as heavy as in Entre Ríos. The days are hot, and the nights cool.

It was the Jesuits who first grew *yerba mate* in plantations; Misiones has always been a large producer of this leaf, and also of citrus, tobacco, timber and tung oil. The province has attracted immigrants from Eastern Europe, from Paraguay and from the rest of Mesopotamia. There is good fishing in many of the small river-towns. In NE Corrientes and in Misiones more Indian tea is now grown than can be absorbed by the internal market.

The Indian-tea industry was started by Sir Herbert Gibson, who sent for seed from Assam in 1929; it was sown in Playadito, Corrientes province. Six seeds developed into sturdy bushes. Year after year their seed was given to anyone interested. All Argentina's tea plantations today have their origin in Sir Herbert Gibson's enterprise.

Communications in the area are by road (now greatly improved) and by the two rivers, the Uruguay and the Paraná, which bound it to E and W. Neither river is very good for navigation. Bridges between Fray Bentos (Uruguay) and Puerto Unzué, near Gualeguaychú, and between Paysandú (Uruguay) and Colón were opened in 1976, and there are a road and railway over the Salto Grande dam, near Concordia.

Up the Río Uruguay

The Río Uruguay is the eastern boundary of Mesopotamia and forms the western border of the Republic of Uruguay. There are no regular passenger shipping services.

Boats leaving Buenos Aires go past Martín García island, and enter the wide estuary. At 193 km from Buenos Aires, the Uruguayan town of Fray Bentos is to the right; there is a bridge (toll US$1) between Fray Bentos and the Argentine town of **Puerto Unzué**, near Gualeguaychú, but pedestrians and cyclists cannot cross it other than on motor vehicles; officials will give lifts on either side (customs formalities take about 10 mins). The river now becomes braided into channels and

NORTH-EAST ARGENTINA

islands. Opposite Fray Bentos, on the left, is the mouth of the Río Gualeguaychú; 19 km up is **Gualeguaychú**, a very pleasant town with a river promenade, an open-air railway museum (in the old railway station) and an attractive cathedral (1863). Lively pre-Lenten Carnival. Population, 80,000, with quite a large German contingent. Since the opening of the bridges between Zárate and Brazo Largo, the journey time from Buenos Aires, 248 km S, has been reduced and Gualeguaychú has become a popular weekend resort for *porteños*. Airport.

Hotels Accommodation is scarce at weekends and during carnival. The tourist office has a list of families. **B** *Embajador*, San Martín y 3 de Febrero, T 24414, casino; **D** *Entre Ríos*, Andrade 1009, T 27214; **D** *Alemán*, Bolívar 535, T 26153, friendly, German-speaking, rec; **D** *París*, Bolívar y Pellegrini, T 26260; **D** *Mayo*, Bolívar 550, T 27661, uncomfortable beds, noisy.

Camping *La Delfina* in the Parque Unzué; *Puerto del Sol* and *Playa Chica*, near the river; *Ñandubaysal*, 15 km E, best.

Exchange Banco Internacional Cooperativa, 25 de Mayo y Perón, changes cash; *Casa de Cambio*: **Daniel**, 3 de Febrero 128.

Tourist Office Av Costanera y 25 de Mayo, open 0800-2000.

Buses Terminus in centre of town at Bolívar y Chile. To **Fray Bentos**, 1 hr, US$3, 4 a day, ETA. To **Mercedes**, 1½ hrs, US$4, 2 a day, ETA; to **Concepción del Uruguay**, **Colón** and **Concordia**; to/from Buenos Aires US$9; companies running these routes are Tigre Iguazú (T Bs As 313-2355), Tata Rápido (T Bs As 313-3836), Singer (T BsAs 313-3915).

Concepción del Uruguay (known locally as Concepción), the first Argentine port of any size on the river, is 74 km N of Gualeguaychú. Founded in 1783, it was until 1883 capital of Entre Ríos province. Population 50,000. Overlooking the main plaza is the church of the Immaculate Conception which contains the remains of Gen Urquiza, whose former residence, the Palacio San José, 35 km W of the town, is now a museum, open daily 0900-1300, 1500-1900, US$1.50 (buses to 3 km from the Palacio), highly rec.

Hotels D *Gran Hotel*, Rocamora y Colón, T 22851; **D** *Virrey*, Aceso Ruta 131 y 15 de Oeste, T 25017; **D** *Ramírez*, Blvd Martínez 50, T 25106; **E** *Hospedaje Los Tres Trenes*, Galarza 1233, clean, friendly. Many hotels of all classes by the bus station.

Restaurants *El Canguro*, opposite bus terminus, good food, reasonably priced; *Rocamora*, Rocamora y Millán.

Tourist Office 9 de Julio 844, T 25820.

Colón (pop 17,000), 350 km from Buenos Aires, is 45 km N of Concepción del Uruguay. The river is more picturesque here with sandy beaches, and cliffs visible from a considerable distance; a road bridge now links Colón and Paysandú. (Toll for cars US$1.40. All border formalities, incl stamping of vehicle carnets, are conducted at both ends of the bridge, easy crossing.) The town is known for *artesanía* shops down San Martín, the main street, and there is a large handicrafts fair at Carnival time (Feb). Tourist office Av Quirós y Gouchón (very helpful).

Hotels L3 *Quirinale*, Av Quirós s/n, T 21978, 5-star, (with casino); **C** *Nuevo Hotel Plaza*, 12 de Abril y Belgrano, T 21043; **C** *Palmar*, Blvd Ferrari 285, T 21952, good; **D** *Holimasu*, Belgrano 28, T 21305; **D** *Vieja Calera*, Bolívar 344, T 21139; **C** *Res Aridan*, Alvear 57 y San Martín, T 21830, clean, hot water; **D** *Ver-Wei*, 25 de Mayo 10. Many families rent rooms—the Boujon family, Maipú 430, E, good breakfast, have been rec. Apartments for rent from Sr Ramón Gallo, Av Paysandú, T 472 3280, with kitchen, bathroom, hot showers, close to bus terminal. Several **campsites** along river bank (municipal site, excellent facilities, cheapest).

Restaurant *Comedor El Rayo*, Paysandú 372; *Pizzería Luisa*, San Martín 346; *La Rueda*, San Martín y 3 de Febrero; *Marito*, Gral Urquiza y Andrade.

Buses Bus terminal on outskirts, but buses also call at bus company offices in town. To **Paysandú**, US$2, 45 mins, but none 1145-1645 and none Sun. To **Buenos Aires**, 4 a day, US$18, 5 hrs, to **Concordia**, US$6 (2½ hrs) and **Paraná** daily. To **Córdoba** 4 a week.

Parque Nacional El Palmar (8,500 ha), 44 km N of Colón off the Ruta Nacional 14. Buses from Colón, 40 mins, US$2.50, will drop you on the road and it is easy to hitch the last 6 km to the park administration. There are camping facilities (US$3 pp, electricity, hot water), a small hotel 8 km N of the Park, with restaurant opposite, and a small shop. The Park (entrance US$2) contains varied scenery with a mature palm forest, sandy beaches on the Uruguay river, Indian tombs and other remains, a good museum and many rheas and other birds. The Yatay palms grow up to 12 m and some are hundreds of years old. It is best to stay overnight as wildlife is more easily seen in the early morning or at sunset. Very popular at weekends in summer.

Concordia, 104 km N of Colón, a little downriver from Salto, Uruguay, is a prosperous city, with a population of 93,800, which has some fine public buildings, a racecourse, rowing clubs, and a 9-hole golf club. Paved roads to Buenos Aires, Paraná and Posadas.

Park, Museums 5 km out is Parque Rivadavia, with a circular road used occasionally as a motor-racing track; there are pleasant views of the river and in the centre of the park is the Palacio San Carlos, inhabited briefly by Antoine de Saint-Exupéry. To get to the park, take colectivo No 2, 1 block from Plaza 25 de Mayo; to corner of Av Justo and Av Salto Uruguay, beyond bus terminal; entrance is 1 block from here. The Regional Museum on Plaza Urquiza is worth a visit; local and natural history collections, entry free.

Hotels A1 *Salto Grande*, Urquiza 575, T 213916; **B** *San Carlos*, Parque Rivadavia, T 216725; **C** *Colón*, Pellegrini 611, T 215510, simple, unusual but run down; **C** *Embajador*, San Lorenzo 75, T 213018, nr bus station, neat and clean; **C** *Palmar*, Urquiza 517, T 216050; **D** *Central*, 1° de Mayo 148, T 212842, reasonable, but shared bathrooms not too clean; **D** *Victoria*, Urquiza next to Esso, 2 blocks from terminal, quite good.

Camping *La Posada de Suárez—Club Viajantes* on Av Costanera near the park, warmly rec, with good *parrillada* alongside.

Restaurants *La Estancia*, good value, and *Gran Mary* (1st floor), both on plaza; *El Abrojito*, Pellegrini 1203, rec. *Comedor Las Dos Naciones*, Plaza 25 de Mayo and Av 1° de Mayo, good, moderate prices, large portions; *Mafalda*, corner of Plaza Urquiza and Av Entre Ríos, very good home made ice cream and cakes.

Services Exchange Banco Río de la Plata, on plaza, no commission on Visa advances; Casa Julio, 1 de Mayo, ½ block from plaza; Casa Chaca, on plaza; *Tourfé* on Mitre. **Post Office** La Rioja y Buenos Aires. **Telephone** 700 block of San Luis (24 hrs).

Tourist Office Plaza 25 de Mayo, open 0700-2400 daily, very friendly; kiosk at bus terminal, lousy map.

Buses Bus terminal 2 km from centre. No 2 bus goes to main plaza. To **Buenos Aires**, 6 daily, US$17, 6½ hrs; to **Córdoba**, US$25 with Expreso Singer, at 2200 and 0300, 9 hrs; to **Paraná** 5, to **Posadas** at 1800 and 2300, with Expreso Singer (8½ hrs, US$32), to **Iguazú** one (1810, 13½ hrs), to **Corrientes** US$11. Bus to **La Paz** (Entre Ríos)—see p 156, 1100, US$10.50, 8 hrs. To **Paso de los Libres** direct, 2300 or take 0755 Empresa Gualeguaychú bus to Curuzú Cuatiá and catch connecting service. Possible to sleep overnight on benches in bus terminal.

The river is impassable for large vessels beyond the rapids of Salto Chico near the town, and Salto Grande 32 km up-river, where there is a large international hydro-electric dam, providing a route for an international road and railway. Above Salto Grande the river is generally known as the Alto Uruguay. There is excellent fishing in the artificial lake. Before Salto Grande lake was filled, the town of Federación (pop 7,000) had to be relocated to higher ground.

To Uruguay Take No 2 or 4 bus from Concordia bus terminal marked "Puerto", for ferry crossing to Salto US$2.50 (tickets obtainable at a small kiosk, which shuts 15 mins before departure, outside customs) departures 0900, 1000, 1200, 1430, 1600, weekdays, 0900, 1200, 1500, Sat but none Sun; takes 15 mins, passengers only.

About 153 km upstream from Concordia lies the small port of **Monte Caseros** (pop 18,400), with the Uruguayan town of Bella Unión, on the Brazilian border, almost opposite (**Hotels** *Paterlini*, Colón y Salta, T 219; *Conte*, Salta 463; *Cortez*, 2 de Febrero 1663).

   Above Bella Unión, the **Alto Uruguay** is the boundary between Argentina and Brazil. Ninety-six km above Monte Caseros is **Paso de los Libres** (pop 25,000), with the Brazilian cattle town of **Uruguaiana** opposite: a bridge joins the two. No bus service on Sun – taxi charges US$20. From Uruguaiana into Brazil the buses are much quicker than trains, though there is a comfortable railway service to Porto Alegre. Paso de los Libres was founded in 1843 by General Madariaga; it was here that he crossed the river from Brazil with his hundred men and annexed Corrientes province for Argentina. Road (paved) to Paraná.

Hotels C *Alejandro* I, Coronel López 502, T 21000, best; *Uruguay*, Uruguay 1252, T 21672.

Transport Líneas Aéreas Entre Ríos (LAER) flies from Aeroparque, Buenos Aires to Paraná, Gualeguaychú and Concordia with very low fares; enquire at Puente Aéreo desk at Aeroparque.

58 km N of Paso de los Libres, on the road to Alvear, is **Yapeyú**, the site of a Jesuit mission and famous as the birthplace of the liberator, José de San Martín. Part of the house where he was born is well preserved, and there is an interesting Jesuit Museum. (**D** *Hosteria ACA*, T 93020; the Carillo family on the main plaza rent rooms, E, good; *cabañas* on the outskirts of town; camping by the river.)

Up the Río Paraná

Navigation River boats carry passengers along various stretches of the river, but there are no long-distance passenger services up the river from Buenos Aires, except those to Asunción, Paraguay. Depending on the tide, boats enter the Paraná river by either the Las Palmas reach of the delta, on which is Zárate, or the Paraná-Guazú reach, on which is Ibicuy.

Most of the important towns of Mesopotamia lie on the E bank of the Paraná, or the S bank of the Alto Paraná.

Zárate, 65,000 inhabitants on the W bank 90 km N of Buenos Aires, is industrially important, with large *frigoríficos* and paper works (**C** *Hotel San Martín*, Ameghino 773, T 2713, clean; *Restaurant La Posta de Correa*, cheap, good service). Along the waterfront are many *parrillas* and restaurants; trips to Palmira in Uruguay are arranged here, $2\frac{1}{2}$ hrs, US$11. There are 2 museums: in the old Urquiza station, local history, and a Boy Scout museum. In Plaza Italia a handicraft market is held on Sun and holidays. It is served from Buenos Aires by bus (US$3, every 30 mins from Plaza Once) and two railways: the Mitre and the Urquiza. Urquiza trains used to be ferried 84 km across the river, but a link including two large and beautiful bridges has been built between Zárate and Brazo Largo, accelerating rail and road journeys alike (the bridge toll is US$6). The picturesque Ibicuy Islands can be visited by boat. About 50 km N of Zárate is **San Pedro** (pop 28,000) where fine riverfront camping can be had at either the *Centro Turístico*, *Club Pescadores* or *Camping Municipal*.

About 108 km N of Ibicuy, on the E bank, is **Gualeguay**, with a population of 26,000. It is the centre of one of the richest cattle and sheep ranching regions in Entre Ríos. The house in which Garibaldi was tortured by the local chief of police in 1837, in the time of Rosas, still exists. Eight km S is its river port, Puerto Ruiz. The road from Gualeguay N along the E bank of the Paraná is paved most of the way to Posadas.

Hotels B *Gran Hotel Gualeguay*, Monte Caseros 217, T 23085; **E** *Italia*, Palacios 1, T 24575, with bath, friendly. There is a municipal **campsite**. In the centre there are practically no **restaurants**, but the *Jockey Club* and the *Club Social*, both on the main square close to the *Gran Hotel Gualeguay*, cater also for non-members. The *Club Social* has a very nice atmosphere, good food, and you might be invited to see films on certain nights.

On the way upstream to Rosario, on the W bank, are two ports which export grain: **San Nicolás** (pop 97,000), 80 km below Rosario, and **Villa Constitución** (pop 34,000), 37 km below Rosario. Both are served by a railway from the capital. At San Nicolás is the General Savio steel plant. **Pergamino**, an important road/rail junction in the pampas, is 72 km S by road or rail.

Rosario, chief city of the province of Santa Fe, 320 km N of Buenos Aires, is the third city of the republic, with a population of well over a million. It is a great industrial and export centre. The streets are wider than those of Buenos Aires, and there are fine boulevards, handsome open spaces and good shopping facilities. In recent years the city has been developing a lively cultural scene. It is the home of many popular rock musicians and modern artists and there are good discothèques and theatres. From Oct to early Mar it is warm, and from Dec to the end of Feb uncomfortably hot. Changes of temperature are sudden.

Points of Interest Monument of the Flag, a memorial on the river bank in honour of General Belgrano, designer of the Argentine flag, who raised it on this spot for the first time (lifts go to the top); **Parque Independencia** (Rose Garden): Boulevard Oroño; **Cathedral** in Calle 25 de Mayo; **St Bartholomew's Church** (Anglican), Calle Paraguay; racecourse, the Alberdi and Arroyito boat clubs, and Saladillo Golf Club, with its own Links station on the Mitre line. The Aero Club is in the suburb of Gral Alvear. The **Museo Histórico Provincial** (open Thur and Sat 1500-1800, and Sun 1000-1200, 1500-1800) is in Parque Independencia. Two art museums: **Museo Municipal de Bellas Artes Juan B Castagnino**, Av Pellegrini 2202, 1,500 paintings, among them El Greco, Goya and Titian; **Museo Municipal de Arte Decorativo Firma y Odilio Estévez**, Santa Fe 748, has some Caravaggios, Goyas and Murillos. A rec pedestrian tour called **"Paseo Centenario"** around Calle Córdoba touches on the interesting buildings and monuments of the "Golden Days of Rosario" (1880-1950). There are explanation signs now installed. Swimming at sandy **Florida beach**, about 8 km N of Rosario.

Local Holiday 7 Oct (Foundation of the City).

Hotels A1 *Riviera*, San Lorenzo 1460, T 213481, a/c; **B** *Presidente*, Av Corrientes 919, T 242545, good; **B** *Plaza*, Barón de Mauá 26, T 47097; many **C** hotels opp bus station (*Embajador*, *Micro*, *Nahuel*, shabby); **D** *La Paz*, Barón de Mauá 36, T 210905, clean, quiet, friendly, rec; **E** *Río*, Rivadavia 2665, T 396421, opp railway station, clean, friendly.

Camping La Florida, near the river.

Restaurants *Don Rodrigo*, Sante Fe 968, and *Fénix*, Santa Fe next to Citibank, are both very good. *Doña María*, Santa Fe 1371, does good Italian food; *Casa Uruguaya*, Alvear 1125 (T 69320), away from centre, good. *Marialronn*, Santa Fe y Pres Roca, rec for dancing. Along the river are good cheap restaurants and fishing club barbeques, good atmosphere.

Exchange Lloyds Bank (BLSA), Calle La Rioja 1205; **Citibank**, Santa Fe 1101; **First National Bank of Boston**, Córdoba esq Mitre. Open 1000-1600. Most banks charge 2% commission on cheques and cash. Amex, Grupo 3 de Turismo, Córdoba 1147, T 244415. *Casas de Cambio*: *Transatlántica*, Córdoba 900; *Carey*, Corrientes 802; *Carbatur*, Corrientes 840.

Laundry Santa Fe 1578.

Post Office Córdoba y Buenos Aires. **Telecommunications** San Luis, between San Martín and Maipú.

Tourist Office At Monument of the Flag, helpful but information inadequate.

Airport at Fisherton, 8 km from centre. Taxi charges vary. Several flights daily to Buenos Aires with AR, 3 a week with Austral.

Buses Bus terminal expanded 1994. There are regular bus services to Arroyo Seco, Casilda, Cañada de Gómez, San Lorenzo and other important centres up to 80 km from the city. To **Buenos Aires**, via San Nicolás on Route 9 (4 hrs) or via Pergamino, less frequent on Route 8 (Chevallier bus every hour, US$20; also Ablo, General Urquiza, La Unión), NW to **Córdoba** and **Tucumán**. To **Santa Fe**, US$10. To **Mendoza**, US$40. To **Puerto Iguazú**, US$50.

Rosario can be reached from Buenos Aires by Route 8 (marked Córdoba) to Pergamino, and then, following signs, by Route 188, and then 178 to Rosario. This is a better way than lorry-packed Route 9. Hitching to Salta along Route 34 is possible.

Ferries to Victoria, in Entre Ríos, which has a municipal **campsite**.

Above Rosario the river is very braided and islanded. Boat trips to river islands can be made at weekends (eg *Ciudad de Rosario* from Estación Fluvial by the Monument of the Flag, Sat 1730, Sun 1600, 1830), or from Florida beach at any time. Canoes can be hired. Some 23 km N of Rosario is *San Lorenzo* (pop 28,700), with one of the largest chemical works in Argentina. See the restored San Carlos monastery on the river bank, where in 1813 San Martín won his first battle in the War of Independence. Visitors are shown a pine tree grown from a cutting of the tree under which the Liberator rested after the battle.

Some 180 km above Rosario, on the E bank, is *Paraná*, capital of Entre Ríos (pop 210,000), founded in 1588. From 1853 to 1862 the city was the capital of the Republic. The centre is situated on a hill offering fine views over the river and beyond to Santa Fe. There are many fine buildings; in the centre is the Plaza Primero de Mayo, where there are fountains and a statue of San Martín. Around the Plaza are the Municipalidad, the Cathedral, notable for its portico and its interior, and the tourist information office. The Casa de Gobierno at Santa Fe y Laprida has a grand façade. The city's glory is Parque Urquiza, to the NW. It has an enormous statue to General Urquiza, and a bas-relief showing the battle of Caseros, at which he finally defeated Rosas; also an open-air theatre. There are pleasant walks along the river bank and around the fishing *barrio* of Puerto Sánchez. Boats sail along the river from near the tourist office.

Museums Museo de Bellas Artes, Buenos Aires 355; **Museo Histórico**, Buenos Aires y Laprida, open Mon-Fri, 0800-1200, 1500-1800, Sat, 0900-1200, 1600-1900, Sun, 0900-1200.

Hotels There is a shortage of hotel space, especially at peak periods (Semana Santa and Jul), when the tourist office arranges accommodation with families. There is a greater selection of hotels—at lower prices—in Santa Fe. **A1** *Mayorazgo*, Etchevehere y Córdoba, on Costanera Alta, T 216111, 5-star, with fine view of park and river, has casino and swimming pool; **C** *Gran Hotel Paraná*, Urquiza 976, T 223900; **C** *Super Luxe*, Villaguay 162, T 212373; **D** *Almafuerte*, Av Almafuerte 1295, T 240644. Cheap hotels near railway station, incl **E** *City*, basic, rec, and **D** *Bristol*, Alsina 221, T 213961, close to the bus terminal, good quality, refurbished rm, and **D** *Plaza*, San Martín 915, T 210122.

Laundry *Laverap*, Belgrano 650.

Tourist Office 25 de Mayo 44, T 221632.

Air Service Airport: General Urquiza, 12 km from town.

Bus E across Entre Ríos to Concordia on Río Uruguay, 5 a day, 5 hours. To/from Buenos Aires, US$18.

Travelling Between Santa Fe and Paraná The 2 cities do not face one another, but are 25 km apart and are separated by several islands. From Paraná the Hernandarias tunnel, toll US$2 per car, passes under the river to connect with the W bank; from here a road runs 23 km W to Santa Fe across two islands and bridges. Trucks with dangerous loads cross the river by a launch which also carries pedestrians and operates Mon-Sat, 0600-2100, 20 mins journey, frequency depending on demand from trucks. Frequent bus service between the 2 cities by Etacer and Fluviales del Litoral, US$2, 1 hr.

Santa Fe, a larger city of some 400,000 inhabitants, is the capital of its province and the centre of a very fertile region (160 km from Rosario). It was founded by settlers from Asunción in 1573, though its present site was not occupied until 1660. It was in its Cabildo (town hall) that the Constitution of 1853 was adopted. The oath of allegiance was taken before the crucifix in the sacristy of the church of San Francisco, built in 1680 from materials floated down the river from Paraguay; this old colonial church has been tampered with but is still fine, especially the carved wooden ceilings, which were fitted without nails.

Most of the best buildings are in the E part of the city near the Plaza 25 de Mayo. On the Plaza itself are the **Cathedral**, the church of **Nuestra Señora de los Milagros** and the majestic **Casa de Gobierno**. The church and convent of **San Francisco** (see above) are a block SE of the Plaza. Opposite it is the **Museo Histórico Provincial**. The **Convent of Santo Domingo**, a block W of the Plaza at 3 de Febrero y 9 de Julio, has a fine patio and museum. In Calle General López is the **Museo de Bellas Artes Rosa Galisteo de Rodríguez**, where local painters hold their exhibitions. The church of **Nuestra Señora de Guadalupe**, with beautifully painted glass windows, is at Javier de la Rosa 623 and may be reached by bus 8, 14 or 16 from the centre. Twice weekly boats from Buenos Aires, 483 km to the south; regular only in winter.

Local holidays 30 Sep (St Jerome); 15 Nov (Foundation of City).

Hotels A2 *Río Grande*, San Gerónimo 2586, modern, rec; **B** *Bertaina*, H Irigoyen 2255, may negotiate; **B** *Corrientes*, Corrientes 2520, T 40126; **B** *El Conquistador*, 25 de Mayo 2676, T 51195; **B** *Hostal de Santa Fe de la Vera Cruz*, San Martín 2954, T 51740, best, genial, well-kept and run; **C** *Avellaneda*, Av Oro Blanco 765, Ruta 11, Km 792, suburban, T 81187, good; **C** *Colón*, San Luis 2862, T 45167, with bath, D without, pleasant, large and clean rooms; **C** *Niza*, Rivadavia 2755, T 22047, very clean, friendly; **C** *Royal*, Irigoyen Freyre 2256, clean, private bath, opp bus station; **C** *Suipacha*, Suipacha 2375, T 21135, clean, safe, rec; **C** *Brigadier*, San Luis 3148, T 37387, two blocks from bus station, good, clean, friendly, 50 rooms, a/c extra but rec if the river is in flood and there are lots of mosquitoes, some English spoken, private parking; **D** *Carlitos*, Irigoyen Freyre 2336, T 31541, clean, friendly; near the bus terminal is **E** *Apolo*, Belgrano 2821, clean, basic.

Camping Possible in free municipal site near town centre, Parque del Sur, bus No 5; beware ferocious mosquitoes. Several sites on the lakes and rivers outside town incl: *Luz y Fuerza*, 7 km N near Lago Guadalupe; *Cámara del Hogar*, 4 km E on Route 168; 2 sites on Río Colastine, 15 km E on Route 168.

Restaurants Many good ones, offering excellent meals with good wine. *El Quincho de Chiquito*, Obispo Príncipe y Almte Brown, excellent and good value, classic fish restaurant, huge helpings. Excellent grills incl *surubí* (local fish) at *Gran Parrillada Rivadavia*, Rivadavia 3299. *Surubí* also at *España*, San Martín 2644. Several good cafeterias around San Martín y 25 de Mayo, incl *Café de la Paix*, San Martín y Santiago del Estero; *Comedor Porky*, Gálvez 2345, eat all you want. *Nochera Española*, opposite railway station.

Exchange Lloyds Bank (BLSA), Calle 25 de Mayo 2501, open 0715-1315; Citibank, San Martín 2609. **Amex** representative, Vacaciones Felices, San Martín 2347. *Casas de Cambio*: *Camsa*, 25 de Mayo 2466; *Carbatur*, San Martín 2520; *Tourfé*, San Martín 2901, changes TCs.

Laundromat *Servi Rap*, Rivadavia 2834 (open Sat 0800-1300); *Laverap*, San Martín 1687.

Swimming On river at Guadalupe beach; local bus.

Tourist Office at the conveniently situated bus terminal: maps, friendly.

Airport At Sauce Viejo, 17 km from the city. Two daily AR flights (1 on Sat and Sun) to and from Buenos Aires, T 20713.

Roads and Buses Fully paved to Rosario, 160 km (3 hours by bus); to Formosa, 894 km; to Roque Sáenz Peña, with spurs S to Villa Angela and General Pinedo and N to San Martín. Large and modern bus terminal. Bus for **Asunción** (Paraguay), La Internacional, express at 0100, 12 hrs, US$45, *convencional* at 1925, 13 hrs, US$32. To **Córdoba**, US$15, 5 hrs. Many buses to **Buenos Aires** (US$25, La Internacional, Tata), **Paraná** and **Rosario**; daily to **Mendoza** (2100) and **Santiago del Estero/Tucumán** (2010).

Upstream from Santa Fe the Paraná rapidly loses depth and is navigable only by river boats and small coastal vessels.

Between Paraná and Goya, on the left bank, is *La Paz (Entre Ríos)*, a small port (pop 15,200) with regional museum, riverside park and golf club. Buses to Buenos Aires, Rosario and Concordia.

Hotels *Milton*, Italia 1029, T 22232, modern; *Plaza*, main square, T 21208; *Rivera*, San Martín 367, T 21032. Small **restaurants** in port and near bus station.

Between Santa Fe and Corrientes the boat calls at several river ports, incl La Paz, Goya and Empedrado. *Goya* (airport 7 km from centre), on the E bank, the second town of the Province of Corrientes, is near the junction of the Paraná with the Santa Lucía river. It is a large tobacco centre on the Urquiza railway, with a population of 47,000. There is a vehicle-ferry service across the river to *Reconquista* (34,800 people). The road N from Goya to Empedrado and Corrientes is paved; many buses. Some stop at Bella Vista where a river crossing is possible at the port 5 km away, US$1.50, closing times unknown. Bus Reconquista-Santa Fe 6 hrs, US$12.

Hotels at Goya *Hotel de Turismo*, Mitre 880, T 22560, modern, rec. *Cervantes*, JE Gómez 723, T 22684; *Goya*, Colón 929, T 22354; **D** *España*, España 345, clean, hot water, friendly, near bus station. *Hoguimarsa*, B Mitre 880/90 (the last-named also has establishments at Curuzú Cuatiá, Empedrado and Mercedes, in Corrientes province). *Restaurant El Colonial* said to be the best, near bus station at Loza 415.

Hotels at Reconquista **B** *Grand*, Obligado 8083, T 20010; **C** *Magui I*, H Yrigoyen 755, T 21470, adequate, excellent restaurant. **C** *Motel Hostal del Rey*, located on the edge of town, clean, with bath. Many around bus station, eg **D** *Olessio*, opposite bus terminal. **D** *Residencial San Martín*, with bath, on B Mitre y Bolívar.

140 km E of Goya is *Mercedes (Corrientes* – pop 20,750) (*Hotel de Turismo*, Caaguazú y Sarmiento, T 317; *Hotel Plaza*, San Martín 699, T 13, E, cheapest), a good base from which to visit the *Iberá marshes*. The marshes are a nature reserve containing more species, it is claimed, than the Pantanal in Mato Grosso, Brazil. Among the species are the endangered aguará-guazú (maned wolf), deer, otters, the Juan Grande stork, kingfishers, snakes, etc. At *Carlos Pellegrini*, 110 km NE of Mercedes (3 buses a week), a new visitors centre to the marshes has been opened (take food, sleeping bag, light, binoculars). Workers at the visitors

centre take boat trips in small punts, a recommended way of discovering the wildlife quietly, or tours can be arranged in Mercedes or Corrientes. The tap water here is not drinkable, but bottled water is sold at the main store in the village.

27 km S of Mercedes are the strange Ita Pucú rock formations, remnants of a mountain massif long disappeared.

Empedrado, further up the river on the E bank, has a population of 5,000. It is on the railway line between Buenos Aires (1,014 km) and Corrientes. Oranges and rice are grown in the neighbourhood. **Hotels** *Turismo*, with swimming pool and fine views; *Rosario*. **Campsite**.

About 600 km upstream from Santa Fe, on the W bank, is the little port of **Barranqueras**, served also from Santa Fe by railway (17 hours). It is on a steep bluff overlooking the Paraná. A paved road connects it with **Resistencia**, the bustling, hot and energetic capital of the Province of Chaco, a galaxy of neon after dark, 6½ km up the Barranqueras stream. Pop 218,000. The road N from Resistencia to Formosa (200 km) and on to Puerto Pilcomayo (137 km) is paved.

In the streets there are many modern statues, promoted by the **Fogón de los Arrieros**, Brown 350, between López and French, a famous club frequented by local artists and full of local art and "*objets*" from abroad. Open to non-members Mon-Sat, 0800-1200, Tues, Wed, Thur only, 2130-0100. Entry US$2. Good place to meet local people.

Museums Museo Histórico Regional, Donovan 475, open Mon-Fri, 0800-1200, 1400-1700, traces the development of the city; **Museo de Ciencias Naturales**, Oturo Illia 658, open Mon-Fri, 0700-1200, 1700-2000, Sat 0900-1200; **Museo de Bellas Artes**, Mitre 163, open Mon 1600-2200, Tues-Fri, 0900-1300, 1600-2200, Sat/Sun 1900-2200, collection of 19th and 20th century local works; **Museo Regional de Antropología**, Las Heras 727 in the Universidad Nacional del Nordeste.

Area Products Cotton, *quebracho*, cattle.

Hotels Many accept Visa cards. **B** *Colón*, Sta María de Oro 139, T 22861, friendly, clean, rec; **B** *Covadonga*, Güemes 182, T 22875, small rooms, clean, a/c, *Tabaré* snack bar; **C** *Esmirna*, H Irigoyen 83 on corner of Plaza, T 22898, with bath, good; **C** *Sahara*, Güemes 169, T 22970. **D** *Celta*, Alberdi 210, T 22986; **D** *Residencial San José*, Rawson 304, clean, decent. Several cheap ones near bus station, eg **D** *Aragón*, Santiago del Estero, 154; **D** *Residencia Alberdi*, Av Alberdi 317, one block from bus station, basic but clean, restaurant, friendly owner, rec.

Camping *Parque Dos de Febrero*, very pretty, near artificial lake, tent US$3, take bus 5 or 9 one block from terminal; adequate free site nearby. *Parque Mitre*, showers and toilets. There is another site, shady but no facilities, NW of Resistencia on Route 16.

Restaurants *Círculo Residentes Santafecinos*, Vadia 150, tasty meals, family style. Try *chupin de surubí*, a sort of bouillabaisse, delightful. *Parrillada Clemente*, Santa María de Oro 399 opp bus station. *Restaurant Sociedad, Italiana*, Yrigoyen 204, excellent cuisine, smart, pricey; *Charly*, Güemes 215, snacks, good breakfast.

Banks and Exchange Banco del Chaco, Güemes on main plaza, cash only; **Banco de Crédito**, Justo 200 block, cash advance on Mastercard. **Banco de Iberá** changes TCs (3% commission). It can take a long time to change TCs on Mon as locals queue for money; **Cambio Dorado**, Güemes, changes TCs at reasonable rate. Try also the *Hotel Sahara* (cash only).

Laundry *Tokio*, Güemes y Brown.

Post Office Plaza 25 de Mayo, Mon-Sat, 0700-1200, 1500-2000. **Telecommunications**, Justo y Paz.

Shopping Sculptured Chaco woods from Domingo Arenas, cubist-type wood-statues. Regionales Pompeya, Güemes 154, sells local handicrafts and has an Indian handicraft display. Excellent leather goods at CHAC, Güemes 166.

Tourist Office Justo 135; kiosk in Plaza 25 de Mayo, very little info.

Car Hire Avis, French 701 and at airport. Localiza, Julio A Roca 460, T 39255.

Air Airport 8 km from town (no bus). AR (T 22859/25360) 3 and Austral 4 times a week to Buenos Aires.

Buses Buses leave every 15 mins to **Corrientes** over the Río Paraná bridge, 40 mins, US$0.55, the Resistencia terminal is on Sta María del Oro, 3 blocks from main plaza. 3 *especiales* a day to **Buenos Aires** (US$47) 14 hrs, 3 *comunes* a day (US$40), 17 hrs La Internacional, El Norte Bus; bus to **Santa Fe** (US$18). 8 a day to **Formosa** (2½ hrs, US$9) and **Puerto Pilcomayo**,

6-7 hrs. To **Iguazú** (US$40), 0700, 2300. To **Posadas**, 1230, 1300, 5$\frac{1}{2}$ hrs (good road), US$15, 4 a day, hot journey with lots of stops. Veloz del Norte and Saenz Peña direct to **Salta** (US$49) at 1700, 13 hrs. To Bolivian border at Aguas Blancas/Bermejo, take bus for Salta, change at Güemes, for direct connection to Orán (5 hrs, US$12, Atahuallpa buses every 2 hrs or so), from where it is a 45 min ride to border. El Rayo to **Tucumán** at 1930 and 2200, 12 hrs, US$21. Bus to **Rosario**, daily, 2015, US$21. Bus to **Clorinda** and Paraguayan border US$13, 5 hrs (walk across bridge then take taxi to Asunción, US$20 per vehicle). Many searches, watch your belongings and make sure everything is there afterwards. Also to **Asunción** daily, via Formosa, with Godoy (at 0300, 0600, 1400) and Brújula, 6$\frac{1}{2}$ hrs, US$18. Easy border crossing. Possible to change money.

Excursion To El Chaco National Park, camping possible, **see p 148**.

On the other side of the river from Resistencia (25 km) is **Corrientes**. The 2$\frac{3}{4}$-km General Belgrano bridge crosses the river (toll US$1 per car); the best view of it is from the Corrientes side. The city, site of Graham Greene's *The Honorary Consul*, is the capital of Corrientes Province. The river can make the air heavy, moist and oppressive, but in winter the climate is pleasant. Population, 200,000. The city was founded in 1588. The church of La Cruz de los Milagros (1897) houses a miraculous cross placed there by the founder of the city, Alonzo de Vera—Indians who tried to burn it were killed by lightning from a cloudless sky. The Cathedral is in the renaissance style. Plaza Sargento Cabral has a statue to the sergeant who saved San Martín's life at the battle of San Lorenzo. A beautiful walk eastwards, along the Av Costanera, beside the Paraná river leads to Parque Mitre, from where there are good views of sunsets over the river. Up river from the bridge to Resistencia, is a zoo with animals of the region. Calle Junín is pedestrianized, with restaurants and shops, crowded at night. Swimming pools in town are open to members only.

Museums Museo Histórico Regional, 9 de Julio 1044; Museo de Bellas Artes, San Juan 634, open Tues-Fri, 0800-1200, 1600-2100, Sat, Sun, 0900-1200, 1800-2000; Museo de Ciencias Naturales, San Martín 850, a once famous collection now sadly neglected; Museo de Artesanía, Quintana 905, Mon-Fri, 0730-1200, 1500-2000, Sat 0900-1200, 1600-1900.

Hotels More expensive than Resistencia, **B** *Gran Hotel Guaraní*, Mendoza 970, T 23663/23090, very good a/c restaurant; **C** *Corrientes*, Junín 1549, T 65025; **C** *Gran Hotel Turismo*, Entre Ríos 650, T 23841, pool US$3 a day to non-residents; **C** *Orly*, San Juan 861, T 27248; **D** *Sosa*, España 1050, T 62151, a little overpriced; **D** *Robert* on La Rioja, nr *Colón* (No 437), basic, clean; **D** *SOS*, Irigoyen 1750, friendly, but noisy.

Camping Near bus terminal and railway station is *Camping-club Teléfono*, hot showers or bath, friendly. There is another campsite on the riverbank, go up through Parque Mitre and continue along the road closest to the river; the site is just past the water works.

Restaurants *El Recreo*, Pellegrini 578, good, reasonable prices, popular with locals. Many others, incl *Raviolandia*, Nueve de Julio 652; *Che Camba*, Av Independencia 1173; and various *pizzerías*. Ice creams at *Italia*, Nueve de Julio 1301 and *Verona*, Av Ferré 1750. Several tea rooms on San Juan, eg *Confitería Viki*, San Juan 721 y Maipú 1198 and on Junín. Try local, baked delicacy called *chipa*.

Banks and Exchange Banco de la Provincia, 9 de Julio y San Juan, cash advance on Mastercard; **Banco de Crédito**, Junín 1326, cash accepted only; street money-changers at SW corner of Plaza Cabral.

Nightclubs *Metal*, Junín y Buenos Aires; *Savage*, Junín y San Lorenzo.

Travel Agency *Turismo Aventura 4WD*, Galería Paseo del Sul, Junín 1062, T 27698, Amex. *Quo Vadis*, Carlos Pellegrini 1140, T 23096.

Tourist Office Plaza Cabral; lots of information about fishing.

Car Hire Avis at *Gran Hotel Guaraní* and airport; only credit cards accepted from foreigners.

Airport Camba Punta, 10 km from city. (Bus No 8 from urban bus terminal at river end of La Rioja) Aerolíneas Argentinas T 27442; Austral, Junín 1301, T 23850. Austral flights to and from Buenos Aires daily.

Bus Terminal 5 km from centre; bus No 6 from terminal to town centre (US$0.20). Corrientes-**Posadas** US$15, 5$\frac{1}{2}$ hrs, road paved. Buses to **Resistencia** US$0.55, Cota, every 15 mins, 40 mins journey, labelled "Chaco", leave from harbour; **Buenos Aires**-Corrientes,

US$50, Chevallier; Tata Rápido; there are many more buses to Buenos Aires, Rosario and Santa Fe from Resistencia than from Corrientes.

At 20 km along Route 12 from Corrientes is **Santa Ana de los Guacaras**, a 17th-century settlement with attractive colonial architecture. To the N of Corrientes is the small town of **Paso de la Patria** (38 km, Route 12), a paradise for *dorado* fishing, with plenty of bungalows to stay. (**B** *Hostería Don Julián*, T 94021, full board.)

A tiny port on the Alto Paraná, **Itatí** (pop 5,700), is reached by bus (73 km on Route 12). Here, on 16 Jul, is held a festival which celebrates jointly the crowning of the Virgin of Itatí (housed in a sanctuary built 1638), and St Louis of France. Thousands of pilgrims arrive on the 16th (when the religious ceremonies begin) from San Luis del Palmar (pop 15,000) in picturesque procession. *Hospedajes* incl *Antártida*, *El Promesero*, *El Colonial*.

Some 250 km E of Corrientes is **Ituzaingó**, pop 10,000, a rapidly growing town serving the Yacyretá-Apipé hydroelectric project (all turbines due to be in place by 1998). Buses run to the Relaciones Públicas centre (free, no stops en route), where a video film is shown and other information given. Several hotels, eg **E** *Hospedaje Dos Hermanos*, Pellegrini y Posadas, clean, friendly.

About 15 km W of Ituzaingó on Ruta Nacional 12, Km 1237, is *Estancia San Gará*, "the perfect place to relax and experience the typical Gaucho life" (Thomas and Petra Sbampato, Switzerland), US$80 pp in double bedroom with rm service, or US$30 pp in dormitory with hammock-style accommodation. Price incl 4 good meals, use of pool and all excursions into the Iberá marshes, by boat, jeep or on horseback (highly rec); a lovely place with extraordinary hospitality. Book in advance: T 0786-20550, in Posadas 0752-27217, in Buenos Aires, 01-811-1132, F 476-2648 (office at Av Alvear 1668, 5 piso); always ask for owner Sr Pablo Prats. Ask to be let off any bus going to or from Posadas via Ituzaingó at the turn-off (drivers know it) and walk 1.5 km to the *estancia*.

210 km SE of Corrientes, on the edge of the Iberá marshes (**see p 156**), is the Estancia of **San Juan Poriahú** (16,500 ha), a wildlife reserve with a superb array of animals and birds. Visitors can explore the estancia on horseback, or in pick-ups or tractors.

Corrientes is 40 km below the confluence of the Paraguay and Alto Paraná rivers. Up the former are Formosa and Asunción; up the latter are Posadas and Iguazú.

The only Argentine port of any note on the Paraguay river is **Formosa**, 240 km above Corrientes. It is the capital of Formosa Province, and has a population of 95,000. There is a colonial museum in the town centre. The surroundings are flat and swampy, the climate and vegetation tropical. From the port a trip can be made to Isla Alberdi, a Paraguayan duty-free spot; no possibility of continuing into Paraguay, and can only be done if you have a multiple entry visa. By road from Buenos Aires; 1,365 km. Airport (5 Austral flights a week).

Hotels A2 *Turismo*, best, San Martín 759, T 26004; **C** *Colón*, Belgrano 1098, T 26547, noisy, a/c, colour TV, spacious, 1st floor, B 2nd floor, good; **C** *Plaza*, J.M. Uriburu 905, T 26747. Several others on San Martín, eg **D** *Rivas*, Belgrano 1395, T 20499, ½ block from old bus station, with bath (E without), cold water, basic, run down, friendly. **D** *Colonial*, San Martín 897, T 26345, near railway station, with private bath (E without), clean, a/c, basic but good value, private parking available. **D** *Casa de Familia*, Belgrano 1056, friendly, good. Many more along Belgrano.

Camping Possible on the river about 2 km from the centre along a dirt road, upstream and over the railway lines.

Restaurant *Ser Bran*, near bus terminal, cheap and good; several others opp bus terminal, eg *17 de Agosto*, good, cheap. *El Alamo*, Av 25 de Mayo 65, good *parrillada*; *Latino American Bar*, 25 de Mayo 55, good Italian food, nice atmosphere, expensive. On same road *Italiano*, excellent food, friendly, reasonable prices, and *Raíces*, good.

Exchange Banks close at about noon and there are no exchange shops; buy pesos in Asunción or Clorinda if en route when they're closed. **Banco de la Provincia de Formosa** changes TCs, but very high commission.

Tourist Office *Hotel Internacional*, San Martín 759. Also at new bus terminal very helpful.

Roads S to Resistencia (200 km); N to Clorinda and Asunción, paved, 150 km, via new toll bridge. Direct road to Salta very bad.

Bus To Asunción, 0400, 0800 and 1730, 3 hrs, US$10.50, delays at frontier common. Easier to go to Clorinda on the border (US$6.50) and then take a micro to Asunción. To Puente Loyola,

US$5, Empresa Godoy, Mariano Moreno 1050 (surcharge for every 5 kg of luggage). Six a day to **Resistencia**, US$9. To/from Buenos Aires US$41, La Internacional.

Bus services to **Embarcación** are frequently cancelled (scheduled daily 1200; do not rely on this as a route to Bolivia, better to go from Resistencia to Salta and then N).

Excursions To nature reserve (flora and fauna) at Guaycotea, incl zoo with animals badly neglected in small cages, 6 buses a day from Formosa, 3/4 hr, US$2. To Estancia Bouvier, 70 km N, an 80,000 hectare estate which incl a wildlife reserve. Accommodation available on the Estancia which is accessible only by motorboat. Details: Santiago de la Vega, T 795-1727.

137 km N of Formosa, almost opposite Asunción (Paraguay), is **Clorinda** (pop 21,200), whence the new Loyola bridge crosses to Puerto Falcón, Paraguay. Border crossing is easy. Many buses from Argentine end of bridge: to Formosa (10 a day), Resistencia (4) and Santa Fe/Rosario/Buenos Aires (3). Clorinda has a banana festival in early Oct. Street money changer at Clorinda bus station gives good rates pesos/guaraní. From Puerto Pilcomayo, close to Clorinda (bus US$0.40) one can catch a ferry to Itá Enramada (Paraguay), a US$0.65 five-minute journey every 20 minutes. Argentine migration office at Puerto Pilcomayo is open 7 days a week.

Hotels C *Embajador*, San Martín 166, T 21148; D *Helen*, San Martín 320, T 21118; E *Residencial 9 de Julio*, San Martín y R Sáenz Peña, T 21221; *Residencial San Martín*, 12 de Octubre 1150, T 21211.

At the confluence of the two rivers above Corrientes the Río Paraguay comes in from the N, the Alto Paraná from the E. The Alto Paraná is difficult to navigate; it is, in parts, shallow; there are several rapids, and sometimes the stream is braided, its various channels embracing mid-stream islands. Much rice is grown on its banks. The shortest and least crowded route from Buenos Aires to the Alto Paraná is along Route 14 from Zárate which follows the Río Uruguay and avoids the main population centres.

The main Argentine port, on the S bank of the Paraná, is **Posadas**, capital of the province of Misiones, 377 km above Corrientes, and very hot in summer. Population 141,000. A good way of seeing the city is to take the No 7 bus ("Circunvalación") from Calle Junín. There is a good Mercado Artesanal at Alberdi 602 in the Parque Río del Paraguay (Mon-Fri, 0800-1700). Yerba mate, tea and tobacco are grown in the area. **NB** All street numberings have been changed: buildings now have both new and old numbers.

Museums Museo Regional, Alberdi 606 in the Parque Río del Paraguay, open 0800-1200, 1400-2000, rather neglected; Museo del Hombre, Gen Paz 1865, open Mon-Fri, 0700-1300, 1400-1900, housing archaeological pieces from the areas to be flooded by the Yacyretá hydroelectric project and a section on the Jesuit missionary era; Museo de Ciencias Naturales, San Luis 384, open Tues-Sun, 0800-1200, 1500-1900, incl artefacts from San Ignacio Miní; Museo de Bellas Artes, Sarmiento 317, open 0700-1230, 1400-1830.

On the opposite bank of the river lies the Paraguayan town of Encarnación (with buses to Asunción): a bridge links the two towns, no pedestrians or bicycles allowed across. Buses every 15 mins from opposite bus terminal, US$1; bus will not wait at frontier so keep your ticket (and your luggage) and catch next bus. A ferry service still runs, apparently for Argentines only. Pesos are accepted in Encarnación, so no need to change them back into dollars.

Hotels Best is **A1** *Libertador*, San Lorenzo 2081, T 37601; **A2** *Continental*, Bolívar 314, T 38966, comfortable, but noisy, reasonable breakfast; **A2** *Posadas*, Bolívar 272, T 30801, with bath and breakfast, good service, snack bar, laundry, highly rec; **C** *Familiar*, Mitre 58; **C** *Turismo*, Bolívar 171, T 32711, modern but poor maintenance; **C** *City*, Colón 280, T 33901, shower, a/c, clean and reasonable, good restaurant (colectivo bus service from airport to this hotel); **C** *Residencial Colón*, Colón, 2169, good and clean; **C** *Horianski*, Líbano 2655, T 22675, with bath, garage, family atmosphere but poor value; **C** *Residencial Córdoba*, Santiago del Estero 171, T 35451; **C** *Residencial Misiones*, Azara 382, simple but good value, bugs; **C** *Residencial Marlis*, Corrientes 234, T 25764, clean, German spoken, highly rec. Many adequate *residenciales* in the centre. **D** *Residencial Andresito*, Salta 1743, T 23850, youth hostel style, clean, noisy.

Camping Municipal camping ground on the river, off the road to San Ignacio Miní, electric showers, dirty, shop, reached by buses 4 or 21 from centre.

Restaurants *El Tropezón*, San Martín 185, good, inexpensive; *El Encuentro*, San Martín 361, good value; *La Ventana*, Bolívar 1725, excellent; *Restaurant de la Sociedad Española*, La Rioja 1848, good food, popular lunches; *El Estribo*, Tucumán y Ayacucho, good cooking in attractive atmosphere, rec; excellent buffet on ground floor of *Hotel Savoy*. There is an excellent restaurant *La Querencia*, Bolívar 322, on Plaza 9 Julio, good value, rec; *Pizzería Los Pinos*, Sarmiento y Rivadavia, excellent and cheap; *Pizzería La Grata Alegría*, Bolívar y Junín, good. *Sukimo*, Azare near San Martín, good for breakfast. The restaurant at San Martín 1788 serves excellent meals, good value. Several cheap places on Av Mitre near the bus terminus, near the market and on the road to the port.

Banks and Exchange Difficult to change cheques. Only **Banco de Iberá**, Bolívar 1821 (main square), changes Amex cheques (4-5% commission). **Banco de La Nación**, Bolívar 1799. Opens very early, 0700-1215. **Banco Francés**, San Martín y San Lorenzo, Visa cash advance (am only) also **Banco Río**, Colón 1950. *Cambio Mazza*, Bolívar 1480 and Buenos Aires 1442. Street money changers on SW corner of Plaza 9 de Julio. If stuck when banks and *cambios* are closed, cross the river to Encarnación and use the street changers.

Paraguayan Consulate San Lorenzo 179. **Brazilian Consulate** Mitre 631, T 24830, 0800-1200, visas issued free, photo required, 90 days given.

Discos on Bolívar between 3 de Febrero y 25 de Mayo (*Power*) and at San Martín y Jujuy, open 0100-0500 Thur-Sun.

Post Office Bolívar y Ayacucho.

Travel Agent *Viajes Turismo*, Colón 1901, ask for Kenneth Nairn, speaks English, most helpful, good tours to Iguazú and local sights. Amex agent, *Express Travel*, Félix de Azara 2097, T 237687.

Tourist Office Colón 1985 y La Rioja, T 24360, helpful, open Mon-Fri, 0630-1230, 1400-2000, Sat/Sun, 0800-1200, 1600-2000; maps and brochures in English of Posadas, Formosa and Iguazú Falls. Hotel listings for Misiones province.

Airport General San Martín (12 km), reached from Posadas by Bus No 8 or 28 from near bus terminal (ask at kiosk opp terminal) in 20 mins, US$0.45, taxi US$13. Daily from **Buenos Aires** with Austral, Ayacucho 264, T 32889/35031, Mon-Fri via Corrientes.

Buses Terminus at Av Uruguay y Av Mitre on W side of town. From **Buenos Aires**, US$40-80, 15 hrs; Expreso Singer and Tigre-Iguazú each have several buses a day: *común* US$47.50, *diferencial* US$58, *ejecutivo* (with hot meal) US$70. Some go via Resistencia, some via Concordia. Expreso Singer (Av Mitre 2447, T 24771/2) and Tigre bus terminal is 5 mins walk from the main bus terminal. From the Argentine side of the international bridge bus tickets to Buenos Aires are sold which incl taxi to bus terminal and breakfast. Frequent services to San Ignacio Miní (1 hr), US$5 and Puerto Iguazú, *servicio común* US$19 (20% student discount), 7 hrs, *expreso*, US$23, 5 hrs. To **Córdoba** with Singer and Litoral on alternate days at 1200, arrive at 0735 next day. To **Corrientes** US$15; to **Formosa**, US$8. La Estrella bus to **Tucumán**, Tues, Thur, Sun at 1720, 16 hrs, US$28. To **Resistencia**, 6-7 hrs, US$15. To **Concordia** (Expreso Singer) US$32, 2100 daily, 10 hrs. To **Concepción del Uruguay**, Singer, US$29, 11 hrs.

International To **Asunción** (Expreso Singer, daily 1400, 7 hrs, and Empresa Godoy), US$14. To **Montevideo**, a roundabout journey because the main Asunción-Montevideo route passes through Corrientes. One can take Expreso Singer bus to the junction for Colón, at Villa San José (ACA hostel, C), local bus to Colón; two local buses over the bridge to Paysandú (US$3), then plenty of buses to Montevideo. If going to Brazil (Uruguaiana) there are 3 daily buses (Singer) to **Paso de los Libres** for Puente Internacional—Argentine customs—the bus from here to the Brazilian border on the other side of the Río Uruguay costs US$0.50. Expreso Singer bus to **Porto Alegre** (via Oberá, Panambí, Santo Angelo and Carazinho), Tues, Thur, Sun at 1400, arriving 0345 next day. If the bus is full it is possible to buy a ticket (without a seat) in Oberá. The bus usually empties before long and you can get a seat.

Excursion To *San Miguel Apóstoles*, 65 km S, a prosperous town founded by Ukrainian and Polish immigrants, where a maté festival is held in Nov (**E** *Hotel Misiones*, clean).

From Posadas a visit should be paid to the impressive ruins of Jesuit settlements and to the magnificent Falls of Iguazú.

Not far from Posadas are the ruins of several old Jesuit missions among the Guaraní Indians, from which the province of Misiones derives its name. On Ruta 12, 25 km E of Posadas, is Candelaria, the oldest Jesuit village in Misiones (not signposted, in grounds of the prison, ask permission to visit). 16 km before San

Ignacio Miní (the best-maintained – see below) are the impressive ruins of *Santa Ana*, more extensive in area than San Ignacio. The turn off to the ruins (signed) is 1 km from the town of Santa Ana; they lie about 15 mins walk off the main road along a path. *Loreto* (not restored) can be visited from San Ignacio. The ruins are 5-6 km before San Ignacio (coming from Posadas), 3 km down a dirt road; there is a sign post. Little remains standing, other than unconnected walls, of a once substantial establishment. Note the number of old trees with stones encased between their buttresses and main trunk.

At *San Ignacio Miní*, founded on its present site in 1696, the grass-covered plaza, a hundred metres square, is flanked N, E and W by 30 parallel blocks of stone buildings with ten small, one-room dwellings to the block. The roofs have gone, but the massive metre-thick walls are still standing except where they have been torn down by the *ibapoi* trees; each block was surrounded by a roofed gallery. The public buildings, some of them still 10m high, are on the south side. In the centre are the ruins of a large church finished about 1724. To the right is the cemetery, to the left the school and the cloisters of the priests. Beyond are other buildings which were the workshops, refectory and storerooms. The masonry, a red or yellow sandstone from the Paraná River, was held together by a sandy mud. There is much bas-relief sculpture, mostly of floral designs. Now maintained by UNESCO as a National Monument (open 0700-1900, entry US$2.50, includes "Museo Vivo", see below – US$10 with guide, tip appreciated if the guards look after your luggage; you have to pay to park by the ruins' fence; park on the other side of the street, it's free!). Opposite the entrance is a shop selling massive homemade ice creams for US$2.50. Allow about 1½ hrs for a leisurely visit. There are heavy rains in Feb. Mosquitoes can be a problem. Go early to avoid crowds; good birdwatching.

The Jesuits set up their first missions among the Guaraní Indians about 1609, in the region of Guaíra, now in Brazil. The missions flourished: cotton was introduced, the Indians wove their own clothes, dressed like Europeans, raised cattle, and built and sculpted and painted their own churches. But in 1627 they were violently attacked by the slave-hunting Bandeirantes from São Paulo, and by 1632 the position of the missions had become impossible: 12,000 converts, led by the priests, floated on 700 rafts down the Paranapanema into the Paraná, only to find their route made impassable by the Guaíra Falls. They pushed for eight days through dense virgin forests on both sides of the river, then built new boats and continued their journey; 725 km from their old homes they founded new missions in what is now Paraguay, Argentine Misiones, and Brazilian Rio Grande do Sul. By the early 18th century there were, on both sides of the river, 30 mission villages with a combined population of over 100,000 souls. Only four of these show any signs of their former splendour: San Ignacio Miní, São Miguel (Brazil), and Jesús and Trinidad (Paraguay). (Note Trinidad can also be visited by bus from Posadas. See Paraguay section for details.) At the height of its prosperity in 1731 San Ignacio contained 4,356 people. In 1767, Charles III of Spain expelled the Jesuits from Spanish territory; the Franciscans and Dominicans then took over. After the Jesuits had gone, there was a rapid decline in prosperity. By 1784 there were only 176 Indians at San Ignacio Miní; by 1810, none remained. By order of the Paraguayan dictator Francia, all the settlements were evacuated in 1817, and San Ignacio was set on fire. The village was lost in the jungle until it was discovered again in 1897. In 1943 an agency of the Argentine Government took control. Some of the craft work produced at the settlement can be seen at two museums in Buenos Aires: the Museo Colonial Isaac Fernández Blanco and the municipal Museo de Arte Colonial. 200m beyond the entrance to the ruins is the Centro de Interpretación Jesuítico-Guaraní, generally known as the "Museo Vivo", with sections on the lives of the Guaraníes before the arrival of the Spanish, the work of the Jesuits, the consequences of their expulsion and a fine reconstruction of the ruins, well laid out, rec before going on to ruins. *Son-et-lumière* show at the ruins, 2000 (not Mon or Tues) US$2.50, weekends only out of season, cancelled in wet weather, Spanish only, tickets from museum. Festival Jul 30-31.

Accommodation B ACA *Hostería*, good, lunches available; **C** Hotel San Ignacio, friendly, good, clean, restaurant with light meals, *cabañas* (closed in Aug/Sep); **D** Hospedaje El Descanso, Pellegrini 270, clean, modern, quiet, owner speaks German, rec, signposted from the main road, also has excellent camping, US$4 pp; **D** Albergue Municipal, San Martín 4040. **E** Hospedaje Alemán Los Salpeterer, Sarmiento y Centenario, 100 m from bus station, kitchen, nice garden, a bit run down, "pool", camping, rec, English and German spoken, owner Peter Sutter is helpful and has good travel information. Gerardo, owner of *Caño 14* restaurant, on left between exit and entrance to ruins, offers cheap lodging, or camping in garden, good. *Hospedaje de la Selva*, 5 km NE on Route 12, D pp with meals, also cabins, horse riding, canoeing and ecological tours, English and German spoken, a good way to experience life on a farm. Ask at *Rest Artemio* (see below) and you will be given a lift there, rec. *Restaurant Artemio I*, good and cheap lunches, open evenings in high season, weekend evenings otherwise (accepts all local currencies, US$ and D-mark, good exchange rate too). There are two *comedores* (lunch only) opposite the entrance to the ruins.

Camping outside the ruins in municipal site; cold showers and toilets. Two pleasant sites by small lake about 5 km S of San Ignacio, on Route 12, cold showers only.

Buses To/from **Posadas** every ½ hr-1 hr, US$5, last return bus at 2100; to Puerto Iguazú, dep 0915, arr 1500, US$14; to **Buenos Aires**, US$35 incl dinner, 24 hrs, dep 1800 or 1900, tickets from restaurant at entrance to town.

Excursions To the house of Horacio Quiroga, the Argentine writer, 2 km outside town. To the Peñón Teyu-Cuare, 11 km S, a 150m high hill overlooking the Río Paraná offering panoramic views. Tours and excursions on foot, on horseback and by canoe are offered by Dante and Eva Perroue, details from tourist information.

At Jardín América, 48 km N of San Ignacio, there is an excellent municipal campsite 2 km off Route 12. Flights can be taken over Misiones province for US$50. At **Capioví** there is a restaurant (*Salto*) and campsite, with a room with beds for budget travellers, pleasant, near Capioví Falls; owner speaks German and English. At **Puerto Rico**, 21 km N of Jardín América, there is a good hotel, **C** *Suizo*; campsite at Club de Pesca; rec restaurants are *Don Luis* and *Churrascaría Flach*, both on main street. In **Montecarlo**, 38 km further N, there is a zoo (ACA *hostería*, T 97023, highly rec; *Hotels Ideal* and *Kayken*, both F, clean, friendly).

The most successful colonization in Argentina of late years has been at **Eldorado** (pop 14,440), 16 km further N. This prosperous small town is surrounded by flourishing *mate*, tung, citrus, eucalyptus and tobacco plantations. There are tung oil factories, sawmills, plywood factories, *mate* drying installations and a citrus packing plant. The ACA office is very helpful and has a large illuminated map of Eldorado and its surroundings. For information on the **Misiones Rainforest Reserve**, contact Daphne Colcombet, T (0751) 21351.

Hotels at Eldorado B *Hostería ACA*, T 21370, pool, good facilities; **C** *Alfa*, Córdoba y Rioja, T 21097; **D** *Atlántida*, San Martín 3087, T 2441, a/c, pool, parking, good restaurants, friendly, rec; **D** *Esmeralda*, Av San Martín, Km 8; **D** *Ilex*, Av San Martín, Km 9, clean, safe; *Gran Riojano*, Av San Martín 314, T 22217, very friendly, 5 min walk from main road crossing, with restaurant; **E** *Ideal*, clean, safe.

Camping Municipal site in Parque Schweim, Av San Martín, Km 1, T 0751-2154, free, good.

Exchange *Cambio Fonseca*.

Near **Wanda**, 42 km further N, there are at least two open-cast amethyst and quartz mines which sell gems, but they are much more expensive than in Brazil. There are free guided tours to one of them, Salva-Irupé, daily, worthwhile. Nearby at **Puerto Esperanza** is the **D** pp *Hotel Las Brisas*, Swiss owned, English and German spoken, discount for Swiss nationals. (Buses between Posadas and Puerto Iguazú stop near the mines and the hotel.) From Eldorado, an interesting trip, especially for lovers of flora and fauna, can be made by following Route 17 W (buses 0800 and 1530), paved to **Bernardo Yrigoyen**, a nice village, lovely vegetation en route (**D** ACA *Motel*, T 0751-92026, Ruta Nacional 14, Km 1435, clean, friendly). The direct (dirt) road from Puerto Iguazú to Bernardo Yrigoyen crosses the National Park of Iguazú, passing Andrecito (**D** *Residencial Los Robles*, clean, quiet, nice), Cabuneí and San Antonio. Local buses ply the route if the weather is dry. From B Yrigoyen follow Route 14 to Tobuna, where you will see the Alegría falls. At **Palmera Boca**, 3 km from San Pedro, SW of Tobuna, is **D** *Posada Itaroga*, T 0751-70165, a family farm with log houses beside a lake, swimming and rowing boats, breakfast incl in price, cooking facilities, peaceful, relaxed and friendly, rec. Continue on Route 14 to the small village of Paraíso, see Moconá falls 82 km from there, then Dos de Mayo (**D** *Hotel Alex*, clean, friendly). Pass through **Oberá**, pop 42,000, the second largest town in Misiones (*Hotel Cuatro Pinos*, Av Sarmiento 853, T 21306, good value; **D** *Hotel Real*, opp bus terminal, basic, hot showers; many others; cheap accommodation at Centro Deportivo; campsite 6 km outside town on road to Santa Ana, with swimming pool and waterfall nearby; *Enqüete* restaurant, Cabeza de Vaca 340, good, excellent *empanadas* at *Bar Terminal* next to bus terminal), and follow Route 103 W to Santa Ana, and the main Puerto Iguazú-Posadas road. In Oberá, there is a Parque de Naciones, with houses to commemorate the nationalities of all the immigrants who founded the town. In the first week of Oct is a Fiesta del Inmigrante; there are about 14 groups of immigrants. Places of interest: Museo de Ciencias Naturales; ceramics workshops; Criadero de Pájaros Wendlinger (with birds of the region); Serpentario, Calle La Paz (with snakes of Misiones), best visited 1000-1200; and the many tea and maté-leaf drying factories can be visited. Tourist information centre at Plazoleta Güemes, close to San Antonio church, open 0700-1900, Sat 0700-1300, very helpful, lots of maps. Bus to Posadas, 2 hrs, US$5.50, Expreso Singer; once a day to/from Iguazú, 5 hrs.

THE IGUAZU FALLS (8)

For specific references to the Brazilian side of the Falls, with accommodation and transport links, see Southern Brazil section, the Paraná River. For a general description, local transport arrangements, and specific Argentine references, see below.

The **Iguazú Falls** are the most overwhelming falls in South America. They lie about 350 km upstream from Posadas where, 19 km above the confluence of the Iguazú with the Alto Paraná, the waters fall thunderously in virgin forest bright with orchids and serpentine creepers festooning the branches. Above the impact of water on basalt rock hovers a perpetual 30-metre high cloud of mist in which the sun creates blazing rainbows. The Río Iguazú (Guaraní for great waters) rises in the Brazilian hills near Curitiba and receives some 30 streams on its course across the plateau. Above the main falls the river, sown with wooded islets, opens out to a width of 4 km. There are rapids for 3½ km above the 60-metre precipice over which the water plunges in 275 falls over a frontage of 2,470m, at a rate of 1,750 cubic metres a second. Their height is greater than Niagara's by 20m or so and their width by one half, but most of the falls are broken midway by ledges of rock. Viewed from below, the tumbling water in its setting of begonias, orchids, fern and palms with toucans, flocks of parrots and cacique birds, swifts (*vencejos*) dodging in and out of the very falls, and myriads of butterflies (at least 500 different species), is majestically beautiful, especially outside the cool season (when the water is much diminished, as are the birds and insects). The first European visitor to the falls was the Spaniard Alvar Núñez Cabeza de Vaca in 1541, on his search for a connection between the Brazilian coast and the Río de la Plata.

Visitors to the Falls should note that the Brazilian side (best visited in the morning because the light then is better for photography) shows the best panorama of the whole falls and should therefore be preferred if your visit is limited to, say, half a day, but the Argentine side (which needs a day or more to explore properly: the area is much greater) shows more close detail of the individual falls and is much more interesting from the point of view of seeing the forest with its wildlife and butterflies. There is a bird hide overlooking a marsh (Bañado), a 4 km-long interpreted (Spanish) nature trail (Macuco) in the jungle, 1½ hrs, US$25, a self-guided trail around the *Circuito Inferior*, and a tour of the jungle by jeep, 1030 and 1500 daily, US$30 (Spanish only), "good fun but not a serious nature experience". There is a natural pool, El Pozón, at the end of the nature trail, fed by a waterfall, and good for swimming (peccaries have been spotted here). Another nature trail leads from the old airstrip, near the start of the Macuco trail, and follows the route of the old dirt road to Puerto Iguazú. The whole park on both sides of the border is an excellent place for seeing birds and wildlife, but to appreciate this properly you need to get well away from the visitors' areas. Many of the roads and trails on both sides need permission to enter. A company like Focus (T Belo Horizonte, Brazil, 031-223-0358, USA 612-892-7830) can arrange guided tours on foot (full details under Belo Horizonte **Travel Agents**). (An advantage in visiting the Argentine side first is that the information provided at the Visitors' Centre is far superior to anything offered in Brazil.) One cannot cross the river at the Falls themselves; this can only be done by bridge between Porto Meira and Puerto Iguazú.

The Devil's Throat, the most spectacular fall, is best seen from Puerto Canoas, to which buses run (see below), or you can drive (parking US$1). On the Argentine side the upper series of catwalks on the river, *Circuito Superior*, are periodically destroyed by floods (they were open in late 1993/1994). Boats from Puerto Canoas to the Devil's Throat catwalk charge US$5, "breathtaking". Recommended in the evening when the light is best and the swifts are returning to roost on the walls, some behind the water. There are no boats when the water level is low.

To walk along the lower series of catwalks, at the level of the midway ledge,

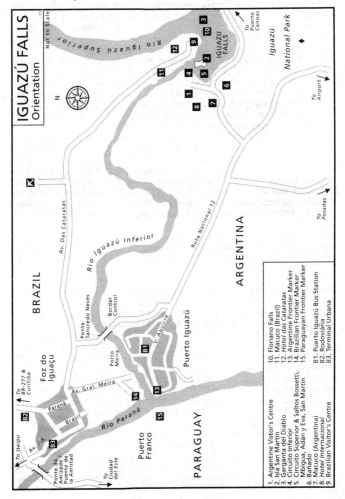

IGUAZÚ FALLS
Orientation

Not to Scale

1. Argentine Visitor's Centre
2. Isla San Martín
3. Garganta del Diablo
4. Circuito Inferior
5. Circuito Superior & Saltos Bossetti, Mbigua, Adán y Eva, San Martín
6. Bañado
7. Macuco (Argentina)
8. *Hotel Internacional*
9. Brazilian Visitor's Centre
10. Floriano Falls
11. Macuco (Brazil)
12. *Hotel das Cataratas*
13. Argentine Frontier Marker
14. Brazilian Frontier Marker
15. Paraguayan Frontier Marker

B1. Puerto Iguazú Bus Station
B2. Rodoviária
B3. Terminal Urbana

waterproof coats or swimming costumes are advisable but not absolutely necessary. Wear shoes with good soles when walking around, as the rocks are very slippery in places. Put your camera in a plastic bag. Take bathing gear in summer to cool off. A trail starting behind the *Hotel Internacional* leads down to the Río Iguazú ferry to Isla San Martín; ferry leaves on demand, takes 2-3 mins, US$5 return (no charge in low season, early 1995); bathing is possible from Isla San Martín, and a circuit of paths gets very close to some of the less-visited falls; well worth the effort but waterproofs essential. The boat trip, Aventura Náutica or Adventurama, is good (US$25); it goes over the rapid water, under a couple of falls, 10-15 mins, life jackets are provided and be prepared to get drenched.

The Argentine Iguazú National Park embraces a large area. The fauna includes the black howler monkey, capybara, jaguar and puma, along with a huge variety of birds; neither hunting nor fishing are allowed. The months to avoid are Jul (holidays) and Dec-Mar (hot); at any time of year the Falls are a very popular tourist destination. Information and permits can be got from the Visitors' Centre information desk, open daily 0800-1200 in the old, Argentine Cataratas Hotel, now converted (very helpful). The Visitors' Centre organizes a 4-hour walk (8 km) through the jungle, beginning at 0900 daily; fixed price US$40 to share among the party (better chance of seeing wildlife, rec). Catch 0825 bus from Puerto Iguazú. It also runs night-time walks between *Hotel Internacional Iguazú* and the falls when the moon is full; on clear nights the moon casts a blue halo over the falls. Mountain bikes and boats can also be hired, US$2.50 an hour. Helicopter rides over the Falls, about 7 mins for US$40, start from both the Brazilian and Argentine sides. The Argentine National Park keepers regard the helicopter rides as a serious noise pollutant. It is also reported that the helicopter noise is a threat to some bird species which are laying thinner-shelled eggs. Also, sadly, a lot of the parkland around the falls is littered, and not a waste bin in sight. Do not add to the rubbish that has to be dredged from the falls each week. There is a museum of local fauna and an auditorium for periodic slide shows (on request for 8 or more people), no commentary, just music. A good guide book on Argentine birds is for sale.

There is a US$3 charge which allows one-day entry to the Argentine Park; pay in pesos or dollars only (guests at *Hotel Internacional* pay and should then get their tickets stamped at the hotel to avoid paying again). Entry is free before 0800 and after 1800. Tenders are out for the private operation of tourist services in the park (mid-1994); if awarded, facilities may alter greatly.

Getting to the Falls Transportes Cataratas buses run every 30 mins from the Puerto Iguazú bus station to the Falls (US$4 return), taking about 30 minutes for the 22½ km. These buses are sometimes erratic, especially when it is wet, even though the times are clearly indicated. They stop at the National Park entrance for the purchase of entrance tickets. Return fare to the Falls and Puerto Canoas for Garganta del Diablo, US$4.40; first bus at 0640, last at 1700; first back at 0915, last at 1900. Inclusive fare, including boat to Isla San Martín and bus to Puerto Canoas is US$10. Fares are payable in pesos, dollars or reais. The bus runs from the Park Administration to Puerto Canoas (for Devil's Throat), US$1, hourly on the half-hour; returning, hourly at twenty-minutes-past-the-hour, but the bus is at 1750 (no buses when water level is low, but hitching is easy). There are fixed rates for taxis, US$30, up to 5 people. A tour from the bus terminal, taking in both sides of the Falls, costs US$40. Hitchhiking to the Falls is difficult, but you can hitch up to the Posadas intersection at Km 11, then it is only 7 km walk. Food and drink are available in the park but are expensive so take bottled water and a snack.

Travel between Argentina and Brazil is by the 480m Puente de la Fraternidad/Ponte Presidente Tancredo Neves, which joins Puerto Iguazú (Route 12) and Porto Meira (BR-469). Buses run every 20 mins (US$3) from the Puerto Iguazú bus terminal on Av Córdoba to Foz do Iguaçu, pausing at the border but not stopping long enough for passport controls; if you want to stay in Brazil, you have to buy a transfer ticket and wait for the next bus after getting your passport stamped (keep the ticket so as not to pay twice). Pluma bus company have been rec. Some companies have a mechanical turnstile and you have to pay again if you get off the bus. On the other hand if you are simply crossing to see the other side of the Falls and returning the same day, just stay on the bus. There is a new free zone being created round the falls so that tourists can tour the Brazilian and Argentine sides without having to worry about border crossings. Note that the Terminal Urbana is not the bus' final destination in Foz, it continues to the Paraguay border bridge; ask for the terminal if you want to alight there. The last bus leaves Puerto Iguazú at 1850. Motorists visiting the Argentine side from Brazil can park overnight in the National Park, free. Taxis between the border and Puerto Iguazú cost US$15 and between the border and *Hotel Internacional Iguazú* cost US$35. Between Oct and Feb (daylight saving dates change each year) Brazil is one hour ahead of Argentina.

Change some money into reais before going into Brazil: they try to charge you triple the true cost if you use Argentine money. Foz do Iguaçu being much the larger town, tends to be cheaper, with more choice than Puerto Iguazú for hotels and food.

It is not possible to go direct by road to Puerto Franco (Paraguay) from Puerto Iguazú; one must go through Brazil. If passing through Foz do Iguaçu en route from Puerto Iguazú to Paraguay, make sure that Brazilian officials stamp your passport. "Ponte-Ponte" buses ply between the Brazilian ends of the bridges into Argentina and into Paraguay, via Foz do Iguaçu. However, there are launches plying on the rivers Paraná and Iguazú between Puerto Franco and Puerto Iguazú: every 2 hours or so. The customs office only opens am on Argentine side.

On the Argentine side is **Puerto Iguazú**, a small modern town above the river (pop 19,000). There is a helpful tourist office (English spoken) at Av Victoria Aguirre and Brasil, open 0800-1200, 1500-2000 Mon-Fri, 0800-1200, 1630-2000 Sat and Sun (also a small office at the bus terminal). At the far end of the Av Tres Fronteras there is a *mirador* overlooking the confluence of rivers Iguaçu and Alto Paraná, with several tourist souvenir and crafts stalls.

Hotels Crowded during summer (Jan-Feb), Easter and Jul holiday periods and busy at other times of the year. Accommodation is generally expensive and in 1994 it was much cheaper to stay in Foz do Iguazu. Outside the high season be prepared to shop around and to bargain. **L2-L3** *Internacional Iguazú*, T 20748, F 20311, five-star, pool, casino, good restaurants, business facilities, overlooking the falls, rooms with garden views cost less, excellent, check-out can take ages. Reservations at Av Eduardo Madero 1020 (T 3114259, or 3136292), Buenos Aires (in UK through Utell Internacional). **A1** *Esturión*, Av Tres Fronteras 650, T 20020, clean, comfortable, swimming pool, good restaurant, reservations at Belgrano 265, 10th floor, Buenos Aires. **A2** *Saint George*, Av Córdoba 148, T 20633, with breakfast, comfortable, pool and garden, good, expensive restaurant, B in low season, highly rec; **B** *La Cabaña*, Av Tres Fronteras 434, T 20564, with shower and breakfast, a/c, good, clean and friendly, with an older part and a new annexe, swimming pool, rec; **B** *El Tropical*, Av Aguirre, out of town, breakfast incl, pool, rec; **B** *Libertador*, Bompland 110, T 20416, modern, central, helpful, large bedrooms and public rooms, rooms at back have balconies overlooking garden and swimming pool, no credit cards; **B** *Alexander*, Córdoba 685, T 20249, opp bus station, incl meagre breakfast, swimming pool; **B** *Las Orquídeas*, Ruta 12, Km 5 (T 20472), very comfortable, clean, set right in the jungle outside Puerto Iguazú, restaurant; **C** *Hostería Casa Blanca*, Guaraní 121, T 21320, 2 blocks from bus station, with breakfast, fan, immaculate rooms with phone, friendly, rec. Behind *Saint George* is **C** *Hostería Los Helechos*, Amarante 76 (off Córdoba), 100 m from bus station, T 20338, with bath and breakfast, owner speaks German, clean, pleasant and friendly, fan, motel-style accommodation, 10% discount for ISIC and youth card holders in high season; **C** *Residencial Gloria*, Av Uruguay 344, with bath (electric showers) and fridge, pool, clean, quiet, friendly; **C** *Residencial Lilian*, FL Beltrán 183, 2 blocks from bus terminal, with bath, clean, helpful, safe, rec; **C** *Residencial Paquita*, Av Córdoba 158, T 20434, opp bus terminal, clean, friendly, nice setting, some rooms with terrace rec; **C** *Residencial Río Selva*, San Lorenzo 147, T 21555, clean, friendly, laundry facilities, large garden, use of swimming pool, communal barbecue, highly rec. **C** *Residencial San Fernando*, Córdoba 693, close to bus station, with bath, clean, popular, D in low season. Two blocks uphill to left of bus station is **C** *Residencial San Diego*, with shower and breakfast, clean, friendly, rec. **D** *Tierra Colorada*, Av Córdoba y El Urú 265, T 20649, very good, clean, with fan and bath, nice restaurant, trips arranged; **D** *Residencial Arco Iris*, Curupy 152, with private shower, basic, cooking facilities, clean; **D** *El Descanso*, Curupy 160; **D** *King*, Aguirre 209, T 20917, pool, hot showers, good value; **D** *Misiones*, Aquirre opp Tourist Office, clean, friendly and less busy than many other hotels. **E** *Hospedaje Uno*, Beltrán, T 20529, toilet and electric shower in all rooms,

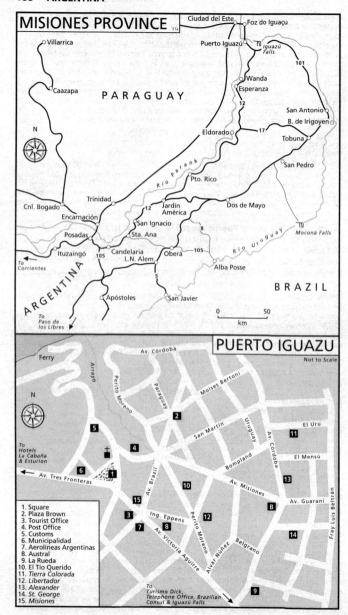

MISIONES PROVINCE

Villarrica

Caazapa

PARAGUAY

N

Ciudad del Este · Foz do Iguaçu

Puerto Iguazú · Iguazú Falls

101

Wanda
Esperanza

12

San Antonio
B. de Irigoyen

Eldorado 17

Tobuna

San Pedro

Río Paraná

Pto. Rico

Cnl. Bogado

Trinidad

12 Jardín América

Dos de Mayo

Encarnación

San Ignacio

8

Posadas

Sta. Ana

Moconá Falls

Ituzaingó

105

Candelaria
L.N. Alem

Obera 105

Río Uruguay

To Corrientes

ARGENTINA

5

Alba Posse

BRAZIL

Apóstoles

San Javier

0   50
        km

To Paso de los Libres

PUERTO IGUAZU

Not to Scale

Ferry

Av. Córdoba

N

Arroyo

Perito Moreno

Paraguay

Moisés Bertoni

2

San Martín

Uruguay

El Uru

11

5

4

Av. Córdoba

El Mensú

To Hotels La Cabaña & Esturion

Bomplant

6

Av. Tres Fronteras

1

10

Av. Misiones

13

15

Av. Brazil

B

Av. Guaraní

3

Ing. Eppens

12

Perito Moreno

7

8

Av. Victoria Aguirre

14

Alvar Núñez

Belgrano

Fray Luis Beltrán

1. Square
2. Plaza Brown
3. Tourist Office
4. Post Office
5. Customs
6. Municipalidad
7. Aerolíneas Argentinas
8. Austral
9. La Rueda
10. El Tío Querido
11. *Tierra Colorada*
12. *Libertador*
13. *Alexander*
14. St. George
15. *Misiones*

To Turismo Dick, Telephone Office, Brazilian Consul & Iguazú Falls

9

friendly, clean, rec. The Tourist Office has a list of *Casas Familiares* (F pp), though it may be reluctant to find private accommodation unless the hotels are full.

Camping Free site 600m past parking area at Puerto Canoas. Tables, but no other facilities. Camping sometimes permitted at the school just inside the Park entrance. Municipal campsite in Puerto Iguazú reported "grim". Camping El Pindó at the edge of town, charges US$1.60 pp, plus charge for tent and for use of pool, friendly, but very run down. There are also facilities at Complejo Turístico Americano, Km 5, Route 12, T 2782 incl pool (open to non-guests, US$2.50) in pleasant, wooded gardens, but no food; US$3 pp, US$3/car, US$3/tent.

Restaurants *La Rueda*, Av Córdoba 28, good food at reasonable prices; *Pizzería Ser*, Victoria Aguirre 453, good pizzas; *Charo*, Córdoba 106, good food, popular with locals, no credit cards; *Don Nicola*, Bompland 555, good. *El Criollito*, Av Tres Fronteras 62, rec; *Casa de Comercio*, Aguirre 327. Good meals in the bus terminal restaurant, *Toma's*, open 24 hrs. *Bar La Plaza*, Av Aguirre, outdoor tables, music, cheap and pleasant. *Chapa*, behind bus station, cheap, highly rec. *Fechonas*, Ing Eppens, good *empanadas*.

Exchange Banco de la Nación, Aguirre, cash only, am only. 3 *casas de cambio* opposite the tourist office (rates may vary between the *casas*; shop around!), only one, **Dick**, Av Aguirre, on outskirts of town towards the falls, changes TCs, at high commission (up to 10%). Kiosk at the bus terminal accepts cheques (high commission). Several *casas de cambio* also on the outskirts of town towards the falls. Alternatively change dollars in Foz do Iguaçu and buy pesos in Puerto Iguazú. Bad rates at bus station.

Brazilian Vice Consulate Aguirre 77, 0800-1200, arrive early with onward ticket and 1 photo for a free, 90-day, multiple entry visa (check Brazil chapter, **Documents** section). Without ticket, only 15 days given. Supplies useful maps of Foz do Iguaçu.

Car Hire Avis at airport. Localiza, at airport and Victoria Aguirre 279, T 20975. Cars may be taken to the Brazilian side for an extra US$5.

Travel Agents *Turismo Dick*, Aguirre on outskirts of town towards the falls, also in Foz do Iguaçu; does not close at lunchtime; *Reinhard Foerster*, Privat Servis, Av Tres Fronteras 335, T 2774, offers naturalists' and birdwatchers' programmes. *Turismo Caracol*, on Aguirre, T 2124, does all-day tour of both sides of falls, incl good meal in Brazil, but mainly for "non-English speaking clients with an interest in shopping". *Turismo Cuenca del Plata*, Paulino Amarantes 76, T 20338, offers 10% discount to ISIC and youth card holders on local excursions. Recommended taxi-guide, Juan Villalba, T 20973 (radiotaxi 044), good value, speaks basic English. Agencies arrange tours to the Brazilian side, lunch in Foz, Itaipú and Ciudad del Este (US$45), or to a Wanda gem mine, San Ignacio Miní and a local zoo (10 hours driving time, US$25, not incl entry fees, may be cheaper for more than 2 in a taxi or hired car). *Africana Tours*, Esmeralda 358, Buenos Aires T/F 394-1720, are rec for their complete package, by plane or bus, incl all tours, hotels and half-board (US$167-598 depending on hotel). Many agencies run tours from Buenos Aires, starting at US$75 for 1-day (Flyer Turismo, T 312-9194).

Airports There is an Argentine domestic airport near the Falls, and a Brazilian international airport about half-way between Foz do Iguaçu and the Falls. Taxi between the two airports over the bridge costs US$25. Expreso A del Valle buses (T 20348) run between Argentine airport and hotels, about 2 hrs before plane departures, US$3; it stops at the bus terminal, check times at Aerolíneas Argentinas office in Puerto Iguazú (Brasil y Aguirre, T 20237/20168, open Mon-Sat until 2000 and on Sun am). (Austral office is at Aguirre 429.) A bus meets each flight on arrival; tickets US$3. Taxis charge US$10 to *Hotel Internacional* and at least US$18 to Puerto Iguazú and US$14 to Foz do Iguaçu.

Air Transport By Boeing 737 (Aerolíneas Argentinas and Austral) from Buenos Aires, mostly direct (1 hr 50 mins), several daily, US$175. Lapa Buenos Aires-Iguazú; Thur and Sun. For best view on landing, sit on left side of aircraft. Flights back to **Buenos Aires** are very crowded.

Road Transport From **Buenos Aires** crossing the Paraná at Santa Fe or Resistencia, taking the paved road to Posadas, and on to the falls, or the more direct run via Zárate and Concordia. Direct buses take some 21 hours, leaving at 1130 (returns at 1200), with Singer (Av Perito Moreno 366, T 2581) no a/c, and Buenos Aires-Posadas-Iguazú (returns at 1600 to Buenos Aires) Expreso Tigre-Iguazú, daily at 1500 and 1945, offices at Plaza Once, Buenos Aires leaving from Retiro terminal (US$56 cheapest fare). Expreso Iguazú and other companies offer discounts to students. From Iguazú to Buenos Aires, it is cheaper to take a local bus to Posadas, and then on from there. To **Santiago del Estero**, Wed and Sat at 0130 (20 hours) with Cotal, gives student discount. To **Córdoba**, daily at 1130, via Posadas 26 hrs, US$40, with Singer or El Litoral. To **Rosario** daily except Thur, 24 hrs, US$50. To **Posadas**, stopping at San Ignacio

Miní, frequent, 5 hrs, US$23, *expreso*, 7 hrs, US$19 *servicio común*. To San Ignacio Miní, US$14 *servicio común*, US$17 *rápido*. To **Resistencia** daily 1430 and 2200, 11 hrs, US$40; change there for Bolivian border at Aguas Blancas/Bermejo, via Güemes and Orán. Puerto Iguazú to **Eldorado**, 2 hrs, US$5 with Cotal. To **Salta**, via Tucumán, Tues, Thur, Sun at 1100, 12 hrs, US$80, with Itatí.

THE LAKE DISTRICT (9)

The **Lake District** contains a series of great lakes strung along the foot of the Andes from above 40° South to below 50° in the Los Glaciares National Park area. In the N the W ends of these lakes cut deeply into the mountains, their water lapping the forested skirts of some of the most spectacular snow-capped peaks in the world; their eastern ends are contained by the frontal moraines deposited there by the ancient glaciers which gouged out these huge lakes. The water is a deep blue, sometimes lashed into white froth by the region's high winds. The area is good for fishing, water-sports, walking, climbing and skiing.

Northern Patagonia has two railway lines. The more northerly runs W from Bahía Blanca to Neuquén and Zapala; the southern line runs from Bahía Blanca southwards across the Colorado to Viedma and then W through San Antonio Oeste to Bariloche and the Lake District. The roads along which buses ply and airlines are mentioned in the text. See the Chilean chapter, section 5 **The Lake District**, for map and details of the system of lakes on the far side of the Andes. These can be visited (unpaved roads) through various passes. The Puyehue route is given on p **182**, with an alternative in the Chilean section.

NB Off season, from mid-Aug to mid-Nov, many excursions, boat trips, etc, run on a limited schedule, if at all. Public transport is also limited.

Fishing The 2 main areas in this region are Junín de los Andes (from Lago Aluminé south to Bariloche), and around Esquel (from Lago Cholila in the N to Río Grande in the S to Río Arroyo Pescado in the E). The latter is the most scenic area. The lakes are full of fish, and the best time for fishing is at the beginning of the season, that is, in Nov and Dec (the season runs from early Nov to the end of Mar). Among the best are: Lagos Traful, Gutiérrez, Mascardi, Futalaufquen (in Los Alerces National Park), Meliquina, Falkner, Villarino, Nuevo, Lacar, Lolog, Curruhué, Chico, Huechulafquen, Paimún, Epulafquen, Tromen (all in Lanín National Park), and, in the far N, Quillén. In the far S, the fishing in Lago Argentino is also good. The Río Limay has good trout fishing, as do the rivers further N, the Quilquihue, Malle, Chimehuín, Collón-Curá, Hermoso, Meliquina and Caleufú. All rivers are "catch and release". They are all in the neighbourhood of San Martín de los Andes. See **Fishing**, p 229.

To the northern lakes: From Bahía Blanca, Route 22 cuts across the southern tip of La Pampa to Río Colorado (campsite with all facilities), on the river of the same name. (Bus to Buenos Aires 0100, 11 hrs, US$30.) It then runs through N Río Negro to **Choele Choel** on the Río Negro itself, 308 km from Bahía Blanca. (**C** *ACA Motel* on edge of town, T/F 0946-2394, Ruta Nacional 22, Km 1006, with bath, good restaurant at bus station, and fine modern *Hotel Choele Choel*; several other hotels; free municipal campsite beside Río Negro, shady, excellent, no showers.) The railway line from Buenos Aires follows the Río Colorado for some distance, then crosses it into the valley of the Río Negro where large fruit growing areas at Choele Choel and Villa Regina (en route to Neuquén) are irrigated from the Río Negro dam. An unbroken series of groves of tall trees shelter the vineyards and orchards.

Neuquén, capital of Neuquén Province, was founded 1904 on the W side of the confluence of the Ríos Limay and Neuquén (223 km from Choele Choel by Route 22). It is a pleasant, clean industrial city of 90,000 people. A major stop on paved

Highway 22, 540 km from Bahía Blanca and 474 km NE of Bariloche, it serves the rich oilfields to the W with heavy equipment and construction materials, and the irrigated fruit-producing valley to the E. There are also many wine *bodegas* nearby. Much farm machinery is sold to the orchards where apples, pears, grapes, hops and plums are grown. At the Parque Centenario is a *mirador* with good views of the city and the confluence of the rivers, where they become the Negro (be sure *not* to take the bus to Centenario industrial suburb). Facing Neuquén and connected by bridge is Cipolletti, in Río Negro province (pop 43,600) a prosperous centre of the fruit-growing region. The Museo Provincial Carlos Ameghino, Yrigoyen 1047, is modest but interesting.

Museums Museo Histórico Provincial, Santa Fe 163; **Museo de Ciencias Naturales**, at entrance to airport (as is the Casino).

Hotels **A3** *del Comahue*, Av Argentina 387, T 22439, 4-star, very good; **C** *Apollo*, Av Olascoaga 361, T 22334, very good; **C** *Cristal*, Av Olascoaga 268, T 22414, adequate; *ACA Cipolletti*, Ruta Nacional 22 y Av Luis Toschi, just outside Neuquén, T 71827; **C** *Hospedaje Neuquén*, Roca 109, T 22403, overpriced; other *Hospedajes* on San Martín, mostly **D**. 13 km S on Zapala road is *Hostal del Caminante*, T 33118, with pool and garden, popular. Municipal camping site near river, free, local police warn that it's dangerous.

Restaurants *Las Tres Marías*, Alberdi 126, excellent. Pleasant bars on Av Argentina; cheap places on Av Mitre opp bus station.

Exchange *Pullman*, Alcorta 163, T 22438.

Tourist Office Félix San Martín y Río Negro. **Post Office** Rivadavia y Santa Fe.

Car Mechanic Normando Toselli, Mitre 801, Neuquén 8300 (former South American superbike champion), for cars or motorbikes, highly rec.

Air Airport 7 km from centre. Taxi US$8. 3 daily flights to and from Buenos Aires, one with AR (T 30841), and 2 with Austral; also Lapa 5 a week. Connecting flights to **San Martín de los Andes** with TAN, Av Argentina 383, T 23076/24834 (30096 at airport), who also fly to **Mendoza** 7 times a week, Córdoba, Bahía Blanca (3 a week each), Comodoro Rivadavia (6 a week), **Bariloche** (8 a week) and **Puerto Montt** and **Temuco** in Chile. Ladeco flies to Temuco and Santiago 3 times a week.

Rail From Cipolletti to **Bahía Blanca** daily except Sat, 1240, a/c, bar, video, waitress service.

Buses La Estrella/El Cóndor (La Estrella), El Valle and Chevallier bus **Buenos Aires**-Neuquén, daily US$44, 18½ hours; paved road throughout. Connections with **Copahue** and **Córdoba**; also with **San Rafael** (US$20) and **San Martín de los Andes** (US$22, 4 hrs). Bus to **Zapala** daily, 7 hours. To **Mar del Plata**, US$40, 12 hrs. To **Bariloche**, take La Estrella or Chevallier (not El Valle as it stops too often), and sit on left. Bus La Unión del Sud to **Temuco** (Chile) via Zapala all year three times a week each way, and Ruta Sur twice a week, US$30, 16 hrs.

Roads If driving from Neuquén to Buenos Aires on Routes 151 and 21, via **Catriel** (rather than on Route 22), fill up with fuel here because there is no other fuel for 323 km of desert before **General Acha**. Driving from Neuquén to **Bariloche**, go via El Chocón hydroelectric lake, Junín and San Martín (both "de los Andes"), taking Routes 237, 40 and 234; route more attractive than that via Zapala. The most direct road to Bariloche (426 km) is by Route 237, then Route 40, missing Junín and San Martín. The road is fast, skirting the entire length of the reservoir formed by the Ezequiel Ramos Mejía dam. Then it drops over an escarpment to cross the Collón Curá river before following the Río Limay valley to Confluencia (**see p 174**) and the Valle Encantado.

Excursions Paved roads lead 33 km N to the artificial and natural swimming pools at the Ballester dam (take bus marked "Banda del Medio" from terminal); nearby is artificial Lago Pellegrini, where watersports are held. A narrow-gauge railway with sporadic services runs via Cipolletti to Contralmirante Cordero, 7 km from the dam. Extensive irrigation has turned the Río Negro valley into a major fruit-producing region, with apples the principal crop. All the towns in the valley celebrate the Fiesta Nacional de la Manzana in the second half of Mar.

Route 22 and the railway go W from Neuquén to **Zapala** (179 km, pop 20,000) through the oil zone at Challacó, Cutral-Có and Plaza Huincul (at the local Carmen Funes municipal museum, there are the vertebrae of a dinosaur, Argentinosaurus Huinculensis, believed to have been the largest that ever lived on Earth; its vertebra are estimated to have weighed 70 kg each; a recovered tibia is 1.60m in length). There is an excellent geology museum in Zapala, visited by specialist groups from all over the world (open only to 1300, entry free, closed weekends). Among the collections of minerals, fossils, shells and rocks, is a complete crocodile jaw, believed to be 80 million years old. There is an airport and an ACA service station.

Accommodation and Food A3 *Hue Melén*, Almte Brown 929, T 22407, good value, restaurant; **C** *Coliqueo*, Etcheluz 159, T 21308, opposite bus terminal, good; **C** *Nuevo Pehuén*, Vidal y Etcheluz, 1 block from bus terminal, T 21360, rec; **D** *Huincul*, Roca 313, restaurant. **D** *Odetto's Grill*, Ejército Argentino 455, 2 mins from bus terminal, OK. There is a municipal camping site.

Buses A Pullman bus, with hostess service, plies 3 times daily between **Bahía Blanca** and Zapala (15 hrs, US$25 with Alto Valle). El Petróleo bus leaves Zapala 0230 and 1630 for **San Martín de los Andes** (5¹/₂ hrs) via Junín de los Andes. In winter the direct route from San Martín de los Andes via the lakes may be impassable, so a bus must be taken back from San Martín to La Rinconada and then round to Bariloche (4 hrs). There is also an overnight (at 2200) Neuquén-Zapala-San Martín bus that comes through Zapala at 0230; same service at 0915 (US$23). From Zapala to **Bariloche** there are direct buses about twice a week. Zapala-**Temuco** (Chile) all year with La Unión del Sud and Ruta Sur, at 0500, US$22, 10-12 hrs, as under Neuquén (see above). Also with Igi-Llaimi Wed and Fri at 0530, return 0330, twice weekly. Buy Chilean currency before leaving.

North of Zapala on the Chilean border is the Copahue National Reservation, best-known for its thermal baths and volcano of the same name. At 1,980m above sea-level in a volcanic region, **Copahue Termas** are enclosed in a gigantic amphitheatre formed by mountain walls, with an opening to the E (several hotels in the town of Copahue, 15 km from the Termas). Near Copahue, Caviahue is being developed; accommodation is available in prettier surroundings (there are trees), and a bus service connect the two. There are bus services from Neuquén (5 hrs) and Zapala to Copahue, which may also be reached by road from Mendoza. TAN flies daily Neuquén-Copahue. The **Laguna Blanca National Park** 35 km SW of Zapala is known for its animal and bird life (notably black-necked swans). The park has not yet become a tourist centre. It can be reached by an unmarked turning off Route 40 about 10 km S of Zapala. The park entrance is 10 km from this turning, and the lagoon lies amid flat and scrubby land 4-5 km beyond. No public transport and little traffic makes hitchhiking difficult. Advice may be available at the park warden's (*guardia fauna*) office on Vidal, next to *Hotel Pehuén*, in Zapala.

Hotels N of Zapala incl those at Churriaca (131 km), Chos Malal (202 km) and Río Barrancas (at 340 km). The road via Las Lajas is paved as far as **Chos Malal**, founded as a military fort in 1889 (restored as a historic monument, with Museo Histórico Olascoaga). ACA service station and hotels (*Chos Malal*, San Martín 89, T 21469; *Hostería El Torreón*, T 21141; *Hospedaje Baal Bak*, T 21495; *Hospedaje Lavalle*, T 21193). Routes 143 and 151 from Neuquén to Mendoza via San Rafael are almost fully paved (apart from 40 km around Santa Isabel) and provide faster, though less scenic alternatives to Route 40 via Zapala, Chos Malal and Malargüe.

Bariloche is 418 km S of Zapala by a road through **Junín de los Andes** and San Martín de los Andes. Junín, known as the trout capital of Argentina, is famous for salmon and rainbow trout. A short detour from Junín leads to the very beautiful lake of Huechulafquen (bus, Kiko, US$6 one way, arrange return journey with driver); from Junín, too, a road runs W over the Tromen Pass through glorious scenery to Pucón (135 km) on Lago Villarrica, in Chile; on the way there are splendid views of Lanín volcano. Between Junín and San Martín is Chapelco civil airport, served by AR and TAN, the provincial airline of Neuquén.

Hotels and Food B *Hostería Chimehuín*, Suárez y 25 de Mayo, T 91132, fishing hostelry; **C** *Alejandro I*, on edge of town, T 91184; **D** *Residencial Marisa*, Rosas 360, cheapest; **D** *Residencial El Cedro*, Lamadrid 409, T 91182, with bath, gloomy. *Posada Pehuén*, Coronel Suárez 560, clean, good value, charming owners, Rosi and Oscar Marconi, rec. *Estancia Huechahue* (reached from the Junín-Bariloche bus), T 0944/91303, run by Jane Williams (English), comfortable, friendly, farmhouse accommodation, horseriding, fishing, river trips, rec. **Restaurant** *Ruca Hueney*, main plaza, good trout and pasta dishes, friendly service, rec. Municipal campsite. 30 km N of Junín is the ACA *Las Rinconadas*.

The Tromen (Chileans call it Mamuil Malal) pass route between Argentina and Chile is much less developed than the Puyehue route, and definitely not usable during heavy rain or snow (Jun to mid-Nov). Parts are narrow and steep. Argentine customs are at the pass. The Chilean *aduana* is at Puesco, 58 km SE of Pucón and 16 km from Tromen. Ferry at Lago Quilleihue, which is halfway between the posts, has been eliminated by a road blasted across cliffs. It is possible to camp in the area (though very windy), but take food as there are no shops at the pass. From the border, it is 24 km to Curarrehue, from where several buses a day go (either at 0600 or at the latest at 1400) to Pucón. The international bus will officially only pick up people at Tromen but at the discretion of the driver can pick up passengers at Puesco (no hotel) at 0900 and Curarrehue stops. Hitchhiking over to the Tromen Pass is difficult.

Lanín Volcano at 3,768m high, is extinct and one of the world's most beautiful mountains. Geologically, Lanín is one of the youngest volcanoes of the Andes. Special permission to visit is not needed; from Junín, during the summer season, trucks carry hikers to Paimún for US$1. A 4-hour hike from the Argentine customs post at Tromen pass (speak to the *guardaparque* at the border) leads to the *refugio* at 2,400m. The climb from *refugio* to summit is easy but crampons and ice-axe are needed. Dr González, President of the Club Andino in Junín, can arrange guides and equipment hire.

San Martín de los Andes, 40 km S of Junín (paved road), and 196 km from Zapala, is a lovely but expensive little town, population 14,000, at the E end of Lago Lacar; Mirador Bandurrias above town for views. It is the best centre for exploring **Lanín National Park**, with its sparkling lakes, wooded mountain valleys and the snow-capped Lanín Volcano (Park Administration on main plaza, helpful but maps poor; entry US$3). The numerous deer in the park are the red deer of temperate Europe and Asia. There is excellent ski-ing on Cerro Chapelco, to which there is a road, and facilities for water ski-ing, windsurfing and sailing on Lago Lacar.

Hotels Single accommodation is scarce. Motel, **L2-L3** *El Sol de los Andes*, very expensive and nice, set above the town (Cerro Cnl Díaz), T 27460, 5-star, shopping gallery, swimming pool, sauna, night club, casino, regular bus service to centre of town. In our **L3-A1** range: *Alihuen Lodge*, Ruta 62, Km 5 (road to Lake Lolog), T 26588, F 26045, incl breakfast, other meals (very good) available, lovely location and grounds, very comfortable, highly rec (owners Tomás Alfredo Sinclair and Barbara Marggraf); *El Viejo Esquiador*, San Martín 1242, T 27690, clean, friendly, rec. *La Cheminée*, Roca y Moreno, T 27617, very good, breakfast incl, but no restaurant; *La Masía*, Obeid 811, T 27688, very good. **A2** *Turismo*, Mascardi 517, T 27592, rec. *La Raclette*, Pérez 1170, T 27664, 3-star, charming, warm, excellent restaurant, rec; *Posta del Cazador*, San Martín 175, T 27501, very highly rec; **B-C** *Curra-Huinca*, Rivadavia 686, T 27224, clean, modern, rec; **B** *Hostería Los Pinos*, with breakfast, Almte Brown 420, T 27207 (cheaper low season), German-run, with a/c and heating, clean, friendly, lovely garden; **B** *Hostería Anay*, Cap Drury 841, T 27514, central, good value, rec; **B** *Hostería Las Lucarnas*, Pérez 632, T 27085/27985, English and French spoken; **B** *Residencial Peumayén*, Av San Martín 851, T 27232, very clean, with bath and breakfast. Also good, **C** *Casa Alta*, Gabriel Obeid 659, T 27456, chalet in rose garden, "beyond comparison and fantastic"; **C** (low season) *Hostería Cumelén*, Elordi 931, T 27304 (or BsAs T 502-3467), B high season, with bath, hot water, breakfast, nice lobby with fireplace, rec; **C** *Cabañas del Sur*, on main road out of town towards Junín, sleeps up to 6 in comfortable cabin, price per cabin, rec; **C** *Casa del Amigo*, Obeid y Cnl Pérez, very friendly. Consult tourist office for other private addresses, but these are only supplied in high season. Cheapest is **E** pp *Posta del Caminante*, Caballería 1164, summer only, basic, friendly, good atmosphere, noisy. The following offer discounts to ISIC and youth card holders: **D** pp *Hospedaje Turístico Caritas*, Capitán Drury 774, T 27313, shared rooms, run by church, friendly, clean, also floor space for sleeping bags in summer; *Albergue Universitario Técnico Forestal*, Pasaje de la Paz s/n, T 27618, youth hostel style, and *Hostería Los Pinos* (see above).

Camping ACA Camping with hot water and laundering facilities, F pp. *Camping Los Andes*, Juez del Valle 611, other side of bridge, accommodation, D, clean, bunk beds, shared bath. Pleasant site by the lake at Quilaquina, 27 km from San Martín, with beaches, and another on the lake at Catritre, just 6 km from town.

Restaurants Try smoked venison, wild boar or trout, at *El Ciervo*, Villegas 724; *Piscis*, Villegas y Moreno, *Betty*, San Martín 1203, and *El Peñón*, Calderón, all good. *La Tasca*, Moreno 866, excellent trout and venison, home-baked bread, rec; *Parrilla La Tranquera*, Villegas 965, good value; and *Parrilla del Esquiador*, Belgrano 885, reasonable home-cooked food. *Mendieta*,

San Martín, *parrillada*, popular; *Paprika*, Villegas 568, venison and trout, excellent, highly rec; *Jockey Club*, Villegas 657, also good. It is difficult to get dinner before 2200, but there are various good restaurants in the area. *Pizzería La Strada*, San Martín 721, good; *Fanfani*, Rodhe 786, has good pasta.

Exchange Banco de la Nación, San Martín 687, exchanges cash only; **American Express** office on San Martín, 1 block from tourist office; **Andino Internacional**, San Martín 876, Piso 1, only place to change cheques, commission 3%.

Laundry *Laverap*, Drury 878, 0800-2200 daily and Villegas 986, cheaper, 0900-1300, 1600-2130 Mon-Fri, 0900-1300 Sat.

Travel Agency *Tiempo Patagónico*, Av San Martín 950, T 27113, excursions and adventure tourism, 10% discount to ISIC and youth card holders; also *Pucará Viajes*, Av San Martín 943.

Tourist Office at Rosas 790, on main square, corner of San Martín, open 0800-2200, very helpful. **Police station** at Belgrano 611.

Car Hire Avis office, San Martín 998. Localiza, at airport and Villegas 977, T 28876.

Air There are 5 flights a week from Buenos Aires with Austral (San Martín 890, Chapelco, T 0972-27003) to Chapelco Airport, 20 km from San Martín, and daily flights except Mon and Thur with TAN from Neuquén. TAN also to Bariloche, and Puerto Montt.

Buses Station at Gral Villegas 251, good toilet facilities. **Buenos Aires**-San Martín, US$60, daily at 1240 (Chevallier) and 2100 with El Valle. To **Bariloche**, Ko Ko, 3 days a week, 0800, 4 hrs, US$22.50. To Villa La Angostura via Seven Lakes, 3 days a week with La Petroule.

Excursions The most popular trips by car are to Lagos Lolog, Alumine, Huechulafquen and Paimún, to a campsite in the shadow of Lanín Volcano. Shorter excursions can be made on horseback or by launch. A small road runs W from San Martín along the S edge of Lago Lacar for 10 km to Quila Quina, where there are Indian engravings and a lovely waterfall. Boat trip on Lago Lacar from San Martín to Quila Quina, 45 mins one way, US$10 return.

Activities Skiing There are several chair-lifts of varying capacity on Cerro Chapelco and a ski-tow higher up. Bus from San Martín to slopes, US$7 return. Very good slopes and snow conditions. As yet uncrowded. Lift pass US$25, ski hire US$5 a day from *Hostería Villa Lagos*. At the foot of the mountain are a restaurant and base lodge. There are three more restaurants on the mountain and a small café at the top. For information on trout **fishing** or duck and geese **shooting**, contact Logaine and David Denies at Trails, Pérez 662, San Martín.

To Chile 1) To Panguipulli via the frontier at Hua-Hum: boat leaves San Martín for Hua-Hum at the W end of Lago Lacar, at 0930, returns 1800, US$20 (T 27380). Camping with shop at Hua-Hum. There is now a road between San Martín and Puerto Pirehueico (Chile). Buses daily at 0800, US$6, 2 hr journey through Lanín National Park. For connections from Puerto Pirehueico to Panguipulli and beyond, see Chile chapter, **Section 5**. This route is open all year round and is an alternative to the route via the Tromen Pass (see above).

2) To Pucón and Temuco via Junín de los Andes and the Tromen Pass: mid-Nov to May Empresa San Martín Mon, Wed and Fri, at 0700, returns from Temuco the following day at 0500, Igi-Llaimi Tues, Thur and Sat at 0700, returns next day at 0630, US$25, 7 hrs, rough journey. When the pass is closed buses go via Hua-Hum and do not pass through Pucón—Empresa San Martín switches its return and forward journey days but not the times. Igi-Llaimi goes Wed and Fri only at 0500, returning from Temuco Tues and Thur at 0330. For Pucón change to JAC bus in Villarrica. JAC also runs a service between Temuco and San Martín, via Junín de los Andes and continuing to Neuquén. The companies will not give information about each other, and do not run buses in winter when the pass is blocked.

There are 2 routes S to Bariloche: one, via Lago Hermoso and Villa La Angostura, known as the "Seven Lakes Drive", is very beautiful. (National Park permit holders may camp freely along this route). On this route, from a bridge 7 km S of San Martín, you can see the Arroyo Partido: at this very point the rivulet splits, one stream flowing to the Pacific, the other to the Atlantic. Some bus services, however, take a rather less scenic route following Río Traful, then Lago Lanín and joining the paved Bariloche highway at **Confluencia** (ACA station and a hotel, also motel *El Rancho* just before Confluencia). El Valle buses, 4 a week, take this latter route; Ko Ko buses, don't follow the Seven Lakes Drive either. Round trip excursions between San Martín along the Seven Lakes Drive, 5 hrs, are operated by several tour companies.

Villa Traful, beside Lago Traful about half-way between San Martín and Bariloche on a side road, is described as a "camper's paradise". Marvellous views, fishing (licence needed) excellent. All roads are dirt; drive carefully, avoiding wild cattle! **D** pp *Hotel Pichi Traful*, and *Hostería Traful* provide accommodation.

National Park Lago Nahuel Huapi with its surroundings, an area of 7,850 sq km, was set aside in 1903 as a National Park. It contains the most diverse and spectacular natural phenomena: lakes, rivers, glaciers, waterfalls, torrents, rapids, valleys, forest, bare mountains and snow-clad peaks. Most of the area is covered with abundant vegetation, though it is notably more abundant on the Chilean side, which gets more rain. Many kinds of wild animals live in the region, but they are extremely shy and seldom glimpsed by the explorer. Bird life, on the other hand—particularly swans, geese and ducks—is seen at any time and everywhere in large flocks.

The outstanding feature of this National Park is the splendour of the lakes. The largest is *Lago Nahuel Huapi*, 531 sq km and 460m deep in places. It is 767m above sea level, in full view of the snow-covered peaks of the Cordillera and of the forests covering the lower slopes. Towering over the scene is Cerro Tronador. Some 96 km long, and not more than 12 km wide, the lake is very irregular in shape; long arms of water, or *brazos*, reminiscent of the Norwegian fjords, stretch far into the land. There are many islands: the largest is *Isla Victoria*, on which stands the forest research station where new species of vegetation are acclimatized. The Zoological Board is adding to the indigenous fauna; the trout and salmon of the lakes, for instance, have been introduced from abroad. Lago Nahuel Huapi is drained eastwards by the Río Limay; below its junction with the Río Neuquén it becomes the Río Negro, Argentina's second largest river.

A mere sand bar in one of the N *brazos* separates Lago Nahuel Huapi from Lago Correntoso, which is quite close to Lago Espejo. Lago Traful, a short distance to the NE, can be reached by a road which follows the Río Limay through the Valle Encantado, with its fantastic rock formations. S of Nahuel Huapi there are other lakes: the three main ones are Mascardi, Guillermo, and Gutiérrez. There is the luxury *Hotel Tronador* on Lake Mascardi, beautiful setting, highly rec, also camping *La Querencia*. On the shore of Lago Gutiérrez, in a grotto, is the Virgen de las Nieves (Virgin of the Snows). There is a road to these lakes from Bariloche.

Bariloche (San Carlos de), on the S shore of Lago Nahuel Huapi, founded 1898, is the best centre for exploring the National Park. Renowned for its chocolate industry, it is a beautifully-situated, Swiss-looking town of steep streets, its wooden chalets perched upon a glacial moraine at the foot of Cerro Otto. To the S lie the heights of the Ventana and the Cerro Colorado (2,135m). The place is full of hotels and *hosterías*. The cathedral, built in 1946, dominates the town; interior unfinished. There is a belvedere at the top of Cerro Otto with wide views of lake and mountain. The main road into Bariloche from the E is paved and in good condition. The town has experienced phenomenal growth and can be very busy. The best time to visit it is out of season either in the spring or autumn, although the weather is unpredictable (the forest is particularly beautiful around May). Mainly in Jul, Bariloche is a major destination for secondary school students, who come to complete courses, ski and enjoy themselves in the evening. The 24 km road to Llao-Llao (bus No 20, ¾ hr) is ribbon-developed, except near Cerro Catedral. Population, over 70,000. Lido swimming pool on the lake shore is beautifully sited but somewhat run down.

Museums The Museo de La Patagonia in the Civic Centre, has a nice collection of stuffed animals, also well worth seeing for its collection of Indian artefacts, open 1000-1200, 1400-1900 Tues-Fri, 1000-1300, Sat US$2.50; the attached **Biblioteca Sarmiento** is open Mon-Fri, 1100-2200. The clock in the Civic Centre has four figures which rotate at noon; photos with St Bernard dogs (incl brandy keg) may be taken in the Civic Centre square and on 12 de

Octubre above the Lido.

Hotels The most complete listing with map is published by the Oficina Municipal de Turismo, which you are advised to consult if you arrive in the high season without a reservation. It also has a booking service at Florida 520 (Galería), room 116, Buenos Aires. Out of season, prices are most reasonable, in all ranges, but in season everything is very expensive. Most hotels outside the town incl half-board, and those in the town incl breakfast. Hotels with lake views normally charge US$3-4 extra, per room per day, for the view in high season; we give lake-view high-season prices where applicable. The best outside town are: **Huemul** (road to Llao-Llao, 1.5 km, T 22181); **Apart-hotel Casablanca** (same road, 23.5 km), T 48117, good, on a peninsula between Lagos Nahuel Huapi and Moreno, both L2. Also at Llao-Llao, 24 km from Bariloche, is **L2 Tunquelén**, T 48233. **Hotel Llao-Llao**, reopened after complete redecoration, run by a US company, visitors welcome. **C** La Caleta, Km 1.9 on Llao-Llao road, bungalows run by Neil Callwood, price for an apartment sleeping 4, shower, open fire, excellent value, self-catering, rec, T 25650. **Pájaro Azul**, Km 10.8 Ruta Llao-Llao, 4 rooms, friendly, bus No 20 passes the door. **A1** La Cascada, Av Bustillo Ku 6, T 41046, La Cascada district, 5-star, rec.

In the town are the following: **L2 Bariloche Ski**, San Martín 352, 4-star, T 22913, Telex 18273, good; **L2 Edelweiss**, Av San Martín 232, 5-star, T 26165, modern, spotless, excellent food, enclosed pool, highly rec; **L2 Interlaken Palace**, VA O'Connor 383, T 26156, lake view, 4-star, small rooms, noisy; **L2 Lagos de la Patagonia**, San Martín 536, T 25846, 5-star, heated swimming pool; **A3 Tres Reyes**, 12 de Octubre 135, T 26121, F 24230, lake view, 4-star. First class: **A2 Bella Vista**, Rolando 351, T 22435, with breakfast, large well-appointed rooms with lake view, 2 good restaurants; **A2 Italia**, Tiscornia 892, new, clean, friendly, good breakfast; **B Aguas del Sur**, FP Moreno 353, T 22995/24329, incl excellent 4-course meal and breakfast; **B Colonial**, Quaglia 281, T 26101, clean, helpful, lake views; **B Concorde**, Pasaje Libertad 131, T 24500, 4-star, parking; **B Internacional**, Mitre 171, T 25938, F 20072, clean, reduction for ACA members; **B La Pastorella**, Belgrano 127, T 24656, with bath and breakfast, English and French-spoken, central, rec; **B Nevada**, Rolando 250, T 22778, with shower, and heating, breakfast incl, nice rm; **B Hostería Tirol**, Pasaje Libertad 175, T 26152, clean, friendly, good, German spoken; **B Ayelén**, same street, No 157, T 23611, 3-star, comfortable, TV, restaurant, rec; **C Fontán**, Palacios 200 block, pleasant, friendly, family-run, new; **C Millaray**, No 195, good, shower, closed off season; **C Casita Suiza**, Quaglia 342, T 23775/26111, comfortable, rec; **C Hostería Ruca Cheli**, 24 de Septiembre 265, T 24528; **C Residencia Elisabeth**, JJ Paso 117, central, clean, quiet, safe; **C Residencial Premier**, Rolando 263, T 23681, ½ block from main street, incl breakfast, clean, hot showers, English and German spoken, small and basic rm, rec; **C Residencia La Sureña**, San Martín, 500m W of Civic Centre, friendly, clean, helpful; **C Hostería Sur**, Beschtedt 101, T 22677, excellent value, with bath and breakfast, gives 10% discount to ISYC and youth card holders; opp is **D Residencial Piuké**, Beschtedt 136, incl breakfast (A in skiing season), clean, friendly, rec. **C Pucón**, Rolando y Mitre, T 26163, clean, helpful, rec; **C Residencial Adquintue**, VA O'Connor 776, T 22084, clean and comfortable; **C Hostería El Ñire** (T 23041), John O'Connor 94, hot showers, clean, very pleasant, good location, heated, Sr Golisch speaks English, prefers longer-stay visitors, highly rec; **C** pp Hostería El Radal, 24 de Septiembre 46, T 22551, clean, comfortable, warm, English spoken, breakfast incl, **D** pp in low season; **D Hotel Le Montague**, Elflein 49, T 22500, comfortable, clean, friendly, restaurant, gives 10% discount to ISYC and youth card holders; **D Punta Nevada**, Onelli 347, rec; **D Venezia**, Morales 446, T 22407, clean, rec; **D Victoria**, price per person, shared rm Mitre 815, friendly, information service helpful. Also rec, **D Hostería Güemes**, Güemes 715, T 24785, with breakfast, helpful; **D** pp Residencial Puyehue, Elordi 243, T 22196, clean, friendly, incl private bath and breakfast, discount for SAH users; **D** pensión of Sra Carlota Baumann, Av de los Pioneros 860 (T 29689), follow 20 de Febrero uphill for 10-15 minutes, kitchen, bath, hot water, laundry service, friendly, Sra Baumann speaks English and German, charges US$1.50 to be collected from bus station. **E Godec**, 24 de Septiembre 218, T 23085, run down but good value, restaurant (reservations in Buenos Aires T 751-4335); **E** pp Residencial No Me Olvides, Av Los Pioneros Km 1, T 29140, half hour walk from centre or Bus 50/51 to corner of Calle Videla then follow signs, nice house in quiet surroundings, friendly, clean, use of kitchen, camping US$5 pp, highly rec; **E El Mirador**, Moreno 652-76, price per person, hot water, owner speaks German, very pleasant, rec; **E** pp Residencial Rosán, Güemes 691, T 23109 (Sra Arco), strongly rec, English and German spoken, cooking facilities, clean, helpful, US$5 to put up tent. Many private homes also offer accommodation, the tourist office keeps a list. Among those rec are: **D/E Familia Dalfaro**, Rolando y Tiscorna (SW corner), clean, quiet, breakfast served in your room US$2, rec; **E Pensión Venus**, Salta 571, heating, clean, cooking facilities; **F Casa Diego**, Elflein 163, T 22556, price pp in dormitory, kitchen facilities, clean; **E Pire-Cuyen**, Anasagasti 840, clean, doubles only; **E Frey** 635, clean, dormitory accommodation, cooking and laundry facilities, motorcycle parking; **E Anasagasti** 348, friendly; **E** pp Sra Iris, Quaglia 526, with bath, rec; **E**

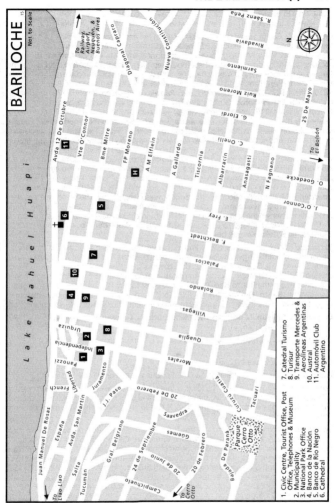

Elouisa Lamuniere, 24 de Septiembre 71, homely, helpful, cooking and washing facilities; **E** pp
Casa Nelly, Beschtedt 658, T 22295, hot showers, kitchen, camping possible, friendly, rec; **E**
Mariana Pirker, 24 de Septiembre 230, T 24873, two 3-bedded apartments with bath and
kitchen. Apartments and chalets—may also be rented—prices vary enormously according to
the season.

Youth Hostels: *Los Andes*, FP Moreno 594, T 22222 (not IYHA affiliated), D pp, cold,
gloomy, overpriced; *Alaska*, T 61564, on the road to Llao-Llao, Km 7.5 (buses 10, 20, 21, get
off at La Florida), IYHA-affiliated, E pp, good atmosphere, cooking and washing facilities,
mountain bikes, pleasant location, English spoken, good information on local treks, highly rec;
both offer 10% discount to ISYC and youth card holders.

Camping List of sites from Tourist Office. Two sites on road to Llao-Llao: *El Yeti*, Km 5.6, good, rec; *Petunia*, Km 14.9, well protected from winds by trees, hot showers, well-stocked shop, rec.

Restaurants *Casita Suiza*, Quaglia 342, excellent but expensive, poor service; *La Marmita*, Mitre 329, small, cosy, excellent mixed fondues particularly rec; *El Mundo*, Mitre 700, excellent, good value; *El Viejo Munich*, Mitre 102, good meat and fish, rec; *La Andina*, Elflein 95, specializes in inexpensive but good "fast food", rec; *Caza Mayor*, Quaglia y Elflein, game and fish, good but expensive; *La Montaña*, Elflein 49, very good value; *Kandahar*, 20 de Febrero 698, T 24702, excellent, run by Argentine ski champion Marta Peirono de Barber; *Parrilla 1810*, Elflein 167, T 23922, good meat, rec; *Parrilla La Vizcacha*, Rolando 279, good value, rec; *Parrilla Los Pioneros*, Quaglia 259, pleasant, historical photographs of Bariloche; *El Rincón*, Villegas 216, good service, cheap, rec; *Lennon*, Moreno 48, small, good food, reasonably priced, English spoken; *La Jirafa*, Palacios 288, good food, good value; *Familia Weiss*, also on Palacios (with delicatessen round corner on Mitre), excellent local specialities. Good pastries and hot chocolate at *Hola Nicolás*, Moreno 66 y Urquiza (see the graffiti-graven tables). *La Rondine*, San Martín 536, Italian, luxurious, good (above *Hotel Panamericano*). *Jauja*, Quaglia 370, good local dishes; *El Ahumadero*, Palacios, good meat and fish; *La Andinita*, Mitre 56, rec, pizzas, reasonable, friendly; *Cocodrilo*, Mitre 5, big choice of good pizzas, good value, take-away service; *Pizzaiola*, Pagano 275, good pizzeria; *La Nueva Estancia*, Elflein 401, good meat and trout, occasional live entertainment. *La Alpina Confitería*, Moreno 98, open fire, good food, reasonably priced, cheese fondue rec, very popular. *Ermitage*, tea rooms, on road to Llao-Llao at Km 18, owner speaks Slovene. Many good delicatessens in the area with take-away food, incl chicken pizzas and cheeses, for picnics.

On Av Bustillo (the road to Llao-Llao), Km 10, is *La Posta del Río*, reasonable, and *La Glorieta*, Av Bustillo, Km 3.8, good.

Exchange There are several banks and exchange shops, which buy and sell virtually all European and South American currencies, besides US dollars; Sat is a bad day. *Kiosko Anri*, Mitre 339 (rear of Galería Arrayanes), US$ cheques and Chilean pesos accepted. *Olano*, Quaglia 238, 2% commission on TCs. **American Express**, B Mitre 387, will not change money and sends you to the **Banco Nación**, Mitre y Villegas, to buy TCs, but does have emergency cash service. **Banco Quilmes**, Mitre 300 block, cash advances on Visa. Beware forged Argentine banknotes. If everything closed try *Kiwanis* (boot rental), Mitre 210, 3% commission.

Consulates Chilean JM de Rosas 180, friendly, helpful; **German**, Ruiz Moreno 45, T 25695; **Swiss**, Quaglia 342, T 26111.

Cinemas Arrayanes, Moreno 39; Cine Club, Tues 2115 only, Biblioteca Sarmiento in the Centro Cívico.

Clinic Cruz Azul, Capraro 1216.

Laundry Laundromats on Palacios, San Martín, Quaglia, and on Villegas nr Mitre.

Post Office Centro Cívico (same building as tourist office). *Poste Restante* US$2.50 per letter.

Telecommunications San Martín e Independencia and Elflein y Frey (3 min minimum charge); cheaper from *Hotel Bariloche*, San Martín 127. Outside the phone office is a telephone with links to several countries (eg UK, Chile, Japan).

Shopping Woollen goods, eg at *Arbol* (expensive) on Mitre. The products of the local chocolate industry are excellent: *Fábrica de Chocolate Cerro León* on Av 12 de Octubre, near railway station. You can watch chocolates being made at *El Turista*, San Martín 252. One block away is *Mamushka*, excellent. Very good chocolate at *Estrella Alpina*, Villegas 216 or Albarracín 146, and *Gallardo*, *Benroth*, Beschtedt 569, and at *Abuela* Goye, Albarracín 157. Smaller shops reported to be better value. Try "Papas de Bariloche", the local chocolate speciality. Local wines are also good. Handicraft shops all along San Martín; some will change money. Artesanía cooperative on Moreno y Rolando, rec. *Burton Cerámica*, ⅔ km on Llao Llao road, Av E Bustillo 4100, T/F 41102, makes and sells "Patagonian pottery". Winter clothing at *Flying Patagonia*, Quaglia between B Mitre and VA O'Connor. **Bookshop** *Cultura*, Elflein 78, has a good range of technical books, some in English and German.

Bicycles may be hired beside the lake in high season (eg A Carlucci, Mitre 723, US$20 full day). Mopeds from Vertigo Rental, San Martín 594.

Tourist Agencies Tour buses pick you up from your hotel. *Catedral Turismo*, Mitre 399, T 25443/5, runs boats to Chile for Peulla-Puerto Montt trip, US$65 one way, rec (10% discount for ISIC and youth card holders on lake crossing to Chile and local excursions); *Turisur*, Quaglia 227, T 26109, organizes trips on lake and on land. *Limay Travel*, VA O'Connor 710, English and German spoken; Hans Schulz, Casilla 1017, T 23835/26508 (speaks Spanish, German and English) arranges tours and guides, highly rec. Arrange trekking with Sr Daniel José Gorgone,

San Martín 127, DT 0706, T 26181. Also rec, **Cumbres y Lagos**, Villegas 222, T/F 23831, skiing, mountain biking, trekking and excursions. Rec guide **Daniel Feinstein**, T/F 42259, speaks fluent English, naturalist and mountaineer, very experienced in both Argentina and Chile. **NB** Check what the cost of your tour incl; funicular rides and chair lifts are usually charged as (expensive) extras.

Tourist Office Oficina Municipal de Turismo in Centro Cívico, open in skiing season Mon-Fri 0800-2000, Sat 0900-1900. Daily at those times in summer but check times out of season (Apr, Oct-Nov) when closed at weekends. Has full list of city buses, and details of hikes and campsites in the area and is very helpful in finding accommodation. The book, *Guía Busch, Turismo y Comercio*, useful, is available free at the Río Negro or national tourist offices in Buenos Aires, but is not free in Bariloche. Also on sale is *El Sur* (Guías Regionales Argentinas, T 61478) which covers the lake district and neighbouring parts of Chile. National Park information (scanty) at San Martín 24, open 0800-2000. Information also from Sociedad Profesional de Guías de Turismo, Casilla de Correo 51, 8400 SC de Bariloche (President: Ama Petroff).

Immigration Office Next to *Hostería Tirol*, Libertad 175.

Taxis Remise Bariloche, T 30222; Auto Jet, T 22408. Some drivers speak English or German.

Car Hire Hertz, Avis, and **A1 International**, at airport and in town (latter at Bartolomé Mitre 26, T 24869, 22038); no flat rates. **Guiñazú del Campo**, Libertad 118, good cars, English spoken, no office at airport but arranges transport to meet flights. **Chapís Car**, Libertad 120, and **Carro's SACI**, Mitre 26, T 24826 (out of season open Mon-Fri, am only) are both said to be cheaper. Localiza, at airport and San Martín 570, reliable, helpful, competitive, better km allowance than others. To enter Chile a permit is necessary, US$50, allow 48 hrs.

Car mechanic Auguen SA, VA O'Connor 1068, fast, reasonable, highly rec.

Air Services Airport, 15 km from town. Many flights to **Buenos Aires**, twice a day with AR (Mitre 119 y Villegas, T 23759/23161) and daily with Austral (Mitre 185, T 22591), and Lapa 3 a week. LADE to **Trelew** and Comodoro Rivadavia, Fri and Mon. Flights, with LADE to **Esquel**, twice a week, and Austral, once. LADE also has other services in the Lake District. (It is reported that it is difficult to obtain LADE flights from Bariloche now, especially the cheaper night flights to Buenos Aires.) TAN (Villegas 142, T 27889) flies to **Puerto Montt** (Chile), twice a week, summer only, and to destinations S of Neuquén. Ladeco also flies to Puerto Montt, and to Temuco and Santiago. Taxi to or from airport, US$12; bus US$3 from Austral or Aerolíneas office.

Rail Services The railway station is 5 km E of centre (booking office closed 1200-1500 weekdays, Sat pm and all Sun), reached by local buses 70 and 71 (US$0.25), taxi US$5-6. Information from the Tourist Office; tickets also available from *Hotel Pagano y Pamozzi*, 3 blocks from Centro Cívico. See under Buenos Aires, **Railways**, for schedule and fares. The train goes via **Bahía Blanca** (about 24 hrs Bariloche-Bahía Blanca). Trip can be extremely dusty, take a wet towel in a plastic bag for face and hands. Scenery only interesting between Bariloche and Jacobacci, (**see p 185**) 4$^1/_2$ hrs. Food on board reasonable (US$7.50 for 3 courses), but not always available and water sometimes runs out.

Buses Buses stop at railway station. Paved road from Buenos Aires via Neuquén, 1,600 km. Chevallier (rec), **Buenos Aires** to Bariloche, daily, 22$^1/_2$ hrs, US$80, incl meals. Also La Estrella daily and El Valle via Neuquén, US$57 (not rec), all have toilet, a/c, video and bar. For **Mar del Plata**, take Buenos Aires bus and change at Bahía Blanca or Tres Arroyos (eg La Estrella, 1500, arrive Tres Arroyos 0555, US$60). To **Mendoza**, TAC (Mitre 86), Tues, Thur and Sat, US$70, 22 hrs, on a paved road via Zapala, Buta Ranquil and San Rafael. To **Córdoba**, TUS, 25 hrs, 4 a week, US$70. To **El Bolsón**, Don Otto (San Martín 283) or Mercedes, daily except Sun, 3$^1/_2$ hrs, US$10. To **Esquel**, Don Otto, daily, 6 hrs, US$30 (direct along Route 40) or Mercedes, US$28.50, 7 hrs (more scenic route through Los Alerces National Park, though the bus may get stuck after rainfall, sit on the right, rec). The Don Otto service continues 4 times a week to Comodoro Rivadavia, US$55. To **Puerto Madryn**, 24 hrs via Esquel (7 hr wait), and Trelew, US$60. To San Martín de los Andes, Ko Ko, Moreno 107, daily except Wed and Sun, 1430, US$22.50, 4 hrs. To **Neuquén** (550 km) US$18 by Transportes Mercedes on Bartolomé Mitre or daily with La Estrella, Palacios 246 at 1415, 6$^1/_2$ hrs (a dull journey). (No direct bus to Río Gallegos; you have to spend a night in Comodoro Rivadavia en route. Don Otto fare to Río Gallegos US$88. If heading for Punta Arenas it may be better value to go to Puerto Montt and take a Chilean bus from there.) To **Santiago** (Chile), Tues, Fri and Sun, 24 hours with tea and breakfast served en route. To **Puerto Montt**, see the route to Chile from Bariloche, **p 182.**

Activities Apart from sailing and boating, there are golf, mountaineering, walking, birdwatching, skiing, and fishing (for which you need a permit). Racquet Club, Ruta Llao-Llao,

Km 13.5, tennis and squash, snack bar. Before going hiking you are rec to buy moisturizing creams for exposed skin areas and lips. Club Andino has sketch maps of hikes, some out of date and incomplete. Excellent trout fishing Nov-Mar; boat hire arranged with tackle shops. Horseflies (*tábanos*) frequent the lake shores and lower areas in summer; lemon juice is good for keeping them away, but can cause skin irritation. For horse trekking trips contact Carol Jones, Casilla 1436 (or through Hans Schulz—see above under **Tourist Agencies**), US$35 half day, US$60 day trips, spectacular, highly rec. Also *Cumbres Patagonia*, Villegas 222, US$40 for 3 hrs, suitable for all levels of experience, enjoyable. Or ask at Club Andino for Valerie, friendly, rec.

Mountain Climbing In the area there is something for every kind of mountaineer. National Park mountain guides are available but can be expensive. Book: *Excursiones, Andinismo y Refugios de Montaña en Bariloche*, by Tonek Arko, available in local shops, US$2, or from the author at Güemes 691. In treks to *refugios* remember to add costs of ski lifts, buses, food at *refugio* and lodging (in Club Andino *refugios*: US$5 per night, plus US$3 for cooking, or US$5 for breakfast, US$8 for dinner). Take a sleeping bag. Best information from Club Andino Bariloche, 20 de Febrero 30, open 0900-1200 and 1500-2000 Mon-Fri and Sat 0900-1200. The Club arranges guides; ask for Sr Ricardo, the secretary, who organizes easy weekend climbs and walks with friendly visitors. Its booklet "Guía de Sendas y Picadas" gives details of climbs and it provides maps (1:150,000) and details of all campsites, hotels and mountain lodges. The climbing may mean a ride on horseback or a skilled ascent of the slopes of Cerro Tronador which looms over the area. The Government has built convenient rest lodges at from 1,000 to 2,000m on the mountains. Firing, light and food are provided at these points. Note that at higher levels, winter snow storms can begin as early as Apr, making climbing dangerous.

Swimming in the larger lakes such as Nahuel Huapi and Huechulafquen is not rec, for the water is cold. But swimming in smaller lakes such as Lolog, Lacar, Curruhué Chico, Hermoso, Meliquina, Espejo, Hess and Fonck is very pleasant and the water—especially where the bottom shelves to a shingly beach—can be positively warm.

Skiing There is good skiing during the winter season (July to early Oct), supervised by the Club Andino Bariloche. It is best organized with a tour company, through whom you can secure discounts as part of an inclusive deal. (Skiing is cheaper, however, at smaller resorts, such as Esquel, though more expensive at San Martín de los Andes.) The favourite skiing slopes are on Cerro Catedral (several hotels), and a new ski-lift is to be built higher up, to permit a longer skiing season. (Regular bus service with seasonal timetable from Mercedes bus company at Mitre 161, US$5 return.) There is a cable car (US$10 single, 13 return) and a chair lift (US$120 full week, US$30 full day, 17.50 afternoon only, discount for students but only if you persevere) from the foot of Cerro Catedral to points high on the ridge. Red and yellow markers painted on the rock mark a trail from the top, which leads to Refugio Frey (well equipped, blankets, meals, US$5-8, bed US$5 pp) on the edge of a small mountain lake (allow 6 hours; one can return through the forest to the ski complex the next day and take a bus back to Bariloche). The seasonal cable car, with a chair lift from its upper terminus, takes one higher than the main (2-stage) chair lift. Check at tourist info if cable car is running, as everything closes in Mar. Bus tours from Bariloche to the foot of Cerro Catedral give time for less than 2 hours on top of the mountain. Entrance to the Cerro Catedral ski slopes, below the snowline, is US$ 0.50. The only disadvantage at Bariloche is that the snow is unreliable except at the top. There are other skiing slopes 5 km out of Bariloche, on Cerro Otto (cable car, US$20 pp; open 0900-1900 Jan, Feb, Jul, Aug, and 1400-1800 rest of year; station at foot reached by bus No 50 "Teleférico", 15 mins, US$1, entry to revolving restaurant at top, US$3.50, nice *confitería* belonging to Club Andino on Cerro Otto, 20 mins walk from main *confitería* on summit). Cerro Otto can be reached in 2-3 hours' walk from the town, rec; take the paved Av de los Pioneros, then switch to the signed dirt track 1 km out of Bariloche (splendid views), or in a minibus which goes every ½ hour from a car park near the National Park headquarters (closed public holidays), between 1400 and 1600, US$7 round trip (local bus US$2.10 return). Also at Piedras Blancas (bus US$7 return); on López (try a car trip, rough road, US$14 for a tour, 1400-1830), Dormilón and La Ventana. Ski hire US$5-9 a day, depending on quality, dearer at Cerro Catedral than in town. Ski clothes can also be rented by the day, at US$1-2 per item, from Kiwanis sport stores, Mitre 210, or El Iglú, Galería Arrayanes II, Rolando 244.

Excursions There are numerous excursions: most travel agencies charge the same price. It is best to buy tours on the spot rather than in advance, although they get very booked up in season. Whole-day trip to Lagos Gutiérrez, Mascardi, Hess, the Cascada Los Alerces and Cerro Tronador (950m) leaves at 0800, US$29, and involves 1 hr walk to the Black Glacier, interesting but too much time spent on the bus. Catedral and Turisur have a 9-hour excursion, leaving at 0900 (afternoon dep also Dec-Mar), to Puerto Pañuelo, sailing down to Puerto Blest and continuing by bus to Puerto Alegre and again by launch to Puerto Frías (US$19.50). A visit to the Cascada de los Cántaros is made (stay off the boat at the Cascada and walk around to Puerto Blest through beautiful forest, 1 hr, rec). Several 12-hour excursions to San Martín de los Andes, US$34, rec, through 2 national parks, passing 7 lakes, returning via Paso de Córdoba and the Valle Encantado. This route is covered by public bus (to Osorno as far as La Angostura before turning W) rec.

The area around the resort of Llao Llao offers beautiful scenery for walking: you can choose between the 15 km Circuito Chico and the 17 km "motor tour" route back to Bariloche. A tour of the Circuito Chico costs US$13. At Km 17.7 on the road to Llao Llao there is a chairlift to Cerro Campanario (0900-1200, 1400-1800 daily, US$5), from the top of which there are fine views of Isla Victoria and Puerto Pañuelo. At Km 18.3 a turning to the left leads to Colonia Suiza and Punto Panorámico, and then along Lago Perito Moreno to Puerto Pañuelo (16 km). A trip that can be done independently is to catch a local bus to Llao Llao, US$1, getting off by the chairlift in front of the mountain (closes at 1900). Chairlift costs US$3 each way; it is possible to walk down on a steep slippery trail, in $1/2$ hr. A recommended one-day walk can be done to the Parque Municipal de Llao-Llao, with a lake, Lago Escondido. Take the Llao Llao bus from Bariloche, and get off at Puerto Pañuelo. From here take the road towards Puerto Llao Llao (signposted) until you reach the park on the left-hand side of the road. A trail leads into the park for 3.5 km to Lago Escondido. Beyond this the trail joins up with the road again. Follow the road to the right and continue until you reach a turning on the left, signposted Cerro Llao Llao. It is a walk of 1-1$1/2$ hrs along an unpaved road and then a track up to the summit. The track uphill is not clear – there are many forks but all of them seem to lead to the top – and you should be rewarded with beautiful views. To return to Puerto Pañuelo retrace your steps back to the road, and follow this to the left back to the village, to catch return buses to Bariloche. There are a couple of hotels in the vicinity: **Hotel Llao Llao**, and *La Caleta* (see p 176).

A two-day walk can be made from **Pampa Linda** over Paso de los Nubes to Laguna Frías and Puerto Frías on the Chilean frontier. To reach Pampa Linda take the Mercedes bus to Villa Mascardi and then hitch the remaining 50 km. Note that the road to Pampa Linda has a one-way system: up only before 1400, down only after 1600. Register at the Ranger station at Pampa Linda and ask their advice about conditions (campsite at Ranger Station). The route is not always well marked, and should only be attempted if there is no snow on the pass (normally passable only between Dec and Feb). Allow at least 6 hrs to reach Puerto Frías from the pass. From Puerto Frías (campsite opposite the customs post) a 30 km road leads to Peulla (see Chile, section 5). From Pampa Linda 2 other paths lead up Cerro Tronador: one leads to Refugio Otto Meiling, 2,000m, on the edge of the E glacier; the other leads to a refugio on the S side of the mountain.

Club Andino provides an inexpensive but sedate rafting trip up the Río Limay (for novices only). There is better rafting in the Chilean lakes district. A half-day excursion is possible taking a bus to Virgen de las Nieves, walking 2 km to arrive at beautiful Lago Gutiérrez; walk along lake shore to the road from El Bolsón and walk back to Bariloche (about 4 hrs).

A recommended one-day trip by car is Bariloche-Llao Llao-Bahía-Colonia Suiza-Cerro Catedral-Bariloche; the reverse direction misses the sunsets and afternoon views from the higher roads, which are negotiable in winter (even snow-covered). If one is staying only 1-2 days in the area the best excursions are to Cerro Tronador the 1st day, and on the 2nd to Cerro Catedral in the morning and Isla Victoria in the afternoon (possible only Dec-Mar when there are afternoon departures for the island). The round trip to Cerro Tronador and Cascada Los Alerces is 230 km, takes a full day starting at 0800, goes up to 950m, costs US$22 in a van for 8 people, and is highly rec. Camping facilities are good. Good walks to the *refugio Italia* at Laguna Negra (16 km trail) and to Cerro López (3 hrs, with a *refugio* after 2); in both cases take Colonia Suiza bus (from Moreno or Rolando) and for the former alight at SAC, for the latter at Picada. For *refugio Italia* allow 6 hrs up (first 4 quite gentle, last 2 steep, beside 2 waterfalls), 4 hrs return. The *refugio* is open all year, supposedly manned during season, but take food and sleeping bags. You can continue from this *refugio* to others for a 3-5 day hike; details from Club Andino.

A half-day excursion (1300-1830) may be taken from Bariloche to Puerto Pañuelo, then by boat to Isla Victoria. The full-day excursion (0900-1830, or 1300 till 2000 in season) US$28 includes the Arrayanes forest on the Quetrihue peninsula further N, and 3 hours on Isla Victoria, picnic lunch advised. It is best to book this trip through an agency, as the boat fare alone is US$21. Some boats going to Arrayanes call first at Isla Victoria, early enough to avoid boat-loads of tourists. These boats carry the names of Paraná river provinces—Corrientes, Misiones, Santa Fe—and they have no open deck. (Turisur have 4 catamarans with a bar and cafeteria.) All boats are very crowded in season, but operators have to provide seating for all passengers. The Arrayanes forest can also be visited by walking 12 km from Villa La Angostura (see next page).

Roads There are 500 km of highways (mostly unpaved) running through the park. The old road to El Bolsón and Esquel (a new, faster, but less interesting road is being built between Bariloche and Esquel) is paved for the first 30 km, then narrow, steep and with many S bends between Villa Mascardi and El Bolsón, but goes past the beautiful lakes of Gutiérrez, Mascardi and Guillermo.

Routes to Chile from Bariloche The preferred route is over Puyehue pass (a third of the cost of the lakes route), on a good broad highway which is paved on the Chilean side up to Termas de Puyehue, and almost entirely paved on the Argentine side (approximately 50 km of gravel road which is difficult in rainy season). Road from Bariloche goes around the E end of Lago Nahuel Huapi, then follows the N side of the lake through the resort town of Villa La Angostura to junction with "Ruta de Los Siete Lagos" for San Martín at Km 94, Argentine customs at Km 109 and pass at Km 125 at an elevation of about 1,280m. (About 22 km from the Argentine customs is Camping Correntoso; 4 km further is Camping El Cruce, ACA, and another 2 km brings you to Camping Osa Mayor, ACA.) Chilean customs at Km 146 in middle of a forest. The frontier is closed at night. *Hotel Termas de Puyehue* is at Km 168. Possible to camp nearby, but take own food as restaurant is expensive. Very pleasant *Motel Ñilgue* on Lake Puyehue (Chile) is at Km 174. A six-hour drive, but liable to be closed after snow-falls. Chilean currency can be bought at customs at a reasonable rate.

The alternative is to go via the lakes. The route is Bariloche to Llao-Llao by road, Llao-Llao to Puerto Blest by boat (2½ hrs), Puerto Blest Lago Frías by bus, cross the lake to Puerto Frías by boat (20 mins), then 1½ hrs by road to Peulla. Leave for Petrohué in the afternoon by boat (2½ hrs), cross Lago Todos Los Santos, passing the Osorno volcano, then by bus to Puerto Montt. This route is not recommended in wet or foggy weather.

Several bus companies run services from Bariloche to Puerto Montt, Osorno and Valdivia, via the Puyehue pass: there is at least one bus every day from Argentine side. The majority go via Osorno (6 hrs) and fares range from US$20-25 (US$35 for a 1-day excursion including city tour and Termas de Puyehue); it is no cheaper to go to Osorno and buy a separate ticket from there to Puerto Montt. Companies include Bus del Norte, San Martín 283, Mercedes, B Mitre 161, and Tas Choapa (at Turismo Algarrobal, San Martín 459, T 22774). Sit on left side for best views. You can buy a ticket to the Chilean border, then another to Puerto Montt, or pay in stages in Chile, but there is little advantage in doing this.

Turismo Catedral sells 1 and 2-day crossings to Puerto Montt via roads and lakes (route as stated above). The one-day crossing costs US$90 + cost of lunch at Peulla (US$10.80), credit cards accepted; this excursion does not permit return to Bariloche next day. (1 Sep-31 Mar, take own food, buy ticket day in advance, departs 0700.) For a two-day crossing (operates all year round), there is an overnight stop in Peulla. Accommodation at *Hotel Peulla* is in our A2 range. You can make reservations independently (*Hotel Peulla*, PO Box 487, Puerto Montt, Chile). More details about accommodation under Peulla, in **Chile, section 5**. Several tour companies sell this tour, incl transport, board and lodging. Book in advance during the high season. The other agencies sell excursions to Puerto Frías using a Mercedes bus to Puerto Pañuelo, a Turisur boat to Puerto Blest and share a bus and boat to Puerto Frías with excursion groups going on to Chile. Request information at Turismo Catedral which owns the exclusive rights to the excursion via the lakes, using their own boats and bus from Puerto Pañuelo to Puerto Frías (Andina del Sud operates with them on the Chilean side). The most satisfactory way of doing the trip full-circle is by car from Bariloche, going first via Puyehue to Puerto Montt, returning via Tromen Pass (see the Villarrica volcano, good road), then Junín and San Martín de los Andes. No cars taken on ferry on Lago Todos Los Santos.

NB You are strongly advised to get rid of all your Argentine pesos before leaving Argentina; it may be useful to have some Chilean pesos before you cross into Chile from Bariloche. The Argentine and Chilean border posts are open every day; the launches (and hence the connecting buses) on the lakes servicing the direct route via Puerto Blest to Puerto Montt generally do not operate at weekends; check. There is an absolute ban in Chile on importing any fresh food—meat, cheese, fruit—from Argentina. Bariloche Tourist Office may not be up to date on lake crossings to Puerto Montt, check details at travel agencies, particularly if travelling to meet connections.

Further information on border crossings in the Lake District will be found in **Chile, section 5**. Parts of road on the Argentine side of the Puyehue route are being rebuilt, and the lake route is long and tiring.

NB Obtain maps and information about the district in Buenos Aires at the National Park Tourist Office at Santa Fe 690, or at the provincial offices (addresses given on **p 77**); it is hard to obtain these in the provinces themselves. Park wardens are also useful sources of information.

Villa La Angostura is a picturesque town (pop 3,000) 90 km NW of Bariloche on Lago Nahuel Huapi. It can be reached by excursion bus (day trip, 8 hrs) or local bus (at 1900 daily, returning 0800, Transporte Mercedes, US$7) which requires staying overnight; hotels a little dearer than Bariloche. The port, 3 km from town, is spectacular in summer. 12 km S of the port at the S end of the Quetrihue Peninsula is **The Arrayanes Forest**, containing 300 year old specimens of the rare Arrayan tree. It is best to return to Bariloche if going on to Osorno (Chile): otherwise you have to pay twice the fare to Osorno from Bariloche and arrange for the bus company to pick you up at La Angostura. Daily bus at 1700 to San Martín de los Andes.

Hotels L2 *Hostería Las Balsas*, small, exclusive, high standard, good location; **A3** *Correntoso*, T 94168, has a chalet next door, C for 2 bedrooms, shared use of kitchen and sitting room, luxurious. *Hotel La Angostura*, T 94151. Cheaper are *La Cabañita* and *Don Pedro* in El Cruce, dirty, both **D**. Ask in the tourist office, opposite ACA, for lodgings in private houses, cheaper than hotels. *Hotel Ruca Malen*, 24 km N on lake shore; *Hotel Pichi Trafal*, 53 km N.

Camping *El Cruce*, 500m from centre, US$2 pp, dirty toilets; *ACA Osa Mayor* (2 km along Bariloche road, pleasant, open late Dec to mid-May), *Autocamping San Martín*, *Municipal Lago Correntoso*.

Travel Agent *Turismo Cerro Bayo*, Av Arrayanes s/n, of 5, T (0944) 94401/94412, 10% discount for ISIC and youth card holders on ski packages, trekking, rafting, lake and adventure tours.

Río Villegas, about 80 km S of Bariloche on the road to El Bolsón, is very beautiful. (**E** *Hostería Río Villegas*, pleasant, friendly, restaurant, just outside the gates of the National Park, by the river.)

El Bolsón is 130 km S of Bariloche on the old road to Esquel (unpaved and very rough). It is an attractive small town (pop 8,000) in beautiful country, with many mountain walks and waterfalls (dry in summer) nearby. As it lies in a hollow at about 200m, it can be very hot in summer. It has good fishing and is fully developed as a tourist resort. Within half an hour's drive are Lagos Puelo (see below) and Epuyén (shops and petrol available). The farms and the orchards sell their produce at Bariloche. Famous local fruit preserves can be bought at the factories in town. Handicraft market Thur and Sat. The Balneario Municipal is 300m from the town centre, pleasant river swimming.

Accommodation Very difficult to find in the high season. **B** *Hotel Cordillera*, San Martín 3210, T 92235, clean, warm; *Motel La Posta*, T 92297, smart and new (Route 258). **D** *Hostería Steiner*, San Martín 300, T 92224, clean and pleasant, wood fire, lovely garden; **D** *Henriquez*, Rivadavia 2950; **D** *Familia Sarakoumsky*, San Martín 3003, good. **D** *Hotel Salinas*, Rocas 641, friendly, clean, rec. **E** *Hospedaje Los Amigos*, Las Malvinas y Balcarce, 2 cabins or camping, hot water, shared bath, cooking facilities, breakfast incl, rec (also have cabins and camping 6 km away on Río Azul, good hiking and swimming in river, owners will provide transport); **E** *Campamento Ecológico*, Pagano y Costa del Río, T 92-954, bunks, US$4 camping, hot water, cooking facilities, friendly. Up to 2 days' stay possible at the Franciscan school, but get recommendation from tourist agent.

20 km N of El Bolsón, at Rinconada del Mallín Ahogado (daily bus from El Bolsón) is **B** *Hostería María y Pancho Kramer*, warmly rec, wholefood meals, hot shower, sauna, swimming pool, chess, volleyball, horseback and trekking excursions to lakes and mountains. At Lago Epuyén, 40 km S of El Bolsón, **E** pp *Refugio del Lago*, with breakfast, also full and half pension; meals with fresh food, tours, trekking, riding, French owned, Sophie and Jacques Dupont, Correo Epuyén, 9211 Chubut, or leave a message, T 0944-92753.

Camping *Del Sol*, ½ km from town, F pp, pleasant, friendly, cheap food; many other sites in surrounding area. Several *residencias* and camping sites nearby; the *Aldea Suiza* camping site, 4 km N on Route 258, rec, tennis courts, hot showers, good restaurant. *Nokan Cani*, 4 km S on road towards Lago Puelo, pleasant site near stream, picnic tables, toilets, hot showers, electricity, owner is an acupuncturist, rec. The paying campsite (US$5) at Lago Puelo has beautiful views across the lake to Tres Picos, but the walking is limited, expensive shop and café; free campsite also at Lago Puelo. Frequent public transport from El Bolsón.

Restaurants *Don Diego*, San Martín 3217, good; *Ricar-Dos*, Roca y Moreno, good coffee (food less good). *Parrilla Achachay*, San Martín y Belgrano, basic, but reasonable value. *El Viejo Maitén*, Roca 359, good. *Confitería Suiza*, Antártida Argentina 569, good homemade food; *Amacuy*, San Mateo 3217, good; *Lustra*, Sarmiento 3212, good value; *Parrilla Las Brasas*, Sarmiento y P Hube, clean, good.

Exchange *Hotel Cordillera*, tourist agency ½ block from plaza, or Inmobiliaria Turneo shop, all cash only. It can take a long time to change TCs on Mon as locals queue for money.

Travel Agent *Turismo Translago*, Perito Moreno 360, T (0944) 92523, 10% discount for ISIC and youth card holders on lake excursions to Chilean border and to Valle del Turbio, trekking to Lago Puelo and Cerro Plataforma.

Tourist Office Office on main plaza, open 0900-200. Ask for sketch maps of the beautiful walks in the neighbourhood incl up Cerro Piltriquitrón, rec (6-7 hrs round trip, great views, food and shelter at *refugio*).

Transport Full-day tours from Bariloche are run by Don Otto and Mercedes, 11 hrs, very crowded and difficult to get on in high season. Also local bus by Mercedes from Bariloche, US$10, 3¼ hrs; Empresa Charter offers 10% to ISIC and youth card holders between Bariloche and El Bolsón.

Horse riding Horacio Fernández, Loma del Medio, Apartado Postal 33, El Bolsón, CP 8430; trips of one or more days into the mountains, US$20 per day, plus US$15 for Horacio and his horse, highly rec for all standards. Cross bridge over Río Azul, follow road to right, at power station turn left, follow path straight ahead and on hill is "Cabalgatas" sign on left.

Excursion To *Lago Puelo*, about 20 km S in the Parque Nacional Lago Puelo. Regular buses from El Bolsón go to the lake via Villa Lago Puelo (*Hostería Enebros*, T 99054; *Hostería Lago Puelo*, T 99059; also *cabañas*) where there is a bank, shops and fuel. From here a path runs 12 km W to Chile. Inside the park is the *Albergue El Turbio*, T (0944) 92523, horse and kayak hire, 10% discount for ISIC and youth card holders (information from Turismo Translago in El Bolsón). Good information on the park is available from the wardens at the entrance. Turismo Translago excursions from the paying campsite, or from office in town: ½-day trip across the lake to Valle Río Turbio below Cerro Tres Picos, US$15; also to the Chilean border and Lago Inferior. Canoes can be rented for US$3/hr to appreciate the beauty of the lake. Use "Fletes" truck transport to get to more remote treks and campsites.

About 80 km S of Esquel is ***Cholila***, with superb views of Lago Cholila, crowned by the Matterhorn-like mountains of Cerros Dos and Tres Picos. A recommended journey for motorists is to spend the night at El Bolsón, enter the Los Alerces park via Cholila and drive right through it to Esquel, travelling the whole length of Lagos Rivadavia and Futalaufquen. Mercedes bus between Bariloche and Esquel passes daily.

Hotel C *El Trébol*, with bath and breakfast, basic evening meal US$5, comfortable rooms with stoves, bus stops in village 4 km away. **Restaurant** *Hue Telén*, 8 km from El Trébol, irregular opening times, 1 km from ACA (which is reported as poor).

Excursion Good walk around Lago Mosquito: continue down the road from El Trébol past the lake then take a path to the left, following the river. Cross the river on the farm bridge and continue to the base of the hills where a second bridge exists. Follow the path to the lake and walk between the lake and the hills, crossing the exit river via a suspension bridge just past El Trébol—6 hrs (Nick Saunders and Sarah Jaggs, London W1).

At La Cholila, 8 km W of Cholila, accommodation is available at the **D** pp *Hostería Estancia Lago Cholila*, views over Cerros Dos and Tres Picos, camping sites. For transport from El Bolsón or Esquel contact Pedro Torres (speaks English) 0944-99039.

Esquel, about 260 km S of Bariloche, was originally an offshoot of the Welsh colony at Chubut, nearly 650 km to the E. It is now a modern town with reasonable amenities (population 18,800). Major skiing location at La Hoya, 7 ski-lifts, 15 km N of Esquel (skiing cheaper than at Bariloche). For skiing information ask at Club Andino Esquel; bus to La Hoya from Esquel, 3 a day, US$7 return, ski pass US$22, gear hire US$7 a day. Esquel is known for its tulips, chocolate, jellies and jams (also for the mazard berry liquor made by the Braese family, interesting, but expensive).

Hotels A2 *Tehuelche*, 9 de Julio 825, T 2421, with shower, heating and breakfast, excellent restaurant, some staff speak English; **B** *Angelina*, Av Alvear 758, T 2763, very friendly and clean good food, warm, run by Italian teacher, highly rec; **C** *Hostería Los Tulipanes*, Fontana 365, T 2748, good rooms and service; **C** *Residencial Esquel*, San Martín 1040, T 2534, clean, friendly, heating, rec; **D** *Hostal La Hoya*, Ameghino 2296, T 2473, on road to airport, 1 km. Also **D** *Hostería La Hoya* at the Centro Deportivo de Ski at La Hoya itself. **D** *Vascongada*, Mitre y 9 de Julio, T 2361, with shower, friendly, good cheap food. **D** *Huentru Niyeu* (no sign), Chacabuco 606, T 2576, clean, quiet, friendly, modern, garage. **D** *Lago Verde*, Volta 1081,

T 2251, doubles only, breakfast incl, modern, comfortable, highly rec; **D** *Zacarias*, Roca 634, T 2270. **D** *Residencial Huemul*, Alvear y 25 de Mayo, T 2149, clean, not very secure, good *confiteria*; **D** *Residencial Argentino*, 25 de Mayo 862, T 2237, no singles, basic, clean, heating, camping in season; **D** *Residencial Gingins*, Rivadavia 1243, T 2452, friendly, grubby; **D/E** Sra Helga Hammond, Antártida Argentina 522, friendly, clean, German spoken; **E** Mrs Megan Rowlands' guesthouse at Rivadavia 330, T 2578, Welsh spoken, rec; **E** Sra Olga Daher, Sarmiento 269, friendly, quiet. Ask at tourist office for lodgings in private houses. Hotels are often full in Feb.

Camping Municipal site 5 km from centre on Trevelin road, near gravel-crushing plant, hot showers, rec. In the Parque Nacional there are numerous paying and free campsites beside the lakes, but a permit may be needed from Intendencia at Villa Futalaufquen and campsites are closed in winter. Free campsite at Laguna Z, 5 km along Calle Fontana. Camping at *Cabañas Tejas Negras* (C), good facilities for US$3.50, by *Pucón Pai Motel*, which has its own campsite. Also at La Colina, on hill overlooking town, Darwin 1400, US$3 pp, hot showers, kitchen facilities, lounge with log fire, highly rec. Those with sleeping bags can go to the Salesian school and sleep in the school classrooms, Dec to Mar; get recommendation from tourist office.

Restaurants *Jockey Club*, Alvear 949, reasonably priced; *Ahla Wasahla*, Sarmiento y San Martín, good cheap, friendly, closed Sun; *Red Fox*, Sarmiento 795 y Alvear, a British-style pub with light, but expensive meals, open from 2200, closed Tues. *Parrilla La Estancia*, 25 de Mayo 541, quite good; *El Mesón*, Rivadavia 1034, reasonable, but slow service; *Pizzería Don Pipo*, Rivadavia 924, good pizzas and *empanadas*. *Atelier*, 25 de Mayo y San Martín, good coffee, cheap, open 24 hrs. *Casa Suiza*, good confitería. Rugby fans will enjoy the *Confitería Las Tejas*, 25 de Mayo 745, which shows videos of the game. Home made chocolate and the famous local mazard berry liquor is sold at the *Braese Store*, 9 de Julio 1540.

Bank and Post Office Banco de la Nación Güemes y San Martín, accepts cheques, no commission on Mastercard, open 0730-1300; **Viajes Sol del Sur**, 9 de Julio 1086, accept cheques; open Mon-Fri, 1000-1300. **Viasur**, 9 de Julio 1027, Amex cheques only accepted. Post and telecommunications office opposite the bus terminal on Fontana and Alvear (open 0800-2000).

Laundry *Laverap*, B Mitre 543, open Mon-Sat, 0900-2100.

Tourist Agencies *Esquel Tours*, Fontana 754, T 2704, and at airport, good for local tours, to Lagos Menéndez and Cisnes. *Fairway Sports and Adventures*, San Martín 1-43, T 3380, varied programme of tours, highly rec.

Tourist Office Alvear y Sarmiento, very friendly, can arrange lodgings in private homes. Closed Sat and Sun off-season.

Car Hire Fiocaci, 9 de Julio 740, T 2299/2704. **Mechanic** Claudio Peinados, Brown 660, T 0945-3462, highly rec.

Airport 20 km E of Esquel, by paved road, US$14 by taxi. US$2.50 by bus; US$4 by Esquel Tours bus 1 hr before each LADE flight. To **Buenos Aires**: 4 a week with Austral (T 3413/3614), via San Martín de los Andes. LADE (Alvear 1085, T 2124) flights to Bariloche, Comodoro Rivadavia, and other towns in the Lake District and Patagonia.

Rail From Buenos Aires, Constitución, train leaves Sun and Wed as for Bariloche (above), arriving in *Ingeniero Jacobacci* (E of Bariloche, pop 6,000), after 31 hrs, returning Wed and Sat 0125. (Infrequent buses from Bariloche to Ing Jacobacci.) Hotel in Jacobacci: **C** *Gran Hotel Argentino*, nearly opp station, with shower and heating, very good, may be closed when late trains arrive, restaurant nearby. Enquire at station for bookings. Sleepers from Jacobacci to BsAs are usually fully booked from Bariloche; only a small quota of first class tickets are available in Esquel for connections to BsAs. The Jacobacci-Esquel branch line, on which runs the steam-operated, narrow gauge train described by Paul Theroux in *The Old Patagonian Express*, was under threat of closure in late 1993. The train (which dates from 1922) is called "El Trencito" and leaves Ingeniero Jacobacci 0430 Fri, arr Esquel 1830. It leaves Esquel Sat 1030, arr El Maitén 1630 (US$7) and Ing Jacobacci 2030 (US$18). If you want to see railway engines, there are only two at Esquel, so go to *El Maitén*, where there is a steam engine cemetery, rec. From El Maitén it is possible to hitch to Bariloche or take the Esquel-Bariloche bus (4 times a week at 1100, US$17, 6 hrs). 2 hotels in El Maitén, same owner, both overpriced, one is *Accomazzo* with good restaurant, the other is **B** *La Vasconia*, nr station, basic, hot showers.

Buses None direct from Buenos Aires to Esquel so travel via Bariloche. To **Comodoro Rivadavia** (paved), Don Otto, 4 times a week, US$25 (but usually arrives from Bariloche full in season) or Angel Giobbi, Tues, and Fri 0600, US$25, via Río Mayo. Don Otto to **Bariloche**, US$30, direct. Empresa Mercedes goes daily (9 hrs) to **Bariloche** at 0800, best bus for views (and at 2200), US$28.50. To **El Bolsón**, 5 hrs, US$10, rough road, goes alternate days via El Maitén (for train buffs) and via Cholila (for views). To **Trelew**, US$32, 9 hrs, leaves 0900 Tues, Thur, Sat, and 2200 Mon, Wed, Fri; other bus companies on Av Fontana and Alvear (bus terminal) are Empresa Don Otto, Chubut, Denis. Bus terminal T 2233, also for taxis.

Los Alerces National Park Sixty km W of Esquel, also reached by road from Rawson, is the Los Alerces National Park, with centuries-old larch trees. An interesting part of the park can be reached from a separate entrance through Trevelin (see below) following the Río Futaleufú, but one can go only 22 km W because of the new Futaleufú hydroelectric dam. Behind it is Lago Amutui Quimei, which has swallowed Lago Situación and 3 others stretching almost to the frontier. (Futaleufú supplies power to the alumina plant at Puerto Madryn, 500 km to the E.) Entrance by car to see Futaleufú dam is only allowed at 1500, under police supervision; photography not permitted, except on top of the dam itself. There is no public transport to the dam, but buses pass the E side of the lake.

The E side of Los Alerces has much the same natural attractions as the Nahuel Huapi and Lanín parks, but is much less developed for tourism. *Lago Futalaufquen* has some of the best fishing in this huge area, season begins Nov 15. Bus (Mercedes) to Lago Verde passing along the E side of Lago Futalaufquen at 0700, 1300 and 1700 daily in season (it passes 3 hotels and drives into 2 camp sites). Buses also from El Bolsón. Off season transport is difficult but the Esquel—Bariloche bus, twice weekly, passes the lake. At the S tip of the lake is the park administration building (or Intendencia); it has a small museum about the park and a slide show of Argentina's National Parks. Petrol station, 2 expensive supermarkets in Villa Futalaufquen and a lady sells bread and vegetables from her house (buy bread early, or order the day before; meat can be hard to get).

Hotels On the E side of Lago Futalaufquen: *Quime Quipán*, T 22272, rec for fishing, closed in winter; **A2** *Hostería Los Tepúes*, simple, rustic, open all year, family bungalow for rent; **A2** *Pucón Pai*, T 3799, good restaurant, rec for fishermen (holds a fishing festival to open the season); open out of season for large groups only; *Cume Hué*, T 2858, also rec for fishing. Camping at Villa Futalaufquen and at Los Maitenes (closed May-Sep), hot water, store.

On the W side, which is untouched by tourism (by law), is **L2** *Hotel Futalaufquen* just N of Puerto Limonao, T 2648, rec, especially rooms 2/3 and 4/5 which have balconies overlooking the lake, open all year (no heating in rooms); good walking around the hotel, eg to Cinco Saltos, and El Dedal. The latter is a 6-hr hike up and back, with great views of the lakes and the cordillera from the top. A good information leaflet describing the flora and fauna encountered along the trail up to Cerro Dedal is available at the park headquarters. Regular full day launch trip from Puerto Limonao (reached by early morning minibus) on Lago Futalaufquen (a sheer delight) through Río Arrayanes to windless Lago Verde (2 campsites, one US$1 pp, one free, very crowded in summer, the free campsite is nicely situated and has a small shop; *Camping Agreste Lago Verde* offers 10% discount to ISIC and youth card holders). From there one can walk out to Lagos Rivadavia and Cholila (see above)—2 days minimum, and to the end of Lago Menéndez, famous for its giant larch trees (US$52 incl launch trip on Lago Menéndez, with Tehuelche Viajes y Turismo, Av Fontana 574, from Esquel); the boat leaves at 1400 but book the day before in Esquel, preferably, as it will not leave if there are not enough passengers; arrive early to claim your space, crossing 90 mins. The dock can be reached by a 30-minute walk across the bridge between lakes Futalaufquen and Verde. There are local guides with outboard motor boats for fishing. Lovely view of Lago Cisne (Swan Lake) to the NW end of Lago Menéndez. One then walks a 3 km nature trail looking across the Andes to Chile before returning. Tours arranged at Esquel (eg Elentur's Lacustre excursion visiting lakes Futalaufquen, Verde, Menéndez and a guided tour around the 2 km walk to Lago Cisne, on which you will see a 2,600-year old alerce, leaves from Puerto Limonao, take food and drink). Other excursion tours offered are less interesting because they only involve short stops in front of points of interest. A road connects all the lakes. The tourist office in Esquel has a pamphlet on all the walks in the Park. **NB** *Refugio Lago Krüger* in the Park offers 10% discount to ISIC and youth card holders, camping and fishing also available.

From Esquel one can also drive to Perito Moreno (**see p 200**) via Teckia (95 km paved), Gobernador Costa (84 km unpaved), La Laurita (last 61 km paved, ACA service station, breakdown truck and snack bar), 65 paved km to join route 22 (60 km) which is being paved, and on to Río Mayo, with 121 km unpaved road to Perito Moreno.

Crossing into Chile Colectivos leave Esquel for the frontier at La Balsa, 70 km SW via Trevelin, 2 hrs, US$3. Campsite (Camping Río Grande) on Argentine side of river. Cross the frontier river by bridge after passing Argentine customs; Chilean customs is 1 km on the other side of river (1 hr for all formalities). Colectivo from Argentine customs to Futaleufú (10 km) is US$3. Very little traffic for hitching. (For transport from Futaleufú to Chaitén (Chile) see Chile chapter.)

NB At the Futaleufú and Palena border crossings, Argentine border officials only give transit visas: legalize your stay within 10 days either by leaving the country or by renewing your entry stamp at an immigration office.

Trevelin (pop 5,000), 23 km SW of Esquel (local bus, US$0.85, every $1/2$ hour, 0700-1900), is an offshoot of the Welsh Chubut colony (**see p 188**). There is a modern Anglican church beside the Catholic church. It has a Welsh historical museum (entrance US$2) in the old mill.

Accommodation and Food *Hostería Estefanía*, Perito Moreno s/n, T 8148; *Hospedaje Trevelin*, San Martín 327, T 8102. Grills at *Che Ferrada*, good mixed *parrillada* at *El Quincho*, and several tea rooms offering *té galés* and *torta negra* (eg *El Adobe* on Av Patagonia; *Nain Maggie*, rec). *La Cabaña*, 7 km out on the road from Trevelin to Lake Futalaufquen, serves Welsh teas. There is a custom of giving a newly-married couple a "black cake" on their wedding day, to be eaten on their first anniversary. Municipal campsite near centre. On the road to Esquel 3 km from Trevelin, signposted on the righthand side, is *La Granja Trevelin*, owned by Domingo Giacci, macrobiotic meals and good Italian cooking, sells milk, cheese and onions; camping US$1, hot water and wc, bungalows US$15 a day; excellent horses for hire.

Tourist Office Good office in central plaza.

Excursion 17 km on road to frontier are Nant-y-fall Falls, entrance US$0.50 pp incl guide to all 7 falls ($1 1/2$ hr walk).

PATAGONIA (10)

The vast, windy, treeless plateau south of the Río Colorado: the Atlantic coast is rich in marine life, most easily seen around Puerto Madryn. In the south of the region is the Parque Nacional de los Glaciares, with journeys on lakes full of ice floes and to the Moreno glacier. In the N of the region is Argentina's Welsh community.

Patagonia is sub-divided into the provinces of Neuquén, Río Negro, Chubut, Santa Cruz and Tierra del Fuego. The area covers 780,000 sq km: 28% of the national territory, but has a population of only 600,000, little over 2.7% of the total population; and 57% of it is urban. Wide areas have less than one person to the sq km, and there are virtually no trees except in the N and the Andean foothills.

Over the whole land there blows a boisterous, cloud-laden strong wind which raises a haze of dust in summer, but in winter the dust can turn into thick mud. Temperatures are moderated by the proximity of the sea and are singularly mild, neither rising high during the summer nor falling low during the winter. Even in Tierra del Fuego, where the warmest summer months average $10 1/2$°C, the winter days' average can reach a high of about 2°C. Make sure you have plenty of warm clothing, and anti-freeze in your car, available locally. Rain falls mostly in the winter, but not more than 200-250mm a year. The whole E part of the area suffers from a lack of rainfall and the land is more or less desert. Deep crevices or canyons intersect the land from E to W. Few of them contain permanent water, but ground water is easily pumped to the surface. The great sheep *estancias* are along these canyons, sheltered from the wind, and in the depression running N from the Strait of Magellan to Lagos Argentino and Buenos Aires and beyond. During a brief period in spring, after the melting of the snows, there is grass on the plateau. Most of the land is devoted to sheep raising. The wool, which is shipped N to Buenos Aires, is mostly the fine and finecrossbred wool used by the Argentine mills, and is often heavy with sand. Over-grazing leads to much erosion. Wild dogs and the red fox are the sole enemies of the sheep. Because of the high winds and insufficient rainfall there is little agriculture except in the N, in the valleys of the Colorado and Negro rivers. Some cattle are raised in both valleys where irrigation permits the growing of alfalfa.

Patagonia is rich in extractive resources: the oil of Comodoro Rivadavia and

Tierra del Fuego, the little exploited iron ore of Sierra Grande, the coal of Río Turbio, the hydro-electric capacity of El Chocón, plentiful deposits of minerals (particularly bauxite) and marine resources, but their exploitation has been slow. Tourism is opening up too. The wildlife is attractive. Guanacos and rheas are a common sight: there are also *maras*, Patagonian hares. On and off parts of the coast, particularly the Valdés peninsula, seals, sea-elephants, right whales and other aquatic mammals may be seen, as well as penguins, especially between Oct and Apr. Further S, particularly in Tierra del Fuego, the antarctic wild goose (*quequén*) is the most commonly seen of the 152 species of birds (rec reading, *Aves de Argentina y Uruguay*, available, in English, from *Librería ABC* in Buenos Aires).

NB In summer hotel prices are grossly inflated (by as much as 100% in Ushuaia, 75% in Calafate); also in some places there may not be enough hotel beds to meet the demand. Camping is increasingly popular, and *estancias* seem hospitable to travellers who are stuck for a bed. During Argentine summer holidays (Jan, Feb, Mar) getting a hotel room in Ushuaia, Río Grande, Río Gallegos and Calafate is practically impossible. In this connection, remember that ACA establishments, which charge the same prices all over Argentina, are a bargain in Patagonia and Tierra del Fuego, where all other accommodation is expensive. As very few hotels and restaurants have a/c or even fans, it can get uncomfortably hot in Jan. TCs are hard to change throughout Patagonia.

Colonization The coast of Patagonia was first visited by a European late in 1519, when the Portuguese Fernão Magalhães (Magellan), then in the service of Spain, was on his voyage round the world. Early in 1520 he turned W into the strait which now bears his name and there struggled with fierce headwinds until he reached that Sea of Peace he named the Pacific. Later European expeditions that attempted to land on the coast were repulsed by the dour and obdurate local Indians, but these were almost entirely wiped out in the wars of 1879-1883, generally known as the "Campaign of the Desert". Before this there had been a long established colony at Carmen de Patagones; it shipped salt to Buenos Aires during the colonial period. There had also been a settlement of Welsh people in the Chubut Valley since 1865 (see below). After the Indian wars colonization was rapid, the Welsh, Scots and English taking a great part. Chilean sheep farmers from Punta Arenas moved N along the depression at the foot of the Andes, eastwards into Tierra del Fuego, and N to Santa Cruz.

The first European to traverse Patagonia S to N was the English sailor, Carder, who saved his life in a 1578 shipwreck in the Strait of Magellan. He crossed the Strait, walked to the Río de la Plata and arrived in London 9 years later.

The Welsh settlement On 28 July 1865, 150 Welsh immigrants landed at Puerto Madryn, then a deserted beach deep in Indian country. After three weeks they pushed, on foot, across the parched pampa and into the Chubut river valley, where there is flat cultivable land along the riverside for a distance of 80 km upstream. Here, maintained in part by the Argentine Government, they settled, but it was three years before they realized the land was barren unless watered. They drew water from the river, which is higher than the surrounding flats, and later built a fine system of irrigation canals. The colony, reinforced later by immigrants from Wales and from the United States, prospered, but in 1899 a great flood drowned the valley and some of the immigrants left for Canada. The last Welsh contingent arrived in 1911. The object of the colony had been to create a "Little Wales beyond Wales", and for four generations they kept the Welsh language alive. The language is, however, dying out in the fifth generation. There is an offshoot of the colony of Chubut at Trevelin, at the foot of the Andes nearly 650 km to the W, settled in 1888 (**see p 187**). It is interesting that this distant land gave to the Welsh language one of its most endearing classics: *Dringo'r Andes* (Climbing the Andes), written by one of the early women settlers.

Gary Luton, of the Welsh Patagonia Expedition 1980, writes: "To me Chubut will always foster memories of horses on an open wind-swept plain, or tethered, with brown sheepskin saddles, outside a *pueblo* inn. It is shuttered houses with poplar windbreaks. Chubut is relative prosperity surrounded by shanties of mud brick and tin; it is Coca-Cola and tea houses, sea lions and right whales sounding a short distance from shore; and *asados* washed down with red wine and *mate*. Chubut is a moonscape of neutral colours where sheep lose themselves in the grey-green saltpans of thornscrub, and dust and wind blow across scattered pockets of civilization. And it is the Eisteddfod at Gaiman, a Welsh festival of the arts in a chapel nestled among the poplars, on a cloudless night, where boys in white shirts recite poetry and choirs sing as a culture fights a subsiding battle to maintain itself."

Recommended Reading *In Patagonia* by Bruce Chatwin, a good introduction to the area and its people. *Patagonia*, by Metzeltin and Buscaini (Dall' Oglio, Milan). *At Home with the*

PATAGONIA

Patagonians, by George Musters (history of 19th century life of Patagonian Indians), ed John Murray, London 1871/1973.

In all Patagonia there is only one town—Comodoro Rivadavia—with a population over 100,000. Most of the towns are small ports, which used only to work during the wool-shipping season but have livened up since the local economy began to diversify. The high tidal range makes it impossible in most of them for ships to tie up at the docks (except at Madryn and Punta Arenas, Chile).

Air Services Aerolíneas Argentinas and Austral from Buenos Aires either direct to Río Gallegos or calling at Bahía Blanca and Trelew or Comodoro Rivadavia on the way. Check if either airline is offering discounts on particular flights, which can result in considerable savings. Beware delays for bad weather. A new company, Almafuerte, flies direct to Puerto Madryn and Calafate.

Many air force LADE flights in the region S of Bariloche must be booked in advance from departure point of flight. The planes are small and fly low; passengers miss little of what there is to be seen, highly recommended for those who enjoy flying. The baggage allowance is 15 kg. Travellers are warned that the flights are often heavily booked ahead, but always check again on the day of the flight if you are told beforehand that it is sold out. Sometimes, through LADE, individual passengers are allowed to fly on air force carriers if planes are full or inopportune. LADE tickets are much cheaper for a long flight with stops than buying separate segments. LADE's computer reservation system is linked to Aerolíneas Argentinas, so flight connections are possible between these airlines. Also LADE's flights synchronize with both AR and Austral flights.

Roads The main road, Route 3, which runs near the coast, is now paved from Buenos Aires via Fitz Roy and down to Río Gallegos. S of this town to Ushuaia is all-weather in a bad state of repair as it is awaiting asphalt. Sometimes passengers going South have to pay for baggage by weight. Many buses do not operate between early Apr and late Oct.

The principal roads in Patagonia roughly form an inverted triangle. Route 3 has regular traffic and adequate services. At the S end, this route enters Chile and crosses the Magellan Straits to Tierra del Fuego by the car ferry at Primera Angostura. The W route (Route 40) zigzags across the moors, is lonely and is good in parts, poor in others (more details given below); there is hardly any traffic except in Dec, Jan and Feb, the tourist season. However, it is by far the more interesting road, with fine views of the Andes and plenty of wild life as well as the Alerces and Glaciares National Parks. Camping is no problem, and there are good hotels at Esquel, Perito Moreno, Calafate and (in Chile) Coyhaique and Puerto Natales. Third class accommodation also at Gobernador Gregores, Río Mayo and Esperanza. The N part of the triangle is formed by the paved highway running from Bariloche through Neuquén to San Antonio Oeste.

Many of the roads in Southern Argentina are gravelled. The price of a good windscreen protector varies according to make of car, but can be US$50 in Buenos Aires. For a VW Kombi they are hard to find at a reasonable price. More primitive versions can be bought for much less—eg US$5 in San Julián, and probably elsewhere—or made from wire mesh, wood and string. The best types to buy are the grid-type, or inflatable plastic ones which are made for some standard-type vehicles, the only disadvantage being some loss of visibility. Drivers should also look out for cattle grids (*guardaganados*), even on main highways. They are signed; cross them very slowly. Always carry plenty of fuel, as service stations may be as much as 300 km apart. Fuel prices are very low in Chubut and Santa Cruz provinces (except Bariloche), US$0.35 per litre, which is about half the price of the rest of the country.

Hitchhiking is generally difficult except on Route 3 in spring and summer; camping equipment is useful as long delays can be expected even in the tourist season.

The upper course of the Río Colorado is the N limit of Patagonia. 160 km S of where it reaches the sea (250 km S of Bahía Blanca), about 27 km from the mouth of the Río Negro, is **Carmen de Patagones** (16,000 people), standing on high ground on the N bank, with **Viedma** (26,000 people) the capital of Río Negro Province, across the river, which is spanned by a connecting rail and road bridge, pleasant setting. There is also a frequent ferry service for pedestrians. On a hill behind Patagones a monument commemorates an attack on the twin towns by a Brazilian squadron in 1827. (Beware of pleasant-looking campsites near this monument; there is an artillery range nearby.) There are three museums, open 1000-1200 only. The swimming is recommended on the Viedma side of the river, where there is a nice shady shore. A law was passed in 1986 nominating Viedma as the site of the new federal capital, but the project is unlikely ever to come to fruition.

Hotels At Viedma: **A1** *Helsingflors Hostería*, San Martín 516, T/F 20719 (BsAs T 824-3634); **C** *Austral*, Villarino 292, T 22019, rec, modern. **D** *Peumayen*, Buenos Aires 334, T 25243; **E** *Hotel Nueva Roma*, basic, fleas. *Restaurant Munich*, Buenos Aires 150, open late.

Camping Good municipal site 500m after crossing the river on the new road bridge on the right, US$14 per tent plus US$4 pp, all facilities incl hot showers, but can be noisy at weekends.

Exchange Travel agency at Namuncurá 78, Viedma, exchanges Amex cheques.

Tourist Office Belgrano 544, 9th floor, Viedma.

Transport Air From Buenos Aires with Austral daily except Sat (the city is also served by LADE). **Buses** Bus terminal at Calle A Zatti y Lavalle about 6 blocks from main plaza. To/from Buenos Aires US$45, La Estrella/Cóndor. To San Antonio Oeste, US$7.50.

Excursion Beautiful beach, El Cóndor, 30 km S of Viedma, 3 buses a day from Viedma in summer, hotel open Jan-Feb, restaurants and shops, free camping on beach 2 km S. 30 km from El Cóndor is a sealion colony (*lobería*); daily bus in summer from Viedma; hitching easy in summer.

Camping Further camping sites on the Río Negro where the main route into Patagonia meets the river (some 170 km from Viedma due NW) with all facilities incl a small shop. Additional shops at General Conesa, 2 km away. Mosquito repellent needed.

Almost due W and 180 km along the coast, on the Gulf of San Matías, is **San Antonio Oeste** (10,000 people). 17 km S is a popular seaside resort, **Las Grutas**, developed in the 1960s with good safe beach (the caves themselves are not really worth visiting); bus from San Antonio hourly US$1.30, ACA has a *Unidad Turística*, with 6-bed rooms, no restaurant. **D** *Tour du Golfe*, friendly, 3-bed rooms, cooking facilities. There are also many good camping sites (eg *La Entrada*, US$5 per tent, on edge of town above beach). Seafood restaurants. The whole of Las Grutas closes down in mid-Mar and retires to Buenos Aires. Between San Antonio and Puerto Madryn is Sierra Grande (ACA garage and café, camping at rear, no facilities but free hot showers at YPF garage in town), where iron-ore deposits are extracted and piped in solution to an ocean terminal 32 km E.

Hotels at San Antonio C *Kandava*, Sarmiento 240, T 21430, with bath, hot water, clean, good. **D** *Golfo Azul*, simple, clean; **D** *Iberia*, Sarmiento 241, with bath, but without breakfast, small rooms, but rec.

Railway via Viedma to **Bahía Blanca** and **Buenos Aires** and W to **Bariloche**. Timetable from Buenos Aires as for Bariloche; train passes through San Antonio Oeste at 1953 en route to Bariloche, 1002 to Bahía Blanca.

Buses From San Antonio N to **Bahía Blanca** and S to **Río Gallegos** and **Punta Arenas** by Transportes Patagónicos. To **Viedma** 0700 daily, US$7.50. To **Puerto Madryn** and **Trelew**, Don Otto, 0200 and 1530, 4 hrs, US$20. To **Buenos Aires**, US$46 via Bahía Blanca, frequent.

Route to Neuquén and Bariloche: paved. From San Antonio Oeste a road runs N 91 km through bush country providing fodder for a few cattle, with a view to the W of the salt flats called

Salina del Gualicho, before joining Route 250 which meets the Zapala-Bahía Blanca highway (Route 22) at Choele Choel, 178 km N of San Antonio Oeste (**see p 170, and Roads p 171**).

About 250 km S, along Route 3 (paved) in Chubut province is **Puerto Madryn**, a port on the Golfo Nuevo. It was founded by the Welsh colonist, Parry Madryn, in 1865. Population, 42,000. Ask at tourist office about visits to the alumina plant. The town is becoming a popular tourist centre, with a casino, skin-diving and nature reserves, both near the town and on the nearby Valdés peninsula. Museo de Ciencias Naturales y Oceanográfico on Domecq García and J Menéndez, informative and worth a visit (open 1600-2000, closed Mon), entry US$2, ask to see video. No Youth Hostel.

Hotels (Often full in summer, make bookings early.) **A1** *Península Valdés*, JA Roca 155, T 71292 4-star, sea view, suites available, comfortable, rec; **A2** *Playa*, Roca 181, T 50732, overpriced but safe, clean, only Spanish spoken; **A3** *Yanco*, Av Roca 626, T 71581, on beach, nightly entertainment programme, free, has rooms for up to 6; **A3** *Gran Madryn I*, L Lugones 40, T 72205, 2-star, friendly, clean, good; **A3** *Hostal del Rey*, Blvd. Brown 681, T 71156, on beach, rec, 2-star, clean, breakfast US$4; **B** *Muelle Viejo*, Yrigoyen 38, T 71284, opposite pier, good restaurant, expensive breakfast, good, clean, quiet; **B** *Hostería Hipocampo*, Bvd Marítimo 33, clean, helpful, but overpriced; **B** *Tolosa*, R Sáenz Peña 250, T 71850, 3-star, friendly, no English spoken, no evening meal, noisy; **C** *Apart-Motel Palma*, Av Roca 7, T 74044, heated, showers, clean, warm, kitchen facilities; **C** *Atalaya*, Domecq García 149, T 73006, with bath, noisy; **C** *Backpackers*, 25 de Mayo 1136, T 74426, clean, friendly, kitchen facilities; **C** *El Dorado*, San Martín 546, T 71026, clean, shower, patio, a bit run down, landlady not keen on backpackers; **C** *Español*, 28 de Julio y San Martín, clean, basic, hot water, restaurant, parking; **C** *Gran Palace*, Av 28 de Julio 390, T 71009, clean; **C** *Motel ACA*, Marcos A Zar e Irigoyen, T 71452; **C** *Residencial Petit*, Alvear 845, T 51460, with bath, clean, quiet, good. **D** *Anciamar*, 25 de Mayo 875, T 51509 clean, quiet, rec; **D** *Antiguo*, 28 de Julio 170, T 71742, good, clean, friendly; **D** *Hospedaje* at 25 de Mayo 763, central, quiet; **D** *Residencial La Posta*, Av Roca 33, T 72422, good, huge rooms, cooking facilities; **D** *Residencial Jo's*, Bolívar 75, T 71433, pleasant; **D** *Vaskonia*, 25 de Mayo 43, T 72581, hot water, friendly, good value.

Camping All closed out of season. At Punta Cuevas, 3.5 km S of town, is ACA site with evening hot showers, good facilities and shady trees (ACA members only, US$8 per tent for 2) but many people camp on beach. There is a swimming pool in the rocks near the ACA camp site, which gets its water at high tide, very pleasant, and free. Two municipal sites: one at Ribera Sur, 1 km before ACA site on same road along beach (gives student discount). All facilities, very crowded, US$3 pp and US$2 per tent for first day. Also rm with bunkbeds, F pp. Bus from town stops 100m before entrance. The other is N of town at Barrio Brown. Camping out can be interesting as one can watch foxes, armadillos, skunks and rheas roaming around in the evening.

Restaurants *Las Aguilas*, MA Zar and RS Peña, rec, good for seafood; *Cantina El Náutico*, Julio Roca and Lugones, good food, especially fish; *París*, RS Peña by Muella Piedrabuena, good and reasonably priced; *Pizzería Roselli*, Peña y JA Roca, cheap, good, with vegetarian selections; *Parrilla Mayoral*, RS Peña 12; *Parrilla Estela*, RS Peña 27, reasonable prices; *Quijote*, Belgrano 138, reasonable prices, very good; *Barbarians*, 25 de Mayo y 28 de Julio, good coffee. For excellent Welsh afternoon teas, *La Goleta*, Roca 87, 1700-1900 (poor sign, but good tea, US$7).

Banks and Exchange Banco de la Nación, 25 de Mayo y 9 de Julio, go early to avoid long queues, high commission. **Banco del Sud**, Calle Sáenz Peña, advances cash on Visa, 4% commission. **Banco Provincia Chubut**, 25 de Mayo, has Mastercard and Diners ATM (will give dollars). There are no *cambios* as such, apart from Turismo Pu-Ma, 28 de Julio 46 (2% commission for TCs), but fair rates from travel agents (eg Safari Submarino, address below; go in the morning). **La Moneda**, Roca y 28 de Julio, will exchange large sums, not very good rates. Some shops will change US$ cash. High commission on changing cheques, incl at **Banco de la Nación** (but not always, it seems).

Laundromat *Laverap*, 25 de Mayo 529, highly rec.

Post Office Belgrano y A Maiz. **Telephone Office** 28 de Julio, also fax.

Sport Puerto Madryn is being promoted as a diving centre. Tours for those who have never dived before are organized by *Safari Submarino*, Mitre 80; *Pimino* in the harbour, all about US$60 per excursion. A few others along the harbour, ask for Fernando Alonso, rec; all show nature videos at about 1930. Swim in the so-called *parque submarino* amid sunken cars and

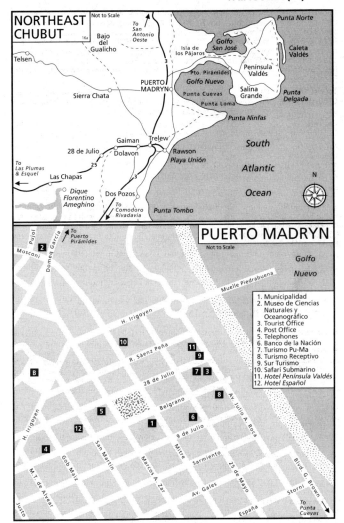

NORTHEAST
CHUBUT

Not to Scale

Bajo
del
Gualicho

To
San
Antonio
Oeste

Telsen

Isla de
los Pájaros

Golfo
San José

Punta Norte

Caleta
Valdés

PUERTO
MADRYN

Pto. Pirámides

Golfo Nuevo

Península
Valdés

Sierra Chata

Punta Cuevas

Punta Loma

Salina
Grande

Punta
Delgada

Punta Ninfas

Gaiman

Trelew

To
Las Plumas
& Esquel

28 de Julio

Dolavon

Rawson

Playa Unión

South

28 de Julio

25

Las Chapas

Atlantic

Dique
Florentino
Ameghino

Dos Pozos

Ocean

To
Comodoro
Rivadavia

Punta Tombo

N

PUERTO MADRYN

Not to Scale

To
Puerto
Pirámides

Mosconi

Golfo

Nuevo

Muelle Piedrabuena

H. Irigoyen

1. Municipalidad
2. Museo de Ciencias
   Naturales y
   Oceanográfico
3. Tourist Office
4. Post Office
5. Telephones
6. Banco de la Nación
7. Turismo Pu-Ma
8. Turismo Receptivo
9. Sur Turismo
10. Safari Submarino
11. *Hotel Península Valdés*
12. *Hotel Español*

R. Sáenz Peña

28 de Julio

Belgrano

9 de Julio

Sarmiento

Av. Gales

España

To
Punta
Cuevas

a few fish! Trained divers seriously interested in marine life who have at least a week's stay should contact the Centro Nacional Patagónico at Av Roca. Windsurfing lessons and equipment hire at Brown 871.

Tourist Agencies Several agencies do tours to the Valdés Peninsula, all are for 12 hours, see below. Prices are fixed by law, but itineraries may differ. Tour rates increase by 75% on 15 Nov and again on 15 Dec by the same amount. By far the largest agency is *Sur Turismo*, JA Roca 175, T 73585, whose tours may have over-large groups and give insufficient time (this applies to other agencies too), reports of reservations not honoured and poor organization, check all details with care. Other agencies incl: *Tur-Mar*, T 74104, 25 de Mayo 167, reportedly sensitive approach to conservation; *Pu-Ma*, 28 de Julio 48, T 71482, mixed reports; *Mar y Valle*, Roca 37, T 72872, rec. *Receptivo*, Roca 303 y Belgrano, T 51048, Amex agent, weekend and off-season tours, their guide Luis speaks excellent English and is an expert on marine biology and ornithology, rec; *Prima Tur*, 28 de Julio; *Coyun Co*, Roca 171, T 51845. *Franca del Sur*, Reconquista 378, T 50710, small groups, Spanish only, rec. **Recommended guide**: Dr Pedro Fuentes Gallardo.

Tourist Office, at Julio Roca 223, T 73029, open until 2400 in the tourist season, but only 0700-1800 Mon-Fri in winter; helpful, has notice board for messages, list of current hotel rates and interesting video on the region, but inaccurate bus information.

Car Hire Very expensive (US$150/day, 1994). *Fiorasi*, on Sarmiento; Localiza, Belgrano 196, T 71660; Cuyun-Co, Roca 171. Filling station in Puerto Pirámides are not rec, untrustworthy.

Air Services Daily from Buenos Aires at 1230 via Trelew with Austral; Mon and Sat from Ushuaia with Kaiken; from Comodoro Rivadavia on Mon with LADE. Airport is 7 km from town, no buses, taxi or *remise* only, US$7-8. LADE office at Roca 117, T 51256; Aerolíneas Argentinas, 25 de Mayo 146, T 50110; Almafuerte, Roca 303, T 51108.

Buses Terminal in old railway station: to **Buenos Aires**, US$79; daily at 1415 and 2030, with El Cóndor, and with Costera Criolla at 2115, via San Antonio Oeste, change at Bahía Blanca, 22-24 hrs. To **Río Gallegos**, about 20 hrs, daily at 1730, US$71 (20% student discount). To **Bahía Blanca** 0800 and 1000 daily, 12 hrs, US$32; 10 1/2 hrs, US25, with La Puntual to **Mar del Plata**, changing at Bahía Blanca. Patagónicos to **San Antonio Oeste** at 0800 and 2230, US$20, 4 hrs. To **Trelew** with 28 de Julio company, every 90 minutes, more frequent in summer, 60 mins at 15 mins past hour, US$3.50; driver will stop at entrance to Trelew airport if asked; direct to Trelew airport hourly at half past the hour, US$3.50, 45 mins journey, or Puma (28 de Julio), US$5, leaves 1 1/2 hrs before flight and takes arriving passengers back to Puerto Madryn (taxi to airport US$45). Don Otto to **Comodoro Rivadavia**, Wed, Thur, Fri, Sun 0915 and daily at 1600, US$26. No direct bus to **Bariloche**, change at Trelew and Esquel (7 hr wait), US$60. Taxi rank on the plaza.

For hitching N, try on the industrial estate road, or take a Trelew bus to the main highway then walk 3 km to the service station/truck stop. With luck it is possible to get to Bahía Blanca in one day.

Excursions There are nature reserves at Punta Loma on Golfo Nuevo (sea-lions), only 15 km S of Puerto Madryn (sea-lions, whales, penguins and flamingoes also frequent the Puerto Madryn area itself, sea-lions even invading the harbour); and also on the Valdés Peninsula at Punta Pirámides (sea-lions) and Isla de los Pájaros (sea birds), Golfo San José and Punta Norte (right whales), see below. (Check opening times of reserves in Puerto Madryn; they vary.) The natural history of the region is most interesting, with other seal and penguin colonies, breeding ground at Golfo Nuevo for right whales, fossils in the cliffs, and guanacos, rheas and armadillos in the countryside. Most animals (except the whale) can be seen in the warm seasons, from Oct to Apr. See whales from perhaps as early as Jun to, at the very latest, end-Dec. Oct-Nov is said to be the time to see the greatest variety of wildlife. There is less wildlife after Dec, a point not made by tour agencies. Past the lighthouse and Naval Zone at Punta Delgada on the other side of the Valdés Peninsula is Salina Grande, 35m below sea level. Naturatur, 9 de Julio 280, have information on local flora and fauna.

The *Punta Loma* sealion reserve is open 0900-1200, 1430-1730, Sep, and Oct, are the best months. Information and video. Entry US$2. Taxis US$25; Tur-Mar does 12-hour US$40 pp trip to Punta Loma and the Florentino Ameghino dam, 110 km inland on the Río Chubut. The dam covers 7,000 ha with water and irrigates 28,000 ha in the lower Chubut valley, as well as producing electric power.

Península Valdés The centre for visits to the Peninsula is **Puerto Pirámides** (pop 100), 90 km E of Puerto Madryn. Entrance fee US$5. About 79 km E of Puerto Madryn, near the entrance to the peninsula, is Isla de los Pájaros. No one is now allowed to visit the island without special permission (only granted to recognized ornithologists). At Punta Norte (176 km) at the N end of the Valdés Peninsula, there are elephant seals (breeding time in first fortnight in Aug, best seen at low tide), late spring and summer (Nov-Mar), reasonably priced restaurant for meals and snacks. At Caleta Valdés, 45 km S of Punta Norte you can see penguins and elephant seals at close quarters, but not at any specific point. Camping at hangar nearby, but take fresh water with you as supplies are unreliable. At Punta Delgada (at the S of the peninsula) most wildlife can be seen except the penguins, which have moved away (*Hotel Faro*, A+, comfortable, excellent food, rec, reservations at *Hotel Península Valdes* in Puerto Madryn). The peninsula is private property. One third belongs to one man, who grazes 40,000 sheep. In theory, the beach on the entire coast is out of bounds, although this is not strictly enforced. A Conservation Officer is permanently stationed at the entrance to the Peninsula (he is very helpful).

Puerto Pirámides Services A2 *ACA Motel*, T 72057, poor restaurant; **B** *Residencial El Libanés*, T 95007; **D** *España*, basic but clean, friendly; *Posada del Mar*, friendly, restaurant; **E** pp *Paradise Pub*, cheapest, good value food and beer, good atmosphere; municipal campsite by the black sand beach (whales may be visible in season) US$5 pp (free out of season), hot showers in evening only, dirty, busy, get there early to secure a place. In summer there are several well-stocked shops, but if staying take sun and wind protection and drinking water. There is a shop that sells original Patagonian Indian work. There is also a small tourist office on the edge of town, useful information for hikes and driving tours. Service station open on Sun. Hydro Sports rents scuba equipment and boats, has a small restaurant, and organizes land and sea wildlife tours (ask for Mariano), boat trips US$20 for 1 hour. Bus (Empresa 28 de Julio) from Puerto Madryn, Thur, Sun at 1000 returns 1800, US$6.50 each way.

Excursions are organized by tourist agencies in Puerto Madryn (addresses above). The usual tour takes in Puerto Pirámides, Caleta Valdés (or Punta Norte) and Isla de los Pájaros (seen through fixed telescopes from a distance of 400m). Shop around, but most agencies charge the same: about US$25-30 pp plus the US$5 entry to the National Park; boat trip to see whales US$20 extra; there are two companies running boat trips from Puerto Pirámides into Golfo Nuevo to see whales, the one on the right as you face the water (Tito Botazzi, T 95016) is better. Trips last about 9 hrs, starting at 0800. On all excursions take drink with you, food too if you don't want to eat in the expensive restaurants (swimsuit, towel and binoculars are also a good idea). Most tour companies stay 50-60 minutes on location, not considered sufficient by some (Siempre Tur are reported to stay longer). Off season tours run regularly only on Thur and Sun, departing at 0955 and returning at 1730. The peninsula is easily reached if one has one's own car, in fact the best way to see the wildlife is by car. Hiring a vehicle is very expensive (US$150 per day), but taking a taxi is worth considering if you can get a group together (taxi US$30 pp for the day). Hitching is very difficult, even at weekends in season. Peninsular roads are variable: from Puerto Madryn to Puerto Pirámides is a good dirt road; from Puerto Pirámides to Punta Norte is degenerating and the road between Punta Norte and Punta Delgada is gravel (tours will not run after heavy rain in the low season).

There are also tours from Puerto Madryn to Punta Tombo **(see p 198)**, US$25 plus US$5 entrance fee with Receptivo, but these usually incl "sight-seeing" in Rawson, Trelew and Gaiman and a lot of time is spent travelling, with only about 1 hr at the Reserve. It is cheaper to visit from Trelew.

NB If possible check all excursion dates in advance; it is very disappointing to arrive in Puerto Madryn only to find that one cannot reach the wildlife reserves. From Mar to Sep (when there is less wildlife to be seen) it may be necessary to take a taxi, but we are informed that the tours run all year, depending on numbers. Tours are cheaper from Madryn than from Trelew, probably because Trelew has the airport.

Along the Río Chubut are several towns. **Rawson** (pop 15,000), the capital of Chubut Province, 7 km from the sea, has law courts, a museum in the Colegio Don Bosco, a fishing port, and a riverside Tourist Office, 9 de Julio 64, T 213. Puerto Rawson is about 5 km down river; you can camp on the beach, and *Cantina El Marinero* serves good seafood (regular buses from Rawson).

Hotels B *Provincial*, Mitre 551, T 81300, clean but dilapidated, good restaurant; *Residencial Papaiani*, A Maiz 377; *Residencial San Pedro*, Belgrano 744.

Some 20 km up the Río Chubut is **Trelew** (pop 61,000), a prosperous town which has lost its Welsh look. There is a pretty red-brick chapel in the centre (rec Sun mornings for Welsh speakers), and a small, interesting museum in the old railway station, open 0700-1300, 1400-2000 Mon-Fri, 1500-1900 Sat, US$3. On the road to Rawson, 500m before the bridge is Chapel Moriah, a beautiful 1880 Welsh chapel, with the graves of many original settlers. The Museo Paleontológico Egidio Feruglio, 9 de Julio 655, open 1600-2300 daily (US$3, Spanish only), has a collection of Patagonian fossils, including some of prehistoric reptiles, and is located in the Parque Paleontológico Bryn-Gwyn. A paved road runs from Rawson through Trelew, Gaiman **(see p 197)** and Dolavon, all on the river, to Las Plumas (mind the bridge if driving) and the upper Chubut Valley, all the way to Esquel **(see p 184)** and Trevelin.

Local Holidays 28 Jul (Founding of Chubut); 13 Dec (Petroleum Day).

Hotels L3 *Rayentray*, San Martín y Belgrano, T 34702, best in town, well run, comfortable; **A2** *Centenario*, San Martín 150, T 30041, expensive restaurant; **A3** *Libertador*, Rivadavia 254, T 35132, without breakfast, 4 blocks from Plaza, good rooms, poor restaurant, quiet, friendly, good value; **B** *Galicia*, 9 de Julio y Rivadavia, T 33803, very warm, without bath, clean; **B** *Parque*, Irigoyen y Cangallo, T 30098, good; **B** *Touring Club*, Av Fontana 240, T 33998, excellent, with bath, a bit dark, book in advance in high season, the social hub of Trelew but run down, chess is played here, colour TV, breakfast rec, coffee the best in town; **C** *Argentino*, Abraham Matthews 186, T 36134, without bath, clean, quiet, breakfast available, good, near bus station; **C** *Provincia*, Yrigoyen 625, T 31544, poor and noisy; **C** *Residencial San Carlos*, Sarmiento 758, T 31538, rec; **C** *Rivadavia*, Rivadavia 55, T 34472, with bath, clean, rec; **D** *Plaza*, with breakfast, on main square, clean, very good rooms; **D** *Residencial Patterson*, Moreno 280, T 31636; **D** *Hostal Avenida*, Lewis Jones 49, T 34172, close to bus station, lots of character, rooms basic but clean, friendly, quiet. Raul G Lerma, Don Bosco 109, offers camping space in garden and local information, speaks English.

Camping By the river, S of the town on the road to Rawson, on right about 200m beyond the bridge over River Chubut, US$12, dirty, run-down, beware of mosquitoes; take Rawson bus, No 7 or 25. The site belongs to the Sports Club and has a public swimming pool.

Restaurants *Don Facundo*, Fontana 213, good, cheap, rec; *Eulogia Fuentes*, Don Bosco 23, good pasta; *El Quijote*, 25 de Mayo 90, good food and service; *Sugar*, 25 de Mayo 247, good fast food; *El Mesón*, Rivadavia 588, seafood; *El Marfil*, Italia 42, good, cheap; *Rotisería La Primera*, San Martín y A P Bell, pasta, pizza, empanadas, good, take-away service; *Cabildo Star*, Roca 88, excellent and cheap pizzas; *Capítulo II*, Roca 393, *tenedor libre*, good and cheap; *La Casa de Juan*, Moreno 360, cosy, good pizzas; *Café Vittorio*, Belgrano 341, good service.

Exchange Lloyds Bank (BLSA), Av 9 de Julio y Belgrano, does not change TCs, unhelpful, cash advance on Visa but high charge for call to verify card; **Banco Provincia del Chubut**, Rivadavia y 25 de Mayo. Local banks. Open 0800-1200. None changes TCs. **Banco del Sud**, 9 de Julio 320, only accepts dollar bills in mint condition; cash advance on Visa, high commission. Difficult to change cheques.

Post Office 25 de Mayo and Mitre. **Telephones** Julio A Roca 1-100 block, open till 2400.

Tourist Agencies *Sur Turismo*, Belgrano 326-330, organize good excursions to Punta Tombo (US$25 pp), Península Valdés (US$58 pp) and Florentino Ameghino dam, T 34550; *Estrella del Sur Turismo*, San Martin 129, T 31282, tours to Valdés Peninsula and Punta Tombo, rec; *Punta Tombo Turismo*, San Martín 150, T 20358; and others. Tours to Valdés Peninsula are more expensive than from Puerto Madryn and take longer, about 12-13 hrs. Best to go in a small tour bus which can get closer to main wildlife viewing sites.

Tourist Office, room 20 on 1st floor of Terminal Terrestre, additionally opens briefly at 0515 for travellers arriving from Esquel, also at airport and at Italia y Rioja, friendly but not always accurate. Free maps and self-guided city tour.

Car Hire Expensive (cheaper to take a tour to Punta Tombo and Península Valdés). 3 companies at the airport; desks are manned only at flight arrival times and cars are snapped up quickly. Localiza, Urquiza 310, T 35344, also at airport.

Air Airport 5 km from centre; taxis cost about US$8. Buses from Puerto Madryn stop at the turning to the airport (10 mins walk; bus from turning to Puerto Madryn, US$3; also hourly buses from terminal to Puerto Madryn, US$3.50, and Puna airport bus, US$5). LADE (Av Fontana 227, T 35925, poor service) flies, **Trelew-Bariloche**, twice a week and to Comodoro Rivadavia twice a week. Aerolíneas Argentinas (25 de Mayo 33, T 34244) flies BsAs-Trelew-Río Gallegos-Ushuaia daily. Austral (same address as AR) also flies to/from BsAs daily. Austral flights from Buenos Aires have a direct bus connection to **Puerto Madryn**. TAN (T 34550) to Neuquén twice a week. LAPA flies BsAs-Trelew-Comodoro Rivadavia-Río Gallegos twice a week and BsAs-Trelew-Comodoro Rivadavia once a week. The Aero Club sells sightseeing flights.

Buses from **Buenos Aires** to Trelew, 4 daily, 21½ hrs (return 0700 and 2130 daily, 1705 Tues, Thur, Fri and Sat, US$83). Bus to **Bahía Blanca**, 734 km, US$32 daily with Don Otto (T 32434), 0600, few a week with La Puntual, 0600; to **Mar del Plata**, changing at Bahía Blanca, US$35 with La Puntual; to **Esquel**, US$32, 2130, 11 hrs with Empresa Chubut (good road, lots of wildlife, spectacular scenery, rec); bus to **Bariloche** daily. Buses to **Rawson** every 15 min; every 1½ hours to **Gaiman** (pop 4,400), US$1.15; every 60 minutes to **Puerto Madryn**, US$3.50 with 28 de Julio; to **Comodoro Rivadavia** daily at 2000, and Sun, Wed, Thur and Fri at 1035, US$26, 4 hrs; to **Río Gallegos**, daily at 1900, US$70. If **hitching** south from Trelew, take the

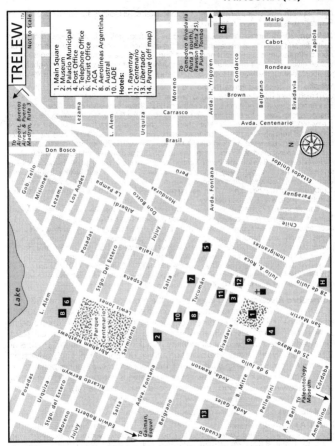

TRELEW
Not to scale

To Airport, Buenos Aires, & Puerto Madryn, Ruta 3

Lake

1. Main Square
2. Museum
3. Palacio Municipal
4. Post Office
5. Telephone Office
6. Tourist Office
7. ACA
8. Aerolíneas Argentinas
9. Austral
10. LADE

Hotels:
11. Rayentray
12. Centenario
13. Libertador
14. Parque (off map)

To Comodoro Rivadavia (Ruta 3 south), Rawson (Ruta 25), & Punta Tombo

To Gaiman, Esquel

Rawson bus to the flyover 5 km out of town; there is a junction N of town for Puerto Madryn traffic.

Gaiman (pop 4,400), 18 km W of Trelew, a pretty place with well-built brick houses but quite touristy, is now the most Welsh of the Chubut valley towns. It has a museum of the colony, US$0.50, in the old railway station (open in summer, Tues-Sat 1600-2000, in winter, Tues-Sat 1500-1800, curator Mrs Roberts is "full of stories"). The only restaurant seems often to be closed, but tea rooms such as *Casa de Té Gaiman*, Yrigoyen 738, excellent, and those opposite the square, *Plas y Coed*, Miguel D Jones 123 (oldest, excellent tea "and enough food for a week", US$10, Marta Rees speaks English and is very knowledgeable about the area, highly rec) and *Ty Gwyn*, 9 de Julio 111, *Ty Nain* Yrigoyen 283 (excellent, US$12, frequented by tour buses), and *Elma*, Tello 571, serve enormous Welsh teas from 1500 for US$8-10. Small municipal campground by river (poor, no facilities). Interesting local agriculture. Welsh-speakers will be interested in the cemetery above town. The Eisteddfod, Welsh festival of arts, is held in early Oct each year. Interesting walking tours led by volunteer guides (Spanish-speaking—meet in main plaza) incl a private, hand-made (out of beer bottles and string!) theme park (El Desafío—US$5, tickets valid 2 months), a seaweed factory and the *Ty*

Nain tearoom which has a nice display of historical items. All facilities are closed out of season. Regular buses from Trelew in season.

Dolavon, 20 km further W is easily reached by bus from Trelew. It still retains some Welsh character and provides an interesting view of the irrigation system built by the settlers. The old flour mill/museum is superb, but not easy to find: it is completely intact and demonstrations will be given. Key kept by owner of nearby tea-room. There is a campsite: turn right by the service station on the way into town, good facilities, free (Wendy Chilcott and Steve Newman).

Wildlife may be seen at **Punta Tombo** and Camarones. Punta Tombo is 117 km S of Trelew, on a dirt road which branches off the road to Rawson, 5 km SE of Trelew: driving time 1¾ hours (this is incorrectly shown on ACA maps). Park entrance US$5. There the wildlife is very varied: penguins, guanacos, etc. Season for penguins, Sep-Mar (Dec-Jan is the time when the young are taking to the water); the Reserve closes after Mar. Check with the Tourist Office that it is all right to visit the penguins as from late Mar they are "off limits" as they prepare to migrate. When visits are permitted it is a fantastic experience. You can share a taxi from Trelew (US$30 pp). Sur Turismo and others run ½ day tours, spending ½ hour at the site for US$25 (standard fee, not incl park entry). About mid-way between Rawson and Punta Tombo, a road leads off Ruta 1 to Isla Escondida (9 km, signed), no facilities, but lovely rock and sand beach with bird and wildlife (badly littered unfortunately); secluded camping. Good place to camp if you are visiting the wildlife at Punta Tombo early am (the best time). When leaving the park, ask the guard for the shortest route back to Ruta 3. There is an E/W road not shown on most maps.

Camarones, 275 km S of Trelew and 300 km N of Comodoro Rivadavia, is less crowded. There is a large **penguin colony** 35 km away at Cabo Dos Bahías along a dirt road (US$5, open all year); free camping is possible there and in the town itself (**C** *Hotel Kau-i-Keuken*, clean, friendly, good food, rec, owner runs trips to penguin colony; 2 others, **D**, the one by the power station is not rec). Local buses very scarce; two a week, US$10, on Mon and Fri from Trelew (Don Otto), book at Uruguay 590, Trelew; bus leaves 0800 from San Martín and Belgrano, arrives 1130, returns to Trelew same day 1600. In Camarones ask the Guardia Fauna on Mon or Fri for a lift, hitchhiking is difficult, but possible at weekends and taxis are unavailable (a private car will charge US$50-60, ask at Busca Vida).

Comodoro Rivadavia, the largest city in the province of Chubut (pop 158,000),

is 387 km S of Trelew. Petroleum was discovered here in 1907 and about 30% of all Argentina's oil production comes from wells to the S and W. A 1,770-km pipeline carries the natural gas to Buenos Aires, and there is a petrochemical plant. Renewed interest in the local oil industry is making the town boom. There is an Oil Museum, with exhibits on exploration and production, 3 km N in Gral Mosconi (bus No 6 from San Martín y Abasolo). From here southward, prices begin to rise very rapidly, so stock up before reaching Río Gallegos (although bear in mind you are not allowed to take food into Chile). Good beach at Rada Tilly, 12 km S (buses every ½ hr) walk along beach at low tide to see sealions.

Local Holidays 28 Jul (Founding of Chubut); 13 Dec (Petroleum Day).

Hotels A3 *Austral*, Rivadavia 190, T 32200, noise from traffic but otherwise comfortable, reasonable restaurant; **A3** *Comodoro*, 9 de Julio 770, T 32300, overpriced, restaurant, night clubs, car rental; **B** *Residencial Azul*, Sarmiento 724, T 24874, comfortable, spotless, rec; **D** *Colón*, San Martín 341, T 22283, run down, but quiet, safe and cheap; **D** *Comercio*, Rivadavia 341, T 22341, friendly, old fashioned, dirty, near bus station, hot showers, good meals; **Pensión Boedo**, Rivadavia 453, cheap restaurant, mediocre food; **D** *Hospedaje Belgrano*, Belgrano 546, T 24313, with bath, clean, hot water; **D** *Diana*, on Belgrano, clean, friendly; **D** *Hospedaje Praga*, España y Sarmiento, shower, clean; **D** *Rada Tilly*, Av Piedrabuena, in Rada Tilly 5 km S, T 51032, modern, clean. *Motel Astra*, access (S) of Route 3, T 25394.

Camping Municipal and ACA, 12 km S at Rada Tilly, may be reached by Expreso Rada Tilly bus from town. Excellent facilities, hot and cold water. There is another, free, campsite at N end of beach, cold water only (watch out for clayslides when it rains).

Restaurants *La Rastra*, Rivadavia 384, very good for *churrasco*, but not much else; *Cocorico* (better) and *El Náutico*, Playa Costanera. *Pizzería El Nazareño*, San Martín y España, good. *Bom-Bife*, España 832, good food, inexpensive. Several *rotiserías*, much cheaper, on 400 block of Rivadavia, in municipal market.

Banks and Exchange Lloyds Bank (BLSA), Av Rivadavia 276. Oct-Mar 0700-1300; Apr-Sep 1200-1800; no exchange transactions after 1000 in summer, 6% commission on TCs, will pay dollars cash on cheques but minimum US$300; the **Banco de la Nación**, San Martín 108, has the best rates on US$ but does not change TCs. Amex agent is **Orbe Turismo Show**, San Martín 488, T 29699, 5% commission for US$ or peso cheques. *Hotel Comodoro* changes US$ at poor rate. Several travel agencies also change money incl **Roqueta Travel**, Rivadavia y Pellegrini, *Ceferino*, 9 de Julio 852, and **CRD Travel**, Moreno 844 (TCs).

Consulates Belgian Vice-Consul, Rivadavia 283; **Chilean Consul**, Sarmiento 936; **Italian Vice-Consul**, Belgrano 1053.

Post Office San Martín y Moreno.

Travel agencies *Puelche EVT*, Rivadavia 527; *Richard Pentreath*, Mitre 952; *San Gabriel* and *Atlas* at San Martín 488 and 263, respectively; *Monitur*, 9 de Julio 948.

Tourist Office On Rivadavia.

VW dealer Comercial Automotor, Rivadavia 380, rec. VW concession in Barrio Industrial, Av Irigoyen, also rec.

Air Services Airport, 9 km. Bus to airport from downtown terminal or opp Aerolíneas Argentinas in main street (T 24781), hourly (45 mins), US$0.40; take bus No 6. Once a day to **Buenos Aires** with Aerolíneas (direct) or Austral, stopping at **Bahía Blanca** daily, except Sun; Austral at 9 de Julio 870, T 22191; Austral daily, except Sun, to **Río Gallegos** and **Río Grande**; LAPA 3 a week to BsAs and Trelew, 2 a week to Río Gallegos; LADE (Rivadavia 360, T 36181) flies once a week (Wed) Comodoro Rivadavia-Perito Moreno-Gobernador Gregores Calafate/Lago Argentino-Río Gallegos-Río Grande-Ushuaia, and on Mon to Puerto Deseado-San Julián-Gob Gregores-Calafate-Río Turbio-Río Gallegos-Santa Cruz; once a week to Bariloche via Trelew and Viedma, or Trelew and Esquel, or via Esquel, El Maitén and El Bolsón; other services to Neuquén via the Lake District (also TAN 6 a week) and to Trelew (also TAN). TAN also flies to Bariloche, Río Gallegos and Puerto Deseado. Kaiken fly to Ushuaia via Río Grande, Río Gallegos and Lago Argentino Tues and Sat. Taxi to airport, US$7.

Buses Bus station conveniently located in city centre; has luggage store, good *confitería* upstairs, lousy toilets, *remise* taxi booth, some kiosks. Bus service to **Buenos Aires** daily at 1200 and 2115, 32 hrs, US$108 (same fare on Costera Criolla; also daily with La Estrella/Cóndor at 1335). Angel Giobbi buses to **Coyhaique** (Chile), US$28.50, 12 hrs, twice a week (Tues and Fri), 0100, Jun-Sep and 3 a week (Mon, Wed, Fri), 0100, Oct-May (weather permitting). Three buses a week to **Bariloche**, US$55 (Don Otto at 2150, Sun, Tues, Thur, stops at Sarmiento midnight, Esquel at 0600 and for ½ hr at El Bolsón at 0900, arrives 0600 at Bariloche). To **Esquel** (paved road) direct, Fri 1230, 10 hrs, via Río Mayo, Mon, Thur, 0100, 15½ hrs, to Río Mayo Tues, Thur, Sun, 1700 and 1900, 5½ hrs. In summer buses heading S usually arrive full. To **Río Gallegos**, Don Otto 2345 daily, and Transportes Patagónica 2200 daily, US$40, reserve or standby. To **Puerto Madryn and Trelew**, US$26, at 1200. La Unión colectivo to **Caleta Olivia**, hourly, US$3.50. To **Sarmiento**, US$7, 2½ hrs at 0700, 1300, 1900. To **Mendoza**, daily at 0130, 20 hrs; to **Córdoba**, Tues, Fri, Sun, 1200, 33 hrs.

Hitchhiking There is a truck stop outside Comodoro Rivadavia on Route 3, the road to Bahía Blanca, where you can contact drivers whether heading N or S. Hitch out of the centre on Ruta 3 to "Astra Km 20", or take any bus going N. Expensive truckdrivers' restaurants along the road; buy food in supermarkets.

The road to Chile runs inland from Comodoro Rivadavia, amid oil wells, to (156 km) Colonia Sarmiento (commonly known just as **Sarmiento**), population: 7,000 (archaeological museum with tourist office next to cathedral, check opening times, may be closed at weekends), on Lago Musters, near the large Lago Colhué Huapi. 32 km by dirt road S of Sarmiento there is a large petrified forest, the Bosque Petrificado José Ormachea (**see p 201**), well worth a visit but difficult to reach (contact Sr Valero, the park ranger, for guided tours, ask at *Hotel Colón*).

Hotels and Restaurants *Lago Musters*, P Moreno y Coronel, T 93097; **C** *Hostería Los Lagos*, Roca y Alberdi, T 93046, good, friendly, heating, restaurant; **E** *Colón*, P Moreno 645, restaurant, cheap, friendly; *San Martín*, San Martín y P Moreno, cheap, good restaurant. Food at *El Gaucho*, Route 20, access Sarmiento. *Ismar*, Patagonia 248; *Oroz*, 200 block of Uruguay. In Dec-Mar you may be permitted to sleep in the Agricultural School (take sleeping bag) on the road to petrified forest, opp the ACA petrol station.

Camping Municipal site 2 km N of centre on Route 24, basic, no shower, US$3 for tent, US$1 pp, beside river.

Travel Agency Julio Lew, Roca and Alberdi.

Bus Overnight buses to **Esquel** on Sun, Tues and Thur, stop at Rio Mayo, 0630, take food for journey as cafés on route tend to overcharge. 3 buses a day to **Comodoro Rivadavia**, 0700, 1300, 1900 and Giobbi buses to **Chile** leave at 0200.

From Sarmiento you can reach Esquel (448 km N along Route 40), at the S edge of the Lake District (**see p 184**). The first 210 km from Sarmiento are paved, then it is mostly a dirt or all-weather road, though short stretches have been paved. Hitching along this road is very difficult, even in summer.

From Sarmiento the road continues W via **Río Mayo** (pop 2,260, 4 hotels, **D** *Covadonga*, very good; **D** *Hotel Pingüino*; **D** *A'Ayones*, T 20044, clean, modern, heating; **F** pp *San Martín*), and the Chilean frontier at Coyhaique Alto to Coyhaique and Puerto Aisén in Chile. The Giobbi buses from Comodoro Rivadavia to Coyhaique, Chile, pass through Río Mayo at 0600 on Mon, Wed and Fri, US$14, 6 hrs, but seats are scarce. Mon and Thur at the same hour Giobbi takes Route 40 N direct to Esquel. From Río Mayo Route 40 runs 130 km S to Perito Moreno; 31 km S of Perito Moreno a turning leads W to Lago Blanco, where there is a small *estancia* community, 30 km from the border with Chile (about 150 km from Río Mayo). No hotel, but police are friendly and may permit camping at the police post; wild but beautiful place. No public transport to Chile. From here the road continues to Chile via Paso Huemules and Balmaceda.

Perito Moreno (pop 1,700), at 400m, is close to Lago Buenos Aires, which extends into Chile as Lago General Carrera. Do not confuse the town with the famous glacier of the same name on Lago Argentino near El Calafate, nor with nearby **Parque Nacional Perito Moreno**, see p 210.

Hotels **C** *Americano*, good restaurant; **C** *Argentino*, Buenos Aires 1236, dirty, no showers; **C** *Belgrano*, San Martín 1001, T 2019, with shower, clean, friendly, no heating, with restaurant, rec; **D** *Santa Cruz*, on Belgrano, heating, shared bath and hot water. 25 km S on ruta 40, **C** pp *Telken*, sheep station of the Nauta family offers accommodation Oct-Apr, discounts for families with 2 children, breakfast incl, other meals extra, English and Dutch spoken. Food is very expensive in Perito Moreno. **Restaurant** *Pipach III*, good pizzas and *empanadas*.

Camping Parque Laguna in town, opposite Laguna Cisnes, well shielded, but dirty, US$0.50 pp. US$1 extra for showers, also cabins (slide shows at the tourist office there, information given).

Exchange US$ cash can be exchanged at **Banco de la Provincia de Santa Cruz**. Better rates from Plácido Treffinger, Av San Martín opposite the town hall. Difficult to exchange TCs, though the *Hotel Belgrano* may do so.

Transport Airport is a long way from town, try to hitch as there is only one taxi; LADE flies from Perito Moreno to **Río Gallegos** on Wed, check in well in advance. Hitch-hikers to the S are warned that, outside the tourist season (Jan-mid-Feb), it is usually quicker to head for the coast at Caleta Olivia and go S from there than to take Route 40 via Gobernador Gregores and Piedrabuena.

Excursions South of Perito Moreno are the famous **Cuevas de las Manos**. The series of galleries with 10,000-years-old paintings of human hands and of animals in red, orange, black, white and green, are interesting even for those not interested in rock art. The canyon in which the caves are situated is very beautiful, especially in the evening light (entrance US$1). 118 km S of Perito Moreno on Route 40, a marked road goes directly to the caves (44 km). A ranger lives at the site; he looks after the caves and is helpful with information. Camping is permitted but very windy. If it is not busy the ranger may let you sleep inside the park building. No buses, but the tourist office at Perito Moreno can supply names of drivers who can take you there, prices between US$80-100, to be split among a party of visitors. On leaving Perito Moreno on the way to the caves you will pass Cerro de El Volcán, its crater is accessible; after passing the Gendarmería on your right, take the first left (dirt road) at the 3-road junction with Route 40. It is 12 km to the path to the crater—ask permission at the Estancia to continue.

Crossing to Chile From Perito Moreno Route 43 runs south of Lago Buenos Aires to **Los Antiguos**, 67 km W, 2 km from the Chilean frontier (**C** *Hotel Argentino*, comfortable, restaurant; outstanding municipal campsite; service station, salmon fishing; annual cherry festival in early Jan). There is a bus connection (Empresa Co-Mi) from Caleta Olivia (see below) through to Los Antiguos every Mon, Thur, and Sat, at 1030 (from Perito Moreno, leaves from

Hotel Argentino) and back to Caleta Olivia every Tues, Fri and Sun at 0830 (1030 from Perito Moreno), daily in Feb (at least), US$10.

At Km 29 **A3** *Hostería La Serena* offers accommodation in *cabinas*, 10% reduction to *South American Handbook* readers, good restaurant and organizes trips in both the Chilean and Argentine Lake Districts, open Oct-June; further details from Geraldine des Cressonières, Estancia La Serena, Casilla 87, 9040 Perito Moreno, Santa Cruz. Nearby is Los Chilcas where Indian remains can be found (trout fishing). From Los Antiguos Transportes VH buses cross the border by new bridge to Chile Chico, 8 km W, US$2.50, 3/4 hr (for routes from Chile Chico to Coyhaique and Puerto Aisén see **Chile section 7**). Another route to Chile is to follow the roads which go around the N side of Lago Buenos Aires to Puerto Ibáñez, but there are no sign posts and it is easy to get lost among the *estancias*.

In Aug 1991, the eruption of Volcán Hudson in Chile buried the area around Lago Buenos Aires in volcanic ash and necessitated its evacuation. The lake itself rose two meters. The effects of the ash were felt as far as the Atlantic coast between Puerto Deseado and San Julián (see below). Much grassland and millions of sheep were killed.

South of Comodoro Rivadavia, Route 3 continues to **Caleta Olivia** (Km 66), pop 13,000. A good start-point for hitching S, Caleta Olivia is the urban centre for important oilfields, and is near Pico Truncado, the gas field which feeds the pipeline to Buenos Aires. On the central roundabout in front of the bus station is a huge granite monument of an oil driller with the tools of his trade.

Hotels **C** pp *Robert*, San Martín 2151, T 61452; **B** *Grand*, Mosconi y Chubut, T 61393; **C** *Capri*, Hernández 1145, T 61132. Camping at Yacht Club.

Buses El Pingüino runs to **Rio Gallegos**, US$34, dep 2100, arr 0900. Many buses to **Comodoro Rivadavia**, 1 hr, US$2.10. To **Perito Moreno** and **Los Antiguos**, Mon, Wed, Fri, 4 hrs, US$18. To **Calafate**, dep 1400, 5 hrs.

73 km further S is **Fitz Roy**, named after the captain of Darwin's ship, *Beagle* (**C** *Hotel Fitzroy*, good, clean, cheap food, camping sometimes possible; petrol station).

This is the area of the **petrified forests**, 70,000,000 years old, of fallen araucaria trees, nearly 3m round and 15-20m long: a remarkable sight. Taxi, Sarmiento to forests, US$39 (3 passengers), incl 1 hr wait, for each extra hour US$9. Hitching is difficult, even in summer, but the Park Warden at Uruguay 43 may give lifts; check return times. There are two sites you can visit: the **Bosque Petrificado José Ormachea**, due W of Comodoro Rivadavia, about 140 km by road (116 km paved—the unpaved part is practically impassable in the wet season), 32 km S of Sarmiento on good gravel road, entry US$5, jeep trip to larger trees US$25 for up to six persons but can be walked in 20 mins; the Víctor Szlapelis park, some 40 km further SW along the same road (follow signposts, road from Sarmiento in good condition). The **Monumento Natural Bosques Petrificados**, W of Puerto Deseado, surrounding the Laguna Grande on a road SW from Fitz Roy, 113 km away, can also be reached from Jaramillo (14 km S of Fitz Roy). This site has the largest examples of petrified trees. A new road has been built from Route 3 about 65 km S of Fitz Roy to the Bosques Petrificados, which reduces the journey by several km.

10 km S of Fitzroy Route 281 branches off Route 3 and runs 123 km SE to **Puerto Deseado**, with a population of 4,100 (airport), at the mouth of the river Deseado which drains Lago Buenos Aires, far to the W. The town was founded on 15 July 1884; its harbour takes large ships. A local tourist attraction is the Cañadón de las Bandurrias, sometimes known as the Grotto of Lourdes, 40m high. Nearby are islands with penguins and other birds, including the unique grey cormorant; local launches available. Lago Buenos Aires is reached by road in 7 hours; 280 km to Las Heras, on to Perito Moreno, near the lake, 177 km, and a further 67 km to the Chilean border at Los Antiguos (see above).

It was at Puerto Deseado that a Welshman in Cavendish's expedition of 1586 gave the name of *pengwyn* (white head) to a certain strange-looking bird. It is only fair to mention the opposing theory that the name is derived from a Spanish word, *pingüe*, meaning fat.

Local holidays 31 Jan (San Juan Bosco); 9 Oct (Coat of Arms day).

Hotels **A3** *Los Acantilados*, Pueyrredón y España, T 70167; **B** *Colón*, Almte Brown 450, T 70304, dormitory-style; accommodation may also be available in the sports centre—ask at the

Municipalidad. **Restaurant** *El Quincho*, Av Costanera Marcelo Lotufu, T 0967 70977, rec.

From Fitz Roy Route 3 runs S 268 km to **San Julián** (founded 1901, pop 4,480), the best place for breaking the 834 km run from Comodoro Rivadavia to Río Gallegos. There is much wildlife in the area: red and grey foxes, guanacos, wildcats in the mountains, rheas, etc. The main activities are sheep raising for export, fish canning, and production of kaolin and clay. Clay grinding can be seen at Molienda Santa Cruz and ceramics made at the Escuela de Cerámica; good handicraft centre at Moreno y San Martín. There is a regional museum at the end of San Martín on the waterfront. The ruins of Florida Blanca, a colony 10 km W of town, founded in 1870 by Antonio Viedma, can be visited. The cascade of San Julián is formed by two different tides. Punta Caldera is a popular summer beach. The first mass in Argentina was held here after Magellan had executed a member of his crew. Francis Drake also put in here to behead Thomas Doughty, after amiably dining with him. Near San Julián (15 km) is Cabo Curioso beach, with an attractive cave.

Hotels B *Municipal*, 25 de Mayo 917, T 2300/1, very nice, well-run, good value, but no restaurant. B *Residencial Sada*, San Martín 1112, T 2013, nice, clean, hot water, own bathroom, but sited on busy main road. Also older C *Colón*, Av San Martín 301 and D *Aguila*, San Martín 500 block, sleazy, cheapest in town. Good municipal campsite on the waterfront, US$2 pp, repeatedly rec, all facilities, Av Costanera betweeen Rivadavia and Roca.

Restaurants *Sportsman*, Mitre y 25 de Mayo, excellent value; *Rural*, Ameghino y Vieytes, good, but not before 2100; a number of others. Also bars and tearooms.

Post Office At Belgrano and Av San Martín; telephone exchange also.

Banks Banco de la Nación, Mitre y Belgrano, and Banco de la Provincia de Santa Cruz, San Martín y Moreno.

Pharmacy *Del Pueblo* on San Martín 570. **Hospital**, Av Costanera entre Roca y Magallanes.

Tourist Office In centre of San Martín.

Air Weekly services (Mon) with LADE to Santa Cruz, Río Gallegos, Puerto Deseado, Gob Gregores, Comodoro Rivadavia, Calafate/Lago Argentino and Río Turbio.

Bus Transportadora Patagónica comes from Río Gallegos en route to **Buenos Aires** (also Pingüino, 6 hrs, US$14 to/from Río Gallegos); Transportes Staller goes weekly to **Lago Posadas** stopping in Gobernador Gregores, Hotel Riera, Las Horquetas, Bajo Caracoles and Río Blanco. Transportes El Cordillerano cover the previous route but also stop at **Caleta Olivia**. For hitching, walk 5 km to petrol station on Ruta 3.

An unpaved road (Route 521) runs NW from San Julián to Route 40 along the foothills of the Andes. About halfway is **Gobernador Gregores** (*Hotel San Francisco*, under repair 1994; municipal campsite; good mechanic in town and all grades of fuel available).

Santa Cruz, 153 km S of San Julián, one of the best of the coastal harbours (airport) is near the mouth of the Santa Cruz river which drains Lago Argentino. Founded on 1 December, 1878 and capital of Santa Cruz province until 1904. A deep-water port is being built 22 km outside Santa Cruz at *Punta Quilla*, pop 3,000 (**Hotels** B *Hostal de la Ría*, 25 de Mayo 645, T 8038; *Hostería Turística*; *Anel Aike*, both C). Isla Monte León, 66 km away (Route 1601, then Route 3 and dirt track) has penguins, beaches, fishing and camping facilities (reported closed to visitors).

At *Piedrabuena* (pop 2,600), 35 km W of Santa Cruz (paved road) are **B** *ACA Motel*, T 7145, simple, functional but good, warm and nice food; **B** *Hostería El Alamo*, Lavalle 08, T 7249, shower, clean, quiet, breakfast extra, rec; *Andalucia*, Belgrano Oeste 170, hotel and restaurant (good pasta); **D** *Residencial Internacional*, Ibáñez 99, T 7197, rec; **D** pp *Hotel Vani*; also campsites N of town on Route 3. ACA breakdown station at Km 247 on Route 3. The *Select* restaurant is very dear for what it offers, but there are several others. Provincial Route 9 (1603 on some maps, unpaved, no petrol) from 43 km S of Piedrabuena to Calafate runs along the edge of a plateau with occasional panoramic views across the valley of the Río Santa Cruz below. Then at about 170 km it drops down into the valley itself to follow the river into the hills and to Lake Argentino. A pleasant run, without being spectacular. Route 288 runs direct to Calafate from Piedrabuena via Tres Lagos. Most traffic to El Calafate goes via Río Gallegos.

Río Gallegos, at the mouth of the Río Gallegos, the capital of Santa Cruz Province, is 265 km S of Santa Cruz; it has a deep-water port with a dry-dock and a large military base. The tidal range here during spring tides is 9.1m. Further N, at Puerto Santa Cruz, maximum tidal range reaches 14.6m. There is a large trade in wool and sheepskins. Population: 75,000. Foundation Day: 9 Dec 1885. The town, although somewhat drab, has a good shopping centre on Roca. "Once beyond Roca and Zapiola, the streets turn to dust, stones and squabbling packs of dogs" (Kevin Healey). The small Plaza San Martín, 1 block from the post office is well tended, with flower beds and statues; outside the post office is the remarkable sight of a balcony (preserved from a demolished house) commemorating the meeting of Presidents Errázuriz and Roca to end Chile and Argentina's 1883 Magellan Strait dispute. The Museo Provincial Mario Echevarría Baleta, Moreno 45 entre Zapiola y Roca, has collections of local history, flora, fauna, rock samples (open 0800-1900, weekends 1500-2000). Museo de los Pioneros, Alberdi y Elcano in the house of a German pioneer family, free, open 1500-2000, rec. Cheap sheepskins (tanned) and very warm leather coats (*gamulanes*) at Puerto Aymond factory of Mr Szasack (half the Buenos Aires price). Argentina's longest road, Route 40, ends at Río Gallegos, or, more precisely, Punta Loyola; it runs from Bolivia for over 4,667 km. **NB** Do not confuse Calle Comodoro Rivadavia with (nearby) Calle Rivadavia. Local holiday 31 Jan.

Hotels L3 *Aparthotel Niza*, Alcorta 190, T 20958, quiet, good breakfast incl, clean, rec; **A1** *Costa Río*, San Martín 673, new, comfortable, discounts for ACA members; **A3** *Alonso*, Corrientes 33, T 22414, simple, very clean, rm very hot; **A3** *Comercio*, Roca 1302, T 20209, clean, poorly lit, noisy, very busy; **A3** *Santa Cruz*, Roca 701, T 20601, with shower and heating, discount for cash, receptionist speaks English, good coffee bar, breakfast; **B** *Covadonga*, Roca 1214, T 20190, clean, with shower, comfortable, warm, rec; **B** *Nevada*, Roca 1040, T 25990 (opp bus station for Punta Arenas), with bath, English spoken, good; **B** *París*, Roca 1040, T 20111, without bath, grubby, friendly; **B** *Piscis*, Avellaneda y Magallanes, T 25064, pleasant rooms, friendly; **C** *Cabo Virgen*, Comodoro Rivadavia 252, with bath, rec; **C** *Colonial*, Urquiza y Rivadavia, T 22329, shower, cheaper without, hot water, heating, friendly, clean, can be noisy; **D** *Laguna Azul*, rundown but clean and good value; **D** *Central*, Av Roca 1127, central, quiet, cold shower, no heating; close by is **D** *Entre Ríos*, Entre Ríos, good; **D** *Pensión Belgrano*, Calle Belgrano 123, dirty, basic but friendly, has good restaurant; **D** *Residencial Internacional*, Sphur 78, with heating, friendly, but insecure; **D** *Río Turbio*, Zapiola 486, T 22155, good value; **D** *Viejo La Fuente*, Vélez Sarsfield 64-70, T 20304, basic, friendly, rooms near bar are noisy, hot water, restaurant; **E** *Puerto Santa Cruz*, Zapiola 238, T 20099, with bath, passable. Private house: Barrio Codepro II, Casa 71, T 23789, E pp, rec.

NB Accommodation is hard to find in Río Gallegos because of the number of transient workers in town. Apparently no **camping** is allowed around Río Gallegos because it is a military zone apart from the authorized municipal site on Italia y Costa Rica, turn off Route 3 at edge of town heading south (small, basic). There is another site 1 block S of bus terminal (Ruta 3 Norte), US$3 pp + US$1 for tent. Ask at tourist office for new site, being developed alongside a children's playground, cheap, free, hot showers. One is not allowed to take photographs either, for the same reason.

Restaurants Plenty and good, some specializing in seafood, but expensive. *Restaurant Díaz*, Roca 1143, good but dirty, cheap; *La Casa de Miguel*, Roca 1284, good food; *Bifería La Vasca*, Roca 1084, good value, young crowd, rock music, open till 0300; *Jardín*, Roca 1315, good, cheap, popular; *Club Británico*, Roca 935, excellent, reasonably priced; *Montecarlo*, Zapiola 558, good seafood, not the cheapest; opp is good *heladería*. *El Palenque*, Corrientes 73, rec. *Café Carrera*, Fagnano y Roca, good but expensive breakfast; *Le Croissant*, Zapiola y Estrada, good bakery.

Banks and Exchange Lloyds Bank (BLSA), Sarmiento 47. Open 1000-1600. Cash advance on Visa and Mastercard. Many banks on Av Roca incl **Banco de Santa Cruz**, 900 block, fair rates, Mastercard. Best rates for TCs, no commission, change cheques here if going to Calafate, where it is even more difficult; fair rates at **Cambio El Pingüino**, Zapiola 469; may also change European and South American currencies. **Cambio Sur**, Av San Martín y Roca, often has good rates. **Banco del Sud**, Calle Alberdi, changes TCs without commission. **Banco de Crédito Argentino**, quick cash advance on Visa upstairs.

Chilean Consulate Mariano Moreno 136, Mon-Fri, 0900-1300; tourist cards issued at border.

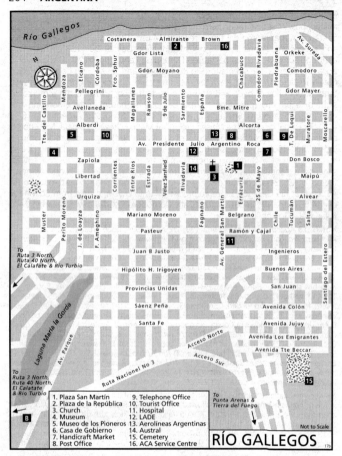

Río Gallegos

1. Plaza San Martín
2. Plaza de la República
3. Church
4. Museum
5. Museo de los Pioneros
6. Casa de Gobierno
7. Handicraft Market
8. Post Office
9. Telephone Office
10. Tourist Office
11. Hospital
12. LADE
13. Aerolineas Argentinas
14. Austral
15. Cemetery
16. ACA Service Centre

Not to Scale

RÍO GALLEGOS

17b

Laundry Alberdi y Rawson. *Laverap* at Corrientes 277.

Post Office Roca 893. Another branch at the airport. **Telephones**, Roca 613.

Shopping *Artesanías Koekén*, San Martín 336, leatherwork, woollen goods, local produce; *Artesanías Santacruceñas*, Roca 658; *Prepop*, an artisan centre, is worth a visit; *Tia* department store, Roca 700 block, good supermarket section; Supermarket *La Anónima*, Roca y España. Most places take a 2-3 hr lunch break.

Tourist Office Roca y Córdoba, Mon-Fri, 0800-1400, friendly, helpful, English spoken. (Also Alberdi 154, and at airport.) They will phone round hotels for you.

Taxis Hiring a taxi for excursions may be no more expensive than taking a tour bus. Try Sr Miguel Caliguiri, Tres Lagos 445; he charges US$200 to Calafate and Moreno glacier. *A1*, Entre Ríos 350, T 22453, for taxis and car rental, not cheap. **Car Rental** *Localiza*, Sarmiento 237, T 24417, and at airport.

Car parts and repairs at Repuestos Sarmiento, on Sarmiento, owner very friendly and helpful.

Motorcycle Mechanic Juan Carlos Topcic, Costa Rica 25, friendly and helpful.

Air Travel In summer, it is best to make your bookings in advance. AR (San Martín 545, T 22342, airport 20163) flies daily to **Buenos Aires** (Austral flies daily except Sun, via Bahía Blanca, LAPA twice a week, via Comodora Rivadavia and Trelew). AR's Buenos Aires-Auckland-Sydney flight (twice a week) stops at Río Gallegos, but the return journey does not. Several flights to **Ushuaia** (Tierra del Fuego), direct (AR, always booked, but standby seats available with AR, US$59). To **Río Grande**, 40 mins, 6 a week with Austral (Roca 917, T 22038). LADE (Fagnano 53, T 20316) to **Río Turbio** (Wed). To **Comodoro Rivadavia** with LADE twice a week, once via Calafate/Lago Argentino Gob Gregores and **Perito Moreno**, once a week, via Calafate, Gob Gregores, San Julián and Puerto Deseado. Pingüino Río Gallegos-Calafate US$46 (office at airport), 1 hr. TAN to Neuquén, Río Grande Trelew and Comodora Rivadavia. Naval flights (Comando de la Marina, T 22600) up and down the coast every Fri, eg to Buenos Aires, but full of navy personnel. Book seats in Buenos Aires to avoid difficulties with departures.

Airport 4 km from town centre and 3 km from bus terminal. Taxi (*remise*) to/from town, eg opp *Hotel Colonial* US$8 (beware overcharging); Interlagos and Pingüino buses stop at airport, leave 1400 for Calafate direct, US$25 (return US$40, 10% ISIC discount on one way only), 4 hrs; hitching from car park is easy. It is permitted to spend the night at the airport prior to early am flights. **NB** Flights may leave early, sometimes up to 40 mins. LADE flights should be booked as far in advance as possible.

Bus company offices: Main companies incl Expreso Pingüino and Interlagos have offices at airport; Pingüino, Zapiola 455, T 22338/25840, open 0800-1300, 1500-2100, Mon-Sat, 0900-1300, 1700-2100, Sun; Transportadora Patagónica, Gobernador Lista 330, T 2330; Mansilla, San Martín 565; Vera, office at bus terminal.

Road Travel New bus terminal at corner of Route 3 and Av Parque, 3 km from centre (no left luggage, small bank, *confitería*, few toilets, kiosks); taxi to centre US$3, bus US$1 (Nos 1 and 12 from posted stops on Roca). To **Calafate**, 4-5 hrs, US$25 (US$40 return), very crowded; turn up with ticket 30 mins before departure: 2 companies—Interlagos and Pingüino—run daily services at 1345 and 1600 between Sep and May, which wait at the airport for incoming flights. In winter both companies operate 3 times a week (El Pingüino has reclining seats, video, toilet, etc, US$50 return, mixed reports). Pingüino offers 2-night excursion to Calafate, sold at airport only, US$93 in single room, credit cards accepted. Route 40, which goes to Calafate (312 km) is paved except the last 40 km; it makes a detour via Río Turbio.

To **Río Turbio**: Expreso Pingüino goes at 1300 daily exc Sat (Sat 1230), $5\frac{1}{2}$-$6\frac{1}{2}$ hrs, US$20 (hitching practically impossible); also Mansilla, Sat 1330, and Vera, Mon-Fri 1200; to **Puerto Natales**, Bus Sur and Pingüino twice a week each, $7\frac{1}{2}$ hrs, US$22. Bus to **Punta Arenas**, 260 km, US$23.50 daily at 1300, by Pingüino, also Ghisoni at 1730, except 1415 Tues and Thur, none on Sat, $6\frac{1}{2}$ hours incl border-crossing process, which is very easy. Make sure your car papers are in order if driving to Chile (go first to Tourist Office for necessary documents, then to the customs office at the port, at the end of San Martín, very uncomplicated). The road to Chile is unpaved but acceptable to the Punta Arenas-Puerto Natales intersection (*hostería* here, D, with restaurant); there is an 11-km paved strip, single lane, southbound from Punta Delgada (just a restaurant) to the turn-off for the Punta Delgada ferry for Tierra del Fuego. Paving is in progress for 10-12 km E of the Punta Arenas intersection. The 55 km S to Punta Arenas on the main road is paved, 2-lane and good.

Pingüino daily at 2100 to **Caleta Olivia**, US$34, 11 hrs. To **Trelew** and **Puerto Madryn** daily (18 hrs), US$71. To **Comodoro Rivadavia**, 834 km, Patagónica at 2100, stops at Fitz Roy daily at dawn, arr 1000 next day, US$40. For **Bariloche**, take this bus to Comodoro Rivadavia, then the 2150 Don Otto bus to Bariloche (fare to Bariloche US$88). A bus (Andesmar) now goes all the way to **Mendoza**, leaves Fri 1300, arrives 0900 Sun, via Comodoro Rivadavia, Puerto Madryn and Neuquén.

To **Buenos Aires**, 2,575 km, 36 hrs, Pingüino, Mon, Wed, Fri, 2200, daily, 2115, with Costera Criolla, US$107. **Hitchhiking** to Buenos Aires is possible in about 5-7 days; appearance important; hitching to Tierra del Fuego possible from service station on Ruta 3 at edge of town, trucks stop here for customs check, be there before 0700. To Calafate, from police control outside town.

Fishing The S fishing zone incl the Ríos Gallegos, Grande, Fuego, Ewan, San Pablo and Lago Fagnano, nr Ushuaia. It is famous for runs of sea trout. See **Fishing** in **Information for Visitors**, p 229.

Excursion 134 km S, there is a penguin colony at *Cabo Vírgenes* (US$3, run by local authority which puts money directly into conservation). Follow Route 3 then branch off on Route 1 for $3\frac{1}{2}$ hrs (unpaved). "Due to recent oil rush this area is now heavily exploited. Many oil workers take the road to the lighthouse, where they stay, and it's quite easy to hitch to the cape. Take transport (taxi) to junction between Route 3 and the gravel road to the cape. Be there around 0700. Take drinking water. It is possible to arrange return with day trippers from Río Gallegos, or ask at lighthouse or naval station" (Rudiger Schultz, Switzerland). (On the way is El Cóndor ranch, where the manager, Mr Blake, is reported to welcome visitors.) The Navy allows visitors to climb up Cabo Vírgenes lighthouse for a superb view.

From Río Gallegos a railway, the southern-most regular line in the world (no longer in operation), runs 260 km to **Río Turbio** (6,000 people), where Argentina's largest coalfield is located; reserves are estimated at 450m tons and the state coal company YCF is building a deep-water port at Punta Loyola to service it. There is a director of tourism, Prof César Cetta, in the municipality on San Martín. Hotels, always almost full: **B** *Hostería Capipe*, Dufour (9 km from town, T 91240); **B** *Gato Negro*, T 91226; *Albergue Municipal*, by ski-run in hills, 6 km from town, US$10 pp. Visitors can see Mina 1, where the first mine was opened in the hills; area good for trekking and horseback riding. The present mining and industrial area, with the school museum, can also be visited. Río Turbio is 39 km by road from Puerto Natales (Chile). This road is open Oct-Mar only. Alternatively, 55 km N of Río Turbio is Cancha Carrera, from where there is a border crossing, also only open during the summer, into Torres del Paine National Park. The Argentine customs are fast and friendly. 8 km beyond at the Chilean border post, open 0830-1200, 1400-2000, Chilean time. You also have to register at the *carabineros'* office. Buses to Puerto Natales, 2 companies, US$3, regular. To Calafate 4 times a week with Pingüino, 7 hrs, US$27. Expreso Pingüino runs daily at 0600 (plus 1300 Tues, Thur, Sat, 6 hrs) in summer or 1300 Wed, Thur, Sat in winter to Río Gallegos, but LADE flights are cheaper and avoid the numerous passport checks. Pingüino also have flights to Calafate, twice weekly (airport 15 km from town, taxi US$15). *Restaurant El Ringo*, near bus station, will shelter you from the wind.

Calafate (properly El Calafate), on Lago Argentino, 312 km NW of Río Gallegos, pop 3,000, is a developing tourist centre. There is a chapel dedicated to Santa Teresa in the centre; behind it Calle Perito Moreno gently climbs the large hill S of the town, from which one can see the silhouette of the southern end of the Andes, the Laguna Redonda and Isla Solitaria on Lago Argentino. It is the southern gateway to the **Parque Nacional de los Glaciares**, which is 50 km away (the northern end is at Lake Viedma). On the alluvial plain by the lake there are many interesting birds, and in the other direction there is scope for good hill-walking. The Lago Argentino area is very popular, booking all transport in advance is a *must*; accommodation can be difficult to find in Jan-Feb. Obtain maps of the area in advance as none is available in Calafate or in the Park. The tourist office has a list of taxis but undertakes no arrangements; it is helpful but some information may be incorrect, so check. Credit cards are not popular, apart from hotels, and high commissions are charged; most places quote in US dollars.

Festivals People flock to the rural show on 15 Feb (Lago Argentino Day) and camp out with much revelry; dances and *asados* (barbecued sides of sheep). There are also barbecues and rodeo etc on Día de la Tradición, 10 Nov.

Hotels Many hotels are open only from Oct to Apr/May. **L2** *Los Alamos*, Moyano y Bustillo, T 91144, F 91186, comfortable, good food and service, rec; **L3** *Hostería Kau-Yatún*, with bath, many facilities, 25 de Mayo (10 blocks from town centre), T 91059, F 91260, old *estancia* house, comfortable, restaurant and barbecues, horse-riding tours with guides; **L3** *El Mirador del Lago*, Libertador 2047, T/F 91176, good accommodation, acceptable restaurant (wines not rec), better not to take half-board; **L3** *Los Notros*, T/F 91438, 40 km from Calafate on road to glacier, half-board, spacious, rm with glacier views, rec; **A2** *Michelangelo*, Espora 1020, T 91045, F 91058, modern, clean, excellent, reasonable, good restaurant, will accept TCs in payment (at a poor rate, though); **A3** *ACA Hostería El Calafate*, Av San Martín, T 91004, F 91027, modern, good view, 16 rooms, open all year; **A3** *Amado*, Av del Libertador 1072, T 91023, good; **A3** *Upsala*, Espora 139, T 91075, incl breakfast, warm, friendly, rec; **B** *Cabañas Del Sol*, Av del Libertador 1956, T 91439 (D in low season), friendly, clean, good meals, highly rec; **B** *Hospedaje del Norte*, Los Gauchos 813, T 91117, open all year, kitchen facilities, clean, comfortable, owner organizes tours, highly rec, a similar place across the street; **A3** *Hostería Schilling*, Roca 895, T 91453, with bath, lovely rooms, manager speaks good English, safe parking for motorcycles; **C** *Hostería Kapenke*, Av del Libertador 1190, opp *Pizzería Onelli*, T 91093, with bath, breakfast incl, good, rec. Rec bed and breakfast at Espora 60, **E** pp. **C** *La Loma*, B Roca y 15 de Febrero (100 m from bus station), T 91016 (can be booked in Buenos Aires at Av Callao 433, 8a "P", T 371-9123), with bath, breakfast incl, excellent view, modern, highly rec, multilingual, restaurant, tea room: the hotel is cheaper in low season, free

EL CALAFATE & Environs 17c

Refugio Onelli
Brazo Upsala
Lago Onelli
Reserva Nacional Zona Centro
Canal Spegazzini
Brazo Norte
Cerro Negro 1650 m
Península Avellaneda
Boca del Diablo
Lago Argentino
Isla Solitaria
Seno Mayo
Canal de los Témpanos
Puerto Bandera
Calafate
To Río Gallegos
Glacier Mayo
Cerro Negro 2011 m
Gl. Ameghino
Península Magallanes
R. Mitre
Glacier Moreno
Cerro Cervantes 2380 m
Brazo Rico
R Rico
ARGENTINA
CHILE
Brazo Sur
Lago Roca
Reserva Nacional Zona Roca
Parque Nacional los Glaciares
CHILE

0 ___ 10
km

EL CALAFATE

Rough Sketch

Lago Argentino
Bahía Redonda
To Cuevas de Gualichú
Los Gauchos
Bustillo
25 de Mayo
9 de Julio
Espora
16
18
19
Gdor Moyano
7 **17**
Perito Moreno
J Pantin
Arroyo Calafate
Cnel Rosales
To Airport
Calle 15
15
Gdor Gregores
14 **12**
11
7 de Diciembre
Guerrero
1 de Mayo
5
2
Av del Libertador
10 **3** **8**
4
6
1
To Glaciar Perito Moreno
B
Av Julio A Roca
To Río Gallegos
9
13
Campo de Desierto
15 de Febrero
To Lago Roca

1. Santa Teresa chapel
2. Bank
3. Market
4. YPF station
5. Automóvil Club de Argentina
6. Tourist Office
7. Telephone Office
8. Post Office
9. LADE
10. Interlagos Travel Agency & El Pingüino
11. Lake Travel
12. Gador Travel Agency

Hotels:
13. *La Loma*
14. *Amado*
15. *Cabañas Nevis*
16. *Los Dos Pinos*
17. *Jorgito*
18. *Belén*
19. *del Norte*

audio-visual of the last breaking of Moreno Glacier in 1988; **C** *Las Cabañitas*, V Feilberg 218, T 91118, cabins, hot water, kitchen and laundry facilities, helpful, rec; **C** *Residencia Dos Lagos*, 25 de Mayo 220, T 91170, with bath, very comfortable and clean, good value, rec; **D** pp *Cabañas Nevis*, about 1 km from town towards glacier, Libertador 1696, T 91180, for 4 or 8, lake view, full board good value. Several slightly cheaper hotels but none less than **E** pp, eg **D** *Lago Azul*, Perito Moreno 83, T 91419, only 2 double rooms, highly rec; **D** *Hospedaje Belén*, Los Gauchos 300 y Perito Moreno, T 91028, clean, warm, hot water, cooking facilities, very friendly, family welcome, highly rec; **D** *Hospedaje Jorgito*, Gob Moyano 943, T 91323, clean, basic, hot water, cooking facilities, heating, breakfast extra, often full, rec; **D** *Hospedaje Los Dos Pinos*, 9 de Julio 358, T 91271, hot water, cooking and laundry facilities, clean, also cabins (D), dormitory accommodation (F pp), and camping (G pp), arranges tours to glacier, popular; **E** pp *Hospedaje Alejandra*, Espora 60, T 91328. **D** *Youth Hostel Albergue del Glaciar*, Calle Los Pioneros, 200m off Av Libertador, T/F 91243 (reservations in Buenos Aires T 541-447 2338 or 54-321 69416), price per person, camping allowed in the grounds (US$5 pp, dirty, exposed), with use of facilities, **E** for ISIC or IYHA members, open 1 Nov—31 Mar, rec, hot water, kitchen facilities, English spoken, travel agency, Perito Moreno Tours, runs tours to Moreno glacier (US$28 pp, constantly rec as good value) and elsewhere, rents camping equipment, free shuttle service from bus station and airport. *Youth Hostel La Loma*, Roca 849, multilingual, restaurant, rm for 2-3 people with bath, or **E** pp sharing, IYHA affiliated, 2 blocks from bus station. Some private houses offer accommodation such as Enrique Barragán, Barrio Bahía Redonda, Casa 10, T 91325, E, rec. **F** pp *Apartamentos Lago Viedma*, Paralelo 158, T 91159, F 91158, hostel, 4 bunks to a room, cooking facilities. **F** pp *La Cueva de Jorge Lemos*, Gob Moyano 839, behind YPF station, bunk beds, bathroom, showers, kitchen facilities, popular and cheap but noisy and dirty. If in difficulty, ask at tourist office from which caravans, tents (sleep 4) and 4-berth *cabañas* may be hired, showers extra.

Camping Campsite behind YPF service station, US$4 pp. 3 campsites in the Park en route to the glacier: *Camping Río Mitre*, near the park entrance, 52 km from Calafate, 26 km E of the glacier, US$3 pp; *Camping Bahía Escondida*, 7 km E of the glacier, toilets and hot showers, US$3 pp; unmarked site at Arroyo Correntoso, 10 km E of the glacier, no facilities but nice location and lots of firewood. Take food to all three. Another campsite is *Camping Río Bote*, 35 km, on road to Río Gallegos.

Restaurants Prices rise during Nov and high season lasts until May. *Pizzería Onelli*, Libertador 1197, reasonable, stays open out of season; *Michelangelo*, Espora 1020, very expensive but absolutely magnificent steaks, rec; *Paso Verlika*, Av Libertador 1108, small, 2 courses with wine US$16, credit cards 10% extra, good value; *El Refugio*, Av Libertador 963, Alpine style; *El Rancho*, 9 de Julio y Gob Moyano, large, cheap and good pizzas, popular, free video shows of the glacier, highly rec; *La Rueda*, Gob Paradelo, friendly, cheap, rec; *La Loma*, friendly, home food, picnic lunches supplied, good cakes and chocolates, beautiful view, reasonable prices, discounts for IYHA; *Comedor Family House*, Av del Libertador. Tea rooms: *Maktub*, Libertador 905, excellent pastries, US$8 pp, pricey; *Bar Don Diego de la Noche*, Av del Libertador 1603, lamb and seafood, live music, good atmosphere.

Exchange Banco de la Provincia de Santa Cruz (Av del Libertador) changes cash (commission 1%) and TCs. Advances on Visa and Mastercard (no commission). Travel agencies such as Interlagos also change notes. YPF garage and **Chocolate El Calafate** and some other shops give good rates for cash; also **El Pingüino** bus company for good rates (but watch the commission); the **Scorpio** snack bar in the main street is reported to give best rates; try also the supermarket in the main street and the *Albergue del Glaciar*. High commission on cheques.

Telephones Public office on Espora, 0700-0100, also has telex and fax facilities.

Travel Agents *Interlagos*, Libertador 1175, tours to Moreno glacier, plenty of time allowed, provide cheapest transport to Fitz Roy (but double check return!), English and Spanish speaking guide, highly rec; *El Pingüino*, Libertador 1025, T 91273, changes TCs, rec; *Los Glaciares*, Libertador 1303, T 91159, rec, prices often cheaper; *Tur Aike*, Libertador 1080, T 91436, and *Gador Viajes*, Libertador 900 block. *Upland Goose*, Av Libertador (1st floor), T 0902-91424, rec. *Hielo y Aventura*, 25 de Mayo, T 91514, organizes 2-hr trek on glacier with champagne, rec. Most agencies charge the same rates for excursions: to the Moreno Glacier US$25 for a trip leaving 0830, returning 1800, without lunch, 3 hrs at glacier; to Lago Roca, at 0930 return 1700, US$25; Cerro Fitz Roy, at 0600 return 1900, US$50; Gualichó caves, 2 hrs, US$8 (see **Excursions**, below). Several hotels also organize tours by minibus incl *Hospedaje del Norte* and *Albergue del Glaciar*, sometimes cheaper and better quality. Jorge Lemos, *Aventrek*, Gob Moyano 839, AP Postal Esp No 7 (9405) El Calafate, Telex Cab pública 86905, runs rec treks with small groups in Glaciares National Park and Fitzroy. *Martín Drake*, Av Roca 2034, T 91364, operates tours in 12-seater minibus throughout the area, as does Dario Serantoni, T

91346. Mountain bikes can be hired from Sr Daniel Alvarez, also rec as source of information, at the Mercado Artesanal on Av del Libertador.

Tourist Information Tourist office on new building by bridge over Río Calafate, friendly. Tour to Moreno glacier information available here. Hotel prices detailed on large chart at tourist office. Sr Jorge Antolín Solache owner of *Hotel La Loma*, Casilla de Correo 36, 9405 Calafate (T 0902-91016, Dec-May), rest of the year Callao 433-8a "P", 1022 Buenos Aires (T 371-9123), has kindly offered to provide any information to travellers in the region. He speaks English, French, Italian and Portuguese. Many shops on main street have maps.

Transport There is a new airport, called Lago Argentino, with an all-weather runway (though flights may be suspended in severe weather). By air from Río Gallegos (LADE twice a week). To Río Gallegos with Pingüino, 1 hr, US$43, daily; to Río Turbio, 3 a week in summer to connect with buses to Puerto Natales and Torres del Paine. Direct flights from Río Gallegos and Ushuaia 3 times a week.

The bus station is on Calle Roca, 1 block from Av del Libertador. Bus Calafate to **Ushuaia** requires four changes, and ferry; total cost of journey US$43. Interlagos Turismo bus runs daily at 0800 (summer) or 0915 Tues, Thur, Sat (winter) to **Río Gallegos** and its airport; in addition El Pingüino runs daily at 0600 and 1630 (Wed, Fri, Sat, in winter) 4½ hrs, US$25, passengers on this bus wishing to go to Chile get off at Güer Aike to catch Pingüino's Gallegos-Río Turbio bus 50 mins later, arriving at 1700. To Río Turbio with Pingüino 4 times a week, 7 hrs, US$27. Taxi to Río Gallegos, 4 hrs, US$200 irrespective of number of passengers, up to 5 people. The Río Gallegos-Calafate road (323 km, all paved) is worth while for the number of animals and birds one sees; however, it is flat and subject to strong winds.

Direct services to Chile: Bus Zaajz Tours, book with Pingüino, Av Libertador (very helpful), Bus Sur and Luis Díaz to **Puerto Natales** via Río Turbio, several times a week, US$25, 7 hrs (rec to book in advance). Travel agencies run regular services in summer, on demand in winter, up to US$50 pp, 5 hrs.

The road trip from Calafate to Punta Arenas is very interesting for wildlife enthusiasts, who will see guanacos and condors at frequent intervals. About 40 km before reaching the border there are small lagoons and salt flats with flamingos. From Calafate take the almost completely paved combination of provincial Route 11, national Route 40 and provincial route 5 to La Esperanza (165 km), where there is a petrol pump and a large but expensive *confitería*. (90 km SE of Calafate Route 40 takes a rough, unpaved and sometimes difficult to follow shortcut which avoids the circuitous La Esperanza route, but even high-clearance vehicles may be unable to cross the unbridged Río Pelque and Chorrillo de Barrancas Blancas after any significant rain. Work has started to improve this section.) East of La Esperanza, gravelled Route 7 joins an improved Route 40 at the Río Coyle. At nearby Fuentes del Coyle, there is a small but acceptable bar/*confitería* with 2-3 rooms for travellers and a Hotel, D pp, cold, dirty. Road continues to Cancha Carrera (border post Dec-Apr, no town), then 14 km to Chilean border post, Cerro Castillo (2 *hosterías* with rooms, expensive, ask to camp in garden—closed Dec-Apr), then unpaved but good road (63 km) to Puerto Natales and 254 km to Punta Arenas, all paved. There is no direct route from Calafate to Torres del Paine National Park, unless you are prepared to hitch, with some patience, from Cerro Castillo. To take the bus coming from Puerto Natales to the Park, you have to board it in Puerto Natales itself. It is not possible to change Argentine pesos once inside the Park.

Road routes to Calafate By a rough but interesting road from Santa Cruz, Provincial Route 9 (Route 288 is 100 km longer with two bridges replacing old ferry crossings), 5 or 6 hrs by car, but not always possible after rain. South of Esquel, Route 40 is paved south through the towns of Tecka and **Gobernador Costa** (*Hotel Jair*, *Hotel Vega*, both D; free municipal campsite with all services) in Chubut province; to the W, on the Chilean border, is Lago General Vintter, plus smaller lakes with good trout fishing. 34 km S of Gobernador Costa, gravelled Route 40 forks SW through the town of Alto Río Senguer, while provincial Route 20 heads almost directly south for 81 km (ACA petrol station at isolated La Laurita), before turning E toward Sarmiento and Comodoro Rivadavia. At La Puerta del Diablo, in the valley of the lower Río Senguer, Route 20 intersects provincial Route 22, which joins with Route 40 at the town of Río Mayo (**see p 200**). This latter route is completely paved and preferable to Route 40 for long-distance motorists; good informal campsites on the W side of the bridge across the Río Senguer.

South of Río Mayo Route 40 becomes quite rough, with no public transportation and very few vehicles of any kind even in mid-summer; persistent enquiries around town may locate a lorry heading to the town of Perito Moreno (**see p 200**) 124 km to the S, E of Lago Buenos Aires. While there is an excellent paved road connecting Perito Moreno to Caleta Olivia, on the coast, and Los Antiguos, on Lago Buenos Aires, corrugated Route 40 is dismal until tiny, forlorn **Bajo Caracoles** (D *Hotel Bajo Caracoles*, decent but relatively expensive meals). There is a

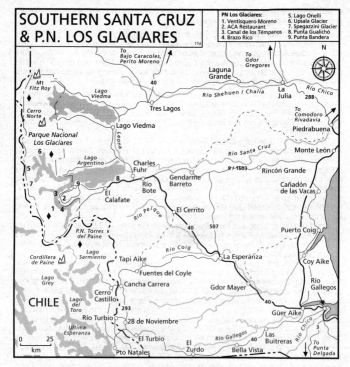

SOUTHERN SANTA CRUZ & P.N. LOS GLACIARES

PN Los Glaciares:
1. Ventisquero Moreno
2. ACA Restaurant
3. Canal de los Témpanos
4. Brazo Rico
5. Lago Onelli
6. Upsala Glacier
7. Spegazzini Glacier
8. Punta Gualicho
9. Punta Bandera

good grocery store here. 92 km further S of Bajo Caracoles is the town off W to Lago Belgrano. 7 km E, along Route 521 is *Hotel Las Horquetas* with a café/bar, and 15 km beyond this is the Tamel Aike village (police station, water). "Super" grade fuel is available in most places; carry extra, since the only other available source of fuel before Tres Lagos involves a 72-km detour to Gobernador Gregores (**see p 202**).

Midway between Perito Moreno and Gobernador Gregores, at the end of a 90-km spur, is **Parque Nacional Perito Moreno**, one of the Argentine park system's wildest and most remote units, where guanaco and other wildlife roam among a large, interconnected system of lakes below glaciated peaks. The largest of the lakes is Lago Belgrano. Here the mountains are streaked with a mass of differing colours. This is excellent hiking country (ammonite fossils can be found), and a downhill expedition into Chile is possible for intrepid walkers (take all food). On the way to Cerro León is *Estancia La Oriental*, T 0966 2445/2196, guest house and camping site, D pp, A full board, clean, horses for hire. Good chance of spotting condors here. There are few visitors and no formal facilities, but camping (US$2-4 per night) is among the best in South America. The park is situated S of Cerro San Lorenzo, highest peak of the Patagonian Andes. Entrance fee US$5, park ranger has maps and information. Except after heavy rain, the road is better than Route 40 and negotiable by any ordinary vehicle. For more detail, see William C Leitch's *South America's National Parks* (Seattle: The Mountaineers, 1990).

From the Parque Moreno junction to Tres Lagos (accommodation at *Restaurant Ahoniken*, Av San Martín, E pp), Route 40 improves considerably, but after Tres Lagos (one restaurant and supermarket) it deteriorates rapidly and remains very rugged until after the turnoff to the Fitz Roy sector of Parque Nacional Los Glaciares. 21 km beyond is the bridge over Río La Loma, with a hotel which has a bar/café. The remainder of the highway to Calafate, while slow, holds no major problems.

Route 288 runs E from Tres Lagos to Piedrabuena; fuel is available at Laguna Grande, 100 km from Tres Lagos.

NB It is nearly impossible to hitchhike between Calafate and Perito Moreno. There is no public transport, at any time of year along this road. A weekly bus (Sat) from Puerto San Julián goes through Gobernador Gregores, passes *Hotel Las Horquetas*, and on to the village of Bajo Caracoles. There is no public transport into the park but it may be possible to arrange a lift with *Estancia* workers from *Hotel Las Horquetas*.

Excursions Travel by road to the most interesting spots is limited and may require expensive taxis. Tours can be arranged at travel agencies, or with taxi drivers at the airport who await arrivals. Two recommended walks: (1) From the Centro Cívico in Calafate, visit Capilla Santa Teresita in Plaza San Martín; behind it is Calle Perito Moreno; walk to the top of the hill for a view of Calafate. Then go S to the Río Calafate, then to the new section of the town, where the ACA grill is. (2) From the Intendencia del Parque, follow the new road among cultivated fields and orchards to Laguna de Los Cisnes, a bird reserve, with flamingoes, ducks, and abundant birdlife. Walk down to **Lago Argentino**; 15 km along the lakeside are the painted caves at Punta Gualichó. Unfortunately the paintings have greatly deteriorated, but there are fascinating geological formations caused by erosion, on the edge of Lago Argentino, 12 km from Calafate on the road to Río Gallegos. An excursion can also be made to Lago Roca, 40 km S from Calafate. Trout and salmon fishing, climbing, walking, camping and branding of cattle in summer. Good camping here in wooded area, restaurant.

At the far end of Lago Argentino (80 km from Calafate) the **Ventisquero Moreno**, one of the few glaciers in the world that has been growing larger, descends to the surface of the water over a five-km frontage and a height of about 60m. In a cycle of roughly three years it used to advance across the lake, cutting the Brazo Rico off from the Canal de los Témpanos; then the pressure of water in the Brazo Rico would break up the ice and reopen the channel. Owing to rising temperatures from the thinning of the ozone layer, the glacier is reportedly not growing any more (since 1992) and the three-year cycle has been disrupted (it is estimated at 7 years now). Pieces break off and float away as icebergs. The vivid blue hues of the ice floes and the dull roar as they break away from the snout are spectacular, especially at sunset. When visiting the glacier, do not go down too close to the lake as these icebergs can cause great waves when breaking off, and wash people off rocks. New wooden catwalks prevent you from going to the water's edge; there is a fine of up to US$500 for leaving the catwalks.

From Calafate to the glacier's edge there are daily buses by Receptivo Calafate, Pingüino and Interlagos, Sep-May only (daily Nov-Mar, less frequent at other times), return, US$25 from Av Libertador at 0830 returning 1800, giving 3 hrs at glacier; you can use the return fare at no extra cost if you come back next day (student discount available). Trips run by the Youth Hostel cost US$28, go out via the *estancia* and return past the lake. They also do walking tours on the glacier, book ahead. Fares do not incl the US$5 park entrance fee. Taxis, US$80 for 4 passengers round trip. It may be possible to camp in the guardaparque's backyard, but you must ask first. Out of season, trips to the glacier are difficult to arrange, but one can gather a party and hire a taxi; take warm clothes, and food and drink; try asking at hotels or taxis at cooperative, T 91044 (for 4 people). Ask rangers where you can camp out of season, no facilities except a decrepit toilet block. Boat trips are organized by Hielo y Aventura travel agency, T 91414, large boats for up to 60 passengers, US$20 pp on "Safari Náutico" (1 hr), or a day trip ("Minitrekking") incl boat trip and 2½ hrs walk on the glacier, US$70, rec, but not for the fainthearted, take your own lunch.

A worthwhile trip is by motor-boat from Punta Bandera, 50 km from Calafate, to the **Upsala Glacier** at the NW end of Lago Argentino (in early 1995 access to the glacier face was impossible, check in advance if it is possible to go). The trip also goes to Lago Onelli and glacier (restaurant) and Spegazzini glacier. From the dock on Bahía Onelli to Lago Onelli is an easy 2-km trail done with a guide (in English, German or Spanish) through a lovely southern forest wreathed in bearded moss. Small **Lago Onelli** is quiet and very beautiful, beech trees on one side, and ice-covered mountains on the other. The lake is full of icebergs of every size and sculpted shape.

A tour boat usually operates a daily trip to the glacier, the catamaran *Serac*, US$90. The price includes bus fares and park entry fees — pay in dollars and take food. Bus departs 0730 from

Calafate for Punta Bandera. 1 hour is allowed for a meal at the restaurant near the Lago Onelli track. Return bus to Calafate at 1930; a tiring day, it is often cold and wet, but memorable. Out of season it is extremely difficult to get to the glacier. Many travel agencies, eg in Bariloche, make reservations. On the road from Calafate to Punta Bandera, at the foot of Cerro Comisión, is a rock formation that looks like a herd of elephants facing you.

Another worthwhile excursion is to the N end of the Glaciares National Park (entrance US$3.50) to *Cerro Fitz Roy* (Tehuelche name El Chaltén) and Cerro Torre, 230 km NW of Calafate. The Fitz Roy massif can be seen from the village of *El Chaltén*, which is becoming very popular, and one can walk for $2\frac{1}{2}$ hrs to see Cerro Torre (stupendous views: "anyone within 500 miles would be a fool to miss them"—Julian and Cordelia Thomas). It is possible to hike from Chaltén to Cerro Torre base camp and back in one day, crossing the Río Fitz Roy by the new bridge. There are three main trails in the park from the entrance (all well signposted): "Río Blanco" to Fitz Roy glacier, 5 hrs each way, "Cerro Torre" 3 hrs each way and to the Salto, 1 hr each way. Cerro Fitz Roy base camp is 3 hrs easy walk from *Camping Madsen* (which is a better place to stay). Ask at the *gendarmería* (border-police) in Calafate if you can join their truck which goes once or twice a week. On the way to Cerro Fitz Roy (often bad weather) on Route 40, is the Southern Astronomical Observatory, managed by the Observatory of La Plata. Día de la Tradición (10 Nov) is celebrated with gaucho events, riding and barbecue (US$5).

Daily buses in summer from Calafate are run by Caltur, daily at 0600, returning at 1600 (back in Calafate 2000), and Los Glaciares, leaving at 0600 to El Chaltén, at the base of Cerro Fitz Roy, 5 hrs, returns 1600, allowing 2-3 hrs at site, US$50 return. Best to book return before departure during high season (private drivers go off season and charge more). A new road has been built from Route 40 to Chaltén. **Accommodation A3** *Fitz Roy Inn*, 32 beds, restaurant. Cabins sleep 2 (US$50), 3 (US$60) or 4 (US$70). Opposite is *Albergue Patagonia* (US$8 pp private room, US$5 pp communal room, kitchen and laundry facilities, TV and video, book exchange, accepts TCs); **C** pp *Estancia La Quinta*, 3 km from Chaltén, half-board, no heating, prepares lunch for trekkers, rec; **E** pp *Hotel Lago del Desierto*, good, small, showers, new 6-birth cabins D pp with bath. *Confitería La Senyera*, excellent bread, rec; *Josh Aike*, excellent *confitería*, homemade food, beautiful building, rec; *The Wall Pub*. Camping Madsen (free) at end of village near the paths to Cerros Fitz Roy and Torre (the bus from Calafate goes to and from this site), no facilities; *Ruca Mahuida*, 400m N on route to treks, Paula Marechal (guide and owner), very helpful, camping US$5, showers, stores gear, rec.

A stove is essential for camping as firewood is scarce. Take plenty of warm clothes and a good sleeping bag. Buy supplies in Calafate (cheaper and more choice). It is possible to rent equipment in El Chaltén, ask at park entrance. Beware of straying from the paths. A map is essential, even on short walks (the information centre at park entrance provides photocopied maps of treks). The best is one published by Zagier and Urruty, 1992, US$10 (Casilla 94, Sucursal 19, 1419 Buenos Aires, F 572-5766) and is now available in several shops in Calafate.

Climbing Fitz Roy (3,375m) is approached from Chaltén to Río Blanco, 2-3 hrs, walk, then to Laguna Torre (base camp for Cerro Torre), 3-4 hrs walk. Ask the guide Sr Guerra in Chaltén about hiring animals to carry equipment. The best time is mid-Feb to end-Mar; Nov-Dec is very windy; Jan is fair; winter is extremely cold. There are no rescue services; necessary gear is double boots, crampons, pickaxe, ropes, winter clothing; the type of terrain is ice and rock. Possible targets nearby incl Cerro Torre, Torre Eger, Cerro Solo, Poincennot, Guilleaulmet, Saint-Exupery, La Bífida, La Indómita, Cardón Adela and Hielo Continental (Continental Ice Shelf). Ask for a permit to climb at the Parques Nacionales office in Chaltén. There is no access at all from Chile.

Organized trips to the Glaciares National Park are too short to appreciate it fully; either go on a tour bus, then camp (good gear essential) or hire a taxi/minibus. The travel agencies charge US$200 for up to 8 people, US$300 to take you and return later to collect you; private drivers (eg Martín Drake, see under Calafate **Travel Agents**) charge US$300 for up to 8 to take you and collect later (also does similar arrangements for the Moreno glacier).

TIERRA DEL FUEGO (11)

The island at the extreme south of South America is divided between

Argentina (E side) and Chile (W). The S has beautiful lakes, woods and mountain scenery, and there is much birdlife to see. Boat trips can be made on the Beagle Channel; there is skiing in winter.

Tierra del Fuego is bounded by the Magellan Strait to the N, the Atlantic Ocean to the E, the Beagle Channel to the south—which separates it from the southern islands—and by the Whiteside, Gabriel, Magdalena and Cockburn Channels etc, which divide it from the islands to the W. The local Ona Indians are now extinct. Throughout Tierra del Fuego the main roads are narrow and gravelled. The exceptions are the road for about 50 km out of Porvenir (Chile), which is being widened, and Río Grande-Ushuaia, which is being improved. Part of the south is a National Parks Reserve: trout and salmon in nearly all the lakes and rivers, and in summer wild geese, ducks, 152 other species of birds, and imported musk rats and beaver. **Note** that accommodation is sparse and the island is becoming popular among Argentines in summer. Hotel beds and seats on aircraft may begin to run short as early as Nov. Fruit and meat may not be taken onto the island.

Books *Tierra del Fuego* (3rd edition), in English, by Rae Natalie Prosser de Goodall, US$7.50 (obtainable in Ushuaia and Buenos Aires), colourful maps by the same author. Also *Tierra del Fuego: The Fatal Lodestone*, by Eric Shipton, and *Uttermost Part of the Earth*, by E Lucas Bridges. Available in USA: *Birds of Isla Grande* (Tierra del Fuego) by Philip S Humphrey, and *A Guide to the Birds of South America*, by Rodolphe Meyer de Schauensee.

Mar-Apr is a good time to visit because of the beautiful autumn colours.

There are two ways of crossing the Strait of Magellan to Tierra del Fuego. Coming S from Río Gallegos, an unpaved road turns left for **Punta Delgada** (1 hotel, 2 *hosterías*). (On the road Río Gallegos-Punta Delgada is Laguna Azul—3 km off main road in an old crater; an ibis breeding ground, beautiful colours). A 30-minute crossing can be made by fast modern ferry from Punta Delgada to **Punta Espora** (no hotel—if desperate, ask the lighthouse keeper). The boats, which take 4 lorries and about 20 cars, run every hour, with schedule determined by tides. Under normal conditions they run from 0800 to 2100 daily, with tidal breaks lasting 4 hours (autumn and winter timetable). Cost is US$1 pp, US$14 per car, ferry-operators accept US dollars or Argentine or Chilean currencies. If going by car, do not go before 1000, as first crossings are taken by buses, etc. At Punta Delgada office the staff can try to reserve the Porvenir/Punta Arenas ferry. There is no bus service from Punta Espora (or Punta Delgada); buses to and from the island only through Porvenir. From Punta Espora (Bahía Azul is ferry terminal) a road runs through Chilean territory to San Sebastián (Chile) and 14 km further to San Sebastián (Argentina, one restaurant and hotel) (usually 15 min delay in crossing borders), Río Grande (road San Sebastián-Río Grande is now paved) and Ushuaia. There is an Esso service station 38 km from Punta Espora. Accommodation is scarce in the Chilean part (except for Porvenir—see **Chilean Patagonia**), and it is not always possible to cross it in one day because of the irregularity of the ferry. It is sometimes possible, coming and going, to spend the night at the guest house of ENAP at Cerro Sombrero (petrol there for employees only, but if you are running out, they may help), but do not count on it. Try *Hostería Karu-Kinka*.

The road from Río Gallegos goes on to Punta Arenas, from where (dock at Tres Puentes 5 km E of town) there are is a daily crossing to Porvenir (passenger US$5, motor car US$30, 2½-3 hours, T Punta Arenas 227020; there is a passenger saloon with small cafetería; get on first and you are invited on the bridge, get on last and you stand outside in the cold). Return from Porvenir at 1400 (Sun 1630). If crossing with car, don't allow it to be parked too close to other vehicles; the ferry company will not accept responsibility for damage caused by onboard "crashes". If you want to continue, Senkovic buses to Río Grande leave at 1400 on Sat and Tues. A 225-km road runs from Porvenir E to Río Grande (6 hours) via San Sebastián; or by alternative route through Cerro Sombrero (see previous paragraph). Border police at San Sebastián will sometimes arrange lifts to Ushuaia or Río Grande. Hitching after San Sebastián is easy. Distances are roughly as follows in this area: Border with Chile at Monte Aymont; to Río Gallegos 73 km; road to Río Grande via Kimiri-Aike (114 km from Río Gallegos)—no buses; from here to Punta Delgada 30 km; Punta Delgada-Punta Espora (ferry, free for pedestrians) 20 km; from Punta Sombrero (60 km) and San Sebastián (60 km) reaching Río Grande 80 km on. The best way to hitch from Río Gallegos to Punta Arenas is to take any lorry as far as the turn-off for Punta Delgada ferry. Then there is plenty of Chilean traffic from Punta Delgada to Punta Arenas. *Hotel San Gregorio* will put you up if you get stuck near the turn-off.

Entering Argentina from Chile, be firm about getting an entry stamp for as long as you require. Going in the other direction, don't stock up with food in Argentina, as Chilean border guards will confiscate all fruit, vegetable, dairy and meat products coming into Chile.

Río Grande (pop 35,000), is a port in windy, dust-laden sheep-grazing and oil-bearing plains. The oil is refined at San Sebastián in the smallest and most southerly refinery in the world (**B ACA** motel; service station open 0700-2300). The *frigorífico* (frozen meat) plant in Río Grande is one of the largest in South America; so is the sheep-shearing shed. Government tax incentives to companies in the 1970s led to a rapid growth in population; the subsequent withdrawal of incentives has produced increasing unemployment and emigration. The town is now full of empty temporary housing. Accommodation is difficult if arriving at night. Food is cheaper here than in Ushuaia (*Tía* supermarket rec, good choice). ACA garage on sea-front has free hot showers for men, as has the gymnasium. Fill up with gasoline here.

Local Festivals *Trout Festival*, 3rd Sunday in Feb; *Snow Festival*, 3rd Sun in July; *Woodsman Festival*, 1st week of Dec.

Hotels A3 *Atlántida*, Av Belgrano 582, T 22592, said to be best, always full; **A3** *Los Yaganes ACA*, Av Belgrano 319, T/F 23897, clean, comfortable, restaurant; **B** *Federico Ibarra*, Rosales 357, T 21071, excellent restaurant; **C** *Hospedaje Noal*, Rafael Obligado 557, lots of bread and coffee for breakfast, clean, cosy, friendly, rec; **C** *Residencial Rawson*, Estrada 750, T 21352/24523, with bath, clean, rec; **C** *Villa*, San Martín 277, T 22312, very warm; **D** *Hospedaje Irmary*, Estrada 743, clean and pleasant, rec; **D** *Miramar*, Mackinlay 595, T 22462, without bath, no breakfast, heated, hot water, kitchen facilities, rec; **E** pp *Pensión Stella*, Moreno 835, good, clean.

Restaurants *Yaganes* (good for *centolla*—King crab) expensive; *Don Rico*, Belgrano y Perito Moreno, in ultra-modern building in centre, interesting, closed Mon; *Pizzería La Colonial*, Rosales 666, home made food, friendly. **Confitería Roca**, Roca 629, open all hours, reasonably priced food and bar; likewise **A** *Todas Horas* in same street. Good workmen's café, *Mary's*, Moyano 373. **Supermarket** *Sados* on San Martín, near 25 de Mayo. Smart place for a drink, *París*, Rosales 448.

Banks and Exchange **Banco de la Nación Argentina**, San Martín 200, high commission on TCs; **Banco del Sur**, San Martín; **Superkiosko**, Piedrabuena y Rosales, cash only. Try *Confitería Roca*, Roca 629. Tends to be difficult: if coming from Chile, buy Argentine pesos there.

Post Office Piedrabuena y Ameghino.

Travel Agency *Yaganes*, friendly and helpful.

Tourist Information at the Municipalidad, Mon-Fri, on Calle Sebastián Elcano.

Car Hire Rent-a-Car, Belgrano y Ameghino, T 22657. Localiza, at airport, T 30482.

Car mechanic and VW dealer Viaval SRL, P Moreno 927.

Airport 4 km W of town. Bus US$0.50. Taxi US$5. Río Grande-Buenos Aires flights with Aerolíneas Argentinas – T 22749, daily, 3 hrs 20 mins direct. Austral daily (except Sun) via Bahía Blanca, Comodoro Rivadavia and Río Gallegos. TAN flies to Neuquén, Trelew, Comodoro Rivadavia and Río Gallegos twice a week. To **Ushuaia**, AR 3 a week, LADE 1 a week, Kaiken, daily. LADE also to **Río Gallegos**, 50 mins (book early in summer, 1 a week, Thur), continuing to **Comodoro Rivadavia** via Calafate, Gob Gregores and Perito Moreno. Telephone LADE office (Lasarre 425) open Mon-Fri, 0900-1200 and 1530-1900, 0700-1200 on Sat, T 22968. Conversely, travel with Aeronaval (if you're lucky), mostly Hercules transports, for half the price – enquire at airport. "Rent-a-plane" at airport. You can now fly to Punta Arenas in Chile, through Kaiken Agency, Perito Moreno 937, T 31513, or Aerovías DAP, 9 de Julio 597, T 30249, dep Tues, Thur, Sat, US$80, dep 1300.

Buses leave at 0630 Tues and Sat US$25 (Senkovic, San Martín 959, T 22345), for **Porvenir**, Chile (about 230 km), no food or drink provided, no toilets, nor stops, for 7 hrs, always heavily booked but especially over Christmas/New Year period, meticulous passport and luggage control at San Sebastián. To Punta Arenas, Pacheco (Bilbao 873), runs buses via Porvenir on Tues, Thur, Sat 0700, US$36, 10 hrs, tickets available on day of departure, also with Los Carlos on Mon, Thur, 0730, same price, but at Christmas and New Year tickets are hard to come by. Best to book bus connection in Ushuaia. Very difficult to hitch to Porvenir. Ferry journey from Porvenir to **Punta Arenas** (2 hrs) can be very rough and cold. Daily bus service with Transportes

Los Carlos, to **Ushuaia**, 234 km on an unpaved road (sit on right for better views), US$25, 4 hours, times vary, stopping at *Hostería El Kaikén*, Lago Fagnano, for a drink (rec for the view). Bus departs from Los Carlos office (Estrada 568); arrive 15 mins early. Summer service also by Tecni Austral, daily (exc Sat) at 0730, 3 hrs, US$22.

Excursion 11 km N lies the Salesian mission and the regional museum housed in the original chapel and first parish church of Río Grande. Although the exhibits are not at all organized or classified, there is a great deal to see. There are Ona Indian materials, Salesian mission works, fossils, handicrafts and flora, fauna and mineral exhibits of the area. Just past the mission, on the right side of the road, is the old cemetery.

With a population of 50,000, **Ushuaia**, 236 km SW of Río Grande, is the most southerly town in Argentina, and among the most expensive. Its steep streets (there are mountains, the Cerro Martial, at the back of the town) overlook the green waters of the Beagle Channel, named after the ship in which Darwin sailed the Channel in 1832, on Captain Fitzroy's second expedition. The old prison, Presidio, at the back of the Naval Base can be visited, interesting (see also **Rail** below): tours start from the Museum daily 1600-2300, US$3 (not incl tip for guide). There are impressive views of the snow-clad peaks, rivers, waterfalls and dense woods. There is a naval station at Isla Redonda. The people are engaged in timber cutting, fishing and, nowadays, in factories. The tourist industry is also expanding rapidly, although hotel prices are higher here than on the mainland. A new road has been built between Río Grande and Ushuaia via Paso Garibaldi. Ushuaia and its environs are worth a 2-3 day visit.

Museum Museo Territorial, Maipú y Rivadavia, T 21863, open Mon-Sat 1600-2000, US$2, small but interesting display of early photos and artefacts of the local Indian tribes; relics from the missionaries and first settlers, etc. Also known as the "museum at the end of the world". Highly rec. Building also contains an excellent library with helpful staff, a good bookshop with books in English, and post office, open afternoons when the main one is closed.

NB Prices double on Dec 12 and accommodation may occasionally be hard to find throughout Dec – the tourist office will help. It is best not to drink tap water in Ushuaia.

Hotels **L3** *Canal Beagle*, ACA, Maipú 590, T 21117, restaurant (catering usually for tour groups), overpriced; **A1** *Tolkeyen*, at Estancia Río Pipo 5 km from town, with rec restaurant Tolkeyen, 100 m (see below); **A2** *Albatros*, Maipú 505, T 22504, clean, modern, incl breakfast, but rooms a bit cold; **A2** *Las Lengas*, Goleta Florencia 1722, T 23366, superb setting, heating, good dining room; **A2** *Malvinas*, Deloqui 615, T 22626, with bath, breakfast incl, pleasant, helpful, central heating, rec; **A2** *Antártida*, San Martín 1600, T 21896, friendly, restaurant with fine views, rec; **A2** *Cabo de Hornos*, San Martín y Rosas, T 22187, comfortable, often full, TV, spotless, good value (but surcharge on credit cards), restaurant not open to non-residents; **A2** *César*, San Martín 753, T 21460, with bath, comfortable, often full (book in advance), friendly, clean, incl breakfast, rec; **A3** *Maitén*, 12 de Octubre 140, T 22745, good value, clean, but 2 km from town centre, 10% discount for ISIC and youth card holders; **A3** *Posada Fin del Mundo*, Valdez 281, T 22530, family atmosphere, rec; **B** *Casa de Gapgin*, Gob Paz 1380, clean, comfortable, friendly, heating, good breakfast, no sign, rec; **B** *Hospedaje Turístico*, Deloqui 271, T 21316, with private bath, very clean, friendly, parking, TV, kitchen, English spoken, rec; **B** *Hostal Julio Linares*, Deloqui 1522, nr airport, new, good value; **B** *Monte Cervantes*, San Martín y Sarmiento, T 30600, rec; **B** *Mustapic*, Piedrabuena 230, T 21718, multi-lingual owner (Sr Miro, from Croatia, his daughter runs travel agency next door, T 23557, rec), 10% discount for ISIC card holders, no singles, highly rec, exceptionally clean, can leave luggage, rooftop restaurant for breakfast; **C** *Familia Cárdenas*, 25 de Mayo 345, T 21954, near top of hill, rec; **C** *Fernández*, Onachaga y Fitzroy, T 21192, very friendly, hot water, good but expensive meals, but cheaper in bunk-bed accommodation; **C** Sra Marta Loncharich, Magallanes 229, T 24150, shared bathroom, good food and comfort, clean, but overpriced; **D** pp *Alojamiento Internacional* (Hilda Sánchez and Pedro Sieczkovsky), Deloqui 395, 1st floor, T 23483/23622, spartan, friendly, dormitory, take sleeping bag, cooking and laundry facilities, no security, good meeting place, changes money; **D** *Hospedaje Turístico*, Magallanes 196, new, comfortable, excursions; **D** pp *Klewel*, Karukinka 22, T 22548, Sandra Gabriela Sainz, tourist information, laundry, café, cocktails, excursions, rec; **D** pp María Guercio, Kuanip 67, T 22234, also large chalet outside town to let; **D** rooms, at home of Ismael Vargas, Kayen 394 (T 21125) 15 mins from centre, clean, doubles only, Sra Vargas speaks English; **E** *Casa Elvira*, Fuegio Basquet 419, T 23123, 10 mins walk from airport, price per person, use of kitchen; Accommodation in private homes (all **C-D**): Familia Beltrame, Gob Valdez 311,

T 22819, rec; Familia Galeazzi, Gob Valdez 323, T 23213, speak English and French, rec; Familia Velásquez, Fadul 361, T 21719, dormitory accommodation, clean, warm, helpful, not enough showers, skimpy breakfast, can leave luggage when hiking. Zulema R Saltzmann, Roca 392 (esq Campos), **D** pp, clean and friendly; Sr Ueno, 12 de Octubre 432, T 24661, full board US$10 pp, rec. The following gives 10% discount to ISIC card holders: Marta Lebhian, Deloqui 641, T 22669, **D** pp, clean, hot water, cooking facilities. There is no YHA in Ushuaia. Hostel for sporting groups only at Sports Complex. Lodging in Ushuaia has recently become rather a problem esp Jan-Mar, but even in winter hotels are very expensive. Enquire at Tourist Office for accommodation in private homes, and for campsites, some of which are free. Many people go to the airport to offer rooms in private houses, in our **E** pp range (minimum).

Camping None in town. After paying US$3.50 entrance fee to park, there are 4 camping sites to choose from, of which 3 are free, but have few or no facilities. The fourth is Camping Lago Roca, at Lapataia, by forested shore of Lago Roca in Parque Nacional, with facilities for car and tent, US$5, dirty, noisy, caters for travellers without car, Dec-Mar, incl gas (18 km from Ushuaia; weather can be bad). Can be reached by bus Jan-Feb. Hot showers evenings (US$3), toilet (US$1), small shop, cafeteria. One free site is by restaurant, with no facilities, on road to Parque Nacional about 4 km from Ushuaia at Río Pipo, and another, 2 km from the Lago Roca campsite close to a beaver dam. The third free site is at Monte Susana, 10 km W. Hot showers at Sports Centre on Malvinas Argentinas.

Restaurants *Tía Elvira*, Maipú 349, very popular, make advance booking, good seafood; *Moustacchio*, San Martín 298, sea food, warmly rec; *Asturias*, Rosas 45, pleasant, reasonable, open 1200-1500, 2030-2300. *Barcleit 1912*, Fadul 148, cordon bleu cooking at reasonable prices. *Kaupé*, Roca 470, English spoken, excellent food and wine, rec, expensive. Best place to eat lamb is at *Tolkeyen*, Estancia Río Pipo, 5 km from town, meal US$15, taxi US$7. *El Viejo Marino*, Maipú 229, nice ambience, excellent food; *Mi Viejo*, Campos 758, good *parrillada* and buffet, highly rec; *Cafetería, pizzeria Ideal*, San Martín 393, good, cheap, hot buffet US$13, very popular with travellers, 10% discount for ISIC card holders; *Los Amigos*, San Martín 130, quick service, some cheap dishes; *Volver*, Maipú 37, interesting decor, good food and service, not cheap; *El Aborigen*, Antártida Argentina 75, inexpensive; *Quick*, San Martín 130, clean, good service, rec, 10% discount for ISIC card holders; also *Split*, Piedrabuena 238, pizzería, offers same discount, cheap. *Turco*, San Martín between Onas y Patagonia, cheap, popular with locals. *Der Garten, confitería*, San Martín 638, in Galería shopping arcade. Excellent homemade chocolate sold at a shop at San Martín 785. *Helados Massera*, San Martín 270-72, good. The coffee bar at the airport is very expensive. Ask around for currently available *centolla* (king crab) and *cholga* (giant mussels). Food and drink (apart from the duty-free items) in Ushuaia are very expensive. A popular spot at night is the disco *Extasis* at 9 de Julio y Maipú; another disco is *Barny's*, Antártida Argentina just off San Martín. *Café Latino*, Deloqui y Rivadavia, bar with live music (Argentine and contemporary), in summer gets going around 0200, great atmosphere, high standard.

Banks and Exchange Banks open 1000-1500 (in summer). Useful to have credit cards here as difficult to change cheques and very high commission (up to 10% reported), but Banco del Sud, Maipú 600 block, will change cheques (downstairs), also at Shopping Centre Lapataia, San Martín y 9 de Julio, commission US$8. Cash advance on Mastercard at Banco de Santa Cruz and Banco de Tierra del Fuego, San Martín 1044. Tourist agencies and the Hotel Albatros also give poor rates. *Listus* record shop, San Martín 973, sweet shop next door, or *Caminante*, Deloqui 368 for better rates for cash.

Consulates Chile, Malvinas Argentinas y Jainen, Casilla 21, T 21279. Finland, Paz y Deloqui; Germany, Rosas 516; Italy, Yaganes 75.

Laundromat Rosas 139, between San Martín and Deloqui, open weekdays 0900-2100, US$8.

Post Office San Martín y Godoy, Mon-Fri 0900-1300 and 1700-2000, Sat 0830-1200. **Telephones** and fax on Roca next to Aerolíneas Argentinas.

Shopping Good boots at *Stella Maris*, San Martín 443. Bookshop at San Martín y 9 de Julio (Lapataia Arcade). Film is cheaper in Chile. Supermarkets: Surty Sur (with clean toilets, San Martín y Onas) and Sucoop, Paz 1600. Most things are more expensive than elsewhere but some cheap imported goods, eg electrical equipment and cigarettes.

Sport Sports Centre on Malvinas Argentinas on W side of town (close to seafront). Ice skating rink at Ushuaia gymnasium in winter (when lagoon is frozen). Beachcombing can produce whale bones. Fishing: trout, contact Asociación de Caza y Pesca at Maipú y 9 de Julio, with small museum. Fishermen may be interested in visiting the fish hatchery 7 km E of Ushuaia, visiting hours daily 1400-1700. There are brook, rainbow and brown trout and land-locked salmon. Take No 1 bus E-bound on Maipú to the end of the line and continue 2½ km on foot

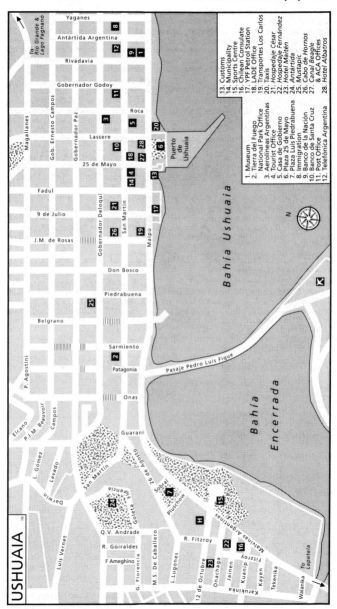

USHUAIA

1. Museum
2. Tierra del Fuego
3. National Park Office
4. Aerolíneas Argentinas
5. Tourist Office
6. Casa de Gobierno
7. Plaza 25 de Mayo
8. Plaza Luis Piedrabuena
9. Immigration
10. Banco de la Nación
11. Banco de Santa Cruz
12. Post Office
13. Telefónica Argentina

14. Customs
15. Municipality
16. Sports Centre
17. Chilean Consulate
18. YPF Petrol Station
19. LADE Office
20. Transportes Los Carlos
21. Taxis
22. Hospedaje César
23. Hospedaje Fernández
24. Hotel Maitén
25. Antártida
26. Mustapic
27. Cabo de Hornos
28. Canal Beagle
    & ACA Offices
29. Hotel Albatros

to the hatchery. Birdwatchers will also find this ride rewarding. Skiing, hiking, climbing: contact Club Andino, Solís 50, or Caminante. Skiing: A downhill ski run (beginner standard) on Cerro Martial. There is another ski run, Wallner, 3 km from Ushuaia, open Jun-Aug, has lights for night-skiing and is run by Club Andino. The area is excellent for cross country skiing; Caminante organizes excursions "off road". 20 km E of Ushuaia is Valle Tierra Mayoria, a large flat valley with high standard facilities for cross country skiing, snow shoeing and snowmobiling; rentals and a cafeteria; bus am and 1400 from Antartur, San Martín 638.

Travel Agents All agencies charge the same fees for excursions; with 3 or 4 people it is often little more expensive to hire a *remise* taxi. *Rumbo Sur*, San Martín 342, T 21139, runs a range of tours on water and on land and offers a two-day package to Cafayate, US$150 incl transport and hotel, good value. Also organizes bus to ski slope, very helpful. *Antartur*, San Martín 638, T 23240. *All Patagonia*, 25 de Mayo 31, of A, T 24432, F 30707, Amex agent; *Onas Tours*, 25 de Mayo 50, T 23429, just off main street, very friendly. *Aventura Austral*, Maipú 237, catamaran trip to Estancia Harberton, highly rec; *Tiempo Libre*, San Martín 863, T 21017, rec, English spoken. *Caminante*, Don Bosco 319, T 32723, F 31040, organizes walking, climbing tours and horse riding to suit all levels of experience, provides food, tents, equipment, outdoor clothing, detailed map, very friendly and helpful, English and German spoken, highly rec. *Kilak*, Kuanip 67, T 22234, for horse-riding tours. Recommended guide: Domingo Galussio, Intervú 15, Casa 211, 9410 Ushuaia, bilingual, not cheap (US$120), rec.

Tourist Office San Martín 660, T/F (0964) 24550, "best in Argentina", literature in English, German and Dutch, helpful, English spoken. Large chart of hotels and prices and information on travel and staying at Estancia Harberton, off road to Río Grande. Open Mon-Fri 0830-2030, Sat and Sun 0900-2000. National Park Office, on San Martín between Patagonia y Sarmiento, has small map but not much information. The ACA office on Maipú also has maps and information.

Car Hire Tagle, San Martín y Belgrano, T 22744, good, also **Río Grande**, Elcano 799, T 22571, and **Localiza**, in *Hotel Albatros* and at airport, rec, T 30663.

Airport Aerolíneas Argentinas, daily to BsAs via Río Gallegos and Trelew, all year round, over 4½ hrs. To **Río Grande**, AR 3 a week, US$26, LADE once a week (irregular, US$24), Kaiken (T 23049/22620), daily, US$27. To **Río Gallegos**, LADE once a week, US$39 incl airport tax, Kaiken, daily, US$49, AR, daily, US$56 (same price as bus). LADE to Comodoro Rivadavia via Río Grande, Río Gallogos, Calafate/Lago Argentino, Gob Gregores and Perito Moreno on Thur. Kaiken to **Punta Arenas** via Río Grande, Mon-Sat, 1100, US$90. Also with Ladeco, Tues and Fri 1540, US$120, continuing to Puerto Montt and Santiago.

   Services are more frequent in high season; in winter weather often impedes flights. In the summer tourist season it is sometimes difficult to get a flight out. Since Río Grande airport can take larger planes than Ushuaia (until the new airfield is built), it may be easier to get a flight to Río Grande and travel on from there. At the airport ask around for a pilot willing to take you on a ½ hr flight around Ushuaia, US$38 pp (best to go in pm when wind has dropped). Alternatively ask about flights at the tourist office in town. Taxi to airport, US$3, or 30 mins walk (no bus).

   New airport being built, but some say it won't be ready until 2000.
   Airline Offices LADE, Av San Martín 564, T 21123, airport T 21700; Austral, Barberis agency, Av San Martín 638, T 23235; Aerolíneas Argentinas, Roca 160, T 21093, airport 21265; Kaiken, San Martín 857, T 23663, or at airport, T 22620/23049.

Rail A Decauville gauge train for tourists runs along the shore of the Beagle Channel between the Fin del Mundo station in Ushuaia to the boundary of the Tierra del Fuego National Park, 2.2 km, US$15; it is planned to continue to Lapataia, 3.8 km. Run by Ferrocarril Austral Fueguino with new locomotives and carriages, it evokes the early "trencito de los presos" (train for prisoners).

Buses run daily between Ushuaia and Río Grande 4 hrs, 0600, 0700, 1900, US$21, Transportes Los Carlos, Rosas 85, T 22337, and Tecni Austral, San Martín 657, T 21945. There are bus services between Río Grande and Porvenir in the Chilean part of the island (242 km, 6-8 hrs) but no air connection. There is a twice-weekly service to Punta Arenas on Mon and Fri, dep 0300 with Transportes Los Carlos, 14 hrs, US$46, a comfortable and interesting ride via Punta Delgada. Trucks leave Ushuaia for the refinery at San Sebastián Mon-Fri, but hitching is very difficult (easier via Bahía Azul and Punta Delgada where there is more traffic). A good place to hitch is from police control on Route 3.

Excursions To the *Parque Nacional Tierra del Fuego*, W of Ushuaia on the Chilean frontier (entrance is 12 km W). At Km 30 from Ushuaia is *Lapataia Bay*. US$3.50 National Park fee (free before 31 Oct). Minibus to National Park from Turismo Pasarela, Fadul 40, T 21735, US$10 return, 4 times a day, first at 1000, last back 2000 from Lago Roca in the Park. In summer Caminante run minibuses to the National Park, departing from Don Bosco 319, 2 or 3 a day, US$15 return. A similar service is operated by two other agencies. Caminante also runs a one day excursion to the Parque Nacional, incl trek, canoeing, *asado* lunch, US$70 inclusive (small groups, book early). Ask at the tourist office about cycling tours in the park, US$65 full day, also "Eco Treks" available and cultural events (ask for Ricardo Araujo, Fundación Antártica). See above for **Camping** possibilities. In winter the temperature drops to as low as -12°C, in summer it goes up to 25°C. Even in the summer the climate can often be cold, damp and unpredictable. It is possible to hitch-hike, as far as Lapataia. Rangers in the park are friendly and will sometimes put people up for a couple of days (as will police) and help with places to visit. A ranger truck leaves Ushuaia every weekday at 1300 and picks up hitch-hikers. Beaver inhabit the Parque Nacional near the Chilean border; one may see beaver dams and with much luck and patience the beavers themselves stand still and down-wind of them: their sense of smell and hearing are good, but not their eyesight. There are many beautiful walks. No maps of the Park are available and hiking can be interrupted by the Chilean border. Good climbing on Cerro Cóndor, rec. Reports that most of the park has been closed off to preserve nature (Feb 1994).

There are excursions to the Cerro Martial and the glacier (itself unspectacular but fine views down the Beagle Channel and to the N) about 7 km behind the town; take road behind *Hotel Antártida*, 2 km to small dam, then 3-4 hour walk along trail to get to chairlift, camping possible. (In winter the Cerro is inaccessible, even on foot; a bus leaves at 1030, 1200, 1400, 1600, 1800, returning 1100, 1230, 1430, 1630, 1830, in summer from in front of Rumba Sur office, US$5 return.) Also to the falls of the Olivia river.

Accommodation At Lago Fagnano: **D** *Hostería El Kaiken*, T 0964-24427 (ACA) also bungalows, nice site, well-run facilities, cheap drinks, on a promontory 93 km from Ushuaia, has real bath. At Lago Escondido **C** *El Petrel Inn*, 54 km from Ushuaia after a spectacular climb through Garibaldi Pass, on the road to Río Grande (bus dep 0900, returns 1500, US$17 return, min 4 people), T 24390, trout fishing possible, boat rides, friendly staff. Facilities at *Kaiken* and *Petrel* are open all year round. These inns are rec for peace and quiet.

Los Carlos bus to Lago Fagnano, 2½ hrs, US$10, then from lake to Río Grande 2 hrs, US$11. Tours also arranged to Lagos Fagnano and Escondido, 5-6 hrs, dep 0930, US$25, and aerial excursions over the Beagle Channel (with local flying club, hangar at airport, 3-5 seater planes, 30 mins), Lago Fagnano, Lapataia and Ushuaia Bay. To Lago Escondido/Fagnano US$50; bus to Puerto Almanza (on Beagle Channel), 75 km, 4-5 hrs, US$18.

The Estancia ***Harberton***, the oldest on the island, now run by descendents of a British missionary, Mr Bridges. It offers guided walks through protected forest (not Mon) and tea, in Manacatush confitería (T 22742). You can camp. It can be reached by rented car from Ushuaia and by boat (long trip, most of it on the boat and the sea can be very rough, US$65). By car, leave Ushuaia on Route 3, after 40 km fork right on Route J, passing Lago Victoria, then 25 km through forest before the open country around Harberton (85 km in all). Some parts of the road are bad; tiring driving, 5 hrs there and back. Agency tours to the Estancia, by land cost US$30 plus US$6 entrance, but take your own food as the Estancia is expensive. Tours to the Estancia and to the penguin colony by boat and bus, Mon, Tues, Fri, Sun, US$72 plus US$6 entrance, 12 hrs, from all agents, take own food. Some tour agencies in Ushuaia imply that their excursions go to the Estancia though in fact they only go to the bay; others go by inflatable launch from main beach to shore. Check thoroughly in advance.

Sea Trips Rumbo Sur does a whole-day trip by catamaran down the Beagle Channel to see wildlife, with return by bus, highly rec (see above under **Travel Agents**). Similar tours operated by Aventura Travel, US$70. Take food, on board it is overpriced. *Tres Marías* is a fishing boat, tours are 7 hrs, departing 0900, maximum 8 passengers, incl sea lion and sea bird watching, fishing for king crabs, 2 hr trek on Isla de los Lobos (a private island), lunch and a snack incl, US$70 pp (half day US$40 pp), through agencies Antartur, All Patagonia, Caminante, Tiempo Libre. In summer, chartered trips may be taken to see the sealions on Isla de Los Lobos, US$40, 4-5 hrs, or by catamaran, US$25, dep 0930, 1430, 2½ hrs. Ask at Rumbo Sur; the *Ana B* leaves 0930 and 1430 daily, US$30, English and Spanish-speaking guide, expensive food and drinks on board. Interesting boat trips of 3 weeks' duration on the 2,346 ton *Lindblad Explorer* and others cost from US$6,500.

To Puerto Williams, Chile, with Aventura Austral on *Catamaran 14*, 12 hrs, Wed and Sat (end 1993), US$65 pp, take own lunch, post office and postcards available in Puerto Williams, immigration formalities dealt with on board. El Caminante, Don Bosco 319, has also been recommended for trips to Puerto Williams. Luxury cruises around the horn via Puerto Williams are operated by the Chilean company, Tierra Austral, 7/8 days, US$1,260. Ask at the Club Náutico for trips in private launches or catamaran (US$60 pp in Apr 1993), to Puerto Williams.

Isla de los Estados Robert T Cook writes: "This long (75 km) and guarded island lies E of Tierra del Fuego. Except for the caretakers of the lighthouse and an occasional scientist few people ever set foot on this cloud-shrouded reserve of Fuegian flora and fauna that no longer exist on the main island. During the 18th and 19th centuries large numbers of ships were wrecked or lost in the treacherous waters surrounding this island. Much gold, silver and relics await salvage." Information and tours from Rumbo Sur, San Martín 342, Ushuaia.

Argentina apparently has plans for tourist developments in *Antarctica* (accommodation at Marambio and Esperanza stations). Flights can be arranged in Buenos Aires in Jan-Feb through Surexpress, Esmeralda 629, 4th floor, T 325-0252. The plane goes to Ushuaia and you take a boat from there. Also try Andy Macfarlane at Macren Travel, T 322-7988. Complete trips for US$6,000-8,000 for 11 days can be booked at Corrientes 536, 10th floor, T 394-5399. The National Institute of the Antarctic is at Cerrito 1248, T 816-6313/1689, 0900-1500.

INFORMATION FOR VISITORS

Before you go

Entry requirements

● **Documents**

Check visa requirements as they change frequently. Passports are not required by citizens of neighbouring countries who hold identity cards issued by their own Governments. No visa is necessary for US citizens, British citizens and nationals of other Western European countries (except Spain), Canada, Mexico, El Salvador, Nicaragua, Malaysia, Israel, Hungary, Poland, Slovenia and Japan, who may stay for 3 months, a period which can be renewed for another 3 months at the National Directorate of Migration. For all others there are three forms of visa: a business 'temporary' visa (US$28 for UK passport holders, valid 1 year), a tourist visa (US$28), and a transit visa. Australians, New Zealanders and South Africans need visas. (Australians applying for a visa in London must have a letter from Australia House confirming passport ownership.) Tourist visas are usually valid for three months in Argentina and for any number of exits and entrances during that period. If leaving Argentina on a short trip, check on re-entry that border officials look at the correct expiry date on your visa, otherwise they will give only 30 days. Renewing a visa is difficult and can only be done for 30-day periods. Visitors should carry passports at all times; backpackers are particular targets for thorough searches – just stay calm; it is illegal not to have identification handy. When crossing land frontiers, remember that though the migration and customs officials are generally friendly, helpful and efficient, the police at the control posts a little further into Argentina tend to be extremely bureaucratic in their approach.

At land borders, 90 days permission to stay is usually given without proof of transportation out of Argentina. If you need a 90-day extension for your stay in Argentina, get a new stamp at the first opportunity. Do not be put off by immigration officials in provincial cities who say that the stamp is not necessary, or too complicated to obtain. You can also leave the country, at Iguazú or to Uruguay, and 90 further days will be given on return. Without a valid stamp you will be fined US$40 on leaving.

NB At Argentine/Uruguayan borders one immigration official will stamp passports for both countries. Under Mercosur regulations (1992), borders between Argentina, Uruguay, Paraguay and Brazil are open 24 hrs a day. Argentine immigration and customs officials wear civilian dress. The border patrol, *gendarmería*, in green combat fatigues, operate some borders.

● **Representation overseas**

Australia, 100 Miller Street, Suite 6, Level 30, North Sydney, New South Wales 2060, T 2922-7272, F 2 923-1798; **Belgium**, 225 Avenue Louise B.3, 1050 Brussels, T 2 647-7812, F 2 467-9319; **Canada**, 90 Sparks Street, Suite 620, Ottawa KIP 5B4, T 613 236-2351, F 613 235-2659; **France**, 6 Rue Cimarosa 75116 Paris, T 1 4553-3300, F 1 4553-44633; **Germany**, Wiesenhuetten-platz 26, 8th Floor, 6000 Frankfurt, T 496 923-1050, F 496 923-6842; **Netherlands**, Herengracht 94 1015 BS, Amsterdam, T 2 023-2723/6242, F 2 062-67344; **New Zealand**, 11 Floor, Harbour View Bldg, 52 Quay Street, PO Box 2320, Auckland, T 9 39-1757, F 9 373-5386; **Spain**, Paseo de la Castellana 53, Madrid 1, Madrid, T 1 442-4500, F 1 442-3559; **UK**, 53 Hans Place, London SW1X 0LA, T 071 584-6494, F 071 589-3106; **USA**, 12 West 56th Street, New York 10019, T 212 603-0400, F 212 397-3523.

● **Tourist information**

Addresses of tourist offices are given in the text.

● **Tourist offices overseas**

Delegations abroad: Bonn, Eduardo Piva, Penthouse 1, Suite F, Bldg AmeriFirst, Adenauerallee 52, 5300 Bonn, T 228-222011; New York, López Lecube, 12 West 56 St, NY10019, T 603-0400; Rome, Luis Ruzzi, Via B Ammamati 6, T 963-60-1485; São Paulo, Ruben Eduardo Ali, Av Paulista 2319, Argentine Embassy, F (5511) 881-4063.

● **Specialist tours**

An increasing number of foreign visitors are birdwatchers. Since at least 980 of the 2,926 species of birds registered in South America exist in Argentina, in places with easy access, enthusiasts head for Península Valdés, Patagonia, the subtropical forests in the NW, or the Chaco savannah in the NE. Tours to observe and photograph the animals are led by expert guides.

● **Maps**

The best road maps are those of the ACA (see above). Topographical maps are issued by the Instituto Geográfico Militar, Cabildo 301, Casilla 1426, Buenos Aires (reached by *Subte* D to Ministro Carranza – or Palermo while Min Carranza is closed for repair – where IGM is one block from station – turn right from station, or take bus 152 from Retiro). 1:500,000 sheets cost US$3 each and are 'years old'; better coverage of 1:100,000 and 1:250,000, but no general physical maps of the whole country or city plans. Helpful staff, sales office accessible from street, no passport required, map series indices on counter, open Mon-Fri, 0800-1300. Pirelli publishes a good series of maps (N, Central and S Argentina), with plenty of tourist information.

Health

Argentina is in general a healthy country to visit, with good sanitary services. In some provinces, like Neuquén and Salta, medical assistance, incl operations, X-ray and medication, is free in provincial hospitals, even for foreigners. Sometimes, though, one must pay for materials. All private clinics, on the other hand, charge. Medicines are more expensive than in Europe (eg US$8.20 for Paracetamol drops for children). Smallpox vaccination no longer required to enter Argentina. If intending to visit the low-lying tropical areas, it is advisable to take precautions against malaria. Chagas' disease (**see Health Information**) is found in NW Argentina. To counter the effects of altitude in the NW, chew coca leaves or take *te de coca* (use of coca is legal, its trade is not). In the S take plenty of sunscreen to prevent burning owing to the thinning of the ozone layer. Certain shellfish from the Atlantic coast are affected once or twice a year by red algae (*Marea roja*), at which time the public is warned not to eat them. Buy seafood, if self-catering, from fishmongers with fridge or freezer. To be certain, soak fish for 30 mins in water with a little vinegar. Cholera presents no problem except in some remote villages on the Bermejo and Pilcomayo rivers in the tropical lowlands of the Salta and Jujuy provinces, where the Mataco and Toba tribes have been affected by the disease. If travelling through this region, use bottled water and take your own food.

Money

● **Currency**

In Jan 1992 a new currency – the peso – was introduced at par with the dollar. The peso is divided into 100 centavos. Peso notes in circulation: 1, 2, 5, 10, 20, 50 and 100. All old Austral notes were withdrawn from circulation by 31 March 1993. There is an acute shortage of small denomination notes and coins. Coins in circulation: 5, 10, 25 and 50 centavos and 1 peso. It is often difficult to change TCs, particularly in the smaller towns. There is a 3% tax on cheques and commissions can be as high as 10% and in banks is generally 4%. Commission can be avoided if you go to a branch of the issuing bank, especially if changing small amounts. It can take a long time and many forms to transact these cheques. Cheques are often scrutinized very closely: any variation between signatures can lead to their being refused. It is best to take US$ cash (which is widely accepted in larger, more expensive establishments, but take only utterly unblemished notes, dirty or torn notes are usually refused) and American Express TCs, which can be changed at the American Express bank in Buenos Aires. (In N Argentina, while Amex card is widely accepted, Amex TCs are hard to change.) Citibank TCs have been rec; no commission is charged at their own branches around the country. Buy TCs from Citibank itself if possible, as the name is written more clearly. Emergency cash from Amex is available only in Buenos Aires and Bariloche. Because of TCs fraud there are periodic crackdowns on particular types; take more than one type to avoid being stuck without funds. Thomas Cook Mastercard TC refund assistance point, 25 de Mayo 195, 6° piso, Buenos Aires, T 343-8371. It is not advisable to engage in unsolicited currency transactions on the street as you may be tricked or have problems with the police. Some of the major towns have exchange shops (casas de cambio) and these are given in the text. In Dec 1989, the exchange rate was freed and exchange controls were lifted, so there was no market rate from which travellers could benefit as opposed to the official exchange rate. This régime was in force at the time of going to press, but you are advised to check for changes at the time of your visit. Exchange rates are quoted in major newspapers daily. Money remitted to Argentina from abroad is normally paid out in local currency. It is possible to obtain money from Europe through an express transfer, which takes 2-3 days, and the currency will be subject to tax. For Western Union, T (1) 322-7774. If staying for a long time in Argentina and especially Buenos Aires, you can transfer money from your bank in your home country to a local bank, opening an account in pesos or dollars. Paperwork is not complicated and your money is safe and gaining interest. Check with your bank before leaving.

The provinces of Tucumán, Jujuy and La Rioja have issued bonos (bonds) which circulate at face value alongside the national currency. Two warnings: they are not accepted outside the province of issue and even inside province of issue they are not accepted for some transactions, eg trains, long distance buses. Also, they bear redemption dates, after which they are valueless. Beware!

When crossing a land frontier into Argentina, make sure you have some Argentine currency as there are normally no facilities at the border.

● **Cost of living**
In 1995, Argentina was very expensive for the foreign visitor. Budget travellers should allow US$35-40 a day minimum. High costs can be expected for items such as slide film, and clothing as well as basics, although you can save money by camping and preparing your own food. Imported electronic goods are cheap.

● **Credit cards**
American Express, Diners Club, Visa and Mastercard cards are all accepted. There is a 10% surcharge on credit card transactions in many establishments. Credit cards are readily accepted in all main towns, even in the S, but outside main towns their use is limited. In the S very few service stations accept credit cards (ACA stations only take cards from members) and filling a tank can cost US$40. All shops, hotels and places showing Argencard (head office, H Yrigoyen 878, Buenos Aires, T 331-2088) signs will accept Eurocard and Access, but you must state that these cards are affiliated to Mastercard. Argencard will not permit cash advances on these cards in outlying regions, and is itself very slow in advancing cash. Lloyds Bank, in many cities, handles Mastercard.

● **Value-added tax**
VAT is not levied on most medicines and some foodstuffs but on all other products and services 18% (raised "temporarily" to 21% 1 April 1995).

Getting there

By Air
● **From Europe**
British Airways (non-stop, 3 times a week) and Aerolíneas Argentinas (AR once, via Paris and Madrid) each fly from London. Aerolíneas also fly to the following European destinations (with other carriers in parentheses): Frankfurt (once a week, Lufthansa, 3 times); Madrid (7 a week, Iberia, daily); Paris (4 a week, Air France, 4 a week); Rome (3 a week, also Alitalia); Zurich (once, Swiss Air, 3 times). KLM flies 3 times a week from Amsterdam. Aeroflot flies from Moscow on Mon with a stopover in Cape Verde Islands.

● **From North America**
Aerolíneas Argentinas fly from the following US destinations (with other carriers in brackets): Los Angeles (6 times weekly, United); Miami (daily, LanChile, American, United); New York (daily, Lan Chile, American, United). Ladeco flies 3 times a week from Baltimore, New York and Miami; American from Dallas daily via Miami; United from Chicago daily. Canadian Air International, fly 3 times a week from Toronto; Aerolíneas fly twice a week from Toronto, once a week from Montreal. **NB** AR is part of Continental's frequent flier programme.

● **From Australasia and South Africa**
Aerolíneas Argentinas fly from Sydney, Australia, via Auckland, New Zealand, on Tues and Fri. On the outward flight from Argentina (Mon), Aerolíneas stop at Río Gallegos, but it is difficult to board there in high season. Malaysia Airlines fly twice a week from Johannesburg and Cape Town.

● **From Latin America**
Aerolíneas Argentinas and Lapsa daily from Asunción; AR (4) and Avianca (4) from Bogotá; Viasa from Caracas (5 a week); Saeta from Quito and Guayaquil, AR from the latter only; AR and LAB twice a week from La Paz via Santa Cruz, once a week from Santa Cruz;

from Lima, AR (3), AeroPerú daily; AR 4 a week from Mexico City; from Montevideo (apart from those given in the Buenos Aires section), AR, Pluna, Varig, United and Iberia (operated by AR); frequent flights also to Punta del Este, with many more in holiday season; from Santiago, Chile, daily with AR, Ladeco and LanChile and other Latin American, European and North American carriers on various days; from Panama City, AR once a week.

From Brazil, AR, Varig and Vasp fly daily from Rio de Janeiro and São Paulo (plus European airlines stopping over at both cities); Varig stops over in Porto Alegre, Transbrasil flies daily from São Paulo and Porto Alegre; AR also fly from Porto Alegre, via Montevideo. See under Brazil, or **Introduction and Hints**, for the Mercosur Air Pass.

By Road

For entering Argentina by automobile see **Motoring, Additional Notes** in **Introduction and Hints**. Tourists can bring into Argentina their own cars, vehicles bought or hired in neighbouring countries for up to 8 months under international documentation. No specific papers are usually required to bring a Brazilian registered car into Argentina.

Customs

No duties are charged on clothing, personal effects, toilet necessities, etc. Cameras, typewriters, binoculars, radios and other things which a tourist normally carries are duty-free if they have been used and only one of each article is carried. This is also true of scientific and professional instruments for the personal use of the traveller. Travellers may only bring in new personal goods up to a value of US$200 (US$100 from neighbouring countries); the amount of duty and tax payable amounts to 50% of the item's cost. There are red and green divisions at airport customs. Baggage claim tags are inspected at the exit from the customs inspection area. All incoming baggage is normally inspected. Keep US$20 notes separate from main money supply; they may be asked for as 'payment'.

2 litres of alcoholic drinks, 400 cigarettes, 40 cigars and 4 kg of foodstuffs are also allowed in duty-free; for tourists originating from neighbouring countries the respective quantities allowed are 1 litre, 200, 20 and 2 kg. You can buy duty-free goods *on arrival* at Ezeiza airport.

If having packages sent to Argentina, do not use the green customs label unless the contents are of real value and you expect to pay duty. For such things as books or samples use the white label if available.

When you arrive

● **Airport information**

Do not send unaccompanied luggage to Argentina; it can take up to 3 days of form-filling to retrieve it from the airport. Paying overweight, though expensive, saves time.

● **Clothing**

Shorts are worn in Buenos Aires and residential suburbs in spring, summer and autumn, but their use is not common outside the capital. Bermuda-type shorts are very fashionable, as are jogging suits. In general, dress tends to be formal (unless casual wear is specified on an invitation) in Buenos Aires and for evening outings to shows, etc. The general standard of dress among Argentines is very high: collar and tie, with jacket, are very much the standard for men, and women 'should always err on the side of elegance' – David Mackintosh. Men wearing earrings can expect comments, even hostility, in the provinces.

● **Hours of business**

Banks, government offices, insurance offices and business houses are not open on Sat. *Government Offices*: 1230-1930 in the winter and 0730-1300 in summer. *Banks*: generally 1000-1500 but time varies according to the city, and sometimes according to the season. (See under names of cities in text.) *Post Offices*: 0800 to midnight for telegrams. Stamps on sale during working days 0800-2000 but 0800-1400 on Sat. *Shops* are open from about 0900 to 1900, though many close at midday on Sat. Outside the main cities many close for the daily afternoon siesta, reopening at about 1700. 24-hr opening is allowed except on Mon; this applies mainly to restaurants, foodshops, barbers, newspaper shops, art, book and record stores.

Dance halls open at 2300 but don't fill up till after midnight; night clubs open after midnight. In city centre, cafés and restaurants are busy till after midnight and many evening events, such as lectures, may not start before 2200.

● **Official Time**

3 hrs behind GMT.

● **Safety**

Argentina is one of the safest countries in South America but in Buenos Aires and other major cities beware of the increasingly common trick of spraying mustard (or ketchup) on you and then getting an accomplice to clean you off (and remove your wallet). If you are sprayed, walk straight on.

NB Never carry weapons, or drugs without prescriptions.

● **Shopping**

Local leather goods in Buenos Aires, eg coats (leather or suede), handbags and shoes. *Ciudad del Cuero*, Florida 940, has clothing, footwear and luggage from 40 manufacturers. **NB** Leather from the *carpincho* is from the capybara and should not be purchased. A gourd for drinking *yerba mate* and the silver *bombilla* which goes with it, perhaps a pair of *gaucho* trousers, the *bombachas*. Ponchos (red and black for men, all colours for women). *El Guasquero* in Calle Anasagasti specializes in old *gaucho* objects, saddlery, *bolas*, horn items, all genuine and reconditioned by Sr Flores, the owner. The shop is N of Av Santa Fe, near Calle Bulnes, Buenos Aires (postcode 2028). Articles of onyx, specially in Salta. Silver handicrafts. In Buenos Aires, there is a good, reasonable and helpful souvenir shop on Av de Mayo near Chacabuco. Knitted woollens, especially in Bariloche and Mar del Plata. If you like honey, the Casa de la Miel has different honeys from every province. Try Mendoza or Tucumán varieties.

● **Voltage**

220 volts (and 110 too in some hotels), 50 cycles, AC, European Continental-type plugs in old buildings, Australian 3-pin flat-type in the new. Adaptors can be purchased locally for either type (ie from new 3-pin to old 2-pin and vice-versa).

● **Weights and measures**

The metric system is used.

On departure

● **Airport tax**

US$15 for all international flights, except to Montevideo, which is subject to US$3 tax; US$3-6, payable only in pesos also for internal flights (US$1.75 in Ushuaia). When in transit from one international flight to another, you may be obliged to pass through immigration and customs, have your passport stamped and be made to pay an airport tax on departure. There is a 5% tax on the purchase of air tickets.

Where to stay

● **Camping and youth hostels**

Camping is very popular in Argentina (except in Buenos Aires) and there are sites with services, both municipal, free, and paying private campsites in most tourist centres. Most are very noisy and many are closed off-season. Camping is allowed at the side of major highways and in all national parks (except at Iguazú Falls). Wild camping in deserted areas is possible, but note that in Patagonia strong winds make camping very difficult. Many ACA service stations have a site where one can camp, and in general service station owners are very friendly to campers, but ask first. Service stations usually have hot showers. A list of camping sites is available from ACA (labelled for members, but should be easily available and from the main tourist office in Av Santa Fe, BsAs); see Autoclub magazine. References to sites will be found in the text. ACA campsites offer discounts to members, and to holders of the International Driving Licence; European automobile clubs' members are allowed to use ACA sites. The Danmark Organization, Junín 1616, 3rd Flr, Buenos Aires, T (54-1) 803-3700, has a network of clean, cheap youth hostels throughout Argentina (no age limit, but card needed): in Bariloche, El Bolsón, Pinamar, Calafate and the Tigre Delta. There are few other youth hostels (many open only Feb to Mar), but some towns offer free accommodation to young travellers in the holiday season, on floors of schools or church halls; some fire stations will let you sleep on the floor for free (sometimes men only). Many garages have showers that you can use. Good lightweight tents are now available, eg Cacique. Regular (blue bottle) Camping Gaz International is available in Buenos Aires, at an electrical goods store on Av 9 de Julio, near Teatro Colón, and Suntime, Lima 225, Guatemala 5908 (Palermo), Juramento 2452 (Belgrano) and América Pesca, Alfredo Pollini Alvear 1461. Camping Center, Acoyte 1622, Buenos Aires, T 855-0619, rents camping, fishing and backpacking equipment, 5% discount for ISIC holders.

Food and drink

Food

National dishes are based in the main upon plentiful supplies of beef. Many dishes are distinctive and excellent; the *asado*, a roast cooked on an open fire or grill; *puchero*, a stew, very good indeed; *bife a caballo*, steak topped with a fried egg; the *carbonada* (onions, tomatoes, minced beef), particularly good in Buenos Aires; *churrasco*, a thick grilled steak; *parrillada*, a mixed grill, mainly roast meat, offal, and sausages, *chorizos* (incl *morcilla*, black pudding to the British, or blood sausage), though do not confuse this with *bife de chorizo*, which is a rump steak (*bife de lomo* is fillet steak). A *choripán* is a roll with a *chorizo* inside. *Arroz con pollo* is a delicious combination of rice, chicken, eggs, vegetables and strong sauce. *Puchero de gallina* is chicken, sausage, maize, potatoes and squash cooked together. *Empanada* is a tasty meat pie; *empanadas de humita* are filled with a thick paste of cooked corn/maize, onions, cheese and flour. *Milanesa de pollo* (breaded, boneless chicken) is usually good value. *Ñoquis* (gnocchi), potato dumplings normally served with meat and tomato sauce, are tasty and often the cheapest item on the menu; they are also a good vegetarian option when served with either *al tuco* or Argentine roquefort (note that most places only serve them on the 29th of the month, when you should put a coin under your plate for luck). *Locro* is a thick stew made of maize, white beans, beef, sausages, pumpkin and herbs. Pizzas come in all sorts of exotic flavours, both savoury and sweet. **NB** Extras such as chips, *puré* (mashed potato), etc are ordered and served separately, and are not cheap. Almost uniquely in Latin America, salads are quite safe. A popular sweet is *dulce de leche* (especially from Chascomús), milk and sugar evaporated to a pale, soft fudge. Other popular desserts are *almendrado* (ice-cream rolled in crushed almonds), *dulce de patata* (sweet potato preserve), *dulce de membrillo* (quince preserve), *dulce de zapallo* (pumpkin in syrup); these *dulces* are often eaten with cheese. *Postre Balcarce*, a cream and meringue cake and *alfajores*, maize-flour biscuits filled with *dulce de leche* or apricot jam, are also very popular. Sweets: the Havana brands have been particularly rec. Excellent Italian-style ice-cream with exotic flavours. For local recipes (in Spanish) *Las Comidas de Mi Pueblo*, by Margarita Palacios, is rec.

Offices close for 2 to 2½ hours for lunch between 1200 and 1500. Around 1700, many people go to a *confitería* for tea, sandwiches and cakes. Dinner often begins at 2200 or 2230; it is, in the main, a repetition of lunch. Budget travellers should note that especially in Buenos Aires a number of cheaper restaurants are advertised as *tenedor libre* – eat all you want for a fixed price. Those wishing to prepare their own food will find supermarkets fairly cheap for basics.

Drink

Argentine wines (incl champagnes, both charmat and champenoise) are sound throughout the price range. The ordinary *vinos de la casa*, or *comunes* are wholesome and relatively cheap; reds better than the whites. Among the wines highly praised by correspondents, are Etchart Cabernet Sauvignon and Torrontés (white), Michel Torino Torrontés, Weinert, Flickemann, and Santa Ana Cabernet Sauvignon. The local beers, mainly lager-type, are quite acceptable. In restaurants wines have become more expensive (up to US$20/bottle for a good quality wine). Hard liquor is relatively cheap, except for imported whisky. *Clericó* is a white-wine *sangría* drunk in summer. It is best not to drink the tap water; in the main cities it is often heavily chlorinated. It is usual to drink soda or mineral water at restaurants, and many Argentines mix it with their cheaper wine, with ice, as a refreshing drink in summer. *Yerba mate*, a very popular home-grown tea, is widely drunk, especially in the interior, continuing the old *gaucho* custom. The tea is called *mate*; the gourd from which it is drunk is called *un mate*.

Getting around

Air transport

Internal air services are run by Aerolíneas Argentinas (AR), Austral, Lapa (reliable turbo-prop and Boeing 737 services from Buenos Aires to Córdoba, Tucumán, Salta, Mendoza, Iguazú, Bariloche, Villa Gesell, Mar del Plata, Necochea, cheaper than main airlines), TAN (Transporte Aéreo Neuquén) in the S (book tickets through Austral), LAER (Entre Ríos, Mesopotamia), Aeroposta in the S and the army airline LADE (in Patagonia), which provides a good extended schedule with new Fokker F-28 jets. **NB** LADE will not accept IATA MCOs. Inter Austral is a subsidiary of Austral. Deregulation and privatization has permitted the introduction of discounts by the major carriers. Ask at a travel agency. (Even though sometimes offices in various towns may tell you the flights are full, it is usually worth a try out at the airport.) The naval air passenger service, Aeronaval, carries paying civilian passengers, one third cheaper than LADE. No firm schedule though; 2 flights a week between Ushuaia, Río Grande and Río Gallegos; once a week between Ushuaia and Buenos Aires. Some airlines, like Air Kaiken operate during the high season, or are air taxis on a semi-regular schedule. Check with main airlines about discounts on certain flights. All airlines operate standby systems, at half regular price, buy ticket 2-3 hrs before flight. It is only worth doing this off season. *Plan familiar* tickets allow couples to travel with a 25%

discount for the spouse. Children under 3 travel free. LADE also operates discount spouse (65%) and children (35%) tickets. If travelling by AR or Austral a long linear distance, eg Río Gallegos-Buenos Aires, but wishing to stop en route, it is cheaper to buy the long flight and pay extra (about US$2) for stopovers. **NB** All local flights are fully booked way in advance for travel in Dec. Don't lose your baggage ticket; you won't be able to collect your bags without it. Some travellers have rec checking in 2 hrs before flight to avoid being 'bumped off' from overbooking.

Visit Argentina fare Aerolíneas Argentinas sells a Visit Argentina fare: 4 flight coupons costing US$450, with US$120 for each extra coupon up to a maximum of 8. It is valid for 30 days and must be purchased outside Argentina and in conjunction with an international flight ticket. Austral sell similar tickets (known as Jetpaq) and they are interchangeable (but cannot be used on Inter Austral). Routing must be booked when the coupons are issued: one change of date and destination is free (but subsequent changes cost US$50). One stop only is permitted per town; this incl making a connection (as many flights radiate from Buenos Aires, journeys to and from the capital count as legs on the airpass, so a 4-coupon pass might not get you very far). If you start your journey outside Buenos Aires on a Sun, when Aerolíneas Argentinas offices are closed, you may have difficulty getting vouchers issued at the airport. If you wish to visit Tierra del Fuego and Lago Argentino it is better fly on the Visit Argentina pass to Río Grande or Ushuaia and travel around by bus or LADE from there than to stop off in Río Gallegos, fly to Ushuaia and thence back to Buenos Aires, which will use 3 coupons. Children travel at a 50% discount, infants 10%. Domestic timetables are given in *Guía Argentina de Tráfico Aéreo* and *Guía Internacional de Tráfico*. It is unwise to set up too tight a schedule because of delays which may be caused by bad weather. Flights between Buenos Aires and Río Gallegos are often fully booked 2 to 3 weeks ahead, and there may be similar difficulties on the routes to Bariloche and Iguazú. If you are 'waitlisted' they cannot ensure a seat. Reconfirmation at least 24 hrs ahead of a flight is important and it is essential to make it at the point of departure. Extra charges are made for reconfirming LADE flights (useful in Santa Cruz and Tierra del Fuego) but they are not high.

Land transport

● **Train**
See under Buenos Aires, **Railways**: the future of rail services in Argentina is most uncertain.

● **Bus**
Fares are charged at about US$4.50 per 100 km. Sleeper services from the capital to Mendoza, Córdoba and Bariloche cost US$7/100 km. There are also 'ómnibus truchos' (fake buses), which do not start or end services at bus stations and which have less reliable equipment or time-keeping; they charge less than US$4/100 km (ask at travel agents or hotels). Most bus companies give a 20% student discount if you show an international student card; a YHA card is also useful. The same discount may also be given to foreign, as well as Argentine, teachers and university professors but you must carry documentary proof of your employment. It can be difficult to get reductions between Dec and Mar. Express buses between cities are dearer than the *comunes*, but well worth the extra money for the fewer stops. When buying tickets at a bus office, don't assume you've been automatically allotted a seat: make sure you have one. Buses have strong a/c, even more so in summer; take a sweater for night journeys.

● **Motoring**
All motorists are required to carry two warning triangles, a fire-extinguisher, a rigid tow bar, a first aid kit, full car documentation together with international car driving licence (for non-residents, but see **Car Hire** below), and the handbrake must be fully operative. Safety belts must be worn if fitted. Although few checks are made in most of the country, with the notable exceptions of roads into Rosario and Buenos Aires, checks have been reported on cars entering the country. **NB** Police checks around Buenos Aires can be very officious, even to the point of charges being invented and huge 'fines' demanded. You may not export fuel from Argentina, so use up fuel in spare jerry cans while you are in the country. Always fill up when you can in less developed areas like Chaco and Formosa and especially in Patagonia as filling stations are infrequent. Diesel fuel 'gas-oil' prices are US$0.27 per litre. Octane rating for gasoline ('nafta') is as follows: regular gasoline 83 (US$0.65/litre); super 93(US$0.78/litre). Unleaded fuel is not widely available but its use is increasing (it is called Ultra SP and costs a little more than super). ACA sells petrol vouchers (*vales de nafta*) for use in ACA stations. Shell and Esso stations are slightly more expensive.

To obtain documents for a resident (holder of resident visa, staying at least 6 months in the country) to take a car out of Argentina, you can go to ACA in Buenos Aires, which may take up to 4 working days, or you can ask for a list of other ACA offices that can undertake the work; take forms with you from Buenos Aires, and papers may be ready in 24 hrs. You will need at least one passport-size photo, which you can have taken at ACA at a fair cost. If the car is not your own (or is hired), you require a special form signed by the owner and witnessed by a notary public. **NB** Non-residents may buy a car in Argentina but are in no circumstances allowed to take it out of the country; it must be resold in Argentina, preferably in the province where it was purchased. If buying a used car, the procedures are complicated and expensive, and must be handled correctly to ensure that the possessor of the vehicle is actually the owner. The vehicle must be checked by a trustworthy mechanic to see that the motor and chassis numbers agree with those in the ownership documents; the purchaser and owner must go to the local Registro de Automotores to review the documents and then to the Municipalidad to check that tax (*patente*) has been paid. Employ a *gestoría* to undertake all the paperwork, which will cost about US$150 in all, and take you to *gendarmería* to check the vehicle's identification numbers (US$8) and then to the Registro de Automotores to obtain certificate of ownership (*cédula verde*), with your name and local address on it. The new owner has to pay tax at the municipality where it was paid last; if you pay up to the end of the year you will receive a 'libre de deuda' (US$10). At control posts drivers have to show the *cédula verde*, proof of payment of tax, sometimes a driver's licence, the items required mentioned above, and all lights and tyres may be checked. If you move to another province, your new address has to be registered on all the vehicle documents with a 'cambio de radicamiento'. Third party insurance is obligatory; best obtained from the ACA, for members only.

Most main roads are paved, if rather narrow (road maps are a good indication of quality), and roadside services are good. Road surface conditions vary once one leaves main towns: high speeds are quite possible on the dirt and gravel roads, as long as you have the essential guard for the windscreen. Most main roads now have private tolls, ranging from US$2 to US$10; tolls are spaced about every 100 km. Secondary roads (which have not been privatized) are generally in poor condition. Sometimes one may not be al-lowed to reach a border if one does not intend to cross it, stopping eg 20 km from the border.

Automóvil Club Argentino (ACA), Av Libertador General San Martín 1850, 1st flr, touring department on 3rd flr, 1425 Buenos Aires, T 802-6061/9, open 1000-1800 (take colectivo 130 from LN Alem and Corrientes down Alem, Libertador and F Alcorta, alight opp ACA and walk 1 block through park; to return take the 130 from corner of Libertador on left as you leave building), office on Florida above Harrod's, 2nd flr, has a travel document service, complete car service facilities, insurance facilities, road information, road charts (*hojas de ruta*-about US$2.35 each to members, if available) and maps (dated with the code letters in the bottom corner – road map of whole country, with service stations and *hosterías* shown, US$4 to members, US$9.50 to non-members, and of each province), a hotel list, camping information, and a tourist guide book sold at a discount to its members and members of other recognized, foreign automobile clubs upon presentation of a membership card. (YPF, the state oil agency, also produces good maps for sale.) **NB** Members of other recognized automobile clubs are advised to check if their club has reciprocity with ACA, thus allowing use of ACA facilities and benefit from lower prices for their rooms and meals at ACA *hosterías*. The Club has service stations, some with parking garages, all over the country. If you are not a member of ACA you will not get any help when in trouble. ACA membership permits you to pay with Eurocard (Argencard) for fuel at their Service stations, gives 20% discount on hotel rooms and maps, and discounts at associated hotels, and 10% discount on meals.

ACA accommodation comes in 4 basic types: *Motel*, *Hostería*, *Hotel*, and *Unidades Turísticas*, and they also organize campsites (see below). A *motel* may have as few as 3 rooms, and only 1 night's stay is permitted. *Hosterías* have very attractive buildings and are very friendly. *Hotels* are smarter and more impersonal. All have meal facilities of some kind. Anyone can get in touch with the organization to find out about accommodation or road conditions.

Hitch-hikers, as well as motorists, are rec to contact the ACA for its wealth of information.

Touring Club Argentino, Esmeralda 605 and Tucumán 781 3rd flr, T 392-6742 has similar travel services but no service stations.

● **Motorcycle**
Repairs at Eduardo Olivera, Mecánica Ruben SA, Lavoiser 1187-1674, Sáenz Peña, Buenos

Aires, T 757-4285, excellent BMW mechanic with good selection of spares. Juan Carlos Topcic, Costa Rica 25, casa 48, 9400 Río Gallegos, T 0966-23572, all makes.

● **Motorhomes**

Casa Import Trailer, Av Juan de Garay 331, T 361-5674, sells articles for motorhomes. Casa Car, Humberto Primo 236, T 30-0051, rents motorhomes. Rancho Móvil, Luis Viale 2821, T 59-9470, is club for motorhome owners; all in Buenos Aires. Porta-Potti toilets are widely sold in Argentina, sometimes under a different name.

● **Car hire**

To rent a small car (for four plus luggage) costs from US$40 to US$110 a day, not incl mileage, fuel, insurance and tax (20%); highest prices are in Patagonia. Discounts are available for several days', or weekly rental. Minimum age for renting is 25 (private arrangements may be possible). A credit card is useful. You must ensure that the renting agency gives you ownership papers of the vehicle, which have to be shown at police and military checks. At tourist centres such as Salta, Posadas, Bariloche or Mendoza it may be more economical to hire a taxi with driver, which includes the guide, the fuel, the insurance and the mechanic. Avis offers a good and efficient service with the possibility of complete insurance and unlimited mileage for rentals of 7 days or more, but you should prebook from abroad. No one-way fee if returned to another Avis office, but the car may not be taken out of the country. Localiza, a Brazilian company, accepts drivers aged at least 21 (according to Brazilian rules, but higher insurance). They also offer 4WD vehicles, though only from Buenos Aires. Taking a rented car out of Argentina is difficult with any company. Other companies are given in the text.

If you do not have an international driver's licence, you can get a 3-month licence from Dirección de Transportes de la Municipalidad, Av Roca 5225, Buenos Aires, T 602-6925, Mon-Fri 0800-1300; bring documentation from home.

● **Hitchhiking**

Argentina seems to be getting increasingly difficult for this. Ask at petrol stations. Traffic can be sparse, especially at distances from the main towns, and in Patagonia. It may be useful to carry a letter from your Consulate. Though they tend to be more reserved in manner than most Latin Americans, Argentines are generally friendly and helpful, especially to foreigners (display your flag, but not the Union Jack).

Communications

● **Language**

Spanish, with variant words and pronunciation. English comes second; French and Italian (especially in Patagonia) may be useful.

The chief variant pronunciations are the replacement of the "ll" and "y" sounds by a soft "j" sound, as in "azure" (though note that this is not done in Mendoza), the omission of the "d" sound in words ending in "-ado" (generally considered uncultured), the omission of final "s" sounds, the pronunciation of "s" before a consonant as a Scottish or German "ch", and the substitution in the N and W of the normal rolled "r" sound by a hybrid "rj". In grammar the Spanish "tú" is replaced by "vos" and the second person singular conjugation of verbs has the accent on the last syllable eg *vos tenés, podés*, etc. In the N and NW, though, the Spanish is more akin to that spoken in the rest of Latin America.

● **Newspapers**

Buenos Aires dailies: *La Nación, La Prensa.* Tabloids: *Clarín, La Razón.* Evening papers: *Crónica.* English language daily: *Buenos Aires Herald.* Magazines: *Noticias, Gente, Redacción, Mercado, El Gráfico* (sports). The daily, *Página Doce,* is very popular among students and intellectuals. English language magazines: *The Review of the River Plate* (commercial, agricultural, political and economic comment), and *The Southern Cross* (Irish community). German-language weekly, *Argentinisches Tageblatt,* available everywhere, very informative. There is a weekly international edition of *La Nación,* priced in Europe at US$1.30. Write for further information to: La Nación, Edición Internacional, Bouchard 557, 1106 Buenos Aires.

● **Postal services**

Letters from Argentina take up to a month to get to the UK and the USA (but service is improving). Rates for letters up to 20 grams: US$0.75 Mercosur, US$1 rest of Latin America, US$1.25 rest of world (add US$2 for *certificado*); up to 150 grams, US$1.50, US$2.25, US$3 respectively.

Small parcels only of 1 kg at post offices; larger parcels from Encomiendas Internacionales, Centro Postal Internacional, Av Antártida Argentina, near Retiro Station, Buenos Aires, and in main provincial cities, about US$40 for 5 kg. Larger parcels must first be examined, before final packing, by Customs, then wrapped (up to 2 kg, brown paper; over 2 kg must be sewn in linen cloth), then sealed by Customs, then taken to Encomiendas Internacionales for posting. Cheap packing service available. Open 1100-1700 on weekdays. Used clothes have to be fumigated before they will be accepted. Having parcels sent to Argentina incurs a customs tax of about US$3/package. *Poste restante* is available in every town's main post office, fee US$1.

● **Radio**
English language radio broadcasts can be heard daily on short wave: 0100-0130 on 6060 KHz 49m, 0230-0300 on 11710 KHz 25m, 0430-0500 and 2230-2300 on 15345 KHz 19m; Radiodifusión Argentina al Exterior, Casilla de Correo 555, 1000, Buenos Aires. This is a government station and broadcasts also in Japanese, Arabic, German, French, Italian and Portuguese. Broadcasts by foreign radio stations (incl the BBC) are receivable on short wave.

● **Telephone services**
Two private companies operate telephone services, Telecom in the N and Telefónica Argentina in the S. Buenos Aires Federal District and the country as a whole are split roughly in two halves. For the user there is no difference and the two companies' phone cards are interchangeable. For domestic calls public phones operate on *cospeles* (tokens) which can be purchased at news stands. On weekdays, 2200-0800, and from Sat 1300 to 0800 Mon inland and local calls cost one third (Telefónica Argentina) and international calls are reduced by 20%; other offices have different reduced rate hours. Rates per minute for international calls, full rate (Mar 1995): USA US$3.52; Paraguay, Chile US$3.55; Spain, Italy US$4.22; Canada, UK, Germany, France US$5.10; Japan, Hong Kong US$6.37. All charges are payable only in pesos. In main cities there are also privately-run 'Centros de Llamadas', offering a good telephone and fax service. International public phones display the DDI sign (Discado Directo Internacional); DDN (Discado Directo Nacional) is for phone calls within Argentina. Provide yourself with enough tokens or phone cards in Buenos Aires because, in the regions, phone booths exist, but the tokens and cards are not on sale. Most telephone company offices in principal cities have a phone for USA Direct; if they do not, they can direct you to one. There is frequently a high mark-up on calls made from hotels; beware of erroneous charges for international calls on hotel bills. No reverse-charge calls to South Africa. It is now easy to call reverse charge to Australia. Operator speaks English. Fax: American Express in Buenos Aires allows card holders to receive Faxes at US$1 per sheet and to send them at

US$8/sheet (to Europe). Telefónica and Telecom send faxes abroad for US$1.23/page, plus cost of the call, and US$1.82/page to receive.

NB Owing to modernization, many 2- and 3-digit prefixes are being changed (**see p 75**).

Sport

Fishing The three main areas for fishing are the Northern Zone, around Junín de los Andes, extending S to Bariloche; the Central Zone around Esquel; the Southern Zone around Río Gallegos and Río Grande. To fish anywhere in Argentina you need a permit, which costs US$10/day, US$30/week, US$100/year. In the Northern Zone forestry commission inspectors are very diligent. For tours arranged from the UK, contact Sport Elite (JA Valdes-Scott), Woodwalls House, Corscombe, Dorchester, Dorset, DT2 0NT.

Walking and skiing Details on outdoor activities in Argentina can be found in *Weekend* (Spanish), good photos and excellent maps. Information on trails in NW Argentina, the Lake District, Patagonia and Tierra del Fuego is given in *Backpacking in Chile and Argentina*, 3rd edition 1994 (Bradt Publications, 41 Nortoft Road, Chalfont St Peter, Bucks, SL9 0LA, UK). Note that Bradt Publications' *South America Ski Guide* (1992) gives details of Argentine ski resorts.

The skiing season is May to end-Oct; best sites are Las Leñas (Mendoza, which has many other small sites), Chapelco, San Martín de los Andes, Bariloche and La Hoya (nr Esquel, cheapest, but shorter runs).

Holidays and festivals

The main holiday period, generally to be avoided by business visitors, is Jan-Mar, though some areas, such as Tierra del Fuego, begin to fill up in Nov/Dec. Winter school holidays, in which travelling and hotels may be difficult, are the middle two weeks of Jul. No work may be done on the national holidays (1 May, 25 May, 20 June, 9 July, 17 Aug, 12 Oct and 25 Dec) except where specifically established by law. There are no bus services on 25 and 31 Dec. On 1 Jan, Holy Thursday and Good Friday, and 8 Dec employers are left free to decide whether their employees should work, but banks and public offices are closed. Banks are also closed on 31 Dec. There are gaucho parades throughout Argentina, with traditional music, on the days leading up to the Día de la Tradición, 10 Nov. On 30 Dec (not 31 because so many offices in centre are closed) there is a ticker-tape tradition in downtown Buenos Aires: it snows paper and the crowds stuff passing cars and buses with long streamers.

Further reading

Federico B Kirbus has written the highly informative *Guía de Aventuras y Turismo de la Argentina* (with comprehensive English index – 1989), obtainable at El Ateneo, or from the author at Casilla de Correo 5210, 1000, Buenos Aires. Kirbus has also written the *Guía Ilustrada de las Regiones Turísticas Argentinas*, 4 volumes, NW, NE, Centre, S, with about 300 black and white photos, colour pictures and colour plates on flora and fauna (published by El Ateneo); also *La Argentina, país de Maravillas*, Manrique Zago ediciones (1993), a beautiful book of photographs with text in Spanish and English. *Nuestros Paisanos Los Indios* by Carlos Martínez Sarasola is an excellent compendium on the history and present of Argentine Indian communities, rec. The Fundación Vida Silvestre (conservation organization and bookshop), Defensa 245/251, has information and books on Argentine flora and fauna. Field guide to Argentine birds: *Guía para la identificación de las aves de Argentina y Uruguay* by T Narosky and D Yzurieta, with drawings and colour illustrations. Among a number of guide books to the country, recent rec additions are *Travel Companion: Argentina* by Gerry Leitner, the *Pirelli Guide* by Diego Bigongiari, US$18, incl maps, rec for cultural, historical and nature information, and the *Insight Guide* to Argentina.

British business travellers are strongly advised to read '*Hints to Exporters: Argentina*', obtainable from DTI Export Publications, PO Box 55, Stratford-upon-Avon, Warwickshire, CV37 9GE. Similar information is provided for US citizens by the US Department of Commerce.

Acknowledgements

We wish to offer our profound thanks to Alan Murphy for doing the updating. For their generous assistance we wish to thank Federico Kirbus, Herbert S. Levi and Brad Krupsaw (all from Buenos Aires), and Carola Burton (Bariloche). Thanks are also due to the following residents and travellers: Anika Absolan (Vienna, Austria), Daniel Aeberhard (Slough, UK) an excellent contribution, Louise Bach (Vestbjerg) and Tine Tang Kleif (Aarhus, Denmark), David Barton (Willenhall, UK), Niki Beattie (Cobham, Surrey), Janie Bergeron and François Vitez (Longueuil, Canada), Phil and Jenny Blackman (Bath, UK), Stephen Bone (Lingfield, UK), Ruth Brandt (Israel), Anke Brednich (Frieburg, Germany), Terrie Catlow (Buenos Aires, Argentina), Ludovic Challeat (Lamastre, France), Diego Puls (Amsterdam, The Netherlands), Carmelita Chávez (Vista, USA), Etienne Claes (Brugge, Belgium), Bernard Cloutier (Montreal, Canada), Judith Stanton and Mark Collins (London, UK) a helpful up-date, Mary Crow (Ft Collins, USA), Kathrin and Henning Dictus (Neuwied, Germany), Karl Dokter (Munich, Germany), Jae and Gerry Duffy (Elizabeth, USA), Olivier Dumoulin (Buenos Aires, Argentina), Jayne Dyer and Nicholas Hird (Bexhill-on-Sea, UK), Eddie Edmundson (British Council, Recife, Brazil), Urs Eggli (Zurich, Switzerland), Jakob Engström and Richard Björlin (Brussels, Belgium), Gonzalo I Fernández (Viña del Mar, Chile), Stefanie Floegel (Vilsbiburg, Germany), Valerie Fraser and Tim Butler (Lima, Peru) many long and informative letters, Gisa Gericke (Wetzlar), Nicole Hofmann (Weisbaden), and Tanja Wirth (Flörsheim, Germany), Mariecke van der Gias (Utrecht, The Netherlands), Michael Gonin (Canberra, Australia), Nicole Gotze (Bariloche, Argentina), Loukas Grafakos (Papagou, Greece), Herbert Gramm (Cambridge, USA), Matt Griffin (Seattle. USA), Sylvia Grisez (Warren, USA), Erez Guilatt (Jerusalem, Israel), John W Guinee (Reston, USA), Jay Hassani (Baltimore, USA), Sibylle Hössler (Munich, Germany), Carlos and Seba Orellana (Buenos Aires), A Jachnow and A Kuhn (Berlin, Germany), Marten H Jacobsen and Brit R Lauritsen (Denmark), Guy Jarvi (Bondi, Australia), Kate Jenikes (Eugene, USA), Patrick J Paludan (Valby) and Erik Hassenkamm (Valby and Skanderberg, Denmark), Sonja Jovanovic and Andrew Thompson (London, UK) a helpful letter S and Othmer KamerGüntert (Uetikon, Switzerland), Mark Kent (Asunción, Paraguay), May-Britt Koopman (Triesen, Switzerland), Kato and Mark Kostrzewa (Mountain View, USA), M Leufgens and M Jollands (Alsdorf, Germany), Riika Levoranta (Vammala) and Vesa Lampiner (Möjärvi, Finland), Thomas Lüscher (Rümikon, Switzerland), Claire Marin and Jean-Claude Praz (Baar/Nendaz, Switzerland), Egon Otto Mayer (Mendoza, Argentina), Peter McFadden (Conwy, UK), Oliver Meiser (Pfullingen, Germany) a very detailed contribution Mr Max Mizejewski (Kerby, USA), Rachel Morán (Ruxton, USA), Christiane Moser (Frieburg, Germany), Christina Müller (Hanau, Germany), Martijn Mugge (Enschede, The Netherlands), Mark Muhlbacher (Lucerne, Switzerland) for many letters Hans-Peter Neusch (Stuttgart, Germany), Holly O'Callagnan (Durazno, Uruguay), Paul Olai-

Olssen (Oslo, Norway), T P O'Sullivan (Loughborough, UK), Serge Ouddane (Paysandú, Uruguay), Luzia Portmann and Rolf Studer (Lucerne, Switzerland), Margorie Powell (Cambridge, UK) extensive contribution, Cindy Raider (Concepción del Louguay, Argentina), Lawrence Railton and Susan Boyd (London, UK), Guillermo Ramires (Kings Cross, Australia), Urs Riegger (Zurich, Switzerland), Thomas and Petra Sbampato (Wallisetten, Switzerland), Burkhard Schack and Michael Zickgraf (Seelbach, Germany), Doris Schmittat (Weisbaden, Germany), Herbert K Schmitz (Potomac, USA), Therese Schöb (Zurich) and Urs Steinmann (Gruningen, Switzerland), Rüdiger Schultz (St Gallen, Switzerland), Ken Simons (London, UK), Jorge Antolín Solache (Calafate, Argentina), Marianne and Jürg Weber, Claudia Hess Steiner and Thomas Steiner (Lyss, Switzerland), Patrick Sterckx (Grez-Doiceau, Belgium), J R Stourton (Cirencester, UK), Alexandra Strickner and Peter Buda (Vienna, Austria), Urs and Verena Stuber (Schindellogi, Switzerland), Astrid Studer and Andreas Hediger (Reinach, Switzerland), Pim and Irma Sybesma (Leiden, The Netherlands), Ilay Tamari (Ramat-Hasharon, Israel), Rainer Teck (Solingen, Germany), Ron and Dorothy Thyer (Blackburn, Australia), A.ndrios Tieleman and Ditty Bakker (Haarlem, The Netherlands), Peter Titz (Oberwil, Switzerland), Jean Tremlett (Carshalton, UK), Arnaud Troost and Fenna den Hartog (Rotterdam, The Netherlands), Samuel Urech (Niederhasli, Switzerland), Eric and Ingrid Van den Broeck (Leuven, Belgium), Ruben Vázquez (Santa Cruz, Argentina), Margot Verhagen and Carel van der Velden (Holland), Infanger Vinzenz (Erstfeld, Switzerland) an extensive contribution Dre Visscher (Tilburg, The Netherlands), Ron Wain (Teddington) and Steve 'Ribs' Harrop (Cardiff, UK), Noemi Wallingre and Al Bianco (Buenos Aires, Argentina), Dr Volker Weinmann (Blumenau, Brazil), Jane Westlake (London, UK), Jacqui White (Salta, Argentina), Marc Williamson (Melbourne, Australia) an extensive contribution, Natalie and Derek Windsor (Durham, UK), Christian Leonards and Sandra Winterhalter (Insel Reichenau, Germany) and P Lamartine Yates (Cuvat, France).

BOLIVIA

INTRODUCTION

BOLIVIA, straddling the Andes, is a land of gaunt mountains, cold desolate plateaux and fertile, semi tropical lowlands. In area it is about twice the size of Spain. It is land-locked, with Chile and Peru to the W, Brazil to N and E, and Argentina and Paraguay to the S.

The Andean range is at its widest, some 650 km, in Bolivia. The Western Cordillera, which separates Bolivia from Chile, has high peaks of between 5,800 and 6,500m and a number of active volcanoes along its crest. The passes across it are above 4,000m. To the E of this range lies the bleak, treeless, windswept Altiplano, much of it 4,000m above sea-level. It has an average width of 140 km, is 840 km long, and covers an area (in Bolivia) of 102,300 sq km, or nearly 10% of the country. Its surface is by no means flat, for the Western Cordillera sends spurs into it which tend to divide it into basins. The more fertile northern part is the more inhabited; the S part is parched desert and almost unoccupied, save for a mining town here and there. Nearly 70% of the population lives on it, for it contains most of the major cities; almost half of the people are urban dwellers.

Lake Titicaca, at the northern end of the Altiplano, is an inland sea of 8,965 sq km at 3,810m: the highest navigable water in the world. Its maximum length and breadth are 171 and 64 km, and the greatest known depth is 280m. There are large annual variations between high and low water levels; 95% of the water flowing into it is lost by evaporation, making it more salty than most freshwater lakes. The immense depth of the water keeps the lake at an even all-the-year-around temperature of 10°C. This modifies the extremes of winter and

Legend:
1. La Paz, Titicaca & the Peruvian Frontier
2. The Yungas
3. Oruro & Routes to Chile and Argentina
4. Potosí, Sucre and the Southern Highlands
5. The Cochabamba Basin
6. The Northern Lowlands
7. Eastern Bolivia

BOLIVIA

Not to Scale

night temperatures on the surrounding land, which supports a large Aymara indian population, tilling the fields and the hill terraces and tending their sheep and llamas.

The Altiplano is a harsh, strange land, a dreary grey solitude except for the bursts of green after rain. The air is unbelievably clear—the whole plateau is a bowl of luminous light. A cold wind blows frequently in the afternoons, causing dust storms. During the winter temperatures fall below freezing point; there is frost every night in July and August, but during the day the tropical sun raises temperatures over 20°C.

The animals of the Altiplano are fascinating. Llamas serve as pack animals. They carry up to 22 kg loads up to 20 km a day and yield about 2½ kg of wool when sheared at intervals of from two to five years. The alpaca, bred not for work but for wool, belongs to the same group; the two may be distinguished by differences in the texture of their coats and shape of their tails. The vicuña, chinchilla and red fox are the main wild animals. The vicuña, an untamed smaller member of the family to which the llama and the alpaca belong, is found, though in diminishing numbers, on the bleak pampas. It may not be hunted, but its fine silky, tawny coloured wool may be sold.

Agriculture in the Altiplano is also interesting: the potato and the oca (another tuber), eaten in the dehydrated form of chuño and tunta, are the main crops. Quinoa, a kind of millet, and cañava, a smaller and darker grain, are the main cereals; both are extremely nutritious. Chicha, the national intoxicant, is brewed from maize (corn). Edible fish (small *boga*, large white-fleshed *pejerrey* and the rainbow and salmon trout with which Lake Titicaca has been stocked) are widely sold in the towns of the Altiplano.

Since the colonial period mining has been far more important to the economy of the Altiplano than agriculture. In 1545 the Spanish discovered Indian mine workings and vast reserves of silver, tin, bismuth and tungsten in a mountain which they called Cerro Rico (the "rich hill"). Interested only in silver, they built Potosí at its base, 4,070m above sea level. Today a much more important mining centre is Oruro, 210 km S of La Paz at the base of the Eastern Cordillera, where a low belt of hills supplies tin, copper, silver and tungsten. Nearby are the mines of Huanani, formerly owned by the tin magnate Simón Patiño, and Colquiri. Since the collapse of the world tin market in 1986, most of the other mines in the area have been closed or are now worked as small-scale cooperatives, including the ex-Patiño mines at Catavi, which used to produce nearly half the tin of Bolivia. Lack of investment and the high cost of producing Bolivian tin was a major contributor to the industry's decline. Silver is still mined or extracted from the tailings left by past generations, and variable amounts of lead, bismuth, antimony, tungsten and zinc from pockets in the Cordillera are exported. Large deposits of silver have been found S of the Altiplano, near López, and mines are being reopened, and their tailings reprocessed, two centuries after the Spaniards abandoned them.

Recommended reading: *We Eat the Mines and the Mines Eat* Us by June Nash, New York, 1979, and *The Potosí Mita* 1573-1700 by Jeffery Cole, Stanford University Press, 1985.

From the Altiplano rises, to the E, the sharp façade of the Eastern Cordillera. As luck would have it there is a gently graded passageway along the plateau at the foot of the Eastern Cordillera from Lake Titicaca, in the N, to the Argentine frontier, in the S. From Viacha, near La Paz, a railway line runs S along this passageway to Villazón on the Argentine border with connections to Chile (from Uyuni). The giant masses of the northern parts of the Eastern Cordillera rise to very great heights in the Cordillera Real to the E of Lake Titicaca: four peaks soar to above 6,000m. This magnificent sight can be seen on a clear day from the top of a ridge on the more S Titicaca-La Paz road, which goes past Tiahuanaco. The far sides of the Cordillera Real fall away to the NE, very sharply, towards the Amazon basin.

These heavily forested north E slopes are deeply indented by the fertile valleys of the Nor Yungas and Sud Yungas, drained by the Río Beni and its tributaries, where cacao, coffee, sugar, coca and tropical fruits are grown. The problem of transport from here to the consuming centre of La Paz is formidable: the connecting all-weather road, hair-raising in places, climbs 3,430m in 80 km to surmount La Cumbre pass, at 4,725m within 24 km of La Paz.

Further S, from a point just N of Cochabamba the Eastern Cordillera is tilted, not to the NE, but to the E. This part of the Eastern Cordillera rises abruptly in sharp escarpments from the Altiplano, and then flattens out to an easy slope E to the plains: an area known as the Puna. The streams which flow across the Puna are tributaries of the Río Grande flowing NE to the basin of the Amazon, and of the Pilcomayo flowing SE through the Chaco to the Río de la Plata system. They cut increasingly deep incisions as they gather volume until, to the E, the Puna is eroded to little more than a high remnant between the river valleys. These valleys are densely inhabited; a variety of grain crops and fruits is grown. All these semi-tropical mountain valleys are known as Yungas: the generic name is not confined to the valleys of the Provinces of Nor and Sud Yungas to the E of La Paz. Rainfall in the Yungas is from 700 to 800 mm a year, as opposed to the 400 to 700 mm of the northern Altiplano and much less further S. The heaviest rain is during December, January and February. The mean average temperature is between 16° and 18°C, with high humidity.

The very fertile basins in which Cochabamba, Sucre, and Tarija lie send food and cattle to the towns of the Altiplano, but the other valleys have, until recently, lacked the communications to do so.

The lowland tropics, stretching from the foothills of the Eastern Cordillera to the frontiers with Brazil to the NE and E and with Paraguay and Argentina to the SE and S, take up 70% of the total area of Bolivia, but contain only about 20% of its population. Rainfall is high but seasonal, and large areas suffer from alternate flooding and drought. The climate is hot, ranging from 23° to 25°C in the S and to 27°C in the N. Occasional cold dust-laden winds from the S, the *surazos*, lower the temperature considerably. In the N and E the Oriente has dense tropical forest. Open plains covered with rough pasture, swamp and scrub occupy the centre. Towards the end of the 18th century this was a populous land of plenty; for 150 years Jesuit missionaries had controlled the area and guided it into a prosperous security. A symbol of their great effort is the cathedral at San José de Chiquitos: a gem of elegance and dignity. But the Jesuits were expelled in 1767; years of maladministration, spoliation and corruption reduced the area to lethargy.

This once rich land, drained by the Madre de Dios, Beni and Mamoré rivers into the Madeira, a tributary of the Amazon, has been isolated from the rest of the country. It is as difficult to get at from the E as from the W, for there are rapids and falls in the Madeira which limit navigation. In its heart lie the seasonally inundated tropical Llanos de Mojos, ringed in by rain forest or semi-deciduous tropical forest: 230,000 sq km with only 120,000 people. Roads and river connections are being improved; roads link Trinidad with La Paz and Santa Cruz, Guayaramerín and Riberalta with La Paz and Todos Santos and Puerto Villarroel with Cochabamba. Meat is now shipped from Trinidad, capital of Beni Department, and from airstrips in the area, to the urban centres of La Paz, Oruro, and Cochabamba.

The forests and plains beyond the Eastern Cordillera sweep S towards the Río Pilcomayo, getting progressively less rain and merging into a comparatively dry S land of scrub forest and arid savanna. The main city of this area is Santa Cruz de la Sierra, founded in the 16th century, now the second city of Bolivia and a large agricultural centre. Here conditions favour the growing of sugar-cane, rice, oil plants and citrus fruit. The plains to the E are mainly used as grazing lands with small areas under cultivation, but in this area are extensive oil, gas, and iron-ore deposits, possibly Bolivia's greatest asset when developed.

Climate There are four distinct climatic zones: (1) The tropical departments of Santa Cruz and Beni, drained by the Amazon; altitude between 150 and 750m; average temperature, 29°C. (2) The Yungas north of La Paz and Cochabamba, among the spurs of the Cordillera; altitude, 750-1,500m; average temperature, 24°C. (3) The Valles, or high valleys and basins gouged out by the rivers of the Puna; average temperature, 19°C. (4) The Puna and Altiplano; average temperature, 10°C, but above 4,000m may get down to -25°C at night in June-August. The period from December to April is considered the rainy season throughout Bolivia. Little rain falls upon the western plateaux between May and November, but the rest of the year can be wet. There is rain in all seasons in the E part of the country, heaviest from November to March.

History At Tiwanaku (Tiahuanaco), near Lake Titicaca, stand the impressive remains of a pre-Inca civilization. The Aymara speaking Indians in this area emerged around 1000 BC into a civilization characterized by massive stone buildings and monuments, exquisite textiles, pottery and metalwork. This phase seems to have been ended abruptly by some unexplained calamity around AD 900 (possibly the failure of the agricultural system). When the Quechua-speaking Incas of Cuzco conquered the area around AD 1200, they found the Aymaras at Tiahuanaco living among ruins they could no longer explain. The Aymaras resisted obstinately and were not finally conquered until the latter part of the 15th century in the reign of Inca Túpac Yupangi (1471-93). Even so, they kept their traditional social structures and language, and fought for the Incas under their own leaders. Only religion was formally imposed by the Incas. Kollasuyo, Inca Bolivia, was only a small part of the Inca empire and lasted only about 80 years.

Francisco Pizarro landed in Peru in 1532. Six years later Spain conquered Bolivia, and the next year La Plata, now Sucre (still the official capital), was founded. The excellent Inca communications system and economic organization fell into ruin. In 1559 La Plata became capital of the *audiencia* of Charcas, in the Viceroyalty of Peru. As a result of the discovery of silver at Potosí in 1545, Charcas became one of the most important centres of the Spanish colonial economy, sending a constant supply of silver to Spain. By 1610 Potosí, with a population of over 160,000 was the largest city in the Americas, but, as the richest deposits were exhausted and new mines opened in Mexico, Alto Peru, as present day Bolivia was known, went into decline.

Revolutionary movements against Spanish colonial rule began early; there were revolts at La Paz in 1661, at Cochabamba in 1730 and at Sucre, Cochabamba, Oruro and La Paz from 1776 to 1780. In 1809 the University of San Francisco Xavier, at Sucre, called for the independence of all Spain's American colonies. Finally, on 9 December 1824, Simón Bolívar's general, Gen Antonio José de Sucre, won the decisive battle of Ayacucho in Peru and invaded Alto Peru, defeating the Spaniards finally at the battle of Tumusla on 2 April 1825. On 9 February 1825, when he first entered La Paz, Sucre had already promulgated the decree of independence, but his second in command, Santa Cruz, was for retaining links with Peru; Bolívar was in two minds. Sucre had his way and Bolivia was declared independent.

For most of the period since independence, three main features have dominated Bolivian history: the importance of mining; the loss of territory through disputes and wars with neighbouring countries; and chronic political instability. Although silver had been so important in the colonial period, the Bolivian economy has depended for much of this century on exports of tin. The construction of railways and the demand for tin in Europe and the USA (particularly in wartime) led to a mining boom after 1900. By the 1920s the industry was dominated by three entrepreneurs, Simón Patiño, Mauricio Hochschild and the Aramayo family, who exercised great influence over national politics. The importance of mining and the harsh conditions in the isolated mining camps of the Altiplano led to the rise of a militant miners movement.

Bolivian politics have been even more turbulent than elsewhere in Latin America. Although in the nineteenth century the army was very small, officers were key figures in power-struggles, often backing different factions of the landowning elite. Between 1840 and 1849 there were 65 attempted coups d'etat. The longest lasting government of the nineteenth century was that of Andrés Santa Cruz (1829-1839), but when he tried to unite Bolivia with Peru in 1836, Chile and Argentina intervened to overthrow him. After the War of the Pacific (1879-1883) there was greater stability, but opposition to the political dominance of the city of Sucre culminated in a revolt in 1899 led by business groups from La Paz and the tin-mining areas, as a result of which La Paz became the centre of government.

Since independence Bolivia has suffered continual losses of territory, partly because of communications difficulties and the central government's inability to control distant provinces. The dispute between Chile and Peru over the nitrate-rich Atacama desert in 1879 soon dragged in Bolivia, which had signed a secret alliance with Peru in 1873. Following its rapid defeat in the War of the Pacific Bolivia lost her coastal provinces. As compensation Chile later agreed to build the railway between Arica and La Paz. Railways traded for valuable territory has been Bolivia's fate. A railway to Yacuiba was Argentina's return for annexing some of the Chaco. When Brazil annexed the rich Acre Territory in 1903, Bolivia was compensated by yet another railway, but this Madeira-Mamoré line never reached its destination,

Riberalta, and proved of little use; it was closed in 1972.

There was not even an unbuilt railway to compensate Bolivia for its next loss. A long-running dispute with Paraguay over the Chaco erupted into war in 1932. Defeat in the so-called Chaco War (1932-1935) resulted in the loss of three quarters of the Chaco (**see Paraguay chapter, p 1065**).

The Chaco War was a turning point in Bolivian history, increasing the political influence of the army which in 1936 seized power for the first time since the War of the Pacific. Defeat bred nationalist resentment among junior army officers who had served in the Chaco and also led to the creation of a nationalist party, the Movimiento Nacional Revolucionario (MNR) led by Víctor Paz Estenssoro. Their anger was directed against the mine owners and the leaders who had controlled Bolivian politics. Between 1936 and 1946 a series of unstable military governments followed. This decade witnessed the apparent suicide in 1939 of one president (Germán Busch) and the public lynching in 1946 of another (Gualberto Villarroel). After a period of civilian government, the 1951 elections were won by the MNR but a coup prevented the party from taking office.

In April 1952 the military government was overthrown by a popular revolution in which armed miners and peasants played a major role. Paz Estenssoro became president and his MNR government nationalized the mines, introduced universal suffrage and began the break-up and redistribution of large estates. The economy, however, deteriorated, partly because of the hostility of the US government. Paz's successor, Hernán Siles Zuazo (president 1956-1964), a hero of the 1952 revolution, was forced to take unpopular measures to stabilize the economy. Paz was re-elected president in 1960 and 1964, but shortly afterwards in November 1964 he was overthrown by his vice president, Gen René Barrientos, who relied on the support of the army and the peasants to defeat the miners.

The death of Barrientos in an air crash in 1969 was followed by three brief military governments. The third, led by Gen Torres, pursued left-wing policies which alarmed many army officers and business leaders. In August 1971 Torres was overthrown by Hugo Banzer, a right-wing general who outlawed political parties and trade unions. Banzer's government, though repressive, was mild by comparison with contemporary regimes in Argentina and Chile. After Banzer was forced to call elections in 1978, there was another period of short-lived military governments, which overruled elections in 1978 and 1979 giving victories to Siles Zuazo. One of these, led by Gen García Meza (1980-1981) was notable for its brutal treatment of opponents and its links to the cocaine trade which led to its isolation by the international community. In August 1982 the military returned to barracks and Dr Siles Zuazo assumed the Presidency in a leftist coalition government with support from the communists and trade unions. Under this regime inflation spiralled out of control. The elections of 14 July 1985 were won again by Víctor Paz Estenssoro, who imposed a rigorous programme to stabilize the economy. In the elections of 7 May 1989, Gonzalo Sánchez de Lozada of the Movimiento Nacionalista Revolucionario, MNR (chief architect of the stabilization programme) won most votes but the result was so close that Congress had to choose a president from the three leading contenders. Jaime Paz Zamora of the Movimiento de la Izquierda Revolucionaria (MIR) who came third in the elections, was inaugurated as President on 6 August 1989 after having made an unlikely alliance with the former military dictator, Gen (retired) Hugo Banzer (Acción Democrática Nacionalista), in return for certain cabinet posts.

At the end of Paz Zamora's term, the former military dictator General Luis García Meza was sentenced to 30 years in prison at a much-publicized trial. Although several of his accomplices were imprisoned at the same time on human rights charges, García Meza himself managed to escape during the trial. He was captured in Brazil in early 1994 and held there by the military until February 1995, when he was extradited to Bolivia. He is now held in solitary confinement in a prison outside

La Paz.

The presidential election of 6 June 1993 was fought between Acuerdo Patriótico, led by Hugo Banzer, a coalition of MIR, Banzer's own ADN and two other parties, Gonzalo Sánchez de Lozada of the MNR, Unidad Cívica Solidaridad (UCS), led by the brewery owner Max Fernández, and the populist Conciencia de Patria (Condepa) of Carlos Palenque. Gonzalo Sánchez de Lozada won the greater number of votes but failed to gain the required 51% majority to win the presidency outright. Shortly afterwards, however, the other candidates recognized Sánchez de Lozada's victory and withdrew from the contest.

The People Of the total population some two thirds are Indians, the remainder being *mestizos*, Europeans and others. The racial composition varies from place to place: Indian around Lake Titicaca; more than half Indian in La Paz; three-quarters *mestizo* or European in the Yungas, Cochabamba, Santa Cruz and Tarija, the most European of all. Since the 1980s, regional tensions between the "collas" (*altiplano* dwellers) and the "cambas" (lowlanders) have become more marked. Under 40% of children of school age attend school even though it is theoretically compulsory between 7 and 14.

About two-thirds of the population lives in adobe huts, and medical services are sketchy outside the towns and mining camps. Epidemics are comparatively rare on the Altiplano, but malaria and yellow fever are still problems in the Oriente and Santa Cruz, and hepatitis and Chagas disease (**see Health Hints in Introduction**) are endemic in the warmer parts of the country.

The most obdurate of Bolivian problems has always been that the main mass of population is, from a strictly economic viewpoint, in the wrong place, the poor Altiplano and not the potentially rich Oriente; and that the Indians live largely outside the monetary system on a self-sufficient basis. Since the land reform of 1952 isolated communities continue the old life but in the agricultural area around Lake Titicaca, the valleys of Cochabamba, the Yungas and the irrigated areas of the S, most peasants now own their land, however small the plot may be. Migration to the warmer and more fertile lands of the E region has been encouraged by the Government.

The highland Indians are composed of two groups: those in the N of the Altiplano who speak the guttural Aymara (an estimated 1 million), and those elsewhere, who speak Quechua, the Inca tongue (3 million). Outside the big cities many of them speak no Spanish, but knowledge of Spanish is increasing. In the lowlands are some 150,000 people in 30 groups, including the Ayoreo, Chiquitano, Chiriguano, Garavo, Chimane and Mojo. The lowland Indians are, in the main, Guaraní. About 70% of Bolivians are Aymara, Quecha or Tupi-Guaraní speakers. The first two are regarded as national languages, but were not, until very recently, taught in schools, a source of some resentment. There are also about 17,000 blacks, descendents of slaves brought from Peru and Buenos Aires in 16th century, who now live in the Yungas.

The Indian women retain their traditional costume, with bright petticoats, and in the highlands around La Paz wear, apparently from birth, a flattish brown or grey bowler (locally called a *bombín*). In Cochabamba they wear a white top hat of ripolined straw. In Potosí, the women's hat is like a "stove-pipe". According to Peter McFarren (*An Insider's Guide to Bolivia*) there are over 100 styles of hat. The angle at which it is worn is significant, the variety is evidence of the strength of traditional costume, but the hat is also practical (protection against the sun and wind). Indians traditionally chew the coca leaf, which deadens hunger pains and gives a measure of oblivion. Efforts to control the cultivation of coca is one of many sources of friction between the indigenous population and the authorities; others include landlessness, and exploitation of labour. On feast days they drink with considerable application, wear the most sensational masks and dance till they drop.

NB Remember to refer to rural Indians not as "indios" (an insult) but as "campesinos" (peasants).

The Economy Bolivia is the poorest country on the South American mainland. Its poverty is partly attributable to its rugged terrain, which makes communications between the various parts of the country extremely difficult, and to its landlocked position.

The agricultural sector employs over one third of the working population and contributes 17% to gdp. Employment in agriculture has fallen since the mid-1960s because of increasing urbanization. Production of crops for food takes place primarily in the Altiplano, mainly by subsistence farmers, while crops for industrial use (cotton, sugar and soya) are concentrated around Santa Cruz. Most commercial agriculture is in the E, where there are a number of food-processing plants: vegetable oils, a maize mill and sugar refineries. The controversial area in agriculture is the cultivation of the coca leaf, used for chewing by the Indians and to make the drug cocaine. In the 1980s the extreme economic depression and rising unemployment drove increasing numbers in search of the lucrative cocaine trade. Coca is easy to grow, up to four crops a year can be harvested, and Bolivia's production is believed to be worth about US$2bn a year, although less than a third of that actually returns to the country.

In contrast to agriculture, mining, including oil, contributes 7.7% of gdp, yet about half of export earnings. Bolivia is a major producer of tin, antimony, wolfram and bismuth. Silver, lead and zinc are also produced and there are large unexploited reserves of lithium and potassium. Tin used to be the major mineral export, but because of the collapse of the world tin market, it has lost its dominant position in overall exports to natural gas and zinc.

Estimated reserves of natural gas are 111bn cu m, sufficient to meet domestic demand and export commitments for 30 years, but oil reserves, at 108 million barrels in 1994, were being exploited faster than the rate of discovery. Production of around 19,175 b/d was just sufficient to meet domestic demand, but would be insufficient were there to be a general economic recovery.

The recession which afflicted most Latin American countries from 1980 hit Bolivia with six consecutive years of contraction of gdp, accompanied by accelerating inflation, massive and frequent devaluations of the currency and social unrest. Government spending to support key export sectors was hampered by widespread inefficiency, corruption and strikes in state enterprises, which led to massive public sector deficits and external indebtedness. Economic problems were compounded in 1983 by a severe drought in the Altiplano and floods in the E lowlands, which devasted farming. The resulting food shortages exacerbated existing inflationary pressures and led to hyperinflation with annual rates reaching over 20,000%.

In the mid-1980s the government of President Paz Estenssoro introduced severe austerity measures to stabilize the economy, in which price controls were lifted, subsidies removed, public sector wages frozen and the currency linked to the US dollar in a controlled float. Tax reform was passed, a new currency, the boliviano, was created, worth 1 million pesos, the IMF agreed to disburse a standby credit, bilateral and multilateral lending began to flow again and steps were taken to buy back the external commercial bank debt. Inflation came down to 10-20% a year, although unemployment continued to rise and living standards to fall. Nevertheless, by the 1990s there were encouraging signs that growth and employment were recovering and structural adjustment had put Bolivia on a firmer footing (gdp grew by 4.2% in 1993 with inflation at 9.3%, 7.5% in 1994). Growth was insufficient, however, to relieve Bolivia's profound poverty and this, combined with widespread corruption, continues to fuel discontent. In 1994 President Sánchez de Lozada initiated a plan to privatize six state companies: private investors would take up to half the equity in each company without payment, but would agree to substantial, long-term investment. The remaining shares would be divided among the adult population, to be held in pension funds. The aim of the scheme, due to start in 1995, is to generate investment, jobs and economic growth.

Government The Constitution of 1967 vests executive power in the President, elected by popular vote for a term of 4 years; he cannot be immediately re-elected. Congress consists of two chambers: the Senate, with 27 seats, and the Chamber of Deputies, with 130 seats. There are nine departments; each is controlled by a Delegate appointed by the President.

Bolivia has, in effect, two capitals. Although Sucre is the legal capital, La Paz is in almost all respects the actual capital, being the seat of the Government and of Congress. The Supreme Court, however, still holds its sessions in Sucre.

Communications After centuries of isolation new roads are now integrating the food-producing eastern zones with the bulk of the population living in the towns of the Altiplano or the W-facing slopes of the Eastern Cordillera. Under Spanish rule there were four great trails in use within the country: three of them led through passes in the western Cordillera to the Pacific; the fourth led from La Paz S into Argentina. At the turn of the century, railways replaced the llamas and mules. By far the shortest line is the one from La Paz to Arica (Chile), completed in 1913. Arica ships a large part of the exports together with Antofagasta (Chile) and Matarani (Peru).

Bolivia has 3,774 km of railway. There are two private railways: Machacamarca-Uncia, owned by the Corporación Minera de Bolivia (108 km) and Uyuni-Pulacayo (52 km) owned by the Empresa Minera Pulacayo. A railway to link Cochabamba and Santa Cruz, as part of a Pacific-Atlantic rail network, has been under study with Inter-American Development Bank assistance since 1989. Bolivia has over 14,000 km of navigable rivers, which connect most of the country

Bolivia : fact file

Geographic
Land area	1,098,581 sq km
forested	51.2%
pastures	24.5%
cultivated	2.2%

Demographic
Population (1994)	7,888,000
annual growth rate (1989-94)	2.4%
urban	57.7%
rural	42.3%
density	7.2 per sq km
Religious affiliation	
Roman Catholic	92.5%
Birth rate per 1,000 (1993)	32.8
	(world av 26.0)

Education and Health
Life expectancy at birth,	
male	60.3 years
female	65.3 years
Infant mortality rate	
per 1,000 live births (1990-95)	75.1
Physicians (1991)	1 per 2,561 persons
Hospital beds (1990)	
	1 per 1,183 persons
Calorie intake as %	
of FAO requirement	84%
Population age 25 and over	
with no formal schooling	23.3%
Literate males (over 15)	84.7%
Literate females (over 15)	70.7%

Economic
GNP (1992 market prices)	US$5,084mn
GNP per capita	US$680
Public external debt (1992)	
	US$3,694mn
Tourism receipts (1991)	US$90mn
Inflation (annual av 1988-93)	14.8%
Radio	1 per 1.9 persons
Television	1 per 12 persons
Telephone	1 per 38 persons

Employment
Population economically active (1992)	
	2,530,409
Unemployment rate	19.0%
% of labour force in	
agriculture	38.9
mining	2.1
manufacturing	8.8
construction	5.1
Military forces	33,500

Source *Encyclopaedia Britannica.*

with the Amazon basin. The national highway system at the end of 1988 totalled 41,642 km, of which only 4% were paved and under 25% gravel-surfaced.

Music and Dance The heart of Bolivia is the 2-mile (3¼ km) high Altiplano and it is the music of the Quechua- and Aymara-speaking Indians of this area that provides the most distinctive Bolivian musical sound. Although there is much that is of Spanish colonial origin in the Indians' dances, the music itself has more Amerindian style and content than that of any other country in South America. It is rare to find an Indian who cannot play an instrument and it is these instruments, both wind and percussion, that are quintessentially Bolivian. The clear sounds of the *quena* and *pinkullo*, the deeper, breathier notes of the *tarka*, *pututo* and *sicuri* accompanied by *huankaré*, *pululu* and *caja* drums can be heard all over the Altiplano, the *charango* being virtually the only instrument of European origin. The Indian dances are mainly collective and take place at religious fiestas. The dancers wear colourful costumes with elaborate, plumed headdresses and some of them still parody their ex-Spanish colonial masters. Such are the Auqui Auquis and Pakhochos dances. The Khachua dance on the other hand dates from the time of Inca Túpac Yupangi. Other notable dances are the Wititis, Wila Khawani, Jucumaris, Takiri de Kharmisa and Sikuris de Ayata.

The principal popular dances that can be regarded as "national" in their countrywide appeal are the Cueca and Huayño. The Bolivian Cueca is a close relative of the Chilean national dance of the same name and they share a mutual origin in the Zamacueca, itself derived from the Spanish Fandango. The Huayño is of Indian origin and involves numerous couples, who whirl around or advance down the street, arm-in-arm, in a "Pandilla". Other similar, but more regional dances are the Bailecito Chuquisaqueño, Khaluyo Cochabambino, Rueda Tarijeña from the SE and Carnavalito Cruceño and Taquirari Beniano from the tropical lowlands. Justly celebrated is the great carnival Diablada of Oruro, with its hordes of grotesquely masked devils, a spectacle comparable to those of Rio in Brazil and Barranquilla in Colombia.

The region of Tarija near the Argentine border has a distinctive musical tradition of its own, based on religious processions that culminate with that of San Roque on the first Sunday in September. The influence is Spanish, the dance is the Chapaqueada and the musical instruments are the *caña*, *erke* and *violin chapaco*. The first named is an immensely long bamboo tube with a horn at the end, aimed at the sky, on which different "Toques" are played.

There are many professional folk groups on record, the best known being Grupo Aymara, Los Runas, Los Laris, Los Masis, Kolla Marka and Bolivia Manta, some of which have now established themselves in Europe and North America.

Recommended reading: Herbert S Klein, *Bolivia: The Evolution of a Multi-Ethnic Society* (Oxford University Press). Latin American Bureau's *Bolivia in Focus*, on history, culture, politics and economics.

LA PAZ (1)

La Paz, Lake Titicaca and Mount Illimani are probably the three most familiar sights of Bolivia, set amid high Andean Altiplano and the Cordillera Real. The region around La Paz is known as Little Bolivia, containing snow-peaks, desert and sub-tropical jungle in Coroico, just one day's breathtaking bus-ride away.

La Paz, the highest capital in the world, lies in a steep canyon; Plaza Murillo in the centre, at 3,636m, is about 370m below the level of the Altiplano and the new city of El Alto. Mount Illimani, with its snow-covered peaks (6,402m), towers over the city. One of the best ways to appreciate the setting is from the air. East-west flights pass by Illimani with beautiful views of the summit; the rim of the Altiplano, with El Alto built up to the edge, the old city descending the canyon, is very dramatic. The Spaniards chose this odd place for a city on 20 October 1548, to avoid the chill winds of the plateau, and because they had found gold in the Río Choqueyapu, which runs through the canyon. Beware of *soroche* (altitude sickness), especially if arriving from much lower altitudes by air. The mean average temperature is 10°C, but it varies greatly during each day, and the nights are cold. It rains almost every day from December to February, but the sun usually shines for several hours. The rest of the year is mostly clear and sunny. Snow is rare.

In 1993, the population of La Paz was estimated at 1.2 million, over half of it Indian. Orientation is relatively simple; a major avenue, changing its name from Av Mariscal Santa Cruz to Av 16 de Julio (this section is generally known as Prado) runs SE from Plaza San Francisco down to the Plaza del Estudiante. The business quarter, government offices, university and many of the main hotels and restaurants are situated in this area. On the hills above Plaza Mendoza are the poorer parts of the city. From the Plaza del Estudiante, Av Villazón and its extensions lead further SE towards the wealthier residential districts, which run from Sopocachi to the bed of the valley at Obrajes, 5 km from the centre and 500m lower than Plaza Murillo. Sopocachi, through which runs Av 6 de Agosto, has many restaurants, discos, bars, etc; the Mercado Sopocachi, on F Guachalla, is good but not cheap (a bimonthly *Sopocachi* magazine of cultural events, with map, is sold at newsstands). Beyond Obrajes are the upper-class districts of Calacoto and La Florida. The main sports and social clubs are in these districts.

El Alto is now a city in its own right. Apart from the district known as Ciudad Satelite, it is almost 100% indigenous; almost everyone is an emigrant from the countryside. It is growing at 10% per year, compared with 4% growth in the wealthier districts of La Paz. Costs are much lower than in La Paz, but construction, etc is much more basic. There is a market on Thursday and Sunday in Avenida Alfonso Ugarte, more interesting for its size than the items for sale. El Alto is connected to La Paz by motorway (toll US$0.50, cycles free). Buses from Plaza Aguino and Pérez Velasco leave regularly for Plaza 16 de Julio, El Alto.

There are few colonial buildings left in La Paz; probably the best examples are in the Calle Jaén. Late 19th/early 20th century architecture, often displaying heavy European influence, can be found in the streets around Plaza Murillo, but much of La Paz is modern. Emilio Villanueva added local features to European styles, eg the Tiwanaku-style decorations on the University building, but much 20th-century architecture was influenced by Frank Lloyd Wright, eg the new Correo. The Plaza del Estudiante (Plaza Franz Tamayo), or a bit above it, marks a contrast between old and new styles, between the traditional commercial and the more elegant. The Prado itself is lined with high-rise blocks dating from the 1960s and 1970s. Plaza

---

La Paz: Key to map

1. Plaza Murillo; 2. Congreso Nacional; 3. Museo Nacional de Arte; 4. Cathedral; 5. Palacio Quemado; 6. General Post Office; 7. Iglesia La Merced; 8. Museo de Costumbres; 9. Museo y Casa de Murillo; 10. Iglesia Santo Domingo; 11. Museo Nacional de Etnografía y Folklore; 12. Entel; 13. Casa de la Cultura; 14. Basílica de San Francisco; 15. Mercado de Hechicería; 16. Parque Prehistórico Tiahuanaco (Museo Semisubterráneo); 17. Alcaldía; 18. US Embassy and Citibank; 19. Banco Central; 20. Tourist Office; 21. TAM; 22. Museo Arqueológico de Tiahuanaco; 23. Lloyd Aéreo Boliviano; 24. Biblioteca Municipal. Hotels: 25. *Presidente*; 26. *Sucre Palace*; 27. *Gloria*; 28. *Libertador*; 29. *Plaza*; 30. *El Dorado*; 31. *Panamericano*; 32. *Res Rosario*; 33. *Milton*; 34. *La Paz*. 35. *Plaza*; 36. *Sagárnaga and Alem*; 37. *Hostal República*; 38. *Continental*; 39. Restaurant/Peña *Los Escudos*; 40. *Casa del Corregidor*. Markets: 41. Rodríguez; 42. Camacho; 43. Lanza; 44. Main Indian Market; 45. Negro. Parks and Squares: 46. Plaza del Estudiante; 47. Plaza Venezuela; 48. Plaza Sucre; 49. Garita de Lima; 50. Plaza Mendoza; 51. Plaza Velasco; 52. Plaza Riosinio; 53. Plaza Antofagasta; 54. Plaza Vicenta Eguino; 55. Estadio Hernando Siles; 56. Universidad Mayor San Andrés; 57. Immigration Office.

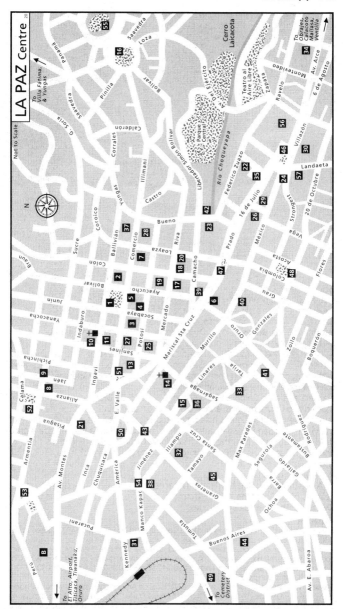

LA PAZ Centre

Not to Scale

To Villa Fátima & Yungas

To Obrajes, Calacoto, Mallasa, Ventilla

To Alto, Airport, El Alto, Tiwanaku, Oruro

To Cemetery District

Murillo, 3 blocks N of the Prado, is the traditional centre. Facing its formal gardens are the huge Cathedral (modern but very graceful); the Palacio Presidencial in Italian renaissance style, usually known as the Palacio Quemado (burnt palace) twice gutted by fire in its stormy 130-year history; and on the E side the Congreso Nacional. In front of the Palacio Quemado is a statue of former President Gualberto Villarroel who was dragged into the plaza by an angry mob and hanged in 1946. Across from the Cathedral on Calle Socabaya is the Palacio de los Condes de Arana, dating from 1775, now the Museo Nacional del Arte. Calle Comercio, running E-W across the Plaza, has most of the stores and shops. On Av Libertador Simón Bolívar (to which Mount Illimani provides a backdrop), is the Central Market (called "Mercado Camacho"), a picturesque medley of Indian victuals and vendors presiding raucously over stalls, their black braids topped by hard-brimmed bowler hats. Further E is the residential district of Miraflores. Another good view of Illimani can be had from the top of the rise on Calle Illimani.

At the upper end of Av Mariscal Santa Cruz is the Plaza San Francisco with the church and monastery of San Francisco, dating from 1549, well worth seeing: the church is richly decorated on native religious themes (the mestizo baroque façade clearly displays how the traditional baroque vine motif is transformed into an array of animals, birds, fruits and plants), the interior contains huge, square columns and gilt altars on which stand many saints; Indian weddings can be seen on Sats 1000-1200. Behind the San Francisco church a network of narrow cobbled streets rise steeply. Much of this area is a permanent street market. Handicraft shops line the lower part of Calle Sagárnaga; further up, from Illampu to Rodríguez and in neighbouring streets, is the local Rodríguez market. Turning right on Max Paredes, heading W, is Avenida Buenos Aires, one of the liveliest streets in the Indian quarter, where small workshops turn out the costumes and masks for the Gran Poder festival. Continuing W along Max Paredes towards the cemetery district, the streets are crammed with stalls selling every imaginable item, household goods, clothing, hats, food, festive goods. Transport converges on the cemetery district (for more information see **Buses** below). Do not expect to go anywhere in a hurry in this part of the city; there are good views of Illimani from these heights.

Other churches of more than passing interest are Santo Domingo (originally the cathedral) on the corner of Calles Ingavi and Yanacocha, with its decorative 18th-century façade (next door is the University Pacensis Divi-Andreae, 1826, and the Colegio Nacional San Simón de Ayacucho, a pink building); La Merced, on a plazuela at Calles Colón and Comercio; San Juan de Dios, on Loayza between Merced and Camacho, with a carved portico, circular paintings of the life of Christ and, above the altar, figures holding lighted (electric) candles around a statue of the Virgin; and San Sebastián, the first church to be built in La Paz, in Plaza Alonso de Mendoza (named after the church's builder). On Plaza Sucre (with trees, benches and photographers) is San Pedro church, Av 20 de Octubre y Colombia, built 1720; large paintings of the life of Christ along the nave, a huge chandelier below the dome and a gilt altar.

A worthwhile walk is to Mirador Laicacota on Avenida del Ejército: one of the delights of La Paz is the change from day to night, when all the lights begin to twinkle on the surrounding hillsides.

Museums

Museo Nacional de Arte, across from the Cathedral at Calle Socabaya 432, housed in the 18th century baroque palace of the Condes de Arana, with beautiful exterior and patio. It has a fine collection of colonial paintings including many works by Melchor Pérez Holguín, considered one of the masters of Andean colonial art, and also exhibits the works of contemporary local artists. Open Tues-Fri 0930-1230, 1500-1900, US$0.25, Sat 0930-1330, entry US$0.50, students US$0.25.

Museo Tiahuanaco (Tiwanaku), or Museo Nacional de Arqueología, easily reached by going down the flight of stairs by María Auxili church on the Prado. This modern building, simulating the Tiwanaku style, contains good collections of the arts and crafts of ancient Tiwanaku and items from the E jungles. It also has a 2-room exhibition of gold statuettes and objects found in Lake Titicaca. Tues-Fri 0930-1230, 1500-1900, Sat 1000-1230, 1500-1800, Sun 1000-1400. Entry US$1.20.

Museo Semisubterráneo, or Templete del Estadio, in front of National Stadium, with restored statues and other artefacts from Tiahuanaco. It's in a sunken garden and much can be seen from street level. No explanations are given and the statues are being badly eroded by pollution.

Museo Nacional de Etnografía y Folklore, on Calle Ingavi 916, is housed in the palace of the Marqueses de Villaverde, worth seeing (exhibits on the Chipaya and Ayoreo Indians), quite good library adjoining. Mon-Fri 0830-1300, 1430-1800.

The following four museums, all on Calle Jaén, are included on a single ticket, which costs US$0.75 (free on Sat), from Museo Costumbrista. All are open Tues-Fri 1000-1200, 1430-1830, Sat and Sun 1000-1230, and all are delightful, with well-displayed items in colonial buildings. Calle Jaén, a picturesque colonial street with many craft shops, is well worth seeing for itself.

Museo Costumbrista, Plaza Riosinio, at top of Jaén. Miniature displays depict incidents in the history of La Paz and well-known Paceños. Also has miniature replicas of reed rafts used by Norwegian, Thor Heyerdahl and Spaniard, Kitin Muñoz, to prove their theories of ancient migrations, T 378478.

Museo Casa Murillo, on Jaén, T 375273 was originally the home of Pedro Domingo Murillo, one of the martyrs of the abortive La Paz independence movement of 16 July 1809. This colonial house has been carefully restored and has a good collection of paintings, furniture and national costumes of the period; there is also a special room dedicated to herbal medicine and magic (Kallawaya) along with two rooms of paintings. Warmly rec.

Museo de Metales Preciosos, Jaén 777, well set out with Inca gold artefacts in basement vaults, also ceramics and archaeological exhibits, warmly rec, T 371470.

Museo de Litoral, Jaén 789, with artefacts of the War of the Pacific, and interesting selection of old maps.

Mineral Museum, Banco Minero, 6 de Agosto 2382, esq Belisario Salinas. Open Mon-Fri 0900-1300, 1430-1630. Good gold and silver exhibits; free.

Núñez del Prado, Ecuador 2034, Mon-Fri, 0900-1200, 1400-1800, excellent sculpture.

Museo Tambo Quirquincho, Calle Evaristo Valle, nr Plaza Mendoza (Tues-Fri, 0930-1200, 1500-1900, Sat-Sun, 1000-1230, US$0.50, Sat free), in a restored colonial building, displaying modern painting and sculpture, carnival masks, silver, early 20th century photography and city plans, highly recommended.

Museo de Historia Natural, Calle 26, Cota Cota, ½ hr from centre by micro-bus marked Cota Cota from Plaza San Francisco, small but quite well-presented. Check for opening times.

Festivals Particularly impressive is the Alacitas Fair held from last week of Jan to first week of Feb, on the upper part of Plaza Villarroel, mostly on Calle Tejada Zorzano (take *micro* B, K, H, 131 or X). "It is dedicated to Ekeko, an Indian household god. You can buy plaster images of him at many of the booths. He is a red-nosed cheerfully-grinning little personage laden with an assortment of miniature cooking utensils, coins, balls of wool, tiny sacks of sugar, coffee, salt, rice and flour; a kind of Bolivian Santa Claus. Ekeko is said to bring prosperity and to grant wishes. If you buy a toy house, or a cow, or a sheep at the Alacitas, you will get a real one before the year is out. There are also model motor-cars and planes, for the extreme optimists." (Christopher Isherwood, "The Condor and the Cows.") Beginning of May, Corpus Christi. End May/early June, Festividad del Señor de Gran Poder, the most important festival of the year, with a huge procession of costumed and masked dancers. Fiestas de Julio, a month of concerts and performances at the Teatro Municipal, offers a wide variety of music, including the University Folkloric Festival 8 December, festival around Plaza España, not very large, but colourful and noisy. On New Year's Eve fireworks are let off and make a spectacular sight, and a din, view from higher up. **See also p 333** for festivals outside La Paz.

Hotels Try to arrive in La Paz early in the day as accommodation, especially at the cheaper end of the market, can be hard to find. Prices include tax and service charge (20% in all).

Expensive Hotels: **L3** *Radisson Plaza*, formerly *Hotel La Paz* (still referred to as *Sheraton*), Av Arce 2177, T 316163, F 343391, good 5-star hotel with all facilities; **L3** *Plaza*, Av 16 de Julio 1789, T 378317, F 343391, excellent, restaurant is good value and open to the public, fine view (check bill); peña show on Fridays; **L3** *Presidente*, Potosí 920 y Sanjines, T 368601, F 354013, including breakfast, "the highest 5-star in the world", pool, gymnasium and sauna all open to non-residents, bar, disco, excellent service, comfortable, good food, rec; **A1** *El Rey Palace*, Av 20 de Octubre 1947, T 393016, F 367759, inc breakfast, large suites, excellent restaurant, stylish, modern; **B** *Sucre Palace*, Av 16 de Julio 1636, T 363453, F 392052, hot water is a problem, overpriced, *Karin* snack bar on ground floor, excellent, expensive, disappointing restaurant on 1st floor; **A2** *Camino Real*, Ravelo 2123, T 314542, F 365575, self-catering apartments, incl breakfast, TV, parking, new; **A3** *Gloria*, Potosí 909, T 370010/18,

F 391489, central, 2 restaurants, one on top floor with good view, one vegetarian, excellent food and service, rec; **B Eldorado**, Av Villazón, T 363355, F 391438, with breakfast, may be able to bargain for longer stays, safe luggage deposit, secure parking nearby; **B Libertador**, Obispo Cárdenas 1421, T 351792, F 391225, very good value, colour TV, good cheap restaurant, helpful (baggage stored), highly rec; **B Max Inn**, Plaza Sucre 1494, T 374391, F 341720, all rooms with bath, heating, TV, smart, very clean, poor service; **C Hostería Blanquita**, Santa Cruz 242, T 352933, "baroque", incl breakfast, hot showers, comfortable; **C Hostal Embajador**, Juan de la Riva 1438, T 392079, with bath, TV, heating, breakfast included, German spoken, helpful; **C Hotel Copacabana**, Av 16 de Julio 1802, T 352244, with bath, central, restaurant and grill room (lunch only at latter), good service, safe deposit, rooms a bit small and fusty, rec; **C Residencial Rosario**, Illampu 704, T 326531, F 375532, Turisbus travel agency downstairs (see under Travel Agents), with bath (electric shower—safe design), D without, very popular with foreigners, avoid noisier rooms near foyer, sauna, laundry, good restaurant, "superb", stores luggage, most highly rec; **C Sagárnaga**, Sagárnaga 326, T 350252, F 360831, with bath, E without, basic breakfast included, good location, laundry, English spoken, rec.

For people staying several weeks, often looking for permanent residences, boarding houses (**pensiones**) are popular, eg Illimeier, Sopocachi, Calle Resequin 1978, D with breakfast, English and German spoken.

Medium-priced hotels: **D Continental**, Illampu 626, T 378226, with bath, hot water, clean; **D España**, Av 6 de Agosto 2074, T 354643, hot water, TV, quiet, friendly, rec; **D Hostería Claudia**, Av Villazón 1965, T 372917, with bath, E without, breakfast extra, clean, secure, friendly, rec; **D La Joya**, Max Paredes 541, T 324346, F 350959, with bath and TV, phone, E without bath or TV, breakfast incl, clean, modern and comfy, helpful, restaurant, bar, in the heart of market district, highly rec; **D Latino**, Perú 171, T 358341, near bus terminal, with bath; **D Milton**, Illampu y Calderón No 1124, T 368003/353511, F 365849 (PO Box 5118), with bath, hot water, popular with travellers, will store luggage, excellent views from roof, good restaurant, rec, local market outside, so no taxis to the hotel at weekends; **D Neumann**, Loayza 442, T 325445, with bath (E without), bargaining possible for students; **D Residencial Copacabana**, Illampu 734, T 367896/375378, hot water, clean but basic and run down, changes TCs; **D Residencial La Estancia**, Mexico 1559, T 324308, with bath and breakfast,

helpful, good restaurant; **D** *Hostal República*, Comercio 1455 (T 357966), with bath, E without, breakfast, beautiful old house of former president, very clean, hot water, luggage stored, helpful, laundry service, rec, also a separate house is available, sleeps 6, all facilities, US$25 a night; **D** *Tambo de Oro*, Armentia 367, T 322763, near bus station, hot showers, clean, friendly, helpful and safe for luggage; **D** *Viena*, Loayza 420, T 323572, with bath, E without, beautiful old building with elegant entrance and patio, gloomy rooms, friendly staff, clean, rec, arrive early, often full, tours with Vicuña Tours, good.

E *Alem*, Sagámaga 334, T 367400, hot water, cheaper without bath, clean, helpful, rec; **E** *Andes*, Av Manco Kapac 364, T 323461, clean, good beds, hot water 24 hrs a day, good value (one of the few that offers single rooms at F), discount for IYHA card holders; rec; **E** *Austria*, Yanacocha 531, T 351140, without bath, clean, hot water, but insufficient showers, safe deposit, very cosy, good for longer stays, use of kitchen, laundry, TV, friendly and helpful staff, very popular, arrive early, highly rec; opposite is **E** *Hostal Yanacocha*, large clean rooms, dirty bathrooms, hot water, secure; **E** *Bolivia*, Manco Kapac 287, T 375030, opp railway station, clean, shared tepid showers, good views from back, upper rooms; **E** *Italia*, Av Manco Kapac 303, T 325101, with bath, try upper floor for quieter rooms, clean but showers usually cold; **E** *Alojamiento Illimani*, Av Illimani 1817, T 325948, hot water, friendly, clean and safe, uncomfortable beds, laundry facilities, often full; **E** *Ingavi*, Ingavi 727, nice rm, poor service, good value; **E** *Hostal Latino*, Junín nr Sucre, clean, hot water, motorcycle parking, luggage stored, helpful; **E** *Panamericano*, Manco Kapac 454, T 340810/378370, with hot showers, near railway station and main bus terminal, helpful, good restaurant, rec; **E** *Res Plaza*, Plaza Pérez Velasco 785, T 322157, a bit run-down, but clean and hot water, F without bath, washing and luggage storage facilities; **E** *Res Sucre*, Colombia 340, opp Plaza San Pablo, T 328414, cheaper without bath, warm water, big rooms, clean; **E** *Torino*, Socabaya 457, T 341487, central, hot water on request (electric showers) with bath (F without), formerly *the* gringo hotel but run down, poor beds, dirty, noisy, from disco especially at weekends till 0300, 2400 curfew, has noticeboard, stores luggage, book exchange, bar; **E** *Max Paredes*, Max Paredes 660, T 362726, with bath (cheaper without), modern, clean; **F** *Hostal Chiquiago*, Plaza San Francisco, simple, friendly, secure, luggage stored; **F** *Alojamiento Illampu*, Illampu 635, T 342274, hot water, laundry facilities, very small rooms with poor soundproofing, check prices carefully; *Alojamiento París*, Sucre 949, T 356836, hot showers, friendly but not very clean, and noisy; **F** *Alojamiento Universo*, Inca 175, dormitories, basic, motorcycle parking. Cheapest possibly is **F** *Posada El Carretero*, Catacora 1056, y Pichincha y Sanjinés, T 322233, 5 beds to a room, helpful, pleasant, hot shower extra, can use kitchen for breakfast.

Youth Hostel association, **Asociacón Boliviana de Albergues Juveniles**, ABAJ, Edif Alborada piso 1, of 105, Calle Juan de la Riva 1406 y Loayza, T 361076/321597, has hostels at *Hostal Duendes*, Av Uruguay 470, T 351125, Casilla 8765, and *Hotel Andes*, Manco Kapac 364, US$3.50 and 2.80 respectively, pp, without breakfast; other hostels around the country are given in the text. To use hostels you must have a Bolivian YHA card, US$2, two photos needed, available from ABAJ, which also sells international cards, US$20.

Camping No organized site, but Mallasa (Municipal Park, unmarked, turn left at Aldeas Infantiles SOS), Valencia and Palca below the suburb of La Florida have been recommended. Club Andino Boliviano (T 794016) rents equipment. *Caza y Pesca*, Edif Handal Center, Av Mcal Santa Cruz y Socabaya, *Sajama*, Sagárnaga 177, 2° piso, or *Epcot*, Av 6 de Agosto 2190, local 9, T 342424, for camping equipment and camping gas. Kerosene for pressure stoves is available from a pump in Plaza Alexander. Public showers at Duchas La Paz, 20 de Octubre 1677.

Restaurants in La Paz can be roughly divided into two categories: either they serve international cuisine and are expensive or they serve local dishes and are fairly cheap. The restaurants with international cuisine are to be found mainly on three streets, Av 16 de Julio (the Prado), Av 6 de Agosto and Av 20 de Octubre. Service charges and tax of up to 23% are usually included on the bill but it is customary to leave a tip of 10% anyway. Always check prices before ordering, and then your bill and change.

Av 16 de Julio: (street numbers given in brackets). There are many snack bars, including *Confitería Elis* (1497), with good plate lunches, excellent soups, breakfasts (waffles, pancakes, French toast, pay extra for coffee refills) and pastries, not cheap, also *Eli's Pizza Express* in same block (very good), English spoken, highly rec; *Denny's*, No 1605, US-style, one of a chain; *La Mía Pasta* (1665 and Áv Salinas at Plaza Abaroa) good pasta, salad buffet; *Patito Pekín* (1687), good Chinese, reasonably priced; *California Donuts II* (1695), American-style food, expensive, US$2-10, opens 1230 (*No I* is at Av Camacho 1248, *No III* is on Av Arce); *Utama*, in *Plaza* hotel (1789) excellent salad bar, highly rec; *Tokio* (1832), good, also has tea room and patisserie and rec for *salteñas*, but look out for high prices not written on menus, expensive; *Super 10* (1991 y Villazón), very good, *almuerzo* US$4, open Sun evenings. On Plaza Estudiante, *Pizza I'Passo II*, good but expensive; *Il Fiore*, snacks, ice cream, pizza; *Café Ciudad*, 24 hr coffee shop, full menu, good, pricey. *Mary's Tee*, near Plaza Estudiante, for excellent pies and cakes.

S of Plaza del Estudiante and Av Arce: *El Batau*, Landaeta 402, T 342518, German owner, Bolivian and international cuisine, rec; *Don Francisco*, Av Arce 2312, good steaks, especially à la Pepe; *Pizzeria Morello*, Av Arce 2132, very good but very expensive, also *La Suisse*, Av Arce 2164, good steaks and raclette, fair fondue, closed Sat and Sun, gourmet restaurant on first floor, expensive; *Viva La Pizza*, J José Pérez 322, rec, expensive; *Kranky*, Av Villazón 1987, good, cheap sandwiches, burgers, ice cream, rec; *Chifa Emy*, Cordero 257, best Chinese, very good service, takes credit cards, US$12.50 pp with drinks; *Rigo's*, Plaza Organo, near Museo Semisubterráneo, pleasant and good set lunch; *Vienna*, Federico Zuazo 1905, T 391660, German, Austrian and local food, excellent, at moderate prices, very fashionable with Bolivians and popular with foreigners too.

In the Sopocachi district: up-market Italian cuisine at *Pronto*, Jauregui 2248, T 355869, Mon-Sat 1830-2230 (below Imprenta Quipus behind 6 de Agosto between Guachalla and Rosendo Gutiérrez), beautiful decor, about US$7 pp, serves three different types of pasta: regular, integral and "pasta de quinoa", "must be unique in South America", popular, good service, poor coffee; *Montesano*, Sánchez Lima 2329, nr Plaza Abaroa, excellent Italian US$35 for 2, also fish and steaks. Several restaurants on Belisario Salinas, eg *El Honguito* (steak sandwiches), *Bar Pub*, and others. Among those **on Av 6 de Agosto**: *El Arriero* (No 2535, Casa Argentina), best barbecue with large portions, but quite expensive; *Mocambo*, 6 de Agosto y L Gutiérrez 319, good food and service, Spanish, US$15 pp; *Oriental*, good, cheap, Chinese; while **on Av 20 de Octubre** there is *Mamma Mia*, art gallery by day, good Italian restaurant at night, expensive but good pizzas; *La Quebecoise*, near Plaza Abaroa, French Canadian, good value, pleasant atmosphere; *El Gaucho*, No 2041, steakhouse, good, about US$20 pp. Close to 20 de Octubre: Brazilian *feijoada* on Sat and Sun, at *Ipanema*, Av Ecuador 2139, between Aspiazu and F Guachalla, T 372306, rec, closed Mon. *Gringo Limón*, Plaza Abaroa, good but expensive steaks; *Filippo*, just off Plaza Abaroa, for good *salteñas*. *La Caldera Mágica*, JJ Pérez 322 y 20 de Octubre, nice atmosphere, good lunches, bar. Rec Mexican place: *Tacos Teru K*, Ignacio Cordero 1294, San Miguel (behind Loreto College) T 794513.

On the continuation of the **Prado going west**, in Av Mariscal Santa Cruz, is *Los Escudos* (Edif Club de La Paz, T 322028/350586), Munich-type bierkeller with fixed 4-course lunch, food and shows, Fri and Sat nights

(2000-2400). On the corner of Colón with Santa Cruz is *Restaurant Verona* for good economical *plato del día*, very popular in the evenings; *La Fiesta*, Santa Cruz 1066, excellent, good lunches, rec. On Plaza Velasco is *Kory Punku*, which serves excellent *parrilladas*, cheap and popular, live music some evenings.

On Calle México, running parallel S of the Prado: *La Estancia*, No 1553, good *almuerzo*, rec; *Capullito*, No 1490, pleasant café and *confitería*. México continues W as Murillo: at No 1040 is *Casa del Corregidor*, T 353633, centrally heated, behind Correo, Spanish colonial restaurant with Bolivian and European dishes, food not cheap, bar *El Horno*, open Mon-Sat, lunches from US$2.50 including vegetarian, *peña* at nights (see **Entertainments** below); *Crístal*, No 726, outdoor, quite cheap, good.

On Sagárnaga: *Naira*, next to *Peña Naira* (No 161 downstairs), which serves good food (see **Entertainments** below), and above the Peña, is *Resolana*, often confused with the *Naira* restaurant. Next to *Naira*, at street level, is *Panadería San Jorge*. *El Montañés* (No 323), opposite *Hotel Sagárnaga*, good, clean, family-run, homemade dishes. *Imperial*, Sagárnaga y Murillo, good and inexpensive local food, clean, balcony tables, cheap *almuerzo*, vegetarian dishes, frequently rec. In same area, *El Lobo*, Santa Cruz 441, good, clean, rec (Israeli dishes, good meeting place, noticeboard, limited menu, very popular); good cheap meals at Illampu 773, closed Sun evening. *Snack América*, Av América 192, good hamburgers; also *Los Laureles*, Av América 67, rec. On Calle Evaristo Valle there are several inexpensive typical restaurants. Excellent set lunch at *Clávida*, opp train station, including potatoes and cheese in peanut curry sauce.

In the shopping and business district N of the Prado: there are numerous snack bars and cheap restaurants. *Club de la Prensa*, Calle Campero, set in a pleasant garden, the limited menu is typical Bolivian—meat only, in copious quantities—and the company is lively; *Confitería Club de la Paz*, Camacho 1202, on the corner where Ayacucho joins Av Mcal Santa Cruz, good tea room, traditional, serious atmosphere, meeting place for businessmen and politicians, great coffee, expensive; *Torino*, at the hotel in Socabaya, is rec for excellent set lunch, US$1.50; next to *Torino*, *Chifa Jardín*, Socabaya 48, good, cheap Chinese; nearby, also in Socabaya is *Salteñería Super Salteña*; *Confitería California*, Potosí 1008, Centro Comercial Cristal, does good set lunches for US$2, also on Potosí, *Repostería Alemana* (*Nollo*)

Restaurant – Peña
Los Escudos

- TYPICAL MUSIC
- TYPICAL DRINKS
- TYPICAL DANCES
- TYPICAL FOODS

IN FOLKLORIC SHOW
Los Escudos

Every day from Monday to Saturday
**AV. MARISCAL SANTA CRUZ
EDIFICIO CLUB DE LA PAZ**
(Opposite the Post Office)

RESERVACIONES:
32 - 2028
35 - 0586

La Paz   Bolivia

for breakfasts, *La Kantuta*, in *Hotel Presidente*, No 920, excellent food, good service, *Subterráneo* (No 1120), cheap and OK, *Chez Pierre* (1320) good lunches, US$1.25, *Rincón Tarijeño La Choza*, good food at reasonable prices, and *Hogar Austriaco*, good lunches, pleasant. On Yanacocha, *La Fregata* (No 525), good value, and *La Tertulia*, near Ingavi, small, simple, charming, hot drinks and pastries. *Dumbo*, Camacho y Loayza, large portions, clean, very good; *Confitería Arabesque*, Mercado y Loayza, excellent *café con crema*; *Snack Conny*, Loayza opp San Juan de Dios, confitería, lunches, etc; *Casa Chang*, Juan de la Riva y Bueno, good set course Chinese meals, highly rec; *Los Pinochos*, Sanjines 553, excellent cheese empanadas and steaks, good food in large portions, popular café; *La Casa de los Paceños*, Sucre 856, very good, especially its *fritanga*. There are many other snack bars and Chinese restaurants on Calles Comercio (eg *Café Comercio*, next to *Hostal República*, *La Fuente de Soda*, No 801, good burgers, and *Salteñería Comercio*, No 1439, excellent *salteñas* and Bolivian food, outdoor seating) and Colón. *Taiwan*, opp Mercado Camacho, large portions, excellent. *Confitería Rivoli*, Colón 415, small and pleasant snack bar, good and cheap food. At Av Ayacucho 206 is the *Internacional*, a lunch-time favourite of local businessmen and has good shows Friday and Saturday nights.

Cheap vegetarian restaurants to recommend are the *Hotel Gloria Naranjos*, Potosí 909, buffet lunch, US$2, very popular, be there by 1200 for a table, closed Sun; *Andromeda*, Arce 2116, French, pricey but good, live music; *La Huerta*, Plaza Isabel La Católica, Av Arce, 1st floor, excellent salads, lunchtime and early evening, rec; *Natur Center*, Cañada Strongest 1852, lunches only, closed Sun; *Viscachani*, México 1290, lunches only, closed Sun. Vegetarian dishes served at *Palacio del Buen Gusto*, 18 de Julio 1698, closed weekends, not cheap.

Burgers: A good chain is *Clap's*, Centro Comercial El Patio, Av Arce, Calle Ayacucho, Calle Belisario Salinas, another chain is *Denny's*. Stalls in the Indian quarter sell hamburgers for US$0.75 each including chips, egg and tomato, have 2 for a filling meal, but don't have aji, mayonnaise or mustard if worried about hygiene and watch your burger being cooked.

Comedor Popular, often referred to as *Comedor Familiar*, for strictly limited budgets, cheap but filling local meals around US$0.80-1.50, available at Camacho and Lanza markets. The foodstalls at the top of Jiménez sell good T-bone steak cheaply. Bread from street vendors and Cochabamba wholemeal bread (*pan integral*) sold at the main markets, is rec. Fresh dairy produce at *Pil* on Bueno y Cárdenas. *Kremrik* is a chain of ice-cream parlours, with outlets at Plaza Murillo 542, and on Av Villazón, just off Plaza del Estudiante, good ice-cream. Good coffee at *Solo Café*, Potosí 1108, esq Socobaya and *Café Pierrot*, in *Hotel Gloria*. Patisseries: a good one at Bueno y Camacho, with apple pie and cakes; *Kuchen Stube*, Rosendo Gutiérrez, Ed Guadelquivir (closed Mon), and Edificio Mcal Ballivián, Mercado 1328 (hard to find), Mon-Fri 0930-1230, 1500-1900, very good cakes, coffee and German specialities.

The **Calacoto** district situated in The Valley 15 mins S of the city, "La Zona Sur" (US$0.40 by *trufi* or minibus), is home of the resident foreign community. Calacoto has recently developed into an important area in its own right: international shopping centres, supermarkets stocked with imported items and some of the best restaurants and bars in La Paz. The area begins after the bridge at La Florida where there is an attractive park, Plaza Humbolt – exhibitions of local art work on Sun and a collection of kiosks selling cheap snacks. The main road, Av Ballivián begins here at Calle 8 and continues up the hill to the shopping district of San Miguel on Calle 21 (about a 20 min walk). On the main avenue, corner of Calle 8 is *El Viejo Tonel*, Brazilian rodizio restaurant, bar and disco (young crowd). Next, on the right side of the avenue, between Calle 9 y 10 is *Rumors*, an American/Mexican bar, restaurant, excellent music, popular late night place. *Puerto del Sol*, good Chinese on the left on the corner of Calle 11. Opposite, still on the main road, is an excellent arts and handicrafts shop, weavings, ceramics, silver etc. Continuing up the hill on Av Ballivián between Calle 15 y 16 on the left is *The Britannia*, Bolivia's only authentic English pub, open Tues-Sun from 1700, cosy, popular with regular ex-pat crowd. Batemans XXXB best English bitter, bar snacks, darts etc. English owner, Tom Clough, moved this well-known local from its former location on the shores of Lake Titikaka in Dec 1994. Highly rec. Next door to The Britannia on the avenue is *Abracadabra*, open 7 days for lunch and dinner, great ribs, best hamburgers and pizza in La Paz, American owner, rec. Five minutes walk further up the hill on the right is Calle 21 – the church of San Miguel on the corner of the avenue is an easy landmark – which has a huge variety of shops, fast-food cafés, banks and a post office. Back on the main avenue and continuing up the hill between Calle 24 y 25 is *The Suisse Chalet*, excellent fondue, steaks, expensive but rec, and almost next door *The Galeon* for some of the city's best seafood.

Airline Offices Lloyd Aéreo Boliviano (LAB), Camacho 1460, T 367701/7/367718/371020; Aero Sur, 16 de Julio 1607, T 371834, F 390457; British Airways at Martín Travel, Av 20 de Octubre 2164, T 340831/355541, F 391641; KLM, Av Arce 2355; American Airlines, Av 16 de Julio 1440, Edificio Herman, T 372009. In Edif Avenida, 16 de Julio 1490 are AeroPerú, 2nd floor, T 370002-4, and Viasa, planta baja, T 327223. Aerolíneas Argentinas, Edificio Banco de la Nación Argentina, Av 16 de Julio 1486, T 351711/351624; Qantas, Av 16 de Julio, Ed Cosmos, planta baja, T 322903. Varig, Av Mcal Santa Cruz 1392, Edif Cámara de Comercio, T 314040, F 391131.

Banks Money is changed in hotels or *casas de cambio* rather than in banks. **Citibank**, on the Prado (cashes its own TCs, very high commission and will receive money sent from any US bank), but will not advance cash to holders of Citibank Mastercard. **Banco Industrial**, Av Gral Camacho 1333, open 0830-1700, Sat 1000-1300, good service, changes cash and TCs. Cash advance (in bolivianos) on Visa and Mastercard at **Banco de La Paz** on Prado (limit US$300 per day, no commission). **Banco Santa Cruz de la Sierra, Banco Mercantil**, ground floor, **Banco Popular, Banco Nacional** and **Banco Boliviano Americano**, among others; Banco Santa Cruz branch in Shopping Norte is open Sat pm. **Visa** has an office on Av Camacho 1448, 11th and 12th floors, T 369975/357014, F 354066, for cancelling cost or stolen credit cards. Automatic cash dispensers for Visa and Mastercard can be found at several sites in the city including Av Camacho 1223, the airport and Shopping Norte shopping centre (look for the sign Enlace – Visa at branches of ATC). **Amex**, Av 16 de Julio 1490, piso 5, T 323954/341201.

Exchange Houses Sudamer, Colón 256, good rates also for currencies other than US$ (1% commission on TCs into dollars, frequently rec); **Unitours**, Mercado 1300, 1% commission on TCs. **Casa de Cambio Silver**, Mercado 979, charges 1% commission to change TCs into dollars; similarly **D'Argent**, Mercado 1328, free coffee and drinking water, US$ only (will change TCs into dollars at 1% commission).**Kantuta**, Av Mcal Santa Cruz 1326. Some *cambios* verify passports. Some deal in Argentine and Chilean pesos. Street changers can be found at corners around Camacho, Colón and Prado. It is not worth dealing on the black market since there is virtually no difference between black and official rates. NB if arriving on Friday night, bring bolivianos or US dollars cash as it is difficult to change TCs at the weekend (try *El Lobo* restaurant, which usually changes TCs at any time, good rates, or *Hotel Gloria* which gives good rates for most western currencies). If you leave Bolivia with bolivianos you may not be able to change them in neighbouring countries. Watch out for forged currency, especially dollars and Chilean pesos.

Embassies and Consulates Argentine Consulate, Sánchez Lima 497, T 353089/343516; **Brazilian Consulate**, Av 20 de Octubre, 20-38 Edificio Fonconain, Embassy piso 11, visa office, piso 9, T 352108, 0900-1300, Mon-Fri (visas take 2 days). **Chilean Consulate**, H Siles 5843, corner of Calle 13, Obrajes district, T 785269, open Mon-Fri 0830-1130 (visa same day if requested in the morning, take microbus N, A or L from Av 16 de Julio). **Ecuador** 16 de Julio 1440, piso 14, T 321208. **Paraguayan Consulate**, 7th floor Edificio Venus, Av Arce 2105, just below Calle Montevideo (very good visa service), T 322018; **Peruvian Consulate and Embassy**, 6 de Agosto 2190 y Calle F Guachalla, Edif Alianza, T 353550, 0930-1300 (a visa costs US$10 in US$ bills, issued same day if you go early); **Venezuelan Embassy and Consulate**, Av Arce 2678, Ed Illimani, 4th floor, T 375023 (consulate open Mon, Wed, Fri 0900-1200 – visas are only given to Bolivian residents, if you need one, get it in your home country).

United States Embassy and Consulate, Av Arce 2780, opp Edif Illimani, T 350120/430251, F 359875, Casilla 425. **Canadian Consulate**, Av 20 de Octubre 2475, Plaza Avaroa, T 375224, Mon-Fri. 0900-1200. **Japanese Embassy**, Rosendo Gutiérrez 497, esq Sánchez Lima, PO Box 2725, T 373151.

Austrian Consulate, Edif Petrolero, 7th floor, Oficina 1, Av 16 de Julio 1616, T 326601, 1600-1800; **British Embassy and Consulate**, Av Arce 2732-2754, T 357424, F 391063, Casilla 694, Mon-Thur 0900-1200, 1400-1600, Fri 0900-1300, has a list of travel hints for Bolivia, doctors, etc; **Danish Consulate**, Federico Zuazo 1598, Edif Park Inn, Piso 11, Casilla 662, T 360655/1, F 376380; **Finnish Consulate**, Mercado 1004, c/o Sibo SA, T 350900/367227; **French Consulate**, Av Hernando Siles 5390, esq Calle 08, Obrajes, T 786114 (take bus No 11 or microbus N, A or L down Av 16 de Julio); **Belgian Embassy** is 1 block from French at No 5290, T 784925; **German Embassy**, Av Arce 2395, T 390850, slow service, Mon-Fri 0900-1200; **Italian Embassy**, 6 de Agosto 2575, PO Box 626, T 323597, F 391075; **Netherlands Consulate**, Av Arce 2031, Edif Victorio, 2nd floor, T 355701; **Norwegian Consulate**, Calle Presbítero Medina 2516, T 322528; **Spanish Consulate**, Av Arce y Calle Cordero, T 343518; **Swedish Consulate**, Av Arce 2856, Casilla de Correo 852, T 327535, open 0900-1200; **Swiss Embassy**, Av 16 de Julio 1616, 6th floor, T 353091, F 391462, Casilla 9356, open 0900-1200, 1400-1500; **Israeli Embassy**, Av Mcal Santa Cruz, Edificio Esperanza, 10th floor, T 358676/371287, Casilla 1309/1320.

Entertainment Best entertainment for visitors are the folk shows (*peñas*). Outstanding folk show at *Peña Naira* (US$5, includes first drink), Sagárnaga 161, T 325736, every night about

2215. Various restaurants have shows worth seeing. At these, visitors will be able to listen to the wide variety of local musical instruments, the different types of flutes, including the *quena*, and the *charango*, a small guitar with five strings, the body of which was originally made from the shell of an armadillo. Enquire at the *Rumillajta* shop (in the *galería* close to San Francisco church) about future performances by the famous folk group of that name. Good *peña* at *Casa del Corregidor*, Calle Murillo 1040 (T 363633), dinner show Mon-Thur, no cover charge, Fri and Sat *peña* US$4, colonial atmosphere, traditional music and dance (see also under **Restaurants**); nearby is *La Luna*, Oruro y Murillo, great live bands, contemporary music. See also under restaurants for *Los Escudos*. Another *peña* is *Marko Tambo* on Calle Jaén, US$7 (all incl) repeatedly rec (also sells woven goods). Indian dance halls, for example on Max Paredes, should only be visited in the company of Bolivians. If you wish to learn a local indstrument, contact *Academia "Walisuma"*, Av Apumalla 512 (old Cemetery District between José M Asin and José M Aliaga): Pedro Mar teaches bi-lingual courses, English/Spanish, for *quena*, *zampoña* and *charango*.

Good salsa at *El Loro en su Salsa*, on Rosendo Gutiérrez on corner of Av 6 de Agosto, open Thur, Fri and Sat pm. *Bar Socavón*, Aspiazu y 20 de Octubre 2172, Sopocachi, T 353998, has live music Thur-Sat, music videos Wed, very popular. On Calle Belisario Salinas in Sopocachi Bajo, is *Piano Bar*, cosy, with a fireplace, live piano music, good drinks and snacks. On the same street in *Panyco*, live music, rec; and *Caras y Caretas*, live music, food, good atmosphere. *Café Montmarte*, Fernando Guachalla, off Av 6 de Agosto, next to Alliance Française, set lunch US$4, bar with live music Thur, Fri, Sat. Excellent jazz at *Marius Club*, Presbitero Medina y Salazar (near Plaza Avaroa). Local radio station, *Radio Fides*, Calle Sanjines y Sucre, Andean music on Thur, when it is open to public (2000, US$0.75), not all year round, check in advance, T 359191.

La Paz has a resident ballet and symphony orchestra, but no theatre company. There are some good **cinemas**, films being mainly in English. For film buffs there is the excellent Cinemateca Boliviana, Pichincha y Indaburo, La Paz's art film centre with festivals, courses, etc (entry US$0.75 for students). **Casa Municipal de la Cultura "Franz Tamayo"**, almost opp Plaza San Francisco, hosts a variety of exhibitions, paintings, sculpture, photography, videos, etc, most of which are free. The **Palacio Chico** (Ayacucho y Potosí, in old Correo), operated by the Secretaría Nacional de Cultura, also has exhibitions (good for modern art), concerts and ballet. The SNC is also in charge of many regional museums. Listings available in Palacio Chico.

There are clown and mime shows in Parque del Ejército on Sunday, colourful and popular; the Parque Central has a children's amusement park, US$0.20.

Hospitals *Clínica del Accidentado*, Plaza Uyuni 1351, T 328632/321888 offers first aid. Efficient and well run nursing homes such as *Clínica Americana* (Av 14 de Septiembre 78, T 783509), *Clínica Alemana* (6 de Agosto 2821, T 323023/327521/373676, good), *Clínica Rengel* (T 390792/8), *Clínica Santa María*, Av 6 de Agosto 2487, efficient and not too expensive, *Clínica del Sur*, Av Hernando Siles y Calle Siete, Obrajes. **Red Cross** opposite Mercado Camacho will give inoculations if required, T 323642. *The Methodist Hospital* (12th block of Obrajes, T 783809, take "A" *micro* from the Prado) runs clinic at US$5, telephone for appointment.

Health and Hygiene If suffering from *soroche*, ask in chemists/pharmacies for suitable medication. Malaria pills and yellow fever vaccination, US$15.50 including certificate are available at *Centro Piloto de Salva*, Av Montes y Basces, T 369141 about 10 mins walk from Plaza San Francisco, N of the main bus station, rec as helpful and friendly. *Laboratorio Inti*, Socabaya 266, has been recommended, also for vaccines (human immunoglobulin, cholera, rabies vaccine - but make sure you know precisely how it should be administered). Tampons may be bought at most *farmacias* and supermarkets; others say they are impossible to find, especially outside La Paz. The daily paper, *Presencia*, lists chemists/pharmacies on duty (*de turno*). For contact lenses, *Optaluis*, Comercio 1089, a stock of 5,000 lenses, including "semiduros".

Doctors Check that any medical equipment used is sterilised. Dr Ricardo Udler, Edificio Mcal de Ayacucho, Calle Loayza, T 360393/327046, speaks very good German, rec. Dr César H Moreno, Pinilla 274, Edif Pinilla, T 433805/792665 (home), rec. Dr Eduardo Fernández, Edif Avenida, Av 16 de Julio, 9th floor of 3, T 370385 (surgery)/795164 (home), speaks English, rec. **Dentists** Dr and Dra Osorio at *Hostal Austria*, Yanacocha 531. Dr Horacio M Rosso, Av 20 de Octubre, Edificio Guadalquivir, T 35475, his wife speaks German, rec. Also rec: Dr Benjamín Calvo Paz, Edificio Illimani, Av Arce esq Campos, T 343706, and Dra Esperanza Eid, Edificio Libertad, Potosí, Piso 9, No 909, both speak English. Tourist Office has a list of doctors and dentists who speak foreign languages.

Language Schools *Centro Boliviano Americano* (address under **Libraries** below) US$140 for

2 months, 1¹/₂ hrs tuition each afternoon. *Alliance Française* (see also below). *Fastalk*, T 812341, offers Spanish and Portuguese courses, 1 week or 1 month, 3 hrs a day; *Instituto de La Lengua Española*, Calle 14 Final Derecha Esq Aviador No 80, Achumani, T 796074. For English language teaching try *Pan American English Centre*, Av Villazón y Pasaje Bernardo Trigo 429, T 379654, Casilla 5244, native speakers only, minimum stay 3 months.

Laundromats Wash and dry, 6-hour service, at *Gelmi-Lava-Sec*, 20 de Octubre 2019, suite 9, T 352930, helpful service, US$1.40 for 1 kg; *Lavandería Cinco Estrellas*, 20 de Octubre 1714, US$3 for 3 kg. *Limpieza Rosario*, Av Manco Kapac, nr Hotel Andes; *Lavandería Bandel*, Av Mcal Santa Cruz 1032, local 10, T 353563; *Lavandería Select*, Av Arce, down from *Hotel La Paz*; 3-hour service, rec; *Limpieza Finesse*, Illampu 865. Usual charge US$1 per kg. Normally leave laundry early morning and collect same evening. Laundry service at *Oficina Gregoria Apazá*, Colombia y Almirante Grau, T 369607, phone first. Sra Elena Aranda offers laundry and repairs service, meets people on ground floor of Post Office. Dry cleaning, Calle Murillo 1366, US$.15 per kg, *La Esmeralda*, Colón 558.

Libraries *Centro Boliviano Americano* (CBA), Parque Zenón Iturralde 121, T 351627/342582 (10 mins walk from Plaza Estudiante down Av Arce), has public library and recent US papers (Mon-Fri 0900-1230, 1500-1930). *USIS* has lending library and 2nd-hand paperbacks. *Alliance Française*, F Guachalla 399 y Av 20 de Octubre, T 324075 (open Mon-Fri 1600-2000), has an old library. *Goethe-Institut*, Av 6 de Agosto 2118, T 374453 (Mon-Thurs, 1600-2000), good library, recent papers in German, videos in German and Spanish.

Post Office Correo Central, Av Mariscal Santa Cruz y Oruro (Mon-Sat 0800-2200, Sun 0900-1200 only). Stamps are sold only at the post office. Good philately section on first floor. There are a number of shops selling good postcards, etc. Poste Restante keeps letters for 3 months, good service, no charge. Procedure for sending parcels: all is arranged downstairs (open office hours only, Mon-Fri 0800-1200, 1430-1830); you must buy official packaging, US$1 for each parcel. Find out the price of postage before mailing parcels as the service is very expensive. Don't forget moth balls (difficult to buy – try Calle Sagárnaga) for textile items. To collect parcels costs at least US$0.50. Express postal service is on the top floor, expensive.

DHL, Av Mcal Santa Cruz 1297.

Telecommunications Entel (T 367474) office for telephone calls is at Ayacucho 267 (the only one open on Sun), and in Edif Libertad, Calle Potosí. Pay for overseas calls in advance. Long wait for incoming calls. Fax also from Ayacucho 267.

Places of Worship Protestant Community Church (inter-denominational), in English, American Co-operative School, Calle 10 Calacoto (T 795639 or 792052). Sunday service at 1100, but there are "lots of activities during the week". Anglican-Episcopalian services are held at the Community Church on the third Sunday of each month. **Synagogues** Calle Landaeta 330 (Sat am services only); Colegio Boliviano Israëlito, Cañada Strongest 1846 for Friday service—it looks like a private house.

Shopping Look around and bargain first. There are good jewellery stores throughout the city (eg *Joyería Cosmos*, Handal Center, Loc 13, Socabaya y Camacho, Inca and Bolivian designs in gold and silver, colonial objects) but visit the gold factories for lower prices and special orders. There is inexpensive silver and jewellery in the little cabinets outside Lanza market on Av Santa Cruz. Up Sagárnaga, by the side of San Francisco church (behind which are many handicraft stalls in the Mercado Artesanal), are booths and small stores with interesting local items of all sorts, best value on Sunday am when prices are reduced. The lower end of Sagárnaga is best for antiques. At Sagárnaga 177 is an entire gallery of handicraft shops: *Artesanía Nacional Tiwanaku*, for paintings, silver jewellery and woven goods, and, although there have been complaints about quality and price, a visit is a must. Upstairs is *Artesanía Sajama*, rec for woollens. *Millma*, Sagárnaga 225, and in *Hotel Radisson*, for alpaca sweaters (made in their own factory) and antique and rare textiles. *Wari* on Sagárnaga will make to measure very quickly, English spoken, prices reasonable; also *Toshy* on Sagárnaga for top quality knitwear. *Artesanía Sorata*, Linares 862, and Sagárnaga 311, 0900-1930, Mon-Sat, specializes in dolls, sweaters and weavings made by a women's cooperative and handmade textiles. Along Murillo and between Sagárnaga and Santa Cruz are various little shops selling old ponchos and rugs. For musical instruments: *Rumillajta*, one of the Galería shops adjacent to the San Francisco church entrance; many shops in Linares, eg *Sumaj Supay*, No 851, also sell woollen goods, also *Coral* at No 852 (very good waistcoats, rugs, etc.). Other music shops (LPs, CDs, cassettes) on Evaristo Valle. Alpaca goods are about 50% dearer than in Puno; sweaters are much more expensive than Peru (beware of moths in woollen goods). The maximum you can bargain prices down is 20%. Handmade clothing for children is good value. Most shops close Saturday afternoon and Sunday. Very cheap rubber stamps are made on Sagárnaga, to your own, or local designs. See also the "witchcraft market" on Calles Melchor Jiménez, and Linares, which cross Calle Santa Cruz above San Francisco, fascinating items for sale.

Artículos Regionales in Plaza de los Estudiantes is rec. *Suma Ampara*, Av Villazón 1958, wide variety of woven goods, but prices not as low as in street markets. The rec *Casa Fisher* (see Cochabamba **Shopping**) has an outlet in Handal Center, Store No 2, Calles Mcal Santa Cruz y Socabaya, T/F 392948. Antique stores at El Prado 1615, Javier Núñez de Arco downstairs, his father upstairs, nice items, very expensive, also old photographs.

The Indian market is a good place for ponchos and local handicrafts. Many Indian objects are sold near Av Buenos Aires, and Indian musical instruments on Calle Granier, near the General Cemetery. On Calle Los Andes, above Buenos Aires, there are several embroidery shops. At Gallardo 1080, 1 block above Buenos Aires, there is the small workshop of the late master mask maker, Antonio Viscarra, now run by his daughter and son-in-law. Costume, mask and trinket shops for Gran Poder abound above Buenos Aires. Food market is the Mercado Camacho (Camacho y Bolívar). The Tourist Office has a full list of all markets.

Shopping Norte, Potosí y Socabaya, is a new, modern mall with restaurants and expensive merchandise.

Bookshops Large stock of English, French and German books, and US magazines, at *Los Amigos del Libro*, Mercado 1315, also Edificio Alameda, Av 16 de Julio (1 block from *Plaza Hotel*) and El Alto airport, rec; they also sell a few tourist maps of the region from Puno to the Yungas, and walking-tour guides. Amigos del Libro will ship books. *Gisbert*, Comercio 1270, books, maps, stationery, will ship overseas, rec. *Multi-Libro*, Loayza 233, T 391996, small, good for maps, politics, religion, psychology etc (ask if you don't see what you want), open till 2100 Mon-Fri, and am Sat and Sun. *El Umbral*, Potosí 1375, T 361282, and *Hisbol*, Zapata 178, for academic subjects. *Librería La Paz*, Colón y Ballivián (wide selection of maps). Historian Antonio Paredes-Candia has a kiosk selling rare historical works on Villazón, opp San Andrés University. *Librería Martínez Acchini*, Arce 2132, good for technical books. There are 2nd-hand stalls on Av Ismael Montes; there are occasional book fairs on the Prado. German books available at Goethe Institut (see below).

Films For Kodak, Casa Kavlin, Calle Potosí 1130; Laboratorio Fuji Color, Potosí 1316; Foto Linares, Mercado y Loayza, will develop both Ansco and Agfa colour film, 1-day service on black-and-white, rec. *Foto 88*, Ayacucho 224, quick for slide developing (24 hrs), prints in 2 hrs, colour not so good. *Full Color* is the cheapest chain for developing but quality is variable; *Fotoplan* on Calle Graneros highly rec. Fuji transparency film available at half shop price in

market, and Agfa transparency film for about US$5. Cheap Fuji, Kodak and Konika film from stalls nr San Francisco. In all cases check dates on film. **Repairs** at Av Sánchez Lima 2178 by Rolando Calla C, just ring bell (1400-1700), there is no sign; also at Potosí 1316, between 1000-1200, T 373621, very helpful, professional, fair prices.

Sport There are two golf clubs (Mallasilla, the world's highest, and Pinos). Non-members can play at Mallasilla on weekdays: club hire is possible, green free, clubs, balls, and caddie US$37, the course is empty on weekdays, no need to book; it is in good condition and beautiful. After your round have a drink in the small outside bar. There are two tennis clubs (La Paz Tennis and Sucre Tennis); and two riding clubs. Football is popular and played on Wed and Sun at the Siles Stadium in Miraflores, two clubs (Micro A); there are reserved seats. Basketball is played in Plaza del Estudiante on Mon, Wed and Fri in season. YMCA sportsground and gymnasium, opposite the University of San Andrés, Av Villazón, and clubhouse open to the public, Av 20 de Octubre 1839 (table tennis, billiards, etc); regular meetings Tues and Thurs 1930 of a mountaineering group which runs weekend excursions. **Snooker/Pool** *San Luis*, Edificio México, 2do Sótano, Calle México 1411, *Picco's*, Edificio 16 de Julio, Av 16 de Julio 1566, both places rec for good tables and friendly atmosphere. See also under **Skiing** and **Mountaineering** under **Excursions** below.

Cycle Spares Try the shop at the Velódromo in Alto Irpavi, about 10 km out of town; the cheap cycle chains made in India and sold in shops in the centre of La Paz are not rec.

Tour Companies and Travel Agents *Crillon Tours*, Av Camacho 1223, Casilla 4785 (T 374566, F 391039), with 24-hr ATM for cash on credit cards; in USA, 1450 South Bayshore Dr, suite 815, Miami, FL 33131, T (305) 358-5853, F (305) 372-0054. *Transturin*, Camacho 1321 (T 328560/363654, F 391162, Telex 2301 TRTURIN BV): these two agencies offer full travel services, with tours ranging from La Paz to the whole country; full details of their Lake Titicaca services will be found on p 274. *Turismo Balsa*, Capitán Ravelo 2077 (T 357817, F 391310) and Av 16 de Julio 1650 (T 354049), PO Box 5889, city and local tours (rec), **see also under Lake Titicaca, p 274**; *Turisbus* (Illampu 702, Casilla 442, T 325348/369542, F 375532), helpful, trekking equipment rented, agent for Peruvian railways, ENAFER, tickets (to Puno and Cuzco—US$12 and US$31, also local and Bolivian tours), rec. *Exprinter*, Edificio Herrman, Plaza Venezuela (also operates exchange facilities) to Cuzco via Copacabana, US$30.

Magri Turismo, Av 16 de Julio 1490, 5th floor, T 323954/341201, F 366309, Amex representative: gives TCs against American Express card, but cannot give cash or exchange TCs; offers all other Amex emergency services and clients' mail, recommended for tours in Bolivia, travel services. *Pachamama Tours*, Av Mcal Santa Cruz y Colón, Galería Ed Litoral, subsuelo, of 17, T 322311, recommended for tours of La Paz, Tiwanaku, Titicaca, etc, also arranges tours throughout Bolivia; *Diana Tours*, Sagárnaga 328, T 340356/375374/350252, F 360831, some English spoken, good tour to Coroico but Tiwanaku expensive; *Titikaka Tours*, Loayza between Riva and Camacho, good for flights; *Tawa Tours*, Sagárnaga 161 and Rosenda Gutiérrez 701, T 325796, run jungle tours to their own camp as well as the Salt Lake areas, friendly, good guides (also charter flights to Europe and USA). *Shima Tours*, Potosí 1310, very helpful, good for flight tickets; *Cóndor Tours*, Sagárnaga, cheap; *Combi Tours*, Illampu 734, T 367896; *Seul Travel*, Plaza San Francisco, arranges tours to the Yungas for more than one day, helpful; *Transamazonas*, Edificio Cosmos, Piso 10, Oficina 3, Av 16 de Julio 1800, T 350411, tours to Salt Lakes and the Beni (also at the *Restaurant El Lobo*). *Fremen*, Plaza Abaroa, T 327073/376336, F 367329, range of tours incl to the Beni. *Paititi SRL*, Calle Pedro Salazar 848, T 353558/341018/342759, F 329625, organizes adventure tours, rec, Javier Prudencio is helpful and speaks several languages. *Peru Bolivian Tours*, Loayza, Ed Mcal de Ayacucho PB - Of 8, T 363720, F 365845. *Expediciones Guarachi*, Plaza Alonso de Mendoza, Edif Santa Ana, of 314, T 320901/310655, F 392344, treks and mountaineering to many lesser-known and remote destinations, highly rec for their expertise and efficiency. Also *Carmoar Tours*, Calle Bueno 159, which is headed by Günther Ruttger (T/F 340633), has information and maps for the Inca Trail to Coroico, rents trekking gear. For information on and arrangement of climbing and adventure tours, *Colibrí*, Sagárnaga 309, see under **Mountaineering** below. *Reinaldo Pou Munt*, Capitán Ravelo 2401, T 327226, Casilla 13632, expensive, offers excellent tours of the city and environs, speaks English and German. *Nuevo Continente*, Manco Kapac 366, T 373423/812479, rec for trip to Zongo, Clemente is a good driver, cheap service to airport, very friendly and helpful. Roberto Méndez, speaks English, rec for private tours, contact through Marta in the Mercado de Hechicería, Calle JM Linares, near Sagárnaga, opp No 896. Many agencies arrange excursions or travel to Peru (Puno, Cusco, Arequipa), as well as local tours. A one-day tour to Coroico is popular, US$22. See also names and addresses under "Exchange Houses", p 253.

NB Unless indicated in the list above, services offered by travel agents are expensive, some being criticised as overpriced. We have also been told that many services to Peru and beyond deteriorate markedly once Bolivia has been left (commitments unfulfilled, buses changed, extra passengers taken on—but **see also Peru to Bolivia—Peru, Section 5**). Note also that flight tickets can be bought more reliably from airlines than through agencies.

Tourist Office Secretaría de Turismo, Mercado 1328, between Loayza and Colón, Edif Mcal Ballivián, 18th floor, T 358213, F 374630, open Mon-Fri 0830-1200, 1430-1830. Information office at the bottom end of Av 16 de Julio (Prado) on Plaza del Estudiante on corner with C México, free leaflets, map of La Paz US$2.25. Telephone directories in La Paz have economic and tourist information in English on all the provinces.

Maps Instituto Geográfico Militar, Av 16 de Julio 1471, T 364416, open Mon-Fri 0900-1200, 1500-1900. The IGM head office is at Estado Mayor General, Av Saavedra Final, Miraflores. You must show your passport to enter the head office, but any map can be delivered to the Prado office, which has copies of all those available, within 24 hours. Topographic maps cost US$5.25 per sheet, US$4 for a photocopy (scale 1:50,000) and US$8, US$7 photocopy (scale 1:250,000). A 3-sheet map of La Paz costs US$5.25 per sheet; a 3-sheet map of La Paz Department, including Lake Titicaca, costs US$9.20; 1-sheet national communications map, US$6; 4-sheet country map, political 1988, 1:1,500,000 US$10.50; 9-sheet hydrographical map, 1990 1:1,000,000, US$17. Departmental road maps are meant to be available in the tourist offices in the capitals of each department but often they are out of stock. Senac (the national road service) publishes a Red Vial 1989 map, which is probably the best, but is still inaccurate, about US$4.50 from the office on 8th floor of Ministerio de Transporte y Communicaciones, Av Mcal Santa Cruz, tall building behind Correo, open till 1800, have to show passport. Also reported as inaccurate are the maps of the Automóvil Club Boliviano. Maps are generally hard to find. Maps are sold at Ichthus bookshop on the Prado, No 1800; also at Librería La Paz and Amigos del Libro (**See p 256**). Tourist map of La Paz, US$2.25.

Useful Addresses Instituto Nacional de Arqueología de Bolivia, Calle Tiwanaku 93. **Immigration**, to renew a visa go to Migración Bolivia, Av Camacho 1433 (opp Banco de Santa Cruz), T 359665, Mon-Fri 0900-1200, 1600-1800. **Tourist Police**, Mercado 1328, Edif Ballivián 18° piso, for insurance claims after theft, English spoken, helpful. YMCA, 20 de Octubre 1839, Casilla 963. **Asociación Boliviana de Agencias de Viajes y Turismo**, Edif Litoral, Mariscal Santa Cruz 1351, Casilla 3967.

Local Buses There are three types of city bus: large Fiat buses run by the city corporation, on fairly limited routes; *micros* (Bluebird-type buses), which charge US$0.30; and minivans, marginally more expensive, but quicker than *micros*.

Taxis US$1-1.25, for short trips within city limits. *Trufis* are fixed route collective taxis which charge US$0.35 within city limits. Fares out of town are given under **Excursions** below. Taxi drivers are not tipped. Don't let the driver turn the lights out at night. Radio taxis, many companies, eg Alfa T 322427, La Rápida 392323 (standard fare in centre US$1.10, to suburbs US$2.20).

Car Hire Cars may be hired direct from **Imbex**, Av Montes 520, T 379884, F 322947, well maintained Suzuki jeeps (US$45/day, highly rec); **National**, F Zuazo 1935, T/F 376581, rec; **Avis** at Martin Travel, Plaza del Estudiante 1920; **Rent-a-Car International**, F Suazo 1942, T 357061; **Kolla Motors**, Rosendo Gutiérrez 502, T 341660/351701 who have well-maintained four-wheel drive Toyota jeeps (which seat 6), insurance and gasoline extra. **Petita Rent-a-car**, Cañada Strongest 1857-A, T 379182, F 322596, Swiss owners Ernesto Hug and Aldo Rezzonico, rec for well-maintained VW "beetles" and 4WD jeeps, etc, also offer adventure tours, **Jeeping Bolivia**, German, French, English spoken, rec. One can also hire experienced drivers for US$25 a day plus accommodation and meals. Eduardo Figueroa, T 786281, taxi driver and travel agent, recommended. Adolfo Monje Palacios, in front of *Hotel El Dorado* or T 354384 highly rec for short or long trips. Oscar Vera, Simón Aguirre 2158, Villa Copacabana, La Paz, T 230453, specializes in trips to the Salar de Uyuni and the Western Cordillera, speaks English, rec.

Motorcycle rental: Moto Rent, Av Busch 1255, Miraflores Norte, T 357289, 650 Kawasaki endurance type, US$50/day unlimited mileage, US$250/week.

Garage for VW and other makes: Ernesto Hug, Av Jaime Freyre 2326, T 342279 (see also **Car Hire** above) highly rec. *Car Park* on corner of Ingavi and Sanjines, US$1.75 for 24 hrs, safe and central.

Airport El Alto, above La Paz, the highest commercial airport in the world (4,018m) connected to the city by motorway, T 810122. A taxi between the centre and airport takes about 30 mins, US$8 but may be negotiated down; current prices, including luggage, should be on display at the airport exit (enquire at the tourist office in town, or at the airport). Cotranstur minibuses, white with "Cotranstur" and "Aeropuerto" written on the side and back, go from anywhere on the Prado and Av Mcal Santa Cruz to the airport between 0800-0830 to 1900-2000, US$1.50, best to have little luggage, departures from the airport every 5 mins or so; colectivos from opposite *Hotel Crillón* (Plaza Isabel La Católica) charge US$2.65 pp, carrying 4 passengers. Micros marked "El Alto", "Río Seco", "Alto Lima", "Ceja", 30 mins to summit, then $1/2$-hr walk to airport. There is a duty-free shop but it can sometimes forget to open. Bank in international departures hall will change cash. The international departures hall is the main concourse, with all check-in desks and is the hall for all domestic arrivals and departures. Small tourist office at the Airport, some maps available, English spoken, helpful (when staffed). The coffee shop inexpensive and serves good breakfasts.

Air Taxis Contact Major Pericón of Taxi Aéreo Urkupiña, T 350580, 812099. Aero Inca, T 361018. Alas Doradas T 354070.

Air Services LAB, Aero Sur (T 371833), TAM and Kantuta (T 390290) fly to the main cities and towns. Fares are comparatively low for internal flights. (For details, see under destinations.)

Bus Services (for information, T 367275/367274); buses to: **Oruro, Potosí, Sucre, Cochabamba, Santa Cruz, Tarija** and **Villazón**, leave from the main terminal at Plaza Antofagasta (micros 2, M, CH or 130), see under each destination for details. Beware of taxi rip-offs, false police and theft from buses as they pull in at the bus station. The terminal (open 0700-2300) has a post office, ENTEL, restaurant, luggage store and agencies, such as Turisbus, Diana, Vicuña (cheaper than their offices in town).

Buses to **Sorata, Copacabana** and **Tiahuanaco** do not leave from the bus station but from the Cemetery district. Companies located here include Flota Copacabana, Manco Kapac, 2 de Febrero, Ingavi, Morales. To get to the Cemetery district, take any bus or kombi marked "Cementerio" going up Calle Santa Cruz; the route is Santa Cruz, Max Paredes, Garita de Lima, Mariano Bautista, Plaza Félix Reyes Ortiz/Tomás Katari (look out for the cemetery arch on your left). On Plaza Reyes Ortiz are Manco Kapac (T 350033) and 2 de Febrero (T 377181) for Copacabana and Tiquina. From the Plaza go up Av Kollasuyo and at the 2nd street on the right (Manuel Bustillos) is the terminal for kombis to Huatajata and Huarina, and buses for Sorata (Trans Tur Sorata and, nearby, Larecaja). Several micros (20, J, 10) and kombis (223, 252, 270, 7) go up Kollasuyo; look for "Kollasuyo" on the windscreen in most, but not all, cases.

Buses to **Coroico and the Yungas** leave from Villa Fátima (25 mins by micros B,V,X,K, 131,

135, or 136, or *trufis* 2 or 9, which pass Pérez Velasco coming down from Plaza Mendoza, and get off at the service station, Calle Yanacachi 1434).

International Buses To Buenos Aires, daily at 1800, Expreso Panamericano, 3 days, US$135 incl meals, 10% student discount, but you have to insist. Service advertised as direct, but you have to change at Villazón and walk across the border. (Cheaper to book to Villazón and rebook in Argentina). To **Arica** via the frontier at Tambo Quemado and Chungará the only reliable service is at 0500 Tues and Fri, US$20, with Litoral, T 358603 (office No 19 bus terminal), 18-19 hrs; there is also Tues and Fri at 2030, US$21, Expreso Panamericano. To Arica via the frontier at Charaña and Visviri in stages (no direct service), Senobus (Calle Hujutri, 400 m from train station in direction of Cementerio), Tues, Fri, Sat evenings (US$8.50) or (cheaper) El Cariñoso. In Charaña take taxi to Visviri (US$0.50), then colectivo taxi to Arica US$10. It is a beautiful, exhausting trip, but doing it in stages, rather than straight through, involves extra waiting at the border, all companies involve several changes of bus ("an 18-hr passage, swallowing dust all the time, but worth it at half the cost of the *ferrobus*"). Military checks can be expected both sides of the frontier. To **Iquique** and Arica, Tues, Thurs and Sat at 1830, US$32, Geminis (T 378255, when office in bus station is closed, Diana Tours at office No 5 also sell tickets), Iquique 20 hrs, Arica 24 hrs. To **Tacna**, also with Litoral, Thurs or Sun 0700, US$17.50, 13-16 hours; a very bad road, but an alternative if all other routes to Arica are truly booked (there are no Bolivian customs or immigration at the border for exit stamp, Peruvian entry is given in Tacna). Colectivos and agencies to **Puno** daily with different companies (eg Colectur) most easily booked through travel agencies, US$10-12, 10 hrs. **NB** Of the various La Paz-Puno services, only Transturin does not make you change to a Peruvian bus once over the border. For luxury and other services to Peru see under **Lake Titicaca** below.

Trains It is imperative to check times before travelling as changes are frequent and timetables contradictory. For this reason, schedules given in the text (under destinations) should be treated with caution. For information T 353510/352510/373069. Towns served are Oruro, Potosí, Sucre, Cochabamba, Villazón and intermediate stops. In early 1994, many services, including *ferrobuses*, had been withdrawn. Micros which go to the station are A, M, N, P, 130, 131, C. The ticket office, at the rear of the building at the N end of main station, opens 0700, but get there at least 2 hrs beforehand.

To **Villazón** (minimum 20 hrs) for Argentina, dep Fri at 1300. Trains also leave Oruro Mon and Thur at 1900; no sleepers; restaurant car. Book ahead at central station; queue at 0600 on previous day (queuing numbers are given out), take passport. If all train tickets are sold out, go to station 2 hrs before departure for returned tickets, try Exprinter travel agency, try and board train anyway and pay the guard, or fly to Tarija and then go by road to Villazón.

Railways to/from the Coast (1) By the Southern Railway of Peru from Arequipa to Puno, on Lake Titicaca then by road to La Paz, incorporating if desired one of the lake crossings described below under **Lake Titicaca** and **Crossing the Peruvian Frontier**.

(2) **La Paz-Arica International Railway**, 447 km: In the Bolivian section the line climbs to El Alto and then runs SW to Viacha (Km 32) the junction of lines to Antofagasta, Guaqui (freight only) and Villazón. It continues to Corocoro, the copper mining town, crosses the Río Desaguadero at Calacoto (Km 98) and then runs SW to the border at Charaña (Km 208 – see below) a very cold place to change trains or wait for a bus. The mountain peaks visible include Illimani, Sorata, Huayna-Potosí, Mururata, and many others. For description of the Chilean part, **see Chile, The Desert North, Section 1. NB** Chilean pesos can be bought in La Paz at a better rate of exchange than in Arica.

There is a Bolivian *ferrobus* service straight through to Arica, on Mon and Fri at 0700, arrives 1900, US$52, US$95 return, incl breakfast and lunch, meals and refreshments after this charged extra ("bill in bolivianos, paid for in US dollars, change given in Chilean pesos"), max 20 kg baggage is free, extra charge for excess, worth it for the views, change money on train (poor rates), book ticket one-two weeks in advance, especially in high season (when extra trains are added). Alternatively take a train to Charaña every other Thur from Viacha at 0300 (no chance of seeing the spectacular scenery), then change to a colectivo to Arica (US$10), or, on 2nd and 4th Wed of each month a train leaves Charaña at 0930, arriving Arica at 1800 (every Wed Jan-Mar). The return from Charaña to Viacha is in daylight. Fares: Viacha-Charaña: US$3.05 pullman. Bus Charaña-La Paz US$7.50.

(3) La Paz-Antofagasta, by Antofagasta and Bolivia Railway, 1,173 km, now definitely a trip for the adventurous who are impervious to cold at night, or blazing sunshine at tedious daytime border changes. The train is full of contrabandistas, impromptu folk music, but the ride is very rough and subject to long delays. The train starts at Oruro (but check in La Paz in advance), to where you must go by bus, then train as far as Calama in Chile, then by bus (240 km) to Antofagasta. This, the most S of the three railway routes connecting La Paz with the Pacific

coast, passes through magnificent scenery. The train leaves Oruro at 1930 on Sun only (schedules often change), reaching Uyuni sometime after 0300 on Mon (US$4.10 Oruro-Uyuni), then there is a wait of up to 11 hrs, then another 4 hrs to Avaroa, the border (US$5 Uyuni-border, US$6.65 Oruro-border); 1 hr to change trains, then 40 minutes to Ollagüe, where Chilean customs take 4-12 hrs. As Cathy and Alan Hook of Bromley say, there is a ridiculous line-up in Chile, with officious checks (including a blood-pressure test for cholera), then "battle to get searched, all for the prize of waiting on the windswept railway line for the train to reappear." After that it is 6 uncomfortable hours to Calama (US$16 Oruro-Calama, US$5 border-Calama). In Bolivia, seats can be reserved as far as the border; tickets are sold in Oruro 0730-1100 on day of departure, in Uyuni 30 minutes before train arrives, or at 1800 the day before. Restaurant car and waiter service. If taking your own food, eat fresh things first as the Chileans do not allow dairy produce, teabags (of any description), fruit or vegetables to be brought in. There are no exchange facilities at the border. It is advisable to buy Chilean currency and sell bolivianos before journey, or on the train. All passports are collected and stamped in the rear carriage, they should be ready for collection after 1-2 hours; queue for your passport, no names are called out (beware, as the train goes down to Chile, carriages are added; the reverse happens in the other direction).

(4) La Paz-Buenos Aires: No trains now run to Argentina as this service was suspended in March 1993.

By Road from La Paz to the Pacific Coast
There are 2 routes: the shortest and most widely used is the road from La Paz to Arica via border towns of Tambo Quemado (Bolivia) and Chungará (Chile). The majority of Bolivia's imports, including foreign cars, jeeps and large vehicles from Chile's Pacific sea-ports, Arica and Iquique, are brought to La Paz by truck via this route. From La Paz take the main highway S towards Oruro to *Patacamaya* (104 km – about 1½ hrs from central La Paz on good paved road – 130 km N of Orwo); Sun market, no tourist items; **G** *Los Angeles*, basic, no electricity, candles provided, other cheap accommodation and restaurants. At Patacamaya (ask for directions – no road signs) turn right (W towards the cordillera) towards Tambo Quemado. From Patacamaya, the "road" which climbs to altitudes of around 5,000m and which is, at times, unmarked except for the tracks of heavy lorries, becomes dirt, sand, stones, mud and water. Allow 6-8 hours to cover the next 220 km to Tambo Quemado. Four-wheel drive obligatory. Take extra petrol (none available after Chilean border until Arica) food and water. Watch out for river crossings and seek advice before travelling during or just after rainy season (Dec-April).

"In the right vehicle, the journey is, in itself, a worthwhile adventure; the views, particularly to the W, of the volcanoes in distant Lauca National Park, Chile (see Chile - **The Desert North** (1) are breathtaking" (Tom Clough, La Paz). There are plans to pave this section: when completed the journey time between La Paz and Arica is expected to be about 7 hrs.

Mid-way between Patacamaya and Tambo Quemado is the town of Curahuara de Carangas. Watch for speed restrictions upon entering town past military school. Police control point in main plaza. Possible overnight stop in Sajama Village (4,200m) 22 km E of Tambo Quemado at the foot of Mt Sajama (see **South from La Paz (2) - Excursions from Oruro**). Lagunas, 12 km further on is a popular "truck-stop". Petrol available. Restaurant/bar *Lagunas* offers cheap set menu, helpful, friendly. Owner can usually find accommodation somewhere in the village, US$1, take your own sleeping bag, extra blankets, warm clothing. Facilities are at best very basic; you may well be sleeping on a straw mattress on a dirt floor. No water or electricity, gas lamps or candles are usual. Nights can be bitterly cold and very windy but the array of stars in crystal clear skies makes it worthwhile. In the daytime there are spectacular views of nearby snowcapped Mt Sajama.

The Bolivian border control at Tambo Quemado consists of customs, "tránsito" (highway police), immigration, and international police. Approx US$3.50 per "particular" (private non-commercial) vehicle. Check with Autómovil Club Boliviano, La Paz for any special documents which may be required, depending on the registration of your vehicle. Bolivian vehicles require a Temporary Export Certificate in order to leave Bolivia (to be obtained in La Paz prior to travel), and Temporary Import Certificate approx US$2.50 from customs at Chungará on entering Chile. Best to change a small amount of currency into Chilean pesos in La Paz. Temporary Import/Export Certificates are normally valid 90 days. It is worth double checking all documents including visa requirements with the Consulate of Chile in La Paz before travelling. From Tambo Quemado there is a stretch of about 16 km of "no-man's land" (the road is more appalling than ever) before you reach the Chilean frontier at Chungará. Here the border crossing, which is set against the most spectacular scenic backdrop of Lake Chungará and Volcán Parinacota is strictly controlled. Open: 0800-1200; 1430-1800. Expect a long wait behind lines of lorries; avoid Sundays; best to travel midweek. Drivers must fill in "Relaciones de Pasajeros", US$0.25 from kiosk at border, giving details of driver, vehicle and passengers.

Border control consists of Ministry of Agriculture and Livestock (SAG - control of animals entering Chile is rigidly enforced; do not take any fruit, vegetables, or dairy products, into Chile). Immigration, Customs and Police.

From Chungará, the road is paved; the first 50 km section to Putre goes through spectacular Lauca National Park. Look out for some treacherous bends as the road descends dramatically to sea-level where it meets the Pan Amerian Highway (Route 5) 12 km North of Arica.

An alternative, on which there are no trucks, is to go by good road from La Paz via Viacha to Santiago de Machaco (130 km, petrol); then 120 km to the border at **Charaña** (*Galojamiento Aranda*; immigration is behind the railway station, only 30-day permit given on entry), very bad road. In Visviri (Chile) there is no fuel, accommodation, bath or electricity, ask for restaurant and bargain price. From Visviri a regular road runs to Putre, then as above.

A variation from Viacha is take the roads which more-or-less follow the railway to Charaña (4WD essential). On this scenic route, with interesting rock formations, you pass Comanche (puya raimondii flowers grow near here) and General Campero in the Ciudad de Piedra (near the football field in Gen Campero is a house which lets a room and has water). From Gen Campero roads go to Gen Pérez, Abarao and Charaña. From this route treks can be made S to the mountains towards Sajama and, from Charaña, to Sajana itself.

Excursions from La Paz   There is trout fishing in the many glacial lakes and streams near La Paz.

The best near-by excursion is to Río Abajo and Mallasilla golf course: through suburbs of Calacoto and La Florida follow the river road past lovely picnic spots and through some weird rock formations, known as the **Valle de la Luna**, "Moon Valley". Kombi A, Nos 231 and 273 pass the Valle de la Luna en route to the Mallasa recreation area, a large weekend excursion area near Mallasa village. (No 231 can be caught at Plaza Belzu; if you do not want to walk in the valley, stay on the bus to the end of the line and take a return bus, 2 hrs in all.) About 3 km from the bridge at Calacoto the road forks; sharp right leads to the Caza y Pesca Club and Mallasilla golf course. Get out of the minibus at the turning and walk a few minutes E to the Valle entrance, or get out at the football field which is by the entrance. Take good shoes and water. Alternatively take Micro 11 ("Aranjuez"-large, not small bus) from Calle Sagárnaga, near Plaza San Francisco, US$0.50, and ask driver where to get off. Just before the Valle are the Aranjuez Forest, the Aniceto Arce cactus gardens (badly eroded) and the *Playa de Aranjuez*, a bathing spot popular for lunch at weekends. Most of the local travel agents organize tours to the Valle de la Luna (which are very brief, 5 minutes stop for photos in a US$12 tour of La Paz and surroundings); taxis are not dear (US$12), especially if shared; make sure the price is per car and not per person. Just past the Valle de la Luna and the Mallasilla Golf Course is Mallasa where several small roadside restaurants and cafés have opened; also *Oberland*, T 796818, a Swiss-owned, chalet-style restaurant (good meat) and resort, popular at weekends, especially with the expat community: cabañas, sauna, swimming pool, racket ball, tennis. It has been recommended for superb fondue, raclette, pasta and salads. Book in advance. Also *Los Lobos*, highly rec for *churrasco* steaks, US$4.50.

Zoo, on road to Río Abajo, entrance just past Mallasa, well-housed animals in beautiful, wide open park-like setting. The climate in this valley is always much warmer than in the city, where the zoo previously was. Open daily 0900-1200, 1430-1800, US$0.60 adults, US$0.40 children.

To Achumani (past Valle de la Luna) for good views of the valley and houses of the wealthy. Walk back along the valley and catch frequent buses into town. Further beyond Ashumani is the new residential zone of Chasquipampa on the Palca road, near which is the Valle de las Animas. Here the eroded landscape is similar to, but much larger than, the Valle de la Luna; good for walking and picnics. Take Kombi 239 from University to Chasquipampa. On the way back there are good views of the S districts and the city above.

To La Muela del Diablo, a gigantic, tooth-shaped rock which can be seen from the Valle de la Luna road, take Micro "Ñ" from Murillo y Sagárnaga or from the University (last stop Cota Cota) minibus 213 to Rosales, or *trufi* 288 from Cementerio, Plaza Isabel La Católica to

Urbanización Pedregal (ask driver where to get off). Cross the river and climb through the village to the cemetery; from there it is 1½ hrs easy climb to the rock, "more impressive especially if the wind is blowing than Moon Valley". The road continues to Ventilla, the start of the Inca trail.

To the Zongo Valley: a steep but scenic ride down past several of La Paz's electric power plants. Either take taxi for US$4/hr, allow at least 5 hrs, or take Micro 52, EMTA or 101 to Plaza 16 de Julio, El Alto (US$0.50) from where you can hire a taxi for US$2.25-4.50 pp or take Trans 16 de Julio (Plaza Ballivián) on Tues, Thurs and Sat, 0600. It is quite safe to drive yourself (in suitable vehicle) and hike. The road passes a series of lakes and a water course (on left); at each junction en route turn left. 20 minutes past a miners' cemetery (also on left) and a large deserted mining camp, you come to the last hydroelectric dam and on the right, a white guard house (4,750 m). Alight here. Walk up and over the small hill on the righthand side of the road until you meet the water channel again. Follow the water course for 45 minutes; this needs special care as it is cut into the side of a sheer cliff in places. You eventually come to an aqueduct which you can either cross, straddling the water, or walk beneath to the other side. At the end of the bridge, turn right up hill to a marker of rocks piled one on top of the other. Continue over the hill, cross a stream and go straight up the next hill at a similar rock marker. From the top of the hill, it is only a few minutes down to the site of the former ice cave (about 1¼ hour's walk in all). Global warming has completely destroyed the ice cave, which used to be the main attraction of the valley.

For the acclimatized only: A climb to **Corazón de Jesús**, the statue at the top of the hill reached via the steps at the N end of Calle Washington, then left and right and follow the stations of the cross. Worth the climb for the views over the city and the Altiplano, but watch out where you put your feet. Do not go alone, there is a risk of robbery; beware of dogs. Take a bus to Ceja El Alto (eg No 20 or 22) to save yourself some of the walk.

To see Puya Raimondii flowers, go to the village of Comanche, 2½ hrs from La Paz (micros from railway station to Viacha—1 hr—then truck to Comanche—rough, dusty and cold, or by train, Tues 2200, back on Wed only at 1500, US$1.50 each way); some travel agencies arrange tours.

Hikes near La Paz For the *Takesi* (Inca) road hike, take a Sector Bolsa Negra bus at 1000, US$1.25, daily from between Calles Riobamba and Burgoa, 2 blocks N of Plaza Líbano (another location may be Boquerón y Rodríguez, by the Mercado Rodríguez) to Ventilla on Palca road, arrive 1 hr early for seat, 3 hrs, return 0930 (alternatively take a Cota Cota bus Ñ to the end of the line or a taxi to Ovejura vehicle checkpoint above Cota Cota, US$6.35, then truck to Ventilla). Take the track to the left, parallel to the Río Palca for 10 km track to San Francisco mine. At Choquecota, before San Francisco, there are shops. If you leave Ventilla before 1300, you should reach Takesi village before nightfall (it's worth seeing the village). The "camino de Takesi" goes over the pass (4,650m), passes the Laguito Loro Keri and then follows the valley which ends at Chojlla (colectivo to La Paz US$2, 0730 and 1200 daily) and on 5 km to Yanacachi (one hotel, one *alojamiento*), meals available in private homes (only colectivo to La Paz at 0700 US$2.85, daily except Sat—or Sun, check, buy ticket day before), 4 hrs (if you miss that, it's a 45-min walk down to Santa Rosa, which is on the main La Paz-Chulumani road). One powerful river can be crossed by asking at houses on the bank, where they will rig up a pulley for you for US$1-2. *Backpacking in Peru and Bolivia* (Bradt Publications), and the La Paz tourist office leaflet with sketch map both describe this 3-5 day walk, which shows exceptionally fine Inca paving in the first part. Several reports say that it is much tougher than descriptions suggest (especially for the the less-than-fit), and is very unpleasant in the wet season. Please take care not to add to the litter already on the route. The highest point is 4,650m and the lowest 2,100. The scenery changes dramatically from the bitterly cold pass down to the humid Yungas. At Chojlla one can sleep at the school house for US$0.80, or the *Sheraton Inn*, basic, US$1 or less. At the village of Kakapi (3 hrs beyond Takesi, 2½ hrs before Chojlla) Don Pepe provides campsite or you may also be able to stay in the schoolhouse. Ask for Señor Genaro Mamani, a very helpful local expert and guide. The trail can also be used as a starting point for reaching Chulumani or Coroico.

Another trail is the **Choro** hike from La Cumbre pass to Coroico, descending from the snow-covered heights to tropical vegetation. Take any early bus to the Yungas from Villa Fátima (see p 246 for transport details) to the statue of Christ at La Cumbre, US$1, where the trail starts (a pick-up is unlikely to take you). Look out for condors at the start of the trail. The speedy can do the hike in under 3 days, lesser mortals will need about 4 days. The start of the trail is signposted. It is 4-5 hrs from La Cumbre to Chucura (campsite; reports of theft and begging); 5-6 hrs further to the village of Choro (campsite; on this stretch is Challapampa where Doña Juana lets rooms, G, also campsite); 8-9 hrs further along a very overgrown path and across a major river without a bridge (cross in a group; do not attempt in the wet season) to **Sandillani** (camping possible at 3 places beyond Choro, after 1 hr, 1 hr 20 mins next to water, and 1½ hrs near big empty house. In Sandillani a Japanese man welcomes visitors and will let you camp in his orchard, an excellently situated campsite, clean water, fire pit, and small shelter for packs and drying laundry. He likes postcards, stamps, old magazines or money from your home country, he keeps a log-book for any hikers to sign. Another family sell food and drinks. Thereafter it is 3 hours/7 km to Chairo. Be sure to cross the river as you enter Choro (the path resumes clearly on the other side after 200 m); the trail rises high above here to Chairo. Water is available all the way, but take water purification pills. A tent is essential. (The tourist office has a map of the trail, but it is unreliable.) From Chairo (accommodation—US$2.50,or sleep under eaves of the school, and food with Familia Paredes de la Tienda, very friendly, swimming pool), there is a daily truck to Coroico at 0500. It is a stiff, 3-hr climb up to the main road below Coroico (occasional jeeps). From this junction hitch to Yolosa (1½ hrs walk), or take a truck to Coroico. From Yolosa there are minibuses to Chuñavi and trucks from there to Chulumani (see below and p 276).

Take all supplies with you. See the warning in **Hiking**, p 332.

For both hikes, Carmoar Tours in La Paz (address above) has been recommended for equipment rental (tents US$4.10/night) and maps. Also the Club Andino Boliviano, México 1638.

A third hike is **Yunga Cruz**, from Chuñavi to Chulumani in the Sud Yungas (sketch map available from La Paz tourist office, though not very accurate or helpful). 5-7 days walking and spectacularly beautiful, many birds to be seen en route, from condors to hummingbirds. H-W Neumann and Gabi Zahn from Frankfurt, Germany, reported that it "needs a minimum of 5-6 days hard walking, mostly uphill. Great views but little water after passing the highest point". Simone Fecht from Stockach, Germany, adds that "it takes nearly a day to get to **Chuñavi** from La Paz. A bus leaves at 0800-0830 from Plaza Líbano on the corner of Calle Venancio Burgoa, go early as it is often full and no reservations possible. Accommodation in Chuñavi at the school or in the garden, ask for permission. There are two campsites near Chuñavi, one 35 mins walk and another 45 mins walk away. After these there are no more camping sites for another 6-8 hours walking, until you reach a small plain after the first river crossing".

Mountaineering Increasing numbers are visiting the Cordillera Real, to the E of La Paz. The range has the marked advantages over many high massifs of settled weather from end April-Sept, easy access via numerous mine tracks, and favourable starting altitudes (4,200-4,700 m). The Cordillera Real is 150 km long with six peaks over 6,000 m (20,000 ft)—Illampu 6,380 m (see under Sorata, below), Ancohuma 6,420 m, Chearoco 6,100 m, Chachacomani 6,100 m, Huayna Potosí 6,090 m, Illimani 6,460 m. All can be reached relatively easily from La Paz, the latter two within a few hours' driving. There are also a large number of impressive 5,000m-plus peaks.

The route to **Illimani** is via Calacoto and Huancapampa. Trucks leave Calle Zoilo Flores (behind *Hotel Milton*) 0600, 4½ hrs to Estancia Uno. From here you can hire mules, US$6 (Antonio Limachi rec), 4 hrs to base camp (4,400m), then climb to Nido de Cóndores (5,750 m) and set out for summit at 0300. The route to **Huayna Potosí**, an attractive peak (2 days) starts from Zongo Lake. (Minibus from Plaza Ballivián in El Alto Mon, Wed, Fri 0800-0900, US$4 one way, taxi US$35; trucks from Plaza Ballivián each morning. On Sundays a truck belonging to Corpac, the state electricity company, goes from Av Montes, near the bus station, to its plant by the lake.) Huayna Potosí requires mountaineering experience for ice and crevasses on the way to the top; however, bad weather, apart from mist, is rare. (*Refugio Huayna Potosí*, at base camp, 60 km, 2 hrs, from La Paz, has bedrooms, kitchen, electric light, water and food, accommodation for 20, contact Hugo Berrios, Calle Illampu 626, *Hotel Continental*, T 795936/323584, Casilla 731; transport and guiding service available.) Climbing on this mountain is now well-organized and, with a guide (recommended) it is good for gaining experience in mountain climbing. Before setting out you must register at *Refugio Huayna Potosí*.

Condoriri or Pequeño Alpamayo are reached in one or two days from Tuni at Km 21 on the La Paz-Tiquina road. Base camp is at 4,700m. From here recommended walks are to summit of Apacheta (5,300m) and Paso Jallayco (5,100m). If climbing in the Condoriri area, make sure return transport is arranged in advance; there is no traffic apart from the odd tour. People at Tuni are very friendly, but expect payment for guarding base camp. Theft from tents has been reported.

Quimza Cruz, "the future of Bolivian mountaineering", rock climbing, some ice-climbing, the highest point is 5,300 m, starting at 3,000 m. Any excursion there requires 4 days minimum, plus one day there and one back. In the N part, the Araca group, there are good rock climbs on solid granite. Snow and ice-climbing can be found in the central part. There is no direct road from La Paz; either drive to Mocoya, 280 km, 8 hrs by car, or take a bus from La Paz to

Veloco, 5 km before Mocoya, a tin mine at 4,100 m. The route, also made by truck, is to take the autopista towards Oruro. At Pan Duro take an unpaved road, direction Inquisivi, to Caxata. From Caxata it is 4 hrs to Veloco. In this region there is nowhere to buy food.

For the Western Cordillera with the peaks of Sajama, Parinacota and Pomerape, **see under Sajama, p 284, below**. The Cordillera Apolobamba, the N extension of the Cordillera Real, with many 5,000m-plus peaks, can be reached by public transport from La Paz, the main starting out points being **Charazani**, see p 275 (trucks from La Cancha del Tejar on Calle Reyes Coronados, 10 hrs in dry weather) and Pelechuco (buses and trucks from La Paz).

Normal alpine experience and equipment will enable most peaks to be ascended, and many new routes remain to be explored. Several peaks can be climbed in a day, but the 6,000 m mountains usually require 2-4 days. There are no huts (except Chacaltaya ski-lodge and the *refugio* at Huayna Potosí). Do not underestimate altitude problems: at least 1-2 weeks' acclimatization is usually necessary before exceeding 5,500 m. (A visit to Chacaltaya and its ski-slopes is an easy way of judging one's reaction to altitude). Also, rescue services are virtually non-existent; prudence, proper gear and experience (incl crevasse rescue abilities) are indispensable. Note that mountaineering gear and high altitude camping equipment cannot normally be bought in Bolivia, though you may be able to buy it from climbers leaving the country. Club Andino Boliviano will be very pleased to accept, or buy, good "surplus" gear after climbing is finished.

A good guidebook is *The Southern Cordillera Real*, R Pecher & W Schmiemann, Plata Publishing Ltd (1977), possibly obtainable in La Paz; distributor: Los Amigos del Libro (W Guttentag), Casilla 450, Cochabamba. Also numerous expedition reports. Maps covering most of the range are the photo-surveyed 1:50,000 IGM Series, US$5 each. The Royal Geographic Society in London has an excellent map of the Cordillera Apolobamba, copies of which are available for US$6. Colonial Travel, Mexico 1733, provide information and advice on routes, organizes transport.

Guides *Alfredo Martínez* at the **Club Andino Boliviano**, Calle México 1638, T 365065, Casilla 5879, is the country's foremost guide, or contact *Hugo Berrios*, the Club secretary, T 795938, F 326724, who is also a guide. Also rec is: *Bernardo Guarachi*, Plaza Alonso de Mendoza, Edif Santa Anita, oficina 314, T 320901, Casilla 20886, La Paz (he has equipment for hire). *Colibrí SRL*, Sagárnaga 309, T 371936, F 355043 att Colibrí, *Oscar Sainz* and *Juan Villarroel*, specialize in climbing, with up-to-date information, trips arranged for all levels of experience and adventure tourism in all parts of Bolivia, very helpful, rec, full range of equipment hire. *Andes Expediciones*, Plaza Alonso de Mendoza, Edif Santa Anita, 3° piso, of 314, experienced guides, rec. *Sajama*, Calle Sagárnaga, La Paz, rec for equipment. *Iván Blanco Alba, Asociación de Guías de Montaña y Trekking*, Calle Chaco 1063, Casilla 1579, La Paz, T 350334, has been recommended (the association has about 10 guides in all and arranges climbing and hiking expeditions). Also recommended, *José Camarlinghi* (licensed by the German Alpine Club), Casilla 3772, Pedro Kramer 924, La Paz (T 352266) and *Ricardo Albert* at Inca Travel, Av Arce 2116, Edificio Santa Teresa. *Dr Juan Pablo Ando*, Casillo 6210, T 783495, trained in Chamonix, for mountaineering, rock climbing, trekking and ecological tours. In Europe the following have been recommended for group tours: *Adventura Ultimos*, Arzgruben weg 1, 8102 Mittenwald, Germany, and *Dr Erich Galt*, A-6020 Innsbruck, Amraser Str 110a, Austria. For guiding, *Norbert Kloiber*, Herrenstrasse 16, 8940 Memmingen, West Germany (T 08331-5258). *Trek Bolivia*, Sagárnaga 392, T/F 317106. The experienced Alex Munroy organizes expeditions in the Cordillera as well as trips to Peru.

The **Club de Excursionismo, Andinismo y Camping**, CEAC, helps people find the

cheapest way to go climbing, trekking, etc; foreigners may join local groups, T 783795, Casilla 8365, La Paz, or ask at the University or for Catherina Ibáñez at Plaza Tours, Av 16 de Julio 1789, T 378322, F 343301 (she has an information service for CEAC). Each week there is a meeting and slide show.

Skiing Ninety minutes by car from La Paz (36 km) is **Chacaltaya**, the highest ski run in the world. Season: November to March, sometimes longer. Skiing equipment may be hired, and a rope-tow reaches a maximum altitude of 5,221m. The facilities are sub-standard, emergency services non-existent and the rope tow should be used with extreme caution (it is of a design no longer permitted in Europe). Midweek skiing is often not possible owing to the absence of staff. Taxi or minibus US$30 (whole car) for a half-day trip, or similar to the top by rented car costs about US$60, and really only at weekends; no visitor should miss the experience and the views. However the trip can be hair-raising, buses carry no chains. Often the buses and tours only go half way. The Club Andino Boliviano, México 1638 y Otero de la Vega, runs its own Saturday and Sunday buses (mixed reports, Marco is a good guide); the day trip, beginning at 0730 and returning at 1600, comes to about US$30 for bus ticket, ski pass and equipment for the day; your bus ticket (US$13) gives free access to the ski station restaurant, otherwise US$2 entrance, hot drinks only. Equipment for hire is available (US$13 skis and boots from the Ski School—in the same building as the Ski Club, very limited, poor equipment for hire, queue at once), but better take your own. A good tip is to share equipment since, at that altitude, you will need a long break between activities. The lift pass costs US$1.50—out of season the lift only goes if there are 5 or more people. Reports suggest that Club Andino's Chacaltaya programme is not totally reliable; people have been stranded at the run, resulting in a 5-hr walk back to La Paz in the dark. (NB Club Andino's oxygen bottle at the Chacaltaya station may not always be full.) Many agencies do day trips, US$12.50, often combined with Valle de la Luna. Club Andino also occasionally arranges trips to Mount Illimani. One can walk to the summit of Chacaltaya for views of Titicaca on one side, La Paz on the other, and Huayna Potosí. Tiring, as it is over 5,000m, but one has most of the day to do the climb. Laguna de Milluni, near Chacaltaya, is a beautiful lake to visit, but do not drink its water; it is dangerously contaminated by acid residues from mining. For the really hardy, accommodation costs US$3 at the Chacaltaya ski station, but take very warm clothes and sleeping bag, food and water, as there is no heating, or bedding and the caretakers are unhelpful. (Chacaltaya skiing is described in Bradt's *South America Ski Guide*.)

Take plenty of mineral water when going to the mountains as it's thirsty work in the rarefied air. To avoid *soroche* after skiing drink *mate de coca*.

Urmiri Take road S towards Oruro, turn left at Urmiri sign at Km 75. To get this far take Flota Bolivar or Flota Copacabana bus; lifts from the crossroads are few and far between. A steep scenic descent leads to pool filled by mineral springs and a pleasant primitive inn. Worth visiting, it's a 2½ hour trip one way. The La Paz Prefectura runs buses to Urmiri, where they have a hotel (D), price includes food.

Tiahuanaco (Tiwanaku) The ruins of Tiwanaku, not far from the village of Tiahuanaco, are 72 km W of La Paz, near the S end of Lake Titicaca. The road from El Alto is graded and dusty. It passes through the village of **Laja** (Laxa), the first site of La Paz, at the junction of the roads between Potosí and Lima and Potosí and Arica. Because there was no water, La Paz was moved to its present site on the Río Choquepayu. Laja's church was the first cathedral of the region. On its mestizo baroque façade, note the fruits and plants, the monkey (an Indian symbol of reconstruction), the double-headed Habsburg eagle (the Spanish king, Charles I, was also Habsburg Emperor), and the faces of King Ferdinand and Queen Isabella as Indians on the left bell tower (the right bell tower was built in 1903). The church has a solid silver altar, but is closed to visitors. Simple meals at US$0.80 available in village. At the highest point on the road between Laja and Tiwanaku are wide views of the Cordillera and a site where offerings to Pachamama are made.

Many archaeologists believe that Tiwanaku existed as early as 1600 BC, while the complex visible today is estimated to have been built between the 8th and 10th centuries AD. Recent research suggests that the site was a ceremonial complex at the centre of an empire which covered almost half Bolivia, S Peru, N Chile and NW Argentina. It was also a hub of trans-Andean trade. The reason for the demise of the Tiwanaku civilization is not entirely clear, although studies by Alan Kolata of the University of Illinois indicate that the area had an extensive system of raised fields, capable of sustaining a population of 20,000, which may have been flooded by rising water levels in Lake Titicaca. This could have precipitated the empire's fall. The Pumapunka section, 1 km S of the main complex may have been a port, as the waters of the lake used to be much higher than they are today. The raised field system is being reutilized in the Titicaca area.

The main structures are: Kalasasaya, meaning "standing stones", referring to the statues found in that part. Two of them, the Ponce monolith (centre of inner patio) and the Fraile monolith (SW corner), have been re-erected. In the NW corner is the Puerta del Sol, originally at Pumapunku: the split in the top probably occurred in the move. Its carvings, interrupted by being out of context, are thought to be either a depiction of the creator God, or a calendar. The motifs are exactly the same as those around the Ponce monolith. This figure displays many of the typical Tiwanaku features: puma faces looking downwards, condor faces, two left hands, the snake with a human face on his left arm, the crying god. The Templo Semisubterráneo is a sunken temple whose walls are lined with faces, all different, according to some theories depicting states of health, the temple being a house of healing. The Akapana, originally a pyramid, was the largest structure, but is now no more than a hill. At Pumapunku, some of whose blocks weigh up to 100 tonnes, the widespread confusion of fallen stones suggests a natural disaster putting a sudden end to the construction before it was finished.

The entrance ticket to Tiwanaku costs US$2.50 for foreigners, including entry to museum; the site opens at 0900. There is a small museum at the ticket office; it has a toilet. An older museum, the other side of the railway from the main site, on the way to Pumapunku, is due for relocation. Most of the best statues are in the Museo Tiahuanaco or the Museo Semisubterráneo in La Paz. Indians trade arrowheads and bronze figures (almost all fakes); the llamas paraded at the site for photo opportunities spit and attack people. Allow 4 hours to see the ruins and village.

Tiahuanaco, the present-day village, has arches at the four corners of its square, dating from the time of independence. The church, built 1580-1612, used precolumbian masonry. In fact, Tiwanaku for a long while was the "quarry" for the altiplano. There is a very basic *alojamiento* on Calle Bolívar, cheap, good views. There is little chance of buying a meal, except food on market day. Across the Pan-American Highway from the ruins, a café sells refrescos, sandwiches, etc.

Fiestas At Tiwanaku, 21 June, before sunrise, colourful dances, llama sacrifices, etc. In Tiahuanaco village, on the eighth day of carnival (Sunday), local carnival, colourful, souvenirs for sale, bargain hard, do not take photographs. Market day in Tiahuanaco is Sunday; do not take photos then either.

Guidebook in English *Tiwanaku*, by Mariano Baptista, Plata Publishing Ltd, Chur, Switzerland, or *Discovering Tiwanaku* by Hugo Boero Rojo. They are obtainable from Los Amigos del Libro (or 2nd-hand from stalls in Av Ismael Montes). *Guía Especial de Arqueología Tiwanaku*, by Edgar Hernández Leonardini, a guide on the site, recommended. Written guide material is difficult to come by; hiring a good guide costs US$10.

Transport Transportes Ingavi, José María Azú y Eyzaguirre (take any Micro marked 'Cementerio') US$1.20, 2 hrs, 4 daily (frequency may change according to demand—the earlier you go the better). They are usually full. Tickets can be bought in advance. Taxi for 2 costs about US$20 (can be shared), return, with unlimited time at site. (US$30-40 inc El Valle de la Luna). Some buses go on from Tiahuanaco to Desaguadero; virtually all Desaguadero buses stop at Tiahuanaco, US$0.50. Return buses (last one back 1730-1800) can be caught at the crossroads in the village at the "Tránsito" sign. They are always very crowded and cannot be booked in advance, but there are usually plenty available.

Tours La Paz cost US$15 return; they stop at Laja and the highest point on the road before Tiwanaku. Some tours include El Valle de la Luna.

If driving between Tiwanaku and La Paz, especially if en route from Desaguadero, note that the police checkpoint at Tambillo is not above bribery for trumped-up charges.

Lake Titicaca

Lake Titicaca is two lakes joined by the Straits of Tiquina: the larger, N lake (Lago Mayor, or Chucuito) contains the Islas del Sol and de la Luna at its S end; the smaller lake (Lago Menor, or Huiñamarca) has several small islands. The waters are a beautiful blue, reflecting the hills and the distant cordillera in the shallows of Huiñamarca, mirroring the sky in the rarified air and changing colour when it is cloudy or raining. Periodically the water level rises, inundating low-lying land, but its size is much reduced from prehispanic times. There are various legends concerning the origin of the name, some surrounding the *titi*, a wild cat of the lake shore, whose pelt is much prized by witch doctors. The trout fished in the lake and served in many restaurants is not native. There is some trout farming but stocks are low enough for trout to have become too expensive for many locals, who catch *pejerrey* and *karachi*. Also beginning to be farmed are the Lake's giant frogs, whose legs are served, fried, with chips, in several places. The totora-reed boats are still made, more as museum pieces than for practical purposes. Wood and fibreglass vessels last much longer. Totora reed, harvested on the shore, as well as for boatbuilding, can be used for thatching, straw, animal feed, and the young shoots can be eaten as a salad vegetable. A trip on the lake is a must if in the area; boat services are given below.

Tristan Jones, who crossed South America in his sailing cutter *Sea Dart*, spent over eight months cruising Lake Titicaca (see his book *The Incredible Voyage*, Futura Publications). He says "the Titicaca Indians' most interesting music, and quite rare, is at masses held for the dead". *An Insider's Guide to Bolivia*, by Peter McFarren, gives a good historical background, including an interesting article about archaeological discoveries in Lake Titicaca, by Johann Reinhard (available in many bookshops and large hotels in La Paz). Reinhard also contributed a chapter on "Underwater Archaeological Research in Lake Titicaca" to *Ancient America, Contributions to New World Archaeology*, edited by Nicholas J Saunders (Oxford: Oxbow Monograph 24, 1992).

Copacabana, 158 km from La Paz, is an attractive little town on Lake Titicaca. It has a heavily restored, Moorish-style cathedral containing a famous 16th century miracle- working Dark Virgin of the Lake, also known as the Virgin of Candelaria, the patron saint of Bolivia. Candlelight procession on Good Friday. The cathedral itself is notable for its spacious atrium with four small chapels; the main chapel has one of the finest gilt altars in Bolivia. The basilica is clean, white, with coloured tiles decorating the exterior arches, cupolas and chapels. Vehicles are blessed in front of the church daily, especially on Sunday. An *hospicio* (serving now as an almshouse) with its two arcaded patios is worth a visit; ask permission before entering. There are 17th and 18th century paintings and statues in the sanctuary and monastery. Good food and drink at the hotels and in the market.

There are good walks beside the lake, or on the hills around the town. On the headland which overlooks the town and port, Cerro Calvario, are the Stations of the Cross. On the hill behind the town (Cerro Sancollani) overlooking the lake, roughly SE of the Basilica, is the Horca del Inca, two pillars of rock with another laid across them (probably a sun clock rather than a gallows, now covered in graffiti). With the church entrance behind you turn right up PD Murillo towards the green house at the street end. At the green house turn right and immediately left up a rocky hill. There is a path marked by white stones. Boys will offer to guide you: fix price in advance if you want their help. Above the Horca, on the other side of the ridge, is the Flecha del Inca, an arrow-shaped hole in a rock. Back down at the green house, turn left instead of right to the cemetery at the Asientos (Seats) del Inca, close to town. Further from town is El Baño del Inca, about 2 km (an hotel and museum are under construction here). Ask for directions on reaching the woods. Copacabana's water supply can be intermittent. Beware of sunburn especially on the lake, even when it does not feel hot. **NB** The local police have been known to accuse travellers of "photographing secret buildings" and "fine" them US$10-20, or confiscate "false" US$ bills or travellers cheques. New arrivals may also be pressurized into paying for 'entry' to the town; the fee is in fact for the sanctuary.

Fiestas 2-5 May, very colourful; 5-8 August, when the town gets very full, hotel prices quadruple and theft is common in broad daylight.

Hotels C *Playa Azul*, 6 de Agosto, full board (rooms fair, but chilly, half-board a possibility),

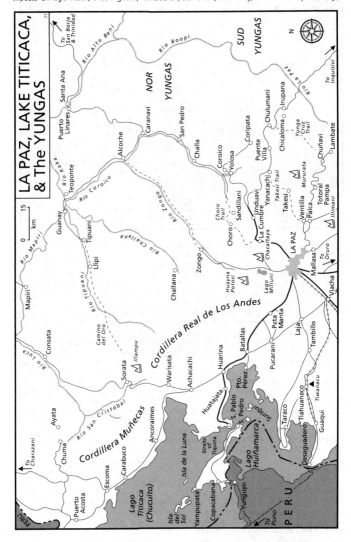

LA PAZ, LAKE TITICACA, & The YUNGAS

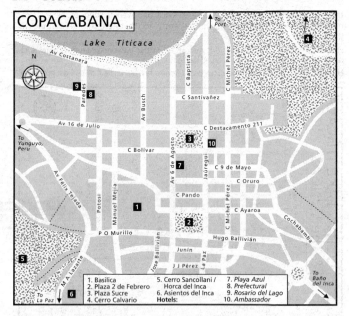

COPACABANA 21a

Lake Titicaca

N

Av Costanera

Av 16 de Julio

To Yunguyo, Peru

To La Paz

C Baptista

C Santiváñez

C Destacamento 211

C Bolívar

C 9 de Mayo

C Oruro

C Pando

C Ayaroa

P O Murillo

Hugo Ballivián

Junín

J J Pérez

To Port

To Baño del Inca

1. Basílica
2. Plaza 2 de Febrero
3. Plaza Sucre
4. Cerro Calvario
5. Cerro Sancollani / Horca del Inca
6. Asientos del Inca
7. Playa Azul
8. Prefectural
9. Rosario del Lago
10. Ambassador

Hotels:

tepid electric showers, water supply poor, good food, T 320068; **C** *Residencial Rosario del Lago*, Rigoberto Paredes between Av Costanera and Av 16 de Julio, same ownership as *Res Rosario*, La Paz, inc breakfast, colonial style, hot water (solar power), Turisbus office, due open Jan 1995; **D** *Prefectural*, with good meals, some rooms have lake view, very mixed reports; **F** *Alojamiento Aransaya*, Av 6 de Agosto 121, T 229, basic but clean and friendly, hot shower, with good restaurant (specializes in trout), about US$2 a dish; **F** *Alojamiento Aroma*, Av Jauregui, towards beach, clean, hot showers, very helpful and informative owner; **F** *Alojamiento Imperio*, Calle Visconde de Lemos, some hot water (shower US$0.50 extra), will change money; **F** *Residencial Sucre*, Murillo 228, T 2080, hot water, bath, parking, quiet, clean; **F** *Ambassador*, Bolívar y Jauregui, T 216, balcony, request heater, clean, with bath, cheaper without, good restaurant, reduction with YHA card; **F** *Kota Kahuaña*, Av Busch 15, blue house, hot showers (water not available all day), cheap, clean, some rooms with lake view, rec. **F** *Residencial Copacabana*, Oruro 555, T 220, warm water, reasonable; **F** *El Turista*, Pando 378, rec, friendly, cheap and clean, inadequate shower facilities; **F** *Residencial Porteña*, by market on Jauregui, clean, safe, rec; **F** *Solar*, Jauregui, new, clean; **F** *Emperador*, Calle Murillo, behind the Cathedral, clean, popular with travellers, laundry service and laundry facilities, communal baths, hot showers all day (electric), breakfast served in your room, very highly rec; many others on Murillo, eg **G** *Illimani*, basic, clean, Cochabamba. **G** *Las Playas*, overlooking beach, hot showers, dirty, laundry facilities; **G** *San José*, next to *Ambassador*, T 215, 1 block from lake, clean, basic, hot water, some rooms with lake view; *Alojamiento Bolívar*, Jauregui 158, bright blue, good views, hot shower, pleasant, simple, clean, rec. Many other residencials in F and G categories. Prices increase at Easter and during fiestas.

Restaurants On Plaza 2 de Febrero (main square) are *Napolés*, clean, reasonable prices, "cold rice and tough meat on plastic plates", changes money; *La Patria*, very good *pique* dish, not too expensive; *Colonial*, decent lunch, good trout. Several on 6 de Agosto inc *Snack 6 de Agosto*, good trout, salad and chips, big portions, serves breakfast, closed in evenings, *Tourist Palace*, cheap, reasonable, *Puerta del Sol*, good, and *Pensión Flores*, lunch only. Watch out for gringo pricing of food and in restaurants. *Peña Clima* has music on Saturdays, behind the market. Many other restaurants offer acceptable US$2 meals; trout rec; good breakfasts and other meals, especially fish, in the market.

Services ENTEL, behind the church on road from La Paz. Motorcycles and bicycles can be hired; ask boys at the beach, but bargain. (If planning to cycle far hire mountain bikes.) Bank only opens Wednesday-Sunday (does not change TCs or sell soles); a few restaurants and shops give poor rates for US$, but not for soles, so, if coming from Peru, buy bolivianos in Yunguyo (beware, much counterfeit money here, poor rates) before crossing frontier. Difficult to change TCs (try David Suxo's *artesanía* shop on the plaza, or *Bidesa*, 6 de Agosto, poor rates). Post Office on Plaza 2 de Febrero. Open Wed to Sun 0900-1200, 1400-1700. Many shops are closed on Mon and Tues, as they are open on Sundays.

Transport By car from La Paz to Copacabana (direct), 4 hrs, take exit to "Río Seco" in El Alto; the road is paved as far as Tiquina. Bus from La Paz: either take an agency bus for US$12-15 approximately (pick up at your hotel; eg Turisbus, Diana Tours); or public bus: 2 de Febrero, T 377181, 6 a day; Manko Kapac, T 350033, 3 a day, 4½ hrs, US$3, last bus 1700, book day before; both companies' offices in La Paz are in Plaza Reyes Ortíz, opposite entrance to cemetery. Note that buses for La Paz are very full on Sunday afternoons. One day trips from La Paz are not recommended as they allow only 1½-2 hrs in Copacabana. To reach Copacabana you cross the lovely straits of Tiquina (for details of the ferry crossing see below). Bus Copacabana-Yunguyo (Peru), hourly when full, US$0.40, from Plaza Sucre below *Hotel Playa Azul*. Agency buses between La Paz and Puno can be picked up (slightly cheaper to pay La Paz-Copacabana and Copacabana-Puno separately). No public bus services to Puno: you have to go to Yunguyo and catch a bus from there. Bus to Huarina (difficult connection for Sorata), US$2.50. **NB** It is impossible to travel from Copacabana to Guaqui direct, because of border crossings.

Isla del Sol. The site of the Inca creation legend is a short distance by boat from Copacabana. A sacred rock at its NW end is worshipped as the birthplace of Manco Kapac and Mama Huaca, the first Incas. On the E shore near the jetty for Crillon Tours' hydrofoils and other craft is the Fuente del Inca, a pure spring, and Inca steps leading up from the water. A 2-km walk from the landing stage takes one to the main ruins of Pilko Caima (the Sun Gate from the ruins is now kept in the main plaza in Copacabana), a two-storey building with false domes and superb views, entry US$1.20. Southeast of the Isla del Sol is the Isla de la Luna (or Coati), which also may be visited—the best ruins are an Inca temple and nunnery, but they have been sadly neglected. It is worthwhile staying overnight on the Isla del Sol for the many beautiful walks through villages and Inca terraces, some still in use. It is not possible to see all the sites on the Isla del Sol (a 4-hour round trip on foot) and return to Copacabana in one day. Take camping equipment, all food and water (or water sterilizers), or ask Don Juan, next to the school on the beach at Challas (NW coast) for lodging in one of his rooms (US$0.80). He serves thirsty walkers with beer or refrescos. Also enquire near the Inca steps for lodging. **G** *Casa Blanca* in the main village above the landing area, rec as clean and comfy, owners will cook meals to order. Also *Albergue Inca Sama*, next to Pilko Caima, restaurant serving fish dishes, excellent views, basic accommodation (G pp) at Yumani, 30 mins walk from Pilko Caima, campsite (contact via *Hotel Playa Azul*, Copacabana, or La Paz T 356566/357817). The owner, Sr Pusari, offers boat service from Copacabana, US$33 one way, US$50 return, or the 15-min crossing Yampupata-Pilko Caima.

Boats can be hired in Copacabana, at the beach or through many *residenciales* (including *Emperador*), to go to Islas del Sol and de la Luna. Few boats are available in the low season. You can go either to the S end of Isla del Sol, or to the N, or both, and on to La Luna. Whatever you choose to do it is imperative to agree with the boatman what is included in the price, how long you will stay ashore and, if staying overnight, when you will be collected (preferably in writing). Fares vary according to type of boat (motor or sail), its capacity, length of trip, etc; by sail to the S end costs US$15, by motor US$30, by motor boat to N and S US$40, similar to include Isla de la Luna. Between Islas del Sol and de la Luna, US$10 return. All prices for 5-7 passengers. Note that sailing boats may suffer from lack of wind and that motor boats generally hold more passengers. Warning: Several reports have been received of boat excursions giving less than value for money, and often giving free rides to the owner's friends and relatives encountered en route. Many boat owners are also reluctant to do more than a morning trip (0730-1300). Don't always take the cheapest possible offer, ask around and check what is included for your money. Cheaper boats can be found by walking 15 km N along the lakeside from Copacabana to Yampupata where fishermen cross the narrows in rowing boats to Isla del Sol in ½ hour, US$3, return. This is a lovely walk in itself (allow 3½ hrs), through unspoilt countryside, but it is too rough for cycling. At the village of Sequañe ask for Señor Hilario Paye Quispe who will row you across and bring you back another day if you plan to stay on the Isa del Sol.

Tour boats to Isla del Sol often stop only briefly at the jetty by the Fuente del Inca. All the time visitors are ashore they are pestered by people with llamas and children for photographs to be taken, after which payment is demanded.

To hire a rowing boat in Copacabana costs US$4.50 per hour.

From Copacabana to La Paz: the unpaved road from the Peruvian border and Copacabana goes to San Pedro, the W side of the Straits of Tiquina, the main base of the Bolivian navy. On the E side is San Pablo. Vehicles are transported across on barges, US$3. Passengers cross separately, US$0.20 (not included in bus fares) and passports are checked. Expect delays during rough weather, when it can get very cold. In San Pablo there is a clean blue restaurant with excellent toilets. After the crossing, the route is through *Chúa*, where there is fishing, sailing and Transturin's catamaran dock (see below). The public telephone, Cotel, office is on the plaza just off the main road. No restaurants or accommodation. About 2 km further along the main road is a turning to the right (signed) to *La Posada del Inca* restaurant, open Sat, Sun and holidays for lunch only, in a beautiful colonial *hacienda* setting (good trout, average prices). After another 4 km the road passes through *Huatajata*, with restaurants, *Yacht Club Boliviano* (restaurant open to non-members, open Sat, Sun lunch only, sailing for members only) and Crillon Tours International Hydroharbour and *Inca Utama Hotel* (see also below). At Huarina, 42 km E of Tiquina, is the turn off for Achacachi, Sorata and the road along the E shore of Titicaca to Puerto Acosta (see below). Between Huatajata and Huarina (at Km 65 from La Paz) is the **B** *Hotel Titicaca*, T La Paz 374877, F 391225, beautiful views, friendly, sauna, pool, good restaurant, very quiet during the week (address in La Paz, Potosí y Ayacucho 1220, 2° piso). The main road to the capital continues through Batallas (see below). Bus La Paz—Huatajata/Tiquina, US$0.80, Transportes Titikaka, Av Kollasuyo 16, daily from 0400, returning between 0700 and 1800.

In Huatajata, next to Crillon's *Inca Utama*, is *Restaurant Huatajata Utama*, highly rec, then *Inti Raymi*, with boat trips, *El Lago*, *Panamericano*, *La Playa* and *Hostal Restaurante Lago Azul* (cramped rooms, basic, overpriced). The restaurants are of varying standard, most offering trout and *chairo* (chuño soup with meat or quinoa or barley). Most seem to come to life at weekends and in the high season. Beside *Lago Azul* is Máximo Catari's *Inti Karka* restaurant on the road (full menu, open 7 days, average prices, good fish but small portions), and hotel, a 3-storey building on the waterfront (F pp, breakfast extra, basic, shower, water unreliable, some rooms with lake view, ask for extra blankets, T 813212). Catari arranges boats to the islands in Lago Huiñamarca, Pariti, Kalahuta and Suriqui: prices, to Suriqui US$22 for 4-5 people, to all 3 islands US$40, 1-hr boat trip US$7.50, sailing boat for 3 US$16 for a day (Catari's prices, boat trips rec). Paulino Esteban (see below) is also rec, contact through Servitur, PO Box 8045, La Paz, T 340060, F 391373. On *Suriqui* (1½ hrs from Huatajata) you can visit the museum/craft shops of the Limachi brothers (now living at the *Inca Utama* cultural complex) and Paulino Esteban, who helped in the construction, out of totora reeds, of Thor Heyerdahl's *Ra II*, which sailed from Morocco to Barbados in 1970. Heyerdahl's *Tigris* reed boat, and the balloon gondola for the Nazca (Peru) flight experiment (see Peru chapter, Section 4), were also constructed by the craftsmen of Suriqui. Reed boats are still made on Suriqui, probably the last place where the art survives. On *Kalahuta* there are *chullpas* (burial towers), old buildings and the town of Kewaya (no one lives there). On *Pariti* there is Inca terracing; the weaving on the island is very good. Boats can also be hired in Tiquina for trips to Suriqui, US$3 pp in a group. No food is available on Suriqui.

Three major La Paz travel agents base their Titicaca operations on the shores of Lago Huiñamarca: 1) Crillon Tours (address under La Paz **Travel Agents**), run a hydrofoil service on Lake Titicaca with a bilingual guide – "excellent and willing to resolve any problem". Among Crillon's vessels is the *Glasnost Arrow*, a gift from Leonid Brezhnev to Richard Nixon. All Crillon's tours stop at the cultural complex at *Inca Utama*: in the daytime visitors see the archaeological and ecological museum (recorded commentary, quite brief, but interesting), in the evening the

Kallawaya (Native Medicine) museum, including a meeting with a Kallawaya fortune teller. The *Inca Utama* hotel has a health spa based on natural remedies; the rooms are comfortable, with heating, good service, bar, good food in restaurant (5-star accommodation, **A**, reservations through Crillon Tours, T La Paz 374566/350363). Also at *Inca Utama* are an observatory (*Alajpacha*) with retractable thatched roof for viewing the night sky, a new panoramic restaurant, a bar on the lake, a new colonial-style building with 12 de-luxe suites and 2 conference rooms. Health, esoteric, mystic and ecological programmes are offered. Leaving La Paz at 0600, you get to Huatajata for breakfast and a visit to the "admirable" museum 0800. The hydrofoil sets off at 0830, moves past reed fishing boats, and stops in the Straits of Tiquina for a few minutes to watch the wooden ferry boats crossing. Only the Isla del Sol is visited to see the ruins (30 mins). You arrive at Copacabana for sightseeing and a trout lunch. The short tour returns to La Paz from Copacabana via *Inca Utama*; the longer one continues to Puno (Peru) to connect with the Puno-Cuzco rail service (customs and immigration handled by Crillon). Trips can be arranged to/from Cuzco and Machu Picchu, hydrofoil and train one way, flight the other; other combinations of hydrofoil and land-based excursions can be arranged (also jungle and adventure tours). Charge: US$156 from La Paz to Puno, US$119 for day excursion from La Paz (US$114 for day trip to Tiwanaku and Huatajata). Expensive but fascinating, not least for the magnificent views of the Cordillera on a clear day. All facilities and modes of transport connected by radio.

2) Transturin (see also La Paz **Travel Agents**) run catamarans on Lake Titicaca, either for sightseeing or on the La Paz-Puno route (US$127 La Paz-Puno; day trips US$70-90; overnight at *Hotel Titicaca* and tour US$130). From their dock at Chúa, 3-hour trips go to Copacabana, with bar, video, sun deck and music on board. One-night tours to Copacabana are also available. The catamarans are slower than the hydrofoils of Crillon so there is more room and time for on-board entertainment. Transturin runs through services to Puno without a change of bus, and without many of the usual formalities at the border. Transturin has offices in Puno, Av Girón Tacna 149-147, T 352771, and Cuzco, Av Portal de Panes 109, of 1, T 222332.

3) **Hotel Las Balsas**, owned and operated by Turismo Balsa (see La Paz **Travel Agents**), T La Paz 357817, F 391310, in a beautiful lakeside setting at Puerto Pérez, with views of the cordillera; all rooms have balcony over the lake. Large new salon caters for groups, seminars. Hotel is advertised as 5-star; **A3**, but willing to negotiate to reduce price out of season; fitness facilities incl massage. jacuzzi, sauna, racket ball; T/F (2) 813226; restaurant expensive, but fixed price lunch or dinner good value at US$12. Turismo Balsa operate boat trips to Suriqui and Kalahuta, and services to Puno and Cuzco.

Note: these three travel agencies also offer a full range of packages and travel services; contact their La Paz offices.

Puerto Pérez is the closest point to La Paz on Lake Titicaca (72 km, less than 1 hr by car). The road to the port turns off the main road at ***Batallas***, a typical Altiplano market town so named because of the final battles between Almagro and Pizarro. The views of the lake and mountains from Puerto Pérez are superb; the sunsets are spectacular, too. The port was the original harbour for La Paz, founded in the 19th century by British navigators as a harbour for the first steam boat on the Lake (the vessel was assembled piece-by-piece in Puno). Colourful fiestas are held on New Year's Day, Carnival (Mon and Tues before Ash Wednesday), 3 May and 16 July. For transport to Puerto Pérez there is a regular minibus service from La Paz Cementerio district: across from the cemetery, above the flower market, ask for buses to Batallas, price US$0.75.

Crossing the Peruvian Frontier

There are 3 routes from La Paz to Puno: 1) Along the W side of Lake Titicaca. The road and railway (no passengers) go from La Paz 91 km W to **Guaqui**, formerly the port for the Titicaca passenger boats. Guaqui was flooded by a 3-metre rise in the lake's water level in 1985. The line was repaired in 1990. **G** *Residencial Guaqui*, good value, basic, friendly; tiny restaurant on the Plaza de Armas has been rec. On the last weekend of July, Guaqui celebrates the festival for the Apóstol Santiago. Arrive early morning to join in the end of all-night carousing (what little accommodation there is, is all fully occupied). The road crosses the border at ***Desaguadero*** 22 km further W (*Hotel Bolivia*, near Bolivian customs, reasonable 4-course meals) and runs along the shore of the lake to Puno. A side road which branches off to the N leads to Yunguyo and back across the border to Copacabana. The route La Paz-Guaqui-Puno is being paved so that, eventually La Paz to the Peruvian ports of Matarani/Mollendo will be paved throughout.

Transport Buses from La Paz to Guaqui and Desaguadero depart from Ignavi office (José María Asu y Eyzaguirre) 0830 and 1000, US$1.50, 3½ hrs, avoid putting luggage on roof. From Desaguadero to La Paz 1430. To Puno US$6.50, 3 hrs. To Puno from La Paz US$15, 8 hrs.

2) Via Copacabana (see under Copacabana for description of the route to Copacabana). From Copacabana an unmetalled road leads S to the frontier near Yunguyo. For La Paz tourist agency services on this route **see under International Buses (p 260)** and under Lake Titicaca above.

This is now a very straightforward border crossing, with customs and immigration posts at either side of the border; the buses/colectivos stop at each one (or you can walk, 400m, and a small hill, between the two posts; transport does not start till Yunguyo, a further 600m). Taxis and tricycles run between the border and Yunguyo. Make sure, if arranging a through ticket La Paz-Puno, that you get all the necessary stamps en route, and ascertain whether your journey involves a change of bus. Note the common complaint that through services La Paz-Puno (or vice versa) deteriorate once the border has been crossed, eg smaller buses are used, extra passengers taken on, passengers left stranded if the onward bus is already full, drivers won't drop you where the company says they will.

At Yunguyo, do not photograph the border area. Beware of "out of hours" charges on the Peruvian side; if returning immediately to Bolivia, with a new visa, a US$5 bribe is asked for by Peruvian officials to avoid the statutory 72 hours outside Bolivia. There are many money changers on the Peruvian side. When leaving Peru, take as few soles as possible since they are very difficult to change. Arrive at the Peruvian border in the morning to ensure transport into Bolivia.

If crossing into Bolivia with a motorcycle, do not be fooled into paying any unnecessary charges to police or immigration.

3) Along the E side of Lake Titicaca. The Peruvian authorities do not officially recognize the road as being a border crossing. (Officially, you must get your entry stamp in the Department of Puno, but as this is next to impossible on this route, you will run into difficulties later on.) The road passes through Achacachi (**see p 280**), Ancoraimes (small Sun market), Carabuco (with colonial church), *Escoma*, which has a large Aymara market every Sunday (it finishes before 1300, watch out for drunks in the afternoon) and *Puerto Acosta*. The area around Puerto Acosta is good walking country and the locals are friendly. From La Paz to Puerto Acosta the road is fine during the dry season (approximately May to Oct). North of Puerto Acosta towards Peru the road deteriorates rapidly and should not be attempted except in the dry season.

There is an immigration office, beware extortionate demands by guards, but it is advisable to get an exit stamp in La Paz first. **G** *Alojamiento Espinosa*, basic, friendly, but no restaurants. Bus La Paz (Cementerio district)-Puerto Acosta, US$2.50, Fri 1130, Sat/Sun 0630. Many trucks travel La Paz-Puerto Acosta on Tues and Fri afternoons. The only transport beyond Acosta is early on Wed and Sat mornings when a couple of trucks go to the markets, some 25 km from Puerto Acosta on the border (no formalities); the Peruvian and Bolivian markets are completely different.

At Escoma a road branches N, roughly parallel with the border, going to Chuma, and to **Charazani** (Juan José Pérez; Ulla-Ulla *fiesta*, 16 July, witch doctor; **G** pp *Hotel Charazani*, good, clean, friendly; 2 restaurants; one bus a week from La Paz, otherwise trucks; by car 2 days from La Paz). The road ends at Apolo.

The road from Escoma to Charazani is very scenic, climbing to 4,500m. At the highest point is a sign to the **Reserva Ulla Ulla**, where llamas, alpacas, vicuñas, vizcachas and many birds can be seen, with the backdrop of the Cordillera de Apolobamba. Camping is possible (but cold), ask for the thermal springs, or for permission at farms (payment welcome). Sendero Luminoso activity was reported in the area in late 1994. Ulla Ulla-Charazani by car 3-4 hrs. Charazani is in the Yungas, with thermal springs. 2-3 hrs away is Curva, one of the bases of the Kalawaya (native medicine doctors), now reported to be unwilling to practice for visitors (too many of the latter). Also in the area is *Iskanwaya*, a major archaeological site on the eastern Andean slopes. A road from the Escoma-Charazani road crosses a 5,000m pass before descending to Aucapata; continue down a very poor jeep track then hike 1 hr down a cactus-filled canyon to the ruin (at about 1,500m). The city stands on two built-up platforms, with delicate walls, plazas, narrow streets, storerooms, niches, pot shards, etc. Admission to the museum in Aucapata is by donation. Great care is needed not to damage this site. (With thanks for information to Gregory W Frux, New York, and Dr J Kleinwächter, AM Wetzelsberg, Germany.)

THE YUNGAS (2)

Lush forested slopes behind the mountains to the N of La Paz; this is the main production area of citrus, bananas, coffee and coca leaves for the capital. It is also a favourite retreat for those escaping the Andean chill.

NB The Yungas are a coca-growing region, so it is advisable not to wander too far off the beaten track.

The Yungas can be approached either via La Cumbre, NE of La Paz, or by turning off the road which skirts the E shore of Lake Titicaca and crossing the Cordillera to Sorata. Both routes join at Caranavi, so a circular route can be made (**see map, p 269**).

The route NE out of La Paz circles cloudwards over La Cumbre pass at 4,725m; the highest point is reached in an hour; all around stand titanic snowcapped peaks and snowfields glinting in the sun. At Unduavi the paving ends; the road becomes "all-weather" and drops over 3,400m to the luxuriant green rain forest in 80 km. The roads to Coroico and Chulumani divide just after Unduavi, where there is a *garita* (check point), the only petrol station, but no good place to eat. Police may ask drivers of private vehicles for a voluntary contribution at the checkpoint near Unduavi. Note, if travelling by truck from La Paz to the Yungas via La Cumbre, the best views can be seen in May and June, when there is least chance of fog and rain on the heights. If you want to alight at La Cumbre, ensure you tell the driver beforehand for it is easy to miss in fog or cloud. It is very cold at La Cumbre and, further down, there are waterfalls at San Juan that baptise open vehicles—be prepared. For details of the La Cumbre-Coroico hike (Choro), **see p 263**.

Chulumani, the capital of Sud Yungas, is the main regional centre. Citrus fruits are the main products from this area as well as some coffee.

Hotels B *Motel San Bartolomé* (T 358386), pleasant, some family rooms and cabins cheaper, superb jungle setting with fabulous views of mountains, swimming pool, can be booked through the *Hotel Plaza*, La Paz, T 378311, Ext 1221 (or Plaza Tours in La Paz); **C** *Motel San Antonio*, pleasant cabins and swimming pools (both Motels are out of town, a taxi ride or long walk away). **D** *Prefectural*, on outskirts, full board, swimming pool (not always full, open to non-residents for US$0.50). **D** *Residencial El Milagro*, good views, at entrance to town by *tránsito*, very clean, very attentive landlady, garden; **D** *La Hostería*, Junín, T (0811) 6108, with bathroom, breakfast included, clean and friendly, restaurant; **E** *Panorama*, with pool, basic rm, poor service, restaurant; **F** pp *García*, on main square, with toilet, cheaper without, basic, clean and cheap, rec, but noisy at weekends from disco; *Hotel Bolívar*, cheap, clean and friendly.

C *Hotel Tamapaya*, 95 km from La Paz, just outside Puente Villa (the lowest point on the road), is in a beautiful setting, with shower, good rooms, swimming pool, rec.

Restaurants *Don Miguel* on main street, doesn't look much, but very good. Cheap food at *García* and at *Pensión Viviana*, Calle Lanza, for freshly-squeezed orange juice.

Bus From La Paz, Flota Yungueña, Av Las Américas 354, Villa Fátima, 120 km, Sat 0830, 6 hours, US$3.30. Minibus from Villa Fátima, La Paz, 0830/1430 daily, and returns early afternoons daily, US$3.50, 3-4 hrs, more comfortable than the bus.

Excursion From Chulumani you can continue to *Irupana* (fiesta 5 August, hotel F, clean with pool); the road passes through fruit, coffee and coca plantations. Bus from Chulumani less than US$1, or take any passing truck. In Irupana you can hire transport for **Chicaloma**, the centre of Bolivia's black population (½ hr, US$13 with waiting; 2 hrs walk). The village is in a tremendous location.

The other branch from Unduavi leading to Yolosa, the junction 7 km from Coroico, has been described as "life-endangering". True, it is steep, twisting, clinging to the side of sheer cliffs, and it is very slippery in the wet, but the danger lies in not knowing the rules of the road, especially at weekends. Uphill vehicles always have right of way; downhill must wait or reverse to a passing place. Uphill drives on the cliff side, be it left or right, downhill on the outside. Speed and ignorance on the narrow road leads to drivers plunging over the edge.

The little town of **Coroico** is perched on a hill at 1,525m; the scenery is beautiful. The hillside is covered with orange and banana groves; there are delightful walks through paths down to the river where warm pools are ideal for bathing (and if you're not up to 2-3 hrs walk each way, lifts are usually available in Coroico). The trail to the river starts at the left corner of the football pitch, looking downhill; it forks often, keep right. Another pleasant short walk starts at El Calvario (follow the Stations of the Cross by the cemetery, off Calle Julio Zuazo Cuenca which leads uphill from the main square). Facing the chapel at El Calvario, with your back to the view of the town and its setting, look for a path on the left, which soon becomes well-defined. It leads in 1 hour to the Cascada y Toma de Agua de Coroico (the source of the town's water supply); the path runs quite level along the hill's edge.

Festivals There is a colourful four-day festival on 19-22 October, when accommodation is hard to find. It is great fun, but wait a day or two before returning to La Paz (hung-over drivers). On 2 November, All Souls' Day, the local cemetery is festooned with black ribbons.

Hotels *San Carlo*, 1 km outside town, 3-star, T 813266 (La Paz T 372380), with restaurant, pool and sports facilities, modern, rec. Also out of town is off *El Viejo Molino*, 4-star, with pool, T 0811 6004 (or represented in La Paz by Valmar Tours, T 361076, F 352279). **D** *Don Quijote*, 800 m down Coripata road (up from square, then left, then right), new, pool, restaurant. **D** *Prefectural*, down the steps from the square, past the convent and beyond the football pitch, building a bit dated, but clean and pleasant, nice garden, good views, swimming pool (may not have water), full board (E without food), food quite good, has bus service to La Paz. **E** *Lluvia de Oro*, on street off square by Entel, good value (but confirm price), food rec, cheap, swimming pool, top floor rooms are best, opp is **G** pp *Res Coroico*, dormitory accommodation. **E** *Sol y Luna*, uphill past cemetery, and Umopar (narcotics police) station, 1/2-hr walk from town (ask for La Alemana, La Gringa, Victoria or Sigrid Fronius—all the same person!), dormitory accommodation **G** pp, meals available (Indonesian food), cooking facilities, also 2 *cabañas* for rent **D**, camping US$1 pp, swimming pool, garden, laundry service, highly rec (also, Sigrid offers Shiatsu massage for US$7), in La Paz reserve through Chuquiago Turismo, Planta Baja, Edif La Primera, Av Santa Cruz 1364, Casilla 4443, T 362099/359227. On road to *Sol y Luna* is **E** pp *Esmeralda*, T 811-6017, with bath (**F** pp without), German owner, good views, hot showers, TV, restaurant, changes money, rec. **E** *Hostal Kori*, at top of steps leading down from square, swimming pool (open to all, US$1), with bath, cheaper without (weekly rates available), very popular, not very clean, top floors most highly rec, restaurant. **E** *La Casa*, just down the hill from *Hostal Kori*, small, swimming pool, clean, with restaurant (below), rec; **G** pp *Residencial de la Torre*, next to Veloz del Norte office, showers, nice garden. *Res 20 de Octubre* is ABAJ youth hostel affiliate, US$2.50 pp. Camp site by the small church on the hill overlooking the town—a stiff climb though. Hotels can be difficult at holiday weekends and as the area is a popular retreat for the rich from La Paz, prices are higher.

Restaurants *La Casa* is German-run, good food and setting but not cheap, excellent salads, vegetarian dishes, fondue and raclett for dinner (reserve in advance), wonderful views, rec. The convent opposite *La Casa* has been rec for its biscuits, peanut butter and coffee liqueurs, and interesting cheap white wine. *Don Pasante*, J S Cuenca, up the hill to *Hotel Esmeralda*, local and international food, breakfasts, rec. Also try second to last stall on right in Mercado Municipal, highly rec. *Daedalus Bar*, main plaza, for cocktails. Honey is sold in various places.

Horse Riding Patricio and Dany (French), who live at *Rancho Beni* by the new hospital in Comunidad de Aparto, have 6 horses for hire, US$5/hr, US$9 for 2 hrs inc guide, US$30 for all-day trek, with breakfast, lunch and swim at Río Vagante, also trekking in the mountains or just a few hours' riding; very friendly, rec. Dany makes excellent, home-grown coffee. Reservations in La Paz: Shuriya, Plaza Abaroa, Av 20 de Octubre 2463, T 322041, 1100-1300, 1530-1930.

Services Entel, main plaza, for international and local calls; Cotel next to church, phones, public TV. No banks; nowhere to change TCs. Pío Rolando Gutiérrez Linares rec as knowledgeable about local plantlife (Spanish only).

Transport Buses, minibuses, trucks and pick-ups from La Paz all leave from Villa Fátima, where transport companies have their offices: Flota Yungueña, Av Las Américas 354; Trans Tours Hotel Prefectural, Yanacachi 1434; Veloz del Norte, Virgen del Carmen 1329, T 311640; Don Juan, Av Las Américas y Ocobaya. Three buses a day, 2 companies, US$3, 3-5 hrs; several companies eg Trans Tours Hotel Prefectural, Don Juan, Turibus Totai, Turismo Nuevo Continente, run 14 seater minibuses, US$4, 3-4 hrs and perhaps slightly less hair-raising, worth booking in advance; trucks (best for views) US$2. Also pick-ups, usually from company offices. Sit on right in the mountains, on left hand side on the descent to Yungas. In Corcoico: Flota Yungueña in

Comedor Municipal, on road to Caranavi; Trans Tours Hotel Prefectural at *Restaurant Las Peñas/Res 20 de Octubre*; Veloz del Norte, next to *Restaurant Disco Safari* uphill from square; Don Juan, on square next to Artesanías Arco Iris. Extra services run on Sundays. It can be difficult to book journeys to La Paz on holidays and on Sun evenings/Mon mornings (though these are good times for hitching). Trucks and pick-ups may drop you at Yolosa, 7 km from Coroico; there is usually transport Yolosa-Coroico, US$0.50, or you can walk, uphill all the way, 2 hrs. In Coroico trucks leave from the market. Buses and pick-ups run from Yolosa to **Caranavi**, 3-4 hrs, US$2.50, **Guanay**, 7 hrs, US$4 and **Rurrenabaque**. Also trucks.

On the road from Puente Villa to **Coripata** (F *Hotel Florida*), which is also reached by road from Coroico, you enter the main coca growing area of N Bolivia. The countryside is quite different from that near Coroico, where coffee, as well as coca and fruits, is the main crop.

From the road junction at Yolosa the lower fork follows the river NE to **Caranavi**, a very ugly town 164 km from La Paz, 75 km from Yolosa, at times along a picturesque gorge, towards the settled area of the Alto Beni . Market day is Saturday; lots of transport in late afternoon.

Hotels   Mainly along Av Mcal Santa Cruz, the main street: E *Landivar*, most expensive, pool; F *Caranavi*, clean and friendly, rec; F *Residencial Avenida*, friendly, basic and cheap; F *Alojamiento Capitol*, basic; F *México*, basic.

Restaurants   *Paradiso*, cheap; *Tropical*, good set menu and cheap.

Bus   From Villa Fátima in La Paz, Veloz del Norte and Yungueña buses, US$4, daily, 6-7 hrs; also Turibus Totai, 4 a day, US$4.50 and trucks, 12½ hrs. Trans Tours Hotel Prefectural Coroico (address above) 0900 and 1400 to Caranavi, 0900 continues to Guanay, US$2.50; to Rurrenabaque, 2000, 12 hrs, US$9. Direct bus Coroico-Caranavi on Sundays, or you can take a truck, US$1.65. If you want to continue into the Beni Lowlands without going into Caranavi, wait at the checkpoint before the town where all transport has to stop and ask for a ride there. Rurrenabaque and Trinidad can be reached by road.

Some 70 km NW of Caranavi lies the gold mining town of **Guanay**, an interesting, friendly place at the junction of the Tipuani and Mapiri rivers. Other gold mining sites are Tipuani and Mapiri (see below). Buses direct from La Paz, Yungueña and Estrella Azul, about US$8, also trucks, which make frequent stops and diversions. The bridge just before Guanay was washed away in 1994: travellers change buses and cross by a temporary footbridge. (Transport from Caranavi is very erratic: buses run if there are enough passengers, if not take a pick-up.)

Hotels, Restaurants, Services   E *Panamericana*, helpful, popular with tour groups; F pp *Perla Andina*, clean, friendly, cold water, rooms on street less hot than those on courtyard, fans in rooms but electricity 1800-2400 only; F *Hotel Ritzy*, on main plaza, very clean, with mosquito nets; G pp *Alojamiento Los Pinos*, opp football pitch, cold water, basic, clean, may arrange exchange of TCs (with commission — cash can be changed with shopkeepers or gold dealers); G pp *Estrella Azul*, basic, friendly; G pp *Pahuichi*, clean, nice restaurant. Camping is possible next to the football field. *Restaurant La Bamba*, opp *Panamericana*, good value, English spoken. Many other eating places on main street have fixed-price meals; one, with courtyard, monkey and parrot, serves excellent value breakfast of steak, eggs and tomato for US$0.75. Electricity is rationed—every 10 mins or so – and water is available before 1200 only.

Boats go down the Río Beni from Guanay to Rurrenabaque (see p 314), 8-12 hrs, US$11-18 depending on how successfully you negotiate and availability of vessels. Cargo is now carried by road so you have to wait till the boat is full, which can take several days. Latest reports suggest that boatmen are unwilling to go with fewer than ten passengers. "Expreso" boats can also be hired from Flota Fluvial, opposite *Perla Andina*, at a price (US$150-300 depending on size and your ability to bargain). The journey goes through gold mining settlements, then narrow, fertile river banks sown with peanuts.

From Guanay boats leave from the dock 3 blocks from the square for **Mapiri**, a mining town on the river of the same name (Accommodation **F**). Boats leave daily at 0700, or later if not full, US$10, 5-7 hrs; cargo boats may run at other times, but do not rely on it. Mines can be seen along the way, in among the tropical vegetation.

From Mapiri, an adventurous route goes up into the mountains via Sorata Limitada (a mining town, not to be confused with Sorata) and Santa Rosa to Sorata, thence, completing the Yungas circuit, back to La Paz. *Camionetas* run to Santa Rosa (**G** *Hotel Las Cinco Estrellas*, small rooms, tiny beds, cleanish, pool), US$2. At Sorata Limitada there are 2 basic *alojamientos*, both G, the one beside the football pitch is quieter than the one beside the bar. *Camionetas* leave for Sorata from Sorata Limitada, US$10, 14 hrs and from Santa Rosa, US$8, 10 hrs. The scenery is superb, but the road is narrow, slippery, dangerous and dirty, especially in the rainy season. Try to get yourself as comfortable a seat as possible; the driver usually carries carpet to protect passengers against rain, but there is also a lot of dust. Have warm clothing handy for the road crosses the pass at 4,700m before dropping to Sorata.

Rather than going straight through to La Paz, it is worth breaking the journey at **Sorata**, a beautiful place at 2,695m. There is also good transport from La Paz (see below). All around Sorata are lovely views and ideal country for hiking and climbing since it is in a valley at the foot of Illampu. The town square, with its trees and, on a clear day, the snow-capped summit of Illampu as a backdrop, is delightful. The market area is beside the square; market day is Sunday. Fiesta 14 September.

Hotels D *Prefectural*, at entrance to town, C full board, bath, hot water, good but dear food, bar, pool (US$0.80 for non-residents), nice building and garden, rec; **E** *Paraíso*, Villavicencio 117, with bath, breakfast extra, hot water, smart, restaurant; **F** pp *Copacabana*, down the hill from the centre (look for the signs), shared hot showers, meals (including vegetarian and German breakfast – called "Americano" – but not cheap), clean, simple rooms; **F** pp *San Cristóbal*, Muñecas 350, near market, basic, shared bath, meals available, friendly; **G** *Alojamiento Central*, main square No 127, basic, no showers, but nice rooms. **G** pp *Residencial Sorata*, just off main square, mansion (formerly major export/import house) in process of renovation, shared bathrooms, hot water unreliable, clean, large reading room and table-tennis, good restaurant, laundry facilities, friendly staff incl Louis from Quebec, highly rec.

Restaurants *Casa de Papaco*, follow signs from main square, pizzas, homemade pasta, meat and vegetarian dishes, Bolivian dishes, good food, nice building, friendly, not cheap but worth it. *La Terraza*, good, friendly, cheap, good breakfast; *Santa Rosa*, main square, cheap meals; *El Tigre*, main square, cheap lunches. Good and cheap set meals at *Pensión Larecaja*, just off the main square.

Services Two Entel offices for telephones. Money exchange in the hotels, or good rates for cash at the Oficina Parroquial, next door to the church. For handicrafts, *Artesanía Sorata* on the main square.

Transport Buses from La Paz with Transtur Sorata (Bustillos 670, Cemetery district; in Sorata, just off square at No 101) and Larecaja (Bustillos y Angel Bobia, Cemetery district; in Sorata, 14 de Septiembre 206, just off square on road into/out of town), both have departures at 0700-0715, return from Sorata 1130-1300, US$2, 4 hrs "directo", 6 hrs stopping (Larecaja). On Mon there is a 0530 bus to La Paz. Plenty of trucks in am from Cemetery district, La Paz, to Sorata. Sit on left from La Paz.

Hiking and Climbing The climbing season is end-April to beginning-September. Sorata is the starting point for climbing *Illampu* (experience and full equipment necessary).

Hotel Copacabana rents equipment and can arrange treks, guides and mules – at a price. Much cheaper to make arrangements yourself.

When trekking in this area do not trust any water, it may be infected by vizcacha urine or with micah from the snow melt; it is best to filter it.

There are lots of walking possibilities. The most popular is to San Pedro cave, most easily reached by road, a 12 km walk (2 hrs) each way. The cave is beyond the village of San Pedro (where the road splits, take the lower road and look for the white building above). You can swim in the underground lake, which is 20.6°C. Entry US$1.25; do not go alone, do not swim alone. Latest reports say the cave is filthy and vandalized (1994). It is also possible to walk to the cave along the Río San Cristóbal; on leaving Sorata on the San Pedro road, look for the round sign to the Seminario. Go down that road and join the river. Initially you may have to walk on the river bed, or through fields (only for a short way), then the path becomes clearer, following the gorge. After 2 hrs, you come to a small plain with white boulders. After 3 hrs, you reach a bigger plain with scrub, above which is a large, whitish rock. In about the middle of the plain is a small gorge, on the far side of which, by a tree, a path leads right through the scrub up to the white rock. Just follow this path steeply up until you reach the road. The last part is difficult to follow. It is imperative to take water, at least 1 litre per person (or else take sterilizing tablets and fill up at the tap in San Pedro). Ask for the house selling refrescos by the litre in San Pedro.

A highly recommended hike is to Laguna Chillata and Inca Marka, a strenuous full-day walk, climbing from Sorata to 4,207m (either take plenty of water, or a water filter). Go with a guide because this is a sensitive area; the lake is sacred and Inca Marka is a burial place, dating back to the precolumbian Mollu culture. Camping is forbidden; do not touch anything, not even bits of paper, bottles, etc, which may be offerings.

Werner Bischoff from Steffisburg in Switzerland recommends the "Circuito Illampu", a 7-day high-altitude trek (5 passes over 4500 m) around Mt Illampu. "It can get very cold and it is a hard walk, though very beautiful with nice campsites on the way. Food can be bought in Cocoyo on the third day. A very good trek for getting acclimatized if you intend to climb a high peak".

Sorata is the starting point for two treks into the Yungas. The **"Camino del Oro"** or "Gold Digger's Trail", a 7-8 day hike to Guanay (see above), rises to 4,800m before going to Ancoma (1½ days from Sorata), then Wainapata, Chusi, 18 hrs from Ancoma (shop), Llipi, 8 hrs from Chusi and Unutulumi (2-3 hrs from Llipi, from here a *camioneta* runs daily to Guanay, US$5, 0930, winding through the many gold-digging towns in the Tipuani valley). After Ancoma it is very hot. The Ancoma-Llipi section is the most interesting, following the Tipuani river, climbing Inca staircases, crossing rivers on precarious plank bridges and going through an Inca tunnel. Very strenuous, not much flat ground for camping. See the warning in **Hiking**, p 332.

The **Mapiri Trail** opens up a road; claimed by some to be prehispanic and paved since Mollu times and used by explorer Colonel Faucett, but certainly used by quinine and rubber traders, gold miners as well as the Bolivian army on the way to defeat by Brazil in 1903. It is 150 km, 7-8 days, and tough; a guide is essential. Travel light, take water purification and capacity for at least 3 litres pp. From Mapiri, you continue to Guanay by boat.

Anne Girardet (Nyon, Switzerland) writes: "It starts in the freezing cold town of Ancoma at 4,200m, follows for much of its length a ridge allowing beautiful views and ends in tropical Mapiri at 800m" adding "It is not a luxury to hire mules to carry the heavy load for the first three days." Matthew Parris (London E14) adds: "Your camps must be waterproof and insect-excluding. If you don't like flies, wasps, bees and ants, don't go. Much of your time will be spent crawling along rock-bottomed trenches and under logs. You will be rewarded with parrots, butterflies, flowers, tree-ferns, millions of tons of moss and with unbelievable views over thousands of square miles of near-vertical cloud forest, utterly unpenetrated by man."

It is also possible to hike from Sorata to Lake Titicaca. It is much cheaper to go to Sorata and ask about trekking there than to book up a trek with an agency in La Paz.

Sorata to La Paz The road to the capital leaves Sorata, descends to the river, crosses a bridge and climbs up the side of the valley. It continues climbing, in a landscape of huge valleys and ridges, to a pass in fields with stone walls and boulders before reaching the openness of the altiplano. Between Warisata and Achacachi is a tremendous marsh, with sheets of water, dykes, farms, cattle, people working the fields and many birds; in the distance snow-capped peaks can be seen. At *Achacachi*, there are 3 *alojamientos: Huancayuno*, opposite school, bathroom, water, *San Pedro*, no bathroom, *Tu Residencial*, all G, none too clean and all reported hostile, better stay somewhere else; 2 restaurants to the left of *Huancayuno*; market behind the main plaza (which looks as if it was once prosperous). Interesting Sun market. Fiesta 14 September. There are good views of Lake Titicaca from the church up the hill from the left side of the plaza. It is also possible to walk to the lake in 1½ hrs. Plenty of buses to La Paz in the morning, US$1; from La Paz to Achacachi every 15 mins from Cemetery district (opposite side of Av Kollasuyo from Sorata buses). Achacachi is a good place for connections if coming from Peru to Sorata: from Copacabana take a bus to Huarina, change there for a bus to Achacachi, then take a truck for Sorata. Sorata to Peru: take a La Paz bus and get out at Huarina; from there take a bus to Copacabana (best done in the morning).

ORURO AND ROUTES TO CHILE AND ARGENTINA (3)

Flamingoes shimmering in the glare of salt-flats, geysers and volcanoes on the Chilean border and, around Oruro, the poverty of the mines belies former wealth.

Oruro, 230 km SE of La Paz, is built on the slopes of a hill at an altitude of 3,704m. The population, mostly Indian, is 195,000. Although Oruro is famous as a mining town, there are no longer any working mines. It is, however, an important railway junction and the commercial centre for the mining communities of the altiplano. Several fine buildings in the centre hint at the city's former importance, notably the baroque concert hall (now a cinema) on the main square (Plaza 10 de Febrero) and the Casa de la Cultura (**see below under Museums**) built as a mansion by the tin "baron" Simón Patiño. There is a good view of the city from the Cerro Corazón de Jesus, near the church of the Virgen del Socavón, 5 blocks W of Plaza 10 de Febrero at the end of Calle Mier. Excellent daily market, near railway station. The zoo is not really worth a special visit. Along Calle La Paz, the continuation N of Soriano Galvaro, are many of the workshops in which costumes and masks for the Diablada are made. The disused San José mine, worked for over 450 years for silver, tin and other minerals, lies 3 km W of the city and can be visited with a permit (permit and guide arranged through the tourist office). A 20,000 tons-a-year tin smelter has been built nearby at Vinto; open to visitors, but a permit has to be applied for, 24 hours in advance, in Oruro.

La Diablada   At carnival on the Saturday before Ash Wednesday, Oruro stages the Diablada ceremony in gratitude to Pachamama, the Earth Mother. Two figures, a bear and a condor, clear the way for a procession of masked dancers, led by two luxuriously costumed masqueraders representing Satan and Lucifer. Alternating with them in the lead are St Michael the Archangel and China Supay, the Devil's wife, who plays the role of carnal temptress. Behind them come hundreds of dancers in ferocious diabolical costumes, leaping, shouting, and pirouetting. The parade ends in the crowded football stadium, where the masqueraders perform various mass and solo dances. These are followed by two masques: the first is a tragic re-enactment of the Conquest, in the second the golden-haired Archangel conquers the forces of evil in battle.

In the contest between good and evil, the result is in favour of the good is pronounced by the Virgen del Socavón, the patroness of miners, and after the performance the dancers all enter her chapel, chant a hymn in Quechua and pray for pardon. The Diablada was traditionally performed by Indian miners, but three other guilds have taken up the custom.

The costume always features the heavy, gruesome mask modelled in plaster, with a toad or snake on top; huge glass eyes; triangular glass teeth; a horsehair wig; and pointed, vibrating ears. Tied around the neck is a large silk shawl embroidered with dragons or other figures, and the dancer also has a jewelled, fringed breastplate. Over his white shirt and tights he wears a sash trimmed with coins, and from it hang the four flaps of the native skirt, embroidered in gold and silver thread and loaded with precious stones. Special boots equipped with spurs complete the elaborate outfit. Satan and Lucifer wear scarlet cloaks, and carry a serpent twisted around one arm and a trident. The working-class Oruro district known as La Ranchería is particularly famous for the excellence of the costumes and masks made there. One of the most famous folklore groups is the stately Morenada. The opening procession begins at around 0800 on Saturday and dancing continues until 0300 the following day. Carnival lasts 8 days with displays of dancing by day and night often superior to those given on the opening Saturday. There are two options for seating: municipal seats around the main plaza and on Av Cívica, which cost US$5 a day, booked in advance; Av Cívica is a good spot because the street is wide and the dancers are unrestricted. The alternative is seating outside shops (US$4 a day, also booked beforehand) where the streets are narrower so you are closer to the dancers, and to the water-bombers. To wander among the dancers you are officially supposed to purchase a professional photographer's ticket for US$15, but little checking seems to be done (amateurs need pay only US$1.50, show your small camera and insist). Seats can be booked at the town hall.

Tony Baker writes, "Do not wear a raincoat as protection against water bombs; you will merely become a prime target, or rather more of a prime target since gringos get soaked as a matter of course. The best thing to do is buy a water-cannon and arm yourself to the teeth, try to buy seats near a water supply, wear few clothes as possible, and, though you will get soaked, at least you will get some revenge... Fortunately hostilities cease as it gets dark, so you can get changed into something warm and dry and really enjoy the nights' entertainment. *Leche de tigre* is drunk against the cold: hot milk with a heavy shot of singani."

Latest reports suggest that the processions on the opening Saturday are fine, but degenerate thereafter as all the participants are drunk; also participants now have to be wealthy to afford to take part, so *campesinos* have been forced to the periphery (selling food, etc). The Friday before carnival, traditional "challa" ceremonies are held at mines, including the slaughter of a white llama. It is essential to go with a guide and get permission to visit (eg Pepé-Elmer Chávez at the Tourst Office). The weekend before carnival the groups practise, which is almost

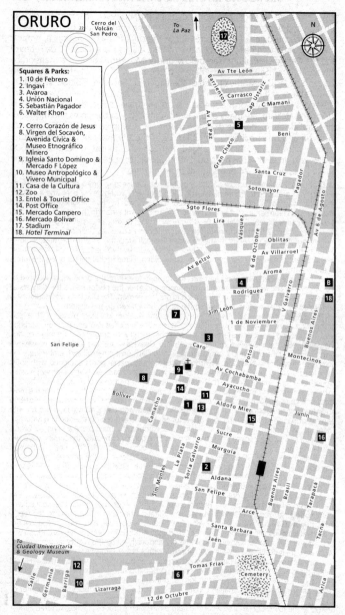

ORURO

Cerro del
Volcán
San Pedro

To
La Paz

Squares & Parks:
1. 10 de Febrero
2. Ingavi
3. Avaroa
4. Unión Nacional
5. Sebastián Pagador
6. Walter Khon

7. Cerro Corazón de Jesus
8. Virgen del Socavón,
   Avenida Cívica &
   Museo Etnográfico
   Minero
9. Iglesia Santo Domingo &
   Mercado F López
10. Museo Antropológico &
    Vivero Municipal
11. Casa de la Cultura
12. Zoo
13. Entel & Tourist Office
14. Post Office
15. Mercado Campero
16. Mercado Bolívar
17. Stadium
18. Hotel Terminal

Av Tte León

Barrientos Carrasco

Cap Ustariz

C Mamani

Av La Paz

Gran Chaco

Beni

Santa Cruz

Sotomayor

Pagador

Av 6 de Agosto

Sgto Flores

Lira

Vásquez

Oblitas

6 de Octubre

Av Villarroel

Av Belzu

Aroma

Rodríguez

V Galvarro

Buenos Aires

Sim León

1 de Noviembre

Caro

Potosí

Montecinos

Av Cochabamba

Ayacucho

Aldofo Mier

Junín

Bolívar

Camacho

Sucre

Murguia

La Plata

Soria Galvarro

Aldana

San Felipe

Buenos Aires

Brasil

Tarapacá

Tacna

Arce

Santa Barbara

Jaén

To
Ciudad Universitaria
& Geology Museum

Salle

Germania

Barriga

Lizarraga

Tomas Frias

12 de Octubre

Cemetery

Sim Montes

San Felipe

Arica

as good as the main event. On the Saturday after Carnival all the groups perform in the football stadium, less atmosphere, less crowded, but good for photos. Beware of sharp practices during the period of carnival. Accommodation, increases in the prices of which are officially controlled, must be booked in advance for carnival; the Senatur office in the Edificio Prefectural will find accommodation with families, US$5 pp; book a few days in advance. Transport prices from La Paz triple. Organized tours from La Paz cost US$50, including transport, food and a seat in the main plaza, but it is probably more interesting to go independently.

Museums Museo Etnográfico Minero, under the Church of the Virgen del Socavón, W end of Calle Mier, containing mining equipment and other artefacts from the beginning of the century as well as a "tío", entry via the church 0900-1200, 1430-1800, US$0.50; **Casa de la Cultura**, Galvarro 5755, formerly one of the Patiño residences, now run by the Universidad Técnica de Oruro, contains European furniture and a coach imported from France, also houses temporary exhibitions, open Mon-Fri 0900-1200, 1430-1800, US$1; **Museo Antropológico**, S of centre on Av España (take micro A heading S or any trufi going S) has a unique collection of stone llama heads as well as impressive carnival masks, open Tues-Sun 1000-1200, US$0.75, no guide, all in Spanish; **Museo Mineralógico**, part of the University (take micro A South to the Ciudad Universitaria), with over 3,000 mineral specimens, claimed as one of the best in South America, open Mon-Fri 0800-1200, 1430-1700.

Guide Carnival de Oruro. Dance costumes and masks, Calle La Paz, 400 block.

Hotels In the centre: **C** Nikkei Plaza, Plaza 10 de Febrero, T 54799, with bath and breakfast, modern, comfortable; **D** Repostero, Sucre 370 y Pagador, T 50505, with bath, hot water, clean, pleasant, comedor; **D** Gran Sucre, Sucre 510, T 53838, run-down but pleasant, has new wing; **D** América, Bolívar y Pagador, T 60707, with bath, **E** without, clean, restaurant; **E** Ideal, Bolívar 386, T 52863, with bath, **F** without, basic but clean, poor beds; **E** Gloria, 15 de Octubre, with bath, **F** without, basic, clean, hot water. **Near the bus terminal: C** Terminal, above bus terminal, T 53797, modern, heating, good views, expensive restaurant, higher rates charged for foreigners, noisy; **E** Bolivia, Rodríguez 131 y 6 de Agosto, T 41047, with bath, **F** without, hot water, clean restaurant; **E** Lipton, Av 6 de Agosto 225, T 41538, with bath, **F** pp without, clean, secure, parking extra; **E** Residencial Verano, 200 m from bus terminal, T 41742, without bath, modern, clean; **F** pp Residencial El Turista, 6 de Agosto 466, T 41888, without bath, unhelpful, safe parking. **Near the railway station:** all on Galvarro, all **G** pp and very basic, no hot water: Hispano-Americano (No 6392, T 61117); **Alojamiento Copacabana** (No 6352, T 54184); Ferroviario (No 6278, T 60079); 5 blocks N is **F** F85MIAlojamiento 15 de Octubre, 6 de Agosto 890, T 40012, without bath, hot shower US$2 extra, clean, good value.

Restaurants La Casona, Pres Montes 5970, opp Post Office, good pizzería; La Tarantella, Bolívar y 6 de Octubre, pizzas and Chinese dishes; La Gaviota, Junín 676, reasonable; Nayjama, typical Oruro cuisine; Club Social Arabe, Junín 729 y Pres Montes, good value lunches; Los Escudos, Montecinos y 6 de Agosto, good value; good salteñas at **Super Salteñas**, Bolívar 490. Bamin, Potosí 1640, excellent and not expensive, friendly; Libertador, Bolívar 347, excellent set lunch for US$1; Cafetería París, just off main square, excellent cakes. Vegetarian: El Huerto, Bolívar 359, cheap. Cheap meals in the Mercado Fermín López.

Banks and Exchange Cash advances on credit cards at **Banco de La Paz**, US$3.75 authorisation charge. TCs can be changed at **Banco Boliviano Americano**, 5% commission and at **Banco de Santa Cruz**, Bolívar 670 (also office at Pagador y Caro, open Sat 0900-1200). It is quite easy to change dollars (cash) on the street: good rates on Av V Galvarro, opposite train station, or at Ferretería Findel, Calle Pagador 1491, near the market (large hardware store), or try Don Ernest at Av V Galvarro 5998, T 60520.

German Consulate at Adolfo Mier y Galvarro.

Laundry Alemania, Aldana 280.

Post Office Presidente Montes 1456. **Telecommunications** Entel, Bolívar, 1 block E of plaza.

Sauna Ayacucho y Galvarro, wet or dry, showers US$0.75. Duchas Oruro, 500 block of Av 6 de Agosto (near bus terminal); Santa Bárbara, Pagador 6801.

Shopping Infol, Ayacucho 426 for alpaca, high quality but not cheap nor a large selection and Reguerín on the junction with Mier; also sell devil masks. An un-named shop at Av La Paz 4999 is recommended for all kinds of masks, good quality and prices. The municipal market has an interesting witchcraft section, said to be far better than the one in La Paz. A good handicraft shop is on Av Cochabamba, opposite the market, although handicrafts are generally cheaper in Cochabamba.

Travel Agent Jumbo Travel, 6 de Octubre 6080, T 55005/55203, friendly and efficient. A recommended driver and guide is Freddy Barron, Casilla 23, Oruro, T (052) 41776, who offers a programme of excursions and aventure tours. Juan Carlos Vargas, T 40333, also rec as tour guide, contact via tourist office.

Tourist Office The kiosk at Bolívar y Galvarro, 1 block E of Plaza 10 de Febrero, T 50144, open Mon-Fri 0900-1200, 1400-1800, Sat/Sun 0900-1000, supplies a map of the city.

Trains Check in advance which services are running, T 60605. 4 hrs 20 mins from/to **La Paz** Wed only. To **Cochabamba**, Wed and Fri at 0800. To **Potosí**, Wed at 2100, US$4.25 *especial*, US$5.75 *pullman*. To **Villazón**, Mon and Thur, 1900, 16-19 hours (US$6.80 *especial*, US$9 *pullman*), exhausting but exhilarating to the hardy traveller. Ticket office opens at 0700, best to be there early. **Calama**, for Antofagasta (Chile), 30-36 hrs, very prone to delay. Sun 1930, US$16, be at ticket office at 0700. For details **see above** under La Paz, **Railways to/from the Coast** (3).

Buses Terminal 10 blocks N of centre at Buenos Aires y Aroma, T 53689. To/from **La Paz**, 3 hours, seven bus lines work the route, hourly in the day, US$2.50, also at night US$3.10; to **Potosí**, 8-10 cold and rough hours, US3.15-3.75; to **Cochabamba**, 4½-6 hrs, US$4, Cometa frequent, several other companies. To **Sucre**, best to go via Cochabamba if wet as the road to Potosí is so bad. Roads to **Río Mulato** and **Uyuni** are very bad, Panasur and 11 de Julio, 2 days a week each, US$6.30 and US$4.20, some trucks work the route; train (4½-8 hours) recommended. Trucks to Potosí and Sucre leave from Av Cochabamba near the Mercado Bolívar. Note: if coming to Oruro and travelling on a tight budget, do not take a bus which arrives late at night as cheap accommodation will be shut; only the expensive *Hotel Terminal* will be open.

Excursions To the hot springs at **Obrajes**, 23 km N, where there is the choice of private baths or swimming pool, both hot (not very clean, but excellent for the dirty traveller), entry US$1.20. Also to springs at Capachos, less good. Free facilities for clothes washing in the natural hot water. Wait at the bus stop at Calle Caro for the (intermittent) bus to both places, US$0.50 to Capachos. Go early as return transport difficult after 1600. Taxis sometimes make the run. Take picnic lunch. Avoid Sun when it is very crowded.

To **Lago Poopó**, about 80 km S, and the **Santuario de Aves Lago Poopó**, an excellent bird reserve. Moreno Ortelli from Como, Italy, writes "If you do not have your own transportation, stay in Challapata (120 km S of Oruro), accessible by bus or train from either Potosí or Oruro. There is a basic *alojamiento* where you can rent a bike or motorbike to ride the approx 10 km to the lake-shore. Some Uro indians live in the region, belonging to the Muratos sub-group."

To **Llallagua**, 3,881m, 95 km SE, a mining town at which visitors are not always made welcome (**F** *Hotel Bustillo*; *Santa María*; **G** *Hotel Llallagua*, small beds, no bath, seldom has water, perhaps the best, but not really rec; few restaurants). *Fiesta*: Asunción. Nearby is the famous Siglo Veinte, once the largest tin mine (ex-Patiño) in the country (now closed), but being worked by small cooperatives. There is an acute water shortage. Llallagua can be reached by bus from Oruro (Bustillo, 7 a day, Enta 0900, 1700 daily, 3 hrs, US$2), continuing twice a week to Sucre (Bustillo), buses also to Potosí, beautiful but uncomfortable. Also buses 1900 from La Paz. Nearby at **Uncia** (Km 102; small *alojamiento* near the prison, G, clean, safe, basic; poor restaurants, eat at the market) there are more former Patiño mines and good hot springs (reached by *trufi*).

Travellers with a 4WD vehicle might explore the country SW of Oruro towards the Chilean frontier. It's a day's drive to the western mountains following tracks rather than roads. There are no hotels in any of the towns, but lodging can often be found by asking a local school-teacher or mayor. At Toledo, 38 km SW, there is a colonial church. **Escara**, further SE, is a lovely village with a beautiful square; it is a friendly place, has bike rental. From Escara it is only 25 km S to **Chipaya**, 190 km from Oruro, which is less welcoming, the main settlement of the most interesting Indians of the Altiplano. They speak a language closely related to the almost extinct Uru; their distinctive dress and unique conical houses are beginning to disappear as the community changes. This is a very difficult trip without your own transport; there is transport once a week in either direction from Huachacalla on the Oruro-Sabaya road. In Chipaya, the town council charges visitors US$50 for free access and hospitality. For a smaller, or no, contribution you will be much less welcome. There is very little for the visitor to do and it is very cold.

A one-day drive to the W is the **Parque Nacional Sajama**, established in 1945 and covering 60,000 hectares. The park contains the world's highest forest, consisting mainly of the rare Kenua tree (Polylepis Tarapana) which grows up to 5,200m. The scenery is wonderful and includes views of three volcanoes (**Sajama** – Bolivia's highest peak at 6,530m – Parinacota, Pomerape). The road is very bad. Take the Litoral La Paz-Arica bus (La Paz 0500 Tues and Fri;

from Arica same days 0900), ask for Sajama. and pay the full fare. A cheaper way is to take a La Paz-Oruro bus as far as Patacamaya (1½ hrs from La Paz), then take a truck to Estación Tomarapi (dusty, but very interesting, US$2). There are restaurants in the park but no fresh food, so take plenty from La Paz (water no problem, but take purifying tablets). If continuing into Chile (same buses) remember that no meat, dairy products, fruit or vegetables may be taken across the border. Crampons, ice axe and rope are needed for climbing the three volcanoes which are not technically difficult; the routes to base camp and beyond are fairly obvious. In Sajama village (altitude 4,200 m, population 500), Peter Brunnhart (Señor Pedro) and Telmo Nina have a book with descriptions of the various routes to the summit (Telmo Nina keeps the visitors book, Park entry fee US$1); basic accommodation available. It can be very windy and cold at night (good sleeping bag essential). Mules can be hired, US$6/day. Good bathing in hot springs 5 km N of village, interesting geothermic area 6 km W of village. The Sajama area is a major centre of alpaca wool production and llama meat is still the main food. This area will become more accessible when the new La Paz-Arica highway is completed.

A road and railway line run S from Oruro, through Río Mulato, the junction for trains to Potosí, to Uyuni (323 km). The road is sandy, and after rain very bad, especially S of Río Mulato.

Uyuni, population about 10,000, lies bitterly cold and unprotected at 3,665m near the eastern edge of the Salar de Uyuni, claimed to be the largest salt lake in the world. Still a commercial and communication centre, Uyuni was, for much of this century, important as a major railway junction. A giant statue of an armed railway worker, erected after the 1952 Revolution, dominates Av Ferroviaria. Most services are near the station. Uyuni's main point of interest is as a centre for excursions to the Salar de Uyuni, Laguna Colorada and Laguna Verde (see below). Note that water is frequently cut off and may only be available between 0600 and midday. Market Sun. **Fiesta** San Miguel.

Hotels and Services D *Avenida*, Av Ferroviaria, opp station, T 878, in renovated wing, rooms with bath, hot water, F without bath in old wing, clean, hot showers (timed) US$1 extra, bar, breakfast, unfriendly, has a book for comments on trips to the Salar and Lagunas. **F** *Residencia Sucre*, new, clean, padlocks on doors, glass in windows. Three *Residenciales* all on Av Arce, all **G** pp: *Copacabana*, no hot water, basic, clean rrn, dirty bathrooms; *Urkupiña*, basic and quite clean, hot water; *Uyuni*, small rooms, basic, dirty, hot showers extra. *Restaurant 16 de Julio*, Av Arce, best in town, good cheap meals, friendly. *Salteñas* go on sale about 0900 daily. The stalls around the municipal market are well-stocked with regional contraband. Banco del Estado will not change money, best rates at *Restaurant 16 de Julio*, or try the pharmacy on Av Arce, or shops. Nowhere to change TCs but tour agencies and some shops accept payment in TCs. The Immigration Office is on Calle Potosí; only issues 30-day stamps, for 90 days go to Potosí. The tourist office opposite is helpful.

Transport The train service to Calama, Chile, is described under **Railways To/From the Coast,** (3), p 260. Uyuni is also a stop on the La Paz-Oruro-Villazón line: Oruro-Villazón (Mon, Thur at 1900) and Oruro-Tupiza (1 *ferrobus*) all stop here. Uyuni-La Paz (Expreso del Sur, Sat 1430, US$11.55; to Oruro, *ferrobus*, Tues, Wed 1330, local train Mon, Thur 1430. Fares: Oruro-Uyuni US$3.15 *especial*, US$4.25 *pullman*, 8 hrs. Daily freight train to Ollagüe, US$4.50, 6 hrs.

Bus to **La Paz** and **Oruro**, Panasur, Wed, Sun 1800, US$8, 15 hrs, terrible road as far as Huari (US$6.30 to Oruro), 11 de Julio also to Oruro, Mon and Fri 1800, US$4.20; to **Tupiza**, Wed 1530, US$4, 7½ hrs; to **Potosí**, American, daily 1030, other companies, 6 hrs, US$5, spectacular journey on unpaved roads. Trucks to Potosí are unpredictable, umpteen different versions of what's going on, but a great 8-9 hr trip when you get it, US$4.

By Road to Chile Motorists must be warned against the direct route from Uyuni into Chile by way of Ollagüe. There is the danger of getting lost on the many tracks leading over the deserted salt lakes, no gasoline between Uyuni and Calama (Chile), and little hope of help with a breakdown on the Bolivian side unless you don't mind waiting for perhaps a week. After rain the route is impassable and even experienced guides get lost. Maps give widely differing versions of the route. "Where the road has been built up, *never* forsake it for the appealing soft salt beside it. The salt takes a man's weight but a vehicle breaks through the crust into unfathomable depths of plasticine mud below."—Andrew Parkin.

To hitch to Chile via Ollagüe, trucks first go N, then across the Salar de Ollagüe. The scenery on this route is amazing and, once in Chile, you will see lakes similar to Lagunas Colorada and Verde. There is nowhere to stay in Ollagüe, but police and border officials will help find lodging and transport for hitchers.

Excursions To *Llica*, the capital of Daniel Campos Province, 5 hrs W of Uyuni across the Salar de Uyuni by truck, daily, 1100, bus daily, 1200. There is a new, basic **F** *Alojamiento Municipal* in town. Also Angel Quispe in the plaza has 3 beds. Meals are available in private houses. There are no shops and no electricity. There is a teachers' training college but not much special to see. Two fiestas: July 26 and August 15. Good for llama and other wool handicrafts. To *Pulcayo*, 20 km E on the road to Potosí, a largely abandoned mining town with a railway cemetery and alpaca wool factory (**G** *Hotel Rancho No 1*, without bath, large old rooms, hot water, good meals).

The standard excursions are NW to the *Salar de Uyuni* and S to *Laguna Colorada* and *Laguna Verde*. "When it still has water in it (up to 4 or possibly 6 inches), being in the middle of the Salar de Uyuni is like being an ant on a gigantic mirror. The blue sky merges into the blue water, the islands are perfectly reflected and since there is no horizon they appear suspended in space. Some areas may be dry, in which case the salt crust is as blinding-white and featureless as the most perfect snowfield (sunglasses essential)."—Stephen Saker.

Dan Buck and Anne Meadows write (with additional details from other travellers): *Laguna Colorada*, about 350-400 km SW of Uyuni, 12 hours' straight driving over unmarked, rugged truck tracks, is featured in Tony Morrison's two books, *Land Above the Clouds* and *The Andes*. It is one of Bolivia's most spectacular and most isolated marvels. The rare James flamingos, along with the more common Chilean and Andean flamingos, breed and live in its red algae-coloured waters. The shores and shallows of the lake are crusted with gypsum and salt, a bizarre arctic-white counterpoint to the flaming red waters. From afar, with their loping, John Cleese walks and pinkish feathers, the flamingos look alike. The leg and bill colorations are the easiest way to distinguish the three breeds. Chilean: brownish-blue legs with red knee-joints; almost white bill with brown-black tip. Andean: bright yellow legs; black front half on yellow bill. James: dark, brick-red legs; small black tip on bright yellow bill. See: *The Birds of Chile*, AW Johnson, or *Land Above the Clouds*, Tony Morrison.

The standard outing (see below for operators) lasts four days and takes visitors from Uyuni N to the Salar de Uyuni, S on to Lagunas Colorado and Verde, and then back to Uyuni. Day one: Uyuni to Colchani, thence to the Salar, including a salt-mine visit, lunch on the cactus-studded Isla Pescado, and overnight at a village, eg, San Juan, S of the Salar (simple lodging, ask around, electricity 1900-2100, running water). Between Colchani and Isla Pescado is **D** *Hotel Playa Blanca* run by Teodoro Colque, new in 1994, warm, well-designed. Day two: To Laguna Colorada (4,775m), passing active Volcán Ollagüe and a chain of small, flamingo-specked lagoons. Overnight at Laguna Colorada. (Eustaquio Berna runs the *campamento* and still appreciates small gifts – cigarettes, oranges, etc, US$1 to stay, dirty, windy. Permission to lodge at the nearby, modern ENDE, electricity company, facilities must be obtained in writing from Cochabamba headquarters.) Day three: Drive past belching geysers at Sol de Mañana (do not walk over the geysers) and through the Pampa de Challviri (4,800m, via a pass at 5,000m) where telluric outcroppings sprout from sand dunes surrounded by wind-scoured mountains, to the wind-lashed, frothy jade waters of the *Laguna Verde* (4,600m) at the foot of Volcán Licancábur, and back to Laguna Colorada. *Refugio* at Laguna Verde, US$2, small, mattresses, running water, view of lake. Day four: Return to Uyuni. A three-day version eliminates the Salar de Uyuni.

The excursion price from Uyuni depends on the size of the vehicle, the number of days and the demand. Expect to pay up to US$100 per day, divided by the number of passengers. (Whether you return to Uyuni or proceed into Chile, you pay for a round-trip.) For example, the four-day trip is US$300 in a double-cab Datsun pickup (one to four passengers) with Uyuni Tours or US$400 in a Toyota Land Cruiser (one to seven passengers) with Transamazonas. Although some haggling is allowed, don't get your hopes up. Price includes gas but excludes lodging, which costs about US$1 pp per night, and food. Tents are not required, but a warm sleeping bag is essential. Packing your vehicle with the maximum number of passengers will lower the per-head tariff, but bouncing cheek-by-jowl for several days over dusty, corrugated roads is tedious.

Tour Agencies Tours can be organized in Uyuni, or in Potosí or La Paz (some of the Uyuni companies are connected with Potosí and La Paz travel agencies). In Uyuni most agencies are on Av Ferroviaria, including: Transamazonas; Uyuni Tours, T 878, owners Ciprián and Antonia Nina, rec; Brisa Tours, frequently rec; Transandino Tours (Wilma Ignacio Apala) has been recommended (Casilla 18, T 0693-2132, or La Paz 820353); Tunupa Tours (Elias Cruz Romero, warmly rec), good value; Koala Tours (see under Potosí for head office). Prices are reported to be much higher in La Paz. Reports disagree on the ease of arranging a tour by turning up in Uyuni and hunting for others to form a group (this can take several days). Do not try to form a group at Carnival; everyone is at Oruro.

Temperatures at Laguna Colorada can easily drop below -20°C even out of the persistent strong winds. It is imperative that trips carry sufficient food, water and fuel and that the vehicle is equipped with spares and is up to the task. Take warm bedding, candles, hat, swimming costume and high factor sun tan lotion. **NB** Reports vary on the quality of tours. Obtain a written contract and be firm. Try to check the vehicle before agreeing terms. Insist on taking spares and try to ensure the vehicle is filled with fuel the evening before (in case of power cuts). It is worth taking two drivers and choosing an agency with experienced drivers and radio contact. Drivers are reported habitually to try to cut a day off a 4-day tour. Tour agencies will, if requested, leave travellers at Hito Cajones on the border with Chile (see below for the problems of travelling between Hito Cajones and San Pedro de Atacama). They can also arrange for a Chilean company to meet you at Hito Cajones (eg *Nativa:* see San Pedro de Atacama **Tourist Agencies**, p 639, and **To Bolivia**). Check whether the cost of this service is per person or per vehicle. Tours do not run at Christmas/New Year.

If you plan to enter Chile via one of the unattended border crossings in the SW region, you must get an exit stamp at the Bolivian immigration office on Calle Potosí (Mon-Fri only). There are (reportedly) no immigration offices SW of Uyuni. The stamp is valid for three days, ie, you have 72 hrs to get out of Bolivia, but reports suggest that more than 72 hrs is permitted if you state the exact date you intend to leave Bolivia. Before issuing the exit stamp, Bolivian immigration requires that you present proof of travel, ie, your excursion contract. Your tour company can run your passports over to immigration, which opens at 0900, the morning you are leaving.

To **San Pedro de Atacama (Chile)** From Laguna Verde it is 7 km to Hito Cajones, the frontier post with Chile and a further 8 km to La Cruz, the junction with the E-W road used by trucks carrying borax and sulphur from the mines to San Pedro. There are reports of a daily bus Hito Cajones-San Pedro, but the frequency of other traffic and the ease of finding transport is uncertain. Tour guides may be very over-optimistic: if you are unlucky you will have to walk a long way in difficult conditions. Adequate, food, water and clothing essential. **Do not underestimate the dangers of getting stuck without transport or lodging at this altitude**.

South of Uyuni, 200 km, is ***Tupiza*** (2,990m, 20,000 people), a centre of the silver, tin, lead, and bismuth mining industries. The statue in the main square of Tupiza is to Victor Carlos Aramayo, the founding member of the Aramayo mining dynasty, pre-eminent in the late 19th, early 20th centuries, together with the Patiños and the Hoschilds. Chajra Huasi, a palazzo-style, abandoned home of the Aramayo family across the Río Tupiza, may be visited. It was expropriated by the government after the 1952 revolution. An archaeology museum, part of the University of Tupiza, has been opened just off plaza (US\$1.75). IGM office, for maps, is in the Municipal building.

Hotels and Services F *Hotel Mitru*, run down, private shower and bath, water unreliable, poor plumbing, downstairs rooms might be better, laundry can take 3 days, but still the best, restaurant has good *almuerzo*, but no dinner, annex has snack shop and restaurant, both open for dinner; next to it is F *Residencial Crillón*, very run down, with good motorcycle parking; much better for motorcyclists is F *Res Valle Hermoso*, Av Pedro Arraya, T 589, hot showers, good, will let you park bikes in restaurant; **G** pp *El Rancho*, Av Arrayo 200 block, without bath; also **G** pp *Residencial Monterrey*, opposite railway station, clean, hot water, and 2 blocks from the station, F *Hotel Centro*, clean, friendly and quiet; *Restaurant Gallo de Oro*, Calle Chorloque, cheap *parrillada*; *Restaurant Chicheño*, near market, typical food; *Picantería Las Brisas*, on opposite side of river, open Sat and Sun only, large helpings.

TCs can be changed at Empresa Bernall Hmnos, but only in the presence of the owner, good rates, many shops will also change dollars at better rates than in Villazón. Good food market on Sat and Sun. Hospital Ferroviário (nr *Hotel Mitru*), Dr Rolando Llano Navarro and staff, very helpful.

Transport Trains to **Villazon**, 3 a week, 3 hrs. Trains to **Uyuni**, *expreso* US\$9. Bad road from Potosí which goes on S to Villazón; often closed in rainy season because road fords the Río Suipacha. Bus to **Villazón** 3 hrs, US\$2, 1000 and 1500; to **Potosí**, US\$5.25, Expreso Tupiza and Flota Chicheño, both daily. To **Uyuni**, US\$4, 7½ hrs. No direct bus to La Paz, only via Potosí. A new road is being built from Uyuni to Atocha.

Wendy Chilcott and Steve Newman (Sussex) write: "Follow the road to the left of the cathedral out of town between the cemetery and a barracks. Continue as road curves right until you reach a dry river bed. Follow this to the left towards the hills. After 200 m take the right fork in the river bed. Here are some superb rock formations... huge pinnacles of rock and soil, only 4 inches thick—seem to defy gravity! The valley narrows rapidly but the path follows a stream bed for several hundred metres to a picturesque waterfall. Any further progress requires difficult scrambling but will eventually lead to the altiplano. " The whole walk takes 2 hrs, worth it for the rock formations alone, take water and food. Beautiful sunsets over the fertile Tupiza can be seen from the foot of a Christ statue on a hill behind the plaza.

Tupiza is the centre of Butch Cassidy and the Sundance Kid country. On 4 November 1908, they held up an Aramayo company payroll N of Tupiza. (Aramayo *hacienda* in Salo, one hour N of Tupiza, still stands. Roadside kiosks serve excellent roast goat, *choclo*, *papas*, soup.) Two days later they encountered and were killed by a four-man military-police patrol in **San Vicente** (pop 400, 4,500 m), 103 km, 4 to 6 hours on a good dirt road, NW of Tupiza. Supposedly truck transport from Tupiza on Thur early am from near football stadium. Alternatively hire a vehicle: Fermín Ortega at Taller Nardini, Barrio Lourdes, rec; Don Manuel at *Hotel Mitru* can suggest others, US$30 to US$80 one-way. (Also accessible and a bit closer from Atocha, but fewer vehicles for hire.) Travel up spectacular canyon with red and white, wind-carved rock formations. Basic *alojamiento* on main street marked "Hotel;" restaurant "El Rancho" next-door; several *tiendas* sell beer, soda, canned goods, etc. Shootout site off main street—ask locals. Cassidy and Sundance are buried in an unmarked grave in the cemetery, but the grave has yet to be found. An investigation of the supposed grave, by the Nova project in 1991, proved negative, but see *Digging Up Butch and Sundance*, by Anne Meadows (New York: St Martin's Press, 1994). Whether Butch and Sundance did die here or not, San Vicente has been described by one correspondent as "a very sad place to die".

Dr Félix Chalar Miranda, President of the local historical society offers jeep tours to the hold-up site near Salo, the escape route and San Vicente. He can also arrange excursions to Laguna Colorada and Laguna Verde, T 467 (office), 509 (home) or contact via *Inquietud* newspaper office at Av Cul Arraya 205.

The Argentine border is at **Villazón**, population 13,000, altitude 3,443 m, 81 km S of Tupiza. From Villazón there is an improved road to Tarija. The road linking Potosí with Villazón via Camargo is in poor condition and about 100 km longer than the better road via Tupiza. For information on border crossing with Argentina **see Argentina Section 3**; remember Jujuy province, Argentina is 1 hour ahead. Little to see in Villazón (has two cinemas) and not at all welcoming; border area must not be photographed. Entering Bolivia, guards will let you pass through after hours to sleep in Villazón, but you must get your passport stamped next day. There is an entry/exit tax of US$4.

Hotels at Villazón E *Residencial El Cortijo*, clean, good value, intermittent hot water, restaurant; **F** pp *Grand Palace*, behind bus station, safe, sheets taken at 0700 for washing; **F** *Hotel Bolivia*, one block from border, clean small rooms, good value breakfast, hot showers extra; **F** *Panamericano*, clean, laundry facilities, rec. **F** *Residencial Martínez*, ½ block from bus station, well signed, hot water when town's supply is on, basic but clean and well-maintained; **F** *Residencial 10 de Febrero*, next door, very basic. Restaurants opposite bus station and on first floor of covered market, for example *Repostería*, about US$1 a head. The Mercado Municipal de Vivanderos is near the frontier, parallel with main street, across the railway.

Banks and Exchange Money-changing at Cambio Porvenir or other *cambios* on main street, rates said to be good (some take TCs), also at Cambio Trébol, shop by border that sells train tickets (see below) but with 6% commission on TCs; Banco del Estado does not change TCs. Out of hours try the Ciné Rex. No exchange facilities in La Quiaca. **Warning** Do not show passport or money to men claiming to be plainclothes police.

Argentine Consulate in main plaza, open 1400-1700, Mon-Fri; not very helpful.

Buses To Potosí several between 0830 and 1830, 10-15 hrs, US$4.20-5.25 (unsurfaced road—terrible in the wet, can take 24 hrs); to **Tupiza**, 0700 and 1500, US$2; to **Tarija**, beautiful journey but most buses overnight only, daily at 1900/2000, US$5, 6 hrs, very cold on arrival but passengers can sleep on bus until daybreak; trucks for Tarija leave from beside bus station. From **La Paz**, several companies: journey takes 25 hrs, costs US$13.25, eg Panamericana and Chicheña, even though buses called "direct", you may have to change in Potosi, perhaps to another company, eg Villa Imperial. 1830 depart La Paz, 0700 arrive Potosí, 0830 leave Potosí, 1930 arrive Villazón. The same procedure applies from Villazón to La Paz. Bus station is near the main square, behind Ciné Teatro Libertador Bolívar; it is 5 blocks from the border. Taxi to border, US$0.20 or hire porter, US$1, and walk across.

Trains Station about 1 km N of frontier on main road, taxi US$1.80. To **Oruro** for La Paz (very dusty and cold journey), twice a week (US$9 Pullman, US$6.80 special). Train stops at Tupiza, Atocha, Uyuni and Oruro. The express from La Paz/Oruro connects with a bus to **Tarija** (in theory), tickets from railway station. Ticket office opens 0800, long queues, or tickets to La Paz can be bought (US$1 commission per ticket) at the first shop on the right next to the border.

POTOSI, SUCRE AND THE SOUTHERN HIGHLANDS (4)

The World Cultural Heritage Sites of Potosí, with its rich mining past and its current mining misery, and Sucre, the white city. In the S of this region, Tarija is known for its fruit and wines and its traditions which set it apart from the rest of the country.

Potosí (pop 110,000), 551 km SE of La Paz, stands at 4,070m, the highest city of its size in the world. The climate is often bitterly cold and fireplaces are few; warm clothes essential. It was founded by the Spaniards on 10 April 1545, after they had discovered Indian mine workings at Cerro Rico, the hill at whose foot it stands.

Immense amounts of silver were once extracted from this hill. In Spain "éste es un Potosí" (it's a Potosí) is still used for anything superlatively rich. By the early 17th century Potosí was the largest city in the Americas, but over the next two centuries, as its lodes began to deteriorate and silver was found elsewhere, Potosí became little more than a ghost town. It was the demand for tin—a metal the Spaniards ignored—that lifted the city to comparative prosperity again. Silver, copper and lead are also mined.

Large parts of Potosí are colonial, with twisting, narrow streets and an occasional great mansion with its coat of arms over the doorway. UNESCO has declared the city to be "Patrimonio de la Humanidad." Some of the best buildings are grouped round the Plaza 10 de Noviembre, the main square. The old Cabildo and the Royal Treasury—Las Cajas Reales—are both here, converted to other uses. The Cathedral (open Mon-Fri 0930-1000, 1300-1500, Sat 0930-1000, guided tour only, US$1) faces the square, and near-by is the Mint—the Casa Real de Moneda (founded 1572, rebuilt 1759-1773)—one of the chief monuments of civil building in Hispanic America (Calle Ayacucho, T 22777). The Moneda (entrance US$2, US$3 to take photos), has a museum in many sections occupying 30 of its 160 rooms. The main art gallery is in a splendid salon on the first floor. One section is dedicated to the works of the 17th-18th century religious painter Melchor Pérez de Holguín, one of Bolivia's most acclaimed artists (and dubbed "the El Greco of America"). Elsewhere are coin dies and huge wooden presses which made the silver strip from which coins were cut (there are plans to resume minting in Potosí – on a different site). The smelting houses have carved altar pieces from Potosí's ruined churches. There are also sections on armaments and on minerology. You cannot fail to miss the huge, grinning mask over an archway between two principal courtyards; its significance is uncertain, perhaps to hide a coat of arms at the time of Independence. You are advised to wear warm clothes, as it is cold inside; a guided tour (obligatory) starts at 0900 and 1400 approximately, and lasts for 2 hours, Spanish only (if you want an English guide, get a group together, or turn up at opening time and hope that others arrive). The rooms are only opened for the tours. Open Mon-Sat 0900-1200 and 1400-1700. The Convento y Museo de Santa Teresa at Chicas y Ayacucho, T 23847 (entry US$1.50, Mon-Fri 0900-1200, 1300-1800, Sat 0900-1200, but check at Tourist Office) has an interesting collection of colonial and religious art, obligatory guide. Among Potosí's baroque churches, typical of the Andean or "mestizo" architecture of the 18th century, are the Compañia (Jesuit) church, on Ayacucho, with an impressive bell-gable (1700, closed for restoration in 1992), San Francisco (Tarija y Nogales) with a fine organ

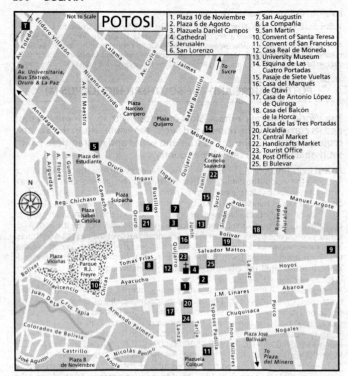

POTOSI

1. Plaza 10 de Noviembre
2. Plaza 6 de Agosto
3. Plazuela Daniel Campos
4. Cathedral
5. Jerusalén
6. San Lorenzo
7. San Augustín
8. La Compañía
9. San Martín
10. Convent of Santa Teresa
11. Convent of San Francisco
12. Casa Real de Moneda
13. University Museum
14. Esquina de Las Cuatro Portadas
15. Pasaje de Siete Vueltas
16. Casa del Marqués de Otavi
17. Casa de Antonio López de Quiroga
18. Casa del Balcón de la Horca
19. Casa de las Tres Portadas
20. Alcaldía
21. Central Market
22. Handicrafts Market
23. Tourist Office
24. Post Office
25. El Bulevar

(can be visited in morning and evening, worthwhile for the views from the tower and roof, museum of ecclesiastical art, underground tunnel system, open 1400-1600, Mon-Fri, entry US$1), and San Lorenzo, with a rich portal (1728-1744, Calle Héroes del Chaco); fine views from the tower. San Martín on Calle Hoyos, with an uninviting exterior, is beautiful inside, but is normally closed for fear of theft. Ask the German Redemptorist Fathers to show you around; their office is just to the left of their church. Other churches to visit include Jerusalén, close to the *Hotel Centenario*, and San Agustín (only by prior arrangement with tourist office) on Bolívar y Quijarro, with crypts and catacombs (the whole city was interconnected by tunnels in colonial times). Tour starts at 1700, US$0.10 admission. From San Cristóbal, at Pacheco y Cañete, one gets a fine view over the whole city. Teatro Omiste on Plaza 6 de Agosto is under restoration; it has a fine façade. The University has a museum with some good modern Bolivian painting (Mon-Fri, 1000-1200, 1500-1700, entrance US$1, Calle Bolívar, T 22248).

In Potosí, 2,000 colonial buildings have been catalogued. The city is being repainted in traditional colours of teracotta, cream and blue. A suggested tour round the town is to start at San Agustín at the corner of Bolívar and Quijarro and walk down Quijarro which, in colonial times, was Calle Ollería - potmakers - and Calle de los Sombreros. The whole block behind San Agustín belonged to the monastery; there are many wooden balconies, many houses retain colonial interiors with balconies, patio, rings for tying horses, etc, but much restoration is needed. At Quijarro and Omiste is the Esquina de las Cuatro Portadas (four houses with double doors), or Balcón de Llamacancha. Quijarro is one of Potosí's best preserved streets, with many emblems over doorways. Go right up Omiste for one block then turn right again into Junín, at Plaza Cornelio Saavedra (Mercado de Artesanías). See the Pasaje de Siete Vueltas (the passage of the seven turns) on your left. There is a fine stone doorway (house of the Marqués de Otavi) in Junín between Matos and Bolívar. Cross Plaza 10 de Noviembre diagonally to Lanza to see at No 8 (now a school) the house of José de Quiroz and of Antonio López de Quiroga. Turn up Chuquisaca and after 3 blocks right into Millares: here on the left is a sculpted stone doorway and on the right a doorway with two rampant lions in low relief on the lintel. Turning left up Nogales you come to an old mansion in a little square. Turn left along La Paz and one block along there is another stone doorway with suns in relief. At the corner with Bolívar is the Casa del Balcón de la Horca. Turn left and you reach the Casa de las Tres Portadas, then it's 2½ blocks back to San Agustín.

Festivals San Bartolomé, or the Fiesta de Chutillos, is held from the middle of August, with the main event being processions of dancers on the last weekend, Saturday featuring Potosino, and Sunday national, groups. Costumes can be hired in artesanía market on Calle Sucre. In May there is a market on Calle Gumiel every Sunday, with lotteries and lots of fun things for sale. On three consecutive Saturdays at the end of May, beginning of June llama sacrifices are made at the cooperative mines in honour of Pachamama; the same occurs on 1 August, the Ritual del Espíritu. Other mining festivals are the Carnaval Minero and the Fiesta de los Compadres in February, for decorating El Tío (the Dios Minero) and one's work place. Potosí is sometimes called the "Ciudad de las Costumbres", especially at Corpus Cristi, Todos Santos and Carnaval, when special cakes are baked, families go visiting friends, etc. In October, Festival Internacional de la Cultura, in Potosí and Sucre.

Hotels Unless otherwise stated hotels have no heating in rooms. **C** *Claudia*, Av Maestro 322, 3-star, 22242, helpful, modern, highly rec; **C** *Hostal Colonial*, Hoyos 8, a pretty colonial house (T 24809) near the main plaza, rec, with heating, has names and T numbers of guides, even if you're not staying there very helpful, very expensive for long-distance phone calls; **C** *Hostal Libertador*, Millares 58, T 27877/24629, Casilla 324, heaters in rooms, with bath, hot water, clean, quiet, comfortable, viewpoint, parking, highly rec (owner is Sr Wilson Mendieta Pacheco, director of Casa Real de la Moneda); **D** *Hostal Felimar*, Junín 14, T 24357, 2-star, hot water, breakfast, 2 roof-top suites, solar-powered, 1st floor rm have no exterior windows but warm, quiet; **D** *Santa María*, Av Serrudo 244, T 23255, clean, hot water; **D** *Jerusalem*, Oruro 143, T 22600, recently modernized, pleasant, helpful, *comedor*, with bath, F without, parking, laundry, highly rec; **D** *El Turista*, Lanza 19 (T 22492), also LAB office, helpful, hot showers all day, breakfast (US$1) highly rec; **D** *Hotel IV Centenario*, Plaza del Estudiante, T 22751, hot water all day, large cold rooms, central, very run down, poor service, apparently cheaper for Israelis and Danes; **E** *Central*, Bustillos 1230 y Linares, T 22207, hot shower, breakfast, basic, very mixed reports; **E** *Hotel Carlos V*, Linares 42 on Plaza 6 de Agosto, T 25151, friendly, breakfast, without bath, occasional hot water, clean, luggage store, rec; **E** *Residencial Sumaj*, Gumiel 10, T 23336, small rm, double rm on top floor good, with windows and views, hot water, shared bathrooms only, good value, clean and friendly, highly rec; **F** *Alojamiento La Paz*, Oruro 262, T 22632, central, basic, clean; **E** *Residencial Copacabana*, Av Serrudo 319, T 22712, individual or shared rooms, restaurant, clean, hot showers, will change $ cash, safe car park (owner, Dr Hugo Linares Fuentes will give medical assistance), rec; **E** *Res Felcar*, Serrudo 345 y Bustillos, T 24966, 1-star, clean, hot water, friendly, rec; **G** *Alojamiento Ferrocarril*, Av E Villazón 159, T 24294, basic, clean (hot showers US$0.55), friendly, close to the railway station; **G** *Alojamiento San Lorenzo*, Bustillos 967, T 24842, close to market, very basic, no shower or hot water; **G** pp *Casa de María Victoria*, Chuquisaca 148, T 22132, clean, stores luggage, popular, friendly, kitchen and laundry facilities, unpredictable plumbing, rec. In times of drought there may be rationing of water for showers etc. **Youth hostels D-E** *Res San Antonio*, Oruro 136, T 23566, US$2 pp without breakfast, dirty and **F** *Alojamiento El Barquito*, Oruro 7, T 22600 (not obviously spotted, good, rustic, rec).

5 km from Potosí in the village of San Antonio is *Hotel El Tambo*, Km 5 Carretera a Oruro, T 25597, F 22985, 3-star, colonial/rustic architecture, 3 restaurants, Bodega Bar, all details from Hidalgo Tours (see below).

Restaurants *Sumaj Orcko*, Quijarro 46, excellent food including fried vizcacha, large portions, cheap set lunch, reasonably priced Chilean wine, very popular with foreigners and locals, heating, slow service; *Plaza*, next door, serves a cheap set lunch, good and friendly; *Confitería Royal*, just off main plaza, small selection of good snacks and cakes; *El Aldabón*, Linares 35, good set meal, US$1; *El Mesón*, corner of Plaza 10 de Noviembre near Tarija, irregular opening, European-style, very pricey (prices not written on menus, beware of overcharging), variously reported as excellent, poor, or pretentious; *Pizzería Argentina*, Linares 20, rec, cheap, tasty *salteñas* and pizzas, good service; *Las Vegas*, Padilla y Linares, 1st floor, cheap *almuerzos*, dinner more expensive, good; *La Tranquita*, Bolívar 957, good; *Anexo El Criollo*, Bolívar 581, good, excellent steaks; *Don Lucho*, Bolívar 765, large and tasty servings, but not cheap, meat good, *peñas* on Fri, check entrance fee for show before eating. *The Sky Room* at Bolívar 701 has interesting views of the town and the Cerro, pricey. On Sucre, *Confitería Capricornio*, good sandwiches, light meals, cheap, clean, rec. *La Carreta*, Gumiel, excellent, pleasant service, mid-price range; *Quillahuasi*, Junín 56, good. *Snack bar Bamby*, just off top of main square, good cheap lunches. Breakfast can be a difficult meal to find, but it is available in the Mercado Central, Calle Bolivar from 0700 (also other meals – not always hygienic): worthwhile to see if the hotel serves it as most restaurants seem to be closed at this time. *Coffee Shop*, Plaza Alonso Ibáñez, good coffee and cakes and *Confitería Cherys*, Padilla 12 y Linares, friendly, good cakes, coffee, burgers, very popular, attractive, breakfast. Other *confiterías*: *Kivo's*, Quijarro 12, *Santa Clara*, Plaza Principal (nice and clean), and *Chaplin*, Bustillos 979.

Banks and Exchange Banco Nacional, Sucre near Plaza, exchange for US$ cash. Many shops and restaurants around main plaza on Padilla and on Bolívar between Sucre and Junín (most display "compro dólares" signs). Amex cheques may only be changed at Morales, Bertram y Schuett, Matos 19; TCs may also be changed at Distribuidora Cultural Sud, same address. **Casa de Cambio Fernández**, Sucre 10. **Banco La Paz** on Plaza 10 de Noviembre, for cash withdrawals on Visa and Mastercard, with US$1.25 authorization charge Mon-Wed only. **Banco Popular**, Bolívar y Junín, cash withdrawals on Visa, friendly.

Clinic Clínica Británica, on Oruro near *Alojamiento La Paz*, clinics am and pm English spoken.

Sauna Bath and showers in Calle Nogales. Sauna Florida, Plaza Chuquimina, near bus station, open Thurs and Fri, US$1.50 (also has racquetball).

Laundry *Limpieza la Veloz*, Calle Quijarro, corner of Mattos, Edificio Cademin, and at Camacho 258, US$1.3 per kilo.

Post Office Lanza 3, open Sat till 1900, Sun 0900-1200; unreliable for overseas mail. **Telephone** Entel, Calle Camacho, T 43496; also at Av Universitaria near bus terminal.

Shopping Silver (sometimes containing nickel) and native cloth. Silver coins, jewellery and coca leaves in market between Av Camacho and Héroes del Chaco. Coca leaves (for *soroche*) also available in streets near the market. There is an interesting gift shop in the post office. Silver is sold in the main market near the Calle Oruro entrance. There is an informal swap market every Friday night at the Plazuela, at Bolívar and Quijarro. There is a small handicraft market at the junction of Calle Sucre and Plaza Saavedra (rec) but very expensive. Some Fridays the merchants organize music, food and drink (*ponche*), not to be missed. Almost opposite is *Andina*, Sucre 94, for handicrafts and antiques. The Triángulo Productivo, in front of San Lorenzo, has handicrafts for sale. For musical instruments, Arnaud Gerard (Belgian), Los Alamos 18, workshop *Killay* behind Mercado Artesanal, makes beautifully made and tuned pieces, designed to be played, will make to order. Art gallery of Carlos Cornejo L, Simón Chacón 19, open every afternoon and some evenings, very good (also does trips to, and gives information on, Tarapaya; see **Excursions**). The best bookshop is at the University, open Mon-Fri, 1000-1200, 1500-1700.

Tourist Agents Hidalgo Tours, Junín y Bolívar, T 28293, F 22985, Casilla 310, *ferrobus* tickets for La Paz/Sucre, specialized services within the city and to Salar de Uyuni (with all meals, accommodation at Albergue San Juan, aperitifs, wine, radio-controlled), highly rec for mine visits (see below); *Potosí Tours*, corner of Padilla, on the Plaza, good tours of the city and mine (see below); *Transamazonas*, Quijarro 12, Edif Cámara de Minería, T 27175, F 24796; *Cerro Rico Travel*, Plaza Alonso Ibáñez 21, T 25552; *Koala Tours*, Ayacucho 5, frente a la Casa de Moneda, PO Box 33, T 24708, F 22092 mine tours (see below) and has a branch in Uyuni for Salar trips; *Turismo Balsa*, Plaza Alonzo de Ibáñez, T 26272, English spoken, daily city and mine tours (see also La Paz **Travel Agents**).

Some agencies offer trips to the Salar de Uyuni, Laguna Colorada and Laguna Verde (**see above p 286**) but reports suggest that this is more expensive and more time-consuming than excursions to these places from Uyuni. Tours from Potosí cost US$160-180 pp and last 5-6 days. It is essential to get a written contract (a tourist police requirement) and make sure that the guide is approved by the police. The trip needs a suitable vehicle, sufficient fuel, food and water (if not included in the price, take your own or tell the guide precisely what you need), first aid, and proper organization.

Tourist Office On 2nd Floor, Cámara de Minería, Calle Quijarro (T 25288), ½ block from main plaza, and booth on main plaza (both closed Sat and Sun and unreliable opening times during the week); sells town maps (US$0.25), information booklet (US$2.50), helpful. Instituto Geográfico Militar, Calle La Paz, possible to buy maps, 0900-1200, 1400-1800.

Useful Addresses Police station On Plaza 10 de Noviembre. **Migración** La Paz 1001, can renew tourist permit here for 1 month, 10 bolivianos.

Local Transport Taxi within city limits US$0.60; approx US$1/km for longer journeys. Buses US$0.10.

Airport Aerosur (Bolívar y Junín, T 22087) to La Paz daily except Sun at 1005 (US$130 return), with connections to Cobija, Cochabamba, Guayaramerín, Santa Cruz, Tarija and Trinidad. LAB fly to La Paz (US$120 return), also Santa Cruz (US$100 return), Sucre and Cochabamba. Book flights well in advance. Airport is 5 km out of town on the Sucre road.

Trains Potosí is on the La Paz, Oruro, Potosí, Sucre line; latest report is of a *ferrobus* twice a week to Potosí from Oruro/La Paz, Tues and Sat at 1820 (US$11), continues to Sucre (US$14.50). Full information from Enfe at the station, T 23101 (ask at Hidalgo Tours, who sell Enfe tickets, about Hidalgo Express, special service).

Buses Bus terminal out of town, on Av Universitaria, below railway station, 30 min walk, steeply uphill to main plaza (or *micros* C, I or L); through buses from La Paz call here at the toll gate, as they are not allowed to enter city limits. There is an information office at the terminal, T 26075, an express mail service, and a terminal tax, 50 centavos. To **Tarija**, Andesbus Mon, Thur, Sat 1400, US$10.50, rec, or San Jorge (T 26214), San Lorenzo or *Emperador* (T 25580), all daily, US$10.50 at 1600 or 1630 from bus terminal; Tarija is reached by car or lorry leaving Plaza Minero (Bus "A"), full range of scenery. To **Villazón**, several companies daily, usually departing 1800-1900, 12 hrs (but O'Globo 0800), US$4.20-5.25 (Trans Tupiza, T 24264, rec). To **Cochabamba**, US$5.25-7.35, 12 hrs, several companies inc Copacabana, T 24041, 1900. Many buses to **La Paz** (mostly overnight in either direction, 10-14 hrs, US$5.25-8.50, you get what you pay for), Trans Copacabana luxury service with heat and video, US$12.60, 10 hrs, spacious, rec. Avoid Flota Copacabana. To **Oruro**, US$3.15-3.75, Bustillos, T 25672, Universo and Imperial, 8 hrs, leaving between 1900 and 1930. To **Uyuni**, at least 4 companies: Diana Tours, American (T 27162), 11 de Julio (T 28126, rec), Expreso Parco, all have offices around Av Toledo y Av Antofagasta, at least 1 a day 1100-1215, 6-8 hrs, unpaved road, OK in dry season, US$4, book in advance, especially on the day when the bus connects with the Oruro-Calama train. To **Sucre**: two types of service, the more luxurious being Andesbus, Bustillos 1094, T 25050, 3½ hrs, US$5, rec, similar service with Transtin, Cochabamba 104, T 22056, Alave, Bustillos 1066, T 27655, and Emperador, Camacho 281, all at 0700 and 1700. Less comfortable are companies such as 10 de Noviembre (not rec, not safe), all US$3.15. The road to Sucre is being paved, so a lot of dust, or mud, depending on the weather; all but 30 km have been paved. To **Santa Cruz**, Trans Copacabana, 1900, and Flota Copacabana, 1930, both US$12.55. Trucks for **Tarabuco** leave from Plaza San Francisco. Heavy overbooking reported on buses, also, timetables change frequently; the trucks from the plaza are an alternative.

Excursions to the mines: The state mines in Cerro Rico were closed in the 1980s and are now worked as cooperatives by small groups of miners. A 4½ hr morning tour to the cooperative mines and ore-processing plant involves meeting miners and seeing them at work in conditions described as "like stepping back into the nineteenth century". Visitors need to be reasonably fit as parts are very hard going, not recommended for claustrophobics or asthmatics. Guided tours are offered by former miners. By law all guides have to work with a travel agency. Guides recommended include: Eduardo Garnica Fajardo, Hernández 1035, Casilla 33, T 24708/22092 (Koala Tours), he speaks English, French and some Hebrew (frequently rec, and sometimes impersonated by unprofessionals). Also highly rec as an English-speaking guide for small groups is Julio César Morales of Koala Tours. Koala Tours offer breakfast at 0600, "plato típico" with llama meat; they also donate part of their fee to buy medicines (donations can be sent to Eduardo Garnica). Raul Braulio, Millares 147 (Transamazonas Tours), T 25304, experienced guide, speaks some English; David Almendras, Colombia 631, T 25552 (Cerro Rico Travel), highly rec; Santos and Marco Mamami, Pacheco 60, T 27299 (Cerro Rico Travel); Roberto Méndez E, Campamento Pailaviri 4, T 26900 (Turismo Balsa), speaks English, very knowledgeable, rec; Salustio Gallardo, Calle Betanzos 231, near Plaza Minero; Juan Carlos González, Av Japón 10, T 26349 (Turismo Balsa), rec, Spanish spoken only. Efraín Huanca (Hidalgo Tours) warmly rec as friendly and very informative. Guides provide essential equipment – helmet, lamp and usually protective clothing (but check when booking). Wear old clothes and take torch and a handkerchief to filter the dusty air. The price of tours is regulated (US$5 pp) and includes transport. A contribution to the miners' cooperative is appreciated as are medicines for the new health centre (*Posta Sanitaria*) on Cerro Rico. New projects (a radio, drinking water) have been, or will shortly be realized. You will also be asked to contribute towards buying presents for the miners – dynamite, coca leaves, cigarettes. The size of tour groups varies – some agencies, eg Koala, limit groups to 8, some groups are as large as 20 people, which is excessive. The Pailaviri State mine is closed temporarily as of April 1995.

Thermal Baths at *Tarapaya*, on the road to Oruro. Trucks go straight to Tarapaya where there are public baths, US$0.30, and private, US$0.60; the private baths, higher up, may be cleaner. If you get out of the truck or bus at the bridge at Km 25, cross the bridge and take any trail up, you reach the 50 metre-diameter crater lake on the other side of the river from Tarapaya. The temperature of the lake is 30°C, a beautiful spot; take sun protection. Below the crater lake are boiling ponds. Bus from market nr train station, Av Antofagasta, US$0.50. Taxi US$6 for a group, hitch back; do not go in late afternoon, there is no transport back to Potosí (no problem at weekends). A good place to spend a lazy day resting, or to freshen up after visiting the mines (mine guides often offer transport after a mine tour). On the way to Tarapaya is the village of El Molino (15 km), in a green valley; no accommodation or shop, but nice landscape. Take a colectivo from Plaza Chuquimia. Also baths at Chaqui (by truck or bus from Plaza Uyuni, 1 hr, clean, pleasant baths, closed Wed), Tora and San Diego (on the main road to Sucre, it also has a restaurant).

The following walk, originally proposed by Hallam Murray, has proved popular. It takes 8-9 hrs at a gentle pace and covers about 24 km (map Hoja 6435, serie H631, from Instituto Geográfico Militar, and a compass are useful). Take Av Hoyos E out of Plaza 10 de Noviembre and continue beyond the Iglesia San Martín. Aim initially for Laguna San Ildefonso SE of the city. Ask directions: after a brickworks on the paved road to the ore-processing plant by Cerro Rico, a footpath heads E over a gentle hill planted with young trees. Follow this path until the second junction with a dirt road, then turn left/N and continue to the W shore of the lake. It was built in 1767 to provide water for the city and is in a wonderful position. It has duck, and fish deep down in the clear water. Beyond, to the E, are lumpy hills and mountains. Go round the W shore, cross a small river at the lake's N end and at the next intersection turn left. Follow up the valley, passing herds of llama and old mine openings. This valley is full of fascinating plants, animals, and rock formations.

Continue along the left side of the valley beyond a second unnamed, and possibly dried-up lake (visible only when close to it) and turn S to climb steeply to the adjoining valley (very tough for the unacclimatized), just beyond the peak of Cerro Masoni (4,920m). The time from the Plaza to the highest point between the two valleys is 5-6 hrs. The views from this point are spectacular, with mountain peaks to the S towards Argentina. Closer at hand is moon-like scenery. This is an excellent spot for a picnic. Continue down and back to Potosí via the small lake which can be seen from the high point. Probably best to keep high to the left (S) of Lagunas San Sebastián and to approach Cerro Rico on its E flank. The walk back into Potosí is depressing and bleak, passing miners' houses, close to a heavily polluted stream and with the most extensively worked face of Cerro Rico to your left, but this is a side of Bolivia which should also be seen.

A recommended Sunday trip is to Manquiri, a sanctuary in the mountains. Wait from 0730 at Garita de San Roque or at Plaza Uyuni for a truck. At **Betanzos** (1 hr on the Sucre road; **G** nameless *alojamiento*, basic), the Feria de Papas is held within the first two weeks of May: folk dances, music and costumes (buses from Plaza Uyuni, Potosí).

Another trip is to **Caiza** on a road which forks off the Tarija road at Ingenio Cucho; there is one small hotel, near main square, *San Martín de Porres*, clean, with restaurant. Two buses a day from Potosí, from Plaza del Minero at 1330 but they are sometimes late. Caiza is where cooperatives produce handicrafts in tin and some silver. Silverware is being encouraged. On 4 August, the entry of the Virgen de Copacabana is celebrated with dancing and traditional costumes. For information go to the tourist office in Potosí, or Programa de Autodesarrollo Campesino, Av Argentina y Gareca, Ciudad Satélite, Potosí, T 32013/32028. Caiza is about 2 hrs from Potosí, at a much lower altitude, so it is hotter and can provide relief from *soroche*.

Sucre (pop 112,000), the official capital of Bolivia, is 164 km NE of Potosí. A branch road runs to it from Epizana on the old Cochabamba-Santa Cruz highway. The altitude is 2,790m, and the climate is mild (mean temperature 12°C, but sometimes

24°C in November-December and 7°C in June).

Founded in 1538 as the city of La Plata, it became capital of the audiencia of Charcas in 1559. Its name was later changed to Chuquisaca. The present name was adopted in 1825 in honour of the first president of the new republic. In 1992 UNESCO declared the city a "Patrimonio Histórico y Cultural de la Humanidad". The city is an important administrative and educational centre: there are 2 universities, the oldest dating from 1624. Long isolation has helped it to preserve its courtly charm; by tradition all buildings in the centre are painted in their original colonial white. It is sometimes referred to as La Ciudad Blanca. Throughout the city, the public buildings are impressive. The main square is Plaza 25 de Mayo, which is large, spacious, full of trees and surrounded by elegant buildings. Among these are the Casa de la Libertad, formerly the Assembly Hall of the Jesuit University (open Mon-Fri 0900-1130 and 1430-1830, Sat, 0930-1130, US$0.30, US$0.65 to take photographs, US$2.65 to use video), where the country's Declaration of Independence was signed (it contains a famous portrait of Simón Bolívar by the Peruvian artist Gil de Castro "... hecho en Lima, con la más grande exactitud y semejanza" - the greatest likeness); also on the Plaza is the beautiful 17th century Cathedral, entrance through the museum in Calle Ortiz (open Mon-Fri 1000-1200, 1500-1700, Sat 1000-1200, entry US$1, if door is locked wait for the guide). Worth seeing are the famous jewel-encrusted Virgin of Guadalupe, 1601, works by Viti, the first great painter of the New World, who studied under Raphael, and the monstrance and other church treasures including giant lanterns of pure silver weighing 46 kilos. Four blocks NW of Plaza 25 de Mayo is the modern Corte Suprema de Justicia, the seat of Bolivia's judiciary (entry free but must leave passport with guard, no photographs allowed). The nearby Parque Bolívar contains an obelisk, a small triumphal arch and a miniature of the Eiffel tower which can be climbed (the park used to be a lovers' meeting place but improved lighting has turned it into a favourite place for students to revise at night). The obelisk opposite the Teatro Gran Mariscal, in Plaza Libertad, was erected with money raised by fining bakers who cheated on the size and weight of their bread. Also on this plaza is the Hospital Santa Bárbara. Sucre University was founded in 1624. Early 17th century wooden ceilings (*alfarjes*) are found in San Miguel (see below) and San Francisco (0700-0930 and 1600-1930).

SE of the city, at the top of Calle Dalence, lies the Franciscan monastery of La Recoleta (see below under **Museums**) with good views over the city. Behind the monastery a road flanked by Stations of the Cross ascends an attractive hill, Cerro Churuquella, with large eucalyptus trees on its flank, to a statue of Christ at the top. The cemetery is worth a visit, to see mausoleums of presidents and other famous people, boys give guided tours; take Calle Junín S to its end, 7-8 blocks from main plaza.

Churches Church opening times seem to change frequently, or are simply not observed. **San Miguel**, completed in 1628, has been restored and is very beautiful with Moorish-style carved and painted ceilings, pure-white walls and gold and silver altar. In the Sacristy some early sculpture can be seen. It was from San Miguel that Jesuit missionaries went S to convert Argentina, Uruguay and Paraguay (open 1130-1200, no shorts, short skirts or short sleeves). **San Felipe Neri**, church and monastery, neoclassical, attractive courtyard with cloisters (note above the crucifix an inscription in Hebrew letters saying, from right to left, TALE - lamb, one of the signs for Christ in the zodiac, on each side of the cross are two replicas of the Israeli *menora*, the lamp from the Temple). The monastery is used as a school. The church, sadly is closed. Access to the roof (note the penitents' benches), which offers fine views over the city, is only open for an hour between 1600 and 1800 (times change) US$0.50 entrance with a free guide from Universidad de Turismo office, opposite the convent, at N Ortiz 182. **Santa Mónica** (Arenales y Junín) is perhaps one of the finest gems of Spanish architecture in the Americas, note the main altar and pulpit in filigree (it is no longer a church but may be visited when functions are being held inside or daily 1500-1800). **San Francisco** in Calle Ravelo has altars coated in gold leaf; the bell is the one that summoned the people of Sucre to struggle for independence (open 1800 most days). **Capilla de la Rotonda** (Av L Cabrera, near the railway

SUCRE

Not to Scale

1. Plaza 25 de Mayo
2. Plaza Zudáñez
3. Plaza Monteagudo
4. Casa de la Libertad
5. Corte Suprema de Justicia
6. Cathedral
7. San Miguel
8. San Lázaro
9. Santa Mónica
10. San Francisco
11. San Felipe Neri
12. Santa Rita
13. San Sebastián
14. Museo de Historia Natural
15. Santo Domingo
16. Santa Clara
17. Museo Charcas, Modern Art & Anthropology
18. Teatro Mariscal de Ayacucho
19. Post Office
20. ENTEL - communications
21. Tourist Office
22. LAB
23. Hostal Sucre
24. Central Market
25. Hotel Cruz de Popayán

station), **Santa Rita**, **San Sebastián** (reconstructed in 1990). **Santo Domingo**, corner of Calvo and Bolívar (1545), open only Frid and Sun night. Next door at Calvo 212 is the **Santa Clara museum** (see below). **San Lázaro**, Calvo y Padilla, built in 1538, is regarded as the first cathedral of La Plata (Sucre). On the nave walls are six paintings attributed to Zurbarán; it has fine silverwork and alabaster in the Baptistery, open daily for mass 0700-0745. **La Merced** (Azurduy and Pérez) has gilded altar pieces.

Museums These include the University's anthropological, archaeological, folkloric, and colonial collections at the **Museo Universitario Charcas** (Bolívar 698), and its presidential and modern-art galleries (open Mon-Fri 0830-1200, 1500-1800, Sat 0830-1200, US$1, photos US$1.50). The **Museo de Santa Clara** (Calle Calvo 212), displays paintings, books, vestments, some silver and musical instruments (including a 1664 organ); there is a window to view the church; small items made by the nuns on sale, entry US$1, open Mon-Sat 1000-1130, 1430-1700. The **Museo de la Recoleta** (Calle Pedro de Anzúrez, open Mon-Fri 0900-1130, 1500-1630, US$0.55 for entrance to all collections, guided tours only) is at the Recoleta monastery, on a hill above the town, notable for the beauty of its cloisters and gardens; the carved wooden choirstalls above the nave of the church are especially fine (see the martyrs transfixed by lances); in the grounds is the Cedro Milenario, a thousand-year old cedar. **Museo de Historia Natural**, Calle San Alberto 156 (open Mon-Fri 0830-1200/1400-1800), US$0.50. **Caserón de la Capellanía**, San Alberto 413, houses the textile museum run by Antropológicas del Surandino. Rec for explanations of Indian groups and their distinctive textiles, open Mon-Fri 0830-1200, 1500-1800, Sat 0900-1200, free.

Warning Police all wear uniform and carry ID cards with photographs. Note: you do not have to show your passport to anyone on the street, be they in or out of uniform. On arrival at a hotel your passport number is registered and then given to the tourist police; each hotel's list is handed to the tourist office. If in doubt call 110 radio patrol or the tourist office (see below). Insist on going to the police station, if possible with a witness, before showing passport or money to anyone without credentials. Common targets are lone tourists who don't speak

Spanish; places where scams frequently occur are the plaza, Cerro Churuquella, Recoleta and Santa Clara. Cons can be very elaborate, involving an initial approach from a fellow "tourist from Peru" who is in league with the false "policeman" who later approaches, demanding inspection of passport, luggage, etc, and with the "taxi driver" enlisted to take you all to the police station.

Festival Independence celebrations, 24-26 May, most services, museums and restaurants closed. **Oct**: Festival Internacional de la Cultura, 10 days, shared with Potosí.

Hotels A3 *Real Audiencia*, Potosí 142, T 32809, F 30823, excellent restaurant, modern, rec; **C** *Hostal Cruz de Popayán*, Loa 881, T 25156/31706, rec, a beautiful colonial house with interior courtyard, no heating, colour TV, excellent breakfast served in rm or patio; **C** *Colonial*, Plaza 25 de Mayo 3, T 24709/25487, F 21912, expensive but rec all round and for good breakfast; **C** *Hostal Libertad*, Arce y San Alberto, 1st floor, T 23101/2, clean, spacious and comfortable rooms, friendly and efficient with excellent restaurant, highly rec; **D** *Hostal España*, España 138, T 25765, inc breakfast, TV, clean, pleasant; **D** *Hostal Sucre*, Bustillos 113, T 21411/31928, good, clean, dining room, patio, friendly staff, rec; **C** *Municipal*, Av Venezuela 1052 (T 21216), rec, restaurant; **D** *Hostal los Pinos*, Colón 502, T 24403, clean, comfortable, hot showers, TV in room, garden, quiet, peaceful, good breakfast; **D** *Londres*, Av H Siles 949, T 24792, 3 blocks uphill from station, with shower, restaurant, good; **D** *Hostal San Francisco*, Av Arce 191 y Camargo, T 22117, bath or shower, with bath, E without, pleasant, meals available, clean, quiet, comfortable, safe motorcycle parking, rec; **E** *Alojamiento Austria*, Av Ostria Gutiérrez 518, T 24202, hot showers, good value, restaurant, near bus station as well as **E** *Alojamiento Central*, Ostria Gutiérrez 456, T 23935, hot showers charged extra, and **F** *Alojamiento Chuquisaca*, Ostria Gutiérrez 33, T 24459, shared bathrooms, clean, friendly, safe car parking (US$0.50 per day). **E** *Residencial Avenida*, Av H Siles 942, T 21245, clean, hot showers, breakfast extra, laundry, friendly and helpful, rec; **E** *Residencial Bolivia*, near plaza, San Alberto 42, T 24346, with electric showers, cheaper without bath, spacious rooms, hot water, breakfast included (clothes washing not allowed); **E** *Residencial Bustillo*, Calle Ravelo 158, T 21560, without bath (D with bath), tiny rooms, clean, hot water, will store luggage at a price; **E** *Residencial Charcas*, Ravelo 62, T 23972, with bath, F without, good value breakfast, hot showers, some rooms small, quiet except for first floor (best rooms nos 15-19), clean, helpful, opp market, laundry facilities, rec; **E** *Residencial Oriental*, Calle San Alberto 43, T 21644, with bath, F without, clean, friendly but basic, tiny rooms, unlockable interior windows, hot water, motorcycle parking; **F** *Alojamiento Abaroa*, Loa 419, hot showers, uncomfortable beds, friendly, basic; **F** *Alojamiento El Turista*, Ravelo 118, T 23172, clean, hot showers 0700-1200 only, safe, basic, laundry facilities, cheap meals, terrace, doors closed at 2300; **F** *Alojamiento La Plata*, Ravelo 26, T 22102, without bath, limited shower facilities, clean, central, opp market, noisy, very friendly; **F** pp *Grand*, Arce 61, T 22104, large rm, with bath, restaurant, laundry service. Many cheap and basic places opp central market. **Youth hostel**, *Hotel Londres*, Av Hernando Siles 949.

Restaurants *Piso Cero*, Venezuela 241, good but expensive; *Las Vegas* on SE side of Plaza, Nos 31 and 37, main restaurant and annex (less grand), mixed reports but generally good (icecream, no breakfast, at lunchtime no drink without food, evening meals); *Pizzería Napoletana*, on Plaza, 25 de Mayo 30, excellent pizzas (evenings and some lunchtimes) and good home-made ice cream, not cheap; *Plaza*, also on main square, with balconies, good food and pisco sours, good live music on Friday nights, very popular with locals. *Kactus*, on Calle España, just off the main square, nice bar and restaurant, pizzas, not expensive, highly rec. *Pecos Bill Pizza*, Argentina 27, between plaza and *Hostal Sucre*, serves *almuerzo*, mixed reports. *La Taverne* of the *Alliance Française*, Aniceto Arce 35, 1/2 block from main square, closed Sun, good value, soft music—also regular films and cultural events, good meeting place; *Picolíssimo*, San Alberto entre Avaroa y Bolívar, rec, good value lunch, otherwise expensive, popular; *Alcázar*, Av Arce 105, opp San Francisco, attractive, popular, a bit more expensive than others. On Ortiz, near Plaza 25 de Mayo, are *Snack Paulista* (No 14), no food but excellent fruit juices and milk shakes; *Bibliocafé Sureña* (No 30) good pasta and light meals, music, opens 1800, closed Mon; and *Arco Iris* (No 42), good service, pricey but good, peña on Sat, excellent *roesti*, Swiss potato dish, live music some nights; *Kultur-Café Berlin*, Avaroa 326, opens 1530, good food but limited selection and small portions, German newspapers, peña every other Friday, closed Sunday (in same building as Instituto Cultural Boliviano Alemán—ICBA), popular meeting place. *Rainbow Room Café*, Calvo y Potosí, cheap meals, live music, English language magazines (next to Centro Boliviano Americano). *El Germen*, Av Arce near San Francisco church, good lunches, cosy. *Don Sancho*, Ostria Gutiérrez 130, good, clean, rec. *Confitería Palet*, Plaza 25 de Mayo 6, good coffee. *Le Repizza*, Calvo 70, very good value lunches, small but good pizzas in evening, rec; *Café Cupido Corazón*, Olañeta 77, nice coffee shop, snacks available. *Los Bajos*, Loa 759, serves special sausages (*chorizo* *chuquisaqueño*), good, daytime only. *Doña Máxima*, Junín 411, usually only cold food; *El Solar*, Bolívar 800, good but expensive and no prices written on menus (Sun closed); *Snack Miryam*, España 67, good *salteñas*; also on España, No 140 is *Snack Lucy*, recommended for snacks; *Tucanito* on Estudiantes, wide choice of sandwiches, hot and cold drinks, pleasant, popular with local students; *Amanecer*, Pasaje Junín 810-B, German *pastelería*, run by social project supporting disabled children, excellent. *New Hong Kong II*, 25 de Mayo 29, good Chinese; a good Chinese restaurant is *Canton*, San Alberto 242, clean, large portions and tea, reasonable prices. *El Tropezón*, Junín, 1/2 block from Post Office, good set meal for US$1. *Bunkers*, Ravelo next to *Res Charcas*, good breakfasts; *Chop Clock Café*, Audiencia Grau, 1 block from plaza, good breakfasts; *Café Hacheh*, Pastor Sainz 241, coffee bar and art gallery near university, interesting to visit, tasty sandwiches and fresh fruit juices, highly rec. *La Carreta*, Estudiantes 34, good fruit juices, cakes, coffee. Good chicken and chips cafés on Camargo between Arce and Loa; many others on Calles Loa and H Siles. Typical of many Bolivian cities, not many restaurants open for breakfast, but there are many fruit juice and snack stalls in the market (No 24 on map); stall No 11, Rosa, is rec for her *vitaminico*; stalls also sell cheap lunches until 1400. The local brewery produces an interesting sweetish porter or stout. The local sausages (eg at *Chorizería*, Loa between Estudiantes y Olañeta, not cheap but good) and the local chocolate, Taboada and Para Tí, are recommended.

Banks and Exchange Banco Nacional, Calle España, cash given on Visa card, good rates. TCs changed, 1% commission. **Banco de la Paz**, Plaza 25 de Mayo, for cash on Visa and Mastercard. Travel agencies' rates are good and at **casa de cambio** on corner of Calvo y Plaza Monteagudo. **Ambar**, *casa de cambio*, San Alberto 7, T 31339, good rates, TCs cashed for US$ cash at 1.5% commission. Most shops and hotels will change money. Street changers on Hernando Siles/Camargo between España and Junín, and in market.

Cultural Institutes The **Instituto Cultural Boliviano - Alemán** (Delegación de Enseñanza del Goethe Institute), Avaroa 326, Casilla 304, T 22091, shows films, has German newspapers and books to lend (0930-1230 and 1530-2000), runs Spanish, German, Portuguese and Quechua courses and it has the *Kulturcafé Berlin* (see above). Spanish lessons cost from US$3.50 for 45 mins for one person, with reductions the more students there are in the class. The ICBA also runs a folk music *peña* on Fridays. **Alianza Francesa**, Aniceto Arce 35, T 23599, noticeboard on Plaza 25 de Mayo (Casa de Libertad side) announces events. **Centro Boliviano Americano**, Calvo y Potosí, in the Colegio Simón Rodríguez. The *Café Hacheh* (see above), is run by Felix Arciénega, Bolivian artist of national fame. He organizes folk and jazz concerts, conferences and discussions, and is the editor of an art and poetry journal "Hacheh". The cafe also puts on exhibitions by other local artists, has an extensive library and a large collection of native, jazz and classical records.

Folklore Centro Cultural Masis aims to promote the traditional Yampara culture: textiles, ceramics, figurines and music. It offers instruction in Quechua, traditional Bolivian music (3 hrs a week for US$12 a month, rec) and handicrafts; once or twice a week there are musical events and the snack bar holds exhibitions of textiles and photographs. Items are for sale, including musical instruments to the highest professional standard. Open 1530-2130. The director, Roberto Sahonero, who will give further details, is to be found at Bolívar 561 DS (T 23403, Casilla 463); he is usually at the centre Mon, Wed and Fri, 1900.

Consulates West German, Arenales 215 (T 21862). **Spain**, Pasaje Argandoña (T 21435); Italy, Vice Consul, Dalence 33.

Hospital Recommended, staffed by Japanese and locals. **Doctor** Dr Gaston Delgadillo Lora, Colón 33, T 21692, speaks English, French, German, highly rec. **Dentist** Dr Carlos Sánchez C, San Alberto 75.

Laundry *Laverap*, Bolívar 617, between Audiencia and Dalence, quick, US$2.50 wash and dry. *Lavandería Paola*, Bolívar 543, T 32477, rec.

Motorcycle Mechanic Sr Jaime Medina, Motorservi Honda, Calle René Calvo Arana, T 25484. Will service all makes of machine. **Car Mechanic** at Camargo 450, rec for Toyotas.

Post Office Junín y Ayacucho/Estudiantes, open till 2000. **Poste Restante** is organized separately for men and women. **Telephone and Fax** Entel, España 271, open till 2245.

Saunas Acuario, San Alberto 680; El Tropical, Calle Guillermo Andrade.

Shopping Permanent market is bounded by Ravelo, Loa, Camargo and Junín, for food and household goods. A bus from the central market will take you to the *campesino* market. *Artesanías Calcha*, Arce 109, in same arcade as *Hostal Libertad* (San Alberto 13 other entrance), rec, very knowledgeable proprietor. *ASUR*, Antropológicos del Surandino, have a museum and project shop at San Alberto 413, Caserón de la Capellanía, T 23841, weavings from around Tarabuco and from the Jalq'a (Chuquisaca and Potosí departments); weavings are more expensive, but of higher quality than elsewhere (see above for the museum). Good selection in arcade at Junín 403 also at 417 and *Winai*, 465. Doña Máxima can be found at the *Alojamiento Guadalupe*, Junín 411, opp Central Market; she will take you to an Aladdin's Cave of superb weavings and textiles, upstairs 2 doors away; best to know what you're looking for, not especially cheap. *Charcas*, Camargo 481 y España, high quality hats. *Charangos* and weavings from Tarabuco and Candelaria are obtainable in the main plaza. Prices for souvenir items tend to be much higher than in La Paz. Camping gas can be bought at Alberto 25.

Sport Sucre Tennis Club, Av Venezuela, good clay courts, US$5 pp inc equipment hire. Swimming pool also on Av Venezuela, US$1 pp.

Travel Agents *Fremen*, Plaza 25 de Mayo 15, T 30351/32211, rec; *Tarco Tours*, España 66, German and English spoken, very friendly and helpful; *Teresita's Tours*, Arenales 9; *Sur Andes*, N Ortiz 6, T 21983, F 21677, organizes trekking from ½ day to 5 days, including the Camino Prehispánico (must take sleeping bag and good shoes, all else provided, but no porters); for groups of 3 or more US$14 pp for 1 day to US$30 for 3 days; also tours to Salar de Uyuni, Laguna Colorada and Laguna Verde. *Highland Pioneer*, T 2-5659, English, Dutch, French, German, Spanish spoken, safe 4WD jeep tours, rec, good value.

Tourist Office Calle Potosí 102 esq San Alberto, T 25983, map for sale; it is in the same building as the ASUR textile museum, the Caserón de la Capellanía, but has a different entrance. Check church and museum opening hours. Sub-office at airport, helpful. Tourist information office opp San Felipe Neri, at Nicolás Ortiz 182 (open 0800-1200, 1400-1800 Mon-Fri), is run by students studying tourism, who will show you around tourist sites for free (see above under **Churches**). All offices closed Sat and Sun. For country maps Instituto Geográfico Militar, Dalence, 2, 1° piso, T 25514, open 0830-1200, 1430-1800, Mon-Fri.

Useful Addresses Immigration Plaza 25 de Mayo, Ayacucho y Bustillos in Palacio de Gobierno, for visa extensions.

Taxis US$0.30 pp within city limits.

Air Service By LAB there is a Mon, Wed, Fri La Paz-Sucre direct air service (US$100 return), to Cochabamba (US$67 return) on Tues, Thur and Sat and to Santa Cruz Mon, Wed and Fri (US$75 return). To Puerto Suárez, for Brazil, you have to go via Santa Cruz, then take Aero Sur's daily flight. There are also LAB flights to Tarija (US$80 return, Tues, Thur). The private Aero Sur (Arenales 204A, T 064-24895) flies from Sucre to La Paz and Santa Cruz. All flights heavily booked but some "stand by" available. Your best chance is to lie in wait at the airport; they know nothing in town. Tucsupaya Airport 5 km NW of town (T 24445). LAB office is at Bustillos 131 (T 21140/21943 for reservations, poor information), from where free bus for passengers leaves 1½ hrs before flight (not always). Taxi US$3 (US$1.50 shared); buses from main road (difficult to get on with luggage). *Trufis* No 1 and F go from entrance to H Siles y Loa, 1 block from main plaza, US$0.25, 25 mins. Beware of pickpockets at airport.

Train Service Enfe information, T 31115; station is on Plaza Aniceto Arce. A *ferrobus* runs twice a week to Potosí (US$14.50), Oruro and La Paz. Warning of bag-slashing thieves on trains, highest risk just before departure.

Bus Terminal is on N outskirts of town, 3 km from centre on Ostria Gutiérrez, T 22029; closed 1900-0700; taxi US$0.50; Micro A or *trufi* No 3. Information T 22029. Daily to/from **La Paz** via Cochabamba (21 hrs, US$11), several companies, Chuquisaca and Trans Copacabana rec (Unicatur not rec), all leave about 1800-1830, first hour out of Sucre bad then the road is OK, 3 hour wait at Cochabamba at 0500, you may have to pay for each journey separately, waiting rooms; or via Potosí, US$10 (20-24 hrs) at least 4 companies, departures in am (Trans La Paz not rec). To **Cochabamba** daily, several companies 1800-1830 departures (San Francisco not rec), 10-12 hrs, US$7.50 (also by truck for about US$4, night trip caught at cement works 1½ km off Cochabamba road—Micro A goes as far as turning); **Potosí**, a number of companies operate from the centre of town: Andesbus, Bolívar 621, T 24251/30751, daily 0700 (complimentary breakfast, snack meal en route), 1700, 3½ hrs, US$5, Transtin (on Loa, but tickets etc from Sur Andes Travel Agency), all with same timetable and fares; from the bus terminal several companies, either en route to Oruro and La Paz, or solely to Potosí, average fare US$3.15 (10 de Noviembre not reliable). Trans O'Globo goes daily at 0830 to Potosí, continuing to Tupiza (US$9.50) and Villazón (US$10). Trucks from the end of Bustillos, US$2.50-3.50, 6 hrs, also *micros* leave from the bus terminal at about 0800, US$3.50, 5 hrs. To **Uyuni** via Potosí, US$8.50, Emperador. Bus to **Santa Cruz**, direct Tues, Fri, Sun, 15 hrs, or via Cochabamba, Flota Unificada, highly rec with video, Tues and Fri, 1700, also Mopar, Tues, Fri, Sun (rec) and others, US$10-13 (but bargain) most departures 1130-1300. Once a week to **Tarija** 10 de Noviembre, Tues, US$15.50, Andesbus' service to Potosí on Mon, Thur and Sat at 0700 continues to Tarija, US$15.50, 19-20 hrs. To **Camiri**, El Chaqueño, Tues and Fri, US$16. To **Monteagudo**, Thurs and Sun, 1500, US$5.30. **Oruro**, via Potosí or Cochabamba, none direct. To **Llallagua**, with Bustillo, Thur, US$10, continuing to Oruro, 10 hrs.

Excursions To the **Castillo de la Glorieta**, 5 km S on the Potosí road (*trufi* 4 or E from Arce y Siles), the former mansion of the Argandaña family, built in a mixture of contrasting European styles with beautiful painted ceilings and standing in attractive gardens. Badly damaged by years of military use and sadly neglected, there are plans for its restoration. It is in the military compound, entry free, passports surrendered at the gate, do not cross the river, open daily 0900-1200, 1500-1700.
  Tarabuco, 3,295m, 64 km by good road SE of Sucre, has a most colourful Indian market on Sundays, starting about 0930. Buses (US$1.50) and trucks (US$1) leave from 0630 or when full from top of Calle Calvo (Plaza Huallparimachi), take bus C from Mercado), 2 ½ hr journey (or taxi, US$40). Shared *trufi* taxis can be arranged by hotels, with pick-up service, starting at 0700, US$2.25, one-way, US$4 return. First bus back 1300. You can walk some of the way back and get a lift when you are tired. Transport more difficult on weekdays; take an early bus and return by truck. Guide to Tarabuco, Alberto from Sucre tourist office, US$37 for a full day in a car for 4 people.
  There are at least 2 budget hotels, including **G Residencial Florida**, basic, cold, dirty but friendly, lovely garden and display of butterflies and Bolivian bank-notes since 1911, restaurant not rec; try *Bar California*, basic, or other restaurants. Festival with fair: Virgen de Rosario, 1st Sunday in October and 12 March. The Phujllay independence celebration in March, is very colourful and lively with even more costume and dance than the Rosario. Travel agencies organize special excursions and hotels fill up quickly. If you are hardy take a sleeping-bag and sleep in the only restaurant.
  Although the market is popular with tourists, it is still worth a visit (comments range from "excellent" to "totally spoilt"). Best bargains are to be had on weekdays or on Sun either before the bulk of tourists arrive (from 1030), or late in the day. Our latest reports indicate that prices at the market are high, but that the real appeal is the Indians in their authentic dress. Note: the market is not held at Carnival (when all Tarabuco is dancing in Sucre), Easter Sunday or on a holiday weekend in November.
  The villages where weavers live include Candelaria (two hours by truck from Tarabuco) or Macha (8 hours from Sucre); Pocata (one hour from Macha), or Ravelo (59 km NW of Sucre; travel to Ravelo: by truck between 0900-1000 from departure point near airport, 3 hrs; *micro*, US$1.30, check at shop at Hernando Siles 843 if it's running, it's supposed to leave at 0900, return 1600—lorries back to Sucre invariably full). At Punilla, on the road to Ravelo, there is a 2 ½ hr walk to **Incamachay** where there are precolumbian drawings. Punilla is also where you leave the truck for Challanaca and thence to Potolo, where they weave red animals on a black or brown background. You can buy direct from the weavers, no stores. Trucks (Thurs and Fri in the dry season) go direct from near Sucre airport; in the wet, you can only get to Challanaca and you walk for 3 hours to get there—the prices will probably be lower in the wet season.
  Besides Incamachay, there is a precolumbian site at Pumamachay, where cave drawings can be seen; "very hard to find", recommended to ask at student tourist office (address above). Also in the vicinity is the prehispanic road at Chataquila, possibly Inca. Tours to these sites are run by Sur Andes Travel Agency in Sucre.

East and South of Sucre

A main road runs SE from Sucre through Tarabuco to the frontier with Paraguay at Villazón (not to be confused with the other Villazón on the frontier with Argentina, see above p 288). At Padilla (Km 190, altitude 2,080m, hotels on plaza), a turn-off heads N 20 km to **Villa Serrano**, where the musician Mauro Núñez lived. A music festival is held on 28-29 December. (The journey is beautiful through wild mountains.) At **Monteagudo** (Km 323, altitude 1,138m) there are direct buses to Santa Cruz, twice a week, US$8, 14 hrs. Several basic hotels: **F** *Alojamiento los Naranjos* behind plaza, hot showers, *Alojamiento las Tablitas*, and *Alojamiento Oriental*, both on the main road.
  Further SE at Km 456 is **Camiri** (altitude 827m, pop 20,000), growing rapidly because of nearby oilfields—the oil refinery may be visited. Flota El Chaqueño runs from Sucre to Camiri twice a week in each direction, at least 20 hrs, US$16, service also by Andesbus. From Camiri there is a bus to Santa Cruz which should be booked up well in advance as it is always crowded, office on Av Busch next to *Gran Hotel Londres*, goes 4 times a week if enough passengers, 8 hrs, US$11; *camioneta* leaves from in front of the market when there are enough passengers, US$10-12, 7 hrs (dusty). Aero Sur (T 2880) flies to Santa Cruz daily, with connections to all major airports. As a garrison town it has some hotels (**E** *Hotel Ortuño*, Calle Comercio; **E** *Residencial Marieta*, Av Petrolera 15; **E** *Residencial Premier*, Av Busch 60; **E** *Gran Hotel*

Londres, Av Busch 36, a dump, unhelpful, expensive, terrible beds; **F** pp *Residencial Chaqueña*, Calle Comercio, clean, good; **F** *Residencial Familiar*, Calle Comercio), restaurants, bars (nothing is cheap). There is a post office, but no parcels sent abroad. Immigration is at Av 1 de Mayo 158 (no sign), 0800-1200, 1300-1800 daily. If you arrive by car: at Tránsito checkpoint pick up a slip of paper with instructions on how to reach Guardia where you collect permits to stay overnight. Next visit army post on Plaza de Armas to be checked there. Before leaving town visit Guardia again to collect a permit to proceed—all permits cost about US$0.50 each. Hotels will *not* accept car passengers without a permit. A very bad road (being paved, 1994) heads S from Camiri, through Boyuibe (see below), Villa Montes (**see p 305**) and Yacuiba to Argentina (**see p 327**). By bus, this route is very rough "bus times unknown even by locals and the chance of actually managing to squeeze on is pretty remote" (Peter Gedge).

It is possible to drive from Camiri into Paraguay direct in a truck or 4-wheel-drive, high clearance vehicle, carrying insect repellent, food and water for a week. No help can be relied on in case of a breakdown; a winch is advisable, especially after rain. There are some rivers to ford and although they are dry in the dry season they can be impassable if there is rain in the area. Bernd Proissl (Wernau, Germany) writes "All travellers going through the Chaco are smuggling something". At Camiri, obtain a US$3 permit from the Guardia to go 63 km (1½ hours) over a rough road to **Boyuibe**, Km 519, altitude 817m, the last town in Bolivia (*Hotel Guadalquivir*, or *Hotel Chaqueño* next door, both F, both serve meals). Colectivo from Av Bolívar 1215, daily at 1500, US$2. Occasional buses run as far as Boyuibe. Once there pay US$2 at Customs for an exit stamp. Passports must be stamped by commander of the army post S of the town. Fuel and water are available, and it is on the Yacuiba railway (rail fare Santa Cruz-Boyuibe: *ferrobus* US$13 and US$10, *expreso* US$9 and US$5.50; *rápido* US$5.50 and US$4).

¾ km after the military checkpoint turn left past a large water tower. From then on just follow the most used road; accurate directions may be obtained from the army before leaving Boyuibe. If hitching be at customs post before 0600. It is 134 km from Boyuibe to the Bolivian border post at Villazón. At one point there is a disconcerting S trend for several km; for the first 70 km a few estancias are seen, but nothing else except a total of 3 Bolivian customs posts. This section takes between 6 hrs and up to 3 days if there are unseasonable storms. There are no immigration facilities at Villazón for giving exit stamps (customs agents are still there - they are armed). The Bolivian consulate in Asunción confirms that exit stamp is not required; entry stamp for Paraguay is essential. The army goes to Villazón once or twice a month; you can camp at Villazón, but no food is available, nor is there much water. The nine soldiers at each of the fly-infested lonely posts on either side of the border will vie for your company if you arrive at nightfall. Enormously appreciated by these poor fellows are small gifts of soft drinks, beer, cigarettes or canned fruit. They do six month stints here.

The frontier is 3 km E of Villazón at Guaraní and the Paraguayan post is 13 km further E at Fortín General Eugenio A Garay. Camping is possible here and for a small contribution the troops may give you use of showers and kitchen. The road is somewhat better from here on, sandy and bumpy but straight. There is a military post (water) at Fortín Mister Long, Km 26. It can take 9 hrs to get to Mariscal Estigarribia, where there's a large military base. Passports are stamped at Fortín Gen Garay or at any one of the other posts. Be sure to state whether entering or leaving Bolivia. (For Mcal Estigarriba and the continuation of this route see **Paraguay: The Paraguayan Chaco**.)

A road runs S from Potosí to Tarija. At *Camargo*, 186 km from Potosí, is an excellent restaurant, *Media Luz*. Guest rooms have been built for overnight stop. Around Camargo, vines are cultivated, using the traditional method of training them up pruned *molle* trees. The road continues for 182 km to Tarija.

Tarija, at 1,840m (pop 100,000) was founded 4 July 1574, in the rich valley of the Guadalquivir river. The city had a tumultuous struggle against Spain, declaring itself independent in 1807, and has a strong cultural heritage. Its people are markedly religious and strongly individualistic, and the Indian strain is less marked here than elsewhere in Bolivia. Tarija is a delightful small city, a nice, peaceful place to enjoy the sun. The streets and squares are planted with flowering trees, quite a contrast if coming from the treeless altiplano. The main square, Plaza Luis de Fuentes, has palm trees, jacarandas, orange trees (both in flower/fruit in October), and roses. There is a statue, erected in 1991, to the city's founder, Capitán Luis de Fuentes Vargas. The modern Avenida Las Américas, or Costanera gracefully flanks the curves of the river.

The Cathedral, on Calle La Madrid, is open in the morning and from 1700. San Francisco church (La Madrid y Daniel Campos), is beautifully painted inside, with praying angels depicted on the ceiling; note the four evangelists at the four corners below the dome. The library is divided into old and new sections, the old containing some 15,000 volumes, the new a further 5,000. The oldest book is a 1501 *Iliad* incorporating other works. There are also old manuscripts and 19th century photograph albums. To see the library, go to the door at Ingavi 0137 (open 0830-1130, 1530-1730, Sat 0830-1130). Tarija's university was founded in 1946. There is a palaeontological collection (dinosaur bones, fossils, remains of an Andean elephant), and archaeological and historical collections; the entrance is at the corner of the building at Trigo y V Lema (open Mon-Fri 0800-1200, 1500-1800, brochure US$0.65). The Casa Dorada, Trigo y Ingavi (entrance on Ingavi), also called the Maison d'Or, has been reconstructed and is now the Casa de Cultura. It is open 0830-1200, 1430-1800, Sat 0900-1200, but visitors may see round on guided tours only (voluntary donation). The house and emporium of importer/exporter Moisés Narvajas and his wife Esperanza Morales was begun in 1886, inaugurated 1903, but had fallen into disrepair by 1980. It has been repainted in original colours, silver and ochre on the outside, cerise, green and dark blue, with white trim, inside; it has Italian murals, art nouveau copies on ceiling panels and much gold in the rooms. Tours view the private oratory, with a wooden altar covered in a plaster and gold leaf, sacristy with beautiful vestments, etc; the reception room ("a terrible mixture of styles" –damask curtains, Persian carpets, Victorian chairs, Venetian mirrors, red cedar piano, bronze peacock with original tungsten illumination in the tail, and so on); the photography room (pictures of Tarijan history and the restoration of the house); the dining room (note the opal table lamps in the form of bunches of grapes and lilies). Near Parque Bolívar (shady, pleasant) is another of Narvajas' houses, the Castillo de Beatriz, painted bright blue and white (Bolívar between Junín and O'Connor; ask the owner if it is possible to visit).

A good view can be had from La Loma de San Juan; follow Calle D Paz to the top of the rise where the buses gather, turn right on the cobbled street, then right through the gate and follow the Stations of the Cross to the top (124 steps up, equestrian statue of Moto Méndez, see **Excursions** below, at the top).

Maize, vegetables, wheat, potatoes and splendid grapes thrive in the basin. The best time to visit Tarija is from January onwards, when the fruit are in season. Bolivia's best wines are produced here; see **Excursions** below.

Zoo On Av Costanera, a tatty park for children, but worth the US$0.15 to see the condors.

The city is famous for its *niño* (child) processions: colourful and charming. During processions of San Roque in a 3-day festival from the first Sunday in September the richly dressed saint's statue is paraded through the streets; wearing lively colours, cloth turbans and cloth veils, the people dance before it as it goes, and women throw flowers from the balconies. Dogs are decorated with ribbons for the day. On the second Sunday in October the flower festival commemorates the Virgen del Rosario, and another takes place in Easter week. Also in October, on two weekends mid-month, there is a beer festival on Av de las Américas. Colourful processions take place on 15 April, Day of Tarija.

Hotels A3 *Los Ceibos*, Av Víctor Paz Estenssoro y La Madrid, T 34430, F 42461 (formerly *Prefectural*), inc excellent buffet breakfast, large rooms with bath, TV, phone, mini-bar, good restaurant, outdoor pool and cocktail bar, free transport to airport, rec; **B** *Victoria Plaza*, La Madrid y Sucre, T 42700, F 22600, on square, with bath, hot water, TV, phone, inc buffet breakfast, laundry service, highly rec; **B** *Grand Hotel Tarija*, Sucre 0770, T 42684, F 44777, modernized, comfortable, central; **B** *Hostal Costanera*, Av Las Américas, T 42851, modern, with breakfast; **B** *Hostal Cristal*, 15 de Abril 363, on square, T 45533/4, with breakfast, hot water, phone, TV, transport from airport; **D** *Hostal Libertador*, Bolívar 649, T 44231, with bath, phone, sporadic hot water, breakfast extra, family-run, close to cathedral, rec; **D** *Hostal Carmen*, Ingavi 0-0784 y R Rojas, T 43372/44342, shower, clean, good value, some ground floor rooms without exterior windows, good breakfast, sometimes has transport to/from airport, organizes tours of the area, rec; opposite is **F** pp *Residencial Rosario*, Ingavi 0777, with bath, cheaper without breakfast, clean and friendly, highly rec; **D** *Gran Hotel Max*, Junín 930, T 24549, with bath, **E** without, cheaper still in 3, 4-bedded rooms, inc breakfast, 20 mins walk from main plaza; **D** *Hostal Bolívar*, No 0256, T42741, with bath, highly rec, clean, comfortable, hot water, breakfast US$1, laundry, state clearly when you intend to leave; **E** *América*, Bolívar 257, T 42627, hot showers, good, run down but quiet, small breakfast included, restaurant attached (good); also on Bolívar, No 138, is *Alojamiento El Turista*, OK; **F** *Hostería España*, Alejandro Corrado 546, T 43304, clean, hot showers, pleasant; **F** *Hostal 15 de Abril*, Campos 1079, without bath, bright; **F** pp *Residencial Familiar*, Sucre 656, with bath, cheaper without, most downstairs rooms without windows; **F** *Alojamiento Ocho Hermanos*, Sucre 782, near main plaza, clean, collective rooms only. *Terminal*, behind bus station, family-run, good lunches, suitable for a night's stop-over; **F** *Alojamiento El Hogar*, across Av Las Américas from bus terminal, clean; **F** *Residencial Zeballos*, Sucre 0966, T 42068, clean.

Restaurants   Best is *Milano*, Trigo e Ingavi, T 34093, opp Casa de Cultura, on 2 floors, downstairs European/Italian specialities, home-made pastas, pizzas, schnitzels, gulasch, upstairs more formal, variety of fondues, radette, excellent meat, good wine list, not cheap, rec. In the evening lots of eating places can be found around the square. *La Cabaña de Don Pepe*, Campos 2681, near Av Las Américas, some way from centre, has excellent steaks at reasonable prices; *Cabaña Don Pedro*, Av Las Américas, good typical food, outdoor patio overlooks river, moderate prices; *Don Ñato*, in Mercado La Paz, near La Madrid and Rojas, good food and service, US$3-4; *Café Show*, Ingavi 278 y Mariscal Sucre, superb cakes; *Snack Te Ve*, Sucre 622, just off plaza; *Tonmy*, La Madrid 178, local food; *Palma's Center*, Madrid 0358, on the plaza, good *confitería*, pizzas, ice cream, popular meeting place, bar atmosphere in evening, good food, rec. Also on the plaza: *La Taberna Gatopardo*, pizza, *parrillada* with Argentine beef, hot dogs, snacks, local wines, good value, lively atmosphere; next door is *Punto de Encuentro*, local dishes; *Chingos*, popular with young crowd, hamburgers; on other side of plaza, next to Prefectura, *Pizzería Issabella* and *Fechorias*, good *salteñas* in am. *El Solar*, Campero y V Lema, vegetarian, US$1.50 set lunch; *Heladería Gloria*, Trigo e Ingavi, tea, refrescos, sandwiches, etc at Trigo 655; *Empanadas Chapacas*, Colón y V Lema (Plaza Sucre). *Iscela*, La Madrid 259, cakes, coffee, pizzas. For breakfast either try the market (which also does good lunches, but get there before 1300) or *Hostal Bolívar*, excellent breakfast, open to non-residents. Typical dishes include *keperi*, meat that is first boiled, then fried, *saice*, beef and chickpeas spiced with cumin and picante, *ranga-ranga*, tripe, *chancao*, a chicken soup. Viscachani mineral water is sold by the delicatessen at Domingo Paz y Sucre. Try the local wines, eg Aranjuez, Santa Ana de Casa Real or Kohlberg, the *singani* (a clear brandy, San Pedro de Oro y Rugero are recommended labels), also local beer, Astra. **NB** Many restaurants (and much else in town) close between 1400 and 1600.

Banks and Exchange   Banco del Estado will change money. Banco Mercantil de Bolivia, Sucre y 15 de Abril, exchanges cash and gives cash against Visa and Mastercard (US$5 authorization charge). Cash also advanced on Visa cards at Banco Popular del Perú, Sucre. TCs can be changed at Organización Pulido, Bolívar 220, T 42938, reasonable rates at *Ferretería El Lorito*, nr Bolívar and Trigo, 5% commission, or at *Internacional Tarija Travel Agency*, address below. Dollars and Argentine pesos cash at: Campos y Bolívar 202, *Casa de Cambio San Juan*, Bolívar 246, and Bolívar Nos 235, 258 and 278.

Consulates   German Sucre 665, helpful. Argentine Ballivián 0699, Mon-Fri, 0800-1300.

Dentist   Dra Marta Bass-Werner, opp Casa Dorada, highly rec, inexpensive and good.

Laundry   at D Campos 420, US$1 per kg.

Post Office V Lema y Sucre. **Telecommunications** next door at V Lema y D Campos, T 42676.

Shopping   The market is in the block encompassed by Domingo Paz, Sucre, Bolívar and Trigo. Craft goods in market and in co-operative shop in plaza; some cheap stuff, shoddy. Felt for hats at *La Nueva Italia*, Ingavi y Sucre; they will show you where to have your hat made up for US$3.50. Cheap Kodak Gold film is available.

Swimming   Municipal swimming bath down the hill from the Mercado Negro. Tomatitas, trip of 5 km, popular picnic area (same transport as for San Lorenzo, see below). At lunchtime on Sunday in Tomatitas, many courtyards serve very cheap meals. For those with their own transport El Rincón de la Victoria, 18 km, or Tolomosita, 7 km, sandy beach on river bank, or the Ancón gorge. Sauna at Acuario, 15 de Abril 679.

Travel Agents   *Internacional Tarija*, Sucre 721, T 44446/7, helpful. *Mara Tours*, Gral Trigo 739, T 43045/43490, most helpful.

Tourist Office   On main plaza in Prefectura, very helpful, free map (which you may have to photocopy).

Air Service   LAB to Santa Cruz and La Paz (Mon, Wed, Fri), Sucre (Tues, Thur), and Salta (Wed). Aero Sur flies to Santa Cruz. Flights are frequently cancelled and/or delayed. LAB office at

Suipacha 750; TAM office La Madrid 470, T 45899, Aero Sur office, Ingaví 339, T 45820. Taxi to airport, US$1 pp, or *micro* drops you 2 blocks away. Some hotels have free transport to town, you may have to phone for it. On arrival at Tarija, reconfirm you return flight immediately. Airport information T 43135.

Buses Daily on the 935-km route **Potosí-Oruro-La Paz**, leaving 1700 (26 hrs, US$17.50; check which company operates the best buses, San Lorenzo, for example, has heating). To **Potosí** (386 km), daily, US$10.50 with San Lorenzo, San Jorge and Emperador; for Sucre, you must change buses in Potosí. To **Villazón**: EMTV, Tues, Thur, Sat, 0830, US$6.50, Veloz del Sud, 3-4 times a week, 1900, 6½ hrs, US$7; Cristal, 3 times a week, 0630 Gran Chaco or Golondrina, daily at 2000, very cold on arrival; otherwise you need to take a local truck (US$5). On Tues and Fri there is a combined bus/train service to **Villazón** and **La Paz**, US$18.80, leaves Tarija 0630; seat guaranteed on both services. To **Santa Cruz**, US$15, 32 hrs over incredibly bad roads. To **Villa Montes (see below)**, 12 hrs, Mon, Thurs, 0730, US$11. To **Bermejo**, 9 hrs, US$6, rough ride. The new bus station is in the outskirts on Avenida de Las Américas (30 mins walk from centre, 7-8 mins from airport). Cía El Chapaco and Expreso del Sur use poor quality vehicles. Trucks to all destinations leave from Loma, near the market.

To Argentina The road to Villazón, 189 km, is the shortest route to Argentina. There is no railway (see above for transport). The alternative route to Argentina via Bermejo is the most easily reached from Tarija, 210 km, the views are spectacular (sit on right); not recommended in the rainy season or a month or so after. The road is in an appalling condition apart from 50 km which are paved. Do not try to cycle. Daily buses, usually at night, some early am, take 5-9 hours (4 hrs in a car), US$6, truck US$3.50. At *Bermejo* (altitude 415, pop 13,000, at least three hotels, 2 *casas de cambio* on main street, thorough customs searches) cross river by ferry to Agua Blanca, Argentina. From Tarija to Yacuiba/Pocitos border is 290 km. Buses to Yacuiba, 4 times a week at 2000 by Flota Tarija. **NB** Crossing to Argentina, expect up to 4 hrs to pass through customs and immigration. Electronic goods must be entered in your passport for later checks. Also note there is a 1-hr time difference between Bolivia and Argentina (Bolivia 1 hr behind).

Excursions Recommended tours of Tarija, the city, surrounding areas and vineyards, are offered by *Hostal Carmen* (see **Hotels**, above).

The outskirts of the city can be a good place to look for fossils: take a micro or taxi in the direction of the airport. 5 km out of town, before the police control (*garita*), you see lovely structures of sand looking like a small canyon (*barrancos*). Here have been found bones, teeth, parts of saurian spines, etc; things come to the surface each year after the rains. You may have to go a long way from the city. If in luck, compare your finds with the objects in the University museum.

At San Jacinto (8 km, *trufi* from Ingavi y Daniel Campos, by Palacio de Justicia, every 30 mins, 35 mins' journey, US$0.35), is a tourist complex beside the lake formed by a dam completed in 1991. At the dam there is a café, several shacks selling food and drink, boats for hire. There is a level lakeside walk which is very pleasant. Cross the dam, go past the food stalls and follow the clear track to the head of the lake. The track passes farms and animals in the fields. It takes about an hour until climbing a shoulder and then descending to more houses. Either return the same way (in which case you miss the best part), or climb the hill to the left (a bit of a scramble to the top) for a good, all-round view. Walk back along the ridge path which descends directly back to the steep ravine which is blocked by the dam (take care on the final descent, in particular do not walk over the cliff where the dam is; keep left, the lake side).

To *San Lorenzo* (15 km, *trufis* from top of Domingo Paz, return from San Lorenzo square, 45 mins, US$0.30). The road passes Tomatitas river bathing (5 km), and the **Parque Nacional Los Barrancos**, an area of erosion. San Lorenzo's plaza is very pleasant, with palms, oranges and flowers; the church is huge and unadorned. Around the town the land is agricultural; you can walk down to the river (head N and turn right) and, if it is low enough, you can ford the water and ask directions in the fields for the way up the eroded cliffs (45 mins, fine views). Just off the square is the Museo Méndez, the house of the independence hero Eustaquio Méndez, El Moto (he lost his right hand, many stories as to how it happened). The small museum exhibits his weapons, his bed, his "testimonio", entry US$0.30, open Mon-Fri 0900-1230, Sat 0900-1200, 1500-1700, Sun 1000-1200. Los Chorros de Jurina with natural rock pools, 22 km from Tarija, are beyond San Lorenzo, you need a guide to walk there (check first if there is water in the falls).

To visit the Aranjuez bodega, ask Sr Milton Castellanos at the Agrochemical shop at Trigo 789. To the Rugero Singani bodega at *El Valle de Concepción*, an appointment must be made with Ing Sergio Prudencio Navarro, Bodegas y Viñedos de la Concepción, Casilla 99, Tarija, La Madrid y Suipacha s/n, T 25040. Ing Prudencio will show visitors round the vineyards and the bodega. To El Valle, 15 km S of Tarija, *trufis* go from Plazuela Sucre with no fixed schedule; may be better to take Radio Taxi Moto Méndez, T 24480, US$12 there and back, plus wait.

The route to El Valle de Concepción takes the road past the airport, at the *garita* the road forks left to Yacuiba/Pocitos, right to Bermejo. Take the latter and after a while take an unmade road to the right. This area is called Santa Ana. Look on your left for the ex-Russian observatory (signpost; a good place to go at night to see the stars). Then you pass the Colonial winery, the Santa Ana bridge and Santa Ana Grande vineyards and the Centro Vitivinicola, Cooperación Española, before reaching El Valle (also referred to as Concepción). The town is a mixture of the old and new; the square is filled with bitter orange and ceibo trees. The houses on the road that leads out to Rugero are of adobe or stone-clad.

Santuario Chaguaya, S of El Valle, beyond Padcaya by road, is 76 km S of Tarija. At the fiesta for La Virgen de Chaguaya, 15 August, people walk all the way from the city (the pilgrimage route is 45 km).

Villa Montes, 260 km E of Tarija is famous for the highest temperatures in Bolivia; take mosquito repellent. It is renowned for fishing and holds a Fiesta del Pescado in August. Opposite the railway station 2 km out of town is **F** *Hotel El Rancho*, with bungalow-type accommodation; the food is expensive so eat in town. It is on the edge of the Gran Chaco and is on the road and rail route from Santa Cruz to the Argentine border at Yucuiba. Another dry-season road runs E to Paraguay which is OK for high clearance vehicles. We have received no recent reports about this latter route which some maps show as a main road. **G** *Residencial Tropical*, clean, friendly. Bus from Tarija leaves Tues, Fri and Sat at 0700, US$11; to Tarija, 1700, 12 hrs.

THE COCHABAMBA BASIN (5)

The fertile foothills surrounding the colonial city of Cochabamba provide much of the country's grain, fruit and coca. Colonial villages and precolumbian sites are also within reach.

It is 394 km from La Paz to Cochabamba by road, now completely paved.

Cochabamba, Bolivia's third largest city (population 300,000) was founded in 1571. Situated at an altitude of 2,570m, it has an excellent climate with an average temperature of 18°C. Located in one of the richest agricultural regions in Bolivia, the Cochabamba valley attracted settlers from Spain who prospered as landowners producing foodstuffs for the mining areas. Land reform since 1952 has created a class of relatively prosperous and conservative small farmers. Today Cochabamba is an important commercial and communications centre with a greater vitality than the cities of the altiplano.

At the heart of the old city is the arcaded **Plaza 14 de Septiembre**, with the Cathedral dating from 1571, but much added to (open mornings only). Nearby are several colonial churches: **Santo Domingo** (Santiváñez y Ayacucho) begun in 1778 and still unfinished; **San Francisco** (25 de Mayo y Bolívar) 1581, but heavily modernized in 1926; the **Convent of Santa Teresa** (Baptista y Ecuador) original construction 1753; and **La Compañia** (Baptista y Achá), whose whitewashed interior is completely innocent of the usual riot of late Baroque decoration. From **Plaza Colón**, at the N end of the old town, the wide Av Ballivián (known as **El Prado**) runs NW to the wealthy modern residential areas. To the S of the old town lie the bus and train stations and some of the best produce markets in Bolivia. Overlooking the bus station is the **San Sebastián hill**, offering grand views of the city. From here you can walk to the adjoining **La Coronilla hill**, topped by an imposing monument commemorating the defence of Cochabamba by its womenfolk from Spanish troops in 1812. (Beware of robbery and of bogus policemen.) At the E end of Av Heroínas is another hill the **Cerro de San Pedro**, with a statue to Cristo de la Corcordia.

Cochabamba was the birth-place of Simón Patiño, the tin baron, who built two houses in the city. One of these, in the centre, is now part of the **Universidad San**

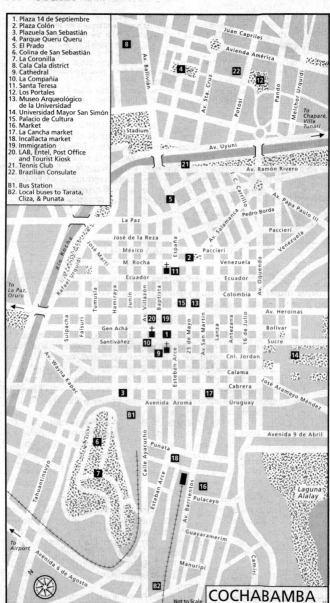

1. Plaza 14 de Septiembre
2. Plaza Colón
3. Plazuela San Sebastián
4. Parque Queru Queru
5. El Prado
6. Colina de San Sebastián
7. La Coronilla
8. Cala Cala district
9. Cathedral
10. La Compañía
11. Santa Teresa
12. Los Portales
13. Museo Arqueológico
    de la Universidad
14. Universidad Mayor San Simón
15. Palacio de Cultura
16. Market
17. La Cancha market
18. Incallacta market
19. Immigration
20. LAB, Entel, Post Office
    and Tourist Kiosk
21. Tennis Club
22. Brazilian Consulate

B1. Bus Station
B2. Local buses to Tarata,
    Cliza, & Punata

COCHABAMBA

Not to Scale

Simón; next door on the corner of Calama and Aguirre is his bank, the Banco Mercantil (see the domed interior of the main banking hall). To the N of Plaza Colón at Av Potosí 1250 (T 43137) lies **Los Portales**, the Patiño mansion, reached by micro H or G from Av San Martín to Recoleta. Built in French renaissance style, furnished from Europe and set in 10 hectares of gardens inspired by Versailles, the house was finished in 1927 but never occupied; open Mon-Fri 1700-1800. Guided tours daily, starting at opening times, entrance US$0.75, don't be late; useful library. There is a modern art museum in the basement (open Mon-Sat 1430-1830). It is also an educational centre for teachers and students, promoting literacy in the surrounding countryside. For Patiño's country mansion at Pairumani, see below under **Excursions**.

Museums Museo Arqueológico, 25 de Mayo between Heroínas and Colombia, part of the Universidad de San Simón, open Mon-Fri 0900-1200, 1400-1800, Sat 0900-1300, entry US$1.50, free student guide (Spanish or English) small but interesting display of artefacts including amerindian heiroglyphic scripts and pre-Inca textiles, good 1½ hr tour; **Museo de la Casa de la Cultura**, 25 de Mayo y Heroínas, open Mon-Fri 0900-1200, 1400-1800, entry free, exhibitions of paintings, occasionally shows films.

Street Numbering Street numbering works as follows: a code of one letter, indicating the block in one direction, plus two numbers to indicate the block in the other direction, plus two further numbers to indicate the door. On longitudinal streets each house has the same letter and different numbers; on transversal streets the letters change with each block, but the same numbers appear in each block (eg A0350 and H0350 are in the same street, but 8 blocks apart). Street names and numbers are frequently written over each doorway, rather than on street corner signs.

Festivals *Fiestas* are frequent and fascinating. Carnival is celebrated 15 days before Lent. Rival groups (*comparsas*) compete in music, dancing, and fancy dress, culminating in El Corso on the last Saturday of the Carnival. Beware the rains around and after Carnival, and water-throwing the day after, when you are likely to get drenched. *Mascaritas* balls also take place in the carnival season, when the young women wear long hooded satin masks.

Fiesta de la Virgen de Urkupiña, Quillacollo, see below; and 14 September, dancing.

Hotels L3 *Portales*, Av Pando 1271, T 48700, F 42071, 5-star, swimming pool, a long way from centre; **A1** *Aranjuez*, Av Buenos Aires E-0563, T 41935, F 40158, Casilla 3056, 4-star, rec, 2 blocks from Los Portales, small, colonial style, good restaurant, jazz in the bar, Fri and Sat night; **A1** *Caesar's Plaza*, 25 de Mayo S-210 y Bolívar, T 50088/54092, F 59324, modern, 4-star, good buffet breakfasts US$2.50; **A2** *Gran Hotel Cochabamba*, Plaza Ubaldo Anze, T 82551, F 42823, beautifully set in the N part of the city (2 blocks from Los Portales at La Recoleta), with garden, swimming pool (guests only) and tennis courts, remodelled, popular with tour groups, rec. In the city: **A3** *Ambassador*, Calle España N-0349 (T 48777, F 28778), private bath, hot water, telephone, modern, central and reasonable, good restaurant; **B** *Americana*, Av Aroma y Esteban Arce, T 50554. F 50484, clean, TV, fridge, fan, helpful, good service; **C** *Boston*, Calle 25 de Mayo 0167, T 28530, clean and friendly, restaurant, luggage deposit, noisy, but quiet rooms at back, safe parking, rec; **C** *Capitol*, Colombia 0415 y Mayo, T 24510, private bath, TV, clean and friendly but rather scruffy, no parking; **C** *Regina*, Calle Reza, well-run, friendly, popular, good room service; **C** *Unihotel*, Baptista S-0111 Esq Av Heroínas, T 51228, with bath and breakfast, pleasant, helpful, modern, clean, central; **D** *City Hotel*, Jordán E-341, T 22993, near centre, with shower but without breakfast, cheaper rooms on upper floors, clean, noisy but modern; **D** *El Dorado*, 25 de Mayo 1034, T 21940, rec, clean, hot water; **D** *Hostal Central*, Gral Acha 0235, T 23622, with bath, modern; **D** *Res Buenos Aires*, 25 de Mayo 329, T 29518, with bath, E without, pleasant, clean communal baths; **D** *Residencial Escobar*, Uruguay E-0213, T 29275, with bath, hot shower, modern, mediocre; **D** *Hostería Jardín*, Hamiraya 248 (between Colombia and Ecuador), T 47844, with or without bathroom, garden, very friendly, safe car-park; **D** *Residencial Elisa*, Agustín López, S-0834, T 27846, with bath, E without, good breakfast, modern, clean, garden, 2 blocks from bus station, laundry service, friendly, highly rec; **D** *Venecia*, Aroma 0136, T 26165, run down but clean; **E** *Colonial*, Junín 134 between Colombia and Heroínas, T 21791, with garden and terrace, rooms with big balcony, peaceful and secure, laundry facilities, breakfast served on terrace, US$0.80, "can't recommend highly enough, absolutely brilliant little hotel"; **E** *Florida*, 25 de Mayo S-0583, T 27787, clean and friendly, but noisy, popular, laundry service, safe deposit box, quite clean, breakfast, rec (hot showers, shared bathrooms only); **E** *Residencial Copacabana*, Arce 0875, without bath, large rooms, clean, friendly, motorcycle parking; **E** *Res El Salvador* Montes E-0420, T 27307, with electric shower, clean, will store luggage, rec, close to market but inconvenient for restaurants; **E** *Residencial Familiar*, Sucre E-0554, T 27988, with annex at 25 de Mayo S-0234, T 27986, old fashioned, pleasant, clean; **E** *Jerusalem*, Aroma y 25 de Mayo, with bath, warm water, clean, friendly; **F** *Residencial Agustín López*, Agustín López 0859, T 27250, near bus station, basic, without bath, clean, hot water; **F** *Residencial Virgen de Copacabana*, Av Arce S-0876 y Brasil, T 27929, near bus station, hot showers, spotless, friendly, rec; **F** *Residencial Kennedy*, Av Aroma, T 24732, hot water, good, clean, with washing facilities; **F** *Residencial Urkupiña*, Av Arce 750, T 23502, very clean, basic, hot water, shared bathrooms only; **F** *Alojamiento Escobar*, Aguirre S-749, clean, a good budget place (not to be confused with *Residencial*, above). Many cheap and basic places to stay near the bus station, eg **F** *Alojamiento Sucre*, Aroma 256, T 24761, not very clean. **Youth hostel** ABAJ affiliate, **F** pp *Residencial Jordán*, Calle Antesana S-0671, without breakfast, modern, clean, basic. For long-term accommodation, Sra Nora de Durán, Ecuador E-0479, entre 25 de Mayo y San Martín, full board available, good value.

Restaurants *Las Tablitas*, Plaza 14 de Setiembre 0209, lunch or set dinner good value, otherwise expensive; *Lose*, also on main square, good and cheap set meals. *Suiza*, Av Ballivián 820, T 45485, popular, rec for international cuisine, good value. *BJ*, Av Libertador Bolívar 1580, T 48629, excellent, international cuisine, well prepared, rec; *La Hacienda*, Av Aniceto Padilla s/n, good buffet meals, good value but good value, rec. Outdoor restaurants: *Guadalquivir*, Cala Cala district, very good food of all types (also has dining room); *Chop América*, Bolívar E-0971, a bit simpler and cheaper; *Miraflores*, Av Tarija nr football stadium, Bolivian food, large, popular, weekend speciality roast pig; *El Caminante*, Arce S-0628, pleasant patio, excellent food including duck with salad and vegetables; *El Grill*, next to Los Portales, good, not expensive, you can eat in the garden; *La Estancia* serves best steak in town, also grilled fish and chicken (inside street off Plaza Recoleta), also has a salad bar, rec; *Los Troncos*, Junín 0-0942, barbecued meats, stylish, good; *Gallo de Oro*, Calle Lanza Sur 0567, rec; *Las Palmeras*, Lanza 248, very good food; *Paso de Loro*, Junín y Aroma, cheap and good; *Papichín*, also on Aroma, cheap and friendly, very good chicken and *churrasco*; *Salteñería Social*, Plaza Santa Ana, Cala Cala, Sat and Sun only for *salteñas* and beverages. A recommended vegetarian restaurant is *Gopal*, Calle España 250, Galeria Olimpia, hare-krishna, hence no smoking or alcohol, Indian-style lunch, US$1, good spiced bread, and Italian in the evenings, pleasant garden, English spoken; *Piñami*, España 0250, also vegetarian, rec. *La Cantonata*, España y Mayor Rocha, Italian, highly rec, though expensive; *Pisa Pizza*, Hamiraya 135, tiny but good; *Cozzolisi*, Heroínas y Lanza, pizzas. *Lai-Lai*, Aniceto Padilla 729 and another branch, best Chinese, also takeaway service; also good is *Chifa Rosa Roja*, Oqueño. Many good and varied restaurants along the Prado, eg *Don Pollo*, top of the Prado next to the roundabout, good ceviche, US$1.50, friendly management; *El Jamaica*, local dishes, good food but not very cheap; *Los Escudos*, Heroínas 0460, good food but not cheap, set meal US$3-4; *España*, España 0272, limited menu, good value; *Carajillo*, España 0386, Spanish-style, snacks and drinks, highly rec. Excellent pastries and ice cream at the *Zurich Tea Room*, Av San Martín Norte 143, closes 2000; *Pastelería Oriental*, Av Mayor Rocha entre 25 de Mayo y España, Santa Cruz-style, popular for tea; *El Pahuichi 2*, Av España nr Colombia, *empanadas* and pastries and *Confitería Continental*, 25 de Mayo and Heroínas, good and not expensive; *La Casa del Panadero* Aguirre 0730, rec. *California Burgers*, 25 de Mayo y Heroínas, good burgers; also at *Snack McDon'Alb*, 25 de Mayo N, near Ciné Capitol, good food and pleasant place. Good ice-cream parlours on Av Heroínas: *Dumbo* 0440, popular eating and meeting spot, also does cheap meals; *Kivon 2000*, 3 doors away, similar but smaller and quieter; *Unicornio*, Heroínas y Baptista, large, attractive, popular gringo hangout. Good salteñas at *Salteñería Illimani*, 25 de Mayo, cheap. *Imperial*, Sucre, a short way beyond Plaza de Armas and Cathedral, excellent ice cream, good value. *La Chatarra del Cronopio*, Ballivián 0674, pleasant bar.

Banks and Exchange Cash on Visa or MasterCard from many banks; no commission on bolivianos. Visa and Mastercard at "Enlace" cash dispensers in *Hotel Portales*, Centro Comercial Cavero (Av Heroínas), bus terminal and Av Heroínas y Tumusla. US dollars obtainable from **Banco Boliviano Americano**, Jordán E-0224, 2½% commission. **Exprint-Bol**, Plaza 14 de Septiembre 252 (will change TCs into dollars at 2% commission); **América**, Acha 0162, good rates. **Universo**, España 153, 1 block from plaza. Money changers congregate at most major intersections, especially outside the Post Office, safe, good rates. Also **Unicornio Cafetería**.

Cultural Centres At 25 de Mayo 25698, T 21288, is the **Centro Boliviano Norteamericano** with a library of English-language books, open 0900-1200 and 1500-1900. **Alliance Française**, Santiváñez 187. **Goethe Institute**, Sucre, corner of Antezana.

Useful Addresses Immigration Office Plaza 14 de Septiembre, will extend tourist visas. **Andean Information Network**, Casilla 4817, or contact via Brian Johnson, T 21707/23456, is a volunteer group composed mainly of foreigners who run educational tours on coca/cocaine to the Chapare, rec.

Consulates Germany, Edif Promotora, 6° piso, Oficina 602, T 25529; **USA**, Avenida Libertador Bolívar 1724, T 43216, 0900-1200 (will also attend to needs of British and Canadian travellers); **Switzerland**, Comaco SA, Av Uyuni 1140, T 42441. **Brazil**, Edificio BIB, Av Oquendo y Av Ramón Rivero, open 1400-1800; **Argentina**, Av Pando 1329, visa applications 0900-1300; **Perú**, Av Pando 1143.

Entertainment Frequent concerts and plays at the elegant *Teatro Achá*; more popular stage productions (stand-up comedy, music and dance) at *Tra La La*, Plazuela 4 de Noviembre, opp Chilean consulate, or *Champagne*, Calle Ballivián 0658. Discos: *Arlequín*, Uyuni between Plaza Recoleta and stadium, big, popular, young crowd; *Reflejos*, Libertador y América, both popular. Nightlife is moving to the N area on América between Libertador and Pando. *Wunderbar* in the centre (Antesana 2 blocks from Plaza Colón), good music, darts upstairs.

Health Doctors recommended by the Tourist Office include: Ariel Quesada, T 48591, who speaks some English, and Jean Koller, Calle Bautista 386, T 24191, call between 1700-1800.

Language Classes *Sra Blanca de La Rosa Villareal*, Av Libertador Simón Bolívar 1108, esq Oblitas, Casilla 2707 (T 44298) charges US$5 for a 45 minute lesson. *Instituto de Lenguaje* (Idelco), Plaza Busch, Bolívar 826, T 44868. *Runawasi*, J Hinojosa, Casilla 4034, T/F 48923, Spanish and Quechua, also arranges accommodation, rec. *Sra Alicia Ferrufino*, T 81006, US$10/hour, is a recommended Spanish teacher. *Profesora Elizabeth Siles Salas*, Av Guillermo Urquidi esq Armanda Méndez 01190, Casilla 4659, T 32278, private and group lessons in Spanish, Quechua and Aymara, highly rec. *Lupe Cardozo*, a guide at the University archaeology museum teaches Spanish, US$3/hr, T 50010, Casilla 3186. Courses available at the Centro Boliviano – Norteamericano (address below).

Laundry *Superclean*, 16 de Julio y Jordán, US$0.65 per kg; *Jet*, 16 de Julio, between Ecuador and Venezuela, US$0.70 per kg; *Kodama*, España 151, and two others, similar prices, at Cabrera 485 and Av Humboldt 313.

Post Office Av Heroínas y Ayacucho, next to LAB office; Mon-Sat 0800-1900, Sun 0800-1200.
Telecommunications Entel, same location, phone, cable, Fax, open till 2245, T 25210.

Shopping *Artesanías Casa Fisher*, Calle Ramón Rivero 0204, opp the Tennis Club, PO Box 3782, T and F 49846, beautiful woollen goods, prices about US$85 locally, US$225-265 in USA, Casa Fisher will be happy to provide information for visitors. *Fotrama* Cooperative for alpaca sweaters, stoles, rugs, alpaca wool, etc (expensive—run by Maryknoll Mission, factory at Grainvalación 0413); there is also a branch at Av de Heroínas. *Amerindia* for good rugs and lengths of alpaca material, as well as ponchos and jumpers, T 49994 to visit offices and purchase items; or picturesque Indian market and nearby shops. *Asarti*, Mayor Rocha 375, beautiful hand-made and machine-knitted sweaters, can make to order, expensive. For leather try *Confecciones Gamucuer*, Destacamento 317. For made-to-measure leather goods and alpaca, *Chenza*, España 0416 and on 25 de Mayo, mostly modern designs, highly rec; similarly rec is *Arizona*, Ayacucho y Colombia. Peruvian pottery is sold at *Artesanías Kay Huasy*, Arce 348.

Markets are very good for tourist items and souvenirs. The main market is called San Antonio. La Cancha market (near railway station) is packed on Wed and Sat with campesinos, " huge and well worth a visit"; woollen items are expensive but high quality, US$35-50 for an alpaca sweater. There is a Sat market at Av América y Libertador, best before 0900. Mercado Incallacta for fruit and vegetables excellent and very cheap, but on more expensive articles do not expect prices to drop very much when bargaining. Try local hot drink, *api*, made from maize. Kiosks behind the post office sell interesting crafts.

A very good **bookshop** is *Los Amigos del Libro*, Av de Heroínas 311 y España, Gral Achá 110, in *Hotel Portales* and *Gran Hotel Cochabamba*, and in the new Torres Sofer shopping centre, stocks US and English magazines as well as *South American Handbook*.

Cycle repairs: parts in market at Lanza 700 Sur. **Camera repairs** recommended at shop on General Achá, next door to *Cromos* and *Maxell* on Plaza 14 de Setiembre, reasonable prices rec. For developing film *Foto Broadway*, España y Colombia, reasonable prices, including slide transparencies. *Germán Grunbaum*, 25 de Mayo N-0345, good quality, rec. **Camping Equipment** available at shop on 25 de Mayo, just before plaza Colón; wide variety of goods, very helpful owner, speaks English and perhaps German. Also try Heroínas 225, T 29711. Camping gas available at several shops on San Martín.

Sports **Swimming** *El Paraíso*, halfway to Quillacollo (Km 10), sauna and pool, US$0.50 entrance, accessible by bus or train. Tourist complex *El Carmen*, road to Quillacolla, US$2, popular, sauna, catch micro on Junín. Pool at Club Social, Calle Méjico y Plaza Colón (US$1.50), is open to the public as well as La Rivera on Simón López (Micro A) or Los Chorrillos, both US$1, crowded on Sunday (Micro G), or outside town there is *Posada de Los Cisnes* at Quillacollo, at Km 13 on Cochabamba road (entrance US$1.60). Pool, sauna, restaurant at Estancia El Rosedal at Tiquipaya, take bus number 12 from Antezana y Cabrera to end of line. See also Sipe Sipe, under **Inka-Rakay**, below. Most are open only at weekend in summer only ("too cold" in winter, check before going).

Tennis Club de Ténis de Cochabamba admits non-members for US$5 per day.

Fishing Excellent trout fishing in lake formed by the Corani dam, 48 km N of Cochabamba.

Travel Agents *Fremen*, Tumusla 0245, T 41873, F 47126, city and local tours, but specializes in travel in Bolivian Amazonia, using the *Reina de Enin* floating hotel out of Puerto Varador near Trinidad; *Tai Tours*, Av Heroínas E-0620, T 23891/25373, adventure tourism. *Turismo Balsa*, Av Heroínas 0184, T 27610/27065, daily city tours, excursions to Quillacollo, Inca-Rakay, Samaipata, Torotoro, etc, airline reservations (see also under La Paz **Travel Agents**); *Martín*, Heroínas E -620, T 340831, Trans Al rep, rec.

Tourist Office Kiosk on Gral Achá between Baptista y Ayacucho, near Entel building, open Mon-Fri 0900-1200, Mon, Tues, Thurs 1430-1800. Also at Jorge Wilstermann airport; sells poor map of the city, little other information. A useful guidebook and city map (not very reliable) can be obtained from Los Amigos del Libro. Instituto Geográfico Militar, Antezana 0684.

Local Transport Micros and colectivos, US$0.10; *trufis* (vans), US$0.12; anything marked "San Antonio" goes to the market. Trufis C and 10 go from bus terminal to the city centre. Taxis: agree fare before getting in and beware overcharging; about US$0.50 from anywhere to the Plaza; double after dark.

Drivers in Cochabamba should note that, when approaching a junction, the driver who blows his/her horn first has right of way.

Air Service Jorge Wilstermann airport. Airport bus is Micro B from Plaza 14 de Septiembre, taxis from airport to centre US$1.25, from centre to airport US$0.75 (no set rates, so bargain). Reconfirm all flights (and obtain reconfirmation number), and arrive early for international flights. Daily by LAB to and from **La Paz** (US$36, ½ hour, 20 kg baggage allowance), book early for morning flights, and to **Santa Cruz** (US$47, 40 mins). Three flights a week to **Sucre**, US$30, and 2 a week to **Trinidad**, US$42.50 (connects with Riberalta flight). LAB in town at Ayacucho and Heroínas, open 0800; at airport LAB office, T 50750/50650, opens 0500. There are no direct flights to/from Argentina but there is an Aerolíneas Argentinas office at 25 de Mayo 233. Aero Sur (Av Ayacucho S-0170, T 28385), has daily flights to La Paz and Santa Cruz, with connections to Camiri, Cobija, Guayaramerín, Potosí, San Ignacio de Velasco, Puerto Suárez, Sucre, Tarija, Trinidad and Yacuiba.

Train service Twice weekly, Wed and Fri, to Oruro at 1400, US$3.40.

Bus Services The main bus terminal is at Av Aroma y Ayacucho. Buses (early am and evening) to **Santa Cruz**, taking 8-15 hrs, US$7-12; the road goes via Villa Tunari, the junction for Puerto Villarroel, Buena Vista and Montero, a more N and lowland alternative to the old mountain road via Epizana. **See p 312, below**. To/from **La Paz** many companies, shop around for best times, services and prices (about US$7.50), either via Oruro, 8-11 hrs (change buses in Oruro and get a new ticket, luggage is automatically transferred to the new bus) or via Caracollo, by night or by day, 6 hrs. The road to La Paz is paved. Bus to **Oruro**, US$4, 4½ hrs, Nobleza bus company recommended for safe drivers. To **Potosí**, US$5.25-7.35 via Oruro, several companies. Daily to **Sucre**, US$7.50, several companies eg Flotas Bolívar (meal and coffee stops), Unificada (warning of negligence over luggage), Azul or Mopar—free drink and videos, rec, between 1800 and 1830, 10 hrs, overnight only, all but the first 2 hours are very bad. To Sucre by day; take a bus or truck to Aiquile (bus every other day 1300), spend the night there (see **Excursions** below), then take a truck to Sucre. Local buses leave from Av 6 de Agosto y San Martín, near **La Coronilla** for **Tarata, Punata** and **Clisa**; Av Oquendo (at the edge of Lake Alalay) to **Villa Tunari**, US$3.50 (usually leave when full); **Chimoré**, US$4.50; **Eterazama**, US$4.50; **Puerto Villarroel**, US$6 (1000 daily); **Puerto San Francisco**, US$5. Trucks to Oruro leave from Plaza San Sebastián. Trucks to Sucre leave from Km 0 on old road to Santa Cruz, 11 hrs, US$3. Trucks to Puerto Villarroel from Av República, US$3.

Excursions To the N, in a high fault-block range of mountains, is Cerro Tunari, 5,180m. A road runs to within 300m of the top, usually sprinkled with a little snow. There are beautiful views of the Cochabamba valley from the mountain road which goes into the Parque Tunari from Cala Cala, ending at the lake which supplies drinking water; best in the afternoon, but no public transport. Another somewhat difficult mountain road to the N, with little local traffic, climbs from Tiquipaya (take bus No 12 from Cochabamba, US$0.15) to Chapisicca. Trucks leave Mon and Thur, returning Tues and Fri with potatoes and wool for the Cochabamba market. Beautiful views on the ascent: good walks on the plateau to mountain lakes in lovely scenery.

Quillacollo (20,000 people), 13 km W, is a 20 minute bus ride, US$0.25, from Heroínas y Ayacucho, buses No 201-211, or micro 2 (good Sunday market but no tourist items; the *campesinos* do not like being photographed). Fiesta de la Virgen de Urkupiña lasts 4 days with much dancing and religious ceremony, its date varies each year between June and August. Plenty of transport from Cochabamba, hotels all full throughout the festivities.

"In 1992 there were about 50 groups in the parade", writes Moreno Ortelli, from Como, Italy, "be there before 0900 to be sure of a seat, as you are not allowed to stand in the street. The first day is the most colourful with all the groups in costumes and masks, parading and dancing in the streets till late at night. Many groups have left by the second day and dancing stops earlier. The third day is dedicated to the pilgrimage (at midnight on the second day pilgrims leave Cochabamba carrying the statue of the Virgin, and walk to El Calvario hill in Quillacollo, the place where the Virgin appeared to a local girl, arriving there at about 0600). The poor take stones from El Calvario, representing money, as a loan from the Virgin. They ask her to change the stones into real money. The following year they return the stones to the hillside, offering the Virgin "interest" on her loan if they have struck it rich".

2-3 km beyond Quillacollo is a road to the beautiful Pairumani *hacienda*, centre of the Patiño agricultural foundation. Known also as Villa Albina, it was built in 1925-32, furnished and inhabited by Patiño's wife, Albina. The house may be visited (T 60082 to arrange visit, open Mon-Fri 1500-1600, Sat 0900-1130, Bus 7 or 38, or *trufi* 211 from Cochabamba); the Patiño mausoleum may be visited if one is accompanied by a member of the family.

At Marquina (US$0.50 by bus from Quillacollo, US$8 taxi from Cochabamba) is **D-E** *Hostal Los Nuevos Inkas*, PO Box 318, Cochabamba, T (042) 41505, F 61234, cheaper rate involves community work. All meals included. It is an ecological Indian hostal, part of the Movimiento Pachamama Universal, solar heating, gardens, swimming pool.

The *Inka-Rakay* ruins are near the village of Sipe-Sipe, 27 km W of Cochabamba; the main attraction is the view from the site over the Cochabamba valley, as well as the mountains ringing the ruins. Take a bus to Quillacollo where the bus for Sipe-Sipe waits until there are enough passengers (about every 20 mins), shared *trufi* taxis also go, more frequently than the buses. *Trufi* No 145 goes direct to Sipe-Sipe from Cochabamba and back. From Sipe-Sipe to the ruins there is either a 4 km footpath, or a 12 km road with almost no traffic, which, to walk, takes three to four hours. Either hitch or hire guides and Land Rover in Cochabamba. Several letters indicate that it might be less terrifying to walk but all admit that this is a beautiful trip. Start early for it is a full day. Leave the Square at Sipe Sipe going up the street past the church, then left at the top and then right when you come to the wider road. Follow this road out of town; while doing so, look upwards for the area of whitish rock, you will be heading for this. When the road crosses the stream and makes a sharp left, continue on the path to the left for 150m and then take the path uphill to the right, cross country, to the white rock. (At the stream, do not take the obvious trail to the right, it leads to the mountains on the right of the valley.) At the rock, turn about 45° to the right as you climb, then you need to stay close to the valley to pick up a distinct trail to the ruins. These will appear first as a rough outcrop of rocks. If you hit the road, you have gone too far left: turn right and climb the road to an obvious sign, from where it's 5 minutes on wide path downhill. It may, of course, be easier to walk there all the way by road and return on the path, which can be found from the road a few hundred metres from the ruins. **NB** Take food and plenty of water as there is none available and beware of theft on the footpath. Also worth taking a hat and sun-block as there is no shade on the path or road. In Sipe Sipe are *La Cabaña* thermal baths, open all year, with restaurant, good food, book in advance. Norberto Rojas Mariscal, who runs a shop in the plaza, is rec as guide to the ruins, speaks English.

Tarata, 33 km SE, is a colonial town centred on a traditional arcaded plaza on which stand the church, containing an 18th-century organ and other colonial artefacts (open 0800-1300 daily), the Casa Consistorial, and the Municipalidad. There is a monastery 1 km out of town on the other side of the river. Large procession on 3 May, day of Santa Vera Cruz, with fireworks and brass band. Market day Thursday (bus also from Av 6 de Agosto, US$0.50, 1 hr, frequent, last return 1800). Ask for Doña Prima Fernández who sells sweaters at "amazing prices"; she lives opposite the monastery. At *Clisa*, 6 km further SE, there is a large Sunday market (buses from Av 6 de Agosto; **G** *Alojamiento*, near bus terminal). *Punata*, 48 km E of Cochabamba, has an interesting, lively market on Tuesday. Behind the main church, new vehicles are lined up to be blessed by the priest. The local speciality is *garapiña*, a mixture of *chicha* and icecream. Beyond Punata, at Villa Rivera, woven wall hangings are produced. At *Arani*, 7 km E of Punata, there is an *artesanía* market on Thursday. For those interested in *charangos* (of wood) a visit to *Aiquile*, 215 km S, is recommended, *charango* festival in Oct or Nov, ask tourist office; weekend market (by bus US$3.50, daily except Thur, Flota Aquile, Calle Montes, Cochabamba; **F** *Hostal Campero*, Bolívar 960, clean, water all day, good food; **F** *Hotel Escudo*, basic, no water in toilets, cooking water unsafe but clean beds).

In the province of Potosí is *Torotoro*, a small village best reached from Cochabamba (120 km), set amid beautiful rocky landscape. The village is in the centre of the **Torotoro National Park**, writes Linda Slater, a peace corps worker from Cochabamba. Attractions include caves, a canyon, waterfalls, pictographs, ruins, dinosaur tracks and fossils. Tourist information is available at the national park office in Torotoro. Dinosaur tracks (fossilised?) can be seen by the stream just outside the village. Ask at Santiago, the only shop, for the key to the Umajalanta cave, about 8 km NW of Torotoro; a guide is necessary for both the cave and the dinosaur tracks, US$2.50 pp for whole day. Trucks and *micros* go to Torotoro from Av República y Punata, near the market in Cochabamba, at 1800 Sun and Thur, US$3, 12 hrs, or a truck also goes from the market at Clisa at about 0800, 10 hrs. Trucks return to Cochabamba every Monday and Friday. Alternatively, hire a jeep, US$220 for 3 days including mileage and fuel; quite an adventure. Take your own food as only a limited range is sold at the shop. New *alojamiento* near bus terminal, **G,** friendly; ask the priest for other places to sleep, rooms are available in locals' homes, cheap and friendly. The village has no electricity. A small travel agency on Calle 25 de Mayo in Cochabamba offers 5-day trips for US$80 pp including transport, highly rec "for the adventurous traveller with time and energy". From 24-27 July, the Fiesta de Santiago, the people from surrounding communities congregate here to sing, dance, and drink. **NB** Travel to Torotoro is all but impossible in the wet season (end Nov-May), as flooded rivers wash out roads. Check bus schedules in advance at all times of year.

The 500-km road via the mountains and Epizana to Santa Cruz (p 319) is paved, but the new lowland route is preferred by most transport. Before the Siberia pass, 5 km beyond Montepunco (Km 119), the 23-km road to Pocona and *Inkallajta* turns off. The Inca ruins, on a flat spur of land at the mouth of a steep valley, are extensive and the main building of the fortress is said to have been the largest roofed Inca building.

To get there without your own transport, take a micro to the checkpoint 10 km from Cochabamba, then a truck to Km 119, walk towards Pocona or take a truck for 15 km, to where a large yellow sign indicates the trail. After approx 10 km the trail divides, take the downhill path and the ruins are a further 2 km. Take food and camping gear. There are several good camping sites. The Cochabamba Archaeological Museum has some huts where visitors can stay, free, but take sleeping bag and food. Water available at nearby waterfall.

Another delightful camping spot is Sehuencas, reached by turning E at Montepunco. About ½ hr by car along a winding, rock and dirt track, the landscape changes from highland puna to subtropical. There is a lovely camping spot by a metal bridge. The Cochabamba Country Club has cabins, for members only. To hike from Montepunco takes a couple of hours. No public transport runs on this road.

At **Epizana**, 13 km beyond Montepunco, Km 128 (**F** *Hotel España*; other so-called hotels are restaurants; also service stations), a branch road, right—dusty, stony, and narrow in parts, but very scenic—goes 233 km to Sucre, 7-8 hours drive. **Totora**, described as one of the loveliest sleepy, friendly colonial villages, is said to be better to stay in than Epizana, with two hotels (**F** *Gran Hotel Totora*, colonial style, huge rooms) and restaurants (truck to Sucre daily 1100, 11 hrs). At Km 386 are the ruins of Samaipata, worth a stop (see p 325).

Cochabamba to Santa Cruz via Chapare The lowland road from Cochabamba to Santa Cruz, which most buses take, is under construction in the mountains (completion date unknown, conditions appalling in the wet). From Villa Tunari to Sinahota is surfaced; Sinahota to Chimoré being paved; Chimoré to Santa Cruz fully paved. This being cocaine country, there are checkpoints at Sacaba, near Cochabamba, Chimoré, before Ivirgarsama and at Bulo Bulo. All occupants may have to leave the vehicle during searches.

Lodging, Food and Services About an hour's drive from Cochabamba is an artificial lake, beside which is *Hotel Poseidon*, cabins for rent; large restaurant popular at weekends. In **Villa Tunari** (Chapare bus from Cochabamba, Av Oquendo 985, 1030, US$3.50, leaves when full, at least 5 hrs; some Santa Cruz buses pass by) ask for the Piscinas Naturales for beautiful swimming. **D** *Hotel Las Palmas*, T 47554, 1 km out of town, clean, friendly, with pool and good restaurant, rec; **D** *Hotel El Puente*, Av de la Integración, with bath in cabins from 2 people to family-size (book in advance at Fremen Travel Agency in Cochabamba or La Paz), to get there continue on the highway through town, cross the second bridge, turn right on the first road to the right, then go 1 km, the turn is clearly marked, the hotel has a beautiful stream and 14 natural pools; *Sumuqué*, cheaper, away from main road, decent, pool; *Hotel Las Vegas*, basic but clean; **F** *Pilunchi*, quiet and rundown in centre; **F** *La Querencia*, pleasant terrace on river front, friendly, good cheap food, clothes washing facilities, insect repellent provided, and toads; *San Martín*, basic, noisy from traffic. On eastern outskirts, *Country Club Los Tucanes*, new. Prices usually pp, not per rm. In **Chimoré**: *Hotel Copacabana*, used by military and prostitutes; water cuts common Jun-Sept; *Restaurants El Tamarindo*, on right entering village from Cochabamba, and *El Curichi*, on left, mostly for bus passengers, token system, limited menu, but OK. In **Ivirgarzama**, *Hotel El Torero*, very basic; *Restaurant Punata*, 100m from bus station, popular. Throughout the Chapare drink only bottled water and check restaurant hygiene.

Exchange One bank in Villa Tunari, then none until Yapacaní, the first town in Santa Cruz department, across the Río Ichilo from Bulo Bulo. (With thanks to Mary J Rodríguez, Cochabamba.)

THE NORTHERN LOWLANDS (6)

From scrubby E lowlands to dense tropical jungle in the N, this is pioneer country: missionaries, rubber tappers and cocaine refiners. Improved roads to Rurrenabaque and Trinidad are opening up the area and wildlife expeditions are becoming increasingly popular.

Bolivia's Northern lowlands, the Cuenca Amazónica, account for about 70% of national territory. Beni department has 53% of the country's birds and 50% of its mammals, but destruction of forest and habitat is proceeding at an alarming rate. A **Beni Biosphere Reserve**, under the auspices of Unesco, has been set up. As much archaeological work is taking place in Beni as in the altiplano; the same efforts to reinstate precolumbian agricultural methods are being made in each zone.

There are two main land routes into the northern lowlands: one from La Paz and one from Villa Tunari on the Cochabamba-Santa Cruz road.

From Caranavi, a road runs N to **Sapecho**, where there is a cocoa, cooperative (**G** *Alojamiento Rodríguez*, "thoroughly basic, thoroughly delightful", S and M Hayden, Gloucester, UK; trucks from Caranavi), where there is a bridge over the Río Beni. This bridge has cut off Puerto Linares, the old port for river access to the lowlands. What little accommodation there was has closed down, there are still a few shops but hardly any river traffic. It may still be possible to hire a boat, but very expensive and only likely in the wet season. Across the river is Santa Ana, originally an Indian village, more interesting than Puerto Linares, but again no services exist now. Aero Sur flies daily Trinidad-Santa Ana. Beyond Sapecho, the road passes through Palos Blancos 20 km from the bridge (market day, Saturday; *Doña Luisa's* restaurant, good non-alcoholic *chicha*), from where a road branches off to Yucumo, the centre of a large area of colonization. This road is passable only with 4 wheel drive, but there are occasional buses from Caranavi (13-15 hrs). There are *hospedajes* (F) and restaurants in **Yucumo**. 550,000 ha of jungle are under cultivation, rice, sugar, corn and fruit being planted. The Chimanes indians are trying to survive the influx of settlers from the altiplano. From Yucumo it is 50 km to **San Borja**, a small, dusty cattle-raising centre with hotels and restaurants clustered near the plaza. It is also a cocaine district and in the centre are three identical, ugly cocaine mansions. From San Borja it is 7-11 hrs E by pick-up, US$12, to Trinidad via San Ignacio de Moxos, or hitch a lift on a timber truck; there are 5-6 river crossings and, in the wetlands, flamingoes, blue heron and a multitude of waterfowl.

Hotels F *Victoria*, 3 blocks from plaza, dirty, no hot water; **F** *Trópico*, 1 block from main plaza, clean, rec; **F** *San Luís*, 2 blocks from plaza, friendly, hot water, car parking in patio; **G** *Jaropa*, clean, basic, friendly. **Restaurants** *Taurus*, good food, cheap; *El Conquistador*, cheap; exchange on plaza, poor rates.

Transport Flota Yungueña from La Paz, Wed, Fri, Sat 1400, US$10; to La Paz Mon, Wed, Fri, book 24 hrs ahead. Aero Sur flies San Borja-Trinidad and from there, to most main cities. Trans Al flies to La Paz and Santa Cruz.

At Yucumo, the other road branches NW, fording rivers 21 times on its way to Rurrenabaque.

Rurrenabaque is a small, picturesque jungle town, on the Río Beni, with San Buenaventura on the opposite bank. Plans to build a brewery are enforcing change. The main square was remodelled in 1989. Mosquito nets can be bought here much more cheaply than in La Paz.

Hotels, Restaurants and Services Most hotels in Rurrenabaque are noisy owing to all night discos. **E** *Santa Ana*, with bath, F without, near main square, clean, basic, cold water, clothes washing facilities, rec, good cake in kiosk; **E** *Porteño*, with bath, less without, quite good; *Safari*, on outskirts, for tours, all rooms with bath, not open all year round; **F** *Rurrenabaque*, clean, safe, cooking and laundry facilities; **F** *Trapiche* in San Buenaventura, PO Box 1314, La Paz, owner speaks German, very helpful, quiet, cooking and laundry facilities, good meals, highly rec, also runs boat trips to Riberalta every two weeks; **F** *Tuichi*, kitchen and laundry facilities, fan, very clean; **G/F** *Berlín*, near wharf, all rooms dirty, insanitary, cold water, to be avoided. Best meals at *Club Social Rurrenabaque*, vegetarian dishes on request; *Snack Horeb*, no sign, run by Jorge Pacheco, friendly, helpful, a good meeting place. Several restaurants offer fixed-price meals which are good value; several "shanty" type restaurants, 1½ blocks up from canoe dock, offer beef or chicken kebabs with rice, empanadas and chicha, all under US$1 an item. Try banana or papaya milk shakes from shop opp *Hotel Berlín*. **Exchange** at Agencia Fluvial, 5% commission on TCs.

Transport Bus to/from La Paz via Caranavi Mon-Sat (leaves La Paz 1300), Flota Yungueña, 18 hrs, but can take 72 hrs especially if the only bridge en route is washed away, US$12. Bus to Riberalta, Fri and Sun 1000, 16 hrs, continues to Guayaramerín; trucks also go to Riberalta but few boats. To Trinidad, 3 a week, 2200, reservations not possible, very poor road.

Excursion *Agencia Fluvial*, at *Hotel Tuichi* runs jungle tours on the Río Tuichi, normally 4 days, but shorter by arrangement, for a group of 5 or more, US$15 pp per day (payable in dollars) including food, transport and mosquito nets. (Write to Tico Tudela, Agencia Fluvial, Rurrenabaque.) 3 nights are spent in the jungle, learning about plants, survival and the foods of the region. You must take swimming costume, insect repellent to ward off sandflies and mosquitoes and a camera. Fluvial also run 1-day (and longer) "Pampas Tours" on a boat, US$20 pp, lots of wildlife incl mosquitos. Fluvial is repeatedly rec for its expert knowledge and well-organised, friendly trips. Leo and Billy also offer guided tours, contact them through *Hotel Santa Ana*, enjoyable. The jungle is very hot in the rainy season with many more biting insects and far fewer animals to be seen. One day trips are reportedly a waste of time as it takes 3 hrs to reach the jungle. Note that an increase in tourism is putting pressure on animal populations.

From Rurrenabaque an all-weather road leads via **Santa Rosa** (F *Hotel Oriental*, changes dollars. *Restaurant and Confitería El Triángulo*, very friendly, recommended) to **Riberalta**, only 175m above sea level, an expanding town (pop 40,000), at the confluence of the Madre de Dios and Beni rivers, which together flow into the Mamoré a few km N of Guayaramerín. The town, with the whole region, attained temporary importance during the natural-rubber boom of the late 19th century; the cattle industry is providing a new boost.

Hotels are not cheap: ask for a fan and check the water supply. **E** *Residencial Los Reyes*, near airport, with fan, clean, safe, pleasant and friendly but beware of noisy disco nearby on Saturdays and Sundays. **F** pp *Comercial Lazo*, Calle NG Salvatierra, D with a/c, clean, basic, comfortable, washing facilities; *Noreste*, clean, friendly, *Cochabamba, Residencia, Santa Rita*, all F (without breakfast). **F** *Colonial*, Plácido Méndez 1, dirty, cold showers, poor; **F** *Residencias Julita*, small rooms, hot, no fan.

Restaurants *Club Social Progreso*; *Club Social Riberalta*, better, on Maldonado; *El Chinito*, Sucre opp market, English spoken, reasonable; *Restaurant Popular Cochabamba*, US$0.50. *Quatro Ases*, Calle Arce, good, cheap; *Heladería Eslavia*, corner of main square, great cheese empanadas and salteñas, superb *jugo de guineo* (banana milk shake) and the best ice-cream in town, try *copoazo*, tropical fruit flavour. Restaurants on main square are mediocre; good meals in market, about US$1 for 2 courses; food stalls outside *Comercial Lazo*, tasty meals.

Exchange Banco Big Beni US$ cash only.

Transport Aero Sur (T 2798), flies daily to Trinidad with connections to Cobija, Guayaramerín, La Paz, San Borja and Santa Cruz. Also flights with Kantuta to Guayaramerín (US$14) and Cochabamba (US$82) Tues and Wed. Expect delays in the wet season. LAB office Linares 31, TAM office is opposite LAB. Air taxi Riberalta-Cobija, US$400 in dollars. 2 bus companies (inc Flota Yungueña) run to La Paz only after the wet season (ie after September); usually twice weekly, US$30, take plenty of food and drink (can take 36 hrs to Rurrenabaque alone and no meals available until there), male passengers are required to dig bus out of the mud ("42 hrs including mud-pushing and mosquito-hunting"). A motorcycle can be hired for US$2 an hour (no licence or deposit required) for visits to jungle; taxi drivers can give you the address.

Cargo boats carry passengers along the Río Madre de Dios, but they are infrequent. There are few boats to Rurrenabaque.

From Riberalta the road continues E, crossing the Río Yata before reaching **Guayaramerín**, a prosperous little town (pop 12,500) and centre for gold prospectors on the bank of the Mamoré river, opposite the Brazilian town of Guajará-Mirim. Passage between the two towns is unrestricted, but if going from Brazil into Bolivia you need your passport stamped by the Bolivian consul in Guajará-Mirim before leaving Brazil, and by the Bolivian immigration office (closed 1100-1400). Similarly, if you are travelling into Brazil and not just visiting Guajará-Mirim, get your passport stamped when leaving Bolivia and entering Brazil (for those who need a visa to enter Brazil, see **Documents** in Brazil chapter: consulate next to *Restaurant Orly*, open 0900-1300, quick service). Exchange money (cash and TCs 2-4% commission normally charged) in Bolivia, as this is very difficult in the State of Rondônia in Brazil. Boat trip, US$1, speed boat US$5 during day, more at night. If you don't want to stay, check the notice of boats leaving port on the Port Captain's board, prominently displayed near the immigration post on the river's bank. Boats up the Mamoré to Trinidad are fairly frequent—a three-day wait at the most.

Hotels B *San Carlos*, 6 de Agosto, a few blocks from launch dock, for a suite, **C** for other rooms, some a/c, hot showers, clean; money exchange (dollars cash and TCs and reais), swimming pool, reasonable retaurant; **E** *Mexo Plaza*, on the main Plaza. **E** *Santa Ana*, clean, with bath, **F** without, close to airport, rec. **F** *Central*, just off the Plaza, very dirty, **F** *Litoral*, cold water only, friendly.

Restaurants Try the old municipal market, two blocks W of the main square. At mid-day try the port area, where rapid short-order meals can be had for US$1-1.50.

Buses To/from **La Paz**, Flota Yungueña, 40 hrs in theory, US$33; to **Riberalta** 2 hrs, US$4.75, 0800 and 1530 daily (first return bus at 0700). Also trucks available from the 1100 block of Gral Federico Román.

Air Transport Aero Sur (T 2493) to Trinidad (daily) and connections to Santa Cruz and La Paz. TAM at airport, 10 minute walk from town. From the airport walk straight on all the way to the river, turn left and immigration is about 2 blocks along (money changers outside); immigration is open all day Sat.

Cobija, capital of the lowland Department of Pando, lies on the Río Acre which forms the frontier with Brazil. It is a small town (pop 7,000; 252m), with brick buildings and paved streets in the centre, thatched buildings on the outskirts. Electricity service is quite erratic, but water and sewage services are OK. The rainy season is November to March; the rest of the year is dry and hot. Temperatures average 29°C but can reach 40°C, or fall to 15°C when the *surazo* blows. This area has many Brazilian residents. Cobija has a produce market and a clothes market, as well as main street shops. Foodstuffs are much dearer than in La Paz. It is difficult to get more than a month-long entry stamp in your passport here; if needing longer, press for it. (We are grateful to Sarah Bruce of the Iglesia Evangélica Metodista en Bolivia for much information on Cobija.)

Hotel F *Prefectural*, Av 9 de Febrero, T 2230, central, cold showers, manager Sr Angel Gil, helpful; **F** *Residencial Frontera*, clean, fan; **F** *Crocodila*, clean.

Services Entel for telephone calls internal and abroad; it may be cheaper to phone abroad from Brazil, check current rates. Post to/from La Paz once a week. There is an old hospital, a recently built one (Japanese-funded), and the Red Cross. Tourist office is at Calle Germán Busch 541, T 22572.

Transport Local: taxis are very expensive, charging according to time and distance, eg US$10 to the outskirts, US$12 over the international bridge to Brasileia. Besides taxis there are motobike taxis (much cheaper). Brasileia can also be reached by canoe, US$0.25.

To reach Cobija by road is just possible, involving 200-300 km of dirt road; the route depends on the weather and is usually done via Brazil. The town can also be reached by river. The US army is building a new airport with tarmac runway, to replace the present grass strip. Aero Sur (T 2230) flies daily except Sun to Trinidad, with connections for La Paz, Santa Cruz. Kantuta flies to La Paz, Mon (US$105).

From Villa Tunari to the Lowlands Another route into Beni Department is via the new road between Cochabamba and Santa Cruz. A few km E of Villa Tunari (see above), 157 km NE of Cochabamba, a road branches N to Todos Santos, on the Chapare river, a tributary of the Mamoré.

The Cochabamba-Santa Cruz lowland road continues E from Villa Tunari and, at Ivirgazama, passes the turn-off to **Puerto Villarroel**, 27 km further N. *Camionetas* go from the junction to Puerto Villarroel a few times a day, 1 hr, US$1.20. (*Hotel Hannover*, no fans, dirty toilets, facilities shared with late night disco; *Alojamiento El Jazmín*, 4 rooms, 11 beds, helpful, pleasant, meals served, restaurant planned; also *Alojamiento Petrolero*) from where cargo boats ply irregularly to Trinidad in about 4-10 days (see below). You can get information from the Capitanía del Puerto notice board, or ask at docks. (There are very few stores in Villarroel. Sr Arturo Linares at the Cede office organizes boat trips to the jungle—not cheap.) The Cochabamba-Villa Tunari run is highly recommended for scenery, and fishing at San Fernando.

From Cochabamba you can get a bus to Puerto San Francisco (US$5), Todos Santos or Puerto

Villarroel. Bus Cochabamba—Puerto Villarroel US$5.30, from 0800 when full, 6 hrs, occasional searches and 5 checkpoints. As this is coca-growing territory the police advise: don't stray from the main road, don't talk to strangers and don't guard or carry other people's luggage. From Puerto Villarroel you can go by road to Santa Cruz, or by boat down the Securé, Chapare or Mamoré rivers to Guayaramerín, then by road to Riberalta and back up river to Santa Ana on the Río Santa Elena, or Rurrenabaque, thence by road to Coroico and back to La Paz.

Boat trip from Puerto Villarroel to Trinidad Puerto Villarroel is the main port for the river transport to the N of Bolivia. The road network is being extended, but many roads can only be used in the dry season, so river transport is still an important means of communication. There are boats running between Puerto Villarroel, Trinidad and Guayaramerín on the Brazilian border, taking passengers. This trip is only for the hardy traveller. In the rainy season when the river is high it takes about 3 to 5 days to go from Puerto Villarroel to Trinidad (45 hrs sailing, but boats stop from sunrise to sunset); in the dry season, ie between May or Jun and Aug-Dec, it may last 8 to 10 days (the river is lower, cleaner and there may be more animals to see on the shore – there may be no boats Oct-Dec). It is another 5 days to Guayaramerín. The launches do not provide berths; you just have to sleep on the cargo which, if you are lucky, may be sugar bags, or cement sacks covered in homemade straw mattresses. Many boats carry Brazil nuts. The fare to Trinidad is about US$15 for 3 days and nights, including meals (prices and quality vary). The food is native, that is to say all kinds of fish, dishes like *massaca* (stewed yuca with cooking bananas, *charque* or dried meat, oil and salt) and turtle eggs. If you are concerned about wildlife preservation, do not eat the turtle eggs; if you are fussy about food in general, don't make the trip because the kitchen is beyond description and the toilet facilities, too. Take your own drinking water, or water sterilizing tablets as the water served is taken from the river. The food served is very starchy and heavy because it is nearly always fried in oil, so supplement the diet with fruit and any other interesting food you can find beforehand (you can also take cigarettes and drink for the crew if you want). The trip is not as exciting as those in the real jungle; the countryside between Puerto Villarroel and Trinidad is more or less cultivated, with plantations of bananas and cattle ranches, some with 20-30,000 head. There is no jungle with orchids, alligators, etc, but one can see *petas*—small turtles basking in the sun, capibara, river dolphin, jumping fish, now and then monkeys playing on the beach, and many types of birds. At night, there are never-ending frog concerts. If one does not know how to enjoy the "green symphony" as it is passing by, one should take a good book, as the trip might otherwise get very long! A mosquito net is a "must", a hammock a good idea, and binoculars for watching the wildlife a useful extra.

Bathing in the river can be done without any harm.

Trinidad, the capital of the lowland Beni Department (237m), founded 1686, population 50,000, is reached by air from La Paz, Cochabamba, Riberalta or Santa Cruz, by road from Santa Cruz or by river from Puerto Villarroel (no boats to Villarroel in the dry season, Oct-Dec). There are two ports, Almacén and Varador, check which one your boat is docking at. Puerto Varador is 13 km from town on the Río Mamoré on the road between Trinidad and San Borja; cross the river by the main bridge by the market, walk down to the service station by the police checkpoint and take a truck, US$1.30. Almacén is 8 km from the city. The main mode of transport in Trinidad (even for taxis) is the motorbike. Motorcycle rental in the plaza, or ask at the tourist office, costs US$4/hr, US$10/$^1/_2$ day. In the dry season it is a dusty city, with many streets still unpaved.

Hotels B *Ganadero*, Av 6 de Agosto, Edificio Big Beni, T 21099/21644, small (shares building with a bank and a US DEA office), rec, friendly, good restaurant, roof top pool; **C** *El Bajío*, Av Nicolás Suárez 632, T 21344/20203, with bath and fan, breakfast extra, modern, swimming pool; **C** *Mi Residencia*, Manuel Limpias 76, near plaza, T 21529/21376, friendly, clean; **C** *Monteverde*, 6 de Agosto 76, T 22342/22738, with or without a/c, all rooms have TV and mini-fridge, daily excursions organised to Balneario Topacare, rec. **D** *Hostal Triny*, Calle Sucre, near Santa Cruz, good value, fan, clean, plenty of safe drinking water (a great rarity here); **F** *Yacuma*, La Paz y Santa Cruz, T 20690, upstairs rooms rec, fairly basic but clean and helpful, restaurant, washing facilities, fan, rec. Some cheaper alternatives on Calle 18 de Octubre. **F** *Residencial Loreto*, Calle La Paz, long way from centre, smelly, basic. **F** *Brasilia*, nearby, dark and dirty; **F** *Residencial Palermo*, Av 6 de Agosto 123, T 20472, clean with hot water, friendly.

Restaurants *Dragón China*, Calama 700, good Chinese food; **Pacumutu**, Nicolás Suárez, for *plato común* and kebabs; **Snack Brasilia**, Av 6 de Agosto, serves a good dinner. *Carlitos*, on main square, rec. *Pescadería El Moro*, Bolívar and 25 Diciembre, excellent fish and another fish restaurant, out of town on the road to the airport, is *El Tiburón*, about US$2 for a main course. *La Casona*, on the main plaza, for good pizzas, set lunch US$1, closed Tuesdays; *La Estancia*, Pl Muiva, excellent steaks. Burgers, ice cream and snacks at *Kivón* cafeteria on main square, and cheap snacks also at *El Cabalino*, on 18 Noviembre. *Balneario Topacare* is a restaurant and bathing resort 10 minutes out of town on Laguna Suárez; delicious local specialities, lunch or dinner, about US$5 a head, beautiful location, excellent bird spotting, favourite spot for locals at weekends, highly rec. It is hard to find a good cheap restaurant, but cheap meals, inc breakfast, are served at the fruit and vegetable market. Try sugar cane juice with lemon—delicious.

Exchange cash dollars at Farmacia, Santa Cruz 470. TCs changed at Big Beni, 6 de Agosto. Street changers are nearby on 6 de Agosto.

Tourist Office Calle Sucre 941, T 21703, free map.

Travel Agents All on 6 de Agosto: *Tarope Tours*, No 731, T 21468. *Paraíso Travel*, No 138, T 20692, Casilla 261, does "Conozca Trinidad" packages. *Moxos*, No 745, T 21141, rec; *Fremen*, No 140, T 22276, F 21400. Most agents offer excursions to local *estancias* and jungle tours down river to Amazonia. Most *estancias* can also be reached independently in 1 hr by hiring a motorbike. It is worth shopping around for jungle tours – prices around US$25 pp/day. Do not be surprised if, whoever you book with, Moxos runs the tour. Fremen operate speed boat trips along the Mamoré and Iboré rivers and to Isiboro National Park. *Flotel Reina de Enin* (of Fremen Tours) offers tours of more than one day, US$70 pp per day, good food, ensure that the itinerary is fixed in advance and adhered to. *CPIB*, a local indigenous organization, runs its own jungle trips to the **Isiboro National Park**, ask for Marcial Fabricano at the Cabildo Indígena, highly rec.

Transport A road links La Paz with Trinidad (via Sapecho, San Borja and San Ignacio), and occasional colectivos and trucks use it (the latter attempt it all year, 24 hrs if you're lucky, ask for El Bonchi at La Grigota hardware store, Trinidad). There is no direct bus from La Paz; either go via Cochabamba and Santa Cruz (through tickets are sold for this route, US$26), or via San Borja, San Ignacio de Moxos (10 hrs) and then to Trinidad, another 4 hrs. The latter route is of typical "penetration" standard, not for use during the rainy season, and gasoline is very difficult to come by. Take water, and a compass. Trucks and minibuses run daily to San Borja if there are enough pasengers, US$12, via San Ignacio de Moxos, US$5, 7 hrs including 2 hr "beautiful" boat trip on the Mamoré River. Buses may cancel (or get stuck) in rainy weather. Bus service to Cochabamba leaves 0700. Trinidad to Santa Cruz by road: 2 companies, Flota Puñata, US$13.50, and Trans Beni, US$12.50, each runs twice a week in the dry season, March-October; the route (Federal No 9) is 612 km, via Casarabe (56 km), Villa Banzer (68 km), Santa María (208 km), Ascención (250 km), El Puente (312 km), San Ramón (372 km), San Julián (382 km) and Montero (564 km—all distances from Trinidad). From Casarabe to Villa Banzer is poor gravel, then it's dirt, tough going and impassable in the wet to San Julián, from where a good gravel surface goes to the Río Guapay and thereafter it is paved. Motorbike taxis will take people with backpacks from bus station to centre for US$0.35; bus station is on Mendoza, between Beni and Pinto, 9 blocks E of main square.

LAB flies between La Paz and Trinidad Tues, Fri and Sun, US$49 (book early). To Guayaramerín, Santa Cruz, Riberalta, La Paz, San Borja and Cobija, daily with Aero Sur (Cipriano Baraci 51, T 20765/21117). LAB also flies Mon, Wed, Sat and Sun to Cochabamba (US$45), and to Santa Cruz (Tues, US$50). A fleet of over 20 air taxis also provides local transport. Ask around at airport for private-hire air fare prices. Taxi to airport US$1.50 pp. Airport, T 20678.

Cargo boats down the Río Mamoré to Guayaramerín take passengers, 3-4 days, assuming no breakdowns, best organized from Puerto Varador (speak to the Port Captain). *Argos* is recommended as friendly, US$22 pp, take water, fresh fruit and toilet paper. Ear-plugs are also recommended as hammocks are strung over the engine on small boats. Monique Wong (Artamon, NSW) writes, "Cargo gets first preference for space but hammock space isn't too difficult to come by ... you just have to hope it doesn't rain. Meals will not be the highlight of your journey. The food was cooked in river water – don't look when they collect water because the kitchen is next to the toilet and everything from the toilet goes straight into the river."

Excursions Interesting for wildlife, as is the river trip (hire a motorbike or jeep to go to the river; good swimming on the opposite bank; boat hire US$5). 5 km from town is the Laguna Suárez, with plenty of wildlife; the water is very warm, the bathing safe where the locals swim, near the café with the jetty (elsewhere there are stingrays and alligators); *Balneario Topacare*, see **Restaurants** above. Motorbike taxi from Trinidad, US$1. 14 km N is *Chuchini* with the Museo Arqueológico del Beni, containing human remains, ceramics and stone objects from precolumbian Beni culture, said to be over 5,000 years old. There is also a tourist centre, with swimming, fishing, walking in the forest, regional meals. Access is by road or river. Contact

Efrém Hinojosa, Carmelo López 510, for details.

San Ignacio de Moxos, 90 km W of Trinidad, is known as the folklore capital of the Beni Department. The traditions of the Jesuit missions are still maintained with big *fiestas*, especially during Holy Week and on 31 July, the town's patron saint's day. 60% of the population is Indian, speaking its own language. There are a few cheapish *residencias*: **E** *Don Joaquín*, on the main plaza, without bath, very clean, fan, family atmosphere; **E** *Residencial 14 de Setiembre*, on main plaza, with or without bath, clean and friendly, rec. Electricity is supplied in town from 1900 to 2400. Several restaurants, including *El Sireri*, corner of the main square, good and cheap set lunches and delicious fruit juices; *Snack Yarepa*, on main plaza, good meat dishes and set lunch, US$1, and *Don Chanta*, also rec for tasty meat dishes. *Camionetas* and trucks run to Trinidad and San Borja.

Magdalena is a charming town NE of Trinidad on the banks of the Río Itonama (pop 5,000). It was founded by Jesuit missionaries in 1720, made a city in 1911 and is now the capital of the province of Iténez. Beef is the main product of the region and the river is the means of transporting cattle and other agricultural produce. 7 km upriver is the Laguna La Baíqui, popular for both swimming and fishing. Around the city is an abundance of wildlife and birds. A road is planned to Bella Vista on the Río Blanco, considered by many to be one of the prettiest spots in NE Bolivia. The city's main festival is on 22 July, Santa María Magdalena, attracting many groups and visitors from all over Beni and beyond. There is an airport with daily flights by Aero Sur, via San Ramón. An unpaved road goes to Trinidad via San Ramón, passable only in the dry season.

    Accommodation, food and services Three *pensiones*: **E** *San Carlos*, private toilet, shower and water bed! Cheaper are *Residencial 72* and *Sylvana*; all are modest but clean. Restaurant *Edén*, near airport, good food (chicken or beef) and *chicha*; *El Gato*, behind the church on the municipal park, drinks and nightly dancing; *Colmena*, between church and airport attracts a younger crowd for modern dance music. Drinking water is available and electricity runs from 1800-2400. There is a bank and an Entel office for phone and fax anywhere in the world. (With thanks to H W Zintzmeyer of Herisau, Switzerland, and Magdalena, for this information.)

EASTERN BOLIVIA (7)

The vast and rapidly developing plains to the E of the Eastern Cordillera are Bolivia's richest area in natural resources. It probably has least to offer most visitors, but the Inca ruins of Samaipata, and the beautiful churches of former Jesuit missions E of Santa Cruz are worth a visit and the "Death Train" (Santa Cruz—Corumbá, Brazil) is a unique experience, dull, erratic but a most convenient land route.

Santa Cruz de la Sierra (437m) is the only other city of note, capital of the Department of Santa Cruz, 851 km by road, 552 km by air from La Paz. Founded in 1561 by the Spaniard Ñuflo de Chávez, who had come from Paraguay, Santa Cruz now has a population of 615,125, making it Bolivia's second city. It is usually hot and windswept from May to August. When the cold *surazo* blows from the Argentine pampas during these months the temperature drops sharply. The rainy season is December-February.

    The Plaza 24 de Septiembre is the city's main square with the Cathedral (interesting hand-wrought colonial silver), the Casa de Cultura (see **Museums** below) and the Prefectura set around it. Look for the five sloths who live in the trees of the plaza. The Cathedral museum is open on Tuesdays and Thursdays (1000-1200, 1600-1800), and Sunday (1000-1200, 1800-2000). Worth seeing if only to wonder how such an isolated community maintained such high artistic standards; it has collections of silver, vestments, painting and some furniture (entry US$0.75). The heart of the city, with its arcaded streets, retains a colonial air, despite the variety of modern shops and the new building that surrounds it. 5 blocks N of the Plaza is Parque El Arenal with a lake and a mural by Lorgio Vaca depicting Santa Cruz' history. Pleasant residential areas are being developed on the outskirts of town. About 7 km E of town new Botanical Gardens are being developed. At the N edge of town (Barrio Equipetrol, Tercer Anillo, W of road to airport) is an excellent zoo with a variety of tropical animals, birds and reptiles, a few of them in small concrete cases, but there is a big lake in the centre for capibara and other creatures, and they all seem quite well kept and content (entry US$1). Take micro 12 or 76 (taxi from centre US$1). The water supply is very good, though typhoid and hepatitis are still a danger outside the city.

Cruceños are famous for their gaiety, their music, the *carnavalitos*, can be heard all over South America. Of the various festivals, the brightest is Carnival, celebrated for the 15 days before Lent: music in the streets, dancing, fancy dress and the coronation of a queen. Beware the following day when youths run wild with buckets and balloons filled with water—no one is exempt. The *mascaritas* balls also take place during the pre-Lent season at *Caballito Blanco*: girls wear satin masks covering their heads completely, thus ensuring anonymity.

Until recently Santa Cruz was fairly isolated, but new rail and road links in the 1950s ended this isolation and now there is an ever-increasing flow of immigrants from the highlands as well as Mennonites mostly from USA and Canada and Japanese settlers, such as the Okinawan colony 50 km from Montero, to grow soya, maize, cotton (now declining in importance), sugar, rice, coffee and other crops, which yield profusely. Cattle breeding and timber projects are also important. A trip out of Santa Cruz to see these newly-settled areas is interesting, especially towards the Río Grande or Yapacaní (beautiful birds and butterflies; the fish are highly recommended).

Museums **Casa de la Cultura**, on the plaza, with occasional exhibitions and also an archaeological display; has plays, recitals, concerts and folk dancing. **Museo de Historia Natural** in the university campus. **Museo Etno-Folklórico**, on the island in the Parque Arenal, entry free, very small collection of artefacts from lowland cultures.

The exploitation of oil and gas in the Department of Santa Cruz has greatly contributed to the city's rapid development. There are several oil fields: at Caranda, 50 km to the NW, at Colpa, 32 km to the N and a large gas field at Río Grande, 40 km to the SE. YPFB has an oil refinery at Santa Cruz.

Fair International Trade Fair held each September.

NB The city has made a big effort to improve its image and it is now a friendly, generally safe place. Nevertheless you should always carry your passport with you as there are constant checks by Immigration (beware imposters). Failure to do so will result in extra hours at the police station. If troubled by the police, you may be able to get advice from Radio Santa Cruz, Calle Marioflores y Güenda.

Hotels **L1-L3** *Yotaú*, Av San Martín y James Freyre, T 367799, new 1994, suites, 5-star, a/c, all services; **A1** *Los Tajibos*, the biggest, Av San Martín 455 in Barrio Equipetrol out of town, 5-star, T 421000, F 426994, a/c, restaurant good (*ceviche* is rec), swimming pool for residents only; **A1** *Cortez*, Av Cristóbal de Mendoza 280, out of town, on 2nd Anillo near the Cristo, T 331234, F 351186, has pool and good reputation, a/c, rec for medium or long stays; **A2** *Caparuch*, Av San Martín 1717, T 423303, F 420144, incl breakfast, a/c, clean, comfortable, friendly, inadequate swimming pool. *Las Palmas*, Av Trompillo, near airport, T 520366, F 330533, 4-star, a/c, friendly, rec; *La Quinta*, 4-star, Arumá, Barrio Urbari, T 342244, F 342667, has individual chalets, a/c, good for families but out of town. In the centre of town is the **B** *Asturias*, Moldes 154, T 339611, F 350897 with 2 pools, a/c, rec for families also has cabins; **B** *Gran Hotel Santa Cruz*, Pari 59, T 348811/348997, F 324194, pool, open to non-residents, fully restored to its 1930s glory, a/c, spacious, friendly, rec; **B** *Hostal Confitería Cañoto*, Florida 45-7, T 331052/3, with breakfast, a/c, TV, small, open air pool, central; **C** *Colonial*, Buenos Aires 57, T 323568, central, comfortable, warmly rec; **D** *Res Cañada*, Cañada 145, T 345541, with bath, E without, clean, good, near bus station; **D** *Brasil*, Santa Bárbara 244, T 323530, breakfast, bath and friendly; **D** *Copacabana*, Junín 217, T 339937, with bath (E without), clean, friendly, cheap laundry service, rec; **D** *Excelsior*, René Moreno 76, good rm, good lunches; **D** *Italia*, René Moreno 167, T 323119, with bath, a/c, phone, TV, E without bath, breakfast included; **D** *Roma*, 24 de Septiembre 530, T 338388, pleasant, good value, helpful, no restaurant; **D** *Viru-Viru* Junín 338, T 322687, including breakfast and a/c, cheaper with fan, clean and pleasant, rec; **E** *Alojamiento Oriente*, Junín 362, T 321976,

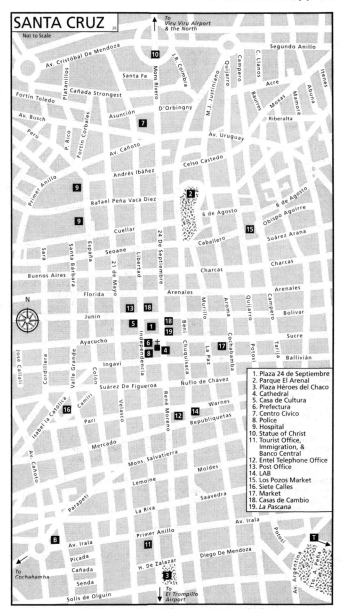

SANTA CRUZ 26
Not to Scale

To Viru Viru Airport & the North

Segundo Anillo

Av. Cristóbal De Mendoza

10

J.R. Cumbra

Campero

C. Llanos

Acre

Itenes

Santa Fe

Mons Rivero

Quijarro

Bauures

Moxas

Mamoré

Abuna

Platanillos

Cañada Strongest

D'Orbigny

T.M. Justiniano

Fortín Toledo

Av. Busch

Perú

P. Rico

Fortín Corrales

Asunción

7

Riberalta

Av. Cañoto

Av. Uruguay

Andrés Ibáñez

Celso Castedo

Primer Anillo

9

Rafael Peña Vaca Diez

2

6 de Agosto

6 de Agosto

Obispo Aguirre

9

Cuellar

Caballero

15

Suárez Arana

Sara

Santa Bárbara

España

Seoane

24 De Septiembre

Libertad

Charcas

Charcas

Buenos Aires

21 de Mayo

Arenales

Arenales

Florida

N

Junín

13

18

Murillo

Aroma

Quijarro

Campero

Bolivar

5

1

18

Beni

Sucre

José Callali

Cordillera

Valle Grande

Ayacucho

Independencia

6

8

19

Chuquisaca

La Paz

Cochabamba

17

Potosí

Tarija

Ballivián

4

Ingavi

Colón

Suárez De Figueroa

Velasco

René Moreno

Ñuflo de Chávez

Isabel la Católica

16

Camiri

Pari

Warnes

12

14

Republiquetas

Av. Cañoto

Mercado

Mons. Salvatierra

Moldes

Parapeti

Lemoine

Saavedra

La Riva

Av. Irala

B

Av. Irala

Picada

Primer Anillo

11

Diego De Mendoza

Potosí

T

Av. Argentina

Tte. A. Peña

Cañada

Senda

H. De Zalazar

3

Solis de Olguin

To Cochabamba

To El Trompillo Airport

1. Plaza 24 de Septiembre
2. Parque El Arenal
3. Plaza Héroes del Chaco
4. Cathedral
5. Casa de Cultura
6. Prefectura
7. Centro Cívico
8. Police
9. Hospital
10. Statue of Christ
11. Tourist Office,
   Immigration, &
   Banco Central
12. Entel Telephone Office
13. Post Office
14. LAB
15. Los Pozos Market
16. Siete Calles
17. Market
18. Casas de Cambio
19. *La Pascana*

shared hot showers, rec; **E** *Alojamiento Santa Bárbara*, Santa Bárbara 151, T 321817, cold showers, helpful, clean, will store luggage, rec; **E** *Santa Clara*, Cañoto y Isabela La Católica, without bath, clean; **E** *Res Ballivián*, Ballivián 71, clean, friendly, hot showers, nice patio, central, rec; **E** *Residencial Bolívar*, Sucre 131, T 342500, breakfast extra, hot showers, some rooms with bath, nice courtyard with hammocks, "absolute silence required after 2200", repeatedly rec; **F** *Posada El Turista*, Junín 455, small basic room, clean, central, quiet; **F** *Residencial Comercio*, Quijarro 439, T 321127, opp Los Pozos market, dirty, shared bathrooms, very friendly and helpful.

In vicinity of Siete Calles market: **C** *Mediterráneo*, Vallegrande y Camiri 71, T 338804, F 361344, bath, a/c, TV, fridge, breakfast included, cheaper with fan; **D** *Ejecutivo*, Camiri 118, T 338654, F 332843, with bath, a/c, TV; and **D** *Residencial 26 de Enero*, Camiri 32, T 321818, E without bath, extra clean, with patio. For those taking buses, **F** *Alojamiento San José*, Cañada 136, T 328024, hot showers, clean, about 1½ blocks. Near train station, **F** *Alojamiento Ferrocarril*, Av Capitán Arrien 131, T 321061, clean, friendly, stores luggage. For all hotels there is 3-tier pricing: locals, South Americans and others. All prices include taxes.

Restaurants The best restaurants are the *Floresca*, Av Velarde 136, which has a good discotheque upstairs; the *"85"* at Bolívar 85 is good with reasonable prices; *Victory* in Casco Viejo (old quarter), near Plaza, is expensive, but rec for lunch and cakes. *Amadeo*, 21 de Mayo, just off Junín, Spanish, good value, rec. *El Fogón*, Av Viedma 436 and *La Buena Mesa*, 2nd Anillo near Cristo, both excellent for *parrillada* and *churrasquería*, and there are many other barbecue restaurants all around the 2nd Anillo; *Churrasquería El Palenque*, Av El Trompillo y Santos Dumon, good; *Michelangelo*, Chuquisaca 502, T 348403, excellent Italian, not cheap; *Amadeus Pizzería*, Tercer Anillo 761, Barrio Equipetrol, T 45319, good and another branch at Primer Anillo 311 (closed Sun lunchtime, open Sun pm); *Machi's*, René Moreno 165, for pizzas; *Pizzería Mesón de René*, 24 de Septiembre 285, bright and clean, good; *Pizzería La Bella Rapoli*, Independencia 635, good selection, pricey. *El Surubí*, Av Irala 515, serves only *surubí* (fish); *El Boliche*, Bení 222, serves good crêpes. Chinese restaurants include; *El Patito Pekín*, 24 de Septiembre 307, excellent, authentic Chinese (open Sun pm); *Shanghai*, Av 27 de Febrero 27, or the expensive *New Hong Kong* on Ballivián 131. *El Mandarín*, Av Irala 673, and *Mandarín 2*, Av Potosí 793, both excellent. *La Plaza*, Libertad y Junín (main square), good; *Café España*, Junín y Colón España, good coffee, *salteñas* (am only), snacks all day; *Hawaii*, Sucre y Beni, good breakfasts and coffee. Many cheap restaurants near the bus terminal on the main avenida. Also on the extension of Calle 6 de Agosto beyond Los Pozos market (daytime). Excellent *empanadas* are sold in the food section of Los Pozos market. The bakeries on Junín, Los Manzanos and España look scruffy but sell the local specialities: *empanadas de queso* (cheese pies), *cuñapés* (yuca buns), rice bread and *humitas* (maize pies). *Ciné Palace* on the main square sells good snacks. *La Pascana* on the Plaza is a favourite of tourists and locals alike for meals, ice-cream and snacks, nice atmosphere, not cheap. *California*, Independencia 481, burgers, donuts, hot dogs. *Dumbos*, on Independencia and on Ayacucho, burgers, ice-creams and full meals, rec. Wholefood at *La Alternativa*, Antonio Vaca Diez 75; *Familiar Vegetariano*, Velasco 225, excellent cheap lunches, good service. *Heladería Pastelería Manolo*, 24 de Septiembre 170, for meals, cakes and ice cream; *Heladería Patty*, Quijarro 409, good and at *Kivón*, Ayacucho 267, highly rec. Good unnamed restaurant at Calle Charcas 64, cheap set lunch for US$0.75.

Airline offices LAB, Warnes y Chuquisaca, T 343998/9; **Aero Sur**, Junín 273, T 331008; **TAM**, Aeropuerto Trompillo, T 342102/351993; **Varig**, Junín 284, T 349333/7, open till 1200 on Sat; **Aeroperú**, Galería Casco Viejo, oficina 105, T 344511; **KLM**, Galería Casco Viejo oficina 106, T 348032; **British Airways**, Casco Viejo, T 361403/5.

Banks and Exchange Bank of America, Velasco 19; **Banco Popular del Perú**, 24 de Septiembre 156; **Banco de la Nación Argentina**, Sucre 31; **Banco de Santa Cruz**, Junín 154 will pay bolivianos on Visa and Mastercard, no commission. Open 0830-1130, 1430-1730. Enlace cash dispensers accept Mastercard and Visa at Comercial Cañoto, Comercial Oriental, Slam supermarket and Floresca restaurant. Use *casas de cambio* for money exchange: **Mendicambio** on Plaza 24 de Septiembre will change TCs into dollars at 3% commission; also on main plaza **Alemana** and **Sudamer**. **Cambios** can also be found on Libertad, eg **Latina** and **Oriente** in 1st block. **Magri Turismo**, Ingavi 14, T 345663, 2 blocks from main plaza, the American Express agent doesn't change American Express TCs, but you may have to go there to have cheques certified before a *casa de cambio* will accept them. Street money changers on Plaza 24 de Septiembre and around bus terminal.

Consulates Brazil, Av Busch 330, near Plaza Estudiantes, T 337368, opens at 0830, 24 hrs to process visa applications; **Argentina**, Banco de la Nación Argentina building main plaza, Sucre 31, T 324153. **Uruguay**, Carretera Cochabamba, Quarto Amillo, T 350184, Mon-Fri

0900-1100; **Paraguay**, Cristóbal de Mendoza 441, T 425233, colour photo required for visa; **Peru**, Libertad 349, T 330482; **USA**, Chuquisaca y Ballivián, Edif Oriente, 3° piso, of 313, T 330725; **British**, Parapetí 28, 2° piso, T 345682; **French**, Avaroa 69, T 334818; **Dutch**, Buenos Aires 168-197, T 330710; **Italian**, La Paz 532, T 322949; **Swiss**, Florida 48, T 346404; **Danish**, Calle Arequipa 164, Casilla 4, T 2928, Mon-Fri, 0830-1200, 1430-1800. **German**, Equipetrol, Calle 5 Este, T 425469.

Entertainment Discotheques: *El Mau-Mau*, open only during Carnival (a vast auditorium). *Reginne*, Av Velarde, is a smart nightclub, entrance US$3, live music Mon, Wed, Fri. *Rincón Salteño*, nr 2nd Anillo, Andean music Fridays and Saturdays 2200, friendly and homely atmosphere. The bar at *Hotel Los Tajibos* usually has live music. *Wiskerías* are popular, for instance *Doña Icha*, René Moreno 239, 2 blocks from plaza, "pub" atmosphere, rec. There are numerous cinemas in town; see local press for details.

Hairdresser *Pippo*, Colón 58, T 326868, "an experience", very good.

Health *Clínica Lourdes*, René Moreno 362, T 25518. Dr Pepe Arzabe, Quiroga Felix Romero 65, is reported to have specialised knowledge of regional illnesses.

Laundry Bolívar 490, no sign, knock on door, US$1 per kg, same day service. *Rápido*, Pasaje Callejas 70, side street on Republiquetas, Plaza Callejás, rec, cheap and quick.

Post Office Calle Junín 146. **Telecommunications** Entel, Warnes 83 (between Moreno y Chuquisaca), T 325526, local and international calls, telex and fax; open Mon-Fri 0730-2300, Sat, Sun and holidays 0800-2100. There is also a small Entel office at Quijarro 267.

Shopping Many smart shops in Galería Casco Viejo, 21 de Mayo y Junín. Cameras and lenses are a good buy, same prices as in USA. Artesanía shops on Libertad and on Plaza 24 de Septiembre y Bolívar. Artecampo, Salvatierra esq Vallegrande, T 341843, run by a local NGO, sells handicrafts made in the Bolivian lowlands, high quality, rec. Leather goods (Dorian, Florida 39, esq Libertad, honest), baskets, fine quality hammocks. Carvings and other objects made from beautiful *guayacán* and *jacarandá* wood (though reported these crack in drier climates). The *Los Pozos market*, taking up the whole block between 6 de Agosto, Suárez Arana, Quijarro and Campero, is clean, good for mid-day meals, food aisles serve local and Chinese food, and worth going to in summer for its exotic fruits: *ambaiba* (looks like a glove and the fruit is sucked out of the "fingers"), *guaypurú* (like a cherry), *ocoro* (like a prickly mandarin), *achachayrú* (mandarin-like with hard skin), *pitón* (like sour grapes) as well as better-known tropical fruits. The market is open daily. Beware of bag-snatching. There are plenty of smuggled Brazilian goods on sale, exchanged for Bolivian coca. Another market (nothing for tourists, mainly for clothing, but food and fruit is sold outside) is *Bazar Siete Calles*: main entrance is in 100 block of Isabel La Católica, also on Camiri and Vallegrande, past Ingavi. There is a fruit and vegetable market at Sucre y Cochabamba.

Film processing *ABC*, Junín 467, top quality, 36 prints, plus new film, US$9.50.

Books *Los Amigos del Libro*, Velasco 37, sells foreign language books and magazines, inc *Time* and *Newsweek*. International magazines and newspapers often on sale in kiosks on main square, eg *Miami Herald*, US$2, after arrival of Miami flight.

Sports/Clubs Tennis Club; Club Las Palmas, 2½ km on road to Cochabamba, has 18-hole championship golf course and olympic-length pool; Club Hípico, riding club, nearby. Racquet Club, Barrio Ubari, racquet ball courts and saunas; Club de Caza y Pesca, Av Argentina 317, T 35707, advice on fishing, hunting and safaris.

Travel Agents *Santa Cruz Tours*, René Moreno 145; *Sudamer*, T 342909 and *Orientur*, Plaza 24 de Septiembre; *Exprinter*, Independencia y La Riva; *Magri Turismo*, address under **Exchange**, helpful, rec; *Chovy Tours*, A Vaca Diez 210, T 322439, rec; *Camba Tur*, Sucre 8; and *Turismo Balas*, Arenales 117, rec. *Fremen*, Libertad 320, T/F 360265; *Anavin*, 21 de Mayo 208, T 352009, rec; *Amazonas Adventure Tours*, Andrés Manso 342, T 324099, F 337587, PO Box 2527, operates tours to Perseverancia, a centre for ecotourism and scientific research, in the **Ríos Blanco y Negro Wildlife Reserve**, NE Bolivia; contact AAT for all details. Mario Berndt, *Kayara Tours*, Casilla 3132, home address Tapiosí 113 (near zoo), T 420340, is highly rec for tours in the high Andes and the lowlands; he is a professional photographer, is knowledgeable about culture, flora and fauna, speaks English, German and Spanish, is safe and attentive. Ed Olde Wolbers, Casilla 5865, gives guided tours of the Santa Cruz area, speaks Dutch, English, rec.

Tourist Office Edif Cordecruz 2nd floor, Irala, 1st Anillo, between Independencia and Velasco, same building as **Migración**, T 334803, very little information but helpful. Open Monday-Friday, business hours only, no city maps. Also kiosk at bus station and airport. *Guía de Santa Cruz*, published by Rede, available in bookshops, gives all details on the city.

Taxis About US$0.80 inside 1st Anillo, US$1.20 inside 2nd Anillo, fix fare in advance.

Air Services LAB flies at least twice daily to La Paz (US$80) and Cochabamba (US$47). International flights are given in **Information for Visitors**, but note that flying is the only straightforward way from Santa Cruz to Paraguay. LAB flies to Trinidad (US$48), Sucre (US$35), Puerto Suárez (3 times a week, US$74), book well in advance, Tarija and other Bolivian destinations. Aero Sur flies to La Paz, Potosí (via La Paz), Cochabamba, Trinidad (for connections to the N Lowlands), Camiri, Yacuiba, San Ignacio de Velasco, Puerto Suárez, Sucre and Tarija.

The international airport is at Viru-Viru, about 16 km from the town. Information on 181; has Emigration/Immigration office, Entel office, luggage lockers, duty free shop, restaurant, bank – when closed, small amounts of cash may be exchanged at LAB *caja*, or at the very helpful Tourist Information kiosk in Check-In hall, English spoken, free map. Airport bus every 30 minutes from the bus terminal, 35 mins (US$0.70). Taxi, US$4 (beware of overcharging). From Trompillo airport in the S part of the city, companies offer flights in small planes to local destinations, eg US$100 to Puerto Suárez.

Train services To Puerto Suárez, for Brazil, and Yacuita, for Argentina, see below.

Buses Bus terminal on corner of Av Cañoto and Av Irala, T 338391 or 340772 (taxi to centre US$0.80). Daily buses to **Cochabamba** (US$7-12, 10 hrs, sit on left for best views), many *flotas* leave between 0730 and 0845, and 1700 and 2000 (Empresa Bolivia not rec). Most buses to Cochabamba now take the new, lowland route, via Montero, Buena Vista and Villa Tunari, which is no quicker than the old mountain route via Epizana and much less scenic. Direct to **Sucre** Mon, Wed, Sat 1700, 12-20 hrs. Unificado, US$13.50, otherwise daily via Cochabamba, which adds 300 km to the journey (it is much quicker to fly). **Oruro** and **La Paz** (US$12, 23 hrs-Copacabana company to La Paz leaves 0900 and 1900, 13 hrs to Cochabamba, 1 hr change-over, then 7 hrs to La Paz). For travel by truck to Cochabamba or Sucre: either take Micro 17 to Km 12 where there is a police checkpoint at which all the trucks stop, or go to the office of Transportes Peco in Av Landívar, half a block W from the Cañoto statue, on Calle Ayacucho. The fare after negotiation will only be marginally less than that for the bus, but at least you will get good views. Note that trucks to Cochabamba (if taking the old road) and Sucre traverse 3,000-metre plus mountains at night, so it's very cold: to Cochabamba 22 hrs, Sucre 32 hrs. Flota Chiquitana leaves for **San Ignacio** Mon, Wed and Fri (US$12), 18 hrs, more if raining. To **Yacuiba** and **Tarija** Wed and Sat afternoon, US$12 and US$15 respectively. To **Camiri**, bus US$11, 8 hrs, *camioneta*, 7 hrs, US$10-12. To **Trinidad**, several daily including Transportes Tropicales, 13 hrs, US$7.50-10, all buses go overnight; in the wet season, Nov-Feb, the service may be cancelled.

Excursions The new road route to Cochabamba passes through fertile lowland to the NW of Santa Cruz. It goes N through Warnes (note the statue of a man leading an ox-cart-load of bananas at the town entrance), then N to **Montero** (37 km, pop 30,000), where sugar and cotton are grown and processed, and on to Puerto Grether, high on the Río Ichilo, a tributary of the Mamoré. It then connects at Todos Santos with the 200-km road to Cochabamba. A non-stop shuttle minibus service leaves from Santa Cruz bus station for Montero when full; US$0.80, 50 mins. The town is named after the Independence hero, Marceliano Montero; the statue to him in the main square is in the same style as the statue of Bolívar in Santa Cruz, the horse supported by broken cannon. From Santa Cruz buses and from Montero minibuses run to Buena Vista (2 *alojamientos*). Near Buena Vista is the **Amboró National Park** (180,000 hectares)—walk to Cerro Amboró (guide required) recommended. There is a national park office in Buena Vista (permit free; guide US$7). The park is home to butterflies, humming birds, macaws, hoatzin and other native fauna (many of them endangered species). Beware of the insects—do not wear shorts or short-sleeved shirts; much wading is required to get around the park (see also below). Transport to the park from Buena Vista: either truck to El Terminal and then walk to the Río Surutú, the park's E boundary, or daily bus to Santa Fe, 0800, then motorcycle taxi to the river, US$5, 1 hr, very rough. At the park guardhouse there are 3 beds (free), avoid weekends, take own food. To return ask park guard to radio for a motorcycle taxi.

The country surrounding the city is flat and scenically uninteresting—except to the agriculturist. The sand-dunes (**Las Lomas de Arena del Palmar**) 20 km to the S are worth a visit; the scenery has been described as similar to deserts in a Walt Disney cartoon. You may be able to get there by taxi, but private transport is best. It may be possible to hitch at weekends, but a 4-wheel drive vehicle is normally required. 20 km E of the city is **Cotoca** (20 mins), whose church has a miraculous virgin, associated with which is a religious handicraft tradition (**fiesta** 8 December). Eat *sonzos* in the market. Swimming is possible during the wet season in the Piray river (weekends very crowded), 10 mins by bus from town centre. A favourite day trip is to the Yapacaní bridge where *surubí* from the river or *jochi* and *tatú* (armadillo) from the forest may be eaten in one of the riverside eating houses.

Excursions can also be made to several places along the old Cochabamba road. **Los Espejillos**, where a mountain stream plunges over a waterfall and carves its way through limestone rocks down a beautiful green and forested valley is well worth the effort to get to—4-wheel drive, only in the dry season. Turn right at Km 26, cross the Piray river and drive some 12 km up a forested valley. At a green field on the left (football goal posts) stop and walk a few hundred metres up to the stream. The drive up to **Samaipata**, 120 km from Santa Cruz (several cheap hotels; try the local wine), takes a full day. Visit the Inca site, El Fuerte (entry US$1), near the town, an exhausting 3-hr walk, but the drive up the Piray gorge and "over the top" makes a splendid trip. The ruins are some kilometres before Samaipata, coming from Santa Cruz; the side road to the left is signed to El Fuerte (take left fork when road appears to divide early on; cross river then uphill). A taxi from the town will go part of the way to the ruins. Travel agency tours from Santa Cruz to Samaipata, with an overnight stay, cost US$45 all inclusive. Close by the archaeological site is *Achira Kamping*, Km 113, 6 km from Samaipata village, 6 km also from one of the access points to the Amboró National Park (information in Santa Cruz at Igmiri 590, Barrio Urbari, Casilla 1020, T 343836): cabin prices ranging from US$12 to 30, camping US$1.35 pp, electricity 1830-2230, horse riding (US$1.35/hr), sports facilities, restaurant. It is not possible to go to Samaipata and back to Santa Cruz by public transport in one day as daily buses to Samapaita or to Vallegrande, which pass the site (2½-3 hrs), leave Santa Cruz at 0800 and 1600, returning 0400 and 1100 US$3, but there are colectivos from outside the *Hotel España*, 2 hrs, US$3.50. Alternatively, you can take a direct Sucre bus on the old Cochabamba road, but they only go three times a week.

South of Vallegrande (some 45 km S of the Santa Cruz-Cochabamba road; Sun handicraft market) is Pukara, from where a 4-5 km walk will take you to the village of **Higuera**, where Che Guevara was killed. On 8 October each year, many people gather there to celebrate his memory; ask at the Universidad Gabriel René Moreno or Radio Santa Cruz about collective transport.

A recommended round trip taking about a week starts by arriving by train at **San José de Chiquitos**, E of Santa Cruz and about half-way to the Brazilian border. San José's beautiful Jesuit church that looks like a candle is definitely worth visiting. It is a Unesco World Heritage site (as are the Jesuit churches in the villages of San Miguel, San Javier, Concepción, and San Rafael, see below). Two hotels on the plaza, **Victoria** and **E Raquelita**, clean, good; also **F Hotel San Sebastián Silvestre**, basic, clean, good food (open 24 hrs, take torch or candles, no electricity 2400-0600, near railway station) good, cheap restaurant on main square. Swimming pool open at weekends, clean, 45 mins walk, or get a lift. Train fares from Santa Cruz range from US$10.50 *ferrobus* Pullman to US$3 *rápido* 1st class. Trains pass through in the middle of the night and it is very difficult to get tickets (impossible for the *ferrobus* to Santa Cruz). Daily bus to Santa Cruz, weather permitting, at 0700 usually, 8 hrs, US$7.

On Monday, many Mennonites bring their produce to sell to shops and to buy provisions in San José de Chiquitos; the colonies, mainly settled by Mennonites from Belize, are 50 km W of San José. They speak English, German, plattdeutsch and Spanish and are happy to talk about their traditional way of life. A visit may be possible. Another interesting place on the railway line to stop (check if the train will halt there) is **Los Cochis**, between San José and Roboré; pop 1,000, no pensión but ask locally (and pay). El Santuario is being built near La Torre mountain, beautiful red stone, columns and local woods and carving, 30 mins' walk. From San José by truck N to San Rafael (134 km), San Miguel (169 km) and then San Ignacio, and Concepción, all with interesting old churches. These Jesuit missions are also connected to Santa Cruz by bus, 4 times a week with Flota Chiquitana. LAB flies twice a week from Santa Cruz to San Ignacio, Aero Sur daily except Sun. There are *micros* from San Ignacio to San José three times a week at 1000 from the market. From **Concepción** there are daily tours to San Javier or Santa Cruz. Accommodation is limited, but best at **San Ignacio** (*Hotel Santa Cruz*; also luxury bungalows, contact Lucy Hartmann, Cochabamba, T 24258, and **E Casa Suiza**, run by Señora Christina (speaks German), full board; visits arranged to *haciendas* with fishing and horse riding). Concepción is roughly 300 km NE of Santa Cruz. Still reasonably wild though being opened up. Accommodation at **F Grand Hotel Guarayas**; *Residencial 6 de Agosto*, shower, clean.

Travel to Brazil The Santa Cruz-Corumbá railway has recently been improved and a new station has been built on the E edge of Santa Cruz on Calle Cochabamba at the Cuarto Anillo, T 348883, No 12 bus to/from centre, taxi US$1. Toilets on the train are still dirty but there is an adequate dining car on most passenger services (food reasonable, coffee and cold drinks all twice normal prices). All trains stop at Quijarro near the frontier. From there travellers must go by taxi to Corumbá in Brazil; these meet the trains as they arrive and try to overcharge (fare should be about US$0.55 per seat; it's a further US$0.50 by bus from the border to Corumbá). The *ferrobus* train service, the fastest, leaves Santa Cruz at 1800 Tues, 12-hr trip, returning from Quijarro the following day at 0900 (meals served at seats). *Ferrobus* tickets are only available at the station (T 348488), and are sold out 1 week in advance; ticket office opens 0800-0830, but queuing starts at 0500 and touts try to pass on tickets (often forged) at double the proper price. Don't buy tickets for seats 2c and 2d, they don't exist. Fares Pullman US$22, 1st US$18. All other trains are scheduled to take 18 hrs (3-5 days in wet weather). An *expreso* train, with food but no a/c, leaves Santa Cruz on Mon and Fri at 1400, returning Tues and Sat 1530; a *rápido* leaves Santa Cruz Wed and Sun at 1350, returning Mon and Thur 1230; a *tren especial* leaves Thur 1800. Fares: *expreso* Pullman, US$28 (comfortable, but sways a lot), *rápido* Pullman US$15, 1st US$10, 2nd US$8; *tren especial* Pullman US$19. Check *all* times before setting out (above schedules 1994). Take food, drinking water and a torch, whichever class you are travelling. Only men are allowed to ride on the roof of the train. From March-August take a sleeping bag for the cold and delays. It is a monotonous journey through jungle except for the frequent stops at trackside towns, where the train's arrival is the chief event in life, and for the company of your fellow passengers who may provide some entertainment. A rail flat-car can be hired to transport cars, US$318 for the whole car; you may have to wait several days for a flat-car, however.

Tickets for trains other than the *ferrobus* go on sale on day of travel and are also sold from an office at Florida 11 in the centre of town, T 463388. Take passport. Trains are very crowded. Book early (queue at 0400-0500 and earlier for the *rápido* as locals travel on this). Failing that you can try to buy a ticket on the platform ½ hr before train departure. Foreign exchange at the border; you will probably only be able to sell bolivianos in Bolivia, and a few dollars in cash have been known to make irritating border formalities less troublesome. However do beware of showing large quantities of money around. If there are heavy rains check that the line has not been washed out.

The customs and emigration post at Quijarro closes very soon after the arrival of the *ferrobus*. At Quijarro station there is a left luggage room run by Willy Sollis Cruz, who is very helpful and speaks English. He will help you purchase the ticket you want and has been known to let people sleep in the luggage room. The train ticket office opens at 0830, queuing starts at 0700; tickets are sold only the day of departure.

It is possible to go by road between Santa Cruz and the Brazilian border, but this is not recommended, especially in the rainy season. Take water, map, food and compass. The stretch between Santa Cruz and San José de Chiquitos has been washed away, so road traffic must go via Concepción and San Ignacio de Velasco (see above). After San José the road heads S from the railway at 7 de Mayo in a 128 km detour until the railway is rejoined at Roboré (check compass because many tracks go to Paraguay). At Roboré the road narrows and deteriorates, being the worst stretch, to Corumbá. It is a 1,050 km journey in all, without paving; in the wet allow 2 weeks.

Travellers who need a visa for Brazil are advised to obtain a visa before arriving in Santa Cruz (without it they will be refused entry to Brazil). The Brazilian consulate in Santa Cruz normally takes 24 hrs to process applications (if you apply at 0900, may be ready by 1200). Yellow-fever certificates are often asked for. Reports of attempts by "police" to plant drugs at the border.

Puerto Suárez Beware thieves. **F** *Hotel Sucre* on main plaza, barely adequate; *Hotel Banidi* (more comfortable and the most obvious), and **E** *Residencial Puerto Suárez*, clean, fans and showers. **D** *Hotel Bolivia*; **E** *Hotel Beby*, Av Bolívar 111, clean, welcoming. Beware the water, it is straight from the river. There are several hotels and cheap snack bars near the **Quijarro** train station, eg **E-F** *Yoni*, new, clean, mosquito netting on windows; **G** *Hotel Frontera*, T 2010, mildly rec as clean and OK and **F** *Hotel Cochabamba*, 100m from the station, basic, friendly, not too clean, quiet, also **D** *Santa Cruz*, T 2113, with bath, E without, clean, good rooms, nice courtyard, highly rec. Most people prefer to go on to Corumbá where hotels are better.

The simplest way to Brazil is to fly to Puerto Suárez, then share a taxi to the border, US$7.50 (per car). According to Feb 1995 schedules, Aero Sur (T 2155) flies daily to Santa Cruz. LAB to Santa Cruz 3 times a week. **NB** Do not buy tickets for flights originating in Puerto Suárez in Corumbá, you will have to pay more. There is an airport immigration office where they will issue Bolivian exit/entry stamps.

A tip if travelling from Brazil to Bolivia is to arrive a week in advance, take a day trip from Corumbá to Puerto Suárez to purchase a train ticket at a travel agency (or book a flight), return to Brazil (to the Pantanal, say) and prepare yourself for the journey.

An alternative route to Brazil from Santa Cruz is further N via San Ignacio (see above). From here there are regular daily buses to Cáceres (Brazil). Bolivian passport facilities in San Ignacio; Brazilian facilities in Cáceres.

Travel to Argentina To Salta by train takes 40 hrs minimum and is a long and tiring trip via

Yacuiba (11,000 people; **B** *Hotel París*; many cheap hotels in town centre: **E** *Hotel Monumental A*, the best in town; **G** *Monumental B*; several restaurants including *Swins*, rec for its food and videos). Passengers must disembark at Yacuiba, taking taxi (US$0.50) to Pocitos on the border and walking across to the Argentine side. In 1995 the schedule from Santa Cruz to Yacuiba was: *ferrobus* Sat 0800, Pullman US$17 (10 hrs); *expreso* Wed 1900, Pullman US$17 (15 hrs). From Pocitos on the Argentine side of the border take a bus to Salta, or to Güemes for connections to Buenos Aires; Veloz del Norte runs a direct Pocitos-Buenos Aires bus service. From Yacuiba to Santa Cruz, tickets go on sale at 0500; there are lots of touts if you fail to get a ticket from the office. Such details must be verified on the spot. There are flights to Yacuiba from Santa Cruz (twice daily with Aero Sur, T 2089), make connections in Santa Cruz for elsewhere. The Yacuiba/Pocitos crossing is very straightforward. Entry tax to Bolivia, US$4, have bolivianos ready. Road transport links into Bolivia are not good: Flota San Lorenzo runs to Santa Cruz daily, or trucks may be taken from the Lourdes market (not advisable after rain); there are daily buses to Tarija (taxi from border to bus stop US$0.50, beware overcharging). Flota San Jorge runs to Potosí daily, US$16.75. There is no direct transport to Oruro or La Paz.

INFORMATION FOR VISITORS

Before you go

Entry requirements

● **Documents**

According to the Ministerio de Gobierno, April 1995, a passport only is needed for citizens of UK, Germany, Austria, Denmark, Finland, Ireland, Iceland, Italy, Norway, Spain, Sweden, Switzerland, Israel, Argentina, Chile, Colombia, Ecuador, Paraguay and Uruguay. All these countries are granted 90 days on entry. Nationals of other countries not requiring a visa are given only 30 days. Among those countries whose nationals require a visa are Canada, France, Middle Eastern and SE Asian countries, Cuba, the former Soviet Union and Yugoslavia, India, Pakistan and most of North Africa (for Canada and France, the visa is issued at once; for some countries it takes 7-10 days). Visas can be renewed at any Migración office (cost US$25 to renew). Visas are normally given for 30 days. A one year visa costs US$50, or US$25 for those under 21. On arrival check whether you are given 30 or 90 days; also ensure that visas and passports are stamped with the same, correct date of entry or this can lead to "fines" later. Beware also of illegal charging on entry into, or exit from Bolivia. Business visitors (unless passing through as tourists) are required to obtain a Determined Object Visa quoting reference Tasa-03.03. D from a Bolivian consulate. This costs £48 (US$85), is valid for one year and is multiple entry.

● **Representation overseas**

Australia, 210 Queen St 5 Floor, Penneys Bldg, Suite 517, Queensland; **Austria**, Doblhoffgasse 316, A-1010 Vienna; **Belgium**, Av Louse N 176 Boite 6, 1050 Brussels; **France**, 12 Avenue Du Presidente Kennedy, 75016 Paris 16; **Germany**, Konstantinstrasse N 16, D-5300 Bonn-2; **Italy**, Via Toscana 30 Int 28, 00187 Roma; **Netherlands**, Hacquartraat 4, 1071 SH Amsterdam; **Sweden**, Sveav Gen 31e TR 11134, Estocolmo; **Switzerland**, 2 Rue Du Lyon D'Or 2/do Piso Gusa, CH 1003 Lausanne; **USA**, 3014 Massachusetts Avenue N.W., Washington DC.

When to go

● **Best time to visit**

The best time to visit is May to Nov, the dry season. May, June, and July are the coldest months.

Health

Whatever their age, travellers arriving in La Paz by air (too quickly, that is, for a progressive adaptation to the altitude) should rest for half a day, taking very little food and alcoholic drink (drink plenty of non-alcoholic beverages). They will be up and doing the next morning. In Bolivia, do as the Bolivians do: above 3,000m, walk slowly, very slowly uphill. Some of the most notable effects of *soroche* (altitude sickness) are headache, sleepiness, ness and flatulence; breathlessness lasts much longer than other symptoms. Local remedies are *maté de coca* and *Micoren* capsules. Never go out for the whole day without taking an outer garment: the temperature drops sharply at sunset. Inoculate against typhoid and paratyphoid (also have yellow-fever inoculation and anti-malaria tablets if visiting the lowlands) and stock up on necessary medicines; they are dear in Bolivia. Visitors should have yellow-fever vaccination when visiting Santa Cruz or the Oriente. A yellow fever vaccination certificate, at least 10 days old, is officially required for leaving the country. Hepatitis is very common. Chagas disease is endemic in the Yungas and other warmer parts of Bolivia. There is no known cure, so that adobe huts with thatched, or leaf-protected, roofs should be avoided as sleeping places because they play host to the *vinchuca* beetle which is the vector; half Bolivia's population has the disease, which leads to heart failure but shows few other immediate symptoms (see **Health Hints**, at the beginning of the book). Public hospitals charge 5 bolivianos for consultation, compared with up to and over US$100 in private hospitals. A good remedy for stomach amoebas is Tinidizol. Contact lens solution is hard to find.

Money

● **Currency**

The unit of currency is the boliviano (Bs), divided into 100 centavos. There are notes for 200, 100, 50, 20, 10, and 5 bolivianos, and coins of 2 and 1 boliviano and 50, 20, 10 and 5 centavos. Bolivianos are often referred to as pesos; expensive items, including hotel rooms, are often quoted in dollars. When changing money, try to get notes in as small denominations as possible. Change is often given in forms other than money: eg cigarette, sweet, or razor blade. Try to refuse torn or damaged notes as these may be difficult to get rid of. It is almost impossible to buy dollars at points of exit when leaving or to change bolivianos in other countries. Inflation is low; there is no need to buy bolivianos in small amounts to avoid depreciation. The black market is more-or-less dead, since rates are no different on the street and in *casas de cambio*. *Cambios* in all the major cities will change TCs, but outside these it can be impossible. Changing US$ cash presents no problems anywhere. It is not worth trying to change other currencies. All the larger, recognized *casas de cambio* will give US$ cash in exchange for TCs, usually with 1% commission.

● **Credit cards**

Credit cards are commonly used in most cities, but usually in the more expensive places; you should expect to have to show your passport; an extra charge, up to 10%, may be made. American Express is not as useful as Visa, or, to a lesser extent, Mastercard. It is possible to get cash against Visa and Mastercard in La Paz and other large cities in some major banks (see p 253). In La Paz, Cochabamba and Santa Cruz automatic cash dispensers displaying the "Enlace" sign ac-cept Visa (ATC outlets) and Mastercard. Many shops displaying credit card signs do not, in fact, accept them.

● **Cost of living**

Bolivia is cheaper than most neighbouring countries. Rents, appliances, and some clothing, and especially toilet goods and medicines, are high priced. Food, accommodation and transport are not expensive however. Budget travellers can get by on US$25-30 a day for two. For basic hotel rates, see above; *almuerzos* cost from US$1-2.

Getting there

By Air

● **From Europe**

Either fly to Lima by Air France, etc, whence 12 flights a week to La Paz, 6 to Santa Cruz (see below), or fly with Lufthansa from Frankfurt, with a change of aircraft in Lima; or via Rio de Janeiro, São Paulo or Buenos Aires, or via Miami.

● **From North America**

American from Miami daily to La Paz and Santa Cruz. LAB (no 1st class on international flights, but good service), daily except Mon from Miami via Caracas, Manaus, Santa Cruz, or Panama (various combinations of stops) to La Paz. Otherwise, connections via Lima.

● **Within South America**

From Caracas twice weekly by LAB to La Paz, 3 a week to Santa Cruz. From Lima to La Paz, 12 a week by AeroPerú, LAB (restricted baggage allowance of 20 kg, but full allowance of 35 kg is permissible if you don't leave transit), or Lufthansa; 6 a week (LAB or AeroPerú) to Santa Cruz. From Santiago and Arica to La Paz, 3 times weekly by LAN-Chile, 3 times by LAB (once a week each to Santa Cruz). From Buenos Aires, 2 direct flights by Aerolíneas Argentinas to La Paz, continuing to Santa Cruz; Aerolíneas also flies BsAs-Córdoba-Salta-Santa Cruz once a week. LAB has weekly flights BsAs-Santa Cruz-La Paz, BsAs-Montevideo-Santa Cruz and Salta-Tarija-Santa Cruz. LAB from Montevideo also once a week to Santa Cruz, via Asunción (two other LAB flights Asunción-Santa Cruz, also one by AeroPerú en route to Lima). Varig flies daily Rio de Janeiro-São Paulo-Santa Cruz, continuing 5 days a week to La Paz; LAB flies São Paulo-La Paz once a week, São Paulo-Santa Cruz (3) and Rio-Santa Cruz (2). LAB flies twice a week Santa Cruz-Mexico City.

By Train

From Argentina and Chile (see p 260).

By Road

From Puno (Peru) via border stations at De-saguadero (for Guaqui and La Paz) or Yun-guyo (for Copacabana, the straits of Tiquina, and La Paz). Border details are given in this or the Peru chapter.

From Salta-Jujuy-La Quiaca (Argentina) to Potosí or Tarija. Roads ford many rivers in Bolivia and are impassable in wet weather (Argentine section is unpaved to Huma-huaca).

Alternative routes lead from the Argentine province of Salta via Bermejo or Yacuiba to Tarija. Dry weather only.

From Ollagüe (Chile) to Uyuni, **see p 285**.

From Arica (Chile) via Tambo Quemado or via Visviri (**see By Road from La Paz to the Pacific Coast, p 261**).

Travel to Paraguay Apart from the adventurous journey described on **p 301**, a cheap way of getting to Paraguay is to travel by bus to Salta or Orán (Argentina), and then on to Asunción via Resistencia (Argentina).

Customs

● **Duty-free imports**
200 cigarettes, 50 cigars and 1 lb tobacco; one opened bottle of alcoholic drink.

When you arrive

● **Clothing**
Visitors to the Altiplano and the Puna should be prepared for it to be particularly cold at night. The climate in the Eastern Lowlands is tropical. Oruro and Potosí are colder than La Paz; Cochabamba can be very warm.

● **Hours of business**
Hours of business are normally 0900-1200 (sometimes 1130 in La Paz), and 1400-1800. Saturday is a half day. Opening and closing in the afternoon are several hours later in the provinces. Government offices are closed on Saturday. Banks 0900-1200, 1400-1630, but closed on Saturday.

● **Official time**
4 hrs behind GMT.

● **Security**
Bolivian law states that the police may only search bags at a police station, not on the street. Identity must be checked only by immigration officials; see their identity card and verify the date. Insist on going to the police station, or call the uniformed police if in doubt. In La Paz and Sucre particularly tourists are often approached by bogus policemen. If at all possible, insist on your rights as outlined

above and in the Sucre section.

The procedure for reporting a robbery is to go to the Departamento de Criminalística, or the office for stolen property, in the town where the theft took place. Purchase official paper from the police for them to write the report, then, with patience and politeness, you may get a report costing between US$1.30 and US$5.25.

NB In some cities there is hostility to foreigners, mainly out of resentment to foreign involvement in anti-narcotics policies.

● **Shopping**
Best Buys Llama-and alpaca-wool knitted and woven items are at least as good as those from Peru. Ponchos, *mantas*, bags, *chullos* (bonnets). Gold and silverware. Musical instruments such as the *charango* (mandolin traditionally with armadillo-shell sound-box, now usually of wood) and the *quena* (Inca flute), and other assorted wooden items.

● **Tipping**
Up to 10% in restaurants; in all other cases a tip is given in recognition of a service provided, eg to a taxi driver who has been helpful (an extra Bs 0.50-1), to someone who has looked after a car, carried bags, etc. Usual tip Bs 0.50-1. In hotels up to 10%, depending on service given.

● **Voltage**
Varies considerably. Generally 110 volts, 50 cycles AC in La Paz, 220 volts 50 cycles AC elsewhere, but check before using any appliance. (You may even find 110 and 220 in the same room). US-type plugs can be used in most hotels.

● **Work opportunities**
In La Paz: teaching English at Pan American English Centre, Pasaje Bernardo Trigo, near Plaza del Estudiante, contact Edmundo. Voluntary work at the Hogar Mixto La Paz, Av Arce, nr British Embassy, beside Centro Boliviano Americano.

On departure

● **Airport and border taxes**
Tax of US$20, payable in dollars or bolivianos, cash only (no change given), is levied on leaving. On internal flights B$15 is paid at La Paz and Santa Cruz, B$10 at smaller airports. Tax on airline tickets 18%. Entry/exit tax at land borders is US$4. If you stay in Bolivia less than 24 hrs, no tax is charged.

Where to stay

● **Camping**
One can camp almost anywhere in safety.

Warm sleeping gear essential, even in the lowlands in the winter. Sleeping bags are also useful for getting some sleep on the buses or long distance trains, especially those crossing the Andes. Mosquito nets can be purchased in La Paz, but they are not cheap. Beware sandstorms S of Oruro. Camping gas is available in La Paz and all large cities. Kerosene is much easier to find outside La Paz, even in small towns.

● **Hotels**

Throughout Bolivia the cheaper hotels impose their own curfews. In La Paz it tends to be midnight (check) but it can be as early as 2130 in Copacabana. These locking up times are strictly adhered to by hotel keepers. Ask for the hot water schedule, it changes with the season, water pressure, etc. Clothes washing is generally not allowed. Many midrange hotels will keep money and valuables in the safe if there are no safety-deposit boxes. Cheaper hotels rarely have heating in the rooms. Youth Hostels are not necessarily cheaper: many middle range *residenciales* are affiliated to the IYHA.

Food and drink

Food

The normal international cuisine is found at most good hotels and restaurants. Local dishes are described below. Be very careful of salads; they may carry a multitude of amoebic life as well as vile green bacteria.

In the *pensiones* and cheaper restaurants a basic lunch (*almuerzo*—usually finished by 1300) and dinner (*cena*) are normally available. The *comida del dia* is the best value, in any class of restaurant. Good cheap and clean breakfasts are served in the markets in most towns (most restaurants do not open very early in the morning). Lunch can also be obtained in many of the modern market buildings in the main towns; eat only what is cooked in front of you. Dishes cooked in the street are not safe. Llama meat contains parasites (similar to those in pork), so make sure it has been cooked for a long time and is hot when you eat it.

Salteñas are meat stew pies (originating from Salta, Argentina, but popular throughout the Andean countries), eaten regularly by Bolivians, mostly in the morning. Some are *muy picante* (very hot) with red chili peppers, but *medio picante* and *poco picante* ones can normally be obtained. *Marraqueta* is bread from La Paz, crusty, with a soft centre; *pan de Batallas* is a sandwich loaf.

In the N lowlands, many types of wild meat are served in tourist restaurants and on jungle tours. Bear in mind the turtles whose eggs are eaten are endangered and that other species not endangered soon will be if they stay on the tourist menu.

NB Bolivian highland cooking is usually very tasty and often *picante*. Local specialities, which visitors should try, include *empanadas* (cheese pies) and *humitas* (maize pies); *pukacapas* are *picante* cheese pies. Recommended main dishes include *sajta de pollo*, hot spicy chicken with onion, fresh potatoes and *chuño* (dehydrated potatoes), *parrillada* (a Bolivian kind of mixed grill), *fricase* (juicy pork dish served with *chuño*), *silpancho* (fried breaded meat with eggs, rice and bananas), *saice*, a dish of minced meat with picante sauce, served with rice, potatoes, onions and tomatoes, *pique macho*, roast meat with chips, onion and pepper, and *ají de lengua*, ox-tongue with chilis, potatoes and *chuño* or *tunta* (another kind of dehydrated potato). The soups are also good, especially a *chairo* soup made of meat, vegetables, *chuño* and *ají* (hot pepper) to which the locals like to add *llajua* or *halpahuayca* (hot sauces always set on restaurant tables) to make it even more *picante*. Fried vizcacha is eaten in some places, mostly outside the main towns and cities.

In the lowland Oriente region, the food usually comes with cooked banana and yuca; for example, *Pollo Broaster* is chicken with rice, chips, yuca and fried banana. The bread in this region is often sweet with cheese on top, and the rice bread is also unusual.

Drink

The several makes of local beer, lager-type, are recommendable; El Inca is a dark beer, sweet, like a stout; the local hot maize drink, *api* (with cloves, cinnamon, lemon and sugar), should be tried (usually US$0.12), as well as *singani*, distilled from grapes, good, cheap and bracing. *Chuflay* is *singani* and 7 Up or Canada Dry (or whatever carbonated drink is available). *Chicha* is a fermented maize drink, popular around Cochabamba. It is not always alcoholic. In the countryside, look for the white flag outside the houses selling *chicha*. Bottled water, Viscachani, is easily available but make sure the seal is unbroken (rain water is sometimes offered as alternative); there are also several brands of flavoured mineral water, Cayacayani, La Cabaña, Mineragua. The local tap water should not be drunk without first being sterilized. Local water purifier is "Lugol Fuerte Solución", an iodine-based product, US$1.75 per small bottle. For milk, try sachets of Leche Pil (plain, chocolate or strawberry-flavoured), at US$0.25 each.

Getting around

Air transport

Internal air services are run by Lloyd Aéreo Boliviano (LAB), Aero Sur, TAM and Kantuta between the main towns. LAB uses American Airlines Sabre computer system with immediate access to worldwide flight information. Boarding passes are issued only at airports; after obtaining one, pay airport tax (internal, "AASANA", approx US$2, or international). LAB offers a 28-day unlimited domestic flight ticket for US$135 for international travellers using LAB, which must be bought outside Bolivia (only one stopover per city is allowed, except for connecting flights; note that many flights radiate from La Paz, Santa Cruz or Cochabamba). To avoid paying the 18% tax on the air-pass, purchase it as an MCO outside the country, then exchange this for flight tickets later. You must enter Bolivia using LAB or on a foreign carrier with whom LAB may have a pooling arrangement. Also LAB is promoting limited stay tickets as well as the normal Apex type fares. Spouse fares (ie one goes free with one paying full fare) available on certain international flights. There are also reductions for special excursion flights. LAB and Aero Sur offer discounts of 25% to students and passengers over 60. Delays are common on LAB; a "through" flight may require a change of plane, or be delayed waiting for a connecting flight coming from elsewhere. Only on international flights is overnight lodging provided during delays. Insure your bags heavily as they tend to get left around.

NB If your internal flight is delayed keep your baggage with you and do not check it in until the flight is definitely announced. There have been robberies of prematurely checked-in baggage.

Land transport

● Train

Trains are operated by Empresa Nacional de Ferrocarriles (ENFE), which is due to be privatized. Schedules change frequently. Always check departure times in advance. Tickets can be bought in advance.

● Road

La Paz-Oruro, paved and dusty; Oruro-Challapata, paved first 30 km, then dirt (or mud in the wet season); La Paz-Tiquina: *autopista* to El Alto (toll US$0.25), then paved to Tiquina; La Paz-Cochabamba now completely paved; Cochabamba-Santa Cruz, mountain route paved, but in a very bad state, lowland route under reconstruction Cochabamba to Chimoré, Yapacaní to Montero, very good Chimoré to Yapacaní and Montero to Santa Cruz; Cochabamba-Sucre via mountain route towards Santa Cruz, paved for 127 km to Totora, then dirt (bad in rainy season). Potosí-Sucre, paved for 120 km. Oruro-Potosí, dirt, very bad in rainy season. La Paz-Yungas, well-engineered and surfaced to Unduavi, but most roads in the Yungas offer "hair-raising driving". La Paz-Beni-Trinidad, mixed reports. Santa Cruz to Trinidad: paved from Santa Cruz to Puerto Banegas on Río Guapey, then gravel to San Julián, thereafter dirt (impassable in the wet) to Casarabe, whence poor gravel to Trinidad. Puerto Suárez-Arroyo Concepción open. Nearly all Bolivian road surfaces, even the paved sections, are bad, and after flooding or rough weather they are even worse. Even main roads may be closed in the rainy season.

NB On election day no public transport runs whatsoever; only cars with a special permit may be on the road.

● Buses

Buses ply on most of the roads (interurban buses are called *flotas*, urban ones *micros*, also minibuses and *trufis*). Reporting time is half an hour before the bus leaves, but you should always try to reserve, and pay for, a seat as far as possible in advance and arrive in good time. In the wet season, bus travel is subject to long delays and detours at extra cost. On all journeys, take food and toilet wipes. They can be very dusty. The services of transportes Copacabana bus company have been recommended, especially for night journeys, as they are more comfortable and have heating, although they are more expensive (not to be confused with Flota Copacabana). Bus companies are responsible for any luggage packed on the roof. A small charge is made for use of major bus terminals; payment is before departure.

● Motorists (including motor-cyclists)

For necessary documents, see **Introduction and Hints – Motoring**: motorcyclists may be asked for a *carnet de passages* (*tríptico*), but it is not officially necessary. If hiring a car, the company can arrange a "blanket" driving permit for tourist purposes which is valid for several days and destinations. Tolls vary from US$0.50 to US$2.50 for journeys up to 100 km. In theory, you need an International Driving Permit (and, since a driving licence number is requested, also your national driving licence, or some ingenuity). Just a national licence will do when hiring a car and the rental document usually suffices at police controls. Two authorisation certificates are required in La Paz: the first from the Automóvil Club Boliviano, corner of 6 de Agosto and Arce, T/F 372139, and the second from the traffic police at the Comando Departmental, Organismo Operativo de Tránsito, corner of Mcal Santa Cruz and Plaza San Francisco. For hints on high-altitude motoring, see **Introduction and Hints** at front of book.

Take great care when driving at night (it is best not to): cyclists do not usually have lights; truck drivers almost never dip their headlights (keep your own on full beam to make the truck dip his); some truck drivers are drunk, or fall asleep at the wheel; at the slightest sign of danger, pull out of the way. Day or night, watch out for people asleep at the roadside in lowland areas; they tend to lie with head and torso in the road where there are fewer mosquitoes.

Petrol (gasoline) 2 grades: 85 and 92 octane. 85 octane costs B\$1.90/US\$0.40 per litre. Gas oil is slightly cheaper. Costs are higher in Guayaramerín, Riberalta and Puerto Suárez. Around Lake Titicaca, there are no petrol stations as such, the only two that exist frequently run out; ask in villages for where petrol is sold from the drum.

● **Trucks**
Trucks congregate at all town markets, with destinations chalked on the sides, they are not much less comfortable than buses or ordinary trains, but can be very dusty. They are normally about half the cost when there is competition. Otherwise they charge what they judge the market will bear and can therefore seem expensive.

Communications

● **Media**
In La Paz: morning papers—*Presencia*, daily, the largest circulation, largely Catholic; *La Razón* (founded 1990), *Hoy* and *El Diario*. *Meridiano* (midday): *Ultima Hora*, and *Jornada* (evenings). In Cochabamba—*Los Tiempos*, *Extra*. In Oruro—*La Patria*, mornings (except Mondays). *El Mundo* and *El Deber* are the Santa Cruz daily papers; *Deber* also appears in Trinidad. In Sucre, *El Correo*. *Presencia*, *El Diario*, *El Mundo*, *La Razón* all have good foreign coverage. La Paz papers are on sale in other cities. English language weekly *The Bolivian Times*, published Fridays, US\$1, available in major cities, many local reports (details T 340062, F 390700, address Jauregui 2248, Sopocachi, La Paz, casilla 1696). International papers are available in La Paz. Also, there are about 85 radio stations, a commercial government TV station as well as a university TV service.

● **Postal services**
Post offices use the post box (*casilla*) system. Items sent by post should therefore bear, not the street address, but the *casilla* number and town. Hours are Mon-Sat 0800-2000, Sun 0800-1200. For security, send mail "certificado". There is a national and international express post system; special counters and envelopes provided. Air-mail letters to and from Europe take between 5 and 10 days. To send a letter up to 20 grammes to USA/Canada costs US\$0.50, to Europe US\$0.60, to Australia/New Zealand US\$0.75. Parcels to Europe can only be sent by air. There are 2 classes – fast (taking 7-10 days) and slow (taking a month): slow rates – US\$16 for 1 kg, US\$90 for 5 kg, US\$120 for 20 kg. Parcels are checked by customs officers before being wrapped in special packaging (US\$1). Several reports of customs officers attempting to charge for inspecting parcels: refuse to pay (politely).

● **Telecommunications**
The national telecommunications company is Entel, which handles all phone, telex and fax services. In the Department of La Paz, Cotel operates local services, alongside Entel. There is now direct satellite communication with Bolivia. Direct calls possible from major cities to Europe, USA, Australia and elsewhere, clear lines, delays minimal; US\$8.70/3 mins to Europe and Mexico, US\$6.75 to USA and South America, US\$9.80 to Australia. Collect calls can only be made to the USA. When making overseas calls, you must deposit the price of the call in advance. At the La Paz exchange you can pay by credit card and the phone shows the cost as you speak. Outside La Paz you may have to wait a while for an overseas connection, but otherwise there are no problems. Fax to Europe costs US\$5 per page, to the USA US\$4, to Australia, New Zealand US\$6. Phone calls within city limits are free for private calls; for public phones, coins/fichas or phone cards are necessary. Fichas and phone cards only work in the city in which they are bought.

Sport

● **Hiking**
Various treks are described in the text, especially near La Paz and from Sorata. Note that all these trails are remote in parts and that robbery and violent attacks have been made on tourists and Bolivians alike. It is advisable

to hike these trails in large, organized groups. *Backpacking and Trekking in Peru and Bolivia* (new edition due spring 1995), published by Bradt Publications, describes 3-9 day hikes in the Cordillera Real within easy reach of La Paz (Bradt Publications also publish *South America Ski Guide*). The local tourist office also produces leaflets with sketch maps on walks available from La Paz. There are also some excellent guides available through local clubs.

Holidays and festivals

● **Public holidays**

1 January, New Year's Day; Carnival Week, Monday, Shrove Tuesday, Ash Wednesday; Holy Week, Thursday, Friday and Saturday; 1 May, Labour Day; Corpus Christi (moveable); 16 July, La Paz Municipal Holiday; 5-7 August, Independence; 12 October, Columbus Day; 2 November, Day of the Dead; Christmas Day.

There are local holidays at Tarija, on 15 April; at Sucre on 25 May; at Cochabamba, 14 Sept; at Santa Cruz and Cobija 24 Sept; at Potosí, 10 Nov; in the Beni, 18 Nov, and at Oruro, 22 Feb.

● **Festivals**

January (last week), La Paz, "Alacitas". 2 Feb. May/June, La Paz, "Gran Poder". 25 Aug: Virgen Copacabana. 3 May: Fiesta de la Invención de la Santa Cruz, various parts. In La Paz El Gran Poder, end May/early June, at the "Calvario". 23 June: San Juan, all Bolivia. 29 June: San Pedro y San Pablo, at Tiquina. 28 July: Fiesta de Santiago (St James), Altiplano and lake region; Achocalla a convenient place to go to. 16 August: San Roque, patron saint of dogs, the animals are adorned with ribbons and other decorations. First weekend in October: San Francisco, dancing on the streets in Copacabana. 1 and 2 Nov: All Saints and All Souls, any local cemetery. For other festivals on the Altiplano enquire at hotels or tourist office in La Paz. Remember that the cities are very quiet on national holidays, but colourful celebrations will be going on in the villages. Beware of water-filled balloons thrown during carnival in most cities—even the coldest. Unsuspecting tourists are favourite targets. Hotels are often full at the most popular places, for instance Copacabana on Good Friday, worth booking in advance.

Further reading

An Insider's Guide to Bolivia, by Peter McFarren (Fundación Cultural Quipus, Casilla 1696, La Paz, 3rd edition, 1992, US$25) has been recommended, especially for its section on culture. *Descubriendo Bolivia*, Hugo Boero Rojo, 1989 on archaeology and precolumbian history, with road routes (also available in English). *La Pintura En los Museos de Bolivia*, by José de Mesa and Teresa Gisbert, published 1991 by Los Amigos del Libro. *Guía Boliviana de Transporte y Turismo* (GBT) published monthly at Plaza del Estudiante 1920, T 321027, F 391641, US$6 a month, US$65 a year, gives information on transport, accommodation, restaurants, useful data etc, with town plans, for the whole country.

British Business Visitors are strongly advised to consult "Hints to Exporters: Bolivia", which can be obtained from DTI Export Publications, PO Box 55, Stratford-upon-Avon, Warwickshire, CV37 9GE. Similar publications for US business visitors may be obtained from the Department of Commerce.

Acknowledgements

For updating this chapter, we are most grateful to Charlie Nurse and, for additional help, to Alan Murphy. Our warmest thanks are also due to Tom Clough, resident correspondent in La Paz, and to Eduardo Garnica for details on Potosí. We should also like to thank the following travellers: Elizabeth Allison (Powys) & Sebastian Cooper (Monmouth, Gwent), Janet Arnold (Melbourne, Australia), Pascale Babillot (Paris), Hans & Lena Bengtsson (Güteborg, Sweden), Sally & Chris Bentley (Boston, Lincolnshire), Kathrin Beutler & Neven Bartel (São Paulo, Brazil), Christine Beyeler & Jurg Roth (Liebefeld, Switzerland), Pascal & Dorothea Bischofberger (Ennenda, Switzerland), Kathrine Breistl & Ole Faye (Oslo, Norway), Judith Brügelmann (St Niklausen, Switzerland), Simon Calne (London W8), Sergio Cebrián, Miguel Cebrián (Spain), Nadia Christinet (Geneva, Switzerland), Julie Chistiansen & Kenneth Kristensen (Copenhagen, Denmark), Nicolas Dubois & Julie Collombat (St Germain du Puy, France), Marty & Anne Marie Cook (Whargarei, New Zealand), Jeremy & Eleanor Jane Cox (Orford, Suffolk), Jacquie Crossland (London, W4), Fiona Dear (Droitwich Spa, Worcestershire), Dr Dieter Sell (Germany), Andrew Dobbie (Swansea), Cedric Domeniconi (Vevey, Switzerland), Florence Dougoud (Fribourg, Switzerland), Monika Eder (Söchtenau, Germany), Fran & Michael Edmunds (London SE24), Jed Ela (Madison, Wisconsin, USA), Richard Engel (Oakland CA), Marc Ermer (Langenselbold, Germany), Rachel Ben Ezra (Ashekelon, Israel), Ariane Fàssler (Wettswil, Switzerland), Joy Hale & Derek Fess (Columbus, Ohio), Suzanne Fischer (Sursee, Switzerland), Karin Frei (Dagmesellen, Switzerland), Armin Fricke

& Jasmin Troll (Berlin), P D Gadd & R del Tufo (London N1), Geert Klein Geltink & Helene Keur (Zwolle, Holland), Natasha George (London W4), Gisa Gericke, Nicole Hofmann & Tania Wirth (Wiesbaden, Germany), Yossi Ghinsberg (Manina del Rey, LA, USA), Patrik Gille-Johnson (Eskilstuna, Sweden), Tracy Gorman (Newport NSW, Australia), Robin Greenall (Colchester, Essex), Adolf Grote (Hannover, Germany), Beatrice Guttman & Rolf Keller (Wattwil, Switzerland), Nicola Hall & Graham Firth (East London, South Africa), Derek Hamilton-Gibbs (London SW19).

Blanche Hampton & Peter Ross (South Coogee, Australia), M Hanselmann & friends (Zurich, Switzerland), Jane A Harries (Dyfed, Wales), Ingrid Hauptmann (Tutzing, Germany), Hauptmann (Tutzing, Germany), Sally & Mike Hayden (Cheltenham, Glos), Samuel Heermann (Bonn, Germany), Dr Ken Heffernan (Turner, ACT, Australia), Carsten Heuser (Germany), Myriam Heusser & Patrick Holleis (Zürich, Switzerland), Said Campos Hinojosa (Cochabamba, Bolivia), Steve Hitov & Tillie Lacayo (Lakeland, FL, USA), Peter Hollmann & Christina Heimsch (Beuerberg, Germany), Harriet Horniman (London SW12), Daniel Höuger (Melchnau, Switzerland), Bee Hughes (Hong Kong), Heike Jakob & Michael Scharfe (Dresden, Germany), Steven Jarard (Calgary, Alberta) & Shir Goldberg (Natanya, Israel), Robert Jensen (Ridgewood, NJ, USA), Carol Jodrell (North Perth, W Australia), Pete Johnston (Sucre, Bolivia), Helen Jönsson (Akarp, Sweden), Doug Joseph (New York City), Svein-Bruno Kallkovel (Egersund, Norway), Yaron Kapitulnik (Jerusalem) & Smadar Sikron (Negev), Roman Karas (Vienna, Austria), Ingrid Keil (Germering, Germany), Oliver Kempe (Enskede, Sweden), an extensive and valuable report, M Kiefer (Landau, Germany), Tina & Lene Kimet (Nykbing F, Denmark Dr Jürgen Koch (Leonburg, Germany), Charles and Betty Konopa (Yuma, Arizona), Stefan Kraus (Feldkirchen-Westerham, Germany), Michael Kreutle (Munderkingen, Germany), Bob Kuehn (New Orleans), Vesa Lampinen (Tampere) & Riikka Levoranta (Vammala, Finland), Curt Larson (Pittsburgh, USA), Knut Lebang (Aachen, Germany), Iolanda Lourenço Leite & Maria Dora Ruy Evangelista (Paraná, Brazil), Anja Lenze & Frank Shillig (Berlin, Germany), Frank Löwen (Rosengarten, Germany), Johann Lubienski (Graz, Austria), Ana María Madrid (Rancagua, Chile), Sabine Magnin (Marly, Switzerland), Claude Martin (Montréal, Canada), Daniel Buck & Anne Meadows (Washington DC), Julia Meller & Richard McIntosh (UK), Liz Minehan & Helly Perwick (London W14),

Sharon Morgan (Melbourne, Australia), Nicoletta & Lionello Morganti (Iseo, Italy), Helmut Moser (ZellamSee, Austria), Olivier Müller (Switzerland), Thomas Kump, Catherine Gerin (Belgium), Inês Oliveira (Brazil), Dr Wolfgang G Müller (Bonn, Germany).

Dr William R C Munro (Stanley, Perth), Alan Murphy (Arncroach, Scotland), Carlo Muttoni (Italy), Nicole Neumaier (Lübeck, Germany), Matthew Parris (London E14), Marco Petznick (Neu-Isenburg, Germany), Marjorie Powell (La Paz), Eckard Quitmann (Argentina), Martin Raaflaub (Zwieselberg, Switzerland), Anne Line V Rasmussen (Copenhagen, Denmark), (Sandy), Alexandra Reid (Leichhardt, NSW, Australia), Philip Rihs (Biel, Switzerland), Rita Roclofs & Nico Floris (San Francisco, CA & Netherlands), Arbel Ronen & Jaffe Michal (Tel Aviv, Israel), Felix Röpcke (Bremen, Germany), Tony Rosenberg (Australia) & Burke Moffat (Canada), Uwe Sacherer (Mannheim, Germany), Helen Saunders (Redruth, Cornwall), Anne Marie Scattarreggia (Basel, Switzerland) & Marcelo Bruno (Buenos Aires, Argentina), Martin Schauera & Ina Greger (Berlin), Hans-Ruedi Schürmann (Emmen, Switzerland), Gudrun Schädler (Jockgrim, Germany), Claudia Schaerer & Fernand Baigle (Stratford, Ontario, Canada), Peter Scharhag (Billigheim-Ingenhem, Germany), Florian Schindelmann (Bad Reichenhall, Germany), Kathy Schmid (Margenmuhle Bussnang, Switzerland), Thomas Schmitt & Marion Lege (Aalen, Germany), Mary Nicoll & Charlie Schreiber (London NW5), Wolfgang Schröppel & Friedemann Bär (Urbach & Plüderhausen, Germany), Roger Schwab (Biel, Switzerland), Kirsten Sehnbruch (Kirchen/Sieg, Germany), Hannelore Seibert (Vachendorf, Germany), Reto Senn (Baden), Shai Shelhav (Izora, Israel) & Laura Radow (Washington DC), Julian Stanley (Stow-in-Wold, Gloucestershire), Helmuth Otto Stuven & Stella Domky oer Dolby Nielsen (Copenhagen), Hellmuth-Chr Stuven & Stella Nielsen (Roskilde, Denmark), Darcy Thomas (Wellfleet, MA, USA), Mike Truman (Burnham-On-Sea, Somerset), Richard D Tucker, Andrew Tune & Maggie Frize (Tunbridge Wells, Kent), Jill Ulmanis (Sheffield, UK), Bill Vallis (Surbiton, Surrey), A Vandermissen (Brussels, Belgium), Edwin van der Werf & Harold Bierens (Holland), Floris van de Tak (Leiden, Holland), Isabelle Vulliard & Jean Christophe Poncetta (La Ravoire, France), Averil Wachman (Carbury, Co Kildare, Ireland), Jutta Werling Durejka (La Paz), Monique Wong (Artarmon, NSW, Australia), Mag Martin & Dr Waltraud Zausner (Vienna, Austria), and Kristin Zeller (Paris).

BRAZIL

INTRODUCTION

BRAZIL, the fifth largest country in the world, has the sixth largest population. It is almost as large as the United States of America and its area is nearly half that of South America. For neighbours it has all the South American countries save Chile and Ecuador. Distances are enormous: 4,320 km from N to S, 4,328 km from E to W, a land frontier of 15,719 km and an Atlantic coast line of 7,408 km. Its population is over half that of all South America, and over 65% is under 30 years of age. It was named for the tropical redwood, *pau do brasil*, exported by the first settlers.

Brazil's topography may be divided roughly into five main zones: the Amazon Basin; the River Plate Basin; the Guiana Highlands N of the Amazon; the Brazilian Highlands S of the Amazon; and the coastal strip. The two great river basins account for about three-fifths of Brazil's area.

The Amazon Basin, in northern and western Brazil, takes up more than a third

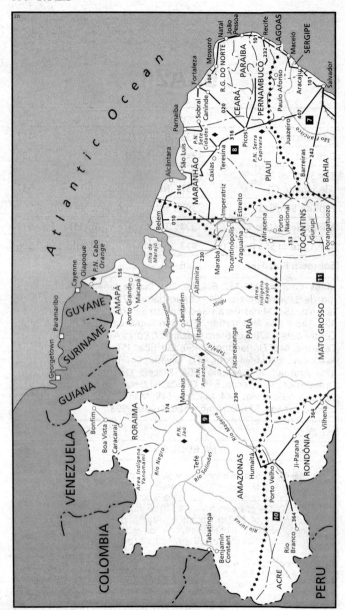

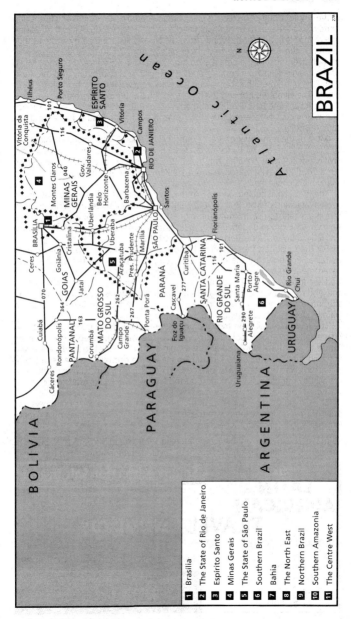

BRAZIL

Atlantic Ocean

N

1 Brasília
2 The State of Rio de Janeiro
3 Espírito Santo
4 Minas Gerais
5 The State of São Paulo
6 Southern Brazil
7 Bahia
8 The North East
9 Northern Brazil
10 Southern Amazonia
11 The Centre West

of the whole country. This basin is plain, broadly based on the Andes and funnelling narrowly to the sea; most of the drained area has an elevation of less than 250m. The rainfall is heavy, for the winds from the NE and SE lose their moisture as they approach the Andes. Some few places receive from 3,750 to 5,000 mm a year, though over most of the area it is no more than from 1,500 to 2,500 mm. Much of the basin suffers from annual floods. The region was covered by tropical forest, with little undergrowth except along the watercourses; it is now being rapidly cut down. The climate is hot and the humidity high throughout the year.

The River Plate Basin, in the southern part of Brazil, has a more varied surface and is less heavily forested than the Amazon Basin. The land is higher and the climate cooler.

Most of the remainder of Brazil's territory is highland. The Guiana Highlands, N of the Amazon, are partly forested, partly hot stony desert. Those that face the NW winds get heavy rainfall, but the southern slopes are arid. The rainfall, which comes during the hot season, is about 1,250 mm a year. The summers are hot and the winters cool.

The Brazilian Highlands lying SE of the Amazon and NE of the River Plate Basin form a tableland of from 300 to 900M high, but here and there, mostly in SE Brazil, mountain ranges rise from it. The highest peak in southern Brazil, the Pico da Bandeira, NE of Rio de Janeiro, is 2,898M; the highest peak in all Brazil, the Pico da Neblina on the Venezuelan border, is 3,014M.

For the most part the Highlands cascade sharply to the sea. South of Salvador as far as Porto Alegre the coast rises steeply to a protective barrier, the Great Escarpment. In only two places is this Escarpment breached by deeply cut river beds—those of the Rio Doce and the Rio Paraíba; and only in a few places does the land rise in a single slope making for comparatively easy communication with the interior. Along most of its course, the Great Escarpment falls to the sea in parallel steps, each step separated by the trough of a valley.

The few rivers rising on the Escarpment which flow direct into the Atlantic do so precipitously and are not navigable. Most of the rivers flow deep into the interior. Those in southern Brazil rise almost within sight of the sea, but run westward through the vast interior to join the Paraná. In the central area the Escarpment rivers run away from the sea to join the São Francisco river, which flows northwards parallel to the coast for 2,900 km, to tumble over the Paulo Afonso Falls on its eastward course to the Atlantic.

The Great Escarpment denies to most of Brazil the natural valley outflows and lines of travel from the interior to the sea. Of its rivers the Amazon alone is directly navigable for a great distance inland.

Climate The average annual temperature increases steadily from S to N, but even on the Equator, in the Amazon Basin, the average temperature is not more than

27°C. The highest recorded was 42°C, in the dry north-eastern states. From the latitude of Recife S to Rio de Janeiro, the mean temperature is from 23° to 27°C along the coast, and from 18° to 21°C in the Highlands. From a few degrees S of Rio de Janeiro to the boundary with Uruguay the mean temperature is from 17° to 19°C. Humidity is relatively high in Brazil, particularly along the coast.

It is only in rare cases that the rainfall can be described as either excessive or deficient: few places get more than 2,000 mm—the coast N of Belém, some of the Amazon Basin, and a small area of the Serra do Mar between Santos and São Paulo, where the downpour has been harnessed to generate electricity. The rainy season in Amazonia is Mar-May, but is getting steadily shorter and less severe, possibly as a result of deforestation. The north-eastern droughts are caused by irregular rainfall.

The rainy season in the S is from Dec to Mar; this is also the holiday season when Brazilians flock to the coastal resorts, and when prices are higher.

Political and Social History The Portuguese, Pedro Alvares Cabral, landed in Brazil in 1500. He left after a week, shortly followed by Amerigo Vespucci who had been sent to explore further. The first system of government adopted by the Portuguese was a Capitânia, a kind of feudal principality—there were thirteen of them, but these were replaced in 1572 by a Viceroyalty. In the same year it was decided to divide the colony into two, N and S, with capitals at Salvador and Rio de Janeiro; it was not until 1763 that Rio became the sole capital. The Portuguese crown expected both a personal and a state revenue from its colony.

Three hundred years under the paternal eye of Portugal had ill-prepared the colonists for independent existence, except for the experience of Dutch invasion (1624 in Salvador, and 1630-1654 in Recife). The colonists ejected the Dutch from Brazil with little help from Portugal, and Brazilians date the birth of their national sentiment from these events. Resentment against Portuguese government and trade intervention led to the Inconfidência, the first revolution, masterminded by Tiradentes with eleven other citizens of Minas Gerais. They were unsuccessful (Tiradentes was executed), but when France invaded Portugal in 1807, King João VI was shipped to safety in Brazil, escorted by the British navy. Rio was temporarily declared the capital of the Portuguese empire. The British, as a price for their assistance in the Portuguese war, forced the opening of Brazil's ports to non-Portuguese trade. King João VI returned to the mother country in 1821, leaving his son, the handsome young Pedro, as Regent. Pedro refused to return control of Brazil to the Portuguese Côrtes (parliament), and on 13 May 1882, by popular request, he agreed to stay and assumed the title of "Perpetual Defender and Protector of Brazil". On 7 Sep he declared Brazil's independence with the cry "Independence or Death" by the Rio Ipiranga; on 12 Oct he was proclaimed constitutional emperor of Brazil, and on 1 Dec he was crowned in Rio de Janeiro.

Dom Pedro the First had the misfortune to be faced by a secession movement in the N, to lose the Banda Oriental (today Uruguay) and to get too involved in his complicated love life. Finally, he abdicated as the result of a military revolt in 1831, leaving his five-year-old son, Dom Pedro the Second, in the hands of a regent, as ruler. On 23 July 1840, the lad, though only 15, was proclaimed of age. Dom Pedro the Second, a strong liberal at heart, promoted education, increased communications, developed agriculture, stamped on corruption and encouraged immigration from Europe. Under his rule the war with the dictator López of Paraguay ended in Brazilian victory. Finally, he declared that he would rather lose his crown than allow slavery to continue, and on 13 May 1888, it was finally abolished by his daughter, Princess Isabel, who was acting as Regent during his temporary absence.

There is little doubt that it was this measure that cost him his throne. Many plantation owners, who had been given no compensation, turned against the

Emperor; they were supported by elements in the army and navy, who felt that the Emperor had not given due heed to their interests since the Paraguayan War. On 15 November 1889, the Republic was proclaimed and the Emperor sailed for Europe. Two years later he died in a second-rate hotel in Paris, after steadfastly refusing a pension from the conscience-stricken revolutionaries. At the time of the first centenary of independence in 1922 the imperial family was allowed to return to Brazil, and the body of Dom Pedro was brought back and buried in the cathedral at Petrópolis.

The history of the "Old Republic" (1889-1930), apart from the first ten years which saw several monarchist rebellions, was comparatively uneventful, a time of expansion and increasing prosperity. Brazil declared war on Germany during both wars and Brazilian troops fought in the Italian campaign in 1944-45. In 1930 a revolution headed by Getúlio Vargas, Governor of Rio Grande do Sul, who was to become known as "the Father of the Poor" for the social measures he introduced, deposed President Wáshington Luís. Vargas assumed executive power first as provisional president and then as dictator. He was forced to resign in Oct 1945. In 1946 a liberal republic was restored and the following 18 years saw considerable economic development and social advance.

An increase in government instability and corruption lead to growing military intervention in civil affairs. This culminated in the military movement of Mar 1964, which ruled until Mar 1985 with the use of political repression and torture, yet achieving great economic success (up to 1980). The economic miracle of 1964-74 brought average growth of 10% a year but deepened the divide between rich and poor. Labour leaders were oppressed, dissenters were jailed and *favelas* mushroomed. Political reform did not occur until 1980 and free elections were not held until 1989. In Jan 1985 a civilian, Tancredo Neves, representing a broad opposition to the military regime, was elected President by the electoral college introduced under the military's 1967 constitution. He was unable, because of illness, to take office: the vice-president elect, Sr José Sarney, was sworn in as acting President in Mar 1985, and became President on Sr Neves' death in Apr. After complete revision by a Constituent Assembly in 1987-88, Brazil's new constitution of 1988 permitted direct presidential elections in Nov 1989. The elections were held in two rounds, the final result giving Fernando Collor de Melo, of the small Partido da Reconstrução Nacional, 53% of the vote, narrowly defeating his left-wing rival, Luis Inácio da Silva (Lula). President Collor took office on 15 March 1990 for a five-year term. Just over half way through his term, Collor was suspended from office after a landslide congressional vote in favour of him being impeached over his involvement in corruption. He avoided impeachment by resigning on 29 December 1992. The presidency was taken over by vice-president Itamar Franco, whose administration showed scant success in tackling poverty and inflation until the introduction of an anti-inflation package which introduced the new *real* currency. The plan's success in cutting inflation was the principal reason for its architect, finance minister Fernando Henrique Cardoso, winning the presidential elections of Oct 1994. After trailing Luis Lula da Silva of the Workers Party (PT), Cardoso's popularity grew so rapidly between July and Oct that a second round of voting was not required. Cardoso represented an alliance of the Brazilian Social Democrat Party (PSDB), the Liberal Front (PFL) and the Labour Party (PTB), which failed to gain a majority in either house of congress.

Settlement and Economic History The first European settlement was at Salvador da Bahia, and the settlers came mainly from southern Portugal, with its feudal tradition of great estates. For the first few years Portugal, then much concerned with the Orient, paid little attention to Brazil. In about 1507 a second colony was settled at São Vicente, near Santos, and in 1537 a third at Olinda, near Recife. The settlers at São Vicente, who founded the first settlement in the highlands at São Paulo in 1534, were unlike those at Salvador and Recife: they came from the poorer and more energetic N of Portugal. All of them were attracted less by the prospect of earning their living by self-supporting labour than by opportunities of speculative profit. To do the work they used the primitive Tupi-Guaraní Indians, many of whom died from European diseases (see *Red Gold*, by John Hemming). They cohabited freely with the Indians and, later, with slaves imported from Africa to run the huge estates.

Sugar cane had been introduced at São Vicente in 1532, but it was the wealthy settlers of the NE who had the necessary capital to establish the crop and to buy African slaves to work it; the Indian, with his hunting-and-gathering culture, was a disappointment as a labourer. In the matter of sugar, Salvador and Recife had the advantages over São Vicente of being very much nearer home, and of having better ports and easier access to the interior. During the latter half of the 16th and the whole of the 17th centuries, the provinces of Bahia, Pernambuco, and Paraíba were the world's prime source of sugar.

The settlers at São Paulo, envious of the more fortunate NE, sent out expeditions to explore the interior for gold, which had already been found in small quantities in their own streams. These hardy Bandeirantes pushed as far S as Colonia, opposite Buenos Aires, as far W as the Río Paraguay, and N into the area W of the sugar plantations of the NE. In 1698 they struck gold in central Minas Gerais. More was found soon after in central Mato Grosso, and in 1725 in Goiás. Diamonds were discovered in 1729 N of the goldfields of Minas Gerais.

There followed a great gold and diamond rush. The gold boom started early in the 18th century, lasted a hundred years, and then petered out. Minas Gerais was transformed from a wilderness into a well populated agricultural, pastoral, and mining region. It was as an outlet for this area that Rio de Janeiro was developed. Some of the wealth went to create the extraordinarily beautiful city of Ouro Preto, to-day a national monument of superb building, painting and sculpture, and the similarly attractive cities of São João del Rei, Mariana, Congonhas do Campo, Diamantina and others.

Brazil was ready for the next speculation, coffee, introduced about 1720 from French Guyane. Coffee planting began near Rio de Janeiro and at many places round the coast as far as the Amazon, but by 1825 it had mainly been concentrated in the Paraíba valley, W of the capital. From there it spread into São Paulo, where its cultivation attracted a large number of immigrants after 1850.

There have been many other typical Brazilian booms and recessions. The best known is the rubber boom in the Amazon valley; competition from SE Asia wiped it out after 1912. Sugar, coffee, and cocoa were alike the subject of booms. In each case Brazil was challenged by other sources of supply, where more intensive methods of production were applied.

This boom tradition still holds, but it is shifting from agriculture to industry: Brazilians today prefer to think of themselves as a rising industrial nation. Nevertheless, a great increase in production and export of manufactured goods has not prevented oases of prosperity being edged by deserts of poverty and wilderness.

The People At first the new colony grew slowly. From 1580 to 1640 the population was only about 50,000 apart from the million or so indigenous Indians. In 1700 there were some 750,000 non-indigenous people in Brazil. Early in the 19th century Humboldt computed there were about 920,000 whites, 1,960,000 Africans, and 1,120,000 Indians and *mestiços*: after three centuries of occupation a total of only four millions, and over twice as many Africans as there were whites.

Modern immigration did not begin effectively until after 1850. Of the 4.6 million immigrants from Europe between 1884 and 1954, 32% were Italians, 30% Portuguese, 14% Spanish, 4% German, and the rest of various nationalities. Since

1954 immigrants have averaged 50,000 a year. There are some 1 million Japanese-descended Brazilians; they grow a fifth of the coffee, 30% of the cotton, all the tea, and are very active in market gardening.

Today the whites and near-whites are about 53% of the population, people of mixed race about 34%, and Afro Brazilians 11%; the rest are either Indians or Asians. There are large regional variations in the distribution of the races: the whites predominate greatly in the S, which received the largest flood of European immigrants, and decrease more or less progressively towards the N.

Most of the German immigrants settled in the three southern states: Santa Catarina, Rio Grande do Sul, and Paraná. The Germans (and the Italians and Poles and other Slavs who followed them) did not in the main go as wage earners on the big estates, but as cultivators of their own small farms. Here there is a settled agricultural population cultivating the soil intensively.

The arid wastes of the Sertão remain largely uncultivated. Its inhabitants are people of mixed Portuguese and Indian origin (*mestiço*); most live off a primitive but effective method of cultivation known as "slash and burn", which involves cutting down and burning the brushwood for a small patch of ground which is cultivated for a few years and then allowed to grow back.

The decision to found a new federal capital, Brasília, deep in the interior, was a symbolic act of faith in the future of the Sertão: a bold attempt to deflect population from the coastal regions to the under-developed central and western plateaux of the country.

Though there is no legal discrimination against black people, the economic and educational disparity—by default rather than intent of the Government—is such that successful Afro Brazilians are active almost exclusively in the worlds of sport, entertainment and the arts.

It is estimated that, when the Portuguese arrived in Brazil, there were more than 5 million Indians living in the area. Today there are only about 200,000. Tribal groups number 221; each has a unique dialect, but most languages belong to four main linguistic families, Tupi-Guarani, Ge, Carib and Arawak. A few tribes remain uncontacted, others are exclusively nomadic, others are semi-nomadic hunter-gatherers and farmers, while some are settled groups in close contact with non-Indian society. The struggle of groups such as the Yanomami to have their land demarcated in order to secure title is well-documented. The goal of the Statute of the Indian (Law 6.001/73), for demarcation of all Indian land by 1978, is largely unmet. Funai, the National Foundation for the Support of the Indian, a part of the Interior Ministry, is charged with representing the Indians' interests, but lacks resources and support. There is no nationwide, representative body for indigenous people. Most of Brazil's indigenous people live in the Amazon region; they are affected by deforestation, encroachment from colonizers, small-and large-scale mining, and the construction of hydroelectric dams. Besides the Yanomami, other groups include the Xavante, Tukano, Kreen-Akrore, Kaiapó, Arawete and Arara.

The population has historically been heavily concentrated in a comparatively small area—chiefly along the coastal strip where the original Portuguese settlers exploited the agricultural wealth, and further inland in the states of Minas Gerais and São Paulo where more recent development has followed the original search for gold, precious stones and slaves. Much of the interior of Pará, Amazonas, Goiás and the Mato Grossos has densities of one person per sq km or less. Brazil's attention is officially focused on these relatively underpopulated regions as a means of syphoning off some of the population excess in the urban centres.

The urban population of Brazil increased at rates more than double the overall average rate, until the 1980s, and much of this growth has been concentrated in the larger cities. Internal migration is the major cause of these phenomenal growth rates, bringing to the cities problems of unemployment, housing shortage, and pressure on services which are already stretched to breaking point; shanty towns—or *favelas, mocambos, alagados*, according to the region—are an integral part of the urban landscape and a constant reminder of the poverty of some of the rural areas from which these people come. But while the NE, because of its poverty, has lost many workers to the industries of the SE, many rural workers from southern Brazil have moved N, drawn by the rapid development of Amazonia, creating unprecedented pressures on the environment.

Of the 13 million children between 7 and 14, 2 million have no school to go to. Of those who go to school, not all stay long enough to learn how to read and write. Adult literacy campaigns have, however, recently improved the picture.

The Economy Brazil is the world's tenth largest economy. It has abundant and varied natural resources and a long-standing development record, the most striking features of which since 1945 have been state intervention and industrialization, particularly in the areas of energy, heavy industry, transport equipment and capital goods. The vast majority of consumer goods are now manufactured locally, as well as a wide range of capital goods. Since the 1970s there has been a rapid expansion of technology-based industries. Manufactures now account for almost 60% of total exports. Manufacturing accounts for 23% of gdp.

Brazil remains a large farming country and is generally self-sufficient in food production. It is the world's largest producer and exporter of coffee. Since the mid-1970s soya and orange juice production have been developed, so that dominant positions in international markets in these products have been secured. Agriculture produces about a third of exports and 11% of gdp. However, the sector is backward in its use of techniques and yields are low. Something of an agricultural revolution is taking place, led mainly by foreign investors attracted by cheap land, but mechanization is largely limited to southern areas.

The country is richly endowed with metals and other minerals. Brazil has up to a third of the world's total iron ore reserves, found mainly in Minas Gerais and certain parts of the Amazon basin, especially the Serra dos Carajás region (Pará). Brazil is also a significant exporter of manganese and gold and produces increasing amounts of tin and copper.

Energy sector development has aimed at substituting local for imported energy. Since the discovery of the Campos basin off the coast of Rio de Janeiro state, oil production has steadily risen to 0.7 million barrels a day, and this satisfies just over half of local requirements. Large investments have been made in hydroelectricity, alcohol and nuclear power. Hydroelectric plants produce 93% of electricity and several major schemes are in preparation. A 620-Mw nuclear reactor at Angra dos Reis (Rio de Janeiro) came on stream in 1985, but financial restrictions have slowed nuclear power development.

High inflation in the 1980s and 1990s was caused by (among other things) urbanization and food supply bottlenecks, energy consumption patterns heavily dependent on oil imports, public accounts disequilibrium, and generalized indexation covering wages, prices and financial instruments. Various stabilization programmes introduced since Feb 1986 met with limited success. The principal cause of failure was the lack of political will to tackle the structural causes of inflation. The Collor Government in 1990 introduced yet another currency, the cruzeiro, and sweeping economic reforms. The chosen tactic of using tight fiscal and monetary policies coupled with liberalization of foreign trade and the exchange rate, pushed the economy into deep recession while inflation remained intractable in the absence of a reduction of the public sector deficit. After the demise of Collor, President Franco's government appeared to lack direction as Franco and successive economy ministers disagreed over policy. His fourth minister, Fernando Henrique Cardoso, appointed in May 1993, announced the Plano Verdade which contained stringent measures to strengthen the public accounts and thus reduce inflation. The widespread cooperation needed for the plan to build on the return to economic growth recorded in the first quarter of 1993 did not materialize, and by Jun 1994 inflation had reached 51% a month. Soaring interest rates caused great hardship for the middle classes, and deepened the divide between rich and poor. Further changes to the currency were announced: in Sep

Brazil : fact file

Geographic

Land area	8,547.404 sq km
forested	57.7%
pastures	22.1%
cultivated	7.0%

Demographic

Population (1994)	159,000,000
annual growth rate (1989-94)	1.7%
urban	75.5%
rural	24.5%
density	18.7 per sq km
Religious affiliation	
Roman Catholic	76%
Birth rate per 1,000 (1991)	25.3
	(world av 26.0)

Education and Health

Life expectancy at birth,	
male	63.5 years
female	69.1 years
Infant mortality rate	
per 1,000 live births (1994)	60
Physicians (1988)	1 per 848 persons
Hospital beds	1 per 270 persons
Calorie intake as %	
of FAO requirement	114%
Population age 10 and over	
with no formal schooling	18.1%
Literate males (over 15)	82.1%
Literate females (over 15)	81.2%

Economic

GNP (1993 market price)	
	US$470,511mn
GNP per capita	US$3,010
Public external debt (1992)	
	US$86,251mn
Tourism receipts (1992)	
	US$1,307mn
Inflation (annual av 1989-93)	1,315%
Radio	1 per 2.6 persons
Television	1 per 5.2 persons
Telephone	1 per 11 persons

Employment

Population economically active (1990)	
	64,467,981
Unemployment rate (1993)	14.9%
% of labour force in	
agriculture	22.0
manufacturing	14.6
mining and public utilities	1.3
construction	5.9
Military forces	336,800

Source *Encyclopaedia Britannica*
InterAmerican Development Bank

1993 the value of the cruzeiro was reduced by 1,000 to create the cruzeiro real. In Mar 1994 a transitional unit of value, the URV (real unit of value) was introduced at par with the US dollar. From that date all prices and contracts were denominated in URVs prior to the introduction of a new currency, the *real*, on 1 July 1994. With the *real* fixed at par with the dollar, inflation in the following months plummeted. By Feb 1995 it was below 1% a month. At the same time, the *real* appreciated by 15% against the dollar as interest rates stayed high. Gdp grew (by 5.7% in 1994), so did consumption. Consequently, imports rose while exports declined leading to Brazil's first trade deficit since the mid-1980's. The worsening trade balance and its impact on the current account alarmed officials in the wake of Mexico's end-1994 financial crisis. The exchange rate regime was relaxed to a range of floating bands within which the *real* would trade. High levels of foreign reserves supported the *real*, but the crisis undermined confidence, led to stock market instability and inspired emergency measures to balance the 1995 budget.

During the 1970s large-scale, high-cost projects and current account deficits were financed by foreign borrowing, and Brazil accumulated the region's largest external debt. From 1982 annual rescheduling agreements were concluded with creditors, with new money and, in 1983-85, IMF standby facilities. The World Bank and Inter-American Development Bank granted large loans for sectoral development. These arrangements did not, however, help to reduce the burden of interest payments and in Feb 1987 Brazil declared a moratorium on interest in order to preserve foreign exchange reserves and halt the net transfer of resources to creditors. The plan did not prosper and a year later reserves were even lower as lenders declined to extend credit and favourable terms were being awarded to other borrowers. In 1988 Brazil returned to the international financial community and negotiated a financing package from all creditors aimed at restoring its creditworthiness, but by 1989 it had moved back into arrears to preserve foreign reserves. In 1992 Brazil successfully negotiated an IMF standby facility, which led to an agreement on rescheduling debt to the Paris Club group of debtor countries. The IMF deal collapsed later the same year, but Brazil continued to negotiate with its commercial bank creditors. Despite failing to win IMF approval for its new economic reforms and without signing a new accord with the Fund, Brazil reached agreement with the banks to restructure US$49bn of debt in April 1994.

Government The 1988 constitution provides for an executive president elected by direct popular vote, balanced by a bicameral legislature (81 seats in the Federal Senate, 513 seats in the Chamber of Deputies) and an independent judiciary. The vote has been extended to 16-year-olds and illiterates. Presidential elections are held every 5 years, with a second round one month after the first if no candidate wins an outright majority. Congressional elections are held every four years, the deputies being chosen by proportional representation.

Local Administration Each state has a popularly-elected Governor who exercises the executive power, and a Legislative Assembly which legislates on all matters affecting provincial administration and provides for state expenses and needs by levying taxes. Each municipality has a similar structure, with a mayor (*prefeito*), also popularly elected, and a local council (*câmara de vereadores*).

Railways There are about 30,282 km of railways originally built to supply export markets, but not combined into a unified system. Brazil has two gauges and there is little transfer between them (some sections have been made mixed gauge). Three more gauges exist for the isolated Amapá Railway, the tourist-only São João del Rei line and the abandoned Perus-Pirapora line. About 2,450 km have now been electrified. Many lines have been closed in recent years.

Roads Though the best paved highways are still heavily concentrated in the SE, those serving the interior are now being improved to all-weather status and many are paved. Brazil has over 1.5 million kilometres of highways, of which 150,000 km are paved, and several thousand more all-weather. Recent road-building programmes have emphasized inter-regional connections and the opening up of the Centre, N and W of the country. Nationwide bus services are frequent and good.

Air Services The first commercial flight in Brazil was in 1927. Because of the great distances and the comparative paucity of good highways and railways, aircraft have eased the traveller's lot more spectacularly in Brazil than in any other country. The larger cities are now linked with each other several times a day by air, and even the more remote points in the country can now be reached by light aircraft.

National Parks This chapter gives details on many of Brazil's national parks, which are run by Ibama (the Brazilian Institute of Environmental Protection). The Institute is underfunded, often understaffed and visitors may find it difficult to obtain information. National parks are open to visitors, usually with a permit from Ibama. Ecological Stations and Biological Reserves are open to researchers and educational groups, but not tourists.

Music and Dance Perhaps because of its sheer size, Brazil has a greater musical inventory than any other Latin American country, not only reflected in the immense regional spread of folk music but also in its successive waves of urban popular music. The Brazilian expresses him/herself through music and dance to an extraordinary degree and the music covers the whole spectrum from the utmost rural simplicity to the ultimate state-of-the-art commercial sophistication. The far N of the country is virtually in the Caribbean, while the extreme S shares its culture with the Rio de la Plata countries and it is here we will start. In Paraná, Santa Catarina and Rio Grande do Sul, the music is strictly European in origin, rhythm and instrumentation. Rio Grande do Sul shares Gaucho dances such as the Pericom and song styles such as the Milonga, Trova and Pajada with neighbouring Uruguay and Argentina. The Chula is a competitive dance for men to show off with (comparable to the Argentine Malambo), while the Pexinho is for men and women. The guitar and the accordion are the favourite instruments, also true for Santa Catarina and Paraná, where the names of the dances denote their European origins: Mazurcas, Valsas, Chotes, Polquinhas and Rancheiras. The Chimarrita is a song style that came straight from the Azores. If you are feeling sentimental, you sing a Toada, if energetic, you stamp your feet to a Fandango. Except for the

Batuque de Rio Grande do Sul in Porto Alegre, closely related to the Candombe of nearby Montevideo, there is no African influence in the music of this region and none of that classic Brazilian syncopation.

Moving N into São Paulo, we enter an area rich in traditional folk dances and music, with the African admixture beginning to show up. At many religious festivals will be found the Congadas (European "Moors & Christians", but danced by blacks) and Moçambique (a stick dance for men), while the Samba de Lenço, Fandango and Batuque are recreational dances for one or more couples. The instrumental accompaniment branches out into shakers (the *ganzá*), drums (*caixas* and *tambores*) and above all the guitar (*viola*). Try the great pilgrimage church at Aparecida do Norte on a Sun. You might well see a group of religious dances. In the hinterland of Rio de Janeiro the Folias de Reis are out on the street from Christmas to Epiphany, singing from house to house, accompanying themselves on the *caixa* and *adufe* drums and the guitar, while in the old coastal towns of Parati and Angra dos Reis are to be found the Dança de Velhos (the old men), performed to the accordion. The Jongo is a dance of African origin for men and women, naturally with a drum accompaniment. And there is hardly need to mention Rio de Janeiro at carnival and its Samba Schools. Further N again, we come to the states of Espíritu Santo, Minas Gerais and Goiás. In colonial Ouro Preto, in Minas, you can hear the old Modinha sung to the Portuguese guitar as a serenade and be transported into the past. Espíritu Santo is home to the Ticumbi, a kind of Congada, danced to the guitar and shakers (*chocalhos*). Goias shares with Minas Gerais a very rich heritage of Portuguese derived religious folk song and dance, centred on Folias, Modas and Calangos.

Bahia is the heart of African Brazil and a very musical heart it is, born of the Yoruba religion that came with the slaves from what is now Nigeria. The resulting syncretic religion is known as Candomble in Bahia and the gods or "Orixás" are worshipped through song, dance and possession in the "Terreiros", directed by the priests (Pães-de-Santo) and priestesses (Mães-de-Santo). The mainly female adepts, dressed entirely in white, circle gracefully to the background chant of "Pontos" and the thunderous pounding of the *atabaques*, the tall drums. The two most revered priestesses are Mãe Olga de Alakêto and Mãe Menininha de Gantois. Similar syncretic African religions are found elsewhere in Brazil. Macumba in Rio, Xangô in the NE and Umbanda all over. Another vital African element in Bahian folk music is the spectacular dance-cum-martial arts form of Capoeira. Bodies whirl and cartwheel around each other to the sound of the *berimbau* (a one-stringed bow with resonator) and the accompanying chant. Related to the Capoeira is the stick dance Maculelê. Two of the best *berimbau* groups on record are Camafeu de Oxossí and the Cordão de Ouro. Bahia has a carnival almost as celebrated as that of Rio and here you can see the Afoxé, a serious religious dance, performed to drums alone.

North of Bahia is the Nordeste, with music that runs the whole gamut from black African to mediaeval Portuguese. In colonial times the church directed the peoples' musical energies into religious plays, songs and dances and a large number of these are still performed. The Bumba-Meu-Boi is a folk drama in the course of which a bull is killed and then brought back to life. Particularly popular in Piauí and Maranhão, its variants are found as far afield as Amazônia, where it is called the Boi-Bumbá, and Paraná in the far S, where it is known as Boi-Mamão. Also popular along the coast from Ceará to Paraíba is a nautical drama of Portuguese origin called Marujada or Nau Catarineta, a version of Moors and Christians, accompanied by Portuguese guitar (*violão*), drums and the *ganzá* scraper. In Alagoas, Sergipe and Pernambuco we find the sword dance called Reisado, danced after Christmas, the Caboclinhos, who are dressed like Indians and dance with bows and arrows, and the Guerreiros Alagoanos, a mixture of both. The last named are accompanied by the classical northeastern musical group called Terno de Pífanos, with the *pífano* vertical flute, accompanied by *maracas* and *ganzá*. The Banda de Pifanos of Caruaru in Pernambuco can be found on record. Recreational dance music in the Nordeste goes under the generic name of "Forró", said to be derived from the expression "For All", because the English companies operating at the turn of the century organized week-end dances for their workmen to which all comers were invited. Four very popular recreational folk dances of this region are the Ciranda (a round dance), the Coco, the Bate-Coxa (where the dancers bump bellies) and the Bambelô. Carnival in Recife, the largest city, is when and where to see the energetic and gymnastic Frevo, danced by young men with an umbrella in their hands, and the very stately and superbly costumed Maracatu dancers, with their queen and king. The Nordeste is equally rich in song styles, notably the Desafios, Emboladas, Cocos and Aboios. The Desafios are performed by so-called Repentistas or Violeiros, who accompany themselves on the Portuguese guitar and whose repertoire includes a large inventory of verse styles. They will sing about individual spectators, who then pay willingly for the compliment. The Emboladas and Cocos are similar, but faster and accompanied solely by tambourines, while the Aboios are haunting songs related to cattle and cattlemen. Repentistas and Emboladores can normally be found at work in markets throughout the region. The premier Repentista is Otacílio Batista do Pajeú, who sang to the Pope during the latter's visit to Brazil.

The music of the Nordeste has also been well propagated by more sophisticated groups that have based themselves on folk roots, such as the Quinteto Violado, Ariano Suassuna's Orchestra Armorial and Cussy de Almeida's Quinteto Armorial, not forgetting the veteran accordionist Luiz Gonzaga and the popular Alçeu Valença. As a result of the huge migration of *nordestinos* to the urban S, moreover, it is just as easy to hear this regional music in São Paulo as it is in Recife.

Finally to Pará and the Amazon in the far N, where the music has been heavily influenced from the Caribbean. The most popular musical genre here is the Carimbó, danced to a Merengue-type rhythm and played on drums, wind or brass (usually the clarinet) and strings, particularly the banjo. Notable performers are Pinduca ("O Rei do Carimbó"), Veriquete and Vieira. It is the last-named who thought up the term "Lambada" for his particular version of the Carimbó and the spectacular, thigh-entwining dance form introduced to the world in Paris by Karakos and Lorsac in 1988 had already been popular among young people at "Forrós" throughout the region for some years. The very traditional island of Marajó in the mouth of the Amazon has preserved versions of 18th century dances, such as the Lundú and Chula.

The vast range of Brazilian regional folk music is only equalled by the chronological depth of its urban popular music, which surges like endless waves on a beach. For the origins we have to go back to Jesuit missions and Portuguese folk music, influenced and blended by African slaves, from which emerged the l9th century Lundús, Polcas and Maxixes that in turn gave way to the romantic and sentimental Choro song genre (from *chorar*, to weep) , accompanied by guitar, flute and *cavaquinho* (small guitar), which became all the rage and indeed still has its adepts in Brazil today. Around the turn of the century the instrumentation turned to brass and Rio's urban Samba was born, a birth that was announced by the recording in 1917 of Donga's "Pelo Telefone". Names from this early period are Pixinguinha, Sinhô, Heitor dos Prazeres, Ary Barroso, Noel Rosa and of course Carmen Miranda, who took the Samba to Hollywood and the rest of the world. It also became intimately connected with the carnival in the form of Marcha Ranchos and Sambas de Enredo as the first samba schools were formed, of which Salgueiro, Mangueira, Partido Alto, Portela, Mocidade Independente and Beija-Flor are some of the most famous. With the Escolas de Samba came the Batucada or percussion groups playing the *pandeiro* (tambourine), *atabaque* and *tamborim* (drum), *agogô* (cowbell), *reco-reco*, *chocalho*, *afoxê* and *cuíca*. This is the real engine room of Samba. Listen to Lucio Perrone or Mocidade Independente de Padre Miguel. A new phase was ushered in with an invasion from Bahia and the Nordeste in the early 50's. From Bahia came Dorival Caymmi, who dropped his fishermen's songs in favour of the Samba, and Luiz Gonzaga, who brought his accordion, *zabumba* drum and *triangulo*, with which to play his Baiãos (his "Asa Branca" is a classic) and almost put the Samba itself into eclipse for several years. Almost, but not quite, for out of the ashes there soon arose Bossa Nova – white, middle class and silky smooth. Vinicius de Moraes and Tom Jobim were its heroes; 1958 to 1964 the years; Copacabana, Ipanema and Leblon the scene; "Samba de uma Nota Só", "A Garota de Ipanema" and "Desafinado" the songs and Nara Leão, Baden Powell, Toquinho, João Gilberto, Luis Bonfá and Astrud Gilberto the main performers. Stan Getz, the American jazz saxophonist, helped export it to the world. What was now being called MPB (Música Popular Brasileira) then took off in several directions. Chico Buarque, Edu Lobo and Milton Nascimento were protest singers. Out of Bahia emerged "Tropicalismo" in the persons of Gilberto Gil, Caetano Veloso and his sister Maria Bethânia, Gal Costa, João Gilberto and "Som Livre". The words were important, but the rhythm was still there. Brazilian rock also now appeared, with such stars as Roberto Carlos, Elis Regina, Rita Lee, and Ney Mattogrosso. Recently, in turning towards international black consiousness, the Bahianos have mixed Reggae and samba to produce "axé". Still, Samba has survived, although now called "Pagôde" and amazingly, 40% of all Brazilian records sold are of Música Sertaneja, a highly commercialized pseudo-folk genre which is closer to American Country and Western than to most other Brazilian music. Listen to the "Duplas" of Tonico & Tinoco, Jaco e Jacozinho or Vieira & Vieirinha and you'll see. In the meantime a series of brilliant Brazilian instumentalists have become international names and often live abroad—Sergio Mendes, the guitaritst Sebastião Tapajos, flautist Hermêto Paschoal, saxophonist Paulo Moura, accordionist Sivuca, percussionists Airto Moreira and Nana Vasconcelos, singer Flora Purim and all-rounder Egberto Gismonti are but a few. On the top of a huge recording industry, we're now a long way from the grassroots and the haunting flute music of the forest Indians.

NB Under each city, we give latest population figures, the CEP, which is the postal code, and DDD, the dialling code.

BRASILIA (1)

The purpose-built capital of Brazil, with its late 20th century design and its overflow communities.

Brasília On 21 April 1960, Rio de Janeiro ceased to be the Federal Capital of Brazil; as required by the Constitution, it was replaced by Brasília, 960 km away in the unpopulated uplands of Goiás, in the heart of the undeveloped Sertão. The official name for central Brasília is the Plano Piloto. Pop 411,000 (census); 1,600,000 (1992 est).

The new capital lies 1,150m above sea-level on undulating ground; the Federal District has an area of 5,814 sq km. The climate is mild and the humidity refreshingly low, but trying in dry weather. The noonday sun beats hard, but summer brings heavy rains and the air is usually cool by night.

The creation of an inland capital had been urged since the beginning of the last century, but it was finally brought into being after President Kubitschek came to power in 1956, when a competition for the best general plan was won by Professor Lúcio Costa, who laid out the city in the shape of a bent bow and arrow. (It is also described as a bird, or aeroplane, in flight.)

Along the curve of the bow are the residential areas made up of large six-storey apartment blocks, the "Super-Quadras". They lie on either side (E and W) of the "bow" (the Eixo Rodoviário) and are numbered according to their relation to the Eixo and their distance from the centre. Thus the 100s and 300s lie W of the Eixo and the 200s and 400s to the E; Quadras 302, 102, 202 and 402 are nearest the centre and 316, 116, 216 and 416 mark the end of the Plano Piloto. The numbering applies equally on either side of the centre, the two halves of the city being referred to as Asa Sul and Asa Norte (the N and S wings). Thus, for example, 116 Sul and 116 Norte are at the extreme opposite ends of the city. Each Super-Quadra houses 3,000 people and has a primary school and playgroup. Each group of four Super-Quadras should have a library, police station, club, supermarket and secondary school. All Quadras are separated by feeder roads, along which are the local shops. There are also a number of schools, parks and cinemas in the spaces between the Quadras (especially in Asa Sul), though not as systematically as was originally envisaged. On the outer side of the 300s and extending the length of the city is the Avenida W3 and on the outer side of the 400s is the Avenida L2, both of these being similarly divided into N and S according to the part of the city they are in.

Asa Sul is almost complete and Asa Norte is growing very fast, with standards of architecture and urbanization that promise to make it more attractive than Asa Sul in the near future. The main shopping areas, with more cinemas, restaurants and so on, are situated on either side of the old bus station. There are now several parks, or at least green areas. The private residential areas are W of the Super-Quadras, and on the other side of the lake.

At right angles to these residential areas is the "arrow", the 8-km long, 250-metre wide **Eixo Monumental**. At the tip of the arrow, as it were, is the **Praça dos Tres Poderes**, with the Congress buildings, the Palácio do Planalto (the President's office), the Palácio da Justiça and the Panteão Tancredo Neves (a memorial to the president-elect who died in 1985 before taking office). The Cathedral and the Ministry buildings line the Esplanada dos Ministérios, W of the Praça. Where the bow and arrow intersect is the city bus terminal (Rodoviária), with the cultural and recreational centres and commercial and financial areas on either side. There is a sequence of zones westward along the shaft of the arrow; a hotel centre, a radio city, an area for fairs and circuses, a centre for sports, the **Praça Municipal** (with the municipal offices in the Palácio do Buriti and, lastly (where the nock of the arrow would be) the combined new bus and railway station (Rodoferroviária) with the industrial area nearby. The most impressive buildings are all by Oscar Niemeyer, Brazil's leading architect.

The main N-S road (Eixo Rodoviário), in which fast-moving traffic is segregated, follows the curve of the bow; the radial road is along the line of the arrow—intersections are avoided by means of underpasses and cloverleaves. Motor and pedestrian traffic is segregated in the residential areas.

The **Palácio da Alvorada**, the President's residence, which is open to visitors (1500-1630, free), is close to the lake. The 80-km drive along the road round the lake to the dam is attractive. There are spectacular falls below the dam in the rainy season. Between the Praça dos Tres Poderes and the lake are sites for various recreations, including golf, fishing and yacht clubs, and an acoustic shell for shows in the open air. The airport is at the eastern end of the lake. Some 395 hectares between the lake and the northern residential area (Asa Norte) are reserved for the Universidade de Brasília, founded in 1961. South of the university area, the Avenida das Nações runs from the Palácio da Alvorada along the lake to join the road from the airport to the centre. Along it are found all the principal embassies. Also in this area is the attractive vice-presidential residence, the **Palácio do Jaburu**, not open to visitors. This area is almost completed and very scenic.

Sightseeing A fine initial view of the city may be had from the **television tower**, which has a free observation platform at 75m up; also bar and souvenir shop; closed for repairs early 1995. A general impression can be gained in a day by bus or taxi tour—don't try walking much unless fit and fairly impervious to heat. This impression is best gained at weekends when the city is quieter, though then there are fewer buses to move you around (some say the city is "totally dead" at

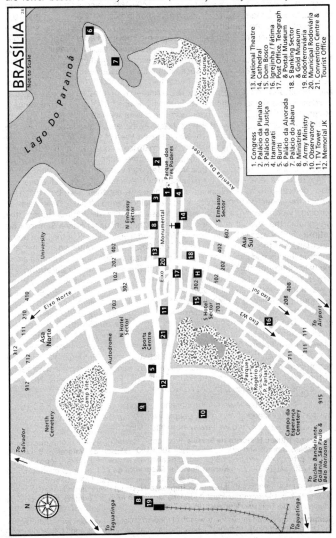

BRASÍLIA
Not to Scale

Lago Do Paranoá

1. Congress
2. Palácio da Planalto
3. Palácio da Justiça
4. Itamarati
5. Buriti
6. Palácio da Alvorada
7. Palácio do Jabaru
8. Ministries
9. Army Ministry
10. Observatory
11. TV Tower
12. Memorial JK
13. National Theatre
14. Cathedral
15. Dom Bosco
16. Igrejinha / Fátima
17. Post Office, Telegraph & Postal Museum
18. Banking Sector & Gold Museum
19. Rodoferroviária
20. Municipal Rodoviária
21. Convention Centre & Tourist Office

weekends). The city can also be seen at night by taking the Alvorada circular bus from the old Rodoviária. Bus maps are not available although buses are plentiful; each bus stop has a list of the services that stop there, but you still need to know which one you require. It is worth telephoning addresses away from the centre to ask how to get there. An urban railway, Metrô, is under construction.

Congress is open to visitors Mon-Fri 0930-1130 and 1400-1700 (take your passport), guides free of charge (in English 1400-1600), and visitors may attend debates when Congress is in session (Fri morning). Excellent city views from the 10th floor in Annex 3. The **Planalto** may be visited on special occasions only. Opposite the Planalto is the Supreme Court building, **Supremo Tribunal Federal**. The marvellous building of the Ministry of Foreign Affairs, the **Itamarati**, has modern paintings and furniture and beautiful water gardens (guided visits Mon-Fri at 1600, free). Opposite the Itamarati is the **Palácio de Justiça**, with artificial cascades between its concrete columns, visiting hours Mon-Fri, 0900-1130, 1500-1700. The **Catedral Metropolitana**, on the Esplanada dos Ministérios, a most spectacular circular building in the shape of the crown of thorns, is open 0900-1700. Three angels, sculpted by Alfredo Ceschiatti, hang from the ceiling; see also the Ceschiatti statues of the evangelists outside and the baptistery in the shape of a large pebble. The outdoor carrillon was a gift from the King of Spain. West of the TV tower on Avenida W3 Sul, at Quadra 702, is the Sanctuary of **Dom Bosco**, a square building with narrow windows filled with blue glass mosaics, purple at the four corners; the light inside is most beautiful. The **Templo da Boa Vontade**, Setor Garagem Sul 915, lotes 75/76, T 245-1070, is a seven-faced pyramid topped by the world's largest crystal, a peaceful place dedicated to all philosophies and religions (to get there take bus 151 from outside the Centro do Convenções or on Eixo Sul to Centro Médico). Other religious buildings worth seeing are the **Igreja Nossa Senhora de Fátima** church (the Igrejinha) in the Asa Sul at Quadras 307-308, the **Santuário Nossa Senhora de Fátima**, the "orange caterpillar" on Av W5, Quadra 906, a little S of the Dom Bosco sanctuary, and the chapel (**Ermida**) of Dom Bosco, on the other side of the lake opposite the Alvorada, though the site is not well maintained. Some 15 km out along the Belo Horizonte road is the small wooden house, known as **"O Catetinho"**, in which President Kubitschek stayed in the late 1950s during his visits to the city when it was under construction; it is open to visitors and most interesting. A permanent memorial to Juscelino Kubitschek, the **"Memorial JK"**, containing his tomb and his car, together with a lecture hall and exhibits, is worth visiting (open daily 0900-1800, entry US$0.50, has toilets and *lanchonete*). The **Quartel-General do Exército**, Brazilian Army headquarters, designed by Oscar Niemeyer, is interesting; the **Monumental Parade Stand** has unique and mysterious acoustic characteristics (the complex is N of the Eixo Monumental, between the "Memorial JK" and the Rodoferroviária). There are remarkable stained glass panels, each representing a state of the Federation, on the ground floor of the Caixa Econômica Federal. **NB** Town clothes (not shorts or minis) should be worn when visiting all the above.

Only light industry is allowed in the city and its population was limited to 500,000; this has been exceeded and more people live in a number of shanty towns, with minimal services, located well away from the main city.

Museums Museu Histórico de Brasília Praça dos Tres Poderes, really a hollow monument, with tablets, photos and videos; open daily 1000-1800. **Museu de Valores** at the Banco Central exhibits old and new notes and coins and gold prospecting in Brazil; open Tues-Fri 1000-1730, Sat 1400-1730. **Museu Postal e Telegráfico da ECT**, Setor Comercial Sul, Ed Apolo, quadra 13 bloco A, stamps, telegraphic equipment, etc. Entry, US$0.30, Tues-Fri 0900-1800, Sat 0900-1300. **Museu da Imprensa Nacional**, Setor de Indústrias Gráficas, Quadra 6; bus 152 from municipal Rodoviária: admission free. Old printing and embossing equipment, etc. Open working days 0800-1700.

Sculptures Brasília is famous for its wealth of modern sculpture. Examples are: "Cultura" (on the University campus), "Meteoro" (above the Itamarati water-mirror), and "Os Candongos"

(The Warriors, in front of the Planalto)—all by Bruno Giorgi; "A Justiça" (in front of Palácio da Justiça), the four evangelists in front of the Cathedral and "As Banhistas" (The Water-Nymphs, above the Alvorada water-mirror)—all by Alfredo Ceschiatti; "Rito dos Ritmos" (Alvorada gardens), by Maria Martins; and the beautiful "Sereia" (Mermaid) in front of the Navy Ministry on the Esplanada dos Ministérios. A statue of Juscelino Kubitschek stands above the "Memorial JK". A short distance W of here is a huge wooden cross marking the site of the first Mass said in Brasília (3 May 1957), at the city's highest point.

Ceremonies The guard is changed ceremonially at the Palácio do Planalto on Tues, 0830 and 1730. The President attends if he is available.

Local Holidays Ash Wed; Maundy Thur, half-day; 8 Dec (Immaculate Conception); Christmas Eve.

Telephone code and Postal address CEP 70000, DDD 061.

Hotels Prices include breakfast, but 10% must be added. Weekend discounts of 30% are often available, but must be asked for. In the Southern Hotel Sector: **L2** *Nacional*, Quadra 1 bloco A, T 321-7575, F 223-9213, 4-star, pool; **A1** *Bristol*, Quadra 4 bloco F, T 321-6162, F 321-2690, 3-star, pool; **A1** *Carlton*, Quadra 5 bloco G, T 224-8819, F 226-8109, 4-star, pool; **A2** *Brasília Imperial*, Quadra 3 bloco E, T 321-8747, F 223-7252, 2-star, deposit for room requested, good breakfast, motel-style; **A2** *Riviera*, Quadra 3 bloco I, T 225-1880, F 224-8115, 3-star; **A3** *Planalto*, Quadra 3 bloco A, T 322-1828, F 225-1406, rooms in front noisy, city tours.

In the Northern Hotel Sector: **L2** *Eron Brasília*, Quadra 5 bloco A, T 321-1777, F 226-2689, 5-star; **A2** *Aracoara*, Quadra 5 bloco C, T 321-9222, F 226-9067, 4 star. All reached from the same access road are: **A2** *Bittar Plaza*, Quadra 2 bloco M, T 225-7077, F 225-1406; **A2** *Diplomat*, Quadra 2 bloco L, T 225-2010, good; **A3** *El Pilar*, Quadra 3 bloco F, T 224-5915, a/c or fan, TV, friendly; **A2** *Aristus*, Quadra 2 bloco O, T 223-8675, good, a/c, TV, phone, money exchange, small restaurant; **A2** *Byblos*, Quadra 3 bloco E, T 223-1570; **A2** *Casablanca*, Quadra 3 lote A, T 321-8586, some rooms noisy; and **C-D** *Mirage*, Quadra 2 lote N, T 225-7150, fan, good, clean, good value. Moderately-priced hotels can be found in the Northern Hotel Sector only. At weekends discounts can be obtained, worth bargaining.

D *Cury's Solar* (Pousada), Neusa Batista Ribeiro, Av W3 Sul, HIGS707, bloco L, casa 15, T 243-6252, cramped but popular (take bus 107 from Rodoviária). Teresa Tasso, SQS413-"K"-306, T 243-5251 or 347-4601, offers accommodation in an apartment in the Asa Sul at US$35 for the flat (sleeps 5, kitchen, bath, laundry facilities), excellent value, Teresa gives city tours for US$40 and will collect you at the airport if you phone in advance (bus to flat from centre, 5 mins). Rooms to let near the TV tower, D with bath, cheaper without, from Getúlio Valente, warmly rec, Av W3 Sul, HIGS 703, Bl.O-C 61/67, good, cheap meals available; Portuguese speakers, T 226-8507/9639 and Getúlio will pick you up. Otherwise, turn right off Av W3 Sul between 703 and 702, then take first left (an unpaved driveway).

The hotels outside the city in **Taguatinga** (take 102 or 106 bus, EIXO, or 304 from new Rodoviária) and Núcleo Bandeirante, though fairly basic, tend to be recommended for cheapness, but reported very difficult to get single rooms. Núcleo Bandeirante: **D** *Hotel Rio de Janeiro*, Av Dom Bosco 720, lt 8, T 552-1295, just about OK for "young and hearty" but many mosquitoes; **D** *São Judas Tadeu*, 2 Av lt 1605, T 552-2068, noisy, clean but cockroaches, poor breakfast; Taguatinga is pleasanter than the Núcleo, which is full of shanties; there are many cheap hotels and restaurants of a reasonable standard, for example, **E** *Solar*, C 7, lt13, sobreloja, T 563-5660, near Jumbo Supermarket, basic and clean; **C** *Colorado*, Setor Hoteleira, Projeção B, T 561-3500, with bath, fridge, TV, good, in the centre; **D** *Pousada Brasília*, next door at Projeção L, T 562-5055, with bath and breakfast; **D** *Globo*, CNB4, lote 1, T 561-1716, without breakfast, friendly, basic. Bus "Estrutural" from Brasília Rodoferroviária to Taguatinga Rodoviária where you change, without extra charge to 700 bus which passes, in order: **D** *Camará*, QNE 16, lt 8, T 561-2597 (hourly rentals also); **D** *Palace*, CNB 11, clean, basic, hot water, communal shower; **D** *Taguatinga*, C 9, lt 10, T 351-1191, by roundabout near clocktower, about 10 mins from Rodoviária, hot showers, TV, back rooms are quieter, clothes-washing facilities, used by prostitutes. Bus 700 or 800 (marked "Eixo") goes from opp Jumbo Supermarket in Taguatinga to old Rodoviária in Brasília. Very cheap accommodation in Formosa (see p 356).

Youth Hostels Associação do Distrito Federal de Albergues de Juventude, in Centro de Convenções, Mon-Fri 1100-1700, T 321-3318, ext 222/247/249.

Camping The city's main site is 2 km out, by the Centro Esportivo, near the motor-racing track, with room for 3,100 campers, mixed reports. Take bus 109 (infrequent) from municipal Rodoviária. Agua Mineral Parque, 6 km NW of city, direct buses only at weekend; US$1 pp, mineral pool, showers. Associação Brasileira de Camping (Edif Márcia, 12th floor, Setor

Comercial Sul, T 225-8768) has two sites: one at Km 19 on the Belo Horizonte road and one 25 km NE of Brasília at Sobradinho. Camping Clube do Brasil has a site at Itiquira waterfall, 100 km NE of the city, near Formosa; information from Edif Maristela, room 1214, Setor Comercial Sul, T 223-6561. There is a Forestry Commission site 10 km out of Brasília on the BR-041. There are signs to the sites. "Wild" camping is possible.

Restaurants The Southern Hotel Sector tends to have more restaurants than the N; there are many cheap places on Av W3 Sul, eg at Blocos 502 and 506. At weekends few restaurants in central Brasília are open. The following are classified by their speciality:

International Cuisine: *Aeroporto*, terrace of international airport, very pleasant, food reported very good. Most of the big hotels' restaurants. *Restaurant Gaf*, Centro Gilberto Salomão, Lago Sul (very good, especially meat, but expensive).

For Brazilian food, there are several churrascarias (barbecues), for example *Churrascaria do Lago*, SHTN, Conj 1-A, by Palácio da Alvorada; a number of Brazilian restaurants and some serving Amazonian food.

Seafood/Fish: *Panela de Barro*, Galeria Nova Ouvidor, Setor Comercial Sul, Quadra 5; and others.

For European cuisine: Portuguese: *Cachopa*, Galeria Nova Ouvidor, loja 127; Spanish: *O Espanhol*, Av W3 Sul, quadra 506, bloco A; French: *Le Français*, Av W3 Sul, quadra 404, bloco B; *La Chaumière*, Av W3 Sul, quadra 408, bloco A. Italian/Pizzerias: *Kazebre 13*, Av W3 Sul, quadra 504; *Roma*, Av W3 Sul, quadras 501 and 511, good, quite cheap.

Chinese: *China*, Av W3 Sul, quadra 103 bloco D; *New China*, Av W3 Sul 209 bloco A (the best according to Chinese diplomats); *Fon Min*, Av W3 Sul 405; *Fon Pin*, Av W3 Sul 402; Japanese: *Nipon*, Av W3 Sul 413 and at 112. Also *El Hadj*, in Hotel Torre Palace, Setor Hoteleiro Norte, quadra 4 bloco A, Arabic, very good.

Macrobiotic/Vegetarian: *Coisas da Terra*, Av W3 Norte, quadra 703; *Boa Saúde*, Av W3 Norte Quadra 702, Ed Brasília Rádio Center, open Sun-Fri 0800-2000, lunch 1100-1400.

Local: *Bom Demais*, Av W3 Norte, Quadra 706, comfortable, inexpensive, serving fish, beef and rice, etc, live music at weekends (cover charge US$0.50).

Pubs There are two "English style" bars: *Gates Pub*, Av W3 Sul 403 and *London Tavern*, Av W3 Sul 409. The *Grenada* bar near the *Hotel Nacional* (pedestrian area across road, 250m away) has good pavement atmosphere in early evening.

Snack Bars (ie those serving *prato feito* or *comercial*, cheap set meals) can be found all over the city, especially on Av W3 and in the Setor Comercial Sul. Other good bets are the Conjunto Nacional and the Conjunto Venâncio, two shopping/office complexes on either side of the municipal bus station (rodoviária), which itself provides the best coffee and *pásteis* in town (bottom departure level). Tropical fruit flavour ice cream can be found in various parlours, eg Av W3 Norte 302. Freshly made fruit juices in all bars.

Banks and Exchange Lloyds Bank, Av W3 Sul, quadra 506, bloco B; First National Bank of Boston, Setor Comercial Sul, quadra 6 bloco A; Citibank, Edifício Citibank, Setor Comercial Sul; Banco Francês e Brasileiro, Av W3 Sul, quadra 506; local banks. Open 0930-1630. Foreign currency (but not always Amex cheques) can be exchanged at these banks and at the branches of: Banco Regional de Brasília and Banco do Brasil, Setor Bancário Sul, latter also at airport. Banco Econômico, Setor Comercial Sul, Subterraneo (currency and Amex cheques), 1045-1630; American Express, Buriti Turismo, CLS 402 Bloco A, Lojas 27/33, T 225-2686. Diners Club office, Av W3 Norte 502. Mastercard, for cash against a card, SCRN 502, bl B, lojas 30 e 31, Asa Norte. Good exchange rates at *Hotel Nacional*. Good exchange rates from hotels with "exchange-turismo" sign.

Cultural Institutes British Council: SCRN 708/709 B1 F No 1/3, T 272-3060, F 272-3455. Cultura Inglesa, SEPS 709/908 Conj B, T 243-3065. American Library: Casa Thomas Jefferson, Av W4 Sul, quadra 706, T 243-6588. Aliança Francesa, Sul Entrequadra 707-907, Bloco A, T 242-7500; Instituto Cultural Goethe, Edifício Dom Bosco, Setor Garagem Sul 902, Lote 73, Bloco C, T 224-6773, Mon-Fri, 0800-1200, also 1600-2000, Mon, Wed, Thur.

Embassies British: SES, Quadra 801, Conjunto K (with **British Commonwealth Chamber of Commerce**), or Av das Nações, Caixa Postal 070586, T 225-2710. USA: SES, Av das Nações 3, T 321-7272. Australian: Caixa Postal 11-1256, SHIS QI-09, Conj 16, Casa 1, T 248-5569 (in residential district, S of the lake). Canadian: SES, Av das Nações 16, T 223-7665. Danish, Av das Nações 26, CP 07-0484, T 242-8188, open 0900-1200, 1400-1700. German: SES, Av das Nações 25, T 243-7466. Netherlands: SES, Av das Nações 5, T 321-4769. Swiss: SES, Av das Nações 41, T 244-5500; Austrian: SES, Av das Nações 40, T 243-3111; Finnish: SES, Av das Nações, suite 27, T 242-8555; Swedish: Av des Nações 29, Caixa Postal 07-0419, T 243-1444. Venezuela: SES, Av das Nações 13, T 223-9325; Guyana: SDS, Edifício Venâncio III, 4th Floor, sala 410/404, T 224-9229.

Electric Current 220 volts, 60 cycles.

Entertainment There are three auditoria of the Teatro Nacional, the Sala Villa-Lobos (1,300 seats), the Sala Martins Pena (450), and the Sala Padre José Maurício (120); the building is in the shape of an Aztec pyramid.

The Federal District authorities have two theatres, the Galpão and Galpãozinho, between Quadra 308 Sul and Av W3 Sul. Concerts are given at the Escola Parque (Quadras 507-508 Sul), the Ginásio Presidente Médici (Eixo Monumental, near TV tower), the Escola de Música (Av L2 Sul, Quadra 602) and the outdoor Concha Acústica (edge of lake in the Setor Hotelero Norte). Planetarium, on the Eixo next to the TV tower, gives shows Sat and Sun at 1600 and 1700.

There are 15 cinemas in the Plano Piloto; programmes are available daily by dialling 139 on the telephone, entrance is half price on Wed.

Information about entertainment etc is available in two daily papers, *Jornal de Brasília* and *Correio Brasiliense*. Any student card (provided it has a photograph) will get you into the cinema/theatre/concert hall for half price. Ask for "uma meia" at the box office.

Nightclubs in Conjunto Venâncio; in Centro Gilberto Salomão and in the main hotels.

Post Office Poste restante, Central Correio, 70001; SBN-Cj 03, BL-A, Ed Sede da ECT, the central office is in the Setor Hotelero Sul, between *Hotels Nacional* and *St Paul*. Another post office is in Ed Brasília Rádio, Av 3 Norte.

Shopping There are eight big shopping complexes, including the vast *Conjunto Nacional* on the N side of the rodoviária, the *Conjunto Venâncio* on the S side, the *Centro Venâncio 2000* at the beginning of Av W3 Sul, the *Centro Venâncio 3000* in the Setor Comercial Norte, *Parkshopping* and the *Carrefour* hypermarket just off the exit to Guará, 12 km from centre. For fine jewellery, *H Stern* has branches in the *Nacional* and *Carlton* Hotels and at the Conjunto Nacional and Parkshopping. The embassy sector is good for low-priced, high quality men's wear. For handicrafts try *Galeria dos Estados* (which runs underneath the *eixo* from Setor Comercial Sul to Setor Bancário Sul, 10 mins walk from municipal Rodoviária, S along Eixo Rodoviário Sul) with shops selling handicrafts from all the Brazilian states; for Amerindian handicrafts, *Artíndia* in the bus station and at the airport. Dried flowers (typical of the region) outside the Cathedral (but not always). There is a *feira hippy* at the base of the TV tower every Sat, Sun and holiday: leather goods, wood carvings, jewellery, bronzes. English books (good selection) at *Livraria Sodiler* in Conjunto Nacional and at the airport.

Tourist Offices at the Centro de Convenções (Detur, helpful, good map of Brasília, open to public 1300-1800); small stand at rodoferroviária, friendly but not very knowledgeable (open 24 hrs, every day). Tourist office at the Air Terminal is on the international arrival side only, will book hotels, generally helpful; French and English spoken. Detur publishes a book called *Brasília, Coração Brasileiro*, which is full of practical information. Tours by bus (US$12-20), may be booked at the airport or *Hotel Nacional*: check that you will be taken back to the airport if you have a flight to catch. Touring Club do Brasil, on Eixo, has maps (members only).

Tours A good and cheap way of seeing Brasília is by taking bus rides from the municipal rodoviária at the centre: the destinations are clearly marked. The circular bus route 106 goes right round the city's perimeter (you can also take buses 108 or 131). If you go around the lake by bus, you must change at the Paranoá dam; to or from Paranoá Norte take bus 101, "Rodoviária", and to and from Sul, bus 100, bypassing the airport. Cheaper tours, from 1300-1700, start from the downtown hotel area and municipal rodoviária. Many hotels arrange city tours. All tour operators have their offices in the shopping arcade of the *Hotel Nacional*; Toscana has been recommended as cheap and good. Presmic Turismo, Galeria do Hotel Nacional, lojas 33/34, T 225-5515, offers full-, half-day and nighttime tours (0845, 1400 and 1930 respectively). Kubitschek Turismo (Lucas Milhomens—speaks English), T 347-1494, recommended for city tour and information. Some tours have been criticised as too short, others that the guides speak poor English, and for nighttime tours, the flood lighting is inadequate on many buildings. Tour guides meet arriving air passengers at the airport, offering city tours, ending at a destination of your choice (3-4 hrs, English commentary, inexpensive but negotiate)—a convenient way of getting to your hotel if you have heavy baggage. Teresa Tasso, T 243-5251, rec.

Immigration Office at end of W3 Sul.

Car Hire About 9 agencies, including Budget, Hertz, Locarauto.

Air Services Varig to Rio and São Paulo regular service (1½ hrs in both cases); daily flights to other main cities; regional services to the interior of Goiás, São Paulo, Pará, etc. Varig flies daily to Manaus direct, 2½ hrs. Varig night flight to Manaus with 30% discount at 2340, arrives

0140. Very few services for individual travellers. Airline offices are in the *Hotel Nacional* building. Bus 102 or 118 to airport, regular, US$0.65, ½ hr. Taxi is US$10 after bargaining, worth it. Left luggage facilities at airport (tokens for lockers, US$0.50). Airport tax US$1.25.

Roads From Saída Sul (the southern end of the Eixo) the BR-040/050 goes to Cristalina where it divides; the BR-040 continues to Belo Horizonte and Rio de Janeiro, the BR-050 to Uberlândia and São Paulo (both paved).

Also from Saída Sul, the BR-060 to Anápolis, Goiânia and Cuiabá; from Anápolis the BR-153 (Belém-Brasília) heads N to Belém (paved—for a description of this road, **see p 577**) and from Goiânia the BR-153 goes S through the interior of the states of São Paulo and Paraná (also paved).

From Saída Norte (the northern end of the Eixo) the BR-020 goes N to **Formosa** (1½ hrs by frequent buses from Brasília, **E** *Hotel Mineiro* and one other, G, clean and friendly; cheap restaurants), Barreiras, and after Barreiras on the BR-242 (all paved) to Salvador and Fortaleza. The BR020 is in good condition for 120 km. At Alvorado do Norte (130 km) there are cheap but very basic hotels. *Posse* (295 km) is picturesque: **Hotels**: **F** *Posse*; **F** *Hoki Mundial*, friendly; **E** *Rex*, all in Av Padre Trajeiro. The road is slow with many potholes until Barreiras.

Road distances in km: Belém, 2,120; Campo Grande, 1,134; Corumbá, 1,531; Cuiabá, 1,133; Foz do Iguaçu, 1,573; Goiânia, 209; Manaus, 3,490; Porto Alegre, 2,027; Recife, 2,220; Rio, 1,148; Salvador, 1,531; São Paulo, 1,015.

Buses To Rio: 17 hrs, 6 *comuns* (US$38) and 3 *leitos* (about US$74) daily. To **São Paulo**: 16 hrs, 7 *comuns* (about US$24) and 2 *leitos* (about US$48) daily (Rápido Federal rec). To **Belo Horizonte**: 12 hrs, 9 *comuns* (US$23) and 2 *leitos* (US$46) daily. To **Belém**: 36 hrs, at 0715, 1200, 1915, 2400 (US$66, Trans Brasília, buses poorly maintained, but no alternative), *leito* (US$132) Tues, Wed and Sat. To **Recife**: 40 hrs. To **Salvador**: 24 hrs, daily at 0900, 1200 and 2100 (US$45). Manaus via Porto Velho and Cuiabá involves several changes, taking up to 6 days (road is good as far as Porto Velho). All major destinations served. Bus tickets for major companies are sold in a subsidiary office in Taguatinga, Centro Oeste, C8, Lotes 1 and 2, Loja 1; and at the city bus terminal. Left luggage, post office (0800-1700, Sat 0800-1200), telephone and telegram facilities available at new bus terminal (rodoferroviária) beside the railway station, from which long-distance buses leave; bus 131 between rodoviária, the terminal for city buses, and rodoferroviária, US$1; taxi rodoferroviária to Setor Hotelero Norte, US$7. The waiting room at the rodoferroviária is very comfortable, but one is not permitted to sleep stretched out. There are showers (US$0.50). Both bus stations have large luggage lockers.

Of the seven *cidades satélites* that contain between them over half the Federal District's population, five are new and two (Brazlândia and Planaltina) are based on pre-existing settlements. **Planaltina**, 40 km N of the Plano Piloto via Saída Norte, was originally a settlement on the colonial pack route from the mines of Goiás and Cuiabá to the coast. The old part of the town (50,000 inhabitants) still contains many colonial buildings. There are two good *churrascarias* on the main street and it is a good place for a rural Sun lunch. 5 km outside Planaltina is the Pedra Fundamental, the foundation stone laid by President Epitácio Pessoa in 1922 to mark the site originally chosen for the new capital.

Just before Planaltina, at Km 30 on the road from Brasília, lies the point known as **Águas Emendadas**: from the same point spring two streams that flow in opposite directions to form part of the two great river systems—the Amazon and the Plate. Permission from the biological institute in Brasília is now required to visit the site. Continuing along the same road (BR-020), at Km 70 is the town of Formosa (see above). Some 20 km N of the town is the Itiquira waterfall (158m high). From the top are spectacular views and the pools at the bottom offer good bathing. It is crowded at weekends. There are four smaller falls in the area. Camping is possible. To get there take the road into the centre of Formosa and follow the signs or ask. It is not possible to get by bus to the Itiquira falls from Brasília in one day; the only bus from Formosa to Itiquira leaves at 0730 and returns at 1700.

In the other direction (S) is the Cristalina waterfall; take the BR-040 (Belo Horizonte road) and at Km 104 take a left turn along a dirt road just after the highway police post. The waterfall is 11 km along this road. The town of **Cristalina** (pop 24,900) is famous for its semi-precious stones, which can be bought cheaply in local shops. The panning and mining sites amid magnificent rock formations are about 6 km away, an interesting excursion. **D** *Hotel Goyás*, R da Saudade 41, fan, fridge, OK. Small municipal museum R 21 de Abril 156, 0800-1100, 1300-1700, except Tues.

Nearer Brasília, good bathing can be had at Água Mineral, two mineral pools 10 km from the centre of the city. The newer pool is the better; turn right immediately after entering the main gate.

Northwest of Brasília, but only 15 mins by car from the centre is the **Parque Nacional de**

Brasília (about 28,000 hectares), founded in 1961 to conserve the flora and fauna of the Federal Capital. Only a portion of the park is open to the public without a permit. There is a swimming pool fed by clear river water, a snack bar and a series of trails through gallery forest (popular with joggers in early am and at weekends). The rest of the park is rolling grassland, gallery forest and *cerrado* vegetation. Large mammals include tapir, maned wolf and pampas deer; birdwatching is good (especially Brasilia Tapaculo, Horned Sungem, Yellow-faced parrot, Least Nighthawk). Contact Focus Tours, Belo Horizonte (**p 402**) for birding and nature tours. For information, contact Delegacia Estadual do Ibama, Av W3 Norte, Quadra 513, Edif Imperador, rooms 301-320, or T 233-4055/234-9057.

For information on the State of Goiás, which surrounds the Federal District, **see p 574**.

STATE OF RIO DE JANEIRO (2)

The world-renowned Rio, with its beautiful location, carnival and much more besides (not all of it delightful), plus the hill and beach resorts nearby.

The State of Rio de Janeiro covers 43,305 sq km (the size of Denmark) and in 1991 had a population of 12.6 million, 88% of whom lived in metropolitan areas. The State is Brazil's second-largest industrial producer.

Rio de Janeiro is on the S-western shore of Guanabara Bay, 24 km long and from 3 to 16 km wide. The setting is magnificent. The city sweeps twenty kilometres along a narrow alluvial strip between the mountains and the sea. The combination of a dark blue sea, studded with rocky islands, with the tumbling wooded mountains and expanses of bare grey rock which surround the city is very impressive. Brazilians say: God made the world in six days; the seventh he devoted to Rio (pronounced Heeoo by locals). God's work is now under threat from too many high-rise buildings and failure to maintain or clean the city adequately.

The best known of these rocky masses are the Pão de Açúcar (Sugar Loaf, 396m), the highest peak of a low chain of mountains on the fringe of the harbour, and the Corcovado (Hunchback), a jagged peak rising 710m behind the city. There are other peaks, including Tijuca (1,012m), the tallest point in the foreground, and 50 km away rise the strangely shaped Serra dos Órgãos.

Rio has one of the healthiest climates in the tropics. Trade winds cool the air. Jun, Jul and Aug are the coolest months with temperatures ranging from 22°C (18° in a cold spell) to 32°C on a sunny day at noon. Dec to Mar is hotter, from 32°C to 42°C. Sunstroke is uncommon, but humidity is high. It is important, especially for children, to guard against dehydration in summer by drinking as much liquid as possible. Oct to Mar is the rainy season, and the annual rainfall is about 1,120 mm. The population in 1991 was estimated at 5,336,180.

History The Portuguese navigator, Gonçalo Coelho, arrived at what is now Rio de Janeiro on 1 January 1502, but it was first settled by the French, who, under the Huguenot Admiral Veillegaignon, occupied Lage Island on 10 November 1555, but later transferred to Sergipe Island (now Villegaignon), where they built the fort of Colligny. The fort has been demolished to make way for the Naval College (Escola Naval), and the island itself, since the narrow channel was filled up, has become a part of the mainland. In Jan 1567, Mem de Sá, third governor of Brazil, defeated the French in a sea battle and transferred the Portuguese settlement to the São Januário hill—the Esplanada do Castelo covers the site today. Though constantly attacked by Indians, the new city grew rapidly, and when King Sebastião divided Brazil into two provinces, Rio was chosen capital of the southern captaincies. Salvador became sole capital again in 1576, but Rio again became the southern capital in 1608 and the seat of a bishopric. There was a further French incursion in 1710-11.

Rio de Janeiro was by now becoming the leading city in Brazil. On 27 January 1763, it became the seat of the Viceroy. After independence, in 1834, it was declared capital of the Empire, and remained the capital for 125 years.

Points of Interest Two of the main streets are particularly impressive. The Avenida Rio Branco, nearly 2 km long and 33m wide, is intersected by the city's main artery, the Avenida Presidente Vargas, $4\frac{1}{2}$ km long and over 90m wide, which starts at the waterfront, divides to embrace the famous Candelária church, then crosses the Avenida Rio Branco in a magnificent straight stretch past the Central do Brasil railway station, with its imposing clock tower, until finally it incorporates the palm-lined, canal-divided avenue formerly known as the Avenida Mangue. The Avenida Rio Branco is lined with ornate buildings, including the Brazilian Academy, National Art Museum, National Library, Municipal Council Chamber, and Municipal Theatre. The R do Ouvidor, crossing the Avenida Rio Branco half way along its length, contains the centre's principal shops. Other shopping streets are the RR Gonçalves Dias, Sete de Setembro, Uruguaiana, Assembléia, and also the arcade running from Av Rio Branco to the R Gonçalves Dias. The most stylish shops, however, are to be found in Ipanema, Leblon and in the various large shopping centres in the city (see under **Shopping** below). (The quality of souvenirs is higher in Ipanema and Leblon than in the centre, and higher still in São Paulo.) The Av Beira Mar, with its royal palms, bougainvilleas and handsome buildings, coasting the Botafogo and Flamengo beaches (too polluted for bathing), makes a splendid drive; its scenery is shared by the urban motorway along the beach over reclaimed land (the Aterro), which leads to Botafogo and through two tunnels to Copacabana, described on **p 377**. Some of the finest modern architecture is to be found along the Avenida Chile, such as the Petrobrás and National Housing Bank buildings, and the new Cathedral, dedicated in Nov 1976. There are many fine trees in the city. The photogenic Abricot de Macaco (Monkey's Apricot) has multi-coloured flowers, and large ball-shaped seeds hanging from the trunk, it originally came from the Guianas.

Carnival Carnival in Rio is spectacular. On the Fri before Shrove Tues, the mayor of Rio symbolically hands the keys of the city to King Momo, a sequinned Lord of Misrule, signifying the start of a five-day party. Imagination runs riot, the main avenues are colourfully lit, full of people, and children wear fancy dress. Special bandstands throughout the city are manned for public street-dancing (see local press for where and when) and organized carnival groups, the *blocos carnavalescos*, are everywhere, dancing, drumming and singing (among others, look out for the entertaining Banda da Ipanema, a parade of transvestites, most evenings in that suburb). There are numerous samba schools in Rio. There are 5 divisions. The first three parade in the Sambódromo; on the Thur, the better of the lower-division schools parade while final sound and lighting checks are made. Group 1 (16 schools) parades on Fri and Sat, the 16 Special Group schools on Sun and Mon; 8 schools per night. The order of appearance is determined by lottery, so both days are good. 12 Group 2 schools parade on Shrove Tues. Each school parades with 3,000-5,000 participants, divided into 40 sections and as many as 30 floats. Each school has 90 mins to parade, and will lose points if it takes longer. The 10 selected winners (5 each from the Special Group and Group 1) perform a celebratory parade the following Sat night at the Sambódromo. The third and fourth divisions parade on Av Rio Branco (less spectacular, but free).

Each school chooses a theme, then composes a samba, and designs costumes and floats to fit it. All the schools are judged on each element, the best ones being promoted to a higher division, those with fewest points being relegated, as in a football league. Competition is intense. For the winners there is a monetary prize, funded by the entrance fees. It may be possible to join a Samba school if you are in Rio prior to Carnival (see below).

The Carnival parade is by no means created as a tourist attraction; it is the culmination of months of intense activity by community groups, mostly in the city's poorest districts. To understand the traditions of the schools, the meanings of the different parts of the parade, and carnival as a whole, visit the carnival museum

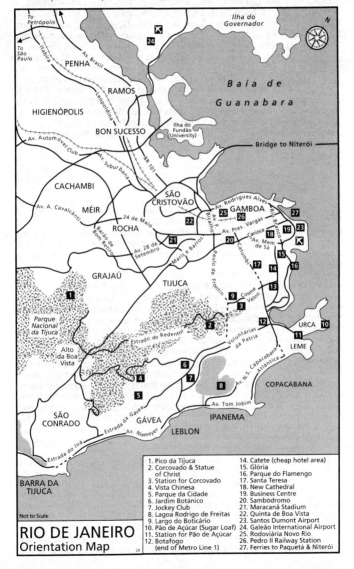

To Petrópolis
To São Paulo

PENHA
RAMOS
HIGIENÓPOLIS
BON SUCESSO
Av. Brasil
Leopoldina
Itabira
Av. Automóvel Club
Av. Suburbana
BR 101

Ilha do Governador
Baía de Guanabara
Ilha do Fundão (University)
Bridge to Niterói

CACHAMBI
MÉIR
ROCHA
GRAJAÚ
Av. A. Cavalcánti
Barão de Bom Retiro
24 de Maio
Av. 28 de Setembro
Marîs e Barros
Paulo de Frontin

SÃO CRISTOVÃO
Av. Rodrigues Alves
Av. Pres. Vargas
Catumbi

25 GAMBOA
26
22
21
20
27
19 23
18
15
16
14
13
17

Carioca
Rio Branco
Av. Mem de Sá

Parque Nacional da Tijuca
TIJUCA
Estrada do Redentor
Alto da Boa Vista
Cosme Velho
Voluntárias da Patria

1
2
9
3
12
URCA 10
LEME 11

6
4
7
5
8
COPACABANA
Av. N.S. Capacabana
Av. Atlantica

SÃO CONRADO
GÁVEA
LEBLON
IPANEMA
Estrada da Gávea
Av. Niemeyer
Av. Tom Jobim

BARRA DA TIJUCA
Estrada do Joá

Not to Scale

RIO DE JANEIRO
Orientation Map

1. Pico da Tijuca
2. Corcovado & Statue of Christ
3. Station for Corcovado
4. Vista Chinesa
5. Parque da Cidade
6. Jardim Botánico
7. Jockey Club
8. Lagoa Rodrigo de Freitas
9. Largo do Boticário
10. Pão de Açúcar (Sugar Loaf)
11. Station for Pão de Açúcar
12. Botafogo (end of Metro Line 1)
14. Catete (cheap hotel area)
15. Glória
16. Parque do Flamengo
17. Santa Teresa
18. New Cathedral
19. Business Centre
20. Sambódromo
21. Maracanã Stadium
22. Quinta de Boa Vista
23. Santos Dumont Airport
24. Galeão International Airport
25. Rodoviária Novo Rio
26. Pedro II Railway Station
27. Ferries to Paquetá & Niterói

in the Sambódromo; although small, it has lots of photographs and the English-speaking staff are very informative (entrance in R Frei Caneca; T 293-9996; Tues-Sun 1000-1700; free). Suggested reading: *The Insider's Guide to Rio* (in English; Christopher Pickard, from Rio bookshops); *Samba* (paperback; a personal account by Alma Guillermoprieto, Bloomsbury Press). The **Sambódromo**, a permanent site at R Marquês de Sapucaí, Cidade Nova, not far from the centre, has a length of 600m, with seats for 60,000 people. Designed by Oscar Niemeyer, it handles sporting events, conferences and concerts during the rest of the year; it also houses a public education centre which presently teaches 5,000 children.

The Sambódromo parades start at 1900 and last about 12 hrs. Gates (which are not clearly marked) open at 1800. Spectator accommodation comprises seats ("cadeiras") at ground level, terraces ("arquibancadas") and boxes ("camarotes"). The best boxes, which are reserved for tourists and VIPs, sell for around US$1,000 pp. Seats are closest to the parade, but you may have to fight your way to the front. Seats and boxes reserved for tourists have the best view; sectors 4, 7 and 11 are preferred (they house the judging points); 6 and 13 are least favoured, being at the end when dancers might be tired, but have more space. The terraces, while uncomfortable, house the most fervent fans, tightly packed; this is where to soak up the atmosphere (but not take pictures – too crowded). Tickets (maximum 4) are sold through Banco do Brasil or the Banco Meridional in most big cities, and start at about US$30; they are also sold at the Maracanã Stadium box office, but not during Carnival weekend: touts outside will try to sell you places at double the price. Check availability, even if they say all tickets are sold. Samba schools have an allocation of tickets which members sometimes sell off; if you are offered one of these, check its date. Tourist tickets start at US$100; available through Riotur or travel agencies. Taxis to the Sambódromo are negotiable (around US$10) and will find your gate; nearest metrô is Praça 11: an enjoyable ride in the company of costumed samba school members. Main metrô and bus routes run all night during Carnival (erratically).

Most Samba schools will accept a number of foreigners: you will be charged double for your costume (US$100 upwards); your money helps to fund a poorer member of the school. You must be in Rio for at least 2 weeks before Carnival. Portuguese speakers can telephone the schools direct, others can be introduced by hotel staff, tour guides, etc, who are school members: ask around. It is essential to attend fittings and rehearsals on time, to show respect for your section leaders, and to enter into the competitive spirit of the event. For those with the energy and the dedication, it will be an unforgettable experience. The "concentration area" at the entrance to the Sambódromo, where schools line up before their parade, is an excellent point from which to see the chaotic preparations on the night; people who cannot afford tickets gather here to see the costumes: Av Presidente Vargas (drinks and food on sale; canal can be unpleasant in hot weather). All schools hold a preview of their entire parade in their own neighbourhood, usually the week before Carnival; well worth seeing, admission around US$1, photography OK but don't take valuables; listed in local press under "ensaios". A new (1993) group called Carnaval Off arranges a series of events for those who prefer rave to Samba; also listed by the press.

Carnival week comprises an enormous range of official contests and events, as well as many unofficial ones. Exhibitions and competitions reach a peak on the Tues; Riotur's guide booklet (also available from better hotels) gives concise information in English; *Veja*, *Manchete* (weekly magazines) and the Jornal do Brasil's *Programa* (Fri) are also invaluable sources: an equally wide programme exists for those looking for entertainment but not wishing to 'play' at Carnival.

Rio's fancy-dress balls range from the sophisticated to the wild. The majority of clubs and hotels host at least one. The *Copacabana Palace* hotel's is elegant and expensive (US$250), with costumed mime artists parading on a backlit terrace for

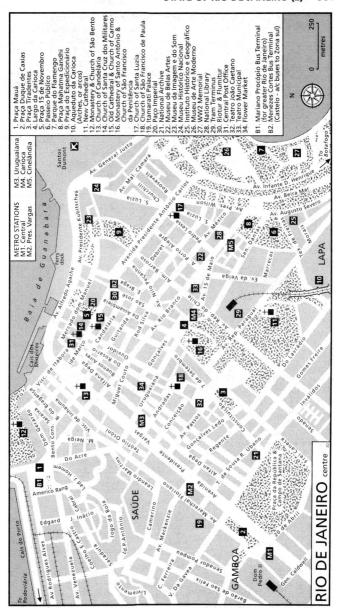

1. Praça Mauá
2. Praça Duque de Caxias
3. Praça Tiradentes
4. Largo da Carioca
5. Praça 15 de Novembro
6. Passeio Público
7. Parque do Flamengo
8. Praça Mahatma Gandhi
9. Praça do Expedicionário
10. Aqueduto da Carioca (Arches, or arcos)
11. New Cathedral
12. Monastery & Church of São Bento
13. Church of Candelária
14. Church of Santa Cruz dos Militares
15. Old Cathedral & Church of Carmo
16. Monastery of Santo Antônio & Church of São Francisco da Penitência
17. Church of Santa Luzia
18. Church of São Francisco de Paula
19. Itamarati Palace
20. Paço Imperial
21. National Archive
22. Museu de Belas Artes
23. Museu da Imagem e do Som
24. Museu Histórico Nacional
25. Instituto Histórico e Geográfico
26. Museu de Arte Moderno
27. WW2 Memorial
28. National Library
29. Tram Terminus
30. Riotur & Flumitur
31. Central Post Office
32. Teatro João Caetano
33. Teatro Municipal
34. Flower Market

B1. Mariano Procópio Bus Terminal (for greater Rio de Janeiro)
B2. Menezes Cortes Bus Terminal (Castelo - a/c buses to Zona sul)

METRO STATIONS
M1. Central
M2. Pres. Vargas
M3. Uruguaiana
M4. Carioca
M5. Cinelândia

RIO DE JANEIRO centre

the benefit of spectators on the Av Atlântica below; the *Scala* club's licentious parties are televised nightly, as are the *Monte e Lîbano*'s. It is not necessary to wear fancy dress; just join in, although you will feel more comfortable if you wear a minimum of clothing to the clubs (crowded, hot and rowdy). Two of the most famous (both at *Scala*) are the Red & Black Ball (Fri) and the Gay Ball (Tues). Prices vary: from about US$15 pp; US$100 per table for 4; US$750 for a box. Drinks are expensive. The clubs give free tickets to attractive young women, which their boyfriends then sell outside the entrance: expect to pay about US$7, and check the date. The tourist office has a full list of balls.

Copacabana Palace Hotel, T 255-7070, ext 187 (reservations); *Monte e Lîbano*, Av Borges de Medeiros, Lagoa, T 239-0032; *Scala*, Av Afrânio de Mello Franco, Leblon, T 239-4448.
   The expensive hotels offer special Carnival breakfasts from 0530 at US$10-12, all good; *Caesar Park* (Ipanema) highly rec, wonderful meal, top-floor view of sunrise over beach.

Visitors wishing to attend the Carnival are earnestly advised to make sure of their accommodation well in advance. Virtually all hotels raise their prices during Carnival, although it should be possible to find a room.
   Your property should be safe inside the Sambódromo, but the crowds outside can attract pickpockets: as ever, don't brandish your camera, and take with you only as much money as you need for fares and refreshments (food and drink are sold in the Sambódromo, glass and cans are not allowed if you take your own). It gets hot! Wear as little as possible (shorts or Bermudas and a T-shirt).

Samba Schools Salgueiro (Andaraí) T 238-5564; Beija-Flor (Nilópolis) T 791-2866; Mangueira (Mangueira) T 234-4129; Estácio de Sá (Cidade Nova) T 293-8944; Imperatriz (Ramos) T 270-8037; Mocidade Independente (Padre Miguel) T 332-5823; Portela (Madureira) T 390-0471; Tradição (Campinho) T 350-5868; União da Ilha (Ilha do Governador) T 396-4951; Vila Isabel (Santa Isabel) T 268-7052; also see local press and Riotur booklet.

If you can't be there at Carnival time, rehearsals are held at various places from Nov onwards; eg the Portela *escola* at R Arruda Câmara 81, Madureira, late Sat nights. Beija Flor, one of the best samba schools, performs on Mon nights at Urca (half-way up to Sugar Loaf Mountain), dinner available at 2000, show, US$10, starts 2200. Reservations required (on Fri and Sat at this venue is the "Noite Carioca" show, or a disco). When buying a video, make sure the format is compatible (Brazilian format matches the USA; VHS PAL for most of Europe).

Carnival dates 18 Feb 1996; 9 Feb 1997; 22 Feb 1998; 14 Feb 1999; 5 Mar 2000.

Other Festivals Less hectic than Carnival, but very atmospheric, is the festival of Iemanjá on the night of 31 Dec, when devotees of the spirit cults brought from Africa gather on **Copacabana, Ipanema and Leblon beaches**, singing and dancing around open fires and making offerings, and the elected Queen of the Sea is rowed along the seashore. There is a firework display on Copacabana beach at midnight, so the crowds tend to concentrate there, in front of the Copacabana Palace and Meridien hotels. At midnight small boats are launched as sacrifices to Iemanjá.

The festival of São Sebastião, patron saint of Rio, is celebrated by an evening procession on 20 Jan, leaving Capuchinhos Church, Tijuca, and arriving at the cathedral of São Sebastião. The same evening an *umbanda* festival is celebrated at the Caboclo Monument in Santa Teresa.

Museums and other Public Buildings

All museums and the Jardim Botânico are closed over Carnival.

The **Museu Nacional** in the Quinta da Boa Vista is said to be one of the most important museums in South America but is disappointing, and the park surrounding it is dangerous. The building was the principal palace of the Emperors of Brazil, but only the unfurnished Throne Room and ambassadorial reception room on the 2nd floor reflect past glories. In the entrance hall is the famous Bêndego meteorite, found in the State of Bahia in 1888; its original weight, before some of it was chipped, was 5,360 kg. Besides several foreign collections of note, the Museum contains collections of Brazilian Indian weapons, dresses, utensils, etc, of minerals and of historical documents. There are also collections of birds, beasts, fishes, and butterflies.

Open 1000-1630, closed Mon; entrance US$1. Buses: 472, 474, 475 from centre, Flamengo and Copacabana, 583 from Largo do Machado. Nearest metro São Cristóvão, but thieves operate by park entrance and in the park, taxi to the main door is safer. Some of the collections are open to qualified research students only.

Museu de Fauna also at Quinta da Boa Vista, contains a most interesting collection of Brazilian fauna. Open Tues-Sun 1200-1700.

The **Biblioteca Nacional** (National Library), at Avenida Rio Branco 219, was founded in 1810. Its first collection came from the Ajuda Palace in Lisbon, and today it houses over 2 million volumes and many rare manuscripts. Open Mon-Fri 0900-2000, and Sat 0900-1500.

Museu Nacional de Belas Artes (National Museum of Fine Art) , at Avenida Rio Branco 199. There are about 800 original paintings and sculptures and some thousand direct reproductions. Exhibitions of works by contemporary Brazilian artists are often held here. Open Tues-Fri 1200-1800; Sat, Sun and holidays 1500-1800; US$1.

Those interested in contemporary art will also visit the former Ministry of Education (Le Corbusier designs modified by Oscar Niemeyer), to see the great murals of Cândido Portinári, whose canvas, "Café", is in the Museum of Fine Art.

Opposite the Art Museum is the **Teatro Municipal**. Opera and orchestral performances are given here; the small museum that used to be below the theatre is now at R São João Batista 103/105, Botafogo, open 1300-1700 Mon-Fri.

The **Paço Imperial** (former Royal Palace on Praça Quinze de Novembro), a beautiful colonial building begun in 1743, has been restored. It has a gallery for temporary exhibitions and the occasional free concert.

The **Museu de Arte Moderna** (Museum of Modern Art) is a spectacular building at Avenida Infante D Henrique 85, near the National War Memorial (**see p 366**). It suffered a disastrous fire in 1978; the collection is now being rebuilt, and several countries have donated works of art. There is also a non-commercial cinema. Entrance US$1, Tues-Sun 1200-1800.

The **Museu Histórico Nacional** on Praça Rui Barbosa (formerly Praça Marechal Âncora) contains a most interesting collection of historical treasures, colonial sculpture and furniture, maps, paintings, arms and armour, silver, and porcelain. The building was once the old War Arsenal of the Empire, part of which was built in 1762. Open Tues to Sun, 1000-1730; Sat, Sun and holidays 1430-1730; admission US$0.30.

Museu Naval e Oceanográfico, R D Manoel 15, daily 1200-1630. There is a particularly large collection of paintings and prints, besides the more usual display of weapons and figureheads.

Museu da Imagem e do Som, also on Praça Rui Barbosa, has many photographs of Brazil and modern Brazilian paintings; also collections and recordings of Brazilian classical and popular music and a non-commercial cinema open Fri-Sun. Open Mon-Fri, 1300-1800.

The **Museu do Índio** (Museum of the Indian) is at R das Palmeiras 55, Botafogo, T 286 0845, closed for renovation in 1994. Small, concise, well displayed; has handicrafts shop, which closes for lunch 1200-1400. It contains 12,000 objects from many Brazilian Indian groups.

The **Chácara do Céu**, or Fundação Raymundo Ottoni de Castro Maia, R Murtinho Nobre 93, has a wide range of art objects and particularly modern painters, including Brazilian. Take Santa Teresa tram to R Dias de Barros, then follow signposts. Open Tues-Sat 1400-1700, Sun 1100-1700, US$1.25. Castro Maia's former residence on the Estrada do Açude in the Tijuca Forest has same name and is also a museum, currently under restoration.

Museu do Instituto Histórico e Geográfico, Av Augusto Severo 8 (10th floor), just off Av Beira Mar, has a very interesting collection of Brazil's products and the artefacts of its peoples. Open Mon-Fri 1200-1700.

The **São Cristóvão Pavilion**, designed by Sérgio Bernardes, has the world's largest open floor space without columns or transverse walls, but is now closed to the public. It is in very poor condition. Sunday market is worth visiting for North Eastern food and hammocks. Bus 472 or 474 from Copacabana or centre.

The **Museu de Astronomia/National Observatory** (founded 1827) is on São Januário hill, R Gen Bruce 586, São Cristóvão. Hours: Tues-Fri 0900-1700, guided tours 1000-1200; 1400-1600. Visitors advised to call 580-7010 after 1700 to arrange a night viewing.

The **Casa de Rui Barbosa**, R São Clemente 134, Botafogo, former home of the Brazilian jurist and statesman, containing his library and other possessions, is open Tues-Fri 1000-1630, Sat, Sun and holidays 1400-1700. The large garden is also open to the public. Buses 106, 176, 178 from centre; 571 from Flamengo; 591 from Copacabana.

Palácio do Itamarati, the former Foreign Ministry, at Avenida Marechal Floriano 196, T 291-4411, contains much interesting old furniture, tapestry and other objects of art. Now called **Museu Diplomático** closed for restoration since 1992.

Museu da República, in Palácio do Catete (R do Catete 153), entrance in R Silveira Martins, was the official residence of the President for 63 years when Rio was the Federal Capital (Tues-Sun 1200-1700).

Museu do Folclore Edison Carneiro, R do Catete 179, displays present-day popular arts and crafts. Explanatory booklet in English: enjoyable. Tues-Fri 1100-1800. Bus 571 from Copacabana, and close to Catete metro station.

Palácio Guanabara, once the residence of the Princess Isabel, daughter of Dom Pedro II, is now the office of the Governor of the State of Rio de Janeiro.

Museu Carmen Miranda, Tues-Fri 1300-1600, Flamengo park area in front of Rui Barbosa 560 (small display of the famous singer's gowns etc); US$0.30, Sun free, but not always open Sun. **Museu de Imagens do Inconsciente**, Ramiro Magalhães 521, Engenho de Dentro, Mon-Fri 0900-1600. **Museu Villa-Lobos**, R Sorocaba 200, Botafogo, Mon-Fri 0930-1730 with instruments, scores, books, recordings. **Capão do Bispo Estate**, Av Suburbana 4616, Del Castilho, Mon-Fri 1400-1700 with archaeological exhibition.

Planetarium, Padre Leonel Franco 240, Gávea, Wed 1830, Sat and Sun at 1530 and 1830: inaugurated in 1970, sculpture of Earth and Moon by Mario Agostinelli. Free choro concert Fri at 2100. Buses 176 and 178 from centre and Flamengo; 591 and 592 from Copacabana.

Museu Aeroespacial, Av Marechal Fontenelle 2000, Campo dos Afonsos, Tues-Fri 0900-1600, Sat, Sun and holidays 0930-1600, early Brazilian civil and military aircraft.

Museu do Carnaval, Passarela do Samba, entrance by R Frei Caneca, Tues-Sun 1000-1700, good.

Museu Antônio Lago, R Andradas 96, centre, Mon-Fri 1400-1900. Reproduction of historical apothecary's shop.

Amsterdam Sauer Museum, Garcia d'Avila e Visconde de Pirajá 105, reproduction of a Brazilian mine and exhibition of gemstones. Open Mon-Fri 1000-1700, Sat 0930-1300.

Churches and Religious Foundations

Check opening hours before attempting to visit.

The oldest foundation is the convent of the **Ordem Terceiro do Monte do Carmo**, built early in the 17th century on R Primeiro de Março close to Praça 15 de Novembro, now used as a school. Its present church, the Carmo Church in R Primeiro de Março, next to the old cathedral, was built in the 1770s and rebuilt between 1797 and 1826. It has strikingly beautiful portals by Mestre Valentim, the son of a Portuguese nobleman and a slave girl. He also created the main altar of fine moulded silver, the throne and its chair, and much else.

The second oldest convent is the seventeenth-century **Convento de Santo Antônio**, on a hill off the Largo da Carioca, built between 1608 and 1615. Its church has a marvellous sacristy adorned with blue tiles. St Anthony is a particular object of devotion for women who want to find husbands, and many will be seen in the precincts.

The crypt contains the tomb of a Scottish soldier of fortune known as "Wild Jock of Skelater". He was in the service of the Portuguese Government during the Napoleonic War, and had the distinction of being appointed the first Commander-in-Chief of the Army in Brazil. The statue of St Anthony was made a captain in the Portuguese army after his help had been sought to drive out the French in 1710, and his salary paid to the monastery. In 1810 the statue became a major, in 1814 a lieutenant-colonel, and was granted the Grand Cross of the Order of Christ. He was retired without pay in 1914.

Separated from this church only by some iron railings is the charming church of **São Francisco da Penitência**, built in 1773. The carving and gilding of walls and altar are superb. In the ceiling over the nave is a fine panel painted by José de Oliveira. There is a museum attached to the church, open first and third Sun of the month, 0700-1000.

The **Mosteiro** (monastery) **de São Bento** (1641); entrance at R Dom Gerardo 68, contains much of what is best in the 17th and 18th century art of Brazil. "O Salvador", the masterpiece of Brazil's first painter, Frei Ricardo do Pilar, hangs in the sacristy. The carving in the church is particularly good. The Chapels of the Immaculate Conception and of the Most Holy Sacrament are masterpieces of colonial art. The organ is very interesting. The monastery is a few mins' walk from Praça Mauá, turning left off Av Rio Branco. Open 0730-1130, 1430-1830 (shorts not allowed).

The **Old Cathedral** of São Sebastião, in the R Primeiro de Março, was built between 1749 and 1770. In the crypt are the alleged remains of Pedro Alvares Cabral, the discoverer of Brazil (though it is only fair to note that Santarém, Portugal, also claims to be his last resting-place).

The **New Cathedral**, on Avenida República de Chile not far from the Largo da Carioca, dedicated in 1976, is a cone-shaped building. Its internal height is 68m, diameter 104m, external height 83m; capacity 5,000 seated, 20,000 standing. The most striking feature is four enormous stained-glass windows (60m high). It is still incomplete.

The Church of **São Francisco de Paula**, at the upper end of the R do Ouvidor, was built in 1759. It contains some of Mestre Valentim's work—the carvings in the main chapel and the lovely Chapel of Our Lady of Victory. Some of the paintings, and probably the ceiling, are by Manuel da Cunha. The beautiful fountain at the back plays only at night.

The Church of **Nossa Senhora da Candelária** (1775-1810), on Praça Pio Dez, at the city end of Avenida Presidente Vargas, is well worth a visit to see its beautiful ceiling decorations and paintings. It is on the site of a chapel founded in 1610 by Antônio da Palma after he had survived a shipwreck, an event depicted by paintings inside the present dome.

In the R de Santa Luzia, overwhelmed by tall office buildings, is the attractive little church of **Santa Luzia**. When built in 1752 it had only one tower; the other was added late in the 19th century. Feast day: 13 Dec, when devotees bathe their eyes with holy water, considered miraculous.

In the R Primeiro de Março, at the corner of Ouvidor (near the Old Cathedral), is the church of **Santa Cruz dos Militares**, built 1780-1811. It is large, stately and beautiful.

The beautiful little church on the Glória hill, overlooking the Parque do Flamengo, is **Nossa Senhora da Glória**. It was the favourite church of the imperial family; Dom Pedro II was baptized here. Built in 1791, it contains some excellent examples of blue-faced Brazilian tiling. Its main altar, of wood, was carved by Mestre Valentim. The church, open 0900-1200 (only Sat-Sun) and 1300-1700 weekdays, is reached by bus 119 from the centre and 571 from Copacabana. The adjacent museum of religious art is open on application to the priest.

The church of **Nossa Senhora da Penha**, in the N suburb of Penha (early 20th century), is on a bare rock in which 365 steps are cut. This staircase is ascended by pilgrims on their knees during the festival month of Oct; there is a funicular for those unable to do this. Bus 497 from Copacabana, 340 and 346 from centre.

When the Morro do Castelo was levelled to build the Esplanada do Castelo, the old church of São Sebastião had to be demolished. Its successor, the Capuchin church of São Sebastião in the R Haddock Lobo, Tijuca, built in 1936, contains the tomb of Estácio de Sá, founder and first Governor of Rio de Janeiro.

Places where worship is conducted other than in Portuguese:
Christ Church, R Real Grandeza 99, Botafogo (Church of England/American Episcopalian). The British School, for children of 5-16, is nearby.
Chapel of Our Lady of Mercy, R Visconde de Caravelas 48, Botafogo (Roman Catholic, with primary school).
Union Church (Protestant undenominational) Services held at R Parque da Lagoa de Marapendi, CP 37154-CEP 22609 Barra da Tijuca.
International Baptist Church, R Desembargador Alfredo Russel 146, Leblon.
First Church of Christ Scientist, Av Marechal Câmara 271, room 301.
Masonic Temple, in the British School at R da Matriz 76, Botafogo.
Synagogues, R Pompeu Loureiro 48, Botafogo, T 257-4299; R Barata Ribeiro 489, Copacabana. Includes kosher bakery.
Swedish Church, Igreja Escandinava, Av Rui Barbosa 170, Bloco B 1, 5 And, T 551-6696, open 1300-2200, Sun 1700-2100, will store luggage.
British Cemetery, R da Gamboa 181, granted to the British community by Dom João, Regent of Portugal, in 1810. It is the oldest cemetery in Rio.

Parks, Squares and Monuments

On the Glória and Flamengo waterfront, with a view of the Pão de Açúcar and Corcovado, is the **Parque do Flamengo**, designed by Burle Marx, opened in 1965 during the 400th anniversary of the city's founding, and landscaped on 100 hectares reclaimed from the Bay. Behind the War Memorial (see below) is the public yacht marina. In the park are many sports fields and a botanical garden; for children, there are a sailboat basin, a marionette theatre, a miniature village and a staffed nursery. There are night amusements, such as bandstands and areas for dancing. Security in the park is in the hands of vigilante policemen and it is a popular recreation area.

The National War Memorial to Brazil's dead in World War II (Monumento aos Mortos na Segunda Guerra) and the Museu de Arte Moderna (**see p 363**) are at the city end of the park, opposite Praça Paris. The Memorial takes the form of two slender columns supporting a slightly curved slab, representing two palms uplifted to heaven. In the crypt are the remains of the Brazilian soldiers killed in Italy in 1944-45. It is well worth a visit, but beach clothes and rubber-thonged sandals will get you ejected—and don't sit on the wall. The crypt and museum are open Tues-Sun 1000-1700.

Those who want to see what Rio was like early in the 19th century should go by bus to the **Largo do Boticário**, R Cosme Velho 822, a charming small square in pure colonial style. Buses to Cosme Velho from all parts of the city. The square is close to the terminus for the Corcovado rack railway (**see p 380**).

(Jardim Botânico) **Botanical Gardens** founded 1808, open 0800-1730 (US$1); well worth a visit. The most striking features are the transverse avenues of 30-metre royal palms. There are over 7,000 varieties of plants, herbarium, aquarium, and library (some labels are unclear). Many improvements were carried out before the 1992 Earth Summit, including a new Orquidário, an enlarged bookshop, a *lanchonete*, replanting and cleaning up. Visitors needing information in English should ask for Beatriz Heloisa Guimarães, of the Society of Friends of the Garden. The Gardens are 8 km from the centre, 140 hectares in area; take any bus from the centre, eg 104, to Leblon, Gávea or São Conrado marked "via Jóquei". From Copacabana take bus 592.

Bird-watchers should visit the Botanical Gardens, preferably early in the morning. 140 species of birds have been recorded there. Flycatchers are very prominent (the social flycatcher, great and boat-billed kiskadees, cattle tyrant); also tanagers (the sayaca and palm tanagers, and the colourful green-headed tanager), and over 20 different kinds of hummingbird. Birds of prey include the roadside hawk, the laughing falcon and the American kestrel, and there are doves, cuckoos, parakeets, thrushes and woodpeckers, and occasional flocks of toucans. (John and George Newmark, Eastbourne.)

Parque Laje, near the Jardim Botânico at R Jardim Botânico 414, almost jungle-like, has small grottoes, an old tower and lakes, pleasant. (The Institute of Fine Arts is housed in the mansion.) Open daily, 0730-1730, admittance free.

Quinta da Boa Vista, formerly the Emperor's private park, contains the zoo (see below) and many specimen trees. The Palace now houses the Museo Nacional (**see p 362**).

Jardim Zoológico, which contains Brazilian and imported wild animals, and a fine collection of birds (as well as many "visitors"—also good for bird-watchers), is in the Quinta de Boa Vista (admission US$2). Open 0800-1800 daily, except Mon (best in the morning). The gateway is a replica of Robert Adam's famous gateway to Syon House, near London. Near the Zoological Gardens is the Museu da Fauna (see above). Take bus 474 or 472 from Copacabana or Flamengo; bus 262 from Praça Mauá.

Parque da Cidade A pleasant park a short walk beyond the Gávea bus terminus. It was previously the grounds of the home of the Guinle family, by whom it was presented to the City. Admission to the park is free; open Tues-Fri 0730-1730, Sat, Sun and holidays 1100-1700. The proximity of the Rocinha favela means that the park is not very safe. It is advisable to carry a copy of your passport here because of frequent police checks.

Jockey Club Racecourse, at Praça Santos Dumont, Gávea, meetings on Mon and Thur evenings and Sat and Sun 1400, entrance US$1-2, long trousers required, a table may be booked. Take any bus marked "via Jóquei". Betting is by totalizator only.

Praça da República and **Campo de Santana** is an extensive and picturesque public garden close to the Central Railway station. At Praça da República 197 lived Marshal Deodoro da Fonseca, who proclaimed Brazil a republic in 1889 (plaque). The Parque Júlio Furtado in the middle of the square is populated by playful agoutis (or gophers), best seen at dusk; there is also a little artificial grotto, with swans.

Passeio Público (turn right at S end of Avenida Rio Branco) is a garden planted by the artist Mestre Valentim, whose bust is near the old former gateway. Coin and stamp market on Sun, am.

Praça Quinze de Novembro contains the original royal palace (**see p 363**). Every Sat 0900-1900, flea market; nearby on the waterfront is a Sun antiques market, 1000-1800.

Praça Tiradentes, old and shady, has a statue to D Pedro I, first Emperor of Brazil. Shops in nearby streets specialize in selling goods for *umbanda* and *macumba*—African-based religion and magic respectively. Several theatres nearby.

Praça Mahatma Gandhi, at the end of Avenida Rio Branco, is flanked on one side by the cinema and amusement centre of the city, known as Cinelândia. The fountain (1789) by Mestre Valentim in the ornamental garden was moved here from Praça Quinze de Novembro in 1979.

Parque do Catete is a charming small park between the Palácio do Catete (Museum da República) and Praia do Flamengo; it has many birds and playful monkeys.

Praça Paris, built on reclaimed ground near the Largo da Glória, is much admired for the beauty of its formal gardens and illuminated fountains.

Fountains The oldest, the Fonte da Glória (1789), has eight bronze spouts. Possibly the finest, although now sadly neglected, is at the back of the church of São Francisco de Paula, at the inland end of the R do Ouvidor. These, and nine other old fountains, are illuminated by night.

Security The majority of visitors enjoy Rio's glamour, and the rich variety of experience it has to offer, without any problems. It is worth remembering that, despite its beach culture, carefree atmosphere and friendly people, Rio is one of the world's most densely populated cities. If you live in London, Paris, New York or Los Angeles and behave with the same caution in Rio that you do at home, you will be unlucky to encounter any crime. There is extreme poverty in Rio: most robberies that occur are committed out of desperation. Overseas visitors are an obvious target: simply by having been able to afford the ticket, you are comparatively wealthy. Brazilians can usually tell you are foreign just by the way you carry yourself, but there is no sense in looking as if you have something worth stealing (by wearing expensive clothes, valuable jewellery, a large daypack, or your camera – put it in your shoulder bag, worn in front of you, or buy disposable cameras as often as you need them). If you are unfortunate enough to be threatened, try to remember that the assailant is probably as scared as you are, and will not hurt you if you give him what he's asking for (keep some money easily accessible, just in case). If you see someone having trouble, don't interfere, but try making a lot of noise to frighten the attacker away; if you think you are being followed, go up to a policeman. The streets are not excessively dangerous at night, but if you're going out in your best clothes, don't know the way, or are drunk, it's wisest to get a taxi. All the above advice comes from the **tourist police**: Delegacia do Turista, Av Afrânio de Melo (opp Scala nightclub), Leblon, T 511-5112, who publish a sensible advice leaflet (available from hotels and consulates: consulates also issue safety guidelines). Recognisable by their white T-shirts ("we're here to help you"), officers are indeed helpful, efficient, and multilingual. All the main tourist areas are patrolled. If you have any problems, **contact the tourist police first**.

The following are risky places: the tunnels are not safe to walk through; the city centre on Sun when it is deserted; quiet alleyways; jostling crowds; dark corners. Locals don't walk on the beaches at night: if you must, do not go out of sight of the pavement. The Tijuca forest is best explored with a group of 6 or more, except the stretch between Afonso Vizeu square and Cascatinha which is well policed during the day; the tram (**see p 376**) attracts pickpockets; robberies sometimes happen in city buses: don't use them if guarding your property is essential (private "frescão" buses are more secure). The main bus station is patrolled inside, but uncomfortable outside. If you go to the North Zone at night, use a taxi; wandering around *favelas* at any time of day is both ill-advised and in questionable taste. Street vendors and children working the tables at your bar or restaurant will have been permitted by the management and there is little risk, though children can be light-fingered, so watch your wallet.

It seems that far too many crimes against tourists are the result of thoughtlessness: remember that you are in a busy city, and that the beaches are a pivot of daily life; leaving things unattended on the sand is equivalent to leaving them on Times Square while you go for a walk. We have been asked to advise male readers that all the usual risks apply if hiring prostitutes of either sex (police may well take your companion's side in a dispute over prices – don't argue). The 'red light' districts of the South Zone are unlikely to offend anyone walking about at night, even children or unaccompanied women. Do, however, be suspicious of any club that you are invited into by a stranger (have your drink opened in front of you), and of anyone offering drugs. You have the most to lose when carrying all your belongings and as you go in and out of banks, exchange houses, and expensive shops, so take extra care then. At other times, put your passport, TCs, etc in the hotel safe. Don't take too much out with you, have some sense, and relax.

Telephone code and Postal address CEP: 20000, DDD 021.

Hotels All hotels in the following list are air-conditioned. A 10% service charge is usually added to the bill and tax of 5% or 10% may be added (if not already included). Note that not all higher-class hotels include breakfast in their room rates. The following list begins with expensive hotels and then gives economy establishments, by area.

Centre Well placed for transport, 30 mins from the beaches. Most offices and commerce are located here, but no night life, so not a secure area and not rec for tourists: **L2** *Luxor Hotel do Aeroporto* at Galeão Airport, T 398-5960, F 398-3983 (3-star); **A1** *Ambassador*, Senador Dantas, 25, T 297-7181, F 220-4783; **A1** *Grande Hotel OK*, Senador Dantas, 24, T 292-4114, F 533-0163; **A2** *Othon Aeroporto*, Av Beira Mar, 280, T/F 210-3253, somewhat run-down and expensive (3-star).

Flamengo Residential area midway between centre and Copacabana: **L3** *Glória*, R do Russel, 632, T 205-7272, F 245-1660, stylish and elegant old building, two swimming pools, highly rec; **L2** *Novo Mundo*, Praia Flamengo 20, T 205-3355, F 265-2369, well rec but noisy; **A1** *Flamengo Palace*, Praia Flamengo 6, T 205-1552, F 265-2846, appears a bit old-fashioned.

Copacabana The famous seaside residential and commercial area: many hotels on Av Atlântica charge about 30% more for a room with a sea view, but some town-side upper rooms have equally fine views of the mountains. 5-star hotels (**L1-2**): *Copacabana Palace*, Av Atlântica 1702, T 255-7070, F 235-7330, British-owned, swimming pool, very good; *Meridien*, Av Atlântica 1020, T 275-9922, F 541-6447, Air France hotel, world-renowned, but very expensive, pool, rooms quite small; *Rio Othon Palace*, Av Atlântica 3264, T 521-5522, F 521-6697, pool, very good, as is *Rio Palace*, Av Atlântica 4240, T 521-3232, F 247-1752, all rooms locked by central system at 0130. There are two excellent suites hotels: **L3** *Rio Atlantica*, Av Atlântica 2964, T 255-6332, F 255-6410 with pool, 2 restaurants and other facilities (Swiss management, very high standards); and *International Rio*, Av Atlântica 1500, T 295-2323, F 542-5443, pool.

4-star hotels in Copacabana: there are 4 Othon hotels in this category, all in the **L3-A1** range (some rooms more): *Califórnia Othon*, Av Atlântica 2616, T/F 257-1900, good; *Savoy Othon*, Av Copacabana 995, T/F 521-8282, very central, popular, commercial, quite noisy; *Olinda*, Av Atlântica 2230, T/F 257-1890, also good, and the *Lancaster*, Av Atlântica 1470, T/F 541-1887, rec, easy to change TCs, helpful management. Next door to the *Lancaster* is *Ouro Verde*, Av Atlântica 1456, T 542-1887, F 542-4597, excellent all round; 3 Luxor hotels: *Luxor Continental*, Gustavo Sampaio 320, T 275-5252, F 541-1946, *Luxor Copacabana*, Av Atlântica 2554, T 235-2245, F 255-1858, *Luxor Regente*, Av Atlântica 3716, T 287-4212, F 267-7693, all good hotels in this range, well-placed. *Leme Palace*, Av Atlântica 656, T/F 275-8080, also good, but poorer location, popular with tour groups. *Royalty Copacabana*, Toneleros 154, T/F 235-5699, 4 blocks from beach, a/c, swimming pool on 13th floor with view.

Copacabana 3-stars (except where indicated A1-A2): *Apa*, República do Peru, 305, T 255-8112, F 256-3628; *Castro Alves Othon*, Av Copacabana 552, T/F 255-8815, central, very comfortable and elegant, rec; *Debret*, Av Atlântica 3564, T 521-3332, F 521-0899, good, helpful staff, some inner rooms dark, but well-furnished; *Plaza Copacabana*, Av Princesa Isabel 263, T 275-7722, F 275-8693, highly rec as most hospitable. Copacabana 2-stars: *Praia Leme*, Av Atlântica 866, T 275-3322, Austrian run; **B** *Atlantis Copacabana*, Av Bulhões de Carvalho 61, T 521-1142, F 287-8896, a/c, TV, very good, close to Ipanema and Copacabana beaches; *Biarritz*, R Aires Saldanha 54, T 521-6542, F 287-6062, good, accepts American Express; *Canadá*, Av NS de Copacabana 687, T 257-1864, TV, a/c, fridge, clean, rec; **B** *Santa Clara*, R Décio Vilares 316, T 256-2650, rec, quiet; **B** *Toledo*, R Domingos Ferreira 71, T 257-1990, one block from beach, good breakfast, single rooms are gloomy, but excellent value; **B** *Acapulco Copacabana*, R Gustavo Sampião 854, T 275-0022, F 275-3396, a/c, TV, simple, rec.

Ipanema/Leblon Outer seaside residential and commercial area: all the following are good, starting with the most luxurious, **L+** *Caesar Park*, Av Tom Jobim (ex Vieira Souto) 460, T 287-3122, F 521-6000, pool; **L** *Everest*, Prudente de Morais 1117, T 287-8282, F 521-3198, pool; **L** *Marina Palace*, Av Delfim Moreira 630, T 259-5212, F 259-0941, and **A+** *Marina Rio*, Av Delfim Moreira 696, T 239-8844, F 259-0941; **A+** *Praia Ipanema*, Av Vieira Souto 706, T 239-9932, F 239-6889, pool; **A+** *Sol Ipanema*, Av Tom Jobim 320, T 267-0095, F 521-6464; **A3** *Arpoador Inn*, Francisco Otaviano 177, T 247-6090, only hotel on beach, rec; **A** *Vermont*, Visc de Pirajá 254, T 521-0057, F 267-7046, rec.

São Conrado and further out Spectacular settings, but isolated and far from centre: the first three are luxury hotels with pools: **L1** *Intercontinental*, Av Litorânea 222, T 322-2200, F 322-5500; **L1** *Sheraton*, Av Niemeyer 121, T 274-1122, F 239-5643; **L** *Nacional*, Av Niemeyer 769, T 322-1000, F 322-0058; **A** *Atlântico Sul*, Av Sernambetiba 18000 (Recreio), T 437-8411, F 437-8777.

Economy Hotels are found mainly in three districts of Rio: Flamengo/Botafogo (best), Lapa/Fátima and Saúde/Maúa. Rates are for doubles, and include continental breakfast.

Flamengo/Catete (Residential area between centre and Copacabana, with good bus and metro connections.) From the centre, you will come across the hotels in this order: **E** *Opera*, Santa Amaro 75, T 242-3585, recently reopened. On the hillside is Ladeira da Glória:

D *Turístico*, Ladeira da Glória 30, with bath, incl breakfast, a/c, tourist information provided, mixed reports, some highly favourable. **D** *Victória*, R do Catete 172, with breakfast, bath and hot water, a/c, clean and friendly, rec; also on R do Catete: No 233, **D** *Rio Claro*, small rooms, breakfast, shower, a/c, safe, rec; No 160, **D** *Monte Blanco*, breakfast, bath, a/c, radio, refurbished, clean, friendly (try for a room about 1200). To the left is R Silveira Martins: No 20, **D** *Inglês*, reasonable breakfast; **D** *Hispano Brasileiro*, No 135, clean, friendly, rec. Walking down Praia de Flamengo you will come across the next streets: Ferreira Viana: **A3** *Florida*, No 71/81, T 245-8160, F 285-5777, sauna, pool, safe, quiet, good views, great breakfast, highly rec; **C-D** *Regina*, No 29, T 225-7280, 2-star, a/c, bath, rooms vary; No 58, **D** *Ferreira Viana* (with bath, basic but always heavily booked, valuables may be left safely). **D** *Unico*, Buarque de Machado 54, T 205-9932, bath, TV, a/c, fridge, clean, friendly, rec (nr Largo do Machado metro). **E** *Monterrey*, R Artur Bernardes 39, with bath, musty but OK; at No 29, **E** *Rio Lisboa*, with bath, a/c, cheaper rooms without bath, clean, safe, rec—both hotels in this quiet street are family hotels. R Paissandu: No 34, **D** *Venezuela*, with bathroom, very clean, but rooms small and breakfast poor; **D** *Paysandu*, opp *Venezuela* at No 23, T 225-7270, very clean, comfortable and good value. Beyond Largo de Machado: R Gago Coutinho: No 22, **D** *Serrano*, pleasant, helpful; and **C** *Argentina*, Cruz Lima 30, T 225-7233, F 285-4573, rec.

Lapa/Fátima Between Lapa and Praça Tiradentes is an inner residential area, less desirable than Flamengo. Parts of this area are deserted from 2200 on. Near Cinelândia metro station are a lot of cheap hotels, but many are short stay. In Lapa itself, near the Arches just beyond Passeio Público, is R Joaquim Silva: No 99, **D** *Marajó*, with breakfast, varied rooms, clean; also **E** *Love's House*, R Joaquim Silva, ask for room with window, safe, respectable, good value. Passing under the Arches you come to Av Mem de Sá (bus 127 from bus terminal): No 85, **E** *Mundo Novo*, clean, a/c. Turning towards Praça Tiradentes is R Resende, No 31, **D** *Estadual*, good; No 35 **D** *Pouso Real*, T 224-2757, good, but the area is dubious. **D** *Marialva*, Gomes Freire 430 (nr New Cathedral, convenient for Av Rio Branco, buses etc), 2 star, with bath, a/c, breakfast in room, rec Praça Tiradentes; **D** *Rio Hotel*, clean, noisy rooms near Praça, quieter overlooking São Sebastião cathedral, with breakfast (only served in rooms).

Saúde/Mauá (area between the railway station and the docks): the very cheapest hotels in town are in this area, but it is not too safe at night.

In the traditional **Santa Teresa** district, R Almirante Alexandrino 660, is the **B** *Santa Teresa Hotel*, with swimming pool. Also Dona Ana's hostel on the same street at No 501, B, T 232-9603. Take the "Dois Irmãos" tram from Largo da Carioca or bus 206/214.

Youth Hostels R Almte Alexandrino 2840, Santa Teresa (*Pousada do Garuda*, T 225-0393/236-1419), Santa Amaro 162, Glória, T 222-8576, noisy; *Chave do Rio de Janeiro*, General Dionísio 63, Botafogo, T 286-0303, US$12, clean, washing facilities, superb breakfast, noisy but frequently rec; *Copacabana Praia* (also called *Indy*), R Ten Marones de Gusmão 85, Bairro Peixoto, CEP 22041, T 235-3817/237-5422, US$6; *Saint Roman*, R Saint Roman 48, Copacabana, T 227-7685; *Copacabana Chalet*, R Pompeu Loureiro 99, T 236-0047, US$23, noisy, near beach, shops, YHA card not necessary, but you pay a bit more without it. Associations: both at R da Assambleia 10: ALBERJ, (for Rio), room 1616, T 531-1302/2234; Federação Brasileira (Brazil), room 1211, T 531-1129. Youth hostels are fully booked between Christmas and Carnival; if intending to stay at this time reserve well in advance. Remember that "motels" are mainly for the use of very-short-stay couples.

The city is extremely noisy. An inside room is cheaper and much quieter. (If you are desperate and it is late, some smaller hotels and hostelries may let you sleep on the floor.)

Self-catering apartments are a popular form of accommodation in Rio, available at all price levels: for example, furnished apartments, accommodating up to 6, cost US$240 per month in Maracanã, about US$360 per month in Saúde, Cinelândia, Flamengo. Copacabana, Ipanema and Leblon prices range from about US$15 per day for a simple studio, up to US$2,000 a month for a luxurious residence sleeping 4 to 6. Heading S past Barra da Tijuca, virtually all the accommodation available is self-catering. Renting a small flat, or sharing a larger one, can be much better value than a hotel room. Blocks consisting entirely of short-let apartments can attract thieves, so check the (usually excellent) security arrangements; flats in residential buildings (described as "prédio familial") have fewer anti-theft devices but would be less at risk. Higher floors ("alto andar") are considered safest.

The following rent apartments in residential blocks: *Hamburg Imobiliária*, Av Copacabana 195, Loja 104, T 542-1446, F 236-4541, German run, specialize in flats, very reasonable, helpful, highly rec, also offer tours at good rates; *Yvonne Reimann*, Av Atlântica 4.066, Apto 605, T 227-0281, rents apartments, all with phone, near beach, a/c, maid service, English, French, German spoken, all apartments owned by the agency, prices from US$48; *Yolanda Thiémard*, Av Prado Junior 165 CO2, T 295-2088, multilingual, good value, rec; *Dona Lígia*, R Ministro Viveros de Castro 141 apto 101, T 541-6367, speaks English, lower-price apartments. European agent: Mr Peter Corr, Friedrichsplatz 6, D-6816, Mannheim, Germany, T 0049-621-402721, F 0049-6234-801177, rec. "Apart-Hotels" are listed in the Guia 4 Rodas and Riotur's booklet; the *Praia Leme Hotel*, Av Atlântica 866, has apartments (expensive), with maid and laundry service at Av Princesa Isabel 7, close to the beach; in high season reservation is necessary; *Rio Beach*, R Prado Junior 48, Loja 2, Copacabana, T 547-2395, well-equipped flats for US$18 per day and US$400 per month; *Rio Flat Service*, Almirante Guilhém 322, Leblon, reservations through SASS Ltda, Ataulfo de Paiva 566/305, T 274-9546, Telex: 30245. Also try *Copacabana Holidays* at R Barata Ribeiro 90, room 204, Copacabana, T 542-1597/542-1525, and at R Barata Ribeiro 87/ 202, T 255-2016 or 237-1133; *New Rio Home Service*, Visconde de Pirajá 414, sala 522, Ipanema, T 521-2332, F 267-6090, Swedish-run, rec; *Mellow Holidays*, R Paula Freitas 45/1101, T 256-5061, have apartments at a range of prices in the Copacabana and Ipanema districts. Agents and private owners advertise in *Balcão* (like *Exchange and Mart*), twice weekly, *O Globo* or *Jornal do Brasil* (daily); under "Apartamentos – Temporada"; advertisements are classified by district and size of apartment: "vagas e quartos" means shared accommodation; "conjugado" (or "conj") is a studio with limited cooking facilities; "3 Quartos" is a 3-bedroom flat. There should always be a written agreement when renting.

Camping Camping Clube do Brasil has beach site at Av Sernambetiba 3200, T 493-0628 (bus 233 from centre or 554 from Leblon, US$1.20—a long way from the centre), Barra da Tijuca (half price for members). During Jan and Feb this site is often full and sometimes restricted to members of the Camping Clube do Brasil. Also at Recreio dos Bandeirantes: Estrada do Pontal 5900, T 437-8400; *Ostal*, Av Sernambetiba 18790, T 437-8350; and *Novo Rio*, at 17.5 km on Rio-Santos road, T 437-6518. If travelling by trailer, you can park at the Marina Glória car park, where there are showers and toilets, a small shop and snack bar. Pay the guards to look after your vehicle. Camping gear for sale at Montcamp, Teixeira de Melo 21, Ipanema, T 287-1143.

Restaurants In Rio, avoid mussels! In 1994-95, meals in 1st and 2nd class restaurants cost between US$20 and 35 per head. The best restaurants in Rio are those at the quality hotels (good value for world-class food and service); most close at midnight. There are much cheaper places to eat as well if going out for an evening meal, Cariocas eat late (2200; later at weekends). **Centre**: *Café do Teatro*, Rio Branco, Teatro Municipal, good food in grand manner; shorts and scruffy gear not admitted; *Mosteiro*, R São Bento 13/15, Portuguese, closed Sat-Sun; *La Tour*, R Santa Luzia 651, 34th floor, revolving restaurant, varied menu; *Alba Mar*, fish, very good and reasonable, Praça Mal Ancora 184-6; *A Cabaça Grande*, Casa das Peixadas, R do Ouvidor 12, best for fish, closed Sun/holidays; *Rio Minho*, R do Ouvidor 10, for seafood, expensive, old-fashioned, very good. *Spaghetti*, Av Rio Branco 26, Italian, self-service, good salads, cheap. There are several Arab restaurants on Av Senhor dos Passos, also open Sat and Sun. *Taberna Carioca*, R Carioca, reminiscent of a Basque bar, interesting dishes; *La Table*, R do Rosário, pancakes, good and cheap; *Luciano*, R das Marrecas 44, all you can eat at buffet, and others on this street. Many *lanchonetes* for good, cheap meals in the business sector. Cheap eating places and juice bars on Praça Tiradentes.

Santa Teresa: *Bar do Arnaudo*, Alm Alexandrino 316, B, rec; *Spirits*, Alte Alexandrino 1458, small, friendly, European food, rec. **Lapa**: *Semente*, R Joaquim Silva 138, vegetarian. **Glória**: *Casa da Suíça* in same building as Swiss Consulate, R Cândido Mendes 157, bar/restaurant, good atmosphere; several others on this street; *Hobby Lanches*, R da Glória, near Metro, good, cheap; good Brazilian food in 1st floor cafeteria and adjoining restaurant (good views) at Santos Dumont airport.

Flamengo and Catete: there are a lot of eating places on R do Catete: *Bar KTT*, excellent; No 239, *Pastelaria Wong*, very cheap, good; No 234B, *Amazônia*, downstairs, one-price counter service, upstairs for good, reasonably-priced evening meals, rec; *Catelandia*, No 204, excellent and cheap; *Restaurante e Pizzaria Guanabara*, No 150, excellent value and selection; *Rio Galícia*, No 265, very good pizza, good service; *Machado*, No 286, good Italian food at reasonable prices; *Parmé*, No 311, one of a chain, friendly and reasonable; *No 128*, no name, lunch only, communal tables, rec; *Rio's*, Parque do Flamengo, "continental" food, nice location; *Alcaparra*, Praia do Flamengo 144, elegant Italian, reasonable; *Lamas*, Marquês de Abrantes 18-A, excellent value, good food, great atmosphere, popular with Brazilian arts/media people; *Gaúcha*, R das Laranjeiras 114, good. **Largo do Machado**: *Adega Real*, R Gago Coutinho, very good. Plenty of pizza places.

Botafogo: *Maxim's*, 44th floor of Rio Sul shopping centre, French, closed Sun; *Neal's*, R Sorocaba, US-style, burgers, chili, steaks, good value; *Manolo*, Bambina e M de Olinda, very good value; *Raajmahal*, R General Polidoro 29, Indian, reasonable; *Zen Japanese Restaurant*, Praia de Botafogo 228, highly rec.

Copacabana and Leme: The main hotels (see above); most expensive is *Le Saint Honoré* at the *Meridien*, Leme, good food and wonderful view; *Churrascaria Marius*, at Leme end of Av Atlântica, all you can eat US$15 with drinks, excellent; *Churrascaria Palace*, R Rodolfo Dantas 16-B, 22 different kinds of meat, very good; *Churrascaria do Jardim*, R República do Peru, excellent; *Nino*, R Domingos Ferreira 242-A, good but not cheap; *Arataca*, Figueiredo de Magalhães 28, try *carne-de-sol* and *lagosta ao molho*; *A Marisquera*, Barata Ribeiro 232, good seafood; *Ponto d'Encontro* at 750, Portuguese, try baked *bacalhau*; *Rian*, Santa Clara 8 (international), excellent and reasonable, very popular; *Arosa*, No 110, *lanchonete*, very good and cheap. *Enotria*, R Constante Ramos 115, Italian and 4 star. Cheap and good inclusive meal at *Frango na Brasa*, R Constante Ramos 35; *La Tratoria*, Av Atlântica (opp *Hotel Excelsior*), Italian, good food and service very reasonable, rec.

Ipanema: *Bardo Beto*, R Farme de Amoedo 51, excellent food, big servings, good value; *Il Capo*, Visconde de Pirajá 276, rec; *Le Streghe*, R Prudente Morais 129; *Banana Café*, Barão da Torre 368, trendy, rec, lively nightclub upstairs after 2400; *Porção*, Barão de Torre 218, a very good *churrascaria*, US$8; *Pax Delícia*, Praça Nossa Senhora de Paz, good food, lively crowd; *Mostarda*, Av Epitácio Pessoa 980, not cheap but food excellent, nightclub upstairs, rec. Ipanema is quieter than Copacabana, many nice places round main square, Praça General Osório, such as *Romanos*. *Del Mare*, rec, at corner of Prudente de Morais and Vinícius de Morais. *Vinícius*, R Vinícius de Morais, a good place to meet young people. *Casa da Feijoada*, Prudente de Morais 10, serves an excellent *feijoada* all week. Health food at *Restaurante Natural*, R Barão de Torre 171. *Delicats*, Av Henrique Dumont 68, good Jewish deli.

Leblon: *Un, Deux, Trois*, R Bartolomeu Mitre 123, very fashionable, restaurant, nightclub; *Antiquarius*, R Aristides Espínola 19, restaurant-cum-antique shop, seafood and international cuisine. *Mediterráneo*, R Prudente de Morais 1810, excellent fish, reasonable prices. In **São Conrado**, *El Pescador*, Praça São Conrado 20, Spanish-style fish restaurant, excellent value and variety of paellas.

Grill or barbecue houses (*churrascarias*) are relatively cheap, especially by European standards. There are many at São Conrado and Joá, on the road out to Barra da Tijuca (**see p 380**). Look for the "Churrascaria Rodízio", where you are served as much as you can eat. There are plentiful hamburger stands (literally "stands" as you stand and eat the hamburger) and lunch counters all over the city. *McDonalds* and *Big Bob's* (similar) can be found at about 20 locations each. *Galetos* are lunch counters specializing in chicken and grilled meat, very reasonable. In the "shopping centres" there is usually a variety of restaurants and snack bars grouped around a central plaza where you can shop around for a good meal. Most less-expensive restaurants in Rio have basically the same type of food (based on steak, fried potatoes and rice) and serve large portions; those with small appetites, and especially families with children, can ask for a spare plate, and split helpings. *La Mole*, at 11 locations, serves good, cheap Italian food: very popular. There are many juice bars in Rio with a wide selection. Most restaurants are closed on 24 and 25 Dec.

Tea Rooms For those who like their teas served English style, the sedate Belle Epoque (100 years old in 1994) *Confeiteria Colombo*, R Gonçalves Dias 32 near Carioca metro station, is highly rec for atmosphere, being the only one of its kind in Rio, with the original décor, open 0900-1800, lunch available, no service charge so tip the excellent waiters. More modern but similar establishments in some of the main hotels, and at *Casarão*, Souza Lima 37A, Copacabana; *Traiteurs de France*, Av Copacabana 386, delicious tarts and pastries, not expensive; *La Bonne Table*, Visc de Pirajá 580 sala 407, Ipanema; and *Ponto de Encontro*, Barata Ribeiro 750B, Copacabana. *Café de la Paix*, Av Atlântica 1020; *Chá e Simpatia*, Av Atlântica 4240; *Um Chorinho Chamado Odeon*, Gávea Shopping Centre; *Bolo Inglês*, Cassino Atlântico

Shopping Centre; *Concorde*, Av Prudente de Morais 129. These establishments have become very fashionable.

Bars Wherever you are, there's one near you. A beer costs around US$1.25, rarely more than US$2 even in expensive bars. A cover charge of US$1.25-5 may be made for live music. Snack food always available. Single drinkers/diners are usually welcome, though you may not remain alone for long unless you stick your nose in a book. The seafront bars on Avenida Atlântica are great for people-watching; the big hotels have good cocktail bars (*Copacabana Palace*, poolside, rec); *Alla Zingara*, corner of Min Viveiros de Castro and Belfort Roxo, is friendly. There are only 4 seafront bars in Ipanema: *Barril 1800*, Av Tom Jobim 110, highly rec, nice place to watch the sunset. *A Garôta de Ipanema*, R Vinicius de Morais 49, is where the song "Girl from Ipanema" was written, very lively; the *Lord Jim* pub, R Paul Redfern 63, charmingly English-style but does attract prostitutes. Lots more bars opening in districts to the S: *Praça do Chopp*, Barra da Tijuca, rec (good Baiano seafood). *Bar Lagoa*, Av Epitácio Pessoa 1674, Lagoa, rec ("arty crowd", evenings only). In Flamengo, *A Garôta de Flamengo* and *Caneco 2* have been rec. British ex-pats meet at *Porão*, under the Anglican church hall, R Real Grandeza 99, Botafogo, Fri only.

Banks Lloyds Bank, R da Alfândega 33; **Banco Internacional** (Bank of America and Royal Bank of Canada), R do Ouvidor 90; **Banco Holandês Unido**, R do Ouvidor 101; **Citibank**, R Assembléia 100, changes large US$ TCs into smaller ones, no commission; **The First National Bank of Boston**, Av Rio Branco 110; **Banco de Crédito Real de Minas Gerais**, SA, Av Rio Branco 116; **Banco Lar Brasileiro**, R do Ouvidor 98; and many others. **Banco Noroeste**, R Buenos Aires 56, advances cash on Eurocard/Mastercard. Banks are open 1000 to 1630. Closed on Sat. Banco do Brasil at the International Airport is open 24 hrs a day. Banks use the legal tourist exchange rate. See **Currency** p 598.

Exchange Houses American Express, Av Atlântica 1702, Loja B, *Hotel Copacabana Palace*, T 255-2148/2677. Most large hotels and reputable travel agencies will change currency and TCs. Copacabana (where parallel market rates are generally worse than in centre) abounds with *câmbios*; Visa cash withdrawals at **Banco do Brasil** (also TCs) and **Bradesco** (machines); Mastercard and Diners at **Credicard** outlets. **NB** Many *câmbios* will give you the parallel rate for cash, but a worse rate for cheques; some will also change US$ cheques for US$ cash with a 4% commission. These transactions are not strictly legal, so you will have to look around for the *câmbios* that do them.

Electric Current 110-220 volts, 60 cycles, AC.

Cultural and Trade Institutions The **British Council**, R Elmano Cardim 10, Urca, T 295-7782, F 541-3693. The **British School of Rio de Janeiro**, R Real Grandeza 99. **Sociedade Brasileira de Cultura Inglesa**, Av Graça Aranha 327, and in Copacabana, T 227-0147. **American Chamber of Commerce for Brazil**, Praça Pio Dez 15, 5th floor. **American Society and American Club**, Av Rio Branco 123, 21st floor. **USICA Reference Library**, US Consulate General, Av Presidente Wilson 147. The **American School of Rio de Janeiro**, Estrada da Gávea 132. **German Cultur-Institut** (Goethe), Av Graça Aranha 416, 9th floor; open Mon-Thur 1200-1900, Wed-Thur 1000-1100. **Centro Cultural Banco do Brasil**, R Primeiro de Março 66, free concerts. **Australian Trade Commission**, R Voluntários da Pátria 45, 2°, Botafogo, T 286-7922; for visas etc you must go to Brasília.

Consulates Argentine, Praia de Botafogo 228, T 551-5498, very helpful over visas, 1130-1600; Uruguay, R Artur Bernardes 30, T 285-0195; Paraguay, Av NS de Copacabana 583, room 404, T 255-7572, visas US$5; Venezuela, Praia de Botafogo 242, 5th floor, T 551-5698 (will not issue visas, see under Manaus and Boa Vista).

US Consulate General, Avenida Presidente Wilson, 147, T 292-7117. Canada, R Dona Gerardo 46, 11th floor, T 233-9286.

UK, Praia do Flamengo 284, T 552-1422; Ireland, Av Princesa Isabel 323, 1208, T 275 0196; Switzerland, R Cândido Mendes 157, 11° andar, T 242-8035; German Consulate-General, R Presidente Carlos de Campos 417, T 553-6777; France, Av Pres Antônio Carlos, 58, T 210-1272; Austria, Av Atlântica 3804, T 227-0040/048/049; Netherlands, Praia de Botafogo 242, 7th floor, T 552-9028 (Dutch newspapers here; also at KLM office on Av Rio Branco); Swedish Consulate-General, Praia do Flamengo 344, 9° andar, T 552-2422; Denmark, Av das Américas 3333, Apt 805, T 431-2080.

Israel, Av NS Copacabana 680-C, T 255-5432; S Africa, Av Pres Antônio Carlos 607, T 533-0216.

Nightclubs Rio nightlife is rich and infinitely varied, one of the main attractions for most visitors. If you are not in Rio for Carnival, it's worth seeing a samba show, cheaper if you buy at the door. *Hotel Nacional* at São Conrado has the most lavish show in town. Other good samba shows at: *Oba-Oba*, Humaitá 110, T 286-9848, eg US$20 without dinner, telephone to confirm price in advance; *Scala*, Av Afrânio de Melo Franco 296, Leblon, T 239-4448; *Plataforma I*, R Adalberto Ferreira 32, Leblon, T 274-4022, arrive by 2000, show finishes 2300. For about 2 months before Carnival, samba schools give public rehearsals, cheap and great fun (see p 362).

Many young Cariocas congregate in Botafogo for live music. There are free concerts throughout the summer, along the beaches, in Botafogo and at the parks: mostly samba, reggae, rock and MPB (Brazilian pop): information from local press (see below). January sees Hollywood Rock, a vast 3-day open air concert featuring international bands, Praça da Apotese; there are live concerts every weekend at the Arpoador park, between Copacabana and Ipanema.

Trendiest clubs in 1994 (contemporary dance music) included: *Dr Smith*, R da Passagem 169, Botafogo, T 295-3135, Wed-Sun; *Banana Café*, Barão da Torre 368, Ipanema; *Mostarda*, Av Epitácio Pessoa 980, Ipanema; *Resumo da Ópera*, Av Borges de Medeiros 1426, Lagoa, T 274-5875 ("rich Brazilians at play"); *The Basement*, Av NS de Copacabana 1241, new, alternative; also rec is *Torre de Babel*, Visconde de Parajá (close to hippy market), Sats only; and at the *Jardim Botânico* (weekends). There are dozens of other good clubs, most open Wed-Sun, action starts around midnight, lone women and male-only groups may have trouble getting in.

Canecão is a big, inexpensive venue for live concerts, most nights, see press for listings: R Venceslau Braz 215, Botafogo, T 295-3044, often hosts famous names, as does *Circo Voador*, in a tent under Arcos da Lapa (flyover), Centro.

Rio's famous jazz, in all its forms, is performed in lots of enjoyable venues, see press. The following are sophisticated sit-down places (you have to eat something, budget around US$20 each, comfortable for lone women): *Jazzmania*, Av Rainha Elisabeth, Ipanema, T 227-2447; **Mistura Fina**, Av Borges de Medeiros 3207, Lagoa, T 286-0195; *Rio Jazz Club*, above *Meridien Hotel*, Av Atlântica, Leme, T 541-9046. Check time of show, usually around 2200.

Gafieiras, for Samba dancing, include **Elite Club**, R Frei Caneca 4, 1st floor, Centro, T 232-3217; *Estudantinha*, Praça Tiradentes 79, T 232-1149, Thur-Sun: there are many cheaper *gafieiras*: one, enthusiastically rec, under the beach highway at Botafogo. All types of music and entertainment are represented: *Forró da Copacabana*, Av NS de Copacabana 435, has been rec for forró fans (safe, disco upstairs); *Reggae Rock Cafe*, Largo de São Conrado 20, T 322-4197; *Raizes*, Av Sernambetiba 1120, T 389-6240, for Afro-Brazilian beats.

Copacabana is full of discos where the girls are for hire: biggest and most entertaining is *Help*. Entry charge includes a drink. Music is usually good, trade is low-pressure, women with female friends and a sense of humour can have a lot of fun (but not rec for couples). Sleazier shows are concentrated around Leme, as are gay clubs; many gay clubs also around Lapa (Cinelândia), but good ones exist all over the city. *Stop-Night*, a disco bar at Av Atlântica (near *Copacabana Palace* hotel) is a popular gay pick-up joint: please be extremely careful.

Many people look for Macumba religious ceremonies. Those offered on the night tours sold at hotels are not genuine, and a disappointment. You need a local contact to see the real ones, which are usually held in *favelas* and are none too safe for unaccompanied tourists.

Theatres There are about 40 theatres in Rio, presenting a variety of classical and modern performances in Portuguese. Seats about US$5; some children's theatre is free, Rio's stages attract top-name Brazilian artists—check local papers.

Cinemas New American releases (with original soundtrack), plus Brazilian and worldwide films, and classics. A very few give cheaper tickets to students, but not at weekends. See local press. Normal seat price US$3.50, discount on Wed and Thur.

Health Vaccinations at Saude de Portos, Praça 15 de Novembro (international vaccination book and ID required). Policlínica, Av Nilo Peçanha 38, rec for diagnosis and investigation. Hospital Miguel Couto, Mário Ribeiro 117, Gávea, has a casualty ward (free), but no eye doctors T 274-2121; these can be found at Hospital Souza Aguiar, Praça da República III (casuality ward also free), T 296-4114. The Rio Health Collective will help you contact an English-speaking doctor: dial 294-0282/325-3327/239-7401; ask for the "dona da casa".

Take note of local advice on water pollution; air pollution also occurs.

Dentist English-speaking, Amílcar Werneck de Carvalho Vianna, Av Pres Wilson 165, suite 811. Dr Djorup, Av Beira Mar Mauro Suartz, R Visconde de Pirajá 414, room 509, T 287-6745, speaks English and Hebrew, helpful.

Public Conveniences There are very few in Rio de Janeiro, but many bars and restaurants (eg Macdonalds) offer facilities; just ask for the "banheiro" (banyairoo). Good conveniences are to be found in the Shopping Centres.

Portuguese Language Courses Instituto Brasil-Estados Unidos, Av Copacabana 690, 5°

andar, T 255-8332, offers 8-week courses, 3 classes a week, US$200, 5-week intensive course US$260. Good English library at same address. Curso Feedback, branches in Botafogo, Centre, Barra and Ipanema, T 221-1863.

Laundromats *Fénix*, R do Catete 214, Loja 20; R Marques de Abrantes, about No 80 (Flamengo); Praça G Osório, Ipanema; *Lavlev Flamengo*, RC de Baepinédi 78, or R das Laranjeiras 43, L28; Laundromat at 1216 Av NS de Copacabana; R Barata Ribeiro 662, Copacabana, self-service, US$1.50 per machine. In Rio Sul are self-service laundrettes such as *Lavlev*, about US$3-4 for a machine, including detergent and drying, 1 hr, also at R Voluntário da Patria 248, Botafogo, Av Prado Jnr 6313, Copacabana.

Local press *Balcão*, an advertising newspaper, US$1.25, twice weekly, offers apartments in and around Rio, language lessons, discounted tickets, items for sale, and advertises shops; similar advertisements in the classified sections of *O Globo* and *Jornal do Brasil*, daily. Both dailies have entertainments pages. *O Globo* includes a travel section on Thur; the *Jornal do Brasil's* Friday *Programa* is an essential "what's-on" magazine, as is the *Rio* supplement to *Veja*, a weekly news magazine (*Veja* publishes similar supplements in other major cities). *Riotur's* monthly booklet listing main attractions; *Rio This Month* (less reliable), free from hotels. *TurisRio's* free magazine about the State of Rio de Janeiro is interesting; if your hotel does not have the above 3 publications, just ask at the reception of one of the larger establishments.

Post Office Central Post Office, R Primeiro de Março 64, at corner of R do Rosário; Av NS de Copacabana 540, and many other locations; all handle international post. There is a post office at the airport. **Poste Restante** American Express, Av Atlântica 1702 loja B, Copacabana (for customers), and all large post offices (letters held for a month, rec, US$0.10 per letter); Kontik Franstur will forward mail to their branches in Brazil without charge. Federal Express, Av Catalogeras 23 (near Sta Luzia church) T 262-8565, is reliable.

Telephones International calls at Av Copacabana 540, 2nd floor, international airport, international telephone booths (blue), rodoviária, R Dias da Cruz 182-4, 24 hrs, 7 days a week, or at Santos Dumont airport, 1st floor (0530-2300).

Cables Embratel, Av President Vargas 1012. Telegrams may be sent through any post office. Larger offices have telex and fax.

Shopping Buy precious and semi-precious stones from reputable dealers. *H Stern* have shops at the airport, and all over Copacabana and Ipanema; they also offer a tour, with head-phone commentary, of their lapidary and designing workshops, on request; *Roditi* and *Amsterdam Sauer* offer free taxi rides to their workshops. There are several good jewellery shops at the Leme end of Av NS de Copacabana. For mineral specimens as against cut stones, try *Mineraux*, Av Copacabana 195, Belgian owner. *Saara* is a multitude of little shops along R Alfândega and R Sen dos Passos (between city centre and Campo Sant'ana) where clothes bargains can be found (especially jeans and bikinis). Little shops on Aires Saldanha, Copacabana (one block back from beach), good for bikinis and cheaper than in shopping centres. *Malamada*, R da Carioca 13, rec for rucksacks. **Shopping centres**: Rio Sul, at Botafogo end of Túnel Novo, Cassino (Copacabana), Norte Shopping (Todos os Santos), Plaza Shopping (Niteroi), Barra on Barra de Tijuca (**see p 380**). At São Conrado The Fashion Mall is smaller and more stylish.

Cameras and Film Processing *Dino's*, R Buenos Aires 241; others in same street. Camera repair, Av Rio Branco 151, 2nd floor, room 204. Kodachrome slide film difficult to get in Rio. For processing, Flash Studio, R Viscondede Piraiá 156, expensive; *One Hour Foto*, in the Rio Sul and Barra shopping centres, is rec; also a laboratory at R do Russel 344, Glória (1 hr for transparencies). Honório, R Vinícius de Moraes 146-E, stocks lithium batteries. Nikon camera repairs, T Tanaka (via Jda, Av Franklin Roosevelt 39, of 505, T 220-1127.

Electronics repair (radio, walkman, etc), *Eletrônica Tekron*, R Figueiredo Magalhes 870, Copacabana, T 235-4096, efficient, friendly.

Bookshops For international stock, *Livraria Kosmos*, R do Rosário 155, good shop (in the centre and Av Atlântica 1702, loja 5) and there are many others, eg *Livros Técnicos*, R Miguel Couto 35, wide selection; *Nova Livraria Da Vinci*, Av Rio Branco 185 loja 2/3, all types of foreign books, *SAH* available; *Livrarias Siciliano*, Av Rio Branco 156, loja 26, European books, also at NS de Copacabana 830 and branches; French books at No 298. Unilivros, Largo do Machado 29C, French and English bestsellers (7 branches); *Livraria Nova Galeria de Arte*, Av Copacabana 291D, international stock. *El Dorado*, Av das Américas 4666, loja 207. Second-hand books also at **Livraria São José**, R Carmo 61 (only a few in English); *Livraria Brasileira*, Av Rio Branco 156, S/Loja 229; Aimée Gilbert, R da Carioca 38 (some in English); *Livraria Antiquário*, Sete de Setembro 207 and in R Pedro I, all in centre. Also on Av Marechal Floriano, near Av Rio Branco, especially at No 63. On S side of Praça Tiradentes, **Casa dos**

Artistas trades in second-hand paperbacks. Second-hand English books at the Anglican church, R Real Grandeza 99, Botafogo.

Markets North-eastern market at Campo de São Cristóvão, with music and magic, on Sun mornings. Saturday antiques market on waterfront, near Praça 15 de Novembro (1000-1800), rec, and flea market Sat (0900-1900) in Praça 15; another in Largo da Carioca. Sunday stamp and coin market in Passeio Público. Sunday open-air handicrafts market (hippie fair) at Praça General Osório, Ipanema, 0800-1300 or 1400, touristy but fun. Markets on Wed 0700-1300 on R Domingos Ferreira and on Thur, same hours, on Praça do Lido, both Copacabana; also on Thur, good leather and jewellery market on 1 de Março in centre. Sunday market on R da Glória, colourful, cheap fruit, vegetables and flowers. Excellent food and household-goods markets at various places in the city and suburbs (see newspapers for times and places).

Sports There are hundreds of excellent gyms and sports clubs; most will not grant temporary (less than 1 month) membership: big hotels may allow use of their facilities for a small deposit. Paissandu Athletic Club, Av Afrânio de Melo Franco 330, Leblon—tennis, bowls, swimming, Scottish dancing, Tues, Apr-Oct, 2000-2230, may admit non-members. Sociedade Hípico Brasileiro, Av Borges de Medeiros 2448, T 246-8090, Jardim Botânico—riding; horse racing Sat, Sun, entrance US$1-2, long trousers required. Iate Clube do Rio de Janeiro, Av Pasteur, Urca, T 295-4482 – yachting. Cycling tours (hire available) with Rio Bikers, R Domingos Ferreira 81, room 201, T 274-5872. Rock climbing and hill walking: ECA, Av Enasmo Braga 217, room 305, T 242-6857/571-0484, personal guide US$100 per day, owner Ralph speaks English; Clube Excursionista Carioca, also rec for enthusiasts, R Hilário Gouveia 71, room 206, T 255-1348, meets Wed, Fri. Hang gliding with Rejane Reis (US$100), T 322-6972. Paragliding from Leblon beach with Sr Marra, T 226-5207 or find him at the beach: "Just fantastic!"

Golf Clubs There are both 18-hole and 9-hole courses at the Itanhangá Golf Club, Jacarepaguá, visiting cards from Avenida Rio Branco 26, 16th floor. The Gávea club, São Conrado, T 399-4141 and the Teresópolis Golf Club, Estrada Imbuí (Várzea) both have 18 holes. 9 holes at Petrópolis Country Club, Nogueira.

Travel Agents *American Express*, see **Exchange Houses** above; *Roxy*, Av Winston Churchill 60, helpful, rec (ask for Michael Oeary who speaks English); *Exprinter*, Av Rio Branco, 128; *Manhattan Turismo Ltda*, R da Assembléia 10, GR 3503, Centro, T 242-3779/3064, very helpful, English spoken; *Tour Brazil*, R Farme de Amoeda 75/605, nr Ipanema, T 521-4461, F 021-521-1056, very good English spoken; *Victor Hummel*, Av Presidente Vargas 290/4, T 223-1262, Swiss-run, rec, T 231-1800. *Marlin Tours*, Av Copacabana 605/1201, T 255-4433, rec, Robin and Audrey speak English. *Quality Travel*, Av NS Copacabana 387, T 235-6888, F 236-6985, helpful with hotel bookings.

The tourist office in Praça da República offers hourly tourist buses for US$0.50: leave the bus at sites you wish to visit, and rejoin the next one. Organized trips to Samba shows cost US$50 including dinner, good but it's cheaper to go independently. Regular sightseeing tours operated by *Gray Line* (294-0393), *American Sightseeing* (236-3551), *Sul América* (257-4235), *Canbitur* (of Copacabana), *Passamar Turismo*, Av Rio Branco 25 (233-8883, 233-4833, 253-1125; also at *Hotel Nacional*). *Adrianotour*, T 208-5103, for guided tours, reservations and commercial services (English, French, German and Spanish spoken).

For a good, private walking tour of Rio's cultural sights, contact Prof Carlos Roquette, a professor of history, who charges US$20 pp, T 322-4872, 24 hrs, write to R Santa Clara 110/904, Copacabana, Rio de Janeiro, RJ 22041, English and French spoken. Prof Roquette also organizes singles parties.

Tourist Information There are several information centres. Embratur, R Mariz e Barros 13, near Praça da Bandeira, T 273-2212, gives information on the whole country. Riotur (for the city of Rio): Official information stands at Pão de Açúcar cablecar station (0800-2000); Marina da Glória, Flamengo; Rodoviária Novo Rio (the bus station—0600-2400; very friendly and helpful in finding accommodation). Riotur also has a multilingual telephone service operating 24 hrs, T 580-8000. English information service, T 242-8000. Flumitur (for the state of Rio de Janeiro) at Rio International Airport, helpful with hotel information and booking, can sometimes arrange discounts, and R da Assembléia 10, 8th floor, very helpful. **Touring Clube do Brasil**, Pres Antônio Carlos 130 and Av Brasil 4294 (out of town) no English spoken. Centro Cultural Banco do Brasil, Primeiro Março 66, has a free, computerized information service.

NB Tourist packs are sold for US$25 at the International Airport—they are completely unnecessary. Best guide to Rio, with excellent map, *Guia Quatro Rodas do Rio* in Portuguese and English (the *Guia Quatro Rodas do Brasil*, published annually in Nov also has a good Rio section). *Guia Rex* street guide. *Guia Schaeffer Rio de Janeiro* is a good map. Also, *The Insider's Guide to Rio de Janeiro*, an annual guide book by Christopher Pickard, available from Rio bookshops, or enquire at Marlin Tours (T 255-4433). Many hotels provide guests with the weekly *Itinerário* (*Rio This Month*); also see **Local Press**, above.

Maps are available from Riotur information desks, Touring Clube do Brasil, newsstands, touring agencies and hotels; Geomapas tourist map is clear. Paulini, R Lélio Gama 75 (outside the entrance of the downtown tram station): topographical and other maps of Brazil and of South America. **NB** Tourist agencies do not normally provide lists of cheap accommodation for travellers; some initiative is required.

Tourist Police Av Afrânio de Melo Franco, Leblon (opp Casa Grande theatre), for renewal of 90-day visa, US$4.

Buses Good services to all parts, very crowded, not for the aged and infirm during rush hours. Hang on tight, drivers living out Grand Prix fantasies. Fare normally about US$0.40. Bus stops are often not marked. The route is written on the side of the bus. Private companies operate air-conditioned buses which can be flagged down practically anywhere: Real, Pegaso, Anatur. They run from all points in Rio Sul to the city centre, Rodoviária and the airports. Fares about US$2 (US$5 to international airport).

Trams The last remaining tram runs from Largo da Carioca (where there is a museum, open only Fri 0830-1700) across the old aqueduct (Arcos) to Dois Irmãos or Paula Matos in Santa Teresa— historical and interesting, US$0.10. Service is cut in low season. The trams are open sided, do not carry valuables.

Taxis The fare between Copacabana and the centre is US$7. Between 2300 and 0600 on Suns and holidays "tariff 2" is used. Taxis have red number plates with white digits (yellow for private cars, with black digits) and have meters. Smaller ones (mostly Volkswagen) are marked TAXI on windscreen or roof. Meters measure in "taxi units" (UT), which are converted to the *real* fare according to updating sheets (make sure the updating sheet is not folded over and is an original in black and red, and not a photocopy—this is a well-known fiddle); all the same, beware of overcharging, which is rife (**see also p 377** in Rodoviária section). Make sure meters are cleared and on tariff 1, except at those times mentioned above. Only use taxis with an official identification sticker on the windscreen. Don't hesitate to argue if the route is too long or the fare too much. Radio Taxis are safer and not much more expensive, eg Cootramo, 270-1442, Coopertramo, 260-2022, Cooper-Transpa, 593-2598, Transcoopass, 278-4888. Luxury cabs are allowed to charge higher rates. Inacro de Oliveira, T 225-4110, is a reliable taxi driver for excursions, only speaks Portuguese, rec. Grimalde, T 267 9812, has been rec for talkative daytime and evening tours, English, Italian, negotiate price.

Underground Railway Line 1 operates between Tijuca and Botafogo, via the railway station and Glória, with 19 km in operation; it is being extended 1 km at the Tijuca end and 7 km at the other. It will go from Botafogo via Copacabana and on to Ipanema and Leblon (Jardim de Allah); due to open in 1994, the extension was still far from completion in Nov. Line 2, running past the Maracanã stadium northward to Irajá, will eventually run from Praça 15 de Novembro (Estação das barcas Rio-Niteroi), through the city centre, to Estácio. Operates 0600-2300, closed Sun and holidays. Fare US$0.50; integrated bus/metro tickets available (cheaper if bought in bulk). Substantial changes in bus operations are taking place because of the extended metro system; buses connecting with the metro have a blue-and-white symbol in the windscreen. If you speak Portuguese, apply to the Municipality and allow 10 days for arranging a sightseeing tour.

Car Hire For self-drive, try **Avis**, Rio International airport, less helpful than office at Praia do Flamengo 224 (205-5796); **Nobre**, Gustavo Sampaio 826 (275-5297) and Av Princesa Isabel 350 (T 541-4646) Copacabana. **Telecar**, R Figueiredo Magalhães 701 (257-2620). Many agencies on Av Princesa Isabel, Copacabana. Credit card virtually essential. Recent reports suggest it is cheaper to hire outside Brazil, you may also obtain fuller insurance this way. Remember service stations are closed in many places on Sat and Sun.

Car Repairs Kyoso Team Mecânico Siquero Campos, at the entrance to the old tunnel, T 255-0506, a good mechanic who enjoys the challenge of an unusual car, rec.

Cycle Repairs For bicycles and repairs, the shop in R Aires Saldanha, Copacabana is rec.

Airports Rio has two airports. The Santos Dumont airport on Guanabara Bay, right in the city, is used exclusively for Rio-São Paulo shuttle flights (US$300 return), air taxis and private planes. The shuttle services operate every ½-hr throughout the day from 0630 to 2230. Sit on right-hand side for views to São Paulo, other side coming back, book in advance for particular flights. The main airport (Galeão), on Governador Island, some 16 km from the centre of Rio, is in two sections, international and domestic (including Vasp and Transbrasil's jet shuttle from Rio to São Paulo). Duty-free shops are well-stocked, but not especially cheap. Uniquely, duty-free at Galeão is open to arrivals as well as departures. The Real company runs an air-conditioned bus (*frescão*) from the first floor of Galeão to Santos Dumont Airport, via the Rodoviária and city centre, every half-hour, US$3 (for Flamengo/Catete hotel area, take this bus, then a taxi - US$2.50 - from Santos Dumont); it continues to Copacabana (stopping at Av Atlântica e Santa Clara) US$3. Stops on Av Atlântica for return to the airport. Air-conditioned taxis (Cootramo and Transcopass) have fixed rates (US$10 downtown, US$35 Copacabana), buy a ticket at the counter near the arrivals gate before getting into the car. The hire is for taxi, irrespective of number of passengers, and therefore the possibility of sharing with other passengers arises. Ordinary taxis also operate with the normal meter reading—make sure you are given the card which gives the number to phone if you are overcharged (about US$17 downtown, US$18 Copacabana). A good policy is to check at the Riotur counter before leaving, for folders, maps and advice. Do not negotiate with a driver on arrival, unless you are a frequent visitor. Town bus No 322 goes to Rio International airport, first one with direction Bananal. There are *câmbios* in the departure hall of airport; there is also a *câmbio* on the first floor of the international arrivals area, but it gives worse rates than the Banco do Brasil, 24-hr bank, 3rd floor, which gives close to parallel rate and will give cash advances against Visa card (beware "officials" who say there are no *câmbios* or banks). There is a wider choice of restaurants before passport control. We have been told that X-ray machines at Galeão are not safe for film.

Rail There are suburban trains to Nova Iguaçu, Nilópolis, Campo Grande and elsewhere. Buses marked "E Ferro" go to the railway station. A consortium led by Montmar is planning to re-establish trains to São Paulo in 1995; a cabin on the 9-hr journey will cost approximately US$80 single.

Buses Rodoviária Novo Rio, T 291-5151. Some travel agents sell interstate tickets, or will direct you to bus ticket office in centre. Buses run from Rio to all parts of the country; it is advisable to book tickets in advance. Details of journey times and fares are given under destinations throughout the chapter.

    International Asunción, 1,511 km via Foz do Iguaçu, 30 hrs (Pluma), US$42; **Buenos Aires** (Pluma), via Porto Alegre and Santa Fe, 44 hrs, US$163 (book 2 days in advance); **Montevideo**, only from São Paulo; **Santiago** de Chile, with Pluma or Gral Urquiza, about 70 hrs. The Buenos Aires and Montevideo services are fully booked a week in advance.

    The main bus station (the rodoviária, at Av Rodrigues Alves, corner with Av Francisco Bicalho, just past the docks, reached by buses 104 from the centre, 127 and 128 from Copacabana and 136, 456, 172 from Flamengo, and 170 from Largo do Machado and Flamengo, or taxi), has a Riotur information centre, very helpful. Left luggage, US$2.50. From rodoviária, take bus 104 to Largo do Machado or to Catete for central location with buses and cheap hotels. The local bus teminal is just outside the rodoviária: turn right as you leave and run the gauntlet of taxi drivers. The rodoviária attracts thieves; exercise caution. The Real bus goes along the beach to São Conrado and will take luggage. **If you do need a taxi collect a ticket**, which ensures against overcharging, from the official at the head of the taxi queue. The fare to Copacabana in 1994 was US$10. On no account give the ticket to the taxi driver.

Hitchhiking To hitch to Belo Horizonte or Brasília, take a C-3 bus from Av Presidente Antônio Carlos to the railway station, cross through the station to a bus station, and catch the Nova Iguaçu bus. Ask to be let off at the Belo Horizonte turn off. For the motorway entrance N and S take bus 392 or 393 from Praça São Francisco.

Roads Distances in km to some major cities with approximate journey time in brackets: Juiz de Fora, 171 (2¾ hrs); Belo Horizonte, 429 (7 hrs); São Paulo, 434 (6 hrs); Vitória, 519 (8 hrs); Curitiba, 839 (12 hrs); Brasília, 1,148 (20 hrs); Florianópolis, 1,154 (20 hrs); Foz do Iguaçu, 1,500 (21 hrs); Porto Alegre, 1,603 (26 hrs); Salvador, 1,690 (28 hrs); Recife, 2,309 (38 hrs); Fortaleza, 2,861 (48 hrs); São Luís, 3,093 (50 hrs); Belém, 3,187 (52 hrs).

The Suburbs of Rio de Janeiro

Copacabana, built on a narrow strip of land—only a little over 4 square kilometres—between mountain and sea, has one of the highest population densities in the world: 62,000 per square kilometre, or 250,000 in all. Its celebrated curved beach backed by skyscraper apartments is an unforgettable "must" for visitors. On all Rio's beaches you should take a towel or mat to protect you against sandflies; in the water stay near groups of other swimmers; there is a strong undertow. Tourist police patrol Copacabana beach until 1700.

    Copacabana began to develop when the Old Tunnel was built in 1891 and an electric tram service reached it. Week-end villas and bungalows sprang up; all have now gone. In the 1930s the Copacabana Palace Hotel was the only tall building;

it is now one of the lowest on the beach. The opening of the New Tunnel in the 1940s led to an explosion of population which shows no sign of having spent its force. Unspoilt Art Deco blocks towards the Leme (city) end of Copacabana are now under preservation order.

There is almost everything in this "city within a city". The shops, mostly in Av Copacabana and the R Barata Ribeiro, are excellent; this is the area in which to watch, or participate in, the city's glamorous night life. A fort at the far end of the beach commands the entrance to Rio Bay and prevents a seashore connection with the Ipanema and Leblon beaches. Parts of the military area are now being handed over to civilian use, the first being the Parque Garota de Ipanema at Arpoador, the fashionable Copacabana end of the Ipanema beach. Buses to and from the city centre are plentiful and cheap, about US$0.40. If you are going to the centre from Copacabana, look for "Castelo", "Praça 15", "E Ferro" or "Praça Mauá" on the sign by the front door. "Aterro" means the expressway between Botafogo and downtown Rio (not open Sun). From the centre to Copacabana is easier as all buses in that direction are clearly marked. Aterro bus does the journey in 15 mins.

Beyond Copacabana are the beautiful seaside suburbs of **Ipanema** (a good place from which to watch the sunset) and **Leblon**. They are a little less built-up than Copacabana, and their beaches tend to be cleaner. Backing Ipanema and Leblon is the middle-class residential area of Lagoa Rodrigo de Freitas, by a salt-water lagoon on which Rio's rowing and small-boat sailing clubs are active; too polluted for bathing. Beyond Leblon the coast is rocky; the Avenida Niemeyer skirts the cliffs on the journey past Vidigal, a small beach where the *Sheraton* is situated, to the outer seaside suburbs of São Conrado (beach polluted) and Barra da Tijuca (see below). The flat topped Gávea rock can be climbed or scrambled up for magnificent views, but beware snakes. Buses from Botafogo Metro terminal to Ipanema: some take integrated Metro-Bus tickets; look for the blue signs on the windscreen. Many buses from Copacabana to Ipanema (buses 154 and 158 from Flamengo) and Leblon (buses 158, 434 and 488 from Flamengo, continuing to Barra da Tijuca).

Santa Tereza, a hilly inner suburb SW of the centre, well known as the coolest part of Rio, boasts many colonial and 19th-century buildings, set in narrow, curving, tree-lined streets. See particularly the Convent (only the outside; the Carmelite nuns do not admit visitors), the Chácara do Céu Museum (**see p 363**), the Hotel Santa Teresa (the oldest house in the area), Vista Alegre, the R Aprazível, and Largo de Guimarães. Santa Tereza is best visited on the traditional open-sided tram, described on **p 376.**

Maracanã Stadium is one of the largest sports centres in the world. The football ground has seating capacity for 200,000 spectators (matches are worth going to for the spectators' samba bands, even if you're not a football fan; **NB** Agencies charge much more for tickets than at the gate). Bus 455 from Copacabana; 434 from Flamengo; from Leblon, 464 via Ipanema and Copacabana; also Metro from Botafogo and centre. Guided tour of stadium (in Portuguese), US$2.50, and museum, US$0.50, highly rec to football fans. Maracanã, sadly, is now used only for major games; Rio teams play most matches at their home grounds (still a memorable experience). Hotels can arrange visits to football matches: good idea Sun when the metro is closed and buses very full. If you want the real football experience, take a bus 3 hrs before the game, buy a ticket (about US$5) in the upper ring (*arquibancada*), people very friendly.

Corcovado (710m) is the hunch-backed peak surmounted by a 40-metre high statue of Christ the Redeemer completed in 1931, weighing, with its base, 1,200 tons. There is a superb view from the top (sometimes obscured by mist), to which there are a cog railway and a road; both car and train put down their passengers behind the statue—there is a climb of 220 steps to the top, near which there is a café. To see the city by day and night ascend at 1500 or 1600 and descend on the last train approx 1815. Mass is held on Sun in a small chapel in the statue pedestal. The floodlighting was designed in 1931 by Marconi himself.

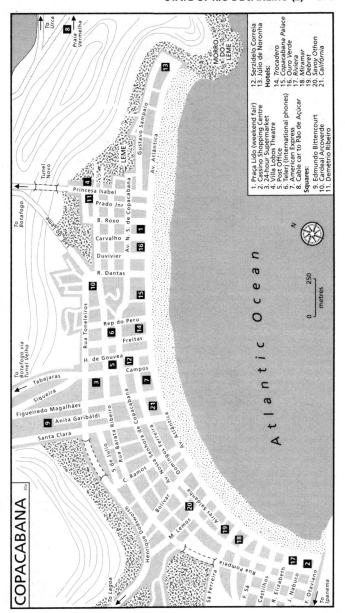

COPACABANA

1. Praça Lido (weekend fair)
2. Cassino Shopping Centre
3. 24-hour Supermarket
4. Villa Lobos Theatre
5. Post Office
6. Teleri (International phones)
7. American Express
8. Cable car to Pão de Açúcar

Squares:
9. Edmundo Bittencourt
10. Cardeal Arcoverde
11. Demétrio Ribeiro

12. Serzidelo Correia
13. Júlio de Noronha

Hotels:
14. Trocadero
15. Copacabana Palace
16. Ouro Verde
17. Riviera
18. Miramar
19. Debret
20. Savoy Othon
21. Califórnia

Atlantic Ocean

0   250
metres

Take a Cosme Velho bus (180, 184 from Centro or Flamengo) to the **cog railway station at R Cosme Velho 513**; from Copacabana take No 583, 584 back. Service every 20-30 mins according to demand between 0800 and 1830, journey time 10 mins (cost: US$12; single tickets available). Minibuses also operate from the station, return trip (1 hr stop) US$5, tickets obtained from office. Also, a 206 bus does the very attractive run from Praça Tiradentes (or a 407 from Largo do Machado) to Silvestre (the railway has no stop here now). An active walk of 1 hr will bring one to the top, and the road is shady. (Best done in company.) Coach trips tend to be rather brief, but for 2 or more it can be economical to share a taxi.

Pão de Açúcar (Sugar Loaf, 396m) is a massive granite cone at the entrance to Guanabara Bay. The bird's eye view of the city and beaches is very beautiful. There is a restaurant (excellent location, mixed reports on food, closes 1900) and a playground for children on the Morro da Urca, half way up, where there are also shows at night (weekends and Mon, 2200). You can get refreshments at the top. On the small path that leads down in the direction of Morro Cara de Cão there are toucans and macaws in cages. Bus 107 (from the centre or Flamengo) and 511 or 500 "jardinière", or those marked "Urca" (from Copacabana) take you to the cable-car station, Av Pasteur 520, at the foot.

The cable car timetable: Praia Vermelha to Urca: first car goes up at 0800, then every 30 mins (or when full), until the last comes down at 2200. From Urca to Sugar Loaf the first connecting cable car goes up at 0815 then every 30 mins (or when full), until the last leaves the summit at 2200; the return trip costs US$10 (US$5 to Morro da Urca, half-way up). The old cableway has been completely rebuilt. Termini are ample and efficient and the present Italian cable cars carry 75 passengers. Even on the most crowded days there is little queuing. There are 35 rock routes up the mountain, with various degrees of difficulty (best months for climbing: Apr to Aug; see **Sports**, above, for climbing clubs).

It is possible to walk or jog on the S side in the military area at the foot.

Tijuca National Park, open 0600-2100, is for those interested in taking a forest walk through mountain scenery. An approximately 2-3 hr walk will bring you to the summit of the Pico da Tijuca (1,012m), which gives a good idea of the tropical vegetation of the interior and a fine view of the bay and its shipping. On entering the park at Alto de Boa Vista, follow the signposts (maps are displayed) to Bom Retiro, a good picnic place (1½ hrs walk), passing by the Cascatinha Taunay, Mayrink Chapel (built 1860) and the restaurant *A Floresta*. At Bom Retiro the road ends and there is another hour's walk up a fair footpath to the summit; take the path from the right of the Bom Retiro drinking fountain; not the more obvious steps from the left. The last part consists of steps carved out of the solid rock; take care of children at the summit as there are several sheer drops, invisible because of bushes. The route is shady for almost its entire length. The panels painted in the Mayrink Chapel by Cândido Portinari have been replaced by copies and the originals will probably be installed in the Museu de Arte Moderna. Maps of the Park are available.

Take a 221 from Praça 15 de Novembro, 233 or 234 bus from the Rodoviária or 454 from Copacabana or from Praça Sáenz Pena, Tijuca (reached by metro) to Alto da Boa Vista, for the park entrance. Other places of interest not passed on the walk to the peak are the Paul and Virginia Grotto, the Vista do Almirante and the Mesa do Imperador (viewpoints). Allow at least 5 to 6 hrs for the excursion. Also, one of the Raymundo Castro Maia museums is nearby (**see p 363**).

Barra da Tijuca This rapidly developing residential area can be reached from the Tijuca Forest by continuing on the 233 or 234 bus (from Praça Sáenz Pena, very good views of São Conrado and Barra), or from the city bus station at R São José, from Santos Dumont airport, bus 591 or 592 from Leme, and from Copacabana via Leblon beach (bus 523). Taxi to Zona Sul, US$15 (US$22.50 after midnight). From Botafogo, Glória or Flamengo take bus 179. A comfortable bus, Pegasus, goes along the coast from the Castelo bus terminal to Barra da Tijuca and continues to Campo Grande or Santa Cruz, or take free "Barra Shopping" bus.

Barra da Tijuca is also one of the principal recreation areas of Rio, with its 20-km sandy beach and good waves for surfing. Bus 700 from Praça São Conrado (terminal of bus 553 from Copacabana) goes the full length of the beach to Recreio dos Bandeirantes. There are innumerable bars and restaurants, clustered at both ends, campsites (**see p 370**), motels and hotels: budget accommodation tends to be self-catering. On Av Sernambetiba (the beach boulevard), **A1** *Aparthotel Barraleme*, No 600, T 389-3100, has been rec. Travel agency and car hire in same building. The facilities include Riocenter, a 600,000 sq m convention complex and the huge Barra Shopping and Carrefour shopping centres. The stylish Fashion Mall is oppsite the golf club. Hang-gliders jump from the hilltops at weekends. View the beaches and hills from the air, Ultra Força Ltda, Av Sernambetiba 8100, T 399-3114, 15 mins. Live concerts on São Conrado beach during summer (Nov-Feb).

The Autódromo (motor racing track) is beyond Barra in the Jacarepaguá district. The Brazilian Grand Prix is held here or at Interlagos, São Paulo, alternately in Jan.

The beaches South of Barra Recreio dos Bandeirantes (small, ocean very rough), Prainha (a little cove, good for surfing) and Grumari (very attractive, rustic beach bar) are inaccessible by public transport, therefore less crowded and safer. They attract heavy traffic at weekends, though, and this stunning coastal road (the start of the legendary Costa Verde highway) is becoming obliterated by executive housing developments – visit soon, if you can.

Viewpoints Apart from the Pico da Tijuca, Corcovado and Pão de Açúcar, splendid views of different parts of Rio can be seen from the Vista Chinesa (420m), where from a Chinese-style pavilion one can see the inland lake (the Lagoa), Ipanema and Leblon; the Mesa do Imperador and Vista do Almirante in the Tijuca Forest; and the Mirante de Dona Marta (340m) off the Corcovado road, with the same direction of view as the Corcovado, but as it is lower the details can be seen more clearly. There is no public transport to these places.

Paquetá Island in Guanabara Bay can be visited by more or less two-hourly ferry services from Praça Quinze de Novembro, none between 1015 and 1300, last back at 1900 (fare US$1.25 by boat, 1 hr, US$6.25 by hydrofoil, 20 mins journey, which more than doubles its price Sats, Suns and holidays). Bus to Praça Quinze: 119 from Botafogo; 154, 134, 455, 474 from Copacabana or 415 passing from Leblon via Ipanema. Horse-drawn carriages hire (many have harnesses which cut into the horse's flesh); they do not stop at the interesting Parque Darke de Mattos. Tour by "trenzinho", a tractor pulling trailers, US$1.25, or on foot, quieter and free. Bicycles also can be hired. The island is noted for its gigantic pebble shaped rocks, butterflies and orchids. The house of José Bonifácio, the opponent of slavery, may be seen. Very crowded at weekends and public holidays, but usually very quiet during the week, though there can be aircraft noise. Reasonable food and drink prices.

Other boat trips, Aquatur (T 230-9273), Brazilian Marina Turismo, Camargo (T 275-0643), Passamar, Siqueira Campos 7 (T 236-4136), Greyline (T 274-7146), Soletur (Bay trips Sat and Sun only) and American Sightseeing, Av NS de Copacabana 605, Sala 1204 (T 236-3551). The last three offer a day cruise, including lunch, to Jaguanum Island (**see p 389**, under Itacuruçá) and a sundown cruise around Guanabara Bay, also deep-sea fishing expeditions and private charters.

Entering Rio from the W, an alternative to the BR-101 and Avenida Brasil, is to leave BR-101 on the road to Santa Cruz, continuing 6 km to the fishing village of Sepetiba, quiet other than at weekends. Along the coast is Pedra de Guaratiba, from where you join Avenida das Américas, turning off right soon afterwards to Ponta do Picão and Guaratiba, a pretty seaside resort on a rocky, narrow, steep ledge between mountain and sea (good beaches and a playground for the rich). Another 2 km along the main road is another (unmarked) right turn leading to a restaurant at the summit, with fantastic views, then down to Praia de Grumari (see above). It is then 30 km to Copacabana, via Recreio dos Bandeirantes.

The State of Rio de Janeiro: East from Rio

Niterói (pop 416,125, CEP 24000, DDD 021), founded in 1573, the ex-capital of the State of Rio de Janeiro, is reached across the bay by bridge or ferries,

Of the frequent ferry boat and hydrofoil services from Praça 15 de Novembro, Rio, the slow, cheaper ferry gives the best views. There is a Flumitur tourist information booth to the right of the ferry-boat station. Nearby you can take the 33 bus (marked "via Froes") to the beaches of Icaraí, São Francisco and Jurujuba on the bay, a beautiful ride. Sit on the right-hand side. A few minutes' walk from where the bus route ends at Jurujuba are the attractive twin beaches of Adão and Eva, with lovely views of Rio across the bay. From Praça General Gomes Carneiro, take a 38 or 52 bus to Piratininga, Itaipu and Itacoatiara, fabulous ocean beaches and the best in the area, about 40 mins' ride through picturesque countryside (buses leave from the street directly ahead of the ferry entrance, at right angles to coast street). The undertow at Itacoatiara is dangerous, but the beach itself is safe. The beaches inside the bay, though calm, are often overcrowded and polluted, but no more so than those opposite in Rio. The forts on this side of the bay include Santa Cruz (16th century, still a military establishment), Barão do Rio Branco (1633), Gragoatá and Nossa Senhora da Boa Viagem.

You should also visit the church of Boa Viagem (1633), built on an island connected to the mainland by a short causeway, a few minutes' walk from Icaraí beach. Nearby, on R Tiradentes, is the Antônio Parreira Museum, opens 1300, dedicated to the eponymous artist. The Museu de Arqueologia de Itaipu is in the ruins of the 18th century Santa Teresa Convent, and also covers the archaeological site of Duna Grande on Itaipu beach.

Ferry Service From the "barcas" at Praça 15 de Novembro, ferry boats and launches cross every 10 mins to Niterói (20-30 mins, US$0.40). There are also hydrofoils ("aerobarcas") every 10 mins (about 10 mins, US$4.50). The Niterói ferry service is still being maintained, despite the competition from the 14 km bridge linking the two sides of Guanabara Bay.

The Rio-Niterói bridge (Ponte Costa e Silva) has a length of 14 km. Toll for cars, US$0.50. (The approach to the bridge is on the elevated motorway from the centre, or via Av Rio de Janeiro, in the Caju district; take Av Rodrigues Alves past the docks.) Bus 999 from the corner of Senador Dantas and Av Beira Mar, Rio, crosses the bridge to Niterói and Icaraí (US$0.75); also 996 and 998 from the Jardim Botânico (all three go to the Rodoviária in Rio).

Hotels **A2** *Bucsky*, R Cel Tamarindo 150, Praia do Gragoatá, T 717-3322, F 717-3841; **C** *Niterói Palace*, R Andrade Neves 134, T 719-2155, F 719-2800; *Icaraí Praia*, R Belisário Agusto 21, T 714-1414, F 710-6142, similar price. Youth Hostel, *AJ Solar dos Díos*, R Santo Eduardo 63, T 709-0686.

Clubs Rio Cricket, bus 57 from ferry. Rio Sailing, bus 33 marked "via Froes".

Electric Current 110 volts, AC, 60 cycles.

Laundromat *Lavlev*, R Presidente Backer 138.

To the E of Niterói lie a series of salt-water lagoons, the Lagos Fluminenses. Two small lakes lie behind the beaches of Piratininga, Itacoatiara and Itaipu near Niterói, but they are polluted and ringed by mud. The next lakes are much larger, those of Maricá and Saquarema; though they are still muddy, the waters are relatively unpolluted, and wild life abounds in the scrub and bush around the lagoons. At the outlet to the lake of Saquarema (turn right off the main road at Bacaxá) is the holiday village of **Saquarema**. Of particular interest is the little white church of Nossa Senhora de Nazaré (1675) built atop a green promontory jutting into the ocean. Saquarema is the centre for surfing in Brazil, and the national championships are held here each year in May. Beware of strong currents, though. Mil e Um bus Rio-Saquarema, every 2 hrs 0730-1800, 2 hrs, US$3.60.

The largest lake is **Araruama**, famous for its medicinal mud. The salinity is extremely high, the waters calm, and almost the entire lake is surrounded by sandy beaches, making it very popular with families looking for safe, unpolluted bathing. The major industry of the area is salt, and all around one can see the saltpans and the wind pumps used to carry the water into the pans. At the eastern end of the lake is **São Pedro de Aldeia**, which, in spite of intensive development, still retains much of its colonial charm and has a lovely Jesuit church built in 1723.

Hotels in the lake district: **Saquarema**: **C** *Pousada do Holandés*, Av Vilamar 377, at Itaúna beach, highly rec, many languages spoken by Dutch owner and his Brazilian wife (who runs the local day-care centre), good meals—follow the signs, or take a taxi (US$0.80), from Saquarema. Restaurant in Saquarema, *Tem Uma Né Chama Teré*, very good, in main square. Araruama: **A1** *Chalés do Coqueiral*, chalets on lake beach, T 65-1159; **A1** *Parque Hotel* R Argentina 502, T 65-2129; **A1** *Senzala*, on Iguabinha beach, 10 km from Araruama, T 24-2230, F 24-1212, with meals; **B** *La Gondola*, on the lake beach, T 65-1364, overpriced; **São Pedro de Aldeia**: **B** *Solar de Iguaba*, T 24-2162. At **Ponta Negra** are **A3** *Pousada Colonial*, suites and bungalows in this range, breakfast incl, T Rio, 451-6254 for reservations, and **A3** *Solar Tabauna*, T 748-1626, pool, both highly rec.

The ocean beaches beside these lagoons, except for the sheltered coves of Ponta Negra and Saquarema, are rough and lonely. The whole area is perfect for camping; there are campsites (including Camping Clube do Brasil) at Araruama (close to the *Parque Hotel*) and São Pedro de Aldeia. A very steep road connects the beaches of Itaipu and Itacoatiara with BR-106 (and on to Araruama) via the village of Itaipu-Açu, with beach and good camping. Most maps do not show a road beyond Itaipu-Açu; it is certainly too steep for buses.

An alternative to the route from Niterói to Araruama through the lagoons is via Manilla, Itaboraí and Rio Bonito, on the BR-101 and RJ-124; this is a fruit-growing region.

Cabo Frio (pop 86,615), 156 km from Rio, is a popular holiday and week-end haunt of Cariocas because of its cool weather, beaches, scenery, sailing and good under-water swimming (but mosquitoes are a problem). The ocean beach is much less frequented than the bay beach. The São Mateus fort nearby was built by the French; it is in a state of disrepair. If in the area, take a look at the huge church under construction at Arraial do Cabo nearby; it totally dominates the town (bus every 20 mins from Cabo Frio). There are random car searches for drugs on the road to Búzios.

Hotels A wide selection, from expensive down to **C** *Colonial*, R José Watzl Filho 96. **C** *Jangada*, Granaola 220, near canal, very friendly, good breakfast, rec. Youth Hostel, both sexes, open all year to IYHF members (E pp, more for non-members), on R Kubitschek, 1 block from bus station, very friendly. 3 youth hostels in the area around Cabo Frio and one in Arraial do Cabo, at R Joaquim Nabuco 23, near Praça de Bandeiras.

Camping Camping Clube do Brasil sites at Estrada dos Passageiros, near town; at Km 135 on the Rio road, 4 km outside town, in Palmeiras; and at Arraial do Cabo on Praia dos Anjos, crowded beach. Also site at Cabo Yacht club.

Buses Rodoviária is 2 km from centre. Bus from Rio every ½ hr, 2½ hrs, US$7.20. To Búzios, from local bus terminus in town centre, every hour, US$1.

Búzios (pop 26,000, CEP 28905, DDD 0246), NE of Cabo Frio, is an expensive, fashionable resort sprawling with low-rise (but attractive) development. It has 27 sandy coves, best seen by boat (*Queen Lori*, rec), US$22 – schooner trips of 2-3 hrs around the bay are very popular, calm unpolluted waters (superb for windsurfing), beautiful scenery, thriving nightlife. Tourist information office near bus stop. Very crowded during Brazilian holiday season and extremely difficult to get hotel bookings. Notable beaches are: Ossos, close to town; Azeda, very relaxed, topless OK; Geriba, about 2½ km out of town (turn left down the path between two Shell stations—it is marked); Tartaruga, not marked and not developed (take dirt road up small hill opp *Pousada Baer Búzios*); there is a restaurant and snack bar in season.

Accommodation Plenty of good hotels and *pousadas*: eg **A1** *Pousada Happy*, on road to Raza on opp side of crossing to Rio, on beach, breakfast incl, rec, good windsurfing, German owner; **A2** *Pousada Hibiscus Beach*, Rua 1 No 22, Quadra C, Praia João Fernandes, T/F 23-6221, run by its British owners, 15 nice bungalows, garden, pool, breakfast inc, light meals available, help with car/buggy rentals and local excursions; *Casa D'elas Pousada*, and *Pousada do Sol*, Praia da Armação; **C** *Pousada Casa de Pedra*, Trav Lúcio A Quintanilha 57, T 231499, TV, fridge, safe; **C** *Pousadinha em Búzios*, T 231448, very pretty, friendly; **C** *Pousada dos Búzios*, T 231155, a/c, terrace bar with lovely view; all central, rec; private rooms can be rented in family homes from US$15. Camping is allowed but dangerous.

Restaurants Several good restaurants (try the *camarão tropical*) and popular bars (*Chez Michou*, R das Pedras, is reportedly the mecca for trendy travellers).

Transport Best route from Rio (2 hrs by car) is the paved road towards Macaé, with a paved turnoff to Búzios (1001 bus from Rio, 4-5 a day, 2½ hrs, US$7). Direct road from Cabo Frio (bus 45 mins) is unpaved.

Continuing to the N, one comes to the seaside resorts of Barra de São João, **Rio das Ostras** (**C** *Hotel Mirante do Poeta*, T 64-1910, and others) and **Macaé** (Hotels: **B** *Colonial*, Av Elias Agostinho 140, T 62-5155, friendly, helpful, comfortable; **B** *Panorama*, same avenue No 290, T/F 62-4455; **D** *Central*, R Rui Barbosa, clean, nice, friendly, good breakfast, secure parking), all containing sheltered coves with good swimming and scuba diving. Macaé is also the supply centre for the offshore oil industry.

From Rio and Niterói a first class highway, the BR-101, runs NE past Macaé to Campos (bus Rio-Macaé 2½-3 hrs, every ½ hr, Mil e Um or Rápido Macaense; bus Macaé-Campos, 1¾ hrs, US$3). At Km 222 is the **Biological Reserve of Poço das Antas** (2 hrs drive from Rio; it is not open to the general public, for details, Delegacia Estadual do Ibama, Av Pres Antônio Carlos 607-12°, CEP 20.000, Rio de Janeiro). Many animals (including the *mico-leão*, Golden Lion Tamarin—this is its only natural habitat) roam in the forest. Tours are very restrictive: visitors must be accompanied by Reserve staff to track radio-collared tamarins. Once an animal is seen, the tour ends, with no further opportunity for birdwatching, or looking for the maned sloth (also endangered).

Campos (pop 368,800) is a busy industrial city, some 276 km (4½ hrs by Mil e Um bus, hourly) from Rio de Janeiro (70 km from Macaé). It stands 56 km from the mouth of the Rio Paraíba, up which coffee planting originally spread to São Paulo state. Coffee is still grown near Campos, though the region is now one of the largest sugar-producing zones in Brazil. Important offshore oil discoveries have been made nearby. Town is quite interesting.

Hotels C *Palace*, Av 15 de Novembro 143, T 22-7755, F 22-3661; **C** *Planície*, R 13 de Maio 56, T 23-4455; **C** *Terrazo Tourist*, Joaquím Tavora 22, T 22-1405, 2-star; **D** *Silva*, some way behind church on municipal square, breakfast, clean, safe parking.

Travelling N, as an alternative to BR-101 to Vitória, one can take a detour inland, going through São Fidélis, Cambiasca, Itoacara and on to **Santo Antônio de Pádua** (pop 36,330), 130 km from Campos, a pleasant town on the Rio Pomba. (**C** *Hotel das Aguas*, a short walk from the centre, a resort hotel in a park with pool, health centre and bottling plant for the local mineral water which is used for treating cardiovascular illness; **D** *Braga*, in town, clean, friendly, good food.) Take road No 393 to Itaperuna, Bom Jesus do Itabapoana and into Espírito Santo, then road No 484 to **Guaçuí** (**E** *Grande Hotel Minas*, friendly, clean; *Restaurant Kontiki*, very good), one of the starting points for the Parque Nacional do Caparaó (see p 411). Then take the road 482 to Cachoeira do Itapemirim and the BR-101 (see p 392).

Petrópolis (pop 255,210, CEP 25600, DDD 0242) is a summer hill resort and industrial city at 840m, 68 km N of Rio. It is reached by bus along a steep, scenic mountain road. Until 1962 Petrópolis was the "summer capital" of Brazil; it was founded in 1843 as a summer refuge by Dom Pedro II. Now it combines manufacturing industry (particularly textiles, which may be bought cheaply) with floral beauty and hill scenery. The Imperial Palace (Museu Imperial), which seems to express very faithfully what we know of Dom Pedro II's character, is a modest but elegant building, fully furnished and equipped, containing the Crown Jewels and other imperial possessions. It is assiduously well-kept: one might think the imperial family had left the day before one's visit, rather than in 1889. Open Tues-Sun, 1200-1730. Entry US$1. Well worth a visit is the Gothic-style Cathedral, completed in 1925, which contains the tombs of the Emperor and Empress (guide in English, US$0.50).

Attractions and Excursions Museu Ferreira da Cunha, Fernandes Vieira 390 (old road to Rio) shows large collection of arms, open Sat and Sun (only to groups; need to arrange in advance) 0900-1700. Summer home of air pioneer **Santos Dumont**, showing early inventions. Palácio de Cristal in Praça da Confluência, former imperial ballroom and now exhibition centre. **Orquidário Binot**, R Fernandes Vieira 390 (take bus to Vila Isabel; open Mon-Sat, 0800-1100, 1300-1700), a huge collection of orchids from all over Brazil (plants may be purchased).

Hotels A3 *Casa do Sol*, T 43-5062, 4-star hotel 8 km out on road to Rio; **A3** *Casablanca Center*, General Osório 28, T 42-2612, F 42-6298; **B** *Casablanca*, R da Imperatriz 286, T 42-6662, F 42-5946, good atmosphere in older part, pool, very clean; **B** *Casablanca Palace*, 16 de Março 123, T 42-0162; **B** *Margaridas*, R Bispo Pereira Alves 235, T 42-4686, chalet-type hotel set in lovely gardens with swimming pool, charming proprietors; **B** *Riverside Parque*, R Hermogéneo Silva 522, T 43-2312, F 43-2430; **C** *Dom Pedro*, on main square, pleasant; **E** *Comércio*, opp bus station, with breakfast.

Camping Associação Brasileira de Camping and YMCA, Araras district. Can reserve space through Rio YMCA, T 231-9860.

Restaurants *Churrascaria Majórica*, Av do Imperador (ex 15 de Novembro) 754; *Dom Giovanni*, same street, rec; *Maloca*, Wáshington Luís 466; *Bauernstube*, João Pessoa 297.

Whitewater rafting at Três Rios, on the junction of rivers Paraibuna, Piabanha and Paraíba do Sul, is arranged by *Klemperer Turismo*, T 43-4052 (also from Rio, T 252-8170), highly rec. (It is cheaper – but complicated – to book direct with the owners of the restaurant at Pontal, no phone).

Buses leave from Rio every 15 mins throughout the day (US$3.50), Sun every hour, 1½ hrs, sit on the left hand side for best views. Return tickets are not available, so passengers must buy tickets for the return bus as soon as they arrive in Petrópolis. Journey 75 mins each way. The ordinary buses leave from the rodoviária in Rio; a/c buses, hourly from 1100, from Av Nilo Peçanha, US$4.25. There is a direct overnight bus from São Paulo.

Teresópolis (pop 120,700; 910m), near the Serra dos Órgãos, is 124 km NE of Rio. It was the favourite summer residence of the Empress Teresa Cristina. In recent years there has been a lot of building which has destroyed some of the city's character. See the Colina dos Mirantes hill (½-hr steep climb, sweeping view of the city and surroundings, a taxi up is not dear), the Sloper and Iaci lakes, the Imbui and Amores waterfalls, and the Fonte Judith. Waterfalls in the area are reported too dirty for bathing, but about 10 km from town, on the Rio road, just after the bridge over the Rio Soberbo, on the left, is a nice waterfall with clean water. São Pedro festival on Jun 29 is celebrated with fireworks.

Hotels L3 *São Moritz*, Swiss-style, outside on the Nova Friburgo road, Km 36, T 741-1115, F 741-1135, with meals; **A1** *Montebello*, at Km 17, same road, T/F 742-2116, modern hotel with pool, friendly, with 3 meals, rec; **A2** *Alpina*, Parque Imbui, on Petrópolis road, T/F 742-5252; **D** *Florida*, Av Lúcio Meira 467, with bargaining; **D** *Várzea Palace*, R Sebastião Teixeira 41, T 742-0878, highly rec. Many cheap hotels in R Delfim Moreira, near the Praça. Youth hostel: Retiro da Inglesa, 20 km on road to Friburgo, Fazenda Boa Esperança (reservations, R Papa Pio XII 50, Jardim Cascata, 25963 Teresópolis).

Camping National Park, entrance to Teresópolis from Rio, full facilities; Quinta de Barra, Km 3 on Petrópolis road, T 742-1825; Vale das Choupanas, Km 30 on Rio road.

Restaurants *Taberna Alpina*, Duque de Caxias 131; *Bar Gota d'Água*, Praça Baltasar da Silveira 16 for trout or *feijoada* (small but rec and for *batidas*). Cafeteria in the ABC supermarket, clean and cheap, rec.

Tourist Office in the bus station, T 742-0999.

Exchange Cash or TCs at *Teretur*, Trav Portugal 46 (English spoken).

Bus, Rio-Teresópolis Buses leave every ½-hr from rodoviária. As return tickets are not issued, book for the return journey as soon as you arrive at Teresópolis. Fare US$3. From Teresópolis to Petrópolis, every 2 hrs from 0900-2100, US$3.50.

Leave Rio on the 0800 bus or before (Viação Teresópolis) for the 1¾-hr ride and up into the mountains to Teresópolis (sit on right side of bus). Upon arrival at the bus station, buy another ticket right away for Petrópolis (Viação Teresópolis) for the 1200 bus in order to get a good seat, as the bus fills rapidly. This gives you 2¾ hrs to wander around.

The 90-min drive from Teresópolis to Petrópolis is beautiful. (Sit on left side.) The views on either side are spectacular. Again, upon arrival in Petrópolis at 1330, buy your ticket to Rio (Facil or Unica). Take the 1715 bus "via Quitandinha", and you might catch the sunset over the mountains (in May, Jun, Jul, take the 1615 bus). This gives you time to visit most of the attractions listed in the city description.

About 30,000 hectares of the **Serra dos Órgãos**, so called because their strange shapes are said to recall organ-pipes, are now a **National Park**. The main attraction is the precipitous Dedo de Deus (God's Finger) Peak. There is also the rock formation Mulher de Pedra 12 km out on the Nova Friburgo road, and the Von Martius natural-history museum. The highest point is the Pedra Açu, 2,400m. A path leads up the 2,260-metre Pedra do Sino, 3-4 hrs' climb. The park is the home of the very rare and endemic grey-winged cotinga, as well as a number of other cotingas, berryeaters and other rare endemics. Anyone can enter the park and hike the trails from the Teresópolis gate, S of the town. Entrance to park, US$1, US$1.65 for the path to the top. Ibama (T 742-0266/0260) has some hostels, US$5.75 full board, or US$3.75 first night, US$2 thereafter, a bit rough. Camping, US$1. A good way to see the Park is to do the Rio-Teresópolis-Petrópolis-Rio circuit; a scenic day trip. Tours of the park with Francisco of Lazer Tours are recommended, T 742-7616, or find him at the grocery shop on R Sloper 1. Focus Tours of Belo Horizonte (**see p 402**) offers birdwatching tours.

Nova Friburgo (pop 166,940, 850m above sea-level), is a popular resort during summer months (around 30 hotels; restaurants), in a beautiful valley with excellent walking and riding possibilities. Founded by Swiss settlers from Fribourg, it can be reached by bus (US$5) from Rio (every hour) in 2 hrs or by car in 1 hr 45 min. Cable car from Praça dos Suspiros 650m up the Morro da Cruz, for view of rugged country. Road to Teresópolis paved.

Hotels A2 *Bucsky*, T 22-5052, F 22-9769; 5 km out on Niterói road, with meals; **A2** *Garlipp*, German-run, in chalets, with meals, at Muri, km 70.5 from Rio, 10 km from Nova Friburgo, T 42-1330, F 42-1444; **A2** *Mury Garden*, T 42-1120, with swimming pool, with meals, reasonable, 10 km away at Muri (Km 70 on Niterói road); **A2** *Sans-Souci*, T/F 22-7752, 1 km out, with meals, **C** without; **B** *Fabris*, Av Alberto Browne 148, T 22-2852, central, TV, hot showers, plentiful breakfast buffet. Under same ownership as *Garlipp* is **B** *Fazenda São João*, T 42-1304, 11 km from *Garlipp* up a side road (impassable in the wet), riding, swimming, sauna, tennis, hummingbirds and orchids; owner will meet guests in Nova Friburgo or even in Rio. Also **C** *Everest*, R Manoel António Ventura 75, T 22-7350, comfortable, good breakfasts; **C** *Maringá*, R Monsenhor Miranda 110, T 22-2309, with bath, D without, good breakfast, rec.

Camping Camping Clube do Brasil has sites on Niterói road, at Caledônia (7 km out) and Muri (10 km out). Cambrás site also at Cônego, and private site at Fazenda Sanandu, 20 km out on same road.

The State of Rio de Janeiro: West from Rio

Volta Redonda (pop 220,085, CEP 27180, DDD 0243) stands on a broad bend of the Rio Paraíba at an altitude of 565m, 113 km W of Rio along the railway to São Paulo. In 1942 it was a little village; today it has one of the largest steel works in Latin America. The mills are on the river bank and the town spreads up the surrounding wooded and gardened slopes.

Hotels A2 *Bela Vista*, Alto de Boa Vista, on a hill overlooking town, T 43-2022, F 42-4190; **B** *Sider Palace*, R 33 No 10, T 42-0885/1032, F 42-6116; **D** *Embaixador*, Tr LA Félix 36, T 42-3665, 1-star.

Visitors who have a permit from the Companhia Siderúrgica Nacional, Av Treze de Maio 13, Rio de Janeiro (apply ten days in advance), or locally from the *Bela Vista* hotel, are allowed to inspect the mills. Visits start at 0900, and last 2¹/₂-3 hrs. The town can be reached from Rio by buses or minibuses in 2¹/₂ hrs, US$3.

North of Volta Redonda is **Miguel Pereira**, set in the mountain region with an excellent climate; nearby is the Javari lake, a popular recreational spot. Two *Hotel-Fazendas* (both B) near Miguel Pereira are *Quindins* and *Javari* (T 84-3611), both with restaurant, swimming pool, sports grounds, etc. In town is the **D** *Rei dos Montanhas*, Swiss-chalet style, clean, chilly at night. A tourist train runs 56 km to Conrado on Sat, Sun and holidays, 0945, 3¹/₂ hrs, US$18 round trip, beautiful views of mountains, rivers and waterfalls. Further N, and still in the mountains are the university centres of **Vassouras** and **Valença**; both are historical monuments. 35 km from Valença is **Conservatória**, another colonial town. This region can also be reached via the Japeri turn-off on the BR-116 (a beautiful mountain drive). Some 30 km W of Volta Redonda, in the town of Resende, is the Military Academy of Agulhas Negras. Grounds, with captured German guns of World War II, are open to the public. **Resende** (pop 91,575) can be reached by bus from Aparecida do Norte (**see p 436**), several daily, US$2.50, or from Rio, frequent, 1³/₄ hrs, US$3.60, also from São Paulo and Volta Redonda.

Hotels E *Leme*, R Dr Cunha Ferreira, 100m from rodoviária, clean, basic, pp; *Dormitórios Amazônica*, Dr Cunha Ferreira esq. Praça Oliveira Botelho. Shops across river before railway station.

In the same region, 175 km from Rio, is the small town of **Penedo** (5 buses a day from Resende) which in the 1930s attracted Finnish settlers who brought the first saunas to Brazil. This popular weekend resort also provides horseback riding, and swimming in the Portinho river. (Hotels: **A3** *Bertell*, T 51-1288, with meals; **C** *Pousada Penedo*, T 51-1309, safe, clean, pool, rec, and others, 2 campsites.) Some 33 km beyond Penedo (part of road unpaved) is the small village of **Visconde de Maúa**, where the tourist officer speaks no English but plays guitar (closed out of season). There are lots of alternative places (acupuncture, shiatsu massage, macrobiotic food, etc). Limited cheap lodgings: enquire at *Vendinha da Serra*, excellent natural food restaurant and store; next door is **F** pp *Dona Mariana*, rec, shared bath. *Pousada Beira Rio*, T 54-1801; *Pousada Vale das Horténsias*, T 54-3030, both provide all meals, rec; ¹/₂ km on road to Maringá is *Hotel Turístico*, with handicrafts and homemade food, Italian owner, Nino, and his Brazilian wife, run excursions. Everywhere in town shuts at about 1900, except *Adega Bar*, open till midnight, live music and dancing (Sat only), reasonable pizza, and a restaurant in Lote 10, open till 2200. Youth Hostel, 5 km along the road to Maringá. Fine scenery and walks, lots of holidaymakers, pleasant atmosphere; roads to 3 other small hill towns: delightful 2 hrs' walk to **Maringá**, which is more touristy (several D hotels), *Bar do Jorge* cafe, (US$3); *Forró da Marieta* for forró dancing, Marumbá and Mirantão, at about 1,700m, with semitropical vegetation. The Rio Preto, the border between Rio de Janeiro and Minas Gerais states, runs through the region. 6 km up river from Maringá are the well-known Santa Clara falls; between Visconde de Maúa and Maringá is a natural pool in the river (turn left before crossing the bridge). After Marumbá follow signs to Cachoeira Escorrega, a small fall with cold natural swimming pool, 2 km. Horse rental in Visconde de Maúa from Berto (almost opp *Vendinha da Serra*), or Pedro (Lote 10); many places in Maringá. Buses to Visconde de Maúa from Resende, 1500 and 1630, 2 hrs, return 0900-0830, US$1.25; from Resende buses go to Barra Mansa

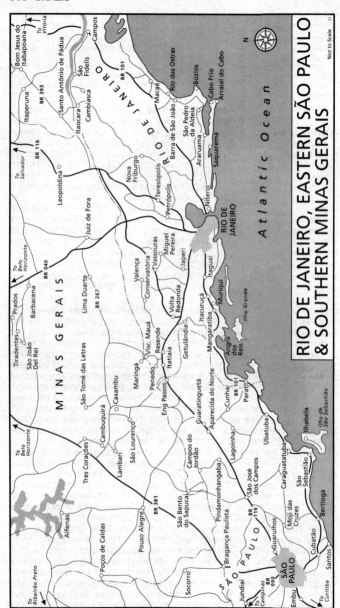

RIO DE JANEIRO, EASTERN SÃO PAULO & SOUTHERN MINAS GERAIS

Not to Scale

(Resendense, 40 mins, US$1.25) where you can change for Belo Horizonte (Util 1230, 8-9 hrs, US$14.50). Direct bus Rio-Visconde de Mauá, Cidade de Aço, 0900 daily, plus one in evening, 3½ hrs, US$8.50.

Further along the Dutra Highway (186 km from Rio) is the small town of **Engenheiro Passos**, from which a road (BR-354) leads to São Lourenço and Caxambu in Minas Gerais (**see p 411**), passing **Agulhas Negras**. One can climb Agulhas Negras from this side by taking the road from Registro pass (1,670m) to the Abrigo Rebouças refuge, which is manned all year round (take your own food, US$1.25 to stay), at 2,350m.

Hotels **A2** *Villa Forte*, 1 km from town, T 52-1219, with meals. Nine campsites in the area.

The **Itatiaia National Park** (founded 1937), on the Serra de Itatiaia in the Mantiqueira chain of mountains, is a few km N of the Via Dutra (Rio-São Paulo highway). The road to it is paved. The town of Itatiaia is surrounded by picturesque mountain peaks and lovely waterfalls. This is a good area for climbing (Pico das Agulhas Negras 2,787m, Pico da Prateleira 2,540m), trekking and birdwatching (specialities include swallow-tailed, shrike-like and black-and-gold cotingas, white-bearded antshrike, black-capped manakin, various tanagers and humming birds). The southern masked titi monkey is common, recognizable by its loud hee-haw-like call. Information and maps can be obtained at the park office. Worth seeing are the curious rock formations of Pedra de Taruga and Pedra de Maçã, and the waterfall Véu de Noiva (many birds). Basic accommodation in cabins and dormitories is available in the park; you will need to book in season, say 30 days in advance, by writing to Administração do Parque Nacional de Itatiaia, Caixa Postal 83657, Itatiaia 27580-000, RJ, T (0243) 52-1652. The Administração operates a refuge in the park which acts as a starting point for climbs and treks: information on these from Clube Excursionista Brasileira, Av Almirante Barroso 2, 8th floor, T 220-3695, Rio. Tres Picos wildlife trail near *Hotel Simon*; very difficult to visit park without a car (70 km from *Hotel Simon* to other side), but hotel is helpful. There is a Museum of Flora and Fauna, closed Mon. Entrance to Park, US$1. A bus from Itatiaia, marked *Hotel Simon*, goes to the Park, 1200, returns 1700; coming from Resende this may be caught at the crossroads before Itatiaia. Through tickets to São Paulo sold at a booth in the large bar in the middle of Itatiaia main street.

Hotels **A2** *Repouso Itatiaia*, Km 11 park road, T 52-1110, F 52-1509, with meals; **A2** *Simon*, Km 13 park road, T 52-1122, with meals, lovely views; **A3** *Fazenda da Serra*, Via Dutra Km 151, T 52-1611, with meals; **A3** *Hotel do Ypé*, Km 13 park road, T 52-1453, with meals; **B** *Pousada do Elefante*, 15 mins' walk back down hill from *Hotel Simon*, good food, swimming pool, lovely views, may allow camping for US$2; **C** *Jahu*, Via Dutra Km 156, very friendly, clean, comfortable. **Camping Clube do Brasil** site is entered at Km 148 on the Via Dutra.

The new **Rio-Santos highway**, BR101, is widely acclaimed as one of the world's most breathtakingly beautiful highways, hugging the forested and hilly "Green Coast" SW of Rio. It is now complete right through to Bertioga (**see p 430**), which has good links both with Santos and (avoiding Santos) to São Paulo. There are direct Rio-Santos buses, and direct services from Rio to Angra dos Reis, Parati, Ubatuba, Caraguatatuba, and São Sebastião. Hotels and *pousadas* have sprung up all along the road, as, unfortunately, have expensive housing developments, though these have not spoiled the views. The coast is littered with islands, beaches, colonial settlements and mountain fazendas: the drive should take 7 hrs, but it would be better to break the journey and enjoy some of the distractions.

Itacuruçá, 91 km from Rio, is a delightful place to visit if you like fine scenery and peace and quiet, with islands off the coast.

Hotels On Ilha de Itacuruçá, is *Hotel Pierre*, reached by boat from Coroa Grande, N of Itacuruçá on the mainland, 5 mins (boats also go from Itacuruçá); hotel has 27 rm in price range L2, restaurant, bars, sporting facilities. For bookings T/F 788-1560, T Rio 247-8938, or

Saveiros Tours, 267-2792. The *Hotel Jaguanum*, Ilha de Jaguanum, Itacuruçá, has apartments and chalets with private bathrooms. There are beautiful walks around the island. Reservations for the hotel, which incl the boat trip to and from the island (at 1000 and 1700), cost US$120-130 per day for two with all meals. The only extra is the bus, US$6 return, which picks you up at your hotel. Book by calling 235-2893 or 237-5119, in Rio, or enquire at Sepetiba Turismo, Av NS de Copacabana 605, s 202.

The sea is now reported to be too polluted for bathing, but you can walk along the railway to Castelo where the beach is cleaner. Ilha de Itacuruçá can also be reached from **Muriqui**, a popular beach resort 9 km from Itacuruçá; bathing also in the Véu de Noiva waterfall. The next beach along the coast is Praia Grande.

Mangaratiba (pop 17,920), a fishing village half-way from Rio to Angra dos Reis, has muddy beaches, but pleasant surroundings and better beaches outside town, for example Ibicuí, São Brás, Praia Brava, Saco, Guiti and Cação.

Hotels D *Moreira*, and *Mendoza* (both have same owner), without breakfast, without bath, good, clean; 2 others, more expensive. None is crowded because the town is not a tourist resort; G *Sítio Santo Antônio 12*, T 789-2192, family run, owner Carlito is proud of his shell collection, rec. At Rio das Pedras is *Club Med*, Km 55, Mangaratiba, CEP 23880, RJ, T 021-789-1635, F 021-789-1312.

Daily ferry (Conerj) to Ilha Grande island (see below), at 0800 daily, 1½ hrs, highly rec; return ferry Mon, Wed, Fri at 1700, Tues, Thur at 1100, Sat, Sun at 1600. Fare US$3.60. Tues and Thur departures continue on to Angra dos Reis. Ferry departures and destinations can be checked at ferry station at Praça Quinze de Novembro, Rio. Buses from Rio Rodoviária 7 a day, US$3.

Angra dos Reis (pop 85,220, CEP 23,900, DDD 0243), said to have been founded in 1502, is 197 km SW of Rio by road. A small port with an important fishing and shipbuilding industry, it has several small bays with good bathing within easy reach and is situated on an enormous bay full of islands. Boat trips around the bay are available, some with a stop for lunch on the island of Jipóia (5 hrs, US$9 pp; boats for hire US$12/hr). Of particular interest are the convent of Nossa Senhora do Carmo, built in 1593, the parish church (1626), the ruins of the Jacuecanga seminary (1797), and the Senhor do Bonfim church (1780).

Hotels L3 *Frade*, road to Ubatuba (Km 123 on BR-101, 36 km), T/F 65-1212; L3 *Porto Aquarius*, Saco de Itapirapuã, T 65-1642, F 65-1766, out of town (access from Km 101 on BR-101, 13 km) lots of facilities, pleasant, helpful staff, but expensive for what is offered. At Km 115 on BR-101 is **A2** *Hotel Porto Bracuhy* (T 65-3939) with lots of facilities for watersports, nightly shows and dancing, restaurant, etc (23 km from Angra dos Reis). B *Londres*, R Pompéia 75, T 65-0044, F 65-0511; and B *Palace*, Carvalho 275, T 65-0032, F 65-2656; B *Solar dos Geranios*, rec; C *Caribe*, R de Conceição 255, T 65-0033, F 65-3450, central, rec; C *Marendaz*, clean, good breakfast; D *Porto Rico*, without breakfast, clean, quiet. Youth Hostel at Km 115 on Estrada Rio-Santos.

Restaurants For meat, *Adega dos Dragos*, good. *Taberna*, Raul Pompéia 33, good, popular, moderate prices; *Jacques*, R de Comércio, good for seafood, also *Tropicalitá*, Largo do Convento do Carmo.

Diving Aquamaster, Praia da Enseada, US$60 for two dives with drinks and food, take bus marked "Retiro" from the port in Angra.

Railway The historic *trem da mata atlântica* has been reopened, making the coastal trip to Lidice on weekends only, 1030 (has restaurant car).

Bus Hourly from Rio's rodoviária, Viação Eval, take the "via litoral" bus and sit on the left, US$7, 2½ hrs. Tourist information opposite the bus station, very good.

A road runs inland (about 18 km beyond Angra), through Getulândia, to join the BR-116 either just S of Pirai or near Volta Redonda, through nice mountain scenery.

2 hrs by ferry boat, US$3.75 (Mon, Wed, Fri at 1500, return 1000—so you have to stay 2 nights; for day trips, go from Mangaratiba) takes you on a most attractive trip through the bay to Abraão, on *Ilha Grande*, once an infamous pirate lair, and now occupied principally by fishermen and one of Brazil's larger prisons, with two good hotels, **A1** *Paraiso do Sol* (inclusive of meals, 2 hrs' walk from Abraão, or

hire a boat, reservations, Rio, T 262-1226) and **A2** *Mar da Tranqüilidade* (reservations T 780-1861 or Rio, T 288-4162). Hotel reservations are necessary. Many new *pousadas* are under construction, generally reported good (try **B** *Pousada da Vanda*, T 285-2429, friendly and clean in green surroundings; **C** *Beto's*, T 780-1202, friendly, central, rec; **D** *Hotel Ori*, R Prof Lima; **D** *Albatroz*, R das Flores 108, T 627-1730, both rec); alternatively you can camp on beaches, or rent a room (E) from Abraão householders. Ask in the port at Angra dos Reis for a fishing boat going to Proveta, where you can stay in boat sheds or, if lucky, with a fisherman. It is a beautiful village, from which you can walk through tropical forest on a mountain to Praia do Aventureiro (a day's leisurely walk each way). Take mosquito precautions and register with police post in Abraão. Note that exchange is difficult on the island.

Beyond Angra dos Reis, the road continues 100 km along the coast, past the nuclear-power plant at Itaorna, to *Parati* (pop 23,870, CEP 23,970, DDD 0243), a charming colonial town only recently accessible. The centre has been declared a national historic monument in its entirety. It used to be the chief port for the export of gold in the 17th century. The churches were built separately for each race, Indian, black and white. There is a great deal of distinguished Portuguese colonial architecture in delightful settings. On the northern headland is a small fort, 15 mins' walk, pleasant views. There is reputedly health-giving mud at one end of Jabaquara beach behind the fort (lively, safe for children). A festival of sacred music is held in Sep. The town centre is out of bounds for motor vehicles, in spring the roads are flooded, while the houses are above the water level. It is now very popular with tourists, and an expensive place to visit (money changing facilities are to be found at the Banco do Brasil). Local patchwork is for sale in the community centre on the waterfront, quilts for sale in gift shop in Santa Rita de Cassia church. Boat trips round the bay daily from 1100, returning 1700, US$14.50 pp, beautiful trip; alternatively you can hire small boats by the hour. Take mosquito repellent. Scuba-diving trips from a schooner owned by Frederico are available from the shops around the quay, US$50 for $^1/_2$ day. Highly rec, especially at weekends.

Hotels A1 *do Ouro*, Dr Pereira 145, T 71-2033, F 71-1311; **A1** *Pousada Pardieiro*, Ten Francisco Antônio 74, T 71-1370, F 71-1139, attractively housed in colonial building with lovely gardens, but always full at week-ends, does not take children; **A1** *Pousada Parati*, R do Comércio, T 71-1205, F 71-2111, reasonable value; **A2** *Coxixo*, Ten Francisco Antônio 362, T 71-1460, F 71-1568, central, pool, attractive patio, rec; **A2** *Pousada do Príncipe*, Roberto Silveira 289, T 71-2266, F 71-2120, all facilities, pool, highly rec; **B** *Pousada del Arte*, R Dona Geralda 79, artist owner Urquijo speaks English, Spanish, rec; **B** *Aconchego*, Domingos Gonçalves de Abreul, T/F 71-1598; **B** *das Canoas*, R Silveira 279, T 71-1133, F 71-2005, rec, clean, swimming pool, a/c; **B** *Pescador*, Av Beira-Rio, T 71-1154, F 71-2145, central; **C** *Estalagem Colonial*, R de Matriz 9, T 71-1626, clean, rec; **C** *Hotel Solar dos Gerânios*, Praça da Matriz, clean, friendly, good breakfast; **C** *Marendaz*, R Patitiba 9, T 71-1369, with breakfast, simple, charming; **C** *Morro do Forte*, R Orlando Carpinelli, T/F 71-1211, lovely garden, good breakfast, pool, German owner Peter Kallert offers trips on his yacht, rec; **C** *Pouso Familiar*, R J V Ramos 262, run by Belgian (Joseph Yserbyt) and his Brazilian wife (Lucia), near bus station, laundry facilities, English, French, German and Flemish spoken, T 71-1475, rec; **C** *Santa Rita*, R Santa Rita 2, good, with bath and breakfast; **D** *Pousada Patitiba*, without bath or breakfast, basic, hot; **E** *Pousada Miramar*, Abel de Oliveira 19, T 71-2132, friendly, good value, 1 room has own kitchen, rec; **E** *Tia Palminas*, opp Entel caravan, basic.

Good **restaurants**, oldest and most famous is *Verde Mar*, on the sea front at Praça Lopes Trovão 35, T 65-2065, expensive but worth it. Rec cheaper places are *Paulinho*, a "sort of shed" on the waterside, *churrascaria*; *Cavallino*, R da Lapa, enjoyable atmosphere; away from older centre: *Ceu de Boca*; *Couto Marquese*, small portions. Snack bars, *Maré Alta*, *Sem Nome* (expensive).

There is a small Camping Club site on the fine Pontal beach, good, very crowded in Jan and Feb, US$8 pp, and also a private camping site and a site next to the police station after the bridge, hot showers, US$2.50 pp. Apart from camping, very little cheap accommodation.

Tourist Information Praça Chafariz.

Bus 7 a day to **Rio** (4 hrs, US$12) and to **Angra dos Reis** (1$^1/_2$ hrs, every 2 hrs, US$4.20); 3

a day to **Ubatuba** (70 km), **Taubaté** (170 km) and **Guaratinguetá** (210 km); 4 a day to **São Paulo** (5½ hrs, US$12, booked up quickly) and São Sebastião.

Excursions Enjoyable walk through a wood (lots of mosquitoes) to Trinidad beach. Also visit Muricana Fazenda: 6 km walk, or buses: zoo, restaurant and rum refinery with 10 different varieties of rum. 7 km from town is the natural water slide of Tubarão.

The coast road continues from Parati into the State of São Paulo. Another road, rough but scenic, climbs the Serra do Mar to Cunha and Guaratinguetá, also in São Paulo.

ESPIRITO SANTO (3)

The coastal state, N of Rio de Janeiro, which has a mountainous interior and a hot, damp seaboard. It is an important grower of coffee. In the N there are large forests containing hardwoods.

North of Campos (**see p 384**) is the State of Espírito Santo (pop 2,598,230) with its capital at Vitória. The people are known as Capixabas, after a former Indian tribe. Just across the frontier between the states is the resort town of **Marataízes**, with fair hotels and good beaches.

Hotels A2 *Praia*, Av Atlântica 99, T 532-2144, F 532-3515, on beach; **A2** *Saveiros Palace*, Av Miramar 119, T 532-1413, F 532-1285, on beach. **B** *Dona Judith*, Av Lacerda de Aguiar 353, T 532-1436, F 532-1305; **Camping** Municipal site on Praia do Siri, 10 km from centre; Xodó private site, Av Atlântica, 2 km from centre.

The main road N passes **Cachoeiro do Itapemirim** (pop 140,400), a busy city on both banks of the fast-flowing Rio Itapemirim; many hotels of all classes.

Further N, 58 km S of Vitória, is **Guarapari**, (pop 61,600) whose beaches attract many people seeking cures for rheumatism, neuritis and other complaints, from the radioactive monazitic sands. Bus from Vitória, 1 hr, US$1.25. (Both Marataízes and Guarapari are very crowded mid-Dec to end Feb).

Hotels A1 *Porto do Sol*, Mediterranean style village on rocky point overlooking a calm beach, pool, sauna, etc, rec, T 361-1100, F 261-2929; **A3** *Coronado*, Av Lourival de Almeida 312, T 261-1709, F 261-1444; **A3** *Hostess*, R Joaquim Silva Lima 701, T 261-0222; **C** *Atlântico*, Av Edísio Cirne 332, T 261-1237 on beach, rec.

Camping Camping Clube do Brasil, Setiba beach, 9 km from centre, T 262-1325. Cambrás site off Vitória highway close to beach, 4 km from centre. Private site near Cambrás site.

1 hr S of Guarapari, is the fishing village of **Ubu** with **A3** *Pousada Alba Ubu*, R Aleixo Neto 1762, T 361-1320, fully equipped, incl lunch and breakfast. A little further S is Praia dos Castelhanos, near **Anchieta** (**A3** *Hotel Thanharu Praia*, T 536-1246, F 536-1466, good; **Restaurant Moacyr**). Fishing/diving boat hire from Sr Romildo, Peixaria da Onça (2 km N of Anchieta) eg to Ilha dos Franceses. Also near Anchieta: is Praia Iriri, 30 km from Guarapari, served by a regular bus; 2 beaches, beautiful setting, lodging in private houses is possible. Coquera has a bar and trees for hammocks; 1 hr's walk S is a deserted beach, you must be self-sufficient, but shellfish and driftwood are plentiful.

There are coastal and inland road routes to **Vitória** (pop 258,245, CEP 29,000, DDD 027) 509 km from Rio de Janeiro, reached several times a day by plane (80 min), and by bus (9 hrs). Two bridges connect the island on which it stands with the mainland. The town is beautifully set, its entrance second only to Rio's, its beaches quite as attractive, but smaller, and the climate is less humid. On Avenida República is the huge Parque Moscoso, an oasis of quiet, with a lake, playground and tiny zoo. The Teatro Carlos Gomes, on Praça Costa Pereira, often presents plays, also jazz and folk festivals. The upper, older part of town, reached by steep streets and steps, is much less hectic than the lower harbour area which is beset by dreadful traffic problems. Vitória is a growing centre for the sport of sea fishing. Its importance is due to its connection westwards with Minas Gerais by the

Vitória-Minas railway, which transports for export millions of tons of iron ore and a large tonnage of coffee and timber. Ships drawing 11m and 240m in length can enter the port. A supplementary iron-ore port has been built at Ponta do Tubarão, near Vitória, to load ships up to 250,000 tons. These installations have led to some beach and air pollution at places near Vitória, such as Camburi (quite a pleasant beach, though, partly built up, palms, drink stands, fair surf).

See the fortified monastery of Nossa Senhora da Penha, on a high hill above the small settlement of Vila Velha. Most of the (unremarkable) structure, now in ruins, is of the 17th and 18th centuries; the views are superb. The Dutch attacked it in 1625 and 1640. Vila Velha has an excellent beach, but it is built up and noisy: take bus from Vitória marked Vilha Velha. A fine bridge has been built across the bay to Vila Velha; for bigger waves go to Barra do Jucu. Pleasant excursions in ferry-boats to Vila Velha.

Warning Robberies on the street are common.

Hotels A1 *Best Western Porto do Sol*, Av Dante Michelini 3957, Praia de Camburi, T 327-2244, F 327-2711, 7 km from centre, overlooking sea; **A3** *Senac Hotel* (Government-run hotel school), luxurious, swimming pool, restaurant, guests attended by student staff, on the ocean at R Bráulio Macedo 417, Ilha do Boi, T 325-0111, F 325-0115; **B** *São José*, Av Princesa Isabel 300, T 223-7222, F 223-5746; **D** *Avenida*, Av Florentino Avidos 350(ish) (T 223-4317/0770), with breakfast, friendly, clean, rec; **D** *Vitória*, Cais de São Francisco 85, near Parque Moscoso, with bath, excellent restaurant, changes money, good, clean, rec; **E** *Europa*, Sete de Setembro, corner of Praça Costa Pereira, clean, noisy but cheap, good value restaurant (nearby is a good value vegetarian restaurant and a money changer, ask at the hotel); **E** *Minister*, Av Cleto Nunes, off Parque Moscoso; *Walter*, across from Rodoviária, adequate, but *Lisboa*, opp Rodoviária, is not rec. Hotels located in beach areas, Camburi to the N, Vila Velha to the S, both about 15 mins from city centre.

Youth Hostel R Hugo Viola 135, T 325-6010, take "Universitário" bus, get off at first University stop.

Camping Serra Verde and Dalla's, private sites with some facilities, about 30 km N of the city on Manguinhos beach.

Restaurants *Mar e Terra* opp Rodoviária, good food, live music at night; *Lavacar* and many others at Praia Camburi offer food and live music; *Lambahias* is a lively dancing place for the young, 1/2 km W of Bambini, buses each hour on the hour.

Banks Local banks. **Casa de Câmbio** at Vitur, Av Getúlio Vargas; **Plumatur**, Av Governador Bley 465, Edif Glória, Loja 101. **Mastercard**, cash against card, Av Jeronimo Monteiro 1000, Grupo 414/424, Ed Trade Center, Centro. **BEMGE**, Thomas Cook agent, Av Princesa Isabela.

Consulates Danish, R do Sol 141, Sala 210, T 222-4075, open 0900-1300, 1500-1900.

Telecommunications Embratel, Palácio do Café, Praça Costa Pereira 52.

Tourist Information Emcatur, Av Getúlio Vargas (corner of Av Jerônimo Monteiro), and at rodoviária (friendly, good free map). Plumatur, Av Governador Bley (first floor), tourist information, coffee and parallel exchange rate.

Rail Daily passenger service to Belo Horizonte, 14 hrs, US$10 1st class, US$7 2nd.

Buses Rodoviária is 15 mins' walk from centre. **Rio**, 8 hrs, US$14.25 (*leito* 18.50). To hitch to Rio, take Itapemirim bus to Aracatiba (26 km). **Salvador**, 18 hrs, US$30; **Porto Seguro** direct 11 hrs with lots of stops, US$15.50 (also *leito* service); alternatively, take bus to Eunápolis, then change buses which run every hour, US$2. To hitch to Salvador, take a bus to Sara, which is beyond Carapina; alight where the bus turns off to Sara. Daily to Porto Velho, 61 hrs. Enquire at rodoviára for other destinations.

Excursions Visit **Santa Leopoldina** or **Domingos Martins**, both around 45 km from Vitória, less than an hour by bus (2 companies run to the former, approx every 3 hrs). Both villages preserve the architecture and customs of the first German and Swiss settlers who arrived in the 1840s. Domingos Martins (also known as Campinho) has a Casa de Cultura with some items of German settlement (Hotels **D** *Campinho*, clean, breakfast; **C** *Imperador*, 2 star). Santa Leopoldina has a most interesting museum (open Tues-Sun, 0900-1100 and 1300-1800) covering the settlers' first years in the area, and a large number of fascinating constructions dating from the end of the last century showing Swiss and German influence.

To *Santa Teresa* (pop 39,365), a charming hill town 2½ hrs by bus from Vitória, US$3.60 (beautiful journey). Two hotels, **E** *Pierazzo*, **E** *Glebo*, clean, and many restaurants. There is a unique hummingbird sanctuary at the **Museu Mello Leitâo**, which is a library including the works of the hummingbird and orchid scientist, Augusto Ruschi. Hummingbird feeders are hung outside the library (open Sat-Sun 1200-1700, at other times with permission). Also the Nova Lombardia National (renamed **Dr Augusto Ruschi**) **Biological Reserve**, a forest rich in endemic bird species (eg Salvadori's Antwren, Cinnamon-vented Pina, Russet-winged Spadebill, Oustalet's Tyrannulet, Rufous-brown Solitaire and Hooded Berryeater). Previous permission must be obtained to visit from Bento Ferreira at Ibama, Av Mal Mascarenhas de Moraes 2487, CP 762, Vitória ES, CEP 29.000.

75 km N of Vitória is the town of *Aracruz* (pop 52,425). A whole new town is being built beside the impressive Scandinavian/Brazilian cellulose plant, surrounded by vast new eucalyptus forests.

136 km N of Vitória is *Linhares* (pop 119,500) on Rio Doce, with good hotels, for example **B** *Linhares*, best in town; **D** *Grande*, pleasant, and others; *Restaurant Mocambo*, good and cheap. Linhares is the nearest town to the **Linhares Reserve** owned by CVRD (the state-owned mining company). Possibly the largest remaining lowland tract of Atlantic forest, permission from the reserve's director must be obtained to visit (very good birdwatching).

Mid-way between Linhares and Vitória, 5 km off BR-101 between Fundâo and Ibiraçu, is a Zen Buddhist monastery.

84 km N of Linhares is *São Mateus*, a pleasant town with no decent hotels, 13 km from good beaches (buses). The **Comboios Biological Reserve**, just S of Linhares, is designed to protect the species of marine turtles which frequent this coast (for information, contact Ibama at address above). Similarly the **Sooretama Biological Reserve**, also in the vicinity of Linhares, NW of the CVRD Reserve, on left of highway; this protects tropical Atlantic rain forest and its fauna and birds (it contains several bird species not found in CVRD Reserve).

Focus Tours, Belo Horizonte (p 402) offers one-week birding and general nature tours combining Museu Mello Leitâo, Nova Lombardia, CVRD Reserve and Sooretama; many bird and orchid species are found in these reserves and apparently nowhere else.

The most attractive beaches (described as "a must") in the State are around *Conceição da Barra* (pop 22,290) 242 km N of Vitória. Basic hotels *Cricaré*; *Nanuque*; and **D** *Rio Mar*. **D** *Sombra e Água Fresca*, Rodovia Bento Daher 1800, *pousada*, and campsite, US$3 pp, both with excellent facilities, many languages spoken, enthusiastically rec; nearby Camping Clube do Brasil site with full facilities. Corpus Christi (early Jun) is celebrated with an evening procession for which the road is decorated with coloured wood chips, a recommended experience if you are in the area. An interesting excursion is to Itaúnas, 21 km up the coast; the small town has been swamped by sand dunes, so it has been moved to the opposite river bank. There is now a fantastic landscape of huge dunes and deserted beaches. A few *pousadas* and a small campsite can be found. Bus from the *padaria* in Conceição da Barra at 0700, returns 1700.

MINAS GERAIS (4)

A state with a number of fine colonial cities built during the gold rush in the 18th century, some splendid caves, the Rio São Francisco in the N, and several spas and hill resorts. The capital is Belo Horizonte, the country's first modern planned city, now a major industrial centre.

The inland State of Minas Gerais (pop 15,746,200) somewhat larger than France, is mountainous in the S, rising to the 2,787-m peak of Agulhas Negras in the Mantiqueira range, and in the E, where there is the Caparaó National Park containing the Pico da Bandeira (2,890m). From Belo Horizonte N are undulating grazing lands, the richest of which are in the extreme W: a broad wedge of country between Goiás in the N and São Paulo in the S, known as the Triângulo Mineiro. Most of the upland is also good grazing country. Being frost-free, Minas Gerais is again becoming one of the main producers of coffee.

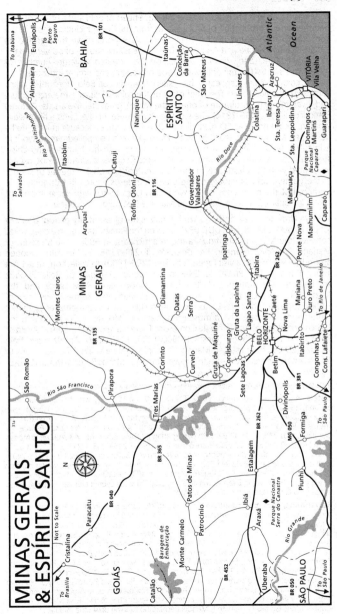

MINAS GERAIS & ESPÍRITO SANTO

Not to Scale

Minas Gerais was once described as having a heart of gold and a breast of iron. Half the mineral production of Brazil comes from the State, including most of the iron ore. Diamonds and gold are still found. Its exports move through Rio de Janeiro, Santos, Vitória and Angra dos Reis. The easy availability of power and the local agricultural and mineral production has created a large number of metal-working, textile, mineral water, food processing and timber industries.

The colonial cities can easily be visited from Rio or Belo Horizonte; many companies provide tours. The chief glory of the colonial cities is the architecture and, even more, the sculpture of one of the world's great creative artists, Antônio Francisco Lisboa (1738-1814), the son of a Portuguese architect and a black slave woman. He is known as "O Aleijadinho" (the little cripple) because in later life he developed a maiming disease (possibly leprosy) which compelled him to work in a kneeling (and ultimately a recumbent) position with his hammer and chisel strapped to his wrists. His finest work, which shows a strength not usually associated with the plastic arts in the 18th century, is probably the set of statues in the gardens and sanctuary of the great Bom Jesus church in Congonhas do Campo, but the main body of his work is in Ouro Preto, with some important pieces in Sabará, São João del Rei and Mariana (see following pages).

129 km N of Rio by air and 155 km by road is the pleasant city of **Juiz de Fora** (pop 378,500, CEP 36,100, DDD 032). It lies on the Paraibuna river, in a deep valley between the Mar and Mantiqueira mountain chains, at 695m. The Museum of Mariano Procópio, Mariano Procópio s/n, T 211-1145, in beautiful wooded grounds, is well worth a visit (open Tues-Sun 1200-1800); its collections date from Imperial Brazil. The Praça da Estação has good examples of Belle Epoque architecture, the station hall, the hotels *Príncipe* and *Renascença* and the Associação Comercial building. Also see the Portinári mural of tiles in the foyer of Edifício Clube Juiz de Fora; Banco do Brasil building by Oscar Niemeyer, both in R Halfeld where there is also a museum of banking (Mon-Fri 1300-1600) and the French neo-classical Academia de Comércio. There is a railway museum at Av Brasil 2001, next to the station; Tues-Sat 0900-1200, 1330-1800. An attractive train journey (25 km) from Estação Mariano Procópio (opp museum, Mon-Sat), runs to South America's first hydro-electric power station at Matias Barbosa (return by bus, hourly).

ındustries Steel-making, textiles, brewing, timber sawing, sugar refining.

Hotels A1 *Ritz*, Av Rio Branco 2000, T 215-7300, F 215-1892, with bath, sauna, pool, parking, takes all credit cards except Amex; **A1** *Center Park*, Av Getúlio Vargas 181, T/F 215-4898, with bath, sauna, pool, parking, accepts credit cards; **A3** *Centenário*, Av Francisco Bernardino 33, T 215-3700, with bath and TV, D without; **A3** *César Palace*, Av Getúlio Vargas 335, T 215-6599, with bath, parking, takes credit cards; **A3** *Joalpa*, R Afonso Pinto Mota 29, between Avs Rio Branco and G Vargas, T 215-6055, F 215-3446, with bath, sauna, pool, parking, credit cards accepted; **B** *Imperial*, R Batista de Oliveira 605, T 215-7400, with bath; **C** *São Luiz*, R Halfeld 360, T 215-1155, with bath, art deco lobby, winter garden; **D** *Majestic*, R Halfeld 284, T 215-5050, with bath and TV, cheaper without bath. Many cheap hotels on Av G Vargas, in E range, mostly short-stay. Travellers should take care when walking betwen Av G Vargas and the railway at night.

Restaurants, Bars, Entertainment The *Fogão de Serra* restaurant, 16 km from the city, serves typical Minas food. *Berttu's*, R Santo Antônio 572, best in town, mineira and international food (about US$20 incl wine); *Cantão Suíço*, R Santa Rita 557/59, good self-service; others on same street and R São João; *Marrakech*, R Espíritu Santo 1081, bar and Arab cuisine; *Barroco*, R Batista de Oliveira 1126, restored cellar with live music, *feijoada* on Sat, good cocktails; *I Due Fratelli*, R São Mateus 144, Italian; *La Belle Bistrot*, R Delfim Moreira 22, French bar/restaurant; *Chez Moi*, R Tietê 40, Swiss-style chalet, live music. Best nightclub is *Clube Noturno Vila das Tochas*, R Roberto Stigert 4, Bairro São Pedro, crêperie, American bar, dance floor; *Bar do Bené*, Pres Costa e Silva 2305, Bairro São Pedro, friendly pub; *Prova Oral*, R A Braga 210, bar with live music, highly rec. For lots of bars, restaurants, pizzerias and night life, visit the Bairro São Mateus, bounded by Av Independência, R Sã Mateus, R Padre Café, R Mons Gomes Freire with R Manoel Bernardino running down the middle.

Language Courses at the federal university, UFJF, T 229-3732, F 231-1342. Students may be able to stay at the *república*, R Dimas Bergo Xisto 155 (bairro São Pedro, 36037-510 Juiz de Fora, 7 km from centre), T 231-1263. From Juiz de Fora rodoviária, take bus 630 to Av Getúlio Vargas esq R Marechal Deodoro, walk to corner of Bargas e R São João, take bus 530 to the *república*, or 532 to corner of Av Senhor dos Passos e Dimas Bergo Xisto.

Health Doctor Alberto Moutinho, R António Dias 475-A, Granbery, T 213-5083 (no English); **Dentist** Dr Elsom Braga de Mello, Av Barão do Rio Branco 25555 sala 1203 (some English); **Hospital** Reunidos, R Delfim Moreira 62, T 215-6400, serious injuries only.

Shopping Locally produced clothing, try bargain shops in R Fonseca Hermes; *Priscila Joiais*, gold and silver workshop, Galeria Solar, loja 228; many interesting antique shops; plentiful regional foods.

Travel Agencies *Serra Branca*, R Aristóteles Braga 186, Cidade Universitária, T 231-1245, local tours and to further afield in Minas Gerais. *Beijaflor*, Shopping Santa Cruz, loja 1148, T 215-0249, French, Italian, some English spoken.

Bus To/from Rio, 19 a day, Útil, US$6, 2¾ hrs (a spectacular trip through mountains and tropical forest); Útil to Belo Horizonte, 10 a day, US$8 (Viaçao Útil, T 215-3976, Rodoviária, or in town H Henrique Surerus 22, T 215-6759, Mon-Fri 0800-1800, Sat 0800-1200). To São João del Rei via Conselheiro Lafaiete, 6 hrs, US$6. Bus station outside town, Av Brasil 4501, T 215-7696, take bus 630 to town.

Airport Av Guadalajara, T 233-1089; bus 520 on the hour to centre. Nordeste Linhas Aéreas, T 233-1040, once a day Mon-Fri to São Paulo and Ipatinga.

85 km from Juiz de Fora, in the municipality of Lima Duarte is the **Parque Florestal de Ibitipoca** at 1,760m, which preserves birds, animals and vegetation of the region, plus several quartzite caves and rock formations. Access by unpaved road (4WD rec) from Lima Duarte to Conceição de Ibitipoca. Bus Rio Preto from Juiz da Fora to Lima Duarte, T 221-4461, then seek out Sr Pedro Moreira's taxi, T 281-1200 (Banco do Brasil) or 281-1296 (home); US$18 to Conceiçao and US$23 to the park, one way. Local guide US$10. For guided tours contact Dale Jaume, T (032) 211-7008, US$70 for full day incl transport and lunch, US$80 with simple overnight accommodation and breakfast. In the nearby village of Conceição de Ibitipoca, hand-dyed and woven bedspreads are made; **B** *Pousada do Rodrigo*, T Juiz da Fora, 032-215-8659.

Within reach of Juiz de Fora: *Mar de Espanha*, 62 km E, charming 19th-century colonial town (tame sloths in the trees, restaurant Nectar, open Fri-Sun 1800); *Torreões*, 33 km, lime hills; *Rio Novo*, 48 km N, nice colonial architecture, renowned for dairy produce; *Monte Verde*, 33 km, for waterfalls and natural swimming pools.

From **Barbacena** (pop 100,050), 103 km on (with an important horse and cattle fair, and a rose festival in Oct), a paved road runs W to the colonial city of *São João del Rei* (pop 72,740, CEP 36300, DDD 032), at the foot of the Serra do Lenheiro, with a fine bridge and three splendid 18th century churches, open most mornings: **Pilar** (the Cathdral, R Getúlio Vargas), the earliest, with rich altars and bright ceiling, and good *azulejos* in choir, and a sacristy with portraits of the Evangelists, new sacred art museum next door, entry US$0.50; **São Francisco de Assis** (1764), Praça Frei Orlando, with two sculptures by Aleijadinho, and others of his school (recent restoration has removed the plaster from the altars, revealing fine carving in sucupira wood) and the **Carmo**, Largo do Carmo, designed by him and with interior sculptures by him, recently very well restored, all in white. Near São Francisco is the house of **Bárbara Heliodora** (1759-1819), one of the Inconfidentes (**see p 405**), which also contains the municipal museum. The **railway museum** (Av Hermílio Alves 366, T 371-2888 see below) is well worth seeing. **Museu de Arte Sacra**, Praça Gastão da Cunha 8, small but well recommended (Tues-Sun 0900-1700). There are also the **Tancredo Neves Museum**, R Padre José Maria Xavier 7 (weekends and holidays 0900-1700, rec to students of Brazilian history); the **Museu de Arte Regional do Patrimônio Histórico**, in Praça Severiano de Resende (open Tues-Sun, 1200-1730, US$0.50), and a **pewter factory** (with exhibition and shop) Av Leite de Castro 1150, T 371-4422, run by an Englishman, John Somers. Tourist office in old bus station. The streets "are paved with fossil plants: almost sacrilegious to walk on them". A good view of the town and surroundings is from Alto da Boa Vista, where there is a Statue of Christ

(Senhor dos Montes). São João del Rei is very lively at weekends, its nightlife brings young people from neighbouring towns.

Festivals The morning masses on Sun and religious festivals at São Francisco (0915) and Mercês (1030)—behind and above Pilar— are accompanied by choir and orchestra who maintain a tradition of over 200 years of local composition.

Barbacena Hotel B *Grogotó*, excellent, operated by Senac, T 331-7755, F 331-4430.

São João del Rei Hotels A3 *Porto Real*, Av Eduardo Magalhães 254, T/F 371-1201, comfortable; **B** *Lenheiro Palace*, Av Pres Tancredo Neves 257, T/F 371-3914, good; **B** *do Hespagnol*, R Marechal Deodoro 131, T 371-4677; **B** *Pousada Casarão*, opp São Francisco church, converted mansion, Ribeiro Bastos 94, T 371-1224, swimming pool, delightful; **B** *Pousada do Sol*, 6 km out on road to Tiradentes, T 371-1004; **C** *Colonial*, Manoel Anselmo 22, T 371-1792, clean and comfortable; **E** *Brasil*, Av Pres Tancredo Neves 395, T 371-2804, lovely colonial house, opp railway station so back rooms much quieter, clean, friendly, cheap, rec, no breakfast (*Cafeteria Globo* in the same street, 2 blocks away, is good, though). Cheap *pousadas* in R Marechal Deodoro: **F** *S Benedito*, No 254, clean but not so friendly; **F** *Santa Rita*, No 242, clean, friendly, shared rooms; **F** *Pousada Ramón*, opp bus station. *Hotel Porto Real* restaurant and *Restaurant Quinta do Ouro*, also good vegetarian restaurant, all rec. Good *Churrascaria* next to railway station.

Buses Rodoviária is 2 km W of centre of São João. Buses to **Rio**, 3 daily, 5 hrs, Sun 0800 only, **São Paulo**, 8 hrs, US$12, and **Belo Horizonte**, 3½ hrs. To **Ouro Preto** via Congonhas, US$13, **Juiz de Fora**, US$6, frequent service to Tiradentes.

John Parsons writes: *Tiradentes* (originally São José del Rei; pop 10,220, CEP 35325, DDD 032). The centre of this charming little town, 15 km from São João, with its nine streets and eight churches, at the foot of the green Serra São José, hardly belongs to this century. The **Santo Antônio** church, first built in 1710, contains some of the finest gilded wood carvings in the country and a small but fine organ brought from Oporto in the 1790s. The reconstructed façade is said to follow a design by Aleijadinho. There is also a sun-dial by him. Also of unusual interest and charm are the **Rosário** church, with fine statuary and ornate gilded altars; this and **Nossa Senhora das Mercês** have interesting painted ceilings and the latter a notable statue of the Virgin.

At the bottom of the stone paved road which descends from Santo Antônio is the fine fountain (*chafariz*), installed in 1749. The water is brought by a stone aqueduct from springs in the forest at the foot of Serra São José, which offers fine walks including the lane beside the aqueduct. The **museum**, housed where Padre Toledo (another Inconfidente) once lived, is of particular interest and there are some good pieces of furniture exhibited. The simple pilgrimage church of **Santíssima Trindade** is also well worth seeing. Tourist Office in the Prefeitura, R Resende Costa 71. See the artists' lithographic printing shop of Largo do Ó. There are attractive walks in the neighbourhood, and a 1½-hr walk to the fountains and pools of Águas Santas.

The town is very busy during Holy Week, when there are numerous religious processions.

Tiradentes Hotels A1 *Solar da Ponte*, Praça das Mercês (prop John and Anna Maria Parsons) T 355-1255, F 355-1201, atmosphere of country house, including breakfast and tea, only 12 rm. Fresh flowers in rooms, bar, sauna, garden, swimming pool, light meals for residents only, for larger meals, the hotel rec five local restaurants listed below. Also *Pousada Maria Barbosa*, **C** *Antônio Teixeira*, Carvallio 134, T 355-1227, pool, very pleasant, *Hotel Wellerson*, T 355-1226, **E** *Pousada Tiradentes*, *Hotel Ponto do Morro*, *Pousada de Laurito*, Direita 187, T 355-1268.

Restaurants Local food: *Quinta de Ouro*, rec; *Churrascaria Ramón*, reasonable prices; *Estalagem*; *Padre Toledo*. Meat: *Thé*. Italian: *Donatelli*; *Aluarte*, Largo do ô 1, cheap, garden, sells handicrafts, rec. Vegetarian: *Opção Saúdavel*, Av Tiradentes 792, tiny, cheap, rec.

Recommended is the train trip between São João del Rei and Tiradentes (13 km). The train has been in continuous operation since 1881, using the same locomotives and rolling stock, running on 76 cm gauge track, all now lovingly restored and cared for. Maximum speed is 20 km per hr. Price: US$2.50 return, one class only. Fri, Sat, Sun and holiday steam train service to Tiradentes, 1000 and 1415, returning 1300 and 1700. Railway museum at the railway station in São João del Rei; open daily 0900-1130, 1300-1700, entrance included in rail fare; there are also a round house which has 16 vintage locomotives in superb condition, an engine shed and a steam-operated machine shop, still working.

From Belo Horizonte, the shortest road to São João del Rei is via Lagoa Dourada. Just past Lagoa Dourada is the turning (12 km) for **Prados**, a small town 15 km from Tiradentes (local bus, 1/2 hr) known for its musical and handicrafts traditions, excellent leather clothing, good prices from *Mara e Café*, R Magachães Gomes 90. Near the turn is Entre Rios de Minas (*Hotel Camapuã*).

Belo Horizonte, the capital of Minas Gerais, is the third largest city in Brazil (pop 2,048,861, CEP 3000, DDD 031). It is situated over 800m above sea-level, surrounded by mountains, and enjoys an excellent climate (16°-30°C) except for the rainy season (Dec-Mar). It was founded 12 December 1897. Sights to be seen are the **Praça da Assembléia**, with three fine modern buildings: Legislative Assembly, church and Banco do Brasil; the **Palácio da Liberdade**, in Praça da Liberdade amid other fine *fin-de-siècle*-style public buildings (every Sun morning and Thur evening an open-air craft market operates here—very good, also a flower market each Fri from 1800 and an antique and occultism market each Sun: at night the fountain is illuminated in a variety of colours, optimistically described as "psychedelic"); the **Palácio das Artes**, Afonso Pena 1567, which is in the Parque Municipal and contains the Centro de Artesanato Mineiro (craft shop open 0900-1700, Tues-Sun); the **Museu Mineiro**, Av João Pinheiro, 342, religious art in old Senate building near centre (open Tues, Wed, Fri 1230-1830, Thur 1500-2100, Sat, Sun 1000-1600); the **Museu da Mineralogia Prof Djalma Guimarães**, R da Bahia 1149, a Gothic building near the park, with interesting exhibits (closed pending renovation in 1994); the **Museu Histórico Abílio Barreto**, R Bernado Mascarenhas, in an old *fazenda* house which is the last reminder of Belo Horizonte's predecessor, the village of **Arraial do Curral d'el Rey**, built by João Leite da Silva Ortiz in the 18th century, with most interesting historical exhibits (open 1000-1700 Wed-Mon, take bus 2902 from Av Pena); the **Museu da Telecomunicaçao**, Av Afonso Pena 4001, Mangabeiras (open Mon-Fri, 0800-1700); the **railway station**, with museum on 2nd floor showing a model railway and the railway headquarters in a mansion on the hill above the station, with locomotive and railway coach used by Dom Pedro II; the **Parque Municipal** (an oasis of green, right in the centre of the city, small amusement park and playground, closed at night and on Mon, except for a small section in the SW corner). **Museo Histórico Natural**, in the Instituto Agronómico, R Gustavo da Silveira 1035, T 461-7666, has a local geological and palaeontological display and good archaeological exhibits (take bus 3803A from Praça Rio Branco). An obelisk in Praça Sete de Setembro commemorates Independence, it is the centre for political protest.

Eight km from the centre is the picturesque suburb of **Pampulha**, famous for its modern buildings and the artificial lake (many infestations, do not swim in it), many buildings designed by the renowned Brazilian architect Oscar Niemeyer (who later designed much of Brasília); in Pampulha the glass and marble **Museu de Arte de Belo Horizonte** may be visited (Av Octacílio Negrão de Lima, open 0800-1800 daily, reported disappointing), as well as the Chapel of São Francisco (the interior of which was decorated by the Brazilian painter Cândido Portinári). There is a bus (not the 4403) from the city centre to the **Jardim Zoológico** (at the far end of the lake from the dam—small selection of birds with some rarities, animals well kept for the most part) that passes the chapel and also the **Mineirão** stadium about 3/4 km away (the second largest in Brazil after the Maracanã stadium in Rio); bus 2004 goes from Av Afonso Pena to the chapel.

In the southern zone of the city, on the Serra do Curral, the **Parque de Mangabeiras** has a good view of the city, forest trails, sports facilities and snack bars. The natural amphitheatre where the Pope spoke in 1982 is nearby; there is an iron monument marking the occasion (take bus 2001 from Afonso Pena between Av Amazonas and R Tamóios, closed Mon). In 1984, the **Minascentro**, a convention centre for exhibitions and congresses, was opened in the city centre. Belo Horizonte is one of the fastest growing of Brazil's main cities; atmospheric pollution has recently been reported.

The industrial area, about 10 Km from the centre, has now become the third largest industrial centre of Brazil, and apart from being the traditional centre of mining and agricultural industries (as well as diamond cutting and precious stones), it has steelworks and an automobile industry. The city has a good public transport system (red buses serve central and express routes, yellow circular routes, and blue diagonal routes), and taxis are plentiful, although hard to find at peak hours.

Local Holidays Maundy Thursday; Corpus Christi; 15 Aug (Assumption); 8 Dec (Immaculate Conception).

Electric Current 120-220 AC 60 cycles.

Warning Blonde visitors should be especially careful of gangs of children who cut off women's hair for wigs. The area around the bus station is dangerous; take a taxi to/from there if travelling with a lot of luggage or valuables.

Hotels (number of stars in brackets) **L2** *Brasilton* (4), out of town at Km 3.65 on Rodovia Fernão Dias, Contagem, T 396-1100, F 396-1144, very good restaurant, discount possible; **L3** *Boulevard Plaza* (3), Av Getúlio Vargas 1640, Savassi district (chic), T 223-9000, F 225-8438, very nice; **L3** *Del Rey* (4), Praça Afonso Arinos 60, T 273-2211, F 273-1804; **L3** *Othon Palace* (5), Av Afonso Pena 1050, T 273-3844, F 212-2318, deluxe, excellent, safe deposit boxes, pool on roof, helpful staff; **L3** *Real Palace* (4), R Espírito Santo 904, T 273-3111, F 273-2643; **A1** *Internacional Plaza Palace* (3), R Rio de Janeiro 109, T 201-2300, F 212-2347, good but seedy part of town; **A1** *Normandie* (3), R Tamóios 212, T 201-6166, F 222-6133, excellent grill; **A1** *Serrana Palace* (3), R Goitacases 450, T 201-9955, F 226-0285, pleasant restaurant but hotel rather run down, seedy area; **A1** *Wembley Palace* (3), R Espírito Santo 201, T 201-6966, F 224-9946, excellent, central, clean, but poor rate for TCs; **A2** *Casa dos Municípios*, R Rio Grande do Norte 1017, Funcionários (in Savassi, chic shopping area), T 226-5177, clean; **A3** *Estoril*, R Carijós 454, T 201-9322, with bath, comfortable, pleasant; **A3** *Itatiaia* (2), Praça Rui Barbosa 187, T 212-3300, near railway station, central, clean, a/c, with bath and good breakfast; **B** *Ambassy* (3), R Caetés 633, near bus station, T 201-0222, helpful, English spoken, clean, a/c, noisy, good restaurant; **B** *Sul América Palace* (2), Av Amazonas 50, T 201-1722, clean, friendly, TV and fridge in rooms, run down; **C** *Continental* (2), Av Paraná 241, T 201-7944, central, clean, friendly, interior rooms rec, those on the street very noisy; **C** *Esplanada* (2), Av Santos Dumont 304, T 273-5311 (E without bath), clean, good restaurant, own garage, good value; **E** *Vitória*, Curitiba 224, without bath, good. Cheaper places are: **E** *Maciel*, Av Ol Maciel 95, basic, clean; **F** *Madrid*, opp rodoviária, rec. Near bus station and in R Curitiba many hotels are for very-short-stay couples: **D** *Magnata*, R Guarani 124, with breakfast, near bus station, cheap and clean, bath, good hot shower, safe deposit, rec; **E** *Minas Bahia*, No 173, friendly. Within 10 mins walk of Rodoviária, turn left along main road to R Espírito Santo, No 284, **D** *Majestic*; No 227, **E** *São Salvador*; No 237, rec; **E** *Magalhães*, basic, clean, friendly, cheap laundry service, good restaurant over the road; **E** *Lux*, corner of Av Santos Dumont, rec. You may spend the night in the bus station only if you have an onward ticket (police check at midnight, but see above).

Youth hostels *Pousadinha Mineira*, R Januária 206, T 446-2911, 15 mins from rodoviária, rec; *Chalé Mineiro*, R Sta Luzia 288, Sta Efigênia, T 467-1576, attractive, splash pool, highly rec.

Camping Wild camping near Alto do Palácio, near river and waterfalls.

Restaurants *Tavares*, R Santa Catarina 64 (local dishes), excellent value. Chinese: *Yun Ton*, R Santa Catarina 946, rec. Churrascarias: *Carretão Guaiba*, Av do Contorno 8412; *Farrounilha*, Afonso Pena 3300; *Picanha na Tábua*, R Curitiba, unprepossessing but highly rec, and *Dona Lucinha*, R Sergipe; *Chico Mineiro*, R Alagoas, corner of Av Brasil, local chicken specialities, good, closed Sun; *Santa Felicidade*, R Dr Morais, good; *Te Par Mi Kadu*, R Paraíba, Japanese, rec; *Arroz com Feijão*, typical food, Av Contorno 6510, Av Contorno 7438 and R Antônio de Albuquerque 440, all friendly, reasonably-priced; *Pizzaiolo*, Av Contorno 8495, good for pizzas; *Naturalmente*, Av Andradas 367; *Superbom* (vegetarian), R São Paulo, 971, 1100-1500, Mon to Fri. *Mangueiras*, at Pampulha, next to Niemeyer chapel of São Francisco, very popular; *Dona Derna*, behind the Palácio de Liberdade, highly rec, and *Dona Lucinha*, R Sergipe; *Buona Távola*, R Sta Rita Durão 309, Funcionários, excellent Italian; *Alpino* (German), R Tupinambás 173, good value and popular, corned beef and fresh boiled vegetables available,

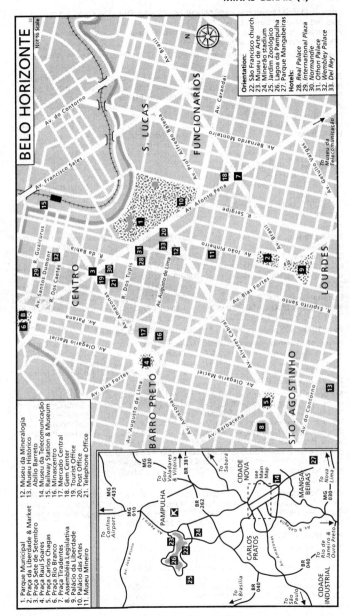

BELO HORIZONTE

Not to Scale

1. Parque Municipal
2. Praça da Liberdade & Market
3. Praça Sete de Setembro
4. Praça Raul Soares
5. Praça Carlos Chagas
6. Praça Rio Branco
7. Praça Tiradentes
8. Assembléia Legislativa
9. Palácio da Liberdade
10. Palácio das Artes
11. Museu Mineiro
12. Museu da Mineralogia
13. Museu Histórico Abílio Barreto
14. Museu da Telecomunicação
15. Railway Station & Museum
16. Minascentro
17. Mercado Central
18. Tourist Office
19. Telemar Center
20. Post Office
21. Telephone Office

Orientation:
22. São Francisco church
23. Museu de Arte
24. Mineirão stadium
25. Jardim Zoológico
26. Lagoa da Pampulha
27. Parque Mangabeiras

Hotels:
28. Real Palace
29. International Plaza
30. Normandie
31. Othon Palace
32. Wembley Palace
33. Del Rey

CENTRO

S. LUCAS

FUNCIONARIOS

BARRO PRETO

LOURDES

STO. AGOSTINHO

open-air; *Flor de Líbano*, opp *Hotel Magalhães* at Espírito Santo 234, cheap and good. Many bars and restaurants around Praça Raúl Soares; more on Av Rio de Janeiro. Two rec bars are *Americana*, R Pernambuco 1025; *Janis*, Av Getúlio Vargas 809. Very cheap and friendly *lanchonete* near rodoviária, Acre 164.

Tea rooms   *Era Uma Vez Un Chalezinho*, R Paraíba 1455; *Tia Clara*, R Antônio de Albuquerque 617.

Banks and Exchange   Lloyds Bank, Av João Pinheiro 580; **Citibank**, R Espírito Santo 871; **Banco do Brasil**, R Rio de Janeiro 750, Av Amazonas 276; **Banco Econômico**, R Bahia 360, 9th floor, and other local banks, 1000-1630. **American Express**, Master Turismo, Av Afonso Pena 1967, T 273-3122. **Mastercard**, cash against card. **Banco Meridional**, R dos Inconfidentes 1051, 4°-6° anadares, Funcionários. **H Pichiommi**, R Espírito Santo and R Guajajanas; Sr Cláudio, R Espírito Santo 466, 16th floor, office 1608, very good rates. **São Paulo Joios**, Amazonas 105 offers a good rate; **Nascente Turismo**, Rio de Janeiro 1101, T 224-3334, ask for Luiz Carlos de Oliveira, changes money at a good rate. Changing TCs is difficult, but hotels will change them for guests at a poor rate.

Consulates   British Vice-Consulate: Av Afonso Pena 952, s 500, Caixa Postal 576, T 222-6318; **German**, R Carijós 244, T 222-3411; **Austrian**; R José Américo Cancado Bahia 199, T 333-3622. **French**, R Prof Antônio Aleixo 843, 5th Floor, T335-5563; **Italian**, Praça Carlos Chagas 49, 2nd floor, T 335-5394; **Netherlands**, R Alagoas 1460, 11th floor, T 221-0615; **Finland**, Av Contorno 6283, sala 604/8, T 227-2725; **Denmark**, R Prof Jerson Martins 166, T 441-4755. **US**: Serviço de Divulgação e Relações Culturais, Av Alvares Cabral 1600, 3rd floor, T 335-3555.

Entertainment   Nightlife *Drosophila*, R Ouro Preto, Bairro Preto, bar, dancing, said to be the best; *L' Apogee*, R Antônio de Alberquerque 729; *Pantheon*, Rio Grande do Norte 1470; *Máscaras*, R Sta Rita Durão 667; *Ao Bar*, R Cláudio Manoel; *Sausalito*, R Tomé de Souza 912, street café. *Teatro da Cidade* theatre, R da Bahia 1341, for Portuguese speakers. *Music school*, Av Afonso Pena, opp Palácio das Artes: "brilliant" classical concerts, entrance free or nominal (US$2).

Hospital   Mater Dei, R Gonçalves Dias 2700, T 335-2200, has been rec; Alfredo Balena MedCentre, R dos Otoni 927, a new private hospital. Dr Ricardo Queiroz Guimarães, Av Brasil 1474, Funcionários, T 224-2020 for contact lenses and eye problems.

Post Office   with poste restante, Av Afonso Pena 1270. **UPS** Salima T 222-9002.

Places of Worship   Synagoga Beth Yacou, R Pernambuco 326, T 224-6013; **Catholic Church**, Av Antônio Carlos 2747, T 442-7743, R Bahia 1596, T 222-6059; **Presbyterian Church**, R Ceará 1434, T 226-1844; **Baptist Church**, R Joaquim de Figueredo 332, T 384-1322; **Mormon Church**, R Levindo Lopes 214, T 233-7883; **Adventist Church**, R Timbras 683, T 226-6144.

Shopping   Mercado Central, Av Aug de Lima 744, large and clean, open every day, Sat social centre. Market for fruit, vegetables, meat and other items at corner of R Santa Catarina and Av Amazonas (near Praça Raúl Soares). There are huge hypermarkets just outside the city on the highways to Rio and to São Paulo. Splendid delicatessen with foreign food and wines—and liquors—*Au Bon Gourmet*, R Tupinambás 187. Gemstones are a good buy here, try *Manoel Bernardes*, R Espírito Santo 835, very reasonable, ask for US saleswoman Manuela, who can arrange tours of workshops. For records, *Cogumelo*, Av Augusto de Lima 399. "**Hippie fair**" Thur evenings in Praça da Liberdade. **Food and Antique fair**, Av Afonso Pena, opp park, Sun; good home-made food; **other fairs** on Fri and Sat. Belo is said to be very good for slide film, cheese and chocolate.

Bookshop   *Daniel Vaitsman*, R Espírito Santo 466, 17th floor, for English language books. Foreign language books at *Livraria Van Damme*, R das Guajajaras 505, also good local and Portuguese selection (and said to change TCs); *Acaiaca*, R Tamóios 72, good for dictionaries. Used foreign-language books at *Livraria Alfarrábio*, R Tamóios 320.

Golf   Morro do Chapeú, 9 holes.

Travel Agent   *Focus Tours*, Rua Alagoas 1460/s 503, Savassi, 30130 Belo Horizonte, T 223-0358, F (031) 223-0599, telex 039 1976, run by Douglas and Nancy Trent, offer specialized tours all over Brazil and have a special interest in ecology and tours to the Pantanal. Tours in Minas to see a great variety of wildlife. Reliable information and a portion of their profits is used for conservation project in Brazil (office in USA 14821 Hillside Lane, Burnsville, MN 55306, T/F 612-892-7830). *Mangabeira Turismo*, R Goitacases 71-8° andar, and *Unitour*, Av Tupis 141, organize river trips on the São Francisco (see p 410).

Tourist Information Belotur (municipal information office), R Tupis 149, 17th floor, T 222-5500; Turminas, Av Augusto de Lima 785, T 201-0122/201-3875; Praça Sete de Setembro; at rodoviária (particularly polyglot, reasonable free map of centre) ask for the Guia Turístico for events, opening times etc, airport (very helpful). Touring Clube do Brasil, Av Afonso Pena 1913.

Car Hire Nobre, Confins Airport and Av Francisco Sales 1424, T 227-5700; and others.

Airport A new international airport near Lagoa Santa, at Confins, 39 km from Belo Horizonte, has been opened. Taxi to centre, US$24; airport bus, either *executivo* from the exit, US$6, or comfortable normal bus from far end of car park every hr on the $1/2$-hr, US$2.40, both go to/from rodoviária.

Closer to the city is the national airport at Pampulha, which has shuttle services from several cities, including Rio and São Paulo. Flights, as well as transportation to/from this airport, are cheaper. From airport to town blue bus 1202 leaves across the street from the aiport, 25 mins, US$0.15, bus passes the rodoviária and cheaper hotel district.

Railway To Vitória, daily 0700, tickets sold at 0530, US$10 1st class, US$7 2nd, 14 hrs.

Buses Rodoviária is by Praça Rio Branco at end of Av Afonso Pena (left-luggage lockers, attended service 0700-2200). To **Rio**, 7 hrs, US$14.25 (ordinary), to **Brasília**, 10 hrs, 9 a day incl 2 *leitos*, only one leaves in daylight (0800), US$23, *leito* US$46. To **São Paulo**, 10 hrs, US$7.25; route passes the great Furnas reservoir. To **Salvador** US$39, 24 hrs, at 1800 and 1900 daily. **Porto Seguro** 18 hrs, direct, via Nanuque and Eunápolis; **Recife**, US$60; **Belém**, US$91. To **Campo Grande** 2000, with Gontijo, a good route to Bolivia, avoiding São Paulo. All major destinations served. For buses within Minas Gerais, see under destination.

Hitchhiking to Rio or Ouro Preto, take a bus marked "Shopping", to the shopping centre above Belo Horizonte on the Rio road.

Excursions Within easy motoring distance from Belo Horizonte are several of the 400 caves and grottoes for which Minas Gerais is famous. The best and most famous is the **Gruta de Maquiné** with 6 chambers open to visitors, well lit, but hot—26°C (entry US$2), 126 km NW of Belo (well signposted and with restaurants nearby, which greet potential customers with combined history and menu leaflet; bus at 0915, return at 1500, $3^1/2$ hrs, US$4.50). In the nearby town of **Cordisburgo** is a museum to the writer Guimarães Rosa. The **Gruta de Lapinha**, almost as good, is only 51 km N of the city (entrance to caves and small museum, US$1); bus at 1015, $1^1/4$ hrs, US$2 one way. Lapinha cave is closed Mon. Local bus stop for Lagoa Santa is 2 km downhill from caves.

10 km before Lapinha is the town of *Lagoa Santa* (pop 24,890), a weekend resort for Belo Horizonte. The sandy beach on the lake (close to the town centre and bus station) is used for fishing, sun-bathing and boating (do not swim, the water is infected with schistosomiasis). Along the beach are bars and restaurants, while in the nearby main square which also has two small hotels and an interesting modernistic church. The road to Belo Horizonte ($1/2$-hrly bus service, US$1) passes Belo Horizonte's new international airport. Bus Lagoa Santa-Lapinha every $1/2$-hr.

To the NE of the city, a few km off the BR-262, is the **Serra de Piedade**, a high peak giving spectacular views over the surrounding countryside. A popular excursion point but only accessible by car or special bus service. There are a small chapel and a *churrascaria*. From the peak can be seen the small town of **Caeté** (pop 33,440), which has one or two interesting churches and the remains of an old ironworks near the railway station. Take the Conceição do Mato Dentro bus to Alto do Palácio; near there are waterfalls and campsites. Further from Belo, turn off the BR-262 (towards Vitória) at Km 73 and go via Barão de Cocais and Brumal to Caracá (120 km), where the seminary, at 1,220m, has been converted into a hotel (B), the site and region highly recommended. Reservations through Instituto São Vicente in Belo, T 031-441-5399 (space is very limited and there is no public transport). Focus Tours (above) runs tours to the **Caracá Natural Park**, which contains many bird species, some rare, and the endangered masked titi monkey, the common marmoset, the black-capped capuchin and the very rare maned wolf (which the monks feed at dusk). Focus Tours will advise on how to get to Caracá. It is possible to stay in Santa Bárbara, **D** *Hotel Karaibe*; **D** *Sta Inés*, 25 km away on the road to Mariana and hitch-hike to Caracá.

The road from Belo Horizonte to the picturesque colonial cities described below follows the Rio das Velhas in which, at points, one can see the *garimpeiros* waist-deep washing for gold.

Nova Lima (pop 52,200), about 27 km SE of Belo by a good road, is set in eucalyptus forests. Its houses are grouped round the gold mine of Morro Velho, opened by a British firm in 1834 but sold to Brazilians in 1959, the deepest mine in the Americas. The shaft has followed a rich vein of gold down to 2,591m (not open to tourists). There are interesting carvings by Aleijadinho, recovered from elsewhere, in the (modern) parish church.

A paved road branching off the Belo Horizonte-Brasília highway leads (30 km, ½-hr) to the colonial gold-mining (and steel-making) town of **Sabará** (pop 89,680). Return by the old road over the mountain range of Serra do Curral for fine views. Sabará is strung along the narrow steep valleys of the Rio das Velhas and Rio Sabará. Its old churches and fountains, its rambling cobbled streets, its simple houses with their carved doors, and its museum of 18th century gold mining in the **Intendência de Ouro** (built 1732, closed for repairs, 1995) are of great interest. Bus from Belo Horizonte, US$0.60, ½ hr, from separate part of Belo Rodoviária from main departure hall. The mineral museum in the **Escola da Minas** is worth a visit for those interested in minerals and rock formations.

Passeio a Sabará, by Lúcia Machado de Almeida, with splendid illustrations by Guignard, is an excellent guide to the place. The main sights are the **Prefeitura**, in R Pedro II, an old mansion, with oratory and main reception room (*salão nobre*) to be seen; the **Teatro Municipal** (former Opera House) (1770, restored 1960) in the same street, for its fine interior; the **Casa Azul**, in the same street, for its portal; the Churches of **Nossa Senhora do Carmo** (1774), with doorway, pulpits and choirloft by Aleijadinho and paintings by Athayde; **Nossa Senhora do Rosário dos Pretos** (left unfinished at the time of the slaves' emancipation); **São Francisco**; **Nossa Senhora da Conceição** (1720) with much gilding, and paintings by 23 Chinese artists brought from Macau; and, last of all, **Nossa Senhora do Ó**, built in 1698 and showing unmistakable Chinese influence (paintings much in need of restoration), 2 km from the centre of the town (take local bus marked "Esplanada" or "Boca Grande"). Also the fountains of Kaquende (1757), and Rosário.

Hotel D *Hotel de Ouro*, overlooking town, or ask for Senhor Sérgio at the Sports Centre, he may have accommodation. **E Pensão Bobagato**, above an art gallery, **Restaurants**: *O Quinto do Ouro*, close to the bus station; *314*, Comendador Viana 314, near main praça; *Imperial Restaurant/Pizzaria*, in R Pedro II; *Ce Kí Sabe*, R Mestre Caetano 56, rec.

At 27 km S along the Belo Horizonte-Rio de Janeiro highway a 68 km road, the Rodovia dos Inconfidentes, branches off to Ouro Preto. On the way (48 km) it passes **Cachoeira do Campo**, which was the centre of the regional mining administration in colonial times: now a sleepy, unspoilt village.

Ouro Preto (pop 62,485, CEP 35400, DDD 031), the famous former capital of the State, was founded in 1711. There is a famous **Escola de Minas** (School of Mining), founded in 1876, in the fortress-like **Palácio dos Governadores** (1742), facing the main square (Praça Tiradentes); it has the interesting **Museo de Mineralogia e das Pedras**, a must, the only one open on Mon (1200-1700), but closed Sun. Opposite the Palace, next to Carmo Church, is the **Museu da Inconfidência**, a fine historical and art museum which has some drawings by Aleijadinho and the Sala Manoel da Costa Athayde, in an annex; the building, begun in the eighteenth century, has been a prison and also the local chamber of commerce (open 1200-1730, entry). See the **Casa das Contas**, now also a museum (open 1230-1700), Sun 0800-1300. All the above US$1. Another museum, the **Casa Guignard**, R Conde de Bobadela 10, displays the paintings of Alberto da Veiga Guignard, open Tues-Sat 0900-1700, Sun 1200-1700, free. The **Mina do Chico Rei**, R D Silvério, open 0800-1700, entrance US$0.75, does not have as much to see as some of the other old mines in the area, but is "fun to crawl about in"; restaurant attached.

The city, built on rocky ground 1,000m above sea-level (cold and wet Oct-Feb) was declared a national monument in 1933. Its cobbled streets wind up and down steep hills crowned with 13 churches. Mansions, fountains, churches, vistas of terraced gardens, ruins, towers shining with coloured tiles, all blend together to maintain a delightful 18th century atmosphere.

Ouro Preto displays many superb baroque carvings, in wood and in soapstone, of the sculptor Aleijadinho. The church of São Francisco de Assis and the façade of the Carmo church are his work, and so are the two pulpits in the church of São Francisco, and much else.

In the **Praça de Independência** there is a statue of José Joaquim da Silva Xavier, known as Tiradentes, leader of the **Inconfidentes** (unsuccessful revolutionaries of 1789), and regarded in Brazil as the precursor of independence. Another Inconfidente, the poet Tomás Antônio Gonzaga (whose house at R Cláudio Manoel 61 is close to São Francisco de Assis), was exiled to Africa. (Most Brazilians know his poem based on his forbidden love affair; visitors are shown the bridge and decorative fountain where the lovers held their trysts.) On 24 Jun of each year Ouro Preto again becomes, for that day only, the capital of the state of Minas Gerais.

Churches The following churches are all closed Mon, but are open at following times on other days: **Santa Efigênia** (1720, decorated with gold dust washed out of slaves' hair), Lad Santa Efigênia e Padre Faria, 0800-1200; **Francisco de Assis** (1766-96), Largo de Coimbra (shared ticket with NS Conceição), beautiful interior and exterior with work by both Aleijadinho and Athayde, 0830-1100, 1300-1700 (keep your ticket for admission to the museum); Senhor Bom Jesus, R Alvarenga (closed since 1992); **NS Carmo**, R Brig Mosqueira (museum of sacred art and Aleijadinho sculptures), 0830-1100, 1300-1700, shared entry ticket with **NS Pilar** (1733, heavily gilded work of Aleijadinho's father, Manuel Lisboa), 1200-1700; **NS do Rosário**, Largo do Rosário (simple altar, interesting side altars), 1200-1700; **das Mercês e Perdões** (1740-73) R das Mercês, 1000-1400, are open in afternoons only. The Antônio Dias parish church, **Nossa Senhora da Conceição** (1722), heavily gilded, contains Aleijadinho's tomb, and a museum devoted to him, Aleijadinho Paróquia, 0800-1130, 1300-1700. São Francisco de Paula (1804), R Padre Rolim, near rodoviária, closed for restoration since 1993. There are a number of other churches and chapels. At least two days are needed to see them all; the tourist office on Praça Tiradentes (opens 0800, Portuguese only spoken) and the hotels offer a leaflet showing the opening times; also sells good map for US$2.50. Most of the churches now charge for admission, usually about US$0.75.

The mid-18th century paintings by Mestre Athayde (1732-1827), to be seen in S Francisco de Assis, Sta Ifigênia and elsewhere, are of particular interest: the pigments were obtained from local iron ore and from forest fruits. They are also very fine artistically; he was a worthy colleague of Aleijadinho.

NB In most churches and museums, tourists' handbags and cameras are taken at the entrance and guarded in lockers (visitors keep their own key).

Ouro Preto is famous for its Holy Week processions, which in fact begin on the Thur before Palm Sun and continue (but not every day) until Easter Sun. The most famous is that commemorating Christ's removal from the Cross, late on Good Fri. This is very much a holiday period and many shops are shut—as indeed they are on winter weekends. Attracting many Brazilians, but few foreigners as yet, Carnival here is also memorable, with samba on the streets.

Hotels L2 *Pousada do Mondego*, Largo de Coimbra 38, T 551-2040, F 551-3094, beautifully kept colonial house, rec; **A1** *Grande*, R Sen Rocha 164, T 551-1488, largest hotel in town and the only modern structure, designed by Oscar Niemeyer; **A1** *Luxor Pousada*, Praça Antônio Dias 10, converted colonial mansion, no twin beds, friendly, clean, comfortable, T 551-2244, reservations in Rio, T 256-2680, restaurant good; **A1** *Priskar da Barra*, R Antonio Martins 98, T and F 551-2666, good facilities; **A2** *Solar das Lajes*, R Conselheiro Quintiliano 604 (T and F 551-3388), with bath, excellent view, swimming pool, friendly and well run; **B** *Pouso Chico Rei*, a fascinating old house with Portuguese colonial furnishings, very small and utterly delightful, book in advance, R Brig Mosqueira 90, T 551-1274 (room No 6 has been described as a "dream"); **B** *Pousada dos Bandeirantes*, R das Mercês 167, T 551-1996, F 551-1962, clean, beautiful views; **C** *Pousada Nello Nuno*, R Camilo de Brito 59, T 551-3375, with bath, cheaper without, charming owner Annamélia speaks some French, highly rec; **C** *Pousada Ouro Preto*, Largo Musicista José dos Anjos Costa 72, T 551-3081, 4/5 rm, clean, laundry facilities, hot showers, English spoken by owner, Gérson Luís Cotta (most helpful), tasty home-made cake, rec; **C** *Conde*, R Direita, old furniture, clean, rec; **C** *Hospedária Antiga*, R Xavier da Veiga 3, T 551-2203, a restored colonial house, friendly, rec; **C** *Pensão SR* in same street, bath, good cheap *pratos*, rec; **D** *Pousada Ciclo do Ouro* Felipe dos Santos 241, T 581-3201/2210, clean, laundry facilities, rec; **D** *Pousada e Galeria Panorama Barroco*, R Conselheiro Quintiliano 722, T 551-3366, shabby, outside centre; **E** at No 26, same street, Rosana lets rooms, basic, clean, friendly, clothes washing; *Pensão* at R Coronel Alves 2, T 551-2393, clean reasonable, friendly; **E** *Hospedaria* of Consuêlo Perdigão, R Pandiá Calógeras 59, Barra, T551-2318, price pp in shared room, use of kitchen, living room, shared bathroom, very good, English spoken, rec; **E** *Pousada São Francisco*, next to the church of that name, stunningly clean, repeatedly rec, no sign outside, enter through garden; *Pousada*

Tropicão, São José, very basic but cheap; **E** *Villa dos Pilares*, Praça Monsenhor C Barbosa 19, T 551-1324, very relaxed, "slightly weird"; **E** *Vermelha Dormitório*, Praça São Francisco de Assis 30, T 551-1138, quiet, clean, shared shower, laundry facilities. Youth hostel in R das Mercês, accepts student cards as membership. Also try *casas de família*, reasonably-priced, more expensive if booked through tourist office. People offering accommodation meet travellers on Praça Tiradentes. Some correspondents report good experiences staying at family houses found in this way, but choose carefully.

Difficult to get hotel rooms at weekends and holiday periods; a good idea to telephone ahead. In the low season prices can be negotiated. A number of travellers have recommended staying in Mariana where hotels are cheaper; two buses an hour to Ouro Preto (some correspondents point out that the return bus fare more or less equals the difference in hotel prices).

Students may be able to stay, during holidays and weekends, at the self-governing student hostels, known as *repúblicas* (very welcoming, "best if you like heavy metal music"). Many are closed between Christmas and Carnival. Enquire at the city's tourist office.

Camping Camping Clube do Brasil, 2 km N of city, is quite expensive but very nice. Also a site reached by car up a very steep hill at the top end of town: about 5 km. Also at picnic site 4 km W of Ouro Preto, and at Rio Acima nearby.

Restaurants *Pasteleria Lampião*, Praça Tiradentes, good views at the back, US$1.40 (better at lunchtime than in evening); *Casa Grande* (watch your belongings) and *Forno de Barro*, both on Praça Tiradentes, good local dishes; *O Inconfidente*, R Direita nr Praça Tiradentes, quite good, but slow service; *Café & Cia*, R São José 187, closes 2300, very popular, *comida por kilo* at lunchtime, good salads, juices; *Chafariz*, R São José 167, good local food; *Garrapinha*, R São José, good snack bar with cheap meals and many fruit juices; *Calabouço*, good, Conde de Bobadela 132, with an antique shop; *Sobrenatural* on the same road, rec; *Tacho de Ouro Preto*, Conde de Bobadela 76, good lunch buffet, popular; *Casa do Ouvidor*, Conde de Bobadela 42, above De Bernardis jewellery shop (good), near main square, good. *Adega*, R Teixeira Amaral, 1130-1530, vegetarian smorgasbord, US$6, all you can eat, highly rec. Cheap *lanchonetes* on opp side of square to *Hotel Pilão*. Try the local *licor de jaboticaba*. A candlelit bar, *Acaso 85*, Praça Largo Rosário, is not cheap but marvellous for romantics.

Banks and Exchange Banco do Brasil, R São José, good rates, also for TCs.

Electric Current 110 volts AC.

Post Office on R Direita, opp *Hotel Miranda*.

Shopping For precious stones, *Videmaju*, owned by Vincente Júlio de Paula, a professor at the School of Mines, sells stones at very good prices from his house at R Conselheiro Santana 175. Buy soapstone carvings at roadside stalls and bus stops rather than in the cities; they are much cheaper. Many artesans sell soapstone carvings, jewellery and semi-precious stones in the square in front of São Francisco de Assis church. Gems are not much cheaper from freelance sellers in Praça Tiradentes than from the shops around the square, and in the shops themselves, the same quality of stone is offered at the same price—*Brasil Gemas* and *De Bernard* are rec.

Tourist Office Praça Tiradentes 41. Enquire here for details of accommodation in *casas de família*, *repúblicas* and other forms. Note, though, that foreigners are expected to want expensive hotels. The tourist office at the bus station is sometimes open, map US$1.10 from either office. **Guides** Bandeira's *Guia de Ouro Preto* in Portuguese and English (US$3.50 with coloured map, US$1 with black and white one), normally available at Tourist Office. Also available is Lucia Machado de Almeida's *Passeio a Ouro Preto*, US$6 (in Portuguese, English and French). A local guide for a day, Associação de Guias de Turismo, T 551-2655, is more expensive if obtained through Tourist Office (rec guide: Cassio Antunes). Ourotur runs a tour of Ouro Preto in a vintage-style bus, 0900 and 1430, from the bus station (T 551-2764).

Transport There is a new bus station (rodoviária) at Ouro Preto, above the town near the São Francisco de Paula church. It's an easy downhill walk to the centre (10 mins), or a town bus passes every ½ hr; taxis charge exorbitant rates. An early plane from Rio to Belo Horizonte and a bus (11 a day) gets to Ouro Preto by lunch (2 hrs); bus fare, each way, US$4, taxi US$50. Day trips are run; alternatively take bus from **Rio**, Util at 2300 (US$18, 6½ hrs), return bus to Rio leaves at same time. Book your return journey to **Belo Horizonte** early if returning in the evening; buses get crowded. There are also buses to **Conselheiro Lafaiete** for connections to Belo Horizonte and Congonhas, and direct to **Congonhas** at 1400 and 1530, or to Rio via Barbacena and Juiz da Fora (direct bus to Rio is often fully booked 2-3 days, or weekends, in advance). Direct bus Ouro Preto to **Vitória** at 2100, US$13, 5½ hrs (connection to Porto Seguro), daily. To **Salvador** with Gontijo (change at Belo Horizonte), 1945, 24 hrs, US$40, buy ticket at Util desk. Direct bus to **São Paulo**, 1900, 11 hrs, US$24. Check that your bus ticket from Ouro Preto is in fact from Ouro Preto and not from Belo Horizonte. Two buses an hour to Mariana, if returning buses are full walk to the next village. Hitch-hiking to Mariana is said to be easy, start in Praça Tiradentes.

Excursion The Cachoeira das Andorinhas, a nearby waterfall, is reached by taking a bus to Morro de Santana and then walking 25 mins. To walk all the way (N of town) takes 1½ hrs. Do not camp beside the waterfall, there have been robberies there. It may be possible to visit the Zen monastery near the waterfall, apply in advance: Mosteiro Zen Pico de Rajos, Morro de São Sebastião, CP 101, 35400-000, Ouro Preto. The town is dominated by a huge cross, easily reached from the road to Mariana. Lovely sunsets, but don't go alone as it's in a poor district.

Mariana (pop 38,115, CEP 35420, DDD 031, 697m above sea level), another old mining city, founded 1696, much less hilly than Ouro Preto, is 12 km E of Ouro Preto on a road which goes on to join the Rio-Salvador highway. See the beautiful old prison on Praça João Pinheiro (**Cadeia**, 1768, now the Prefeitura Municipal); on the same square the **Carmo** church (1784, steatite carvings, Athayde paintings, chinoiserie panelling – closed for repairs since 1992), next to it is the fine **São Francisco** church (1762, pulpits designed by Aleijadinho, Athayde paintings and tomb, fine sacristy, one side-altar by Aleijadinho, entry, US$0.50) and the old **Palácio dos Governadores** connected with it; the **Museu Arquidiocesano** for its church furniture, gold and silver collection, Aleijadinho statues and ivory cross (R Frei Durão 49, open 0900-1300 except Mon and 1400-1645; entrance US$1, good guide book), **Capela de Santo Antônio**, wonderfully simple and the oldest. The **Cathedral**, Basílica de NS da Assunção, built 1711-1760, Praça da Sé, has a wooden German organ (1701), façade by Aleijadinho, beautiful interior and side altars (entry US$0.50). Organ concerts are given on Fri, 1100 and Sun, 1200 (US$5). Between the old prison and São Francisco is a stone monument to Justice, at which slaves used to be beaten. The house of the poet Afonso de Guimarães (buried behind the Igreja Santuaria), R Direita 35, is open to visitors: photographs and letters (free). There are viewpoints at the churches of NS do Rosário, R do Rosário (1752, with work by Athayde and showing Moorish influence) and São Pedro dos Clérigos (built in 1753), Largo de São Pedro. Some people still pan for gold in the river running through the town. Between Ouro Preto and Mariana is the Minas de Passagem gold mine, dating from 1719.

Minas de Passagem A guided tour visits the old mine workings and underground lake (take bathing suit), entrance US$10, visiting hours 0900-1800, T Ouro Preto 551-1068, Mariana 557-1340/1255. Buses leave Ouro Preto from beside the Escola de Minas, nr *Restaurante Casa das Contas*, for Mariana, US$0.75, all passing Minas de Passagem, US$0.25; bus from Belo Horizonte (via Ouro Preto), US$2, 2¼ hrs. Taxi from Ouro Preto, US$7.80. There is a waterfall, Cachoeira Serrinha, where swimming is possible, ¾ hr walk from the bus stop to the mine. Ask for directions. Initially you have to walk 100m towards Mariana then ask.

Hotels C *Faisca*, R Antônio Olinto 48, T 557-1206, incl breakfast; **C** *Müller*, Av G Vargas 34, T 557-1188; **D** *Providência*, R Dom Silverio 233, T 557-1444, run by nuns, small rooms, pool, clean, quiet; **E** *Central*, R Frei Durão 8, on attractive square, pleasant, quiet, rec but avoid downstairs rooms. The modern service station (*posto*) on the highway above the town offers good clean rooms at E, with hot showers.

Restaurants *Alvorada*, Praça Cláudio Manoel 42 *Tambaú*, Praça da Sé; *Papinha della Nonna*, D Viçoso 27, Italian, rec. *Portão da Praça*, Praça Gomes Freire 108, excellent.

Tourist Office Terminal Turístico, 500m beyond rodoviária towards colonial centre, Praça Tancredo Neves, guides' association, small tourist office, map US$1.50. Tourist agency, Transcolta, Praça JK, T 557-2056; enquire also at Embratur, Praça Neves, T 557-1533.

24 km N of Mariana (infrequent bus US$0.50), is the small village of Antônio Pereira where the imperial topaz is mined. Tours of an interesting cave with stalactites: pay local children a few centavos to show you round.

Congonhas do Campo (pop 41,070, CEP 36404, DDD 031, alt 866m) is a hill town with a good road through pleasant farming country connecting with Ouro Preto (a worthwhile day trip, taking 0900 bus to Cons Lafaiete and changing at

Murtinho), and a paved 3½-km road link with the Rio-Belo Horizonte highway. The town is dominated by the great pilgrimage church of Bom Jesus do Matozinho (1773), which opens at 0815; indeed there is little else of architectural interest. There is a wide view of the country from the church terrace, below which are six small chapels set in attractive sloping gardens, showing scenes with life-size Passion figures carved by Aleijadinho and his pupils in cedar wood. The church is mainly famous for its group of prophets sculpted by Aleijadinho, standing on the parapets of the terrace. These twelve great dramatic statues (thought of as Aleijadinho's masterpieces), carved in soapstone with dramatic sense of movement, constitute one of the finest works of art of their period in the world—not just in Latin America. Inside the church, as well as the Room of Miracles, there are paintings by Athayde and the heads of four sainted popes (Gregory, Jerome, Ambrose and Augustine) sculpted by Aleijadinho for the reliquaries on the high altar. (Bus "Basílica", on the hour from opposite the Rodoviária to Bom Jesus, US$0.20.) Pleasant excursion to waterfall with park and swimming, at Cachoeira Santo Antônio.

Congonhas is also celebrated for its Holy Week processions, which have as their focus the Bom Jesus church. The most celebrated ceremonies are the meeting of Christ and the Virgin Mary on the Tues, and the dramatized Deposition from the Cross late on Good Fri. Pilgrimage season, first half of Sep, draws many thousands.

Hotels **D** *Colonial*, Praça da Basílica 76, opp Bom Jesus, T 731-1834, good and comfortable, breakfast extra, no showers/toilets in room, blankets only, fascinating restaurant downstairs full of colonial handicrafts and good local food; **E** *Freitas*, R Marechal Floriano 69, T 731-1543, basic. There are handicraft shops selling soapstone artefacts.

Bus Rodoviária is 1½ km outside town. To/from **Belo Horizonte**, 1½ hrs, US$3.25, 6 times a day, best to buy a return ticket. None direct from Rio; you have to change buses at **Conselheiro Lafaiete** (**C** *Rhud's Hotel and Restaurant*, R José Nicolau de Queiroz 11, T/F 721-4199; **B** *Hotel Cupim*, on main Rio road, 18 km, T 721-5022, F 721-5375). To **São João del Rei**, either direct (US$13), or go via Murtinho. Bus to **Ouro Preto**: direct (US$13), or go via Belo Horizonte, Murtinho or Conselheiro Lafaiete.

Diamantina, the most remote of these cities, is reached from Belo Horizonte by paved road (289 km, 6 daily buses via Pássaro Verde, US$7.75, 5½ hrs) but there is no scheduled air service. Take the road to Brasília almost as far as the turnoff for **Curvelo** (a lively town, *Hotel Sagarana*—5-star, very good; *Restaurant Denise* with sleeping accommodation, on main highway, very clean), then through the impressive rocky country of the Serra do Espinhaço. 30 km N of Belo Horizonte on this road, is the *Hotel Fazenda* at Ipê Amarelo—horses to ride, etc. Further on, between Paraopeba and Caetanópolis, is the *Flora Eunice* (*Leite ao Pé de Vaca*) snackbar (good toilets) with small private botanic garden and zoo with contented animals, recommended. About 120 km N of Belo Horizonte, 33,400 square km of the Serra do Espinaço has been named as the **National Park of Serra do Cipó**, in view of its scenic beauty and rich variety of plant and animal life. The park is between 1,140 and 1,560m, with rocky outcroppings, although there are more outcroppings, better scenery and rich birdlife outside the park. There are several endemic plants, insects and birds (the Cipo Canestero – only found outside the park in one small area). There are also several carnivorous plants (Ibama office: Av do Contorno 8121, Cidade Jardim, CEP 30.110-120, Belo Horizonte, T 335-6611).

Diamantina (pop 42,980, CEP 39100, DDD 037) centre of a once active diamond industry founded in 1729, has excellent colonial buildings. Its churches (difficult to get into, except for the modern Cathedral) are not so grand as those of Ouro Preto, but it is possibly the least spoiled of all the colonial mining cities, with carved overhanging roofs and brackets; try walking through the lower part of the town. This very friendly town is in the deep interior, 1,120m up amid barren mountains; it is the birthplace of President Juscelino Kubitschek, the founder of Brasília. His house has been converted into a museum. An airport was due for completion in 1995.

After repeated thefts, the diamonds of the Diamond Museum, in the house of Padre Rolim, one of the Inconfidentes (see under Ouro Preto) have been removed to the Banco do Brasil. Diamonds are still sought; see traditional methods at Guinda, 7 km away. *Passeio a Diamantina*, an excellent guide, is written by the author of *Passeio a Sabará*. The town's latest industry is the making of Portuguese Arraiolos-style tapestry carpets by hand, at a cooperative in the centre; it was started by a diplomat, Sr Flecha da Silva, who was perturbed by the amount of local unemployment, and it has become very successful. Also etchings on leather are made locally.

The house of Chica da Silva, an 18th-century slave who married a rich diamond contractor, is at Praça Lobo Mesquita 266, entry free; Chica has become a folk-heroine among Brazilian blacks.

Hotels B *Tijuco*, Macau do Melo 211, T 931-1022, best, good food; **D** *Dália*, Praça JK (Jota-Ka) 25, T 931-1477, fairly good; **E** *JK*, opp bus station, with breakfast, clean, friendly; **E** *Pensão Comercial*, Praça M Neves 30, basic. Wild camping near waterfall just outside town.

Restaurants *Bar-Restaurant Confiança*, R da Quitanda 39, good. *Capistrana*, R Campos Carvalho 36, near Cathedral square, rec. *Sarumba* bar, live music at weekends. *Serestas* (serenades) Fri and Sat nights; many young people in bars in Beco da Mota.

Voltage 110 AC.

Tourist Information Dept de Turismo in Casa de Cultura in Praça Antônio Eulálio 53, 3rd floor, pamphlets and a reliable map, also information about churches opening times, friendly and helpful, will arrange free tour of churches with guide who has access to keys (tip guide).

Buses 6 a day to **Belo Horizonte**, via Curvelo, for connections to Brasília, with Pássaro Verde: 2½ hrs to **Curvelo**, US$3.25, to **Belo Horizonte**, US$10.75. A slow but interesting trip to the N is possible by taking the bus to **Aracuaí**, 6 hr, then to **Itaobim**, 1½ hr, from where there are connections along the BR116 to **Bahia**.

Excursion Walk along the Caminho dos Escravos, the old paved road built by slaves between the mining area on Rio Jequitinhonha and Diamantina. A guide is essential (ask at the Casa de Cultura—cheap), and beware of snakes. Along the river bank to (12 km) Biribiri, a pretty village with an abandoned textile factory. About half-way, swimming pools in the river; opposite them, on cliff face, animal paintings in red, age and origin unknown. Interesting plant life along river, and beautiful mountain views.

Serro (pop 19,445, CEP 39150, DDD 037) 92 km by paved road from Diamantina and reached by bus from there or from Belo Horizonte, is an unspoiled colonial town on the Rio Jequitinhonha with six fine baroque churches, a museum and many beautiful squares. It makes *queijo serrano*, one of Brazil's best cheeses, being in the centre of a prosperous cattle region. The most conspicuous church is Santa Rita, on a hill in the centre of town, reached by steps. On the main square, by the bottom of the steps, is the Carmo, arcaded, with original paintings on ceiling and in choir. The town has two large mansions: those of the Barão de Diamantina, now in ruins, and of the Barão do Serro across the river, beautifully restored and used as the town hall and Casa de Cultura; there are old mine entrances in the hillside behind the courtyard.

Hotels C *Pousada Vila do Príncipe*, T 941-1485, very clean, in old mansion on main street, contains own museum, the artist Mestre Valentim is said to have been born in slave quarters; other cheap hotels (eg **F** *Dormitório*, R Rio Branco, opp Banco do Brasil). **Restaurants**: *Itacolomi*, Praça João Pinheiro 20, fair; good one on main square, also *Churrascaria Vila do Príncipe* nearby on main street.

Just by the Serro turnoff is the town of ***Datas***, whose spacious church (1832) decorated in red and blue, contains striking wooden image of Christ with the crown of thorns.

Tres Marias (pop 21,410) Some 240 km NW of Belo Horizonte is a lake five times as large as Rio de Janeiro bay, formed by the Tres Marias dam on the upper reaches of the São Francisco river. There is a motel, and the power company, Cemig, runs a guest house (book in advance through its head office at Belo Horizonte). At Barreiro Grande is the Clube Náutico Tres Marias, D, simple. There are plans to develop the Tres Marias area for tourism.

Almost the same distance SW of Belo is the even larger lake formed by the

Furnas dam. It can be seen from the BR-381 road to São Paulo.

Also N of Belo Horizonte is **Pirapora** (pop 46,230, CEP 39270, DDD 037) terminus for boat journeys on the River São Francisco (see also p 498). The cutting down of trees, in part as fuel for the boats, and the low rainfall in recent years, has greatly reduced the flow. The Sobradinho lake, which was meant to save the river, is only one third full and it is feared that, in the long term, the production of energy will be reduced. The town itself is a tourist attraction because of the falls in the river which make for excellent fishing: catches weighing 73 kg (160lb) have been reported. The fishermen use punt-like canoes. The sandy river beaches are used for swimming. The grotesque figureheads of the riverboats, *carrancas*, are made in the workshops of Lourdes Barroso, R Abaeté 390.

Hotels **C** *Canoeiras*, Av Salmeron 3, T 741-1946, used by river-tour parties; **B** *Pirapora Palace*, on Praça Melo Viana (7 blocks W and 1 block S of Rodoviária), T 741-1330, ask for room on garden, clean, friendly, safe; **C** *Daila*, Praça JK 13, with breakfast but without bath; **D** *Grande*, R da Quintande 70, with bath but without breakfast; **E** *Carajas*, basic, friendly, and **E** *Hotel Rex*, R Antônio Nascimento 357, small breakfast, not very good. Camping near the Praça on riverside.

Restaurants *Lá em Casa*, "meals by the kilo, huge *caipirinhas* US$0.50, excellent value"; *Borretos* on the riverfront, and *Barrenko*, next door, better value.

The old river passenger service of the Companhia de Navegação do São Francisco (Franave) to Juazeiro has been discontinued, but it is still sometimes possible to arrange journeys down the river on cargo boats if you talk to the masters, in the port. If you can get on a cargo boat, the regular stops are at Januária (famous for Brazil's reputed best cachaça) and Bom Jesus da Lapa (a pilgrimage centre with a church built in a grotto inside a mountain, but a very poor town; hotels incl **B** *Hansão das Pedras*, **C** *Real*, **F** *Brasília*; a choice of bars on the river beach). Between Pirapora and Januária is the colonial town of **São Francisco**, with many attractive houses and a good handicraft market in the town hall; the boats do not always stop there. If you want to see the real Sertão, get off at Xique-Xique and take a bus to Utinga, Rui Barbosa and Itaberaba, then on to Salvador. Of the two remaining wood-burning stern-wheel boats, allegedly built for Mississippi services in the 1860s and imported from the USA in 1922 to work on the Amazon, one, the *Gaiola*, has been restored for tourist-agency use. An expensive weekly trip (starting Sun) is made downriver visiting various ports as far as São Francisco, organized by **Unitour or Mangebeira Turismo**, of Belo Horizonte.

If you can't get a boat, an adventurous journey to the Bahia coast is as follows: bus 0730 Pirpora-Montes Claros, next morning bus Montes Claros—Almenara (12 hrs) then bus Almenara-Salto da Divisa (2½ hrs), then after night in Salto at hotel facing bus station, take 0600 bus to Porto Seguro. **Montes Claros** is a pleasant town with many hotels, restaurants and cinemas, reportedly very welcoming to its few foreign visitors (**E** *Hotel Giovanni*, close to rodoviária, clean, modern). Bus from Diamantina, weekdays 0600, US$10, 6 hrs. An alternative route to Bahia is the daily 1000 bus to Vitória da Conquista (see p 484, Gontijo line US$13); interesting journey through hilly country, pine and eucalyptus plantations, and many remote towns.

Eastern Minas

Eastern Minas Gerais is not of great cultural or historical interest, but is a centre of semi-precious stone processing and crystal carving, and also contains the Serra do Caparaó, where are found several of Brazil's highest mountains. The two principal towns, Governador Valadares and Teôfilo Otôni, are both on the BR-116 inland Rio-Salvador road, and both have good connections with Belo Horizonte. Only through **Focus Tours (see Belo Horizonte, p 402)** can the private Caratinga Biological Station be visited, 880 hectares of mountainous, inland Atlantic forest which is home to four rare primates: the muriqui (formerly called the woolly spider monkey, the largest primate in the Americas and the largest mammal endemic to Brazil), the black-capped capuchin, the brown howler monkey and the buffy-headed marmoset. Also at the station are brown-throated, three-toed sloths and an incredible array of birds. The primates and many of the birds are not bothered by human presence. Entrance fee is US$20 pp per day.

Douglas Trent writes:

Governador Valadares (pop 230,490, CEP 35100, DDD 0332), 324 km from Belo Horizonte, $5\frac{1}{2}$ hrs by bus (US$9.50, US$19 leito) and also by regional air service, is a modern planned city. It is a good place to break the Belo Horizonte-Salvador journey. The altitude is 170m. It is a centre of semi-precious stone mines and lapidation, as well as for the cut-crystal animals one finds in tourist shops all around Brazil.

Hotels A3 *Governador Palace*, Av Minas Gerais 550, T 271-7474, F 271-4750; **B** *Panorama*, Mal Floriano 914, T 221-7833; **B** *Real Minas*, Praça Serra Lima 607, T 271-6751; **C** *São Salvador*, R Prudente de Morais 915; **E** *Kennedy*, R Minas Gerais, good breakfast. Many **F** hotels near bus station.

Restaurants Main hotels; *JB*, R Bárbara Heliodora 384, rec, huge servings; *Joazeiro*, R Pessanha 639; *Tabu* in town centre, US$5 churrascaria, rec.

Airport is on the BR-381, 6 km from the city centre with flights to Belo Horizonte and Ipatinga.

Excursion to the top of the Pico de Ibituruna, 960m.

Teófilo Otôni (335m, pop 140,640, CEP, DDD 033), 138 km from Governador Valadares, is a popular buying spot for dealers of crystals and semi-precious stones. The best prices in the state are found here (try K Eluwar Ltda, R Epamin 458—change money also).

Hotels *Nobre Palace*, Av Francisco Sá 43, T 521-5824, F 522-3272; *Teófilo Otôni*, BR-116 Norte km 275, 5 km from centre, T 521-4822; **C** *Lancaster*, R Frei Gonzaga 142, T 522-3131; **C** *Metrópole*, Av Francisco Sá 14, T 521-3753; **D** *Beira-Rio*, Av Israel Pinheiro 671, T 521-4653; **E** *Presidente*, Av Getúlio Vargas 183, clean, good breakfast, laundry facilities.

Restaurant *Amigo do Rei*, R Benedito Valadares 161, T 521-4927.

Bus To Porto Seguro via **Nanuque** (can break Belo Horizonte-Salvador journey here; **F** *Hotel Minas*, at rodoviária, adequate, and others nearby).

Caparaó National Park, 49 km by paved road from Manhuaçu (about 190 km S of Governador Valadores) on the Belo Horizonte-Vitória road (BR-262), has the Pico da Bandeira (2,890m), Pico do Cruzeiro (2,861m) and the Pico do Cristal (2,798m). The park features rare Atlantic rainforest in its lower altitudes and Brazilian alpine on top. It is best to visit during the dry season (Apr-Oct). Camping is permitted within the park at two spots and it can be quite crowded in Jul and during Carnaval. Contact via Caixa Postal 17, alto Jequitibá, MG, CEP 36976-000, T 255, via operator on 101, Alto do Caparaó.

Hotel C *Caparaó Parque*, near park entrance 15 mins walk from the town of Caparaó, nice, T (032) 741-2559.

How to get to Caparaó There are buses from Belo Horizonte, Ouro Preto or Vitória to **Manhumirim**, 15 km S of Manhuaçu (pop 27,625, **E** *Hotel São Luiz*, good value, but *Cids Bar*, next door, Travessa 16 do Março, has better food). From Manhumirim, take a bus direct to Caparaó, 0930, 1630 US$0.80, or to Presidente Soares (several, 7 km), then hitch 11 km to Caparaó. By car from the BR-262, go through Manhumirim, Pres Soares and Caparaó village, then 1 km further to the hotel, which is 2 km from the park entrance (small entry fee). Coming from Rio, leave BR-116 at Fervedouro and take BR-482 to Carangola. Just before this town branch N to Espera Feliz. About half way turn left again to Pres Soares. From the park entrance it is 6 km on a poorly-maintained road to the car park at the base of the waterfall. From the hotel jeeps (US$20 per jeep) run to the car park at 1,970m ($2\frac{1}{2}$ hrs' walk), then it's a 3-4 hrs' walk to the summit of the Pico da Bandeira, marked by yellow arrows; plenty of camping possibilities all the way up, the highest being at Terreirão (2,370m). It is very difficult to get to the Pico da Bandeira from Manhumirim and back in a day. This is good walking country. It may also be possible to visit local fazendas, for example Fazenda Modelo, 8 km from Manhumirim.

Southern and Western Minas

The spas of southern Minas Gerais are easily reached by road and in some cases by air from Rio de Janeiro and São Paulo. They are also popular holiday places with a great many hotels; the high season is from Dec through Mar.

São Lourenço (pop 29,510, CEP 37470, DDD 035) easily accessible from Rio de

Janeiro (5-6 hrs by bus) or São Paulo (6-7 hrs by bus), stands at 850m above sea-level. There is a splendid park, tennis, boating, swimming, a flying field, and fishing from the Ilha dos Amores in a lake ringed by gardens and forests. Its rich mineral waters are used in the treatment of stomach, liver, kidney and intestinal complaints. There is an up-to-date hydro establishment for douches and for the famous carbo-gaseous baths, unique in South America. There is a grand ride through fine scenery to the Pico de Buqueré (1,500m). On Sat and Sun a tourist train goes to São Lourenço from Cruzeiro (São Paulo state), 0900, US$15 incl guide and snack.

Caxambu (pop 19,470, CEP 37440, DDD 035), N of São Lourenço, at 900m, is one of the more sophisticated of these resorts. Its waters are used for treating stomach, kidney and bladder diseases, and are said to restore fertility. They seemed to work for Princess Isabel, daughter of Dom Pedro II, who produced three sons after a visit. The little church of Santa Isabel da Hungária stands on a hill as a thank-offering. The mountains and forests around are very beautiful. View over the city from Morro Caxambu, 1,010m. Excellent hotels.

Lambari (pop 16,080, CEP 37480, DDD 035) is 56 km W of Caxambu by road at 900m. Hotels are not luxurious but fairly comfortable. The Parque das Águas has seven springs and a swimming pool. There are boat trips on the Lago Guanabara. Casino.

Cambuquirá (pop 11,600, CEP 37420, DDD 035) a little N of Lambari by road at 946m, very popular, with friendly atmosphere and picnic sites close by.

Poços de Caldas (1,180m; pop 110,150, CEP 37700, DDD 035), in western Minas, is reached by road or plane from São Paulo (272 km), Rio (507 km) or Belo Horizonte (510 km). The city is sited on the crater of an extinct volcano in a mountainous area. Venetians from Murano settled here and established a crystal-glass industry. A well-known resort, it is a traditional honeymoon centre and has complete and up-to-date thermal establishments for the treatment of rheumatic, skin and intestinal diseases; you need a local doctor's certificate to use these facilities. Excursions include several lakes within a few km of the city with boating and restaurants; the Véu das Noivas with its three waterfalls illuminated at night; the tall statue of Cristo Redentor at an altitude of 1,678m, which can be reached by cable car; nearby is an 80-metre granite rock, Pedra Batão. There are also the lovers' well, Fonte dos Amores, and the Japanese teahouse at the Recanto Japonês. A tourist train runs from Poços de Caldas to Aguas da Prata and back each Sat (dep 0915 and 1500, return 1130 and 1700, 1 hr 15 mins journey). Hippie fair every Sun in Praça Pedro Sanches. Festivals include Carnival, São Benedito ending on 13 May, and the Festival de Música Popular Brasileira (Festa UAI, 2nd half of Aug). Excellent climate. There is now a small industrial estate.

Hotels Some 80 hotels and pensions. **A1** *Palace*, Praça Pedro Sanches, T 722-1392, old fashioned but well run, with sulphur baths; **A1** *Pousada Vale das Rosas*, Av W Brás 4500, T 713-1759, F 713-1315; **A3** *Continental*, Av Francisco Salles 235, T 722-1166. The following are **F** pp and good: *Pensão Central*, R Rio Grande, nr city centre bus terminal; *Real*, R Minas Gerais 390, T 721-4152; *Virginia*, R Minas Gerais 506, T 722-2694.

Restaurants *Sem-Sem*, R Assis Figueiredo 1080; *Cantina do Araújo*, R Assis Figueiredo 1705. Local specialities: smoked cheese, sausages, sweets and jams (try squash-and-coconut).

Buses Rodoviária 3 km from centre. **Rio**, 8 hrs, US$11.50; **São Paulo**, 4½ hrs, US$6.60.

Tres Corações (pop 57,040), also in southern Minas but not a spa, is the birthplace of Pelé, the legendary football star (statue). Hotels: **D** *Italian Palace*; **E** *Capri*; good food at *Cantina Calabresa*. Reached by daily buses from Rio, São Paulo and Belo Horizonte. 2 daily buses to (35 km, US$1.80, 2 hrs) *São Tomé das Letras*, beautiful hilltop village, one of the five highest places in Brazil (1,291m, pop 5,710). A traditional quarry town, it has some charming old-style buildings with frescoed 17th-century church and many caves in surrounding hills. Cave inscriptions have lent the town a mystical reputation, attracting 'new age' visitors, very popular at weekends. Waterfalls: Cachoeira de Eusebiose, 4 km; Véu de Noiva 8 km. Hotel: *Hospedaria* *do Gê*, R Gabriel Luis Alves 28; restaurant opp, *Das Letras*, both rec. **Pocinhos de Rio Verde**, a friendly hill resort, bus 1 hr; *Hotel Bosque das Fontes*, rec, at entrance to town, chalets, camp sites, restaurant, low cost steam and mineral baths; *O Portal*, R Armando Vilela 7, camping, good lasagne on offer; lake, horses and many trails. Rainy season Oct-Mar. Downhill, on road to Sobrachinha is the quiet community of Harmonia, 'new age', cheap vegetarian food, clean accommodation (F pp).

Note that there are also mountain spa resorts (Serra Negra, Lindóia, Campos do Jordão) in São Paulo State (**see p 435**).

Araxá (pop 69,860) in the Minas Triangle, about 193 km before Uberaba at 970m, is a quiet little place with thorium and radio-active waters and sulphur and mud baths. It can be reached from Rio (848 km), São Paulo (549 km) or Belo Horizonte (374 km), by bus. Airport.

Hotels A1 *Grande de Araxá*, luxury, 8 km away, T 661-2011; **A3** *Colombo*, same location, T 661-3016, F 661-5367; *Pinto*, Pres O Maciel 284, T 661-2551.

South of Araxá is the **Serra da Canastra National Park**, in which the Rio São Francisco rises. It is a cool region (temperatures in May and Jun average 18°C), best reached from Piumhi, on state road 050, 267 km W of Belo Horizonte. (Ibama, address as for Serra do Cipó, above.)

Uberaba (pop 210,800, CEP 38100, DDD 034), also in the Minas Triangle, is on the Rio da Prata, 718 km from São Paulo. It is an important rail and road junction, being on the direct highway between São Paulo and Brasília, and serves a large cattle raising district. At the beginning of May each year the Rural Society of the Minas Triangle holds a famous cattle and agricultural exhibition at Uberaba. Altitude, 700m. Hotels: *Palácio*; *Grande*. Bus from Belo Horizonte, US$11.50 (leito US$23), 7 hrs.

To the N of Uberaba is **Uberlândia** (pop 366,710, CEP 38400, DDD 034), founded in 1888 as São Pedro do Uberabinha (the current name was adopted in 1929); good communications by air and road (buses to Brasília, 6 hrs, US$9; to Belo Horizonte, 9 hrs, US$14.50, to São Paulo, US$15.25). **D** *Hotel Nacional*, Higino Guerra 273, T 235-4983, opp rodoviária, with view (cheaper without), shower and breakfast, clean; many others, also restaurants. In the rodoviária is a helpful tourist information kiosk.

THE STATE OF SÃO PAULO (5)

The state is the industrial heart of Brazil, with much agriculture too; the city is the financial centre. The metropolis does have much of cultural interest in the way of museums, and the famous Butantã Snake Farm. On the coast there are many fine beaches, although pollution is a problem; inland there are hill resorts.

The State of São Paulo (pop over 31,000,00), with an area of 247,898 square km, is larger than the states of New York and Pennsylvania together and about the same size as Great Britain and Northern Ireland. A narrow zone of wet tropical lowland along the coast rises in an unbroken slope to the ridge of the Great Escarpment—the Serra do Mar—at from 800 to 900m above sea level. The upland beyond the Great Escarpment is drained westwards by the tributaries of the Rio Paraná. The broad valleys of the uplands are surmounted by ranges of low mountains; one such range lies between the São Paulo basin and the hinterland of the state. West of the low mountains between the basin and the rest of the state lie the uplands of the Paraná Plateau, at about 600m above the sea. One of the soils in this area is the terra roxa, the red earth in which coffee flourishes. When dry it gives off a red dust which colours everything; when wet it is sticky and slippery. There is ample rainfall in São Paulo State; indeed, the highest rainfall in Brazil (3,810

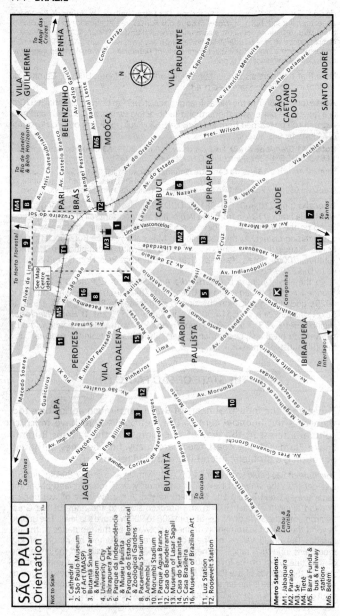

SÃO PAULO
Orientation

Not to Scale

1. Cathedral
2. São Paulo Museum of Art (MASP)
3. Butantã Snake Farm & Museum
4. University City
5. Ibirapuera Park
6. Parque da Independência & Museu Paulista
7. Parque do Estado, Botanical & Zoological Gardens
8. Pacaembu Stadium
9. Anhembi
10. Morumbi Stadium
11. Parque Água Branca
12. Casa do Bandeirante
13. Museum of Lasar Sagall
14. Casa do Sertanista
15. Casa Brasileira
16. Museum of Brazilian Art

T1. Luz Station
T2. Roosevelt Station

Metro Stations:
M1. Jabaquara
M2. Paraíso
M3. Sé
M4. Tietê
M5. Barra Funda & bus & railway stations
M6. Belém

N

See Map Centre detail

mm) is over a small area between Santos and São Paulo; at São Paulo itself it is no more than 1,194 mm. Temperatures on the plateau are about 5°C lower than on the coast, but it is only S of the latitude of Sorocaba that frosts occur and then not frequently. Temperatures are too low for coffee in the São Paulo basin itself, but the State produces, on average, about 7 million bags a year.

Between 1885 and the end of the century a boom in coffee and the arrival of large numbers of Europeans transformed the State out of all recognition. By the end of the 1930s there had arrived in São Paulo State a million Italians, half a million each of Portuguese and immigrants from the rest of Brazil, nearly 400,000 Spaniards and nearly 200,000 Japanese. It is the world's largest Japanese community outside Japan. Today the State produces some 20% of Brazil's agricultural output and 65% (40% in São Paulo city alone) of its industrial production, being also responsible for 60% of the country's industrial consumption of electric energy. São Paulo provides 33% of the total exports of Brazil and takes 40% of the total imports: nearly all pass through the port of Santos.

São Paulo (pop 10,998,000—metropolitan population est 19,000,000) is 429 km from Rio de Janeiro, and is connected with it by air, the Via Dutra highway, and the Central do Brasil railway. It was founded in 1554 by two Jesuit priests from São Vicente, Blessed José Anchieta and Padre Manuel Nóbrega, as a mission station. The original settlement, not yet effectively preserved, was at the Pátio do Colégio in the centre of the city, where a copy of Anchieta's original church has been built, using one of the surviving mud-packed walls of the original 16th century structure (it is open Tues to Sun, 1300-1700).

São Paulo (altitude 730m) is one of the fastest growing cities in the world. It is already the most populous city in South America, and the continent's leading industrial centre. Until the 1870s it was a sleepy, shabby little town known as "a cidade de barro" (the mud city), as most of its buildings were made of clay and packed mud. The city was transformed architecturally at the end of the 19th century when wealthy landowners began to invest in São Paulo as a financial and residential centre. Nowadays, it covers more than 1,500 square km—three times the size of Paris—but little remains of its 19th century architecture. Although most of its citizens are proud of its skyscrapers, of its well-lit streets, and especially of its Metro system, they also mourn the loss of innumerable historical buildings and green areas through shortsighted planning policies in the 1980s. The traffic pattern is extremely exasperating: you may have to drive around 10 blocks to reach a point half a block away. Buy a *Guia de São Paulo* from a newstand if you plan to stay any length of time, it gives bus routes which are equally confusing. Also exasperating is the amount of air pollution: in dry weather eyes and nose are continually troubled.

The main reasons for the city's development lie in its position at the focus of so much agricultural wealth, while a strong tradition of work and industry and relatively low temperatures combine to make the Paulistanos the most hard working and energetic people in Brazil. Visitors, however, find the characteristic sharp changes of temperature troublesome and even Paulistanos seem to catch cold often. (Incidentally, one differentiates between Paulistas—inhabitants of the State—and Paulistanos— inhabitants of the city.) There is another and a most potent factor which explains its industrial growth: the availability of plentiful hydro-electric power.

The shopping, hotel and restaurant centre embraces the districts of Av São Luís, the Praça da República, and R Barão de Itapetininga. The commercial quarter, containing banks, offices and shops, is contained within a central district known as the Triângulo, bounded by R Direita, Quinze de Novembro, São Bento and Praça Antônio Prado, but it is already rapidly spreading towards the apartment and shopping district of Praça da República. R Augusta begins close to Avenida São

Luis, extends as far as **Avenida Paulista**, and continues beyond into one of the most affluent areas, Jardins. Both sides of R Augusta have a variety of shops, snackbars and restaurants, but the Jardins side contains the more exclusive boutiques and fashion houses, while the part which leads to the centre is a rather curious but colourful mix of seedy bars, saunas (mixed, or men only) and 5-star hotels. Cinemas are found on both sides as well as a number of shopping malls (close to Paulista). Avenida Paulista, once the home of coffee barons and São Paulo's wealthy citizens, is now Brazil's largest financial centre housing most banking head offices (most consulates as well), and the **Museu de Arte de São Paulo** (MASP—opened by Queen Elizabeth II in 1968). It is becoming a new downtown area, more dynamic, but considerably less colourful than the old centre with its maze of bustling pedestrianized streets. Another new centre is Av Faria Lima, 8 km from **Praça da República**. Other popular areas are Vila Madalena and Pinheiros; in the latter is Espaço Paulista on Depto La Cerda Franco 87, with entertainers on Fri and Sat pm.

The park in Praça da República is worth going into between 0800 and 1400 on Sun: birds, trees and Brazilians in all their variety, and a famous handicrafts fair; on Sat pm there is live music, and stalls sell sweets and salgados. Near the Praça is the city's tallest building, the **Edifício Itália** on the corner of Av Ipiranga and Av São Luís. There is a restaurant on top (pricey, but worth it), and a sightseeing balcony, you have to buy a drink or two as "entrance fee" (US$6). Also worth a visit is the **Martinelli building**, the city's first skyscraper, R Líbero Badaró and Av São João, Mon-Sat, 0900-1600, entry to 26th floor, free.

The **Viaduto do Chá**, which bridges the central avenue, Anhangabaú, leads to the **Teatro Municipal**, one of the few distinguished 19th-century survivals that São Paulo can boast. The Av Paulista and the "jardins" América, Paulista and Paulistano still contain some mansions of beauty and interest and are on the 702U Cidade Universitária bus route to the Butantã Institute or "snake farm". About 10 mins' walk from the centre of the city is the old **Mercado Municipal** at R Cantareira 306, covering an area of 27,000 sq metres (open Mon-Sat 0400-1600); a new Mercado Municipal has been built in the outskirts. The **Biblioteca Municipal**, surrounded by a pleasant shady garden, is well worth visiting.

The **Cathedral's** foundations were laid over 40 years before its inauguration during the 1954 festivities commemorating the 4th centenary of the city. This massive building in neo-Gothic style, with a capacity for 8,000 worshippers, is in the heart of the city. Two central parks are **Parque da Luz**, Av Tiradentes (110,000 square metres) and **Siqueira Campos (Parque Trianon)**, Peixoto Gomilde 949 and Av Paulista, open daily 0700-1830, a welcome green area in the busiest part of the city.

The large municipal stadium in the **Pacaembu** valley, a flourishing residential district, is well worth seeing. Built on Olympic lines in an area of 75,500 square metres, it holds nearly 70,000 spectators. Besides the flood-lit football ground and athletics field and basketball court, there are also a covered gymnasium, open-air and covered tennis courts, an illuminated 50-metre long swimming pool, and a great hall for receptions and rallies. There is a larger stadium holding 100,000 people in **Morumbi**, one of the more elegant residential districts. Motor racing fans might like to visit the Morumbi cemetery, last resting place of Ayrton Senna.

Typical of modern development are the huge Iguatemi, Ibirapuera and Morumbi **shopping centres**. They include luxurious cinemas, snack bars and most of the best shops in São Paulo. Parking in each for over 1,000 vehicles. On a rather humbler level are the big supermarkets of El Dorado (Av Pamplona 1704) and Pão de Açúcar (Praça Roosevelt, near the *Hilton*); the latter is open 24 hrs a day (except Sun).

The palatial **Jockey Club** racecourse is in the Cidade Jardim area with easy access by bus (Butantã from República, among others). Race meetings are held on Mon, Wed and Thur at 1730 and Sat and Sun at 1500. The new town premises of the Jockey Club (R Boa Vista) are well worth a visit.

Ibirapuera Take a Monções bus (675-C) from Ana Rosa metro station to Ibirapuera Park (designed by architect Oscar Niemeyer and landscape artist Burle Marx) for the architecturally impressive new **Legislative Assembly**. There is also a **planetarium** equipped with the most up-to-date machinery (shows at 1600-1800 weekends and holidays, during the week for groups only, T 544-4606); a velodrome for cycle and motor-cycle racing; an all-aluminium covered stadium for indoor sports which seats 20,000 people. The **Museu de Arte Contemporâneo**, founded in 1963, has an important collection of Western and South American modern art. The collection is divided between the Bienal building, 3rd floor, in Parque Ibirapuera (entrance at back of building, open Tues-Sun, 1200-1700, closed holidays, free) and a building at R da Reitoria, 109, Cidade Universitária, open Wed-Sun 1000-1700, closed holidays, students free (it is hoped to unite the collection in a building under construction in the Cidade Universitária). Buses to Ibirapuera, 6414 (Gatusa) from Praça da Bandeira; to Cidade Universitária 702U or 7181 from Praça da República.

In this park, too, are the museums of **Modern Art** (Arte Moderna—MAM, Tues-Fri 1300-1900, Sat-Sun 1100-1900), **Aeronáutica** (showing the Santos Dumont plane; closed 1995), and **Folklore** (Tues-Sun 1400-1700). There is also a unique display of nativity scenes and scenes of the life of Christ. (Concerts held at Christmas-time.) At the entrance is a majestic monument to the Bandeirantes, or pioneers. All the Ibirapuera museums (except Aeronáutica) are open Tues-Sun, 1400-1700. (For other museums see p 417.)

Anhembi (Av Assis Chateaubriand e R Olava Fontoura, Santana) is the largest exhibition hall in the world. It was inaugurated in 1970 and all São Paulo's industrial fairs are held there. It has a meeting hall seating 3,500 people, three auditórios, 24 conference rm (*salas de reunião*) and two restaurants. Parking space is provided for 3,500 cars. It may be reached by underground (short walk from Tietê station).

Galleries and Museums   The **Museu de Arte de São Paulo** (founded by Assis Chateaubriand, Av Paulista 1578, immediately above the 9 de Julho tunnel, nearest metro is Paraíso on the N-S line, or MASP-Trianon on the new line, or bus 805A from Praça da República) has a large group of French Impressionists, Florentine and Umbrian painters (including Botticelli and Raphael), several Hieronymus Bosch and Frans Post, sculptures by Rodin, a collection of 73 sculptures by Degas and paintings by Modigliani, Renoir, Toulouse-Lautrec, and some interesting work by Brazilian artists, including Portinári. Particularly interesting are the pictures of the NE done by Dutch artists during the Dutch occupation (1630-54): the exotic tropical landscapes— even the Paulo Afonso falls!—have been made to look incredibly temperate. (Exhibitions vary, not all the artists above may be on view.) Temporary exhibitions are held in the basement. Entrance US\$0.50, Tues-Fri 1300-1700, Sat-Sun 1400-1800. The **Museu de Arte Brasileira** is at R Alagoas 903, Pacaembu, entrance free, Tues-Fri 1400-2200, Sat-Sun 1300-1800, houses collections of Brazilian artists such as Portinári, Anita Malfatti and Brecheret. Here also there are copies of Brazilian sculptures, including those of Aleijadinho. The **Museu de Arqueologia e Etnologia** is on the fourth and fifth floors of Bloco D in the students resident blocks (known as Crusp) in the main Arts Complex of the Universidade de São Paulo (USP), bus stop before the entrance to the Butantã Institute (see p 427); open Tues-Fri 0900-1700. Every odd-numbered year the São Paulo Bienal at Ibirapuera has the most important show of modern art in Latin America, open from beginning of Sep till Nov. For the other museums at Ibirapuera, see above, and for the Museu Paulista and Casa do Grito at Ipiranga, see p 427. In the Parque Modernista, R Santa Cruz 325, Vila Mariana, is the first Modernist house, built by the Russian born architect Warchavchik; it was frequented by members of the modernist movement (closed 1995).

There are two museums on Av Tiradentes, near the Jardim da Luz; the **Museu de Arte Sacra** in the Convento da Luz, No 676 (open Tues-Sun 1300-1700, US\$0.20) and the State Art Collection (**Pinacoteca do Estado**) at No 141 (open Tues-Sun 1300-1800, free).

Not far from the Butantã Institute (see p 427) are the **Casa do Bandeirante** (being renovated) at Praça Monteiro Lobato, the reconstructed home of a pioneer of 400 years ago; and the **Casa do Sertanista**, a museum of Indian folklore and handicrafts mounted by the famous expert on the Indians, Orlando Villas Boas, at Av Prof Francisco Morato 2200, Caxingui, T 211-5341, open Tues-Sun, 0900-1700, same hours, entrance free.

The **Casa Brasileira**, Av Faria Lima 774, has been established as a museum of Brazilian furniture, Tues-Sun, 1300-1700. **Museo Padre Anchieta**, Pátio do Colégio, is a restored mission house; inside are examples and relics of the Jesuit era, same hours, entrance US\$0.50. The **Museu da Imagem e do Som** (MIS) is at Av Europa 158, Tues-Sun 1400-2200, regular photographic exhibitions and archives of Brazilian cinema, video and music, which can be consulted by the public, nice café on ground floor. The **Museu de Lasar Segall**, at R Alfonso Celso 362, Vila Mariana (near Santa Cruz metro station), shows the works of a German expressionist painter who emigrated to Brazil, with cinema and library, holds free courses and seminars (arrive early), Tues-Fri 1430-1800, Sat 1430-2000, Sun 1430-1830. **Museu da Imigração Japonesa**, R São Joaquim 381, Liberdade, Tues-Sun 1330-1730, excellent, nice

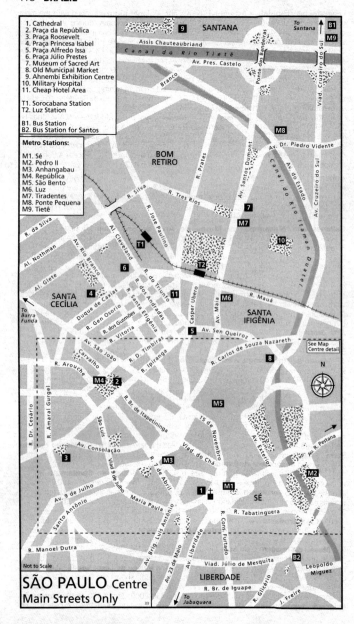

1. Cathedral
2. Praça da República
3. Praça Roosevelt
4. Praça Princesa Isabel
5. Praça Alfredo Issa
6. Praça Júlio Prestes
7. Museum of Sacred Art
8. Old Municipal Market
9. Anhembi Exhibition Centre
10. Military Hospital
11. Cheap Hotel Area

T1. Sorocabana Station
T2. Luz Station

B1. Bus Station
B2. Bus Station for Santos

Metro Stations:
M1. Sé
M2. Pedro II
M3. Anhangabau
M4. República
M5. São Bento
M6. Luz
M7. Tiradentes
M8. Ponte Pequena
M9. Tietê

SÃO PAULO Centre
Main Streets Only

Not to Scale

roof garden, ask at desk for English translation of the exhibits. **Museu da Fundação Maria Luisa e Oscar Americano**, Av Morumbi 3700, Morumbi, a private collection of Brazilian and Portuguese art and furniture, well-displayed, Tues-Fri 1100-1700, Sat-Sun 1000-1700. There is a **Museu da Discoteca e Biblioteca da Música** at R Catão 611, 5th and 6th floors, open Mon-Fri, 0900-1300 (take bus 819 P from Praça Princesa Isabel to Lapa district). **Museu do Telefone**, Martiniano de Carvalho 851, Paraíso, Tues-Fri 0900-1730, Sat-Sun 1400-1800, quite good, but you're not allowed to operate anything. **Museu CMTC dos Transportes Públicos**, Av Cruzeiro do Sul 780, Tues-Fri, 0900-1700. **Museu de Veterinária**, Cidade Universitária, Facultade de Veterinária, bloco 7, T 210-2122, ext 475, Mon-Fri 0900-1200, 1400-1700. **Museu do Papel** (Paper), R Mauá 836, casa 25, Tues-Fri 1330-1700, Sat-Sun 1000-1400; **Museu do Relógio** (clocks and watches), rec for enthusiasts, Av Diógenes R de Lima 2333, Pompéia, Mon-Fri 0800-1130, 1300-1700; **Estação Ciência**, R Guaicurus 1274, Lapa, Tues-Wed 1200-2200, Thur and Sun 1000-2000.

The **Centro Cultural São Paulo**, R Vergueiro 1000 (metro Vergueiro) has art and photographic exhibitions, a library, music and dance shows (often regional) and films; open daily until 2200. **Memorial da América Latina**, designed by Oscar Niemeyer, built in Mar 1989, at Av Mário de Andrade 664, next to Barra Funda metro station, relief map of Central and South America under a glass floor in the section which houses a permanent exhibition of handicrafts from all over Latin America, library of photographs, books, magazines, newspapers and films shown on video, very impressive, restaurant, at weekends there are free concerts with Brazilian and Latin American musicians, programme available on request, entrance free (open Tues-Fri 0900-2100, Sat 0900-1800, Sun 1000-1800).

Local Holidays 25 Jan (Foundation of City). Note that during carnival most museums and attractions are closed.

Warning Beware of assaults and pickpocketing in São Paulo. Thieves often use the mustard-on-the-back trick (see Introduction and Hints, **Security**). The areas around Luz station and Centro are not safe at night, and visitors should not enter *favelas*.

Telephone code and Postal address CEP 01000, DDD 011.

Hotels Among the most luxurious (corporate rates available), all with swimming pools, nightclubs and convention halls, are the **L1** *Caesar Park*, R Augusta 1508, T 253-6622, F 288-6146; **L1** *Maksoud Plaza*, Alameda Campinas 150, T 253-4411, F 253-4544; **L1** *Mofarrej Sheraton*, Alameda Santos 1437, T 253-5544, F 280-8670 (rec); **L2** *Grand Hotel Cà d'Oro*, R Augusta 129, T 256-8011, F 231-0359; **L2** *Brasilton*, R Martins Fontes 330, T 258-5811, F 258-5812; **L1** *Hilton*, Av Ipiranga 165, T 256-0033, F 257-3137; **L3** *Holiday Inn Crowne Plaza*, R Frei Caneca 1360, T 253-2244, F 251-3121, 5-star, central, small swimming pool, very comfortable; the **L2** *Della Volpe Garden*, R Frei Caneca 1199, T 285-5388, F 288-8710, is rec; **A1** *Eldorado Boulevard*, Av São Luís 234, T 214-1833, F 256-8061 (excellent); **A1** *Linson*, R Augusta 440, Consolação, T 256-6700, F 258-5371, all apartments with double bed, kitchenette, sitting room, bath, TV security system, restaurant, pool; **L3** *Grand Corona*, Basílio da Gama 101, T 259-8177, F 257-5025, very fairly priced; **A1** *Planalto*, Cásper Líbero 117 (Varig-Tropical chain), T 227-7311, F 227-7916, secure, helpful, good service, good dining room.

There are many other good hotels, incl **L2** *Bristol*, R Martins Fontes 277, T 258-0011, F 231-1265; **A1** *Othon Palace*, R Líbero Badaró 190, T 239-3277, F 37-7203; **A1** *Samambaia*, R Sete de Abril 422, T 231-1333 (discounts for cash and at weekends); **A1** *Jaraguá*, R Major Quedinho 44, T 256-6633, F 256-1377; **A1** *Solar Paulista*, R Francisca Miquelina 343, T 257-2800, F 257-2800; **A3** *Terminus*, Av Ipiranga 741, T 222-2266.

A residential hotel, rec for longer stays, is **A1** *Metropolitan Plaza*, Alameda Campinas 474, T 287-4855, F 285-3158. A rec "Apart-hotel" for longer stays is *Residencial Alameda Nothman* (Santa Cecília), Al Nothman 682, T 222-6144; **A2** *Hores Belgrano*, R Marquês de Paranaguá, 88, T 258-0255, F 257-7803, central, English spoken, special rates for long stays. *Service-Flat Monterey*, Alameda Itu 265, Jardim Paulista, T 285-6111, F 283-3247, has been rec for longer stays; safe parking, comfortable accommodation.

B *Banri*, R Galvão Bueno 209, T 270-8877, F 278-9225, good, near metro station Liberdade (Japanese quarter); **B** *Center Bela Vista*, 13 de Maio 198, T 255-4042, near plenty of restaurants in an old Italian suburb (R Santo Antônio/R 13 de Maio, nr Praça da Bandeira). There are scores of cheaper hotels, of which we append a selection: **D** *Continental*, R Vitória 223, clean, safe, highly rec; **D** *Itauna*, Av Rio Branco 280, well furnished, rec; **D** *Las Vegas*, R Vitória 390 (corner Av Rio Branco); **D** *Lincoln*, Av Rio Branco 47, excellent breakfast, friendly, safe, rec; **D** *Joamar*, José de Barros, Centro, in the pedestrian area, hot showers, clean, safe, TV, room service, rec; **D** *Serrano*, R Gago Coutinho 22, T 285-3233, warmly rec; **D** *Natal*, R Guaianazes 41, T 220-6722, recently rebuilt, very well rec; **D** *Itamarati*, Av Viera de Carvalho

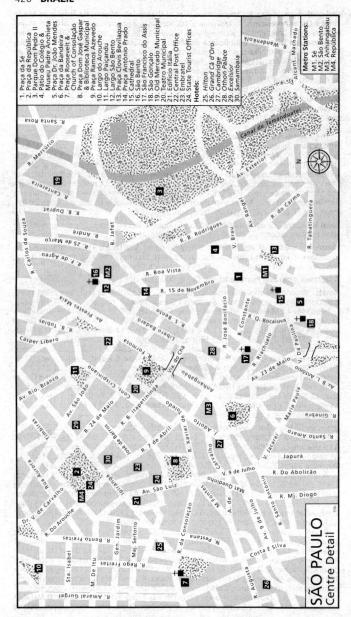

1. Praça da Sé
2. Praça da República
3. Parque Dom Pedro II
4. Pátio do Colégio & Museu Padre Anchieta
5. Praça Dr. João Mendes
6. Praça da Bandeira
7. Praça Roosevelt & Church of Consolação
8. Praça Dom José Gaspar & Biblioteca Municipal
9. Praça Ramos Azevedo
10. Largo do Arouche
11. Largo Jaraguá
12. Largo São Bento
13. Praça Clovis Bevilaqua
14. Praça Antonio Prado
15. Cathedral
16. São Bento
17. São Francisco do Assis
18. São Gonçalo
19. Old Mercado Municipal
20. Teatro Municipal
21. Edifício Itália
22. Central Post Office
23. Edifício Itália
24. State Tourist Offices

Hotels:

25. *Hilton*
26. *Grand Cã d'Oro*
27. *Cambridge*
28. *Othon Palace*
29. *Excelsior*
30. *Samambaia*

Metro Stations:

M1. Sé
M2. São Bento
M3. Anhangabau
M4. República

SÃO PAULO
Centre Detail

150, T 222-4133, ½ block from Praça da República, good location, friendly, safe, highly rec; **D** *Plaza Marabá*, Av Ipiranga 757, T 220-7811, very clean, rec. Also suggested: **C** *Riviera*, Av Barão de Limeira 117, T 221-8077, excellent value, highly rec; **D** *Ofir*, R dos Timbiras 258, T 223-8822, with bath, stores valuables but not money, big rooms, TV, well equipped, good value; **D** *S Sebastião*, 7 de Abril 364 (T 257-4988/255-1594), with bath, rec, cheap and clean; **E** *Metro*, R Vergueiro 1563, nr Paraíso, T 549-8531, without breakfast, quiet, convenient. In Av São João **B** *Cineasta*, No 613, T 222-5533, 80 rm, a/c; **C** *Plaza*, No 407, 42 rm; **E** *Central*, No 288, with shower, F without, clean, good, helpful, central; many others in the district. Very many of the cheap hotels accommodate short-stay couples.

Take the metro to Luz station and in the block behind the old Rodoviária, off Av Rio Branco, there are scores of cheap hotels with prices ranging from category E to category C; try: R Santa Ifigênia: **C** *Uai*, No 66, clean and pleasant, rooms on street are good, rec; **D** *Luanda*, No 348, with breakfast, English-speaking owner, helpful, rec; **E** *Trinidade*, No 737, clean, friendly, good value; **E** *Aliança*, R Gral Osório 235, crnr Sta Ifigênia, nice; **E** *Saturno*, Largo Osório 39, T 223-9561, hot water, soap and towel. R dos Gusmões: **E** *Galeão*, No 394, clean, safe, helpful, hot showers; **E** *Itaipu*, No 467, good, clean; **F** *Hotel Ideal da Luz*, cheap at the price with shower; **E** *Lepanto*, R Cásper Líbero 359, shower, TV, clean; **E** *Lima*, Ipiranga 770, friendly, rec; **E** *Tatuí*, Praça Princeza Isabel 171 (on corner of Av Duque de Caxias, 2 blocks from old bus station), clean with bath. **NB** The redlight district is in the blocks bounded by RR Santa Ifigênia, dos Andradas, dos Gusmões and Av Ipiranga, and is definitely not rec for women travelling alone. The whole area around Av Rio Branco is rather seedy and not entirely safe late at night.

E *Comendadore*, Largo Santa Cecília, safe, quiet; **E** *Casa do Politécnico*, R Afonso Pena 272, cheap accommodation; **E** *São José*, Alameda Barão de Piracicaba 221, without breakfast, basic. Accommodation of the youth-hostel type is available at the Pacaembu Stadium at a fee in (our) category E. A letter addressed to the Secretário de Esportes is required. Youth hostel at Rua Mariz e Barros 350, Vila Santa Eulália (bus 4491 from Parque Dom Pedro in the centre), F, cooking and washing facilities, good fruit and vegetable market directly across R Ricardo Jafet on Tues. YHA for membership, 15 de Novembro e Av São João—office in centre, about US$5 a year. International youth hostel at Parque Estadual do Jaguaré. Also Magdalena Tagkiaferro, Estrada Turística do Jaguará 651, Km 18, via Anhanguera, 05173 São Paulo (T 229-3787/3011), and *Sampa City*, R dos Franceses 100, T/F 288-1592, 500m from Brigadeiro metro station, US$6.50.

Camping Cemucam, at Cobia (Rodovia Raposo Tavares, Km 27). List of sites can be obtained from Camping Clube do Brasil, R Minerva, 156—Perdizes (T 864-7133).

Restaurants Apart from the international cuisine in the first-class hotels listed above, here are only a few out of many (the average price of a meal in 1st or 2nd class restaurants in 1995 was US$35-65 without drinks; US$15-30 in mid-range establishments).

The best (all accounts): *Bassi*, R 13 de Maio 334, T 34-2375, Bela Vista, for meat; *Don Curro*, R Alves Guimarães 230, T 852-4712, Piaheiros, closed Mon, for seafood, especially paella; *Le Bistingo*, Al Franca 580, T 289-3010; *Massimo*, Al Santos 1826, T 284-0311, international cuisine; *Antiquarius*, Al Lorena 1884, T 282-3015, Portuguese; *La Tambouille*, Av 9 de Julho 5295, Itaim Bibi, T 883-6276, French and Italian, closed Mon, reserve in advance.

Portuguese *Abril em Portugal*, R Caio Prado 47, reasonable and good; *Bocage*, Al Joaquim Eugênio de Lima 1377, excellent.

Italian *San Genovese*, R Bela Cintra 1849, very reasonable, US$29 pp, *salada Lellis* is a must, and fresh squid in batter; *Famiglia Mancini*, R Avanhandava 81, Bela Vista, excellent, especially lads and cold dishes, always queues between 2000-2400; *Gigetto*, Avanhandava 63, good pasta, reasonable prices; *Trattoria del Sargento*, Al Pamplona 1354, Jardim Paulista, good, popular; *Leonardo*, Al Santos 1508, Bela Vista (opp *Sheraton*), good; *Da Fiorella*, R Bernardino de Campos 294, Brooklin (closed Mon and Sun pm), top quality vegetarian pasta; *Don Cicillio*, Praça Tomás Morus 185, Perdizes, good homecooking in traditional surroundings; *Via Veneto*, Al Barros 909, Sta Cecília, good pasta and meat, very popular; *La Trattoria*, R Antônio Bicudo 50, Pinheiros, closed Mon, midweek until 1900, Fri, Sat till 0100, very good, reasonably priced food, *strozzapreti* a must, portions usually enough for 2; *La Farina*, Av Ipiranga 924, for good cheap pasta, popular. Many Italian restaurants in Bela Vista/Bixiga area, especially R 13 de Maio; good pizzerias are *Torre do Bixiga*, 13 de Maia, *Capuano*, R Consarrão 416, *Margherita*, Al Tietê 255.

French *L'Affiche*, R Campos Bicudo 141, small, intimate, décor includes owner's collection of antique French posters; *La Casserole*, Largo do Arouche 346, (centro), best known bistro in São Paulo, closed Mon (US$40-60 pp). *Freddy*, Praça Dom Gastão Liberal Pinto 11; *Marcel*, Al Lorena 1852, sensational soufflés.

German *Jucalemão*, R Álvaro Rodrigues 320; *Bierhalle*, Av Lavandisca 249, Indianópolis; *Arnold's Naschbar*, R Pereira Leite 98, Sumarezinho, *Eisbein peruruca*, rec; *Bismarck* (excellent draught beer) and *Paprika* (very reasonable), on Av Ibirapuera 3178 and 573 respectively.

Swiss *Chamonix*, Al Lorena 1052, and *Le Jardin Suisse*, Al Franca 1467, both in Jardim Paulista, expensive, very good.

Russian *Samovar*, R Baronesa de Bela Vista 602, Aeroporto, good food, typical shows at weekends, closed Sun. **Hungarian** *Hungaria*, Al Joaquim Eugênio de Lima 776, Jardins, old world décor, good food, expensive; *Hungaria Express*, Av Jaú 310, cheap and good.

Greek *Zorba*, R Henrique Monteiro 218.

Arabic *Almanara*, good and reasonable, Av São João 1155 (Centro), Oscar Freire 523 (Cerqueiro César), R Basilio da Gama 70 and Av Vieira de Carvalho 109 (Consolação), *Mandalun*, Al Itú 1564, Jardim Paulista, mainly Lebanese, high standard, not cheap; *Bambi*, Al Santos 59, cheapish, good; *Rubayat*, Av Vieira de Carvalho 116, Al Santos 86 and Av Faria Lima 583, excellent meat, fixed price meals.

Oriental (Japanese tends to be expensive) *Sino-Brasileiro*, R Alberto Torres 39 (Perdizes); *Iti Fuji*, Al Jaú 487, typical Japanese, excellent; *Sushigen*, Av Brig Luis Antônio 2367, Lojas 13 and 14, very good *sushi* and *sashimi* but a bit overpriced; *Komazushi*, same street No 2050, Loja 7, reasonably priced and good; *Korea House*, Galvão Bueno 43 (Liberdade). *Kar Wua* Chinese restaurant, at R Mourato Coelho 30, highly praised. Many other Chinese and Japanese restaurants in Liberdade, the Japanese quarter, where there is a Japanese food market in the square by the metro station.

Indian *Govinda*, R Princesa Isabel 379, good, expensive.

Vegetarian Almost always the cheapest option in São Paulo. *Sattva*, R da Consolação 3140; *O Arroz de Ouro*, Largo do Arouche 42-44 (shop as well, central); *Cheiro Verde*, Peixoto Gomilde 1413, Jardins, very good, more expensive than most; *Nutri Som*, R 9 Júlio 160, new, rec; *Intergrão*, R Joaquim Antunes 377, macrobiotic; *Delícia Natural*, Av Rio Branco 211 (4th floor), corner Av Ipiranga, lunch only, good; *Sabor Natural*, same building, 1st floor, lunch only, good; *Folhas e Raizes*, Líbero Bádaro 370, buffet lunch US$3.20; *Saúde Sabor*, São Bento 500, lunch only; *Vegetaliano*, D Sampaio 155, Sto Amaro, Italian vegetarian. "Vida Integral" newspaper gives details of all health food restaurants and stores in São Paulo.

General *Terraço Itália*, on top of Edifício Itália (Ipiranga e São Luis), 41 floors up, good fixed price lunch, dancing with excellent band and superb view (must consume to be allowed to see the view), expensive, shorts and flip flops not allowed; *Mexilhão*, R 13 de Maio 626, Bela Vista, very good seafood. *Paulista*, João Moura 527, Pinheiros, top quality meat, popular; *Horse's Neck*, Av Juscelino Kubitschek, Haim Bibi, near *Runner* sports centre, good Brazilian, English and international food. *Dinho's Place*, Al Santos 45 and Largo do Arouche 246, Fri excellent seafood buffet, good meat, US$45, has daily bargains; *Mate Amargo*, Av Pompéia 1603, *churrascaria*, live music, rec; *Paddock*, Av São Luís 258 and Av Faria Lima 1541, traditional fare, excellent *feijoada*; *Planeta*, R Augusta, includes Brazilian dishes, rec; *Um, Dois, Feijão e Arroz*, Praça de Sé 42 and R Ipiranga 940, modest but very good traditional food; *Cantina Amigo Piolin*, R Augusta 89, good, US$20; *Novo Olido*, Largo do Arouche 193, closed Sat, regional dishes from interior of São Paulo; *Bolinha*, Av Cidade Jardim 53 for *feijoadas* (on Wed and Sat); *Oxalá*, Tr Maria Antônia 72, just off Consolação, Bahian specialities at modest prices; *Bronx*, R Haddock Lobo 1576, very reasonable traditional home cooking.

McDonalds and other fast food chains can be found all over the city as well as many other not quite so fast, but infinitely more interesting alternatives. *Frevinho Lanches*, R Augusta 1563, famous for its *beirute* (speciality of São Paulo), as well as many other toasted sandwiches with pitta bread; *Baguette*, Consolação 2426, nr Paulista, opp Belas Artes cinema, good sandwiches, especially lively around midnight; *Absolute*, Al Santos 843, best hamburgers in town; *Rock Dreams*, Al Tietê 580, good hamburgers and sandwiches; delicious *pão de queijo* in *Lanchonete* of same name on Augusta (between Antônio de Queirez and Marquês de Paranaguá—Centro). *Restaurante do MASP*, Av Paulista 1578, in basement of museum, reasonably priced, often has live music.

Bars and Cafés *Ritz*, Al Franca 1088, Jardins, a bit overpriced but always lively, friendly, predominatly gay clientèle; *Riviera*, R da Consolação 2450, traditional haunt of students and "counter" revolutionaries since early 60s, noisy, a bit rough but kept under control by surly waiters. *Café com Arte*, R Oscar Freire 1051 (Jardins), small coffee shop, 1000-2000 (later weekends); *Fran's Café*, open 24 hrs, Av Paulista 358; R Heitor Penteado 1326 (Sumaré); R Haddock Lobo 586; Estac Alameda Lorena 1271 (Jardim Paulista); *Café Columbia*, R Augusta 3008 (Jardim América); *Café das Flores*, R dos Pinheiros 953; *Café Paris*, Av Waldemar Ferreira 55, Butantã; *Café do Bixiga*, 13 de Maio 76 and lots of others in Bixiga/Bela Vista area with live music, eg *Café Piu Piu* and *Café Pedaço*, at 13 de Maio 134 and 140. Bixiga is traditionally known as the "Bohemian" area and bars here are usually cheaper than Jardins and Pinheiros areas. *Euro Bar*, R Min José Geraldo R Alkimin 2338, quiet; *Baguette*, good breakfasts, R

Consolação 2426 (Consolação) and R 13 de Maio (Bela Vista); in Itaim Bibi: *Hard Rock Café*, R Brigadeiro Haroldo Veloso 707, fake but still sells the T-shirts; *Blue Note Jazz Bar*, Av São Gabriel 558, as the name describes.

Banks Opening hours vary from bank to bank, but most are open between 1000-1600, **Banco do Brasil**, R 7 de Abril, near República. **Banco Internacional**, R Quinze de Novembro 240. **Banco Holandês Unido**, R Quinze de Novembro 150. **Citibank**, Av Ipiranga 855, or Av Paulista 1111 (T 576-2211) will receive money from abroad (US$20 charge, takes 5 days). **First National Bank of Boston**, R Líbero Badaró 487. **Banco Lar Brasileiro** (Chase Manhattan owned), 131 R Alvares Penteado, and other national banks. **Banco Mercantil de São Paulo**, Av Paulista 1450, for cash advances on Access/Mastercard. Thomas Cook/Mastercard TC refund assistance point: Rua Haddock Lobo 337, 2 andar, 01414 São Paulo, T 259-3022. **Western Union** at Banco Itamarati, T 0800-11-9837.

Exchange Many *câmbios* near Praça da República; none near rodoviária or Tietê hotels. **American Express**, Al Santos 1437 (*Hotel Mofarrej Sheraton*) T 284-2515 and Kontik Franstur (address below) very helpful; **Mastercard**, cash against card, R Campo Verde 61, 4° andar, Jardim Paulistano; **Exprinter**, Barão de Itapetininga 243, also deals in foreign currencies (cash only). **Boreal Turismo**, Praça da República, opp Tourist Office, on Ipiranga. **Tourist Cambio**, R Badaró (turn left off Viaduto do Chá); **Agency Faro**, Av São Luis 157, for TCs; **Interpax**, Praça da República 177, loja 13, changes cash but not cheques; **Amoretur**, Praça da República 203, will change cheques. For parallel rates ask at tourist kiosks for details. Most travel agents on Av São Luis change TCs and cash at good rates.

Electric Current 110-220 volts AC, 60 cycles.

Culture and Education There are three universities: the official university of São Paulo, the Pontifical Catholic University, and the Mackenzie University. The official University of São Paulo is now situated in the Cidade Universitária (buses from main bus station), outside the city beyond Pinheiros. There are a number of architecturally interesting buildings housing different faculties and the four museums of archaeology, ethnology, anthropology and mineralogy. (All keep different hours, but all are open Mon-Thur 1400-1700.) They have courses available to foreigners, including a popular Portuguese course, registry is through the International Bureau, Comissão de Cooperação Internacional, R do Anfiteatro 181, Bloco das Colmdias 05508, Cidade Universitária, São Paulo.

Trade and Cultural Institutions British Chamber of Commerce of São Paulo, R Barão de Itapetininga 275, 7th floor; Caixa Postal 1621. T 255-0519. **British Council**, R Maranhão 416, Higienópolis, Caixa Postal 1604, T 826-4455, F 66-3765, library at R Dep Lacerda Franco 333, Pinheiros, T 814-4155. **Sociedade Brasileira de Cultura Inglesa**, Avenida Higienópolis 449, has cinema (films US$1.50). **American Chamber of Commerce for Brazil**, R Formosa 367, 29th floor, T 222-6377. **American Library**, União Cultural Brasil-Estados Unidos, R Coronel Oscar Porto 208, T 287-1022. **Goethe-Instituto**, R Lisboa 974, T 280-4288 (open Mon-Thur 1400-2030). **Instituto Hans Staden**, R Cons Crispiniano 53, 12th floor. See under **Entertainment** for Alliance Française Theatre.

Consulates Argentine, Av Paulista 1106, T 284-1355 (open 0900-1300, very easy to get visa here); **Bolivian**, R da Conso lação 37, 3rd floor (open 0900-1300), T 255-3555; **Chilean**, Av Paulista 1009, T 284-2044; **Paraguayan**, Av São Luiz 50, 10th floor, T 255-7818; **Peru**, R Laplace 739, T 531-0943; **Uruguayan**, Al Campinas 433, 7th floor, T 284-5777; **Venezuelan**, R Veneza 878, T 887-4583.

American Consulate General, R Padre João Manuel 933, T 881-6511; **Canadian Consulate General**, Av Paulista 854, 5th floor, T 287-2122; **British Consulate General**, Av Paulista 1938, 17th floor, Caixa Postal 846, T 287-7722; **Irish**, Av Paulista 2006, 5th floor, T 287-6362; **Danish Consulate General**, R João Tibiriçá 900, T 831-9799, open 0900-1200, 1300-1700, Fri until 1400 only; **German**, Av Brig Faria Lima 1383, 12th floor, T 814-6644; **Swiss Consulate-General**, Av Paulista 1754, 4th floor, Caixa Postal 30588, T 289-1033; **Austrian Consulate-General**, R Augusta 2516, 10th floor, T 282-6223; **French**, Av Paulista 1842, T 287-9522; **Swedish Consulate-General**, R Oscar Freire 379, 3rd floor, T 883-3322 (Caixa Postal 51626); **Dutch**, Av Brigadeiro Faria Lima 1698, T 813-0522.

Entertainment The Teatro Municipal (magnificent interior) is used by visiting theatrical and operatic groups, as well as the City Ballet Company and the Municipal Symphony Orchestra who give regular performances. There are several first-class theatres: Aliança Francesa, R General Jardim 182, T 259-0086, Itália (Av Ipiranga 344, T 257-3138), Cacilda Becker (R Tito 295, T 864-4513), Paiol (R Amaral Gurgel 164, T 221-2462), Ruth Escobar (R dos Ingleses 209, T 251-4881) among others. Free concerts at Teatro Popular do Sesi, Av Paulista 313, at midday under MASP (Mon-Sat) and at weekends at the Memorial América Latina. Free films are shown at the Centro Cultural São Paulo, R Vergueiro 1000, and the Museu Lasar Segall, R Afonso Celso 362. The biggest cinema is reckoned to be the Marabá, Av Ipiranga 757, which has 1665 seats. In cinemas entrance is usually half price on Wed; normal seat price is US$2.50.

See *Ilustrada* section of *Folha de São Paulo* for listings of concerts, theatre, museums, galleries and cinema. *Veja São Paulo* of weekly news magazine *Veja* lists bars, restaurants, clubs and shows as well as the above.

Nightclubs São Paulo is teeming with clubs catering to most preferences. We list below some of the most popular in 1994-95: **Disco bars**: Entrance/cover charges US$5-10: *Banana-Banana Café*, Av 9 de Júlio 5872 (Itaim Bibi), closed Mon; *HB Club*, R Cardeal Arcoverde 2958 (Pinheiros), closed Sun, bar, snooker, and informal dance lessons; test your new skills at *Blen-Blen*, same address weekends, live Latin bands; *Cervejaria Continental*, packed, mixed music, R dos Pinheiros 1275 and R Haddock Lobo 1573. **Clubs**: Entrance US$5-20 which may include a drink: *Columbia* upstairs, R Estados Unidos 1570, lively; *Hell's Club* downstairs, opens 0430, techno, wild; *Cha-Cha-Cha*, R Tabapuã 1236, closed Mon, trendiest in 1994-95, no Brazilian music, art on walls, candles, gay and straight; *Balafon*, R Sergipe 160, Wed-Sun, small, Afro-Brazilian; *Reggae Night*, Av Robert Kennedy 3914, Thur-Sun, outdoors on lakeside; *Limelight Industry*, R Franz Schubert 93, pop hits, Japanese restaurant upstairs; *Café Piu-Piu*, R 13 de Maio 134, closed Mon, unpretentious, live blues, bossa nova, rock; *Plataforma 1*, Av Paulista 424, dinner and folkloric show, very touristy but extremely popular.

Health Doctors (English-speaking) Edwin Castello, José Maria Lisboa 861, s/104, T 884-9132; Ruy Silva, Conselheiro Brotero 1505, No 64, T 67-2470; Wilson Frey, Barão de Jacegua 1103, T 241-4474. Christel Schlúnder, R Alvares de Azevedo 127, Sto Amaro, T 247-5963, German speaking, and for children. Also Samaritans' Hospital, R Conselheiro Brotero 1486, T 825-1122.

Post Office Correio Central, Praça do Correio, corner Av São João and Prestes Máia, T 831-5222. Booth adjoining tourist office on Praça da República, weekdays only 1000-1200, 1300-1600, for letters and small packages only. **UPS** office, Brasinco, Alameda Jaú 1, 1725, 01420 São Paulo, T 852-8233, F 853-8563; *Federal Express*, Av São Luiz 187, is reliable.

International Telephone R 7 de Abril 295, near Praça da República. **Telecommunications** Embratel, Av São Luís 50, and Av Ipiranga 344.

Places of Worship St Paul's Anglican (Episcopal) Church, R Comendador Elias Zarzua 1231, Santo Amaro, T 246-0383. **Igreja Metodista**, Av Liberdade 659, T 278-5895. **Adventist**, R Jaguá 88, T 279-8206. **Presbyterian**, R Néstor Pestanha 106, T 255-6111. **Mormon Church**, Av Prof Francisco Morato 2430, T 570-2483. **Synagogue** Congregação Shalom, R Comendador Elias Zarzur 568, Israelita Paulista, R Antonio Carlos 553. **Templo Budista**, Av do Cursino 753, T 63-4015. **Lutheran church**, Av Rio Branco 34. **Swedish Church**, Igreja Evangelica Luterana Escandinava, R Job Lane 1030, T 247 88 29.

Shopping All types of stores at **Shopping Centers Iguatemi, Ibirapuera** and **Morumbi**, (see p 416), also **El Dorado Shopping Centre** (corner of Av Rebouças and Marginal Pinheiros). Souvenirs from *Mimosa*, Joaquim Nabuco 275, Brookin Paulista; *Artindia*, R Augusta 1371, loja 119 (Galeria Ouro Velho), T 283-2102; *Coisarada*, R Tabapuã 390, Itaim Bibi (T 881-4810); *Casa dos Amazonas*, Av São Luis 187, Galeria Metrópole, loja 14; *Ceará Meu Amor*, R Pamplona 1551, Loja 7, good quality lace from the NE. *H Stern*, jewellers, at Praça da República 242, R Augusta 2340 and at Iguatemi, Ibirapuera and Morumbi shopping centres and main hotels; designer jewellery, *Our Collection*, R São Benedito 1747, Alto da Boa Vista. *Tatuagem Polaco*, R 24 de Maio, is a professional and hygienic tattoo parlour, who will work to your own designs. Haggling with the price is suggested, but maybe not too much. Open air markets: **"Hippy" fair**, Praça da República, daily 0800-1400, very varied, many tourists, good selection of inexpensive fossils, Bahian food, lots of artists, items from Peru and Bolivia; **"Oriental" fair**, Praça de Liberdade Sun pm, good for Japanese snacks, plants and some handicrafts, very picturesque, with remedies on sale, tightrope walking, gypsy fortune tellers, etc. Below the Museu de Arte de São Paulo, an **antiques** market takes place on Sun, 0800-1700. There are **flea markets** Suns in the main square of the Bixiga district (Praça Don Orione) and in Praça Benedito Calixto in Jardim América. **Embu** is an enjoyable, touristy market ½ hr from Eldorado shopping by special bus. São Paulo is relatively cheap for film and clothes (especially shoes). The **Ceasa flower market** should not be missed, Av Doutor Gastão Vidigal 1946, Jaguaré, Tues and Fri 0700-1200. **Handicraft market** at Praça Campos de Bagatelle, Sun 0800-1300.

Bookshops *Livraria Cultura*, Av Paulista 2073, Conjunto Nacional, new books in English; *Ilco*, Barão do Triúnfo 371, Brookin Paulista, books in English. *Livraria Kosmos*, Praça Dom José Caspar 134, loja 30, international stock. *Livraria Alemã*, R Laplace 159, Brooklin; *Librairie Française*, R Barão de Itapetininga 275, 6th floor, wide selection. *Free Book*, R da

Consolação 1924, T 256-0577, ring bell for entry, wide collection of art books. *Letraviva*, Av Rebouças 2080, Mon-Fri 0900-1830, Sat 0900-1400, specializes in books and music in Spanish. *Book Centre*, R Gabus Mendes 29 loja 5, Consolação area books in English and German. *Duas Cidades*, R Bento Freitas 158, nr República, good selection of Brazilian and Spanish American literature. *Cinema Elétrico*, R Augusta 973, Centro, and *Sola Cinemateca*, R Fradique Coutinho 361, sell postcards and books on cinema and art.

Camera Repairs T Tanaka Cia Ltd repair Nikon cameras, very helpful. Canon and other makes: *Cine Camera Service*, R Cons Crispiano 97, 2nd floor.

Sport The most popular is association football. The most important matches are played at Morumbi and Pacaembu grounds. At Interlagos there is a first-class racing track (see p 428). There is yachting, sailing and rowing on the Santo Amaro reservoir. For nature trails, etc, Free Way, R Leôncio de Carvalho 267, Paraíso, T 285-4767/283-5983.

Golf Courses About half an hour's drive from the centre there are 18-hole golf courses, at the São Paulo Golf Club, Praça Dom Francisco Souza 635, in Santo Amaro, in beautiful surroundings; Clube de Golf de Campinas, Via Anhanguera, Km 108, Campinas; Clube de Campo São Paulo and Guarapiranga Golf e Country, both at Reprêsa Guarapiranga, Estrada Paralheiros, Km 34; São Fernando Golf Club, Estrada de Cotia, Km 29; a lakeside club at Km 50 on the Santos road. Outside the city are Terras de São José, Itú, 110 km; PL Golf in Arujá; Bastos golf club, 400 km.

9-hole courses at São Francisco club, Estrada de Osasco, Km 15; Anglo Sports Center, Barretos; International golf club, Via Dutra Km 232, Guaratinguetá; PL Golf and Arujá Golf Club, in Arujá; Lago Azul Golf Club, Araçoiaba da Serra, 120 km. from city. There are also two 9-hole courses in Santos (see p 429).

Travel Agents *Woehrle Turismo*, R do Tesouro 47, CEP 01013, T 37-7594, USA T (011) 532-1105, helpful, German spoken; *Lema Turismo*, Av Marquês de Itú 837, personalised excursions, Marta Schneider speaks 8 languages, including Hungarian; *Tunibra*, Praça da Liberdade 63, T 36-0101, helpful; *Itatiaia Publicidade e Turismo*, Cons Crispiniano 69 (for hotel reservations especially); *Transatlântica Turismo*, R Coronel Xavier de Toledo 98 (for local excursions); *AmEx* office in *Hotel Sheraton Mofarrej*, Al Santos 1437, T 284-3515; *Kontik-Franstur* (American Express representative), R Marconi 71, T 259-4211. *Royal Turismo*, Manoel da Nóbrega off Av Paulista, helpful to budget travellers; *Student Travel*, Estados Unidos 153, T 887 4242; *Audiotur* (ask for Janice Kawasake), Estados Unidos 627, T 887-3400, gives information about trains. *Ambiental Viagens e Expedições*, Av Brigadeiro Faria Lima 1684-S/L 40, Jardim Paulista, T 814-8809, English and Spanish spoken, helpful, rec for trips to less well known places; *Terra Expedições*, Osmar e Valdir, R Silva Jardim 429, Sta Terezinha, Santo André, T 446-3381/447-3535, rec for motocycle tours and information, Spanish and Italian spoken (English improving). Visits to coffee fazendas (May-Jun) and round trips into the surrounding country are organized by the travel agencies.

Tourist Offices Praça da República (very helpful, most regularly open), Praça da Sé and Liberdade metro entrances, Praça Dom José Gaspar (corner Av São Luis); Av Augusta esq Av Paulista, R Barão de Itapetininga, near Teatro Municipal; excellent free map at all these offices. Office at Guarulhos airport is helpful. For information on São Paulo State, Praça Antônio Prado 9, 6th floor, Av São Luís 115. Very cheap tours leave tourist office at Praça da República every 1/2-hr Tues-Sat from 0900 to 1700 and Sun 0900-1600; there are 8 different itineraries visiting places of cultural interest. Each tour lasts approximately 3 hrs, tickets and full programme from tourist office in Praça da República, T 267-2122, ext 627/640, Mon-Fri, CMTC tours by metro on Sat-Sun from 0900-1000, 1400-1500 from Praça da Sé; information at Praça da Sé, T 229-3011. Tourist offices have free magazines in Portuguese and English: *Where* and *São Paulo This Month* (also available from most travel agencies and better hotels). Also recommended is Quatro Rodas guide to the City.

Maps of São Paulo in train timetables at news-stands (US$3.50), and in the monthly tourist guide published by the Prefeitura (US$0.70 - poor map but good for what's on). Also obtainable from the tourist offices, the rodoviária (upstairs), the better hotels, American Express and H Stern, the jeweller. Map shops: **Mapolândia**, 7 de Abril 125, shop 40; **Metrópole Mapas**, Av São Luís 153, Loja 1 (Galeria Metrópole). 2 private map producers: Geo Mapas, R Libero Badaró 336, CEP 01008, T 259-2166 (40% discount for volume purchases, excellent 1988 1:5,000,000 map of Brazil, town maps), and Editorial Abril, R do Cartume 769, bl G, 11° andar, Lapa, CEP 05066-900, T 831-0599, F 831-0599 ext 2270.

Police T 228-2276; Radio Patrol, T 190. Federal Police, Av Prestes Maio 700, open 1000-1600 for visa extensions.

Emergency and Ambulance T 192, no charge. **Fire** T 193.

Local Transport Local buses are normally crowded and rather slow, but clean. Maps of the bus and metro system are available at depots, and eg Anhangabaú. Taxis display cards of actual tariffs in the window, for "especial taxis", dearer but fewer hassles, T 223-1975 (Tele Taxi), call out charge US$1, calls not accepted from public phones.

Metro The metro, the first in Brazil, began operating in 1975. It has two main lines intersecting at Praça de Sé: N-S from Santana to Jabaquara; E-W from Corinthians Itaquera to Barra Funda (the interchange with Fepasa and RFFSA railways and site of the São Paulo and Paraná Rodoviária). A third line runs from Clínicas in the W, along Av Paulista, to Ana Rosa in the S, joining the Jabaquera line at Paraíso and Ana Rosa. The system is clean, safe, cheap and efficient; it operates from 0500-2400. Fare US$0.50, book of ten tickets US$5; backpacks are allowed. Combined bus and metro ticket are available, eg to Congonhas airport.

Motorcycle repairs BMW São Paulo, R Funchal 551, CEP 04551, São Paulo, T 820-8633, few parts but helpful and they have all BMW motorcycle special tools; can order parts from Miami.

Air Services There are air services to all parts of Brazil, Europe, North and South America from the new international airport at Guarulhos, also known as Cumbica, Av Monteiro Lobato 1985, T 945-2111 (30 km from the city). Varig has its own, new terminal for international flights, adjoining the old terminal which all other airlines use. Money exchanges open 0800-2200 daily, post office, etc, 2 information booths. The local airport of Congonhas, 14 km from the city centre, is used for the Rio-São Paulo shuttle, some flights to Belo Horizonte and Vitória and private flights only. From Guarulhos there are airport taxis which charge US$27 on a ticket system (go to the second booth on leaving the terminal and book a Co-op taxi at the Taxi Comum counter, the best value). Fares from the city to the airport are higher and vary from cab to cab. Emtu bus service every 30 mins to Guarulhos from Praça da República (NW side, corner of R Arouche), US$8.50, very comfortable (in airport buy ticket at booth in Domestic Arrivals); the same company runs services from Guarulhos to Tietê (hourly), Congonhas airport (hourly 0600-2200) and Av Paulista (hourly 0600-0700 from airport to 2100, passing in front of, or near many major hotels on its route to the city: *Bristol, Brasilton, Cá d'Oro, Caesar Park, Della Volpe, Crowne Plaza, Sheraton, Maksoud Plaza*). Cheap buses from Bresser and Jabaquara bus terminals to Guarulhos, without luggage space, usually crowded. Inter-airport bus US$12. There are about four hundred flights per week to Rio de Janeiro (US$300 return). All airline offices in triangle formed by Av São Luís, Av Ipiranga and R da Consolação.

Air freight Varig will send anything, anywhere, but involves some red tape.

Railways São Paulo has four stations: **1) Estação da Luz**, T 225-0040/991-3062, for long-distance trains to **Ribeirão Preto** and **Campinas**; trains from Campinas go to **Araguari** via **Uberlândia**, dep 2345 (the Campinas-Brasília line had no passenger service in 1994-95). Express trains to **São José do Rio Preto**. The rail link to Bauru, Campo Grande and Corumbá was, in 1994, only running on the Campo Grande-Corumbá section, beyond which, after crossing frontier by road, trains run from Quijarro (Bolivia) to Santa Cruz de la Sierra by the Estrada de Ferro Brasil-Bolívia (**see p 582**). Also from Luz, 8 trains a day to Campinas.

2) A new terminal, **Barra Funda**, T 991-3043, has a metro station and handles Sorocabana and Santos a Jundiaí commuter services; all long distance trains into and out of Luz stop at Barra Funda; a new, weekend service "down the hill" to **Santos** dep Barra Funda 0820, arr Santos 1205, return—in the dark—1700 (superb scenery); express from Barra Funda to **Presidente Prudente**, about 15 hrs, daily at 2135, all facilities, reservations essential.

3) **Júlio Prestes station**, T 702-1400, for commuter services to SW of the state (former Sorocabana); **4) Rosevelt**, T 292-5417, for commuters to Mogi das Cruzes (ex Central do Brasil) and eastern suburbs. Slower meter guage trains to Pres Prudente.

Buses To get to the main rodoviária (T 235-0322), take the metro to Tietê, very convenient. Left luggage US$0.80 per day per item. You can sleep in the bus station after 2200 when the guards have gone; tepid showers US$2.50. Bus to centre, US$0.60. Buses to the interior of São Paulo state, all state capitals and international buses (see next paragraph): to **Rio**, 6 hrs, every 30 mins, US$12 (leito, 24), special section for this route in the rodoviária; request the coastal route ("via litoral") unless you wish to go the direct route; to **Porto Alegre**, 18 hrs, US$30 (leito, 60); **Belo Horizonte**, 10 hrs, US$7.25; buy ticket and get on bus at Terminal Bresser; **Salvador**, 30 hrs, US$58 (leito, 16); **Recife**, 40 hrs, US$80 (leito, 160); **Cuiabá**, 24 hrs, US$40; **Porto Velho**, 60 hrs (or more), US$90; **Brasília**, 16 hrs, US$24 (leito, 48); **Foz do Iguaçu**, 16 hrs, US$29 (leito, 58); **São Sebastião**, 4 hrs US$7.80 (say "via Bertioga" if you want to go by the coast road, beautiful journey but few buses take this route—ferry from São Sebastião for Ilhabela). To **Santos**, US$3 (there is a bus station for Santos and São Vicente at the southern end of the Metro line, at Jabaquara, buses from here leave every 5 mins, taking about 50 mins). There are two other bus terminals, Barra Funda, T 235-0322 or 66-4682 (same as metrô and rail station), to cities in southern São Paulo state and many destinations in Paraná;

Bresser, T 299-0177 (Cometa) or 267-7411 (Transul), for destinations in Minas Gerais.

To **Montevideo**, via Porto Alegre, with TTL, departs 2200, 31 hrs, US$58 (leito 116—early booking recommended) cold a/c at night, plenty of meal stops, bus stops for border formalities, passengers disembark only to collect passport and tourist card on Uruguayan side. To **Buenos Aires**, Pluma, 36 hrs, US$145; to **Santiago**, Pluma or Gral Urquiza (both start from Rio), 56 hrs, US$110 (leito US$220), Chile Bus, Av Paulista 1009, SL 1909, T 251-5388, or Terminal Tietê, T 267-6239, US$107 (poor meals, but otherwise good, beware overbooking); to **Asunción** (1,044 km), 18 hrs with Pluma or RYSA, US$33 (leito US$48); to **Puerto Suárez** (Quijarro, Bolivia), 22 hrs.

Roads   To take the beautiful coast road to Rio, take the Via Anchieta to the Guarujá turn, before Guarujá take Bertioga turn and you're on the Santos-Rio highway. Motorists leaving the ring road for Curitiba and Iguaçu should follow Regis de Bittencourt signs. To hitch to Rio, take the metro to Ponte Pequeno, then a bus to Guarulhos, alighting where the bus turns off the Rio road for Guarulhos.

City Excursions   The Butantã Snake Farm and Museum   Av Dr Vital Brasil 1500, Pinheiros, is the most popular tourist attraction. The snakes are milked for their poison six times a day but you may not witness this; the antidotes made from the venom have greatly reduced deaths from snakebite in Brazil. It also deals with spider and scorpion venom, has a small hospital and is a biomedical research institute. Open daily from 0900-1700 (except Mon), entrance US$1.50. Informative museum; details in English and Portuguese. From Praça da República take bus marked "Butantã" or "Cidade Universitária" (Nos 701U or 792U) along Av Paulista, and ask to be let out at Instituto Butantã.

Parque da Independência, in the suburb of Ipiranga, contains the famous Ipiranga Monument to commemorate the declaration of Brazilian independence; beneath the monument is the Imperial Chapel, with the tomb of the first emperor, Dom Pedro I, and Empress Leopoldina (open Tues-Sun, 1300-1700). Take bus 4612 from Praça da República. The **Casa do Grito**, the little house in which Dom Pedro I spent the night before his famous cry of Ipiranga— "**Independence or Death**"—is preserved in the park (open Tues-Sun 0930-1700). The **Museu Paulista**, housed in a huge palace at the top of the park, has old maps, traditional furniture, collections of old coins and of religious art and rare documents, and a department of Indian ethnology. Behind the Museum is the Ipiranga Botanical Garden. Open Tues-Sun and holidays, 0900-1700. Take bus 478-P (Ipiranga-Pompéia for return) from Ana Rosa. There is a *son et lumière* show on Brazilian history in the park on Wed, Fri and Sat evenings at 2030.

Parque do Estado   (Jardim Botânico), out at Água Funda (Av Miguel Estefano 3687), has a vast garden esplanade surrounded by magnificent stone porches, with lakes and trees and places for picnics, and a very fine orchid farm worth seeing during the flowering season, Nov-Dec. Over 32,000 different kinds of orchids are cultivated. Open Tues-Fri, 0900-1130, 1230-1700, Sat-Sun 0900-1600. The astronomical observatory nearby is open to the public Thur afternoons. Take metro to São Judas on Jabaquara line, then bus.

Zoological Gardens   Av Miguel Estefano 4241, near the Jardim Botânico, not more than half an hour's drive from the city centre. A very large variety of specimens can be seen in an almost natural setting of about 35 hectares of forest: a most interesting site. Open 0900-1700, admission US$0.45 (bus 4742, "Jardim Celeste", from São Judas). There is a wild-life park, Simba Safari, nearby, admission US$0.80 per pedestrian, US$3 pp with a car (children under 11 free), open Tues-Fri 1000-1630, Sat-Sun 0900-1630 (1730 in summer).

Parque Água Branca   (Avenida Água Branca 455) has beautiful gardens with specimens of tropical plants, Brazilian birds and wild life. Pavilions house a well stocked aquarium, a zoo, and exhibitions of food produce.

In Tremembé, a little beyond Cantareira, $1/2$-hr from the down-town area, is the **Horto Florestal** (R do Horto, in Parque Estadual da Cantareira, 7,900 ha), containing examples of nearly every species of Brazilian woodland flora, 15 km of natural trails, museum with exhibits of regional flora and fauna, view of São Paulo from Pedra Grande on the right of entrance to the park (admission US$0.80, daily, 0700-1730).

Miraporanga Botanical and Wildlife Sanctuary in the foothills of the Serra do Mar, is 1 hr's drive from São Paulo city centre. It is a 100 ha botanist's paradise, with a vast collection of orchids, carnivorous and aquatic plants, waterlily pools, a lake and 20 glasshouses. It also contains armadilloes, deer and other mammals, monitor lizards and a variety of hummingbirds, T Sr Samuel Jorge de Mello, 816-0817, weekends 476-6716 for information on times and prices of admission.

Santo Amaro Dam   (Old Lake), is 3 km from the centre of Santo Amaro suburb. This is a popular boating resort with several sailing clubs and many attractive cottages along the shore. There is a bus (30 min) from São Paulo to Santo Amaro.

Interlagos (Av Interlagos, T 577-0522), which has a motor-racing circuit with 18 km of track, is São Paulo's lake resort on the Santo Amaro dam. It can be reached from Santo Amaro by bus. Close to the track, where the Brazilian Grand Prix takes place every second year, usually in Feb, is the 32-km long Guarapiranga artificial lake with good restaurants and several luxurious sailing and sports clubs (Av Guarapiranga 575, open 0600-1700 daily). Camping Clube do Brasil site. Guarapiranga is less polluted than the other artificial lake, Billings, which also has restaurants.

Pico de Jaraguá (1,135m) the highest peak in the neighbourhood, gives good views of Greater São Paulo on a fine day. Lots of hang gliding here at weekends, many people go to watch. This peak is reached from Km 18 on the Campinas highway (Via Anhanguera) by a good road through Taipas and Pirituba.

Embu (pop 138,520), 28 km from São Paulo, is a colonial town which has become a centre for artists and craftsmen. On Sun afternoons there is a large and popular arts and crafts fair (0900-1800); not to be missed. Buses from close to the Largo de Pinheiros, São Paulo, or Santo Amaro bus.

The Coast of the State of São Paulo

Santos, (pop 428,525, CEP 11000, DDD 0132) 63 km SE of São Paulo and 5 km from the open sea, is the most important Brazilian port. (Over 40% by value of all Brazilian imports and about half the total exports pass through it.) It is reached from Rio by ship (320 km) in 12-15 hrs, and a direct highway between the two cities has been completed (see p 389 and 430). A railway and the Anchieta and Imigrantes highways run to São Paulo. A free-port zone for Paraguay, 1,930 km by rail or road, has been established. A few km outside the city there is an important industrial area round the steelworks, oil refinery and hydroelectric plant at Cubatão (once known locally as the Valley of Death because of the pollution from chemical factories, now largely cleaned up).

The plain upon which the city of Santos stands is an island which can be circumnavigated by small boats. The city has impressive modern buildings, wide, tree-lined avenues, and wealthy suburbs. The streets around Praça Mauá are very busy in the daytime, with plenty of cheap shops. In the centre, an interesting building is the Bolsa Oficial de Café, in R 15 de Novembro. The night-life is best in the Gonzaga area which has the large hotels. Although best known for its commerce, Santos is also a holiday resort, with magnificent beaches, all declared polluted at the end of 1990, and views. The port is approached by the winding Santos Channel; at its mouth is an old fort (1709). It is sometimes possible to visit naval ships, for details see the local press.

There are many monuments: one in Avenida Ana Costa to commemorate the brothers Andradas, who took a leading part in the movement for independence; one in the Praça Rui Barbosa to Bartolomeu de Gusmão, who has a claim to the world's first historically recorded airborne ascent in 1709; one in the Praça da República to Bras Cubas, who founded the city in 1534; and one in the Praça José Bonifácio to the soldiers of Santos who died in the Revolution of 1932. There are a disappointing municipal aquarium on Av Bartolomeu de Gusmão (Ponta da Praia) and a Museu do Mar, R República do Equador 81. In the eastern district of José Menino are the orchid gardens in the Praça Washington (flowering Oct-Feb). There is an open-air cage containing humming-birds of 20 different species and the park is a sanctuary for other birds.

Local Holidays (in addition to national): 26 Jan (Foundation of Santos); Good Fri; Corpus Christi.

Hotels A2 *Mendes Plaza*, Av Floriano Peixoto 42, T 37-4243, F 4-8253; **A2** *Parque Balneario*, complex at the centre of Gonzaga, Ana Costa 555, T 34-7211, F 4-0475, with shopping centre; **B** *Mendes Panorama*, R Euclides da Cunha 15, T 37-2627, F 4-8253; **B** *Atlântico*, Av Pres Wilson 1, T 37-8823, F 37-8837, good value. Beach front hotels on Av Pres Wilson: **A3** *Gonzaga*, No 36, T 4-1411, with bath, poor value; **B** *Avenida Palace*, No 10, T 4-1166; **B** *Maracanã Santos*, No 172, T 37-4030; **B** *Indaiá*, Av Ana Costa 431, T 4-1134; *Transmontana*, R Marechal Floriano Peixoto 202, rec; **B** *Santos*, Bartolomeu de Gusmão 16, with bath; small, family-style hotels can be found in this area. Many cheap hotels near the Orquidário Municipal (Praça Washington), 1-2 blocks from the beach. **E** *Vilazul*, Av Sen Feijo, clean, a/c, breakfast.

Restaurants *Cibus*, Av Vicente de Carvalho 1, beach end, considered the best; *Hong Kong Palace*, Av Conselheiro Nébias 288 (Chinese food); *Penhasco*, Ilha Porchat; first class *Pizzaria Zi Tereza*, Av Ana Costa 449; *Churrascaria Tertúlia*, Av Bartolomeu de Gusmão 187, T36-1461.

Banks Banco Internacional, R General Câmara 24; Banco Holandês Unido, Citibank, Banco do Brasil, all in the R 15 de Novembro. The First National Bank of Boston, Praça Visc de Mauá 14. Banks open: 1000-1630.

Exchange Houses Casa Faro, R 15 de Novembro, 80 & 260; Casa Bancaria Branco, Praça de República 29 and Gonzaga, R Galeão Carvalhal 52/4.

Consulates British, R Tuiuti 58, 2nd floor, Caixa Postal 204, T 33-6111/34-6656. Danish, R Frei Gaspar 22, 10th floor, 106, CP 726, T 355-165, open 1000-1100, 1500-1700.

Electric Current 220 AC 60 cycles.

Telecommunications Embratel, Largo Senador Vergueiro 1 and 2.

All Saints Church Praça Washington 92, José Menino. Services in English held every Sun.

Golf Courses Two 9-hole courses: Santos Golf Club, Av Pérsio de Queiroz Filho, São Vincente; Guarujá Golf Club (see below and, above, under São Paulo).

Tourist Information Praça dos Expedicionários 10, 10th floor; booths at Aquarium (Av Bartolomeu de Gusmão, Ponta da Praia), rodoviária, Casa do Café, Orquidário Municipal.

Taxis All taxis are supplied with meters. The fare is a fixed charge of US$0.50 plus US$0.20 per km. Taxi, Gonzaga to bus station, US$4.

Air Services At São Paulo; Santos has no airport.

Rail The British-built Santos a Jundiaí up the hill to São Paulo is one of the railway wonders of the world; it passes through Cubatão and then, running on toothed tracks up the escarpment, interesting hill scenery. The schedule for weekend passenger services is given under São Paulo. From Ana Costa station, a Fepasa (mixed) train may be taken to Embu Guaçu from where there is a bus to São Paulo.

Coastal Shipping Irregular services to Brazilian ports by Companhia de Navegação Lóide Brasileiro. Consult their agents, R General Câmara 22, 2nd floor, conjunto 34.

Bus Services Buses start for most suburbs from Praça Mauá, in the centre of the city. There are buses to **São Paulo** (50 mins, US$2.40) at intervals of approximately 15 mins, from the rodoviária near city centre. Enquire about being picked up or put down outside usual terminal points. Express cars also run to São Paulo at regular intervals. Fare, US$4.50 each way, per passenger. (The two highways between São Paulo and Santos are sometimes seriously crowded, especially at rush hours and weekends.) Buses for Santos are caught in São Paulo in the Jabaquara bus station, not the Tietê rodoviária. There are direct buses to **Rio** (Normandy company, 6 a day, 7½ hrs, US$10, leito at 2230, US$19); to Rio along the coast road is via São Sebastião, Caraguatatuba, Ubatuba and Parati.

Excursions The *Ilha Porchat*, a small island reached by a bridge at the far end of Santos/São Vicente bay, has beautiful views over rocky precipices, of the high seas on one side and of the city and bay on the other. The Praias dos Milionários and São Vincente were officially declared polluted at the end of 1990. At the summit is a splendid nightclub, the *Top House Restaurante e Discoteca*. No entrance fee but there is a minimum charge of US$10.

To **Alto da Serra**, the summit of the forest-clad mountain range; magnificent views. The return journey can be done in under 2 hrs by road.

Monte Serrat A funicular railway to the summit, where there is a semaphore station and look-out post which reports the arrival of all ships in Santos harbour, has not been operating since 1992. There is also a quaint old church, dedicated to Nossa Senhora da Monte Serrat, said to have performed many miracles. The top can be reached on foot. Seven shrines have been built on the way up; annual pilgrimages are made by the local people. Fine views.

Guarujá (pop 206,750).The route from Santos to the resort of Guarujá is along Av Conselheiro Nébias to the seafront, continuing along the beach to the Guarujá ferry (every 10 min, free for pedestrians) at Ponta da Praia. On the other side proceed as far as Enseada das Tartarugas (Turtle Bay). During the season and weekends there is a long delay at the Ponta da Praia vehicle ferry; to avoid this take the ferry on foot and get the bus on the Guarujá side; motor boats also cross for US$0.10. There is a strong undertow on nearly all the Guarujá beaches; the

Jequiti-Mar beach (officially called Praia de Pernambuco) is the safest. The beaches are built-up and polluted. Golf club at Guarujá. (Trolleybus from Praça Mauá in Santos to the ferry, then buses.)

Turn left in centre of Guarujá and drive less than 1 km to reach **L2** *Delphin Hotel* and its restaurant *La Popote* at the beginning of the long beach of Praia da Enseada. Close by, at Av Miguel Stefano 999, is **L2** *Casa Grande Hotel*, luxury, in colonial style, with clean beach. Facing sea is the luxurious **A1** *Ferraretto Hotel* (nightclub, swimming pool). Camping Clube do Brasil site at Praia do Perequê (where the best fish restaurants are), near municipal nursery. Good *churrascaria* opposite Rodoviária.

The Jequiti-Mar holiday complex, 8 km beyond Guarujá on the road to Bertioga, is extremely attractive. There are private beaches (excellent swimming and boating) and very fine fishing grounds, and chalet accommodation, A1-3, according to size and situation. There is an excellent restaurant and two nightclubs; they are open each weekend and every night from Dec to Mar, in the holiday season. 2 km further N is a beach where fishing boats land their catch—a number of good seafood restaurants line the seafront.

There are good sea-food restaurants on the road to **Bertioga**, an overcrowded place, where the fort of São João houses the João Ramalho museum (bus Guarujá-Bertioga, 1 hr, US$0.30). (Hotels: *Marazul*, Av Tomé de Souza 825; *Indaiá Praia*, same street, No 1079, both **A2**; restaurants include *Zezé e Duarte*.) The coastal road beyond Bertioga is paved, and the new Rio-Santos highway, 1-2 km inland, is completed, and provides a good link to São Sebastião. Going NE, the beaches are Praia de Bertioga, Praia São Lourenço, Praia Guaratuba and Praia Boracéia (campsite, meals served). 30 km beyond Boracéia is the beach resort of Maresia (hotels, campsite), from where it is 21 km to **São Sebastião** (pop 32,845, CEP 11600, DDD 0124). There is a Museu de Arte Sacra in the chapel of São Gonçalo in the town centre. Tourist Office: Av Dr Altino Arantes 174, friendly and helpful except regarding Ilhabela. The beaches within 2-3 km of São Sebastião harbour were officially declared polluted at the end of 1990; others, Barra do Una, Boiçucanga, Praia da Balcia, are clean and very inviting. Ilhabela tends to be expensive in season, when it is cheaper to stay in São Sebastião.

Accommodation Foreigners can stay in the Camping Clube do Brasil grounds for US$4 a night. 6 km S of São Sebastião is Camping do Barraquecaba Bar de Mar de Lucas, hot showers, English spoken, cabins available, rec. **D** *Hotel Roma*, on the main square, T 52-1016, has more expensive rooms, excellent, very well rec; **B** *Recanto dos Pássaros*, Porto Grande, T 52-2046; **A2** *Arrastão*, T 62-0099, most facilities.

Transport Two buses a day from Rio, 0830 and 2300, to Rio 0600 and 2330, heavily booked in advance; 4 a day from Santos, 3½ hrs; buses from São Paulo (US$8) run inland via São José dos Campos, unless you ask for the service via Bertioga, only 2 a day. Free ferry to Ilhabela (4 hrs by bus from Santos, 3 a day, US$6).

Halfway between Bertioga and São Sebastião, on the Praia de Juqueí beach, are **B** *Hotel Timão*, German-owned, with excellent fish meals; **L3** *Encanto da Praia*, with dinner, on the hill leading to Barra da Una, rec. 45 km S of São Sebastião is **Camburi**, surrounded by the Mata Atlântica. The sea is clean and good for bathing and watersports, including surfing. There are a number of good hotels and restaurants (**A2** *Pousada da Rosa*, R das Rosas 139, T 0124-651412, **B** in low season, with bath and breakfast, clean, friendly, pool). 3 daily buses from São Paulo, 160 km, en route to São Sebastião/Ilhabela, US$6. You can walk on the Estrada do Piavú into the Mata Atlântica to see streams, vegetation and wildlife (bathing in the streams is permitted, but use of shampoo and other chemicals is forbidden). 5 km from Camburi is Praia Brava, reached by 45 mins' walk through the forest, camping and nude bathing possible. Between Juquey and São Sebastião, **Maresias** is an in-place for surfers; fashionable young crowd. Several hotels in town: **A2** *Maresias Praia*, on beach. *Mr Harris Jazz Bar*, rec.

Ilha de São Sebastião (Ilhabela). The island of São Sebastião, known popularly as Ilhabela, is now easily accessible by car or bus from Santos. A bus runs along the coastal strip facing the mainland. Cavendish, the English pirate, had his secret anchorage in one of the sheltered caves there. Last century it was used as a landing place for illegal slave-traffic.

The island is of volcanic origin, roughly about 390 sq km in area. Its highest peak, Morro do Papagaio, rises 1,300m above sea-level, with its bare peak often obscured by mist; the slopes are densely wooded. There are many beautiful waterfalls, easily accessible to the enterprising walker. Most of the flatter ground is given over to sugar-cane.

The only settled district lies on the coastal strip facing the mainland, the Atlantic side being practically uninhabited except by a few fisherfolk. The place abounds in tropical plants and flowers of the most extraordinary variety, and many fruits grow wild, whose juice mixed with cachaça and sugar makes as delicious a cocktail as can be imagined.

No alterations are allowed to the frontage of the main township, *Ilhabela* (pop 9,500). Visitors abound during summer week-ends; motorists are warned to avoid those days as the car-carrying capacity of the ferry is very limited. It is, however, a nice place to relax on the beach, with good food and some good value accommodation.

The energetic can climb over the hump of the island down towards the Atlantic, sometimes through dense tropical forest following the old slave trail, but for this 50-km return journey a local guide is required. There is a rough road to the Atlantic side, but it is very difficult to drive. A visit to the terraced Toca waterfalls amid dense jungle close to the foot of the 970-metre Baepi peak will give you cool freshwater bathing (entry, US$0.50). In all shady places, especially away from the sea, there abounds a species of midge known locally as *borrachudos*. A locally sold repellant (Autan) keeps them off for some time, however. Those allergic to insect bites should remain on the inhabited coastal strip. There is a small hospital (helpful) by the church in town.

Hotels in Ilhabela: **L2** *Ilhabela*, Av Pedro Paulo de Morais 151, T 72-1083, F 72-1031, good breakfast, rec; **L2** *Mercedes*, T 72-1071. Next door to *Ilhabela* is **A1** *Itapemar*, T 72-1329, F 72-1329, windsurfing equipment rented. **A3** *Colonial*, Av Brasil 1541, T 72-1033; **A3** *Petit Village*, Morro da Cruz 241, T 72-1393; **A3** *Pousada dos Hibiscos*, Av PP de Morais 714, T 72-1375, good atmosphere, swimming pool, rec; **B** *Solar dos Bandeirantes*, Bertini 165, T 72-1065. There are several other less expensive hotels in B-C range, mostly on the road to the left of the ferry. *Camping Porto Seguro*, accessible by two-hourly bus from Ilhabela.

Restaurant *Perequê*, Av Princesa Isabel 337, reasonable. *Farol*, Av Princesa Isabel 1634, Perequê, good, especially seafood, rec.

Sightseeing Visit the old Feiticeira plantation, with underground dungeons. The road is along the coast, sometimes high above the sea, towards the S of the island. You can go by bus, taxi, or horse and buggy. *Gipsy Tur*, T 72-1518, helpful.

Pedras do Sino (Bell Rocks) These curious seashore boulders, when struck with a piece of iron or stone, emit a loud bell-like note. Another campsite nearby.

Bathing Bathing on the mainland side is not recommended because of oil, sandflies and jelly fish on the beaches and in the water. Praia dos Castelhanos, reached by a rough road over the island (no buses), is recommended.

Transport Passenger ferry every 2 hrs; stops at Perequê and Ilhabela; car ferry runs through the night and serves Perequê only (fare for cars is US$7 weekdays, double at weekends).

North of São Sebastião, on the Santos-Rio road, is São Francisco, a village with *Pontal Hotel* (not rec, expensive, noisy), good beaches. Further on is *Caraguatatuba* (pop 52,915) with 17 good beaches to the NE and SW (several hotels, popular at weekends, good restaurants). Good camping site on beach and other sites. Direct buses to Caraguatatuba from Rio de Janeiro, São Paulo and Santos; direct buses from São Paulo do not use the coast road. Further E is *Lagoinha*, 34 km W of Ubatuba, with chalets and sailing boats for hire. Exotic birdlife and virgin forest. *Maier's Mar Virado* is owned by Hans Maier, who speaks English and arranges hirings. Next is *Ubatuba*, (pop 47,295, CEP 11680, DDD 0124) with two Camping Clube do Brasil sites at Maranduba and Perequê-Açu beaches. In all, there are 72 beautiful beaches (Iperoig, Itaguá and Saco da Ribeira were officially declared polluted at the end of 1990), quite spread out, most with campsites (Grande, just S, and one 6 km N of Ubatuba are rec). There is also a yacht haven. The area gets very crowded at Carnival time as people from Rio come to escape the crowds in their city. At all holiday times it is expensive, with camping costing US$8 and no hotels less than US$15. Jewellery market on beach, Sats.

Ubatuba hotels A1 *Saveiros*, Praia do Lázaro T 42-0172, pool, restaurant, run by a Rumanian, Lucian Strass, who welcomes users of *South American Handbook*, English spoken; **A2** *Solar das Aguas Cantantes*, Praia do Lázaro, T 42-0178, reached by local bus, swimming pool, restaurant; **A3** *Tropicana*, Praia da Enseada, T 42-0461; **C** *Xaréu*, JH da Costa 413, T 32-1525, central near beach, clean, quiet, friendly, rec; *Mauricio*, Av Abreu Sodre 607, nr Praia do Perequê-Açu, has cheap rooms, friendly, clothes washing possible. **Youth Hostel** Cora Coralina, Rodovia Oswaldo Cruz, Km 89, T 229-3787/3011, ext (ramal) 286 for details. Furnished flats and cottages may be rented from Lúcio Martins Rodrigues, R Amaral Gurgel 158, Apto 121—CEP 01221, Vila Buarque, São Paulo; T 853-8101, 532-0496.

The road from São Sebastião is paved, so a journey from São Paulo along the coast is possible,

5 buses daily. 25 km S of Ubatuba at Baia Fortaleza is *Refugio de Corsário*, T 43-1126, C and up, a clean quiet hotel on the water front, sailing and swimming, a good place to relax. Ubatuba is 70 km from Parati (**see p 391**), several buses daily, on the hour, from *Lanchonete Nice*, near Rodoviária. If driving from Ubatuba along the coast to Rio, one can stop for lunch at Porto Aquarius, where there is a cave and hotel in a beautiful setting (not cheap). Direct buses from Rio, São Paulo and Santos.

Straddling the border of São Paulo and Rio de Janeiro states is the **Parque Nacional Serra da Bocaina**, which rises from the coast to heights of over 1,900m, encompassing three strata of vegetation (Ibama, T 021-294-6497, or 0125-77-1225).

In the opposite direction (SW) from Santos, it is 50 km beside the Praia Grande to the town of *Itanhaém* (pop 33,210) with its pretty colonial church and semi-ruined Convento da Conceição on a small hill. There are several good sea-food restaurants along the beach, and a Camping Clube do Brasil site nearby at Peruíbe beach, and many others which are cheaper. There are many attractive beaches here, and hot springs with medicinal mud (hotels *Maison Suisse*, *Príncipe*, *Glória*). The whole stretch of coast is completely built up with holiday developments. The beaches of Praia Grande and Itanhaém were officially declared polluted at the end of 1990. Frequent buses from Santos US\$1.50, 1 hr.

Further S is the town of *Iguape* (pop 27,890) founded in 1538. Typical Portuguese architecture, the small municipal museum is housed in a 16th century building. Buses from São Paulo, Santos, or Curitiba, changing at Registro (see below). It has a market, hotels and restaurants. (**C** *Hotel Silvi*, R Ana Cândida Sandoval Trigo 515, T 41-1421, with bath and breakfast, good; **C** *Hotel Rio Verde*, R Antônio José de Morais 86, T 41-1493, good rooms but humid; **D** *Hotel Pousada Aguape*, R Padre Homer). Camping Clube do Brasil site on beach. Opposite Iguape is the northern end of the Ilha Comprida with 86 km of beaches. A continuous ferry service runs from Iguape (passengers free; cars at a small charge); buses run until 1900 from the ferry stop to the beaches and campsite Britânia (clean, friendly, drinkable tap water, tastes bad). The island is being developed as a resort; good restaurants, hotels, supermarket—fresh fish is excellent. At the southern end **Cananéia** (pop 9,905) is more commercialized than Iguape; it has 3 or 4 hotels (mostly **C**).

From Iguape it is possible to take a boat trip down the coast to Cananéia and Ariri. Tickets and information from Dept Hidroviário do Estado, R Major Moutinho 198, Iguape, T 41 1122. Boats leave Iguape on Mon, Thur (but check in advance), returning next day, or bus back from Cananéia. It is a beautiful trip, passing between the island and the mainland. The boat has a toilet, fresh water, and meals. In wet weather, the cabin gets crowded and uncomfortable. Ariri has no road connections; there is a hostel, E, run by the shipping line.

Caves Inland, W of the BR-116 are the caverns of the Vale do Ribeira; among the best known is the 8-km **Gruta da Tapagem**, known as Caverna do Diabo (Devil's Cave—as huge "as a cathedral" with well-lit formations), 45 km from Eldorado Paulista. The caves are open 0800-1100 and 1200-1700; bar and toilets. **D** *Hotel Eldorado*, friendly, clean, with breakfast. Bus to Eldorado Paulista from Santos or São Paulo, US\$4.75, 4-5 hrs, then hitch-hike on banana trucks or tourist buses (which run from both cities); most traffic on Sat and Sun. From Curitiba, change buses at Jacupiranga for Eldorado Paulista. A suitable stopping place for visiting the caves area is *Registro* (pop 48,860) on BR-116, in the heart of the tea-growing region, populated mainly by Japanese Brazilians. (**C** *Lito Palace Hotel*, Av J Banks Leite 615, T 21-1055, F 21-4470; **F** *Hotel Brasília*, R Brasília, round corner from rodoviária, no breakfast, shower, clean, airy; good *Churrascaria* next to bus station, international telephone exchange in town centre). 43 km from Caverna do Diabo is **Caverna de Santana**, 10 km from the town of *Iporanga*; it has 5.6 km of subterranean passages and three levels of galleries. (Iporanga is the most convenient town for visiting both sets of caves; it is 42 km from Apiaí, which is 257 km SW of São Paulo.)

Towns in the State of São Paulo

About 13% of Brazil's population lives within 200 km of São Paulo city, a circle which includes 88 municipalities. Four of them—the big ABCD towns— sharing a population of over a million, are Santo André, São Bernardo, São Caetano and

Diadema; they have many of the largest industrial plants. There are some 70 cities in the State with populations of over 50,000 and São Paulo is linked with all of them by road, and several of them by railway. One important line, the broad-gauge Santos a Jundiaí, runs from Santos to São Paulo and across the low mountains which separate São Paulo city from the interior to its terminus at **Jundiaí** (pop 312,520, CEP 13200, DDD 011), 58 km from São Paulo, which has textile factories and other industries. The district grows coffee and grain and there is an annual Grape Festival.

Hotel *Grande Hotel*, R do Rosário 605, T 434-5355, with good restaurant.

Campinas (pop almost 1 million, CEP 13100, DDD 0192), 88 km from São Paulo by the fine Via Anhanguera highway (many buses, US$3), is important as a clearing point for coffee, for its Agricultural Institute, and its rapidly growing industries. The Viracopos international airport is 11 km from Campinas, which also has its own airport.

See fine cathedral, old market, colonial buildings, several museums (including Arte Contemporânea, Arquidiocesano, Carlos Gomes and, in the Bosque de Jequitibás, Histórico and Folclore), arts centre (noted symphony orchestra; the city is the birthplace of the noted 19th century Brazilian composer Carlos Gomes), and the modern university outside the city. Visits can be made to the Agricultural Institute to see all the aspects of coffee. A tourist train operates in Parque Taquaral.

Hotels L2 *Royal Palm Plaza* Praça Rotatória 88, T 2-9085, F 2-7085; **L2** *Solar das Andorinhas*, a health farm with pool, sauna, horses, sports, etc 18 km outside city on the Mogi-Mirim road, with meals, T 39-4411, F 39-5899. **L2** *Vila Rica*, R Donato Paschoal 100, T 31-5242; **A1** *Savoy*, R Regente Feijó 1064, T 32-9444, F 2-9207; **B** *Opala Avenida*, Av Campos Sales 161, T 8-4115, F 31-6983, central; **B** *Parati Palacio*, R Bernardino de Campos 426, T 32-0395/8368, German spoken, bath, TV, clean, rec.

Restaurants *Bar Restaurante Barão*, Barão de Jaguará 1381 and *Churrascaria Gaúcha*, Av Dr Campos Sales 515, excellent for Brazilian food. *Cenat*, R Barão de Jaguara 1260, 2nd floor, closed Sat (and Fri for dinner). *Nutrir*, R Dr Quirino 1620, vegetarian, very good value. *Sucão*, R Benjamin Constant 1108, good variety of juices.

Banks and Exchange The **First National Bank of Boston**, Av Francisco Glicério 1275, and local banks. Open 1000-1630. Good rates at Valortec, T 311-555.

Entertainment Nightlife on weekends is busy around the Centro de Convivência, Praça Imprensa Fluminense, in city centre. There are cinemas in the city centre and the Iguatemi and Galleria shopping centres.

Community Church Services in English at School of Language and Orientation, R Eduardo Lane 270.

Shopping H Stern jewellers at Shopping Centre Iguatemi. **Bookshops** *Pontes Editores*, R Dr Quirino 1223, has English books; second-hand at *Sebo Comércio*, R Bareto Leme 1265, and *O Livrão*, R B Jaguara 936, Loja 11.

Transport Trains and buses to São Paulo, Ribeirão Preto and Araguari, buses to Rio de Janeiro, 7 hrs, US$11.50. The metre-gauge Mogiana line, connecting with the broad-gauge Paulista at Campinas, serves the north-eastern part of the state. It goes through Ribeirão Preto to Uberlândia and Araguari in the Triângulo of Minas Gerais, a great area for fattening cattle which are trucked to the *frigoríficos* of São Paulo. No São Paulo-Ribeirão Preto tickets are sold, so you may have to wait a day at Campinas for a connection (or go by bus). From Araguari there is a line into the state of Goiás and to Brasília (no passenger services in 1995). 25 km from Campinas, at Jaguariúna, is a railway preservation group with steam engines and wagons; hourly bus from Campinas US$1, or take the steam train itself from Campinas (station behind Carrefour, Anhumas, reached by town bus), Sat and Sun, T 53-6067 for schedule. Tourist train one Sat a month to Peruibe, 0700, 6 hrs, run by Pettená-Tur.

Americana (pop 142,580), an interesting town, is 42 km from Campinas. This area was settled by Confederate refugees from the S of the USA after the Civil War. Most of the original settlers soon returned to the States, but some stayed, and there still exist reminders of their occupation here. A visit to the cemetery reveals an unusual number of English surnames. (**D** *Hotel Cacique*, R Wáshington Luís 143.)

Ribeirão Preto (pop 430,805, CEP 14100, DDD 016), the centre of a rich coffee-growing district, also has a steel industry. The town is 300 km from São Paulo by rail via Campinas or paved road (4 hrs by bus); airport has TAM flights to São Paulo, Rio, Poços de Caldas. Altitude, 420m. It is a distribution centre for the interior of São Paulo State and certain districts in Minas Gerais and Goiás. Products: coffee, cotton, sugar, grain and rice.

Hotels L3 *Holiday Inn*, R Alvares Cabral 1120, T 625-0186, F 635-1279; **A3** *Stream Palace*, R General Osório 850, T 636-0660, F 636-7834, with TV; **B** *Umuarama Recreio*, Praça dos Cafeeiros 140, T 637-3790, 6 km from centre, very pleasant, pool, gardens; **D** *Brasil*, R General Osório 20.

Some 115 km NW of Ribeirão Preto is **Barretos**, where, in the third week in Aug, the *Festa do Peão* is held. This is the biggest annual rodeo in the world. Trips from the UK are run by Last Frontiers, Swan House, High St, Long Crendon, Bucks, HP18 9AF, T/F 01844-208405.

All the southern part of the state and most of its western part are served by the metre-gauge Sorocabana railway. The main line runs from São Paulo through Sorocaba to Bauru, where it connects with the Noroeste, to Corumbá, 1,223 km. The line from a junction near Sorocaba extending (through connections with other lines) across the southern states to the border with Uruguay is for freight only.

Sorocaba (pop 377,270, CEP 18100), 110 km W of São Paulo, is an important industrial centre. The altitude is 540m, and the climate temperate. It has textile mills; produces cement, fertilizers, footwear, hats, alcohol, wines; there are railway workshops, extensive orange groves and packing house installations. It is an important cotton centre. Other products are timber, sugar, cereals, coffee, and minerals. Communications with São Paulo are better by road than by rail; the Castello Branco highway passes nearby.

Hotels B *Terminus*, Av General Carneiro 474, T 21-6970; **D** *Manchester*, R 15 de Novembro 21, basic, friendly.

There is a picturesque paved road along the Tietê valley from São Paulo to Bauru, via the colonial towns of Pirapora and Itu.

Pirapora de Bom Jesus (pop 7,935) is a popular place of pilgrimage, in a most attractive setting on both sides of the river. *Itu* (pop 106,870) was founded by the Bandeirantes in the 17th century. The beautiful falls of Salto de Itu, 8 km N, are flanked by a park and a textile mill.

Itu Hotels C *International*, R Barão do Itaím 93; **D** *Sabará*, Praça Padre Miguel 90.

Camping *Casarão do Carmo*, km 95 on the Jundiaí road; Itu, at km 90 on the Cabreúva road.

Bauru (pop 260,380, CEP 17100, DDD 0142) was founded at the end of the last century. Its points of interest include the Horto Florestal, an experimental forestry station opened in 1928, the Vitória Regia amphitheatre in the Parque das Nações and the Tenrikyo temple, R Newton Prado. It is used by Paulistanos as a weekend resort. Currency exchange is difficult.

Hotels A3 *Bekassin*, Av Duque de Caxias 1717, T 24-3700, swimming pool; **B** *Alvorada Palace*, R Primeiro de Agosto 619, T 22-5900. **C** *Colonial*, Praça Rui Barbosa 248, T 22-3191. Cheaper ones too, such as *Hotel Português* near bus station. To right of railway station exit is **D** *Cariani*, clean, good breakfast, rec; **D** *Estoril*, in alley behind *Cariani Hotel*, clean, safe, shared bath, family-run; opp railway station **D** *Lisboa*, clean, hot shower, restaurant, rec, very friendly; **E** *Phenix*, near railway station.

Restaurant *H 2 Churrascaria*, Piauí 8-55; *Cantina Bello Nápoli*, 1º de Agosto 6-52, cheap. Homemade ice-cream at sorveteria near *Hotel Lisboa*.

Transport Passenger services to Bauru were not running in 1995. Connections with São Paulo and Campo Grande (for Corumbá and Bolivia) must be made by bus.

Marília (pop 151,760), W of Bauru, is a pleasant clean town with a good hotel, **A3** *Sun Valley Park Hotel*, friendly. Texaco garage rec for car repairs, top of hill, Japanese owner. Express trains run to São Paulo, 2 a day, 1 night train with sleeper.

Ourinhos (pop 76,900), founded in 1924 near the border with Paraná state, is surrounded by sugar cane plantations. It is a possible stop-over on the road from São Paulo to Foz do Iguaçu or Campo Grande, although Londrina in Paraná is perhaps a more interesting city. (**Hotels**: **C** *Pousada Ourinhos*, R Mons Córdova 333, T 22-5898, good value; **D** *Comercial*, R Amornio Prado 38, friendly; a *dormitório* near the railway station. **Restaurants**: *Donna Maria*, rec; money exchange impossible.) It is on the railway which runs to Presidente Epitácio (**see p 466**) on the Paraná river. Further W is **Presidente Prudente** (pop 165,450) another useful place to make bus connections for Campo Grande (US$17), Porto Alegre, São Paulo, Ribeirão Preto, US$15, 9 hrs. **A1** *Hotel Aruá*, single rooms poor but doubles said to be nice; **D** *Hotel Alves* opp bus station, clean, nice but noisy.

Serra Negra (pop 21,660) is a very pleasant spa town and summer holiday resort up in the mountains at 1,080m, 145 km from São Paulo. Visitors tour the countryside in horse-drawn buggies. There are many first class hotels, a balneário and a small zoo.

Hotels **L2** *Rádio Hotel*, T 92-3311, very nice indeed, and several others.

Near Serra Negra is the even better-known spa town of Lindóia (pop 4,665), whose still waters are bottled and sent all over Brazil.

Another weekend resort, 70 km N of São Paulo on the Dom Pedro I highway, is **Atibaia** (pop 86,190); nearby is the strangely-shaped Pedra Grande mountain summit. There are two campsites, Pedra Grande, and Taba, which is near the *Hotel Village Eldorado* (with sports facilities, American-plan accommodation).

Campos do Jordão (pop 36,850), between Rio de Janeiro and São Paulo, is a mountain resort at 1,710m, in the Serra da Mantiqueira. It is prettily set in a long valley. The climate is cold and dry in winter and cool in summer, a great relief from the coastal heat and humidity. There are many hotels; but no airport, as yet.

The resort, about 190 km from São Paulo, is reached by an 87 km paved road from São José dos Campos, 100 km from São Paulo, on the Presidente Dutra (BR-116) highway. By car it takes about 3 hrs from São Paulo, 6 to 7 from Rio.

Places of Interest Palácio Boa Vista, 4 km from Abernéssia Centre, Governor's residence and museum, open Wed, Sat, Sun, 1000-1200, 1400-1700; Pedra do Baú (1,950m), to get there take a bus to São Bento do Sapucaí at 0800 or 1500, then walk to Paiol Grande and then on an unmarked path to the Pedra. Return buses from São Bento at 0915 and 1615. Near Paiol Grande is the small waterfall of Cachoeira dos Amores. Pico do Itapeva (2,030m) and Imbiri (1,950m) command a beautiful view of the Paraíba valley; see also Morro do Elefante (chairlift available); Gruta dos Crioulos; nature reserve at Horto Florestal (20 km), signposted from chairlift station, very pretty —go in the morning to avoid crowds; lots of streams with bridges, waterfalls nearby. Campos do Jordão is a popular place for hikers; most of the roads leading off the main avenue lead to quiet areas with nice views, eg up Av Dr Antônio Nicola Padula, turn left 500m past Refúgio na Serra for waterfalls and Pico do Itapeva. The villages of Emílio Ribas and São Cristóvão are connected by a railcar which runs frequently, US$0.15.

Hotels *Toriba*, Av E Diederichsen, T 62-1566, F 63-2793; *Vila Inglesa*, Sen R Simonsen, T 63-1955, F 63-2699; *Refúgio Alpino*, T 63-1660, and others at Capivari. **B** *Refugio na Serra*, Av Dr Antônio Nicola Padula 275, T 63-1330, comfortable, good breakfast, very helpful owners (some English spoken), rec. Youth Hostel, R Diogo de Carvalho 86, T 229-3787/3011, ramal 286; membership card and permission from Dr Fernando at Tourist Office in the bus terminal required. Camping Clube do Brasil site in the Descansópolis district. Book accommodation in advance if going Jun/Jul.

Restaurants *Sole Mio* (on road to Horto Florestal), Italian, big portions; *Baden Baden*, German, good. Good cheese on sale at a shop just past sports centre on way out of town, also jams and chocolates; plenty of other chocolate shops. "Milbaho" mineral water is produced here.

Stalls on main square Thur-Sun sell local produce. Exchange at Geneve Sweater shop, or Cadij Imóveis, "if they want to", check rates.

Transport Bus from São Paulo, US$6, 3 hrs; from Rio, changing at São José dos Campos, US$9.50. No through rail service: railcars make round trips between Campos do Jordão and Santo Antônio do Pinhal, in season between 0800 and 0900 and at 1310, out of season (Oct-Nov, Mar-Apr) at 1310 only, a bit bumpy, but beautiful views (sit on the right on the way there, left coming back): hills, valleys, tight corners. The train is very crowded even though you are assigned a seat; fare US$1.50 (buy ticket in advance, and get return immediately on arrival in San Antônio; watch your belongings on board). Whole trip takes about 3 hrs: 1 hr each way on train, 40 mins-1 hr in Santo Antônio (not much on offer there: a few snack bars, nice views, statue of Madonna and Child). There is a local railcar service within São José (very crowded but cheap). From **Pindamonhangaba** buses run to **São Paulo** and **Taubaté**; also to **Aparecida do Norte**, 1030, US$2. The short road down to "Pinda", starting from the paved road 24 km SW of Campos do Jordão, is now paved (5 buses daily, 50 mins). Railcar to **Pinda** leaves 1705 Mon-Thur and weekends, from Pinda 0600 Tues-Fri, 0930 weekends. A new road branching off the BR-116 near Caçapava provides a quicker drive from Rio, or São Paulo, than the route via São José dos Campos.

Nearer to Rio than the Pindamonhangaba turn, just off the BR-116, is **Aparecida do Norte** (pop 35,060), Brazil's chief place of pilgrimage and the seat of its patron saint, Nossa Senhora Aparecida. This small black image of the Virgin is said to have been taken by a fisherman from the nearby River Paraíba, and quickly acquired a miraculous reputation. It is now housed in a huge modern basilica in Romanesque style on top of a hill, with the clean white-walled, red-roofed town below.

For the route to the Paraná River, from São Paulo to Presidente Epitácio, **see p 466**.

SOUTHERN BRAZIL (6)

This consists, from S to N, of the three states of Rio Grande do Sul, Santa Catarina and Paraná. Rio Grande do Sul is *gaúcho* (cowboy) country; it is also Brazil's chief wine producer. Throughout the S European settlement, especially from Germany, heavily influences cultural and agricultural activity. The coast offers a variety of beaches and scenery while in the far W is one of Latin America's major natural attractions, the Iguaçu falls, and one of its largest manmade constructions, the Itaipu dam.

The conformation of the land is not unlike that further N; the Great Escarpment runs down the coastal area as far as Porto Alegre, receding from the coast in a wide curve between Paranaguá and Florianópolis. South of Tubarão to the borders of Uruguay the hills of southern Rio Grande do Sul, which never rise higher than 900 to 1,000m, are fringed along the coast by sand bars and lagoons.

Rio Grande do Sul

North of the Rio Uruguai the land is deeply forested, but the area of prairie, small in São Paulo, Paraná and Santa Catarina, grows more extensive than the forest in Rio Grande do Sul, S of the Uruguai valley. In southern Rio Grande do Sul, S and W of the Rio Jacuí (draining into the Lagoa dos Patos) there are great grasslands stretching as far as Uruguay to the S and Argentina to the W. This is the distinctive land of the *gaúcho*, or cowboy (pronounced ga-oo-shoo in Brazil), of the flat black hat, of *bombachas* (the baggy trousers worn by the *gaúcho*), of the poncho and *ximarão* (or *mate* without sugar), the indispensable drink of southern cattlemen. There are many millions of cattle, sheep and pigs, and some 75% of all Brazilian wine comes from the state. Its population (who all call themselves *gaúchos*) now number over 9 million. Rio Grande do Sul has the highest proportion of literate people in Brazil. The *gaúcho* culture is quite vigorous, increasingly developing a sense of distance from the African-influenced culture of further N. This separationist strain was most marked in the 1820s and 1830s when the Farroupilha movement, led by Bento Gonçalves, proclaimed the República Riograndense in 1835. The subsequent war with the federal government ended with the Treaty of Ponche Verde in Feb 1845.

There are three sharply contrasted types of colonization and land owning in Rio Grande do Sul. During the colonial period, wars with the Spaniards of Uruguay were frequent, and the Portuguese government brought into the grasslands of

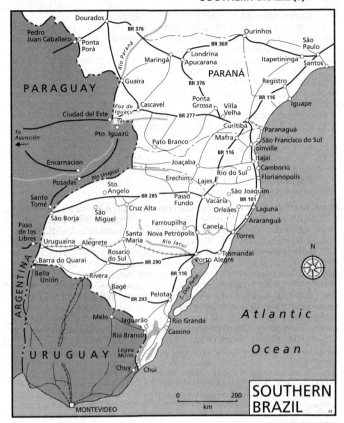

SOUTHERN
BRAZIL

the S a number of military settlers from the Azores; these soldiers inter-married with the Brazilian herdfolk in the area. In the colonial period, also, the Jesuits built several settlements to acculturate the local Indians; relics of this process include the impressive ruins of the **Sete Povos das Missões Orientais** (São Borja, São Nicolau, São Luiz, São Lourenço, São Miguel, São João, Santo Ángelo). West from Porto Alegre, in the floodlands of the Rio Jacuí and its tributary, the Rio Taquari, rice is cultivated in typical Brazilian fashion: large estates with tenant workers.

At São Leopoldo, N of Porto Alegre, a group of Germans were settled in 1824 on their own small farms, and during the next 25 years over 20,000 more were brought into the area by the Brazilian Government. The Germans concentrated on rye, maize, and pigs. Between 1870 and 1890, settlers from northern Italy arrived, bringing viticulture with them, and settled N of the Germans at Alfredo Chaves and Caxias do Sul.

Porto Alegre (pop 1,262,630, CEP 90000, DDD 0512), capital of Rio Grande do Sul, lies at the confluence of five rivers which flow into the Rio Guaíba and thence into the great fresh-water lagoon, the Lagoa dos Patos, which runs into the sea.

It is the most important commercial centre S of São Paulo.

Standing on a series of hills and valleys on the banks of the Guaíba, with its business centre jutting out into the water on a promontory, Porto Alegre is one of the most up-to-date cities in Brazil. The older residential part of the town is on a promontory dominated previously by the **Palácio Piratini** (Governor's Palace), the imposing modern cathedral, and the two high white towers of the old church of **Nossa Senhora das Dores**, but Governor and God have now been utterly dwarfed by the skyscraper of the **Assembléia Legislativa**. The streets in the centre are famous for their steep gradients. The climate is temperate through most of the year, though the temperature at the height of summer can often exceed 40°C and drop below 10°C in winter. The surrounding suburbs are very pleasant. For instance, Ipanema, on the banks of the Guaíba, has a selection of bars and small restaurants; a popular rendezvous, with spectacular sunsets over the river.

Do not miss that section of the **R dos Andradas** (R da Praia) that is now permanently closed to traffic. It is the city's principal outdoor meeting place, the main shopping area, and by around 1600 it is full of people; at the peak hour of 1900 the street is jammed for about 6 blocks.

Points of Interest The **Parque Farroupilha** (called Parque Rendação) is a fine park near the city centre; the interesting cathedral of the **Anglican-Episcopal church** of Brazil; the **Jardim Zoológico do Estado** near São Leopoldo (bus US$0.80), the **Botanic Gardens** (Bairro Jardim Botânico, bus 40 from Praça 15 de Novembro) and the **Cidade Universitária** are well worth a visit. The **Mercado Público** is next to the Prefeitura, in the centre of town. In the Cidade Baixa quarter are the colonial **Travessa dos Venezianos** (between RR Lopo Gonçalves and Joaquim Nabuco) and the house of **Lopo Gonçalves**, R João Alfredo 582, which houses the Museu do Porto Alegre, free, 0900-1700 Tues-Sun. The 5-km wide Rio Guaíba lends itself to every form of boating and there are several sailing clubs. Boat trips leave from Av Mauá opp the Ministério de Fazendo, US$3.50, 1 hr. A good view of the city, with glorious sunsets, may be had from the **Morro de Santa Teresa** (take bus 95 from the top end of R Salgado Filho, marked "Morro de Santa Teresa TV" or just "TV").

Porto Alegre is a fresh-water port for ocean-going vessels of up to 7,000 tons and 4.87m draught. Vessels must come up through Rio Grande and the Lagoa dos Patos, some 275 km from the open sea. Large areas of reclaimed land have been used for residential building and to extend the port facilities and quays, now among the most up-to-date in Brazil. Mosquitoes are plentiful.

Porto Alegre's most important industries are food and farm products, textiles, metal-processing, chemicals and leather products. Chief exports are pinewood, rice, wheat, soya, meat, hides, wool, animal hair, semi-precious stones, wine and tobacco. A visit to Varig's installations and workshops is well worth while.

Museums The **Museu Júlio de Castilhos**, Duque de Caxias 1231, has an interesting historical collection (Tues-Sun 0900-1700), and there is the **Museu do Trem** in the old railway station of São Leopoldo, decrepit but interesting exhibits: entrance free, Mon-Fri 1400-1800, sometimes closed Mar-Nov. **Museu de Arte do Rio Grande do Sul**, Praça Senador Florêncio (Praça da Alfândega), Tues 1000-2100, Wed-Sun 1000-1700, entry free, is interesting. **Varig airline museum**, open all day Tues-Fri and 0900-1300 on Sun.

Festivals 2 Feb (local holiday) is the festival of Nossa Senhora dos Navegantes, whose image is taken by boat from the central quay in the port to the industrial district of Navegantes. Semana Farroupilha, celebrating *gaúcho* traditions, main day 20 Sep.

Warning The market area in Praça 15 de Novembro and the bus terminal are dangerous at night; thefts have been reported in Voluntários da Pátria and Praça Parcão.

Hotels L2 *Plaza São Rafael*, Av Alberto Bins 514, T 21-6100, F 21-6883; *Conceição-Center*, Av Senador Salgado Filho 201 (T 26-0610), good; **L3** *Alfred Executivo*, Av Otávio Rocha 270, T 21-8966; **L3** *Embaixador*, Jerônimo Coelho 354, T 28-2211, F 28-5050, 4-star, comfortable, unexciting restaurant; **A1** *Porto Alegre Residence*, Av André da Rocha 131, breakfast, large rooms, TV, a/c, friendly, rec; **A1** *Ritter*, lgo V J Veppo 55, T 21-8155, F 28-1610, opp rodoviária, good service, English spoken, conveniently located; **A2** *Everest*, R Duque de Caxias 1357, T 24-7355, F 28-4792; *Umbu*, Av Farrapos 292, T 28-4355, not far from rodoviária, good restaurant.

B *Praça Matriz*, Praça Mal Deodoro; **B** *São Luiz*, Av Farrapos 45, T 24-9522, spotless, good service, but near rodoviária and so a bit noisy; **B** *Terminaltur*, opp rodoviária, T 27-1656, with bath, a/c, TV, breakfast, heating, but small rooms and tiny bathrooms; **C** *Palácio*, Av Vigário José Inácio 644, central, clean, friendly, hot water, rec; **C** *Savoy*, Av Borges Medeiros 688, T 24-0511, good value; **C** *Santa Catarina*, R Gen Vitorino 240, T 24-9044; **D** *Coliseu*, Voluntários da Pátria, with shower, clean; **D** *Minuano*, Farrapos 31, without breakfast or bath (more with bath), noisy but otherwise good, and **D** *Elevado*, Av Farrapos 63, with hot shower, both near bus station; *Marechal*, R Andrade Neves 123, basic, clean (not far from Mercado

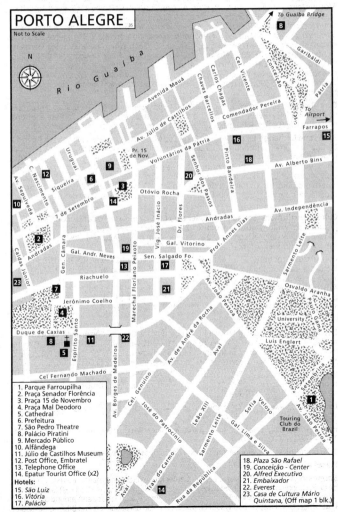

PORTO ALEGRE

Not to Scale

To Guaiba Bridge

1. Parque Farroupilha
2. Praça Senador Florência
3. Praça 15 de Novembro
4. Praça Mal Deodoro
5. Cathedral
6. Prefeitura
7. São Pedro Theatre
8. Palácio Piratini
9. Mercado Público
10. Alfândega
11. Júlio de Castilhos Museum
12. Post Office, Embratel
13. Telephone Office
14. Epatur Tourist Office (x2)
Hotels:
15. São Luiz
16. Vitória
17. Palácio
18. Plaza São Rafael
19. Conceição - Center
20. Alfred Executivo
21. Embaixador
22. Everest
23. Casa de Cultura Mário Quintana, (Off map 1 blk.)

Municipal); **D** *Ritz*, André da Rocha 225, friendly, central, helpful, Spanish spoken; next door is *Finks*, same price range; **D** *Uruguay*, Dr Flores 371, clean, simple, rec. Two *Casas dos Estudantes* (for those with student cards), at Av João Pessoa 41, and R Riachuelo 1355 (both not far from bus station), night free, breakfast and evening meal US$0.40, lunch US$0.60, if there's room. **E** *Porto Alegre*, Pinto Bandeirantes 339, good, clean, quiet, rec. Hotels in the area around R Garibáldi and Voluntários da Patria between Av Farrapos and rodoviária are used for very short stays. Youth hostel *Laçador*, R Aurora Nunes Wagner 148, Morro Santa Tereza, T 287717.

Camping Do Cocão, 10 km out on Viamão road; Praia do Guarujá, 16 km out on Av Guaíba.

Restaurants Many good ones. **General:** *Everest Roof*, Duque de Caxias 1357; *Mosqueteiro*, Estádio Olímpico; *Rancho Alegre*, Cristóvão Colombo 2168, good "gaúcho" music; *Gauchão* at Rodoviária, good, quality meats, with live entertainment nightly; *Churrascaria Quero-Quero*, Praça Otávio Rocha 47; *Grumete*, 24 de Outubro 905; *Barranco*, Av Protásio Alves 1578; *Farroupilha*, Fernando Machado 973 (corner of Borges de Medeiros), delicious *prato feito* US$3. Chinese: *Tai Seng Nhe*, Andradas 1097. German: *Printz*, Protásio Alves 3208; *Steinhaus*, Paulino Teixeira 415; *Floresta Negra*, 24 de Outubro 905. Portuguese: *Casa de Portugal*, João Pessoa 579; *Galo*, João Alfredo 904. Italian: *Copacabana*, Praça Garibáldi; *Cantina do Peppe*, Getúlio Vargas 273. *Pizzeria 4 Climas*, Av Vigario José Inacio 695. The many Italian restaurants on Cristóvão Colombo are probably the best option for vegetarians.

Bars (beer and sandwiches, music.) *Cia Sandwiches*, Getúlio Vargas 1430; *João de Barro*, R da República 546, Cidade Baixa, good jazz; *Julius*, José de Alencar 1348; *Sgt Peppers*, Dona Laura 329. *Elo Perdido*, R Garibáldi 1330 (Bom Fin), avant-garde bar with 50's décor.

Banks and Exchange Exchange on Av Borges de Medeiros, good rate, cash only (eg **Agência Platina**, on corner with Andradas). Many câmbios in the centre will change TCs at parallel rates; eg **Platino Turismo**, Dos Andrades e Av Borges de Medeiros (only one to change TCs, Amex, but 6% less than cash), **Exprinter**, Sen Salgado Filho 247 (best for cash); **Mastercard**, cash against card, R 7 de Setembro 722, 8° andar, centro; for other addresses consult tourist bureau brochure. **Lloyds Bank**, R General Câmara 249 (open 1000-1630). **Banco do Brasil**, Uruguai 185, 9th floor (open 1000-1500), good rates for TCs. **Citibank**, R 7 de Setembro (open 1300-1700).

Cultural Institutions Sociedade Brasileira da Cultura Inglesa, Praça Mauricio Cardoso 49, Moinhos de Vento. **Instituto Goethe**, 24 de Outubro 122 (open Mon-Fri, 0930-1230, 1430-2100), occasional concerts, bar rec for German Apfelkuchen. **Instituto Cultural Americano Brasileiro**, Mon-Fri, 0800-2000 (Sat 0800-1700).

Consulates Argentine, R Prof Annes Dias 112, 1° andar, T 24-6799/6810/6786. **Uruguayan**, R Siquera Campos 1171, 6th floor, T 224-3499. **US**, Genuino 421, corner of Mendeiros, T 226-4288. **British**, R Itapeva 110, Sala 505, Edif Montreal Bairro D'Areia, T 41-0720; **Austrian**, R 7 de Setembro 1069, conj 1714, Caixa Postal 1771, T 2460 77/85. **Danish**, Av Ipiranga 321, 5th floor, Bairro Menino Deus, CP 10105; T 512-339966, open 0800-1200, 1400-1800. **Finnish**, R Commendador Azevedo 224, T 222-7188.

Electric Current 110-120 AC 50 cycles.

Entertainments The old Hotel Majestic has become the **Casa de Cultura Mário Quintana**, at R dos Andradas 736: this is a lively centre for the arts, with exhibitions, theatre etc. Plays by local and visiting companies at the theatres of São Pedro (opposite Government Palace) free noon and late afternoon concerts Sat, Sun, art gallery, café, and Leopoldina (Av Independência). Modern cinemas. Centro de Tradição Gaúcha has *gaúcho* shows every Sat, starting at 2200.

Nightclubs *Crocodillo's*, 24 de Outoubro (Auxiliadora), disco, rec. *Descretu's*, Venâncio Aires 59, gay disco, shows at 0230.

Language Courses Portuguese and Spanish, Matilde Dias, R Pedro Chaves Barcelos 37, apto 104, T 31-8235. US$10 for 90 mins, rec.

Post For sending parcels abroad: R Araújo Ribeiro 100; bring parcel unopened. **UPS** T 43-4972/42-4602 (Alvaro).

Telecommunications Embratel, R Siqueira de Campos 1245. T 41233.

Places of Worship Sibra, R Mariante 772.

Shopping H Stern jewellers at Shopping Center Iguatemi and international airport. The Praia de Bello shopping centre, claimed to be the largest in Latin America, is a US$1.50 taxi ride from town. There is a street market (leather goods, basketware, etc) in the streets around the central Post Office. Good leather goods sold on the streets. Sun am handicraft and bric-a-brac market (plus sideshows) Av José Bonefácio (next to Parque Farroupilha). Very good food market.

Bookshops *Livraria Kosmos*, R dos Andrades 1644 (international stock); *Livraria Lima*, Borges de Medeiros 539; *Papyrus*, R dos Andrades e Caldos Jnr, cheap English books; *Livraria Globo*, Andradas 1416; airport bookshop. *Livres e Artes* bookstall in book market, Praça Senador Florêncio, English books. Brasil-America Cultural Centre has free English library, next door used books are sold and exchanged.

Sports The Jockey Club at which races are held on Sat and Sun; the Country Club (picturesque 18-hole golf course). British Club, Av Carlos Gomes 534 (Montserrat). Weights and aerobics at Academia do Parcão, 24 de Outoubro 684.

Golf Porto Alegre Country Club, Av Líbero Badaró, 18 holes. Several 9-hole courses in nearby towns, see p 445.

Swimming from the beaches near or in the city is forbidden because of pollution. See "Beaches", below for out-of-town beaches.

Tourist Information Epatur, Travessa do Carmo 84 (head office), helpful as is branch in Praça 15 de Novembro. Branch offices: Salgado Filho airport; interstate bus station, very helpful (free city maps); R General Câmara 368; Av Salgado Filho 366. CRTur (Companhia Riograndense de Turismo), R dos Andradas 1137, 6th floor. Epatur maintains information booths at the frontier towns. A monthly booklet is available. City bus tour US$6, Regional tour US$18, Spanish or Portuguese only. **Touring Clube do Brasil**, Av João Pessoa 623.

Local transport First-class minibuses (*Lotacão*), red, stop on request. Safer and pleasanter than normal buses, fare about US$0.75. There is also a metrô service, the Trensub, from the southern terminal at the Mercado Modelo (station beside the market) going as far N as Canoas. The second station serves the rodoviária and the fifth the airport (10 mins), 0500-2300, single journey US$0.20.

Air Services There is a large modern international airport, Salgado Filho, 8 km from the city, connected to the centre by train (see above). There are daily flights to Rio, São Paulo, Curitiba, Buenos Aires and Montevideo, and many other Brazilian cities. The airport is served by all Brazilian airlines, Pluna and Aerolíneas Argentinas.

Rail The only long-distance passenger service from Porto Alegre is the line W to (386 km) *Santa Maria* (pop 217,565, **A1** *Hotel Itaimbé Palace*, R Venâncio Aires 2741, T 222-1144, F 221-2051; **E** *Jantzen*, R Rio Branco, central, noisy on disco nights; *Imperial*, R Manoel Ribas 1767, near station, clean, garden; **E** *Popular*, also near station, clean amenities, not so rooms, basic; fruit and vegetable market Sat am R 13 de Maio; useful junction for road connections N to São Miguel mission ruins and Iguaçu, and S direct to Pelotas) and on to Cacequi, where the line branches for Uruguaiana (see p 446), for connections to Argentina, and for Santana do Livramento, for connections to Uruguay (Planalto buses run Santa Maria-Montevideo). On Fri a standard train (no sleepers) leaves Porto Alegre at 0800 to Santa Maria (11 hrs, US$3.60 1st class, US$3, 2nd), thence to Santana or Uruguaiana, arriving 0605 next day, returning Sat 1930 to Porto Alegre. (Bus Porto Alegre - Santa Maria 4³⁄4 hrs, frequent service, US$9.50.)

Buses Bus to Rio, US$46.20 (*leito* 92.50), 26 hrs; **São Paulo**, US$30 (*leito* 60), 18 hrs; **Uruguaiana**, US$17, 8 hrs; **Florianópolis**, US$10.50, 7 hrs with Viação São Cristóvão (beware of overbooking and of stopping buses—eg Santo Anjo—on this route); **Curitiba**, US$19.25, 11 hrs; **Rio Grande**, US$11.50, 8 per day, 0600 to 2000, 4¹⁄2 hrs. **Foz do Iguaçu**, US$24, 15 hrs. Very many other destinations. To **Cascavel** (Paraná) for connections to Campo Grande, Cuiabá and Porto Velho: daily except Sat with Aguia Branca, 21 hrs, or Unesul, 19 hrs. To **Jaguarão** on Uruguayan border at 2400, 6 hrs, US$10.50.

Bus to **Montevideo**, with international buses TTL (daily 1700 and 2000, US$36; **see p 447**) alternatively take bus to border town of Chuí at 1200 daily, 7¹⁄2 hrs, US$13.25, then bus to Montevideo (US$8, cheaper bought in Porto Alegre or Chuí than in Uruguay). Leito to **Punta del Este** (Uruguay), departs Fri 2100, arriving Sat 0700, US$70. Ouro o Prata operates a 2-3 times weekly service to Salto and Paysandú (Uruguay), via Santana do Livramento/Rivera. To **Asunción** with Unesul at 1900 daily via Foz do Iguaçu. Expresso Singer bus Porto Alegre-**Posadas** (Argentina) via Oberá, Alba Posse, Porto Maúá, departs 2100 on Tues, Thur, and Sun arriving following day at 1135. There are bus services to **Buenos Aires**, US$71, 19 hrs (depending on border) with Pluma, 1400 or 1500, 1900 and 2300, route is Uruguaiana, Paso de los Libres, Entre Ríos and Zárate. **NB** Take your passport when purchasing international bus tickets.

The new and excellent bus terminal on Av Maúá with Garibáldi has good facilities, including a post office and long-distance telephone service until 2100. A regular bus runs from the rodoviária to the airport, also the suburban train service (see above).

Roads Good roads radiate from Porto Alegre, and Highway BR-116 has a paved surface to

Curitiba (746 km). To the S it is paved (though some stretches are in poor condition), to Chuí on the Uruguayan frontier, 512 kms. In summer visibility can be very poor at night due to mist, unfenced cows are a further hazard. The paved coastal road to Curitiba via Itajaí (BR-101), of which the first 100 km is a four-lane highway, is much better than the BR-116 via Caxias and Lajes. The road to Uruguaiana is entirely paved but bumpy.

Excursions Cervejaria Brahma, Av Cristovão Colombo 545, offers tours of its brewery (but not Dec-Mar). To Foz do Iguaçu and Ciudad del Este, overnight journey each way (12 hrs in Paraguay), offered by several tour companies. 3-day trips with 1 night's hotel accommodation, US$56 including sightseeing (time at the falls may be limited). See Turismo section in "Zero Hora" classifieds (Thur, Sat, Sun) for tour companies' ads.

Beaches The main beach resorts of the area are to the N of the city. The towns of *Tramandaí* (126 km, pop 20,070) and *Torres* (209 km, pop 37,505) are the most popular, with lots of luxury (and more reasonable) hotels and motels, bars, restaurants, and other standard requisites associated with seaside resorts. To celebrate independence in 1836, a cavalcade of horses reaches Torres on 16 Sep from Uruguay. To reach Florianopólis, take a bus from Torres to Araranguá and change. There is no lack of cheap accommodation, but hotels tend to be very full during the summer season. There are fully equipped campsites at both towns, and camping is also allowed on some beaches.

Tramandaí Hotels C *São Jorge*, F Amaral 19, T 661-1154, quiet, clean, bath, rec. Many more.

Torres Hotels A1 *Dunas da Praia*, on beach, T 664-1011, F 664-2080; **A3** *A Furninha*, R Joaquim Porto 281, good service, T 664-1655, F 664-1437; **B** *Grande Hotel Torres*, R Júlio de Castilhos 124, T 664-1887, with bath, balcony and breakfast; **B** *Farol*, R José A Pirasol 240, T 664-1240, with full board; **C** *Central*, Borges de Medeiros 296, T 664-2580, clean and friendly; **C** *Salth*, Borges de Medeiros 209, T 664-1881, with bath, friendly, clean, Dec-Feb; **E** *São Domingo Youth Hostel* in a school building, Júlio de Castilhos 875, T 664-1865, clean. Other hotels, D, bath and breakfast are available.

Restaurants *Bom Gosto*, Rio Branco 242, churrascaria; *Sol Macrobiótico*, J Castilhos 746, good cheap vegetarian with a cosy, personal atmosphere; *Casa de Peixe do Souza*, by the river, very good fish.

Banks and Exchange In Torres, Banco do Brasil and at Rodoviária.

Between the two towns are the resorts (heading S to N) of *Atlântida* (Hotel Azul), *Capão da Canoa* (Hotel Kolman, R Sepé 1718; **youth hostel** *Riveira di Fiori*, Av Venâncio Aires 711, T 265944, pool, rec; and others), *Arroio Teixeira* (Camping Clube do Brasil) and *Arroio do Sal* (**D** *Hotel D'Itália*, Av Assis Brasil 11, T 09, on beach, highly rec; *Casa da Sogra*, good food).

Roads There is a paved road from Torres and Tramandaí (mostly prohibited to trucks) along the coast to Quintão, giving access to many beaches. A track continues to Mostardas, thence along the peninsula on the seaward side of the Lagoa dos Patos to São José do Norte, opposite Rio Grande. There is accommodation in *Palmares do Sul* (across the peninsula from Quintão) and Mostardas. South of Mostardas is *Tavares* on the **Lagoa do Peixe**, a national park, which is a resting place for migrating birds (details from Praça Luís Martins 30, Mostardas, CEP 96270-000, T 051-673-1464). The road to the park is called the Estrada do Inferno. In Tavares, the red house on the praça is a hotel, no sign, rec; several buses a week Tavares—São José do Norte (130 km) and several daily to Porto Alegre and to Buenos Aires (US$35).

Another popular beach area is S of Porto Alegre, around Cassino, near Rio Grande (**see p 445**). 40 km to the S (towards Rio Grande) begins the Costa Doce of the Lagoa dos Patos; noted bathing points are Tapes, Barra do Ribeiro, Arambaré, *São Lourenço do Sul* (rec camping site 1 km out of town on lake shore) and Laranjal.

At São Lourenço do Sul is *Hotel Vilela*, R Almirante Abreu 428, family hotel, clean, friendly. The town is a good place to enjoy the lake, the beaches, fish restaurants and watersports.

Inland is the pleasant Serra Gaúcha, the most beautiful scenery being around the towns of *Gramado* (pop 22,045) and *Canela* (pop 24,375), about 130 km from Porto Alegre (chocolate factory between the two towns). There is a distinctly Bavarian flavour to many of the buildings. In spring and summer the flowers are a delight, and in winter there are frequently snow showers. This is excellent walking and climbing country among hills, woods, lakes and waterfalls. There are many excellent hotels at all prices in both towns, but it is difficult to get rooms in the summer. Local crafts include knitted woollens, leather, wickerwork, and chocolate. Gramado has two fine parks, Parque Knorr and Lago Negro, and Minimundo, a collection of miniature models. The town is decorated and, on Sat, about one week before 24 Dec there is outdoor Christmas music; book hotels in good time as the town is crowded. The two towns are linked by frequent buses (10 mins).

Gramado Hotels **L3** *Serra Azul*, R Garibáldi 152, T 286-1082, F 286-3374; **L3** *Serrano*, Costa e Silva 1112, T 286-1332; **A1** *Hortensias*, R Bela Vista 83, T 286-1057; **A1** *Ritta Höppner*, R Pedro Candiago 305, T 054-286-1334, in cabins, very good value, friendly, good breakfasts, German owners, cabins have TV, fridge, pool and miniature trains in grounds; **A2** *Pequeno Bosque*, R Piratini 486, T 286-1527, with bath, fridge, TV, good breakfast, located in wood close to Véu da Noiva waterfall; **A3** *Pousada Zermatt*, A Acorsi e R da Fé, T 286-2426, rec; **B** *Luiz*, Senador Salgado Filho 432, T 286-1026, good breakfast, clean, among the cheapest; **B** *Parque*, Leopoldo Rosenfeldt 818, T 286-1326, bungalows, good breakfast, friendly, maid will do laundry reasonably; **C** *Dinda*, R Augusto Zatti 160, T 286-1588, one of the cheapest; **C** *Tia Hulda*, Av Borges de Medeiros 1653, T 286-1813, friendly; try the *Planalto*, Borges de Medeiros 2001, T 286-1210, opp rodoviária, clean and friendly; a private house in this street, No 1635, rents rooms, rec.

Restaurants *Saint Hubertus*, R da Caixa d'Água; *Nápoli*, Av Borges de Medeiros, good Italian; *Lancheira*, R Garibáldi 321, cheap and good. Coffee shop, *Tia Nilda*, Av Pres Costa e Silva. *Pyp* yoghurt factory, Av S Diniz 1030, has snack bar serving health food sandwiches and yoghurt. The local speciality is *café colonial*, a 5 o'clock meal of various dishes, including meats, rec at *Café da Torre* (very filling). Visitors should also sample hot *pinhões* (nuts from the Paraná pine) and *quentão* (hot red wine, cachaça, ginger, cloves, sugar and cinnamon, often topped with gemada—beaten egg yolks and sugar).

Banks and Exchange Banco do Brasil, R Garibáldi esq Madre Verónica, Gramado.

Tourist Offices Corner of Borges de Medeiros and Coronel Diniz, Gramado (2 blocks from Rodoviária, no English spoken) and on main square in Canela, good maps and hotel lists.

Canela Hotels **L2** *Laje de Pedra*, Av Pres Kennedy Km 3, T 282-1530, F 282-1532; **A1** *Vila Suzana Parque*, Theoboldo Fleck 15, T 282-2020, chalets, heated pool attractive; **C** *Bela Vista*, R Oswaldo Aranha 160, T 282-1327, near rodoviária, clean, good breakfasts. Cheap hotels: **E** *Jubileu*, Oswaldo Aranha 223 (acts as Youth hostel, T (054) 282-2133); *CNEC*, youth hostel, R Melvin Jones 151, T 282-1134 and **D** *Central*, Av Júlio de Castilhos 146, clean, safe, rec; **D** *Pousada do Viajante*, R Ernesto Urbani 132, price pp, clean, kitchen facilities, friendly, rec, T 282-2017.

Camping Camping Clube do Brasil, 1 km from waterfall in Parque do Caracol, 1 km off main road, signposted (6 km from Canela); excellent honey and chocolate for sale here, highly rec. Sesi, camping or cabins, 2½ km outside Canela, T (054) 282-1311/1697, clean, restaurant, rec.

Restaurant *Cantina do Nono*, Av Oswaldo Arantia, near petrol station, good *churrascaria*.

Wine merchant in Canela, Joliment, Estrada de Morro, Calçado.

Electric Current 220 volts AC.

Bus Several daily **Canela-Caxias** do Sul, 2 hrs, US$3. From **Florianópolis**, you have to go via Porto Alegre.

6 km from Canela is the **Parque Estadual do Caracol** (closed for upgrading in 1994); a well-marked nature trail leads to the foot of the falls, which are 130m high (allow 1½ hrs of daylight), and to smaller falls above Caracol. From the high point at Ferradura, 7 km from the park, there is a good view into the canyon of the River Cai. Good views also from Moro Pelado, follow signs from behind the town (nice walk through forest).

80 km from São Francisco de Paula is the **Parque Nacional de Aparados da Serra**, where the major attraction is the 7.8-km canyon, known locally as the Itaimbezinho (check in advance if open—Ibama, R Miguel Teixeira 126, Cidade Baixa, Caixa Postal 280, Porto Alegre, CEP 90050-250, T 225-2144). Here, two waterfalls cascade 350m into a stone circle at the bottom. There is a free campsite and a restaurant, which has a few rooms, in the park. From the restaurant one can walk to the canyon of Malacara. For experienced hikers (and with a guide) there is a difficult path to the bottom of Itaimbezinho. One can then hike 20 km to Praia Grande in Santa Catarina (see p 447). As well as the canyon, the park and surrounding region have several bird specialities (eg speckle-breasted Antpitta, Black-and-White Monjita, Hellmayr's Pipit, Giant Snipe, Straight-billed Reed haunter, and others). Red-legged Seriema, a large conspicuous bird, can be seen on the way to the park, and there are two fox species. Tourist

excursions, mostly at weekends, from *São Francisco de Paula*, which is 38 km E of Canela and 117 km N of Porto Alegre (Hotel: **A1** *Veraneio Hampal*, RS-235 road to Canela, Km 73, T 644-1363). At other times, take a bus to Cambará, get off at the crossroads, from where it is 15 km to the park—walk or hitchhike if you're lucky. *Pousadas* in Cambará: **D** *Fortaleza*, with bath; **F** *São Jorge*.

24 km W of Gramado (99 km from Porto Alegre, 30 km from Caxias do Sul) is **Nova Petrópolis** (pop 16,715) (bus US$0.65), another city with strong German roots; there is a Parque do Imigrante, an open-air museum of German settlement. (Hotels incl *Veraneio dos Pinheiros*, RS-235, Km 3.5; *Recanto Suiço*, Av 16 de Novembro 2195, T 281-1229, on Parque dos Imigrantes, Av 15 de Novembro 2195, T 281-1229, on Parque dos Imigrantes, 3 star, Petrópolis; *Veraneio Schoeller*, one-star; youth hostel *Bom Pastor*, at Km 14, Linha Brasil RS 235, T 281 1195 ext 14.) N of Nova Petrópolis is *Jammerthal*, a valley in the Serra Gaúcha with German farms, many of whose inhabitants still speak German (go to Joanette and walk from there).

Caxias do Sul (pop 290,970, CEP 95100, DDD 054) 122 km from Porto Alegre, is the centre of the Brazilian wine industry. The population is principally of Italian descent, and it is an expanding and modern city. Vines were first brought to the region in 1840 but not until the end of the century and Italian immigration did the industry develop. The church of São Pelegrino has paintings by Aldo Locatelli and 5 metre-high bronze doors sculptured by Augusto Murer. Good municipal museum at R Visconde de Pelotas 586 (open Tues-Sat, 0800-1200, 1400-1800), with displays of artefacts of the Italian immigration. The best time to visit is Jan-Feb.

Hotels L3 *Alfred Palace*, R Sinimbu 2302, T/F 221-8655; **L3** *Samuara*, 10 km out on RS-122, road to Farroupilha, T 227-2222, F 227-1010. **A1** *Alfred*, R Sinimbu 2266, T 221-8655; **A1** *Cosmos*, 20 de Setembro 1563, T/F 221-4688; **A1** *Volpiano*, Ernesto Alves 1462, T 221-4744, F 221-4445; **A3** *Itália*, Av Júlio de Castilhos 3076, T/F 225-1177; **B** *Real*, R Marquês de Herval 606, T 221-4400, F 221-2911; **D** *Bandeira*, R Sinambu 2435, with TV and bath; **D** *Peccini*, R Pinheiro Machado 1939, shared bath, good breakfast; **D** *Pérola*, corner Ernesto Alves and Marquês de Herval (No 237), clean, good value. Hotels fill up early pm.

Good **restaurants**: *Fogo de Chão*, Os 18 do Forte 16, reasonably priced, live music (not touristy), "gaúcho"-style; also *Cantina Pão e Vino*, R Ludovico Cavinato 1757, Bairro Santa Catarina, Caxias, good value; *Dom Rafael*, on main square, good value.

Camping Municipal campsite, 4 km out on R Cons Dantas; Palermo, 5 km out on BR-116 at Km 118, T 222-7255; Belvedere Nova Sonda, 38 km out in the district of Nova Pádua. At Garibáldi, near the dry ski slope.

Exchange Ask for Joel at Viagens e Turismo Galâxia, good rates.

Tourist Office Praça do Centro Administrativo; kiosk in Praça Rui Barbosa, also in Ed Bonifa, Júlio de Castilho 1634, 2nd floor.

Caxias do Sul's festival of grapes is held in Feb-Mar. One should not miss the opportunity to visit the many *adegas* (but do not always expect free tasting), and the neighbouring towns of *Farroupilha* (Hotels *Don Francesco*, R Dr J Rossler 88, T 261-1132, 2 star; *Grande*, Júlio de Castilhos 1064) and **Bento Gonçalves** (hotels **B** *Dall'Onder*, R Erny Hugo Dreher 197, T/F (054) 451-3555; **C** *Vinocap*, R Barão do Rio Branco 245, T 452-1566) and *Garibáldi* (pop 25,900): hotels **A3** *Pietá*, João Pessoa 1728, T 262-1283; **A3** *Estação de Esqui*, cabins without breakfast; dry ski slope and toboggan slope—equipment hire, US$2.50/hr. A good *adega*, with free tasting, is Cooperativa Viti Vinícola Emboaba Ltda, in Nova Milano (bus to Farroupilha, then change—day trip). Good tour and tasting (6 wines) at Adega Granja União, R Os 18 de Forte 2346, US$0.30.

A restored steam train leaves Bento Gonçalves Sat at 1400 for Carlos Barbosa; called "a rota do vinho" (the wine run), it goes through vineyards in the hills. US$10 round trip; reserve in advance through Giodani Turismo.

On the road N, 112 km from Porto Alegre, is *Osório* (pop 36,775) a pleasant town near sea and lakes, with a good cheap hotel, **E** *Big Hotel*.

Rio Grande (pop 172,435, CEP 962000, DDD 0532) at the entrance to the Lagoa dos Patos, 274 km S of Porto Alegre, was founded in 1737. The city lies on a low, sandy peninsula 16 km from the Atlantic Ocean. Today it is the distribution centre for the southern part of Rio Grande do Sul, with significant cattle and meat industries.

During the latter half of the 19th century Rio Grande was an important centre, but today it is a rather poor town, notable for the charm of its old buildings. (Museu

Oceanográfico, US$0.50, 0900-1100, 1400-1700 daily, interesting, 2 km from centre; bus 59 or walk along waterfront.) At Praça Tamandaré is a small zoo.

Hotels A1 *Charrua*, R Duque de Caxias 55, T 32-8033, rec for good value; **B** *Europa*, R Gen Neto 165, main square,T 32-8133; **D** *Paris*, R Marechal Floriano 112, T 32-8944, old, charming; **D** *City, Iria* (latter clean, friendly), on R Luís Loréa; **D** *Ritter*, Silva Paes 373; **E** *Novo Mundo*, nearby.

Restaurants *Recanto Doce*, Silva Paes 370, cheap, friendly, and *Junior's*, good, big pizzas, cheap and quick; *China Brasil*, R Luís Loréa 389, good but not cheap; *Pescal*, Mal Andréa 389, for fish, fairly expensive; *Angola*, Benjamin Constant 163 e Luís Loréa, very good and reasonable; *Caumo's*, Dr Nascimento 389, good churrascaria; *Jensen*, Al Abreu 650, near rodoviária, good and cheap; *Bar Brejeiro*, Andrades 193, jazz upstairs.

Exchange *Hotel Charrua* for US$ notes.

Consulates British, R Francisco Marques 163, Caixa Postal 455, Centro, 96-200 Rio Grande, T 32-7788. Danish, R Mal Floriano 122, CP 92-96200, T 532-32-4422, open 0800-1200, 1330-1800.

Telecommunications Embratel, R Andrade Neves 94.

Golf Clubs 9-hole clubs in the following towns: Club Campestre de Pelotas, Bairro da Fragata, Pelotas; Country Club da Cidade de Rio Grande, Km 12 Estrada Rio Grande, Cassino; Club Campestre de Livramento, Santana de Livramento. Also at Swift Golf & Country Club, Rosário do Sul, and Santa Cruz Country Club.

Tourist Office R Riachuelo, on the waterfront, behind the Cámera de Comércio and beneath the Hidroviária; good map and information.

Transport Frequent daily buses to and from **Pelotas** (56 km), **Bagé** (280 km), **Santa Vitória** (220 km), and **Porto Alegre** (US$11.50, 4½ hrs). To **Itajaí**, 14 hrs, US$24. Road to Uruguayan border at **Chuí** is paved, but the surface is poor (5 hrs by bus, at 0700 and 1430, US$7.75). Bus tickets to Punta del Este or Montevideo at Bentica Tourismo, Av Silva Paes 373, T 32-1321/32-1807. All buses to these destinations go through Pelotas.

Boat Trip By boat across mouth of Lagoa dos Patos, to pleasant village of São José do Norte, US$0.30, every hour from Porto Velho.

Excursions To *Cassino*, a popular seaside town on the Atlantic Ocean, 24 km, over a good road. The Cassino beaches are populous, but have no restaurants, hotels or facilities (note the statue of Yemanjá); those further N are mainly used in summer.

Hotels B *Atlântico*, Av Rio Grande, 387, T 36-1350, clean, refurbished, special rates for students; **B** *Marysol*, Av Atlântica 900, T 36-1240, near beach, friendly. Private campsite on Avenida 33, on the way out to Rio Grande. Camping Clube do Brasil site near town.

The breakwater (the Barra), 5 km S of Cassino, no bus connection, through which all vessels entering and leaving Rio Grande must pass, is a tourist attraction. Barra-Rio Grande buses, from E side of Praça Ferreira pass the Superporto. Very good fishing. The coastline is low and straight, lacking the bays to the N of Porto Alegre; unfortunately the beach is used as a roadway. One attraction is railway flat-cars powered by sail, settle the price in advance; the railway was built for the construction of the breakwater.

Pelotas (pop 289,495, CEP 96100, DDD 0532), on the BR-116, 56 km N of Rio Grande, is the second largest city in the State of Rio Grande do Sul, on the left bank of the Rio São Gonçalo which connects the Lagoa dos Patos with the Lagoa Mirim. Its proximity to Rio Grande has hindered the development of its own port. Pelotas is prosperous, with an array of shops and pleasant parks. Like Rio Grande, it is rather damp.

Within a radius of 60 km, say an hour's drive, there are numerous excursions into the hilly countryside. Simple and clean accommodation and cheap, good and plentiful food can be found on the farms of settlers of German descent. 5 km from Taím there is an ecological station with a small museum of regional animals; some accommodation for interested visitors.

Hotels B *Estoril*, R Gen Osório 718, T 25-2411, a/c, reasonable; **C** *Rex*, Praça Pedro Osório 205, T 22-1163, friendly, dowdy; **D** *Germano*, next bus station, owner speaks some German;

D *Grande*, Praça Pedro Osório 51, T 25-8139/6659, "wonderful colonial hotel", some rooms with electric shower.

Camping Municipal camp site on coast N of town, take bus Z3 from centre, superb site, fresh fish in village 2 km away. 60 km out at the Arco Iris waterfall, no facilities; *Cascata*, 25 km out on the Cangussu road. Between Pelotas and Chuí, 1 km S of junction with Rio Grande road, 1,200m from road at a working ranch, rec, clean, meals included.

Restaurant Tyrolean restaurant, opp *Hotel Rex*, excellent, cheap. 29 km out of town, on the road to Rio Grande, is an excellent restaurant owned by Tia Laura, who specializes in home cooking and *café colonial*.

Exchange Banco do Brazil will change TCs. Try Sr Jesus Faria at 15 de Novembro 626 for good cash rate. It is difficult to change money at weekends.

Communications One plane a day Mon-Fri to Porto Alegre and Rio Grande. Rodoviária is far out of town, with bus every 15 mins to centre. Frequent daily buses to **Porto Alegre**, 244 km (US$8.50, 3-4 hrs, paved road); **Rio Grande**, 90 mins (paved but in poor condition) buses stop at Praça 20 de Setembro; **Jaguarão**, on frontier with Rio Branco, Uruguay (police post 3 km before the bridge), paved; and inland to **Bagé** (**D** *Hotel Medronha*, near bus station, without breakfast, clean) and other towns. The road to the Uruguayan frontier at **Chuí** (paved), has international bus service, but only a couple of daily buses Pelotas-Chuí. TTL bus services (Montevideo-Porto Alegre) stop at the bus station for Montevideo (RR Chile and Venezuela); tickets must be purchased from agency during day. Bus service to Buenos Aires via Uruguaiana. From Bagé, where there is a police post, the Uruguayan company Núñez runs buses 3 times a week to Melo, via Aceguá. Good direct road NW to Iguaçu via **São Sepe** (**C** *Trevo Parque Hotel*, a/c, very friendly), Santa Maria (**see p 441**) and São Miguel mission ruins (see below).

The southern interior of the state is the region of the real gaúcho. Principal towns of this area include ***Santana do Livramento*** (pop 80,215; train once a week and bus to Porto Alegre, 2 daily, 7 hrs, US$18; 3 daily to Urugaiana (4 hrs, US$8.50), services also to São Paulo and other destinations). Its twin Uruguayan city of Rivera has a great attraction in its casino. Rivera is considered to have the better hotels and better exchange facilities. Duty free shopping.

Hotels **A3** *Jandaia* R Uruguai 1452 T 242-2288, rec; **A3** *Portal*, Av Tamandaré 2076, T 242-2533, garage, clean, rec; **D** *Piranga*, clean; **D** *Uruguaiana*, close to bus station. **Youth hostel**, **F** *Hotel Palace*, R Manduca Rodrigues 615, with breakfast, single rooms available, old and grimy.

In the extreme W are ***Uruguaiana***, pop 117,460, a cattle centre 772 km from Porto Alegre (**A1** *Hotel Glória*, R Domingos de Almeida 1951, T 412-4422, good; **D** *Progresso*, Flores da Cunha 1856, garage, friendly; **D** *Palace*, Praça Rio Branco, without breakfast; *Fares Turis Hotel*, Pres Vargas 2939, T/F 412-3358, may let you leave your bags while you look around town) and its twin Argentine town of Paso de los Libres, also with a casino. A 1,400-metre bridge over the Rio Uruguai links the two cities; taxi or bus across about US$3.50. Buses connect the railway and bus stations, and centres of each city every half-hour; if you have to disembark for visa formalities, a following bus will pick you up without extra charge. Brazilian customs and immigration are at the end of the bridge, 5 blocks from the main praça exchange and information in the same building. Exchange rates are better in the town than at the border. There are trains (once a week) and bus services to Porto Alegre.

The W of Rio Grande do Sul also contains the Sete Povos das Missões Orientais (**see p 437**). The only considerable Jesuit remains in Brazilian territory (very dramatic) are at *São Miguel* (church, 1735-45, and small museum; **D** *Hotel Barichello*, highly rec, **E** *Hotel Nova Esperança*, behind bus station, without breakfast;) some 50 km from *Santo Ângelo*, pop 76,375 (*Hotel Turis*, R Antônio Manoel 726, T (55) 312-4055, helpful, rec; **D** *Maerkli*, Av Brasil 1000, rec; other cheap central hotels near old railway station). At São Miguel there is a son et lumière show, weekdays at 2000, weekends at 1930, but ends too late to return to Santo Ângelo. *Gaúcho* festivals often held on Sun afternoons, in a field near the Mission (follow the music). East of Santo Ângelo is *Passo Fundo*, "the most *gaúcho* city in Rio Grande do Sul", so much so that the town's square boasts a statue of a maté gourd and bombilla—otherwise not much of interest (pop 147,215; **E** *Hotel dos Viajantes* opp bus station.) Planalto buses run from Uruguaiana via Barra do Quarai/Bella Unión to Salto and Paysandú in Uruguay. *São Gabriel*, a small town just W of Planalto, boasts very interesting amethyst mines.

Entering Uruguay Those requiring a visa face problems: a medical exam is required before a visa can be issued, cost approximately US$20 and US$10 respectively. All buses, except those originating in Pelotas, stop at customs on both sides of the border; if coming from Pelotas, you must ask the bus to stop for exit formalities. You must have a Brazilian exit stamp to enter Uruguay. The Brazilian immigration office (and tourist caravan) is about $2^{1}/_{2}$ km from the border, on Av Argentina. International buses, eg TTL from Porto Alegre, make the crossing straightforward: the company holds passports; hand over your visitors card on leaving Brazil and get a Uruguayan one on entry. Have luggage available for inspection. Make sure you get your stamp; or walk back from town at your leisure. The Brazilian border town is **Chuí** (pop 20,060).

At Santana do Livramento all one need do is cross the main street, but the Uruguayan immigration is hard to find, in a side street. No customs formalities, but luggage is inspected on boarding bus for Montevideo, and there are checkpoints on the roads out of town. Bus to Montevideo, US$8. For motorists there are 3 customs offices in Santana do Livramento, about $1/2$ hr needed for formalities. Plenty of exchange offices on the Uruguayan side. Banco do Brasil on Av Sarandí; best rates for Amex TCs at **Val de Marne**.

Entering Brazil from Uruguay, on the Uruguayan side, the bus will stop if asked, and wait while you get your exit stamp (with bus conductor's help); on the Brazilian side, the appropriate form is completed by the rodoviária staff when you purchase your ticket into Brazil. The bus stops at Polícia Federal (Av Argentina) and the conductor completes formalities while you sit on the bus. **NB** Change all remaining Uruguayan pesos into *reais* before leaving Uruguay since not even black marketeers in Brazil want them. Note that you cannot obtain US$ cash in Brazil. Also, if entering by car, fill up with petrol in Brazil, where fuel is much cheaper.

Chuí hotels **C** *Cairo*, Av Uruguai, T 65-1076 opp Atlantic petrol station, shower, breakfast, clean, TV lounge; **C** *Turismo* Av Rio Branco 1078, T 63-1431. **D** *San Francisco*, Av Colombia e R Chile, shower, clean, restaurant; on R Chile, **D** *Itaipú*, No 1169, 1 block from rodoviária, shared showers, clean, friendly; *Hospedagem Roberto* at No 1631; **E** *Pensão* in private house at No 767. *Atlantico*, Barra do Chuí, Km 11. In Chuy (Uruguay), there is a *hospedaje* on Av Brasil, opp the Atlantic petrol station.

Post Offices Av Uruguay, between Colombia and Argentina (Chuí); Av Brasil, 4 blocks from Gen Artigas (Chuy).

Telephones in Brazil, corner of R Chile and Av Argentina; in Uruguay one block behind plaza, between Calles L Olivera and Gen Artigas.

Tourist Information On Av Argentina (Chuí), $2^{1}/_{2}$ km from border; Uruguayan office in middle of Av Brasil/Uruguay, at Av Argentina/Calle Gen Artigas junction.

Transport Rodoviária on R Venezuela. Buses run from Chuí to **Pelotas** (6-7 daily, US$7.25, 4 hrs), **Rio Grande** (0700, 1400, 5 hrs, US$7.75) and **Porto Alegre** (1200, 2400, $7^{1}/_{2}$ hrs, US$13.25); also from Chuí to **Santa Vitória** nearby, where there are a few hotels and rather quicker bus services to the main cities.

Santa Catarina

Further up the coast, in Santa Catarina (pop 4,536,435), a group of Germans settled at Lajes in 1822. In 1848 a new German-speaking settlement was founded at Blumenau. The Germans spread inland over the mountains from the port of São Francisco to Joinville (censuses have revealed that some isolated families still speak only German, understanding little Portuguese). The Italians came later. Over northern Rio Grande do Sul and Santa Catarina the vast majority of people today can trace their origin to these immigrants.

In Santa Catarina, a state of smallholdings, the farmer owns his land and cattle: the familiar European pattern of mixed farming worked by the family. Sixty per cent of the population is rural. There is coal in the S, and flourishing food processing (notably poultry and soyabean) and knitted textile industries. Itajaí and São Francisco do Sul are the main ports, handling 90% of the trade. Except for the summer months of Jan and Feb, the beaches of Santa Catarina are pleasant and uncrowded.

Just across the border from Rio Grande do Sul (but not on the main highway—BR101) is **Praia Grande** (hotel, E, and churrascaria, just off praça, good and cheap; cheap hotel at bus station, E). Buses from Praia Grande go to **Araranguá** (pop 48,220), on the BR101, 13 km from which is the beautiful beach of **Arroio do Silva** (**D** *Hotel Palace Scaini*, T/F 22-1466, good food, clean, rec). Some 75 km N of Araranguá is the coalfield town of **Tubarão** (pop 95,060;

D *Hotel Mossi*, in centre, excellent). Inland from the main road are the coalfields of Criciúma and Içara, all interesting, and the nearby beaches are good.

From Tubarão one can visit the **Termas do Gravatal**. (There is one first class hotel, and two others: **E** *Petit Village*, a/c, mineral pool, good value, quiet, good food.) Also, buses go inland to Lauro Müller, then over the Serra do Rio do Rastro (beautiful views of the coast in clear

1. Forte São José da Ponta Grossa
2. Forte Nossa Senhora da Conceição
3. Universidade Federal
4. Morro da Cruz
5. Lagoa da Conceição
6. Lagoa do Peri
7. Tourist Office

0   5
km

ILHA SANTA CATARINA

weather). At **Bom Jardim da Serra** there is an apple festival every Apr. A dirt road continues to São Joaquim (see p 452), and over Pericõ to **Urubici** (E *Pensão Anderman*, clean, friendly, big meals). A new paved road is being built, as far as Santo Amaro da Imperatriz. There are direct buses from São Joaquim to Florianópolis.

About 60 km inland from Tubarão is **Orleães**. It has one of the most interesting and least known museums in the area, which has an original water-powered workshop and sawmill, complete with waterwheel. It dates from the original settlers (late 19th century), and is still in working order. To get there one must get off the bus at the junction about 3 km from the town.

386 km NE of Porto Alegre, 15 km from Tubarão, is the small fishing port of **Laguna** (pop 44,825; *Hotel Laguna Tourist*, first class; *Hotel Itapirubá*, 4-star with beach and pool; **B** *Turismar*, Av Rio Grande do Sul 207, view over Mar Grosso beach, TV; several others, medium-priced, **D** *Grande*, opp post office, clean, without breakfast, **E** *Recanto*, close to bus terminal, clean, basic), in southern Santa Catarina. At Laguna is the Anita Garibáldi Museum, containing documents, furniture, and the personal effects of the Brazilian wife of the hero who fought in the 1840s for the independence of Rio Grande do Sul and later helped to unify Italy (US$0.10). Laguna's beach, 2 km from the centre, is not very good, but 16 km away (by ferry and road) are beaches and dunes at Cavo de Santa Marta. Also from Laguna, take a Lagunatur or Auto Viação São José bus to Farol (infrequent, US$0.85). You have to cross the mouth of the Lagoa Santo Antônio by ferry to get to Farol; look out for fishermen aided by dolphins (*botos*). Here is a fishing village with the alleged third oldest lighthouse in the world (Farol Santa Marta)—guided tours available (taxi, US$10, not including ferry toll). No hotels, but it is possible to bargain with fishermen for a bed. (Bus to/from Porto Alegre, $5\frac{1}{2}$ hrs, with Santo Anjo Da Guarda; same company goes to Florianópolis, 2 hrs, but you can't buy a ticket before the bus arrives in Laguna—as soon as it comes in, follow the driver to ticket office.) Another 32 km to the N of Laguna is the port of **Imbituba** (pop 30,975) where there is a carbo-chemical plant, from which air pollution is very bad. Imbituba sends the coal mined in the area between Araranguá and Tubarão in coastal vessels to Rio de Janeiro, where it is railed to the steel mills at Volta Redonda for coking. The rail link between Imbituba and Tubarão is one of the busiest steam services in South America (freight only apart from an occasional tourist steam train on Sun, probably summer only). There are good beaches (particularly those near Garopaba and Araçatuba), and bus services to Porto Alegre.

The 124 km N of Laguna is **Florianópolis** (founded in 1726, pop 254,945, CEP 88000, DDD 0482) capital of the State, on the Ilha de Santa Catarina joined to the mainland by two bridges, one of which is Ponte Hercílio Luz, the longest steel suspension bridge in Brazil (closed in 1994). The newer Colombo Machado Salles bridge has a pedestrian and cycle way beneath the roadway. It is a port of call for coastal shipping, 725 km from Rio de Janeiro and 420 from Santos. The natural beauty of the island, beaches and bays make Florianópolis a popular tourist centre (only Jan and Feb are very crowded and expensive). The southern beaches are usually good for swimming, the E for surfing, be careful of the undertow. It seems a pity that the city's waterfront, scene of a traditional market, has been filled in and reclaimed and that the city is not in general better maintained. The **cathedral** on Praça 15 de Novembro has a life-size sculpture in wood of the flight into Egypt, originally from the Austrian Tyrol. Forts include the **Santana** (which houses a **Museu de Armas de Policia Militar**), **São José da Ponta Grossa** (at the N end of the island) and **Nossa Senhora da Conceição** (at the S end). There are three other museums, the **Museu Histórico** in the old Palácio Cruz e Souza, on Praça 15 de Novembro (1000-2000, Tues-Fri, 1000-1800 Sat-Sun), the **Museu de Antropologia** at the Federal University (0900-1700 Mon-Fri 1300-1800 Sat-Sun) and the **Museu do Homem Sambaqui** at the Colégio Catarinense, R Esteves Júnior 159 (open 0800-1100, 1400-1700, Mon-Sat). There is a look-out point at **Morro da Cruz** (take Empresa Trindadense bus, waits 15 mins). Carnival is recommended as beautiful.

Hotels L3 *Florianópolis Palace*, R Artista Bittencourt and R dos Ilhéus 26, T 22-9633,

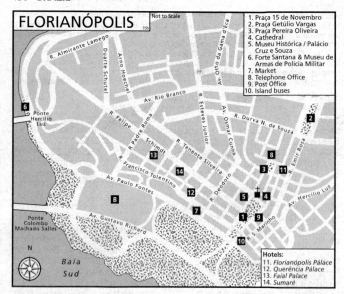

FLORIANÓPOLIS

Not to Scale

1. Praça 15 de Novembro
2. Praça Getúlio Vargas
3. Praça Pereira Oliveira
4. Cathedral
5. Museu Histórica / Palácio Cruz e Souza
6. Forte Santana & Museu de Armas de Policia Militar
7. Market
8. Telephone Office
9. Post Office
10. Island buses

Hotels:
11. Florianópolis Pálace
12. Querência Pálace
13. Faial Palace
14. Sumaré

F 23-0300, best, a/c, clean, TV, rec, but check bill; **A1** *Ivoram*, Av Hercílio Luz 652, T 24-5388, F 24-5890, discount in off season; **A3** *Royal*, Trav João Pinto 34, T 22-2944, F 22-2537, good; **B** *Oscar Palace*, Av Hercílio Luz 90, T 22-0099 watch the bill carefully; **B** *Pousada dos Tucanos*, Estra Geral da Costa de Dentro 2776, T 237-5084, English, French, Spanish, spacious bungalows in garden setting, excellent organic food, owner will collect, very highly rec; **C** *Veleiro*, R Silva Jardim 234, T 23-6622, with breakfast, a/c and TV, rec, clean, friendly, pier for yachts, 10 mins from bus station, take Cidade Universitária bus.

Within 10 mins' walk of the rodoviária: **A3** *Querência Palace*, R Jerônimo Coelho 95, T 24-2677, F 22-3874, highly rec; R Felipe Schmidt, **A1** *Faial Palace*, No 603, T 23-2766, F 22-9435, good restaurant; **D** *Cacique*, No 53, good, clean, good value but rooms vary; **B** *Felippe*, one block from 15 de Novembro at R João Pinto 25, good, clean, friendly, small rooms, 10% off to Youth Hostel members. *Dormitória Estrela*, R Mafra, nr R Bento Gonçalves, very basic but cheap. *Pousada do Sol*, 7 km from airport, T 222-2869, on the beach, pool, rec. On the mainland: **B** *Bruggeman*, R Santos Saraiva 300, T 44-2344, F 44-2045 (bus 236 or 226 from Terminal Urbano do Aterro), motel-type rooms and 2-star accommodations; **C** *Filadelfia*, Santos Saraiva 8, does a good breakfast; *Noblis* and *Continental* in the same road are cheaper; **C** *Oasis*, R Gral L Bittencourt 201, T 44-2440, with breakfast, clean, good (take bus 201 from here to bus terminal); **D** *Carvalho*, Fúlvio Adduci 184-186, good views, clean, rec. To rent a room, contact Leny Saboia, R J Colago 525, Jardím Santa Mônica, T 33-4684 (take a bus to Beira Mar Norte, alight at Santa Mônica supermarket); Apartment to let, Term Tur Joaquina, T 32-0059. Houses to let from Federico Barthe, Ponta das Canas, Lagoinha, T 66-0897; also Ricardo at R Manoel Severimo de Oliveira 8, Lagoa da Conceição. There are plenty of cabins and apartments for rent outside the Jan-Feb season.

Youth hostels on the island: Ilha de Santa Catarina, R Duarte Schutel 59 (T 22-3781, clean, rec, cooking facilities, breakfast extra, low rates for IYHA cardholders, US$4/night); Barra da Lagoa (T 22-6746) and Fortaleza da Barra (T 32-0169), both on Estrada Geral da Barra da Lagoa; Praia do Campeche (T 22-6746) and Praia dos Ingleses (T 22-6746 also).

Camping Camping Clube do Brasil, São João do Rio Vermelho, near the lagoon, 21 km out of town; also at Lagoa da Conceição, Praia da Armação, Praia dos Ingleses, Praia Canasvieiras. "Wild" camping allowed at Ponta de Sambaqui. Beaches of Brava, Aranhas, Galheta, Mole, Campeche, Campanhas and Naufragados. 4 km S of Florianópolis, camping site with bar at Praia do Sonho on the mainland, beautiful, deserted beach with an island fort nearby. "Camping Gaz" cartridges from Riachuelo Supermercado, on R Alvim with R São Jorge.

Restaurants *Manolo's*, R Felipe Schmidt 71, near centre, good, but not cheap. *Lindacap*, R Felipe Schmidt 178 on outskirts (closed Mon), rec, good views. *Pim-Pão*, R Marechel Deodoro, good cheap breakfast, lunches; *Don Pepé Pizza*, Almirante Lamego, giant helpings; *Papparella*, Av R de Arruda Ramos 1560, excellent giant pizzas; *Snack Bar Doll*, R Vidal Ramos, open 0900-1900. Shrimp dishes are good everywhere. *Polly's*, Praça 15 de Novembro, good food and service, reasonable prices; *Macarronada Italiana*, Av Beira Mar Norte 196, good. *Pirão*, upstairs in market, very popular; *Recaka* churrasceria, Av Beira Mar, highly rec. *Churrascaria Ataliba*, Rúa Jaú Guedes da Fonseca s/n, 2 km from centre at Coqueiros, excellent rodízio. *Garagem Sopas e Panquecas*, R Duarte Schutel. Vegetarian: *Vida*, R Visconde Ouro Preto 62 (closed Sun). *Padaria União*, R Tenente Silveira, very good; *La Cucina*, R Padre Roma 73, buffet lunch, Mon-Sat, pay by weight - good, vegetarian choices, rec.

Banks and Exchange Banco do Brasil, R dos Ilheus; Banco do Estado de São Paulo, Tenente Silveira 55; Banco Estado de Santa Catarina, Trajano 33, cheques and cash. Turismo Holzmann, R Conselheiro Mafra 53, parallel exchange rate in adjoining room. Lovetur, Av Osmar Cunha 15, Ed Ceisa and Centauro Turismo at same address. Money changers on R Felipe Schmidt.

Electric Current 220 volts AC.

Post Office Praça 15 de Novembro 5, T 22-3188.

Telecommunications Telesc, Praça Pereira Oliveira 20, T 23-3700 (interstate and international telephones).

Tourist Office Head office: Portal Turístico de Florianópolis (Setur), at the mainland end of the bridge, 0800-2000 (Sat, Sun 0800-1800); Praça 15 de Novembro, 0800-1800 (2200 in high season), reliable for leaving messages; at bus terminal and airport, 0700-1800, (0800 Sat, Sun); maps available, free.

Car Hire Auto Locadora Coelho, Felipe Schmidt 81, vehicles in good condition.

Transport Daily flights to Porto Alegre, São Paulo, Curitiba, Rio de Janeiro, Belo Horizonte, Vitória, Aracaju, Maceió, Salvador and Recife; also flights on weekdays from many southern Brazilian cities. International flights from Buenos Aires daily (several at weekends); once a week from Montevideo. Bus terminal at the E (island) end of the Ponte Colombo Machado Salles; the Terminal Urbano do Aterro for the island nearby, is on R Proc A Gomes between R Paulo Fortes and R Antônio Luz, 2 blocks from Praça 15 de Novembro. Regular daily buses to Porto Alegre (US$10.50, 7 hrs), São Paulo, (US$19.25, *leito* US$38.50), Rio, 20 hrs (US$31 ordinary, 62 *leito*), Brasília, (3 a week at 0300, US$43); to Foz do Iguaçu (US$20, continuing to Asunción), to most other Brazilian cities and to Montevideo, US$50, daily 0900, by TTL. Buenos Aires, US$115, Pluma, buses very full in summer, book 1 week in advance. The coastal highway (BR-101) is preferred as an alternative to the congested inland BR-116; it runs close to Florianópolis but it is bad in places and has many lorries.

Excursions There are 42 beaches around the island almost all easily reached by public buses: northern beaches from the Terminal Urbano do Aterro, southern beaches from the nearby Praça 15 de Novembro (schedules from Tourist Office). Buses (US$0.15-0.35) run hourly to virtually every place on the island. To **Lagoa da Conceição** for beaches, sand dunes, fishing, church of NS da Conceição (1730), boat rides on the lake (Ricardo, R Man S de Oliveira 8, CEP 88062, T 320107, rents self-contained apartments, can arrange houses also, rec; restaurants: *Oliveira*, excellent seafood dishes; *Leca*, try *rodízio de camarão*, prawns cooked in a dozen ways; *Caminho das Índias*, Av das Rendeiras 69, warmly rec; Tandem hang gliding, Lift Sul Vôo Livre, T 32-0543. Across the island at **Barra da Lagoa** is a pleasant fishing village and beach, lively in the summer season, with plenty of good restaurants, which can be reached by "Barra da Lagoa" bus (US$0.50, every ½ hr from Terminal Urbano, platform 5, or *seletivo* vans, US$1; **E** *Hotel Camping Duvalerim*, on beach, overpriced; *Camping da Barra*, beautiful site, clean, helpful owner). The same bus goes to beaches at Mole and at Joaquina (surfing championships in Jan, **A1** *Hotel Cris*, T 32-0380, F 32-0075, luxurious, rec). At Barra da Lagoa, **A3** *Cabañas Verde Limão*, on the beach, small cabins with bath, fan, fridge, friendly; **C** *Cabanas da Barra*, R Geral 23, good, German and English spoken. Hotel near Barra da Lagoa: **C** *Gaivota* T 32-0177 (Familia Coelho), Praia do Moçambique, closed off season, not rec; nearby is **D** *Pousada-Lanchonete Sem Nome*, in 4-bunk rooms, bathrooms separate, kitchen, laundry, rec; **E** *Albergue do Mar*, basic, friendly, good for lone travellers; **E** *Pousada Ale-Pris*; *Dormitório Beira Rio*, noisy; **C** *Mini-Hotel Caiçara*, good, clean, near beach; **D** *Pousada Floripaz*, 2-bedroom apartments with kitchen, restaurant and bar, T 32-3089, highly rec; *Pousada Sol Mar* operates as a youth hostel but only 2 bathrooms for all. Mussels can be collected at the rocky headland, 1 km further on there are clams, and, for the enthusiast, cannibal clams and sand urchins. Also visit the "city of honey bees" with a Museo da Apicultura, closes 1600 Sat, and the Church of Sto Antônio Lisboa; take Trinidadense bus 331 or any bus going N, to the turn off, on the way to Sambaqui beach and fishing village. There is a pleasant fishing village at *Ponta das Canas*, walk 1 km to Praia Brava for good surfing, and the beach at *Canasvieiras* is good (B *Hotel Moçambique*, T/F 66-1857, in centre of village, noisy at weekends). In the N of the island, at *Praia dos Ingleses* (bus 602) is B *Sol e Mar*, T 62-1271, excellent, friendly, rec. Other northern beaches: Jureré, Daniela and Forte (with fort and beautiful views). In the S of the island are *Praia de Campeche*, 30 mins by bus from Florianópolis (*Hotel São Sebastião da Praia*, T/F 37-4247/4066, resort hotel on a splendid beach, offers special monthly rate Apr to Oct, excellent value; *Natur Campeche Hotel Residencial*, T 37-4011, 10 mins walk from beach), *Praia da Armação* with, just inland, **Lagoa do Peri** (a protected area). Further S is *Pantano do Sul*, an unspoilt fishing village. D *Pousada Sítio dos Tukanos*, Caixa Postal 5016, T 375084; take bus to Pantano do Sul, walk 6 km or telephone and arrange to be picked up, German owner speaks English, beautiful, warmly rec. Praia dos Naufragados and Fora beaches: take bus to Caieira da Barra do Sul and take 1-hr walk through fine forests.

Excursions can be made on the mainland to the hot springs at *Caldas da Imperatriz* (41°C) and *Águas Mornas* (39°C); at the former are 2 spa hotels (B *Caldas da Imperatriz*, meals and baths incl, built in 1850 under the auspices of Empress Teresa Cristina, houses public baths; from **A3** *Plaza Caldas da Imperatriz*, with baths, swimming pools, very well appointed), at Águas Mornas, the **A1** *Palace Hotel* is on the site of the springs, baths open to public Mon-Fri am only. Boat trips can be made from Florianópolis in the bay, T 22-1806, from US$4.50.

From Florianópolis a partly paved road runs SW inland via São Joaquim (see below) to *Lages* (formerly spelt Lajes; pop 150,865, CEP, DDD 0492) a convenient stopping place on BR-116 between Caxias do Sul and Curitiba. Despite the poor road, however, this journey is perhaps the most interesting in the State, with scenery changing as the road climbs out of coastal forest (3 buses a day do this journey in summer, 1 in winter, 5 hrs, via Alfredo Wagner, otherwise go via Blumenau). (*Grande Hotel*, good, but no heat; cheaper is D *Presidente*; *Natal*, cheap, adequate; *Rodalar*, *Centauro*, clean, friendly, restaurant, both E, near bus station. Bus station is ½-hr walk SE of centre. Voltage 220 AC.)

São Joaquim (pop 22,285) at 1,360m, the highest town in Southern Brazil, regularly has snowfalls in winter; very pleasant town with an excellent climate (Camping Clube do Brasil site). East of the town, in the Serra Geral is the **São Joaquim National Park** (33,500 ha), with canyons containing sub-tropical vegetation, and araucaria forest at higher levels (local Ibama office, T 0482-22-6202, Secretaria de Turismo de São Joaquim, T 0492-33-0258). The park has not been officially designated, it is still all privately owned. There is no bus. To visit, ask landowners if you may see the beautiful scenery.

Hotels: *Nevada* (expensive meals) and D *Maristela*, (good breakfast) both on R Manoel Joaquim Pinto, 213 and 220 respectively (5 mins' walk from Rodoviária). Bus to Florianópolis 0830 and 2230, 7½ hrs, US$9.50. To Caxias do Sul, 4½ hrs, US$7.25. The bridge over the Rio Pelotas on the road to Cambará do Sul and Bom Jesús is closed, a new bridge is being built.

On the coast N of Florianópolis there are many resorts. They include *Porto Belo*, a fishing village of 9,700 people on the N side of a peninsula settled in 1750 by Azores islanders, with a calm beach and a number of hotels and restaurants (bus Florianópolis—Porto Belo with Praiana or Biguaçu, 8 daily, 3 on Sun). West of Port Belo is Praia de Perequê (Hotels: **E** *Tati*, T 69-4363, across from beach, and **E** *Blumenauense*, with bath and breakfast, on beach, T 69-4208). In Porto Belo itself is *Hotel Baleia Branca* (T 69-4011), with camping. Around the peninsula are wilder beaches reached by rough roads: Bombas (2 hotels), Bombinhas (*Pousada do Arvoredo*, T 69-4355, up on a hill), Mariscal, and, on the southern side, Cantinho (B *Pousada Zimbros*, T 69-4225, less off season, on beach, sumptuous breakfast, restaurant, highly rec, spear fishing guide). *Itapema* (66 km, many hotels). *Camboriú* (pop 25,715, 86 km) once beautiful, now has 4 blocks of concrete jungle behind the beach, which is very safe. From 15 Dec to end-Feb it is very crowded and expensive; the resort is popular with Argentines, especially the over 40s. At other times of the year it is easy to rent furnished apartments by the day or week (try Bom Pastor agency, Av Brasil 1861, T 0473-66-0769, reliable). There are a great many hotels, restaurants and campsites (an excellent hotel, opp the rodoviária, is D *Jaitur*, with bath and hot water, clean, safe). Note that from mid-Jul to mid-Aug it can be chilly. Buses run from

Florianópolis, Joinville and Blumenau. TTL buses Montevideo-São Paulo stop here at about 2000-2200, US$50, a good place to break the journey. A few km S, at Lojas Apple, there is a museum, zoo and aquarium; and Meia Praia, which is quieter and cleaner than Camboriú. Pinho beach, 15 km out of the city, is one of Brazil's few legal nudist beaches; 2 campsites and a small hotel. Between Itajaí and Camboriú is the beautiful, deserted (and rough) beach of Praia Brava.

One hundred km up the coast N of Florianópolis by the BR-101 paved road or by sea is the most important port in Santa Catarina: *Itajaí* (pop 119,585, CEP 88300, DDD 0473) at the mouth of the Itajaí river. It is well served by vessels up to 5^{1}/$_{2}$m draught, and is the centre of a district largely colonized by Germans and Italians. It is one of Brazil's main fishing ports and also handles exports of timber, starch, tapioca, sassafras oil, and tobacco. Airport. You can walk to Cabeçudas beach, which is quiet and small.

Hotels A1 *Marambaia Cabeçudas*, at Cabeçudas beach, best, 6 km out of town, T 44-0999; **C** *Grande*, R Felipe Schmidt 44, T 44-0968, good value; *Maringá*, N of town, friendly, cheap and clean, with Shell service station next door, providing good food, open all night. *Rex*, *Cacique*, both on R Asseburg, cheap, near market. Rec. **Bar** *Trudys*, on riverfront at end of main street, a good place for changing cash.

Finnish Consulate R Almirante Tamandaré 100, T 44-6511.

Resorts N of Itajaí include Piçarras, with sandy beaches interspersed with rocky headlands (ideal for fishing), and *Barra Velha* (**D** *Hotel Mirante*, good, cheap restaurant, and 2 dearer hotels).

There is a 61 km paved road to *Blumenau* (pop 211,175, CEP 89100, DDD 0473), 47 km up the Itajaí river. It is in a prosperous district settled mostly by Germans; see Museo da Família Colonial, German immigrant museum, Av Duque de Caxias 78, open Mon-Fri, 0800-1130, 1330-1730, Sat am only, US$0.15. German Evangelical Church. A clean, orderly city with almost caricatured Germanic architecture, Blumenau offers a charming alternative to the less-organized Brazilian way of life. It is very popular with people from São Paulo. Places of interest include the houses, now museums (open 0800-1800) of Dr Bruno Otto Blumenau and of Fritz Müller (a collaborator of Darwin), who bought the Blumenau estate in 1897 and founded the town, which is a notable textile centre. A "traditional" Oktoberfest beer-festival was started in 1984 here, and was expected to become the second largest in the world after Munich's (bands come from Germany for the event). Visitors report it is worth attending on weekday evenings but weekends are too crowded. It is repeated, but called a "summer festival", in the 3 weeks preceding Carnival ("5 visitors").

Hotels Reservations essential during Oktoberfest. **L2** *Plaza Hering*, 5-star, 7 de Setembro 818, T 26-1277, F 22-9409, heating and a/c; **A1** *Garden Terrace*, R Padre Jacobs 45, T 26-3544, F 26-0366; **A1** *Garden Convention Center*, Alameda Rio Branco 21, T 26-0145; **A1** *Himmelblau Palace*, R 7 de Setembro 1415, T/F 22-5800; **A3** *Glória*, R 7 de Setembro 954, T 22-1988, F 22-5370, German-run, excellent coffee shop; **C** *Blumenau Tourist Hotel*, R Francisco Margarida 67, T 23-4640, 200m from bus station, helpful (all aforementioned hotels have heating in rooms); **D** *Central*, R 7 de Setembro 1036, T 22-0570, basic, with bath, E without, both without breakfast, clean, but not safe for luggage; **D** *City*, R Ángelo Dias 263, T 22-2205; **E** *Herrmann*, central, Floriano Peixoto 213, T 22-4370, rec, shower, clean. Many cheap hotels do not incl breakfast. Most hotels and restaurants very clean. Youth Hostel at R Paraíba 66 (T 22-8420).

Camping Municipal campsite, 3 km out on R Pastor Osvaldo Hesse; Paraíso dos Poneis, 9 km out on the Itajaí road, also Motel; Refúgio Gaspar Alto, 12 km out on R da Glória.

Restaurants Good German food at *Frohsinn*, Morro Aipim (panoramic view) and *Cavalinho Branco*, Av Rio Branco 165, huge meals; international eating at *Moinho do Vale*, Paraguai 66. *Amigo*, Peixoto 213, huge cheap meals; *Caféhaus Glória*, in *Hotel Glória*, excellent coffee shop. On R Alwin Schrader, *Biergarten*, with a "German" band on Sun afternoon, and nearby *Bar Kriado*, with authentic Brazilian music, Mon-Fri only; dancing and good atmosphere at *Adega Espanhola*, R 7 de Setembro; *Deutsches Eck*, same street No 432, rec, esp *carne pizzaiola*; *Gruta Azul*, Rodolfo Freygang, good, popular, not cheap. *Internacional*, Nereu Ramos 61, Chinese, very good, not particularly expensive; good Chinese food at R 15 de Novembro 346, near Tourist office; vegetarian lunches, R Curt Herring, near *Herrmann* hotel.

Exchange At *Câmbios*/travel agencies: *Vale do Hajaí Turismo e Cambio*, Av Beira Rio 167, very helpful, German spoken; *International Turismo*, 1 block away. *President Turismo*, 7 de Setembro, 2nd floor; also *Turismo Holtzmann* nearby; *Ilhatur Turismo*, Rodolfo Freygang 5, 1st floor. *Tilotur Turismo*, Alameda Rio Branco e 15 de Novembro, 2nd floor; *Casa Rowder*, R Curt Herring 20.

Voltage 220 AC.

Amenities *Teatro Carlos* Gomes is also exhibition centre; public library open 0800-1800; German bookshops, *Librerias Alemãs*, at bus station and RR 7 de Setembro (also stocks English books), and 15 de Novembro. Craft shop, *Casa Meyer*, 15 de Novembro 401.

International Telephones Corner of Av Brasil and República Argentina.

Bus Bus to rodoviária from Av Pte Castelo-Branco (Beira Rio). Good bus connections in all directions from Blumenau. Blumenau to **Caxias do Sul** at 1930 only, arrives 0400, US$14.50.

Excursions By bus to Timbo and Pomerode (from riverside road opp Prefeitura) past rice fields and wooden houses set in beautiful gardens. At *Pomerode* (pop 18,790) 32 km, US$1 (**D** *Hotel Central*, big lunches) there is an interesting zoo. Tourist office. The N German dialect of Plattdeutsch is still spoken here. The *Tortenparadies* serves excellent German cakes. Rex Bus goes to Iraguã from Pomerode; change for connection to Joinville, US$3. ½-day excursion to Gaspar to visit the cathedral set high above the river (Verdi Veli bus company from stop outside the huge supermarket on R 7 de Setembro in the centre).

To Iguaçu As an alternative to a direct bus, daily from Florianópolis and Itajaí to Iguaçu via Blumenau, you can travel through rich and interesting farming country in Santa Catarina and Rio Grande do Sul, stopping at *Joaçaba*, a town of German immigrants (pop 28,145 *Hotel Colonial*, at bus station, *Lotus*, across bridge, both E), *Erexim* (**D** *Hotel Rex*, strong *gaúcho* influence), or *Iraí* Italian immigrant area, town with thermal springs (pop 11,595; **D** *Hotel São Luís*, with full board, town good for semi-precious stones), thence from any of these places to Pato Branco and Cascavel (see p 461 for connections to Foz do Iguaçu).

2 hrs from Joaçaba is *Treze Tilias*, a little village where 19th-century Tyrolean dialect is still spoken and the emigrant culture is perfectly preserved.

São Francisco do Sul (pop 29,550) 80 km up the coast is the port for the town of Joinville, 45 km inland at the head of the Cachoeira river. Most of the colonial architecture has been replaced by modern buildings. There are some excellent beaches nearby, such as Ubatuba, Enseada (hotels, pensions and 3 camp sites, Pascerella rec) and Cápri. (At weekend trips to Ilha do Farol in port's supply boat.) Petrobrás oil refinery, but oil pollution has been reported, take mosquito repellent. (**B** *Hotel Kontiki*, on Camacho 33, T 44-0232; **D** *Hotel Avenida*, with breakfast, clean, friendly; **B** *Zibamba*, R Fernandes Dias 27, T 44-0077, F 44-0823, central, good restaurant. The *Restaurante Franciscano*, on the Praia dos Coqueiros, is rec, so are the *Metralhas* and *Flutuante* (good seafood.) Bus terminal is 1½ km from centre. Direct bus (Penha) daily to Curitiba at 0730, US$6, 3½ hrs. Men are not allowed to wear shorts.

Joinville (pop 346,095, CEP 89200, DDD 0474) the state's largest city lies 2 km from the main coastal highway, BR-101, by which Curitiba and Florianópolis are less than 2 hrs away. To Guaratuba (see p 460) by bus, 1¼ hrs, US$2 (connections to Paranaguá).

See the **Museu Nacional da Imigração e Colonização** in the Palácio dos Príncipes, R Rio Branco 229 (Tues-Fri 0900-1800, Sat-Sun 0900-1200, 1400-1800), which has a collection of objects from the original German settlement. The interesting **Museu de Arte** is in the old residence of Ottokar Doerfell, R 15 de Novembro 1400 (open Tues-Sun, 0900-1200, 1400-2200). The **Museu Arqueológico do Sambaqui**, R da Francisca 600, has a collection dating back to 5000 BC (open Tues-Fri, 0900-1200, Sat, Sun, and holidays, 0900-1200, 1400-1800; US$0.25). **Museum** of the sculptor **Fritz Alt**, R Aubé (0800-1800, closed Mon).

At **Expovile**, 4 km from centre on BR-101 (continuation of 15 de Novembro) is an exhibition of Joinville's industry. The industry does not, however, spoil the considerable charm of the city. There is an annual flower festival in the first fortnight of Sep.

Hotels *Tannehof*, Visconde de Taunay 340, T/F 22-8011, 4 stars, restaurant on 14th floor;

B *Anthurium Parque*, São José 226, T/F 22-6299, colonial style, good value, English spoken, friendly; **F** *Novo Horizonte*, at bus station, basic, clean; **D** *Konig*, 15 de Novembro 937; same street No 811, **D** *Mattes*, T 22-3582, good facilities.

Camping Camping Clube do Brasil, R Saguaçu, Horto Florestal. Municipal site, same road, 1 km from centre.

Restaurants *Pinheiro*, Rio Branco 299, is well worth a visit for excellent fish and shrimp dishes. For meat or German specialities, *Churrascaria Rex*, Blumenau 3097, *Churrascaria Ataliba*, near Expoville, *Bierkeller*, 15 de Novembro 497. Vegetarian: *Cozinha Natural*, R Marinho Lobo 38. The cheapest place to eat is the *Sociedade Ginástica*, R Ginásticos—you don't have to be a member.

Banks Banco do Brasil. Open 1000-1630.

Tourist Office corner Praça Nereu Ramos with R Príncipe; no information on cheap hotels. Good exchange rates

Air Service Airport 5 km from city. Daily flights to major cities.

Buses To Blumenau, US$3.50, 2¼ hrs. The bus terminal is 2½ km outside the town (regular bus service).

Excursions Four daily buses go to *Ubatuba* beach, a week-end resort (see above under São Francisco do Sul). The Sambaqui site of Rio Comprido can be reached by Gideon Bus, but there is not much to see. It is a pleasant trip to Jaraguá do Sul, European, hilly landscape.
　　The festival of São João in Jun can be seen best in Santa Catarina at *Campo Alegre*, the first town on the road inland to Mafra. There are bonfires, a lot of (German) folk dancing, and large quantities of *quentão* and *pinhões* (see under Gramado **Restaurants** above). It is a beautiful climb on the road from the BR-101 to Campo Alegre. The road continues through São Bento and Rio Negrinho to Mafra, from where a good road (the BR-116) goes to Curitiba.

The State of Paraná

The Italians were first in Paraná, but apart from a few Germans most of the later settlers were of Slavonic origin—Poles, Russians, Ruthenians and Ukrainians. Paraná is now the leading producer of wheat, rye, potatoes and black beans, but its population, 8,415,660, no longer expands as quickly as it did, partly because of the displacement of rural workers following the uprooting of coffee plants in the more frost-prone areas and the turning of the land over to cattle. The recent boom crop, soya, also employs fewer workers throughout the year than coffee.

Curitiba, capital of Paraná state (pop 1.3 million, CEP 80000, DDD 041), is a modern city at 900m on the plateau of the Serra do Mar. It has won a prize as one of the 3 cleanest cities in Latin America. A panoramic view can be had from the telecommunications tower, **Telepar**. The commercial centre is busy **R 15 de Novembro** (old name: R das Flores), which has a pedestrian area where there are Sat morning painting sessions for children. Another pedestrian area is behind the cathedral, near **Largo da Ordem**, with sacred art museum, flower clock and old buildings, very beautiful in the evening when the old lamps are lit - nightlife is concentrated here. Art market Sat morning in **Praça Rui Barbosa**, and on Sun morning in **Praça Garibáldi** (rec), beside the attractive Rosário church. The **Civic Centre** is at the end of Avenida Dr Cândido de Abreu, 2 km from the city centre: a monumental group of five buildings dominated by the **Palácio Iguaçu**, headquarters of the state and municipal governments. In a patio behind it is a relief map to scale of Paraná. The **Bosque de João Paulo II** behind the Civic Centre contains the Polish immigrants' museum: both are worth a visit. In contrast to the Civic Centre is the old municipal government building in French Art Nouveau style, now housing the **Museu Paranaense** in Praça Generoso Marques. Nearby, on Praça Tiradentes, is the **Cathedral** (1894). The most popular public park is the **Passeio Público**, in the heart of the city (closed Mon); it has a little zoo, a network of canals with boats, and a small aquarium. On the NE edge of the city is **Parque do Barigui**, take bus 450 "São Braz" from Praça Tiradentes. Near the shores of Lake Bacacheri on the northern edge of the city (R Nicarágua 2453) is an

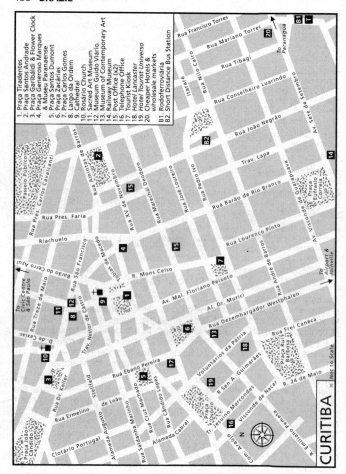

Key to map:

1. Praça Tiradentes
2. Praça Santos Andrade
3. Praça Garibáldi & Flower Clock
4. Praça Generoso Marques & Museu Paranaense
5. Praça Santos Dumont
6. Praça Cajarias
7. Praça Carlos Gomes
8. Largo da Ordem
9. Cathedral
10. Rosário Church
11. Sacred Art Museum
12. Museum Guido Viário
13. Museum of Contemporary Art
14. Railway Museum
15. Post Office (x2)
16. Telephone Office
17. Tourist Kiosk
18. Hotel Lancaster
19. Hotel Tourist Universo
20. Cheaper Hotels & wholesale markets
B1. Rodoferroviária
B2. Short Distance Bus Station

CURITIBA

unexpected Egyptian temple (the Brazilian centre of the Rosicrucians—visits can be arranged—take Santa Cândida bus to Estação Boa Vista, then walk). 4 km E of the rodoferroviário, the **Jardim Botânico** is worth visiting. There are three modern theatres, the Guaíra for plays and revues (also has free events—get tickets early in the day), one for concerts and ballet, and the Teatro Paiol in the old arsenal. Many of the main streets have been widened and the city is being rapidly transformed.

Museums Museu Paranaense, Praça Generoso Marques (open Tues-Fri 1000-1800, other days 1300-1800, closed first Mon of each month). **Museu David Carneiro**, on R Comendador Araújo 531, Sat, 1400-1600. **Museu Guido Viário**, R São Francisco 319, painter's house, Tues-Fri 1400-1830; **Museu de Arte Contemporânea**, R D Westphalen 16 (Tues-Fri 0900-1900, Sat-Sun 1400-1900). **Casa Andersen**, R Mateus Leme 336, house of painter, open Mon-Fri, 0900-1200, 1400-1800. **Arte Paranaense**, R Dr Keller 289, new, in restored house, Mon-Fri 1000-1800. **Museu do Expedicionário** (Second World War Museum), Praça do

Expedicionário, open daily 0800-1800; **Museo do Automóvel**, Av Cândido Hartmann 2300 (Sat 1400-1800, Sun 1000-1200, 1400-1800), all worth a visit.

Local Holidays Ash Wed (half-day); Maundy Thur (half-day); 8 Sep (Our Lady of Light).

Hotels L2 *Bourbon*, Cândido Lopes 102, T 322-4001, F 322-2282, most luxurious in centre, newly restored; **L2** *Mabu*, Praça Santos Andrade 830, T 234-2277, F 233-7963; **L2** *Grand Hotel Rayon*, R Visconde de Nacar 1424, T 800-8899, rec; **L3** *Slaviero Palace*, Sen Alencar Guimarães 50, T 322-7271, F 222-2393, central; **A1** *Iguaça Campestre*, on BR116, 8 km from centre (road to São Paulo), T 262-5313, F 262-5775, set in park, swimming pool, tennis, mini golf, horse riding. The following, in our categories **L3-A1**, are rec: *Caravelle Palace*, R Cruz Machado 282, T 322-5757, F 223-4443, first class; *Del Rey*, Ermelino de Leão 18, T/F 322-3242, good restaurants; *Lancaster*, R Voluntários da Pátria 91, T 223-8953, F 233-9214, tourist class; *Ouro Verde*, R Dr Murici 419, T 322-5454, F 225-6165, standard class. In the **A2-A3** categories: *Araucária Palace*, Amintas de Barros 73, T 224-2822, F 262-3030, good commercial hotel; *Curitiba Palace*, Ermelino de Leão 45, T 224-1222, central, very pleasant; *Jaraguá*, Av Pres A Camargo, T 362-2022, F 264-7763, opp station, very clean, noisy, good breakfast, rec (but not the buffet supper); *Tibagi*, Cândido Lopes 318, T 223-3141, F 234-4632, central, business hotel; *Tourist Universo*, Praça Gen Osório 63, T 223-5816, F 223-5420, Sky TV, good restaurant, rec. **B** *Climax*, R Dr Murici 411, T 224-3411, F 225-6165, good value, popular; **D** *Regência*, R Alfredo Bufrem 40, T 223-4557, with breakfast, excellent; **C** *Novo Roma*, R Barão do Rio Branco 805, T 224-2117, with bath, cheaper without; **D** *Cervantes*, R Alfredo Bufrem 66, T 222-9593, amazing breakfast, rec.

There are hotels in categories C downwards in the vicinity of the Rodoferroviária, but the cheaper ones are close to the wholesale market, which operates noisily throughout the night (there are many hotels so don't settle for a bad one), those listed are **C-D** unless stated otherwise: *Condor*, Av 7 de Setembro 1866, T 262-0322, a/c, TV, clean, breakfast, rec; *Costa Brava*, R Francisco Torres 386, T 262-7172, well rec; *Doral*, Mota 1144, T 222-1060, TV, frigobar, good breakfast; *Filadélfia*, Gen Carneiro 1094, T 264-5244, clean, good breakfast, 4 blocks from station through market; *Maia*, Av Pres Afonso Camargo, with bath, incl breakfast, clean and quiet; on same street **D** *Cristo Rei*, with bath, basic, clean; *Inca*, R João Negrão, German spoken; same street **F** *La Rocha*, No 528, basic; *Turismo*, Tibagi 950, 500m from rodoferroviária, clean, with bath, E without, fan, friendly, garage, good breakfast but some mixed reports; *SR*, Mariano Torres e Visc Guarapuava, rooms OK but noisy and poor service; **D** *Nova Lisboa*, Av 7 de Setembro 1948, with breakfast, bargain for cheaper rates without breakfast, clean; **E** *Ouro Preto*, Pedro Ivo, more expensive with bath, basic, not very helpful. Cheap hotel in N of city, **F** *Solar*, Jaime Reis 445, basic but adequate.

F *Casa dos Estudantes*, Parque Passeio Público, N side, with student card, 4 nights or more; **F** *Casa do Estudante Luterano Universitario*, R Pr Cavalcanti, T 223-8981, good. Youth hostels in Paraná state: Asociação Paranaense de Albergues de Juventude, Av Padre, Agostinho 645, Curitiba PR, CEP 80.410; in the city, *Hans Staden*, R Vol da Pátria 475, 2nd floor, T 232-9012.

Apart Hotel C *King's*, Av Silva Jardim 264, T 223-5953, good, secure, highly rec.

Camping Official site 7 km N of city, on São Paulo road. Camping Clube do Brasil, 14 km out on same road.

Restaurants *Ile de France* (French), Praça 19 de Dezembro 538; *Matterhorn*, Mateus Leme 575, centre (Swiss). **A** *Sacristia*, R João Manuel 197, restaurant, pizzeria, bar, very good; *Oriente*, R Ebano Pereira 26 (1st floor), excellent, huge Arab lunch. *Salão Italiano*, R Padre G Mayer 1095, Cristo Rei, good Brazilian and Italian food. *Cantina do Eisbein*, Av dos Estados 863, Agua Verde, owner Egon is friendly, duck specialities highly rec (US$15 for 2). Local and Italian food and local red wine in nearby Santa Felicidade (10 km out of town on road to Ponta Grossa), eg *Madalosso*, Av Manoel Ribas 5875, enormous Italian self-service, cheap, rec, and *Dom Antônio*, same street No 6121, excellent. *Sukiyat*, Yuasa 1923, cheap and good, rec. *Nakaba*, R Nunes Machado 56, Japanese, huge set meal under US$10.

Vegetarian: (most closed at night) *Transformação* (macrobiotic, shop also), Al Augusto Stellfeld 781; *Vegetariano*, Carlos de Carvalho 127, 13 de Maio 222; *Vherde Jante*, R Pres Faria 481, very good, US$2.85 (open in evening); *Super Vegetariano*, R Pres Faria 121, Cruz Machado 217, R Dr Murici 315, lunch and dinner Mon-Fri, very good and cheap (buffet US$1.35). *Kisco*, 7 de Setembro near Tibagi, good, huge *prato do dia*, US$4, friendly. *Panini*, R da Glória 307, rec for buffet lunches (US$4 with meat; US$2.50 vegetarian) in a charming house.

On Barão Rio Branco, *Pandulius*, self service, offers a full meal with juice for only US$1, rec. Av 7 de Setembro near Tibagi, good, huge *prato do dia*, US$4, friendly. Cheap food also near old railway station and a good meal in the bus station. Close to the Rodoferroviária is the market, where there are a couple of *lanchonetes*; also opp the fruit market *Chammoróco*, good meat dishes. Students can eat at University canteen (student cards required). Hot sweet wine sold on the streets in winter helps keep out the cold. Rec tea house: *Chez Arnold*, Av Manoel Ribas 526, in the Mercês district.

Bars At R Visconde de Nacar is the *Rua 24 Horas*, an indoor street full of bars and cafés, open all night. *Dallas*, R 7 de Setembro, is fun; *Francis Drake*, Alameda Dr Muricy 1111, pub; *London Pub*, São Francisco 294, rec.

Banks and Exchange Banco Noroeste, 15 de Novembro 168, advances on Eurocard/Master Card. **ABN/AMRO**, Dutch bank, Av Cândido Abreu 304, Centro Cívico, T 252-2233, changes TCs, also arranges money transfer from Netherlands, paid in Brazilian currency (2-3 days). **Triangle Turismo Travel**, Praça General Osório 213, cash and TCs; **Diplomata**, R Presidente Faria 145 in the arcade. Sydney Turismo, R Marechal Deodoro 301. **Credicard**, cash with Mastercard, R Saldanha Marinho 1439, Bigorrillo.

Cultural Institutes Centro Cultural Brasil-Estados Unidos (Mon-Fri, 0800-1200, 1400-2100); **Sociedade Brasileira de Cultura Inglesa** (British Council), R General Carneiro 679 (Caixa Postal 505). **Instituto Goethe**, Rua Schaffenberg, nr Military Museum, Mon-Thur 1500-1900, Library, Mon-Tues till 2130.

Consulates Austria, R Marechal Floriano Peixoto 228, Edif Banrisul, 17 andar, Caixa Postal 2473, T 224-6795. **Germany**, Av J Gualberto 1237, T 252-4244; **Swiss**, Av Mal F Peixoto, T 223-7553; **Netherlands**, R Mal Floriano Peixoto 96, conj 172, T 222-0097, consul Tony Bruinjé, open 1400-1700, except emergencies. **Uruguay**, R Vol da Pátria 475, 18th floor.

Electric Current 110 v 60 cycles.

Entertainment Pedeira Paulo Leminski, was a disused quarry in R J Gava, Pilarzinho district, now used for outdoor concerts, nearby is the new **Opera de Arame**.

Laundry R C Laurindo 63, next to theatre, US$3 for 5 kg. 2 laundries on Nilo Cairo about 3 blocks from *Hotel Hamarati*, US$2.80 for 4 kg wash and dry.

Post Office Main post office is at Marechal Deodoro 298; post offices also at R 15 de Novembro and R Pres Faria. **Telecommunications** Embratel, Galeria Minerva, R 15 de Novembro. UPS, T 262-6180 (Waldomiro).

Church services held in German at the Evangelical Church.

Shopping Curitiba is a good place to buy clothes and shoes. *H Stern* jewellers at Mueller Shopping Centre. Bookshop: *O Livro Técnico*, Shopping Itália, R João Negrão e Mal Deodoro.

Golf Graciosa Country Club, Av Munhoz da Rocha 1146: 9 holes.

Tourist Office *Guía Turística de Curitiba e Paraná*, annual, US$4, on sale at all kiosks, has been rec. Paranatur has booths at Rodoferroviária, and at airport, helpful, English spoken, but no maps. Free maps from R Ebano Pereira 187, 5th floor. Free weekly leaflet, *Bom Programa*, available shops, cinemas, paper stands etc. **Visa extensions** Federal police, Dr Muricy 814, 1000-1600.

Local Transport The city has a very efficient bus system; all bus stops have maps. Express buses on city routes are orange: eg from centre (Praça Rui Barbosa) take Leste bus marked "Villa Oficinas" or "Centenário" for Rodoferroviária (combined bus and railway station). A tourist bus, US$3, stops at the Botanic Garden, the Opera, the University and other sites; 4 stops permitted.

Transport Rodoferroviária at end of Av 7 de Setembro (bus to centre US$0.15); short-distance bus services (up to 40 km) begin at old bus station at R João Negrão 340. Passenger trains to Paranaguá, see below. Also tourist train on first Sun of month to Lapa, 85 km, 3 hrs, tickets from travel agencies or from the railway station at Praça Eufrásio Correa (Railway Museum here is officially closed, but permission may be given to see the steam locomotives).
   Frequent buses to São Paulo (6 hrs, US$7.25; *leito* 14.50) and Rio de Janeiro (12 hrs, US$24, *leito* 50). To Foz do Iguaçu, 10 a day, 10 hrs, US$27.50; Porto Alegre, 10 hrs; Florianópolis, 4½ hrs; good service to most destinations in Brazil. Pluma bus to Buenos Aires US$128 and to Asunción US$32. TTL runs to Montevideo, 26 hrs, US$50, 0300 departure (*leito*) US$100. If travelling by car to Porto Alegre or Montevideo, the inland road (BR-116) is preferable to the coastal highway (BR-101).
   An international air terminal is under construction (1995).

Excursions The beautiful Ouro Fino estate (34 km) is open to the public every day except Mon, Dec-Mar, and every second Sun the rest of the year. The nearest bus stop is 16 km away at Campo Largo, so car is the best way to get there. Advance permission needed, from R Silva Jardim 167, Curitiba, T 232-7411, or phone Ouro Fino (041) 292-1913. Near Lapa (about 80 km SW) is a free, secure campsite from which the Groto do Monge can be visited.

20 km from Curitiba (at Km 119) on the road to Ponta Grossa is the Museu Histórico do Mate, an old water-driven mill where mate was prepared (free admission). On the same road is *Vila Velha*, now a national park, 97 km from Curitiba: the sandstone rocks have been weathered into most fantastic shapes. There is a Camping Clube do Brasil site near Vila Velha, 85 km from Curitiba. Alternatively, stay in Ponta Grossa (**see p 461**, last bus back, stops near Furnas at 1800). The park office is 300m from the highway and the park a further 1½ km (entrance—also to Furnas, keep the ticket—US$2—opens at 0800). If taking a bus from Curitiba, make sure it's going to the Parque Nacional and not to the town 20 km away. Transport from the Park to a swimming pool (free—costumes can be rented for US$2), 2 km away. Princesa dos Campos bus from Curitiba at 0730 and 0930, 1½ hrs, US$2.40 (return buses pass park entrance at 1500 and 1700). The Lagoa Dourada, surrounded by forests, is close by. Nearby are the Furnas, three water holes, the deepest of which has a lift (US$1—not always working) which descends almost to water level (the same level as Lagoa Dourada); entrance US$0.20. Bus from Vila Velha at 1310, 1610 and 1830, US$1, 4½ km to turn-off to Furnas (another ¼-hr walk) and Lagoa Dourada (it's not worth walking from Vila Velha to Furnas because it's mostly uphill along the main road). From the turn-off buses to Curitiba pass 10 mins before they pass Vila Velha. Allow all day if visiting all 3 sites (unless you hitch, or can time the buses well, it's a lot of walking). Since the afternoon buses which pass en route to Curitiba are often full, it may be advisable to go to Ponta Grossa and return to Curitiba from there.

Popular expeditions during the summer are by paved road or rail (4½ hrs) to Paranaguá. The railway journey is the most **spectacular** in Brazil. There are numerous tunnels with sudden views of deep gorges and high peaks and waterfalls as the train rumbles over dizzy bridges and viaducts. Near Banhado station (Km 66) is the waterfall of Véu da Noiva; from the station at Km 59, the mountain range of **Marumbi** can be reached: see below. Trains leave Curitiba twice daily during the summer and in Jul. For the rest of the year, there are return services on Sun only, plus one-way trains to Morretes on Tues and Thur. On Sun the year round ordinary service is at 0730, arriving in Paranaguá at 1030 (US$4 one class, tickets on sale at 0630, except for Sun when the ticket office is closed: buy ticket for weekend as early as possible (Mon); sandwiches, chocolate and drinks for sale on board; the schedule may vary, ask at the station). Avoid the front coach and sit on the left hand side. A modern air-conditioned rail-car (the Litorina, called the automotriz) leaves at 0900, daily in summer; winter Sun, arriving at 1130 (US$8 each way, reserved seats bookable 2 days in advance; latest reports suggest the service varies) with recorded commentary (in Portuguese, French, Spanish and English) and stops at the viewpoint at the Santuário da NS do Cadeado and at Morretes (only a few minutes). Sit on the left-hand side on journey from Curitiba. If Litorina is full, take bus to Paranaguá, US$3.50, then take Litorina back: return journeys start at 1500 (Litorina) and 1600 (ordinary train) so remember that in winter part of the ordinary train's journey is covered in the dark (also, on cloudy days there's little to see on the higher parts). The train is usually crowded on Sat and Sun. Many travellers recommend returning by bus (1½ hrs, buy ticket immediately on arrival), if you do not want to stay 4½ hrs. A tour bus meets the train and offers a tour of town and return to Curitiba for US$6.

You can also visit *Antonina* (a port, not on main route, pop 17,055) and *Morretes* (on main route, pop 13,130), two sleepy colonial towns which can be reached by bus on the old Graciosa road, which is almost as scenic as the railway. Bus Paranaguá to Morretes at 1830, US$1.25, to Antonina, stopping en route at Morretes, 6 a day (US$2). 12 buses daily Morretes-Curitiba US$2; 20 buses a day Curitiba-Antonina.

Morretes hotel: C *Nhundiaquara*, in town centre, well located but hot and cramped, good restaurant; good restaurants in town (try "barreado", beef cooked for 24 hrs, especially good in the two restaurants on the river bank) and a river beach. 14 km N of Morretes is the beautiful village of São João de Graciosa, 2 km beyond which is a flower reserve. The Graciosa road traverses the Marumbi range for 12 km, with 6 rest stops with fire grills, shelters and camping. Marumbi is very beautiful; you can also hike the original trail which follows the road and passes the rest-stops. Take food, water and plenty of insect repellent.

Paranaguá (pop 107,585, CEP 83200, DDD 041), and chief port of the state of Paraná and one of the main coffee-exporting ports, was founded in 1585, 268 km S of Santos. It is on a lagoon 29 km from the open sea and is approached via the Bay of Paranaguá, dotted with picturesque islands. The fort of Nossa Senhora dos Prazeres was built in 1767 on a nearby island; 1 hr's boat trip. The former Colêgio dos Jesuitas, a fine baroque building, has been converted into a Museu de Arqueológia e Artes Populares (Tues-Sun 1200-1700; entrance US$1). Other attractions are a 17th century fountain, the church of São Benedito, and the shrine of Nossa Senhora do Rocio, 2 km from town. There are restaurants and craft shops near the waterfront. The part of town between the waterfront, railway station and new bus station has been declared a historic area. Paranaguá is a free port for Paraguay. The paved 116-km road to Curitiba is picturesque, but less so than the railway (see above).

Hotels C *Auana*, R Correia de Freitas 110, T 422-6531, good value, rec; **D** *Karibe*, F Simas 86, T 422-1177, good value; **D** *Litoral*, R Correia de Freitas 66, without breakfast, clean and comfortable; **D** *Monte Líbano*, R Júlio da Costa 152, T 422-2933, overpriced; **E** *Rio Mar*, on waterfront; **E** *Santa Ana*, very clean.

Camping Camping Clube do Brasil site at Praia de Leste, on the beach, 29 km S of Paranaguá, 30 mins (beach said to be better than Matinhos, see below).

Restaurants *Bobby's*, Faria Sobrinho, highly rec, esp for seafood. *Danúbio Azul*, 15 de Novembro 91, good, not cheap, view of river, classical piano music; *Aquarius*, Av Gabriel de Lara 40, good but not cheap seafood; there are cheap restaurants in the old market building, and plenty of cheap ones near the markets on the waterfront; the *Yacht Club*, beyond *Danúbio Azul* is impressive and has a good bar.

Exchange Banco do Brasil, Largo C Alcindino; *Câmbio*, R Faría Sabrintio, for cash.

Tourist Information kiosk outside railway station.

Bus Station All buses operated by Graciosa. To **Curitiba**, US$3.50, many, 1½ hrs (only the 0745 in either direction and the 1545 to Curitiba take the old Graciosa road); direct to **Rio** at 1915, 15 hrs, US$38.50.

Excursions *Matinhos* (pop 11,315) is a Mediterranean-type resort, invaded by surfers in Oct for the Paraná surf competition; several cheap hotels, incl *Bolamar* (**E**, basic, cheapest) and *Beira Mar*. 3 camp sites, but the municipal site is closed until Nov. Cruises on Paranaguá Bay by launch, daily from Cais do Mercado. Bus from Paranaguá at 1000, 1400 and 1615, US$1. 6 buses a day to Guaratuba, US$1.25 (2 hrs via ferry). *Guaratuba* (pop 17,990 less built up than Caiobá) has **E** *Pensão Antonieta*, clean, dangerous showers; and other hotels; campsite. 12 buses daily, incl beautiful ferry crossing. All Guaratuba buses pass *Caiobá* (**D** *Hotel Caiobá*, cheapest). Caiobá to Guaratuba by ferry, free for pedestrians, US$1.50 for cars, 10 mins, frequent departures.

To *Ilha do Mel*, take bus to Pontal do Sul (many daily, direct from/to Curitiba, 1 hr, US$2), then wait for a bus to the ferry, US$2; if one does not leave soon, take a taxi or walk; turn left out of the bus station and go 25m to main road, turn right for 1½ km and bear left along a sandy road for 2 km to fishermen's houses from where a ferry runs (US$3). Alternatively, go the small harbour in Paranaguá and ask for a boat to the Ilha do Mel, 2-3 hrs, US$5 one way (no shade). Make sure the ferry goes to your chosen destination (Nova Brasília or Ecantados are the developed areas; ferries to the S go to an area with only a camping site, 2-3 hrs' walk to Nova Brasília at low tide only).

On the island, which is an ecological reserve (no cars permitted), well-developed for tourism, there are two beach villages, 5 km apart. From Praia dos Encantados to Nova Brasília there are boats (US$10, or US$2 pp if more than 5), or you can walk on a track (1½-2 hrs) or follow the coast, walking in the sea. From Nova Brasília, a 20-min walk leads to El Farol for good views. Praia dos Encantados is more suitable for swimming than Brasília. Camping is possible on the more deserted beaches (good for surfing). At Praia dos Encantados, one can camp or rent a fisherman's house—ask for *Valentim's Bar*, or for Luchiano; behind the bar is *Cabanas Dona Maria*, shared showers, cold water; Dona Maria and Dona Ana sell bread and cakes, and meals if you ask in advance; *Lanchonete Paraiso*, nice meeting place, good food and music; more expensive restaurant next door to *Forró Zorro* (see below). At Praia da Brasília, try *Pousadinha*, on road to Praia do Farol, excellent breakfast, delightful rooms, clean, good beds, fan, bath, mosquito nets, staff speak various languages; *Pousada Praia do Farol* or *Estalagem Ancoradouro*, both with breakfast (*Ancoradouro*, clean, friendly, meals cooked if required); *Estalagem Pirata*, Nova Brasi'lia, wonderful house on beach, music, easy atmosphere, run by Roberto and Darlene, all accommodation is **E**; restaurant *Toca do Abutre* and bar *Barbeiria*. The beaches, caves, bays and hill walks are beautiful. 4 hrs' walk from the villages is an old Portuguese fort. If camping, watch out for the tide, watch possessions and beware of the *bicho de pé* which burrows into feet (remove with a needle and alcohol) and of the *borrachudos* (discourage with Autan repellent). In summer and at holiday times the island is very crowded with an active nightlife and *Forró* dancing (eg *Forró Zorro*, Praia dos Encantados, Thur-Sun, lively, popular); at other times it is very quiet. Electricity on the island 1000-0200.

About 117 km from Curitiba the road inland (which passes Vila Velha— see p 459) reaches **Ponta Grossa** (pop 233,515, CEP 84100, DDD 0422, 895m). It now calls itself the "World Capital of Soya" (as does Palmeiras das Missões, in Rio Grande do Sul). Roads run N through Apucarana (Camping Clube site) and Londrina to São Paulo, and S to Rio Grande do Sul and the Uruguayan border.

Hotels **A2** *Vila Velha Palace*, R Balduino Taques 123, T 25-2200, F 24-4348; **C** *Planalto Palace*, R 7 de Setembro 652, T 25-2122, plain and clean; **C** *Scha Fransky*, R Francisco Ribas 104, T 24-2511, very good breakfast; almost next door, same street No 162, is **D** *Central*, with fan and basin; **E** *Esplanada*, in bus station (quiet, however), with bath and breakfast, clean, safe. **F** *Luz*, basic, near railway station; **F** *Casimiri*, next door, often full. Try area around Praça Barão de Garaúna.

Camping Camping Clube do Brasil, 26 km out at the entrance to Vila Velha.

Restaurants *Casa Verde*, near the *Central*, lunch only, rec; there are cheap restaurants near the railway station.

Buses Princesa dos Campos to **Curitiba**, 6 a day, 2 hrs, US$3.50; same company to **Iguaçu**, 4 daily, 11 hrs, US$14.50. To **Vila Velha** at 0700 and 0900 (return bus at 1800).

In Alto Paraná in the extreme NW of the State, connections have traditionally been with São Paulo rather than with Curitiba. Large new centres of population have risen in a short time. In 1930 four Japanese and two Germans arrived in **Londrina** (pop 388,330), developed by a British company. Today it is a city with skyscrapers, modern steel and glass cathedral, and wide streets; small museum at Sergipe e Rio de Janeiro (**C** *Hotel Coroados*, Sen Souza Naves 814, T 23-7690, standard; **C** *Hotel Triunfo*, R Prof João Cândido 39, T 23-5054, with bath, clean, friendly, laundry, restaurant; **E** *Hotel dos Viajantes*, Av São Paulo 78, clean, quiet, safe, friendly; **E** *Hotel Cravinho*, R Minas Gerais 88, clean, friendly. Youth Hostel, R Gomes Carneiro 315, centro Esportivo Moringão). Bus Londrina-Ponta Grossa, US$8.50, 5½ hrs. *Maringá* (pop 239,930, about a third Japanese) is 80 km W of Londrina, founded in 1947. There is a small conical cathedral; Parque Ingá is shady, with a Japanese garden. Londrina and Maringá are good points for connections between the S (Porto Alegre), Foz do Iguaçu and Mato Grosso do Sul (Campo Grande). Bus from Londrina to Porto Alegre takes 22 hrs; to Campo Grande 11 hrs, via Presidente Prudente (see p 435). A number of bus services from Paraná state to Porto Alegre (Aguia Branca, Unesul) and to Campo Grande, Cuiabá and Porto Velho (Eucatur) commence at **Cascavel** (pop 218,410) further S on the Curitiba-Iguaçu road (hotels: **F** *Vila Paraguaya*, clean, simple; **D** *Grand Prix*, Av Brasil 5202, clean, good value; **D** *Príncipe*, Av Brasil, good). 47 km NW of Cascavel on the BR 467 is the quiet agricultural town of Toledo (Hotel *Monte Sion*, good).

If driving from Curitiba to Foz do Iguaçu (or vice versa), **Guarapuava** makes a useful stopover town (258 km from Curitiba, 389 km from Foz); **C** *Hotel América*, excellent value, and others.

The Paraná River

In the extreme SW of the State, on the Argentine frontier, are the **Iguaçu Falls**, approached by a good paved road from Curitiba, through Guarapuava and Cascavel, with frequent bus services. There is an international airport about 14 km from the Falls, and 32 km from the Falls is the city of Foz do Iguaçu, with excellent road connections with Argentina and Paraguay.

For a detailed description of the Falls as a whole, and the Argentine side in particular, together with maps and an account of road links between the Argentine and Brazilian sides, **see the Argentine chapter, Section 8.**

If one has the time, first visit the Brazilian side to get some idea of the size and magnificence of the whole, and take introductory photographs in the morning, and then cross to the Argentine side to see the details (quickest to get some Argentine pesos on the Brazilian side). This can all be done in a day, starting at about 0700, but the brisk pace needed for a quick tour is very exhausting for the non-athletic in the heat. Sunset from the Brazilian side is a worthwhile experience.

A 1½ km paved walk runs part of the way down the cliff near the rim of the Falls, giving a stupendous view of the whole Argentine side (the greater part) of the falls. It ends up almost under the powerful Floriano Falls; a new catwalk leads right to the edge of one of the lower waterfalls. Waterproof clothing can be hired although it is not absolutely necessary. An elevator (from 0800) hoists the visitor to the top of the Floriano Falls (US$1.50) and to a path leading to Porto Canoa, if there is a queue it is easy and quick to walk up. A safari, Macuco, near the falls, costs US$25 for a guided tour, but it is better on the Argentine side. Helicopter flight over Falls—US$40/head—lasts 7 mins, departing from *Hotel das Cataratas*. (There is pressure for the helicopter rides to stop: the noise is seriously disturbing the wildlife - altitude has been increased, making the flight less attractive.) There is a small museum 10 km from the Falls (1 km from park entrance is side road to museum, look for sign "Centro de Visitantes" near the Policia Militar post – closed 1995) and opposite it are some steps that lead down the steep slope to the river bank. Beautiful walk. It can be misty early in the morning at the Falls. Entry to the Brazilian side of the Falls is US$2, payable only at the National Park entrance. If possible, visit on a weekday when the walks are less crowded.

From Foz do Iguaçu, Dois Irmãos buses (from local bus station—*Terminal Urbana*—on Av Juscelino Kubitschek, opp Infantry Barracks) marked "Cataratas" run the 32 km to the falls every 2 hrs Sat, Sun, hourly Mon-Fri, past airport and *Hotel das Cataratas*: schedule is usually 0800 to 1800, but sometimes buses start and finish earlier, journey takes 40 mins; those marked "Parque Nacional" stop at the park entrance, take a "Cataratas" bus the rest of the way (this works out more expensive). Buses of either route can also be picked up at any of the stops on Av Juscelino Kubitschek, sometimes more convenient than going to the Terminal Urbana. At weekends, holidays and other high seasons, frequency increases to every hour. Buses return 0700-1800, US$1 one way, payable in *reais* only. The driver waits at the Park entrance while passengers purchase entry tickets. (The taxi fare is US$6, plus US$2.50 for each hour of waiting.) The tours of the Falls organized by the various hotels have been recommended in preference to taxi rides.

Buses between Foz do Iguaçu and Puerto Iguazú (Argentina) run half-hourly along Av Juscelino Kubitschek, crossing the frontier bridge; 20 mins journey, no stops for border formalities (Pluma and Tres Fronteiras companies, tickets interchangeable between the two, US$1.50). There are many advantages in staying in Foz and commuting to the Argentine side (better and cheaper hotels and restaurants, for example). If you decide to stay in Brazil, do not rely on spending *reais* in Argentina; they are accepted, but at very poor rates. It is better to change dollars into pesos for the day, which is easily done at Puerto Iguazú bus station or nearby before taking the bus to the falls. A poorer rate for pesos is given in Brazil. **NB** Be sure you know when the last bus departs from Puerto Iguazú for Foz (usually 1900) and remember that in summer Argentina is an hour earlier than Brazil. Combined tickets to Puerto Iguazú and the falls cost more than paying separately; when returning from Puerto Iguazú, ask to be let off in Foz. Taxi Foz-Argentina US$33. Crossing the frontiers in a private vehicle, if only intending to visit the National Park, presents no problems.

Be sure to get a stamp on your passport if intending to stay in Brazil, but if going nowhere other than Iguaçu there is no need for citizens of countries requiring visas to have one. There is an entry tax on the Brazilian side for car passengers only, not for bus passengers. If driving into Brazil insist on visiting customs. You must get entry papers for your car here or you'll have serious problems later.

There are Brazilian immigration offices on the Brazilian sides of the bridges into Paraguay and Argentina; if you are just visiting Ciudad del Este (formerly Ciudad Stroessner) or Puerto Iguazú and the Argentine side of the Falls and returning to Brazil the same day, you must take your passport; no need to have it stamped. There are Brazilian customs patrols looking for undeclared goods on the roads past the frontier. Note that if entering or leaving a country and you have to visit customs and immigration, buses won't wait; take a taxi instead.

Foz do Iguaçu (CEP 85890, DDD 0455) is a rapidly developing and improving town of 188,190 people, with a wide range of accommodation and good communications by air and road with the main cities of southern Brazil, and with Asunción, Paraguay.

NB There are increased reports of night-time assaults at Foz, with thieves carrying knives or guns. Also, taxis are expensive and not worth the money for short distances in town. At bus terminals watch out for pickpockets who pose, with a coat over their arm, as taxi drivers.

Hotels On a height directly overlooking the falls, 32 km from Foz, is the **L3** *Hotel das Cataratas*, T 23-2266, F 574-1688 (but 15% discount for holders of the Brazil Air Pass) highly rec, an attractive colonial-style building with nice gardens and a swimming pool not without insects. Much wildlife can be seen in the grounds at night and early am. It is reported money is exchanged only at the official rate, check before paying. Non-residents can have US$15 lunch here (midday and evening buffets, or else wait 45 mins for *à-la-carte* dishes), dinner (churrasco) with show, US$30.

In 1994, **many street numbers were changed**. Old numbers (lower) and the new higher ones were still in use. We have altered numbers where known: best advice is to bear changes in mind when looking for your hotel. If you know which hotel you wish to stay in (there are over 180), do not be put off by touts who say it no longer exists. Note that touts quote room rates below what is actually charged; in high season (eg Christmas-New year), you will not easily find a room under US$15.

Many out-of-town hotels on the Falls road state their address as km from Foz. On road to Falls (Rodovia das Cataratas) are the **L2** *Bourbon*, all facilities, excellent buffet dinner, open to non-residents (US$12), km 2.5, T 23-1313, F 574-1110; **L3** *Colonial* (Km 16.5), T 574-1777, F 76-1960, near airport, swimming pool, fine location. **A1** *Belvedere* (Km 10.4), T 23-1123, F 574-1050; **A1** *Carimã* (Km 16), T 23-1818, F 574-3531, 3-star, very good value, a/c, pool, restaurant, bars, rec; **A1** *Dom Pedro I* (Km 3, T 23-2177, F 574-5677); **A3** *Panorama* (Km 12), good value, pool, T 23-1200, F 574-1490.

L2 *Internacional*, Almirante Baroso 345, T 23-1414, F 574-5201, good; **A1** *Continental Inn*, Av Paraná 485, T/F 574-4122, good restaurant; **A1** *Salvatti*, R Rio Branco 651, T 23-1121, F 574-3674, all a/c (with restaurant and cinema); *Rafahin Palace*, Br 277-Km 727, T 22-3434, F 22-3131, bungalows to rent nearby; **A2** *Foz Presidente*, R Xavier da Silva 918, T/F 574-5155, shower, a/c, overpriced, restaurant, swimming pool, trips arranged to Falls, convenient for buses; **A2** *Lanville*, Jorge Schimmelpfenig 827, T 23-1511, F 23-1636; **A2** *Rafahin*, Mal Deodoro 984, T 23-1213, F 23-2007, good restaurant, pool, well spoken of; **A2** *Suiça*, Av Felipe Wandscheer 3580, new, Swiss manager, helpful, rec. on Av Brasil: **A1** *Bogari Palace*, No 106, T 23-2243, F 23-1125, excellent restaurant, swimming pool; **A3** *Foz do Iguaçu*, No 97, T 574-4455, F 574-1775, good (expensive) laundry, wonderful, breakfast, will look after luggage, fair; **B** *City*, No 938, T 574-2074, own bathroom, fan, hot water, clean; **B** *Diplomata*, No 678, T 23-1615, some a/c, with shower, own bathroom, swimming pool, arranges taxi tours to Argentine side; **C** *O Astro*, No 660, T 72-3584, clean, OK, a/c; **C** *Dani Palace*, No 509, comfortable, good buffet breakfast, bath, clean; **C** *Imperial*, No 168, T 574-2422, with bath, clean; **D** *Ortega*, Av Brasil 1140, T 574-1288, good breakfast; **C** *Syaden*, Av Brasil, friendly, a/c, rec; **B** *Estoril*, Av República Argentina 694, T 23-1233, F 23-2311, breakfast, pool, TV, rec; **C** *Bastos*, Castelo Branco 931, T 574-5839, a/c with bath, clean, secure, helpful, rec; **C** *Luz*, Almte Barroso, T 73-1891, near Rodoviária, clean, rec; **C** *San Remo*, Kubitschek e Xavier da Silva 467, T 72-2956, good, bath, good breakfast, a/c; **D** *Pousada Pôr do Sol*, R Santos Durmont 41, T 574-3122, family-run, helpful, rec; **D** *Goya*, Kubitschek 969, T 574-3955; **D** *Ninhos*, Av Argentina, shared bath, fair; **D** *Hospedaria Britos*, Santos Dumont e Xavier da Silva, shared shower, large breakfast, clean, good value; **D** *Hospedaria Janice*, Santos Dumont 1222, very friendly and helpful; **D** *Riviera*, Mal Deodoro 559 with Bartolomeu de Gusmão, clean, friendly; **D** *Senhor do Bonfim*, Almte barroso 6, clean, not very secure; **E** pp *Pousada Laura*, R Naipi 629, T 574-1799, clean, safe, friendly, hot water, kitchen, laundry, English, French, Spanish spoken, rec; **E** *Hospedaje Paraiso*, near *Hotel King*, clean, cheap, safe,

1. Post Office &
   Tourist Office
2. Paranatur
3. Argentine Consulate
4. Paraguayan Consulate
5. Prefeitura
6. Banco do Brasil
7. Infantry Barracks

Hotels:

8. *Internacional*
9. *Salvatti*
10. *Continental Inn*
11. *Lanville*
12. *Bogari*
13. *Foz do Iguaçu*
14. *Pousada Verde Vale*

B1. Terminal Urbana
B2. Rodoviária, (off map)

FOZ DO IGUAÇU

showers; **F** *Holiday*, Xavier da Silva 1407, T 574-5948, good, breakfast. Lots of cheap (**F**) accommodation on Almirante Baroso, Nos 2000-2200.

In R Rebouças: **B** *Pietá*, No 84, T 574-5581, pool, clean, friendly, good breakfast, car and guide, rec; **D** *German Pension*, No 907, friendly, rec; **C** *Minas*, No 641, T 574-5208, clean and basic, hot water, safe, TV downstairs, no breakfast; **E** *Trento*, No 665, T 574-5111, a/c and bath, clean, rec; **E** *Pousada Verde Vale*, No 335, T 574-2925, youth hostel style, cramped but popular, buses to falls stop outside; **D** *Piratini*, No 101, hot showers, shabby but friendly. Rec accommodation: house of Gertrudis Roth, Rebouças 1091, T 574-5603, E incl breakfast, 3 rm, highly rec; *Pousada da Laura*, Rua Naipi 629, T 574-1799, secure, friendly, Spanish, English and French spoken; Maria Schneider, Av Jorge Schimmelpfeng 483, T 574-2305, E, German spoken. Be sure to leave hotels punctually, or you will be charged an extra day. Many hotels have a minibus service to the airport for guests for a small fee and also offer excursions to Falls.

Warning There is a scam in which children will escort you to a cheap hotel, receiving commission for doing so. Your luggage is then stolen from the hotel.

Camping (pretty cold and humid in winter). By National Park entrance Camping Clube do Brasil, 17 km from Foz, US$10 pp a night (half with International Camping Card), swimming pool, clean; park vehicle or put tent away from trees in winter in case of heavy rain storms, no restaurants; food there not very good, closes at 2300. *Camping Ecológico*, Fazenda São João Batista (W Keller), T 574-1794, 8 km from Foz, turn left just before park entrance, basic, nice scenery, dormitory and space for tents. Not permitted by hotel and Falls. Sleeping in car inside the park also prohibited. Avoid *Camping Internacional*, where several assaults have been reported, 5 km from Foz centre.

Restaurants Many open till midnight, most accept a variety of currencies. *Rafahin* before the policia rodoviária post at Km 533, with Paraguayan harp trio, good *alcatra* (meat), excellent buffet, but expensive. *Rafain Center*, Rebouças, next to *Minas Hotel*, a collection of food stalls for different tastes and budgets, with live music and dancing 2000 to 0200, lively, rec; *Calamares*, No 686, all you can eat buffet US$5, closes 2300, rec; *Santos Delavy*, Av J

Kubitschek 393, Argentine owner, cheap and friendly; *Ali Baba*, No 998, very good Arabic food; *Churrascaria Cabeça de Boi*, Av Brasil 1325, large, live music, buffet US$9, also for coffee and pastries. *Cantina*, Av Rodrigues 720, buffet, all you can eat, rec; *Clarks*, No 896, excellent food, reasonable. *El Club Caxos*, No 249, cheap; *Lanches Sol*, Av Brasil 86; *Scala*, Santos Dumont e Xavier da Silva, good atmosphere and value. *Barbarela*, Av Júlio Pasa, highly rec for juices and healthy snacks; *Vegetaránio*, next door, also rec; *Supermercado Maringo*, lunch counter US$2.

Beware of overcharging at *lanches* (small restaurants)—sometimes three times the posted price; have the right change available.

Consulates   Argentina, R Don Pedro II, close to Paranatur, open 0800-1300; **Paraguay**, Bartolomeu de Gusmão 480.

Electric Current   110 volts a/c.

Entertainment   Discotheque *Whiskadão* with three different dance halls, Alm Barroso 763, reasonable, lively at weekends. Fun fair, Centro de Diversões Imperial, on Av Brasil. There is a cinema on Barão do Rio Branco, also a late-opening supermarket.

Health   There is a free 24-hr clinic on Av Paraná, opposite Lions Club. Few buses: take taxi or walk (about 25 mins). Ask for Sra Calça: friendly and helpful. Her son speaks English.

Post Office   Praça Getúlio Vargas 72, next to Tourist Office. **International phone** calls from the office on Rui Barbosa.

Travel Agents and Currency Exchange   Beware of overcharging for tours by touts at the rodoviária. There are many travel agents on Av Brasil. *Dicks Tours* is said to change up to US$100 per day, 10% charge, and has been rec for its all-day tour to the Brazilian side of the Falls, to Paraguay (Ciudad del Este) and to the Itaipú dam. Recommended guides, *Wilson Engel*, T 574-1367, friendly, flexible. Ruth Campo Silva, *STTC Turismo Ltda*, Av Brasil 268, T 574-3122; *Chiderly Batismo Pequeno*, R Almirante Barroso 505, Foz, T 574-3367. Very difficult to exchange on Sun, but quite possible in Paraguay where US dollars can be obtained on credit cards. **Banco do Brasil**, Av Brasil, good rates for TCs (note that you cannot obtain US dollars in Brazil); **Bradesco**, Av Brasil 1192, cash advances on Visa. Mastercard cash advances only available in Paraguay (Aug 1994).

Tourist Office   Praça Getúlio Vargas 56; Paranatur, very helpful, Almirante Barroso 485. Kiosk on Av Brasil, by Ponte de Amizade (helpful), will book hotels. Airport tourist information is also reported to be very good, open for all arriving flights, gives map and bus information. Helpful office, free map, at rodoviária, English spoken. A newspaper, *Triplice Fronteira*, carries street plans and other tourist information.

Airport   The Iguaçu international airport has daily flights from Río, São Paulo, Curitiba, Salvador and other Brazilian cities. Three flights a week to Buenos Aires. Tourist office (see above). Taxis to town from the Brazilian airport 18 km from Foz, are expensive (up to US$54); Dois Irmãos town bus for US$0.20, first at 0530, does not permit large amounts of luggage (but backpacks OK). Varig office in Foz: Av Brasil 821, T 23-2111; staff speak foreign languages; Vasp, T 574-2999.

Buses   Rodoviária, Av Costa e Silva, 4 km from centre on road to Curitiba; bus to centre, Anel Viario, US$0.35. Book departures as soon as possible. Foz is reached by buses from **Curitiba** (Sulamericana, 9-11 hrs, paved road, US$27.50), from Guaíra via Cascavel only (5 hrs, US$5), and from **São Paulo** (15 hrs, about US$29 with Pluma, *leito* US$58). To **Campo Grande**, 15 hrs by Maringá company (3 hrs to Cascavel, and 12 from there to Campo Grande); to **Brasília**, 26 hrs, 1800, US$50; to **Rio** 22 hrs, several daily, US$37 (*leito* 74). **Buenos Aires**, Pluma daily 1630, 18 hrs, US$45. It is cheaper to go to **Posadas** through Paraguay than through Argentina. Very many other destinations.

Travel From Paraguay   By 3 flights a week from Asunción to Foz do Iguaçu, or by paved road from Asunción (book in advance to take the 0730 bus from Asunción, arriving at 1300 at the Brazilian border and at the bus terminal at 1500). (If you wish to return to Asunción the same day, take a bus to the falls and return at 1730 to the rodoviária, to be back at 2400.) Several bus companies ply the route: Nuestra Señora, Rysa, Pluma etc, US$14. From Ciudad del Este, take a bus or walk across the Ponte de Amizade (Friendship Bridge, Brazilian post open until 0200, pay US$2 in dollars, guaraníes or reais at the Paraguayan end) past Brazilian Customs and take Ponte-Cidade bus (US$0.12) to local bus station where buses go to the Falls or to Argentina. Do use the buses to cross no-man's-land. Taxi from Ciudad del Este to centre of Foz, US$12.

Travel to Paraguay   Visas are free. A tourist charge of US$3 is made at the border.

Excursions   From Foz, you can make an excursion to the 12,600-megawatt *Itaipú* dam, the largest single power station in the world, which Brazil and Paraguay have built nearby. The dam is 8 km long. The power house 1½ km. Paraguay does not use all its quota of power so this is sold to Brazil, which powers all of Southern Brazil and much of Rio, São Paulo and Minas Gerais from Itaipú. Bus marked Canteira da Obra from Terminal Urbana (stand 50 Batalhão) goes every 40 mins to the Public Relations office at the main entrance (US$0.35), Conjunto C-via Norte or via Sul bus goes more frequently to within 250m, visits free (but in groups only)—film in Portuguese (half of which is about protecting animals and the environment) and then the dam (one stop for taking photos), ask in reception if you may see turbines. Four tours daily. 300m before Public Relations is the Eco Museum, about the Itaipú dam, free visit with guide, rec (closed Sun). There are also an "executive" bus and agency tours but these are an unnecessary expense. You get a better view sitting on the right-hand side. If it's sunny, go in the morning as the sun is behind the dam in the afternoon and you will get poor photographs. You cannot go alone to the site as it is fenced in and guarded by its own security force. You can also visit the Paraguayan side, bus from Av J Kubitschek beside the military area to Ciudad del Este. Santa Helena on Lake Itaipu, has an artificial beach and relaxing leisure park, US$2.50.

Good reports on the Parque das Aves bird park, entrance US$8, at Rodovia das Cataratas Km 10.5, just before the falls. To book a guided tour, T 523-1007. Several other excursions, by bus or boat, into the surrounding countryside, enjoyable, book with a reputable company. **Fishing** for dourado and surubi with Simon Williams at Cataratas late Club, Av Gen Meira, Km 5, T 23-2073.

In the far NW of the state, also on the River Paraná, were the tremendous waterfalls known in Brazil as Sete Quedas (the Seven Falls), and in Spanish Latin America as the Salto de Guaíra; they were drowned by the filling of the lake behind the Itaipu dam in 1982. Guaíra (about 130 km N of Iguaçu by air or road) will not be flooded, but much of its agricultural land and its clay beds have been. *Presidente Epitácio* (pop 34,740) on the Paraná can be reached by bus from São Paulo, several daily, US$30. A luxury passenger vessel, the *Epitácio Pessoa*, sails twice monthly (weekly during holiday periods) on Wed at 1700 downstream to **Guaíra** (pop 30,965) 400 km S, getting there at 1900 Thur evening. Return trips on Sat at 1100, arrive at Pres Epitácio at 2200 Sun. (**NB** These schedules appear to be variable.) Cabins or cheaper accommodation available on lower decks. Bookings should be made in advance with: Comércio e Navegação Alto Paraná Ltda, Praça da República 177, Loja 15, São Paulo, T 259-8255, Telex: 011-32400. Passages can also be purchased (subject to space available) at the office by the port in Presidente Epitácio, and in Guaíra from Ernst Mann, Americatur, R Alvorada 253. Alternatively it may be possible to obtain passage on a cargo boat.

The 4 km from Guaíra to the lake can be walked or done by car (US$2.50 one way, return taxi up to US$12). Entrance to park US$0.35; small museum three blocks from Guaíra bus terminal, 0800-1100 and 1400-1700.

Presidente Epitácio Hotel E *Itaverá*, Curitiba 622, good value, near station.

Guaíra Lodging and Food Near the bus station: **C** *Palace Hotel*, Rui Barbosa 1190, T 42-1325; **D** *Hotel Itaipu*, with bath, hot showers, good food (restaurant closed Sun); **D** *Ichapena*, not very clean but very friendly; **D** *Majestic*, opp bus station, with or without bath, with breakfast, good; **D** *Sete Quedas*, Otávio Tosta 385, with breakfast and sandwich lunch, not too clean; and others. **Camping** Municipal site at Bosque do Kartódromo, 2 km out of town on the road from the bus station; ask at the Prefeitura for details. Basic facilities at each. **Restaurant** *O Chopão*, Otávio Tosta 69, pleasant.

Buses Guaíra-Campo Grande: buy a ticket (US$32) at the Guaíra bus terminal, take ferry to Ponta Porã, then bus to Mondo Novo, change bus there for Campo Grande; morning and night bus, 12 hrs in all. There is a bus service between **Curitiba** and Guaíra, US$23, 10 hrs; bus to **São Paulo**, US$30, 16 hrs; Guaíra to **Presidente Epitácio**, US$3.50. Other destinations include Iguaçu (bumpy, but interesting) 5 hrs but may be cancelled in the wet, US$9.50. There are also flights.

NB If entering Brazil from Paraguay in the Guaíra region, make sure to get passport stamped at the nearest available location (probably Foz do Iguaçu)—there is no passport control when coming off the boat from Salto Guaíra, Paraguay. There is an hourly passenger ferry service from Porto de Lanchas and Porto Guaíra to Paraguayan side, US$0.60, and hourly car ferry from Porto Guaíra (US$4 for car with 2 people). The car ferry runs until 1800 (Brazilian time); customs and immigration for documentation close at 1700. There is a time change when you cross the Paraná. The area is intensively patrolled for contraband and stolen cars, ensure that all documentation is in order.

BAHIA (7)

Salvador, the capital of Bahia, is one of Brazil's most historic cities, with a wealth of colonial architecture. It is also dubbed "Africa in exile": the mixture of African and European finds its most powerful expression in Carnival. The state itself is a producer of cacao, sugar and oil. Its coast has many fine beaches, particularly in the S around Porto Seguro. Inland is the harsh Sertão, traversed by the Rio São Francisco.

Bahia is the southernmost of the nine states of the north-eastern bulge of Brazil. The other eight are Sergipe, Alagoas, Pernambuco, Paraíba, Rio Grande do Norte, Ceará, Piauí, and Maranhão. They cover 2.6 million square km and contain a third of Brazil's people. The birthrate is the highest in Brazil, but so is the infant mortality rate. The average annual income from subsistence farming is deplorably low. Despite the misery, both regional and state loyalty remain ineradicable.

The nine states by no means form a homogeneous unity, but may be roughly divided into three contrasting parts. One is the sugar lands of the Zona da Mata along the coast between Salvador (Bahia) and Natal, where the rainfall can be depended upon. This was the first part of Brazil to be intensively colonized; hence the number of 16th century buildings and the density of old settlements are way above the national average. Inland from the Zona da Mata is the Zona do Agreste, with less rainfall, but generally enough for cattle raising. Inland again is the true interior, the Sertão, where rainfall cannot be depended upon; there is a little agriculture where water allows it but the herding of goats, and occasionally cattle, is more important. There are few blacks in the interior; the inhabitants are mostly

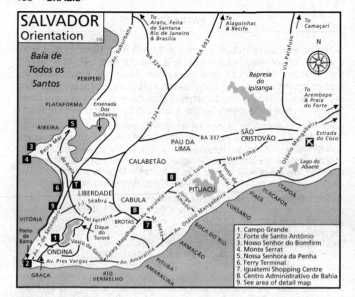

SALVADOR
Orientation

Baía de Todos os Santos

To Aratu, Feira de Santana Rio de Janeiro & Brasília

To Alagoinhas & Recife

To Camaçari

PERIPERI

PLATAFORMA

Ensenada Dos Tainheiros

Represa do Ipitanga

To Arembepe & Praia do Forte

RIBEIRA

Beira Mar

Av. de Areia

SÃO CRISTÓVÃO

PAU DA LIMA

Estrada do Coco

CALABETÃO

Viana Filho

Lago do Abaeté

LIBERDADE

J.J. Seabrá

Av. Gov. Luís

Pinto de Aguiar

PITUAÇU

ITAPOÃ

CABULA

Av. Paralela

Av. M. Neto

PLACAFOR

PIATÃ

VITÓRIA

Leal Ferreira

BROTAS

Av. Otávio Mangabeira

CORSARIO

Porto da Barra

Dique do Tororó

Vasco da Gama

Juraci Magalhães

BOCA DO RIO

ONDINA

Av. 7 de Setembro

Av. Pres Vargas

Av. Amaralina

ARMAÇÃO

GRAÇA

RÍO VERMELHO

PITUBA

AMARALINA

N

BR 324

BA 093

Via Parafuso

BA 337

Av. Suburbana

Av. Otávio Mangabeira

Jorge Amado

1. Campo Grande
2. Forte de Santo Antônio
3. Nosso Senhor do Bomfirm
4. Monte Serrat
5. Nossa Senhora da Penha
6. Ferry Terminal
7. Iguatemi Shopping Centre
8. Centro Administrativo de Bahia
9. See area of detail map

of Portuguese-Indian stock, one of the most distinctive in Brazil. They are known as the *flagelados*, the scourged ones.

When there is rain, food in the zone is plentiful and varied. Manioc is a basic food; in addition, there are goat's milk and cheese, beef, beans, and sweet potatoes. But in the years of drought, when the hot dry winds from Africa scorch the earth, the effects can be tragic. Migration towards the coast and the southern towns begins, and the people are exposed to castigation of yet another sort: exploitation by grasping labour contractors. But at the first news that there is rain, the *flagelado* heads for home.

The main export crops of the NE are sugar, cotton and cacao. Sugar and cotton have long been in decline, and now the southern states grow more than half of the Brazilian total. But cacao is grown almost entirely in southern Bahia, inland from the port of Ilhéus.

Some of Brazil's main oilfields are in the State of Bahia; there are also offshore wells in the coastal waters of Alagoas, Sergipe and Rio Grande do Norte.

Salvador (often known as Bahia), is the capital of the state of Bahia. It is the third largest city in Brazil with a population of over 2 million. The population of the state is 14 million in an area about that of France. It rains somewhat all the year but the main rainy season is between May and Sep. The climate is pleasant and the sun is never far away. Temperatures range from 25°C to 32°C, never falling below 19° in winter.

Salvador stands on the magnificent Bahia de Todos os Santos, a sparkling bay dotted with 38 islands. The bay is the largest on the Brazilian coast covering an area of 1,100 sq km. Rising above the bay on its eastern side is a cliff which dominates the landscape and, perched on top, 71 metres above sea level, are the older districts of Salvador with buildings dating back to 17th and 18th centuries. The bay was discovered by Amérigo Vespucci on 1 November 1501, All Saints Day. The first Governor General, Tomé de Sousa arrived on 23 March 1549 to build a fortified city to protect Portugal's interest from constant threats of Dutch and French invasion. Salvador was the capital of Brazil until 1763 at which stage it was the most important city in the Portuguese empire after Lisbon, ideally situated in a safe, sheltered harbour along the trade routes of the New World.

The city's first wealth came from the cultivation of sugar cane and tobacco, the plantations' workforce coming from the W coast of Africa. For three centuries Salvador was the site of a thriving slave trade and this major influx is responsible for Salvador being described as the most African city in the Western Hemisphere. The influence permeates the city: food sold on the street is the same as in Senegal and Nigeria, Bahian music is fused with pulsating African polyrhythms, men and women nonchalantly carry enormous loads on their heads, fishermen paddle dug out canoes in the bay, the pace of life is a little slower than elsewhere. The pulse of the city is *candomblé*, an Afro-Brazilian religion in which the African deities of Nature, the Goddess of the sea and the God of creation are worshipped. These deities (or *orixás*) are worshipped in temples (*terreiros*) which can be elaborate, decorated halls, or simply someone's front room with tiny altars to the *orixá*. *Candomblé* ceremonies may be seen by tourists—but not photographed—on Sun and religious holidays. Contact the tourist office, Bahiatursa, or see their twice monthly calendar of events.

Salvador today is a city of 15 forts, 166 Catholic churches, 1,000 *candomblé* temples and a fascinating mixture of old and modern, rich and poor, African and European, religious and profane. It is still a major port exporting tropical fruit, cocoa, sisal, soya beans and petrochemical products. Its most important industry, though, is tourism; after Rio it is the second largest tourist attraction in the country, very popular with Brazilian tourists who see Bahia as an exotic destination. It is mostly a rundown, poor and dirty city, but most visitors feel that the richness of its culture is compensation enough for any problems they encounter.

The centre of the city is divided into two levels, the Upper city (or Cidade Alta) where the Historical Centre lies, and the Lower city (Cidade Baixa) which is the commercial and docks district. The two levels are connected by a series of steep hills called *ladeiras*. The easiest way to go from one level to the other is by the *Lacerda* lift which connects Praça Municipal (Tomé de Sousa) in the Upper city with Praça Cairu and the famous Mercado Modelo. There is also the Plano Inclinado Gonçalves, a funicular railway which leaves from behind the Cathedral going down to Comercio, the commercial district.

There is much more of interest on the Upper city. From Praça Municipal to the Carmo area 2 km N along the cliff is the **Centro Histórico** (Historical Centre), now a national monument and also protected by Unesco. It was in this area that the Portuguese built their fortified city and where today stand some of the most important examples of colonial architecture in the Americas. The historic centre is undergoing a massive restoration programme funded by the Bahian state government and UNESCO (1993-94). With this restoration the old centre has taken on a new lease of life with many shops, restaurants and bars opening in the area. The colonial houses have been painted in their original pastel colours. Crime, once a major issue in this part of town, has diminished greatly. Many of the bars have live music which spills out onto the street on every corner. Patios have been created in the open areas behind the houses with open air cafés and bars. Artist ateliers, antique and handicraft stores have brought new artistic blood to what was once the bohemian part of the city. Many popular traditional restaurants and bars from other parts of Salvador have opened new branches in the area.

Dominating the **Praça Municipal** is the old **Paço Municipal** (Council Chamber—1660), while alongside is the **Palácio Rio Branco** (1918), once the Governor's Palace now the headquarters of Bahiatursa, the state tourist board. Leaving the square with its panoramic view of the bay, R Misericôrdia goes N passing the **Santa Casa Misericôrdia** (1695—see the high altar and painted tiles) to **Praça da Sé**. This square with its mimosa and flamboyant trees leads into **Terreiro de Jesus** (under reconstruction until 1996/7), a picturesque square named after the church which dominates the square. Built in 1692, the **church of the Jesuits** became the property of the Holy See in 1759 when the Jesuits were expelled from all Portuguese territories. The façade is one of the earliest examples of Baroque in Brazil, an architectural style which was to dominate the churches built in the 17th and 18th centuries. The whole church was built with Portuguese Lioz marble. The interior is particularly impressive, its vast vaulted ceiling and 12 side altars in Baroque and Rococco, framing the main altar completely leafed in gold. The tiles in blue, white and yellow in a tapestry pattern are also from Portugal. It houses the tomb of Mem de Sá and coloured marble and inlaid furniture. The church is now the city Cathedral and is open Tues to Sun, 0800-1100 and 1500-1800. Across the square is the church of **São Pedro dos Clérigos**, while alongside is the church of the **Ordem Terceira de São Domingos** (Dominican Third Order), both rarely open to the public.

Facing Terreiro de Jesus is Praça Anchieta and the church of **São Francisco**. Its simple façade belies the treasure inside. The entrance is by a small door to the right of the main doors and leads to a sanctuary with a spectacular painting on the wooden ceiling, by local artist José Joaquim da Rocha (1777). The main body of the church is the most exuberant example of Baroque in the country. The cedar wood carving and later gold leaf was completed after 28 years in 1748. The cloisters of the monastery are surrounded by a series of blue and white tiles from Portugal. The church is open from 0800 to 1115 and 1400 to 1700 (entry to cloisters US$0.20, church free). Next door (and with the same opening hours, entry US$0.20) is the church of the **Ordem Terceira de São Francisco** (Franciscan Third Order—1703) with its façade intricately carved in sandstone. Inside is a quite remarkable Chapter House with striking images of the Order's most celebrated saints.

Leading off the Terreiro de Jesus is R Alfredo Brito, a charming, narrow cobbled street lined with fine colonial houses painted in different pastel shades. This street leads into the **Largo do Pelourinho**, which was completely renovated in 1993. Considered the finest complex of colonial architecture in Latin America, it was once the site of a pillory where slaves were publicly punished and ridiculed. It was also the site of the slave market. After the cleaning of the area and the eviction of less desirable elements, new galleries, boutiques and restaurants are opening, and at night the Largo is lively, especially on Tues (see **Nightlife** below). **Nosso Senhor Do Rosario Dos Pretos** church, the so-called Slave Church, dominates the square. It was built by former slaves, with what little financial resources they had, over a period of 100 years. The interior is much simpler than the Cathedral of São Francisco, with side altars in honour of black saints. The painted ceiling is also very impressive, the overall effect being one of tranquillity in contrast to the complexity of the other two churches. A small entrance fee is charged.

At the corner of Alfredo Brito and Largo do Pelourinho is a museum to the work of Jorge Amado (**Casa da Cultura Jorge Amado**, mainly photos, book covers and a lecture room, Mon-Fri 0900-1800), who lived in, and set many of his books, in this section of the city. His works have been published in 47 languages. A good way to get a feel of the city and its people is to read *Dona Flor and her two husbands*. The Carmo Hill is at the top of the street leading out of Largo do Pelourinho. The **Carmo** (Carmelite Third Order) church (1709) houses one of the sacred art treasures of the city, a sculpture of Christ made in 1730 by a slave who had no formal training, Francisco Xavier das Chagas, known as O Cabra. One of the features of the piece is the blood made from whale oil, ox blood, banana resin and 2000 rubies to represent the drops of blood. Opening hours are 0800 to 1200 and 1400 to 1730, entry US$0.30.

South of the Praça Municipal, in the direction of the mouth of the bay, is the more modern section of the city with many skyscrapers. R Chile leads to **Praça Castro Alves**, with its monument to Castro Alves, who started the campaign which finally led to the Abolition of Slavery in 1888. Two streets lead out of this square, Avenida 7 de Setembro, a bustling street of shops and street vendors selling everything imaginable, and, parallel to it, R Carlos Gomes. **São Bento** church (rebuilt after 1624, but with fine 17th century furniture) is on Av 7 de Setembro. Both eventually come to **Campo Grande** (also known as Praça Dois de Julho). In the centre of the square is the monument to Bahian Independence, 2 July 1823. The British Club is just off the square on R Banco dos Ingleses. Av 7 de Setembro continues out of the square towards the Vitória area, indeed this stretch is known as Corredor da Vitória (Vitória Corridor). There are some fine homes along this street built during the last century as the city expanded in this direction. The Corredor da Vitória comes to Praça Vitória and continues down Ladeira da Barra (Barra Hill) to **Porto da Barra**. The best city beaches are in this area. Also in this district are the best bars, restaurants and nightlife. A little further along is the **Forte de Santo Antônio**, 1580, built on the spot where Amérigo Vespucci landed in 1501. It is right at the mouth of the bay where Bahia de Todos Os Santos and the South Atlantic Ocean meet.

The promenade leading away from the fort and its famous lighthouse is called Av Oceânica, which goes along the coast to the new beach suburbs of Ondina, Amaralina and Pituba. The road is also called Avenida Presidente Vargas, but the numbering is different. Beyond Pituba are the best ocean **beaches** at Jaguaripe, Piatã and Itapoan (take any bus from Praça da Sé marked Aeroporto or Itapoan, about one hour, sit on right hand side for best views). En route the bus passes small fishing colonies at Amaralina and Pituba where *jangadas* can be seen. A *jangada* is a small raft peculiar to the northeastern region of Brazil used extensively as well as dug out canoes. Near Itapoan is the **Lagoa do Abaeté**, surrounded by brilliant, white sands. This is a deep, fresh water lake where local women traditionally come to wash their clothes and then lay them out to dry in the sun. The road leading up from the lake offers a panoramic view of the city in the distance, the coast, and the contrast of the white sands and fresh water less than a kilometre from the sea and its golden beaches. Near the lighthouse at **Itapoan** there are two campsites on the beach. A little beyond the campsites are the magnificent ocean beaches of Stella Maris and Flamengo, both quiet during the week but very busy at the weekends. Beware of strong undertow at these beaches.

See also the famous church of **Nosso Senhor do Bomfim** on the Itapagipe peninsula in the suburbs, whose construction began in 1745; it draws endless supplicants (particularly on Fri and Sun) offering favours to the image of the Crucified Lord set over the high altar; the number and variety of ex-voto offerings—often of parts of the body deemed to have been cured by divine intervention—is extraordinary. The processions over the water to the church on the third Sun in Jan are particularly interesting.

Also on the Itapagipe peninsula is a colonial fort on Mont Serrat point, and at Ribeira the church of **Nossa Senhora da Penha** (1743). The beach here has many restaurants, but bathing from it is not recommended because of pollution (bus from Praça da Sé or Av França).

Museums The city has 27 museums. The **Museu de Arte Contemporânea**, converted from an old estate house and outbuildings off Av Contorno, is only open for special exhibitions. The good restaurant(*Solar do Unhão*) is still there, and the buildings are worth seeing for themselves (take a taxi there as access is dangerous).

There is a remarkable **Museu de Arte Sacra** in the 17th century monastery and church of Santa Teresa, at the bottom of the steep Ladeira de Santa Teresa, at R do Sodré 276 (off R Carlos Gomes). Many of the 400 carvings are from the Old World, but a number are local. Among the reliquaries of silver and gold is one of gilded wood by the great Brazilian sculptor Aleijadinho. Open Mon-Fri 0700-1800, US$0.40. Many of the treasures which used to be in an old mansion, the Casa de Calmon, Av Joana Angélica 198, are here now. This important collection is well worth a visit. Opposite is **Tempostal**, a private museum of postcards, open

Tues-Sat, 1000-1130, 1400-1600, at R do Sodré 276 (proprietor, Antônio Marcelino do Nascimento).

The **Museu do Carmo**, in the Convento do Carmo, has a museum with a collection of icons and colonial furniture, open Mon-Sat 0800-1200, 1400-1800, Sun 0800-1200; don't miss the carving of Christ by Francisco Xavier das Chagas (see above), entry US$0.10. **Museu Abelardo Rodrigues**, in the Solar Ferrão, Pelourinho (R Gregório de Mattos 45, open Mon-Fri 1000-1200, 1400-1700, closed Tues, Sat-Sun 1100-1700), is another religious art museum, with objects from the 17th, 18th, and 19th centuries, mainly from Bahia, Pernambuco and Maranhão.

Museu Costa Pinto, Av 7 de Setembro 2490, US$0.50, daily 1430-1800, is a modern house with collections of crystal, porcelain, silver, furniture etc. It also has the only collection of *balangandãs* (slave charms and jewellery), highly rec.

Museu de Arte da Bahia, Av 7 de Setembro 2340, Vitória, Tues-Fri 1400-1900, Sat-Sun 1430-1830, poor.

Museu Afro-Brasileiro, in former Faculty of Medicine building, Terreiro de Jesus, open Mon-Sat, 0900-1700, US$0.30 (sometimes closed by strikes), comparing African and Bahian Orixás (deities) celebrations, beautiful murals and carvings, highly rec. Medical and ethnographic museums in same complex.

Casa do Benin, below Igreja dos Pretos, shows African crafts, photos, video show on Benin and Angola, open Tues-Sat 1000-1800.

Museu da Cidade, Largo do Pelourinho (centre of old upper city), arts and crafts, old photographs, entrance free, Tues-Fri 1000-1800, Sat, Sun, 1300-1700. **Museu Hidrográfico**, Forte de Santo Antônio (Mon-Fri 0700-2100, Tues and Wed free, Thur-Sat US$0.50); recently restored and housed in the upper section of the fort, fine views of the bay and coast, rec.

Thirty-six km from the city is the **Museu do Recôncavo** (Museu do Vanderlei do Pinho) in the old Freguesia mill—1552 (open Tues, Thur and Sun 0900-1700), in which one can find artefacts and pictures of three centuries of the economic and social life of this region. The Casa Grande e Senzala (the home of the landowner and the combined dwelling and working area of the slaves) is still intact. It is a peaceful way to spend an afternoon, but difficult to get to by public transport, the museum is near the town of São Francisco do Conde, 7 km from main highway. The **Museu Geológico do Estado** is at Av 7 de Setembro 2195, Vitória, open Mon-Fri 1330-1830.

NB Many guides offer their services in museums, but their English is poor and their expectations of a tip high.

Local Holidays 6 Jan (Epiphany); Ash Wed and Maundy Thur, half-days; 2 Jul (Independence of Bahia); 30 Oct; Christmas Eve, half-day. An important local holiday is the Festa do Nosso Senhor do Bomfim; it takes place on the second Sun after Epiphany, but the washing or *lavagem* of the Bomfim church, with its colourful parade, takes place on the preceding Thur (usually mid-Jan). The Festa da Ribeira is on the following Mon. Another colourful festival is that of the fishermen of Rio Vermelho on 2 Feb; gifts for Yemanjá, Goddess of the Sea, are taken out to sea in a procession of sailing boats to an accompaniment of *candomblé* instruments. The Holy Week processions among the old churches of the upper city are also interesting.

The **pre-Carnival festive season** begins towards the end of Nov with São Nicodemo de Cachimbo (penultimate Sun of Nov), then comes Santa Bárbara (4 Dec), then the Festa da Conceição da Praia, centred on the church of that name (open 0700-1130 normally!) at the base of the Lacerda lift. (8 Dec is the last night—not for those who don't like crowds!) The last week of Dec is the Festa da Boa Viagem in the lower city; the beach will be packed all night on the 31st. On 1 Jan is the beautiful boat procession of Nosso Senhor dos Navegantes from Conceição da Praia to the church of Boa Viagem, on the beach of that name in the lower city. The leading boat, which carries the image of Christ and the archbishop, was built in 1892. You can follow in a sailing boat for about US$1; go early (0900) to dock by Mercado Modelo. A later festival is São Lázaro on the last Sun in Jan.

Carnival in Bahia

It is said that few things start early in Bahia. Carnival is one exception. Carnival officially starts on Thur night at 2000 when the keys of the city are given to the Carnival King "Rei Momo". The unofficial opening though is on Wed with the Lavagem do Porto da Barra, when throngs of people dance on the beach. Later on in the evening is the Baile dos Atrizes, starting at around 2300 and going on until dawn, very bohemian, good fun. Check with Bahiatursa for details on venue, time etc (see under Rio for carnival dates).

Carnival in Bahia is the largest carnival in the world. Unlike Rio de Janeiro (very much a spectator event), Salvador encourages active participation. It's a time for dancing in the street. It is said that there are 1½ million people dancing on the streets at any one time.

There are two distinct musical formats to be seen and heard during carnival. The **Afro Blocos** are large drum based troupes (some with up to 200 drummers) who play on the streets accompanied by singers atop mobile sound trucks. The first of these groups was the Filhos de Gandhi (founded in 1949), whose participation is one of the highlights of Carnival. Their 6,000 members dance through the streets on the Sun and Tues of Carnival dressed in their traditional costumes, a river of white and blue in an ocean of multicoloured carnival revellers. The best known of the recent drum based **Afro Blocos** are Ilê Aiye, Olodum, Muzenza and Malê Debalê. All of these are groups which operate throughout the year in cultural, social and political areas. Not all of them are receptive to foreigners among their numbers for Carnival. The roots of the so-called axé music comes from these groups who have looked to their African and Brazilian origins, creating exciting new rhythms. The basis of the rhythm is the enormous *surdo* (deaf) drum with its *bumbum bumbum bum* anchorbeat, while the smaller *repique*, played with light twigs, provides a crack-like overlay. Ilê Aiye take to the streets on Sat night and their departure from their headquarters at Ladeira do Curuzu in the Liberdade district is not to be missed. Their departure time is around 2100. The best way to get there is to take a taxi to Curuzu via Largo do Tanque thereby avoiding traffic jams. The ride is a little longer but much quicker. A good landmark is the Paes Mendonça supermarket on the corner of the street from where the bloco leaves. From there it's a short walk to the departure point.

The enormous **trio eléctricos** 12m sound trucks with powerful sound systems that defy most decibel counters, are the other format to be heard during the festivities. These trucks, each with its own band of up to 10 musicians, play songs influenced by the **afro blocos** and move at a snail's pace through the streets, drawing huge crowds of revellers. Each of the **Afro Blocos** and **blocos de trio** have their own distinct costume. Each has its own security personnel who cordon off the area around the sound truck, thereby permitting **bloco** members to dance in comfort and safety. Entrance to this area is only permitted to those wearing the relevant costume.

Carnival becomes more decentralized as years go by. The traditional route is from Campo Grande square (by the *Tropical Hotel da Bahia*) to Praça Castro Alves near the old town. The **blocos** go along Avenida 7 de Setembro and return to Campo Grande via the parallel Rua Carlos Gomes. Many of the trios no longer go through the Praça Castro Alves, once the epicentre of Carnival. The best night at Praça Castro Alves is Tues (the last night of Carnival) when the famous "Encontro dos trios" (Meeting of the Trios) takes place. Trios jostle for position in the square and play in rotation until the dawn (or later!) on Ash Wednesday. It is not uncommon for major stars from the Bahian (and Brazilian) music world to make surprise appearances.

There are grandstand seats available at Campo Grande throughout the event. Day tickets for these are available the week leading up to Carnival. Check with Bahiatursa for information on where the tickets are sold. Tickets are US$10. These can be bought on the black market for three times this price on the day. The blocos are judged as they pass the grandstand and are at their most frenetic at this point. There is little or no shade from the sun so bring a hat and lots of water. Best days are Sun to Tues. For those wishing to go it alone, just find a friendly *barraca* in the shade and watch the blocos go by. Places to avoid are the Piedade Square and Relogio de São Pedro. Both of these areas are on Av 7 de Setembro where the street narrows creating human traffic jams.

The other major centre for Carnival is Barra to Ondina. This area has become very popular in recent years. The **blocos alternativos** ply this route. These are nearly always **trios electricos** connected with the more traditional blocos who have expanded to this now very popular district. Not to be missed here is Timbalada, the drumming group formed by the internationally renowned percussionist Carlinhos Brown.

Recommended Blocos Traditional Route (Campo Grande): *Mel*, T 245-4333, Sun, Mon, Tues; *Cameleão*, T 336-6100, Sun, Mon, Tues; *Pinel*, T 336-0489, Sun, Mon, Tues; *Internacionais*, T 242-6211, Sun, Mon, Tues; *Cheiro de Amor*, T 336-6060, Sun, Mon, Tues. **Afro Blocos**: *Ilê Aiye*, T 241-4969, Sat, Mon; *Olodum*, T 321-5010, Fri, Sun. **Blocos Alternativos**: *Timbalada*, T 248-3412, Fri, Sat; *Nana Banana*, T 235-0113, Fri, Sat; *Melomania*, T 245-4570, Fri, Sat.

Prices range from US$180 to US$450. The quality of the **bloco** often depends on the act that plays on the **trio**. Best acts are Araketu, Margareth Menezes, Timbalada, Daniela Mercury, Geronimo, Chiclete Com Banana, Banda Mel, Asa de Águia, Cheiro de Amor and Netinho.

Culture   The Bahianas—black women who dress in traditional 18th century costumes—are street vendors who sit behind their trays of delicacies, savoury and seasoned, made from the great variety of local fish, vegetables and fruits.

See Capoeira, a sport developed from the traditional foot-fighting technique introduced from Angola by African slaves. The music is by drum, tambourine and *berimbau*; there are several different kinds of the sport. If you want to attempt Capoeira, the best school is Mestre Bimba in Terreiro de Jesus, at R Francisco Muniz Barreto 1. Classes are held in evenings (if you want to get the most out of it, knowledge of Portuguese is essential). There are two more schools in Forte de Santo Antônio behind Pelourinho, but check addresses at tourist office. Exhibitions take place in the Largo do Pelourinho, very picturesque, in the upper city (cost: US$2). You can also see the experts outside the Mercado Modelo on most days, around 1100-1300, and at Campo Grande and Forte de Santo Antônio on Sun afternoons; they often expect a contribution. Negotiate a price before taking pictures or demands may be exorbitant. At the Casa da Cultura at Forte de Santo Antônio there is also free live music on Sat night.

Music in Bahia   Whilst the music industry elsewhere in Brazil is going through difficult times, it is booming in Bahia where a number of artists and groups are to be found. The best time to hear and see these is during carnival but they are also to be seen outside the carnival period. Olodum, Ilê Aiye, Muzenza and Araketu are the most famous of the numerous drumming troupes where up to 100 drummers form the powerful rhythms for the sweet melodies. For Olodum, see **Nightlife** below; Ilê Aiyê practises on Sat from 2200-0400 in the Forte de Santo Antônio, Santo Antônio Além do Carmo, small admission fee.

Artists and bands using electronic instruments and who tend to play in the *trios eléctricos* draw heavily on the rich rhythms of the drumming groups creating a new musical genre known as *Axé*. The most popular of such acts is Daniela Mercury who is set to become the next local act to be successful abroad, following the steps of Caetano Veloso, Maria Bethânia, João Gilberto, Gilberto Gil. Other newer, interesting acts are Margareth Menezes who has travelled extensively with David Byrne. Gerónimo was one of the first singer/songwriters to use the wealth of rhythms of the Candomblé in his music and his song "E d'Oxum" is something of an anthem for the city. Other artists worth investigating are Roberto Mendes, Carlinhos Brown and his vibrant drumming group called "Timbalada", a major success during Carnival 93. The most famous of the trio bands are Chiclete com Banana, Banda Mel, Banda Beijo and Banda Reflexus.

All of the above have albums released and you can find their records easily in most record stores. *Mini Som*, in Praça da Sé has a wide collection in a very small store, but has a good collection of older recordings upstairs (watch the steep steps) and is more than willing to let you hear the records before buying. Another good record store is *Billbox* in the Shopping Barra on the third floor. See also **Shopping in the Pelourinho**, below.

Warning   Be very careful of your money and valuables at all times and in all districts. Avoid the more distant beaches out of season, when they are empty (eg Itapoan, Piatã, Placafor); on

Sun they are more crowded and safer. At night, the area around and in the lifts, and buses are unsafe. On no account change money on the streets; this is a guaranteed way to be robbed. Leave valuables securely in your hotel (inc wristwatch and cameras if possible: disposable cameras are widely available), particularly at night. Be wary. Carry a small amount of money that you can hand over if you are threatened. One is warned not to walk down any of the links between the old and new city, especially the Ladeira de Misericôrdia, which links the Belvedere, near the Lacerda lifts, with the lower city. Should a local join you at your table for a chat, leave at once if drugs are mentioned. The civil police are reported to be very sympathetic and helpful

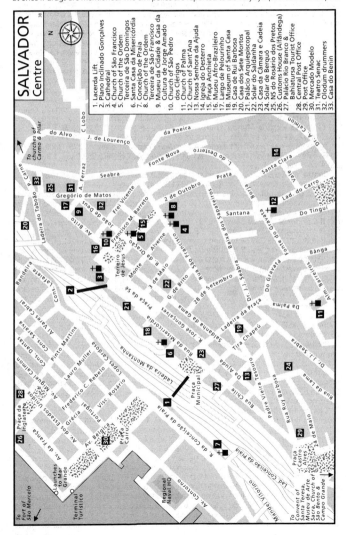

SALVADOR Centre

1. Lacerda Lift
2. Plano Inclinado Gonçalves
3. Cathedral
4. Church of São Francisco
5. Church of the Ordem Terceira de São Domingos
6. Santa Casa da Misericôrdia
7. Conceição de Praia
8. Church of the Ordem Terceira de São Francisco
9. Museu da Cidade & Casa da Cultura de Jorge Amado
10. Church of São Pedro dos Clérigos
11. Church of Palma
12. Church of Santana
13. Nossa Senhora da Ajuda
14. Igreja do Desterro
15. Praça Anchieta
16. Museu Afro-Brazileiro
17. Largo de Pelourinho
18. Museum of Santa Casa
19. Casa de Rui Barbosa
20. Casa dos Sete Mortos
21. Palácio Arquiepiscopal
22. Solar do Saldanha
23. Casa da Câmara e Cadeia
24. NS do Rosário dos Pretos
25. Customs House (Alfândega)
26. Palácio Rio Branco & Bahiatursa Tourist Office
27. Central Post Office
28. Post Office
29. Mercado Modelo
30. Teatro Senac
31. Olodum drummers
32. Casa do Benin

and more resources have been put into policing the old part of the city, which is now well-lit at night. Police are little in evidence after 2300, however.

Telephone code and Postal address CEP 40000, DDD 071.

Hotels Those listed below are in the categories L2-A1. A 10% service charge is often added to the bill. Check which credit cards are accepted. All have swimming pools. **L2** *Enseada das Lajes*, Av Oceânica 511, Rio Vermelho, T 336 1027, family run, 9 rm in what used to be a private house, antique furniture, excellent pieces of art, wonderful setting, 2 mins beach. **L3** *Bahia Othon Palace*, Av Oceânica 2456, Ondina, T 247 1044, F 245 4877, 5 star, nice rooms and views, excellent swimming pool, next to beach, average service; **L3** *Grande Hotel da Barra*, Av 7 de Setembro 3564, Barra, 4 star, T 336 6011, F 247 6223, excellent location on beach, small, friendly, ask for room with sea view; **L3** *Hotel da Bahia* (Tropical), Praça 2 de Julho 2, Campo Grande, T 321 3699, F 321 9725, 5 star, refurbished well run hotel, owned by Varig, location noisy but convenient for city centre, daily courtesy bus to beach; **L3** *Marazul*, Av 7 de Setembro 3937, Barra, T 336 2110, F 235 2121, 4 star, on seafront, heartily rec, good discounts for longer stays; **L3** *Meridien*, R Fonte do Boi 216, Rio Vermelho, 5 star, T 248 8011, F 248 8902, well run, ocean views, no beach, nothing within walking distance so taxis must be used. **L3** *Ondina Apart Hotel*, Av Oceânica 2400, Ondina, T 203 8000, 5 star, new, self-contained apts, on beach, highly rec; **L3** *Sofitel* (Quatro Rodas), R da Passargada, Farol de Itapoan, T 249 9611, F 249 6946, 5 star, is a complete resort hotel 22 km from city centre, extensive grounds, peaceful but plenty of activities available eg golf, tennis, etc, shuttle bus to city centre; **L3** *Victória Marina Apart Hotel*, Av 7 de Setembro 2068, Vitória, T 336 7736, F 336 0507. **A1** *Itapoan Praia*, Jardim Itapoan, Placafor, T 249 9988, F 248 7111, 3 star, 20 km from centre near excellent beaches; **A1** *Ondina Praia*, Av Oceânica 2275, Ondina, T 336 1033, F 247 9434, 3 star, near beach; **A1** *San Marino*, Av Oceânica 889 Barra, T 336 4363, 3 star, on ocean.

Centre (includes old city and main shopping area): **B** *Bahia de Todos os Santos*, Av Sete de Setembro 106 (Ladeira de São Bento), T 321 6344; **B** *Palace*, R Chile 20, T 243 1155, F 243 1109, rec; **D** *Chile*, opp, clean, big rooms, some have harbour view; **C** *Pousada do Boqueirão*, R Direita do Santo Antônio 48, T/F 241 2262, family run, beautiful house overlooking the bay, relaxed atmosphere, most European languages spoken, great food, especially breakfast, highly rec; **B-C** *Imperial*, Av 7 de Setembro 751, Rosario, T 321 3389, a/c, helpful, breakfast, highly rec; **D** *Internacional*, R da Faisca 88, T 243 6151, clean, convenient, good value; **D** *Paris*, R Ruy Barbosa 13, T 321 3922, a/c rooms more expensive, shared showers, breakfast, restaurant in same building, rec; also **E** *Pousada da Praça*, at No 5, T 321 0642, breakfast, rooms with and without bath, clean, friendly, rec; **D** *São Bento*, Largo de São Bento 3, T 243 7511, friendly, good cheap restaurant. Cheaper hotels on Av 7 de Setembro: **E-D** *São José*, No 847, T 321 4928, safe, rec; **F** *Madrid*, No 186, Mercês, T 321 9505, very cheap and basic, damp, not too secure; **E** *Pousada Pampulha*, No 76, 1st floor, São Pedro, 243 1240, breakfast, restaurant, laundry service; **F** *Pousada*, No 2349, price pp, warmly rec. **F** *Joana Angélica* in street of same name, friendly, no breakfast.

There are many hotels near the Praça da Sé. The following have been rec: **C** *Pelourinho*, R Alfredo Brito 20, T 321 9022, run down but central and charismatic; **D** *Solara*, R José Alencar 25, Largo do Pelourinho, T 321 0202, with shower, toilet, breakfast, clean, laundry facilities; **D** *Themis*, Praça da Sé 398, Ed Themis, 7th floor, T 243 1668, bath, fan, wonderful views over bay and old city, rec restaurant with French chef; Spanish is spoken in all of the following: **D-E** *Ilheus*, Ladeira da Praça 4, 1st floor, T 243 2329, breakfast; **E** *Colón*, Praça Anchieta 20, T 321 1531, breakfast, laundry facilities, variable cleanliness, will keep luggage, changes money, decor in both the above is depressing; **E** *Vigo*, R 3 de Maio 18, 2 blocks from Praça da Sé, with bath and breakfast (F without), fairly clean; **F** *Jequié*, off Praça da Sé at Ciné Liceu, clean, no breakfast, mixed reports, some rooms better than others.

Campo Grande/Vitória This is a much quieter area, still central and convenient for museums: **B** *Bahia do Sol*, Av 7 de Setembro 2009, T 336 7211, F 336 7776, comfortable, safe and frigobar in room, clean, family run, good breakfast, rec; **D** *Mater Café Teatro*, R Marechal Floriano 5, Canela T 235 1958, with breakfast, clean (but poor locks on doors); **D** *Caramuru*, Av Sete de Setembro 2125, Vitória, T 336 9951, breakfast, very friendly, clean, safe parking, rec; **D** *Do Forte*, R Visc de São Lourenço 30, Campo Grande, T 321 6915, breakfast, bath; **D** *Santiago* at No 52, breakfast, bath, T 245 9293.

Barra The best location to stay in: it is safe, has good beaches (but the sea may be polluted), is a short bus ride from the centre, has good restaurants in all price ranges and good nightlife (but note that the bars around Porto da Barra have become meeting places for prostitutes and European tourists). On Av 7 de Setembro: **B** *Barra Turismo*, No 3691, Porto da Barra, T 245 7433, breakfast, bath, a/c, TV, fridge, on beach, rec; **C** *Porto da Barra*, No 3783, Porto da Barra, T 247 7711, friendly, clean, some rooms very small, on beach; **C** *Solar da Barra*, No

2998, Ladeira da Barra, T 336 4917, some rooms with bay view; **C** *Pousada Malu*, No 3801, T 237 4461, small and friendly with breakfast, on beach; **C** *Villa da Barra*, No 3959, Porto da Barra, T 247 7908, F 247 9667, chalets in front of the beach, English spoken, rec. **B** *Barra Praia*, Av Alm Marqués do Leão 172, Farol da Barra, T 235-0193, a/c, clean, one street from beach, rec; **B** *Summer Blue*, R Cezar Zama 122, T 237 6399, a/c, mini fridge, mixed reports; **C** *Enseada Praia da Barra*, R Barão de Itapoã 60, Porto da Barra, T 235 9213, breakfast, clean, safe, friendly, money exchanged, accepts credit cards, laundry bills high otherwise good value, near beach; **C** *Pousada Village Paulista*, R Lord Cochrane 148, Barra, T 245 9099, fan, clean, English spoken, mixed reports, annexe opp is cheaper but not as good; **C** *Seara Praia*, R Belo Horizonte 148, Barra Avenida, T 235 0105, good breakfast; **D** *Bella Barra*, R Afonso Celso 439, T 237 8401, a/c, good, rec; **E** *Pousada da Carmen Simões*, R 8 de Dezembro 326, safe, friendly, helpful; **E** *Pousada Marcos*, Av Oceânica 281, T 235 5117, youth hostel style, great location nr lighthouse, very busy, many notices in Hebrew for potential travelling companions; also very good value, **F** *Pousada do Porto*, R Barão de Sergy 197, Porto da Barra, T 247 8228, hostel-type but more luxurious than normal in beautiful turn-of-the-century house, inc breakfast, near beach, convenient, English spoken, highly rec. Also rooms to let in private apartment, rec, from Gorette, R 8 de Dezembro 522, Apt 002, T 237-3584.

Atlantic Suburbs This is the modern suburban area built along the coast from Ondina to Itapoan stretching for 20 km towards the airport. The best beaches are in this area. **A3** *Catharina Paraguaçu*, R João Gomes 128, Rio Vermelho, T 247 1488, charming, small, colonial-style, tastefully decorated, rec; **A3** *Maravista*, R H C Ribeiro 1, Ondina, T 247 3866, rec, near beach; **A3** *Ondina Plaza*, Av Pres Vargas 3033, Ondina, T 245 8188, a/c, pool, good value, on beach, rec. **B** *Amaralina*, Av Amaralina 790, Amaralina, T 248 6347, a/c, near beach. Two in Pituba: **B** *Paulus*, Av Otavio Mangabeira, T 248 5722, a/c, pool; **D** *Pituba*, Av Manoel Dias da Silva 1614, T 248 5469, no breakfast. Two near excellent beach, in Placaford: **B** *Praia Dourada*, R Dias Gomes 10, T 249 9639, a/c, rec; **B** *Praia dos Coqueiros*, Av Otavio Mangabeira 25, Placaford, T 249 9828, a/c, rec. **A3** *Pituaçu Praia*, Jardim Iracema, Lote 27, Corsario, T 371 9622, a/c, 2 blocks from good beach. In Itapoan: **A3** *Praia da Sereia*, Av Dorival Caymmi 14, T 249-4523, F 249-4550, very good, pool, clean, friendly, safe; **B** *Grão de Areia*, Loteamento Jardim Piatã, Quadra 25, Lote 23/24, T 249 4818, a/c, pool, near good beach; **B** *Pousada de Itapoan*, Av D Caymmi, V dos Ex Combatentes, Quadra 1, Lote 3, T 249 9634, with bath, D without, excellent breakfast, clean, good value, laundry, parking; **C** *Europa*, R Genibaldo Figuereido 53, T 249 9344, breakfast; **D** *Pousada Glória*, R do Retiro 46, T 249 1503, with bath, no breakfast, near beach.

A1 *Solar Diana*, Av Yemanjá, Rua U, Lote 16, Jardim Armação, near Convention Center, T 231 1017, F 231 7927, sophisticated, small, most European languages spoken, highly rec; **A3** *Portal Da Cidade*, Av Antonio Carlos Magalhães, 4230, next to bus station, T 371 0099, a/c, pool.

Youth Hostels are called Albergues de Juventude. They cost E-F pp incl breakfast but cheaper if you have a YHA membership card. In Pelourinho: *Albergue Solar*, R Ribeiro dos Santos 45-47, T 241 0055; *Albergue do Pelô*, same street No 5, T 242 8061; *Albergue das Larangeiras*, R Iñácio 13, T 321-1366 (English spoken); *Pousada do Passo*, R Ribeiro dos Santos 3, T 321-3656, both highly rec. *Casa Grande*, R Minas Gerais, 122, Pituba, T 248 0527; *Albergue da Barra*, R Florianopolis 134, Jardim Brasil, Barra, T 247 5478, good location.

Pensionatos are places to stay in shared rooms (up to 4 persons/room) eg *Pensionato No 20*, Av Cerqueira Lima; part or full board available. Houses or rooms can be rented for US$5-35 a day from Pierre Marbacher, R Carlos Coqueijo 68A, Itapoan, T 249 5754 (Caixa Postal 7458, 41600 Salvador), he is Swiss, owns a beach bar at Rua K and speaks English, French and German. At Carnival is a good idea to rent a flat; the tourist office has a list of estate agents (eg José Mendez T 237 1394/6). They can also arrange rooms in private houses, however caution is advised as not all householders are honest.

Apart Hotels These are self-contained apartments with fully equipped kitchen and a/c, with all the facilities of a hotel, which can be rented by the day; standards are generally high. *Jardim Paraiso*, Av Dunas 259, Itapoan, T 249 3397, pool, near beach; *Bahia Flat*, Av Pres Vargas 235, Barra, T 336 4233, on beach, pool, sauna; *Barra Apart Service*, R Marques de Caravelas 237, Barra, T 247 5844; *Flat Jardim de Alã*, Av Otavio Mangabeira 3471, Armação, T 371 5288, beautiful location by beach, pool, sauna, rec; *Manhattan Residence Service*, R Maranhão 445 Pituba, T 248 9911, pool, gym, popular with business visitors; *Parthenon Farol da Barra Flat*, Av Oceânica 409, Barra, T 336 6722, pool, sauna, on beach, rec; *Pituba Apart Hotel*, R Paraíba 250, Pituba, T 240 7077, pool, sauna; *Barra Summer Flat*, Av Princesa Isabel 526, Barra, T 336 3699; all in A1-A3 range.

Camping Near the lighthouse at Itapoan, take bus from Praça da Sé direct to Itapoan, or to Campo Grande or Barra, change there for Itapoan, about 1 hr, then ½ hr walk; two campsites, one Camping Clube do Brasil, at US$6 pp/night (members half price); Ecológica, opposite, bar, restaurant, hot showers, highly rec at US$2 pp/night. Camping de Pituaçu, Av Prof Pinto de Aguiar, Jardim Pituaçu. Sea bathing is dangerous off shore near campsites.

Bahian cuisine is spiced and peppery. The main dish is *moqueca*, seafood cooked in a sauce made from coconut milk, tomatoes, red and green peppers, fresh coriander and *dendê* (palm oil). It is traditionally cooked in a wok-like earthenware dish and served piping hot at the table. Served with *moqueca* is *farofa* (manioc flour) and a hot pepper sauce which you add at your discretion, it's usually extremely hot so try a few drops before venturing further. The dendê is somewhat heavy and those with delicate stomachs are advised to try the *ensopado*, a sauce with the same ingredients as the *moqueca*, but without the palm oil.

Nearly every street corner has a Bahiana (see above under **Folklore**) selling a wide variety of local snacks, the most famous of which is the *acarajé*, a bean dumpling fried in palm oil. To this the Bahiana adds *vatapá*, a dried shrimp and coconut milk paté (also delicious on its own), fresh salad and hot sauce (*pimenta*). For those who prefer not to eat the palm oil, the *abará* is a good substitute. *Abará* is steamed, wrapped in banana leaves. The Bahianas are being given lessons on hygiene, but seek local advice on which are safest.

Three good Bahianas are *Chica*, at Ondina beach (on street at left side of *Mar A Vista Hotel*), *Dinha* at Largo da Santana (in a newly opened public square, very lively late afternoon), serves *acarajé* until midnight, extremely popular, and the one in front of *Tiffany's* restaurant on R Barão de Sergy at Porto da Barra. The Bahians usually eat *acarajé* or *abará* with a chilled beer on the way home from work or the beach at sunset.

Another popular dish is *Xin-Xin de Galinha*, chicken on the bone cooked in dendê, with dried shrimp and squash.

Restaurants Pelourinho (Historical Centre): *Cantina da Lua*, Terreiro De Jesus, open daily, popular but hangers-on can sometimes be a nuisance; *El Mesón*, Alfredo Brito 11 (upstairs), open Mon-Sat, 1100-2330, Sun 1800-2330 good seafood, meat, English spoken; *Pizzaria Micheluccio*, Alfredo Brito 31, best pizzas in Pelourinho, open daily 1200 till late, rec (T 321 5884). *Senac*, Praça José Alencar 8 (commonly known as Pelourinho Square), state run catering school, a selection of 40 local dishes, buffet, lunch 1130-1530, dinner 1830-2130, all you can eat for US$12, inconsistent quality but very popular, folkloric show Thur-Sat 2030, US$5. *Casa do Benin*, Praça José Alencar 29, Afro-Bahian restaurant, great surroundings, try the shrimp in the cashew nut sauce, closed Mon, open 1200-1600, 1900-2300, expensive but highly rec (closed until Sep 1994). *Bar Banzo*, Praça José Alencar 6 (upstairs) Mon-Sat 1100 to 2300, Sun 1800 to 2300, reasonably priced, good view of streetlife in Largo do Pelourinho below, friendly, good music. *Celina*, R dos Passos nr Casa do Benin, good, cheap, popular with locals.

First right on Alfredo Brito is R J Castro Rabelo: *Atelier Maria Adair*, No 2, specializing in various kinds of coffee, interesting cocktails, Maria is a well known artist, the café gives a glimpse of her highly original work, rec. Good wholemeal snacks and juices at *Saúde Brasil*, No 16, open daily 0900-2330, rec; *Dona Chika-Ka*, No 10, 1100-1500 and 1900-0200, good local dishes. Open gates beside *Dona Chika-Ka* lead to an open square (known locally as Quadra 2M) with many bars and restaurants. On the next block down is *Tempero da Dadá*, R Frei Vicente 5, open daily 1130 till late, closed Tues, the best Bahian cuisine in the Pelourinho, owners Dadá and Paulo are genial hosts, extremely popular, try the *bobó de camarão* (shrimp in yam sauce) and the shrimp *moqueca* which is served with the best *pirão* (thick manioc gravy) in Bahia, highly rec. Next door is *Mustafá*, R Frei Vicente 07, open 1200-2400 except Sun 1200-1500, closed Tues, Middle Eastern dishes, try the *mezze*, a selection of starters and main dishes, enough for two people. Across the street is *Abará da Ró*, specializing in *acarajé* and *abará*, popular late afternoon and early evening.

Uauá, R Gregório de Matos 36 (upstairs), 1130-1500 and 1900-2330, closed Tues, has the best in northeastern Brazilian cuisine, try the *carne de sol*, very reasonably priced, highly rec. Next door is the new branch of the famous *Casa da Gamboa*, R João de Deus 32, 1st floor, 1200-1500 and 1900-2400, closed Mon; *Uauá*, same street above *Bar do Reggae*, good Bahian and NE food, good value.

Good *feijoado* at *Alaide do Feijão*, R Fransisco Muniz Barreto 26, open daily 1100-2400. Also at *da Dinha* on Praça José Alencar 5, Mon-Sat 0800-2000.

Between Historical Centre and Barra: At Praça Da Sé, *Café Brasil*, good breakfast; also *Hotel Themis* (see above). *Bar Padrão*, R José Gonçalves, near Praça Da Sé, rec. There are some good snack bars on Av 7 de Setembro; *Nosso Cantinho*, nr *Hotel Madrid*, good value; *Kentefrio*, No 379, the best, clean, counter service only, closed Sun, rec; on same street, 600 block, *La Portuguesa*, good, cheap; *Casa D'Italia*, corner of Av 7 and Visconde de São Lourenço, reasonable prices, good service; *Grao de Bico*, No 737, very good vegetarian. *Suave Sabor*, R Cons Lafaiete, vegetarian, US$2.50 for all you can eat. Another good vegetarian restaurant nearby is *Nutrebem*, Av Joana Ângélica 148. Also on same street is *Bela Napoli*,

Italian, reasonable. *Casa Da Gamboa*, R da Gamboa, beautifully located in old colonial house overlooking the bay, good reputation, open Mon to Sat 1200-1500 and 1900-2300, not cheap. *Manjur*, R Banco dos Ingleses 20, Campo Grande, good, friendly, vegetarian dishes, 0900-1900, great view of bay. An excellent Japanese restaurant is *Gan*, Praça A Fernades 29, Garcia, intimate atmosphere, Tues-Sun 1900 till midnight, rec. The best churrascaria in Salvador is *Baby Beef*, Av AC Magalhães, Iguatemi, top class restaurant, excellent service, extremely popular, not expensive, highly rec, open daily 1200-1500 and 1900-2300.

At the bottom of the Lacerda Lift is Praça Cairu and the famous *Mercado Modelo*: on the upper floor of the market are two very good restaurants, *Camafeu De Oxossi* and *Maria De São Pedro*, both specializing in Bahian dishes, great atmosphere, good view of the port, daily 1130 till 2000, Sat lunchtime particularly busy. Opposite Mercado Modelo, the Pães Mendonça supermarket self-service counter is good value, 1100-1500, 1st floor. At the base of the Lift is *Cinquenta Saladas*, not only salads, very reasonable. On Av Contorno, *Solar Do Unhão*, beautiful manor house on the edge of the bay, lunch and dinner with best folklore show in town, expensive. *Juárez*, Mercado de Ouro, Comércio, good steaks, cheap, rec.

Barra Section *Xangai*, Avenida 7 de Setembro, 1755 (Vitória) Chinese, reasonable; *Nan Hai*, No 3671, good Chinese, lunch and dinner (Porto da Barra); good cheap snacks at Goethe Institute and American Institute, also restaurant at *Hotel Bahia Do Sol*, No 2009, on first floor, good, reasonably priced; *Tiffany's*, Barão do Sergy 156, 1900-2400, French, rec; on same street are *Alface e Cia*, wide range of salads and juices; *Via Brera* No 162, T 247-6973, upmarket Italian; *Unimar* supermarket, good cheap meals on 2nd floor. Good cheap meal at *Sorbon*, Av Doutora Praquer Fries, Porto da Barra.

Near the lighthouse at the mouth of the bay (Farol Da Barra area) there are a number of good fast food places: *Micheluccio*, Av Oceânica 10, best pizza in town, always busy, friendly, rec; next door is *Baitakão*, good hamburger and sandwiches; *Speed Lanches*, nearby, good snack bar. *Mon Filet*, R Afonso Celso, 152, good steaks, pastas, open 1830 till midnight; on same street, *Pastaxuta*, pizza, pasta, reasonable prices; a number of other good cheap restaurants on R Afonso Celso, eg *Maná*, opens 1100 till food runs out, different menu each day, closed sun, popular, owner Frank speaks a little English; also *Luar da Barra*, No 447; Shopping Barra has good cheapish places to eat, *Pizza e Cia* on ground floor, good selection of fresh salads, also good pizzas, good value, rec; opp is *Perini*, great ice cream, chocolate, savouries and cakes; *MacDonald's* also on this floor; *Saúde Brasil*, on the top floor (L3, above C&A's), for very good wholefood snacks, cakes and a wide variety of juices, rec. The best Bahian restaurant in the area is *Frutos Do Mar*, R Marques de Leão 415. A very good vegetarian restaurant is *Rama*, R Lord Cochrane, great value. *Don Vitalone*, D M Teixeira 27, nr lighthouse, off seafront, excellent Italian, open daily for lunch and evening meal, highly rec.

In Ondina: *Double Gula*, in *Mar A Vista Hotel*, and *Baby Beef Martínez*, in *Ondina Apart Hotel*, for excellent meat. Further along Av Oceânica towards the Rio Vermelho district is *Sukiyaki*, No 3562, an excellent Japanese restaurant, open 1200-1500, and 1900 till midnight, not cheap, rec. Also highly rec is *Extudo*, Largo Mesquita 4, T 237-4669, good varied menu, lively bar at night, attracts interesting clientele, open 1200-0200, closed Mon, not expensive. *Manjericão*, R Fonte do Boi (the street leading to *Meridien Hotel*), excellent wholefood menu, Mon-Sat 1100-1600, highly rec. *Philippe Camarao*, same street, bar and restaurant, specializes in shrimp dishes, expensive. *Marisco*, at Paciencia Beach nearby, good seafood, 1100-1500 and 1800-2100, good value. Zona Franca, Largo da Santana, top floor of Free Shopping Center, open air, varied menu, popular, Mon-Sat lunch and dinner.

There is an interesting fish market at Largo Da Mariquita with a number of stalls serving food from noon until the small hours, recently built, clean, good atmosphere, popular with locals. A good kiosk is *Riso e Nega* (kiosk with green tables), friendly, good basic food; nearby is *Brisa*, R Augusto Severo 4, Mon-Sat 1100-1500, excellent wholefood restaurant, small, simple, cheap, owner Nadia is very friendly.

Further along Avenida Oceânica at Jardim Armação are three very good restaurants: *Yemanjá*, excellent Bahian seafood, open daily from 1130 till late, very typical, always busy, reasonably priced, good atmosphere, highly rec. Nearby is *Tamboril*, busy seafood restaurant, 1200-1600 and 1900-2400. *Deutsches Haus*, Av Otávio Mangabeira 1221, good German cooking. The very best Bahian restaurant in the city is *Bargaço*, open daily 1200-1600 and 1900-2400, great selection of starters, oyster, lobster, fresh water shrimp, crab meat, etc, highly rec, expensive but worth it. *A Porteira* at Boca do Rio specialises in northeastern dishes including *carne do sol* (beef dried in the sun), 1200-1600 and 1800-2300, seafood dishes also served. A popular bar/restaurant is *Casquinha De Siri* at Piatã beach, daily from 0900 until last customer leaves, live music every night, cover charge US$2. The beaches from Patamares to Itapoan are lined by Barracas, thatched huts serving chilled drinks and freshly cooked seafood dishes, ideal for lunch and usually very cheap. Try *Ki-Muqueça*, Av Oceânica, for large helpings of excellent Bahian food in attractive surroundings. At Itapoan the road goes left towards the airport along Av Dorival Caymmi. *Restaurant Uauá*, Av Dorival Caymmi 46 specialses in northeastern dishes, meat based, seafood also served, open Thur to Sun. Fri and Sat are very busy with forró dancing till 0400.

Banks and Exchange Do not be tempted to change money on the street (see above) especially in the Upper City where higher rates are usually offered. Changing at banks can be bureaucratic and time-consuming. Banks are open 1000-1600. All major banks have exchange facilities but these are only available at selected branches. **Citibank**, R Miguel Calmon 555, Comércio, centre, good rates, will charge large denomination TCs into smaller ones with a commission: **Lloyds Bank**, Rua Miguel Calmon 22, Comércio. **Banco Econômico**, R Miguel Calmon 285, Comércio is the American Express representative; VISA at **Banco do Brasil**, Av Estados Unidos 561, Comércio, in shopping centre opposite Rodoviária (also a *câmbio* here), and at Rua Miguel Bournier 4, Barra. Mastercard at **Credicard**, 1st floor, Citibank building, R Miguel Calmon 555, Comércio. **Banco do Brasil** is to open an exchange office in Shopping do Pelô on R Francisco Muniz Barreto 2; also at the airport is open 0830-1530 and 1600-2100 Mon-Fri and 0900-1600 Sat, Sun and holidays. **Carlos**, Bazaar Colon, Praça Anchieta 17, in front of São Francisco church in the old city gives the best black market rates, but doesn't always accept TCs (will require passport when he does). In the Barra section, exchange at **Banco do Brasil**, R Miguel Bournier and in Shopping Barra; also in Ondina. **Banco do Nordeste**, R Marquês de Leão 41. Banking hours only. **Figueiredo**, opp *Grande Hotel da Barra* on Ladeira da Barra will exchange cash at good rates. Also in Ondina is **Banco Econômico** in the parade of shops under *Ondina Apart Hotel*. If stuck, all the big hotels will exchange, but at poor rates.

Consulates British Vice-Consulate, Av Estados Unidos 4, Salas 1109/1113, Ed Visc de Cairu, Caixa Postal 38, Comercio, T 243-9222, Mon-Fri, 0800-1200, 1400-1730. **USA**, Av Antonio Carlos Magalhães, Ed Cidadella Center 1, Sala 410, Itaigara, T 358 9166, Mon-Fri, 1430-1630. **Germany**, R Lucaia 281, Rio Vermelho, T 247 7106, Mon-Fri 0900-1200. **Austria**, R Alm Marquês do Leão 46, Apto 33, Barra, T 247 6013, Mon, Wed, Fri 1400-1700. **Belgium**, Centro Empresarial Iguatemi, Bloco B, Sala 809, Iguatemi, T 358 9542, Tues and Thur 1430-1800, Fri 0900-1700. **Denmark**, Av Sete de Setembro 3959, Barra, T 247 9667, Mon-Fri 0900-1200, 1400-1700. **Spain**, R Marechal Floriano 21, Canela, T 336 9055, Mon-Fri 0900-1300. **Finland**, C Portinári 19, Barra, T 247 3312, Mon-Fri 1000-1600, closes for lunch. **France**, Trav Francisco Gonçalves 1, Sala 805, Comércio, T 371-0410, Mon-Fri 0800-1130. **Holland**, R Lauro Miller 8, Sala 503, T 241 7645 Mon-Fri 0800-1130, 1400-1730. **Italy**, Av Sete de Setembro 1238, Mercês, T 321-8335, Mon, Wed, Fri, 0900-1100, 1500-1700. **Norway and Sweden**, R Quintino de Carvalho 153, Apto 601, Jardim Apipema, T 247 0528, Mon-Fri 0800-1200. **Portugal**, Praça Piedade, Gabinete Português de Leitura, T 241-1633, Mon-Fri 0800-1400. **Chile**, R Chile 22, Sala 401, T 321 9457, Mon-Fri 1330-1630.

British Club, Inglesa 20B, just off Campo Grande. **Cultura Ingelsa**, R Plinio Moscoso 357, Jardim Apipema. **Associação Cultural Brasil-Estados Unidos**, Av 7 de Setembro 1883, has a library and reading room with recent US magazines, open to anyone, and at No 1809 on the same avenue is the German **Goethe Institut**, also with library and reading room with recent papers.

Electric Current 110-220 AC, 60 cycles.

Nightlife In the historical centre, there is live music on the streets on Tues and Sun evening (especially the first and last Tues of the month) and Fri and Sat nights (particularly lively, especially in the summer months). *Pagóde*, a samba style from Rio, is becoming very popular, and bands play in the Pelourinho Square in front of the Casa de Jorge Amado. The main attraction is the rehearsal of the Olodum drummers on Tues; these are the most innovative of the carnival drumming groups and have attracted much attention after being featured on Paul Simon's 1990 album, *Rhythm of the Saints*. They rehearse in an open space known as the Quadra behind Teatro Antônio Miguel on R João de Jesus from 1900-2300, tickets on sale from 1700, US$12, buy tickets in advance from Casa do Olodum on R Gregório de Matos and go early. They usually also rehearse on Sun in Largo de Pelourinho from 1800-2300, but these rehearsals can be very crowded (at both, beware pickpockets and fights, police use tear gas to quell trouble). Another drumming group, Levado do Pelo, plays for free on Tues at the same time as Olodum in the Largo do Pelourinho. It is recommended to get as close as the crowds permit by taxi at night.

Araketu, a fusion of samba and African rhythms, was the hit of Carnival '95. The band rehearses in R Chile on Fri night; very popular, US$12. Two more squares in Pelourinho were renovated in 1995: Praça Teresa Batista, behind the Sebrae building, usually hosts a good jazz band called *Garagem* on Wed night in the summer months (entry free). A good bar on the square is *Oratório*. The *Cailleur Bar* across the street leads onto the Praça Pedro Arcanjo. The best night here is Sat, when a local big band under the baton of the great local musician Fred

Dantas plays to a packed square. Check with Bahiatursa for details on both squares.

Good bars are *Atelier Maria Adair* (see above), *Casa do Olodum*, *Estação Pelô* and *Bar Do Reggae* and *Alamabique Cachaçaria*, all on R João de Deus, the latter has a great selection of cachaças from all over Brazil, watch out for the steep stairs, especially after a few cachaças! Many bars on the Quadra 2M (see above), *Dom Crepe*, *Habeas Copos* are very busy. There is often live music in this square. Also good is *Café Impresso* on Rua João de Deus 3, interesting clientele, rec. Good bars in the Pelourinho Square are *Bar Banzo* and *Kalundo*. Good café and great chocolate at *Cailleur*, R Gregório de Matos 17, open daily 0930-2100, bar service continues till 0100. Popular disco is *Gueto*, R Alfredo Brito, plays techno mainly, but does vary.

Barra Section: *Mordomia Drinks*, Ladeira Da Barra, enter through narrow entrance to open air bar with spectacular view of the bay, very popular. Most Barra nightlife happens at the Farol da Barra (lighthouse). R Marques de Leão is very busy, with lots of bars with tables on the pavement: *Habeas Copos*, R Marques de Leão 172, famous street side bar, very popular; also *Aladim*, *Bali*, *Ponte de Safena* and *Psicoanalista*, all busy. In the next street, R Afonso Celso, is *Casco Grosso*. *Barril 2000*, on Av Oceânica, is very busy, with live music (MPB – popular Brazilian music) at weekends; *Flashdance*, on Av 7 de Setembro leading into Barra, was the hottest club in 1993; *Barra Vento* 600, popular open air bar on the beach front.

Further along the coast at Ondina is the *Bahia Othon Palace Hotel* with a good disco called *Hippotamus*, busy at weekends. In **Rio Vermelho** district are *Rio de Janeiro Bar*, Largo Mesquita, small bar attracting bohemian clientele, few tables, most people drink in the street, Thur-Sat, very busy. *Via Brasil*, rooftop bar in *Bahia Park Hotel*, Largo da Mariquita, open Wed-Sun 2130-0300, live music, cover charge. In same square, *Bar Canoa* at the *Meridien Hotel* has live music every night, jazz, popular Brazilian music, cover charge US$6, 2100 till 0100. Dancing at *Carinhoso*, Av Otavio Mangabeira, T 248-9575; *Champagne* at *Salvador Praia Hotel*, T 245-5033; *New Fred's*, Av Visc de Itaboraí 125, T 248-4399 (middle-aged market, singles bar). *Bell's Beach* disco at Boca Do Rio, open Tues to Sat 2200-0400, up-market, expensive; *Concha Acústica*, Ladeira da Fonte (behind Teatro Castro Alves, Campo Grande), concerts every weekend with best Brazilian musicians. Rock, MPB, mainly during summer months, usually very cheap, open air, good venue.

Theatres Castro Alves, at Campo Grande (Largo Dois de Julho), frequent concerts; Teatro da Gamboa; Teatro Vila Velha; Senac; Instituto Cultural Brasil-Alemanha (ICBA): Teatro Santo Antônio, part of the Escola de Teatro da Universidade Federal da Bahia; Teatro de Arena.

Health Clinic: Barão de Loreto 21, Graça. Dr Argemiro Júnior speaks English and Spanish. First consultation US$40, second free. Dr Manoel Nogueira (from 1000-1200), Av Joana Angélica 6, T 241-2377, English-speaking. Yellow fever vaccinations free at Delegação Federal de Saúde, R Padre Feijó, Canela. Ensure that a new needle is used. Israeli travellers needing medical (or other) advice should contact Sr Marcus (T 247-5769), who speaks Hebrew and is glad to help. German-speaking doctor, Dr Josef Stangl, R Conselheiro Pedro Luiz 179, Rio Vermelho, T 237-1073.

Language school Casa do Brasil, R Milton de Oliveira 231, Barra, T 245-5866.

Laundry *Lavanderia Lavalimpo*, R do Pilar 31, Comércio, Mon-Sat 0800-1800. *Lavanderia Comficha*, Av Doutora Praquer Fries, Porto do Barra, automatic, not too dear.

Post Office Main post office and poste restante is in Praça Inglaterra, in the Lower City, open Mon-Fri 0800-1700, Sat 0800-1200. Other offices at Praça da Sé in Ed Associação Bahiana de Imprensa on R Guedes de Brito 1, T 240-6222; R Alfredo Brito 43, Mon-Sat 0800-1700, Sun

0800-1200, has philatelic section (only pink post office in Brazil!); Rodoviária, Mon-Sat 0800-1800 (till 1200 on Sun); airport; Barra and Iguatemi Shopping Malls (Mon-Fri); Av Princesa Isabel, Barra, and R Marqués de Caravelas; in Ondina by the hotels there is a booth by the beach next to *Ondina Apart Hotel*.

Communications Embratel, Rua do Carro 120. Telebahia has branches at Campo da Pólvora, on R Hugo Baltazar Silva (open 0700-2200 daily), Barra and Iguatemi Shopping Centres (Mon-Fri 1000-2200 and Sat 0900-2000), airport (daily 0700-2200) and rodoviária (Mon-Sat 24 hrs and Sun 0700-2200).

Shopping *H Stern* jewellers at *Hotels Meridien, Othon* and *Bahia*, also at Barra and Iguatemi Shopping centres. Visit the stone-cutting workshops at *Breis* in the Largo do Carmo; best prices for cut stones and jewellery made to order in 24 hrs with a genuine guarantee; *Simon Joalheiros*, Praça Anchietal, European designs. The Barra and Iguatemi shopping centres are big, modern and a/c with big department stores. Quality *artesanato* at the 3 official FIEB-SESI shops: Av Tiradentes 299 (Bonfim); Av Borges dos Reis 9 (Rio Vermelho); Av 7 de Setembro 261 (Mercês).

Shopping in Pelourinho There are many new shops in the area. The major carnaval *afro blocos* have boutiques selling tee-shirts etc. *Boutique Olodum*, on Praça José Alencar, *Ilê Aiyê*, on Rua Fransisco Muniz Barreto 16 and *Muzenza* next door. On the same street is *Modaxé*, a retail outlet for clothes manufactured by street children under the auspices of the pioneering and highly successful Projeto Axé, expensive but these are the trendiest T-shirts in town. Also on this street at No 18 is *Brazilian Sound*, latest in Brazilian and Bahia music, CDs mainly. Another good record store is *Mini Som* in nearby Praça de Sé (see **Music in Bahia**, above).

Instituto Mauá, R Gregorio de Matos 27 (T 321 5638), open Tues-Sat 0900-1800, Sun 1000-1600, good quality Bahian handicrafts at fair prices, better value and better option for traditional crafts than the Mercado Modelo. A similar store is *Loja de Artesanato do SESC*, Largo Pelourinho (T 321 5502), Mon-Fri 0900-1800 (closed for lunch), Sat 0900-1300. Both stores recommended.

Trustworthy, reliable jewellery stores are *Lasbonfim* (T 242 9854) and *Simon* (T 242 5218), both in the Terreiro de Jesus. They both have branches in the nearby Carmo district. Excellent hand-made lace products at *Artesanato Santa Barbara*, R Alfredo Brito 7. For local art the best stores are *Atelier Portal da Cor*, Ladeira do Carmo 31 (T 242 9466), run by a cooperative of local artists, Totonho, Calixto, Raimundo Santos, Jô, good prices, rec. Also across the street at *Casa do Indio*, Indian artefacts and art, restaurant and bar open here till late, good surroundings. Also good *naif* art at *Koisa Nossa* on R Alfredo Brito 45. Good wood carvings next door by a cooperative of sculptors, Palito and Negão Barão being the most famous. Hand-made traditional percussion instruments (and percussion lessons) at *Chez Lua*, Alfredo Brito 27, made by percussionist Dilson Lua. Also percussion lessons at *Oficina de Investigação Musical*, Alfredo Brito 24 (T 321 0339), Mon to Fri, 0800-1200 and 1300-1600. *Shopping do Pelô*, Rua Fransisco Muniz 02 (T 321 4200), is run by SEBRAE, the Brazilian small business authority, open daily until 1800, stalls with varied goods, clothes, jewellery etc.

Markets The Mercado Modelo, at Praça Cairu, lower city, offers many tourist items such as wood carvings, silver-plated fruit, leather goods, local musical instruments. Lace items for sale are often not handmade (despite labels), are heavily marked up, and are much better bought at their place of origin (eg Ilha de Maré, Pontal da Barra and Marechal Deodoro, **see p 507**). Cosme e Damião, musical instrument sellers on 1st floor, has been rec, especially if you want to play the instruments. Bands and dancing, especially Sat (but very much for money from tourists taking photographs), closed at 1200 Sun. Photograph exhibition of the old market in basement. (Many items are often cheaper on the Praça da Sé in the nearby Cidade Alta.) Largest and most authentic market is the **Feira de São Joaquim**, 5 km from Mercado Modelo along sea front: barkers, trucks, *burros*, horses, boats, people, mud, all very smelly, every day (Sun till 1200 only), busiest on Sat morning; interesting African-style pottery and basketwork; very cheap. (Car ferry terminal for Itaparica is nearby.) Instituto Mauá at Porto da Barra and the Iguatemi Shopping Centre sells good handicraft items, it is run by the government so prices are fixed and reasonable. Every Wed from 1700-2100 there is a handicrafts fair in the 17th century fort of Santa Maria at the other end of Porto da Barra beach. On Fri from 1700-2100, there is an open air market of handicrafts and Bahian food in Porto da Barra, a popular event among the local young people. Daily market of handicrafts in Terreiro de Jesus in the old city from 1000-1800. Mosquito nets from *Casa dos Mosquiteiros*, R Pedro Sá 6F, Calçada, T 226 0715.

Bookshops *Livraria Brandão*, R Ruy Barbosa 104, Centre, T 243 5383, secondhand English, French, Spanish and German books. *Livraria Civilizaçao Brasileira*, Av 7 de Setembro 912,

Mercês, and in the Barra, Iguatemi and *Ondina Apart Hotel* shopping centres have some English books; also *Graúna*, Av 7 de Setembro 1448, and R Barão de Itapoan 175, Porto da Barra, many English titles; *Livraria Planeta*, Carlos Gómez 42, loja 1, sells used English books. The bookshop at the airport has English books and magazines.

Photography and repairs *Pepe*, R da Ajuda, ed Triunfo, first floor Centre. *Maxicolor*, R Estados Unidos (Mercado Modelo), for cut-price developing.

Tourist Agencies Bus tours are available from several companies: *LR Turismo*, *Itaparica Turismo* and *Alameda Turismo*: city tour (US$25 pp), Bahia by Night includes transport to Moenda restaurant, show and dinner (US$45 pp). All day boat trip on Bahia de Todos Os Santos from 0800-1700 including visit to Ilha das Frades, lunch on Itaparica (US$10 extra) US$35 pp. *Tatu Tours*, Ed Victória Center, Sala 1108, Av Centenário 2883, 40147-900 Salvador, BA, in front of Shopping Barra, T 245 9322, F 237 7562, run by an Irishman, specialise in Bahia, give private guided tours and can make any necessary travel, hotel and accommodation arrangements. They are represented in the USA by Brazil Nuts, 1150 Post Road, Fairfield, CT 06430, T (203) 259-7900, F 259-3177. *Submariner*, R de Paciência 223, Rio Vermelho, T 237-4097, hire diving equipment, friendly.

Tourist Office (with lists of hotels and pension stays in private homes) Bahiatursa, Palácio Rio Branco (former government palace, which may be viewed), R Chile on Praça Municipal, open 0800-1830, Mon-Fri, English and German spoken, helpful. Visitors can obtain weekly list of events and itineraries (on foot or by car) planned by the city, well worth doing. Map, US$2, good; offices have noticeboard for messages. Also at R Francisco Muniz Barreto 12, Historical Centre, T 321 2463, open daily 0830-1930; at bus station (good, English spoken), airport (T 204-1244, open daily 0800-2000), friendly (but inefficient), in the Mercado Modelo (T 241-0242, Mon-Fri 0800-1800, Sat 0800-1200), Porto da Barra (T 247-3195, Mon-Fri, 0800-1800, Sat-Sun 0800-1200). Also details of travel throughout Sate of Bahia. Phone 131 0600-0030 for tourist information in English. Emtursa, at airport, T 377 2262, Mon-Sat 0800-2200, has good maps. **Maps** from Departamento de Geografia e Estatística, Av Estados Unidos (opp Banco do Brasil, lower city): also from newsstands including airport bookshop, US$1.50.

Tourist Police R Gregório de Matos 16.

Immigration (for extensions of entry permits), Policia Federal, Av O Pontes 339, Aterro de Agua de Meninos, Lower City, T 321-6363, open 1000-1600. Show an outward ticket or sufficient funds for stay, visa extension US$7.

Local Transport Taxi meters start at US$0.60 for the "flagdown" and US$0.15/100 metres. They charge US$15/hr within city limits, and "agreed" rates outside. Taxi Barra-Centro US$3 daytime; US$4 at night. Watch the meter, especially at night; the night-time charge should be 30% higher than daytime charges. Teletaxi (24-hr service), 321-9988. Local buses US$0.30, *frescões* (or *executivos*) US$1. On buses and at the ticket-sellers' booths, watch your change and beware pickpockets. To get from the old city to the ocean beaches, take a "Barra" bus from Praça da Sé to the Barra point and walk to the nearer ones; the Aeroporto *frescão* (last 2130) leaves Praça da Sé, passing Barra, Ondina, Rio Vermelho, Amaralina, Pituba, Costa Azul, Armação, Boca do Rio, Jaguaripe, Patamares, Piatã and Itapoã, before turning inland to the airport. A new bus service, the Jardineira, goes to Flamengo beach (30 km from the city) following the coastal route. A glass-sided bus, it passes all the best beaches; sit on right hand side for best views. It leaves from the Praça da Sé daily 0730-1930, every 40 mins, US$1.50. For beaches beyond Itapoã, take the *frescão* to Stella Maris and Flamengo beaches. These follow the same route as the Jardineira. During Carnival, when most streets are closed, buses leave from Vale do Canela (O Vale), nr Campo Grande.

Car Rental Avis, Av Sete de Setembro 1796, T 237-0155, also at airport, T 377-2276 (toll free 0800-118066); **Budget**, Av Presidente Vargas 409, T 237-3396; **Hertz**, R Baependi, T 245-8364, **Unidas**, Av Oceânica 2456, Ondina, T 336 0717. If renting a car check whether credit card or cash is cheapest. National Car Rentals allow decision at the end of the rental.

Hitchhiking out of Salvador, take a "Cidade Industrial" bus from the bus station at the port; it goes on to the highway.

Air Daily flights to Rio, São Paulo, Recife, Aracaju, Belém, Belo Horizonte, Brasília, Curitiba, Fortaleza, Foz do Iguaçu, Goiania, Ilheus, João Pessoa, Maceió, Manaus, Natal, Porto Alegre, São Luis, and Vitoria. Nordeste Regional Airlines, Av Dom João VI 259, Brotas T 244 3355 has daily flights to Porto Seguro and several flights a week to Barreiras, Bom Jesus da Lapa, Guanambi, Paulo Afonso and Vitória da Conquista in the interior of Bahia. Varig flies daily to Petrolina. Dois de Julho Airport is 32 km from city centre. Buses from airport to Centre Aeroporto-Campo Grande US$0.35, at least 1 hr. Special *Executivo* bus Aeroporto-Praça da Sé along the coast road for hotels, US$1.30. Special taxi (buy ticket at airport desk) US$30; taxis airport to city are controlled by certain drivers. From the city to airport is less restricted, fare US$17.50.

Shipping National coastal vessels.

Rail From Salvador there are only local train services.

Buses Bus station 5 km from city but regular services to centre (US$0.30); bus RI or RII, "Centro-Rodoviária-Circular"; in centre, get on in lower city at foot of Lacerda lift; buses also to Campo Grande; journey can take up to 1 hr especially in peak periods. Executive bus, quicker, from Praça da Inglaterra (in front of MacDonalds), Comércio, runs to Iguatemi Shopping Centre, weekdays only, from where there is a walkway to the bus station (take care in the dark, or a taxi, US$10). To **Recife**, US$24 (*leito*, 47), 13 hrs, 4 a day and 1 *leito*, Itapemerim, T 388-0037, all at night; plenty to **Rio** (28 hrs, US$47, *leito* 115, Itapemirim, good stops, clean toilets, rec), **São Paulo** (30 hrs), US$58, *leito* US$116 (0815 with Viação Nacional, 2 in pm with São Geraldo, T 533-0188), to **Fortaleza**, 19 hrs, US$40 at 0900 with Itapemerim; **Ilhéus**, 7 hrs, Aguia Branca, T 533-1515, *comercial* US$14, *expresso* US$17, *executivo* US$19, *leito* US$28, several; **Belo Horizonte**, Gontijo T 358-7448, at 1700, US$40, São Geraldo at 1800, US$39. Foz do Iguaçu, 52 hrs, US$65. There are daily bus services to **Brasília** along the fully paved BR-242, via Barreiras, 3 daily, 23 hrs, Paraíso, T 358-1591, US$45. Frequent services to the majority of destinations; a large panel in the main hall of the terminal lists destinations and the relevant ticket office.

Motorists to Rio can do the trip on the BR-116 highway in 3 days, stopping at *Vitória da Conquista* (524 km from Salvador), a busy town with large market Mon-Sat, and a man-made lake with fountains and waterfalls: **D** *Hotel Aliança*, **D** *Hotel Livramento*, with restaurant, and **F** *Tel-Aviv Palace*, good breakfast, one block from final stop of urban bus from rodoviária; also Camping Clube do Brasil site at Km 1,076 (bus to Salvador, 8 hrs, US$10; to Feira Santana; to Itaobim, 6 hrs, US$4.50; to Lençois—change at Bominal—8 hrs); Teôfilo Otôni, 946 km, or Governador Valadares, 1,055 km (see p 411), and Leopoldina (1,402 km). There are also various motels; two in the State of Bahia are at Vitória da Conquista; and at Feira de Santana; also between Feira and Salvador. Fairly good hotels are also available in *Jequié* (*Itajubá*, *Rex*, and motels), and basic ones in Milagres. Stopovers on the BR-101 coastal road can be made at Vitória and Itabuna (or Ilhéus), and there are many other towns on or near the coast.

Excursions From the lower city the train (Trem do Leste) leaves Calçada for a 40 min journey through the bayside suburbs of Salvador—Lobato, Plataforma (canoes and motor boats for Ribeira on the Itapagipe peninsula), Escada (17th century church), Praia Grande, Periperi and Paripe (take bus for 17th century church at São Tomé de Paripe). The train runs Mon-Fri only; the same trip can be made by bus, less picturesquely. From Ribeira a small boat goes 25 km to *Ilha da Maré* between 0900 and 1100, connecting the island's villages of Itamoaba, Praia Grande and Santana (US$0.70); boat returns next day from Santana at 0400-0500. Santana is a centre for lace making, Praia Grande for basket-weaving. None of the villages has a hotel, but there are restaurants and bars and camping is possible. From São Tomé de Paripe, near the naval base at Aratu, irregular boats go to *Ilha dos Frades*, sparsely populated, no electricity, one *pousada* (**C** *Ponta de Nossa Senhora de Guadalupe*, beachfront, T Salvador 245-8536). The beach is busy lunchtimes with excursions from Salvador, but otherwise is quiet, good snorkelling.

Across the bay from Salvador lies the island of *Itaparica*, 29 km long and 12 km wide. The island is reached from the main land by two ferries. The main passenger ferry leaves for Bom Despacho from São Joaquim (buses for Calçada, Ribeira stop across the road from the ferry terminal; the "Sabino Silva—Ribeira" bus passes in front of the Shopping Barra). The first ferry from Salvador leaves at 0600 and, depending on demand, the ferries leave at intervals of 45 mins and 90 mins alternately. Last ferry from Salvador is at 2230. Returning to Salvador the first ferry is at 0515 and the last one is at 2230. During the summer months the ferries are much more frequent. Enquiries at the Companhia de Navegação Baiano (CNB), T 321 7100 from 0800 to 1700. One way ticket for foot passenger is US$0.70.

From Bom Despacho there are many buses, kombis and taxis to all parts of the island. The best beaches are at Ponta de Areia, Mar Grande (US$0.50 by kombi), Berlinque, Aratuba and Cacha Pregos. Kombi and taxis can be rented for trips around the island but be prepared to bargain, US$20-30 for a half-day tour.

The town of Itaparica is very picturesque, with a fair beach in the town, and well worth a visit. Take a bus or kombi by the coast road (Beira Mar) which passes through the villages of Manguinhos, Amoureiras and Ponta de Areia. A good simple *pousada* at Amoureiras is **C** *Pousada Pé na Praia*, good breakfast, good sized rooms, English and French spoken (T 831 1389). The beach at Ponta de Areia is one of the best on the island and is very popular. There are many *barracas* on the beach, the best and busiest is *Barraca Pai Xango*, always very lively.

In Itaparica there are many fine residential buildings from the 19th century, plus the church of São Lourenço, one of the oldest in Brazil, a delightful walk through the old town. During the summer months the streets are ablaze with the blossoms of the beautiful flamboyant trees. There is a popular *Club Med* on the island (Fazenda Boca do Rio, 44470 Vera Cruz, Bahia, T 071-833-1141, F 071-241-0100). There are few *pousadas* in the town. The best is **L3** *Quinta Pitanga* (T 831 1554), beautifully decorated by the owner Jim Valkus, 3 suites and 2 singles, beachfront property, a retreat, excellent restaurant, expensive but highly rec. Accepts day visitors. **A1** *Grande Hotel da Itaparica* (T 831 1120). **A3** *Pousada Iemanjá*; **C** *Pousada Santa Rita*, and **E** *Restaurant/Pousada Cantinha da Ilha*, clean. **C** *Pousada Icarai*, charming, good location.

Mar Grande can be reached via minibus from Bom Despacho, or by a smaller ferry (Lancha) from the Terminal Marítimo in front of the Mercado Modelo in Salvador. The ferries leave every 45 mins and the crossing takes 50 mins, US$0.45. They ask that no swimming costumes be worn on board. The beaches here are fair but can be dirty at times. There are many *pousadas* in Mar Grande and the nearby beaches of Ilhota and Gamboa (both to the left as you disembark from the ferry).

A3 *Pousada Arco Iris*, Estrada da Gamboa 102, T 833 1130, magnificent building and setting in mango orchard, expensive, good if slow restaurant, *Manga Rosa*. They have camping facilities next door, shady, not always clean. **C** *Pousada Estrela do Mar*, Av NS das Candeias 170 (T 833 1108), good rooms, clean, fan or a/c, rec. Next door is **C** *Pousada Mar da Ilhota* (T 833 1486). **E** *Pousada Samambaia*, same street , No 61, good breakfast, French spoken, rec. **C** *Pousada Sonho do Verão* (R São Bento 2, opposite *Pousada Arco Iris*), chalets and apartments, cooking facilities, French and English spoken, T 833 1616. Like other *pousadas* they rent bicycles (US$3/hr); they also rent horses (US$5/hr). Near the church in the main square is the **C** *Pousada Casarão da Ilha*, (T 833 1106), spacious rooms with a great view of Salvador across the bay, swimming pool, a/c, rec.

At Gamboa is **B** *Hotel Pousada Ponta Caieira* (T 833 1080), beachfront, take bus to Gamboa and it's a 5 mins walk to the *pousada*, quiet.

Good restaurants in Mar Grande are *Philippe's Bar and restaurant*, Largo de São Bento, good French and local cuisine, information in English and French. *O Pacífico* is good, friendly, peaceful. *Restaurant Rafael* in main square for pizzas and snacks. Also pizzas at *Bem Me Quer*, opp *Pousada Samambaia* down alley. There are many Baiana's selling *acarajé* in the late afternoon and early evening in the main square by the pier.

At Aratuba there is an excellent hostel, *Albergue da Juventude*, F (for students)—E, on the beach, clean, friendly, shady, rec.

At Cacha Pregos the good **D** *Pousada Cacha Pregos*, next to the supermarket, with fan, bath, no breakfast, T 839 1594. Also **C** *Pousada Casa da Praia*, T 837 1058.

From Bom Despacho there are many buses to other towns such as Nazaré das Farinhas, Valença (see below) and also *Jaguaribe*, a small, picturesque colonial port. Both of these towns are on the mainland connected by a bridge on the SW side of the island, turn off between Mar Grande and Cacha Pregos (bus company is Viazul). There are good beaches across the bay on the mainland, but a boat is needed to reach these (US$8.25). Visits to the marine reseach Station on Ilha do Medo, a project run by the Federal University of Bahia, have to be arranged through their visitors' centre beside the handicraft centre in the historical centre of Itaparica.

Small boats for trips around the bay can be hired privately at the small port by the Mercado Modelo called Rampa do Mercado. A pleasant trip out to the mouth of the bay should take an hour and a half as you sail along the bottom of the cliff. When arranging to hire any boat ensure that the boat is licensed by the Port Authority (Captânia dos Portos) and that life-jackets are on board. Boats are regularly checked to ensure that they are sea worthy and boats not complying with these regulations are not permitted to carry paying passengers. The Companhia de Navegação Bahiana (T 321 7100) sails 5 times a week to **Maragojipe** on the Rio Paraguaçu to the W (see under **The Recôncavo** below). The trip takes 3 hrs. It sails across the bay and then up the valley of the river. There are some very beautiful views along the trip. The ship makes two stops along the way, at Barra do Paraguaçu and also at Mutuca where locals row out to the ship in dug out canoes to disembark passengers leaving the ship at that point. A good trip would be to continue to Cachoeira by bus from Maragogipe and return to Salvador the following day. Departure from Salvador from Terminal Turístico in front of the Mercado Modelo Mon-Thur 1430 (Brazilian Summer time departs 1530). Fri departure is at 1130. Departure Maragogipe Mon-Thur 0500 and Fri 0830, US$3.

Itaparica Turismo (T 248 3187/248 3433) and LR Turismo (T 248 3333) run daily schooner trips to islands in the bay visiting Frades and Itaparica islands; boats leave from Terminal Turístico at 0830. American yachtsman Steve Lafferty is highly rec for enjoyable sailing trips, US$120 a day for up to 4 people: R do Sodre 45, apt 301, T 241-0994.

Nazaré das Farinhas (pop 25,940), 60 km inland from Itaparica, and reached over a bridge by bus from **Bom Despacho**, is an 18th-century town celebrated for its market, which specializes in the local ceramic figures, or *caxixis*. There is an especially large market in Holy Week, particularly on the Thur and Good Fri. 12 km from Nazaré (taxi US$5.50, also buses) is the village of ***Maragojipinha***, which specializes in making the ceramic figures. Bus from Salvador, 1530, takes 5 hrs.

Feira de Santana (pop 405,690), 112 km NW of Salvador on both the coastal BR-101 and the inland BR-116 roads to Rio, the centre of a great cattle breeding and trading area; its Mon market, known as Feira do Couro (leather fair), said to be the largest in Brazil, attracts great crowds to its colourful display of local products. The permanent Artesanato market in the centre has a bigger selection, including leather, than the Mon market. Bus every half hour from Salvador, 2 hrs, US$3. (Bus station has a wall of painted tiles made by Udo-Ceramista, whose workshop is Brotas, Av Dom João VI 411, Salvador.)

Hotels **A1** *Luxor*, BR-116 Sul, Km 437, T 221-5922; **C** *Flecha Motel Feira*, about 20 km away at Km 171 BR-101; several cheap ones in Praça da Matriz and near the bus station, which is quite near the centre; **C** *Senador*, R Senador Quintano, rec, Bahian restaurant in same street, No 259, *Panela de Barro*, good.

The Recôncavo The area around Salvador, known as the Recôncavo Baiano, was one of the chief centres of sugar and tobacco cultivation in the 16th century.

Leaving Salvador on the Feira road, at Km 33 one forks left on the BR-324 to the **Museu de Recôncavo Vanderlei de Pinho** (see p 472). Further W, round the bay, is ***São Francisco do Conde***, 54 km from Salvador, with a church and convent of 1636 and the ruins of Don Pedro II's agricultural school, said to be the first in Latin America.

At 60 km from Salvador the BA-026 road branches off the BR-324 to Santo Amaro, Cachoeira and São Félix. Seventy-three km from Salvador is ***Santo Amaro da Purificação*** (pop 54,145) an old sugar centre sadly decaying, noted for its churches (often closed because of robberies), municipal palace (1769), fine main square, house of the poet and singer Caetano Veloso (his sister, the singer Maria Bethânia, is also from here), and ruined mansions including Araújo Pinto, former residence of the Barão de Cotegipe. Other attractions include the splendid beaches of the bay, the falls of Vitória and the grotto of Bom Jesus dos Pobres. Festivals in Jan and Feb (Santo Amaro and NS da Purificação) are interesting. Craftwork is sold on the town's main bridge. No good hotels or restaurants.

3 km beyond Santo Amaro on BR-420, turn right onto BA-878 for ***Bom Jesus dos Pobres***, a small, traditional fishing village with a 300-year history. One good

hotel: **B** *Agua Viva*, T (075) 696 1178, reservations (Salvador 071) 359 1132, beach front, chalets or apartments, a/c or fan, good breakfast and restaurant, on one of the oldest farms in the region, good beach, rec. Bus from Salvador rodoviária 4 a day (Camurjipe), US$3.75.

At 54 km from Santo Amaro, and only 4 km from the BR-101 coastal road, are the twin towns of **Cachoeira** (Bahia's "Ouro Preto", pop 28,255), and *São Félix* (pop 12,095) on either side of the Rio Paraguaçu below the Cachoeira dam. Cachoeira, recently declared a national monument, was twice capital of Bahia: once in 1624-5 during the Dutch invasion, and once in 1822-3 while Salvador was still held by the Portuguese. It was the birthplace of Ana Néri, known as "Mother of the Brazilians", who organized nursing services during the Paraguayan War (1865-70). There are beautiful views from above São Félix. Cachoeira's main buildings are the **Casa da Câmara e Cadeia** (1698-1712), the **Santa Casa de Misericórdia** (1734—the hospital, someone may let you see the church), the 16th-century **Ajuda** chapel (now containing a fine collection of vestments), and the Convent of the **Ordem Terceira do Carmo**, whose church has a heavily gilded interior. Other churches: Carmo (1548) and its Third Order (fine *azulejos* and gilding), the **Matriz** with 5-metres-high *azulejos*, and **Nossa Senhora da Conceição da Monte**. Beautiful lace cloths on church altars. All churches either restored or in the process of restoration. Ruined Jesuit seminary. Tourist office in the Casa de Ana Néri. Craftwork in ceramics and wood readily available. Buses from Salvador (Camurjipe) every hour or so; Feira Santana 2 hrs US$1.70.

Festivals São João (24 Jun) "Carnival of the Interior" celebrations, well-attended by tourists, Boa Morte (early Aug), and a famous *candomblé* ceremony at the Fonte de Santa Bárbara on 4 Dec.

Hotels Cachoeira: **B** *Pousada do Convento de Cachoeira* (run by Bahiatursa), T 725-1716, in newly restored 16th-century convent, good restaurant; *Pousada do Guerreiro*, 13 de Maio 14, T 724-1203, no restaurant; **E** *Santo Antônio* near the rodoviária, basic, clean, safe, friendly, laundry facilities, rec; **E** *Colombo*, near the river, basic, friendly, meals available, rec. *Youth Hostel*, Av Parnamirim 417, T 268-4844/3390. **Restaurants:** *Cabana do Pai Thomaz*, excellent Bahian food, good value, also an hotel, D with private bath and breakfast; *Recanto de Oxum*, nearby, *Gruta Azul*, lunch only; *Do Nair*, R 13 de Maio, delicious food and sometimes Seresta music. São Félix: *Xang-hai*, F, good, cheap food, warmly rec. Try the local dish, *maniçoba* (meat, manioc and peppers).

Excursion 6 km from Cachoeira, on the higher ground of the Planalto Baiano, is the small town of Belém (turning 2½ km on road to Santo Amaro). Church and seminary of Carmo. Healthy spot: people from Salvador have summer homes.

The tobacco centre of Cruz das Almas can also be visited, although transport is poor. The São João celebrations here (24 Jun) are not rec: very dangerous games with fireworks are involved.

Maragojipe (pop 38,800) a tobacco exporting port 22 km SE of Cachoeira along a dirt road (BA-123), can also be reached by boat from Salvador. See the old houses and the church of São Bartolomeu, with its museum. The main festival is São Bartolomeu, in Aug. Good ceramic craftwork.

Inland from Salvador Motorists to Brasília can save a little time by taking the ferry to Itaparica, book in advance to avoid long queues, and then going across country to Itaberaba for the BR-242 highway. The journey can be broken at Itaberaba (*pousada*), Lençóis (see below), at Ibotirama on the Rio São Francisco; at Barreiras on the Rio Negro, where buses stop for 2-3 hrs (**C** *Hotel Vandelena*, full board); or at Alvorada do Norte (several poor-looking places), Sobradinho (**C** *Hotel Alvimar*) or at Posse (Goiás). The road is paved from Salvador to Brasília, but it is reported full of potholes between Alvorada do Norte and Barreiras and poor between Salvador and Lençóis.

400 km W of Salvador on the BR-242 to Brasília is *Lençóis* (pop 7,590, DDD code 075), a historical monument and a colonial gem, founded in 1844 because of diamonds in the region. There are still some *garimpeiros*. In the town, Artesanato

Areias Coloridas, R das Pedras, owned by Tourino, is the best place for local sand paintings made in bottles. These are inexpensive and fascinating to see being done. They will make one as you wait. For ceramic work, the best is *Jota*, who has a workshop which can be visited. Take the steps to the left of the school near the *Pousada Lençois*. His work is very original, rec. Market day is Mon, in the morning, rec.

Hotels A3 *Pousada de Lençóis*, T 334-1102, with breakfast, swimming pool, rec; **B** *Estalagem Alcino e Silvinha*, R Gen Vieira de Morais 139, T 334-1171, with bath, D pp shared bath, beautiful, restored 19th-century house, superb breakfast, highly rec; **B** Ze Carlos and Lia Vieira de Moraes have 2 excellent chalets in their huge garden at the entrance to the town, R Gen Viveiros 187, T 334 1151, English spoken, good breakfast (he is a keen birdwatcher and an authority on the region, she makes excellent jams). **B** *Canto de Águas*, Av Senhor dos Passos s/n, T 334-1154, F 334-1188, comfortable, good location, swimming pool, a/c or fan, good service, rec; **C** *Colonial*, T 334-1114; **C** *Pousada do Parque*, quiet, by first bridge before town; **C** *Pousada Village Lapāo*, nearby, chalets of various size, quiet, T 334-1117; **E** *Pensão Diamantina*, R Miguel Calmon; **D** *Pousalegre*, R Boa Vista 95, T 334-1124, with good regional breakfast, friendly, hot showers, good vegetarian restaurant; **D** *Repousada*, R Boa Vista, rec; **D** *Tradição*, with bath, breakfast, fridge, mosquito net, pleasant; **E** *Casa de Hélia*, R das Pedras 102, English and some Hebrew spoken, good facilities, renowned breakfast, rec; 2 campsites, one 2 km before Lençóis, one in the town centre (friendly, rec). There are also houses to rent in the town. Most of these are basic, with cooking and washing facilities. Juanita on R do Rosário rents rooms with access to washing and cooking facilities, US$3.50 pp. Isabel rents a house on the main square in front of the Correios, US$4 pp without breakfast.

Restaurants *Lajedo*, good food with good view of town, popular meeting place at night; *Goody*, R da Rodaviária s/n, good simple cooking, reasonably priced. A busy local bar is *Ynave*, with live music on weekends. The busiest spot at weekends is *Amigo da Onça*, R José Florêncio, near municipal market, lambada, forró and samba-reggae until the small hours, good fun.

Communications Telebahia, open daily 0800-2200.

Tourist Information Sectur, near *Pousada Lençois*, open daily 0800-1200, 1400-1800. A new tourist office is on Praça Oscar Maciel, next to the church across the river from town, T 334-1121. There are many guides offering their services at most *pousadas*, about US$18; most of them are very young. A reliable guide is Edmilson (known locally as Mil), who can be found at Sectur; he knows the region extremely well and is very knowledgeable for his age. It is difficult to change money in Lençóis. Reliable tour company: *Pé de Trilha Turismo Aventura*, Praça Horácio de Matos s/n, T/F 334-1124, near Banco do Brasil, guiding, trekking, rents camping equipment, etc, represented in Salvador by Tatu Tours (071-245-9322, F 071-237-7562).

Buses Paraíso bus from Salvador 0730, 1200 and 2200, US$14 (bus goes to Seabra, 80 km beyond Lençóis, make sure driver knows you want to go to Lençóis); Feira de Santana, returns at 0900, 2100; buses also from Recife, Ibotirama, Barreiras or Brasília, 16 hrs, US$22.

Excursions Near the town, visit the Serrano with its wonderful natural pools in the river bed, which give a great hydro massage. A little further away is the Salão de Areia, where the coloured sands for the bottle paintings come from. Ribeirão do Meio is a 45-min walk from town; here locals slide down a long natural water shute into a big pool. Care should be taken when doing this; it is best to be shown the way it is done and to take something to slide in.

Lençóis is the headquarters of the **Parque Nacional da Chapada Diamantina** (founded 1985), which contains 1,500 sq km of mountainous country, with waterfalls, large caves (take care, and a strong torch, there are no signs and caves can be difficult to find without a guide), rivers with natural swimming pools and good walking tours. Information, T (075) 332-2175, or Ibama, Av Juracy Magalhães Jr 608, CEP 40295-140, Salvador, T (071) 240-7322. Roy Funch, the ex-director of the National Park, is an excellent guide and can be found at his craft shop, Funkart, in the main square. Morro de Pai Inácio, 30 km from Lençóis, has the best view of the Chapada, rec at sunset (bus from Lençóis at 0815, 30 mins, US$0.75). In the park is the Cachoeira de Glass (or Smoke Waterfall), 400 metres, the highest in Brazil. To see it, go to Palmeiras, from where it is 18 km on a dirt road to the point where you then walk 2 hrs to the falls. The view is astonishing; the updraft of the air currents often makes the flow of water stand up. Well worth the effort of getting there. The village of *Capão* is near the base of the climb. Hotels: **C** *Candombá*, good breakfast, excellent food, home-grown vegetables, run by Claude and Suzana (Claude speaks French and English and guides in the region); F (075) 332 2176, or through Tatu Tours in Salvador (address above); **D** *Pousada Verde*, at entrance to town, very good breakfast, rec; **E** *Tatu Feliz*, no breakfast; **E** *Pouso Riacho do Our*, friendly, rec. Pé de Trilha Turismo can make reservations for most of the *pousadas* in the Chapada Diamantina. Southwest of the park is **Mucujé** (*Hotel Mucujé*, opp rodoviária, good food, basic, take mosquito coils), lovely walks among hills or along Rio Paraguaçu. It is possible to walk from Mucujé to Lençois, about 50 km, but seek expert advice on the route through the park before doing so. Buses from Mucujé to Seabra run Tues, Thur, Sat at 0500; frequent service from there to Lençois and Palmeiras.

Other excursions are: Lapa Doce, a cave with fine stalagmites and stalactites, 70 km, Andaraí, 101 km, and the diamond ghost town of **Igatu**, a further 14 km on the other side of the Rio Paraguaçu. There is a bridge across the river. The town has a new *pousada* (1994). Recommended. A good day trip from Lençois to this part of the Chapada is to **Poço Encantado**, a mountain cave with a lake of crystal clear water, 60m deep, very spectacular, known locally as the 8th wonder of the world. From Apr to Aug, the sunlight entering the cave from the mountain side and hits the water and is dispersed into the colours of the spectrum. A visit is highly recommended and can be followed by a trip to Igatu on the return to Lençois. Local guides can often arrange transport to the more remote excursions, certainly this is possible when groups are involved.

South from Salvador 271 km from Salvador, on an asphalted road, is **Valença** (pop 66,785) a small, attractive and bustling town at the mouth of the Rio Una. Two old churches stand on rising ground above the town; the views from Nossa Senhora do Amparo are recommended. The town is in the middle of an area producing black pepper, cloves and *piaçava* (used in making brushes and mats). Other industries include the building and repair of fishing boats (*saveiros*). Tourist office opposite rodoviária on other side of river, friendly. Valença and the beaches towards Ilhéus are being developed and are becoming less attractive to those wanting to get away from it all. The Rio Una enters an enormous region of mangrove swamps. The main attraction of Valença is the beaches on the mainland (Guabim, 14 km N) and on the island of Tinharé. Avoid touts at the rodoviária, they give misleading information and then offer an overpriced alternative.

Hotels *Rio Una*, T 741-1614, fairly chic, expensive, swimming pool; **C** *Cabana*, on road to Guabim, in high season, friendly, chaotic; **C** *Guabim*, Praça da Independência, T 741-1110, modest, rec, good *Akuarius* restaurant; next door, **D** *Rafa*, new, large rooms, well rec; **E** *Tourist Hotel*, Mal Floriano 167, good, friendly; **E** *Valença*, clean, comfortable, good breakfast, rec.

Transport Long-distance buses run from the new rodoviária, while the old one is for local buses. Eight buses a day to/from Salvador, 5 hrs, US$9, Camarujipe (T 071 358-0109) and São Jorge companies; São Jorge to Itabuna, 5 hrs, US$7, very slow.

A new road has been opened, greatly shortening the journey to Valença; take the ferry from São Joaquim to Bom Despacho on Itaparica island. From there it is 130 km to Valença via Nazaré das Farinhas (**see p 402**). To/from Bom Despacho on Itaparica, Camarujipe and Águia Branca companies, 16 a day, 1 hr 45 mins, US$7.

Tinharé is a large island (with good walking, beaches and camping, but no banks or exchange) separated from the mainland by the estuary of the Rio Una and mangrove swamps, so that it is hard to tell which is land and which is water. Boats (US$1.50) leave every day from Valença for Galeão (1½ hrs), Gamboa (1½ hrs) and Morro de São Paulo (1½ hrs). The best beaches and *pousadas* are at Morro de São Paulo. Boats to the Morro leave from the main bridge in Valença 5 times a day (signalled by a loud whistle). The fare is US$2.50. Only buses between 0530-1100 from Salvador to Valença connect with ferries. Private boat hire can be arranged outside these times. A responsible local boatman is Jario, T (075) 741 1681; he can be contacted to meet travellers arriving at the bus station for transfer to the Morro. He also offers excursions to other islands, especially **Boipeba**, a small simple fishing village. Overnight excursions to this village are possible; **D** *Pousada Luar das Águas* (T 741 2238), simple, good.

From Salvador, a direct ferry service sails from the Terminal Marítimo in front of the Mercado Modelo to Morro de São Paulo (*Lancha Executiva*): daily in high season, Fri, Sat, Sun in low season, 0830, returns 1730, US$30 one way, 2½ hr trip. There is also a less expensive schooner which makes the crossing daily from in front of the Mercado Model. Part of the trip is on the open sea, which can be rough (not rec for those who suffer from seasickness).

Morro de São Paulo is very popular in summer, situated on the headland at the northernmost tip of the island, lush with ferns, palms and birds of paradise, dominated by the lighthouse and the ruins of a Dutch colonial fort (1630). The village has a landing place on the sheltered landward side, dominated by the old gateway of the fortress. From the lighthouse a path leads to a ruined lookout with cannon, which has panoramic views. The place is expensive Dec-Mar, crowded at holiday times, but cheaper during the rest of the year. All roads are unmade, but beaches are good. Fish can be bought from the fishermen in summer, or borrow a pole and catch your own at sunset. Secondhand books (English, German, and others) sold at the back of the craft shop: the bearded owner will trade 2 for 1 if he's in the mood.

Hotels and Beaches E pp *Pousada Bora Bora*, shared bath, OK; *Pousada da Tia Glória*, friendly, quiet; next door is **D** *Pousada da Praça*, clean, friendly, fan, rec. There are many cheap *pousadas* and rooms to rent near the fountain (Fonte Grande) but this part of town is very hot at night. Senhora Preta rents rooms E, ask at quay. **D** *Pousada Village da Ponte*, Rua da Fonte Grande, T in Salvador 071-248 2699, a/c fridge, fan, rec. Highly recommended are **C** *Pousada Porto da Cima* (200 metres past **D** *Pousada Casarão*) chalets with fans, very friendly, and **E** *Pousada Gaúcho*, huge breakfast, shared bath. A little further along and up some steep steps to the left is **B** *Pousada Colibri*, cool, always a breeze blowing, excellent views, only six apartments, Helmut, the owner, speaks German and German, highly rec.

The beaches on Morro de São Paulo are at the bottom of the main street where one turns right on to the first beach (Primeira Praia). **B** *Pousada Vistabella*, is very clean, owner Petruska is extremely friendly, good rooms with bathroom, rooms to the front have good views and are cooler, all have fans, hammocks, rec (T 073 254 1272); **C** *Pousada Farol do Morro*, all rooms with sea view, cool, T (071) 243 4144, F 243 4207. **D** *Pousada Ilha da Saudade*, good breakfast, simple, friendly. **C** *Pousada Ilha do Sol*, good views, rec. On second beach (Segunda Praia) is **C** *Pousada Oxum*. On third beach is **B** *Pousada Gaimu*, 14 rm, in lush tropical setting, secluded (T 071-321 1936). Nearby is **B** *Pousada Fazenda Caeira*, large grounds, private, well stocked library with snooker and other games, friendly (T 075-741 1272), both of these are rec. A new 5 star hotel, *Hotel Ville Gaignon*, has opened, swimming pools, games rooms, convention rooms, etc. On fourth beach (Quarta Praia) is **C** *Pousada Catavento*.

Restaurants *Restaurant Gaúcho* for good, reasonably priced, typical regional cooking. *Ebano* offers a good varied menu. *Belladonna* on the main street is a very good Italian restaurant with great music, a good meeting point; owner Guido speaks Italian, English and French and is a willing source of information on the Morro; open daily from 1800 till the small hours, rec. Across the street in a very good pizzeria called *Pizzas!*, rec. *Casablanca* is a good simple restaurant, open daily till late. Good breakfasts at *Doceria da Paula* on main street and at *Pousada Ilha da Saudade*, on first beach. The second beach is the liveliest with many beach huts offering cool drinks, meals etc. *Barraca Caita* opens till late with good music, dance music at weekends. They have snorkelling equipment for hire, popular meeting point, potent cocktails! Another *barraca* is *Ponto da Ilha* alongside. There are many other *barracas* on the third beach but a short walk to the fourth beach is *Barraca da Piscina*, good swimming in front, good ambience, dominos, draughts etc, reasonable seafood menu, open till late during summer months.

Galeão is another village in the island, but has no beach, only mangrove swamps. The church of São Francisco Xavier looks imposing on its hill. It is sometimes possible to get a direct boat from Salvador, 2-3 times a week in summer, 6-7 hrs, ask for Sr Cacu and the *Natureza* at the fishing port next to the Mercado Modelo.

On the coast, S toward Ilhéus, is the picturesque fishing village of *Itacaré*. It is a beautiful area with a protected beach with crystal-clear water to the right of town; across the river there are beaches with good surfing. It is becoming a popular weekend spot, especially for surfers.

Hotels **C** *Pousada Litoral*, R de Souza 81, 1 block from where buses stop, with bath, owner João Cravo, speaks English and can organize tours to out of the way beaches, hiring fishing boats, etc, rec; **E** *Bela's Casa de Família*, nice rooms (next to *Hotel Santa Bárbara*); *Pousada Iemanjá*, near praça; **E** *San Miguel*, 1 street from waterfront, nr the cannon at N end of town, basic, uncomfortable; *Pousada da Paz*, nr waterfront, S end of town. Camping site.

Restaurant *Marconi*, bar also, good, cheap, friendly.

Buses To Ilhéus, 3-4 hrs, US$4.75; to **Salvador**, change at Ubaituba (3 hrs, US$2), Ubaituba-Salvador, 6 hrs, US$9.50, several daily.

Ilhéus (pop 223,350, CEP 45660, DDD 073), near the mouth of the Rio Cachoeira, 462 km S of Salvador, serves a district which produces 65% of all Brazilian cocoa. Shipping lines call regularly. A bridge links the Pontal district (airport) to the mainland. The town is the scene of the famous novel by Jorge Amado, *Gabriela, Clove and Cinnamon*. The local beaches are splendid (but the central beach is polluted) and the place is highly recommended for a short stay. Among the churches to visit: **Nossa Senhora da Vitória**, in Alto da Vitória, built in 17th century to celebrate a victory over the Dutch; **São Jorge**, in city centre; and the cathedral of **São Sebastião** on sea shore; **Santana**, in Rio de Engeho is one of the 3 oldest in Brazil. Tourist office on Av Soares Lopes, near cathedral.

Local Festivals include Festa de São Sebastião (17-20 Jan), Carnival, Festa de São Jorge (23 Apr), Foundation day, 28 Jun, and Festa do Cacau (Oct).

Hotels A3 *Hotel Barravento* on Malhado beach, R NS das Graças, T 231-3223, ask for the penthouse—usually no extra charge, including bath, breakfast and refrigerator; **A3** *Ilhéus Praia*, Praça D Eduardo (on beach), T 231-2533, pool, helpful, rec; **A3** *Pontal Praia*, T 231-3033, Praia do Pontal, swimming pool; **C** *Britânia*, T 231-1722, R 28 de Junho 16, and at 29 the **D** *San Marino*, T 231-3668, friendly, clean. **D** *Pousada GG*, Praça Cairu 18, without breakfast (restaurant next door), clean, near beach; **D** *Pousada Kazarão*, Praça Coronel Pessoa 9, clean, friendly, no breakfast, noisy; *Tio San*, R Antonio Levigne de Lemos, T 231-3668, **E** *Pousada Cravo e Canela*, near beach; on R Carneiro da Rocha are **D** *Tropical*, No 129, basic, and **D** *Bahiano*, No 94 (helpful, clean, friendly), and two *dormitórios*. Plenty of cheap hotels near municipal bus station in centre.

Campsite *Estancia das Fontes*, on road S to Olivença, cheap, shady, rec.

Restaurants *Tokyo*, 2 de Julho, Japanese, very good, not cheap. At Pontal, *Cabana Cinco Estrellas*, excellent, cheap Bahian food. *O Velho Marinheiro*, on the waterfront, rec; *Come Ben*, nr Praça Cairu, cheap and good; *Vesúvio*, Praça D Eduardo, next to Cathedral, made famous by Amado's novel (see above), now Swiss-owned, very good but pricey; *Nogar*, Av Bahia 377, close to the sea, good pizzas and pasta. Local drink, *coquinho*, coconut filled with cachaça, only for the strongest heads! Also try *suco de cacau* at juice stands. *Carlos Twity's* in Una, 40 km S, for *shrimp muceca*, which Michael de Lapa opines "will knock your socks off".

Buses Station is some way from centre, but Itabuna-Olivença bus goes through centre of Ilhéus. Several daily to **Salvador**, 7 hrs, US$14-19 (*leito* US$28, Expresso São Jorge); 0620 bus goes via Itaparica, leaving passengers at Bom Despacho ferry station on the island—thence 50-mins ferry to Salvador. To **Itacaré**, 4 hrs, US$4.75; to **Eunápolis**, 7 hrs, US$6, this bus also leaves from the central bus terminal. Other destinations also served; local buses leave from Praça Cairu. Insist that taxi drivers have meters and price charts.

Buses run every 30 mins to *Itabuna* (32 km; pop 185,180), the trading centre of the rich cocoa zone (also many lumber mills). Bus from Salvador, $6\frac{1}{2}$ hrs, US$8.50. Of the hotels, the *Príncipe*, *Lord* and **A3** *Itabuna Palace* (Av Cinquentenário 1061, restaurant) are probably the best (**D** *Rincão Gaúcho*, small, friendly, overlooking river; opposite rodoviária is **E** *Dormitório Rodoviária*, basic; several motels on the outskirts). The paved BA-415 links Itabuna to Vitória da Conquista (275 km) on the BR-116. Ceplac installations at Km 8 on the Itabuna-Ilhéus road show the whole processing of cocoa. Tours of cocoa plantations can be arranged through the *Ilhéus Praia* hotel; Jorge Amado's novel *The Violent Lands* deals with life on the cocoa plantations.

The beaches between Ilhéus and Olivença are good, eg Cururupe, and frequent buses run to Olivença. For the good beaches at Pontal, take "Barreira" bus and get off just past *Hotel Jardim Atlântico*. Hot baths (*balneário*) 18 km away, are reached by Viação São Jorge or Canavieiras buses. 115 km S is **Canavieiras** (pop 32,960), a developing beach resort (**B** *Pousada Maria*; **C** *Mini-Hotel*; Camping at Praia de Atalaia).

About 400 km S of Ilhéus on the coast is the old town of **Porto Seguro** (pop 34,520, CEP 45820, DDD 073), now developed for tourism; the airport has been enlarged to take jets, frequent buses from the new rodoviária. Building is, however, subject to controls on height and materials, in keeping with traditional Bahian styles (colonial or Indian). In the area are remains of original Atlantic coastal forest, with parrots, monkeys, marmosets and snakes. There are *borrachudos*, little flies that bite feet and ankles in the heat of the day; coconut oil keeps them off; at night mosquitoes can be a problem (but there is no malaria, dengue or yellow fever). (For the routes from Vitória **see p 393** and from Belo Horizonte **p 403**). At Brazilian holiday times, all transport N or S should be booked well in advance.

It was N of the site of Porto Seguro that Cabral first landed on 22 Apr 1500; a cross marks the supposed site of the first mass in Brazil on road between Porto Seguro and Santa Cruz Cabrália (see **Excursions** below). A tourist village, Coroa Vermelha, has sprouted at the site, 20 mins by bus to the N, with souvenir shops selling Pataxó-Tupi Indian items, beach bars, hotels and rental houses, all rather uncoordinated. From the roundabout at the entrance to Porto Seguro take a wide, steep, unmarked path uphill to the historical city (Cidade Histórica), three churches (NS da Misericórdia-1530, NS do Rosário-1534, and NS da Pena-1718), the former jail and the cross; a small, peaceful place with lovely gardens and panoramic views.

Hotels The town is a popular holiday resort—prices rise steeply Dec-Mar. **A3** *Porto Seguro Praia*, 3 km N of city on coast road, T 288-2321, F 288-2069; *Cabanas do Tio João*, BR-367, Km 64, 2 km N of Porto Seguro, T 288-2315, a/c, pool, English and French spoken, rec; **A3** *Phonécia*, Av 22 de Abril 400, T 288-2411; **B** *Estalagem Porto Seguro*, R Mal Deodoro 66, T 288-2095, old colonial house, a/c, fan, rec; **B** *Pousada Albatroz*, Av dos Navegantes 600, a/c, pool, rec, T 288-2394, F 288-2047; **B** *Pousada Casa Azul*, 15 de Novembro 11, T 288-2180, with bath, English spoken, good, swimming pool; **B** *Pousada Chauá*, same Av No 800, T 288-2894, a/c; **B** *Pousada Coquéiro Verde*, Rua "A" No 01, T 288-2621, F 288-2623, a/c, pool, sauna; **B** *Pousada do Cais*, Portugal 382, T 228-2111, with bath, colonial house on sea-front, good; several others on same street; **B** *Pousada Gaivota*, Av dos Navegantes 333, T/F 288-2826, a/c, pool, sauna; **B** *Pousada Solar da Praça*, Praça da Bandeira, bath, a/c, good seafront location; **B** *Vela Branca*, Cidade Histórica, T 288-2316, top of cliff, good; **C** *Chica da Silva*, Av dos Navegantes 94, T 288-2280, friendly, family run; **C** *Pousada Aquarius*, R Pedro Alvares Cabral 176, T 288-2738, bath, fan, English, French, Italian spoken, rec; *Pousada Coral*, R Assis Chateaubriand 74, T 288-2630, good breakfast, fan; **C** *Pousada Saveiros*, Av Navegentes 151, T 288-2122, good breakfast, will change TCs; **D** *Mar Azul* at No 109, with bath, breakfast, clean, friendly, rec. A number of good *pousadas* on Av Getúlio Vargas, most without breakfast: **C** *Pousada da Praia*, No 153, T 228 2908, a/c, fridge, showers, nice and clean, no breakfast; **C** *Pousada Raizes*, Praça dos Pataxós 196, T 288-2198, with bath, fan, rec; same square No 278 is **C** *Pousada Travessia*, T 288-2616, with good breakfast. **C** *Pousada Mar e Sol*, No 223, T 228-2137, clean, safe, filtered drinking water, very helpful manager (who teaches *lambada*), highly rec; **D** *Pousada Peixinho*, No 228, attractive, friendly; **D** *Pousada Coroa Vermelha*, No 12, T 288-2132, with bath, no breakfast, clean, good, friendly owners; **D** *Pousada São Luíz*, rec. **D** *Porto Brasília*, Praça Antonio Carlos Magalhães 234, with breakfast, E without; **D** *Pousada Navegantes*, Av 22 de Abril 212, T 288-2390, rec; **D** *Pousada Vera Cruz*, Av 22 de Abril 100, T 288-2162, with bath, good breakfast, clean.

Some good, cheap *pousadas* on R Mal Deodoro at the port; *Pousada Sol Poente*, No 40, T 288-2451, member of IYHA, US$5 pp in dormitory with card, US$7 without; **D** *Cavalo Marino*, No 100; **D** *Estalagem da Yvonne*, No 298, with breakfast, more with a/c, T 288-2045; **D** *Hospedaria do Pirata*, No 249, with good breakfast, bath, rec; **D** *Pousada de Sagres*, R 15 de Novembro, T 288-2031, with good breakfast, family run; **D** *Pousada Sonho Meu*, same street No 86, with bath, breakfast, fan, good; **E** house of Luisiana Silva Mercedes, No 214, T 288-1137.

Outside Dec-Feb rooms with bath and hot water can be rented for about US$150/month.

Camping *Camping dos Marajas*, Av Getúlio Vargas, central; *Camping Gringa*, Praia do Cruzeiro, T 288-2076, US$2.50 pp/night, laundry, café, pool, excellent; *Camping do Sitio*, R da Vala, mosquitoes can be a problem here.

Restaurants *Cruz de Malta*, R Getúlio Vargas 358, good seafood; *Preto Velho*, on Praça da Bandeira, à la carte or self-service, good value; also good value is *Hall of Hunger*, R Rui Barbosa 194, home cooking daily from 1200 to 2200, cheap; good breakfast at *Pau Brasil*, Praça dos Pataxós, and *Club dos Sem Casa*, R Pedro Alvares Cabral 185, open 0800-2100, good, cheap lunches here also; *do Japonês*, Praça dos Pataxós 38, excellent value with varied menu, open 0800-2300, rec; *Ponto do Encontro* on same square, No 106, good simple food, friendly, owners rent rooms, open 0800-2400; *Sambuca*, on Praça dos Pataxós is good for pizzas; on same square is *Prima Dona*, No 247, Italian, good. *Anti-Caro*, R Assis

Chateaubriand 26, good, rec, also antique shop, good atmosphere; *Casa da Esquina*, on same street, French, good, moderately priced. The best meat restaurant is *Churrascaria do Maça*, R Mal Deodoro 342, open 1500-2400, very good *picanha*, enough for 3 people, not expensive, rec; *Les Agapornis*, Av dos Navegantes 180, wide selection of crêpes and pizzas; *Tres Vintens*, Av Portugal 1246, good imaginative seafood dishes, rec; *Ninô*, 22 de Abril 100, good pizzas; *Grilhadaz*, same street, moderate prices; *New Jersey*, nearby, good, reasonable prices; *Vida Verde*, R Dois de Julho 92, good vegetarian, open 1100-2100 except Sun, T 288 2766, rec.

Banks and Exchange Banco do Brasil, Av 22 de Abril e Av Carlos Alberto Paracho, Dec-Mar for exchange 1800-2200, but not Sun. Other banks will not change money, but managers may privately. *Sergio Vanni*, Praça da Bandeira 100, 1st floor; good rates at *Agência do Descobrimento*, Av Getúlio Vargas, lower rate for TCs, also arranges flight tickets and house rental. Rates are not as good as in the big cities.

Entertainment Porto Seguro is famous for the *lambada* (see **Music and Dance**). The best place to see it is at *Boca da Barra* at Praia do Cruzeiro. Instructors are on hand from 1800-2000, then the locals take the floor until the small hours. No entry charge, not to be missed, nightly throughout the year. The strong local liqueur, *guarachaça*, a mixture of guaraná and cachaça, keeps the dancers going during the long hours; don't underestimate its strength. Another place to see *lambada* is *Lambaporto*, busy only at weekends.

A good bar for live music is *Porto Prego* on R Pedro Alvares Cabral, small cover charge. *Sotton Bar*, Praça da Bandeira, is lively. There are lots of bars and street cafés on Av Portugal.

Telephones Telebahia service post, Praça dos Pataxós beside ferry terminal, open daily 0800-2000, cheap rates after 2000 so can be very busy at this time.

Tourist Information Casa de Lenha, Praça Visconde de Porto Seguro, near port, has basic information.

Rentals Car hire, Itapoan, Av Portugal 1350, T 288-2710; **motorcycles**, Lupa Motos, Praça dos Pataxós, T 288-2868, expensive, heavy deposit required; **bicycles**, Oficina de Bicicleta, Av Getúlio Vargas e R São Pedro, about US$10 for 24 hrs; also at Praça de Bandeira and at Dois de Julho 242. **Diving equipment**, Portomar Ltda, R Dois de Julho 178, also arranges diving and snorkelling trips to the coral reefs offshore, professional instructors.

Buses from Porto Seguro: **Salvador** (Águia Branca), daily, 12 hrs, US$28 (*leito* 44), once a day each service; **Vitória**, daily, 11 hrs, US$15.50; **Ilhéus** daily 0730, 5½ hrs, US$12; **Eunápolis**, 1½ hrs, US$2. For **Rio** direct buses (São Geraldo), leaving at 1745, US$36, 18 hrs, from Rio direct at 1600, or take 1800 for Ilhéus and change at Eunápolis. To **Belo Horizonte** daily direct. To **São Paulo** direct, 1045, 25 hrs, US$45, not advisable, very slow, much better to go to Rio then take Rio-São Paulo express. Other services via Eunápolis (those going N avoid Salvador) or Itabuna (5 hrs, US$7.80). There is new rodoviária, with reliable luggage store and lounge on 3rd floor, on the road to Eunápolis, 2 km from the centre, regular bus service (30 mins) through city to the old rodoviária near port. For local trips a taxi is an economic proposition for two or more passengers wishing to visit various places in one day.

Air Nordeste daily except Sun from Rio, direct on Sat 2 hrs, otherwise 2 hrs 45 mins with 2 stops, also Rio Sul 3 times a week via Campos; Nordeste daily except Sat to Salvador (also Vasp twice a week), São Paulo Rio Sul daily (also Vasp and Pantanal), Belo Horizonte (once a week each Vasp and Taba) and other local destinations.

Excursions Guided tours of the area with BPS, at the Shopping Centre, T 288-2373. Companhia do Mar (Cia do Mar, Praça dos Pataxós, T 288-2981) does daily trips by schooner to coral reefs off the coast. The most popular is to Recife de Fora, with good snorkelling; leaves daily 1000, returns 1630, about US$18, US$3 extra for snorkelling gear. Other good trips to Coroa Vermelho and Coroa Alta, and S to Trocosso. 10 mins N of Coroa Vermelha, **Santa Cruz Cabrália** is a delightful small town with a splendid beach, river port, a 450-year old church with a fine view, and several hotels (eg *Pousada Xica da Silva* near bus stop, cheap, nice, good restaurant *Coqueiro Verde*—try *pitu*, a kind of crayfish). Across the river (dugout US$1) is Santo André, a small village on the ocean, also with a beach and inns. Hourly buses from Santa Cruz to Porto Seguro (23 km). Schooner trips to the reef also from Santa Cruz. For equipment hire, see above.

Across the Rio Buranhém S from Porto Seguro (10 mins, US$0.25, ferries take cars day time only, every ½-hr day and night), and a further 5 km (US$0.45 in bus), is the village of *Arraial da Ajuda*; about 15 mins walk from the beach (better for camping than Porto Seguro). Pilgrimage in Aug to the shrine of Nossa Senhora da Ajuda (interesting room in church, full of ex-voto offerings—fine view from behind church). Ajuda has become very popular with tourists and there are many *pousadas*, bars and small shops. Known as a "hippie" resort: drugs are said to be widely available, but easily avoided. Parties almost every night, on the beach or in the *Broadway*. At the *Jatobar* bar the *lambada* is danced, on the main square, by the church (opens 2300—*pensão* at the back is cheap, clean and friendly). There is also a *capoeira* institute; ask for directions. Beach protected by coral reef. At Brazilian holiday times it is very crowded and, with the coastline up for sale, it may become overdeveloped in a few years. The beaches in this neighbourhood are splendid, for instance Pitinga, also protected by coral reef, Lagoa Azul and Mucugê. Porto Belo or Sta Cruz Cabrália buses go to the beaches frequently from the port.

Hotels B *Pousada das Brisas*, T 875-1033, clean, panoramic views, English, German, French and Spanish spoken; **B** *Ivy Marey*, nr centre on road to beach, T 875-1106, 4 rm and 2 bungalows, showers, nice décor, good bar, French/Brazilian owned, rec; nearby *Le Grand Bleu*, T 875-7272, same French owner, similar prices, good *pizzaria*; **B** *Sole Mio*, T 875-1115, just off beach road leading from ferry to Arraial, different French owners, English spoken, laid back, 4 chalets, excellent *pizzaria*; **B** *Pousada Canto d'Alvorada*, on road to Ajuda, T 875-1218, in season, D out of season, Swiss run, 7 cabins, restaurant, washing facilities; **C** *Villa do Beco*, beautiful garden, good value; **C** *Pousada Caminho do Mar*, T 875-1099, English spoken, rate depending on season, owners very informative and helpful, also highly rec; **C** *Pousada Natur*, run by German environmentalist, clean, friendly, rec, English spoken T 288-2738; **D** *Pousada Le Cottage* (across ferry from Porto Seguro, but before Ajuda, T 875-1023), French owner, Sr Georges, with bath, C in chalet; **C** *Thaina Plage*, highly rec, reserved in São Paulo, T 011-533-5898, or in Paris T 43-26-31-41, and **C** *Pousada Torrorão*, between village and beach, T 875-1260, restaurant, rec; **C** *Pousada Erva Doce*, T 875-1114, owners very friendly, good restaurant, well appointed chalets, highly rec; **C** *Pousada Girasol*, with good breakfast, bath; **C** *Pousada Tubarão*, R Bela Vista, beyond the church on the right, T 875-1086, good view of the coastline, cool, good restaurant, rec; **C** *Pousada Altomar*, next door, without breakfast; **C** *Pousada Maravilha*, Av São João, with good breakfast; **D** *Pousada Aberta Mar*, on road to beach, with bath, good breakfast; **D** *Pousada Flamboyant*, pleasant, good breakfast, rec; **D** *Pousada Flor*, also on square, T 875-1143, owner Florisbela Valiense takes good care of female guests, warmly rec; **E** *Pousada Mangaba*, on way to the beach, bath, washing facilities, without breakfast, friendly, rec; **E** *Pousada Nova Esperança*, nearby, without breakfast, bath, rec; **E** *Pousada Tamarind*, on Praça Brigadeiro Eduardo Gomés, near church, without breakfast, bath; **E** *Pousada Tio Otto*, without breakfast, alongside church; **F** *Pousada Miramar*, without breakfast, cheapest accommodation in town, rec; also, next door, **F** *La Nuit des Temps*.

   NB Above prices are high season prices unless otherwise stated, if staying for a long period they are negotiable; this is certainly true in the low season.

Camping *Praia*, on Mucugê Beach, good position and facilities, US$1 pp/night; *Chão do Arraial*, 5 mins from Mucugê beach, shady, good snack bar, also hire tents, rec. Also *Camping do Gordo*, on left shortly after leaving ferry, on beach but beach is not as good as Mucugê.

Restaurants *São João*, near the church, is the best typical restaurant; *Asa Branca*, R Santa Rita, very good *carne do sol de picanha*; *Manda Brasa*, on Broadway, good *prato feito*, cheap; *Le Gourmet*, R São João, good international cuisine, specialise in French dishes, not cheap, rec; *Mão na Massa*, an excellent Italian restaurant, behind the church; also recommended is *Varanda Grill*, good grilled fish, meat and chicken; *Paulinho Pescador*, open 1200-2200, excellent seafood, also chicken and meat, English spoken, good service, *bobó de camarão* highly rec. *Erva Doce*, on way to the beach, good pizzas and lasagnes, rec; *Tubarão*, behind the church has also been rec, regional and international dishes; *Café das Cores*, on way to the beach, good cakes and snacks, expresso coffee. Two good "barracas" on Pitinga beach are *Bar da Pitinga* and *Bar do Genésio*, fresh fried fish, shrimp etc.

Telephone Telebahia has a service post on the main square, open 0800 until 2200.

25 km to the S of Porto Seguro and 15 km from Ajuda is *Troncoso*, reached by bus, 5 a day (US$0.60, 50 mins, last returns at 1630, more buses and colectivos in summer), by colectivo, hitch-hiking or by walking along the beach; the road bridges are not safe, bus passengers alight and walk across. The village is simple but also popular with Brazilian tourists, beautiful beaches (some nude) and many Europeans have built or bought houses there. There are good restaurants around the main square. From the end of Praça São João there is a fine coastal panorama.

Trancoso has a historic church. Colectivos run from Trancoso to Ajuda (US$1.90). Between Ajuda and Trancoso is the village of Rio da Barra. Caraíva with beautiful beaches, no electricity, can be reached by boat, 4 hrs from Porto Seguro, 2 hrs from Trancoso, or by bus, two daily. The sandy road from Trancoso is a difficult drive, ending at the river which must be crossed by boat. There are pousadas and restaurants with electricity generators, but no exchange facilities.

Trancoso Hotels A3 *Hotel de Praça*, bath, games room, good breakfast (T São Paulo 211-2239); **B** *Pousada Calypso*, good apartments, comfortable, rooms at lower price also available, good library, German and English spoken, rec (T Rio 267-3741); **C** *Caipim Santo*, to the left of main square, with breakfast, the best restaurant in Trancoso (natural cuisine), very friendly, bath, rec. **C** *Posada Canto Verde*, with breakfast, bath, restaurant only in high season, rec (T 0242-43-7823). Also on main square, **C** *Gulab Mahal*, oriental style, lovely garden, vast breakfast, highly rec; **C** *Pousada do Bosque*, on the way to the beach, English, German and Spanish spoken, with breakfast, camping facilities also available, good value; **D** *Pousada Sol da Manhã*, with breakfast; **E** *Pousada Terra do Sol*, without breakfast, good, rec. About 500 metres inland away from main square (known as the "quadrado") lies the newer part of Trancoso (known as the "invasão") with two good value *pousadas*: **D** *Pousada Quarto Crescente*, English, German, Dutch and Spanish spoken, cooking facilities, washing also, very friendly and helpful owners, library, highly rec, about 15 mins from beach. Another good *pousada* is **D** *Luna Pousa*, further along on the left, with breakfast, well ventilated, only 4 rm. There are many houses to rent, very good ones are rented by Clea who can be contacted at *Restaurant Abacaxi* on main square on right. You can leave a message for any one of the above mentioned *pousadas* by calling the Telebahia service post 867-1116, most people in town check there for messages on a daily basis. As in Porto Seguro and Ajuda if you stay for a longer period you can nearly always negotiate a better price, this is certainly true in the low season.

Restaurants *Urano*, just before the main square is also rec, good portions, usually enough for two; *Rama* has also been recommended; *Abacaxi* on main square does good breakfasts, light snacks and very good crêpes; *Galub Mahal* for Eastern dishes; good breakfast also at *Pé das Frutas*, *Maré Cheia* next door good simple dishes. Good ice cream at *Tão Vez*. Apart from restaurants which serve breakfast most others open at 1500 until 2200 or so.

South of Porto Seguro, reached by a paved access road from the BR-101 16 km N of Itamaraju, is the **Parque Nacional de Monte Pascoal**, set up in 1961 to preserve the flora, fauna and birdlife of the coastal area in which Europeans made landfall in Brazil (Caixa Postal 076, CEP 45830-000 Itamaraju, T 073-281-2419). The Pataxó Indian reservation is located at Corombau village, on the ocean shore of the park. Corombau can be reached by schooner from Porto Seguro. A small luxury resort has been built at Corombau. From Itamaraju (93 km S of Eunápolis) the coastal towns of **Curumuxatiba** (**D** *Pousada Guainamby*, R Bela Vista, CEP 45983, German and Brazilian owned, small, clean, comfortable chalets, good views to long beach, good breakfast and fish and Italian meals, rec) and Prado. Also reached from Itamaraju is the *Jacotoka* holiday village, which offers diving, surfing and riding in a tropical paradise. US$50/day, reservations at 7 de Setembro 149, Porto Seguro, T 288-2291, F 288-2540; it can also be reached by boat from Porto Seguro.

Further S still is **Caravelas** (pop 21,650) 130 km S of Porto Seguro, a charming little town, rapidly developing for tourism, but a major trading town in 17th/18th centuries. It had a rail connection to Minas Gerais. Caravelas is in the mangroves; the beaches are about 10 km away at Barra de Caravelas (hourly buses), a fishing village.

Hotels A1 *Marina Porto Abrulhos*, on beach front, very luxurious; **C** *Pousada Caravelense*, 50m from rodoviária, T 297-1182, bath, TV, fridge, good breakfast, clean; **E** *Grande Hotel São Benedito*, close by, breakfast, dirty, noisy; **D** *Shangri-la*, Barão do Rio Branco 216, bath, breakfast, clean. At Barra de Caravelas: **C** *Pousada das Sereias*, French-owned; **E** *Pousada Jaquita*, use of kitchen, clean, big breakfast, bath, airy rooms, owner is Secka who speaks English; some food shops, restaurants and bars.

Teresa and Ernesto (from Austria) organize boat trips (US$40/day), jeep and horse hire (turn left between bridge and small supermarket). "Alternative" beach holidays (organic vegetarian food, yoga, meditation, other activities) with Beky and Eno on the unspoilt island of Coçumba, rec; contact Abrolhos Turismo. Helpful **tourist information** at Ibama Centro de Visitantes, Barão do Rio Branco 281; Banco do Brasil does not change money (Praça Dr Imbassahi); on same square, No 8, Abrolhos Turismo rents diving gear and arranges boat trips. Buses to Texeira de Freitas (4 a day), Salvador, Nanuque and **Prado**, where the proprietors of the *Casa de Maria*, R Seis, Novo Prado, T (073) 298-1377, claim to serve the best breakfast in the region. Prado (pop 20,000) has some 16th-century buildings and beautiful beaches N and S. It is 200 km S of Porto Seguro.

John Raspey writes: The **Parque Nacional Marinho dos Abrolhos** is 70 km E of Caravelas: 5 small islands (Redonda, Siriba, Guarita, Sueste, Santa Bárbara), and several coral reefs. The archipelago is administered by Ibama, and a navy detachment mans a lighthouse on Sta Bárbara, which is the only island that may be visited. Permission from Parque Nacional Marinho dos Abrolhos, Praia do Kitombo s/n, Caravelas, Bahia 45900, T (073) 297-1111, or Ibama, Av Juracy Magalhães Jr 608, CEP 40295-140, Salvador, T (071) 240-7322. The islands and surrounding reefs are home to birds, whales, fish turtles, and giant fire corals (also goats). Darwin visited them in 1830. A master authorized by the Navy to take tourists is Mestre Onofrio Frio in Alrobaça, Bahia, T (073) 293-2195. Tours also available from Abrolhos Turismo, see above, Caravelas, T 297-1149 (about US$170 for a slow 2½ day tour by *saveiro*). One-day tours in a faster boat (US$100) from Abrolhos or the Marina Porto Abrolhos.

North from Salvador   The paved BA-099 coast road from near the airport is known as the Estrada do Coco (Coconut Highway, because of the many coconut plantations) and for 50 km passes some beautiful beaches. The best known from S to N are Ipitanga (with its reefs), Buraquinho, Jauá, Arembepe, Guarajuba, Itacimirim, Castelo Garcia D'Avila (with its 16th century fort) and Forte. Buses serve most of these destinations. The Estrada do Coco was extended in 1994 to the state of Sergipe. The road is called the Linha Verde (Green Line), because of the concern to disturb the environment as little as possible.

Some 50 km to the N of Salvador is the former fishing village of **Arembepe**, now a quiet resort. *Pousada da Fazenda* on the beach, thatched huts, good seafood, not cheap; **E** *Pousada*; and restaurant *Mar Aberto*, T 824-1257, rec, food very good, English and French spoken; Verá's restaurant, try *pastel de banana*. There is an "alternative" village of palm huts, ½ hr walk along the beach, behind the sand dunes, café and swimming. Best beaches 2 km N of town. Bus from Terminal Francés, Salvador, every 2 hrs, 1½ hrs, US$1.20, last one back at 1700; or from Itapoan.

Praia do Forte is a small fishing village, 80 km N of Salvador. The village takes its name from the castle built by a Portuguese settler called Garcia D'Ávila in 1556. He built the fortification as a lookout post to warn the city to the S of any attempt of invasion by enemy forces. Garcia D'Ávila was given a huge area of land which extended from Praia do Forte to Maranhão on the northern coast of Brazil. His was the first farm in Brazil and it was he who brought the first heads of cattle to the country. To create pasture lands for these cattle he cleared the virgin Atlantic forest; he also brought the first coconut and mango trees to Brazil. Praia do Forte is now a tranquil resort with a strong emphasis on preservation of the local flora and fauna. Inland from the coast is a *restinga* forest, which grows on sandy soil with a very delicate ecosystem. *Restinga* forests are found in very few areas in Brazil. Near the village is a small *pantanal* (marshy area) and this is host to a large number of birds, caymans etc. Early morning and late afternoon the *pantanal* resounds to the calls of snail kites, kingfishers, cormorants and chattering parakeets. Trips on the *pantanal* in small boats are rewarding for the keen birdwatcher. The Tamar Project was set up 12 years ago to preserve the sea turtles which lay their eggs in the area. Praia do Forte is now the headquarters of the national turtle preservation programme and is funded by the Worldwide Fund for Nature. There is a visitors centre at the project which explains the aims and success of the programme.

Hotels   (prices rise steeply in summer season) Most hotels were in the **A1** price range during 1994. It may prove difficult to find cheaper accommodation. *Praia do Forte Resort Hotel*, apartment with seaview, very good sports facilities, 4 swimming pools, water sports equipment for hire, T 832 2333 or 835 1111, F 832-2100; *Pousada Praia do Forte*, 18 chalets in peaceful setting, more private than larger *Resort Hotel*, rec, T 835 1410, F 876-1050; *Pousada Solar da Lua*, R do Forte, T 876-1029, good location, spacious rooms; *Pousada Sobrado da Vila*, on main street, T 876-1088, F 235-7886, pleasant, good value restaurant; *Pousada*

Tatuapara, 876 1015, friendly; **B** *Pousada João Sol*, R da Corvina, T 876 1054, owner speaks English, Spanish and German, good, friendly, rec, only 6 apts, great breakfast. **B** *Pousada Canto da Sereia*, R da Corvina, all apartments with ventilator, good breakfast; **C** *Pousada Oxumaré*, verandah; **B** *Pousada Sol Nascente*, on street parallel to main street, clean, friendly, good, bath, frigobar, fan, breakfast; **E** *Pousada e Restaurant Doce Mania*, basic rooms, good simple food, cheap, rec. Two-bedroom apartments at *Solar dos Arcos*, on beach, US$90, with pool, gardens, lawns, warmly rec.

Restaurants *Bar Da Souza*, on the right as you enter the village, best seafood in town, open daily from 1000 until last customer leaves, live music at weekends by excellent local musicians, highly rec, reasonably priced; *Brasa Na Praia*, specializes in grilled seafood and meat, open daily from 1100 till midnight, peaceful setting, rec. *La Crêperie*, excellent crêpes, Tues to Sun, 1100 until the early hours, good music, a very popular meeting place, owner Klever very friendly, highly rec; *Pizzaria Le Gaston*, good pizza and pasta, also good home made ice-creams, open daily from 1000 until midnight. There are many other restaurants in the village: good ones are at *Pousada Solar Da Lua*, open daily until late, *Nora*, on main street, and *Restaurant Tropical* can also be recommended.

Tours Odara Turismo, in the *Resort Hotel*, T 876 1080, F 876 1018, do imaginative tours to surrounding areas and outlying villages and beaches using 4WD vehicles. They are very friendly and informative, rec. The owners, Norbert and Papy, speak English and German. Praia do Forte is ideal for windsurfing and sailing owing to constant fresh Atlantic breezes.

Bus To Praia do Forte from Salvador (US$2.50): Santa Maria/Catuense leaves 5 times daily from rodoviária, 1½ hrs.

The Linha Verde runs for 142 km to the Sergipe border, the road is very scenic, especially near Conde. There are very few hotels or *pousadas* in the more remote villages. The most picturesque are **Imbassaí**, Subaúma, **Baixios** (very beautiful, where the Rio Inhambupe meets the sea) and **Conde**. Sítio do Conde on the coast, 6 km from Conde, has many *pousadas*, but the beaches are not very good. Sítio do Conde is a good base to explore other beaches at Barra do Itariri, 12 km S, at the mouth of a river (fine sunsets). The road passes unspoilt beaches (the best are Corre Nu and Jacaré). You can also go to Seribinha, 13 km N of Sítio do Conde (the road goes along the beach through coconut groves and mangroves; at Seribinha are beach huts serving cool drinks or food, one *pousada* reported on beach). The last stop on the Linha Verde is **Mangue Seco**. Access from Sergipe is by boat or canoe on the Rio Real from Pontal (10 min crossing). A steep hill rising behind the village to tall white sand dunes offers a superb view of the coastline. The encroaching dunes have caused the mangrove to dry up. Bus Salvador-Conde (São Luis, T 071 358-4582), 3 a day, 4 on Fri, US$7.50.

Accommodation Imbassaí: **C** *Pousada Imbassaí*, T 235-3599, chalets and apartments of varying sizes, operates as an apart hotel; **B** *Pousada Anzol de Ouro*, T 971-9025, reservations, T/F 243-2614, 12 chalets, ventilation, swimming pool; **B** *Pousada Lagoa da Pedra*, T 971-7095, reservations 359-3512/245-2506, large grounds, a little English spoken, friendly. Subaúma: **B** *Pousada da Praça*, new, simple, clean. Sítio do Conde: **A3** *Hotel Praia do Conde*, T (075) 429-1229, reservations (071) 321-2542, a/c, pool; **C** *Pousada Oasis*, T (075) 421-2397, simple; **C** *Pousada Beira Mar*. Cheaper are **D** *Pousada do Boliviano* and **E** *Pousada de Dona Dulce*. **Restaurants** *Bar e Restaurante Zeca*, typical dishes; *Pizzaria Marcos*; *Restaurante Harmonioso*. Mangue Seco: **B** *Pousada Mangue Seco*, T (071) 359-8506, in main square, ceiling fan; further away, left from boat landing, 15 mins walk, **B** *Pousada Village Mangue Seco*, T (071) 241-7355, swimming pool, fan. Seafood restaurants at boat landing.

Inland, North from Salvador **Monte Santo** About 270 km N of Feira de Santana, and 38 km W of Euclides da Cunha on the direct BR-116 road to Fortaleza, is the famous hill shrine of Monte Santo in the Sertão, reached by 3½ km of steps cut into the rocks of the Serra do Picaraça (about 45 mins' walk each way—set out early). This is the scene of pilgrimages and great religious devotion during Holy Week. The shrine was built by an Italian who had a vision of the cross on the mountain in 1765. One block N of the bottom of the stairs is the Museu do Sertão, with pictures from the 1897 Canudos rebellion. **Canudos** itself is 100 km away at the junction of the BR-116 and BR-235 (direct buses from Salvador); religious rebels led by the visionary Antônio Conselheiro defeated three expeditions sent against them in 1897 before being overwhelmed. These events are the theme of two great books: *Os Sertões* (Revolt in the Backlands) by Euclides da Cunha, and *La Guerra del Fin del Mundo* (The War of the End of the World) by the Peruvian Mario Vargas Llosa. The Rio Vaza Barris, which runs through Canudos has been dammed, and the town has been moved to Nova Canudos by the dam. Part of the old town is still located 10 km W.

Hotels D *Grapiuna*, Praça Monsenhor Berenguer 401 (T 275-1157), with bath (cheaper without, downstairs), rec; **E** *Santa Cruz*, opp Banco do Brasil, shared bath, basic but clean; pleasant bars. At Euclides da Cunha, on the BR-116 and 39 km from Monte Santo, are *Hotel Lua*, simple and *Hotel Conselheiro*.

Part of the northern border of Bahia is the Rio São Francisco; on the opposite bank are Pernambuco and Alagoas. From Salvador, the BR-110 runs N to the river at Paulo Afonso; the road is paved for all but 71 km between Cícero Dantas and Jeremoaba (turn W here on BR-235 to Canudos, 111 km). 76 km N of Jeremoaba is the **Parque Nacional de Paulo Afonso**. The Falls of *Paulo Afonso*, once one of the great falls of the world but now exploited for hydroelectric power, are 270 km from the mouth of the São Francisco river, which drains a valley 3 times the size of Great Britain. There are 2,575 km of river above the Falls to its source in Minas Gerais. Below the Falls is a deep, rock gorge through which the water rushes. The national park is an oasis of trees and the lake amid a desert of brown scrub and cactus. The best time to visit the Falls is in the rainy season (Jan-Feb); only then does much water pass over them, as almost all the flow now goes through the power plant. The best view is from the northern (Alagoas) bank. The Falls are in a security area; no admission for pedestrians, so you need to visit by car or taxi (US$4.50 an hour). Admission is from 0800 onwards, but it depends on the availability of guides, without whom one cannot enter; go to the tourist information office in the centre of the town and sign up for a tour of the hydroelectric plant, 2 hrs, US$6/car.

Accommodation and Services A3 *Hotel Casande*, **A3** *Grande Hotel de Paulo Afonso* (a/c, TV, pool, T 281-1914) and a guest house (apply for room in advance) at the Falls.

The town of Paulo Afonso (pop 86,560) is some distance from the Falls, reached by bus from Salvador, by paved road from Recife, bus, 7 hrs, US$8, or from Maceió (306 km) via Palmeira dos Índios, partially paved. Hotels *Guadalajara* and *Paulo Afonso*, friendly, cheap; **C** *Belvedere*, T 281-1814, a/c, swimming pool and **C** *Palace*, T 281-1521, with bath, a/c, swimming pool, "best value in town", next door to each other on R André Falcão; **F** *Hospedagem Lima*, very basic, near *Hotel Guadalajara*; **F** *Hotel Dormitório*—all hotels within walking distance of bus terminal. Plenty of restaurants, eg *Kilanche*, next to Tourist Office. For information about Paulo Afonso and the *sertão*, ask the Italian fathers (Mario, Antonio and Riccardo) who are most helpful. Handicrafts (embroidery, fabrics) from Núcleo de Produção Artesanal, Av Contorno s/n.

It is possible, with plenty of time, to go upstream from Penedo (see p 502) to about Pão de Açúcar or Piranhas, but on to the Falls is complicated and involves non-connecting buses. *Piranhas* (Alagoas), 80 km from Paulo Afonso (road almost completely paved, buses difficult), is a charming town with good beaches on the Rio São Francisco; it has picturesque houses and an old railway station which is now a *Pousada* (3-4 rm, E, restaurant) with a small museum (photographs of the severed head of Lampião, the Brazilian "Robin Hood").

Travel on the River São Francisco (see p 410). The river is navigable above the Falls from above the twin towns (linked by a bridge) of *Juazeiro* (128,380 people), in Bahia, and *Petrolina* (174,970), in Pernambuco (buses from Salvador, 6 hrs, also from Recife, Fortaleza, Teresina) to Pirapora in Minas Gerais, linked by road to the Belo Horizonte-Brasília highway. Like Pirapora, Petrolina is famous for the production of *carrancas* (boat figureheads, mostly grotesque) of wood or ceramic. River transport has changed rapidly in the past few years; for information telephone Juazeiro (075) 811-2465. The BR-253 runs W from Canudos to Juazeiro, alternatively, from Salvador go to Feira de Santana, take the paved BR-324, then the BR-407, which continues through Petrolina to Picos in Piauí (see p 533) junction for Fortaleza or Teresina. On the BR-324, 124 km S of Juazeiro is **Senhor do Bonfim** (pop 83,260), a busy market town with lots of life (also banks and post office).

John Hale writes: Juazeiro and Petrolina are thriving towns compared with many others on the upper São Francisco. Petrolina has its own airport and close to this is the small Museu do Sertão—relics of rural life in the NE and the age of the "coronéis" and the bandit Lampião. **B** *Grande Rio*, R Padre Praga; **D** *Pousada da Carranca*, BR-122, Km 4, T 961-3421; **E** *Hotel Newman*, Av Souza Filho 444, T 961-0595; **E** *Espacial*, EF Leste Brasileiro Km 2; and *Restaurante Rancho Grande*. *Restaurante Panorâmico*, the only one on the river front, is good. Juazeiro is the poorer of the two cities. Hotels: *Grande Hotel*, R Pititinga, T 811-2710, *Vitória*, T 811-2712, and *União* (rec) and *Oliveira*, the last two in R Conselheiro Saraiva. **B** *Hotel Pousada de Juazeiro*, 6 km S on BR-407, T 811-2820, with bath, a/c, pool, restaurant, bar, pleasant. Unique restaurant known as the *Vaporzinho* is high and dry on the river front, a side-wheel paddle steamer (poor food), the *Saldanha Marinho*, built at Sabará in 1852. Market on Fri and Sat.

Margy Levine and Jordan Young (Lexington, MA) write:
There are three wineries in the area: one in Casa Nova (Bahia); Ouro Verde in Lagoa Grande (Pernambuco); and Fazenda Milano in Santa Maria da Boa Vista (Pernambuco), on the N shore of the Rio São Francisco. Fazenda Milano (24 km from Lagoa Grande, towards Santa Maria da Boa Vista) was the first winery in the NE, and makes wine from European grapes, with 150 hectares of vines. Owned by Forestier, a winemaker from the S, they make red, white and rosé, blended and varietals. You can visit the winery on Thur, if you call in advance on (081) 961-4669 or, in Recife (081) 251-2200. Wine can be bought at US$3 for 3 bottles. When you get to the Fazenda Milano sign on the Lagoa Grande-Santa Maria road, turn S towards the river, and drive 8 km on a dirt road to the gate.

THE NORTHEAST (8)

The eight northeastern states are generally poor economically, but are neither poor historically (see Recife, Olinda, São Luis), nor culturally (eg "Forró" and other musical styles, many good museums, lacework, ceramics). There is a multitude of beaches: those in established resorts tend to be polluted, but you don't have to travel far for good ones, while off the beaten track are some which have hardly been discovered.

South of Cabo São Roque (Rio Grande do Norte) there is abundant rainfall, but in Pernambuco the zone of ample rain stretches only 80 km inland, though it deepens southwards. São Luís in Maranhão also gets plenty of rain, but between eastern Maranhão and Pernambuco lies a triangle, with its apex deep inland, where the rainfall is sporadic, and occasionally non-existent for a year. Here the tropical forest gives way to the *caatinga*, or scrub forest bushes which shed their leaves during drought. In this area grow the palms that produce carnauba wax and babaçu nuts, and the tree that produces oiticica oil.

There was a brief period of colonization from northern Europe in the NE, when the Dutch West India Company, based at Recife, controlled some seven captaincies along the coast. They gained control in 1630, when Portugal was subject to Spain. After 1640, when Portugal freed itself, the colonists fought the Dutch and finally expelled them in 1654.

Sergipe and Alagoas

247 km N of Salvador, on BR-101, almost midway between the Sergipe-Bahia border and Aracaju is **Estância**, with pleasant hotels: **E** *Turista*, and **E** *Dom Bosco*, opposite, slightly cheaper, bath and breakfast. The town boasts a small Jorge Amado museum, and the June festival of São João has a good reputation. Many buses stop at the

Rodoviária, which is on the main road. Bonfim buses on the Aracaju-Salvador run make a mandatory stop at Entre Rios on the Bahia-Sergipe border.

Aracaju (pop 401,245, CEP 49000, DDD 079), capital of Sergipe (state pop 1,492,400), 327 km N of Salvador, founded 1855, is a clean and friendly town. It stands on the S bank of the Rio Sergipe, about 10 km from its mouth, and can be reached from Salvador or Maceió by road. The city—unusually for coastal Brazil—is laid out in the grid pattern. In the centre is a group of linked, beautiful parks: Praça Olímpio Campos, in which stands the cathedral, Praça Almirante Barroso, with the Palácio do Governo, and Praças Fausto Cardoso and Camerino. Across Avenida Rio Branco from these two is the river. The streets are clean (parts of Laranjeiras and João Pessoa in centre reserved for pedestrians). There is a handicraft centre, the Centro do Turismo, open 0900-1300, 1400-1900, in the restored Escola Normal, on Praça Olímpio Campos; the stalls are arranged by type (wood, leather, etc). The commercial and banking area is on Ruas Itabaianinha and João Pessoa, leading up to Rua Divina Pastora and Praça General Valadão. At Rua Itabaianinha 41 is the Instituto Geográfico e Histórico de Sergipe (Mon-Fri 0800-1200, 1400-1700).

A 16-km road leads to the fine *Atalaia* beach: oil-drilling rigs offshore. Beaches continue S down the coast. There is an even better beach, Nova Atalaia, on Ilha de Santa Luzia across the river, reached by boat from the Hidroviária (ferry station), which is across Av Rio Branco from Praça General Valadão. Boats cross the river to Barra dos Coqueiros every 15 mins (US$0.25); the boats at a quarter past the hour combine with a bus to Nova Atalaia (US$0.35). Buses return to Barra on the hour. Services are more frequent at weekends, when it is very lively. The river at Barra dos Coqueiros is busy with fishing and pleasure craft.

Festivals   On 8 Dec there are both Catholic (Nossa Senhora da Conceição) and Umbanda religious festivals.

Hotels   In Atalaia (Velha) there are many hotels and aparthotels, mostly mid-to-high priced. **L2** *Parque dos Coqueiros*, Atalaia beach, Rua F R Leite Neto 1075, T 243-1511, F 243-2186, large pool, luxurious, attractive, only hotel on beach; **A1** *Beira Mar*, Av Rotary, T 243-1921, F 243-1153; **D** *Pousada da Praia*, R Niceu Dantas 667, T 223-1700. At Atalaia Nova is the *Da Ilha*, T262-1221, F 262-1359.

In the centre: **A2** *Palace de Aracaju*, Praça Gen Valadão, T 224-5000, 3-star, a/c, TV, fridge, central, restaurant, pool, parking. **A2** *Grande*, R Itabaianinha 371, T 211-1383, F 222-2656, a/c, TV, fridge, central, *Quartier Latin* resturant; **B** *Aperipê*, R São Cristóvão 418, T 211-1880, central, a/c, phone, fridge, restaurant; **A3** *Serigy*, R Santo Amaro 269, T 211-1088, same management and facilities, comfortable. **C** *Brasília*, R Laranjeiras 580, T 224-8022, good value, good breakfasts, rec; **C** *Oásis*, R São Cristóvão 466, T 224-2125, with good breakfast, hot water, fair, a bit tatty; **D** *Amado*, R Laranjeiras 532, a/c (less with fan), clothes washing facilities; **D** *Aragipe Praia*, with bath, parking, rec; **E** *Turista*, R Divina Pastora 411, noisy, mosquitoes, no hot water or breakfast, friendly. **F** *Youth Hostel*, T 223-2802, on road to Atalaia (take bus Os Campos, from Centre), no card needed, clean, friendly; new *youth hostel*, R Braulio Costa 675, with pool, rec.

Camping   Camping Clube do Brasil site at Ataláia beach.

Restaurants   Very many in Ataláia; on Av Oceânica try *Chapéu de Couro*, No 128, rec; *Cantinha da Bahia*, No 180, rec for fresh crab. In town, there is a good bar and restaurant, *Cacique Chá*, in the cathedral square, lively at weekends; also on Praça Olímpio Campos is *Rancho Gaúcho*, No 692, quite good, very friendly; *Bar e Lanchonete Dom Qui Chopp*, Laranjeiras opp Telergipe, popular.

Post Office   Laranjeiras e Itabaianinha. **Telephones**   Telergipe, Laranjeiras 296, national and international calls until 2200.

Shopping   *Artesanato* interesting: pottery figures and lace particularly. Fair in Praça Tobias Barreto every Sun. Municipal market is a block N of the Hidroviária.

Tourist Information   Emsetur, Av Tancredo Neves s/n, T 231-9166, in the Centro Integrado Comunitário, a long way from the centre. In the centre, go to *Aracatur*, R Maruim 100, Sala 10, T 224-1226, which has leaflets and maps such as *Aracaju no bolso* and *Onde?*, helpful, English spoken.

ARACAJU   Not to scale

1. Praça Olímpio Campos & Cacique Chá restaurant
2. Praça Fausto Cardoso
3. Praça General Valadão
4. Praça da Bandeira
5. Cathedral
6. Palácio do Governo
7. Assembléia
8. Centro do Turismo
9. Ponte do Imperador
10. Market
11. Terminal Hidroviário
12. Old Rodoviária
13. Post Office
14. Telergipe (telephones)

Hotels:
15. Grande
16. Pálace
17. Aperipê & Serigy
18. Brasília
19. Oásis
20. Amado

Buses The new rodoviára for interstate buses is 4 km from the centre, linked by local buses from the adjacent terminal (buy ticket before going on to the platform). Bus 004 "T Rod/L Batista" goes to the centre, US$0.25; look for route plates on the side of buses and at termini in town. The old bus terminal in town is at Santo Amaro e Divina Pastora, Praça João XXIII: buses from here to new rodoviária, Laranjeiras and São Cristóvão (45 mins, US$0.70). Buses to the rodoviária also can be caught at the terminal near the Hidroviária and from Capela at the top of Praça Olímpio Campos.

To **Salvador**, 6-7 hrs, 11 a day with Bonfim, US$10.50, executive service at 1245 US$14.50, saves 1 hr. To **Maceió**, US$8.50 with Bonfim. Many coastal destinations served; also Vitória (US$44), Rio (US$60), São Paulo, Belo Horizonte (US$50).

São Cristóvão (pop 41,300), SW of Aracaju on the road to Salvador, was the old state capital of Sergipe, founded in 1590 by Cristóvão de Barros. It is the fourth oldest town in Brazil. Built on top of a hill, its colonial centre is unspoiled, the majority of buildings painted white with green shutters and woodwork. Worth visiting are the Museu de Arte Sacra e Histórico de Sergipe in the Convento de São Francisco (open Tues-Sun 0800-1800), and the Museu de Sergipe in the former Palácio do Governo, both on Praça de São Francisco. Also on this square are the churches of Misericórdia (1627) and the Orfanato Imaculada Conceição (1646, permission to visit required from the Sisters). On Praça Senhor dos Passos are the churches of Senhor dos Passos and Terceira Ordem do Carmo (both 1739), while on the Praça Getúlio Vargas (formerly Praça Matriz) is the Igreja Matriz Nossa Senhora da Vitória (all are closed Mon). Also worth seeing is the old Assembléia Legislativa on R Coronel Erundino Prado. Outdoor arts festival in second half of Oct. Buses (São Pedro) from Aracaju, from old rodoviária in centre, see above. A tourist train runs between Aracaju and São Cristovão each Sat and Sun, 0900, 3½ hrs. (No hotels, but families rent rooms near the bus station at the bottom of the hill, straight down from Praça G Vargas.)

15 km NW from Aracaju is *Laranjeiras* (pop 15,600), reached by São Pedro bus, from old rodoviária in centre, 30 mins-1 hr. A small pleasant town, with a ruined church on a hill, it has three museums (Museu Afro-Brasileiro, Centro de Cultura João Ribeiro, and Sacro in the Conceição church), and the 19th century Capela de Sant'Aninha with a wooden altar inlaid with gold. **C** *Pousada Vale dos Outêiros*, rec.

70 km W of Aracaju is *Itabaiana* , which has a famous gold market on Sat.

The Rio São Francisco marks the boundary between Sergipe and Alagoas. The BR-101 between Aracaju and Maceió—the next port to the N—is paved, crossing the São Francisco by bridge between Propriá and Porto Real do Colégio.

Another crossing can be made by boat from **Neópolis** in Sergipe, to **Penedo** (pop 40,665) in Alagoas, near the mouth of the Rio São Francisco. Neópolis has a small market place by its central landing stage and, up the hill, a square with two churches.

Penedo is a charming town, with a nice waterfront park, Praça 12 de Abril, with stone walkways and walls. Originally the site of the Dutch Fort Maurits (built 1637, razed to the ground by the Portuguese), the colonial town stands on a promontory above the river. Among the colonial architecture, modern buildings such as the Associação Commercial and *Hotel São Francisco*, both on Av Floriano Peixoto, do not sit easily. On the Praça Barão de Penedo is the neoclassical **Igreja Matriz** (closed to visitors) and the 18th century **Casa da Aposentadoria**. East and a little below this square is the Praça Rui Barbosa, on which are the **Convento de São Francisco** (1783 and later) and the church of **Santa Maria dos Anjos** (1660). As you enter, the altar on the right depicts God's eyes on the world, surrounded by the three races, one Indian, two negroes and the whites at the bottom. The church has fine *trompe-l'oeil* ceilings (1784). The convent is still in use. Guided tours are free. The church of **Rosário dos Pretos**, on Praça Marechal Deodoro, is open to visitors, while **Nosso Senhor da Corrente** (1764), on Praça 12 de Abril, and **São Gonçalo Garcia** (1758-70) on Floriano Peixoto are closed, the latter for restoration to its façade. Also on Floriano Peixoto is the pink **Teatro 7 de Setembro** of 1884; between it and the old covered market are fruit and vegetable stalls. The **Casa de Penedo**, at R João Pessoa 126 (signs point the way up the hill from F Peixoto), displays photographs and books on, or by, local figures such as the Barão de Penedo (Francisco Ignácio de Carvalho Moreira), Elysio de Carvalho (writer and poet), and others. It also has a few historical exhibits and a small lecture room.

Very few of the long two-masted sailing vessels that used to cruise on the river can be seen now, although there are plenty of smaller craft. Boats can be rented at the waterfront for excursions to the river islands, the mouth of the river and to beaches (eg Praia do Peba).

Hotels **C** *São Francisco*, Av Floriano Peixoto, T 551-2273, standard rooms have no a/c, others have a/c, TV, fridge, rec except for poor restaurant; **C** *Pousada Colonial*, Praça 12 de Abril 21, T 551-2677, all rooms with bath, *luxo* and suite have phone, TV and fridge, suites have a/c, spacious, clean, good cheap restaurant, front rooms with view of Rio São Francisco; **E** *Turista*, R Siqueira Campos 143, T 551-2237, with bath, fan, hot water, rec; **F** *Impérial*, Av Floriano Peixoto, basic.

Restaurants *Forte da Rocheira*, R da Rocheira (take either of the alleys running W off the hill between Praças Barão de Penedo and 12 de Abril, turn right), good food, especially *ensopada de jacaré* (alligator stew); continue along the cliff walkway to the riverside for *Churrascaria O Scala*, at the end of R 15 de Novembro.

Banks and Exchange Banks open 0830-1300. **Banco do Nordeste do Brasil** on Av F Peixoto; **Banco do Brasil** and **Bradesco** on Av Duque de Caxias, opp Bompreço. *Restaurant e Bar Lulu*, Praça 12 de Abril, will change cash if conditions suit the owner, fair rates.

Post Office Av Floriano Peixoto, opp *Hotel Imperial*. **Telephones** Telasa on Barão de Penedo.

Shopping Daily market on streets off Av Floriano Peixoto. Good hammocks. Ceramics for sale outside Bompreço supermarket on Av Duque de Caxias.

Tourist Office in Casa da Aposentadoria, Praça Barão de Penedo (if open).

Transport Frequent launches for foot pasengers and bicycles across the river to Neópolis, 25 mins, US$0.35. The dock in Penedo is on Av Duque de Caxias, below Bompreço. The ferry makes three stops in Neópolis, the second is closest to the rodoviária (which is near the Clube Vila Nova, opp Texaco station). Heading S, if you take the 0730 ferry from Penedo, you will have plenty of time to get out at the third stop, walk through Neópolis and catch the 0900 bus to Aracaju. Also half-hourly car ferry (US$1; take care when driving on and off).

451 km from Salvador (US$16, 10 hrs, by daily bus at 0600, book in advance), at same time for Aracaju (US$8.50); buses S are more frequent from Neópolis, 6 a day (0630-1800) to Aracaju, 2 hrs, US$5. 115 km from Maceió, 5 buses a day in either direction, US$5-6, 3-4 hrs. One bus to São Paulo daily, 1500, 2 a day to Recife, 0700, 2100. The Penedo rodoviária is on Av Duque de Caxias, behind Bompreço, little information; timetables posted in *Pousada Colonial*.

Maceió (pop 527,440, CEP 57000, DDD 082), capital of Alagoas state (pop 2,513,000), is about 287 km NE of Aracaju by road, and 244 km S of Recife. It is mainly a sugar port, although there are also tobacco exports and a major petrochemical plant. A lighthouse stands in a residential area of town (Farol), about one km from the sea.

Two of the city's old buildings, the Palácio do Governo, which also houses the Pierre Chalita museum (see below), and the church of Bom Jesus dos Mártires (covered in tiles), are particularly interesting. Both are on the Praça dos Martírios (or Floriano Peixoto). The recently restored cathedral, Praça Dom Pedro II, is also interesting. The Associação Comercial has a museum on R Sá e Albuquerque, Jaraguá, near the sea, in a beautiful, though deteriorating building.

The commercial centre stretches along the seafront to the main dock and climbs the hills behind. An enjoyable lagoon, Lagoa do Mundaú, whose entrance is 2 km S at **Pontal da Barra**, limits the city to the S and W: excellent shrimp and fish at its small restaurants and handicraft stalls; a nice place for a drink at sundown. Boats make excursions in the lagoon's channels.

Museums Instituto Histórico e Geográfico, R João Pessoa 382, T 223-7797, good small collection of Indian and Afro-Brazilian artefacts. **Fundação Pierre Chalita**, Praça Floriano Peixoto 49, centre, T 223-4298, Alagoan painting and religious art. **Museu do Folclore Theo Brandão**, Praça Sinimbu 206, centre. All closed Sat and Sun.

Alagoas is one of the poorest and least developed states. Be prepared for delays, cancellations and changed opening times. Maceió, however, is a friendly city with a low crime rate.

Local Holidays 27 Aug (Nossa Senhora dos Prazeres); 16 Sept (Freedom of Alagoas); 8 Dec (Nossa Senhora da Conceição); Christmas Eve; New Year's Eve, half-day.

Hotels Many hotels on Praia Pajuçara, mostly along Av Dr Antônio Gouveia and R Jangadeiros Alagoanos. **A1** *Enseada*, Av A Gouveia 171, T 231-4726, F 231-5134, rec; **A1** *Pajuçara Othon*, R Jangadeiros Alagoanos 1292, T 231-2200; **A2** *Sete Coqueiros*, Av A Gouveia 1335, T 231-8583, F 231-7467, 3-star, a/c, TV, phone, restaurant, pool; next door is the smaller **B** *Velamar*, T 231-5888, a/c, TV, fridge, safes in rooms. Many good *pousadas* R Jangadeiros Alagoanos, one block back from the beach (it can be hard to find a room during the Dec-Mar holiday season, when prices go up): **B** *Verde Mar*, No 1, with bath, a/c, hot water, TV, T 231-2669, very good; **B** *Maceió Praia*, No 3, T 231-6391, highly rec; **B** *Pousada Sete Coqueteiros*, No 123, T 231-5877, rec; **B** *Laguna Praia*, No 1231, T 231-6180, clean, highly rec; **C** *Buongiorno*, No 1437, T 231-7577, F 231-2168, a/c, fridge, clean, English-speaking owner, helpful; **D** *Costa Verde*, No 429, bath, fan, good family atmosphere, English, German spoken, rooms on 1st floor are best, T 231-4745; **D** *Casa Grande da Praia*, No 1528, T 231-3332, with bath, a/c and TV, cheaper without, rec; *Amazona*, No 1095, clean, friendly, great breakfast; **D** *Pousada Quinta Pruma*, No 597, T 231-6065, clean, friendly. In Antônio de Mendonça: **E** *Pousada Rex*, No 311, with bath, clean, friendly, honest, helpful, highly rec (esp the breakfast); **E** *Pousada Maramar*, No 343, clean and bright, some rooms with sea view, exchange library; **E** *Pousada Shangri-La*, No 1089, T 231 3773, clean, friendly and safe; *Mandacaru*, Almte Maranenhas 85, 2 corners from beach, clean, safe, good value.

At Ponta Verde, the next beach: **A1** *Tambaqui Praia*, R Eng Mário de Gusmão 176,

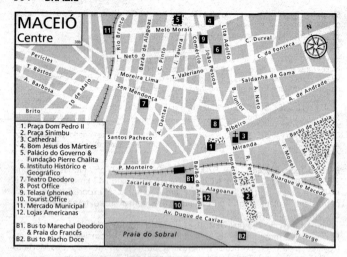

MACEIÓ
Centre

1. Praça Dom Pedro II
2. Praça Sinimbu
3. Cathedral
4. Bom Jesus dos Mártires
5. Palácio do Governo & Fundação Pierre Chalita
6. Instituto Histórico e Geográfico
7. Teatro Deodoro
8. Post Office
9. Telasa (phones)
10. Tourist Office
11. Mercado Municipal
12. Lojas Americanas

B1. Bus to Marechal Deodoro & Praia do Francês
B2. Bus to Riacho Doce

T 231-0202, a/c, TV, phone, restaurant; **C** *Dos Corais*, R H Guimarães 80, helpful; **C** *Hotel do Mar*, Av R Kennedy 1447, T 231-3171, good; **D** *Baleia Azul*, Av Sandoval Arroxeias 822, a/c, fridge, TV; **D** *Sol de Verão*, R Eng Mário do Gusmão 153, with bath, E in small rooms without, clean, friendly.

Further from centre, **L2** *Matsubara*, on Cruz das Almas beach, T 231-6178, F 235-1660, pool, tennis, all facilities, rec; **L2** *Jatiúca*, R Lagoa da Anta 220, T 231-2555, F 235-2808, a/c, on Jatiúca beach, swimming pool, heavily booked, but small rooms with thin walls; *Pousada Des Basques*, Av Jatiúca 694, T 231-8984, on beach, pool; **D** *Hospedaria de Turismo Costa Azul*, Av João Davino and Manoel Gonçalves Filho 280, T 231-6281, clean, hot shower, fan, English spoken, discounts over a week.

C-D *Pousada Cavalo Marinho*, R da Praia 55, Riacho Doce (15 km from centre), facing the sea, T 235-1247, F 235-3260, use of bicycle, canoes and body boards included, hot showers, clean, German and English spoken, tropical breakfasts, Swiss owner, very highly rec (nearby is *Lua Cheia*, good food and live music at night).

In the centre: **A1** *Beiriz*, R João Pessoa 290, T 221-1080, comfortable, pool; **A3** *Sobral Praia*, Av Assis Chateaubriand 8022 (Praia do Sobral), T 221-6665, shower, a/c, restaurant, pool, run down; **B** *Praia Avenida*, Artur Jucá 30, T 221-5050, 2 star; **C** *Parque*, Praça Dom Pedro II 73, T 221-9099, a/c; **D** *Pousada Sol e Mar*, Av Rosa da Fonseca s/n, T 221-2615, with bath, helpful owners, safe, rec; **E** *Golf*, R Prof Domingos Moeda 38A (near the Cathedral), clean. Cheap hotels (mostly without windows) in R Barão de Ataláia. Owing to polluted beaches, few visitors now stay on Avenida or Sobral: hotels in the area are being allowed to run down.

Youth hostel **F** *Nossa Casa*, R Prefeito Abdon Arroxelas 177, T 231-2246.

Camping There is a Camping Clube do Brasil site on Jacarecica beach, T 235-3600, a 15-min taxi drive from the town centre. Camping Pajuçara at Largo da Vitória 211, T 231-7561, clean, safe, food for sale, rec.

Restaurants *Ao Lagostão*, Av Duque de Caxias 1348, seafood, fixed price (expensive) menu; *Pizzeria Sorrisa*, Av Alagoana e J Pessoa Imperador, very cheap, good food, popular with Brazilians; *Bar das Ostras*, R Cruzeiro do Sul 487, Vergel do Lago, expensive but good. Vegetarian: *O Natural*, R Libertadora Alagoana (R da Praia) 112; *Nativa*, Osvaldo Sarmento 56, good views. *Spettus*, Av R Kennedy 1911, Ponta Verde, *churrascaria rodizio*. Many good bars and restaurants in Pajuçara: recommended places on Av Antônio Gouveia are: *Paraíso*, No 631, vegetarian, open late; *O Dragão*, No 21, Chinese; *Comes e Bebes*, No 981, Italian and Arabic, good, take-away service; *Tempeiro Paulista*, No 1103, typical food, good service, cheap. *Massarella*, Jangadeiras Alagoanas 1255, Italian, small, good. *Sete Coqueiros*, on Pajuçara beach, is popular. *Mello's Bar*, R Epaminondas Gracindo 194, excellent food and value. The beaches for 5 km from the beginning of Pajuçara to Cruz das Almas in the N, are lined with *barracas* (thatched bars) providing music, snacks and meals until midnight (later at weekends). Vendors on the beach sell beer and food during the day: clean and safe. At Ponto da Barra, on the lagoon side of the city, *Alípio*, and many others. Local specialities include oysters, *pitu*, a crayfish (now becoming scarce), and *sururu*, a kind of cockle. Local ice cream, Shups, rec.

Banks and Exchange Banco do Brasil, etc. Open 1000 to 1500. **Aeroturismo**, R Barão de Penedo 61 or **Pajuçara Turismo** on same road, which begins opposite ferroviária at Praça Valente de Lima (but not named on all maps); best rates reckoned to be at the **Banespa bank**.

Electric Current 220 volts AC, 60 cycles.

Entertainment *Teatro Deodoro*, Praça Marechal Deodoro, in centre; *Cinema São Luiz*, R do Comércio, in centre; *Arte 1* and *2* Pajuçara and Iguatemi shopping centre; the other cinemas tend to be fleapits. *Bar Chapéu de Couro*, José Carneiro 338, Ponto da Barra, is a popular music bar for young people.

   Nightlife is relaxed and varied. The beach *barracas* offer live music, especially good at weekends: popular ones are *Bar Lampião* (or *Tropical*) and *Ipaneminha* on Pajuçara (Brazilian pop), and *Fellini* on Ponta Verde (varies: good blues and jazz). There are nightclubs to suit most tastes; *Calabar*, in Pajuçara, for *forró* and *lambada*, *Lambadaõ* at Cruz das Almas (excellent *lambada*, weekends only). **Carnival** at Barra de São Miguel (see **Excursions**) has gained a very good reputation in recent years.

Post Office R Joã Pessoa 57, centre, 0700-2200. **Telecommunications** R do Comércio 508, almost opposite Bandepe. Small Telasa office on Pajuçara beach, opposite *Othon* hotel. Also at rodoviária.

Tourist Information Ematur, Duque de Caxias 2014, Centro, T 221-8987. Also at airport and rodoviária (latter not always open). Helpful, has good maps and leaflets. The municipal tourist authority is Emturma, R Saldanha da Gama 71, Farol, T 223-4016; information post on Pajuçara beach, opp *Hotel Solara*.

Local transport Frequent buses, confusingly marked, serve all parts of the city. Bus stops are not marked, best to ask where people look as if they are waiting. The "Ponte Verde/Jacintinho" bus runs via Pajuçara from centre to rodoviária, also take "Circular" bus (25 mins Pajuçara to rodoviária, the stop in Pajuçara is opposite the petrol station by Bompreço supermarket); "Feitosa" also goes to the rodoviária, by a different route. See also **Beaches**, below.

Airport 20 km from centre, taxi about US$15. Buses to airport from near *Hotel Beiriz*, R João Pessoa 290 or in front of the Ferroviária, signed "Rio Largo"; alight at Tableiro dos Martins, then 7-8 mins' walk to airport, bus fare US$0.50. Tourist flights over the city.

Train The ferroviária is in the centre, R Barão de Anádia 121. 5 trains a day, Mon-Sat, from 0630-1855 to Rio Largo (35 km, US$0.12), via Fernão Velho, Satuba and Utinga. Worth taking in one direction at least since it passes beside the Lagoa Mundaú, through places where buses do not go.

Buses Rodoviária is 5 km from centre, on a hill with good views and cool breezes. Luggage store. Take bus marked "Ouro Preto p/centro" or see above (taxi quicker, US$3.50) to Pajuçara. Bus to Recife, 10 a day, 3½ hrs express (more scenic coastal route, 5 hrs) US$7; to Aracaju, US$8.50, 5 hrs (potholed road); to Salvador, 10 hrs, 4 a day, US$19 (*rápido* costs more). Buses to most large cities including Belém, Fortaleza, Brasília, Belo Horizonte, Rio, São Paulo.

Beaches Beyond the city's main dock the beachfront districts begin; within the city, the beaches are posher the further from the centre you go. The first, going N, is Pajuçara beach, where there is a nightly craft market. At weekends there are wandering musicians and entertainers and patrols by the cavalry on magnificent Manga Larga Marchador horses. There are periodic *candomblé* and *axé* nights and rituals to the goddess Iemanjá. Next is Ponta Verde, then Jatiúca, Cruz das Almas, Jacarecica (9 km from the centre), Guaxuma (12 km), Garça Torta (14 km), Riacho Doce (16 km), Pratagi (17 km) and Ipioca (23 km). Jatiúca, Cruz das Almas and Jacarecica are all good for surfing. Taxis from town go to all the northern beaches (eg 30 mins to Riacho Doce), but buses run as far as Ipioca. The Jangadeiras bus marked "Jacarecica-Center, via Praias" runs past all the beaches as far as Jacarecica. From there you can change to "Riacho Doce-Trapiche", "Ipioca" or "Mirante" buses for Riacho Doce and Ipioca. These last three can also be caught in the centre on the seafront avenue below the Praça Sinimbu (US$0.25 to Riacho Doce). To return take any of these options, or take a bus marked "Shopping Center" and change there for "Jardim Vaticana" bus, which goes through Pajuçara. Beaches fronting the old city, between Salgema terminal and the modern port area (Trapiche, Sobral) are too polluted for swimming. The beaches, some of the finest and most popular in Brazil, have a protecting coral reef a kilometre or so out. Bathing is much better three days before and after full or new moon, because tides

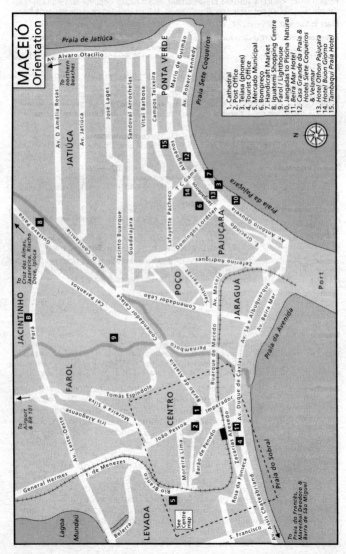

MACEIÓ
Orientation

1. Cathedral
2. Post Office
3. Telasa (phones)
4. Tourist Office
5. Mercado Municipal
6. Bompreço
7. Handicraft Market
8. Iguatemi Shopping Centre
9. Farol/Lighthouse
10. Lançadas do Piscina Natural
11. Beira Mar Hotel
12. Casa Grande da Praia & Hotels Siete Coqueiros
13. Hotel Othon Pajuçara & Velamar
14. Hotel Buon Giorno
15. Tambaqui Praia Hotel

are higher and the water is more spectacular. For beaches beyond the city, see **Excursions** below.

Jangadas take passengers to a natural swimming pool 2 km off Pajuçara beach (Piscina Natural de Pajuçara), at low tide you can stand on the sand and rock reef (beware of sunburn). You must check the tides, there is no point going at high tide. *Jangadas* cost US$2.50 pp/day (or about US$12 to have a *jangada* to yourself). On Sun or local holidays in the high season it is overcrowded, take mask or goggles (at weekends lots of *jangadas* anchor at the reef selling food and drink).

Excursions By bus (22 km S) past Praia do Francês to the attractive colonial town and former capital of Alagoas, **Marechal Deodoro** (pop 31,000), which overlooks the Lagoa Manguaba. The 17th century Convento de São Francisco, Praça João XXIII, has a fine church (Santa Maria Magdalena) with a superb baroque wooden altarpiece, badly damaged by termites. You can climb the church's tower for views, but if you want to take photos you will have to collect your camera from the baggage store at the entrance. Adjoining it is the Museu de Arte Sacra, open Tues-Sun, 0900-1700, US$0.30 (guided tours available, payment at your discretion). Also open to visitors is the Igreja Matriz de NS da Conceição (1783). Remains of other 18th century churches include NS do Rosário, do Amparo and the Convento do Carmo. The town is the birthplace of Marechal Deodoro da Fonseca founder of the Republic; the modest house where he was born is on the R Marechal Deodoro, close to the waterfront, open Mon-Sat, 0800-1700 (entry free). The cleanliness of this little town is exemplary: on Mon everyone is required by local law to sweep the streets. Good local lacework. *Restaurant São Roque*, simple but good. **NB** Schistosomiasis is present in the lagoon.

On a day's excursion, it is easy to visit the town, then spend some time at beautiful **Praia do Francês**. The northern half of the beach is protected by a reef, the southern half is open to the surf. Along the beach there are many *barracas* and bars selling drinks and seafood; try *agulhas fritas*. Hotels include **A2** *Cumaru*, T 231-2223, 3-star, good; **C** *Agua Praia*, good, clean; **C** *Pousada Bougainville e Restaurant Chez Patrick*, T 231-1079, a/c, TV, pool, seafood and international cooking, very nice; **C** *Pousada Manguaba*, good; **D** *Pousada Le Baron*, T 235-3061, on road from beach to highway, good; **D** *O Pescador*, T 231-6959, with restaurant. Recommended restaurant *Panela Mágica*; several others.

Further out from Maceió is the beach of **Barra de São Miguel**, entirely protected by reef, now very popular, crowded at weekends, with *Pousada da Barra*, good, new, and **A3** *Village Barra Hotel*, T 272-1207, pool, restaurant, excursions to other beaches. Several good, cheap *barracas* for food and drink (*do Amizade*, rec).

Buses and kombis to Marechal de Deodoro, Praia do Francês and Barra de São Miguel leave from R Barão de Anádia, outside the ferroviária, opposite *Lojas Americanas*: bus US$0.50, kombi US$0.55 to Marechal Deodoro, 30 mins, calling at Praia do Francês in each direction. Last bus back from Praia do Francês to Maceió at 1800.

There are many interesting stopping points along the coast between Maceió and Recife. At **Paripueira**, 40 mins bus ride from Maceió (Rodoviária) is the **C** *Paripueira Praia Hotel*, good value, very clean, friendly. The beach is busy only during high season. **Barra de Santo Antônio**, 45 km N, is a busy fishing village, with a palm fringed beach on a narrow peninsula, a canoe-ride away; boats also go to the Ilha da Croa; many beautiful beaches nearby. Restaurants: *Peixada da Rita*, try prawns with coconut sauce, rec for local seafood; *Estrela Azul*, more expensive, good, popular with tourists. Hotel, **E** *São Geraldo*, simple, very clean, restaurant; *Pousada Buongiorno* in Maceió has 6 modest rm to rent in a farmhouse, bathrooms but no electricity, many fruit trees (T Maceió 231-7577, F 231-2168); accommodation can be found through local people. Also **Japaratinga** (**C** *Hotel Solmar*, 2 rm, basic, good restaurant; **E** *Pousada Rei dos Peixes*, rooms for 12 or 24 hrs, bit dirty, fan, toilet, simple, opposite sewer; 3 km S is **B** *Praia Hotel Bitingui*, nicely situated—bus from Maceió at 0515) and **São José da Coroa Grande** (**D** *The Pousada*, Av Pedro Cavalcante 535, T 291-1112, rec; a few families rent rooms); at low tide watch colourful fish in the rock pools on the reef. Along this coast, the protecting reef offshore prevents garbage and silt from being taken out to sea at high tide, so water can be muddy and polluted. Furthermore, accommodation tends to be poor value, especially at the cheaper end of the market.

Pernambuco

About 244 km N of Maceió and 835 km N of Salvador is **Recife** (pop 1,290,150), founded on reclaimed land by the Dutch prince Maurice of Nassau in 1637 after his troops had burnt Olinda, the original capital. It is the capital of Pernambuco

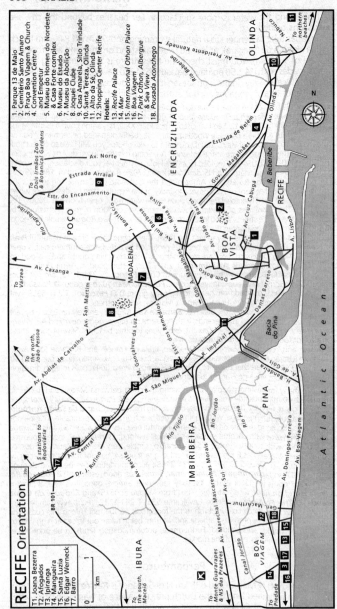

RECIFE Orientation

T1. Joana Bezerra
T2. Afogados
T3. Ipiranga
T4. Mangueira
T5. Santa Luzia
T6. Edgar Werneck
T7. Barro

1. Parque 13 de Maio
2. Cemitério Santo Amaro
3. Praça Boa Viagem & Church
4. Convention Centre and Empetur
5. Museu do Homem do Nordeste & Casa Forte complex
6. Museu do Estado
7. Museu da Abolição
8. Joquei Clube
9. Casa Amarela, Sítio Trindade
10. Santa Tereza, Olinda
11. Alto da Sé, Olinda
12. Shopping Center Recife

Hotels:
13. Recife Palace
14. Mar
15. Internacional Othon Palace
16. Boa Viagem
17. Park Othon, Albergue & Sea View
18. Pousada Aconchego

0   1
km

State (state population 7,110,000). The city centre consists of three portions, Recife proper, Santo Antônio and São José, and Boa Vista and Santo Amaro. The first two are on islands formed by the rivers Capibaribe, Beberibe and Pina, while the third is made into an island by the Canal Tacaruna, which separates it from the mainland. The centre is always very busy by day; the crowds and the narrow streets, especially in the Santo Antônio district, can make it a confusing city to walk around. Recife has the main dock area, with commercial buildings associated with it. South of the centre is the residential and beach district of Boa Viagem, reached by bridge across the Bacia do Pina. Olinda, the old capital, is only 6 km to the N (**see p 516**).

Churches The best of them are the churches of **Santo Antônio do Convento de São Francisco** (1606; beautiful Portuguese tiles), in the R do Imperador, and adjoining it the **Capela Dourada** (Golden Chapel, 1697, the finest sight of all, Mon-Fri 0800-1130 and 1400-1700, Sat 0800-1130: US$0.15, no flash photography; it is through the Museu Franciscano de Arte Sacra, entry US$0.35); **São Pedro dos Clérigos** in São José district (1782), for its façade, its fine wood sculpture and a splendid *trompe-l'oeil* ceiling, open Tues-Fri 0800-1200, 1400-1630, Sat 0800-1000; **Santo Antônio** (1753), in Praça da Independência, rebuilt in 1864, open daily 0800-1200 and Mon-Fri 1400-1800, Sun 1700-1900; **Conceição dos Militares**, R Nova 309 (1708), grand ceiling and a large 18th century primitive mural of the battle of Guararapes (museum next door), open Mon-Fri, 0700-1130, 1330-1600, Sat 0730-1100; **Nossa Senhora do Carmo**, Praça do Carmo (1675), open Mon-Sat 0800-1200, 1400-1800, Sun 1000-1100, 1900-2000; **Madre de Deus** (1706), in the street of that name in district of Recife, with a splendid high altar, and sacristy, Mon-Fri 0800-1100, Sun 1000-1100; the **Pilar Church** (1680), R do Pilar, Recife district; the **Divino Espírito Santo** (1642), the original church of the Jesuits, Praça 17 in Santo Antônio district, Mon-Fri 0730-1630, Sat 0730-1200; **S José do Ribamar** (19th century), in São José, open Thur only. There are many others. Most of them are closed to visitors on Sun, because of services.

14 km S of the city, a little beyond Boa Viagem and the airport, on Guararapes hill, is the historic church of **Nossa Senhora das Prazeres**, open daily 0800-1700. It was here, in 1648-9, that two Brazilian victories led to the end of the 30-year Dutch occupation of the NE in 1654. The church was built by the Brazilian commander in 1656 to fulfil a vow. Boa Viagem's own fine church dates from 1707.

Other Attractions **Forte do Brum** (built by the Portuguese in 1629, before the founding of Recife), is an army museum—open Tues-Fri 1000-1700, Sat-Sun 1400-1700. **Forte das Cinco Pontas** (with Museu da Cidade do Recife—cartographic history of the settlement of Recife—open Mon-Fri 1300-1800, Sat-Sun 1400-1800, free), built by the Dutch in 1630 and altered by the Portuguese in 1677. The two forts jointly controlled access to the port at the northern and southern entrances respectively. The first Brazilian printing press was installed in 1706 and Recife claims to publish the oldest daily newspaper in South America, *Diário de Pernambuco*, founded 1825. The building is on the Praça da Independência.

The artists' and intellectuals' quarter is based on the **Pátio de São Pedro**, the square round São Pedro dos Clérigos (see under **Churches**). Folk music and poetry shows in the square on Fri, Sat and Sun evenings and there are pleasant little restaurants, with good atmosphere, at Nos 44, 46 and 47, and No 20 *Caldeira de Cana e Petisqueira Banguê*. The square is an excellent shopping centre for typical NE craftware (clay figurines are cheapest in Recife). Not far away is the **Praça do Sebo**, where the city's second-hand booksellers concentrate; this Mercado de Livros Usados is off the R da Roda, behind the Edifício Santo Albino, near the corner of Av Guararapes and R Dantas Barreto. Visit the city markets in the São José and Santa Rita sections.

The former municipal prison has now been made into a cultural centre, the **Casa da Cultura** (open Mon-Sat 0900-1900, Sun 1400-1800), with many cells converted into art or souvenir shops and with areas for exhibitions and shows (also public conveniences). Local dances such as the ciranda, forró and bumba-meu-boi are held as tourist attractions on Mon, Wed and Fri at 1700 (T 241-2111 to check in advance). Among other cultural centres are Recife's three traditional **theatres, Santa Isabel** (Praça da República, open to visitors Mon-Fri 1300-1800), **Parque** (R do Hospício 81, Boa Vista, newly restored and beautiful, open 0800-1200, 1400-1800) and **Apolo** (R do Apolo 121, open 0800-1200, 1400-1700).

Boa Viagem is the finest residential and hotel quarter. The 8 km promenade commands a striking view of the Atlantic, but the beach is crowded at weekends and not very clean. In 1995, sharks were becoming a hazard during the Jan breeding season, when they come close to the shore. Go fishing on *jangadas* at Boa Viagem with a fisherman. The main square has a good market Sats, with forró being danced. Bus from centre, take any marked "Boa Viagem"; from Nossa Senhora do Carmo, take buses marked "Piedade", "Candeias" or "Aeroporto"—they go on Av Domingos Ferreira, two blocks parallel to the beach, all the way to Praça Boa Viagem (at Av Boa Viagem 500). Back to centre take buses marked "CDU" or "Setubal" from Av Domingos Ferreira.

Museums The **Museu do Estado**, Av Rui Barbosa 960, Graças (closed am on Sat and Sun, and all day Mon), has excellent paintings by the 19th-century landscape painter, Teles Júnior. The **Museu do Homem do Nordeste**, Av 17 de Agosto 2223 (open Tues-Sun, 1100-1700), Casa Forte (open Tues, Wed, Fri 1100-1700; Thur 0800-1700; Sat, Sun and holidays 1300-1700) comprises the **Museu de Arte Popular**, containing ceramic figurines (including some by Mestre Alino and Zé Caboclo); the **Museu do Açúcar**, which contains models of colonial mills, collections of antique sugar bowls and much else; the **Museu de Antropologia**, the **Nabuco Museum** (at No 1865) and the modern museum of popular remedies, **Farmacopéia Popular**. Take the "Dois Irmãos" bus (check that it's the correct one, with "Rui Barbosa" posted in window, as there are two) from in front of the Banorte building near the post office on Guararapes, half-hour ride 10 km outside the city to the zoo (US$0.20, not very good) and **botanical gardens**; it passes the museum complex, and together with the zoo they make a pleasant day's outing. It is easier to get to the museum complex by taxi. Also the **Museu do Trem**, Praça Visconde de Mauá, small but interesting, especially the Henschel locomotive, built to the Beyer-Garrett pattern (open Tues-Fri, 0900-1200, 1400-1700, Sat 0900-1200, Sun, 1400-1700). **Museu da Abolição (of Slavery)**, R Benfica 150, Madalena, is worth a visit, in an early 19th-century tiled house, once owned by the abolitionist João Alfredo (closed since 1990). **Museu de Imagem e Som**, R da Aurora 379, Boa Vista, open Mon-Fri, 0900-1200, 1400-1800. You may like to visit **Cerámica Brennand**, a factory in the western suburbs at Várzea, 16 km from the centre, on the Camaragibe road, T 271-2784 (take a taxi, or walk the 3 km along R Gastão Vidigal—past hotels *Costa Azul* and *Tropical*—from the end of the bus line along Av Caxangá). They make ceramic tiles, and one of the brothers is a sculptor of idiosyncratic works on display, for those interested in the wilder shores of artistic endeavour. Entry is free, and it is very friendly. They also have a shop at Av Conselheiro Aguiar 2966, loja 4, convenient for Boa Viagem.

Local Holidays 1 Jan (Universal Brotherhood). 12-15 Mar, parades to mark the city's foundation. 24 June (São João). 16 July (Nossa Senhora do Carmo, patron saint of the city). São João, though cancelled by the Pope, is still celebrated with bonfires and fireworks on 24 June all over the State of Pernambuco—and, indeed, throughout Brazil. 8 Dec (Nossa Senhora da Conceição).

Carnival The carnival groups dance at the doors of all the churches they pass; they usually go to the Church of Nossa Senhora do Rosário dos Pretos, patron saint of the slaves (R Estreita do Rosário, Santo Antônio), before proceeding in procession into the downtown areas. A small car at the head bears the figure of some animal; it is followed by the king and queen under a large, showy umbrella. The *bahianas*, who wear snowy-white embroidered skirts, dance in single file on either side of the king and queen. Next comes the *dama do passo* carrying a small doll, or *calunga*. After the *dama* comes the *tirador de loas*: he chants to the group which replies in chorus, and last comes a band of local percussion instruments.

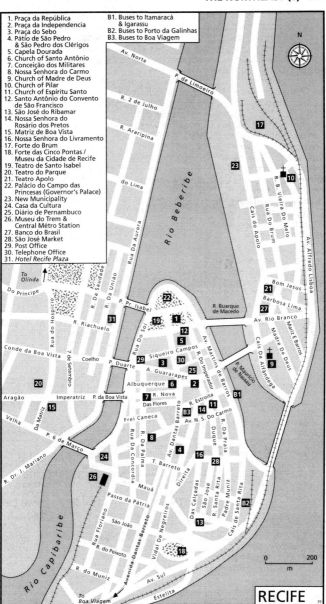

1. Praça da República
2. Praça da Independencia
3. Praça do Sebo
4. Pátio de São Pedro
   & São Pedro dos Clérigos
5. Capela Dourada
6. Church of Santo Antônio
7. Conceição dos Militares
8. Nossa Senhora do Carmo
9. Church of Madre de Deus
10. Church of Pilar
11. Church of Espíritu Santo
12. Santo Antônio do Convento
    de São Francisco
13. São José do Ribamar
14. Nossa Senhora do
    Rosário dos Pretos
15. Matriz de Boa Vista
16. Nossa Senhora do Livramento
17. Forte do Brum
18. Forte das Cinco Pontas /
    Museu da Cidade de Recife
19. Teatro de Santo Isabel
20. Teatro do Parque
21. Teatro Apolo
22. Palácio do Campo das
    Princesas (Governor's Palace)
23. New Municipality
24. Casa da Cultura
25. Diário de Pernambuco
26. Museu do Trem &
    Central Métro Station
27. Banco do Brasil
28. São José Market
29. Post Office
30. Telephone Office
31. Hotel Recife Plaza

B1. Buses to Itamaracá
    & Igarassu
B2. Buses to Porto da Galinhas
B3. Buses to Boa Viagem

RECIFE

Still flourishing is the dance performance of the *caboclinhos*. The groups wear traditional Indian garb: bright feathers round their waists and ankles, colourful cockades, bead and animal teeth necklaces, a dazzle of medals on their red tunics. The dancers beat out the rhythm with bows and arrows; others of the group play primitive musical instruments, but the dance is the thing: spinning, leaping, and stooping with almost mathematical precision.

There is a *pre-carnavalesca* week, followed by the main days Sun to Tues; on the Sat the *bloco* "Galo da Madrugada" officially opens carnival (wild and lively), see local press for routes and times. The groups taking part are *maracatu*, *caboclinhos*, *trocas*, *blocos*, *ursos*, *caboclos de lança*, *escolas de samba* and *frevo*. Usually they start from Av Conde da Boa Vista and progress along R do Hospício, R da Imperatriz, Ponte da Boa Vista, Praça da Independência, R 1° de Março and R do Imperador. During Carnival (and on a smaller scale throughout the year) the Casa de Cultura has frevo demonstrations where visitors can learn some steps of this unique dance of Pernambuco (check press for details of "Frevioca" truck and frevo orchestras during Carnival in the Pátio de São Pedro). The best place to see the groups is from the balconies of *Hotel do Parque*. Information from Casa de Carnaval, office of Fundação da Cultura de Recife, Pátio de São Pedro, lojas 10-11.

In the "Festivais Juninos", the Jun *festas* of São João and São Pedro, the forró is danced. This dance, now popular throughout the NE, is believed to have originated when the British builders of the local railways held parties that were "for all".

Warning Opportunistic theft is unfortunately common in the streets of Recife and Olinda (especially on the streets up to Alto da Sé). Keep hold of bags and cameras, and do not wear a watch. The police in Olinda are reported to be far less helpful than those in the city.

Telephone code and Postal address DDD 081, CEP 50000.

Hotels (for Olinda hotels **see p 516**). In general, there is a shortage of good, mid-range hotels, plenty of multi-star hotels and plenty of flea-pits.

Hotels in the **centre** and away from the beach: in Casa Forte, NW of centre, is **A1** *Pousada Casa Forte*, Av 17 de Agosto 735, T 268-0524, 3-star; **A3** *Recife Plaza*, R da Aurora 225, T 231-1200, Boa Vista, 3-star, overlooking the Rio Capibaribe, every comfort, highly rec, fine restaurant (very popular lunchtime); **B** *4 de Outubro*, R Floriano Peixoto 141, Santo Antônio, T 424-4477, 4 standards of room, with bath, hot water, TV, phone, a/c.

In the cheaper categories: **C** *Interlane*, R do Hospício 186, T 221-1363, good value in town centre; **D** *América*, Praça Maciel Pinheiro 48, Boa Vista, T 221-1300, 2-star, with a/c (cheaper without), front rooms pleasanter, clean, quiet; **D** *Lido*, R do Riachuelo 547, T 222-4660, good breakfast, hot water, friendly, rec; **D** *Nassau*, Largo do Rosário 253, T 224-3977/3520, clean, hot showers, but a bit noisy (breakfast only, served on 7th floor, with a balcony overlooking the city); **E** *Parque*, R do Hospício 51, T 222-5427, good value, safe, good bars and restaurants nearby; **E** *Recife*, R do Imperador 310, T 224-0799, with bath (cheaper without), central, OK but grubby.

Hotels on or near the beach in **Boa Viagem**: **L2** *Recife Palace*, Av Boa Viagem 4070, T 325-4044, F 326-8895, 5-star; **L2** *Vila Rica*, No 4308, T 326-5111, F 326-5511, 4-star; **A1** *Do Sol*, No 978, T 326-7644, F 326-7166, 4-star; **A1** *Internacional Othon Palace*, No 3722, T 465-5022, F 326-7661, 4-star; **A1** *Savaroni*, No 3773, T 325-5077, F 326-4900, 4-star; **A3** *Boa Viagem*, No 5000, T 341-4144, F 341-1627, 4-star, near beach; *Castelinho Praia*, No 4520, T 326-1186, F 465-1150, 3 stars, pool, bar, restaurant. Also in Boa Viagem, **L2** *Mar*, near beach at R Barão de Souza Leão 451, T 341-5433, F 341-7002, 5-star; **A3** *Casa Grande e Senzala*, Av Conselheiro Aguiar 5000, T/F 341-0366, 3-star; **A3** *Arcada*, Av Cons Aguiar 3500, T 326-9922, F 326-9622, hotel, fondue restaurant and travel agency with exchange.

There are several cheaper hotels in Boa Viagem (check all prices carefully—beware of sudden price increases); **A3** *Aguamar Praia*, R dos Navegantes 492, T 326-4604, a/c, TV, safe, good breakfast; **B** *Setúbal*, R Setúbal, clean, helpful, good breakfast; **B** *Uzi Praia*, Av Cons Aguiar 942, T 325-2741, a/c, bath, rec; **C** *Pousada Aconchego*, Félix de Brito 382, T 326-2989, F 326-8059, 3 levels of tariff, all with bath, a/c, pleasant, swimming pool, good meals, safe is closed on Sun and in evening, English-speaking owner, previously rec but going downhill, will collect you from the airport. **C** *Sea View*, R Navegantes 101, T 326-5891, Dutch-owned (Dutch, English, French spoken), a/c, small, very friendly, rec; **B** *Pousada da*

Praia, Alcides Carneiro Leal 66, T 326-7085, with bath, a/c, fridge, TV, safe, rooms vary (some tiny), new owner, Emilia, helpful; **C** *Praia Mar*, Av Boa Viagem 1660, T 326-6905, small, clean, rec; **C** *200 Milhas*, No 865, T 326-5292, safe, highly rec; **C** *Saveiro*, R Conselheiro Aguiar 4670, T 326-6073, no pool, mosquitoes, but clean, a/c; **D** *Guest House Pousada*, Luis Marques Teixeira 155, T 341-0559, a/c, secure, proprietor Ricardo Teixeira is a Sevagtur guide, helpful, highly rec, English and German spoken; **D** *Solar da Tia Cléo*, R Joaquim Carneiro da Silva 48, T 326-3460/1090, no sign outside, fans, family atmosphere, fine garden, English spoken, clean, rec. **D** *Guest House Pousada*, R Luiz Marques Teixeira 155, T 341-0559, nr Av Barão de Souza Leão, not far from airport, English, German spoken, helpful, security boxes.

Youth Hostel: **E** *Albergue do Mar 81*, R dos Navegantes 81, T 326-2196, cheaper for IYHA members, good breakfast and atmosphere; **E** *Albergue Mandacaru*, R Maria Carolina 75, T 326-1964, stores luggage, English and German spoken, good breakfast, rec; *Maracatus do Recife*, R Maria Carolina 185, T 326-1221, good breakfast, pool, clean, safe, friendly, open summer only. Membership information from Associação Pernambucano de Albergues da Juventude (APEAJ), from Empetur (see below – take 2 photos).

For longer stays, rooms may be rented in the centre for about US$25-30 a month, make inquiries on the streets. For example, contact Dr Bezerra dos Santos, R Floriano Peixoto 85, Edif Vieira da Cunha S/511, T 224-1098 (English-speaking dentist); Paulo Bezerra de Mello, DHL, R do Riachuelo 201, T 221-2000, rents an apartment for 3 at Boa Viagem, rec. Hotels in the Santa Rita area are not rec as this area is dangerous at night.

During Carnival, private individuals rent rooms and houses in Recife and Olinda; Lins Turismo has listings as does the *Diário de Pernambuco*, or ask around the streets of Olinda. This accommodation is generally cheaper, safer and quieter than hotels. Many hotels sell 5-day Carnival packages (at high prices), which you must take regardless of the length of time you wish to stay. Shop around.

Restaurants   There are many good restaurants, at all prices, in the city, and along beach at Boa Viagem.

City: *Leite* (lunches only), Praça Joaquim Nabuco 147/53 near Casa de Cultura, old and famous, good service, smart (another branch in Boa Viagem, at Prof José Brandão 409). *Le Buffet*, R do Hospício 147-49, good, helpful, friendly, English-speaking owner; *Fuji* (Japanese), No 354, economical, good tofu dishes; *Lisboa á Noite*, Hospício nr Conde da Boa Vista, good, reasonable, open Sun evenings (unlike many); *Tivoli*, R Matias de Albuquerque, Santo Antônio, lunches downstairs, a/c restaurant upstairs, good value; *Galo D'Ouro*, Gamboa do Carmo 83, rec, good value; at No 136, *Casa de Tia*, lunch only, must arrive by 1215, try *cosido*, a meat and vegetable stew, enough for 2, highly rec. *O Vegetal*, R Cleto Campelo e Av Guararapes (2nd floor) behind Central Post Office, lunch only, highly rec, closed Sat-Sun. *Casa dos Frios*, da Palma 57, loja 5, delicatessen/sandwich bar, salads, pastries etc, very good. Good baker *Nabuco* opposite park at R do Sol and R Concórdia.

Boa Viagem: Main hotels. *Maxime*, Av Boa Viagem 21, is where the locals eat seafood; *O Porcão*, Av Domingos Ferriera 4215, very good rodizio and salad bar, expensive; *Oficina da Massas*, No 2232, Italian; pizzas at *Mr Pizza*, Av Cons Aguiar 3553 and *Fiorentino*, R Laete Lemos 60 (another branch at Av Bernardo Vieira de Melo 4738, Candeias); *Mediterráneo*, R Setúbal, 100m from *Hotel Setúbal*, Italian, pasta, fish, reasonable, rec; *Shangai Palace* (Chinese), Av Domingos Ferreira 4719, excellent, plenty of food, another branch at Av Boa Viagem 5262; *China Especial*, Av Domingos Ferreira 3470, good value, large helpings; *Futuba*, R Mauoel de Brito 44, a tiny side street towards beach from Av Conselheiro Aguiar 1313, Japanese, good; *Chinés*, Herculano Bandeiro 875, Pina (just after bridge, on Boa Viagem side), good value, another branch at Av Bernardo Vieira de Melo, Piedade; *Prá Vocês*, Av Herculano Bandeira 115, Pina (town end of Boa Viagem beach), good but pricey seafood. *Snack Bar Flamingo*, Av Cons Aguiar 542, good hamburgers and ice cream.

(For Olinda restaurants see under Olinda, p 518). Be careful of eating the local small crabs, known as *guaiamum*; they live in the mangrove swamps which take the drainage from Recife's *mocambos* (shanty towns).

Bars   The Graças district, W of Boa Vista, on the Rio Capibaribe, is popular for bars and evening entertainment. Recommended is *Depois do Escuro*, R da Amizade 178, Graças, but there are many others. The cafe/ice cream parlours *Fri-Sabor* and *Eskimo*, both close to Praça Boa Viagem, are suggested. *O Beliscão*, Av Boa Viagem, by Sea View Hotel, rec; *Bar Sem Nome* at Jangada; *Shoparia*, 2 doors from *Maxime* restaurant, rec for beer and atmosphere, live rock music after 2200; *Mustang*, Av Conde de Boa Vista, Boa Vista, also rec for a beer and watching the "movimento". *Highlander*, English pub at Av Domingos Ferreira 2222, Boa Viagem.

Banks and Exchange   Banks open 1000-1600, hours for exchange vary between 1000 and 1400, sometimes later. **Banco do Brasil**, next to shopping centre, Boa Viagem (Visa), very helpful. In Boa Viagem, **Banorte** branches on Avs Domingos Ferreira and Cons Aguiar.

Mastercard, cash against card, Av Cons Aguiar 3621, Boa Viagem. **Lloyds Bank**, R do Fogo 22; **Citibank**, Av Guararapes, not very helpful. Moneychanger hangs out at *Casa dos Frios* deli, R da Palma corner with Guararapes. **Edifício Bancomércio**, 3rd floor, R Matias de Alberquerque 223, takes cash and TCs. *Restaurante Leite*, Praça Joaquim Nabuco 147/53, good rates for TCs and cash.

Consulates British, Domingos Ferreira 222, sala 203, Boa Viagem, T 326 3733, open 0800-1130. **Danish**, Av M de Olinda 85, Ed Alberto Fonseca 2°, CP 3450030, T 224-0997, open 0800-1200, 1400-1800. **Swedish**, Av Marquês de Olinda 126, sala 101, T 326-3144. **Finnish**, Av Conde da Boa Vista 708. **German**, Dantas Barreto 191, Edif Santo Antônio, 4th floor, T 424-3488. **French**, Av Dantas Barreto 1200, 9° floor, Edif San Diego, São José, T 224-6722. **US**, Gonçalves Maia 163, Boa Vista, T 221-1412.

Cultural Institutes British Council, Domingos Ferreira 4150, Boa Viagem, CP 6104, T 272-3060, F 272-3455, 0800-1500, new reading room with current English newspapers, very helpful. **Instituto Brasileiro Alemã**, R do Sossego 364. **Alliance Française**, R Amaro Bezerra 466, Derby, T/F 222-0918.

Electric Current 220 volts AC, 60 cycles.

Entertainment The following have live regional music: *O Catedral da Seresta*, R Real da Torre 1435, Bairro Torre, T 228-0567; *O Pirata*, Av 17 de Agôsto 1738, Bairro Casa Forte; *Maria Bonita*, R Jack Ayres s/n, Boa Viagem, T 325-5402. Also visit a typical N-Eastern "Forró" where local couples dance to typical music, very lively especially on Fri and Sat: several good ones at Candeias. **Recife Ballet** shows in the Recife/Olinda Convention Center, US$10, traditional dances in full costume, rec. **Discotheques** tend to be expensive and sophisticated—best of these are in Casa Forte. Best times are around midnight on Fri or Sat. Take a taxi.

Language Courses Baynsches Institut, Av Domingos Ferreira, Portuguese classes.

Laundrette Av Conselheiro Aguiar 1385, Boa Viagem. *Úosh*, Av Domingo Ferreira.

Post Office including poste restante, Central Correios, 50001, Av Guararapes 250 (or American Express, R Félix de Brito 666, T 465 5000 for poste restante). In Boa Viagem, Av Cons Aguiar e R Cel Sérgio Cardim.

Telecommunications Embratel, Av Agamenon Magalhães, 1114, Parque Amorim district, T 221-4149; also Praça da Independência. Telpe, Av Cons Aguiar e R Padre Carapuceiro, closes 1200 on Sun. Telex, public booth, Av Guararapes 250. **International Telephones** R Diário de Pernambuco, 38 (closes 2230); also at airport (first floor), noisy.

Church Episcopalian, R Carneiro Vilela 569.

Markets Permanent craft market in **Casa da Cultura** (see above); prices for ceramic figurines are lower than Caruaru (see below). Also in the Casa da Cultura is *Sucos da Terra*, Ralo Norte, wide selection of juices made with mineral water. Mercado São José (1875) for local products and handicrafts. **Casa Amarela** for a truly typical market on Sat and Sun evening; "hippy fair" at Praça Boa Viagem, on the sea front, life-sized wooden statues of saints (a good meeting place is the *Bar Lapinha* in the middle of the square). Sat craft fair at **Sítio Trindade**, Casa Amarela: during the feast days of Jun 12-29, fireworks, music, dancing, local food. On Apr 23, here and in the Pátio de São Pedro, one can see the *xangô* dance. Herbal remedies, barks and spices at Afogados market.

Bookshops *Livraria Brandão*, R da Matriz 22 (used English books and some French and German) and bookstalls on the R do Infante Dom Henrique. *Livro 7*, a huge emporium with a very impressive stock, R Sete de Setembro 329. *Solider* at Guararapes airport has books in English, newspapers, magazines. *Livraria do Nordeste*, between cells 118 and 119, Ralo Leste, Casa da Cultura, for books in Portuguese on the NE. *Livraria Nordeste*, R Imperatriz 43, Boa Vista. *Síntese*, R do Riachuelo; *Ao Livro Técnico*, R Princesa Isabel, has thrillers in English and beginners' readers. A great local character, *Melquísidec Pastor de Nascimento*, second-hand bookseller, at R Bispo Cardoso Aires, 215; also has a second-hand stall at Praça de Sebo (see p 509).

Golf Caxangá Golf & Country Club, Av Caxangá 5362: 9 holes.

Travel Agency *Trilhas*, T 222-6864, rec for ecologically oriented excursions.

Tourist Offices Empetur (for the State of Pernambuco), main office, Centro de Convençôes, Complexo Rodoviário de Salgadinho, T 241-2111, F 241-9011, between Recife and Olinda, branch at airport—24 hrs (will book hotels if phones are working, helpful but few leaflets, English spoken). Maps available, or can be bought at newspaper stands in city; also sketch maps in monthly guides *Itinerário Pernambuco* and *Guia do Turista*.

Hours of opening of museums, art galleries, churches etc are published in the daily newspaper *Diário de Pernambuco*.

Local Transport   City buses are clearly marked and run frequently until about 2230. Many central bus stops have boards showing routes. On buses, especially at night, look out for landmarks as street names are written small and are hard to see. Integrated bus-**metrô** (see **Rail** below) routes and tickets (US$0.75) are explained in a leaflet issued by CBTU Metrorec, T 251-5256. See below for buses to Olinda and other destinations outside the city. Trams run in the city centre. Taxis are plentiful; fares double on Sun.

Air Services   The principal international and national airlines fly to Guararapes airport, 12 km from the city. Direct flights from Europe with Air Portugal and Varig from Lisbon, and Varig from Rome and Frankfurt. Bus to airport, No 52, US$0.60, 30 mins from NS do Carmo, or "Aeroporto" from city centre and Av Domingos Ferreira, Boa Viagem (US$0.25, 10 mins). Tourist taxis at the airport cost US$5 to Boa Viagem, while ordinary taxis picked up on the main road cost about US$1 less. There is a bank desk before customs which gives much the same rate for dollars as the moneychangers in the lobby.

Rail   Recife is the centre of the Rede Ferroviária do Nordeste, with lines N to Paraíba and Natal (no passenger services). Commuter services, known as the **Metrô** but not underground, leave from the central station; they have been extended to serve the rodoviária (frequent trains, 0600-2300, US$0.25). If going to Boa Viagem from the rodoviária, get off the Metrô at Joanna Bezerra (20 mins from bus station) and take a bus or taxi (US$5.25) from there.

Coastal Shipping   Lóide Brasileiro ships run frequently between Brazilian coastal ports. They have several up-to-date vessels, some de luxe. Recife is an international port; customs (closed Sat, Sun) reportedly can be obstructive.

Buses   The rodoviária, mainly for long-distance buses, is 12 km outside the city at São Lourenço da Mata (it is called Terminal Integrado dos Passageiros, or TIP, pronounced "chippy"). T 455-1999/1503. There is a 30-mins metrô connection to the central railway station, entrance through Museu do Trem, opp Casa da Cultura (US$0.25), 2 lines leave the city, take train marked "Rodoviária". From Boa Viagem a taxi all the way costs US$18, or go to Joana Bezerra Metrô station and change there. Bus US$0.60, 1 hr, from centre or from Boa Viagem. The train to the centre is much quicker than the bus. Tickets for long and short distances may be bought from Lins Turismo (no commission) on Av Guararapes, or in R La Palma in São José, English spoken. Real Alagoas bus tickets (for Maceió and Aracaju) also sold at Cais de Santa Rita (opp EMTU) and Fruir Tur, Av Sigismundo Gonçalves 487, Carmo, Olinda.

To **Salvador**, 13 hrs, 4 a day (all at night) US$24 (1 *leito*, 47); 12 hrs to **Fortaleza**, US$22, and 4 hrs to **Natal** US$9.25. To **Rio**, 50 hrs (the road is severely pot-holed), US$59 (118 *leito*); to **São Paulo**, 40 hrs; to **São Luís**, 28 hrs, Progresso at 1430 and 1945, US$48.50; to **Belém**, 34 hrs (Boa Esperança bus rec). Good roads N to **João Pessoa** (buses every 30 mins, US$3.60), Natal and Fortaleza, W to Arcoverde and Caruaru (US$4.75, 2 hrs). South to **Maceió**, US$7, 3½ hrs, either by the main road or by the coast road "via Litoral". Efficient service to most Brazilian cities.

Buses to the nearby destinations of Igarassu (every 15 mins) and Itamaracá (every 30 mins) leave from Avenida Martins de Barros, in front of *Grande Hotel*; to Olinda, see below; those to beaches beyond Olinda from Av Dantas behind the post office. To Cabo (every 20 mins) and beaches S of Recife from Cais de Santa Rita.

Excursions   Any bus going S of Boa Viagem passes the Ilha do Amor; ask a fisherman to row you out to it and collect you at a set time, US$2.50. Walk across the island (10 mins) to the Atlantic side for a fine, open, uncrowded beach. Take care here as it is a little isolated. About 30 km S of Recife, beyond Cabo, is the beautiful and quiet *Gaibu* beach (take bus "Centro do Cabo" from airport, frequent buses – 20 mins – from Cabo), *Pousada Beto Qualhado*; rooms, E, at *Oliver y Daniel*, Av Laura Cavalcante 20, German, very relaxed, cheap restaurants; 1 km on foot from Gaibu is Praia Calhetas, which is very nice. Itapuama beach is even more empty, both reached by bus from Cabo. *Cabo* (pop 121,000), Pernambuco's main industrial city, has interesting churches and forts and a Museu da Abolição, and at nearby Suape are many 17th-century buildings and a biological reserve. *Porto de Galinhas*, further S still, is a beautiful beach, reached by bus from Cais de Santa Rita, Recife US$2, via the town of Nossa Senhora do Ó, 2 hrs, 0900, 1230, 1530 (not Sun), 0740 Sun only, take 0900 since others don't allow enough time; last back at 1600, packed out. It has cool, clean water, and waves. **A1** *Solar Porto de Galinhas*, T 325-0772, F 325-1331, on beach, many facilities, beautiful place; *pousada* of Dona Benedita in the street where the bus stops, very basic, clean; several other hotels and *pousadas*; food at *Rang Bem* in same street as Benedita. Further S (80 km from Recife) are the beaches of *Barra do Sirinhaém*, with little tourist development as yet, 3 hotels including **E** *dos Cataventos*; fishermen make trips to offshore island (good views).

Biological Reserves For information on Pernambuco's two reserves, contact Ibama, Av 17 de Agosto 1057, Casa Forte, CEP 50.000, Recife. They are **Saltinho**, which preserves some of the last vestiges of Atlantic Forest in the NE, and **Serra Negra**, which has some of the last remaining forest at higher altitude in the interior.

Olinda (pop 340,675, CEP 53000, DDD 081), the old capital, founded in 1537 and named a "Patrimônio da Humanidade" by Unesco in 1982, 6 km to the N, is served by buses and taxis. A programme of restoration, partly financed by the Netherlands government, was initiated in order to comply with the recently conferred title of National Monument. Despite adoption by Unesco and the Dutch, the need for restoration and cleaning has grown.

Of particular interest are: on R São Bento, the **Prefeitura**, once the palace of the viceroys, and the monastery of **São Bento**, founded 1582 by the Benedictine monks, restored 1761, the site of Brazil's first law school and the first abolition of slavery (paintings, sculpture, furniture; the monastery is closed to anyone without written permission to visit); the convent of **Santa Teresa** (1687), Av Olinda 570; the **Convento de São Francisco** (1585), with splendid woodcarving and paintings, superb gilded stucco, and azulejos, in Capela de São Roque, also church of **NS das Neves**, Ladeira de São Francisco (visits permitted only with prior written application); the **Igreja da Misericórdia**, built 1540, R Bispo Coutinho, fine tiling and gold work, and Acadêmia Santa Gertrudes; the **Cathedral** (1537), Alto da Sé, the first church to be built in the city, of simple and severe construction; the **Graças** church (seminary) built 1582, also in Alto da Sé; **São João Batista dos Militares** (1581), R da Saudade, the only church not burnt by the Dutch; **Nossa Senhora do Monte**, built early 16C; the **Carmo** church (1588) overlooking Praça Carmo (under restoration, guides may be able to get you in), and the colonial public fountain, the **Bica de São Pedro**, R Joaquim Cavalcanti. None of the historic buildings has fixed opening hours.

There are some houses of the 17th century with latticed balconies, heavy doors and pink stucco walls, including a house in Moorish style at Praça João Alfredo 7, housing the *Mourisco* restaurant. There is a colony of artists and excellent examples of regional art, mainly woodcarving and terracotta figurines, may be bought in the Alto da Sé, the square on top of the hill by the cathedral, or in the handicraft shops at the **Mercado da Ribeira** (the former slave market), R Bernardo Vieira de Melo (Vieira de Melo gave the first recorded call for independence from Portugal, in Olinda in 1710). Handicrafts are also sold at good prices in the Mercado Eufrásio Barbosa, by the junction of Av Sigismundo, Gonçalves and Santos Dumont, Varadouro; the bars serve good value meals. There is a **Museu de Arte Sacra** in the former Palácio Episcopal (1696) at Alto da Sé 7, open Mon-Fri, 0700-1300. At R 13 de Maio 157, in the 18th-century jail of the Inquisition, is the **Museu de Arte Contemporânea** (Tues-Fri 0900-1700, Sat-Sun 1400-1700). The **Museu Regional**, R do Amparo 128, is excellent (same hours).

NB Olinda has been severely afflicted by rapidly-worsening poverty, the effects of which are perhaps more noticeable in this attractive and comparatively prosperous area. Please exercise caution, and sympathy.

Guides Guides with identification cards wait in Praça do Carmo. They are former street children and half the fee for a full tour of the city (about US$20) goes to a home for street children. If you take a guide you will be safe from mugging which, unfortunately, occurs (see above). If in doubt about this system, ask at the *Pousada Flor da Manhã*.

Hotels At Casa Caiada, Av José Augusto Moreira 2200 (T 431-2955, F 431-0670), is **L2** *Quatro Rodas* with swimming pool, excellent restaurant, tennis courts, gardens, very good. A *Pousada dos Quatro Cantos*, R Prudente de Morais 441, in a converted mansion, very good, highly rec, prices rise to L2 for 5-night package during Carnival, T 429-0220, F 429-1845, sometimes has live entertainment, expensive restaurant; **B** *Marolinda*, Av Min Marcos Freire (Beira Mar) 1615, Bairro Novo, T 429-1699, F 326-6934, 2 star, rec, rooms at front very noisy at weekends; **B-E** *Pousada d'Olinda*, P João Alfredo 178, T/F 439-1163, happy, warmly rec, 10% discount with *South American Handbook*, 5 luxury a/c apartments, 2 colonial suites, 16

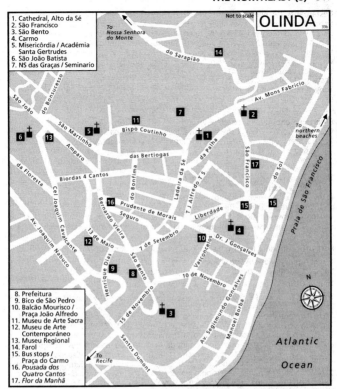

Map key (left side):
1. Cathedral, Alto da Sé
2. São Francisco
3. São Bento
4. Carmo
5. Misericórdia / Académia Santa Gertrudes
6. São João Batista
7. NS das Graças / Seminario

Map key (lower left):
8. Prefeitura
9. Bico de São Pedro
10. Balcão Mourisco / Praça João Alfredo
11. Museu de Arte Sacra
12. Museu de Arte Contemporáneo
13. Museu Regional
14. Farol
15. Bus stops / Praça do Carmo
16. Pousada dos Quatro Cantos
17. Flor da Manhã

OLINDA 39b
Not to scale
To Nossa Senhora do Monte
To northern beaches
To Recife
Atlantic Ocean

rm with shared bath, two communal rooms with good view, pool, breakfast, other meals if requested in advance, English, French, German and Spanish spoken. **B** *Pousada São Francisco*, R do Sol 127, T 429-2109, F 429-4057, clean, comfortable, pool, rec, modest restaurant; **B** *Quatorze Bis*, Av Beira Mar 1414, T 429-0409, friendly, helpful, clean, run by Dutchman; **C** *Circular do Bonde*, Av Min Marcos Freire 223, T 429-3485, shared bath, sea views, communal breakfast, garage, pool, friendly, rec; **D** *São Pedro*, Praça Cons João Alfredo 168, T 429-2935, cosy, helpful, laundry, Danish run, English spoken, rec; **D** *Hospedaria do Turista*, Av Beira Mar 989, excellent, T 429-1847; **D-E** *Flor da Manhã*, R São Francisco 162, T 429-2266, clean, good food, beautiful views, friendly, safe, multilingual, consistently rec; **E** *Albergue da Olinda*, R do Sol 233, T 429-1592, reasonable, clean, friendly, popular with gringos, suites with bath and communal bunk rooms, clothes washing facilities, discounts for IYHA members. Several **youth hostels**: *Portalinda*, Av Min Marcos Freire (Beira Mar) 295, Bairro Novo, T 429-3198; **E** *Cheiro do Mar*, No 95, T 429-0101, more expensive for non-members, very good small hostel with some double rooms (room No 1 is noisy from disco), cooking facilities, ask driver of "Rio Doce/Piedade" or "Bairra de Jangada/Casa Caiada" bus (see below) to drop you at Albergue de Juventude on sea front; *Palanquim*, Prof Cândido Pessoa 1833, Bairro Novo, T 429-0101. **E** *Do Bomfim*, R do Bomfim 115, Carmo, T 429-1674, more for non-members, clean, safe, breakfast, cooking and laundry facilities. **NB** Hotels on R do Sol and in Bairro Novo are below the old city and on the roads heading N.

At Carnival, the price of accommodation rises steeply. Houses or rooms may be rented at this time for 5-10 days. Ask also at the Amex office in Recife about lodging.

Camping Olinda Camping, R Bom Sucesso 262, Amparo, T 429-1365, US$5 pp, space for 30 tents, 5 trailers, small huts for rent, quiet, well-shaded, town buses pass outside, rec.

Restaurants *L'Atelier*, R Bernardo Vieira de Melo 91, Ribeira, small converted workshop with beautiful view, run by Swiss tapestry artists, excellent international food, local dishes with reservation (necessary) T 429-3099, open Wed-Sun evenings. *Mourisco*, R João Alfredo 7, calm and pleasant, discotheque attached; *Samburá*, Av Ministro Marcos Freire 1551 (with terrace) rec to try *caldeirada* and *pitu* (crayfish), also lobster in coconut sauce or daily fish dishes, very good; on Av Beira Mar, *Ouriço*, local food good; *Gouiaba*, charcoal grill, facing sea, good value, rec; *Cantinho da Sé 305*, lively, good view of Recife, views just as good and prices lower upstairs; *O Rei do Vatapá*, on seafront near Praça do Carmo, friendly, good, quite cheap; *Tony*, 2 blocks from Praça do Carmo towards Recife, good, reasonable; *Chin Lee*, excellent Chinese food; many others, mostly for fish. The traditional Olinda drinks, *Pau do Índio* (which contains 32 herbs) and *Retetel*, are both manufactured on the R do Amparo.

Entertainment At Janga beach on Fri and Sat, you can join in a *ciranda* at the bar-restaurant *Ciranda de Dona Duda*. For the less active, there is the *Casa da Seresta*, also in Janga on the beach side of the main road. On Praça do Carmo is *Clube Atlântico*, a *forró* dance hall. *Capoeira* is practised on Sun at about 1800 in the Mercado da Ribeira.

Beginning at dusk, but best after 2100, the Alto da Sé becomes the scene of a lively street fair, with arts, crafts, makeshift bars and barbeque stands, and impromptu traditional music. The fair becomes even more animated at Carnival.

At Olinda's **carnival** thousands of people dance through the narrow streets of the old city to the sound of the Frevo, the brash energetic music which normally accompanies a lively dance performed with umbrellas. The local people decorate them with streamers and straw dolls, and form themselves into costumed groups to parade down the R do Amparo; Pitombeira and Elefantes are the best known of these groups. Foundation Day is celebrated with 3 days of music and dancing, 12-15 Mar, night time only.

Post Office In Santa Tereza, nr Santa Tereza church, on way out of Olinda to Recife.

Travel Agency *Viagens Sob O Sol*, Prudente de Moraes 424, T 429-3303/432-5109, 24 hrs, transport offered to all parts, any type of trip arranged, contact Mauro and Felipe.

Tourist Office Secretaría de Turismo, R do Sol 127, Carmo, T 429-1039.

Transport from Recife Take any bus marked "Rio Doce", No 981 which has a circular route around the city and beaches, or No 33 from Av NS do Carmo, US$0.60 or "Jardin Atlântico" from the central post office at Siqueiro Campos; from Boa Viagem, take bus marked "Piedade/Rio Doce" or "Bairra de Jangada/Casa Caiada" (US$0.65, 30 mins). From airport to Olinda by bus, take "Aeroporto" bus to Av Domingos Ferreira, Boa Viagem, ask to be let off, and catch a "Piedade/Rio Doce" or "Bairra de Jangada/Casa Caiada" bus; from the Recife Rodoviária, take the metrô to Joana Bezerra station and then catch a "Piedade/Rio Doce" or "Bairra de Jangada/Casa Caiada" bus. In all cases, alight in Praça do Carmo. Taxis between Olinda and Recife put their meters onto higher rates at the new Convention Centre (between the two cities), best to start a journey either way there (taxi to Recife US$6, US$10.75 to Boa Viagem at night).

Beaches The beaches close to Olinda are reported to be seriously polluted. Those further N from Olinda, beyond Casa Caiada, are beautiful, usually deserted, palm-fringed; at Janga, and Pau Amarelo, the latter can be dirty at low tide (take either a "Janga" or "Pau Amarela" bus). At many simple cafés you can eat *sururu* (clam stew in coconut sauce), *agulha frita* (fried needle-fish), *miúdo de galinha* (chicken giblets in gravy) and *casquinha de caranguejo* (seasoned crabmeat and *farinha de dendé* served in crabshells). Visit the Dutch fort on Pau Amarelo beach; small craft fair here on Sat nights. Near the fort is *Bar Lua Cheia*, which has music and dancing.

Igarassu (pop 79,400), 32 km N of Recife on the road to João Pessoa, has the first church built in Brazil (SS Cosme e Damião), the Livramento church nearby, and the convent of Santo Antônio with a small museum next door. The church of Sagrado Coração is said to have housed Brazil's first orphanage. Much of the town (founded in 1535) has been declared a National Monument; it is an attractive place, with a number of colonial houses and Brazil's first Masonic hall. Hotel: **A2** *Fazenda Praia da Gavoa*, Estrada do Ramalho (Nova Cruz), T 543-0110, F 541-1088; Camping Clube do Brasil has site nearby at Engenho Monjope, an old sugar estate, now a historical monument and interesting (it is 3 km before Igarassu coming from Recife—bus US$0.65—alight at the "Camping" sign and walk 5-10 mins, T 543-0528). Igarassu buses leave from Av Martins de Barro, Recife, 45 mins, US$0.70. North of Igarassu you pass through coconut plantations to Itapissuma, where there is a bridge to *Itamaracá* island, where, the locals say, Adam and Eve spent their holidays (so does everyone else on Sun, now). It has the old Dutch Forte Orange; an interesting penal settlement with gift shops, built round the 1747 sugar estate buildings of Engenho São João, which still have much of the old machinery; charming villages and colonial churches, and fine, wide beaches. Buses from Recife (Av Martins de Barros opp *Grand Hotel*, US$0.75, very crowded) and Igarassu.

Itamaracá Hotels **A2** *Itamaracá Parque*, Estrada do Forte, T 544-1030; **B** *Caravela*, Praça João Felipe de Barros Dias, T 544-1130, with shower, good restaurant, on beach, rec; **B** *Pousada Itamaracá*, R Fernando Lopes 205, T 544-1152, pool etc, some minutes from beach; *Hospedaria do Turismo*, Pilar 9, fan, clean; **C** *Santa Ina*, on main square, with good restaurant, *Barretinha*; **D** *Rancho Ecológico*, R Rios 355 (close to bus terminal), pool, friendly, not too clean.

Those with a car and above budget means should have lunch and a swim at *Porto Brasílis*, a restaurant at tiny, hidden, charming Vilha Velha (T 081-543-0366 for reservation); allow all afternoon. There is good, relaxing music, fine artefacts and furnishings and a majestic panorama.

Pleasant trips by *jangada* to Coroa do Avião, a recently-formed sandy island (developing wildlife, migratory birds) with rustic beach bars, crossing (US$2 return) from Forte Orange, S of Igarassu bridge; Praias do Sossego and da Enseada, quiet, some bars but relatively undiscovered, crossing 3 km N of Itamaracá town, rec for sun worshippers.

Further N again, 2 hrs from Recife by bus, is *Pontas de Pedra*, an old fishing village, nice beach, fishing and diving expeditions, lots of bars; try **C** *Pousada Calanda*, R do Meio 269, T 626-0500.

Goiana (pop 64,060, CEP 55900, DDD 081), on the Recife-João Pessoa road, founded 1570, is one of the most important towns for ceramics. Carmelite church and monastery, founded 1719, impressive but poorly restored; Matriz do Rosário, only open for 1800 mass, Soledade convent (1755); Amparo church with sacred art museum; Misericórdia church (1723). The uniformity of many of the dwellings is due to their construction, for his workforce, by the owner of a now-defunct textile factory. *Hospedaria Durma Bem*, open weekends only; ask at Prefeitura at other times. Visit the workshop of Zé do Carmo, opposite the *Buraco da Giá* restaurant (excellent seafood; owner has tame crab which will offer you a drink), R Padre Batalha 100. Just N of Goiana is a sugar-mill, Usina Nossa Senhora das Maravilhas, which can be visited during the week; ask for Dr Jairo. Profesor Bartolomeu R de Jesus, at the International Center for Specific Studies, has been recommended as a very helpful Portguese teacher who speaks excellent English.

At the Pernambuco-Paraíba border, a 27 km dirt road to the fishing village of Pitimbu, with *jangadas*, lobster fishing, surf fishing, lobster-pot making. No tourist facilities but camping is possible; food from *Bar do Jangadeiro*. Bus from Goiana, US$0.60.

Carpina, 54 km from Recife, 71,950 people, is well known for its carnival and for the traditional Epiphany festival early in Jan, and also for the carpets made in nearby village of Lagoa do Carro. There is a historical museum. Hotels (**A3** *Pousada das Acácias*, BR-408, Km 77, T 621-0594; **C** *São João da Escócia*, Av João Alfredo 136, T 621-0365) and restaurants. *Tracunhaém* (pop 13,700), is a peaceful town where fine ceramics are made; there are two interesting early 19th-century churches. It is just N of Carpina, on to the road to Nazaré da Mata.

Caruaru (pop 250,000), is 130 km W of Recife. The paved road there passes through rolling hills, with sugar cane and large cattle fazendas, before climbing an escarpment. As the road gets higher, the countryside becomes drier, browner and rockier. Caruaru is a busy, modern town with a big Fri to Sun market: a combination of the feira da Sulanca (clothes), feira do Gado (livestock), feira de Artesanato, feira do Troca-Troca (barter market), and feira de Antigüidades (antiques). A separate site, Feira do Artesanato, across the river for leather goods, ceramics, hammocks and basketware, although now disappointingly tourist-oriented, is open daily. See the hand-painted textiles of Sr Valério Cristóvão, R 13 de Maio 94, 1st floor; he is very helpful and his work depicts local history. The little clay figures (*figurinhas de barro*) originated by Mestre Vitalino, and very typical of the NE, are a local speciality;

many local potters live at Alto da Moura 6 km away, where a house once owned by Vitalino is open, but has no examples of his work. Bus, $\frac{1}{2}$ hr, bumpy, US$0.35.

Festivals São João, month of June, huge *forró* festival; 15-22 Aug, folklore week; 18-22 May, city's anniversary; carnival; holy week.

Hotels A1 *Do Sol*, Cidade Alta, T 721-3044, F 721-1336 (3-star) on hill outside town, good restaurant, pool; **B** *Grande Hotel São Vicente de Paulo*, Av Rio Branco 365, T 721-5011, bar, restaurant, laundry, a/c, pool, TV; **C** *Centenário*, 7 de Setembro 84, T 721-9011, clean, friendly, restaurant; also *Trevo*, opposite rodoviária, and *Village*, on road to Recife from rodoviária, food rec. Cheap *hospedarias* around central square, Praça Getúlio Vargas.

Buses Rodoviária is 4 km from town; buses from Recife stop in the town centre. Alight here and look for the *Livraria Estudiantil* on the corner of Vigario Freire and R Anna de Albuquerque Galvão. Go down Galvão, turn right on R 15 de Novembro to the first junction, 13 de Maio; turn left, cross the river to the Feira do Artesanato. Bus from centre, same place as Recife bus stop, to Rodoviária, US$0.20. Many buses from TIP in Recife, 2 hrs express, US$4.75, also *comum*. Bus to Maceió, 0700, 5 hrs, US$5.50. Bus to Fazenda Nova 1030, 1 hr, returns for Caruaru 1330.

On the way to Caruaru is *Gravatá*, 60,000 people (**A1** *Hotel Fazenda Portal*, BR-232, Km 88, T 533-0288; **C** *Grande da Serra*, BR-232, Km 83, T 533-0014; **C** *Centro*, Av C B de Oliveira/BR-232, Km 82, T 533-0016, 2-star), known as the Switzerland of Pernambuco for its scenery and good hill climate.

During Easter Week each year various agencies run package tours to the little country town of *Fazenda Nova*, 23 km from Caruaru, but 2 hrs by bus (US$2). Just outside the town is *Nova Jerusalém*, where for the week up to Easter Sun, an annual passion play, suggested by Oberammergau's, is enacted. The site is one third the size of the historic quarter of Jerusalem, with 12 permanent stages on which scenes of the Passion are presented; the audience moves from one to another as the story unfolds. Performances begin at 1800, lasting around 3 hrs – well worth a visit if you are in the region at this time of year.

Hotels in Fazenda Nova *Grande*, Av Poeta Carlos Penha Filho, T 732-1137, best; *Mansão Verde; Fazenda Nova*.

Good roads via Caruaru or Palmares run to the city of *Garanhuns* (pop 113,470), 243 km SW of Recife. It claims to be the best holiday resort in the NE, partly because of its cool climate—it stands at 890 metres, and has an average temperature of 21°C—and partly because of its mineral waters and beautiful landscapes and parks.

Hotels A2 *Tavares Correia*, Av Rui Barbosa 296, T 761-0900, 4-star; **B** *Petrópolis*, Praça da Bandeira 129, T 761-0125. **Camping** *Camping Treze*, BR-432, Km 105.

Arcoverde (pop 54,150), about 126 km W of Caruaru (bus $2\frac{1}{2}$ hrs, US$3), is a market town in the Sertão, market every Sat, cool at night. Hotels: **C** *Grande Majestic*, Av Cel Japiassu 326, T 821-1175 (fair), with breakfast; **E** *Dormitório O Barão*, clean.

Triúnfo (pop 28,900), about 200 km W of Arcoverde via Serra Talhada, is a delightful small town in Serra de Borborema, good climate, with great variety of crops, flowers and fruits. There are also a sugar mill that can be visited (Engenho Boa Esperança), waterfalls, sounding rocks, the convent of São Boaventura, and the Museu do Cangaça, showing the lives and relics of the traditional bandits of the Nordeste. Stay at **B** *Pousada Baixa Verde*, nice rooms, good breakfast; **B** *Hospedaria Santa Terezinha* (Centro), abundant and good meals; **D** *Pousada Baixa Serote*, superb breakfast, friendly, highly rec. Two buses daily to and from Recife ($6\frac{1}{2}$ hrs).

Fernando de Noronha is a small archipelago 345 km off the NE coast. It was declared a Marine National Park in 1989 (T Parnamar 081-619-1210). Only one island is inhabited. It used to be an independent dependency under military control but is now part of the state of Pernambuco administered from Recife. The islands were discovered 1503 and were for a time a pirate lair. In 1738 the Portuguese built the Forte dos Remédios, later used as a prison in this century; remains still exist as well as a semi-deserted village nearby. Sea landing is difficult but an airport has been built. Three flights daily from Recife, four on Sat and Sun, some flights via Natal, on 13 and 17 seater planes by Nordeste, T 341-3187, 1 hr 40 mins. An entry fee of US$5 a day is payable at the airport. Many locals are now dependent on tourism and it can be difficult to find fish as the fishermen are busy taking tourists on boat trips. Most food is brought from the mainland and prices are about double. Repellent is not available for the many mosquitoes. The island, which is dominated by a 321-metre peak, has many unspoilt beaches, interesting wildlife and fishing; scuba-diving and snorkelling are excellent. It is now prohibited to swim with the dolphins but they can be seen from the beach.

The only hotel, **Pousada Esmeralda**, T 619-1355, is expensive and none too comfortable. Large a/c apartments at **Solar dos Ventos** (full board), have been rec, ask for "o capitanão". Overpriced packages from mainland travel agents usually place visitors in the *Esmeralda*. Beware of similar packages at lower prices in other "pousadas" because they turn out to be rooms in family homes. Aeroporto Turismo in Recife offers such "deals". Independent travellers can go much cheaper as many local families rent out rooms with full board, US$20 pp/day. The best known is that of Suzanna and Rocha, rooms with fan and bathroom, but they never refuse a reservation and farm people out to other families with much inferior levels of accommodation. Vanilda across the street has been highly recommended. Boat trips and jeep tours around the island are available; also possible to hire a jeep or beach buggy. You can hitch everywhere as everyone stops. Scuba-diving is organized by Aguas Claras (T 619-1225, US$50) in the hotel grounds, staff are regarded as entertaining but unqualified; 2 dives (with superannuated equipment). There is only one restaurant, called *Ilha Encantado*, near the hotel. Bars: *Bar da Vila* in the village of Remédios, only open in the daytime; *Bar Idade* on the Conceição beach, daytime only with loud rock music; *Mirante Bar*, near the hotel, with spectacular view over Boldró beach, has loud music and at night is an open-air disco and the only nightlife on the island. Take sufficient *reais* as dollars are heavily discounted. The time is one hour later than Brazilian Standard Time.

Paraíba and Rio Grande do Norte

It is a bus ride of 2 hrs through sugar plantations over a good road from Recife (126 km) to **João Pessoa** (pop 497,215, CEP 58000, DDD 083), capital of the State of Paraíba (pop 3,200,620), on the Rio Paraíba. Ocean-going ships load and unload at Cabedelo (see **Excursions**). The old monasteries are worth seeing, and the 18th century church of São Francisco is a beauty (open 0800-1700). At São Francisco is an excellent cultural centre with a magnificent collection of colonial and popular artefacts. This is also the best point to see the sun set over the forest. Other tourist points include the Casa da Pólvora, an old gunpowder store which has become the city museum; the city parks; and trips on the Rio Paraíba. Airport for internal services. See the booklet *Relíquias da Paraíba*, by Padre Antônio Barbosa.

Hotels L3 *Tropical Tambaú*, Av Alm Tamandaré 229, Tambaú, T 226-3660, F 226-2390, comfortable, good service, rec, though sometimes they pretend no standard rooms are available when they are. Also in Tambaú: **B** *Costa Bela Praia*, Av Négo 131, T 226 1570, rec, small; **B** *Sol-Mar*, Rui Carneiro 500, T 226-1350, F 226-3242, pool, superb restaurant, highly rec; **D** *Gameleira*, Av João Maurício 157, T 226-1576, good breakfast, dirty, noisy at night. Central hotels: **D** *Aurora*, Praça João Pessoa 51, T 241-3238. with a/c and bath, clean, friendly; **D** *Guarany*, R Almeida Barreto 181 e 13 de Maio, T 241-2161 (more with a/c and TV), clean, safe, friendly, rec as good value, good breakfast; **D** *Pedro Américo*, Praça Pedro Américo, 109, clean (no breakfast on Sun); cheap hotels near the old bus station, eg **E** *São Pedro*, R Irineu Pinto 231, clean, basic, friendly. **Youth hostels**, on Av das Trincheiras, at Palácio dos Esportes, T 221-7220/1, and R Bezerra Reis 82, T 226-5460/1988.

Restaurants Two good restaurants on Tambaú beach are *Adega do Alfredo* (Portuguese) and *Wan Li* (Chinese); *Pescador*, near Cabo Branco lighthouse; *Pavilhão do Chá*, pleasant, drinks, sandwiches, TV, open air, in centre.

Banks and Exchange Banco do Brasil, near Praça João Pessoa, 3rd floor, helpful.

Electric Current 220 volts AC, 60 cycles.

Shopping Crafts at Casa do Artesão, R Maciel Pinheiro near city bus station; very good new *Mercado de Artesanato* in Tambaú, almost opposite *Hotel Sol Mar*.

Telecommunications Embratel, R das Trincheiras 398.

Tourist Information In Tambaú shopping centre (helpful).

Tourist Agencies *Planetur*, Av Miguel Couto 5, Loja 12, and *Hotel Tropical*. *Agência de Viagens e Turismo Arnaldo von Sohsten*, R Gama e Melo 100.

Bus Station is 10 mins from centre; luggage store. To **Recife**, every 60 mins, US$3.60, 2 hrs. To **Natal**, every 2 hrs, US$4.75, 3 hrs; to **Fortaleza**, 4 daily, 16 hrs, US$15.25.

Excursions The principal beach and seaside resort is Tambaú, 7 km from João Pessoa, take a taxi or bus (No 510 "Tambaú" from outside the rodoviária, or "Lagoa" from city centre, alight at *Hotel Tropical*); excellent bathing. North of Tambaú is Manaira beach, but the section near *Hotel Tropical/Tambaú* is too polluted for bathing. Cabo Branco club on Tambaú beach, open to visitors: good food, beautiful views. 14 km S down the coast is the **Cabo Branco** lighthouse at Ponta do Seixas, the most easterly point of continental Brazil and South America; there is a panoramic view from the cliff top. The beaches below are palm-lined but oil-polluted. (Hotel: *Pousa das Águas*, Praia do Cabo Branco, T 226-5103/7268, seafront; youth hostel **Cabo Branco**, Av Pe-José Trigueiro 104, Praia de Cabo Branco, T 221-2903/226-6171). Take bus 507 "Cabo Branco" from outside the rodoviária, or "Lagoa" bus from centre and get out at last stop; hike up to the lighthouse. The Fundação José Américo de Almeida, halfway between Tambaú and Cabo Branco, on the esplanade, should be visited by those interested in modern literature and politics; it is in the former house of the novelist and sociologist. At **Cabedelo** (pop 28,925), 18 km by road or rail, are the impressive walls of the 17th-century fortress of Santa Catarina. If you take a Cabedelo bus and alight at Jacaré, about 12 km from João Pessoa, there is an excellent beach with food stalls at weekends. In Jacaré, where the yachts tie up, is a bar run by an Englishman.

Campina Grande (pop 326,155), the "Porta do Sertão", is 120 km from João Pessoa (bus 2 hrs), a rapidly growing centre for light industry and an outlet for goods from most of the NE. There is a museum of modern art, and another of the cotton industry. Most genial climate. Near Campina Grande is Lagoa Seca, where the local craft is the making of figures in wood and sacking.

Hotels *Rique Palace Hotel* (excellent) is on the top floors of the tallest building in town, Venâncio Neiva 287, T 341-1433: the restaurant is on the 11th floor. Other hotels: **B** *Ouro Branco*, João Lourenço Porto 20, T 341-2929, F 322-5788; **E** *Barborema*, near old bus station, friendly; **E** *Dormitório São Paulo*, also near bus station, cheap, clean. Many others near old bus station.

West of Campina Grande the main highway, still paved, leads on through *Patos* (pop 81,300, **E** *Hotel JK*) to Ipaumirim (Ceará). Here a left turn leads to the twin towns of *Crato* (pop 90,360) and *Juazeiro do Norte* (Ceará, pop 173,300), oases of green in the dry Sertão. Mosquitoes can be a problem at night.

Juazeiro do Norte is a small pilgrimage town; it was the home of Padre Cícero, one of the unofficial saints of the NE. A statue to him stands in the Logradouro do Horto, a park overlooking the town; either take the pilgrim trail up the hill or go by bus. **Hotels**: **C** *Panorama*, R Sto Agostinho 58, T 511-2399, F 511-2173, good value; **D** *Vieira*, corner of R São Pedro and R Santo Antônio, private bathroom and breakfast; and **D** *Municipal*, Praça P Cícero, T 511-2299, rec.

Many small fishing villages along the coast, often difficult to reach; one of the most popular is *Baía Formosa* in Rio Grande do Norte (daily bus from Natal, 2 1/2 hrs). No hotel; ask in town for accommodation in fishermen's houses, infinitely preferable to the overpriced accommodation at the *Miramar* bar.

Natal (pop 606,540, CEP 59000, DDD 084), capital of Rio Grande do Norte (pop 2,413,620), on the estuary of the Rio Potengi, is about 180 km to the N of João Pessoa. It is served by weekly coastal vessels and there is a railway S through the State of Paraíba to Recife and Maceió (only suburban passenger services). There is a large airport 13 km from the city (taxi US$12). The old part of the city is called **Cidade Alta**. The main square, the **Praça João Maria**, oblong in shape, has a traditional cathedral at one end and a fine modern bank building at the other. The city is centred on the Av Rio Branco. The church of **Santo Antônio**, R Santo Antônio in the centre, dates from 1766, and has a fine, carved wooden altar and a sacred art museum. The **Museu Câmara Cascudo**, Av Hermes de Fonseca 1440 (T 222-2860), has exhibits on archaeological digs, Umbanda rituals and the petroleum industry (open Tues-Fri, 0800-1100, 1400-1600, Sat 0800-1100, US$1.40). The **Forte dos Reis Magos** (16th-century) on the coast at Rocas is open Tues-Sun 0900-1700; between it and the city is a military installation. It is possible to walk along the beach to the fort, or to go in a tour, or by taxi; it is worth it for the views (entry US$1.40). The **Marine Research Institute** at the Praia da Areia Preta can be visited; bus marked "Areia Preta" from Av Rio Branco. Good local craftware Sat at **Mercado do Alecrim**, along R Quaresma near R Gonçalves. At Mãe Luiza is a lighthouse with beautiful views of Natal and surrounding beaches (take city bus marked Mãe Luiza; get key from the house next door). In mid-Oct there is a country show, Festa do Boi, bus marked Parnamirim to the exhibition centre, it gives a good insight into rural life. Mid-Dec sees *Carnatal*, a lively 4-day music festival with dancing in the streets. Dance is an important pastime in Natal. The **Casa da Música Popular Brasileira** has dancing on Fri and Sat night and Sun from 1700, very popular. Daily shows also at *Mandacaru*, Av do Jiquí 21, Neopolis, T 217-3008 (US$8) and *Zás-Trás*, R Apodi 500, Tirol, T 222-6589; many other enjoyable venues where visitors are encouraged to join in.

Hotels *Marsol Natal*, Via Costeira 1567, Km 7, Parque das Dunas, T/F 221-2619, 3-star; Via Costeira is a good place to stay, but hotels mostly in **A1-A3** range: eg *Barreira Roxa Praia*, T/F 222-1093, clean, helpful, good; *Imirá Plaza*, Costeira 4077, T 211-4105, F 211-5722, on beach, pool, tennis, rec; **B** *Oásis*, R Joaquim Fabrício 291, Casa 08, Petrópolis, T 221-3570, F 221-5699, Swiss-owned, pool, massive breakfasts, exceptional value; **B** *Praia do Sol*, Av Pres Café Filho 750, Praia do Meio, T/F 211-4562, opp beach, renovated, clean, quiet, a/c, TV, friendly, rec; **B** *Samburá*, R Prof Zuza 263, T 221-0611, rec; **E** *Fenícia*, Av Rio Branco 586, T 222-1366 (more with a/c), with breakfast and shower, friendly, English spoken; **D** *Beira Mar*, Av Pres Café Filho, Praia dos Artistas, T 222-4256, on the beach front, with breakfast, but no a/c, small, good value, popular; **D** *Pousada Marina*, at No 860, T 222-0678, a/c, TV, fridge, "lovely"; **D** *Farol*, Av Gouv Silvio Pedrosa 174 (on beach), T 222-4661, with a/c; **D** *Le Bateau*, Praia de Areia Preta, on beach front, clean, helpful, good breakfast, English and French spoken. **E** *Casa Grande*, R Princesa Isabel 529, T 222-1513, with a/c, F without bath, good breakfast, pleasant, excellent value; **E** *Flat*, R 31 de Março, Morro de Careca, T 219 2541, breakfast, fridges in rooms, fans, hot showers and a nice garden, warmly rec; **E** *Natal*, Av Mar Floriano Peixoto 104, clean, English spoken; *Bom Jesús*, Av Rio Branco 384, good value, popular; **E** *Pousada Bejo Tropical*, R Valentim de Almeida 10, T 221-5361, clean, helpful, warmly rec; **E** *Pousada Esquina de Mar*, Av Roberto Freire, T 236-2843, rec, baths, pool, breakfast, meals available; **E** *Pousada Zur Kurve*, Avenida Silvio Pedrosa 97, good breakfast, clean, safe, rec. *Praia dos Artistas* on beach, clean, helpful, good breakfast, rec; *Papa Jerimum*, R Rodrigues Dias 445, Praia do Meio, English spoken, rec. *Pousadas* at Ponta Negra and Genipabu beaches, see **Beaches**. **Youth hostels** *Lua Cheia*, Av Estrela do Mar 2215, Conj Algamar, Ponta Negra, T 236-3696; *Verdes Mares*, R das Algas 2166, Conj Algamar, T 236-2872; *Ladeiro do Sol*, R Valentin de Almeida 10, Praia dos Artistas, T 221-5361. Head office of Associação Potiguar de Albergues da Juventude, Av Deodoro 249, Petrópolis, T 221-3751, open 1300-1730.

Camping on the Praia do Forte beach, near the Forte dos Reis Magos, not rec because unsafe. Camping Clube do Brasil site at Sítio do Jiqui, expensive. Vale das Cascatas, Ponta Negra beach, swimming pool, leisure facilities, US$4 pp.

Restaurants *Casa de Mãe*, R Pedro Afonso 153 (Petrópolis), regional food, rec; *Bom Demais*,

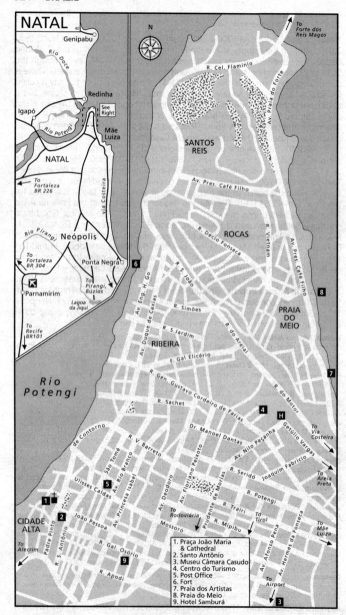

NATAL

40

Genipabu

Rio Doce

Redinha

Igapó

Rio Potengi

See Right

Mãe Luiza

NATAL

To Fortaleza BR 226

Rio Pirangi

Neópolis

To Fortaleza BR 304

Ponta Negra

Parnamirim

To Pirangi, Búzios

To Recife BR101

Lagoa da Jiqui

N

Rio Potengi

R. Cel. Flaminio

Av. Praia do Forte

To Forte dos Reis Magos

SANTOS REIS

Av. Pres. Café Filho

R. Décio Fonseca

R. Vietnam

ROCAS

Av. Pres. Café Filho

Av. Eng. H. Go

R. S. João

R. Simões

R. S. Jardim

RIBEIRA

F. Gal Elicério

R. Gen. Gustavo Cordeiro de Farias

R. Sachet

Av. Duque de Caxias

R. do Areial

R. do Motor

PRAIA DO MEIO

Dr. Manoel Dantas

de Contorno

R. V. Barreto

São Tomé

Av. Rio Branco

Ulisses Caldas

Av. Princesa Isabel

Padre Pinto

R. S. Antônio

João Pessoa

R. Gal. Osório

R. Apodi

CIDADE ALTA

To Alecrim

Av. Floriano Peixoto

Av. Deodoro

Mossoró

Prudente de Morais

R. Traíri

R. Mipibu

To Rodoviária

Av. Nilo Peçanha

R. Seridó

R. Potengi

Joaquim Fabrício

Getúlio Vargas

To Via Costeira

To Areia Preta

To Tirol

Av. Afonso Pena

Av. Hermes da Fonseca

To Mãe Luiza

To Airport

1. Praça João Maria & Cathedral
2. Santo Antônio
3. Museu Câmara Casudo
4. Centro do Turismo
5. Post Office
6. Fort
7. Praia dos Artistas
8. Praia do Meio
9. Hotel Samburá

R Princesa Isabel No 717-C, cheap, good; same street, *Casa Grande*, good value; *Pietro's*, Av Marechal Deodoro, opp cathedral, cheap, good; *Raizes*, Av Campos Sales, with C Mossoró, good regional dishes; *Thin-San*, Av Hermes da Fonseca 890, Tirol, Chinese, quite good, not expensive; *Farol Rest-e bar*, Avenida Silvio Pedrosa, cheap, huge helpings. Vegetarian (with shops): *Amai*, General Varela 624, and *A Macrobiótica*, Princesa Isabel 524. Good, inexpensive lanchonetes on R Judas Tadéu, just off Rio Branco. For snacks try the stalls on Praia do Meio, there are also various restaurants along the beach road nearby, where itinerant musicians play. Try the restaurants on the point that separates Praias dos Artistas and da Areia Preta (eg *Calamar*), *Chaplin*, Av Pres Café Filho 27 (Praia dos Artistas), very good seafood, sociable.

Banks and Exchange   Cash advances against Visa card at **Banco do Brasil**, Av Rio Branco 510.

Electric Current   220 volts AC, 60 cycles.

Telecommunications   Embratel, Av Duque de Caxias 99, T 221-2209. International phone calls, Telern, R João Pessoa e Princesa Isabel.

Tourist Information   Centro de Turismo (a converted prison with wide variety of handicraft shops), R Aderbal de Figueiredo s/n, off R General Cordeiro, Petrópolis (only Portuguese spoken, poor information); Rodoviária and Aeroporto Augusto Severo.

Airport   Augusto Severo, 15 km from centre; flights to Belém, Brasília, Cuiabá, Fernando de Noronha, Fortaleza, Manaus, Recife, Rio, Salvador, São Paulo and other cities. Bus every 1/2-hr from old bus station near centre US$0.65, taxi US$15.

Bus   (terminal, with luggage store, is about 6 km out of town, bus "Cidade de Esperança Av 9", "Areia Preta via Petrópolis" or "Via Tirol" to centre); to **Recife**, 4 hrs, US$9.25; to **Fortaleza**, 5 hrs, US$9; to **Maceió**, buses go either direct, or via Recife, 4-6 hrs; to **João Pessoa**, US$4.75, 3 hrs.

Excursion   At *Pirangi*, 25 km S, or 30 mins by bus from new rodoviária, is the world's largest cashew-nut tree (*cajueiro*); branches springing from a single trunk cover an area of some 7,300 square metres. From Natal (Viação Campos), US$0.60, 5 times a day from 0630 to 1815, 3 on Sun, 0730, 0930, 1645; the snack bar by the tree has schedules of buses back to Natal. A number of good beaches and attractive villages may be found along this coast. North of Natal are extensive cashew plantations.

Beaches   Natal has excellent beaches: *Ponta Negra*: many hotels: **C** *Maria Bonita 2*, T 236-2941, rec; *Caminho do Mar*, nr Ponta Negra beach, clean, very friendly (R Des HH Gomes 365, T 219-3363); **C** *Ponta Negra*, R Des João V da Costa 8896, T 219-3264, pool, friendly, rec; **C** *Pousada do Mar*, T 236-2509, pool; *Miramar* (Av da Praia 3398, T 236-2079), *Bella Napoli* (Av da Praia 3188, T 219-2666). Also restaurants. It is 20 mins by bus from centre; pleasant and "quaint" atmosphere (not safe to wander alone on the dunes as there are robberies). Some beaches are on the far side of the Potengi river, for example Redinha and *Genipabu*—where you can toboggan down the sand-dunes—reached by direct bus from old Rodoviária, last bus back from Genipabu at 1830. **NB** Muggings have been reported in Genipabu. (**D** *Hotel Aldeia*, caixa postal 274, T (084) 225-2011, has five luxury bungalows and a restaurant, double room around $50; **D** *Hotel Genipabu*, 2 km from beach, marvellous views, isolated; **D** *Mar-Azul*, T 225-2065; **E** *Pousada Ponta Alberta*, on beach, good breakfast), few people are there from Jun-Oct. You can hire buggies to drive on the dunes for US$30 a day, or by the hour, these are making the most popular beaches very noisy. More beautiful beaches to the S: Pirangi, Tabatinga, *Búzios* (**C** *Hotel Balneário Rio Doce*, pool, games, highly rec; *pousadas* and bars at all beaches; **C** *Pousada da Lagosta*, rec). Litoral Sul bus from rodoviária follows coastline, US$1. The friendly village of *Pipa* lies 80 km S of Natal, with lovely beaches and several pousadas (try **F** *Pousada do Pipa*, French-owned; **F** *Tropical*). Hotels arrange transport to the stunning bay N of the village, visited most mornings by dolphins. Reached by the Natal-Goianinha bus.

The state of Rio Grande do Norte (whose people are called "Potiguares" after an Indian tribe that now resides at Jacaré de São Domingos, municipality of Rio Tinto in neighbouring Paraíba state) has three main paved roads radiating from Natal: S to São João Pessoa and Recife, SW to Caicó and W to Mossoró and Fortaleza. Between *Caicó* (pop 50,660, **D** *Hotel Guanabara*, rec) and *Mossoró* (pop 191,960)— (**A3** *Hotel Termas*, comfortable, with a hot, mineral water pool system, each pool on a terrace, with temperatures ranging from 54°C at the top to 30°C at the bottom; **D** *Hotel Grand*, *Hotel Pax* next to market; **D** *Hotel Zenilândia*, highly rec) there is a turning to *Patu* with its huge basilica on a hillside, with passable "hotels", rather primitive. From Mossoró you can visit the salt pans at Grossos on the coast, but get written permission from the administrative offices in Mossoró. Bus Mossoró-Aracati at 0800 with Emp Nordeste, 2 hrs, US$2.

Ceará and Piauí

From Mossoró the main road, BR304, enters Ceará and continues about 50 km to **Aracati**, pop 60,710 (**E** *Hotel Litorânea*, clean, nr Rodoviária: bus from Natal via Mossoró, 6 hrs, US$9; São Benedito bus 11 a day from Fortaleza 174 km, US$3.50).

From this town take a VW Combi-Bus to **Canoa Quebrada** (US$1, from corner of Gen Pompeu e Tableau João Paulo—taxi US$6), a fishing village on a sand dune, 10 km from Aracati. The village is famous for its *labirinto* lacework and coloured sand sculpture, for sand-skiing on the dunes, for the sunsets, and for the beaches, though beware of jiggers (*bicho de pé*), best to wear shoes. Canoa Quebrada has been "discovered" and is becoming rather busy and dirty; basic tours (no food) from Fortaleza, 12 hrs, US$18.

Accommodation and Services **D** *Pousada Alternativa*, with or without bath, central, clean, rec; **D** *Pousada Cultural*, basic, clean, friendly; **D** *Pousada Ma Alice*, clean, safe, friendly; **D** *Pousada do Rei*, highly rec; **D** *Lua Morena*, chalets; 2 rm **E** behind *Sol de Manhã* café on mainstreet, clean, with shower, good breakfast in the café; **D** *Tenda do Cumbe*, at end of road on cliff, thatched huts, restaurant, warmly rec; also on cliff above beach, **D** *Pousada Ao Nascer do Sol*, clean, shower, friendly, hammocks for rent; villagers will let you sling your hammock or put you up for about US$2 (Brendan is rec, but his food is expensive, European books exchanged; Sr Miguel rents good clean houses for US$10 a day). **Youth hostel** *Lua Estrela*, T 421-1401, restaurant and café. Bars and restaurants, vegetarian food in *Espácio Cultural*, cheap seafood (don't drink the water); only a few places have running water. Nowhere to change money except Banco do Brasil in Aracati.

Beyond Canao Quebrada is **Majorlândia**, reached by paved road from the main highway (bus from Fortaleza, 4 a day, US$5). A very nice village, with many-coloured sand dunes (used in bottle pictures) and a beach; the arrival of the fishing fleet in the evening is an important daily event. Food and lodging: **D** *Apartamento Beira Mar*, on beach; **C** *Pousada Dunas Praia*; **D** *Pousada do Gaúcho*; **E** *Pousada e Restaurante Reouinte*, 100m before beach on main road, clean, airy rooms, friendly, use of kitchen, rooms with or without bath, rec. 4-5 km S along the beach is the village of Camo.

87 km from Fortaleza (too far for a day trip) is **Morro Branco** (4 km from Beberibe— bus from Aracati, 2 hrs), with spectacular beach, craggy cliffs and beautiful views. *Jangadas* leave the beach at 0500, returning at 1400-1500; hotel-restaurants; **D** *Cabana do Morro*, *Pousada do Morro*, clean, but mosquitoes, fan and shower, **D** *Novo*, clean, noisy at weekends and **C** *Recanto Praia*, clean, good breakfast, rec (first two have swimming pool); **D** *Pousada Sereia*, on the beach, clean, good breakfast, friendly, highly rec; **F** *Rosalias's*, with use of kitchen, 50 metres from bus stop, strongly rec; or you can rent fishermen's houses; meals can also be arranged at beach-front bars (try *O Jangadeiro*). Double room for rent at **F** *Bar São Francisco*, or 7-rm house for rent. Beach buggies and taxi for hire, Marrambaia can be visited, some accommodation. São Benedito bus from Fortaleza, US$2; 2½ hrs, 4 a day. To get to Natal, take 0600 bus to Beberibe, then 0800 bus (only one) to Aracati, US$1, then on to Natal. Town is very crowded at holiday time. No money exchange available.

Caponga beach, further up the coast, is reached by direct bus from Fortaleza (2 a day) or by taking a bus from Fortaleza to Cascavel (80 mins, US$1.50) then a bus from Cascavel (20 mins, US$0.45); accommodation at *Caponga Praia*, on the beach front, simple rooms and good meals, **D** *Mon Kapitan*, on the square, very helpful, good restaurant, and at **C** *Pousada Sereia*, very friendly, good. A ½-hr walk S along the deserted white-sand beach leads to a river mouth, offering a combination of fresh-and salt-water bathing. *Jangadas* set sail in the early morning (arrangements can be made to accompany fishermen on overnight trips); there is a fish market on the beach. Weekend houses now being built here.

40 km before Fortaleza, along the coast, is **Prainha**, a fishing village and weekend resort near the town of Aquiraz (bus terminal in Fortaleza opp Escola Normal at 1430 and 1700, return 1530 and 1800). You can see *jangadas* coming in daily in the late afternoon. The beaches are clean and largely empty. **C** *Prainha Solex Hotel*, R Pericich Ribeiro 5, T 361-1000/01/02, ramal 156.7, pool, comfortable; also **C**, the *pousada*, near rodoviária, no name and no breakfast, owner lives on beach, noisy but clean. Good fish restaurant, *O Leonção*, on same street. There are several small, cheap and good restaurants, where it is possible to see displays of the Carimbó, one of the N Brazilian dances.

Fortaleza (pop 1,758,335, CEP 60000, DDD 085), capital of the State of Ceará, is about 520 km from Natal, NW along the coast (population of Ceará state

6,353,345). It is 1,600 km by road from Belém and 885 km from Recife. There are fair dirt roads throughout the State, and paved roads W to São Luís and SE to Recife; the federal highway S to Salvador (BR-116) is now largely paved but much is in poor condition.

A fine tourist centre in the old prison on the waterfront (Av Senador Pompeu 350) includes the **Museu de Arte e Cultura Popular** (open Mon-Fri, 0700-1800, Sat-Sun 0800-1200, most interesting), shops and restaurants. Other museums: **Museu Histórico e Antropológico do Ceará**, Av Barão de Studart 410 (open Mon-Fri, 0800-1200, 1400-1800; take bus marked "Dom Luís"); **Museu de Minerais**, R Monsenhor Tabosa 777 (open Mon-Fri, 0800-1200, 1400-1800). **Museu das Secas**, Pedro Pereira 683, Mon-Fri, 0800-1100, 1400-1700, collections of photographs and anti-drought equipment. Also visit **Forte Nossa Senhora da Assunção**, originally built by the Dutch. The mausoleum of President Castello Branco (1964-67), next to the state government building, may be visited. The new cathedral, in gothic style but built in concrete, stands opposite the **Mercado Central**, open 0600-1000; it has beautiful stained glass windows.

The local dance, forró, can be experienced at the *Clube dos Vaqueiros* out on the BR-116 road S, Wed 2230; or at *Viva Maria*, Vieira e Estados Unidos, Sat at 2200 (check by phone first).

Local Holidays 6 Jan (Epiphany); Ash Wed; 19 Mar (São José); Christmas Eve; New Year's Eve, half-day.

A festival takes place on the last Sun in Jul, during which the traditional *jangada* (raft) races take place. On 15 Aug, the local Umbanda *terreiros* (churches) celebrate the Festival of Iemanjá on Praia do Futuro, taking over the entire beach from noon till dusk, when offerings are cast into the surf. Well worth attending (members of the public may "pegar um passo"— enter into an inspired religious trance—at the hands of a *pai-de-santo*). Beware of pick-pockets and purse-snatchers.

NB At night the centre of town is dead, but by day it is very busy with vendors and crowds. Still, it is not over-agitated. Crime is reported to be on the increase in this previously safe city but there is a large police presence, except in the centre at night.

NB The road which runs along the sea front (Av Pres Kennedy) is often known as Av Beira Mar. Many new hotels and apartment blocks have been built along this stretch.

Hotels *L2 Marina Park*, Av Pres C Branco 400, T 252-5253, F 253-1803, huge new luxury leisure complex with all facilities, modern mooring for yachts at reasonable prices, day rates available for non-residents, strongly rec; *L2 Esplanada Praia*, Av Presidente Kennedy 2000, T/F 224-8555; *L3 Beira Mar*, on Meireles beach, Av Pres Kennedy, T 244-9444, F 261-5659, swimming pool; *L3 Colonial Praia*, 4-star (Best Western), R Barão de Aracati 145, T 211-9644, F 252-3501, pleasant grounds and big pool, laundry service (10 mins walk from Av Kennedy); *L3 Novotel*, Av Pres Kennedy 2380, T 244-9122, F 261-2793; *A1 Othon Palace*, 5-star, Av Pres Kennedy 2500, T 244-9177, F 224-7777, beach front location; *Nordeste Palace*, R Assunção 99 in centre, T 221-1999, large rooms, friendly, good value; *A2 Pousada Jardim*, run by Sr Abelardo Bezerra at Ildefonso Albano 950, no sign outside (T 231-7991) in Aldeota district, by Iracema beach, very clean, friendly, nice garden, excursions arranged, many languages spoken, warmly rec, 20% discount to *South American Handbook* users; another on same street, No 644, E, clean and friendly (T 226-9206); *A2 Samburá Praia*, Av Pres Kennedy 4530, T 263-1999, F 263-2177, cheaper than most beach hotels, friendly; *B Pousada d'Antonietta*, Carlos Vasconcelos 660, T 224-3454, clean, quiet, 5 mins from beach, buses to centre and other beaches nearby, with bath; *B Cabana Praia II*, at R João Lourenço 441 (T261-1399) and No I at Av Rui Barbosa 555, T 261-4954, both small, friendly; *B Caxambu*, General Bezerril 22 (T 231-0339), a/c, with breakfast, and bath, clean, but poor food, central (opp Cathedral, in market area); *B Paraíso da Praia*, R dos Pacajus 109, Iracema, small, on beach, helpful and friendly, good *trattoria* next door; *B Pousada da Praia*, Av Mons Tabosa 1315, Iracema, 2 blocks from beach, best rooms on 2nd and 3rd floors, a/c, clean, friendly, also cheaper rooms, fan, rec, buses to centre stop at door; *B Apart-hotel Aquidabá*, Av Raimundo Girão (was Aquidabá) 630, T 226-1405, at beginning of Praia Iracema, 20 mins' walk from centre, with bath, pool and bar, clean, quiet; *C Amuarama*, T 227-4744, pool, sauna, by rodoviária (6 km from centre), entrance by service station; *C Ondas Verdes*, Av Pres Kennedy 934, T 226-0871, fan, TV, shower, clean, rec; *C Passeio*, R Dr João Moreira 221, with bath, fan, good breakfast, safe, storage, good value; *C Pousada Central*, Av Dom Manuel,

FORTALEZA

N

Hotels:
21. Esplanada Praia
22. Imperial Othon Palace
23. Colonial Praia
24. Novotel
25. Nordeste Palace
26. Cabana Praia
27. Ondas Verdes
28. Cabana Praia
29. Pousada da Praia
30. Zen Praia
31. Nossa Pousada
32. Chevalier

Praças:
1. Castro Carreiro
2. Passeio Público
3. Ferreira
4. Coração de Jesus
5. Carmo
6. Figueira de Melo
7. Bandeira
8. Portugal
9. Cathedral
10. Museu Histórico e Antropológico
11. Teatro José de Alencar
12. Centro de Turismo, Museu de Arte e Cultura Popular & Tourist Office
13. Forte Nossa Senhora da Assunção
14. Palácio do Governo
15. Mausoléu ou Castelo Branco
16. Palácio Municipal
17. Central Market
18. Centro de Artesanato Luiza Távora
19. Post Office
20. Telecearà telephone office

Praia de Meireles

Praia dos Diários

Praia do Ideal

Praia de Iracema

Praia Formosa

Praia do Futuro

Pres. Kennedy
Antônio Justa Abolição
Silva Jatai
Oswaldo Cruz
Pereira Valente
Vis. de Mauá
Moreira
Ana Bilhar
Canuto de Aguiar
Joaquim Nabuco
Dom Luiz
Marcos M.
Maria Tomásia
Macedo
Nunes Valente
Tibúrcio Cavalcante
Av. Santos Dumont
R. Desembargador
Costa Barros
Torres Câmara
José Vilar
Silva Paulet
Av. Barão de Studart
Dr. José Lourenço
Av. Rui Barbosa
Monsenhor Bruno
Carlos Vasconcelos
Barão de Aracati
Fluza de Pontes
J. Carvalho
Eduardo Salgado
República do Líbano
Thomaz Pompeu
Antonele Bezerra
Monsenhor Tabosa
Av. Raimundo Girão
Deputado Moreira da Rocha
Tenente Benévolo
Pereira Filgueiras
Ildefonso Albano
Augusto
Pe. Climério
Gonçalves Ledo
Noguèira Acioly
Dom Joaquim
Dona Leopoldina
Rodrigues Júnior
Antônio
R. João Cordeiro
J. Alves
José Avelino
Dragão de Mar
Poço da Draga
Pessoa Anta
Monsenhor Tabosa
Boris
dos Tabajaras
Alm. Barroso
Tamandaré
Pres. Castelo Branco
Adolfo Caminha
Gen. Sampaio
24 de Maio
Senador Pompeu
R. Senador Pompeu
Castro e Silva
Floriano Peixoto
Barão do Rio Branco
Rufino de Alencar
Av. A. Nepomuceno
Baturité
Gov
Borges
Sampaio
Sena Madureira
Vic. de Sabóia
Franklin Távora
Pinto Madeira
Av. Santos Dumont
de Março
Dom Manuel
Manuel
Rio Branco
Sólon Pinheiro
Clarindo de Queiroz
Liberato Barroso
Pedro Pereira
Pedro Primeiro
Antônio Pompeu
BR 116 to the South & to East Coast
Rodoviária & Airport
Br 222, to the West
To Praia do Futuro

near Costa Barrios, T 252-5040, good value; **C** *Pousada Village Mar e Sol*, R Idelfonso Albano 614, Praia Iracema, T 252-3206, with or without bath, friendly, rec; **D** *Chevalier*, Av Duque de Caxias 465, T 231-4611, with bath and fan, pleasant; **D** *Pousada Vida da Praia*, José Vilar 252, T 244-6444, in Aldeota district, clean, safe, helpful, English spoken; **D** *Pousada Osvaldo Cruz*, R Osvaldo Cruz, rec; **E** *Pousada Abril em Portugal*, Av Almirante Barroso 1006, with bath, breakfast, fan, good value, rec; **D** *Pousada Tropicália*, No 617, T 244-4019, laundry, kitchen, English-run, rec.

On Av Abolçião, Meireles, **C** *Zen Praia*, No 1894, clean, friendly, rec; **D** *Nossa Pousada*, No 2600, T 261-4699, without bath, near beach, friendly, helpful; **C** *Pousada Aoncheo Da Praia*, Xavier de Castro 50, rec, will pick you up if you call from rodoviária.

Several hotels along R Senador Pompeu, eg **D** *Universo*, at No 1152, without breakfast, clean, friendly, may rent by the bed (ie single sex clients 3 to a room), smokers unwelcome, some rooms have mosquito nets. Try student houses on Av Universitários, cheap or even free. **Youth Hostel** *Albergue Praia de Iracema*, Av Al Barroso 998, T 252-3267, US$12 for members, US$20 for non-members, use of kitchen and laundry, clean, helpful, good location; another at R Rocha Lima 1186, Aldeota, T 244-1850.

Camping Official site about 10 km S of city, 2 kms along a bumpy road off the highway, signposted, expensive US$4.50 pp.

Restaurants Several good fish restaurants at far end of Av Presidente Kennedy, where the boats come ashore between 1300 and 1500, for example, *Trapiche*, No 3956 (seafood, expensive, but excellent except for wine list). At Praia de Iracema, a collection of cafés on the beach serve good fast food and great coffee; on Av Kennedy *Alfredo* (good fish) and, next door, *Peixada do Meio* (better). Italian are *La Trattoria*, Praia de Iracema between Tabajaras and Av Kennedy, *Sandras*, Av Eng Luis Vieirra 555, Praia do Futuro, lobster has been specially rec, as has *Francés-Italiano*, Av Desem Moreira 155. *Churrascaria Tourão*, Av Mons Tabosa 825, all you can eat at fair prices. Good restaurant in Clube Náutico. A short taxi ride from Clube Náutico is *O Ozias*, R Canuto de Aguiar 1449 (T 224-9067), good for seafood, but hard to find. Good Chinese: *HongKong*, Av Pres Kennedy 4544, Mucuripe. Vegetarian: *Alivita*, Barão do Rio Branco 1486, good, has fish, lunch only, Mon-Fri; *Céu da Boca*, R Franklin Távora 136, lunch and 1800-2000 Mon-Fri, good and inexpensive; *Fonte de Saúde*, R Pedroi 339, excellent vegetarian food, sold by weight, and a wide range of fruit juices; *Kury*, R Senador Pompeu 959, good food at reasonable prices; opp is a good Chinese restaurant. Another good place in centre is *Belas Artes*, Major Facundo 82, just up from Passeio Público. Cheap meals at railway station. Emcetur restaurant, *Xadrez*, in old prison, good atmosphere, open to 2400, reported safe to 2100. Good view of Fortaleza from *Restaurant Panorámico*, R Mirante, in Mucuripe district, near the lighthouse. At *Pirata* club, Praia de Iracema, forró is danced. Many good bars and clubs along the beach. *El Mirante*, on a hill with spectacular views has many lively bars and restaurants, accessible by car or taxi.

Banks and Exchange Banco do Nordeste, Major Facundo 372, a/c, helpful, rec; and other national banks; **Banorte** gives good rates. Open 0900-1630. **Mastercard**, cash against card, Av Dom Luiz 880, Aldesta. **Banco Económico**, R Major Facundo 322, T 211-1834, sells TCs on Amex card; TCs exchanged and cash with Visa at **Banco do Brasil**, R Barão do Rio Branco 1500. Exchange at **Tropical Viagens**, R Barão do Rio Branco 1233, English spoken, **Libratur**, Av Abolição 2794, rec; **Ari**, Sapataria Brasileira, R Gen Bezerril 259, or at the **Zely** shop in the old prison.

Electric Current 220 volts AC, 60 cycles.

Consulate Danish, Av da Nações 26, CP 07-0484, 70416, T 242-8188, open 0900-1200, 1400-1700.

Theatre Teatro José de Alencar, near railway station in centre, built 1810, building contains also newer theatre built 1910.

Health R Vincente Leite 631, English-speaking doctor.

Post Office Praça Ferreira in centre. Parcels must be taken to Receita Federal office at Barão de Aracati 909, Aldeota (take "Dom Luiz" bus).

Telephone International calls from Emcetur hut on Iracema beach and from Teleceará offices (R João Moreira esq R Floriano Peixoto). **Telecommunications** Embratel, Av Pontes Vieira 1554.

Shopping Fortaleza has an excellent selection of textiles at reasonable prices (among the cheapest in Brazil) and some handicrafts. The local specialities are lace (some hand-made) and embroidered textile goods; also hammocks (US$3-20), fine alto-relievo wood carvings of NE scenes, basket ware and clay figures (*bonecas de barro*). Bargaining is OK at the **Mercado**

Central in the Praça da Sé, and the **Emcetur tourist market** in the old prison (more expensive). The *SINE* shop, at R Dr João Moreira 429, is part of a state government initiative to promote small independent producers, high quality traditional handicrafts at reasonable prices. Every night (1800-2300), there are stalls along Av Pres Kennedy (the beach), lively, fair prices. The **Centro de Artesanato Luiza Távora**, Av Santos Dumont 1589, has been rebuilt and is worth a visit. Boutiques along Monsenhor Tabosa between Senador Almino and João Cordeiro. Cashew nuts at the Mercado Central are excellent.

Golf The Ceará Golf Club has 9 holes.

Tourist Agencies *Hippopotamus Turismo*, Prai de Iracema, tour to Jericoacoara rec, as is the tour by *Ondas Verdes pousada* (US$90). Advised that, in other cases, it is best to book beach trips through Emcetur.

Tourist Information Emcetur, in ex-municipal prison, helpful, has maps (sometimes). Open 0700-1800, Sun 0700-1200. Also at Praça Ferreira and on Iracema beach.

Car Hire Beach buggies rentable from **Junna's Buggy**, Av Abolição 2480, T 244-7872.

Air Service Direct flights to Belém, Recife, Rio and other cities in Brazil; international flights: Miami, Rome, Milan (Varig), Vienna (Trans Brazil), all once a week. Bus 404 from airport to Praça José de Alencar, taxis US$5. The airport is near the rodoviária.

Rail South to Baturité (tourist train round trip Sun).

Bus Service New rodoviária 6 km from centre, bus from Av Grl Sampaio marked Aguanambi 1 or 2, or Bairra de Fátima-Rodoviária bus from Praça Coração de Jesus, US$0.35 (and others); no luggage store, only lockers. The Expresso de Luxo runs daily to **Recife** (12 hrs, US$22, leave at night), book early for weekend travel; also **Rio de Janeiro**, 48 hrs, US$86 (*leito* 110), **São Paulo**, 48 hrs, US$88 (*leito* 176); **Salvador**, daily 0900, US$40, and many other cities. **Belém** US$42, 5 buses a day, 23 hrs (2 companies, Exp Timbira good: also sells Belém-Manaus boat tickets). Piripiri, for Parque Nacional de Sete Cidades, US$9.50, 9 hrs, a good stop en route to Belém.

To hitch to Teresina, take a bus W to the BR-222, the Teresina road.

Beaches are fine (take bus marked "P Futuro" from Praça Castro Carreira, "Praia Circular" bus which does a circular route to Praia Futuro, or bus marked "Caça e Pesca", which passes all SE beaches on its route), and you can watch the boats coming in before sundown with their catch. The majority of high class hotels are on the beach from Praia de Iracema (which is the most popular beach, though now unsuitable for swimming; in the evenings everyone promenades along this beach). Other beaches not suitable for bathing are Diarios, Meireles, Volta da Jurema and Mucuripe all to the SE. Praia do Futuro is 8 km to the SE (no shade). Iguape beach is recommended, but is at end of 90 min bus ride—São Benedito bus marked "Iguape" from Praça F de Melo (trips on *jangadas* for US$8.50). Northwest of the centre is Praia Barra do Ceará, 8 km, where the Ceará river flows into the sea. Praia de Icaraí 22 km to the NW is under development. Beyond Icaraí, 12 km, is Cumbuco, a lively beach with good swimming, bars, buggies, horse riding, dunes, palm trees; *Teto do Praia*, cooking facilities, on beach, *jardineira* bus from Av Pres Kennedy and other points in Fortaleza, US$1.40.

Two hours NW of Fortaleza by bus is **Paracuru**, a small fishing port (fish readily available), pop 20,940, which is being developed as Ceará's carnival city (restaurant *Ronco do Mar*, good fish dishes, also *Balança do Mar* and a pizzaria; breakfast at Dona Luci's *sítio*, No 25 in the market; *Boca do Poço* bar is scene of *forró* at weekends). It has some lovely deserted white sand beaches with good bathing, and the people are very friendly. Some 7 hrs from Fortaleza, passing lovely Lagoinha and Fleixeras beaches, is the sleepy fishing village of *Almofala*, served by many buses. There is electricity, but no hotels or restaurants, although locals rent hammock space and cook meals. Bathing is better elsewhere, but the area is surrounded by dunes and is excellent for hiking along the coast to explore beaches and lobster-fishing communities. In Almofala, the church with much of the town was covered by shifting sands and remained covered for 50 years, reappearing in the 1940s.

Nestled in the dunes near the border with the state of Piauí is the fishing community of *Jericoacoara* (known as Serrote by locals). It is becoming increasingly popular with travellers and Brazilians, crowded Jan to Mar. It is now accessible by bus. The visitor is rewarded with towering sand dunes, deserted beaches with little shade, cactus-covered cliffs rising from the sea, and a chance to savour village life, although it is becoming ever more geared to tourism. Pigs, chickens and donkeys roam the streets at will; electricity depends on generators. Ice-cold beer is available in several tiny lantern-lit bars and there is forró nightly.

Hotels A2 *Papagaio*, is said to be the best (has organized tours); **A2** *Hippopotamus*, with pool; **A3** *Matusa*, pool and bar; **B** *Isalana*, R São Francisco, light and shower. On R do Forró: **C** *Acuara*, by beach, gas lamps; **C** *Isabel*, light and shower, rec; **E** *Estrela do Mar*, light and shower, no breakfast; **E** *Pousada Parahiso*, friendly, clean; on R São Francisco, **F** *Dona Belinha*, the oldest *pousada*, very basic; **F** *Natur*, basic, hammocks, friendly. Other rec *pousadas* **F** *São Francisco*; **F** *do Coqueiro*; **O** *Alemão*. Many locals rent hammock space, hammocks, and cook food.

There are several **restaurants** serving vegetarian and fish dishes: *Laricau*; *Acuara do Jèrico*, reasonable; for *pratos feitos* try *As Paulistas*; *Pousada São Francisco*; *Verandhao*; pasta and pizza at *Casinha da Barra*; juices, snacks and beer until late at *Jacaré*; *Tenda Popular* for the cheapest breakfast; *Espaço Aberto* also rec for breakfast. Fresh banana tart available most days at about 1300. Several shops sell basic provisions, so camping is possible. *Restaurante Central*, in Jijoca, is rec.

Nightlife is interesting: *Forró e Lambateira* has dancing every night (unless raining); *Cabaret do Lopez*, video shows, dancing when Lambateira rained off; *Tochas (bar do Loco)*, on beach by church, reggae, salsa and rock by candlelight; *GP Rangos Biritas* for blues and jazz.

Horses can be hired to visit beautiful lagoons, but the animals may be badly treated. A jeep meets buses at Jijoca da Cruz for the hour-and-a-half onward journey to Jericoacoara. If coming from Belém (20 hrs, US$30, difficult journey) you may be able to change at Sobral for Jijoca, but it is much more reliable to go to Fortaleza, from where there are regular buses to Jijoca, 3 hrs, US$4. Jeep transfer is free with some bus lines, eg Redenção, otherwise about US$3, less if the bus is full. Returning, the bus leaves Jijoca for Fortaleza at midnight and 0600. A direct journey from Fortaleza on a 2 or 3-day tour is possible in a VW Kombi, book through an hotel or T 244-5974, Maria do Carmo. You can also get there by boat "seasickness guaranteed", or bus from **Camocim** (a little further W; **F** *Hotel Lusitania*). Take a truck from Camocim to Guriú where hammock space can be found. The village musician sings his own songs in the bar. Walk 4 hrs, or take boat across the bay to Jericoacoara. Many other marvellous beaches in this region; some like Nova Tatajuba, recently discovered, with simple *pousadas*; others like Maceió, also reached from Camocim, an unspoilt paradise.

The Serra de Maranguape with tropical growth and distant views back to the city is 30 km inland from Fortaleza. The pilgrimage centre of **Canindé** may be visited, 108 km SW of Fortaleza, 3-hr bus ride from Box 21 of the rodoviária (Viação Nova Esperança). Large modern church on hill with carved baptistery doors, many ex-votos, interesting dry-land vegetation along route. (Hotels: *Plaza*, by basilica, food OK; *Santo Antônio*). Another inland town, **Baturité**, can be seen, 3 hrs from Rodoviária (Box 45) by Redenção bus, mornings only, also a tourist train round trip Sur.

The road to Sobral and Teresina, BR-222, is paved, but in poor condition. **Sobral** (pop 127,450), the principal town in western Ceará and well-known for straw hats, has **C** *Hotel Visconde*, 10 mins from rodoviária, friendly, good breakfast, and **D** *Francinet's Hotel*. At **Tianguá**, 311 km from Fortaleza on the Teresina road, is **B** *Serra Grande* hotel, all amenities, good (bus from Fortaleza US$9, from Belém, US$32.50).

The Ubajara caves in the **Ubajara National Park** are worth seeing; they are 18 km off the road to Teresina, on a good paved road, 3 km from Ubajara town. A cablecar descends the cliff to the cave entrance, 0830-1600, US$3.50. Lighting has been installed in the nine caverns of the complex, but a torch and spare batteries may be useful. Ibama office at the park entrance, 5 km from the caves; not always helpful, T 634-1388. There is a 3-km cobbled path from the cablecar (take drinking water). The views of the *sertão* from the upper cablecar platform are superb, beautiful ,walks among forest and waterfalls, some barely discovered, and old sugar-mills scattered around the plateau. To walk all the way up to the top of the plateau takes 14 hrs; if you want to do this take plenty of water, from the trail entrance the walk is 3 hrs. Nearby is the **C** *Pousada Neblina*, T 634-1270, in beautiful cloud forest, with swimming pool, rustic campground (US$1.25), with breakfast and private shower (**D** without breakfast) restaurant open 1100-2000, meals rec; opposite is **F** *Pousada Gruta da Ubajara*, with bath, clean, friendly, rustic, restaurant, rec. Near the park, at Sítio Santana (ask taxi driver for "Sítio do Alemão"), is the coffee plantation of **Herbert Klein**, on which there are 3 small chalets, D, warmly rec, with full facilities, excursions, bicycle hire offered (postal address Caixa Postal 33, CEP 62.350, Ubajara, Ceará), if chalets are full the Kleins accommodate visitors at their house. In **Ubajara** town (pop 23,350, 2 hotels; **C** *Le Village*, on Ibiapina road, T 634-1364, restaurant, pool, sauna, good value; **D** *Ubajara*, R Juvêncio Luís Pereira 370, T 634-1261, small restaurant). Most restaurants US$10, big meals in the old market cost US$3. An interesting Sun morning market sells produce of the *sertão*. Buses to Fortaleza.

South of Sobral is the remote town of **Crateús** (pop 66,635), paved road all the way to Fortaleza, with the **D** *Crateús Palace Hotel*, very reasonable and clean, with breakfast. Good restaurant, *Churrascaria Pequena Cabana*, at back of hotel. Bus service from Crateús over very bad road to Teresina, every 2 days.

Between the states of Maranhão and Piauí runs the river Parnaíba. Near its mouth is the anchorage of Luís Correia, where ships unload for final delivery by tugs and lighters at **Parnaíba** (pop 127,990, CEP 64200, DDD 086) 15 km up river, the collecting and distributing centre for the trade of Piauí: tropical products and cattle. There is a regular connection here to Tutóia, for boats across the Parnaíba delta (see p 533).

Hotels B *Cívico*, Av Gov Chagas Rodrigues, T 322-2470, with bath and a/c, good breakfast, friendly, rec; **E** *Rodoviária*, and other basic hotels in the centre.

Beaches at Luís Correia, which with Parnaíba has radioactive sands. Some 15 km from Parnaíba is Pedra do Sal: dark blue lagoons and palm trees. At Lagoa de Portinho there are bungalows, a bar and restaurant and it is possible to camp; canoes for hire.

Teresina (pop 598,450, CEP 64000, DDD 086) about 435 km up the Parnaíba river, is the capital of the State of Piauí (pop 2,581,055), possibly the poorest in Brazil. There are paved road and rail connections (freight only) with the neighbouring state capitals. The city itself is reputed to be the hottest after Manaus (temperatures rise to 42°C). The Palácio de Karnak (the old governor's palace), just S of Praça Frei Serafim, can be visited, Mon-Fri, 1530-1730; it contains lithographs of the Middle East in 1839 by David Roberts RA. Also see the Museu do Piauí, Praça Mal Deodoro, Mon-Fri 0800-1730, Sat, Sun, 0800-1230, US$0.60. There is an interesting open market by the Praça Marechal Deodoro and the river is picturesque, with washing laid out to dry along its banks. The market is a good place to buy hammocks, but bargain hard. Every morning along the river bank there is the *troca-troca* where people buy, sell and swap; an under-cover complex (Mercado Central do Artesanato) has been built at R Paissandu 1276 (Praça Dom Pedro II), open daily 0800-2200 (not weekends). Most of the year the river is low, leaving sandbanks known as *coroas* (crowns).

Hotels A1 *Luxor Hotel do Piauí*, T 222-4911, F 222-4171, and **Teresina Palace**, Paissandu 1219, T 222-2770; **B** *Sambaíba*, R Gabriel Ferreira 230-N, 2-star, T 222-6711, central, good; **B** *São José*, João Cabral 340, T 223-2176, F 223-2223, reasonable restaurant; **E** *Fortaleza*, Felix Pacheco 1101, Praça Saraiva, T 222-2984, fan, basic, rec; many cheap hotels and *dormitórios* around Praça Saraiva; **E** *Grande*, Firmino Pires 73, very friendly and clean. Many cheap ones in R São Pedro: **E** *Bom Clima*, No 890; **E** *Globo*, No 861; **E** *São Pedro*, No 905; and in R Alvaro Mendes; **E** *Glória*, at 823 (clean, best), and at 860, 906.

Restaurants For fish dishes, *Pesqueirinho*, near the confluence of the rivers in Poti Velho district. Many eating places for all pockets in Praça Dom Pedro II (*Típico do Piauí*, good value).

Exchange For parallel market try **Alda Tur**, R A de Abreu 1226. Larger hotels may be helpful.

Laundry *Tintoraria São Paulo*, Rui Barbosa 431, nr *Luxor Hotel do Piauí*.

Shopping Supermarket on **Praça Marechal Deodoro 937**, clean, good, fresh food. Local handicrafts include leather and clothes.

Tourist Information Piemtur, R Alvaro Mendes 2003, Caixa Postal 36, information office at R Magalhães Filho s/n (next to 55 N -English spoken); kiosks at rodoviária and airport.

Buses The bus trip from **Fortaleza** is scenic and takes 9 hrs (US$12.25, *leito* US$24.50). Another road, very bad, leads inland to Porto Franco and **Imperatriz** on the Belém-Brasília highway (see p 536); daily bus takes 26-40 hrs for the trip to Imperatriz (US$17), depending on the state of the road; these buses are very crowded. There are direct buses to Belém (16 hrs, US$20), Recife (16 hrs, US$30) and to **São Luís** (7 hrs, US$9.50). Another main road, runs SE to **Picos** (pop 78,425, **E** *Hotel Picos*, basic, but a/c); from there a good road runs via Salgueiro (many *pousadas*) to Recife (800 km) and another to **Petrolina**, on the River São Francisco opposite the Bahian town of Juazeiro. Buses from Petrolina/Juazeiro (**see p 498**) SE to Salvador.

Rail Local services only, on a diesel service called the "metrô".

Air Flights to Fortaleza, Brasília, Rio de Janeiro, São Paulo, Goiânia, São Luis.

Excursion Some 190 km NE of Teresina and 12 km from Piracuruca is the interesting 20-sq km Parque Nacional de **Sete Cidades** with its strange eroded rock formations, just off the Fortaleza-Teresina road. From the ground it looks like a medley of weird monuments. The inscriptions on some of the rocks have never been deciphered; one Austrian researcher in the 1920s suggested links with the Phoenicians, and the Argentine Professor Jacques de Mahieu, considers them to be Nordic runes left by the Vikings. There is plenty of birdlife, and iguanas, descending from their trees in the afternoon. If hiking in the park, beware of rattlesnakes. Ibama provides a free bus, returns 1700, or else walk (takes all day, very hot, start early). Ibama, Av Homero Castelo Branco 2240, Teresina, CEP 64048-400, T 232-1142. Small booklet with sketch map (not really good enough for walking), entrance US$1.25. There are camping facilities (US$2) and two natural swimming pools, although several years of drought have lowered their water level drastically. Local food is limited and monotonous: bring a few delicacies, and especially fruit. Guided tours with Tropicália Turismo, Piracuruca, T (086) 343-1347.

6 km from the park entrance is the hotel **B** *Fazenda Sete Cidades*, with private bathroom, swimming pool, good restaurant and bicycle or horse transport (it is at Km 63 on BR-222, T (086) 261-3642); also has a free pick-up to the park (and a most unpleasant zoo). In the park is an Ibama hostel, **G** pp, rooms with bath, pleasant, good restaurant, natural pool nearby, rec.

A free bus service leaves the Praça in **Piripiri** (in front of Telpisa office), 26 km away (pop 63,015), at 0700, passing *Hotel Fazenda Sete Cidades* at 0800, reaching the park 10 mins later; return at 1630, or hitch-hike. Taxi from Piripiri, US$14, or from Piracuruca, US$18. Bus Teresina-Piripiri and return, throughout the day 2½ hrs, US$3.50. Bus São Luis-Piripiri, 1200, 1630, 2130, 10 hrs, US$12. Several daily buses Piripiri-Fortaleza, 9 hrs, US$12. Bus Piripiri-Ubajara (see above), marked "São Benedito", or "Cratéus", 2½ hrs; US$3.60, first at 0700 (a beautiful trip). Hotels in Piripiri: **F** *Dos Viajantes*, basic and clean; *Piripiri*, both near bus offices and behind the church. Exchange at the bank only. Piripiri is a cheap place to break the Belém-Fortaleza journey. 50 km away Pedro Segundo is a good place to buy opals.

In the S of the state is **Oeiras** (pop 51,890) old capital of Piauí, where the state government is restoring some of the old buildings, such as the bishop's palace and the church of Nossa Senhora da Vitória.

Maranhão

Maranhão state (pop 4,922,340) is about the size of Italy; its land is flat and low-lying, with highlands to the S. The Atlantic coastline—a mass of sandbanks and creeks and sandy islands on one of which stands São Luís—is 480 km long. A quarter of Maranhão is covered with *babaçu* palms, and by far the most important products are *babaçu* nuts and oil. Rice often takes second place, but well behind *babaçu*. There are salt pans along the coast. The huge Boa Esperança hydroelectric plant on the Parnaíba river now floods the State with energy, and some petroleum has been discovered. The main road from Teresina passes through the Maranhense town of Caxias, which has a good churrascaria, *Selva do Braz* (Av Central 601), live music in the evening.

It is possible to cross the Parnaíba delta, which separates Piauí from Maranhão, by boat arriving in **Tutóia**: an interesting trip through swamps sheltering many birds. Trucks from Tutóia go to Barreirinhas, gateway to the Parque Nacional dos Lençóis Maranhenses, a vast protected area of sand dunes with rare birds and other wildlife (see below).

São Luís (pop 695,780, CEP 65000, DDD 098) the capital and port of Maranhão state, founded in 1612 by the French and named for St Louis of France, is about 560 km W of Fortaleza (1,080 km by road) and 400 km SE of Belém (830 km by road) in a region of heavy tropical rains, but the surrounding deep forest has been cut down to be replaced by *babaçu* palms. The city stands upon São Luís island between the bays of São Marcos and São José. The urban area extends to São Francisco island, connected with São Luís by three bridges. An old slaving port, the city has a large black population and has retained much African culture. The old part, on very hilly ground with many steep streets, is still almost pure colonial. Part of it, known as the Reviver, has been restored with generally splendid results: the damp climate stimulated the use of ceramic tiles for exterior walls, and São Luís shows a greater variety of such tiles than anywhere else in Brazil, in Portuguese, French and Dutch styles. See the **Palácio dos Leões** (Governor's Palace — closed in Jan 1995), beautiful floors of dark wood (*jacarandá*) and light (*cerejeira*), marvellous views from terrace, and the old slave market. The best colonial churches to see—some of them rebuilt and not improved by it—are the **Cathedral** and the churches of **Carmo**, **São João**, **Rosário**, and **Santana**. On Largo do Desterro is the church of **São José do Desterro**, finished in 1863, but with some much older parts. The restored **Fortaleza de Santo Antônio**, built originally by the French in 1614, is on the bank of the River Anil at Ponta d'Areia. The **Fonte do Ribeirão**, Largo do Ribeirão, was begun in 1796. The **Cafua das Mercês**, R Jacinto Maia 43, is a museum housed in the old slave market (open Mon-Fri 1330-1700), well worth the effort to find it: a small building opposite the Quartel Militar. Also visit the Casa dos Negros, next door. The **Museu Histórico e Artístico do Estado**, in a fine early 19th century mansion (complete with slave quarters) at R do Sol 302, closed for renovations (Jan 1995). Also on the R do Sol is the **Teatro Artur Azevedo** (1816). Visit the **Fábrica Canhamo**, a restored factory now housing an arts and crafts centre, near Praia Grande. The **Centro da Creatividade Odylo Costa Filho**, Praia Grande, is an arts centre with theatre, cinema, exhibitions, music, etc, with a bar and café, a good meeting place. Near the Travessa Ladeira there is live music at night. **Museu de Artes Visuais**, Av Portugal 289, shows ceramics and post war art (Mon-Fri 0800-1300, 1600-1800, US$0.65 entry). The commercial quarter (Rua Portugal, also called Rua Trapiche) is still much as it was in the 17th century; best shopping area is R de Santana near Praça João Lisboa.

Festivals On 24 June (São João), the Bumba-Meu-Boi, see **Music and Dance**. For several days before the festival street bands parade, particularly in front of the São João and São Benedito churches. There are dances somewhere in the city almost every night in June. The São Benedito, at the Rosário church in Aug. Festival in Oct, with dancing, at Vila Palmeira suburb (take bus of same name).

Hotels **L2** *Quatro Rodas*, 8 km from centre on Calhau beach, T 227-0244, F 227-4737, excellent, with all facilities; **L2** *Vila Rica*, 5-star, Praça D Pedro II, T 232-3535, F 222-1251, central, many amenities; rec; **C** *Deodoro*, R de Santaninha 535, T 222-1196, clean, friendly; **C** *São Marcos*, Saúde 178, T 232-3763, restored colonial house, a/c, family-run, rec; **D** *Pousada Solar do Carmo*, Praça João Lisboa 400, T 222-2455, pleasant, friendly, light and airy, excellent food; **C** *Pousada Colonial*, R Afonso Pena 112, T 232-2834, in beautiful restored, tiled house, rec; **D** *Lord*, R Nazaré 258, T 222-5544 facing Praça Benedito Leite, comfortable, clean, rec, good breakfast; **D** *Solar Imperador*, good value. Many cheap hotels in R das Palmas, very central, and R Formosa; *Ribamar*, Praça João Lisboa; **E** *Pousada da Praia*, R dos Magistrados 10, helpful owner, mosquitoes; **E** *Praia Grande*, R 14 de Julho, central; **E** *Estrela*, R da Estrela 370, Centro (T 222-1083), noisy, not too clean, safe; Casa do *Estudante*, R do Passeio, 2 km from centre; **E** *Lusitano*, R da Palma 220 (also called R Dr Herculano Parga), with breakfast, cheaper without bath, cheaper still without window.

At Ponta d'Areia: **A1** *Praia Mar*, T 227-4477, on the beach, 5-star, all amenities, opp *São Francisco*, T 227-1155.

Restaurants *Solar do Ribeirão*, R Ribeirão 141, T 222-3068, good buffet lunch and seafood, good value but not cheap, regional cuisine, closed Sat pm and Sun; *La Bohème*, R Isaac Martins 48, very good food, live music, expensive, popular; *Candelabro*, R do Egito, very expensive but excellent international cuisine; *Base de Edilson*, R Paulo Kurger de Oliveira 31, shrimp only, excellent; *Hibiscus*, Av dos Franceses, and *Tia Maria*, Av Nina Rodrigues (Ponta d'Areia), seafood, rec; *Base do Germano*, Av Wenceslau Bras in Canto da Fabril district, excellent *caldeirada de camarão* (shrimp stew), about US$4/head. *Tia Dadi*, Praça Manuel Beckman,

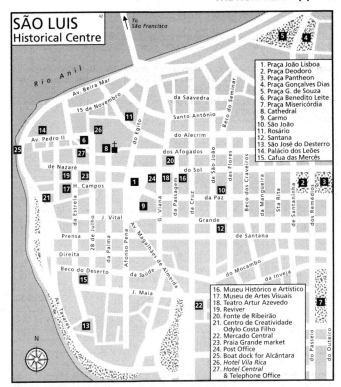

SÃO LUIS
Historical Centre

To
São Francisco

Rio Anil

Av. Beira Mar

15 de Novembro

da Saavedra

Santo Antônio

Beco do Seminar

do Egito

do Alecrim

dos Afogados

Av. Pedro II

de Nazaré

H. Campos

do Sol

de São João

dos Flores

do Sol

da Cruz

da Paz

da Passagem

G. Viana

J. Vital

Av. Magalhães de Almeida

Afonso Pena

28 de Julho

da Palma

Prensa

Direita

Beco do Deserto

da Saúde

J. Maia

Grande

de Santana

do Mocambo

da Inveja

da Mangueira

Sta Rita

de Santaninha

dos Remédios

do Passeio

do Outeiro

N

1. Praça João Lisboa
2. Praça Deodoro
3. Praça Pantheon
4. Praça Gonçalves Dias
5. Praça G. de Souza
6. Praça Benedito Leite
7. Praça Misericórdia
8. Cathedral
9. Carmo
10. São João
11. Rosário
12. Santana
13. São José do Desterro
14. Palácio dos Leões
15. Cafua das Mercês

16. Museu Histórico e Artístico
17. Museu de Artes Visuais
18. Teatro Artur Azevedo
19. Reviver
20. Fonte de Ribeirão
21. Centro de Creatividade
    Odylo Costa Filho
22. Mercado Central
23. Praia Grande market
24. Post Office
25. Boat dock for Alcântara
26. *Hotel Vila Rica*
27. *Hotel Central*
    & Telephone Office

Beira Mar Centre, good regional dishes; *Senac*, R Nazare (next to hotel *Lord*), tourism school restaurant, good local cuisine in a beautifully restored mansion; *Seu Nacib*, R do Trapiche 260, opp Museo de Artes Visuais, kilo restaurant, excellent; *São Luís*, R de Palma, rec; *Kanto Lanches*, Nazaré y de Palma, cheap snacks, friendly. *Base da Lenoca*, R Don Pedro II 187, good view, seafood, big portions; *Naturalista Alimentos*, R do Sol 517, very good, natural foods shop and restaurants, open till 1900. Said to be more choice in new São Francisco district, just across bridge, eg *Oriental*, Av Pres Castelo Branco 47, good Chinese, and *Agapê*, good pizzas. Try the local soft drink called *Jesús* or *Jenève*.

Banks and Exchange TCs at **Banco do Brasil**, Praça Deodoro; **BFB**, R do Sol 176; **Agetur**, R do Sol 33.

Consulates Danish, R do Sol 141, Ed Colonial, Sala 210, T 222-4075, open 0900-1300, 1500-1900. **French**, Rua do Passeio 495, centro, T 222-7412.

Health Clínica São Marcelo, R do Passeio 546, English speaking doctor.

Portuguese Lessons Sra Amin Castro, T 227-1527. rec.

Telecommunications Embratel, Avenida Dom Pedro II 190.

Tourist Offices Maratur, R Djalma Dutra 61-A, also at R Isaac Martins 141, Centro Av dos Franceses, good information on walks in city. *Taguatur* and *Babaçu Viagens*, both in R do Sol shopping gallery, good. Town maps from agencies and office in Praça João Lisboa, opp post office. Funai shop at R do Sol 371. Centro do Artesanato in main street of São Francisco suburb, over bridge from the city.

Airport Internal flights only. 15 km from centre; buses ("São Cristovão") to city until midnight, US$0.40.

Rail Three trains a week on Carajás railway to Parauapebas, 13½ hrs, 890 km, leave São Luís 0800, Mon, Wed, Fri, return 0600, Tues, Thur, Sat (crowded, take own food); for station take "Vila Nova" or "Anjo da Guarda" bus.

Road Bus station 12 km from centre on airport road, "Rodoviária via Alemanha" bus to centre (Praça João Lisboa), US$0.20. Bus to **Fortaleza**, US$24, 4 a day, 18 hrs. Also to **Recife**, US$45, 25 hrs, all other major cities and local towns.

To Belém Direct road via *Santa Inês* (convenient stopping place, **E** *Hotel Novo Horizonte*, nr rodoviária, with bath, others nearby with restaurants) and Alto Bonito paved, in reasonable condition (sometimes washed out but still passable—fascinating swamplands), with petrol stations not far apart (about 9 hrs driving with stop for lunch). There is a bus service 13 hrs, US$22, Transbrasiliana at 1900 and 2000 (no *leito*). There are occasional coastal ships of the Costeira line.

Excursions Calhau is a huge beach, 10 km away, excellent *Churrascaria Pavan*; Ponta D'Areia is nearer to São Luís but more crowded. An hour's bus ride from São Luís is Raposa, a fishing village built on stilts; another fishing village is Ribamar, a half hour's bus ride from São Luís, from in front of the market.

To the E of the city, on the Atlantic Coast is the **Parque Nacional Lençóis Maranhenses**, 155,000 hectares of beaches, lakes and dunes, with very little vegetation and largely unstudied wildlife. For information, phone the Ibama office, T 221-2125/2776, or Baluz Turismo, T 222-6658, or Jaguarema Turismo, T 222-4764.

Some 22 km away by boat is *Alcântara* (city population 4,000, municipality 19,620) the former state capital, on the mainland bay of São Marcos. Construction of the city began at the beginning of the seventeenth century and it is now a historical monument. There are many old churches (eg the ruined Matriz de São Matias) and colonial mansions (see the Casa, and Segunda Casa, do Imperador, also the old cotton barons' mansions with their blue, Portuguese tiled façades), the traditional pillory, the Pelourinho, in the Praça Gomes de Castro, also a small museum in the square (US$0.20) and the Forte de São Sebastião (1653) now in ruins. See also the Fonte de Mirititiva. Good beaches, good walking around the coast (can be muddy after rain), mosquitoes after dark. A rocket-launching site has been built nearby. Principal festival: Festa do Divino, at Pentecost (Whitsun).

Transport Ferries cross the bay daily, leaving São Luís at about 0800, returning from Alcântara about 1400: check time and buy the ticket at the *hidroviária* (W end of Rua Portugal, São Luís) the day before as departure depends on the tides. The journey takes 90 mins, return US$12 and rising in 1995, worth paying extra for "panorámica" seat. Sea can be very rough. There are also catamaran tours bookable through tour operators in São Luís, meals not included.

Hotels B *Pousado do Mordomo Régio*, R Grande 134 (T 337-1221 or São Luís 227-0110), rooms with bath, TV, refrigerator, good restaurant. One can also stay cheaply in houses (eg Dona Maria, 3rd house on left on R Neto Guterres, near harbour, hammock space and 2 meals). **C** *Pousado do Imperador*, R Grande 13, some rooms with bath; **C** *Pousada do Pelourinho*, Praça Gomes de Castro (**E** without breakfast), clean, friendly, good restaurant, communal bathroom. Try bargaining for hammock space in private houses. Children who offer themselves as guides can help arrange accommodation in private houses, friendly but no great comfort; provide your own mineral water.

    Restaurante Tijupa has very good home cooking but meals must be ordered in advance, owner Claudio is the best guide in town; *Bar do Lobato*, on the praça, is pleasant, with good, simple food, fried shrimps highly rec. All restaurants around US$15, take a picnic if on a tight budget.

On the Eastern bank of the Rio Tocantins, at Maranhão's western border with Tocantins, is *Imperatriz* (pop 276,450), a city serving a large cattle region. Go down Av Getúlio Vargas and see the range of goods on offer. It is also in an area of violence over landholding; in 1986, a priest was shot in his church. To get to the ferry across the river, go along R Luis Domingues, which runs parallel to Av Getúlio Vargas. **Hotels**: **B** *Poseidon*, R Paraíba 740, T 721-4466, central, best, a/c, TV, swimming pool, rec; **D** *Anápolis*, BR-010, Km 1345, T 721-2255, opp rodoviária, a/c, fridge, swimming pool, friendly; a lot of cheap hotels near rodoviária. Restaurant *Bar Central* is OK. There is a good, expensive discotheque at Beira Rio, N of the ferry crossing,

Fly Back Disco Club; it has two dance floors, one fast, one slow (for couples only). Telephone office on R Rio Grande do Norte, a side street off Av Getúlio Vargas, near *Hotel Poseidon*. Lying on the Belém-Brasília highway, Imperatriz has bus connections with both cities; there is a slow, crowded bus service to Teresina. To get to Marabá on the Transamazônica, you can either take a Transbrasiliana bus direct, 7-10 hrs (starting on the Belém highway, the bus then turns W along a poorer road, passing finally through destroyed forest, new fazendas and unplanned cities), or, a faster route, involving taking a ferry across the river in the early morning (0600-0700) to catch a pick-up on the other side, takes about 5 hrs, but is more expensive.

NORTHERN BRAZIL (9)

Brazilian Amazonia, from the mouth of the great river to the Colombian and Peruvian borders. The cities of Belém, Santarém and Manaus are described, together with river travel between and excursions into the jungle. Also dealt with are the land and water routes to Venezuela and the Guianas.

Northern Brazil consists of the states of Pará, Amazonas, Amapá and Roraima. The northern states of Rondônia and Acre are dealt with under Section 10, Southern Amazonia.

The area is drained by the Amazon, which in size, volume of water—12 times that of the Mississippi—and number of tributaries has no equal in the world. At the base of the Andes, far to the W, the Amazonian plain is 1,300 km in width, but E of the confluences of the Madeira and Negro rivers with the Amazon, the highlands close in upon it until there is no more than 80 km of floodplain between them. Towards the river's mouth—about 320 km wide—the plain widens once more and extends along the coast S-eastwards into the state of Maranhão and northwards into the Guianas.

Brazilian Amazonia, much of it still covered with tropical forest, is 56% of the national area. Its jungle is the world's largest and densest rain forest, with more diverse plants and animals than any other jungle in the world. It has only 8% of Brazil's population, and most of this is concentrated around Belém (in Pará), and in Manaus, 1,600 km up the river. The population is sparse because other areas are easier to develop; the rainfall is heavy, the humidity high and the climate hot; and the soil, as in all tropical forest, is poor.

Successive Governments have made strenuous efforts to develop Amazonia. Roads have been built parallel to the Amazon to the S (the Transamazônica), from Cuiabá (Mato Grosso) northwards to Santarém (Pará), and NE from Porto Velho through Humaitá to the river bank opposite Manaus. Some maps show a road N of the Amazon, marked Perimetro (or Perimetral) Norte; this road does not exist, never has and probably never will. Agricultural settlements are being established along these roads; major energy and mining projects for bauxite and iron ore are bringing rapid change. Much environmental damage has been caused to the region by gold prospectors (*garimpeiros*), especially by their indiscriminate use of mercury. The most important cause of destruction, however, has been large scale deforestation to make way for cattle ranching. Choosing the best path towards development in Amazonia remains the subject of much controversy throughout Brazil, and foreign interference in the matter (there has been no shortage of it) is generally not welcome. Nonetheless, there is a gradually growing awareness among many Brazilians that their northern hinterland is a unique treasure and requires some form of protection. Most recently, much attention has been focused on ecotourism as a potentially non-destructive source of income for the region. Just how benign this activity actually is, remains to be confirmed. There are increasing numbers of Brazilians from the S taking holidays in Amazonia.

Anyone interested in the Amazonian development programme and its ecological, social, economic and political effects should read Richard Bourne's masterly *Assault on the Amazon* (London, Gollancz, 1978), *Dreams of Amazonia*, by Roger D Stone (Penguin, 1986), or *Amazon* by Brian Kelly and Mark London (Harcourt Brace Jovanovich, New York, 1983). *The Fate of the Forest* by Suzanne Hecht and Alexander Cockburn (Penguin, 1991) has also been rec.

Along the Transamazônica

The Transamazônica, about 5,000 km in length, represents the greater part of a direct road connection between Brazil's furthest E and furthest W points. It skirts the southern edge of the Amazonian plain, linking the following places: Estreito (junction with the Belém-Brasília highway, N of Araguaína, see p 578), Marabá (on the Tocantins river), Altamira (on the Xingu), São Luís do Tapajós, near Itaituba (on the Tapajós), Jacarèacanga, Humaitá (on the Madeira), Rio Branco, and Japim, in the far W of the State of Acre. The road was officially opened in Dec 1973. Parts of it have been paved, but the harsh climate and inadequate maintenance have caused much deterioration. Some sections are often totally intransitable throughout the rainy season (eg Santarém to the Belém-Brasília Highway). Others may require 4WD and winch. There are stretches with regular truck traffic and scheduled bus services, but as conditions are constantly changing, detailed local inquiry is essential before heading out. Also ensure that you have sufficient *reais* for your journey. Despite all the resources invested in road construction, the rivers remain the principal avenues of transport throughout Amazonia. In April 1995 the government announced plans to extend and pave the Transamazonian highway system, to improve the road links with Peru and Venezuela, and to Cuiabá in Mato Grosso.

Near **Marabá** (pop 121,815, alt 84m), are beaches on the Rios Tocantins and Itacaiúnas, best Jun-Oct. Hotels: **B** *Vale do Tocantins*, Folha 29, Cidade Nova, 7 km, T 322-2321, modern, restaurant, travel agency; of similar standard are **B** *Itacaiúnas*, nearby, T 322-1715, and *Del Príncipe*, Av Mal Rondon 95, Cidade Nova, T 324-1175; **C** *Plaza*, Nova Marabá, by rodoviária, T 322-1610, a/c, pleasant, helpful, some English spoken; **C** *Keyla*, Rod Transamazônica 2427, 3 km, a/c, some cheaper rooms; *Victoria*, Av Espírito Santo 130, 2 km, both similar to *Plaza* but not as friendly. Others near rodoviária. Restaurants: *Kome Aki no Chikão*, Av Antônio Maia 997, central, a/c, modest, 1200-1500, 1800-2300 (in theory); *Bambu*, Pedro Cameiro 111, Cidade Nova, 3 km, mainly fish, clean, good value, 1100-1500, 1800-2300; *Restaurant O Calmon* for fish. Buses leave daily for Belém (654 km, paved), for Santarém (34 hrs) and many daily for Imperatriz (7-10 hrs, US$9.50, there is also a pick-up to the bank of the Tocantins opp Imperatriz, 5 hrs, but more expensive, US$12); buses can be caught going S at Toncantinópolis, opposite Porto Franco on the Belém-Brasília road. Also a bus can be taken to Araguaína, 12½ hrs, US$19; bus Marabá-Goiânia (change at Araguaína), US$48. Bus to Santa Inês (Maranhão, on Belém-Teresina road), 19 hrs, US$23. On these bus trips take plenty of food and drink—local supplies are expensive. Rodoviária in Nova Marabá, 4 km on PA-150, T 321-1892. Airport in Cidade Nova, 3 km, flights to Brasília, Belém and regional centres; boat trips to Belém (24 hrs), Altamira (6 hrs) and Santarém (18 hrs). With the filling of the Tucuruí dam the town has been moved; even so it suffers from flooding. There is a bridge across the Toncantins at Marabá. Banco do Brasil will not cash TCs; parallel market in larger stores, eg *Supermercado Bato Logo*.

To visit the **Serra Pelada** gold mines, now worked by individuals on a very diminished scale, take a bus to Km 6, change there to bus to Serra Pelada (US$3, 3 hrs, last bus back 1400). (The mine was described on British Channel 4 television as "the largest swimming pool on Earth"). 11 km before the town is a police post: search for weapons and alcohol (forbidden); second search at airport 2 km from the mine. **E** *Hotel Serra de Ouro*, all of wood, shower; good *Churrascaria* in main square near public TV set; juice bars and *DiscoTony* discotheque. No prior permission needed to visit the mines. The miners are usually friendly and like being photographed, but enquire about the conditions before going there.

From Marabá, or from São Luis or Belém, one can reach the **Carajás** iron mine (the largest mineral development in Brazil) by road or train (see under São Luis above, train can be caught at station 12 km from Marabá, Mon, Wed, Fri approx 2300; to São Luis Tues, Thur, Sat 0420). Plenty of Transbrasiliana buses daily Marabá-Carajás, 4-5 hrs, US$5.75; Military Police check for weapons and drugs at Curianópolis. Many unplanned towns along the road. To get into

Carajás (checkpoint 35 km from the project), you must have a permit, available from Companhia Vale Rio Doce (CVRD) in Marabá, São Luis, São Paulo or Rio: Av Groça Aranha 26, 16° andar, Centro, Rio 20030000 – attention Dr Hugo Mourão (hotel bookings handled here too); apply in advance and have a good reason. There are flights from Belém, Imperatriz, Marabá, Tucuruí and São Luis by Brasil Central and Varig has a flight Porto Alegre-Curitiba-Brasília-Carajás-Belém once a week and Brasília-Carajás-Belém once a week. Between Marabá and Belém, on the Tocantins river, is the Tucuruí hydroelectric scheme (which is causing much ecological damage), reached either by bus or by day and night riverboat from Belém. *Hotel Transamérica* best in Tucuruí (pop 81,655); **E** *Marajoara*, R Lauro Sodré 685, T 787-1776, simple but OK. Floating bar (light meals), *Fluente*, 1½ km N, take a taxi or motorboat, or walk, popular. To go to the dam, take bus "V Temp I II" or " Vila Temporávia"; it is difficult to obtain a permit to visit the inside of the hydroelectric plant. From Marabá to Tucuruí, take Transbrasiliano bus, 3 a day, 8 hrs, US$9.50, road good to Itupiranga, deteriorates thereafter; also boat from Belém (32 hrs).

The Transamazônica crosses the river Xingu at Favânia, 41 km E of *Altamira* , a busy, booming Amazonian town with many gold dealers (pop 120,565— **C** *Alta Palace*, Av Tancredo Neves 3093, bar/restaurant, a/c, good, T 515-2057; **D** *Lisboa*, Lindolfo Aranha 405, a/c, TV, good value, slightly better than **D** *Globo*; good pizzeria opp; *Hotel Imperatriz*, R Beto Somez near market, bath, a/c, rec; good *churrascos* and shopping in the market; *Restaurante Casa Grande*, R Anchieta, centre, good *churrascos*, cheap, 1130-1430, 1930-2330. The town is served by jets, the airport is 8 km from centre, no bus, exchange is difficult. Rodoviária on Av Perimentral, T 515-1879, no left luggage. Buses run from Tucuruí via Ripartimento. New road is being paved 46 km N to fishing village of Vitória on the lower Xingu, from which boats go to Belém; a good place to watch the *garimpeiros* working below the last rapids. No organised trips but a boat can be hired, US$25/day, for a trip up the Xingu. Many animals. The area is an Assurine Indian reservation and it is not allowed to enter villages; buy food in Altamira.

Rurópolis (Presidente Medici) lies at the junction of the Transamazônica and the Santarém highway. Hotel run by Incra, "by all accounts, like the rest of the place: cracked, empty, dreaming of a future that never came" (Kevin Healey).

At *Itaituba* (the jumping-off place for the **Amazonia National Park**; see Father Paul Zoderer, who may help to arrange a visit, at church on waterfront—nearest Ibama information, T (091) 224-5899/2621) the Transbrasiliana company has a bus station on the Rio Tapajós, near the ferry docks (**E** *Hotel 3 Poderes*, clean, friendly, rec). Bus to Marabá, about 34 hrs, US$30.

In *Humaitá* (pop 38,755) there are several basic hotels on the eastern edge of town; try *Hotel Meire*, on main street. The Soltur bus station is in the centre.

There is very little traffic on the Transamazônica between Itaituba and Humaitá (1,028 km); local drivers may give lifts. A ferry crosses the Rio Aripuanã at Vila do Carmo. The road is good for about 350 km from Humaitá, then it deteriorates badly. It is hilly, narrow, and the jungle usually grows over the side of the road. Expresos Humaitá daily bus takes 24 hrs from Humaitá to Jacarèacanga, 597 km (the town is 8 km off the highway). One must stay overnight and catch the Transbrasiliana bus to Itaituba (24 hrs, schedule erratic; the bus is replaced occasionally by a truck). There are two insanitary and expensive hotels in Jacarèacanga (try the filling station on the Transamazônica near the Jacarèacanga turn-off, they may have hammock space). Bus fare Humaitá-Jacarèacanga, US$30; Jacarèacanga-Itaituba, US$14.50; travel time depends on the weather conditions, the condition of the bus, and whether the driver decides to stop somewhere for the night.

Up the Amazon River

The Amazon system is 6,577 km, long, of which 3,165 km are in Brazilian territory. Ships of up to 4/5,000 tons regularly negotiate the Amazon for a distance of about 3,646 km up to Iquitos, Peru. Distances upstream from the river mouth to Manaus in nautical miles are:

Belém	80	Santarém	538
Narrows (entrance)	225	Óbidos	605
Narrows (exit)	330	Parintins	694
Garupa	334	Itacoatiara	824
Prainha	452	Manaus	930

River Transport in Amazonia Although air service is widespread throughout the region, and road transport is gradually increasing, rivers remain the arteries of Amazonia for the transport of both passengers and merchandise. The two great ports of the region are Belém, at the mouth of the Amazon, and Manaus at the confluence of the Rio Negro and Rio Solimões. The strategic location of the latter makes it the hub of river transport. From Manaus there is regular shipping service E to Santarém and Belém along the lower Amazon, S to Porto Velho along the Rio Madeira, W to Tabatinga (the border with Colombia and Peru) along the Rio Solimões, NW to São Gabriel da Cachoeira along the Rio Negro, and N to Caracaraí (for Boa Vista) along the Rio Branco. There is also a regular service connecting Belém and Macapá, on the N shore of the Amazon Delta, Santarém and Macapá, as well as Santarém and Itaituba S along the Rio Tapajós. All of the above services call at many intermediate ports and virtually every village has some form of riverboat service. There is no regular direct service between Belém and Tabatinga, or Manaus and Iquitos (Peru).

The size and quality of vessels varies greatly, with the largest and most comfortable ships generally operating on the Manaus—Belém route; however acceptable conditions can be found on some boats to almost all destinations. Since 1991 there has been more stringent government control (see **Health** below) as well as increased competition among ship owners. Thus conditions have generally improved, with less overcrowding, better hygiene, better food, and friendlier service. Many of the larger ships now offer a/c berths (not really necessary), and even suites with double beds and private bath, in addition to first class (upper deck) and second class (lower deck) hammock space. Most boats have some sort of rooftop bar serving drinks and snacks (generally overpriced).

Riverboat travel is not a substitute for visiting the jungle. Except for a few birds and the occasional dolphin, little wildlife is seen. However it does offer an insight into the vastness of Amazonia and a chance to meet some of its people. It can be a very pleasant and satisfying experience.

The vessels operating on a particular route and their schedules are frequently changing and it is generally not possible to book far in advance. Extensive local inquiry and some flexibility in one's schedule are indispensable for river travel. The following are some suggestions on how to choose a riverboat. Refer to the appropriate city sections for details of port facilities in each.

Whenever possible, avoid purchasing tickets from agents or touts (hawkers) for a boat you have not seen. See the vessel yourself and have a chat with the captain or business manager to confirm departure date and time, length of voyage, ports of call, price, etc. Have a careful look around, inspecting cleanliness in the kitchen, toilets and showers. All boats are cleaned up when in port, but if a vessel is reasonably clean upon arrival then chances are that it has been kept that way throughout the voyage. You can generally arrange to sleep onboard a day or two before departure and a day or two after arrival, but be sure to secure carefully your belongings when in port. If you take a berth, choose exactly the one you want, lock it and keep the key even if you will not be moving in right away. If you are travelling hammock class, it is best to board ship at least 8 to 12 hrs before sailing in order to secure a good spot (away from the toilets and the engine). Be firm but considerate of your neighbours as they will be your intimate companions for the duration of the voyage. Always keep your gear locked. Take some light warm clothing, it can get chilly at night in the hammock area.

Compare fares for different ships. As a general rule of thumb they will be about half of the prevailing one-way airfare, including all meals. (Drinks not included. Many ships sail in the evening and the first night's supper is not included.) Shop around and bargain for the best fares. Payment is usually in advance. Insist on a signed ticket indicating date, vessel, class of passage, and berth number if applicable.

All ships carry cargo as well as passengers and the amount of cargo will affect the length of the voyage because of weight (especially when travelling upstream) and loading/unloading at intermediate ports. All but the smallest boats will transport vehicles, but these are all too often damaged by rough handling. Insist on the use of proper ramps and check for adequate clearance. Vehicles can also be transported aboard cargo barges. These are usually cheaper and passengers may be allowed to accompany their car, but check about food, where you will sleep, and adequate shade.

The following are the major shipping routes in Amazonia indicating intermediate ports, average trip durations, and fares. Not all ships stop at all intermediate ports. There are generally more vessels sailing each route than are listed here, several are regularly added to and withdrawn from service each year, and it is not unusual for ships to switch from one route to another in response to changing cargo or passenger traffic. There are many other routes and vessels providing extensive local service. All fares shown are one-way only and include all meals unless otherwise stated. Information is identical for the respective reverse voyages (eg Belém-Manaus and Manaus-Belém).

Belém-Manaus via Breves, Almeirim, Prainha, Monte Alegre, Curua-Uná, Santarém, Alenquer, Obidós, Juruti, and Parintins on the lower Amazon. 5 days upriver, 4 days downriver, including 12 hr stop in Santarém, suite US$245, double berth US$180, 1st class hammock space US$70 pp, 2nd class hammock space US$45 pp, vehicle up to pickup or combi size US$500 usually including driver, other passengers extra. *Nélio Correa* is best on this route. *São Francisco* is largest, also new and modern. *Cisne Branco* of similar quality. *Benjamin* is ageing but known for its good food, friendly service, and pleasant atmosphere onboard, as is *Lider II*.

Belém-Santarém, same intermediate stops as above. 2 days upriver, 1½ days downriver, fares are slightly more than half Belém-Manaus. All vessels sailing Belém-Manaus will call in Santarém and there are others operating on only the Belém-Santarém route.

Santarém-Manaus, same intermediate stops as above. 2 days upriver, 1½ days downriver, fares slightly more than half Belém-Manaus. All vessels sailing Belém-Manaus will call in Santarém and there are others operating on only the Santarém-Manaus route, including: *Cidade de Terezinha III* and *IV*, good. *Miranda Dias*, family run and friendly.

Belém-Macapá (Porto Santana) non-stop, 24 hrs on large ships, double berth US$60-100, hammock space US$8-22 pp, meals not included but can be purchased onboard (expensive), vehicle US$100, driver not included. *Silja e Souza* (Weds) is best. *Almirante Solon* (Thur, Sat) is state run, slightly cheaper, crowded and not as nice. Same voyage via Breves, 36 to 48 hrs on smaller riverboats, hammock space US$25 pp including meals. *ENAL* (Sat); *Macamazónia* (every day except Thur), slower and more basic; *Bartolomeu I* of Enavi, food and sanitary conditions OK, 30 hrs; *JK I, II, III, Cidade de Santarém* and others, none too clean.

Macapá (Porto Santana)-Santarém via Vida Nova, Boca do Jari, Almeirim, Prainha, and Monte Alegre on the lower Amazon (does not call in Belém), 2 days upriver, 1½ days downriver, fare slightly more than half Belém-Manaus.

Santarém-Itaituba along the Rio Tapajós, 24 hrs.

Manaus-Porto Velho via Borba, Manicoré, and Humaitá on the Rio Madeira. 4 days upriver, 3½ days downriver (up to 7 days when river is low), double berth US$136, 1st class hammock space US$48 pp, 2nd class hammock space US$30 pp. *Anna-Maria* is very good, as is *Almirante Mendonça*. *Cometa Halley* also OK.

Manaus-Tefé via Codajás and Coari, 24 to 36 hrs, double berth US$80, 1st class hammock space US$30 pp, 2nd class hammock space US$25 pp. *Capitan Nunes* is good. *Jean Filho* also OK. Note that it is difficult to continue W from Tefé to Tabatinga without first returning to Manaus.

Manaus-Tabatinga via Fonte Boa, Foz do Mamaria, Tonantins, Santo Antônio do Ica, Amataura, Monte Cristo, São Paulo de Olivença and Benjamin Constant along the Rio Solimões. Up to 8 days upriver (depending on cargo), 3 days downriver, double berth US$175, 1st class hammock space US$75 pp, 2nd class hammock space US$50 pp. *Almirante Monteiro*, *Voyagers*, *Avelino Leal*, and *Capitão Nunes VIII* all acceptable, *Dom Manoel*, cheaper, acceptable but overcrowded.

Manaus-Caracaraí (for Boa Vista) along the Rio Branco, 4 days upriver, 2 days downriver, many sandbars, impassable during the dry season. Now that the BR-174 (Manaus-Boa Vista road) has been improved and remains open almost all year, river service is erratic.

Manaus-São Gabriel da Cachoeira via Novo Airao, Moura, Carvoeiro, Barcelos, and Santa Isabel do Rio Negro along the Rio Negro. Infrequent service to/from this remote and isolated area.

What to wear Light cotton or poplin clothing for the day and at night put on a sweater or coat, for it gets quite cold. Leather sandals fall apart in the wet, rubber ones are better, but proper shoes or boots are best for going ashore: there are many foot-attacking parasites in the jungle. (2 pairs of trainers, so you always have a dry pair, is a good idea.) Also take a hat and rain gear, such as a poncho with hood.

A hammock is essential on all but the most expensive boats; often too hot to lie down in cabin during day. Light cotton hammocks seem to be the best solution. Buy a wide one on which you can lie diagonally; lying straight along it leaves you hump-backed.

Health   There is a danger of malaria in Amazonia. Mosquito nets are not required when in motion as boats travel away from the banks and too fast for mosquitoes to settle, though repellent is a boon for night stops. From Apr to Oct, when the river is high, the mosquitoes can be repelled by Super Repelex spray or K13. A yellow-fever inoculation is strongly advised; it is compulsory in some areas and may be administered on the spot with a pressurized needle gun. In response to the 1991 cholera outbreak, the authorities have greatly tightened the enforcement of sanitary regulations onboard the riverboats and hygienic conditions are much improved. The larger ships must have an infirmary and carry a health officer. There are regular sanitary inspections at all ports of call. All drinking water is now treated (usually by adding chlorine bleach), but taking your own mineral water is still not a bad idea. Micropur brand water purification tablets are available in Belém pharmacies.

Food   is ample but monotonous. Fresh fruit is a welcome addition also take plain biscuits, tea bags, seasonings, sauces and jam. Fresh coffee available; most boats have a bar of sorts. Plates and cutlery may not be provided. A strong fishing line and a variety of hooks can be an asset for supplementing one's diet; with some meat for bait, *piranhas* are the easiest fish to catch. Negotiate with the cook over cooking your fish. The sight of you fishing will bring a small crowd of new friends, assistants, and lots of advice—some of it useful.

Exchange   facilities are sparse in Amazonia: banks and and parallel market exchange can be found in Belém, Macapá, Santarém and Manaus. Small amounts of US$ cash can usually be exchanged in many other towns.

Food in Amazonia   Inevitably fish dishes are very common, including many fish with Indian names, eg *pirarucu, tucunaré,* and *tambaqui*, which are worth trying. Also shrimp and crab dishes (more expensive). Specialities of Pará include duck, often served in a yellow soup made from the juice of the root of the manioc with a green vegetable (*jambú*); this dish is the famous *pato no tucupi*, highly rec. Also *tacaca* (shrimps served in *tucupi*), *vatapá* (shrimps served in a thick sauce, highly filling, simpler than the variety found in Salvador), *maniçoba* (made with the poisonous leaves of the bitter cassava, simmered for 8 days to render it safe—tasty). *Caldeirada*, a fish and vegetable soup, served with *pirao* (manioc puree) is a speciality of Amazonas. There is also an enormous variety of tropical and jungle fruits, many unique to the region. Try them fresh, or in ice creams or juices. Avoid food from street vendors.

Belém   (do Pará—population of city 1,246,435, CEP 66000, DDD 091, of state 5,084,725), founded in 1616, 145 km from the open sea and slightly S of the equator, is the great port of the Amazon. It is hot (mean temperature, 26°C), but frequent showers freshen the streets. There are some good squares and fine buildings. The largest square is the Praça da República; the main business and shopping area is along the wide Avenida Presidente Vargas leading to the river and the narrow streets which parallel it. The **Teatro da Paz**, one of the largest theatres in the country, is of neo-classical splendour, worth visiting, free concert and theatre performances are given (recently restored, open Mon-Fri 0800-1200, 1400-1800, tours cost US$0.50). There was much renovation of public places in 1985-87, and a building boom in the early 1990s sent up many new apartment towers.

Places to visit are the **Bosque Rodrigo Alves**, Av Almirante Barroso (0900-1700 closed Mon), a public garden (which is really a preserved area of original flora), with a small animal collection, yellow bus marked "Souza" or "Cidade Nova"—any number—30 mins from "Ver-o-Peso" market, and the **Museu Emílio Goeldi**. Both can be reached by bus from the Cathedral. The Museu Goeldi, Av Magalhães Barata 376, takes up a city block and consists of the museum proper (with a fine collection of Marajó Indian pottery, an excellent exhibition of Mebengokre Indian lifestyle), a zoological garden (including manatees), and botanical exhibits including Victoria Régia lilies; open Tues-Sat 0900-1200, 1400-1700, all day Sun, closed Wed and Fri pm. Entry US$1, additional charges for specialist areas, now renovated. The **Murucutu ruins**, an old Jesuit foundation, are reached by the

Ceará bus from Praça República, through an unmarked door on the right of the Ceará bus station.

The Belém market, known as **"Ver-o-Peso"** (see the weight), now has lots of gift shops selling charms for the local African-derived religion, *umbanda*; the medicinal herb and natural perfume stalls are also interesting. It is one of the most varied and colourful markets in South America; you can see giant river fish being unloaded around 0530, with frenzied wholesale buying for the next hour. The area around the market swarms with people, including many armed thieves and pickpockets. In the old town, too, is the fort, which you can enter on request; the site also contains the *Círculo Militar* restaurant (entry US$1; drinks and *salgadinhos* served on the ramparts from 1800 to watch the sunset, restaurant is good). At the square on the waterfront below the fort the *açaí* berries are landed nightly at 2300, after picking in the jungle (*açaí* berries ground up with sugar and mixed with manioc are a staple food in the region). Visit the **Cathedral** (1748) with several remarkable paintings (closed Tues-Fri 1130-1400, Sun 1200-1600, all day Mon), and directly opposite the 18th-century **Santo Aleixandre** church (now being restored) noted for its wood carving. The 17th-century **Mercês** church (1640), near the market, is the oldest church in Belém; it forms part of an architectural group known as the Mercedário, the rest of which was heavily damaged by fire in 1978 and is being restored. The **Basilica of Nossa Senhora de Nazaré** (1909), built from rubber wealth, is an absolute must for its beautiful marble work and stained glass windows (closed 1200-1500, Mon-Fri). The **Lauro Sodré palace**, praça Dom Pedro II, a gracious 18th-century Italianate building, contains Brazil's largest framed painting, "The Conquest of Amazonia" by de Angelis (Mon-Fri 0800-1200, 1400-1800).

Local Holidays Maundy Thursday, half-day; 9 June, Corpus Christi; 15 Aug, accession of Pará to independent Brazil; 7 Sept, Independence Day, commemorated on the day with a military parade, and with a students' parade on the preceding Sun (am); 30 Oct, half-day; 2 Nov, All Souls Day; 8 Dec, Immaculate Conception; Christmas Eve, half-day.

Círio, the Festival of Candles in Oct, is a remarkable festival based on the legend of the Virgin of Nazaré, whose image is kept in her Basilica; it apparently was found on that site around 1700. To celebrate, on the second Sun in Oct, a procession carries a copy of the Virgin's image from the Basilica to the cathedral. On the Mon, two weeks later, a further procession takes place, to return the image to its usual resting-place. There is a Círio museum in the crypt of the Basilica, enter at the right side of the church; free. Exhibits from the celebrations of the past 100 years; enthusiastic guide. (All hotels are fully booked during Círio.)

Hotels Expensive: **L2** *Hilton*, Av Pres Vargas 882, T 223-6500, F 225-2942, swimming pool, sauna, restaurants (the *Açaí* is rec for regional dishes and others, Sun brunch, desserts, expensive); **L2** *Novotel*, Av Bernardo Sayão 4808, T 229-8011, F 229-8709, with bath, a/c, TV, swimming pool, unprepossessing neighbourhood, far from centre (take Universidade bus); **A2** *Cambará*, 16 de Novembro 300, esq Tamandaré, T 224-2422, a/c, good, mosquitoes. Less expensive: **A3** *Sagres*, Av Gov José Malcher 2927, opp bus station, T 228-3999, F 226-8260, a/c, good meals, swimming pool, English-speaking manager, reported run down; **A3** *Vanja*, Av Benjamin Constant 1164, T 222-6688, F 222-6709, good service, inexpensive rooftop restaurant, pool, rec; **A3** *Verde Oliva*, Boaventura da Silva 1179 (T 224-7682), 10 mins from centre, a/c, TV, good value, rec; *Regente*, Av Gov José Malcher 485, T 241-1222, F 224-0343, 3-star, modest, comfortable, friendly, good breakfast; **A3** *Zoghbi Park*, R Padre Prudencio 220, T/F 241-1800; **B** *Itaoca*, Av Pres Vargas 132, T 241-3434, F 241-0891, with bath, TV, a/c, new, clean, charming, breakfast incl; **C** *Novo Avenida*, No 404, T 222-9953, central, some rooms better than others, no backpackers, good breakfast; **D** *Auberge L'Amazone*, Tv Campos Sales 542, commercial district, French owned, clean, safe, highly rec; **D** *Ver-o-Peso*, Castilhos Franco 208, T 224-2267, opposite Ver-o-Peso market, rooftop restaurant, TV and fridge in room, rec; **E** *Central*, Av Presidente Vargas 290 (T 222-3011), with bath and a/c (F without bath), some rooms noisy, but friendly, clean, comfortable, good meals, a must for art-deco fans (one reader suggests checking doors for peep-holes); **C** *Vidonho*, same ownership, a/c, fridge, shabby, abundant breakfast, R O de Almeida, 476, T 225-1444, in a side street opp; **D** *Plaza*, Praça da Bandeira, T 224-2800, 2-star, a/c, bath, fridge, restaurant good value, take care in this area, especially at night; **D** *São Geraldo*, R Padre Prudéncio 56, T 223-7800, central, clean, rec; **E** *Vitória Rêgia*, Frutuoso Guimarães 260, T 224-2833, F 241-3475, with breakfast, more with

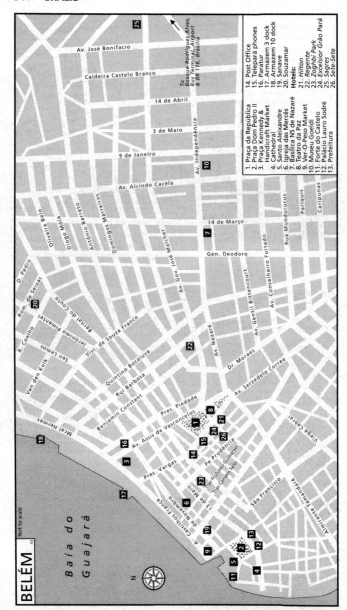

BELÉM

Not to scale

Baía do Guajará

N

1. Praça da Republica
2. Praça Dom Pedro II
3. Praça Kennedy & Handicraft Market
4. Cathedral
5. Santo Alexandre
6. Igreja das Mercês
7. Basílica N S de Nazaré
8. Teatro da Paz
9. Ver-O-Peso Market
10. Museu Goeldi
11. Forte do Castelo
12. Palácio Lauro Sodré
13. Prefeitura
14. Post Office
15. Teleparà phones
16. Paratur
17. Armazem 3 dock
18. Armazem 10 dock
19. Sanave
20. Souzamar

Hotels:
21. Hilton
22. Regente
23. Zoghbi Park
24. Excelsior Grão Pará
25. Sagres
26. Sete-Sete

Av. José Bonifacio

Caldeira Castelo Branco

14 de Abril

3 de Maio

9 de Janeiro

Av. Alcindo Cacela

To Bosque Rodrigues Alves, Bus Terminal, Airport & BR 116, Brasília

Av. Independência

14 de Março

Gen. Deodoro

Av. Gov. José Malcher

Rua Mundurucus

Pariquis

Caripunas

D. Pedro

Rom. de Seixas

R. Coelho

Van den Kolk

Sen. Lemos

Jerônimo Pimentel

Bernal do Couto

Oliveira Belo

Diogo Móia

Antônio Barreto

Domingos Marreiros

Quintino Bocaiuva

Rui Barbosa

Benjamin Constant

Visc. de Souza Franco

Av. Nazaré

Dr. Moraes

Av. Gentil Bittencourt

Av. Conselheiro Furtado

Av. Serzedelo Correa

Pres. Piedade

Av. Assis de Vasconcelos

Pe Prudência

Trav Frutuoso Guimarães

Trav Campos Salles

Pres. Vargas

Av. Castilhos França

de Novembro

15 de Maio

São Francisco

Viega Cabral

Almirante Tamandaré

Mcal Hermes

a/c, bath, fridge (F without), refurbished, safe; next door is **F Fortaleza**, Frutuoso Guimarães 276, very basic (ferry tickets to Manaus, Macapá, etc, sold); **E Palácio das Musas**, same street No 275 (cheaper without fan or breakfast), clean, friendly, built round a courtyard, large rooms; **D Sete-Sete**, Trav 1 de Março 677, T 222-7730, comfortable, with breakfast, rec. Many cheap hotels close to waterfront, none too safe. Near the rodoviária, all OK, all **F**, **Akemi, Duas Irmãs, Real**.

Camping nearest at Mosqueiro, 86 km away.

Restaurants All the major hotels have good but expensive restaurants. **Círculo Militar** rec for Belém's best Brazilian food and situation in the grounds of the fort with view over river (good choice, try *filete na brasa*, expensive). **Churrascaria Sanambaia**, Quai Kennedy; **Churrascaria Rodeio**, Rodovia Augusto Montenegro, excellent meat, salad bar, reasonable prices. **Augustos**, Av Almirante Barroso, past rodoviária, a/c, good food, reasonable prices, piano music; **Cristal**, R Benjamin Constant e R dos Mundurucus, very good, nice décor, expensive; **Roxy Bar e Restaurante**, Av Sen Lemos 231, delicious dishes named after Hollywood stars, pleasant, nice music, no a/c, open late, reasonable prices; **Casa Portuguesa**, R Manoel Barata 897, good, inexpensive; **Lá em Casa**, Av Gov Malcher 247, try *menu paraense*, good cooking, fashionable, expensive; **Okada**, R Boaventura da Silva, past R Alcindo Cacela, Japanese, excellent, try "Steak House", various types of meat, rice and sauces, vegetables, all you can eat, also try *camarão à milanesa com salada*, good prices; **Miako**, Travessa 1 de Março 766, behind Praça de República (very good medium-priced oriental food); **Kyoto 294**, Trav Dr Morais 294, Chinese and Japanese, mixed reports; **Livorno**, Dr Morais 314, good, mid-price; **Germania**, R Aristides Lobo 604, Munich-style, mid price, rec; **Pizzaria Napolitano**, Praça Justo Chermont 12 (in particular pizzas and Italian dishes); **Cantina Italiana**, Benjamin Constant 1401, very good Italian, enthusiastically rec; **Churrascaria Tucuravi**, on the highway leading out of Belém, BR316, Km 3. Vegetarian: **Nectar**, Av Gentil Bittencourt; Travessa P Eutíquio 248, pedestrian zone, good, lunch only; **Chez Jacques**, R Silva Santos 102 (behind Hilton), delicious French food: knock on the window to enter, and check your bill as Jaques makes mistakes.

Specially rec for tourists are also some very good snack-bars (mostly outdoors in Belém) where you can buy anything up to a full meal, much cheaper than restaurants: **Charlotte**, Av Gentil Bittencourt 730, at Travessa Quintino Bocaiuva, for best *salgadinhos* in the city, also good desserts, very popular. Many buffet-style restaurants along R Santo Antônio pedestrian mall and elsewhere in the *Comércio* district, generally lunch only, good variety, pay by weight, prices average US$4/kg. **La Crème**, snack bar on Praça Nazaré, sells exotic fruit ice creams, view of Basilica; **Sorveteria Cairu** in Umarizal has excellent ice creams, including 30 fruit flavours. **Casa dos Sucos**, Av Presidente Vargas, Praça da República, serves 41 types of juice (including Amazonian fruits) and delicious chocolate cake (vegetarian restaurant upstairs, rec for lunches). **Navegante**, R Barata, **Tip-Top**, Trav Pedro Catiquio and R Pariquis (40 mins' walk from harbour), excellent ice cream. **Bar do Parque**, next to Municipal Theatre, excellent place for meeting local people, the more flamboyant stroll here after 2100. **Cosanostra Café**, Trav Benjamin Constant 1507, "pub" atmosphere, a/c, expensive. There are also many street and market vendors, who, although they should be viewed with care, often sell delicious local food.

Banks and Exchange Banco do Brasil, Av Presidente Vargas (near *Hotel Central*), good rates, and other Brazilian banks (open 0900-1630, but foreign exchange only until 1300). **Banco de Amazônia** (Basa), on Pres Vargas, gives good rates for TCs (Amex or Citicorp only), but does not change cash. **American Express**, R Gen Gurjão e Av Vargas, No 676, also representative office in *Hilton Hotel*, helpful. **Mastercard**, cash against card, Trav 14 de Março 1155, Nazaré. *Casas de câmbio*: **Carajás**, Av Pres Vargas 762, Galeria da Assambléia Paraense, Loja 12, also at Pres Vargas 620; **Casa Francesa**, Trav Padre Prudêncio 40; **Monopólio**, Av Pres Vargas 325, térreo do Ed Palácio do Rádio; **Turvicam**, Av Conselheiro Furtado 1558A, also at Av Pres Vargas 640, Loja 04; **Loja Morpho**, Presidente Vargas 362. *Hilton*, *Central* (cash only), *Ver-o-Peso* (cash and cheques, reasonable rates) and *Victória Rêgia Hotels*. French francs are readily available, but rates vary markedly between different *câmbios* and change rapidly.

Consulates Venezuelan, opposite French Consulate, Av Pres Pernambuco 270, T 222-6396 (Venezuelan visa takes 3 hrs, costs US$30 for most nationalities, but we are told that it is better to get a visa at Manaus; latest reports indicate that a yellow fever vaccination certificate is not required but best to check in advance—see also **Health** below). British, Robin Burnett, Ed Palladium Centre, room 410/411, Av Gov José Malcher 815, T 222-8470; Swedish, R Santo Antônio 316, mailing address Caixa Postal 111, T 222-4788, open 1600-1800; French, Av Pres Pernambuco 269, T 224-6818 (also for French Guiane; South Africans must apply in South Africa); German, Trav Piedade 651, sala 201, T 222-5634/5666; Finnish, Rodovia Arthur Bernardes 1393, Bairro Telégrafo, T 233-0333; Danish (Consul Arne Hvidbo), R Senador Barata 704, sala 1503, T 223-5888 (PO Box 826); US, Av Oswaldo Cruz 165, T 223-0800.

Electric Current 110 AC, 60 cycles.

Entertainment *Eskapuli*, Rodovia Augusto Montenegro, huge dance hall with various types of music, live and recorded, frequented by all age groups, open Wed-Sat from 2200 (take a radio taxi for safety), no a/c, dress informally. *Bar Teatro Maracaibo*, Av Alcindo Cacela 1289, informal place with live Brazilian popular music, moderate prices. *O Lapinha* discotheque/nightclub, good floor show, out of town, take taxi. *Rhinos*, Av Nazaré 400, good discotheque, also *Pink Panther*, R Aristedes Lobo 92. *Brasília Disco*, between the Hilton and Av Nazaré, expensive, good, most of the girls are working.

Health A yellow fever certificate or inoculation is mandatory. Best to get yellow fever vaccination at home (always have your certificate handy) and avoid the risk of recycled needles. Medications for malaria prophylaxis are not sold in Belém pharmacies. You can theoretically get them through the public health service, but this is hopelessly complicated. Such drugs are sometimes available at pharmacies in smaller centres, eg Santarém and Macapá. Bring an adequate supply from home. Clínica de Medicina Preventativa, Av Bras de Aguiar 410 (T 222-1434), will give injections, English spoken, open 0730-1200, 1430-1900 (Sat 0800-1100). Hospital Ordem Terceira, Trav Frei Gil de Vila Nova 2, doctors speak some English, free consultation but a bit primitive. British consul has a list of English-speaking doctors.

Post Office Av Presidente Vargas 498, but international parcels are only accepted at Post Office on the praça at the corner of Trav Frutuoso Guimarães e R 15 de Novembro, next door to NS das Mercês (hard to find).

Telecommunications Telegrams and Fax at the Post Office, Av Presidente Vargas. For phone calls: Telepará, Av Presidente Vargas.

Shopping in Av Presidente Vargas; also try the Indian handicrafts shop at Praça Kennedy, set in a garden with Amazonian plants and animals. *Parfumaria Orion*, Trav Frutuoso Guimarães 268, has a wide variety of perfumes and essences from Amazonian plants, much cheaper than tourist shops. Belém is a good place to buy hammocks, look in the street parallel to the river, 1 block inland from Ver-O-Peso. Also good for secondhand English books, in the Trav Campos Sales.

Camera Repairs Neemias Texeira Lima, R Manoel Barata 274, Sala 211, T 224-9941.

Golf Maracangalha Golf Club has 9 holes.

Travel Agent *Ciatur*, Av Presidente Vargas 645, T 224-1993, good half-day tour on water and in forest and 32-hr trip to Marajó.

Tourist Office Municipal office, Detur, in airport and Rodoviária. Hotel reservations made, including low-priced hotels. Map, US$1, from bus station bookshop. Paratur, Praça Kennedy on the waterfront, by the handicraft shop, helpful, many languages spoken; has a good map of Belém in many languages (but some references are incorrect). Town guidebook, US$2.75.

Police For reporting crimes, R Santo Antônio e Trav Frei Gil de Vila Nova. Robberies seemed to be on the increase in 1994-95. Take sensible precautions and stay out of dark corners.

Air Services Bus "Perpétuo Socorro-Telégrafo" or "Icoaraci", every 15 mins (even on public holidays) from Prefeitura, Praça Felipe Patroni, to airport, 40 mins, US$0.30. Taxi to airport, US$10 (ordinary taxis cheaper than Coop taxis, buy ticket in advance in Departures side of airport). Airport has a hotel booking service but operated by, and exclusive to, 5 of the more expensive hotels, discounts offered. Regular flights N to **Miami** by Varig, S to **Brasília** and other Brazilian cities, and W to **Santarém** and **Manaus**. To **Paramaribo**, four, and **Cayenne** 7 times weekly. Air France, R Boaventura Da Silva 1457, T 223-7547/7928. Suriname Airways, R Santo Antônio 432, Edif Antonio Velho, 4th floor, English spoken, help with information and documentation. To **Oiapoque** on French Guyane frontier by Taba (R O de Almeida 408, T 223-8811). Travellers entering Brazil from Guyane may find it necessary to obtain a 60-day visa (takes two days) before airlines will confirm their flights.

Shipping Services Regular coastal services to Southern Brazil. Agency for international services, Agências Mundiais Ltda, Av Pres Vargas 121, T 224 4078.

 To **Santarém, Manaus**, and intermediate ports (see **River Transport in Amazonia, p 539**). The larger ships berth at Portobrás/Docas do Pará (the main commercial port) either at Armazem (warehouse) No 3 at the foot of Av Pres Vargas, or at Armazem No 10, a few blocks further N (entrance on Av Marechal Hermes corner Av Visconde de Souza Franco). The guards will sometimes ask to see your ticket before letting you into the port area, but tell them you are going to speak with a ship's captain. Many touts will spot you as you approach the area, they are best ignored. Many smaller vessels (sometimes cheaper, but usually not as clean, comfortable or safe) sail from several small docks along the Estrada Nova (not a safe part of town). Take a Cremacao bus from Ver-o-peso.

To **Macapá (Porto Santana)**. *Silja e Souza* of Souzamar, Trav Dom Romualdo Seixas corner R Jeronimo Pimentel, T 222-0719, and *Almirante Solon* of Sanave (Servico Amapaense de Navegação, Castilho Franca 234, opposite Ver-o-Peso, T 222-7810). ENAL, T 224-5210; *Macamazónia*, R Castilho Franca (see **River Transport in Amazonia**, p 539). There is a desk selling tickets for private boats in the rodoviária; some hotels (eg *Fortaleza*) also sell tickets. They are good for information on the boats for which they sell tickets, but will not tell you anything about alternatives. Purchase tickets from offices 2 days in advance. Smaller boats to Macapá also sail from Estrada Nova.

There is weekend service to **Souré** on Ilha Marajó, for beaches, departing from the old ENASA dock next to Ver-o-Peso market.

Bus Services The rodoviária is located at the end of Av Gov José Malcher 5 km from centre, take Aeroclube, Cidade Novo, No 20 bus, or Arsenal or Canudos buses, US$0.35, or taxi, US$3 (at rodoviária you are given a ticket with the taxi's number on it, threaten to go to the authorities if driver tries to overcharge). It has a good snack bar and showers (US$0.10). Regular services to all major cities. There are direct buses from Belém to Marabá (16 hrs), on the Transamazônica, via Porto Franco and Toncantinópolis, and then change to Santarém (Marabá-Santarém 34 hrs). Direct bus Belém-Santarém once a week (US$75, more expensive than by boat and can take longer). To **São Luís**, 2 a day, 13 hrs, US$22, interesting journey through marshlands. If going to Campo Grande or Cuiabá, it may be better change in Goiânia than in Brasília.

Hitchhiking Going S, take bus to Capanema, 3½ hrs, US$3.80, walk ½ km from rodoviária to BR-316 where trucks stop at the gas station.

Roads A good asphalted road leads E out of the city to the coast town of Salinópolis, some 223 km, at the extreme end of the eastern part of the Amazon Delta. Various paved roads branch off: 118 km out of Belém one turns right on to the paved highway S to Brasília (2,120 km). Straight on, the road leads to Bragança, the centre of an early, unsuccessful, attempt in the 1900s to transfer population to Amazonia. At *Capanema* (E *Hotel São Luís*, good), on the road to Bragança, the road for São Luís, Teresina, Fortaleza and Recife branches right.

Excursions Travel agents offer short and longer visits to the rivers and jungle (Ciatur's ½ day trip, US$25, rec). A passenger ferry (*foca*) to the small town of Barcarena makes an interesting ½ day trip, departures from Ver-O-Peso, US$1. A return trip on the ferry from Ver-o-Peso to *Icaoraci* provides a good view of the river. Several restaurants here serve excellent seafood; you can eat shrimp and drink coconut water and appreciate the breeze coming off the river. The nearest beach is at *Outeiro* (35 km) on an island near Icoaraci, about an hour by bus and ferry (the bus may be caught near the Maloca, an Indian-style hut near the docks which serves as a night-club). To visit the ceramics workshops where marajoara and tapajônica wares are made, take the bus from Av Presidente Vargas to Icoaraci (1 hr). Open all week but best on Tues-Fri. Artisans are friendly and helpful, will accept commissions and send purchases overseas. A further bus from Icoaraci to Outeiro takes 30 mins. Further N is the island of **Mosqueiro** (86 km) now accessible by toll bridge (US$0.20) and an excellent highway, with many beautiful sandy beaches and jungle inland. It is popular at weekends and the beaches can get crowded and polluted.

Many hotels and weekend villas at the villages of Mosqueiro and Vila; rec. **C** *Hotel Farol*, on Praia Farol, 1920s architecture in good repair, small restaurant, good views; **C** *Hotel Marésia*, Praia de São Francisco, on beach, pool, helpful owner, agree prices for excursions in advance; **C** *Hotel Murumbira*, on Praia Murumbira, pool, restaurant. Restaurants at Mosqueiro: in *Hotel Ilha Bela*, Av 16 de Novembro 409, rec for fish, no evening meals; highly rec at Praia Chapeu Virado is *Marésia*; *Pizzeria Napolitana*; *Sorveteria Delícia*, Av 16 de Novembro, good local fruit ice creams, owner buys dollars. The traffic is heavy in Jul and at weekends, and hotels are full. Camping is easy. Buses Belém-Mosqueiro every hour from rodoviária, US$1.45, 80 mins.

Marajó is the world's largest river island (a claim disputed by the Bananal). Flooded in rainy Dec-Jun, it provides a suitable habitat for the water buffalo, said to have swum ashore after a shipwreck. They are now farmed in large numbers (try the cheese and milk). It is also home to many birds, crocodiles and other wildlife, and has several good beaches. It is becoming crowded at weekends and in Jul holiday season. The island was the site of the precolumbian Marajoaras culture.

Boats leave Belém (near Porto do Sal, seat US$3.60, cabin US$38 for 2, 5 hrs) most days for **Ponta de Pedras** (E *Hotel Ponta de Pedras*, good meals, buses for Souré or Salvaterra meet the boat). Bicycles for hire (US$1/hr) to explore beaches and the interior of the island. Fishing boats make the 8 hr trip to Cachoeira do Arari (1 hotel, E) where there is a Marajó museum.

A 10 hr boat trip from Ponta de Pedras goes to the Arari lake where there are two villages, Jenipapo (1 *pousada*, E) built on stilts, forró dancing at weekends and Santa Cruz which is less primitive, but less interesting (a hammock and a mosquito net are essential). There are water buffalo on the lake. There is a direct boat service to Belém twice a week.

Trips to the island are arranged by the *Grão Pará Hotel* (rec) and travel agents in Belém. Alternatively, a light aircraft may be hired to see Marajó from the air eg from Kovacs, Av Dr Freitas, opposite the airfield of the Aero Clube do Pará.

The Enasa service to **Souré** (pop 17,200), "capital" of the island, sails weekends only (4 hrs, US$5). Flights to Souré (infinitely preferable), Mon and Wed, 0700 and 1600, US$30 (return Mon, Wed, Fri). Colectivos into town, US$2. **E** *Hotel Soure* (3a Rua, Centro: walk straight on from Enasa dock, then take 3rd street on left), with bath, a/c, basic; *Pousada Marajoara*, and **E** *Pousada Parque Floresta*, nearby, friendly and clean, good meals. **D** *Cosampa*, Travessa 14, T 229-3928, hot showers, clean, friendly, free transfer from docks; **D** *Waldeck*, Trav 12, T 741-1414, clean, friendly, only 4 rm, Taba representative can be found here. **F** *Pensão* at 2nda Rua 575 (*Bar Guarani*), simple, rec. *Canecão*, Praça da Matriz, sandwiches, meals, rec. Changing money is only possible at very poor rates. Take plenty of insect repellent. There are fine beaches, Araruna (2 km—take supplies and supplement with coconuts and crabs, beautiful walks along the shore), do Pesqueiro (bus from Praça da Matriz,1030, returns 1600, eat at *Maloca*, good, cheap, big, deserted beach, 13 km away) and Caju-Una (15 km). Small craft await passengers from the Enasa boats, for Salvaterra village (good beaches and bars: seafood), US$12, 10 mins, or trips bookable in Belém from Mururé, T 241-0891, **B** *Pousada das Guarãs* (on beach, well-equipped), or at *Hotel Marajó*, T 741-1396 (Belém 225-2880), cheaper.

Salinópolis (228 km, pop 22,688) about 4 hrs by bus (US$5.50) on an excellent highway, is also worth a visit. Seaside resort with many small places where you can eat and drink at night by the waterfront, and fine sandy beach nearby (buses and cars drive on to the beach), a peaceful place mid-week. Best during holiday month of Jul. Atalaia, opposite Salinópolis, is pleasant, reached by taxi (US$10) or with a fisherman.

Hotels **C** *Atalaia*, on island of Atalaia, 15 km from Salinópolis, T 724-1122, simple, clean, beautiful setting, reserve in advance and take a taxi; **C** *Solar*, Av Beira Mar s/n, with bath, best in town, good restaurant; **D** *Jeanne d'Arc*, with breakfast; **E** *Salinas*, on beach.

Restaurants *Bife de Ouro* opp filling station, simple, but excellent fish and shrimp, always crowded for lunch; *Gringo Louco*, further out than Atalaia (take taxi or hitch), at Cuiarana beach, follow signs, gringo owner serves good, unusual dishes, and some "wild" drinks known as "bombs", popular.

For a view of life on a smaller river than the Amazon, take a bus to **Tomé-Açu**, S of Belém on the Rio Acará-Mirim, 3 buses a day, US$8.75. **E** *Hotel Las Vegas*, owner Fernando is very friendly. Boat back to Belém on Sun at 1100, arriving 1800, US$7.50.

There are ferries and daily flights from Belém to **Macapá** (pop 179,610, CEP 68900, DDD 096) a town on the northern channel of the Amazon Delta, which used to be decrepit but is now improving, particularly along the riverfront. Macapá is the capital of Amapá (agriculture, gold, manganese, coal, timber), one-quarter the size of France but with only 289,050 inhabitants. Each brick of the Fortaleza de São José do Macapá, built 1764, was brought from Portugal as ballast. The Fortaleza is used for concerts, exhibits, and colourful festivities on the anniversary of the city's founding, 4 Feb. The handicraft complex (*Núcleo de Produção Artesanal*) is located on Av Azárias Neto e Av JM Lombaerd, T 222-3681, daily 0800-1200 and 1500-2000. Craftsmen produce their wares onsite. A feature is pottery decorated with local manganese ore, also nice woodcarvings and leatherwork; staff are very friendly and helpful. São José Cathedral, inaugurated by the Jesuits in 1761, is the city's oldest landmark. Its aisles are lined with gravestones. The riverfront has been landscaped with trees, lawns and paths. It is a very pleasant place for a stroll in the evening, when the whole town is out doing the same. There are food and drink kiosks, and a nice lively atmosphere. The main avenue along the river is closed to vehicles on weekends. The pier (*trapiche*) is decaying, but is still a lovely spot for savouring the cool of the evening breeze, or watching sunrise over the Amazon. There is a monument to the equator, Marco

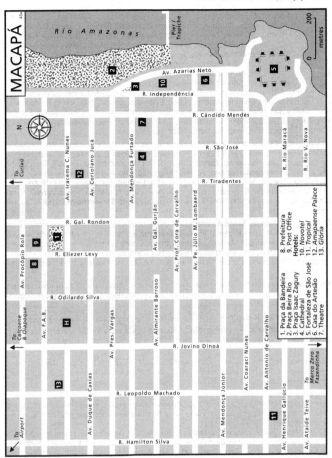

Zero (take Fazendinha bus from Av Mendonça Furtado). The equator also divides the nearby football stadium in half, aptly named O Zerão. South of these, along the road to Fazendinha, are the zoo and botanical gardens. Fazendinha itself is a popular local beach, very busy on Sun.

Lagoa dos Indios, 4 km W of the city along the Duque de Caxias road is a lake with snowy egrets and water buffaloes. Also fishing and swimming. **Curiau** is a town located 8 km from Macapá. Its inhabitants are the descendants of African slaves who have maintained many of the customs of their ancestors. Analogous to the Bush Negroes of Suriname, but apparently the only such village in Brazil.

Marabaixo is the traditional music and dance of the state of Amapá, festival held 40 days after Easter.

Macapá was declared a customs free zone in Jan 1993, raising hopes for an economic boom. So far, though, nothing has happened.

Hotels   A1 *Novotel*, French-owned, Av Azarias Neto 17, on waterfront, T 223-1144, F 231-1115, small, 4-star, all rooms a/c, swimming pool; **A3** *Ekinox*, R Jovino Dinoá 1693, T 231-4925, central, a/c, clean, helpful, excellent restaurant, highly rec; **D** *Santo Antônio*, Av Coriolano Jucá 485, T 222-0226, near main square, very clean, fan, shower, good breakfast extra; **D** *Tropical*, Av Antônio Coelho de Carvalho 1399, 20 mins from centre, one star, T 223-4899, with a/c (cheaper without), rec; *Glória*, Leopoldo Machado 2085, T 222-0984; **D** *Amapaense Palace*, R Tiradentes 109, T 222-3366, F 222-0703, 2 star, a/c, cold showers, comfortable, clean (*lanchonete* in same building, poor); **E** *Kamilla*, Av Padre JM Lombaerd, behind *Novotel* tennis courts, clean, friendly, with fan and bath, **F** hotel above churrascaria at Av Cora de Carvalho e R Independencia, basic; **E** *Meruno*, central, good value. The following are 10-mins walk from port and from Praça São José (where bus from Porto Santana stops): **E** pp *Mara*, R São José 2390, with bath, a/c, TV, fridge, good, clean, breakfast; **E** *Mercúrio*, R Cândido Mendes, 1300 block (no sign), T 223-4123.

Restaurants *Kamilla*, below hotel of same name, good buffet, pay by weight. Another buffet is *Kilo's*, Hamilton Silva 1398, T 223-1579, elegant, overpriced; *O Boscão*, Hamilton Silva 997, no sign, quite good; *Portenho*, Hamilton Silva 1390; *O Paulistano*, Av Henrique Galúcio 412, a/c, good; *Churrascaria Tropeiro*, Av Pres Vargas 450; *Clip*, Av Duque de Caxias 848; *Pizza San Carlos*, Cândido Mendes 1199, good for lunch; *Lennon*, good pavement café, no meals, at R Gen Rondon esq IC Nunes. Excellent ice cream sold in Macapá, eg *Sorveteria Santa Helena*, Av Feliciano Coelho 1023, Bairro do Trem, excellent; *Sorveteria Macapá*, R São José 1664, closer to centre.

Banks and Exchange Banco do Brasil, Av Independência 250, cash and TCs. Cambios (cash only): *Lantur*, Cândido Mendes 1085, *Casa Francesa*, on same street, *Monopólio*, Av Isaac Alcoubre 80. The rates in Macapá are similar to other cities in northern Brazil. Both US$ and French francs can be exchanged here. Best to buy francs in Belém if heading for Guyane as *câmbios* in Macapá are reluctant to sell them and they are more expensive and hard to obtain at the border.

Consulate There is a French consular agent in Macapá, some distance from town (ask taxi drivers or at *Novotel*), but visas are not issued for non-Brazilians. Only French and Portuguese spoken.

Post Office Praça da Bandeira.

Car Rentals National, Av Independência 30, near Praça Beira Rio, T 223-2799, at airport 231-4799. Localiza, Alameda Serrano, T 223-2799. Locauto, Av Pres Vargas 519, T 222-1011/1511.

Air Service Taba, office on Almirante Fracisco Serra 21, T 222-2083, has daily flights to Belém and 3 a week to Oiapoque and Cayenne. Varig, office on R Cândido Mendes 1039, T 223-1755, flies to Belém, Iguaçu, Rio and São Paulo.

Shipping Service Most ships now dock at Porto Santana, 30 km from Macapá (frequent buses US$0.55, shared taxis US$3.60 pp), however some smaller vessels still arrive at the pier in Macapá itself. This pier is also used when all of Porto Santana's dock space has been occupied by ore freighters.

To **Belém**, *Silja e Souza* of Souzamar, R São José S of cathedral, and *Almirante Solon* of Sanave (Servico Amapaense de Navegação, Av Azárias Neto, Praça Beira Rio). Both ships operate twice a week (see **River Transport in Amazonia**, p 539). Purchase tickets from offices 2 days in advance. Clean, smaller boats.

There is also regular direct service to **Santarém**, not going via Belém.

Overland Transport Buses to Oiapoque: Estrela de Ouro has its office on the main square, in front of the cathedral; it leaves daily at 2000. Cattani, office on Nunes between São José and Cândido Mendes, leaves daily at 0630. Journey time about 12 hrs (dry season) with several rest stops, 14-24 hrs in rainy season. Both leave from opposite Policia Técnica, 30 mins from centre, take bus "Jardim" and get out at Policia Técnica. Fare US$40. The Oiapoque bus does not go into Amapá or Calçoene and it is therefore difficult to break the trip at these places. One would have to walk several km from town to the main highway to catch the northbound bus when it passes in the small hours of the morning. Bus fare to Amapá and Calçoene US$25, 7 hrs, daily at 0700.

Pickup trucks (office Av Pres Vargas between São José and Tiradentes, can reserve in advance) also run daily to various locations throughout the state of Amapá, crowded and dusty on narrow benches in the back, or pay more to ride in the cab. Despite posted schedules, they leave when full. To **Oiapoque** at 0800, 10-12 hrs, US$40 cab, US$25 in back. To **Lourenço** at 0900, to **Laranjal do Jari** at 1000.

Rubber was almost the only product of Amapá until the 1950s, when manganese was discovered 150 km NW of Macapá. A standard-gauge railway, 196 km long, the only one in Brazil, has been built from the mining camp to Porto Santana, from which there is an excellent road. Malaria is rampant in the state; the illiteracy rate is 85%; smuggling goes on in a big way. The mining area—Icomiland, pop 4,000—is a startling exception: swimming pools, football fields, bowling alleys, supermarkets, dance halls, movies, a healthy oasis in the wilderness.

Ibama office, R Hamilton Silva 1570, Santa Rita, CEP 68.900, Macapá, has details on the **Cabo Orange National Park** in the extreme N of the Territory, and the **Lago Piratuba Biological Reserve**, neither accessible by road.

The road N to the Guyane border (BR-156) has been improved and although still precarious in places, it is now open throughout the year with both bus and pickup truck service continuing to operate even in the wet season. At all times however, it is prudent to take food and water for the journey as services are scarce in this sparsely populated region. Gasoline and diesel (not alcohol) are available along the road but there are occasional shortages. Those driving should take extra fuel from Macapá.

North of Macapá the road passes through **Porto Grande** (Recanto Ecológico Sonho Meu, resort at Km 108, Macapá T 234-1298) and on to **Ferreira Gomes** on the shores of the Rio Araguari, where the pavement ends. Further on are the towns of **Amapá** (formerly the territorial capital; **D** *Tourist Hotel* and one other, clean, comfortable, one block from square towards docks, turn right, 2nd house on left) and **Calçoene** (**D** government-owned hotel by bus stop, expensive food in adjoining canteen; sleeping space advertized in a café on Oiapoque road, very cheap). North of Calçoene a road branches W to **Lourenço**, whose gold fields continue to produce even after various decades of prospecting. The main road continues N across the Caciporé River and on to **Oiapoque**, on the river of the same name, which is the border with French Guyane. It is 90 km inland from Cabo Orange, Brazil's northernmost point on the Atlantic coast. 7 Km to the W is Clevelândia do Norte, a military outpost and the end of the road in Brazil.

Oiapoque is a remote border town, with its share of contraband, illegal migration, and drug trafficking. It is also the gateway to gold fields in the interior of both Brazil and Guyane. Quite a rough place, and the visitor should be cautious, especially late at night. Prices here are at least double those of anywhere else in Brazil, but still substantially lower than in neighbouring Guyane. The **Saut Maripa** rapids can be visited, 20 mins upstream along the Oiapoque River.

Hotels and Restaurants **D** *Government Hotel*, at E end of riverfront, now privately operated, refurbished, best in town, restaurant; **E** *Kayama*, on riverfront street above Taba office, with fan, 1 rm has private bath, good. Another **F** next door, basic. **F** *Sonho Meu*, one street back from river, basic. *Restaurant Paladar Drinks*, one block up from river, very expensive. There are several cheap hotels (**F**) along the waterfront. They are often full of Brazilians waiting to cross to Guyane.

Exchange It is possible to exchange US$ and *reais* to francs, but dollar rates are low. Visa users can withdraw *reais* at Bradesco, exchanging these to francs. Gold merchants, some shops, and one cambio in the market will sell *reais* for US$ or French francs, but are reluctant to sell francs. Rates are even worse in St-Georges. Best to buy francs in Belém, or abroad.

Flights Taba (office on riverfront) three times weekly to Macapá and Belém.

Buses Estrela de Ouro leaves for Macapá from the waterfront, daily at 1000, 12 hrs (dry season), 14-24 hrs (wet season), US$40, also Cattani. Pickup trucks depart from the same area when full, US$40 in cab, US$25 in the back.

Boats Occasional cargo vessels to Belém or Macapá (Porto Santana). A regular boat departs Wed for Cayenne, about 8 hrs, US$30. *Catraias* (decrepit canoes) carry illegal migrants for nighttime landing expensive, dangerous, definitely not rec.

Crossing to Guyane Motorized canoes cross to St-Georges de L'Oyapock, 10 mins downstream, slightly cheaper in *reais*, bargain. There is no vehicle ferry and no bridge; nor a road from St-Georges to Cayenne, you must fly or take a boat (very infrequent). Flights to Cayenne are usually booked several days in advance, and it is much cheaper to wait on the Brazilian side. Policia Federal for Brazilian exit stamp is on the road to Calçoene, about 500 meters back from the river. Gendarmerie in St-Georges at the E end of town, follow signs.

Belém to Manaus

A few hours up the broad river the region of the thousand islands is entered. The passage through this maze of islets is known as "The Narrows". The ship winds through 150 km of lanes of yellow flood with equatorial forest within 20 or 30 metres on both sides. In the Furo Grande the vessel rounds a hairpin bend almost touching the trees, bow and stern.

After the Narrows, the first point of special interest is formed by the curious flat-topped hills, on one of which stands the little stucco town of **Monte Alegre** (airport), an oasis in mid-forest.

Monte Alegre has some simple hotels (E), offering lagoon cruises to see lilies, birds, pink dolphins; boat trips to ancient cave paintings; village visits (US$25-40 per day), rec guide lives next door to a small brown and white hotel near the end of terrace at E side of docks.

Santarém (pop 265,105, CEP 68100, DDD 091) 2-3 days upstream on the southern bank, stands at the confluence of the Rio Tapajós with the Amazon, just half-way between Belém and Manaus. It was founded in 1661, and is the third largest town on the Brazilian Amazon. The yellow Amazon water is mottled with greenish patches from the Tapajós; the meeting of the waters is said by some to be nearly as impressive as that of the Negro and Solimões near Manaus. A small museum was opened in Jan 1993 in the old city hall on the waterfront, downriver from where the boats dock. It has a collection of ancient Tapajós ceramics, as well as various 19th century artefacts and publications. There is a movement for statehood for the Tapajós region, with Santarém as its capital. There is now a road southwards to Cuiabá (Mato Grosso), meeting the Transamazônica at Rurópolis (see p 539). (The southward leg from the Transamazônica to Cuiabá begins about 90 km W of this point, or 20 km from Itaituba.) Timber, bauxite and gold discoveries promoted very rapid growth, but the gold is running out and the city is no longer expensive. It is the jumping off point for gold prospectors in the Mato Grosso territories to the S. It is reported that prospectors are exploited by high prices, and that lawlessness abounds in the goldfields. Santarem itself, though, has an air of calm prosperity with good shops and a thriving business district centred around the *Hotel Tropical*. The unloading of the fish catch between 0500 and 0700 on the waterfront is an interesting scene. There are good beaches nearby on the river Tapajós.

Hotels A1 *Tropical*, Av Mendonça Furtado 4120, T 522-1533, F 522-2631, swimming pool seems to be unrestricted, friendly staff; **B** *Brasil Grande Hotel*, Trav 15 de Agosto 213, T 522-5660, clean, family-run, with restaurant; **B** *Santarém Palace*, close to city centre, Rui Barbosa 726, T 522-5285, good, with bath and TV; **C** *City*, Trav Francisco Correia 200, T 522-4719, with bath, a/c, TV, radio, frigobar, good, will collect from airport; **C** *Central Plaza*, Praça Rodrigues dos Santos 877, with bath and fan, run-down, friendly; **D** *Brasil*, Travessa dos Mártires, 30, including breakfast, good meals served, clean, good service, English spoken, owner plays chess; **E** *Equatorial*, good value, friendly, but noisy, thin partition walls, some rooms without windows; **D** *Greenville*, Av Adriano Pimenal 44, T 522-5820, good bathroom facilities and balcony view across the river; **E** *Horizonte*, Travessa Lemos 737, clean.

Restaurants *Mascotinho* bar/pizzeria, on beach, popular, good view; *Storil*, Travessa Turiano Meira, 2 blocks from Rui Barbosa, good fish, live music, takes credit cards; *Ritz*, Praça do Pescador, good; *Lanchonete Luci*, Praça do Pescador, good juices and pastries; *Sombra do Jambeiro*, Trav 15 de Novembro, Norwegian-owned bar and lanchonete, excellent meals; *Maxote*, bar with live Pagode on Sat afternoons.

Banks and Exchange It is very difficult to change dollars (impossible to change TCs anywhere), try **Farmácia Java** or travel agencies. Cash withdrawals on Visa at **Banco do Brasil**, good rate.

Health Dr Ihsan Youssef Simaan, T 522-3886/3982, speaks English and Spanish.

Travel Agents *Amazon Tours*, Trav Francisco Corrêa 17, 2 rm, T 522-1098, res 522-2620, run by Steve Alexander (from Alaska), specializes in half-day ecological tours and has a property in the jungle for overnight tours, pre-booking appreciated. Highly rec. *Gil Serique*, Praça do Pescador 131, T 522-5174, English-speaking guide, rec. *Coruá-Una Turismo*, 15 de Novembro 185-C, T 522-6303/7421 offers various tours, Pierre d'Arcy speaks French, rec.

Airport 15 km from town. Internal flights only. Buses to centre or waterfront. From centre bus leaves in front of cinema in Ruy Barbosa every 80 mins from 0550 to 1910, or taxis (US$12 to waterfront); *Hotel Tropical* has a free bus for residents; you may be able to take this.

Shipping Services To Manaus, Belém, Macapá, Itaituba, and intermediate ports (**see River Transport in Amazonia**, p 539). Most boats dock at the waterfront by the centre of town, but at times they may dock at the Cais do Porto, 4 km W, take "Circular" or "Circular Externo" bus. Check both places for departures to your destination. Also local service to **Obidós, Oriximiná, Alenquer**, and **Monte Alegre** (US$10, 5-8 hrs).

Buses Rodoviária is on the outskirts, take "Rodagem" bus from the waterfront near the market, US$0.25. Santarém to **Itaituba**, 8 hrs, US$10.25; there connecting service E to **Marabá on the River Tocantins**, 28 hrs (if lucky; can be 60 hrs, or even 6 days), US$48, with Trans Brasiliana. Also to **Imperatriz**, 46 hrs, US$54, office on Av Getúlio Vargas and at rodoviária. Enquire at rodoviária for other destinations. (Beware of vehicles that offer a lift, which frequently turn out to be taxis.) Road travel during the rainy season is always difficult, often impossible.

Excursion to *Altar do Chão*, a village set amid Amazonian vegetation on the river Tapajós, at the outlet of Lago Verde; hotel (D), comfortable; *Pousada* near the church, quiet, clean; luxury hotel to be built shortly; *Restaurant Mongote*, Praça 7 de Setembro, good fresh fish, huge portions; *Lago Verde*, try *calderada de tucunaré*; good swimming in the Tapajós from the beautiful, clean beach; bus from Mercado Municipal, Santarém, leaves 0500, 1100, 1600, 1½ hrs, returns 0630, 1230 and 1730 approx (rugged, but fun). Boat tour from *Hotel Tropical* US$30. Also by 0800 (0930 on Sun) bus to Porto Novo, 3 hrs into jungle by a lake, bus returns 0500 next morning and at 1230 Sun, Tues, Wed (you can sleep in it). Interesting wildlife on lake; canoe also can be hired.

37 km S from Santarém on a dirt road is *Belterra* (pop about 8,000), where Henry Ford established one of his rubber plantations, in the highlands overlooking the Tapajós River. Ford built a well laid-out new town; the houses resemble the cottages of Michigan summer resorts. Many of the newer houses follow the white paint with green trim style. The town centre has a large central plaza that includes a band stand, the church of Santo Antônio (circa 1951), a Baptist church and a large educational and sports complex. A major hospital, which at one time was staffed by physicians from North America, is now closed. Ford's project was unsuccessful: now the rubber forest is in bad condition. (**E** *Hotel Seringueira*, with about 8 rm and pleasant restaurant).

Fordlândia was the Ford Motor Company's first rubber plantation, founded in 1926; it is a friendly town since there are few visitors. *Hotel Zebu*, in old Vila Americana (turn right from dock, then left up the hill); one restaurant, two bars and three shops on town square. There is a little pebble beach N of the town.

Bus from Santarém to Belterra (from unmarked *Café Amazonas*, Travessa Moraes Sarmento between Rui Barbosa and São Sebastião), 1000 and 1230, Mon-Sat, return 1300 and 1530, US$2, about 2 hrs—note: one hour time difference between Santarém and Belterra so if you take the 1230 bus you'll miss the 1530 return bus). If driving, take Av Santarém-Cuiabá out of town, which is paved for 8 km. At Km 37 is a small Shell station; fork right and stop at the guardhouse; it's 15 km in town, following the electricity cables. Boats from Santarém to Itaituba may stop at Fordlândia if you ask (leave Santarém 1800, arrive 0500-0600, US$12 for 1st class hammock space); ask the captain to stop for you on return journey, about 2300. Boats may stop for Belterra, but it's a walk of several km from the river to town.

110 km up-river from Santarém is *Óbidos* (pop 42,195) a picturesque and clean city with many beautiful, tiled colonial buildings. It is located at the narrowest and deepest point on the river. For many kilometres little is seen except the wall of the great Amazonian forest. Small airport.

Manaus, the next city upstream, was at one time an isolated urban island in the jungle. It is the collecting-point for the produce of a vast area which includes parts of Peru, Bolivia and Colombia. There is superb swimming in the natural pools and under falls of clear water in the little streams which rush through the woods, but take locals' advice on swimming in the river; electric eels and various other kinds of unpleasant fish, apart from the notorious *piranhas*, abound and industrial pollution of the river is growing.

Until recently Manaus' only communications were by river and air. A road SW to Porto Velho, which is already connected with the main Brazilian road system, has been completed, but officially closed since 1990. Another, not yet fully paved, has been built due N to Boa Vista, from where other roads already reach the Venezuelan and Guyanese frontiers.

Manaus (pop 1,010,560 CEP 69000, DDD 092) is the capital of the State of Amazonas, the largest in Brazil (1.6 million square km), which has a population of 2.1 million. Though 1,600 km from the sea, it is only 32 metres above sea-level. The average temperature is 27°C. The city sprawls over a series of eroded and gently sloping hills divided by numerous creeks (*igarapés*). Dominating the centre is a Cathedral built in simple Jesuit style on a hillock; nothing distinguished inside or out. Nearby is the main shopping and business area, the tree-lined Avenida Eduardo Ribeiro; crossing it is Av Sete de Setembro, bordered by ficus trees. The area between Av Sete de Setembro and the rear of *Hotel Amazonas* is now reserved to pedestrians. There is a modern air-conditioned theatre. Manaus is building fast; 20-storey modern buildings are rising above the traditional flat, red-tiled roofs. It was the first city in South America to instal trams, but they have now been replaced by buses. A rather heavy-handed clean-up campaign between 1989 and 1993 brought major changes to the Zona Franca, the old city and the port area: better public sanitation; the eviction of street vendors (*camelos*) and beggars; the enforcement of building and hygienic standards in cheaper hotels; the completion of a concrete retaining wall from behind the market to Montecristi, improving the waterfront; opening one of the floating docks to regional shipping.

The main attractions are the **Botanic Gardens**, the well stocked public library, and the legendary Opera House, the **Teatro Amazonas**, completed in 1896 during the great rubber boom following 17 years of construction and rebuilt in 1929. It seats 685 people; for information on programmes, T 622-2420 (open Tues-Sun, 0900-1500, guided tour US$3 but same price to attend a concert). Another interesting historic building is the **Mercado Adolfo Lisboa**, commonly known as the Mercado. It was built in 1902 as a miniature copy of the now demolished Parisian Les Halles. The wrought ironwork which forms much of the structure was imported from Europe and is supposed to have been designed by Eiffel. It was restored in 1978. There is a curious little church, the **Igreja do Pobre Diabo**, at corner of Avs Borba and Ipixuna in the suburb of Cachoeirinha; it is only 4 metres wide by 5 metres long, and was built by a worker (the "poor devil" of the name); take Circular 7 Cachoeirinha bus from cathedral to Hospital Militar.

The remarkable **harbour installations**, completed in 1902, were designed and built by a Scottish engineer to cope with the up to 14 metre annual rise and fall of the Rio Negro. The large passenger ship floating dock is connected to street level by a 150-metre long floating ramp, at the end of which, on the harbour wall, can be seen the high water mark for each year since it was built. When the water is high, the roadway floats on a series of large iron tanks measuring 2½ metres in diameter. The material to build the large yellow **Alfândega** (customs building) near the harbour was brought block by block from Scotland as ballast. Tourists can visit the docks 0730-2000 daily.

Museums Museu do Índio (Indian Museum), kept by the Salesian missionaries, this interesting museum's collection includes handicrafts, ceramics, clothing, utensils and ritual objects from the various Indian tribes of the upper Rio Negro, R Duque de Caxias (nr Av 7 Setembro); excellent craft shop, rec; open Mon-Fri 0800-1200 and 1400-1700, Sat 0800-1200, T 234-1422, US$1.20; **Museu do Porto de Manaus** (Harbour Museum), holds various historical pieces, documents, letters, diaries and charts, R Vivaldo Lima 61 (nr Harbour); open Mon-Sat 0700-1100 and 1300-1700, Sun 1200-1700, T 232-0096; **Museu Tiradentes**, kept by the Military Police, holds selected historical pieces and old photographs, Praça da Policia; open Mon 1400-1800, Tues-Fri 0800-1200 and 1400-1800, T 234-7422; **Museu de Minerais e Rochas** (Geological Museum) contains a large collection of minerals and rocks from the Amazon region, Est do Aleixo 2150; Mon-Fri 0800-1200 and 1400-1800, T 236-1582; **Museu do Homem do Norte** (Anthropological Museum) reviews the way of life of the Amazonian population; social, cultural and economic aspects are displayed with photographs, models and selected pieces, Av 7 de Setembro 1385 (nr Av J Nabuco); closed 1994 for renovation T 232-5373; **Instituto Geográfico e Histórico do Amazonas**, located in a fascinating older district of central Manaus, houses a museum and library of over 10,000 books which thoroughly document Amazonian life through the ages, R Bernardo Ramos 117 (nr Prefeitura); open

Mon-Fri 0800-1200, T 232-7077, US$0.20; **Museu de Ciências Naturais da Amazônia** (Natural Science Museum), has a pavilion with insects and fish of the region, Est Belém s/n (difficult to get to, "São José-Acoariquarape/Tropolis" bus 519 to Conjunto Petro, then 2 km walk, best take a taxi), US$3.50, Tues-Sun 0900-1700, T 244-2799. The **Centro Cultural Chaminé**, R Isabel, near R Q Bocaiuva bridge, has occasional art exhibitions mounted in a restored water treatment works, built by the British in 1896.

Jardim Botânico "Chico Mendes" (Horto Municipal) The botanical gardens contain a collection of plants from the Amazon region. Unfortunately the plants are not well named. Av André Araujo s/n (Buses Aleixo, Coroado). Daily 0800-1200 and 1400-1700.

Zoo Run by CIGS, the Brazilian Army Unit specializing in jungle survival. About 300 Amazonian animals are kept in the Gardens (reported run-down with small cages). Est Ponta Negra 750 (no sign). Bus 120 or 207 (marked "Ponta Negra"), US$0.45, every ½ hr from R Tamandaré, opp cathedral in centre, alight 400 metres past the 1st Jungle Infantry Barracks (a big white

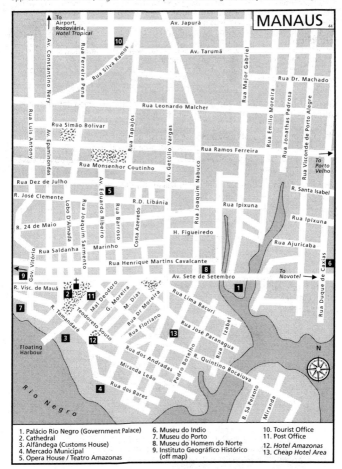

MANAUS 44

1. Palácio Rio Negro (Government Palace)
2. Cathedral
3. Alfândega (Customs House)
4. Mercado Municipal
5. Opera House / Teatro Amazonas
6. Museu do Indio
7. Post Office
8. Museu do Homem do Norte
9. Instituto Geográfico Histórico (off map)
10. Tourist Office
11. Post Office
12. *Hotel Amazonas*
13. *Cheap Hotel Area*

building), look for the sentries. Open 0800-1700. Entrance for foreigners, US$0.75, free on Sun. Small zoo also at *Hotel Tropical*, see above. Instituto Nacional de Pesquisas Amazonas (INPA), Estrada de Aleixo, at Km 3, not far from the Natural Science Museum (any bus to Aleixo), has named trees and manatees (best seen Wed and Fri at 0830 when water is changed), caimans and giant otters; worth a visit and good for birdwatchers.

Local Holidays 6 Jan (Epiphany); Ash Wednesday, half-day; Maundy Thursday; 24 June (St John); 14 July; 5 Sept; 30 Oct; 1 Nov, All Saints Day, half-day; Christmas Eve; New Year's Eve, half-day.

14 Jan: Anniversary of Praça 14 de Janeiro, commemorates the founding of the bairro; Samba Schools, street market, and fun fair. **Feb**: Carnival dates vary—5 days of Carnival, Amazonense culminating in the parade of the Samba Schools (see below). **3rd week in April**: Week of the Indians, Indian handicraft, talks, photographic exhibition, various localities. **First fortnight of June**: Festival Marquesiano, three days of festival, regional and Afro-Brazilian dancing, Arabian, Russian and European folklore, held at the Campo da Amizade, São Raimundo; Festival Folclórico do Amazonas, **second fortnight**, Praça Francisco Pereira da Silva, Bola da Suframa. **Second fortnight of Aug**: this is reported to be second only to Carnival. **10 Sept**: Travessia Almirante Tamandaré, swimming race across the Rio Negro (8500 metres) leaving from Praia da Ponta Negra; **also in Sept**: Festival de Verão do Parque Dez, **second fortnight**, summer festival with music, fashion shows, beauty contests, local foods, etc, Centro Social Urbano do Parque Dez; Festival da Bondade, **last week**, stalls from neighbouring states and countries offering food, handicrafts, music and dancing, SESI, Est do Aleixo Km 5. **Nov**: Festival Universitário de Cultura (entire month) with music, art and book exhibition, organized by the students on the University Campus. **8 Dec**: Procissão de Nossa Senhora da Conceição, from the Igreja Matriz through the city centre and returning to Igreja Matriz for a solemn mass.

Carnival in Manaus is rapidly becoming one of Brazil's most famous. It is a carnival of samba, with spectacular parades in a sambadrome modelled on Rio's, but with 3 times the capacity. Brazil's most famous performers appear at the Manaus carnival. Tourists may purchase grandstand seats, but admission at ground level is free, with every samba school member guaranteed entrance. This may make it rather unsafe for those carrying valuables, but ensures a memorable occasion with plenty of dancing.

NB Manaus time is one hour behind Brazilian standard time (2 hrs behind during Oct-Mar when the rest of Brazil is on summer time).

Crime Since 1991, Manaus has suffered a more serious economic downturn than the rest of Brazil. As lower national customs duties have undermined the Zona Franca, leading to increased unemployment, many people are seeking greener pastures, and there has been a substantial rise in crime and prostitution. The tourist industry continues to flourish, making the visitor a common target. One should take appropriate precautions, but also bear in mind that Manaus is still a good deal safer than the big cities of southern Brazil. (see **Information for Visitors**).

Hotels 10% tax and service must be added to bills. There is a hotel booking service at the airport. The Zona Franca is reported to be safer than the area around Av Joaquim Nabuco.

L1-L2 *Tropical*, Praia de Ponta Negra, T 658-5000, F 658-5026, a lavish, 5 star Varig hotel 20 km outside the city (taxi to centre, US$20), very expensive, discount with a Varig air pass, *Restaurant Tarumã* open for dinner only, *churrascaria* by pool, open to non-residents on weekdays only (well-dressed non-residents may use pool on weekdays, US$3 for non-residents, take bus from R José Paranaguá in front of Petrobras building esq Dr Moreira 0830, 0930, 1130 to Hotel, 1200, 1400, 1500, 1800 to town, or take Ponta Negra bus, US$0.35, then walk to hotel). It is rarely full, except in Jan-Feb. Parkland setting, pools, artificial ocean beach, small zoo with animals in small cages, new dock, departure point for many river cruises, tennis. Exchange at official rate only. Also away from centre, **L2** *Novotel*, Av Mandii 4 in the Industrial Area, T 237-1211, F 237-1094, 4 star, luxurious, T 663-1213/3323, F 611-3721, pool, US$1.75 taxi ride from centre, less good than *Tropical*; **A2** *Da Vinci*, R Belo Horizonte 240, 3 km from centre, T 663-1213/3323, F 611-3721, pool, friendly service.

Central hotels: **L3** *Best Western*, Marcílio Dias 217/225, T 622-2844, F 233-5984, some rooms a/c, expensive for what they offer, with good breakfast, good service; has a cheaper annex; **L3** *Amazonas*, Praça Adalberto Vale, T 622-2233, F 622-2064, 4 star, the ground floor is not rec, but rooms are reasonable, hot water, a/c; opp is **A1** *Ana Cassia Palace*, expensive, R dos Andradas 14, T 622-3637, F 622-4812; **L3** *Imperial*, Av Pres Vargas 227, T 622-3112, F 622-1762. A highly rec Aparthotel is **L3** *St Paul*, R Ramos Ferreira 1115, T 622-2131/36, F 622-2137, best in town, suites with bath, kitchen, living room, has pool, gym and sauna.

A2 *Mônaco*, R Silva Ramos 20, T 622-3446, F 622-3637, 3 star, rooms have good view, pleasant (some rooms noisy), rooftop restaurant/bar, delicious breakfast; **C** *Premier*, Av Eduardo Ribeiro 124, T 234-0061, some rooms with TV and fridge, friendly, good value; **D** *Janelas Verdes*, Leovegildo Coelho 216, T 233-1222, a/c, shower, TV, small, quiet (except Sun), safe, rec; **C** *Nova Avenida*, Av Pres Vargas, helpful, rec; **D** *Especial* at 198, T 234-0389, a/c, fridge, TV, bath, breakfast included; **D** *Fortaleza*, R dos Bares 238, with bath, a/c, fridge, reasonable, rec, cheaper without a/c, also dormitory (G), next door are *Allison* and *Asa Branca*, both a little cheaper; **D** *Hospedária Turístico 10 de Julho*, Dez de Julio 679, T 232 6280, a/c, clean, rec; **D** *Sun*, R Lima Bacuri 67B, centre, T 233-5668.

In R G Moreira (Zona Franca): **B** *Internacional* (168), (2-stars), T 234-1315, F 234-5396, a/c, friendly, central, coffee most of the day, good exchange rates; **B** *Rey Salomão* (No 119, T 234-7374), clean, breakfast; **B** *Central* (202), T 232-7887, some a/c, quiet; **B** *Nacional* (59), T 233-0537, with bath, fridge, a/c; **B** *Rio Mar* (325, T 234-7409), incl breakfast and bath, poor service reported, central.

In Av Joaquim Nabuco (by no means a safe area): **E** *Arteiro*, No 471, T 622-1343, near corner with R Lima Bacuri, with a/c or fan, clean, large rooms with bath; **E** *Aurora* (120) F 234-5121, with bath, a/c, friendly, clean, noisy TV in front rooms, refurbished 1993, good, simple breakfast; **E** *Luz* and **E** *Iguaçu*, T 232-9339 (Nos 779 and 711 respectively) are better than most on this street: the former is singles only above a gym, clean, breakfast included at *Iguaçu*; **E** *Manauara*, No 129, with bath, a/c, fridge, coffee all day, friendly, has TV; **E** *Dona Joana*, R dos Andradas 553, T 233-7553, a/c, clean, good value, insecure; **E** *Ideal*, No 491, a/c, F with fan, bath, no windows; **E** *Rio Branco*, No 484, T 233-4019, rec, avoid damp rooms on ground floor, clean, safe, laundry facilities, a/c, popular, friendly; **F** *Cheap*, R dos Andrades, friendly, clean, safe and cheap; **F** *Jangada*, No 473, cooking allowed, laundry facilities, very basic, fan, without bath. Other cheaper places in same area. **E** *Turista*, R Miranda Leão 356, basic; **F** *Hospedaria Olinda*, R L Coelho y J Paranaguá, rec, has soccer evenings; **F** *Nadie*, opp rodoviária.

NB When taking a taxi from the airport, insist on being taken to the hotel of your choice, and not to the one which pays the driver commission.

10 km E of the city is the small but growing town of *Iranduba*, cheaper than Manaus and with a good beach. *Hotel Verdes Matas*, T 367-1133, rec (US$15). Easy bus ride from Manaus, includes ferry crossing.

Camping There are no campsites in or near Manaus; it is difficult to find a good, safe place to camp wild. It is possible to camp wild on the bank of the Rio Negro near the *Hotel Tropical*; through outskirts of city via Tarumã bathing waterfalls to Ponta Negra bathing beaches, 20 km. Good swimming. Bus daily (US$0.45). Camping Praia Dourada, showers, toilets, restaurant, boat hire, good swimming, busy at weekends.

Restaurants *Novotel* serves a rec *feijoada completa* on Sat; *La Barca*, R Recife 684, wide variety of fish dishes, classy, popular, often has live music; *São Francisco*, Blvd Rio Negro 195, $1/2$ hr walk from centre (or bus 705), in Educandos suburb, good fish, huge portion, highly rec; *Panorama* next door, No 199 (also good for fish, cheap, highly rec). *Caçarola*, R Maués 188, Cachoerinha, T 233-3021, very good local fish dishes (take a taxi); Japanese at *Miako*, R São Luís 230, also *Suzuran*, Blvd Álvaro Maia 1683, Adrianópolis, good, closed Tues, taxi US$2; *Búfalo*, churrascaria, Joaquim Nabuco 628, all you can eat (of high quality); *Fiorentina* R José Paranaguá 44 (Praça da Policia), Italian, very good, half price on Sun; *Mister Pizza*, R José Paranaguá 104 (Praça da Policía), good pizza and sandwiches, a/c, upstairs; *Esquina do Lanche*, corner Paranaguá and Dr Moreiro, good, cheap; *Fiorella*, R Pará 640, good Italian; *Olinda*, Pedro Botelho 93, nr Miranda Leão, good regional dishes, *caldeirada* rec; *Frangolandia*, Joaquim Nabuco nr 7 de Setembro, good grill. *Chapaty*, Saldanho Marinho 429B; also R Costa Azevedo 105, vegetarian, closed eves. *Mandarin*, Av Eduardo Ribeiro 650, all you can eat lunches; *Schnaps bar and restaurant*, R Recife 1005, Casa 17-A, typical German, friendly, evenings only, closed Sun; *Skina dos Sucos*, corner of E Ribeiro and 24 de Maio, rec for juices; pizzeria next door also good; *Casa do Guaraná*, R Marcilio Dias, marvellous juices mixed with *guaraná*; *Casa dos Sucos*, 7 de Setembro between Joaquim Nabuco and G Vargas, regional fruit juices and snacks; *Maté Amargo*, R Saldanha Marinho 603, good buffet, all you can eat; *Veneza*, Av Getúlio Vargas 570, good Sat *feijoada*; *Floresta*, R dos Andradas 335, friendly, English-speaking, good vegetables; *Jangada Bar*, opp *Hotel Amazonas*, good for snacks; good, but expensive snacks in *Hotel Amazonas* itself; *Alemã*, cafeteria, R José Paranaguá/Praça da Policía, good for juices, sandwiches; good *pratos* at Brasileiros department store, Av 7 de Setembro. *Sorveteria Glacial*, Getúlio Vargas 161 and other locations, highly rec for ice cream. *Restaurante Natalia*, Av Epaminondas s/n, downtown, with garden, has Pagode music and dancing on Fri nights. The floating reurant in the harbour below the market building is rec for best *tucunaré* fish. Many restaurants close on Sun nights and Mon. City authorities grade restaurants for cleanliness: look for A and B. Good juice bars along Av Joaquim Nabuco, try *cupuaçu*. *Lanchonete Pigalle* particularly rec.

The fishing catch is brought to the waterfront between 2300-0100, including the giant *pirarucu*. Good fruit and vegetable market by the port.

Banks and Exchange Banco do Brasil, R Marechal Deodoro (5th floor) and Airport (basement—24 hrs) changes dollars cash at tourist rate, efficient; many local banks. Open 0900-1600. Most offices shut afternoons. Foreign exchange operations 0900-1200 only, or close even as early as 1100. **Banco Meridional**, 7 de Setembro 691 (Mastercard). Thomas Cook cheques changed by *Banespa* (good rates, cheques and cash). **B**amerindus, R Marcílio Dias 196, TCs only, good rates, fast and friendly service; **Credicard**, Av Getúlio Vargas 222 for Mastercard and Diner's cash advances, also at R Joaquim Nabuco. **American Express** for money transactions and mail, Selvatur, Praça Adalberto Valve, T 622-2577, adjacent to *Hotel Amazonas*. Cash at main hotels, at Souvenirs de Manaus shop and at Minitur (good rates); Sr Lima, R Quintino Bocaiúva 189, Sala 34; Câmbio Cortez, 7 de Setembro e Getúlio Vargas, converts TCs into US$ cash at 3-5% commission. It is not safe to change money on the streets.

Electric Current 110 volts AC; some hotels 220 volts AC, 60 cycles.

Consulates Most open am only. **Peruvian**, Conjunto Aristocratais, Chapada, R A, Casa 19 (T 656-3267, open 0800-1400). **Colombian**, R Dona Libânia 62, near opera house, T 234-6777, please note that apparently a Colombian tourist card can be obtained at the border. We advise double-checking. **Venezuelan**, Ferreira Pena 179, T 233-6004, 0800-1400; everyone entering Venezuela overland needs a visa: in late 1994 the requirements were: 2 passport photos, US$30, and an onward ticket, while in early 1995 the tourist visa was free; a yellow fever certificate and a flight ticket into Venezuela have also been requested. **Bolivian**, the consulate is now apparently run from a restaurant, *Los Palmas*, R Rio Jauari.

British, Eduardo Ribeiro 520, Sala 1202, T 622-3879. **United States**, Geral Recife 101, T 234 4546 (office hours) and 232 1611 (outside office hours). Will supply letters of introduction for US citizens. **Spain**, R Monsenhor Coutinho, T 234-0842; **Dutch**, R M Leão 41, T 234-8719/223-6874; **Austria**, Av Eduardo Ribeiro 500, 1st floor; **Italy**, R Belo Horizonte 240, T 611-4877; **Japanese**, R Ferreira Pena 92, T 234-2521; **Danish**, R M Leão 45, T 622-1356; also handles **Norway**; **Finnish**, T 234-5084; **Belgium**, 13 qd D conj Murici, T 236-1452; **Portugal**, R Terezina 193, T 234-5777.

Entertainment For *Teatro Amazonas*, see above. *Spectrum*, R Lobo D'Almada 322, very young. Cachoeirinha has a number of bars offering music and dancing, liveliest at weekends. *Kalamazon Night Club*, Km 12 on Torquato Tapajós road, T 651-2797, Wed-Sat, all kinds of music, disco; *Studio 5* disco, R Contorno, Distrito Industrial, T 237-8333. *Superstar*, next to the terminal; *Orvalho da Noite*, R Santa Isabel 1000; *Nostalgia Clube*, R Ajuricaba 800; *Clube de Samba*, R Manicoré.

Cinema Six screens at the new Amazonas shopping centre, bus Cidade Nova 5, or 204, 207, 208, 307. Most foreign films are shown with original soundtrack and Portuguese sub-titles. Afternoon performances are recommended as long queues often form for the evening performances.

Hospital of tropical medicine, treatment free, some doctors speak a little English: gives out mefloquine malaria prophylaxis free. Take "Dom Pedro" bus from main terminal, about 20 min ride.

Laundromat Blvd Álvaro Maia 1570, Mon-Sat 0800-2200, coin operated, take mini bus ROTA 05 from Av 5 de Setembro.

Post Office Main office including poste restante in Marechal Deodoro. On the first floor is the philatelic counter where stamps are sold, avoiding the long queues downstairs. Staff don't speak English but are used to dealing with tourists. For airfreight and shipping, Alfândega, Av Marones Santa Cruz (corner of Mal Deodoro), Sala 106. For airfreight and seamail, Correio Internacional, R Monsenhor Coutinho e Av Eduardo Ribeiro (bring your own packaging). **UPS** office, T (092) 232-9849 (Custódio).

Telephone TeleAmazon on R Guilherme Moreira, opp Banco do Brasil; Av Getúlio Vargas, about 7 blocks N of 7 de Setembro.

Markets and Souvenirs Go to the *Mercado Adolfo Lisboa* (see above) early in the morning when it is full of good quality regional produce, food and handicrafts, look out for *guaraná* powder or sticks, scales of *pirarucu* fish (used for manicure), and its tongue used for rasping *guaraná* (open daily 0500-1800). In Praça da Saudade, R Ramos Fereira, there is a Sun *Festa de Arte* from 1700; try prawns and calaloo dipped in *tacaca* sauce. In the Praça do Congresso, Av E Ribeiro, there is a very good Sun craftmarket. See the two markets near the docks, best in the early morning. The *Central Artesanato* Handicraft Centre (R Recife s/n, nr Detran) has local craft work. *Casa de Beija-Flor*—The House of the Hummingbird, in the *Hotel Tropical*, good. *Selva Amazônica*, Mercado Municipal, for wood carvings and bark fabric. For hammocks go to R dos Andrades where there are many shops. In R Duque de Caxias is a rubber factory open to the public. Since Manaus is a free port, the whole area a few blocks off the river front is full of electronics shops. Note that all shops close at 1400 on Sat and all day Sun.

Bookshop *Livraria Nacional*, R 24 de Maio, stocks some French books, the *Livraria Brasília* has some English books.

Photographic Highly rec for camera repairs: *Oficina Kawasky*, R Floriano Peixoto; film processing at *Studio Universal*, R 24 de Mai 146, cheap, good quality.

Sports For **swimming**, go to Ponta Negra beach by Soltur bus for US$0.35, though beach virtually disappears beneath the water in Apr-Aug. The whole area has been remodelled with a new sidewalk and snack bars; popular by day and at night with outdoor concerts and samba in the summer season. Good swimming at Bolívar Falls in the river Tarumã, where lunch is available, shade, it is crowded at weekends, and not too nice; take Tarumã bus from R Tamandaré or R Frei J dos Inocentes, ½ hr, US$0.35 (very few on weekdays), getting off at the police checkpoint on the road to Itacoatiara.

Tourist Information Emamtur, Praça 24 de Outubro, R Tarumã 379 helpful, 0730-1330, weekdays only, at Teatro Amazonas, corner of Eduardo Ribeiro, and airport. Town map from *Hotel Amazonas* or from Amazon Explorers. *Guide Book of Manaus*, US$3, available from *Hotel Amazonas* and other places, in English, useful. *A Notícia*, newspaper, lists local entertainments and events. *Mananara Guia*, a very detailed Manaus street index and guide, is available from news kiosks, US$18. Tucumaré Turismo, R Henrique Martins, T 234 5071, will give information and make reservations.

Police Take bus from *Hotel Amazonas* to Kissia Dom Pedro for Policia Federal post, people in shorts not admitted.

Car repairs Mavel VW, highly recommended, English spoken.

Bicycle repairs 3 shops on R Com Clementino, near Av Alvaro Maia.

Air Services International flights: Varig to Miami once a week; LAB twice weekly to La Paz (via Santa Cruz), Miami and Caracas. Vasp twice a week to Aruba. To the Guyanas, connection must be made in Belém. Transbrasil to Buenos Aires daily (2-3 stops). Make reservations as early as possible, flights may be full. Do not rely on travel agency waiting lists; go to the airport 15 hrs early and get on the airport waiting list. Varig, M Dias 284, T 622-3161, English spoken, helpful; LAB, T 232-7701; Vasp, T 622-1141/3470.

Internal flights: There are frequent internal flights with Varig, Vasp and Transbrasil (T 622-3738). The most frequent routes are Brasília-Rio, Brasília-São Paulo and the NE Coast milk run Santerém-Belém-São Luís-Fortaleza-Recife. Varig flies to Boa Vista, midnight, US$99. For other Amazon towns call Taba (232-0806/5605). Taba flights can be irregular and often reservations cannot be changed. Return reservations cannot be made with Taba when purchasing ticket.

The taxi fare to or from the airport is US$12, fixed rate, buy ticket at airport and in most hotels; or take bus 608 or hourly bus 201 marked Aeroporto Internacional from R Tamandaré near cathedral, US$0.45, or 1107 from Ed Garagem on Av Getúlio Vargas. No buses 2200-0700. (Taxi drivers often tell arrivals that no bus to town is available, be warned!) It is sometimes possible to use the more regular, faster service run by the *Tropical Hotel*; many tour agenices offer free transfers without obligation. Check all connections on arrival. **NB** Check in time is 2 hrs in advance. Allow plenty of time at Manaus airport, formalities are very slow. The restaurant serves good à la carte and buffet food through the day. It is possible to sleep on the airport observation deck if catching an early morning flight. Local flights leave from airport terminal 2: make sure in advance of your terminal.

Shipping To Santarém, Belém, Porto Velho, Tefé, Tabatinga (for Colombia and Peru), Caracaraí (for Boa Vista), São Gabriel da Cachoeira, and intermediate ports (see **River Transport in Amazonia**, p 539). Almost all vessels now berth at the first (downstream) of the floating docks which is open to the public 24 hrs a day. A ticket sales area has been built by the pedestrian entrance to the port (bear left as you enter) where bookings can be made up to 2 weeks in advance. The names and itineraries of departing vessels are displayed here as well as on the docked boats themselves; travellers still recommend buying tickets from the captain on the boat itself. The port is relatively clean, well organized, and has a pleasant atmosphere.

ENASA (the state shipping company) sells tickets for private boats at its office in town (prices tend to be high here). A few local boats and some cargo barges still berth by the concrete retaining wall between the market and Montecristi.

NB See introduction to **Up the Amazon River** section on **Health**. You may need a visa to travel to Peru; consulate address above. Those arriving from Leticia should go to the police for their immigration entrance stamp, but you should get this in Tabatinga. Departures to the less important destinations are not always known at the Capitânia do Porto, Av Santa Cruz 265, Manaus. Be careful of people who wander around boats after they've arrived at a port: they are almost certainly looking for something to steal.

Passports For those arriving by boat who have not already had their passports stamped, the immigration office is on the first of the floating docks next to the tourist office. Take the dock entrance opposite the cathedral, bear right, after 50 metres left, pass through a warehouse to a group of buildings on a T section.

Roads Manaus rodoviária is 5 km out of town at the intersection of Av Constantino Nery and R Recife; take local bus from centre, US$0.45, marked "Aeroporto Internacional" or "Cidade Nova" (or taxi, US$7.50). Local buses to Praça 14 or airport leave from opposite *Hotel Amazonas* (take airport bus and alight just after Antártica factory) or take local bus to Ajuricaba. To *Itacoatiara*, 285 km E on the Amazon, with Brazil-nut and jute processing plants (bus service 8 a day, 4 hrs); now paved route AM-010, 266 km, through Rio Preto da Eva.

The road N from Manaus to Boa Vista (770 km) is described on **p 564**. Hitch-hiking with truckers is common, but not recommended for women travelling alone. To hitch, take a Tarumã bus to the customs building and hitch from there, or try at "posta 5", 2 km beyond rodoviária.

The Catire Highway (BR 319) from Manaus to Porto Velho (868 km), has been officially closed since 1990, several bridges are out, and there is no repair in sight. It may, however, be passable in the dry season with a 4-wheel-drive and winch (ask Embratel, whose vehicles use the road to maintain the telephone lines). Those who would undertake such an expedition must be entirely self-sufficient and obtain a permit from the military in Manaus. Without this you will be turned back at the second ferry crossing. The 250 km middle stretch is uninhabited: if taking this route, sling your hammock high and check your shoes for spiders. The alternative for drivers is to ship a car down river on a barge, others have to travel by boat (see below). There is, at present, no bus service on this road.

Tours There are many different kinds of tours: "luxurious", which are comfortable but "set up" for tourists; some aiming at seeing lots of animals, and others at seeing how the people in the jungle live. Be sure to ascertain in advance the exact itinerary of the tour, that the price includes everything (even drink and tips), that the guide is knowledgeable and he himself will accompany you, and that you do not want to kill anything rare. Be very clear about what you want from your trip, and ensure that others in your party share the same expectations, and are going for the same length of time. Choose a guide who speaks a language you can understand. A shorter tour may be better than a long, poor one. It is worth shopping around for the best service and bargaining may reduce prices. **NB** Guides must be officially registered with Embratur and must carry an identity card. It is potentially very dangerous to go with an unofficial guide. Do not employ freelance guides touting at the airport or the river port. Wait until you get to your hotel and seek advice on reputable companies there. Then book direct with the company itself. Ask for a detailed, written contract.

Flights over the jungle give a spectacular impression of the extent of the forest.

Bill Potter, resident in Manaus, writes: opposite Manaus, near the junction of the Rio Negro and the Rio Solimões, lies the Lago de Janauri, a small nature reserve. This is where all the day or half-day trippers are taken usually combined with a visit to the "meeting of the waters". Although many people express disappointment with this area because so little is seen and/or there are so many "tourist-trash" shops, for those with only a short time it is worth a visit. You will see some birds and with luck dolphins. In the shops and bars there are often captive parrots and snakes. The area is set up to receive large numbers of tourists, which ecologists agree relieves pressure on other parts of the river. Boats for day trippers leave the harbour constantly throughout the day, but are best booked at one of the larger operators such as Amazon Explorers or Selvatour. Remember that in the dry season, 1-day tours may not offer much to see if the river is low.

Those with more time can take the longer cruises and will see various ecological environments, but bear in mind that most tour operators will make a trip up the Rio Negro because it is easier to navigate, generally calmer and there are many fewer biting insects. There is also much less animal life in general, so to see any patience and luck are needed. To see virgin rainforest a 5 day trip by boat is needed. On the Rio Solimões there is more wildlife, but you are less likely to see anything because you'll be constantly fighting the mosquitoes and sandflies.

Another alternative is to go up river to one of the jungle hotels. From the base, you can then take short trips into the forest or along the river channels.

Taking a transport boat from Manaus is not a substitute for a tour as they rarely get near to the banks and are only interested in getting from A to B as quickly as possible. The passengers see very little of the forest.

Prices vary. The recommended companies charge within the following ranges: 1 day, US$30-60; 2 days, US$100-150; 4 days, US$200-250; longer, specialized, or more luxurious excursions will cost significantly more. It is more economical to incorporate the meeting of the waters in a longer trip than to make a separate excursion.

Amazon Explorers Manaus Ltda, run by Manoel (Bebê) Barros, R Quintino Bocaiúva 189, T 232-3052 his day's tour including "meeting of the waters", Lago do Januauri and rubber collecting and lunch has been highly recommended by most users; 32-hr trips, require a minimum of 4 people; other tours available. Boat *Amazon Explorer* available for hire at about US$230/day. Next door is *Swallows and Amazons*, R Quintino Bocaiúva 189, andar 1, Sala 13, T/F 622-1246 (or Box 771, Eastham, Mass 02642, T 508-255-1886, F 508-240-0345, or 1-800-356-1121), Mark and Tania Aitchison, wide range of riverboat tours and accommodation (up to 9 days). *Transamazonas Turismo*, Leonardo Malcher 734, T 622-4144 (reservations through South American Turismo, Av NS de Copacabana 788, T 255-2345, 22050 Rio de Janeiro), for parties of 10 or less offers a 3-days-plus stay at *Amazon Lodge*, a floating lodge on Lake Periquitão, 80 km from Manaus, or *Amazon Village*, on dry land, rec. *Ariaú Jungle Tower*, Rio Amazonas Turismo, at *Hotel Mônaco*, R Silva Ramos 41, T 234-7308, 35 km from Manaus on a side channel of the Rio Negro, jungle hotel with observation tower and a walkway across a swamp, trips to Anavilhanas islands in groups of 10-20, rec. The better hotels also arrange tours (ask for Joe Sears in *Hotel Tropical*), and so do *Selvatur* (office in *Hotel Amazonas*, T 622-2577), Rio Negro trip, 0800-1500, with lunch at *Janaurylândia* floating hotel. *Exotic Amazon Tours*, Av 7 de Setembro 1367A; *Queiroz Tours*, Av Joaquim Nabuco 681, sala 02, T 233-3354, both rec.

Safari Ecológico, Av Marechal Câmara 160, Sala 621, Caixa Postal 3321, CEP 20.010, Rio de Janeiro, T (021) 240-6785, has been recommended for its ecological tours. (Manaus address: R Monsenhor Coutinho 119, T 233-6910, bookings also through Carretour du Brésil, Paris; Brazil Nuts, Fairfield CT, USA; Jolivac, Montreal.) All tours are accompanied by guide, scientific adviser and doctor. The **Amazon Monkey Jungle**, 30 mins up Rio Tarumã from the Rio Negro confluence, is part of a new *Amazon Ecopark* initiative where many monkey species are treated and rehabilitated in natural surroundings. For day tours T 234-0939. The Living Rainforest Foundation, which administers the ecopark, also offers educational jungle trips and overnight camps (bring own food). Entrance US$15.

There appears to be an endless supply of guides. Those listed below have been recommended by travellers in 1994 and 1995, but bear in mind that different tourists have different expectations and recommendations can change: for trips on the Amazon and Rio Negro, **Moacir Fortes**, R Miguel Ribas 1339, Santo Antônio, Manaus, T 232-7492 or through Amazonia Expeditions Ltd, Houston, T (713) 660-8115 (has his own 18-metre boat *Amazonia Expedition*), he speaks English and German. Also **Gerry Hardy**, very warmly rec, contact through Chris at *Hotel Rio Branco*, or T 237-6981, Chris, who charges up to 30% commission, also deals with Elmo de Morais Lopez, Carlos Colares (see below), and **Carlos Grandes Perez**, enthusiastically rec. Carlos Grandes Perez can also be contacted through the *Hotel Turístico* at Lad da Glória in Rio de Janeiro, and *Hotel Nunes*, Porto Velho, T 069-221-1389. **Elmo de Morais López**, R Henrique Martins 364, Centro, T 233-8927, speaks English, German, Spanish, Italian, French, rec for 2-5 day tours, 2-4 people, sleeping in hammocks (Elmo works for agencies as well). *Jangal Tours*, R Quintino Bocaiuva 371 esq R Floriano, 1st floor, T 232-5884, F 232-4843, has been rec as efficient; **Sandro Gama**, Miranda Leão 591, speaks English, good on environment, indigenous peoples, plants; *Amazon Wild*, R Quintino Bocaiúva 425, T 233-9308, frequent good reports, with rec guides Cláudio Gonzaga and Robert, speaks English and French; Ananacis of *Guaraná Native Tours*; **Francisco da Silva**, T 625-1905, has his own boat, rec.

Thérèse Aubreton, director of *Alternatur Amazônia*, R Costa Azevado 9, sala 203, works with Carlos Jorge Damasceno (see below) to provide ecologically sensitive tours away from the usual routes, T 232-5541, F 233-5941. For those prepared to spend around 10 days in the interior on a real expedition, contact **Carlos Colares**, Av Atlântica 91, Raiz, 69.000 Manaus, T 092-237-1961, Telex 092-165 XPMNA, or PO Box 360, who conducts private excursions, with fishing, hunting and exploring in the more remote regions of the Rio Negro. Carlos Colares speaks good English. A colleague of his, **Sebastião Dimas**, also rec, can be reached at R Elisabeth 6, Bairro de Flores. Similar tours arranged by **Sabrina Lima de Almeida**, R Boa Esperança 6, T 237-7359, Portuguese speaking only, rec. Serious deep jungle exploration with an ecological slant and visits to remote historical and Indian settlements: **Carlos Jorge**

Damasceno, Jaguar, R Belém 1646, Cachoeirinha, T 234-0736; multilingual, very highly rec.

Generally, between Apr and Sep excursions are only by boat; in the period Oct-Mar the Victoria Regia lilies virtually disappear. Fishing is best between Sep and Mar (no flooding). If using a camera, do remember to bring a fast film as light is dim.

Bird-watchers can see many kinds of birds in and around the grounds of the *Hotel Tropical* (for instance: fly catchers—kingbirds and kiskadees, swallows, yellow-browed sparrows, aracaris—member of the toucan family, woodpeckers, woodcreepers, thrushes, anis, three species of tanager, two of parrots—the dusky and blue-headed). Sloths and monkeys may also be seen. For further information contact Moacir Fortes.

The enterprising go to the Capitânia do Porto and find out what boats are making short trips; eg, Manaus-Itacoatiara, US$10 first-class.

About 15 km from Manaus is the confluence of the Solimões (Amazon) and the Rio Negro, which is itself some 8 km wide. Here you can see the meeting of the blue-black water of the Rio Negro with the yellow-brown Solimões flood; the two rivers run side by side for about 6 km without their waters mingling. Tourist agencies run boat trips to this spot (US$50). The simplest way to see the waters meeting is to take a taxi or No 617 "Vila Buriti" bus to the Careiro ferry dock, and take the car ferry across. The ferry goes at 0700, returning 0900 and 1500, returning 1830 (approx). You can also take small private launches across, 40 mins journey, about US$12/seat, ask for the engine to be shut off at the confluence, you should see dolphins especially in the early morning. Alternatively, ask in the dock area for boats which may be going to the confluence, or hire a motorized canoe from near the market (US$15 approx); allow 3-4 hrs to experience the meeting properly). A 2-km walk along the Porto Velho road from the Careiro ferry terminal will lead to a point from which Victoria Regia water lilies can be seen in April-Sept in ponds, some way from the road. If you continue over the Capitari bridge, you reach unspoilt jungle. There are several small restaurants on the S bank in Careiro, where the road SW to Porto Velho and the S begins.

To **Manacapuru** to see a typical Amazon town, 84 km on AM-070 by bus, 4 daily, US$5, 2 hrs including ferry crossing. A small market town on the Solimões W of Manaus, with three basic hotels, *Rio Branco*, clean, friendly, and *Il Maccarone* pizzeria, Av Eduardo Ribeiro 1000, with its friendly Italian owner Mário. Another village one can visit is **Araçá**, a 3-hr bus ride from Rodoviária in the direction of Castanho; the journey includes a ferry crossing at the confluence of the Negro and Solimões (fare to Araçá US$0.85, bus leaves 0600 and 1100). The village is on the banks of the Rio Mamori; canoes can be hired for US$5 for a day (night trips also possible) and you may be able to sling your hammock in a private house. Plenty of wildlife close at hand. 3 buses a day return to Manaus. A recommended trip is from São Raimundo to Barcelos on the Rio Negro, in the boat *Emerson Medeiros*, 2 days, and a night at *Hotel Oasis*.

Tefé (pop 26,000) lies approximately halfway between Manaus and the Colombian border. The waterfront consists of a light sand beach; waterfront market Mon am; the nuns at the Franciscan convent sell handicrafts and embroidery; there are three small hotels and five pensions (**D** *Anilce*, Praça Santa Teresa 294, clean, a/c, do not leave valuables in your room, very helpful; *Hotel Panorama*, rec, good restaurant), the restaurant *Au Bec d'Or* by the port, French/Amazonian cuisine. Airport with connection to Manaus. If travelling on to Tabatinga, note that Manaus-Tabatinga boats do not usually stop at Tefé. You must hire a canoe to take you out to the main channel and try to "flag down" the approaching ship.

Benjamin Constant (pop 15,000) on the frontier with Peru, with Colombian territory on the opposite bank of the river. Several hotels, including, **B** *Benjamin Constant*, beside ferry, all a/c, some with hot water and TV, good restaurant, arranges tours, postal address Apartado Aéreo 219, Leticia, Colombia; *Mar Azur*, a/c, friendly; **D** *Benjamin*, very basic; **E** *Hotel São Jorge*, rec, meals available; **F** *Hotel Lanchonete Peruana*, good food; **D** *Márcia Maria*, with bath, a/c, fridge, clean, friendly, rec. Eat at *Pensão Cecília*, or *Bar-21 de Abril*, cheaper. Clothes shop on road reaching to port (left hand side) changes US$ cash. Exchange best in Leticia. Boat services from Manaus, 7 days, or more; to Manaus, 4 days, or more. Boats from Manaus to Benjamin Constant normally go on to Tabatinga, and start from there when going to Manaus. Boats usually stop 1-2 days in both Tabatinga and Benjamin Constant before returning to Manaus; you can stay on board during the wait.

Ferry (Recreio) to Leticia (Colombia) twice daily, US$2.50, 1½ hrs, ferry calls at **Tabatinga** (pop 27,950), only 4 km from Leticia. (*Hotel Martins*, good but expensive; **E** *Residencial*

Aluguel Pajé, with bath, fan, clean; **D** *Solimões*, run by the military—close to the airport—with breakfast, other meals available if ordered in advance, excellent value, clean—some taxi drivers are unaware that this hotel accepts non-military guests, but there is a VW colectivo minibus from the barracks to town centre, harbour and Leticia; excellent *Tres Fronteiras* restaurant. Better accommodation is available in Leticia, there are no border formalities if you go no further into the country. Hammock (good) will cost US$15 in Tabatinga (try Esplanada Teocides) or Benjamin Constant. It is difficult to change TCs in Tabatinga (try Casa Branca, Casa Verde or Casa Amarela on main road, or general manager of the main shopping centre), and far harder to purchase Peruvian soles than in Leticia. Good rates found at Câmbio Cortez, Av da Amizade 2205 (near Banco do Brasil). Airport to Tabatinga by minibus, US$0.75. The Port Captain in Tabatinga is reported as very helpful and speaking good English. **NB** The port area of Tabatinga is called Marco. Mosquito net for hammock essential if sailing upstream from Tabatinga; much less so downstream.

Entering Brazil from Colombia Get your exit stamp at Leticia airport. Cross frontier between Leticia and Tabatinga. Boats to Manaus also depart from Benjamin Constant (see preceding paragraph and below). Brazilian exit/entry formalities at Marco (Tabatinga) are essential: walk through docks and follow road to its end, turn right at this T-junction for one block, white Policia Federal immigration building is opp *Café dos Navegantes*, 10 mins walk from docks, Mon-Fri, 0800-1200, 1400-1800 (immigration also at airport, open Wed and Sat only), proof of US$500 or exit ticket may be required. This is a frontier area: carry your passport at all times, but travel between Leticia and Tabatinga is very informal. Taxi to Leticia, US$7.50, colectivo US$0.45. Brazilian Consulate in Leticia, Calle 8, No 8-71, Mon-Fri, 1000-1600, requires two black-and-white passport photos and 36 hrs for visa (best to get your visa beforehand); go there if you have entry problems coming from Peru into Brazil. It may be possible to obtain entry stamp at Policia Federal in Manaus.

Entering Brazil from Peru Boats from Iquitos to the Brazilian border stop at Islandia, a mud-bank anchorage off Benjamin Constant (passengers are ferried by canoe between the two: Peruvian boats are not allowed to stop at Benjamin Constant). You must have a Peruvian exit stamp (obtained on the boat, or at Peruvian consulate in Leticia, or at Puerto Alegría; practice seems to vary so check first in Iquitos). You must also get an entry stamp in Tabatinga (yellow fever certificate needed); without either you will be sent back to Peru. Don't wear shorts in the Brazilian immigration office. Take one of the ferries from Benjamin Constant to Tabatinga (1½-2 hrs, US$2, or hire a canoe, US$5.50), get off at first stop, walk 1 km to the main road, police offices are on the right, the larger will stamp your passport. To get on to the ferry in Tabatinga it is necessary to walk the plank, narrow, muddy and without a handrail. Tans flies Islandia to Iquitos, but there are no guarantees of flights.

To Peru and Colombia NB Exit stamps in Tabatinga are given at the Policia Federal office (address above), whether you are leaving by air or by boat; you are permitted one week in transit. Entering Colombia from Brazil, you must have a tourist card to obtain a stamp to go beyond Leticia, but there appears to be no problem in staying in Leticia without a stamp (but you cannot change TCs without a stamp); check these details on arrival. Colombian consulate on unnamed street opp Restaurant *El Canto de las Peixadas*, open 0800-1400. Frequent sailings from Peruvian border jetties (Santa Rosa/Islandia) to Iquitos, US$24, 3 days, speedboat (2 days), 3 a week at 0500, US$50, book ahead. Peruvian tourist cards obtained from Puerto Alegría, 2 hrs up river where boats stop for police checks (these formalities may change).

It is possible to get a launch from Manaus up the Rio Negro; see **River Transport in Amazonia, see p 539**. There are hardly any villages of more than a few houses; these places are important in terms of communications and food resources. It is vital to be self-sufficient in food and cash and to be able to speak Portuguese or have a Brazilian guide. *Nova Airão*, on the W bank of the Negro, is about two days upstream. It has a large boat-building centre at the S end, and a fish and vegetable market at the N end. Ice and bread can also be purchased here. The town has many similar houses of wood and corrugated-iron construction. It has a telephone (from which calls to Europe can be made—after a fashion). Airão is the starting point for the **Parque Nacional Jaú** (Ibama office in Manaus, BR-319, Km 01, Distrito Industrial, Caixa Postal 185, CEP 69.000, T 237-3721). Moura is about 5 days upstream from Manaus; it has about 120 people based around the military-run granite quarry. There are basic medical facilities and the military base has an airstrip (only usable Sep to Dec) and telecommunications. About a day further upstream is *Carvoeira*, almost opposite the mouth of the Rio Branco; although small, it has a vibrant festival in the first week of Aug. More than a day beyond is *Barcelos*, with an airstrip (Hotel *Oasis*, German spoken; *Macedo*). A great distance further upstream is *São Gabriel da Cachoeira*, from where you can continue to Venezuela (see Venezuela section). São Gabriel is near the **Pico de Neblina National Park** (Pico de Neblina is the highest mountain in Brazil, 3,014 metres, Ibama office in Manaus, see above); in São Gabriel, Tom Hanly, an Irish Salesian brother, is helpful, friendly and informative. Hotels: **E** *Valpes*; another (better class) on the island, restaurant colonial, rec, shops, 2 banks, no exchange, beautiful white beaches and, in the river, rapids for 112 km. Cargo boats ply to *Cucuí* at the Brazil/Colombia/Venezuela border, also twice-weekly bus, US$2.50 (1 hotel, ask for Elias, no restaurants); with your embassy's assistance it may be possible to fly with the military (airport 8 km from São Gabriel). From Cucuí daily boats to Guadalupe (Colombia), infrequent boats to Santa Lucía (Venezuela).

Many of the gold prospectors (*garimpeiros*) expelled from the Yanomami reserves in Roraima have begun to move W into the middle and upper reaches of the Rio Negro, bringing conflict and destruction in their wake. The environment and indigenous populations in the area have been affected and relations with Venezuela strained. Get detailed local information and exercise considerable caution if travelling to this region.

About two days up the Rio Branco is Santa Maria de Boiaçu, a village of about 30 families. There is a military airstrip which is in use in Jul and Aug, very basic medical facilities and an indirect radio link with Manaus. There are three small shops selling basic necessities (but they aren't often open), and several tiny, but lively churches. The Rio Branco is yellowish in colour, and less acidic than the Negro. Therefore, biting insects and their associated diseases are more prevalent outside the wet season. The river is better for fishing, though, and there is more wildlife to see.

River traffic on the Rio Branco connects Manaus with *Caracaraí*, a busy, but unattractive river port with modern installations. It is also on the the Manaus-Boa Vista road (see below). If this road is washed out, the Rio Branco is the only route through to Venezuela. In the rainy season, Apr-Sep, river transport is quite easy to arrange (bargain for your fare, and sling your hammock under a truck); empty trucks offer cheaper fares for cars, talk to the drivers; it's an interesting journey, 96 hrs upstream, 48 down, take water or purifying treatment. The river banks are closer, so there is more to see than on the Amazon and stops in the tiny riverside settlements are fascinating. Bus on from Caracaraí to Boa Vista costs US$6, 3 hrs.

Hotels, Food, Services D *3 Irmãos*, behind rodoviária, clean, rec; **E** *Caracaraí*, down street from bus station, friendly but dirty; **E** *Márcia*, next to bus stop, a/c, breakfast, clean; **E** *Roraima*, cold shower, basic; *Pizzeria Delícia*, good, English spoken; *Sorveteria Pizzaria Lidiany*, rec. Silas in the Drogaria on S side of town will change dollars.

NB The Perimetral Norte road marked on some maps from Caracaraí E to Macapá and W to the Colombian frontier does not yet exist; it runs only about 240 km W and 125 km E from Caracaraí, acting at present as a penetration road.

The road which connects Manaus and Boa Vista (BR-174 to Novo Paraíso, then the Perimetral, BR-210, rejoining the BR174 after crossing the Rio Branco at Caracaraí, ferry during daylight hours) is of dirt between Manaus and Caracaraí, but is regularly maintained and in better shape than in the past. It is generally passable, even during the rainy season (when it is slower, bus takes between 1 and 3 days: good idea to pack food, drink and a raincoat). The road is fully paved from Caracaraí to Boa Vista. For drivers on this route, some advise being defensive with regard to lorry drivers (who drive for too long, haul too much and drink), but they can be very helpful to anyone in difficulties. There are service stations with toilets, camping, etc, every 150-180 km, but all petrol is low octane; take a tow cable and spares. At Km 100 is Presidente Figueiredo, with shops and a restaurant. About 100 km further on is a service station at the entrance to the Uaimiri Atroari Indian Reserve, which straddles the road for about 120 km. Private cars and trucks are not allowed to enter the Indian Reserve between sunset and sunrise, but buses are exempt from this regulation. Nobody is allowed to stop within the reserve at any time. At the northern entrance to the reserve there are toilets and a spot to hang your hammock. Usually crowded with truckers overnight. At Km 327 is the village of Vila Colina with *Restaurante Paulista*, good food, clean, can use shower and hang hammock. At Km 359 there is a monument to mark the equator. At Km 434 is the clean and pleasant *Restaurant Goaio*. Just S of Km 500 is *Bar Restaurante D'Jonas*, a clean, pleasant place to eat, you can also camp or sling a hammock. Beyond here, large tracts of forest have been destroyed for settlement, but already many homes have been abandoned.

Boa Vista has road connections with the Venezuelan frontier at Santa Elena de Uairen (237 km, a dirt road, improved in 1993 but still difficult, the only gasoline 110 km S of Santa Elena) and Bonfim for the Guyanese border at Lethem. Both roads are open all year.

Boa Vista (pop 142,815, CEP 69300, DDD 095), capital of the extreme northern State of Roraima (pop 215,790), is 759 km N of Manaus. Mount Roraima, after which the Territory is named, is possibly the original of Sir Arthur Conan Doyle's "Lost World". There is swimming in the Rio Branco, 15 mins from the town centre (too polluted in Boa Vista), reachable by bus only when river is low. This town has a modern functional plan, which often necessitates long hot treks from one function to another. Industrial estate S of town. A new government district is being built on the NW edge of town. Interesting modern cathedral; also a museum of local Indian culture (poorly kept). Taxi from airport should cost no more than US$12 (45 mins' walk). Under heavy international pressure, the Brazilian government expelled some 40,000 gold prospectors (*garimpeiros*) from Yanomami Indian Reserves in the W of the state of Roraima in 1991/92 and again in 1993. Although some have since returned, the economic consequences have been very severe for Boa Vista, which went from boom to bust. There has been some increase in cattle ranching in the area, but this has not taken up the slack.

Hotels   Generally expensive. **A1** *Aipana Plaza*, Praça Centro Cívico 53, T 224-4800, F 224-4116, modern, friendly service; **A1** *Praia Palace*, on river, with beach, hard beds but service friendly, T 224-8111, F 224-8496 (good food in restaurant next door); **A1** *Uiramutam*, Av Cap Enne Garcez 427, T 224-9912; **C** *Eusêbio's*, R Cecília Brasil 1107, T 224-0300, always full, book ahead, demand single if on your own, very good restaurant, swimming pool, free transport to bus station or airport, rec; **C** *Casa Nova*, Av Sebastião Diniz, with a/c, E with fan; **D** *Roraima*, Av Cecília Brasil e Benjamin Constant, with bath, rec, restaurant opp is also rec; **D** *Colonial*, Ajuricaba 532, T 224-5190, near Consolação church, a/c with bath and breakfast, clean; **E** *Joelma*, Av NS da Consolata, corner of Av Gulana S Vincento, T 224-5404, with bath, near rodoviária; **E** *Monte Líbano*, Benjamin Constant 319 W, without a/c, dearer with a/c, clean (bus from rodoviária to centre passes by); next door is **E** *Brasil* in R Benjamin Constant 331 W near Drogafarma, good meals (do not confuse with dirty, overpriced *Hotel Brasa* in same street); **E** *Neto*, opposite rodoviária, rec; **E** *Tres Nações*, Av Ville Roy 1885, T 224-3439, also close to bus station, some rooms a/c, refurbished, clean, basic, often rec; at No 1906-24 Carlos Alberto Soares lets a room, warm shower, friendly, rec; **E** *Lua Nova*, R Benjamin Constant 591, without a/c, more expensive with, English spoken, noisy, seedy, often full; **F** *Terraço*, Av Cecília Brasil 1141, without bathroom, noisy, friendly; and **E** *Universo*, No 997, only 4 rm, with bath, rec. There are also two missions who offer hospitality to those in need. If all else fails, sling your hammock in the trees around the rodoviária.

Camping   Rio Caaumé, 3 km N of town (unofficial site, small bar, clean river, pleasant).

Restaurants   *Senzala*, Av Castelo Branco 1115, where the town's high society eats; *Casa Grande*, Av Ville Roy, good; *Churrascaria Venezuela*, bus station; *Churrascaria La Carreta*, Av Ville Roy, very good value; *Bigode*, on waterfront, fish, music at weekends; *Café Pigalle*, just off central square, next to *Eusêbio's*, good food, drinks and atmosphere, open till all hours; *Góndola*, Benjamin Constant and Av Amazonas, good; restaurant and bar in Parque Anana, near airport; *Vila Rica*, R Ville Roy, near rodoviária, good cheap lunch. Snacks at *Top Set*, Av Jaime Brasil, *Catequeiro*, Araújo Filho with Benjamín Contant, rec *prato feito*.

Banks and Exchange   US$ and Guyanese notes can be changed in Boa Vista; try *Ramiro Silva*, Rimpex, Av Jaime Brasil. TCs and cash in **Banco do Brasil** (minimum US$200). There is no official exchange agency and the local rates for bolívares are low: the Banco do Brasil will not change bolívares. Best rate for dollars, **Casa Pedro José**, R Araújo Filho 287, T 224 4277, also changes TCs and bolívares; try the chemist/drugstore on main square for dollar exchange or the Compra e Vende Ouro shop on Av Araújo Filho, or the gold dealers in front of *Hotel Paraíso*.

Health   Yellow fever inoculations are free at a clinic near the hospital.

Tourist information   at rodoviária. **Tour Guide**   Boat trips on Rio Branco and surrounding waterways (jungle, beaches, Indian reservations), *Acqua*, R Floriano Peixoto 505, T 224-6576. Guide Elieser Rufino is rec.

Bus   (See also Border Crossings below.) To **Manaus**, by União Cascavel, US$36, 18-24 hrs, can be very crowded, leaves 0830, 1000 (leaves 1800, 1900 from Manaus), advisable to book because sometimes buses are fully booked days in advance, but extra buses may run when scheduled service is full, check times. Buses often run late, and the night bus has to wait up to 4 hrs for the Rio Branco ferry. **Boa Vista-Caracaraí** US$6, 3 hrs. To **border**, see below. União Cascavel to **Bonfim**, 1630, Mon, Wed, Fri, 2 hrs, returning next morning, US$6. Rodoviária is on town outskirts, 3 km at end of Av Ville Roy; taxi to centre, US$5, bus US$0.45, 10 mins (marked "13 de Setembro" or "Joquey Clube" to centre). Local bus terminal is on Av Amazonas, by R Cecília Brasil, near central praça. Note that it is difficult to get taxi or bus to rodoviária in time for early morning departures; as it's a 25 mins walk, book a taxi the previous evening.

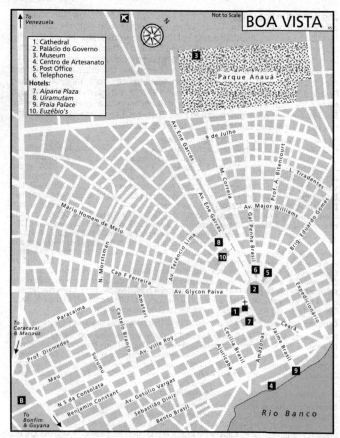

BOA VISTA

1. Cathedral
2. Palácio do Governo
3. Museum
4. Centro de Artesanato
5. Post Office
6. Telephones
Hotels:
7. Aipana Plaza
8. Uiramutam
9. Praia Palace
10. Euzébio's

Parque Anauá

Rio Banco

Hitchhiking to Santa Elena, Venezuela, is not easy; either wait at the bridge and police checkpoint on the road to the border, or try to find a Venezuelan driver on the square. Hitching from Boa Vista to Manaus is fairly easy on the many trucks travelling to Manaus; try from the service station near the rodoviária. You may have to change trucks at Caracaraí. At the ferry crossing over the Rio Branco there is usually a long queue of waiting hikers; try to arrange a lift on the ferry. Truck drivers are asking approx half the bus fare to take passengers in the cab (bargain), much cheaper or free in back. The view from the truck is usually better than from the bus and you can see the virgin forest of the Indian Reserve in daylight. Take some food and water.

If you have a vehicle but do not want to expose it to the rigours of the Boa Vista-Manuas road (although improved it would still be rough on a sedan car), you can arrange to have it loaded onto an empty lorry for the journey S, approx US$170 includes vehicle and all passengers, negotiable.

Air Travel To and from Manaus; confirm flights before reaching Boa Vista as they are fully booked. Aircraft maintenance, baggage checking and handling are unreliable; Guyanese come to Boa Vista to buy goods unavailable in Guyana—make sure your luggage is not among the excess that has to be taken off the plane. No left luggage, information or exchange facilities at airport. Bus "Aeroporto" from centre is US$0.40. Taxi to rodoviária, US$9.

Border Crossing, Guyana Get exit stamp at police station in Lethem, Guyana, then take rowing-boat over border river Tacutu. No car ferry, but river can be forded in dry season. Once in Brazil, register at military camp at Bonfim (hotels: **E** *Blessing*, *Frontera*, and *Bonfim*) and get entry stamp (closed for lunch). English-speaking Bonfim teacher, Tricia Watson, has been helpful to bewildered travellers. Phone Bonfim 2290 (for one G$) for car to take you to Boa Vista (US$50), or if lucky, take a colectivo (US$18, 3 hrs) or bus at 0800, Tues, Thur, Sat. The bus leaves Boa Vista for Bonfim at times given above; luggage is checked at the Ministério da Fazenda checkpoint, before Bonfim, from where a jeep takes travellers to the Brazilian immigration post (US$1) and then walk the short distance to the river, 5 km in all. To cross the river, yell "Boat" and a motor boat will come (no boats at night). It is very difficult to hitch between Boa Vista and Bonfim. From Bonfim to Boa Vista the road is passable all year; bridge over Rio Branco. There is another border crossing at Laramonta from where it is a hard, but rewarding walk to the Guyanese town of Orinduik. A weekly jeep connects Laramonta with Boa Vista (US$30), also flights once a week, to Georgetown, often fully booked. A good rate for *reais* is reported in the Guyana border area. *Reais* can be changed into G$ in the shop at Brazilian immigration post; Bonfim is not much better than Lethem for exchange, but Boa Vista is best. If you need a visa to enter Guyana, you must get it in Brasília or São Paulo; no consulate in Boa Vista (see Guyana **Documents**, in **Information for Visitors**).

Border Crossing, Venezuela Everyone who crosses the border from Boa Vista, regardless of nationality, requires a visa (passport must be valid for 1 year). These can be obtained from the Venezuelan Consulate in Boa Vista, Av Benjamín Constant 525E (T 095-224-2182, open Mon-Fri 0830-1300 but may close earlier). In 1995, it was possible to cross without a visa and obtain one in Santa Elena; best to enquire beforehand. The consulate in Manaus was issuing one-year multiple visas (**see p 558**). Visitors with dual nationality may have problems gaining entry. Health requirements are reported to have been relaxed: a malaria test certificate, yellow-fever vaccination certificate and certificate of medical checkup are no longer necessary, but be prepared for them anyway as regulations change. Border officials may also insist on US$20 a day—however, regulations state that a visa is sufficient. Buses leave the rodoviária in Boa Vista for Santa Elena at 0700 and 0800, US$18 (stopping at all check points), take water, journey anything from 4 to 6 hrs. Through tickets Boa Vista-Ciudad Bolívar are sold, but are more expensive than paying separately; there are no through buses. Border searches are thorough and frequent (there are also road checks in Venezuela and fresh fruit and vegetables must be left on the Brazilian side, because of cholera). Entry stamp can be obtained only in Santa Elena; border closes at 1700. Trucks leave for Venezuela from R Benjamin Constant, drivers are not officially supposed to take passengers. For the price of the bus ticket you can pay for a lift in a truck and avoid an overnight stay. There are a bank, a basic hotel, *Pacaraima Palace*, and a guest house on Brazilian side and you can camp. The road from the frontier into Venezuela is paved; it passes through some very scenic countryside.

SOUTHERN AMAZONIA (10)

Rondônia and Acre, frontier areas, not just between Brazil and Peru and Bolivia, but also between the forest and colonization, between those who live off the forest and ranchers.

Porto Velho (pop 286,400, CEP 78900, DDD 069), capital of the State of Rondônia with a population of 862,000 in 1985, which had reached 1,130,400 in 1991. The city stands on a high bluff overlooking a curve of the River Madeira; at the top of the hill is the cathedral, built in 1950. The principal commercial street is Av Sete de Setembro, which runs from the railway station and market hall to the upper level of the city, past the Rodoviária. Parks are under construction. Rondônia is the focus of experimental development in agriculture, with concomitant colonization of the area. At the same time, much of the state is being reserved for Indians and national forests. Porto Velho is expensive, but quieter now the local gold rush has slowed. About 20 km from Porto Velho, the Samuel hydroelectric scheme is under construction, with a new town to house the workers. When it comes on stream in the 1990s, it will be insufficient to provide power for the states of Rondônia and Acre as was originally intended. The population has grown too rapidly. Malaria is common; the drinking water is contaminated with mercury (from gold panning). With the growth in population, crime has increased in the city and outside.

The Madeira is one of the major tributaries of the Amazon. The four main rivers which form it are the Madre de Dios, rising a short distance from Cuzco (Peru); the Beni, coming from the southern Cordillera bordering Lake Titicaca; the Mamoré, rising near Sucre, Bolivia; and the Guaporé, coming out of Mato Grosso, in Brazil.

Hotels L2 *Vila Rica*, Av Carlos Gomes 1616, T 221-2333, F 221-2900, tower block, "flashy, flamboyant and mechanically efficient"; nearby *Central*, T 221-0787; *Selton*, T 221-3159, both **C**, central, rec. Also on Av Carlos Gomes: **E** *Erica*, opp rodoviária, convenient but short-stay; much better is **E** *Líder*, nr rodoviária, honest, reasonably clean, fan, coffee, rec for new arrivals; *Ouro Fino*, No 2844, *Amazonas*, No 2835, both E; **D-E** *Karme (Tia Carmen)*, No 2995, very good, honest, good cakes in *lanche* in front of hotel, highly rec. From rodoviária, take bus No 301 "Presidente Roosevelt" (outside *Hotel Pontes*), which goes to railway station at riverside, then along Av 7 de Setembro, passing: **D** *Guaporé Palace*, No 927, a/c, restaurant; **D** *Sonora*, No 1103, clean, fan, clothes washing facilities; **D-E** *Cuiabano*, No 1180, friendly, good, clean, shared bath, fan, rec; **E** *Nunes*, No 1195, very cheap but basic, probably best value; **F** *Rio*, Av Joaquim Nabuco 2110, T 223-1430, basic, good breakfast, friendly, fairly good cheap meals; **E** *Laira*, same street, just off 7 de Setembro, good, clean, cheap; **F** *Ubatuba*, R Dom Pedro II 3140, near rodoviária, T 223-2249, breakfast included, other meals US$2, good coffee, motorcycle parking.

Restaurants *Churascaria Natal*, Av Carlos Gomes 2783, good meat and chicken; *Assados na Brasa*, Carlos Gomes 2208, similar; *Mister Pizza II*, Carlos Gomes e José de Alencar, good. A number of good restaurants around the intersection of Dom Pedro II and Av Joaquim Nabuco: *Champagne*, rec for pizzas, and a good Chinese. Many *lanches* in town: rec are *Loja Japonesa*, Av 7 de Setembro e Joaquim Nabuco, excellent juices; *Panificadora Popular*, Av Mal Deodoro between 7 de Setembro e Dom Pedro II, good juices and soups; *Xalezinho*, opp, for an even bigger bowl of soup. *Banana Split*, Av 7 de Setembro, popular, also *Sorvette Pinguim* for ice creams. Avoid eating much fish because of mercury contamination.

Exchange Banks in mornings only; **Banco do Brasil**, Dom Pedro II e Av José de Alencar. *Marco Aurélio, câmbio* at R José de Alencar 3353, quick, efficient. Local radio news and papers publish exchange rates; try local businesses too. Difficult elsewhere in Rondônia.

Electric Current 110 volts AC, elsewhere in Rondônia 220 volts.

Health Dentist at Carlos Gomes 2577; 24-hr clinic opposite.

Laundry *Lavanderia Marmoré*, Pinheiro Machado 1455b.

Post Office Av 7 de Setembro e Av Pres Dutra. **Telephones** Teleron, Av Pres Dutra e Dom Pedro II.

Shopping Bookshop *Livraría de Rosa*, Av Rogério Weber, near the port, a few English paperbacks; manageress speaks English; other bookshops nearby. Indian handicrafts at *Casa do Índio*, R Rui Barbosa 1407. Hammocks more expensive than in Manaus. *Supermercado Maru*, 7 de Setembro e Joaquim Nabuco. Camping supplies and gas at *Casa do Pescador*, J Nabuco e Pinheiro Machado. Film developer at 7 de Setembro e José de Alencar.

Voluntary work Rondonia Reforestation Project, Caixa Postal 50, 78900-970, Porto Velho, at Santa Bárbara, Km 601.5 BR364, T 069-221-0385, F 221-0582, invites anyone interested in a working holiday researching methods of reforesting Rondonia (min 4 weeks), project director Kurt Sartorius.

Tour Guide Carlos Grandes Peres, at *Hotel Nunes*, rec for jungle trips, speaks English.

Immigration To extend entry permit go to Policia Federal on Av Campos Sales on way to airport, then go to Guajará-Mirim (4 hrs), get exit stamp from Policia Federal, cross border and get Bolivian entry stamp. Wait in Bolivia till you can return, get exit stamp and then new entry stamp from Policia Federal in Brazil.

Car hire Silva Car, R Almirante Barroso 1528, Porto Velho, T 221-1423/6040, Telex (069) 1129 SLVL US$30/day.

Air Services Airport 8 km W of town, take bus marked "Aeroporto" (last one between 2400-0100). Twice daily Varig flights to Manaus, daily to Brasilia (Vasp), Cuiabá (several airlines), Rio Branco (Varig); 3 times a week to Cruzeiro do Sul, via Rio Branco; also flights to other Brazilian destinations.

River Services See River Transport in Amazonia, p 539. The Rio Madeira is fairly narrow so the banks can be seen and there are several "meetings of waters". Shipping a car: São

Matheus Ltda, Av Terminal dos Milagros 400, Balsa, takes vehicles on pontoons, US$250 inc passengers, meals, showers, toilets, cooking and sleeping in car permitted. Wait at the Capitânia do Porto in the centre of town for a possible passage on a cargo boat; these boats leave from Porto Bras, down river from Porto Velho. Porto Velho-Humaitá US$16.20 (boat *Dois de Junho*). **NB** From Manaus to São Paulo is cheaper by boat Manaus-Porto Velho, then bus to São Paulo, than by flying direct or by boat to Belém then bus.

Six days a week a boat leaves at 1800 for Manaus from Manicoré, at the confluence of the Rios Madeira and Manicoré, two nights and one day's journey, food included; boats from Porto Velho to Manicoré on Mon, Wed and Sat (1800, arr 0200, but you can sleep on the boat), connecting with Manicoré-Manaus boats (a rec boat is *Orlandina*). **Manicoré** (37,810 people) is a pleasant town; the Praça de Bandeira is at the corner of Av Getúlio Vargas and Av Pedro Tinoco (one block to left of road that goes up from the dock). **E** *Hotel Silviani*, 4 blocks left from Praça on Av Vargas, just before the big church; *Restaurant Tapuia*, 1 block from Praça in opp direction to river on Av Tinoco; slow but good restaurant at floating dock. Fruit market on Av Vargas.

If you want to see a typical river community, get off at Calama, about 10 hrs from Porto Velho. Stay with Dona Morena in her "hotel" and eat *en famille* (F). The people are friendly and Tyer, the school teacher, enjoys a chat. From Calama you may be able to get a boat up the Ji-Paraná river; very attractive with waterfalls and a few isolated settlement schemes.

Buses New rodoviária is on Jorge Teixeira between Carlos Gomes and Dom Pedro II. From town take "President Roosevelt" bus No 301 (if on Av 7 de Setembro, the bus turns at Av Mal Deodoro); "Aeroporto" and "Hospital Base" (No 400) also go to rodoviária. Bus to **Humaitá**, US$5.75; to **São Paulo**, change at Cuiabá, 60-plus hrs, US$80; to **Cuiabá**, 23 hrs, US$40, take plenty of food and drink. Fast bus at 2030, Colibri, drug controls in operation. To **Rio** US$85; **Belo Horizonte** US$60; **Curitiba** US$90; **Fortaleza** US$130. To Guajará-Mirim, see below. To **Rio Branco**, twice daily, 12 hrs, US$18. Daily bus with Eucatur from **Cascavel** (Paraná, connections for Foz do Iguaçu) via Maringá, Presidente Prudente, Campo Grande and Cuiabá to Porto Velho (Porto Velho-Campo Grande 36 hrs, US$50). To **Cáceres** for the Pantanal, Colibri, 18 hrs, US$23. To **Vitória**, daily, 61 hrs. Hitching difficult, try at the *posto* 2 km out of town. In 1995 there was no bus service to **Manaus** as the road was closed. Try asking for transport at the ferry crossing just outside town.

Roads to Cuiabá (BR-364—Marechal Rondon Highway, 1,450 km, fully paved; **see below and p 592**); Rio Branco, 490 km, following Madeira-Mamoré railway, paved; to Humaitá (205 km) on the Madeira river (fully paved), connecting with the Transamazônica Highway, and on to Manaus (Catire Highway, 877 km). This road is frequently closed (eg in 1995). Road journeys are best done in the dry season, the second half of the year.

A result of the paving of BR-364 is the development of towns along it: **Ariquemes** (159 km from Porto Velho, pop 83,660, buses hourly from 0600, 3-4 hrs, Banco do Brasil, some hotels, **E** *Valerius Palace*); Nova Vida (200 km), Jaru (257 km), Ouro Preto d'Oeste (297 km). About 250 km S of Porto Velho it is possible to stay on a working *fazenda*, the **Rain Forest Lodge Rancho Grande** at Caixa Postal 361, Ariquemes, Rondônia 78. 914, T (069) 535-4301 (reservations and tours can be arranged through Focus Tours, Belo Horizonte). Not cheap but rec, esp for butterfly lovers. About 450 bird species and numerous mammals can be seen on the 20 km of trails. Harald Schmitz speaks English, German and Spanish, highly rec.

Ji Paraná (337 km, municipal pop 200,000—bus to Porto Velho, US$17, 18 hrs; to Cuiabá, 15 hrs, US$20, 40 *leito*; hotels **D** *Horizonte*, rec with reasonable restaurants, **E** *Sol Nascente*, with *churrascaria*, **A3** *Hotel Transcontinental*, rec; cheap hotels in front of rodoviária for the hardy only; trips to frontier towns possible, eg Nova Colina), Presidente Médici (373 km, 50,000 people), **Cacoal** (404 km, 67,000 people, Hotels **C** *Cacoal Palace*, **D** *Ramadas*, safe parking, rec, and **Amazonis**), Pimenta Bueno (440 km, pop 50,000) and **Vilhena** on the Rondônia-Mato Grosso border (658 km from Porto Velho, 710 km from Cuiabá, pop 35,400; **D** *Diplomata Hotel*, near bus station; **E** *Rodoviária*, rec; **F** *Gastão*). At Vilhena proof of yellow-fever inoculation required: if no proof, new shot. Two cities have grown without prior planning: **Rolim de Moura**, W of Pimenta Bueno, with a population of 110,000 and a *Transcontinental Hotel*, and Itarua do Oeste, 91 km S of Porto Velho, at what used to be a bus waiting station (population about 5,000).

The **Pacaás Novos National Park**, 765,800 hectares, lies W of the BR-364; it is a transitional zone between open plain and Amazonian forest. Details from Ibama, T (069) 223-2599/3597, Porto Velho; also enquire here about the Jaru and Guaporé Biological Reserves in the State.

Porto Velho was the terminus of the Madeira-Mamoré railway of 367 km (closed 1971), Brazil's price to Bolivia for annexing the Acre territory during the rubber boom. It cost a life for every hundred sleepers, 6,208 in all, during construction. The line, built 1907-12, by-passed the 19 rapids of the Madeira and Mamoré rivers, and gave Bolivia an outlet of sorts to the Atlantic. It was supposed to go as far as Riberalta, on the Rio Beni, above that river's rapids, but stopped short at **Guajará Mirim** (pop 32,530), a charming town. It still runs the 7 km to the Madeira river rapids at Santo Antônio. Woodburning steam trains, built in 1925 in Philadelphia, use a narrow-gauge track which gave the line its nickname "the devil's railroad" because of its cost in lives. The line works all week but tourist excursions are on Sun only, 7 departures. The roundhouse, recently restored, has two other antique locomotives on display. Besides the railway there is a real road, partly paved, which uses the rail bridges (in poor condition); the 370-km bus ride is far faster than the train (6 buses a day from rodoviário, 30 mins walk from the town, US$18, takes 5½ hrs or more depending on season—road, in poor condition S of Abunã, is often closed Mar-May). The Bolivian town of Guayaramerín is across the Mamoré river; it is connected by road to Riberalta, and there are air services to other Bolivian cities. An ancient stern wheeler plies on the Guaporé; 26-day, 1,250 km trips (return) can be made on the Guaporé from Guajará Mirim to Vila Bela (see p 596) in Mato Grosso, fare includes food. 170 km from Guajará Mirim, on the Guaporé river, is the Forte Príncipe da Beira, begun in 1777 as a defence of the border with Bolivia. The fort, which is being restored, can be reached from Costa Marques (20 km by road), which can only be reached by air or by river.

If travelling by road between Porto Velho and Guajará Mirim, two possible stops are at Maluca dos Índios, from where you can visit villages of gold prospectors by the Madeira river; the other is from the railway bridge just before Vila Murtinho where you can see gold panners, and, walking a few hundred metres, the rapids on the Mamoré river.

Museum Museu Municipal at the old Guajará-Mirim railway station beside the ferry landing—small, with railway memorabilia and a few specimens of regional wildlife.

Guajará Mirim Hotels *Central Palace*, Av Marechal Deodoro 1150, T 541-2610, rec. *Alfa*, Av Leopoldo de Matos 239, T 541-3121; C *Mini-Estrela*, Av 15 de Novembro 460, T 541-2399; E *Fénix Palace*, Av 15 de Novembro 459; F *Mamoré*, clean, friendly; F *Hudson*, friendly, safe. **Youth Hostel** Av 15 de Novembro, Centro Deportivo Afonso Rodrigues, T 541-3732. There is a basic *dormitório*, F, opposite rodoviária.

Restaurant Best is *Oasis*, at Posto Nogueira service station, Av 15 de Novembro 464.

Services Exchange Banco do Brasil (foreign exchange am only). **Loja Nogueira**, Av Pres Dutra, esq Leopoldo de Matos (cash only). There is no market in Brazil for bolivianos. **Post Office** on Av Pres Dutra. **Telephone** office: Av B Ménzies 751.

To Bolivia Speedboat to Bolivia, US$1.20, tickets at waterside, Bolivian immigration open 0800-1200, 1400-1800. Before crossing into Bolivia you may need a visa from the Bolivian consul in Guajará Mirim in Av C Marqués 495, Western Europeans can cross river and visit the Immigration Office; which closes at 1100 on Sat. You will need a Brazilian exit stamp from Policia Federal, Av Pres Dutra, corner of Av Q Bocaiuva.

NB If you need a visa to enter Brazil, apply to the Brazilian Consul at Guayaramerín (Bolivia), open 1100-1300, before crossing the Rio Mamoré into Brazil. You must get your passport stamped at the Policia Federal office in town, address below.

From *Abunã*, 220 km from Porto Velho (E *Hotel Thalita*; F *Dormitório Oliviera*, however town is best avoided if at all possible) the road from Porto Velho continues W, paved all the way, to *Rio Branco* (pop 196,925, CEP 69900, DDD 068) the capital of the State of Acre (pop 417,440). The city has a cathedral, an airport and an agricultural research centre.

Museums Rubber Museum, Av Ceará 1177 (*pizzaria* opposite), and Casa do Seringueiro on the corner of Av Getúlio Vargas and Av Brasil, which has a good exhibit on rubber tappers and on Chico Mendes in particular. Trips to see rubber tapping, or the religious colony at Colonia Cinco Mil, can be made by taxi.

Hotels always crowded: B *Inacio Palace*, R Rui Barbosa 72, T 224-6397, F 224-5726, overpriced, fair restaurant; B *Pinheiro Palace*, Rui Barbosa 91, T 224-7191, F 224-5726, a/c, pool, friendly, rec; B *Rio Branco*, R Rui Barbosa 193, T 224-1785, F 224-2681, on park, nice but simple; C *Cuzco*, near airport, T 224-4348; C *Veloso*, R Benjamin Constant, highly rec; E *Lux Palace*, R Quintino Bocaiúva 397, T 224-7340, clean, friendly, 20 mins from centre; *Amazonas* (best of a bad bunch of budget hotels, F, not clean), *Fortaleza*, F *Novo Hotel Fontes*, freshly renovated, highly rec, all on W bank. On E bank, E *Sucessor*, showers, fan, clean, comfortable, friendly. **Youth Hostel**, Fronteira Verde, Trav Natanael de Albuquerque, T 224-3997.

Restaurants Cheap meals at *Dos Colonos* near market. *Marayina*, for pizzas, sandwiches, cakes, ice cream, popular at night; *Casarão*, next to telephone office, popular with human rights workers, good food and drink; *Churrascaria Triângulo*, near airport, as much charcoal-grilled meat as you can eat, rec; *Churrascaria Modelo*, R Marechal Deodoro 360, less good.

Post Office on corner of R Epaminondas Jacome and Av Getúlio Vargas. **Telephone** International calls at Av Brasil, by the Governor's palace.

Market West bank, off R Epaminondas Jacome.

Bus station on Av Uirapuru, on E bank in Cidade Nova. Bus to Guajará Mirim, Mon, Wed, Fri, 0900, 9 hrs, US$13.25.

Warning The road from Porto Velho to Rio Branco should be travelled with caution; the area is seriously affected by malaria. We have also received reports of lawlessness on the BR-364 after dark; to be safe, be in a city before nightfall.

At Rio Branco the Transamazônica Highway meets the road from Brasília and goes on to Cruzeiro do Sul and Japim; it is expected to reach the Peruvian frontier further W when completed; it is hoped that it will be continued by the Peruvians to Pucallpa. It is very difficult to get from Rio Branco to Cruzeiro do Sul by road because there is no bus service, and the occasional lorry goes mainly in the dry season; the road is frequently impassable (it is open, on average, 20 days a year). There are daily flights Manaus-Rio Branco with Varig, continuing to Cruzeiro do Sul on Mon, Wed and Fri.

Cruzeiro do Sul (pop 66,600) an isolated Amazonian town, is situated on the river Juruá; cheap excursions can be made on the river, for example to the village of Rodrigues Alves (2-3 hrs, return by boat or by road, 15 km). In the jungle one can see rubber-tapping, and collecting the latex into "borrachas" which weigh up to 45 kg. Hotels: **D** *Sandra's*; **E** *Novo do Acre*, rec, a/c, clean; **F** *Hospedaria Janecir*; *dos Viajantes*; **E** *Flor de Maio*, facing river, clean, showers, full board available. Restaurant *O Laçador*, good food. Money changing is very difficult; none of the banks will change dollars. Try the airline staff (poor rates).

A road from Rio Branco (the BR-317), paved as far as *Xapuri* (the location of the Fundação Chico Mendes in memory of the environmentalist and union organiser murdered in 1989—only go there if very keen, "the hotel is horrible and so is the food"), goes to *Brasiléia* (bus twice daily, 6 hrs, US$7.80, basic hotel, Federal Police give exit stamps), opposite the Bolivian town of Cobija on the Acre River, and finally to Assis Brasil where the Peruvian, Bolivian and Brazilian frontiers meet; across the Acre River are Iñapari (Peru) and Bolpebra (Bolivia). There is no public transport, and little else, beyond Brasiléia to Iñapari, but hitching is possible. *Quixadá*, 30 km W of Brasiléia has no facilities, poor roads, crossing to Bolivia unreliable, but a friendly community. In *Assis Brasil*, there is one small hotel (basic but clean, friendly, E), one restaurant, some shops, a bank which does not change US dollars (the hotel owner may be persuaded to oblige) and river transport only, which is dependent on the seasons. You get between Iñapari and Assis Brasil by wading across the river. The Brazilian side is reported to be somewhat more expensive, but much pleasanter and offering more variety. Note that there is no passport office in the village.

NB Rio Branco time is one hour behind Manaus time; this means two hours behind Brazilian Standard Time.

THE CENTRE-WEST (11)

The so-called Centre-West (*Centro-Oeste*) of Brazil, occupied by the states of Goiás, Mato Grosso and Mato Grosso do Sul (divided from Mato Grosso in 1977), was the most isolated part of the nation until President Vargas' "Drive to the West" in the 1940s (when many of the Xingu Indian tribes were first contacted). Today Goiás, with an area of 364,714 sq km and 4,024,550 inhabitants, is one of Brazil's most rapidly-developing frontier agricultural areas, producing coffee, soya and rice, most of Brazil's tin and tungsten, and raising beef on the country's largest cattle ranches. The Federal District of Brasília was subtracted from its territory in 1960, which was further split in half in 1990 to form the new state of Tocantins in the N (see p 577). Old colonial mining towns in the state sprang from gold rushes which began in 1722, as Paulistas and Bandeirantes pushed out from Minas Gerais in search of precious stones and new mineral wealth. The eroded Brazilian Plateau, clothed in woodland savannah and varying from 600m to 900m in height, ripples across the S of the state; most of its clearwater rivers flow N to feed the Araguaia and Tocantins rivers. Elsewhere, the climate is sub-tropical, with distinct wet and dry seasons.

The Centre West, with rich, fertile soil, provides 6% of the country's internal income, mainly from farming and cattle raising. With over 100 mn fertile hectares, the region produces 10% of national bean production, while Goiás alone has about 12% of the nation's cattle (about 18mn head) and produces 7% of Brazil's milk (about 1bn litres). Goiás accounts for 36% of the Centre West's gdp. Corn (maize) is abundant the year round, so much so that many regional corn dishes have been created: cakes, ice cream, soufflés and *pomonhas* (see under Goiânia, **Restaurants**).

Goiânia (pop 920,840, CEP 74000, DDD 062) just off the BR-060, 209 km SW of Brasília, the second (after Belo Horizonte) of Brazil's planned state capitals, was founded in 1933 and replaced Goiás Velho as capital four years later. It is a spacious and modern city, with many green spaces and well-lit main avenues, ornamented with plants, radiating out from the central **Praça Cívica**, on which stand the Government Palace and main Post Office. In general, commercial and industrial sectors are to the N, with administration in the centre and residential zones to the S. 1½ km out along the Avenida Araguaia (which runs diagonally NE from the Praça) is the shady **Parque Mutirama**, with recreational and entertainment facilities and a planetarium (Sun sessions at 1530 and 1630); there is also a pleasant **Parque Zoológico** (formerly called the Parque Educativo e Horto Florestal), Av Anhangüera, some distance W of the main square, with good zoo, zoological museum, playground, lake and sports fields (park open Tues-Sun 0900-1830). Other pleasant places to visit are Bosque dos Buritis, just W of the Centro Cívico, and the Lagoa das Rosas, also W of the centre. Because of its youth, Goiânia has few historical sights, but there are several interesting museums: the **Museu Antropológico do UFG** on the Praça Universitária (1 km E of Praça Cívica) with wide-ranging ethnographic displays on the Indians of the Centre-W (Mon-Fri 0900-1700), and the **Museu de Ornitologia**, Av Pará 395 (Sétor Campinas), with more than 8000 stuffed birds and animals from many countries (open 0900-1900, except Mon). Just off the Praça Cívica is the **Museu Estadual "Zoroastro Artiaga"**, Praça Dr P L Teixeira 13, with a collection of local handicrafts, religious objects, animals and Indian artefacts. The unremarkable **Metropolitan Cathedral**, corner Ruas 14 e 19, stands two blocks E of the Praça. Walk due N on broad Avenida Goiás to see the painted walls of the **Projeto Galería Aberto**; many city buses are also painted with colourful and eye-catching designs.

Hotels Many hotels located along Avenida Anhangüera, which runs E-W 4 blocks N of the Central Plaza; as one of the main arteries through the city it is busy and noisy. **L3** *Castro's Park*, Av Rep do Líbano 1520, Setor Oeste, T 223-7766, F 225-7070, warmly rec; **A1** *Papillon*, Rep do Líbano 1824, T 223-8511, F 223-8381, good. *Samambaia*, Av Anhanguera 1157, T/F 261-1444; *Bandeirantes*, same street No 3278, T/F 224-0066; *Umuarama*, R 4 No 492, T 224-1555, F 224-1673, all three good; **A3** *Karajás*, Av Goiás e R 3, T 224-9666, F 229-1153, 3 blocks N of Praça, convenient and comfortable; **A3** *Cabiúna Palace*, Av Parnaíba 698 (close to Parque Mutirama), T/F 224-4355, 40 rm, good value; **B** *Augustus*, Praça Antônio Lizita 702, T 224-1022, F 224-1410, good; *San Conrado*, R 3 No 652, T/F 224-2411; **A3** *Tucanotel*, Anhangüera 1756, 4 km W of centre, T 261-2100, F 261-7691; **B** *Vila Rica*, Anhangüera 3456, T 224-0500, F 225-0551, 2-star Embratur hotel, a/c, convenient; **C** *Mundial*, R 10A No 69 (nr airport), T 224-6629; **C** *Presidente*, Anhangüera 5646, T 224-0500. Cheaper (**C-D**) are: *Príncipe*, Anhangüera 2936 e Av Araguaia, T 224-0085, fans, clean, good value; *Paissandú*, Av Goiás 1290 e R 55, T 224-4925, fans, clean, 8 long blocks N of Praça; *Hotel del Rey*, R 8 No 321, T 225-6306, good location on pedestrian mall, fans, good value. Several cheap hotels (**D-E**) near the bus station: eg *Star*, R 68 No 537, basic, interesting clientele; *Itaipú*, R 29A No 178 at the old bus station (Setor Aeroporto), T 212-4055, *J Alves*, opp rodoviária. NW of the rodoviária are many *dormitorios*, for those on a shoestring budget. **Camping** at *Itanhangá* municipal site, Avenida Princesa Carolina, 13 km, attractive wooded location, reasonable facilities, US$5.50 pp.

Restaurants Goiânia is much cheaper for eating than Brasília, and the variety of eating places is too wide to list here. Many *churrascarias*, eg *Boi na Brasa*, on Praça Germano Roriz (the first large square due S of Praça Cívica on R 84), open 1100-0100, and the more expensive *Lancaster Grill*, R 89 No 117, a/c, live music; *Le Steak*, Av 85 No 352, excellent, a/c, good atmosphere, expensive by Brazilian standards; *Fim de Tarde*, Av 85 No 301, good meat dishes (inc *picanha* and *kibe*, Arabic appetizer) and beer, open from 1700; *Costelería do Marcão*, Av 31 de Março, past Praça do Cruzeiro, best ribs in Goiás, rec, also open only after 1700; *Bom Gourmet*, Av 85 No 1676, for meat and chicken dishes, very good, seats on street or in a/c room. Varied menu at *Cliff Piano Bar e Restaurante*, Rua 23 No 72, esq Av Rep do Líbano, expensive, elegant, good food and service, nice atmosphere, highly rec. *Palatinum*, in *Hotel Augustus*, Italian, very good, elegant, a/c, piano music. Good array of restaurants and watering holes around the Praça Tamandaré (Ruas 8 e 5, just beyond the Bosque dos Buritis, 1 km W of Praça Cívica), including *Modiglianni* for good pizzas. Vegetarians are well-catered for: eg *Arroz Integral*, R 93 No 326 (1100-1400, 1800-2100, self-service), or *Naturalmente Natural*, R 15 No 238, one block from the cathedral. Many small eating places near the rodoviária, which also has good food at low prices.

For regional specialities try the *Centro de Tradições Goiánas*, R 4 No 515 (above the Parthenon Centre), traditional rice and fish cuisine. *Piquiras*, Av Rep do Líbano 1758 (nr *Castro's Hotel*) and Rua 139 s/n, Setor Marista, try the *pastelzinho de piquí* as an appetizer: *piquí* is a regional fruit used in many traditional Goiás dishes, the most famous of which is *galinhada* (fried chicken, *piquí*, rice cooked with saffron). If eating *piquí*, be very careful of the little thorns on the inside. Street stands (*pamonharias*) throughout the city sell *pamonha* snacks, tasty pastries made with green corn, some are sweet, some savoury, some *picante*/spicy; all are served hot and have cheese in the middle, some include sausage. rec *pomonharias* are: *Pomonharia 100*, R 101 esq R Dr Olinto Manso Pereira, behind the Forum, Setor Sul; *Frutos da Terra*, Av Perimetral 669, for home delivery T 233-1507/281-4049; *Pura*, Av 83 No 193, Setor Sul. Local meat pies (*empadões de Goiás*) are also delicious.

Bars and Dancing Goiânia is famous for its street bars, some with live music, some with just a pleasant atmosphere. *People Club* and *Académia da Birita*, Rua 7 No 1000, Sector Oeste, dance club, bar and restaurant, very popular, Thur, Fri, Sat pm; *Cave Bar*, Av 85, Caravelo Center, entrance through back of Center, access by narrow R 85C, on left, small pub, nice drinks and decor, foreign owner Gisela, romantic, good soft music; *Café Madrid*, Rua 101, No 353, Setor Sul, behind the Forum. a/c, bar and restaurant, best *paella* in Goiânia, famous for *margaritas*, live music (MPB, saxophone groups), open daily from 2100. Av Ricardo Paranhos, Setor Sul, is full of bars and crowds of young people after 2000.

Exchange National banks. Travel agents will exchange cash, poor rates for TCs.

Shopping Ceramic, sisal and wooden handicrafts from *Centro Estadual do Artesanato*, Praça do Trabalhador (0800-1800); Sun handicrafts markets at the Praça Cívica (am) and Praça do Sol (pm). The latter starts after 1530, until 2100, known as the Honey Fair as all types of honey are sold; also good for a Sun snack, with many sweets and tarts sold along the street. Two shopping centres: *Flamboyant*, the largest, is some way from the centre (take a bus); *Bougainville*, near R 9, Setor Marista, newer; both have cinemas, snack bars (*McDonalds* in Flamboyant, also at Av 85, Praça do Ratinho). **Bookshop** on R 4 has some secondhand English stock, will exchange.

Recreation Motor racetrack (Brazilian Formula 3 Championships held here in Jun) and racecourse. Many sporting facilities throughout Goiânia, visitors welcome; for sunbathing, swimming and water skiing go to the Jaó Club (T 261-2122), on reservoir near the city.

Tourist Office Goiastur, the state tourist agency, on 3rd floor of Serra Dourada football stadium in Jardim Goiás; friendly staff but remote location and difficult to get to. Extensive information, maps and bus routes in *Nova Guia Turístico de Goiás*, readily available at news stands, US$2.25.

Immigration Office R 235, Setor Universitário.

Airport Santa Genoveva, 6 km NE off Rua 57 (T 207-1288). Daily flights to main cities and many provincial centres, such as Barra do Garças, Miracema do Tocantins, Araguaína, etc. Airtaxi companies (not cheap) serve airstrips throughout the region. Several car hire firms at the airport. Taxi from centre US$6. Varig, Av Goiás 285, T 224-5040; Vasp, R 3 No 569, T223-4266.

Roads and Buses Huge new rodoviária on Rua 44 No 399 in the Norte Ferroviário sector, about a 40-mins walk to downtown (T 224-8466). Buses "Rodoviária-Centro" (No 404) and "Vila União-Centro" (No 163) leave from stop on city side of terminal, US$0.80; No 163 goes on to the Praça Tamandaré. To **Cuiabá** (Mato Grosso), 916 km on BR-158/070 via Barra do Garças, or 928 km on BR-060/364 via Jataí (both routes paved, most buses use the latter route), 4 buses a day, US$30, 15-16 hrs, continuing to Porto Velho (Rondônia) and Rio Branco (Acre)—a very trying journey indeed. At Iporá, 200 km W of Goiânia on BR-158, there is a good hotel. At **Rio Verde** (pop 95,895), on the BR-060 some 240 km W of Goiânia, are several possible hotel stops on the way to Cuiabá, **D** *Rio Verde Palace*, R Gusmão 599, and **D** *Vitória*, Praça 5 de Agosto, a/c, are the best of a poor lot. To **Brasília**, 207 km, part divided freeway, at least 15 departures a day, 2½ hrs, US$7.80, and **São Paulo**, 900 km via Barretos, US$36, 14½ hrs, *leito* services at night. To **Goiás Velho**, 136 km, hourly from 0500, 2½ hrs, US$7.20; **Campo Grande**, 935 km, four services daily, 18 hrs, US$36.50. Pirenópolis 0700 and 1700, 2 hrs, US$7.50.

Excursions To Goiás Velho, Caldas Novas and Pirenópolis (see below), the thermal springs at Cachoeira Dourada (240 km S on the Paranaíba River), the fantastic rock formations of the Serra das Galés at **Paraúna** (160 km SSW off BR-060) and a host of delightful, forgotten colonial mining villages within 2 hrs drive of Goiânia on good (often paved) roads. Travel agents in town can arrange day tours, eg *Turisplan Turismo*, R 8 No 388, T 224-1941 (which also sells regular bus tickets).

Anápolis (pop 239,050, CEP 77100, DDD 062), a busy trading centre 57 km nearer Brasília, has little to detain the traveller, although accommodation is cheaper than the capital and more convenient than Goiânia. The **Centro de Gemologia de Goiás**, Quadra 2, Módulo 13, Daia, about 10 km out on the Brasília highway (near the Embratel tower), has a fine collection of gemstones, library, sales and lapidary courses, will show visitors how real and synthetic gemstones are distinguished, open Mon-Fri 0730-1630. At Anápolis the BR-153 (Brasília-Belém) turns N and begins the long haul (1964 km) through Tocantins, Maranhão and Pará to Belém, a bumpy, monotonous trip of 35 hrs or more, US$60. There are regular bus services to Pirenópolis (66 km N).

Hotels B *Estância Park*, in parkland setting 6 km NE, T 324-7624, F 324-1226, pool, tennis, minizoo, etc, best in town; *Príncipe*, Rua Eng Portela 165, T 324-0611, F 324-0936, and *Itamaraty*, Rua Manoel d'Abadia 209, T 324-4812, both **C** and comfortable. Many cheap ones around the bus station (Avenida Brasil-Norte), eg **D** *Serra Dourada*, Av Brasil 375, T 324-0051, restaurant, parking, fans, good value. *Restaurante Caiçara*, 14 de Julho 905, serves good *churrascos*.

Goiás Velho (pop 27,780), the former state capital 144 km NW of Goiânia, is a picturesque old gold-mining town (founded 1727 as Vila Boa) with narrow streets, seven baroque churches and many well-preserved 18th-century colonial mansions and government buildings; the oldest church, **São Francisco de Paula** (1761), Praça Alves de Castro facing the Market, is undergoing restoration. There is a good view of the town from **Santa Bárbara** church (1780) on the Rua Passo da Patria. Also worth visiting are: the **Museu da Boa Morte**, in the colonial church of the same name (a small, but interesting collection of old images, paintings, etc). The **Museu das Bandeiras** is in the Casa da Câmara e Cadeia (old town hall and prison), by the colonial fountain. The old **Government Palace** is next to the red-brick Cathedral in the main square. The **Palacio Conde dos Arcos**, Praça Castelo Branco (across from the Cathedral), still has its original 1755 furniture on display (Tues-Sat 0800-1700, Sun 0800-1200). Most churches and museums are closed on Mon. The rodoviária is next to the **Mercado Municipal** (18th century) beside the trickling Rio Vermelho, ½ km W of the central Praça do Coreto; regular bus services to Goiânia (2½ hrs), Aruanã, Barra do Garças and Jussara.

The streets of Goiás Velho blaze with torches during the solemn Fogaréu processions of Holy Week, when hooded figures re-enact Christ's descent from the cross and burial.

Hotels B *Vila Boa*, 1 km SE on the Morro do Chapéu do Padre, T 371-1000, pool, bar, restaurant, a/c, good views, rec; **D** *Araguaia*, Av Ferreira de Moura (the road into town from the S), T 371-1462, best budget place, fans, comfortable, rec; similar is the nearby *Serrano* (no phone), parking, bar.

Attractive, well-run "*Cachoeira Grande*" campground, 7 km along the BR-070 to Jussara (near the tiny airport), with bathing place and snack bar. More basic site (*Chafariz da Carioca*) in town by the river.

Restaurants *Pito Aceso*, grills; *Pedro's Bar*, good cold beef; *Dona Maninha*, R Dom Cândido, regional food, good value; *Sobradinho*, simple good food.

Shopping *Centro de Tradições Goianas*, in *Hotel Vila Boa*, and (cheaper) *Associação dos Artesãos de Goiás*, at the Rosario Church and in the Municipal Market, for local crafts and *artesanía*; many types of sugary sweets are made in the town and can be purchased direct from the bakeries.

Pirenópolis, a lovely colonial silver-mining town (pop 25,010, altitude 770m) in the red hills of Goiás, 122 km due W of Brasília, was founded in the same year as Goiás Velho and declared a National Heritage Site in 1989; as the nation's unofficial silver capital, shopping for jewellery and related items here is unsurpassed. The **Igreja Matriz NS do Rosário** is the oldest church in the state (1728), but that of **Nosso Senhor de Bonfim** (1750-54), with three impressive altars and an image of the Virgin brought from Portugal, is the most beautiful. A museum of religious art is housed in the church of **NS de Carmo** (daily 1300-1700), and another displays regional historical items, the **Museu Família Pompeu** (Rua Mestre Propício 29, open only 1300-1500, not Mon). The **Theatro de Pyrenópolis** on Rua Com Joaquim Alves is a testament to turn-of-the-century optimism. Pirenópolis was the birthplace of José Joaquim da Veiga Valle, the "Aleijadinho of Goiás", many of whose works are in the Boa Morte museum in Goiás Velho. An excursion may also be made to the **Fazenda Babilônia**, 25 km SW by paved road, a fine example of an 18th-century sugar *fazenda* now listed as an historical site, small museum, original mill, no public transport.

Festival *Festa do Divino Espírito Santo*, 45 days after Easter (Pentecost), is one of Brazil's most famous and extraordinary folkloric/religious celebrations, lasting three days, with medieval costumes, tournaments, dances and mock battles between Moors and Christians, a tradition held annually since 1819.

Hotels **A3** *Hotel Fazenda Quinta da Santa Bárbara*, in garden setting at Rua do Bonfim 1, T 331-1304, all facilities inc *Restaurante Brasília*; **A3** *Pousada dos Pirineus*, Chácara Mata do Sobrado, Bairro do Carmo, T 331-1345, a/c, TV, restaurant, bar, 2 pools, gym, tennis and other sports, boat hire; **C** *Pousada das Cavalhadas*, Praça da Matriz, T 331-1261, central, fans, fridges in rooms, best of the budget choices. More basic are: **D** *Rex*, also on the Praça da Matriz, T 331-1121, 9 sparse rm, small restaurant; *Pousada Tavares*, *Pensão Central* and *Dormitório da Geny* are all **F** and mostly for the desperate. All accommodation is filled during the Festa (see above) and even the downtown municipal camping site beside the Rio das Alvas overflows; better to visit from Brasília at this time.

Caldas Novas (pop 24,060, CEP 76940, DDD 062), 187 km SE of Goiânia (many buses; best reached via Morrinhos on the BR-153 Goiânia-São Paulo highway) is a newly developed thermal resort with good hotels and camp sites with hot swimming pools. Daily bus from Morrinhos, US$1, 1½ hrs. There are three groups of springs within this area: Caldas Novas, Fontes de Pirapetinga (7 km from the town) and Rio Quente (29 km from the town, bus from Caldas Novas); water temperatures are 37-51°C.

Hotels 48 in all. Very fashionable is **L2** *Hotel Turismo* (5-star) - *Pousada do Rio Quente* (4-star) complex at Rio Quente, T 452-1122, F 452-1177, or F São Paulo 282-5281, T 852-5733, or Brasília 224-7166, breakfast and lunch, transportation to main pools and recreation facilities included in price, other extras paid for with hotel's own currency, good hotel, accommodation in main buildings or chalets. (The *Turismo* has a private airstrip; flights from Rio and São Paulo with agencies.) **L3** *Parque das Primaveras*, R do Balneário, T 453-1355, F 453-1294, rec by locals, cheaper than the Rio Quente place. **A1** *Tamburi*, R Eça de Queirós, 10, T 453-1455, OK; **C** *Serra Dourada*, Av Correia Neto 574, T 453-1300, rec; **E** *Goiás*, with breakfast, rec; **E** *Imperial*, near Rodoviária, clean, friendly. Camping at Esplanada, and Camping Clube do Brasil site on the Ipameri road, 1 km from the centre. Many other "Clubes e Campings": *Tropical*, US$2 pp, 2 sites in town, can use both in 1 day, others mostly US$2.50 a day, all have snack bars.

Restaurants *Hotel José*, cheap good food; *Caminho do Natural*, vegetarian, good, but expensive; *Berro d'Água* in Bairro do Turista rec.

Goiás has two major National Parks. In the elevated region 200 km N of Brasília is popular **Chapada dos Veadeiros**, reached by paved state highway 118 to Alto Paraíso de Goiás, then gravel road W towards Colinas for 30 km where a sign marks the turnoff (just before the village of São Jorge). Buses Brasília-Alto Paraíso 1000 and 2200, US$6; occasional local buses Alto Paraíso-São Jorge, inc 1600 departure, 5-km walk to park entrance (US$0.60 fee). The main attractions are a number of high waterfalls (including a series along the Rio Negro, 7 km from São Jorge by rough track) complete with palm-shaded oases and natural swimming pools, and the varied wildlife: capibara, rhea, tapir, wolf, toucan, etc (Ibama address as for Emas, below, or T 061-646-1109). There is a small hotel (E) by the bus station in Alto Paraíso and a very basic *dormitório* in São Jorge (take sleeping bag or hammock), but camping in the park is the most pleasant option, about US$2/night and busy on weekends in the best visiting season (May-Oct). By jeep it is possible to cross from Alto Paraíso to the Brasília-Salvador highway (BR-242) via Nova Roma (ferry crossing) and Posse, a very slow but beautiful journey of 220 km.

In the far SW of the state, covering the watershed of the Araguaia, Taquari and Formoso Rivers, is the small **Emas National Park**, 110 km S of Mineiros, a town of 33,600 just off the main BR-364 route between Brasília and Cuiabá (112 km beyond Jataí). The park is most easily reached from Campo Grande (approx 6 hrs by car, compared with about 20 hrs from Goiânia, paved road poor). In *Mineiros* are: **C** *Pilões Palace*, Praça Alves de Assis, T 661-1547, restaurant, comfortable; and **D** *Boi na Brasa*, Rua Onze 11, T 661-1532, no a/c, good *churrasco* restaurant attached; next door **E** *Mineiros Hotel*, with bath and huge breakfast, good lunch, rec. The road to the National Park is now paved; there is no regular transport but tour operators can organize 4WD trips. The São José monastery, Mineiros, can arrange the necessary permission to visit, turn left out of rodoviária and walk ½ km along dirt road (or from Ibama, R 219 No 95, Setor Universitário, 74605-800 Goiânia, T 062-224-2488), also from Secretaria de Turismo, Praça Cel Carrijo 1, T 661-1551. A 4-day, 3-night visit to the Park can be arranged through agencies (eg Focus Tours, Belo Horizonte, see p 402). Camping within the park costs about US$2 pp and there is simple, dormitory accommodation at the park headquarters; kitchen and cook available but bring own food.

Douglas Trent of Focus Tours writes: The near 132,868 hectares of undulating grasslands and "campo sujo" cerrado forests host the world's largest concentration of termite mounds. They provide a surreal setting for large numbers of pampas deer, giant anteater and greater rhea, or "ema" in Portuguese. Maned wolf are frequently seen roaming the grasses in search of tinamou and other prey. Other animals which may be seen include yellow and giant armadillos, Amazonian anaconda, Brazilian tapir, grisons and white-lipped peccary. The park holds the greatest concentration of blue-and-yellow macaws outside Amazonia, and blue-winged, red-shouldered and red-bellied macaws can also be seen. Other bird specialities include the endemic white-winged nightjar, cock-tailed tyrant, white-vented violetear, lesser tinamou and the rare lesser northura, dwarf tinamou, and crested eagle. A pair of bare-faced currasow, white-woodpeckers, streamer-tailed tyrants and other showy birds visit the park HQ building daily.

Along with the grasslands, the park supports a vast marsh on one side and rich gallery forests on the other. The crystal clear waters of the Rio Formosa pass right by the headquarters and wander through the park. Many have compared this park with the African savannas. As many of the interesting mammals are nocturnal, a spotlight is a must.

Of Goiás' many natural attractions it is the Rio Araguaia which is most being promoted as a vacation destination. Brazilians are firmly convinced that the 2630-km-long river is richer in fish than any other in the world; a visit to the 220-km stretch between Aruanã and the Ilha do Bananal during the fishing season is quite an experience. As the receding waters in May reveal sparkling white beaches along the Araguaia, thousands of Brazilian and international enthusiasts pour into the area, intent on getting the best camping spots. As many as 400 tent 'cities' spring up, and vast quantities of fish (*pirurucu, pintado, pacu, suribim, tucanaré* and various types of catfish) are hauled in before the phenomenon winds down in Sep, when the rivers begin to rise again and flood the surrounding plains. Without Brazilian contacts, the traveller's best way of experiencing this annual event is with one of the specialist tour operators; rec are *Transworld*, R 3 No 560, Goiânia, T 224-4340 (one week group trips in a 'botel' out of Aruanã to Bananal), and *KR International Travel*, R Mexico 11-Gr 1701, Rio de Janeiro, T 210-1238, ex-Peace

Corps manager, good for info on the Centre-W region. Boats (US$10-25 an hour) and guides can also be hired in Aruanã, Britânia, Barra do Garças or **Porto Luis Alves** (**A1** *Pousada do Jaburu*, including meals), guide Vandeir will arrange boat trips to see wildlife, take food and water. Interesting walks in surrounding jungle with Joel, ask at the hotel. There is good fishing for *tucunaré* in the Rio Cristalino. Beware of currents and do not swim where the bed is muddy or where sting rays are said to lurk. Piranhas are reported not to be a problem where there is a current and provided swimmers have no open wounds. Yellow-fever vaccination is also rec for the region. *Borrachudas*, tiny biting insects, are an unavoidable fact of life in Central Brazil in Jun and Jul; repellent helps a little.

The Araguaia is most readily accessible from **Aruanã**, a port of 5,400 people 165 km NW of Goiás Velho by paved highway, which sees little excitement outside the winter fishing season (when its comfortable hotels are booked out for months). Boats can be rented to visit some of the beautiful lakes and beaches nearby. Buses from the rodoviária serve Araguapaz, Britânia and Goiânia; Hotels: **A2** *Recanto Sonhado*, on river at end of Av Altaimoro Caio Pacheco (2 km), T 376-1230, self-service restaurant, boutique, lunch included in tariff, no hardships whatever (reservations can be made through T (062) 241-7913 in Goiânia); **C** *Araguaia*, Praça Couto Magalhães 53 (opposite the docks), T 376-1251; both have pools, a/c, and meals available; restaurants in town rather poor, but try *Columbia*, Rua João Artiaga 221 (opp Municipal Stadium), clean, good menu. The official campground is a 20-min boat ride away on Ilha Redonda, but open (and full) only in Jul. The Brazilian Canoeing Championships are also held along the river in Jul, enthusiastic turn-out.

A direct dirt road (250 km, via Jussara) and a more circuitous paved route through Iporá (340 km) connect Goiás Velho with Aragarças (on the Goiás side) and **Barra do Garças** (on the Mato Grosso side of the Araguaia). Barra (pop 45,600) is the pleasanter of the two and has the better facilities, including several banks and Hotels: **C** *Esplanada Palace*, Rua Waldir Rabelo 81, T 861-2515, a/c, safe parking; various **D-E** hotels along Avenida Min João Alberto, eg *Novo Mundo*, *Presidente* and *Avenida*, all clean and a/c. Churrascarias also on this avenue and near the bridge (eg *Del Fronteyra*, live music, 1100-1400, 1900-2200); pleasant river beach with bars and snacks; campsite on island in river; nighttime entertainment by the port. In *Aragarças* (4 km) is the new **A1** *Hotel Toriuá Park*, T 861-2232, pool, minizoo, own launch, lakeside location. 6 km E of Barra on the road to Araguaiana is **Parque Balneário das Águas Quentes**, with thermal pools (42°C), river bathing and recreational opportunities. The abrupt 600m-high Morro do Cristo (10 km) gives a wide view over the Araguaia and surrounding country. A *Festival de Praia* is held locally in Jul: fishing tournaments, displays, boat races, etc. Buses to Barra to/from São Paulo direct, 20 hrs, US$30; to São Felix do Araguaia at 2000, US$24, arrives early afternoon, wildlife may be seen in early am.

The road N to Marabá, paralleling the Araguaia on the Mato Grosso and Pará side, leaves Barra do Garças and runs 140 km to *Xavantina* on the Rio das Mortes, the famous "River of Deaths" which once marked the territorial boundary of the intractable Xavante Indians. The road is paved for a further 120 km to Serra Dourada, then marginal dirt (485 km) as far as the Pará state border; it is again paved for the remaining 650 km to Marabá via Xinguara and Redenção and the turnoff for the Ilha do Bananal (see below). At Xavantina (pop 13,000) is **E** *Hotel Xavantina*, basic but nothing better; *Churrascaria Arca de Noé*, highly rec.

On the other (E) side of the Araguaia, the Brasília-Belém highway (BR-153) runs N through the heart of Goiás and Tocantins states.

The new state of Tocantins (277,321.9 sq km, pop 920,135) is technically an Amazonian state, the boundary of the Norte region running along the border between it and Goiás. Its main attractions are the Ilha do Bananal and the Araguaia National Park, and fishing, although additional sites of interest might be the various diamond workings in the state and the Kraolândia and Xerente Indian Reserves between Miracema and Carolina. Miracema do Tocantins is the provisional capital until the purpose-built **Palmas** is complete (pop in 1993,

6,000, mostly government personnel and construction workers). The small town of *Gurupi* on the BR-153, 90 km N of the Tocantins border, has been rec as a pleasant place to break the journey. Hotel (E) near the bus station. Entry to the Bananal is not permitted from here.

At Fátima, on the BR-153, a paved road heads E 52 km to a new bridge over the Rio Tocantins to *Porto Nacional* (pop 43,225). From here a road is being built N to Palmas, 55 km, a few km inland from the village of Canela (which is opposite Molha—ferry across the Tocantins). Porto Nacional has 3 habitable hotels, 3 restaurants, an airport with regional flights, 7 banks, the regional hospital and a small rodoviária on Praça do Peso Boiadeiro. The church of Nossa Senhora das Mercês (1903) on the main square is probably the only major point of interest; a regional festival of N Sra das Mercês is on 24 Sep. 2-hr boat trips up the Tocantins from the old ferry port go the Carreira Comprida rapids and island beaches (best May-Sep).

77 km upriver from Palmas, on the W bank, *Miracema do Tocantins* (pop 20,850) has 5 hotels, an airport, sightseeing at nearby Cachoeiras do Lajeado Grande and a 24-hr ferry to Tocantínia on the E bank. From the BR-153 to Miracema is 23 km. Much of the area is under threat of flooding if a hydroelectric dam is built at Lajeada (Miracema): Canela would vanish, and Palmas and the bridge at Porto Nacional have been designed with the hypothetical lake in mind. (We are grateful to Kevin Healey, Melbourne, for most of this information.)

At Guaraí the road forks, one branch continuing W into Pará, then turning N to Marabá on the Transamazônica and on to Belém. The other branch goes to Araguaína, whereafter the BR-226 goes to Estreito in Maranhão, from where the BR-010 runs N through Imperatriz to Belém. A pleasant overnight stop on the road to Araguaiana is the hilly town of *Uruaçu*, cheap hotels near Rodoviária.

Araguaína (pop 103,395) in Tocantins, is on the Brasília-Belém road (Brasília, 1,102 km; Belém 842 km; Imperatriz, 174 km). Several hotels near rodoviária including **D** *Esplanada*, may have to share a room, friendly, clean, fan, no breakfast, good; *Líder*, *São Jorge*, *do Norte* and *Goiás* (all **E**). Bus leaves Araguaína for Marabá 0700 and 1400. Ordinary bus to Goiânia takes 24 hrs: try to get an express. If travelling to Belém or Brasília by bus, reservations are not normally accepted: be at the terminal 2 hrs before scheduled departure as buses tend to leave early; as soon as bus pulls in, follow the driver to the ticket counter and ask if there are seats. Brasília 1200, 2400, US$36 (22 hrs). Buses also to Santarém. Varig flights twice a week from Brasília, Imperatriz and São Luiz.

Off the Brasília-Belém road are fast-developing frontier regions between the lower Araguaia and Xingu rivers. Kevin Healey writes: There is now a soaring concrete bridge spanning the Araguaia just S of Conceição do Araguaia, and the road connection to the Belém highway at Guaraí is being paved. (This is the only bridge across the Araguaia between Barra dos Garças and Marabá.)

North and W of Conceição are many new townships and ranches. Places like Redenção (pop 54,365) and Xinguara are raw, dusty and not very salubrious for tourists, especially at night. At Xinguara (pop 40,315 already) is the **E** *Hotel Rio Vermelho*, not too bad. To the W, Cumaru is a *garimpeiro* settlement, from where the local military governor keeps "law and order" over the gold mining centres near the Rio Fresco. Here, the miners and prospectors are already on the edge of the Gorotiré Indian Reserve and a road is poised to enter the Indian land. To the S is Campo Alegre (pop 8,400), the centre of cow country, with a huge new slaughterhouse serving the corporate ranches around the region (eg the experimental ranch of Cristalino, owned by VW Brasil). This is a perfect place to see the destruction of the rainforest and the changing climate pattern.

At *Conceição do Araguaia* (pop 54,490) the best hotel is the **B** *Taruma Tropical* (T 421-1205), pool, conference centre, garage, sauna, frigobars, expanded restaurant, clean and functioning bathrooms, a/c—when it works; the hotel is well patronized by ranchers and absentee landowners from Brasília; also *Marajoara*, Av JK 1587, T 421-1220, some a/c, safe parking, breakfast; *Araguaia*, R Conto de Magalhães 2605, breakfast, both small, overpriced. Best place to eat is *Café Taboquinha*, Av Francisco Vitor, well-prepared fish, open 1200-1500, 1800-2300. The town has a frontier atmosphere, although mudhuts are being replaced by brick: cowboy hats, battered Chevrolet pick-ups, skinny mules and a red light district. Airport 14 km SW. Conceição would be a useful base for visiting the Ilha do Bananal.

Douglas Trent, of Focus Tours, Belo Horizonte (who arrange tours, see p 402), writes: *Bananal* is the world's largest river island, located in the state of Tocantins on the northeastern border of Mato Grosso. The island is formed by a division in the S of the Rio Araguaia and is approximately 320 km long. The entire island was originally a national park (called **Parque Nacional Araguaia**), which was then cut in half and later further reduced to its current size of 562,312 ha (of an original 2 million). The island and park are subject to seasonal flooding and contain several permanent lakes. The island, and especially the park, form one of the more spectacular wildlife areas on the continent, in many ways similar to the Pantanal. The vegetation is a transition zone between the *cerrado* (woody savanna) and Amazon forests, with gallery forests along the many waterways. There are several marshlands throughout the island.

The fauna is also transitional. More than 300 bird species are found here, including the hoatzin, hyacinthine macaw, harpy eagle and black-fronted piping guan. The giant anteater, maned wolf, bush dog, giant otter, jaguar, puma, marsh deer, pampas deer, American tapir, yellow anaconda and South American river turtle also occur here. The island is flooded most of the year, with the prime visiting (dry) season being from Jun to early Oct, when the beaches are exposed. Unfortunately, the infrastructure for tourism aside from fishing expeditions (the island is a premier spot for big fish) is very limited. Access to the park is through the small but pleasant town of **Santa Teresinha** (pop 8,900) which is N of São Felix (see below), and is the gateway to the park. A charming hotel is the **A3** *Bananal*, Pça Tarcila Braga 106, CEP 78395 (Mato Grosso), with full board. There is room only for 10; make your reservations well in advance, either by mail, allowing several months for the mail to get through, or by phoning the town's telephone operator, asking the hotel to call you back and hoping that you hear from them.

Permission to visit the park should be obtained in advance from Sr Levi Vargas, Director of the Park, Ibama, R 219, No 95, Setor Universitário, 74605-800 Goiânia. There is some simple accommodation for scientists at the park, which can sometimes be reserved at the address above or from IBDF, the National Parks department in Brasilia. Bring your own food and bedding, and the severely underpaid but dedicated staff would appreciate any extra food or financial help, although it will not be solicited. A boat to the park can be lined up at the *Hotel Bananal*.

São Félix do Araguaia (pop 14,365) is a larger town with more infrastructure for fishing. A very simple hotel with the best view in town is the **D** *Mini Hotel Araguaia*, Av Araguaia 344, T (065) 522-1154, inc breakfast. They have a/c rooms, not rec, electricity is turned off at night and the closed-in room gets very hot. Rec is **D** *Xavante*, Av Severiano Neves 391, T 522-1305, a/c, shower, frigobar, excellent breakfast, delicious *cajá* juice, Sr e Sra Carvalho very hospitable. A good restaurant is the *Pizzaria Cantinho da Peixada* on Av Araguaia, next to the Texaco station, overlooking the river: the owner, Klaus, rents rooms, **E**, better than hotels, T 522-1320, he also arranges fishing trips rec. *Bar Paralelos* has live music. Many Carajás indians are found in town; a depot of their handicrafts is between the *Pizzaria* and *Mini Hotel* on Av Araguaia. Rodoviária is 3 km from centre and waterfront, taxi US$3; buses to Barra do Garças at 0500, arr 2300, or 1730, arr 1100 next day; also to Tucumã, 6-8 hrs, and to São José do Xingu, 10 hrs. No buses to Marabá.

Many river trips available for fishing or to see wildlife. Juracy Lopes, a very experienced guide, can be contacted through *Hotel Xavante*; he has many friends, inc the chief and council, in Santa Isabela (see below). Morning or afternoon trips to the village or to see wildlife, cost US$15 for 2; longer trips can be made to the meeting of the waters with the Rio das Mortes, or spending a night in the jungle sleeping in hammocks. *Icuryala* is recommended, T (062) 223-9518 (Goiâna), excellent food, drink, and service, US$100/day, independent visitors also welcomed. Fazenda owners may invite you as their guest—do not abuse this privilege, and remember to take a gift.

Bananal can be visited from São Félix (with permission from Funai in the town) by crossing the river to the Carajá village of **Santa Isabela de Morra** and asking to see the chief, who can tell you the history of the tribe. The island can be crossed from São Félix to **São Miguel de Araguaia** by taking an 8-hr trip (departures twice a week) with Zico in his van (contact him at the *Bar Beira*). From São Miguel a 5-hr bus trip brings you to **Porangatu** (**E** *Hotel Mauriti*, shower, restaurant) on the Belém-Brasilia highway.

Access to both Santa Teresinha and São Félix is by Brasil Central/TAM flights, and to São Félix by bus from Barra do Garças, see above. The air service is unreliable and, as the planes hold just 15 passengers, it is common to get held over for a day or two. There is a daily Votec flight from São Felix to Belém, stopping at Redenção, Tucumã, and many other places. In Sta Teresinha look out for a man in a yellowish taxi who kindly offers a free ride and then tries to collect outrageous sums from foreigners. There are legitimate taxis available—use them. Mosquito nets are highly recommended: high incidence of malaria.

Klaus Brandl (Rio de Janeiro) has sent us the following details on how to get from São Félix do Araguaia to the Rio Xingu. Bus São Félix to Posto da Mata at 0700, 3 hrs; change to bus to **Vila Rica** (5 hrs), stay in *Hotel Casa Verde*, from F to C, small rooms. A bus at 0500 makes a tiring trip on a gruesome road to Redenção, via Santana do Araguaia, arrives 1830, then take 2000 bus to Xinguara (2½ hrs—Redenção and Xinguara are described above). Bus Xinguara to **Tucumã**, 4 hrs, at 0600 and 0900, best to take the earlier one to catch the 1500 bus to São Félix do Xingu (in Tucumã is the dingy **D** *Hotel D'Oro Palace*, noisy, dusty room with a/c, TV, minibar, and excellent *Churrascaria Tucumã*, Praça do Posto). Am buses to São Félix do Xingu leave at 0600 and 0800; arrival depends on Rio Fresco ferry, usually about 1500. The road is horrible and impassable in the wet season, Nov-Mar; then you have to fly or go by river from Altamira on the Transamazônica.

São Félix do Xingu is a dusty, sleepy town with 3 hotels and some *dormitórios*. The best is **D** *Dallas*, a small, concrete building with cell-like rooms, with and without bath and fan, electricity from 1800-0400. The owner, José de Oliveira, promises everything, but his son Waldemir is more reliable, very helpful and sympathetic. The **E** *Hotel Diplomat* is "a rathole", very dirty, but there is a very good restaurant opposite, *Churrascaria Giovenard*, highly rec, proprietor gives 15% discount to SAHB owners.

It seems that from São Miguel de Araguaia you can head S on GO-164 for about 140 km; turn left to Peixe and cross the Rio Araguaia by ferry to Cocalinho. From here drive to the BR-158, crossing both the Rios Cristalino and das Mortes by more ferries (spectacular limestone caverns have been reported 20 km before the Rio das Mortes ferry and 6 km after the limestone quarry). At BR-158 turn left to **Agua Boa** (pop 16,570, **C** *Palace Hotel*; *Manga Rosa*, good churrascaria), then continue to Barra do Garças. If heading for the Pantanal, note that BR-070 from Barra to Cuiabá is in poor condition after the turn to Poxoréo; better to go to Rondonópolis, either for Cuiabá or Campo Grande.

To the W of Goiás are the states of Mato Grosso and Mato Grosso do Sul, with a combined area of 1,231,549 sq km and a population of only about 3.8 million, or about three persons to the sq km. The two states are half covered with forest, with a large wetland area (220,000 sq km) called the Pantanal (roughly W of a line between Campo Grande and Cuiabá, between which there is a direct road), partly flooded in the rainy season (**see p 587**). East of this line the pasture plains begin to appear. The Noroeste Railway and a road run across Mato Grosso do Sul through Campo Grande to Porto Esperança and Corumbá, both on the Rio Paraguai; much of the journey is across the wetland, offering many sights of birds and other wildlife.

Campo Grande (pop 525,620, CEP 79100, DDD 067) the capital of the State of Mato Grosso do Sul (pop 1,778,500) is a pleasant modern city. It was founded in 1899 and became state capital in 1979. Because of the *terra roxa* (red earth), it is called the "Cidade Morena". In the centre is a shady park, the Praça República, commonly called the Praça do Rádio after the Rádio Clube on one of its corners. Three blocks W is Praça Ari Coelho. Linking the two squares, and running through the city E to W, is Avenida Afonso Pena; much of its central reservation is planted with yellow ypé trees. Their blossom covers the avenue, and much of the city besides, in spring. The city also has a great many mango trees, consequently it is very leafy and clean. The Parque dos Poderes, a long way from the centre, extends for several hectares; as well as having the Palácio do Governo and state secretariats, it has a small zoo for the rehabilitation of animals from the Pantanal (phone the Secretaria do Meio Ambiente to visit), lovely trees and cycling and jogging tracks.

Museums **Museu Regional Dom Bosco (Regional Indian Museum)**, R Barão do Rio Branco 1843 (open daily 0700-1100, 1300-1700, US$0.50, T 383-3994), is a superb museum with the following collections: exhibits from the 5 Indian groups with which the Salesian missionaries have had contact in the 20th century, the Bororó, Moro, Xavante, Carajá and tribes of the Rio Uaupés in Amazonia, all with explanatory texts; fossilized shells, malacology (shells), entomology, 2,800 stuffed birds, 7-8,000 butterflies, mammals, minerals and "monstruos" (2-headed calves, etc). Each collection is highly rec. **Museu do Arte Contemporâneo**, Mal Rondón e Calógeras, modern art from the region.

NB The important street in the centre, R Marechal Cândido Mariano Rondon, is called either Marechal Rondon, or Cândido Mariano.

Hotels **L2** *Exceler Plaza*, Av Afonso Pena 444, T 382-0102, F 382-0141, 4-star, very good, luxury, art gallery, pool, tennis, all-you-can-eat business lunches; **L3** *Campo Grande*, R 13 de Maio 2825, T 384-6061, F 624-8349, central, a/c, luxury; **A1** *Concord*, Av Calógeras 1624, T 384-3081, F 382-4987, very good, swimming pool, a/c; **A1** *Indaiá Park*, Av Afonso Pena 354, T 384-3858, F 721-0359, a/c, pool, restaurant; **A3** *Fenícia*, Av Calógeras 2262, T 383-2001, a/c; **C** *Anache*, Marechal Rondón 1396, T 383-2841, with TV.

Near the rodoviária: **B** *Iguaçu*, T 384-4621, F 721-3215, opposite bus station, modern, clean, pleasant, rec; next door is **C** *Cosmos*, Dom Aquino 771, T 383-4271, good value; **C** *Novo*, opp bus platforms, with bath, clean, rec; **E** *Nacional*, R Dom Aquino 610, 1 block W of bus station, basic, shabby but friendly, clean; **E** *Rocha*, Barão do Rio Branco 343, 1 block

CAMPO GRANDE
Not to Scale

1. Praça Repúbica
2. Praça Ari Coelho
3. Museu Regional Dom Bosco
4. Museu do Arte Contemporâneo
5. Igreja São José
6. Casa do Artesanato
7. Telephone Office
8. Post Office
9. CODEMS, Tourist Information

Hotels:

10. Campo Grande
11. Fenícia
12. Gaspar
13. União
14. Iguaçu
15. Cosmos

16. Rádio Clube
17. Peña Eme-Ene

from rodoviária, without breakfast, fan, clean, T 383-6874; **D** *Vania*, near rodoviária, with bath, laundry, clean, rec. There is a wide variety of hotels in the streets around the rodoviária; if you have time, leave bags in the *guarda volumes* and shop around.

Near the railway station: **C** *Gaspar*, Av Mato Grosso 2, T 383-5121, opp station, with bath, ask for quiet room, good breakfast, clean; next door is **D** *União*, Calógeras 2828, good breakfast (most days), clean, ask for quiet room, friendly; **D** *Continental*, R Maracaju 229, 2 blocks from railway, 5 from bus terminal, clean, comfortable; **E** *Rio Negro*, R Maracaju 171, with fan, clean; **E** *Esperança*, R Dr Temistocles 100, at station, hot and cold showers, no a/c or fan, clean, very helpful; **E** *Paulista*, António Maria Coelho 1085, basic but adequate facilities, cheap café (on the street behind *Gaspar*); on same street, **E** *Caçula*, basic, hot showers, laundry; others in R Maracaju.

Restaurants *Vitório*, Av Afonso Pena 1907, *churrascaria*, live music evenings; *Terracus Gaúcho*, at bus station, huge meal; *Churrascaria Campo Grande*, Av Calógeras 2199, good value; *Carinca*, SE corner of main *praça*, modern, clean, good plain food. *Optimus*, Shopping Center Campo Grande, 2nd floor, T 726-1020. *Shanghai*, Rio Branco 1037, rec; *Hong Kong*, R Maracaju 131, centre, good Chinese food, also a legal outlet for *jacaré* meat, closed Mon; *Maracaju*, on same street, cheap good food; *Cafeteria Lojas Americanas*, Marechal Rondón 1336, in a supermarket, and *Meio Kilo* opposite, good value buffet; *El Café*, R Dom Aquino 1248, both rec. *Nutre Bem*, vegetarian, Pedro Celestino 1696, good. Plenty of good places in R Barão de Rio Branco. *Confidência Mineira*, 14 de Julho 945, Mineiro food and 49 types of *cachaça* on sale, open daily, shows Sun and Tues; *Casa Grande Restaurante e Bar*, R 14 de Julho.

Regional specialities include *caldo de piranha* (soup), *chipa* (cheese bread), sold on the streets, delicious when hot, and the local liqueur, *piqui com caju*, which contains *cachaça*.

Banks and Exchange Banco do Brasil changes TCs, several branches, eg 13 de Maio e Av

Afonso Pena, and 13 de Maio e Dom Aquino. Parallel rate hard to find, try at *Hotel Fenícia*, check notes carefully, rodoviária, *Hotel Caranda*, 1 block from rodoviária; Sr Abdala in the clothes shop at 14 de Julho 2581; or try in Las Vegas billiard hall, Barão do Rio Branco 1130.

Entertainment See below for Peña Eme-Ene. *Cameleão*, 15 de Novembro 1131, Wed-Sat, bar with shows, live music, entrance US$1-5 depending on what's on; owned by local artist, Humberto Espíndola, who specializes in depicting and criticizing cattle culture (*boicultura*). Ask at *Cameleão* if you want to find out more.

Health Yellow and Dengue fevers are both present in Campo Grande. There is a clinic for both at the railway station, but it's not very hygienic (take precautions in advance).

Post Office on corner of R Dom Aquino and Calógeras; fax office here. **Telephone** R Dom Aquino, between P Celestino e Rui Barbosa.

Shopping The *Casa do Artesanato*, Av Calógeras e Av Afonso Pena, has a good collection of Indian jewellery and arrows on sale. *Eme-Ene*, Av Afonso Pena 2303, T 382-2373, regional handicrafts, open 0700-1900, Sat 0700-1700, Sun 0800-1200, good, has a *peña* (folk music show) each Wed at 2100, rec. A local speciality is Os Bugres da Conceição, squat wooden statues covered in moulded wax. There is a market (Feira Livre) on Wed and Sat. Mato Grosso do Sul is a good region for buying cheap, good leather shoes. **Bookshop** R 15 de Junho e R Dom Aquino, highly rec, English spoken, will exchange English books.

Tourist Agencies *Tainá Turismo*, R Mal Rondon 1636, T 384-6544, Telex 067-2607; *Vax Tour*, Rui Barbosa 3014, English spoken; *Coelho e Neto*, R Dom Aquino 542, T 624-3616; *Impacto*, R Padre João Crippa 1065, sala 106, T 624-6363; *Nativa*, R 13 de Maio 2825, T 384-6061; *Regina*, R João Pedrossian 128, T 624-2214; *Sansitour*, Av Mato Grosso 2850, T 726-2579; *Origem e Destino*, R Dom Aquino 1682, T 721-1430, English, French and Spanish spoken.

Tourist Information, maps, etc at Codems (Companhia de Desenvolvimento Econômico de Mato Grosso do Sul), R Marechal Cândido Mariano Rondon 1500, CEP 79.002-200, T 721-3385/6/4781. Extremely helpful. Kiosk at airport. Town information in Secretaria de Turismo, Indústrias e Comércio, Parque dos Poderes.

Air Daily flights to São Paulo, Rio, Corumbá, Cuiabá, Brasília, Manaus, Porto Velho. City bus No 158, "Popular," stops outside airport. Taxi to airport, US$6. Banco do Brasil at airport exchanges dollars. Post office, fax and phones in same office.

Rail The railway station is not far from the bus terminal. **Ponta Porã** (9 hrs) Mon, Wed, Fri at 0920, US$13.20 1st class, US$9 2nd, ticket office opens at 0800 on same day. To **Corumbá**: train leaves twice a week, 0700, US$17 1st class, US$12 2nd, US$46 double cabin (office open 0600, a very tiring 12 hr journey but fascinating views, mosquitoes after dark). The trains to **Bauru** were withdrawn in 1994.

Buses Rodoviária is in the block bounded by Ruas Barão do Rio Branco, Vasconcelos Fernandes, Dom Aquino and Joaquim Nabuco, T 383-1678, all offices on 2nd floor; at the V Fernandes end are town buses, at the J Nabuco end state and interstate buses. In between are shops and *lanchonetes*. 8 blocks' walk from Praça República; cinema in bus station, US$1.20; fun fair one block away. (Taxi to rodoviária, US$3.60.) **São Paulo**, paved road, US$33.50 14 hrs, 9 buses daily, 1st at 0800, last at 2400, 3 *leito* buses. **Cuiabá**, US$31, 10 hrs, 12 buses daily, *leito* at 2100 and 2200. To **Brasília**, US$49 (Motta rec), 23 hrs at 0900 and 1900. To **Goiânia**, São Luis company 1100, 1630, 1900, 2300, 15 hrs on 1900 service, US$37, others 24 hrs, US$1 cheaper. **Rio de Janeiro**, US$48, 21 hrs, 4 buses daily, *leito* at 174$. **Corumbá**, with Andorinha, 8 daily from 0600, 6 hrs, US$14.50. Campo Grande-Corumbá buses connect with those from Rio and São Paulo, similarly those from Corumbá through to Rio and São Paulo. Good connections to all major cities. **Ponta Porã**, 5½ hrs, 9 buses daily, US$13. **Dourados**, 4 hrs, 14 daily (Queiroz), US$9. Beyond Dourados is Mundo Novo, from where buses go to Ponta Porã (0530) and to Porto Frajelli (very frequent); from Mundo Novo ferries for cars and passengers go to Guaíra for US$0.50. Twice daily direct service to **Foz do Iguaçu** (17 hrs) with Integração, 1200, 1600, US$24; same company goes to Cascavel, US$23. To **Pedro Juan Caballero** (Paraguay), del Amambay company, US$10.

The Campo Grande-São Paulo journey can be broken at *Três Lagoas* (pop 68,070), 9½ hrs from São Paulo (motorway) and 6 hrs from Campo Grande by paved highway BR-262 (buses dep Campo Grande 0800, 1200, 2230, US$15.75, an interesting journey, "especially for cattle farmers"). Hotels: **B** *Três Lagoas*, Av Rosário Congro 629, T 521-2500, a/c, best; **C** *Regente Palace*, R Paranaíba 580, a/c, good value; **E** *Hotel Novo*, Av Antônio de Souza Queiroz, near bus station, friendly. *Restaurant Casarão*, R Munir Tomé 30, has good selection of dishes; *Boi na Brasa*, Av Antônio Trajano 487, for *churrascos*, rec.

16 km E of Três Lagoas is the massive **Jupiá** Dam on the Rio Paraná, which can be visited with prior permission (T 521-2753) on weekends and holidays only, 0800-1800. Further N are other hydroelectric dams, most impressive of which is at **Ilha Solteira** (50 km, several hotels and good fish restaurants on São Paulo state side); guided tours at 1000 and 1500 weekends and holidays. Overlooking the river 35 km S is restored **Fort Itapura**, built during the War of the Triple Alliance, with beach and restaurants nearby. Excellent swimming is to be had at **Praia Catarina**, with bars, playground and kiosks (6 km).

The paved road from Campo Grande to the Paraguayan frontier at Ponta Porã passes through **Dourados** (224 km, pop 135,780, 430m), the supply centre of a developing agricultural region carved from the red *sertão*, in large part by Japanese immigrants. Apart from a couple of pleasant parks and lakes for swimming there is little of note for the casual traveller. Good bus connections for Campo Grande, Ponta Porã, Mundo Novo, and Presidente Prudente and Maringá to the E of the Rio Paraná; scheduled flights to Campo Grande, Ponta Porã, Ourinhos, Pres Prudente and São Paulo from the small airport (10 km). Hotels: **B** *Alphonsus*, Av Pres Vargas 603, T 421-5211, F 421-9178, best; **C** *Figueira Palace*, Rua Toshinobu Katayama 553, T 421-5611, a/c, pleasant; **C** *Bahamas*, Rua Cândido da Câmara 750, T 421-4714, a/c, simpler but excellent value. *Restaurante Boxexa*, R Araújo 780, good pizzas; *Churrascaria Guarujá* (No 595 same street) for *churrascos* in enjoyable surroundings.

The highway continues 115 km to **Ponta Porã**, separated from Pedro Juan Caballero in Paraguay only by a broad avenue. With a population of 55,830, paved streets, good public transport and smart shops, Ponta Porã is decidedly more prosperous than its neighbour, although Brazilian visitors flock across the border to play the casino and buy cheaper "foreign" goods. At the **Parque das Exposições**, by the rodoviária (see below), an animal show is held each Oct.

Hotels **B** *Porta do Sol Palace*, Rua Paraguai 2688, T 431-3341, F 431-1193, a/c, pool, very nice; **B** *Pousada do Bosque*, Av Pres Vargas 1151, 3 km out of town, T 431-1181, F 431-1741, good motel type, a/c, pool, restaurant; **B** *Guarujá*, R Guia Lopes, T 431-1619, rec; opp is **C** *Barcelona*, maze-like building, a/c, restaurant, pool; **C** *Alvorada*, Av Brasil 2977, T 431-5866, good café, close to post office, good value but often full; **C** *Internacional*, R Internacional 1267, T 431-1243, with a/c and bath, **D** without a/c, hot water, clean, good breakfast, rec; **D** *Grande*, Av Brasil 1181; **E** *Dos Viajantes*, across park opp railway station, very basic, clean. Brazilian hotels inc breakfast in tariff, Paraguayan ones do not.

Restaurants *Top Lanches*, beside *Hotel Barcelona*, cheap and friendly. *Chopão*, good food at reasonable prices. *Pepe's Lunch e Pizzeria*, good, fairly cheap; *Karina Lanches*, near Federal Police office, good, cheap; *Santa Antônia*, rec.

Banks and Exchange Banco do Brasil changes TCs. Several *cambios* on the Paraguayan side. Many in the centre of town (but on Sun change money in hotels or the gambling hall beneath Livraria Sulamérica).

Electric Current 220 volts AC.

Transport **Air** services to São Paulo and points in western Paraná and São Paulo states, more natural connections for Mato Grosso do Sul than Cuiabá or Brasília. A **railway** also connects the city with Campo Grande, a 9-hr trip through rolling hills, departures 3 times a week more-or-less at 1640, US$13.20 1st class, US$9 2nd class; the station is some 8 blocks from the centre, take "Ferroviária" bus (US$1). **Buses** to Campo Grande: nine a day from 0100-2130, 6 hrs, US$13; the rodoviária is 3 km out on the Dourados road ("São Domingos" bus, taxi US$5).

There are no actual border posts between the two towns and people pass freely for local visits. The Brazilian Federal Police office (for entry/exit visas) is on the 2nd floor of the white engineering supply company building at Rua Marechal Floriano 1483, T 431-1428, officially open 24 hrs but weekdays 0730-1130, 1400-1700 is more realistic. See p 1088 for address and hours of Paraguayan control. Taking a taxi between offices can speed things up if pressed for time; drivers know border crossing requirements. The two nations' consulates face each other on R Internacional (border street) a block W of Ponta Porã's local bus terminal; some nationalities require a visa from the Paraguayan consul (next to *Hotel Internacional*), open only 0800-1200 Mon-Fri. Check requirements carefully, and ensure your documents are in order: without the proper stamps you will inevitably be sent back somewhere later on in your travels.

A new area of tourist interest in Mato Grosso do Sul is being established in the municipality of **Bonito** in the Serra do Bodoquena, which yields granite and marble and is clad in forest. (Town pop 15,500, distance from Campo Grande 248 km.) The area's main attractions are in its rivers and caves (the formations are comparable to those found in the Lagoa Santa region of Minas

Gerais). Most excursions require authorization; this is not an obstacle to those with their own transport but as there is no public transport, those without a car will need to use an agency (see below).

Two of the first caves to be opened are the **Lagoa Azul** and **NS Aparecida**, both 26 km from Bonito. Lagoa Azul has a lake 150 metres long and 70 metres wide, 180 metres below ground level. The water, 20°C, is a jewel-like blue as light from the opening is refracted through limestone and magnesium. The startling blue, in combination with the browns and yellows of the stalactites, is beautiful. Prehistoric animal bones have been found in the lake. The light is at its best Jan-Feb, 0700-0900, but is fine at other times. A 25-ha park surrounds the cave. You must visit with a guide and pay a municipal tax, US$3; if not using your own transport, a car for 4 costs US$20. A guide is obligatory also for NS Aparecida, which has superb stalactites and stalagmites, max 5 people allowed at a time; no tourism infrastructure.

River excursions (always take swimwear) include: the Balneário Municipal on the Rio Formoso (7 km on road to Jardim), with changing rooms, toilets, camping, swimming in clear water, plenty of fish to see (strenuous efforts are made to keep the water and shore clean). Horminio waterfalls, 13 km, eight falls on the Rio Formoso, suitable for swimming; bar and camping, entry US$0.15. Rafting on the Rio Formoso: 7km, 2½ hrs, min 4 people, US$15 pp, a mixture of floating peacefully downriver, swimming and shooting 4 waterfalls, lifejackets available; arranged by Hapakany Tour, see below. The Aquário Natural is one of the springs of the Rio Formoso; to visit you must have authorization from Hapakany Tour (a guide is not necessary, but would be helpful for finding the way there through beautiful *fazenda* scenery); you can swim and snorkel with 5 types of fish (*piraputanga, corimba, lambari, mato grosso* and *piau*). Do not swim with suntan oil on. Another tour is from the springs of the Rio Sucuri to its meeting with the Formoso (permission from Hapakany or TapeTur), about 2 km of crystal-clear water, with swimming or snorkelling, birdwatching, very peaceful. The fishing season is from 1 Mar to 31 Oct. In late Oct, early Nov is the *piracema* (fish run), when the fish return to their spawning grounds. Hundreds can be seen jumping the falls. There are spectacular walks through mountains and forest; wildlife includes birds, rheas, monkeys, alligators and anaconda. The wet season is Jan-Feb; Dec-Feb is hottest, Jul-Aug coolest.

Hotels **B** *Tapera*, on hill above Shell station on road to Jardim, T 255-1700, new, fine views, cool breezes, a/c, comfortable, good; **C** *Bonanza*, R Cel Pilad Rebuá (main street) 628, T 255-1315, F 255-1235, suites and family rooms available, a/c, TV, frequently rec, opp is parking lot, with bar from 1800, darts and *churrascaria* on Fri; **C** *Canäa*, Pilad Rebuá 1293, T 255-1255, parking, TV, a/c, fridge, phone, restaurant and *churrascaria*; **D** *Gemila*, R Luis da Costa Leite 2085, clean, bath, fan, hot water, laundry; **D** *Pousadinha da Praça*, Pilad Rebuá 2097, T 255-1135, 2-4 bedded rooms (latter cramped), fan, hot water; also *Alvorado*, with shared baths.

Camping at *Ilha do Padre*, 12 km N of Bonito, very pleasant, no regular transport (Hapakany's raft trip ends here), T/F 255-1430; 4 rustic cabanas with either 4 bunk beds, or 2 bunks and a double, US$10 pp, youth hostel with two sets of 12 beds, US$6 pp, same price as for camping, toilets, showers, clothes washing, meals available, bar, electricity, lots of trees, can swim anywhere, to enter the island for a day US$3. Managers are Henrique Ruas and Jane Tatoni; Henrique has built the **A2-B** *Pousada Olho d'Agua*, just outside Bonito, Km 1 on road to Três Morros, T (067) 255-1430, F 255-1470, accommodation in cabins, breakfast inc, fan, showers with solar-heated water, fruit trees, fresh vegetables, small lake, own water supply, horseriding, bicycles. Camping also at *Poliana* on Rio Formosa, 100m past Ilha do Padre, very pleasant.

Restaurants *Tapera*, Pilad Rebuá 480, T 255-1110, good, home-grown vegetables, breakfast, lunch, pizzas, meat and fish dishes, opens 1900 for evening meal; *Comida Caseira*, Luis da Costa Leite e Santana do Paraíso, good local food, lunch and dinner, not open Sun pm; *Verdo-Frutos e Sucos Naturais*, Pilad Rebuá 1853, next to *Bonanza* carpark, good juices and fruits.

Services No banks but some hoteliers may change money. Post Office on R Cel Pilad Rebuá; telephones on Santana do Paraíso.

Tourist Information and Agencies Sérgio Ferreira Gonzales, R Cel Pilad Rebuá 628, T 255-1315 (opp *Bonanza*), is the Codems representative and an authority on the caves, rec. *Hapakany Tour*, Pilad Rebuá 628, T 255-1315, F 255-1235, Jason and Murilo, for all local tours, rec. *TapeTur*, next to *Tapera* restaurant, guides, information, tours, clothes shop, also rec. For information in English and French, contact Henrique Ruas, T/F 255-1430, see *Ilha do Padre/Pousada Olho d'Agua* above.

Roads and Buses Rodoviária is on edge of town. Road to Jardim is paved; paving due to Bodoquena for Miranda. From Campo Grande, US$12, 5½-6 hrs, 1500, returns at 0530. Bus uses MS-345, with stop at Autoposto Santa Cruz, Km 60, all types of fuel, food and drinks available. For Aquidauana, take Campo Grande bus. Daily bus Corumbá- Miranda-Bonito-

Jardim-Ponta Porã, leaves either end at 0600, arriving Bonito 1230 for Ponta Porã, 1300 for Miranda; can change in Jardim (1400 for 1700 bus) or Miranda (better connections) for Campo Grande. Also connections on 1230 route in Bela Vista at 2000 for Asunción and Coronel Oviedo. Ticket office opens at 1200.

In *Jardim*, which has a wide, tree-lined main street, there is a rodoviária for Cruzeiro do Sul buses. A few blocks uphill is *Panificadora Massa Pura*, clean and bright, and other eating places. Buses: to Campo Grande 0730, 1300, 1700 and 2 in middle of night, US$10.15; Aquidauana 0730 and 1700; Bonito (US$5), Miranda and Corumbá at 1130; Dourados 0600; Bela Vista (Paraguayan border) 0200, 1030, 1500, 1930; Porto Murtinho 0010 and 1530 (bus from Bonito connects); Ponta Porã 0600, 1500; Sun only at 1400 to São Paulo.

From Bonito there is a road to **Porto Murtinho** where a boat crosses to Isla Margarita in Paraguay (entry stamp available on the island). Hotels **E** *Eldorado*, friendly, clean, good food; **E** *Beira Rio*, basic; **E** *Caicaras*; **E** *Americano*, 2 lanchonetes, *Churrascaria Gaspão*. Elia, taxi driver, will change money.

BR-262 is paved all the way from Campo Grande to Corumbá and the Bolivian border, also served by rail. Best to make this journey during the day, to take advantage of marvellous scenery. 131 km W of Campo Grande, just N of the road but on the railway, is **Aquidauana** (pop 39,300, several daily buses from Campo Grande). BR-412 heads S from here to Jardim, with connections to Paraguay (see above). Also turn S here for one route to Bonito. There is an Ibama-controlled *jacaré* farm here, Olhos d'Água, but it is not open to visitors. Aquidauana is a gateway to the Pantanal (see below), excursions in fishing boats negotiable around US$42 pp a day, or via Chalanatur, T 241-3396, 6-day trips rec. *Pousada Cachoeira do Campo*, T (067) 383-2972, 14 km on road to Paxixi; *Fazenda Toca da Onça*, lovely place, rec; take horse-drawn or motor taxi from station, owner also has a camp site. In town, several hotels around railway station, including **E** *Fluminense*, with fan and breakfast, a/c more expensive.

77 km further W is **Miranda** (pop 14,255), another entrance to the Pantanal (see also below for hotels, etc). Here too is a *jacaré* farm, Granja Caimã, which is open to visitors, US$1 entry. A road heads S to Bodoquena and on to Bonito. Bus Campo Grande-Miranda, 7 a day with Expresso Mato Grosso, US$8.50, and others.

Corumbá (pop 88,300, CEP 79000, DDD 067) on the Rio Paraguai, with Bolivia on the opposite bank and beautiful views of the river, has millions of mosquitoes in Dec, Jan and Feb, but is a pleasant place nevertheless. River boats ply occasionally between it and Buenos Aires. The Forte Junqueira, the city's most historic building, which may be visited, was built in 1772. In the hills to the S is the world's greatest reserve of manganese, now being worked. From the Bolivian border town of Quijarro a 650-km railway is open westwards to Santa Cruz de la Sierra, and there is a road of sorts. The Campo Grande-Corumbá road, via Aquidauana, crosses the Paraguai (now mostly paved, two service stations before the Rio Miranda bridge). The scenery between Campo Grande and Corumbá is most interesting, the road and railway follow different routes, but the train is slower than the bus. Corumbá is the best starting point for the southern part of the Pantanal, with boat and jeep trips and access to the major hotel/farms.

Warning Police have very strict controls on drug-trafficking in Corumbá; there are many drug-runners, searches are very thorough.

Climate Hot and humid (70%); cooler in June-July, very hot from Sept to Jan.

Hotels A1 *Nacional*, R América 936, good pool, T 231-6868, F 231-6202; **A3** *Santa Mônica*, R Antônio Maria Coelho 369, T 231-3001, F 231-7880, a/c, good restaurant; **B** *Hotel Premier*, R Maria Coelho, small rooms for maid and TV; **C O** *Laçador*, R América 482, T 231-6933, without breakfast, rec; **C** *Santa Rita*, Dom Aquino 860 (unsigned), T 231-5453, with bath, E without, clean but basic, noisy, good meals in restaurant; *La Siesta*, Dom Aquino 47, good, helpful, restaurant; **D** *Campus*, R Antônio João 133, clean, good value; *Lincoln*, R 15 de Novembro, and *Pousada de Marieta*, América 243; **D** *Dom Diego*, clean, fairly spacious, cheaper than the other hotels on the Paraguai River waterfront; **D** *Internacional*, in sight of rodoviária, clean, friendly, simple breakfast; **D** *Grande Corumbá*, Frei Mariano 468, no breakfast, shared bath, clean, old; **D** *Salette*, R Delamaré 893, T 231-3768, safe, friendly, variable rooms, rec; **D** *Pousada Tucanos*, R 13 de Junho 1297, Centro, T 231-6648, inc breakfast, clean, secure, friendly, garden, laundry, book swap, safety deposit, rec; **E** *Londres*, Joaquin Murtinho 1047, good value with private bath and breakfast; **E** *Cóndor*, R Delamaré; in same street **E** *Nelly*, good breakfast; **E** *Nova Horizonte* on steep street down to port, friendly and clean; **E** *Pousada Pantaneira*, R Ladário 271, private house, friendly old lady, clean, rec; **E** *Esplanada*, opp railway station, clean, cold shower, basic. Other small clean hotels: *Irure*, R 13 de Junho 776; **F** *Paradiso*, Frei Mariano 1150, clean, shared room. **Youth Hostel** R Antônio Maria, rec, the owner, Sr Pontis, organizes jungle trips, cheaper for a group, negotiate price.

Restaurants Several rec restaurants in R Frei Mariano: *Churrascaria Gaúcha*, good value; *Tarantella* (Italian), large helpings, not cheap, but rec; *Barril de Ouro*, good; *Palácio das Pizzas*, at No 468, friendly and cheap; *Batidão*, excellent meat; *Peixaria de Lulu*, R Antônio João, nr centre, good fish; *El Dorado*, on waterfront, good for fish; *Churrascaria Rodeio*, 13 de Junho 760, very good; *Casa Mia*, R Dom Aquino; *Trivial*, R 15 de Novembro, Centro, good, reasonably-priced buffet; good Arabic food on R América, next to *Hotel Nacional*; good local food at corner of R Delamaré and Antônio João; on the waterfront you can eat good fish at *Portal do Pantanal* and *El Pacu*, highly rec, piranha on menu, run by a German, Hermann, and his Brazilian wife; lots of open-air bars on the river front. Good beer in *Xaraes*, R Gen Rondon; Bolivian snacks in *'Sslato*, R Dom Aquino. Lanchonetes tend to overcharge—check prices.

Banks and Exchange Banco do Brasil changes TCs from 1100 only. Many money changers at the border—cash only, good rates.

Shopping Arts and Crafts Centre, R Dom Aquino Correa, in a converted prison.

Air Daily flights to Campo Grande, two airlines, TAM and Pantanal; TAM also to Cuiabá, 6 a week, Londrina and São Paulo, 6 a week. Pantanal twice a week to Vilhena. See Bolivia, **Section 5**, for flights between Puerto Suárez and Santa Cruz. Daily private flights (US$70, "entertaining") to Santa Cruz, Bolivia, especially in rainy season—cheaper to travel overland to Asunción and fly from there.

Shipping Passenger service to Asunción is run by Cruceros srl, every 15-20 days (see **Paraguay** chapter). It may be possible to get a boat to Porto Esperança and continue from there. Seek information at travel agents, *El Pacu* restaurant, or from small cargo boats at the waterfront. (See p 592, under Cáceres.)

Trains and Buses The day train from Corumbá to **Campo Grande** leaves Mon and Fri 0700, arriving in Campo Grande in the evening, single US$17 1st class, US$12 2nd. Trains serve food. These times have been subject to frequent changes and are scheduled for reduction, check in advance (T station 231-2876). The Corumbá-**São Paulo** bus journey takes at least 22 hrs (US$43). As there is no fixed timetable the year round, confirm bus times in advance

CORUMBÁ *46b*

Not to Scale

Rio Paraguai

1. Praça
2. Forte Junqueira
3. Post Office
4. Telephone Office
5. Docks
6. Bus to Frontier
7. Hotel Nacional
8. Hotel Santa Mónica

Av. Gral. Rondon
Rua Delamaré
Rua 13 de Junho
Rua Dom Aquino
Rua Cuiabá
Rua América
Rua Colombo
Rua Cabral
Rua Joaquim Murtinho
Rua Porto Carreiro
Av. Santa Cruz

Rua Mal. Deodoro
Rua José Fragelli
Rua Ciríaco de Toledo
Rua Edu Rocha
Rua 12 de Setembro
Rua Operária
Rua Firmo de Matos
Rua Major Gama
Rua 7 de Setembro
Rua 15 de Novembro
Rua Frei Mariano
Rua Antônio Maria
Rua Antônio João
Rua Tiradentes
Rua Ladário
Rua 1 de Abril
Rua Oriental
Rua Cáceres
Rua Melgaço

N

(T 231-3783); it is best to go Corumbá-**Campo Grande**, 6 hrs, US$14.50, many buses, interesting journey ("an excursion in itself")—take an early bus to see plentiful wildlife, then connections to all parts of Brazil. Two buses (Andorinha, rec) to **Rio** daily 0800 and 2300, US$56, 28 hrs, with change Campo Grande (Andorinha leaves Rio for Curumbá at 1230— *leito* service only as far as Campo Grande). To **Cuiabá**, 18 hrs, US$29; to **Ponta Porã** (get your passport stamped here), for Paraguay, daily, 12 hrs. Bus station is on R Porto Carrero, next to the railway station and a few blocks from town centre (also for Andorinha buses; Viação Motta bus terminal is nearby). Taxis from both stations to centre are extortionate.

There are four train services to **Santa Cruz** in Bolivia, the *ferrobus, rápido, expreso oriente* and *tren especial*; all leave from Quijarro, the Bolivian frontier station, not from Corumbá. The schedule of each appears to change frequently so check on arrival in Corumbá. There is a Bolivian railway office at Corumbá railway station for all details, tickets may be booked through travel agencies or *Pousada Tucanos*, but agencies charge high prices, however. Tickets must be purchased in Quijarro on day of departure, except *ferrobus*, which can be bought the day before, go as early as possible (it may be best to stay in Quijarro to get a good place in the queue; 2 or 3 cheap hotels opp station, basic). If the ticket office has "sold out", ask around on the platform as people buy up tickets and sell them for a few bolivianos more: the money-exchange women know all about it. See Bolivia, **Section 5**, for fares and schedules Quijarro-Santa Cruz. Colectivo Corumbá-Quijarro, US$3, from in front of Dona Aparecida's store, *A Favorita*, R Antônio Maria Coelho (Dona Aparecida changes money outside banking hours; bargaining recommended). Also taxis, US$14.50/taxi; colectivo border—Quijarro US$1.50. Note that buses from São Paulo to Puerto Suárez go only as far as the border. The railway to Santa Cruz is liable to flood damage.

Going to Bolivia Immigration and emigration formalities are constantly changing so check procedure in advance. Have passport stamped by Brazilian Policia Federal at Corumbá bus station (often open other than at the published opening hours, 0730-1130, 1500-1600). Brazilian exit stamp is valid for 5 days. Take bus from port end of R Antônio Maria to Bolivian border (15 mins), walk over the bridge to the Bolivian border post (white building), go through formalities, then take colectivo to Quijarro for train. At the border Bolivian police stamp passport free. At the frontier, it is not necessary to pay any money to anyone. Show ticket at border to return to Corumbá (if exiting Brazil merely to obtain a new visa, remember that exit and entry must not be on the same day). Money changers at the border and in Quijarro offer same rates as in Corumbá. Bolivian Consulate in Corumbá: R Antônio Maria Coelho 852 (colectivos may be caught nearby for frontier), Mon-Fri, 0700-1100, 1500-1730, Sat and Sun closed. Check Bolivian section "Information for Visitors" for document requirements. Those who need a visa must pay US$5; a yellow fever vaccination certificate is required.

Coming from Bolivia If you arrive at the border when the Bolivian offices are closed (eg at night) and you therefore have no exit stamp, be prepared to be sent back for an exit stamp by Brazilian officials in Corumbá (the Bolivian border post opens at 0700). If you arrive in Brazil without a yellow fever vaccination certificate, you may have to go to R 7 de Setembro, Corumbá, for an inoculation. When travelling from Quijarro, take a taxi (bargain fare) or walk to the Bolivian border, go through formalities, outside office take bus to Corumbá Rodoviária (US$0.30), don't believe taxi drivers who say there is no bus. Find a hotel then take a taxi or walk to railway station for Brazilian formalities (some buses go direct to the station): if you're in luck the office will be open.

Pantanal This vast wetland, located between Cuiabá, Campo Grande and the Bolivian frontier, is one of the world's great wildlife preserves, slowly being opened up to tourism. The flora and fauna are similar in many ways to those of the Amazon basin, though because of the more veldt-like open land, the wildlife can be viewed more easily than in the dense jungle growth. Principal life seen in this area is about 300 species of birds, including the hyacinth macaw, jabiru stork (the *tuiuíu*, almost 1.2 metres tall), plumbeous ibis, yellow-billed cardinal, great rufous woodcreeper, buff-bellied hermit, Mato Grosso antbird, Chaco suiriri, white-naped xenopsaris, white-eyed atilla, Chaco chachalaca, bare-faced currasow, both blue-throated and red-throated piping guans, chestnut-bellied guan, red-billed scythebill, black-hooded and yellow-chevroned parakeets, and turquoise-fronted parrot. There are some 230 varieties of fish, from the giant *pintado*, weighing up to 80 kilos, to the voracious *piranha*. Fishing here is exceptionally good (best May-Oct). Animal life is represented among others by giant and collared anteaters, 4 species of opossum, 5 armadillo species, black-tailed marmoset, brown capuchin, black howler monkey, maned wolf, crab-eating raccoon, South American coati, grison, tayra, southern and giant river otters, ocelot, margay, jaguarundi, puma, 3 peccary species, marsh deer and two other species, Brazilian porcupine, yellow anaconda and the ubiquitous *capivara*, a species of giant aquatic guinea-pig. Probably the most impressive sight is the *jacaré* (Yacare Caiman). The extraordinary thing is that man and his domesticated cattle thrive together with the wildlife with seemingly little friction. Local farmers protect the area jealously. (Only one area is officially national park, the Biological Reserve of Cará-Cará in the municipality of Poconé, 135,000 hectares of land and water, only accessible by air or river. Permission to visit at Ibama, R Rubens de Mendonça, Cuiabá, CEP 78008-000, T 644-1511/1581.) Hunting in any form is strictly forbidden. Fishing is allowed with a licence (controlled by Ibama, issued by Banco do Brasil, enquire at travel agents); it is not permitted in the spawning season (Nov to Feb). The International Union for the Conservation of Nature is concerned at the amount of poaching, particularly of *jacaré* skins and *capivaras*. Recently, the Forestry Police have built control points on all major access roads to the Pantanal.

There are two distinct seasons. In the rainy season (Dec-Mar, wettest in Feb), most of the area floods, flies abound, and cattle crowd on to the few islands remaining above water. In the southern part, the wild animals leave the area, but in the N, which is slightly higher, the animals do not leave. An ordinary vehicle should be able to manage the Transpantaneira out of Cuiabá throughout the year, but in the wet season you should be prepared to get muddy pushing your car from time to time. The dry season (July to Oct) is the nesting and breeding season. The birds form vast nesting areas, with hundreds and thousands crowding the trees creating an almost insupportable cacophony of sounds; the white sand river beaches are exposed and *jacarés* bask in the sun.

The Pantanal is not easy to visit. The best starting points are Campo Grande, Corumbá and Cuiabá, from where one finds public transport all around the perimeter, but none at all within. Hitching is not advised because of the amount of drug smuggling in the area. Litter is becoming a problem; don't contribute to it. Wild camping is possible if you have your own transport. Remember that the longer you stay and the further you go from the edges (where most of the hotels are located), the more likely you are to see rare wildlife. Wear long sleeves and long trousers and spray clothes as well as skin with insect repellent (less of a problem Jul-Aug). In winter temperatures fall to 10°, warm clothing and covers or sleeping bag are needed at night, but it's hot and humid during summer. Further reading: *The Pantanal: Brazil's Forgotten Wilderness*, Vic Banks (Sierra Club Books, 1991, 730 Polk St, San Francisco, CA 94100).

There are several lodges with fair to good accommodation, some only approachable by air or river; most are relatively expensive. The best plan is to hire a car and check accommodation for yourself: in Jun-Sep, especially Jul, it is necessary to book accommodation in advance. Following is a list of some of those presently operating:

From Campo Grande: **A1** *Cabana do Pescador*, 65 km from Aquidauana on the Rio Miranda, T (067) 241-3697, access by Bonito bus from Campo Grande (**see p 583**), includes breakfast. *Pousada Agua Pek*, near Aquidauana, farmhouse hotel, horseriding, boat trips, trekking, full board, friendly and clean. **B** *Pousada Aguas do Pantanal*, Av Afonso Pena 367, Miranda, T/F (067) 242-1314, F 242-1242, contact Fátima or Luis Cordelli, very good, clean, friendly, good food, restaurant serves *jacaré* legally (also connected with **B** *Pousada Arara Azul*, a farm 130 km NW of Miranda in Nhecolândia, lots of wildlife to observe, manager Luzia Wendt); *Refúgio Ecológico/Caimã*, 36 km from Miranda, first class, full board, excursions, T (067) 242-1102, or 725-5267, or São Paulo 246-9934; **A1** *Fazenda Salobra*, T (067) 242-1162, 6 km from Miranda, 209 km from Corumbá, 198 from Campo Grande, is rec, including all meals; it is by the Rio Salobra (clear water) and Rio Miranda, with birds and animals easily seen. Take bus from Campo Grande to Miranda, and alight 50m from the bridge over Rio Miranda, turn left for 1,200m to the *Fazenda*; by train, coming from Campo Grande, get out one stop after Miranda, 250m to the *Fazenda*. *Fazenda Beira Rio*, 8 km from Miranda, T (067) 242-1262. There is a good campsite 30 km past Miranda. Alternatively, hire a car in

Corumbá and drive to Miranda, but note that the dirt road is bad after rain (consequently not much traffic and more wildlife can be seen). Car with driver can be hired at Salobra for US$25.
A1 *Hotel dos Camalotes*, Porto Murtinho, T (067) 287-1160, 440 km from Campo Grande; access by bus long, tedious, bumpy and dusty; best access by air taxi; 4-star luxury hotel on the shores of the Paraguai river, favoured by wealthy Paulistas, full board.

To see the Pantanal cheaply, get off the bus from Campo Grande to Corumbá at the ferry across the Rio Paraguai (Porto Esperança). On the Corumbá side is a small hotel on the river bank, negotiate price. Walk down the road early am, or late pm (better on the Campo Grande side), or take a small boat from the hotel (may be included in the price) to see a wide variety of animals and birds. Porto Esperança is on a spur line from the main Campo Grande-Corumbá railway, from Agente Inocêncio, but as rail services are being reduced, the option of going by train is limited. You can walk back along the track, but this is dangerous on the bridges, which have gaps between the sleepers.

From Corumbá: One day river trips available on river boats with a capacity of 80 passengers, US$15 half day; US$28 full day, transfers and hot fish meal inc. Tickets at travel agents. Good fishing for piranha, pintado and dourado—prohibited during Nov-Feb spawning season. Boats may be hired, with tackle and guide, at the port (US$100/day, up to 3 people). *Pousada do Pantanal*, T (067) 231-5797, 125 km from Corumbá near the Campo Grande road at Fazenda Santa Clara (still a working cattle ranch), very comfortable, easy access by bus, reservations from all agencies in Corumbá; US$100 pp for groups of 4-6 for 3 days/2 nights, good food (but drinks not included), with horseback, car and boat excursions, guides included, canoes, simple fishing gear, motor boats for rent (try bargaining in the off-season for reduced rates). **A2** *Fazenda Santa Blanca*, on the Rio Paraguai, 15 mins by boat S of Porto Esperanza, full board, very clean and friendly, good kayak excursions, horseriding, information from R 15 de Novembro 659, 79300 Corumbá, T (067) 382-5926, or Flins Travel (Walter Zoss), R do Acre 92, 6th floor, 602, CEP 20.081, Rio de Janeiro, T (021) 253-8588/0195, Telex 021 32971 ATDA or Safári Fotográfico, R Frei Mariano 502, Corumbá, T 231-5797. *Fazenda Leque*, Roberto Kassan (contact through R América 262, Corumbá, T 231-1598); take mosquito coils; unlimited use of horses and boats, on small lake behind the farm, good food; plenty of wildlife to be seen. Also near Corumbá: *Pousada Do Castelo*, 3 hrs by boat, T (067) 231-5151; *Pousada Quero-Quero*, T (067) 382-5926, *Pousada Curupira*, T (067) 725-6407, and *Hotel Fazenda Xaraés*, T (067) 231-6777, Rio Abobral, 130 km from Corumbá. The going rate for a 3-day photosafari by jeep is US$60-75 pp for 4-6 people; US$80/day for 9 people, 4 days; also fishing trips for 4 days with Hotelboat for 8 (eg *Pérola do Pantanal* and *Pantanal Tours*, Corumbá—must be booked in advance). Hotels specializing in fishing, all reached from Corumbá by road: **A1** *Pesqueiro Cabana do Lontra*, including meals T (067) 383-4532, 180 km from Aquidauana on the Corumbá road. *Pesqueiro Tarumã*, Rio Paraguai, T (067) 231-4197, and *Pesqueiro Paraíso dos Dourados*, 72 km from Corumbá, Rios Paraguai e Miranda, T (067) 231-3213. José Paraguaio, R Manoel Cavassa 331, T (067) 231-1721, 3 day tours to *Fazenda São Joaquim*, US$60; *Karine Tours* at No 111, T (067) 231 2629, also rec.

Travel Agents in Corumbá: Receptivo Pantanal, R Frei Mariano 502, T 231-5795, helpful (1-day tour US$50, 3-day US$100, 4-day US$130); **Pantanal Tours**, R Manoel Cavassa 61, T 231-4683, fishing trips by hotel boat, stays at *Fazenda Santa Clara*, happily rec; tours at *Pantanal Hotel*, R Frei Mariano, highly rec; **Pérola do Pantanal Viagens e Turismo**, R Manoel Cavassa 219, T 231-1460, good one-day river tour with *Lancha Pérola*. Turismo Sandino, R Firmo de Matos, T 231-3345, rec tours, good food; **Pantur**, R América 969, T 231-4343 helpful; **Transpantanal**, R Dom Aquino 99, F 231-4834.

On arrival in Corumbá you will be met by private tour guides offering a tour on the spot. The tours are of 3-4 days, costing between US$50-90 (includes all food, accommodation and transport). Bear in mind that a well-organized 3-day tour can be more rewarding than 4 days with an ill-prepared guide. There is fierce competition between guides who provide similar services, but with very different styles. Travel is in the back of a pick-up (good for seeing animals), up to a maximum of 6. Accommodation is in a hammock under a palm thatch on a *fazenda*. Food is good. If you want flushing toilets, showers or luxury cabins, approach an agency. Guides provide bottled mineral water (make sure enough is carried), but you must take a hat, sun screen and mosquito repellent. Some accredited guides go to *fazendas* without permission, have unreliable vehicles, or are inadequately equipped, so try to check their credentials. If unsure, it is advisable to pay only half the amount in advance. One of these tours could be the highlight of your travels, so it is best to do some research before contracting a guide. Many guides are freelance, therefore it can be more important to seek out a guide by name, than his agency.

Guides will generally not make the trip with fewer than 5 people, so if you have not already formed a group, stay in touch with several guides (most important during Mar-Oct, when fewer tourists are around). Decide on your priorities: try to ensure that your guide and other group members share your ideas. Many guides chase, catch and even kill the animals; pressure from paying customers is an effective way to reduce this harassment. Similarly, make sure that no litter is left behind.

We list below those guides who have received positive reports from travellers: *Natureza Tours*, Durvanil Pereira Rodrigues, R Dom Aquino 255, T 231-1218, or contact through Sr Pontis at the Youth Hostel, 2-4 day trips, including boat trip, fishing, horse riding; *Tucantur*, guides Mario and Pedro rec, R 13 de Junho 1297, T 231-6648, 3-5 day trips; *Katu*, R Dom Aquino 220, T 231-1987; Carlos; Walter. *Carlos Grandes Perez*, who could hardly be more highly rec, is reachable through *Hotel Nunes* in Porto Velho, T (069) 221-1389. The Danish guide Morgens Trolle can be contacted at *Hotel Santa Rita*, R Dom Aquino Corrêa 860; he promotes responsible tourism in the Pantanal. *Gil Tours*, R Porto Carrero 612, T 231-1772, generally rec, tours with Gil himself, guide Elísio Rodríguez da Silva rec; the company has a commitment to preservation. *Pantaneira*, R Frei Mariano 1335, connected with *Pousada Pantaneira* (see above), run by Claudine (Swiss), good guides. There are many other guides not listed here; lots have received criticisms (some repeatedly) from correspondents. There may be others on whom we have received no feedback.

Camping out is preferable to staying in *fazendas* because less driving (which scares animals) is involved, and you can see the wildlife at its greatest period of activity—dawn and dusk (protection against mosquitoes essential). Only in the very wettest periods is travel into the Pantanal from Corumbá impossible by vehicle; trucks can usually make access the year round. Cattle boats will take passengers on their round trips to farms in the Pantanal, 3 days, US$8 but take your own food—it is not possible to disembark. Ask at Bacia da Prata, 10 mins out of Corumbá on the Ladário bus (the gatekeeper is unhelpful). Road trips from Corumbá into the Pantanal US$35 for 6 hrs/vehicle.

From Cuiabá: The Transpantaneira Highway, originally projected to connect Cuiabá with Corumbá, goes only as far as Porto Jofre on the Rio Cuiabá. Work has been suspended indefinitely because of difficulties, costs and ecological considerations. A paved road turns S off the main Cuiabá-Cáceres road to *Poconé* (pop 27,330, 135 km from Cuiabá, US$5 by TUT bus, 6 a day between 0600 and 1900, T 322-4985). **D** *Hotel Skala*, in the main square; **E** *Pousada Pantaneira*, good restaurant, clean and simple, on Transpantaneira, T 721-1220, to hitchhike to Pixaim or Porto Jofre (see below), start at 0600 outside the hotel; **E** *Hotel Joá*, with bath, basic, acceptable, car parking; *3 Poderes Restaurant*, R Beri, cheap good food. All types of fuel are available in Poconé.

From Poconé the Transpantaneira runs 146 km S to Porto Jofre (just a gas station, gasoline and diesel, but no alcohol available). At the entrance to the Pantanal, a gate across the road, cars have to pay US$3, jeeps US$7 and buses US$14.50; drivers are given a list of rules of conduct. The road is of earth, in poor condition, with ruts, holes and many bridges that need care in crossing. Easiest access is in the dry season (Jul-Sep), which is also the best time for seeing birds and, in Sep, the trees are in bloom. In the wet, especially Jan-Feb, there is no guarantee that the Transpantaneira will be passable. The wet season, however, is a good time to see many of the shier animals because more fruit, new growth and other high calorie foods are available, and there are fewer people. It is easier to see the animals listed above from the Transpantaneira than from other areas of the Pantanal, but you need to go to the last 40 km of the road to gain the full benefit. In Poconé one can hire a car from *Hotel Skala*, or hitch (easy, but bumpy, especially in a truck) to Porto Jofre, or hire a vehicle in Cuiabá.

105 km from Poconé is *Pixaim* (2 hrs in the dry, up to 5 in the wet season), a bridge across the Rio Pixaim, where there are two hotels, with a fuel station (all types available, check that the pump is set to zero) and a tyre-repair shop (*borracheria*). **A2** *Hotel Pixaim*, built on stilts, T Cuiabá 322-8961, full board (meals also available separately), rooms with fan, mosquito-netted windows, hot water, electricity 24 hrs, boat trips—US$30/hr, rec. On the opposite bank of the Rio Pixaim is **A1** *Hotel Beira Rio*, 35 rm for 3-6 people, with full board, fan, clean, hot water (also family-size apartments with a/c), good home-grown food, in radio contact with office on R Barão de Melgaço in Cuiabá. 2 km beyond Pixaim is **A2** *Fazenda Santa Teresa*, pp full board, extension planned, fishing trips. **A2** *O Pantaneiro*, pp full board, 4 mm with 2 bunk beds each, bath, simple, owned and operated by *pantaneiros* (reservations through *Focus Tours*, Belo Horizonte, **see p 402**), about 60 km from Pixaim, not as far S as **A1** *Hotel Fazenda Santa Rosa*, 150 km from Poconé, near Porto Jofre, with full board, no electricity, an old *fazenda*, undergoing improvement, occasional water problems, river trips not included and expensive, breakfast-eating parrot (reservations through Focus Tours, Belo Horizonte).

L2 *Pousada dos Araras*, Km 30 on Transpantaneira, 10 rm with bath, good food, home-made *cachaça*, book through Expeditours in Cuiabá; **A1** *Hotel-Fazenda Cabanas do Pantanal*, 142 km from Cuiabá, 50 km from Poconé by the rivers Pixaim and Cuiabá, on the northern edge of the Pantanal, 10 chalet bedrooms with bath, restaurant, boat trips (few in dry season), horse-riding, fishing, helpful proprietor and staff, everything except boat trips and bar drinks included in price (booking: Confiança, Cuiabá). *Sapé Pantanal Lodge*, Caixa Postal 2241—CEP 78020.970, Cuiabá, T/F (065) 322-3426/361-4069, 8 rm, 4-day, 3-night all-inclusive programme US$490, fishing, wildlife observation and photography excursions, holder of the Embratur "Ecológico Especial" classification. A complete programme includes road transport from Cuiabá airport to Barão de Melgaço (wet season), or Porto Cercado (dry season) with onward river transportation (2 hrs and 1½ hrs respectively), and return; full board; outboard powered boats with experienced guides at guests' disposal during entire stay; optional trekking in dry season, paddling in wet; English, French, Spanish spoken. *Sapé* is closed 20 Dec-31 Jan.

You will get more out of this part of the Pantanal by going with a guide; a lot can be seen from the Transpantaneira in a hired car, but guides can take you into *fazendas* and will point out wildlife. Take 8x40 binoculars and insect repellent from home (mosquitoes in this region are becoming immune to local brands). Recommended guides in Cuiabá are listed below.

Barão de Melgaço, 130 km from Cuiabá (TUT bus at 0730 and 1500, US$6.50) on Rio Cuibá, is reached by two roads: the shorter, via Santo Antônio de Leverger, unpaved from Sto Antônio to Barão, or via São Vicente, longer, but more pavement. As you approach Barão, the hills which limit the eastern edge of the Pantanal come into view and the last part of either route skirts the *mata* (forest), with babaçu and açori palms. In the town are *Barão Tour Hotel*, apartments with a/c, restaurant, boat trips and excursions (T Cuiabá 322-1568, or Melgatur), and, much humbler, *NS do Carmo Hotel* on the waterfront, and *Pousada e Lanchonete Francisco de Asis* on main road down to waterfront. Along the river is the *Tuiuiú Hotel Club*. *Mercadinho do Povo* minimarket sells provisions, including cheap hats.

The way to see the Pantanal from here is by boat down the Rio Cuiabá. Boat hire, for example from *Restaurant Peixe Vivo* on waterfront, up to US$85 for a full day; or enquire at Joel Souza Safari in Cuiabá (see below). The best time of day would be sunset, but it would need some organizing to be in the best part at the best time, without too much boating in the dark. Protect against the sun when on the water. Initially the river banks are farms and small habitations, but they become more forested, with lovely combinations of flowering trees (best seen Sep-Oct). After a while, a small river to the left leads to the Baia and Lakes Chacororé and Sia Mariana, which join each other. Boats can continue beyond the lakes to the Rio Mutum, but a guide is essential because there are many dead ends. The area is rich in birdlife and the waterscapes are beautiful.

On Sia Mariana are *Pousada do Barão*, 6 chalets with bath, swimming pool, 1st class, boat and trekking expeditions (book through Melgatur); *Restaurant Flamingo*, simple food, rooms, camping with permission, popular with fishermen; one other restaurant. Barão de Melgaço is also the starting point for the *Pousada Passargada*, programmes from 3 days up, full board, boat, car and trekking expeditions, transport from Barão de Melgaço, owner speaks English, French and German, food excellent, highly rec, closed Dec to Feb; reservations in Barão de Melgaço on riverside, through Nature Safaris, Barão de Melgaço, or Av NS de Copacabana 330, Rio de Janeiro, CEP 22020, T 235-2840, F 236-5285. Much cheaper if booked direct with the owner, Maré Sigaud, Mato Grosso, CEP 786807, *Pousada Passargada*, Barão de Melgaço. On the Rio Mutum is the *Pousada Mutum*.

Travel Agents in Cuiabá *Confiança*, Mariano 434, T 321-4142, very helpful travel agency, tours to Pantanal are expensive. Also recommended *Expeditours*, Av Gov Ponce de Arruda 670, T 381-4959/5674, sightseeing, fishing trips for 4-5 days by boat; *Ametur*, R Joaquim

Murtinho 242, T 624-1000, very helpful, advice on Pantanal tours (also run their own tours, from 12 hrs to 5 days, not cheap); Adriana Coningham of *Ararauna Turismo Ecologica*, R Barão de Melgaço, highly rec. All these agencies arrange trips to the Pantanal; for longer or special programmes, book in advance. Focus Tours of Belo Horizonte (**see p 402**) specializes in tours in this part of the Pantanal and, starting from Cuiabá, to the southern Amazon, with bases at Alta Floresta and on the Rio Cristalino (**see p 596**).

Recommended guides (in alphabetical order): **Cesar Magallon Arias**, "the Panamanian", R-065 C-04, Parque Cuibá, 78000, T 361-2115, or contact through the *Aurea Palace Hotel*, knowledgeable, fluent English, small groups. **Laércio Sá**, *Fauna Tour, Hotel Mato Grosso*, R Cdte Costa 2522, T 321-9121, F 321-2386, CEP 78.025-200, Cuiabá, or Av Beira Rio, Quadra 28, Casa 21, CEP 78.065-780, has own car, well-informed. **Joel Souza**, Av Getúlio Vargas 155-A, T/F 624-1386, PO Box 1514, 78005-600 Cuiabá, MT, speaks English well, checklists for flora and fauna provided, will arrange all transport, farm accommodation, fishing, horse riding, trekking, night excursions (US$140 for 2-night tours). Most guides await incoming flights at airport; compare prices and services in town if you don't wish to commit yourself at airport. The research station 40 km from the end of the Transpantaneira is for Brazilian scientists only.

River trips from Cuiabá to Corumbá are very difficult since boats on the Cuiabá river are few and irregular. You can get to Corumbá by river from *Cáceres* (pop 92,670), on the banks of the Rio Paraguai, 200 km W of Cuiabá, very hot but clean and hospitable. There is a yacht club, with swimming pool, volley ball and children's playground. Annual cattle fair at the airport. Hotels: *Comodoro*, Praça Duque de Caxias; *Charme*, Col José Dulce; *Ipanema*, R Gen Osório 540, good restaurant; **C** *Fênix*, R dos Operários 600, fridge, a/c, TV; **E** *Santa Terezinha*, R Tiradentes 485, with fan, breakfast, not clean, friendly. Many other cheap hotels, eg *Hispano*, clean. *Hotel Barranquinho*, outside Cáceres, book in advance through Ametur, Cuiabá. Good restaurants: *Corimbá* on main square (fish specialities); *Bisteção*, on the waterfront; restaurant on stilts on opposite bank, good lunch. *Casa de câmbio*, next to main square, changes cash and TCs at good rates. For information on boat sailings, ask at the Capitânia dos Portos, on the corner of the main square at the waterfront. If possible phone in advance to Cáceres, Posto Arrunda, 221-1707 to find out which boats are going. Also Portobrás on the outskirts at the waterfront (T 221-1728), you may (with a lot of luck) be able to get passage on a boat; 3 days to Corumbá (8 the other way). These boats are officially not allowed to take passengers. You may have a better chance of getting a boat in Corumbá since there are more head offices and river traffic. In the dry season there are practically no boats to Corumbá. Colibrí buses Cuiabá-Cáceres, US$9.50, 9 a day between 0630-2400 (book in advance, very crowded), 3½ hrs now that the road is paved, one stop in the jungle at a restaurant; also 10 União Cascavel buses a day. At the waterfront you can hire a boat for a day trip.

From Cáceres to the Bolivian border: Get passport stamped by the Federal Police then take the 0730 or 1600 bus to San Matías, Bolivia, where you must have your passport stamped (**E** *Residencial Génova*, rec; military flights on Fri and Sun to Santa Cruz via Roboré—book in advance).

From Bolivia to Cáceres: Obtain exit stamp at San Ignacio, then take bus (US$22, 15 hrs, leaves about 0900) to Cáceres where you must have your passport stamped.

Cuiabá (pop 401,110, unofficially 800,000, 1992, CEP 78000, DDD 065) the capital of Mato Grosso state (pop 2,020,580) on the Rio Cuiabá, an upper tributary of the River Paraguai, is in fact two cities: Cuiabá on the E bank of the river and Várzea Grande, where the airport is, on the W. Alt: 165 metres. It is very hot; coolest months for a visit are June, July, and Aug, in the dry season. Cuiabá has an imposing government palace and other fine buildings round the green Praça da República. On the square is the Cathedral, with a plain, imposing exterior, two clocktowers and, inside, coloured-glass mosaic windows and doors. Behind the altar is a huge mosaic of Christ in majesty, with smaller mosaics in side chapels. Beside the Cathedral is another leafy square, Praça Alencastro. On Praça Ipiranga, at the junction of Avs Isaac Póvoas and Ten Cel Duarte, a few blocks W of the central squares, there are market stalls and an iron bandstand from Huddersfield. On a hill below the square is the church of Bom Despacho (closed for restoration).

Museums Museus de Antropologia, Historia Natural e Cultura Popular in the Fundação Cultural de Mato Grosso, Praça da República 151, US$0.10, historical photos, documents, furniture, one room of religious art, contemporary art gallery, stuffed fauna, stones and woods from the region, Indian items and weapons, archaeological finds and pottery, open Mon-Fri 0800-1730. **Museu de Arte Sacra**, beside Bom Despacho church. **Museu das Pedras**,

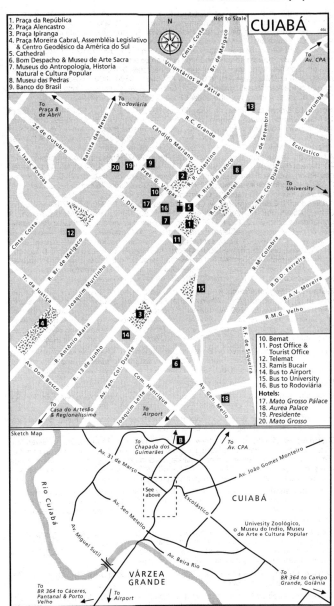

CUIABÁ

Not to Scale

1. Praça da República
2. Praça Alencastro
3. Praça Ipiranga
4. Praça Moreira Cabral, Assembléia Legislativo & Centro Geodésico da América do Sul
5. Cathedral
6. Bom Despacho & Museu de Arte Sacra
7. Museus do Antropologia, Historia Natural e Cultura Popular
8. Museu das Pedras
9. Banco do Brasil

10. Bemat
11. Post Office & Tourist Office
12. Telemat
13. Ramis Bucair
14. Bus to Airport
15. Bus to University
16. Bus to Rodoviária
Hotels:
17. *Mato Grosso Pálace*
18. *Aurea Palace*
19. *Presidente*
20. *Mato Grosso*

Sketch Map

CUIABÁ

Univesity Zoológico, o Museu do Indio, Museu de Arte e Cultura Popular

VÁRZEA GRANDE

US$0.70 entry, in shop on pedestrian part of R Ricardo Franco, exhibits stones from the Chapada dos Guimarães. At the entrance to Universidade de Mato Grosso, 10 mins by bus from the centre, is the **Museu do Índio/Museu Rondon** (by swimming pool), small, well-displayed exhibits. Carrying on along the road through the campus, signed on the left before a right turn in the road, is the **Zoológico**, open 0800-1100, 1330-1700 (closed Mon), free; the jacaré, capivara, tortoise and tapir pen can be seen at any time, but best early am or late pm, also has coatis, otters, emu, monkeys, peccaries, birds, etc. Opposite the zoo is the theatre with the **Museu de Arte e Cultura Populares**, 0800-1800, closed Sat pm and Sun. In front of the Assembléia Legislativa, Praça Moreira Cabral, is a point marking the Geogedesic Centre of South America (see also under Chapada dos Guimarães, below).

Hotels **L3** *Eldorado Cuiabá*, Av Isaac Póvoas 1000, T 624-4000, F 624-1480, very smart; **L3** *Mato Grosso Palace*, Joaquim Murtinho 170, T 624-7747, F 321-2386, 4-star (Best Western), with bath and breakfast, central, good; **L3** *Taiamã Plaza*, Av Rubens de Mendonça 1184, Bosque de Saúde, T/F 624-1490, 3-star, very good, pool, excellent breakfast; **A1** *Aurea Palace*, Gen Melo 63, T 322-3377, pleasant rooms, restaurant, swimming pool, good; **A1** *Jaguar*, Av Getúlio Vargas 600, T 322-9044, F 322-6698, use of swimming pool; **A1** *Veneza Palace*, Av Cel Escolástico 738, T 321-4847, F 322-5212, 3-star, rec; **A3** *Las Velas*, opp airport, with breakfast, clean, pool, good value. Opp rodoviária and both **B**, *Skala Palace* (T 322-4347) and *Colorado Palace* (T 323-3170), Av Jules Rimet 26 and 22 respectively, both have smart lobbies and restaurants. **C** *Almanara*, Av Cel Escolástico 510, T 323-1244; opposite but less good is **C** *Bandeirantes*, Av Cel Escolástico 425, T 321-0920, F 624-2366, a/c, out of centre; *Abudi Palace*, Cel Escolástico 259, T 322-7399, good; **D** *Mato Grosso*, R Comandante Costa 2522, T 321-9121, 2-star, clean, good restaurant, good value; *Panorama*, R Barão de Melgaço, beyond Telemat from centre, rec; **D** *Presidente*, Barão de Melgaço e Av G Vargas, T 321-6162, on a busy central corner, convenient but lots of traffic outside, a/c or fan, TV, fridge, being refurbished 1995; **D** *Lord*, Av G Vargas, by Praça 9 de Abril; **D** *Samara*, R Joaquim Murtinho 150, central, hot shower, fan, basic but good, clean, friendly; **E** *Lagunas*, Av Gen Mello 166, small rooms, basic; the following are all **E-F**: *Dormitório Cézar*, *Brazil*, *San Francisco*, rec, near bus terminal, price pp; others in same area.

Restaurants *Regionalíssimo*, R 13 de Junho by Casa de Artesão (see below), regional food, fixed price, rec (closed Mon); *Churrascaria Recanto do Bosque*, R Cândido Mariano; *Bierhaus*, Isaac Póvoas 1200; *Naturama*, R Comandante Costa 770; *Sachimi*, Av Ipiranga 740, Japanese. *O Choppão*, Praça 9 de Abril, very good, popular. Av Getúlio Vargas, between Praças Santos Dumont and 9 de Abril, about 10 mins walk from centre, has several popular pizza and other restaurants. On Av CPA are many good restaurants and small snack bars.

Banks and Exchange Banco do Brasil, Av Getúlio Vargas e R Barão de Melgaço, very slow for TCs, but best rates; fewer people at Banco do Estado de Mato Grosso (Bemat), Av G Vargas e R Joaquim Murtinho, but may not change TCs every day. Hours 1000-1500.

Electric Current 110 volts AC, 60 cycles.

Entertainment Cuiabá is quite lively at night, bars with live music and dance on Av CPA; *Tucano* bar/restaurant, Av CPA, beautiful view, rec. 4 cinemas in town.

Post Office Praça da República. **Telecommunications** Telemat, R Barão de Melgaço, 0700-2200, also at rodoviária, international service.

Shopping Handicrafts in wood, straw, netting, leather, skins, Pequi liquor, crystallized *caju* fruit, compressed *guaraná* fruit (for making the drink), Indian objects on sale at airport, bus station, craft shops in centre, and daily market, Praça da República, interesting. The *Casa de Artesão*, Praça do Expedicionário 315, T 321-0603, sells all types of local crafts in a restored building, rec. Fish and vegetable market, picturesque, at the riverside.

Tourist Information Fundação de Cultura e Turismo (Funcetu, T 322-5363), Praça República, next to post office building, T 624-9060, Mon-Fri, 0800-1800. Good maps, friendly, helpful regarding general information, hotels and car hire. Ramis Bucair, R Pedro Celestino 280, is good for detailed maps of the region.

Local Buses Many bus routes have stops in the vicinity of Praça Ipiranga. To/from airport, see below; bus 501 or 505 (Universidade) to University museums and zoo (ask for "Teatro") from Av Ten Cel Duarte by triangular park just E of Praça Ipiranga. To rodoviária, No 202 from R Joaquim Murtinho behind the cathedral, about 20 mins.

Car Hire Unidas, Av Isaac Póvoas 720, T 321-4646; **Nobre**, at airport, T 381-1651; **Localiza**, Av Dom Bosco 963, T 321-0846.

Air Services Airport in Várzea Grande. By air to Corumbá, São Paulo, Manaus, Campo Grande, Goiânia, Brasília, Rio de Janeiro, Belém and Porto Velho. Also many smaller Brazilian cities. No bank at airport; there is a post office and a Turimat office (not always open). Taxi to centre US$8.50, bus US$0.40 (take any white Tuiuiú bus, name written on side, in front of airport to Av Ten Cel Duarte; to return take "Aeroporto" bus from Praça Ipiranga).

Buses and Roads There is a paved road to Campo Grande (712 km); the 2,400 km BR-364 road from Brasília to Porto Velho and Rio Branco passes through Cuiabá; it is paved all the way between Brasília, Cuiabá (1,127 km) and is in good condition, but between Cuiabá and Porto Velho there are many pot-holes. Service stations often provide free hot showers and the *prato comercial* is a cheap meal. The more direct road to Brasília through Barra do Garças and Goiás Velho (the BR-070) is paved also. Several paved feeder roads connect the BR-070 and BR-364.

Rodoviária is on outskirts; town buses (see above) stop at the entrance. Comfortable buses (toilets) to **Campo Grande**, 10 hrs, US$29, 12 buses daily, *leito* at 2000 and 2100. **Goiânia**, 14 hrs, US$29; direct to **Brasília**, 24 hrs, US$48. To **Porto Velho**, 6 União Cascavel buses a day, US$39, road paved, 1,450 km, bus journey takes 21 hrs. Andorinha 1700 bus São Paulo-Cuiabá connects with Porto Velho service. Eventually a paved road from Brasília to Caracas is envisaged. Several to **São Paulo**, eg Motta, US$40. Integração buses go to Ponta Porã, Foz do Iguaçu and Cascavel; União Cascavel also go to the NE and Fortaleza via Imperatriz, to Curitiba via Londrina and Ponta Grossa, with a service continuing to Florianópolis. To **Barra do Garças**, Xavante 0800, 1300 and 2030, US$17, also Barattur. Connections to all major cities. Belo Horizonte bus passes through Ituiutaba (**E Hotel São Luiz**, rec), Nova São Simão (a new dam nearby), and Jataí.

Excursions Good fishing in the Cuiabá and smaller Coxipó rivers. The Águas Quentes hot springs, 86 km, can be visited; *Hotel Águas Quentes* at the springs (reservations through *Hotel Mato Grosso Palace*, address above, T 322-9304). The waters fill pools of 42° and 36° C; no buses go there, arrange transport through *Hotel Mato Grosso Palace*.

To **Chapada dos Guimarães** (pop 12,765), 68 km NE of Cuiabá, where a new National Park has been established on one of the oldest plateaus on earth. The town itself is a base for many beautiful excursions in the area; it has the oldest church in the Mato Grosso, NS de Santana (1779), a bizarre blending of Portuguese and French baroque styles, and a huge spring-water public swimming pool. It is still inhabited mainly by *garimpeiros* (diamond prospectors). Hotels: **A3** *Pousada da Chapada*, 2 km out on Cuiabá road, T 791-1171, very comfortable, restaurant, bar, sports facilities; **C** *Turismo*, R Fernando Corrêa 1065, a block from bus station, T 791-1166, a/c, restaurant, very friendly and popular, German-run; **D** *Rio's Hotel*, R Tiradentes 333, clean, good breakfast, rec; **F** *São João*, R Vereador José de Souza 50, friendly but very basic; **E** *São José*, hot showers, good, owner Mário sometimes runs excursions. *Costelão*, near the *Pousada da Chapada* in the old town, music, good *churrascos*, 1100-1500, 1900-2100; *Nivios* on main square for regional food, good value. Crafts, indigenous artefacts, sweets and locally-made honey from *Casa do Artesão* (R Quinco Caldas 192) and *Arte Nativa* (R Fernando Corrêa 392). There are bus services from the rodoviária to Brasilândia and Paranatinga (350 km away to the N by seasonal road in the headwaters of the Xingu River), and 6 departures daily to and from Cuiabá (Rubi, 0800-1900, last back 1630), 1½ hrs, US$3. The Festival de Inverno is held in last week of Jul, when accommodation is scarce and expensive.

The Chapada is an immense geological formation rising to 700m, with rich forests, curiously-eroded rocks and many lovely grottos (eg Caverna do Francês, 35 km from town, fresh, crystal-clear water), peaks and waterfalls. 22 km before the town is the Salgadeira tourist centre, with bathing, camping and restaurant. The beautiful 85-metre Véu da Noiva waterfall (Bridal Veil), 12 km before the town near Buriti (well-signposted, ask bus from Cuiabá to let you off), is reached by a short route, or a long route through forest. Other sights include the Mutuca beauty spot, Rio Claro, the viewpoint over the breathtaking 80m-deep Portão do Inferno (Hell's Gate), and the falls of Cachoeirinha (small restaurant) and Andorinhas, all unspoilt. The Ponto Geodésico, a monument officially marking the Geodesic Centre of South America, overlooks a great canyon with views of the surrounding plains and Cuiabá's skyline on the horizon; to reach it take the last road in town to the right (S), drive 8 km then turn right at the "Centro Geodésico" sign. The Chapada dos Guimarães is one of the most scenic areas of Brazil and retains much of the mystery attributed to it for centuries. In the 1920s Colonel Fawcett was told of many strange things hidden in its depths, and an unusual local magnetic force which reduces the speed of cars has been reliably documented. The birdwatching is very good and mammals, such as puma, giant river otter and black-tailed marmoset, live here. Unfortunately, the national park is not regulated so that soil erosion, mercury used by the *garimpeiros* and uncontrolled tourism are threatening both the Chapada's own features and the waters that run from it into the Pantanal.

Hiring a car in Cuiabá is the most convenient way to see many of the scattered attractions; the small Tourist Office at the W entrance to the town provides a useful map of the region (weekdays 0800-1100, 1300-1600). Rec tours with Jorge Belfort Matos (*Ecoturismo*, Praça

Dom Wunibaldo 464, Chapada town, T 791-1393), who speaks English, knows the area well and meets the 0800 bus from Cuiabá daily; several 4- to 6-hr itineraries from US$20-56 pp (min 4 people or prices increase). Also with Cássio of AC tours, who often waits at the rodoviária. Tours from Cuiabá cost US$35-40 pp.

The road due N to Santarém (1,777 km) has been completed and is all-weather, through Sinop (pop 38,330), with a branch W to Colíder (pop 31,155), and **Alta Floresta** (pop 66,735): daily bus at 2000. Yellow fever inoculations insisted on when travelling this route. Outside Alta Floresta, the *Cristalino Jungle Lodge*, on the Cristalino river, is a basic lodge, with shared baths, in a very rich and well-preserved section of southern Amazonia. Many rare mammals are found here (including the short-eared dog), as well as 5 species of macaw, Harpy Eagle and a few hundred other bird species. *Focus Tours* of Belo Horizonte can make reservations or arrange guided tours.

From **Rondonópolis** (pop 125,110, many hotels, **A1** *Novotel*, R Floriano Peixoto 711, T 421-9355, try for a discount; *Dormitório Beija Flor*, near bus station, or *Sumaré*, clean but unfriendly, both **D**) about 215 km SE of Cuiabá on the road to Goiânia, a paved road branches southwards to Campo Grande and thence to the western parts of the State of São Paulo.

Airport for internal flights.

Buses from Rondonópolis Brasília, US$23, 14$\frac{1}{2}$ hrs; **Goiânia**, US$19, 11 hrs; **Campo Grande**, US$9.50, 6$\frac{1}{2}$ hrs; **Presidente Epitácio**, US$7.75; **Presidente Prudente**, US$11.50. Beware of overbooking on Viação Motta buses.

Indians The Bororo tribe, on a reservation 3 hrs by truck from Rondonópolis, have long been "civilized". It may be possible to visit the Xavantes at one of the Reservas Indígenas along the BR-158, N of Barra do Garças (see p 577). Funai is reluctant to permit travellers to visit Indian reservations without recommendations, qualifications or a compelling reason; the office in Cuiabá is at R São Joaquim 1047, T 321-2325.

A journey along the Porto Velho road from Cuiabá (BR-364) demonstrates the amount of development along Brazil's "Far West" frontier, see p 569. A side road off the BR-364 goes to **Vila Bela** on the Rio Guaporé, which used to be the capital of Mato Grosso. It has a ruined church, cannon balls lying around, and is very interesting.

NB When travelling N of Cuiabá, yellow fever vaccination is obligatory; if you do not have a certificate, you will be (re)vaccinated.

INFORMATION FOR VISITORS

Before you go

Entry requirements

● **Documents**

Consular visas are not required for stays of up to 90 days by tourists from Western European (except for French nationals) or South American (except Bolivia and Guyana) countries, Finland, Morocco, Bahamas, Barbados, Trinidad and Tobago, and the Philippines. For them, only the following documents are required at the port of disembarkation: valid passport (or *cédula de identidad* for nationals of Argentina, Chile, Paraguay and Uruguay); and a return or onward ticket, or adequate proof that you can purchase your return fare, subject to no remuneration being received in Brazil and no legally binding or contractual documents being signed. Some consulates (eg Frankfurt) insist that your passport be valid for at least 6 months from date of entry. If coming from Bolivia, Colombia or Peru (or certain African countries), you must have a valid yellow fever vaccination certificate. Venezuelan passport holders can stay in Brazil for 60 days on filling in a form at the border. (Some consulates, eg Santiago, ask to see an onward ticket: persistence, adequate money and showing a credit card may overcome this.) 90-day renewals are easily obtainable, but only at least 15 days before the expiry of your 90-day permit, from the Policia Federal: the procedure is; give your name, passport data and Brazilian address to the clerk, who will type this on the form for extension (US$0.50); take this to a bank; pay US$3 tax; then return to Policia Federal who will stamp the extension in your passport after they have seen onward flight tickets and receipt from the bank for the tax; sometimes proof of sufficient funds for your continued stay is requested. Some points of entry refuse entry for longer than 30 days, renewals are then for the same period, insist if you want 90 days.

For longer stays you must leave the country and return (not the same day) to get a new 90-day permit. If you overstay your visa, or extension, you will be fined US$1/day, up to US$75. After paying the fine to Policia Federal, you will be issued with an exit visa and must leave within 8 days. If you cannot pay the fine you must pay when you next return to Brazil. US, Canadian and French citizens and people of other nationalities, and those who cannot meet the requirements above, *must* get a visa before arrival, which may, if you ask, be granted for multiple entry. (Visa fees vary, eg free for USA, US$32 for Canadians, US$40 for French and Russians; for most others a tourist visa costs US$16.) Do not lose the emigration permit they give you when you enter Brazil. Leaving the country without it, you may have to pay up to US$100 pp.

Officially, if you leave Brazil within the 90-day permission to stay and then re-enter the country, you should only be allowed to stay until the 90-day permit expires. Usual practice, though, is to give another 90-day permit, which may lead to charges of overstaying if you apply for an extension.

You must always carry identification when in Brazil; it is a good idea to take a photocopy of the first 5 pages of your passport, plus that with your Brazilian immigration stamp, and leave your passport in the hotel safe deposit. Always keep an independent record of your passport details. In Rio it is a good idea to register with your consulate to expedite document replacement if yours gets lost/stolen.

● **Vaccinations**
Vaccination against smallpox is no longer required for visitors, but vaccination is necessary against yellow fever if you are visiting Amazonia and the Centre-W, or are coming from countries with Amazonian territories, eg Bolivia, Colombia, Ecuador, Peru. It is strongly rec to have a yellow fever inoculation before visiting northern Brazil since those without a certificate will be inoculated on entering any of the northern and centre-western states, probably in unsanitary conditions. Poliomyelitis vaccination is required for children from 3 months to 6 years. If you are going to Amazonia, or to other low-lying forested areas, malaria prophylaxis is advised (this can be difficult to obtain in some areas – the local name for paludrine is doroprim) and water purification tablets are essential. Dengue fever is now endemic in Brazil, and Rio is one of the worst places: protect yourself against mosquitoes. Sporadic outbreaks of cholera have occurred in the Amazon region and on the NE coast (eg Recife), but numbers have been in the tens, rather than the hundreds. Take care to drink only sterilized water. Also, in the Amazon basin, sandflies abound; take a good repellent and get inoculations against hepatitis and typhoid.

Yellow fever (see p 596) and some other vaccinations can be obtained from the Ministério da Saúde, R Cais de Pharoux, Rio de Janeiro. Less common vaccinations can be obtained at Saúde de Portos, Praça 15 de Novembro, Rio de Janeiro. It is reported that shots of immunoglobulin against hepatitis are not screened against Aids, which is widespread.

● **Representation overseas**
Canada, 2000 Mansfield, Suite 1700, Montreal H3A 3AS, T 514-0499; **Denmark**, Ryvangs Alle 24, 21 Copenhagen, T 20-6478; **France**, 34 Cours Allert IER, 75008 Paris, T 4225-9250; **Germany**, Stephanstrasse 3, 4 Stock, 6000 Frankfurt, T 290709; **UK**, 32 Green Street, London WIY 4AT, T 0171-499-0877, consulate at 6 St Albans St, London SW1Y 4SQ, T 0171-930-9055; **USA**, 630 Fifth Avenue, 27 Floor, New York NY 10111, T 212 916-3251/3200; **USA**, 8484 Wilshire Blvd, Suites 730-711, Los Angeles, California, T 213 651-2664.

● **Tourist information**
All Brazil's States, and most cities and towns have their own tourist information bureaux. They are not usually too helpful regarding information on very cheap hotels, tending to imagine that no foreign tourist should consider staying in anything of that kind. It is also difficult to get information on neighbouring states. *Quatro Rodas*, a motoring magazine, publishes an excellent series of maps and guides in Portuguese and English from about US$10. Its *Guia Brasil* is a type of Michelin Guide to hotels, restaurants (not the cheapest), sights, facilities and general information on hundreds of cities and towns in the country, including good street maps. These guides can be purchased at street newspaper vendors throughout the country. Quatro Rodas Guides may be bought in Europe from 33 rue de Miromesnil, 75008 Paris, T 42.66.31.18, F 42.66.13.99, or Distribuidora Jardim, Quinta Pau Varais, Azinhaga de Fetais, Camarate 2685, Lisbon, Portugal, T Lisbon 947-2542. In USA: Lincoln Building, 60 East 42nd St, Suite 3403, New York, NY 10165, T 557-5990/3, F 983-0972. Note that telephone yellow pages in most cities (but not Rio) contain good street maps which, together with the Quatro Rodas maps, are a great help for getting around.

Many of the more expensive hotels provide locally-produced tourist information magazines for their guests. Travel information can be very unreliable and it is wise to recheck details thoroughly.

When to go

● Best time to visit

The best time for a visit is from April to June, and Aug to Oct, inclusive. Business visitors should avoid from mid-Dec to the end of Feb, when it is hot and people are on holiday. In these months hotels, beaches and means of transport tend to be crowded. July is a school holiday month.

Conditions during the winter (May to Sept) are like those of a N European summer in Rio de Janeiro (including periods of rain and overcast skies), but more like a N European autumn in São Paulo and the southern states. Summer-weight woollens can be worn without discomfort in winter in Rio de Janeiro (temperatures vary at this season from 14°C to the high 20s), but further S something heavier is often required. It can get very cold in the far S. In São Paulo, which is in the Highlands, light-weight clothing is only required in the summer; the climate can be treacherous, however, with large temperature changes in a brief space of time. It can get surprisingly cold S and W of Rio, and on high ground anywhere in Brazil, at night; warm clothes are needed. The season of heavy rains is from Nov to Mar in Rio and São Paulo, Jan to April in the N, and from April to Aug around Recife.

Summer conditions all over the country are tropical, but temperatures of 40°C are comparatively rare. On the coast there is a high degree of humidity. The luminosity is also very high; sunglasses are advisable.

Health

Be very careful about bathing in lakes or slow rivers anywhere in Brazil: harmful parasites abound (including the snails that carry schistosomiasis – this disease is rampant in Minas Gerais and most of central Brazil). South of the Amazon beware of *borrachudos*, small flies with a sharp bite that attack ankles and calves; coconut oil deters them. Water should not be drunk from taps unless there is a porcelain filter attached or unless you have water sterilizing tablets ('Hydrosteril' is a popular local brand); there is mineral water in plenty and excellent light beer, known as 'chopp' (pronounced 'shoppi'), and soft drinks. For those who have been in Brazil for a while, *água gelada* (chilled water) is usually safe to drink, being filtered water kept in a refrigerator in most hotels, restaurants and stores. Avoid ice in cheap hotels and restaurants; it is likely to be made from unfiltered water. Colestase is the rec local treatment for upset stomachs.

Brazilians are famous for their open sexuality: appearances can be deceptive, however, and attitudes vary widely. To generalize, the coastal cities are very easy-going, while in smaller towns and the interior, traditional morals are strictly enforced. Aids is widespread, commonly transmitted by heterosexual sex, and tolerance of male homosexuality is diminishing. You should take reliable condoms with you, even if you are sure you won't be needing them. The primary means of HIV infection in Brazil is now heterosexual sex. Local condoms are reported not to be reliable.

Tampons are available, as are Hydrocare contact lens products (expensive).

● Medical facilities

An excellent hospital, supported by the American and British colonies in São Paulo, is Hospital Samaritano, R Conselheiro Brotero 1486, São Paulo (T 51-2154). If staying in Brazil for any length of time, it is rec to take out Brazilian health insurance; Banco Econômico and Citibank are reported to provide good advice on this matter.

Money

● Currency

Until 1 July 1994, the currency unit was the cruzeiro real (called 'cruzeiro'), introduced in Sep 1993, and having 1,000 times the value of the cruzeiro introduced in Mar 1990. A new currency unit, the *real*, R$ (plural *reais*), was introduced on 1 July 1994. The value of the *real* was the same as one Real Unit of Value (URV), a transitionary accounting unit introduced on 1 March 1994 at a par with the US dollar. By Dec 1994 the *real* had risen to US$0.84, but revaluations in early 1995 permitted it to float between R$0.91 and 0.99 to the dollar. Any amount of foreign currency and 'a reasonable sum' in *reais* can be taken in; residents may only take out the equivalent of US$4,000. Notes in circulation are: 100, 50, 20, 10, 5 and 1 *real*; coins 1 *real*, 50, 25, 10, 5, 2 and 1 centavo.

Money sent to Brazil is normally paid out in Brazilian currency, so do not have more money sent to Brazil than you need for your stay in the country itself. Banco do Brasil now offers US$ accounts for temporary visitors, with the option to withdraw half in dollars cash, half in TCs. In most large cities Citibank will hold US personal cheques for collection, paying the day's tourist dollar rate in *reais* with no charge. Banco do Brasil offers the same service with small charge. From the UK the quickest method of having money sent is Swift Air. Tourists cannot change US$ TCs into US$ notes (though some exchange houses will do this illegally), but US$ TCs obtained on an American Express card (against official policy).

● **Cost of living**
Since the introduction of the *real* in Jul 1994, prices for residents and visitors have increased. Until early 1995, tourists also had to contend with the depreciation of the dollar against the *real*, making Brazil one of the most expensive South American countries for foreigners. Eating in smart restaurants became very costly; hotel accommodation rose steeply in price, although budget hotels responded by cutting extras, cramming more beds into rooms, etc. A cheap room cost about US$10. Shopping prices were equivalent to Europe. Hotel price categories and transport fares in this chapter reflect the appreciation of the *real*, but travellers may find variations as the *real* fluctuates within the floating exchange rate system introduced in 1995. Prices are higher in Amazonia than elsewhere.

● **Exchange**
Banks in major cities will change cash and TCs. For the latest exchange rate, see tables near end of book. If you keep the exchange slips, you may convert back into foreign currency up to 50% of the amount you exchanged. This applies to the official markets only; there is no right of reconversion unless you have an official exchange slip. The parallel market, found in travel agencies, exchange houses and among hotel staff, was of no benefit compared with bank rates in early 1995. TCs are a safer way to carry your money, but rates for cheques are usually lower than for cash and they are less easy to change, commission may be charged. In 1995, many banks would only change US$300 minimum in cash, US$500 in TCs. Dollars cash are becoming more frequently used for tourist transactions and are also useful for those places where TCs cannot be changed and for when the banks go on strike; damaged dollar notes may be rejected. Black market and official rates are quoted in the papers and on TV news programmes.

● **Credit cards**
Credit cards are widely used; Diners Club, Master Card, Visa and American Express are useful. Master Charge/Access is accepted by Banco Econômico, Banco Meridional and Banco Real. Overseas credit cards need authorization from São Paulo, this can take up to 2 hrs, allow plenty of time if buying air tickets. Mastercard and Diners are equivalent to Credicard, and Eurocheques can be cashed at Banco Alemão (major cities only). Banco Bradesco handles the international Visa automatic teller machine (ATM) network, Visa cash advances also at Banco do Brasil (in case of lost or stolen cards T 000-811-933-5589). Mastercard/Cirrus ATMs can be found at 16 branches of Credicard; Citibank plan to extend their ATM facility to Brazil in 1995. Credit card transactions are charged at the tourist official rate. Cash advances on credit cards will only be paid in *reais* at the tourist rate, incurring a 1½% commission; banks in small remote places may still refuse to give a cash advance, if you have run out of cash and TCs, try asking for the manager ('gerente'). Automatic cash dispensers are now common in Brazil: you need only a passport and address to open an account with a large Brazilian bank, and you can then draw cash from a machine as required; worth considering since queues can be extremely long.

Getting there

By Air

● **From Europe**
Brazil is connected with the principal cities of Europe by Air France, KLM, Lufthansa (operated by Varig), Alitalia, Iberia, Aerolíneas Argentinas, Varig and TAP. Varig flies from London to Rio and São Paulo 3 times a week. British Airways flies 3 times a week London-São Paulo-Rio. Varig fly to Salvador from Amsterdam, Milan, Rome and Paris. Vasp flies to Brussels from Rio, São Paulo, Salvador and Recife. There are flights with Varig to Recife from Frankfurt, Lisbon (also TAP), Madrid, Milan and Rome. Transbrasil flies from Vienna to Rio and São Paulo.

● **From USA**
Brazil is connected to the USA direct by Varig, Transbrasil, American Airlines, United, Aerolíneas Argentinas and Vasp (LA-Rio and São Paulo, Miami-São Paulo and Rio). The cheapest route is probably from Miami.

● **From Latin America**
All South American capitals are connected by air services to Rio. Caracas, 6 weekly (Varig, Viasa); Bogotá, 4 weekly (Varig, Avianca); Lima, 4 weekly (AeroPerú, Varig); La Paz, 5 weekly Varig, via Santa Cruz and São Paulo; Quito/Guayaquil, twice a week with Varig and Lacsa joint operation; Asunción, daily with Varig (American flies Asunción-São Paulo daily; Lapsa flies Asunción-São Paulo 5 times

a week); Santiago, several (Ladeco, LAN-Chile, Varig, Iberia; São Paulo is also served, LAN-Chile and European carriers in addition); Montevideo, about 15 weekly (incl KLM, Pluna, also Varig to São Paulo); Buenos Aires, several daily. Paramaribo, 4 a week by Suriname Airways to Belém via Cayenne. If buying a ticket to another country but with a stop over in Brazil, check whether two tickets are cheaper than one.

Varig and Aerolíneas Argentinas operate the Mercosur Airpass, in conjunction with other carriers in Brazil, Argentina, Uruguay and Paraguay. Valid for a minimum of 10 and maximum of 30 days, the pass is for a maximum of 8 flight coupons, no more than 4/country. At least two countries must be included; rerouting is not permitted. The airpass must be bought outside the region by holders of an international return ticket. Price is worked out on a kilometre basis: the further you go and the more countries you visit, the cheaper it is: prices range from US$225 to US$870. Varig also has an extensive 'Stopover' programme which gives reduced rates on transfers and hotel rooms in many cities in Brazil and throughout South America (plus San José, Costa Rica).

● **From elsewhere**

Varig (twice a week) and SAA (once) fly between Rio and Johannesburg. Varig and Japan Airlines fly several times a week between Tokyo and Rio and São Paulo, some flights stopping in Los Angeles. Airline tickets are expensive in Brazil, buy internal tickets with *reais* (you can pay by credit card). External tickets must be paid for in dollars.

NB Regulations state that you cannot buy an air ticket in Brazil for use abroad unless you first have a ticket out of Brazil.

By Road

To drive in Brazil you need either a translation of your home driving licence, or an international licence. There are agreements between Brazil and all South American countries (but check in the case of Bolivia) whereby a car can be taken into Brazil (or a Brazilian car out of Brazil) for a period of 90 days without any special documents; an extension of up to 90 days is granted by the customs authorities on presentation of the paper received at the border, this must be retained; this may be done at most customs posts and at the Serviço de Controle Aduaneiro, Ministerio da Fazenda, Av Pres A Carlos, Sala 1129, Rio.

This now applies to cars registered in other countries; the requirements are proof of ownership and/or registration in the home country and valid driving licence (international or from home country). It is better to cross the border into Brazil when it is officially open (from 1300 to 1800 Mon to Fri) because an official who knows all about the entry of cars is then present. The motorist should in any case insist on getting the correct paper 'in accordance with Decree No 53.313/63', or he/she might find it impossible to get the 90-day extension. You must specify which border station you intend to leave by, but application can be made to the Customs to change this. If you want to leave by ship the Touring Club in Rio (possibly also elsewhere, but this is less definite) will arrange it at a cost; you can also arrange the paper yourself by taking your car away by ship, but it takes about two days and costs about US$15 in port and police charges; the Touring Club provides information on how to go about it. (Klaus Elgner, of Hannover, reports this can be done with a letter in Portuguese saying you wish to leave by ship plus passport number, vehicle number, entry forms data plus an *ordem de embarque* supplied and stamped by the shipping agent. These should be presented to the Customs.) Crossing by a land border is, in any case, easier and probably cheaper.

By Sea

For shipping lines that carry passengers to Brazil, see **Introduction and Hints**. **NB** There is an 8% tax on international shipping-line tickets bought in Brazil.

Customs

Clothing and personal articles are free of import duty. Such articles as cameras, movie cameras, portable radios, tape-recorders, typewriters and binoculars are also admitted free if there is not more than one of each. Tourists may also bring in, duty-free, 12 bottles of alcohol, 400 cigarettes, 25 cigars, 280 grams of perfume, up to 10 units of cosmetics, up to 3 each of any electronic item or watch, up to a total value of US$500. Duty free goods may only be purchased in foreign currency.

When you arrive

● **Clothing**

Fashions are provocative, and while women are advised to dress in the local style, this can have unnerving effects. It is normal to stare and comment on women's appearances, and if you happen to look different or to be travelling alone, you will undoubtedly attract attention. You are very unlikely to be groped or otherwise molested: this is disrespectful, and merits a suitable reaction. Be aware that Brazilian men can be extraordinarily persistent, and very easily encouraged; it is safest to err on the side of caution until you are accustomed.

In general, clothing requirements in Brazil are less formal than in the Hispanic countries. It is, however, advisable for men visiting restaurants to wear long trousers (women in shorts may also be refused entry), trousers and jackets or pullovers in São Paulo (also for cinemas). As a general rule, it is better not to wear shorts in official buildings, cinemas, inter-state buses and on flights.

● **Conduct**
Men should avoid arguments or insults (care is needed even when overtaking on the road); pride may be defended with a gun. Gay men, while still enjoying greater freedom than in many countries, should exercise reasonable discretion.

Colour The people of Brazil represent a unique racial mix: it is not uncommon for the children of one family to be of several different colours. Individuals are often described by the colour of their skin (ranging through several shades of brown), and 'white' can refer to people who would not necessarily be thought white in Europe or North America. Generally speaking, the emphasis is on colour rather than racial origins.

Racial discrimination is illegal in Brazil. There is, however, a complex class system which is informed both by heritage and by economic status. This effectively discriminates against the poor, who are chiefly (but by no means exclusively) black due to the lack of inherited wealth among those whose ancestors were servants and slaves. Some Brazilians might assume that a black person is poor, therefore of low status. Black visitors to the country may encounter racial prejudice. We have also received a report from a black North American woman who was the subject of sexual advances by non-Brazilian, white tourists. Black women travelling with a white man may experience some problems, which should disappear with the realisation that your partnership is not a commercial arrangement. A surprising number of Brazilians are unaware that black Europeans exist, so you could become the focus of some curiosity.

Brazilian culture is rich in African influences. Those interested in the development of Afro-Brazilian music, dance, religion, arts and cuisine will find the whole country N of São Paulo fascinating, and especially the cities of Bahia and São Luis which retain the greatest African influences. Black Pride movements are particularly strong in Bahia. Further reading: *Samba* by Alma Guillermoprieto, paperback, Bloomsbury Press; *Towards the Abolition of Whiteness* by David Roediger, Verso, £11.95 (a sociological study of how 'colour' is determined by economic status, mostly in the USA and UK).

● **Hours of business**
Hours of business are 0900-1800 Mon to Fri for most businesses, which close for lunch some time between 1130 and 1400. Shops are open on Sat till 1230 or 1300. Government departments are open from 1100-1800 Mon to Fri. Banks 1000-1500, but closed on Sat.

● **Official time**
Brazilian standard time is 3 hrs behind GMT; of the major cities, only the Amazon time zone, Manaus, Cuiabá, Campo Grande and Corumbá are different, with time 5 hrs behind GMT. The State of Acre is 4 hrs behind GMT. Clocks move forward one hour in summer for approximately 5 months (usually between Oct and Feb or Mar) but times of change vary. This does not apply to Acre.

The days of the week are: segunda feira (Mon), terça feira (Tues), quarta feira (Wed), quinta feira (Thur), sexta feira (Fri), sábado (Sat), domingo (Sun).

● **Police**
There are 3 types of police: Policia Federal, civilian dressed, who handle all federal law duties, including immigration. A subdivision is the Policia Federal Rodoviária, uniformed, who are the traffic police. Policia Militar is the uniformed, street police force, under the control of the state governor, handling all state laws. They are not the same as the Armed Forces' internal police. Policia Civil, also state-controlled, handle local laws; usually in civilian dress, unless in the traffic division.

● **Safety**
Personal safety in Brazil has deteriorated of recent years, largely because of the economic recession, and crime is increasing. Some recommend avoiding all large cities; the situation is far less insecure in smaller towns and in the country. The police are reported to be charging for documents reporting crimes if these are required quickly.

Apart from the obvious precautions of not wearing jewellery (wear a cheap, plastic *digital* watch), do not camp or sleep out in isolated places and if you are hitch-hiking, never accept a lift in a car with two people in it. Money belts are safer than bags for your valuables. Consider buying clothing locally to avoid looking like a gringo. If you are held up and robbed, it is worth asking for the fare back to where you are staying. It is not uncommon for thieves to oblige. Do carry some cash, to hand over if you are held up. Do not leave valuables in hotel rooms, except where a safe is provided. Hotel safe deposits are generally (but not always) secure. If you cannot get a receipt for valuables in a hotel safe, seal the contents in a plastic bag and sign across the seal. Always photocopy your passport, air ticket and other documents, make a record of TC and credit card numbers and keep them separately from the originals. Leave another set of records at home. Never trust anyone telling 'sobstories' or offering 'safe rooms', when looking for a hotel, always choose the room yourself. Take only your towel and lotion to the beach, tuck enough money for your cold drinks into your trunks/bikini bottom. A few belongings can safely be left at a bar. Ted Stroll of San Francisco advises, "remember that economic privation has many Brazilians close to the edge, and that they are probably as ashamed of exploiting you as you are angry at being exploited". The corollary is be generous to those who give you a good deal. Travellers are most vulnerable when carrying baggage, if possible take a taxi, but don't leave the driver in the car with your bags.

● **Shopping**
Gold, diamonds and gemstones throughout Brazil. Innovative designs in jewellery: buy 'real' at reputable dealers (best value in Minas Gerais); cheap, fun pieces from street traders. Interesting furnishings made with gemstones, marble; clay figurines from the NE; lace from Ceará; leatherwork; strange pottery from Amazonia; carvings in soapstone and in bone; tiles and other ceramic work, African-type pottery and basketwork from Bahia. Many large hotel gift shops stock a good selection of handicrafts at reasonable prices. Brazilian cigars are excellent for those who like the mild flavours popular in Germany, the Netherlands and Switzerland. Recommended purchases are musical instruments, eg guitars, other stringed, and percussion instruments.

Excellent textiles: good hammocks from the NE; other fabrics; design in clothing is impressive, though unfortunately not equalled by manufacturing quality. Buy your beachwear in Brazil: it is matchless. For those who know how to use them, medicinal herbs, barks and spices from street markets; coconut oil and local skin and haircare products (fantastic conditioners) are better and cheaper than in Europe, but known brands of toiletries

are exorbitant. Other bad buys are film (including processing), cameras and any electrical goods (including batteries). Sunscreen, sold in all department stores and large supermarkets, is expensive.

As a rule, shopping is easier, quality more reliable and prices higher in the shopping centres (mostly excellent) and in the wealthier suburbs. Better prices at the small shops and street traders; most entertaining at markets and on the beach. Bargaining (with good humour) is expected in the latter.

● **Tipping**
Tipping is usual, but less costly than in most other countries, except for porters. Restaurants, 10% of bill if no service charge but small tip if there is; taxi drivers, none; cloakroom attendants, small tip; cinema usherettes, none; hairdressers, 10-15%; porters, fixed charges but tips as well; airport porters, about US$0.50/item.

● **Weights and measures**
The metric system is used by all.

● **Working in Brazil**
Work-permit restrictions are making it harder to find work as an English language teacher than it used to be, though many people do it unofficially and leave Brazil every 90 days in order to re-enter as tourists. One's best bet would be in a small language school. Or advertise in the Press.

On departure

● **Airport tax**
The equivalent of about US$20 is charged for international flights and, for internal flights, US$10 depending on the class of airport. It must be paid on checking in, in *reais* or US$. Tax is waived if you stay in Brazil less than 24 hrs.

Where to stay

● **Hotels**
The best guide to hotels in Brazil is the *Guia Brasil Quatro Rodas*, with good maps of towns. Motels are specifically intended for very short-stay couples: there is no stigma attached and they usually offer good value (the rate for a full night is called the *pernoite*), though the decor can be a little unsettling. The type known as *hotel familiar*, to be found in the interior – large meals, communal washing, hammocks for children – is much cheaper, but only for the enterprising. *Pousadas* are the equivalent of bed-and-breakfast, often small and family run, although some are very sophisticated and

correspondingly priced. Usually hotel prices include breakfast; there is no reduction if you don't eat it. In the better hotels (our category C and upwards) the breakfast is well worth eating: rolls, ham, eggs, cheese, cakes, fruit. Normally the *apartamento* is a room with a bath; a *quarto* is a room without bath. The service stations (*postos*) and hostels (*dormitórios*) along the main roads provide excellent value in room and food, akin to truck-driver type accommodation in Europe, for those on a tight budget. The star rating system for hotels (five-star hotels are not price-controlled) is not the standard used in North America or Europe. For information about Youth Hostels contact Federação Brasil Albergues Juventude, R da Assambleia 10, room 1211, T 531-1129, Rio de Janeiro; its brochure provides a full list of good value accommodation. Low-budget travellers with student cards (photograph needed) can use the Casa dos Estudantes network. Leave rooms in good time so frigobar bills can be checked; we have received reports of overcharging in otherwise good hotels.

Business visitors are strongly rec to book accommodation in advance, and this can be easily done for Rio or São Paulo hotels with representation abroad. Varig has a good hotel reservation service, with discounts of up to 50% for its passengers.

NB Taxi drivers will try to take you to the expensive hotels, who pay them commission for bringing in custom. Beware!

● **Camping**

Members of the Camping Clube do Brasil or those with an international campers' card pay only half the rate of a non-member, which is US$10-15 pp. The Club has 43 sites in 13 states and 80,000 members. For enquiries, Camping Clube do Brasil, Divisão de Campings, R Senador Dantas 75° andar (T 262-7172), Rio de Janeiro. It may be difficult to get into some Camping Clube campsites during the high season (Jan-Feb). Private campsites charge about US$5 pp. For those on a very low budget and in isolated areas where there is no camp site, service stations can be used as camping sites (Shell stations rec); they have shower facilities, watchmen and food; some have dormitories; truck drivers are a mine of information. There are also various municipal sites; both types are mentioned in the text. Campsites often tend to be some distance from public transport routes and are better suited to those with their own transport. Never camp at the side of a road; wild camping is generally not possible.

Good camping equipment may be purchased in Brazil and there are several rental companies. Camping gas cartridges are easy to buy in sizeable towns in the S eg in HM shops. *Guia de Camping* is produced by Artpress, R Araçatuba 487, São Paulo 05058; it lists most sites and is available in bookshops in most cities. Quatro Rodas' *Guia Brasil* lists main campsites. Most sizeable towns have laundromats with self service machines. *Lavanderias* do the washing for you but are very expensive.

Food and drink

Food

The most common dish is *bife (ou frango) com arroz e feijão*, steak (or chicken) with rice and the excellent Brazilian black beans. The most famous dish with beans is the *feijoada completa*: several meat ingredients (jerked beef, smoked sausage, smoked tongue, salt pork, along with spices, herbs and vegetables) are cooked with the beans. Manioc flour is sprinkled over it, and it is eaten with kale (*couve*) and slices of orange, and accompanied by glasses of *aguardente* (unmatured rum), usually known as *cachaça* (booze), though *pinga* (drop) is a politer term. Almost all restaurants serve the *feijoada completa* for Sat lunch (that means up to about 1630). Bahia has some excellent fish dishes (**see note on p 478**); some restaurants in most of the big cities specialize in them. *Vatapá* is a good dish in the N; it contains shrimp or fish sauced with palm oil, or coconut milk. *Empadinhas de camarão* are worth trying; they are shrimp patties, with olives and heart of palm. A mixed grill, including excellent steak, served with roasted manioc flour (*farofa*; raw manioc flour is known as *farinha*) goes under the name of *churrasco* (it came originally from the cattlemen of Rio Grande do Sul), normally served in specialized restaurants known as *churrascarias* or *rodizios*; good places for large appetites. Minas Gerais has two splendid special dishes involving pork, black beans, *farofa* and kale; they are *tutu á mineira* and *feijão tropeiro*. A white hard cheese (*queijo prata*) or a slightly softer one (*queijo Minas*) is often served for dessert with bananas, or guava or quince paste. Meals are extremely large by European standards; if your appetites are small, you can order, say, one portion and one empty plate, and divide the portion. However, if you are in a position to do so tactfully, you may choose to offer the rest to a person with no food (many Brazilians do – observe the correct etiquette). Many restaurants now serve *comida por kilo* where you serve yourself and pay for the weight of food on your plate. Unless you specify to the contrary many restaurants will lay a *coberto opcional*, olives, carrots, etc, costing US$0.50-0.75. **NB** The main meal is usually taken in the middle of the day; cheap restaurants tend not to be open in the evening. **Warning** Avoid mussels, marsh crabs and other shellfish caught near large cities: they are likely to have lived in a highly polluted environment. In a restaurant, always ask the price of a dish before ordering.

For vegetarians, there is a growing network of restaurants in the main cities. In smaller places where food may be monotonous try vegetarian for greater variety. We list several. Most also serve fish. Alternatives in smaller towns are the Arab and Chinese restaurants.

There is fruit all the year round, ranging from banana and orange to mango, pawpaw, custard-apple (*fruta do conde*) and guava. One is especially rec to try the *manga de Uba*, a non-fibrous small mango. Also good are *mora* (a raspberry that looks like a strawberry), *jaboticaba*, a small black damson-like fruit, and *jaca* (jackfruit), a large yellow/green fruit.

The exotic flavours of Brazilian ice-creams should be experienced. Try *açaí, bacuri, biribá, buruti, cupuaçu* (not eveyone's favourite), *mari-mari, mucajá, murici, pajurá, pariri, patuá, piquiá, pupunha, sorva, tucumá, uxi* and others mentioned below under 'drinks'.

If travelling on a tight budget, remember to ask in restaurants for the *prato feito* or *sortido*, a money-saving, excellent value *table-d'hôte* meal. The *prato comercial* is similar but rather better and a bit more expensive. *Lanchonetes* are cheap eating places where you generally pay before eating. *Salgados* (savoury pastries), *coxinha* (a pyramid of manioc filled with meat or fish and deep fried), *esfilha* (spicey hamburger inside an onion-bread envelope), *empadão* (a filling – eg chicken – in sauce in a pastry case), *empadas* and *empadinhas* (smaller fritters of the same type), are the usual fare. In Minas Gerais, *pão de queijo* is a hot roll made with cheese. A *bauru* is a toasted sandwich which, in Porto Alegre, is filled with steak, while further N has tomato, ham and cheese filling. *Cocada* is a coconut and sugar biscuit.

Drink

Imported drinks are expensive, but there are some fair local wines. Chilean and Portuguese wines are sometimes available at little more than the cost of local wines. The beers are

good and there are plenty of local soft drinks. *Guaraná* is a very popular carbonated fruit drink. There is an excellent range of non-alcoholic fruit juices, known as *sucos: caju* (cashew), *pitanga, goiaba* (guava), *genipapo, graviola* (= *chirimoya*), *maracujá* (passion-fruit), *sapoti* and *tamarindo* are rec. *Vitaminas* are thick fruit or vegetable drinks with milk. *Caldo de cana* is sugar-cane juice, sometimes mixed with ice. Remember that *água mineral*, available in many varieties at bars and restaurants is a cheap, safe thirst-quencher (cheaper still in supermarkets). Apart from the ubiquitous coffee, good tea is grown and sold. **NB** If you don't want sugar in your coffee or *suco*, you must ask when you order it.

Among the better wines are Château d'Argent, Château Duvalier, Almadén, Dreher, Preciosa and Bernard Taillan. The red Marjolet from Cabernet grapes, and the Moselle-type white Zahringer have been well spoken of. It has often been noticed that a new *adega* starts off well, but the quality gradually deteriorates with time; many vintners have switched to American Concorde grapes, producing a rougher wine. Greville Brut champagne-type is inexpensive and very drinkable. A white-wine *Sangria*, containing tropical fruits such as pineapple and papaya, is worth looking out for. The Brahma, Cerpa and Antárctica beers are really excellent, of the lager type, and are cheaper by the bottle than on draught. Buying bottled drinks in supermarkets, you may be asked for empties in return.

Some genuine Scotch whisky brands are bottled in Brazil; they are very popular because of the high price of Scotch imported in bottle; Teacher's is the most highly regarded brand. Locally made gin, vermouth and campari are very good. The local firewater, *aguardente* (known as *cachaça* or *pinga*), made from sugar-cane, is cheap and wholesome, but visitors should seek local advice on the best brands; São Francisco, Praianinha, Maria Fulô, '51' and Pitu are rec makes. Mixed with fruit juices of various sorts, sugar and crushed ice, *cachaça* becomes the principal element in a *batida*, a delicious and powerful drink; the commonest is a lime batida or *batida de limão*; a variant of this is the *caipirinha*, a *cachaça* with several slices of lime in it, a caipiroska is made with vodka. *Cachaça* with Coca-Cola is a *cuba*, while rum with Coca-Cola is a *cuba libre*.

Getting around

Air transport

Internal air services are highly developed. A monthly magazine, *Guia Aeronáutico*, gives all the timetables and fares. All national airlines – Varig, Vasp and Transbrasil – offer excellent service on their internal flights. Between 2200 and 0600, internal flights cost 30% less than daytime flights. (Ask for the *vôo coruja*.) On some flights couples can fly for the price of one-and-a-half. A 30% discount is offered on flights booked 7 days or more in advance; there are also seasonal and other discounts. It is well worth enquiring in detail. Double check all bookings (reconfirm frequently) and information given by ground staff as economic cutbacks have led to pressure on ground service (but not to flight service).

Varig, Vasp and Transbrasil offer a 21-day Airpass, which costs US$440 (Varig has more flights and destinations). The Airpass must be purchased outside Brazil by holders of an international flight ticket to Brazil, no journey may be repeated, it may not be used on the Rio-São Paulo shuttle. The airpass is limited to 5 coupons, to which a maximum of 4 may be added (purchased outside Brazil) at US$100 each. No sector may be repeated in the same direction; the itinerary may be changed in Brazil. Make sure you have two copies of the Airpass invoice when you arrive in Brazil; otherwise you will have to select all your flights when you book the first one. Remember that domestic airport tax has to be paid at each departure. Hotels in the Tropical and Othon chains, and others, offer discounts of 10% to Airpass travellers; check with Varig, who have a hotel reservation service. Promotions on certain destinations offer a free flight, hotel room, etc; enquire when buying the airpass. We have been told that it is advisable for users of the Airpasses to book all their intended flights in advance or on arrival in Brazil, especially around summer holiday and Carnival time. Converting the voucher can take some hours, do not plan an onward flight immediately, check at terminals that the air pass is still registered, faulty cancellations have been reported. Cost and restrictions on the Airpass are subject to change. An alternative is to buy an internal flight ticket which includes several stops.

The small feeder airlines have been formed into scheduled domestic airlines, and now operate Brazilian-built *Bandeirante* 16-seater prop-jets into virtually every city and town with any semblance of an airstrip. **NB** Internal flights often have many stops and are therefore quite slow. Foreigners are not allowed to travel on Brazilian air force flights. Most airports have left-luggage lockers (US$1 for 24 hrs). Seats are often unallocated on internal flights: board in good time.

Land Transport

● **Train**

Trains are appreciably slower than buses. There are services in the state of São Paulo and between Campo Grande and Corumbá. There is a service between Porto Alegre and the Argentine frontier at Uruguaiana. More and more services are being withdrawn; travellers are normally advised to go by air or road. Timekeeping is good on the whole.

● **Motoring**

Most main roads between principal cities are now paved. Some are narrow and therefore dangerous. Many are in poor condition.

Any foreigner with a passport can purchase a Brazilian car and travel outside Brazil if it is fully paid for or if permission is obtained from the financing body in Brazil. Foreigners do not need the CPF tax document (needed by Brazilians—you only have to say you are a tourist) to purchase a car, and the official purchase receipt is accepted as proof of ownership. Sunday papers carry car advertisements and there are second-hand car markets on Sun mornings in most cities—but don't buy an alcohol-driven car if you propose to drive outside Brazil. It is essential to have an external intake filter fitted, or dust can rapidly destroy an engine. VW Combi vans are cheapest in Brazil where they are made, they are equivalent to the pre-1979 model in Europe. Be sure to travel with a car manual and good quality tools, a VW dealer will advise. There are VW garages throughout the continent, but parts (German or Latin American) are not always interchangeable. In the main, though, there should be no problems with large components (eg gears). If a lot of time is to be spent on dirt roads, the Ford Chevrolet pickup is more robust. A letter in Spanish from your consul explaining your aims and that you will return the vehicle to Brazil can make life much easier at borders and checkpoints. Brazilian cars may not meet safety regulations in N America and Europe, but they can be easily resold in Brazil.

● **Bus**

There is no lack of transport between the principal cities of Brazil, mostly by road. Ask for window seats (*janela*), or odd numbers if you want the view. Brazilian bus services have a top speed limit of 80 kph (buses are supposed to have governors fitted). They are extremely comfortable (many have reclining seats), stopping fairly frequently (every 2-4 hrs) for snacks; the cleanliness of these *postos* is generally good, though may be less so in the poorer regions. Standards of comfort on buses and in *postos* vary from line to line, which can be important on long journeys. Buses only stop at official stops. Take something to drink on buses in the N. The bus terminals are usually outside the city centres and offer fair facilities in the way of snack bars, lavatories, left-luggage stores ('guarda volume'), local bus services and information centres. *Leito* buses ply at night between the main centres, offering reclining seats with foot and leg rests, toilets, and sometimes in-board refreshments, at double the normal fare. For journeys over 100 km, most buses have chemical toilets. Air conditioning can make *leito* buses cold at night, so take a blanket or sweater (and plenty of toilet paper); on some services blankets are supplied. Some companies have hostess service. Bus stations for interstate services and other long-distance routes are usually called *rodoviárias*. Buy bus tickets at bus stations (most now take credit cards), not from travel agents who add on surcharges. Reliable bus information is hard to come by, other than from companies themselves. It is not easy to sell back unused bus tickets. Some bus companies have introduced a system enabling passengers to purchase return tickets at point of departure, rather than individual tickets for each leg. Buses usually arrive and depart in very good time; you cannot assume departure will be delayed. In the SE and S a *Horário de Ônibus* is available at *rodoviárias* (not available for N or NE). Many town buses have turnstiles which can be inconvenient if you are carrying a large pack. Urban buses normally serve local airports.

● **Car hire**

It is essential to have a credit card in order to hire in Brazil; four agencies accept TCs, dollars cash may not be accepted, but *reais* cash may qualify for a discount. Check insurance carefully, as few policies give full cover, unless purchased outside Brazil. Avis is found only in the major cities and have only a time-and-mileage tariff. National, ie Localiza, is represented in many places, often through licencees; connected with InterRent/Europcar in Europe, will accept credit cards from Inter-Rent/Europcar and offers unlimited mileage if booked in advance from Europe on a fixed US$ rate. Compare prices of renting from abroad and in Brazil. If you intend to hire a car for a long time, buying and re-selling a

vehicle within Brazil may be a reasonable alternative (see above).

NB It is virtually impossible to buy premium grades of petrol/gasoline anywhere. With alcohol fuel you need about 50% more alcohol than regular gasoline. Larger cars have a small extra tank for 'gasolina' to get the engine started; remember to keep this topped up. Fuel is only 85 octane (owing to high methanol content), so be prepared for bad consumption and poor performance and starting difficulties in non-Brazilian cars in winter. Diesel fuel is cheap and a diesel engine may provide fewer maintenance problems for the motoring tourist. Service stations are free to open when they like. Very few open during Carnival week.

● **Hitchhiking**

Information on hitch-hiking (*carona* in Portuguese) suggests that it is difficult everywhere; drivers are reluctant to give lifts because passengers are their responsibility. Try at the highway-police check points on the main roads (but make sure your documents are in order) or at the service stations (*postos*).

● **Taxis**

Taxi meters measure distance/cost in 'taxi units' (UT), not *reais*. Taxi units are converted into *reais* with a price list. In many cities this list is taped to the side window of the taxi; in others the driver has the list. Be sure that the list is not a photocopy. The original either has colours inset on the black and white, or, if black and white only, is laminated. Whether or not you see the conversion sheet, you can work out the price by knowing the *real* value of each UT. This rate will either be posted near the meter in the front window, or written on the bottom of the conversion sheet. The rate varies from city to city, but is consistent within each city. At the outset, make sure the meter is cleared and shows tariff 1, except 2300-0600, Sun, and in Dec when 2 is permitted. Check that the meter is working, if not, fix price in advance. The radio taxi service costs about 50% more but cheating is less likely. Taxis have a 40% surcharge on Sun. If you are seriously cheated note the number of the taxi and insist on a signed bill, threatening to go to the police; it can work.

Communications

● **Language**

The language is Portuguese. Efforts to speak it are greatly appreciated and for the low-budget traveller, Portuguese is essential. If you cannot lay your tongue to 'the language of the angels', apologize for not being able to speak Portuguese and try Spanish, but note that the differences in the spoken languages are very much greater than appears likely from the printed page and you may well not be understood: you will certainly have difficulty in understanding the answers.

One important point of spelling is that words ending in "i" and "u" are accented on the last syllable, though (unlike Spanish) no accent is used there. This is especially important in place names: Parati, Iguaçu. Note also that 'meia' (half) is frequently used for number 6. Audioforum, Microworld House, 2-6 Foscote Mews, London W9 2HH, T 0171-266 2202 does cassette courses on Brazilian Portuguese (US$195/£155 and US$245/£165), orders by mail or phone with credit card no. There are Brazilian tutors in most cities (in London, see *Time Out* for advertisements).

● **Newspapers**
The main **Rio** papers are *Jornal do Brasil, O Globo,* and *Jornal do Commércio.* **São Paulo** Morning: *O Estado de São Paulo, Folha de São Paulo, Gazeta Mercantil* and *Diário de São Paulo.* Evening: *A Gazeta, Diário do Noite, Ultima Hora.*

● **Postal services**
Postal charges are high: the overseas rate for letters, aerogrammes and postcards is the same (we do not publish rates owing to the rapid changes caused by inflation). Air mail takes 4 to 6 days to or from Britain or the US; surface mail takes some 4 weeks. 'Caixa Postal' addresses should be used when possible. Postes restantes usually only hold letters for 30 days. You can buy charge collected stamps, Compraventa de Francamento (CF) for letters only, to be paid on delivery. The Post Office sells cardboard boxes for sending packages internally and abroad (they must be submitted open); pay by the kilo; you must fill in a list of contents; string, but not tape, provided. Franked and registered (insured) letters are normally secure, but check that the amount franked is what you have paid, or the item will not arrive. Aerogrammes are most reliable. It may be easier to avoid queues and obtain higher denomination stamps by buying at the philatelic desk at the main post office. Poste Restante for Amex customers efficiently dealt with by the Amex agents in most large towns. Courier services such as DHL, Federal Express and UPS (rec) are useful, but note that they may not necessarily operate under those names.

● **Radio**
English-language radio broadcasts daily at 15290 kHz, 19m Short Wave (Rádio Bras, Caixa Postal 04/0340, DF-70 323 Brasília).

● **Telephone services**
There is a trunk-dialling system linking all parts: for the codes see DDD in the text, or look in the telephone directory. There are telephone boxes at airports, post offices, railway stations, hotels, most bars, restaurants and cafés, and in the main cities there are telephone kiosks *for local calls only* in the shape of large orange shells, for which *fichas* can be bought from bars, cafés and newsvendors; in Rio they are known as *orelhões* (big ears). Phone cards are being introduced, available from telephone offices. Public boxes for intercity calls are blue; there are boxes within main telephone offices for international calls, make sure you buy a card worth at least 100 international units. Collect calls within Brazil can be made from any telephone – dial 9, followed by the number, and announce your name and city. Local calls from a private phone are normally free. International phone calls are priced on normal and cheaper rates, depending on time of day. Check with the local phone company. Peak rate to Europe is US$4/minute, to USA US$3. There is a 40% tax added to the cost of all telephonic and telegraphic communications, which makes international service extremely dear. Local phone calls and telegrams, though, are quite cheap. **NB** Brazil is now linked to North America, Japan and most of Europe by trunk dialling (DDI). Codes are listed in the telephone directories. Embratel operates Home Country Direct, available from hotels, private phones or blue public phones to the following countries (prefix all numbers with 00080); Argentina 54, Canada 21, Chile 56, France 33, Italy 39, Japan 81, Holland 31, Portugal 35, Sweden 46, UK 44, USA 10 (AT&T), 12 (MCI), 16 (Sprint), Uruguay 59. For collect calls from phone boxes (in Portuguese: 'a cobrar'), dial 107 and ask for the *telefonista internacional.* No collect calls available to New Zealand, though to Australia is OK. To use the telephone office, tell the operator which city or country you wish to call, go to the booth whose number you are given; make your call and you will be billed on exit. Not all offices accept credit cards.

Cable facilities are available at all post offices, and the main ones have public telex booths. Post offices are recognizable by the ECT (Empresa de Correios e Telégrafos) signs outside. Make sure that hotels equipped by telex facilities can send outgoing telexes; some are unable to do so, or only at certain times of day.

Fax services operate in main post offices in major cities, or from private lines. In the latter case the international fax rates are as for phone calls; from the post office the rates are US$14 to Europe and US$12 to the USA.

Holidays and festivals

National holidays are 1 Jan (New Year); 3 days up to and including Ash Wed (Carnival); 21 Apr (Tiradentes); 1 May (Labour Day); Corpus Christi (Jun); 7 Sep (Independence Day); 12 Oct, Nossa Senhora Aparecida; 2 Nov (All Souls' Day); 15 Nov (Day of the Republic); and 25 Dec (Christmas). The local holidays in the main cities are given in the text. Four religious or traditional holidays (Good Fri must be one; other usual days: 1 Nov, All Saints Day; 24 Dec, Christmas Eve) must be fixed by the municipalities. Other holidays are usually celebrated on the Mon prior to the date.

Further reading

British visitors are referred to 'Hints to Exporters: Brazil', obtainable from DTI Export Publications, PO Box 55, Stratford-upon-Avon, Warwickshire, CV37 9GE.

Acknowledgements

This chapter has been updated by Cherry Austin, to whom we are most grateful. We are also grateful to Conor O'Sullivan of Tatu Tours for revising the Bahia section; Eddie Edmundson (British Council, Recife); Tony Burnett (Caruaru); and Joel Souza (Cuiabá). We thank also the following travellers: Daniel Aeberhard (Slough, UK) an excellent contribution, Pierre-Yves Atlan (Paris, France), Tomer Bachar (Herzlya, Israel), Louise Bach (Vestbjerg) and Tine Tang Kleif (Aarhus, Denmark), James Bailey (Croydon, UK), Isabelle Barbier and Astrid Käser (Neuchatel, Switzerland), James Beeker (Wabasha, USA), Phil and Jenny Blackman (Bath, UK), Erich Blum (Rümlang, Switzerland), Colette and Tanya Botha (South Africa), Ruth Brandt (Israel), Evan B Campbell (USA), Ludovic Challeat (Lamastre, France), Derek Chan (San Franciso, USA), Carmelita Chávez (Vista, USA), Bernard Cloutier (Montreal, Canada), Judith Stanton and Mark Collins (London, UK) a helpful up-date, Simon Denyer (London, UK), Gerd Dörner (Darmstadt, Germany), Gunter Dörr (Höopfingen, Germany), Jae and Gerry Duffy (Elizabeth, USA), Jean-Philippe Dumont (Quebec, Canada), Jayne Dyer and Nicholas Hird (Bexhill-on-Sea, UK), Ludwig Eberle (Olching, Munich, Germany), Urs Eggli (Zurich, Switzerland), Yang-Un Eiman (San Francisco, USA), Jakob Engström and Richard Björlin (Brussels, Belgium), Elisabeth Estorilio (Curtiba, Brazil), Holger Fabig (Bonn, Germany), Bernard Fison (on board the yacht ODI), Mark Foley (London, UK), Gisa Gericke (Wetzlar), Nicole Hofmann (Weisbaden), and Tanja Wirth (Flörsheim, Germany), Fred Van Gestel (Deurne, Belgium), Loukas Grafakos (Papagou, Greece), Steven Grigg (London, UK), Sylvia Grisez (Warren, USA), Steve Grist (Santiago, Chile), Erez Guilatt (Jerusalem, Israel), Ora Hartman (Holon, Israel), Dan Heilborn and Maya Schneider (Haifa and Tel-Aviv, Israel), Hannah Holm (Rochester, USA), Lars Hortin (älvsjö, Sweden), Richard Jennen (USA), Erik Jennische (Uppsala, Sweden), Patrick J Paludan (Valby) and Erik Hassenkamm (Valby and Skanderborg, Denmark), Hanne Stadsgaard Jensen (Aarhus, Denmark), S and Othmer KamerGüntert (Uetikon, Switzerland), Hielke Keikke (Breda, Holland), Herbert Klein (Ubajara, Brazil), Eugene and Marlizé de Klerk (South Africa), Kato and Mark Kostrzewa (Mountain View, USA), Peter Krauer (Arisdorf, Switzerland), Al Landry (Parksville, Canada), William Leonard (Alameda, USA), Dr Jeffrey Lesser (Connecticut, USA), M Leufgens and M Jollands (Alsdorf, Germany), Riika Levoranta (Vammala) and Vesa Lampiner (Möjärvi, Finland), Valerie Levrier (London, UK), Teresa Lloyd (Bristol, UK), Robert E Manley (Cincinnati, USA) a very helpful letter, Georgina Matthews (London, UK), Helmut Matuly (Frankfurt, Germany), Cinnamon McGhee (San Francisco, USA), Elke Meinert (Essen, Germany), Oliver Meiser (Pfullingen, Germany) a very detailed contribution Michel Blanes and Kristine Meyer (Copenhagen, Denmark), Alison and David Moran (Oxford, UK), Christiane Moser (Frieburg, Germany), Martijn Mugge (Enschede, The Netherlands), Mark Muhlbacher (Lucerne, Switzerland) for many letters Dominick Nisbett (Sudbury, UK), Trond Nygard-Sture (Ulset, Norway), Holly O'Callagnan (Durazno, Uruguay), Stephen Oiver (Manuas, Brazil), Paul Olai-Olssen (Oslo, Norway), Jonathan Paisner (London, UK), Wilbrod Parent (Quebec, Canada), Per Petersen (Copenhagen, Denmark), Luzia Portmann and Rolf Studer (Lucerne, Switzerland), Margorie Powell (Cambridge, UK) extensive contribution, G Pratt (Encinitas, USA), Dr-Ing Wolfgang Reick (Mulheim-Ruhr, Germany), Mariane Ritte (Igna, Switzerland), Barbara and Peter Roniger (Suberg, Switzerland), Erika Rosch (Siegen, Germany), Bruce Rumage (Pawleys Island, USA), Bruno Schmid (Zurich, Switzerland), Detlev Schrodi (Freiburg, Germany), Inge and Machiel de Schutter (Cologne, Germany), Ludwig Seitz (Dossenheim, Germany), Hedi Shmueli (Ein-

Hod, Israel), Ken Simons (London, UK), Mark and Kit Smit (Hilversum, The Netherlands), Marlies Stabel (Beusichem, The Netherlands), J R Stourton (Cirencester, UK), Jan Stüve (Karlsruhe, Germany), S Nielsen and Hellmuth-Chr Stuven (Copenhagen, Denmark), Ingve Taksdal (Oslo, Norway), Ilay Tamari (Ramat-Hasharon, Israel), Anne Helene Tangen (Norway), Mette and Lotte Thillerup (Hesselager, Denmark), Inger Tingsgard (Abyhoj, Denmark), Arnaud Troost and Fenna den Hartog (Rotterdam, The Netherlands), Origem -& Destino Origem Rejane Reis (Brazil), Eduardo Macedo (Brazil), Jim Turner (Antigua, Guatemala), Bas van Tussenbroek (Aracati, Brazil), Jürgen Urbanski (Dusseldorf,Germany), Gonzalo Valdés (Santiago, Chile), Eric and Ingrid Van den Broeck (Leuven, Belgium), Margot Verhagen and Carel van der Velden (Holland), Jan Vervoort (Mechelen, Belgium), Infanger Vinzenz (Erstfeld, Switzerland) an extensive contribution Dre Visscher (Tilburg, The Netherlands), Adrian Vogel (Lucerne, Switzerland), Thomas Vogel (Passau, Germany), Clive Walker (San José, Costa Rica), Pamela Weekes (Chifley, Australia), Dr Volker Weinmann (Blumenau, Brazil), Jacqui White (Salta, Argentina), Ollo Wiemann (Trier, Germany), Natalie and Derek Windsor (Durham, UK), Rowan Wood (Aspen, USA), Ann Wright (London, UK), Elke Wurtz (Frankfurt, Germany), Piet Ysabie (Mecheler, Belgium), Arne Ystehede (Aas, Norway), and Dan Zoëga-Nielsene (Ribe, Denmark).

CHILE

INTRODUCTION

CHILE is smaller than all other South American republics save Ecuador, Paraguay, Uruguay and the Guianas. Its territory is a ribbon of land lying between the Andes and the Pacific, 4,329 km long and, on average, no more than 180 km wide. Of this width the Andes and a coastal range of highland take up from a third to a half. There are wide variations of soil and vast differences of climate; these are reflected in the density of population and the occupations of its people.

In the extreme N Chile has a frontier with Peru running 10 km N of the railway from the port of Arica to the Bolivian capital of La Paz. Its eastern frontier—with Bolivia in the far N and with Argentina for the rest of its length—is along the crest of the Andes, gradually diminishing in height from Santiago southwards to the southern seas, where the Strait of Magellan lies, giving access to the Atlantic. Chile's western and southern coastline is 4,500 km long.

Down the whole length, between the Andes and the coastal range, there runs a valley depression, though it is less well defined in the N. North of Santiago transverse ranges join the two massifs and impede transport, but for 1,044 km S of the capital the great longitudinal valley stretches as far as Puerto Montt. South

CHILE

1 The Far North
2 South of Antofagasta to Illapel
3 The Heartland & Santiago
4 South through the Central Valley
5 Forest Chile: Temuco to Puerto Montt
6 Chiloe
7 Archipelagic Chile
8 Chilean Patagonia

of Puerto Montt the sea has broken through the coastal range and drowned the valley, and there is a bewildering assortment of archipelagos and channels.

From N to S the country falls into five sharply contrasted zones:

A The first 1,250 km from the Peruvian frontier to Copiapó is a rainless hot desert of brown hills and plains devoid of vegetation, with a few oases. Here lie nitrate deposits and several copper mines.

B From Copiapó to Illapel (600 km) is semi-desert; there is a slight winter rainfall, but great tracts of land are without vegetation most of the year. Valley bottoms are here cultivated under irrigation.

C From Illapel to Concepción is Chile's heartland, where the vast majority of its people live. Here there is abundant rainfall in the winter, but the summers are perfectly dry. Great farms and vineyards cover the country, which is exceptionally beautiful.

D The fourth zone, between Concepción and Puerto Montt, is a country of lakes and rivers, with heavy rainfall through much of the year. Cleared and cultivated land alternates with mountains and primeval forests.

E The fifth zone, from Puerto Montt to Cape Horn, stretches for 1,600 km. This is archipelagic Chile, a sparsely populated region of wild forests and mountains, glaciers, fjords, islands and channels. Rainfall is torrential, and the climate cold and stormy. There are no rail links S of Puerto Montt, but the Carretera Austral now provides almost unbroken road access for more than 1,000 km S of that city. Chilean Patagonia is in the extreme S of this zone. To make the most of this trip, read Darwin's *Voyage of the Beagle* beforehand.

A subdivision of the fifth zone is Atlantic Chile—that part which lies along the Magellan Strait to the E of the Andes, including the Chilean part of Tierra del Fuego island.

There is a cluster of population here raising sheep and mining coal. Large offshore oilfields have now been discovered in the far S, and the area is developing rapidly.

History A century before the Spanish conquest the Incas moved S into Chile from Peru, crossing the desert from oasis to oasis at the foot of the Andes. They reached the heartland and conquered it, but were unable to take the forest S of the Río Maule; there the fierce Mapuches (Araucanians) held them. In 1537 Diego de Almagro, at the head of a hundred Spaniards and some thousands of Indians, took the Inca road from Peru S to Salta and across the Andes. Many of the Indians perished, but the heartland was reached; bitterly disappointed at not finding gold they returned to Peru. The next *conquistador*, who took the desert road, was Pedro de Valdivia; he reached the heartland in 1541 and founded Santiago on 12 Feb. Reinforced by fresh colonists from Peru and Spain, Valdivia pushed S into Mapuche land and founded a number of forts. Valdivia was killed in 1553 and the Mapuches soon overran all the Spanish settlements apart from the town to which he had given his name. The Mapuches were fearsome opponents; they soon mastered the use of horses and were effective guerrilla fighters. In 1598 they began a general offensive which destroyed most of the Spanish settlements S of the Río Biobío. The Spanish were forced to create a special frontier army and to build a string of forts along the Biobío. For the rest of the colonial period the Spanish presence S of the river was limited to the coastal fortress of Valdivia and the Island of Chiloé.

In addition to constant wars against the Mapuches, the colonial period was marked by internal dissensions, particularly between the landowners and the priests who strongly objected to a system of Indian serfdom. There were also natural disasters in the form of earthquakes and tidal waves which wiped out cities again and again. From the end of the 16th century British and French pirates frequented the coasts. For most of the colonial period, Chile formed part of the Viceroyalty of Peru; it was controlled from Lima, and trade was allowed only with Peru. This led to uncontrolled smuggling and by 1715 there were 40 French vessels trading illegally along the coast. It was not till 1778 that trading was allowed between Chile and Spain.

In 1810 a group of Chilean patriots, including Bernardo O'Higgins— the illegitimate son of a Sligo-born Viceroy of Peru, Ambrosio O'Higgins, and a Chilean mother—revolted against Spain. This revolt led to seven years of war against the occupying troops of Spain—Lord Cochrane was in charge of the insurrectionist navy—and in 1817 General José de San Martín crossed the Andes with an army from Argentina and helped to gain a decisive victory. O'Higgins became the first head of state: under him the first constitution of 1818 was drafted. But there was one thing which was dangerous to touch in Chile: the interests of the dominant landed aristocracy, and O'Higgins's liberal policies offended them, leading to his downfall in 1823. A period of anarchy followed, but in 1830 conservative forces led by Diego Portales restored order and introduced the authoritarian constitution of 1833. Under this charter, for almost a century, the country was ruled by a small oligarchy of landowners.

After 1879 Chilean territory was enlarged in both N and S. During the 1870s disputes arose with Boliva and Peru over the northern deserts which were rich in nitrates. Although most of the nitrates lay in Bolivia and Peru, much of the mining was carried out by Anglo-Chilean companies. In the ensuing war (War of the Pacific, 1879-1883) Chile defeated Peru and Bolivia, mainly because her stronger navy gave her control over the sea and even allowed her to land troops in Peru and occupy Lima. Chile gained the Bolivian coastal region as well as the Peruvian provinces of Tarapacá and Arica and for the next 40 years drew great wealth from the nitrate fields.

In the S settlers began pushing across the Río Biobío in the 1860s, encouraged by government settlement schemes and helped by technological developments

including repeating rifles, telegraph, railways and barbed wire. At the end of the War of the Pacific the large Chilean army was sent to subdue the Mapuches who were confined to ever-diminishing tribal lands. The territory was then settled by immigrants – particularly Germans – and by former peasants who had fought in the North.

The rule of the Right was challenged by the liberal regime of President Arturo Alessandri in 1920. Acute economic distress in 1924, linked to the replacement of Chilean nitrates with artificial fertilizers produced more cheaply in Europe, led to army intervention and some reforms were achieved. The inequalities in Chilean society grew ever sharper, despite the maintenance of political democracy, and gave rise to powerful socialist and communist parties. President Eduardo Frei's policy of 'revolution in freedom' (1964-70) was the first concerted attempt at overall radical reform, but it raised hopes it could not satisfy. In 1970 a marxist coalition assumed office under Dr Salvador Allende; the frantic pace of change under his regime polarized the country into Left- and Right-wing camps. Gradually increasing social and economic chaos formed the background for Allende's deposition by the army and his death on 11 September 1973. After the overthrow of President Allende, Chile was ruled by a military president, Gen Augusto Pinochet Ugarte, and a 4 man junta with absolute powers. In its early years particularly, the regime suppressed internal opposition by methods which were widely condemned. Despite economic prosperity and efforts to make the regime more popular, Pinochet's bid for a further eight years as president after 1989 was rejected by the electorate in a plebiscite in 1988.

As a result, presidential and congressional elections were held in 1989. A Christian Democrat, Patricio Aylwin Azócar, the candidate of the Coalition of Parties for Democracy (CPD, or Concertación), was elected President and took office in March 1990 in a peaceful transfer of power. The CPD won 71 of the 120 seats in the Chamber of Deputies, but only 22 seats in the 47-seat Senate, its majority wiped out by eight seats held by Pinochet appointees, who could block constitutional reform. Gen Pinochet remained as Army Commander although other armed forces chiefs were replaced. The new Congress set about revising many of the military's laws on civil liberties and the economy. In 1991 the National Commission for Truth and Reconciliation published a report with details of those who were killed under the military regime, but opposition by the armed forces prevented mass human rights trials. In Dec 1993 presidential elections resulted in the election of the Christian Democrat Eduardo Frei, son of the earlier president, but in congressional elections held at the same time the Concertación failed to achieve the required two-thirds majority in Congress to reform the constitution, replace heads of the armed forces and end the system of designated senators. Soon after taking office, Frei became embroiled in the tensions between the military and the elected government. After a special investigation sentenced 15 former police officers to terms of between 18 years and life in prison for human rights abuse in the 1980s, Frei indicated that police chief Rodolfo Stange should resign. Stange, supported by Pinochet, publicly refused to do so, but later took leave pending a military court decision on whether he should face charges.

The People There is less racial diversity in Chile than in most Latin American countries. Over 90% of the population is *mestizo*. There has been much less immigration than in Argentina and Brazil. The German, French, Italian and Swiss immigrants came mostly after 1846 as small farmers in the forest zone S of the Biobío. Between 1880 and 1900 gold-seeking Serbs and Croats settled in the far S, and the British took up sheep farming and commerce in the same region. The influence throughout Chile of the immigrants is out of proportion to their numbers: their signature on the land is seen, for instance, in the German appearance of Valdivia, Puerto Montt, Puerto Varas, Frutillar and Osorno.

There is disagreement over the number of indigenous people in Chile. The Mapuche nation, 95% of whom live in the forest land around Temuco, between the Biobío and Toltén rivers, is put at 1 million by Survival International, but much less by other, including official, statistics. There are also 15,000 Aymara in the northern Chilean Andes and 2,000 Rapa Nui on Easter Island. A political party, the Party for Land and Identity, unites many Indian groupings, and legislation is proposed to restore indigenous people's rights.

The population is far from evenly distributed: Middle Chile (from Copiapó to Concepción), 18% of the country's area, contains 77% of the total population. The Metropolitan Region of Santiago contains, on its own, about 39% of the whole population.

The rate of population growth per annum is slightly under the average for Latin America. The birth rate is highest in the cities, particularly in the forest zone. The death rate is highest in the cities. Infant mortality is highest in the rural areas.

Since the 1960s heavy migration from the land has led to rapid urbanization. Housing in the cities has not kept pace with this increased population; many Chileans live in slum areas called *callampas* (mushrooms) on the outskirts of Santiago and around the factories.

The Economy Chile is endowed with a diversified environment, allowing the production of all temperate and Mediterranean products. Agriculture, however, supplies only about 8.3% of gdp and contributes about 12% of merchandise exports. Traditional crops, such as cereals, pulse, potatoes and industrial crops (sugarbeet, sunflowerseed and rapeseed) account for about 37% of the value added of agriculture, and vegetables for about 25%. The area showing fastest growth is fresh fruit which now earns about US$1bn a year in export revenues. Another area of expansion is forestry. More than 80% of the 1.6 million ha of cultivated forest is planted with insignis radiata pine, a species which in Chile grows faster than in other countries. Chile is the most important fishing nation in Latin America and the largest producer of fishmeal in the world. Industrial consumption absorbs about 93% of the fish catch; fresh fish and fish products contribute about 10% of merchandise exports. An important area of expansion is salmon farming.

The dominant sector of the economy is mining. Chile has been the world's largest producer of copper since 1982 (production in 1994 was 2.23 million tonnes) and also produces molybdenum, iron ore, manganese, lead, gold, silver, zinc, sulphur and nitrates. Chile has a quarter of the world's known molybdenum ore reserves (3 million tonnes), and is believed to have around 40% of the world's lithium reserves. Mineral ores, most of which is copper, account for half of total export revenue. Fluctuations in world prices for minerals therefore have a great impact on the balance of payments.

Chile is fortunate in possessing reserves of oil, natural gas and coal, and abundant hydroelectricity potential. Almost all the country's hydrocarbon reserves are in the extreme S, on Tierra del Fuego, in the Strait of Magellan and the province of Magallanes. Proven oil reserves are 300 million barrels (1994) and petroleum production at 5 million barrels accounts for 11% of domestic consumption. Natural gas production (1.2 billion cu metres, 1993) accounts for 30% of local needs, while coal production (1.7 million tonnes, 1992) supplies 62% of consumption. Hydropower provides 66% of electricity generation.

Manufacturing has been particularly vulnerable to changes in economic policy: nationalization during the Allende administration in the early 1970s; recession brought about by anti-inflationary policies in the mid-1970s; increased foreign competition resulting from trade liberalization in the early 1980s, and greater exports together with import substitution in the mid-1980s. The contribution of manufacturing to total gdp fell from 25% in 1970 to 18% in 1992 although its share of exports rose. Activity is mostly food processing, metalworking, textiles and fish processing.

The policies used to bring inflation down from over 500% at the end of 1973 to less than 10% by end-1981 resulted in fiscal balance and an overvalued currency.

Freeing the exchange rate in 1982 caused renewed inflation, this was restricted by tight monetary control and a lower public sector borrowing requirement which caused a severe recession and contraction in gdp. IMF help was sought following a sharp fall in international commercial lending in 1982 and a decline in Chile's terms of trade. In the 1980s, Chile successfully negotiated several debt refinancing packages and reduced its foreign debt through schemes which converted debt into equity in Chilean companies. Renewed growth in debt in the 1990s, was offset by rising exports, which meant that the debt: exports ratio fell.

The Government continued to follow anti-inflationary policies, accompanied by structural adjustment and reform. Privatization continued, including that of the pension system, which had the effect of massively increasing domestic savings as a percentage of gdp. Rising investor confidence brought eleven consecutive years of economic growth and the Chile model was held up as an example for other debtor countries to adapt to their own needs. Unemployment began to fall, real wages and productivity both rose, which, together with higher social spending, led to a reduction in the number of people living in poverty from 40% to 28% of the population in 1989-93.

At the end of 1994, foreign exchange reserves stood at US$13.5bn; a trade surplus of US$700mn was due in part to higher than expected earnings from copper and wood pulp; foreign investment reached a record US$4.26bn; the stock exchange continued to perform well and domestic savings to expand, and inflation was cut to 8.9%. With the backing of 1994's positive results, Chile was strongly placed to start negotiations in 1995 to enter the North American Free Trade Association.

Constitution and Government The pre-1973 constitution was replaced, after a plebiscite, on 11 March 1981. This new constitution provided for an eight-year non-renewable term for the President of the Republic (although the first elected president was to serve only 4 years), a bicameral Congress and an independent

Chile : fact file

Geographic

Land area	756,626 sq km
forested	11.8%
pastures	18.1%
cultivated	5.8%

Demographic

Population (1994)	13,805,000
annual growth rate (1989-94)	1.6%
urban	85.3%
rural	14.7%
density	18.2 per sq km
Religious affiliation	
Roman Catholic	80.7%
Birth rate per 1,000 (1991)	21.3
	(world av 26.0)

Education and Health

Life expectancy at birth,	
male	68.5 years
female	75.6 years
Infant mortality rate	
per 1,000 live births (1991)	14.6
Physicians (1992)	1 per 889 persons
Hospital beds	1 per 312 persons
Calorie intake as %	
of FAO requirement	102%
Population age 25 and over	
with no formal schooling	9.4%
Literate males (over 15)	93.5%
Literate females (over 15)	93.2%

Economic

GNP (1992 market prices)	
	US$37,064mn
GNP per capita	US$2,730
Public external debt (1992)	
	US$9,578mn
Tourism receipts (1992)	US$706mn
Inflation	
(annual av 1986-91)	18.5%
Radio	1 per 3.2 persons
Television	1 per 6.8 persons
Telephone	1 per 9.0 persons

Employment

Population economically active (1991)	
	4,794,100
Unemployment rate	5.3%
% of labour force in	
agriculture	17.1
mining	1.9
manufacturing	16.0
construction	6.8
Military forces	91,800

Source *Encyclopaedia Britannica*

judiciary and central bank. In Feb 1994, the Congress cut the presidential term of office from 8 years to 6. Congress is composed of a 120-seat Chamber of Deputies and a 48-seat Senate, eight of whose members are nominated, rather than elected. In 1974 the country was divided into 13 regions, replacing the old system of 25 provinces. The first local elections since 1971 took place in Apr 1993; the Concertación coalition won majorities on 12 of 13 regional councils.

Railways There are 4,470 km of line, of which most are state owned. Most of the privately owned 2,130 km of line are in the desert N, where the northern terminal is Iquique. The main gauge on the Valparaíso and southern lines is 5 ft 6 in (1.676m). Passenger services N of the Valparaíso area have ceased except for the international routes to La Paz.

Three international railways link Chile with its neighbours. There are two railways to Bolivia: between Arica and La Paz (448 km), and from Antofagasta via Calama to La Paz. Between Chile and Argentina there is only one line now in operation, between Antofagasta and Salta, in the Argentine NW. There is no international passenger service on this line. The Ferrocarriles del Estado publish an annual *Guía Turistica*, available in various languages from the larger stations.

Roads About one-half of the 79,593 km of roads can be used the year round, though a large proportion of them is unimproved and about 11,145 km are paved. The region round the capital and the Central Valley are the best served.

The Pan-American (Longitudinal) Highway, from Arica through Santiago to Puerto Montt and recently extended by the Carretera Austral beyond Cochrane to within 30 km of its terminus, is vital to the Chilean economy and is paved to Puerto Montt. From Llay-Llay a branch goes to Los Andes and over La Cumbre (Uspallata) pass to Argentina. Another main international road in the Lake District goes from Osorno across the Puyehue pass to Argentina. Note that any of the passes across the Andes to Argentina can be blocked by snow from Apr onwards.

Chile has an extensive system of protected natural areas, 7 million ha in all. The areas, managed by Conaf (the Corporación Nacional Forestal), are divided into 30 national parks, 36 forest reserves and 10 natural monuments. Of the 76 areas, 46 have public access, and details of the majority are given in the text.

Music and Dance At the very heart of Chilean music is the Cueca, a courting dance for couples, both of whom make great play with a handkerchief waved aloft in the right hand. The man's knees are slightly bent and his body arches back. It is lively and vigorous, seen to best advantage when performed by a Huaso wearing spurs. Guitar and harp are the accompanying instruments, while handclapping and shouts of encouragement add to the atmosphere. The dance has a common origin with the Argentine Zamba and Peruvian Marinera via the early 19th century Zamacueca, in turn descended from the Spanish Fandango. For singing only is the Tonada, with its variants the Glosa, Parabienes, Romance, Villancico (Christmas carol) and Esquinazo (serenade) and the Canto a lo Poeta, which can be in the form of a Contrapunto or Controversia, a musical duel. Among the most celebrated groups are Los Huasos Quincheros, Silvia Infante with Los Condores and the Conjunto Millaray. Famous folk singers in this genre are the Parra Family from Chillán, Hector Pávez and Margot Loyola. In the N of the country the music is Amerindian and closely related to that of Bolivia. Groups called 'Bailes' dance the Huayño, Taquirari, Cachimbo or Rueda at carnival and other festivities and precolumbian rites like the Cauzulor and Talatur. Instruments are largely wind and percussion, including *zampoñas* (pan pipes), *lichiguayos*, *pututos* (conch shells) and *clarines*. There are some notable religious festivals that attract large crowds of pilgrims and include numerous groups of costumed dancers. The most outstanding of these festivals are those of the Virgen de La Tirana near Iquique, San Pedro de Atacama, the Virgen de la Candelaria of Copiapó and the Virgen de Andacollo.

In the S the Mapuche nation, the once greatly feared and admired 'Araucanos', who kept the Spaniards and Republicans at bay for four hundred years, have their own songs, dance-songs and magic and collective dances, accompanied by wind instruments like the great long *trutruca* horn, the shorter *pifilka* and the *kultrun* drum. Further S still, the island of Chiloé, which remained in the hands of pro-Spanish loyalists after the rest of the country had become independent, has its own unique musical expression. Wakes and other religious social occasions include collective singing, while the recreational dances, all of Spanish origin, such as the Vals, Pavo, Pericona and Nave have a heavier and less syncopated beat than in central Chile. Accompanying instruments here are the *rabel* (fiddle), guitar and accordion.

NB Throughout this chapter, beside population figures, the local dialling code, DDD, is given.

NB also See **Cost of Living** in Information for Visitors for Stop Press on price rises in dollar terms.

THE FAR NORTH (1)

A desert zone with various oases: the main cities are Arica, Iquique, Antofagasta and Calama; the main points of interest the Andean landscapes of the Lauca National Park and San Pedro de Atacama (which also has remains of Atacameño culture), the Pacific coastline and mineral workings old and new.

The 1,255 km between Arica and Copiapó (in our Section 2) are desert without vegetation, with little or no rain. The inhospitable shore is a pink cliff face rising to a height of from 600 to 900m. At the bottom of the cliff are built the towns, some of considerable size. The far from pacific Pacific often makes it difficult to load and unload ships. The nitrate fields exploited in this area lie in the depression between Pisagua and Taltal. Copper, too is mined in the Cordillera; there are two large mines, at Chuquicamata, near Calama, and at El Salvador, inland from Chañaral.

Life in the area is artificial. Water has to be piped for hundreds of km to the cities and the nitrate fields from the Cordillera; all food and even all building materials have to be brought in from elsewhere.

There is some difference of climate between the coast and the interior. The coast is humid and cloudy; in the interior the skies are clear. The temperatures on the coast are fairly uniform; in the interior there is often a great difference in the temperature between day and night; the winter nights are often as cold as -10°C, with a cruel wind. Drivers must beware of high winds and blowing sand N of Copiapó.

Arica is Chile's most northerly city, 19 km S of the Peruvian border (pop 174,064; phone code – DDD 058). It is built at the foot of the Morro headland, fringed by sand dunes. The Andes can be clearly seen from the anchorage. The Morro, with a good view from the park on top (10 mins walk by footpath from the southern end of Colón), was the scene of a great victory by Chile over Peru in the War of the Pacific on 7 June 1880. Arica is an important port and route-centre. A 448 km railway runs E to the Bolivian capital La Paz: about half the legal trade of Bolivia passes along this line. An oil pipeline also runs to La Paz. The completion of the international highway to the Bolivian frontier at Tambo Quemado has added to the city's importance. A 63 km railway runs N to Tacna in Peru. Regrettably there are indications that Arica is also becoming a key link in the international drugs trade. There are large fishmeal plants and a car assembly factory. Air pollution at night can be bad. There is no rain, winter or summer. The average, daytime winter temperature is 19°C, and the average summer temperature 24°C. It is frequented for sea-bathing by Bolivians as well as the locals.

At the foot of the Morro is the Plaza Colón with the cathedral of **San Marcos**, built in iron by Eiffel. Though small it is beautifully proportioned and attractively painted. It was brought to Arica from Ilo (Peru) in the 19th century, before Peru lost Arica to Chile, as an emergency measure after a tidal wave swept over Arica and destroyed all its churches. Eiffel also designed the nearby **customs house** which is now the Casa de la Cultura. (Open Mon-Sat 1000-1300, 1700-2000.) Just N of the Aduana is the La Paz railway station; outside is an old steam locomotive (made in Germany in 1924) once used on this line. In the station is a memorial to John Roberts Jones, builder of the Arica portion of the railway, and a small museum (key at booking office).

Museums At San Miguel, 13 km E of Arica in the Azapa Valley, is the **Museo Arqueológico** of the University of Tarapacá, the most important in northern Chile (see under Excursions). **Museo Histórico y de Armas**, on summit of the Morro, containing weapons and uniforms from the War of the Pacific.

Local Festival Fiestas for the Virgen de las Peñas at the Santuario de Livircar in the Azapa Valley (see below) are held on the first Sun in Oct and a lesser festival on 7-9 Dec (on 8 Dec the festival moves to Arica). Take a bus from Av Chacabuco and Vicuña Mackenna, then walk 12 km from where it stops to the sanctuary. The Dec festival is not particularly outstanding but it takes place in a part of the valley not normally accessible. **NB** The arrival of Africans during the colonial period has created an Afro-Chilean folklore here.

Hotels NB In this area, *pensión* means restaurant, not hostel. **L3** *Arica*, San Martín 599, T 254540, best, price depends on season, good value, good and reasonable restaurant, other services expensive, about 2 km along shore (buses No 7, 8, frequent), liable to strong smell from fishmeal plants, tennis court, pool, lava beach (not safe for swimming), but there are two public beaches nearby; **L3** *El Paso*, bungalow style, pleasant gardens, swimming pool, Av Gral Velásquez, 1109, T 231965, with breakfast, good food; **A2** *Azapa*, attractive grounds but several km from beaches and centre: Sánchez 660, Azapa, T 222612, but cheaper cabins available, restaurant; **A1** *Saint Georgette*, Camino a Azapa 3221, T 221914, F 223830, 5 star, pool, tennis court, restaurant, bar; **A2** *Central*, 21 de Mayo 425 (T 252575), central, nicely decorated; **A3** *Amadís de Gaula*, Prat 588, T/F 232994, central, modern; **A3** *Los Hibiscos*, Capitán Avalos 2041, T 221914, motel-style; **L3** *San Marcos*, Sotomayor 367 (T 232970, F 254815), clean, helpful, restaurant, parking; **A3** *Savona*, Yungay 380, T 232319, comfortable, quiet, highly rec; **B** *Diego de Almagro*, Sotomayor 490, T 224444, F 221248, helpful, clean, comfortable, rec, will store luggage; **C** *Lynch*, Lynch 589, T 231581, D without bath, pleasant but poor beds, clean, rec, parking; **C** *Residencial América*, Sotomayor 430, T 254148, clean, friendly, central; **C** *El Refugio*, Km 1½ Valle de Azapa, T 227545; **D** *Jardín del Sol*, Sotomayor 848, T 232795; **D** *Hostal 18 de Septiembre*, 18 de Septiembre 524,

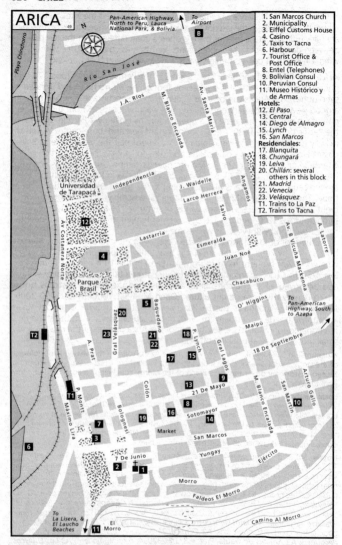

ARICA

Pan-American Highway, North to Peru, Lauca National Park, & Bolivia.

To Airport

1. San Marcos Church
2. Municipality
3. Eiffel Customs House
4. Casino
5. Taxis to Tacna
6. Harbour
7. Tourist Office & Post Office
8. Entel (Telephones)
9. Bolivian Consul
10. Peruvian Consul
11. Museo Histórico y de Armas

Hotels:
12. El Paso
13. Central
14. Diego de Almagro
15. Lynch
16. San Marcos

Residenciales:
17. Blanquita
18. Chungará
19. Leiva
20. Chillán: several others in this block
21. Madrid
22. Venecia
23. Velásquez
T1. Trains to La Paz
T2. Trains to Tacna

Playa Chinchorro

Río San José

J. A. Ríos

Independencia

Universidad de Tarapacá

J. Waidelle

Larco Herrera

Salvo

Lastarria

Esmeralda

Parque Brasil

Juan Noé

Chacabuco

O' Higgins

To Pan-American Highway, South to Azapa

Baquedano

Maipú

18 De Septiembre

21 De Mayo

Sotomayor

San Marcos

Yungay

Morro

Faldeos El Morro

To La Lisera, & El Laucho Beaches

El Morro

Camino Al Morro

7 De Junio

Market

Bolognesi

Colón

Gral Velásquez

A. Prat

P. Montt

Máximo Lira

Av. Cottanera Norte

Gral Velásquez

M. Blanco Encalada

Av. Santa María

Angamos

Av. B. Vicuña Mackenna

A. Latorre

P. Lynch

Gral Lagos

M. Blanco Encalada

San Martín

Arturo Gallo

Ejército

T 251727, clean, hot water, breakfast; **D** *Residencial Caracas*, Sotomayor 867, T 253688, cheap, clean, hot water, TV, breakfast; **D** *Residencial Blanquita*, Maipú 472, T 232064, clean, hot water; **D** *Residencial Chungará*, Lynch 675 (T 231677), with bath, clean, hot water am only, small rooms; **D** *Residencial Las Condes*, Vicuña Mackenna 628, T 251583, helpful, hot water, rec; **D** *Residencial Puerta del Sol*, 21 de Mayo 480, T 252597, 12 rm, shared bath, meals available, clean, quiet, excellent service; **D** *Pensión Donoso*, Baquedano y Maipú, downstairs with bath, gloomy, **E** upstairs without bath, bright; **E** *Res Las Vegas 120*,

Baquedano 120, T 231355, basic, friendly, dark rooms, hot water, safe, central; **E** *Residencial Leiva*, Av Colón 347, T 232008, without bath, French spoken, cooking facilities, motorcycle parking with difficulty; **E** *Casa Blanca*, Gral Lagos 557, modern, clean, rec; **D** *Residencial Ecuador*, Juan Noé 989, T 251573, clean, noisy, helpful, meals available; **E** *Residencial Española*, Bolognesi 340, T 231703, central, clean, basic, quiet; **E** *Residencial Madrid*, Baquedano 685 (T 231479), without bath, clean, good value but poor beds, reductions for IYHA cards; **E** *Residencial Maipú*, Maipú 479, T 252157, basic, clean, hot water, safe; **E** *Hostal Raissa*, San Martín 281, T 251070, without bath, with breakfast. On Velásquez are: **E** *Residencial Valencia*, No 719, T 253479, hot water, cooking and laundry facilties; **E** *Residencial Velásquez*, No 669 (T 231949), central, basic, friendly; **E** *Res Chillán*, No 749, T 251677, safe, friendly, clean, good value; **E** *Residential Ine'sa*, No 725, T 231609, comfortable, breakfast available, kitchen, laundry, good; **D** *Residencial Venecia*, Baquedano 739, T 252877, spotless, hot water, small rooms, rec; **E** *La Posada*, 21 de Mayo 186, small rooms, good beds, central, without bath; **E** *Residencial Tropical*, Gral Lagos 649, friendly, basic; **E** *Residencial Muñoz*, Lynch 565, friendly; **E** *Residencial El Sur*, Maipú 516, very clean, small rooms, hot water, basic; **E** *Casa de Huéspedes Nilda*, Raul del Canto 946, Población Juan Noé, T 227993, family-run, safe, 1 block from bus terminal, rec. Sra Leony Vidiella, Gonzálo Cerda 1030, close to bus station, **E** pp with breakfast, shared bath, cooking facilities, clean, safe, tepid water, English spoken. In Jan-Feb the municipality supplies cheap basic accommodation, ask at the tourist office.

Camping *Gallinazos*, at Villa Frontera, 15 km N, T 232373, and at the *Residencial El Refugio* (see above).

Restaurants *Acuario*, Máximo Lira, Terminal Pesquero, good food and atmosphere, expensive; *El Rey del Marisco*, Maipú y Colón, good seafood, pricey, rec; *Maracuyá*, San Martín 0321, good seafood, splendid location on the coast, pricey; plenty of seafood lunch places in the market; *La Lancha*, Blanco Encalada 470, good value, fish, highly rec; *Los Aleros del 21*, 21 de Mayo 736, very good food and service; *La Genovesa*, Lagos 436, excellent food and service; *Don Floro*, V MacKenna y Chacabuco, good steaks; *Snack Suceso Inn*, 18 de Septiembre 250, good set meal and coffee; *La Jaula*, 18 de Septiembre 293, good cheap lunches; *Casanova*, Baquedano 397, excellent but not cheap; *Yuri*, Maipú 500, good food and service, cheap, rec; *Bavaria*, Colón 613, expensive but good, with delicatessen and expresso coffee, repeatedly rec; *Govinda*, Bolognesi 430, vegetarian, good value lunches, repeatedly rec; *Carpaccio*, Velásquez 510, restaurant and bar, live music from 2330 Wed-Sat; *El Tambo*, in Poblado Artesanal, Huelles 2025, good lunches, folk music and dancing on Sun. Several Chinese restaurants (*chifas*) including *Si Lom*, Sotomayor 593, good; *Chin Huang Tao*, Lynch 317, very good. Several good places for cheap breakfasts and good set meals on Baquedano 700 block. *Casino de Bomberos*, Colón 357, at fire station, good value *almuerzo*; *Schop*, 18 de Septiembre 240, good, cheap sandwiches.

Exchange Many money changers on 21 de Mayo and its junction with Colón. **Fincard** (Mastercard), 21 de Mayo 252, Mon-Fri 0900-1400, 1600-1730, only pesos given, at varying rates. *Casas de Cambio*: **Inter-Santiago** and **Cambio Fides**, Shopping Centre del Pacífico, Diego Portales 840; **Daniel Concha**, Chacabuco 300; **Sol y Mar**, Colón 610; **Tacora**, 21 de Mayo 171, good rates for cash; **Yanulaque**, 21 de Mayo 175, which stay open until 2000 but close all day Sun. Most large hotels also change cash. Rates for TCs are generally poor.

Consulates **United Kingdom**, the only one in Chile N of Valparaíso and Instituto Chileno—Británico de Cultura (library open Mon-Fri 0900-1200, 1600-2100), Baquedano 351, T 231960, Casilla 653. **Brazil**, Las Margaritas 717, Pob Prat, T 231142; **Bolivia**, 21 de Mayo 575, T 231030; **Denmark**, 21 de Mayo 399, T 231399; **Peru**, San Martín 220, T 231020; **Germany**, 21 de Mayo 639, T 231551, open 0900-1300; **Spain**, Av Santa María 2660, T 224655; **Italy**, San Martín y Chacabuco, T 229195; **Norway**, 21 de Mayo 399, T 231298. Instituto Cultural Chileno Norteamericano, San Marcos 581. Instituto Chileno-Alemán de Cultura, 21 de Mayo 816.

Theatre Teatro Municipal de Arica, Baquedano 234, new, wide variety of theatrical and musical events, exhibitions, rec.

Discotheques 3 S of town along front, also *Sunset* and *Swing*, both 3$\frac{1}{2}$ km out of town in the Valle de Azapa, 2300-0430 weekends (taxi US$3).

Cinemas *Colón*, 7 de Junio 190, T 231165; *Cine Arte Universidad*, University Campus, T 251813.

Health Dr Juan Noé, 18 de Septiembre 1000, T 231331 (T 232242 for urgent cases). **Dentist** Juan Horta Becerra, 18 de Septiembre 1154, T 252497, speaks English; Rodrigo Belmar Castillo, 18 de Septiembre 1051, T 252047.

Laundry *Lavandería La Moderna*, 18 de Septiembre 457, 24 hr service, good; *Americana*, Lynch 260, T 231808.

Post Office Prat 375. To send parcels abroad, contents must be shown to Aduana (under main post office) on weekdays, except Tues, between 1500 and 1700. Your parcel will be wrapped, cheaply, but take your own carton.

Telephones Entel-Chile, Baquedano 388, open 0900-2200. CTC, Colón 430 and at 21 de Mayo 211; VTR Telecommunications, 21 de Mayo 477, telex, fax, telegrams.

Shopping *Poblado Artesanal*, Plaza Las Gredas, Hualles 2025 (take bus 2, 3 or 7): local 2, expensive but especially good for musical instruments; Mercado Central, Sotomayor, between Colón and Baquedano, mornings only. *Feria Turística Dominical*, Sun market, W end of Chacabuco extending N on Av Costanera Norte, good prices for llama sweaters. Fruit, vegetable and old clothes market at Terminal Agropecuario at edge of town; take bus marked 'Terminal Agro'. Arica, as a duty free zone, is an important centre for cheapish electronic goods for Bolivian and Peruvian shoppers. Supermarket at San Martín y 18 de Septiembre.

Sports Golf, 18 hole course in Valle de Azapa, open daily except Mon. Tennis: Club de Tenis Centenario, Av España 2640, open daily.

Bathing Olympic pool in Parque Centenario, Tues-Sun, US$0.50; take No 5A bus from 18 de Septiembre. The best beach for swimming is Playa Chinchorro, N of town. Buses 7 and 8 run to beaches S of town – the first two beaches, La Lisera and El Laucho, are both small and mainly for sunbathing. Playa Brava is popular for sunbathing but not swimming (dangerous currents). Strong currents also at Playa Las Machas which is popular with surfers. Playa Corazones, 15 km to S (no buses, take taxi or hitch), rec, not for swimming but picnics and fishing.

Travel Agencies *Turismo Payachatas*, Prat 484, T 251514, poor reports; *Jurasi*, Bolognesi 360 A, T 251696, will hold mail, helpful, good city tour; *Kijo Tour*, Bolognesi 359, T 232245; *Huasquitur*, Sotomayor 470, T 223875, helpful, English spoken, will cater for individual itineraries, rec for flights; *Vicuña Tour*, 18 de Septiembre 399, oficina 215, T 253773, F 252404, rec; *Globo Tour*, 21 de Mayo 260, T 232807, F 231085, very helpful; *Aricamundi*, Prat 358, T 252263, F 251797, for airline tickets; *Parinacota Expediciones*, Lynch 731, T 251309; *Transtours*, Bolognesi 421, T 253927, F 251675; and many others. Agencies charge similar prices for tours: Lauca National Park US$20, Valle de Azapa US$12, city tour US$10.

Tourist Office Sernatur, Prat 305, 2nd floor; open Mon-Fri 0830-1300, 1500-1830, T 232101. Very helpful, English spoken, good map; Kiosk on 21 de Mayo between Colón and Baquedano, open Mon-Fri, 0830-1300, 1500-1900. **Conaf**, Valle de Azapa 3444 (Km 1.5), T 231559, closed weekends (bus 8 to Azapa intersection).

Local Transport Local buses run from Calle Maipú, US$0.25. Collective taxis on fixed routes within city limit, US$0.30 pp (US$0.50 pp after 2000).

Car Hire Hertz, *Hotel El Paso*, Gral Velázquez 1109, T 231487, cheaper; **Budget**, 21 de Mayo 650, T 252978, rec; **Klasse**, Velásquez 762, Loc 12, T 254498; **American Rent a Car**, Gral Lagos 559, T 252234; 4WD and antifreeze are essential for Lauca National Park.

Automóvil Club de Chile Chacabuco 469, T 237780.

Car Service Shell, Panamericana Norte 3456; Esso, Av Diego Portales 2462; Autocentro, Azola 2999, T 241241. **Car insurance** At Dirección de Tránsito; may insist on car inspection.

Air Services Airport 18 km N of city at Chacalluta, T 222831. Taxi to town US$9, shared taxi US$4-5 pp from Lynch y 21 de Mayo. Airline offices: LanChile, 7 de Junio 148, T 224738; Ladeco, 21 de Mayo 443, T 252021; Lloyd Aéreo Boliviano, P Lynch 298, T 251472; AeroPerú, 7 de Junio 148, T 232852; National, 21 de Mayo 627, T 253447, F 251283. Flights: to **La Paz**, LanChile (daily except Sun) and LAB (Tues, Thur, Sat); to **Santiago**, Ladeco (daily via Iquique and Antofagasta), LanChile (at least twice a day via Iquique or Antofagasta) and National (daily via Iquique and Antofagasta). Book well in advance. To **Lima**, AeroPerú and others from Tacna (Peru), enquire at travel agencies in Arica.

Rail To La Paz (Bolivia): direct ferrobus services operated by Enfe (Bolivian Railways) leave Arica Tues and Sat at 0930, 12 hrs, US$52 (in clean US$ bills only) including breakfast, lunch and drinks up to lunchtime (extra food and drinks sold). Book well in advance in Jan-Mar, tickets from the station at 21 de Mayo 51, T 232844. Baggage allowance, 20 kg excluding hand luggage (luggage is weighed and searched at the station). Additional trains may run in Jan-Mar. Local trains run to the frontier towns of Visviri (Chile) and Charaña (Bolivia) every other Tues (every Tues in Jan-Mar) at 2300, 9 hrs, US$12 1st class, US$7 2nd class; from Charaña a service runs to Viacha, 32 km from La Paz, US$3.05 pullman. Check details in advance. (For train and bus connections from Charaña to La Paz see under La Paz, Bolivia.) On all journeys, take plenty of warm clothing; long delays, particularly at the frontier are common. Search for fruit, vegetables and dairy products at Arica station for passengers arriving from Bolivia.

The line from Arica skirts the coast for 10 km and passes into the Lluta Valley, whose vegetation is in striking contrast with the barrenness of the surrounding hills. From Km 70 there is a sharp rise of 2,241m in 42 km through a series of tunnels. At Puquíos station, Km 112, the plateau is reached at 4,168m. The line continues through Coronel Alcérreca (Km 140) and Villa Industrial (Km 165), before reaching its highest point at General Lagos (4,247m). In the distance can be seen the snowcapped heights of Tacora, Putre, Sajama, and their fellows. The frontier station of Visviri is at Km 205, with a customs house. Beyond, the train enters Bolivia and the station of Charaña. In summer a tourist train runs from Arica to Coronel Alcérreca and back on Sun, 0800, returning to Arica 2100.

To **Tacna** (Peru): regular passenger services connect with Tacna, US$1.60, 2½ hrs, from the station at Máximo Lira 889, T 231115. In Tacna there is a customs check at the station but no immigration facilities.

Buses Terminal at Av Portales y Santa María, T 241390, bus or colectivo No 8 or 18 (US$0.15, or US$0.30), taxi to centre US$1.25 (terminal tax US$0.25). All luggage is carefully searched for fruit prior to boarding. All long-distance buses are modern, clean and air-conditioned, but ask carefully what meals are included. Intercity bus company offices at bus terminal. Local services: Flota Paco (La Paloma), Germán Riesco 2071 (bus 7 from centre); Humire, P Montt 662, T 231891; Martínez, P Montt 620, T 232265; Bus Lluta, Chacabuco y V Mackenna. To **Antofagasta**, US$16, 10 hrs. Some services to destinations between Antofagasta and the capital involve a change in Antofagasta. To **Calama** and **Chuquicamata**, 10 hrs, US$16, several companies, all between 2000 and 2200, Tramaca rec. To **Iquique**, frequent, US$6, 4½ hrs. Collective taxis also run to Iquique; several companies, all with offices in the bus terminal. To **Santiago**, 28 hrs, a number of companies, eg Carmelita, Ramos Cholele, Fénix and Flota Barrios (not rec), US$28-43 (San Andrés not rec); also *salón cama* services, run by Fichtur, Flota Barrios, Fénix and others, US$50. Tramaca are rec. Most serve meals and the more expensive, the more luxurious; student discounts available. To **La Serena**, 18 hrs, Fénix, US$25, and other companies. To **Viña del Mar** and **Valparaíso**, US$35-40; also *salón cama* service, Fénix, US$50, including poor meals.

International Buses To **La Paz**, Bolivia, Bolivia Litoral, Chacabuco 454, T 251267, Mon and Thur, 2400, 20 hrs, US$20, no food; service via border towns of Chungará (Chile) and Tambo Quemado (Bolivia, very cold at border—take blanket/sleeping bag, food, water and sense of humour), subject to cancellation in wet season. Also Geminis, Wed 2400, US$32, some food, 20 hrs, more comfortable via Huara and Challapata (Bolivia). To **Salta** (Argentina), Geminis, Tues 2130, US$50, connects at Calama next day with Antofagasta-Salta service. Computerized booking ensures seat reservation; passport details required, book in advance.

To **Tacna**: colectivo taxis run to and from Tacna from bus terminal and bus company offices for about US$4 pp one way and take about an hour for the trip (drivers take care of all the paperwork—it's a normally a fairly uncomplicated border crossing). Four companies: Chile Lintur, Baquedano 796, T 232048; Chasquitur, Chacabuco 320, T 231376; San Marcos, Noé 321, T 252528; Colectivo San Remo, Chacabuco 350, T 251925. Bus costs US$2 and leaves from the bus terminal, as does Taxibus, 2 hourly, US$4. For Arequipa it is best to go to Tacna and catch an onward bus there. Money-changing at frontier, but reported better rates in Tacna.

NB Remember that between Oct and Mar, Chilean time is 1 hr later than Bolivian, 2 hrs later than Peruvian time Oct to Feb or Mar, varies annually (1 hr vis-à-vis Peru the rest of the year).

Motorists At the Chile-Peru frontier drivers are required to file a form, *Relaciones de Pasajeros*, giving details of passengers, obtained from a stationery store in Tacna, or at the border in a booth near Customs. You must also present the original registration document for your car from its country of registration. The first checkpoints outside Arica on the road to Santiago also require the *Relaciones de Pasajeros* from drivers. If you can't buy the form, details on a piece of paper will suffice or you can get them at service stations. The form is *not* required when travelling S of Antofagasta. Since the outbreak of cholera in the region, border controls are very strict (all opened jars and cans will be destroyed).

By road to Bolivia There are 2 routes: 1) Via Chungará (Chile) and Tambo Quemado (Bolivia). This, the most widely used route, begins by heading N from Arica on the Pan-American Highway (Route 5) for 12 km before turning right (E towards the cordillera) on Route 11 towards Chungará via Putre and Lauca National Park (see below). This road is now paved as far as the border. Check with Automóvil Club for any special documents which may be required, depending on the registration of your vehicle (eg a temporary export certificate for Chile, or a temporary import certificate for Bolivia); also double check with the Bolivian consulate in Arica before travelling. For the Bolivian portion of this route and the journey in reverse, see **By Road to the Coast of Chile** in Bolivia, section 1.

2) Via Visviri (Chile) and (Charaña) Bolivia, following the La Paz-Arica railway line. This route should not be attempted in wet weather. Although there are no through bus services, it is possible to travel from Arica to Visviri by colectivo (US$10), take a jeep across the border and then catch a bus between Charaña and La Paz, US$8.50, 7 hrs. There appear to be no regular buses Arica-Visviri.

Excursions To the Azapa valley, E of Arica, by yellow colectivo from P Lynch y Maipú, US$1. At Km 13 is the Museo Arqueológico de San Miguel, part of the University of Tarapacá, containing an important collection of mummies from the Chinchorro culture, reputed to be the oldest collection in the world, as well as sections on Andean weaving, basketwork and ceramics (open Mon-Fri 0830-1300, 1500-1800, Sat, Sun, and holidays 1200-1800, Latin Americans US$1, others US$3, worth a visit). In the forecourt of the museum are several boulders with precolumbian petroglyphs. On the road between Arica and San Miguel images of humans and llamas ('stone mosaics') can be seen to the S of the road. On the opposite side of the valley at San Lorenzo are the ruins of a *pukará* (Inca fortress) dating from the 12th century.

To the Lluta valley, N of Arica along Route 11, bus from MacKenna y Chacabuco, 4 a day: At Km 14 and Km 16 there are ancient images of llamas and humans on the hillside. The road continues through the Lauca National Park and on to Bolivia.

Before proceeding further, we offer the following advice on travelling off the beaten track in this region, kindly supplied by vulcanologist Dr Lyndsey O'Callaghan. In all of the mountain areas of the N of Chile, it is important to note that weather and road conditions are very variable. The *carabineros* and military are very active trying to control the borders with Bolivia and Argentina, so they know about the conditions and are quite willing to tell, but only if asked. Some frontier areas are closed to visitors.

In many villages it is possible to rent a small unfurnished house, if you are planning to stay for a while. Ask for the schoolmaster (or mayor in larger villages). It may also be possible to stay in the small clinics (eg at Socaire or Chiu-Chiu).

If you plan to stay in the mountains for any length of time, it is advisable to take small gifts such as tea, sugar, coffee, salad oil, flour for the locals. If you are driving, a few litres of fuel is also a welcome gift, while carrying a tow-rope will enable you to assist other drivers. It is often possible to get people to bake bread etc for you every day, but you need to supply flour, yeast and salt. If you are planning to do much cooking, then a good pressure cooker is indispensible (remember water boils at only 90°C at these altitudes). You may also get problems with kerosene stoves; petrol ones, though rather dangerous, are much more reliable.

Moreover, anyone travelling in this region should consult the *Turistel Norte* guide (see **Tourist Information** in Information for Visitors).

Lauca National Park A visit to the Parque Nacional Lauca, 176 km E of Arica stretching to the frontier with Bolivia, is highly recommended. Situated at over 3,200m (beware of soroche unless you are coming from Bolivia), the park covers 137,883 ha and includes numerous snowy volcanoes including 10 peaks of over 6,000m, two large lakes (Cotacotani and Chungará) and lava fields at Cotacotani. The park contains over 130 species of birds including a wide variety of waterfowl as well as vicuña, puma and vizcacha. It is administered by Conaf. During the rainy season (Jan and Feb) roads in the park may be impassable although the main Arica-La Paz road is now paved as far as the frontier; check in advance with Conaf in Arica from whom further information and map may be obtained. On the way, at Km 90 there is a pre-Inca *pukará* (fortress) and a few km further there is an Inca *tambo* (inn). At the entrance to the park is **Putre**, 3,500m, a scenic village with a church dating from 1670 and surrounded by terracing dating from Inca times. Putre is a good base for acclimatization. At **Parinacota**, 4,392m, at the foot of the Payachatas volcano, there is an interesting 17th century church—rebuilt 1789—with frescoes and the skulls of past priests. Local residents knit alpaca sweaters, US$26 approx; weavings of wildlife scenes also available. Weavings are sold from a tin shed with an orange roof opposite the church. From here an unpaved road runs N to the Bolivian frontier at Visviri. 20 km SE of Parinacota is **Lago Chungará**, one of the highest lakes in the world at 4,600m, is a must for its views of the Parinacota, Sajama and Guallatire volcanoes and for its varied wildlife. From here it is about 10 km to the Bolivian frontier at Tambo Quemado. About 30 km S of Parinacota by road is Choquelimpie, the highest gold mine in the world, with an attractive colonial church in the precinct.

Services At Putre **A3** *Hostería Las Vicuñas*, T 224466, 3 classes of room, bungalow-type; does not accept TCs, US$ cash or credit cards. *Restaurant Oasis*, several rooms to let, F pp, basic, no showers, cheap, restaurant itself closed early 1994. Rooms are also let by families. At Chucuyo, a village 30 km E of Putre, there are two shops/restaurants, one of which has 2 rooms to let, a good place to stock up on food. In Parinacota cheap accommodation at the local school, G pp, rec. There are three Conaf refuges in the park, but check in advance with Conaf in Arica that they are open: at **Parincota** (there is supposed to be oxygen for those suffering from soroche, but it is often not available), at **Lake Chungará**, and at Chucuyo; all have cooking facilities, US$10 pp, sleeping bag essential, take your own food, candles and matches. Camping US$4 tent. Advance booking rec. On arrival in Putre you are supposed to register with Conaf. Maps of the park (unreliable) are available from Conaf in Arica and from the tourist office.

Transport Buses go daily from Arica to the gold mines in the park at 0600 and 1400. Flota Paco buses (known as La Paloma) leave Arica for Putre daily at 0700, 3½ hrs, US$5, returning 1300; Martínez buses leave Arica at 0930 and 2130 Tues and Fri for Putre, Parinacota and Charaña; Bolivia Litoral bus from Arica to La Paz also runs along this route (charges full Arica-La Paz fare).

One-day tours are offered by most travel agencies in Arica (addresses above), daily in season, according to demand at other times, US$20 pp with breakfast and light lunch; but some find the minibuses cramped and dusty. You spend all day in the bus and, if not acclimatized, you will suffer from soroche. Take food, water, sunglasses and warm clothing. You can leave the tour and continue on another day as long as you ensure that the company will collect you when you want. For 5 or more, the most economical proposition is to hire a vehicle; fuel is available in Putre, ask at the shop, take at least one spare fuel can.

Trucks on the Arica-La Pax road often give lifts. For trucks from Arica the best place to wait is at the Poconchile control point, 37 km from Arica. Most trucks for Bolivia pass Parinacota between 0600-0900. The frontier opens at 0800 and most trucks from La Paz pass Parinacota 1000-1100. You can also hitch from Parinacota to Visviri, further N on the Bolivian border on Tues with lorries going to meet the train; catch the train to La Paz at Charaña.

South of Lauca is the beautiful **Reserva Nacional Las Vicuñas** at 4,300 to 5,600m, which is suitable for 'adventure tourism', to use Conaf's phrase. Be prepared for cold, skin burns from sun and wind, etc; there is no public transport. A high clearance vehicle is essential and, in the summer wet season, 4WD: take extra fuel. Administration is at **Guallatiri**, reached by turning off the Arica-La Paz road onto the A147 2 km after Las Cuevas, where there is also a Conaf office. Open Mar-Nov. The same road leads into the **Monumento Natural Salar de Surire** (4,200m), which is open for the same months and for which the same conditions apply. Administration is in **Surire**, 7 hrs from Arica. This can be reached by getting a ride in a borax truck; these run every day between Jul and Nov from Zapahuira (a road junction between Bolivia and Arica). At Surire there is a Conaf *refugio* (8 beds, very clean, solar heating).

South from Arica The Pan-American Highway runs across the Atacama desert at an altitude of around 1,000m, with several steep hills which are best tackled in daylight (at night, sea mist, *camanchaca*, can reduce visibility). It is illegal to take fruit S from Arica; all vehicles are searched at Cuya (Km 105); 21 km further on, to the right at Km 131 are the **Geoglifas de Chiza** (sign-posted and easily accessible). At Huara, there is a checkpoint for buses and lorries (Km 234; basic accommodation). A sense of humour is required during fruit searches, especially on night buses.

Service stations between the Peruvian border and Santiago can be found at: Arica, Huara, Iquique, Pozo Almonte, Oficina Vitoria, Tocopilla, Oficina María Elena, Chuquicamata, Calama, Carmen Alto, Antofagasta, La Negra, Agua Verde, Taltal, Chañaral, Caldera, Copiapó, Vallenar, La Serena, Termas de Soco, Los Vilos, and then every 30 km to capital.

Detours off the Pan-American Highway: to **Tignamar** (take a turning E about 20 km S of Arica, 100 km to the village) and **Codpa** (turn E about 70 km S of Arica, 40 km to the village on a good dirt road), both interesting villages. The latter is an agricultural community in a deep gorge with interesting scenery.

At Km 185 S of Arica on the Pan-American Highway there is an interesting British cemetery dating from 1876. 10 km further S at Zapiga there is a cross-roads. One branch leads W for 41 km to the run down nitrate port of **Pisagua**. There is little left of this place, though some of the ruins of the nitrate port are still standing. There are a few quite good fish restaurants in the town and it makes a pleasant stop for a meal. Mass graves dating from just after the 1973 military coup were discovered near here in 1990.

The branch which leads E is much more interesting, though the road is not in very good condition, with deep sand and dust causing problems. After 67 km there is the picturesque village of Camiña where there is a basic hostal. 45 km further on is the Tranque de Caritaya, a dam which supplies water for the coastal towns set in splendid scenery with lots of wildlife and interesting botany (especially *llareta*). Travelling further E along mountain roads (not in very good condition) leads through magnificent volcanic scenery to **Isluga** (120 km from Caritaya) and **Colchane**, 6 km further on the Bolivian frontier. This remote area, the **Parque Nacional Volcán Isluga**, contains some of the best scenery in northern Chile. Conaf wardens are at Enquelga in the Park, but the carabineros at Colchane are more helpful. Isluga has an 18th century Andean walled church and bell tower. Colchane can be reached by Kennybus from Iquique, one a week, returns after 2 hrs. Geminis bus from Iquique to La Paz also passes through Colchane. It is, in theory, possible to drive N from Isluga through the Salar de Surire (see above) via Guallatiri to the Parque Nacional del Lauca, and from there to Bolivia, or via Putre and Poconchile to Arica or Peru.

The best way to return to the Pan-American Highway, if going S, is via the road to the village of Cariquima (35 km S of Isluga), and take the road via the thermal springs at **Chuzmisa** (100 km from Cariquima). It is possible to stay in a basic hotel at Chuzmisa. The water here is bottled and sold throughout northern Chile. Chuzmisa lies about 3 km down a side road, but it is signposted. From Chuzmisa a good dirt (last part paved) road leads to Huara on the Pan-American Highway (80 km) passing on the left, at Km 67, the **Giant of the Atacama**, 86m high, reported to be the largest geoglyph in the world (best viewed from a distance). The round trip from Zapiga to Huara is about 540 km, and fuel is not available between Arica and Huara.

Iquique (pop 140,000; DDD 057), the capital of I Región (Tarapacá) and one of the main northern ports, is 304 km by road S of Arica. The name of the town is derived from the Aymara word *ique-ique*, meaning place of 'rest and tranquillity'. It was founded in the 16th century on a rocky peninsula at the foot of the high Atacama pampa, sheltered by the headlands of Punta Gruesa and Cavancha. The city, which was partly destroyed by earthquake in 1877, became the centre of the nitrate trade after its transfer from Peru to Chile at the end of the War of the Pacific. In the centre of the old town is **Plaza Prat** with a clock tower and bell dating from 1877. On the NE corner of the Plaza is the **Centro Español**, built in Moorish style in 1904; the ground floor is a restaurant, on the upper floors are paintings of scenes from Don Quijote and from Spanish history. On the S side of the Plaza is the **Teatro Municipal**, built in 1890; the façade features 4 women representing the seasons. Three blocks N of the Plaza is the old **Aduana** (customs house) built in 1871; in 1891 it was the scene of an important battle in the Civil War between supporters of President Balmaceda and congressional forces. Part of it is now a **Naval Museum**. Five blocks E along Sotomayor is the Railway Station, now disused, built in 1883. Along Calle Baquedano, which runs S from Plaza Prat, are the attractive former mansions of the 'nitrate barons'. Adorned with columns and balconies, these date from between 1880 and 1903 and were constructed from imported oregon pine. The finest of these is the **Palacio Astoreca**, Baquedano y O'Higgins, built in 1903, subsequently the Intendencia and now a museum.

The main exports are fishmeal, fish oil, canned fish and salt. Sealions and pelicans can be seen from the harbour. There are cruises around the harbour from the passenger pier, US$2.65, 45 mins, minimum 10-15 people.

Museums Museo Naval, Sotomayor y Baquedano, focussing on the Battle of Iquique, 1879 (**see p 693**) open Tues-Sat 0930-1230, 1430-1800, Sun and holidays 1000-1300, entry US$0.50; **Museo Regional**, Baquedano 951, containing an archaeological section tracing the development of prehispanic civilizations in the region and a section devoted to the Nitrate Era

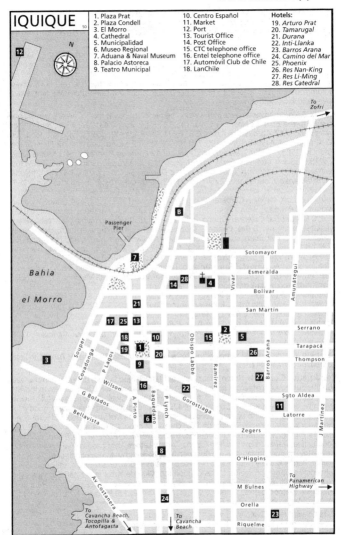

IQUIQUE

1. Plaza Prat
2. Plaza Condell
3. El Morro
4. Cathedral
5. Municipalidad
6. Museo Regional
7. Aduana & Naval Museum
8. Palacio Astoreca
9. Teatro Municipal

10. Centro Español
11. Market
12. Port
13. Tourist Office
14. Post Office
15. CTC telephone office
16. Entel telephone office
17. Automóvil Club de Chile
18. LanChile

Hotels:
19. *Arturo Prat*
20. *Tamarugal*
21. *Durana*
22. *Inti-Llanka*
23. *Barros Arana*
24. *Camino del Mar*
25. *Phoenix*
26. *Res Nan-King*
27. *Res Li-Ming*
28. *Res Catedral*

which includes a model of a nitrate *oficina* and the collection of the nitrate entrepreneur, Santiago Humberstone, open Mon-Fri 0830-1300, 1500-1900, Sat 1030-1300, Sun (in summer) 1030-1300, US$0.50; **Palacio Astoreca**, Baquedano y O'Higgins, fine late 19th century furniture and exhibitions of shells, open Tues-Sun 1000-1300, 1600-2000, entry free.

A short distance N of town along Amunátegui is the Free Zone (Zofri), a giant shopping centre selling mainly imported electronic goods: it is worth a visit (much better value than Punta Arenas), good for cheap camera film (open Mon 1630-2100, Tues-Sun 0930-1300,

1630-2100). Colectivo taxi from the centre US$0.35. Limit on tax free purchases US$650 for foreigners, US$500 for Chileans. All vehicles travelling S from Iquique are searched for duty-free goods at the customs posts at Quillagua on the Pan-American Highway and at Chipana on the coastal road.

Local holiday During the ten days before 16 Jul there is a religious festival at the village of La Tirana (pop 250), 70 km E of Iquique (near Pica, **see p 630**). Over 100 groups dance night and day, starting on 12 Jul, before making their pilgrimage to the church of the Virgen del Carmen. All the dances take place in the main plaza in front of the church; no alcohol is served. Accommodation is impossible to find, other than in organized camp sites (take tent) which have basic toilets and showers.

Hotels Accommodation scarce in the weeks before Christmas as many Chileans visit Iquique to shop in the Zofri. **L3** *Hostería Cavancha*, Los Rieles 250, T 431007, 4 star, S of city, on water's edge; **A2** *Atenas*, Los Rieles 738, T 431100, F 424349, good service and food, rec; **A2** *Arturo Prat*, Av Aníbal Pinto 695, T 411067, F 423309, facing Plaza Prat; **A2** *Playa Brava*, Los Rieles 2503, T 431167, with breakfast, good; **A2** *Primeras Piedras*, street of same name, T 421358, 3 km from city, good food, friendly; **A3** *Tamarugal*, Tarapacá 369, T 424365, central, clean and modern, good restaurant. **B** *Durana*, San Martín 294, T 412511, helpful; **B-C** *Inti-Llanka*, Obispo Labbe 825 (T 412511), helpful; **C** *Barros Arana*, Barros Arana 1330 (T 412840), clean, modern, good value; **C** *Camino del Mar*, Orella 340 (T 420465), restored building, clean, simple; **C** *Hostal Cuneo*, Baquedano 1175, T 428654, modern, clean, pleasant; **C** *Phoenix*, Aníbal Pinto 451 (T 421315) room with bathroom, breakfast, old but nice; **C** *Residencial Catedral*, Obispo Labbe 253, T 423395, clean, friendly, but insecure and breakfast expensive; **D** *Res Condell*, Thompson 684, T 423079, with bath, clean, quiet; **D** *Plaza*, Plaza Prat (bargain), T 414268, clean, friendly; **D** *Res Nan-King*, Thompson 752 (T 423311), clean, good value; **D** *España*, Tarapacá 465, near Plaza Condell, without bath, friendly, warm water, dirty; **D** *Hostal América*, M Rodríguez 550, T/F 427524, near beach, clean, good value; **D** *Hostal San Francisco*, Latorre 990, clean, hot water, noisy; **D** *Res José Luis*, San Martín 601, spacious, clean; **D** *Residencial Marclaud*, Juan Martínez 753, rec, quiet, clean, motor-cycle parking (good cheap restaurant at the corner); **E** *Playa*, Gral Hernán Fuenzalida 938, T 22911, small, friendly; **F** *Res Raluez*, Esmeralda 1008, T 424783, very cheap but very basic with filthy toilets; **E** *Res Araucano*, San Martín 777, T 420211, friendly, cooking facilities, grubby, noisy; **E** *Res Li Ming*, Barros Arana 705 (T 421912), good value; **E** *Res Centro*, Lynch 621, cheap, run down, basic; **E** *Residencial Sol del Norte*, Juan Martínez 852, T 421546, cold water, basic, small rooms. **F** pp *Hospedaje Tarapacá*, Tarapacá 1348, T 426040, clean, friendly, no hot water.

Camping No site but wild camping possible on La Brava beach. Equipment: *Tunset*, in Zofri; *Lombardi*, Serrano 447.

Restaurants *Club de la Unión*, Plaza Prat, roof terrace, good views, good food, not cheap; also, the *Sociedad Protectora de los Empleados de Tarapacá*, Plaza Prat, is open to tourists, reasonable prices. *Centro Español*, Plaza Prat, excellent meals well served in beautiful building, attractive, but expensive; *José Luis*, Serrano 476, good food, pleasant atmosphere, good value *almuerzo*; *Bavaria*, Wilson y Pinto, good but not cheap; *Rapa Nui*, Amunátegui 715, for good, cheap, local food; *Grecia*, Thompson 865, cheap but good; *La Estancia*, Amunátegui 765, good fish, inexpensive; *Balcón*, P Lynch 656, snacks, live music; *Pizzería D'Alfredo*, Vivar 631, good coffee; *Italianissimo*, Edificio España, Vivar y Latorre, very good coffee. Several good, inexpensive seafood restaurants (eg *Bucanero*) can be found on the second floor of the central market, Barros Arana y Latorre; also cafés opp the bus station, on the wharf, sell good, cheap fish lunches. *Bahía*, on seafront, cheap, good fish. *Club de Yates* at the harbour serves very expensive meals. *El Rey del Pescado*, Bulnes y Juan Martínez, very nice local place with good and cheap seafood dishes, 'menú de la casa' a bargain; also *El Pescado Frito*, Bulnes y Juan Martínez, large portions. *Chifa Fu-Wa*, Barros Arana 740, Chinese.

Cafés *Salón de Té Chantilly*, Tarapacá 520; *Café Diana*, Vivar 836; *Pinina*, Ramírez y Tarapacá, juices, ice-cream; *Samoa Grill*, Bolívar 396, good coffee and snacks.

Exchange National banks. **Fincard** (Mastercard), Serrano 372, open Mon-Fri 0900-1400, 1600-1800. Difficult to change TCs in town. Best rates for cheques and cash at *casas de cambio* in the Free Zone.

Consulates Bolivia, Latorre 339, T 421777; Peru, Los Rieles 131, T 431116.

Cinema Cine Tarapacá, Serrano 202, shows foreign films.

Language School Academia de Idiomas del Norte, Ramírez 1345, T 411827, F 429343, Swiss run, Spanish classes, also finds accommodation.

Laundry Bulnes 170, expensive; Obispo Labbé 1446.

Post Office Correo Central, Bolívar 458. **Telecommunications** CTC, Serrano 620, Ramírez 587; Entel, Gorostiaga 287; Diego Portales 840; Telegrams at TelexChile, Lynch y San Martín. **NB** Correos, Telex/Telefax and Entel all have offices in the Plaza de Servicios in the Free Zone.

Bathing Beaches at Cavancha just S of town centre, good, and Huaiquique, reasonable, Nov-Mar. Restaurants at Cavancha. Piscina Godoy, fresh water swimming pool on Av Costanera at Aníbal Pinto and Riquelme, open pm, US$1.

Fishing Equipment: *Ferretería Lonza*, Vivar 738; *Ferretería La Ocasión*, Sargento Aldea 890; fishing for broadbill swordfish, striped marlin, yellowfin tuna, oceanic bonito, Mar till end of Aug.

Travel Agencies *Iquitour*, Tarapacá 465B, Casilla 669, T 422009, no English spoken, tour to Pintados, La Tirana, Humberstone, Pica, etc, 0900-1900, lunch included, a lot of time spent eating and bathing; *Lirima*, Baquedano 823, rec; *Taxitur*, Sgto Aldea 791, 5-6 hr tour to local sites, maximum 5 passengers.

Tourist Information Aníbal Pinto 436, T 411523; open Mon-Fri, 0830-1300, 1500-1800. **Automóvil Club de Chile**, Serrano 154, T 426772.

Car hire Expensive: **Hertz**, Souper 850, T 426316. **Continental**, Thompson 159, T/F 411426; J Reategui, Serrano 1058-A, T 429490/446079, reported as cheapest.

Mechanic Sergio Cortez, *Givet*, Bolívar 684, highly rec for motorcycles. In the Zona Franca there is a wide range of motorcycle tyres.

Air Services Diego Aracena international airport, 35 km S at Chucumata, T 424577. Taxi from outside *Hotel Prat*, Plaza Prat, US$3, T 426184. Airport bus to city centre, US$2. LanChile, Aníbal Pinto 641, T 414378; Ladeco, San Martín 428, T 413038; National, Galería Lynch, Local 1-2, T 427816, F 425158. LanChile, Ladeco and National all fly daily to Arica, Antofagasta and Santiago; to Calama, Ladeco 5 a week, en route to Antofagasta and Santiago.

Buses Terminal at N end of Patricio Lynch (not all buses leave from here); bus company offices are near the market on Sargento Aldea and B Arana. All luggage is searched for duty-free goods before being loaded onto buses. To **Arica**, buses and colectivos, frequent, US$6, 4½ hrs, comfortable in spite of checkpoints. To **Antofagasta**, US$13, overnight only, 8 hrs. To **Calama**, 8 hrs, US$11, Kennybus not rec. To **Tocopilla** along the coastal road, minibuses, several companies, 4 hrs, US$7; also buses to **Tocopilla** along Pan-American Highway. To **La Serena**, 17 hrs, US$20. To **Santiago**, 28 hrs, several companies, US$30 (US$50 for Barrios *salón cama*).

International Buses Geminis (Obispo Labbé y Sotomayor) to **La Paz** (Bolivia) via Oruro, Thur and Sat 2300, 22 hrs, US$30; also Litoral, Esmeraldas y Martínez. To **Salta** (Argentina) via Calama and San Pedro, Geminis, once a week, US$50; Panamericano twice a week to Jujuy via Paso de Jama, US$55.

Excursions To **Humberstone**, a large nitrate town, now abandoned, at the junction of the Pan-American Highway and the road to Iquique. Though closed since 1956, you can see the church, theatre, *pulpería* (company stores) and the swimming pool (built of metal plating from ships' hulls). Entry US$2.65, guided tours Sat-Sun, leaflets available. Opposite, on the other side of the Iquique road, is the Oficina Santa Laura, the earliest nitrate plant in Chile, through which you can walk. Transport to/from Iquique: take any bus to/from Arica or Antofagasta, or a colective taxi for Pozo Almonte from Sgto Aldea y Barros Arana, US$2. To Pintados (see **below p 626**) take any bus S, US$2.50, and walk from the Pan-American Highway (3 km) then hitch back or flag down a bus. Many other sites around Iquique, including the Giant of the Atacama (**see above p 626**), are difficult to visit without a vehicle. Hire a car and drive S along the Pacific coast to see sealions, *guano*, fishing settlements and old salt works, including the ghost town of Guanillos, complete with castle.

From Pozo Almonte on the Pan-American Highway, an unpaved road runs 73 km NE to the hot mineral springs in the mountains at Termas de **Mamiña** (2,700m), where there is also an interesting church (1632), a prehispanic *pukará* (fortress), a mud spring (Baño El Chino; open 0930-1300) and good accommodation for tourists (**C** pp *Hotel Termas de Salitre*, full board, thermal pool in each room, electricity till midnight, swimming pool open 0930-1300; **B** *Termal La Coruña*, T 796298, good, nice views; **C** *Tamarugal*, T 424365, thermal pool in each room; **D** *Residencial Sol de Ipla*, cheapest, 2 others; *cabañas* to let and campsite; basic accommodation may also be available at the military refuge). Electricity till 2230. The rainy season in Mamiña is mainly in Jan and is called *Invierno Boliviano* (Bolivian winter). Transport from Iquique: minibuses from B Arana y Latorre, Mon-Sat 1600; from Mamiña, 0800; Sun from Iquique 0930, from Mamiña 1600, US$4.50.

9 km S of Pozo Almonte a road runs SE to La Tirana 10 km—**see above p 628**, and the fertile oasis of *Pica* (1,300m, pop 1,500) a centre of Spanish settlement during the colonial period. The town is famous for its pleasant climate, its citrus groves and its two natural springs, the best of which is Cocha Resbaladero (open 0700-2000 all year, changing rooms, snack bar, beautiful pool, entry US$0.70).

Services D *Resbaladero*, Ibáñez 57, T 741316, full pension, good pool; E *San Andrés*, Balmaceda 197, T 741319, with large breakfast; E *O'Higgins*, Balmaceda 6, T 741322; E *El Tambo*, Ibáñez 60, T 741320, old fashioned, good restaurant; also *cabañas* for rent. Campsite at *Camping Miraflores*, T 741333. *Restaurant Palomar*, Balmaceda 74, excellent *almuerzo*.

Transport from Iquique: Santa Rosa, Latorre 973, daily bus from Iquique 0930, 2 hrs; from Pica 1800, US$3. Several companies (Flonatur, Sgto Aldea 790; Julia, B Arana 965) operate minibuses but services vary. If travelling by car, a quicker route to Pica is by turning E off the Pan-American Highway at Pintados, 43 km S of Pozo Almonte.

La Tirana and Pintados fall within two of the three areas which make up the **Reserva Nacional Pampa del Tamarugal**, the third part is some 60 km N of Pozo Almonte, straddling the Pan-American Highway.

South From Iquique There are 2 routes from Iquique S to Antofagasta. The Pan-American Highway continues S from the turning to Iquique via Pozo Almonte and, 42 km further S, Pintados, where the **Geoglyphs of Pintados**, some 400 figures on the hillsides, can be seen (3 km W off the Pan-American Highway). At Quillagua, 172 km S of Pozo Almonte there is a customs post: all vehicles are searched for duty-free goods (long delays especially for buses). At Km 262 a road runs W 8 km to *María Elena*, one of the three nitrate mines still functioning in Chile (E *Hotel Chacance*, T 632749, nice, secure; cheap meals at the Casino Social; museum on main plaza; bus to Iquique 6 hrs, US$10). 99 km further S at Carmen Alto a road branches off NE to Calama (see below).

The other route is via Tocopilla offering fantastic views of the rugged coastline and tiny fishing communities. The coastal road, Route 1, is being paved and its completion was expected in 1995. It is 100 km shorter than the Pan-American Highway. When completed, tourist development will follow. From Iquique to the Río Loa (142 km) is paved; customs post at the Río Loa. Paving is in progress on the next 82 km to Tocopilla, with a tunnel being driven through the Cuesta Paquica.

Tocopilla (pop 24,600, DDD 055) is 244 km S of Iquique via the coastal road and 365 km via the Pan-American Highway. The town is dominated by a thermal power station, which supplies electricity to the whole of northern Chile, and by the port facilities used to unload coal and to export nitrates and iodine from two famous nitrate fields—María Elena (68 km), and Pedro de Valdivia (85 km). In the centre is the copper concentrate plant of Cía Minera de Tocopilla. There is a sports stadium and two good beaches: Punta Blanca (12 km S) and Caleta Covadonga. There is also fine deep sea fishing if you can find a boat and a guide.

Hotels C *Chungará*, 21 de Mayo 1440, T 811036, comfortable, clean, rec; C *Vucina*, 21 de Mayo 2069, T 811571, modern, good restaurant; *Casablanca*, 21 de Mayo 2054, T 813222, F 813104, friendly, helpful; D *Hostería Bolívar*, Bolívar 1332, T 812783, modern, helpful, meals served, clean, friendly, highly rec; E *Hostal Central*, Aníbal Pinto 1241, friendly, clean; F *Res La Giralda*, 21 de Mayo 1134.

Restaurants *Club de la Unión*, Prat 1354, good *almuerzo*, cheap; *Kong Jong*, 21 de Mayo 1833, reasonable value, Chinese; *El Pirata*, 21 de Mayo 1999, *parrilladas*. Good seafood at the Muelle Pesquero opposite the old wooden clock tower.

Buses To **Antofagasta** 8 a day, several companies inc Barrrios, Tramaca and Camus, US$2.50, 2½ hrs; to **Iquique**, by bus and minibus along coastal road, Barrios, Tramaca and Turisnorte, 4 hrs, US$2.50, frequent. To **Chuquicamata** and **Calama**, Camus, 2 a day, 3 hrs, US$5. No direct services to **Santiago**, go via Antofagasta or take Tramaca or Flota Barrios to Vallenar or La Serena and change. Bus company offices are on 21 de Mayo.

From Tocopilla a good paved road runs E up the narrow valley 72 km to the Pan-American Highway (with a short spur to María Elena and Pedro de Valdivia nitrate mines). From here the road continues E in a very bad state (requires careful driving) to Chuquicamata.

The coast road S from Tocopilla to Antofagasta, 185 km, is paved all the way, but deteriorates after 78 km, there is no fuel between Tocopilla and Mejillones. The route runs at the foot of 500-metre cliffs, behind which are mountains which are extensively mined for copper, often by *piquineros* (small groups of self-employed miners). There are larger mines, with the biggest concentration inland about 80 km S).

A zig-zag road (very steep) winds up the cliffs to the mine at Mantos de la Luna about 35 km S of Tocopilla. At the top there are rather dead-looking groves of giant cactus living off the sea mist which collects on the cliffs. Wildlife includes foxes (*zorros*).

The coast is rocky though there are good beaches at Poza Verde (70 km S of Tocopilla) and Hornitos (104 km, town is dead except at week-ends). There is also the Tocopilla Yacht Club (45 km) and Punta Blanca (12 km), which have bars and restaurants.

Reminders of the area's mining past can also be seen at several points: at Km 38 S there is an amazing ransacked cemetery. About 5 km further S are the atmospheric ruins of the port of Gatico. The main interest is the ruins of **Cobija** (60 km S), formerly the coastal end of the silver trail from Potosí. This town was destroyed by an earthquake in 1877, and captured by the Chileans in the War of the Pacific two years later. Adobe walls, the rubbish tip (right above the sea) and the wreckage of the port are all that is left of the town.

Mejillones (pop 4,000; DDD 055), 60 km N of Antofagasta (140 km S of Tocopilla), has a good natural harbour protected from westerly gales by high hills. Until 1948 it was a major terminal for the export of tin and other metals from Bolivia: remnants of that past include a number of fine wooden buildings: the Intendencia Municipal, the Casa Cultural (built in 1866) and the church (1906), as well as the Capitanía del Puerto. Today the town lives mainly by fishing, coming alive in the evening when the fishermen prepare to set sail. The sea is very cold because of the Humboldt current. A Mediterranean-style tourist complex is planned for Mejillones Bay, once paving of the coastal road is finished.

Accommodation and Food A *Costa Del Sol*, M Montt 086, T 621590, 4-star, new; **D** *Residencial Marcela*, Borgoñi 150, with bath, pleasant; **F** *Residencial Elisabeth*, Alte Latorre 440, T 621568, friendly, basic, restaurant. Municipal campsite behind the fishing port. *Juanito Restaurant*, Las Heras 241, excellent *almuerzo*; *Sion-Ji*, Alte Latorre 718, Chinese, good value.

Antofagasta (pop 185,000; DDD 055), 1,367 km N of Santiago and 699 km S of Arica, is the largest city in Northern Chile. It is the capital of the Second Region and is a major port for the export of copper from Chuquicamata. It is also a major commercial centre and home of two universities. In the main square, Plaza Colón, is a clock tower donated by the British community. Paseo Prat, which runs SE from Plaza Colón, is the main shopping street. Two blocks N of Plaza Colón, near the old port, is the Ex-Aduana, built as the Bolivian customs house in Mejillones and moved to its current site after the War of the Pacific. Opposite are two other buildings, the former Capitanía del Puerto (now occupied by the Fundación Andrés Sabella, which offers occasional workshops on weaving, painting, etc) and the ex-Resguardo Marítima (now housing Digader, the regional coordinating centre for sport and recreation). East of the port are the buildings of the Antofagasta and Bolivia Railway Company (FCAB) dating from the 1890s and beautifully restored, but still in use and difficult to visit. These include the former railway station, company offices and workers' housing. The former main square of the Oficina Vergara, a nitrate town built in 1919 and dismantled in 1978, can be seen in the campus of the University of Antofagasta, 4 km S of the centre (bus 3 or 4). Also to the S on a hill (and reached by Bus B) are the ruins of Huanchaca, a Bolivian silver refinery built after 1868 and closed in 1903. From below, the ruins resemble a fortress rather than a factory. The climate is delightful (apart from the lack of rain); the temperature varies from 16°C in Jun/Jul to 24°C Jan/Feb, never falling below 10°C at night.

Museums Museo Histórico Regional, in the former Aduana, Balmaceda y Bolívar, Tues-Sat 1000-1300, 1530-1830, Sun 1100-1400, US$0.80, children half-price, fascinating new displays (many in Spanish only) on life on land and in the oceans, development of civilization in South America, minerals, human artefacts, rec. **Museo Geológico** of the Universidad

Católica del Norte, Av Angamos 0610, inside the university campus, open Mon-Fri, 0830-1230, 1500-1800, free (colectivo 3 or 33 from town centre).

Local Holiday 29 Jun, San Pedro, patron saint of the fishermen: the saint's image is taken out by launch to the breakwater to bless the first catch of the day. **Festivals** On the last weekend of Oct, the foreign communities put on a joint festival on the seafront, with national foods, dancing and music.

Hotels A1 *Nadine*, Baquedano 519, T 227008, F 265222, new, bath, TV, bar, café, parking, etc; opp is **A2** *Ancla*, Baquedano 508, T 224814, F 261551, new, bath, TV, bar, restaurant, exchange (see below); **A2** *Antofagasta*, Balmaceda 2575, T 268259, garage, swimming pool, lovely view of port and city, run down, with breakfast (discount for Automóvil Club members); beach; **A2** *Diego de Almagro*, Condell 2624, T 268331, good for the money but a bit tatty; **A2** *Plaza*, Baquedano 461, T 269046, F 266803, modern, clean, comfortable, safes in rooms, but charges foreigners VAT and is unwelcoming, parking 1 block away; **B** *Pieper*, Sucre 509, T 263603, clean, modern, warmly rec; **C** *Latorre*, Latorre 2450, pleasant; **C** *San Antonio*, Condell 2235, T 268857, clean, helpful, modern but noisy from bus station; **B** *San Marcos*, Latorre 2946, T 251763, modern, comfortable, avoid rooms at the back (loud music); **B** *San Martín*, San Martín y Bolívar, T 263503, with bath, TV, parking, clean, safe and friendly; **D** *Residencial La Riojanita*, Baquedano 464, T 268652, basic, old-fashioned, hot water on demand, noisy; **D** *Res El Cobre*, Prat 749, T 225162, central, noisy, basic; **E** *Residencial Paola*, Prat 766, T 222208, shared bathrooms, inadequate water, otherwise clean and neat; **D** *Res O'Higgins*, Sucre 665, T 267596, big, old, dirty, no hot water; **D** *Rawaye*, Sucre 762, T 225399, basic.

B *Tatio*, Av Grecia 1000, T 247561, modern building, out of old town on the beach, has buses converted into caravans, D, friendly, beautiful views, acts as youth hostel, no cooking facilities.

Camping To the S on the road to Coloso are: *Las Garumas*, Km 6, T 247758, US$10 for tent (bargain for lower price out of season), US$15 for cabins; cold showers and beach (reservations Av Angamos 601, casilla 606). *Rucamóvil*, Km 13, T 231913 and 7 *cabañas*, T 221988. Both open year-round, expensive. Also *La Rinconada*, 30 km N of city, off road to Mejillones, between La Portada and Juan López, T 261139.

Restaurants *Marina Club*, Av Ejército 0909, good fish and seafood dishes and a view, expensive but worth it; *Tío Jacinto*, Uribe 922, friendly, good seafood; *El Arriero*, Condell 2644, good value set lunch, meat dishes good but pricey, live music; *Bavaria*, J S Ossa 2428, excellent meat and German specialities, not cheap; *Flamingo*, Condell y Baquedano, rec; *D'Alfredo*, Condell 2539, pizzas, good; *Club de la Unión*, Prat 474 (quite good); *Chicken's House Center*, Latorre 2660, chicken, beef and daily specials, open till 2400; *Casa Vecchia*, O'Higgins 1456, good food, good value. Difficult to find any coffee, etc, before 0900. *Café Bahía*, Prat 452, and *Café Caribe*, Prat 482, good coffee, open 0900; *Piccolo Mondo*, Condell 2685, expresso coffee, snacks, drinks, opens 0930, good; ice cream at *Fiori di Gelatto*, Baquedano 519, in new *Hotel Nadine*, highly rec; *Chico Jaime* above the market, surrealistic decor, seafood, *almuerzo* US$3, mixed reports; good reports of *El Mariscal* in same area. Many eating places in the market. Good cheap lunches at *El Rincón de Don Quijote*, Maipú 642. Good fish restaurants at Coloso, 8 km S near the Playa Amarrilla (take your own wine). *Chez Niko's*, Ossa 1951, restaurant, bar, bakery, *pastelería*, good pizzas, *empanadas* and bread. *Chifa Pekín*, Ossa 2135, Chinese, smart, reasonable prices.

Exchange Banco O'Higgins, San Martín 2541; **Banco de Concepción**, Plaza Colón for Visa. **Banco Edwards**, Prat 461, TCs changed at high commission. Foreign money exchange (all currencies and TCs) is best at new *Hotel Ancla*, Latorre 2478 y Baquedano 508, T 224814, open all day every day. **NB** Impossible to change TCs S of Antofagasta until you reach La Serena.

Consulates Bolivia, Av Grecia 563, Oficina 23, T 221403; **France and Belgium**, Baquedano 299, T 268669.

Theatre *Teatro Municipal*, Sucre y San Martín, T 264919, modern, state-of-the art; *Teatro Pedro de la Barca*, Condell 2495, run by University of Antofagasta, occasional plays, reviews.

Discotheques *Con Tutti*, Av Grecia 421; *Popo's*, Universidad de Chile (far end from town); *Parador 63*, Baquedano 619, disco, bar-restaurant, live shows, good value.

Cinemas *Gran Vía*, Av Angamos, far from centre, take bus or taxi; *Nacional*, Sucre 735.

Laundry *París*, Condell 2455, laundry and dry cleaning, expensive, charge per item; *Laverap*, 14 Febrero 1802.

Post Office on Plaza Colón, 0830-1900, Sat 0900-1300. **Telephones**, Entel Chile, Baquedano, 753; CTC, Condell 2529.

Shopping Galería del Arte Imagen, Uribe 485, sells antiques including artefacts from nitrate plants. **Bookshop** Librería Universitaria, Latorre 2515, owner Germana Fernández knowledgeable on local history; opp is *Multilibro*.

Market Municipal market, corner of Matta and Uribe.

Swimming Olympic pool at Condell y 21 de Mayo, US$1.20, open till 1800, best in am. **Sauna** Riquelme y Condell.

Tennis Club Club de Tenis Antofagasta, Av Angamos 906.

Travel Agencies Many including *Tatio Travel*, Latorre 2579, T 263532, Telex 225242 TATIO CL, English spoken, tours arranged for groups or individuals, highly rec. *Turismo Cristóbal* in *Hotel Antofagasta*, helpful. *Turismo Corssa*, San Martín 2769, T/F 251190, rec. Alex Joseph Valenzuela Thompson, Edif Bulnes, Sucre 220, Piso 4, Oficina 403, T 243322/F 222718, Aptdo Postal 55, offers to guide German speakers around the area.

Tourist Office at Maipú 240, T 264044, very little information of use; kiosk at airport (open summer only). **Automóvil Club de Chile**, Condell 2330, T 225332.

Customs Agent Luis Piquimil Bravo, Prat 272, oficina 202, excellent, fast service, efficient.

Car Rental Rent-a-Car, Prat 810, T 225200; **Avis**, Prat 272, T 221668; **Budget**, Prat 206, T 251745; **Hertz**, Balmaceda 2566 (T 269043), offer city cars and jeeps (group D, Toyota Landcruiser) and do a special flat rate, with unlimited mileage; **Felcar**, 14 de Febrero 2324, T 224468, English spoken, reported to be the cheapest.

Air Services Cerro Moreno Airport, 22 km N. LanChile (Washington 2552, T 265151), Ladeco (Washington 2589, T 269170, F 260440); National, Latorre 2572, T 224418, F 268996. Taxi to airport US$7, but cheaper if ordered from hotel. Bus No 20 from San Martín y Prat, US$0.50, every 2 hrs from 0730. LanChile, Ladeco and National fly daily to Santiago, Iquique and Arica.

Buses The main bus terminal is at S end of town, Av Argentina y Díaz Gana, but each company has its own office in town (some quite a distance from the centre). Some, like Tramaca, go only from their own terminal. Buses for **Mejillones** and **Tocopilla** operated by Barrios, Tramaca, Camus and others depart from the Terminal Centro at Riquelme 513. Minibuses to Mejillones leave from Latorre 2730. Bus company offices as follows: Tramaca, Uribe 936, T 223624; Flota Barrios, Condell 2764; Géminis, Latorre 3099; Fénix Pullman Norte, San Martín 2717; Incatur, Maipú 554; Turis Norte, Argentina 1155; Libac, Argentina 1155; Pullman Bus, Latorre 2805; Chile-Bus (to Argentina and Brazil) and Tur-Bus, Latorre 2751. To **Santiago**, 18 hrs (Flota Barrios, US$40, *cama*, includes drinks and meals); 30% reduction on Inca, Tramaca, and Géminis buses for students, but ask after you have secured a seat; many companies: fares range from US$28-32, book 2 days in advance. If all seats to the capital are booked, catch a bus to **La Serena** (13 hrs, US$15, or US$30 *cama* service), or Ovalle, US$18, and re-book. To **Valparaíso**, US$25. To **Arica**, US$16 (Tur-Bus), 13½ hrs, Tramaca, US$18. To **Chuquicamata**, Tur-Bus leaves at 0700, returns at 1900, as well as many others. To **Calama**, several companies, US$5 (Tramaca, 3 hrs). To **San Pedro de Atacama**, no direct services—go via Calama. Direct to **Copiapó** on Thur and Sat at 2230, US$10.50. Frequent buses to **Iquique**; US$13, 8 hrs.

Buses to Salta, Argentina Géminis, Wed, US$50, 22 hrs; via Calama, immigration check at San Pedro de Atacama, then on to high Cordillera and to San Antonio de los Cobres (Argentine customs) all year round, although Apr-Sep dependent on weather conditions. Also Atahualpa/Tramaca joint service in summer only, Tues, Fri US$50, student discount if you are persistent. Book in advance for these services, take food and as much warm clothing as possible. There is nowhere to change Chilean pesos en route. These services can be picked up in San Pedro, but book first in Calama or Antofagasta and notify but company.

If hitching to Arica or Iquique try at the beer factory a few blocks N of the fish market on Av Pinto, or the lorry park a few blocks further N. If hitching S go to the police checkpoint/restaurant/gas station La Negra, about 15 km S of the city.

NB There are no railway passenger services from Antofagasta. The famous journey to Bolivia starts from Calama (see below)—tickets from Tramaca, Uribe 936 or in Calama, and the line into Argentina carries no passengers.

Excursions There are two favourite spots for picnics: near the town of La Chimba, the fantastic cliff formations and symbol of the Second Region at *La Portada*, 16 km N, reached by taking airport bus No 20 (see above), or any bus for Mejillones from the Terminal Centro. Last bus back leaves at 2030. Taxis charge US$11. Hitching is easy. From the main road it is 2 km to the beach which, though beautiful, is too dangerous for swimming; there is an excellent seafood restaurant (*La Portada*) and café (open lunch-time only). A number of bathing beaches are also within easy reach. *Juan López*, 38 km N of Antofagasta, is a windsurfers' paradise (Hotel *La*

Rinconada, T 268502; *Hostería Sandokan*, T 692031). Buses at weekends in summer only, also minibuses daily in summer (tickets from Latorre 2700 block). For those with their own transport, follow the road out of Juan López to the beautiful cove at Conchilla. Keep on the track to the end at Bolsico. The sea is alive with birds, including Humboldt penguins, especially opposite Isla Santa María.

Several interesting industrial archaeological sites dating from the nitrate era (see History section) can be visited. 72 km NE of Antofagasta (on the Pan-American Highway) is **Baquedano**, formerly an important railway junction. The old railway station (still used by goods trains) and the Museo Ferroviario, a large collection of old (and rusting) locomotives, can be seen. 30 km further N and just off the Pan-American Highway is **Chacabuco**, a large nitrate town, opened in 1924, closed in 1938 and used as a concentration camp by the Pinochet government between 1973 and 1975. Workers' housing, the church, theatre, stores and the mineral plants can be visited. Free guided tour (in Spanish). Take any bus from Antofagasta towards Calama or Iquique, get off at the Carmen Alto junction and walk the last 4 km.

202 km NE of Antofagasta on the Río Loa at an altitude of 2,265m is the oasis town of **Calama** (pop 100,365; DDD 082). The town is modern, expensive and is a commercial and residential centre for workers at nearby Chuquicamata. 2 km from the centre on Av B O'Higgins is the **Parque El Loa** (open 1000-1800 daily), which contains a reconstruction of a typical colonial village built around a reduced-scale reproduction of Chiu Chiu church. Nearby in the park is the **Museo Arqueológico y Etnológico**, with an exhibition of pre-hispanic cultural history (open Tues-Fri 1000-1330, 1430-1800, Sat-Sun 1100-1830; colectivos 4, 5, 6 or 18 from the centre). Although there is little to do, Calama may be a useful point to stay for a day or two to get used to the altitude before going higher.

Travellers by car coming from the N can drive via Chuquicamata, although the road is quite poor on either side of that town, or, from the S, by a paved road leaving the Pan-American Highway 98 km N of Antofagasta at Carmen Alto (petrol and food). This road passes many abandoned nitrate mines (*oficinas*).

Hotels **L3** *Lican Antai*, Ramírez 1937, T 211621, with breakfast, good service and good restaurant, TV, phone, safe, rec; **A1** *Park*, Camino Aeropuerto 1392, T 319900, F 319901, 233-8509 in Santiago, first class, swimming pool, popular, bar and restaurant, rec; **A2** *Alfa*, Sotomayor 2016, T 211565, reasonable; **A2** *Hostería Calama*, Latorre 1521, T 211511, comfortable, good food and service; **A2** *Quitor*, Ramírez 2116, T 211716, good. **B** *Casablanca* on Plaza, Sotomayor 2160, T 211722, clean. **A3** *El Sol*, Sotomayor 2064, T 211235, with bath, C without, clean, rec; **C** *Res John Keny*, Ecuador 1991, T 211430, modern, clean, friendly, car park. **C** *Atenas*, Ramírez 1961, T 212666, dirty, lukewarm showers, airless rooms, run down; **D** *El Loa*, Abaroa 1617, T 212963, English spoken; **D** *Res Splendid*, Ramírez 1960, T 211841, with bath, E without, clean, hot water, good; **D** *Residencial Internacional*, Gral Velázquez 1976, T 211553, hot water, friendly but noisy; **D** *Genesis*, Granaderos 2148, T 212841, near Tramaca and Geminis bus terminals, clean, kitchen, rec; **D** *Residencial Casa de Huéspedes*, Sotomayor 2079, poor beds, basic, clean, hot shower; **D** *Res Toño*, Vivar 1973, T 211185, next to Kenny bus, hot shower, basic, clean; **E** *Le Relais*, Sotomayor 2261, cooking facilities; **E** *Prat*, Vivar 1970, cheap, cold water; **E** *Residencial El Tatio*, P L Galo, 1987, T 212284, basic, friendly, noisy, clean, reasonable; **E** pp *Capri 2*, Ramírez 1880, clean, hot water; **E** *Los Andes*, Vivar, 1920, T 211073, renovated, good beds, noisy; **E** *Luxor*, Vargas 1881, basic.

Restaurants *Bavaria*, Sotomayor 2095, modern, clean, good coffee and delicatessen; *Nueva Victoria*, Vargas y Abaroa, serves early breakfast, good, cheap, other meals; *Club Croata*, Abaroa 1869 (Plaza de Armas), serves good set lunches and evening meals; good, cheap lunches also at *Hotel Quitor*, *Comedor Camarino*, Latorre 2033, *Lascas*, Ramírez 1917, and in the market. *Mariscal JP*, Felix Hoyos 2127, 4 houses from Tramaca bus, good seafood; *Pukará*, Antofagasta 2076, good, rec. Good ice cream at *Fior di Gelato*, Plaza de Armas.

Banks and Exchange Rates are generally poor especially for cheques. **Banco O'Higgins**, Sotomayor; **Banco de Crédito E Inversiones**, Latorre, good rates, no commission (US$100 minimum); **Banco Osorno** (Visa), Sotomayor; **Fincard** (Mastercard), Latorre 1763, 1° piso, Mon-Fri 0900-1400, 1600-2000, Sat 1100-1300. *Casa de Cambio*, Sotomayor 1818, Mon-Fri, 0830-1400, 1500-1900 (closes 2300 for passengers on train to Bolivia). Try also **La Media Luna** clothes store, Ramírez 1992 (poor rates). Money changers selling Bolivian money outside the railway station. At weekends try Tramaca or Morales Moralitos bus offices or *farmacias* (poor rates).

Consul The Bolivian Consulate (Vicuña Mackenna 2020) is open (in theory only) 0900-1230 and 1530-1830, Mon-Fri, friendly, helpful.

Cinemas Central on Latorre and another on Ramírez, near plaza.

Laundry Ramírez 1867, English spoken (Mon-Sat 0900-2100), expensive.

Post Office Granaderos y V Mackenna, 0830-1300, 1530-1830, Sat 0900-1230, will not send parcels over 1 kg. **Telecommunications** CTC, Abaroa 1756; Entel, M Curie 2374.

Travel Agents Several agencies run one-day and longer tours to the Atacama region, including San Pedro; these are usually more expensive than tours from San Pedro and require a minimum number for the tour to go ahead. Reports of tour quality are increasingly mixed – poorly maintained vehicles and poor guides. Agencies include: *Talikuna*, Gral Velázquez 1948, T 212595. good reports; *Payachatas*, Cobija 2030; *Tujina*, Ramírez 2234, T 342261, F 342790; *Turismo El Sol*, Abaroa 1796, T 210152, good reports; *Desierto Diferente*, Sotomayor 2261, T 315111; *Atacama Desert Expeditions*, Latorre 1760, T 312019, F 312064; *Nativa*, Avaroa 1780, T 319834, F 340107, rec; *Livia Tours*, Vivar 1960, T 211664, rec for their 3-day desert tour.

Tourist Office José Latorre 1689, T 211314. Map of town, helpful. Open Mon-Fri 0900-1300, 1430-1900 Sat-Sun (summer only) 0900-1300. **Automóvil Club de Chile**, Av Ecuador 1901, T 212770.

Car Hire **Comercial Maipo SA**, Balmaceda 3950, T 212204; **Hertz**, Latorre 1510, T 211380; **Avis**, Granaderos 2895; **American's**, Latorre 1512, T 211220; **Maxso**, Abaroa 1930, T 212194; **Budget**, Diamante s/n, T 211076, cheapest. A 4WD jeep (necessary for the desert) costs between US$87-118 a day. Rates are sometimes much lower at weekends. A hired car or taxi, shared between several people, is an economic alternative for visiting the Atacama region. **NB** Car hire is not readily available in San Pedro de Atacama.

Air LanChile (Latorre 1499, T 211394/211477), daily, and Ladeco (Mackenna 2020, T 312626/211355), 5 a week to Santiago, via Antofagasta. Ladeco also daily to Iquique. Taxi to town US$6 (courtesy vans from Hotels *Calama, Alfa* and *Lican Antai*).

Buses Daily to **Santiago** (23 hrs, fares from US$28-32, Pullman Bus, with 3 meals, drinks, sleeping car, US$36, Flota Barrios *salón cama* US$40), to **Arica**—often involves a change in Antofagasta (Geminis, 2130 and Tramaca, 4 until 1730 daily, may be more in summer, US$16). To **Valparaíso/Viña del Mar**, US$25. To **Iquique**, 8 hrs, US$11, overnight only (Geminis rec, Kenny Bus not rec). To **La Serena**, 15 hrs, US$18. To **Chuquicamata** (see below). For services to **San Pedro de Atacama** and Tocornal, see below. **Antofagasta**, 3 hrs, several companies, eg Tramaca, hourly on the half-hour till 2130, US$5. Bus company offices: Tramaca, terminal at Granaderos 3048 (colectivo 1A from centre), office at Sotomayor 1961; Morales Moralitos, Sotomayor 1802; Yusmar Antofagasta 2041, T 318543; Geminis, O'Higgins 078; Kenny Bus, Vivar 1954; Flota Barrios, Ramírez 2298.

To **Salta**, Argentina Géminis services from Iquique and Antofagasta call at Calama, details above, book well in advance, US$39, 22 hrs. (Géminis service can also be picked up in San Pedro but book in Calama and tell the booking office).

Rail To Oruro (Bolivia). This, the only section of the old Antofagasta and Bolivia Railway line still open to passenger trains, is a long slow journey but well worthwhile for the scenery. Schedules are subject to change: most common departure time is Wed 2300, but Fri and Sat also occur, US$12 to Uyuni, US$16 to Oruro, passport essential. Book seats in advance from Tramaca in Calama (Sotomayor, 1961) or Antofagasta. (The 2 offices sell tickets for different carriages and do not know of reservations made at the other office). Catch the train as early as possible: although seats are assigned, the designated carriages may not arrive; passengers try to occupy several seats (to sleep on) but will move if you show your ticket. The journey is very cold, both during the day and at night (-15°C). Sleeping bag and/or blanket essential. Restaurant car; food is also available at Ollagüe and Río Mulato (only for the conditioned). The highest point of the line is reached at Ascotán (3,960m) and the line then descends to 3,735m at Cebollar, where it skirts a great borax basin 39 km long. Chilean customs are at Ollagüe, where there is a delay of 5-6 hrs before an engine is sent from Uyuni. The train is searched at Bolivian customs at Avaroa and passengers may be required to disembark. Passports are collected on the train: queue at the restaurant for return. There are money changers at Ollagüe and Avaroa. From the border the line runs NE to Uyuni, 174 km, crossing the Salar de Chiguana and running at an almost uniform height of 3,660m. Uyuni is the junction with the line S to the Argentine frontier at Villazón.

Río Mulato is the junction for Potosí, but it is much quicker to travel by bus from Uyuni. The train terminates at Oruro (see Bolivia chapter: **La Paz Railways to/from the Coast**). **Watch**

baggage at Oruro; the thieves are notorious, even grabbing bags through open windows.

A freight train with one or two passenger cars attached leaves Calama for Ollagüe Sun 1130, return departure 1730, check details beforehand, buy ticket a few hours before departure, US$5 one way, not crowded. Note that there is no connecting passenger train and riding on goods trains from Ollagüe into Bolivia is not allowed. No accommodation in Ollagüe.

NB Remember, if arriving from La Paz between Oct and Mar, Chilean time is 1 hr later than Bolivian.

At **Chuquicamata**, a clean, modern town (pop 20,000), 16 km N of Calama at 2,800m, is the world's largest open-cast copper mine, employing 11,000 workers and operated by Codelco (the state copper corporation). It is an astoundingly large hole, 4 km long, 2 km wide and 600m deep. The giant trucks, carrying 225 ton loads, work 24 hrs a day, extracting rock which is processed in other parts of the plant. Guided tours in Spanish (by bus) leave from the office of Chuqui Ayuda (a local children's charity) near the entrance at the top end of the plaza, Mon-Fri 1000 (though less frequently in low season—tourist office in Calama has details), 3 hrs, US$1.50 donation, be there by 0915. Register in the café near entrance at least 30 mins in advance. Be in good time because space is sometimes limited; passport essential. No filming permitted, but photographs may be taken at specified points in tour. You must wear strong shoes and a long-sleeved garment (shorts and skirts not allowed) if you wish to see the industrial plants; children under 12 are not normally allowed to enter (check details at Calama tourist office).

Services Overnight accommodation is difficult. Cheap lunches available at the *Club de Empleados* and at *Arco Iris*, both facing the bus terminal.

Transport from Calama: yellow colectivo taxis (marked 'Chuqui') from the corner of the main plaza, US$0.75. Buses to **Arica** at 2200 (weekends at 2300), US$16, 9 hrs. To **Antofagasta**, ten a day, US$6. To **Iquique** at 2300. To **Santiago** at 1400, US$28, 24 hrs.

Near Calama there are several small towns and villages in the valley of the Río Loa. 33 km E is the village of **Chiu Chiu**, with a very interesting church, dating from 1611, and nearby a unique, perfectly circular, very deep lake, called Chiu Chiu or Icacoia. Ancient rock carvings are to be found a few km N in the Río Loa valley. 8 km N of Chiu Chiu at **Lasana** are the ruins of a pre-Incaic *pukará*, a national monument, with explanatory tablets (soft drinks and beer on sale). At **Conchi**, 25 km N of Lasana, there is a spectacular view from the bridge over the Río Loa, but it is a military zone, so no photographs allowed. Access to the river is by side tracks, best at Santa Bárbara; interesting wildlife and flower meadows, trout fishing in season (permit from Gobernación in Calama). **Estación San Pedro** (16 km NE of Conchi) has quite an interesting old village and small gorge, away from the railway station. Possible to camp at the station (ask the station master).

From Chiu Chiu a road runs to Ollagüe, 240 km N on the Bolivian frontier. There is a *carabinero* checkpoint at Ascotán, the highest point of the road at 3,900m. North of Ascotán the road becomes worse, especially where it crosses the Salares de Ascotán and Ollagüe (ask at Ascotán or Ollagüe before setting out about the conditions, especially in Dec/Jan or Aug). There are many llama flocks along this road and flamingoes on the salars. **NB** The desert to the eastern side of the road is extensively covered with minefields.

5 km S of Ollagüe is the sulphur mining camp of Buenaventura. It is possible to camp here. The mine at 5,800m (only 150m short of the summit of Ollagüe Volcano) can be reached by hiring a 4WD vehicle or by walking. Amazing views of volcanoes and salt flats.

NB There is no petrol between Calama and Uyuni in Bolivia. If really short try buying from the *carabineros* at Ollagüe or Ascotán, the military at Conchi or the mining camp at Buenaventura. The only real answer is to take enough.

Ollagüe is 419 km from Antofagasta, at 3,690m, on the dry floor of the Salar de Ollagüe, surrounded by a dozen volcanic peaks of over 5,000m. Pop 200; one basic *alojamiento*, one bus a week to Calama.

A 77-km spur railroad of metre gauge runs to the copper mines of Collahuasi, and from there one can reach the highest mine in the world: the Aucanquilcha, at 5,700-5,900m. Its sulphur is taken to Amincha, a town at the foot of the volcano, to be refined. The mine closes for Bolivian winter; it is served by road, which is sometimes impassable. On site are the ruins of an aerial tram system. From the mine you can scramble to the summit of Aucanquilcha at 6,176m, superb views. High clearance vehicle needed to drive to mine. The highest passenger station on this spur is Yuma, at 4,400m. Ollagüe can be reached by taking the Calama-Oruro

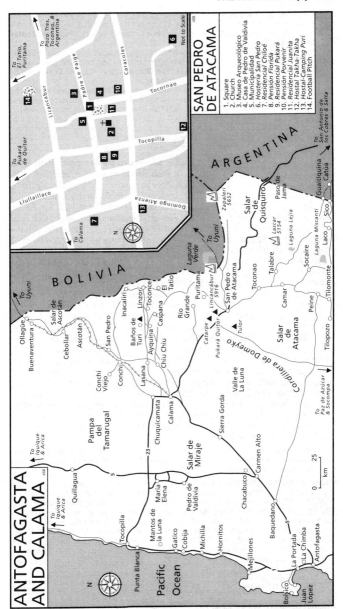

SAN PEDRO DE ATACAMA

1. Square
2. Church
3. Museo Arqueológico
4. Casa de Pedro de Valdivia
5. Municipalidad
6. Hostería San Pedro
7. Residencial Chiloé
8. Pensión Florida
9. Residencial Pukará
10. Pensión Porvenir
11. Residencial Juanita
12. Hostal Takha-Takha
13. Hostal-Camping Puri
14. Football Pitch

ANTOFAGASTA AND CALAMA

Pacific Ocean

BOLIVIA

ARGENTINA

train (see above) but, if you stop off, you will have to hitch back as the daily freight trains are not allowed to carry passengers. (Hitching is difficult but the police may help you to find a truck.) Bad unmade road from Ollagüe into Bolivia (**see Section 3, Bolivia, Oruro and Routes to Chile & Argentina**).

At this altitude nights are cold, the days warm and sunny. Minimum temperature at Ollagüe is -20°C, and at the mine, -37°C. There are only 50 mm of rain a year, and water is very scarce.

An interesting excursion can be made N from Ollagüe to the village of **Coska** with its traditional agriculture and herds of llamas and alpacas.

The main stock animals are llamas and alpacas, whose principal forage is the *ichu* bunch-grass covering the lower slopes. There is no timber. *Taqui*—dried llama dung— and *tola* scrub are used for cooking fires, but the main fuel is *yaretal*, a resinous moss growing in pillow-like masses in rocky outcrops from 3,500 to 5,000m high. Its calorific value is half that of bituminous coal. It apparently is an Ice Age relic, growing very slowly but now worked out in this area. Across the border in Bolivia there is plenty, which is used as fuel for the Laguna Verde sulphur mine. It is broken up with dynamite into chunks for transport.

103 km SE of Calama by a paved road is **San Pedro de Atacama**. There is no fuel, food or water along this road. At Paso Barros Arana (Km 58) there is an unpaved turning to the left which leads through interesting desert scenery to the small, mud-brick village of Río Grande. Look out for vicuñas and guanacos on the pass. The main road skirts the Cordillera de la Sal about 15 km from San Pedro. Spectacular views of sunset over to the Western Cordilleras. The old unmade road to San Pedro turns off the new road at Km 72 and crosses this range through the Valle de La Luna (see **Excursions** below), but should only be attempted by 4WD vehicles. This road is partly paved with salt blocks.

San Pedro de Atacama, at 2,436m, is a small town (pop 1,600; DDD 108) more Spanish-Indian looking than is usual in Chile, now attracting large numbers of visitors. Both Diego de Almagro and Pedro de Valdivia stopped in this oasis. The impressive archaeological museum, the collection of Father Le Paige, a Belgian missionary who lived in San Pedro between 1955 and 1980, is now under the care of the Universidad Católica del Norte (Mon-Fri, 0800-1200, 1500-1900; Sat, and Sun, 1000-1200, 1500-1800, summer, Mon-Fri 0900-1200, 1400-1800, Sat-Sun 1000-1200, 1400-1800, entry US$2.65). It is a fascinating repository of artefacts, well organized to trace the development of prehispanic Atacameño society. Labels on displays are good and there is a comprehensive booklet in Spanish. Graham Greene tells us that "the striking feature of the museum is . . . the mummies of Indian women with their hair and dresses intact dating from before the Conquest, and a collection of paleolithic tools which puts the British Museum in the shade". There is no heating in the museum: wear warm clothing even in warm weather. Nor is there electric light during the day: go when sunlight is strongest. The church has a roof of cactus wood; inside, the statues of Mary and Joseph have fluorescent light halos, quite arresting.

San Pedro has electricity 1800-2230, but take a torch (flashlight) for walking at night. *Residenciales* supply candles, but better to buy them in Calama beforehand. Accommodation is scarce in Jan/Feb and expensive.

Hotels B *Hostería San Pedro*, on Solcor, rec, reserve in advance, swimming pool (residents only), a Copec petrol station (leaded fuel only), tents for hire, cabins, hot water, electricity am, 1200 and 1800-2300, restaurant (good lunch) and bar, T 11. **C** *Kimal*, Atienza y Caracoles, T 30, F 52, good. **D** *Hostal Takha-Takha*, on Tocopilla, T 38, (F camping), hot water, very small rooms, some tents for rent, friendly and clean; **D** *Residencial Andacollo*, Tocopilla 11 T6, clean, basic, laundry facilities, cheap restaurant, rec; **D** *Residencial Licancábur*, Toconao, clean, safe, good; **E** *Pensión Florida*, on Tocopilla, temperamental hot water, basic, clean, laundry facilities, poor beds; **E** *Pukará*, Tocopilla 28, cold water, mixed reports; **D** *Residencial Chiloé*, Domingo Atienza, T 17, hot water, good meals, laundry facilities, good beds, safe, popular; **D** pp *Residencial Solcor*, Domingo Atienza, dormitory accommodation, friendly; **E** *Camping Tulor*, off Domingo Atienza, T 27, good food, camping F pp, rents camping equipment, rec; **D** *Residencial Juanita*, on the plaza, T 39, renovated, hot water on request, friendly, restaurant, rec; **E** *Restaurant Porvenir*, Caracoles y Tocornao, T 8, only 1 rm, rec; **E** *Hostal-Camping Puri*, Caracoles s/n, T 49, restaurant, clean, quiet, camping F.

Restaurants On Caracoles are *Estaka*, good lunches and evening meals, popular; *Tambo Cañaveral*, live music at weekends, own generator, open late. Apart from these try *Hostería San Pedro* and residencials: *Juanita*, good set-course lunch and evening meal; *Andacollo*; *Porvenir*, cheap; try also *Chiloé* for cheap lunches. *Chañar Luminoso*, Caracoles, good coffee and juice. The tap water contains a high level of toxins.

Exchange Cambio Atacama, Caracoles, open daily, poor rates, will change TCs, but best to change elsewhere. If stuck try *Hostería San Pedro* (worse rates still), or *Hostal Takha-Takha*.

Post Office near the museum; sells excellent postcards. **Telephone** office on Tocopilla, 0830-2000.

Horse riding *Galopea*, run by Eleanor Merrill and Roberto Plaza Castillo ("Guatita") run guided horseback tours, US$5 per hr, speak 6 languages, ask *Esteca* or in *Tambo Canaveral*.

Swimming Pool Piscina Oasis, at Pozo Tres, 3 km SE, was drilled in the late 1950s as part of a mineral exploration project, open all year 0500-1730 daily (except Mon). US$1.50 to swim, sometimes empty. Worth asking around before walking there. Camping US$0.55 and picnic facilities, very popular at weekends.

Climbing San Pedro is also a good centre for climbing Mount Lincancábur (5,916m) and other peaks on the Chile/Bolivia border. Allow at least 8 hrs to climb Lincancábur and 4 hrs to descend. Take plenty of water and your passport and hire a 4WD vehicle in Calama.

Tourist Agencies About 10 agencies, though most charge the same rates and organize joint tour groups. Agencies include: *Nativa*, Toconao, T 44, rec; *Cosmo Andino Expediciones*, Caracoles s/n, T/F 340107, English, German, French and Dutch spoken, book exchange in the above languages, wide selection, owner Martin Beeris (Martín El Holandés) rec; *Atacama Inca Tour*, Toconao s/n, T 34, F 52, rec; *Desert Adventure*, Caracoles s/n; *Pachamama*, Toconao, rec; *Ochoa*, Toconao, Spanish only, rec; *Alpacámac*, O'Higgins s/n, run by Sra Ana María Baron, a leading archaeologist of the area, rec; *Antaí*, Caracoles s/n, English and French spoken, also sell handicrafts, rec. *Cactus* offers horseriding with good guides to Valle de la Luna and other sites. Tours are also run by several *residenciales* including *Florida*. Usual tour rates: to Valle de la Luna (best at sunset) US$6; to Toconao and the Salar de Atacama (best at sunset) US$11; to El Tatio (begin at 0400) US$16 (take swimming costume and warm clothing). These run most days in season, subject to demand at other times. Several agencies' tours to Laguna Verde, Mt Lincancábur and other sites in Bolivia no longer run because the Bolivian authorities refuse permits for Chilean tour vehicles.

There has been a boom in travel agencies in since 1993, but many lack experience, dependable vehicles, suitable equipment (eg oxygen for El Tatio) or professionalism. Check that a guide speaks English if so advertised; ask to see the vehicle to be used (4WD land-cruisers are best); check if the company is recognized by the municipality. At the time of writing the first in the above list had formed the Asociación de Operadores Turísticos de San Pedro de Atacama; others are expected to join. Report any complaints to the municipality.

Car Hire is impossible in San Pedro. Try Calama. Pick up truck with 4WD best. Agency authorization essential to go to Bolivia.

Bicycle Hire from next door to *Florida*, *Takha-Takha*, and *Dada Atacama*, US$2.50 per hr, US$10-12 a day.

Buses from Calama Yusmar services leave **Calama** bus terminal daily, 1100, 1600 and 1800, returning from San Pedro 0800, 1400 and 1800. Morales Moralitos buses leave Calama

(Balmaceda y Sotomayor) 1000, 1530 and 1800, returning 0800, 1400 and 1800, 1½ hrs. Fare US$3 one way. Frequencies vary with more departures in Jan/Feb and some weekends, fewer out of season. Book in advance especially to return from San Pedro Sun pm. Geminis buses from Iquique and Antofagasta to Salta (Argentina) stop in San Pedro on Wed and Sat—book in Calama, Iquique or Antofagasta.

To Bolivia A poor road runs E to Hito Cajones, 45 km from San Pedro, the frontier post with Bolivia, 7 km S of Laguna Verde (see Bolivia chapter). There are reports of a daily bus service from San Pedro to Hito Cajones to meet tour vehicles from Uyuni, US$10 pp. At Hito Cajones you may be able to find space in a tour vehicle (about US$20 to Uyuni). Nativa will take people to the frontier, US$120 per vehicle. (**NB** Emigration formalities in San Pedro.)

To Argentina From San Pedro de Atacama there are 2 routes into Argentina: over the pass of Laguna Sico (4,079m) to San Antonio de los Cobres and, further N, via the Paso de Jama (4,200m) along an improved road to Susques and Jujuy, suitable for any vehicle. Travellers by car should make careful enquiries into road conditions (often impassable in rainy season, 1 Jan to mid-Mar, and blocked by snow in winter); gasoline may be bought in Calama or at *Hostería San Pedro*. The Paso de Jama route is the most popular route (1995), but note that there is no accommodation in Susques. Passport control and customs clearance must be undertaken in San Pedro (fruit search of incoming vehicles).

Excursions The **Valle de la Luna**, 15 km W of San Pedro, with fantastic landscapes caused by the erosion of salt mountains, is crossed by the old San Pedro-Calama road. Although buses on the new Calama-San Pedro road will stop to let you off where the old road branches off 13 km NW of San Pedro (signposted to Peine), it is far better to travel from San Pedro on the old road, either on foot (allow 3 hrs there, 3 hrs back; no lifts) by bicycle or by car. Aim to get there just before sunset. Take water, hat, camera and torch. Also consider spending the night to see the sunset (take warm clothes and plenty of water).

3 km N of San Pedro along the river is the **Pukará de Quitor**, a pre-Inca fortress restored in 1981. The fortress, which stands on the W bank of the river, was stormed by the Spanish under Pedro de Valdivia, 1,000 defenders being overcome by 15 horsemen who vaulted the walls (the path involves fording the river several times). A further 4 km up the river there are Inca ruins at Catarpe. The archaeological site at **Tulor**, 12 km SW of San Pedro, is a stone-age village; worth a visit on foot (you can sleep in two reconstructed huts), or take a tour, US$5 pp. Nearby are the ruins of a 17th century Spanish-style village, abandoned in the 18th century due to lack of water. For Toconao, 37 km S of San Pedro, see below.

North of San Pedro A maintained road runs NE, past the Baños de Puritama (28 km), then on a further 94 km to the geysers at **El Tatio** (alt 4,500m). The geysers are at their best 0630-0830, but there is no public transport and hitching is impossible, if going in a hired car, make sure the engine is suitable for very high altitudes and is protected with antifreeze; 4WD is essential. If driving in the dark it is almost impossible to find your way: the sign for El Tatio is N of the turn off. A swimming pool has been built at El Tatio. Nearby is a workers' camp which is empty apart from one guard, who will let you sleep in a bed in one of the huts, G pp, take food and sleeping bag. From here you can hike to surrounding volcanoes if adapted to altitude. Tours arranged by agencies in San Pedro and Calama. **NB** People have been killed or seriously injured by falling into the geysers, or through the thin crust of the mud.

There are 3 alternative routes from El Tatio W to Calama: direct, on an atrocious track, to Caspana (basic accommodation at village store, G pp), beautifully set among hills, with a museum with interesting displays on Atacameño culture, and then W along the valley of the Río Salado.

North of El Tatio to Linzor (Represa Toconce); here you can turn W to **Toconce**, which has extensive prehispanic terraces set among interesting rock formations. Between Toconce and Caspana to the S are valleys of pampas grass with llama herds. If visiting Toconce, check in with the *carabineros* in the square. From Toconce follow the road W to Calama via Lasana and Chiu Chiu. 20 km W of Toconce is **Ayquina**, in whose ancient church is enshrined the statue of the Virgin of Guadalupe. Her feast-day is 8 September, when pilgrims come from far and wide. There is day-long group dancing to Indian rhythms on flute and drum. Towards sunset the Virgin is carried up a steep trail to a small thatched shrine, where the image and the people are blessed before the dancing is renewed at the shrine and all the way back to the village. The poor people of the hills gather stones and make toy houses all along the route: miniatures of the homes they hope to have some day.

6 km N of Ayquina are the luke-warm thermal waters of the **Baños de Turi** and the ruins of a 12th-century *pukará* which was the largest fortified town in the Atacama mountains. A further 35 km N of Turi is **Cupo**, which has a *fiesta* on 19 Mar (San José). Between this village and Turi is a large, ruined prehispanic settlement at **Paniri** with extensive field systems, irrigation

canals (including aqueducts) and a necropolis. Some of the fields are still in use. The area around Cupo is one of the best for seeing the Atacama giant cactus (*Notocereus atacamensis*). Flamingos can be seen on the mudflats. The Vega de Turi is an important site for the llama and sheep herders, who believe it has curative properties. At several times in the year, herders from a wide area congregate with their flocks, especially in Sep.

The third alternative route to Calama is to continue N from Linzor to Inacaliri and the Ojo de San Pedro saltflat. Follow the road along the Río San Pedro Valley and cross the Río Loa at Conchi. The Río San Pedro has been a route for herders and silver caravans for centuries and there are many sites of interest, although access is on foot. For details on Conchi, Lasana and Chiu Chiu, **see p636 above**.

South of San Pedro From San Pedro to Toconao, 37 km S, the road (well-surfaced) runs through groves of acacia and pepper trees. There are many tracks leading to the wells (*pozos*) which supply the intricate irrigation system. Most have thermal water but bathing is not appreciated by the local farmers. The groves of trees are havens for wild life especially rheas (ñandu) and Atacama owls.

About 4 km before you reach Toconao, there are some vehicle tracks heading E across the sand. They lead to a hidden valley 2 km from the road where there is a small settlement called **Zapar**. Here are some well-preserved pre-hispanic ruins on the rocky cliffs above the cultivated valley. The sand is very soft and 4WD is essential. **Toconao**, with some 500 inhabitants is on the eastern shore of the Salar de Atacama. All houses are built of bricks of white volcanic stone, which gives the village a very characteristic appearance totally different from San Pedro. The 18th century church stands next to the colonial bell tower, also built of volcanic stone. East of the village is an attractive oasis called the Quebrada de Jérez. The quarry where the stone (*sillar*) is worked can be visited. Worth visiting also are the vineyards which produce a unique sweet wine, and the tree-filled gorges with their hidden fields and orchards. Three basic *residenciales*—ask around in the village. Camping possible along the Quebrada de Jérez. Yusmar buses daily from San Pedro, 1300 and 2000, return 0700, 1645, US$1.30.

South of Toconao is one of the main entrances to the **Salar de Atacama**, the third largest expanse of salt flats in the world. Rich in minerals including borax, potassium and an estimated 40% of world lithium reserves, the Salar is home to the pink flamingo and other birds. Entry is controlled by Conaf in Toconao, US$1.50.

From Toconao the road heads S through the scenic villages of **Camar** (where handicrafts from cactus may be bought) and **Socaire** (which has domesticated llamas, knitwear for sale). 20 km S of Socaire is the beautiful **Laguna Miscanti** where wildlife abounds; 3 types of flamingo may be seen: Andean, Chilean (white and pink, no black) and James (small, with yellow legs). After Socaire the road goes on to the mine at Laco (one poor stretch below the mine), before proceeding to Sico, which has replaced the higher, more northerly Guaytiquina pass (4,295m, also spelt Huaytiquina) to Catúa, San Antonio de los Cobres and Salta.

10 km S of Toconao the old road branches E towards Guaytiquina. In a deep *quebrada* below Volcán Láscar is the small agricultural settlement of **Talabre**, with terracing and an ancient threshing floor. Above the *quebrada* is an isolated, stone-built cemetery. Large flocks of llamas graze where the stream crosses the road below Láscar. After a steep climb, you reach the **Laguna Lejía** (4,190m), where flamingoes abound. You then pass through the high plains of **Guaytiquina** (4,275m), where only a few herdsmen are found. This crossing is not open for road traffic to Argentina.

67 km S from Toconao, on a road that branches initially W between Camar and Socaire, is the attractive village of **Peine**, which is the site of the offices of the lithium extraction company. There is also a pool filled by thermal springs where you can swim. Woollen goods and knitwear are made here. To the E of the village is a group of beautifully coloured hills (colours best at sunset) with good views over the Salar de Atacama. A path leads across these hills to Socaire (allow 2 days). It is worth asking if the offices' access road can be used to visit the Salar de Atacama's spectacular salt formations. Other villages worth visiting include Tilomonte and Tilopozo, S and W of Peine.

From Peine a road crosses the Salar de Atacama and then runs S until it joins the road to Argentina via the Portezuelo de Socompa, 13 km E of **Pan de Azúcar**. It is possible to stay at Pan de Azúcar (hot showers and water). From Pan de Azúcar a good road leads back to San Pedro de Atacama along the western side of the Salar.

Pan de Azúcar is on the road which leads from the Pan-American Highway, 50 km S of Antofagasta to Socompa on the Argentine border. The road passes the mining centre at La Escondida (owned by RTZ) and continues, after Pan de Azúcar, in bad condition to Monturaqui. This is the source of the green onyx which is much used for carving in northern Chile. Formalities for crossing into Argentina are completed at Socompa. The road carries on to San Antonio de los Cobres and Salta.

SOUTH OF ANTOFAGASTA (2)

Yet more desert before the Heartland is reached. The main oases are the valleys of the Copiapó, the Huasco and the Elqui rivers. The city of Copiapó is a mining and agroindustrial centre. At the mouth of the Elqui is the neo-colonial resort city of La Serena. Nearby is one of the southern hemisphere's astronomical centres.

Some 175 km S of Antofagasta there are ruined nitrate mines at Oficina Alemania and Oficina Flor de Chile (just off the Pan-American Highway). Mining tracks lead off to the E, but there are no real signs. A good one leads E from Aguas Verdes (fuel) to Plato de Sopa, a camp built into caves above a salt flat.

The next important port to the S is *Taltal*, 306 km S of Antofagasta, along the Pan-American Highway. There is also a poor but scenic route which branches off the highway 52 km S of Antofagasta and runs along the coast, passing near the Quebrada El Médano (72 km N of Taltal), a gorge with ancient rock-paintings. Taltal is a town of wooden buildings, many dating from the late 19th century when it prospered as an important mineral port of 20,000. It is now a nitrate and copper ore centre with 9,000 people (DDD 108). There is an archaeological museum on Av Prat. There is an airport, but few flights.

Accommodation and Food **C** *Hostería Taltal*, Esmeralda 671, T 101, excellent restaurant, good value *almuerzo*; **D** *Verdy*, Ramírez 345, T 105, with bath, E without, clean, spacious, restaurant; opp is **E** *Taltal City*, clean, no hot water; **E** *San Martín*, Martínez 279, T 88, without bath, good *almuerzo*. **E** *Viña del Mar*, Serrano 762. **Restaurant** *Caverna*, Martínez 247, good seafood.

Buses To Santiago 2 a day; to Antofagasta Tramaca, 3 a day, US$5.

Chañaral, a neglected looking town with wooden houses perched on the hillside is 146 km S of Taltal and 400 km S of Antofagasta by the Pan-American Highway. In its heyday it was the centre for the nearby copper mines of El Salado and Las Animas. Pop 10,000. Tourist office on coastal road outside town, open summer only.

Accommodation and Food **B** *Hostería Chañaral* Miller 268, T 480055, excellent restaurant; **C** *Mini*, San Martín 528, T 480079, good value restaurant; **D** *Nuria*, Costanera 302, good. **D** *Jiménez*, Merino Jarpa 551, without bath, friendly, clean, rec, restaurant good value; **E** *La Marina*, Merino Jarpa 562, basic. **Restaurants** in hotels; *Rincón Porteño*, Merino Jarpa 567, good and inexpensive. *San Remo*, Torreblanca, good seafood; *Restaurante de los Pescadores*, in La Caleta, good fish, clean, cheap, rec.

Exchange Poor rates for cash; nowhere to change TCs.

Tourist Information Kiosk on the Pan-American Highway at S end of town (closed winter).

Buses Terminal Merino Jarpa 854. Frequent services to **Antofagasta** US$8, 5 hrs, and Santiago.

Excursions N of Chañaral is the **Parque Nacional Pan de Azúcar**, which consists of the Isla Pan de Azúcar on which Humboldt penguins and other sea-birds live, and some 43,700 hectares of coast whose vegetation, mainly cacti, is nourished by frequent sea mists (*camanchaca*). The park is home to 103 species of birds and 26 varieties of cacti. There are some fine beaches (popular at weekends in summer). Access by secondary road from Chañaral (28 km to Caleta Pan de Azúcar), or from the Pan-American Highway (45 km N, then side road 20 km W). Taxi from Chañaral US$15, or hitch a lift from fishermen at sunrise. After rain in some of the gullies there are tall purple lilies. Conaf office in Caleta Pan de Azúcar, maps available; park entry US$1, camping US$5. Fishermen near the Conaf office offer boat trips round Isla Pan de Azúcar to see the penguins which are normally not visible from the mainland. **NB** There are heavy fines for driving in 'restricted areas' of the park.

    12 km E of Chañaral a road branches off the Pan-American Highway and runs 117 km E along the valley of the Río Salado towards the mining town of *El Salvador*. All along the valley there are people extracting metal ore from the water by building primitive settling tanks.

(*Hostería El Salvador*, Av Potrerillos 003, T 472492; *Hotel Camino del Inca*, El Tofo 333, T 472311; *Residencial Linari*, Potrerillos 705). Flights from Santiago and Copiapó 5 times a week. Daily bus from Santiago (Pullman Bus).

93 km S of Chañaral is the port of *Caldera* (pop 12,000; DDD 052), which has a pier of 230m; 1¹⁄₂ km to the S there is a terminal for the loading of iron ore. There is a fruit inspection for all passing through Caldera going S; this applies to bus passengers, whose luggage is searched.

Hotels C *Costanera*, Wheelwright 543, T 316007, takes credit cards, simple rooms, friendly; **B** *Hostería Puerta del Sol*, Wheelwright 750, T 315205, price inc tax, cabins with bath and kitchen, view over bay; **A** *Portal del Inca*, Carvallo 945, T 315252, shower, cabins with kitchen, English spoken, restaurant not bad, order breakfast on previous night; **C** *Pucará*, Ossa Cerda 460, T 315258; **D** *Residencial Fenicia*,Gallo 370, T 315594, eccentric owner, rec; **D** *Los Andes*, Edwards 360, good but no singles; **E** *Residencial Millaray*, main plaza, clean, friendly. **Restaurant** *Miramar*, Gana 090, at pier, good seafood. *El Pirón de Oro*, Cousiño 218, good but not cheap.

Buses Several a day to **Copiapó** and **Santiago**; to travel N, take a bus to **Chañaral** (Inca-bus US$1.60), then change.

Bahía Inglesa (DDD 052), 6 km S of Caldera, 6 km W of the Highway, is popular with Chileans for its white sandy beaches and unpolluted sea (can get crowded Jan-Feb and at weekends). The climate is warm and dry the year round. It was originally known as Puerto del Inglés after the arrival in 1687 of the English 'corsario', Edward Davis. Accommodation: **C** *Los Jardines de Bahía Inglesa*, Av Copiapó, *cabañas*, T 315359, open all year, good beds, comfortable; *Camping Bahía Inglesa*, Playa Las Machas, T 315424, **E** per tent, fully equipped *cabañas* for up to 5 persons, B. *El Coral* restaurant has some cabins (C, T 315331), Av El Morro, overlooking sea, good seafood, groups welcome, open all year. Buses almost hourly to Copiapó with connections from the N; taxis and colectivos US$1 from Caldera all year; frequent micro service Jan and Feb US$0.25.

Copiapó (pop 100,000; DDD 052), capital of III Región (Atacama), is situated 60 km inland in a ribbon of farms and orchards about 150 km long on the river Copiapó, the river generally regarded as the southern limit of the Atacama desert. From Chañaral there are two routes to Copiapó: inland, 212 km, via Diego de Almagro; the coastal route, 167 km, via Caldera (see above). It is an attractive mining centre with an important mining school. There is a monument to Juan Godoy, a mule-driver, who, in 1832, discovered silver at Chañarcillo (see below). The plaza is interesting, with a wooden Cathedral dating from 1851. The best **mineralogical museum** in Chile is at Colipí y Rodríguez, 1 block E from Plaza de Armas; Mon-Fri 1130-1300, 1500-1900, Sat 1000-1300, US$0.50. Many ores shown are found only in the Atacama desert. Also **Museo Regional del Atacama**, Atacama y Rancagua, entrance US$0.75 (free on Sun), interesting. Open Mon-Sat 0900-1245, 1500-1830, Sun 1000-1245. The museum at the **railway station** is dull, but the steam locomotive used in the inaugural journey between Copiapó and Caldera in 1851 (the earliest railway line in South America) can be seen at the Universidad de Atacama on the northern highway.

Hotels A2 *Hostería Las Pircas*, Av Kennedy s/n, T 213220, bungalows, pool, dining room, out of town; **A2** *San Francisco de la Selva* Los Carrera 525, T 217013, modern; **C** *Derby*, Yerbas Buenas, 396, T 212447, clean. **C** *Inglés*, Atacama 337, T 212797, old-fashioned, spacious; **C** *Palace*, Atacama 741, T 212852, patio, pleasant; **C** *La Casona*, O'Higgins 150, T 217277/8, clean, friendly, tours organized; **C** *Marcoan*, Yumbel 351, T 211397, modern. **E** *Residencial Chacabuco*, Calle Chacabuco 271, T 213428, near bus terminal; **E** *Residencial Rodríguez*, Rodríguez 528, T 212861, basic, friendly, good *comedor*, rec. **E** *Residencial Rocío*, Yerbas Buenas 581, T 215360, good value, clean, attractive patio, rec.

Restaurants *La Carreta*, on Carretera de Copayapu, 5 km S, ranch-style, very good meat and fish; *Bavaria Restaurant*, on main square, excellent but not cheap. *Chifa Hao Hua*, Colipi 340, good Chinese; *Pampas*, Maipú y Atacama, smart, pleasant.

Exchange Fincard (Mastercard), Chacabuco 389, open Mon-Fri 0900-1400, 1630-1930, Sat 1030-1300. **Banco Concepción**, cash advance on Visa.

Telephone CTC, Atacama 566.

Travel Agency *Exploration and Adventure Tour*, Rodriguez 771, T 212459, organize a wide range of excursions.

Tourist Office Los Carrera 691, N side of Plaza de Armas, T 212838, helpful.

Car Hire Expensive: Av Kennedy 310, T 2964, **Hertz** at Copayapu 173, T 211333.

Airport LanChile, O'Higgins 640, T 213512, daily to/from Santiago, also to El Salvador; National (Colipi 350, T 218951) direct to La Serena and on to Santiago.

Buses To Santiago US$15, 12 hrs; to **La Serena** US$7, 5 hrs; to **Caldera**, US$1.50, 1 hr.

Excursions 90 km SE up the river valley from Copiapó is the **Centro Metalúrgico Incaico**, an Inca bronze foundry (rebuilt, disappointing), connected by a paved road. By public transport: Take Casther bus, 0845, to Valle del Cerro, US$1.50, 2 hrs and get off at Valle Hermoso (foundry is 1 km walk from main road). Return buses pass about 1400 and 1600. No accommodation in nearby villages of Los Loros, Villa Hermoso, Las Juntas.

59 km S of Copiapó on the Pan-American Highway is a signposted turning to *Chañarcillo*. This was one of the 19th century's richest silver mines, becoming the second largest in the Americas. The tips are being reworked and this has destroyed much of the ruins.

To Argentina A road runs NE via the Salar de Maricunga and Laguna Verde through the pass of San Francisco to Tinogasta, in Argentina (suitable only for 4WD vehicles, open only Nov-Apr, often closed by landslides). South of the pass rises the Ojos del Salado mountain, believed to be the third highest peak in the Americas; its height is now thought to be 6,864m (although the latest Chilean IGM map says 6,879m – 1994; it seems to depend which side of the border you are on).

Climbing **Ojos del Salado**: Allow 12-14 days for a climbing expedition. Base camp for the climb is at the Argentine frontier post (4,500m). There are 2 refuges, at 5,200m (4 beds) and 5,700m (6 beds). From the latter it is 10-12 hrs climb to the summit, approx grade 4. Take water from Copiapó. Guides and equipment can be hired in Copiapó (Rubén E Rubilan Cortes, O'Higgins 330, T 216536 and others) US$450-600 or contact Southern Summits (details under Santiago).

The zone S of the Atacama Desert between the valleys of the Copiapó and the Aconcagua is a transitional zone between the northern desert and the fruitful heartland. South of Copiapó the central valley is cut across by transverse spurs of mountain which link the Andes and the coastal *cordillera*. Between these spurs several rivers flow westwards. Southwards the desert gives way slowly to dry scrub and bush interspersed with sand dunes. This desert is of little interest except after rain. Then it is covered with a succession of flowers, insects and frogs, in one of the world's most spectacular wildlife events. Rain, however, is rare: there is no rain in summer; in winter it is light and lasts only a short time. It is about 115 mm at Copiapó and 500 mm at Illapel. In the river valleys under irrigation, fruit, vines, and barley are grown, and some alfalfa for cattle. There are many goats.

Vallenar (pop 47,000; DDD 054; airport), 144 km S of Copiapó, is the chief town of the Huasco valley. Near the municipal stadium is the Museo del Huasco, containing artefacts from the valley (Tues-Fri 1030-1230, 1530-1900; Sat-Sun 1000-1230).

The valley is an oasis of olive groves and vineyards. There are Pisco distilleries at Alto del Carmen and San Félix; a sweet wine known as Pajarete is also produced.

Hotels L3 *Hostería Vallenar*, Ercilla 848, T 614538, excellent, pool, Hertz car hire office, restaurant reputed to be among the best in Chile; **C** *Real*, Prat 881, T 613963; **D** *Cecil*, Prat 1059, T 614071, with bath and hot water, clean, rec; **D** *Viña del Mar*, Serrano 611, T 611478, clean, *comedor*, smoking disapproved of; several *residenciales* nearby. **Restaurants** *Bavaria*, Santiago 678, good, not cheap; *El Fogón*, Ramírez 944, for meat dishes, *almuerzo* good value; *Shanghai*, Ramírez 1267, Chinese; cheap places along S end of Av Brasil.

Excursions To *Huasco* (pop 7,000), a pleasant town and interesting port 56 km W at the mouth of the river. 1½ km S of Huasco is a terminal for loading iron ore from the deposits at Algarrobal, 52 km N of Vallenar. (**B** *Hostería Huasco*, T 531026; *Restaurant Escorial*, best; cheap seafood restaurants near port.) To *Freirina*, 36 km W of Vallenar, 21 km E of Huasco, easily reached by colectivos from either. Founded 1752, Freirina was the most important town in the valley, its prosperity based upon the nearby Capote goldmine and on later discoveries of copper. On the main plaza are the Municipalidad (1870) and the Santa Rosa church. No accommodation.

Up the rugged and spectacular Huasco valley to Alto del Carmen, 30 km, where the river divides; an unpaved road leads up the Carmen valley to **San Félix** (F *Residencial San Félix*, basic); another runs up the Tránsito valley to **El Tránsito** (F *Pensión Santa Anita*, basic). Buses from Verdaguer 658, Vallenar.

At Domeyko, 51 km S of Vallenar, a turning W goes to Caleta Chañaral on the coast, where is the **Humbolt Penguin Natural Reserve**. On Isla Chañaral, besides penguins, there are seals, sea lions, a great variety of seabirds and, offshore, a colony of grey dolphin. Permission to visit must be sought from Conaf in Caleta Choros.

La Serena (pop 160,000; DDD 051), on the coast 194 km S of Vallenar, 473 km N of Santiago, is the capital of IV Región (Coquimbo). Built on a hillside 2 km inland from Coquimbo Bay, it is thought by some to be one of the pleasantest towns in Chile, with many neo-colonial buildings and pretty gardens. Around the attractive Plaza de Armas are most of the official buildings, including the Post Office, the **Cathedral** (built in 1844 and featuring a carillon which plays every hour) and the Historical Museum (see below). There are 29 other churches, several of which have unusual towers. **San Francisco**, Balmaceda y de La Barra, has a nice façade and is on a small plaza with handicraft stalls and arcades covered with purple flowers. **Santo Domingo**, half a block from the Plaza de Armas is fronted by a small garden with statues of sealions. **La Recova**, the new market, at Cienfuegos y Cantournet, includes a large display of handicrafts and, upstairs, several good restaurants. On the W edge of the old city is the Parque Pedro de Valdivia, which includes a children's zoo. A *moai* from Easter Island can be seen on Av Colo Colo, direction Vicuña, about 15 mins walk from the centre; there is a view of the city from here. A pleasant boulevard, Av Francisco de Aguirre (known as the **Alameda**), runs from the centre to the coast, terminating at the **Faro Monumental**, a neo-colonial style mock-castle (US$0.45 entry). A series of beaches stretch from here to Peñuelas, 6 km S, linked by the Avenida del Mar. Many apartment blocks, hotels, *cabañas* and restaurants have been built along this part of the bay.

History La Serena was founded by Juan de Bohón, aide to Pedro de Valdivia, in 1544, destroyed by Diaguita Indians in 1546, rebuilt by Francisco de Aguirre in 1552, and sacked by the English pirate Sharpe in 1680. Legends of buried treasure at Guayacán Bay, frequented by pirates, persist. The present-day layout and architectural style has its origins in the 'Plan Serena' drawn up in 1948 on the orders of Chilean president, Gabriel González Videla, a native of the city.

Museums Historical museum in the Casa Gabriel González Videla on the Plaza de Armas, including several rooms on the man's life. Open Tues-Sat 0900-1300, 1600-1900, Sun 1000-1300, entry US$0.60, ticket also valid for **Museo Arqueológico**, Cordóvez y Cienfuegos, interesting collection of Diaguita and Molle Indian exhibits, especially of most attractively decorated pottery; open Tues-Sat 0900-1300, 1600-1900, Sun 1000-1300, entrance, US$0.30. There is a **mineralogical museum** in the University of La Serena, Calle A Muñoz between Benavente and Infante (for geologists, open Mon-Fri 0930-1200, free).

Hotels L3 *El Escorial I*, Colón 617, T 224793, F 221433, good; **L3** *Los Balcones de Alcalá*, Av de Aguirre 452, T 225999, F 211800, comfortable, clean, TV; **L3** *Mediterráneo*, Cienfuegos 509, Casilla 212, T 225837, including good breakfast, rec; **A2** *Francisco de Aguirre*, Córdovez 210, T 222991, with breakfast, shower, good rooms, reasonable restaurant; **A2** *Pucará*, Balmaceda 319, T 211966, F 211933, with bath and breakfast, modern, clean, quiet; **A3** *Berlín*, Córdovez 535, T 222927, F 223575, clean, safe, efficient, rec; **C** *Londres*, Córdovez 550, T 214673, with bath, D without, restaurant, old fashioned; **C** *Brasilia*, Brasil 555, T 225248, friendly, small rooms, overpriced; **C** *Hostal Del Mar*, Cuatro Esquinas 0680 (near beach), T 225816, also *cabañas*, clean, friendly; **D** *Alameda*, Av de Aguirre 450, T 213052, run down, clean and comfortable; *Hostal Santo Domingo*, Bello 1067, 10 mins walk from bus station, with breakfast, highly rec; **D** *Lido*, Matta 547, T 213073, hot water, clean, friendly; **D** *Res Chile*, Matta 561, T 211694, basic, small rooms, clean, hot water am only; **D** *El Cobre*, Colón y Matta, large rooms, spotless, friendly owners, highly rec; **D** *Residencial El Loa*, O'Higgins 362, with shower, good inexpensive home cooking, friendly; **D** *Residencial Petit*, de la Barra 586, T 212536, hot water; **D** *Turismo 2000*, Lautaro 960, T 215793, hot water, bargain; **D** *Lautaro 880*, hot water, clean, rec; **D** *Gabriela Matos*, Cienfuegos 230, T 214588, in beautiful old building, use of kitchen, helpful, rec; **D** *Casa del Turista*, Colón 318, clean, hot water, helpful; **D** *San Juan*, Balmaceda 827, clean, central; **F** pp unnamed *residencial* at Av de Aguirre 411, in dormitories, clean; **E** Isabel Ahumada Rolle,

Eduardo de la Barra 315, T 212591, incl breakfast, lovely patio, rec; **E** *Residencial Americana*, Andrés Bello 859, shabby but friendly; **E** Andrés Bello 979A, T 224400, highly rec, clean, friendly, good beds; **E** *Rosa Canto*, Cantournet 976, T 213954, hot water, kitchen, comfortable, family run, rec; private accommodation at **F** pp Cienfuegos 324, dirty, laundry and cooking facilities, friendly; **E** Matta 221, with breakfast, cooking and laundry facilities; **E** pp Alejandro Muñoz, Brasil 720, T 211619, good showers, English and French spoken, helpful, rec; **E** Adolfo Ballas 1418, T 223735; **E** Los Carrera 880, small rooms; similar at No 881. **Motels A1** *Canto del Agua*, Av del Mar 5700, T 242203, F 241767, very good, pleasant cabins; **A3** *Les Mouettes*, Av del Mar 2500, T 225665, F 226278, good restaurant, incl breakfast, rec; **B** *Cabañas Los Papayos*, Huerto 66, 2 km S of city (Vista Hermosa bus), much cheaper out of season, 2 bedroom cabins, rec, pool, gardens; several more motels along the beach. Accommodation in the centre of town is expensive. Route 5 from La Serena to Coquimbo is lined with cheaper accommodation, from hotels to *cabañas*, and restaurants. There are no buses along Av del Mar, but it is only ½ km off Route 5. The tourist office in the bus terminal have accommodation information, helpful.

Campsites *Camping Peñuelas*, Los Pescadores 795, T 313818. *Maki Payi*, 153 Vegas Norte, T 213628, about 5 km N of La Serena, near sea, friendly, rec, self-contained cabins available. *Hipocampo*, 4 km S on Av del Mar (take bus for Coquimbo and get off at Colegio Adventista, US$2.50 pp by Playa El Pescador), T 214276.

Restaurants *Club Social*, Córdovez 516 (first floor), unpretentious but excellent value; *El Rincón Colonial*, Córdovez 578, good fish; *Hotel La Serena*, Córdovez 610, good meat. *Ciro's*, Francisco de Aguirre 431, T 213482, old-fashioned, good lunch, rec; *Rapsodia*, Arturo Prat 470, tea house with good cakes; *Domingo Domínguez*, Prat 572, good Italian, pricey but worth it, repeatedly rec; *Mesón Matias*, Balmaceda 1940, excellent Spanish, elegant, expensive but highly rec; *La Mía Pizza*, O'Higgins 460, Italian, good value, inexpensive (branch on Av del Mar in summer); *Mai Lai Fan*, Córdovez 740, good Chinese, reasonably priced; *Salón Las Tejas*, Francisco de Aguirre 395, cheap, local dishes incl vegetarian; *La Vie Claire*, Cantournet 880, excellent vegetarian, daily 1030-1600, 1700-2230; *Chopería Don Antonio*, Vicente Zorrilla 837-9, 20m from *La Recova*, friendly, good value. For good, fish lunches try the restaurants on the upper floor of the Recova market. Several good cafés: *Tito's*, O'Higgins y Córdovez, popular meeting place; *Café do Brasil*, Balmaceda 461, good coffee; *Casa Miró*, Balmaceda 265, good for coffee and late evening drinks; *Café La Crêperie*, O'Higgins y de la Barra, crêpes, light meals, occasional live music; *Bocaccio*, Prat y Balmaceda, good cakes, modern, smart, popular. *Vadinho*, Balmaceda 545, open late. Note that the quality of restaurants, especially on Av del Mar, varies considerably; often the majority of what is on the menu is not available: a good restaurant is *Puerto de Andaluz* on Av del Mar.

Exchange Fincard (Mastercard), Balmaceda 383, Local 217, Mon-Fri 0900-1400, 1600-2030. Banco Concepción, O'Higgins 529, Visa. *Casas de Cambio*: La Reconquista, in a galería on Córdovez between Balmaceda and O'Higgins, excellent rates; US$100 Money Exchange, Prat 645, Mon-Fri 0900-1400, 1600-2100, Sat 0900-1400; Viajes Val, Prat 540 (open Sat 1100-1400); La Portada, Balmaceda 515; Serena Cambios at bus terminal and airport, open 1100-2300 daily; Cambio Fides, Caracol Colonial, Balmaceda 460, good rates, changes TCs (another *cambio* in the basement, building closed 1400-1600). If heading N note that La Serena is the last place to change TCs before Antofagasta.

Discotheques *La Burbuja*, Balmaceda 677. *Cesare*, Av del Mar.

Laundry *Ro-Ma*, Los Carrera 654; another at Balmaceda y Brasil.

Telecommunications Long distance calls from Córdovez 446 and La Recova market. Entel, Prat 571. CTC administration on Plaza de Armas sells *Turistel.*

Shopping *La Recova* handicraft market, though many items imported from Peru and Bolivia; *Cema-Chile*, Los Carrera 562; *Las Brisas* supermarket, Cienfuegos y Córdovez, food not as cheap as in *La Recova*. 24-hr supermarket on corner of Cienfuegos, 30m from *alojamiento* at No 324.

Sport Gimnasio GFU, Amuñategui 426, T 222420, and Vitalia, Córdovez 756, T 221939.

Travel Agents *Ingservitur*, Los Lirios 300, Coquimbo, T 312943, varied programme of tours, incl Parque Nacional Fray Jorge (see p 650), depending on demand; *San Bartolmé*, Brasil 415, T/F 221992; *Gira Tour*, Prat 689, T 223535; *Turismo Elquitur*, Los Carrera 594, T 227875.

Tourist Office Main **Sernatur** office in Edificio de Servicios Públicos (next to the Post Office on the Plaza de Armas), T 225138, open Mon-Fri 0900-1300, 1500-1730. Kiosks at bus terminal (summer only) and at Balmaceda y Prat (open in theory Mon-Sat 1100-1400, 1600-1900), helpful.

Local transport City buses US$0.25; taxis US$0.75 + US$0.10 per every 200m.

Car Hire Hertz, Francisco de Aguirre 0225, T 225471/226171, **Budget**, Av de Aguirre 0240; **Daire**, Prat between O'Higgins and Cienfuegas, rec as cheapest, good service. **Automóvil Club de Chile**, Eduardo de la Barra 435, T 211504.

Bicycle Repairs *Green Go Club*, Panamericana Norte y Av Francisco de Aguirre, T 224454, North American run, good parts, information on local cycle routes.

Air Services LanChile, T 225981; Ladeco, Córdovez 484, T 225753; National, Eduardo de la Barra 435, T 214460, F 232808. Ladeco flies to **San Juan**, Argentina, in summer only. To **Santiago**, Ladeco daily, National 6 a week; to **Autofagasta**, Ladeco 2 a week; To **Copiagó**, National 5 a week.

Buses Bus terminal, El Santo y Amunategui, (about 8 blocks S of the centre). Buses daily to **Santiago**, several companies, 7 hrs, US$14; to **Arica**, US$25; to **Calama**, US$18, 16 hrs. To **Valparaíso**, 7 hrs, US$10; to **Antofagasta**, 13 hrs, several companies, US$15-18, and to **Iquique**, 17 hrs, US$20. Bus to **Vicuña**, Frontera Elqui, Av Perú y Calle Esmeralda, frequent service, 1 hr, US$1.50; *colectivo* to Vicuña, Empresa Nevada del Sol de Elqui, Domeyko 550, T 21450, others from Av Aguirre y Balmaceda, US$2; to **Coquimbo**, bus No 8 from Av Aguirre y Cienfuegos, US$0.30, every few mins.

Excursion La Serena is at the mouth of the Elqui river valley, where the Nobel Prize-winning poet Gabriela Mistral was born. She described the valley as "confined yet lofty, many-sided yet simple, rustic yet a mining area". The branches of the road up the valley all lead to "fertile nooks, to shady vegetation, to dense groves, to gardens fed by the very sap of the hills". Of the *elquinos*, the people of the valley, she says that "even the most taciturn of them come out with witty and charming remarks". There are still a few descendants of the Diaguitas, the tribe that inhabited the valley at one time. The road up the valley is paved as far as Varillar, 24 km beyond Vicuña, the capital of the valley. Except for Vicuña, most of the tiny towns have but a single street. There are mines, orchards, orange groves and vineyards in the valley, which is the main pisco-producing area of Chile, the climate and soil being ideally suited to the cultivation of grapes with a high sugar-content. Of the 9 Pisco distilleries in the valley, the largest is Capel in Vicuña. Huancara, a delicious liqueur introduced by the Jesuits, is also produced in the valley.

Vicuña (pop 6,000; DDD 051), 66 km E of La Serena, is a small, clean, friendly, picturesque town. On the W side of the plaza are the municipal chambers, built in 1826 and topped in 1905 by a prefabricated medieval-German-style tower—the Torre Bauer—imported by the German-born mayor of the time. Inside the chambers is a gallery of past local dignitaries. Also on the plaza is the Iglesia Parroquial. The Museo Gabriela Mistral is at Calle Gabriela Mistral y Riquelme (open Tues-Sat 0900-1300, 1500-1900, Sun 1000-1300, entry US$0.40). Tourist office on Plaza de Armas. There are good views from Cerro La Virgen, N of town. The Capel Pisco distillery is 1½ km E of Vicuña, to the right of the main road; guided tours (in Spanish) are offered Dec-Feb Mon-Sat 0930-1200, 1430-1800, Sun 1000-1230, 0Mar-Nov Mon-Fri 0930-1200, 1430-1800, Sat 1000-1230, free, 1 hr; no booking required, passport necessary.

Hotels L3 *Hostería Vicuña*, Sgto Aldea 101, T 411301, F 411144, swimming pool, tennis court, excellent restaurant. **A2** *Yunkai*, O'Higgins 72, T 411195, F 411593, cabañas for 4/6 persons, pool, restaurant. On Gabriela Mistral: **C** *Hostel Valle Hermoso*, No 706, T 411206, helpful, rec; **D** *Sol del Valle*, at No 743, hot water, TV, vineyard, restaurant; **E** *Hostal Michel*, No 573, breakfast extra, large gardens; **E** *Residencial Moderna*, at No 718, full board available, no hot water, nothing modern about it, but quiet, clean, very nice; **E** pp *Residencial Mistral*, at No 180, restaurant, basic, hot water, clean.

Camping *Camping y Piscina Las Tinajas*, E end of Chacabuco, swimming pool, restaurant.

Restaurants Mainly on G Mistral: *Club Social de Elqui*, at No 435, good food, attractive patio, good value, *almuerzo*; *Mistral*, at No 180, very good food, popular with locals, good value *almuerzo*; *Halley*, at No 404, good meat dishes, also *choperia*, swimming pool; *Yo Y Soledad*, No 364, inexpensive, good value.

Buses To La Serena, about 10 a day, most by Frontera Elqui, first 0800, last 1930, 1 hr, US$1.50, *colectivo* from Plaza de Armas US$2; to Santiago via La Serena, Expreso Norte at 1145 and 2200; to Pisco Elqui, 4 a day, Vía Elqui and Frontera Elqui, 1 hr, US$2.

From Vicuña the road continues up the valley another 18 km to Rivadavia where it divides: the main route (Route 41) winding through the mountains to the Argentine frontier at Agua Negra. The road over the pass, after years of closure is now open Jan-Apr only between 1100-1700. No public transport on this route: El Indio mine transport may give lifts to the Chilean border post at Juntas (92 km NW of Agua Negra). The other branch of the road runs through Paihuano (camping) and **Monte Grande** (where the tomb of Gabriela Mistral is situated) to **Pisco Elqui** (E *Hosteria de Don Juan*, fine views, excellent breakfasts; E *Elqui*, hot shower, good restaurant, rec, not always open; *Las Vegas* campsite, F pp, Sol de Barbosa, also camping. *Camping El Olivo*, G pp, no hot water. One bus a day to La Serena).

Beyond Monte Grande, on the road to El Colorado, are some Ashram places, some of which welcome visitors; one can camp ("a firm belief in UFOs is a help"—Quentin Crewe). Bus from Vicuña plaza to Monte Grande US$1.20, from Monte Grande you can walk or take a pick-up if one is running to a self-contained community where you can stay up to 4 days (take sleeping bag and food); ask for Gladys or Juanita.

Observatories The La Serena district is one of the astronomical centres of the world, with three observatories: **El Tololo**, 89 km SE of La Serena in the Elqui Valley, 51 km S of Vicuña, which belongs to Aura, an association of US and Chilean universities. This possesses the largest telescope in the southern hemisphere, eight others and a radio telescope. It is open to visitors every Sat 0900-1200, 1300-1600, only by permit obtained from Aura, Calle Mariátegui 2438, Santiago, T 274-5884/496-568, or Casilla 603, La Serena, T 225-415, and then pick up your free permit the day before (the office is at Colina Los Pinos, on a hill behind the new University—personal applications can be made here for all three observatories). During holiday periods apply well in advance. At other times you may be able to book the day before. They will insist that you have private transport; you can hire a taxi, US$33, but you will require the registration number when you book.

La Silla, 150 km NE of La Serena, which belongs to ESO (European Southern Observatory), financed by 8 EC countries, comprising 14 telescopes. Open first Sat of the month, 1430-1730, no permission required; for prior information (essential), Alonso de Córdoba 3107, Santiago, T 228-5006/698-8757, or write to Casilla 567, La Serena, T 213-832. Office also at bus terminal. From La Serena it is 114 km to the turn-off (D *Posada La Frontera*, cabañas), then another 36 km.

Las Campanas, 156 km NE of La Serena, 30 km N of La Silla, belonging to the Carnegie Institute, has 4 telescopes and is altogether a smaller facility than the other two. It is open without permission every Sat 1430-1730, T 213-032, or write to Casilla 601, La Serena. Go to the same junction as for La Silla, then 40 km in a different direction. For La Silla and Las Campanas those without private transport can take the 1100 Pullman Fichtur bus towards Vallenar (2 hrs, US$3.25) and get out at the junction (*desvío*); hitch from there. It is possible to hire a car with driver to visit all three sites in one day for US$22.

Three travel agents in La Serena, Ingservitur, Gira Tour and Turismo Cristóbal, receive tickets from the observatories and arrange tours from US$30 pp, but these are often booked up well in advance and, unless travelling alone, it is cheaper to arrange your own transport.

Coquimbo (pop 106,000; DDD 051), 12 km S of La Serena on the same bay, is a port of considerable importance, with one of the best harbours on the coast and major fish-processing plants. The city is strung along the N shore of a peninsula. Most of the commercial life is centred on 3 streets which run between the port and the steep hillside on which are perched many of the poorer houses. On the S shore of the peninsula lies the suburb of Guayacán, with an iron-ore loading port and a steel church designed by Eiffel. Nearby is **La Herradura**, 2½ km from Coquimbo, which has the best beaches. Also nearby is a resort complex called **Las Tacas**, with beach, swimming pool, tennis, flats, *apart-hotel*, etc.

Museum In 1981 heavy rain uncovered 39 ancient burials of humans and llamas which had been sacrificed. A small museum has been built in the Plaza Gabriela Mistral to exhibit these.

Hotels Generally much cheaper than in La Serena. **B** *Lig*, Aldunate 1577, T 311171, comfortable, friendly, good value, near bus terminus; **C** *Prat*, Bilbao y Aldunate, T 311845, comfortable, pleasant; **C** *Iberia*, Lastra 400 (facing Plaza de Armas), T 312141, friendly, rec; **D** *Punta del Este*, Av Videla 170, T 312768, nice rooms; **E** *Claris*, Aldunate 669, run-down, old-fashioned, rambling hotel with bar and *comedor*, live music on Fri and Sat, popular with sailors; **E** *Mi Casa*, Varela 1653, clean, friendly, good value. Several hotels in La Herradura, including **C** *Hotel La Herradura*, Av Costanera 200, T 321320.

Camping *Camping La Herradura*, T 312084.

Restaurants Lots of good fish restaurants including *Sal y Pimiento del Capitán Denny*,

Aldunate 769, one of the best, pleasant, old-fashioned, mainly fish, US$12-20 pp; *La Picada*, Av Costanera near statue of O'Higgins, excellent, pricey; *Crucero*, Aldunate 1326, excellent; *La Barca*, Ríos y Varela, modest but good; and *La Bahía*, Pinto 1465, excellent, good value. Several good seafood restaurants (known as *pensiones*) at the municipal market, Melgarejo between Bilbao and Borgoño (*El Callejón* has been rec); *Mai Lai Fan*, Av Ossandón 1, excellent Chinese, rec;*Tavola Calda*, Bilbao 451, good Italian, good value; *El Brasero*, Av Alessandri, for meat lovers, pricey.

Telephone CTC, Aldunate 1633.

Tourist Office Kiosk in Plaza de Armas (open summer only).

Buses New bus terminal at Varela y Garriga. To La Serena, every few mins, US$0.30.

Excursions Good beaches at *Totoralillo*, 12 km S (good swimming) and **Guanaqueros**, a fishing village 35 km S (**D** *Hotel La Bahía*, simple, clean; *Restaurant El Pequeño*). Buses (45 mins, US$0.80) and colectivos (US$1.40) from Coquimbo.

Tongoy, 48 km S of Coquimbo, is an old fishing port occupying the whole of a small peninsula. It is now a rapidly growing resort and well worth a visit: to the S the Playa Grande is 14 km long; to the N the Playa Socos is 4 km in length.

Services A2 *Panorámico*, Mirador 455, T 391944, incl breakfast, all rooms with view of bay and fishing boats, excellent, clean, friendly; **A1-B** *Hotel Yachting Club*, Costanera 20, T 391154, good; *Samay*, overlooking fishing port, T 391355; **E** *Plaza*, on main square, T 391184; several basic *residenciales*. Wide range of restaurants—try the *marisquerías* near the fishing port, excellent value. *Restaurant El Buque*, Puesto 17 on seafront, near fishing harbour, fish and meat with superb sauces, good service, highly rec. Bus services from Coquimbo, Ruta Costera, 1 hr US$1, frequency varies according to season and day (more on Sun). Colectivos US$1.70.

From here to Santiago, the Pan-American Highway mainly follows the coastline, passing many beautiful coves, alternatively rocky and sandy, with good surf, but the water is very cold, as is the air. The last stretch before Santiago is through green valleys with rich blue clover and wild artichokes. Beware, the green caterpillars crossing the road in Nov sting!

The good inland road from La Serena or Coquimbo S to Ovalle makes an interesting contrast to Ruta 5, with a fine pass and occasional views of snowcapped Andes across cacti-covered plains and semi-desert mountain ranges. Off this road, 54 km SE is the little town of **Andacollo** (colectivo, US$2.40; bus, US$1.70—last 20 km of road very bad). Here, on 24 to 28 Dec a picturesque religious ceremony is held. The pilgrimage to the shrine of the miraculous Virgen del Rosario de Andacollo is the occasion for ritual dances dating from a pre-Spanish past. The church is huge. Alluvial gold washing and manganese and copper mining in the area. No hotel, but some *pensiones*; during the festival private houses rent beds and some let you pay for a shower. Colectivos run to the festival from Calle Benavente, near Colocolo, in La Serena, but 'purists' walk (torch and good walking shoes essential). 2 villages are passed on the route, which starts on the paved highway, then goes along a railway track and lastly up a steep, dusty hill.

Ovalle (pop 66,000; DDD 053) is 86 km S of Coquimbo in the valley of the Limarí river, inland from the sea. It is the centre of a fruit, sheep-rearing, and mining district. Market days are Mon, Wed, Fri and Sat, till 1600; the market (*feria agrícola*) is by the railway on Benavente. The town is famous for its *talabarterías* (leather workshops) and for its products made of lapis lazuli which is mined locally. The Paloma dam, at the confluence of the Grande and Huatulame rivers, SE of Ovalle, is one of the largest in Chile.

Museum Museo Regional, Calle Independencia, open Tues-Sun 1000-1600, has 3 rm, information on petroglyphs and a good collection of Diaguita ceramics and other artefacts.

Hotels C *American*, V Mackenna 169, T 620722, run down; **D** *Residencial Bristol*, Araucano 224, pleasant spacious building, restaurant. On Libertad: **D** *Buenos Aires*, No 136, no locks on doors, OK; **D** *Francia*, No 231, T 620828, pleasant, friendly, restaurant; **D** *Roxy*, No 155, T 620080, constant hot water, clean, friendly, patio, *comedor*, highly rec; **E** *Venecia*, No 261, T 620968, clean, safe, friendly, rec; **E** *Res Socos*, Socos 22, T 624157, clean, quiet, family run, rec. For cheaper accommodation try **G** *Residencial Lolita*, Independencia 274, without bath, **F** with, clean, basic, rec. Several other cheap *residenciales* in Calle Socos (short stay).

Restaurants *Club Social*, V MacKenna 400 block, excellent fish dishes though pricey; *Club Social Arabe*, Arauco 255, spacious glass-domed premises, limited selection of Arab dishes, good but not cheap; *El Quijote*, Arauco 294, intimate atmosphere, good seafood, inexpensive; *Alamar*, Santiago 259, excellent seafood, good value; *El Bosco*, Benavente 88, good, cheap. Good value *almuerzos* at *Casino La Bomba*, Aguirre 364, run by fire brigade. For drinks and snacks try *Café Caribe Express*, V MacKenna 241; *Yum Yum*, V MacKenna 21, good, cheap, lively; *D'Oscar Bar*, Plaza de Armas; *Pastelería Josti*, Libertad 427. *Club Comercial*, Aguirre 244 (on plaza), open Sun.

Shopping For articles made of Lapis Lazuli try Sr Wellington Vega Alfaro at his workshop at Vicente Ovando 660, Población Yungay, T 621951.

Tourist Offices Two kiosks on the Plaza de Armas. **Automóvil Club de Chile**, Vitacura 8620, very helpful, overnight parking.

Buses To **Santiago**, several, 6½ hrs, US$7. To **La Serena**, 12 a day, 1¼ hrs, US$2. To **Antofagasta**, US$18.

Excursions The **Monumento Nacional Valle del Encanto**, about 22 km SW of Ovalle, has Indian petroglyphs as well as dramatic boulders, its own microclimate, cacti and lizards (open Mon-Fri 0900-1300, 1500-1900, Sat 0900-1300, 1500-1800, Sun 1000-1300, US$2). No local bus service; you must take long distance bus and ask to be dropped off—5 km walk to the valley; flag down a bus to return. Camping facilities are being upgraded. **Termas de Socos**, 35 km SW of Ovalle, has fine thermal springs (entrance US$5), a good hotel (A2, T Ovalle 1373, Casilla 323) and a campsite (US$10 per tent, but bargain) nearby. Bus US$2. The **Parque Nacional Fray Jorge**, 50 km W at the mouth of the Río Limari, is approached by a poor road leading off the Pan-American Highway (very poorly signposted). Its forests, usually covered in fog, contrast with the otherwise barren surroundings. Open Sat, Sun and public holidays only, 0830-1830; visits closely controlled due to risk of fire. (Scientific groups may obtain permission to visit from The Director, Conaf, Cordóvez 281, La Serena, T 211124.) Round trip in taxi, US$30. 2 km N of Ovalle along Monte Patria road is Balnearia Los Peñones, on a clean shallow river.

Some 47 km NE along an unpaved and largely winding road is the **Monumento Nacional Pichasca** (open 0830-1700, US$3). It has petrified tree trunks, archaeological remains, including a vast cave (comparable to the Cueva Milodón outside Puerto Natales) with remains of ancient roof paintings, and views of gigantic rock formations on the surrounding mountains. Daily bus from Ovalle to Río Hurtado passes the turn-off (to San Pedro) about 42 km from the city. From here it is 3 km to the park and about 2 km more to sites of interest.

About 165 km S of Ovalle by road, and 59 km NE by new paved road from Los Vilos, is *Illapel*, in the basin of the river Choapa (Hotel). Pop 25,600. Fruit, grains and cattle are raised in the valley.

Los Vilos, 280 km S of Coquimbo, is a former mineral port, now a small seaside resort with frequent launches to the off-shore Isla de Los Huevos and Isla de Los Lobos and a beautiful nearby beach (26 km S) at *Pichidangui*. (DDD Los Vilos 051, Pichidangui 053.)

Hotels in Los Vilos A2 *Cabañas Antulanquen* (negotiable during off season), good service, own porch, kitchenette, rec; **C** *Hostería Arrayán*, Caupolicán 1, T 541005, clean; **D** *Lord Willow*, Hostería 1444, T 541037, overlooking beach and harbour, with breakfast and bath, pleasant; **D** *Bellavista*, Rengo 20, T 541073, with breakfast, without bath, hot water, clean; **F** pp *Residencial Angelica*, Caupolicán 627, central, warm water, restaurant attached. No campsite. *Restaurant Costanera*, good views over ocean, excellent meals. The *Panamerican Motel* is right on the highway, Km 224, and is a convenient stopping place between La Serena and Viña del Mar or Santiago, quite good. **In Pichidangui**: *Motel El Bosque*, El Bosque s/n, T 541182, rec; **B** *Motel Pichidangui*, Francis Drake s/n, T 594010, swimming pool; **C** *Puquen*, 2 Poniente s/n, attractive, good value; various other hotels and *pensiones* in every price range. Two good campsites, US$10 in season, bargain for lower price off season. Restaurants tend to be pricey although there is a food shop. Only 1 bus daily Pichidangui-Santiago, but N-S buses on the Highway are in walking distance of the beach.

10 km S of Pichidangui is *Los Molles*, a small town where many wealthy residents of Santiago have their summer homes. There are two small hotels, one down at the beach and the other on the cliff overlooking the beach. *Restaurant La Pirata Suiza*, excellent European-style cooking, run by a Swiss couple.

See p 625 for list of service stations between Santiago and the Peruvian border.

SANTIAGO AND THE HEARTLAND (3)

The capital and its surroundings, from N of the Río Aconcagua to the Río Maipo; within easy reach are Andean ski resorts and Pacific beaches, such as the international resort of Viña del Mar. On the same stretch of coast is the port of Valparaíso.

Nearly 70% of the people of Chile live in the comparatively small heartland. The rural population density in the area is exceptional for Latin America: it is as high as 48 to the square km to the S of Santiago.

From a third to half of the width of the area is taken up by the Andes, which are formidably high in the northern sector; at the head of the river Aconcagua the peak of Aconcagua (in Argentina), the highest in the Americas, rises to 6,964m. The region suffers from earthquakes. There is a mantle of snow on the mountains: at Aconcagua it begins at 4,300m. The lower slopes are covered with dense forests. Between the forest and the snowline there are alpine pastures; during the summer cattle are driven up to these pastures to graze.

The coastal range, over 2,130m high, takes up another third of the width. It is lower here than in the northern desert, but the shoreline is still unbroken; it is only at Valparaíso and San Antonio that good harbourage is to be found.

Between the coastal range and the Andes lies the Central Valley; the rivers cross it at right angles and cut their way to the sea through narrow canyons in the coastal range. The valley of the Aconcagua is separated by a mountainous spur from the valley of the Mapocho, in which Santiago lies.

There is rain during the winter in the heartland, but the summers are dry. The rain increases to the S. On the coast at Viña del Mar it is 483 mm a year, but is somewhat less inland. Temperatures, on the other hand, are higher inland than on the coast. There is frost now and then, but very little snow falls.

Santiago, founded by Pedro de Valdivia in 1541, is the fifth largest city in South America, with nearly 5m people, and one of the most beautifully set of any, standing in a wide plain, 600m above the sea. The city is crossed from E to W by the Río Mapocho, which passes through an artificial stone channel, 40m wide, spanned by several bridges. Public gardens, laid out with admirable taste, are filled with flowers and kept in good order. The magnificent chain of the Andes, with its snow-capped heights, is in full view for much of the year, rain and pollution permitting; there are peaks of 6,000m about 100 km away. More than half the country's manufacturing is done here; it is essentially a modern capital, full of skyscrapers, bustle, noise, traffic and smog (tables for which are published in the daily papers, as are the registration numbers of those cars which are not allowed into the city each day).

The centre of the old city lies between the Mapocho and the Avenida O'Higgins usually known as the **Alameda**. From the **Plaza Baquedano** (Plaza Italia) in the E of the city's central area, the Mapocho flows to the NW and the Avenida O'Higgins runs to the SW. From Plaza Baquedano the Calle Merced runs due W to the **Plaza de Armas**, the heart of the city; it lies 5 blocks S of the Mapocho. On the eastern and southern sides of Plaza de Armas there are arcades with shops; on the northern side is the Post Office and the Municipalidad; and on the western side the Cathedral and the archbishop's palace. The Cathedral, much rebuilt, contains a recumbent statue in wood of St Francis Xavier, and the chandelier which lit the first meetings of Congress after independence; it also houses an interesting museum of religious art and historical pieces. In the **Palacio de la Real Audiencia** on the Plaza de Armas is the Museo Histórico Nacional (see **Museums**, below). A block W of the Cathedral is the **former Congress** building now occupied by the

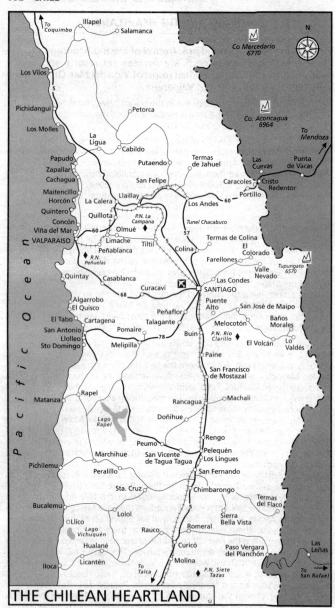

THE CHILEAN HEARTLAND

Ministry of Foreign Affairs (the Congress, which held no sittings after 1973, has been moved to Valparaíso to a purpose-built building). Nearby are the law courts. At Calle Merced 864, close to the Plaza de Armas, is the **Casa Colorada**, built in 1769, the home of the Governor in colonial days and then of Mateo de Toro, first President of Chile. It is now the Museum of the History of Santiago. From the Plaza de Armas Paseo Ahumada, a pedestrianized street lined with cafés runs S to the Alameda 4 blocks away, crossing Huérfanos, which is also pedestrianized.

The Avenida O'Higgins runs through the heart of the city for over 3 km. It is 100m wide, and ornamented with gardens and statuary: the most notable are the equestrian statues of Generals O'Higgins and San Martín; the statue of the Chilean historian Benjamín Vicuña Mackenna who, as mayor of Santiago, beautified Cerro Santa Lucía (see **Parks and Gardens** below); and the great monument in honour of the battle of Concepción in 1879.

From the Plaza Baquedano, where there is a statue of General Baquedano and the Tomb of the Unknown Soldier, the Alameda skirts, on the right, Cerro Santa Lucía, and on the left, the Catholic University. Beyond the hill the Alameda goes past the neo-classical **National Library** on the right, which also contains the national archives. Beyond, on the left, between Calle San Francisco and Calle Londres, is the oldest church in Santiago: the red-walled church and monastery of **San Francisco**. Inside is the small statue of the Virgin which Valdivia carried on his saddlebow when he rode from Peru to Chile. Near the church cloisters is the Museo de Arte Colonial. South of San Francisco is the Barrio París-Londres, built in 1923-1929, now restored and pedestrianized. Two blocks N of the Alameda on Calle Agustinas is the **Teatro Municipal**. A little further W along the Alameda, is the **University of Chile**; the **Club de la Unión** is almost opposite. Nearby, on Calle Nueva York is the **Bolsa de Comercio**.

One block further W is the Plaza de la Libertad. To the N of the Plaza, hemmed in by the skyscrapers of the Centro Cívico, is the **Palacio de la Moneda** (1805), the Presidential Palace containing historic relics, paintings and sculpture, and the elaborate 'Salón Rojo' used for official receptions (guided visits only with written permission from the Dirección Administrativa—3 week notice required). Although the Moneda was damaged by air attacks during the military coup of 11 September 1973 it has been fully restored. In front of the Palace is the statue of former President Arturo Alessandri Palma. (Ceremonial changing of the guard every other day, 1000, never on Sun; Sun ceremony is performed Mon.)

The Alameda continues westwards to the **Planetarium** and, opposite it on the southern side, the railway station (Estación Central or Alameda). On Avenida Matucana, running N from here, is the very popular **Parque Quinta Normal**. About seven blocks W of the Estación Central is the southern bus terminal.

Four blocks N of the Plaza de Armas is the interesting **Mercado Central**, at Puente 21 de Mayo. The building faces the Parque Valenzuela, on which is the Cal y Canto metro station, the northern terminus of Line 2, and, at its western end, the former **Mapocho railway station**, now a cultural centre, which is planned to extend eventually over land currently occupied by the prison (currently in use) and the Terminal del Norte bus station four blocks W. If you head E from Mapocho station, along the river, you pass through the Parque Forestal (see below), before coming back to Plaza Baquedano.

Between the Parque Forestal, Plaza Baquedano and the Alameda is the **Lastarria** neighbourhood (Universidad Católica metro). For those interested in antique furniture, objets d'art and old books, the area is worth a visit, especially the **Plaza Mulato Gil de Castro** (Calle José V Lastarria 305). Occasional shows are put on in the square, on which are the Museo Arqueológico de Santiago in a restored house, a bookshop (Librería Latinoamericana), handicraft and antique shops, and art gallery, the Instituto de Arte Contemporáneo and the *Pérgola de la*

SANTIAGO
Orientation

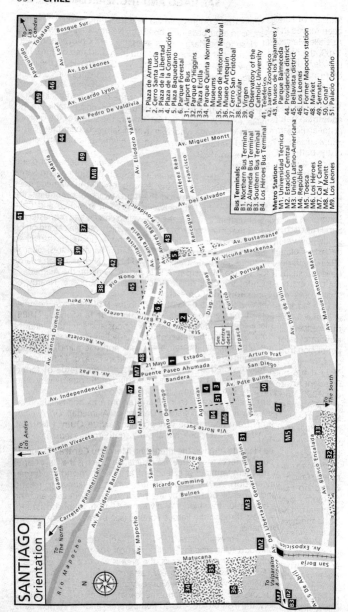

1. Plaza de Armas
2. Cerro Santa Lucia
3. Plaza de la Libertad
4. Plaza de la Constitución
5. Plaza Baquedano
6. Parque Forestal
31. Airport Borestal
32. Parque O'Higgins
33. Plaza Ercilla
34. Parque Quinta Normal, & Museums
35. Museo de Historica Natural
36. Museo Artequin
37. Cerro San Cristóbal
38. Funicular
39. Virgen
40. Observatory of the Catholic University
41. Teleférico
42. Jardín Zoológico
43. Museo de los Tajamares / Parque Balmeceda
44. Providencia district
45. Bellavista district
46. Población
47. Former Mapocho station
48. Market
49. Sernatur
50. Conaf
51. Palacio Cousiño

Bus Terminals:
B1. Northern Bus Terminal
B2. Alameda Bus Terminal
B3. Southern Bus Terminal
B4. Los Héroes Bus Terminal

Metro Station:
M1. Universidad Técnica
M2. Estacion Central
M3. Unión Latino-Americana
M4. República
M5. Toesca
M6. Los Héroes
M7. Cal y Canto
M8. M. Montt
M9. Los Leones

N

Plaza restaurant. Nearby, on Lastarria, are the **Jardín Lastarria**, a cul-de-sac of craft and antique shops (No 293), *Gutenberg, Lafourcade y Cía*, an antiquarian bookseller (No 307), the Ciné Biógrafo (No 131) and, at the corner with Merced, the Instituto Chileno-Francés (see below).

The **Bellavista** district, on the N bank of the Mapocho from Plaza Baquedano at the foot of Cerro San Cristóbal (see below), is the main focus of nightlife in the old city. Around Calle Pío Nono are restaurants and cafés, theatres, entertainments, art galleries and craft shops (especially those selling lapis lazuli, a semi-precious stone found only in Chile and Afghanistan).

East of Plaza Baquedano, the main E-W axis of the city becomes **Avenida Providencia** which heads out towards the residential areas, such as Las Condes, at the eastern and upper levels of the city. It passes the new headquarters of Sernatur (the national tourist board), the modern shopping, office and restaurant areas around Pedro de Valdivia and Los Leones metro stations (collectively known as Providencia), to become Avenida Apoquindo at Tobalaba metro.

Parks and Gardens

Cerro Santa Lucía, bounded by Calle Merced to the N, Avenida O'Higgins to the S, Calles Santa Lucía and Subercaseaux is a cone of rock rising steeply to a height of 70m. It can be scaled from the Caupolicán esplanade, on which, high on a rock, stands a statue of that Mapuche leader, but the ascent from the northern side of the hill, where there is an equestrian statue of Diego de Almagro, is easier. There are striking views of the city from the top (reached by a series of stairs), where there is a fortress, the Batería Hidalgo (the platform of which is its only colonial survival—the building is closed). Even on smoggy days, the view of the sunset is good; the Cerro closes at 2100. It is best to descend the eastern side, to see the small Plaza Pedro Valdivia with its waterfalls and statue of Valdivia. The area is famous, at night, for its gay community.

The great **Parque O'Higgins** (Parque O'Higgins metro station on Line 2, or bus from Parque Baquedano via Avs Mackenna and Matta), is about 10 blocks S of Avenida O'Higgins. It has a small lake, playing fields, tennis courts, swimming pool (open from 5 Dec), an open-air stage for local songs and dances, a discothèque, the racecourse of the Club Hípico, an amusement park, Fantasilandia (admission US$7, unlimited rides, open at weekends only in winter, and not when raining), kite-fighting contests on Sun, and a group of about twenty good 'typical' restaurants, some craft shops, the Museo del Huaso, an aquarium and a small insect and shellfish museum at El Pueblito. Cars are not allowed in the Parque.

In the large **Parque Quinta Normal**, N of the Estación Central, are four museums, details of which are given below.

There are several other parks in Santiago, but perhaps the most notable is the **Parque Forestal**, due N of Santa Lucía hill and immediately S of the Mapocho. The Museo Nacional de Bellas Artes is in the wooded grounds and is an extraordinary example of neo-classical architecture (details below). The Parque Balmaceda (Parque Gran Bretaña), E of Plaza Baquedano, is perhaps the most beautiful in Santiago (the Museo de los Tajamares is here).

The sharp, conical hill of **San Cristóbal**, forming the Parque Metropolitano, to the NE of the city, is the largest and most interesting of the city's parks. A funicular railway goes up the 300m high hill from Plaza Caupolicán at the northern end of Calle Pío Nono every few minutes from 1000-1900 Mon-Fri, 1000-2000 Sat and Sun (closed for lunch 1330-1430), stopping on its way at the Jardín Zoológico (open 1000-1300, 1500-1800 Tues-Fri, 1000-1800 Sat, Sun and holidays), US$2 in week, US$2.25 weekends. The zoo is being extended and has an excellent collection of animals which are well-cared for. (Fares: from Plaza to zoo US$2.40 (easily walked); from zoo to San Cristobal US$3.20.) A *teleférico* ascends from Estación Oasis, Av Pedro de Valdivia Norte (only taxis go there, although it is not a long walk from Pedro de Valdivia metro station), via Tupahue to the summit, near the funicular's upper station. The fare from Oasis is US$2.80 to the top, US$2.85 to Tupahue and US$2.80 return to Tupahue. A combined funicular/*teleférico* ticket is US$6. The *teleférico* runs 1030-1900 at weekends, 1500-1830 weekdays except Tues (in summer only), so to get to Tupahue at other times you must take the funicular up and walk down from the summit (or drive, or take a taxi). An open bus operated by the *teleférico* company runs to Tupahue and the summit from the Pío Nono terminal with the same schedule as the *teleférico* itself. To walk up, head up Calle Pío Nono for 1 km to the sign 'A la Virgen'; the path is shady, tree-lined and has good views.

On the hill's summit stands a colossal statue of the Virgin, which is floodlit at night; beside it is the astronomical observatory of the Catholic University which can be visited on application to the observatory's director. The hill is very well laid out around the Tupahue station, with terraces, gardens, and paths; in one building is a good, expensive restaurant (*Camino Real*, T 232-1758) with a splendid view from the terrace, especially at night, and an Enoteca, or exhibition of Chilean wines from a very limited range of vineyards. (You can taste one of the three 'wines of the day', and buy if you like, though prices are much higher than in shops.) The Casa de la Cultura has art exhibitions and free concerts at midday on Sun. There are two good swimming pools: one at Tupahue; the other, Antilen, can be reached from the road that starts below the Enoteca. Also in the Tupahue vicinity are the Botanical Gardens, with a collection of Chilean native plants, guided tours available.

Things to do and Festivals During Nov there is a free art fair in the Parque Forestal on the banks of the Río Mapocho, lasting a fortnight. In Oct or Nov there are a sumptuous flower show and an annual agricultural and industrial show (known as Fisa) in Parque Cerrillos. Religious festivals and ceremonies continue throughout Holy Week, when a priest ritually washes the feet of 12 men. The image of the Virgen del Carmen (patron of the Armed Forces) is carried through the streets by cadets on 16 July.

Walking tours of the city are offered free by the Municipal Tourist Board, Wed, 1500; details and reservations from the Board's offices (see below) or from the information kiosk in Paseo Ahumada.

Climate Temperatures can reach 33°C in Jan, but fall to 13°C (3°C at night) in Jul. Days are usually hot, the nights cool.

Museums

Note, almost all museums are closed on Mon.

Museo Histórico Nacional, Plaza de Armas 951, covers the period from the Conquest until 1925 (well worthwhile); open Tues-Sun, 1000-1230, 1400-1700 (US$0.75).

Museo de Santiago, Casa Colorada, Merced 860, history of Santiago from the Conquest to modern times, excellent displays and models, guided tours; open Tues-Sat, 1000-1800 (US$1.50), Sun and holidays (free), 1000-1300.

Museo Chileno de Arte Precolombino, Bandera 361, in the former Real Aduana, recommended, representative exhibition of objects from the precolombian cultures of Central America and the Andean region; open Tues-Sun 1000-1800, US$1.25, Sun free. Booklet, US$0.35.

Museo Iglesia de la Merced, MacIver 341, colonial religious art and archaeological collection from Easter Island; Tues-Fri 1000-1300, 1500-1800, Sat 1000-1300, US$1.

Museo de Arte Sagrado, in the Cathedral, open Mon and Fri only, 0930-1230, 1530-1830, free.

Museo de Arte Colonial, Londres 4, beside Iglesia San Francisco, religious art, includes one room with 54 paintings of the life of St Francis; in the cloisters is a room containing Gabriela Mistral's Nobel medal; also a collection of locks; Tues-Sat 1000-1800, Sun 1000-1400, US$1.

The Palacio de la Alhambra, Compañía 1340 corner of Amunátegui, is a national monument sponsored by the Society of Arts; it stages exhibitions of paintings as well as having a permanent display; open Mon-Fri 1100-1300, 1700-1900, T 80875.

Biblioteca Nacional, Moneda 650, temporary exhibitions of books, book illustrations, documents, posters, etc.

At Calle Dieciocho 438, some 5 blocks S of the Alameda, is the **Palacio Cousiño**, a large elaborate mansion amongst crumbling buildings and shanties; it contains some good oriental rugs and 19th-century European furniture. It is run by the Corporación Cultural as a museum; open Tues-Sun 0930-1330, US$3, free, but donations welcome. Visitors must be accompanied by a guide and wear cloth bootees to protect the floors.

In the Parque Quinta Normal are the following museums: **Museo Nacional de Historia Natural**, which has exhibitions on zoology, botany, mineralogy, anthropology, ethnography and archaeology; open Tues-Fri 1000-1230, 1400-1730, Sat-Sun 1100-1300, 1500-1700, US$0.80 (Sun free). The **Museo Ferroviario** containing 13 steam engines built between 1884 and 1953 (open Tues-Fri, 1000-1215, 1500-1700, Sat, Sun and holidays, 1100-1315, 1500-1715, US$1). **Museo Ciencia y Tecnología**, US$1, open same hours as **Ferroviario**. Nearby, at Av O'Higgins 3349, is the excellent **Planetarium**, T 776-2624, US$2.50. Also nearby on Av Portales is the **Museo Artequín**, in the Chilean pavilion built for the 1889 Paris International Exhibition, containing prints of famous paintings and activities and explanations of the techniques of the great masters, rec, daily 1000-1800, US$1.25.

Museo Aeronáutico, Camino a Melipilla 5100, Cerrillos Airport, Tues-Sun 1000-1700, free, in a new building, well displayed, worth a visit.

Museo Arqueológico de Santiago, in Plaza Mulato Gil de Castro, Lastarria 307, temporary exhibitions of Chilean archaeology, anthropology and precolombian art; open Mon-Fri 1030-1400, 1530-1900, Sat, 1030-1400, free.

In the Parque Forestal is the **Museo Nacional de Bellas Artes**, which has a large display of Chilean and foreign painting and sculpture, and contemporary art exhibitions are held several times a year (Tues-Sat 1000-1800, Sun and holidays 1100-1800, US$0.70; free on Sun). In the W wing of the building is the **Museo de Arte Popular Americano**, a collection of N and S American folk art (this wing is awaiting renovation, so only a small part of the exhibition is on display). Similarly, the **Museo de Arte Contemporáneo** is on limited view as it is normally housed in the W wing.

Museo Tajamares del Mapocho, Parque Balmaceda, Av Providencia 222, an exhibition of the 17th and 18th century walls built to protect the city from flooding by the river, and of the subsequent canalization; Tues-Sat 1000-1800, Sun 1000-1330.

Museo Benjamín Vicuña Mackenna, Av V Mackenna 94, recording the life and works of the 19th century Chilean historian and biographer; occasional exhibitions.

In Parque O'Higgins, at Pueblito: **Museo del Huaso**, a small, interesting collection of criollo clothing and tools; Tues-Fri 1000-1300, 1430-1715, Sat, Sun and holidays 1000-1800, free; **Municipal Aquarium** at Local 9, Tues-Fri 1000-2000 (till 2100 Sat, Sun, holidays—small charge); **Museo de Insectos y Caracoles**, Local 12, a collection of indigenous items, same hours as the aquarium but open till 2200 at weekends and holidays.

Museo de la Escuela Militar, Los Militares 4500, Las Condes, with displays on O'Higgins, the Conquest, the Pacific War and a room devoted to the medals of Gen Pinochet (not on general display so ask), Mon-Fri 0930-1230, 1500-1800, Sat 0930-1430, Sun 1430-1800, free (passport essential).

Museo Ralli, Sotomayor 4110, Vitacura, collection of works by modern European and Latin American artists, including Dali, Chagall, Bacon and Miró; open Tues-Sun 1100-1700, free.

Museo de Artes Decorativos, Casas Lo Matta, Av Presidente Kennedy 9350, Vitacura, a new, beautiful museum containing Don Hernán Garcés Silva's bequest to the nation: antique silverplate from South America and Europe, 16th-18th century Spanish colonial and European furniture, 15th century Books of Hours, housed in an 18th century country mansion. Guided tours available; by bus, take Intercomunal No 4 from Mapocho station, or take a taxi; in either case ask to be let out at 'Casas lo Matta'.

The house of Pablo Neruda, the poet, **La Chascona**, is at F Márquez de la Plata 0192, Bellavista, T 777-8741, now restored after earthquake damage in 1985 and headquarters of the Fundación Pablo Neruda. Closed Sun and Mon. Hourly guided visits only, US$2 entry; can book an English guide. (see p 684).

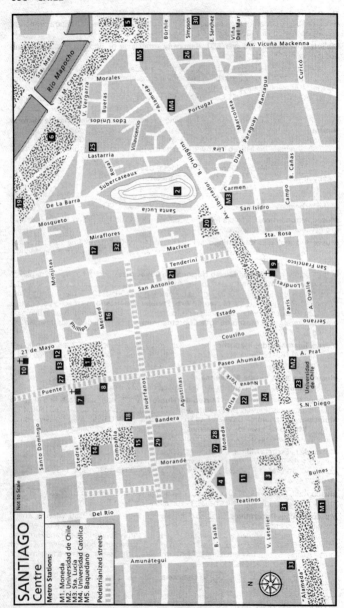

SANTIAGO
Centre

Metro Stations:
M1. Moneda
M2. Universidad de Chile
M3. Sta. Lucia
M4. Universidad Católica
M5. Baquedano

Pedestrianized streets

Not to Scale

53

N

Warning Like all large cities, Santiago has problems of theft. Pickpockets and bagsnatchers, who are often well-dressed, operate especially on the Metro and around the Plaza de Armas. The Cerro Santa Lucía area is reported to be dangerous even in daytime.

Telephone code 02.

Hotels Check if breakfast and 18% tax is included in the price quoted (if foreigners pay in US$ cash or with US$ TCs, the 18% IVA/VAT should not be charged; if you pay by credit card, there is usually a 10% surcharge).

Hotels in the upper price brackets in the Providencia area are: **L1** *San Cristóbal Sheraton*, Av Santa María 1742, T 233-5000, F 223-6656, best in town, good restaurant, good buffet lunch, and all facilities, also *Sheraton Towers*, slightly cheaper; **A1** *Aloha*, Francisco Noguera 146, T 233-2230/7, F 233-2494, helpful, good restaurant; **A1** *Santa María*, Av Santa María 2050, T 232-6614, F 231-6287, excellent, friendly, small, good breakfast, other meals good value, highly rec; all three N of the Río Mapocho. **A1** *Los Españoles*, Los Españoles 2539, T 232-1824, F 233-1048; **A1** *Orly*, Pedro de Valdivia 27, close to Pedro de Valdivia metro station, T 232-8225, but has smaller, cheaper rooms with less comfort, small, comfortable hotel, has apartments for rent on Juana de Arco, just off Av Pedro de Valdivia, 3 blocks S of Av Providencia, good, US$70 a day (reductions may be possible); **A1** *Montebianco*, Isidora Goyenechea 2911, T 233-0427, F 233-0420, small, smart motel; **A1** *Parinacota*, Av Apoquindo 5142, Las Condes, T 246-6109, F 220-5386, 4-star, small, all services, no pool; **A1** *Torremayor*, Ricardo Lyon 322, T 234-2000, F 234-3779, clean, modern, good service, good location; **A3** *Presidente*, T 235-8015, F 235-9148, Eliodoro Yáñez 867, almost at Providencia, good value and good location; **A3** *Posada del Salvador*, Av Eliodoro Yáñez 893, nearest metro Salvador, T 235-9450, F 251-8697, with bath. In Las Condes: **L1** *Hyatt Regency Santiago*, Av Kennedy N 4601, T 218-1234, F 218-2279, superb, beautifully decorated, highly rec.

Expensive hotels in the central area: **L1** *Carrera*, Teatinos 180, T 698-2011, F 672-1083, enormous rooms, pool, rooftop restaurant (good buffet lunch), *El Conquistador*, Miguel Cruchaga 920, T/F 696-5599, and **L1** *Galerías*, San Antonio 65, T 638-4011, F 639-5240, excellent, welcoming; **L2** *Fundador*, Paseo Serrano 34, T/F 632-6261, helpful, good value; **L2** *Holiday Inn Crowne Plaza*, Av B O'Higgins 136, T 638-1042, F 633-6015, all facilities, also good, spacious, a/c (book through travel agent for better rates); **L3** *Hostal del Parque*, Merced 294, just across from Parque Forestal, T 639-2694, F 639-2754, excellent; **L1** *San Francisco Kempinski*, Av B O'Higgins 816, T 639-3832, F 639-7826, Lufthansa affiliated, 5-star, good. **A1** *Foresta*, Subercaseaux 353, T 639-6262; **A2** *Panamericano*, Teatinos 320 y Huérfanos, T 672-3060, F 696-4992, comfortable, serves popular business lunch between 1230 and 1530; **A1** *Tupahue*, San Antonio 477, T 638-3810, F 639-5240, comfortable; **A3** *City*, Compañía 1063, T 695-4526, F 695-6775, old-fashioned, clean, rec; **A3** *Conde Ansúrez*, Av República 25, T 699-6368, F 671-8376, convenient for central station and southern bus terminal, clean, helpful, safe, luggage stored (100m from metro República); **A3** *Don Tito*, Huérfanos 578, T 639-1987, good, English spoken; **A2** *Gran Palace*, Huérfanos 1178, T 671-2551, F 695-1095, overpriced, clean, noisy rooms facing street (others quiet), good restaurant; **A3** *Libertador*, Av O'Higgins 853, T 639-4212, F 633-7128, helpful, rec, will store luggage, good restaurant, bar, roof top pool; **A3** *Majestic*, Santo Domingo 1526, T 695-8366, F 697-4051, with breakfast, pool, English spoken, rec; **A3** *Monte Carlo*, Subercaseaux 209, T 633-9905, F 633-5577, at bottom of Santa Lucía, modern, restaurant, with heating, stores luggage; **B** *Ducado*, Agustinas 1990, T 696-9384/672-6739, F 695-1271, clean, quiet at back, rec, secure parking; **B** *Imperio*, O'Higgins 2879, T 689-7774, F 689-2916, near central station, with bath, good restaurant, parking, clean.

Mid-price hotels in the centre: **B** *Principado*, Arturo Burhle 015, just off beginning of Vicuña Mackenna, T 635-3879, F 222-6065, convenient location, very nice; **B** *Santa Lucía*,

Santiago centre: Key to map

1. Plaza de Armas; 2. Cerro Santa Lucía; 3. Plaza de la Libertad; 4. Plaza de la Constitución; 5. Plaza Baquedano; 6. Parque Forestal; 7. Cathedral; 8. Archbishop's Palace; 9. San Francisco Church and Museo de Arte Colonial; 10. Santo Domingo; 11. Palacio de la Moneda; 12. Municipalidad; 13. Museo Histórico Nacional; 14. Congress; 15. Palacio de la Justicia; 16. Museo de la Santiago/Casa Colorada; 17. Museo de la Merced; 18. Museo de Arte Precolombino; 19. Museo de Bellas Artes; 20. Biblioteca Nacional; 21. Teatro Municipal; 22. Bolsa de Comercio; 23. Universidad de Chile; 24. Club de la Unión; 25. Plaza de Mulato Gil de Castro/Lastarria neighbourhood; 26. Argentine Embassy; 27. Post Offices; 28. CTC Telephone Office; 29. Entel Telephone Office; 30. Federación de Andinismo; 31. Airport bus; 32. Librería Inglesa; 33. Torre Entel.

San Antonio 327 y Huérfanos, 4th floor, T 639-8201, garage 2 blocks away, clean, comfortable, good, has small, quiet restaurant; **Lira**, Lira 314, T 222-2492, F 634-3637, excellent; **B Riviera**, Miraflores 106, T 633-1176, F 633-5988, opp Biblioteca Nacional, without breakfast. **B Hotel Turismo Japón**, Almte Barroso 160, T 698-4500, convenient location, intermittent hot water, helpful, friendly, clean, good breakfast, manager speaks English, best rooms at top, rec; **B Residencia Alicia Adasme**, Moneda 2055, T 696-0787, hot water, friendly, with breakfast; **B Santa Victoria**, Vicuña MacKenna 435, T 634-5753, quiet, small, safe, family run, rec; **B Vegas**, Londres 49, T 632-2514, F 632-5084, clean, TV/radio, large comfortable rooms, friendly, good breakfast; **B Hostal Vía Real**, Marín 066, T 635-4676, F 635-4678, charming, friendly, helpful, small, with bath, TV, laundry, rec; **C Res Alemana**, República 220 (no sign), T 671-2388, nr Metro República, hot water, clean, pleasant patio, central, heating on request, good cheap meals available, rec; **C Residencial Londres**, Londres 54, T/F 638-2215, nr San Francisco Church, former mansion, large old-fashioned rooms and furniture, few singles, cold in winter, English spoken, very popular, rec repeatedly (often full by 0900), breakfast extra; **C París**, Calle París 813, T 639-4037, with bath, no singles, quiet, clean, good value, also short-stay; In Providencia: **C Hostal Parada**, Grau Flores 168, T 460-6640, spacious, clean.

Cheaper central hotels: **D Residencial Mery**, Pasaje República 36, off 0-100 block of República (T 696-8883), big green building down an alley, hot showers, quiet, rec; **D Hostal Aula Magna**, Vergara 541, T 698-0729, laundry facilities, near Metro Toesca; **D España**, Morandé 510, T696-6066, without bath, hot water, clean, run down; **D Residencial del Norte**, Catedral 2207, T 695-1876, incl breakfast, friendly, safe, clean, large rooms, heating, convenient; **D Maury**, Tarapacá 1112, T 672-5889, F 697-0786, clean, friendly, safe, meals, English and French spoken; **D Santo Domingo**, Santo Domingo 735, with bath, E without, cleanish, basic, gloomy; **E Indiana**, Rosas 1339, T714-251, convenient for buses to centre, only front rooms with bath, hot water, back rooms poor, basic, bed bugs; **E Nuevo**, Morandé y San Pablo, T 671-5698, simple but OK, central, hot water, safe, poor beds, use of kitchen, popular, good meeting place.

Convenient accommodation for southern bus terminal and Estación Central: **C Elisa**, Manuel Rodríguez 140, T 695-6464, with bath, clean, quiet; **C Residencial Midi**, Av Unión Americana 134, huge rooms with ancient furniture, basic, clean, hot water, laundry facilities, rec; **E Residencial Sur**, Ruiz Tagle 55, meals available. Those on República (see above) are only 2-3 metro stops away. **E Alojamiento Diario**, Sanfuentes 2258 (no sign), T 699-2938, shared rooms, clean, safe, kitchen facilities, nr Metro República. On F Reich, 100-200 block, behind the bus terminal are **D México**, incl breakfast, and **D Roma**. **F** pp Sra Isaura Tobar Urra, Federico Scotto 130, N side of Alameda opp bus terminal, T 779-9364, can use phone and fax, without breakfast, good meals, cooking facilities, hot water, clean, often full; **E Casa de Vamilia Loreley**, Av 5 de Abril 3729, T 776-2200, German run, laundry facilities, friendly, rec.

Around the northern bus terminal, **D Residencial Buen Hogar**, San Martín 70, T 671-0737, central, old, good clean rooms; **D Residencial Miraflores**, Riquelme 555, T 696-3961, clean, friendly, safe, meals available, rec; **F** pp **Caribe**, San Martín 821, T 696-6681, 'a pit with decaying rooms, showers that are either scalding or freezing, friendly owners and adorable dogs', laundry facilities, luggage store, a bargain, popular; **E Souvenir**, Amunátegui 862, old, rambling place with 'adventurous plumbing' and chatty parrots around entrance; **E Pudahuel**, San Pablo 900 block, beds like rock, noisy but clean. Many on Gen MacKenna (eg **E San Felipe**, at No 1248, T 713816, secure, cheap laundry service, some single rooms are poor, second floor much quieter, poor service, but clean and good beds; **E Ovallino**, No 1477 y San Martín, clean, hot water in communal showers, secure, between the bus terminal and Cal y Canto Metro. **E** pp **Casa Andina**, Recoleta 895, T 737-2831, clean, cheap, across the river from Cal y Canto Metro. **NB** Many hotels on Morandé, Gen Mackenna, San Martín and San Pablo are convenient for northern bus terminal, but are in the red light district.

As the above list shows there is little good accommodation under US$15-20 a night. Travellers can find good accommodation in comfortable family guesthouses through **Amigos de Todo el Mundo**, Av Pdte Bulnes, Paseo, 285, dept 201, Casilla 52861 Correo Central, T 672-6525, F 698-1474, Sr Arturo Navarrete, prices from US$16 with breakfast, other meals extra, monthly rates available, rec; **E** pp **Alberto and Paola Peirario**, Chapultepec 5657, T 218-2101, F 204-4652, offer family accommodation, C pp, minimum 5 days, Spanish classes also **E** pp Sra Marta, same address dep to 401, T 672-6090, similar; **E** pp Sra Lucía, Catedral 1029, piso 10, dept 1001, T 696-3832, central, friendly, safe, cooking and laundry facilities; **E** pp Sra Fidela, San Isidro 261, Apt H, T 222-1246, shared bathroom, breakfast, rec; **D** pp **Casa del Estudiante Americano**, Huérfanos 1891, good dormitory accommodation—acts as youth hostel out of season, must be in bed by 2200 and out by 1000 (Metro Los Héroes—7 blocks from centre over motorway); **D Casa Paxi**, Av Llico 968, T 522-9947, F 521-6328, 1 block from Metro Departamental, washing machine, gardens, quiet, rec; **D** Sra Marta, Amengual 035, Alameda Alt 4.400, T 779-7592, lado Norte (metro Ecuador), good, hospitable, kitchen facilities, motorcycle parking; **E** Sra Eliana Zuvic, Almirante Latorre 617, T 696-8700, Metro República, hot water, nice atmosphere, highly rec; **D** pp Alicia Bravo, Artemio Gutiérrez 1328, T 556-6620, helpful, friendly, clean, not very central.

For longer stay accommodation, read the classified ads in *El Mercurio*, flats, homes and family *pensiones* are listed by district, or in *El Rastro* (weekly), or try the notice board at the tourist office. In furnished apartments; if you want a phone you may have to provide an *aval*, or guarantor, to prove you will pay the bill, or else a huge deposit will be asked for. Estate agents handle apartments, but often charge ⅓ of the first month's rent as commission, while a month's rent in advance and 1 month's deposit are required. Rec apartments are *Edificio San Rafael*, Miraflores 264, T 633-0289, F 222-5629 US$29 a day single, US$46 a day double, minimum 3 days, US$600 a month, very central. Staying with a family is an economical and interesting option for a few months. Providencia and Las Condes are residential districts, but the latter is some way from the centre; the area W of Plaza Baquedano, E of Cerro Santa Lucía and S of Parque Forestal is good and central; or you could try Bellavista, but not Calle Pío Nono where the nightlife goes on until 0300.

Youth Hostel information available from Av Providencia 2594, oficina 420 (metro Tobalaba), T 233-3226 (worth getting list of YH addresses around country as these change year by year—even in Santiago). Supplies student cards (2 photos required and proof of student status, though tourist card accepted), US$11. Hostels in the capital include **E** pp Cienfuegos 151, T 671-8532 (5 mins from metro Los Héroes) new, clean, satellite TV, no cooking facilities, breakfast and snacks, highly rec; **E** pp *Residencial Gloria*, Almte Latorre 447-449, T 698-8315, clean, popular, (price reduced by US$1 for members, not same concept of youth hostel as elsewhere, difficult to use kitchen).

Camping The campsite on San Cristóbal hill has been closed because of muggings. Alternatives are the Farellones road near the river; or S of Santiago near Puente Alto (take Av J Pedro Alessandri S to Las Vizcachas and La Obra where there is a small park on left side of road). At Km 25 S of city on Panamericana, Esso garage offers only a vacant lot near highway. Club Camping Maki, and Casino Camping, both 70 km from Santiago, **see p 672**. **Camping Equipment** Standard camping gas cartridges can be bought at *Unisport*, Providencia 2503, or Santo Domingo 1079. Other equipment for camper-vans from *Bertonati Hnos*, Manuel Montt 2385. Tent repairs: *Juan Soto*, Silva Vildosola 890, Paradero 1, Gran Avenida, San Miguel, Santiago, T 555-8329. *Reinaldo Lippi*, Granados 566 (near Santa Lucía hill), T 639-1180, F 639-9169, makes tents, sleeping bags, back packs, etc, sells secondhand kit, and does repairs, most helpful. Camping goods from *Club Andino* and *Federación de Andinismo* (**see p 667 below**): expensive because these articles are imported. *Lomas*, Santa Rosa y 10 de Julio, good selection of sleeping bags, helpful. Good sleeping bags from *Fuc*, Rengo 1670 (off M Montt), T 225-8862. Repair of camping stoves at *Casa Italiana*, Tarapacá 1120. For second hand equipment try Luz Emperatrie Sanhuela Quiroz, Portal de León, Loc 14, Providencia 2198 (Metro Los Leones).

Restaurants In addition to those at the main hotels and those in Parque O'Higgins there are, in the centre of the city: *Nuria*, MacIver 208, wide selection, US$20 plus; *Da Carla*, MacIver 577, Italian food, good, expensive; and *San Marco*, 2 doors away, better still; *Casa Suiza*, Huérfanos 648, good Swiss food; *Jacaranda*, Huérfanos 614, elegant, good service, good pasta and seafood. *Les Assassins*, Merced 297, French, very good, highly rec; *La Omelette*, Agustinas near Amex, clean and good, closes 2100. *Gran Parrillada la Brasileña*, San Diego, huge portions, rec.

Seafood: *El 27 de Nueva York*, Nueva York 27, central, pricey, good; *Savory Tres*, Ahumada 327, good but limited choice and closed evenings. Some of the best seafood restaurants are to be found in the Mercado Central (by Cal y Canto metro), or at the Vega Central market on the opposite bank of the Mapocho.

For mainly local food in the centre: *Chez Henry*, on Plaza de Armas, restaurant and delicatessen at Alameda 847, which is highly rec; also in Plaza de Armas, *Faison d'Or*, good *pastel de choclo*, pleasant place to have a drink and watch the world go by; *Torres*, O'Higgins 1570, traditional bar/restaurant, good atmosphere, live music at weekends; *Fuente de Soda Orion*, O'Higgins y Manuel Rodríguez, cheap, good pizzas; *Silvestre*, Huérfanos 956, open 0800-2400, good buffet-style; *Mermoz*, Huérfanos 1048, good for lunches; *Bar Nacional No 1*, Huérfanos 1151 and *Bar Nacional No 2*, Bandera 317, good restaurants, popular, local specialities; *Guima*, Huérfanos y Teatinos, good, reasonable prices, good value *almuerzo*; *Café Dante*, Merced 801 y San Antonio, for *pastel de choclo*, lunchtime only; *Bar Central*, San Pablo 1063, typical food, rec; *Fra Diavolo*, París 836 (nr *Res Londres*), local and Italian, excellent food and service, popular; *Verdijo*, Morandé 526, noisy, cheap and popular; *Bar-restaurant Inés de Suárez*, Morandé 558, cheap; *El Lugar de Don Quijote*, café, and *Parrilladas de*

Don Quijote, restaurant, good, Morandé y Catedral; two doors away is *Congreso*, popular at lunchtime. *Círculo de Periodistas*, Amunátegui 31, 2° piso, unwelcoming entrance, good value lunches, rec; *Los Adobes de Argomedo*, Argomedo 411 y Lira, hacienda-style, good Chilean food and floor show including cueca dancing, salsa and folk, Mon-Sat, only place in winter which has this type of entertainment on a Mon. Several cheap *fuentes de soda* for cheap lunches along Av Santa Rosa between the Alameda and Calle París.

Oriental in the centre: *Guo Fung*, Moneda 1549, rec; *Lung Fung*, Agustinas 715, delicious food, pricey, excellent fixed price lunch, large cage in the centre with noisy parrots; *Pai Fu*, Santa Rosa 101, good; *Kam Thu*, Santo Domingo 771, nr San Antonio, good, large helpings; all Chinese. *Izakaya Yoko*, Merced 456, good, Japanese, rec.

Many in the Lastarria and Bellavista neighbourhoods, including: *La Pergola de la Plaza* in Plaza Mulato Gil de Castro, but better and close by are *Quiche Lorraine* in the Instituto Chileno-Francés, Lastarria 345, highly rec for food, drink and ambience; *Gatopardo*, Lastarria 192, good value and *R*, highly rec. *Café Universitario*, Alameda 395 y Victoria Subercaseaux (near Sta Lucía), good, cheap *almuerzos*. Many restaurants/bars on Pío Nono including: *Venezia*, huge servings, good value; *Eladio*, good steaks; *Zingarrella*, Italian, good; *La Puña*, *Los Ladrillos*, popular, lively, and *La Maviola*, speciality pizzas. *Café del Cerro*, Ernesto Pinto Lazarrigue 192, T 778-308, with live music (check *El Mercurio* for programme), door charge, highly rec; *Cipriani*, Pinto Lazarrigue 195, pasta, elegant atmosphere, US$25-30, top class; *Picoroco*, Pinto Lagarrigue 123, good seafood; *Al Mazzat*, de Bello 82, Arab dishes, good; *El Otro Sitio*, Antonio de Bello 53, excellent food, elegant not cheap; *Caramañol*, Purísima 257, good seafood, reasonably priced, ring doorbell; *Les Copains*, Purísima 65, French, good food; *La Tasca Mediterránea*, Purísima 100 block, good food, rec; *La Divina Comida*, Purísima 215, Italian with 3 rm—Heaven, Hell and Purgatory, highly rec; *La Esquina al Jérez*, Mallinkrodt 102, excellent Spanish; *San Fruttuoso*, Mallinkrodt 180, Italian, rec.

Outside the centre, in Providencia: *La Pizza Nostra*, Av Las Condes 6757, Providencia, sells good Italian food as well as pizzas, real coffee, pricey, also at Av Providencia 1975 and Luis Thayer Ojeda 019; *da Renato*, Mardoqueo Fernández 138 (metro Los Leones), Italian, good; *El Parrón*, Av Providencia 1188, *parrilladas*, rec, the local dice game of 'dudo' is played in the bar; *Lomit's*, Av Providencia 1980, good; *Gatsby*, Av Providencia 1984, American food, as-much-as-you-can-eat buffet and lunch/dinner, snack bar open till 2400, tables outside in warm weather, good; *La Mía Pappa*, Las Bellotas 267, Italian, very popular lunches; *Olé Olé*, Guardia Vieja 136, Spanish, good food, wide selection; *Coco*, La Concepción 236, good seafood, expensive, rec, reservation advised; *Centre Catalá*, Av Suecia 428 nr Lota, good, reasonably-priced. *München*, German, Av El Bosque Norte 204, rec. *Carrousel*, Los Conquistadores 1972, very good, nice garden, over US$20.

Many first-class restaurants out of the centre can be found in the Las Condes district, including grills, Chilean cuisine (often with music), French cuisine and Chinese. They tend to be more expensive than central restaurants. Good examples are *Seriatutix*, Av Colón 5137, restaurant and disco, live music, café, great atmosphere; *Delmónico*, Vitacura 3379, excellent, reasonably priced; *Praga*, Vitacura 3917, Czech; *La Tasca de Altamar*, Noruega y Linneo, good seafood, reasonably priced; *Pinpilinpausha*, Isadora Goyenechea 2900, good; *Martín Carrera*, Isidora Goyenechea 3471, good nouvelle cuisine; *Taj Mahal*, Isidora Goyenechea 3215 (Metro El Golf), T 232-3606, only Indian in Santiago, expensive but excellent; *El Club*, Bosque Norte 280 (approx), popular, good value (US$15-20); *Coco Loco*, opposite at No 215, good, US$20-30. On Av Las Londes: *La Estancia*, No 13810 (US$20-25), *La Querencia*, No 14980, a bit cheaper, both good; *Santa Fe*, Las Condes 10690, excellent Mexican.

It is difficult to eat cheaply in the evening apart from fast food. If on a budget make the *almuerzo* your main meal.

Vegetarian restaurants: *El Huerto*, Orrego Luco 054, T 233-2690, rec, open daily, live music Fri and Sat evenings, varied menu, very good but not cheap, popular; *Rincón Vegetariano*, Monjitas 558, fixed price lunch US$2, good, juices, rec.

Cafés and Bars In the city centre: *Bucaneros*, Morandé 564, good value lunches and snacks; *Café Paula*, several branches, eg Estado at entrance to Galería España, excellent coffee and cake, good breakfast, also on San Antonio opp the Teatro Municipal. *Café Colonia*, MacIver 133, rec; *Café Santos*, Huérfanos 830, popular for 'onces' (afternoon tea); *La E*, San Pablo 1310, good coffee. Try *Café Haití*, *Café Brasil* and *Café Caribe*, all on Paseo Ahumada and elsewhere in centre and Providencia, for delicious coffee. *Bon Bon Oriental*, Merced 345, superb Turkish cakes. *Cafetería Berri*, Rosal 321, live music at weekends; *Tip-Top Galetas* rec for freshly baked biscuits, branches throughout the city, eg Merced 867. Many in Bellavista including: *Fausto*, Av Santa María, gay bar; *Café de la Dulcería Las Palmas*, de Bello 190, good pastries and lunches and several on Purísima 100-200, including *La Candela*; *Libro-Café*, candelit, lots of books, highly rec. In Lastarria: *El Biógrafo*, Villavicencio 398, bohemian style, rec.

In Providencia: *Geo Pub*, Encomenderos 83, owner Francisco Valle speaks English, pub and expensive restaurant with travel films once a week in winter, music occasionally, popular with travellers, rec; *Villa Real*, Pedro de Valdivia 079, rec. Many on Av Providencia including: *Phone Box Pub*, No 1670, T 496627; *El Café del Patio*, next door, student hang-out; *Violin Pub*, No 1684, good lunch; *Salón de Té Tavelli*, Drugstore precinct, No 2124, rec. *Golden Bell Inn*, Hernando Aguirre 27, popular with expatriates; *Cross Keys Pub*, Las Bellotas 270 local 5, (opposite *La Mía Pappa*), near Los Leones metro, with darts, pints, etc, good value. Many other good bars nrby on Av Suecia including *Mr Ed*; *Brannigan Pub*, good beer, live jazz; *Red Pub*. In Las Condes: *Las Urracas Tequila Pub*, Vitacura, good margaritas; *El Vikingo*, Rotunda Atena, good atmosphere, cheap. Note that almost all hotel bars are closed Sun.

For snacks and ice cream, try *Coppellia*, Av Providencia 2211, *Bravissimo*, same avenida No 1406, and *El Toldo Azul*, No 1936.

Airline Offices LanChile, *sales office: Agustinas 640, Torre Interamericana, T 699-0505; reservations T 632-3211;* Ladeco, Huérfanos 1157, T 698-2233 and Pedro de Valdivia 0210, T 251-7204; **National Airlines**, Huérfanos 725, piso 3, B, T 633-9288/632-2698; **British Airways**, Isidora Goyenechea 2934, Oficina 302, T 601-8614, 232-9560 (for confirmation); **Aerolíneas Argentinas**, and **Viasa**, Moneda 756; **Varig**, Miraflores, between Agustinas and Moneda, T 639-5976; **Aero Perú**, Fidel Oteiza 1953, piso 5, T 274-3434; **Lacsa**, Av Providencia 2083, Oficina 22, T 233-6400; **KLM**, San Sebastián 2839, Oficina 202, T 233-0011; **Aeroflot**, Agustinas 640, Local 5, T 632-3914; **South African Airlines**, Moneda 970, piso 18, next to Lufthansa (T 698-6490). **LAP**, Agustinas 1141, piso 2, T 671-4404.

Banks and Exchange Banks, open from 0900 to 1400, but closed on Sat. Official daily exchange rates are published in *El Mercurio* and *La Epoca*. **Banco Central de Chile**, one block from Plaza Constitución, demands the minimum of formalities, but may charge commission. **Banco O'Higgins**, Bandera 201, will change TCs into dollars with commission on transactions between US$100-1,000. American Express, Agustinas 1360 (Turismo Cocha, Av El Bosque Norte 0430, Providencia, for travel information and mail collection), no commission, poor rates (better to change TCs into dollars—no limit—and then into pesos elsewhere). **Citibank**, Ahumada 40. Thomas Cook/Mastercard agent, *Turismo Tajamar*, Orrego Luco 23, T 231-5112.

Casas de Cambio (exchange houses) close on Sat except in summer when they open till 1300 (check first). Normally there is no commission on TCs though rates may be lower. Shop around as terms vary. Most exchange houses are on Agustinas and Huerfanos. **Casa de Cambio Blancas**, opp *Hotel Orly* on Pedro de Valdivia, and **Exprinter**, Agustinas 1074, are rec for good rates, low commission, also **Inter**, Moneda 940, upstairs office at Ahumada 131 (oficina 103), **Cambios Andino**, Ahumada 1062 and **Teletour**, Guardia Vieja 55. **Afex**, Moneda 1140, good rates for TCs; **Sr Fernando Sáez** (travel agent), M Cousiño 150, Oficina 322, T 638-2885, for good exchange rates (and australes). **Casa de Cambio**, Calle Bombero A Ossa 1010, Of 214 (near Ahumada/Agustinas), open 0900-2200 (Mon-Fri only), but operates from travel agency next door on Sat am). In Providencia several around Av Pedro de Valdivia eg at Gral Holley 66, good rates; **Mojakar**, Pedro de Valdivia 072. Mastercard at **Fincard**, Alameda 1427, T 698-4260, 2465/7, 3855, 7229, offers its full range of services (even lost or stolen cards are replaced in a couple of days); open 24 hrs. Visa at **Banco Concepción**, Huérfanos y Bandera, but beware hidden costs in 'conversion rate', and **Banco Osorno**, Av Providencia y Pedro de Valdivia, no commission. For stolen or lost Visa cards go to **Transbank**, Bandera 577, piso 9º. Unless you are feeling adventurous avoid street money changers (particularly common on Ahumada and Agustinas): they will usually ask you to accompany them to a Casa de Cambio or somewhere more obscure. Rates for such transactions are no better and there are increasing reports of mugging and violence en route.

Cultural and Trade Institutions Instituto Chileno Británico de Cultura, Santa Lucía 124, T 638-2156, 0930-1900, except 1330-1900 Mon, and 0930-1600 Fri, has English papers in library (also in Providencia, Dario Urzúa 1933, and Las Condes, Renato Sánchez 4369), runs language courses; British Chamber of Commerce, Av Suecia 155-c, Providencia, Casilla 536, T 231-4366; British Council, Av Eliodoro Yáñez 832, nr Providencia, T 223-4622. The British community maintains the **British Commonwealth Society** (old people's home etc), Av Alessandri 557, T 223-8807, the interdenominational Santiago Community Church, at Av Holanda 151 (Metro Tobalaba), Providencia, which holds services every Sun at 1045. English Schools: The Grange, Redlands, Santiago College, Craighouse and The Brandford School, all coeducational.

Instituto Chileno Francés de Cultura, Merced 298, T 639-8433, in a beautiful house; Instituto Chileno Alemán de Cultura, Goethe-Institut, Esmeralda 650, T 638-3185; German Chamber of Commerce, Ahumada 131. Instituto Chileno de Cultura Hispánica,

Providencia 927; **Instituto Chileno Italiano de Cultura**, Triana 843; **Instituto Chileno Israeli de Cultura**, Moneda 812, oficina 613; **Instituto Chileno Japonés de Cultura**, Providencia 2653, oficina 1902.

Instituto Chileno Norteamericano de Cultura, Moneda 1467, T 696-3215, good for US periodicals, cheap films on Fri; also runs language courses and free Spanish/English language exchange hours (known as Happy Hours) which are a good way of meeting people. (Ask also about Mundo Club which organizes excursions and social events).

Instituto Cultural del Banco del Estado de Chile, Alameda 123, regular exhibitions of paintings, concerts, theatrical performances; **Instituto Cultural de Providencia**, Av 11 de Septiembre 1995 (Metro Pedro de Valdivia), art exhibitions, concerts, theatre; **Instituto Cultural Las Condes**, Av Apoquindo 6570, near beginning of Av Las Condes, also with art exhibitions, concerts, lectures, etc.

Embassies and Consulates **Argentine Embassy**, Miraflores 285, T 633-1076; Consulate Vicuña Mackenna 41, T 222-6853, Australians need letter from their embassy to get visa here, open 0900-1400 (visa US$15, free for US citizens), if you need a visa for Argentina, get it here or in the consulates in Concepción, Puerto Montt or Punta Arenas, there are no facilities at the borders; **Brazilian Embassy**, Alonso Ovalle 1665, T 698-2347, 15th floor, visas issued by Consulate, MacIver 225, Mon-Fri 1000-1300, US$10 (visa takes 1 day); take: passport, 2 photos, ticket into and out of Brazil, photocopy of first 2 pages of passport, of tickets, of credit card and of Chilean tourist card; **Bolivian Embassy**, Av Santa María 2796, T 232-8180 (Metro Los Leones), open 0930-1400; **Panamanian Embassy**, Del Inca 5901, T 220-8286 (open 1000-1330); **Paraguayan Consulate**, Huérfanos 886, Oficina 514, T 639-4640, open 0900-1300 (2 photos and copy of first page of passport required for visa); **Peruvian Embassy**, Av Andrés Bello 1751, T 232-6275 (Metro Pedro de Valdivia).

US Embassy, Edif Codina, Agustinas 1343, unit 4127, T 232-2600, F 330-3710; **US Consulate**, T 710133, Merced 230 (visa obtainable here); **Canadian Embassy**, Ahumada 11, piso 10, T 696-2256 (prints a good information book). **New Zealand Embassy**, Av Isadora Goyenechea 3516, Las Condes, T 231-4204. **South African Embassy**, Av 11 de Septiembre 2353, Edif San Román, piso 16, T 231-2862; **Japanese Embassy**, Av Providencia 2653, piso 19

British Embassy and Consulate, El Bosque Norte 0125 (Metro Tobalaba), Casilla 72-D, T 231-3737, F 231-9771, will hold letters, open 0900-1200; **German Embassy**, Agustinas 785 pisos 7 y 8, T 633-5031; **Netherlands Embassy**, Calle Las Violetas 2368, T 223-6825, open 0900-1200; **French Embassy**, Condell 65, T 225-1030; **Norwegian Embassy**, Av Vespucio Norte 548, T 228-1024; **Belgian Embassy**, Av Providencia 2653, depto 1104, T 232-1071; **Danish Embassy**, Av Santa María 0182, T 737-6056; **Austrian Embassy**, Barros Errázuriz 1968, piso 3; **Italian Embassy**, Clemente Fabres 1050, T 223-2467; **Spanish Consulate**, Av Providencia 329, 4th floor, T 40239; **Finnish Embassy**, Sótero Sanz de Villalba 55, Oficina 71, T 232-0456; **Swedish Embassy**, 11 de Septiembre 2353, Torre San Ramón, 4 piso, Providencia, T 231-2733, F 232-4188; **Swiss Embassy**, Av Providencia 2653, Oficina 1602, T 232-2693, open 1000-1200 (metro Tobalaba).

Theatres *Teatro Municipal*, Agustinas y San Antonio, stages international opera, concerts by the Orquesta Filarmónica de Santiago, and the Ballet de Santiago, throughout the year; on Tues at 2100 there are free operatic concerts in the Salón Claudio Arrau; tickets range from US$5.60 for a very large choral group with a symphony orchestra, and US$7 for the cheapest seats at the ballet, to US$80 for the most expensive opera seats. Some cheap seats are often sold on the day of concerts. *Teatro Universidad de Chile*, Plaza Baquedano, is the home of the Orquesta y Coro Sinfónica de Chile and the Ballet Nacional de Chile; prices from US$1.25-3.50 for concerts to US$1.25-13.50 for ballet.

Free classical concerts are sometimes given in San Francisco church in summer; arrive early for a seat.

There are a great number of theatres which stage plays in Spanish, either in the original language or translations, eg *La Comedia*, Merced 349, *Abril*, Huérfanos 786, *Camilo Henríquez*, Amunátegui 31, *Centro Arrayán*, Las Condes 14891, *El Galpón de los Leones*, Av Los Leones 238, *El Conventillo*, Bellavista 173. Four others, the *Opera*, Huérfanos, *California*, Irarrázaval 1546, *Humoresque*, San Ignacio 1249 and *Picaresque*, Recoleta 345, show mostly Folies Bergères-type revues. *Santiago Stage* is an English-speaking amateur drama group. Outdoor rock concerts are held at the *Estadio Nacional*, Av Unión Latino Americana (metro of same name), at the Teatro Teletón, Rosas 325 (excellent sound system), and elsewhere. Events are listed in *El Mercurio* and *La Epoca*. The most comprehensive listings appear in *El Mercurio's Wikén* magazine on Friday.

Cinemas 'Ciné Arte' (quality foreign films) is very popular and a number of cinemas specialize in this type of film: *El Biógrafo* (Lastarria 181), *Alameda Cultural Centre*, Av Providencia 927,

Casa de Extensión Universidad Católica, Av B O'Higgins 390, T 2221157, *Espaciocal* (Goyenechea y Vitacura), *Tobalaba* (Av Providencia 2563), and others, full details are given in the press. Try also Goethe Institut, and Instituto Chileno-Francés (addresses below). Other cinemas tend to show 'sex, violence and war'. Seats cost US$3-5 with reductions on Wed (elsewhere in the country the day varies).

Night Clubs Some of the restaurants and cafés which have shows are given above. Listings are given in *El Mercurio,* or *La Epoca.* Clubs in Bellavista are cheaper and more down market generally than those in Providencia. *La Cucaracha,* Bombero Núñez 159 (Bellavista) is very popular, floorshow at 2330, US$3.50 cover charge, orchestras, dancing. *Varadero,* on Pío Nono, good. Several tango clubs incl *Club Troilo,* Cumming 795, cheap, unpretentious (tango classes 1800-2000, Fri and Sun). *El Tucano Salsateca,* P de Valdivia 1783, 4th floor, Wed-Sun 2200-0600, fashionable. *Peña Nano Parra,* San Isidro 57, good folk club, cheap.

Discotheques *Gente,* Av Apoquindo 4900, also *Baltas,* Av Las Condes 10690, both expensive, but good. *El Baile,* de Bello, Bellavista. Many more, mainly in the Providencia and Las Condes areas.

Health Emergency hospital at Marcoleta 377 costs US$12. If you need to get to a hospital, it is better to take a taxi than wait for an ambulance. For yellow fever vaccination and others (but not cholera), *Hospital San Salvador,* J M Infante 551, T 225-6441, Mon-Thur 0800-1300, 1330-1645; Fri 0800-1300, 1330-1545. Also *Vaccinatoria Internacional,* Hospital Luis Calvo, Mackenna, Antonio Varas 360. *Clínica Central,* San Isidro 231, T 222-1953, open 24 hrs, German spoken. *Clínica Alemana,* Vitacura 5951, Las Condes. Physician: Dr Sergio Maylis, T 232-0853 (1430-1900). Dentist: Antonio Yazigi, Vitacura 3082, Apto 33, T 487962, English spoken, rec. Dr Torres, Av Providencia 2330, Depto 23, excellent, speaks English; **Emergency Pharmacy,** Portugal 155 (T 382439).

Language Courses *Centro de Idiomas Bellavista,* Dominica 25, T 777-5933/227-7137, offers Spanish in groups or individually and organizes accommodation. *Escuela de Idiomas Violeta Parra,* Alberto Reyes 075, Bellavista, T 284-4708, arranges accommodation. *AmeriSpan Unlimited* has an affiliated school in Santiago, details from PO Box 40513, Philadelphia, PA 19106, USA, T 215-985-4522/800-879-6640, F 215-985-4524. Many private teachers (much cheaper), including Carolina Carvajal, T 623-8405, highly rec, and Patricia Vargas Vives, Monitor Araucano 0680, Depto 25AC, Providencia, T 777-0595, qualified and experienced. Lucía Araya Arevalo, Puerto Chico 8062, Villa Los Puertos, Pudahuel, T 236-0531, speaks German and English.

There are many private language institutes. English language teachers should apply in mid-Feb/early Mar with a full curriculum vitae and photo. Most English teachers are badly paid. Work permits are difficult to obtain, but in any case note that employers cannot get your permit for you, whatever they say: you have to do it yourself. It is not unknown for schools to employ teachers with a 90-day tourist visa and then 'discover' as this expires that the teacher is not entitled to work, at which point it becomes very difficult to obtain unpaid wages.

Laundry Wet-wash places in the centre: at Agustinas 1532, also *Nataly,* at Bandera 72, another at Bandera 572, at Catedral y Amunátegni and *Lava Facil,* Huérfanos 1750, Mon-Sat 0900-2000, US$4 per load. There are plenty of dry-cleaners, eg Merced 494. Nearby, just S of Metro Universidad Católica there are several, including *American Washer,* Portugal 71, Torre 7, local 4, US$3, open 0900-2100 including Sun, can leave washing and collect it later; *Maytag,* Portugal 28, Torre 4, Local 4. Diagonal Paraguay 371, about US$1/kg, quick, rec, open till 1930 (closed Sun). Wet wash laundries in Providencia include *Marva,* Carlos Antúñez 1823 (Metro Pedro de Valdivia), wash and dry US$8; Providencia 1039, full load, wet wash, US$5, 3 hrs; Manuel Montt 67. At the corner of Providencia and Dr Luis Middleton there are several self-service dry cleaners (Metro Pedro de Valdivia, 11 de Septiembre exit).

Places of Worship Anglican Church, Holanda 151 (service 1030); Synagogues Tarapacá 870, T 393872 and Las Hortensias 9322, T 233-8868.

Post Office Plaza de Armas (0800-1900), poste restante well organized (though only kept for 30 days), US$0.20, passport essential, list of letters and parcels received in the hall of central Post Office (one list for men, another for women, indicate Sr or Sra/Srita on envelope); also has philatelic section, 0900-1630, and small stamp museum (ask to see it). Another office at Moneda 1155. If sending a parcel, the contents must first be checked at Post Office; paper, tape etc on sale; open Mon-Fri 0800-1900, Sat 0800-1400.

Cables and Telephones Compañía de Teléfonos de Chile, Moneda 1151, closed Sun. International phone calls also from: Entel, Huérfanos 1133, Mon-Fri 0830-2200, Sat 0900-2030, Sun 0900-1400, calls cheaper 1400-2200; Fax upstairs. Fax also available at CTC offices, eg Mall Panorámico, 11 de Septiembre, 3rd level (phone booths are on level 1) and

Telexchile, Morandé 147. There are also CTC phone offices at some metro stations, La Moneda, Escuela Militar, Tobalaba, Universidad de Chile and Pedro de Valdivia for local, long-distance and international calls. International telex service, Bandera 168. Local calls 50 pesos, only 50 peso coins accepted.

Shopping *El Almacén Campesino*, Purísima 303, Bellavista, handicrafts from all over Chile. Best bargains are handicraft articles, pottery (best bought in Pomaire, 50 km away, **see p 672**) and beautiful wrought copper and bronze. The gemstone lapis lazuli can be found in a few expensive shops in Bellavista but is cheaper in the **Centro Artesanal Santa Lucía** (Santa Lucía metro, S exit) which also has a wide variety of woollen goods, jewellery, etc. *Amitié*, Av Ricardo León y Av Providencia (Metro Los Leones); *Dauvin Artesanía Fina*, Providencia 2169, Local 69 (Metro Los Leones) have also been recommended. *H Stern* jewellery shops are located at the *San Cristóbal Sheraton* and *Carrera* hotels, and at the International Airport. *Cema-Chile* (Centro de Madres), Portugal 351 and at Universidad de Chile metro stop, *Manos Chilensis*, Portugal 373, *Artesanía Popular Chilena*, Av Providencia 2322 (near Los Leones metro), and *Artesanía Chilena*, Estado 337, have a good selection of handicrafts. *Talleres Solidarios*, 1st floor Vicaría de la Solidaridad, on Plaza de Armas (next door to the Cathedral), huge variety, highly rec. *Pel y Pel*, Pedro de Valdivia 20, fur and leather articles, good. Antique stores in Plaza Mulato Gil de Castro and elsewhere on Lastarria (Merced end).

Beside and behind the Iglesia de los Dominicos, on Av Nueva Apoquindo 9085, is *Los Graneros del Alba*, or *El Pueblo de Artesanos*, open daily except Mon, 1130-1900; all types of ware on sale, dishes given in some shops. *Restaurant El Granero* is here. To get there, take a small, green Los Dominicos bus from Av Providencia, marked 'Camino del Alba', or an Apoquindo bus, similarly marked, from Metro Escuela Militar; get out at the children's playground at the junction of Apoquindo y Camino del Alba, at the foot of the hill leading up to the church, and walk up.

Mercado Central, between Puente y 21 de Mayo by the Río Mapocho (Cal y Canto metro) is excellent but quite expensive; there is a cheaper market, the Vega Central, on the opposite bank of the river. There are other craft markets in an alleyway, 1 block S of Av B O'Higgins between A Prat and San Diego, on the 600 to 800 blocks of Santo Domingo (including pieces from neighbouring countries) and at Pío Nono y Av Santa María, Bellavista. The shopping arcade at the Central Station is good value, likewise the street market outside. Many charity clothes shops around Bandera 600 block, good for winter clothes for travellers who need them. There is a flea market at Franklin y Santa Rosa on Sun am and a good outside fruit market at Puente 815, by Frutería Martínez. There is an antique fair on Sun (1000-1400) in the summer and a Fiesta de Quasimodo on the first Sun after Easter at Lo Barnechea, 30 min by bus from Santiago. Parque Arauco is a large modern shopping mall on Av Kennedy, N of Metro Escuela Militar.

Bookshops Book prices tend to be high compared with Europe. *Librería Albers*, Vitacura 5648, Vitacura, T 218-5371, F 218-1458, and 11 de Septiembre 2671, Providencia, T 232-7499 (Spanish, English and German—good selection, cheaper than most, helpful, also German and Swiss newspapers); *Librería Altamira*, Huérfanos 669; *Feria Chilena del Libro*, Huérfanos nr McIver, and in Drugstore precinct, Providencia 2124; *Librería Inglesa* (*Librería Kuatro*), Huérfanos 669, local 11, and Pedro de Valdivia 47, good selection of English books, sells *South American Handbook*. There are many bookshops in the Pedro de Valdivia area on Providencia. Second-hand English books from *Librería El Patio*, Providencia 1652, nearest Metro stop Pedro de Valdivia; exchange for best deal. Also, from Henry at Metro station, Los Leones and *Books*, next to *Phone Box Pub*, in the courtyard at Providencia 1670 (the artist's shop in same precinct sells attractive cards). *Librairie Française*, books and newspapers, Calle del Estado 337. As well as the antiquarian bookshop mentioned above in the Lastarria district, there are other good antiquarian bookshops on Merced around the corner from Lastarria, eg *América del Sur Librería Editorial*, No 306, *Libros Antiguos El Cid*, No 344. Many stalls on Paseo Ahumada/Huérfanos sell foreign newspapers and journals.

Camera Repairs and Film Harry Müller, Ahumada 312, Oficina 402, not cheap but good and fairly quick, rec; speaks German and English. For Minolta and Canon repairs, Asatecnic, Nueva York 52, piso 2, rec. Many developers on Ahumada offer 24-hr service of varying quality (some develop, but not mount, slides, slow service). *Tecnofoto*, Ahumada 131, piso 7, Oficina 719, T 672-5004 rec as quick and efficient. *Moretto*, Merced 753, rec as cheap and good. *Fototeknika*, Lira 45, develops and mounts slides on same day, US$5.30 for 36, also handles prints, Mon-Fri 0800-1800. *Black Box*, Gral Flores 229 (Metro Mannel Montt), highly rec. For camera batteries and other spares try *Fotocenter*, Ahumada y Huérfanos.

Swimming Pools Antilen (closed Mon) and Tupahue, better, open daily 1000-1500 (Mon-Fri, US$3, Sat-Sun US$4), both on Cerro San Cristóbal (check if they are open in winter, one usually is). In Parque O'Higgins, 1330-1830 summer only, US$3. Olympic pool in Parque Araucano (nr

Arauco Shopping Centre, closest Metro E Militar), open Tues-Sat 0900-1900 Nov-Mar.

Bicycles For parts and repairs *Importadora Caupolicán*, San Diego 863, T 697-2765, F 696-1937, wide range, helpful. Ask for Nelson Díaz 'a walking encyclopaedia' on bikes.

Football Main teams include Colo Colo who play at the Estadio Monumental, reached by any bus to Puente Alto; tickets from Cienfuegos 41. Universidad de Chile (Estadio Nacional, Av Grecia 2001, T 239-2212) and Universidad Católica who play at San Carlos de Apoquindo, reached by bus from Metro Escuela Militar.

Racecourses Club Hípico, racing every Sun and every other Wed afternoon (at Viña del Mar, Jan-Mar); Hipódromo Chile every Sat afternoon; pari-mutuel betting.

Other Sports Running The Hash House Harriers hold runs every other week; information through the British Embassy and Consulate. **Tennis** Santiago Tennis Club; also, Club de Tenis Jaime Fillol, Rancho Melnichi, Par 4. See also Tenís Centrum Alemán, under **Camping** above. **Bowling** Bowling Center, Av Apoquindo 5012. **Gymnasium** Gimnasio Alicia Franché, Moneda 1481, T 696-1681, aerobics and fitness classes (women only); another at Huérfanos 1313, T 671-1562. **Tai Chi** and other martial arts: Raul Tou-Tin, Irarrázaval 1971, T 204-8082. **Cricket** Sat in summer at Club Príncipe de Gales, Las Arañas 1901 (bus from Tobalaba metro).

Clubs Ñuñoa (T 223 7846), with swimming pool, tennis courts and school; Polo y Equitación San Cristóbal; Chess Club, Alameda O'Higgins 898, Mon-Sat 1800, lively.

Skiing and Climbing Club Andino de Chile, Enrique Foster, 29, ski club (open 1900-2100 on Mon and Fri). **Federación de Andinismo de Chile**, Almirante Simpson 77 (T 222-9140), open daily; has a small museum (1100-1330, 1500-2000, free) and library (open weekday evenings, not Wed), sells equipment and guides to the mountains around Santiago (US$2.50) and the extreme S (eg Paine, US$4.35). Little other information available, apart from the addresses of all the mountaineering clubs in the country, it has a mountaineering school. Club Alemán Andino, Arrayán 2735, open Tues and Fri, 1800-2000. Also try Skitotal, Apoquindo 4900, Oficina 32,33,43, T 246-0156, for one-day excursions, and Anke Kessler, Arzobispo Casanova 25, T 737-1958, F 274-5146, for individually-tailored packages including hotels and transport for budget skiers. Equipment hire is much cheaper in Santiago than in ski resorts. Sunglasses are essential. For equipment see above; for ski resorts in the Santiago area **see below p 672**.

Climbing and Skiing Equipment *Evasión*, Soero Sanz 95, Providencia, T 231-1876, limited selection of good Italian tents, repairs equipment; *Mountain Service*, Ebro 2805, Las Condes (Metro Tobalaba) T 242-9723, English spoken, tents, stoves, clothing, rec; *Señora Lucy*, Portal Royal, Local 14 (opposite Metro Los Leones), large selection of quality imported equipment, rec; *Panda Deportes*, Paseo Las Palmas 2217 (Metro Los Leones), T 232-1840.

Travel Agencies *Wagons-Lits Cook*, Carmencita, Providencia, T 233-0820, rec; *Turismo Cocha* (American Express representatives with mail service), Av El Bosque Norte 0430, PO Box 191035, Providencia, Metro Tobalaba, T 230-1000. *Passtours*, Huérfanos 886, Oficina 1110, T 639-3232, F 562-633-1498, many languages spoken, helpful, rec. *VMP Ltda*, Huérfanos 1160, Local 19, T/F 696-7829, for all services, German, English, French, Italian and Portuguese spoken, helpful, repeatedly rec. *All Travels*, Huérfanos 1160, local 10, T 696-4348, good for flight tickets; *Eurotur*, Huérfanos 1160, local 13, for cheap air tickets to Europe. **Blanco**, Pedro de Valdivia near Av Providencia, good for flight information and exchange. **Rapa-Nui**, Huérfanos 1160, specializes in trips to Easter Island. *Selectours*, Las Urbinas 95, Providencia,

T 234 2838, F 234 2434. *Turismo Grace*, Victoria Subercaseaux 381, T 693-3740, good service. For local tours: *Ace Turismo*, O'Higgins 949, T 696-0391, city tour, US$12 for ½ day. *Tour Service*, Teatinos 333, 10th floor, T 6960415/727166.

For adventure tours and trekking: *Sportstours*, Teatinos 330, piso 10, T 696-8832/698-3058, German-run, helpful, 5 day trips to Antarctica (offices also at Hotels *Carrera*, and *San Cristóbal*); *Altue Expediciones*, Encomenderos 83, T 232-1103, for wilderness trips incl 15 day tour of Patagonia, rec (above *Geo Pub*). Climbing and adventure tours in the Lake District and elsewhere, *Antu Aventuras*, Casilla 24, Santiago, T 271-2767, Telex 440019, RECAL CZ. *Azimut 360*, Monte Carmelo 360, Dept 36, T 777-2375, highly rec, low prices; *Mountain Service*, Ebro 2805, Las Condes, T 242-9723, F 234-3438, and *Evasión*, Sotero Sanz 95, Providencia, T 231-1876 both recommended for climbing trips; *Racies*, Plaza Corregidor Zañartu 761, cultural tours, including Robinson Crusoe Island and Antarctica, T/F 638-2904. *Turismo Grant*, Huérfanos 863, Oficina 516, T 639-5524, helpful, English spoken; *Patagonia Chile*, Constitución 172, Bellavista, T 351871, offer mountain trips, river rafting, trekking. *Turismo Cabo de Hornos*, Agustinas 814, Of 706, T 6338481, F 6338486, for DAP flights (Punta Arenas-Puerto Williams) and Tierra del Fuego/Antártica tours. *Andina del Sud*, Bombero Ossa 1010, Piso 3, Of 301, T 697-1010, F 696-5121, for tours in the Lake District. Ask at *Hotel Maury*, address above, for tours with Fernández (Tony), who speaks English, including riding, rafting and barbecue, US$50 pp, rec. For skiing in the Santiago area **see below page 672**.

Tourist Information Servicio Nacional de Turismo (Sernatur—the national tourist board), Av Providencia 1550 (Casilla 14082), T 236-1416, Telex SERNA CL 240137, between metros Manuel Montt and Pedro de Valdivia, next to Providencia Municipal Library, open Mon-Fri 0900-1900, Sat 0900-1300. English and German spoken and maps (road map US$1.50), brochures and posters are available. Good notice board. Ask for the free booklet, *Paseos en Santiago* (City Walks in Santiago), which is very useful for those with time to explore on foot. Kiosk on Ahumada nr Agustinas (erratic opening times). Information office also at the airport, open 0900-2100 daily. Municipal Tourist Board, Casa Colorada, Merced 860, T 336700/330723. **NB** Many tourist offices outside Santiago are closed in winter, so stock up on information here.

Excellent road maps (US$1.75) and information may be obtained from the **Automóvil Club de Chile**, Vitacura 8620, T 212-5702/3/4 (Metro P de Valdivia then bus to Vitacura, or a US$6 taxi ride from the centre), which also gives discounts to members of affiliated motoring organizations; open Mon-Fri 0845-1815, Sat 0900-1300, very helpful. Geophysical and topographical maps (not cheap) are available from **Instituto Geográfico Militar**, at their sales office, San Antonio 65, or main office Dieciocho 369, T 698-7278, open 0900-1800 Mon-Fri, closed in Jan/Feb. In 1991 the Insituto Geográfico published a *Guía Caminera*, with roads and city plans, for US$8.75 (available only at IGM offices, not 100% accurate). *Turistel* (see **Tourist Information** in **Information for Visitors**) publishes a *Mapa Rutera*. The Biblioteca Nacional, Moneda 650, has an excellent collection of maps which can be photocopied, particularly useful for climbing. *Conaf* (Corporación Nacional Forestal), Presidente Bulnes 259, oficina 206 (main office at No 285), T 696-0783/699-2833, publishes a number of booklets (see **Information for Visitors**) and has documents and maps about the national park system that can be consulted or photocopied (not very useful for walking). CODEFF (Comité Nacional Pro-Defensa de la Fauna y Flora), Santo Filomena 135, Bellavista, T 377290, can also provide information on environmental questions. Walkers' maps are not available outside Santiago. Write to the Departamento de Estudios Vialidad Nacional, Morandé 59, oficina 344, Santiago, to see if their set of 14 maps of the country (scale 1:500,000—border areas 1:1,000,000) is available. Maps on sale from news kiosks: Esso road and town plans, Copec, Inupal and others (see also **Information for Visitors** for details of other publications).

Immigration Moneda 1417, open 0900-1300; extension of tourist card US$8.

Policia Internacional for lost tourist cards, etc, Santo Domingo y MacIver.

Buses and Taxis There are three kinds of buses: the small fast kind called *liebres* (hares) which cost US$0.50 a ride; the regular buses at US$0.30, and the large buses marked Expreso, US$0.40. Taxi drivers are permitted to charge more at night, but in the day time check that the meter is set to day rates. Taxis (black with yellow roofs) are abundant, and not expensive, with a minimum charge of US$0.40, plus US$0.12 per 200m. At bus terminals, drivers will charge more—best to walk a block and flag down a cruising taxi. Large blue taxis do not have meters. Avoid taxis with more than one person in them especially at night. There are also colectivo taxis to the suburbs, US$0.70. For journeys outside the city arrange the charge beforehand. The private taxi service which operates from the bottom level of *Hotel Carrera* has been rec (same rates as city taxis), as has Radio Taxis Andes Pacífico, T 225-3064/2888; similarly

Rigoberto Contreras, T 638-1042, ext 4215, available at *Holiday Inn Crowne Plaza*, but rates above those of city taxis.

Underground Railway The first line of the underground railway system (Metro) runs W-E between San Pablo and Escuela Militar, under the Alameda, and the second line runs N-S from Cal y Canto to Callejón Ovalle. The connecting station is Los Héroes. Line 5, from Baquedano 5 to La Florida is under construction. The trains are fast, quiet, and full. The first train is at 0630 (Mon-Sat), 0800 (Sun and holidays), the last about 2245. Fares vary according to time of journey; there are 3 charging periods: high 0715-0900, 1800-1930, US$0.35; medium 0900-1800, 1930-2100, US$0.30; low 0600-0715, 2100-2230 and weekends, US$0.20. The simplest solution is to buy a *boleto inteligente*, US$3.50; a charge card from which the appropriate fare is deducted. Metrobus services connects with the metro at Lo Ovalle for southern Santiago and at Escuela Militar for Vitacura, Las Condes and Apoquindo.

Car Hire Prices vary a lot so shop around first. Hertz, Avis and Budget available from airport. **Hertz**, Av Andrés Bello 1469, T 225-9328, and airport, T 601-9262, has a good network in Chile and cars are in good condition. **Avis** at La Concepción 334, T 495-757. **Automóvil Club de Chile** car rental, Marchant Pereira 122, Providencia, T 274-4167/6261, discount for members and members of associated motoring organizations. A credit card is usually asked for when renting a vehicle. Tax of 18% is charged but usually not included in price quoted. If possible book a car in advance. Note that in the capital driving is restricted according to licence plate numbers; look for notices in the street and newspapers.

Motorcycles Small BMW workshop, Av San Camilo 185, Sr Marco Canales. BMW car dealer *Frederic*, Av Portugal, has some spares. Also tyre shops in this area. BMW riders can also seek help from the *carabineros* who ride BMW machines and have a workshop with good mechanics at Av Rivera 2003.

Airport International and domestic flights leave from Arturo Merino Benítez Airport at Pudahuel, 26 km NW of Santiago. A new international terminal was opened in 1994. Airport information T 601-9709. No accommodation nearby. Airport taxi, about US$15 but bargain hard and agree fare beforehand: more expensive with meter. Taxi to airport is much cheaper if flagged down in the street rather than booked by phone. Bus service to/from city centre by 2 companies: Tour Express (Moneda 1529, T 671-7380), US$2, and Metropuerto (T 601-9883/695-8058), US$1.30, approx every 15 mins, plenty of luggage space. First bus from city centre 0530, first from airport 0645, last from airport 0030. Buses leave from outside airport terminal and, in Santiago, from Tour Express office at Moneda 1529 and from Plazoleta Los Héroes, calling also at Metro stations República, Estación Central and Universidad de Santiago. Empresa Turismo Bar-C from your house or hotel to airport (or vice-versa), any time day or night, T 246-3600/1 for reservation (cheaper than taxi). Empresa Navett, Av Ejército Libertador 21 (nearest metro Los Héroes), T 695-6868 has a round-the-clock service, US$7. On arrival, get entry card from desk at entrance to arrivals hall before proceeding to immigration, otherwise you will be sent back. Bank and Afex *cambio* (better rates) outside customs hall; Sernatur office in same area will book accommodation. There are some shops, but they are very expensive, as are the bar and restaurant. Buy your wine etc in town. Left luggage US$2.50 per bag per day. For schedules of domestic flights from Santiago, see under destinations.

Rail No passenger trains to northern Chile. All trains leave from Estación Central at Alameda O'Higgins 3322. Buses from northern bus terminal to Estación Central, Nos 34 and 45, 10 mins, US$0.30, or take metro and change at Los Héroes. The line runs S to Rancagua, San Fernando, Curicó, Talca, Linares, Parral and Chillán, thereafter services go to 1) **Concepción**, 2) **Puerto Montt** via **Temuco**, with a bus connection to **Valdivia**. Schedules change with the seasons, so you must check timetables before planning a journey. See under destinations for fares and notes on schedules. *Expreso* services do not have sleepers; some *rápidos* do (in summer *rápidos* are booked up a week in advance). *Dormitorio* carriages were built in Germany in 1930's, bunks (comfortable) lie parallel to rails, US-Pullman-style (washrooms at each end, one with shower-bath—often cold water only); an attendant for each car; bar car shows 3 films—no cost but you must purchase a drink ticket in advance. There is also a newer, *Gran Dormitorio* sleeping car (1984), with private toilet and shower, US$10 extra for 2, rec. For the *expresos* there are no reservations (get your ticket the morning of the day the train leaves and sit on the train as soon as you can get on; otherwise you'll stand for the whole journey). Free hot water supplied, so take own mug and coffee. Also a car-transporter service to Chillán, Temuco and Puerto Montt. Trains are still fairly cheap and generally very punctual, although 1st class is generally dearer than bus; meals are good though expensive. Check for family, senior citizen and student discounts. Trains can be cold and draughty in winter and spring. Booking offices: for State Railways, Alameda O'Higgins 853 in Galería Hotel Libertador, Local 21; T 632-2801, Mon-Fri 0830-1900, Sat 0900-1300; or Metro Esc Militar, Galería Sur, Local 25,

T 228-2983, Mon-Fri 0830-1900, Sat 0900-1300; central station, open till 2230, T 689-5718/689-1682; for Antofagasta-La Paz, Ahumada 11, Of 602, T 698-5536. Left luggage office at Estación Central.

A steam train runs tourist services between Santiago and Los Andes, 5-hr journey, T 698-5536 for details.

Buses There are frequent, and good, interurban buses to all parts of Chile. (**NB** Many leave early because of tight competition: arrive at bus station early.) Check if student rates available (even for non-students), or reductions for travelling same day as purchase of ticket; it is worth bargaining over prices, especially shortly before departure and out of the summer season. Also take a look at the buses before buying the tickets (there are big differences in quality among bus companies); ask about the on-board services, many companies offer drinks for sale, or free, and luxury buses have meals and wine, colour videos, headphones. Reclining seats are common and there are also *salón cama* sleeper buses. Fares from/to the capital are given in the text. On Fri evening, when night departures are getting ready to go, the terminals are murder.

There are 4 bus terminals: 1) Terminal del Norte, Gral Mackenna y Amunátegui, T 671-2141, about 5 mins walk from Cal y Canto metro station (Line 2), due to be relocated, but still operating Jan 1995; from here buses leave for northern destinations, and some international services (see below). 2) Terminal de Buses Sur, Av B O'Higgins 3878, T 791-385, nearest metro Universidad Técnica/Universidad de Santiago (both names are used); buses from here go to Valparaíso, Viña del Mar and southern destinations. 3) Terminal de Buses Alameda, Al B O'Higgins 3712, next to metro Universidad de Santiago, Línea 1 and next to the Terminal Sur: Pullman-Bus and Tur-Bus services go from here to Valparaíso, Viña del Mar and southern destinations. 4) Terminal Los Héroes on Jiménez, just N of the Alameda, has booking offices of about 10 companies for N and S routes as well as some international services. Varmontt buses, who run an expensive service to Puerto Montt, have their own terminal at Av 21 de Septiembre 2212 (office on 2nd floor), metro Los Leones; many companies have offices away from the terminals, at which their buses call.

See the note under **Taxis** about not taking expensive taxis parked outside bus stations. Also, do not change money at the bus terminals; if coming from Argentina, try to get some Chilean pesos before you arrive.

International Buses Long distance: to **Buenos Aires**, from Los Héroes terminal US$70-75, 22 hrs (TAC and Ahumada rec), see below; to **Montevideo**, also from Los Héroes, several companies, most involving a change in Mendoza, eg Tas Choapa, 27 hrs, meals included; to **Córdoba** direct; **Caracas** (Tues and Fri 0900); **Lima**, 51 hrs, it is cheaper to take a bus to Arica (US$28 and up), a colectivo to Tacna (US$4), thence bus to Lima. Services also to **Bogotá** (7 days); **São Paulo** and **Rio de Janeiro** (eg Chilebus, Tues, Thur, Sat, US$100, 52 hrs), **Asunción** (4 a week, US$50-60), **Guayaquil**; and **Quito**. Tramaca, from northern terminal, runs a *combinación* service which links with the train from Calama to **Uyuni** and **Oruro** in Bolivia. Géminis, also from northern terminal, goes on Tues to **Salta**, Argentina, changing in Calama, US$60. Short distance: there are frequent bus and *colectivo* taxi services from the Terminal del Norte over the Andes to **Mendoza** (should be 6 hrs, but in 1994 9 hrs owing to road repairs), US$15-20; taxis also go from the southern terminal, touts will approach you. All buses go through the Cristo Redentor tunnel. Many *colectivos* for Mendoza go from the 800/900 blocks of Morandé, more expensive than the buses, but with shorter waiting time at customs (US$23): Chi-Ar taxi company, Morandé 890, rec, leaves at 0800; Chile-Bus, Morandé 838, at 0830;

Cordillera Nevada, Morandé 870, T 698-4716, or Local 61 at southern terminal, drive very fast.

Shipping Navimag, Av El Bosque Norte 0440, piso 1, T 203-5030, F 203-5025, Telex 240208-240224 NISA CK, Metro Tobalaba for services Puerto Montt-Puerto Natales and Puerto Montt-Puerto Chacabuco. **Transmarchilay**, Agustinas 715, Oficina 403, T/F 633-5959, for services between Chiloé and the mainland, ferry routes on the Carretera Austral and on Lake General Carrera. M/n *Skorpios*: luxury cruise out of Puerto Montt to Laguna San Rafael. Augusto Leguía Norte 118, Las Condes, T 231-1030, F 232-2269. Navimag and Transmarchilay also sail to the Laguna San Rafael in summer. Check shipping schedules with shipping lines rather than Sernatur.

Hitchhiking To Valparaíso, take Metro to Pajaritos and walk 5 mins to W—no difficulty. Or, take bus 'Renca Panamericana' from MacIver y Monjitas. To hitch S, take Metro to Estación Central, then Buses del Paine at Calle Borja as far as possible on the highway to the toll area, about US$1, 75 mins. To Buenos Aires (and Brazil) take a bus to Los Andes, then go to Copec station on the outskirts (lots of trucks early morning).

Excursions from Santiago On the NE outskirts in Las Condes is the Santuario de la Naturaleza Yerba Loca, administered by Conaf, open Sep to Apr (small entrance fee). Several small resort towns are easily reached by car from the capital. Peñalolén, 16 km E, provides opportunities for hiking and a beautiful view of the city if there's no smog (bus in front of Mapocho station at Av Independencia and Balmaceda). ***Termas de Colina*** (915m), an attractive, popular spa in the mountains 43 km to the N: take a bus from Cal y Canto metro station to the town of Colina (hourly in summer only, 40 mins), then another to the military base 1½ km from town. From here a rough road leads 6 km to **E** pp *Hotel Termas de Colina*, T 844-1408, thermal baths, US$6.50, beautiful swimming pool (closed Fri) US$4 (crowded at weekends), last return bus at 1900. On the walk to the hotel, beautiful countryside, do not take photos or even show your camera when passing the military base. Taxis go from Colina to the hotel.

Southeast of Santiago, in the Upper Maipo valley (Cajón del Maipo) are a number of resorts incl: ***San José de Maipo***, some 50 km from the capital (**E** *Alojamiento Inesita*, Comercio 301, good), buses every 30 mins from N end of Parque O'Higgins, Avenida Norte-Sur, or W side of Plaza Ercilla (return fare US$2, 2 hrs each way), particularly beautiful in spring. The mountain town of *Melocotón* (**D** pp *Millahue Hotel*). is 6 km further S, and ***San Alfonso***, 4 km on (**C** *Posada Los Ciervos*, with breakfast and shared bath, **A** with bath and full board, good; **F** pp *Residencial España*, clean, comfortable, restaurant, also others; campsite at the *Comunidad Cascada de las Animas*, T 251-7506, also rents cabins—**C** for 4, hot water, cooking equipment etc—sauna, horseriding). The walk to the *Cascada de las Animas* is pleasant; ask permission to cross the bridge at the campsite as private land is crossed. Buses at hourly or 2-hr intervals from Parque O'Higgins, Santiago. 31 km further SE is ***El Volcán*** (1,400m) reached by three buses a day (US$2) from Parque O'Higgins; there are astounding views, but little else (the village was wiped away in a landslide). **NB** Passports required if visiting this area or continuing further up the mountain. From El Volcán the road (very poor condition) runs 14 km E to the **B** pp *Refugio Alemán Lo Valdés*, stone-built chalet accommodation, full board, good food, rec, a good place to stay for mountain excursions, open all year. A splendid region which deserves the journey required to get there. Nearby are warm natural baths, ***Baños Morales*** (**E** *Pensión Díaz*, friendly, good food; excellent café in the village, serving homemade jam—it closes at Easter for the winter; **D** pp *Refugio Baños Morales*, full board, hot water); open from Oct (bus leaves daily in summer, weekends only off season, from Parque O'Higgins at 0730, arriving at Baños Morales 1100, US$2 each way; returns at 1800—buy return on arrival to ensure seat back; alternatively, hitch back to Santiago on quarry lorries). North of Baños Morales is **El Morado National Park** with a glacier. 12 km further E up the mountain is Baños Colina (not to be confused with Termas de Colina, see above; basic *residencial* and restaurant), hot thermal springs, entry free, horses for hire, served by daily bus to Baños Morales. This area is popular at weekends and holiday times, but is otherwise deserted.

45 km S of Santiago is the **Reserva Nacional Río Clarillo**, reached by Micro No 32 to El Principal, 2 km from the entrance, US$2.50. It is in the precordillera and can be visited at any time of year for its landscapes.

The small towns in the Aconcagua Valley to the N—San Felipe, Jahuel and Los Andes—are described in the section 'To Buenos Aires across the Andes', p 673.

10 km SW of Santiago lies the suburb of *Maipú*. A monument marks the site of the Battle of the Maipú, 5 April 1818, which resulted in the final defeat of the Spanish royalist forces in Chile. Nearby is the National Votive Temple of Maipú, of fine modern architecture and stained glass; interesting (open daily 0800-2100, also daily mass at 1830, 1730 Sat, 1000-1400, 1600-2000 Sun and religious holidays), and so is the attached Museo del Carmen of carriages, furniture, clothing and other colonial and later items, Sat 1600-2000, Sun and holidays, 1100-1400, 1600-2000. Bus from Teatinos y O'Higgins, 45 mins.

Campsites Excellent facilities about 70 km from Santiago at Laguna de Aculeo, called **Club Camping Maki**. Facilities include electricity, cold water, swimming pool, boat mooring, restaurant, but only available to members of certain organizations. An alternative site is El Castaño camping (with casino), 1 km away, on edge of lake. Very friendly, café sells fruit, eggs, milk, bread and kerosene. Good fishing. No showers, water from handpump.

Pottery can be bought in *Pomaire*, a little town 65 km W of Santiago, where the artists can be observed at work. The area is rich in clay and the town is famous for its cider (*chicha de uva*, 3 strengths: *dulce, medio* and *fuerte*) and Chilean dishes; highly rec: *Restaurant San Antonio*, welcoming, semi-outdoor, good food and service. Pomaire may be reached by Melipilla bus from Calle San Borja, Santiago, bus station behind Estación Central metro station, every few minutes, US$1 each way, Rutabus 78 goes on the motorway, 1 hr, other buses via Talagante take 1 hr 25 mins (alight at side road to Pomaire, 2-3 km from town, colectivos every 10-15 mins); en route, delicious *pastel de choclo* can be obtained at Restaurant *Mi Ranchito*. Both Pomaire and Melipilla have been rebuilt after the 1985 earthquake.

Vineyards Several vineyards in the Santiago area can be visited. *Cousiño-Macul*, Av Quilin on E outskirts of the city offer tours Mon-Fri, phone first T 283-3000. At Pirque, near Puente Alto, 40 km S of Santiago is the vineyard of *Concha y Toro*. Entry free, Mon-Sat and Sun pm, short tour (Spanish, English, French, German, Portuguese). Take 'Puente Alto' bus from Santa Rosa y Alameda, then any bus marked 'Pirque' from Plaza Alto in Puente Alto, asking to be dropped at Concha. The *Undurraga* vineyard at Santa Ana, SW of Santiago, also permits visits on weekdays (tours given by the owner-manager, Pedro Undurraga). Take a Melipilla bus (but not Rutabus 78) to the entrance.

Horse-Breeding A specially rec excursion is to *Los Lingues*, a private *hacienda* 120 km S of Santiago, where it is said the best horses in Chile are bred. Rosie Swale was lent two of them for her epic ride from Antofagasta to Cape Horn, described in *Back to Cape Horn* (Collins, London, 1986). Visits can be arranged to the 17th century house, a gift of the King of Spain, at Hacienda Los Lingues, Torre C de Tajamar, Of 205, Santiago, T 235-2458/5446/7604, F 235-7604, Telex 346060 LINGUES CK. To 6060 LINGUE. One-day tours including transport, rodeo and lunch are available, also accommodation with extra charge for breakfast or full board, very expensive (the Hacienda is a member of the French Hotels et Relais et Chateaux).

Skiing There are 6 main ski resorts nr Santiago, 4 of them E of the capital. *Farellones*, 51 km E of Santiago at 2,470m, and reached by car, bus, or truck in under 90 min is an excellent centre: *Motel Tupungato* (Candelaria Goyenechea 4750, Santiago, T 218-2216), **D** pp *Refugio Club Alemán Andino* (El Arrayán 2735, Santiago, T 242-5453, 1800-2000 May-Jun) *Colorado Apart Hotel* (Av Apoquindo 4900, Oficina 43, Santiago, T 246-0660, F 246-1447), and *Posada Farellones*, highly rec. High season: Jun to Sep/Oct, weather permitting. An excellent network of five ski-lifts. There are excursions for a day from Santiago at US$5 plus US$25 ski-lifts ticket; enquire Ski Club Chile, Goyenechea Candelaria 4750, Vitacura (N of Los Leones Golf Club), T 211-7341. Farellones is easily reached by buses from front of Omnium building, Av Apoquindo, 4 blocks from Escuela Militar Metro, daily at 0830, essential to book in advance, US$7. It is easy to hitch from the junction of Av Las Condes/El Camino Farellones (petrol station in the middle): take a Las Condes bus from Calle Merced almost to the end of the line. Beautiful views for 30 km across ten Andean peaks. Incredible sunsets. Busy at weekends. Large restaurants.

6 km further E is *La Parva*. The upper class Santiago weekend resort which has twelve lifts, 0900-1730 (*Condominio Nueva Parva*, good hotel and restaurant, reservations in Santiago:

Roger de Flor 2911, T 220-8510/206-5068), where the runs are a little easier, though the snow may not be as good. In summer, this is a good walking area: a good trail leads to the base of Cerro El Plomo (6,050m, the southernmost Inca sacrificial peak—the ruins nr the summit are in good repair). Allow 3-4 days for the climb; ice axe and crampons necessary. Lift ticket, US$20, and equipment rental, US$10-15 depending on quality. 8 km SE of Farallones is **El Colorado** (accommodation in *Edificios Los Ciervos* and *Monteblanco*, in Santiago, San Antonio 486, Oficina 151), with 3 triple chairlifts and a ski lodge.

Also nearby is **Valle Nevado** (owned by Spie Batignolles of France), the site of the 1993 Pan American winter games. Valle Nevado aims to be the largest ski resort in South America. Although incredibly expensive and not to everyone's taste, the resort is very highly regarded and much less crowded than the nearby resorts at weekends. **L1** *Hotel Valle Nevado*, and more; *Hotel Puerta del Sol*; *Condominium Mirador del Inca*; 6 restaurants. Casa Valle Nevado, Gertrudis Echeñique 441, T 206-0027, F 228-8888. There are 25 runs, 2 chairlifts, 6 skilifts and many more are planned; daily ski lift pass US$25 weekdays, US$35 weekends.

Portillo, altitude 2,855m, 145 km N of Santiago and 62 E of Los Andes, on the route to Argentina, is another great centre for skiing and winter sports in Chile. The weather is ideal, the snow conditions excellent, the runs many and varied; 12 lifts carry skiers up the slopes. The season is from Jun to Sep/Oct, weather depending. Lift pass US$35. Cheap packages can be arranged at the beginning and out of the season. On three sides the mountains soften into snow-clad fields and finally slope gently into the Laguna de Inca, $5\frac{1}{2}$ km long and $1\frac{1}{2}$ km wide; this lake, at an altitude of 2,835m, has no outlet, is frozen over in winter, and its depth is not known. Out of season this is another good area for walking, but get detailed maps before setting out.

In winter Portillo is easily reached from Santiago by daily bus services (except in bad weather). In summer, ask the bus driver to stop, as it is not a routine call and on the way down you may have to hitch to the customs post. Another option is to take a bus to Los Andes (US$2.25), then to Río Blanco (US$0.70), then hitch (see p 674).

Hotels L2 *Hotel Portillo*, cinema, night club, swimming pool, sauna and medical service, on the shore of Laguna de Inca; accommodation ranges from lakefront suites, full board, fabulous view, to family apartments to bunk rooms without or with bath (much cheaper, from C up). Parking charges even if you go for a meal; jacket and tie must be worn in the dining room. Self-service lunch. Open all year. Reservations, Roger de Flor 2911, T 231-3411, F 699-2575, Telex 440372 PORTICZ, Santiago. Cheaper food available at *Restaurant Yuly* across the road, and *Restaurant Los Libertadores* at the customs station 1 km away. **L3** *Hostería Alborada*, including all meals, tax and service. During Ski Week (last in Sept), about double normal rate, all incl. Reservations, Agencia Tour Avión, Agustinas 1062, Santiago, T 72-6184, or Calle Navarro 264, San Felipe, T 101-R.

There are boats for fishing in the lake; but beware the afternoon winds, which often make the homeward pull 3 or 4 times as long as the outward pull. There are some gentle ski slopes for beginners nr the hotel. The major skiing events are in Aug and Sep. Mules for stupendous expeditions to the glacier at the head of the valley or of the Cerro Juncal, to the pass in the W side of the valley.

Lagunillas is a favourite ski-resort 67 km SE of Santiago in the Maipo Valley (see above for details of transport to San José de Maipo). Accommodation in the lodges of the Club Andino de Chile (bookings may be made at Ahumada 47, Santiago).Tow fee US$20; long T-bar and poma lifts; easy field.

To Buenos Aires across the Andes See under Santiago, **International Buses**.
Check in advance on weather and road conditions before travelling beyond Los Andes. Route 57 runs N from Santiago to the rich Aconcagua Valley, the so-called Vale of Chile. North of Llaillay, at Km 69, the road forks—the E branch going to Los Andes, the W branch to **San Felipe**, the capital of Aconcagua Province, 96 km from Santiago and 128 km from Valparaíso. It is an agricultural and mining centre with 42,000 inhabitants, 635m above sea level, with an agreeable climate. Part of the Inca highway has recently been discovered in the city; previously, no traces had been found further S than La Serena. A paved highway (13 km) runs N from San Felipe to the old town of Putaendo.

Hotel C *Hostería San Felipe*, Merced 204, T 510508.

Termas de Jahuel (**L2** hotel, T 511240 or Santiago 393-810), is high in the Cordillera (1,190m) 18 km by road from San Felipe. The hill scenery includes a distant view of Aconcagua.

Curimón, between San Felipe and Los Andes, has a historic church, with a small museum attached.

Sixteen km SE of San Felipe and 77 km N of Santiago is ***Los Andes***, situated in a wealthy agricultural, fruit-farming and wine-producing area, but also the site of a large car assembly plant. There are monuments to José de San Martín and Bernardo O'Higgins in the Plaza de Armas, and a monument to the Clark brothers, who built the Transandine Railway (much of which is now either disused or pulled up). Good views from El Cerro de la Virgen. Trail starts at the municipal picnic ground on Independencia (easy to climb taking approx 1 hr). See also under Valparaíso **Rail** for train service to the coast. Population: 30,500. Altitude: 730m.

Hotels A1 *Baños El Corazón*, at San Esteban, T 421371, with full board, use of swimming pool but thermal baths extra; take bus San Esteban/El Cariño (US$0.50); **B** *Plaza*, Esmeralda 367, T 421929, good but restaurant expensive; **D** *Central*, Esmeralda 278 (1 block from bus station) T 421275, reasonable and very friendly (excellent bakery opp, try the empanadas); **E** pp *Continental*, Esmeralda 211, T 421013; **F** pp *Estación*, Rodríguez 389, T 421026, cheap restaurant; **F** *Valparaíso*, Sarmiento 160, clean; *Restaurante Círculo Italiano*, near bus station, rec. **Exchange: Cambio Inter** at *Plaza Hotel*, good rates, changes cheques. **Telephones** CTC, O'Higgins 405. **Transport** No buses to Argentina. Hitchhiking over Andes possible on trucks from Aduana building in Los Andes.

East of Los Andes the road to Argentina passes into the Cordillera and winds along the Río Aconcagua for 34 km until it reaches the village of ***Río Blanco*** (1,370m), set at the confluence of two rivers which form the Río Aconcagua: the Blanco and the Juncal. There is a fish hatchery with small botanical garden at the entrance of the Andina copper mine. *Hostería Luna*, 4 km before Río Blanco on road from Los Andes, good value, clean, helpful, good food. *Hostería Guardia Vieja*, expensive but untidy, 8 km beyond town. Possible to camp. Buses run daily from Los Andes; from Santiago, Ahumada, at 1930 daily, direct, 2 hrs, US$2.

East of Río Blanco the road climbs to the Chilean customs post at Caracoles, Km 33 (long delays; no fruit can be taken across). From here the road climbs to the Redentor tunnel, open from 0800 to 1800, Chilean time. Toll US$3. The old pass, with the statue of Christ the Redeemer, at an altitude of 4,200m, is 8 km beyond the tunnel and can be reached by a good, unpaved road from Las Cuevas on the Argentine side (from Chilean side access can be made in summer only, according to the Automóvil Club de Chile). On the far side of the Andes the road descends 203 km to Mendoza, where there are road and rail connections for Buenos Aires. The road from the tunnel to Mendoza is in fair condition, all of it paved.

Valparaíso, Viña del Mar and The Coast

Valparaíso (pop 277,000; DDD 032), capital of V Región (Valparaíso), is the principal port and second-largest city of Chile, and an important naval base. With the construction of a new congress building on Plaza O'Higgins, it is now the seat of the Chilean parliament. The city is situated on the shores of a sweeping bay and on a crescent of hills behind. Seen from the ocean, it presents a majestic panorama: a great circle of hills is backed by the snow-capped peaks of the distant Cordillera. The climate is good, for the summer heat is tempered by fresh breezes and sunshine mitigates the unkindness of a short winter. (The mean annual temperature is 15°C, with -1°C and 31°C as the extremes.)

Founded in 1536, the city became in the nineteenth century the major centre of British naval and commercial activity on the Pacific coast of South America, before declining in importance with the opening of the Panama Canal in 1914. Little of its colonial past has survived the sequence of pirates, tempests, fires and earthquakes, although a remnant of the old colonial city can be found in the hollow known as El Puerto, grouped round the low-built stucco church of La Matriz. Until recently, all buildings were low, as a precaution against earthquakes, but during the last few years modern multi-storey blocks have appeared. Most of the principal buildings date from after the devastating earthquake of 1906. There was another serious earthquake in Jul 1971 and, most recently, in Mar 1985.

There are two completely different cities. The lower part, known as **'El Plan'**, is the business centre, with fine office buildings on narrow streets strung along the

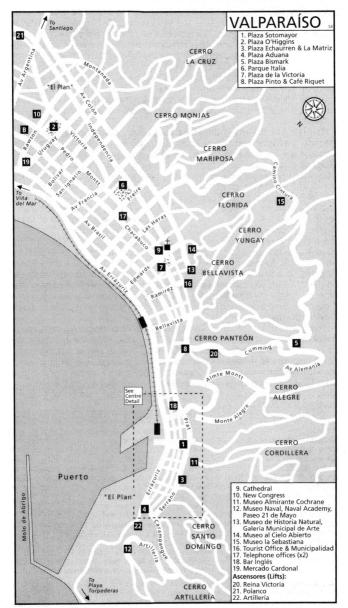

VALPARAÍSO

1. Plaza Sotomayor
2. Plaza O'Higgins
3. Plaza Echaurren & La Matriz
4. Plaza Aduana
5. Plaza Bismark
6. Parque Italia
7. Plaza de la Victoria
8. Plaza Pinto & Café Riquet

To Santiago

CERRO LA CRUZ

Av Argentina

Montaneda

"El Plan"

Av Colón

Independencia

Uruguay

Victoria

Pedro

Rawson

Bolívar

San Ignacio Montt

Av Francia

Freire

Av Brasil

Chacabuco

Las Heras

CERRO MONJAS

CERRO MARIPOSA

Camino Cintura

CERRO FLORIDA

CERRO YUNGAY

CERRO BELLAVISTA

Av Errázuriz

Edwards

Ramírez

Bellavista

CERRO PANTEÓN

Cumming

Almte Montt

Monte Alegre

Av Alemanía

CERRO ALEGRE

CERRO CORDILLERA

See Centre Detail

Puerto

"El Plan"

Errázuriz

Serrano

Prat

Molo de Abrigo

Artillería

Carampangue

To Playa Torpederas

CERRO SANTO DOMINGO

CERRO ARTILLERÍA

To Viña del Mar

9. Cathedral
10. New Congress
11. Museo Almirante Cochrane
12. Museo Naval, Naval Academy, Paseo 21 de Mayo
13. Museo de Historia Natural, Galería Municipal de Arte
14. Museo al Cielo Abierto
15. Museo la Sebastiana
16. Tourist Office & Municipalidad
17. Telephone offices (x2)
18. Bar Inglés
19. Mercado Cardonal
Ascensores (Lifts):
20. Reina Victoria
21. Polanco
22. Artillería

edge of the bay. Above, covering the hills ('cerros'), is a fantastic agglomeration of fine mansions, tattered houses and shacks, scrambled in oriental confusion along the narrow back streets. Superb views over the bay are offered from most of the 'cerros'. The lower and upper cities are connected by steep winding roads, flights of steps and 16 *ascensores* or funicular railways dating from the period 1880-1914. The most unusual of these is **Ascensor Polanco** (entrance from Calle Simpson, off Av Argentina a few blocks SE of the bus station), which is in two parts, the first of which is a 160m horizontal tunnel through the rock, the second a vertical lift to the summit on which there is a *mirador*. Note that the lower entrance is in a slum area which is unsafe: do not go alone and do not take valuables.

The heart of the city is the **Plaza Sotomayor**, dominated by the former **Intendencia** (Government House), now used as the Regional Naval Headquarters. Opposite is a fine statue to the 'Heroes of Iquique' (**see p 693**). The passenger quay is one block away (handicraft shops on quay) and nearby is the railway station, from which passenger services run on the metropolitan line to Los Andes. The streets of El Puerto run on either side from Plaza Sotomayor. Calle Serrano runs NW for 2 blocks to the Plaza Echaurren, nr which stands the church of **La Matriz**, built in 1842 on the site of the first church in the city. Further NW, along Bustamante lies the Plaza Aduana from where there is an *ascensor* to the bold hill of **Cerro Artillería**, crowned by the huge Naval Academy and a park. To the W of the Cerro the Avenida **Playa Ancha** runs to a stadium, seating 20,000 people, on Cerro Playa Ancha. Avenida Altamirano runs along the coast at the foot of Cerro Playa Ancha to **Las Torpederas**, a picturesque bathing beach. The **Faro de Punta Angeles**, on a promontory just beyond Las Torpederas, was the first lighthouse on the W Coast; you can get a permit to go up. On another high point on the other side of the city is the **Mirador de O'Higgins**, the spot where the Supreme Dictator exclaimed, on seeing Cochrane's liberating squadron: 'On those four craft depends the destiny of America'.

Southeast of Plaza Sotomayor Calles Prat, Cochrane and Esmeralda run through the old banking and commercial centre to Plaza Aníbal Pinto, the most attractive square in Valparaíso. Further E is Plaza O'Higgins (flea market on Sat mornings), which is dominated by the imposing new Congress building. Several of the Cerros are worth visiting, notably Cerro Concepción, where the Anglican church dating from 1854 can be visited, and Cerro Bellavista, where you can visit the 'Museo Al Cielo Abierto', a collection of 20 murals painted on the exteriors of buildings (reached from Plaza de la Victoria).

The New Year is celebrated by a firework display on the bay, which is best seen from the Cerros.

Museums Museo Municipal de Bellas Artes, with Chilean landscapes and seascapes and some modern paintings, housed in Palacio Baburizza, Paseo Yugoslavo, art nouveau palace overlooking harbour (free), open Tues-Sun 1000-1800; take *Ascensor El Peral* from Plaza Justicia, off Plaza Sotomayor. **Museo del Mar Almirante Cochrane**, housing collection of naval models built by local Naval Modelling Club, good views over port, Tues-Sun 1000-1800, free, take Ascensor Cordillera from Calle Serrano, off Plaza Sotomayor, to Cerro Cordillera; at the top, Plazuela Eleuterio Ramírez, take Calle Merlet to the left. **Museo Naval**, in the old Naval Academy on Cerro Artillería, Paseo 21 de Mayo, naval history 1810-1880, includes exhibitions on Chile's two naval heroes, Lord Cochrane and Arturo Prat, Tues-Sun 1000-1800, US$0.35 (take Ascensor Artillería from Plaza Aduana). **Museo de Historia Natural**, in nineteenth-century Palacio Lyon, Condell 1546, good collection on the cultures of Easter island and **Galeria Municipal de Arte**, in cellars of Palacio Lyon, both closed Mon. **Museo La Sebastiana**, Pasaje Collado 1, Av Alemania, Altura 6900 on Cerro Florida, T 256606, former house of Pablo Neruda (see also his house at Isla Negra below), Tues-Sun 1030-1430, 1530-1800 (closes 1700 Jun-Aug), US$2 (take Verde Mar Bus O or D along Av Alemania).

Sightseeing Launches run trips around harbour from Muelle Prat, 30 mins, US$1.20, to Playa Las Torpederas and to Viña del Mar; other boats for hire for fishing. **NB** Don't photograph naval ships or installations. The **Camino Cintura** is the only road which connects all the hills

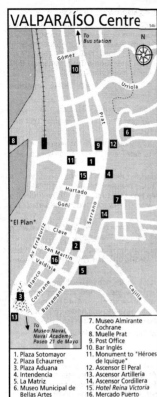

VALPARAÍSO Centre

To Bus station

N

Gómez

Urriola

Prat

Hurtado

Goñi

"El Plan"

Clave

Av Errázuriz

San Martín

Valdivia

Blanco

Cochrane

Bustamante

Serrano

Cajilla

To
Museo Naval,
Naval Academy,
Paseo 21 de Mayo

1. Plaza Sotomayor
2. Plaza Echaurren
3. Plaza Aduana
4. Intendencia
5. La Matriz
6. Museo Municipal de
   Bellas Artes
7. Museo Almirante
   Cochrane
8. Muelle Prat
9. Post Office
10. Bar Inglés
11. Monument to "Héroes
    de Iquique"
12. Ascensor El Peral
13. Ascensor Artillería
14. Ascensor Cordillera
15. Hotel Reina Victoria
16. Mercado Puerto

above Valparaíso; it affords constantly changing views, perhaps the best being from Plaza Bismark. No 9 'Central Placeres' bus gives fine scenic drive over hills to the port; also bus 'Mar Verde' (O) from Av Argentina near the bus terminal to Plaza Aduana.

Warning Robbery is becoming increasingly common in El Puerto and around the *ascensores*, especially on Cerro Santo Domingo.

Hotels A2 *Prat*, Calle Condell 1443, T 253082, 220 beds, gloomy, restaurant; **B** *Reina Victoria*, Plaza Sotomayor 190, T 212203, D on top floor, with small breakfast, hot shower, central but noisy; **C** *Lancaster*, Chacabuco 2362, with bath and breakfast, clean; **D** *Residencial Dinamarca*, Dinamarca 539 (from Plazuela Ecuador—just S of Condell y Bellavista—take any micro marked 'Carcel'; or climb 10 mins up Av Ecuador), hot water, clean, good value, also short stay, car park, not near restaurants but serves full breakfast and snacks; **D** *Garden*, Serrano 501, T 252776, friendly, hot water, use of kitchen; **D** Enzo and Martina Tesser, Av Quebrada Verde, T 288873, with breakfast, German spoken, friendly (reached by bus 1); **E** pp *Residencial Mi Casa*, Rawson 310, near bus terminal, friendly, basic, fleas, also has rooms at Yungay 2842, quiet; **E** pp *Sra Mónica*, Av Argentina 322, Casa B, T 215673, 2 blocks from bus terminus, clean, friendly; **E** pp Sra Silvia, Pje La Quinta 70, Av Argentina, 3 blocks from Congress, T 216592, clean, quiet, kitchen facilities, rec; **E** pp Sra Anita, Higuera 107, Cerro Alegre, with good breakfast, clean, hot water, wonderful views; **E** pp María Pizarro, Chacabuco 2340, Casa No 2, T 230791, clean, lovely rooms, central, quiet, kitchen, highly rec; her neighbours, Francisca Escobar and Guillermo Jones, Chacabuco 2328, T 214193, also rent rooms, same price, equally rec, Guillermo speaks English. Many cheap hotels on Cochrane and Blanco Encalada, S of Plaza Sotomayor, but very few are recommendable, one that is OK is **D** *Residencial Lily*, Blanco Encalada 866, T 255995, 2 blocks from Plaza Sotomayor, clean, safe (despite no locks on doors). Many of the 'cheap' hotels in the Chacabuco area are for short-term occupation only. Youth hostel office at Edwards 695, 3rd floor, will extend membership; nearest hostel in Viña del Mar.

Restaurants *Bar Inglés*, Cochrane 851 (entrance also on Blanco), good food and drink, traditional, rec, not cheap; *Café Riquet*, Plaza Anibal Pinto 1199, also traditional, comfortable, expensive, good coffee and breakfast, rec; *Cinzano*, Plaza Anibal Pinto 1182, old style bar/restaurant, popular; *Los Porteños*, Valdivia 169, near market, lunch only, very good; *Al Galeone D'Oro*, Independencia 1766, Italian, not cheap but good; *Tentazione*, Av Pedro Montt 2484, good, cheap; *La Parrilla de Pepe*, Pedro Montt 1872, good food and service; *Hamburg*, O'Higgins 1274, German management, German beer, beware of overcharging. *Bote Salvavidas*, good, Muelle Prat; *Del Mónico*, Prat 669, good, cheap lunches, popular; *La Rotunda*, Prat 701, good food; *Casino Social de Pescadores*, Altamirano 1480, good, cheap fish meals; *Nahuel*, Donoso 1498, popular, good lunches, cheap; *Mesón del Lord*, Cochrane 800 block, good lunches; *Bambú*, Pudeto 450, vegetarian, cheap fixed price lunches; *Café Westfalia*, Cochrane 847, coffee, breakfasts, vegetarian lunches; *Café do Brasil*, Condell 1342, excellent coffee, juices, sandwiches; *Café Turri*, Templemann 147, on Cerro Concepción, T 259196, overlooking port, good food and service; *Nantón*, Brasil 1368, Chinese, good. Lots of cheap places for lunch between Plaza Sotomayor and Plaza Aduana, and round bus station. Good bars around Plaza Ecuador.

Airlines LanChile, Esmeralda 1048, T 251441; Ladeco, Blanco 951, T 216355.

Exchange National banks. Open 0900 to 1400, but closed on Sat. Rates at **Banco de Santiago** (Prat 816) and **Banco de Crédito e Inversiones** (Cochrane 820) good; **Fincard** (Mastercard), Esmeralda 1087; **Exprinter**, Prat 895 (the building with the clocktower at junction with Cochrane), good rates, no commission on TCs (open 0930-1400, 1600-1900); **Inter Cambios**, Errázuriz 627, near railway station, good rates; **Gema Tour**, Esmeralda 940. When *cambios* are closed, street changers operate outside Inter Cambios.

British Consul, Blanco 725, oficina 26, T 256117, Casilla 82-V; **Instituto Chileno-Norteamericano,** Esmeralda 1069, shows foreign films.

Health Dentist: Dr Walther Meeden Bella, Condell 1530, Depto 44, T 212233.

Telecommunications VTR Telecommunications, Cochrane 825. CTC, Esmeralda 1054 or P Montt 2023.

Bookshop *Librería Universitaria*, Esmeralda 1132, good selection of regional history. *Librería Ivens*, Plaza Aníbal Pinto, specializing in up-to-date French and German newspapers; many others.

Tourist Office in the Municipalidad building, Condell 1490, Oficina 102, open Mon-Fri 0830-1400, 1530-1730. Kiosks at bus terminal (good map available), helpful, open 0900-1300, 1530-1930 (closed Thur, Mar-Nov), Muelle Prat, open Nov-Mar 1030-1430, 1600-2000, and in Plaza Victoria, open 1030-1300, 1430-2000 Nov-Mar. For day trips around Valparaíso and Viña del Mar, Turismo Continental T 6992807.

Addresses YMCA (Asociación Cristiana de Jóvenes), Blanco 1117; YWCA (Asociación Cristiana Feminina), Blanco 967. Valparaíso Seamen's Institute, Blanco 394.

Transport Taxis are more expensive than Santiago: a short run under 1 km costs US$1. Public transport good. Buses and modern electric buses, US$0.20 within city limits. *Funiculares* US$0.15.

Rail Regular service on Merval, the Valparaíso metropolitan line between Valparaíso, Viña del Mar, Quilpue, Limache, Quillota, La Calera, Llaillay, San Felipe and Los Andes (and intermediate stations); to Viña del Mar every 15-30 mins, trains that run the entire route at 1800 daily, 1430 Mon-Fri (not holidays), 0805, Sat, Sun and holidays, fare Valparaíso-Los Andes US$1.50, 3 hrs. *El Porteño* tourist train runs on Sun, 1 Jan-28 Feb and on most public holidays.

Shipping For shipping services from Valparaíso to the Juan Fernández Islands and Easter Island see below under **The Chilean Pacific Islands**.

Buses Excellent and frequent bus service to Viña del Mar (25 min) US$0.25 from Plaza Aduana, passing along Av Errázuriz; colectivos to Viña US$0.40. Terminal is on Pedro Montt 2800 block, corner of Rawson, 1 block from Av Argentina; plenty of buses to/from Plaza Sotomayor. To **Santiago**, 2 hrs, US$2-3 (Tur Bus US$4), frequent (book on Sat to return to the capital on Sun); to **Concepción**, 11 hrs, US$12; to **Puerto Montt**, 17 hrs, US$18. **La Serena**, 8 hrs, US$10. To **Calama**, US$25. To **Arica**, US$35, Fénix *salón cama* service, US$50. To **Mendoza** (Argentina), 4 companies, 6-7 hrs, US$20.

If driving from Santiago the main road passes through two tunnels, toll of US$2.25 paid at the first, but this can be avoided by turning off onto the old road over the mountains about 1 km before the tunnels; several other tolls.

Hitchhiking to Santiago is easy from service station on Av Argentina.

Excursions from Valparaíso About 25 mins from Valparaíso, on the road to Santiago (Ruta 68) is the **Reserva Nacional Peñuelas**, surrounding the artificial Lago Peñuelas. Access is permitted for walking and fishing; administration at park entrance. Laguna Verde, a couple of hours' dusty walk over the hills (or a short road journey bus No 3, marked 'Laguna Verde' from Victoria y Rancagua, hourly) to the S of Valparaíso, is a picturesque bay for picnics. **E** pp *Posada Cruz del Sur*, also camping. Camping site *Los Olivos*, good facilities, well run and friendly. Further S still is Quintay where there is camping; reached by turning left at Peñuelas on the main Santiago- Valparaíso road.

If driving from Valparaíso to the Argentine border, Route 62 runs through Viña del Mar, climbs out of the bay and goes through (16 km) **Quilpue**, 1½ km E of El Retiro, a popular inland resort with medicinal springs and a municipal pool. It crosses a range of hills and reaches the Aconcagua Valley at **Limache**, a sleepy market town, 40 km from Valparaíso (population

22,511). 8 km E of Limache is Olmué, beyond which is **Parque Nacional La Campana**, an area of native woodland, including the Chilean palm (*kankán*), much varied birdlife, and the Cerro La Campana which Darwin climbed in 1836. Extensive views from the top, but a guide may be necessary because there are a number of ascents, some of which are very difficult. Route 62 joins Route 60 just before **Quillota**, an orchard centre (**B** *Balneario El Edén*, 5 km

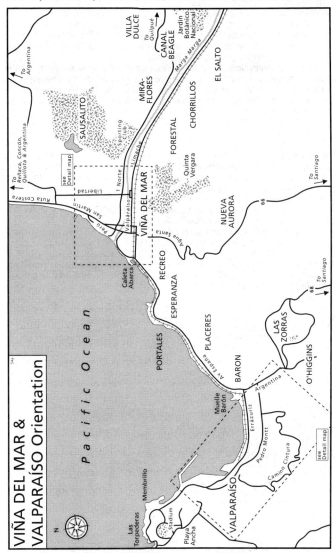

VIÑA DEL MAR &
VALPARAÍSO Orientation

out of town, cabins for rent, up to 6 people, very good restaurant in an old estate building, T 311963, F 312342, good swimming), continuing to La Calera (88 km from Valparaíso), where it joins the Pan-American Highway; turn SE and E for Llaillay, San Felipe, Los Andes and the Redentor tunnel to Mendoza.

Viña del Mar, one of the foremost South American seaside resorts, is 9 km NE of Valparaíso by one of the innumerable express buses, which run along a narrow belt between the shore and precipitous cliffs. Halfway, on the hill of Los Placeres, is the Universidad Técnica. The popular bathing resort of El Recreo is passed, then Caleta Abarca with its crowded beaches, floral clock and big *Hotel Miramar*. Beaches are often closed because of pollution.

Follow the street signs for a self-guided tour of Viña del Mar's sights. At the entrance to Viña del Mar there is a steep bluff, worth climbing for the views over Viña from its *paseos*. Here also is Cerro Castillo, the summer palace of the Presidents of the Republic. Below, to the left, is the lagoon of the Marga Marga, crossed by a bridge which leads direct to the Casino, built in the 1930s and set in beautiful gardens, US$6 to enter, jacket and tie for men required (open all year).

The Teatro Municipal is on Plaza Vergara. The Palacio Rioja, the former mansion of a Spanish banker, dating from 1906, can be visited (Quillota y 3 Norte – see **Museums** below). Near the Valparaíso Sporting Club with its racecourse and playing fields are the Granadilla Golf Club and a large stadium. In the hills behind is a large artificial lake, the Laguna Sausalito, adjacent to Estadio Sausalito (home to Everton soccer team, among many other sporting events). It possesses an excellent tourist complex with swimming pools, boating, tennis courts, sandy beaches, water skiing, restaurants, etc. Entry US$2.50, children under 11, US$1.75; take colectivo No 19 from Calle Viana.

One of the sights the municipally owned Quinta Vergara, superb gardens with a double avenue of palms (highly recommended). The Palacio Vergara, in the gardens, houses the Museo de Bellas Artes and the Academia de Bellas Artes. Part of the grounds is a children's playground, and there is an outdoor auditorium where concerts and ballet are performed in the summer months, and an international song festival is held every Feb.

The Song Festival is lively, with the emphasis more on the 'shows' of the special guests, famous latino singers, and European and local rock bands than on the unknown contestants" (Glyn Fry and Trui Anseeuw). Schedules may be delayed to fit in with TV programming and standards cᶠ organization and performance (with some exceptions) have slipped of late. Take warm clothes if staying till the end. Tickets from the Municipalidad US$3-US$15, seats are numbered so no need to arrive till 2100. For the final evening touts sell tickets outside the Quinta Vergara.

Southeast of the city is the **Jordín Botánico Nacional**, formerly the estate of the nitrate entrepreneur Pascual Baburizza, administered by CONAF. There are over 3,000 species but they are not labelled. Take bus 20 from Plaza Vergara, entry US$1.

Museums Museo de la Cultura del Mar, in the Castillo Wulff, contains a collection on the life and work of the novelist and maritime historian, Salvador Reyes, Tues-Sat 1000-1300, 1430-1800, Sun 1000-1800; **Museo de Bellas Artes**, Quinta Vergara, Tues-Sun 100-1400, 1500-1800, US$0.25; **Palacio Rioja**, Quillota 214, built at turn of century by a prominent local family and now used for official municipal receptions, ground floor preserved in its original state, open to visitors 1000-1400, 1500-1800, Tues-Sun, rec. **Museo Sociedad Fonk**, Calle 4 Norte 784, archaeological museum, with objects from Easter Island and the Chilean mainland, including Mapuche silver, open Tues-Fri 1000-1800, Sat-Sun 1000-1400, entry US$0.20. An Easter Island statue stands on the lawn between the railway and the beach just beyond Caleta Portales, between Viña del Mar and Valparaíso. **Centro Cultural**, Libertad 250, holds regular exhibitions; **Instituto de Oceanografía**, in Montemar, Reñaca (bus No 9).

Festival El Roto, 20 Jan, in homage to the workers and peasants of Chile.

Telephone code 032.

Hotels Many in **L3-A3** range, some with beach. **L3** *San Martín*, Av San Martín 667, T 689191, with breakfast; **L3** *Crown Royal* and *Mount Royal*, 5 Norte 655, T/F 682450 and 1 Norte

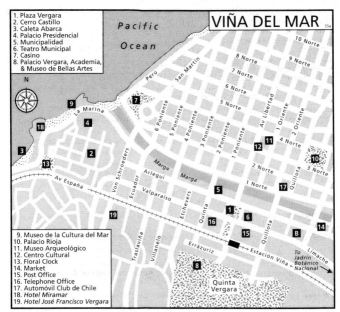

VIÑA DEL MAR

Pacific Ocean

1. Plaza Vergara
2. Cerro Castillo
3. Caleta Abarca
4. Palacio Presidencial
5. Municipalidad
6. Teatro Municipal
7. Casino
8. Palacio Vergara, Academia, & Museo de Bellas Artes
9. Museo de la Cultura del Mar
10. Palacio Rioja
11. Museo Arqueológico
12. Centro Cultural
13. Floral Clock
14. Market
15. Post Office
16. Telephone Office
17. Automóvil Club de Chile
18. Hotel Miramar
19. Hotel José Francisco Vergara

449, T/F 681145; **A2** *Alborada del Mar*, San Martín 419, T 975274, tastefully decorated; **A2** *Español*, Plaza Vergara 191, T/F 685145, with bath, TV, phone and *Restaurante Colonial*; **A2** *José Francisco Vergara*, Calle Dr von Schroeders 392, T 626022, has garden houses for up to 5; **A3** *Residencia Offenbacher Hof*, Balmaceda 102, clean, friendly, rec; **B** *Alejandra*, 2 Poniente 440, T 974404, with shower and breakfast (C in low season, breakfast incl); **B** *Petit Palace*, Paseo Valle 387, T 663134, small rooms, good, central, quiet; **B** *Quinta Vergara*, Errázuriz 690, T 685073, clean, friendly, beautiful gardens; **C** *Capric*, von Schroeders 39, T 978295, with bath, TV, good value; opp is **B** *Balia*, No 36, T 978310, F 680724, bath, TV, phone, parking; **C** *El Escorial*, two places: one at 5 Poniente 114, the other at 5 Poniente 441 (T 975266), with breakfast, shared bath, clean, central. **C** *Residencial Magallanes*, Arlegui 555, T 685101, with breakfast, clean, mixed reports; **D** *Residencial Blanchait*, Valparaíso 82, T 974949, clean, with breakfast, hot water, good service; **D** *Residencial Familiar*, Batuco 147, clean, friendly; **D** *Residencial Tajamar*, Alvarez 884, opp railway station, old-fashioned, central, huge rooms, atmospheric; **D** *Sra Nalda*, 2 Norte 849 (Pasaje Klamer), T 970488, good garden, cooking facilities, rec; **D** *Residencial Agua Santa*, Agua Santa 34, basic, hot shower; **D** *Residencial France*, Montaña 743, clean, safe, helpful; **D** *Residencial Villarica*, Arlegui 172, good, friendly. There are a great many more places to stay incl private accommodation (E pp). Out of season furnished apartments can be rented through agencies (with commission).

Motels Several at Reñaca (6 km N of Viña del Mar).

NB It is cheaper to stay in Valparaíso and commute to the Viña beaches.

Youth Hostels F pp *Residencial La Montaña*, Agua Santa 153, T 622230, for YHA card holders, breakfast included, other meals available, no cooking facilities; family rooms available. **E** pp *Lady Kinnaird Hostal*, 1 Oriente 1096, T 975413, YWCA, central, friendly, English spoken, women only, highly rec.

Camping *Camping Reñaca*, Santa Luisa 401, rec, also cabins. Unofficial site in woods behind Quinta Vergara park. Camping gas and similar articles for sale at Valparaíso 464.

Restaurants At hotels; *Cap Ducal*, Av Marina 51, expensive; *Gipsy*, Av San Martín, excellent; *Raul*, Av Valparaíso 533, live music; *Casino Chico*, Valparaíso 99, Chilean and international dishes; *Panzoni*, Pasaje Cousiño 12-B, good lunches, Italian; *Salón de China*, 4 Norte 201;

Han's Dragón, Libertad y 8 Norte; *Machitún Ruca*, San Martín 529, excellent. *Pizzería Mama Mía*, Av San Martín 435, good, reasonably priced; *Las Gaviotas*, 14 Norte 1248, Chilean meat dishes, not expensive, live music. Many restaurants on Av Valparaíso, try in the Galerías (arcades, eg *Café Big Ben*, No 469, good coffee, good food); also *Alster*, No 225, expensive, and *Samoiedo*, No 637, *confitería*, grill and restaurant. Several pleasant restaurants and cafés along the renovated Muelle Vergara incl *La Mía Pappa*, Italian, good lunches and evening buffets. Many smaller ones along the sea front. *Terminal Pesquero*, 1st floor, interesting.

El Poncho, Av Borgoño 16180, Reñaca, good seafood and service; also at Reñaca, overlooking the sea, are *Anastassia*, Av Borgoño 15000, excellent international menu, expensive; *Hotel Oceanic*, very good, expensive.

Exchange Many *casas de cambio* on Arlegui including **Afex**, 641 (open 0900-1400 Sat); **Cambio Norte**, 610; **Cambio Andino**, 644; also in the tourist office. **Fincard** (Mastercard), Ecuador 259.

British Community The community here maintains several schools, incl: St Margaret's and Mackay. There is also an Anglican church, with a resident English chaplain, postal address Casilla 561. Full details from British Consulate.

Cultural Associations Instituto Chileno-Británico, 3 Norte 824, T 971061; **Instituto Chileno—Norteamericano de Cultura**, 3 Norte 532, T 662145; **Casa Italia** (cultural centre, consulate, restaurant), Alvarez 398; **Goethe Institut**, 3 Norte 599, T 976581; **Instituto Chileno-Francés**, Alvarez 314, T 685908.

Discotheque *Topsy Topsy*, Santa Luisa 501, Reñaca. *El Gato de la Luna*, Arlegui 396, good bar, live music and dancing.

Telephone CTC, Valparaíso 628; Global Telecommunications/Entel, 15 Norte 961.

Market At intersection of Av Sporting and river, open Wed and Sat.

Tourist Office Av Valparaíso 507, T 882285. Arrangements may be made at the Tourist Office for renting private homes in the summer season. **Automóvil Club de Chile** 1 Norte 901, T 971815.

Car Hire Euro Rent-A-Car, in *Hotel O'Higgins*, clean cars, efficient.

Air Ladeco Santiago-Viña del Mar (to naval airfield nr Concón), several daily, 10 mins, US$15, T 978210; National T 883505.

Trains Services on the Valparaíso Metropolitan line (Merval) stop at Viña (details under Valparaíso).

Buses to Santiago, US$2-3, 2 hrs, frequent, many companies (heavily booked in advance for travel on Sun afternoons); to **La Serena**, 6 daily, 8 hrs, US$10, to **Antofagasta**, 20 hrs, US$20. Terminal at Av Valparaíso and Quillota.

Resorts North of Viña del Mar

There is a very fine drive N of Viña del Mar along the coast (many motels) through Las Salinas and Reñaca to Concón, then inland to Quintero. Las Salinas, beach between two towering crags, is very popular. Beyond Reñaca beach (6 km N, very popular with young people; **A3** *Hotel Monte Carlo*, Av V MacKenna 136, very modern, comfortable) is Cochoa with its large sealion colony, 100m offshore. **Concón**, on the S shore of a bay at the mouth of the Río Aconcagua, is 12 km N of Reñaca (from Viña del Mar take bus 9 from Av Libertad between 2 and 3 Norte). Main attractions: tennis, bathing, fishing, and riding. Main eyesore: an oil refinery (not visible from beach). Near the Concón beach there is a very interesting pelican colony. There is also a new inland road, much faster than the coast road, between Viña del Mar and Concón.

Concón Hotels L2 *Hostería Edelweis*, Av Borgoño 19200, T 903600, modern cabins, clean, comfortable, sea views, incl breakfast, excellent food in attached restaurant, German spoken, highly rec; *Playa Amarilla*, T 811915, and several motels; **D** *Cabañas Koala Place*, Los Pescadores 41, T 813026. **Restaurants** Good seafood *empanadas* at bars; *Vista al Mar*, Av Borgoño 21270, T 812-221, good fish restaurant, good value; *Don Chico*, Av Borgoño 21410, good seafood; *Mirador Cochoa*, Av Borgoño 17205, good, pricey; *Restaurant La Picá de Emeterio*, on seafront, excellent fish; *El Rincón de Charlie*, good service and food, good value. *Stella Maris*, on seafront, excellent seafood but pricey.

Campsite Las Gaviotas. Camping Mantagua Playa.

Horse riding Horses for hire from Ernesto Farias Usario, Las Encinas 55, Las Romeras, Concón

Alto (last bus stop on route 9 or 10 from Viña del Mar or Valparaíso). Rides in forest or along sand dunes.

Another 16 km to the N of Concón over the new bridge is the fishing village of **Quintero**, the naval aviation centre. On the N shore of the bay at Las Ventanas are a power station and copper processing plant. **Hotels A2** *Hotel Yachting Club*, Luis Acevedo 1736, T 930061; **D** *Isla de Capri*, Av 21 de Mayo 1299, T 930117, pleasant, sea views; **D** *Monaco*, 21 de Mayo 1530, T 930939, without breakfast, run down but interesting, good views. A number of *residenciales*.

Horcón (also known locally as Horcones), set back in a cove surrounded by cliffs, is a pleasant small village, mainly of wooden houses. On the beach hippies sell cheap and unusual jewellery and trinkets. Vegetation is tropical with many cacti on the cliff tops. Seafood lunches with the catch of the day, sold at any number of stalls on the seafront, are rec. It is best avoided in Jan-Feb when it is packed out. Drinking alcohol on the beach is forbidden—and enforced by the *carabineros*. **Hotels C** *Cabañas* on Playa Cau Cau, good; **D** *Arancibia*, without bath, good views, good food, friendly service, rec; also rooms in private houses. **Restaurants** *El Ancla* rec; *Reina Victoria*, cheap, good.

From Las Ventanas the road continues N past Maitencillo, where there are large numbers of chalets but no hotels, to the fashionable resort of **Zapallar** (33 km N of Las Ventanas). There are several fine mansions along Av Zapallar. Three km S at Cachagua a colony of penguins may be viewed from the northern end of the beach. No cars are allowed on the Zapallar seafront. Excellent bathing, but water is cold. **Hotels A1** *César*, T 711313, very nice but dear; **A3** *Isla Seca*, T 711508, small, pool, good restaurant; good, reasonably-priced food in Restaurant César (different management from hotel), on seafront; no *residenciales*, no campsite. **Papudo**, 10 km further N, formerly connected with Santiago by rail, rivalled Viña del Mar as a fashionable resort in the 1920s but has long since declined. **Hotels D** *Moderno*, T 711496; **D'** *Peppino*, T 711482; **E** pp *La Playa*; many more.

Buses From Valparaíso and Viña del Mar: To Concón bus 9 or 10 (from Av Libertad between 2 and 3 Norte in Viña), US$0.50; to Quintero and Horcón, Sol del Pacífico, every 30 mins, US$1; to Zapallar and Papudo, Sol del Pacífico, 4 a day (2 before 0800, 2 after 1600), US$3.

Resorts Near the Mouth of the Río Maipo The Río Maipo flows into the sea near the port of **San Antonio**, 113 km from Santiago and 112 km S of Valparaíso. San Antonio (pop 60,000, DDD 035) is connected with Santiago by railway and a motorway. Its shipping has grown considerably, mostly at the expense of Valparaíso, and a new fishing port and fishmeal plants have been built. The port exports copper brought by railway from the large mine at El Teniente, near Rancagua. San Antonio was badly damaged by the earthquake of Mar 1985. South of San Antonio are **Llolleo** (4 km) at the mouth of the Maipo, a famous resort for those who suffer from heart diseases, and 7 km further **Rocas de Santo Domingo**, the most attractive and exclusive resort in this area with 20 km of beaches and a golf course; even in high season it is not very crowded.

Hotels At San Antonio: **C** *Jockey Club*, 21 de Mayo 202, T 31302, best good views, restaurant; **D** *Colonial*, Pedro Montt 196; **E** *Patria*, Pedro Montt 194, short stay, dirty, avoid. At Llolleo: **D** pp *Oriente*, Inmaculada Concepción 50, T 32188; *Residencial El Castillo*, Providencia 253, T 373821. At Santo Domingo: **B** *Rocas de Santo Domingo*, La Ronda 130, T 231348; no cheap accommodation—try Llolleo.

Transport Buses from San Antonio: To **Valparaíso**, Pullman Bus, every 45 mins until 2000, US$2; to **Santiago**, Pullman Bus, every 20 mins, US$2. Rail: passenger train, supposedly daily, Santiago-San Antonio-Cartagena 15 Dec—15 Mar only.

Cartagena, 8 km N of San Antonio and the terminus of the railway is the biggest resort on this part of the coast. The administrative centre lies around the Plaza de Armas, situated on top of the hill. To the S is the picturesque Playa Chica, overlooked by many of the older hotels and restaurants; to the N is the Playa Larga. Between the two a promenade runs below the cliffs; high above hang old houses, some in disrepair but offering spectacular views. Cartagena is a very popular resort in summer, but out of season especially it is a good centre for visiting nearby resorts; there are many hotels and bus connections are good.

Hotels **D** *Biarritz*, Playa Chica, T 32246; **D** *La Bahía*, Playa Chica, T 31246; **D** *Violeta*, Condell 140, T 234093, swimming pool, good views; **E** pp *El Estribo*, just off Plaza de Armas, with breakfast, E pp full board, basic, cheap *comedor*; **E** pp *Residencial Carmona*, Playa Chica, T 212199, small rooms, basic, clean, good value.

North of Cartagena are several small resorts including **Las Cruces**, **El Tabo** and **El Quisco**, a small fishing port with 2 beautiful white beaches (very expensive and crowded during Chilean holidays). **Algarrobo**, 29 km N of Cartagena, is the largest of these and the most chic, with its large houses, yacht club, marina and penguin island (no entry). In summer there are boat tours round the island from the jetty. On the road between El Tabo and El Quisco is the village of *Isla Negra* where the house of the Chilean poet Pablo Neruda is located. The beautifully-restored **Museo-Casa Pablo Neruda**, containing artefacts gathered by Neruda from all over the world, is open for guided tours in Spanish, English or French (last two only after 1500), Tues-Sun 1015-1230, 1500-1800, in summer 1000-1745, US$2, T 035-212284 for opening hours or to book English guide (see also his house, La Chascona, under Santiago **Museums**, and La Sebastiaña, under Valparaíso **Museums**). Tours from Santiago, departing at 0900 from Plaza de Armas (Compañia y Ahumada), cost US$23.75 and incl seaside resorts, T 232-2574.

Hotels At Las Cruces, **D** *La Posada*, T 233520, good birdwatching. At El Tabo: **C** *Hotel El Tabo*, T 33719, quite nice, and *Motel El Tabo*, T 212719, next door (overfull in Jan-Feb). At Isla Negra: **B** *Hostería Santa Elena*, beautiful building and location, restaurant, some rooms damp and gloomy. At El Quisco (accommodation generally expensive), **C** *Motel Barlovento*, Calle El Quisco 0520, T 481030; *residenciales* 100-200m from beach in **C** range, eg *Residencial y Restaurant Oriental*, T 481662, with breakfast, good, clean, hot water; **D** *Residencial Julia*, Av Aguirre 0210, esq Independencia, T 481546, very clean, quiet, good value, rec; **D** *Cabañas Pozo Azul*, Capricornio 234, SE of town, quiet; **D** *Hotel El Quisco*, Av Isidora Dubournais 166, with breakfast, clean, open weekends only; others on this avenue. Excellent seafood restaurant *La Caleta*, Av Isidoro Dubournais 166 (main street). At Algarrobo, **C** *Costa Sur*, Alessandri; **C** *Panamericano*, Alessandri; **D** *Uribe*, behind *Costa Sur*, T 481035, pleasant, quiet; **D** *Vera*, Alessandri 1521, with breakfast, good. **E** pp *Residencial San José*, Av Principal 1598, basic, no hot water.

Buses between Algarrobo and Santiago, Pullman Bus, every 20 mins, 2 hrs, US$3, stopping in Cartagena and the resorts along the coast (but not San Antonio). Services between Algarrobo and San Antonio also by Empresa de Buses San Antonio (frequent, last bus around 2000) and Empresa Robles.

SOUTH THROUGH THE CENTRAL VALLEY (4)

One of the world's most fruitful and beautiful countrysides, with the snowclad peaks of the Andes delimiting it to the E, the Central Valley contains most of Chile's population. It is a region of small towns, farms and vineyards, with several protected areas of natural beauty. To the S are the major city of Concepción, the port of Talcahuano and the main coal-mining area.

Road and railway run S through the Central Valley; the railway has been electrified from Santiago to just S of Temuco. Along the road from Santiago to Temuco there are several modern motels. From Santiago to San Javier (S of Talca), the highway is dual carriageway, with two tolls of US$2.50 to pay. The highway between Santiago and Rancagua is dangerous for cyclists (inattentive truck drivers).

Rancagua (pop 167,000; DDD 072), the capital of VI Región (Libertador General Bernardo O'Higgins), 82 km S of Santiago (1 hr 10 mins bus, US$2.10), is an agricultural centre. At its centre is an attractive tree-lined plaza, the Plaza de los Héroes, and several streets of one-storey colonial-style houses. In the centre of the plaza is an equestrian statue of O'Higgins. The Merced church, 1 block N, several times restored, dates from 1758. The Museo Histórico, 3 blocks S of the plaza, housed in a colonial mansion, contains collections of religious art and late 19th century furniture. The main commercial area lies along Av Independencia which runs W from the plaza towards the bus and rail terminals.

Rancagua was the scene of an important battle during the Wars of

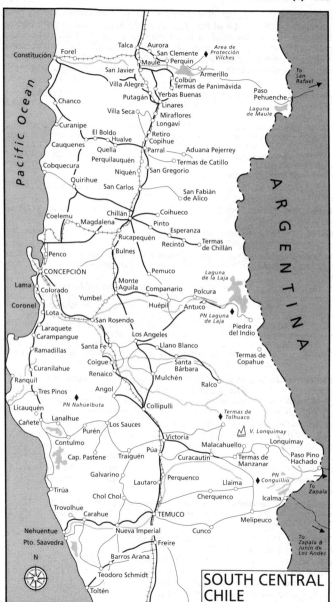

SOUTH CENTRAL CHILE

Independence. On 1/2 Oct 1814 O'Higgins and his 1,700 Chilean patriots were surrounded in the centre of Rancagua by 4,500 Royalist (pro-Spanish) troops; O'Higgins, who commanded his forces from the tower of the Merced church, managed to break out and escape. Defeated, he was forced into exile in Argentina and the Royalists re-established control over Chile. Plaques mark the sites of the battle and a diagram in the main Plaza de los Héroes shows the disposition of the troops.

Festivals at Rancagua The national rodeo championship is held there at the end of Mar (plenty of opportunities for purchasing cowboy items). Festival del Poroto (Bean Festival), 1-5 Feb.

Hotels B *Aguila Real*, Brasil 1055, T 222047, incl breakfast; **B** *Santiago*, Av Brasil 1036, T 230855, poorly maintained, friendly; **C** *España*, San Martín 367, T 230141, with bath, less without, central, hot water, pleasant, clean; **B** *Rancagua*, San Martín 85, T 232663, F 241155, with bath, quiet, clean, secure parking, rec. Many hotels do not accept guests before 2000, or may charge you double if you arrive in the afternoon. Some 50 km S (22 km N of San Fernando) is *Hacienda Los Lingues*, see p 672.

Exchange *Transafex*, Campos 363, local 4, for US$ cash; **Fincard**, Av Campos 376, Mon-Fri 0900-1400, 1530-1930, Sat 1000-1300, for Mastercard.

Tourist Office Germán Riesco 277, T 230413, helpful, English spoken. **Automóvil Club de Chile**, Ibieta 09, T 239930.

Rail Main line services between Santiago and Concepción and Chillán stop here. Also regular services to/from Santiago on Metrotren, 1¼ hrs, 11 a day, US$2.

Excursions To the thermal springs of Cauquenes, 28 km E, reached by colectivo from Rancagua market (**A** *Hotel Termas de Cauquenes*, T 297226, excellent, clean, excellent food, rec).

To the SW of Rancagua, in the valleys of rivers Cachapoal, Claro and Zamorano, the land is given over to fruit growing (including the estates of Viña Concha y Toro). Towns such as Doñihue, San Vicente de Tagua Tagua and Peumo have their roots in an Indian past which has been replaced by the *huaso* (cowboy) and agroindustry. West of Peumo is **Lago Rapel**, the largest artificial lake in the country (camping, water sports, etc at Bahía Skorpios). The lake feeds the Rapel hydroelectric plant, best reached from Melipilla.

The Rio Rapel reaches the Pacific Ocean just N of the town of Navidad. 3 km N of Navidad is the village of La Boca, where the *Restaurant Donde Lucho*, Av El Bosque, serves lunches at US$6 for as much as you can eat, excellent value.

San Fernando (pop 44,500; DDD 074), founded in 1742, capital of Colchagua Province, is 51 km S of Rancagua. It stands in a broad and fertile valley at a height of 340m. A road (buses) runs W to the seaside resort of **Pichelemu** (120 km, 86 paved), with beaches, surfing, camping and a great many hotels and *residenciales*. (**C** *Rex*, Av Ortúzar 34, T 681003, good breakfast, good value; **E** *Bahía*, Av Ortúzar 262, with breakfast, clean). Another road runs E towards the Cordillera and divides: the northern branch runs to the **Termas del Flaco**, nr the Argentine frontier (poor campsite, *cabañas* and hotels, but open only in summer when it attracts large numbers of visitors); the southern branch goes to the resort of **Sierra Bella Vista**, a private *fundo* where many Santiago businessmen have holiday houses. Rodeos in Oct and Nov.

Hotels in San Fernando On Av Manuel Rodríguez: **C** *Español*, No 959, T 711098; **E** *Marcano*, No 968, T 714759; *Imperio*, No 770, T 714595, and **D** *Pérez*, No 1028, T 713328, without bath.

Curicó, 60 km S of San Fernando and 192 km from Santiago, is in the heart of the wine country (pop 85,000; DDD 075). The surroundings are picturesque. In the Plaza de Armas there are lovely fountains with sculptures of nymphs, black-necked swans and a monument to the Mapuche warrior, Lautaro, carved from the trunk of an ancient beech tree. There is a steel kiosk, built in New Orleans in 1904, which is a national monument. The church of San Francisco, also a national monument, partly ruined, contains the 17th century virgen de velilla, brought from

Spain. At the junction of Carmen and Av San Martín is the imposing Iglesia del Carmen. Overlooking the city, the surrounding countryside and with views to the distant Andean peaks is Cerro Condell (100m); it is an easy climb to the summit from where there are a number of walks. The fine, broad and tree-lined Avenida Manso de Velasco leads to Parque Balmaceda, in which is a bust of the poet, Gabriela Mistral. The Torres wine bodega, 5 km S of the city, is worth a visit: take a bus for Molina from Henríquez y O'Higgins and get off at Km 195 on the Pan-American Highway, open 0900-1300, 1500-1800, no organized tour, Spanish only.

There is a toll (US$3) on the Longitudinal Highway S of Curicó. The city has a good road connection with Argentina, via Paso Vergara (Paso del Planchón, 92 km from Curicó) to San Rafael (transport schedules from Turismo Bucalemu, Yungay 621).

Hotels **B** *Luis Cruz Martines*, Prat 301 y Carmen, T 310552, breakfast extra, overpriced; **C** *Comercio*, Yungay 730, T 312442, rec; **E** *Prat*, Peña 427, T 311069, pleasant patio, not all rooms have windows, but clean, hot water, heated lounge; opp is **D** *Residencial Rahue*, No 410, T 312194, basic, meals, hot water, annex rooms have no ventilation; **D** *Res Central*, Av Prat, 2 blocks from station, good value; **E** *Residencial Colonial*, Rodríguez 461, clean, patio, friendly.

Restaurants *El Fogón Chileno*, Yungay 802, good for meat and wines; *American Bar*, Yungay 647, coffee, small pizzas, good sandwiches, pleasant atmosphere, open early am to late pm incl weekends, rec; *Café-Bar Maxim*, Prat 617, light meals, beer and wine; on same street nearby is *Guindalera*, quite good. *Club de la Unión*, Plaza de Armas, good; *Centro Italiano Club Social*, Estado 531, good, cheap meals.

Exchange Fincard, Carmen 498, for Mastercard. Casa de Cambio, Merced 255, Local 106, no TCs.

Laundry/Dry Cleaners *Limpiabien*, Prat 454 (and other branches), quick, efficient.

Telephone CTC, Peña 650-A.

Tourist Office Tourist information supplied by the Mayor's secretary, Gobernación building, 2nd floor, Plaza de Armas, helpful, has street map. **Automóvil Club de Chile**, Chacabuco 759, T 311156. **Conaf** 1st floor of Gobernación, Plaza de Armas.

Buses To **Santiago** US$2 (Pullman del Sur), 3 hrs, from Terminal del Sur in Santiago. To **Temuco**, LIT and Tur Bus both from Panamericana nr Alameda, 7 hrs, US$7. Companies have their own terminals for interprovincial destinations. Local buses, including to coastal towns, from Terminal Rural, O'Higgins y Prat, one block E of railway station. Many southbound buses by-pass Curicó, but can be caught by waiting outside town.

Rail Station is at the end of Prat, 4 blocks W of Plaza de Armas, T 310028. To/from Santiago, 5 a day, US$3 *económico*, US$3.65 *superior*. To/from Concepción 3 a day.

Excursions A road runs W to the mouth of the Río Mataquito and the popular sea beaches of **Iloca**. North of Iloca is a popular resort, **Llico**, reached either by a coastal route or by an inland road which branches off at Hualañe (Km 74). (**C** *Hostería Atlántida 2000*, near beach, good restaurant, bar, friendly, discount for *South American Handbook* readers; *Hostería Llico*; *Residencial Miramar*, good seafood restaurant; **D** *Pensión Chile*, clean, friendly, rooms with bath have hot water, cheap meals. Buses: several from Terminal Rural in Curicó: Brava at 1230, others 1500 or 1700, return 1600-1700.) Just before Llico are Lago Vichuquen (hotels, camping at Bahía Mansa, and watersports) and **Laguna de Torca**, a natural sanctuary for wildlife especially black-necked swans and other water birds (there are *miradores* for birdwatching 5 km before Llico, the administration is 2 km from Llico, take the trail from administration to Puente Llico; open Sep-Apr). South of Curicó is the **Siete Tazas National Park**, where a river flows through seven rock bowls, each with a pool emptying into the next by a small waterfall. The river then passes through a canyon, 15m deep but only 1½m wide, which ends abruptly in a cliff and a beautiful waterfall. Go to Molina, 26 km S of Curicó, from where buses run to the Park, on Tues and Thur returning Wed and Fri. Daily bus from Curicó in summer, 1545, 4½ hrs, returns 0745 (Sun 0700, returns 1900). The park is open Oct to Mar. Accommodation: camping near park entrance; **D** *Hostería La Flor de la Canela*, at Parque Inglés, 5 km away, including breakfast, T 491613, good food, highly rec, camping, open summer only.

Talca (pop 300,000; DDD 071), 56 km S of Curicó (258 km from Santiago, all dual carriageway) is the most important city between Santiago and Concepción and a major maufacturing centre; it is the capital of VII Región (Maule). It was founded in 1692, and destroyed by earthquake in 1742 and 1928; it has been completely rebuilt. Just off the Plaza de Armas at 1 Norte y 2 Oriente is the Museo O'Higginiano (open Tues-Sat, 0915-1245, 1500-1845, US$1) located in a colonial mansion which belonged to Juan Albano Pereira, tutor to the young Bernardo O'Higgins who lived here between the ages of 4 and 10. The house was later the headquarters of O'Higgins Patriot Government in 1813-14 (before his defeat at Rancagua). In 1818 O'Higgins signed the declaration of Chilean independence here: the room (Sala Independencia) is decorated and furnished in period style. 8 km SE is Villa Huilquilemu, a 19th century hacienda, now part of the Universidad Católica del Maule, housing 4 museums, of religious art, handicrafts, agricultural machinery and wine.

Hotels **A3** *Plaza*, 1 Poniente 1141, T 226150, good commercial standard; **C** *Amalfi*, 2 Sur 1265, T 225703, old-fashioned, central, very clean; **D** *Alcázar*, 2 Sur 1359, breakfast and meals available, rec as reasonable and clean; **E** pp *Cordillera*, 2 Sur 1360, T 221812, F 233028, near new bus terminal. On the Panamericana Sur, Km 250, are **A3** *Cabañas Entre Ríos*, T 223336, F 220477 (Santiago San Antonio 486, of 132, T 633-3750, F 632-4791), very good value, excellent breakfast, pool, very helpful owner, highly rec.

Exchange Edificio Caracol, Oficina 15, 1 Sur 898, for US$ cash; **Fincard** (Mastercard), 1 Sur 826.

Post Office 1 Oriente s/n. **Telephone** CTC, 1 Sur 1156 and 1 Sur 835.

Tourist Office 1 Poniente 1234, T 233669. **Automóvil Club de Chile**, 1 Poniente 1267, T 223-2774.

Bus Terminal, corner 12 Oriente and 2 Sur To Chillán, frequent service, US$2; also frequent to Constitución, 2 hrs, US$1.20.

Train Station at 2 Sur y 11 Oriente, T 226254. To/from Santiago, 5 a day; to/from Concepción, 3 a day, to/from Temuco 1 a day; fare from Santiago, US$3.65 *económico*, US$5 *superior*.

Excursion To *Vilches*, 63 km E, the starting point for the climb to the volcanoes Quizapu and Descabezado (3,850m) 2 buses a day, US$1.50, 2-2½ hrs, leave Talca 1300 and late pm, leave Vilches 0700 and 1730. **C** pp *Hostería Rancho Los Canales*, T 223164, bed and breakfast, use of kitchen, log cabins C between 4 people, hospitable, knowledgeable family (postal address: Casilla 876, Talca). 2 km beyond the town is the **Area de Protección Vilches**, with 20 km of beautiful walks; visit the lakes Los Patos, La Encantada and El Toro, and the Piedras Tacitas, a stone construction supposedly made by the aboriginal inhabitants of the region. For walks on Descabezado Grande and Cerro Azul (ice axe and crampons needed) contact rec guide Carlos Verdugo Bravo, Probación Brilla El Sol, Pasaje El Nickel 257, Jalca (Spanish only). The administration is nr the *Hotel Altos de Vilches*; there is a visitors' centre in the park (2 daily buses from Alto Vilches).

South of Vilches a road from Talca runs 175 km SE along Lago Colbún (*Hotel Casa El Colorado*, T/F 221750) and the valley of the Río Maule, passing through some of the finest mountain scenery in Chile before reaching the Argentine frontier at Paso Pehuenche (2,553m). From here you can continue to Malargue and San Rafael.

Constitución (DDD 071), W of Talca and reached by road (89 km) from San Javier, is the centre of a prosperous district producing grain and timber, but its main attraction is as a seaside resort. The beach, an easy walk from the town, is surrounded by very picturesque rocks. There are good views from Cerro Mutrún, at the mouth of the river (access from Calle O'Higgins). The scenery is attractive, despite a nearby factory. There are plenty of hotels and *pensiones*, but accommodation is difficult from Jan to Mar, and bookings must be made well in advance.

Hotels **A2** *Hostería Constitución*, Echeverria 460, T 671450, best; **C** *Avendaño*, O'Higgins 681, pleasant patio, restaurant, friendly, safe; **D** *Residencial Urrutia*, Freire 238, incl breakfast, some rooms gloomy, laundry facilities; **D** *Residencial Fadiz*, Bulnes near bus terminal, clean, laundry facilities.

There are two **Reservas Nacionales** S of Constitución, in the vicinity of Chanco, 63 km S: **Los Ruiles**, protecting woods and flowers (open Oct-Mar, daily buses from Constitución or Cauquenes, on the road to the coast from Parral), and **Federico Albert**, ½ km N of Chanco (bus), which covers a marginal zone of woods and encroaching sand (visitors' centre, 4 paths of 5 km, open Oct-Mar).

About half-way between Talca and Chillán is the road and rail junction of **Parral**, 342 km S of Santiago, celebrated as the birthplace of the Nobel Prize-winning poet Pablo Neruda (**D** *Hotel Brescia*, Igualdad 195, T 422675, without bath, clean, good restaurant; **D** *Santiago*, opposite station, large old-fashioned rooms, clean; **E** *Residencial do Brasil*, Calle 18, clean, quiet; campsite).

Chillán (pop 134,000; DDD 042), 105 km S of the road junction for Linares is an important agricultural centre, capital of Ñuble province. When the city was destroyed by earthquake in 1833, the new city was built slightly to the N; that, too, was destroyed by earthquake in 1939 and there was a further earthquake in 1960. It is a pleasant city with a modern cathedral. Chillán was the birthplace of Bernardo O'Higgins (Arturo Prat, Chile's naval hero, was born 50 km away at Ninhue). In Chillán Viejo (SW of the centre) there is a monument and park in honour of O'Higgins; it has a 60m long mural depicting his life (an impressive, but sadly faded, mosaic of various native stones), and a Centro Histórico y Cultural, with a gallery of contemporary paintings by regional artists (park is open 0900-1300, 1500-1900). In the Escuela México (at Av O'Higgins between Vega de Saldías and Gamero), donated to the city after the 1939 earthquake, are murals by the great Mexican artists David Alvaro Siqueiros and Xavier Guerrero which present allegories of Chilean and Mexican history. In the S of the city, at Av Collin y I Riquelme, is the Museo Naval Arturo Prat, which contains naval artefacts and replicas of Chilean vessels, Tues-Fri 0930-1200, 1500-1730. The Mercado y Feria Municipal (covered and open markets) sells regional arts and crafts, and has many cheap, good restaurants, serving regional dishes; open daily, Sun until 1300. The Chillán area is well-known for its *pipeño* wine (very young) and its *longanizas* (sausages).

Hotels A2 *Isabel Riquelme*, Arauco 600, T 213663; **B** *Cordillera*, Arauco 619, on Plaza de Armas, T 215221, 3-star, small, all rooms with heating and bath, good; **B** *Rucamanqui*, Herminda Martín 590 (off Plaza de Armas), T 222927, clean, spartan; **C** *Quinchamali*, El Roble 634, T 223381, central, quiet, clean, hot water, heated lounge; **C** *Ruiz de Gamboa*, O'Higgins 497, T 221013, with bath, D without, good value; **D** *Libertador*, Libertad 85, T 223155, large rooms, clean, hot water; **D** *Real*, Libertad 219, T 221827, good; these three are a few minutes' walk from the railway station and are much better than the closer hotels such as *Chillán*, Libertad 65, **Santiago**, next door, T 222068, and **D** *Bahía*, opp station, no hot water, clean but basic. **D** *Residencial Su Casa*, Cochrcas 555, T 223931, incl breakfast, clean (owner is a dog- and rose-lover), parking; **D** *Claris*, 18 de Septiembre 357, T 221983, 2 blocks from plaza, friendly, good value, hot water; **D** *Barcelona*, at bus terminal, clean, friendly.

Restaurants *Centro Español*, Plaza de Armas, separate bar with snacks, excellent. *Fuente Alemana*, Arauco 661, for *churrasco*; *Café París*, Arauco 686, expresso coffee. *Club Comercial*, Arauco 745, popular at lunchtime, good value *almuerzo*, popular bar at night; *Quick Lunch*, El Roble 610, open 0800-2400 for good value meals with good service; *O'Higgins*, Constitución 199, good value. 2 good Chinese: *Jai Yang*, Libertad 250 and *Taipe* at No 299. On the plaza: *La Copucha*, 18 de Septiembre y Constitución, inexpensive meals and sandwiches; *Café Madrid*, 5 de Abril 608, good for coffee; *La Masc'a*, 5 de Abril 544, excellent cheap meals, *empanadas de queso*, drinks, rec. In Chillán Viejo, *Los Adobes*, on Parque O'Higgins, good food and service, reasonable prices.

Exchange Both *Banco de Concepción* and *Banco Sudamericano* give poor rates. Better rates at *Casa de Cambio*, Constitución 550, or *Café París* on Arauco (ask for Enrique Schuler). Fincard (Mastercard), El Roble 553.

Tourist Office In Gobernación building on main plaza, central courtyard, left-hand gallery; street map of city, leaflets on skiing, Termas de Chillán, etc. **Automóvil Club de Chile**, O'Higgins 677, T 212550.

Train Station, Av Brasil opp Calle Libertad, 5 blocks from plaza, T 222424. To **Santiago**, 5 daily, 5$\frac{1}{2}$ hrs, *Salón* US$7-7.35 depending on the service, *económico* US$5-5.35. To **Concepción**, 3 a day, US$2, 2 hrs.

Bus Terminal at Maipon and Sgto Aldea for local buses (4 blocks from centre). For **Santiago**, 7 hrs, US$7.50, buses leave from the interprovincial terminal at Constitución 10 y Brasil (opp railway station). Tegualda 860 and Barrios Arana 90, bus to **Concepción**, every $\frac{1}{2}$ hr.

Excursions 27 km SW of Chillán is **Quinchamalí**, a little village famous for the originality of its craftsmen in textiles, basketwork, black ceramics, guitars and primitive paintings (all on sale in Chillán market). To the thermal baths, **Termas de Chillán**, 82 km E, 1,850m up in the Cordillera, reached by a good road (paved for the first 50 km). There is excellent skiing on the slopes and views of the Chillán volcano, E of the Termas; 4 chair lifts, 2 T-bars, lift pass US$30/day, US$20/half-day. Cheaper than centres nearer Santiago; packages available. This ski resort is to be expanded. Season: middle Dec to the end of Mar. Information from Chillán Ski Centre, Barros Arana 261, or from Libertador 1042. Equipment hire from Chillán Ski Centre (about US$25 pp) or on slopes. Ski buses run from Libertador 1042 at 0800 and from Chillán Ski Centre, subject to demand, US$30 (includes lift pass). Taxi US$30 one way, 1½ hrs. At busy periods hitching may be possible from Chillán Ski Centre. Ski Club de Chile has a tourist centre with hotel (2, full board, T 223887 Chillán, Casilla 247, office at Arauco 600, or Santiago T 251-5776, Av Providencia 2237, locales 42-4). On the road to the Termas, 70 km from Chillán are **A2** *Hotel Los Pirineos*, T 293839, and **A2** *Parador Jamón, Pan y Vino*, 18 de Septiembre 661, oficina 23, T 492241, Casilla 22, Chillán (Don Emilio Chamorro), arranges recommended horse riding expeditions. Camping 2 km from the slopes.

From Chillán there are various road routes to Concepción: (1) SW to Penco and S along the coast; (2) along the Longitudinal Highway to Bulnes, where a branch road goes SW to Concepción; or (3) along the Highway past the Salto del Laja to Los Angeles, from which a main road and a railway run NW to Concepción.

Concepción, the capital of VIII Región (Bío-Bío), 15 km up the Biobío river and 516 km from Santiago, is the most important city in southern Chile and the third city of the Republic. Its port, Talcahuano, is 15 km away. Pop 240,000 (with Talcahuano: 468,000); DDD 041.

The climate is very agreeable in summer, but from Apr to Sep the rains are heavy; the annual average rainfall, nearly all of which falls in those 6 months, is from 1,250 to 1,500 mm. Concepción has been outstandingly unfortunate in the matter of earthquakes; it was founded in 1550, but its site has had to be moved more than once during its history.

In the attractive Plaza de Armas at the centre are the **Intendencia** and the **Cathedral**. It was here that Bernardo O'Higgins proclaimed the independence of Chile on 1 January 1818. In the **Parque Ecuador** (on Victor Lamas, at the foot of Cerro Caracol), there is a craft fair every Feb. At the edge of the park, Lincoyán y Víctor Lamas, is the **Galería de la Historia**, covering both Concepción and the region, open Tues-Sun 1000-2000, entrance free (worth a visit).

Cerro Caracol can easily be reached on foot starting from the statue of Don Juan Martínez de Rozas in the Parque Ecuador, arriving at the Mirador Chileno after 15 mins. From here it is another, 45 mins climb to **Cerro Alemán**. Chile's largest river, the Biobío, and its valley running down to the sea lie below. On the far side of the river you see lagoons, the largest of which, **San Pedro**, is a water-sport centre. On the city side, among cypress trees, is the modern **Barrio Universitario**. A stroll through the grounds, which are beautifully kept with geese, ducks, swans, hummingbirds and a small enclosure with *pudu-pudu* (miniature deer) is rec; the **Casa del Arte** here contains a fine allegorical mural, 35m by 6m, the *Presencia de América Latina*, by Jorge González Camerena (closed Mon). La Posada golf club, on the road to Coronel, is beside a picturesque lake.

There are massive rock formations along the banks of the Biobío estuary. Concepción is linked with Talcahuano, on the bay, by railway (no passenger services) and 2 good roads, half-way along one of which is the Club Hípico's racetrack. Races are held on Sun and holidays. A branch road leads to good beaches, including Penco (see below). Two other beaches are Las Escaleras (a private club)—a flight of natural stairs down a sheer 53m sea cliff leads to it—and Ramuntcho, named after a novel by a visitor in 1875: Pierre Loti.

Museum Museo de Concepción, nr Barrio Universitario, Tues-Sat 1000-1300, 1400-1700, Sun 1430-1730; entrance US$0.50; interesting on history of Mapuche nation. See above for Galería de la Historia.

Concepción is one of Chile's industrial centres. It has plenty of the most important industrial raw material, water, and good port facilities at Talcahuano and other places in the bay. It is nr the coalfields, has ample sources of hydroelectric power, good rail and road communications with the consuming centres further N, and plenty of room to expand.

Hotels A1 *Alborada*, Barros Arana 457, Casilla 176, T 242144, good, check prices carefully; **A1** *El Araucano*, Caupolicán 521, T 230606; **B** *Alonso de Ercilla*, Colo Colo 334, T 227984;

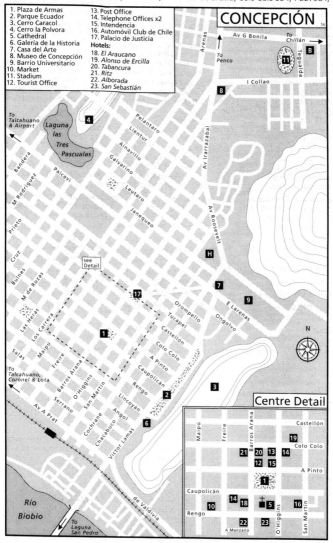

1. Plaza de Armas
2. Parque Ecuador
3. Cerro Caracol
4. Cerro la Polvora
5. Cathedral
6. Galería de la Historia
7. Casa del Arte
8. Museo de Concepción
9. Barrio Universitario
10. Market
11. Stadium
12. Tourist Office
13. Post Office
14. Telephone Offices x2
15. Intendencia
16. Automóvil Club de Chile
17. Palacio de Justicia

Hotels:
18. El Araucano
19. Alonso de Ercilla
20. Tabancura
21. Ritz
22. Alborada
23. San Sebastián

CONCEPCIÓN

B *Ritz*, Barros Arana 721, T 226696, reasonable; **B** *Tabancura*, Barros Arana 790, 8th floor, T 238348, clean, highly rec; **C** *Residencial Antuco*, Barros Arana 741, T 235485, flats 28-33, rec; **C** *Res Colo Colo*, Colo Colo 743, central, hot water, heated lounge, pleasant, welcoming, rec; **C** *Res Metro*, Barros Arana 464, windowless rooms, hot shower, clean; **C** *Residencial Central*, Rengo 673, T 227309, with breakfast, friendly, spacious; **C** *San Sebastián*, Barros Arana 741, flats 34-35, T 242710, rec; **E** *Del Viajero*, Maipú 785, cheap, basic, run down, horrible bathrooms; **E** pp *Pablo Araya*, Salas 643-C; **E** Silvia Uslar, Edmundo Larenas 202, T 227449, good breakfast, quiet, clean, comfortable. Good budget accommodation is hard to find.

Restaurants *El Rancho de Julio*, Barros Arana 337, Argentine parrillada, good value; *Piazza*, Barros Arana 327, good pizzas; *Rincón de Pancho*, Cervantes 469 (closed Sun), excellent for meat, mainly, but also pasta and congrio, good service and ambience; *Novillo Loco*, Portales 539, good food, efficient service. *Le Château* (French), Colo Colo 340, for seafood and meat, but overpriced and closed Sun. Oriental: *Yiet-Xiu*, Angol 515, good, cheap; *Chungwa*, Barros Arana 270. *Big Joe Saloon*, O'Higgins 808, just off plaza, popular at lunchtime, closed Sun am but open in pm, good breakfasts, vegetarian meals, snacks and pizzas. *Saaya 1*, Barros Arana 899, excellent panadería/pastelería/rotisería, highly rec. Vegetarian: *Naturista*, Barros Arana 244, good fresh juices, soups and other dishes, live music at lunchtime, highly rec. Many *fuentes de soda* in centre; *Fuente Alemana*, Av O'Higgins, rec; those on the Plaza de Armas incl *Café El Dom*, Caupolicán side, open Sun 0900, *Café Haiti*, Plaza end of Caupolicán, also open Sun am, and *Café Status*, on first floor, pleasant, reasonable lunches; *Royal Pub*, O'Higgins 796, not a pub but a rather posh snack bar; *Salón Inglés*, next door, is an English tea shop, 'good for expats longing for a cuppa'; *Nuria Café Bar*, Barros Arana 736, serves very good breakfasts and lunches, good value; *Café Colombia*, Pedro Aguirre Cerda, good coffee, good atmosphere; good sandwiches at *Entrepanes*, Caupolicán, between B Arana and Freire. The market place, bounded by Freire, Caupolicán, Maipú and Rengo, has excellent seafood, also good for fruit, vegetables, cheese and sausages (closes 2000, 1400 on Sun).

Exchange Cambios Fides, Barros Arana 565, local 58, Galería Internal, lower ground floor below *Hotel Araucano*, best rates for TCs; **Inter-Santiago**, Caupolicán 521, Local 31, T 228914. Fincard (Mastercard), O'Higgins 412, open 24 hrs. Banks such as **Banco Concepción** (which handles Visa) charge high commission on TCs.

Cultural Institutes Aliance Française, Colo Colo y V Lamas, library, concerts, films, cultural events; **Chilean-British Cultural Institute**, San Martín 531 (British newspapers, library); **Chilean-North American Institute**, Caupolicán 301 y San Martín, has library; Chileno-Italiano, Barros Arana.

British Consul Dr John F Pomeroy, Castellón 317, T (041) 225655, Casilla 452.

Laundry Lincoyán 441; many others in the centre especially in Freire 900 block.

Post Office and telex, O'Higgins y Colo Colo. **Telephone** CTC, Colo Colo 487, Angol 483. Entel, Caupolicán 567, 2nd floor; Colo Colo 487.

Country Club, Pedro de Valdivia, outdoor swimming pool, tennis.

Tourist Office Aníbal Pinto 460 on plaza, T 227976. Will advise on the more expensive hotels and *residenciales*. **Automóvil Club de Chile**, San Martín 519, T 226554, for information and car hire (T 222070).

Car Hire Hertz, Prat 248, T 230152; **Budget**, Arana 541, T 225377.

Bicycle Repairs *Martínez*, Maipú y Lincoyán, very helpful.

Air In the summer, flights daily to and from Santiago (in winter, only four a week) and connections to Temuco, Puerto Montt and Punta Arenas. The new jet airport is by the fast road from Talcahuano and Concepción. LanChile, Barros Arana 541, T 25014/240025; Ladeco, Barros Arana 451, T 248824. National, Barros Arana 348, T 246710.

Rail 3 regular daily trains to/from **Santiago**, plus overnight service, 9 hrs; in summer the service is increased: *salón* US$10-11 depending on service, *económico* US$8-9, sleeper from US$12 to US$33.35 for *departamento*. No regular, direct services to **Temuco** (a seasonal service runs once a day). Station at A Prat y Barros Arana. Ticket office Galería Alessandri, local 6, T 225286, or T 226925 for station.

Buses Main long distance terminal 5 km N, on Av Gen Bonilla, next to athletics stadium. Tur Bus terminal is 2 km E of main terminal on J M García; buses from Av Maipú in centre. To and from **Santiago**, 8½ hrs, US$6-10; to **Loncoche**, 7 hrs, US$6.50; to **Puerto Montt** several companies, US$9-11, about 12 hrs, only one ½ hr stop so take food and drink with you; to **Pucón**, 8 hrs, US$7.35. Igi-Llaima, to **Temuco**, 5 hrs, US$5, and other companies. To **Los Angeles**, US$1.50. Best direct bus line to **Chillán** is Línea Azul, 2 hrs, US$2, at 0700. For a longer and more scenic route, take Costa Azul bus which follows old railway line, through Tomé, Coelemu and Ñipas on to Chillán (part dirt-track, takes 5½ hrs). Frequent service to **Coronel** (US$0.45) and Lota. For Arauco and Bío-Bío region (including **Cañete**) buses leave from railway station on Av Prat. To **Contulmo**, 0745 and 1545, US$2.55. To **Lota**, from Carrera y Prat, every 15 mins, 1 hr, US$0.50 (ask tourist office for details of all services). To **Talcahuano** frequent service from Plaza de Armas (bus marked 'Base Naval'), US$0.15, 1 hr, express US$0.25, ½ hr.

Excursion To the **Museo y Parque Hualpen**, a house built around 1885 (now a national monument) and its gardens, donated to the city by Pedro del Río Zañartu; it contains beautiful pieces from all over the world, 2 hr visit, rec (open Tues-Sun 0900-1230, 1400-1800, free). Take a city bus to Hualpencillo, ask driver to let you out then walk 40 mins, or hitch. You have to go along Av Las Golondrinas to the Enap oil refinery, turn left, then right (it is signed). North of Concepción there are several picturesque coastal villages. At **Penco**, 12 km N, are **D** *Hotel La Terraza*, T 451422, **E** *Hospedaje Miramar*, good, and *Casinoriente*, good seafood restaurant. **Lirquén**, 15 km N, is a small, old, pretty town of wooden houses with a beach (walk along railway to reach it). Recommended. Plentiful cheap seafood for sale (try *Casa Blanca*, on Calle Manuel Rodríguez). 13 km further N is **Tomé**, 1½ hrs, US$0.70, another picturesque village; *Restaurante Piña*, main Plaza (owner speaks English); **D** *Hotel Roxy*, Sotomayor 1077, T 650729, and **E** *Linares*, Serrano 875, T 651284. 7 km before Tomé, on a hill, is *El Edén*, restaurant, bar and *cabañas*, D. An interesting cemetery, Miguel Gulán Muñoz, is set on a cliff overlooking the ocean. **Dichato**, 5 km further N, is also worth visiting: it is a beautiful fishing village and has the oceanographic centre of the University of Concepción. In summer it is a busy holiday resort. **B** *Kalifa*, Daniel Vera 815, T 681027; **D** *Hotel Chicki*, P L Ugalde 410, T 681004, dirty bathrooms, friendly; **E** pp Evaristo Jara Andrades, Ismael Valdés 125, kitchen facilities, friendly, helpful. Camping *Manatial Mar*, T 222933; *Restaurant Monte Carlo*, on beach, good. Private Museo del Mar, by Benjamín Ortega, interesting, free. Take a local bus to the tiny village of Cocholgüe. Buses from Concepción leave from Av Prat 484 and pass through all these villages.

Between Concepción and Lota (see below) are the Lagunas San Pedro Chica (swimming) and Grande (water sports), just across the Río Biobío. Nearer Lota are Playa Negra (small, few people, black sand) and Playa Blanca (bigger, bars, cafés, crowded, white sand, free campsite), both on the Bahía de Coronel (see below).

Talcahuano, on a peninsula jutting out to sea, has the best harbour in Chile. It is Chile's main naval station; its dry docks accommodate vessels of 30,000 tons. Pop 228,000. 1½ km away the steel plant at Huachipato has its own wharf to unload the iron ore shipped from the N.

Hotel **D** *Res San Pedro*, Manuel Rodríguez 22, T 542145. **Restaurants** *Bentotecas*, on seafront, a row of four restaurants sharing one window facing the harbour, superb fish and seafood in each one, rec, reasonable prices. *El Alero de los Salvo*, Colón 3396; *La Aguada*, Colón 912, shellfish dishes; *Domingo Lara*, Aníbal Pinto 450, seafood specialities, excellent.

The *Huáscar*, a relic of the War of the Pacific, is in the naval base. At the outbreak of the war the Chilean navy blockaded Iquique, then an important Peruvian nitrate port. On 21 May 1879, the Peruvian Navy's huge ironclad, the *Huáscar*, and the smaller *Independencia* reached Iquique to lift the siege. Chile sent out two small wooden ships, the *Covadonga* and the *Esmeralda*, under Captain Arturo Prat to challenge them. Prat fought with ferocity. When his damaged vessel, the *Esmeralda*, was rammed by the *Huáscar* Prat called upon his men to follow him, boarded the enemy and continued fighting until he was killed. Chile later captured the *Huáscar* at the battle of Angamos nr Mejillones, on 8 October 1879. The ship is open Tues-Sun 0900-1130, 1400-1700, US$0.60, but the schedules do change. Photography is permitted, but passports must be handed in at main gate.

A road links Concepción with the coal-producing districts to the S of the Río Biobío. The town of **Coronel**, in the heart of the coal area, 29 km from Concepción, was the scene of a British naval defeat in 1914 (the *Good Hope* and *Monmouth* were sunk by the *Scharnhorst*—a monument was dedicated in Nov 1989), which was later avenged at the Battle of the Falklands/Malvinas with the destruction of the German squadron.

Frequent buses to **Concepción** and **Lota**. Between Coronel and Lota the smells of fishmeal processing can be overpowering.

Lota, 8 km S of Coronel, is a coal-mining centre with 52,000 inhabitants. In the church on the main plaza you can see a virgin made of coal. To the W of the town, on a promontory, is the famous Parque de Lota (Cousiño Isidora), laid out with views of the sea by an English landscape architect in the last century. It contains many flower gardens, romantic paths, and peafowl and pheasants roaming freely. (Admission US$1, no picnicking; open 1000-1800 daily, till 2000 in summer.) Guided tours (Spanish only) of the mine, which extends beneath the sea, are available, Tues-Sat 1100 (minimum party of 5) US$15 pp, rec, book at the Park entrance, T 249039, or at Tourist Office in Concepción from whom further details can be obtained. Ask to see the mining museum before you leave. The road is paved beyond Lota as far as the seaside resort of **Laraquete** (an hour's run by car from Concepción), where there are miles of golden sands, and on to **Arauco**, past the Celulosa Arauco wood-pulp plant.

Hotels In Lota: *Residencial Rome*, Galvarino 233, clean, friendly. In Laraquete: **D** *Laraquete*, on Gabriela Mistral, main street, friendly, small rooms, baths in poor repair; **D** *Hostería El Quinto*, helpful, basic, good breakfast. Several *residenciales* close to beach. In Arauco: **B** *Hosteria Arauco*, P de Valdivia 80, T 551131. **D** *Plaza*, Chacabuco 347, T 551265.

Buses to Coronel (20 min), and Concepción (1½ hrs, US$0.50). Many southbound buses by-pass the centre: catch them from the carretera.

From Lota a road runs S, 76 km to Tres Pinos, where a bus can be taken W to **Lebu**, 31 km, a fishing port and coal washing centre with a population of 17,000 (DDD 046) (**C** *Hotel Central*, Pérez 183, T 511904, some cheaper rooms but bargain, clean, good, rec; **D** *Rocha*, Pérez 309, T 511939; **E** *Res Alcázar*, Alcázar 144, with breakfast, cold water, friendly). It lies at the mouth of the Río Lebu, and is the capital of Arauco province (buses S leave from Los Alces, next to train station). The lower river reaches and the beach are popular with tourists in summer. The views from the hill behind the town are majestic.

24 km S of Tres Pinos is **Cañete** (DDD 046), a small town on the site of Fort Tucapel where Pedro de Valdivia and 52 of his men were killed by Mapuche warriors in 1554. Museo Mapuche de Cañete, half-hour walk from town in direction of Contulmo. Open, Tues-Sun 1000-1230, 1400-1800. Entrance US$0.60. Interesting for its architecture, landscape, gardens with flowers cultivated by the Mapuches.

Accommodation **D** *Alonso de Ercilla*, Villagran 641, T 611974, clean; **D** *Derby*, Nariñan 680, T 611960, central, clean, friendly, good restaurant; **D** *Hotel Nahuelbuta*, Villagran 644, T 611073, main street nr plaza, private parking. **E** *Comercio*, 7° de la Línea, T 611218, very pleasant, rec; **E** *Gajardo*, 7° de la Línea 817 (1 block from plaza), old fashioned, friendly, pleasant. Some shops rent rooms, Mormons in Calle Condell offer accommodation, free and friendly.

Buses 3 night buses to and from Santiago, 12 hrs. Buses to Purén, US$1.50; sit on right-hand side to get good views of **Lago Lanalhue**. To Concepción, 3 hrs, US$2.50.

From Lebu or Tres Pinos you can go to Puerto Peleco on Lago Lanalhue, 63 km SE of Lebu (buses S leave Los Alces, next to train station). At Peleco the road forks, the E branch running to the N of the lake to Contulmo (31 km). There is extensive commercial logging around the lake. In **Contulmo** **D** *Hotel Contulmo* is highly recommended. (Millaray 116, Eduardo Videla and family love to break out the wine and guitar with visitors); **D** *Hotel Central*, Calle Millaray 131, no sign, and very hospitable. Taxi from Contulmo to lake beach US$2; swimming good, but fishing not so. Well worth a visit is the wooden Grollmus House and Mill (1920s), 3 km NW of Contulmo, with a fine collection of every colour of copihue (the national flower) in a splendid garden. The mill has original wooden machinery. Bus Contulmo-Temuco, Thiele company, 3 a day, US$3, at least two a day to Concepción, US$2.55 (check times in advance).

From Contulmo the road crosses the Cordillera to **Purén**, where there is a full-scale reconstruction on the original site of the wooden Chilean fort used in the last campaign against the Mapuche (1869-1881). **D** *Hotel Tur*, Dr Garriga

912, T 22, clean, good; *Central Hotel*, on the plaza, meals excellent, rooms in tourist season only.

The W branch of the road from Peleco runs S parallel to the coast. 3 km S a road forks off along the S side of Lake Lanalhue to *Hostería Lanalhue*, beautifully situated 16 km from Peleco. Poor forestry tracks continue to Contulmo, only negotiable in dry weather. *Tirúa*, at the mouth of the Río Tirúa, is 67 km S of Peleco (3 *hospedajes*, all E pp; buses from Cañete). 32 km offshore lies the island of *Mocha*, visited by Juan Bautista Pastenes in 1544 and later by Sir Francis Drake. Most of the island's 800 inhabitants live around the coast, the interior being of forests. The main settlement is La Hacienda where accommodation is available with families. Transport from Tirúa: ferry daily 0600, US$14; plane US$56 (ask the police to radio the plane which is based on Mocha).

Travelling S from Chillán on the Longitudinal Highway, the next major centre is **Los Angeles** (pop 106,000; DDD 043), capital of Bío-Bío province, in a wine, fruit and timber district. Founded in 1739 as a fort, it is now a pleasant, expanding city, with a large Plaza de Armas; Colón is the main shopping street. There is a good daily market.

Hotels A3 *Mariscal Alcázar*, Lautaro 385 (Plaza de Armas), T 311725; **B** *Gran Hotel Müso*, Valdivia 230 (Plaza de Armas), T 313183, good restaurant open to non-residents; **C** *Mazzola*, Lautaro 579, T 321643. **C** *Hotel Winser*, Rengo 138, overpriced but clean and friendly; **C** *Res Santa María*, Caupolicán, hot shower, TV, good beds; **E** *Res Winser*, Colo Colo 335. Private house at Caupolicán 651, E, large breakfast, good value; opposite is another, also No 651, basic, cheaper. 10 km N is **E** pp *Casa de familia/Cabañas El Rincón*, Panamericana Sur Km 494, Cruce La Mona 1 km E, T (09) 441-5019, F 043-317168, Elke and Winfried Lohmar, beautiful property beside a small river, restful, South American and European cuisine, including vegetarian, tours arranged, English, French, German and Spanish spoken, rec.

Restaurants *El Arriero*, Colo Colo 235, T 322899, good *parrillas* and international dishes; *Di Leone*, Colón 265, good lasagna; *Julio's Pizzas*, Colón 542 and *Rancho de Julio*, Colón 720, excellent *parrilla*.

British Cultural Institute Vicuña 648.

Post Office on Plaza de Armas. **Telephone** CTC, Paseo Quilpué, or Valdivia 326; Entel, Colo Colo 393.

Tourist Office Av Caupolicán and Villagrán; also kiosk on Plaza de Armas. **Automóvil Club de Chile**, Villagrán y Caupolicán, T 322149.

Bus Long distance terminal on NW outskirts of town, local terminal at Villagrán y Rengo in centre: to Santiago, 9 hrs, US$7.50. To Viña del Mar and Valparaíso, 10 hrs, US$8.25; 4 daily to Concepción, US$1.50, 2¼ hrs. Hourly buses to Temuco, US$2.30. To Curacautín, daily at 0600, 3 hrs, US$2.25.

Excursion There is swimming in the Río Duqueco, 10 mins S by bus, US$0.80. The *Salto El Laja*, 25 km N, is a spectacular waterfall in which the Laja plunges 47m over the rocks. It costs a few pesos to enter and walk up to the falls, or to walk on the hotel side. There is a good motel (**A1-B** *Motel Salto del Laja*, address: Casilla 562, Los Angeles) with fine restaurant, 2 swimming pools and chalet-type rooms on an island overlooking the falls. Also at or nr the falls are *Camping Los Manantiales*, T 323606, and Motels *El Pinar* and *Los Coyuches*. The falls are 6 hrs drive from Santiago (by bus, US$7.25). Buses (Bus Bio Bio) from Los Angeles (US$0.60, 1/2 hr—fairly frequent buses back to Los Angeles) or Chillán (US$2).

A road runs from Los Angeles to the **Parque Nacional Laguna de Laja**, 88 km E, past the impressive rapids of the Laja river. The lake is surrounded by stark volcanic scenery of scrub and lava, and dominated by the Antuco volcano and the glacier-covered Sierra Velluda. Take a bus to Abanico (**E** pp *Hostería del Bosque*, restaurant, also good campsite), 20 km past Antuco (US$1.35, 2 hrs, 5 a day but only 0830 in am, last return 1730), then 4 km to park entrance, passport retained by guards till you leave (details from Conaf in Los Angeles, José de Manzo 275, 0800-1300, 1430-1800 Mon-Fri). *Cabañas y Camping Lagunillas*, T 314275, 50m from the river, 4 km from the ski slopes, poor campsite US$2.50 pp. Camping not permitted on lake shore. 21 km from the lake is the *Refugio Chacay* offering food, drink and bed (B, T Los Angeles 222651); two other *refugios*: *Digeder*, E, and Universidad de Concepción, both on slopes of Volcán Antuco, for both T Concepción 221561, office O'Higgins 734. Nearby is the Club de Esquí de los Angeles with two ski-lifts, giving a combined run of 4 km on the Antuco volcano (season, May-Aug).

Mulchén, a small, old-fashioned town, 32 km S of Los Angeles, reached by regular buses, 45 mins. It has few cars, no concrete and is a glimpse of a world gone-by.

The road continues from Los Angeles via Collipulli (campsite), Victoria, Púa and Lautaro to Temuco.

From Collipulli and Los Angeles paved roads run W to **Angol** (35,000 people; DDD 045), capital of the Province of Malleco (IX Région), founded by Valdivia in 1552, seven times destroyed by the Indians and rebuilt. Buses from Santiago US$6.50, Los Angeles, US$1.20, or Collipulli. To Temuco US$2.50. Worth seeing are El Vergel experimental fruit-growing station, the Dillman S Bullock regional museum with precolumbian Indian artefacts (open daily 0830-1300, 1500-1800, US$0.50, a 5 km bus-ride from town) and the San Francisco church. 35 km W is the **Parque Nacional Nahuelbuta**, in the coastal mountain range, reached by bus to Vegas Blancas, 0700 and 1600 Mon, Wed, Fri, 11/2 hrs, US$1, 27 km from Angol, then walk (or possibly hitch) 7 km to park gate, and a further 7 km to the campsite (US$0.70 to enter park, US$0.70 to camp—there are many free campsites on the way to the entrance). The park has many araucaria trees (monkey-puzzles) and viewpoints over both the sea and the Andean volcanoes. Rough maps are available at the park entrance for US$0.25.

Hotels **A1** *Millaray*, Prat 420, T 711570; **C** *Olimpia*, Lautaro 194, T 711517; **D** pp *La Posada*, at El Vergel, T 712103, full board, clean, friendly; **D** *Residencial Olimpia*, Caupolicán 625, T 711162; **E** *El Parrón*, O'Higgins 345, T 711370; **E** Vergara 651, chaotic but cheap.

A small town which has hot springs nearby, **Curacautín**, is 56 km SE of Victoria (on the Longitudinal Highway, Ruta 5) by paved road; bus from Los Angeles or Temuco; bus station on Curacautín plaza (timetables posted on window are fiction).

Curacautín Hotels **C** *Hostería La Rotonda del Contiu*, restaurant; **D** *Plaza*, Yungay 157, T 56, restaurant good but pricey; **E** pp *Hostería Abarzúa*, full board C pp, camping; **E** pp *Residencial Rojas*, Tarapacá 249, without bath, good meals, rec; **E** pp *Turismo*, Tarapacá 140, T 116, clean, good food, comfortable, best value. *Camping Trahuilco*, 3 km S, expensive. **Restaurant** *El Refugio*, popular.

The beautiful pine-surrounded **Termas de Tolhuaca** (open 1 Nov-30 Apr), with hot springs, are 35 km to the NE of Curacautín by unpaved road, or 57 km by unpaved road from just N of Victoria (high clearance 4WD essential). (**A2** *Hotel Termas de Tolhuaca*, with full board, use of baths, and horse riding incl, very good, T 164, Casilla 48 Curacautín, or T Temuco 220975; **E** pp *Residencial Roja*, hot water, food, camping nr the river, good.) It is about 9 km from the hotel to the **Parque Nacional Tolhuaca**, in which are the waterfalls of Malleco and Culiebra, and Lago Malleco; superb scenery and good views of volcanoes from Cerro Amarillo (the park is open Dec-Apr). 32 km SE of Curacautín are the hot springs and mud baths of **Termas de Río Blanco** (hotel), at 1,046m on the slopes of the Sierra Nevada and nr Lago Conguillio (bus to Conguillio National Park—see p 702 below—only at 1800). 18 km E of Curacautín are the indoor **Termas de Manzanar** (US$5, open all year), reached by bus from Temuco and Victoria (**B** *Hotel Termas*, but also has simple rooms with bath but not luxurious; **E** *Hostería Abarzúa*, simple, friendly).

Northeast of Curacautín is the **Lonquimay volcano** with the Puelche ski-run, season May-Nov. The volcano begun erupting on Christmas Day 1988; the new crater is called Navidad. To see it, access is made from Malalcahuello, 15 km S and half-way between Curacautín and Lonquimay town. In Malalcahuello, the teacher at the school charges US$8.50 for the car to drive up to the volcano and collect you later (crampons, ice-axe and ropes essential); Sra Naomi Saavedra at *Residencial Los Sauces* also arranges lifts (D pp full board, or F pp with use of kitchen, hot water, good value). In the village is a steam-powered carpenter's shop. You can also stay at a refuge in the **Reserva Nacional Malalcahuello-Nalcas** on the slopes of the volcano (D, hot showers, open ski-season only), 5 km from the summit and 10 km from the bus stop. Bus Erbuc from Temuco, US$2 to Malalcahuello, 4 a day, 4 hrs, 5$\frac{1}{2}$ to Lonquimay town, US$2.80. There is accommodation in Lonquimay, but no public transport to the volcano. The road Curacautín-Lonquimay town, 57 km, passes the Salto del Indio (Km 14), before which is a turnoff to Laguna Blanca (25 km away, take fishing gear, ask Sernatur about trucks), and Salto de la Princesa, just beyond Manzanar.

THE LAKE DISTRICT (5)

Yet more beautiful scenery: a variety of lakes, often with snow-capped volcanoes as a backdrop, stretch southwards to the salt water fjords which begin at Puerto Montt. There are a number of good bases for exploring (Valdivia has the added attraction of colonial forts a river trip away) and many national parks.

South from the Biobío river to the Gulf of Reloncaví the same land formation holds as for the rest of Chile to the N: the Andes to the E, the coastal range to the W, and in between the central valley. The Andes and the passes over them are less high here, and the snowline lower; the coastal range also loses altitude, and the central valley is not as continuous as from Santiago to Concepción. The climate is cooler; the summer is no longer dry, for rain falls all the year round, and more heavily than further N. The rain decreases as you go inland: some 2,500 mm on the coast and 1,350 mm inland. This is enough to maintain heavy forests, mostly beech, but agriculture is also important; irrigation is not necessary. The farms are mostly medium sized, and no longer the huge *haciendas* of the N. The characteristic thatched or red tiled houses of the rural N disappear; they are replaced by the shingle-roofed frame houses typical of a frontier land rich in timber. The farms raise livestock, fruit and food crops, and timber is a major industry.

About 20,000 Mapuches live in the area, more particularly around Temuco. There are possibly 150,000 more of mixed blood who speak the Indian tongue, though most of them are bilingual.

A Mapuche music festival (plus market) is normally held mid-Feb in Villarrica. Enquire at the Santiago or Temuco tourist office.

Crossing to Argentina There are four main routes from the Chilean Lake District to Argentina: 1) The Tromen Pass, from Pucón and Curarrehue to Junín de los Andes (**see p 707**); 2) the Huahum Pass, from Panguipulli via Choshuenco and Lake Pirehueico to San Martín de los Andes (**see p 708**); 3) The Puyehue Pass, from Osorno and Entrelagos via the Parque Nacional Puyehue to Bariloche (**see p 714**); 4) The Lakes Route, from Puerto Montt or Osorno via Ensenada, Petrohue and Lago Todos Los Santos to Bariloche (**see p 720**).

Between parallels 39° and 42° S is found one of the most picturesque lake regions in the world. There are some 12 great lakes of varying sizes, some set high on the Cordillera slopes, others in the central valley southwards from Temuco to Puerto Montt. Here, too, are imposing waterfalls and snowcapped volcanoes. Anglers revel in the abundance of fish, the equable climate, and the absence of

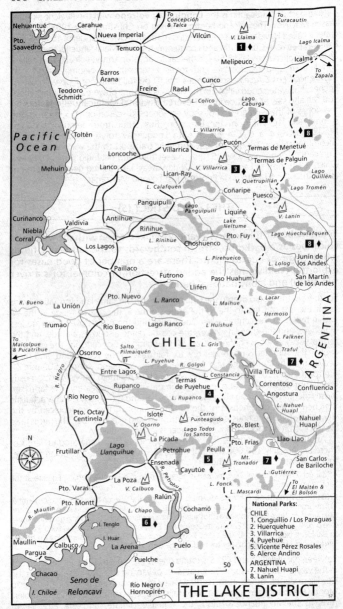

THE LAKE DISTRICT

troublesome insects (except for enormous horseflies, *tavanos*, between mid-Dec and mid-Jan—do not wear dark clothes). Out of season many facilities are closed, in season (from mid-Dec to mid-Mar), prices are higher and it is best to book well in advance, particularly for transport. It is a peaceful area, with fewer tourists than across the border in the Argentine lake district.

The Lake District proper does not begin until we reach Chile's newest city, Temuco, founded 1881 after the final treaty with the Mapuches.

Temuco (pop 225,000; DDD 045), 679 km S of Santiago, is the capital of IX Región (Araucanía), and one of the most active centres in the S. Wheat, barley, oats, timber and apples are the principal products of the area. The **cattle auctions** in the stockyards behind the railway on A Malvoa, Thur mornings, are interesting; you can see the *huasos*, or Chilean cowboys, at work. Also, cattle sales at Feria Agroaustral, just outside Temuco on the road to Nuevo Imperial, on Fri (take bus 4 from Calle Rodríguez), auction starts at 1400, and at Nuevo Imperial, 35 km away, on Mon and Tues. The **Municipal Cultural Centre** at the intersection of Balmaceda, Caupolicán and Prat houses the municipal library, a theatre, and art galleries. Temuco is the Mapuches' market town and you may see some, particularly women, in their typical costumes in the produce market next to the railway station (Lautaro y Pinto). Mapuche textiles, pottery, woodcarving, jewellery etc are also sold inside and around the **municipal market** in centre of town (corner of Aldunate and Diego Portales—it also sells fish, meat and dairy produce), but these are increasingly touristy and poor quality. The *Casa de la Mujer Mapuche*, San Martín 433, sells the textiles made by a co-operative of 135 Mapuche weavers; all items are 100% wool with traditional designs (spinning and weaving demonstrations were due to start in Nov 1994). Also highly recommended is the *Casa de Arte Mapuche*, Matta 25-A, T 213085, Casilla 1682, for information on Mapuche arts and crafts speak to the director Rayen Kvyeh. There is a good view of Temuco from **Cerro Ñielol**, a park (entry US$1), where there is a fine collection of native plants in the natural state, including the national flower, the *copihue rojo*. There is also a bathing pool (US$0.40) and a restaurant (open 1200-2400). On Cerro Ñielol is also La Patagua, the tree under which the final peace was signed with the Mapuches in 1881.

Museum Museo de la Araucanía, Alemania 84, a well-arranged collection devoted to the history and traditions of the Mapuche nation. Open Tues-Sat 0800-1300, 1500-1800; Sun 1000-1400 (at some times of year Tues-Fri 0800-1300, 1500-1900), US$1.

NB Do not confuse the streets Vicuña MacKenna and General MacKenna.

Hotels A1 *Nuevo Hotel de la Frontera*, Bulnes 726, T 210718, incl breakfast, excellent; **A2** *Bayern*, Prat 146, small rooms, clean, helpful; **A2** *Apart Hotel Don Eduardo*, Bello 755, T 215554, parking, suites with kitchen, rec; **B** *Continental*, A Varas 708, T 211395, popular with business travellers, clean, friendly, colonial-style wooden building, excellent restaurant, the bar is popular with locals in the evening, cheaper rooms without bath, rec; **B** *Turismo*, Claro Solar 636, T 210583, near main square, slightly run-down restaurant, good value, with bath, C without, good service; **C** *Espelette*, Claro Solar 492, T 234805, overpriced; **C** *Oriente*, M Rodríguez 1146, T 233232, clean, rec; **C** *Residencial Ginebra*, V Mackenna 361, T 236995, hot water, heating, modern, German and Italian spoken; **D** *Casa de huéspedes Centenario*, Aldunate 864, with breakfast, hot water, clean; **D** *Casablanca*, Montt 1306 y Zenteno, T 212740, good breakfast; **D** *Hostal Montt*, Manuel Montt 965, T 211856, parking, clean, friendly; **E** pp Sra Veronica Kiekebusch, Av Alemania 0649 (T 247287), with breakfast, clean, quiet, rec, buses No 1 or 9 for train and rural bus stations; **D** *Hospedaje Millarey*, Claro Solar 471, simple, basic. Many cheap *residenciales* and *pensiones* near railway station in market area, incl **D** *Rupangue*, Barros Arana 182, hot shower, clean, helpful, good value; **D** *Flor Acoca*, Lautaro 591, hot water, breakfast, clean; **D** *Hospedaje* at Claro Solar 483, clean, friendly; **D** *Hospedaje Adriane Becker*, Estebáñez 881, without bath, good breakfast, basic, friendly; also **D** Alemania 035, hot water, use of kitchen, pleasant, rec; **D** Balmaceda 925, T 237181, with breakfast; **E** pp Bulnes 1006 y O'Higgins, good double rooms, hot water, above drugstore, ask for house key otherwise access limited to shop hours; Rodríguez 1311, friendly, clean, meals served; **D** Claro Solar 151, with breakfast; **D** *Familia Rodríguez*, Lautaro 1149,

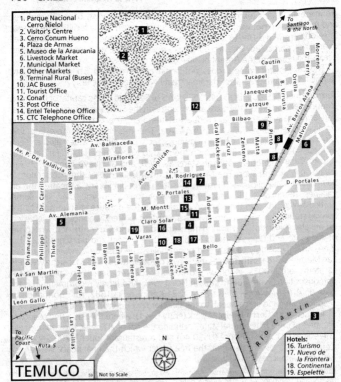

```
1. Parque Nacional
   Cerro Ñielol
2. Visitor's Centre
3. Cerro Conum Hueno
4. Plaza de Armas
5. Museo de la Araucania
6. Livestock Market
7. Municipal Market
8. Other Markets
9. Terminal Rural (Buses)
10. JAC Buses
11. Tourist Office
12. Conaf
13. Post Office
14. Entel Telephone Office
15. CTC Telephone Office
```

Hotels:
16. *Turismo*
17. *Nuevo de
    la Frontera*
18. *Continental*
19. *Espelette*

TEMUCO Not to Scale

very clean, laundry and kitchen facilities; **E** A Bello y Las Heras, basic, clean; **D** Encalada 1078, use of kitchen, friendly, rec; **D** *Alba Jaramillo*, Calbuco 583, T 240042, by Av Alemania, with breakfast, clean; **D** Sra Ruth Palominas, Zenteno 486, T 211269, friendly, clean, hot water, rec; **D** Gral MacKenna 46, clean, Jan-Mar only; other private houses in same street. **E** *Residencial Ensuéno*, Rodríguez 442, hot water, clean; **E** *Hospedaje González*, Lautaro 1160, 2° piso, friendly, safe, clean, rec; **E** Sra Egla de González, San Martín 01760, T 246182, with breakfast, clean. Accommodation in private houses, category D, can be arranged by Tourist Office. Private accommodation is cheaper nearer the railway station.

Camping *Camping Metrenco*, 10 km S on Route 5.

Restaurants *Kim Long*, Portales 1192 and at Bulnes 145, Chinese, excellent; *Café Marriet*, Prat 451, Local 21, excellent coffee; *Café Istanbul*, Bulnes 563, good, especially for coffee; also on Bulnes: *Dino's*, No 360, branch of a chain of good restaurants, rec; *Julio's Pizza*, No 778, wide variety, not cheap; *Centro Español*, No 483; *Della Maggio*, Lautaro No 536, good coffee and light meals; *D'Angelo*, San Martín 1199, good food, pleasant, pricey. Plenty of good eating places inside the municipal market. *Pront Rapa*, Aldunate 421, for take-away lunches and snacks, rec; *Ñam-Ñam*, Portales 802, pizzas, sandwiches etc, good. Outside town: *Hostería La Estancia* (dancing), Rudecindo Ortega, highly rec; *La Cumbre del Cerro Ñielol* (dancing), on top of Cerro Ñielol.

Exchange Good rates for cheques at **Banco Osorno**, Plaza de Armas; also **Turcamb**, Claro Solar 733; *Christopher Money Exchange*, Prat 696, Oficina 419; also at Bulnes 667, Local 202; **Inter-Santiago**, Bulnes 443, local 2. All deal in dollars and Argentine pesos. **Fincard** (Mastercard), Claro Solar 922. **Banco Concepción** (for Visa), M Montt 901; **Banco de Chile**,

A Varas 818, rec for money transfers by Switch.

Consulate Netherlands, España 494, Honorary Consul, Germán Nicklas, is friendly and helpful.

Laundry *Lavajet*, Claro Solar 574; Caupolicán 110, Nos 4 and 5, open 0900-2100 daily, good, cheap, quick; Portales 1185, expensive; M Montt 415 (automatic).

Post Office Portales 839.

Telephones Centro de Llamadas CTC, A Prat just off Claro Solar and plaza, Mon-Sat 0800-2400, Sun and holidays 1030-2400. Entel, Bulnes 303, daily 0830-2200.

Supermarket *Las Brisas*, Carrera 899.

Camera Shop Ruka, Bulnes 394, helpful, owner speaks German.

Tourist Office Bulnes 586, T 211969. Open 0830-2030, all week in summer, 0900-1200, 1500-1800 Mon-Fri in winter. Has full list of places to stay. Also at Balmaceda and Av Prat. **Automóvil Club de Chile**, Bulnes 763, T 213949. **Conaf**, Bilbao 931, T 234420.

Air Airport 6 km from the city. LanChile, Bulnes 667, T 211339, daily to Santiago and Osorno. Ladeco has daily flights to Valdivia; National and Ladeco fly once a week each to Concepción; National flies twice a week to Punta Arenas; Ladeco and TAN fly to Neuquén, Argentina (6 days a week). Ladeco, Prat 565, Local 102, T 214325; National, Claro Solar 780, Local 7, T 215764; Varig, Mackenna 763, T 213120; TAN T 210500

Rail Station at B Arana and Lautaro, T 233416. To **Concepción** once a day, but not all year. To **Santiago**: 2 a day, 12 hrs, fares: *económico* US$8, *superior/salón* US$12-14 (depending on service), sleeper US$16.65-23.35, double compartment US$66. To **Osorno** and **Puerto Montt** daily 0850, 9 hrs; to Valdivia 1 a day (Santiago train combines with bus to Valdivia). Ticket office at Bulnes 582, T 233522, open Mon-Fri 0900-1300, 1430-1800, Sun 0900-1300 as well as at station.

Bus to neighbouring towns from Terminal Rural at Pinto and Balmaceda. Flota Erbuc (also at Miraflores y Bulnes, and Balmaceda 1415), to **Curacautín**, US$1.50, 7 daily, 2³/₄ hrs; also to **Lonquimay**, 4 daily, 5¹/₂ hrs, US$3, **Laguna Captren** Mon and Fri 1645, 4 hrs, US$2.20. No long-distance bus terminal—buses leave from company offices. To **Santiago** US$7-11, *salón cama* US$20, different companies; most overnight (book in advance); Bus LIT, San Martín y Bulnes. Buses Cruz del Sur from V Mackenna 671, 3 a day to **Castro**, 10 a day to **Puerto Montt** (5¹/₂ hrs), to Valdivia US$2; to **Osorno** US$3.30. Other buses in 600 block of V Mackenna (nr Claro Solar): ETTA, Longitudinal Sur, Thiele for **Lebu** and **Contulmo**, 0745, 1310, 1600, 3¹/₂ hrs to Contulmo, US$3, change here for Cañete and Concepción, and JAC for Santiago. JAC's main terminal is at Mackenna y Bello for all other services except to Argentina (see below): **Villarrica** and **Pucón** many between 0705 and 2045, 1¹/₂ hrs, US$2, and 2 hrs, US$2.50 respectively, and **Coñaripe**, 3 hrs, and **Lican Ray** (2 hrs). Several other companies on Claro Solar, 500-600 blocks. Buses to **Puerto Montt** charge US$7-9. Fénix, Pedro Lagos y Claro Solar, to **Arica** (2200 and 2245, arrives 1400 2 days later, US$45 or US$60 *cama*), Iquique, Antofagasta (US$35), **La Serena** and **Santiago** (US$20), also Pucón and Valdivia. Power, Bulnes 174 and Balmaceda 1438 to **Villarrica** and **Pucón** 0730, and **Panguipulli** at 0730, 2 hrs. Also to **Panguipulli**, Pangui Sur, Miraflores 871, 10 a day between 0700 and 1915, 3 hrs, US$2, also to **Loncoche**, **Los Lagos**, **Mehuin** in summer only. Bío Bío bus to **Concepción** (US$5, 4¹/₂ hrs), six daily.

Buses to Argentina JAC from Terminal Rural to **Junín de los Andes** (US$25), San Martín de los Andes (US$25) and Neuquén (US$30), Wed and Fri 0400; Igi Llaima and San Martín both go three times a week to **San Martín**; Nar Bus from Terminal Rural to San Martín and Neuquén, Mon-Fri, (San Martín buses go via Villarrica and Pucón when the Tromen Pass is open); Ruta Sur, Miraflores 1151, to **Zapala** (US$22) and Neuquén (US$28), Wed and Sat daily; La Unión del Sud, Miraflores 1285, same destinations Wed, Fri and Sat Fénix (address above) to **Buenos Aires** and **Mendoza**. Buses on the Zapala route go via the Pino Hachado pass, not Icalma; formalities at Pino Hachado take 2-3 hrs, thorough searches (pleasant scenery, though).

Car Hire Hertz, Las Heras 999, T 235385, US$45 a day. **Budget**, Lynch 471, T 214911; **Automóvil Club de Chile**, Bulnes 763, T 231283; **Puig**, Portales, 779; *Fatum*, Varas 983, T 234199; Eurc, Mackenna 426, T 210311, helpful, good value.

Excursions A paved road runs W to (55 km) *Carahue* (accommodation available). About 30 km further, S of the mouth of the navigable Río Imperial, is **Puerto Saavedra**, where there is a stretch of beach with black volcanic sand. It comprises 3 distinct towns: the first administrative; the second, 2 km away, the fishing port with one poor *residencial*; the third, a further 2 km, the tourist area (**C** *Gran Hotel El Criollito*, clean, good views, rec; **E** Sra Rita

Sandoval Muñoz, Las Dunas 01511, lovely, knowledgeable; many *hosterías* in D-E category). It is reached from Carahue by car (1 hr), or by bus from Temuco Terminal Rural (Nar Bus, 0730, 0800, 0930, 3¼ hrs, US$1.20).

From Puerto Saavedra there are interesting excursions to Nehuentue, on the N bank of the river, and to Trovolhue, reached by a specially chartered launch which takes 4 hrs to go up the Río Moncul.

40 km S of Carahue on an unpaved road is **Puerto Domínguez**, 2 hrs by bus from Temuco; good accommodation at **E** pp *Hostería Rucaleufú*, Alessandri 22, with good meals, clean, lake views, highly rec. Puerto Domínguez, a picturesque little place famous for its good fishing, is on **Lago Budi**, the only inland, salt-water lake in Chile. Over 130 species of bird, aquatic and marine, including black-necked swans, visit it. The *Carlos Schalchli* ferry (free) leaves Puerto Domínguez for Isla Huapi, Mon-Fri 0800 and 1630, returning 1030 and 1700. It takes about 30 mins. The Isla has a Mapuche settlement with traditional thatched houses (*rucas*) and fine views of both the lake and the Pacific.

Another pleasant trip through Mapuche country is to take a minibus from the Central Market to the country town of **Chol Chol**, 30 km unpaved to the NW. There are daily buses (Huincabus from Terminal Rural, 1 hr, 4 times between 1100 and 1800, US$0.60, or García/Gangas from same terminal at 1000), laden with corn, vegetables, charcoal, animals, as well as the locals. The trip traverses rolling countryside with panoramic views. On a clear day it is possible to see five volcanoes. Nearer Chol Chol, a few traditional round *rucas* can be seen. For an overnight stay and information, contact Sra Lauriza Norváez, Calle Luzcano (s/n), who prepares meals, and is very helpful. Daily bus at 1330 to Nueva Imperial and on to Puerto Saavedra, but bus connections few and slow (stay overnight in Puerto Saavedra).

The 3,050m Llaima volcano has at its foot one of the prettiest skiing resorts in Chile: **Llaima**, at 1,500m, 80 km E of Temuco. It stands in the middle of two large **national parks**, **Los Paraguas** (named after the umbrella-like araucaria, or monkey puzzle, pine trees—best visited Aug-Oct according to Conaf) and **Conguillio** (open 20 Nov-13 Mar). The latter, which contains the Laguna Conguillio and the snow-covered Sierra Nevada, is the best place to see araucaria forest, which used to cover an extensive area in this part of Chile. It is one of Chile's most popular parks, but is deserted outside the Jan/Feb season. The best way to get to the park is to drive, preferably in a high-clearance vehicle (roads are very bad, especially after rain) and with clear instructions on which roads shown on maps are suitable and exist. There are three routes, on all of which there is public transport in season only: via Curacautín (N of the Park), via Melipeuco (to the S) or via Cherquenco (to the W). From Curacautín (**see p 696**) take a bus at 1830, Mon and Fri towards the park, 1 hr, US$1, or hitch, to Conaf hut (you can camp nearby). It is then 10 km to Laguna Captren situated in araucaria forest, where you pay a park entrance fee of US$3; campsite (US$8 incl firewood but no other facilities), good hiking. 6 km further on is Laguna Conguillio, with a visitor's centre (closed off-season) campsite (US$15 per tent, hot water, showers, firewood), cheaper campsite (*camping de mochileros*, US$5 pp); *cabañas*, (A3 summer only, sleep 6, no sheets or blankets, gas stove, and café/shop), from where you can hike into the Sierra Nevada, or take a shorter, interesting walk on the Sendero de los Carpinteros (impassable under snow). 15 km S of Laguna Conguillio, mostly across deserted lava fields, is the southern entrance to the park, which is 13 km N by road from the village of **Melipeuco** (**E** *Hotel Central*, basic, good food; **E** *Pensión Hospedaje*, Aguirre 729, rec; **C** *Hostería Hue-Telén*, Pedro Aguirre Cerda 15, Casilla 40, T 693032 and leave message, good; *Restaurant Los Troncos*, Aguirre 352, rec). Bus from Temuco Terminal Rural, Flota Erbuc, 5 daily, 0900-1830, 4 hrs, US$1.30, ask driver to drop you at the road fork, 10 km from park entrance, last back to Temuco at 1630. Transport can be arranged from Melipeuco into the park (ask in grocery stores, US$20 one way). The third entrance is from Cherquenco (road paved to Vilcún, then very poor for the last 40 km, high clearance essential. Daily buses Temuco-Cherquenco). It is then a 2-3 day hike around Volcán Llaima to Laguna Conguillio, dusty, but beautiful views of Laguna Quepe, then on to the Laguna Captren *guardería*.

To climb Llaima, crampons, ice-axe and ropes essential. Climb from W entrance (Cherquenco). There is a *refugio* (very poor condition) 22 km W of Cherquenco. The volacano erupted in May 1994; check in advance if any facilities are closed.

A brief résumé of the route on foot through the park from the S end: from entrance, 600m trail to Rio Truful-Truful canyon and waterfall; 8 km to Laguna Verde (camping possible); 3 km to Laguna Arco Iris (beautiful, camping, possible); 3 km to Laguna Conguillio; 6 km from Centro de Información Ambiental on Conguillio to Laguna Captrén; 10 km to Park limits and *guardería*.

For details of these excursions visit the Corporación Nacional Forestal, IX Región, Caupolicán y Bulnes, Temuco. For best touring, hire a 4WD vehicle in Temuco.

The way from Temuco to Villarrica follows the paved Longitudinal Highway as far as Freire (24 km), then (also paved) runs 63 km SE. Villarrica can also be reached from Loncoche, 54 km S of Freire, but most of this road is in very poor condition. Wooded Lago Villarrica, 21 km long and about 7 km wide, is the most beautiful in the region, with snow-capped Villarrica volcano (2,840m) to the SE.

Villarrica, pleasantly set at the extreme SW corner of the lake, was founded in 1552 but destroyed by the Mapuches in 1602; the present town, population 36,000, dates from 1882 (DDD 045).

Festival Festival Cultural Mapuche in second week of Feb.

Hotels A3 *Hotel El Ciervo*, Gen Koerner 241, T 411215, German-run, beautiful location, pool, rec; **A3** *Yachting Club*, Av San Martín 802, T 411191, pleasant atmosphere, terraced gardens, swimming pool, restaurant, boating and fishing, but cheaper rooms in motel annex; **A3** *Hostería la Colina*, JA Ríos 1177, overlooking town, T 411503, Casilla 382, run by North Americans, with breakfast, large gardens, good service, good restaurant, highly rec; **B** *Hostería Kiel*, Gen Koerner 153, T 411631, D off season, lakeside, clean, friendly, good; **B** *Hotel y Cabañas El Parque*, 3 km out of Villarrica on Pucón road, T 411120, Casilla 65 (or T Temuco 235872), lakeside with beach, tennis courts, without breakfast, good restaurant set meals, highly rec; *Cabañas Traitraico*, San Martín 380, T 411064, 100m from lake, cabins sleep 6, TV, heating, kitchenette, parking; **C** *Hostería Bilbao*, Henríquez 43, T 411452, good restaurant; **C** *Gerónimo de Alderete*, Gerónimo de Alderete 709, T 411370; **C** *Rayhuen*, Pedro Montt 668, T 411571 (B in summer), clean, good restaurant, good breakfast, lovely garden, rec; **D** *Yandalay*, Henríquez 401, small rooms, good; **D** *Casa San Jorge*, Calle Catedral, is a Scouts' hostel, good value dormitory accommodation; **D** *Fuentes*, Vicente Reyes 665, T 411595, basic, clean, friendly, restaurant; **D** *Hospedaje Dalila Balboa*, San Martín 734, clean, cheap; **E** pp *Hospedaje Las Cabañitas*, Henríquez 398, restaurant, poor reports, owner also has *cabañas* nr lake; **D** *Residencial Villa Linda*, Valdivia 327, T 411392, hot water, clean, basic, cheap, good restaurant; **E** pp *Residencial Victoria*, Muñoz 530, friendly, cooking facilities; **E** pp Vicente Reyes 854, near JAC terminal, good breakfast, poor bathroom facilities. **Youth hostel E** pp *Residencial San Francisco*, Julio Zegers 646, shared rooms. Also, rooms in private homes, eg Calle Francisco Bilbao 969, run by Tom Funk, E pp; at No 537 (Eliana Castillo), E pp, clean, friendly; at No 827 and also V Letelier 702, E pp (open throughout the year); **E** pp Urrutia 407, large breakfast, kitchen, clean; **E** pp Matta 469, cooking facilities, clean.

Camping 2 sites just outside town on Pucón road, *Los Castaños* and *du Lac*, quiet, but buy supplies at *Los Castaños* which is cheaper. Many more on S side of Lake Villarrica, see under Pucón (below). Also 25 km S of Villarrica (1 hr, US$1 bus), at Lican-Ray on Lago Calafquén (see below). Bus leaves from near tourist office. Summer houses available in Dec-Feb.

Restaurants *Club Social*, P de Valdivia 640, good; *El Rey de Mariscos*, Letelier 1030, good seafood; *Rapa Nui*, V Reyes 678, good and cheap, closed Sun; *Hotel Yandaly*, Henríquez 401, good food, rec; *Panaderías*, at Gral de Aldunate 632 and 635; *Café 2001*, Henríquez 379, coffee and ice-cream, good.

Exchange Banco de Osorno changes TCs; *Casa de Cambio*, O'Higgins 210, poor rates for TCs; also Carlos Huerta, Anfión Muñoz 417, for TCs and cash (dollars and Argentine pesos—rec that only men deal with him). Rates are generally poor.

Laundry Lavandería y Lavaseco Villarrica, Andrés Bello 348, T 411449.

Post Office Anfión Muñoz y Urrutia, open 0830-1230, 1400-1800 (Mon-Fri), 0830-1230 (Sat). Telex service also available. Entel, Reyes 721. CTC, C Henríquez 430.

Tourist Office Valdivia 1070; information and maps (open all day all week in summer).

Travel Agencies *Pesky Tour*, Leterlier 650, T 411385; *Trigal*, P Montt 365, T 411078.

Buses To **Santiago**, 10 hrs, US$15-20. To **Pucón**, in summer every 30 mins, 40 mins journey, US$1; to **Valdivia** (JAC, Reyes 616), US$2.50, 3 a day, 2½ hrs; daily service to **Panguipulli** at 0700, US$2, scenic ride. To **Coñaripe** (US$1.50) and **Liquiñe** at 1600 Mon-Sat, 1000 Sun. **Temuco**, JAC, US$2. To **Loncoche** (road and railway junction), US$1.15. **NB** JAC has 2 terminals: long distance at Reyes y Montt, local on Reyes between Henríquez y Muñoz. To **Argentina** at 0615 on Tues, Thur and Sat with Empresa San Martín (Av A Muñoz 417) and at 0730 on Mon, Wed and Fri with Igi-Llaima, US$12, but passes can be blocked for four months by snow. If Tromen Pass is closed, buses go via Panguipulli instead of Pucón.

Some 65 km NE of Villarrica is **Lago Colico** in a wild, remote setting. A road follows the lake's northern shore leading to the northern tip of Lago Caburgua (see **Excursions** from Pucón).

Pucón, a most attractive town on the S-eastern shore of Lago Villarrica, is 26 km E of Villarrica. Pucón has a good climate and first-class accommodation. The black sand beach is very popular for swimming and watersports on the lake (prices given below). The season is from 15 Dec to 15 Mar, when the town is crowded and expensive. Off season it is very pleasant but many places are closed. There is a pleasant walk to La Península for fine views of the lake and volcano, pony rides, golf, etc (private land owned by an Apart-Hotel, you must get permission first). There is another pleasant *paseo*, the Otto Gudenschwager, which starts at the lake end of Ansorena (beside *Gran Hotel Pucón*) and goes along the shore. Launch excursion from the landing stage at La Poza at end of O'Higgins at 1500 and 1900, US$4 for 2 hrs. There is a large handicraft centre where you can see spinning and weaving in progress. The town is scheduled for major development, with plans to build on La Península and around La Poza, the yacht harbour. It now supersedes Villarrica as the tourist centre for the lake. There is a suggestion that greater emphasis will be given to watersports with, possibly, the banning of swimming (in Feb 1994, swimming was forbidden because of pollution). Besides the lake, other attractions nearby include whitewater rafting. A Villarrica-Pucón Centro de Ski has been built (see **Skiing** below) so that Pucón is also a winter sports centre.

Hotels In summer, Dec to Feb, add 20% to hotel prices; at this time rooms may be hard to find—plenty of alternatives (usually cheaper) in Villarrica. Off-season it is often possible to negotiate for accommodation. **L1** *Antumalal*, luxury class, 30m above the shore, 2 km from Pucón, T 441011, F 441013, very small (18 rm), picturesque chalet-type, with magnificent views of the lake (take breakfast or lunch on terrace), lovely gardens, excellent, with meals, open year round, good beach and swimming pool, and good fishing up the river; state owned **L3** *Gran Pucón*, Holzapfel 190, T 441001, half board, **L2** full board, remodelled, restaurant, disco, sports and recreation centre (swimming, gym, squash, etc) shared with **L3** *Condominio Gran Hotel* apartments; **L3** *Interlaken*, Caupolicán, on lakeside 10 mins from town, T 441276, F 441242, Swiss run, chalets, rec, water skiing, golf, pool, will exchange TCs (only open Nov-Apr), no restaurant; **A1** *Araucarias*, Caupolicán 243, T 441963, F 441286, clean, comfortable but not luxurious; **A2** *Gudenschwager*, Pedro de Valdivia 12, T 441904, classic Bavarian type, views over lake, volcano and mountains, attentive staff, comfortable, excellent restaurant, (open in summer only); **A2** *Hostería El Principito*, Av Gral Urrutia 291, T 441200, with bath, good breakfast, clean, very friendly, rec; **A3** *La Posada*, Valdivia 191, T 441088, with bath, cheaper without, full board available, also spacious cabins (C low season); **C** *Hostería Suiza*, O'Higgins 112, T 441945, clean, has a small café which is cheap and serves excellent empanadas; **C** *Salzburg*, O'Higgins 311, T 441907, with bath and breakfast, rec, German spoken, some rooms with view over volcano (possible to borrow crampons); **C** *Turista*, O'Higgins 136, T 441153 (D low season), with bath, friendly, clean; **D** *Goldapfel*, O'Higgins 136A, clean, cooking facilities; **D** *Hospedaje De La Montaña*, O'Higgins 472, T 441267, good value, clean, TV, central, restaurant, no heating, next to JAC buses; **D** *Hostería Milla Rahue*, Av O'Higgins 460, T 441904, clean, good inexpensive restaurant, convenient for JAC; **D** *Residencial Lincoyán*, Av Lincoyán, T 441144, with bath, cheaper without, clean and comfortable; **D** pp *Saint John*, hostería and campsite, 2 km on Villarrica road, open Dec-Mar, full board available, Casilla 154, T 441165/92; **D** *Hospedaje La Casita*, Palguín 555, kitchen facilities, motorcycle parking; **D** *Hospedaje Gerlach*, Palguín 460, clean, kitchen facilities, helpful.

The following are all **D**, or **E** pp: *Don Pepe*, Urrutia 592, T 441081, incl breakfast, good, restaurant is quite cheap; Familia Acuña, Palguín 233 (ask at *peluquería* next door), without breakfast, hot water, kitchen and laundry facilities, dirty, good meeting place. On Lincoyán: Juan Torres, No 445, T 441248, clean, cooking facilities (log fires in winter), very friendly, information on climbing Villarrica and the Huerquehue National Park; *El Refugio*, No 348, with breakfast, good; *Hospedaje Sonia*, No 485, T 441269, hot showers, very popular, meals, upper rooms better, friendly, rec; *Casa de Familia*, Don Juan, No 815, cooking facilities (information on climbing Villarrica); Irma Torres, No 545, with breakfast, cooking facilities, clean; No 565, friendly, clean, safe, quiet, rec; next door is Sra Lucila Oliva (Pasaje Chile 225), kitchen facilities, rec; **E** Adriana Molina, No 312, with breakfast, clean, helpful. *Hospedaje Cherpas*, Fresia 161, T 441089, kitchen facilities, warm and friendly; *Hospedaje Graciela*, Pasaje Rolando Matus 521 (off Av Brasil), good food and atmosphere; Irma Villena, Arauco 460, clean, friendly, rec; Perú 720, use of kitchen, helps organize excursions to Volcán Villarrica and Huerquehue National Park; **F** pp Roberto y Alicia Abreque, Perú 170, basic, popular, use of kitchen, laundry facilities, information on excursions; *Casa Richard*, Uruguay 539, basic but friendly, cooking facilities; many other families have rooms, especially on Calles Perú, Uruguay and Paraguay—look for the signs or ask in bars/restaurants, eg next to garage opp *Gran Hotel Pucón.*

Camping Buy supplies in Villarrica (cheaper). Site next to lake, 20 mins walk from town, US$10 for two. There are several campsites between Villarrica and Pucón: *Acapulco, Playa Linda* (Villarrica), *Suyay, Lorena*, 10 km from Villarrica (also rents *cabañas*); *Huimpalay*, 12 km from Villarrica; *Millaray*, 7 km S of Pucón; *Trancura* and *Saltos del Molco*. In fact, there are so many establishments along the lake's southern shore that you cannot get to the water's edge unless staying in one. Camping is also possible in gardens, US$2.50 pp with use of bathroom. On the road to Tromen Pass, *Cabañas El Dorado*, US$18 for 2, good site, poorly maintained. Cheaper sites en route to Caburga. **Camping Equipment:** *Eltit*, O'Higgins y Fresia; *Mawinda*, Ansorena 485.

Restaurants *Pizzería Che Thomas*, Palguín 465, good value, small place run by Jorge; *El Fogón*, O'Higgins 480, very good; *El Refugio*, Lincoyán 348, *Le Demago*, Lincoyán 361 (plus *Pub Naf-Naf*); *Carnes Orlando*, bar/restaurant/butcher's shop, Ansorena nr Urrutia; *Club 77*, Av O'Higgins, excellent trout; *Pastelería Suiza*, next to *Hostería Suiza* at O'Higgins 116, good; *Café de Brasil*, Fresia 477, good, especially pancakes. *Holzapfel Backerei*, Clemente Holzapfel 524, German cafe/restaurant, rec.

Exchange Banco del Estado de Chile, O'Higgins casi Lincoyán, does not change cash or TCs. Many *casas de cambio* on O'Higgins, poor rates. Big supermarket on O'Higgins changes TCs.

Laundry on Calle Fresia close to *Gran Hotel Pucón*; Colo-Colo 475 and 478.

Post Office Fresia 813. **Telephone** International service at O'Higgins 170.

Horse riding Horse hire US$5 per hour.

Watersports Water-skiing, sailing, windsurfing at the beach by *Gran Hotel* and La Poza beach end of O'Higgins (more expensive than hotel, not rec); hotel rates: waterskiing US$10 for 15 mins, Laser sailing US$5/hour, US$25/day, sailboards about the same, rowing boats US$4-8/hr.
  Whitewater rafting is very popular; many agencies offer trips (see below), charging about US$12.50-17.50 pp for 3 hrs.

Skiing on the slopes of the Villarrica volcano, where there are 7 lifts (US$12 full day, US$18 weekends). Season is from Jul to Nov. Equipment rental US$15 per day, US$82 per week; lessons available.

Fishing Pucón and Villarrica are celebrated fishing centres, for the lake and the very beautiful Lincura, Trancura and Toltén rivers. The fishing is now reported to be even better further S, in Lago Ranco (**see p 712**) for example. Local tourist office will supply details on licences and open seasons etc. Some tourist agencies also offer fishing trips, US$12-20.

Travel Agents On O'Higgins: *Sol y Nieve* (esq Lincoyán, also at *Grán Hotel Pucón*), good reports; *Altue*, No 371, *Nacional Travel Club*, No 323, *Trancura*, No 211, T 441959/441189 (good reports); *El Conquistador*, No 323, *Apumanque*, No 412, T 441085. Also *Turismo Florencia*, T/F 441267. All arrange trips to thermal baths, trekking to volcanoes, whitewater rafting, etc (prices: whitewater rafting and riding, see above; climbing Villarrica, US$35-40, 12 hrs, equipment provided; mountain bike hire from US$5/hr to US$20/day; tours to Termas de Huife, US$20 including entry. Shop around: prices vary at times, quality of guides and equipment variable. *Sergio Catalán*, T 441269 (office) or 441142, Gerónimo Alderete 192, tours, excursions and taxi service all year round. *Sherpa*, Ansorena 355, T 441070, rec for climbing expeditions and hire of equipment. Taxi excursions from O'Higgins y Ansorena.

Tourist Information Sernatur, Av Caupolicán y Av Brasil, very helpful, ask here about all types of accommodation; Cema-Chile shop at same location. Municipal Tourist Office at O'Higgins y Palguín will provide information and sell fishing licences (US$1/month). **Ancient Forest International** provides information on Chilean rainforests from its office in the *Hotel Don Pepe*.

Taxis Cooperative, T 441009; individual member Oscar Jara Carrasco, T 411992 (home in Villarrica).

Car Hire Hertz, Fresia 220, US$65 for cheapest car (incl tax, insurance, and 200 km free); same prices per day at *Gran Hotel*. **Bicycle Hire** Taller el Pollo, Palguín 500 block and Trancura, O'Higgins 261, US$10-12 per day. Try also travel agencies, eg *Sol y Nieve*.

Bus JAC terminal: O'Higgins 480, T 441923, for **Villarrica**, **Temuco** (US$2.50, about 20 a day) and **Valdivia** (0630, 1545, 1845, US$3.50) by JAC and others. At Palguín 383, agency for Servi-Tur, Tur-Bus—sleeper bus to the capital, Inter Sur, Fénix, Power (cheapest, least comfortable) and Igi-Llaima. LIT, for Temuco and Santiago, O'Higgins y Palguín. Cordillera, Av Miguel Ansorena (nr O'Higgins, next to minimarket) for **Paillaco** and **Lago Caburgua**—see below. Colectivos to **Villarrica** from O'Higgins y Palguín. **Buses to Argentina**: Buses from Temuco to Junín pass through Pucón, fares are the same as from Temuco.

Excursions from Pucón may be made to the active **Villarrica** volcano in the **Villarrica National Park** 8 km S of the town (entry US$6). Following a number of deaths in recent years, restrictions on access to the park have been imposed: entry is usually only permitted to groups with a guide, charge US$35-40 including transport to park entrance and hire of equipment (but not park entry fee); at the park entrance equipment is checked; entry is refused if the weather is poor. Note that travel agencies will not start out if the weather is bad. Establish in advance what terms apply in the event of cancellation and be prepared to wait a few days. Do not under any circumstances attempt this climb alone. There is a refuge without beds 4 km inside the Park, insecure and in desperate need of renovation. Campsite with drinking water, toilets, below refuge. The volcano can be climbed up and down in 8-9 hrs (go in summer when days are longer), good boots, iceaxe and crampons, sunglasses, plenty of water and sun block essential. Beware of sulphur fumes at the top—take a cloth mask moistened with lemon juice. Guides, see above under Travel Agents. Also Alvaro Martínez, Cristóbal Colón 430; Juan Torres, Lincoyán 445; Juan Carlos, at Oliva's *pensión*, or his pool room on main street, rec. Many others, all with equipment; beware charlatans, ask at the tourist office. Crampons, ice axe, sunglasses can be rented for US$3.60/day from the Taller El Pollo bicycle shop (aaddress above).

To volcanic **Lago Caburgua**, very pretty, to the NE, in wild setting (row-boats may be hired, US$1.50 per hour). Lago Caburgua is unusual for its beautiful white sand beach (3 km from Caburgua village) whereas other beaches in the area are black sand of volcanic origin (campsite, T 236989, expensive in season, US$2.50 car, US$6.50 tent, but cheap out of season, US$2.50 for tent). Visit also the **Ojos de Caburgua**, some 30 km NE of Pucón, beautiful pools fed from underground, particularly attractive after rainfall (entry US$0.50). Cordillera bus departs 1230, returns 1400, 2nd bus (in summer only) leaves 1700 and returns next morning (US$1 single), but there are colectivos or you can try hitching. If walking or cycling to Lago Caburgua, turn left 3 km E of Pucón (sign to Puente Quelhue) and follow track for 18 km through beautiful scenery, rec. No shops, so take own food. Three more beautiful lakes are Verde, Chico and Toro in the **Huerquehue National Park**, W of Lago Caburgua. For all these lakes, the turn off from the main road is 8 km E of Pucón. Paving ends at the bridge over the Río Pucón, by Metreñehue; the road continues as gravel to Lago Caburgua. 3 km before Caburgua a road turns right to Paillaco, after which the surface is yellow earth, very dusty (use lights) and quite slippery in the dry, treacherously slippery after rain. For Huerquehue, take Cordillera bus to Paillaco, beyond Caburgua, 1½ hrs, US$1, from where it's 7 km (3 uphill, 3 down, 1 along Lago Tinquilco) to park entrance (entry US$1.60), where there is a campsite. 1½ km before the Huerquehue Park entrance, two German speaking families—the Braatz and Soldans offer accommodation (F pp, no electricity), food and camping (US$1.50); they also rent rowing boats on the lake. Park open officially only Jan-Mar, but you can get in at other times. Warden very helpful; people in park rent horses and boats. Take your own food.

From the car park at Lago Tinquilco there is a well-signed track to Lagos Verde, Chico and Toro (for those with cars there is a private car park, US$0.50, 1½ km along the track). The track zig-zags up (sign says 5 km, but worth it) to Lago Chico, then splits left to Toro, right to Verde. From Toro you can continue to Lago Huerquehue and Lago de los Palos (camping); there is no connecting path from Toro to Lago Verde, which is beautifully surrounded by trees. In Huerquehue there are 20 lakes in all and their outlines keep changing.

Outside the Huerquehue Park are the *Huife* thermal baths (*Hostería Termas de Huife*, T 441222, PO Box 18, Pucón), US$8, including use of one pool, modern, pleasant, picnicking not allowed (taxi from Pucón, US$23 return with taxi waiting, US$16 one way). Termas de

Quimaico can be reached from the road to Huife: new, less ostentatious than Huife, camping allowed, 2 cabins and *hostería* (*centro turístico* under construction). There are also thermal baths at San Luis, 25 km E of Pucón and N of the road to Curarrehue (bus Pucón-Curarrehue passes 2 km from the baths), small hotel, 1/2 hr walk to Lago del León. South of the same road, and 36 km SE of Pucón, there are further baths at *Palguín* (**A1** *Hotel*—address, Casilla 1D, Pucón, T 441968—full board, B in small huts with bath, run down, poor food, German-speaking owner, cool swimming pool, baths US$5). Taxi rates are same as for Huife. Nearby is the **D** *Rancho de Caballos*, offering accommodation, also *cabañas* and camping, good food, tours (write to Cristina Bonninghoff, *Rancho de Caballos*, Casilla 142, Pucón). There are many hikeable waterfalls in the area; eg, 6-7 km from the turn-off for Termas de Palguín, Salto Palguín can be seen, but not reached, a further 2 km Salto China (spectacular, entry US$0.40, restaurant, camping); one more km to Salto del Puma (free) and Salto del León (US$0.60), both spectacular and 800m from the Termas. From Pucón take Bus Regional Villarrica from Palguín y O'Higgins at 1100 to the junction (10 km from Termas); last bus from junction to the Termas at 1500, so you may have to hitch back. Nearby is the entrance to the **Quetrupillán** section of the Villarrica National Park (high clearance vehicle necessary, horses best), free camping in the park, *refugio* at first campsite. Ask rangers for the route to the other entrance.

Two excursions from Pucón close to Lago Villarrica: 2-km walk N along the beach to the mouth of the Río Pucón, with views of the volcanoes Villarrica, Quetrupillán and Lanín. To cross the Río Pucón: head E out of Pucón along the main road, then turn N on an unmade road leading to a new bridge, upstream from the old ferry crossing to La Reducción de Quelhue, near the N bank. This is supposed to be a Mapuche village, but no traditional dress, language or customs are used, and the children ask for money. From here there are pleasant walks along the N shore of the lake to Quelhue and Travilelfu, or NE towards Caburgua, or up into the hills through farms and agricultural land, with views of the three volcanoes and, higher up, of the lake.

There is a road from Pucón to the Argentine town of Junín de los Andes. The route runs E to Curarrehue, with the volcanoes of Villarrica and Quetrupillán to the S and then turns S to the Chilean customs post at *Puesco* (free CONAF campsite, no facilities, daily bus from Pucón, 1800, 2½, US$2). From here the road deteriorates, running E via Lago Quellelhue, a gem set between mountains at 1,196m above sea level to the frontier at the Tromen Pass. To the S of the Pass is the graceful cone of Lanín volcano (3,747m—see under Junín de los Andes, **Argentina, Section 9**), and beyond the border is Lago Tromen, much visited by Argentine tourists. Conaf campsite 5 km from border, on a good dirt road by Lago Tromen, no amenities. On the Argentine side the road from the border runs S to Junín de los Andes and then continues S to San Martín de los Andes, and via Lago Hermoso and Villa Angostura (a beautiful drive) to Bariloche. There is a more direct road from San Martín de los Andes to Bariloche but it is not so interesting (see under Argentina, **The Route to Chile from Bariloche** in Section 9).

30 km S of Villarrica (fully paved) and 125 km SE of Temuco is **Lican-Ray**, with 2 good beaches, on the N shore of Lago Calafquén, full of islands. Boats can be hired from the beach (US$1.50 an hour). The resort is very crowded in season. Several buses daily in summer from Villarrica (JAC—7 a day, 3 on Sun— and García, Reyes y Henríquez, also frequent colectivos, US$0.60) and, in Jan-Feb, there are frequent direct buses from Santiago and Temuco. 6 km to the E is the river of lava formed when the Villarrica volcano erupted in 1971. Buses Mon-Sat at 0730 from Lican-Ray to Panguipulli.

Hotels (most closed out of season) *Bellavista*, Cacique Punulef 240; **A3** *Refugio*, Canadian-owned, on Playa Grande, open all year, has a Travellers' Exchange Library for English-language books, all donations of paperbacks (in reasonable condition) welcome. **D** *Cabinas Los Pinos*, 3 blocks from lake, nice; **D** *Rio Negro*, Gerónimo 776; **E** pp *Residencia Temuco*, G Mistral 515, clean, hot water, good; *Hospedaje Los Nietos*, on water's edge, by the hire boats; **E** Hugo Linolilli 235; several motels (eg at **C** *Cabañas El Eden*, Huenuman 105, for a chalet for 6 with hot water; *El Conquistador*, Cacique Millaqueo s/n), *hosterías*, and camping sites (eg *Camping Las Gaviotas*, 3 km E). *Café Ñaños*, Gral Urrutia 105, very good, reasonable prices, helpful owner. Also on Urrutia, *Restaurant-Bar Guido's*, good value. Note that by the end of Mar almost everything has closed for the season.

A road runs 14 km SE along the N shore to **Coñaripe**, at the eastern end of Lago Calafquén. At first sight, the village is dusty and nondescript, but its setting, with a black sand beach surrounded by mountains, is very beautiful. There is a good walk from the left-hand side of the beach back through the fields to Coñaripe. This is a popular Chilean tourist spot: the lake is reputedly one of the warmest and is good for swimming. **D** *Hotel Antulafquen*, homely; **E** pp *Hospedaje House*, with breakfast; cheap campsites nr private houses; buses to Panguipulli, 3 a day, US$1 and Villarrica US$1.50. A road around the lake's southern shore leads to Lago Panguipulli (see below).

From Coñaripe a road runs SE to the Carirriñe pass, with a border post for crossing to Argentina en route to San Martín de los Andes. The road climbs the steep Cuesta Los Añiques, with views of Lago Pellaifa. The **Termas de Pellaifa**, (accommodation, restaurant etc at *Centro Termal Coñaripe ex-Pellaifa*), and the **Termas de Liquiñe** (hotel, B pp, cabins, restaurant, hot swimming pool, small native forest; accommodation in private houses, E pp; tours from Lican-Ray in summer, US$17, 0830-1830 with lunch). 6 km before Liquiñe is a road going S (50 km) to meet the Choshuenco-Puerto Fuy road (see below).

The Longitudinal Highway (Ruta 5) runs from Loncoche (81 km S of Temuco, good place for hitching) through Lanco to Paillaco and Osorno. At San José de la Mariquina, a road branches off Ruta 5 to Valdivia, 42 km from the Highway (bus Lanco-Valdivia, Chile Nuevo, US$0.85, 4 a day, fewer at weekends). The road from Valdivia to Ruta 5 going S is not in very good condition; the Highway is rejoined near Paillaco.

Panguipulli, on the W bank of the lake of the same name, is in a beautiful setting, with roses planted in all the streets (the name is Mapuche for 'hill of lions'). It is reached by paved road from Lanco; there are also road connections to Lake Calafquén and Villarrica. For fishermen, daily excursions on Lago Panguipulli are recommended. Excursions can be made to Lagos Panguipulli, Calafquén, Neltume and Pirehueico, and S to the northern tip of Lago Riñihue at **El Desagüe** (**B** *Hotel Riñimapu*, T 388, excellent). There is a new 23-km road around the N shore of the lake to **Choshuenco**, a beautiful coastline, wooded, with cliffs and sandy beaches. Buses daily at 1530 and 1630, US$2, 2½ hrs, but it is not possible to return from Choshuenco on the same day. (Bus returns from Choshuenco at 0645 and 0700.) S of Choshuenco is the Choshuenco volcano, on which Club Andino de Valdivia has ski-slopes and a *refugio*. This can be reached by a turning from the road which goes S from Choshuenco to Enco at the E end of Lago Riñihue (**see p 708**). From Choshuenco another road leads E to **Puerto Fuy** at the N end of Lago Pirehueico. At Km 15 are the waterfalls of **Huilo Huilo**, which are most impressive, the river channels its way through volcanic rock before thundering down into a natural basin. The falls are 4 hrs walk from Choshuenco, or take the bus to Puerto Fuy and get off 1 km before Neltume. Alternatively get off at *Alojamiento Huilo Huilo*, where the road crosses the Huilo Huilo river. From here it is a 1½ hr walk the following day to the falls. From Puerto Fuy a scenic road runs S through rainforest around the Choshuenco volcano to the river Pillanleufú, Puerto Llolles on Lago Maihue and Puerto Llifén on Lago Ranco (see below); we have no up-to-date information on the condition of this road, or whether it is open.

From Puerto Fuy a ferry crosses Lago Pirehueico to **Puerto Pirehueico** US$3, 2-3 hrs. A beautiful crossing (to take vehicles reserve in advance at the *Hotel Quetropillán* in Panguipulli). Schedule varies according to season. From Puerto Pirehueico it is a 4-hr walk to the Argentine frontier crossing at Paso Huahum. Bus daily Puerto Fuy to Panguipulli at 0600, 3 hrs, US$2, except Sun when it runs at 1700.

Hotels Most closed out of season. At **Panguipulli**: **C** *Hostería Quetropillán*, Etchegaray 381, T 348, comfortable, food; **D** *Central*, clean, hot water, friendly, good breakfast, rec; **E** pp *Las Brisas* restaurant, has rooms to let; **E** pp *Residencial La Bomba*, quiet, friendly; **E** pp private house opp *Quetropillán*, clean, good breakfast; **E** pp Sra Pozas, Pedro de Valdivia 251, clean, clothes washing extra; **E** pp Olga Berrocal, JM Carrera 834, small rooms. *Restaurante Valparaíso*, rec; *Café de la Plaza*, O'Higgins 816, good food and coffee; *Café Central*, Martínez de Rosas 880, good cheap lunches, expensive evening meals; several cheap restaurants in O'Higgins 700 block. At **Choshuenco**: **D** *Hotel Choshuenco*, good meals, lovely setting, laundry facilities; various *hosterías*, including **E** pp *Hostería Rayen Trai* (former yacht club), María Alvarado y O'Higgins, good food, open all year, rec; Sra Elena Arrigada, Padre Vernave 198, rec; free camping on the beach. *Restaurant Rucapillán*, lets out rooms. At **Puerto Pirehueico and Puerto Fuy**: beds available in private houses incl the blue farmhouse, **E** pp; camping on the beach, take own food. At **Neltume**, **E** *Pensión Neltume*, meals. At **Huilo Huilo**: **E** pp *Alojamiento Huilo Huilo*, basic but comfortable and well situated for walks, good food, highly rec.

Campsite Chollinco, on Lago Ranco, 8 km from Futrono. Municipal campsite at Panguipulli 1½ km outside town, US$5 with all facilities, rec (closes at end-Feb); free camping on lakeside at Panguipulli possible. Also, at Los Molinos; and at Choshuenco on the lake shore (food shops in the village), and Puerto Fuy on the beach (take your own food, none available to buy).

Exchange Banco de Crédito e Inversiones in Panguipulli changes cash only, minimum transaction US$100. Shops give poor rates.

Tourist Office in plaza next to police station.

Bus from Panguipulli to **Santiago** daily at 1845, US$12; 14 daily (Sun only 4), several lines, from/to **Valdivia**, 2 hrs, US$3 and 9 daily to **Temuco** (eg Power at 1800, 2 hrs, or Pangui Sur, 10 a day, US$2, 3 hrs). To **Puerto Montt**, US$5. To **Calafquén**, 3 daily at 1200, 1545 and 1600. To **Choshuenco** 1530, 1630, US$2, 2½ hrs. To **Puerto Fuy**, 1800, 2½ hrs. To **Coñaripe** (with connections for Lican Ray and Villarrica), 4 a day, 1½ hrs, US$1.40 from depot in Calle Freire, 100m uphill from *Hostería Quetropillán*.

There is a road from Panguipulli to Coñaripe, on Lago Calafquén, which offers superb views of the lake and of Villarrica volcano, whether you are travelling on foot or by bus. Some buses continue to Lican Ray.

Valdivia, 839 km S of Santiago by road, is situated at the confluence of two rivers, the Calle Calle and Cruces which form the Río Valdivia. It is set in rich agricultural land receiving some 2,300mm of rain a year. The capital of Valdivia province, it has a population of 110,000 (DDD 063).

Valdivia was one of the most important centres of Spanish colonial control over Chile. Founded in 1552 by Pedro de Valdivia, it was abandoned as a result of the Mapuche insurrection of 1599 and the area was briefly occupied by Dutch pirates. In 1645 it was refounded as a walled city, the only Spanish mainland settlement S of the Río Biobío. The coastal fortifications at the mouth of the Río Valdivia also date from the 17th century, but were greatly strengthened after 1770 owing to Spanish fears of war with Britain. The capture of Valdivia by the Chilean Navy under Lord Cochrane in 1820, when he seized the forts of Corral, Amargos and San Carlos, was one of the most important stages in the Chilean struggle for independence. From 1850 to 1875 a comparatively small number of German colonists settled in the area; their imprint in terms of architecture and agricultural methods, order, education, social life and custom is still strong. In particular they created numerous industries, some of them on Isla Teja, the island on the N side of the river, where the Universidad Austral de Chile is also situated. On the tree-lined, shady Plaza de la República, a new cathedral is under construction. A pleasant walk is along Avenida Prat (or Costanera), which follows the bend in the river, from the bus station to the bridge to Isla Teja, the boat dock and the riverside market.

Museum Museo Austral, run by University on Isla Teja, cartography, archaeology, history of German settlement (including cemetery), local Indian crafts, etc. Open Tues-Sun, 1000-1300, 1500-1800, US$1. Also on the island, nr the library in the University, a **botanic garden** and **arboretum** with trees from all over the world. 'Lago de los Lotos' in Parque Saval on the island—has beautiful Nov blooms, entry US$0.30.

Festival Semana Valdiviana, 12-18 Feb.

Hotels A3 *Melillanca*, rec, Av Alemania 675, T 212509, F 222740; **A2** *Naguilán*, Gen Lagos 1927, T 212851/52/53, F 219130, clean, quiet, swimming pool, good restaurant; **L3** *Pedro de Valdivia*, Carampangue 190, T/F 212931, with bath, good; **A2** *Villa del Río*, with bath, Av España 1025, T 216292, F 217851, restaurant expensive (try salmon in almond sauce), rents apartments with kitchen; **A3** *Palace*, Chacabuco 308 y Henríquez, T 213319, F 219133, good, comfortable; **A3** *Villa Paulina*, Yerbas Buenas 389, T/F 216372, hot showers, clean, pool,

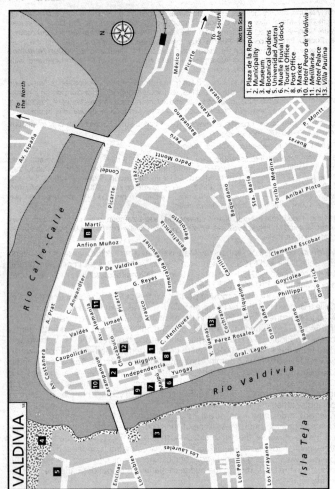

Key:
1. Plaza de la República
2. Municipality
3. Museum
4. Botanical Gardens
5. Universidad Austral
6. Muelle Fluvial (dock)
7. Tourist Office
8. Post Office
9. Market
10. Hotel Pedro de Valdivia
11. Melillanca
12. Hotel Palace
13. Villa Paulina

VALDIVIA

highly rec; **B** *Raitúe*, Gral Lagos 1382, T 212503, with bath; **B** *Hostal Centro Torreón*, P Rosales 783, T 212622, with breakfast, shared bath, old German villa, nice atmosphere, car parking. On Picarte, near bus station, **C** *Hostal Montserrat* (No 849), T 213032, with breakfast, clean, comfortable, highly rec; *Residencial Anilebu*, No 875, T 212186 and **C** *Residencial Germania*, No 873, T 212405, clean but no heat in small rooms, with breakfast; cheaper hotels in same street include No 915, **D** (summer only), Nos 979 and 1005 (no hot water); **E** pp, No 953, opposite bus terminal, with breakfast, good value, clean, heated lounge; **D** *Hospedaje Elsa Martínez*, No 737, T 212587, clean, friendly, highly rec. **D** *Hospedaje Triviños*, Gral Lagos 1080, clean, good beds, cooking facilities, also dormitory accommodation; **D** *Hospedaje* at Arauco 905, clean, friendly; **D** *Prat*, Prat 595, T 222020, with good breakfast, clean; **D** *Unión*, Prat 514, T 213819, central, good value. Student *pensiones* incl Arauco 852; **E** pp *Hospedaje Turismo*, Gral Lagos 874, T 215946, with breakfast, old German house, pleasant family atmosphere, rec; **E** *Hospedaje Universitaria*, Serrano 985, T 218775, breakfast, hot water, clean, cheap meals, rec; **E** pp *Hospedaje Lodging*, Pérez Rosales 1037, T 215607, cooking facilities, family accommodation, clean, highly rec; **E** pp *Hostal Cochrane*, Cochrane 595, with breakfast; **E** pp Baquedano 664, incl breakfast (but avoid laundry service). The house at Aníbal Pinto 1335 (T 3880) is friendly and cheap; also **E** pp in Aníbal Pinto, No 980, use of kitchen; **D** *pensión* of Sra Armida Navarrete Uribe, Phillippi 878, full board if desired, hot water, good value. **E** pp Riquelme 15, T 218909, with breakfast, friendly, clean, good value; **E** pp Henríquez 747, lovely villa in gardens, friendly, large rooms, laundry facilities, clean, highly rec. On A Muñoz, near bus station: **E** pp *Hospedaje* de Señora A de Prussing, No 345, with breakfast, clean, friendly; **E** pp Sra Segovia, No 353, breakfast, hot water, rec. On Beauchef: **E** pp *María Farías Flores*, No 684, T 215826, clean, friendly; **E** pp *Ana María Vera*, No 669, T 218542, clean, friendly, hot water, good breakfast; **E** pp No 620, with breakfast. Sra Paredes, García Reyes 244, D with breakfast, hot water, rec. On Calle Anwandter: **E** pp No 624, with breakfast, comfortable, friendly; **E** pp *Hospedaje Carlos Andwandter*, No 482, clean, hot water; **E** pp No 802.

Campsite Camping Centenario, in Rowing Club on España, E per tent, overlooking river. Also in Parque Saval. White gas impossible to find, other than in pharmacies/chemists.

Restaurants *Centro Español*, Calle Henríquez 436, good, lunch US$3.50; *Club de la Unión*, on Plaza, serves a good, cheap lunch; *Sociedad Protectora de EECC*, Independencia y Libertad, near Plaza, good seafood; *El Conquistador*, on plaza at O'Higgins, on 1st floor, good food, reasonable prices, live music at weekends; *Dino*, good, Plaza de la República (Maipú 191); *Palace*, Arauco y P Rosales 580, popular, good atmosphere, expensive; *Pizzerón*, Henríquez 314, cheap, good, popular; *Delicias*, C Henríquez 372, rec for meals and cakes (open Sun am); *Selecta*, Av Ramón Picarte 1093, pleasant, excellent fish and meat, not cheap; *Shanghai*, Henríquez 326, pleasant Chinese, reasonably priced. *Fértil Provincia*, Maipú 60, café, bookshop, cultural events, good meeting place, rec; *Café Haussmann*, O'Higgins 394 (good tea and cakes); *Phoenix Haus*, Av Viel s/n, on Isla Teja; restaurant in boat house, good seafood; several restaurants on the Costanera facing the boat dock, have good food and good atmosphere: *Bar Olimpia*, Costanera Prat nr Tourist Office, always full, 24 hrs, cheap, good meeting point; *Ipanema*, Picarte 483, good value lunches; *Entrelagos*, Pérez Rosales 622, ice cream and chocolates. Bakery: *La Baguette*, Libertad 110, French-style cakes, brown bread.

Exchange Banco del Estado at Arauca y Camilo Henríquez (huge commission on TCs). Good rates for cash at **Banco Osorno**, P Rosales 585, **Banco Concepción** (Visa), Picarte 370, will change cash and TCs. **Turismo Cochrane**, Arauco y Caupolicán. **Fincard** (Mastercard), Picarte 334, Mon-Fri 0900-1400, 1500-1930, Sat 0900-1330. *Casa de Cambio* at Carampangue 325, T 213305, open 0800-2100 Mon-Fri, also open Sat and Sun. Cash changed at *Restaurant Shanghai* (see above).

Laundry *Au Chic*, Arauco 436; *Lavazul*, Chacabuco 300, slow. Coin laundry *Autoservicio*, Schmidt y Picarte (Mon-Sat 0900-2030).

Film Fotoquideon, Picarte 417 for developing.

Clubs Santa Elvira Golf Club (9 holes); tennis, sailing, motor, and rowing clubs like Phoenix on Teja Island.

Car Hire Hertz, Aguirre Cerda 1154, T 218316; **Turismo Méndez**, Gral Lagos 1249, T 233205.

Tourist Office Calle Arturo Prat 555, by dock, T 213596. Good map of region and local rivers, list of hotel prices and examples of local crafts with artisans' addresses. Helpful kiosk in bus station next to the news stand. **Conaf**, Ismael Valdéz 431. **Automóvil Club de Chile**, Caupolicán 475, T 212378, also for car hire.

Air LanChile, Arauco 159, of 201, T 213042. Ladeco (Caupolicán 579, local 18, T 213392) to/from Santiago every day via Temuco.

Rail Station at Ecuador 2000, off Av Picarte, T 214978. To **Santiago**, one a day, 14 hrs, bus Valdivia-Temuco 2¾ hrs, then change to train.

Bus Terminal is at Muñoz and Arturo Prat, by the river. To **Santiago**: several companies, 13 hrs, most services overnight, US$12-17, *salón cama* US$25; Pullman daily to and from central and southern towns. Half-hourly buses to **Osorno**, 1 hr 40 mins, several companies, US$2-3. 4 a day to **Llifén**, US$2.50. 25 buses daily to **Panguipulli**, US$3. Many daily to **Puerto Montt**, US$7-9, 3 hrs. To **Puerto Varas**, 3 hrs, US$6. To **Frutillar**, on Pullman Sur Temuco-Puerto Montt bus, US$2.75, 3 hrs. To **Villarrica**, by Bus JAC, 6 a day, 2½ hrs, US$2.50 continuing to Pucón, US$3.50, 3 hrs. Frequent daily service to Riñihue via Paillaco and Los Lagos. To **Bariloche** via Osorno (10 hrs) with Bus Norte, US$22, and Tas Choapa, 5 a week. To **Zapala** (Argentina),

Igi-Llaima, Mon, Thur, Sat, 2300, change bus in Temuco at 0200, arrive Zapala 1200-1500, depending on border, US$34.

Excursions The district has a lovely countryside of woods, beaches, lakes and rivers. The various rivers are navigable and there are pleasant journeys to Futa, Putabla, and San Antonio, behind Isla Teja and through the Tornagaleanes, the Isla del Rey (these journeys can only be made in a rented motor boat). Among the waterways are countless little islands, cool and green.

At the mouth of the Río Valdivia are remains of the fortifications built by the Spanish to defend the entry to Valdivia. There are two centres for visiting the area, *Niebla* on the N bank and *Corral* on the S. In all there are the ruins of 17 forts but the principal ones to see are the following: the Fuerte de la Pura y Limpia Concepción de Monfort de Lemus, a substantial earthwork fort on a promontory W of Niebla (entry US$0.75, closed Mon, opens 0900-1000 in winter). It was partially restored in 1992 and has an interesting museum on this area of Chilean maritime history. Opposite it, in Corral, the Castillo de San Sebastián with a museum and battery of 24 guns and a view upriver to Volcán Llaima in the distance; Castillo San Luis de Alba, in poor condition, in Amargos, 40 mins walk along the coast from Corral; and, in midstream, the Castillo de San Pedro de Alcántara on *Isla Mancera*. This last has the most standing buildings; all are national monuments. Niebla is also a bathing resort with seafood restaurants and accommodation (**D** *Hostería Riechers*; *Cabañas Fischers*, C per cabin; 2 campsites, worth bargaining out of season; **E** *Santa Clara Restaurante Jardín Delicias*, with 'a view that would be worth the money even if the food weren't good'); information and telephone office by the fort. 6 km further round the coast is Los Molinos, a seaside resort set among steep wooded hills. The fishing port of Corral has several restaurants (eg *Español*, Av 6 de Mayo, opp the dock, good seafood, note the shell floor), and **E** *Residencial Mariel*, Tarapacá, modern, clean, friendly, good value, and *Hostería La Nave*. Also in Corral is a small tourist office (closed 1300-1400) with a museum attached, entry US$0.25. 4 km along the coast from Corral is San Carlos, with its **E** *Hostería los Alamos*, a delightful hideout for those seeking a quiet life. West and S of San Carlos the coastal walks are splendid. Isla Mancera is a pleasant place to stopover on the boat trips, but it has no accommodation or restaurants and gets crowded when an excursion boat arrives.

The tourist boats (*Neptuno* or *Calle-Calle*) to Isla Mancera and Corral, including a guided half-day tour (US$20 with meals—cheaper without) leave the Muelle Fluvial, Valdivia (behind the tourist office on Av Prat 555), 1330 daily. Cheaper local boats to Corral leave 5 times a day, from 0800, from Muelle Fluvial, Valdivia and return between 0800 and 1900, 1½-hr journey; only twice a day in winter; they usually go out via Niebla (ferry dock is 20 mins walk from the fort, near the Copec station) and call at Isla Mancera (if you want to stop en route, you must first pay full fare, US$0.75 then US$0.75 for each 'leg'; some boats make a 1¼-hr stopover on Isla Mancera en route back to Valdivia). The river trip is beautiful, but you can also take a bus to Niebla from Chacabuco y Yungay, Valdivia, roughly every 20 mins between 0730 and 2100, 20 mins, US$0.70 (bus continues to Los Molinos), then cross to Corral by boat (US$0.50) and return to Valdivia by river. There are occasional buses from Valdivia to Corral.

Mehuin, on the coast, 2 hrs bus ride N from Valdivia, US$2, through San José de La Mariquina; post office, good sea bathing and several hotels: **C** *Hostería Millalafquen*, T 279; **D** *Mehuin*, not very inviting; *Playa*; **E** *Hospedaje Marbella*, clean, cheapest. Queule, 6 km from Mehuin, has two simple *residenciales*. Good beach but bathing dangerous at high tide because of undercurrents; safer to bathe in the river nr ferry.

A beautiful, unpaved route runs E from Valdivia along the Río Calle Calle to *Los Lagos* (61 km; **D** *Hotel Roger*, Lynch 42, T 261, rec; *Turismo Tell*, 10 km E, cabañas and campsite, T 09-653-2440, English, French and German spoken; 2 buses a day in summer), and on to the beautiful **Lago Riñihue** (39 km). The road around the southern edge of the lake from Riñihue to Enco is now closed (except to jeeps in summer only), so Choshuenco at the SE end of Lago Panguipulli can only be reached by road from Panguipulli or Puerto Fuy. Riñihue, a beautiful but very small and isolated village at the western end of the lake, is worth a visit. Campsite by the lake; *Restaurant del Lago* has rooms, **E** (no meals).

Access from the Longitudinal Highway to lovely, island-starred **Lago Ranco** and to **Lago Maihue** further E is made from Los Lagos, or from a point 18 km S of Los Lagos, 11 km N of Paillaco. These two roads join to meet the road around the lake some 5 km W of *Futrono* on the northern shore. From Futrono (accommodation in the Casa Parroquial, F pp) the road curves round the N of Lago

Ranco to **Llifén**, a picturesque place on the eastern shore. From Llifén, a visit can be paid to Lago Maihue (Cordillera Sur bus Valdivia-Llifén twice daily, once Sun).

Hotels A1 *Huequecura*, Casilla 4, T 09-653-5450, including meals and fishing services, good restaurant. **B** *Hostería Chollinco*, 3 km out of town on the road towards Lago Maihue, T 0638-202, limited electricity, swimming pool. **C** *Hostería Lican*, T 09-653-5315, F Valdivia 218921. 4 campsites in the vicinity.

From Llifén the road continues round the lake to **Riñinahue** (*hostería*, A3) and Lago Ranco, an ugly little town on the S shore (several small hotels, *residenciales*, houses to let in summer—see below for bus from Osorno). The road is terrible (lots of mud and animals, including oxcarts), but is worth taking to see an older lifestyle, the beautiful lake, waterfalls and sunsets on the distant volcanoes (if walking, beware the numerous guard dogs in the area). There is excellent fishing on the S shore of the lake. On the western shore is **Puerto Nuevo** (hotel of same name, A1, very good, watersports, fishing on the Río Bueno). Roads from Puerto Nuevo and Lago Ranco run W to La Unión (*Hotel Club Alemán*, Letelier 497, T 322695), which is bypassed by the Longitudinal Highway.

Río Bueno is at the crossroads of the Lago Ranco-La Unión road and the Highway (Ruta 5). Some 42 km S of this point is Osorno, another centre for exploring the Lakes.

Osorno (pop 103,000; DDD 064) , 921 km from Santiago and 105 km N of Puerto Montt, was founded in 1558. It was destroyed shortly after its foundation, and was later settled by German immigrants, whose descendants are still of great importance in the area. The city has some old wooden buildings mixed in with the new (eg on Calle Mackenna). On the large Plaza de Armas stands the modern, concrete cathedral, with many arches, repeated in the tower, itself an open, latticed arch with a cross superimposed. Behind the new railway station is the Fuerte Reina Luisa, constructed 1793, restored 1977, with only the river front walls and end turrets standing. The old railway station, down the line from the new, is almost derelict, but its forecourt is used by some buses and shops.

Museum Museo Histórico Municipal, Matta 809. Entrance in Casa de Cultura, free; Mon-Fri 1000-1200, 1500-1830, Sat 1100-1300, 1600-1800: old photos, archaeology and anthropology, history, natural history.

Hotels L3 *Del Prado*, Cochrane 1162, T 235020, swimming pool, garden, good meals, well-located, charming; **A1** *Waeger*, Cochrane 816, T 233721, PO Box 802, F 237080, 4-star, restaurant, comfortable, rec; **A3** *Inter-Lagos*, Cochrane 515, T 234695; **B** *Gran* (good restaurant), main square, O'Higgins 615, T 233990, with bath, renovated; **B** *Tirol*, Bulnes 630, T 233593, with bath; **C** *Residencial Riga*, Amthauer 1058, T 232945, highly rec but heavily booked in season; **C** *Villa Eduviges*, Eduviges 856, T 235023, good, rec. **D** *Melchor*, Errázuriz 1502, English spoken, basic, also food; **D** *Residencial Aitué*, Freire 546, T 239922, spotless, friendly, TV; **D** *Residencial* at Amunátegui 520, run by Sra Gallardo, near bus terminal, good; **D** *Residencial Hein*, Cochrane 843, T 234116, breakfast US$1.80, pleasant; **D** *Residencial Schulz*, Freire 530, T 237211, with breakfast, hot water, other meals extra; **D** *Hospedaje Eliano del Río Cortés*, Bulnes 876; **D** *Germania*, Rodríguez 741, no hot water, cooking facilities; **D** *Residencial Ortega*, Colón 602, nr Errázuriz, 1 block from bus terminal, parking, basic, clean, terrible beds, toilet facilities limited; **D** *San Fernando*, Bulnes 836; others nr bus terminal: at A Pinto 1758, E incl breakfast and hot water, T 238024; **D** Los Carrera 1387, 50m from bus terminal, basic, friendly, cheap meals; **E** pp Los Carrera 1595 is very friendly, use of kitchen, hot showers, clean, with breakfast; **E** pp Colón 844, with breakfast; *Residencias/Restaurantes La Paloma* (Errázuriz 1599), *Richmond* (Lastarria 500 block) and *Ver-Mar* (Errázuriz y Lastarria, T 234429), are fairly basic. Private houses at Germán Hube, pasaje 1, casa 22, población Villa Dama, E pp, hot water, clean, use of kitchen, rec; **E** pp Lynch 1306, 2° piso (1 block from bus station, use of kitchen, clean).

Camping Municipal site at S entrance to city, open summer only, free.

Restaurants *Peter's Kneipe*, M Rodríguez 1039, excellent German restaurant, not cheap; *Café Dino*, Ramírez 898, on the plaza, restaurant upstairs, bar/cafetería downstairs, good. *Luca's Pizzas*, Cochrane 551, pizzas, pastas, burgers, etc, fair. *Dumbos*, O'Higgins 580, good, rec; *Casa del Atillo*, MacKenna 1011, good food and service, pleasant atmosphere, rec. Good restaurant in the bus station.

Exchange Fincard for Mastercard, Mackenna 877, Mon-Fri 0900-1400, 1530-1900, Sat

0930-1330. For good rates try **Cambio Tur**, Mackenna 1010, T 4846; La Frontera, Ramírez 949, local 5 (Galery Catedral).

Laundry Av Arturo Prat 678 (allow at least a day).

Post Office O'Higgins 645, also Telex. **Phone Office** Ramírez at central plaza and Juan Mackenna y Cochrane.

Shopping *Reinares and Thone*, Ramírez 1100, for good fishing gear. *Las Brisas* supermarket has been rec; adjoining is *Kaffeestube* for good snacks and cakes.

Club Andino Juan Mackenna esq Manuel Bulnes, 3rd floor, better for skiing than mountaineering.

Tourist Office Provincial government office, on Plaza de Armas, O'Higgins s/n, 1st floor, left, T 234104. **Automóvil Club de Chile**, Bulnes 463, T 232269, information and car hire.

Garage Automotriz Salfa Sur SA, Fco Bilbao 857; Automotriz Amthauer, Amthauer 1250.

Air LanChile, Manuel Antonio Matta 862, T 236688, Ladeco, Mackenna 975, T 234355. LanChile operates daily flights Osorno-Santiago, via Temuco.

Rail Station at Juan Mackenna 600, T 232992. Daily train to/from Santiago (18 hrs) and to Puerto Montt (3 hrs).

Buses Most leave from the bus terminal 1 block from municipal market at Errázuriz 1400. Left luggage at terminal open 0730-2030. Bus from centre, US$0.30. Frequent buses to **Santiago**, US$16, *salón cama* US$25, 16 hrs. Cruz del Sur to **Concepción** US$7.65, to **Temuco**, US$3.35, to **Punta Arenas**, US$60-75. Other services to Punta Arenas: Sur, Mon and Sat, Turisbus, Mon and Thur, Eurobus and Bus Norte. Varmontt buses every ½ hr (from about 0700 to 2200) to **Alto Frutillar** (US$1.75), **Llanquihue**, **Puerto Varas** and **Puerto Montt** (US$7). To **Puerto Octay**, US$1.50, Via Octay company 6 daily between 0815-1930 (return 0800-1930) Mon-Sat, Sun 5 between 0800 and 2000 (4 return buses). Buses to **Valdivia**, every half hour, 1½-2½ hrs journey depending on company (eg Trans Norte, Etta, Cruz del Sur), US$2-3. To **Lago Ranco**, Buses Ruta 5, 6 a day from 0810, 2 hrs, US$1.50. To **Entre Lagos**, **Puyehue** and **Aguas Calientes**, Buses Puyehue from the municipal market; to Entre Lagos, 4 a day, 0900-1500, return 1600, 1800, 1900, 1 hr, US$1; Puyehue and Aguas Calientes, 0915, 1130, 1530, return 0730, 0830, 1230 and 1730 (1600 also on Sat, in theory), 2½ hrs, US$2.50. Local bus to **Anticura** (Chilean customs post) leaves at 1620, 3 hrs, 22 km from border.

To Argentina via the Puyehue Pass The Argentine town of Bariloche can be reached by Route 215 through the Puyehue pass (paved most of the way). Although less scenic than the ferry journey across Lake Todos Los Santos and Laguna Verde (**see p 719**) this crossing is cheaper, more reliable (though the pass is liable to closure after snow) and still a beautiful trip. In season daily services to Bariloche from Puerto Montt via Osorno, US$20-25, 7-11 hrs, are run by the following companies: Cruz del Sur, Turismo Lanín (not rec), Tas Choapa and Bus Norte. Tas Choapa services also run to Mendoza, Buenos Aires, Montevideo and Rio de Janeiro. Out of season, services are reduced. Buy tickets for international buses from the bus terminal, not through an agency. If intending to return by this route, buy an open return ticket as higher fares are charged in Argentina.

If entering Chile by car at this point, formalities are quick (about 15 mins), but includes the spraying of tyres and shoes have to be wiped on a mat (pay US$2 to 'Sanidad') and US$1.25 at the documents counter. Passage will be much quicker if you already have Chilean pesos and don't wait to change at the border.

Excursions Route 215 runs E past the Pilmaiquen waterfall (35 km – now dry because of a hydroelectric power project) to *Entre Lagos*, Lago Puyehue and the thermal waters at *Termas de Puyehue* (US$3.50 pp for bathing, 0900-2000); 2 hrs by car, 2½ by bus (schedule under Osorno **Buses**). The bus does not stop at the lake (unless you want to get off at *Gran Hotel Termas de Puyehue* and clamber down), but turns off Route 215 and goes 4 km further to Aguas Calientes. The main road continues to *Anticura* (*Hostería y Cabañas Anticura*; *Camping Catrue*) and the Puyehue pass.

The headquarters of the **Puyehue National Park** are about 80 km E of Osorno at *Aguas Calientes*, where there is an open air pool with very hot thermal water beside the Río Chanleufú, open 0830-1900, US$1.50, children US$1 and a very hot indoor pool, open Mon-Fri 0830-1230, 1400-1800, Sat, Sun and holidays 0830-2030, US$4, children US$2 (information centre open weekends only off-season). There is a Conaf campsite with private sites (US$12 per site), cabin type accommodation (B, T 236988, a small shop—better to take your own food), and an expensive café. Several houses nearby offer beds at E pp, or full board, D, but ask someone who doesn't work in the cabins. In the Puyehue National Park is surviving temperate rain-forest. Three marked paths can be followed: Los Rápidos, 1 km to falls on the Río Chanleufú (the trail starts at the entrance to the outdoor pool, if you don't want to swim, just say you're going to Los Rápidos); El Recodo, a continuation of Los Rápidos up the river bank; El Pionero, 1,800m up to a viewpoint (good for the exercise before you bathe). The trees are lovely: listen to the birds and watch for kingfishers by the river.

The road beyond Aguas Calientes continues 18 km to *Antillanca*, past three of small lakes and through forests. (**A** *Hotel Antillanca*, T 235114, without food, at foot of **Volcán Casablanca**, 4 km from crater, excellent hotel/restaurant/café, with pool, sauna and small ski resort, 3 ski lifts. In winter chains can be hired; a one way traffic system operates, up in am, down pm.) Antillanca is beautiful, especially at sunrise, with the snow-clad cones of Osorno, Puntiagudo, and Puyehue forming a semicircle. The tree-line on Antillanca is one of the few in the world made up of deciduous trees (southern beech). It is possible to hike from Antillanca to Volcán Casablanca for even better views of the surrounding volcanoes and lakes; no path, information from Club Andino in Osorno. No public transport from Aguas Calientes to Antillanca; try hitching—always difficult, but it is not a hard walk.

Hotels at Lago Puyehue L2-A1 pp *Gran Hotel Termas de Puyehue*, hot-springs swimming pool (T Osorno 235157), large and well kept (cheaper May to mid-Dec), meals expensive, in beautiful scenery, heavily booked Jan-Feb (postal address Casilla 27-0, Puyehue, or T Santiago 231-3417); accommodation also in private house nearby, E pp full board). In *Entre Lagos*, *Pub del Campo*, highly rec restaurant, reasonable prices, owner is of Swiss descent; **D** *Hostería Entre Lagos*, Ramírez 65, lake view, T 647225; **D** *Villa Veneto*, Gral Lagos 602, T 647203; **E** pp *Hospedaje Millarey*, with breakfast, excellent, clean, friendly; *Restaurant Jardín del Turista*, very good. On the S lakeshore are: *Chalet Suisse*, Ruta 215, Km 55 (Casilla 910, Osorno, T Puyehue 647208, Osorno 064-234073), *hostería*, restaurant with excellent food; a few km beyond, *hospedaje y cabañas* at Almacén Valenciana; *alojamiento* at Shell station after Km 60, before **A1** *Motel Ñilque*, T Santiago 231-3417, or (0647) 218, cabins, half-price May-Oct, fishing trips, watersports, car hire. **B** *Hostería Isla Fresia*, located on own island, T 236951, Casilla 49, Entre Lagos, transport provided.

Camping *El Manzano*, Route 215, Km 58; *Camping No Me Olvides*, Km 60; *Playa Los Copihues*, Km 60 (hot showers, good), all on S shore of Lake Puyehue; *Camping Playa Puyehue*, Km 75.

A further excursion can be made to the S shore of **Lago Rupanco** (65 km) taking the road from Osorno to Puerto Octay and turning E after 33 km. This lake is very beautiful and much less developed than most of its neighbours. At the western end of the lake is *Hostería y Cabañas El Paraíso*, T 236239; at the eastern end, reached by a 40 km dirt road along the S shore of the lake, is *Hotel Bahía Escocia*, run by Ian and Alice Hamilton (Casilla 1099, T 0647-254, Telex 273002 BOOTH CL), beautiful setting, most hospitable, hot water, good meals, warmly rec; tennis, boating, walking. Access by car only. Bus from Osorno, to Piedras Negras (midway along the southern shore) at either *Minimarket El Capricho*, Mackenna y Colón, or from Estacíon Viejo (old railway station), leaves 1645, 1545 on Sat, returns from Piedras Negras 0700.

Drive or take bus (US$0.60, frequent) N of Osorno to Río Bueno, celebrated for its scenery, to La Unión, and to **Trumao**, a river port on the Río Bueno, whence a launch may be taken to La Barra on the coast; leaves Wed and Sat only at 0900, 5 hrs, US$6; returns Sun at 0900, no service in winter.

The sea beaches at **Maicolpue** (60 km from Osorno—**D** *Hostería Müller*, on the beach, clean, good service, rec, campsite) and **Pucatrihue** (*Hostería Incalcar*, summer only) are worth a visit in the summer (daily bus service).

From Osorno it is 106 km S to Puerto Montt, including 25 km along the shore of **Lago Llanquihue**. Across the great blue sheet of water can be seen two snowcapped volcanoes: the perfect cone of Osorno (2,680m) and the shattered cone of Calbuco, and, when the air is clear, the distant Tronador (3,554m). Lago Llanquihue covers over 540 square km and is the third largest natural lake in South America. There is a road, 187 km long, around it.

At the northern tip of the lake is **Puerto Octay**, just 56 km SE of Osorno. Founded by German settlers in 1851, it is a small town (pop 10,000; DDD 065) in a lovely setting. The Museo El Colono, Independencia 591, includes a small collection of local artefacts. Tourist office Pedro Montt s/n, T 276, open Mon-Fri 1000-1200, 1500-1700 (Jan and Feb daily 0900-2100). 4 km S is the Peninsula of **Centinela** with lodging, camping, a launch dock, bathing beaches, water sports. From the headland are fine views of the volcanoes Osorno, Calbuco, Puntiagudo and the Cordillera of the Andes; a very popular spot in good weather.

Services Puerto Octay: B *Haase*, Pedro Montt 344, T213, very pleasant (rooms with and without bath), US$70 for rooms, breakfast and supper for family of 6; C *Posada Gubernatis*, Calle Santiago s/n, lakeside, clean, comfortable. E pp *Hospedaje La Naranja*, Independencia 361, restaurant; E pp *Hospedaje Fogón de Anita*, 1 km out of town, T 34523, good breakfast; F pp *Hospedaje Raquel Mardorf*, Germán Wulf 712, clean, quiet, comfortable, owners have *Restaurante La Cabaña* at No 713, good; *Café Kali*, Esperanza 497, rec. *Restaurante Bariera*, Germán Wulf 582, cheap and good; campsite US$5. **Centinela**: *Hotel Centinela*, Casa 12, Península de Centinela, T Santiago 232-5376, rooms with or without bath, meals available, nice setting, friendly staff; *Hostería La Baja*, Península de Centinela, Casilla 116, T 269. **Camping** Municipal site at Centinela, US$4 per group.

Buses To Osorno 7 a day; to Frutillar, twice daily Jan-Mar, Mon, Wed, and Fri Apr-Dec; to Las Cascadas (see below) Mon-Fri 1700, return next day 0600.

10 km E of Puerto Octay is Playa Maitén, 'highly recommended, nice beach, marvellous view to the Volcán Osorno, no tourists'. 24 km further on is **Las Cascadas**, surrounded by picturesque agricultural land, old houses and German cemeteries. The small settlement at Las Cascadas also has vacation houses. For a circuit of Lago Llanquihue by car, follow the road from Puerto Octay along the eastern lakeside, with the Osorno volcano on your left, to Ensenada (see below), with a turning to Petrohué with its beautiful falls and Lago Todos los Santos; continue along the S shore of the lake to Puerto Varas, then N along the W side via Frutillar (see below) to Octay. Note that the road round the N and E sides of the lake is narrow with lots of blind corners, necessitating speeds of 20-30 kph at best in places.

Hotels in Las Cascadas *Centro de Recreación Las Cascadas*, T 235377; E *Hostería Irma*, on lake, 2 km past Las Cascadas, run by 3 Marías, good food, very pleasant. Several farms on the road around N and E side of the lake offer accommodation, look for signs.

Camping *Centro de Recreación Las Cascadas* and Villa Las Cascadas picnic area (free); at Playa Maitén, rec.

About half-way down the W side of the lake is **Frutillar** (DDD 06542), in fact two towns: Alto Frutillar, with a railway station, just off the main highway, and Bajo Frutillar on the lakeside, 4 km away. It is 5 mins by colectivo between the two towns, US$0.50.

Bajo Frutillar is possibly the most attractive—and expensive—town on the lake. A beautifully kept town, it offers a highly-regarded classical music festival in late Jan to early Feb (accommodation must be booked well in advance). The Museo Colonial Alemán, including watermill (which does not turn), two replicas of German colonial houses with original memorabilia, a blacksmith's shop (personal engravings for US$5), and a *campanario* (circular barn with agricultural and dairy machinery and carriages inside), gardens and handicraft shop, is well worth a visit. Open 1000-1800, closed Mon, US$1.25 (maintained by the Universidad Austral de Chile). The nearby University collection of native trees and commercially-grown farm produce is worth visiting. There is a large open-air chess board in the square outside the Club Alemán.

Accommodation and Food On the road to Playa Maqui: **L3** *Salzburg*, T 589 or Santiago 2061419, new, excellent, country style, restaurant, sauna, mountain bikes, arranges tours and fishing; *Hostal Cinco Robles*, Km 1, Casilla 100, T 351, with bath, breakfast, other meals on request, parking; **B** *Casona del 32*, with bath and breakfast, comfortable old house, central heating, English and German spoken, T 369, Caupolicán 28, PO Box 101; **C** *Hospedaje El Arroyo*, Philippi 989, T 560, with breakfast, highly rec; **C-D** *Hospedaje Costa Azul*, Philippi 1175, T 388, mainly for families, good breakfasts; also on Philippi: **C** *Winkler*, No 1155, T 388, discount to YHA members, cabins, friendly, rec; **D** pp *Hospedaje Vivaldi*, No 851, T 382, Sra Edith Klesse, quiet, comfortable, excellent breakfast and lodging, also family accommodation, rec; **D** *Las Rocas*, No 1235, T 397, with breakfast; **D** *Residenz/Café am See*, No 439, T 539, good early breakfast; **C** No 451, T 204, clean, good breakfast; **D** *Hotel Philippi*, on lake shore, good rooms, rec; **D** Pérez Rosales 590, excellent breakfast; **D** *Hospedaje Trayén*, Philippi 963, T 346, basic, clean; **E** pp *Hospedaje Kaisersseehaus* (Viola Herbach), No 1333 (Casilla 13, T 387), hot water, good, cheap food, very comfortable and welcoming, English, German, Spanish spoken, highly rec (due to be replaced in 1995 by a condominium complex); **D** *Faralito*, Winkler 245, hot water, cooking facilities (owner can be contacted at shop at Pinker 167, T 440). Many more in the lower town. **D** *Frutillar Alto*, Calle Principal 168, clean.

Camping *Playa Maqui*, 7 km N of Frutillar, T 9139, fancy, expensive; *Los Ciruelillos*, 2 km S, T 9123, most services. Try also Sr Guido González, Casa 3, Población Vermont, T 385, G pp, rec.

Restaurants *Club Alemán*, Av Philippi 747, good but not cheap, hostile to backpackers; there is a Bar Restaurant upstairs at the Fire Station, *Bomberos*, opp *Hotel Frutillar* (which burnt down in 1993), best value, open all year, memorable painting caricaturing the firemen in action. *Bierstube*, A Varas, open 1600-2400. Many German-style cafés and tea- rooms on Calle Philippi (the lakefront, eg *Salón de Te Frutillar*, No 775). *Der Volkladen*, O'Higgins y Philippi, natural products, chocolates and cakes, natural cosmetics. *Café Hermosa*, good breakfast (view of lake and Volcán Osorno). Budget travellers should eat at *Kaisersseehaus* (see **Hotels**) 'and explode'.

Services and Transport Toilet, showers and changing cabins for beach on O'Higgins. Cema-Chile shop, Philippi y O'Higgins. Tourist Office on lakeside opp *Club Alemán*, helpful; Viajes Frutillar in Alto Frutillar (Richter y Alissandre) run tours. To Puerto Varas, Varmontt, US$1. To Osorno, Varmontt 1¼ hrs, US$1.75. All buses leave from Alto Frutillar; 3 times a week to Puerto Octay from Opec station.

Puerto Varas (pop 26,000; DDD 065), a beauty spot on the shore of Lago Llanquihue, has standard roses growing along the streets. It is 996 km from Santiago and only 20 by paved road from Puerto Montt. The church was built by German Jesuits in 1918; it has an orange-coloured exterior and a white and blue interior, worth a visit. Parque Philippi, on top of hill, is a pleasant place to visit; walk up to *Hotel Cabañas del Lago* on Klenner, cross the railway and the gate is on the right. The views are a bit restricted by trees and the metal cross at the top is unattractive (so is the electric clock which chimes the quarter-hours in town). Casino charges US$2.65 entry, including first drink.

Hotels Accommodation is expensive, it is cheaper to stay in Puerto Montt. **L3** *Los Alerces*, Pérez Rosales 1281, T 233039, 4-star hotel, with breakfast, new cabin complex, attractive; **A1** *Colonos del Sur*, Del Salvador 24, T 233369, new, with bath, good views, good restaurant, tea room; **A1** *Cabañas del Lago*, Klenner 195, T 232291, F 232707, rooms or remodelled cabins, central heating, TV, phone, parking, superb location; **A2** *Asturias*, Del Salvador 322, T 232446, friendly, discounts for cash, fine restaurant; **A2** *Bellavista*, V Pérez Rosales 60, T 232012, cheerful, rec, no restaurant, but breakfast service, overlooking lake; **A2** *Cabañas del Lago*, Klenner 195, T 232291, cabins, adequate; **A3** *Motel Ayentemo*, V Pérez Rosales 950, clean, comfortable cabins, friendly, T/F 232270; **A3** *Licarayén*, San José 114, T 232305, F 232955, with bath, overlooking lake, comfortable, highly rec, book in season, C out of season, clean, friendly, 'the perfect place for bad weather or being ill'; **B** *Merlín*, Walker Martínez 584, T/F 233105, quiet, excellent restaurant, highly rec; **B** *Motel Altué*, Av V Pérez Rosales 1679, T 232294, incl breakfast; **C** *Motel Sacho*, San José 581, T 232227. **C** *El Greco*, Mirador 134, T 233388, modern, good; **B** *Hospedaje Loreley*, Maipo 911, T 232226, rec, homely, quiet; **D** *Residencial Hellwig*, San Pedro 210, rooms and bathrooms clean and neat, water usually tepid, not welcoming. Also cheap *residenciales* opposite bus station and in Plaza de Armas.

Residencial at Salvador 423, D, run by a German lady, rec, as is María Schilling Rosas' *hospedaje* at La Quebrada 752; **D** pp *Hospedaje Las Carmelas*, Imperial y Rosario, new, excellent, helpful, good meals, highly rec; **D** *Hospedaje Walker*, Martínez 576, T 232921, with breakfast, clean, quiet; **D** pp *Carmen Bittner*, Martínez 564, with breakfast, German spoken, rec; Sra Elly A Prat 151, D with breakfast; **D** *hospedaje* at Santa Rosa 318, with breakfast; **D** pp Andrés Bello 321, nice atmosphere, good breakfast; **D** *Hospedaje Don Raúl*, Salvador 928, cooking facilities, newly renovated, clean, rec, camping F pp. Familia Niklitschek-Pozas, Imperial 8 (opp *Motel Trauco*), C, good breakfast, good views, highly rec. Many other family *hospedajes* on same street incl **D** *Hospedaje Imperial*, No 653, T 232451, clean, incl breakfast, central, rec. **E** pp Elsa Pinto, Verbo Divino 427, clean.

Camping On S shore of Lago Llanquihue starting at Puerto Varas: Km 10, Playa Hermosa (T Puerto Varas 8283, Puerto Montt 252223), fancy, US$6 pp, take own supplies. Km 11, Playa Niklitschek, full facilities; Km 20, Playa Venado; Km 49, Conaf site at Puerto Oscuro, beneath road to volcano, very good.

Restaurants *Club Alemán*, San José 415, poor service; *Mercado*, next to market, excellent food, good service, not cheap but good value; Donde El Gordito, in the market, small place, immense portions, very popular, rec; *Café Asturias*, San Francisco 302, good empanadas and other food (same management as hotel of same name); *Ibis*, Pérez Rosales 1117, next to *Motel Ayentemo*, warmly rec; *Central*, San José 319, good coffee, cakes, vegetarian dishes, pies and breakfast, opens early. *Domino*, Del Salvador 450, good, cheap; *Café Danés*, Del Salvador 441, good coffee and cakes; *Gato Renzo*, Del Salvador 314, good pizzas; *El Amigo*, San Bernardo 240, large portions, good value; *Costa Azul*, Av Pérez Rosales 01071, 2 km from town towards Puerto Chico, in wooden building (expensive motel restaurants just beyond it aren't worth visiting, eg *Roller*, although service is friendly—this does not apply to *Ibis*, above). *Café del Turismo*, next to Cruz del Sur office, cheap, good; *El Molino*, an excellent coffee house next to an old water mill, on road to Ensenada 22 km from Pto Varas.

Exchange Turismo Los Lagos, Del Salvador 257 (Galería Real, local 11), open daily 0830-1330, 1500-2100, Sun 0930-1330, accepts TCs, good rates. **Banco Osorno**, Del Salvador 399, good rates.

Phone Office Salvador y Santa Rosa.

Shopping *VYH Meistur Supermarket*, Walker Martínez, good selection, reasonably priced.

Fishing The area around Puerto Varas is popular for fishing. A licence costs US$2.50 a year, obtainable from the Municipal offices.

Travel Agents *Andina del Sud*, Del Salvador 243, T 232511, operate 'lakes' trip to Bariloche, Argentina via Lago Todos los Santos, Peulla, Cerro Tronador (see under Puerto Montt, **To Argentina**), plus other excursions, good. Also *Eco Travel*, Av Costanera s/n, T 233222, *Turismo Nieve* (on San Bernardo, rec), *Aqua Motion*, Imperial 0699, T/F 232747, for trekking, rafting and climbing. Several others. Most tours operate in season only (1 Sep-15 Apr).

Tourist Office Del Salvador 328, 0900-2100 in summer, helpful, will find cheap accommodation; also art gallery.

Buses To Santiago: Igi-Llaima (office San Francisco 516) leaves from Salvador at 1830, arrives 1130 (US$11.50). To Puerto Montt, every ¼ hr from Varmontt station (San Francisco 600 block), US$2, 30 mins; same company, same frequency to Frutillar and Osorno. To Osorno US$3.50, 1¼ hrs; to Valdivia US$6.

To Bariloche, for Andina del Sud, see above. Bohle bus from Puerto Montt departs 1130, daily except Sun, from *Res Hellwig* to Petrohué, connecting with the ferry service to Peulla. It is not possible to go by private car from Puerto Varas direct to Bariloche as none of the ferries takes cars; one must go via Osorno.

Excursions Puerto Varas is within easy reach of many famous beauty spots—Desagüe, Totoral, Frutillar, Los Bajos, Puerto Octay (direct bus only from Osorno), Puerto Chico, Puerto Fonck, La Poza, Isla Loreley, Volcán Calbuco, La Fábrica, Puerto Rosales, Playa Venado, Ralún and Río Pescado. The whole countryside with its primeval forest, deep blue rivers and snowcapped volcanoes is very beautiful; interest is added by the timber-frame buildings with shingle roofs—even the churches.

La Poza is a little lake to the S of the main lake and reached through narrow channels overhung with vegetation; a concealed channel leads to yet another lake, the Laguna Encantada. The motor-boats that tour Lago Llanquihue stop at Isla Loreley, very beautiful and well worth a visit.

Buses from Puerto Montt run every day on the southern side of the lake between Puerto

Varas and (50 km) Ensenada, in the S-eastern corner of the lake, continuing to Ralún, Cochamó and Río Puelo (see below). In summer, buses go daily from Puerto Montt and Puerto Varas in the morning to Ensenada, Laguna Verde, Petrohué Falls and Lago Todos Los Santos, US$7, good value. The drive around the lake is very picturesque. On the northern road are Puerto Octay and Centinela (**see above**).

Ensenada is 50 km E of Puerto Varas, beautifully situated at the SE corner of Lago Llanquihue and a good centre for excursions.

Hotels A2 *Hotel Ensenada*, Casilla 659, Puerto Montt, T 232888, with bath, olde-worlde, good food (closed in winter) good view of lake and Osorno Volcano, runs tours, hires out mountain bikes; also *hostal* in the grounds, cooking facilities, much cheaper but not that cheap. **C** *Hostería Los Pumas*, 3 hrs up the hill also highly rec, in season only; about 2 km from town is **C** *Pucará*, also with good restaurant (the steaks are rec); **C** *Ruedas Viejas*, T 312, for room, or **D** in cabin, about 1 km from Ensenada, basic, damp, hot water, restaurant; **D** *Cabañas Brisas del Lago*, T 252363, chalets for 6 on beach, good restaurant next door but one, highly rec for self-catering, but bring your own food; **D** *Hospedaje Arena*, on same road as *Ruedas Viejas* but nearer police station, with breakfast, rec; **D** *Moteles Hostería*, with breakfast, clean, poor service, comfortable; **D** *Hospedaje Ensenada*, T 8278, very clean, excellent breakfast; **D** *Hospedaje Opazo*, with breakfast, friendly; **E** pp *hospedaje* above Toqui grocery, cheapest in town, basic, quiet, hot water, use of kitchen, beach in the back yard, rec. Ensenada has little more than the hotels, restaurants (closed out of season: *Canta Rana* rec for bread and kuchen, *Ruedas Viejas* the cheapest) and a few pricey shops; bring your own provisions.

Camping *Camping Montaña*, opposite *Hotel Ensenada*, US$10, fully equipped, highly rec; also at Playa Larga, 1 km beyond *Hotel Ensenada*, US$10.

Transport Bohle bus from Puerto Montt, via Puerto Varas, continues to Petrohue in summer. Hitching from Puerto Varas is difficult.

Excursions A good hike from Ensenada goes to Laguna Verde, about 30 mins from *Hotel Ensenada*, along a beautiful circular trail behind the lake (take first fork to the right behind the information board), and then down the road to a campsite at Puerto Oscuro on Lago Llanquihue. The site is quiet and secluded, a good spot for a picnic.

Volcán Osorno lies N of Ensenada. It became active in May 1995. It can be reached either from Ensenada, or from a road branching off the Puerto Octay-Ensenada road at Puerto Klocker, 20 km SE of Puerto Octay. The Club Andino Osorno (address under Osorno) has three shelters (US$3 pp): to the N at La Picada (20 km SE of Puerto Klocker), on the ski slopes at 950m; to the S *Las Pumas*, 12 km from Ensenada at 900m, with plenty of beds and cooking facilities, very friendly guards (apply at the Oficina de Turismo de Osorno); also to the S, 1.5 km from Ensenada at 1,200m **Refugio Teski Club**, **E**, bunk accommodation, restaurant and bar, bleak site above the tree line; a good base for walking. *La Burbuja* ski centre, 1,250m, T 2891, 12 km N of Ensenada, **C**, restaurant, bar, ski lessons and equipment hire, open all year (ski season Jun to Sep). Weather permitting, *Travellers* tour agency in Puerto Montt offer guided climbs with local guide Danilo, with transport, food and mountain equipment, US$100, dep 0500, return 2000, all year. Only experienced climbers should attempt to climb right to the top, ice climbing equipment and guide essential: there are many deep crevasses, the weather can change suddenly, never go alone, and set off early in the morning; there is a shelter for hikers. Before setting out ask first at Las Pumas or Refugio Teski for advice.

16 km E of Ensenada, along a scenic, partially paved road, is **Lago Todos los Santos**, a long irregularly shaped sheet of water, the most beautiful of all the lakes in southern Chile. The lake, which lies within the **Parque Nacional Vicente Pérez Rosales**, has no roads round it. The waters are emerald green; the shores are deeply wooded and several small islands rise from its surface. Private launches can be hired for trips, for instance to Cayutué on a southern arm of the lake. In the waters of the lake are reflected the slopes of Volcán Osorno. Beyond the hilly shores to the E are several graceful snow-capped mountains, with the mighty Tronador in the distance. To the N is the sharp point of Cerro Puntiagudo (2,278m), and at

the North-eastern end Cerro Techado (1,720m) rises cliff-like out of the water.

The ports of **Petrohué** at its western and **Peulla** at its eastern ends are connected by boat, costing US$18 return (book in advance); it leaves Petrohué at 1030, Peulla at 1500 (not Sun, 2½ hrs—most seating indoors, no cars carried, cycles half fare). This is the only public service across the lake and it connects with the Andina del Sud tour bus between Puerto Montt and Bariloche (see under Puerto Montt). In season there are also minibuses to Petrohué from Puerto Montt. Local fishermen ask US$13 for the trip across the lake, but will settle for US$5-7. If you prefer to go walking, ask for the park guard, Hernán, who organizes expeditions from Petrohué in the summer months. Trout and salmon fishing at Petrohué are excellent. The Salto de Petrohué (entrance, US$1.50) is 6 km (unpaved) from Petrohué, 10 km (paved) from Ensenada (a much nicer walk from Petrohué). Near the falls is a snackbar; there are also two short trails, the Senderos de los Enamorados and Carileufú. Puella is a good starting point for hikes in the mountains. The Cascadas Los Novios, signposted above the *Hotel Peulla*, are a steep walk, but are stunning once you reach them; don't forget to turn round to see the views. Good walk also to Laguna Margarita, 4 hrs, take water.

Isla Margarita, the largest island on the lake, with a lagoon in the middle, can be visited from Petrohué, boats by Andino del Sud leave 1500, ½ hr each way, ½ hr on island, US$5.

Petrohué and Peulla are infested by *tavanos* in Dec and Jan. Cover up as much as possible with light-coloured clothes.

Services At **Petrohué**: **A2** *Hostería Petrohué*, with bath, modernized and expanded, commercialized for tour groups (lunch with Chilean folksinging), comfortable, also self-service restaurant next door, better value; **A3** *Fundo El Salto*, nr Salto de Petrohué, very friendly, run by New Zealanders, mainly a fishing lodge, good home cooking, fishing trips arranged, Casilla 471, Puerto Varas; **E** pp *Familia Küscher* on other side of river, with breakfast, meals available, cold water, electricity only 3 hrs in pm, dirty, noisy, poor value, camping possible; Refugio above being repaired. There is also a shop in the village. At **Peulla**, on the opp shore: **A1** *Hotel Peulla*, PO Box 487, Puerto Montt, T 253253 (incl dinner and breakfast, direct personal reservations A3, cheaper out of season), beautiful setting by the lake and mountains, restaurant and bar, good but expensive meals, cold in winter, often full of tour groups (tiny shop at back of hotel); **D** pp *Residencial Palomita*, 50m W of Hotel, half board, family-run, simple, comfortable but not spacious, separate shower, book ahead in season, lunches; accommodation is also available with local residents: Elmo and Ana Hernández Maldonado (only house with a balcony), D with breakfast, use of kitchen, helpful, clean. Small shop in Andino del Sud building but best to take your own food.

Camping At Petrohué beside the lake, no services. At Peulla, opp Conaf office, US$1.50. Ask the commander of the military garrison at the beach nearest the hotel if you can camp on the beach; no facilities.

Bus Bohle bus from Puerto Montt to Ensenada continues to Petrohué in summer (from 13 Dec); returns from Petrohué at 1800. At other times of year there is a bus from Puerto Varas to Petrohué US$2, 1 hr, but it only waits 5 mins in Petrohué before returning to Puerto Varas. There are day return bus and boat tours to Peulla from Puerto Montt (Andina del Sud), with

possibility of continuing to Bariloche. If planning to go to Bariloche in stages, book through to Bariloche in Petrohué, not Peulla because onward connections from Peulla may be full and the accommodation is not so good there. It is difficult to hitch from Ensenada to Petrohué.

To Argentina The Argentine frontier at Paso de Pérez Rosales is 30 km E of Peulla. Hitching is impossible along this road. If walking, go to Chilean customs in Peulla for exit stamp, good campsite 1¾ hrs walk E of Peulla, take food. For the route from the frontier via Puerto Frías to Bariloche see under Argentina.

On the S shore of Lago Todos Los Santos is the little village of **Cayutué**, reached by hiring a boat from Petrohué, US$30. From Cayutué it is a 3 hr walk to Laguna Cayutué, a jewel set between mountains and surrounded by forest. Good camping and swimming. From here it is a 5 hr hike S to Ralún on the Reloncaví Estuary (see below). This is part of the old route used by missionaries in the colonial period to travel between Nahuel Huapi in Argentina and the island of Chiloé. It is now part of a logging road and is good for mountain bikes. For further details of this walk see Bradt Publications' *Backpacking in Argentina and Chile*.

A paved road runs 31 km SE from Ensenada along the wooded lower Petrohué valley to **Ralún**, on the salt-water Estuario de Reloncaví. The road continues, unpaved, along the E side of the estuary to Cochamó and Puelo. At Ralún **E** pp *Restaurant El Refugio* rents rooms; also **E** pp *Navarrito*, restaurant and lodging; **E** pp *Posada Campesino*, simple room; **E** pp *El Encuentro*, village shop and post office, with telex. There is also the *Hotel Ralún*, at S end of the village, the main building of which burnt down in 1992; cabins are still available, but no restaurant. Bus from Puerto Montt, 5 a day, Bohle, between 1000 and 1930, 4 on Sat, return 0700-1830, US$2. Also bus from Ensenada daily, US$1.

The road which goes to *Hotel Ralún* continues round the base of the mountains to Lago Chapo, giving access at the eastern end to Parque Nacional Alerce Andino (see p 738). There is, as yet, no connection between the eastern and western shores of Lago Chapo.

The Reloncaví estuary, the northernmost of Chile's glacial inlets, is recommended for its local colour, its sealions and dolphins and its peace. At **Cochamó**, 17 km S of Ralun on the E shore of the estuary, there is the **D** *Hotel Cochamó*, Catedral 19, T 212, basic but clean, friendly, often full with salmon farm workers, good meals, rec, and a large number of *pensiones* (just ask), eg **E** pp *Mercado Particular Sabin*, Calle Catedral 20 (Sra Suni, next to *Hotel*), **E** pp Sra Flora Barrientos offers floorspace in her bar/restaurant/drugstore, same street No 16; also **E pp** *Restaurant Copihue* and **E** pp *Residencial Gato Blanco*; cheapest accommodation in same street, No 2, by the pier (floor space only). *Camping Los Castaños*, T 214 (Reservations Casilla 576, Puerto Montt). Cochamó itself is pretty, with a fine Chiloé-style church in a striking setting, with the estuary and volcano behind. *Campo Aventura*, Correo Cochamó, T/F 232747, specialize in horseback and trekking expeditions, run by Clark Stede and Michelle Poncini. A side trip is to the Termas de Sotomó, but this requires an affinity for mud. (Buses Bohle's 1300 and 1700 services from Puerto Montt to Ralún continue to Cochamó Mon-Fri; US$4, return 0800 and 1800.) Further S, on the S bank of the Río Puelo (ferry crossing) at **Puelo**, lodging is available at the restaurant (F pp) or with families—try Roberto and Olivia Telles, simple, clean, no bath/shower, meals on request or Ema Hernández Maldona; 2 restaurants. This is a most peaceful, pretty place. Daily buses from Cochamó 1515 and 2000. From here the road continues to Llaguepe. In summer boats sail up the Estuary from Angelmó. Tours from Puerto Montt US$30. Off season the *Carmencita* sails once a week, leaving Puelo Sun 1000 and Angelmó Wed 0900 (advisable to take warm clothes, food and seasickness pills if windy).

Puerto Montt, capital of X Región (Los Lagos), 1,016 km from Santiago, is the terminus of the railway (DDD 065). The first German colonists arrived in 1852; they have remained to this day a small but influential percentage of the 130,000 inhabitants. The houses are mostly faced with unpainted shingles; here and there stand structures in the Alpine manner, all high pitched roofs and quaint balconies. The little fishing port of **Angelmó**, 2 km W, has become a tourist centre with many seafood restaurants and handicraft shops (reached by Costanera bus along Portales). Puerto Montt is a popular centre for excursions to the Lake District.

The port is much used by fishing boats and coasting vessels, and it is here that passengers embark for Puerto Chacabuco, Aisén, and for the long haul S to Punta Arenas. A paved road runs 55 km SW to Pargua, where there is a ferry service to Chiloé.

Museum Museo Juan Pablo II at Avenida Diego Portales opp Ancud (nr bus terminal): memorabilia of the Pope's visit, and local history. Open daily 1030-1800, US$0.50.

Hotels Accommodation is expensive in season, much cheaper off season. Check Tourist Office. **A1** *Vicente Pérez Rosales*, Antonio Varas 447, T 252571, Telex 270056, with bath and breakfast, some rooms noisy, excellent restaurant, seafood, tourist and climbing information, rec. **A2** *Burg*, Pedro Montt y Portales, T 253813, modern, central heating, centrally located, good, interesting traditional food in restaurant; **A2** *Club Presidente*, Av Diego Portales 664, T 251666, new 4 star, with breakfast, very comfortable; **A2** *Don Luis*, Urmeneta y Quillota, T 259001, very good, no restaurant, breakfast in room; **A3** *Montt*, Av Varas y Quillota, T 253651, with bath and C without, clean, friendly, good value (good restaurant); **A3** *Raysan*, Benavente 480, T 256151, helpful; **A2** *Viento Sur*, Ejército 200, T 258701, F 258700, excellent, good restaurant, sauna, gym; **B** *Colina*, Talca 81, T 253813, with bath, clean, some rooms with sea view, breakfast extra, restaurant, bar, car hire; **B** *Le Mirage*, Rancagua 350, T 255125, quite good but cheaply built, T 255125; **B** *Millahue*, T 253829, Copiapó 64, good food; **B** *Residencial Millantú*, Illapel 146, T 252758, basic, clean; **C** *Hostal Panorama*, San Felipe 192, T 254094, steep climb up steps, some rooms with bath, some with view, damp, restaurant; **C** *Miramar*, Andrés Bello 972, T 251548, breakfast, hot water, dirty, across Av Diego Portales from museum and bus terminal; **C** *Residencial Embassy*, Valdivia 130, T 253533, clean, will store luggage, few bathrooms and some rooms lack windows, otherwise good; **C** *Residencial Urmeneta*, Urmeneta 290, T 253262, with bath, **D** without, clean, comfortable, rec. **D** *Residencial El Turista*, Ancud 91, T 254767, with and without bath, with breakfast, clean, comfortable, rec. **D** *Residencial La Nave*, Ancud y Varas, clean, pleasant, good inexpensive restaurant; **D** *Residencial Sur*, San Felipe 183, T 252832 (poor breakfast extra), basic, clean; **D** *Residencial Talquino*, Pérez Rosales 114-116, T 253331, nr bus terminal, hot water, clean; **D** *Hospedaje Alemán*, Egaña y Copiapó, with breakfast, good, clean, safe, German spoken, top floor rooms better, luggage stored; **D** *Residencial Calipso*, Urmeneta 127, T 254554, shared bath, hot water, breakfast extra, clean (acts as youth hostel); **E** pp *Res Emita*, Miraflores 1281, incl breakfast with homemade bread, clean, friendly, safe; **D** *Residencia Punta Arenas*, J J Mira 964, with breakfast, hot water, basic but clean. Other *residenciales* around JJ Mira and Lota. Accommodation also available in many private homes, from US$7-8 pp, look for signs in windows, incl **D** *Casa Haraldo Steffen*, Serrano 286 (T 253823), with breakfast, 15 mins walk from centre, small clean rooms, run down, only 1 bathroom; **G** pp *Uncle Renato*, Guillermo Gallardo 621, floor space, very basic, popular, packed in summer; **D** *Alda González*, G Gallardo 552, T 253334, with breakfast, cooking facilities, clean. There are also several inexpensive hostels in Calle Huasco, eg at **E** pp No 16, with breakfast (hot water), but much better is **E** pp No 126, friendly; **E** pp No 130, hot showers, cooking facilities, rec; **E** pp No 151, T 252586, good breakfast, quiet, friendly, hot water; **D** *Hospedaje Polz*, J J Mira 1002, fussy owner, curfew 2300, clean, warm, good beds, breakfast incl, rec; **D** Aníbal Pinto 328, with breakfast, friendly, popular, laundry facilities, 20 mins walk from centre, rec; **E** pp Sr Raúl Arroyo, Concepción 136 (go to the 'inland' end of Concepción, turn right to end of alley), cooking facilities, hot water, English spoken, often packed, small rooms, with breakfast (also has a 3-rm cottage at Chinquihue, 10 km W, with kitchen and living room, toilets, showers, hot water, very peaceful); **D** A Varas 840, incl good breakfast, rec; **E** pp *Hospedaje*, Balmaceda 300, with breakfast, clean, friendly; **E** pp Balmaceda 283, clean, hospitable; *Residencial Familiar*, Egaña 538, picturesque wooden house, friendly, breakfast only; **E** pp *Hospedaje Matzner*, Talcahuanco 153, with breakfast; **E** pp *Vista Hermosa*, Miramar 1486, with bath, quiet, helpful; **E** pp *Walglad*, Ancud 112, with breakfast, clean, friendly; **E** pp Balmaceda, 754 esq Vial, Ida Soto de Arcas, very friendly, good breakfast, safe, clean, rec; **E** pp Sra Mina Barrio, Trigal 309, use of kitchen, clean; **E** pp Casa Perla, Trigal 312, T 262104, with breakfast, French, English spoken, helpful, friendly, meals, Spanish classes offered off season, rec; **E** pp *Hospedaje Reina*, Trigal 361, family run, clean, welcoming; **E** pp Bilbao 380, T 256514, hot water, very clean, comfortable; **E** pp Lota 132, basic, safe, cooking facilities; **E** pp *Residencial Central*, Lota 111, T 257516, newly renovated, clean, central; **E** pp Sra María Oyarzo, Subida Miramar 1184, T 259957, incl

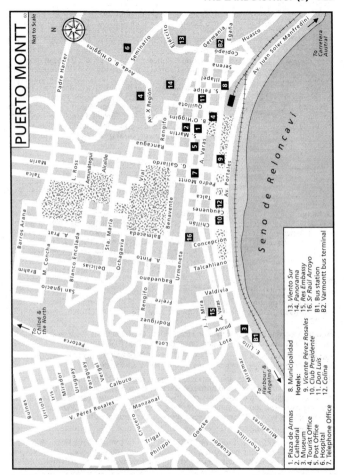

PUERTO MONTT

Not to Scale

N 60

Seno de Reloncaví

To Carretera Austral

To Chiloé & the North

To Harbour & Angelmó

1. Plaza de Armas
2. Cathedral
3. Museum
4. Tourist Office
5. Post Office
6. Hospital
7. Telephone Office
8. Municipalidad

Hotels:
9. Vicente Pérez Rosales
10. Club Presidente
11. Don Luis
12. Colina
13. Viento Sur
14. Panorama
15. Res Embassy
16. Sr Raúl Arroyo
B1. Bus station
B2. Varmont bus terminal

breakfast, friendly, basic (no heating, hot water next door), clean, good beds; **E** pp Vivar 1141, T 255039, incl breakfast, hot water; **E** pp Baquedano 247, T 252862, friendly, clean; on Petorca: **E** pp No 119, T 258638, clean, friendly, rec; **E** pp *Hospedaje Montesinos*, No 121, T 255353, with breakfast, clean, rec; **E** pp No 132, clean; **E** Dr Marín 673, basic, friendly, no hot water. *Albergue* in disused school opp bus station, sleeping bag on floor, very cheap, but no security.

Camping At Chinquihue, 10 km W of Puerto Montt (bus service), about US$1.50 pp. Open Oct-Apr US$8 per site, for any size of tent. Each site has table, two benches, barbecue and plenty of shade. Toilets and showers. Small shop, no kerosene. *Camping Anderson*, 11 km W along coast road at Panitao Bajo, run by an American, hot showers, private beach, home-grown fruit, vegetables and milk products, US$3 pp per night. *Camping Los Alamos* (T 256067 for reservations), on the road W to Panitao and Calbuco. 'Wild' camping possible along the front. 4 km E of Puerto Montt, Copec have a network of 18 'Rutacentas' between Quillagua and Puerto Montt, which, apart from selling petrol and oil, have good shower (US$0.25) and toilet facilities and restaurants.

Restaurants *Embassy*, Ancud 106, very good, pricey; *Club de Yates*, Av Juan Soler s/n, excellent, expensive seafood; *Centro Español*, on Quillota (2nd floor), moderate prices; *Super Yoco*, Quillota 259, good value; *Balzac*, on Rengifo, French and seafood, excellent, pricey; *Kiel*, Capilla 298, excellent food and atmosphere, not cheap; *Club Alemán*, Varas 264, old fashioned, good food and wine; *Café Real*, Rancagua 137, good for *empanadas*, *pichangas*, *congrio frito*, and cheap lunches. *Costa de Reloncaví*, Portales 736, good food at moderate prices, speciality *Pizzeta a la Siciliana*; *Café Central*, Rancagua 117, good atmosphere, food and good pastries; *Suerte Rincón*, Talca, excellent lunches, large portions, popular with locals. *Restaurant Café Dino*, Varas 550, excellent restaurant upstairs, snacks downstairs (try the lemon juice). *Don Pancho*, by the sea, in railway station, good. *Di Napoli Pizzas*, Guillermo Gallardo 119, excellent pasta, but limited choice; *Café Amsel*, Pedro Montt y Portales, superb fish but not cheap; *Plato's*, Av Diego Portales 1014, Galería Comercial España, cheap, good; also in the Galería is *El Rinconcito*, a good bar. *Super Dragon*, Benavente 839, Chinese, good, not cheap. Excellent and cheap food at the central bus depot (all credit cards accepted). Seafood restaurants in Pelluco, 4 km SE and in market at Angelmó, and on the road there (more expensive, poor hygiene but food can be trusted, ask prices first as there is no menu; ask for *té frío blanco*, cold white wine in tea cups, since they are not legally allowed to serve wine). *Asturias*, Angelmó 2448 C, limited menu, friendliest in town, often rec. Try *picoroco al vapor*, a giant barnacle whose flesh looks and tastes like crab; *curanto*, a regional dish (seafood, chicken, sausages and potatoes). In Angelmó, *Rancho Patache*, Pasaje Martí, on corner, 2nd floor, T 252974, very good, simple, informal. Bakery: *La Estrella*, Varas 984, self-service, good.

Exchange Impossible on Sun (but try *Hotel Pérez Rosales*). Change money here if visiting Chiloé as it is difficult outside Castro and rates are poor. Exorbitantly high commission and low rates at Banco del Estado. For Visa try Banco Concepción. Banco Chile (cash only poor rates). Commission charges vary widely. Good rates at Galería Cristal, A Varas 595, El Libertador, Urmeneta 529-A, local 3, and Turismo Latinoamericano, Urmeneta 531. *Travellers* travel agent in Angelmó (address below) has exchange facilities. Fincard (Access), A Varas 437, open Mon-Fri 0845-1400, 1530-1900. La Moneda de Oro at the bus terminal will exchange Latin American currencies (Mon-Sat 0930-1230, 1530-1800). Obtain Argentine pesos before leaving Chile.

Consulates Argentine, Cauquenes 94, 2nd floor, T 253996; German, Chorrillos 1582, Tues-Thur 0930-1230, T253001; Spanish, Rancagua 113, T252557; Dutch, Seminario 350, T 253428.

Laundry Opposite Banco O'Higgins on Pedro Montt; *Center* at Varas 700, one at San Martín 232, and *Unic* at Chillán 149. Laundry prices generally high (US$7 for 3 kg).

Post Office Rancagua 120, open 0830-1830 (Mon-Fri), 0830-1200 (Sat). **Telephone Office** on Pedro Montt between Urmeneta and A Varas, and at Chillán 98.

Shopping Woollen goods and Mapuche-designed rugs can be bought at roadside stalls between port and Angelmó and at tourist shops in town. Prices are much the same as on Chiloé, but quality is often lower. New craft market between bus terminal and Empremar. *Las Brisas* supermarket opp bus station, very good, open 0900-2200 daily; *Mondial*, 2 blocks away is cheaper with better selection; local produce on sale opp bus terminal.

Gymnasium Urmeneta 537.

Travel Agents *Empresa Andina del Sud*, very close to central tourist kiosk, Varas 437, T 257797, sells a daily tour at 0830 (not Sun) to Puerto Varas, Parque Nacional V Pérez Rosales, Petrohué, Lago Todos los Santos, Peulla and back (without meals US$27, with meals US$37), and to other local sights, as well as skiing trips to the Osorno volcano (see below for trip to Bariloche). *Travellers*, Av Angelmó 2270, T/F 258555, Casilla 854, close to 2nd port entrance and Navimag office, open 0830-2000 every day, for information, Osorno volcano trips, bookings for southern Patagonia (has limited allocation of Navimag tickets), sells imported camping equipment, computerized tourist information service, book swap, English-owned and run, rec. *Petrel Tours*, San Martín 167, of 403, T/F 255558, rec. Many other agencies. Most offer a one-day excursion to Puerto Varas, Isla Loreley, Laguna Verde, and the Petrohué falls (reported to be much cheaper from kiosks inside the bus terminal than from agencies in town). One day excursions to Chiloé also offered.

Tourist Office Sernatur is at Edificio Intendencia Regional, Av Décima Región 480 (3rd floor), Casilla 297, T 254580/256999, F 254580, Telex 270008. Open 0830-1300, 1330-1730 Mon-Fri. Ask for information on Chiloé as this is often difficult to obtain on the island. Also kiosk on Plaza de Armas run by the municipality, open till 1800 on Sat. Town maps available, but little information on other places. Telefónica del Sur and Sernatur operate a phone information service (INTTUR), dial 142 (cost is the same as a local call). Dial 149 for

chemist/pharmacy information, 148 for the weather, 143 for the news, etc. The service operates throughout the tenth region. Sernatur in Puerto Montt has a reciprocal arrangement on information with Bariloche, Argentina. **Conaf**: Benaventi y G Gallardo. **Automóvil Club de Chile**, Esmeralda 70, near train station, T 252968.

Car Hire Hertz, Varas 126, T 259585, helpful, English spoken; **Automóvil Club de Chile**, Cauquenes 75, T 254776, and several at airport (shop around). Others are Avis, Egaña 64, T 256575; **Budget**, San Martín 200; **Dollar** (*Hotel Vicente Pérez Rosales*), Varas 447; **First**, Varas 437; **Formula Uno**, Santa María 620, T 254125, highly rec; **Autovald**, Portales 1330, T 256355, cheap rates; **Travicargo**, Urmeneta 856, T 257137/256438; **Automotric Angelmó**, Talca 79, cheap and helpful. *Famas*, Diego Portales y G Gallardo, friendly, helpful, has vehicles that can be taken to Argentina.

Boat hire Lucinda Cárdenas, Manuel Montt Pasaje 7, Casa 134, Angelmó, for trips around the harbour or to Tenglo island.

Air Service To Santiago at least 2 daily flights by LanChile, Ladeco and National (cheaper). To Punta Arenas, LanChile, Ladeco and National run daily flights; in Jan, Feb and Mar you may well be told that flights are booked up; however, cancellations may be available from the airport. Both LanChile and Ladeco offer 50% discounts on standby: these and the lower standard fares charged by National are as cheap as bus fares via Argentina. Flights to Bariloche (Argentina), TAN, Tues, Sat, 40 mins. To Balmaceda, Ladeco, daily. To Coyhaique, LanChile daily. El Tepual airport is 16 km from town, bus to bus terminal hourly, ETC, US$1.50, 20 mins. LanChile, San Martín 200, T 253141/253315, Ladeco, Benevente 350, T 253002; National, Benevente 305, T 258277, F 250664; TAN, T 250071. Don Carlos, Quillota 127, T 253219, flies to Chaitén, 1115 and 1515 Mon-Fri, Sat 1115 (fares under Chaitén), and runs regular charters for 5 passengers to Bariloche, Chaitén, and Coyhaique. Aerosur, Urmeneta 149, T 252523, also flies to Chaitén.

Rail Station at San Felipe 50, T 254908. Daily service to **Santiago**: Rápido with 1930s German-built sleepers, 23 hrs, US$19-25 seat, US$40 bed, US$90 double compartment, bicycles US$10, restaurant car, car transporter, book 3 days in advance, but 2 weeks in advance in high season. Ticket office opens 0830-1130, 1300-1700. Left luggage, US$1.50 per piece.

Bus Service Bus station on sea front, at Av Diego Portales y Av Lota, has telephones, restaurants, *casa de cambio* (left luggage, US$1 per item for 24 hrs). To **Puerto Varas** (US$2), **Llanquihue, Frutillar** (US$2.50) and **Osorno** (US$7) every 30 min between 0750-2050 (2120 Sun), 1½ hrs with Varmontt, either from main terminal or own terminal at Copiapó y Varas. To **Ensenada** and **Petrohué** (US$8), Bohle daily except Sun. To **Pucón**, US$7. To **Santiago**, express 15 hrs, fares US$15-20, 27-35 *cama* (most buses stop ½ hr for dinner); Varmontt are the most expensive, double-decker bus (US$82 including bed, cocktails, cold dinner, breakfast). Bus service to **Punta Arenas**, Austral, Turbus and Ghisoni, between 1 and 3 times a week, US$60-75 depending on company, departing either 0800 or 1100 (bus goes through Argentina via Bariloche—take US$ cash to pay for meals etc in Argentina), 38 hrs; book well in advance in Jan-Feb and check if you need a multiple Chilean visa; also book any return journey before setting out. Many buses daily to **Temuco** US$7-9, to **Valdivia**, US$7-9; **Concepción**, US$9-11. For services to Chiloé, see p 731.

To Argentina There are 2 routes to Bariloche: 1) via Lago Todos Los Santos, involving ferries across Lago Todos Los Santos, Lago Frías and Lago Nahuel Huapi; outstandingly beautiful whatever the season, though the mountains are often obscured by rain and heavy cloud. This route is operated only by Andino del Sud (address above). Bus from company offices daily at 0800, via Puerto Varas, Ensenada and Petrohué falls (20 mins stop) to Petrohué, where it connects with catamaran service across Lago Todos Los Santos to Peulla. Lunch stop in Peulla 2 hrs (lunch not incl in fare: *Hotel Peulla* is expensive, **see p 720** for alternatives). Chilean customs in Peulla, followed by a 2 hr bus ride through the Paso Pérez Rosales to Argentine customs in Puerto Frías, 20 min boat trip across Lago Frías to Puerto Alegre and bus from Puerto Alegre to Puerto Blest. From Puerto Blest it is a beautiful 1½ hr catamaran trip along Lago Nahuel Huapi to Puerto Panuelo, from where there is a 1 hr bus journey to Bariloche (bus drops passengers at hotels, camping sites or in town centre). The fare is US$90 one way. Out of season this trip is done over 2 days with overnight stay in Peulla, add about US$60 to single fare for accommodation in *Hotel Peulla*. (Baggage is taken to *Hotel Peulla* automatically but for alternative accommodation see under Peulla above.) Note that the trip may be cancelled if the weather is poor and there are reports of difficulty in obtaining a refund. Try both Puerto Montt and Puerto Varas offices if you want to do this trip in sections. It is impossible to do this journey independently out of season as then there are buses only as far as Ensenada, there is little traffic for hitching and none of the ferries take vehicles.

2) via Osorno and the Puyehue pass. Daily services are run on this route by several bus

companies (details under Osorno **p 714**) with a reduced service out of season. Although all buses go to Bariloche, other destinations in Argentina vary. Lanín also goes to Neuquén, as does Igi Llaima (also to Zapala). Book well in advance in Jan and Feb. Hitchhiking on this route is difficult and may take as long as four days. When driving N out of Puerto Montt (or out of Puerto Varas, Frutillar, etc), look for signs to 'Ruta 5'.

Shipping Offices in Puerto Montt: Navimag (Naviera Magallanes SA), Terminal Transbordadores Angelmó 2187, T 253318, F 258540. **Constantino Kochifas C**, Angelmó 1660 y Miraflores (Castilla 588), T 252619, Telex 370161 NATUK CL. **Transmarchilay Ltda**, Angelmó 2187, T 254654, F 253683.

Shipping Service Taxi from centre to ferry terminal, US$2. All shipping services should be checked in advance; schedules change frequently. Navimag's *Puerto Edén* sails to Puerto Natales every 8 days, taking 4 days and 3 nights; the fare ranges from US$120 economy (incl meals) to US$165 to US$660 in various classes of cabin (also incl meals), all prices pp. Navimag head office sells international student and hostels cards, which give 10% discount on fares. Economy class accommodation is basic, in 24-berth dormitories and there is limited additional space for economy class passengers when weather is bad. The ship has been remodelled with new cafetería, living room, library, etc. Games, videos, films and classes in history, Tai-Chi, etc are available on board. Optional tours can be booked to Patagonian attractions. Food is good, but only water is served except at breakfast, so take supplementary food and drinks. Economy class and cabin passengers eat in separate areas, but economy class passengers are able to buy extra food and drinks in the cabin class restaurant outside meal-times. Book well in advance, for departures, between mid-Dec and mid-Mar especially for the voyage S (Puerto Natales is less heavily booked). Numerous reports of confusion and difficulty over booking: Navimag office in Santiago sometimes says economy class can only be booked in Puerto Montt and Puerto Natales, but if you insist they can do it for you. Navimag, especially in Puerto Montt frequently say economy class is sold out and only cabins are available, then sell economy tickets just before departure. Try at *Travellers*, see **Travel Agents**, above. (It is well worth going to the port on the day of departure if you have no ticket. Reservations are reported to be worthless unless you have paid. Note that departures are frequently delayed—or even advanced.)

The dramatic 1,460 km journey first goes through Seno Reloncaví and Canal Moraleda. From Bahía Anna Pink along the coast and then across the Golfo de Peñas to Bahía Tarn it is a 12-17 hrs sea crossing, usually rough. The journey continues through Canal Messier, Angostura Inglesa, Paso del Indio and Canal Kirke (one of the narrowest routes for large shipping). The only regular stop is made off Puerto Edén (1 hr S of the Angostura Inglesa), where there are 3 shops, with scant provisions; there is one off-licence, one café, but no hotel or camping facility, nor running water. Population is 180, plus 5 *carabineros* and the few remaining Alacaluf Indians. It is, though, the drop-off point for exploring Isla Wellington, which is largely untouched, with stunning mountains. If stopping here, take all food; maps (not very accurate) are available in Santiago.

The roll on/roll off vehicle ferry m/n *Evangelistas* of Navimag, runs twice weekly to Puerto Chacabuco (80 km to the W of Coyhaique), usually Wed and Sat, returning from Puerto Chacabuco on the following day. From end-Dec to mid, or end-Mar the schedule changes to include a Sun-Tues trip from Puerto Chacabuco to Laguna San Rafael, so Pto Montt to Pto Chacabuco is Wed and Sat, but return to Pto Montt is Tues and Thur (schedules change annually and in 1995-96 *Evangelistas* may sail twice a week to Lajuna San Rafael, with a second ship, *Amadeus*, sailing Puerto Montt-Puerto Chacabuco). The cruise to Puerto Chacabuco lasts about 24 hrs. First class accommodation includes 2 cabins with bath (US$125-250 depending on which cabin and number of occupants); tourist class, 14 bunks (about US$145 double); and third class, 400 reclining seats (US$68, type 'B', US$40, type 'A'). Fare to Laguna San Rafael US$155-220, reclining seat, or US$285-510 in cabin. First class reservations must be made in advance at the Santiago offices (**see p 671**). There are canteens and bars on board.

The *Colono* of Transmarchilay sails to Puerto Chacabuco on Tues and Fri between 1 Jan and early Mar, 26 hrs; passengers US$17.50-200 (double suite), vehicles US$145. Transmarchilay also runs a ferry service on the route Quellón (Chiloé)-Chaitén-Puerto Montt-Chaitén-Quellón (see under Quellón and Chaitén for details). Overbooking and long delays reported.

The m/n *Skorpios 1* and *2* of Constantino Kochifas C leave Pto Montt on Sat at 1100 for a luxury cruise with stops at Puerto Aguirre, Melinka, Laguna San Rafael, Quitralco, Castro (each ship has a slightly different itinerary) and returns to Puerto Montt on Fri at 0800. The fare varies according to season, type of cabin and number of occupants: a double ranges from US$465 (low) to US$660 (high) on *Skorpios 1* and from US$770 (low) to US$1,100 (high) on *Skorpios 2*, which is the more comfortable of the two. It has been reported that there is little room to sit indoors if it is raining on *Skorpios 1*, but generally service is excellent, the food superb and at the glacier, you chip your ice off the face for your whisky.

Patagonia Connection, Fidel Oteíza 1921, Oficina 1006, T 225-6489, F (562) 204-9118, Santiago (D Portales 872, T 259790, Puerto Montt), operates *Patagonia Express*, a catamaran which runs from Puerto Montt to Laguna San Rafael via Termas de Puyuguapi **see p 740** and Puerto Chacabuco. Stops can be made at any of these points on the weekly service, high season Jan-early Mar, low season Mar-mid Apr. High season fares for a 4 day cruise costs US$600, all inclusive. 7-day cruises also available.

The m/n *Bohemia* makes 6 day/5 night trips from Puerto Montt to Río Negro, Isla Llancahué, Baños Cahuelmó and Fiordo Leptepu/Coman, US$545-720 pp depending on season (Antonio Varas 947, T 254675, Puerto Montt).

See also under Chaitén for passenger services on Terminales Marítimos Chilenos.

Excursions   The wooded *Isla Tenglo*, close to Puerto Montt and reached by launch from Angelmó (US$0.30), is a favourite place for picnics. Magnificent view from the summit. The island is famous for its *curantos*, a local dish. Chinquihue, W of Angelmó, has many seafood restaurants, with oysters as a speciality. East of Puerto Montt, Chamiza, up the Río Coihuin, has fine fishing. There is a bathing beach with black sand (polluted) at Pelluco, 4 km E of Puerto Montt (accommodation incl *cabañas*; several good seafood restaurants, incl *Pazos*, best *curanto* in Puerto Montt, rec). *Isla Guar* may be visited by boat from Angelmó harbour (1600, 2 hrs); boat returns from other end of island at 0730. The N shore is rocky. Accommodation, if lucky, at the church; best to camp.

West of Puerto Montt the Río Maullín, which drains Lago Llanquihue, has some attractive waterfalls and good fishing (salmon). The little fishing village of *Maullín*, founded in 1602 (**B** *Motel El Pangal*, 5 km away, T 244), at the mouth of the Río Maullín, is worth a visit. Southeast of here, on the coast, is Carelmapu; 3 km away is an excellent beach, Playa Brava. *Calbuco*, centre of the fishing industry, with good scenery is on an island linked to the mainland by a causeway. It can be visited direct by boat or by road (the old coast road from Puerto Montt is very beautiful).

CHILOÉ (6)

The culture of the island of Chiloé has been heavily influenced by isolation from Spanish colonial currents, the mixture of early Spanish settlers and Mapuche indians and a dependence on the sea. Religious and secular architecture, customs and crafts, combined with delightful landscapes, all contribute to Chiloé's uniqueness.

The Isla de *Chiloé* is 250 km long, 50 km wide, 9,613 sq km, and has a population of 116,000. There are two main towns, Ancud and Castro (airport), and many fishing villages. Seaweed is harvested for export to Japan. The hillsides in summer are a patchwork quilt of wheat fields and dark green plots of potatoes. Inland are impenetrable forests. There has recently been appreciable development, and power and water shortages and poor sanitation are things of the past. Though the weather is often cold and foggy, the island is extremely beautiful when the sun is out. Music is popular, with many players in the waterfront cafés in Castro. The local sailing sloops, *lanchas*, are fast being replaced by diesels, very few can be seen now. Chiloé was claimed for Spain by Martín Ruiz de Gamboa in 1567 and the few Spaniards who settled divided the indigenous population and their lands between them. The rising of the Mapuche after 1598 which drove the Spanish out of the mainland S of the Río Biobío left the small Spanish community on Chiloé (some 200 settlers in 1600) isolated. During the seventeenth century Chiloé was served by a single annual ship from Lima. In 1600 and 1642 the island was attacked by Dutch pirates. Following a violent earthquake in 1646 the Spanish population asked the Viceroy in Lima for permission to leave but this was refused.

Much of the island's distinctive character derives from its 200 years of isolation from the mainstream of Spanish colonial development. A major role in the island's cultural development was played by the Jesuits, who established missions (*reducciones*) for the indigenous population and ordered the building of schools and churches. By 1767, when the Jesuits were expelled, there were 79 churches on the island. Today it is dotted with nearly 150 churches, several of them dating

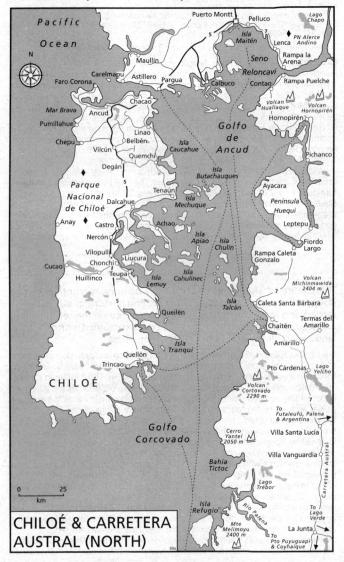

CHILOÉ & CARRETERA
AUSTRAL (NORTH)

from the eighteenth century. Chiloé was also used by the Jesuits as a base for missionary activity on the mainland; from here expeditions were sent out to the Río de la Plata and to the far S. The islanders were the last supporters of the Spanish Crown in South America. When Chile rebelled the last of the Spanish Governors fled to the island and, in despair, offered it to Britain. Canning, the British Foreign Secretary, turned the offer down. The island finally surrendered to the patriots in 1826.

Since independence the relatively high birth rate and the shortage of employment on Chiloé have led to regular emigration. Chilotes have settled throughout Chile, were prominent as shepherds in late nineteenth century Patagonia and are an important source of labour for the Argentine oil industry.

The availability of wood and the lack of metals have left their mark on the island. Some of the oldest churches are built entirely of wood, using wooden pegs instead of nails. Although the earliest houses were thatched, this was replaced by thin tiles (*tejuelas*) made in a wide variety of styles from alerce wood. However another typical feature of the island, *palafitos* or wooden houses built on stilts over the water, is a late nineteenth century innovation. The island is also famous for its traditional handicrafts, notably woollens and basket ware.

Transport to Chiloé From Puerto Montt buses run 15 times a day (US$1.50) to **Pargua** (55 km, 1 hr) on the Straits of Chacao. (At Pargua, *Hotel La Ruta*, on A Prat. At **Chacao**, **E** pp *Pensión Chiloé*; **E** pp *Hospedaje Angelino*.) The ferry terminal in Pargua is in town. Most buses go right through to Ancud (3½-4 hrs) and Castro (eg Trans Chiloé at 0810, 1220 and 1820, Varmontt at 0800, 1230 and 1830, Bus Norte at 1115), but the company with most services is Cruz del Sur, 10 a day between 0730 and 2015 to Ancud and Castro, 5 to Chonchi and Quellón. Cruz del Sur, fares are highest, Trans Chiloé lowest (but fill up quickly). Fares from Puerto Montt: Ancud, Cruz del Sur US$3.50 (Trans Chiloé US$2.50), Castro, Cruz del Sur US$6 (Trans Chiloé US$4.60), Chonchi, US$5, Quellón, US$7. Note that there are direct bus services from Santiago, Osorno, Valdivia, Temuco and Los Angeles to Chiloé. Buses drive on to the ferry (passengers can get out of the bus), foot passengers travel free. Transmarchilay run frequent ferries (two vessels in summer) and Cruz del Sur runs ferries for its buses; the buses have priority, but cars are also taken. There are 24 trips a day by ferry: cars US$7.75 one way (20 mins crossing). The Tourist Office in Ancud has a number of brochures of different circuits on Chiloé which are very useful (eg Circuito Histórico Cultural, Circuito Mitológico, Excursión al Sur de Chiloé), all are free.

Ancud (pop 20,000; DDD 0656) is 30 km W of the Straits of Chacao. The port is dominated by the Fuerte San Antonio, built by the Spanish in 1770, now well-preserved. Close to it are the ruins of the Polvorín del Fuerte (a couple of cannon and a few walls). 1 km N of the fort is a secluded beach, Arena Gruesa. 2 km E is a Mirador offering good views of the island and across to the mainland. Near the Plaza de Armas is the Museo Regional (open Tues-Fri 0900-1300, 1430-1830, Sat 1000-1330, 1430-1800, US$0.70), with an interesting collection on the early history of Chiloé as well as a replica of the small sailing ship *Ancud* which, in 1843, sailed to the Straits of Magellan to claim the Peninsula for Chile. No facilities.

Hotels A1 *Hostería Ancud*, San Antonio 30, T 2340/2350, Telex 275002, with bath and hot water, very comfortable, friendly and helpful, but meals overpriced; **A3** *Galeón Azul*, Libertad 751, T 2567; **B** *Cabañas Las Golondrinas*, end of Baquedano at Arena Gruesa, T 2823, with bath, hot water and kitchenette; **B** *Hostería Ahui*, Av Costanera 906, T 2415, with bath and breakfast, modern, clean, good views; **B** *Montserrat*, Baquedano 417, T 2957, with bath, hot water, breakfast; **B** *Pauldeo*, Ramírez 352, T 2964, rec; **B** *Polo Sur*, Av Costanera 630, T 2200, with bath, hot water, good seafood restaurant, not cheap, avoid rooms overlooking disco next door; **C** *Lydia*, Chacabuco 630, T 2990, with bath and restaurant; **B** *Residencial Weschler*, Cochrane 480, T 2318, clean, view of bay; **D** *Caleta Ancud*, Bellavista 449, good breakfst, good restaurant; **D** *Lacuy*, Pudeto 219 nr Plaza de Armas, T 3019, rec; **D** *Hospedaje Bellavista*, Bellavista 449, with sleeping bag on floor much cheaper, no hot water; **E** *Hospedaje Capri*, Ramírez 325, good breakfast; **D** *Hospedaje Alinar*, Ramírez 348, clean, hot water, hospitable; **D** *Hospedaje Santander*, Sargento Aldea 69, clean, rec; **E** pp *Residencial Montenegro*, Blanco Encalada 531, T 2239, fair, no hot water; **E** pp *Residencial* on Aníbal Pinto 515, good; **E** pp Edmundo Haase Pérez, Ramírez 299, with breakfast, clean,

ANCUD

N

1. Plaza de Armas
2. Fuerte San Antonio
3. Museo Regional
4. Cathedral
5. Municipalidad
6. Market
7. Post Office
8. Tourist Office
9. Transmarchilay
10. Restaurante El Cangrejo
11. Restaurante Coral

Hotels:
12. Hosteria Ancud
13. Galeón Azul
14. Montserrat
15. Polo Sur
16. Lydia
17. Wechsler
18. Montenegro

B1. Buses Cruz del Sur
B2. Bus Terminal

Bahia de Ancud

basic, good value; **E** pp Elverrez 442, with breakfast, cold water; **E** pp Puedto 357, fair, next to watch shop; **E** pp Elena Bergmann at Anibal Pinto 382 (5 rm in private house), clean, friendly, use of kitchen; **E** pp Irma Miguel, Puedto 331, clean, homely; **E** pp Familia Vargas, Puedto 442, friendly; **E** pp Lautaro 947, T 2980, clean, friendly; **E** pp Sra Lucía, San Martín 705; **E** pp Familia Reuter-Miranda, Errázuriz 350, T 2261, with breakfast, clean, spacious, hot showers, rec. In summer, the school on Calle Chacabuco is open for lodging.

Camping *Camping Playa Larga Huicha*, 9 km N of Ancud, **E** per site, bath, hot water, electricity.

Restaurants Seafoods, almejos and cheese in market area. Good lunches at *Hotel Polo Sur*. *Carmen*, Puedto 145, Chilean cooking, pasteles; *Coral*, Puedto 346, good, not cheap; *Jardín*, same street No 263, good local food, not cheap; *Macaval*, Chacabuco 691; *El Trauco*, Blanco y Prat, seafood excellent, highly rec; *La Pincoya*, next to harbour, friendly, good seafood; *Lydia*, café-restaurant, Puedto 254, Chilean and international; *El Cangrejo*, Dieciocho 155, seafood highly rec. *Hamburguería*, Av Prat, much better than name suggests, good seafood; *Mar y Velas*, Serrano 2, 2° piso, beautiful views, good food.

Post Office Puedto y Blanco. **Telecommunications** Plaza de Armas, open Mon-Sat 0700-2200.

Tourist Office Sernatur, Libertad 665, T 2665, open Mon-Fri 0900-1300, 1430-1800.

Travel Agent *Turismo Ancud*, Puedto 219, Galería Yurie, T 2235, Telex 297700 ANCD CL.

Bus Ancud-Castro, US$2.50; frequent (see below), 1½ hrs. No direct Sun bus from Ancud to Dalcahue, need to stay in Castro. To **Puerto Montt**, 2 hrs, Cruz del Sur 10 times between 0710 and 2000, office on Chacabuco nr Puedto, Varmontt 3 a day from *Hotel Polo Sur*, Trans Chiloé also 3. Local buses leave from terminal at Pedro Montt 538.

Shipping Transmarchilay Libertad 669, T 2317/2279, Telex 375007 MARCHI CK.

Excursions Walk from Ancud W along the beach towards Faro Corona (34 km to Punta Corona), good views, interesting birdlife, dolphins can be seen, but the beach is not suitable for swimming. To Pumillahue, 27 km SW, and Mar Bravo on W coast, bus 1230 Mon-Fri. Near Pumillahue there is a penguin colony: hire a fishing boat to see it, US$2.50 pp. To Chepu, further S along the coast, famed for its river and sea fishing. There is a 2 day coastal walk between Ancud and Chepu: you can take the daily bus to Pumillahue or hitch. The route is difficult to follow so take food for 3 days and wear light-coloured clothes in summer to protect against *tavanos*. East of Ancud on the N coast is Caulín, with good beaches; fresh oysters in *Hotel Lyon*. The road goes along the beach, only passable at low tide.

From Ancud, Route 5 leads S to Castro, 88 km in good condition and from there on through Chonchi to Quellón. An alternative route S runs from near Chacao along the E coast of the island through Quemchi and Dalcahue before joining Route 5 N of **Castro** (pop 20,000; DDD 0657) capital of the island and a very friendly town. There is a tremendous variety of styles in housing, including houses on stilts (*palafitos*) above the water, on the northern side of town and by the bridge over the Río Gamboa. Local woollen articles (hats, sweaters, gloves) can be found at **Feria**, or Mercado Municipal de Artesanía on the waterfront. *Palafito* restaurants have been put up behind the market. The large **cathedral** (1906), on the Plaza de Armas, strikingly decorated in lilac and orange, with a splendid wooden interior, was built by Italian architect, Eduardo Provosoli. The **Museo Municipal** on Esmeralda, opp *Restaurante La Bomba*, contains history, folklore, handicrafts and mythology of Chiloé. The **Museo de Arte Moderno** is nr the Río Gamboa (open 1000-2000). Views of the city from **Mirador La Virgen** on Millantuy hill above the cemetery. Conaf at Gobernación, 3rd floor, Plaza de Armas. East of Castro across the estuary at Quilquico there is a wooden church dating from 1767. On the road out of town to Quellón, walk to the Peninsula and Puntilla Ten Ten (2 hrs round trip), through woods and fields, nice views.

Hotels A1 *Unicornio Azul*, Pedro Montt 228, T 2359, in summer, good but expensive for what is offered; **A2** *Cabañas Centro Turístico Nercón*, 5 km S, T 2985, rooms with bath, hot water, heating, restaurant, tennis court; **A2** *Hostería Castro*, Chacabuco 202, T 2301, with bath and breakfast, hot water, good restaurant, interesting building (in summer coach and boat trips are organized to other places on the island); **A3** *Cabañas Truyen*, 5 km S of Castro, B off season, lovely views; **B** *Casita Española*, Los Carrera 359, T 5186, heating, TV, parking, rec; **B** *Gran Alerce*, O'Higgins 808, T 2267, with bath, heating and TV, small rooms, breakfast; **B** *Moteles Auquilda*, Km 2, Panamericana Norte, T 2458; **C** *Plaza*, Blanco Encalada 38, T 5109, F 5477, with bath, D without, rec on 3rd floor, breakfast included, 2 fair comedores, good seafood, not cheap; **C** *Quinta Niklitschek*, Panamericana Norte 331 (3 km N), T 2137, better inside than out. **D** *Costa Azul*, Lillo 67, T 2440, friendly, but no heating, hot water, bed bugs; **D** *Hilton*, Ramírez 385, good value, friendly, restaurant; nr bus terminal, **E** pp *Hospedaje Chiloé*, San Martín, 800 block, breakfast, clean, rec; **D** *Hospedaje Turístico*, O'Higgins 831, good breakfast, pleasant, rec; **D** *Residencial Lidia*, Blanco Encalada 276, T 2331, clean, cold shower, good; **E** pp *Hospedaje* of Jessie Toro at Las Delicias 287, hot shower, nice family and place, clean, spacious, good bathrooms, also cabinas, warmly rec; **D** *La Bomba*, Esmeralda 270, T 2300, without bath, cheaper on 3rd floor, clean, good value, hot water, good 3 course menu; **E** pp *Casa Blanca*, Los Carrera 300, incl breakfast, clean, modern, warm; **E** pp *Residencial Capullito*, San Martín 709, clean, friendly, quiet; **E** pp *Residencial La Casona*, Serrano 488, above TV shop, with breakfast,rec; **E** *Hospedaje* at Serrano 407, Sara Borquez, breakfast, friendly, warm water; **D** *Residencial Mirasol*, San Martín 815, next to bus station, basic, friendly, noisy; **E** pp *Hospedaje Angie*, San Martín 747, small rooms, clean, pretty; **E** pp *Hospedaje Guillermo*, San Martín 700, clean, cheap; **E** pp *Hospedaje Laura Muñoz Sánchez*, O'Higgins 556, hospitable; **E** pp *Res El Gringo*, Av Lillo 51, OK; **E** *Hospedaje Ipallu*, O'Higgins 657, run down, with breakfast; **E** pp Euzaguirre 469, comfortable, rec; **E** pp María Zuñiga, Barros Arana 140, T 5026, incl breakfast, cooking facilities, friendly, secure, rec; Esmeralda 233, with bath; **E** pp Adriana Gutiérrez, Freire 758-9, breakfast, clean, good value; also good, Freire 497; **E** pp O'Higgins 415, Dpto 41, quiet, very clean, hot water; **E** pp O'Higgins 865, clean, friendly, hot water; **E** pp Chacabuco 449, good beds, clean, quiet, friendly, water only warm; **E** pp Los Carrera 560, T 2472, clean, hot water; **E** Sotomayor, 442, hot water, clean, rec; **D** *Hospedaje Sotomayor*, Sotomayor 452, T 2464, with breakfast, quiet, small beds; **E** pp *Hospedaje Tonque*, Pasaje Díaz 170, T 2773, without breakfast, clean, hot water; **E** Gamboa 588. Several on San Martín: **E** pp No 879 (Sra Judith Mancia), with breakfast, central, clean, highly rec; **E** pp Lidia Low, No 890, warm, clean, rec; **E** pp No 638, clean; **E** pp No 581, helpful. **F** *Hospedaje Polo Sur*, Barros Arana 169, T 5212, clean, safe, cooking facilities, wonderful views. Basic accommodation Dec-Feb in the Gimnasio Fisical, Calle Ramírez, F with breakfast, clean.

Camping Camping Pudú, Ruta 5, 10 km N of Castro, cabins, showers with hot water, sites with light, water, children's games. Several sites on road to Chonchi.

Restaurants *Palafito* restaurants nr the Feria Artesanía offer good food and good value, incl *Brisas del Mar*, *Mariela*, *La Amistad*; *Gipsy*, O'Higgins 548, Chinese; *Sacho*, Thompson 213, excellent food, sea views, clean; *Don Camilo*, Ramírez 566, good food, not expensive, rec; *Pizzería La Niña*, Serrano 300 block, good pizzas, welcoming staff; *Stop Inn Café*, Banco del Estado building, 2nd floor, Plaza de Armas, good coffee; *Chilo's*, San Martín 459, rec, good lunches. *Octavio*, Lillo 67, T 2440, seafood incl *curantos*, rec. *Maucari*, Lillo 93, good seafood, not expensive. In the market, try *milcaos*, fried potato cakes with meat stuffing; also *licor de oro*, like Galliano.

Exchange Banco del Estado de Chile on main square accepts TCs (at a poor rate). Better rates from Luis Barrientos Bilisco, who lives at Chacabuco 286, cash and TCs.

Doctor Muñoz de Las Carreras, near police station, surgery 1700-2000 on weekdays, rec.

Post Office On O'Higgins, W side of square; **Phone Office** Latorre y San Martín.

Shopping See above for market. Cema-Chile outlet on Esmeralda, opp *Hotel La Bomba*. *Libros Chiloé*, Serrano y Blanco Encalada, books in Spanish on Chiloé. Cassettes of typical Chilote music are widely available.

Tourist Office O'Higgins 549, T 5699; kiosk on main square opposite Cathedral.

Bicycle Hire San Martín 581.

Tours Varmontt, Plaza de Armas, day trips around the island, Jan and Feb only. Pehuén Expediciones, opp craft market; Chiloé Tours, Blanco Encalada 318; Turismo Queilen, Gamboa 502, good tours to Chonchi and Chiloé National Park, rec. LanChile agency, Thompson 245. Ladeco agency on Serrano, opp *Hostería Castro*. Transmarchilay agency at Suzuki Car Hire, San Martín y Blanco Encalada.

1. Plaza de Armas
2. Plazuela Gamboa
3. Cathedral
4. Museo Municipal
5. Municipalidad
6. Conaf / Gobernación
7. Feria de Artesanía
8. Palafitos
9. Tourist kiosk
10. Post Office
11. Telephone Office

Hotels:
12. Hostería Castro
13. Unicornio Azul
14. Plaza
15. La Bomba
16. Residencia Lidia
17. Costa Azul
18. Hospedaje Ipallu
19. Residencia Mirasol

B1. Bus Terminal
B2. Buses Cruz del Sur

CASTRO

Buses The Municipal Terminal is on San Martín, 600 block, before Sgto Aldea. Bus Norte to Ancud, Puerto Montt, Osorno and Santiago (1815), and daily to Puerto Montt at 0830 with connection to Bariloche; Bus Sur, Mon, Sat 0630 to Punta Arenas; also Ghisoni (to Punta Arenas also) and Varmontt. Local buses: Arroyo and Ocean to Cucao at 1200 daily, Sun 0900, US$2.25, more in season, no advance sales (a minibus usually leaves at 1530 for Huillinco where you can catch the bus on to Cucao, assuming the minibus arrives before the bus); to Chonchi and Huillinco, Mon, Wed, Fri 1130, 1630; Cárdenas to Dalcahue; buses to Puqueldón and Queilén.

Cruz del Sur buses (T 2389) and buses for Achao leave from the terminal behind San Francisco cathedral: Cruz del Sur to Ancud and Puerto Montt 11 a day (0700-1830), also to Osorno, Valdivia, Temuco, Concepción, Santiago (1545 Pullman, 1600 *cama*); 7 a day to Chonchi and Quellón (0700-1845); also daily Cruz del Sur service to Cucao in season. Colectivo US$4 to Chonchi from Esmeralda y Chacabuco. At least 4 buses daily (3 on Sun) to Achao (0700-1700) via Dalcahue and Curaco de Vélez. Turbus for Concepción and Santiago next to *La Bomba*; Trans Chiloé on square; Varmontt, Balmaceda 289, T 2776, next to *Hotel Plaza*.

Dalcahue 21 km N of Castro, the wooden church dates from 1858, on older foundations. Good market on Sun, from 0700 to 1300. Good quality, but bargaining practically impossible. Tourist kiosk in season. Bus from Castro (San Martín 800 block), hourly, 40 mins, US$1. Colectivos also available from 900 block of San Martín in Castro. (E *Pensión Montaña*, M Rodríguez 9, basic; **E** *Casa Puteman*, Freire 305, T 330, clean, cooking facilities; **E** *Residencial San Martín*, San Martín 1, T 207, basic, also meals; **E** *Pensión Niemun*, Freire, clean, pleasant, restaurant; many private houses offer accommodation. *Restaurant La Dalca*, Freire 502, good food and service, rec). Further N still, on the E coast is Quemchi, with *Hospedajes El Embrujo* (Pedro Montt 431, T 262) and *La Tranquera* (Yungay 40, T 250). Tenaún, 40 km E of Dalcahue, is an interesting fishing village with a good 18th-century church.

Achao, on the Island of Quinchao (ferry from Dalcahue, frequent, free for pedestrians and cyclists); is a quiet, pretty fishing village with a wooden church, built in 1730, which inspired most of the other churches in the area.

Services E pp *Cocinería Insular*, friendly, rec excellent breakfast; **E** pp *Hospedaje Sao Paulo*, Serrano 52, basic, not very clean, soft beds, good restaurant, hot water; **E** pp *Hotel Delicia*, Serrano y Delicias, clean, friendly, small restaurant; **E** pp *Hostería La Nave*, very basic, cheap restaurant, poor service; good *pensión* at Riquilme 5, E; *Casa de Familia*, Zañarte 19; *Restaurant Central*, Delicias, simple, cheap, good; *Restaurant Mar y Velas*, on waterfront, good fish, cheap, rec. **Tourist Office**, Serrano y Progreso (Dec-Mar only).

The island of Mechuque can be reached by boat from Dalcahue, dep Tues and Thur 1330, return Mon and Wed 1000, 2¹/₂ hrs, US$2.50 one way. There is one village on the island which offers splendid walks (accommodation either with the schoolteacher's son or with Sra Dina del Carmen Paillacar, E, good meals, rec).

Chonchi, 25 km S of Castro (DDD 06553; bus US$0.75, paved road), is a picturesque fishing village with rambling shingled houses painted in many colours and a lively wharf for fishing (wooden church built 1754, remodelled in neo-classical style 1859—key from handicraft shop next door). There is another eighteenth century church at Vilopulli, 5 km N. Visit Opdech (Oficina Promotora del Desarrollo Chilote), on the waterfront, which has a weaving cooperative. Tourist information kiosk on main square open Jan-Feb only.

Services A3 *Posada Antiguo Chalet*, Irarrazával, T 221, B in winter, charming, beautiful location, very good; *Cabañas Amankay*, Centenario 421, T 367, homely, kitchen facilities,

rec; **D** *Hospedaje Chonchi*, O'Higgins 379, T 288, full board available, good value, rec; **D** *Esmeralda By The Sea*, Irarrazával, large rooms, clean, patio, rec; **D** *Huildin*, Centenario 102, good; **D** *Hospedaje Mirador*, Alvarez 198, with breakfast, friendly, clean, rec; **E** *Hostería Remis*, T 271, lovely position on waterfront, good food, rec; **E** *Pensión Turismo*, Andrade y Alvarez, with breakfast. Rooms available in *Hostería* next to *Provisiones Magallanes*, F pp in shared room, or floor space, use of kitchen; at **E** *Almacén la Patagonia* at Cerda 178, basic, use of kitchen; **E** Baker at Andrade 184, clean, friendly; and Cerda 160. *Restaurant La Parada*, on left half way down hill from centre to quay, very good value. *El Alerce*, on Aguirre, excellent value; *El Trabat*, waterfront, new. **Exchange**, Nicolás Alvarez, Centenario 429, cash only.

A visit to the island of **Lemuy** is rec; 90 sq km, quiet, with good walking through undulating pastures and woodland. Ferry service from Chonchi; terminal at Puerto Huicha, 4 km from Chonchi 8-10 crossings a day, then, once across, 8 km (no bus) to the main town, Puqueldón which offers basic accommodation, clean, E, good food, in Calle J M Carrera. *Restaurant Lemuy* (F pp, basic, clean, good food) is next to the municipal offices and *Café Amancay* opp (bus from Castro). Good walks to Lincay, 5 km, or Lincura, one-day expedition.

Queilén, 46 km SE of Chonchi, is a pretty fishing village with a long beach and wooden pier. Buses from Castro, 1¾ hrs, US$1.50. (*Residencial Segovia*; *Pensión Chiloé*; *Restaurant Melinka*, good.)

From Chonchi an unpaved road leads W to **Cucao**, 40 km, one of two settlements on the W coast of Chiloé. At Km 12 is Huillinco, a charming village on Lago Huillinco (**E** pp *Residencial*, good food, or stay at the Post Office). At Cucao there is an immense 15 km beach with thundering Pacific surf and dangerous undercurrents. Electricity is due to be connected soon.

Services *Hospedaje Paraíso* and *Posada Cucao*, both **E** pp, both provide candles, warm, friendly, open all year, good meals US$5, rec; E pp with full board or *demi-pension* at *Provisiones Pacífico* (friendly, good, clean, candles provided, no hot water), Sra Boreuel or with Sra Luz Vera, next to school (rec); **E** pp *Casa Blanca*, with breakfast; one shop, take candles. For buses from Castro see above; hitching is very difficult. Taxis can be rented for about US$20; for a bit more Alfredo Alvarez will drive out from Castro, wait for several hours and take you back.

The **Chiloé National Park**, which is in 2 sections, includes large areas of forest along the coast N of Cucao. At the entrance to the S sector, 1 km N of Cucao, there is an administration centre (limited information), small museum, guest bungalow for use by visiting scientists (applications to Conaf via your embassy) and a campsite US$1.50 pp, free firewood, no access by car (there are 2 more campsites on the sandy road that runs N past the park entrance). Park entry US$1. A path runs 3 km N from the administration centre to Laguna Huelde and then N a further 12 km to Cole Cole (*refugio*, camping) offering great views, but involving crossing a stream (waist-deep at times) and best done on horseback (return journey from Cucao 9 hrs by horse). The next *refugio* is at Anay, 9 km further N. There are several other walks but signposting is limited. Maps of the park are available from Conaf in Castro (**NB** *refugios* are inaccurately located). Many houses in Cucao rent horses at US$2.50/hour, US$22/day. If you hire a guide you pay for his horse too. Horseflies are bad in summer. The N sector of the park is reached by a path which runs S from Chepu (**see** p 733) and includes a *refugio* at Lar.

Quellón Southernmost port on Chiloé; 92 km from Castro, fishing boats built at wharf, pleasant beaches. **D** *Hotel Playa*, P Montt 245, T 278, good, clean, hot water, restaurant; **E** pp *Residencial Estrella del Mar*, A Gómez García 18, basic; **E** pp *El Chico Leo*, cheap, clean, no hot water; **E** pp *Residencial El Tráfico*, on waterfront, restaurant; **E** pp *La Pincoya*, La Paz 64, T 285; **E** pp *Restaurant Las Brisas*, Miramar 25, cheap, accommodation; **F** pp *Turino Club Deportes*, floor space and camping, cold water, kitchen facilities, basic, open Dec-Feb only. *Restaurant Rucantú* on waterfront, good food, good value. *El Coral*, 22 de Mayo, good, reasonably priced, superb views; *Fogón Las Quilas*, La Paz 053, T 206, famous for lobster, rec. Daily service from Castro to Quellón, US$3,50 2 hrs.

Ferries In summer only (2 Jan-8 Mar), the Transmarchilay ferry *Pincoya* sails from Quellón to Chaitén on the mainland 3 times a week each way (days and times vary, although at the beginning of the month the ship leaves Quellón in am and Chaitén in pm, at the end of the month it leaves Quellón in pm and Chaitén in am), 5 hrs crossing, US$70-80 per car, US$11 pp. The ship continues from Chaitén to Puerto Montt. The *Pincoya* sails from Quellón to Puerto Chacabuco Wed 1400 and Sat 2000, all year round, 18 hrs, cars US$110, passengers US$20-27. If you take this ferry when heading S you miss a large section of the Carretera Austral; if you wish to see the Carretera's scenery, take the ferry to Chaitén. From 15 Mar to 29 Dec ferries go only from Pargua to Chaitén and Puerto Chacabuco. Transmarchilay office, Av Costanera s/n, Quellón T 319. Enquire first, either in Santiago or Puerto Montt.

ARCHIPELAGIC CHILE South from Puerto Montt (7)

The construction of the Carretera Austral has opened up the impressive landscapes of this wet and windy region of mountains, channels and islands. The main town is Coyhaique. A boat journey, either as a means of access, or for viewing the glacier at Laguna San Rafael gives an equally magnificent, but different perspective.

South of Puerto Montt lies a third of Chile, but its land and its climate are such that, until recently, it has been put to little human use: less than 3% of the country's population lives here. There is no real dry season. On the offshore islands and the western side of the Andes it is frequently wet and windy, particularly S of the Río Baker. North of that river, the summers are drier than the winters, but to the S, summers are windier and marginally wetter. Impenetrable forest covers much of the land, although in many parts there is stark evidence of the felling of trees which began in the nineteenth century and has accelerated during the last decade. Wood is used for construction, fencing and fuel; in this last respect it is in such demand in population centres like Coyhaique that in winter it costs as much as petrol. It is also increasingly exported, often as woodchips.

It is only the northern part, as far S as Cochrane, and the far S that are inhabited. South of Chiloé, for 1,100 km, there is a maze of islands—the tops of submerged mountains—separated by tortuous fjord-like channels, a veritable topographical hysteria. It is fortunate for shipping that this maze has a more or less connected route through it: down the channel between Chiloé and the mainland, across about 290 km of open sea beyond the southern tip of Chiloé and then down the Moraleda, Mesier, Inocentes and Smyth channels into the Straits of Magellan. In some places along this route the tide levels change by 12m. In one particular place two sharp-cut walls, 900m high, enclose the constricted channel which leads to Puerto Natales; here the waters are deeper than the cliffs are high and slack water lasts for 30 mins only. The Smyth Channel enters the Straits of Magellan at Cape Thamar. Jan and Feb are probably the best months for a trip to this region.

The original inhabitants were Tehuelches (Tzónecas, or Patagones), who lived on the pampa hunting guanacos, ñandúes (rheas) and huemules (a large indigenous deer, now almost extinct), and Alacalufes (Kaweshour, or Canoeros), who were coast dwellers living off the sea. The arrival of the Spaniards, who called the region Trapananda, led to little more than exploration of the coast by navigators and missionaries. Inland exploration in the nineteenth century was greatly helped by Fitzroy's cartographical surveys; George Charles Muster, Enrique Simpson Baeza and Juan Steffen led the main expeditions, travelling up the rivers. Colonization followed the first commercial enterprises (timber extraction, cattle farming) on an E-W axis, from Argentina or the sea, with Puerto Aisén-Coyhaique becoming the most important route.

With the opening of the **Carretera Austral** (Southern Highway) in 1988, the Pan-American Highway was extended a further 1,098 km through southern Chile to Puerto Yungay. The highway is divided into three major sections: Puerto Montt-Chaitén (242 km) with two-to-three ferry crossings (see next page); Chaitén-Coyhaique (435 km); and Coyhaique-Puerto Yungay (421 km).

Puerto Montt to Chaitén Before setting out on this section, it is imperative to check when the ferries are running. If travelling by car carry plenty of fuel and spares and protect the windscreen and headlamps. It is essential that motorists make a reservation for the ferries: do this in Puerto Montt, rather than Santiago, at the Transmarchilay office, Angelmó 1666, T 254654.

The road (Ruta 7) heads E out of Puerto Montt, through Pelluco, the city's black sand beach, and after an initial rough stretch follows the shore of the beautiful Seno Reloncaví to the first ferry across the Reloncaví estuary at **La Arena** (Km 46). Allow $1\frac{1}{2}$ hrs to get there. The last part of this section passes the southern end of the **Parque Nacional Alerce Andino** which contains tall alerce trees, some over a thousand years old (the oldest is estimated at 4,200 years old), and waterfalls. There are ranger posts at both entrances: 7 km from Correntoso (35 km E of Puerto Montt) at the N end of the park (Fierro bus from Puerto Montt daily 1230, return 1800), and 7 km E of Lenca (46 km S of Puerto Montt) at S end of the park (buses from Puerto Montt to Lenca). Very little information at ranger posts; map available from Conaf in Puerto Montt. Good campsite in the Park, 3 km from the S entrance, *refugio* at Laguna Sargazo.

Ferry La Arena-Puelche: $\frac{1}{2}$-hr crossing, US$4.65 for a car, 7 crossings daily. Ferry leaves Puelche for La Arena 45 mins before it returns from La Arena. Arrive at least 30 mins early to guarantee a place; buses have priority. Roll-on roll-off type operating all year.

58 km S of Puelche is **Río Negro**, also called **Hornopiren** after the volcano above it. Electricity 1900-0100. Buses Fierro run daily 0800 and 1500 from Puerto Montt. Río Negro is at the head of a fjord at the mouth of which is **Isla Llancahué**, good for hiking in the forests amid beautiful scenery. *Hotel Termas de Llancahué* charges C pp full board (excellent food), hot spring at the hotel. To get there, make arrangements by phoning 0965-38345. The hotel will send an open boat for you; the one-hour crossing affords views of dolphins and fur seals. Efforts are under way to preserve areas of ancient emerald araucaria and alerce forest around Volcán Hornopiren, coordinated by Ancient Forest International and Codeff, the Chilean environmental organization.

Hotels at Río Negro: *cabañas* at Copec service station, **B** *Perlas del Reloncaví*, clean, pleasant, good restaurant (may not have fuel), English and German spoken, highly rec; the cabins are usually taken before the rooms in the two other hotels, the **D** pp *Holiday Country*, on the road to Pichanco, hot shower, restaurant, and the *Hornopiren*, at the water's edge, next to the sawmill, highly rec (T Puerto Montt 255243).

There are no buses S from Río Negro. Ferry Río Negro—Caleta Gonzalo, Transmarchilay, 1500 daily, 5 hrs (may be much longer if the ferry cannot dock in rough weather). Going N the ferry leaves Caleta Gonzalo at 0900. Fare for vehicles over 4m US$75, under 4m US$64, passengers US$10. The ferry is very busy during its Jan-Feb season (it may not run outside these months, check with Transmarchilay well in advance. There can be a 2-day wait to get on the ferry). This trip may also use two ferry stages, the first, from Pinchanco up the Fiordo Leptepu, passing a narrow channel in which the German light cruiser *Dresden* hid from the British fleet in 1915. The crew was protected by the local German community. The second stage, after a 10 km stretch of road from Leptepu to Fiordo Largo crosses the Fiordo Reñihue to Caleta Gonzalo.

South of Caleta Gonzalo there is a steep climb on a coarse gravel surface to Laguna Blanca. Caleta Santa Bárbara, a black sand beach with nice camping and swimming, is at Km 44. (**NB** Do not camp close to the water.) It is a further 12 km to Chaitén.

The port of **Chaitén** has grown in importance because of the military camp and the new road. The town is quite well-laid out, but is a typical transit place, either full or empty, depending on the movements of the ferries from Puerto Montt and Quellón. Fuel is available in Chaitén (DDD 06503).

Hotels and services **B** *Hostería Schilling*, Av Corcovado 230, T 295, on waterfront, with bath and heating (hot water is turned on or off on the intuition of the landlady, check your shower before entering), no restaurant; **D** *Hotel Continental*, Juan Todesco 18, T 312, no heating nor private bath, but good meals, very helpful and friendly, rec; **D** *Hotel/Restaurant Cordillera*, Todesco y O'Higgins; **D** *Restaurant/Hotel Mi Casa*, Av Norte, T 285—on a hill—rec, with bath, water heaters in rooms, or F in youth hostel, negotiable, the owners prefer you to eat in their restaurant; **D** *Hostería Los Alerces*, Corcovado s/n, F 266, hot water, clean, restaurant; **D** *Residencial Astoria*, Av O'Higgins 442, T 263, with breakfast, shared bath, clean, bar downstairs; **E** pp *Hospedaje La Watson*, Ercilla 580, use of kitchen, clean, friendly; **E** pp *Pensión*, at Rivero y Prat (F pp for floor space, F pp for camping), use of kitchen, clean, open all year. **E** pp Corcovada 466, family atmosphere, hot shower extra; **E** pp Martín Ruiz, Carretera Austral 1 km N, incl breakfast, friendly, nice views; *Los Arrayanes* campsite 4 km N, with hot showers and close to sea, good. *Café-restaurante Flamengo*, Av Corcovado, T 314, excellent, popular with travellers; *Restaurante Mahurori*, Independencia 141. Shopping and most facilities. Phone office in supermarket next to *Hostería Schilling*.

Transport From 2 Jan to early Mar Transmarchilay ferries *Pincoya* and *Mailen* run between Chaitén, Puerto Montt and Quellón on Chiloé: sailings for Puerto Montt are on Mon 2200 and Fri 0900, 11 hrs; from Puerto Montt to Chaitén Tues 1200 and Fri 2000. Fares to Puerto Montt US$80 per car over 40m, US$70 under 40m, US$11 per deck passenger, seat US$20, bunk US$40. Sailings to/from Quellón and fares under Quellón. At other times of the year ferries from Chaitén go only twice a week to Pargua. Check in advance for exact times; office Av Corcovado 266, T 272. There is also a ferry to Puerto Montt for trucks, Ro-Ro *Mercedes*, Terminales Marítimos Chilenos, which will also take passengers but with no shelter, standing only, unless someone lets you get in their vehicle, once a week (twice a week Jan-Feb), 12 hrs, US$8. Office is in a hardware store (*ferretería*) on Juan Todesco, T 333; in Puerto Montt, Chorillos y Pudeto, T 257259.

Flights Puerto Montt-Chaitén-Puerto Montt with Don Carlos, Juan Todesco 42, T 275, 1220 and 1600, Mon-Fri, 1220 on Sat, US$35. Also Aerosur, same fare.

Artetur (Av Costanera) runs microbuses between Chaitén and Coyhaique, once a week (US$28.50) 12-14 hrs. The service depends very much on demand and in winter especially may not run all the way (ie only to La Junta). On the full service, the bus stops overnight in La Junta in winter but only briefly in summer. Other stops on request, but it is easier to go right through than pick up a bus en route. Similar service by Transportes San Rafael, Mon and Thur 1200, summer only. Hitching the whole route takes about a week, but you must be prepared for a day's wait if you find yourself out of luck.

Excursion 25 km S of Chaitén is *Amarillo* (accommodation in village bar, E, breakfast US$1; meals at *Las Rosas* rec); 5 km E of the village are thermal baths (2 wooden sheds with very hot pool inside, US$3 pp, also outdoor swimming pool), camping possible, and one cabin for hire with woodstove and bath, sleeps 4, B (accommodation is being extended). From the thermal baths it is possible to hike along the old trail to Futaleufú, 4-7 days, not for the inexperienced, be prepared for wet feet all the way. The trail follows the Río Michinmawida (passing the volcano of the same name) to Lago Espolón. A sporadic ferry crosses the lake taking cargo only to Futaleufú. Campsite at this end of the lake also has bungalows (see below).

There is superb salmon fishing in the rivers, and the local people are very friendly.

Chaitén to Coyhaique Puerto Cárdenas 46 km S of Chaitén, lies on the northern tip of beautiful Lago Yelcho (out of 10 houses and a police post, there are 2 places to stay, incl **C** *Residencial Yelcho*, clean, full board available). Campsite (US$8 pp) 3 km S of the river crossing, ask the owners in a little white house nr the lake. At Km 60, on the western side of Lago Yelcho, a path leads to the glacier which can be clearly seen from Puente Ventisquero on the road (2 hrs walk). At *Villa Santa Lucía* (Km 81), a road branches E to Argentina. Santa Lucía has 30 houses, a military camp, one small shop, bread from a private house, and accommodation on main street at No 7 (Sra Rosalía Cuevas de Ruiz, basic, meals available), No 13, breakfast US$1, and No 16, not bad, all F pp, none has hot water.

The road to the border is single track, gravel, passable in a regular car, but best with a good, strong vehicle; the scenery is beautiful. Accommodation can be found at La Cabaña, Puerto Piedra (Camping y Cabañas, T 280) and *Puerto Ramírez* (*Hostería Río Malito*—Sr Soto—nearby, rooms, camping, fishing), whence there are two roads to the Argentine border at *Futaleufú* and Palena (several *pensiones*, Expreso Yelcho bus from Chaitén twice a week, US$12, 5½ hrs). 6 km before Futaleufú, turn left to Lago Espolón for campsite and cabins, E per bed, US$3.75 for a motorhome; gorgeous lake, warm enough for a quick dip (take care with the current). There is superb rainbow trout fishing in Lago Espolón, ask for the Valebote family's motorboat. The fishing is also excellent in Río Yelcho, Lago Yelcho and Río Futaleufú (the *Isla Monita Lodge* offers packages for anglers and non-anglers on a private island in Lago Yelcho, with fishing in many nearby locations; Turismo Grant, PO Box 52311, Santiago, T 639-5524, F 633-7133). See also **Fishing** under **Sport** in Information for Visitors. Aníbal, who owns the campsite, sells meat, bread, beer and soft drinks and will barbecue lamb. The area around Espolón and Futaleufú has a microclimate, 30°C in the day in summer, 5° at night.

Hotels and transport Futaleufú D *Res Carahue*, O'Higgins 322, T 221; **E** pp *Hotel Continental*, Balmaceda 597, T 222, basic, hot water, clean, rec, cheap restaurant. A microbus runs from Chaitén to Futaleufú on Tues, at least. At the small grey store, Kitty, at the school corner on Balmaceda, ask about bus Futaleufú to the border, Tues and Fri 1300 approx, US$3, ½ hr. From the border (new bridge over the Río Grande), bus to Esquel, US$3, 1½ hrs, Mon-Thur 0800. Esquel is the starting point for several Argentine national parks.

Coming from Argentina, allow 1½ hrs for formalities; continue from Futaleufú to Puerto Ramírez, but don't go into Ramírez, take the unsigned right turn to Chaitén (left goes to Palena). **NB** At border points they only issue transit visas, which can cause problems. You must either leave within 10 days or renew your entry stamp at an immigration office.

La Junta (where the buses stop) is at the confluence of Río Rosselot and Río Palena, 151 km from Chaitén, 270 km from Coyhaique. It is a drab, expensive village, but the fishing is good and the walks to Lake Rosselot beautiful. **E** pp *Hostería Copihue*, Antonio Varas 611, T 314140, few rooms but nice, shared bath, hot water, good meals; **D** *Café Residencial Patagonia*, Lynch 331, T 314115, good meals; **C** *Hostería Valderas*, Varas s/n, T 314105, incl breakfast. Fuel is available. Buses to Coyhaique, Artetur (Diego Portales 183), US$14.30, twice a week, also Transaustral twice a week US$15. If desperate to change money try the hotels, but bargain hard. A 74 km road heads E to Lago Verde; at Lago Risopatrón is a Conaf campsite.

Puyuguapi (also spelt Puyuhuapi; DDD 068), 196 km S of Chaitén, at the end of the Puyuguapi Canal, is an intriguing town founded by Germans in 1935. The famous carpet factory can be visited. 18 km SW, accessible only by boat, are Termas de Puyuhuapi, several springs with 50°C water filling two pools nr the beach (baths cost US$6.50 pp, children under 12 US$4.40, take food and drink). The *Hotel Termas de Puyuhuapi* has accommodation at A1-L3 (depending on season and type of room), incl use of baths and boat to hotel, full board US$35 extra, good restaurant. For reservations: Patagonia Connection, Fidel Oteíza 1921, Oficina 1006, Casilla 16417, Correo 9, Santiago, T 223-5567/225-6489, F (562) 274-8111 (in Puyuguapi T 325103). (See also under Puerto Montt **Shipping**.) Boat schedule from jetty, 2 hrs walk from town, 0930, 1000, 1200, 1230, 1830, 1900, residents only, US$3 each way. 10 mins crossing. Sr Alonso runs day-trips from Puyuguapi, US$30. **Parque Nacional Queulat** nearby is, according to legend, the place where the rich town of Césares once was. In the park, 24 km S of Puyuguapi, are the beautiful Ventisquero Colgante (hanging glacier), campsite, and the Salto del Cóndor waterfall. Operation Raleigh opened a number of trails in the park (entry US$1; camping US$3.50).

Accommodation and services **C** pp *Residencial Alemana*, Av Otto Uebel 450, T 325118, a large wooden house on the main road, owned by Sra Ursula Flack Kroschewski, comfortable, highly rec; **C** pp *Hostería Ludwig*, on the road S, T 325131, excellent, often full; **E** pp *Hospedaje El Pino*, Hamburgo s/n, T 325117, homemade bread, friendly; **E** pp *pensión* of Sra Leontina Fuentes, Llantureo y Circunvalación, clean, hot water, good breakfast for US$1; **E** pp *Residencial Elizabeth*, Llantureo y Henríquez, incl breakfast, clean; 300m S at Sur Rolando, stay at Sra Sophía's house; **E** pp *pensión* at Tureo 18. Cabins at Fiordo Quelat, cheap, rec. There is a dirty campsite by the sea behind the general store. The store is behind the service station, which sells fuel until 2100. Opposite is *Café Rossbach* with limited menu, not cheap, excellent salmon (owned by the Kroschewski family). There are 2 bars. Transport out of Puyuguapi is very scarce. Artetur (O'Higgins 039, T 325101) to Coyhaique and La Junta twice a week, Transaustral once a week (Tues), Transaustral twice a week to Coyhaique.

59 km S of Puyuguapi a road branches W and follows the Río Cisne 35 km to **Puerto Cisnes** where you can buy food and find accommodation. (**D** pp *Hostal Michay*, Mistral 112, T 346462; **D** *Residencial El Gaucho*, A Holmberg 140, T 346483, with breakfast, dinner available, welcoming, hot water; *pensión* at Carlos Condell y Dr Steffen, **D** pp, with breakfast, hot shower, friendly. Petrol available. There are buses Wed and Sun at 1100 to Coyhaique with Litoral, 5½ hrs, US$12.85, Trans Mañihuales daily US$12.85, Colectivos Basoli 2 a week, US$11.50. The Río Cisnes is rec for rafting or canoeing; 160 km of grand scenery, with modest rapids except for the horrendous drop at Piedra del Gato; there is a 150m cliff at Torre Bright Bank. Good camping in the forest.

At Cisne Medio (no hotel, restaurant or telephone), 92 km S of Puyuguapi, there is a road to La Tapera and to the Argentine border. A few km N of Cisne Medio provisions and lodging can be found at Villa Amengual. 6 km S is the **Parque Nacional Lago Las Torres**, a wonderful lake with good fishing and a small Conaf campsite (free).

At Km 125 a road branches E to El Toqui copper mine. 23 km further S is *Villa Mañihuales*, connected by bus with Coyhaique (Trans Mañihuales, one a day except Sun). There are at least 3 *pensiones*, incl **E** pp *Pensión Bienvenido*, clean, friendly, and restaurant; **E** pp *Villa Mañihuales*, friendly, breakfast (both right-hand side of road going S at S end). 13 km S of Mañihuales the road forks W to Puerto Aisén, E to Coyhaique. At Villa Ortega on the Coyhaique branch, the *Restaurant Farolito* takes guests, E pp, rec.

Puerto Aisén, 426 km S of Chaitén, used to be the region's major port, but it has been replaced by Puerto Chacabuco, 15 km to the W. They say it rains 370 days a year in Puerto Aisén (pop 13,050; DDD 332), quite an attractive town at the meeting of the rivers Aisén and Palos. There are few vestiges of the port left, just some boats high and dry on the river bank when the tide is out and the foundations of buildings by the river, now overgrown with fuchsias and buttercups. To see any maritime activity you have to walk a little way out of town to Puerto Aguas Muertas where the fishing boats come in. There is a good walk to Laguna Los Palos, 2 hrs. Folklore festival in 2nd week of Nov. A new bridge over the Aisén and paved road lead to *Puerto Chacabuco* (DDD 067); a regular bus service runs between the two. The harbour is a short way from the town. In season the *Patagonia* sails regularly to Termas de Chiconal, about 1 hr from Puerto Chacabuco, offering a good way to see the fjord, US$20, take own food. Services given below are in Puerto Aisén unless stated otherwise.

Accommodation hard to find, most is taken up by fishing companies in both ports. In Puerto Aisén: **D** *Plaza*, O'Higgins 237, T 332784, without breakfast; **D** *Residencial Aisén*, Av Serrano Montaner 37, T 332725, good food, clean, full board available; **E** pp *Roxy*, Aldea 972, T 332704, friendly, clean, large rooms, highly rec, restaurant; **E** pp unnamed *hospedaje* at Serrano Montaner 471, T 332574, very pleasant and helpful, rec; **E** pp *Café-Restaurant Yaney Ruca*, Aldea 369, T 332583, clean, friendly. No campsite but free camping easy.

In Puerto Chacabuco: **A2** *Parque Turístico Loberías de Aisén*, Carrera 50, T 351112/5, F 351188, excellent meals, climb up steps direct from port for drink or meal overlooking boats and mountains before boarding; **D** *Hotel Moraleda*, O'Higgins, T 331155. No other places to buy food or other services.

Exchange on Plaza de Armas will only change cash, not TCs.

Post Office on other side of bridge from Plaza de Armas; **Telephone Office** on S side of Plaza de Armas, next to *Café Rucuray*, which posts boat information.

Tourist Office in Municipalidad, Arturo Prat y Sgto Aldea, 1 Dec to end-Feb only; helpful.

Bus to Puerto Chacabuco, La Cascada on Serrano Montaner, to left of Sgto Aldea (main street) walking away from Plaza de Armas, 6 a day between 0800-1730, 30 mins, US$1, return 0830-1800; colectivo US$1.50 pp.

La Cascada to Coyhaique, 4 a day between 0830-1900 (Sun and holidays between 0845 and 1930), US$3, 1½ hrs; Transaustral, Sgto Aldea next to No 348, 4 a day; Don Carlos taxi-bus, 8 a day, US$3. Transaustral and La Cascada have daily buses between Coyhaique and Puerto Chacabuco.

Shipping Offices Agemar, Teniente Merino 909, T 332716, Puerto Aisén; Navimag, Terminal de Transbordadores, Puerto Chacabuco, T 351111, F 351192; Transmarchilay, Av O'Higgins s/n, T 351144, Puerto Chacabuco. It is best to make reservations in these companies' offices in Puerto Montt, Coyhaique or Santiago (or, for Transmarchilay, in Chaitén or Ancud). For trips to Laguna San Rafael, see below; out of season, they are very difficult to arrange, but try Edda Espinosa, Sargento Aldea 943, or ask at *Restaurant Yaney Ruca* or *Restaurant Munich*.

Ferry Services Transmarchilay's *Colono* runs from Puerto Chacabuco via the Canal Moraleda to Puerto Montt, Mon and Wed, 26 hrs (fares under Puerto Montt); meals are available. This service operates 2 Jan to early Mar only, and in this season the ship also makes an excursion to Laguna San Rafael each Sat at 2200, returning Mon 0800 (fares, incl food, from US$165-440, ranging from economy class to cabin). The *Colono's* schedules for the rest of the year on this route are not given in any timetable; enquire locally. Transmarchilay's *Pincoya* sails to Quellón on Chiloé Thur 1200 and Sun 1600, all year round (fares under Quellón). Navimag's *Evangelistas* sails each Thur and Sun from Puerto Chacabuco to Puerto Montt, taking about 24 hrs (fares under Puerto Montt, the *pionero* seats are quite spacious and comfortable and there is a cafeteria selling burgers, sandwiches, soft drinks, beer, hot beverages, etc); it too diverts from its schedule in summer to run a 5-day trip to Laguna San Rafael, leaving Sat, from US$250. See under Puerto Montt **Shipping** for *Patagonia Express*.

The paved road from Puerto Aisén to Coyhaique passes through the **Parque Nacional Río Simpson**, with beautiful waterfalls and good views of the river. There is a campsite near the turning to Santuario San Sebastián.

Coyhaique, 420 km S of Chaitén (pop put at 38,000; DDD 067), the administrative and commercial centre of the region, is located in a large green valley surrounded by mountains. The town provides a good base for hiking and skiing excursions in the area and has a good Museo Regional de la Patagonia Central in the Casa de Cultura, Baquedano 310 (US$0.75, Tue-Sun 0900-1300, 1500-2000). The museum contains photos of early settlers, history, paleontology, fauna and archaeology. The town's plaza is pentagonal and on it stand the Cathedral, the Intendencia, the Liceo San Felipe Benicio and a handicraft market. When entering Coyhaique from the airport, look left from the bridge over the Río Simpson for the Piedra del Indio, a rock outcrop which looks like a face in profile. Fuel is available in Coyhaique, several stations.

Hotels In summer rooms are in very short supply; the tourist office has a full list of all types of accommodation, but look out for notices in windows since any place with less than 6 beds does not have to register with the authorities (several on Baquedano and Almte Simpson).

A3 Los *Ñires*, Baquedano 315, T 232261, with breakfast, pleasant; **A2** *Cabañas La Pasarela*, T 234520, Km 1.5 Carretera a Aisén, good atmosphere, *comedor*; **A3** *Austral*, Colón 203, T 232522, hot water, clean, tours arranged, friendly, rec; **E** pp *Cabaña San Sebastián*, Freire 554, T 231762, with bath and breakfast; **E** pp *Residencial El Reloj*, Baquedano 444, T 231108, with restaurant; **D** pp *El Serrano*, Ignacio Serrano 91, Sra Berly Pizarro Lara, T 235522, with breakfast, friendly, clean, rec; **D** *Residencial Puerto Varas*, Serrano 168, T 233689, without bath, check which of the bathrooms has hot water, restaurant and bar, basic, tatty; **A2** *Cabañas Río Simpson*, T 232183, Km 3 road to Pto Aysén, cabins for 5, or 2, fully-equipped, horse hire, fishing; **D** *Hospedaje* at Baquedano 20, T 232520, Patricio y Gedra Guzmán, room in family home (also 3 comfortable flats), use of kitchen, breakfast with homemade bread, tent sites with bathroom and laundry facilities down by the river, English spoken, most hospitable, rec; **D** *Hospedaje* Hermina Mansilla, 21 de Mayo 60, with breakfast, highly rec; **E** pp *Cabaña Abedules*, 18 de Septiembre 463, F 232396, at Plaza Angol, cabins for 5, hot water, heating, kitchen, TV, suitable for families; **E** pp Manuel Torres, Barroso 957, hot water, use of kitchen, good; **E** pp *Residencial Navidad*, Baquedano 198, T 235159, without bath or breakfast, comedor, hot showers, use of kitchen, clean. Several cheap places on Av Simpson, eg **F** pp at No 649. **E** pp *Los Cuatro Hermanos* Colón 495, T 232647, without breakfast (more with), hot water, clean; **E** pp Carrera 33-A, rec; **E** pp Gladys Chadil, Baquedano 274, small rooms, very good; **E** pp *Hospedaje* at Lautaro 532, T 231852, good for family groups. Youth hostel in summer at one of the schools (it changes each year), F pp with sleeping bag.

Camping At Baquedano 20, see above. There are many camping sites in Coyhaique and on the road between Coyhaique and Puerto Aisén, eg at Kms 1, 2 (*Camping Alborada*, US$8.50, T 231014, hot shower), 24, 25, 35, 37, 41, 42 (*Camping Río Correntoso*, T 232005, US$15 per site, showers, fishing, Automobile Club discount) and 43. Sernatur in Coyhaique has a full list of all sites in XI Región.

Restaurants *Loberías de Chacabuco*, Barroso 553, good seafood, slow service; *Café Oriente*, Calle 21 de Mayo y Condell 201, good bakery, tea; *Moneda de Oro*, Prat 431, good food, good value; *Café Kalu*, A Prat 402, serves set meals, hamburgers. *Café Ricer*, Calle Horn 48, cheap; *Cafetería Alemana*, Condell 119, nice, excellent cakes and coffee; *Lito's*, Lautaro 147, next to Bus Terminal, good food and atmosphere; *Casino de Bomberos*, Gral Parra 365, wide range, cheap. A good bar is *Pub*, 12 de Octubre 361, nice atmosphere and music; around the corner is *Bar West*, Western style.

Exchange Banco Osorno, Prat 340, T 232214, for cash advance on Visa, and Turismo Prado, 21 de Mayo 417, T/F 231271, both accept TCs. For Argentine pesos, dollars and cheques go to Lavaseco on Gral Parra. Fincard (Mastercard), A Prat 340, local 1, T 233026, Mon-Fri 0900-1400, 1530-1900, Sat 0930-1330; at same address, oficina 208, *El Libertador*, T 233342.

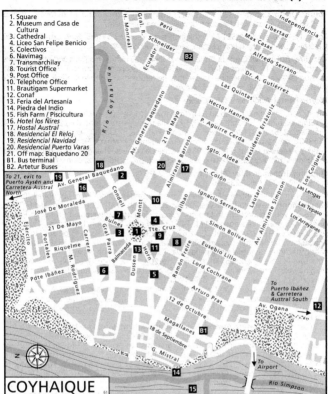

Legend (map):

1. Square
2. Museum and Casa de Cultura
3. Cathedral
4. Liceo San Felipe Benicio
5. Colectivos
6. Navimag
7. Transmarchilay
8. Tourist Office
9. Post Office
10. Telephone Office
11. Brautigam Supermarket
12. Conaf
13. Feria del Artesania
14. Piedra del Indio
15. Fish Farm / Piscicultura
16. Hotel los Nires
17. Hostal Austral
18. Residencial El Reloj
19. Residencial Navidad
20. Residencial Puerto Varas
21. Off map: Baquedano 20
B1. Bus terminal
B2. Artetur Buses

COYHAIQUE

Language School *Baquedano International Language School*, Baquedano 20, at *Hospedaje* of Sr Guzmán (see **Hotels** above), T 212520, F 232500: US$300 per week course including lodging and all meals, 4 hrs a day person-to-person tuition, other activities organized at discount rates, open Jan-Feb.

Laundry *Lavamatic*, Bilbao 198; *QL*, Bilbao 160; *Universal*, Gen Parrá 55; *Lottie*, Baquedano 1259.

Post Office Cochrane 202, open Mon-Fri 0830-1230, 1430-1800, Sat 0830-1200. **Telephone office** at Barroso 626, open till 2200, opens on Sun about 0900.

Shopping *Feria de Artesanía* on the square; *Cema-Chile* on square, between Montt and Barroso. Large well-stocked supermarkets: *Brautigam*, Horn, Prat y Bilbao (closed Sun); *Central*, Magallanes y Bilbao, open daily till 2230; 2 small ones on Prat, Nos 480 and 533, open Sun. Food, especially fruit and vegetables, is more expensive than in Santiago.

Travel Agents *Turismo Prado*, address in **Exchange** above; *Expediciones Coyhaique*, Bolívar 94, T/F 232300. Both offer tours of local lakes and other sights arrange Laguna San Rafael trips, etc; Prado does historical tours, while Expediciones does fishing trips and excursions down the Río Baker. *Turismo Quelat*, 21 de Mayo 1231, T/F 231441, trips to Quelat glacier, adventure and nature tourism, fishing, etc. *Residencial Serrano*, Calle Serrano, organizes trips to Lake Elizalde and Lake Atrevesado, US$15 pp. *Aventura*, Fco Bilbao 171, T 234748, offers rafting; *45 Sur*, 12 de Octubre 253, T 234599, horseriding, good value; *Alex Prior*, T 234732, for fly fishing. Tours only operate in season.

Tourist Office Cochrane 320, T 231752. **Conaf** office, Ogana 1060. Maps (photocopies of 1:50,000 IGM maps) from Dirección de Vialidad on the square.

Taxis US$5 to airport (US$1.65 if sharing); fares in town US$1.35. 50% extra after 2100. Colectivos congregate at Prat y Bilbao, average fare US$0.50.

Car Hire **Automóvil Club de Chile**, Bolívar 254, T 231649, rents jeeps and other vehicles. **Budget**, Parra 215; **Traeger-Hertz**, Baquedano 457; **Economy**, Carrera 339, T 233363, cars may be taken across Argentine border, may be returned to a different office; **Automundo AVR**, Bilbao 509. 4WD rec for Carretera Austral.

Bicycle Rental *Figón*, Simpson y Colón.

Air Airport, Teniente Vidal, about 5 km from town includes a steep climb up and down to the Río Simpson bridge. LanChile flies daily to Santiago and Puerto Montt daily. LanChile office at Gral Parra 215, T 231188. Ladeco, Dussen y Prat 188, T 231300. Air taxi to visit glaciers, US$350 (five passengers), also to southern archipelagic region. Transportes Aéreos 'Don Carlos', Subteniente Cruz 63, T 232981 to Chile Chico (Tues, Thur, Sat), and Cochrane (Wed, Fri, 45 mins, rec only for those who like flying, with strong stomachs, or in a hurry).

Shipping Transmarchilay, 21 de Mayo 417, T 231971, Telex 377003 MARCHI CK. **Navimag**, Ibáñez 347, T 233306, F 233386.

Buses Terminal at Lautaro y Magallanes; most buses leave from here, but not all. To/from **Puerto Montt**, via Bariloche, all year, Turbus, Baquedano 1171, T 231333, Tues and Fri 1600, US$28.50, with connections to Osorno, Valdivia, Temuco, Santiago and Castro. To **Puerto Aisén**, Transaustral, Baquedano 1171, T 231333, 4 a day, 5 on Sun, La Cascada, 4 daily, and Don Carlos taxi-bus, Subteniente Cruz 63, T 232981, US$3, 8 a day, 3 on Sun; to **Puerto Chacabuco**, Transaustral Thur and Sun, La Cascada 3 times daily, US$3.25. **Puerto Cisnes** daily with Litoral, Baquedo e Independencia, T 232903, Tues and Sat at 1130, US$12.85, or Colectivos Basoli, T 232596, Thur and Sun 1200, same price. There are daily buses to **Mañihuales**, Trans Mañihuales (daily 1700) and Litoral. To **Balmaceda**, Buses Libertad, Magallanes y Simpson, T 212244, daily 1700, US$1.70.

To **Puerto Ibáñez** on Lago Carrera, the Chilean section of Lago Buenos Aires colectivos connect with *El Pilchero*, from *El Gran Calaforte*, Calle Prat, 3 hrs, book the day before, US$7; to Bajada Ibáñez, Aerobus from bus terminal, Mon, Wed, Fri 1000, return next day, US$5.45, and Pudú, T 231000/6, Tues and Sat 0815.

Buses on the **Carretera Austral**: N to **Chaitén**, with Artetur, Baquedano 1347, T 233466, F 233367, or bus terminal T 233368, Wed 0900, US$28.50, overnight stop in La Junta, extra service on Sun in summer, in winter may go only as far as La Junta, US$14.30. Similar service by Transportes San Rafael, 18 de Sept 469, T 233408, Mon and Thur 0900 in summer, 11 hrs, US$25. Transaustral goes to La Junta via Puyuguapi, US$15, Tues and Sat. To **Puerto Montt**, Tues and Fri US$35. South to **Cochrane** Pudú, at terminal, T 231008, Don Carlos and Río Baker Taxis, all 3 times a week, charging US$23, 10-12 hrs.

Travel to Argentina To **Comodoro Rivadavia**, Empresa Giobbi, Bolívar 194, T 232067, Tues, Thur, Sat 0830, US$28.50, 12-13 hrs via Coyhaique Alto, Río Mayo and Sarmiento (bus may leave from main bus terminal). Other routes are via Balmaceda or Puerto Ibáñez, but there is no through transport. Alternatively, the routes S of Lago General Carrera, via Chile Chico (public transport—see below), or through Villa Chacabuco and Paso Roballos, N of Cochrane (no public transport, road passable in summer, but often flooded in spring, if hitching allow a week). Beware, many border posts closed at weekends. If looking for transport to Argentina it is worth going to the local Radio Santa María, Bilbao y Ignacio Serrano, and leaving a message to be broadcast.

Excursions Excellent views of the Río Simpson valley from the hill, 4 hrs walk N of town, at **Reserva Forestal Coyhaique**. South to the lakes Elizalde (good salmon fishing), Atravesado, Frío, Castor and Pollux. Skiing at El Fraile, 29 km SE, where there are 5 pistes and 2 lifts, cafeteria, equipment hire (season Jun to Sep). **Reserva Forestal Mañihuales**, 76 km from Coyhaique, was largely destroyed by forest fires in the 1940s, but the views are good. **Monumento Natural Dos Lagunas**, lakes Toro and Bonito, 21 km on the Coyhaique Alto road, is worth a visit. Entry to all 3 parks about US$1; camping US$2.75.

Fishing Excellent opportunities on the Río Simpson and Lagos Frío and Pollux, rainbow trout is the main catch. See **Fishing** under **Sport** in Information for Visitors.

The Carretera Austral continues S of Coyhaique. At Km 35 is *El Blanco*, a hamlet with *pensión* at *Restaurant El Blanco* (or **F** pp *El Nuevo*—breakfast extra) and shop. At Km 41 a branch road E leads to *Balmaceda* on the Argentine frontier (no accommodation, daily bus to Coyhaique, 0800, US$1.70, Ladeco flights from

Santiago via Concepción and Puerto Montt, taxi from airport to Coyhaique, 1 hr, US$6, minibus US$4.50). Further S on the Carretera Austral at Km 88 a branch road S leads to **Puerto Ibáñez**, on Lago Carrera. There are two *residenciales*: **E** pp *Ibáñez*, Bertrán Dixon 31, T 423227 (clean, warm, hot water) and, **D** *Hostería Doña Amalia*, Bajada Río Ibañez. Fuel available at Luis A Bolados 461 (house with 5 laburnum trees outside); it's sold in 5-litre containers. Minibus to Coyhaique, 2½ hrs, US$7. 6 km away are some grand waterfalls on the Río Ibáñez.

There are 3 ways of reaching Chile Chico on the southern shore of Lago Carrera, by boat from Puerto Ibáñez, the newly-opened long route around the lake, or through Argentina. The region prides itself in having the best climate in Southern Chile with some 300 days of sunshine; much fruit is grown as a result. Rainfall is very low but strong winds are common. Annual festival at end-Jan. The lake itself, a beautiful azure blue, covers 2,240 sq km; the Chilean end is predominantly Alpine and the Argentine end (Lago Buenos Aires, 881 sq km) dry pampa.

The major eruption of Volcán Hudson in 1991, polluted parts of the lake and many rivers, but the waters are now clear. The effects can still be seen in a metre-thick layer of ash on the ground.

Ferry The car ferry, *El Pilchero*, sails between Puerto Ibañez and Chile Chico, twice a week, with extra sailings in the summer season. Fares for cars US$33, for passengers US$3.50, 2¾ hr crossing. Number of passengers limited to 70; locals given preference, no reservations possible. Buses and jeeps meet the ferry in Puerto Ibáñez for Coyhaique.

The Carretera Austral branches off the Coyhaique-Puerto Ibáñez road 97 km S of Coyhaique. It goes through Villa Cerro Castillo (small supermarket, *residencial* at Aguirre Cerda 35, D with good meals), named after the fabulous nearby mountain, which looks like a fairytale castle, with pinnacles jutting out of thick snow. This and other peaks in the northern wall of the Río Ibáñez valley, are in the **Reserva Nacional Cerro Castillo** (*guardería* on the Senda Ibáñez, opp Laguna Chinguay, open Nov-Mar, camping US$2.75, picnic entry US$1.15). The Carretera climbs out of the valley, passing the aptly-named Laguna Verde and the Portezuelo Cofré. It descends to the boggy Manso valley, with a good campsite at the bridge over the river, watch out for mosquitoes (this area was seriously affected by the ash from Volcán Hudson). The road then goes on to **Bahía Murta** (the village, 5 km off the Carretera, at Km 198, on the northern tip of the central 'arm' of Lago General Carrera, has **E** pp *Res Patagonia*, Pasaje España; **E** pp *Res y restaurante Lago Gen Carrera*, Av 5 de Abril, welcoming, excellent meals, also has cabin with own store; free camping by lake, good view of Cerro Castillo). The road follows the lake's western shore; the colour of the water is an unbelievable blue-green, reflecting the mountains that surround it and the clouds above. At **Río Tranquilo**, Km 223, where the buses stop for lunch (**C** *Residencial Los Pinos*, 2 Oriente 41, basic; **E** pp *Cabañas Jacricalor*, 1 Sur s/n; **E** pp *Residencial Carretera Austral*, 1 Sur 223), fuel is available at the ECA store from a large drum (no sign).

At the SW tip of Lago Carrera, at El Maitén, 50 km S of Río Tranquilo, a road branches off E along the S shore of Lago Carrera towards Chile Chico. At **Puerto Guadal**, 10 km E, there are shops, post office; **E** pp *Hostería Huemules*, Magnolia 382, T 411212, with breakfast, good views; **E** pp *Residencial Maitén*, Las Magnolias; also at Quemel 'Sade' Guerrero—1st shop you see from jetty, No 382 on corner of Los Pinos. *Restaurant La Frontera*, Los Lirios y Los Pinos. Petrol available. Bus fare Coyhaique-Puerto Guadal (en route to Cochrane) US$17.

Further E along the shore are the villages of Mallín Grande and **Fachinal** (no accommodation though people will let you stay for free if you have a sleeping bag). Beyond Fachinal, take care if driving, there are dangerous, unprotected precipices.

Chile Chico is a quiet, friendly but dusty town on the lake shore, pop 2,200.

Hotels **B** *Hostería de la Patagonia*, Camino Internacional s/n, full board, clean, excellent food, English, French and Italian spoken, trekking, horse-riding and white-water rafting organized (Casilla 91, Chile Chico, XI Region, T 411337, F 411444); rec; **E** pp *Casa Quinta No me Olvides/Manor House Don't Forget Me, hospedaje* and camping (María Sánchez de Campaña), Camino Internacional s/n, clean, cooking facilities, warm, bathrooms, hot showers, honey, eggs, fruit and vegetables for sale, rec, tours arranged to Lago Jeinimeni and Cueva de las Manos; **E** pp *Plaza*, O'Higgins, basic, clean, rec; Private house: O'Higgins 43, E pp, good meals. Free campsite at Bahía Jarra, 15 km E. **Restaurants** Apart from *residenciales*: *Cafetería Elizabeth y Loly* on Plaza serves coffee and delicious homemade cakes, expensive. Supermarket on B O'Higgins, buy wine here. It is very difficult to change dollars (*Café Elizabeth y Loly* changes dollars at bank rate in small amounts); change Argentine pesos in shops and cafés on main street (very poor rates). Ask at the Municipalidad or at the tourist office on O'Higgins for help in arranging tours.

Transport Three companies run minibuses along the S side of the lake between Chile Chico and Puerto Guadal, up to 3 times a week each, US$9. These connect in Puerto Guadal with Pudu service for Cochrane.

Jeeps run from Chile Chico to Los Antiguos, the Argentine border, US$3, ¾ hr including formalities; from here connections can be made to Perito Moreno. Border open 0800-1900. Minibus to Coyhaique, frequency varies, US$9, 2¾ hrs. Lifts to/from Coyhaique (see above).

J M Bibby (The Wirral) writes: "60 km S of Chile Chico lies the **Reserva Nacional Lago Jeinimeni**, covering breathtaking snow-capped peaks, impressive cliffs, waterfalls, small glaciers and Lakes Jeinimeni and Verde. Activities include fishing for salmon and rainbow trout, trekking and rowing. A good map is essential. Entrance fee US$1, camping US$2.75. Access only between November and March owing to high river levels. Lifts may be possible on timber trucks; try Juan Viega in the shop next to the Conaf office in Chile Chico."

The country to the S and W of Chile Chico provides good walking for the mountaineer. The weird rock formations and dry brush-scrub give a 'wild west' feel to the country. The northern and higher peak of Cerro Pico del Sur (2,168m) can be climbed by the agile from Los Cipres (beware of dogs in farmyard). You will need a long summer's day and the 1:50,000 map. Follow the horse trail until it peters out, then navigate by compass or sense of direction until the volcano-like summit appears. After breaching the cliff ramparts at an obvious point, there is some scrambling and a 10-foot pitch to the summit: indescribable views of the Lake and Andes. (Brian Spearing).

South of El Maitén the Carretera Austral becomes steeper and more bendy (in winter this stretch, all the way to Cochrane, is icy and dangerous). Just past *Puerto Bertrand*, a good place for fishing (dormitory-style accommodation available – *Casa de Huéspedes*, and **A3** *Hostería Campo Baker*, one small shop), is a sign to the Nacimiento del Río Baker, with the most abundant water of any Chilean river. Note how the colours of the rivers and lakes change in this region. The road climbs up to high moorland, passing the confluence of the Ríos Neff and Baker, before winding into Cochrane. The scenery is splendid all the way; in the main the road is rough but not treacherous. Watch out for cattle on the road and take blind corners slowly.

Cochrane (2,000 people), 345 km S of Coyhaique, sits in a hollow a little distance W of Lago Cochrane. It is a simple place, sunny in summer, good for walking and fishing. Northeast of the town is the **Reserva Nacional Tamango**, administered by Conaf in two sectors (Tamango, 9 km by dirt track, and Húngaro, 4 km, which reaches down to Lago Cochrane). In the Húngaro sector are a few remaining huemules (deer—two radio-tagged); there are also guanaco in the pampa part, foxes, lots of birds including woodpeckers and hummingbirds and lenga forest. It is inaccessible in the four winter months. Ask in the Conaf office on the square (T 422164) about visiting because some access is through private land and tourist facilities are still in the planning stage, entry US$1. The views from the reserve are superb, over the town, the nearby lakes and to the Campo de Hielo Norte to the West.

Accommodation, food and services **C** pp *Hostería Wellmann*, Las Golondrinas 36, T 522171, hot water, comfortable, warm, good meals, rec; **D** pp *Residencial Rubio*, Teniente Merino 04, T 522173, Sra Elva Rubio, very nice, breakfast included, lunch and dinner extra; **E** pp *Residencial Austral Sur*, Sra Sonia Salazar, Prat s/n, T 522150, breakfast included, hot water, also very nice; **E** *Residencia Cero a Cero*, Lago Brown 464, T 522158, with breakfast, welcoming. In summer it is best to book rooms in advance. Restaurants: *Belén*, Esmeralda 301; *Café* at Tte Merino 502.

Transport Bus companies: *Pudú Bottillería Quiaco*, Tte Merino; *Don Carlos, Residencial*

Austral Sur; **Río Baker Taxis**, Río Colonia. All run 3 buses a week to Coyhaique, US$23. Petrol is available, if it hasn't run out, at the Empresa Comercial Agrícola (ECA). Horses can be hired for excursions in the surrounding countryside, ask around, eg at *Hostería Wellmann*.

The Carretera has been constructed a further 100 km S of Cochrane to Puerto Yungay (opened Feb 1994). En route, it bypasses Tortel, a village built on a hill above the sea. It has no streets, no proper plan, only wooden walkways ('no hay ni una bicicleta'). It trades in wood with Punta Arenas and fishes for shellfish (such as *centolla* and *loco*). Access is by Don Carlos plane, by horse, mountain bike or on foot, several days journey from Cochrane on a good track by the Río Baker (several river crossings by boat), or by kayak down the Río Baker.

Some 150 nautical miles S of Puerto Aisén is the **Laguna San Rafael** glacier, 30m above sea level, and 45 km in length. It calves small icebergs, carried out to sea by wind and tide. The thick vegetation on the shores, with snowy peaks above, is typical of Aisén. The glacier is one of a group of four that flow in all directions from Monte San Valentín. This icefield is part of the **Parque Nacional Laguna San Rafael** (1.74 million ha), regulated by Conaf. The only way there is by plane or by boat: Air Taxi from Coyhaique (Don Carlos), US$110 each if party of 5; some pilots in Puerto Aisén will fly to the glacier for about US$95, but many are unwilling to land on the rough airstrip. The glacier is best seen from the sea: the official cruises are: *Skorpios I* and *II* (under Puerto Montt); Navimag's *Evangelistas* and Transmarchilay's *Colono* (see under Pto Chacabuco); *Patagonia Express* (see under Puerto Montt **Shipping**); *Pamar*, Pacheco Altamirano 3100, T 256220, Puerto Montt, Sep-Mar only; Compañía Naviera Puerto Montt has 2 vessels: the *Quellón*, with 6-day, 6-night tours to the Laguna from Puerto Montt via various ports and channels (US$900 not including flight from Santiago), and *Lago Yelcho*, 2-night trips from Puerto Chacabuco 3 times a week, US$145, in Santiago Av Providencia 199, 5° piso, T 274-8150, F 205-2197; Puerto Montt Diego Portales 882, T/F 252547; Puerto Chacabuco T 351106. *Odisea* and *Visun*, motorized sailing boats, Dec to Mar, in Santiago, Alameda B O'Higgins 108, local 120, T 633-0883, in Puerto Aysén, Sgto Aldea 679, T 332908, 6-day trips from Puerto Chacabuco to Laguna San Rafael. Various private yachts can be chartered in Puerto Montt for 6-12 passengers to Laguna San Rafael. Local fishing boats from Chacabuco/Puerto Aisén take about 18-20 hrs each way, charging the same as the tourist boats. Ask for Jorge Prado at the port (he takes a minimum of 7, more expensive than others); Andino Royas, Cochrane 129; Justiniano Aravena, Dr Steffen 703; Rodrigo Azúcar, Agemar office, T 332716; or Sr Ocuña, ask at the port. These unauthorized boats may not have adequate facilities.

Park entry fee US$4.65. At the glacier there is a small ranger station which gives information; a pier and two paths have been built. One path leads to the glacier. The rangers are willing to row you out to the glacier in calm weather, a 3-hr trip. Robert af Sandeberg (Lidingö, Sweden) describes this journey as follows:

"The trip in the rowboat is an awesome venture. At first it is fairly warm and easy to row. Gradually it gets colder when the wind sweeps over the icy glacier (be sure to take warm clothes—a thick sweater, and waterproof jacket are rec—Ed). It gets harder to row as small icebergs hinder the boat. Frequently somebody has to jump onto an icefloe and push the boat through. The glacier itself has a deep blue colour, shimmering and reflecting the light; the same goes for the icebergs, which are an unreal, translucent blue. The glacier is very noisy; there are frequent cracking and banging sounds, resembling a mixture of gun shots and thunder. When a hunk of ice breaks loose, a huge swell is created and the icebergs start rocking in the water. Then great care and effort has to be taken to avoid the boat being crushed by the shifting icebergs; this is a very real danger."

In the national park are puma, pudu pudu (minature deer), foxes, dolphins, occasional sealions and sea otters, and many species of bird. Walking trails are limited (about 10 km in all) but a lookout platform has been constructed, with fine views of the glacier.

NB If you plan to go to Laguna San Rafael by boat, check first with the Gobernación Marítima in Puerto Aisén that the boat is licensed for the trip (very few are).

CHILEAN PATAGONIA (8)

The glacial regions of southern Patagonia and Chilean Tierra del Fuego. Punta Arenas and Puerto Natales are the two main towns, the latter being the gateway to the Torres del Paine and Balmaceda national parks. In summer, a region for climbing, hiking, boats trips and the southernmost crossings to Argentina.

Magallanes (XII Región), which includes the Chilean part of Tierra del Fuego, has 17.5% of Chile's total area, but it is inhabited by under 1% of Chile's population. In summer the weather is most variable, with temperatures seldom rising above 15°C. In winter snow covers the country, except those parts near the sea, making many roads more or less impassable, except on horseback. Strong, cold, piercing winds blow, particularly during the spring, when they may exceed 100 km an hour. The dry winds parch the ground and prevent the growth of crops, except in sheltered spots and greenhouses. When travelling in this region, protection against the sun's ultraviolet rays is essential.

For much of this century, sheep breeding was the most important industry, before being replaced after 1945 by oil. Although oil production has ceased, large quantities of natural gas are now produced and coal is mined near Punta Arenas. Sheep farming continues to be important: about 50% of all Chilean sheep are in the Magallanes region. Tourism is growing rapidly, making an increasingly important contribution to the area's economy.

Punta Arenas (pop 115,000; DDD 061), the most southerly city in Chile, and capital of XII Región, 2,140 km S of Santiago, lies on the eastern shore of the Brunswick Peninsula facing the Straits of Magellan at almost equal distance from the Pacific and Atlantic oceans. It is the centre of the local sheep farming industry and exports wool, skins, and frozen meat. It is also the home of La Polar, the most southerly brewery in the world. Good roads connect the city with Puerto Natales, 247 km N, and with Río Gallegos in Argentina. Punta Arenas has certain free-port facilities; the Zona Franca is 3½ km N of the centre, on the righthand side of the road to the airport.

Originally founded as a penal colony in the nineteenth century, its heyday was in the years before the opening of the Panama Canal in 1914. The city has expanded rapidly, particularly in recent years, but remains tranquil and pleasant. Several new hotels have been built in response to increased tourism. Although there are many architectural styles, it retains a number of interesting buildings from the turn of the century. See especially the interiors of the Museum of Regional History and of the **Teatro Cervantes** (now a cinema). In the **Plaza de Armas** (Plaza Muñoz Gamero), is a statue of Magellan with a mermaid and 2 Fuegian Indians at his feet. According to local wisdom those who rub the big toe of one of the Indians will return to Punta Arenas. The cemetery, at Av Bulnes 929, is even more fantastic than the one at Castro (Chiloé), with a **statue of Indiecito**, the little Indian (now also an object of reverence, bedecked with flowers, the left knee well-rubbed, NW side of the cemetery), cypress avenues, and many memorials to pioneer families and victims of shipping disasters (open 0800-1800 daily). Walk up Calle Fagnano to the **Mirador Cerro de La Cruz** for a view over the city.

There is an excellent modern museum in the **Colegio Salesiano**, 'Mayorino Borgatello' dealing with the Indians, animal and bird life of the region, and other interesting aspects of life in Patagonia and Tierra del Fuego, at Av Bulnes 374, entrance next to church. Open Tues-Sat 1000-1200 and 1500-1800, Sun 1500-1800, hours change frequently (entry US$1.25). **Museo de Historia Regional, Braun Menéndez**, Calle Magallanes 949, off Plaza de Armas, T 244216, located in a mansion built by one of the early millionaires, is well worth visiting. Part is set out as room-by-room regional history, the rest of the house is furnished (guided tours in Spanish only). Closed Mon, otherwise open 1100-1600 (summer) and 1100-1300 (winter, entry US$1), free booklet in English. The **Instituto de la Patagonia**, Av Bulnes Km 4 N (opp the University), T 244216, outdoor exhibits open Mon-Fri 0800-1800, indoor pavillions: 0830-1115, 1500-1800, has an open air museum with artefacts used by the early settlers, a pioneer home and a naval museum. **Naval and Maritime Museum**, Pedro Montt 981, open Mon-Fri 0930-1230, 1500-1800, Sat 1000-1300, 1500-1800. The

Carrera
To
Patagonian Institute,
Free Port, Airport &
Ferry to Porvenir,
Puerto Natales
Senoret
Cemetery
H
18
Av. Bulnes
Angamos
Carrera
Jorge Montt
Maipú
Armando Sanhueza
Quillota
Chiloé
Sarmiento
Mejicana
Bories
Magallanes
13
Caupolicán
Garay
Mario Toledo
Yugoeslavia
Almte. Senoret
Mejicana
Lautaro Navarro
Senoret
Carrera Pinto
Arauco
J. Menéndez
5
O'Higgins
Av. Colón
N
6 **15**
4 **11**
7
J. Montt
Cerro de
la Cruz
Waldo Seguel
9
17 **14**
Av. Costanera
Fagnano
3
P. Montt
1 **10**
12
2
16
Roca
8
Errázuriz
Balmacedo
Av. España
Av. Independencia
Muelle A. Prat
Bolivian
21 de Mayo
Paraguaya
To
Fuerte Bulnes
& Puerto
del Hambre
Not to Scale
Bellavista

1. Plaza de Armas
2. Cathedral
3. Museo Braun-Menéndez
4. Bus Austral
5. Bus Sur
6. Bus Fernández and
   Pingüino
7. Lan Chile
8. Ladeco
9. Tourist Office
Hotels:
10. *Cabo de Hornos*
11. *Los Navegantes*
12. *Mercurio*
13. *Hostal de la Patagonia*
14. *Ritz*
15. *Monte Carlo*
16. *Plaza* and *Residencial París*
17. *Savoy*
18. *Residencial Sonia Kuscevic*

PUNTA ARENAS

British School on Waldo Seguel, and **St James' Church** next door, are wooden, in colonial style. The **Parque María Behety**, S of town along 21 de Mayo, features a scale model of Fuerte Bulnes and a campsite, popular for Sun picnics. **NB** Calle Pedro Montt runs E-W, while Calle Jorge Montt runs N-S. **NB** All transport is heavily booked from Christmas through to Mar: advance booking strongly advised.

Hotels Most hotels include breakfast in the room price. Prices indicated below include 18% IVA. Most hotels above a certain size will not charge this to foreigners if they pay in US$ cash, but some will if you use a credit card. Hotel prices are substantially lower during winter months (April-Sep). **L2** *Hotel José Nogueira*, Plaza de Armas, Bories 959 y P Montt, in former Palacio Sara Braun, T 248840, F 248832, beautiful loggia, lovely atmosphere, rec; **L3** *Cabo de Hornos*, Plaza Muñoz Gamero 1025, T/F 242134, rec; **L3** *Finis Terrae*, Av Colón 766, T 228200, F 248124, modern, some rooms small but all very nice, fridge, safe in room, rooftop café/bar with lovely views; **L3** *Isla Rey Jorge*, 21 de Mayo 1243, T 222681, F 248220, modern, pleasant, pub downstairs; **L3** *Los Navegantes*, José Menéndez 647, T 244677, F 247545, **L3** *Tierra del Fuego*, Av Colón 716, T/F 226200, comfortable rooms, one floor all with kitchenettes, *Café 1900* downstairs; **A2** *Hostería Yaganes*, Camino Antiguo Norte Km 7.5, T 211600, F 211948, cabins on the shores of the Straits of Magellan, nice setting; **A1-A2** *Apart Hotel Colonizadores*, Av Colón 1106, T 243578, F 244499, clean, fully furnished apartments (2 bedrooms **A1**, 1 bedroom **A2**) discounts for long stay; **A3** *Hostal de la Patagonia*,

O'Higgins 478, T 241079, with bath (B without), good breakfast, excellent; **A3** *Hotel Colonizadores*, 21 de Mayo 1690, T 244144, F 226587, with bath; **A3** *Hostal Carpa Manzano*, Lautaro Navarro 336, T/F 248864, rec; **A3** *Cóndor de Plata*, Av Colón 556, T 247987, F 241149, very good; **A3** *Mercurio*, Fagnano 595, T/F 242300, bath, TV and phone, good restaurant and service, rec; **B** *Savoy*, José Menéndez. 1073, T 241951, F 247979, pleasant rooms but some lack windows, good place to eat; **B** *Ritz*, Pedro Montt 1102, T 224422, old, clean and cosy, rec; **A3** *Plaza*, José Nogueira 1116 2nd floor, T 241300, F 248613 (B without bath), pleasant, good breakfast; **B** *Hostal Kóiuska*, clean, friendly, shared bath; **B** *Hotel El Pionero*, Chiloé 1210, T 248851, F 248263, with bath; **B** *Monte Carlo*, Av Colón 605, T 243438, with bath, C without, good value, rec; **C** *Residencial Central*, No 1 España 247, T 222315, No 2 Sanhueza 185, T 222845, with bath, (D without), comfortable; **B** *Chalet Chapital*, Armando Sanhueza 974, T 242237, F 225698, (cheaper without bath) good, comfortable, doubles only, welcoming; **B** *Hostal de la Avenida*, Colón 534, T 247532, good breakfast, friendly, safe, rec; **C** *Albatros*, Colón 1195, T 223131, without bath, good; **C** *Residencial París*, J Nogueira 1116 4th floor, T 223112, rec, heating, some rooms have balconies, others have no windows; **D** *Casa Dinka*, Caupolicán 169, T 226056, great breakfast, use of kitchen, English spoken, very popular; **E** pp *Residencial Roca*, Magallanes 888 esq J Menéndez, T 243903, clean; **E** pp *Casa Deportista*, O'Higgins 1205, T 225205, F 243438, cheap meals, cooking facilities, several bunks to a room, noisy; **E** pp *Casa Roxas*, Angamos 971, very good, clean, with bath; **E** pp *Residencial Rubio*, España 640, T 226458, dirty, helpful; **E** pp *Hostal Paradiso*, Angamos 1073, T 224212, with bath, parking, use of kitchen, highly rec; **D** *Hospedaje Lodging*, Armando Sanhueza 933, T 221035, good value, clean, heating, modern; **D** pp *Residencial Sonia Kuscevic*, Pasaje Darwin 175 (Angamos altura 500), T 248543, popular; **E** pp *Residencial Internacional*, Arauco 1514 (esq Boliviana, T 223677), dormitory beds and private rooms, hot water, popular, owner and pricing system very eccentric; **F** pp *Alojamiento Prat*, Sgto Aldea 0520, clean, rec; **F** pp *Backpackers*, Carrera Pinto 1022, T 222554, F 226863, hot water, popular, large dormitories, cooking facilities, limited bathroom facilities, TV, luggage store, rec. **D** Sra Carolina Ramírez, at Paraguaya 150, T 247687, nice and friendly, hot water, safe motorcycle parking, meals, rec; **E** pp, Paraguaya 517; **E** Sra Lenka, José Miguel Carrera 1270, heating, clean, use of kitchen, rec; **E** Nena's, Boliviana 366, T 242411, friendly, with breakfast, highly rec; **D** Mireya Cárcamo, Boliviana 375, use of kitchen, good meals, rec; **E** pp Juanita Cofre, Boliviana 533, knowledgeable, helpful; **F** pp Boliviana 238, bunk beds, shared bath, basic, use of kitchen; **E** pp, Casa de Mena, España 1492 esquina Boliviana, T 247422, shared bath, clean, friendly, use of kitchen; **F** pp Armando Sanhueza 712, T 225127, basic, use of kitchen; **E** Sanhueza 750, homely, rec. **F** pp Youth hostel-style accommodation at Bellavista 577, kitchen, hot showers, clean; **D** Sra Inés Ojeda de Alvorado, Av España 1291 y Balmaceda, heaters, shared bath with hot water, pleasant. Accommodation available in many private houses, usually E pp, ask at tourist office. **Camping** in Reserva Forestal Magallanes, 8 km W of Punta Arenas (no public transport, see **Excursions** below). *Camping Pudú*, 10.5 km N on Route 9, G pp, pleasant, good facilities.

Restaurants Main hotels; good value set lunches and dinners at *Cabo de Hornos*, excellent restaurants at *Los Navegantes* and *José Nogueira*. *El Mercado*, Mejicana 617, open 24 hrs, reasonably-priced set lunch, expensive á la carte; *Centro Español*, Plaza Muñoz Gamero 771, above Teatro Cervantes, large helpings, limited selection, reasonably priced; *El Mesón del Calvo*, Jorge Montt 687, excellent, seafood, lamb, friendly service, rec; seafood at *Sotitos*, O'Higgins 1138, good service and cuisine, excellent, rec; *La Taberna del Silver*, O'Higgins 1037, fast and cheap, *La Mama*, Sanhueza 700 block, little Argentine-style pasta house, rec. *Lucerna*, Bories 624, excellent meat, reasonably priced, good; *Dino's Pizza*, Bories 557, cheap, good, big pizzas; *Café Garogha*, Bories 817, open Sun pm, pleasant but busy at night, smoky. *Bianco's Pizza*, Bulnes 1306, excellent pizzas, rec. *El Quijote*, Lautaro Navarro 1087, best café in town, good sandwiches, highly rec; *Asturias*, Lautaro Navarro 967, good food and atmosphere; *Venus*, Pedro Montt 1046, good food, service and atmosphere, reasonable prices; *La Casa de Juan*, O'Higgins 1021, Spanish food; *El Estribo*, Ignacio Carrera Pinto 762, good grill, also fish; *Yaganes*, Camino Antiguo Norte Km 7.5, beautiful setting, weekend buffet. *Golden Dragon*, Colón 529, good Chinese, inexpensive. *La Terraza*, 21 de Mayo 1288, and *El Porteño*, 21 de Mayo e Independencia, sandwiches, *empanadas* and beer, cheap and good; *La Taberna del Club de la Unión*, Plaza Muñoz Gamero Seguel, for drinks. For economic set lunches several along Chiloé: *Restaurant de Turismo Punta Arenas*, No 1280, good, friendly, rec; *Los Años 60 The Mitchel*, No 1231, also serves beer and 26 varieties of sandwiches, open 24 hours; *Parilla Apocalipsis*, Chiloé esq Balmaceda, also grill; Carioca, J Menéndez 600 esq Chiloé, also for snacks and beer; *Lomit's*, Menéndez 722, cheap snacks and drinks, open when the others are closed. *Kiosco Roca* (no sign), Roca 875, early morning coffee. Cheap fish meals available at stalls in the Cocinerías, Lautaro Navarro S of the port entrance. Excellent empanadas, bread and pastries at *Pancal*, 21 de Mayo 1280; also at *La Espiga*, Errázuriz 632;

excellent pastries at *Casa del Pastel*, Ignacio Carrera Pinto y O'Higgins. Try Polar beer. Lobster has become more expensive because of a law banning fishing them with nets, allowing only lobster pots. *Centolla* (king crab) is caught illegally by some fishermen using dolphin, porpoise and penguin as live bait. There are seasonal bans on *centolla* fishing to protect dwindling stocks, do not purchase *centolla* out of season. At times *centolla* fishing is banned because the crabs can be infected with a disease which is fatal to humans. If this ban refers to the marea roja (red tide), it does not affect crabs, only bivalve shellfish. Mussels should not be picked along the shore due to pollution and the *marea roja* (red tide), see p 772.

Banks and Exchange Banks open Mon-Fri 0830-1400. Casas de cambio open Mon-Fri 0900-1230, 1500-1900, Sat 0900-1230; outside business hours try *Buses Sur*, Av Colón y Magallanes, kiosk at Garogha Café, Bories 817 and the major hotels (lower rates). **Fincard** (Mastercard), Pedro Montt 837, T 247864, Mon-Fri 0900-1400, 1530-1730. **Banco Concepción**, Magallanes y Menéndez, for Visa. Argentine pesos can be bought at *casas de cambio*. Good rates at **Cambio Gasic**, Roca 915, Oficina 8, T 242396, **La Hermandad**, Lautaro Navarro 1099, T 243991, US$ cash for Amex TCs; *Sur Cambios,* Lautaro Navarro 1001, T 225656 accepts TCs. *Kiosco Redondito*, Mejicana 613 in the shopping centre, T 247369.

Consulates Argentine, Av 21 de Mayo 1878, T 261912, open 1000-1400. Visas take 24 hrs, US$15; **Belgian**, Roca 817, Oficina 61, T 241472; **British**, Roca 924, T 247020; **Danish**, Colón 819, Depto 301, T 221488; **Dutch**, Sarmiento 780, T 248100; **German**, Pasaje Korner 1046, T 241082, Casilla 229; **Italian**, 21 de Mayo 1569, T 242497 **Norwegian**, Av Independencia 830, T 242171; **Spanish**, J Menéndez 910, T 243566; **Swedish**, Errazúriz 891, T 224107. **Finish**, Av Independencia 660, T 247385; **Brazilian**, Arauco 769, T 241093.

British School founded 1904, co-educational.

Discotheques Discos in the city centre often have a young crowd: *Gallery,* J Menéndez 750, T 247555; *Yordi*, Pedro Montt 937; *Borssalino*, Bories 587. On the outskirts of town, to the S: *Club Boulevard*, Km 5.5, T 265807; *Torreones*, Km 5.5, T 261985; *Salsoteca* Km 5. To the N: *Drive-In Los Brujos*, Km 7.5, T 212600; *Salsoteca*, Km 6. **Nightlife** *The Queen's Club*, 21 de Mayo 1455. Lots of *Whiskerias*: *Sexywoman*, Av España, and *Tentación*, Av Colón rec.

Hospitals *Hospital Regional Lautaro Navarro*, Angamos 180, T 244040, public hospital, for emergency room ask for *La Posta; Clínica Magallanes*, Bulnes 01448, T 211527, private clinic, medical staff is the same as in the hospital but fancier surroundings and more expensive.

Dentists Dr Hugo Vera Cárcamo, España 1518, T 227510, rec; Rosemary Robertson Stipicic, 21 de Mayo 1380, T 22931, speaks English.

Laundry *Lavasol*, the only self-service, O'Higgins 969, T 243067, Mon-Sat 0900-2030, Sun (summer only) 1000-1800, US$6 per machine, wash and dry, good but busy; *Lavaseco Josseau*, Carrera Pinto 766, T 228413; *Lavandería Limpec*, 21 de Mayo 1261, T 241669.

Post Office Bories 911 y J Menéndez, Mon-Fri 0830-1930, Sat 0900-1400.

Telecommunications For international and national calls and faxes (shop around as prices vary): *CTC*, Nogueira 1106, Plaza de Armas, daily 0800-2200, *CTC*, Roca 886, loc 23, daily 0900-2030; *Entel*, Lautaro Navarro 957, Mon-Fri 0830-2200, Sat-Sun 0900-2200; *Telex-Chile/Chile-Sat,* Bories 911 and Errázuriz 856, daily 0830-2200, also offers telex and telegram service. *VTR*, Bories 801, closed Sat afternoon and Sun. For international calls and faxes at any hour *Hotel Cabo de Hornos*, credit cards accepted, open to non-residents.

Shopping For leather goods and sheepskin try the Zona Franca, Mon-Sat 1030-1230, 1500-2000 (bus E or A from Plaza de Armas; many collective taxis; taxi US$3). Handicrafts at *Pingüi*, Bories 404, **Artesanía Ramas**, Independencia 799, **Chile Típico**, I Carrera Pinto 1015, **Indoamérica** Av Colón y Magallanes and outdoor stalls at the bottom of Av Independencia, by the port entrance. Supermarkets: *Listo*, 21 de Mayo 1133; *Cofrima*, Lautaro Navarro 1293 y Balmaceda, *Cofrima 2*, España 01375; *Marisol*, Zenteno 0164. **Chocolate** Hand made chocolate from *Chocolatería Tres Arroyos*, Bories 448, T 241522 and *Chocolatería Regional Norweisser*, José Miguel Carrera 663, both good.

Cameras Wide range of cameras and film, especially slide film, from Zona Franca. *Foto Arno*, Bories 893, for Kodak products *Foto Sánchez*, Bories 768, for Fuji film and *Fotocentro*, Bories 789, for Agfa: all have same day print-processing service. *Lab Todocolor*, Chiloé 1442, for slide processing.

Sport 9-hole golf course 5 km S town on road to Fuerte Bulnes.

Travel Agents *Turismo Lazo*, Angamos 1366, T/F 223771, wide range of tours, highly rec; *Turismo Aventour*, J Nogueira 1255, T 241197, English spoken, helpful, organize tours to Tierra del Fuego. *Turismo Comapa*, Independencia 840, T 241437, F 247514, tours to Torres del Paine, Tierra del Fuego, also trips to the Falklands/Malvinas, charter boats to Cape Horn and Isla Magdalena; *Turismo Runner*, Lautaro Navarro 1065, T 247050, F 241042, adventure tours; *Arka Patagonia*, Lautaro Navarro 1038, T 248167, F 241504, all types of tours, rafting, fishing, etc; *Turismo Aonikenk*, Magallanes 619, T 228332, rec; *Travel Broom*, Roca 924, T 228312, F 228322; *Turismo Pali Aike*, Lautaro Navarro 1129 T 223301; *Traveltur*, Roca 886, T 244159; *Turismo Pehoé*, Colón 782, T 244506, F 248052; *El Conquistador*, Menéndez 556, T 222896, rec; *Turismo Viento Sur*, Fagnano 565, T/F 225167, for camping equipment; *Turismo Paralelo 53*, Armando Sanhueza 745, T 241684, F 225984; *Turismo Patagonia*, Bories 655 local 2, T 248474, F 247182, specializes in fishing trips. And others. Most organize tours to Torres del Paine, Fuerte Bulnes and *pingüineras* on Otway sound: shop around as prices vary.

Tourist Office Sernatur, Waldo Seguel 689, Casilla 106-D, T 241330, at the corner with Plaza Muñoz Gamero, 0830-1745, closed Sat and Sun. Helpful, English spoken. Kiosk on Colón between Bories and Magallanes Mon-Fri 0900-1300, 1500-1900 Sat 0900-1200, 1430-1730, Sun (in the summer only) 1000-1230. Turistel Guide available from kiosk belonging to *Café Garogha* at Bories 831. **Conaf**, J Menéndez 1147, 2nd floor, T 223841, open Mon-Fri.

Taxis Ordinary taxis have yellow roofs. Collective taxis (all black) run on fixed routes, US$0.25 for anywhere on route. Reliable service from *Radio Taxi Austral*, T 247710/244409.

Car Hire Hertz, Colón 798 and Carrera Pinto 770, T 248742, F 244729; **Australmag**, Av Colón 900, T 242174, F 226916. **Autómovil Club**, O'Higgins 931, T 243675, F 243097, **Budget**, O'Higgins 964, T 241696. **Internacional**, Sarmiento 790-B, T 228323, F 226334, rec; **Willemsen**, Lautaro Navarro 1038, T 247787, F 241083, highly rec; *Lubac*, Magallanes 970, T/F 242023/247060. **Note** that you need a hire company's authorization to take a car into Argentina.

Car Repair *Automotores del Sur*, O'Higgins 850, T 224153.

Air Services LanChile, Lautaro Navarro 999, T 241232, F 222366; Ladeco, Lautaro Navarro 1155, T/F 241100/223340. National, Bories 701, T 221634. Aerovías DAP, O'Higgins 891, T 241326/223340 F 221693, open 0900-1230, 1430-1930; Kaiken, Magallanes 974, T 242134 ext 106, F 241321. To Santiago, LanChile, Ladeco and National daily US$220 (discount fares US$150 available for a limited number of seats on each flight), via Puerto Montt (sit on right for views), National flights also stop in Concepción and Ladeco stops Sat in Balmaceda). When no tickets are available, go to the airport and get on the standby waiting list. Aerovías DAP fly to **Porvenir** daily at 0815 and 1730, return 0830 and 1750, (US$20), and to **Puerto Williams** Mon and Fri at 1400, Wed at 0830, return Mon and Fri 1800, Wed 1000, US$64 one way; plus other irregular flights, with Twin-Otter and Cessna aircraft. (Heavily booked with long waiting list so make sure you have your return reservation confirmed.) Military (FACh) flights approx twice a month to Puerto Montt US$30, information and tickets from airforce base at the airport, Spanish essential, T 213559; need to book well in advance. It is very difficult to get space during the summer as all armed forces personel and their families have priority over civilians.

Services to Argentina: Ladeco to Ushuaia Tues and Sat, 1400, return 1540, US$70 one way (Dec 15 to Mar 15 only). Aerovías DAP to Ushuaia, Tues, Thur and Sat at 0845, return at 1015, US$60; to Río Gallegos, Tues, Thur and Sat 1330, return at 1440, US$49, and to Río Grande, daily except Sun, at 0915, return at 1030, US$50. Kaiken to Ushuaia, in the summer daily except Sun, 1300, return 1500, US$75 (schedules change frequently). Reserve well in advance from mid-Dec to Feb. Austral Bus, J Menéndez 565, T 247139, T/F 241708, has service to/from

the airport scheduled to meet flights, US$2.50. LanChile, DAP and Ladeco have their own bus services from town; taxi US$7.50. The airport restaurant is good.

Shipping Navimag, office at Independencia 840, T 224256, F 247514/225804 (confirmation of reservations is advised); Navimag services Puerto Montt—Puerto Natales, see under Puerto Montt; *Comapa* (Compañía Marítima de Punta Arenas), Independencia 830, T 244400, F 247514. Government supply ships are recommended for the young and hardy, but take sleeping bag and extra food, and travel pills. For transport on navy supply ships to Puerto Williams, enquire at Tercera Zona Naval, Lautaro Navarro 1150, or ask the captain direct, but be prepared to be frustrated by irregular sailings and inaccurate information. All tickets on ships must be booked in advance Jan-Feb. **Ferries** For services to Porvenir (Tierra del Fuego), see p 762.

Bus Company Offices Pingüino and **Fernández**, Armando Sanhueza 745 T 242313, F 225984; **Ghisoni**, Lautaro Navarro 975, T 223205; **Pacheco**, Colón 900, T 242174; **Bus Sur**, Colón y Magallanes, T 244464; *Austral Bus*, J Menéndez 565, T 247139 T/F 241708. **Los Carlos**, Magallanes 974, T 241321. Turbus, Errazuriz 932, T/F 225315. Senkovic, C Wood 485. Bus timetables are printed daily in La Prensa Austral.

Bus Service Buses leave from company offices. To **Río Gallegos**, Pingüino daily 1130, return 1300 and Ghisoni, daily except Fri, 1100, book in advance US$23.50, officially 5 hrs, but can take up to 8, depending on customs, 15 mins on Chilean side, up to 3 hrs on Argentine side, including ½ hr lunch at Km 160. All customs formalities now undertaken at the border, but ask before departure if this has changed (taxi to Río Gallegos US$130). To **Río Grande**, Hector Pacheco, Mon, Wed, Fri 0715 via Punta Delgada, return Tues, Thur and Sat, 0700, 10 hrs, US$25, heavily booked. To **Ushuaia** via Punta Delgada or Porvenir, Los Carlos, Tue and Sat, 0700, return Mon and Fri, 0300, 14 hrs, US$46, book any return at same time. Or take Pacheco to Río Grande with overnight stay in *Hotel Avenida* and next day service with Austral, US$65 incl accommodation. **Puerto Natales**, 3½ hrs with Fernández, Austral Bus, and Buses Sur, several every day, US$6. Turbus, Ghisoni and Austral Bus have service through Argentina to Osorno, Puerto Montt and Castro. Fare to Puerto Montt or Osorno US$60-75, 36 hrs, to Castro US$ 67-83; Turbus continues to Santiago US$95 (cheaper in winter), 46 hrs.

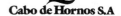

To the Falkland Islands/Islas Malvinas Punta Arenas is now the main South American link with the islands. Aerovías DAP (address above) fly once a week in summer, fortnightly in winter, Fri 1000, 2½-3½ hrs depending on the aircraft, US$350 one way (cheaper in winter, May-Aug), book well in advance (see under the Falklands/Malvinas for conditions). Have warm clothing handy.

To Puerto Williams For details of sea and air service, see p 763.

To Antarctica Punta Arenas is a major starting point for Antarctica. Juanita Cofre, Boliviana 533, is frequently recommended as helpful and knowledgeable about transport to the Antarctic, she has good contacts with the Navy. Alternatively try the Navy Office at Navarro 1150. Three naval vessels make regular voyages: the *Piloto Pardo*, an icebreaker, is the largest, US$80-90 pp per day in a 4-berth cabin. The *Yelcho* and *Galvarino* charge US$50 pp per day, women only accepted if ships officers vacate their cabins. All fares include 3 meals a day. Crews very friendly and helpful. South Pacific Expeditions, San Antonio 486, Piso 18°, Oficina 82, Santiago, T 632-3284, runs tourist cruises to the Antarctic region, US$5,000 for 10 days, US$500 pp group rates, lectures may be by scientists. These budget cruises sell out quickly. For further details, see page 1497.

Overland to Argentina From Punta Arenas there are 3 routes to Calafate and Río Gallegos: 1) NE via Route 255 and Punta Delgada to the frontier at Kimiri Aike (open all year) and then along Argentine Route 3 to Río Gallegos. 2) N along Route 9, turning 9 km before Puerto Natales for Dorotea (frontier open all year, daytime only) and then NE via La Esperanza (fuel, basic accommodation). 3) Via Puerto Natales and Cerro Castillo on the road to Torres del Paine (frontier open 1 Nov-31 Mar) joining the road to La Esperanza at Paso Cancha.

Skiing Cerro Mirador, only 9 km W from Punta Arenas, the most southerly ski resort in the world and one of the few places where one can ski with a sea view. Transtur buses 0900 and 1400 from in front of *Hotel Cabo de Hornos*, US$3, return, taxi US$7. Daily lift-ticket, US$7; equipment rental, US$6 per adult. Mid-way lodge with food, drink and equipment. Season Jun to Sep, weather depending (no suitable snow 1992 to 1994) Contact the Club Andino, T 241479, about crosscountry skiing facilities. Also skiing at Tres Morros.

Excursions Within easy reach are Puerto del Hambre and **Fuerte Bulnes**, a replica of the wooden fort erected in 1843 by a Chilean garrison, 56 km S, tours by several agencies, US$12. The trip can be done in a day. 51 km S of Punta Arenas, at the intersection of the roads to Puerto del Hambre and Fuerte Bulnes, is a small marker with a plaque of the Centro Geográfico de Chile, ie the midway point between Arica and the South Pole.

5 km W of town is the **Reserva Forestal Magallanes**, known locally as Parque Japonés follow Independencia right through town and up the hill, 3 km from the edge of town is the turnoff for Río de las Minas to the right. The entrance to the reserve is 2 km beyond, there you will find a self-guided nature trail, 1 km, free leaflet. The road continues through the woods for 14 km, passing by several small campgrounds. From the top end of the road a short path leads to a lookout over the Garganta del Diablo (Devil's Throat), a gorge formed by the Río de las Minas, with views over Punta Arenas and Tierra del Fuego. From here a slippery path leads down to the Río de las Minas valley and thence back to Punta Arenas. Turismo Pali Aike offers tours to the park, US$ 3.75 pp. Further S, 53 km from Punta Arenas, is the **Reserva Forestal Laguna Parrillar**, which has older forest than the Magallanes Reserve and sphagnum bogs. There is a 3 hr walk to the tree-line along poorly-marked paths. (No public transport, radio taxi US$60.)

A small colony of Magellanic penguins at **Otway Sound**, 60 km N of Punta Arenas, can be visited (Nov-April only); the attentions of some tourists, chasing the birds or trampling over the hatcheries and the illegal use of penguins as bait in fishing for *centolla* (king crab), have led to a decline in the number of penguins. Patience is required to see the penguins since they nest in burrows underground (tread carefully on the soft ground so as not to damage the nests), in the late afternoon they can be seen by the beach where blinds have been built to facilitate viewing. Tours by several agencies, US$12, entry US$3 (small tours better, as large ones frighten the birds).

Comapa (address above) charters boats to **Isla Magdalena**. On the island is a penguin colony, deserted apart from the breeding season, Nov-Jan; the island is administered by Conaf. Magdalena is one of a group of three islands (the others are Marta and Isabel), visited by Drake, whose men killed 3,000 penguins for food.

The most interesting excursions are to the Ultima Esperanza region (see below under Puerto Natales) and to the Torres del Paine National Park. Tours to Torres del Paine are offered by several travel agencies in Punta Arenas and Puerto Natales; Sr Mateo Quesada, Chiloé 1375, T 222662, offers local tours in his car, up to 4 passengers.

The fjords and glaciers of Tierra del Fuego (70 km by schooner) are exceptionally beautiful. Comapa runs a once a fortnight 22-hr. 320-km round trip to the fjord d'Agostino, 30 km long, where many glaciers come down to the sea. The luxury cruiser, *Terra Australis*, sails from Punta Arenas on Sat via Ushuaia and Puerto Williams; details from Comapa. Advance booking (advisable) from Cruceros Australis SA, Miraflores 178, piso 12, Santiago, T 696-3211, F 331871.

Wildlife Arthur Shapiro (Dept of Zoology, Univ of California, Davis) writes that a good place to photograph rheas (ñandúes) is a few km N of the checkpoint at Kon Aiken, near the turnoff for Otway. Antarctic cormorants can be seen sitting on offshore rocks from the road to Fuerte Bulnes. The local skunk (*chingue*) is apparently very docile and rarely sprays. Also look out for foxes and the Great Horned Owl.

North from Punta Arenas

From Punta Arenas a single-track, paved road runs N to Puerto Natales; beside it, the southbound lane is gravel. Fuel is available in Villa Tehuelches, 100 km from Punta Arenas. Along this road are several hotels, including **B** *Hostal Río Penitente*, Km 138, T 331694, in an old *estancia*, rec; **C** *Hotel Rubens*, Km 183, T 226916, popular for fishing; *Hostería Llanuras de Diana*, Km 215, T 248742, F 244729 (Punta Arenas), T 411540 (Puerto Natales) hidden from road, highly rec; **C** *Hostería Río Verde*, Km 90, E off the highway on Seno Skyring, T 311122, F 241008, private bath, heating.

Puerto Natales (14,000 people: DDD 061) is 247 km N of Punta Arenas and close to the Argentine border at Río Turbio. It stands on the Ultima Esperanza gulf amid spectacular scenery, and is the jumping-off place for the magnificent Balmaceda and Torres del Paine national parks. Very quiet in the winter, packed with tourists in the summer.

Museums Museo De Agostini, in the Colegio Salesiano at Padre Rossa 1456, 1 rm, Tierra del Fuego fauna, free. **Museo Histórico**, Bulnes 285, Tues-Sun 1500-1800.

Hotels Most prices include breakfast. **L3** *Eberhard*, Pedro Montt 58, T 411208, F 411209, excellent views, expensive and mediocre restaurant; **L3** *Cost Australis*, Pedro Montt 262, T 412000, F 411881, new in 1994, modern, good views, popular cafeteria; **A2** *Juan Ladrilleros*, Pedro Montt 161, modern, with bath, good restaurant, clean, T 411452, F 412109 rec; **A1** *Palace*, Ladrilleros 209, T 411134, good food, overpriced; **A2** *Hotel Glaciares*, Eberhard 104, T 412189, T/F 411452, new 1994, snack bar. **A2** *Hostal Sir Francis Drake*, Philippi 383, T 411553, F 411300, good views, snack bar; **A3** *Hostal Lady Florence Dixie*, Bulnes 659, T 411158, F 41943, modern; **B** *Blanquita*, Carrera Pinto 409, quiet, rec; **B** *Hostal Melissa*, Blanco Encalada 258, T 411944, private bath; **C** *Hostal Los Antiguos*, Ladrilleros 195 y Bulnes, T/F 411488, shared bath, pleasant; **C** *Residencial Carahue*, Bulnes 370, T 411339, hot water, nice; **B** *Natalino*, Eberhard 371, T 411968, clean and very friendly (tours to Milodón Cave arranged), C without bath; **C** *Bulnes*, Calle Bulnes 407, T 411307, good, stores luggage; **C** *Hostal Puerto Natales*, Eberhard 250, T 411098, private bath; **D** *Residencial Centro*, Magallanes 258A, T 411996, private bath; **D** *Austral*, Valdivia 949, T 411593, clean, friendly, good food, without bath, C with bath and breakfast, hot water, cooking and laundry facilties; **E** pp *Hospedaje La Chila*, Carrera Pinto 442, use of kitchen, welcoming; **E** pp *María José* Magallanes 646, cooking facilities, helpful; **E** pp *Res Termas de Puyehue*, O'Higgins 484, use of kitchen, laundry facilities, dirty, run down, insufficient showers; **E** pp *Hostal Famatina*, Labilleros 370, T 412067, clean, friendly; **E** pp *Hospedaje Gamma*, El Roble 650, T 411420, cooking facilities, evening meals, highly rec; **E** pp *Residencial La Busca*, Valdivia 845, run down, cheap food available; **E** pp *Los Inmigrantes*, Carrera Pinto 480, clean, friendly, kitchen and laundry facilities, luggage store, highly rec; **E** pp *Residencial El Mundial*, Bories 315, T 412476, large breakfast, use of kitchen, meals, luggage stored; **D** *Residencial Sutherland*, Barros Arana 155, with and without bath, welcoming, clean, kitchen facilities; **E** pp *Café Tierra del Fuego*, Bulnes 29, clean, family of Juan Osorno, will store luggage, good; **E** pp *Casa de familia Bustamante*, Bulnes 317, T 411061, clean, good breakfast, helpful, rec; **E** pp *Casa de familia Elsa Millán*, O'Higgins 657, good breakfast, homemade bread, dormitory-style, popular, hot water, warm, friendly, cooking facilities, rec; **E** pp *Casa de familia Dickson*, Bulnes 307, T 411218, good breakfast, clean, helpful, cooking and laundry facilities, rec; **E** pp *Pensión Ritz*, Carrera Pinto 439, full pension available, friendly; **D** pp *Residencial Grey*, Bulnes 90, T 411542, hot water, some rooms with heating, very friendly, good dinners; **E** pp *Residencial Temuco*, Ramírez 202 y Bulnes, T 411120, friendly, reasonable, good food; **F** pp *Residencial Lago Pingo*, Bulnes 808, T 411026, breakfast extra, clean, hot water, laundry, use of kitchen, will store luggage; similar at O'Higgins 70, 431 and Perito 443; **F** pp Bories 206, hostel type, use of kitchen, sleeping bag necessary, friendly; **E** pp Casa Cecilia, Tomás Rogers 54, T/F 411300, 'one of the most famous breakfasts in South America', helpful, clean, friendly, cooking and laundry facilities, English and German spoken, rents camping equipment, information on Torres del Paine, repeatedly rec; **E** pp *Patagonia Adventures*, Tomás Rogers 179, friendly, clean, use of kitchen, good breakfast; **F** pp private house at Magallanes 1, friendly, cheap meals; **E** pp Sra Bruna Mardones, Pasaje Don Bosco 41 (off Philippi), friendly, meals on request; Ana y Ernesto, Barros Arana 175, small and cosy; **E** pp *Casa de familia Alicia*, M Rodríguez 283, clean, spacious, helpful, rec; **E** pp *Don Bosco*, Padre Rossa 1430, good meals, use of kitchen, helpful, rec, motorcycle parking, luggage store; **E** pp Sra Teresa Ruiz, Esmeralda 463, good value, cheap meals extra, quiet, friendly, rec, tours to Torres del Paine arranged.

North from Puerto Natales are: *L3-A2 Cisne de Cuello Negro*, a former guest house for meat buyers at the disused meat packing plant, T 411498, friendly, clean, reasonable, excellent cooking, rec, 5 km from town at Km 275 nr Puerto Bories; **A2** *Patagonia Inn*, Km 26 N, reservations *Hotel Cabo de Hornos*, T/F 242134, Punta Arenas, private bath, restaurant; **C** *Hotel 3 Pasos*, 40 km N, T 228113, simple, beautiful. In Villa Cerro Castillo, 63 km N: **B** *Hostería El Pionero*, T/F 411646, with basin but not bath, country house ambience, good service; *Hospedaje Loreto*; *Hospedaje Kosken*. For accommodation in the Torres del Paine area, see below. **Note**: hotels in the countryside open only in summer months: dates vary.

Restaurants *Nikol's*, Barros Arana 160, seafood and salmon very good; *Don Alvarito*, Blanco Encalada 915, hospitable; *El Marítimo*, Pedro Montt 214, good seafood and salmon, good views, popular, slow service; *Mari Loli*, Baquedano 615, excellent food, good value; *La Ultima Esperanza*, Eberhard 354, rec for salmon, seafood, enormous portions, not cheap; *La Costanera*, Bories y Ladrilleros, good food, superb views; *Andrés*, Ladrilleros 381, good salmon, friendly, rec; *Rey Mar*, Baquedano 414, good food; *La Burbuja*, Bulnes 371, huge portions, reasonably priced; *Tierra del Fuego*, Bulnes 29, cheap, good, slow service; *Café Josmar*, Yungay 743, only cafe open every day, packed lunches sold for boat trips; *Melissa*, Encalada, good crêpes and cakes; *Centro Español*, Magallanes 247, reasonable restaurant. *La Frontera*, Bulnes 819, set meals and à la carte, good value; *La Tranquera*, Bulnes y Blanco Encalada, popular. Cheap meals at *Club Deportivo Natales*, Eberhard 332. *Café Aguila Dorada*, Eberhard 244, T 411982, cheap meals, snacks and ice cream; *Tío Cacho*, Phillipi 553, pizzas and sandwiches. *Delicatessen Pollo Loco*, Baquedano 330, T 411393, good, does packed lunches, rec.

Exchange Travellers' cheques can be changed only into pesos, at 1% commission. **Banco O'Higgins**, Bulnes 633, Mastercard. *Casas de cambio* on Blanco Encalada 226 (Andes Patagónicos) and 266 (Enio América) where Argentine pesos can be changed. **Cambio Stop**, Baquedano 380, good for cash (also arranges tours). Another two at Bulnes 683 and 1087 (good rates); others on Prat. Shop around as some offer very poor rates.

Language School *Natalis English Centre*, Bulnes 1231, T 411193, F 411300, one to one tuition US$4 per hr, good.

Laundry at *Tienda Milodón*, on Bulnes, cheap, or try Sra María Carcamo (at Teresa Ruiz's *hospedaje* at 1000-1200, 1800-2200), good service, more expensive.

Telephones CTC, Blanco Encalada 23 y Bulnes, phones and fax.

Shopping Supermarket *Record* on Bulnes 1,000 block; markets good; food prices variable so shop around. Prices for provisions are better in Punta Arenas.

Shoe Repairs *París*, Miraflores between Blanco Encalada and Baquedano.

Camping Equipment *Onas*, Eberhard 254, best for camping gear, both sale and hire; Luis

Díaz, Encalada 189; Andes Patagónicos, Encalada 226, though less good; Casa de Familia Elsa Millan, O'Higgins 657; Casa Cecilia, Tomás Rogers 54; *Trekatun*, Eberhard 220, T 412177, good equipment; *Urbina Tours*, Eberhard 554, also hire equipment. Check all equipment carefully. Average charges, per day: tent US$6, sleeping bag US$3-5, mat US$1.50, raincoat US$0.60, also cooking gear. (**NB** Deposits required: 1994 rates, tent US$200, sleeping bag US$100.) Camping gas is widely available in hardware stores in Puerto Natales.

Fishing Tackle for hire at Andes Patagónicos, Blanco Encalada 226, T 411594, US$3.50/day for rod, reel and spinners; if you prefer fishing with floats, hooks, split shot, etc, take your own. Other companies up to 5 times as expensive (but see **Camping Equipment**).

Travel Agents *Urbina Tours*, Eberhard 554, T 411965; *Onas*, Bulnes 453, T 411098, tours, trekking, climbing, equipment hire, rec; *Turis Ann*, Tomás Rogers 255, T/F 411141, very helpful, accommodation arranged, tours, equipment hire; *San Cayetano*, Eberhard 145, T 411112; *Michay*, Baquedano 388, T 411149/411957 (Pedro Fueyo rec); *Adventur*, Eberhard y Montt; *Andes Patagónicos*, Eberhard 560, T/F 411176, also horses for hire; *Andescape*, Prat 353, 2°, T 412592; *Knudsen Tours*, Encalada 284, T 411531, rec; *Servitur*, Pratt 353, T411028; *Turismo Zaajh*, Bulnes 459. Patricio Canales, Eberhard 49, rec as a good guide; Eduardo Scott, Valdivia 949. Reports of the reliability of agencies, especially for their trips to Torres del Paine National Park, are very mixed. Several agencies offer tours to the Perito Moreno glacier in Argentina, 2 days including overnight in Calafate, US$70 without accommodation, food and park entry fee. The agencies are reluctant to let tourists leave the tour in Calafate and continue into Argentina. It is cheaper to book tours direct with agents rather than to go through *residenciales* in Puerto Natales as the latter add 10% commission.

Tourist Office in kiosk on waterfront, Av Pedro Montt y Phillipi; maps for US$1 from Eberhard 547. **Conaf**, Carrera Pinto, opp the hospital.

Car Hire Andes Patagónicos, Blanco Encalada 226, T 411594, helpful, US$85/day incl insurance and 350 km free; others US$80/day (San Cayetano, Eberhard 145, not rec), or US$85 with driver. Jeeps, better suited to the road, from US$60/day. Hire agents can arrange permission to drive into Argentina (cheaper than renting a car in Argentina). **Bicycle Hire** Onas, Eberhard 254, US$10 a day; also try *Hotel Eberhard*.

Mechanic Carlos González, Ladrillos entre Bories y Eberhard, rec.

Bicycle Repairs El Rey de la Bicicleta, Arauco 779, good, helpful.

Shipping (See p 728 on services from Puerto Montt). Navimag office: Pedro Montt 380, Terminal Marítimo, T 411421, F 411642.

Buses to **Punta Arenas**, several daily, 3½ hrs, US$6. Bus Fernández, Eberhard 555, T 411111, Bus Sur, Baquedano 534, T 411325 (booking office—buses depart from Turismo Urbina, Eberhard 554, T 411965) and Austral Bus, Baquedano y Valdivia, T 411415. Book in advance. To **Coyhaique** via Calafate, Urbina Tours, 4 days, US$120 (Nov-Mar).

  To **Argentina**: to Río Gallegos direct service by Bus Sur, US$22, Tues and Thur 1830 and El Pingüino, Wed and Sat 1200; hourly to Río Turbio (with Lagoper, Baquedano y Valdivia and other companies), US$3, 2 hrs (depending on Customs—change bus at border). 1000 bus to Río Turbio arrives in time for 1300 El Pingüino bus to Río Gallegos. To **Calafate**, in summer Bus Sur, Turismo Zaajh and Luis Díaz, Patricio Lynch 170, T 411050, run services several times a week, 7 hrs, US$25, reserve one day ahead. Several travel agencies including Knudsen Tours, Scott Tours, Urbina Tours and Servitur run regular minibuses in summer and according to

demand off season, 5 hrs, up to US$50 pp. The cheapest route is to take El Pingüino bus from Río Turbio to La Esperanza and wait there (no more than an hour) for a Río Gallegos bus to Calafate, US$14.

Excursions A recommended walk is up to Cerro Dorotea which dominates the town, with superb views of the whole Ultima Esperanza Sound. Take any bus going E and alight at jeep track for summit (Km 9.5). 25 km NW of Puerto Natales the **Monumento Natural Cueva Milodón** (80m wide, 200m deep, 30m high) can be visited. It now contains a plastic model of the prehistoric ground-sloth whose bones were found there in 1895. (Free camping once US$3 entrance fee has been paid.) Take a taxi (US$15 return) or check if you can get a ride with a tour, both Adventur and Fernández tour buses to Torres del Paine stop at the cave.

At the N end of Ultima Esperanza Sound is the **Parque Nacional Bernardo O'Higgins** (usually referred to as the **Parque Nacional Monte Balmaceda**) which can be reached by sea only. Two boats, the cutter *21 de Mayo* (which carries life jackets and modern navigation equipment) and the motor launch *Alberto de Agostini* sail daily from Puerto Natales in summer and on Sun only in winter (minimum 10 passengers), when weather conditions may be better with less cloud and rain. After a 3 hr journey up the Sound, the boat passes the Balmaceda Glacier which drops from the eastern slopes of Monte Balmaceda (2,035m). The glacier is retreating; in 1986 its foot was at sea level. The boat docks 1 hr further N at Puerto Toro, from where it is a 1 km walk to the base of Serrano Glacier on the N slope of Monte Balmaceda. From here it is possible to walk 35 km to the Torres del Paine National Park. On the trip dolphins, sea-lions (in season), black-necked swans, flightless steamer ducks and cormorants can be seen.

Bookings through Andes Patagónicos (address above) or other agencies, US$40 pp, expensive lunch extra, take own food, drinks available on board. Take warm clothes, hat and gloves. This trip can also be combined with a visit to Torres del Paine. You have to pay full fare on the boat and you need a permit from Conaf. The 35 km walk from Puerto Toro along the Río Serrano to the Torres del Paine administration centre is hard going with no clear path.

145 km NW of Puerto Natales is the ***Torres del Paine*** National Park, covering 1,630 sq km, a 'must' for its wildlife and spectacular scenery. There are 15 peaks above 2,000m, of which the highest is Cerro Paine Grande (3,248m). Nearby, in the centre of the park are the *Torres* (Towers) and *Cuernos* (Horns) of Paine, oddly shaped peaks of over 2,600m, which fall straight down to the valleys, which are filled by beautiful lakes at 50m to 200m above sea level. In the NW of the Park are the glaciers (*ventisqueros*) Grey, Dickson and Zapata, three of the main ones branching off the huge mass forming the Patagonian icecap. The scenery in the Park is superb, with constantly changing views of fantastic peaks, ice-fields, vividly coloured lakes of turquoise, ultramarine and grey and quiet green valleys. The park enjoys a micro-climate especially favourable to wild life and plants: there are 105 species of birds including 18 species of waterfowl and 11 birds of prey. Particularly noteworthy are condors, black-necked swans, rheas, kelp geese, ibis, flamingos and austral parrots. There are also 25 species of mammals including *guanaco*, hares, foxes, *huemules* (a species of deer), pumas and skunks. Over 200 species of plants have been identified. The Park is open all year round, although snow may prevent access in the winter: best time is Dec-Mar. Torres del Paine has become increasingly popular with foreigners and Chileans alike, and despite the best efforts to manage the large influx of visitors rationally, their impact is starting to show. Do your share to protect this unique place: leave nothing but footprints, take nothing but photos!

The park is administered by Conaf: the Administration Centre is in the S of the park at the N end of Lago del Toro (open 0830-1230, 1400-1830). The Centre provides a good slide show at 2000 on Sat and Sun and there are also exhibitions, but no maps or written information to take away. Six ranger stations (*guarderías*) are staffed by rangers (*guardaparques*) who give help and advice and will also store luggage (except at the Laguna Amarga station where they have no room). All visitors are requested to register, show their passport and indicate their intended hiking route when entering the park; they must also inform the rangers when leaving. There are 9 *refugios* and 6 campsites (see below). Park entry for foreigners: US$11, climbing fees US$800. Allow a week to 10 days to see the park properly. The area is very popular in summer and the *refugios* often crowded, and in poor condition (except for Lago del Toro, Lago Pehoe and Grey which are new, privately run and charge a fee). Litter is a problem especially around the *refugios* and camping areas (*campamentos*). Please take all your rubbish out of the park and remember that toilet paper is also garbage.

It is vital not to underestimate the unpredictability of the weather (which can change in a few minutes), nor the arduousness of some of the stretches on the long hikes (the further W you go, the more likely you are to have precipitation). It is essential to be properly equipped against cold, wind and rain. The only means of rescue are on horseback or by boat; the nearest helicopter is in Punta Arenas and high winds usually prevent its operation in the park.

There are about 250 km of well-marked trails. The most popular hike is a circuit ('*El Circuito*') starting from either the Laguna Amarga ranger station or from the administration centre, and going past the spectacular Grey Glacier and round the back of the Cuernos and Torres del Paine. Although the route normally takes 5-6 days, some people do it in less. Strong, fit walkers can complete the circuit using only the *refugios*, but that would be risky and less enjoyable. Consequently, camping gear must be carried. The circuit is often closed in winter due to snow. The longest lap is 30 km, between Refugio Laguna Amarga and Refugio Dickson (10 hrs in good weather), but the most difficult section is the steep slippery slope between Paso John Gardner (1,241m) and Campamento Paso. Although most people go anti-clockwise round the circuit, some advise doing it clockwise so that you climb to Paso John Gardner with the wind behind. Footbridges are occasionally washed away, but in Feb 1995 all were in place. Note that the rangers will not allow solo walkers to attempt '*El Circuito*' and they keep records of those on the route.

Several shorter walks are also recommended including: (1) Up the valley of the Río del Francés between (to the W) Cerro Paine Grande and the Ventisquero del Francés and (to the E) the Cuernos del Paine. Allow 2½ hrs from Refugio Lago Pehoé to Campamento Italiano on the shores of the Río Francés, 2½ hrs further to Campamento Británico. The views from a point 20 mins above the Campamento are superb. (2) To Lago Pingo, S of Ventisquero Zapata (plenty of wildlife, icebergs in the lake), via Refugio Pingo (about halfway) and Refugio Zapata, about 1½ hrs before the Lake.

(3) To the base of the Torres del Paine: from the Park entrance it is 2 hrs to the *refugio*, campsite and ranger station at Laguna Amarga, then 1½ hrs to an *estancia* which includes Hostería Las Torres and a campground. From the *estancia* it is 2 hrs up the valley of the Río Ascensio to *Campamento Chileno* on the river bank, 1 hr further to *Campamento Torres* where many climbers make their base camp and 1 hr more to the base of the Torres where there is a lake: the path is well-marked, but the last ½ hr is up the morraine; if you want to see the towers lit by sunrise (spectacular but you must have good weather), it's well worth humping camping gear up to *Campamento Torres* and spending the night. 1 hr beyond *Camp Torres* is the good site at *Campamento Japonés*.

Descriptions of several walks in the Torres del Paine area are found in *Backpacking in Chile and Argentina* (Bradt Publications).

Refugios are free (except for Refugios Lago Toro, Lago Pehoe and Grey, see below). Most of the *refugios* have cooking areas (wood stove or fireplace) but Laguna Verde and Pingo do not. Rangers know how many people are on each route so you can find out which *refugios* are likely to be full. Take your own food: the small shops at the Andescape *refugios* (see below) and at the *Posada Río Serrano* are expensive and have a limited selection. In most cases a strong, streamlined, waterproof tent is preferable to the *refugios* and is essential if doing the complete circuit. Also essential are protective clothing against wind and rain, strong waterproof footwear, compass, sleeping bag, sleeping mat and cooking equipment. Firewood is scarce nr *refugios* so it is best to take a camping stove. Maps (US$3), are obtainable at Conaf offices in Punta Arenas or Puerto Natales. Most maps are unreliable but the one produced by Sociedad Turística Kaoniken, US$5, has been recommended as more accurate than the Conaf map (available at *Nandú Artesanía* at port end of Bulnes).

Accommodation L3 *Hotel Explora*, new, luxurious and comfortable, at Salto Chico on edge of Lago Pehoé, T 411247, offering spectacular views, pool, gym, tours reservations: Av Américo Vespucci 80, piso 7, Santiago, T 228-8081, F 208-5479; **A1** *Hostería Pehoé*, T 411390, 60 rm, private facilities, cheaper off season, 5 km S of Pehoé ranger station, 11 km N of park administration, on an island with spectacular view across the Lake to Cerro Paine Grande and Cuernos del Paine, daily boat service to *Refugio Pehoé*, at 1300, good meals (reservations: Turismo Pehoé in Punta Arenas or Nataniel 31, office 68, T 671-8709, F 695572, Telex 240875 PEHOE CL in Santiago); **A1** *Hostería Estancia Lazo*, on the E edge of the park, 8 cabins beautifully situated on Laguna Verde with spectacular views, very friendly, comfortable, excellent food, very highly rec, horse riding (reservations: Turismo Lazo, Ignacio Carrero Pinto 443, Punta Arenas, T/F 223771; or T Rogers 255, T/F 41141, Puerto Natales); **B** *Posada Río Serrano*, T 411355, an old *estancia*, some rooms with bath, some with shared facilities, breakfast extra, nr park administration, backpackers sometimes unwelcome, with expensive but good restaurant and a shop (reservations advisable: Serco Ltda, Casilla 19-D, Punta Arenas, T 223395); **L3** *Hostería Las Torres*, head office Chiloé 1212, Punta Arenas, T 226054, F 226473, new, modern conveniences, separate restaurant, English spoken at reception, camping F pp, transport from Laguna Amarga ranger station, rec; **L3** *Hostería Lago Grey*, T/F 222681 (Punta Arenas) new, on edge of Lago Grey, very bad road but due for improvement in late 1994 (reservations through Arka Patagonia or Turismo Runner in Punta Arenas); **F** pp *Refugio Lago del Toro*, nr administration centre, sleeping bag and mattress essential, cooking facilities, in good condition, good meeting place, hot shower US$.75 (open summer only—in the winter months another more basic (free) *refugio* is open near adminsitration centre). The following are run by Andescape (addresses under Puerto Natales and Santiago) and accommodate 32 people in dormitories: **D** pp *Refugio Lago Pehoé*, on the NE arm of Lago Pehoé, new, clean, hot showers, cooking and laundry facilities, meals (breakfast US$2.50, lunch US$5.50, dinner US$8), kiosk with basic food and other supplies, campground (US$3 pp), hot shower for non residents US$2, note the old refugio at the same location is now closed; **D** pp *Refugio Grey*, on the eastern shore of Lago Grey, similar to Refugio Lago Pehoé. Similar *refugios* are to be opened at Campamento Los Perros and Lago Dickson.

Camping *Camping Pehoé* (32 lots, US$2.50 pp, hot shower, am only), *Camping Río Serrano* (25 lots, US$3.50) and *Camping Serón* (US$3.75, hot showers) are operated by Serco Ltda;

Camping Laguna Azul (10 lots) by Conaf (US$3.50). *Camping Lago Pehoé*, by the *refugio* of the same name, US$2.75, hot shower US$2, kiosk with supplies, toilets, boat service to *Refugio Pudeto* (see below); *Camping Grey*, by the refugio, US$3 pp, services as at Lago Pehoé; *Camping Torres*, at the estancia E of the Torres del Paine, US$2.50, hot shower, toilets, picnic tables. Camping and lighting fires are permitted in other locations, but only where indicated by park wardens. (**NB** These restrictions should be observed as forest fires are a serious hazard.) You can camp outside *refugios*, but not nr the Park Administration. Beware mice, which eat through tents. Equipment hire in Puerto Natales (see above).

Boat Trips From *Hostería Grey* at the S end of Lago Grey to the Grey Glacier, minimum 8 passengers, US$25 including refreshments, a stunning trip. From *Refugio Lago Pehoé* to *Refugio Pudeto*, US$10 one way, daily, from Pudeto 0900, 1300, 1600, from Pehoé 1030. 1430, 1730, 1 hr, in high season reserve in advance at the *refugios* on either end or Turismo Tzonka in Puerto Natales.

Transport San Cayetano, Servitur and other agencies (addresses above) run daily bus services to the park from Puerto Natales leaving between 0630 and 0800, returning between 1300 and 1500, 3½ hrs journey, US$5 one way, US$9.50 open return (return tickets are not interchangeable between different companies), from early Nov to end Mar. At other times services by travel agencies dependent on demand, arrange return date with driver and try to arrange your return date to coincide with other groups to keep costs down. A new road to the Park from Puerto Natales has been built to the southern entrance, at Lago Toro, although in Feb 1995, a bridge over the Río Serrano was still missing. Buses now enter the park via Laguna Amarga, not the old portería (park entrance), and stop at the Laguna Amarga ranger station (3 hrs from Puerto Natales) where visitors must register and pay the park entrance fee. They then proceed to *Refugio Pudeto* at Lago Pehoé (30 min) and on to the Administration (30 min); same route for the return trip, departing the Administration between 1300 and 1500 (in high season the buses fill quickly so it is best to board at the Administration). All buses wait at *Refugio Pudeto* until the 1430 boat from *Refugio Lago Pehoé* arrives. Travel between two points within the park (eg Pudeto-Laguna Amarga) US$1.25.

See above for combining a trip to Torres del Paine with a cruise to the Balmaceda Glacier.

To go from Torres del Paine to Calafate (Argentina) either return to Pto Natales and go to Río Turbio for bus to La Esperanza, or take a bus or hitch from the park to Villa Cerro Castillo (106 km S of the administration), the Chilean border point, cross to Paso Cancha de Carreras (Argentina) and try to link with the Río Turbio-La Esperanza-Río Gallegos bus schedule, or hitch. There are a couple *hospedajes* in the village. (See Accommodation **North of Puerto Natales**, above.)

Tours Several agencies in Puerto Natales including *Urbina, San Cayetano* and *Servitur* offer one-day tours by minibus, US$37.50. *Enap* weekend tours in summer cost US$45 including accommodation and meals. *Buses Fernández* offer 2-day tours, US$132 and 3-day tours (which includes trip to the Balmaceda Glacier) US$177. Before booking a tour check carefully on details and get them in writing: increasingly mixed reports of tours. Many companies who claim to visit the Grey Glacier only visit Lago Grey (you see the Glacier in the distance). Taxi costs US$80 per day, run by Sergio Zaley (Arturo Prat 260), but may be cheaper if you catch him when he's going to the Park anyway. After mid-Mar there is little public transport (ask *San Cayetano)* and trucks are irregular.

Hiring a pick-up from Budget in Punta Arenas is an economical proposition for a group (up to 9 people): US$415 for 4 days. If driving there yourself, the road from Pto Natales is being improved and, in the Park, the roads are narrow, bendy with blind corners, use your horn a lot; it takes about 3½ hrs from Pto Natales to the administration, 3 to Laguna Amarga. Petrol may not be available in the park.

Tierra del Fuego is the largest island off the extreme S of South America. It is surrounded by the Magellan Strait to the N, the Atlantic Ocean to the E, the Beagle Channel to the S—which separates it from the southern islands—and by the Whiteside, Gabriel, Magdalena and Cockburn channels etc, which divide it from the islands situated to the W. The western side belongs to Chile and the eastern to Argentina. It produces most of Chile's oil.

In Chilean Tierra del Fuego the only town is **Porvenir**, with a population of 4,500, several hundred from former Yugoslavia (DDD 061). There is a small museum, the Fernando Cordero Rusque, Samuel Valdivieso 402, mainly Indian culture.

Porvenir Hotels **A2** *Los Flamencos*, Teniente Merino, T 580049, best; **C** *Central*, Phillippi 298, T 580077, hot water; **C** *Rosas*, Phillippi, T 580088, with bath, hot water, heating, restaurant and bar, rec; **E** pp *Res Colón*, Damián Riobó 198, T 580108, also full board; **C** *España*, Santos Mardones y Yugoeslavia, good restaurant with fixed price lunch; *Residencial Los Cisnes*, Soto Salas 702, T 580227; **E** pp *Residencial* at Santos Mardones 366 (D with full board), clean, friendly, heaters in rooms, hot water, good; **E** pp *Residencial Cameron*, Yugoeslavia, for shared room, 'friendly folk', good meals, D full board, sleep on dining-room floor for US$1; there is a hotel at the Transportes Senkovic office, Yugoeslavia y Almeyda; many good *pensiones*, D, with full board, but they are often fully occupied by construction workers. *Yugoslav Club* does wholesome and reasonable lunch (about US$5), also *Restaurante Puerto Montt*, Yugoeslavia 1169, for seafood, rec. Many lobster fishing camps where fishermen will prepare lobster on the spot.

Other hotels on Chilean Tierra del Fuego: **E** pp *Hostería de la Frontera*, on the Chilean side of the border, at San Sebastián, in the annex which is 1 km away from the more expensive main building. At Cerro Sombrero, 46 km S of Primera Angostura: **E** pp *Hotel Tuculmen*, rec; **F** *Pensión del Señor Alarcón*, good, friendly. *Posada Las Flores*, Km 127 on the road to San Sebastián, reservations via *Hostal de la Patagonia* in Punta Arenas.

Exchange at *Estrella del Sur* shop, Calle Santos Mardones.

Buses on Tierra del Fuego Two a week between Porvenir and Río Grande (Argentina), Tues and Sat 1400, Transportes Senkovic, Yugoeslavia y Almeyda, T 580100, US$25 heavily booked, buy ticket in advance, or phone. Bus from Río Grande arrives 1300, ferry to Punta Arenas leaves 1400 daily from ferry terminal, 7 km W of Porvenir (schedule is reduced in winter); from bus terminal to ferry, taxi US$6, bus (if running) US$1.50, ferry US$6. Minibus to San Sebastián (Argentine frontier) US$14. Beware: frontier posts are 10 km apart and taxis are not allowed to cross. If you go to the police station and ask for a ride to the border on a truck, you can save the fare to Río Grande. Hitchhiking elsewhere is difficult as there is so little traffic. Argentine time one hour ahead of Chilean time, except Oct-Mar (dates vary each year) when Chile has daylight saving. **NB** If crossing from Argentina, Chile does not allow entry of fruit, vegetables, dairy produce or meat. All stocks will be confiscated. For transport between Río Grande and Ushuaia see under Argentina.

Bus from Calle Manuel Señor, Porvenir, Mon and Fri, 1700, US$10, to Cameron, from where a road runs SE to Estancia Vicuña. Before Vicuña is a scenic fishing-ground; beyond Vicuña a horse trail leads across the Darwin Range to Yendegaia. From there you will have to retrace your steps as it seems impossible to get permission to cross the unmanned border to Ushuaia or to get a Chilean exit stamp.

Transport to Tierra del Fuego There are 2 ferry crossings to Tierra del Fuego. 1) Between Punta Arenas and Puerto Porvenir the *Melinka*, leaving Tres Puentes (5 km N of Punta Arenas, bus A or E from Av Magallanes, US$1; taxi US$3) at 0900 daily (0930 Sun) in season, less frequently off season, depending on tides, 2½ hr crossing, US$5 pp, US$5 per bike, US$30 per vehicle. Reservations essential especially in summer, obtainable from Agencia Broom, Bulnes 05075, T 218100, F 212126. Timetable subject to change: check in advance. It returns from Porvenir (Bahía Chilota) same day at 1400 (1630 Sun). 2) Across the Primera Angostura (First Narrows), 170 km NE of Punta Arenas, between Punta Delgada (**E** pp *Hotel El Faro*; **D** pp *Hostería Tehuelche*, 17 km from port, with restaurant) and Punta Espora: several crossings a day, schedule varies with the tides. Reservations at the ferry. Price US$1 pp and US$14 per car, one way. If hitching, this route is preferable as there is more traffic. By air from Punta Arenas—weather and bookings permitting, Aerovías DAP (O'Higgins 891 y Menéndez, T 243958/223340, F 221693 Punta Arenas and Oficina Foretic, T 80089, Porvenir) fly daily at 0815 and 1730 to Porvenir, return at 0830 and 1750, US$20. Heavily booked so make sure you have your return reservation confirmed.

Puerto Williams is a Chilean naval base on Isla Navarino, S of the Beagle Channel, and about 50 km E of Ushuaia (Argentina) the most southerly place in the world with a permanent population (about 1,500-1,800. Position 54° 55' 41" S, 67° 37' 58" W). It's a small, friendly, remote place (it suffered a serious fire in 1994). The island is totally unspoilt and beautiful, with a chain of rugged snowy peaks, magnificent woods and many animals, including large numbers of beaver which were introduced to the island and have done a lot of damage. Sights include beaver dams, cascades, the Villa Ukika, 2 km E of town, the place where the last descendants of the Yaghan people live, and the local *media luna* where rodeos are held. For superb views, climb Cerro Bandera (3-4 hrs round trip, steep, take warm clothes). Ask the tourist office for details on longer hikes. The *Hotel Walla*, on the edge of Lauta bay, T 223571, 2 km out of town (splendid walks), was closed for repairs in Feb 1994, due to re-open at a future date; **E** pp *Residencial Onashaga* (run by Señor Ortiz—everyone knows him), cold, run down, good meals, helpful, full board available; **E** pp *Pensión Temuco*, Piloto Pardo 224, also full board, comfortable, hospitable, good food, hot showers, rec; you can also stay at private houses. You can camp nr the *Hostería* (closed): collect drinking water from the kitchen. Aeropetrel will charter a plane, if a sufficiently numerous party is raised, to Cape Horn (US$2,600 for 8-10 people).

Museum Excellent **Martín Gusinde** *'Museo del fin del Mundo'* ('End of the World Museum') in Puerto Williams, full of information about vanished Indian tribes, local wildlife, and voyages including Charles Darwin and Fitzroy of the *Beagle*, a 'must'. Open 1000-1300, 1500-1800 (Mon-Thur); 1500-1800 (Sat-Sun), Friday closed (subject to change). Admission US$1.

Offices Post Office (closes 1900), telephone (CTC, Mon-Sat 0930-2230, Sun 1000-1300, 1600-2200), telex, Aerovías DAP, LanChile, Ladeco in the centre of town (maps available). Tourist Office (closed in winter) nr the museum. Ask at the yacht club on the off chance of hitching a ride on a private yacht. Luxury cruises around Cape Horn are run by Tierra Austral for US$800, 6 days. Captain Ben Garrett offers recommended adventure sailing in his schooner *Victory*, from special trips to Ushuaia to cruises in the canals, Cape Horn, glaciers, Puerto Montt, Antarctica in Dec and Jan. Write to Victory Cruises, Puerto Williams (slow mail service); Fax No 1, Cable 3, Puerto Williams; phone (call collect) asking for Punta Arenas (Annex No 1 Puerto Williams) and leave message with the Puerto Williams operator.

Transport to Puerto Williams Ferry from Ushuaia (Argentina), the *Tres Marías*, once a week, 3-4 hrs crossing, US$65 pp, take own lunch; there may be no service in winter, and frequent schedule changes (see under Ushuaia, **p 219**, for other options). From Punta Arenas by air, Aerovías DAP (O'Higgins 891 y Menéndez, T 223958/223340, F221693) on Mon and Fri 1400, Wed 0830, return Mon and Fri 1800, Wed 1000, US$64 single. Book well in advance; 15 seater aircraft and long waiting lists (be persistent). The flight is beautiful, with superb views of Tierra del Fuego, the Cordillera Darwin, the Beagle Channel, and the straits stretching S to Cape Horn. Also army flights available (they are cheaper), but the ticket has to be bought through DAP. Boats from Punta Arenas: *Ñandú* or *Ultragas* leaves on a fixed schedule every 10 days, about midnight, arrives 1700 each way, reclining chairs, no food, US$45 one way. Enquire at the office, Independencia 865, next to service station. The *Navarino* sails from Punta Arenas in 3rd week of every month, 12 passengers, US$150 pp one way; contact the owner, Carlos Aguilera, 21 de Mayo 1460, Punta Arenas, T 228066, F 248848. A small cargo vessel, the *Beaulieu*, sails from Punta Arenas once a month and carries a few passengers, US$300 return, 6 days. Juanita Cofre, Boliviana 533, Punta Arenas, frequently rec as knowledgeable and helpful in arranging transport to Puerto Williams. Navy and port authorities may deny any knowledge, but everyone else in Puerto Williams knows when a boat is due.

THE CHILEAN PACIFIC ISLANDS (9)

Two national park possessions in the Pacific: Juan Fernández Islands, a little easier to reach (and leave) now than in Robinson Crusoe's time, and the unique Easter Island.

Juan Fernández Islands, some 650 km W of Valparaíso, are named after Fernández, the first European to visit, in 1574. They are now a national park administered by Conaf. One of them was the home (1704-09) of Alexander Selkirk (the original of Defoe's *Robinson Crusoe*), whose cave on the beach of Robinson Crusoe island is shown to visitors. The main island has 550 people housed in simple wood frame houses, who fish for *langosta de Juan Fernández* (a pincerless lobster) which they send to the mainland. The only settlement, the village of San Juan Bautista, located on Bahía Cumberland, has a church, schools, post office, and wireless station. The official names of the three islands are: Robinson Crusoe (previously Más a Tierra), Alejandro Selkirk (previously Más Afuera) and Santa Clara (the smallest island).

The climate is mild, the vegetation rich, and there are plenty of wild goats—and some tourists, for the islands are now easily reached by air. There are no beaches to speak of. The boat service, about every three weeks from Valparaíso on the *Río Baker* and *Charles Darwin*, is for cargo and passengers, modest accommodation, 36-hr passage; Agentur, Huérfanos 757, oficina 601, T 337118, Santiago.

Pesquera Chris, Cueto 622, Santiago, T 681-1543, or Cochrane 445 (near Plaza Sotomayor), Valparaíso, T 216800, 2 week trips to the island (5 days cruising, a week on the island), from US$200 return. No fishing or cargo boats will take passengers; the simplest way is to fly. There is an air taxi daily in summer (subject to demand) from Santiago (Los Cerrillos airport, US$395 round trip), by Transportes Aéreas Isla Robinson Crusoe, Monumento 2570, Maipú, Santiago, T 531-4343, F 531-3772 and by Lassa, Av Larraín 7941, La Reina, Santiago, T 273-4354, F 273-4309; also from Valparaíso. The plane lands on an airstrip in the W of the island; passengers are taken by boat to San Juan Bautista (1½ hrs, US$2 one way). In summer, a boat goes once a month between Robinson Crusoe and Alejandro Selkirk if the *langosta* catch warrants it, so you can visit either for a few hours or a whole month.

The anvil-shaped El Yunque, 915m, is the highest peak on Robinson Crusoe and it was upon this hill that Selkirk lit his signal fires. A tablet was set in the rock at the look-out point by British naval officers from HMS *Topaze* in 1868, to commemorate Selkirk's solitary stay on the island for 4 years and 4 months. Selkirk, a Scot, was put ashore from HMS *Cinque Ports* and was taken off by a privateer, the *Duke*. The look-out (Mirador de Selkirk) is the only easy pass between the N and S sides of the island. During the First World War, two British destroyers, HMS *Kent* and *Glasgow*, cornered the German cruiser, *Dresden*, in Bahía Cumberland. The ship, which was scuttled, is still on the bottom; a monument on shore commemorates the event and, nearby, unexploded shells are embedded in the cliffs.

Each Feb, a yachting regatta visits the islands; it originates in Algarrobo, sails to Robinson Crusoe, thence to Talcahuano and Valparaíso. The bay is full of colourful and impressive craft, and prices in restaurants and shops double for the duration. (Thomas G Lammers, Miami University, Department of Botany).

Services C pp *Hotel Selkirk*, clean, good food, full board A pp rec (T Santiago 531-3772); **A3** *Hostería Robinson Crusoe*, full board, plus 20% tax), about 1 hr walk from the village; **A1** *Daniel Defoe Hotel*, at Aldea Daniel Defoe (T Santiago 531-3772); *Hostería Villa Green*, good. Lodging with villagers is difficult. There are no exchange facilities. Only pesos and US$ cash accepted. No credit cards, no TCs. Take insect repellent.

Easter Island (Isla de Pascua, Rapa Nui) is just S of the Tropic of Capricorn and 3,790 km W of Chile; its nearest neighbour is Pitcairn Island. It is triangular in shape, 24 km across, with an extinct volcano at each corner. Its original inhabitants called the island Te Pito te Henua, the navel of the world. The population was stable at 4,000 until the 1850s, when Peruvian slavers, smallpox and emigration (encouraged by plantation-owners) to Tahiti reduced the numbers. Now it is about 2,500, of whom about a quarter are from the mainland, mostly living in the village of Hanga Roa. About half the island, of low round hills with groves of eucalyptus, is used for sheep and cattle, and nearly one-third constitutes a National Park (entry US$10). The islanders, of Polynesian origin, have preserved their indigenous songs and dances, and are extremely hospitable. Tourism has grown rapidly since the air service began in 1967. Paid work is now more common, but much carving is still done. The islanders have profited greatly from the visits of North Americans: a Canadian medical expedition left a mobile hospital on the island in 1966, and when a US missile-tracking station was abandoned in 1971, vehicles, mobile housing and an electricity generator were left behind. The rainy season is from Feb to the end of Aug; the tourist season from Sep to Apr.

The unique features of the island are the 600 (or so) *moai*, huge stone figures up to 9m in height and broad in proportion. One of them, on Anakena beach, was restored to its (probably) original state with a plaque commemorating Thor Heyerdahl's visit in 1955. Heyerdahl's theories, as expressed in *Aku-Aku, The Art of Easter Island* (New York: Doubleday, 1975), are not as widely accepted as they used to be, and South American influence is now largely discounted (see below).

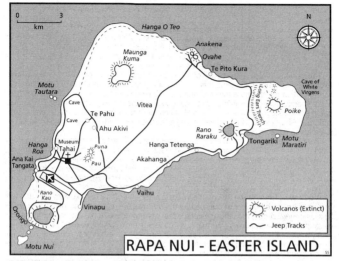

RAPA NUI - EASTER ISLAND

Other *moai*, at Ahu Tepeu and Ahu Tahai, have since been re-erected.

Recommended Reading There is a very thorough illustrated book by J Douglas Porteous, *The Modernization of Easter Island* (1981), available from Department of Geography, University of Victoria, BC, Canada, US$6. See also *Easter Island, Earth Island*, by Paul Bahn and John Flenley (Thames and Hudson, 1992) for a comprehensive appraisal of the island's archaeology. *Islas Oceánicas Chilenas*, edited by Juan Carlos Castillo (Ediciones Universidad Católica de Chile, 1987), contains much information on the natural history and geography of Juan Fernández and Easter Islands.

Anyone continuing into Polynesia or Melanesia from Easter Island will find David Stanley's *South Pacific Handbook* (Moon Publications Inc, PO Box 3040, Chico, CA 95927, USA, F 1-916-345-6751) a useful guidebook.

David Bulbeck, an anthropologist from Adelaide, writes: Far from being the passive recipient of external influences, Easter Island shows the extent of unique development possible for a people left wholly in isolation. It is believed to have been colonized from Polynesia about AD 800: its older altars (*ahu*) are similar to those of (French) Polynesia, and its older statues (*moai*) similar to those of the Marquesas Islands. The very precise stone fitting of some of the *ahu*, and the tall gaunt *moai* with elongated faces and ears for which Easter Island is best known were later developments whose local evolution can be traced through a comparison of the remains. Indigenous Polynesian society, for all its romantic idylls, was competitive, and it seems that the five clans which originally had their own lands demonstrated their strength by erecting these complex monuments. The *moai* were sculpted at the Rano Raraku quarry and transported on wooden rollers over more or less flat paths to their final locations; their red topknots were sculpted at and brought from the inland quarry of Puna Pau; and the rounded pebbles laid out checkerboard fashion at the *ahu* all came from the same beach at Vinapu. The sculptors and engineers were paid out of the surplus food produced by the sponsoring family: Rano Raraku's unfinished *moai* mark the end of the families' ability to pay. Over several centuries from about AD 1400 this stone work slowed down and stopped, owing to the deforestation of the island caused by roller production, and damage to the soils through deforestation and heavy cropping. The birdman cult represented at Orongo is a later development after the islanders had lost their clan territoriality and were concentrated at Hanga Roa, but still needed a non-territorial way to simulate inter-clan rivalry.

Things to See A tour of the main part of the island can be done on foot, but this would need at least two days, either camping at Anakena or returning to Hanga Roa and setting out again the next day (but most correspondents agree that this is far too quick). To see more, hire a vehicle. From Hanga Roa, take the road going SE past the airport; at the oil tanks turn right to

Vinapu, where there are two *ahu* and a wall whose stones are joined with Inca-like precision. Head back NE along the S coast, past Vaihu (an *ahu* with 8 broken *moai*; small harbour with windmill); Akahanga (*ahu* with toppled *moai*); Hanga Tetenga (1 toppled *moai*, bones can be seen inside the *ahu*), Ahu Tongariki (once the largest platform, damaged by a tidal wave in 1960, being restored with Japanese aid). Turn left to Rano Raraku (20 km), the volcano where the *moai* were carved. Many statues can be seen. In the crater is a small lake surrounded by reeds (swimming possible beyond the reeds). Good views.

The road heads N past 'the trench of the long-ears' and an excursion can be made to Poike to see the open-mouthed statue that is particularly popular with local carvers. On Poike the earth is red; at the NE end is the cave where the virgin was kept before marriage to the victor of ceremonies during the birdman cult. The road along the N coast passes Ahu Te Pito Kura, a round stone called the navel of the world. It continues to Ovahe, passing many temple sites and conical houses. At Ovahe, there is a very attractive beach with pink sand and some rather recently carved faces and a cave.

From Ovahe, one can return direct to Hanga Roa or continue to Anakena, site of King Hotu Matua's village and Thor Heyerdahl's landing place. From Anakena a coastal path of variable quality passes interesting remains and beautiful cliff scenery. At Hanga o Teo, there appears to be a large village complex, with several round houses, and further on there is a burial place, built like a long ramp with several ditches containing bones. From Hanga o Teo the path goes W then S, inland from the coast, to meet the road N of Hanga Roa.

A 6-hr walk from Hanga Roa on the W coast passes Ahu Tahai (a *moai* with eyes and top knot in place, cave house, just outside town). Two caves are reached, one inland appears to be a ceremonial centre, the other (nearer the sea) has 2 'windows' (take a strong flashlight and be careful near the 'windows'). Further N is Ahu Tepeu (broken *moai*, ruined houses). Beyond here you can join the path mentioned above, or turn right to Te Pahu cave and the 7 *moai* at Akivi. Either return to Hanga Roa, or go to Puna Pau crater (2 hrs), where the topknots were carved (good views from the 3 crosses at the top).

Rano Kau, S of Hanga Roa, is another important site to visit; one finds the curious Orongo ruins here. The route S out of Hanga Roa passes the 2 caves of Ana Kai Tangata, one of which has paintings. If on foot you can take a path from the Orongo road, just past the Conaf sign, which is a much shorter route to Rano Kau crater. 200m below is a lake with many reed islands. On the seaward side is Orongo (entrance US$11), where the birdman cult flourished, with many ruined buildings and petroglyphs. Out to sea are the 'bird islets', Motu Nui, Motu Iti and Motu Kao. It is very windy at the summit; good views at sunset, or under a full moon (it is easy to follow the road back to Hanga Roa in the dark).

In Hanga Roa is Ahu Tautira, next to a swimming area marked out with concrete walls and a breakwater (cold water). Music at the 0900 Sun mass is 'enchanting'. Museum nr Tahai, US$1, most objects are reproductions because the genuine articles were removed from the island, but it has good descriptions of island life. There is a cultural centre next to the football field, with an exhibition hall and souvenir stall.

Festival *Tapati*, or *Semana Rapa Nui*, end-Jan/beginning-Feb, lasts one week. Dancing competitions, singing, sports (horse racing, swimming, modified decathlon), body-painting, typical foods (lots of small booths by the football field), necklace-making, etc. Only essential activities carry on outside the festival.

Accommodation and Food The airport information desk displays a list of accommodation. In practice this only covers the more expensive places. Flights are met by large numbers of hotel and *residencial* representatives. Accommodation is very expensive, but less so if you are prepared to bargain hard, especially at the airport. Note that room rates, especially in *residenciales* can be much cheaper out of season and if you do not take full board. **L3** *Hotel Hanga Roa*, Av Pont, including all meals (120 beds), does not take credit cards, breakfast incl, T 299 (Santiago 633-9130, F 639-5334); **L3** *Iorana Hotel*, on Ana Magara promontory (5 mins from airport), T 312 (Santiago 633-2650), 14 rm, friendly, excellent food, convenient for visiting Ana Kai Targata caves; **A1** *Easter Island Hotel*, Av Policarpo Toro, Hanga Roa, breakfast and dinner (excellent restaurant), good service, nice garden (T 294, or Santiago 211-6747); **A1** *Hotel Otai*, Te Pilo Te Henua, T 250, comfortable, friendly, run by a family, rec; **A1** *Hotel Victoria*, Av Pont, T 272, friendly, helpful owner Jorge Edmunds arranges tours; **A1** *Topo Ra'a*, Atamu Kekena, T 223, 5 mins from Hanga Roa, very good, helpful, excellent restaurant; **A3** *Hotel Poike*, Petero Atamu, T 283, homely, hot water. Homes offering accommodation and tours (rates ranging from US$18 to US$35, incl meals): **A1** *Residencial Pedro Atán*, T 329, full board, Av Policarpo Toro; **A1** *Res Apina Nui*, Hetereki, T 292 (C low season, but bargain), good food, helpful, English spoken; Yolanda Ika's **A2** *Residencial Taire Ngo Oho*, T 259, with breakfast, rec, modern; Krenia Tucki's **A2** *Residencial Kai Poo*, Av Pont, small, clean, friendly with hot water; **A2** *Residencia Hanga Roa Reka*, T 276, full board, good, friendly, camping US$5; María Georgina Hucke, of Tiki Tours, **B** with half board, rec; Sophia Gomero and María Luisa Pakarati, *Res El Tauke* (Clementina Riroroko Haoa), T 253, same rates as *Hanga Roa Reka*, excellent, airport transfers, tours arranged; *Res Taheta One One*, T 257, same rates, ask here for motorbike rental; **B** *Residencial Tahai*, Simón Paoa s/n (María Hey), T 338, with breakfast, A2 full board, nice garden, rec; **B** pp *Res Holiday Inn* (Viviane Tepano), T 337, half board, excellent food, hot water, rec; **C** Anita and Martín Pate's guesthouse, opp hospital in Hanga Roa, half board in high season, less low season, clean, good food; **D** pp *Res Taniera*, T 290, also camping, horses; **D** pp María Cecilia Cardinale, near Tahai Moai, half board, speaks English and French, excellent food, camping US$5; **D** María Goretti, rooms with breakfast, camping US$6; Sra Inez Pateñárez, Calle Make Make, Hanga Roa, private house accommodation; **D** pp *Ana Rapu*, Calle Apina, T 540, F 318, incl breakfast, evening meal US$7, camping US$5, comfortable, family-run, hot water (except when demand is heavy), English spoken; **C** pp *Residencia Viaka Pua*, Simón Paoa, Hanga Roa, T 377, full board, comfortable, friendly, rec. **A3** Emilio and Milagrosa Paoa, with full board, rec accommodation and tours. Unless it is a particularly busy season there is no need to book in advance; mainland agencies make exorbitant booking charges.

Camping Free in eucalyptus groves near the Ranger's house at Rano Raraku (with water tank), and at Anakena, no water, make sure your tent is ant-proof. Officially, camping is not allowed anywhere else, but this is not apparently strictly enforced. Many people also offer campsites in their gardens, US$5-10 pp (Ana Rapu rec), check availability of water first; some families also provide food. Several habitable caves around the coast: eg between Anakena beach and Ovahe. If you must leave anything behind in a cave, leave only what may be of use to other campers, candles, oil, etc, certainly not rubbish. **NB** There is no camping equipment for hire on the island.

Restaurants *Maitai*, at harbour, friendly, good value; *Copa Cabana*, run down; *Mama Sabina*, Av Policarpo Toro, clean, welcoming; another opp municipal market (which does not sell food). *Pizzería*, opp post office, moderately priced. Most *residenciales* offer full board.

Exchange Best done in Santiago. Bank at Tahai, open 0900-1400 daily. Bank charges US$12 commission on changing TCs, but you can change as many TCs as you like (and they can be in different names). Prices are quoted in dollars, but bills can be paid in pesos and many items, such as food, are priced in pesos; rate of exchange about 10% lower than on the mainland. Amex credit cards are accepted on the island, but credit cards cannot be used to obtain cash. While most places accept TCs, cash dollars are expected. Best rates of exchange at Sunoco service station, also accepts Amex TCs and gives cash on Amex cards. Kia-Koe Land Operator, *Hanga Roa Hotel*, changes Amex cheques. **Post Office** 0900-1700.

Discotheques There are two in Hanga Roa: *Toroko*, near harbour (open Thur-Sun), US$1.25, and *Piditi*, near airport (open Wed-Sun). Both are popular (action begins after 0200), but drinks are expensive: a bottle of pisco costs US$9, canned beer US$2. Coffee is always instant. Beware of extras such as US$3 charge for hot water.

Medical There are a 20-bed hospital, 2 resident doctors, a trained nurse and 2 dentists on the island.

Telephones Code from mainland is 223. Phone calls from the Chilean mainland are subsidized, at US$0.35 per minute. Calls to Europe cost US$10 for 3 mins, cheap rate after 1400.

Shopping There are a couple of expensive supermarkets, cheapest is *Kaikere* on main street, Av Policarpo Toro. Local produce which can be found free (but ask) includes wild guava fruit, fish, 'hierba Luisa' tea, and wild chicken. Food, wine and beer are expensive because of freight charges, but fruit and bread are cheap, and fish bought from the fishermen is good value. Average prices: coffee/tea US$0.50, meals about US$7.50, snacks US$1, beer/cola US$1.50 in most bars and restaurants. Bring all you can from the mainland, but not fruit. Vegetarians will have no problems on the island.

On Av Policarpo Toro there are lots of small shops and market stalls (which may close during rain. **Handicrafts** Wood carvings, stone moais, best bought from the craftsmen themselves, such as Antonio Tepano Tucki, Juan Acka, Hipolito Tucki and his son (who are knowledgeable about the old culture). The municipal market, E of Tahai, will give you a good view of what is available—no compunction to buy. The airport shop is expensive. Good pieces cost between US$30 and 150. Souvenirs at *Hotu Matua's Favorite Shoppe* have been described as 'top dollar and she will not bargain', but she does have the best T-shirts. There is a *mercado artesanal* next to the church and people sell handicrafts at Tahai, Vaihu, Rano Raraku and Anakena. Bargaining is only possible if you pay cash.

Travel Agency *Mahinatur Ltda*, will make your car reservations in advance. Their guide, Christian Walter, is rec.

Tourist Office Kia-Koe, at *Hanga Roa Hotel*, excellent range of excursions which include all the island's sites in 2½ days. Maps are sold on Av Policarpo Toro for US$15-18, or at the ranger station at Orongo for US$10.

Time Zone Easter Island is always 2 hrs behind the Chilean mainland, summer and winter time.

Transport on Easter Island There are no taxis and the only *colectivo* is often off the road. LanChile office on Av Policarpo Toro provides tours of the island (including during stop-overs). Many agencies, residenciales and locals arrange excursions around the island, eg: Aku-Aku Tours, Krenia Tucki of *Residencial Kai Poo*, Michel Fage, Fernando and Marcelo León (Pai Tepano Rano, rec), Hugo Teave (good English, well-informed, polite), Charles Wilkins, Agencia de Viajes Mahinatur Ltda, T 20, English-born guide, rec, as is Victoriano Giralde, Kia-Koe Tours. Some go in jeeps, others will accompany tourists in hired vehicles (eg US$130 for 8), prices up to US$30 pp/day. The English of other tour guides is often poor.

For **hiking**, allow at least a day to walk the length of the island, one way, taking in all the sites. It is 5 easy hours from Hanga Roa to Rano Raraku (camp at ranger station); 5 hrs to Anakena (camp at ranger station, but ask first). You can hitch back to Hanga Roa, especially at weekends though there are few cars at other times. Anyone wishing to spend time exploring the island would be well-advised to speak to Conaf first (T 236); they also give good advice on special interests (biology, archaeology, handicrafts, etc).

The best way to see the island, provided you are fit, is on horseback: horses, US$20-25 a day. Try Emilio Arakie Tepane, who also leads horseback tours of the island (Spanish only) T 504.

Vehicle Rental If you are hiring a car, you should do the sites from S to N since travel agencies tend to start their tours in the N (also a high-clearance vehicle is better-suited to the roads than a normal vehicle). Jeep hire at **Sunoco service station**, Vaihu, T 325 or 239, on airport road, US$10/1 hr, US$20/4 hrs, US$50/day. **Hertz**, opp airport, US$50 a day. Many other vehicle hire agencies on the main street. Chilean or international driving licence essential. There is no insurance available, drive at your own risk (be careful at night, many vehicles drive without lights). Motorbikes may be rented for about US$35 a day incl gasoline (Suzuki or Honda 250 rec because of rough roads). Rentals from Av Policarpo Toro, T 326.

Bicycles, some in poor condition, are available for rent for US$15 on main street or from *residenciales*, or you can buy a robust one in Santiago (LanChile transports bikes free up to a limit of 20 kg) and sell it on the island after 4 days.

How to Get There LanChile fly 4 times a week in high season (Sat, Sun, Tues, Thur), 3 times a week low season (Sun, Tues, Thur) 3½ hrs. Return to Santiago is Mon, Tues, Fri and Sat (Mon, Tues, Fri out of season). LanChile's office on the island is on Av Policarpo Toro, T 279, reconfirm flights here—imperative; do not fly to Easter Island unless you have a confirmed flight out (planes are more crowded to Tahiti, to which LanChile's flights continue, than back to Santiago) and reconfirm your booking on arrival on the Island. For details of LanChile's air passes which include Easter Island and which must be purchased outside Chile, see **Information for Visitors**. The fare in May 1994 was US$852 return. Get to airport early and be prepared for a scramble for seats. Students studying in Chile eligible for 30% discount. If flying to, or from Tahiti, check if you can stay over till another flight or even if there is time for sightseeing before the flight continues—US$10 stop-over sightseeing tours can be arranged (in either case it won't be long enough to take it all in properly). Don't take pesos to Tahiti, they are worthless in French Polynesia. The airport runway has been improved. A US project to extend the airfield, to provide an emergency landing for space shuttles, has been completed.

Airport tax Flying from Santiago to Easter Island incurs the domestic tax of US$5; if flying to Tahiti without stopping on Easter Island you pay the international departure tax of US$12.50. The airport tax for international flights from Easter Island to Tahiti is US$5.

By Sea There are no passenger services to Easter Island. Freight is brought by sea 3 times a year.

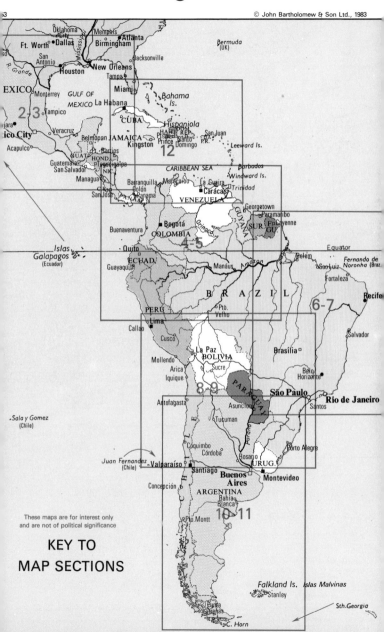

① ③

© John Bartholomew & Son Ltd., 1983

Oklahoma
Ft. Worth • Dallas
Memphis
Atlanta
Birmingham
San Antonio
Houston
Jacksonville
R. Grande
Monterrey
EXICO
Bermuda (UK)
New Orleans
Tampa
GULF OF MEXICO
La Habana
Miami
Bahama Is.
Tampico
jara
ico City
Veracruz
2-3
CUBA
Hispaniola
Acapulco
Belmopan JAMAICA
Kingston
HAITI REP
Prince Santo
Domingo
San Juan
P.R.
Leeward Is.
GUAT
Barrios
Guatemala HOND
Tegucigalpa
San Salvador
NIC
Managua
12
CARIBBEAN SEA
Barbados
Windward Is.
CR
San José
Barranquilla Maracaibo
Colón Panama
La Guaira
Carácas
Trinidad
Georgetown
Paramaribo
Cayenne
GU
SUR
Buenaventura
Bogotá
COLOMBIA
VENEZUELA
Orinoco
4-5
Islas Galapagos (Ecuador)
Quito
ECUAD.
Guayaquil
Manáus
Amazon
Belem
São Luiz
Fortaleza
Equator
Fernando de Noronha (Braz)
Recife
B R A Z I L
6-7
PERU
Lima
Callao
Cusco
Pto. Velho
Salvador
La Paz
BOLIVIA
Sucre
Brasília
Sala y Gomez (Chile)
Mollendo
Arica
Iquique
8-9
Antofagasta
PARAGUAY
Asunción
São Paulo
Santos
Belo Horizonte
Rio de Janeiro
Tucuman
Juan Fernandez (Chile)
Coquimbo
Córdoba
Valparaíso
Santiago
Rosario
URUG.
Porto Alegre
Buenos Aires
Montevideo
Concepción
ARGENTINA
Bahia Blanca
10-11
Pto. Montt

These maps are for interest only
and are not of political significance

**KEY TO
MAP SECTIONS**

Falkland Is. Islas Malvinas
Stanley
Sth.Georgia
Punta
Arenas
C. Horn

ON THE SAME SCALE

OKLAHOMA
City
McAlester
Hot Springs
Little Rock
Memphis
Tennessee
Gadsden
Atlanta
Athens

Durant
Red
Pine Bluff
ARKANSAS
Columbus
Birmingham
Augusta
Orangeburg
Charleston

nson
reenville
Texarkana
Ouachita
Greenwood
Tuscaloosa
Macon
GEORGIA
CAROLINA

Dallas
S T A T E S
Monroe
Jackson
MISSISSIPPI
Meridian
Montgomery
ALABAMA
Columbus
Savannah

Longview
Tyler
Shreveport
LOUISIANA
Vicksburg
Natchez
Laurel
Phenix City
Albany
Waycross
Brunswick

Corsicana
Waco
Alexandria
Baton Rouge
Hattiesburg
Dothan
Valdosta
Jacksonville

Lufkin
Lake Charles
Lafayette
Biloxi
Mobile
Pensacola
Tallahassee
Panama City
Gainesville
St. Augustine

Beaumont
Orange
Pt Arthur
New Orleans
Apalachee Bay
Ocala
Daytona Beach

Houston
Galveston
Orlando

Antonio
ria
ville
Matagorda B.
Clearwater
St. Petersburg
Tampa Bay
Tampa
Lake Okeechobee

Corpus Christi
gsville
Padre I.
Ft. Myers
The Everglades

len
Brownsville
Matamoros
Lag. Madre
C. Sable
Key West
Marquesas Keys

Fernando
La Habana (Havana)
Matanza
CUBA

ia
Pinar del Río
Guane
Guanes
G. de Batabanó
I. de la Juventud

Madero
mpico
Lag. de Tamiahua
C. Rojo
Yucatan Channel
San Antonio
C. Catoche
Pto Juárez
Cancun

Tuxpan
Poza Rica
Papantla
Bahía de Campeche
Progreso
Mérida
Tizimin
Valladolid
I. de Cozumel

Jalapa
an Enríquez
zaba
Córdoba
Veracruz
S Andrés Tuxtla
Frontera
Halachó
Ticul
Peto
B. de la Ascensión

Tierra Blanca
Cuicatlán
Coatzacoalcos
Minatitlán
Cd del Carmen
de Términos
Campeche
Felipe C. Puerto
Yucatán
Escárcega
Chetumal
Bco Chinchorro

Oaxaca
Tlacolula
Cd Ixtepec
Istmo de Tehuantepec
Villahermosa
Tenosique
Hondo
Ambergris Cay
Turneffe I.
Swan (Hond)

Sur
Tehuantepec
Salina Cruz
Tuxtla Gutiérrez
San Cristóbal
Comitán
Flores
Belmopan
BELIZE
Belize
Dangriga
L. de Caratasca

Angel
Golfo de Tehuantepec
Tonalá
Pijijiapan
Huixtla
Tapachula
Pta Gorda
G. of Honduras
Pto Cortés
Trujillo
Is de la Bahía

GUATEMALA
Cobán
Barrios
Tela
La Ceiba
HONDURAS
Patuca
Coco
Segovia
Pto Cabezas

Quezaltenango
Escuintla
STA ANA
Sta Rosa
S Miguel
Comayagua
Tegucigalpa
Juticalpa
Bonanza
Prinzapolc

San José
EL SALVADOR
Sonsonate
Chinandega
San Salvador
La Unión
G. de Fonseca
Matagalpa
León
NICARAGUA
Rio Grande
Bluefields

Managua
Masaya
Granada
L. de Managua
L. de Nicaragua
San Juan del Sur
San Juan

G. de Papagayo
Pen. de Nicoya
Puntarenas
COSTA
RICA
Majuela
San José

G.de Nicoya
Pto Cortés
Pen. de Osa

1:16M

GULF OF MEXICO

100   200   300   400 miles
200   400   600 km.

④

CARIBBEAN SEA

Pta Gallinas
I. de San Andrés (Col)
I.de Providencia (Col)

Aruba (Neth.)   Curaçao (Neth.)
Uribia   Pen. de Guajira   Pto Fijo   Willemstad
Ríohacha   G.de Venezuela   Coro   Riecho
Sta Marta   Maicao   Sa Nevada de Sta Marta 5800   Coro   Tocuyo   Cab
Ciénaga   Machiques   Cd Ojeda   Valencia
Barranquilla   Valledupar   Maracaibo   Cabimas   Barquisimet
Cartagena   L.de Maracaibo   Trujillo   Valera   Acarigua
S.Jacinto   El Banco   Ocaña   Mérida   Guanare
Sincelejo   Magangué   Cúcuta   Barinas
Colón   Monteria   Caucasia   San Cristóbal   Apure   Férr
Panamá   Turbo   Pamplona   Arauca
La Chorrera   Guapá   Barrancabermeja   Bucaramanga   Arauca
Chitré   La Palma   Yarumal   Málaga   Tame   Pto Pá
PANAMA   Quibdó   Bello   Pto Berrio   Barbosa   Pto Carreño
Pen. de Azuero   Itagüí   Medellín   Tunja   Orocué   Vichada
Santiago   Pta Mariato   Manizales   Sogamoso   Meta
David   Chiriqui   Pereira   Chocontá   Ayá
Chiriqui   C. Corrientes   Cartago   Armenia   Bogotá
Buenaventura   Tuluá   Ibagué   Villavicencio   Inírida
G.de Tortugas   Buga   Girardot   Granada   Guania
Palmira   Cali   Guaviare   Salto Angostura
Santander   COLOMBIA
Popayán   Vol. Puracé 4700   Pto Rico   Calamar
Tumaco   Pitalito   Florencia   Yarí   Vaupés   Mitú   Cu
S.Lorenzo   El Divisio   Pasto   Mocoa   Apaporis   Içana
Esmeraldas   Ipiales   Belén   Pto Asis   Caquetá   Icana
Cojimies   Ibarra   Tulcán   Leguizamo   Salto Grande   Japurá
Otavalo   Lago Agrio
Jama   Quito   Coca   Napo
San Lorenzo   Cotopaxi   Tena
Manta   Chone   Ambato   Putumayo   São Paulo de Olivença
Jipijapa   Guaranda   Chimborazo 6287   ECUADOR   Napo   Iquitos   Letícia   Tabatinga
Guayaquil   Babahoyo   Riobamba   Macas   Icá
La Libertad   Milagro   Azogues   Gualaceo   Solimões (Amazonas)   Caxias
I.Puná   Cuenca   Santiago   Jutaí
G.de Guayaquil   Machala   Marañón   Yavari (Javari)
Tumbes   Zaruma   Loja   Tigre   Elvira   Eirunepé
Talara   Zamora   Jutai
Negritos   Sullana   Yuruá   Cruzeiro do Sul
Paita   Piura   Chulucanas   Huancabamba   Tarauacá   Feijó
Pta Aguja   Catacaos   Jaén   Moyobamba   ACRE   Sena
Lambayeque   Ferreñafe   Chachapoyas   Tarapoto   Madureira
Chiclayo   Juanjui   Ucayali   Rio Branco
Chepén   Cajamarca   Cajabamba   Purus   Brasiléia
Pacasmayo   Huamachuco   Uchiza   Cobija   Porvenir
Trujillo   Otosco   Pomabamba   Pucallpa
Huallanca   Huascarán 6768   Tingo Maria   Madre de
Chimbote   Huaraz   PERU   Huánuco
Casma   La Union   Oxapampa   Rio Branco
Huarmey   Cerro de Pasco   La Merced   Porvenir
Pativilca   Tarma   Pto Maldonado   Pto Heath
Barranca   La Oroya   Jauja   Acobamba   Quillabamba
Huacho   Ancón   Huancayo
Callao   Huancavelica
Lima

FOR GALAPAGOS ISLANDS
SEE PAGE 2

⑥

400 miles

600 km.

300

400

Tropic of Capricorn

200

100

1:16M

ALAGOAS Maceió
Propriá Arapiraca Penedo
SERGIPE Estância
Lagarto Aracaju
Sen. do Bonfim
Jacobina
Itabuna Ilhéus
Canavieiras
Belmonte
Pôrto Seguro
Itamaraju
Caravelas
São Mateus
ESPÍRITO Linhares
Colatina
SANTO Vitória
Cariacica Vila Velha
Cachoeiro de Itapemirim
S. João da Barra
Campos
Macaé
Friburgo
Niterói
Rio de Janeiro

Salvador (Bahia)
Alagoinhas
Feira de S.
Cachoeira
Castro Alves Nazaré
Valença Jequié
Iaçu
Itapetinga
Vitória da Conquista
Itambé
Itaberaba
Brumado
Caetité
Salinas
Araçuai
Teófilo Otoni
Nanuque
Gov. Valadares
Diamantina
Fabriciano
Ipatinga
Manhuaçu
Nova Era
Caratinga
Ponte Nova
Barbacena
Juiz de Fora
Além Paraíba
Leopoldina
Muriaé
Carangola
Barra do Piraí
Volta Redonda
Barra Mansa

BAHIA
R. de Jacuipe
Ibotirama
Barra
Xique Xique
Barreiras
Bom Jesus da Lapa
Januária
Montes Claros
Pirapora
Corinto
Curvelo
Sete Lagoas
Belo Horizonte
Ouro Prêto
Conselheiro Lafaiete
São João del Rei
Lavras
Poços de Caldas
Barbacena

TOCANTINS
Taguatinga
Arraias
Formosa
Brasília
GOIÁS
Ceres
Jaraguá
Pirenópolis
Anápolis
Goiânia
Catalão
Araguari
Uberlândia
Ituiutaba
MINAS GERAIS
Patos de Minas
Paracatu
Araxá
Uberaba
Patrocínio
Franca
Ribeirão Prêto
São Carlos
São João da Boa Vista
Limeira

Caldas Novas
Rio Verde
Jataí
Mineiros
Pres. Vargas
Fernandópolis
S. José do R. Prêto
Barretos
Catanduva
Araçatuba
Marília
Bauru
Jaú
Araraquara
Piracicaba
Campinas
São José dos Campos
São Paulo
Santo André
Santos
São Vicente
Itanhaém
Iguape

MATO GROSSO
Pto Artur
Sa Formosa
os Caiabis
Cuiabá
Planalto de Mato Grosso
Rondonópolis
MATO GROSSO DO SUL
Campo Grande
Três Lagoas
Panorama
Pres. Prudente
Pto E. Cunha
Dourados
Ponta Porã
Paranavaí
Umuarama
Maringá
Londrina
Apucarana
PARANÁ
Ponta Grossa
Curitiba
Paranaguá

Fátima du Sul
Caarapó
Guaíra
Cascavel
Toledo
Foz do Iguaçu
Ciudad del Este

Rio de Janeiro

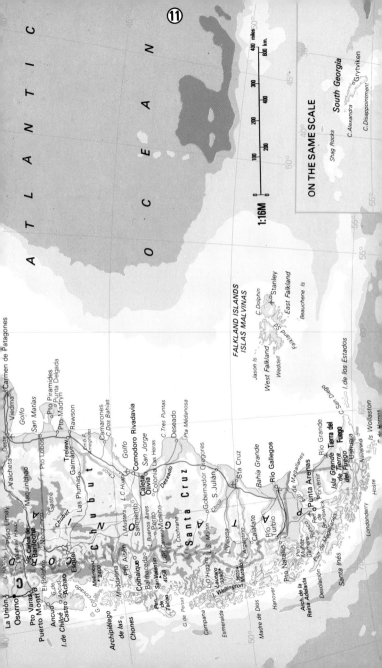

⑪

ATLANTIC

OCEAN

Golfo
San Matías

La Unión
Osorno
Pto Varas
Puerto Montt
Ancud
I.de Chiloé Castro Achao
Chonos

Viedma° Carmen de Patagones
Valcheta°
Maquinchao

Pto Pirámides
Pto Madryn Punta Delgada
Rawson

S.Carlos de
Bariloche
El Bolsón
Esquel

Paso Limay
Ñancu
Manuel Hauri
Ñorquinco
Castre
Pto Lobos

Camarones
C.Dos Bahías

Golfo
San Jorge

C. Tres Puntas

Deseado

Pta Medanosa

C H U B U T

Las Plumas
Gaimano
Trelew

Chubut

L.C.Huapi
L.Musters
Sarmiento
Colonia
Las Heras

Comodoro Rivadavia

Caleta
Olivia

Coihaique
El Maiten
Balmacedao
L.Buenos Aires
Perito
Moreno

Deseado

S a n t a C r u z

Gobernador Gregores

S. Julián

Sta Cruz

L.Fontana
Cochrane
L.San Martín
L.Viedma
Calafate
Río
Turbio

Bahía Grande

Melimoyu
2400
Magdalena

Pen.
de
Taitao

San Valentín
4058
O'Higgins
Lautaro
3380
Moreno

Río Gallegos

Río
Grande

I.Wellington

Archipiélago
de las
Chonos

Pto Natales

Punta Arenas

Isla Grande Tierra del
de Tierra Fuego
del Fuego

G.Corcovado

G.de Penas

Campana

Madre de Dios

Esmeralda

Hanover

Arch.de la
Reina Adelaida

Desolación

Santa Inés

Punta
Dungeness

Porvenir

Estr.de Magallanes

Ushuaia

Londonderry

Hoste

Navarino

Is Wollaston

I.de los Estados

San Diego

C.San Diego

Is Nuevo

FALKLAND ISLANDS
ISLAS MALVINAS

Jason Is

West Falkland

Weddell

Falkland Sd

C.Dolphin

Stanley

East Falkland

Beauchene Is

ON THE SAME SCALE

South Georgia

Shag Rocks

C.Alexandra   Grytviken

C.Disappointment

1:16M

0   100   200   300   400 miles
0   100 200 300 400 500 600 km.

INFORMATION FOR VISITORS

Before you go

Entry requirements

● **Documents**

Passport and tourist card only are required for entry by all foreigners except citizens of New Zealand, Guyana, Haiti, Kuwait, African countries, Cuba and some ex-Communist countries, who require visas. It is imperative to check visa requirements before travel. These details were correct in May 1995 according to the Chilean Consul in London, but regulations change. National identity cards are sufficient for entry by citizens of Argentina, Brazil, Paraguay, and Uruguay. The tourist card is valid for 90 days and is renewable for 90 more (US$8); it is available from Chilean consulates, immigration offices at major land frontiers, airline offices and most aircraft bound for Chile; it must be surrendered on departure and it is essential to keep it safe. If you wish to stay longer than 180 days (as a tourist), it is easier to make a day-trip to Argentina and return with a new tourist card, rather than to apply for a visa, which involves a great deal of paperwork. An onward ticket is officially required but is seldom asked for. 90-day extensions are obtained from any local Gobernación office, which will require proof of funds, then you have to go to Investigaciones for an international record check. A one-year 'visa temporaria' can also be obtained, before one's initial 90-day stay expires, available through the same offices. Proof of financial means or income will have to be shown. On arrival you will be asked where you are staying in Chile. For some nationalities a visa will be granted within 24 hrs upon production of an onward ticket, for others (eg Guyana), authorization must be obtained from Chile. For visitors from New Zealand, a single entry, 90-day visa is free, but a multiple entry is not. For other nationalities who need a visa, a charge is made, but it varies from country to country. Note that to travel overland to or from Tierra del Fuego a multiple entry visa is essential since the Argentine-Chilean border is crossed more than once (it is advisable to get a multiple entry visa before arriving, rather than trying to change a single entry visa once in Chile). A student card is sometimes useful for obtaining discounts on buses, etc. Student cards can be obtained from Providencia 2594, Local 421 and cost US$8, photo and proof of status required.

All foreigners who wish to work in Chile must obtain visas.

● **Tourist information**

The national secretariat of tourism, *Sernatur*, has offices throughout the country (addresses are given in the text). City offices provide town maps, leaflets and much useful information. A rec guide book is *Turistel*, published annually in three parts, *Norte*, *Centro*, and *Sur* (or in a combined edition), sponsored by the CTC telephone company, with information and a wealth of maps covering the whole country and neighbouring tourist centres in Argentina (eg Mendoza, San Martín de los Andes, Bariloche), in Spanish only. Each volume costs between US$6-10, depending where you buy it, but buying the whole set is better value; they can be found in CTC offices, bookshops, but best of all in the news stands in the centre of Santiago. Turistel also publishes a *Mapa rutero* annually, US$4 from news stands and a guide to camping. The publisher is Impresora y Comercial Publiguías SA. **Conaf** (the Corporacíon Nacional Forestal *see p 668*) publishes a series of illustrated booklets in Spanish/English on Chilean trees, shrubs and flowers, rec, as well as **Juventud, Turismo y Naturaleza**, which lists National Parks, their facilities and the flora and fauna of each. Ancient Forest International, Box 1850, Redway, CA 95560, T/F 707-323-3015, USA, can be contacted regarding Chilean forests. Bird-lovers will appreciate *Guía de Campo de Las Aves de Chile*, by B Araya and G Millie.

When to go

● **Best time to visit**

The best time for a visit to Santiago is between Oct and Apr when fine weather is almost assured, but business visits can be made any time during the year. During the holiday season, between mid Dec and early Mar, it is sometimes difficult to make appointments.

Health

Tap water is fairly safe to drink in the main cities but bottled water is safer away from the larger centres. Hotels and restaurants are usually clean. Inoculation against hepatitis and typhoid is a wise precaution. Travellers should not eat salads, strawberries or ground-growing food; hepatitis and typhoid are all too common as the result of the use of untreated sewage for fertilizer. Hepatitis type B inoculation is unavailable. (Check what extra precautions against typhoid are necessary eg 3-pill preventative treatment, available locally.)

Tampons are available but expensive.

Money

● **Currency**

The unit is the peso, its sign is $. Notes are for 500, 1,000, 5,000 and 10,000 pesos and coins for 1, 5, 10, 50 and 100 pesos. There is a shortage of change so keep a supply of small denomination coins.

● **Cost of living**

Shops throughout Chile are well stocked and there is a seasonal supply of all the usual fruits and vegetables. Milk in pasteurized, evaporated, or dried form is obtainable. Chilean tinned food is dear. Food is reasonable, but food prices vary tremendously. Santiago tends to be more expensive for food and accommodation than other parts of Chile. Slide film is very expensive, much cheaper in Bolivia.

In 1994-95 the average cost for a traveller on an economical budget was about US$250 per week. Cheap accommodation in Santiago costs over US$10 pp while N and S of the capital rates are US$5-10 pp. Breakfast in hotels, if not incl in price, is about US$2 (instant coffee, roll with ham or cheese, and jam). In almost every town, private houses offer *alojamiento* (bed, breakfast and often use of kitchen) for US$7-10 pp (bargaining may be possible). Southern Chile is more expensive between Dec 15 and Mar 15.

Stop Press Since the calculations for prices in this chapter were made, the peso has continued to appreciate against the dollar. Unless government policy alters the exchange rate, travellers will find that Chile will become more expensive for those carrying dollars.

● **Exchange**

Travellers' cheques are accepted at reasonable rates if exchanging them for pesos, though rates are better in Santiago than in most other places and this has become more difficult in most towns apart from Arica, Antofagasta and Puerto Montt. TCs can be changed into dollars in Santiago, but is much more difficult elsewhere: check if a commission is charged as this practice seems to vary. Even slightly damaged US dollar notes may be rejected for exchange. Exchange shops (*casas de cambio*) are open longer hours and often give slightly better rates than banks. It is always worth shopping around. Rates tend to get worse as you go N from Santiago. Official rates are quoted in *El Economista* and *El Mercurio*.

Prices may be quoted in US dollars; check if something seems ridiculously cheap. Remember that foreigners who pay with US dollars cash or TCs are not liable for VAT.

The easiest way to obtain cash is by using ATMs (in major cities) which operate under the sign Redbank; they take Visa and Mastercard and permit transactions up to US$250. Diners' Club, Visa and Mastercard are common in Chile (Bancard, the local card, is affiliated to the last two), offices can be found in most cities and will give cash against the cards: Fincard handles Mastercard and Banco Concepción takes Visa, but American Express is less useful (use in American Express banks does not incur commission). US dollars cash are very rarely given against cards or cheques. For Western Union, T (02) 696-8807.

Getting there

By Air

● **From Europe**

To Santiago: British Airways from London via São Paulo (twice a week); Air France from Paris (3 per week); from Madrid LanChile (3 times) and Iberia (4 times a week); KLM from Amsterdam (2), Lufthansa and LanChile from Frankfurt (3 a week each), Alitalia from Rome (2) and Aeroflot (2), via Luxembourg and Shannon, or Stockholm and Shannon. Some flights go via Rio/São Paulo, Montevideo and Buenos Aires; others via New York and/or other points in northern S America. Also, Varig, Aerolíneas Argentinas, Lacsa and Avianca offer services between Europe and Santiago, with connections in Rio, Buenos Aires, San José and Bogotá respectively.

● **From North America**

American Airlines fly daily from Miami, once direct, once via Buenos Aires. LanChile also has daily flights from Miami. Also from Miami, Ladeco flies non-stop; United daily. Also from Miami, Lacsa with connections in San José. From New York, United, Lan Chile and Ladeco via Miami. From Los Angeles there are flights with LanChile via Mexico City and Lima, and Lacsa via Mexico City, San José and Lima. From Dallas with American. From other US cities, connect with LanChile or Ladeco flights in Miami, New York or Los Angeles. CP Air have 2 flights per week from Toronto (changing planes in São Paulo).

● **Transpacific routes**

LanChile flies once or twice a week, depending on season, between Tahiti (making connections from Japan, Australia and New Zealand) and Santiago; they stop over at Easter Island. For excursion fares between Australia/New Zealand and Chile, the stopovers at Easter Island now carry a surcharge of about US$125.

● **Within Latin America**

To/from Buenos Aires (about 75/week) by LanChile, Ladeco, Aerolíneas Argentinas, Saeta, Air France, Alitalia, KLM, Swissair, American, or Avianca (many depart at the same time, check carefully); from Mendoza by Aerolíneas Argentinas or Ladeco. From Montevideo (9 per week) by LanChile, Ladeco, Pluna; from Asunción 3 times a week by Ladeco, 6 days a week by Lapsa, once with National; from Rio de Janeiro with Iberia direct (4 a week), Lan Chile, Varig or Ladeco via São Paulo; from São Paulo non-stop by LanChile, Ladeco, Varig, British Airways; from La Paz 4 per week by Lloyd Aéreo Boliviano (LAB) and 6 a week with LanChile (LAB also from Cochabamba once a week and Santa Cruz 4 a week, Lan Chile once from Santa Cruz); from Caracas, LanChile and Viasa; from Lima (18/week) by Aeroperú, Lacsa and Lan-Chile; from Bogotá (9/week) by Avianca and Ladeco; from Ecuador, Ladeco and Saeta non-stop from Guayaquil (Saeta's flights—3 a week start in Quito) Ladeco also flies to the following: Mexico City, Guatemala City, Cancún, Havana, Purta Cara (Dominican Republic). San José (as does Lacsa) and Montego Bay.

To Arica, from La Paz (10/week) by LAB and LanChile.

● **Overland From Neighbouring Countries**

By land: Roads connect Santiago with Mendoza, and Osorno and Puerto Montt with Bariloche, in Argentina. Less good road connections N and S of Santiago are described in the main text. The main route connecting N Chile with Bolivia. (Arica-La Paz) is paved on the Chilean side. Other routes are poor. In 1995, the possibility of all Chile/Argentina land borders being open 24 hrs a day was under study.

There are railways from La Paz (Bolivia) to Calama for Antofagasta, and to Arica. All passenger services have been suspended on the lines between Chile and Argentina.

Customs

● **Duty free allowance**

500 cigarettes, 100 cigars, 500 grams of tobacco, 3 bottles of liquor, camera, and all articles of personal use. Fruit, vegetables, meat, flowers and milk products may not be imported. It has been reported that bringing a video recorder into Chile involves a great deal of paperwork.

NB There are internal customs checks for all travellers going S on leaving the First Region (ie for duty-free goods from the Zofri free zone in Iquique).

When you arrive

● **Clothing**

Warm sunny days and cool nights are usual during most of the year except in the far S where the climate is like that of Scotland. Ordinary European medium-weight clothing can be worn during the winter (Jun to mid-Sep). Light clothing is best for summer (Dec to Mar), but men do not wear white tropical suits. Chileans are very fashion-conscious. Dress well though conservatively: practical travel clothing makes you stick out as a foreigner.

● **Hours of business**

Banks: 0900-1400, but closed on Sat. Government offices: 1000-1230 (the public is admitted for a few hrs only). Business houses: 0830-1230, 1400-1800 (Mon to Fri). Shops (Santiago): 1030-1930, but 0930-1330 Sat.

● **Law enforcement**

Officers are Caribineros (brown military uniforms), who handle all tasks except immigration. Investigaciones, in civilian dress, the detective police who deal with everything except traffic. Policia Internacional, a division of Investigaciones, who handle immigration.

● **Official time**

GMT minus 4 hrs; minus 3 hrs in summer. Clocks change from mid-Sep or Oct to early Mar.

● **Shopping**

There is an excellent variety of handicrafts: woodwork, pottery, copperware, leatherwork, Indian woven goods including rugs and ponchos in the S. VAT is 18%.

● **Tipping**

10% in restaurants and a few pesos in bars and soda fountains. Railway and airport porters: US$0.10 a piece of luggage. Cloakroom attendants and cinema usherettes: US$0.05. Taxi-drivers are not tipped.

● **Voltage**

220 volts AC, 50 cycles.

● **Weights and measures**

The **metric** system is obligatory but the quintal of 46 kilos (101.4 lb) is used.

On departure

● **Airport and other taxes**

5,300 pesos, or US$12.50 for international flights; US$5, or 2,000 pesos for domestic flights. There is a tourist tax on single air fares of 2%, and 1% on return fares beginning or ending in Chile; also a sales tax of 5% on all transport within Chile.

Where to stay

● **Hotels**

On hotel bills service charges are usually 10%, and taxes on bills are 18%. Prices increase in January. **(If you pay in dollars cash or TCs, you do not have to pay VAT.)** Whether or not the 18% is added to bills in hotel restaurants that are signed and charged to the hotel bill depends on the policy of the establishment. When booking in make certain whether meals are included in the price or only breakfast or nothing at all, and don't rely on the posted sheet in the bedroom for any prices. Particularly in North and Central Chile breakfast is likely to be coffee and bread or toast. Small *residenciales* are often good value. If you are looking for a motel, ask for a *motel turístico*; most motels are short stay.

● **Camping**

Camping is easy but no longer cheap at official sites. A common practice is to charge US$10 for up to 5 people, with no reductions for fewer than 5. 'Camping Gaz International' stoves are rec, since green replaceable cylinders are available in Santiago (white gas – *benzina blanca* – is available in hardware shops, but is expensive; for good value try the *Sodimac* chain of DIY stores). Copec run a network of 33 'Rutacentros' along Ruta 5 which have showers, cafeterias and offer free camping. Free camping is also available at many filling stations.

● **Youth hostels**

There are youth hostels throughout Chile; average cost about US$5-7 pp. Although some hostels are open only from Jan to the end of Feb, many remain open all year round. The IYHA card is usually readily accepted. In summer they are usually crowded and noisy, with only floor space available. Chilean YHA card costs US$4. An additional stamp costing US$4 enables one to use the card in Argentina, Uruguay and Brazil. IYHA card costs US$15. These can be obtained from the Asociación Chilena de Albergues Turísticos Juveniles, Providencia 2594, oficina 420-421, Providencia, Santiago, T 233-3226; together with a useful guidebook of all Youth Hostels in Chile, *Guía Turística de los Albergues Juveniles*. In summer there are makeshift hostels in many Chilean towns, usually in the main schools.

Food and drink

Food

A very typical Chilean dish is *cazuela de ave*, a nutritious stew containing large pieces of chicken, potatoes, rice, and maybe onions, and green peppers; best if served on the second day. *Valdiviano* is another stew, common in the S, consisting of beef, onion, sliced potatoes and eggs. Another popular Chilean dish is *empanadas de pino*, which are turnovers filled with a mixture of raisins, olives, meat, onions and peppers chopped up together. *Pastel de choclo* is a casserole of meat and onions with olives, topped with a maize-meal mash, baked in an earthenware bowl. *Humitas* are mashed sweetcorn mixed with butter and spices and baked in sweetcorn leaves. *Prieta* is a blood sausage stuffed with cabbage leaves. A normal *parrillada* or *asado* is a giant mixed grill served from a charcoal brazier. The *pichanga* is similar but smaller and without the brazier. *Bistek a lo pobre* (a poor man's steak) can be just the opp: it is a steak topped by a fried egg, mashed potatoes, onions and salad.

What gives Chilean food its personality is the seafood. The delicious conger eel is a national dish, and *caldillo de congrio* (a soup served with a massive piece of conger, onions and potato balls) is excellent. A *paila* can take many forms (the *paila* is simply a kind of dish), but the commonest are made of eggs or seafood. *Paila Chonchi* is a kind of bouillabaisse, but has more flavour, more body, more ingredients. *Parrillada de mariscos* is a dish of grilled mixed seafood, brought to the table piping hot on a charcoal brazier. Other excellent local fish are the *cojinoa*, the *albacora* (swordfish) and the *corvina*. Some shellfish, such as *loco* (known to Australians as abalone) and mussels may be periodically banned because they carry the disease *marea roja* (which is fatal in humans). *Cochayuyo* is seaweed, bound into bundles, described as 'hard, leathery thongs'. The *erizo*, or sea-urchin, is also commonly eaten. *Luche* is dried seaweed, sold as a black cake, like 'flakey bread pudding' to be added to soups and stews.

Avocado pears, or *paltas*, are excellent, and play an important role in recipes. Make sure whether vegetables are included in the price for the main dish; menus often don't make this clear. Always best, if being economical, to stick to fixed-price *table d'hôte* meals or try the local markets. A *barros jarpa* is a grilled cheese and ham sandwich and a *barros luco* is a grilled cheese and beef sandwich. *Sopaipillas* are cakes made of a mixture which includes pumpkin, served in syrup (traditionally made in wet weather). *Ice cream* is very good; *lúcuma* and *chirimoya* are highly rec flavours.

Lunch is about 1300 and dinner not before 2030. *Onces* (Elevenses) is tea taken at 1700, often accompanied by a snack. The cocktail hour starts at 1900. Waiters are known as *garzón* – never as *mozo*. Good, cheap meals can usually be found in Centros Españoles or Casinos de Bomberos. By law restaurants have to serve a cheaper set meal at lunchtime; it is called *colación* and may not be included on the menu.

It seems impossible to get real coffee unless you go to expresso bars and specify *café-café, expresso*. If you ask just for *café*, you get soluble coffee. The soluble tea should be avoided. If you order '*café*, or *té, con leche*', it will come with all milk; to have just a little milk in either, you must specify that. After a meal, instead of coffee, try an *agüita* – hot water in which herbs such as mint, or aromatics such as lemon peel, have been steeped. There is a wide variety, available in sachets, and they are very refreshing.

Drink

The local wines are very good; the best are from the central areas. Among the good *bodegas* are Cousiño Macul, Santa Carolina, Undurraga, Concha y Toro, Tocornal, San Pedro and Santa Helena. Santa Elena (no H) is less good. The bottled wines are graded, in increasing excellence, as *gran vino, vino especial* and *vino reservado*. Champagne-style wines are also cheap and acceptable. A small deposit, US$0.30, is charged on most wine bottles. Beer is quite good and cheap (about US$0.75, plus US$0.75 deposit in shops); the draught lager known as Schop is good; also try Cristal Pilsener or Royal Guard in the central regions and Escudo and Polar in the S. Malta, a brown ale, is rec for those wanting a British-type beer.

Good gin is made in Chile. Reasonably good brandy, *anís* and crème de menthe are all bottled in Chile. *Vaina* is worth trying, and so is the traditional Christmas drink, *cola de mono*, a mixture of *aguardiente*, coffee, milk and vanilla served very cold. *Pisco* is worth sampling, especially as a 'Pisco Sour' or with grapefruit or lemon juice. *Manzanilla* is a local liqueur, made from *licor de oro* (like Galliano); *crema de cacao*, especially Mitjans, has been rec. *Chicha* is any form of alcoholic drink made from fruit; *chicha cocida* is 3-day-old fermented grape juice boiled to reduce its volume and then bottled with a tablespoonful of honey. Cider (*chicha de manzana*) is popular in the S. *Chicha fresca* is plain apple juice. *Mote con huesillo*, made from maize and dried fruit, is very refreshing in summer.

Getting around

Air transport

Most flights of LanChile, Ladeco and National, between Santiago and major towns and cities, are given in the text. Try and sit on the left flying S, on the right flying N to get the best views of the Andes.

LanChile and Ladeco offer a 21-day 'Visit Chile' ticket; 5 prices: US$300, valid for Santiago and northern Chile, or Santiago and southern Chile; US$550 for all mainland Chile; Pacific 1, US$812, Santiago-Easter Island-Santiago; Pacific 2, US$1080, valid for a trip to Easter Island and either northern Chile, or southern Chile; Pacific 3, US$1,290 for all mainland Chile and Eastern Island. It must be purchased abroad in conjunction with an international ticket and reservations made well ahead since many flights are fully booked in advance. Rerouting charge US$30. Booked destinations can be left out so it is worth including as many destinations as possible. The airpass is not interchangeable between airlines. It is also possible for the route Santiago – Antofagasta – Arica – Santiago to take a coupon ticket which allows greater flexibility. **NB** Book well in advance (several months) for flights to Easter Island in Jan-Feb. Check with the airlines for matrimonial, student and other discounts. Both LanChile and Ladeco sell out-price tickets (up to 50% off) either as part of special promotions or to stand-by passengers (though the availability of standby fares is often denied). Note that with some fares it is as cheap to fly long distance as take a *salón cama* bus, especially with National, whose fares are usually considerably lower than LanChile or Ladeco.

Land transport

● **Train**
Trains in Chile are moderately priced, and not as slow as in other Andean countries, but dining car food is expensive. There are no passengers services N of Santiago, apart from services to Bolivia from Calama and Arica, and S of the capital passengers are carried as far as Puerto Montt. Student discounts are given on *económico* and *salón* fares, but not on sleepers. There is a railway information office at O'Higgins 853 (at end of arcade), Santiago, for all lines except the Antofagasta-Bolivia (Ahumada 11, Oficina 602, T 698-5536). English spoken.

● **Bus**
Buses are frequent and on the whole good. Apart from holiday times, there is little prob-

lem getting a seat on a long-distance bus. *Salón-cama* services run between main cities (TurBus highly rec). *Salón-cama* means 25 seats, *semi-cama* means 34 and *Salón-ejecutivo* means 44 seats. Stops are infrequent. Prices are highest between Dec-Mar and fares from Santiago double during the Independence celebrations in Sept. Since there is lots of competition between bus companies, fares may be bargained lower, particularly just before departure. Students and holders of IYHA cards may get discounts, but not usually in high season. Most bus companies will carry bicycles, but may ask for payment (on TurBus payment is mandatory).

● **Motoring**
Car drivers require a *Relaciones de pasajeros* document, available at borders, and must present the original registration document of their vehicle, as must motor cyclists. Insurance is obligatory and can be bought at borders. See also **Motoring** in **Introduction and Hints**. The Carta Caminera from the Dirección de Vialidad is the most detailed road map (series of twenty-six) but is only available at Vialidad, Marsende y Alameda, Santiago. Reasonable road maps may also be obtained from the Automóvil Club de Chile, Av Vitacura 8620, Santiago; or other regional offices. You will find several individual maps provide much greater detail than the Club's road atlas. Members of foreign motoring organizations may join the Automóvil Club de Chile (US$58/3months), and obtain discounts at hotels. Town maps from the Automóvil Club and Copec service stations. Shell publish a *Guía caminera y turística de Chile*. The *Turistel* Guides are very useful for roads and town plans, but note that not all distances are exact and that the description 'ripio' (gravel) usually requires high clearance; 'buen ripio' should be OK for ordinary cars. Hydrographic maps from Instituto Hidrográfico, Malgarejo 59, Valparaíso. Gasoline (sold in litres) costs the equivalent of US$2.40 a gallon; it becomes more expensive the further N and further S you go. Unleaded fuel, 93 octane, is available at many service stations, but less frequently outside Santiago and not in the Atacama region. Unleaded 95 and 97 octane are less common. Diesel fuel is widely available. Service stations are frequently reluctant to accept credit cards. Often when they advertise that they accept credit cards, they refuse to do so: always ask beforehand. In Santiago car parts available from many shops on Calle 10 de Julio. For car and motorcycle tyres try Serranos 32, reported to be the best stock in South America.

Carabineros are strict about speed limits: Turistel maps mark police posts, make sure you are not speeding when you pass them. Car drivers should have all their papers in order and to hand since there are frequent checks, but fewer in the S. When driving in the S (on the Carretera Austral particularly), and in the desert N, always top up your fuel tank and carry spare petrol/gasoline (Car hire companies may not have fuel cans. These are obtainable from some supermarkets but not from service stations). Tyres need to be hard-wearing (avoid steel belt); it is rec to carry more than one spare and additional inner tubes.

For motorcyclists the following shops in Santiago have been rec: *Calvin y Calvin*, Av Las Condes 8038, T 224-3434, run by Winston Calvin, friendly, helpful, speaks English, knows about necessary paperwork for buying bikes, Honda and Yamaha parts and service; *Solo Moto*, Vitacura 2760, T 2311178, English spoken, service and parts for Honda and Yamaha; *Moto Service*, Vitacura 2715, new and second-hand Honda and Yamaha dealer; *Guillermo de Freitas Rojas* (Willy), Calle Félix Mendelson, 4740-Santiago, T 521-1853, excellent BMW mechanic; *Miebacc*, Doble Almeda 1040, Nunoa, T 2237533, for BMW parts and service. Mechanics, etc outside Santiago are given in the text.

● **Car hire**
Many agencies, both local and international, operate in Chile. Vehicles may be rented by the day, the week or the month, with or without unlimited mileage. Rates quoted do not normally include insurance or 18% VAT. Make sure you know what the insurance covers, in particular third-party insurance. Often this is only likely to cover small bumps and scratches. Ask about extra cover for a further premium. If you are in a major accident and your insurance is inadequate, your stay in Chile may well be prolonged beyond its intended end. A small car, with unlimited mileage costs about US$500 a week in high season, a pick-up much more. In some areas rates are much lower off-season. (At peak holiday times, eg Independence celebrations, car hire is very difficult.) Shop around, there is much competition. Note that the Automóvil Club de Chile has a car hire agency (with discounts for members or affiliates) and that the office may not be at the same place as the Club's regional delegation. **NB** If intending to leave the country in a hired car, you must obtain an authorization from the hire company, otherwise you will be turned back at the frontier. When leaving Chile this is exchanged

for a quadruple form, one part of which is surrendered at each border control. (If you plan to leave more than once you will need to photocopy the authorization.)

● **Taxis**
Taxis have meters, but agree beforehand on fares for long journeys out of city centres or special excursions. A 50% surcharge is applied after 2100 and on Sun. Taxi drivers rarely know the location of any streets away from the centre. There is no need to tip unless some extra service, like the carrying of luggage, is given. Collective taxis are often little more expensive than buses.

● **Hitchhiking**
Hitchhiking is easy and safe, but in some regions traffic is sparse.

● **Walking**
Serious walkers are advised to get *Backpacking in Chile and Argentina*, (Bradt Publications) 3rd edition 1994. **Skiing** Bradt Publications' *South America Ski Guide*, 1992, gives thorough coverage of all Chile's ski areas.

Boat

Shipping information is given in the text under Santiago and all the relevant southern ports. Local newspapers are useful for all transport schedules.

Communications

● **Language**
The local pronunciation of Spanish, very quick and lilting, with final syllables cut off, can present difficulties to the foreigner. See also Argentine **Information for Visitors**.

● **Newspapers**
Santiago daily papers *El Mercurio, La Nación* (state-owned), *La Epoca* (liberal/left), *La Segunda, La Tercera* and *La Quarta. Las Ultimas Noticias. The Latest Daily News* is an English language paper, published daily except Mon, in Santiago, with international news and tourism details. *El Cóndor*, weekly in German.

Weekly magazines; *Hoy, Qué Pasa, Análisis, Ercilla* and *Panorama Económico* are best economic journals. Monthly: *Rutas* (official organ, Automobile Association).

● **Postal services**
Airmail takes 3-4 days from the UK. Seamail takes 8-12 weeks. There is a daily airmail service to Europe with connections to the UK. Poste restante only holds mail for 30 days; then returns to sender. Lista de Correo in Santiago, Central Post Office, is good and

efficiently organized. Rates: letters to Europe/North America US$1.20, aerogrammes US$0.75. To register a letter costs US$0.75. Surface mail rates for parcels to Europe: Less than 1 kg US$14; 1-3 kg US$18; 10 kg US$30.

● **Telephone services**
National and international calls have been opened up for competition. In early 1995, seven phone companies were in the market, Entel, CTC Mundo, Telefónica del Sur (in regions X and XI), VTR, Chilesat and Bell South and Bell Atlantic of the USA. Full details were not available at time of writing, but in the text above we give the main offices in towns and cities. Through press advertisements, callers find out which company is offering the best rate and make the call via a 3-, or 4- digit company access code. Details were not available on tariffs, cheap rates, ease of making collect calls, or how the multicarrier system works for public phones vis-à-vis private lines. Competition has greatly reduced phone rates.

Telephone boxes can be used to make local and long-distance calls, for making collect calls and receiving calls. Although in theory it is possible to make international calls from these phones, in practice it may be easier to go to a company office. Dial 182 on a yellow phone (not red) for the international operator. Local calls from a public booth are charged at a rate of US$0.20-0.30 a minute. Yellow phones accept only 50 peso coins. Blue phones accept pre-paid phone cards costing 5,000 pesos (*tarjeta telefónica*); available from kiosks. On phone cards, only the time of the call is charged rather than the normal 3 min minimum. There are special phones for long-distance domestic calls which accept credit cards (Mastercard and Visa). Entel has strategically-placed, self-dialling phones, which are white. Users press a button and are instantly connected with the operator from their own country.

Fax is operated by Entel, CTC and VTR, who have offices throughout the country (Entel, US$4 a page world-wide; CTC US$5 a page). VTR also operate telex services. Amex Card holders can often use telex facilities at Amex offices free of charge.

● **Television**
TV channels include TVUC (Universidad Católica) on Channel 13, the leading station; TVN (government operated) on Channel 7; Megavisión (private) on Channel 9 and La Red (private) on Channel 4.

Sport

Sernatur will give all the necessary information about sport.

Skiing Season from Jun to Sep/Oct, weather depending. For information write to: La Federación de Ski de Chile, Casilla 9902, Santiago.

Horse racing is also popular and meetings are held every Sun and on certain feast days at Viña del Mar, Santiago and Concepción throughout the year; horse riding is also popular.

Fishing Santiago and Valparaíso residents fish at the mountain resort of Río Blanco. Some of the world's best fishing is in the Lake District, but this region is very popular. Better still, and relatively, less heavily fished, are the lakes and rivers S of Puerto Montt: Lago Yelcho, Río Futaleufú, Río Yelcho, the rivers and lakes S of Chaitén to La Junta, around Coyhaique and around Cochrane. The licence required can be got from the local police or such angling associations as the Asociación de Pesca y Caza, which gives information on local conditions, or Sernap, San Antonio 427, piso 8, Santiago, open Mon-Fri 0900-1400, US$2 a year. Check with Sernatur on closed seasons. Outside Chile, all information can be obtained from Sport Elite Ltd, Woodwalls House, Corscombe, Dorchester, Dorset, UK, DT2 0NT, T 093589-1477, F 093589-1797 (Major J A Valdes-Scott).

Other popular sports are football and basketball. Viña del Mar has a cricket ground; on Sat there are polo matches at Santiago.

Holidays and festivals

1 Jan, New Year's Day; Holy Week (2 days); 1 May, Labour Day; 21 May, Navy Day; 15 Aug, Assumption; 18, 19 Sept, Independence Days; 12 Oct, Discovery of America; 1 Nov, All Saints Day; 8 Dec, Immaculate Conception; 25 Dec, Christmas Day.

Further reading

British business visitors are advised to obtain 'Hints for Exporters: Chile' from the DTI Export Publications, PO Box 55, Stratford-upon-Avon, Warwickshire, CV37 9GE.

Acknowledgements

Our warmest thanks are due to Charlie Nurse, for updating this chapter. We are most grateful to Robert and Daisy Kunstaetter (Quito), for a thorough review of Chilean Patagonia, to Adrian Turner (Puerto Montt), Patricio Guzmán (Coyhaique), and to the following travellers: Anika Absolan (Vienna, Austria), Antonius Ackermann (Oensingen, Switzerland), Daniel Aeberhard (Slough, UK) an excellent contribution, Maren Althoff (Oberkirch, Germany), Sarah Anderson and Anne Patterson Ishay Attar (Afula, Israel), Alicia Baglietto (Valparaiso, Chile), Hubert Baierl (Augsburg, Germany) most detailed correspondence Andreas Barkentin (Hamburg, Germany), Niki Beattie (Cobham, Surrey), Douglas and Janet Beckers (Armidale, Australia), Ann Beckett (St Petersburg, USA), Janie Bergeron and François Vitez (Longueuil, Canada), Iris Berner (Stuttgart, Germany), Nicole Berry (Columbia, USA), Phil and Jenny Blackman (Bath, UK), Mette Andrea Boesgaard (Greve, Denmark), Stephen Bone (Lingfield, UK), Norman Brust (Richmond, USA), Anke Brednich (Frieburg, Germany), Ludovic Challeat (Lamastre, France), Etienne Claes (Brugge, Belgium), Bernard Cloutier (Montreal, Canada), Alan Cohen (New York, USA), Judith Stanton and Mark Collins (London, UK) a helpful up-date, Ian D R Cox (Weybread, UK), Kathrin and Henning Dictus (Neuwied, Germany), Andrea Dittrich and Thomas Bröhl (Köln, Germany), Paul and Karen Drummond (London), Jae and Gerry Duffy (Elizabeth, USA), Jayne Dyer and Nicholas Hird (Bexhill-on-Sea, UK), Matt Ebiner (Covina) and Suzan Almanza (Westchester, USA), Jakob Engström and Richard Björlin (Brussels, Belgium), Martin Fiems (Brugge, Belgium), Valerie Fraser and Tim Butler (Lima, Peru) many long and informative letters, Patrick Ganahl (Wolfhausen, Switzerland), Helene Keur and Geert Klein Geltink (Zwolle, The Netherlands), Gisa Gericke (Wetzlar), Nicole Hofmann (Weisbaden), and Tanja Wirth (Flörsheim, Germany), Michael Gonin (Canberra, Australia), Loukas Grafakos (Papagou, Greece), Steven Grigg (London, UK), Lea Grinter and Andy Wheeler (Australia), Sylvia Grisez (Warren, USA), Steve Grist (Santiago, Chile), David Guy (Fordingbridge, UK), Maria Chang and Craig Harrison (Arlington, USA), Emma Collingwood and Jim Hart (Edinburgh, UK), Jay Hassani (Baltimore, USA), Dan Heilborn and Maya Schneider (Haifa and Tel-Aviv, Israel), Karin and Ueli Hermann (Reichenburg, Switzerland), Simon Heron (Blackburn, UK), Hotel San Patricio Peter Hunt (Basingstoke, UK), A Jachnow and A Kuhn (Berlin, Germany), Marten H Jacobsen and Brit R Lauritsen (Denmark), Guy Jarvi (Bondi, Australia), Kendra Jones (Wellington, New Zealand), Sonja Jovanovic and Andrew Thompson (London, UK) a helpful letter S and Othmer KamerGüntert (Uetikon, Switzerland), Orna Katz (Be'er Sheva, Israel), Yvonne Kellenberger (Rorschach, Switzerland), David Kergon (Great Yarnmouth, UK), Dr Joachim Kleinwächter (Gorxheimertal), May-Britt Koopman (Triesen, Switzerland), Kato and Mark Kostrzewa (Mountain View, USA), Carsten Leminsky (Hamburg, Germany), William Leonard (Alameda, USA), B W Lessels (Chile), M Leufgens and M Jollands (Alsdorf, Germany), Riika Levoranta (Vammala) and Vesa Lampiner (Möjärvi, Finland), Christoph D Lienke (Munich, Germany), Henning Lösch (Freiburg, Germany), Thomas Lüscher (Rümikon, Switzerland), Franz Mageri (Santiago, Chile), Sandra Maisel (temporarily in La Paz, Bolivia), Eric Mankin (Venice, USA), Daniel Marinello (Cotati, USA), Tammy and Greg McMahon (Fairport, USA), Geraldine and John McQuaid (Ireland), Sylvianne Morlaix (Flobecq, Belgium), Christiane Moser (Frieburg, Germany), Christina Müller (Hanau, Germany), Mark Muhlbacher (Lucerne, Switzerland) for many letters Brian Mullin (Guayaquil, Ecuador), Peter Münch (Mannheim, Germany), Marie-Helene Boone and Ulrich Nanz (Stuttgart, Germany), Hans-Peter Neusch (Stuttgart, Germany), Annesofie Nielsen (Niva, Denmark), Carine Oesterle (Zurich, Switzerland), Paul Olai-Olssen (Oslo, Norway), Paride and Roberta (Switzerland), Sandrine Pocobelli & Alexandra Vernier (Martigny, Switzerland), Margorie Powell (Cambridge, UK) extensive contribution, Lawrence Railton and Susan Boyd (London, UK), K Rascon and S Cummings (Houston, USA), Heidi Reichen (Gsteig) and Roger Strähl (Balsthal, Switzerland), Urs Riegger (Zurich, Switzerland), Eladia Rivera (USA), Geri Robinson and Robyn Stanyon (Burton-on-Trent, UK), Barbara and Peter Roniger (Suberg, Switzerland), Frederic Rouganne (Le Pecq, France), Dr Michael Saxby (Dorking, UK), Burkhard Schack and Michael Zickgraf (Seelbach, Germany), Svenja Schmidt (Germany), Doris Schmittat (Weisbaden, Germany), Therese Schöb (Zurich) and Urs Steinmann (Gruningen, Switzerland), Rüdiger Schultz (St Gallen, Switzerland), Elke Schwichtenberg (Berlin, Germany), Mark E. Smith (Grass Valley, USA), Marianne and Jürg Weber, Claudia Hess Steiner and Thomas Steiner (Lyss, Switzerland), J R Stourton (Cirencester, UK), Alexandra Strickner and Peter Buda (Vienna, Austria), Astrid Studer and Andreas Hediger (Reinach, Switzerland), Pim and Irma Sybesma (Leiden, The Netherlands), Simon Watson Taylor (London, UK), Rainer Teck (Solingen, Germany), Mette and Lotte Thillerup (Hesselager, Denmark), Ron and Dorothy Thyer (Blackburn, Australia), Bezdek Tobija (Salzburg, Austria), Pernilla Tragardh (Stockholm, Sweden), Arnaud Troost and Fenna den Hartog (Rotterdam, The Netherlands), Russell Trounce (Santiago, Chile), Lucie Turgeon and Paul Legros (Maniwaki, Canada), Kim Umemoto (Bangkok), Samuel Urech (Niederhasli, Switzerland), Gonzalo Valdés (Santiago, Chile), Margot Verhagen and Carel van der Velden (Holland), Infanger Vinzenz (Erstfeld, Switzerland) an extensive contribution Dre Visscher (Tilburg, The Netherlands), Claus Voss (Chile), Ron Wain (Teddington) and Steve 'Ribs' Harrop (Cardiff, UK), Rupert A E Walker (Salisbury, UK), Noemi Wallingre and Al Bianco (Buenos Aires, Argentina), Pamela Weekes (Chifley, Australia), Pierre-André Widmer (Céligny, Switzerland), Marc Williamson (Melbourne, Australia) an extensive contribution, Christian Leonards and Sandra Winterhalter (Insel Reichenau, Germany), Sylvia and Norbert Wyder-Amherd (Naters, Switzerland), and Emanuel Zanin (Switzerland).

COLOMBIA

INTRODUCTION

COLOMBIA is the fourth largest country in South America. It has coast lines upon both the Caribbean (1,600 km) and the Pacific (1,306 km). Nearly 55% of the area is almost uninhabited lowland with only 4% of the population; the other 96% are concentrated in the remaining 45%, living for the most part in narrow valleys or isolated intermont basins, or in the broad Caribbean lowlands. The population is infinitely varied, ranging from white, Indian, and black to mixtures of all three.

The 620,000 square km of almost uninhabited land in Colombia lie E of the Eastern Cordillera. Near the foot of the Cordillera the plains are used for cattle ranching, but beyond is jungle. Islands of settlement in it are connected with the rest of the country by air and river, for there are no railways and very few roads: communication is by launch and canoe on the rivers.

In the populous western 45% of the country four ranges of the Andes run from S to N. Between the ranges run deep longitudinal valleys. Of the 14 main groups of population in the country, no less than 11 are in the mountain basins or in the longitudinal valleys; the other three are in the lowlands of the Caribbean.

The first 320 km along the Pacific coast N from the frontier with Ecuador to the port of Buenaventura is a wide, marshy, and sparsely inhabited coastal lowland. Along the coast N of Buenaventura runs the Serranía de Baudó. East of this range the forested lowlands narrow into a low trough of land; E of the trough again rise the slopes of the Western Cordillera. The trough (the Department of the Chocó) is drained southwards into the Pacific by the Río San Juan, navigable for 200 km,

COLOMBIA

1 Bogotá
2 Bogotá to Cucutá
3 The North Coast and Islands
4 Up the Magdalena River
5 The Central Cordillera: Medellín and Manizales
6 The Cauca Valley
7 Popayán, Tierradentro and San Agustín
8 The Llanos and Leticia
9 Southern Colombia

and northwards into the Caribbean by the Río Atrato, navigable for 550 km. The climate is hot and torrential rain falls daily. The inhabitants are mostly black.

From the borders of Ecuador two ranges of mountains, the Western Cordillera and the Central Cordillera, run N for 800 km to the Caribbean lowlands. Five peaks in the Western Cordillera are over 4,000m but none reaches the snowline. The Central Cordillera, 50-65 km wide, is much higher; six of its peaks, snow clad, rise above 5,000m and its highest, the volcano cone of Huila, is 5,439m. Apart from the peaks, mostly inactive volcanoes, there are large areas of high undulating plateaux dissected by deep river gorges giving spectacular scenery. There are narrow ribbons of soil along some of the rivers.

Between the two ranges, as they emerge from Ecuador, lies a valley filled in the S to a height of 2,500m by ash from the volcanoes. Not far from the frontier there is a cluster of self-subsisting Indians around Pasto. Further N between these two ranges lies the Cauca valley; in its northern 190 km, roughly from Popayán N past Cali to Cartago, there is an important agricultural region based on a deep bed of black alluvial soil which yields as many as five crops a year. This valley, which is at a height of about 1,000m and up to 50 km wide, is drained northwards by the Cauca river. Cali, the second city, is the business centre of the valley, and a road and railway run from Cali over a low pass of less than 1,500m in the Western Cordillera to Buenaventura. Sugar cane was the great crop of this valley in colonial times, but has now been varied with tobacco, soya, cotton, pineapple, and every other kind of tropical fruit. There is still some cattle raising. Coffee is grown on the Cordillera slopes above 600m.

At Cartago the two Cordilleras close in and the Cauca valley becomes a deep gorge which runs all the way to the Caribbean flatlands. In the Cordillera Central, at an altitude of 1,540m, is the third largest city and industrial centre in Colombia: Medellín. Much of the coffee and 75% of the gold comes from this area. North of Medellín the Cordillera Central splits into three ranges, separated by streams flowing into the Caribbean.

Near Latitude 2°N, or about 320 km N of the Ecuadorean border, the Eastern Cordillera, the longest of all, rises and swings N and then NE towards Venezuela. About Latitude 7°N it divides; one branch becomes the western rim of the Maracaibo basin and the other runs E into Venezuela, to the S of the Maracaibo basin.

Between this Eastern Cordillera and the Central Cordillera runs the 1,600 km long Magdalena river, with the Caribbean port of Barranquilla at its mouth. There are more intermont basins in the Eastern Cordillera than in the others. Some of its peaks rise above the snow line. In the Sierra Nevada del Cocuy (just before the Cordillera divides) there is a group of snowy peaks, all over 5,200m; the highest, Ritacuba Blanca, reaches 5,493m. The basins are mostly high, at an altitude of from 2,500 to 2,750m. In the Lower Magdalena region the river banks are comparatively deserted, though there are a few clearings made by the descendants of black slaves who settled along the Magdalena after their emancipation. There are oilfields in the valley, particularly at Barrancabermeja.

In a high basin of the Eastern Cordillera, 160 km E of the Magdalena river, the Spaniards in 1538 founded the city of Bogotá, now the national capital. The great rural activity here is the growing of food: cattle, wheat, barley, maize and potatoes.

Roads run N from Bogotá to the basins of Chiquinquirá and Sogamoso, over 160 km away. Both are in the Department of Boyacá, with Tunja, on a mountain between the two, as capital. Both basins, like that of Bogotá, produce food, and there are emerald mines at Muzo, near Chiquinquirá.

There are other basins in the N of the Eastern Cordillera: in the Departments of Santander and Norte de Santander at Bucaramanga and Cúcuta, and a small one at Ocaña. Movement into these basins by Europeans and *mestizos* did not take place until the 19th century, when chinchona bark (for quinine) rose into high demand. By 1885 this trade was dead, but by that time coffee was beginning to be planted. In Bucaramanga coffee is now the main crop, but it has been diversified by cacao, cotton and tobacco, all grown below the altitude suitable for coffee.

There is one more mountain group in Colombia, the Sierra Nevada de Santa Marta, standing isolated from the other ranges on the shores of the Caribbean. This is the highest range of all: its snow-capped peaks rise to 5,800m within 50 km of the coast.

To the W of this Sierra, and N of where the Central and Western Cordilleras come to an end, lies a great lowland which has three groups of population on its

Caribbean shores; at Cartagena, Barranquilla and Santa Marta. The rivers draining this lowland (the Magdalena, Sinú, Cauca, San Jorge and César) run so slowly that much of the area is a network of swamps and lagoons with very little land that can be cultivated. Indeed the whole area E of the channel of the Magdalena is under water at most times of the year. When the floods come, large areas of the land W of the Magdalena—the plains of Bolívar—are covered too, but during the dry season from October to March great herds of cattle are grazed there.

History Before the coming of the Spaniards the country was occupied by Indians, most of whom were primitive hunters or nomad agriculturists, but one part of the country, the high basins of the Eastern Cordillera, was densely occupied by Chibcha Indians who had become sedentary farmers. Their staple foods were maize and the potato, and they had no domestic animal save the dog; the use they could make of the land was therefore limited. Other cultures present in Colombia in the precolumbian era were the Tairona, Quimbaya, Sinú and Calima. Exhibits of their and the Chibcha (Muisca) Indians' gold-work can be seen at the Gold Museum in Bogotá (see p 793).

The Spaniards sailed along the northern coast as far as Panama as early as 1500. The first permanent settlement was by Rodrigo de Bastidas at Santa Marta in 1525. Cartagena was founded in 1533. In 1536, Gonzalo Jiménez de Quesada (who wrote a full account of his adventures) pushed up the Magdalena river to discover its source; mounting the Eastern Cordillera in 1536, he discovered the Chibchas, conquered them, and founded Santa Fe de Bogotá in 1538. In the meantime other Spanish forces were approaching the same region: Pizarro's lieutenant, Sebastián de Belalcázar, had pushed down the Cauca valley from Ecuador and founded Pasto, Popayán and Cali in 1536. Nicolás de Federmann, acting on behalf of the Welser financiers of Germany, who had been granted a colonial concession by Charles V, approached from Venezuela. Belalcázar reached Bogotá in 1538 and Federmann got there in 1539. As in Peru, the initial period of settlement was one of strife between contending *conquistadores*. The royal Audiencia de Santa Fe set up in 1550 gave the area a legislative, judicial and administrative entity. In 1564 this was followed by a presidency of the kingdom of Nueva Granada controlling the whole country and Panama, except Benalcázar's province of Popayán. The Presidency was replaced in 1718 by a viceroyalty at Bogotá which controlled the provinces now known as Venezuela as well; it was independent of the Viceroyalty of Peru, to which this vast area had previously been subject.

The movement towards independence from Spain was set going in 1794 by a translation into Spanish by the *criollo* Antonio Nariño of the French Declaration of the Rights of Man. The movement was given point and force when, in 1808, Napoleon replaced Ferdinand VII of Spain with his own brother Joseph. The New World refused to recognize this: there were several revolts in Nueva Granada, culminating in a revolt at Bogotá and the setting up of a *junta* on 20 July 1810. Other local juntas were established: Cartagena bound itself to a *junta* set up at Tunja. Late in 1812 the young Bolívar, driven out of Venezuela, landed at Cartagena. In a brilliant campaign in 1813 he pushed up the Magdalena to Ocaña, and from there to Cúcuta, and obtained permission from the *junta* at Tunja to advance into Venezuela. In 90 days he marched the 1,200 km to Caracas over mountain country, fighting six battles, but he was unable to hold Caracas and withdrew to Cartagena in 1814.

Napoleon fell in 1815, and the Spanish Government immediately set about reconquering, with some success, Venezuela and New Granada. General Pablo Morillo took Cartagena after a bitter siege of 106 days (Bolívar had withdrawn to Jamaica) and was later "pacifying" Bogotá with a "Reign of Terror" by May 1816.

Bolívar had by now assembled an army of Llaneros, fortified by a British legion recruited from ex-servicemen of the Peninsular wars, in Venezuela at Angostura, or Ciudad Bolívar as it is called today. In the face of incredible difficulties he made a forced march across the Andes in 1819. After joining up with Francisco de Paulo Santander's Nueva Granada army, he defeated the royalists at the battle of the Swamps of Vargas in July and again at Boyacá on 7 August. He entered Bogotá three days later.

Bolívar reported his success to the revolutionary congress sitting at Angostura, and that body, on 17 December 1819, proclaimed the Republic of Gran Colombia, embracing in one the present republics of Venezuela, Colombia, and Ecuador. A general congress was held at Cúcuta on 1 January 1821, and here it was that two opposing views which were to sow such dissension in Colombia first became apparent. Bolívar and Nariño were for centralization; Santander, a realist, for a federation of sovereign states. Bolívar succeeded in enforcing his view for the time being, but Gran Colombia was not to last long; Venezuela broke away in 1829 and Ecuador in 1830. The remaining provinces were named Nueva Granada; it was not till 1863 that the name Colombia was restored.

Almost from its inception the new country became the scene of strife between the centralizing pro-clerical Conservatives and the federalizing anti-clerical Liberals. The Conservative president Tomás Cipriano de Mosquera (1845) encouraged education, began building roads, adopted the metric system, and put steamers on the Magdalena. The Liberals were dominant from 1849 for the next 30 years of insurrections and civil wars. In 1885 the Conservatives imposed a highly centralized constitution which was not modified for over 100 years. A Liberal revolt in 1899 turned into a civil war, "the War of the Thousand Days". The Liberals were finally defeated in 1902 after 100,000 people had died. It was in 1903 that Panama declared its independence from Colombia, following US pressure.

After 40 years of comparative peace, the strife between Conservatives and Liberals was re-ignited in a little-publicized but dreadfully bloody civil war known as *La Violencia* from 1948 to 1957 (some 300,000 people were killed). This was ended by a unique political truce. It was decided by plebiscite in 1957 that the two political parties would support a single presidential candidate, divide all political offices equally between them, and thus maintain political stability for sixteen years. In 1978 the agreement was ended, though some elements of the coalition (representation of the main opposition party in the Cabinet, for instance) were allowed to continue until 1986. Sr Belisario Betancur, the Conservative president from 1982-86, offered a general amnesty to guerrilla movements in an attempt to end violence in the country. Following an initial general acceptance of the offer, only one of the four main guerrilla groups, the FARC, upheld the truce in 1985-7. In May 1986, when the Liberal candidate, Sr Virgilio Barco, won the presidential elections, FARC's newly-formed political party, the Unión Patriótica, won 10 seats in congress; the Liberal party took the majority. Right-wing groups refused to accept the Unión Patriótica and by the beginning of 1990, 1,040 party members had been killed since the UP was formed in 1985. During the campaign for the 1990 presidential and congressional elections violence brought the assassination of the Liberal Party and the UP presidential candidates, Luis Carlos Galán and Bernardo Jaramillo. President Barco pledged to crack down on the drugs barons and an international effort was launched to bring them to justice, but opposition to extradition of suspects to the USA stymied progress.

In the March 1990 parliamentary elections, the Liberal Party won 60% of the seats, against 37% for the Conservatives. Presidential elections were held on 27 May, 1990. The winner was César Gaviria Trujillo (Liberal), a former Finance Minister and Interior Minister, who won a clear majority in the March primaries after taking up the candidacy of the murdered Luis Carlos Galán. Gaviria appointed a coalition government made up of Liberals from rival factions, Conservatives and the M-19 leader. A plebiscite held concurrently with the presidential elections showed clear support for reform of the 1886 constitution. In December 1990, therefore, a 73-member Constituent Assembly was elected, to reform the constitution by 5 July 1991. There was broad agreement that the electoral system, Congress and the judiciary needed modernizing and democratizing. As a result, general elections were held in October 1991 (although not due until 1994), and the Liberals retained a majority in the Senate and the House of Representatives. Voter turnout was low, but many small parties, including M-19 and the indigenous National Indian Organization gained representation in Congress.

Violence erupted again in 1992/93. Having begun in June 1991, peace talks between the government and the Coordinadora Guerrillera (CG, an umbrella group representing all the insurgent factions) collapsed. This was followed by several indecisive, but destructive offensives on the part of both the guerrillas and the armed forces. Pablo Escobar, the alleged leader of the Medillín drugs cartel, who had surrendered under secret terms in 1991, escaped from custody in July 1992. Despite a multi-million dollar reward offered for his recapture and renewed conditional offers of surrender, he remained at large until his death in December 1993. Drug trafficking from Cali continued unabated. The Gaviria government was unable to stem violence, whether perpetrated by drug traffickers, guerrillas or common criminals. Not surprisingly, this was one of the issues in the 1994 election campaign. The two main candidates, Ernesto Samper (Liberal) and Andrés Pastrana (Conservative), supported Gaviria's policy of offering reduced prison sentences for drugs dealers who surrender.

The Liberal party retained its dominance of Congress while Samper won the presidency by a very slim margin after two rounds of voting. The main thrust of Samper's programme was that Colombia's current economic strength should provide resources to tackle the social deprivation which causes drug use and insurgency. Related to this was the widening gap between rich and poor and between urban and rural incomes following the opening of the economy. Early in his presidency Samper placed much emphasis on bringing the FARC and ELN guerrillas to the negotiating table and on public spending on social welfare. Although serious efforts continued in 1995 to eradicate drug plantations and stocks, little progress was made in establishing alternative crops. This left many rural communities without means of support. Much of the current unrest can be traced to this problem.

The People of Colombia The regions vary greatly in their racial make-up: Antioquia and Caldas are largely of European descent, Pasto is Indian, the Cauca Valley and the rural area near the Caribbean are African or *mulato*. No colour bar is legally recognized but it does exist in certain centres. Population figures of cities and towns in the text refer to the 1993 census; except where stated figures are for cities, not municipalities.

The birth and death rates vary greatly from one area to the other, but in general infant mortality is high. Hospitals and clinics are few in relation to the population. About 66% of the doctors are in the departmental capitals, which contain 12% of the population, though all doctors have to spend a year in the country before they can get their final diploma. Deplorable *barrios clandestinos* (shanty-towns) have sprung up around Cali, Barranquilla, Cartagena and Buenaventura.

An estimated 400,000 tribal peoples, from 60 ethnic groups, live in Colombia. Groups include the Wayun (in the Guajira), the Kogi and Arhauco (Sierra Nevada de Santa Marta), Amazonian indians such as the Witoto, the nomadic Nukak and the Ticuna, Andean indians and groups of the Llanos and in the Pacific Coast rain forest. The diversity and importance of indigenous peoples was recognized in the 1991 constitutional reforms when indians were granted the right to two senate seats; the National Colombian Indian Organization (ONIC) won a third seat in the October 1991 ballot. State recognition and the right to bilingual education has not, however, solved major problems of land rights, training and education, and justice.

The Economy Agriculture is an important sector of the economy, contributing about 16% of gdp. It is also the largest earner of foreign exchange, with about half of total legal exports. The traditional crops are coffee, flowers, sugar cane, bananas, rice, maize and cotton. Colombia is the leading producer of mild Arabica coffee and second to Brazil in world production. Output has declined since 1984 as the Government has encouraged diversification, but coffee remains a dominant export item with between 17 and 25% of total revenues, depending on world prices.

Manufacturing contributes 20% of gdp, with agricultural-related activities such as food processing, drink and tobacco accounting for about a third of the sector's value added. Textiles and clothing are also important, and provide an outlet for home-grown cotton. In the second half of the 1980s, strong growth was shown by textiles and clothing, chemicals, transport equipment, cement, metalworking and paper, helping to reduce unemployment. By 1994, the job market had not improved appreciably as the main areas of growth were construction (of office blocks and luxury housing) and services, rather than industry, agriculture and mining.

Although contributing only 7.6% of gdp, mining, mainly oil and coal, was the most dynamic sector of the economy in the 1980s, with growth rates of over 20% a year. With the exception of a few major projects, mining is concentrated in the hands of small scale producers with little technology or organization. Much of their output remains outside the formal economy. Colombia is, however, the largest producer of gold and platinum in Latin America, and these two metals, together with emeralds, have traditionally dominated the mining sector. Mining of precious metals, including silver, is primarily in the Departments of Antioquia and El Chocó; huge gold deposits have also been discovered on the borders of the Departments of Cauca and Valle, while others have been found in the Guairía, Vaupés and Guaviare regions near the Brazilian border.

Colombia: fact file

Geographic
Land area	1,141,748 sq km
forested	48.1%
pastures	39.0%
cultivated	5.2%

Demographic
Population (1994)	34,520,000
annual growth rate (1989-94)	1.7%
urban	67.2%
rural	32.8%
density	30.2 per sq km
Religious affiliation	
Roman Catholic	93.1%
Birth rate per 1,000 (1990-95)	25.8
	(world av 26.0)

Education and Health
Life expectancy at birth,	
male	66.4 years
female	72.3 years
Infant mortality rate	
per 1,000 live births (1990-95)	37.0
Physicians (1989)	1 per 1,078 persons
Hospital beds (1989)	1 per 693 persons
Calorie intake as %	
of FAO requirement	106%
Population age 25 and over	
with no formal schooling	15.3%
Literate males (over 15)	87.5%
Literate females (over 15)	85.9%

Economic
GNP (1992 market prices)	
	US$44,555mn
GNP per capita	US$1,290
Public external debt (1992)	
	US$13,245mn
Tourism receipts (1992)	US$705mn
Inflation (annual av 1988-93)	27.0%
Radio	1 per 1.0 persons
Television	1 per 6.2 persons
Telephone	1 per 8.7 persons

Employment
Population economically active (1985)	
	9,558,000
Unemployment rate	4.3%
% of labour force in	
agriculture	28.5
mining	0.6
manufacturing	13.4
construction	2.9
Military forces	140,000

Source *Encyclopaedia Britannica*

In 1984, rising production of hydrocarbons moved the oil trade into surplus for the first time in ten years. By 1990 oil had replaced coffee as the top export earner. Petroleum productions accounted for 19.2% of total exports in 1992. Development of energy sources has been given high priority to satisfy domestic requirements and to diversify exports. Most of the oil production comes from the Magdalena basin, but these are older fields which are running down. The discovery of the Caño Limón field near Arauca raised output to around 450,000 barrels a day. Another field, Cusiana-Cupiagua, in the Llanos, will be in full production by end-1995 and ensure that the current level of exports, of about 200,000 b/d can be maintained into the next century. Cusiana also has substantial reserves of gas. Ecopetrol, the state oil company, plans to double oil production by 1999 and to invest US$2 bn in new refineries and petro-chemical projects. New pipelines are also being built. As well as oil and gas, Colombia has the largest coal reserves in Latin America, which partial surveys have put at 16.5 bn tonnes. The largest deposits are in the Cerrejón region, where a huge project mines and exports steam coal from a new port at Bahía de Portete. A mine at La Loma (César department) and deposits in the Chocó are also being developed for export markets. Hydroelectricity now accounts for 63% of installed generating capacity. It has an advantage over thermal power because 75% of the nation's hydroelectric potential is in the central zone, where 80% of the population live.

Current account surpluses in the late 1970s during the coffee price boom were turned into large deficits in the first half of the 1980s, reaching over US$3bn in 1982 and 1983, because of lower export receipts and rapidly rising imports. However, Colombia was able to avoid having to reschedule its foreign debts, and took steps to adjust its external accounts. The devaluation of the peso was speeded up, reinforced by import restrictions and export incentives. The fiscal accounts were also turned around and the public sector deficit was reduced from 6.9% of gdp in 1984 to 0.3% in 1990 while economic growth remained positive throughout the 1980s and the early 1990s (gdp grew by 5.7% in 1994). The World Bank and the IMF endorsed the Colombian economic strategy and commercial banks continued to lend to the country to refinance loans falling due. The Gaviria Government accelerated the economic opening of the country and liberalized financial, investment, foreign exchange and tax legislation. High real interest rates encouraged capital inflows and economic stability encouraged foreign investors, who had previously been deterred by civil unrest. A strong peso against the dollar restricted all exports, which, accompanied by soaring imports, greatly expanded the trade deficit, but President Samper's first development plan included large investments in infrastructure in the hope of attracting imports to soak up foreign exchange. Samper also aimed for a budget surplus of 0.7% of gdp and to cut inflation from 1994's 22.6%.

Constitution and Government Senators and Representatives are elected by popular vote. The Senate has 102 members, and the Chamber of Representatives has 161. The President, who appoints his 13 ministers, is elected by direct vote for a term of four years, but cannot succeed himself in the next term. Every citizen over 18 can vote. Reform of the 1886 Constitution was undertaken by a Constituent Assembly in 1991 (see above, **History**).

Administratively the country is divided into 23 Departments, 4 Intendencias, 5 Comisarias, and the Special District of Bogotá.

Liberty of speech and the freedom of the press are in theory absolute but in practice more limited. The language of the country is Spanish. Its religion is Roman Catholicism. There is complete freedom for all other creeds not contravening Christian morals or the law.

Education Education is free, and since 1927 theoretically compulsory, but many children, especially in rural areas, do not attend. There are high standards of secondary and university education, when it is available.

Communications The three Cordilleras, separated by valleys often no more than 1,500m above sea-level, make internal communications extremely difficult. The 3,235 km of narrow-gauge railways and the 106,220 km of roads have eastern and western systems, with inter-communicating laterals (see maps and text). Only about 10% of the road system is paved. Given these difficulties it is natural that Colombia, which ran the first airline in South America, has taken ardently to the air.

Music and Dance No South American country has a greater variety of music than Colombia, strategically placed where the Andes meet the Caribbean. The four major musical areas are (a) the mountain heartland, (b) the Pacific coast, (c) the Caribbean coast and (d) the Llanos or eastern plains. The heartland covers the Andean highlands and intervening valleys of the Cauca and Magdalena and includes the country's three largest cities, Bogotá, Cali and Medellín. It is relatively gentle and sentimental music, accompanied largely by string instruments, with an occasional flute and a *chucho* or *carángano* shaker to lay down the rhythm. The preferred instrument of the highlands and by extension Colombia's national instrument, is the *tiple*, a small 12-stringed guitar, most of which are manufactured at Chiquinquirá in Boyacá. The national dance is the Bambuco, whose lilting sounds are said to have inspired Colombian troops at the Battle of Ayacucho in 1824. It is to be found throughout the country's heartland for dancing, singing and instrumentalizing and has long transcended its folk origins. The choreography is complex, including many figures, such as la Invitación, los Ochos, Los Codos, Los Coqueteos, La Perseguida and La Arrodilla. Other related dances are the Torbellino, where the woman whirls like a top, the more stately Guabina, the Pasillo, Bunde, Sanjuanero and the picaresque Rajaleña. Particularly celebrated melodies are the "Guabina Chiquinquireña" and the "Bunde Tolimense". The following fiestas, among others, provide a good opportunity of seeing the music and dance:- La Fiesta del Campesino, ubiquitous on the first Sunday in June, the Fiesta del Bambuco in Neiva and Festival Folklórico Colombiano in Ibagué later in the month, the Fiesta Nacional de la Guabina y el Tiple, held in Velez in early August, the Desfile de Silleteros in Medellín in the same month and Las Fiestas de Pubenza in Popayán just after the New Year, where the Conjuntos de Chirimía process through the streets.

On Colombia's tropical Pacific coast (and extending down into Esmeraldas, Ecuador) is to be found some of the most African sounding black music in all South America. The Currulao and its variants, the Berejú and Patacoré, are extremely energetic recreational dances and the vocals are typically African-style call-and-response. This is the home of the *marimba* and the music is very percussion driven, including the upright *cununo* drum plus *bombos* and *redoblantes*. Wakes are important in this region and at these the Bundes, Arrullos and Alabaos are sung. Best known is the "Bunde de San Antonio". The Jota Chocoana is a fine example of a Spanish dance taken by black people and tuned into a satirical weapon against their masters. The regional fiestas are the Festival Folklórico del Litoral at Buenaventura in July and San Francisco de Asís at Quibdó on 4 August. Quibdó also features a "Fiesta de los Indios" at Easter.

The music of Colombia's Caribbean lowlands became popular for dancing throughout Latin America more than 30 years ago under the name of "Música Tropical" and has much more recently become an integral part of the Salsa repertory. It can be very roughly divided into "Cumbia" and "Vallenato". The Cumbia is a heavily black influenced dance form for several couples, the men forming an outer circle and the women an inner one. The men hold aloft a bottle of rum and the women a bundle of slim candles called "espermas". The dance probably originated in what is now Panama, moved E into Cartagena, where it is now centred and quite recently further E to Barranquilla and Santa Marta. The most celebrated Cumbias are those of Ciénaga, Mompós, Sampués, San Jacinto and Sincelejo. The instrumental accompaniment consists of *gaitas* or *flautas de caña de millo*, backed by drums. The *gaitas* ("male" and "female") are vertical cactus flutes with beeswax heads, while the *cañas de millo* are smaller transverse flutes. The most famous conjuntos are the Gaiteros de San Jacinto, the Cumbia Soledeña and the Indios Selectos. Variants of the Cumbia are the Porro, Gaita, Puya, Bullerengue and Mapalé, these last two being much faster and more energetic. Lately Cumbia has also become very much part of the Vallenato repertoire and is therefore often played on the accordion. Vallenato music comes from Valledupar in the Department of Cesar and is of relatively recent origin. It is built around one instrument, the accordion, albeit backed by *guacharaco* rasps and *caja* drums. The most popular rhythms are the Paseo and the Merengue, the latter having arrived from the Dominican Republic, where it is the national dance. Perhaps the first virtuoso accordionist was the legendary "Francisco El Hombre", playing around the turn of the century. Today's best known names are those of Rafael Escalona, Alejandro Durán and Calixto Ochoa. In April the Festival de la Leyenda Vallenata is held in Valledupar and attended by thousands. Barranquilla is the scene of South America's second most celebrated Carnival, after that of Rio de Janeiro, with innumerable traditional masked groups, such as the Congos, Toros, Diablos and Caimanes. The Garabato is a dance in which death is defeated. Barranquilla's carnival is less commercialized and more traditional than that of Rio and should be a "must" for anyone with the opportunity to attend. Other important festivals in the region are the Corralejas de Sincelejo with its bullfights in January, La Candelaria in Cartagena on 2 February, the Festival de la Cumbia in El Banco in June, Fiesta del Caiman in Ciénaga in January and Festival del Porro in San Pelayo (Córdoba). To complete the music of the Caribbean region, the Colombian islands of San Andrés and Providencia, off the coast of Nicaragua, have a fascinating mix of mainland Colombian and Jamaican island music, with the Calypso naturally a prominent feature.

The fourth musical region is that of the great eastern plains, the so-called Llanos Orientales between the Arauca and Guaviare rivers, a region where there is really no musical frontier between the two republics of Colombia and Venezuela. Here the Joropo reigns supreme as a dance, with its close relatives the Galerón, the slower and more romantic Pasaje and the breathlessly fast Corrido and Zumba que Zumba. These are dances for couples, with a lot of heel tapping, the arms hanging down loosely to the sides. Arnulfo Briceño and Pentagrama Llanera are the big names and the harp is the only instrument that matters, although normally backed by *cuatro*, guitar, *tiple* and *maracas*. Where to see and hear it all is at the Festival Nacional del Joropo at Villavicencio in December.

BOGOTA (1)

The capital, with its wealth of museums and historic buildings, and nearby towns for a weekend excursion out of the city.

Bogotá, capital of the Republic (population 6.3 million, 1993), is on a plateau at 2,650m. Its full name is Santa Fe de Bogotá. The average temperature is 14°C (58°F). It is built on sloping land, and covers 1,587 square km. The central part of the city is full of character and contrasts: La Candelaria is the historic centre, occupying the area to the S of Av Jiménez de Quesada and N of Cra 10. There is some modern infill but many of the houses are well preserved in colonial style, of one or two storeys with tiled roofs, projecting eaves, wrought ironwork and carved balconies. Few are brightly painted. The churches, museums and palaces are concentrated around and above the Plaza Bolívar. There are also many intriguing cobbled streets further out from this nucleus. Some hotels are found in this part, more along the margins, eg Av Jiménez de Quesada. The streets are relatively uncrowded and safe; care should be exercised after dark. South of Cra 10 is seedier; the streets accommodate market stalls.

Downtown Bogotá, the old commercial centre with shops, offices and banks, runs in a band northwards from Av Jiménez de Quesada. It is very patchy, with a thorough mix of styles including modern towers and run down colonial and later

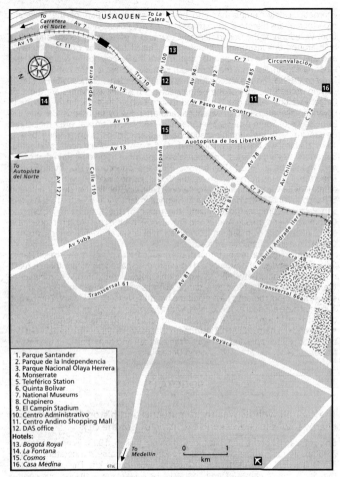

1. Parque Santander
2. Parque de la Independencia
3. Parque Nacional Olaya Herrera
4. Monserrate
5. Teleférico Station
6. Quinta Bolívar
7. National Museums
8. Chapinero
9. El Campín Stadium
10. Centro Administrativo
11. Centro Andino Shopping Mall
12. DAS office
Hotels:
13. *Bogotá Royal*
14. *La Fontana*
15. *Cosmos*
16. *Casa Medina*

buildings, together with a few notable ones. This commercial hub narrows to a thin band of secondary shops extending between Cra 7 and Av Caracas to around C 60. The streets are full of life; they are also paralyzed by traffic and laden with fumes much of the time. The pavements can be very congested too, particularly C 7 and Av 19. Many of the budget hotels and some of the better ones are found in this area, which is rated as low to moderate risk.

North of C 60 and E of Cra 13 (the extension of Av Caracas which eventually becomes the Autopista del Norte) is an expanding band of wealthy suburbs, shopping malls and classy restaurants. The best hotels are scattered through this area, which is regarded as relatively safe.

The area in which to exercise most caution is generally SW of Av Caracas. Away from the centre, the whole of the S of the city should be avoided unless there were

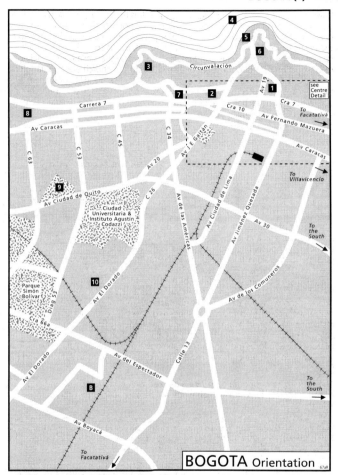

BOGOTA Orientation

specific reasons for a visit.

Visitors should not be too active for the first 24 hrs. Some people get dizzy at Bogotá's altitude. Be careful with food and alcoholic drinks for the first day also.

The Calles (abbreviated "Cll", or "C") run at right angles across the Carreras ("Cra" or "K"). It is easy enough to find a place once the address system, which is used throughout Colombia, is understood. The address Calle 13, No 12-45 would be the building on Calle 13 between Carreras 12 and 13 at 45 paces from Carrera 12; however transversals and diagonals (numbers with letters appended) can complicate the system. The Avenidas, broad and important streets, may be either Calles (like 19) or Carreras (like 14). Av Jiménez de Quesada, one of Bogotá's most important streets, owes its lack of straightness to having been built over a river-bed. Part of Carrera 7, one of the main shopping streets, is now closed to motor traffic on Sundays and holidays when cycles, roller skates and skateboards take over.

There is a very good view of the city from the top of **Monserrate** (3210m), the lower of the two peaks rising sharply to the E. It is reached by a funicular railway and a cable car. The new convent at the top is a popular shrine. At the summit, near the church, a platform gives a bird's-eye view of the city's tiled roofs and of the plains beyond stretching to the rim of the Sabana. Also at the top are several restaurants and snack bar (good *tamales*, US$1), and the Calle del Candelero, a reconstruction of a Bogotá street of 1887. Behind the church are popular picnic grounds. The fare up to Monserrate is US$3.20 adult return (US$1.60 child). The funicular works only on Sun and holidays (expect to have to queue for an hour if you want to go up before about 1400, and for coming down); the cable car operates 0600-2400 daily.

A good time to walk up is Sat or Sun about 0500, before the crowds arrive. There are enough people then to make it quite safe and the view of Bogotá at sunrise is spectacular. The path is dressed stone and comfortably graded all the way up with refreshment stalls at weekends every few metres. It takes about 1¼ hrs up (if you don't stop). Sunset is also spectacular from the top. On no account walk down in the dark; also, take a taxi from the bottom station into town. There are usually taxis waiting by the footbridge across the road. Although the area is reportedly safer than it used to be, it is still best not to go alone. On weekdays, it is not recommended to walk up and especially not down. You should also take a bus or taxi to the foot of the hill Mon-Fri. The walk up to Guadalupe, the higher peak opposite Monserrate, is said to be more dangerous and not recommended at any time.

At the foot of Monserrate is the **Quinta de Bolívar**, a fine colonial mansion, with splendid gardens and lawns. There are several cannons captured at the battle of Boyacá. The house, once Bolívar's home, is now a museum showing some of his personal possessions and paintings of events in his career. (Open 0900-1700, Tues-Sun; its address is C 20, No 3-23 Este; charge US$0.50.)

The **Plaza Bolívar**, with a statue of the Liberator at its centre, is at the heart of the city; around the Plaza are the narrow streets and massive mansions of the old quarter (known as the **Barrio La Candelaria**), with their barred windows, carved doorways, brown-tiled roofs and sheltering eaves. The district is popular as a residential area and has an artists' community. Most of the mansions and best colonial buildings are in this district: the Palacio de San Carlos, the house of the Marqués de San Jorge (housing an archaeological museum), the Palacio Municipal, the Capitolio, and the churches of San Ignacio, Santa Clara, San Agustín, and the Cathedral.

The street map of Bogotá on **p 791** is marked with numerals showing the places of most interest for visitors. Each place will be described under the numeral for it in the map.

1 The Plaza Bolívar, heart of the city, coeval with the city's foundation. On the eastern side is the Palacio Arzobispal, with splendid bronze doors. To one side of it is the colonial Plazuela de Rufino Cuervo. Here is the house of Manuela Sáenz, the mistress of Bolívar. On the other side is the house in which Antonio Nariño printed in 1794 his translation of "The Rights of Man" which triggered off the movement for independence.

See the Casa del Florero or Museo 20 de Julio in a colonial house on the corner of Plaza Bolívar with Calle 11. It houses the famous flower vase that featured in the 1810 revolution and shows collections of the Independence War period, including documents and engravings. Entry fee US$0.40, open Tues-Sat, 0915-1830. On the northern side of the Plaza is the Corte Suprema de Justicia, wrecked in a guerrilla attack in 1985. A new Corte Suprema de Justicia is under construction.

2 The Cathedral, rebuilt in 1807 in classical style. Notable choir loft of carved walnut and wrought silver on altar of Chapel of El Topo. Several treasures and relics; small paintings attributed to Ribera; banner brought by Jiménez de Quesada to Bogotá, in sacristy, which has also portraits of past Archbishops. There is a monument to Jiménez inside the Cathedral. In one of the chapels is buried Gregorio Vásquez Arce y Ceballos (1638-1711), by far the best painter in colonial Colombia. Many of his paintings are in the Cathedral.

3 The beautiful Chapel of El Sagrario, built end of the 17th century. Several paintings by Gregorio Vásquez Arce.

4 Alcaldía Mayor de Bogotá.

5 The Capitolio Nacional, an imposing building with fine colonnades (1847-1925). Congress

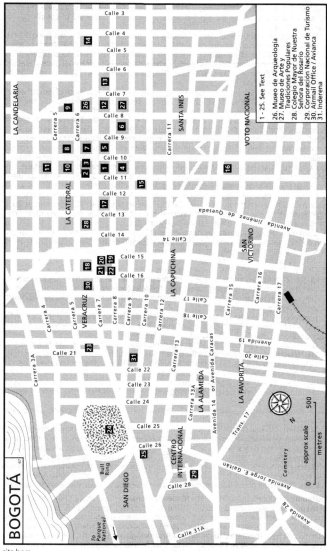

Calle 3
Calle 4
Calle 5
Calle 6
Calle 7
Calle 8
Calle 9
Calle 10
Calle 11
Calle 12
Calle 13
Calle 14

LA CANDELARIA

Carrera 5
Carrera 6

LA CATEDRAL

SANTA INES

Carrera 11

VOTO NACIONAL

Avenida Jiménez de Quesada

SAN VICTORINO

LA CAPUCHINA

Calle 14

Calle 15
Calle 16

VERACRUZ

Carrera 4
Carrera 5
Carrera 7
Carrera 8
Carrera 9
Carrera 10
Carrera 12

Calle 17
Calle 18
Avenida 19
Calle 20

Carrera 15
Carrera 16
Carrera 17

Calle 21

Carrera 3A

Calle 22
Calle 23
Calle 24

Carrera 13
Carrera 13A

LA ALAMEDA

Avenida 14 or Avenida Caracas

LA FAVORITA

Trans. 17

Calle 25
Calle 26

CENTRO INTERNACIONAL

Calle 28

Cemetery

Avenida Jorge E. Gaitán

Avenida 28

SAN DIEGO

Bull Ring

To Parque Nacional

Calle 31A

approx scale
0   500
metres

N

1 - 25. See Text
26. Museo de Arqueología
27. Museo de Arte y Tradiciones Populares
28. Colegio Mayor de Nuestra Señora del Rosario
29. Corporación Nacional de Turismo
30. Airmail Office / Avianca
31. Inderena

BOGOTÁ

sits here.

6 The church of Santa Clara, another colonial church; religious museum and concert hall.

7 San Ignacio, Jesuit church built in 1605. Emeralds from the Muzo mines in Boyacá were used in the monstrance. Paintings by Gregorio Vásquez Arce.

8 The Palacio de San Carlos, where Bolívar lived. He is said to have planted the huge walnut tree in the courtyard. On 25 September 1828, there was an attempt on his life. His mistress,

Manuela, thrust him out of the window and he was able to hide for two hours under the stone arches of the bridge across the Río San Agustín. Santander, suspected of complicity, was arrested and banished.

The Museo de Arte Colonial, across from the Palacio de San Carlos (Carrera 6, No 9-77) is one of the finest colonial buildings in Colombia. It belonged originally to the Society of Jesus, and was once the seat of the oldest University in Colombia and of the National Library. It has a splendid collection of colonial art and paintings by Gregorio Vásquez Arce, all kinds of utensils, and 2 charming patios. Open Tues to Fri 1000-1700; Sat and Sun 1100-1700. Entry fee US$0.40 for adults; students US$0.20.

9 Church of María del Carmen, with excellent stained glass and walls in bands of red and white.

10 **Teatro Colón**, C 10, No 5-32 (operas, lectures, ballets, plays, concerts, etc), late 19th century with lavish decorations. Seating for 1,200, and very ornate.

11 The Casa de la Moneda (Mint), built in 1720, is at C 11, No 4-93. The courtyard is worth seeing. Open Mon-Sat 0900-2100, Sun and holidays, 0900-1800. In the same street, No 4-14, is the Banco de la República's Biblioteca de Luis Angel Arango formerly one of the best endowed and arranged in South America, though showing signs of decline, with 3 reading rooms, research rooms, art galleries on the 1st and 3rd floors and, the best, across the street. There is also a splendid concert hall. There are exhibitions and regular concerts (free on Mon pm, US$0.75 on Sun am, and full-price on Wed, student tickets at US$0.75). The architecture is impressive and the lavatories are recommended. There is a fine cafeteria on the 6th floor.

12 Palacio de Nariño (1906), the presidential palace. Spectacular interior, fine collection of modern Colombian paintings. Free tours Sat morning with guide, 0930 in Spanish, 1000 in English, though not on a regular basis (enquire). It is not open to the public any other time. The guard is changed—full-dress uniform—daily at 1700.

13 Church of San Agustín, strongly ornamented (1637). Fine paintings by Gregorio Vásquez Arce and the Image of Jesus which was proclaimed Generalísimo of the army in 1812.

14 Santa Bárbara church (mid-16th century), one of the most interesting colonial churches. Paintings by Gregorio Vásquez Arce.

15 Church of San Juan de Dios, well worth a visit.

16 Parque Mártires (Park of the Martyrs) with monument, on the site of the Plaza in which the Spanish shot many patriots during the struggle for independence.

17 Palacio de Comunicaciones (postal and telegraph), built on the site of the old colonial church of Santo Domingo.

18 The Banco de la República, next to Parque Santander. Next to the Bank is the wonderful Museo del Oro (see p 793). In Parque Santander there is a bronze statue of Santander, who helped Bolívar to free Colombia and was later its President.

19 Gobernación de Cundinamarca, almost as imposing as the Capitolio. Corinthian style.

20 San Francisco church (mid-16th century), with paintings of famous Franciscans, choir stalls, and a famous high altar (1622). Remarkable ceiling is in Spanish-Moorish (*mudéjar*) style.

21 Church of La Veracruz, first built five years after the founding of Bogotá, rebuilt in 1731, and again in 1904. In 1910 it became the Panteón Nacional e Iglesia de la República. José de Caldas, the famous scientist, was buried along with many other victims of the "Reign of Terror" under the church. Fashionable weddings.

22 La Tercera Orden, a colonial church famous for its carved woodwork, altars, and confessionals.

23 Las Nieves, colonial church, has been demolished and replaced by an ugly modern church.

24 Planetarium, Museo de Historia Natural and Museo de Arte Moderno, in Parque de la Independencia. Two daily showings of best foreign modern painters, US$0.30 (see also p 792).

25 *Tequendama Hotel*. Nearby (on Cra 7 and C 26) are the church and monastery of San Diego, a picturesque old building recently restored. The Franciscan monastery with fine *mudéjar* ceiling was built in 1560 and the church in 1607 as its chapel. It is now used as a crafts shop by Artesanías de Colombia. Southeast of the *Tequendama Hotel* is the Biblioteca Nacional, with entrance on C 24.

Museums (all closed on Mondays) The **Museo Nacional**, on Cra 7, No 28-66, the Panóptico, an old prison converted into a museum (to the NE of the map), founded by Santander in 1823. Its top floor houses a fine art section, comprising national paintings and sculptures. Open Tues-Sat 0930-1730, Sun 1000-1600, US$0.60 (pensioners free). Many of its pre-conquest exhibits have been transferred to the **Museo Arqueológico** at Cra 6, No 7-43, see below. See map: 8 for **Museo de Arte Colonial**, under 1 for **Museo 20 de Julio** and 11 for the Banco de la República's Luis Angel Arango library (US$0.20, half price for students).

The **Museo de Arte Moderno**, C 24, No 6-55, entry US$0.60, half price for students (open Tues-Sat 1000-1900, Sun 1200-1800), good café. If you want to photograph in the museum you must obtain permission from the office. The **Planetarium** and **Museo de Historia Natural**, C 26 y Cra 7, open Tues-Fri 0900-1800, Sat, Sun, and holidays, 1000-1800 (see map, No 24). Planetarium, last show 1630.

The **Museo Mercedes de Pérez**, formerly the Hacienda de El Chicó, a fine example of colonial architecture, is at Cra 7, No 94-17. It contains a world-wide collection of mostly 18th century porcelain, furniture, paintings, etc. Open Tues-Sun, 0930-1230, 1430-1700.

The **Museo de Arte y Tradiciones Populares** is at Cra 8, No 7-21 in an old monastery and exhibits local arts and crafts. It has a shop, selling handicrafts at higher prices than Artesanías de Colombia, and a reasonably-priced bar and restaurant (dishes typical of different regions of Colombia served in colonial setting, usually with regional traditional music). Open 0900-1700, Tues-Sat. Entry fee US$0.50.

Museo Siglo XIX, Cra 8, No 7-91, founded by the Banco Cafetero, has a collection of 19th-century painting, clothes and furniture. Open: Mon-Fri, 0830-1730, Sat, 0900-1300. US$0.30.

The **Museo Arqueológico** (belonging to the Banco Popular) is a fine and extensive collection of precolumbian pottery, assembled in the restored mansion of the Marqués de San Jorge, Cra 6, No 7-43. The house itself is a beautiful example of 17th century Spanish colonial architecture. US$0.60 entry. Open: Mon-Sat 0900-1230, 1315-1700, Sun 1000-1300.

Museo Militar, C 10, No 4-92, history of Colombian armed forces and good collection of weapons, T 281-3086, Tues-Sat 0900-1200, 1400-1800, US$0.30.

Quinta de Bolívar (Simon Bolívar museum), see p 790.

Casa-Museo Jorge Eliécer Gaitán, C 42, No 15-52, is former residence of the populist leader whose assassination in April 1948 triggered the infamous "Bogotazo", at the outset of La Violencia.

Instituto Nacional de Investigaciones Geológico-Mineras has a library and pleasant museum at Diagonal 53, No 34-53. Entrance US$0.10.

Museo de los Niños, Cra 48, No 63-97, natural sciences explained for children, created by Sra Ximena Rosas with funding from industry, Tues-Sun 0900-1200, 1400-1700.

Museo Colsubsidio, C 26, No 25-42, exhibitions of contemporary artists.

Museo del Oro (the Gold Museum), is in splendid premises at the Parque de Santander (corner of C 16, No 5-41, see No 18 on map). This collection is a "must", for it is unique. No less than 30,000 pieces of precolumbian gold work are shown. Open: Tues to Sat 0900-1630; Sun and holidays, 1000-1630. (People in shorts not allowed). Charge, US$1.85 (US$1.25 on Sat and Sun). There are tours and films in Spanish and English, enquire for times. Do not miss the Salón Dorado, a glittering display inside an inner vault.

The ancient gold objects discovered in Colombia were not made by the primitive technique of simple hammering alone, but show the use of virtually every technique known to modern goldsmiths.

The **Universidad Nacional** (about 13,000 students) is housed in the Ciudad Universitaria shown on the orientation map. The oldest centres of learning are in the old centre: oldest of all is the Colegio Nacional de San Bartolomé (C 10, No 6-57), in the same block as the Chapel of El Sagrario (3 on map), founded 1573. The second oldest, founded on 18 December, 1653, is the Colegio Mayor de Nuestra Señora del Rosario (C 14, No 6-25); its beautiful colonial building is well worth a look (you can buy a good cheap lunch at the cafeteria; it is not far from the Gold Museum).

There is an interesting and well organized **Botanical Garden**, José Celestino Mutis, Cra 66, No 56-84. It has a collection of over 5,000 orchids, plus roses, gladioli and trees from all over the country.

Warning Any "officials" in uniform asking to register your money are almost certainly thieves. Under current legislation police may shoot and kill a suspect during any narcotics operation and it will be automatically classified as self-defence.

The Judicial Unit for Tourism (Tourist police) offers 24-hour service for tourists at Cra 7, No 27-42, T 283-4930 or 334-2501. If you are robbed of documents, contact police at C 46 y Cra 14, of valuables, police at C 40, No 8-09.

Hotels Book hotels in advance whenever possible. IVA tax of 14% is additional to the bill.

Hotels in New Bogotá, Calles 76 and upwards: L1 *Bogotá Royal*, Av 100, No 8A-01, T 610-0066, F 218-3362, said to be one of the best in South America; **L2** *Bogotá Plaza*, C 100, No 18A-30, T 236-4940, F 218-4050, pricey, good restaurant, *Atrium*; **L2** *Charleston*, Cra 13, No 85-46, T 257-1100, F 218-0605, handsome building, close to restaurants and clubs, but reported not to honour bookings; **L1** *Victoria Regia*, Cra 13, No 85-80, T 621-2666, F 610-3516, PO Box 250-718, superior rm and suites, all services, pool, restaurant; **L2** *La Fontana*, Av 127, No 21-10, T 274-0200, F 216-0449, distinctive, very good (*Los Arcos* restaurant in hotel, superb, elegant); **L2** *La Bohème*, C 82, No 12-35, T 617-1177, F 618-0003, well-equipped rooms, attractive, good location and **L2** *Hacienda Royal*, C 114, No 64-02, T 612-0888, F 620-0958, CCH Santa Bárbara, very well-appointed; **L3** *El Belvedere*, Tr 18, No

100-16, T 257-7700, F 257-0331, modern, redecorated, very good value, excellent restaurant *Balmoral*; **L2** *Cosmos 100*, C 100, No 21 A-41, friendly staff, great view, good breakfasts US$6, T 257-4000, F 257-1035, new tower block added 1993, rec; **L2** *Los Urapanes*, Cra 13, No 83-15, T 218-1188, F 218-9242, very pleasant, smart, but friendly, smaller hotel; **L3** *Portón 84*, C 84, No 7-65, T 616-4006, F 616-3905, very good, excellent restaurant; **B** *Rincón Chico*, C101, No 13-32, T 214-7430, hot water, clean, safe, family atmosphere, TV, helpful, good restaurant; **L2** *Dann Norte*, Av 15, No 114-09, T 215-9655, F 215-4144; **L3** *Travelodge*, Cra 14, No 81-20, T 621-8691, F 218-8890, all services, restaurant; **A2** *Neuchatel*, C 90, No 7A-66, T 236-1568, F 218-3892, quiet, safe district, good restaurant but poor plumbing, unfriendly receptionists. **A1** *Apartamentos 82*, Cra 14, No 81-34, T 256-6751, self catering flatlets, good service, pleasant safe part of the city, rec. **C** *Hostal Residencias Moreno*, Transversal 33 No 95-28, T 218-1226, inc two meals, two house taxi drivers, nearby frequent bus service to town centre, very friendly, safe for left luggage, quiet, comfortable, hot water, highly rec.

Between Calles 31 and 75: **L1** *Casa Medina*, Cra 7, 69A-22, T 217-0288, F 212-6668, nice interior, chic; **L1** *María Isabel*, C 33, No 15-05, T 245-9040, F 288-6563, old, but very good; **L2** *Orquidea Royal* Cra 7, No 32-16, T 285-6020, F 287-7480, restaurant, pool; **A1** *Centro Internacional*, Cra 13A, No 38-97, T 288-5566, F 288-0850, popular but pricey, good location; **A3** *Las Terrazas*, C 54A, No 3-12, 2-star, T 255-5777, very clean, "rustic charm", pleasant, nice view of city; **B** *Hostal Linden*, C 36, No 14-39, T 287-4239, central, small, 2 rooms with kitchenette, breakfast, credit cards accepted; **C** *Casa Berlinesa*, C 45A, No 21-40, T 232-8504, German and English spoken, full breakfast available US$5; **D** *La Cabaña*, C 58, No 9-55, safe, good value; **D** *Hospedaje Turístico 61*, C 61, No 10-18, T 217-0383, clean, friendly, discounts for stays over 3 days, also has short-stay section. **D** *Fiesta Avenida*, Av Caracas, No 47-28, T 285-3407, rec.

In Old Bogotá (up to Calle 31): **L3** *Tequendama*, Cra 10, No 26-21, T 286-1111, F 282-2860, restaurant serves excellent *ajiaco*, good for breakfast (though not cheap); **A1** *Nueva Granada*, Av Jiménez, No 4-77, T 286-5877, F 284-5465, relaxed atmosphere. **L3** *Bacatá*, C 19, No 5-20, T 283-8300, F 281-7249, downtown on busy street, cheaper at weekends, worth asking at other times, restaurant not rec; **L3** *Dann*, C 19, No 5-72, T 284-0100, F 282-3108, very helpful; **A2** *El Presidente*, C 23, No 9-45, T 284-1100, F 284-5766. **L3** *Del Parque*, C 24, No 4-93, T 284-2200, F 283-2315, good commercial hotel; **B** *Quiratama*, C 17, No 12-44, T 282-4535, F 341-3246, very nice rooms, TV, telephone, good service, restaurant; **B** *Regina*, Cra 5, No 15-16, with private bath, TV, phone, friendly, good; **A3** *Del Duc*, C 23, No 9-38, T 334-0080, friendly, clean, good French restaurant; **C** *Virrey*, C 18, No 5-56, T 334-1150, modern, with hot shower, TV, good value restaurant, friendly, rec.

On C 14 near Cra 4 are: **B** *Dann Colonial*, No 4-21, T 341-1680, not reliable in honouring reservations; opposite is **D** *Santa Fe*, No 4-48, shower, good service, quiet, clean, friendly, safe, good restaurant, popular with locals, best value in the Candelaria area, warmly rec; **F** *Residencia Aragón*, Cra 3, No 14-13, clean and safe, friendly and honest, hot water, will store luggage, parking facilities, warmly rec; **F** *El Dorado*, Cra 4, C 15, hot water, safe, clean, noisy, upstairs rooms better (cheap taxi to airport can be arranged).

A3 *Santa Mónica*, Cra 3, No 24-11, T 341-9570, a/c, cable TV, comfortable, good location, rec; **B** *San Diego*, Cra 13 y C 24, T 284-2100, friendly, clean, large rooms, good value, accepts credit cards but not Amex TCs; **C** *La Hostería de la Candelaria*, C 9, No 3-11, T 342-1727, Aptdo Aéreo 15978, highly rec for comfort, atmosphere and service, charming patio, no heat, breakfast extra, dinner available if ordered in am (good for longer stays); **C** *Bogotá Internacional*, Cra 7, No 21-20, T 342-9428, very central, comfortable, noisy, restaurant and bar, a little run down but very helpful; **C** *La Sabana*, C 23, No 5-23, T 284-4830, F 284-6552, central, quiet, clean, English spoken, small restaurant, menu US$2, Visa accepted; **D** *Los Cerros*, C19, No 9-18, pleasant, good restaurant; **D** *Zaratoga*, Av Jiménez de Quesada, No 4-56 (opp *El Turista*, not rec), with bath, no hot water, quite nice; **D** *Residencia Dorantes*, C 13, No 5-07, very clean (cheaper without bath), hot water, rooms on Cra 5 side noisy, reasonable, safe, rec; **D** *Residencias Ambala*, Cra 5, No 13-46, T 241-2376, cheap, clean, friendly and central; **D** *Avenida Jiménez*, Av Jiménez, No 4-71, T 243-6685, helpful, friendly, sauna, safe.

E *Hollywood*, C 18, No 8-68, clean but small rooms with bath; **E** *Italia*, Cra 7, No 20-40, convenient, safe, T 334-6629, hot water, TV lounge, friendly, laundry, safe, rec; **E** *Panamericana*, C 15, No 12-70, T 242-1802, good, with bath, helpful; **E** *Platypus*, C 16, No 2-43, T 341-2874, clean, pleasant, kitchen facilities, hot water, free coffee, friendly informative owner, excellent travellers guest house, highly rec; **E** *Regis*, C 18, No 6-09 (also known as *Residencias María*), C with shower, sometimes hot water, old-fashioned, run down but safe, clean, safe parking for car or motorcycle; **E** *Virgen del Camino*, C 18A, No 14-33, friendly, clean, quiet, safe, T 282-4450; **E** *International*, Cra 5, No 14-45, friendly, hot water, good value, T 341-8731, safe deposit (care, taxi drivers may take you to the *Bogotá International* if you do not specify the address); **E** *Lima*, Cra 4 y C 16, with bath, clean, secure, TV, phone, hot water, good views from upstairs rooms.

F *Príncipe de Viena*, C 19, No 15-35, T 286-5901, big old rooms, with bath, TV, restaurant; **F** *María Luisa*, Cra 14, between Cs 15 and 16, hot water, very reasonable and food is good; **F** *Asturias*, C 16, No 15-36, T 242-0931, safe, good value but no hot water; **F** *Francés*, C 22, No 15-83, T 282-7492, room with shower, clean, safe; **F** *Residencia Bucamaranga*, C 15, No 16-68, with bath, cold water, basic; **F** *Residencias Americana*, C 13 and Cra 16, clean, safe, but only cold water; **F** *Residencias Avenida Fénix*, Cra 15, No 15-74, T 341-6237, with bath, friendly, family atmosphere, clean; many other cheap hotels in the C 15, Cra 10 area, which is dangerous especially for women alone.

There are a number of small, unregistered *hostales* in the N of the city, ask at tourist offices at airport or in the centre. From C 12 southwards, Cra 13 westwards is not salubrious: visitors are therefore advised to pick hotels in streets NE of C 12, with higher numbers. There are certainly many hotels between Cs 13 and 17 and Cras 15 and 17, many of which are cheap, some of which are clean. Private vehicles should be parked in lockable, guarded parqueaderos.

Youth Hostel Association Alcom, Apartado Aéreo 3220, Cra 7, No 6-10, behind Presidential Palace, safe area, T 280-3041/280-3202, F 280-3460; IYHA member, has a full list of 16 hostels around the country. There is a hostel at this address with 90 beds, US$4 pp members, US$4.50 non-members per night. Ask for full information at Alcom. Reservations for all hostels must be made through Prosocial, Bogotá 16, No 33-29, T 285-9296/285-9351, 0800-2000.

Restaurants 14% value-added tax is charged. For hotel restaurants, see above.

Recommended restaurants in New Bogotá (Calles 76 and above) include: *El Arko de los Olivos*, Tr 22, C 122-13, new, rustic style, excellent cooking; *La Fragata*, C 100, No 8A-55, 12th floor of World Center, revolving; also at Cra 13, No 27-98 and Diag 127A, No 30-26, L1, expensive, excellent fish; *La Academia de Golf*, Cra 15, No 85-42, and Cra 15, No 102-20, international, very good; *La Bodega Marina*, Cra 11A, No 93A-46, Cra 9, No 81-49, and 2 other branches, superb; *Il Giardino*, C 93, No 18-25, Italian; *Il Piccolo Caffe*, Cra 15, No 96-55, pasta etc, very good quality; *Las Tapas*, Av 19, No 114-13, Spanish bar-restaurant; *Zeukadi*, C 82, corner of Cra 11, fire lit at 2200, candlelight, rec. *Na Zdarovia*, Cra 14, No 80-71, Russian, very good, same owners, *Tandoor*, Cra 11, No 84-53, good Indian; *Viva Villa*, C 82, No 12-70, Mexican, good food, rec; *Casa de Cultura de México*, Cra 14, No 80-44, good Mexican food on second floor; *El Mondongo y Algo Más*, Cra 11, No 97A-38, local food; *El Buque*, Cra 18 y C 101, excellent; *Fulanitos*, C 81, No 9-13, good Valle Cauca food, friendly atmosphere; *Fridays*, C 82, No 12-18, US$10-12, superb value, rec; *Le Bilbouquet*, C 83, No 12-19, excellent French, nice atmosphere, rec; *L'Epicurien*, Cra 30, No 89-56, French chef, 1960 décor, very good, rec; *Il Pomeriggio*, Cra 11 y C82 in Centro Andino, popular, good atmosphere; *Welcome*, Cra 14, No 80-65, Japanese, good cooking supervised by perfectionist owner; *Hatsuhana*, Cra 13, No 93A-27, Japanese; *Casa Brava*, Km 4.5, Vía La Calera, steak house, superb view, very good food. In these restaurants meals cost from US$20/25 to US$40.

Tony Roma's, C 93, No 13-85, good quality food and excellent service. *Café Libre*, Cra 15, near Universidad Católica, bar with live music, also serves lunches; *Café Oma*, several locations, inc Cra 15, No 82-58, Av 19, No 118-78, Cra 5, No 14-71, and airport Muelle Nacional local 2-33, good food and coffee, nice atmosphere but relatively expensive, open till 0100; *Café y Crepes*, Transversal 10, 106-35, T 2140884, moving in 1995 to Cra 16, No 82-17, T 236-2905, good food, good atmosphere, climbers meet here; *Shamua*, Av 19, No 114-70, good cocktails, small selection of well prepared food, US style.

Central Bogotá (note that in the colonial centre very little is open after 2000 any day of the week): *Refugio Alpino*, C 23, No 7-49, is an excellent international restaurant; *Casa San Isidro*, on Monserrate, good, not cheap; *Casa Vieja*, Av Jiménez 3-73, traditional Bogotá food, live music, atmosphere better than the food (and the toilets), also at C 116, No 20-50 in New Bogotá; *Eduardo*, C13, No 8-66, T 243-0118, good business restaurant upstairs, more popular downstairs; *Doña Herta*, C 19, No 8-61, the best goulash in town, friendly, Swiss owned; *Donde Canta la Rana*, Cra 24C, No 20-10 Sur, a few km from centre, is refreshingly local and unspoilt, open 1400-1900; *Tierra Colombiana*, Cra 10, No 27-27, good, expensive food, evening floor show; *Cafetería Romana*, Av Jiménez, No 6-65, all meals, very clean, reasonable pasta, but excellent, expensive breakfast menu; its sister restaurants *Sorrento* (round the corner from *Romana*) and *Salerno*, Cra 7, No 19-43, good value. For excellent, inexpensive Arab food, *Ramses*, Cra 7, No 18-64. *Bambú*, Cra 7 y C 61/62, good Chinese, reasonable prices.

Punta Roja, Cra 7 y C 22, good 3-course meal for US$2, open 24 hrs; *Punto Rápido*, Cra 7; No 19-49, self service, good meals, reasonable, friendly, 24 hrs service; *Salón Fontana*, C 14, No 5-98, busy, good, inexpensive; *La Tienda de Don Zoilo*, Cra 4, No 19-56, student pub, good food, friendly atmosphere; *Crepes y Waffeles*, restaurant chain, good value; also *La Boliche*, C 27, No 5-64, Italian and good crepes; *Empanadas La 19*, Av 19, No 8-56, good, cheap meals and snacks. A cheap two-course meal can be had in the cafeteria of the Ley and Tía supermarkets. For the traveller on a budget, *bandeja* (the local *plato del día*) can cost US$1.50-2 for a 2-course meal at the right places.

Vegetarian: *El Champiñon*, Cra 8, No 16-36, 2 other branches, good vegetarian lunches; *Govindas*, Cra 8, No 20-56, set (vegetarian) meal US$1, good quality; *Samovares*, Cra 11, No 69-89 (T 249-4549—lunch only, fixed menu, nice atmosphere), also Cra 11, No 67-63 (T 249-6515) and Av Caracas No 32-64 (T 285-6095). *El Integral Natural*, Cra 11, No 95-10, health food shop with a few tables at street level, restaurant downstairs, fixed menu US$1.50. Vegetarian food excellent at Cra 8, No 11-19, near Plaza Bolívar.

Tea Rooms (Pastelerías) *Benalcázar*, near Plaza de las Nieves on Cra 8, No 20-25, excellent pastries; *La Suiza*, C 25, No 9-41, excellent pastries; *Panadería Florida*, Cra 7, No 20-82, also has good pastries; *La Espiga*, Cra 15 esq C 82, and other locations, excellent bread and pastries.

Airline offices The Avianca office is at Cra 7, No 16-36, T 295-4611/243-1613, airport 413-8295. Satena, Centro Tequendama, Cra 10 y C27, T 286-2701, airport 413-8158, military airline, not best for comfort and delays. SAM, Cra 10, No 27-91, T 286-8402, airport 413-8868. Many international airline offices are closed on Sat and Sun. **See p 899** for procedure to obtain refunds on unused tickets.

Banks All banks, except **Banco de la República**, are authorized to exchange TCs and cash; banks are everywhere in Bogota where there is commercial activity. Many head offices are grouped around the Avianca building at the corner of Plaza San Francisco. You may need your passport rather than a notarized photocopy. **Banco Anglo Colombiano**, Cra 8, No 15-46/60, and 18 local agencies, will cash Thomas Cook and Amex TCs (US$200 min, passport will be stamped) and will give advances against Visa, good rates. **Banco Unión Colombiana** (Cra 10, No 26-55 – take passport, not a copy) and other banks (eg **Banco Popular, Banco del Occidente**) will in theory change TCs, but obtaining cash against a credit card is best (your passport will be photocopied). Mastercard useful, **Banco Industrial de Colombia** (BIC), Cra 7, No 32-32, is the agent, which gives good rates for TCs. See **Hours of Business** and **Currency** in **Information for Visitors**.

Exchange American Express, Tierra Mar Aire Ltda, edif Bavaria Torre B, Local 126, Cra 10, No 27-91, T 283-2955, does not change TCs, but will direct you to those who do, eg Banco Unión. Also very helpful in replacing lost Amex TCs provided you have full details and preferably proof of purchase. Other offices at C 92, No 15-63, T 218-5666 and Cra 8 y C 15 are reported as helpful. **International Money Exchange**, Cra 7, No 32-29, open Mon to Fri till 1600, check all transactions carefully; opposite, at *Hotel Orquidea Real*, you can exchange on Sat. Also exchange at Av 19, No 15-35. **Exprinter** on Av Jiménez and Cra 6. Inside you can only get pesos and no TCs are exchanged, but the black market operates on the pavement outside, or try the kiosk right there; Peruvian and Ecuadorean currencies available (rates generally little different from official rates). **Orotur**, Cra 10, No 26-05 (very small, below *Hotel Tequendama*) is quick and efficient, cash only; **Money Point**, Cra 10, No 27, in Centro Internacional, unit 161, good rates, take passport photocopy. Other *cambios* on Av Jiménez de Quesada, between Cras 6 and 11, and in the N of the city. On Sun exchange is virtually impossible except at the airport.

Cultural Institutions British Council, C 87, No 12-79, T 236-2542/257-9632 has a good library and British newspapers. **Anglo-Colombian School**, Transversal 30, No 152-38; postal address: Apartado Aéreo 52969, Bogotá 2. **English School**, C 170, No 31-98 (T 254-1318 or 254-8874), Apartado Aéreo 51284, Bogotá. **American School**, Colegio Nueva Granada, Cra 2E, No 70-20, T 212-3511. **Centro Colombo Americano**, C 109A, No 17-10, T 214-4960, Spanish courses similar to those below, but only if enough students, rec. **Goethe Institut**, Cra 7, No 81-57, T 255-1843. **Biblioteca Luis Angel Arango**, C 11, No 4-14, see under No 11 on map.

Embassies and Consulates Venezuelan Consulate, Av 13, No 103-16, T 256-3015, hrs of business 0900-1230, 1300-1500, visas cost US$30, but allow 3 days (they will tell you to get your visa at the border, which may not be easy; it is hard to persuade them to give visas to overland travellers). **Ecuadorian Consulate**, C 100, No 14-63, T 257-9947, open 0830-1230; **Brazilian Embassy**, C 93, No 14-20, T 218-0800; **Peruvian Consulate**, C 90, No 14-26, T 257-3147. **Bolivian Embassy**, Tr 12, No 119-95, Apto 101, T 215-3274. **Panamanian Consulate**, C 92, No 7-70; Mon-Fri, 0900-1300. **Costa Rican Consulate**, Cra 15, No 80-87, Mon-Fri 0900-1300, T 236-1098. **Guatemalan Consulate**, Transversal 29A, C 139A, No 41, T 258-0746, Mon-Fri, 0900-1200, visa takes 48 hrs, US$10 (cash only), one photo, one airline ticket (does not have to be return), tourist visa free for Canadians; takes 48 hrs. **Mexican Consulate**, C 99, No 12-08, T

616-3462, Mon-Fri, 0900-1300. **El Salvador Embassy**, Cra 9, No 80-15, T 212-5932.

US Embassy, C 38, No 8-61 (mailing address: Apartado Aéreo 3831, Bogotá 1, DE), T 285-1300. **Canadian Embassy**, C 76, No 11-52; T 217-5555, open 0800-1630 (mailing address: Apartado Aéreo 53531, Bogotá 2, DE).

British Embassy, C 98, No 9-03, 4th floor, T 218-5111, postal address: Apartado Aéreo 4508. **German Embassy**, Cra 4, No 72-35, 6th floor, T 212-0511. **French Embassy**, Cra 11, No 93-12. **French Consulate**, Cra 7, No 38-99, T 285-4311. **Belgian Embassy**, C 26, No 4A-45, piso 7, T 282-8881/2. **Dutch Embassy**, Cra 9, No 74-08, 6th floor, T 211-9600. **Finnish Consulate**, Cra 10, No 95-26, Of 223, T 610-1830. **Norwegian Consulate**, Cra 13, No 50-78, Oficina 506, T 235-6920. **Swedish Embassy**, C 72, No 5-83, T 255-3777. **Danish Consulate General**, Cra 10, No 96-29, of 611, T 610-0918/0887, 0900-1300 Mon-Thur, 0900-1200 Fri. **Swiss Embassy**, Cra 9, No 74-08, oficina 1101, T 255-3945, open Mon-Fri 0900-1200. **Italian Consulate**, C 70, No 10-25 (Aptdo Aéreo 50901), T 235-4300. **Israeli Embassy**, Edificio Caxdac, C 35, No 7-25, piso 14, T 287-7783/808/962. **Japanese Embassy**, Cra 7, No 74-21, piso 8.

Entertainment Night Life There are many popular bars, discos etc in the Cra 15, C 82 region, known as the Zona Rosa. Also many popular bars and dancing places on Cra 5 with C 25, relatively safe area. Try *El Viejo Almacén*, Cra 5 y C 13-14, run by an aged Argentine lady who plays 78 tango records and sells reasonably priced beer and *aguardiente* (on Fri and Sat only). *Disco del Teatro de Candelaria*, C 15 between Cras 4 and 5, good atmosphere especially Friday and Saturday. Gay bars: *Adonis*, C 33 y Cra 13A; *Alex*, C 22 y Cra 7, and three bars on Cra 7 between C 17 y 18, all no cover, expensive drinks.

Theatre Many of the theatres are in the Candelaria area. Teatro Colón details on **p 792**. Teatro Libre de Bogotá, C 62, No 10-65, T 217-1988; Nacional, C 71, No 10-25, T 235-8069; La Candelaria, C 12, No 2-59, T 281-4814; Teatro Popular de Bogotá, C 5, No 14-71, T 342-1675.

Cinema Cinemateca Distrital, Cra 7 No 22-79; good films. Also on Cra 7: Teatro Municipal, No 22-53; Metro, No 21-78; Tisquesa, No 27-29; Av Chile shopping centre cinema, C 71, between Cras 11 and 13 (usually prize-winning films); Centro Comercial Andino, Cra 12, C82/83, modern, expensive, especially at weekends. Ciné Club Latino, Auditorio Comfenalco, Cra 4, No 19-85, US$0.75. The Museo de Arte Moderno shows different films every day, all day. Foreign films old and new are shown on weekend mornings at 1030 in commercial cinemas and there are many small screening rooms which run the occasional feature. Consult *El Espectador* or *La Prensa*, and handbills all over town for what is on; frequent programme changes. Admission, US$3.

Health Cruz Roja Nacional, Av 68, No 66-31, T 250-661/231-9027/231-9008, open 0830-1800. Instituto Nacional de Salud, Av El Dorado y Cra 50, will give you vaccinations, T 222-0577. Centro Médico La Salud, Cra 10, No 21-36, 2nd floor, T 243-1381/282-4021. Clínica Bogotá, Cra 17, No 12-65 (not a safe area to walk in), discourages travellers from having gamma-globulin shots for hepatitis. Walter Röthlisberger y Cía Ltda, C 26, No 13-37, T 283-6200, imports medicines, including Vivotif for typhoid and gamma globulin, and stores them correctly; trade prices. The US Embassy will advise on doctors, dentists. etc. Profamilia, C 34, No 14-46, for contraceptives. For ambulances, T 115. Clínica Marly, C 50, No 9-67, T 287-1020 (bus runs along Cra 4 - C 14) and Clínica del Country, Cra 15, No 84-13, T 257-3100, are well-equipped private hospitals. Dr Arturo Corchuelo at C 89, No 12-21, T 218-8710, recommended for orthopaedic problems. Clínica Barraqer, Av 100, No 18A-51, internationally known eye clinic.

Language Courses Pontificia Universidad Javeriana, Centro Latino Americano de Relaciones Humanas e Interculturales, Cra 10, No 65-48, T 212-3009, recommended for full Spanish language and cultural courses; short, one-month courses in June, July and August, and mid-November to mid-December, US$150. At other times of the year courses last 3 months, 2 hrs a day. Accommodation with local families can be arranged, but this is cheaper through the small ads section of *El Tiempo*. All other schools in Yellow Pages offer one-to-one private tuition at US$10/hr. Cheaper lessons can be found through *El Tiempo*.

Laundry *Piccadilly*, C 63, No 7-10; *Burbujas*, Edificio Procoil, Av 19, No 3A-37, open Mon-Sat 0730-1930, US$3.65 per machine load for wash, dry and iron, 24-hr service, manager speaks English. *Panorama*, Cra 7, C 67; *Lava Viente*, C 20, No 4-90. Drycleaners: *Lavaseco*, Av Jiménez, No 4-30.

Postal Services Main airmail office and foreign *poste restante* in basement of Ed Avianca, Cra 7, No 16-36, open 0730-1900 Mon to Sat, closed Sun and holidays (0730-1800, Mon-Fri, 0730-1500, Sat for *poste restante*, letters kept for only a month, bureaucratic, have to buy 100 peso stamp for each each letter retrieved). At weekend the Post Office only franks letters;

stamps for postcards are not sold. Pharmacies and newsagents in Bogotá have an airmail collection. Parcels by air, contact Avianca. To send film abroad pay for recorded delivery, use regulation envelope and get glue from counter 15.

International Telephone Calls from several Telecom offices in centre of Bogotá (eg C 12 y Cra 8, C 23, No 13-49, in the *Tequendama Hotel*/Centro Internacional complex); all close within half an hour of 2000.

Sauna Los Andes, Cra 4, No 16-29, good service, open daily 1000-2200. Sauna San Diego, Cra 7 near C 25, massage, turkish bath and sauna rec.

Shopping 14% value-added tax on all purchases. *Artesanías de Colombia* (state-owned), Almacén San Diego, in the old San Diego church, Cra 10, No 26-50, Almacén Las Aguas, next to the Iglesia de las Aguas, Cra 3A, No 18-60, has good selection of folk art and crafts, at fair prices. There is a shop in the **Museo de Artes y Tradiciones Populares**, which is recommended. A street market on Av Jiménez and Cra 14 (Av Caracas) sells cheaper *ruanas*, blankets, leatherware, etc. Woollen *ruanas* at **Galerías Nariño** (Mercado La Victoria), or *Almacén Fascinación*, local J36-38, T 281-0239. Mercado de Pulgas (fleamarket) on Cra 3, from C 19, N, on Sunday afternoons and holidays. It is a popular place and bar at the N end sells cheap beer and has a reggae band playing all afternoon (on no account wander around here other than on Sunday). Another, also only Sun, Cra 7 y C 19.

Galerías Cano, Ed Bavaria, Cra 13, No 27-98 (Torre B, Int 1-19B), Unicentro, Loc 218, Airport, sell textiles, pottery as well as gold and gold-plated replicas of some of the jewellery on display in the Gold Museum. *Galería Alfred Wild*, C 82, No 12-35, has excellent but pricey drawings and paintings.

The pavements and cafés along Av Jiménez, below Cra 7, Parque de los Periodistas, and C 16 and Cra 3, are used on weekdays by emerald dealers. Great care is needed in buying: bargains are to be had, but synthetics and forgeries abound. (Beware of stones that seem too perfect or have a bluish colouring.) *La Casa de la Esmeralda*, C 30, No 16-18, wide range of stones; *Joyas Verdes Ltda*, Cra 15, No 39-15 also. Other jewellery shops in the *Hotel Tequendama*. See *H Stern's* jewellery stores at the International Airport, and *Tequendama Hotel*. Modern textiles and knitwear can be bought at low prices at *Unicentro*, a large shopping centre on Cra 15, No 123-30 (take "Unicentro" bus from centre, going N on Cra 10—takes about 1 hr). *Centro Granahorrar*, Av Chile (C 72), No 10-34, is another good shopping centre; also *Metropolis*, Av 68, No 75A-50 (with *Exito* supermarket opposite), *Hacienda Santa Bárbara*, Cra 7 y C 115, and *Bulevar Niza*, Cra 52, No 125A-59. *Centro Comercial Andino*, Cra 12 entre C 82 y C 83 (near *Hotel La Bohème*) is a fine, new centre.

Heavy duty plastic for covering rucksacks etc is available at several shops around C 16 and Av Caracas; some have heat sealing machines to make bags to size.

Bookshops *Librería Aldina*, Cra 7, C 70-80, most helpful on books and Bogotá alike, excellent stock of English-language books including this *Handbook*, open 0930-1930, Sat 0930-1700. *Oma*, Cra 15, No 82-58 (and other branches), good art and literature books, international newspapers, also sells this *Handbook*, open late including Sun. *Librería Nacional*, Cra 7, No 17-51 (has small selection of English novels). *Librería Francesa*, Cra 8, No 63-45. *Librería Lerner*, Av Jiménez, No 4-35 (no English books). *Librería Buchholz*, Cra 7, No 27-68 (opp *Hotel Tequendama*), also at C 59, No 13-13 (Chapinero), most books in Spanish; useful advice in a number of languages. *Ateneo*, C 82, No 13-19, in the N of the city, good selection of Colombian titles, knowledgeable staff; *Librería Tercer Mundo*, Cra 7, No 16-91, knowledgeable; *Librería Cultural Colombiana*, C 72, No 16-15; *Casa de Libro*, C 18 between Cras 7 and 6. *Panamericana*, Cra 7, No 14-09, disorganized, but has some guidebooks and maps. Books in Colombia are generally expensive.

Maps The best current map of Bogotá is by Cartur, scale 1:25,000, 1994, and of Colombia, Mapa Vial de Colombia by Rodríguez, scale 1:2,000,000, also 1994, about US$4 each. You may have to try several bookshops. Hiking, topographical and general **maps** from Instituto Geográfico, Agustín Codazzi, Av Ciudad de Quito y C 45 (topographical details are generally accurate, but trails and minor roads less so). Esso road maps from service stations, US$0.40.

Photography *Foto Japón*, branches all over the city, gives free film, branch at Cra 7, No 50-10, develops slides in 1 hr. *Poder Fotográfico*, Cra 5, No 20-70, T 342-4130, for good developing in 2-3 hrs. Film tends to be cheaper in Colombia than in Ecuador and Peru.

Sports Bull fighting on Sat and Sun during the season, and every 2-3 weeks for the rest of the year, at the municipally owned Plaza de Santamaría, near Parque Independencia. In season, the bulls weigh over 335 kg; out of season they are "comparatively small and unprofessional". (Local bullfight museum at bullring, door No 6.) Boxing matches are held here too. Horse races at Hipódromo los Andes, on Autopista Norte, races at 1400 (entrance US$1 and US$0.35), and at the Hipódromo del Techo, in the SW, on Sat, Sun and public holidays. Nearby is the Municipal Stadium, which can hold 50,000 spectators. Football matches are played here.

Football Tickets for matches at El Campín stadium can be bought in advance at *Cigarrería Bucana*, C 18, No 5-92. It is not normally necessary to book in advance, except for the local Santa Fe-Millonarios derby. Take a cushion; matches Sun at 1545, Weds at 2000.

Tour Companies recommended: *Tierra Mar Aire*, Cra 10, No 27-91, is Amex agent; does city tours from *Hotel Tequendama* (T 286-1111). Similar tours of the City (4 hrs) can be arranged from *Hotel Nueva Granada*. *Expedición Colombia*, Edificio KLM, piso 9, C 26, No 4A-45, T 284-8284/8456, runs tours to the Llanos by private, chartered plane. *Interamerican Tours*, C 17, No 6-57 very helpful arranging flights to Central America via San Andrés. *Viajes Chapinero*, Av 7, 124-15, T 612-7716, F 215-9099, with branches at C63, No 13-37, Chapinero, and Cra 40C, No 57-08, bloque A1, manager David Krech, helpful with information in English.

Tourist Offices Corporación Nacional de Turismo (CNT), C 28, No 13A-59, admin offices at C 28, No 13A-15, T 413-8202/9830, Ed Centro de Comercio Internacional (the name at the top of the building is Banco Cafetero), Mon-Fri, 0830-1300, 1400-1700, closed Sat and Sun, take passport; they will tell you which parts of the country are unsafe, good maps of major cities available; at Eldorado Airport (also open Sat, Sun and holidays, 0700-1430) and new bus terminal (both helpful, will book hotel rooms). Municipal tourist office, Instituto Distrital de Cultura y Turismo, Cra 10, No 3-6, T 286-6555, with office at Plaza Bolívar, T 334-6010 (also at airport, Mon-Fri 0700-2100, Sat 0800-1700, and bus terminal, T 295-4460). Corporación de Cultura y Turismo de Cundinamarca, C 16, No 7-76, T 242-8587, for details of towns around Bogotá. The Coordinadora de Turismo de Bogotá (Cra 13, No 27-95) has daily tours of the city with interpreters. For information on 24-hr chemists (pharmacies), events, attractions, etc, T 282-0000.

Inderena, the National Parks Office, is at Cra 10, No 20-30 in Caja Agraria building (office also at airport) for information and permission to visit the parks (very helpful), some permissions may take a day or two (must leave passport at reception). They publish a National Parks Guide, attractive and informative, US$10 (pay in Tesorería, 7th floor, collect book on 2nd floor). Information on individual parks 8th floor, also on possibilities to work as volunteer rangers (minimum 30 days).

Thefts Most hotels charge US$0.25 a night for insurance against theft. If you have something stolen go to the Corporación Nacional del Turismo for help and collect the insurance; this will probably take a few days of strenuous effort, but it has been known to work.

Useful Addresses DAS Immigration office, Cra 27, No 17-85, open 0730-1530; Dirección de Extranjería (for renewing entry permits), C 100, No 11B-27, open Mon-Thur 0730-1600, Fri 0730-1530. T 610-7371 (División de Extranjería) or 277-6666 (emergency). DAS will not authorize photocopies of passports; look in Yellow Pages for notaries, who will.

Transport Travel in Bogotá Bus stops in centre by red and yellow "Paradero" boards; otherwise flag buses down. Bus fares are from US$0.20 up, depending on length of route and time of day. Most buses have day/night tariff advertised in the window. *Busetas* charge a little more. There are some "super-executive" routes with plush seats and videos, at US$0.40 (if traffic is heavy you might see the whole film). Fares are a bit higher at night and on holidays. Urban buses are not good for sightseeing because you will be standing as likely as not. A metro is planned.

Car Rental Dollar Rent-a-Car, airport and Diag 109, No 14-61, T 612-8295; **Hertz**, at airport, and at Cra 10, No 26-35, T 284-1445; **Avis**, C 99, No 11-26, T 610-4455, and at airport.

Taxis have meters; insist that they are used. If the driver tries to charge more than the meter reading (eg from airport to hotel), tell the driver to wait, take your luggage into the hotel and ask hotel representative to deal with the driver. Starting charge, US$0.40, plus US$0.07 for every 90m, minimum charge US$0.85. Additional charge of US$0.40 after 2000 and on public holidays and Sun (a list of legal charges should be posted in the taxi). At busy times, empty taxis flagged down on the street may refuse to take you to less popular destinations.

Tan and green tourist taxis can be rented by the hour or the day from major hotels, most of the drivers speak English and are very helpful (T 284-0856). Radio taxis are rec for safety and reliability; when you call the dispatcher gives you a cab number, confirm this when it arrives (eg Proturismo T 224-2198; Radio Taxi Aeropuerto, T 211-1111). Taxis are relatively cheap, so it is worthwhile taking one if you are carrying valuables, or at night. Tipping is not customary, but is appreciated. If you are going to an address out of the city centre, it is helpful to know the section you are going to as well as the street address, eg Chicó, Chapinero (ask at your hotel). See also under **Airport** and **Buses** below.

Airport The airport at El Dorado has the world's second largest landing field. There are two terminals, the Puente Aéreo terminal (T 413-8103) being 1 km before the main terminal (T 413-9500) on Av El Dorado. Frequent buses run between the two. Avianca international flights use both terminals (usually Miami and New York). Puente Aéreo is more comfortable but there is not as much duty-free shopping (there is a 100 pesos tax payable at this terminal). **You must check which terminal your flight will use**. "Tourist Guide" policemen have white armbands. For **Tourist Offices**, see above. The main terminal is being slowly modernized. The departure areas with the usual duty-free shops are of a high standard and comfortable. The entrance foyer is run down and crowded. Free Colombian coffee inside the customs area, between gates 2 and 3. Many snack bars and restaurants on first floor. International calls can be made from Telecom on 1st floor, credit cards accepted; post office in main arrivals lounge. Hotel reservations can be made at the airport but their hotel rates are often out of date. The cheapest is in our Category D. Exchange rates are marginally lower than in the city, but pesos cannot be changed back into dollars at the airport without receipts. Airport bank changes TCs, but is not open at holiday times. When closed, ask airport police where to change money. Allow 1½ hrs for checking in and security. There is no baggage deposit.

The taxi fare from airport to city is a fixed charge, by zones. Ask for a fare slip from the taxi office by airport exit. The cost is usually about US$5 (30% more at night and early am). Make sure you get a registered taxi, normally yellow, found at right (from inside) side of main terminal or Avianca terminal (drivers try to overcharge all the same). Unofficial taxis not advisable. Use only uniformed porters. There are colectivos (US$0.75 plus luggage pp) from airport to centre; also buses in the daytime, US$0.15 (not easy with bulky luggage and they may refuse to take you). You have to cross eight busy lanes of traffic to get a bus into town, and negotiate two drainage ditches. In the city centre buses and colectivos can be picked up on Av 19, anywhere between Cras 3 and 10 at which they turn right for the airport; colectivos can also be taken from the corner of C 13 (Av Jiménez de Quesada) and Av 14 (Av Caracas); buses marked "Aeropuerto" or "Universitaria Dorado"; colectivos marked "Aeropuerto". Watch belongings inside and outside airport, especially at night.

For internal flights, which serve all parts of the country, **see p 904**. For domestic shuttle flights to Medellín/Montería, Cali/Pasto, and Barranquilla, go to Puente Aéreo terminal. As a rule, all flights are overbooked, so check in well in advance.

Rail There are no passenger services at present from Bogotá station at C 13 y Cra 20. Long distance services were suspended in 1992. A tourist steam train runs on Sun and holidays starting at present at Usaquén, C 110, Transversal 10, in the N of the city (see map), due to substantial roadworks toward the city centre. The train departs at 0930 from Usaquén to Nemocón (1212) leaving at 1500 and back in Bogotá at 1740. Cost: adult US$12.50, child up to 10, US$7.50. Information, Turistrén Ltda, Transversal 17 A, No 98-17, T 257-1459, or travel agents.

Buses There is a long-distance bus terminal, Terminal de Transportes, near Av Boyacá (Cra 72) between El Dorado (Av 26) and Av Centenario (C 13). There is also access from Cra 68. Exact address C 33 B, No 69-59, T 295-1100. The terminal is divided into modules serving the 4 points of the compass; each module has several bus companies serving similar destinations. If possible, buy tickets at the ticket office before travelling to avoid overcharging. **Fares and journey times are given under destinations below**. If you are travelling N, enquire if the bus company has a pick-up point on the Autopista del Norte around C 160. Velotax busetas are slightly quicker and more expensive than ordinary buses, as are colectivos, which go to several long-distance destinations. To get to the terminal take bus marked "Terminal" from "Terminal Transportes" bus stop at corner of Av Jiménez de Quesada and Cra 15, or *buseta* on Cra 10 before *Hotel Tequendama*. At night take a colectivo taxi from Av 13 y Av Caracas, US$0.35 (no buses). To get into town take Route No 1 or No 3 "Centro" at the terminal: the bus goes through the S of the city, then N on C 13, turning right on Cra 14, closest to the centre (from this junction "Germania" bus goes to the centre). A *buseta* (US$0.05) runs from Cra 68 to the terminal and back. Taxi around US$3, depending on destination, surcharge at night, passengers are given a computer slip showing the cab's registration number and the exact fare (avoid the unofficial taxis, normally touting for particular hotels). The terminal is well-organized and comfortable, but, as usual, watch out for thieves. Free self-service luggage trolleys are provided. There are shops and restaurants. There are showers at the terminal (between Nos 3 and 4), US$0.40, soap and towel provided.

Bus to Venezuela It is better not to buy a through ticket to Caracas with Exp Berlinas as this does not guarantee a seat and is only valid for 2 Venezuelan companies; moreover no refunds are given in Cúcuta. Ideally, if you have time make the journey to Cúcuta in two stages to enjoy the scenery to the full. Bus connections from San Antonio de Táchira in Venezuela to Caracas are good.

Excursions from Bogotá

If you have a car, drive round the Av Circunvalación for splendid views.

Hiking Sal Si Puedes is a hiking group based in Bogotá, walking every weekend and sometimes midweek on trails in Cundinamarca; a very friendly group which welcomes visitors. Hikes are graded for every ability, from 3 km to 4-day excursions of 70 km, camping overnight. Reservations must be made and paid for a week in advance at Cra 7 No 17-01, offices 640 and 641, T 283-3765 or contact Justo Alfonso Gamboa, Diagonal 123, No 50-30, Bogotá, T 283-9980 office, 253-6228 home.

To the E of Bogotá is **Choachi**, an attractive village set in a valley, where there are hot springs (good food at *El Colonial*, 1½ blocks from main square). Flota Macarena bus, several a day. A turnoff from the Choachi road brings one to the Santuario de San Francisco, with better views of Bogotá than one can get from Monserrate.

South-West: The Simón Bolívar Highway runs from Bogotá to Girardot (**see p 849**); this 132-km stretch is extremely picturesque, running down the mountains within 5 km of the Salto de Tequendama (take the exit marked to El Colegio).

At the **Salto de Tequendama**, the water of the Río Bogotá or Funza falls 132m over the lip of the Sabana; the water is dirty with sewage but the falls are still a spectacular sight though the smell can be most unpleasant. The site is 31 km from Bogotá in an amphitheatre of forest-clad hill sloping to the edge of a rock-walled gorge. There is a good bus service from Bogotá.

After the Tequendama Falls turning is **Fusagasugá** which lies in a rich wooded valley famous for its fruits. A few kilometres beyond is the *Hotel Catama*. Fusagasugá is noted for its good climate and Sunday market. Population: 58,215, with an admixture of the wealthier families from Bogotá during the summer. A visit should be paid to the Jardín Luxemburgo for its splendid orchids, best flowering Nov-Feb but it is a long walk out of town; the Jardín Clarisa for orchids, and that at the Casa de la Cultura are pleasant. There are bathing spots on the Sumapaz river. Altitude: 1,740m. From Bogotá, Autos Fusa and Cootransfusa, US$1.20. 25 km from Bogotá, on the old road to Fusagasugá, is the beautiful artificial lake of Muña, formed by a dam.

Hotels E *Castillo*, rec; **F** *La Scala*, rec. There are many luxury hotels on the road to Melgar. Near Fusagasugá is **C** *Hotel Miramonti*, Italian-run family place, very quiet.

Down the main road from Fusagasugá is El Boquerón, below which is a spectacular rock overhang known as El Nariz del Diablo (Devil's Nose), near which is a side road left to **San Bernardo**, a pretty little town. The cemetery has a macabre attraction; looking through a window near the central "altar" you see mummified figures, including a woman and child, assembled in the dimly lit cellar, entry US$0.25. Off this road go right about 10 km to **Pandi** where there is a park with ancient stones. Nearby, on the road to Icononzo, is a famous natural bridge in a spectacular and very deep gorge through which runs the Sumapaz river. This can also be reached from the road to San Bernardo (above) by turning right 3 km short of the village. Bus: from Fusagasugá to San Bernardo, 1½ hrs.

Melgar, near Girardot, is a popular weekending place for Bogotanos who like a little warmth. There are lots of hotels in the area most of which have swimming pools; it is best to try whichever you like the look of and move on to another if it is full; **D** *Plaza Crillón* and *Nuevo Guadaira* have been recommended; there are also camping sites and the state-subsidized Cafam vacation centre, best visited in mid-week. There are three tolls between Bogotá and Melgar (not always manned). For those driving S towards Neiva there is a new bypass avoiding Girardot. There are good places to stop for snacks and meals, often with good family facilities, eg *Parador Las Villas*, near the Girardot bypass.

North-West: The Sabana de Bogotá is dotted with white farms and groves of eucalyptus. The road passes through two small towns, Fontibón and Madrid. **Fontibón**, 10 km from Bogotá, has a good colonial church, and about 3 km outside the town are stones with Indian pictographs; nearby, on the road from the old Techo airport to Bogotá, there are replicas of San Agustín statues.

Facatativá (pop 61,590) is 40 km from Bogotá. Some 3 km from Facatativá, on the road to the W, is the Piedras de Tunja, a natural rock amphitheatre of enormous stones; it has numerous Indian pictographs and has now been established as a park with an artificial lake. A road goes SW from Facatativá through Tocaima to Girardot. From *Tocaima* (pop 8,520), a small, attractive holiday town (several hotels; **D** *Bella Vista*, clean, friendly, good simple food, swimming pool, no hot water), a road runs through beautiful mountain country, via La Mesa, to Mosquera on the road between Madrid and Fontibón. This is a good alternative to the Simón Bolívar highway from Girardot to Bogotá.

71 km from Facatativá is *Villeta* (12,465 inhabitants), which has become a popular weekend resort for the Bogotanos. Not far away are the waterfalls of Quebrada Cune. Hotels: *Pacífico* and *Mediterráneo* (both have swimming pools and are expensive); less expensive is the *Colonial Plaza*, Cra 4, No 6-07 (corner of main square), good restaurant, with swimming pool, pleasant. On the road to Bogotá is *Balneario El Descanso*, swimming pool, safe parking. Near the centre is *Llamarade* restaurant, good value; many good ice cream parlours around the square. The road continues to Honda (see p 847).

Midway between Villeta and Honda is *Guaduas*; in the main square is a statue of the liberator Policarpa Sala Varrieta. Also in the main square is a delightful colonial hotel. Public swimming pool in town. There is a Sunday market. Best local dish is *quesillos*. Bus to Honda, US$1.45, 1 hr. The surrounding countryside is beautiful, including waterfalls at Versalles (10 km). Hotels: **B** *Tacuara*, swimming pool, riding, *cabañas*; *Cacique*, 1 km outside village, and *Real Agrada*, in resort area.

North: Interesting day trips can be made to the attractive rolling antiplano, leaving Bogotá on the Autopista del Norte (extension of Av 13), or on the parallel Carretera del Norte (the old road, extension of Av 7). On the latter, once out of Bogotá, there are many old fincas and good typical restaurants, eg *El Pórtico*, a converted *hacienda*, much visited at weekends. The two roads join at Km 24 at La Caro where a road leaves left (west) to Chía and Zipaquirá. At this junction you will see the 'castle' of Rodríguez Gacha with a sinister history connected to this drug baron. By contrast, there is opposite the graceful colonial bridge over the Río Bogotá, now preserved and bypassed by the road to Chía.

Chía has a typical Sunday market (bus from Av Caracas, Bogotá US$0.30). Near Chía is Terijo, whose metalworks is famous. On the way there you pass through Fonqueta, where tapestries are made. Walk, or take a bus to La Barbanera church on a hill overlooking the Sabana de Bogotá. Good restaurant just outside Chía, *Andrés Carne de Res*, good music, good atmosphere, good food from 1600.

From Chía (via Cájica, pop 15,315, pleasant town with good shopping for ponchos and carpets) to *Zipaquirá* (62,130 people), centre of a rich cattle farming district, and famous for its rock salt mine, which has enough salt to last the world 100 years, though it has been exploited for centuries. The church in the attractive central Plaza is also worth a visit for its stonework (despite its external appearance, it has a modern interior).

Zipaquirá is famous for the underground cathedral constructed by miners inside the huge main salt mine, dedicated in 1954 to Nuestra Señora del Rosario (patron saint of miners). A road was opened into the galleries and originally cars were allowed in, but continuing deterioration has made the whole cave unsafe and it is closed. Although you will be told that it will soon be reopened, no restoration work is being done (Feb 1995) and political difficulties (it is now owned by the local municipality) compound the problem. You can walk up to the entrance to the cave in hills to the W of the town in about 20 mins and you will pass the entrance to a second cave which also "will open shortly". Here some activity is evident. However, the state of the town itself is not encouraging.

Many buses from Av Caracas, Bogotá, marked "Zipa", US$0.60 each way, 1¼ hrs. The Zipaquirá bus station is 15 mins' walk from the mines and cathedral. Zipaquirá can also be reached from Tunja (**see p 805**), by taking a Bogotá-bound bus and getting off at La Caro for connection to Zipaquirá, US$2.40. Leave plenty of time for the return journey as it can be difficult to stop Bogotá-Tunja buses at La Caro. It can also be difficult to get on a bus from Zipaquirá going N towards Villa de Leiva.

C *Hostería del Libertador*, near the mine, good food, T 3060; **E** *Hotel Colonial*, without bath, clean and friendly. Restaurants on main square, *El Mesón del Zipa*, good, cheap food, US$1.50-2.00; *Los Pijaos*, pleasant.

Not far from Zipaquirá, at **Nemocón**, there are salt mines and a church, but the mines are sometimes closed to visitors, following accidents. Restaurant, *El Colonial*, 100m from the station. A side (dirt) road connects with the Bogotá-Cúcuta highway.

A steam-hauled *tren turístico* runs on Sundays and holidays from Usaquén in N Bogotá to Zipaquirá and Nemocón. See under Bogotá, **Rail.**

Ubaté is 48 km by road to the N. On Sunday, the market in the big plaza has nothing of interest for the tourist. It is the cheese-making centre of the Sabana. Here a branch road runs E to Lenguazaque. Close by, at Chirbaneque, is a worked-out emerald mine in lovely scenery. A spur from this road branches left to Guachetá, 21 km from Ubaté, and slightly larger than Lenguazaque. Nearby is the **Laguna de Fúquene** (Devil's Lake) hotel, about 4,850 hectares of water with four cultivated islands.

Chiquinquirá, 32,585 people, 134 km by road from Bogotá, is on the W bank of the Suárez river at 2,550m. It is a busy commercial centre and the focus of a large coffee and cattle region. In December thousands of pilgrims honour a painting of the Virgin whose fading colours were restored by the prayers of a woman. In 1816, when the town had enjoyed six years of independence and was besieged by the Royalists, this painting was carried through the streets by Dominican priests from the famous monastery, to rally the people. The town fell, all the same.

Hotels F *Moyba*, Cra 9, No 17-53, facing square, with bath (cheaper without); **F** *Residencias San Martín*, Cra 9, No 19-84, basic; **G** *Residencias Viajero*, opposite Banco de Colombia, good, cheap meals. Many others.

Restaurant *El Escorial*, good but expensive.

In the shops of Chiquinquirá are displayed the toys made by local Indians: some ceramics painted in gay colours and others white and porous as they come from the kiln; tops and teetotums and other little things carved from tagua nuts; orange-wood balls to catch on a stick; the most durable tambourines in the world; shining, brightly coloured gourds; diminutive nine-stringed guitars on which children try the first measures of the *bambuca*; many scapularies and a good place for raw emeralds; but better than anything else, the little pottery horses from Ráquira, or, by the same Indian craftsmen, little birds that whistle, hens with their chicks, and enchanting little couples dancing to an orchestra of guitars and mandolins.

Bus from Chiquinquirá to Villa de Leiva takes 1¾ hr, US$2.70 (**see p 806**). Bus to Tunja, 3 hrs, US$4; to Zipaquirá, US$3.30; to Bogotá, 2½ hrs, US$3.60 (last returns at 1730); all from bus station.

Excursion A poor road, dangerous in the rainy season, runs 105 km SW to *Muzo*, on the banks of the Río Carare, 600m above sea-level. Population: 5,000. Hotels: **E** *Colonial*; **E** *El Castillo*; **F** *Hospedaje El Occidente*, all reasonable in the circumstances. Sixteen km away a famous open-cast emerald mine has been worked since 1567, and long before that by the Muzo tribe of Indians. You can visit the mine; check at your hotel, which may be able to fit you out with boots and spade and arrange for you to seek your fortune.

There are roads from Chiquinquirá to Tunja, the capital of the Department, and to Barbosa. Both are on the Bogotá-Cúcuta highway and are described below. On the Tunja road a short branch right at Tinjacá leads to **Ráquira**, where Indians make the pottery described above (sold in about 10 shops on the main street, including branch of Artesanías de Colombia). There are 2 good hotels, **E** *Nequeteba*, converted colonial house, pool, restaurant, craft shop, helpful owner, and **E** *Norteño*, nice and clean (both on plaza). Avoid the *Carlos Andrés* restaurant on the main plaza. At weekends it is possible to eat at the Museo de Arte y Tradiciones Populares. Market day Sunday. 1½ hrs' walk along a very rough road is a beautiful 16th-century monastery, the Convento de la Candelaria, with anonymous 17th-century paintings of the life of San Agustín; they sell honey to finance the monastery (visiting times 1400-1700). **C** *Parador La Candelaria*, adjoining monastery, picturesque, good food. Also nearby are some waterfalls. The old colonial town of Villa de Leiva is also on this road. Ráquira is best reached from Tunja although there are direct buses from Bogotá (Rápido El Carmen, 0545, 0715, US$3, 6 hrs, returning 1300) on an appalling road. Last bus to Tunja 1330. If stuck after 1330, walk 5 km to Tres Esquinas on Villa de Leiva-Chiquinquirá road, where buses pass between 1530-1630, mostly going E. There are 2 direct buses to and from Villa de Leiva daily.

BOGOTÁ TO CÚCUTA (2)

The main road route from Bogotá to Venezuela has some beautiful stretches. It passes through, or near, several colonial towns and gives access to the Sierra Nevada del Cocuy, excellent climbing and hiking country.

A 618-km road runs NE from Bogotá to Cúcuta, near the Venezuelan border, through Tunja, Moniquirá, Barbosa, Socorro, San Gil, Bucaramanga and Pamplona. It is good most of the way. The road out of Bogotá is the *autopista* to La Caro (**see p 802**), then follow Tunja signs.

From La Caro, the road goes through rich agricultural country with many crops including fruit and flowers. At Km 32.5 is the Alpina Yogurt factory and the Parque Puerto de Sopó with artificial lake. 30 km E into the Sabana is *Sopó* where there is an image of the Saviour which has appeared in an eroded stone; the paintings of angels in the church are very strange and worth seeing (ask at the Casa Cural for entry to church – give a tip). Sopó can also be reached on a difficult road that climbs E out of Bogotá through La Calera (see Bogotá orientation map). Continuing N from Puerto de Sopó is the large Jaime Dugue amusement park created by one of Colombia's pioneer pilots. A replica of the first Avianca aircraft is the centrepiece. The railway (freight only) returns to parallel the road at Tocancipá and Gachancipá, Muisca Indian names. The large new (1995) brewery of Cervecería Leona is here, now competing with the Bavaria monopoly. A few km short of the turning to Sequilé is *El Carajo* restaurant, typical menu, good. 2 km E of the main road is *Sesquilé*, several restaurants, no accommodation. On your right beyond the town is the large Tominé lake and dam. There is a campsite on the lakeside. 17 km from Sesquilé, overlooking the lake is:

Guatavita Nueva This modern town, 75 km from Bogotá, was built in colonial style when the old town of Guatavita was submerged by the reservoir. Although the blend of old and new is fascinating, Guatavita Nueva has failed as a social experiment. Almost all the country folk have left and it is now a week-end haunt for Bogotanos and tourists. (During the week the town is empty.) Cathedral, artisan workshops and small bull-ring for apprentices to practise Sun afternoons. There are also two small museums, one devoted to the Muisca Indians and the other to relics of the old Guatavita church, including a delightful Debain harmonium (Paris 1867). Sun market best in morning, before Bogotanos get there. Bus from Bogotá (Flota Valle de Tenza, Cra 25, No 15-72, rec; Flota Aguila, Cra 15 No 14-59), US$1.45, 2-3 hrs, departures 0730, 0800 and 0930; last return bus at 1730. There are no hotels in Guatavita Nueva. You can walk (or ride, US$7 per horse) from the town to the **Laguna de Guatavita** (also called Lago de Amor by locals), where the legend of El Dorado originated, but it is a long (2-3 hr) walk. It is easier to approach the lake from a point on the Sesquilé-Guatavita Nueva road (the bus driver will let you off at the right place) where there is a sign "via Lago Guatavita". Nearby, on the main road, are good places to eat at weekends, recommended is *Pinos*, 3 km S of the laguna turning, trout, *carne asada* and *chorizos* are specialities. There is a good campsite nearby. From the main road to the lakeside the road is paved as far as a school, about half way. Follow the signs. This road and subsequent track can be driven in a good car to within 300m of the lake where there is a car park and good restaurant, *Hostería Caminos a El Dorado*, open at weekends. There are usually drinks on sale near the lake during the week, but don't count on it. The lake is a quiet, beautiful place; you can walk right round it close to the water level, 1½ hrs, or climb to the rim of the crater in several places. Opinions differ on whether the crater is volcanic or a meteorite impact, but from the rim at 3100m there are extensive views over the varied countryside.

The basis of the El Dorado (Gilded Man) story is established fact. It was the custom of the Chibcha king to be coated annually with resin, on which gold dust was stuck, and then to be taken out on the lake on a ceremonial raft. He then plunged into the lake and emerged with the resin and gold dust washed off. The lake was also the repository (as with the *cenotes* in Yucatán, Mexico) of precious objects thrown in as offerings; there have been several attempts to drain it (the first, by the Spaniards in colonial times, was the origin of the sharp cut in the crater rim) and many items have been recovered over the years. The factual basis of the El Dorado story was confirmed by the discovery of a miniature raft with ceremonial figures on it, made from gold wire, which is now one of the most prized treasures of the Museo de Oro in Bogotá. Part of the raft is missing; the story is that the gold from it ended up in one of the finder's teeth! (Read John Hemming's *The Search for El Dorado* on the subject.)

Beyond Sesquilé, the main road goes through Chocontá (pop 13,650), 88 km from Bogotá, the route is across the western slopes of the Eastern Cordillera to Tunja, 137 km from Bogotá.

Tunja, pop 113,945, capital of Boyacá Department, stands at 2,820m in an arid mountainous area. The climate is cold; mean temperature, 12°C. One of the oldest cities in Colombia, it was refounded as a Spanish city by Gonzalo Suárez Rendón in 1539. It was then the seat of the Zipa, one of the two Chibcha kings. The city formed an independent Junta in 1811, and Bolívar fought under its aegis during the campaign of the Magdalena in 1812. Six years later he fought the decisive battle of Boyacá, nearby (see below).

Museums and churches Of the many colonial buildings the most remarkable is the church of **Santo Domingo**, a masterpiece begun in 1594; the interior is covered with wood most richly carved. Another is the **Santa Clara chapel** (1580), now the hospital of San Rafael, with some fine wood carving. In **Parque Bosque de la República** is the adobe wall against which three martyrs of the Independence were shot in 1816. The **house of Don Juan de Vargas** has been restored as a museum of colonial Tunja, entry US$0.25 includes guided tour in several languages, open 0800-1200, 1300-1800. About 7 km along the road to Duitama there is a huge bronze statue called "El Pantano de Vargas", which appears on the back of the 1,000 peso note. The **Casa del Fundador Suárez Rendón**, Plaza Bolívar, dates from 1540-43 and is one of the few extant mansions of a Spanish *conquistador* in Colombia; open as a museum (except Mon and Tues); see the unique series of colonial paintings on the ceilings. The church of **Santa Bárbara** is full of colonial woodwork, and in the nearby parish house are some notable religious objects, including silk embroidery from the 18th century. Some houses still have colonial portals. There are some fine colonial buildings on Plaza Bolívar opposite the Cathedral. Also impressive is the church of **San Ignacio**. Ask the tourist police guarding these buildings for information; they are helpful and often knowledgeable. For the Piedras de Tunja see under Facatativá **p 802**.

Festival During the week before Christmas, there is a lively festival with local music, traditional dancing and fireworks.

Hotels **D** *Hostería San Carlos*, Cra 11, No 20-12, T 423716, colonial style, good restaurant, highly rec; **D** *San Francisco*, Cra 9, No 18-90, T 426645, on Plaza Bolívar, near cathedral, clean, friendly; **E** *Conquistador*, C 20, No 8-92, on the corner of Plaza Bolívar, hot water, safe, clean, but many rooms don't have outside window; **F** *Príncipe*, limited hot water, small rooms but clean, near bus station, 5 mins from Plaza Bolívar, rec; **E** *Tunja*, just off plaza, private bath; **D/E** *Lord*, C 19, No 10-64, small rooms but hot water, friendly; **Res Dux**, near Res Lord, nice old hotel, good rooms, cold water, good value; **E** *Americano*, Cra 11, No 18-70, friendly, hot water, attractive lobby; **G** *Colonial* , Cra 8, No 20-40, clean, safe, friendly; **G** *Imperial*, C 19, No 7-43, clean, basic, use of kitchen; **G** *Bolívar*, opp bus station, clean, basic. Area around bus station said not to be safe at night.

Restaurants *San Ricardo*, C 19, No 8-38, good; *Surtipan*, C 20, No 12-58, good cakes and coffee; *Estar de Hunzahúa*, C 20, No 11-20 (2nd floor), good food and value, rec; *Pollo Listo* Cra 11, No 19-30, good food; *Santo Domingo*, Cra 11, No 19-66, good food, menú for US$1.30; *Bodegón de los Frayles,* beside the church of San Ignacio, one block from the Plaza Bolívar, good food.

Shopping Market, near Plaza de Toros on outskirts of town, open every day (good for *ruanas* and blankets). Friday is main market day.

Tourist Office In Casa del Fundador, Plaza Bolívar, helpful but not always accurate. Guide for the town: Carlos Julio, will take you to major monuments. Ask at the Tourist Office.

Bus Station is a steep 500m down from city centre; from **Bogotá** 2¹/₂-4¹/₂ hrs, US$4.20, Villa de Leiva, colectivos, 1 hr, US$1.65, **Duitama**, Cotrans, and others. To **Bucaramanga**, hourly, 7¹/₂ hrs, US$10.

Excursions from Tunja The battle of Boyacá was fought about 16 km S of Tunja, on the road to Bogotá. On the bridge at Boyacá is a large monument to Bolívar. Bolívar took Tunja on 6 August 1819, and next day his troops, fortified by a British Legion, the only professional soldiers among them, fought the Spaniards on the banks of the swollen Río Boyacá. With the loss of only 13 killed and 53 wounded they captured 1,600 men and 39 officers. Only 50 men escaped, and when these told their tale in Bogotá the Viceroy Samao fled in such haste that he left behind him half a million pesos of the royal funds. There is now a huge modern restaurant overlooking the site.

On a hillside outside Tunja is the carved rock throne of the Chibcha king, the Zipa; ask for directions from the Tourist Office.

At **Paipa**, between Tunja and Duitama, there are popular municipal thermal baths, US$1.75 (disappointing), 15 mins bus ride from Tunja, US$1.20, then 30-min walk from plaza (taxi from plaza US$0.70, from hotel US$1—taxi drivers are likely to take you to a hotel of their recommendation, not yours). **A** *Hotel Sochagota*, T 850012, overlooking the lake, has a swimming pool fed by hot springs, cabins for hire, with 2 bedrooms, bathroom, log fires and private hot spring pools. Among the many other places to stay are **C** *Panorama* (T 850076, huge swimming pool, Turkish bath, sauna), **D** *Casablanca*, and *cabañas*, hotels and *residencias* ranging from our **D** range to **F** pp. There are 7 restaurants.

Villa de Leiva (also spelt Leyva, pop 3,310), an extremely pretty place, is reached either by a direct road from Tunja or by a branch road, left, at Arcabuco. (Toll at Arcabuco, US$0.40.) Although the surface is not good, the drive affords some beautiful views and, near the fork to Sáchica there is a campsite, bathrooms, swimming pool, refreshments. At Km 20 from Villa de Leiva, there is a left turn for the **Iguaque National Park** (3 km) run by Inderena, which is the site of interesting oak woods, flora, fauna and several lakes. Entrance US$0.70 students US$0.55, cars US$1.35. There is a tourist centre with accommodation for 60 and a restaurant. There are guided paths and a marked trail to Lake Iguaque, a walk of 2¹/₂ hrs. Getting there can be difficult; most likely day for a lift is Saturday, market day, but there is a daily bus at 0700 from Villa de Leiva to the turn off to the Park. It returns at 1300. (Camping is allowed, safe.)

The town dates back, like Tunja, to the early days of Spanish rule, but unlike Tunja, it has been declared a national monument so will not be modernised. The first president of Nueva Granada (see p 781), Miguel Venero de Leiva, lived in the town. There are **two colonial houses** which are worth a visit: the house in which Antonio Nariño lived (Cra 9, No 10-39, open Tues-Sun 0900-1230, 1400-1800)—he translated the *Rights of Man* into Spanish—and the building in which the first Convention of the United Provinces of New Granada was held, C 13 y Cra 9, on corner of plaza, now also a good place for tourist information, local maps available at US$0.25. Also worth a visit is the restored birthplace of the independence hero Antonio Ricaurte (Cra 8 y C 5). A **palaeontological museum** has been opened 15 mins walk N of the town on Cra 9, entrance US$0.55. The shops in the plaza have an excellent selection of Colombian handicrafts, while the Saturday market, not yet geared to the tourist trade, still offers many bargains. On the Plaza Mayor is the **Casa-Museo Luis Alberto Acuña**, housing fascinating examples of Acuña's work (recommended, entry US$0.70, extra to take photographs). The **Monasterio de las Carmelitas** has one of the best museums of religious art in Colombia, open Sat and Sun 1400-1700.

The mountains around Villa de Leiva abound in fossils. 5 km along the road to Santa Sofía can be seen the complete fossil of a dinosaur now housed in a room, entry US$0.50, there are road signs to it, ask for El Fósil (open 0800-1200, 1300-1600, Thur only 1300-1600); the children sell fossils and rough emeralds. 2 km from El Fósil along this road is the turning for (1 km) the archaeological site known as **El Infiernito**, where there are several huge carved stones believed to be giant phalli and a solar calendar (0900-1200, 1400-1700, closed Mon, admission US$0.50). 6 km after the

1. Plaza Mayor
2. Plaza de Mercado
3. Casa de Antonio Nariño
4. Casa del Primer Congreso
5. Museo Luis Alberto Acuña
6. Iglesia del Carmen
7. Iglesia Parroquial
8. San Francisco
9. San Agustín
10. Alcaldía
11. Tourist Office
12. Telecom & Post Office

VILLA DE LEIVA

Infiernito turning is the **Monastery of Ecce-Homo** (founded 1620), which is worth a visit; note the fossils on the floor at the entrance. There are buses from Villa de Leiva at 0645, 0930 and 1345, going to Santa Sofía, US$0.50; it's half an hour to the crossing, then a 2 km walk to the monastery. A tour including most of these attractions leaves the plaza at 0930, Sat/Sun, US$6, rec.

A festival of light is held every year in mid-December which attracts many visitors.

NB The town tends to be full of visitors at weekends and bank holidays and is generally expensive. It is better not to visit Villa de Leiva on Mondays or Tuesdays as many places are closed. Also there are few services in Villa de Leiva, buy fuel etc in Tunja. The houses are closed Monday-Friday out of season, but the trip is worth while just for the views. In any event, the town and surrounding hills are excellent for long, peaceful walks.

Hotels B *El Molino la Mesopotamia*, C del Silencio, T 320235, a beautifully restored colonial mill (meals US$4, breakfast US$3), 10% rebate for booking 10 days ahead (closed during the first weeks of January), swimming pool, home cooking, excellent food with good *menú* at US$7.50, beautiful gardens, rec; **B** *Mesón de la Plaza Mayor*, Cra 9, No 13-51, T 218-7441 (Bogotá), beautifully restored *hospedaría*, owner, Mauricio Ordóñez, speaks English, helpful; **B** *Hospedaje El Mesón de Los Virreyes*, Cra 9, No 14-51, T 320252, with bath, good restaurant; **C** *Molino del Balcón*, Cra 12, No 11-51, colonial building, garden, friendly; **D** *Residencial de Los Angeles*, 1 block from plaza, good value; **D** *Los Llanitos*, C 9, No 12-31, T 256-1643 (Bogotá), 5 min walk from main plaza, quiet, hot water, very friendly, good food; **E-D** *Hostería La Roca*, C 13, No 9-54, clean and pleasant, with some rooms overlooking main square and reasonable breakfast, noisy at night because of bar music; **E** *Hospedaría Colonial*, C 12, one block from main plaza, with bath; **E** *Estancia el Olivo*, Fósil, clean, hot water, use of kitchen, friendly. Accommodation with Familia Fitata, C 12, No 7-31, **E** (F in week), breakfast extra, friendly, clean, safe. **E** *Hospedaje El Sol de la Villa*, Cra 8, No 12-28, T 320-224, safe, quiet, clean, hot shower. new, very good breakfast, cooking facility, rec; **E** *Hospedaje La Villa*, C 6 just off plaza, shared bath, rooms with balcony, upstairs rooms best, can be noisy. The telephone connection from Bogotá is poor and most hotels have reservation numbers in

Bogotá. Booking essential during holidays, and advisable at weekends (try bargaining Mon-Thurs). **Camping** Inderena's *Vivero*, 15 mins walk N of plaza on road to Arcabuco (just before palaeontological museum), nice place with bathroom, warm shower, ask for Juan; also Los Olivares near village of Sáchica, 4 km from Villa de Leiva (no services). Ask for advice on other sites at the Tourist Office.

Restaurants Several on the main square, in, and opposite, the bus station. *Nueva Granada*, Cra 9, No 13-69, good value, friendly, owner Jorge Rodríguez, plays classical music; *El Parrilón de los Caciques*, W side of town on Cra 9, No 9-05, warmly rec, good value; *Los Portales*, just off plaza, cheap, early breakfasts; *Freilon*, nearby, large servings; *El Estar de la Villa*, C 13, No 8-89, good; *Donna Mia*, C 9, No 11-102, good pizzas and crêpes, good helpings, Swedish owners, very knowledgeable; *Giorgio*, C 12 between Cra 8 and 9, Italian, good atmosphere, reasonable prices; *La Dicha Buena*, near the Plaza, good vegetarian place, cakes, real Twinings tea, also good breakfasts; *Ricos Pizzería*, Cra 9 y C 14, good pizzas, reasonable prices. Good value restaurant opp bus station.

Post Office in Telecom building, C 13, No 8-26.

Tourist Office Cra 9 y C 13 on plaza. At the bus station; gives advice on cheaper accommodation; city map US$0.35.

Transport Bus station in 8th block of Cra 9. It is recommended to book the return journey on arrival. Buses to **Leiva** from Tunja, 1 hr, US$1.65 with Flota Reina or Valle de Tenza company. (From Bogotá to Villa de Leiva, via Tunja, takes 4 hrs, US$5, several companies, and via Zipaquirá and Chiquinquirá, US$5.70.) Colectivo taxis leave the bus station in Tunja for **Villa de Leiva** every hour, US$1.20, and return from the main square. Bus at 1000 from Leiva to **Moniquirá** (see p 810) connects with bus to Bucaramanga, thus avoiding Tunja. If driving from Tunja, watch out for rockfalls. Another way of getting to Villa de Leiva is via Sáchica, either directly from Tunja or, coming from Bogotá, turning left (W) at the Boyacá monument, via Samacá.

From Tunja there are two possible routes to Cúcuta; the main road, almost entirely paved, goes via Bucaramanga, but the other via Duitama and Málaga, rejoining the main road at Pamplona, is also interesting, though there are few filling stations N of Duitama. In *Duitama* there is the interesting tourist complex Punta Larga, close to a furniture manufacturer. (**E** *Isobel*, Cra 18, No 18-60, clean, quiet; many others nearby). About 7 km from Duitama, on the road to Belencito, there is another hotel, also in an old *hacienda*, the **B** *Hostería San Luis de Ucuenga*. Bus Duitama to Bucaramanga at 0900, 9 hrs, US$9; to Málaga at 0800, sit on right side for best views, 6 hrs. At Duitama turn right for *Sogamoso*, where a good museum of archaeology has been opened on the site of the centre of the precolumbian city. This was an important Chibcha settlement; destroyed by the Spaniards, but it has been reconstructed on site. Their arts of mummification, statuary, and gold working are shown in the museum (closed Mon). It is possible to camp in the museum grounds if you ask permission. A museum of religious art is open on the road from Duitama to Sogamoso. Many hotels near bus station eg **G** *Hostal Aranjuez*, basic, safe, very helpful, **F** *Residencia Embajador*, clean, friendly, rec; **G** *Residencia El Terminal*, basic, clean, safe. (Bus Bogotá-Sogamoso US$4, 4 hrs.) East of Sogamoso the churches of *Mongua* (a pleasant colonial town, 20 km) and Tópaga are worth a visit, and so is the mountain-ringed *Lago de Tota* (3,015 metres above sea level), S of Sogamoso. The *Refugio el Pozo Azul*, on the lakeside, is a private club run by Gary Clements and his Colombian wife, who will extend membership to readers of *The South American Handbook*; an excellent place to stay, in C price range, also has cabins for up to 7 people, US$40. Good food, fresh trout caught in the lake, suitable for children, very friendly atmosphere. Boats and fishing tackle for hire; good walking in pastoral surroundings, and bird-watching country; recommended to book in advance, postal address: Apartado Aéreo 032, Sogamoso, Boyacá (in Bogotá, T 211-2828). Also on the lake is *Las Rocas Lindas*, D with bath and hot water, US$2.50 for each extra person, 2 cabins for 7 (US$30), one for 8 at Playa Blanca across the lake (US$40), boats for hire, dining room, bar, fireplaces, recommended. The owner, Sr Mauricio Moreno Arenas, is very friendly. *Aquitania*, a cold, expensive town on the lake, is a centre of onion growing, with a nice camp ground called Playa Blanca nearby, with services and cafeteria. It is reached by bus from Sogamoso, US$0.90, 1 hr; bus from Bogotá (Rápido Duitama), via Tunja and Sogamoso, goes round the lake to Aquitania, passing Cuitiva, Tota and the *Rocas Lindas* and *Pozo Azul* hotels (3 hr wait in Aquitania). In Aquitania, **F** *Residencia Venecia*, C 8, No 144, with restaurant *Lucho* below, reasonable. Above the town is a hill (El Cumbre) with beautiful views. On the opposite side of the lake from Aquitania is the colonial town of *Iza* with several hotels.

Just before the descent to the Lago de Tota, a road branches left, leading in 4 hrs to *Yopal*, capital of the Intendencia of Casanare in the Llanos. (Pop 10,000.) The road passes through *páramo* and virgin cloud forest. A fine waterfall can be reached in one hour's walk from the

DAS checkpoint just above Pajarito. The best *residencias* in Yopal are usually full; direct buses from Sogamoso and Bogotá (US$13). **NB** Casanare and Arauca beyond are centres of guerrilla activity.

Northeast of Duitama, on the road to Málaga, is the turning at Belén for Paz de Río, where Colombia's national steelworks is sited; visitors can see over it. The road goes N to **Soatá** (*Residencias Colonial*, excellent, good restaurant; **D** *Hotel Turístico*, swimming pool) and then descends to the very dry, spectacular valley of the Río Chicomocha.

By the bridge over the river at **Capitanejo** is the turning to the very attractive **Sierra Nevada del Cocuy** in the Eastern Cordillera. Guerrillas were reported in 1993 as active in this area, **see p 901** for security advice and ask locally before going into the mountains. In Capitanejo are several hotels where the bus stops: **F** *Residencias El Oasis*, **G** *Residencia El Córdobes*, *Residencia El Dorado* and *Villa Del Mar*, and more on the *parque* on block below bus stop, all are basic. The Sierra extends in a half circle for 30 km, offering peaks of rare beauty, lakes and waterfalls. The flora is particularly interesting. Everyone wears ponchos, rides horses and is very friendly. The area is good for trekking and probably the best range in Colombia for rock climbers. The most beautiful peaks are Cocuy (5,100m), Ritacuba Negra (5,200m), Ritacuba Blanca (5,200m) and El Castillo (5,400m). The main towns are **Cocuy**, to the W of the Sierra (tourist office on Cra 3, No 8-06, very helpful, run by Pedro Moreno; **F** *Residencia Cocuy*, cold water, meals, laundry); and **Guicán**, 30 km to the N, a friendly place. There are 3 hotels, **F** *Hotel La Sierra*, good, owner "Profe" (Orlando Corea) has good maps of the region, informative visitors' book for trekkers, roof terrace, meals available; **F** *Las Montañas*, basic, but pleasant, meals available, laundry facilities, overlooks main plaza, thin walls (guests leaving for the 0400 bus will wake you); and **F** *Del Norte*, on opposite corner. At *Las Montañas*, Teresa Cristancho or Jorge Ibáñez can arrange a stay in *Cabinas Kanwara* at 3,920 m, about 1000m above Guicán, **E**, restaurant, 9 beds, well furnished, open fires, electrically-heated showers; or camping (US$1.25), horse rental (US$4.55/day) and guide service included, with Dionisio and Berthilda López at the last house before the Nevado on Ritacuba Blanca, highly rec. From here it is 3 strenuous hours' walk on a clear trail to the snowline on Ritacuba Blanca. This would also be the best base for the 2-3 day walk round the N end of the Sierra and into Ratoncito valley, which is surrounded by snow-capped mountains. A milk truck ("el lechero") leaves Guicán between 0600 and 0700 via Cocuy for La Cruz, 1 hr walk below the cabins, arriving 1100, getting back to Guicán around 1230, a rough but interesting ride. Both towns are 1-1½ hrs drive by jeep from the mountains, so it is recommended to stay higher up (jeep hire about US$17 from José Riaño or "Profe" in Guicán).

Above Cocuy, accommodation is available at Estadero Don Pastor and the farmhouse above Hacienda La Esperanza (8 hrs from Guicán) US$6 with 2 meals. Horses can be hired at both places. La Esperanza is the base for climbing to the Laguna Grande de la Sierra (7 hrs round trip), a large sheet of glacier-fed water surrounded by 5 snow-capped peaks, and also for the 2-day walk to the Laguna de la Plaza on the E side of the Sierra, reached through awesome, rugged scenery. Between Cocuy and La Esperanza is Alto de la Cuera where you can stay at El Himat meterological station for US$5, basic, including 2 meals. There is a fine walk from here to Lagunillas, a string of lakes near the S end of the range (5 hrs there and back). Permission to camp can easily be obtained from the friendly people. Maps available in Cocuy from the tourist office. It takes 8-10 days to trek from one end to the other through a central rift, but equipment (crampons, ice axe, rope etc) is necessary. Be prepared for unstable slopes and rockfalls, few flat campsites and treacherous weather. The perpendicular rock mountains overlooking the Llanos are for professionals only. The best weather is from December to April.

Transport 6 buses a day Bogotá-Cocuy, 2 with Tricolor, 2 with Paz de Río, 1 Libertadores and 1 Gacela, either 0300 or 0400 or between 1000-1800, 13 hrs, US$12; Paz de Río or Libertadores

Capitanejo-Cocuy at 0400 and 1200, US$2.15, to **Guicán**, 3-4 hrs, US$2.75, Libertadores Tunja-Cocuy/Guicán 0730, 10 hrs, US$9.75. From Guicán buses leave at 0400, 1600 and 1800 for **Capitanejo**, **Duitama** (US$6.15), **Paipa** (9 hrs, US$6.65) and points N. For points N, or to get to this area from the N, change at Capitanejo. From Capitanejo 3 buses a day to Bucaramanga, 4 to Cúcuta.

The area around *Málaga* is very picturesque: pretty red-tiled villages, riders in ponchos and cowboy hats, and mountains (some covered in flowering trees). The roads are twisty but spectacular.

Hotels E *Santander*, friendly, good value; E *Arizona Plaza*, with bath, modern, clean, friendly; E *Brasilia*, reasonable; F *Príncipe*, near main square, shared bathroom, clean, friendly, good meals, rec, and restaurants, eg *La Riviera*, Cra 8, No 13-61, good food; nearby, *La Esperanza*, good Colombian food.

Transport Good bus services to Duitama (6 hrs), Bucaramanga (6-7 hrs, US$6) and Pamplona. The road from Málaga to Bucaramanga is another spectacular trip through the mountains, but the road is not good and is very tortuous.

The main road from Tunja goes on to *Moniquirá* (64 km) 1650m, a pleasant place to stay. Hotels (all on central plaza) D *Mansión*, good; E *Clara Luz*, OK; E *Casablanca*, with swimming pool; F *Tairona*, clean, friendly. 10 km beyond is *Barbosa* in the Department of Santander (E *Hotel Príncipe*, clean rooms with private bath); youth hostel at *Parador Turístico Barbosa*; *El Palacio del Pollo*, good, simple roadside restaurant).

A road runs NW from Barbosa to the Magdalena at Puerto Olaya, opposite Puerto Berrío. 18 km from Barbosa is *Vélez*, a charming little town where horses and mules are raised.

The road (toll at Santana, US$0.40) goes NE for 84 km to *Socorro* (pop 23,020), with steep streets and single storey houses set among graceful palms. It has a singularly large and odd stone church. The local museum, La Casa de la Cultura, is worth seeing, as is the market which is open every day.

At Socorro, in 1781, began the revolt of the peasant *comuneros*: not a movement for independence but a protest against poverty. It was led at first by a woman, Manuela Beltrán, and then, when other towns joined, by Juan Francisco Berbeo. They marched as far as the salt town of Zipaquirá, N of Bogotá; rebel terms were accepted by the Spaniards, and sworn to by the Bishop of Bogotá, but when they had returned home troops were sent from Cartagena and there were savage reprisals. Another woman from Socorro, Antonia Santos, led guerrillas fighting for independence and was captured and executed by the Spaniards in 1819; her statue is in the main square. The Casa de Cultura museum (opening hours vary according to season) has disappointingly little information on these local heroines, but is still worth a visit.

Hotels C *Tamacara*, C 14, No 14-15, T 273517, swimming pool; E *Colonial*, Cra 15, good, TV; F *Venezia*, shower, dining room, nice old rooms, good value. **Restaurants** *Panadería Imperial*, C 14 y Cra 13, very good, simple; *La Gran Parrilla*, C 9, Cra 15, good steaks.

From Socorro, a road leads N and W to Barrancabermeja. 21 km along, there is a dirt track off to *Barichara*, a beautiful colonial town at 1,336m, population 7,175, founded in 1714 and designated as a national monument to preserve its character. A better road connects Barichara to San Gil. In Barichara there are many places of historical interest, the most important being the house of the former president Aquiles Parra (the woman next door has the key). An interesting excursion is to *Guane*, a town 9 km away by road, or 1½ hrs delightful walk by trail, where there are many colonial houses and an archaeological museum in the priest's house, collection of coins and a mummified woman (admission, US$0.25). The valley abounds with fossils. There are buses from Barichara, but not every day. Another interesting trip is to the waterfall Salto de Mica, a 30 min walk along a trail following the line of cliffs near Barichara.

Hotels D *Santa Barbara*, C 5, No 9-12, T 7163, old colonial house refurbished in 1989 owned by two British Council scholars Mario and Nubia de Gallegos; quiet, clean showers in rooms, all meals available; E *Corata*, Cra 7, No 4-02, with private bath, charming courtyard, restaurant and lovely cathedral views, rec; F *Posada Real*, Cra 7, No 4-78, restaurant. You can make reservations in Bogotá, at Cra 16A, No 79-61, T 610-3425. Ask at the Casa de Cultura about staying in private homes.

Restaurants *La Casona*, C 6, Cras 5-6, cheap, good food, friendly; *Bahía Chala*, near the Central Square, goat-meat speciality.

Another 20 km N of Barichara is **Zapatoca** a sleepy town which at one time controlled the traffic between highland Santander and the Magdalena. Local products include juicy sweets (*cocadas*) and *pauche*, a balsa type wood painted and carved into many forms. There is also a small museum. Nearby are the Cuevas del Nitro which include the cave "El Salto de la Monja", a sheer drop where a nun is believed to have fallen to her death and was never retrieved. There are many bats in the caves. On the outskirts of the village there is a natural pool for swimming with a small waterfall called Pozo del Ahogado. There are buses to Bucaramanga, 2 hrs US$4.20. The road continues to Barrancabermeja, **see p 847**.

About 21 km beyond Socorro, NE on the main road to Bucamaranga, is **San Gil**, a friendly colonial town with a good climate, which has the tourist attraction of El Gallineral, a riverside spot whose beautiful trees are covered with moss-like tillandsia. (Entrance US$0.50.) Good view from La Gruta, the shrine overlooking the town (look for the cross). The town has become a truck stop on the Bogotá-Bucaramanga road, and accommodation facing the main road is noisy.

Hotels E *Alcantuz*, Cra 11, No 10-15, T 3160, clean, free coffee, good location, pleasant but noisy facing street; **E** *Residencia Abril*, Cra 10, C 8, T 3381, secure parking, refrigerators in rooms (contents overpriced), relatively quiet; **E** *Residencias Señorial*, C 10, No 8-14, T 4442, pleasant and quiet; **F** *Residencias Royal*, C 10 y Cra 10, with bath but no a/c; **F** *Victoria*, near bus terminal, with bath. **G** *San Gil*, C 11, or F with bath, clean, friendly, upstairs rooms are preferable, basic.

Between Socorro and San Gil, there is a *Balneario Campestre El Raizon*, swimming pool, showers, restaurant, car campers allowed and a few small rooms.

Restaurants   Just outside Pinchote on the road from Socorro to San Gil is the *Mesón del Cuchicote*, which specializes in dishes from the Santander region (also has rooms, D). A good restaurant in San Gil is *Herberduc*, Cra 11, C 8, US$2-5; *Central*, C 10, No 10-70, good and cheap; *La Mama*, Cra 9, good vegetarian; *Antojos*, Cra 9, No 11-19, good juices; *La Palma*, across from *Residencias Abril*, rec; *Bambi*, Cra 10—at night it is a discotheque; open air restaurant in Parque Gallineral, good in evening, music at weekends; *Dusi's King*, on plaza, fast food. *Aphrodite*, a night club built inside a cave with a lake and waterfall outside.

Transport   Bus station 5 mins out of town by taxi on road to Tunja. Bus to **Bogotá**, US$7.20; to **Bucaramanga**, US$2.30, 2½ hrs; to **Barichara** from C 12, US$1, 1 hr. Flights to Bogotá.

A road runs E from San Gil to Onzaga (bus), through Mogotes and San Joaquín, dropping from high mountain ridges to tropical valleys. From Onzaga it is 20 km to Soatá (**see p 809**); no regular public transport, if walking make sure you take the right road. 1 hour E of San Gil is **Charalá**, which has a beautiful plaza with a statue of José Antonio Golán, leader of the 1781 Comunero revolt. Also an interesting church and Casa de la Cultura; very attractive lush scenery. **E** *Hotel El Refugio*, with private bath, clean, safe. Bus San Gil-Charalá, US$1.

About 24 km beyond San Gil, a little off the road, is the picturesque village of **Aratoca**, with a colonial church. 10 km further on, the descent from the heights along the side of a steep cliff into the dry Río Chicamocha canyon, with spectacular rock colours, is one of the most dramatic experiences of the trip to Cúcuta, but, if driving, this is a demanding and dangerous stretch.

Bucaramanga (pop 464,585), 420 km from Bogotá, is the capital of Santander Department. It stands at 1,018m on an uneven plateau sharply delimited by eroded slopes to the N and W, hills to the E and a ravine to the S. The city was founded in 1622 but was little more than a village until the latter half of the 19th century. The metropolitan area has a population of 782,345, which has expanded rapidly because of the success of coffee, tobacco and staple crops. The Parque Santander is the heart of the modern city, while the Parque García Rovira is the centre of the colonial area. Just off Parque García Rovira is the Casa de Cultura. Casa Perú de la Croix, C 37, No 11-18, is a beautiful colonial mansion (closed, temporarily it is hoped, since 1989). There is a pleasant park where the market next to the bus station used to be. The city's great problem is space for expansion. Erosion in the lower, western side topples buildings over the edge after heavy rain. The fingers of erosion, deeply ravined between, are spectacular. The Club Campestre is one of the most beautifully set in Latin America. There is an amusement park, Parque El Lago, in the suburb of Lagos I, SW of the city on the way to Floridablanca. On the way out of the city NE (towards Pamplona) is the Parque Morrorico, well-maintained with a fine view. There is a sculptured Saviour overlooking the park, a point of pilgrimage on Good Friday.

Museums *Museo de Arte Moderno*, C 37, Cra 26, US$0.20. Also *Casa de Bolívar*, C 37, No 12-15, an interesting museum (0900-1200, 1400-1700, entry US$0.15, closed Sat and Sun).

Average maximum temperature is 30°C; average minimum, 19.4°C. Rainfall is about 760 mm, and humidity is high (68% to 90%).

The annual international piano festival is held here in mid-September in the Auditorio Luis A Calvo at the Universidad Industrial de Santander, one of the finest concert halls in Colombia. The university is worth a visit for beautiful grounds and a lake full of exotic plants and alligators.

Hotels **A2** *Chicamocha*, C 34, No 31-24, luxury, a/c, clean, swimming pool (non guests US$1.50); **A2** *Bucarica*, C 35 y Cra 19, T 301592, F 301594, spacious, on main plaza, private bathroom, telephone, good restaurant and snack bar; **D** *El Pilar*, C 34, No 24-09, T 453147, clean, hot water, quiet, good service and food, rec; **E** *Tamana*, Cra 18, No 30-31, with bath, F without, clean, friendly, rec. Wide variety of hotels on C 31, between Cras 18-21. A few blocks uphill from the bus terminal are several *residencias*; **E** *Las Bahamas*, opposite Copetran terminal, friendly, good value; **F** *Las Islas*, also by the bus terminal, clean, good value; **E** *Nutibara*, C 55, No 21-42, shower, fan; **F** *Residencias Solo Suite*, C33, No 24-43, clean, friendly; **F** *Residencias Tonchala*, C 56, No 21-23, with bath, good; **F** *Residencias Amparo*, C 31, No 20-29, with bath; **F** *Hostal Doral*, C 32, No 21-65, rooms with bath F, family business, clean, safe, several nice tiny rooms but varying reports. Accommodation at the **A** *Club Campestre*, is good, but you must have an introduction; try the mayor's office or Chamber of Commerce. **Note**: Since Bucaramanga is the site for numerous national conventions, it is sometimes hard to find a room.

Camping Half-an-hour drive S of Bucaramanga, on left of dual carriageway, with swimming pool and waterside restaurant.

Restaurants *Di Marco*, C 48, Cra 29 esquina, excellent meat; *La Casa de Spagheti*, Cra 27, No 51-18, cheap and good; *La Tranquera*, Cra 33, C 40, good Baby Beef, US$6; pizzas at: *Piz Pan Pum*, Cra 33, No 31-107 (next to Cinema Rivera); *Tropical*, C 33, No 17-81; *Fonda*, C 33, No 34-42, good, cheap, vegetarian; *Zirus*, C 56, No 30-88, friendly, owner speaks a little English; *Super Pizza*, Centro Comercial Cabecera (pizza by the slice, hamburgers, etc). Good snack bars including *Mucho Pinchos* (C 54, No 31-07). Oriental: *Tokio*, Cra 18 between C 33 and 34; *Oriental*, same street.

Vegetarian: *Maranatha*, Cra 24, No 36-20, good lunches and dinners, reasonable prices; *El Toronjil*, Cra 33, No 52-123, a bit dear; *Govinda*, Indian vegetarian, Cra 20, C 35/36, excellent lunch US$2.50; *Berna*, C 35, No 18-30, best pastries in town. Try the *hormigas calonas* (large black ants), a local delicacy mainly eaten during Holy Week (sold in shops, not restaurants).

Banks Banco Anglo Colombiano, Cra 19 No 36-43, and 4 agencies. **Banco Industrial Colombiano**, by Parque Santander, will cash Thomas Cook and Amex TCs. Long queues (cheques and passports have to be photocopied). Many other banks. Cash changed at *Distinguidos*, C36, No 17-52 local 1A33.

Discotheques On road to Girón are *El Pulpo* and *Capricornio*; *Ulisses 2000*, Av Quebrada Seca y Cra 28, gay. Many on Cra 33, try *Silver Rose*. Drinks are expensive. Worth taking a look at : *Barbaroja*, Cra 27, No 28, a *salsa* and *son* bar set in a renovated red and white, gothic-style mansion, happy hour 1700-1800.

Shopping Camping equipment, *Acampemos*, C 48, No 26-30, last place in Colombia to get camping gas cartridges before Venezuela. Handicrafts in Girón (expensive—see below) and typical clothing upstairs in the food market, C 34 y Cras 15-16. Similar articles (*ruanas*, hats) in San Andresito. *Feria de artesanías* in first 2 weeks of September, usually near the Puerta del Sol.

Tourist Office On main plaza in *Hotel Bucarica* building, C 35, No 18-70A, friendly and knowledgeable, T 338461 (closed 1200-1400). City maps free.

City Transport Most taxis have meters; beware of overcharging from bus terminals. Buses charge US$0.35.

Airport Palonegro, on three flattened hilltops on other side of ravine S of city. Spectacular views on take-off and landing. At least 3 Avianca flights a day to **Bogotá**, regularly overbooked; also daily to **Cúcuta**. Flights to **Medellín** (daily) are better value and less hassle than going by bus. Taxi, US$4; colectivo, US$1. Buses are scarce despite the fact that some bus boards say "Aeropuerto" (direction "Girón/Lebrija" from Diagonal 15). Avianca, C 37, No 15-03, T 27534.

Roads To the Magdalena at Barrancabermeja, 174 km; to Cúcuta, 198 km; to Bogotá, 420 km; to Medellín, 1,010 km; to Santa Marta, 550 km, all paved.

Buses The terminal is on the Girón road, with cafés and showers. Taxi to centre, US$1.20; bus US$0.15. To **Bogotá**, 8-11 hrs, US$18 (Pullman) with Berlinas del Fonce, Cra 18, No 31-06 (this journey is uncomfortable, there are no relief stops, and it starts off hot and ends cold in the mountains, be prepared); Copetran, C 55, No 17B-57, recommended for advance bus reservations, has 3 classes of bus to Bogotá including Pullman, 10 hrs, and to Cartagena, leaving at 1930 daily; Expreso Brasilia, C 31, Cra 18-19, T 422-152, runs to Bogotá but they sell tickets only half an hour before departure. **Tunja**, 7½ hrs, US$10; **Valledupar**, 8 hrs, US$17; **Barranquilla**, 9 hrs (US$18 first class with Copetran); to **Pamplona**, Copetran, 3 a day, US$3.25 (Pullman), US$2.75 (*corriente*); **Cúcuta**, 6 hrs, US$5 (Pullman), Berlinas buses often arrive full from Bogotá, Copetran US$6 and colectivo US$7.20. The trip to Cúcuta is spectacular in the region of Berlín (see below). **Santa Marta**, 9 hrs, maybe more according to season, US$20 with Copetran; **Barrancabermeja**, 3 hrs, US$2.30, a scenic ride with one rest stop permitted; this road is paved. To **El Banco** on the Río Magdalena, US$10, several companies, direct or change at Aguachica. Hourly buses to **San Gil**, US$2.30. To **Berlín**, US$1.20. Other companies with local services to nearby villages on back roads, eg the colourful folk-art buses of Flota Cáchira (C 32, Cra 33-34) which go N and E.

Excursions The suburb of *Floridablanca*, 8 km SW, has the famous El Paragüitas gardens (also known as the Jardín Botánico), belonging to the national tobacco agency, reputed locally as "a replica of the Garden of Eden"; look for the caymanes round the lake. The gardens have been recently reconstructed and open at weekends 0800-1100 and 1400-1700. Entrance US$0.25. There are plenty of buses: take the Cotandra bus (US$0.30) from Cra 22, Bucaramanga, either Florida Villabel which goes by El Paragüitas, or Florida Autopista (continuation of Cra 33) which goes direct to the square in Florida and you have to walk about a km. Toll on road to Floridablanca, US$0.20. *Rincón Santanera* restaurant, Cra 8, No 4-41, good local food.

Lebrija (pop 19,130), 17 km to the W, is in an attractive plain. Rionegro (pop 28,415) is a coffee town 20 km to the N with, close by, the Laguna de Gálago and waterfalls. *Girón* (pop 75,155) a tobacco centre 9 km SW of Bucaramanga on the Río de Oro, is a quiet and attractive colonial town, filled with Bumangueses at weekends, with a beautiful church. The buildings are well preserved and the town unspoilt by modernization. By the river are *tejo* courts and popular open air restaurants with *cumbia* and *salsa* bands; in the square at weekends, sweets and *raspados* (crushed ice delights) are sold. (Hotels: **B** San Juan de Girón, outside town on road from Bucaramanga, T 466430, swimming pool, restaurant uninspired; **F** Río de Oro, in centre, but make sure you get a lock for the door. Restaurants: *Mansión del Fraile* on the square, in a beautiful colonial house, good food—Bolívar slept here on one occasion, ask to see the bed; *La Casona*, Cra 28, No 27-47, friendly, rec; try their "fritanga gironesa". It seems no food is available after 1900.) Take the bus from Cra 15 or 22 in Bucaramanga, US$1.75. In **Piedecuesta**, 18 km SE of Bucaramanga (bus from Cra 22, US$0.45, 45 mins, Hotel: **F** *Piedecuesta*, good, safe, clean). Here you can see cigars being hand-made, furniture carving and jute weaving—cheap, hand-decorated *fique* rugs can be bought. There are frequent buses to all these dormitory towns for the city; a taxi costs US$6. Corpus Christi processions in these towns in June are interesting.

Another excursion is to *California*, about 60 km NE of Bucaramanga, where there are gold mines that tourists can visit, but check for safety before setting out.

The road (bad and narrow) runs E to Berlín, and then NE (a very scenic run over the Eastern Cordillera) to Pamplona, about 130 km from Bucaramanga.

Berlín has been recommended to the hardy camper as challenging and rewarding. The village lies in a valley at 3,100m, the peaks surrounding it rise to 4,350m and the temperature is constantly around 10°C, although on the infrequent sunny days it may seem much warmer. The scenery is awesome. The inhabitants are tolerant of visitors; ask a farmer for permission to camp in his field. There is a tourist complex with cabins and there are several basic eating places. It has been recommended as an ideal place to appreciate the grandeur of the Eastern Cordillera and the hardiness of the people who live on the *páramo*. At the highest point on the road between Bucaramanga and Berlín, 3,400m, is a café where you can camp on the covered porch. They have a friendly woolly dog.

Pamplona (pop 43,645), Department of Norte de Santander, lies amid mountains at 2,200m. The town is definitely worth seeing. Founded in 1548, it became important as a mining town but is now better known as a university city. Few modern buildings have as yet broken its colonial harmony. Cathedral in the spacious central plaza. The earthquake of 1875 played havoc with the monasteries and some of the churches: there is now a hotel on the site of the former San Agustín monastery, but it may still be possible to visit the ex-monasteries of San Francisco and Santo Domingo. The Iglesia del Humilladero, adjoining the cemetery, is very picturesque and allows a fine view of the city. Museum of religious art at C 5 y Cra 5. See the Casa Colonial archaeological museum, C 6, No 2-56, open Tues-Sat, 0900-1200, 1400-1800; Sun, 0900-1200, "a little gem". The town's Easter celebrations are famous throughout Colombia.

Hotels C *Cariongo*, Cra 5, C 9, T 682645, very good, excellent restaurant, US satellite TV (locked parking available); E *Residencia Doran*, Cra 6, No 7-21, with bath (F without), large rooms, good meals, US$1.50; E *Imperial*, Cra 5, No 5-36, T 682571, on main plaza (cheaper without carpet), large sparse rooms, noisy; E *Lincoln*, on the Plaza, simple, but good beds, private bath and hot water; F *Orsua*, on main square, clean, friendly, cheap, good food also available (good, cheap restaurant also to left of hotel); F *Llanos*, C 9 y Cra 7, shared bath, cold water, motorcycle parking, rec. Hotel accommodation may be hard to find at weekends, when Venezuelans visit the town.

Restaurants *El Maribel*, C 5, No 4-17, cheap lunch; *La Casona*, C 6, No 6-57, limited but good menu; *La Garza de Oro*, C 6, No 5-46, good food; *Fuente de Sifón*, on main square, student-run, good music. *El Rincón Paisa*, also on main plaza, good; *Portal Alemán*, C 7 y Cra 6, good meals, especially breakfasts; *Angelitas*, C 7 y Cra 7, best coffee in town; *Piero's Pizza*, C 9 y Cra 5, good pizza.

Exchange At banks, or try the store at C 6, No 4-37, where "Don Dolar" will change cash and TCs; also Cochabamba store on Cra 6, one block from the square.

Shopping Pamplona is a good place to buy *ruanas*. Good indoor market.

Tourist Office C 5 y Cra 6, on main plaza.

Buses To Bogotá, US$13.80, 13-16 hrs; to Cúcuta, US$3, 2½ hrs; to Bucaramanga, US$3.45, 4 hrs, great views; to Málaga from main plaza, 5 a day from 0800, 6 hrs, US$3.75, beautiful but very hard journey (continues to Capitanejo); to Tunja, US$10.75, 12 hrs (leaving at 0600). To Berlin, US$2.10.

It is a run of 72 km from Pamplona through sparsely populated country, descending to an altitude of only 215m, to *Cúcuta*, capital of the Department of Norte de Santander, and only 16 km from the Venezuelan frontier. It was founded 1734, destroyed by earthquake 1875, and then rebuilt, elegantly, with the streets shaded by trees, and they are needed for it is hot: the mean temperature is 29°C. The cathedral, Av 5 between C 10 and 11, is worth a visit. Note the oil paintings by Salvador Moreno. Population: 525,465. Coffee is the great crop in the area, followed by tobacco. There are also large herds of cattle.

Cúcuta, because it is the gateway of entry from Venezuela, was a focal point in the history of Colombia during the wars for independence. Bolívar captured it after his lightning Magdalena campaign in 1813. The Bolívar Column stands where he addressed his troops on 28 February 1813. At El Rosario de Cúcuta, a small town of 8,000 inhabitants 14½ km from Cúcuta on the road to the frontier, the First Congress of Gran Colombia opened on 6 May 1821. It was at this Congress that the plan to unite Venezuela, Ecuador, and Colombia was ratified; Bolívar was made President, and Santander (who was against the plan) Vice-President. (Santander was born at a *hacienda* near El Rosario which is now being developed as a tourist centre.) The international bridge between Colombia and Venezuela is a few km from El Rosario; just beyond it is San Antonio del Táchira, the first Venezuelan town, and 55 km on is San Cristóbal.

Hotels A3 *Tonchalá*, C 10, Av 0, T 712005, good restaurant, swimming pool, a/c, airline booking office in hall; C *Casa Blanca*, Av 6, No 14-55, T 721455, good, reasonable meals, rec; C *Lord*, Av 7, No 10-58, T 713609, a/c, nice rooms, good restaurant and service, safe; D *Cacique*, Av 7, No 9-66, a/c, cold showers only, reasonable; D *Tundaya*, C 10, No 6-21, T 716161, 1-star, clean, safe, very good restaurant, breakfast US$10; E *Amaruc*, Av 5, No 9-37, T 717625, with fan, private bath, no hot water; F *Flamingo*, near Venezuelan Consulate, bath, fan, clean, private bathroom, noisy; **F** *Imperial*, Av 7, No 6-28, with bath, clean, secure, highly rec; **F** *Residencia Leo*, Av 6A, No 0-24 N, Barrio La Merced, T 41984, run by family Mogollón de Soto, private bath, clothes washing, free coffee all day, rec; **F** *Residencia Los Rosales*, near bus station, C 2, 8-39, fan, private bath, good. **G** *Residencias Nohra*, C 7, No 7-52, common bathroom, quiet. **Youth Hostel** at El Rosario de Cúcuta in *Hotel El Saman*, T 700411, with bar, restaurant, disco and pools. Details from Alcom in Bogotá.

Restaurants *"M"*, also called *Chez Esteban*, on road to Venezuela, very good; *La Brasa*, Av 5, C 7, good *churrascos*, modest prices; *Don Pancho*, Av 3, No 9-21, local menus, try *lengua criolla* (beef tongue); *Bahía*, just off main square, pleasant; other good restaurants at reasonable prices are *El Pollo Especial*, *Cantón* (Chinese) and *Las Acacias*, Av 5, rec.

Exchange A good rate of exchange for pesos is to be had in Cúcuta, at the airport, or on the border. **Banco Ganadero** and **Banco de Los Andes** near the plaza will give cash against Visa cards. There are money changers on the street all round the main square and many shops advertise the purchase and sale of bolívares. Change pesos into bolívares in Cúcuta or San Antonio—difficult to change them further into Venezuela.

Shopping A good range of leather goods at possibly the best prices anywhere in Colombia. Try C 10, Av 8 for leather boots and shoes. *Cuchitril*, Av 3 No 9-89, has a selection of the better Colombian craft work.

Tourist Office C 10, No 0-30, helpful, has maps, etc. At bus station (1st floor), and at airport. Other maps obtainable from Instituto Geográfico, Banco de la República building, in the main plaza.

DAS Office Av Primera, No 28-55, open 0800-1200 and 1400-2000 daily. Bus ride from town centre to Barrio San Rafael. Taxi from border US$1 (shared), will wait for formalities, then US$0.80 to bus terminal. Women should **not** visit this office alone. There is also an office at the airport which will deal with land travellers and a new building before the international bridge, on the left.

NB Cúcuta and the surrounding area is a great centre for smuggling. Be careful.

Airports At Cúcuta for Colombian services to Bogotá (twice a day with Avianca; also SAM and Intercontinental de Aviación) and other Colombian cities. Airport 10 mins by taxi from the town and the border, US$2. It is cheaper to buy tickets in Colombia than in advance in Venezuela. Avianca, C 13, No 5-09, T 277758. Also at San Antonio, Venezuela (30 mins) for Venezuelan domestic lines. At latter, be sure all baggage is sealed after customs inspection and the paper seals signed and stamped. **NB** Do not buy airline 'tickets' from Cúcuta to Venezuelan destinations, all flights go from San Antonio.

Transport For Venezuela: to San Cristóbal colectivo, US$2.40; bus, US$1.20 (Bolivariano); to San Antonio taxi US$7.20; bus and colectivo from C 7, Av 4, US$1. Bus to Bogotá, hourly, 17-24 hrs, US$21.40, Berlinas del Fonce 1000, 1400, 2 stops, including 15 mins in Bucaramanga (US$2.50 extra for *cochecama*), or Bolivariano, 20 hrs. There are frequent buses, even during the night (if the bus you take arrives in the dark, sit in the bus station café until it is light). To Bucaramanga, US$5, 6 hrs, with Berlinas del Fonce Pullman, several departures daily; from there a connection to Barranquilla can be made. To Tunja, US$11. The road is bad for the first part of the journey. Bus station: Av 7 and C 0 (a really rough area). Taxi from bus station to town centre, US$2.40.

Warning All travellers report that the bus station is overrun with thieves and conmen, who have tried every trick in the book. You must take great care, there is little or no police protection. On the 1st floor there is a tourist office for help and information and a café/snack bar where you can wait in comparative safety. Alternatively, go straight to a bus going in your direction, get on it, pay the driver and don't let your belongings out of your sight. Don't put your valuables in bus company "safety boxes". Make sure tickets are for buses that exist; tickets do not need to be "stamped for validity". For San Cristóbal, only pay the driver of the vehicle, not at the offices upstairs in the bus station. If you are told, even by officials, that it is dangerous to go to your chosen destination, double check. If the worst happens, the victimized should report the theft to the DAS office, who may be able to help to recover what has been stolen.

There are good roads to Caracas (933 km direct or 1,046 km via Mérida), and to Maracaibo (571 km). Bus to Caracas, 14 hrs, Expreso Occidente, two daily, or taxi colectivo.

From Venezuela to Colombia It is cheaper to fly Caracas-San Antonio, take a taxi to Cúcuta (US$7.20), then take an internal Colombian flight, than to fly direct from Caracas to Colombia. It will, of course, take longer. The airport transfer at San Antonio is well organized, with taxi drivers calling at necessary immigration offices, and at exchange places, the trip taking 25 mins. You do not have to buy your Colombian ticket in Cúcuta, you can make a reservation and purchase a ticket in a travel agency in Venezuela some days in advance (check exchange rates to see whether it is better to pay in Venezuela or Colombia). With a computer (*localizador*) reference number, you can avoid queues.

If arriving by bus, make sure bus stops at border for Venezuelan exit formalities. If you need one, obtain your Colombian tourist card and entrance stamp from the DAS office at the international bridge (before the bridge on the left). It is essential to obtain entry stamps (passport and/or tourist card) at the border. You will otherwise have problems with police checks, banks and leaving the country. You can also be fined. Border checks in Cúcuta are very strict. Air travellers can undertake all Colombian formalities at Cúcuta airport.

From Colombia to Venezuela All visitors need a visa and tourist card to enter Venezuela. There is a Venezuelan Consulate at Cúcuta (Av O, C 8, T 713983/712107—open 0800-1300, Mon-Fri) which supplies these—same applies at Venezuelan Embassy in Bogotá (may send you to Cúcuta for visas, etc). You must also provide two photographs for a visa; evidence of onward transportation out of Venezuela, often with a date, is officially required (but often not asked for in Cúcuta—it is necessary in Bogotá), and proof of funds is sometimes requested. In 1993/94 applicants had to pay US$30 for a visa in pesos only at the Banco Comercial Antioqueño on Av 6 (open until 1100 only), then take the receipt back to the Consulate (other banks are also used). Start at 0800 to get visa by 1400. You are strongly advised to obtain visa and card from the Venezuelan embassy in your own country, if you know in advance when you will be arriving at the frontier. (Just to visit San Antonio de Táchira in Venezuela, no documents are required.) Colombian exit/entrance formalities are at the international border bridge. If you do not obtain an exit stamp, you will be turned back by Venezuelan customs officials, and the next time you enter Colombia, you will be subject to a fine of US$7.50. You may be asked to pay further amounts at the Venezuelan border "because your visa is incorrect". Resist.

Entering or leaving Colombia by car, you must have your passport stamped at the DAS in town and the car papers stamped at the Customs (Aduana) office on the road to the airport—watch hard for the small sign. At the Customs Office is a restaurant serving excellent, large meals for US$2. Venezuelan car documentation is checked at the DIEX office in San Antonio. You must have a *carnet de passage* to enter Venezuela at this border, but **see Additional Notes on Motoring, p 27.**

7 km from Cúcuta is Zulia (Petróleo *buseta*), worth a visit if waiting for a Venezuelan tourist card.

The Andes chain N of Cúcuta is the branch which sweeps N to the Guajira Peninsula after the bifurcation of the Eastern Cordillera near Cúcuta: the other branch crosses into Venezuela. This western branch is the Sierra de Perijá y Motilones, in which live the Motilones Indians, the only Indians in Colombia who have refused to accept absorption into the larger nation. Little is known of them; they have killed many of the missionaries sent to convert them, and the anthropologists sent to study them.

THE NORTH COAST AND THE ISLANDS (3)

Caribbean Colombia, very different in spirit from the highlands: the coast stretches from the Darién Gap, through banana plantations, swamplands and palm plantations to the arid Guajira. The main resorts are Cartagena, which is also steeped in colonial history, and Santa Marta, near which is the Tairona national park with precolombian remains and the unique Sierra Nevada de Santa Marta coastal range.

The climate is much the same for the whole area: the heat is great—ranging from 26° to 36°C and there is a difference of only 2° between the hottest and coolest month. From November to March the heat is moderated by trade winds.

Character, like climate, seems to change in Colombia with the altitude. The *costeños* (the people of the coast) are gayer and more light-hearted than the more sober people of the highlands. (The contrast is sharply drawn in the great modern Colombian novel, *Cien años de soledad*, by Gabriel García Márquez.) The coastal people talk very fast, slurring their words and dropping the final s's.

NB In this region hotel prices are subject to high and low season variations: high season is 15 December-30 April, and 15 June-31 August.

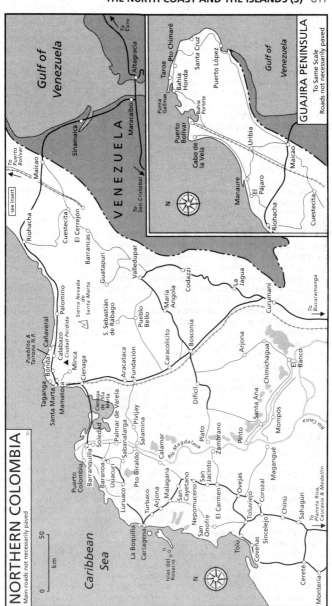

NORTHERN COLOMBIA
Main roads not necessarily paved

0   50
km

Caribbean Sea

Gulf of Venezuela

VENEZUELA

To Coro

Altagracia

Maicao

Sinamaica

Maracaibo

To Puerto Bolívar

see insert

Riohacha

Cuestecita

El Cerrejón

Barrancas

Guatapurí

Valledupar

Codazzi

La Jagua

Curumaní

To Bucaramanga

Palomino

Cañaveral

Pueblo & Tairona N.P.

Calabazo

Bonda

Taganga

Santa Marta

Mamatoco

Minca

Ciénaga

Ciénaga de Sta Marta

Sierra Nevada de Santa Marta

Ciudad Perdida

S. Sebastián de Rabago

Pueblo Bello

María Angola

Bosconia

Arjona

Chimichagua

El Banco

Aracataca

Fundación

Caracolicito

Difícil

Santa Ana

Mompós

Rio Cauca

Palmar de Varela

Pivijay

Salamina

Calamar

Plato

Zambrano

Pinto

Soledad

Sabanalarga

Barranquilla

Puerto Colombia

Baranoa

Usiacurí

Luruaco

La Boquilla

Cartagena

Islas del Rosario

Turbaco

Arjona

Pto Giraldo

Malagana

San Cayetano

Nepomuceno

San Jacinto

El Carmen

San Onofre

Tolú

Coveñas

Toluviejo

Ovejas

Corozal

Magangué

Sincelejo

Chinú

Sahagún

To Planeta Rica, Caucasia & Medellín

Cereté

Montería

N

Rio Magdalena

GUAJIRA PENINSULA
To Same Scale
Roads not necessarily paved

Gulf of Venezuela

Pto Chimaré

Taroa

Santa Cruz

Bahía Honda

Puerto López

Punta Gallinas

Bahía Portete

Puerto Bolívar

Cabo de la Vela

Uribia

Maicao

Manaure

El Pájaro

Riohacha

Cuestecita

N

Cartagena, old and steeped in history, is one of the most interesting towns in South America. Its population is 661,830. An arm of the river, 145 km long, canalized in 1650 by Spain—the Canal del Dique—from Calamar to Cartagena allows free access for ships from the up-river ports.

What interests the visitor is a comparatively small part of Cartagena, the old walled city almost completely surrounded by the Caribbean sea on the W, the waters of the Bay of Cartagena on the S, and lakes and lagoons to the N and E. Cartagena was one of the storage points for merchandise sent out from Spain and for treasure collected from the Americas to be sent back to Spain. A series of forts protecting the approaches from the sea, and the formidable walls built around the city, made it almost impregnable.

Cartagena was founded by Pedro de Heredia on 13 January 1533. There were then two approaches to it, Bocagrande, at the northern end of Tierra Bomba island—this was a direct entry from the Caribbean—and Boca Chica. Bocagrande was blocked after Admiral Vernon's attack in 1741, and thereafter the only approach was by the narrow channel of Boca Chica from the S. Boca Chica leads into the great bay of Cartagena, 15 km long and 5 km wide. The old walled city lies at the head of it.

Entering Boca Chica by sea, the island of Tierra Bomba is to the left. At the tip of a spit of land is the fortress of San Fernando (entrance fee, US$0.60; guide, US$1.50 for one to five people; if closed, ask around for the key). Boat trips to it (1 hr) are worth while (last one back is at 1830). Opposite it, right on the tip of Barú island, is the Fuerte San José. The two forts were once linked by heavy chains to prevent surprise attacks by pirates. North of Barú island stretches Manga island, much larger and now an important suburb. At its northern end a bridge, Puente Román, connects it with the old city. This approach was defended by three forts: San Sebastián del Pastelillo built between 1558 and 1567 (the Club de Pesca has it now) at the N western tip of Manga Island; the fortress of San Lorenzo near the city itself; and the very powerful Castillo San Felipe de Barajas inland on a height to the E of the city. Yet another fort, La Tenaza, protected the walled city from a direct attack from the open sea. The huge encircling walls were started early in the 17th century and finished by 1735. They were on average 12m high and 17m thick, with 6 gates. They contained, besides barracks, a water reservoir.

In spite of its daunting outer forts and encircling walls Cartagena was challenged again and again by enemies. Sir Francis Drake, with 1,300 men, broke in successfully in 1586, leading to a major reconstruction of the ramparts we see today. Nevertheless the Frenchmen Baron de Pointis and Ducasse, with 10,000 men, beat down the defences and sacked the city in 1697. But the strongest attack of all, by Sir Edward Vernon with 27,000 men and 3,000 pieces of artillery, failed in 1741 after besieging the city for 56 days; it was defended by the one-eyed, one-armed and one-legged hero Blas de Lezo, whose statue is at the entrance to the San Felipe fortress.

Cartagena declared its independence from Spain in 1811. A year later Bolívar used the city as a jumping-off point for his Magdalena campaign. After a heroic resistance, Cartagena was retaken by the royalists under Pablo Morillo in 1815. The patriots finally freed it in 1821.

The old walled city was in two sections, inner and outer. Much of the wall between the two was razed some years ago. Nearly all the houses are of one or two storeys. The houses in El Centro were occupied by the high officials and nobility. San Diego (the northern end of the inner town) was where the middle classes lived: the clerks, merchants, priests and military. The artisan classes lived in the one-storey houses of Getsemaní in the outer city. Today, the streets of the inner city are relatively uncrowded; budget hotels and restaurants are sprinkled thinly throughout the area. Immediately adjoining is the downtown sector, known as La Matuna, where vendors crowd the pavements and the alleys between the modern commercial buildings. Several middle range hotels are in this district, between Avs Venezuela and Urdaneta Arbeláez. South of the latter is Getsemaní, the outer city, where many colonial buildings survive; the greatest concentration of budget hotels and restaurants is here. Just under a kilometre from the old city, along an ocean boulevard, Bocagrande is a spit of land crowded with hotel and apartment towers. Thousands of visitors flock to the beach with its accompanying resort atmosphere, fast food outlets, shops and dirty seawater.

The old city streets are narrow. Each block has a different name, a source of confusion, but don't worry: the thing to do is to wander aimlessly, savouring the street scenes, and allow the great sights to catch you by surprise. Our map is marked with numerals for the places of outstanding interest. The most attractive streets have been given a star (*). Most of the "great houses" can be visited. Churches generally open to the public at 1800.

The numbers stand for the following places:

1 The Puente Román, the bridge which leads from the island of Manga into the Getsemaní district. Visitors should on no account miss seeing the *casas bajas* or low houses of Getsemaní, but be careful; it is not a very safe neighbourhood.

2 The chapel of San Roque (early 17th century), near the hospital of Espíritu Santo.

3 In an interesting plaza, the church of Santísima Trinidad, built 1643 but not consecrated till 1839. North of the church, at number 10, lived Pedro Romero, who set the revolution of 1811 going by coming out into the street shouting "Long Live Liberty".

4 The monastery and church of San Francisco. The church was built in 1590 after the pirate Martin Côte had destroyed an earlier church built in 1559. The first Inquisitors lodged at the monastery. From its courtyard a crowd surged into the streets claiming independence from Spain on 11 November 1811. The Iglesia de la Tercera Orden is now the Teatro Colón.

Immediately to the N is Plaza de la Independencia, with the landscaped Parque del Centenario just off it. At right angles to the Plaza runs the Paseo de los Mártires, flanked by the busts of nine patriots executed in the square on 24 February 1816 by the royalist Morillo when he retook the city. At its western end is a tall clock tower. Passing through the tower's arches (the main entrance to the inner walled city) we get to

5 The Plaza de los Coches. Around almost all the plazas of Cartagena arcades offer refuge from the tropical sun. On the W side of this plaza is the famous Portal de los Dulces, a favourite meeting place.

6 Plaza de la Aduana, with a statue of Columbus and the Palacio Municipal.

7 Church of San Pedro Claver and Monastery, built by Jesuits in 1603 and later dedicated to San Pedro Claver, a monk in the monastery, who was canonized 235 years after his death in 1654. He was called the Slave of the Slaves (El Apostol de los negros): he used to beg from door to door for money to give to the black slaves brought to the city. His body is in a glass coffin on the high altar, and his cell and the balcony from which he sighted slave ships are shown to visitors. Entry, US$0.60. Guides charge US$2. Open daily 0800-1800.

8 Plaza de Bolívar (the old Plaza Inquisición), modest, and with a statue of Bolívar. On its W side is

9 The Palacio de la Inquisición, established in 1610, but the building dates from 1706. The stone entrance with its coats of arms and well preserved and ornate wooden door is very notable. The whole building, with its balconies, cloisters and patios, is a fine example of colonial baroque. There is a modest historical museum at the Palacio, and a library. Entry charge US$0.75; good historical books on sale. Open Mon-Fri, 0800-1130, 1400-1700.

On the opposite side of the Plaza to the Palacio de la Inquisición, the Museo del Oro y Arqueológico has been installed in an old building. Gold and pottery, very well displayed. Entrance US$1, but closed on Sunday. There is a Naval Museum with maps, models and display of armaments a short way towards the city wall along C Baloco, entry US$0.75.

In the NE corner of Plaza de Bolívar is

10 The Cathedral, begun in 1575 and partially destroyed by Francis Drake. Reconstruction was finished by 1612. Great alterations were made between 1912 and 1923. A severe exterior, with a fine doorway, and a simply decorated interior. See the guilded 18th century altar, the Carrara marble pulpit, and the elegant arcades which sustain the central nave.

11 Church and convent of Santa Teresa, founded 1609.

12 The church and monastery of Santo Domingo, built 1570 to 1579 and now a seminary. The old monastery was replaced by the present one in the 17th century. Inside, a miracle-making image of Christ, carved towards the end of the 16th century, is set on a baroque 19th century altar. Most interesting neighbourhood, very little changed since the 16th century. In C Santo Domingo, No 33-29, is one of the great patrician houses of Cartagena, the Casa de los Condes de Pestagua, now the Colegio del Sagrado Corazón de Jesús. North of Santo Domingo, at

13 C de la Factoria 36-57 is the magnificent Casa del Marqués de Valdehoyos, now owned by the tourist authority and containing a Tourist Office; open to visitors.

14 The church and convent of La Merced, founded 1618. The convent—a prison during Morillo's reign of terror—was occupied by the Law Courts and its church is the Teatro Municipal,

but now appears to be in disrepair.

15 The monastery of San Agustín (1580), now the Universidad de Cartagena. From its chapel, now occupied by a printing press, the pirate Baron de Pointis stole a 500-pound silver sepulchre. It was returned by the King of France but the citizens melted it down to pay their troops during the siege by Morillo in 1815. Adjoining the university is the Edificio Ganem, which offers a good, free view of the city from the 9th floor.

16 The church of Santo Toribio de Mongrovejo. Building began in 1729. In 1741, during Admiral Vernon's siege, a cannon ball fell into the church during Mass and lodged in one of the central columns; the ball is now in a recess in the W wall. The font of Carrara marble in the Sacristy is a masterpiece. There is a beautiful carved ceiling (*mudéjar* style) above the main altar. Opens for Mass at 0600 and 1800, closed at other times.

17 Casa del Consulado (C Sargento Mayor) was one of the great houses but has now become a teachers' college.

18 Church and monastery of Santa Clara de Assisi, built 1617-21, now the Hospital de Santa Clara, but being converted into a hotel.

19 Plaza de las Bóvedas. The walls of Las Bóvedas, built 1799, are some 12m high and from 15 to 18m thick. Cars can drive along the rampart, from which there is a grand view of the harbour. At the base of the wall are 23 dungeons, now containing tourist shops. Both a lighted underground passage and a drawbridge lead from Las Bóvedas to the fortress of La Tenaza on the sea shore.

20 Casa de Núñez, just outside the walls of La Tenaza in El Cabrero district opposite the Ermita de El Cabrero and 5 mins from the old bullring; here lived Rafael Núñez, president (four times) and poet (he wrote Colombia's national anthem). His grandiose marble tomb is in the adjoining church. Mon-Fri 0800-1200, 1400-1800.

Three of the sights of Cartagena are off our map. One of them is the Fortress of San Fernando, already mentioned.

The Castillo San Felipe de Barajas, across the Puente Heredia (21) from the outer walled city, stands on the hill of San Lázaro, 41m above sea-level. Building began in 1639 and it was finished by 1657. Under the huge structure are tunnels lined with living rooms and offices. Some are open and lighted; visitors pass through these and on to the top of the fortress. Baron de Pointis, the French pirate, stormed and took it in 1697, but Admiral Vernon failed to reach it in the abortive attack of 1741. Entrance fee US$4 (half price for students and Colombians). Guide US$1.50 for one to five people. Open daily 0800-1800.

A lovely road leads to the summit of La Popa hill, nearly 150m high, from which there is a fine view of the harbour and the city (entry US$1); open daily 0800-1745. Here are the church and monastery of Santa Cruz and restored ruins of the convent dating from 1608. In the church is the beautiful little image of the Virgin of La Candelaria, reputed a deliverer from plague and a protector against pirates. Her day is 2 February. For nine days before the feast thousands of people go up the hill by car, on foot, or on horseback. On the day itself people carry lighted candles as they go up the hill. The name was bestowed on the hill because of an imagined likeness to a ship's poop. It is dangerous to walk up on your own; either take a guided tour, or take a public bus to Teatro Miramar at the foot of the hill (US$0.50), then bargain for a taxi up, about US$2.50. You can tour the old town and Bocagrande in a *chiva*, a brightly coloured wooden seated bus with a live band in the bus.

Festivals The other great feast, apart from Candlemas, is on in the second week of November to celebrate the independence of Cartagena. Men and women in masks and fancy dress roam the streets, dancing to the sound of *maracas* and drums. There are beauty contests and battles of flowers and general gaiety. This festival tends to be wild and can be dangerous. **Caribbean Music Festival** for 5 days in March, groups from all over the Caribbean region and beyond perform salsa, reggae, etc; loud and fun. There is a **film festival** at the end of April. Avianca offices everywhere have details of festival dates.

Art Gallery and Museum Contemporary Latin American paintings, **Banco Ganadero**, Plaza de la Aduana. Nearby is the **Museo de Arte Moderno** (open Mon-Fri, 0900-1200, 1500-1800, Sat, 1000-1200), opposite the San Pedro Claver church.

Warnings Carry your passport (or, safer, a notarized photocopy of it) at all times. Failure to present it on police request can result in imprisonment and fines. Regarding sea passages, see warning under Barranquilla (p 833). In addition, if offered a job on a ship to the USA, Central America, San Andrés or wherever, it is almost certainly a "con". Should you nevertheless believe it is genuine, insist on full documentation at the Seamen's Union office and do not make any arrangements on the street.

Beware also of self-appointed tourist guides who charge very highly for their services, and can turn nasty if thwarted. Bus travellers are met by people offering to recommend a hotel; their services are not necessary and may lead to "coincidental" theft later. See also **Security**

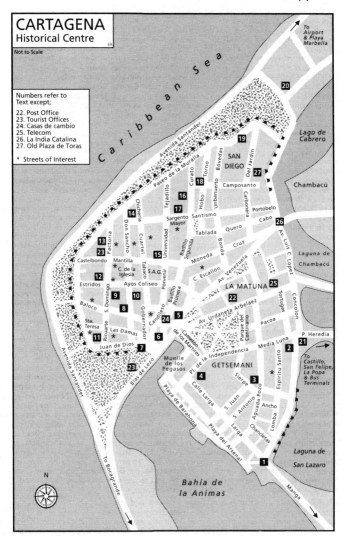

CARTAGENA
Historical Centre

Not to Scale

Numbers refer to
Text except;

22. Post Office
23. Tourist Offices
24. Casas de cambio
25. Telecom
26. La India Catalina
27. Old Plaza de Toras

* Streets of Interest

Caribbean Sea

To
Airport
& Playa
Marbella

Lago de
Cabrero

Chambacú

Avenida Santander

Paseo de la Muralla

Bovedas

SAN
DIEGO

Del Jardín

Camposanto

Laguna de
Chambacú

Chicheria

Curato

Torno

Hobo

Unbanuerto

Carbonera

Portobelo

Cabo

Tejadillo

Santismo

Tablada

Quero

Cruz

Av. Luis C. Lopez

Don Sancho

Cuartel

Universidad

Badillo
Segunda

Moneda

Bonda

Sargento
Mayor

Factoria

Castelbondo

Mantilla

C. de la
Iglesia

Tabaco

S.A.G.

Porvenir

C. Escallón

Av. Venezuela

LA MATUNA

Estridos

S. Domingo

Ayos Coliseo

Badillo
Primera

Baloco

Gobernador

Candilejo

Av. Urdaneta Arbeláez

Parque del
Centenario

Concolon

Sta.
Teresa

Las Damas

Pacoa

Ricaurte

Juan de Dios

Comercio
de los Mártires

Media Luna

P. Heredia

Blas de Lezo

Muelle
de los
Pegasos

Pl. de la Independencia

GETSEMANI

Sierpe

Espíritu Santo

To
Castillo,
San Felipe,
La Popa
& Bus
Terminals

Avenida Santander

Playa de Barahona

Calle Larga

S. Juan

Aguada Pozo

Ancho

Lomba

To Bocagrande

Playa del Arsenal

S. Antonio

Larga

Chancleras

Manga

Laguna de
San Lazaro

N

Bahía de
la Animas

---

in **Information for Visitors**. Expert pickpockets reported in crowded areas in town and on the beaches. Quiet Sunday mornings require special care, cameras a particular target. Generally, the central areas are reported safe and friendly, but should you require the police, there is a station in Barrio Manga. You may be offered drugs on the beaches, beware.

Hotels   On Bocagrande beach, 10 mins by bus from city: at the extreme tip is **L1-2** *Cartagena-Hilton*, El Laguito, T 650666, F 650661 (Apto Aéreo 1774, best equipped); **L2** *Hotel del Caribe*, Cra 1, No 2-87, T 650155, F 653707, colonial style with newer annexes, comfortable, all rooms a/c, stylish, nice grounds, swimming pool in the (expensive) restaurant, pancakes rec; **L3** *Capilla del Mar*, C 8, Cra 1, T 651140, F 655145, resort hotel, excellent French restaurant, swimming pool on top floor, be careful of their travel desk and check any reservations they make for you, no connection with restaurant of same name ½ km away; **L3** *Cartagena Real*, Av del Malecón, T 655590, F 654163, all suites, highrise. **A2-3** range hotels: *Decamerón*, Cra 1, No 10-10, T 654400, F 653738, all-inclusive resort; *Barlovento*, Cra 3, No 6-23, T 653965, smaller scale, 400m from beach; *Las Velas*, Av de las Velas 1-60, T 650590, F 650530, 3 nights min, holiday resort, good restaurant; *Costa del Sol*, Av 1 y C 9A, T 650866, tower with rooftop pool, very comfortable. **C** *India Catalina*, Cra 2, No 7-115, T 655392, very good, with a/c, safe, clean (acts as youth hostel); **C** *Residencias Internacional*, Av San Martín 4110, T 650675 (D in low season), small rooms, small bath, a/c, cold water, TV, uncomfortable beds, convenient location, friendly; opposite at No 5-86 is **B** *Flamingo* (D in low season), T 650301, with bath and a/c, clean, helpful, pleasant, eat on the terrace, highly rec; **D** *Leonela*, Cra 3, 7-142, T 654761, quiet, comfortable; **C** *Playa*, Av 2, No 4-87, T 650552, all rooms with private bathroom, a/c, very clean, open air bar, restaurant (breakfast, US$1), swimming pool, noisy disco next door; **D** *La Giralda*, Cra 3, No 7-166, T 654507, clean, friendly, with bath, fan, a/c dearer; **D** *Succar*, Cra 2, No 6-40, clean, helpful. **E** *Residencia Punta Canda*, C 7 between Cras 2 and 3, reasonable and everything works. **F** *La Sultana*, Av San Martín, No 7-44, clean, pleasant atmosphere. On Cra 3, there are plenty of small, pleasant **D** *residencias*, for instance *Mary*, Cra 3, No 6-52, T 652822, small, respectable, and Cra 3, No 5-29, cheaper in low season, clean and friendly.

In La Matuna: **C** *Del Lago*, C 34, No 11-15, T 653819, more for a/c, phone, no singles, reasonable restaurant, laundry, credit cards accepted, no parking; **D** *Montecarlo*, C 34, No 10-16, T 645835, more with a/c, good value, big neon sign on the roof, good reliable laundry next door, fair restaurant; **D** *San Felipe*, Cra 9, No 13-72, T 645439, central, close to old city, big café. In Old City: **D** *Hostal Baluarte*, Media Luna No 10-81, T 642208, with bath and fan, converted colonial house, family run, helpful, will arrange day trips, well-priced restaurant; **D** *Hostal Santo Domingo*, C Santo Domingo, No 33-46, basic but clean and quiet, well located, rec; **D** *Veracruz*, C San Agustín, No 6-15, opp San Agustín church (more with a/c), clean, safe, helpful but noisy from disco on ground floor. **E** *Doral*, Media Luna, No 10-46, nice, fan, large rooms, safe courtyard where you can park cycles/motorbikes, noisy at night, good cheap restaurant; **E** *Holiday*, Media Luna, No 10-47, clean, fan, friendly, hot water; **E** *Roma*, Tripita Media, with bath, basic; **E** *Hotel Familiar*, C del Guerrero, No 29-65, near Media Luna, T 648374, clean, friendly, rec; **F** *Lina*, San Andrés y Tripita, clean with restaurant; **F** *Viena*, San Andrés, No 30-53, T 646242, Belgian run, clean, safe, cooking facilities, washing machine, book exchange, excellent value, rec, restaurant *Algo Diferente* nearby under same management, profits help street children; **F** *Magdalena*, C Pacoa, with bath, cold water, fan, clean but small rooms; **F** *Media Luna*, Media Luna y Centenario, without bath, clean, good value; **F** *Monterrey*, Camellón de los Mártires (opposite the clocktower), clean, friendly, central, good Colombian meals in restaurant; **F** *Residencias Venecia*, C del Guerrero No 29-108, friendly, some rooms with fan, garden, washing facilities, clean and secure; **F** *Tropicana*, Plaza Independencia, run down but friendly, helpful and clean. The following are used frequently, but recently none has received good reports (ie insecure, poor value): **F** *Bucarica*, San Agustín 6-08, quite popular with travellers, but rooms vary a lot and acts as a brothel; **F** *El Refugio*, C Media Luna, No 10-35, clean, friendly; **F** *Hostal Valle*, C Media Luna, No 10-15, some rooms with private bath, free coffee, discounts for long stay, check the room before paying. Many cheap hotels on C Media Luna are brothels; area not advisable for women on their own. *Turístico Margie*, Av 2A, 63-175, Crespo district, convenient for airport, walking distance to old city (or bus), family-run, clean, modern. On the road to the airport are several hotels and **pensiones**, particularly at Marbella beach, eg **D** *Bellavista*, Av Santander, clean, fans, nice patio, English-speaking owner, Enrique Sedó, secure, nice atmosphere; right behind is **F** *Mirador del Lago*, clean, large rooms, fan, friendly owner.

NB Hotel prices rise for high season, 1 Nov-31 March, and June-July. From 15 Dec to 31 Jan they rise by as much as 50 per cent (ie increase Bocagrande hotels by at least a letter in our range at this time; in town nothing is below E, but price increases are not so steep); hotels tend to be heavily booked right through to March. Either book well in advance yourself, or avoid the city at this time. For hotel insurance, add 5%, plus US$0.05 pp per day.

Camping People camp on the beach, but may be troubled by thieves—and the police. Vehicle parking overnight possible at the Costa Norte Beach Club, 2 km NE on coast beyond the airport, US$4 per night.

Restaurants *Nautilus*, facing the statue of La India Catalina, seafood; another *Nautilus* (same menu and service) on road to airport in Marbella; and yet another *Nautilus*, Cra 3, Bocagrande, good but expensive; *Capilla del Mar*, rec, sea food dinner for 2, US$20-30;

all-you-can-eat buffet on Tues (shrimp) and Fri (seafood). Also in Bocagrande, Av San Martín, *Fontana di Trevi*, Italian; *Italia*, Av San Martín 7-55, good Italian food, excellent ice creams and sorbets; *Palacio de las Frutas*, Av San Martín y C 6, good *comida corrida*; *La Fonda Antioqueña*, Cra 2, No 6-161, traditional Colombian, nice atmosphere; *La Piragua*, Cra 2, an open-air bar with live music, dancing, pleasant. Good reasonably priced food in the chain restaurants: *Crepes y Waffles*, *Pizza por Metro* and *La Loca*.

Away from Bocagrande: *Pacos*, good bar/restaurant on Plaza Santo Domingo; *El Zorba*, Plaza Fernández, small, cosy, good music. On C Quero, close to *Zorba*, *La Tablada*, arty, usually good music, basic; *Mesón Taurino*, No 9-23, good, cheap. *Dalmacia*, C Santo Domingo, just off square, charming, run by a Croatian, rec, closes 2000. *La Langosta*, Av Venezuela, just outside old city walls, good food, reasonable prices; *La Crepería*, Plaza de Bolívar 3-110, excellent salads, fruit drinks, crêpes, gets busy around 1230; *Nuevo Mundo*, C 30, No 8B-62 serves typical menu, cheap, good sized servings. *El Koral*, next to *Hotel Doral*, Media Luna, good, cheap; *El Ganadero*, also on Media Luna, good value; *Bucarest*, Marbella, next to *Hotel Bellavista*, for seafood and juices. Many restaurants around Plaza Independencia have good value meals. eg *Fonda El Socorro*, C Larga on Plaza Independencia. Restaurants in C San Andrés are usually cheaper, with plenty to eat. Several Chinese restaurants in the old city, eg *WingWah*, C Ayos, good food, rec, *Dragón de Oro*, C Venezuela, good, inexpensive and *Jumbo*, C Tabaco, good Chinese and local food, *churrasco*, large portions, reasonable prices. Vegetarian restaurant and health food shop, *Santísimo*, C Quero, lunch under US$1; *Tienda Naturista*, C Quero 9-09, good cheap vegetarian; *Govinda*, C de Necesidad, No 36-50, also vegetarian, mixed reports. *Panadería La Mejor*, Av Arbeláez, good for breakfast, fine wholemeal bread, coffee, yoghurt, expensive; *Panificadora la Española*, C 8, No 7-61, fresh bread and pastries.

At cafés try the *patacón*, a biscuit made of green banana, mashed and baked; also in Parque del Centenario in early morning. At restaurants ask for *sancocho* a local soup of the day of vegetables and fish or meat. Also try *obleas* for a snack, biscuits with jam, cream cheese, or caramel fudge, and *buñuelos*, deep-fried cheese dough balls.

Banks and Money Changers Banco Unión Colombiana, Av Venezuela (C 35), No 10-26, La Matuna, changes American Express TCs up to a maximum of US$300, without commission. **Banco Industrial**, good rates for TCs; **Banco Cafetero**, gives money on Visa cards. There are many *cambios*; many in the arcade at Torre Reloj and adjoining streets change Amex TCs; also *Caja de Cambio Caldas*, Av San Martín, No 4-118, Bocagrande, and on the corner of Plaza de los Coches, downtown. Be sure to count the pesos yourself before handing over your dollars. Never change money on the street, they are nearly all crooks and will short-change you. **American Express** (Tierra Mar Aire), Bocagrande, Cra 4, No 7-196, is a travel agency downstairs, will change TCs and give cash against credit cards upstairs. TCs can be changed Sat am (arrive early) at **Joyería Mora**, Román 5-39, and at El Portal nearby, in the old city.

Consulates Venezuelan, C 5, No 10-106, open to 1500, possible to get a visa the same day (US$30): you need onward ticket, two photos, but ensure you get a full visa not a 72-hour transit unless that is all you need. **Canadian Honorary Consul** (for emergencies only), C de la Inquisición con Santo Domingo, esq, No 33-08, Apto 201. **Danish**, Cra 10, No 5-68. **Finnish**, Av San Martín, Centro Comercial Bocagrande, 3 piso, 308, T 657672. **Norwegian Consulate**, Edif Banco Central Hipolecario, La Matuna, T 654639. **Panamanian Consulate**, Calle 69, No 4-97, T 662079.

Entertainment Casino Turístico, Av San Martín and Casino de Caribe at Pierino Gallo shopping centre, Bocagrande.

Good discos in Bocagrande eg *La Escollera*, also in Old City, Parque La Marina, upmarket, in stately building. Bar *La Muralla* on the city wall W of Plaza Bolívar, open at night only, live music at weekends, romantic, but drinks about US$6; for salsa, *Quiebra Canto*, C Media Luna at Parque Centenario, nice atmosphere.

Post Office beside Avianca office between Avs Venezuela and Urdaneta Arbeláez. **Telecom** Av Urdaneta Arbeláez nr corner of C 34; long distance phones behind this building; long distance also in Bocagrande.

Places of Worship Anglican Church, C Ricuarte, services in English can be arranged.

Shopping A good selection of *artesanías* at *Compendium* on Plaza Bolívar, but in general (except for leather goods) shopping is much better in Bogotá. Handicraft shops in the Plaza de las Bóvedas. Woollen *blusas* are good value; try the *Tropicano* in Pierino Gallo building in Bocagrande. Also in this building are reputable jewellery shops. *H Stern* has a jewellery shop in the Pierino Gallo shopping centre and at the *Hilton Hotel*. Suntan oils and lotions can vary in price as much as 100%—shop around. Comercial Centro Getsemaní, C Larga between San Juan and Plaza de la Independencia, a large new shopping centre has many establishments. *Magali París*, Av Venezuela y C del Boquete, is an a/c supermarket, with cafetería (pizza, good café con leche), good for escaping the heat when exploring old Cartagena. Good badges for backpacks from the shops along the wall of the old prison.

Market There is a new market out of town, which is disappointing; bus from Av Urdaneta Arbeláez. The fish market is in the SE suburbs of the old city.

Watersports Fishing; yachting. Windsurf rental, Bocagrande, US$6.50 per hour. Diving: *Catagena Divers*, Marina Todomar, Cra 2 No 15-346, Bocagrande, T 654493, 2 dives incl all equipment US$60, also snack and drinks; *La Tortuga Dive Shop*, Edif Marina del Rey, 2-23 Av del Retorno, Bocagrande, T 656995, 2 dives US$70, faster boat, same price at Hotel Caribe Dive Shop. Recompression chamber at the naval hospital, Bocagrande.

Bullfights and Cockfights The former take place mainly in January and February in the new Plaza de Toros on Av Pedro de Heredia away from the centre; the old, wooden Plaza de Toros (no 27 on the map) is a fine structure, but is no longer in use. Cockfights are held throughout the year on Sat, Sun and holidays. On Sat and Mon at 1500 cockfighting takes place at the Gallerita Popular de la Quinta and on Sun at 1600 at Club Gallístico Pedro Rhenals in El Bosque.

Tourist Office Empresa Promotora de Turismo de Cartagena, Av Blas de Lezo, Ed Muelle de los Pegasos, T 651843; also in Parque Flanagan, Bocagrande, T 654987, and at the airport, who will call cheaper hotels (all 3 open 0700-1900 daily, allegedly). There is also a hotel reservations office at the airport but you will only be given information on the more expensive hotels. Town plan for US$0.20. CNT, Calle de la Factoría, Casa del Marqués de Valdehoyos, Cra 3, No 36-57, T 647015/9, open daily till 1730, US$0.25 to tour the house. For information T 113. Recommended guide, Fernando Vargas Osorio, C de Magdalena, No 7-52.

DAS just beyond Castillo San Felipe, behind the church (ask), Plaza de la Ermita (Pie de la Popa), T 664649, helpful. DAS passport office is in C Castelbondo, near Plaza de la Artillería.

Local Transport Within the city large buses (with no glass in windows) cost US$0.10, short-wheelbase type (with glass windows), US$0.25. Taxis from Bocagrande to the centre should be less than US$1.50; for airport, see below. Try to fix price before committing yourself. A horse-drawn carriage can be hired for US$10, opposite *Hotel El Dorado*, Av San Martín, in Bocagrande, to ride into town at night (romantic but rather short ride).

Car Rental National and Hertz at airport; Avis at *Hilton Hotel*.

Airport Crespo, 1½ km from the city, reached by local buses from Blas de Lezo, SW corner of inner wall. Bus from airport to Plaza San Francisco US$0.25. Taxi to Bocagrande US$2.45, to town US$1.55 (official prices). Tourist information desk gives list of taxi prices. Good self-service restaurant. No exchange facilities. Commuter flights to Barranquilla. SAM and Avianca (T 644446) offices both near the post office. From December to March all flights are overbooked—even reconfirming and turning up 2 hrs early doesn't guarantee a seat; don't book a seat on the last plane of the day.

Shipping There are modern wharves. It is possible to ship a car from Cartagena to Panama. For the new ferry service to Panama, **see p 827**. Two other companies which will ship vehicles to Panama: Hermann Schwyn, Edif Concasa, 10th floor, T 647450, and Mundinaves, Cra 53, No 64-72, of 301, T 454691. Cargo ships are not allowed to take passengers to San Andrés; some may risk it, charging about US$25. You have to ask the captain; ships leave from Embarcadero San Andrés, opp Plaza de la Aduana. There are boats leaving most days for points S along the coast, for example to Turbo cargo boats take 24 hrs, all in cost about US$15 pp, and up the river Sinú to Montería, and the Atrato as far as Quibdó. For the trip to Quibdó **see p 860**. See also under **Warning**, above.

Buses A new bus terminal opened in 1995, 30 mins from town, take city buses "Terminal de Transportes", or "Puzón"; previously, all long-distance buses left from C 32, with Av Pedro Heredia, near foot of San Felipe fortress. Pullman bus from Cartagena to **Medellín** 665 km, US$29 (Brasilia, or Rápidos Ochoa, slightly cheaper, rec). Several buses a day, book early (2 days in advance at holiday times), takes 13-16 hrs. The road is now paved throughout, but in poor condition. To **Santa Marta**, US$8.40 (with Brasilia, C 32, No 20D-55), 4 hrs, also cheaper lines, US$7.20. To **Barranquilla** US$2.75 with Transportes Cartagena, 3 hrs, or US$5 with Expreso Brasilia pullman or La Costeña, US$3.10, 2 hrs. To/from **Bogotá** via Barranquilla and Bucaramanga with Expreso Brasilia pullman or Copetran, eight a day, US$48, may take 21-28 hrs, depending on number of check-points. To **Magangué** on the Magdalena US$8.50, 4 hrs with Brasilia; to **Mompós**, Unitransco, 0530, 12 hrs inc ferry crossing from Magangué, US$9.50. To **Valledupar** with Expreso Brasilia, pullman US$10 (with a ½ hour stop in Barranquilla), for Sierra Nevada and Pueblo Bello. To **Riohacha**, US$12. Bus to **Maicao** on Venezuelan frontier US$16.75 (with Expreso Auto Pullman, Expreso Brasilia at 2000, or Unitrasco), 12 hrs; the road is in good condition, except for 30 km.

Beaches Take bus from Plaza de la Independencia to Bocagrande, whose beaches can be dirty and often crowded. Marbella beach, just N of Las Bóvedas (the locals' beach, and therefore quieter than Bocagrande) is good for swimming, though subject at times to dangerous currents. The Boca Chica beach is dirty, and the boat service there unreliable. Boats leave from Muelle de los Pegasos; the round trip can take up to 2 hrs each way. *Ferry Dancing*, about half the price of luxury boats, carries dancing passengers; the much faster launches are more expensive. You can take a tour round the fort of San Fernando in a dugout canoe. There are boats from the city; the last return trip is at 1230. Swimming is good. Boats taking in Boca Chica and San Fernando include Alcatraz, which runs a daily trip from the Muelle Turístico leaving at about 1000, returning at 1530 (very good juice stands along the wharf which also sell *patacones con queso*, fried plantain with a slice of cheese). Boats to the Islas del Rosario (see below) may stop at the San Fernando fortress and Playa Blanca on the Isla de Baru for 1 hr (bargain with boatman to leave you, camp on the beach, and continue the cruise next day, or later, take a hammock, food and water since these are expensive to obtain on the island, if at all. Playa Blanca is crowded am, but peaceful after the tour boats have left). There are several restaurants on the beach, the best *La Sirena* run by Carmen (La Española), good food, lunch US$4.50, hammocks for hire US$2.50, if available. Another is run by a French/Colombian couple. You can also reach Playa Blanca by taking the bus to Puerto Caballo, crossing the Canal de Dique by canoe and thence by truck to the beach; if walking, 2½ hrs in all. If staying the night at Playa Blanca in cabañas or tents, beware of ferocious sandflies. **NB** Pay for boat trips on board if possible, and be certain that you and the operator understand what you are paying for. You are taking a risk if you buy tickets on shore.

Islas del Rosario

The National Park of **Corales del Rosario** embraces the archipelago of Rosario (a group of 30 coral islets 45 km SW of the Bay of Cartagena) and the mangrove coast of the long island of Baru to its furthest tip. Isla Grande and some of the smaller islets are easily accessible by day trippers and those who wish to stay in one of the hotels. Permits are needed for the rest. The islands represent part of a coral reef, low-lying, densely vegetated and with narrow strips of fine sand beaches. Rosario (the largest and best conserved) and Tesoro both have small lakes, some of which connect to the sea. There is an incredible profusion of aquatic and bird life here. An Aquarium in the sea is worth visiting, US$2, not included in boat fares. Many of the smaller islets are privately owned.

Travel agencies and the hotels offer launch excursions from the Muelle Turístico, leaving 0800-0900 and returning 1600-1700, costing from US$10 to US$25, lunch included; free if staying at one of the hotels. Book in advance. Rec are Excursiones Roberto Lemaitre, C 8, No 4-66, Bocagrande, T 652872 (owner of *Club Isla del Pirata*). They have the best boats and are near the top end of the price range. *Yates Alcatraz* are more economical; enquire at the quay (a modern, 2-storey circular glass building, half way along, is the departure point; it's also the Tourist Information Office). Apart from fish and coconuts, everything is imported from the mainland, fresh water included. *Hotel del Caribe* in Bocagrande has scuba lessons in its pool followed by diving at Islas del Rosario, US$230 and up.

Hotels A2 *Club Isla del Pirata*, mainland booking office at C 8, No 4-66, Bocagrande, T 652873, F 652862, complex occupies a tiny islet in the archipelago. There is a daily launch service to and from Cartagena operated by the hotel, it also carries day trippers. Room price pp inc meals, add 14% tax. **L3** *San Pedro de Majagua*, mainland office at Cra 5, No 8-59, Bocagrande, T 652745, F 652745, inside *Restaurant Capilla del Mar*, under the same ownership. Complex occupies part of Isla Grande, in the Rosario archipelago. Hotel provides free (for guests) daily launch service to and from Cartagena. Price pp, inc meals. *Casa Blanca*, white with arched windows, former family home, converted to luxury 5-star hotel.

Excursions from Cartagena To the little fishing village of *La Boquilla*, E of Cartagena, about 20 mins past the airport. A luxury hotel has been built nearby. One small hotel, **E** *Los Morros* (clean, good food) and campsite, well appointed and maintained, clean, showers, restaurant and small market, tents rented with matresses. On Sat and Sun nights people dance the local dances. Go there by taxi, US$3 (there is a reasonable bus service, and Carlos drives a green Dodge regularly to the bus terminal, US$0.50); can be dangerous for pedestrians and cyclists. Visit the mangrove swamps nearby to see the birds. Golf courses are under development here. On the coast, 50 km NE is Galera Zamba, no accommodation but good local food. Nearby are the clay baths of Volcán del Totumo, in beautiful surroundings. To **Turbaco**, 24 km SE by road; Botanical Garden, 1½ km before village on the left, superb guides, worth a visit for ½-day excursion. To **San Jacinto**, 1½ hrs (73 km) by road S of Cartagena, good place for local craft work, eg hand woven hammocks. Bus from Cartagena US$2.45.

South of Cartagena

About 60 km SE of Cartagena is *Malagana* (**G** *Residencia Margarita*, friendly, fan, basic). *Sincelejo*, capital of Sucre Department, is a cattle centre 193 km S of Cartagena on the main road to Medellín (pop 148,420). It is well known for the dangerous bull-ring game in January, likened to the San Fermín festivities in Pamplona, Spain, in which bulls and men chase each other. Also at Eastertime there is the "Fiesta del Burro" where they dress up donkeys and prizes go to the best and the funniest. A big party for three days. The town is hot, dusty and power cuts are common.

Hotels B *Marsella*, C 21, No 23-59, T 820729; **D** *Majestic*, Cra 20, No 21-25, T 821872; same range *Ancor*, Cra 25, No 20A-45, T 821125; **E** *Panorama*, Cra 25, 23-108, a/c; **E** *Santander*, corner of Plaza Santander, with bath, balconies, good restaurant, *La Olla*, opposite.

20 mins from Sincelejo, on the coast is *Tolú* (several friendly *residencias*, D-F, and many fish stalls along the beach) with unsigned beaches—ask to be let off the bus. Bus to Medellín, US$20, 8-10 hrs, Brasilia or Rápido Ochoa. A good trip from Tolú is by boat 3 hrs to Múcura island in the Islas de San Bernardo. Good for camping but take your own supplies. Trips to the mangrove lagoons also rec. There are better beaches at *Coveñas*, 20 mins further SW (196 km S of Cartagena). It is the terminal for the crude oil pipeline from the Barco oilfields N of Cúcuta, 420 km away. (Hotels: *La Fragata*, on beach; better is **D** *Cabañas La Coquera*, 1½ km N of bridge, cabins on beach, fully equipped; **E** *Cabañas El Tesoro*, clean, good atmosphere but plenty of mosquitos; **E** *Mediterráneo*, next to beach, restaurant, friendly, modern.) W of Coveñas are beautiful beaches at Porvenir, no food available, afternoon buses infrequent. Tolú and Coveñas can be reached by turning off the main road at Ovejas, 40 km N of Sincelejo.

127 km S of Sincelejo is *Planeta Rica*, 60 km beyond which there is a camping site in the grounds of the *Parador Chambacú* (T 226946, US$4 per tent); next door is the **C** *Mesón del Gitano* (T Medellín 268-3408); **F** *Residencia Bonaire*, good, quiet, clean, TV in lounge. Eleven km further on is *Caucasia*, which makes a good stopping point if you want to break the journey from Cartagena to Medellín. *Auto Hotel*, Cra 2, No 22-43, T 226355, best, quiet, heavily booked; **F** *Hotel Catalina*, good food, friendly, noisy; **D** *Hostería Horizontes*, calm, spacious, two swimming pools, good restaurant; **E** *Residencias San Francisco*, Cra 49 y C 45, with bath, good value; Chinese restaurant, 3 doors up, good cheap food; **F** *Del Río*, with bath, clean, close to bus station, free morning coffee but avoid front rooms on street; **F** *Residencia El Viajero*, Cra 2, No 23-39, near centre, quiet, clean, ceiling fan; **F** *Londres*, very clean, good value, good restaurant; **G** *San Martín*, close to market. A nice place to visit is the Jardín Botánico, entrance fee US$0.25. Buses to Medellín US$8.50, 7 hrs; to Cartagena US$16 (Brasilia), US$15 (Rápido Ochoa), US$10 (2nd class, 17 hrs). 50 km S of Caucasia is *Taraza* (**G** *Residencia Magdalena*, friendly, fan, basic but noisy bar). About half way between Caucasia and Medellín is *Valdivia* with a spectacular bridge over the Cauca. The road continues to Yarumal (**see p 856**).

Montería (municipal population 266,850), capital of Córdoba Department, on the E bank of the river Sinú, can be reached from Cartagena by air, by river boat, or from the main highway to Medellín. (Bus from Cartagena—dual carriageway almost completed, US$11, 5 hrs, with Brasilia, has own terminal in Montería, or colectivo, US$10, also 5 hrs.) It is the centre of a cattle and agricultural area turning out tobacco, cacao, cotton and sugar. Compared with other Caribbean cities there is little to attract the tourist except for the one fine church, picturesque street life and the extremely friendly people. Average temperature: 28°C. Road to Planeta Rica (airport).

Hotels A3 *Sinú*, Cra 3, C 31 y 32, T 823355, F 823980, a/c and swimming pool, TV, restaurant; **D** *Alcázar*, Cra 2, No 32-17, T 824900, comfortable, friendly, restaurant not always open; **F** *Brasilia*, clean, friendly, good value; **F** *Embajador*, fan, OK; many cheap dives around; **F** *Residencias Imperial*, Cra 2.

67 km W of Montería, on the coast, is *Arboletes* a small quiet town with a mud lake nearby of volcanic origins, worth a visit. **Hotels**: **E** *Ganadero*, fan, bath, good beds; **E** *Aristi*, very clean but small windows; **F** *Julia*, on the main square, no private bathrooms. Other accommodation along the beach. *Guido's* restaurant is probably the best. You can "swim" in

the mud lake, then wash off in the ocean, 100m away. Buses: 4 a day to Turbo, 5-6 hrs, US$5.40, 10 a day to Montería, 3 hrs, US$2.40.

The unmade road continues to Turbo (see below), **Chigorodó** (F *Residencial Tobi*, fan), **Dabeiba**, 186 km S of Turbo (F *Residencial Diana*, on main street, simple, clean, helpful), **Cañasgordas** (G *Doña Concha*, private bath, modern, good value), Antioquia (**see p 856**) and Medellín. Scenic, but a long, bumpy ride.

On the Gulf of Urabá is the port of **Turbo**, now a centre of banana cultivation, which is booming. It is a rough frontier community, not too law-abiding. Turbo may be reached from Cartagena and from Medellín (6 buses a day, a gruelling 17 hrs, US$12; to Montería, 8 hrs, US$9, bad road, several army checkpoints). Boats are available to Cartagena and up the Río Atrato to Quibdó, but you need plenty of time; services are intermittent and unreliable. **Hotels**: **D** *Castillo de Oro*, best, reliable water and electricity; **D** *Playa Mar*, good, but somewhat run down; **D** *Sausa*, running water in early morning only, helpful owners, pleasant dining room; **F** *Residencia Sandra*, good; **F** *Residencia Turbo*, friendly, good; **F** *Residencia Marcela*, friendly, quiet, secure, best value; **G** *Residencia El Golfo*, friendly, good; in Playa district: *Miramar*, *Rotitom*, both D. No banks are open for exchange of TCs on Monday or Tuesday; try exchanging money in stores.

There is a DAS office at the Postadero Naval, Cra 13 between Cs 101 and 102, open 0800-1630.

To visit the **Los Katíos National Park** (see below), go first to the Inderena office in Turbo, where all necessary information is available (recommended trip). The office is 1 km along the road to Medellín.

A description of routes by boat and overland from Colombia to Panama will be found below; note that if going from Colombia to Panama via Turbo you should get an exit stamp from the DAS office. There is also a DAS office in Capurganá (see below), opp *Hotel Uvita*, and a Panamanian consultate, but best not to leave it that late. If leaving Colombia, check the facts in Cartagena (or any other place with a DAS office). If arriving from Panama, go to the DAS in Turbo for your entry stamp. We have been informed that the immigration office at the Panamanian port of Puerto Obaldía is sometimes obstructive (all baggage will be checked for drugs, adequate funds for your stay may have to be shown—US$400, TCs or credit card; a ticket out of Panama is required, although a ticket from another Central American country may do). Think twice about taking a trip in a small boat between Panama and Colombia other than the regular boats shown below: the majority are contraband, even arms runners and if stopped, you will be in trouble. (Even if not stopped you will have difficulty obtaining a DAS entry stamp because the captain of the boat must state officially that he is carrying passengers into Colombia.) If taking a reputable cargo boat be sure to arrange with the captain the price and destination before departure. Boats may also be stopped outside Turbo for medical checks: yellow fever inoculations will be given (free) to all without a certificate. Spend your surplus pesos in Colombia, they are impossible to change at fair rates in Panama.

NB If travelling from Panama to Colombia by coastal boat or land, we strongly advise you to aim for Turbo (or Buenaventura) and obtain your entry stamp from the DAS office there. We have had many reports from travellers being fined or accused of illegal entry who have requested entry stamps at other DAS offices. A police stamp is no substitute.

From Colombia to Panama

The simplest way is to fly from Barranquilla, Bogotá, Cali, Cartagena, Medellín or San Andrés. By sea, there is a new ferry service (Dec 1994) from Cartagena (Terminal Marítimo beyond the Muelle Turístico) to Colón (Cristóbal). The ship, the *Crucero Express* is operated by Promotora de Navegación SA of Panama City, subsidiary of Flota Mercante Grancolombiana. Sailings from Cartagena are Tues, Thur and Sun 1630 arriving the following morning at 1000. From Colón, Mon, Wed and Fri, same times. Prices are: US$70 pp for 4 people in a quadruple cabin (US$80 pp for 3), US$95 pp, 2 travellers, one way (one person min, US$135), including cabin, dinner and breakfast, US$195 pp for a suite. Motor cycles US$50, cars US$125, with trailer US$180; bicycles free. This is a typical ro-ro ferry with disco, casino, jacuzzi, duty free etc, capacity for 1600 passengers and 400 metres of vehicle deck space (which could be over 200 cars but commercial vehicles and freight will also be carried). Latest information is that, so far, the passenger service is operating, but conditions for the transport of wheeled traffic have not been agreed by the two governments. Some cars and larger vehicles (eg campers) are being transported from Panama to Colombia. On arrival in Colombia, entry is straightforward, car registration, fumigation and customs no problem. Permit for 90 days granted if requested, no *carnet* or bond asked for, only passport and car ownership certificate. Also rec to stock up with film on board at US$4 for 36 exposures. For further information: T 286-3050 (Bogotá), reservations: T 342-1330, F 336-2714 (Bogotá), or T 607722 for information in Cartagena, or any major travel agent. In Panama City, reservations T 633322, F 633326.

There are also various routes involving sea and land crossings around or through the **Darién Gap**, which still lacks a road connection linking the Panamanian Isthmus and South America. Detailed descriptions of these routes are given in the *Mexico and Central American Handbook* (although in the direction Panama-Colombia). While maps of the region are available, there is no substitute for seeking informed local advice. In all cases, it is essential to be able to speak Spanish. See also **Notes and Cautions** below.

On the Caribbean side, the starting point is Turbo on the Gulf of Urabá. From Turbo boats sail to Acandí, 3 hrs, Capurganá and Zapzurro (all in Colombia) and Puerto Obaldía (Panama), normally at 0900 daily, US$25, via Capurganá (emigration formalities). Enquire for the best passage. There are also cargo boats from Cartegena to Capurganá which take passengers, 30-50 rough hours, US$25-30, take hammock. From Puerto Obaldía (see above on immigration), boats go to Colón, planes to Panama City (daily except Sun). **Acandí**, a town of about 7,000 people, has several *residencias*, eg **F** *Central*, clean, safe; **G** *Pilar*, clean; **F** *Acandí*, OK. Most have their own electricity generators. A little further N is **Capurganá**, now a small tourist resort with several hotels: **B** *Calipso*, a/c, good facilities; **D** *Náutico*, cabins, clean and friendly; **E** *Al Mar*; **E** *Uvita*, with bath, clean and safe, by harbour; and cheaper accommodation: **G** *Don Blas*, basic. Across the Panamanian border, **E** *Residencial Cande* in Pto Obaldía is good with meals at US$1.50. There is an overland route from Puerto Obaldía which involves a 4-hour walk to the foot of the Darién range (guide essential, US$10), crossing the hills to the Río Tuquesa (3 hrs) and following the river downstream with a great many crossings and one night camping out, to Maranganti (immigration post). From here a dugout can be taken to B Vigía; walk to the next village, Villa Calleta (take care with directions on this stretch). From Villa Calleta you walk along the Río Chucucanaque to join the Yaviza-Panama City road near La Pinita. Note that locals on this route are very wary of foreigners (much illegal immigration).

Two alternative routes from Turbo cross the central Gap to Paya, from where there is a well-trodden route to Yaviza: Paya-Pucuro, 6 hrs on foot; Púcuro-Boca de Cupe, by dugout, US$20-50; Boca de Cupe-Pinogana, also by dugout, US$15 pp, plus a walk, 2 hrs in all; Pinogana-Yaviza, walk and ferries/dugouts. From Yaviza (one hotel, **E** *Tres Américas*, basic) buses can be caught to Panama City, US$15, 10-14 hrs, road subject to wash-outs.

The first route to Paya: motorboat from Turbo across the Bahía de Colombia, through the Great Atrato Swamp and up the Río Atrato, with much birdlife to be seen (US$10 if scheduled, US$130 to hire a boat). At Travesía, also called Puente América, at the confluence of the Río Cacarica, you can buy limited provisions. There is a restaurant and rooms to stay in Travesía. From Travesía you go by another boat to Bijao (3 hrs, up to US$120). **NB** Both Travesía and Bijao are very expensive places to buy supplies, but worse still they have become anti-gringo (1994); we have been told of robbery by officials. From Bijao you have to get by boat to Cristales in the Los Katios National Park; the Inderena rangers may take you for up to US$100 per boat. At Cristales there is an Inderena hut; 7-8 hrs through the Park on foot is Palo de los Letras, the frontier stone, from where it is 4-6 hrs to Paya. A guide is strongly recommended. It is best to take two days for this section. You can approach this route from Quibdó down the Río Atrato to Travesía (see Section 6). Get your Panamanian entry stamp in Boca de Cupe or Púcuro (enquire: it can be very difficult to get an entry stamp anywhere before Panama City on this route; try at every opportunity as hikers have been detained in the capital for not having an entry stamp. It may help to prove you have adequate funds for your stay). Between Travesía and Yaviza there are some walking alternatives to taking river boats, detailed in the *Mexico and Central American Handbook*.

The Katios National Park (**Warning**: entry by motorized vehicle is prohibited), extending in Colombia to the Panamanian border, can be reached by boat from Turbo most days, charging US$8. The boats, normally going up the Atrato to Riosucio, or beyond, will leave you at the Inderena headquarters of the Park in Sautatá. Ask in Turbo harbour when they are leaving. You should have a permit from Inderena in Turbo for the Park, US$0.75, or you can pay in the park. Arrange your return trip Sautatá—Turbo with the park guide at Sautatá beforehand. Boats do not normally stop. The Park can be visited with mules from the Inderena headquarters in Sautatá (cabins US$5.50 pp, or rangers may offer free space for your hammock, very friendly). Food can be ordered half a day in advance. In the park is the Tilupo waterfall, 125m high; the water cascades down a series of rock staircases, surrounded by orchids and fantastic plants. This is 6 hrs return trip. A 5 hr trip passing through splendid jungle is required for two other fine waterfalls, the Salto de La Tigra and Salto de La Tendal. A full day's hike is recommended to Alto de Limón for a fine view of primary forest. You can stay overnight in a hut. Also in the park are the Alto de la Guillermina, a mountain behind which is a strange forest of palms called "mil pesos", and the Ciénagas de Tumaradó, with red monkeys, waterfowl and alligators.

The second route to Paya: take a boat from Turbo across the Gulf of Urabá into the Río Tarena to **Unguía**, F *Residencias Viajero*, with bath; **G** *Doña Julia*, also with bath. Also basic restaurants. From here it is 3-4 hrs to the frontier, then 3 hrs to the Río Paya. You then hike down the Paya river through dense jungle to Paya itself (about 12 hrs). Do not attempt the Unguía-Paya route without a guide. We have heard of a number of other routes successfully attempted across the land frontier. It is also possible to trek from the coast through Unguía and Paya (Inderena cabin) to the waterfalls and Sautatá (2 days), but good guides are essential. Guides in this area cost around US$12 for a full day. Well-equipped groups using local paths and information, armed with compass and machete, can more-or-less make their own way. However, accident or illness could be very serious, much of the area is sparsely inhabited, and getting lost is usually fatal.

On the Pacific side, one sea route is from Bahía Solano (**see p 862**) or Jurado in Chocó Department (Jurado can be reached by plane from Turbo). Canoes go from both towns to Jaqué, 50 km N of the Colombian border (Jurado-Jaqué 1½ hrs, US$20), from where you can take a boat to Panamá City, US$12, 12 hrs, or fly, US$37 or fly to La Palma, capital of Darién in Panama (one *pensión* F, cooking and laundry facilities, English spoken). Launches and dugouts go from La Palma to Puerto Lardo on the Río Sabanas, from where it is a 2-hour walk (or hitch on a truck) to Santa Fe on the Panamá-Yaviza road. (Bus Santa Fe-Panamá 6-8 hrs; flight with Parsa, T Panamá 26-3883/3808, La Palma—Panama City 3 times a week). Alternatively from La Palma take a boat to Puerto Quimba, then transport to Metetí, from where a bus can be taken to Panama City.

Jurado can be reached overland from Riosucio by the Trans-Isthmus route, using both boat and walking (30-36 hrs in all). Serious advance planning is essential, although the Trans-Isthmus route is well-trodden by local traders (legal or otherwise). The Embera and Wounan Indians encountered en route are wary, but hospitable. The route passes through Riosucio, Tamboral/finca (outboard 4-5 hrs), Leta (aka Belencito, or Unión de Embera y Katío, foot-3 hrs), Peñita shelter and Espavé shelters (both stretches 4 hrs on foot, both uninhabited), Pueblo Antioquia (foot-1hr), Val de Rama cabin (foot 5-6 hrs), Amparradocito (foot 3 hrs), Doboka and Jurado (outboard 2½ hrs from Amparradocito – also a difficult path, 6-8 hrs). Besides the boat Jurado-Jaqué, there is an overland route involving at least one night camping between Santa Teresita (Wounan village, Colombia) and Mamey (Embera, Panama), detailed local instructions are essential. Transport out of Jaqué is frustrating; you must obtain a DAS stamp in either Turbo or Buenaventura, without it you will have problems in Jaqué or Panama City.

Notes and Cautions Anyone considering crossing the Darién Gap overland should bear in mind that the area is becoming less safe because of drug trafficking, banditry and guerrilla activity on both sides of the border, but especially in Colombia (as far into the country as Turbo). The New Tribes Mission, after the kidnap of 3 missionaries, has withdrawn its staff from the area, thus removing one of a travellers' main sources of assistance. Follow these points of advice: 1) travel only in the dry season; 2) travel with a reliable companion or two; 3) hire at least one Indian guide, but do it through the village *corregidor*, whose involvement may add to the reliability of the guide he selects (budget up to US$12/day per guide and his food); 4) travel light and move fast.

Dr Richard Dawood, author of *Travellers' Health: How to Stay Healthy Abroad*, and photographer Anthony Dawton, crossed the Darien Gap at the end of the wet season (November). We are pleased to include Dr Dawood's health recommendations for such a journey: **Heat** Acclimatization to a hot climate usually takes around 3 weeks. It is more difficult in humid climates than in dry ones, since sweat cannot evaporate easily, and when high humidity persists through the night as well, the body has no respite. (In desert conditions, where the temperature falls at night, adaptation is much easier.) Requirements for salt and water increase dramatically under such conditions. We had to drink 12 litres per day to keep pace with our own fluid loss on some parts of the trip.

We were travelling under extreme conditions, but it is important to remember that the human thirst sensation is not an accurate guide to true fluid requirements. In hot countries it is always essential to drink beyond the point of thirst quenching, and to drink sufficient water to ensure that the urine is consistently pale in colour.

Salt losses also need to be replaced. Deficiency of salt, water, or both, is referred to as heat exhaustion; lethargy, fatigue, and headache are typical features, eventually leading to coma and death. Prevention is the best approach, and we used the pre-salted water regime pioneered by Colonel Jim Adam and followed by the British Army; salt is added to all fluids, one quarter of a level teaspoon (approx 1 gram) per pint—to produce a solution that is just below the taste threshold. Salt tablets, however, are poorly absorbed, irritate the stomach and may cause vomiting; plenty of pre-salted fluid should be the rule for anyone spending much time outdoors in the tropics.

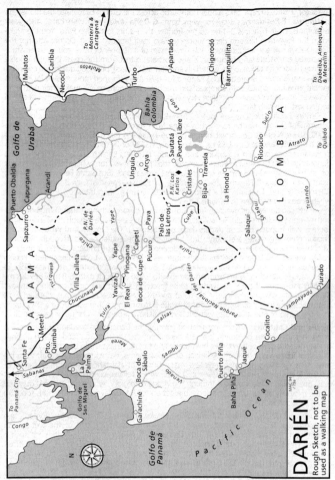

DARIÉN
Rough Sketch, not to be
used as a walking map

Sun Overcast conditions in the tropics can be misleading. The sun's rays can be fierce, and it is important to make sure that all exposed skin is constantly protected with a high factor sun screen—preferably waterproof for humid conditions. This was especially important while we were travelling by canoe. A hat was also essential.

Food and Water Diarrhoea can be annoying enough in a luxurious holiday resort with comfortable sanitary facilities. The inconvenience under jungle conditions would have been more than trivial, however, with the added problem of coping with further fluid loss and dehydration.

Much caution was therefore needed with food hygiene. We carried our own supplies, which we prepared carefully ourselves: rather uninspiring camping fare, such as canned tuna fish, sardines, pasta, dried soup, biscuits and dried fruit. In the villages, oranges, bananas and coconuts were available. The freshly baked bread was safe, and so would have been the rice.

We purified our water with 2 per cent tincture of iodine carried in a small plastic dropping bottle, 4 drops to each litre—more when the water is very turbid—wait 20 mins before drinking.

This method is safe and effective, and is the only suitable technique for such conditions. (Another suggestion is a water purifying pump based on a ceramic filter. There are several on the market, eg Katadyn. It takes about a minute to purify a litre of water. When water is cloudy, eg after rain, pumps are less effective and harder work. Take purification tablets as back-up – Ed) It is also worth travelling with a suitable antidiarrhoeal medication such as Arret.

Malaria Drug resistant malaria is present in the Darien area, and antimalarial medication is essential. We took Paludrine, two tablets daily, and chloroquine, two tablets weekly. Free advice on antimalarial medication for all destinations is available from the Malaria Reference Laboratory, T 0891-600-350 in the UK. An insect repellent is also essential, and so are precautions to avoid insect bites.

Insects Beside malaria and yellow fever, other insect-borne diseases such as dengue fever and leishmaniasis may pose a risk. The old fashioned mosquito net is ideal if you have to sleep outdoors, or in a room that is not mosquito-proof. Mosquito nets for hammocks are widely available in Latin America. An insecticide spray is valuable for clearing your room of flying insects before you go to sleep, and mosquito coils that burn through the night giving off an insecticidal vapour, are also valuable.

Ticks It is said that ticks should be removed by holding a lighted cigarette close to them, and we had an opportunity to put this old remedy to the test. We duly unwrapped a pack of American duty-frees that we had preserved carefully in plastic just for such a purpose, as our Indian guides looked on in amazement, incredulous that we should use these prized items for such a lowly purpose. The British Army expedition to Darien in 1972 carried 60,000 cigarettes among its supplies, and one wonders if they were for this purpose! The cigarette method didn't work, but caused amusement. (Further discussion with the experts indicates that the currently favoured method is to ease the tick's head gently away from the skin with tweezers.)

Vaccinations A yellow fever vaccination certificate is required from all travellers arriving from infected areas, and vaccination is advised for personal protection.

Immunization against hepatitis A (with gammaglobulin) and typhoid are strongly advised.

Attacks by dogs are relatively common: the new rabies vaccine is safe and effective, and carrying a machete for the extra purpose of discouraging animals (and warding off snakes) is advised.

In addition, all travellers should be protected against tetanus, diptheria and polio.

You can get some food along the way, but take enough for at least 5 days. Do take, though, a torch/flashlight, and a bottle of rum, or present of equal worth for the ranger at Cristales. It is highly recommended to travel in the dry season, when there is no mud and fewer mosquitoes. Wet season travel is not impossible, but with heavy rain every afternoon, the rivers are full and dangerous, and there is mud beyond belief making progress painfully slow. Only for the masochistic.

Taking a motorcycle through Darién is not an endeavour to be undertaken lightly, and cannot be recommended. Ed Culberson (who, in 1986 after two unsuccessful attempts, was the first to accomplish the feat) writes: "Dry season passage is comparatively easy on foot and even with a bicycle. But it simply cannot be done with a standard sized motorcycle unless helped by Indians at a heavy cost in dollars...It is a very strenuous, dangerous adventure, often underestimated by motorcyclists, some who have come to untimely ends in the jungle".

Northeast from Cartagena

Cartagena-Barranquilla, a good paved road but driving is violent, and cyclists have reported muggings. The main road goes via Sabanalarga (50 km from Barranquilla). From Sabanalarga an all-weather road continues to Puerto Giraldo, a port on the Río Magdalena linked by ferry with the small town of Salmina (ferry 0500 to 1800). An all-weather road leads to Fundación, on the Atlántico Railway, and a junction point with the road from Santa Marta to Bucaramanga and Bogotá, which is now paved throughout, though the surface is somewhat uneven. From Baranoa a branch road runs to Usicurí (72 km from Barranquilla), known for its medicinal waters and for the grave of the popular Colombian poet, Julio Flores. A spectacular new bridge over the Río Magdalena gives a fine view of Barranquilla and the river.

Barranquilla (pop 1.09 million), is Colombia's fourth city. It lies on the western bank of the Río Magdalena, about 18 km from its mouth, which, through deepening and the clearing of silted sandbars, makes it a seaport (though less busy than Cartagena or Santa Marta) as well as a river port. Those who know the people say they are the most friendly in Colombia.

Barranquilla is a modern industrial city with a dirty, colourful, polluted central area near the river, and a good residential area in the NW, beyond C 53. The principal boulevard is **Paseo Bolívar**; there is a handsome church, San Nicolás, formerly the Cathedral, in Plaza San Nicolás, the central square, and before it stands a small statue of Columbus. The new **Catedral Metropolitana** is at Cra 45, No 53-120, opposite Plaza de la Paz. This was visited by the Pope in 1986. There is an impressive statue of Christ inside by the Colombian sculptor, Arenas Betancourt. The commercial and shopping districts are round the Paseo Bolívar, a few blocks N of the old Cathedral, and in C Murillo. The colourful and vivid **market** is between Paseo Bolívar and the river, the so-called Zona Negra on a side channel of the Magdalena. Good parks in the northern areas; the favourite one is **Parque Tomás Surí Salcedo** on C 72. Stretching back into the northwestern heights overlooking the city are the modern suburbs of El Prado, Altos del Prado, Golf and Ciudad Jardín, with the German-run *El Prado Hotel*. There are five stadia in the city, a big covered coliseum for sports, two for football and the others cater for basketball and baseball. The metropolitan stadium is on Av Murillo, outside the city.

Museum Small **archaeological** collection, C 68 No 53-45 (Mon-Fri 0900-1200, 1400-1700), with big physical relief map on front lawn. Also, Museo Romántico, Cra 54, No 59-199, history of Barranquilla.

Zoo There is a well-maintained zoo with some animals not often seen in zoos, but many are in small cages, C 77, Cra 68 (bus "Boston/Boston" or "Caldes/Recreo"), entrance US$0.60, 0830-1200, 1400-1800. All the trees are labelled.

Festivals Carnival, lasting four days, parades, floats, street dancing and beauty contests.

Hotels L2 *El Prado*, best, the social centre, swimming pool and tennis courts, good restaurant, sauna, original 1920s building is national monument, new annex behind, some distance from the centre (Cra 54, No 70-10, T 456533, F 450019); **L3** *Dann Barranquilla*, Cra 51B, No 79-246, T 450099, F 450079, highrise, in smart residential Altos del Prado; **L3** *Puerta del Sol*, C 75, NO 41D-79, T 456144, F 455550, totally refurbished; **B** *Royal*, Cra 54, No 68-124, T 453058, good service, with swimming pool, modern; **C** *Capricornio*, Cra 44B, No 70-201, T 340240/565045, very clean, good service, with bath, a/c; **D** *Canadiense*, C 45, No 36-142, fan, shower, noisy but convenient for bus station 2 blocks away; **D** *El Golf*, Barrio El Golf, Cra 59b, No 81-158, T 342191; **D** *Villa Venecia*, C 61, No 46-41, T 414107, clean, TV, a little noisy but rec; **E** *Alianza*, C 34, No 43-110, with bath; **E** *Victoria*, C 35, No 43-140, downtown, large, scruffy rooms with fan; **E** *Diplomático*, Cra 38, No 42-60, with private bath, fan, TV room, washing facilities, cafetería; **F** *Horizonte*, C 45 y Cra 44, with bath, clean, quiet, fan; **F** *California*, C 32 y Cra 44, pleasant but about to fall down, enjoy the chickens. **NB** Hotel prices may be much higher during Carnival. Watch for thieves in downtown hotels.

Restaurants *La Puerta de Oro*, C 35, No 41-100, central, a/c good for meals (inc breakfast); *El Huerto*, Cra 52, No 70-139, good vegetarian; *Jardines de Confucio*, Cra 54, No 75-44, good Chinese food, nice atmosphere; various Lebanese with belly-dancers; several Chinese and *pizzerias*. Many places, for all tastes and budgets, on C 70 from *Hotel El Prado* towards Cra 42; at C 70 y 44B are several *estaderos*, bars with snacks and verandas for watching the passers-by.

Banks and Exchange Banco Anglo Colombiano, C 34, No 44-43, and 3 agencies; Banco Internacional de Colombia, cash against Mastercard. Casa de cambio El Cacique, C 34, No 43-108, T 326392, reliable.

Consulates Venezuelan, C 70, No 53-74 (Centro Financiero El Prado, 4° piso), T 580048/582832, 0800-1500 (take "Caldes/Recreo" or "Boston/Boston" bus), visa issued same day, but you must be there by 0915 with photo and US$30 cash; onward ticket may not be requested; **US**, Centro Comercial Mayorista, C 77, No 68-15, opposite zoo (Apartado Aéreo 51565), T 457088 or 457181 (visas obtainable only in Bogotá); **British**, Cra 44, No 45-57, T 326936; **German**, C 80, near Vía 40 (ask for Herr Schnabel); **Norwegian**, C 72, No 57-33, T 581043; **Dutch**, Cra 42H, No 85-33, T 341282; **Spanish**, C 51, No 37-64, T 313694; **Finnish**, Vía 40 de las Flores, Cementos del Caribe, T 350080.

Entertainments Teatro Amira de la Rosa. **Night Life** *La Cabaña* at *Hotel El Prado*. Famous disco *Agua Sala* at beach.

Post Office in Plaza Bolívar.

Market San Andrecito, or "Tourist Market", Vía 40, is where smuggled goods are sold at very competitive prices; a good place to buy film. Picturesque and reasonably safe. Any taxi driver will take you there.

Bookshop *Librería Nacional*, Cra 53, No 75-129, English, French and German books. Maps from Instituto Agustín Codazzi, C 36, No 45-101.

Travel Agent *Tierra Mar Aire*, AMEX agent, C 74, No 52-34, very helpful for flights to Central America.

Tourist Information at main hotels and at C 72, No 57-43, of 401, T 454458 or 336658. CNT is at Cra 54, No 75-45, T 454458.

Useful Addresses Police (for declarations of theft, etc), Policia F2, C 47 y Cra 43; **DAS**, C 54, Cra 43.

Local Transport Taxis within the town cost US$1.25 (eg downtown to northern suburbs).

Airport Ernesto Cortissoz airport is 10 km from the city; there is plenty of transport of all types. City bus from airport to town, US$0.15 (US$0.20 on Sunday). Taxi to town, US$4.50 (taxis do not have meters, fix fare in advance). To town, take only buses marked "centro" from 200m to right when leaving airport; the bus to the airport (marked Malambo) leaves from Cra 44 up C 32 to Cra 38, then up C 30 to Airport. Taxi to Cartagena US$40. Avianca (C 72, No 57-79, T 454355) and SAM to Aruba as well as Colombian destinations; Lacsa to Caracas, Panama and San José, and connections to Mexico City, other Central American capitals and Los Angeles. Copa also to Panama. American Airlines to Miami and Houston.

Warnings When leaving by air for the USA, you may be searched by drug squad police; they are very civil, but acquisitive—check your belongings afterwards. Beware also of people claiming to be ships' officers who say they can arrange a passage if you pay in advance; buy a passage only in a recognized shipping office or agency. If shipping a car into Barranquilla allow 2 days to complete all paperwork to retrieve your car from the port, unless you have a *carnet de passages*, which opens all doors and dispenses with all othe paperwork.

Buses Most bus companies operate from C 34 and Cra 45 (Brasilia and Copetran at C 45 y Cra 35: Brasilia links all N coast towns and S as far as Bogotá, rec a/c buses). To **Santa Marta**, US$3.25, Pullman (less in non-a/c, Coolibertador), about 2 hrs, also direct to Santa Marta's famous Rodadero beach; to **Valledupar**, 4½ hrs, US$6; to **Montería**, US$11, 8 hrs; to **Medellín** by Pullman, US$19, 16hrs; to **Bucaramanga**, US$18 with Copetran, a/c, first class, departures at 1130 most days, arriving 2030; to **Bogotá**, 20-24 hrs, US$25 direct; to **Caucasia**, US$10.75, 11 hrs. To **Maicao**, US$7.80, 5 hrs (with Brasilia, every ½ hour from 0100-1200); to **Cartagena**, 3 grades of bus, 3 hrs (US$2.75 with Transportes Cartagena, US$5 with Expreso Brasilia, by Brasilia Van Tours mini-bus, from their downtown offices as well as the bus terminals), 2 hrs by colectivo, US$3.10.

Roads Regular buses from Paseo Bolívar and the church at C 33 and Cra 41 to the attractive bathing resort of **Puerto Colombia**, 19 km (US$0.60, ½ hr). Beach clean and sandy, water a bit muddy. South along the Magdalena to the little town of Palmar de Varela. On this road, 5 km from the city, is the old colonial town of **Soledad**, with 16,000 inhabitants. The cathedral and the old narrow streets round it are worth seeing.

Santa Marta, capital of Magdalena Department (municipal pop 279,960), the third Caribbean port, is 96 km E of Barranquilla, at the mouth of the Río Manzanares. It is best reached from Barranquilla by the paved road along the coast, which passes salt pans and skirts an extensive and most interesting lagoon, the Ciénaga de Santa Marta, in which all types of water birds, plants and animals may be seen. (There has been an ecological disaster there, as a result of cutting off the egress to the sea to build the coast road. A National Environment Programme, funded with the help of IDB, is working to reopen the canals and restore the area's fish and vegetables. The former Solanca National Park appears now to be abandoned although there is still a large tank containing caimanes etc.) There is a paved road S to Bucaramanga (**see p 811**) and Bogotá.

Santa Marta lies on a deep bay with high shelving cliffs. The climate ranges seasonally from hot and trying to hot but pleasant in February and March; occasionally one can see snow-clad peaks of the Sierra Nevada to the E, less than 50 km away and 5,800m high.

Its sandy beaches stretch from the Simón Bolívar airport to Punta Aguja across the Rodadero de Gaira and the little fishing villages of Villa Concha, surrounded

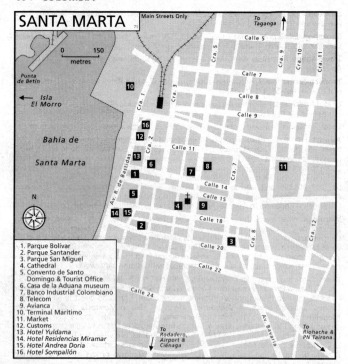

SANTA MARTA
Main Streets Only

Map labels:
To Taganga
Calle 5
Calle 7
Calle 8
Calle 9
Calle 11
Calle 14
Calle 15
Calle 18
Calle 20
Calle 22
Calle 24
Cra. 1
Cra. 2
Cra. 3
Cra. 5
Cra. 7
Cra. 8
Cra. 9
Cra. 10
Cra. 11
Cra. 12
Av. R. de Bastidas
Av. Bavaria
Punta de Betín
Isla El Morro
Bahia de Santa Marta
N
0 150 metres
To Rodadero, Airport & Ciénaga
To Riohacha & PN Tairona

1. Parque Bolívar
2. Parque Santander
3. Parque San Miguel
4. Cathedral
5. Convento de Santo Domingo & Tourist Office
6. Casa de la Aduana museum
7. Banco Industrial Colombiano
8. Telecom
9. Avianca
10. Terminal Marítimo
11. Market
12. Customs
13. Hotel Yuldama
14. Hotel Residencias Miramar
15. Hotel Andrea Doria
16. Hotel Sompallón

by meadows and shady trees, and Taganga (see below). A jutting rock—the Punta de Betín—rises from the sea in front of the city and is topped by a lighthouse. Rugged Isla del Moro, 3 km off Santa Marta, completes the panorama. Playa El Rodadero is the most fashionable and tourist-oriented part of Santa Marta, though it lies some distance W of the city (local bus service, taxi, US$1.80). Many of the buses coming from Barranquilla and Cartagena stop at Rodadero on the way to Santa Marta. There is also a dirty, unsafe beach with a seaside promenade close to the centre of town. The promenade itself offers good views of the bay and is lined with restaurants, accommodation and nightlife, not of very high quality. The main shops and banks are on Cra 5.

Santa Marta was the first town founded (1525) by the *conquistadores* in Colombia. Founder: Rodrigo de Bastidas. Most of the famous sea-dogs—the brothers Côte, Drake and Hawkins—sacked the city in spite of the two forts built on a small island at the entrance to the bay. It was here that Simón Bolívar, his dream of Gran Colombia shattered, came to die. Almost penniless he was given hospitality at the *hacienda* of San Pedro Alejandrino, 5 km to the SE. He died on 17 December 1830, at the age of 47, and was buried in the Cathedral, but his body was taken to the Pantheon at Caracas 12 years later. The simple room in which he died and his few belongings can be seen today (admission, US$2, open daily 0900-1700): take the "Mamatoca" bus from the waterfront (Cra 1C) to the *hacienda*, US$0.20.

Museum Casa de la Aduana, C 14 y Cra 2, displays an excellent archaeological collection, including a large number of precolombian gold artefacts; visit strongly recommended before going to Ciudad Perdida. Open Tues-Sat, 0800-1200, 1400-1800, Sun 0800-1200, during the tourist season, Mon-Fri, 0800-1200, 1400-1800, the rest of the year; entry free.

Warning The N end of town, beyond the railway station, and areas near, especially S of, Rodadero beach are very dangerous and travellers are advised not to go there alone. We have received reports of tourists being robbed at gunpoint of everything including their clothes in daylight. If you arrive by bus, beware taxi drivers who take you to a hotel of their choice, not yours (no doubt for a commission). Also beware of "jungle tours", or "boat trips to the islands" sold by street touts in Santa Marta.

Hotels In town: Av Rodrigo de Bastidas (Cra 1) has several seaside holiday hotels while Cra 2 and connecting Calles have many budget *residencias* in our F range. **B** *Yuldama*, Cra 1, No 12-19, T 210063, clean, probably best in the city, a/c, reasonable food; **D** *Bermuz*, C 13, No 5-16, T 210004. F 213625, good, clean, also good vegetarian restaurant; **D** *Costa Azul*, C 17, No 2-09, T 232036, with bath and shower, some rooms with a/c, impeccably clean with good mattresses, fan, windows into courtyard, very friendly, cafeteria, rec; **D** *Saratoga*, C 11, No 2-29, T 210644, a/c, less with fan, average, plain; **D** *Sompallón*, Cra 1, No 1 B-57, T 237195, modern, with *pizzeria* and *casa de cambio*; **D** *Hostal Yuldama*, C 12, No 2-70, T 230057, a/c, cheaper without, modern, plain, safe deposit, clean, rec; **D** *Tairona*, Cra 1, No 11-41, T 32408, with fan, bath, friendly, no frills, not too secure; **E** *Residencia Park Hotel*, Cra 1C, No 18-67, T 37215, on sea front, with shower, fan, reasonable, friendly, phone, popular with young Colombians; **E** *Hotel Residencias Yarimar*, Cra 1A, No 26-37, clean, fan, noisy; **E** *Andrea Doria*, C 18, No 1C-90, T 234329, clean, friendly with bath and fan; **E** *Residencias Bahía Blanca*, Cra 1, No 11-13, T 234439, private shower, friendly, clean, will store luggage; **F** *Residencia Jomar*, Cra 2, No 18-22, fan, quiet, will store luggage, clean; **F** *El Prado Residencia*, C12, No 3-01, quiet, clean, large rooms, use of kitchen; **F** *Residencial Familiar*, C 10 C No 2-14, bath, very friendly, clean family-run, cooking facility, highly rec; **F** *Miramar*, C 10C, No 1C-59, "gringo hotel", tends to be crowded, robberies have often been reported, and be warned this is a dump, its popularity only because it is cheap, motorbike parking, restaurant, 2 blocks from railway station and beach, can arrange trips (not to be confused with **D** *Hotel Residencias Miramar*, Cra 1C, No 18-23, a/c, clean, tidy, holiday hotel); *Marely*, opposite the *Miramar* should be avoided, we have received many bad reports; **F** *Res Marinas*, C 10, No 1C-83, clean, friendly, fan, bath. **Youth Hostel** *Hotel Nabusimake*, details from Alcom in Bogotá.

At Rodadero Bay: **L2** *Irotama*, Km 14, between airport and Rodadero Bay, T 218021, all inclusive, has bungalows; **A2** *La Sierra*, Cra 1, No 9-47, T 227197, disorganized, not currently rec, though relatively inexpensive restaurant; **A2** *Arhuaco*, Cra 2, No 6-49, T 227234, 200m from beach, quiet, pool, bar; **A2** *Santamar* (Travelodge), 8 km from Rodadero towards airport, price is pp all inclusive (about half the price low season), T 218486, or 1-800-255-3050 toll free; **A2** *Tamacá*, Cra 2, No 11A-98, T 227015, direct access to beach, fair rooms, good service, fine pool; **C** *La Riviera*, Cra 2, No 5-42, Aptdo Aéreo 50-69, small, clean, safe, a/c; **C** *Mar Azul*, Cra 3, No 5-146, a/c; **C** *Residencias Edmar*, Cra 3, No 5-188, T 227874, a/c, clean, cafeteria, welcoming; **D** *Valladolid*, Cra 2, No 5-67, T 227465, good value, large clean rooms, helpful, rec; **F** *Residencial Bastidas*, Cra 2, shower, friendly, laundry facilities. Bungalows for 8 for rent from Isidro Ramos, casa 5, Manzana G, Rodadero del Mar, Santa Marta.

Motels **D** *El Rodadero*, C 11, No 1-29, T 227262, swimming pool, English-speaking manageress (Marina Salcedo), very helpful; and others.

Restaurants *Yarimar*, Cra 1A, No 26-37, next to hotel of same name, good seafood; opp is *La Terraza Marina*, also rec for seafood. *El Platanal*, C 13, No 1-33, good cheap food, good service. *La Gran Muralla*, Cra 5, No 23-77 and *Oriental*, C 22, No 3-43, both good Chinese. *Toy San*, C 22, Chinese, good, big portions and *El Gran Wah Yuen*, C 14, No 3-74, good Chinese *à la carte* and *comida corriente*, plenty of fresh vegetables. *Cafetería del Calle*, Cra 3A, No 16-26, good *empanadas*.

At Rodadero there are a number of good restaurants, some pricey, some good value; there are also very good juice kiosks along the seafront.

Banks and Exchange Change money at Banco de Occidente, good rates for Mastercard. Banco Industrial Colombiano, C 13 y Cra 5 for Amex TC exchange, but in am only. Amex office Tierra del Mar, C 15, No 2-60, T 33497. *Casas de cambio* in 3rd block of C 14, many others on this street. In Rodadero, Apto 201, Cra 1, No 9-23.

Laundry Lavandería Paraiso, C 14, No 8C-47.

Tourist Office in the former Convent of Santo Domingo, now Casa de Cultura, Cra 2, No 16-44, T 35773, open office hours Mon-Fri (has library and art exhibitions). There is also an office at Rodadero, C 10, No 3-10. **Inderena** office, Cra 1, No 22-77, T 233-0960, and at the Quinta de San Pedro Alejandrino. **DAS Office** Corner of C 26 y Cra 9.

Airport Simón Bolívar, 20 km from city; bus, US$0.25, taxi from Santa Marta, US$8.50, from

Rodadero, US$3. During the tourist season, get to the airport early. Note, planes are full, book well ahead. Avianca, Cra 5A, No 17-09, T 34958.

Train All services, to La Dorada, Bogotá and Medellín, were suspended in 1992. Enquire locally about resumption of services.

Buses A new bus terminal was opened in 1994 S of the city, towards Rodadero, taxi US$1.50 to centre, minibus US$0.30. To/from **Bogotá**, 22 hrs, US$36, 4 a day; coming from the capital check that if the bus is continuing to Barranquilla, you will be dropped in Santa Marta, not short of it. The Copetran bus to **Bucaramanga** takes about 9 hrs (US$18). Journey time will be affected by the number of police checks. There is a good meal stop at Los Límites. From Bucaramanga the buses take 8 hrs to Bogotá (11 minimum by 2nd class). Buses to **Barranquilla**, 2 hrs (US$3.25); to **Cartagena**, 4 hrs (US$7.20, or US$8.40, Brasilia). To **Riohacha** US$3.45, 3 hrs; Pullman to **Maicao**, US$5.50, 4-5 hrs, these non-airconditioned buses continue to the Venezuelan border on the way to **Maracaibo**. There are three buses a day (Brasilia) direct to **Rodadero Beach** from Barranquilla, taking 2 hrs and costing US$1.80. They return to Barranquilla at 1300, 1530 and 1730. Fastest service to Barranquilla and Cartagena reported to be Transportes la Costeña.

Port Without a *carnet de passages*, it can take up to 4 working days to get a car out of the port, but it is usually well guarded and it is unlikely that anything will be stolen. (See also under **Motorcycles** in **Information for Visitors**.)

Sightseeing Tours in air-conditioned jeeps by Airline travel agency at centre. Launches leave Rodadero beach every hour for the Aquarium, modest, not as good as the one at Islas del Rosario near Cartagena, US$3 return (includes admission). From the Aquarium, one can walk (10 mins) to the Playa Blanca (White Beach) where one can swim in less crowded conditions than elsewhere—food available at the beach. Small Indian figures are sculptured at José Pertuz, C 38, up the hill beyond Cra 17. They cut stone with traditional instruments and will chisel animals etc to order. They are sold on Rodadero beach. Punta Betín, small fishing harbour, marine eco-system research centre run by Colombian and German universities. Ask for details at the Tourist Office.

Diving Diving shops operate at Rodadero: *Buceo y Salvamento*, Edif Libertador, Cra 2 y C8 local 13, 2nd floor, T 228179, 2 dives US$44 inc equipment; *Tienda de Buceo*, C10 y Cra 2, Ed Playa Blanca, local 3, sells good equipment, but for trips sends you to *Pro-Buzos de Colombia*, C14 No 9-170, Santa Marta, T 236383, 2 dives US$55, PADI certification US$150. There are many dive shops in Taganga: *Scuba Sport*, Apartado 1275, T 231393, English and German spoken, offers bed and breakfast, 2 dives US$50; *Oceano Scuba Club*, Frente a la Playa, T 230325 (also at Carrera 44 No 70-56, Barranquilla, T 340857); *Centro de Buceo*, T 232422, 2 dives US$45, English spoken. You must check that a fully qualified dive master is present.

Excursions Close to Santa Marta (minibus US$0.30, taxi US$2.50, 10 mins) is the fishing village and beach of **Taganga**, with hotel **B** *La Ballena Azul*, most attractive, friendly, comfortable, clean, restaurant, also run boat tours to secluded beaches, ask Mauricio about tours, horses for hire (postal address: Aptdo Aéreo 799, Santa Marta, Telex 38886 CCSMT CO, or Bogotá T 2178606). **D** *Playa Brava*, fan or a/c, quiet, basic beds; **E** *El Delfín*, fan, basic. One can stay with Joselito Guerra on the beach, **G** for hammock space, may charge for use of kitchen, secure for luggage, or rent houses on beach (not secure). Restaurants expensive, but a good one is *Tibisay*, seafood. Swimming good, especially on Playa Grande, 25 mins' walk round coast, but thieving is common there. Taganga is quiet during week, but trippers from Santa Marta pour in on Sun. On the E shore of the Ciénaga de Santa Marta, is **Ciénaga**, a town of 75,000 people (see **Music and Dance** for festival). Cotton, bananas, tobacco and cacao are grown in the area. Hotels in Ciénaga: *Tobiexe*; *Naval*. South of Ciénaga, just before Fundación, is **Aracataca**, birthplace of Gabriel García Márquez, fictionalised as Macondo in some of his stories (notably *Cien años de soledad*). His home, called a museum, may be seen in the backyard of La Familia Iriarte Ahumada—just ask for directions. As a museum, it is disappointing. There are *residencias* (**G**), but it is better to stay in **Fundación**. Best hotel is *Caroli*, Cra 8, No 5-30; **F** *Fundación* (**E** with a/c); **E** *Aparte*; **E** *Centro del Viajero*, with a/c, good value; others all in this price range. Do not walk between Aracataca and Fundación at night, otherwise it is safe. Bus Fundación-Aracataca, US$0.20; Fundación-Ciénaga, US$1; Fundación-Barranquilla, US$4.20. Banana growing in the area has now been replaced almost entirely by African palm plantations.

To go to the **Ciudad Perdida**, discovered in 1975, permission is required from Inderena, Cra 1, No 22-77, Santa Marta, T 36355; it is not always given because the area is dangerous. The site covers 400 hectares, at 1,100m altitude, near the Río Buritaca.

Ciudad Perdida was founded between 500 and 700 AD and was surely the most important centre of the Tairona culture. It stands on the steep slopes of Cerro Corea, which lies in the northern part of the Sierra Nevada de Santa Marta. It consists of a complex system of buildings, paved footpaths, flights of steps and perimetrical walls, which link a series of terraces and platforms, on which were built cult centres, residences and warehouses. Juan Mayr's book, *The Sierra Nevada of Santa Marta* (Mayr y Cabal, Apartado Aéreo 5000, Bogotá), which deals beautifully with the Ciudad Perdida, is recommended.

You can reach Ciudad Perdida by helicopter from Santa Marta in about 20 mins, by arrangement. Ask at Helicol, at the airport, at Tourist Office in Santa Marta (address above), or at Aviatur, Edif Centro Ejecutivo, piso 2, Santa Marta, T 213840, 15 days advance booking may be required. Price: about US$350 there and back with a 3 hour stay.

More adventurous trekkers can reach Ciudad Perdida in a six/eight days' excursion, leaving about 0700 from Santa Marta market, at the corner of Cra 11 and C 11.

Toyota jeeps go up to La Tagua (about 3 hrs), where it is possible to rent mules and pay local guides (but see below). You can go on alone, but route finding is difficult. You need to take a tent or a hammock and mosquito net (probably supplied if you take a guide), a good repellent, sleeping bag, warm clothing for the night, torch, plastic bags to keep everything dry, and strong, quick drying footwear. Check conditions, especially information on river crossings, and ensure you have adequate food, water bottle and water purifying tablets before you start. The first day's walking is about 4 hrs mostly uphill, through fine wild scenery. The first night will be spent in a hammock in a typical farmhouse. The second day takes you through hilly country and to a ridge with fine views of the Sierra Nevada de Santa Marta. After 6 to 8 hrs walking you reach the heights of Alto de Mira where you stay the night in a hammock in a typical "bohío". The third day will bring you down to the Buritaca river which you cross several times and then, through impressive scenery, up to the steps which bring you to the archaeological site of Ciudad Perdida. Be warned, there are over 1200 steps to climb when you get there. The visit to the town will take you the fourth day; there are now several shelters with room for about 6 hammocks in each with use of fireplace. There is a waterfall nearby, perfect for bathing. The return to Santa Marta will take you two to three days. Make sure you have sufficient "energy" foods with you. You may be able to buy bananas and other produce from settlements along the way.

Archaeologists and army guards will ask you for your permit. Don't forget that Ciudad Perdida is a National Park: it is strictly forbidden to damage trees and cut flowers or insects.

One week trips organized by the tourist office in Santa Marta cost about US$140 if you take your own food to US$200 all inclusive: price includes mules, guide and food, 3 days' hike there, 1 day at site, 3 days back. Hotels in Santa Marta or Taganga may charge up to US$400 pp. Recommended guides: Frankie Rey, known to German tourists as "die graue Eminenz", very knowledgeable (ask at the tourist office about him), Donaldo, Wilson Montero, Edilberto Rey and Jairo García, who lives at the *Residencia Miramar*, in Santa Marta. *Hotel Miramar* is reported as arranging the 6 day trip for around US$100 pp upwards depending on the service required. Food supplied is inadequate and not rec. You go with Carlos or Gabriel as a guide. If you are prepared to shop around and cook and carry your supplies and belongings, a guide could cost you less. Care: there are many unscrupulous guides about, checking with the Tourist Office is recommended. Try to leave no rubbish behind and encourage the guides to ensure no one else does. Make sure the parts of the ruins you want to see are open. If you want to see rainforest on the trek, insist on going via La Tagua (more beautiful, but more strenuous).

A circuitous route to the site can be arranged through *Hotel La Ballena Azul* (above). It costs about US$250 pp for the 6-day round trip, all inclusive. Its advantage is that it avoids all settlements, especially in the drug-growing lower valleys and Kogi villages which may not welcome foreigners.

It is generally thought that there are more Tairona sites known, but they are being secretly searched for gold and artefacts, some of which may already have reached the market place. The local name for these "researchers" is *guaqueros* (tomb thieves). Unfortunately there is very little true archaeological research being done in this area and much of these cultural remains may be destroyed before they are recorded.

The **Tairona** national park, 35 km E of Santa Marta in the Riohacha direction, wild woodland on the coast, is beautiful and unspoilt. To get to the park entrance at the E end of the park (opens 0800, US$2), take a minibus from the market at C 11 y Cra 11 in Santa Marta, about US$1, or go to the Riohacha road police checkpoint (taxi US$1 or bus to Mamatoca) and catch a bus there. The big, a/c buses en route to Riohacha from Santa Marta bus station do not stop at the entrance. If you arrive before 0800, you may be able to pay at the car park just before **Cañaveral**, 1 hr's walk into the park from the gate. Bathing is not recommended as there is often heavy pounding surf and the tides are treacherous, but the beach is less crowded and cleaner than Rodadero. (There are splendid and deserted sandy beaches, to which you have to walk, about 5 km E of Cañaveral, but take care, the park borders drug growing areas and

SANTA MARTA
Environs

71a

N

Punta de Neguange
Pt. de Cinto
Punta Guachiquita

Isla de la Aguja

Punta Chengue

Parque Nacional Tairona

Arrecifes

Cabo de la Aguja

Gayroca

Pueblito ▲

Cañaveral

Villa Concha

Park boundary

Calabazo

Taganga
Pájaro

Quebrada Concha

Park entrance

To Riohacha

SANTA MARTA

Bonda

San Pedro Alejandrino

Río Manzanares

Mamatoco

Playa el Rodadero
Gaira

Río Gaira

Pt. la Gloria

La Tigresa

0   5
km

Punta Brava

To Ciénaga & Barranquilla

Minca

El Campano

Sierra Nevada de Santa Marta

can be dangerous.) Relics of ancient Tairona culture abound. A guided tour round the **Pueblito** archaeological site is free, every Sat or as arranged, under escort of a park guard. Walking beyond Cañaveral, it is 40 mins to Arrecifes; follow the beach for 1/4 hour to Rancho Viejo from where a clear path leads S to Pueblito (1 1/2 hrs). You may be able to hire a donkey, US$5 each way to Arrecifes, but watch the donkeys, they eat donkeys. On the way to Pueblito, there is a huge mango tree, useful in season since there is little fruit in the park; there are also many camping and hammock places. At the site there are Indians; do not photograph them. From Pueblito you can either return to Cañaveral, or continue for 2 hrs to Calabazo on the Santa Marta-Riohacha road. A circuit Santa Marta, Cañaveral, Arrecifes, Pueblito, Calabazo, Santa Marta in one day is arduous, needing a 0700 start at least. It is advisable to inform park guards when walking in the park; also wear hiking boots and beware of bloodsucking insects. Take no valuables to the park; be vigilant against robbers at all times. Best also to take your own food and water. You will see monkeys, iguanas and maybe snakes. In the wet, the paths are very slippery.

There are cabins for 4-6 persons at Cañaveral for US$18 per night pp, great views over sea and jungle, good restaurant. Camping at Cañaveral costs US$3 per site. The camp at Cañaveral has facilities but there is only one restaurant with a tiny store, so take all supplies. There are plenty of mosquitoes, but a very attractive site. Beware of falling coconuts and donkeys that will eat any food left in tents. Two good camping sites at Arrecifes, the first US$2.50 for tent, US$1.50 for hammock space, US$2 to hire hammock, US$3 for hut, fresh water shower and toilets, the second cheaper, but no electricity or showers, one restaurant, *El Paraíso* (but not cheap), a basic shop and guardroom for gear, soft drinks available (eg from Alberto), beautiful beach nearby (sea dangerous). 15-20 mins' walk, left, along the beach at Arrecifes is La Piscina, a beautiful, safe natural swimming pool, excellent snorkelling.

You need to obtain permission from Inderena to camp in the park if you are not staying in Cañaveral, but this is normally forthcoming if you specify where you intend to stay. Hotels in Santa Marta will help to arrange your trip to Tairona, but there is no need to take guides (who charge US$20 or more pp for a day trip). Tours arranged by *Hotel Miramar*, Santa Marta, cost between US$80-100, very interesting but little care is taken over waste disposal. Note: Tairona park was reported closed for part of 1994 because of water shortages. Check with Inderena office in Santa Marta before visiting.

Riohacha, capital of Guajira Department, 160 km E of Santa Marta, is a port of 79,600 people at the mouth of the Río César: low white houses, concrete streets, no trees or hills. It was founded in 1545 by Nicolás Federmann, and in early years its pearling industry was large enough to tempt Drake to sack it (1596). Pearling almost ceased during the 18th century and the town was all but abandoned. (It is best to travel from Riohacha in a luxury bus, early am as these buses are less likely to be stopped and searched for contraband.)

Hotels B *Arimaca*, C 1 y Cra 9, T 273481, clean and friendly; **D** *Gimaura* (state-owned), Av La Playa, T 272234, including breakfast, they allow camping (free) in their grounds, with outside shower; **E** *Hostal Ota*, opposite the bus station, fan, clean, friendly, expensive food; **E** *Los Delfines*, clean, friendly, one block from sea and central plaza, two from Venezuelan consulate. **F** *International*, Cra 7, No 12A-35, friendly, patio, free iced water, rec; **F** *Residencia Yatoonia*, Cra 7, No 11-26, T 73487, private bath, clean, safe, helpful, half way between beach and bus station.

Many small **restaurants** along sea-front. *Tizones*, opp *Los Delfines*, Cra 2 y Cra 10, rec for food and juices (takes Visa and Diners Club); *Golosinas*, café near the beach, good food, friendly service. No hotel or *pensión* costs less than US$5; food is expensive. You can sling your hammock for free at the police station. There are an airport, a cinema, a tourist office on the beach front and a bank, which changes dollars cash, but not if you're in your beachwear. Good hammocks sold in the market. The best place for buying mantas and other local items is *La Casa de la Manta Guajira*, Cra 6, No 9-35, be prepared to bargain. At the weekend, Riohacha fills up, and bars and music spring up all over the place. The sea is clean, despite the red silt stirred up by the waves.

Venezuelan Consulate C 7, No 3-08 (hours 0900-1300, and closed from 1500 Fri to 0900 Mon). With two passport photographs, photocopy of passport and an exit ticket with date most can get a visa on the same day, if you get there early, but be prepared for an interview with the consul himself; visas cost US$30 and should not be a transit visa, valid for 72 hrs only. Travellers report it is easier to get a Venezuelan visa in Barranquilla.

Tourist Office Cra 7, No 1-38. **DAS Office** (immigration) C 1 y Cra 6, T 72407.

Going S from Riohacha on an alternative road to Maicao and the Venezuelan frontier, you come to **Cuestecita** (*Hotel Turismo*; *Restaurant La Fogata*), where you can turn SW to **Barrancas**. Here a large coal mine (one of the largest in the world—El Cerrejón) came into operation in 1986. A good dirt road and an industrial railway (no passengers) have been built between the mine and the new Puerto Bolívar in the Bahía Portete, many millions of tons of coal are being exported annually. Visitors are apparently welcome, but it would probably be best to make arrangements first at the El Cerrejón main office in Barranquilla.

Continuing on this road, which takes you either round the Sierra Nevada to Barranquilla and Santa Marta via Fundación (see above) or S to Bucaramanga, you come to **Valledupar**, capital of César Department (municipal pop 247,940). Valledupar claims to be the home of the *vallenato* music, in which the accordion features prominently. Each year there is a *vallenato* festival from 29 April to 1 May. You can change money at *casas de cambio* on C 16.

Hotels A3 *Vajamar*, Cra 7, No 16A-30, T 725121, pool, expensive food; **A3** *Sicarare*, two-star, Cra 9, No 16-04, T 722137; cheaper 2-star hotel is **B** *Kurakata*, C 19C, No 7-96, T 724425; **F** *Residencia El Triunfo*, Cra 7, No 19-31, with bath, fan, clean, good; next door is *Hotel/Restaurant Nutibara*, excellent cheap meals and breakfast, excellent fruit juices; several other hotels in this street.

Transport Bus from Santa Marta, 6 hrs, from Cartagena, US$10 (with Expreso Brasilia); to Barranquilla, 4½ hrs, US$6; to Bucaramanga, 8 hrs US$17. You can fly to Bogotá and Riohacha.

The Sierra Nevada, covering a triangular area of 16,000 sq km, rises abruptly from the sea, or from lowlands which nowhere reach over 300m above sea-level. "Indeed, the N slope is one of the most striking anywhere, lifting from the Caribbean to 5,800-metre snow peaks in about 45 km, a gradient comparable with the S face of the Himalaya, and unequalled along the world's coasts. The interior is made up of some eight E-W ranges with their intervening valleys. The lower parts of these interior valleys are flanked by forests—the homes of Indians as well as of pumas, jaguars, and a variety of snakes and birds—but for the most part the Sierra is almost lunar in its sterile grandeur, bleak *páramos* leading to naked crag and scree and glacier, where only an occasional questing condor moves. In the rocky heart of the area are a large number of small, beautiful lakes, many in cirques."—Frank F Cunningham, in an excellent illustrated article on exploring the Sierra in *The Geographical Magazine*. The rainy season in these mountains ends November; January is best month for a visit.

It is necessary to obtain a safe-conduct pass from the Casa Indígena (45 mins out of town) and the police in Valledupar before visiting the Sierra Nevada, if you are going further than San Sebastián. From Valledupar the best route is along the Guatepuri valley. Jeeps run from Valledupar, Cra 7A, C 18, Nos 37-55, to Pueblo Bello, 2 hrs US$4.80 (US$2.40, 1 hr, from turn off main road to Pueblo Bello). In **Pueblo Bello** (**G** *Hotel El Encanto*, good meals US$1, friendly, but poor beds, hot, small, dark, dirty; **F** *El Hogar de Mercedes*), enquire for jeeps to **San Sebastián de Rábago** (also called **Nabusimake**), the central village of one of the four tribes of Indians living in the Sierra, the Arhuacos (jeep owners Quico and Gudar Neader are the only ones who go frequently, US$5 per seat, 2-2½ hrs). It is set in beautiful surroundings and is the epitome of an Indian village. Ask for El Salto, a 2-hr walk, guide US$4.50 (not really needed). The jeep driver may be able to arrange for you to stay on a farm; Doña Inés recommended, F, clean, friendly, good food. Also recommended is Noco, a mestizo who has lived in the valley for over 30 years; he has floor space, free camping (cold) and can arrange mules for trips in the Sierra (US$8.50 per mule including guide, per day). Noco himself may act as guide if he is free (he runs a grocery store); he is very knowledgeable. Camping is also permitted in the valley.

Before hiking in the Sierra, visitors must pay a "tourist tax" to the Arhuaco chief in San Sebastián (at the police HQ); this ranges from US$7 to US$15, depending on what you want to do. (Do not leave litter or disrespect the Indians' sacred grounds.) **The Indians of the Sierra** distrust strangers (stay on paths; do not stray on to private land) and do not take kindly to being photographed, especially without permission. However they like to be given sea-shells which can be ground into powder and mixed with coca leaves and such a gift may improve their reaction to strangers and cameras. **NB** The Sierra Nevada is a marijuana-growing area—take care.

A recommended guide to the Sierra Nevada is Mauricio Guevera (T Bogotá 213-7002), who organizes treks (but not all year). You need to be fit for his 12-day hikes through the villages, valleys alive with butterflies, flowers and waterfalls, and to the lakes and the snowfields and summit of Pico Colón at 5,800m. There is plenty of drinking water, but Pueblo Bello is the only place to stock up with food. A tent is necessary for the trek, there are more for hire or purchase in the Valledupar region. The best place for maps is Bogotá. It is also possible to hike on the coastal side of the Sierra, but it is absolutely essential to take a guide through the marijuana districts. Recommended is Juancho at the village of Bonda, half an hour from Santa Marta by taxi. Juancho is an ethnologist (formerly of Medellín) who has lived with Kogi Indians for many years, owns a farm and speaks the different dialects. You need to be fit for his treks too. Trekking tours to the Nevada de Santa Marta can also be arranged in Santa Marta, check with the Tourist Office.

From Valledupar on to Codazzi is asphalted, to the paved Bucaramanga-Santa Marta highway. There is a possible overnight stay at **Curumaní** (*Hotel Himalaya*), or at Aguachica, just off the road.

Beyond Riohacha to the E is the arid and sparsely inhabited **Guajira Peninsula**. The Indians here live primitively, collecting dividivi, tending goats, and fishing. They are Guajiros, and of special interest are the coloured robes worn by the women. To visit a small part of the Peninsula you can take a bus from Riohacha (they leave twice a day from the Indian market) to Manaure for US$2.40. It is an uncomfortable 3-hr drive through fields of cactus but offers fine views of flamingos and other brightly coloured birds. If you are going in your own transport, check on safety before setting out. **Manaure**, which is known for its salt flats, has a *residencia* (**G** *Hotel Flamingo*). From Manaure there are *busetas* to **Uribia** US$1 (one basic *residencia*, no running water, but fresh water is a problem throughout the Guajira) and thence to Maicao. In Uribia you can buy handicrafts intended for local, not tourist, use by asking around. You can get *busetas* from Uribia to Puerto Bolívar (from where the coal is exported) and from there transport to Cabo de Vela, where the lagoons shelter vast flocks of flamingos, herons and sandpipers. It costs about US$3 from Uribia to Cabo de Vela. There are fine beaches and, in Cabo de Vela, a basic but friendly, Indian-run hotel, *El Mesón* (rooms, hammock veranda, showers, good meals—excellent fried fish), or sling a hammock at *El Caracol* where there is an expensive restaurant (better value next door at *La Tropicana* if you order food in advance). Also Conchita will hire out a large hut, hammocks for up to 5, cook food with prior request, along the coast, ask anyone. Sunsets in the Guajira are magnificent.

The Caribbean coastal highway, now paved, runs direct from Santa Marta along the coast to Riohacha, and the Riohacha-Maicao road (also paved) has been greatly improved. Now that there are no flights from Barranquilla to Maracaibo, taxi or bus to Maicao, and colectivo to Maracaibo is the most practical route.

NB The Guajira peninsular is not a place to travel alone, parties of 3 or more are recommended. Also remember it is hot, it is easy to get lost, there is little cover and very little water. Locals, including police, are very helpful in giving lifts.

Maicao is full of Venezuelan contraband, and is still at the centre of the narcotics trade. Its streets are unmade and it has a considerable reputation for lawlessness; most commercial premises close before 1600 and after 1700 the streets are highly unsafe. If at all possible travellers should avoid Maicao and the road services that go there, which are liable to ambush.

Entering Venezuela, everyone travelling overland needs a visa; a transit visa will only suffice if you have a confirmed ticket to a third country within 3 days. There is now no Venezuelan Consul in Maicao. You must get a visa in Barranquilla, Cartagena or Riohacha; with all the right papers, border crossing is easy. Entering Colombia, immigration is at the border. If you enter by *por puesto*, make sure the driver stops at the Colombian entry post. If not you will have to return later to complete formalities.

Hotels in Maicao D *Maicao Juan Hotel*, Cra 10, C 12, T 8184, the only safe one; several others on Cra 10 (*El Dorado*, No 12-45; *Medanos*, No 11-25) and elsewhere; no reports.

Buses (basic): to **Riohacha**, US$1.35; **Santa Marta** (Expreso Occidente), US$5.50; **Maracaibo**, US$6 (Expreso Maicao, 0400-1800); **Barranquilla**, last one at 1600, US$10.75. **Cartagena**, US$16.75. Colectivos, known as "por puestos" in Venezuela, Maicao-Maracaibo, US$5 pp, or infrequent microbus, US$3.30, very few buses to Venezuela after midday.

San Andrés and Providencia

San Andrés and *Providencia* are two small and attractive, but very expensive, islands in the Caribbean Sea. They are 400 km SW of Jamaica, 180 km E of Nicaragua, and 480 km N of the Colombian coast. The original inhabitants, mostly black, speak some English, but the population has swollen with unrestricted immigration from Colombia. There are also Chinese and Middle Eastern communities. The population in 1993 was officially put at 61,050. The main problem is deteriorating water and electricity supplies (in most hotels the water is salty).

Places to see: the beautiful Keys, like Johnny Key with a white beach and parties all day Sunday (US$3 return, you can go in one boat and return in another), and the so-called Aquarium (US$3 return), off Haynes Key where, using a mask and wearing sandals as protection against sea-urchins, you can see colourful fish. Boats to these places all leave am; none pm. Snorkelling equipment can be hired on San Andrés for US$4-5, but it is better and cheaper on the shore than on the key. Pedalos can be hired at US$4 per hour. Diving trips to reef cost US$60 with Pedro Montoya at Aquarium diving shop, Punta Hansa, T 26649, or Buzos del Caribe, Centro Comercial Dann, T 23712. Diving off San Andrés is very good. From Tominos Marina, 2-hr boat trips round the bay cost US$8.75, 4-hr trips US$17.50 (both inc 3 free rum-and-cokes); also trips round the island.

The Hoyo Soplador is a geyser-like hole through which the sea spouts into the air most surprisingly when the wind is in the right direction. Less spoilt parts of the island are San Luis (good beach), Sound Bay and the W side (but no beaches this side). A road circles the island, of coral, some 11 km long rising to 104m. Buses, which cover the eastern side of the island all day (15 min intervals) cost US$0.25. There is a "tourist train" (suitably converted tractor and carriages) which tours the island in 3 hrs for US$3. Bicycles are a popular way of getting around on the island and are easy to hire, eg opposite *El Dorado Hotel*—usually in poor condition, choose your own bike and check all parts thoroughly (US$1.10 per hour, US$6 per day); motorbikes also easy to hire, US$3.50 per hour. Cars can be hired for US$15

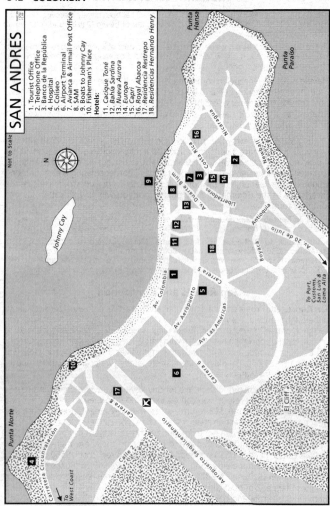

SAN ANDRES

Not to Scale

1. Tourist Office
2. Telephone Office
3. Banco de la República
4. Hospital
5. Coliseo
6. Airport Terminal
7. Avianca & Airmail Post Office
8. SAM
9. Boats to Johnny Cay
10. Fisherman's Place

Hotels:
11. Cacique Toné
12. Bahía Sardina
13. Nueva Aurora
14. Europa
15. Capri
16. Royal Abacoa
17. Residencia Restrepo
18. Residencias Hernando Henry

Punta Hansa

Punta Paraíso

Johnny Cay

Punta Norte

To West Coast

To Port, Customs, San Luis, & Loma Alta

El Cliff

for 2 hrs, with US$6 for every extra hour.

The islands are a customs-free zone; they are very crowded with Colombian shoppers looking for foreign-made bargains. Although alcoholic drinks are cheap, essential goods are extremely costly, and electronic goods are more expensive than in the UK. In July and August, it is very difficult to get on flights into and out of San Andrés; book in advance if possible. Checking in for flights can be difficult because of queues of shoppers with their goods. There is a customs tax of 15% on some items purchased if you are continuing to mainland Colombia.

Culture San Andrés and Providencia are famous in Colombia for their music, whose styles include the local form of calypso, soca, reggae and church music. A number of good local groups perform on the islands and in Colombia. Concerts are held at the Old Coliseum (every Saturday at 2100 in the high season); the Green Moon Festival is held in May. There is a cultural centre at Punta Hansa in San Andrés town (T 25518).

Carry your passport (or photocopy) at all times.

Hotels **NB** Some hotels raise their prices by 20-30% on 15 December. *Bahía Marina*, road to San Luis Km 5, T 23539, luxury resort; **A1** *Aquarium*, Av Colombia 1-19, T 23120, F 26174, all suites; **A1** *Casablanca*, Av Colombia y Costa Rica, T 25950, central, food; **A1** *Casa Dorada*, Av Las Américas, T 24008, salt water washing, reasonable food; *Decamerón*, road to San Luis Km 15, book through *Decamerón Cartagena*, T 655-4400, F 653-738, all-inclusive resort, pool, a/c, TV, good restaurant, rec; **A2** *Royal Abacoa*, Av Colombia No 2-41, good restaurant, T 24043; **A2** *Cacique Toné*, Av Colombia, No 5-02, T 24251, deluxe, air conditioning, pool, on sea-front. **A3** *Tiuna*, Av Colombia No 3-59, T 23235, a/c, swimming pool. New expensive hotel, *Mary Land*, nr airport and beach (no details, 1994); **B** *Abacoa*, Av Colombia, T 4133/4, with bath and a/c; **A3** *Bahía Sardinas*, Av Colombia No 4-24, T 23793, across the street from the beach, a/c, TV, fridge, good service, comfortable, clean, no swimming pool; **B** *Capri*, Av Costa Rica No 1A-64, T 24315, with bath and a/c, good value; **A2** *El Isleño* Av de la Playa 3-59, T 23990, F 23126, 2 blocks from airport, in palm grove, good sea views; **C** *Nueva Aurora*, Av de las Américas No 3-46, T 23811, fan and private bath, pool, restaurant; **A3** *El Dorado*, Av Colombia No 1A-25, restaurant, casino, swimming pool; **D** *Coliseo*, Av Colombia No 1-59, T 23330, friendly, noisy, good restaurant; **A** *Verde Mar*, Av 20 de Julio, T 25525, quiet and friendly, a/c, rec; **C** *Mediterráneo*, Av Los Libertadores, T 26722, clean, friendly, poor water supply.

D *Residencias Hernando Henry*, Av de las Américas 4-84, T 26416, restaurant, fan, clean, good value, often full, on road from airport; also near airport, **D** Olga and Federico Archibold, C de la Bodega Marlboro, No 91-18, T 25781, have 3 self-contained apartments, modern, clean, friendly; *Residencia Restrepo*, "gringo hotel", Av 8 near airport, noisy ("share a room with a Boeing 727"—till midnight), much cheaper than others, E, or less for a hammock in the porch, but you get what you pay for, the accommodation is in a poor state and the grounds are a junkyard, not rec. On the way to *Restrepo* you pass a good food shop, breakfast, juices, snacks. Campsite at South End said to be dirty and mosquito-ridden.

Restaurants *Oasis* (good), Av Colombia No 4-09; *Popular*, on Av Bogotá, good square meal; *El Pimentón*, Av de las Américas, good *menú*, cheap; *El Zaguán de los Arrieros*, Av 20 de Julio (50m after cinema), good food and value; *Bahía*, good food; *Fonda Antioqueña Nos 1 and 2*, on Av Colombia near the main beach, and Av Colombia at Av Nicaragua, best value for fish; *Sea Food House*, Av 20 de Julio, at Parque Bolívar, good cooking, not expensive, second floor terrace; excellent fruit juices at *Jugolandia*, C 20 de Julio; *Jugosito*, Av Colombia, 1½ blocks from tourist office towards centre, cheap meals; *Nueva China*, next to *Restrepo*, reasonable Chinese. *Fisherman's Place*, in the fishing cooperative at N end of main beach, very good, simple. Cheap fish meals can be bought at San Luis beach.

Banks and Exchange Banco Industrial Colombiana, Av Costa Rica; Banco de Bogotá will advance pesos on a Visa card. Banco Occidente for Mastercard. **Aerodisco** shop at airport will change dollars cash anytime at rates slightly worse than banks, or try the **Photo Shop** on Av Costa Rica. (Rates are lower than in Bogotá.) Many shops will change US$ cash; it is impossible to change TCs at weekends. (Airport employees will exchange US$ cash at a poor rate.)

Post Office Airmail, Avianca office, Av Duarte Blum. **Telecommunications** Av de las Américas 2A-23.

Tourist Information, Av Colombia No 5-117, English spoken, maps.

Taxis round the island, US$8; to airport, US$3; in town, US$0.60; *colectivo* to airport, US$0.50.

Only cruise ships and tours go to San Andrés; there are no other passenger services by sea. To ship a vehicle costs well over US$1,000 (exact 1995 price not known) and is difficult. Immigration insists on seeing a return air ticket on arrival with your car. To ship a vehicle to Panama costs over US$700. Interoceánica cargo ships, T 6624-6625. Beware of agents who, having a monopoly, overcharge for shipping services. Beware also of offers of tickets on ships to/from San Andrés, or of a job on a ship, these are con tricks. Officially, ships may not carry passengers to the mainland; if you want to leave by sea, speak only to the ship's captain.

There are Panamanian and Costa Rican consulates on San Andrés.

Airport Flights to most major Colombian cities: to Bogotá and Medellín with Aces, Intercontinental de Aviación, Aeorepública, SAM (you can arrange a stop-over in Cartagena, which is good value, the onward flight from Cartagena to Bogotá, Cali or Medellín does not cost much more than the bus fare and saves a lot of time); Intercontinental also flies to Barranquilla, Cali, Cartagena, Medellín, while Aces flies to Medellín. SAM flies to Cartagena, Barranquilla, Cali, Medellín and Pereira. Also to Guatemala City and San José (also Aero Costa Rica). Intercontinental flies to Panama City. Note that Panama, Costa Rica and Honduras all require onward tickets which cannot be bought on San Andrés, can be in Cartagena. For advice on purchasing tickets to Colombia via San Andrés, **see p 900**. Care: SAM office in San Andrés will not issue officially one way tickets to Central America. You buy a return, and SAM office on the mainland will refund once you show an onward ticket. The refund (less 15%) may not be immediate. However travellers report that you can purchase a one-way ticket at the SAM desk at the airport. Sunday flights are always heavily booked, similarly July-Aug, Dec-Jan. If wait-listed, don't give up hope. 15 mins walk to town (taxi US$3 pp). All airline offices in town, except Satena at airport. SAM offers hotel packages as well as the airfare, but booking a hotel and meal plan outside San Andrés through a travel agent is not always a satisfactory arrangement. It is best to see the hotel for yourself. However, if you are willing to take the risk, travel agents in Cartagena in 1994 were offering 4 nights, half board, trips, all inclusive US$250 or US$310 with flight to Bogotá.

Providencia, commonly called Old Providence (3,835 inhabitants), 80 km back to the NNE from San Andrés, is 7 km long and is more mountainous than San Andrés, rising to 610m. There are waterfalls, and the land drops steeply into the sea in places. It is also an expensive island. The 3 main beaches are Bahía Manzanillo/Manchincal Bay, the largest, most attractive and least developed, Bahía del Suroeste/South West Bay and Bahía Agua Dulce/Freshwater Bay, all in the S W.

Most of the accommodation is at Playa Agua Dulce (Freshwater): **B** *Cabañas El Recreo* (Captain Brian's, T 48010); **A+** *Cabañas El Paraíso* (T 26330), a/c, TV, fridge; and **B** *Cabañas Aguadulce*, T 41860. *Miss Elma's* rec for cheap food and *Morgan's Bar* for fish meals and a good breakfast. Several houses take in guests. Camping is possible at Freshwater Bay. Truck drivers who provide transport on the island may be able to advise on accommodation. Take cash with you, the two banks do not cash TCs, though one will accept Visa credit cards. English is widely spoken. The sea food is good, water and fresh milk are generally a problem. Superb views can be had by climbing from Casabaja/Bottom House or Aguamansa/Smooth Water to the peak. Horse riding is available, and boat trips can be made to neighbouring islands such as *Santa Catalina* (an old pirate lair joined to the main island by a wooden bridge), and to the NE, Cayo Cangrejo/Crab Key (beautiful swimming and snorkelling), and Cayos Hermanos/Brothers Cay: day trip from 1000 to 1500, about US$7 pp. On Santa Catalina, on the W side, is a rock formation called Morgan's Head. Accommodation: the German-owned *Cabañas Santa Catalina*, friendly, use of small kitchen. Day tours are arranged by the Providencia office in San Andrés, costing US$35 inclusive. SAM flies from San Andrés, US$30, 25 mins, 6 times a day, bookable only in San Andrés. Satena flies twice a day from San Andrés. (Return flight has to be confirmed at airport. Tourist office at airport.) Boat trips from San Andrés take 8 hrs, but are not regular.

UP THE MAGDALENA RIVER (4)

The old waterway from the Caribbean, now superseded by road and air, leads from Barranquilla to the limit of navigation at Girardot. The route passes snow-capped volcanoes and *tierra caliente* weekend resorts before climbing to the river's upper reaches entering Huila Department.

The Magdalena is wide but shallow and difficult to navigate because of surface eddies, and there are little whirlpools over submerged rocks. Away to the NE, in the morning, one can see the high snow-capped peaks of the Sierra Nevada de Santa Marta. Passenger travel by the lofty paddle boats on the river has now come to an end, though the adventurous traveller may still find an occasional passage by cargo paddle boat. In general the only way of getting from one place to the other along the river is by motor launch (*chalupa*), and this is more expensive. The river trip from the N coast (bus to Magangué) to Puerto Berrío or Puerto Boyacá and thence by bus to Bogotá can be completed in about 4 days (1994).

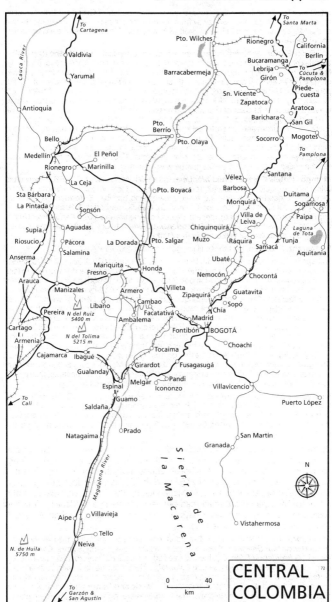

CENTRAL COLOMBIA

Insect repellents should be taken, for mosquitoes are a nuisance. Guerrilla activity has been reported in the Magdalena valley away from the river and the main roads. The upper reaches of the Magdalena, beyond Neiva, are dealt with in Section 7; this includes the archaeological site of San Agustín.

At Tenerife Bolívar had his first victory in the Magdalena campaign. At **Zambrano** (pop 8,210), a cattle centre 96 km beyond Calamar, there are tobacco plantations. There is a road W to the N-S Cartagena-Medellín road, and a trail E to the oil fields at El Difícil. Near Pinto the river divides: the eastern branch, silted and difficult, leads to **Mompós**, an old town of 10,810 people: cattle farming and tobacco, and the scene of another victory for Bolívar: "At Mompós", he said, "my glory was born." Mompós was founded in 1537 and, thanks to its comparative isolation, preserves its colonial character more completely than any other town in Colombia. Old buildings are the Casa de Gobierno, once a home of the Jesuits, and the Colegio de Pinillos. There are 7 churches and the Easter celebrations are said to be among the best in Colombia. The cemetery has considerable historical interest. The town is well known in Colombia for handworked gold jewellery. Airport. Malaria is endemic in the surrounding countryside. If staying overnight, mosquito nets and/or coils are a must. Caution: Drinking fruit juices is not recommended near the river, glasses may be washed in river water.

Mompós Hotels C *Hostal Doña Manuela*, C Real del Medio, 17-41, T 55620, a converted colonial house, quiet and peaceful, restaurant is the best in town; **D** *Residencias Aurora*, shower, fan, good meals, nice and friendly, bargaining possible; **E** *Residencias Villas de Mompós*, 500m E of Plaza Tamarindo, family run, friendly, free coffee; **E** *Posada de Vinney*, opp *Doña Manuela*, shared bath, modern, clean, above medical practice; **E** *Residencias Unión*, C 18, No 3-43, with bath and fan; **F** *Residencias Solmar*, C Cra 18-22, near main square, friendly, basic, but you are welcomed with a "tinto".

Restaurant *El Galileo*, next to the Plaza, good *comida corriente*.

Transport Bus from **Cartagena** with Unitransco (0530, returns 0700), daily, 12 hrs, US$9.50, otherwise take Brasilia bus to **Magangué** 4½ hrs, US$8.50. From Magangué you have to take a *chalupa* (launch) either direct to Mompós, 2 hrs, US$3.30, or to **Bodega** and thence by jeep or taxi, 1½ hrs, US$2. You can also reach Mompós in 2 hrs, US$4 by *chalupa* from **El Banco** to the SE (buses to Santa Marta, Barranquilla, Bucaramanga etc). Plenty of willing hands to carry your luggage to and from the launch, jeep and bus—for an outrageous fee! From Magangué, buses also go to **Barranquilla** and **Sincelejo**. There is a Mon to Fri air service (Aces) from Barranquilla to Mompós. It is also possible to reach Mompós from Barranquilla by *chalupa* changing at Plato, but we do not have good information on the time needed or the price. Note: most *chalupas* and buses run in the morning. There is little public transport after 1100.

To **Valledupar** and **Santa Marta**, either go from El Banco (see below), or cross the river at **Talaigua** (between Mompós and Magangué, *carritos* leave Mompós early am) to **Santa Ana**. Buses leave Santa Ana 0700 for Santa Marta and Valledupar, first 2½ hrs unpaved, then paved; US$8 to Valledupar. For Sierra Nevada alight at Pueblo Bello crossroads.

Most vessels go by the western arm of the loop to **Magangué** (pop 61,265), the port for the savannas of Bolívar. A road runs W to join the N-S Cartagena-Medellín highway. 5 hotels inc **D** *Hans Burchardt*, a/c, private bath, fridge, friendly; *Avenida*; *Rivera*; 10 *residenciales*, cheapest *Londres*, *Brasil* or *Hotel Medellín*, all G pp. Few places to eat, *Terraza*, to the left of plaza, reasonable.

Upstream from Magangué, the Río San Jorge, 379 km long, 240 km of it navigable, comes in from the Western Cordillera. Further up the Río Cauca, 1,020 km long, comes in from the far S. Its Caribbean end is navigable for 370 km, and it is navigable again for a distance of 245 km in the Cauca Valley above the gorge. It is possible to get small boats from Magangué up the Cauca, via Guaranda and Nechi to Caucasia on the main road between Montería and Medellín. This trip costs about US$20 and takes 2 days allowing for unforseen breakdowns etc. A very attractive trip if you have time.

At **El Banco**, 420 km from Barranquilla (airport, one flight each weekday), the river loops join (**F** *Residencias Las Delicias*, C 9 near jeep terminal, basic; also, nearby, **E** *Hotel Continental*, friendly; **G** *Residencia Edén*, C 9, friendly, free coffee; **E** *Casa del Viajero*, C 8, colour TV, fan, bath, clean, fridge with Cokes, safe; **F** *Colonial*, 1 block from harbour, with bath and fan; **G** *Residencia Ocaña*, price pp, basic, clean, noisy; about a dozen others). This is an old, dirty and beautiful town of 10,250 people (see under *Music and Dance* for festival). Along the river front are massive stone stairways. The Cordilleras are in the distance, a blue range on either side of the valley. Egrets, various species of heron, ringed kingfishers much in evidence.

There are many sandy islands in the river to complicate navigation. Daily buses from El Banco to Bucaramanga, US$10, Cúcuta and Valledupar. Don't get conned into taking an expensive boat across the river instead of the bus ferry. *Chalupa* service El Banco-Barrancabermeja with Cootransfluviales, 0800, 7 hrs, US$14.50. A difficult trail leads N of El Banco to the small town of **Chimichagua** (pop 5,000), on the shores of the large lake of Zapatosa.

Continuing upriver are the small towns of **Puerto Boca**, **Tamalameque** (basic *residencia* and restaurant), La Gloria, **Gamarra** (pop 3,700), San Pablo and **Puerto Wilches** (5,600). All are connected by launch.

Some 30 km above Puerto Wilches is **Barrancabermeja** (or more commonly Barranca – pop 135,955), so called because of the reddish-brown oil-stained cliffs on which it stands. It is an important oil centre, with a prominent refinery. It is also a warm, humid place with an interesting indoor market. Owing to recent violence, enquire about conditions before stopping here.

Hotels C *Achue*, Cra 17, No 9-12, T 222500, a/c, private bath, restaurant, friendly, safe; **F** *Iris*, just up road from port, clean, friendly; **F** *Residencias Ferroviario*, with bath, opp railway station, friendly. **F** *Santa Fe*, in town, clean and friendly; many more around the train station and in town. A shop at C 19, Avs 18 y 19 sells good bread and muesli.

Transport Air   10 min by taxi from centre, 2 daily flights to Bogotá, Aces. **Buses** Bucaramanga, 3 hrs, US$2.30. **Boats** *Chalupa* to Puerto Boyacá, 0845, 6 hrs, US$12.

Puerto Berrío (airport; 25,200 inhabitants) is on the W bank 100 km above Barrancabermeja and 756 km from Barranquilla. It is the river port for Medellín and the rich Antioquia Department. A railway from Medellín runs down the slopes of the Cordillera Central and over a low pass to Puerto Berrío, where it connects with the Bogotá-Santa Marta line.

Hotels at Puerto Berrío E *Hotel Magdalena*, pleasant, on a hilltop near river; **F** *Residencias El Ganadero*, with bath, clean, modern, with ceiling fans. Many other hotels, *residencias* and *apartamentos*. **Restaurants**: *La Buena Mesa*, good big meals; *Heladeria Joi*, good ice cream and sundaes.

Rail   To Santa Marta, Bogotá and Medellín, check at **Grecia** station, 4 km from the town and hotels (taxi service only) if trains are running.

75 km upriver (5 hrs by road) from Puerto Berrío is **Puerto Boyacá**. The road is mostly unpaved, passing zebu *fincas*, swamps and oil fields. There are army checkpoints on the road, owing to guerrilla activity in the area. (Hotels: *Residencias Lusitania*; *Santa Fe*; *Hotel* and *Heladería Embajador*.)

River Transport   Puerto Berrío to Puerto Boyacá US$4.10. **Buses**   Rápido Tolima has regular buses to Honda (3 hrs, US$2.70) and to Puerto Berrío.

It is 151 km up river from Puerto Berrío to **La Dorada** (pop 56,220) on the W bank, but only 134 km by rail (7½ hrs) along the W bank. This railway crosses the Magdalena by a bridge from La Dorada to **Puerto Salgar**, on the E bank, from which the Cundinamarca Railway (198 km) goes up the slopes of the Eastern Cordillera to Bogotá. (Bus La Dorada-Bogotá, 5 hrs, US$4.80, La Dorada-Medellín, US$5.) The Lower Magdalena river navigation stops at La Dorada as there are rapids above, as far as Honda. Cargo is taken by railway to Honda, where it is re-embarked. The Upper Magdalena is navigable as far as Girardot (see below).

Hotels La Dorada: **F** *Rosita*, C 17, No 3-28, T 72301, with bath, friendly, pleasant, rec; on highway to Honda, *Magdalena Motel*; others near railway station; youth hostel at *Centro Vacacional La Magdalena*, 3 km from La Dorada—details from Alcom in Bogotá—*Parador Turístico* next door. **Puerto Salgar**: *Salgar*; **G** *Residencia Antioquia*, with fan.

Honda (pop 25,481; average temperature: 29°C; altitude 230m; airport) on the W bank of the river, is 32 km upstream from La Dorada (149 km from Bogotá). It is a pleasant old town with many colonial houses. The streets are narrow and picturesque, and the town is surrounded by hills. El Salto de Honda (the rapids which separate the Lower from the Upper Magdalena) are just below the town. Several bridges span the Magdalena and the Guali rivers, at whose junction the town lies. In February the Magdalena rises and fishing is unusually good. People come from all over the region for the fishing and the festival of the Subienda, as the season is called.

Hotels C *Campestre El Molino*, 5 km from Honda on Mariquita road, T 3130, swimming pools, fans in rooms, friendly; **C** *Ondama*, C 17 y 13A, T 3565, swimming pool; **D** *Club Piscina*, Cra 12, No 19-139, T 3273, fan, swimming pool, clean, friendly, arranges safe parking at reasonable rates with neighbours, rec; **E** *Residencias Las Mercedes*, with bath, clean and friendly.

Restaurants *La Cascada*, overlooking river, good. There is a row of good cheap restaurants across the Magdalena River bridge in Puerto Bogotá.

Buses from **Bogotá** by Velotax US$4.80, and Rápido Tolima, US$3, 4 hrs. **Manizales**, US$3.60. Rápido Tolima run half-hourly buses to **La Dorada** (1 hour), and beyond, to **Puerto Boyacá** (3 hrs), US$2.70. To **Puerto Berrío**, 8 hrs, departures at 0300 and 0800 with San Vicente. The new Bogotá-Medellín highway passes round the town.

West from Honda a paved road goes 21 km to ***Mariquita*** the centre of a fruit-growing country (13,000 people; *Hotel Bocaneme* and others; campsites; **C** *Motel Las Acacias*, outside Mariquita, on the Armero road, T 522016.) Buses depart from Honda every half hour, US$0.35, ¹/₂ hr with Rápido Tolima. On the way is the clean and pleasant bathing pool of El Diamante. On again is the Club Deportivo: private, but visitors are welcome to its swimming pool, a blessing in this climate. There is another, El Virrey, in Mariquita. The town has several old houses and buildings: a mint, the viceroy's house, the parish church. Here José Celestino Mutis lived for 8 years during his famous Botanic Expedition towards the end of the 18th century (when he and his helpers accumulated a herbarium of 20,000 plants, a vast library, and a rich collection of botanical plates and paintings of native fauna). The collection was sent to Madrid, where it remains. Mariquita was founded in 1551, and it was here that the founder of Bogotá, Jiménez de Quesada, died in 1579. From Mariquita a road runs W up the slopes of the Central Cordillera to Manizales.

Fresno, in the heart of a big coffee growing area, is 30 km from Mariquita. The road to Honda is appalling. Bus to Manizales (83 km) US$3.40 (Rápido Tolima).

From Mariquita the road turns S to (32 km) ***Armero***, which used to be a cotton growing centre. This town and surrounding villages were devastated by the eruption of the Nevado del Ruiz volcano (**see p 863**) in November 1985. Over 25,000 people were killed as approximately 10% of the ice core melted, causing landslides and mudflows. (Armero can be reached by colectivo from Honda; no lodging in Armero, nearest at *Lérida*, 12 km S—Hotels **F** *Central*, cheapest, not too clean, unfriendly, **F** pp *Colonial*, *Tundama*, Mariquita or possibly Guayabal; no drinks available in Armero; there are lots of mosquitoes, though.) A branch road runs 35 km W to ***Líbano***, 24,320 inhabitants. Coffee is the great crop here, with potatoes in the uplands. Away to the W looms the peak of Nevado del Ruiz, which before its eruption was the second highest in the Cordillera Central. **F** *Hotel Dorado*, one block from plaza. Bus from Líbano to Ibagué, US$2.70, 4 hrs; to Manizales, US$5.40, 4 hrs daily at 0430.

From Armero a branch road runs down to the Magdalena past Gambao to ***Ambalema***. At Gambao the river is crossed for the road to Bogotá. The main road from Armero goes direct for 88 km to Ibagué.

Ibagué, capital of Tolima Department, is a large city (386,425 inhabitants), lying at the foot of the Quindío mountains at 1,250m. It is cooler here (22°C) than in the valley. Parts of the town are old: the Colegio de San Simón is worth seeing, and so is the market. The Parque Centenario is pleasant. The city specializes in hand-made leather goods (there are many good, cheap shoe shops) and a local drink called *mistela*. There is an excellent Conservatory of Music.

The National Folklore Festival is held during the third week of June. The Departments of Tolima and Huila commemorate St John (24 June) and Sts Peter and Paul (29 June) with bullfights, fireworks, and music.

Hotels There are many hotels of reasonable quality which are quite comfortable. **A3** *Ambala*, C 11, No 2-60, T 610982, F 633490, with bath, TV, pool, restaurant; **D** *Ambeima*, Cra No 13-32, T 634300; **D** *Farallones*, C 16, No 2-88, good, fan, clean and opposite **D** *Cordillera*, also good; **E** *Bolívar*, C 17 y Cra 4, good, clean, TV; **E** *Bram*, C 17 y Cra 4, convenient, clean, secure, and insect-free, cold water; **E** *Raad*, next door; both good; **E** *Residencia Puracé*, opposite Tolima bus station; nearby **F** *La Paz*, C 18, No 3-119, friendly, tinto free in the morning; **F** *Montserrat*, C 18, Cra 1 y 2, price pp, clean, quiet, rec; **F** *Residencia Perón*, good for an overnight stop; **F** *Boston*, near bus station clean, basic.

Restaurants *Toy Wan*, Cra 4, Chinese. 24 hr restaurants inc *Punto Rojo*, in the shopping precinct on Cra 3, good lunch US$3; *El Espacio*, Cra 4, No 18-14, large helpings, good value; *Punto Fácil*, C 15 y Cra 3. Vegetarian, *Govinda*, Cra 2 y C 13.

Tourist Office Cra 3, between Cs 10 and 11; helpful; closed Sat and Sun. The Instituto Giográfico Agustin Codazzi has an office at C 14A, No 3-14, 3rd Floor, for maps.

Buses Terminal is between Cras 1-2 and Calles 19-20. Tourist police at terminal helpful. To Bogotá, US$8 Expreso Palmira 0915, 4 hrs.

Just outside, on the Armenia road, a dirt road leads to the slopes of the **Nevado del Tolima**. Gerhard Drekonja of Vienna writes: For climbing the Nevado del Tolima (5,215m) go from Ibagué to Juntas and El Silencio (2 hrs by train if running). From there half-an-hour walk to the fabulous natural thermal waters of El Rancho (simple sleeping accommodation and food available). The climb starts from El Rancho. It takes 8 to 10 hrs to the top; equipment (crampons and pica) indispensable. The final climb has to be done at sunrise because clouds and mist invariably rise around 0800. From the top is a breathtaking view across the other snowcapped mountains of the Cordillera Central. For information contact Cruz Roja Colombiana in Ibagué, Zona Industrial El Papayo, near the E entrance to the city, T 646014, who can put you in touch with a climbing group, Asociación Tolimense de Montañistas y Escaladores. Another helpful guide is Claus Schlief, who speaks German and English. Nevado del Tolima is the southernmost "nevado" in the **Parque Nacional Los Nevados** which extends up to Nevado del Ruiz overlooking Manizales (see under Manizales and Pereira). A local mountain guide with some Himalayan experience and well rec is Manolo Barrios, Barrio La Francia, Casa 23, Ibagué, T 646726.

There is a road to Girardot, 79 km E on the Magdalena, going on to Bogotá which is 224 km by road from Ibagué. On this road is the village of **Gualanday**, with **F** *Hotel Rozal*, clean, friendly, safe for motorcyclists and 4 good roadside restaurants (*Dona Eva's* also has accommodation). **Espinal**, pop 42,780, is an important agro-industrial town, but of little interest to the tourist. **F** *Bucaros*, in centre of town, private bath, clean, with restaurant. Bus to Ibagué, 1 hr, US$0.90, just flag one down; bus to Neiva, US$2.40. Toll between Ibagué and Espinal, US$0.50; between Espinal and Girardot, US$0.40. West of Ibagué the road runs over the 3,350-metre high Quindio Pass to Armenia, 105 km from Ibagué across the Cordillera Central. The bus trip from Ibagué to Pereira takes 4 hrs and costs US$3. To Cali, on Flota Magdalena pullman, 7 hrs, US$6.90; ordinary buses US$4.80; Velotax US$6. To Bogotá, 4$^{1}/_{2}$ hrs, US$5 with Velotax, US$6.20 by bus. Bus to Popayán, US$8.

Between Ibagué and Armenia, on the E side of the Quindio Pass, is **Cajamarca**, a friendly town in a beautiful setting; **G** *Residencia Central*; *Nevado*, expensive, somewhat noisy; both on same street, friendly and clean. Interesting market on Sunday. 6 km from Cajamarca on a paved road is Anaime, a quiet colourful village with a small plaza de toros. Beyond, the road climbs past *fincas* (food and camping) to 3,500m. Many *palma de cera* trees, the national tree of Colombia that grows to 40m. Jeep transport available.

Girardot (airport) is on the Upper Magdalena. Altitude, 326m; pop 80,040. The climate is hot and there are heavy rains. Here the navigation of the Upper Magdalena ends, although in dry weather boats cannot get this far; walk across the fine steel bridge to see merchandise being loaded and unloaded—coffee and hides are the main items, although shipments of the former have declined considerably. Launch rides on the river can be taken, starting from underneath the bridge. A 1-hour trip to Isla del Sol is rec (US$5). Large cattle fairs are held on 5-10 June and 5-10 December. There is a two-storey market, at its best in early morning but nevertheless good all day, and another good market on Sun mornings. Bogotanos come down here at weekends to warm up.

Hotels **A2** *El Peñón*, on site of former *hacienda* just outside town, Cra 16, No 79-31, T 26981, fashionable bungalow complex, casino, huge pool, lake, price per bungalow; **B** *Bachué*, Cra 8, No 18-04, T 26791, modern large cooled pool, excellent, rooms a/c with bath and TV, restaurant; **D** *Nuevo Río*, Cra 10, No 16-31, TV, fan, restaurant, laundry, friendly, English and German spoken; **D** *Los Angeles*, on main plaza, clean, friendly, rec; **E** *Miami*, Cra 7, No 13-57, large rooms, clean, fan, good, central location safe; **E** *Residencias La Paz*, Cra 1, No 11-3. Opp new bus terminal, **F** *El Cid*, with fan and **F** *Maroti*; **F** *Rincón*, on main street, C 19, No 10-68, balcony, fan; **F** *Colonial*, Cra 11, 16, showers; bath; **F** *El Dorado*, shared bath, basic.

Roads To **Bogotá**, 132 km, bus costs US$3.60, about 3½ hrs; bus to **Neiva**, US$3, 3½ hrs; to **Ibagué**, 78 km. To **Fusagasugá**, US$2.

Another centre of population in the Magdalena Valley lies upstream from Girardot, with Neiva as its capital. Coffee and tobacco are grown on the slopes here, and cattle, mainly Brahman, are raised in the valley. The road, and its short branches E and W, runs through a number of small towns of under 25,000 people. One of these, 35 km from Girardot, is **Guamo**, with 13,340 inhabitants. Just before Guamo is a marked turn off to **La Chamba**, where internationally famous pottery is made and sold. The pottery is fired in the afternoon; lots of mosquitoes here. Eight km beyond Guamo is **Saldaña**, where there are irrigation works that have made 15,000 hectares available for rice, sorghum, sesame and cotton. There are also oil fields in this area of the Magdalena river.

Hotel at Guamo *Lemayá*, Cra 8 y C 9, T 270230, modern, swimming pool, best in region. At El Espinal, before the road to La Chamba is **B** *Hotel Yuma*, T 4323. At **Saldaña**, *Hotel Saldaña*, not too good.

A pretty spot is the reservoir located near **Prado**, Tolima. Turn off the Girardot-Neiva road at Saldaña for 25 km; it is well signposted. There is a dirt road for the last 12 km past Purificación, where you cross the Magdalena. Buses can be caught in Bogotá, Ibagué and all intermediate towns. A pleasant government hotel is at the lake (D, B for cabin for 6-10, free camping on the shoreline, water-skiing, short trip with a boat). The pretty part of the lake is hidden from the end of the road and must be seen from a boat. Official boat trips to the islands are about 3 times cheaper than those of "sharks" operating here; the official mooring-point is down the slope at the end of the road. Swimming is good and the water is warm, but wading is not advisable because of the fresh-water stingray. Cheap hotels and basic restaurants are available in Prado, 4 km from the lake. Food can be obtained at the end of the road at the dock.

A little beyond the 50 Km stone from Neiva you can turn to the left, cross a fence, and see the **Piedra Pintada de Aipe**, a stone not in fact painted but carved by precolumbian Indians with designs akin to the shapes of some of the pieces in the Museo del Oro at Bogotá.

Neiva, capital of Huila Department, has a population of 248,000. It was first founded in 1539, when Belalcázar came across the Cordillera Central from Popayán in quest of El Dorado. It was soon after destroyed by the Indians and re-founded in 1612. It is now a pleasant, modern city on the E bank of the Río Magdalena. There is an interesting monument to the struggles for independence by the riverside. There are rich coffee plantations around Neiva, for here the valley bottom is high enough to be in the coffee zone. The cathedral was destroyed by earthquake in 1967. There is a large and colourful market every day. Tourist information is given at the cultural centre with museum and gallery on the main square. Altitude: 470m; very hot.

Fiesta 18 to 28 June, when the Bambuco Queen is elected: folklore, dances and feasting.

Hotels **C** *Hostería Matamundo*, in old *hacienda* 3 km from centre, on road to Garzón and San Agustín, T 727778, a/c, swimming pool, restaurant, disco; **B** *Tumburagua*, C 5A, No 5-40, T 729165, rec; **B** *Sulicam*, Cra 3, No 5-51, T 713062, F 710159, restaurant; **B** *Anayaco*, C 8, No 3-26, T 713044, a/c, TV; **D** *Americano*, Cra 5, No 8-67, T 729240, clean, swimming pool; **D** *Plaza*, C 7, No 4-62, T 723980, swimming pool, fan, pleasant, restaurant, disco; **E** *Central*, Cra 3, No 7-82, meals, near market, good value, rec; **F** *Residencias Astoria*, C 6, No 1-41, shared bath, clean, big rm; **F** *Res JR*, shared bath, basic but clean and secure; **F** *Residencia Magdalena*, C 1A Sur, No 8A-57, T 733586, close to new bus station, restaurant; **F** *La Posada*, tall building near central plaza and market, private showers.

Restaurants *Hostería Los Cerros*, C 11, No 32-39; *El Caimo*, C 8, No 7A-22; *Los Gauchos*, Cra 15, No 5-12; *Neiva Viejo*, C 9, No 6-49; *Heladería La Pampa*, Pasaje Camacho 8, excellent juices.

Tourist Office Inderena, C 10, No 6-61, T 722580 (Sra María Cristina Sánchez).

Airport La Marguita, 1½ km from city. Aires and Satena fly from **Bogotá** (Aires to Bogotá daily); to **Medellín**, direct once a week. Satena flies to **Leguizamo**, via Florencia twice a week, Aires once. Taxi to bus terminal about US$0.85 (overcharging probable).

Bus New bus station out of town; bus from the centre leaves from the old terminal (Cra 2, Cs 5 y 6). To **Bogotá** (331 km, paved road), 5½ hrs, US$10.50. Regular bus service with Autobuses Unidos del Sur, Cootranshuila (0600) and Coomotor to **San Agustín**, US$6, 5½ hrs (US$5.40 by colectivo). To **Garzón**, US$3.60; to **Pitalito**, US$5. To **La Plata**, for Tierradentro. To **Espinal**, 3 hrs, US$2.40, good road except for stretch between Nataguima and Aipe. To **Pasto**, US$10.75; to **Popayán**, US$9.25, ordinary bus at 0330, 1000, 1930, to **Florencia**, US$7.80.

Warning At the bus stations, both off and on buses, in Neiva, Garzón and especially Pitalito, theft is rife.

Excursions To *Rivera*, a ½ hr drive S, with thermal springs and swimming pools to cool off, entrance US$1.25; to the *Tatacoa* desert to the N, past Tello and Villavieja, where there is a museum showing prehistoric finds in the area; and also S to the Betania dam project with boat trips on the lake formed by the dam, from the village of Yaguará.

Beyond Neiva lie the plains of Huila Department, arid, but still capable of supporting cattle, dominated by the snow-capped Nevado del Huila to the NW (**see p 878**).

THE CENTRAL CORDILLERA: MEDELLIN AND MANIZALES (5)

Medellín and Manizales are both busy, industrial centres yet, for all the commerce and coffee, the surrounding countryside is green, mountainous and pleasant. From the Cordillera Central to the Pacific stretches Chocó Department, thickly wooded, mountainous and undeveloped, but rewarding to explore.

The Central Cordillera lies W of the Magdalena River. In it are two of the most important cities in Colombia: Medellín, the second largest city in the country, and Manizales. Manizales can be reached by a road (309 km) passing through Facatativá and Honda; or through Girardot to Ibagué, then over the high crest of the Quindío pass via Armenia. (For the road from Manizales to Medellín, **see p 859**.) Medellín can be reached from Bogotá by road three ways: the highway opened in 1982 (**see p 855**); the old direct road (478 km) with a 207-km unpaved stretch from La Dorada to La Unión; and the third via Manizales.

The town of Antioquia was founded in 1541, but the Spaniards, eager for gold, were not interested in the hinterland, which was then very sparsely inhabited by nomadic Indians who made very poor agricultural labourers. But during the 17th century a new wave of settlers came to Colombia from Spain; many of them were Jewish refugees who were deliberately seeking isolation, and found it in the little valley of the Río Aburrá, where they founded the city of Medellín in 1616. They were farmers with their families rather than *conquistadores*: they had an extraordinarily high birth rate; they intermarried very little with either Indian or black; and they divided the land into small farms which they worked themselves. Their exports were small: a little gold and silver from their streams. They lived on the food they themselves produced: maize, beans, sugar-cane, bananas, fruit.

In the early 19th century the settlement began to expand and to push out in all directions, particularly to the S. The settlers followed the forested slopes on the western side of the Central Cordillera and occupied all the cultivable land. Manizales, 120 km S, was founded in 1848. In the second half of the century new lands were occupied further S.

It was coffee that brought stability to this expansion, but they were slow to adopt it. Coffee appeared in the Magdalena Valley about 1865, but none was being exported from Antioquia before the end of the century. It was the 1914-18 war that suddenly gave a fillip to the industry: within 20 years the Departments of Antioquia and Caldas were producing half the coffee of Colombia, and they are by far the most important producers today. The industrialization of Medellín followed the coffee boom. There has been little immigration since the original settlement, but the natural growth in population has been extraordinary. Antioquia is considered by many to be the cultural heartland of Colombia. Its residents, referred to as Paisas, are renowned for their distinctive accent and customs. They are also extremely hospitable and courteous.

Medellín, capital of Antioquia Department, is a city of 1.7 million people, at an altitude of 1,487m. It could hardly be less advantageously placed, for it faces forbidding mountain barriers in nearly all directions. Its climate alone, that of an English summer day (21°C), is in its favour, despite a certain amount of smog. Yet Medellín is one of the main industrial cities of Colombia, and seethes with energy. The first looms arrived in 1902. Today the city produces more than 80% of the textile output of the country, and textiles account for only half its industrial activity. A metro is under construction. Excellent views from **Cerro Salvador** (statue on top), SE of the city, and from **Cerro Nutibara**, S of the city, where there are an outdoor stage for open air concerts, sculpture park, miniature village, souvenir shops and restaurants. Cerro Nutibara is a popular gathering place late into the night at weekends.

Medellín is a well-laid-out industrial city. There are four universities, together with other higher educational institutions. The old colonial buildings have nearly all disappeared, but there are still some 17th century churches left: the old Cathedral on Parque Berrío and the churches of **San Benito**, **La Veracruz**, and **San José**. The new **Cathedral of Villanueva** (Catedral Metropolitana), built between 1868 and 1931, one of the largest brick buildings in the world, is on Parque Bolívar, an attractive place. Below the statue of Bolívar in the park are inscribed the words of the conquered Indian leader Choquehuanca to his visitors: "With the centuries, your glory will grow as the shadows grow when the sun sets". Three churches of the 18th century survive: **San Ignacio**, in Plaza San Ignacio, **San Juan de Dios**, and **San Antonio**. The city's commercial centre, **Villanueva**, is interesting for its blend of old and modern architecture, including many skyscrapers. There is a fine sculpture, **Monumento a la Vida**, next to the Edificio Seguros Suramericana on C 50, where exhibitions of work by leading South American artists are held on the ground floor. Entertainments, concerts, clowns etc take place outside the Cathedral on Sun. The cattle auctions on Tues and Thurs, held in specially built cattle yards on the outskirts, are interesting.

Botanical and Zoological Gardens Joaquín Antonio Uribe gardens, Cra 52, No 73-298, near the new campus of the University of Antioquia, which include an orchid garden, are open daily, 0900-1730, US$0.40 entrance, well worth a visit (some of the plants are named); there is a restaurant, pleasant but not cheap. There is also a zoo **Zoológico Santa Fe**, at C 77 y Cra 68, mainly of South American animals and birds (admission US$0.80). In the zoo grounds is the **Museo Santa Fe** (closed Mon and Tues), costing an extra US$0.20 to enter. Also visit El Ranchito, an orchid farm between the towns of Itagüí and La Estrella (entry US$0.50; April to June is the best time to visit).

Museums Museo Etnográfico **Miguel Angel Builes**, Cra 81, No 52B-120, has an extensive collection of artefacts housed in beautiful new building. The **Museo de la Madre Laura**, Cra 92, No 33B-21, has a good collection of indigenous costumes and crafts from Colombia, Ecuador and Guatemala. Museo **El Castillo**, C 9 Sur, No 32-260, formerly a landowner's home, has interesting objects and beautiful grounds; entry US$1.20; take bus to Loma de los Balsos, El Poblado (US$0.07), then walk 1 km up the hill until you see the road lined with pine trees to the right. Open 1300-1700, closed Sun. The **Museo de Antioquia**, Cra 53 y C 52, opp main post office, shows contemporary pictures and sculptures, including works by Fernando Botero, Colombia's leading contemporary artist (now living in USA) US$0.50. Museo de Arte Moderno, Cra 64B, No 51-64, small collection, open Tues-Fri, 0900-1300, 1500-1800. Casa Museo **Maestro Pedro Nel Gómez**, Cra 51B, No 85-24, T 233-2633, house of the contemporary painter and sculptor. **Museo Antropológico** at University of Antioquia, C 67, No 53-108 (new campus). **Museo Filatélico**, on 4th floor of Banco de la República building. Most museums are closed on Mondays.

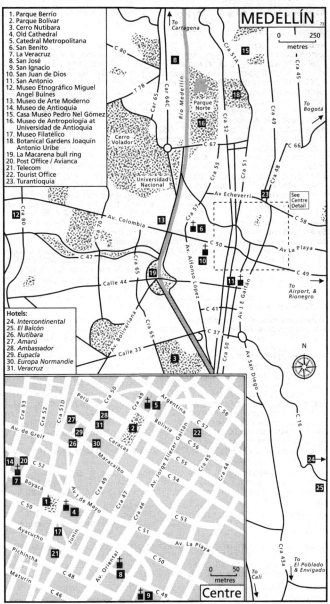

1. Parque Berrío
2. Parque Bolívar
3. Cerro Nutibara
4. Old Cathedral
5. Catedral Metropolitana
6. San Benito
7. La Veracruz
8. San José
9. San Ignacio
10. San Juan de Dios
11. San Antonio
12. Museo Etnográfico Miguel Angel Bulnes
13. Museo de Arte Moderno
14. Museo de Antioquia
15. Casa Museo Pedro Nel Gómez
16. Museo de Antropologia at Universidad de Antioquia
17. Museo Filatélico
18. Botanical Gardens Joaquín Antonio Uribe
19. La Macarena bull ring
20. Post Office / Avianca
21. Telecom
22. Tourist Office
23. Turantioquia

Hotels:
24. Intercontinental
25. El Balcón
26. Nutibara
27. Amarú
28. Ambassador
29. Eupacla
30. Europa Normandie
31. Veracruz

MEDELLÍN

Centre

Travellers should take the same safety precautions as they would in any large city, particularly at night, but remember that Medellín has been the centre of narcotics, and anti-narcotics operations. It is, nevertheless, a friendly place.

Hotels **L2** *Intercontinental*, C 16, No 28-51, Variante Las Palmas, T 266-0680, the best, some distance from the centre, excellent; **L2** *Poblado Plaza*, Cra 43A, No 4 Sur, T 268-5555, F 268-6949, also excellent; **L3** *Las Lomas*, Km 26 Cra Medellín-Sta Elena, T 536-0440, close to airport; **L3** *Nutibara* (casino and swimming pool), C 52A, No 50-46, T 241-4622, F 231-3713, best in centre; *Residencias Nutibara*, an annex facing hotel of same name, slightly cheaper with all the same facilities; **A2** *Amaru*, Cra 50A, No 53-45, T 511-2155, central, quiet, good, expensive restaurant with excellent service; **A2** *El Balcón*, Cra 25, No 2-370, near *Intercontinental*, in Transversal Superior, T 268-2511, beautiful view of the city, good meals; **A2** *Ambassador*, Cra 50, No 54-50, T 511-5311, in connection with **A2** *Veracruz*, Cra 50, No 54-18, T 511-5511, with bath, swimming pool, very good, restaurant on 11th floor gives fine view over city; **A3** *Gran*, C 54, No 45-92, T 251-9951, F 251-6035, commercial hotel; **C** *Eupacla*, Cra 50, No 53-16, T 231-1844, central, noisy, mosquitoes, but helpful staff; **C** *Europa Normandie*, C 53, No 49-100, T 241-9920, restaurant, cafeteria, sauna, disco, central, good value; **C** *Horizonte*, Cra 47 No 49A-24, T 511-6188, good and popular restaurant; **C** *Santelmo* aparthotel, nr bus stop for airport, central, safe, clean, TV, hot water; **D** *Arod*, C 44, No 69-80, T 260-1427, small, secure, clean, friendly, 1½ km from centre. **E** *Casa Blanca*, Cra 45, No 46-09, clean, small restaurant, safe but noisy; **E** *Mariscal*, Cra 45, No 46-49, T 251-5433, hot shower, good service, clean; **E** *Cannes*, Cra 50, No 56-17, T 242-7329, clean, well run; **E** *Comercial*, C 48, No 53-94, friendly, clean, hot water available in some rooms, the best of which are on the top floor, doors barred to all but residents after 1800, good meals US$2; **E** *Holiday*, Cra 45, No 50-25, with bath, clean, safe for bicycles, 5 mins walk from centre; **E** *Linton*, Cra 45, No 47-74, with bath, very clean, TV, safe parking nearby US$0.50 per night, central; **E** *Samaritano*, Cra 45, No 45-25, T 251-8011, clean and friendly, but noisy; **F** *Gómez Córdoba*, Av Oriental between Cs 50 y 51, good value, renovated, safe, clean, central; **F** *Residencias Doris*, Cra 45, No 46-23, family run, clean sheets every day, laundry facilities, locked night and day, good value, rec; **F** *Romania*, Av Echeverri, C 58, No 50-46, with bath, clean, a bit noisy. Many *residencias* on Cras 54 and 55, but this is not a safe area; a safer area for accommodation is around Cra 43. C 45 is said to be an unsafe street.

Restaurants *Hato Viejo*, opp *Intercontinental Hotel*, good local cuisine (another branch on Cra Junín); *La Sombrilla*, *La Yerra* and *Los Cristales* are all on the same road, good. *Asados La 80*, Cra 81, No 30-7, very good, large steaks for about US$3. In El Poblado *Frutos del Mar*, Cra 43B, No 11-51, good seafood; *La Crêperie*, opposite (No 11-88), French; on Av Poblado (Av 43A): *Piemonte* (No 5A-170); *La Bella Epoca*, C 4 Sur, No 43A-9, very good and expensive, on road to Envigado; *Aguacatala*, Cra 43A, No 7 Sur-130 (an old country house with patio and wandering musical trio, *comida típica*, quiet surroundings), and *La Posada de la Montaña*, Cra 43-B, No 16-22, both outside off road to Envigado, good, Colombian food. *Carbón*, Variante a las Palmas, Km 1, T 262-5425, good grills, steaks at US$8, good view over city, live music at weekends. Many vegetarian restaurants, eg *Centro Integral Vegetariano*, C 51, No 45-72; *Govinda*, C 51 No 52-17. There are several round-the-clock cafés in the vicinity of Cra Junín between Maturín and Amador which serve cheap meals. Two good self-service restaurants are *La Estancia*, Cra 49, No 54-15, on Plaza Bolívar, and *Contenalco*, C la Playa, between Av Oriental and El Palo, clean, cheap, very busy in rush hours. Good local food at *Don Edoardo*, Cra 45, No 48-57, central, modest prices. Many good, cheap restaurants on Cra 49. Excellent pastries at *Salón de Té Astor*, Cra 49, No 53-39. Many cheap cafés near bus station.

Banks and Exchange Banco Anglo Colombiano, C 50, No 51-06; 3 agencies; **Banco Industrial de Colombia**, cash against Mastercard, good rates for TCs and cash; and various other Colombian banks. Main hotels will cash TCs for residents when banks are closed, but at less favourable rates.

Consulates British, C 9, No 43-893, T 246-3114. Danish, C 51, No 42-61, T 239-7696. German, C 52, No 47-28. Addresses of others in the phone book. **NB** the **Venezuelan** consul will not issue visas.

Discotheques in central hotels, and in El Poblado district. Many discos and popular dance halls on C 50, between Cras 65 and 75, and Cra 70, between Cs 36 and 44, also in Envigado, near Plaza Envigado. For a dark, underground and lively young place, try *Puf* or *Bar Tolomé* next to each other on autopista Palmas, Km 5. Couples only allowed in to many discos.

Music Monthly concerts by the Antioquia Symphony Orchestra. Band concerts in the Parque Bolívar every Sun at 1130. Open air concerts, on Sundays, of Colombian music on Cerro Nutibara.

Health There is a clinic with free consultations and basic treatment in the airport buildings.

Post Office Main airmail office in Avianca building, Cra 52, No 51A-01, Mon-Sat, 0700-2200, has *poste restante*. **Telecommunications** Pasaje Junín and on corner of C 49 and Cra 50.

Shopping Silver seems cheaper than in Bogotá. Poor selection of handicraft shops in the city, but there are *artesanía* shops on the top of Cerro Nutibara and there is a small handicrafts market at C 52 near Cra 46 with many hippy stalls. **Mercado San Alejo**, Parque Bolívar, open on the first Saturday of every month except January, and before Christmas it is there Sat and Sun (handicrafts on sale at good prices). Good shopping generally around Parque Bolívar. Many of the textile mills have discount clothing departments attached where good bargains can be had; ask at your hotel. *La Piel*, at C 53, No 49-131, has an excellent selection of leather goods at very reasonable prices (the selection and price of leather goods in Medellín is better than Bogotá). *Supermarket Exito* (Cra 66, No 49-01, C 10, No 43E-135, Poblado) is reasonable for cheap leather bags. There are several shopping centres.

Bookshop *Librería Continental*, Cra 50 y C 52; *Librería Científica*, C 51, No 49-52, T 231-4974, large selection, some foreign books.

Photography For developing, Almacenes Duperly (several branches, eg C 52, No 46-28), good quality. Camera repairs: Clínica de Cámeras, Centro Coltejer, Local 120.

Bullfights at the bull-ring of La Macarena, C 44 and Cra 63, in February.

Travel Agents *Tierra Mar Aire* (American Express agents), C 52, No 43-124, T 513-0414, helpful. *Viajes Marco Polo*, C 48, No 65-94, T 230-5944, recommended; also *Terra Nova*, C 5A, No 39-107, T 266-5000, who run an excursion by train to Cisneros, 3 hrs journey, with 3-4 hrs for a picnic and swim.

Tourist Office C 57 No 45-129, T 254-0800, in bus station (some English spoken, helpful), and in airport (will book hotel rooms), free maps, and Turantioquia, Cra 48, No 58-11, T 254-3864, good information on Antioquia and owns 5 good hotels in the Department. For a cheap tour of the city take any "Circular" bus, for US$0.10. **Inderena**, C 43 A No 12A-111, El Poblado.

Useful Addresses DAS, T 341-5900, also at C 19, No 80A-40 in Belén la Nubia section, T 34-1451; Tourist Police at airport, T 287-2053; police T 112; general information T 113.

Taxis They have meters, make sure they are used.

Airport José María Córdoba, 28 km from Medellín by new highway, and 13 km from Rionegro; *Presto* restaurant, shops, Telecom, Fax service, no left luggage, but Turantioquia may oblige. Taxi to town US$12.50, colectivo US$3.60, *buseta* to centre, US$2.40, frequent service, about 1 hr journey, sit on right going to town (catch *buseta* or colectivo in small road behind *Hotel Nutibara* to go to airport). To Rionegro, bus US$0.20, taxi US$10.20. By air to **Bogotá**, 45 mins with Avianca (Cra 52, No 51A-23, T 245-2099), SAM, Aces, Satena or Intercontinental, several daily. Also to many other Colombian cities; Avianca to Miami (also Aces) and New York. Daily flight to **Panama** with SAM or Copa, but you will have to buy a return unless you have another exit ticket out of Panama. There is also a small municipal airport, 10 min by taxi with flights to Quibdó (3 flights daily, US$33), Bahía Solano etc.

Rail For long-distance travel to Barrancabermeja, Bogotá and Santa Marta, check if services have resumed after 1992 suspension. For the tourist train from and to Cisneros, see above under Travel Agents.

Buses The bus terminal for all long-distance buses is about 3 km NW of the town centre, with shops, cafeterias, left luggage (US$0.50 per day) and other facilities. Quite safe. Bus service to city centre, US$0.15, buses to station from C 50, marked: "Terminal de Transporte" via A Echeverría and Jorge Eliécer Gaitán. To/from **Bogotá**, 9-12 hrs, US$15.50, every 40 mins or so, with 5 companies; to **La Dorada**, US$5.10. To **San Agustín**, Rápidos Tolima, 0600, US$21.50. Frequent buses for **Cali**, Flota Magdalena US$17, 10-12 hrs. Frequent buses to **Manizales**, 6 hrs (US$9 1st class, 5.40 2nd, by Empresa Arauca). To **Cancasia**, US$8.50, 7 hrs. To **Cartagena**, Brasilia, 17-20 hrs, or 14 hrs, by Pullman bus, US$27.50 (take food with you, the stops tend to be at expensive restaurants); road paved throughout but poor. To **Barranquilla**, US$19.25 by Pullman, 16 hrs. To **Cartago**, 8 hrs, Flota Magdalena, US$8.50. To **Pereira**, 8 hrs, US$9.50 by Flota Occidental Pullman. To **Sincelejo**, 9½ hrs. To **Popayán**, US$19.50, 12 hrs, Flota Magadalena at 1400 and 1800. To **Ipiales**, US$36, 22 hrs, Expreso Bolivariano (takes Visa). To **Turbo**, US$12 with Gómez (the best), 17 hrs. To **Quibdó**, 11-13 hrs, US$13.

Roads The new **Medellín-Bogotá highway** suffers from landslides in wet weather. The road is totally paved but there are potholes, waterfalls and detours between Medellín and Honda.

There are many campgrounds along the route, for example 130 km and 150 km from Medellín. On the way from Honda to Medellín is **Doradel** with a large zoo called Hacienda Nápoles and several hotels, eg C *La Colina*, pool, rec. 13 km beyond Doradel, a dirt road to the left (badly signposted) leads to **La Danta** where there is a cave with *guácharos* (oilbirds) and bats. Village boys will lead you there for a tip, take torches. At **Marinilla** 40 km from Medellín, there is a reservoir in picturesque surroundings, swimming possible, accommodation nearby.

A paved road, 665 km long, goes N to Cartagena, and another S to Manizales, which provides an alternative route to Bogotá. This road crosses the Río Cauca at **La Pintada**, 38 km S of Medellín, where there is a campground and hotels (**D** *Mi Rey*, T 274008, OK; **G** *Residencia Cosina*, basic, clean, fan, mosquitos, restaurant), followed by a good open air cafeteria at **La Felisa**, 40 km further on, with excellent breads, *buñuelos* and the **D** *Hostería Mayba*, with pool. There are two other important roads: one, 383 km NW through Antioquia to Turbo, on the Gulf of Urabá; and another, 478 km SE from Medellín through Sonsón and La Dorada and on to Bogotá. The latter is paved as far as Rionegro, but from Rionegro to Sonsón is in a bad state of repair. The scenery compensates for this to some extent. Also attractive is the road to Quibdó through coffee, tobacco and pineapple plantations. About half way along this road is **Bolívar**, in the centre of this coffee region where the evening's entertainment is to watch the local horsemen and women showing off their riding skills around the plaza. **E** *Residencias Bahía*, the best available, *Grillo's* restaurant nearby, good for fried chicken, dishes and local food.

Excursions A run N through beautiful landscape along the Cartagena road to (132 km) **Yarumal** in a cool mountain climate (23,515 people, friendly town with fine views from Paroquia La Merced; many *hosterías*; **E** *Residencias Horizontes*, hot showers, clean, quiet, welcoming; next door is *Cafetería La Estancia*, excellent; **G** *Residencia Ensueño*, basic, clean; *Restaurante La Nena*), or NW (many hotels and resort areas, crowded weekends) to (80 km) **Antioquia** (11,000 people) will give a good idea of the very beautiful countryside, excellent walking. Antioquia (full name Santa Fé de Antioquia) lies just W of the Río Cauca; it was founded as a gold mining town by the Spaniards in 1541, the first in the area, and still retains its colonial atmosphere, with interesting Christmas/New Year fiestas. Until 1826 it was the capital of the Department. The fine old Cathedral is worth seeing, as is the church of Santa Bárbara. There are two small museums close to the church. There is an interesting wooden bridge, 300m long, 3 km downstream from the steel bridge which the buses use—ask for directions or take a taxi. Hotels: **C** *Mariscal Robledo*, Cra 58A, No 29-39, T 235-2250, 37 rooms, swimming pool, good; **D** *Hostería Real*, 2 km from town, T 61048, full board, good food, pool; **F** *Hostal del Viejo Conde*, C Mocha 10-56, T 82-61091, friendly, good food; *Del Río*, also outside, *San Pedro* in resort area, or you can stay en famille with Marta Merizalde de Roldán, Cra 11, No 9-39, very friendly and informative, pretty garden. There is good food in the main square, US$1 for a full meal. Bus from Medellín US$1.80 (Flota Urbara or Transporte Sierra), 2½ hrs. Halfway between Medellín and Antioquia is **San Jerónimo** with several places to stay, including **F** *Ben Hur*, without bath, satisfactory. The road goes on to Turbo (daily bus at 0900), on the Gulf of Urabá (see p 827).

Another interesting excursion from Medellín is along the Sonsón road SE to (39 km) the town of **Rionegro**, in a delightful valley of gardens and orchards. Here was born one of Bolívar's generals, José María Córdoba, the hero of the battle of Ayacucho. Medellín's new airport has been built 13 km away. The **Casa de Convención** (where the 1863 Convention took place) is now an archive museum, entry US$0.20. The cathedral, with its gold and silver altar, deserves a visit. A museum of religious artefacts is behind the altar (entry US$0.20); it includes a virgin's robe with 300,000 pearls, not to be missed, and you can climb up behind the Virgin donated by Philip II to look down into the cathedral. There are processions in Easter Week. Many interesting pottery and ceramics factories in Rionegro area, hardly mechanized, as well as leather working; they welcome visitors and explain the processes. Prices of leather goods are high. A day trip can cost US$15, but the Medellín-Rionegro *rápido* taxi service is very cheap. Bus to Rionegro, from Cra 42 y C40, US$1, one hr; bus back to Medellín from plaza every ½ hr. 10 km from Rionegro (15 mins by colectivo, leave when full from plaza, US$0.60; buses every 2 hrs, US$0.20) is **Carmen de Viboral**, well-known for its pottery; there are several factories just N of the market place.

Rionegro Hotels **D** *Oasis*, Cra 50, No 46-23, T 271-0531, with restaurant, bar, laundry, TV in rooms. **E** *Rionegro*, friendly, dark rooms, cold water; **F** *Residencias Onassis*, with bath, good value; **E** *Gutier*, Cra 49, No 50-32, T 271-0106, central, with restaurant; *Residencias David*, same price, both near market. Good restaurant above the bakery in central plaza.

Beyond Rionegro to the E is **El Peñol** , a precipitous, bullet-shaped rock which towers above the surrounding hills and lakes. It has been eroded smooth, but a spiral staircase has been built into a crack from the base to the summit. Entrance to rock, US$0.30. A snack bar has been built at the summit, and the views are very fine (meals available only in holiday seasons). Bus to the rock and to the pretty town of Guatapé with Cía Fco López, US$1.45. Bus back to Medellín is harder to catch; best take a colectivo to town of Peñol and bus from there. From Rionegro, take a colectivo to Marinilla (US$0.30, leaves from near market), then wait for the San Rafael bus which passes El Peñol (US$1.45); from Marinilla you can also take a colectivo to the new town of Nuevo Peñol (US$0.85), then another to El Peñol (US$0.60)—in all about 2 hrs, either route.

On the road to El Retiro is *Fizebad*, an old estate house, restored with original furniture and artefacts, and a display of flowering orchids; entry, US$1.75. In *El Retiro* itself is a small colonial church and an even older chapel which is seldom open: ask for the caretaker. On the road to La Ceja, have lunch in *Parador Tequendamita*, in a beautiful setting by a waterfall. The route is through splendid scenery, and one can see typical Antioquian life and costume. (To Fizebad by bus, catch a La Ceja or El Retiro bus.)

La Ceja, also on the Sonsón road, is well worth a visit. Transportes La Ceja cover the route; the journey takes 1¾ hrs. For the energetic, any one of the surrounding hills affords an excellent view of the area. F *Hotel Primavera* and one other, both delightful, have rooms. Youth hostel at *Centro Vacacional La Montaña*, details from Alcom in Bogotá. At *Sonsón*, there are the F *Tahami* (very good value) and I *Imperio* hotels. Ask for the Casa de los Abuelos, an old house with a printing press, which produces a weekly newspaper, and many other historical objects.

At *Bello*, 6½ km N of Medellín (pop 260,360), is the hut in which Marcos Fidel Suárez, President 1918-1922, was born. It is completely covered in with glass for its preservation.

A good trip is by car to *Hatillo*, 32 km along a road which parallels the railway to Puerto Berrío, and then another 80 km along a new road to Caldas. There are many restaurants along this road.

To the SW of Medellín, the towns in the coffee-growing district (Fredonia, Jericó, Jardín, Venecia) are worth visiting; all have basic inns. The scenery is beautiful.

At *Envigado*, 10 km S of Medellín, craftsmen have for generations turned out the traditional *antioqueño* pouch called *carriel*, carried by the men. Now used for money, its original use was for coffee samples. Envigado is the site of the "maximum security prison" which failed to hold Pablo Escobar.

55 km S of Medellín is *Santa Bárbara*, at 1,857m on a green hill top, with stunning views in every direction of coffee, banana and sugar plantations, orange-tiled roofs and folds of hills. F *Hotel Palomares* on main square, clean, well-maintained; restaurants and cafés also on square, as is the large church. Bus to Medellín, US$1.20. 140 km S of Medellín is *Supia*, a pleasant little town with hotel, F *Mis Ninietas*, near plaza, no sign, with bath, clean and good. Supia is 13 km N of Riosucio (see p 859).

Manizales is dominated by its enormous (still unfinished) concrete Cathedral and the Nevado del Ruiz volcano, which erupted so catastrophically in November 1985. The city was founded in 1848 by settlers from the Department of Antioquia; it has a population of 378,890 and is the capital of the small Department of Caldas, which originally (until 1965) contained what are now the Departments of Quindío and Risaralda. The old Department, now known as Viejo Caldas, produces about 30% of all Colombian coffee and picturesque coffee farms abound.

Manizales, at 2,153m above sea level, rides its mountain saddle uncompromisingly, the houses falling away sharply from the centre of the city into the adjacent valleys. The climate is extremely humid—average temperature is 17°C, and the annual rainfall is 3,560 mm—and frequently the city is covered in cloud. The best months of the year are from mid-December through to early March, and early in January the Fair and Coffee Festival is held, with bullfights, beauty parades and folk dancing. The city looks down on the small town of Villa María, "the village of flowers", now almost a suburb.

Several earthquakes and fires have destroyed parts of the city over the years, so the architecture is predominantly modern with high-rise office and apartment blocks. Traditional architectural styles are still seen in the suburbs and the older sections of the city. The departmental government building, the Gobernación, opposite the Cathedral in the Parque Bolívar, is an imposing example of neo-colonial architecture; the bull-ring built 25 years ago is an impressive copy of the traditional Moorish style. The suburbs stretch away N (with best shopping around C 59) and S of the city centre and are reached by a four-lane highway lined with flowers—marguerites—which grow to enormous proportions (as also the geraniums) because of the damp and the altitude. Chipre, a recreational park, provides a good view of the city (well-visited on Sundays); El Tanque, near Chipre, is another vantage point.

Museums Banco de la República, Cra 23, No 23-06, gold and anthropology museum open during banking hours, classical music every afternoon in the Bank. Universidad de Caldas, natural history museum with good selection of butterflies, moths and birds; open every day from 0800 to 1200 and 1400 to 1800 (take a "Fátima" bus to the University). La Galería del Arte, Av Santander at C 55, exhibitions of work by local artists, pictures can be bought.

Hotels NB in January, during the fiesta, hotel prices are grossly inflated. **A2** *El Carretero*, C 36, No 22-22, T 840225, good but slow restaurant, business clientele, comfortable; **A2** *Las Colinas*, Cra 22, No 20-20, T 842009, three-star, two bars, good restaurant, very comfortable; **C** *Villa Kempis*, Cra 23, No 19-22, T 830187, on road to Pereira, about 2 km past bull-ring, old religious retreat house, beautiful view over the valley, very quiet, hot water am only, restaurant and bar, good food at moderate prices; **D** *Europa*, Av Centenario, No 25-98 (T 822253), near the bull-ring, restaurant for breakfast only, comfortable and clean; **D** *Rokasol*, C 21, No 19-16, T 823307, near bus station so noisy, hot water, clean, all rooms have bathrooms, good restaurant; **E** *Tamá Internacional*, C 23, No 22-43, T 832594, next to Cathedral, with bath, meals, clean and cheap, but noisy. Cheaper: **F** *Cosmos*, opp bus terminal, clean, hot water with luck; **F** *Consol No 4*, Cra 20, No 21-10, clean, friendly, large rooms; **F** *Residencias Avenida No 2*, C 21, No 20-07, T 835251, clean, safe; **F** *Residencias Avenida No 3*, C 19, No 16-35, T 844130, opp bus terminal, bath, clean, quiet, safe, friendly, rec (next door is **E** *California*, No 16-37, T 824217, modern, clean); **F** *Residencias Caldas*, Cra 19, No 22-45, near bus station, US$1 surcharge on holidays, hot water, quiet, but not too clean; **F** *Residencias Margarita*, C 17 between Cras 22 and 23, quiet, good, safe, private parking opposite US$0.75 per night; **F** *Residencias Nueva York*, C 20, No 20-17, extremely clean, hot water, clothes-washing facilities, some bar noise in front but rec; several **F** range hotels around C 18, Cra 22-23; **F** *Marana*, C 18, No 17-34, T 843872, one min from bus station, bath, hot water only am, clean, friendly.

   D *Hotel Termales Arbeláez*, 25 km, from Manizales on the road to the Nevado El Ruiz, hot swimming pool, private bathrooms, restaurant.

Restaurants *Las Redes*, Cra 23, No 75-97, predominantly sea food, good but pricey; *Las Brasas*, Cra 23, No 75A-65, good grill and *comida típica*; *Fonda Paisa*, Cra 23, No 72-130, nice local dishes with local Andean music; *Vitiani*, on outskirts of town, Italian and European food, quite smart, food and wine fairly expensive, has good trout and excellent crab-claws (*muellas de cangrejo*); *La Suiza*, Cra 23, No 26-57, good fruit juices and cakes, but overpriced; unnamed restaurant with pink façade on Cra 23 nr C 31, economical, huge portions, highly rec; *Caballo Loco*, Cra 61, No 23-07, good; another with the same name at C 21, No 23-40 is mainly a bar but serves expensive pizzas; *El Ruiz*, Cra 19, No 22-25, filling 3-course meal.

Banks and Exchange Banco Anglo Colombiano, Cra 22, No 17-04, and other banks. Exchange not possible Sat and Sun.

Teatro de los Fundadores is a modern cinema-theatre auditorium. Interesting wood-carved mural by local artist, Fernando Botero, who also has murals in the entrance hall of the Club Manizales and *Hotel Las Colinas*. Events held here and at other locations during Theatre Festival in first two weeks of September.

Dry Cleaners *La Bruja*, Cra 22 near C 25.

Tourist Office Parque Bolívar, opp Cathedral, good, helpful. **DAS Office**, Cra 23 y C 24.

Airport Manizales has a small airport, La Nubia, and the regional airline Aces provides an efficient and punctual service to Bogotá, Medellín, and Cali.

Buses New terminal with good restaurant, C 19 between Cras 15 and 17. Buses to **Medellín**: Autolegal via Neira and Aguadas, 6 hrs, US$5.40; Empresa Arauca via Anserma, 10 hrs, 1st class US$8, ordinary US$5.40; colectivo to Medellín US$10.25. Both routes offer impressive scenery, but the shorter route is largely unpaved between Aranzazu and La Pintada. Bus to **Bogotá**, Expreso Bolivariano Pullman, US$12, 9 hrs; 7½ hrs by Flota El Ruiz *buseta*, US$13.50—beautiful scenery. To **Honda**, US$3.60 (Expreso Bolivariano). **Cali** by bus Expreso Palmira, 5½ hrs, US$5.40 ordinary; Pullman 6 hrs US$7.20. To **Cartago**, 4 hrs, every 20 mins, US$1.50; **Pereira**, Expreso Palmira, Expreso Trejos, half-hourly, 1½ hrs, excellent road, beautiful scenery, US$1.80 ordinary. **Armenia**, Expreso Palmira, 3 hrs, US$2.40. To **Quibdó**, Transportes Arauca, via Pereira, La Virginia, Pueblo Rico and Tadó, Mon, Wed, Fri, Sat 0600, 14-17 hrs, US$14.

Excursion To see the full process of coffee growing, apply to the Comité Departmental de Cafeteros de Caldas, Cra 22, No 18-21, T 41706; recommended.

Roads To Medellín direct, 265 km via the winding mountain road through the picturesque towns of *Salamina* (*F Residencia Puerto Nuevo*, opp bus office, clean, good meals), Pácora and Aguadas, all perched on mountain ridges, to La Pintada (**see p 856**); it is further if we go W across the Cauca river via Arauca, Anserma, *Riosucio* (a delightful old town with fine mountain views all round and a large colonial church next to the Arauca bus terminal; many restaurants, bars and shops); and then on to La Pintada. Manizales-Honda-Bogotá: all paved but in poor condition. The road climbs to 3,000m, with most superb scenery and little traffic. First accommodation is in Padua, then Fresno (cheap hotels), Mariquita and Honda (**see p 19**).

Parque Nacional Los Nevados: The park comprises 58,300 hectares and straddles the departments of Caldas, Quindio, Risaralda, and Tolima. You must check in advance if entry to the park is permitted. For information in Manizales contact Inderena, C 20A, No 21-45, 2nd floor, T 848457 (not too helpful); or the tourist office, which organizes day trips to Nevado del Ruiz at weekends (expensive; a rec guide is Javier Echeverría, T Manizales 857239). **See under Pereira, p 863**, for access from that city and under Ibagué, **p 849**, for **Nevado de Tolima**. For those planning an independent visit to Nevado del Ruiz (5,399m) with a vehicle, either take the Bogotá road from Manizales, then a branch road to a viewpoint (22 km). La Esperanza is the point to leave the main road for excursions towards the volcano. An alternative route follows the road to Villa María for 6 km, turning left to Barrio La Enea and continuing on an unpaved road for 22 km to Termales del Ruiz at 3,500m (**B Hotel Termales del Ruiz**, comfortable, with restaurant and thermal pools on premises). Five km further on, this road meets the road coming from La Esperanza. Turning right, and continuing 2 km brings you to Las Brisas (**D Hotel Restaurant Brisas del Cumanday**, very cold, best to have your own sleeping bag, basic, but beautiful surroundings and the only accommodation near the park entrance).

Past Las Brisas the road forks. To the left it continues over enormous landslides caused by the 1985 Nevado del Ruiz eruption to the village of Ventanas (a very scenic drive) and on to Murillo in the department of Tolima. To the right it climbs steeply for 1 km to reach the park entrance and visitors center at 4,050m. 5 km from the entrance is a new chalet at 4,400m run by Carlos Alberto, D, food, hot showers, friendly. The turnoff (left) to Nevado del Ruiz is 10 km beyond the park entrance and one can drive to within 2 km of the snow line (if the road is open). On foot from 4,050m to the summit takes 11 hrs. Near the foundations of a large shelter (destroyed by fire before the eruption), there is a basic hut, no water, no beds nor any facilities, ask at the entrance if it is open. A guide is recommended if you wish to climb to the crater. Another excellent climb nearby is La Olleta (4,850m), the ash cone of an extinct volcano. You can descend into the crater, but note your route well as fog can obliterate landmarks very quickly. The principal road continues (S) below the Nevados del Cisne and de Santa Isabel between which you can visit the Laguna Verde. You can stay at the *Refugio El Cisne*, a small farm at 4,200m, where a farmer lives with his family. He lets you sleep in his warehouse (very cold, but less so than outside) for US$2.50 and offers you milk and coffee. His son will guide you to Laguna Verde. 20 km further along the road and 39 km beyond the turnoff to Nevado del Ruiz is Laguna del Otún at the southern end of the park, trout fishing and camping with permission of Inderena.

If you do not have a car, it is still possible to reach Las Brisas and the park entrance with a milk truck that leaves the Celema dairy in Manizales, Cra 22, No 71-97, between 0600 and 0700 daily, returning in the early afternoon, or the Rápido Tolima bus at 1430 from the Terminal in Manizales to Murillo goes through Las Brisas, US$2.50, 2 hrs. One can also walk from Las Brisas down to Manizales in a day, stopping along the way at the Termales del Ruiz, ask about short cuts.

Visitors to the park should come prepared for cold damp weather, and remember to give themselves time to acclimatize to the altitude. Maps of the area are available at the Instituto Geográfico in Manizales, just behind the Club Manizales on Carrera 24.

Chocó

Stretching like a ribbon between the Cordillera Occidental and the Pacific Coast, from Panama to Valle del Cauca, Chocó is one of Colombia's least developed and most beautiful departments. It is also one of the rainiest regions on earth (dry season: December to March). In the northern $^3/_4$ of the department, the mountain ranges of the Serranía de Los Saltos and Serranía del Baudó rise directly from the ocean to reach a height of about 500m. The scenery of pristine rainforest descending the mountain slopes to the sea is spectacular. The principal transport routes are along the Pacific coast from Buenaventura in the S and up the Río Atrato from the Gulf of Urabá and Cartagena to the N. The Baudó and San Juan rivers flow to the Pacific in the S of the department. Road access is via two unpaved routes across the Cordillera Occidental, the one from Medellín in the NE via Amaga and El Carmen, the other from Pereira to the SE via La Virginia and Pueblo Rico.

Chocó is very sparsely populated. The coastline is dotted with fishing villages whose inhabitants, although also of African origin, are culturally distinct from the Caribbean Afro-Colombians of the N. Inland along the rivers are Indian communities leading a largely traditional lifestyle based on hunting, fishing, and subsistence farming. Along the Río San Juan, in the S, there is much gold prospecting around the towns of Tadó and Istmina.

Several development schemes have been proposed for Chocó over the years. Work is currently in progress to build a road to the Pacific, with plans for a deep sea port and industrial complex at the mouth of the Río Tribuga. This is seen as a vital alternative export terminal for the coffee produced in neighboring Caldas, Risaralda, and Quindío, since the port of Buenaventura has reached its maximum capacity. It also represents a serious threat to Chocó's unique environment and to its inhabitants' way of life.

For historical and geographic reasons, Chocó's ties are closer with Medellín than with Bogotá. A number of "Paisas" (Antioqueños) have moved to the area, and virtually all outsiders are referred to as such.

Malaria, yellow fever, and dengue remain endemic throughout Chocó, and the appropriate precautions (prophylaxis, vaccination, mosquito nets, etc) are recommended. Vampire bats are also common in the region, but fortunately, rabies is not.

Quibdó, located on the eastern shore of the Río Atrato, has an interesting mural in its cathedral and is noted for the hordes of birds which fly in to roost at dusk. There are magnificent sunsets. A good place to view them is the permanently moored boat which houses the civil defence authority (bright orange roof, take insect repellent). The large Jorge Isaacs auditorium is used for cultural activities (see under **Music and Dance** for festivals). Prices are higher here than in central Colombia, but they are higher still in the coastal villages, so it is a good place to get supplies. The shops are well stocked. Despite its frontier town appearance, Quibdó is one of the safest cities in Colombia.

Accommodation and Food E *Cristo Rey*, bath, fan, clean, safe; E *Del Río*, good, with bath, safe, free coffee, its restaurant, *Club Naútico* on 2nd floor has an excellent bar, good food and views; F *Dora Ley*, with bath, cheaper without, fan, rooms vary in quality, meals; F *Pacífico*, good rooms and beds; F *Residencia Darién*, Cra 4, No 26-68, T 712997, bath, fan, space to park motorcycle; F *Las Palmas*, with bath, cheaper without; F *Oriental*, no private showers, clean, quiet, charming elderly proprietor. Restaurant *El Paisa*, Cra 4, No 25-54, excellent; *Chopán* bakery, good pastries and coffee.

Exchange Banks do not change. *Restaurant El Paisa, Farmacia Mercedes*, and a few shopkeepers sometimes change US$ cash, but rates are poor. Best to buy pesos in larger centres before arriving.

DAS Office C 29, Cra 4. No entry or exit stamps (see note under **Los Katios National Park**, p 827).

Air Service Aces and Satena fly daily to Medellín, Bogotá, and Cali.

Shipping From Buenaventura up the Río San Juan to Istmina and on by road; services infrequent. Irregular cargo service down the Río Atrato to Turbo and Cartagena takes passengers. Cost to Turbo US$26, food included; to/from Cartagena US$40-53, 4 days, take drinking water. Deal directly with boats, *La Veran II* recommended in 1994. Also 20-seater power boats, 7 hrs to Turbo, about US$30. The lower Atrato was a very dangerous area in 1994 (guerrillas, kidnappings, drug running). Much caution and detailed advance inquiry are strongly recommended.

Buses and Roads Transportes Ochoa to Medellín via El Carmen and Bolívar (sporadic guerrilla activity reported along this route in 1994), 5 daily, 10-12 hrs, US$7.50 regular, US$13 luxury coach. Transportes Arauca to Manizales via Tadó, Pueblo Rico, La Virginia and Pereira, Tues, Thur, Sat, Sun at 0600, 14-17 hrs, US$14. Flota Occidental along same route to Pereira, daily at 0700, 8-10 hrs, US$9.60. Occasional buses to Cali, US$14 otherwise change at La Virginia. Bus to Bogotá US$24. Local service to Santa Cecilia and Tadó.

The road to Manizales goes 60 km S towards Istmina on the Río San Juan to Las Animas where it turns E to cross the San Juan at Yuta (ferry). A few km further is *Tadó*, with a silver-fronted church. E *Hotel Macondo*, very basic but restaurant OK; E *Residencias Confort*, without bath, clean, friendly; good café/bar on corner of plaza. Further on is Playa de Oro, a very depressing area where people have been panning for gold. After crossing into Risaralda Department, the road improves before reaching the Cauca Valley. The first part of this road is in a very poor state, very slow, and you can be stuck in mud for hours. Most is through pure jungle with luxuriant broad-leaf vegetation, flowers mostly red and yellow, colourful butterflies, waterfalls and few people.

Towns along the Pacific Coast *Nuquí*, on the Gulf of Tribuga, is surrounded by estuaries and virgin beaches. It is gaining popularity among Colombian sports fishermen and vacationers alike, and a number of luxury homes have been built nearby. To the S lies the wide curve of Playa Olímpica and the fishing village of Pangui (cross first estuary by canoe, the second at low tide or swim). To the N is the even smaller hamlet of Tribuga, by the mouth of the Río Tribuga, a splendid beach and the proposed site of a deep sea port and industrial complex (see above). Nuquí remains relatively pleasant and friendly but has already been affected by tourism, act accordingly (see Responsible Tourism in **Introduction and Hints**).

Accommodation Along the beach at the N end of town, fully booked during the vacation period, are **C** *Playa del Mar* and **D** *Rosio del Mar*, cabins with private bath. **E** *Doña Jesusita*, at S end of town, basic. Felipe and Luz Largacha will sometimes rent rooms in their home (along main street S of town centre), **F**, basic, friendly. On Playa Olímpica, Guillermo and Doralina Moreno, run a small hotel, **E/F** range, shared bath, pleasant, very friendly. You can also pitch your tent in their coconut grove for a small fee, hammock not recommended because of heavy rains and vicious sandflies at night (mosquito net recommended, repellent a must). Meals available if arranged in advance. **Food** Several small restaurants on road to airport serving mostly fish. Shops are well stocked with basic goods, prices somewhat higher than in Quibdó.

Transport By air from Quibdó (20 min) and Medellín (45 min). Aces flies on Mon, Wed, Fri, and Sun; with extra flights added around Christmas and Easter. There are launches S to Arusi (Mon, Wed, Fri), and N to El Valle (Tues, Thur, Sat), as well as occasional coastal vessels (small fuel barges) to Buenaventura. Construction is continuing on a road from Las Animas (see above) to Nuquí, which will eventually connect the port planned for Tribuga with the interior. At present, it is a strenuous 3 day trek along a jungle trail from the roadhead, through several Indian villages, to Nuquí.

El Valle, located 50 km N of Nuquí along the coast, has the best bathing and surfing beaches in the area, and has been most developed for tourism. Many outsiders have taken up permanent residence here, the locals can be less than friendly, and crime is increasing. El Almejal, N of town, is the best beach. There are several large but simple tourist complexes here, with rooms and cabins (**D/E** range), as well as bars and restaurants (deserted on weekdays off-season). The entrance to El Valle's harbour is very tricky at ebb tide and many boats have been swept onto the rocks here.

Transport A rough road runs 18 km from El Valle to Bahía Solano (passes by airport before town). Jeeps leave every morning, 1 hr ride, tickets can be purchased one day in advance. There are launches S to Nuqui on Tues, Thur and Sat.

Between Nuqui and El Valle lies **Ensenada de Utria National Park**, the jewel of the Pacific Coast. It was created in 1985 to preserve several unique aquatic and terrestrial habitats. Day trips may be arranged from El Valle or Nuquí, and special permits are sometimes granted for longer stays by Inderena in Bogotá. The ranger also welcomes volunteer assistants to help in clearing garbage from the beaches and other tasks (also best arranged in advance from Bogotá).

The park is named for a large inlet (*ensenada*) at its centre, which is home to two varieties of whales, corals, needlefish, and many other aquatic species. Motorboats are not allowed past the park headquarters, located half-way up the inlet, and the area is best appreciated if you paddle through in a canoe (try to rent or borrow). The surrounding hillsides are covered with pristine rainforest and there are several magnificent white sand beaches. Boats hired from El Valle take 45 mins and cost approx US$12 return, from Nuquí 1½ hrs, US$24. The launch which does the run from Nuquí to El Valle can sometimes (depending on tides) leave you at Playa Blanca, a small island near the park boundary. Here Sr Salomon Caizamo runs a simple restaurant and rents space for one or two tents (a nice spot). The park headquarters are 5 mins away by motorboat and you can generally hitch a ride with fishermen or park employees. There is also a road and trail leading through the jungle from El Valle to the head of the inlet (9 km, 4-5 hrs, can be very muddy), but you must arrange for a boat to pick you up as it is not possible to reach the park headquarters on foot.

The park headquarters and visitors centre has a display of whale bones and several other exhibits. There are simple but comfortable accommodation for about 15 people in a guest house (camping prohibited) and an outdoor kitchen with a wood stove. No restaurant or shops. Fresh fish can sometimes be purchased, but all other provisions should be brought from town. Mosquito nets are essential for nighttime protection against insects and vampire bats alike. Across the inlet from the headquarters is a private research station run by Fundación Natura as a base for biologists carrying out studies within the park. There are no facilities for visitors.

Bahía Solano, also known as Ciudad Mutis, lies on a large bay set against jungle covered hills. It is a popular resort and gets quite busy during holiday periods when prices rise. The bay is rather muddy and there are no beaches by the town itself. Good bathing beaches may be reached by launch or by walking about 1½ hrs at low tide (eg Playa Mecana. Be sure to return before the tide rises or you will be stranded).

Hotels B *Balboa* T (816) 27074, best in town, pool, boat service to bathing beaches. **E** *Bahía*, in same street as Satena office, with fan and private bath, good restaurant. Another hotel across the street, **F**, basic. Several others. 2 youth hostels, ask at Alcom in Bogotá. Good food at *Las Delicias*.

Transport Aces flies from Quibdó (US$32) and Medellín on Tues, Thur, and Sat. Satena has service to the same destinations on Mon, Wed, and Fri, slightly cheaper. Cargo flights on Tues and Fri will occasionally take passengers, no bookings, inquire with pilot or crew at the airport. There is daily jeep service to El Valle (18 km, 1 hr). Occasional coastal cargo vessels N to Jurado and S to Buenaventura.

THE CAUCA VALLEY (6)

Modern and colonial cities line the fertile but narrow Cauca valley, whose focus is Cali, the country's southern industrial centre. From here the Pacific port of Buenaventura is reached.

From Manizales a road runs SW to Pereira (fine scenery) and then to Cartago, at the northern end of the rich Cauca Valley, which stretches S for about 240 km but is little more than 30 km wide. The road goes S up this valley to Cali and Popayán, at the southern limit of the valley proper. There it mounts the high plateau between the Western and Central Cordilleras and goes through to Ecuador. From Cali a railway (no passengers) and a road run W to the Pacific port of Buenaventura. The Valley is one of the richest in Colombia. From Cartago S the Río Cauca is navigable by barges up to Cali.

22 km SW of Manizales is **Chinchina** (**F** *Hotel Pielroja*, basic, but clean), followed by **Santa Rosa de Cabai**; 15 km away. A poor 11-km road branches off to Los Termales, where waters from a hot spring cascade down a mountain into a swimming pool, entry US$3 (unpleasant at weekends; hotel and restaurant). There are also cold showers fed from a natural spring. Bus Pereira-Santa Rosa, US$0.25; then bargain for a jeep ride, US$4.80, to the springs. Package tours from Santa Rosa to Los Termales, including meals and one night's lodging, are available, but an afternoon excursion is the best value.

Pereira, capital of Risaralda Department, 56 km SW of Manizales, stands overshadowed by green mountains, at an altitude of 1,476m, above the Cauca Valley. Population, 412,135; a centre for coffee and cattle. It is a pleasant modern city, founded in 1863, with an undistinguished cathedral and four parks: the best is the Parque del Lago, with an artificial lake; a fountain is illuminated several times a week. (Good Christmas illuminations, too.) There is a lively market. Adjacent is the Matecaña zoo but in poor condition and not recommended, a feature is the "ligre", a cross between a lion and a tiger (bus from town centre to zoo, US$0.10.) The Tzobota orchid gardens can also be visited. **NB** Pereira and surrounding areas were hit by an earthquake in Feb 1995.

Hotels L3 *Meliá Pereira*, Cra 13, No 15-73 (T 350770/353970, F 350675, Apartado Aéreo 4050), 5-star (taxes not included), restaurant, bars, swimming pool; **B** *Gran*, C 19, No 9-19, T 359500, restaurant, bar, travel agency, etc; **B** *Sorotama*, Cra 7, No 19-20, T 338809; **D** *Royal*, C 16, No 7-56, T 352501, with bath and hot water, clean, highly rec; **F** *Residencia Edén No 1*, C 15, Cra 10, near market, clean, friendly, but not a safe area; **F** *Residencia Ocmara*, C9, T 356675, good, clean; **F** *Los Reyes*, C 4, No 16-23, clean, efficient, good value. Plenty of *residencias* in C 19, eg **F** *Savoy*, with bath. Youth hostel, *Centro Vacacional Viejo Caldas*, 10 mins by car from Pereira, details from Alcom in Bogotá.

Restaurants *La Ricura*, Cra 8, No 22-21, very good meal; *El Manolo*, C 20, No 8-22, good meals near the market; vegetarian restaurant *Naturista No 2*, C 19, No 5-73, good. *Pastelería Lucerna*, C 19, Cra 6, good Swiss restaurant with excellent ice cream, clean, safe; *El Balcón*, Cra 8 y C 24, reasonable food; *El Mirador*, on a hill overlooking the town (ask Tourist Office for directions), good food and views.

Banks Banco Anglo Colombiano, Cra 7, No 18-70, Suite 201. **Banco Internacional**.

Tourist Information Corporación de Turismo de Risaralda, C 20, No 8-73, T 342503; Oficina de Fomento y Turismo, Cra 7, No 18-55, T 344804.

Transport Matecaña airport is 5 km to the S (bus, US$0.10). Aces (T 353248), Intercontinental and Avianca (T 334863) flights to and from **Bogotá**, Avianca to **Miami**, **New York** (change planes in Bogotá); Avianca and Aces to Medellín.

New bus terminal, clean, with shops, outside city centre. Bus to **Armenia**, 1 hr, US$2, a beautiful trip; to **Cali**, US$8.75, 4½-5 hrs, buses by night, take colectivo by day, same price; **Manizales**, US$1.80, 1½ hrs; to/from **Bogotá**, US$9, 7 hrs, rough journey, not recommended for motorbikes (bus route is via Girardot, Ibagué and Armenia).

Excursion A nice ride can be taken through the heart of coffee country along the road NW to Chocó. The Río Cauca is crossed before **La Virginia** (**F** *Hotel New York*, Cra 9, No 7-45, several others). The road then climbs the eastern slopes of the Cordillera Occidental to reach **Pueblo Rico** (basic hotels and restaurants). The many *veredas cafeteras* with their colourfully painted balconies decorated with flowers and the mountain scenery along the way are beautiful.

From Pereira, a 2 to 4-day excursion to the beautiful **Ucamari Park** is recommended. This is one of the few places where the Andean spectacled bear survives. Above 4,000m in the park are spectacular *frailejón* plants. Permission to visit must be obtained from Edif El Lago, piso 12, C 25 between Cras 7 and 8. There is excellent camping (US$1.30), good meals and rooms for rent at the *Pastora* refuge. The Manager, Carlos, is very helpful. At La Pastora, Andean bears are kept in a compound in natural surroundings (you won't see them anywhere else in the park). From La Pastora it is a 1-2 day hike to Laguna de Otún through beautiful scenery of changing vegetation (**see p 859**). It is possible to walk down the same way, or continue to Manizales by trying to hitchhike from the first farm, about 2 hrs walk from the Laguna (very slim chance of finding a lift).

Hikes can be made to the **Nevado del Ruiz** (see also p 848 y p 859). Take a bus from Pereira (Transportes Florida, C 12, No 8-82) at 0900 and 1440, to *El Cedral* (1½ hrs—return at 1130 and 1630), then walk 2 hrs to the Inderena *refugio* through lush forest. Reservations for the *refugio* must be made in advance at Edif El Lago, see above. Enquire at Edif El Lago if a guide, eg Wilson Cardona, is available for tours to the volcano. Camping is possible in the park, check with the rangers.

Armenia, capital of Quindío Department, is in the heart of the Quindío coffee district (pop 231,745; alt 1,838m; mean temperature 19°C). This modern city, founded in 1889, is the seat of Quindío University. Its economy suffered badly when international coffee prices fell in 1992; unemployment, homelessness and the crime rate rose as a result. The Quindío countryside is dotted with tall wax palms, the national tree. The Bogotá-Armenia-Cali road is fully paved, but slow through the mountains; fog at night, reckless drivers and stray animals make the

Quindío Pass (3,350m) a hazard at night. A newer, more direct road from Armenia to Cali, joining the Panamericana S of Zarzal, has heavier traffic than the old road.

Museum The Museo Quimbaya is on the edge of town on the road to Manizales (take a city bus or taxi); fine collection of ceramics and gold pieces from the Quimbaya culture, well-displayed.

Hotels **B** *Maitama*, Cra 17, No 21-29, T 443400; **B** *Zuldemayda*, C 20, No 15-38, T 443580; **C** *Izcay*, C 22 No 14-05, T 449400; **C** *Palatino*, C 21, No 14-49, T 448730, central, comfortable, renovated 1993; **E** *Moderno Aristi*, C 18, Cra 20, with bath, hot water, clean; **E** *Residencial El Viajero*, opp bus station, but 15 blocks from the centre of town; **E** *Imperial No 2*, Cra 19, C 21, central, safe, good but sometimes noisy; **F** *Imperial*, C 21, No 17-43, T 449151, clean, safe, rec; **G** *Pensión Nueva York*, Cra 19, No 23-52, basic but clean and cheap; **F** *Aymora*, Cra 19, opp *Nueva York*, clean, safe, private bath, radio.

Restaurants *Frisby*, Cra 16, No 20-22, good pizza or fried chicken; *Cafetería Punto Rojo*, C 21, open 24 hrs. Vegetarian: *Manjar*, C 18, No 15-52 and *Rincón*, Cra 16, No 18-28, closed Sun.

Tourist Information Corporación de Fomento y Turismo, C 20, No 15-31, T 449441.

Airport El Edén, 13 km from city. Fog often makes air services unreliable.

Transport To Neiva, Flota Magdalena, 0100, 0400, 2230, US$5.75. To Ibagué, US$2.40. To/from **Bogotá**: Velotax bus, US$7.20, hourly, 9 hrs; Velotax colectivo, US$9.50, 7 hrs.

Excursions NE of Armenia is Salento and the *Acaime Natural Reserve* on the Río Quindío with a visitor centre and cafe. There are lots of humming birds, a wax palm zone and cloud forest. Contact Fundación Herencia Verde, C Real, No 2-15, Salento, T 967 593142. Trips can be arranged with guides and extended to the Parque Nacional de los Nevados and Nevado del Tolima (**see also p 849**). 12 km NW of Armenia is **Montenegro**, near which is a park with an interesting Museo de Café, opened in 1994. You can tour a coffee finca and see a fine view of the area from a tower in the park. There are restaurants and a botanical garden. The tourist office in Armenia will also advise on visits to other coffee farms.

Before the road drops into the Cauca Valley, between Armenia and Buga is *Caicedonia*, near which is a coffee finca owned by Dolly and Umberto Samin de Botero, T 458530, who will show you around their plantations, make arrangements first. Further on is *Sevilla*; **C** *Hotel Sevilla*, good, C 49, No 49-70, T 6434; **F** *Residencias Soratama*, Cra 49, No 51-48, secure parking; others similar. 30 mins' bus-ride from Armenia is Montenegro, a coffee centre (ask at FNC office on Plaza Bolívar about visits to *fincas* in the district); Plaza Bolívar is now the site of a modern church.

Cartago, 98,640 people, about 17 km SW of Pereira, is on a small tributary of the Cauca river before it takes to the gorge separating the two *cordilleras*. Coffee, tobacco and cattle are the main products. Founded in 1540, it still has some colonial buildings, particularly the very fine Casa de los Virreyes. Visit the cathedral, with the cross apart from the main building.

Hotels Around Plaza Bolívar: **D** *Don Gregorio*, Cra 5, No 9-59, T 27491, swimming pool, a/c; **F** *Río Pul*, Cra 2, No 2-146, fan and bath, clean, rec. Many others in area around bus terminals (Cra 9) and railway station (Cra 9 y C 6); **F** *Central*, Cra 6, No 11-51, safe, good parking; **F** *Montserrat*, TV, good; **F** *Residencias El Dorado*, Cra 6, No 11-16; **F** *Casa Turista*, Cra 6 y C 11, clean, fan. Those in the same block as Flota Magdalena office are better value than the others.

Restaurants *Mullipán*, Cra 6 y C 12, good cheap *meriendas*; *El Portal*, Cra 6 y C 11, good *churrascos*.

Exchange Banco Popular, and Banco Cafetero in Plaza Bolívar will exchange cash, but not TCs.

Cinema Roblero, C 11 between Cras 5 and 6 (opp *Hotel Don Gregorio*).

Post Office on Plaza Bolívar.

Transport Bus to Cali, US$4.20, 3½ hrs; to Armenia, US$1.75, 2-3 hrs; to Pereira, US$0.50, 45 mins.

About 27 km S of Cartago is *La Victoria* (the Pan-American Highway bypasses it to the E), a pleasant, small colonial town with a shady plaza. There is **F** *Hotel Turista* (family atmosphere, clean and friendly, will change US$ cash) one block from the plaza, and several restaurants.

La Victoria is in the centre of a scenic area where cattle are raised, and cotton, sorghum, maize and soya are grown. You can cross the Río Cauca by turning right off the road going to the S (good fishing Jan, Feb and July) and 10 km (paved road) further on is **La Unión** at the foot of the mountains on the W side of the valley. La Unión is a small agricultural town, a centre for grape production. The countryside around offers good walks. Just S of La Unión is Rondanillo, a small town in the hot Cauca Valley, with a museum of paintings by the Colombian artist, Omar Rayo. A road runs E to the main highway at Zarzal.

About 50 km S of Cartago is Zarzal, followed by Andalucía (30 km), where the Balneario Campestre allows car camping. 18 km S of Andalucia is **Tuluá (G Mariscal Sucre**, clean, fan and vegetarian restaurant Vivamejor, Cra 26, No 31-64, good) and 23 km S again is **Buga**, an old colonial city of 87,450 people and a centre for cattle, rice, cotton, tobacco and sugar cane. Founded in 1650, its modern Cathedral contains the image of the Miraculous Christ of Buga to which pilgrimages are made. Bus to Cali, US$1.80. Toll 22 km S of Buga, US$0.50.

Hotels B Guadalajara, C 1, No 13-33, T 272611, swimming pool, rec, cabins for families, excellent restaurant, self-service cafeteria; **E** La Casona, good; residencias around Cathedral usually good value. **G** Res Palermo, C 9, No 9-82, T 72552, with bath, clean.

Excursion If you take the road from Buga to Buenaventura you come to the man-made **Lago Calima**. The northern route round the lake goes through **Darién** at 1,500m with a new archeological museum, open Tues-Fri 0800-1700, Sat-Sun 1000-1800, with good displays of Calima and other Colombian cultures. Hotels: **A1** Los Veleros, swimming pool; **C** Hostal El Carmen; **E** Darién, clean, cold showers, good, friendly; **E** Sulevar, clean, cold showers, restaurant, parking; also cabins available at a Centro Náutico on the lakeside. There are a growing number of weekend houses and many leisure activities on the lake. Camping possible near the village. Tourist office at C 10, No 6-21. There are direct buses from Buga, 2 hrs, and Cali, 4 hrs. Taking the southern route round the lake, 42 km from Buga is the **D** Hotel del Lago Calima set in very pleasant surroundings on the edge. There is no swimming pool, but some brave people swim in the lake, which is cold at about 16°C. Many treasures of the Calima culture are said to have been left, to be flooded by the lake, when the dam was built. Closer to Buga on this road, before the Río Cauca, is the **Laguna de Sonso Reserve**, which is good for birdwatching.

47 km S from Buga is **Palmira**, in the Department of Valle del Cauca; population, 189,485. Good tobacco, coffee, sugar, rice and grain are grown, and there is a College of Tropical Agriculture. The Pan-American Highway runs direct to Popayán via Pradera, but the road through Cali is preferable. The best road S is from Palmira through Candelaria and Puerto Tejada, avoiding Cali, to Popayán; paved, straight, not much traffic. (Taxi connection with Cali, 29 km S, US$6.65; bus US$0.55, Transportes Palmira, terminal on C 30, near Cra 33)

Hotels C Las Victorias, Cra 32, T 22666; **F** Pacífico No 1, C 30, No 32-55, T 25633, with bath, simple but nice; **F** Residencias Belalcázar, C 30, No 31-29, with bath, G without, clean, friendly, good value; many other cheap places. **Restaurants** Paradero los Parrales, good breakfast, good service, clean loos. Very good meals at restaurant on C 30 nr Cra 30.

At La Manuelita, 5 km N of Palmira, is a famous sugar estate. Beyond La Manuelita any of 3 roads running E will reach, in 12 km, the fine restored colonial hacienda of El Paraíso, where the poet Jorge Isaacs (author of María, a Colombian classic) lived and wrote. Entry US$0.50; there is a café. To visit the hacienda, take a bus from Palmira, Cra 25 y C 26, at 1230 (another in am), which passes the hacienda ½-an-hour later (US$0.65); returns about 1515. 9 km from El Paraíso is a sugar cane museum in the Hacienda Piedechinche (open 0930-1600, closed Mon; admission, US$0.20), 42 km from Cali, take a bus to Palmira, then taxi, or take bus from Cali to Amaime, a small place on the road to Cartago, US$0.60, then wait for bus to Santa Elena, which passes the turn off to the Hacienda. You can walk from Amaime: take the turning marked "El Paraíso" and walk for one hour to the turn off to the Hacienda (marked "Museo de Caño"), then it's another ½ an hour. There is no public transport connection between the two haciendas. Tours of this and Hacienda El Paraíso arranged by Comercializadora Turística Ltda, Cra 4, No 8-39, local 101, Cali (US$12, including transport, entrance fee, guided tour and lunch).

Cali, capital of Valle del Cauca Department (1.78 million people), is the second largest city in Colombia, set in an exceptionally rich agricultural area producing sugar, cotton, rice, coffee and cattle. Altitude: 1,030m; average temperature: 25°C, hot and humid at mid-day but a strong breeze which blows up about 1600 makes the evenings cool and pleasant. It was founded in 1536, and until 1900 was a leisurely colonial town. Then the railway came, and Cali is now a rapidly expanding industrial complex serving the whole of southern Colombia. South of Cra 10 are many one- and a few two-storey houses, tiled and wide-eaved. Through the city runs the Río Cali, a tributary of the Cauca, with grass and exotic trees on its banks. On one overlooking mountain, from which the best views are obtained, there is a statue of Christ visible for 50 km and there are three large crosses on another mountain. The statue of Belalcázar, the city's founder, is worth a look, beautiful views of the city. It is also worth while going up the skyscraper Torre de Cali for a view of the city, but you have to buy an expensive meal as well. Two nearby *haciendas*, El Paraíso (see above under Palmira) and Cañas Gordas, have important historical associations.

The church and monastery of **San Francisco** are Cali's best buildings. Inside, the church has been renovated, but the 18th century monastery has a splendidly proportioned domed belltower. The 18th century church of **San Antonio** on the Colina de San Antonio is worth seeing and there are fine views. Cali's oldest church, **La Merced** (C 7, between Cras 3 and 4), has been well restored by the Banco Popular. The adjoining convent houses two museums: **Museo de Arte Colonial** (which includes the church) and the **Museo Arqueológico** with precolumbian pottery (US$1, but well worth it). More Indian pottery can be seen in the **Sociedad de Mejoras Públicas**, across the street from La Merced; this collection belongs to the Universidad del Valle. Another church worth seeing is **La Ermita**, on the river between Cs 12 and 13.

The city's centre is the **Plaza de Caicedo**, with a statue of one of the independence leaders, Joaquín Caicedo y Cuero. Facing the square are the **Cathedral**, the **Palacio Nacional** and large office buildings. Across the river, which is 2 blocks from the Plaza de Caicedo, is the Centro Administrativo Municipal (CAM) and the main post office.

Other Museums Museo de Arte Moderno La Tertulia, Av Colombia, No 5-105 Oeste (10 mins from centre) has an exciting exhibition of S American art, open Tues-Sat 0900-1300, 1500-1900, Sun and holidays, 1500-1900. Museo de Historia Natural, Cra 2 Oeste, No 7-18, precolombian exhibits as well as biological specimens from the area, similar opening hours. Museo de Oro, Cra 4, C 8, similar to the one in Bogotá but much smaller, opened 1994.

Parks and Zoos There is a zoo on the South bank some distance from the centre, entrance US$0.50. There is an orchid garden, **Orchideorama**, Av 2N, No 48-10, T 664-3256, worth seeing, free.

Fair from 25 Dec to 3 Jan at Plaza Canaveralejo; bullfights, horse parades, masquerade balls, sporting contests. National Art Festival in June (painting, sculpture, theatre, music, etc). Also in June Feria Artesanal at Parque Panamericano, C 5, handicrafts and excellent leather goods.

Security Although a centre of both guerrilla and counter-insurgency activity and drug and anti-drug operations, the atmosphere in Cali is quite relaxed. However, carry your passport (or notarized photocopy) at all times and be prepared for police checks. Avoid C 15 S of the river and Cra 10, especially near its junction with C 15, at night.

Hotels L1 *Intercontinental*, Av Colombia, No 2-72, T 882-3225, F 882-2567, tennis and pool, pleasant garden, service disappointing, *Los Farallones* restaurant with shows, good barbecues and buffets (weekend discounts); **L3** *Aristi*, Cra 9, No 10-04, T 882-2521, F 883-9697, weekend discounts, rec, art-deco style, large and old by Cali standards, unmodernized rooms much cheaper, turkish baths, rooftop pool, restaurant; **L3** *Dann*, Av Colombia, No 1-40, opposite *Intercontinental* (with weekend discounts), T 882-3330, F 883-0129, all suites, large units, 2nd block under construction, good; **L3** *Obelisco*, Av Colombia, No 4 Oeste-39, T 883-7420, F 883-0219, smart, riverside location, small but good; **A1** *Torre de Cali*, Av de las Américas, No 18-26, T 667-4949, restaurant on top floor; **A3** *Don Jaime*, Av 6, No 15N-25, T 668-1171, good, restaurant rec; **B** *Americana*, Cra 4, No 8-73, T 823063, for businessmen, a/c; **B** *Hotel Residencias Stein*, Av 4N, No 3-33, full board, C bed only, friendly, very good, quiet, excellent food, French, German and English spoken, Swiss-run,

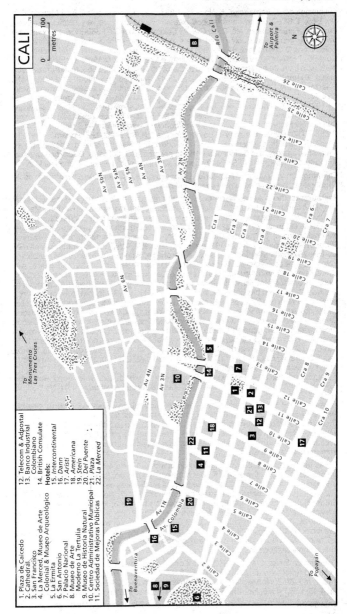

CALI

metres
0   100

N

To
Airport &
Palmira

Río Cali

Calle 26

Calle 25

Calle 24

Calle 23

Calle 22

Calle 21

Calle 20

Calle 19

Calle 18

Calle 17

Calle 16

Calle 15

Calle 14

Calle 13

Calle 12

Calle 11

Calle 10

Calle 9

Calle 8

Calle 7

Calle 6

Calle 5

Calle 4

Calle 3

Calle 2

Cra 1
Cra 2
Cra 3
Cra 4
Cra 5
Cra 6
Cra 7
Cra 8
Cra 9
Cra 10

Av 5b N
Av 5a N
Av 5 N
Av 4 N
Av 3 N
Av 2 N
Av 1 N
Av 6 N

Av Colombia

To
Monumento
Las Tres Cruces

To
Buenaventura

To
Popayán

1. Plaza de Caicedo
2. Cathedral
3. San Francisco
4. La Merced, Museo de Arte
   Colonial & Museo Arqueológico
5. La Ermita
6. San Antonio
7. Palacio Nacional
8. Museo de Arte
   Moderno La Tertulia
9. Museo de Historia Natural
10. Centro Administrativo Municipal
11. Sociedad de Mejoras Públicas
12. Telecom & Adpostal
13. Banco Industrial
    Colombiano
14. British Consulate

Hotels:
15. Intercontinental
16. Dann
17. Aristi
18. Americana
19. Stein
20. Del Puente
21. Plaza
22. La Merced

swimming pool; **C** *Ramader*, C 5, No 5-25, T 883-4219, friendly, central; **B** *La Merced*, C 7, No 1-65, T 882-2520, swimming pool, pleasant young staff are very helpful, restaurant expensive, English spoken, rec; **C** *Río Cali*, Av Colombia, No 9-80, T 880-3156, all rooms have own bath, good, reasonably priced meals available, old colonial building, popular with Colombians; **D** *Centralia*, C 31 near bus terminal, clean, mosquitos, safe; **D** *del Puente*, C 5, No 4-36, T 887-1490, with bath, clean, will store luggage, rec; **D** *María Victoria*, C 10, No 3-38, with bath, 24 hr restaurant; **D** *Plaza*, Cra 6, No 10-29, T 882-2560, friendly, reasonably priced; **E** *Amoblador las Américas*, C 25, 2S-47, with bath, F without, cold water, safe; **E** *Sartor*, Av 8 N, No 20-50, T 668-6482, rooms with bath, central, TV available, Italian spoken; **E** *La Familia*, C 14 N, No 6-42, T 661-2925, safe, good area; **D** *Los Angeles*, Cra 6, No 13-109, good; **F** *Canaima*, Cra 6, No 12-61, T 776-1998, some rooms with bath, cold water, clean, front rooms noisy; **F** *Paseo Bolívar II*, Av 3N, No 13N-43 (T 668-2863), cold water, clean, safe (cheaper rates for long stay); and **F** *Residencial Paseo Bolívar*, Av 3 Norte, No 13N-51 (T 668-5067), friendly but noisy. **G** pp *del Río*, Cra 2 N, No 24-82; **G** *El Porvenir*, Cra 1, Nr 24-29, shared bath, cold water, no keys, no windows but clean and quiet. It is possible to rent a furnished apartment in Cali for about US$45 per month. Out of town: **C** *Turístico La Luna*, Autopista Sur, No 13-01, T 558-7449, friendly, safe, large pool, restaurant, good parking.

Camping On S outskirts *Balneario Campestre*, Brisas Tropicales, swimming pools, refreshments, car camping, armed guards and dogs.

Restaurants Cali is a good place for eating (but restaurants close early, and many close on Sun): *Don Carlos*, Cra 1, No 7-53, excellent seafood, elegant and expensive; *Hostería Madrid*, C 9, No 4-50, European specialities, good service, above-average price; *Restaurante Suizo*, Cra 30 y Diagonal 29, Swiss, excellent fondue bourguignonne, pleasant atmosphere, reasonably priced; *El Quijote*, Cra 4, No 1-64, atmospheric, European dishes, expensive; *Simonetta*, Diagonal 27, No 27-117, pleasant, reasonable, Italian dishes; *Dominique*, Av 6N, No 15N-25, good Italian food and service, reasonable; *Balocco*, Av 6, No 14-04, Italian and Colombian, good value; *La Terraza*, C 16, No 6N-14, elegant, music and dance, nice atmosphere; *El Cortijo Andaluz*, Cra 38 and C 53, atmospheric (converted residence), Spanish food; *Los Girasoles*, Av 6N, C 35, steaks, other meat grills, good atmosphere; *Aragonesa*, Av 6 N, No 13N-68, good breakfasts; *Guacamole*, Av 6 N, No 14-73, Mexican, good quality, good portions; *El Rancho*, S end of Av 6, near municipal building, good local food, draught beer, pricey, closed Sun; *Cali Viejo*, in the Bosque Municipal, good Colombian food; *Los Panchos*, Carretera a Meléndez with Autopista Sur, very good Colombian food, a favourite of Caleños; *Gloria*, Cra 6, C 14, good and cheap; *Mauna Loa*, Centro Comercial del Norte, seafood a speciality, reasonably priced, Lebanese food too; *Mac Club*, Centro Comercial Imbanaco (C 5a and C 39), hamburgers and hotdogs, excellent, cheap, good hamburgers also at *Primos*, near C 5, Cra 34; *La Calima*, Cra 3, No 12-06, good meal US$1.30, always open. At least 10 eating places in the bus station, *Doble Vía* is the best.

Vegetarian: *Raices*, C 18N, No 16-25, open Mon-Sat lunch and dinner, good; *Govindas*, C 14, No 4-49, lunch at 1300, dinner 1900. *Centro Naturista Salud*, C 17N, No 6-39, set lunch US$2.

You can find lots of European-style side-walk places along Av 6 at good prices. Cheaper are the *fuentes de soda*, mostly with Colombian-style cooking, a decent meal for US$3-4. There also *Masserna* on Cra 7 between Cs 10 and 11 and *La Sultana*, C 10, on the corner with *Hotel Aristi*. Try their *buñuelos* (cheesy fritters) and the *pandebono* (cheesy buns) next door at *Montecarlo*. Cafés and ice-cream parlours abound near the university, across the river from the main part of town.

Banks and Exchange Banco Anglo Colombiano, C 11, No 4-48 (Plaza de Caicedo), and agencies in La Tertulia, Sur, and Av 6, does not serve backpackers; **Banco Royal de Colombia**, C 3; and other national banks. **Banco de Bogotá** on the Plaza de Caicedo quickest in giving Visa cash advances. **Banco Industrial de Colombia**, C 11, No 6-24, cashes Amex TCs. **Credencial** in Unicentro, Cra 5, advances against Mastercard. Money can be changed at *Almacén Gerado*, C11, No 5-39, *Almacén Stella*, Cra 8, No 9-64 (by *Hotel Aristi*) open 0800-1200, 1400-1800, very helpful, or at travel agents (eg at bus terminal, open Sat am). **Universal de Cambios**, Edif Lloreda, Plaza de Caicedo, rec. **Intercontinental de Cambios**, C6 Norte, No 2N-36, oficina 536, cash only. At present cash dispensers do not accept international credit cards.

Consulates Swiss, Cra 5, No 8-50; **US Consul** from Bogotá visits monthly at the centro Colombo-Americano, C 13N, No 8-45, T 667-3539; **British**, Ed Garcés, C 11, No 1-07, No 409, T 783-2752; **Norwegian**, Av de las Américas 23-33, T 668-6735; **Danish**, Av 4 N, No 4-46, T 661-4368; **Finnish**, C 4 Norte, No 1N-52, piso 3, Barrio Centenario, T 661-1161.

Entertainments Teatro Experimental, C 7, No 8-63, T 778-1249; films Wed nights at Centro

Colombo-Americano (see above). Also films on Fri nights at the Alianza Colombo-Francesa, Av 6 N, No 21-34. Club Imbanaco, C 5A, No 38A-14, old, popular movies. Good films also shown at the Museo La Tertulia (see above).

Nightclubs and Dancing   Locally known as "Grills". The ones along Av 6 N and C 5a are safest and best known. Try: *Tin Tin Deo*, C 5 y Cra 22, good atmosphere, salsa at weekends; *Nuestra Herencia*, C 5, Cra 34, popular, reggae and salsa; *Taberna Latina*, C 5, Cra 36, small and friendly; *Café Libro*, C 17 N, No 8N-49, very popular, more expensive; *Classicos*, C 22 N, No 2-58, good jazz concerts, drinks more expensive than C 5. There is a nightly tour on a *chiva* (open-sided bus) to various discos. Cali is claimed by some to be the capital of Salsa, which can be heard everywhere. There is a school, Profesional Academía de Baile, Cra 4B, No 44-24, T 446-2275, director Oscar Borrero, where you can perfect your Salsa.

Health   Good clinic for women, Grupo Mujeres, C 6, No 3-64, T 880-0050. Optica Cali, Cra 5, No 13-105, good optician service.

Laundry   *Lavandería x kilo*, C 23 Norte, No 7N-08, T 661-2184.

Post Office   Adpostal for national service, C 10, No 6-25; Avianca for international service, C 12N, No 2a-27. **Telecom**   C 10, No 6-25. Faxes sent to TELECOM 0057-2-883-0797 with name and local phone number will reach you. Small charge for receiving, about US$8 per page to send fax to Europe.

   NB   In 1995 the city code for Cali changed from 23 to 2, and all city phone numbers became 7-digit, with the first digit of the old number repeated (eg 63-2145 becomes 663-2145).

Shopping   *Platería Ramírez*, Cra 11b, No 18-64, for gold, silver, brass, jewellery, table settings, etc. *Artesanías de Colombia*, C 12, No 1-20 and for larger purchases Av 6 N, No 23-45. For boots and shoes *Chaparro* (*Botas Texanas*), Av 6, No 14N-14, T 665-1007, good, owner Edgar speaks a little English. Best shopping districts are: Av 6N, from Río Cali to C 30 Norte and on Cra 5 in the S with new shopping malls: Unicentro and Holguines Trade Center, open also Sun 1000-1300.

Bookshop   *Librería Nacional*, on main square, has a café, as do branches elsewhere in the city. Bookstalls on the sidewalk on Cra 10 near C 10.

Sports   Within its Villa Olímpica in San Fernando, Cali has three stadia: the Pascual Guerrero Stadium, holding 50,000 people, the Olympic Stadium, holding 7,000 people and the Piscinas Olímpicas, 3,000. Another stadium holding 18,000, the Monumental de Cali, is 10 mins from the city on the road to Meléndez. Outside the city also is the new, first-class bullring.

Travel Agent   *Viajes Sinisterra*, Edif Colseguros, 2nd Floor, T 889-3121, good service especially for airline advice. *Viajes Camino Real*, Av 4 N, No 22 N-32, T 661-6840, trips locally and to Popayán, Puracé, Leticia etc. *American Express* at Tierra Mar Aire SA, C 22N, No 5BN-53, PO Box 44-64, T 667-6767, clients' mail service, helpful. There is a Thomas Cook office at Wagons-Lits, Cra 4, No 8-20.

Tourist Information   Office C 16 N, No 4N-83, T 667-5613/667-5614.

Useful Addresses   DAS office, Av 3N, No 50N-20 (T 664-3809).

Taxis   Black taxis are the most reliable; ensure that meters are used. Prices, posted in the window, start at US$0.15. On holidays an extra charge is made.

Airport   Palmaseca, 20 km from city, has *casa de cambio*. International standard, with good *Hotel Aeropuerto Palmaseca*. Frequent services to Bogotá, Medellín, Cúcuta, Ipiales, Cartagena, Barranquilla, San Andrés, and other Colombian cities. Minibus from airport, from far end of pick-up road outside arrivals, to bus terminal (2nd floor), every 10 mins up to 2100, approx 30 mins, US$1.50. Colectivo to city about US$1.20; taxi, US$7.75, 30 mins. Direct flights (Avianca, Intercontinental and Copa) to Panama; also to Miami (Avianca, Aces and American) and New York (Avianca). Avianca, Av 1N, No 7-59, T 889-4018.

Rail   passenger services to **Cartago** and **Armenia**, via Palmira and Buga were reported suspended in 1995 (only freight services running).

Buses   New bus terminal (connected by tunnel to railway station) is at C 30N, No 2A-29, 25 mins walk from the centre (leave terminal by the taxi stands, take first right, go under railway and follow river to centre). Hotel information available left luggage US$0.60 per item, good food at terminal. *Casa de cambio*, cash only. Showers on second level (US$0.40). There are plenty of local buses between the bus station and the centre, which charge US$0.10. Taxi from centre to bus station, US$1.20. Buses to **Popayán**, US$6, 2½-3 hrs, also colectivos, US$7.50. To **Pasto**, US$9.50, 9 hrs; to **Ipiales** (direct), US$12, 12 hrs or by Bolivariano Pullman US$9.50, departures at 0400 and 0615 and 0800; Coomotor have a direct service to **San Agustín** via

Popayán, Coconuco and Isnos, US$12.75, and a service at 0900 to San Agustín via La Plata (much slower than the new road via Isnos); Sotracauca also run Cali-Popayán-Coconuco-Isnos at 0500, 9 hrs, US$10. To Cartago, 3½ hrs, US$4.20; to Armenia, US$6; to Ibagué, US$7.50, 7 hrs; to Buenaventura, US$3.75, 4 hrs; to Manizales, US$5.40, 5 hrs; to Medellín, US$17, 10-12 hrs; to Bogotá, 10-15 hrs, by Magdalena (rec) and Palmira, US$18 (sit on left hand side of the bus). *Busetas* (Velotax and others) charge about 50% over bus prices but save time; taxi-colectivos about 2½ times bus prices and save even more.

145 km by (US$1 toll) road from Cali (4 hrs) over a pass in the Western Cordillera is **Buenaventura**, Colombia's only important port on the Pacific. It was founded in 1540, but not on its present site. It stands on the island of Cascajal, 16 km inside the Bay of Buenaventura. Beaches such as La Bocana, Juanchaco and Ladrilleros (many small hostels and restaurants) may be reached by motor launch, but they are not very safe. Trips to beaches cost between US$10-40 for 10-person launch (rate per launch, not per person).

Buenaventura is 560 km by sea from Panamá, 708 km by road from Bogotá. Population, 186,935, mostly black. Mean temperature, 27°C. It rains nearly every day, particularly at night; the average annual rainfall is 7,400 mm (relative humidity 88%). There are still problems with malaria. The port handles 80% of Colombia's coffee exports, and 60% of the nation's total exports, including sugar and frozen shrimps.

The commercial centre is now entirely paved and has some impressive buildings, but the rest of the town is poor, with steep unpaved streets lined with wooden shacks. It is more expensive than Cali and it is difficult to eat cheaply or well. Festive atmosphere every night (see under **Music and Dance** for festivals). South of the town a swampy coast stretches as far as Tumaco (**see p 893**); to the N lies the deeply jungled Chocó Department, where the most important gold and platinum mines are found.

Hotels A3 *Estación*, C 2, No 1A-08, T 23903, good restaurant; **D** *Del Mar*, Cra 4 y C 3, T 23883, restaurant, TV, phone in rooms; **D** *Felipe II*, C 3 y Cra 3, T 22820, a/c, with bath, restaurant; **E** *Balmoral*, with bath, clean, friendly. Several F and G hotels on Cra 5, eg *Comfort*, a/c; *Colombia*, bath, clean, fan; **E** *Continental*, Cra 5, No 4-05, with bath; opposite is **F** *Europa*, without bath; **F** *Las Gaviotas*, C 3, No 3-83, clean, friendly. **F** *Niza*, C 6, No 5-38, with bath and fan.

Restaurants *Los Balcones*, C 2 y Cra 3, very good, but expensive. Self-service restaurant on main plaza, clean, modern, open 24 hrs. *Listo Auto Services*, C 4, good *tamales*; *La Sombrita de Miguel*, on road to El Piñal, good seafood, reasonable prices; *La Sazón de Merceditas*, opposite Edificio de Café, good seafood, soups, friendly, reasonable prices. Chinese restaurant in street leading NE from telephone building. Good seafood at Pueblo Nuevo market, but not very cheap.

Exchange Do not change money in Buenaventura, but in Cali.

Tourist Office C 1, No 1-26, Mon-Fri, 0800-1200, 1400-1800. Cámara de Comercio nearby is also helpful; maps at CAM, 3rd floor of office block at the far end of the seafront.

Shipping Agent Navemar, C 1, No 2A-25, T 22571, for Sudamericana de Vapores, for shipping vehicles to/from Panama.

Transport Air Services Local airport only; flights to Cali.

The toll **road** to Cali is fully paved; the toll is about US$1.30 for cars and US$0.30 for motorcycles. The ordinary road is not paved. There are plenty of buses to Cali, US$3.75 each way, 3 hrs. Colectivos run at half-hourly intervals to Cali, US$5.75 pp.

Both the toll and ordinary roads give beautiful views of mountains and jungle, and from the old road you can reach the **Parque Nacional Farallones**. To reach the park, take the dirt road S from the plaza in Queremal, at 1,460m, about 1 hr from Cali, 3½ hrs from Buenaventura. There is good walking and bathing in the park and peaks to climb. Busy at weekends, camping possible at US$0.55 pp per day. Information from CVC, Cra 56, No 11-36, Cali, T 309755.

From Buenaventura to Quibdó (**see p 860**) on the Río San Juan: boats are scarce out of Buenaventura (lumber boats from El Piñal only go about a day and a half upstream, and port authorities are strict about allowing passengers on cargo boats). One way is to take a bus from Pueblo Nuevo, Buenaventura, to San Isidro on the Río Calima (28 km, 6 hrs, terrible road), then a motorized dugout (*panga*) to Palestina on the Río San Juan. From there take a dugout going upstream; they rarely go as far as Istmina, which is connected by road and bus to Quibdó. Try to get as far as Dipurdú (no hotels, but friendly locals who offer sleeping space, shops with tinned goods), from where daily boats go to Istmina.

Boats can also be found going S to Tumaco.

The island of **Gorgona** is about 150 km down the coast from Buenaventura. Until a few years ago, it was Colombia's high security prison (a sort of Alcatraz), convicts were dissuaded from escaping by the poisonous snakes on the island and the sharks patrolling the 30 km to the mainland. It was made a nature reserve in 1985, controlled by Inderena. All visitors, research students, scientists and tourists must obtain a (free) pass to go there. Facilities on the island are run by Inderena employees. Many parts are unspoilt with deserted sandy beaches. Some parts have been closed to visitors owing to excessive traffic. There is an abundance of birds (pelicans, cormorants, geese, herons) that use the island as a migration stop-over. There are paths to follow to see monkeys, iguanas, and a wealth of flora and fauna. Rubber boots are provided and recommended. Snorkelling is rewarding, equipment can be hired, exotic fish and turtles to be seen. Collect your own coconuts, but there is no other fruit on the island. There is a good hike across the island through the jungle via a series of lakes, now dry due to earthquake activity. July to September, killer whales visit the area. You can stay in cabins on the island (US$5) and there is a restaurant with a mainly fish menu. Full board about US$14 per day. You can take your own food but all non-biodegradable items must be taken off the island. Don't take alcohol, it will probably be confiscated. Do take drinking water, it is in short supply and expensive on the island. There are organized tours now, one company is Panturismo, C 8, No 1-38, Cali, T 889-3135, who offer a 4-day visit via Guapi for US$240, or 6 days for US$165 via Buenaventura, but better to arrange on your own, including finding a boat at Buenaventura.

If you want to volunteer your services as a Park guard, contact Inderena, Bogotá and speak to Dr Carlos Castaño Uribe, or Dr Luis Emiro Matallana.

To get there, apply for a pass at the office of Inderena in Bogotá (their offices elsewhere in Colombia will advise you). Permits for 4 day visits available on application; at holiday times you must apply 4 weeks in advance and you pay for 3 nights accommodation at the time (about US$30). Boats leave most days at 1600 from the El Piñal dock (Bodega Liscano) in Buenaventura. The trip, US$40 return, takes up to 10 hrs depending on conditions and can be an experience in itself. Try to book a bunkbed in advance. If you can't prepare for a scramble. You may be able to make arrangements in **Guapi** on the mainland to make the 1¹/₂ hour boat trip to Gorgona Island, and Guapi can be visited from Gorgona with Inderena staff going to the market, but don't count on it. A launch costs US$100 to be shared by up to 10 passengers.

Local basket-weaving is on sale in Guapi, as are musical instruments such as the guaza (a hollow tube filled with seeds) and the marimba (about US$15). The only passable place to stay in Guapi is the **Hotel El Río** run by Pedro Arroyo, who speaks a little English, and his brother Camilo. The only way out of Guapi is by boat or by plane to Cali, US$36.

POPAYAN, TIERRADENTRO, SAN AGUSTÍN (7)

The Pan-American Highway climbs out of the valley to Popayán, a richly historic city which gives access to the *páramo* of the Cordillera Central and the burial caves of Tierradentro—excellent walking country. This section also contains the upper reaches of the Magdalena river and the remarkable archaeological site of San Agustín.

The paved Pan-American Highway (142 km) runs S through the Cauca Valley from Cali to Popayán. (Toll, US$0.40.) It takes 2¹/₂-3 hrs by bus through splendid scenery. At first we pass through a land of rich pastures interspersed with sugar-cane plantations. To left and right are the mountain walls of the two Cordilleras. The valley narrows and we begin to climb, with occasional glimpses E of the Nevado del Huila (5,750m).

Warning Both Valle del Cauca and Cauca departments have had guerrilla problems in the recent past. Enquire locally before travelling on minor roads in the area.

Popayán is in the valley of the Pubenza, at 1,760m, in a peaceful landscape of palm, bamboo, and the sharp-leaved agave. (Pop 201,000.) The early settlers after setting up their sugar estates in the hot, damp Cauca valley, retreated to Popayán to live, for the city is high enough to give it a delightful climate. To N, S, and E the broken green plain is bounded by mountains. To the SE rises the cone of the volcano Puracé (4,646m).

Popayán was founded by Sebastián Belalcázar, Francisco Pizarro's lieutenant, in 1536. After the conquest of the Pijao Indians, Popayán became the regional seat of government, subject until 1717 to the Audiencia of Quito, and later to the Audiencia of Bogotá. It is now the capital of the Department of Cauca. The equestrian statue of Belalcázar on the Morro de Tulcán overlooks the city; it is worth climbing this hill, which is the site of a precolumbian pyramid, or even better the one with the three crosses on top, for the views. The streets of two-storey buildings are in rococo Andalusian style, with beautiful old monasteries and cloisters of pure Spanish classic architecture. Look for the Puente Chiquito, a colonial bridge constructed in 1713 (C 2, Cra 6). It is said that Simón Bolívar marched over this bridge.

In March 1983, an earthquake devastated the city. Following restoration work, Popayán has come fully back to life and has managed to retain its colonial character. **The Cathedral** (C 5, Cra 6), beautifully restored, has a fine marble madonna sculpture behind the altar by Buenaventura Malagón. Other churches are **San Agustín** (C 7, Cra 6), note the gilt altar piece and the unusual statue of Christ kneeling on the globe; **Santo Domingo** (C 4, Cra 5), used by the Universidad del Cauca, **La Ermita** (C 5, Cra 2), **La Encarnación** (C 5, Cra 5), also used for religious music festivals, **San Francisco** (C 4, Cra 9—restoration continuing) and **El Carmen** (C 4, Cra 3). The town centre has been fully restored. Walk to **Belén** chapel, which is also open (C 4 y Cra 0), seeing the statues en route, and then continue to **El Cerro de las Tres Cruces** if you have the energy, but best not to go alone (there are plenty of guides offering their services). Popayán was the home of the poet Guillermo Valencia; it has given no fewer than eleven presidents to the Republic.

The scientist Francisco José de Caldas was born here in 1771; it was he who discovered how to determine altitude by variation in the boiling point of water, and it was to him that Mutis (of the famous *Expedición Botánica*) entrusted the directorship of the newly founded Observatory at Bogotá. He was a passionate partisan of independence, and was executed in 1815 during Morillo's "Reign of Terror".

Museums Not open Mondays: **Museo Negret**, C 5, No 10-23, US$0.40, with works, photographs and furniture of Negret. **Museo Guillermo Valencia**, Cra 6 y C 3, birthplace of the poet; **Casa Museo Martínez**, C 3 out of town; **Museo Casa Mosquera**, C 3, No 5-14; **Museo de Historia Natural**, Cra 2, No 1A-25. Small collection in **Banco de la República**.

At weekends you will find people playing "sapo", see under **Sports** in **Information for Visitors**. A good place is along the La Plata road near Belén Church. During the week, the open markets are interesting—Bolívar market, C 1N, Cra 5 is best in the early morning—local foods such as *pipián*, *tamales* and *empanadas*. At the Universidad del Cauca, Cra 3, there is a good, clean swimming pool, entry US$0.50.

Festivals Easter processions, every night of Holy Week until Good Friday, are spectacular; the city is very crowded. The childrens' processions in the following week are easier to see. The children assume all the rôles of the official processions to the delight of parents and onlookers. As at Pasto (but less violent), there are the Día de los Negros on 5 Jan and Día de los Blancos on 6 Jan; drenching with water is not very common, but don't walk under windows when you see people on the first floor.

Warning Take care if you cross any of the bridges over the river going N, especially at night.

Hotels Note: Hotel prices include taxes, but are subject to a 30% increase in some cases for Holy Week and festivals, eg 5-6 January. Continental breakfast is included in most category E and above hotels. Central area: *Monasterio*, C 4, No 10-50, in what was the monastery of San Francisco, lovely grounds, swimming pool, very good, T (939) 232191/6, F 243491, closed but expected to reopen in 1995; **A2** *Camino Real*, C 5, No 5-59, T 241546, PO Box 248, good service, excellent restaurant (try their 6 course dinner US$13), friendly, rec; **A2** *El Herrero*, Cra 5 No 2-08, T 241637, opened 1994, converted large colonial house, family owned, good

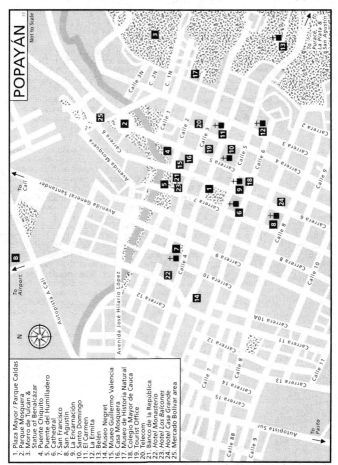

POPAYÁN

Not to Scale

1. Plaza Mayor / Parque Caldas
2. Parque Mosquera
3. Morro de Tulcán &
   Statue of Benalcázar
4. Puente Chiquito
5. Puente del Humilladero
6. Cathedral
7. San Francisco
8. San Agustín
9. La Encarnación
10. Santo Domingo
11. El Carmen
12. La Ermita
13. Belén
14. Museo Negret
15. Museo Guillermo Valencia
16. Casa Mosquera
17. Museo de Historia Natural
18. Colegio Mayor de Cauca
19. Tourist Office
20. Telecom
21. Banco de la República
22. Hotel Monasterio
23. Hotel Los Balcones
24. Hotel Casa Grande
25. Mercado Bolívar area

restaurant, friendly, highly rec; **B** *La Casona del Virrey*, C 4, No 5-78, T 231836, hot water, big rooms with bath, friendly, nice colonial house, warmly rec; **A3** *Hostal Santo Domingo*, C 4, No 5-14, T 240676, with bath, friendly, good value, in recently restored colonial building; **A3** *Los Balcones*, C 3, No 6-80, T 242030, F 241814, hot water, Spanish-style restaurant for breakfast and lunch, good, will change TCs, rec; **C** *Pakandé*, Cra 6, No 7-75, T 240846, clean, good beds, hot shower, rec; **C** *Los Olivares*, Cra 7, No 2-38, T 242186, quiet, good local and international restaurant; **E** *Casa Grande*, Cra 6, No 7-11, T 240604, family run, attractive, friendly, hot water, convenient, will store luggage, highly rec; **E** *Don Blas*, Cra 6 y C 8, T 240817, with bath, clean, modern, rec; **E** *Ermita*, near Capilla Ermita, T 241936, private bath, TV, good breakfast, accepts Visa, rec; **F** *Casa Suiza*, C 4, No 7-79, friendly, hot water, clean, secure; **F** *Casa Familiar Haydée de Varela*, Cra 5 No 2-41, clean, good breakfast for US$1.80, hot water, no sign, highly rec; **F** *Casa Familiar Turística*, Cra 8, No 3-25, T 242100, clean, hot water, family-run, no sign, rec; **F** *Diana*, Cra 6, No 8-58, very comfortable, hot water, friendly; **F** *Bolívar*, Cra 5, No 7-11, T 244844, clean, pleasant, good restaurant, spacious flowery courtyard, safe motorcycle parking, car parking across street, rec; nearby **G** *Residencia Panamá*, Cra 5, No 7-33, good, laundry service, good food, rec. Private accommodation at C 3, No 2-53, T 240602, with Karin and Luis Cabrera, G, food available, Spanish lessons arranged.

Outside the central area, not safe walking alone at night: there are many hotels in the Mercado Bolívar area on Cra 6 to the N of the river, eg **F** *Plaza Bolívar*, Cra 6, No 2N-12, with bath, good cheap restaurant, clean, safe, good value; **G** *Residencia Líder*, Cra 6, No 4N-70, friendly, good; **G** *Residencias San Agustín*, Cra 6, No 1N-15, family run, clean, good beds, laundry facilities. Also, on and S of Calle 8: **D** *Berioska*, C 8, No 5-47, T 223145, with bath, clean, well run; **F** *Residencias El Viajero*, C 8, No 4-45, T 243069, with bath, clean, otherwise basic, popular, watch your belongings, modern; **F** *Residencias Cataluña*, Cra 5, No 8-21, clean, popular, friendly; **G** *Diana*, Cra 6, No 8-58, hot water, same owners as *Berioska*, clean, cooking and laundry facilities, good base for young travellers, rec. For longer stays, finca accommodation near Popayán suitable for families is available, enquire at the Tourist Office.

Restaurants The best restaurants are attached to hotels. If you want good food at more reasonable prices, take a short taxi ride to the road to Cali to *Rancho Grande*, Autopista Norte 32N-50, T 235788, two thatched restaurants, delicious *chuzos* (barbecued beef), credit cards accepted, rec, or *Torremolino*, Autopista Norte 33N-100, similar, also evening entertainment. In the centre, the best are: *La Viña*, C 4, No 7-85, open 24 hrs, good set lunch US$1.65, dinner US$2.25; *Pizzería don Sebastián*, C 3, No 2-54, good food in a colonial mansion; *Cascada*, Cra 7, No 6-46, good for breakfast; *La Oficina*, C 4, No 8-01, huge servings, good value; *La Brasa Roja*, Cra 8 No 5-90, has a set lunch and evening meal for US$1.20, not much atmosphere, but good food; *Jengibre*, Cra 8, No 7-19, T 242732, vegetarian; *Belalcázar*, Cra 6, No 7-55, T 241911, good value, set meal US$2; *Caldas*, Cra 6 y C 8, filling 3-course set meals, their *sancocho* rec; *Mey Chow*, Cra 10, No 10-81, good Chinese; *Chung Wah*, Cra 6, No 9-64, huge, good Chinese meals, also vegetarian; *La Fontana*, C 6, No 7-72, excellent bakery with café serving meals, pizzas and sandwiches; *El Gato Goloso*, Cra 6, No 6-12, for good yogurts, fruit salads and try *champús* (fruit juice with corn, local speciality). For light refreshments: *Peña Blanca*, Cra 7, No 6-73, best bread and cakes, rec; *Comamos*, C4, No 8-41, in front of cinema, friendly, cheap, good meal for US$1, try the excellent *arepas de queso*; *Delicias Naturales*, C 6, No 8-21, good, cheap, set meals for US$1.50, vegetarian; *Olafo*, No 7-42, good pizzas and *patacones con guacamol* and great vanilla ice cream. Near bus station: *Lo Máximo*, Cra 9A, sit outside, good, cheap.

Bars *Los Balcones*, Cra 7, No 2-20; *Salón Azteca*, Cra 9, C 2 y 3; *Café Galería*, Cra 3 y C 4. **Discos:** *Apocalipsis*, Cra 8, C 5 y 6; *Acrópolis*, Vía Panamericana. *El Trapiche 2* and *Maxim's* on the road out to Cali are the best nightclubs.

Banks and Exchange Banks in Popayán will not change TCs (1993/4). Some, eg *Banco Popular*, will give cash advances against Visa cards or Banco del Occidente against Mastercard. **Salvador Duque** at Diana shop on the main plaza, near the cathedral. Cash dollars can be changed at a *casa de cambio* on Cra 5 between C 5 and 6, also open on Saturdays. There are other *cambios*, but their rates are poor. Change dollars elsewhere; if coming from the S, Pasto is a good place.

Cinemas Teatro Popayán, C 4, Cra 8/9, best; Teatro Anarkos, Cra 5, Cs 6/7.

Post Office Cra 7, No 5-77. **Telephone Office** Telecom, Cra 4 y C 3. International calls US$2 a minute, cheaper after 1900, closes 2100.

Tourist Office Casa Caldas, C 3, No 4-70 (T 242251), has good maps of the city, prices of all hotels and pensions, and bus schedules and prices. Ask for Sra Haydée de Varela about accommodation. All staff are very friendly and helpful, giving information on places of interest, will tell you where horses may be hired for exploring, and will store your luggage. In addition to normal hours, they are open Sun until 1200. Ask at the Tourist Office about which areas of the city are unsafe. (For information on travel beyond Popayán ask elsewhere and check with other travellers.) They also sell local crafts at good prices; telephone and mail service. The Tourist Office and the Colegio Mayor de Cauca have details on art exhibitions and concerts. Try also the Casa de la Cultura, C 5, No 4-33, for information on cultural events.

Taxis No meters; normal price within city is US$0.75, or US$0.90 at night.

Air Services Airport is 20 mins walk from the centre. Service to **Bogotá** with Intercontinental, daily at 0915 (office on main plaza). Satena to **Cali** twice a week. Avianca office for airmail, Cra 7, No 5-77.

Buses Popayán's bus terminal is next to the airport, 15 mins walk from the centre (Ruta 2-Centro bus, terminal to centre, US$0.15, or taxi, US$0.75). Luggage can be stored safely (receipt given); there is a charge to use the toilets, and a US$0.07 departure tax. From the bus station, turn left to statue of Bolívar, then take second right to Parque Bolívar; here are the market and cheap hotels. To/from **Bogotá**, Expreso Bolivariano, US$23, 16 hrs. To **Cali**, US$6, 2½-3 hrs, or Velotax microbus, US$7.50, colectivos leave from the main plaza; to **Pasto**, with Coop de Nariño, Cra 6, No 2-16, 1130, Cootranar (cheapest US$9, 1030, but not too reliable), Flota Magdalena, Exp Bolivariano, 0930 and Supertaxis del Sur, US$11.25, 5-8 hrs, spectacular scenery (sit on right); to **Medellín**, US$19.50, 12 hrs; to **Ipiales**, something runs every hour but many buses arrive full from Cali, book in advance; Supertaxis at 1230, US$9, or bus, up to US$10.30 (Transportes Ipiales at 0700, Bolivariano at 0530 or 0900 the best), 7½-10 hrs. To **San Agustín** (confusing routes and schedules), La Gaitana, 11 hrs, at 0900 and 2000, Coomotor, 13 hrs, US$10.75 each once a day. Cootranshuila buses run over the new road via Isnos to San Agustín from bus terminal, twice a day (0600 and 1300), US$9.50, 6 hrs or more depending on the weather; also Sotracauca at 0900, 6 hrs, US$7.80. Sit on the left side for the best views. To **Tierradentro** (Cruce de Pisimbalá, also known as Cruce de San Andrés), with Sotracauca, 5 a day between 0500 and 1500, US$5.50, 4-6 hrs (**see p 878**) continues to La Plata. Flota Magdalena to **La Plata**, US$4.50, 5 hrs, also Unidos del Sur (not via Tierradentro) and Sotracauca at 0730. To **Puracé**, US$1.20, 2 hrs (Pullman is slightly more, Sotracauca at 0600, La Gaitana 0700, Coomotor later in am). To **Silvia** (see below), daily Coomotorista *buseta* at 0800 and 0930 (US$2) or: take Expreso Palmira bus to Piendamó on Cali road, every ½ hour, US$0.75; from there, colectivo to Silvia, US$0.85. On market day (Tuesdays) buses leave directly to Silvia at 1100.

Excursions A favourite is the drive NE to Silvia, at 2,521m, one way through Totoró (partly paved) and the other through *Piendamó* (paved) two beautiful routes. In Piendamó there is **E** *Hotel Central* behind the former railway station (clean, quiet, dubious electrics, has seen better days).

Silvia lies in a high valley. The Indian market on Tues mornings seems to be full of Otavalo Indians from Ecuador and their goods—more expensive than in Otavalo, but sucres accepted. The market is at its best between 0600 and 0830. Not much to buy, but very colourful. A typical Indian settlement, La Campana, is ½ hour on the bus; 1½ hrs' walk downhill back to Silvia. The Indians wear their typical blue and fuchsia costumes, and are very friendly and communicative. It is not safe to park cars in the street at night in Silvia. Tourist information 1½ blocks up from plazuela on righthand side. Horse hire from Sr Marco A Mosquiro, US$1 per hour. On market days you can take a bus to Totoró (on the Popayán-Tierradentro road), departs 1200, US$1.50, 1 hr and then a bus from Totoró to Tierradentro, 5 hrs, US$8.50. Direct bus also to Cali, US$3.50, 3 hrs.

Hotels D *Casa Turística*, helpful, hot shower, good food, beautiful garden; **E** *Cali*, an old house, with good craft shop, including food, a little primitive, but very pleasant; **F** *Ambeima* (3 beds per room), clean, friendly, efficient, rec, good meals; **F** *Cali*, good meals but poor plumbing; **F** *La Parrilla*, water supply erratic, basic, restaurant has reasonable, cheap food; **G** *Residencias La Villa*, about 200m up main road, basic but friendly, negotiate your price; *Taberna El Buho*, friendly, with live music Sats pm.

Road to Neiva (p 850) from Popayán across the Central Cordillera, which is paved from Puerto Seco to Neiva, has interesting sights off it (best seen from left-hand side of the bus). At Km 18 from Popayán, the road turning up to the right (S) leads to Coconuco and San Agustín (see below). Continuing along the valley the road then climbs to the small town of *Puracé*, at Km 12 (ie 30 km from Popayán), which has several old buildings. **F** *Residencias Cubina*, clean, safe, friendly, cold showers, secure parking. *Restaurant Casa Grande* just above the church, meals around US$3. Further up the hill on the left is the school, behind which a ½ km path leads to Chorrera de las Monjas waterfalls on the Río Vinagre, notable for the milky white water due to concentrations of sulphur and other minerals. There are several buses daily to Puracé from Popayán, the last returning around 1730.

At Km 22, look for the spectacular San Francisco waterfall on the opposite side of the valley. At Km 23 is the turning right to Puracé sulphur mines (6 km) which can be visited by applying to Industrias Puracé SA, C4, No 7-32 Popayán, best through the Popayán tourist office. 1 km along this road is a turning left leading in 1½ km to **Pilimbalá** in the **Puracé National Park** at 3,350m. Saloon cars will struggle up this last section. Here there is a Park office, 7 sulphur baths at 28°C (2 in operation 1995), entrance US$0.75, children ½ price, bring your own towels. The centre also has picnic shelters, a good restaurant (rainbow trout a speciality) and 3 *cabañas* that hold 8, US$37.50 minimum for up to 6 and US$50 for 8 people. Firewood is provided. Camping costs US$3. Sleeping bags or warm clothing recommended to supplement bedding provided. They are reintroducing the Andean Condor to the wild here from Californian zoos. There are many birds to be seen. The Park's fauna include the spectacled bear and mountain tapir. The Park is open all the week, but reduced service on Mon.

Pilimbalá is a good base from which to explore the northern end of the park. The hike to the summit of Volcán Puracé, 4,640m, is demanding. A marked trail goes from behind the park office and eventually joins the road leading to a set of telecommunications antennae. These installations are guarded by the military and the area around them is mined, don't take shortcuts. Land mines are placed on the road itself at night, so climb only during daylight hours. The soldiers have been helpful to climbers in need of assistance. The summit is about 1 hr beyond the garrison, total time from Pilimbalá at least 4 hrs up and 2½ down. The volcano is steep; loose ash makes footholds difficult. Avoid getting down wind of the fumaroles, and do not be tempted to climb down into the crater. Although the best weather is reported to be Dec-Mar and July-Aug, this massif makes its own climate, and high winds, rain and sub-zero temperatures can come in quickly at any time. In spite of the internal heat of this volcano, you may find frost on the rim in the early morning. An alternative route is from the sulphur mine (at 3,000m), or driving with permission to the military base. It is also possible to walk round the crater (¾ hr) or make a strenuous 2 day round trip along the line of 9 craters, known as the Volcanes los Coconucos, to Pan de Azúcar, 4,670m, with its permanent snow summit. High altitude camping and mountaineering equipment required and a guide is strongly recommended. A descent over the páramo to Paletará on the Popayán-San Agustín road is also possible. The Puracé National Park extends for 60 km SW and encompasses the sources of four of Colombia's greatest rivers: the Magdalena, Cauca, Caquetá and Patía. Virtually all the park is over 3,000m.

Continuing on the main road to Neiva, at Km 31 there is a viewpoint for Laguna Rafael, at Km 35 the Cascada de Bedón (also chemically charged water) and at Km 37 the entrance to the most northerly part of the Puracé National Park. Here there is a visitor centre, a geology/ethnology museum (entrance US$0.75), a cafeteria (arrange meals beforehand through Popayán Tourist Office) and the very interesting Termales de San Juan, 700m from the road, entry US$0.40, where 112 hot sulphur springs combine with icy mountain creeks to produce spectacular arrays of multi-coloured mosses, algae and lichens—a must if you are in the area. Power for the centre is generated from a small artificial lake of crystalline water 1 km short of the Centre. At Km 42 is the Cueva de los Guácharos. Unfortunately, the bridge to this cave inhabited by oilbirds has been damaged and a visit is not at present possible. All these places from Puracé village to Cueva de los Guácharos can be reached by any bus from Popayán to La Plata or Garzón. In 1995 the last bus returning to Popayán in daylight left the visitor centre at about 1700. As implied in the text, a walk of 2½ km from Km 23 will reach Pilimbalá.

Further E along the main road, at Km 62, a trail leads through humid forest to Laguna del Buey, about 1½ hrs round trip.

At **Santa Leticia**, on the road between Puracé and La Plata (see below) there is a cheap *hospedaje*, F, basic, to the right of the church.

Coconuco, at 2,734m, has beautiful landscapes. Turn to the right off the Popayán-Neiva road at Km 18, then 7 km along is Coconuco (**B** *Hotel de Turismo*, ½ km out of town on the way to the baths, full service, colonial style hotel run by

Cali Tourist authority, restful atmosphere; **E** *Coconuco*, in town, basic; **F** *Casa Familiar*, basic. Several other modest hotels and restaurants in town). Coconuco is known for its baths, Aguas Hirviendos, $1\frac{1}{2}$ km beyond the hotel on a paved road (mostly), which has one major and many individual pools with an initial temperature of at least 80°C. Entry US$0.60. There is one pool where you can boil an egg in 5 mins. 3 cabins are available at US$25/day that will hold up to 6. There is a track from town which is quicker than the road). Coconuco and the baths are crowded at weekends, but during the week it is a fine area for walking and relaxing in the waters. 6 km beyond Coconuco are another set of hot springs, near the road, called Aguas Tibias, warm rather than hot water, with similar facilities for visitors. 24 km S of Coconuco is **Paletará** with high grassland on a grand scale with the Puracé/Pan de Azucar volcanoes in the background. Below the village (roadside restaurant and an Inderena post) flows the infant Cauca river. 10 km S of Paletará, the road enters the Puracé National Park and there is a track NE to Laguna del Buey. The road then enters a long stretch of virgin cloud forest. This section was completed in 1985, linking Paletará with Isnos and San Agustín. Heavy rain, particularly in 1994, has weakened this stretch, 25 km of which is impassable to light vehicles and very tedious for buses and trucks. No efforts are being made currently to improve this road. For bus services and the conclusion of this road, see under San Agustín.

Beyond Totoró, the turn-off for Silvia, is **Inzá**; hotels *Inzá*, *Sayonara* and *Ambalá*. Nine km beyond Inzá is the Cruce de Pisimbalá, sometimes known as the Cruce de San Andrés, where a road turns off to **San Andrés de Pisimbalá** (4 km), the village at the far end of the Tierradentro Park.

At Pisimbalá there is a unique and beautiful colonial church with a thatched roof; for the key ask behind the church. Some few km before reaching Pisimbalá you pass the Tierradentro Museum of indigenous culture, hours: 0700-1100 and 1300-1700, camping is not allowed. Make sure you see both parts of the museum. The museum is 20 mins downhill walk E of Pisimbalá.

At the archway directly opposite the museum or at Pisimbalá village you can hire horses (US$2 an hr, but make sure they are in good condition)—or you can walk—for visiting the **Tierradentro** man-made burial caves painted with geometric patterns. There are four cave sites—Segovia, El Duende, Alto de San Andrés and El Aguacate. The main caves are now lighted, but you are well advised to have your own torch. If you don't have one, try to borrow one from the park administration office. Entry to Park and Museum US$7.50 good for 4 days (less for Colombian nationals). The surrounding scenery is splendid. It is very crowded at Easter-time. Steven Gilman from Georgia, USA, says: "Go to Tierradentro for a week, walk in the hills, people are very friendly. You can stop and ask at almost any house to buy *guarapo*, a local slightly fermented drink. Delicious to sit and talk and enjoy the hospitality." If you do not have that much time, two days is adequate.

Cathy and Alan Hook (Bromley, Kent) say it is possible to visit all the sites in a tough 7-hour walk (take a hat and plenty of water): First visit the museum then walk up behind it, N, across the river to Segovia (15 mins walk). The guard is very helpful and turns lights on in the main tombs; he also gives information about them in Spanish. Segovia has over 20 tombs, 5 of which are lit (these 5 are not opened until 0800-0900). Nos 9, 10 and 12 are best decorated; Nos 8 and 28 are also impressive. Continue up the hill to El Duende (two of the four tombs are very good), 15 mins beyond Segovia. From El Duende continue directly up until you meet a rough road which descends into Pisimbalá (40 mins). El Tablón, with 8 stone statues, is just off the road 20-30 mins walk down. Visit Pisimbalá church before taking a path from the far side of the village down to the river (you will be tempted to have a dip), then up to El Alto de San Andrés, 20 mins (Nos 1 and 5 tombs the best—the guard is very helpful). Leave from the back of El Alto to join the main path; it's $1\frac{1}{2}$ hrs up and down hill, with a final long climb to El Aguacate. Only one tomb is maintained although there may be 30 more. It is possible to scramble down a few more that are not overgrown. The views from El Aguacate are superb. The route carries on a long way on a ridge, fairly overgrown, before a steep descent into the rear of the museum. **NB** The whole area is good for birdwatching.

There are several stone statues in the new plaza at Inzá. The surroundings have spectacular natural beauty; see small Indian villages in the mountains, eg Santa Rosa, 2 hrs' hard walk beyond El Duende (get exact directions before setting out).

The Páez Indians in the Tierradentro region can be seen on market days at Inzá (Sat), and Belalcázar (Sat); all start at 0600. The second floor of the museum at Pisimbalá is dedicated to their work: not to be missed. Take bus (US$0.55) from Tierradentro to Inzá market, on Sat (buses leave from 0200); best to go into Pisimbalá and out again to be sure of getting a seat. On Saturdays there is plenty of transport going to and from Inzá on the Tierradentro road.

NB Single women are advised not to wander around this area at night unaccompanied.

Hotels at Tierradentro A short way up from the museum (see above), state-owned **E** *Albergue de San Andrés (El Refugio)*, good, restaurant and swimming pool (also available to non-residents, US$0.80). Houses on either side of the Albergue offer accommodation, F, meals for US$1.50; green house next to museum, 2 rooms available, G, clean, friendly, rec; **F** pp *Residencia Turista*, also in the village, basic, clean, insufficient bedding; between Pisimbalá and museum, *hospedaje* of Sra Pola Angel de Velasco; **G** *Hospedaje Los Lagos de Tierra Adentro*, good restaurant, hot water, clean, pleasant, rec; **G-F** *Hospedaje Luzerna*, next to museum, clean and friendly, cold showers, quiet, excellent fresh orange juice, free coffee in am, laundry facilities, highly rec, will let you camp for US$0.50. **F** *Residencias Pisimbalá*, "opposite the museum and up a bit", good, clean, set meal and good other meals, laundry facilities, mosquitos. Other cheap accommodation in village: **F** *El Cauchito*, clean, pleasant, family atmosphere, meals available, will arrange horse rentals, rec; camping; **F** *Residencia El Bosque*, cold showers, cheap meals, friendly dueña collects coins, rec; **F** *Residencias El Viajero* (Marta Veláquez), meals US$1, clean, friendly, rec; **F** pp *Residencias Las Veraneras*, 2 houses, 300m from Archaeological Park, clean, run by friendly young couple, restaurant, attractive garden and murals painted by locals; **F** *Residencias Murujuy* (breakfast, US$0.65, lunch and dinner, US$1). Ask about others who will rent rooms.

Restaurants *Pisimbalá*, good food, cheap, rec; good fruit juices at the *Fuente de Soda y Artesanía* store and at *Los Alpes* (try their *mora con leche*), also good breakfasts. *Restaurante 56*, next to *Lucerna*, good meals, also vegetarian dishes. The house of Nelli Parra de Jovar, opposite the museum with the long antenna, is rec for abundance; you must book meals in advance. She can also give up to date information on accommodation.

Transport The road from Popayán to Tierradentro is difficult and narrow, but this is compensated by the beautiful scenery. There are possibly three buses a week from Pisimbalá to Popayán, Mon, Wed, Fri, 0800, but on other days buses go from the Cruce (schedule from Popayán to Pisimbalá unknown). Sotracauca buses from Popayán, US$5.50, 4-6 hrs to Cruce Pisimbalá. Best to take the 0500 or 1000 bus, as the 1300 and 1500 will land you at the Cruce when it's dark, leaving you with a long unlit uphill walk. Walk (about 2 km) to the museum and on, 20 mins, to the village. Bus Cruce Pisimbalá-Popayán, 0600 (unreliable), 0800 and 1300, 4 hrs. If you want to go to Silvia, take this bus and change to a colectivo (US$1.50) at Totoró. There are buses on market day, or trucks (US$1.50). Buses from Tierradentro to La Plata leave at 0900 and 1500 (unreliable) from the Cruce, US$3, 4-5 hrs; if you cannot get a direct Cruce-La Plata bus, take one going to Belalcázar (US$1.20), alight at Guadalejo from where there is a more frequent service to La Plata; or one can hitch. On Fri only, a bus leaves from Pisimbalá village for La Plata at 0400. Similarly, on Fri only, a bus from La Plata to Pisimbalá goes at 1200, otherwise the only La Plata-Tierradentro bus (Sotracauca) leaves daily at 0500 for Inzá; alight at Cruce. Private jeep hire La Plata-Tierradentro, US$32, or less if you agree to pick up other passengers. The road follows the spectacularly beautiful Páez valley.

17 km E of Inzá is Guadualejo, where a road heads N to Belalcázar (12 km, a dusty drive). A further 23 km N along this road to Santander de Quilichao is **Tóez** on the Río Páez from where there is an access track, following the upper reaches of the river, to the **Nevado del Huila** National Park. At 5,750m, this is the second highest massif in Colombia and one of the least accessible. Near the source of the Páez is an Inderena hut with some facilities. There is heavy rain and snow in this area, especially April-June and Oct-Dec. There is also thermal activity which makes the area unstable. There have been a number of 'alerts' recently (1995) when heavy precipitation has led to dangerous slides and flooding below. The snow and ice climbing on Huila is particularly dangerous. Seek professional and Inderena advice before visiting the area.

Another road from Guadualejo goes SE to **La Plata** (municipal pop 37,275), whose central plaza has an enormous tree. 147 km from Popayán, 210 km from San Agustín.

Hotels E *Berlin*, by church on square, 3 blocks from the bus office, with bath, F without, friendly, but unappealing toilets and bugs in the beds; F *Brisas de la Plata*, near bus station, clean, door locked at 2300; F *Brooklyn*, clean, and *Norteño*, in the same price range; *Pensión Murucuju*, basic place to sleep and eat; F *Hospedaje Exclusivo*, near bus station, clean, friendly; F *La Familia*, dirty, unfriendly; F *Residencias Nariño*; next door to *Berlin* is G *Residencias Tunubalá*, OK, friendly; G *Viajero*, opp Sotracauca office, basic but convenient; G *Residencia Orense*, near bus offices, clean, friendly, meals available; G *El Terminal*, clean, friendly, basic, near bus station.

Restaurants most closed by 2000. *Es Aquí*, good meals for US$2; *Noche y Luna*, just off main square, very good. Good set meals opp Banco Cafetero. Excellent bakery on main plaza. There is a café in the house where Bolívar stayed in 1829. *Patolandia*, good, cheap fruit juices. There is a cinema (2030).

Buses Direct bus service with Coomotor from La Plata to Bogotá, via Neiva, 10 hrs, at 0900 and 2100, with Cootranshuila, 1100 and 2030, US$11; to San Agustín at 0600 and 0700, US$5; to Popayú (Sotracauca) 0500 and others, US$5.50, 5^{1}/$_{2}$ hrs.

A site of archaeological interest is **La Argentina**, reached from La Plata (some direct buses), 8 km off the La Plata-Popayán road. Gillian Handyside writes: It is set in beautiful surroundings but is largely ignored by the archaeological authorities and the tourist board. The Museo Arqueológico de la Platavieja contains statues and ceramics as interesting as those found at San Agustín. Ask for Sr Carlos Hernández, who runs the museum almost singlehanded and is extremely knowledgeable about the archaeological aspects of the area. (He also keeps bees and sells honey.) The Universities of Los Andes, Cauca and Pittsburgh run an archaeological project at La Argentina during the dry season: contact Carlos Hernández for details.

Southeast of La Plata is Pital where the road forks, SE to Garzón, and S to near Altamira (jeep or bus La Plata-Garzón, US$3, 1^{1}/$_{2}$ hrs).

The Upper Magdalena

Garzón, a pleasant cathedral town set in mountains, is 92 km S of Neiva (**see p 850**). At Altamira, 29 km further SW, a road heads SE to Florencia, capital of the Intendencia of Caquetá (**see p 887**). SW leads to **Timaná** (G *Hotel Tairona*, basic, dirty; G *Residencias Central*, cold water) and continues paved past Pitalito to San Agustín. **Pitalito** (municipal pop 62,890), has little to offer the tourist.

Hotels at Garzón: The E *Abeyma*, a state hotel, is rec, Cra 10 y C 12, T 2022; it is possible to camp in the grounds. D *Damasco*, C 16, No 10-67, T 2091, colonial building, rec, good meals; E *Cecil*, near bus station, with private bath. E *Residencias Pigoanza*, on main square, with bath, rec. 32 km before Garzón, at El Gigante, is D *Posada La Casona*, T 385072, swimming pool, hot shower, restaurant, good views between El Gigante and Garzón. At **Pitalito** there are 2 hotels with swimming pools: C *Calamó*, Cra 5, No 5-41, T 360600, hot water, and D *Timanco*, a 3-star hotel, C 3 Sur, No 4-45, T 360666; F *Grand Hotel*, bath, good food; F *Residencia Pitalito*, without shower, reasonable, C 5 round corner from police station; *La Laroyano*, on main street, cheap, adequate; F *Residencial El Globo*, main street, clean, basic. *Crêperie*, 1 block S of main plaza, good value, excellent; *Restaurant Cando* rec; also *Napolitano*, good, cheap.

Transport If you hitch you'll find it fairly easy to Garzón; slower on to San Agustín, but plenty of buses and colectivos (US$1.20). Buses in Pitalito go from C 3a; Taxis Verdes from the main square (US$14 to Bogotá). Bus to Mocoa (in the Putumayo), US$8.50, 7 hrs, also jeeps from market square, 2 in am. Aires fly from Bogotá to Pitalito, via Neiva, on Sun at 1300, 1^{3}/$_{4}$ hrs, returning to Bogotá Thur 1645, but the plane only goes if there are enough passengers (confirm tickets 24 hrs in advance).

South of Pitalito is the **Cueva de los Guácharos** National Park; take a bus to Palestina, US$1.20, 1 hour, and then walk for 6 hrs along an eroded, muddy path. Between December and June swarms of oilbirds (*guácharos*) may be seen; they are nocturnal, with a unique radar-location system. The reserve also contains many of the unusual and spectacular cocks-of-the-rock. The rangers are particularly friendly, providing tours and basic accommodation; permission to visit the park must be obtained from the Inderena offices in Pitalito, Neiva or Bogotá.

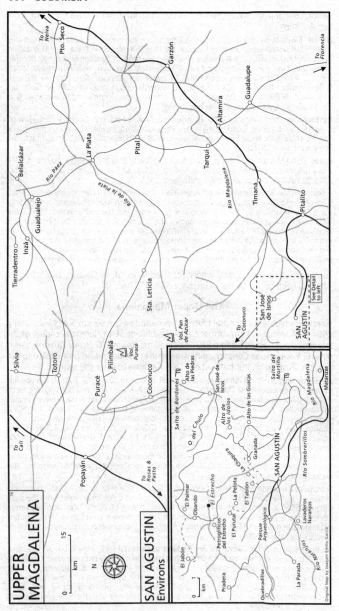

UPPER MAGDALENA

0 — 15 km

N

SAN AGUSTÍN Environs

0 — 1 km

To Neiva

Pto. Seco

Garzón

To Florencia

Altamira

Guadalupe

La Plata

Pital

Tarqui

Belalcázar

Río Páez

Guadualejo

Río de la Plata

Río Magdalena

Timaná

Tierradentro

Inzá

Pitalito

Sta. Leticia

San José de Isnos

SAN AGUSTÍN

See Detail to left

Silvia

Pilimbalá

Vol. Pan de Azúcar

To Coconuco

Totoro

Puracé

Vol. Puracé

Coconuco

To Cali

Popayán

To Rosas & Pasto

Salto de Bordones

Alto de las Piedras

San José de Isnos

Salto del Mortiño

Río Magdalena

Matanzas

Q. del Chulo

Alto de los Ídolos

Alto de las Guacas

El Palmar

El Estrecho

Granada

La Chaquira

El Tablón

SAN AGUSTÍN

Río Sombrerillos

Obando

Petroglíficos del Estrecho

La Pelota

El Purutal

Lavaderos Naranjos

El Jabón

Parque Arqueológico

Pradera

Quebradillas

La Parada

Río Naranjos

Original Map by Joaquín Emilio García

San Agustín (altitude 1,700m) is 27 km from Pitalito (all paved). Here, in the Valley of the Statues, are some hundreds of large rough-hewn stone figures of men, animals and gods, dating from roughly 3300 BC to just before the Spanish conquest. Nothing is known of the culture which produced them, though traces of small circular bamboo straw-thatched houses have been found. Various sculptures found here are exhibited in the National Museum at Bogotá, and there are some life-sized copies of San Agustín originals along the highway from Bogotá to the superseded Techo airport, near Fontibón. There are about 20 sites; information can be obtained from the tourist office, C 5, No 15-47, T 373019, open 0830-1230, 1330-1730, Mon-Fri, 0900-1200, 1300-1700, Sat and Sun, Sr Joaquín Emilio García is most helpful in all matters, he speaks English, French, Italian and a little German. Free maps to the area can only be obtained here or in Bogotá. It is recommended that visitors arriving in San Agustín should go initially to the tourist office which has a list of all hotels, their prices and quality, and a price list for guides, taxi rides and horse hire. Tours can be arranged at the office (see below).

The nearest sites are the Parque Arqueológico, which includes the Bosque de las Estatuas (open 0800-1600 daily, entrance to both costs US$2.50 (less for Colombian nationals) and the ticket is also valid for the museum and the Alto de los Idolos—see below, tickets valid for 2 days), about 2½ km from San Agustín, 1½ km from the *Hotel Yalconia*, and less than 1 km from the *Hotel Osoguaico*. **NB** Make sure the guards return your tickets to you. The statues in the Parque are *in situ*, though some have been set up on end and fenced in with wire; those in the Bosque (a little wood) have been moved and rearranged, and linked by gravel footpaths. Of particular interest are the carved rocks in and around the stream at the Fuente de Lavapatas in the Parque, where the water runs through the carved channels (visitors should not miss the Cerro de Lavapatas, above the Fuente, which has an extensive view, closes at 1600); refreshment stands at "Fuente" and on the way up to Lavapatas. Guides: Spanish US$12.50, other languages US$20. Guidebook in Spanish/English US$3.75. There is a museum in the Parque which contains pottery and Indian artefacts (entry included on Parque ticket, closes at 1700). You can get a very good idea of the Parque, the Bosque and the museum in the course of three hours walking, or add in El Tablón and La Chaquira (see below) for a full day. The whole site leaves an unforgettable impression, from the strength and strangeness of the statues, and the great beauty of the rolling green landscape. The further sites are a very long walk away: use of a jeep or a horse appears advisable. Museo Arqueológico, Cra 11, No 3-61, open Mon-Sat until 2300, opened 1995, with cultural events in the evenings, books and videos in Spanish and English, light refreshments.

Rainy season April-June/July, but it rains somewhat during most of the year, hence the beautiful green landscape; the driest months are Nov-March. The days are warm but sweaters are needed in the evenings; average temperature 18°C.

The *fiesta* of Santa María del Carmen is held in mid-July (not on a fixed date) in San Agustín. Two festivals in June are San Juan (24th) with horse races and dances, and San Pedro (29th) with horse races, dances, fancy dress, competitions and other events. In the first week of October, the Casa de Cultura celebrates La Semana Cultural Integrada, with many folklore events from all parts of the country. There are cockfights in San Agustín on Sun 100m behind the church at 1600.

Warning Beware of "guides" and touts who approach you in the street. Have nothing to do with anyone offering drugs, precolumbian objects, gold, emeralds or other precious minerals for sale; drugs will lead to problems with the authorities, other items will be fakes.

Hotels A2 *Yalconia*, outside town, full board, some rooms with hot water, very pleasant, swimming pool, T (980) 373001 (camping allowed next door, sheltered tents available). Between San Agustín and the Parque Arqueológico is the **B** *Osoguaico*, T 373069, friendly, warm water, very clean, restaurant, laundry, swimming pool, camping site US$1 pp. **E** *Cabañas Los Andes*, Cra 11, No 3-70, cabins, hot water and rooms with excellent views, cooking facilities, owner Sra María Muñoz de Hoyos; **E** *Central*, C 3, No 10-54, T 373027, near bus offices, with bath (cheaper without, or G if you want a room just to dump your luggage in during day's visit), good meals at US$1.50, it is possible to do laundry here (but keep an eye on your clothes), clean and friendly, secure motorcycle parking, will hire horses, English and French spoken; **E** *Colonial*, C 3, No 10-54, T 373159, hot shower, clean, pleasant, good restaurant, parrots in the garden, rec; **E** *Mi Terruño*, C 4, No 15-85, 12 rooms, colonial house, some rooms with bath, hot water, friendly, morning coffee, attractive garden, motorbike parking, rec, but check your bill, owner Carlos Arturo Muñoz also has 3 cabins, *Los Andaqui*, for rent; **E** *Residencias Eduardo Motta*, C 4, No 15-71, T 373031, has five rooms, friendly, clean, hot water, hard beds, but with morning coffee, quiet, rec, similar establishment run by Luis who runs the post office; **E** *Residencias El Imperio*, Cra 13, No 3-42, without bath, good; **E** *Residencia Familiar*, C 3, No 11-14, one block down from Coomotor-Autobuses Unidos del Sur office, 7 rooms, hot water, laundry, friendly, book meals in advance or eat next door at the *Colonial*, horses for hire, but noisy disco nearby at weekends; **E** *Residencias Náñez*, C 5 with Cra 16, T 373087, singles may have to share room, hot water (usually), friendly and clean; guests may use the kitchen; also the owners have horses for rent (US$5 for 5 hrs, check them first) and will act as guides to the archaeological sites; **E** *Residencias Luis Tello*, C 4, No 15-33, run by a teacher, hot water, pleasant and friendly, laundry facilities, good value; **D** *Cabañas Los Andes*, C 4 y Cras 10 y 11, clean, showers, good view of town. There is accommodation in private houses for about US$2 pp, which is often preferable (ask, for example, for Sra Elena Rojas de Llanos, "La Gorda", near the church, whose house is clean, safe, but no hot water). Ask at Tourist Office about cabins for rent for about US$5, with hot showers and cooking facilities. Accommodation at the farm of Constantino Ortiz is rec, 3½ km from town, first turn on left after the Parque Arqueológico, 4 rooms, best to take a sleeping bag, meals and horses available, peaceful, inexpensive, good cooking, plenty of morning coffee, also has camping, reservations at C 5, 11-13 in town. Another farmhouse rec is **G** *Posada Campesina*, Cra 14, Camino al Estrecho (on the way to El Tablón), owned by Doña Silviana Patiño, who makes good pizza and cheese bread, meals with family, simple working farm, camping possible, good walks nearby; **G** *Casa de Nelly*, Vía la Estrella, 1½ km W along 2 Av, T 373221, attractive peaceful finca run by Nelly Haymann (French), hot water, good food nearby, free coffee; **G** *Donde Clemencia*, Vía Antigua just beyond *Pizzeria Cataluña,* friendly, rustic finca, clean, good views, family atmosphere, riding available. Youth Hostel: *Albergue Juvenil Síndayo*, Cra 12, No 5-23, T 373208, F non-members, G members 1 YHA, dormitory, 50 beds, all inclusive 2 and 3 day programmes available.

Camping *El Camping* and *Camping Ullumbe* both provide tents or charge per site, both good, about US$2. Next to *Yalconia* is *Camping San Agustín*, US$2 pp with your own tent, US$3 pp with theirs, clean, pleasant, toilets, lights, laundry service, horse hire (see below).

Restaurants *La Brasa*, opposite *Yalconia Hotel*, good steaks, rec; *Brahama*, C 5, No 15-11, vegetarian meals and *comida* including soup and drink (also meat dishes), good fruit salads, not expensive, rec; *Surabhi*, C 5, No 15-10, friendly, vegetarian dishes or meat, pizzas, *menú* US$2, good juices, desserts etc, rec; *Superpollo*, Diagonal a la Iglesia, US$2.50 for half chicken, good; *Acuario*, C 3, very good, breakfasts and juices, sandwiches etc, good music; *Arhuac*, C 3, Cra 13, filling meals, good quality steaks and meat dishes; *Los Idolos*, good also; *La Negra*, Cra 12, No 3-40, good tamales, weekends only; *Nayn*, Cra 11 y C 3, across from bus offices, good *comida*; *Palacio de Jugos*, Cra 13, No 3-32, excellent fruit juices; also at *Heladería Tauro*, Cra 14, No 2-23, friendly, excellent salads and fruit juices with at least a half glass refill on request; next to *Osoguaico* is *Mulales*, very good; opp *Yalconia*, *Villadolly*, local and international food. *Santa Catalina*, up Cra 13, past brickworks and to right 1 km on Vía Antigua, closed Mon and all December, very good pizzas, crepes, vegetarian, French/Austrian couple, choose your own music, highly rec. Tap water in San Agustín is not safe to drink.

Exchange Travellers are warned to change TCs before arriving in San Agustín; the **Tourist Office** and the small shop opp police station will exchange cash only, at a poor rate. Caja Agraria will give cash advances against Visa card.

Shopping Film is available here in several shops. Leather goods are beautiful and priced reasonably. Machetes are good value here. Many local shops make boots to your own design (double-check the price beforehand); *Calzado Lider* (José Pepicano) is highly recommended, but if you want made-to-measure, he will need at least a couple of days, or *Artesanías El Viajero*, C 3 No 11-33. Recommended handicraft shop is *Taller Orfebrería*, C 5, No 14-28, for masks using precolombian designs, copper and gold items. Market day in San Agustín is Mon.

Transport San Agustín may be reached directly from Bogotá by colectivo (Taxis Verdes at 0300 and 0600, US$20, 8-9 hrs will pick you up at your hotel in Bogotá—ticket must be bought one day in advance—from San Agustín, C 3, No 11-57, 0500 direct, or 0400 and 0600, change at Neiva, just as quick, pickup at your hotel) or by bus (Coomotor, from new bus terminal, 4 a day, am buses US$15.50, pm buses US$12, 10-12 hrs; from San Agustín, C 3, No 10-71). Alternatively there are frequent services from Bogotá to Neiva (approx hourly, US$9.50, 6 hrs) as well as some to Pitalito (Taxi Verde costs US$14, leaving Bogotá at 0730 and 1030). From Neiva there are 6 buses a day to San Agustín, inc Coomotor and Cootranshuila, taking 6 hrs and costing US$6; to Neiva the 1000 Autobusco bus arrives in time for 1630 flight to Bogotá. The journey from Pitalito takes 1½ hrs, costs US$1.20 by jeep. To **Popayán** and **Cali**, Coomotor daily via Pitalito, Garzón and La Plata, US$10.75 to Popayán, US$12.75 to Cali. The bus stops at La Plata, 5-6 hrs, US$6. To **Tierradentro**, take the daily bus to **La Plata** at 1700, stay half a night at a hotel, then, next morning, take the 0500 Sotracauca bus from La Plata to Cruce de Pisimbalá, arrives 0900 or so (continues to Inzá and Popayán). Alternatively, on arrival in La Plata, take a pick-up to Guadualejo (US$1.20), then hitch, or try to get a bus going past Tierradentro (about 3 per day). Buses to **Garzón** at 1230, 1430 and 1730, US$4, 3 hrs, from where more buses go to La Plata for Tierradentro. To appreciate the scenery, do not take a night bus to Tierradentro. Rápido Tolima (C 3, No 10-53) goes to Medellín at 2100, 15 hrs, US$21.50.

A new 130-km direct route has been opened between **Popayán and San Agustín (via Isnos**, Coconuco and the Puracé National Park); it is very scenic, but unpaved. From San Agustín, the road turns left off the main road to Pitalito, crosses, dramatically, the Magdalena river and climbs steeply to Isnos, from which it is a long 62 km to Paletará. There is one stretch of 25 km single track, suitable only for jeeps and trucks. There are also bus services, daily, with Cootranshuila at 0700 and 1300 (office on C 3, No 10-58), slow, 6 hrs, US$9.50; also Sotracauca (C 3, No 10-53) at 0600, continuing to Cali (US$12) and Coomotor on this route to Cali at 1700, 9 hrs. It may be advisable to book seats the day before. (For information ask in the tourist office; the services are sometimes cut.)

NB Avoid travelling by night between Popayán and San Agustín, the roads have been reported dangerous in the past. Cyclists should avoid the new direct route. Also we have received many reports of theft on the buses between these towns; do not trust "helpfuls" and do not put bags on the luggage rack.

There is good riding in the neighbourhood. You are strongly advised to hire horses for trips around San Agustín through hotels or the Tourist Office. The centre for horses is 3 blocks beyond the Tourist Office on the road to the Park (Asociación de Acompañantes y Alquiladores de Caballos) and costs about US$12 per day and US$3 per hour, per rider. If you require a guide, you must add the hire cost of his horse. There are fixed tariffs for 20 or so standard trips. There are 25 guides available at any one time authorized by Turismo at US$15 for a half day, US$30 for a full day, up to 10 people for guide. You can make your own arrangements, and it may cost less, but we have received many letters from visitors with unsatisfactory experiences of unregistered guides. Always ask to see a guide's identity badge; if you have any problems, ask at the Tourist Office.

Alternatively, jeeps may be hired for between 4-5 people. Prices vary according to the number of sites to be visited, but the daily rate is about US$70. The Tourist Office will often be able to fill the vehicle, make arrangements the day before. To be safe, book through the Tourist Office which runs its own, popular tour in a brightly-painted *chiva*, daily at 0900, book the day before. US$10 pp to the narrows, Obando, El Palmar, Alto de los Idolos (entry not included), Isnos (lunch US$1.20), Alto de las Piedras, Saltos de Bordones and Mortiño.

The area offers excellent opportunities for hiking, although some trails to remote sites are not well marked. El Tablón is reached up Cra 14, over the brow of the hill and 250m to a marked track to the right. El Tablón (5 sculptures brought together under a bamboo roof) is shortly down to the left. Continue down the path, muddy in wet weather, ford a stream and follow signs to the Río Magdalena canyon. La Chaquira (figures carved on rocks) is dramatically set half way down to the river. Walking time round trip from San Agustín, 2 hrs. Plenty of houses offer refreshments as far as El Tablón. At the site of La Pelota, two painted statues were found in 1984 (well worth a visit, a 3-hr return trip, 6 hrs if you include El Tablón and La Chaquira, 15 km in all). The latest archaeological discovery (1986) in the area is a series of at least 30 stones carved with animals and other designs in high relief; they are on the right bank of the Río Magdalena, near the Estrecho (narrows) to which jeeps run. This trip is especially recommended. For accurate route information, seek advice from Joaquín Emilio García at the office. Probably best for several people to organize their trips together; prospective horseriders and jeep passengers tend to congregate at the restaurants near the Tourist Office.

The best books on the subject are *Exploraciones Arqueológicas en San Agustín*, by Luis Duque Gómez (Bogotá, 1966, 500 pages) or *San Agustín, Reseña Arqueológica*, by the same author (1963, 112 pages); a leaflet in English is obtainable from tourist offices. The Colombian Institute of Archaeology has published a booklet (English/ Spanish), at US$1.80, on San Agustín and Tierradentro (**see p 877**), available at museums in San Agustín and San Andrés (also available at the Tourist Office).

The visitor with time to spare should visit Alto de los Idolos, about 10 km by horse or on foot. Inexperienced riders should be warned that the path is very steep in places. On foot it is a lovely (if strenuous) walk via Puente de la Chaquira, but 27 km by road via San José de **Isnos** village (which is 5 km from Alto de los Idolos), and to which a bus can be taken, US$1.20, 0500 on Sat return bus at 1100, 1300, or catch a bus from the *cruce* on the Pitalito road or hitch, well signposted (the site is open until 1600, entry included on Bosque Arqueológico ticket). Here on a hill overlooking San Agustín are more and different statues known as *vigilantes*, each guarding a burial mound (one is an unusual rat totem). The few excavated have disclosed large stone sarcophagi, some covered by stone slabs bearing a sculpted likeness of the inmate. Alto de las Piedras, 6 km from Isnos, has a few interesting tombs and monoliths, including the famous "Doble Yo". The Director of the Parque (Sr Alvaro León Monsalve) can arrange transport and guide to outlying sites. Only less remarkable than the statues are the orchids growing nearby. In Isnos (market day Sat) are **E** *Casa Grande*, in centre, with bath, cheaper rooms without; **E** *El Balcón*, also in centre. Nearby there is the **D** *Parador de los Idolos* (3 rooms), ½ km from Alto de los Idolos, hot water, with bath; **D** *Parador Salto de Bordones*, near waterfalls, hot water, restaurant. From San Agustín the Bordones waterfalls can be visited; best with a car.

From Isnos many of the sites can be visited by road. As you come S into Isnos from Popayán, turn left just after the bridge (sign Salto de Bordones). 6 km on right is Alto de las Piedras, and 8 km further is Bordones village. Turn left at end of Bordones and there is (½ km) parking for the falls with a restaurant nearby. Coming S through Isnos, turn right off main street to Alto de los Idolos (5 km). From Isnos it is about 20 km to San Agustín; after 7 km turn left (½ km) to Salto del Mortiño, 300-metre falls.

It is possible to walk from San Agustín to the Lago Magdalena, involving a bus ride or 6-hour walk the first day, 7-hour walk the second, and 8-10 hrs walking on the third, either to the lake and back to the second *refugio*, or on to Valencia. From Valencia, there are buses to Popayán. Good bases for this excursion are **F** *Residencias El Paraíso*, at Puerto Quinchana, 30 km away on the road to the source of the Río Magdalena, 2 km from the Cementerio Indígena de Quinchana, owned by Sr Arsenio Guzmán, friendly, peaceful, restaurant; **F** *Residencias El Páramo* at Juntas, beautiful countryside, owner Alvaro Palechor, clean, safe, friendly, restaurant. San Antonio farm, owned by Sr Wilevaldo, riding, fishing. If walking in the opposite direction, take a bus from Popayán to Valencia, a dismal village with a very basic place to stay, but food available. A recommended guide for the way to San Agustín is Marnix Beching, Cra 7, No 2-56, Ap 7, Popayán, T 241850. He is a Dutchman working at the University of Popayán as a biologist. It is also possible to ride from San Agustín via Lago Magdalena to Popayán, some 100 km, in 5 days or less. A recommended guide is Jorge Caitán, ask at the San Agustín Tourist Office, cost about US$70. Get good advice from several sources on safety etc before committing yourself.

THE LLANOS AND LETICIA (8)

The extensive cattle lands from the Cordillera Central to the Orinoco are a good place to get away from it all—in the dry season. Leticia is Colombia's foothold on the Amazon.

A spectacular 110-km road runs SE from Bogotá to **Villavicencio**, capital of Meta Department in the Llanos at the foot of the eastern slopes of the Eastern Cordillera. Population: 273,510. Rice is grown near Villavicencio and milled there for transport to Bogotá. Altitude: 498m. The town fills up at weekends. It is also full of military police owing to guerrilla activity to the SE.

Festivals See under **Music and Dance**.

Hotels **A3** *Del Llano*, Cra 30, No 89-77, T 41119, F 41125, a/c, TV, bar, restaurant, pools; **B** *Villavicencio*, Cra 30, No 35A-22, T 26434, suites available, a/c, hot water, very comfortable, good restaurant; **D** *Centauros*, C 38, No 31-05, T 25106, small rooms, reasonably clean and quiet, central; **E** *Residencias Don Juan*, Cra 28, No 37-21 (Mercado de San Isidro), attractive family house, with bath and fan, sauna, safe, rec; **F** *Residencias Medina*, C 39D, 28-27, common shower, fair, washing facilities; **F** *Residencia Ejecutiva*, near market, fan, private bath.

Restaurants Some on main square: others, some with swimming pools, on the road to Puerto López.

Airport Satena flies to Bogotá, Mitú and a number of other towns in the Llanos. Aires also to Bogotá. To **Puerto Carreño**: Satena twice a week; Urraca, a freight service with some seats, 3 times a week, arrive early to get a seat, 1½ hrs. Taxi to town, US$2; bus US$0.30.

Buses Station outside town, taxi US$1. La Macarena and Bolivariano run from Bogotá about every half-hour, US$3.30, 4 hrs; alternatively there are colectivos (eg Velotax, US$4.20, or Autollanos who run every hour, US$6.30). Be prepared to queue for tickets back to Bogotá.

Villavicencio is a good centre for visiting the Llanos stretching 800 km E as far as Puerto Carreño, on the Orinoco, with Venezuela across the river. Cattle raising is the great industry on the plains, sparsely inhabited by *mestizos*, not Indians. The cattle town of San Martín to the S of Villavicencio may be visited by bus, 1½ hrs, US$1.50 each way.

A good asphalt road has been built E from Villavicencio to **Puerto López** on the Meta river, a port of call for large river boats. You can, with some patience, arrange to go downstream by boat to Puerto Carreño, US$35 pp, including food, 6 days with night stopovers, or 3 days non-stop, interesting trip. There are hotels and *residencias*, eg **F** *Doña Empera*, friendly, but a bit run down; **F** *Llano Cruz*, private bath, restaurant; **G** *Hospedaje Popular*, near bus station, basic, mosquito nets; also restaurants. The road E (unpaved) continues through horse and cattle country for another 150 km to **Puerto Gaitán**, where there are hotels and restaurants (**F** *Hotel Mi Llanura*, opposite the church between the two squares, clean, friendly, mosquito nets). There are several buses a day from Puerto López to Puerto Gaitán, 3 hrs, US$3.20. Good views from the bridge across the Río Manacacías and great sunsets. The road goes on a further 150 km through San Pedro de Arimena where the road branches: one road goes N to the Río Meta at El Porvenir, where a ferry (dry season only) crosses the river to the Orocue tourist centre, E, swimming pool, excursions. The main road, now degenerated to a rough track impassable in the wet season, continues E for more than 500 km down the Río Meta to its junction with the Orinoco at **Puerto Carreño** (population about 5,000).

Pico de la Bandera, a black rocky outcrop, can be climbed. It offers an excellent view over the Llanos and the confluence of the Ríos Meta and Orinoco. There are good beaches and bathing during the dry season at Tiestero, 15 mins from town by taxi, 1½ hrs walk. Popular with locals on weekends.

Banks will not change cash or TCs. Shopkeepers will change cash, good rates for Venezuelan bolívares, extremely poor rates for US$. Try *Almacén Safari* on Av Orinoco. If arriving from Venezuela, best to bring enough bolívares to be able to pay for your onward transport into Colombia.

The DAS agent meets all flights arriving from Bogotá or Villavicencio. Foreigners must show passport and register with him. DAS office is 2 blocks from the plaza, walking away from the river. Entry/exit stamps are given here. The Venezuelan consulate is on Av Orinoco, one block from the plaza, walking towards the river. Official requirements are onward ticket, 2 photos, and US$30, visa issued the same day, but procedures are extremely arbitrary. Only single entry visas are given here, maximum 30 days. Try to obtain visa in Bogotá.

Hotels E *Martha Helena*, 2 blocks from plaza near navy headquarters, T 54086, clean, friendly, family run, with private bath and fan; **E** *La Vorágine*, off Av Orinoco near plaza, T 54066, with bath, **F** without. Along Av Orinoco going from the plaza to the waterfront are the following: **E** *Apart Hotel Las Cabañas*, T 54018, new, with private bath, fridge and TV; **E** *Safari*, T Bogotá 430-2926, with private bath, fan or a/c, clean, friendly, tame birds in courtyard, fridge facilities; **E** *Residencias Mami*, T 54046; **E** *Samanaré*, T 54181, rooms and 1 cabin for large group, disco-bar next door, a bit run down but clean and friendly, set menu is good value, other food and drinks expensive. Several restaurants along the same street, *Dona Margarita* is rec; also *Donde Mery*, which serves breakfast, *Kitty*, near *Hotel Safari*, and *Oasis*, on main street, for refreshing juices.

Transport Satena tickets are sold at *Hotel Safari* and *Residencias Mami*, US$75 to Bogotá, payable only in pesos; flights on Tues and Sat, 1½ hrs. There is a weekly bus to Villavicencio during the dry season, but the trip is considered dangerous as it passes through guerrilla-held territory.

To Venezuela There are two possible routes. Launches run throughout the day to El Burro (US$1.20) via Pto Páez, where Venezuelan entry stamp must be obtained (take taxi from landing to DIEX office next to military garrison, then back to landing for crossing to El Burro). From El Burro, *por puestos* leave when full for Pto Ayacucho, total time from Pto Carreño is 2-3 hrs. Alternatively you can take an 0700 boat to **Casuarito** (often full, buy ticket the day before at the foot of Av Orinoco) and then cross directly to Pto Ayacucho, reporting to the DIEX office there for your Venezuelan entry stamp (closes 1500). This is a slightly longer trip (3-4 hrs) but an interesting ride along the river. There is no DAS in Casuarito, so that you must, in all cases, get your exit stamp in Pto Carreño before leaving.

For fishing excursions from Puerto Carreño, contact Jairo Zorro, owner of the *Samanaré Hotel* or Sr Feleciano Morán, owner of *Almacén Safari* on Av Orinoco. Equipment can be bought in Puerto Carreño or Puerto Ayacucho.

The **Parque Nacional Tuparro** is in Colombia, but has to be reached via Venezuela. Follow the procedure as above for going to Pto Ayacucho, including having all documents stamped. You may have to wait in Pto Ayacucho until next day before going to Agua Blanca by taxi (US$6.50 pp), where a fire has to be built to send smoke signals to a boatman on the opposite bank. Cross over to Garcita in Colombia (no formalities) and wait while Mateo finds fuel for his *bongo*. He will take you upstream to the Park for about US$60 for the boat, and will return for you when requested. A visitors' centre and lodge is under construction. The warden, Gustavo, is very helpful and friendly. Bring your own food, which can be supplemented with local fish. In the park you can see birds, orchids, bromeliads and dolphin; there are excursions to beaches, rapids and the burial site of the now extinct Maypure Indians. An Indian community on the Isla Carestía (Venezuela) can be visited; the island can be reached from Pto Ayacucho by taking a truck on the paved road to Alcaldía Guayibo, then walking to the river. Call to the island for a ferry. The Indians go shopping in Pto Ayacucho every Sat (Laurie E Henderson, Cali).

The road S from Villavicencio is surfaced as far as San Martín. It runs on to **Granada** and from there deteriorates rapidly. **Vistahermosa** (Macarena bus from Bogotá, 0845, US$6, 9 hrs), situated near the break-point between the Llanos and the jungle, lies further S along this road (**G** *Pampa Llanura*, opposite the Flota La Macarena office, very clean and friendly). It is normally a good place from which to visit the National Park, **Sierra de la Macarena**, a Tertiary outcrop 150 km long by 35 km broad. Its vegetation is so remarkable that the Sierra has been designated a national park exclusively for scientific study, although the flora is under severe threat from colonization and drug cultivation. The road from Vistahermosa to the Sierra de la Macarena is very muddy in the wet season (March-Nov). For more than a quick visit you will need to camp. For the energetic, a worthwhile trip is to the Sardinata or Cañones falls. Both can be reached from Maracaibo, which is a day's walk from Vistahermosa. If you wish to visit the Sierra de la Macarena, seek advice on conditions in advance, preferably from Inderena in Bogotá. There is also an office in the Park where you can hire guides. The Caño Cristal is a spectacular river within a day's reach of the village of Macarena. Take supplementary food, a hammock and normal hiking gear. Satena fly from Villavicencio 3 times a week.

To the SE of Villavicencio, along the river Vaupés, and near the border with Brazil, is **Mitú**, which can be reached by air three times a week from Villavicencio and Bogotá (Satena). Ask around for guides. In the wet season, traders will take you down river to Brazil (July-August). After several hundred km, the Vaupés joins the Rio Negro. Good local buys are baskets and bark paintings. There is a small hospital near the airport.

Hotels E *La Vorágine*, shower, fan, clean, owned by Sr León who will help you to arrange trips; **F** *JM*, friendly, helpful, morning coffee, next to Satena office. Plenty of **restaurants** around; recommended: *de la Selva*, a meeting place of the pilots who fly into Mitú.

Plenty of reserve gasoline should be carried when travelling by car in the Llanos, as there are few service stations. Take food with you, unless you can live by gun and rod. Everybody lets you hang up your hammock or pitch your tent, but mosquito nets are a must. "Roads" are only tracks left by previous vehicles but easy from late December till early April and the very devil during the rest of the year. More information on the Llanos can be obtained from the office of the Gobernación del Departamento de Meta, C 34 and Cra 14, Bogotá.

Caquetá

Lying to the E of the Cordillera Oriental is the Intendencia of Caquetá, reached by air, or by road from Neiva or Garzón. This region, although still sparsely populated, is an area of intensive settlement as people move down from the highlands to raise livestock. The natural forest cover around Florencia, the capital of the Intendencia, has been cleared, creating well-established, undulating pasturelands, dotted with tall palms—the fruits of which are a delicacy for grazing cattle. To the SE, beyond the cleared lands, lie little-touched expanses of tropical forest inhabited by indigenous tribes and wide varieties of Amazonian flora and fauna.

The road Neiva-Florencia is 260 km: possible in one day, but it is recommended that travellers should try to complete the last 100 km over the mountains into Florencia by daylight. From the Garzón-San Agustín road, the only route for vehicles into Caquetá branches off at Altamira. Here the surfaced road ends and becomes a single-track dirt road, originally engineered in 1932 during the Leticia dispute between Colombia and Peru. The climb up over the mountains passes through a region of small farms (some of their cultivated fields appear to be on almost vertical valley sides), through sugar-cane cultivation and up into cloud at the higher points of the route. Soon after the summit, and on a clear day, there are extensive views out over Caquetá and then the road winds down through substantial forests—ablaze with the colours of tropical flowers in the dry season (Jan-March) and into the lowlands. The lower section of the road into the lowlands is prone to frequent landslides (or *derrumbes*).

The roads in Caquetá run from Florencia along the foothills of the Cordillera. Other routes are difficult and seasonal (although tracks, or *trochas*, are laid out as part of the settlement scheme) and the main lines of communication into the lowlands are by boat along the rivers Caquetá and Guayas and their tributaries.

Florencia (pop 101,275), the capital of the region, was originally established in 1908. The square contains sculptures, fountains, a large forest tree (*saba*) and flower beds. Overnight, cars are best left in the care of the fire-station (US$0.20 a night).

Fiesta The local Saint's day is 16 July: candlelight procession in the evening.

Hotels located around the central square are reputed to be the more salubrious. **C** *Kamani*, C 16, No 12, T 4101; **D** *Metropol*, Cra 11, No 16-52, T 6740; **D** *Royal Plaza*, Cra 11, No 14-64, T 7504; **F** *Residencias Don Quijote*, Cra 11, No 13-28, T 3190; and others in same price range. **Cafés, Restaurants** Plenty, but prices tend to be high because much food is trucked in. Vegetarian restaurant on main street for good *patacones*.

Buses There are regular services from Neiva (US$7.80, 7 hrs), Garzón and Altamira to Florencia (bus Altamira to Florencia, US$3.75) and frequent services as far as Puerto Rico and Belén. Bus to **Bogotá** costs US$23.50.

Air Services To **Puerto Asís**, with Satena, on Mon, Wed, Fri, Aires on Tues; daily to **Neiva** (Satena and Aires) and to **Leguizamo** (except Fri and Sun), with Satena and Aires. Several planes a week to **Bogotá**; Aires to **Medellín** Tues.

From Florencia the road runs northeastwards as far as San Vicente del Caguán: it is paved for 67 km to El Doncello. It passes through **El Paujil** (2,750 pop), where the *residencias* are unnamed and are situated alongside the road into the town. Then comes **El Doncello** (10,660) a very pleasant town, overlooked by the church which has a brightly painted steeple. **F** *Residencias Americanas*, highly rec. Popular Sun market. Next comes Esmeralda, a small settlement located on a ford that is too deep for cars, although trucks and buses may cross, and there is a wooden suspension bridge over the river for which the toll is US$0.20. The hotel there provides a very plain but excellently cooked breakfast.

Puerto Rico (pop 8,325) is on the Río Guayas, which is crossed by ferry (US$0.10). Buses then go as far as San Vicente where a mule-track goes over the Cordillera to Algeciras in Huila Department. Puerto Rico is a river port; ferries travel downstream to Río Negro (1½ hrs) and Cartagena (4½ hrs). Houses built down by the river are raised on stilts above possible flood levels. River boats are made and repaired by the riverside. **Hotels** and *residencias* are full on Sat nights—book a room early in the day. *El Gran Hotel*, despite its name, provides basic amenities. *Hotel Almacén* is the only place in Puerto Rico serving fresh fruit juices.

The road SW from Florencia to San José is paved as far as Morelia, where a poor branch road goes S to the Río Pescado, where a ferry will take you across the river to the town of **Valparaíso** (1,175). *Hotel Ceilán* is cheap and friendly; there is also the *Hotel Turista*. From Valparaíso mule tracks go further into the lowlands. If travelling to Valparaíso by car, make sure it is left well away from the river when catching the ferry as, during times of flood, the river may rise rapidly overnight. Morelia to Belén de los Andaquíes is an unsurfaced road, passing through interesting scenery, and crossing fast-flowing rivers by metal bridges. In **Belén** (1,615), hotels fill up quickly, and mosquito nets are not always provided. From Belén an unsurfaced road runs to Albania (1,285) a frontier settlement with only one hotel. Semi-surfaced roads run from here to new areas of settlement.

Anyone wanting to look at wildlife in Caquetá must travel beyond the settlement area. Toucans, monkeys, macaws etc are kept as pets, but there is little wild-life. Boats and canoes are easily hired, but horses and mules are more difficult, especially in the dry season when they are needed to transport the harvest.

Leticia and the Amazon

Leticia, is on the southern tip of a spur of territory which gives Colombia access to the Amazon, 3,200 km upstream from the Atlantic. There is a land frontier with Brazil a short distance to the E beyond which are Marco and Tabatinga. Directly S across the river is another important Brazilian port, Benjamin Constant, which is close to the border with Peru. On the N side of the Amazon, Colombia has a frontage on the river of 80 km to the land border with Peru. Leticia is a fast-growing community of 23,200, clean, modern, though typically run down near the river. It is rapidly merging into one town with neighbouring Marco in Brazil. There is a modern, well equipped hospital. The best time to visit the area is in July or August, the early months of the dry season. At weekends, accommodation may be difficult to find. Tourist services are better than in Tabatinga or Benjamin Constant.

Museum Set up by Banco de la República, covers local ethnography and archaeology, a beautiful building at Cra 11 y C 9 with a library and a terrace overlooking the Amazon. Small Amazonian **zoo**, entry US$0.90 (huge anacondas) and **botanical garden** on road to airport, within walking distance of town (20 mins). The cemetery is near the zoo.

Leticia is a good place to buy typical products of Amazon Indians, but the growth of Leticia, Tabatinga, Marco and Benjamin Constant has imposed an artificiality on the immediately surrounding Amazon territory.

Hotels A2 *Anaconda*, Cra 11, No 7-34, T 27119, F 7005, large a/c rooms but beds on the short side, hot water, restaurant, good terrace and swimming pool; **B** *Parador Ticuna*, Av Libertador (Cra 11), No 6-11, T 27241, 19 spacious apartments (all with bathrooms which have hot—usually—and cold running water, and a/c, when working) which can each sleep up to 6, swimming pool, bar and restaurant. The owners of the *Ticuna* also operate the *Jungle Lodge*, on Monkey Island, 2 hrs' boat ride from Leticia (see below) and, in town, **B** *Colonial*, C 10, No 7-08, T 27164, 16 double rooms and one triple, all with a/c or fans, power and water unpredictable, swimming pool, cafeteria, noisy, not including tax and insurance. **D** *Residencias Marina*, Cra 9 No 9-29 (T 27201/9), TV, some a/c, cold water, good breakfast and meals at attached restaurant, clean; **D** *Residencias Fernando*, Cra 9, No 8-80, T 27362, well equipped but electricity only at night, clean, rec; **E** *Residencia Internacional*, Av Internacional, basic, bath, between centre and Brazilian border, fan, friendly, hard beds, clean; **E** *Primavera*, C 8 between Cras 9 and 10, with bath and fan, noisy; opp is **E** *Residencias La Manigua*, C 8, No 9-22, T 27121, with bath, fan, clean, friendly, preferable; **F** *Residencias Colombia*, Cra 10 y C 8, good value, shared bath.

Restaurants *Sancho Panza*, Cra 10, No 8-72, good value, good meat dishes, big portions, Brazilian beer. Several small sidewalk restaurants downtown, good value *plato del día*. *Señora Mercedes*, C 8 near Cra 11, serves good, cheap meals until 1930; *Viejo Tolima*, C 18 between Cras 10-11; *Heladería Bucaros* offers *empanadas*, sandwiches, juices, etc. Cheap food (fried banana and meat, also fish and pineapples) is sold at the market near the harbour. Also cheap fruit for sale. Many café/bars overlook the market on the river bank. Take your own drinking water and anything stronger that you desire.

Exchange The *cambio* next to the *Anaconda Hotel* has good exchange rates for dollars, reais or soles. There are street money changers, plenty of *cambios*, and banks for exchange. Shop around. TCs cannot be changed at weekends, and are hard to change at other times, but try Banco de Bogotá.

Brazilian Consulate C 13 y Cra 10, 1000-1600, Mon-Fri, efficient and helpful; onward ticket and 2 black and white photos needed for visa (photographer nearby); allow 36 hrs.

Post Office Avianca office, Cra 11, No 7-58. **Telecom** Cra 11, nr Parque Santander.

Tourist Office C 10, No 9-86. **Inderena**, Cra 11, No 12-05. **DAS** office, C 9, No 8-32, T 27189, which will send you to the airport for an exit stamp to leave Colombia by air or overland. Check both offices for entry stamps before taking flights into Colombia.

Transport Avianca (C 11, No 7-46, T 27762), Satena and Aerorepública each fly to **Leticia** (Tabatinga airport if Leticia's is closed) from Bogotá, 2-4 days a week, US$100. Varig has 2 flights a week from Manaus to Tabatinga. It was reported in 1994 that Aerosucre cargo planes will take passengers for US$70, or possibly less if you bargain. Also, US military flights will, from time to time, take civilians free. Airport is 1½ km from town, taxi US$1.60; small terminal, few facilities. Expect to be searched before leaving Leticia airport, and on arrival in Bogotá from Leticia. If arriving in Leticia by plane with a view to leaving for Brazil or Peru, get your exit stamp at the airport while you are there. If you are entering Colombia via Tabatinga airport, you can get stamped out of Brazil at the airport.

The cheapest way to get to Leticia is by bus to **Puerto Asís**, and then by boat (see p 894). There are twice-daily ferries between Leticia, Tabatinga and Benjamin Constant, Brazil (US$2, 1½-2 hrs, US$5.50 in private launch), or take a taxi to Tabatinga (US$3), obtain your Brazilian entry stamp and then cross the river. If leaving Brazil by this route, disembark at Tabatinga and obtain exit stamp from office which is 1 km from dock: turn right one block at main street, office is on the left. There is a Colombian Consular Office near the border on the road from Tabatinga, where Colombian tourist visas are issued on presentation of 2 passport photographs. Most boats down to **Manaus** take passengers, leaving from Tabatinga or Benjamin Constant, none from Leticia. Departure times are uncertain, and the boats tend to be overcrowded. The trip takes at least 3 days; there is a better selection of provisions in Leticia, but purchases are much cheaper in Benjamin Constant. Boats to **Peru** from Tabatinga wharf La Ronda sail daily at 1800 and take passengers and cargo. For boats travelling on the Brazilian and Peruvian Amazon (to Manaus and Iquitos), **see under the relevant sections of the Brazil and Peru chapters**. Remember to get your passport stamped by the DAS office at Leticia airport before you leave the area; there are no customs formalities for everyday travel between Leticia and Tabatinga in Brazil, taxis cost US$3 from a rank (more if you want to stop to change money, immigration, etc en route to harbour), or US$0.80 as colectivos (NB colectivos increase their charges after 1800); bus, US$0.25. 24-hour transit stamps can be obtained at the DAS office for one-night stays in Leticia, although it appears that these are not necessary if you are not going beyond Leticia—best to check. If you are going further into Brazil from Colombia, check the details under Brazil, Benjamín Constant/Tabatinga. If crossing the border, check if there is a time difference (summer time in Brazil).

NB If entering Colombia at Leticia, from Brazil en route to Peru, you should try to get your tourist card before Manaus because the Colombian consul there will tell you that a card is not needed just for passing through Leticia. This is not true: you must have a card. If you do have to see the consul in Manaus tell him you are going further into Colombia—you may have to show an onward ticket, or money—this may get you a card.

It is reported that for travellers interested in Amazonian wild life the Putumayo is more accessible than Leticia; it is best reached from Pasto (**see p 894**).

Excursions If you choose to go on an organized tour, do not accept the first price and check that the supplies and equipment are sufficient for the time you will be away. It is cheaper and better to find yourself a local guide, but make sure he has a good reputation and fix a definite price before you set out. Dug-outs or motorboats can be hired. *Turamazonas*, *Parador Ticuna*, Apto Aereo 074, T 7241, offers a wide range of tours including day visit to Yagua and Ticuna Indians, jungle walk and stop at **Monkey Island**; provisions and bedding for overnight safaris are supplied by the agency, whose staff are all expert, at Monkey Island. There are not many monkeys on Monkey Island now, those left are semi-tame. The Inderena office (see above) will plan a trip for you and put you in touch with guides. You can also stay at their centre in the **Parque Nacional Amacayacu** US$12 for full board, safe, friendly and efficient, about 2 hrs by boat from Leticia, US$7.80. Entry to the park is US$1. There is a jungle walk to a lookout, best to take a guide if only to avoid some of the more unfriendly plants. Take a boat to a nearby island to see Victoria Regia water lilies. Accommodation is clean, mess-style meals available, but useful to take some provisions with you. Lights out 2130. There are two boat operators to the Parque, and if you buy a return ticket check your operator runs the day you wish to return. Other reputable tour companies are *Amaturs* (in lobby of *Hotel Anaconda*), *Amazonian Adventures* (ask for Chiri Chiri) and *Kapax*. The following tours are available: to Benjamin Constant to see a rubber plantation, 8 hrs; to Monkey Island to see Ticuna and Yagua Indians, overnight trip, with full board. Turamazonas offers tours up the river to visit Indian communities, 3 days (price depends on number of people in group). Recommended tours from Leticia to **Puerto Nariño**, a small attractive settlement up the Amazon, are run by *Punto Amazónico*, Cra 24, No 53-18, 2° piso, Bogotá, T 249-3618 (guides Fernando and José), including fishing, visits to Indians, alligator watching for 4-5 days. You can arrange a 3-hr trip from Leticia to Puerto Nariño for US$25. There is an Inderena centre at Mata Mata, a few rooms with hammocks available. Nearby is a huge tree, La Selva, which you can climb. From its crown you can see over the River Amazon. Many independent guides can be found on the river front; for one day excursions to Victoria Regia waterlilies, Monkey Island and more (check that those recommended by posher hotels do not overcharge). A recommended guide is Luis Daniel González, Cra 8, No 9-93 (he can either be found at the airport, or contacted through *Hotel Anaconda*); he runs a variety of tours, is knowledgeable and speaks Spanish, Portuguese and English). Another recommended is Daniel Martínez, speaks good English and is knowledgeable about the jungle and the Indians. Make sure the guides bring rubber boots as it can be quite muddy. Cheap guides do not have the experience or first aid equipment of the main tour companies, and there have been many instances of boats breaking down and guides getting drunk and abandoning their clients. If you choose to go on a night excursion to look for cayman make sure the boat has powerful halogen lights.

When going upstream remember that the slower and dirtier the boat, the more mosquitoes you will meet. (You can swim in the Amazon and its tributaries, but do not dive; this disturbs the fish. Also do not swim at sunrise or sunset when the fish are more active, nor when the water is shallow in the dry season, nor if you have a wound, however slight, which might open up and bleed.) Take water purification tablets, almost all the water used here comes straight out of the river.

SOUTHERN COLOMBIA (9)

From Popayán to Ecuador, including the mangrove swamps of the Pacific coast and the Amazonian-type lowlands of the Río Putumayo.

The Pan-American Highway continues S from Popayán to Pasto. The entire road is now paved. After *El Bordo* (**E** *Hotel Patía*, fan, cold water, rec; **F** *Residencias Confort*, on main road, simple but recommended; **G** *Residencias Central*, on Panamericana, basic, clean, fan) the road takes a new route and the 294-km drive takes 5 hrs. The express bus takes 7 hrs in ordinary conditions, though landslides occasionally block the road. The road drops to 700m in the valley of the Río Patía before climbing to Pasto with big temperature changes. 93 km S of Popayán is a tourist complex, *El Patio*, including hotel, swimming pool and campsite with showers, toilets, barbecues, good.

If one has time, the old route via La Unión and Mercaderes can be done by bus; enquire at Popayán or Pasto bus terminals. There are three basic hotels at La Unión and, 68 km N of Pasto at *El Tablón*, 3 basic hotels, **G** *Residencial Ambala*, the best, noisy from passing traffic but convenient for cyclists.

143 km S of Popayán is *Mercaderes*, a small town with a pleasant climate. Hotels (F) are good and the *Restaurante Tropical* is recommended. 30 km before Pasto is *Chachagui*: **E** *Hotel Imperio de los Incas*, T 218054, with bath, friendly, swimming pool, 2 km from Pasto airport, rec; cheaper is **G** *Casa Champagnat*, with bath, cold water, swimming pool, friendly and helpful. There is also a tourist centre, **D** *Coba Negra*, with *cabañas*, swimming pools and a restaurant.

Pasto, capital of the Department of Nariño, stands upon a high plateau (2,534m) in the SW, 88 km from Ecuador, with a population of 282,310. It is overlooked from the W by Galeras Volcano (when not in cloud) and to the E by green hills not yet suburbanized by the city, a very attractive setting. The city, which retains some of its colonial character, was founded in the early days of the conquest. Today it is a centre for the agricultural and cattle industries of the region, which exports little. Pasto varnish (*barniz*) is mixed locally, to embellish the strikingly colourful local wooden bowls. A visit to the church of **Cristo Rey** (C 20, No 24-64, near the centre), with striking yellow stone W front with octagonal angelic turrets, is recommended. Also **La Merced**, C 18 y Cra 22, is worth seeing for its rich decoration and gold ornaments. From the church of **Santiago** (Cra 23 y C 13) there is a good view over the city to the mountains; **San Felipe** (C 12 y Cra 27) has green tiled domes. The interior courtyard of the **municipal building** on the main square (corner of C 19 and Cra 24) has 2 tiers of colonnaded balconies. The **Museo de Oro del Banco de la República**, C 18, No 21-20, T 239100, has a small well-displayed collection of precolumbian pieces from the cultures of S Colombia, a library and auditorium. **Museo Zambrano**, C 20, No 29-78, houses indigenous and colonial period arts.

During the new year's *fiesta* there is a Día de los Negros on 5 Jan and a Día de los Blancos next day. On "black day" people dump their hands in black grease and smear each other's faces. On "white day" they throw talc or flour at each other. Local people wear their oldest clothes. Things can get quite violent. On 28 December and 5 Feb, there is also a Fiesta de las Aguas when anything that moves—only tourists because locals know better—gets drenched with water from balconies and even from fire engines' hoses. If you try to escape to other places nearby (eg Sandoriá) you will not succeed. The whole region is involved in this legalised water war! In Pasto and Ipiales (**see p 895**), on 31 December, is the Concurso de Años Viejos, when huge dolls are burnt; they represent the old year and sometimes lampoon local people. On

Sun a game of paddle ball is played on the edge of the town (bus marked San Lorenzo) similar to that played in Ibarra, Ecuador.

During the wars of independence, Pasto was a stronghold of the Royalists and the last town to fall into the hands of the patriots after a long and bitter struggle. Then the people of Nariño Department wanted to join Ecuador when that country split off from Gran Colombia in 1830, but were prevented by Colombian troops.

Hotels A1 *Morasurco*, Av de los Estudiantes, y C 20, T 235017, F 235639, rec, reasonable restaurant; **A1** *Agualongo*, Cra 25, No 17-83, T 235216, central, comfortable, reasonable restaurant, courteous staff, credit cards; **A2** *Don Saul*, C 17 No 23-52, T 230618, F 230622, comfortable, good restaurant, rec; **B** *Chambu*, Cra 20 y C 17, T 213129, modern; **A3** *Cuellar's*, Cra 23, No 15-50, roomy, T 232879, well-furnished, some noise from bowling centre underneath, but rec; **A3** *Galerías*, Cra 26, No 18-71, above new shopping mall, comfortable, good restaurant, rec; **B** *Eldorado*, Pasaje Dorado No 23-42, T/F 233260, good; **C** *San Diego*, C 16 A No 27-27, T 235050, good; **B** *Sindagua*, C 20, No 21B-16, T 235404, rec; **E** *Canchala*, C 17, No 20A-38, T 213337, big, safe, clean, hot water, TV, central; **C** *El Duque*, Cra 20, No 17-17, T 217390, including TV and shower, comfortable, rec; **C** *El Paisa*, Cra 26, No 15-37, T 234592, F 239664, good restaurant, bar, laundry facilities; **D** *Isa*, C 18, No 22-23, T 236663, with bath, clean, helpful, safe; **D** *Río Mayo*, Cra 20, No 17-12, T 214905, small rooms, with bath, restaurant downstairs; **D** *Premier*, C 17, No 19-54, T 217594, F 212913, clothes washing facilities; **D** *Metropol*, C 15, No 21-41, T 212636, restaurant, laundry facilities; **D** *Bariloche*, Cra 26, No 15-80, T 233022, F 233120; **E** *El Prado*, Cra 22, No 14-42, T 210544; **F** *Embajador*, C 19, No 25-57, quiet, private bath, patio where you can park motorbikes, cold water; **F** *Koala Inn*, C 18, No 22-37, T 221101, cheaper without bath, laundry facilities, helpful English speaking, well-travelled owner, popular, hot water, book exchange, pleasant, good base for young travellers, highly rec; **F** *Nueva York*, Cra 19 bis, 18-20, hot shower, friendly, near Magdalena bus company, you can put a motorcycle inside; **F** *Residencias Colón*, Cra 22, No 19-61, clean, friendly, hot water; **F** *Residencia Indi Chaya*, C 16, No 18-23 (corner of Cra 19 and C 16, up the steps), T 234476, good value, clean, good beds, carpets, safe; **F** *María Belén*, C 13, No 19-15, clean, safe, quiet, friendly, hot water; **G** *Residencia Aica*, C 17, No 20-75, T 235311, safe, shared bath, but dirty; **G** *Viena*, clean, Cra 19B, No 18-36, cheap, restaurant downstairs, clean, noisy.

Restaurants Central: *La Esquina del Barril*, C 19, No 28-12, good; *Pollorrico*, Cra 25, 17-50, good. *Mister Pollo*, C 17 y Cra 26, good, clean fast food. *La Merced*, Cra 22, No 17-37, pizzas and local dishes, good; *Punto Rojo*, Cra 24, Parque Nariño, self service, 24 hrs, good choice of dishes; *El Mundo de los Pasteles*, Cra 22, No 18-34, cheap *comidas*; *Rancho Grande*, C 17, No 26-89, cheap and open late; *El Vencedor*, C 18, No 20A-40, good value meals, open 0600-1900. *Las Dos Pavrillas*, Pasaje Dorado, No 23-22, steaks, chicken, reasonable prices; *La Cabaña*, C 16, No 25-20, varied menu; *Riko Riko*, various locations, good fast food. **Away from centre:** *El Chalet Suizo*, C 20, 41-80 (T 234419), high class food, rec; *Sausolito*, Cra 35A, No 20-63, seafood, good; *La Casa Vasca*, C 12A, No 29-10, Spanish; rec; *Cokorin*, Bus terminal, T 212084, meat, chicken, local dishes.

Bar/Discotheque *Honey Bar*, C 16, No 25-40, T 234895, pleasant atmosphere.

Banks and Exchange For changing TCs, **Banco Industrial de Colombia**, C 19, No 27. **Banco Anglo Colombiano**, C 17, No 21-32 (best rates), Visa advances. **Banco de Bogotá** will change TCs. If going to Tumaco, this is the last place where TCs can be cashed. **Casas de cambio**, at Cra 25, No 18-97, T 232294, and C 19, No 24-86, T 235616, by the main square, changes sucres into pesos and vice versa, and will change US dollars into either.

Ecuadorean Consulate C 17, No 26-55, 2nd floor. Four photos needed if you require a visa (but this office is not very knowledgeable about requirements for visas).

Cinema Cra 25 and Cs 17 and 18, good.

Airmail Cra 23, 18-42 and C 18, No 24-86. **Telephones** Long distance calls from Telecom, C 17 y Cra 23.

Shopping *Casa del Barniz de Pasto*, C 13, No 24-9, *Artesanías Nariño*, C 26, No 18-91; *Artesanía-Mercado Bombona*, C 14 y Cra 27; *Artesanías Mopa-Mopa*, Cra 25, No 13-14, for *barniz*. Leather goods are cheaper here than in Bogotá, Ecuador or Peru. Most of the shops are on Cs 17 and 18. Try the municipal market for handicrafts. *Mercado Campesino*, southern end of C 16, esq Cra 7. *Supermercado Confamiliar de Nariño*, C 16b, No 30-53, rec; *Ley* on C 18, next to Avianca postal office. On main square (C 19 y Cra 25) is a shopping centre with many types of shops and restaurants.

Tourist Office Just off the main square, C 18, No 25-25, T 234962, friendly and helpful, open

0800-1200 and 1400-1800 Mon-Fri, closed Sat-Sun. It will advise on money changing. **Maps** of Colombia and cities from Instituto Geográfico Agustín Codazzi, in Banco de la República building, C 18, No 21-20, limited selection. The **DAS** office in town, C 16, No 28-11, T 235901, will give exit stamps if you are going on to Ecuador.

Buses All interurban buses leave from the new terminal, Cra 6, C16. To **Bogotá**, 23 hrs, US$26 (Bolivariano Pullman). To **Ipiales**, 2 hrs, US$2.40, Cooperativo Supertaxis del Sur; by bus, US$1.80, sit on left hand side for the views. To **Popayán**, ordinary buses take 10-12 hrs, US$9; expresses take 5-8 hrs, cost US$11.25. To **Cali**, US$9.50, expresses, 8½-10 hrs. To **Tumaco**, 11 hrs by bus, 10 hrs by minibus, US$7.75. To **Puerto Asís**, 11 hrs, US$5.75 with Trans Ipiales or Bolivariano (both C 18), 0500 and 1100. To **Mocoa**, 8 hrs, US$4.80.

Air Services Daily to **Bogotá** (Avianca, US$70, Intercontinental); to **Cali** also with Avianca and Intercontinental, also to Tumaco and Cúcuta. Avianca to **Leticia** via Bogotá or Cali, about US$180, cannot be done in 1 day. The airport is at Cano, 40 km from Pasto; by colectivo (beautiful drive), 45 mins. US$2.40 or US$13.50 by taxi. There are no currency exchange facilities, but the shop will change US$ bills at a poor rate. Avianca, C 18, No 25-86, T 232044; Intercontinental, Cra 25, No 18-53, T 235747.

Excursions There are some gold mines in the area. The volcano, **Galeras** (4,276m), quiescent since 1934, began erupting again in 1989. A British geologist, Geoffrey Brown, died in January 1993 when the volcano erupted just as he was setting up equipment in the crater to measure gravity changes which, it is hoped, will help to predict volcanic activity. Check at the tourist office on whether it is safe to climb on the mountain and whether you need a permit. A highway traversing all kinds of altitudes and climates has been built round it; the trip along it takes half a day. A rough road goes to the summit where there is an army post guarding a TV relay station. A taxi (arrange previous day, if possible) will take you to about 200m from the top; there is a fine view and the soldiers are glad to see people. If you can't get a taxi, take a bus to the village of San Vicente, then hitch as far up as you can, which will probably leave a 3-hour, but pleasant walk to the top. On the N side of the volcano lies the village of **Sandoná** where Panama hats are made; they can be seen being made in the streets in the process of being finished. Sandoná market day is Saturday. (It is a worthwhile trip to Sandoná, 4 buses daily, US$1.50, the last back to Pasto is at 1700.) There are good walks on the lower slopes through Catambuco and Jongovito where there is an interesting brick-making business.

There is interesting country to the SW of Galeras through Yacuanquer and **Consacá** (one hotel/restaurant on the road) to **Ancuya** which is on a tableland on the edge of a gorge. Here there is a restaurant at the right of the church (no sign) and one *residencia*. 30 km through spectacular scenery is **Samaniego**, a big village with several hotels and restaurants, a service station and a hospital. 45 km S to Túquerres (see below). This is an itinerary, mainly dirt roads, for those who like to get off the beaten track in mountain country. 23 km SE of Pasto is the Laguna de la Cocha, a popular place at weekends (see p 894).

The highway N to the airport and Popayán crosses a pass just after leaving town and then descends to a warm valley filled with country homes, restaurants and swimming pools (crowded at weekends). Try the *arepas de choclo*, made with fresh ground sweet corn, at one of the many roadside kiosks (*Choclo Listo* rec).

Tumaco Region

The 250-km road W from Pasto to Tumaco is paved for most of the way but is subject to landslides—check in Pasto. At **Túquerres**, **F *Residencias Santa Rita***, C 4, No 17-29 and several restaurants including ***Cafetería La 14***, Cra 14, C 20 near the Trans Ipiales bus office. Bus to Pasto US$1.70, 2 hrs; regular jeep service to Ipiales from Cra 14, C 20, US$1.45, 1½ hrs. Excellent market on Thur, good for ponchos. A short distance beyond Túquerres is a track to the right which leads in 1½ hrs to Laguna Verde, beyond which is the Volcán Azufral. For information on walking and climbing in this area, enquire in Túquerres. The road continues to El Espino where it divides, right to Tumaco and left 36 km to Ipiales, with splendid wide views to the volcanoes close to the Ecuador border.

About 90 km from Túquerres, before the town of Ricaurte, is the village of **Chucunez**. A dirt road branches S here, and after crossing the river climbs for 7 km to **Reserva Natural La Planada**, a private 3,200 hectare nature reserve (a World Wildlife Fund project). It is a patch of dense cloud forest situated on a unique flat-topped mountain and home to a wide variety of flora and fauna. The area is intended principally for scientific research and there are a number of biologists in residence. Day visitors are welcome but camping is prohibited. For further information contact Reserva Natural La Planada, Apartado Aéreo 1562, Pasto.

At **Ricaurte** is **F *El Oasis***, in the centre, reasonable. Avoid *residencias* in Altaquer and El Diviso between Ricaurte and **Junín**, 36 km further on. The road passes through beautiful cloud forest, excellent for birdwatchers (many species of tanager to be seen). There are restaurants but nowhere to stay in Junín.

At Junín you can turn N, and in 57 km come to the interesting town of **Barbacoas** on the Río Telembí, a former Spanish gold-producing centre which still retains the remains of an extensive water-front, a promenade and steps coming down through the town to the river. Gold is still panned from the rivers by part-time prospector-farmers. **F** *Hotel Telembí*, basic, friendly; **F** *Residencial*, poor, unfriendly. Restaurant *Telembí* on the river front, good food. Problems with water and electricity supplies. River trips on the supply boats are possible, about US$8 for 8 hrs. Bus to Pasto, US$7.20, rough trip. The road to Barbacoas is limited to one-way traffic in places—enquire at the chain barring the road at Junín and the operator will telephone down the line to see if the route is clear for you to pass.

The region is very different from highland Colombia, with two-storey Caribbean-style wooden houses and a predominantly black population. Small farms are mixed with cattle ranches, rice farms and oil-palm plantations. Cocoa is grown. The coastal area around Tumaco is mangrove swamp, with many rivers and inlets on which lie hundreds of villages and settlements; negotiate with boatmen for a visit to the swamps or the beautiful, newly-developed island tourist resort of **Boca Grande**, the trip takes 30 mins, US$8 return; ask for Señor Felipe Bustamante, C Comercial, Apto 224, T 465, who rents canoes and cabins, has a good seafood restaurant on the island, where water and electricity supplies are irregular. There are several places to stay in the F category.

Tumaco has a population of 71,370; the unemployment rate is very high, the living conditions are poor, and the services and roads in the town are not good. It is in one of the world's rainiest areas; the yearly average temperature is in the 25-35°C range. The movement of the tides governs most of the activities in the area, especially transport. A natural arch on the main beach, N of the town and port, is reputed to be the hiding place of Henry Morgan's treasure. Swimming is not recommended from the town's beaches, which are polluted; stalls provide refreshment on the beach. Swimming is safe, however, at El Morro beach, N of the town, only on the incoming tide (the outgoing tide uncovers poisonous rays). Hotels are well subscribed and of varying quality: it is advisable to get a bed early in the day. The northern part of the town is built on stilts out over the sea. Visit it during the daylight as it is reported to be dangerous at night, and not just because you could fall through the holes in the wooden pavements into the sea. The area is also noted archaeologically for the finds associated with the Tumaco culture. Ask for Pacho Cantin at El Morro Beach who will guide you through the caves. The town has problems with water and electricity supplies. There are no money exchange facilities (except in some shops that will buy dollars and sucres at a poor rate; change money in Cali or Pasto).

Hotels **D** *Villa del Mar*, C Sucre, modern, clean, with shower, toilet and fan, no hot water, good café below, also has well equipped cabins at El Morro Beach; **E** *Claudia*, C Mosquera, with restaurant; *Residencias Don Pepe*, Calle de Comercio, near water-front and *canoa* dock, friendly but basic; **F** *Barranquilla*, friendly, safe, good restaurant; **G** *Porvenir*, far from luxurious, most of the family friendly. Children meet arriving buses to offer accommodation; most cheap places are in C del Comercio, many houses and restaurants without signs take guests—nearly all have mosquito nets. Try opp Trans Ipiales, under Cootranor sign, or 2 doors from Trans Ipiales (Barbería Nueva), both F. **Food:** The main culinary attraction of the town is the fish, in the market and restaurants, fresh from the Pacific. A number of good restaurants on the main streets, Cs Mosquera and del Comercio, though the best is probably *Las Velas* on C Sucre. **NB** Be very careful of food and water because there are many parasites.

Entertainment Many discos specializing in Afro/S American rhythms; try *Candelejas*.

Transport Tumaco to Pasto, 9 hrs, US$7.80, with Supertaxis del Sur or Trans Ipiales (better), 4 a day, 8 hrs interesting ride. An alternative is to catch a bus from Ipiales to Espino (US$0.75, colectivo, US$1.15) and there change buses for Tumaco (US$4.80, 7½ hrs). There are no hotels in Espino. There are daily **flights** to and from **Cali** with Intercontinental and 3 a week with Satena, 35 mins. Flights also to **Pasto**, US$60, and Bogotá, US$70.

There are water taxis N up the coast, across the bay to Salahonda and further to La Vigía and beyond. At La Vigía is the **Parque Nacional Sanquianga** ranger headquarters. The park was founded in 1977 and extends for some 30 km along the coast and a similar distance inland consisting of mangrove covered sandbanks formed by rivers flowing down from the Andes. There are fresh and salt water fish in abundance and a rich variety of bird life. It can also be reached from Guapí and Górgona. If you have the time, you can make your way up the coast as far as Buenaventura. Cost about US$20 from Tumaco.

To Ecuador It is possible to travel to Ecuador by motorized canoe, about US$20, or by launch US$50. Part of the trip is by river, which is very beautiful, and part on the open sea, which can be very rough; a plastic sheet to cover your belongings is essential. Take suncream. Daily service at 0800 to San Lorenzo, 7 hrs (but can take 14) tickets from C del Comercio (protective plastic sheeting provided). Señor Pepello, who lives in the centre of Tumaco, owns two canoes: he leaves on Sat at 0700 for San Lorenzo and Limones in Ecuador—book in advance. Also enquire for Señor Lucho, or ask around the water-front at 0600, or try at the fishing centre, El Coral del Pacífico for a cheaper passage, but note that this can be a dangerous trip and you should try to seek advice before taking a boat. DAS stamp for leaving Colombia should be obtained from the **DAS** office in Tumaco, which is in the Alcaldía Municipal, C 11, Cra 9, office open on weekdays only. Visas for Ecuador (if required) should be obtained in Cali or Pasto. Entry stamps for Ecuador must be obtained in the coastal towns. If coming into Colombia through Tumaco, you will have to go to Ipiales to obtain the entry stamp. Apparently the 24/48 hrs "unofficial" entry is not a problem, but do not obtain any Colombian stamps in your passport before presentation to DAS in Ipiales. DAS in Pasto is not authorized to give entry stamps for overland or sea crossings, and the DAS office in Tumaco seems to be only semi-official.

The *Putumayo*

One hour E of Pasto, on the road to Mocoa (capital of the Intendencia of Putumayo) is **Laguna La Cocha**, the largest lake in S Colombia (sometimes called Lago Guámez). By the lake, 3 km from the main road, is the Swiss-run **C Chalet Guámez**, well recommended, particularly for the cuisine, cabins sleeping up to six can be hired; free van-camping allowed. The chalet will arrange a US$22 jeep trip to Sibundoy, further along the road. Boats may be hired for US$2.50 per hour. La Cocha may be reached by taking a bus to El Encano and walking the remaining 5 km round to the chalet area, or 20 mins from the bus stop direct to the fishing village of El Encano, where you can enjoy trout at very low prices at one of the many small restaurants, and from here take a *lancha* to the chalet for US$3. There is also a government hotel nearby, **B Sindamanoy**, chalet style, good views, inviting restaurant with good but expensive food, free van-, and tent camping allowed with manager's permission. There are also cheap and friendly places to stay in and near El Encano. From the hotel you can take a 10-min boat trip to the **Isla de la Chorota** nature reserve; interesting trees, but little wildlife.

The road from Pasto to the Putumayo deteriorates rapidly after El Encano. It is steep but spectacular. It is also dangerous between Sibundoy and El Pepino (the junction for Mocoa) and care should be taken (especially by cyclists), but there is a magnificent view out over the Putumayo by a large statue of the Virgin, just before the final descent.

Sibundoy There is a beautiful church on the main plaza, completed in 1968. About a quarter of the valley is now reserved for Sibundoy Indian occupation. Market Sunday. Best handicraft shop is Fudak, C 16 No 16-73, a cooperative run by the Kamza Indians. Bus from Pasto (3 hrs, US$2.50), passing through Colón (*residencias*) and Santiago.

Hotels and Restaurants E *Hotel Turista*, clean, friendly; better meals at **F** *Hotel Sibundoy*, but hotel dirty, unhelpful, not rec; **F** *Residencia Valle*, clean double rooms, hot water. *Restaurant Viajero*, just off main street. You can camp in the hills, where there are lovely walks and you can see all kinds of flora and fauna.

Mocoa, the administrative capital of the Intendencia of Putumayo, is small (18,960 people), with a number of hotels (**F** *Viajero*, **D** *Central*, off main plaza, very clean and friendly) and *residencias*, eg **G** *Residencia Colonial*, Cra 6, No 8-10, spartan but safe. The town has a very modern square, new offices and modern developments. sugar-cane is grown in the area. The main DAS office for the region is in Mocoa.

Buses 8-12 hrs by bus and jeeps to Pasto, US$4.80; bus to Pitalito, 7 hrs, US$8.20. Bus to Sibundoy, US$2.40, 5 a day; to Puerto Asis, US$5, a few police checks.

The road continues from El Pepino, through cattle-ranching country, to **Puerto Asís**, the main town and port of the Putumayo. The water front is 3 km from the centre. River traffic is busy. All boats that leave for Leticia (with connections to Manaus) are cargo boats, and only sail when they have cargo. They leave from the Hong Kong wharf (muelle), or the nearby Bavaria and Esmeraldas wharves: taxi from town US$4. Local information in town is poor, you must check with the boat personnel yourself. Those carrying gasoline (and most do) are not supposed to take passengers. Only one company, Navenal, normally takes passengers, and it can be weeks between their sailings. One can also try the army for a passage. Fares are about US$100; at least 10-15 days; it is best to see the Jefe de la Marina, or the Oficina de Transporte Fluvial, about a passage. By boat to Leguízamo takes 2-3 days, or by speedboat (canoa), 7 hrs, US$27 one way, twice a week. For those interested in flora and fauna it is necessary to travel down river, beyond new areas of settlement or by canoe up the river for monkeys and many birds. Boats will not go unless the rivers are high; sometimes, they get stuck halfway. Take supplementary food and water with you, meals on the boats are uninspired. One traveller found canned fruit cocktail mixed with local rum went down well.

There are regular flights to and from Puerto Asís three times a week by Satena to Bogotá, US$50, via Florencia. Aires fly to Leguízamo, Neiva, Cali and Lago Agrio in Ecuador. Bus to Bogotá US$24, 18 hrs; to Mocoa US$5.

NB Puerto Asís is a marketing centre for cocaine and has been the scene of much guerrilla and counter-insurgency activity.

Hotels F *Residencias Gigante*, C 10, 24-25, clean; F *Residencias Nevado*, Cra 20, close to the airport, well kept and comfortable, a/c optional, without board; F *Residencias Liz*, C 11, with bath, very friendly; F *Residencia Volga*, C 10, No 23-73, basic, safe; F *Mery*, private bath, clean; G *Residencias Patiño*, rec; G *Residencia Paraíso*, clean except for a few cockroaches. There are plenty of cheap hotels in the port, but it is hard to find a room late in the day.

Buses may be taken to **Pasto** (a 10 hr journey, at 0500, 0600 and 0900 daily, on mostly mountainous roads, US$5.40, be prepared for military checks). Jeep NE to Pitalito, book in advance through bus company. Bus **Sibundoy**-Puerto Asís, US$3.90. Five buses a day to **San Miguel**, 4 hrs, near the Ecuadorean border (US$3.60) where the Sun market provides a meeting place, and where *canoas* may be hired to visit villages 2-4 hrs away on the river.

San Miguel There are several very basic hotels, eg F *Mirador*, safe and *Residencias Olga* which has 6 single rooms. You can cross to Ecuador from here, get your exit stamp from the DAS office in Puerto Asís or Mocoa. The boat trip up the San Miguel river via Puerto Colón to La Punta takes 1 hour and costs US$2.20. There is a bus to Lago Agrio (US$0.60).

Leguízamo, downstream from Puerto Asís, can also be reached by air from Florencia, Neiva and Bogotá, with Satena, several times a week. Aires flies from Neiva via Puerto Asís three times a week. A national park (**Parque Nacional de Paya**) has been established between Puerto Asís and Leguízamo, but so far in name only. There are boats to Leticia and to Peru, but transport on all boats carrying gasoline is forbidden. For information go to Naval at the port, Transporte Fluvial Estrella del Sur (Cra 27, off C 10) or Transporte Fluvial Amazonas (Cra 20, 14-59—English spoken). There is a helpful Inderena office in town. Hotels: *Leguízamo*, *Madrago*, *Marlene*, *Viajero*, *San Pablo* and *Caucaya* (comfortable, nice owners), all G, basic. Further downstream are El Encanto and the nearby village of *San Rafael*.

It is possible to carry on down the Putumayo which forms the boundary between Colombia and Peru, then crosses into Brazil, becoming the Rio Iça to join the Amazon at Santo Antônio. Leticia is 300 km upstream on the Amazon towards Peru. From El Encanto to Leticia is about 10 days, but getting a passage beyond the Brazilian border is problematical. The border town is **Tarapacá** (airport). There is a basic *Residencial*, plenty of spiders and mosquitoes. It can be quite cold at night.

There is a road of a sort from Mocoa to Puerto Limón, on the Río Caquetá (see Caquetá section, p 886).

South to Ecuador

Passing through deep valleys and a spectacular gorge, buses on the paved Pan-American Highway cover the 84 km from Pasto to Ipiales in $1\frac{1}{2}$-2 hrs. The road crosses the spectacular gorge of the Río Guaitara near El Pedregal, 40 km from Pasto. Stop in El Pedregal for *choclo* (corn) cooked in many forms by the roadside. The road to Túquerres and Tumaco goes up to the right here, past brick factories to the high plains of the Cordillera Occidental (**see p 893**). A detour via Túquerres (part unpaved) takes over an hour more; it reaches 3,050m at Túquerres, dropping to 2,440 at Guachucal, and rising again to 2,740m at **Ipiales**, "the city of the three volcanoes", with about 30,000 people; famous for its colourful Friday morning Indian market. The Catedral Bodas de Plata is worth visiting.

Museum Small, set up by Banco de la República.

Hotels B *Mayasquer*, 3 km on road to frontier, modern, nice restaurant, very good, swings for children, T (92725) 3984; **D** *Korpawasy*, Cra 6, No 10-47, T 2634, good food, plenty of blankets; **D** *Dinar*, Cra 4A, No 12A-18, T 3659, cafeteria, private parking; **D** *Angasmayo*, C 16, No 6-38, clean, comfortable; **E** *Bachué*, Cra 6 y C 11-68, safe; **E** *Pasviveros*, Cra 6, No 16-90, T 2622, bath, hot water, clean; **E** *Rumichaca Internacional*, C 14, No 7-114, T 2692, clean, comfortable, good restaurant with reasonable prices. **F** *Belmonte*, Cra 4, No 12-111 (near Transportes Ipiales), very clean, hot water, parking opposite, rec, but crowded; **F** *Colombia*, C 13, No 7-50, hot water, parking for motorbikes; **F** *Bahamas*, 3 doors from Transportes Ipiales, hot water, clean, good value; **F** *San Andrés*, Cra 5, No 14-75, clean, TV, hot water; **G** *India Catalina*, Cra 5a, No 14-88, T 4392, hot shower, run down, 2 blocks from main plaza; **G** *Nueva York*, C 13, No 4-11, near main square, run down, plenty of blankets, friendly; **G** *Oasis*, Cra 6, No 11-34, 1 block from main plaza, shower, ask for hot water, quiet after 2100, clean, helpful.

Camping Free behind last Esso station outside town on road N.

Restaurants *Don Lucho (Los Tejados)*, Cra 5, No 14-13 (*antioqueño*); *Don José*, Cra 5, No 14-53. Plenty of cheap restaurants, better quality ones on Cra 7. Meals in Almacenes Ley cost US$1. Many good bakeries on Cra 6, or *Panadería Galaxia*, C 15, No 7-89, for a good cheap breakfast. Outside town towards the frontier, *La Herradura*, good food, reasonable prices, try their excellent *trucha con salsa de camarones* (rainbow trout with shrimp sauce), rec.

Exchange It is not possible to cash TCs, but cash is no problem eg Banco Anglo Colombiano, Cra 6, No 16-59, T 2331. *Casa de Cambio* at Cra 6, No 14-09, other *cambios* on the square. There are money changers in the street, in the square and on the border, but they may take advantage of you if the banks are closed. Better rates are to be had in Quito. Coming from Ecuador, peso rates compare well in Ipiales with elsewhere in Colombia.

A visit to the nearby Sanctuary of the Virgin of **Las Lajas** , 7 km E of Ipiales on a paved road, is definitely recommended. On days set apart for religion, Indians come down from the hills in their traditional bright colours. Seen from the approach road, looking down into the canyon, the Sanctuary is a magnificent architectural conception, set on a bridge over the Río Guáitara: close to, it is very heavily ornamented in the gothic style. The altar is set into the rock face of the canyon which forms one end of the sanctuary with the façade facing a wide plaza that completes the bridge over the canyon. There are walks to nearby shrines in dramatic scenery. It is a 10-15 min walk down to the sanctuary from the village. There are great pilgrimages to it from Colombia and Ecuador (very crowded at Easter) and the Sanctuary must be second only to Lourdes in the number of miracles claimed for it. The Church recognizes one only. Colectivo from Cra 6 y C 4, Ipiales, US$0.40 pp, taxi, US$6 return (it's about a 1½-hour walk, 7 km); 3 basic hotels and a small number of restaurants at Las Lajas. Try local guinea pig and boiled potatoes for lunch (or guinea pig betting in the central plaza may be more to your taste).

15 km NW of Ipiales is **Cumbal** which sits beneath two 4,700m volcanoes, Cumbal, immediately above the town and Chiles, further S and close to the Ecuador border. There is accommodation, F, at Cra 8, No 20-47 (no name), basic, and very good food at *Rincón de Colombia*, C 18, No 8-48, good value. Jeep from Ipiales (C 15, No 7-23) US$1, 1 hr.

Frontier Ipiales is 2 km from the Rumichaca bridge across the Carchi river into Ecuador. The frontier post stands beside a natural bridge, on a concrete bridge, where customs and passport examinations take place from 0600 to 2100.

To Ecuador All Colombian offices are in one complex: DAS (immigration, exit stamp given here), customs, INTRA (Dept of Transportation, car papers stamped here; if leaving Colombia you must show your vehicle entry permit), ICA (Dept of Agriculture for plant and animal quarantine), and the Ecuadorean consulate (open weekdays 0830-1200, 1430-1800). There is also a restaurant, Telecom for long-distance phone calls, clean bathrooms (ask for key, US$0.10) and ample parking. See p 962 for the Ecuadorean side and see also **Documents** in Ecuador, Information for Visitors. If entering Colombia by car, the vehicle is supposed to be fumigated against diseases that affect coffee trees, at the ICA office; the certificate must be presented in El Pedregal, a village 40 km beyond Ipiales on the road to Pasto. (This fumigation process is not always carried out.) You can buy insurance for your car in Colombia at Caja Agraria, in the plaza. There are frequent police checks on the buses going to Popayán and neighbouring areas.

Transport From Ipiales to Tulcán: colectivo from C14 y Cra 11 (waits till all seats are full), US$0.80 to the frontier (buses to Ipiales arrive at the main park – they may take you closer to the colectivo point if you ask). Colectivo from frontier to Tulcán US$0.75 (ask the fare at the tourist office at the border); to go to bus terminal, take blue bus from central plaza, US$0.05. Taxi to or from border, US$3.50. From Ipiales airport to the border by taxi, about US$6.50; to centre of Ipiales US$4.

Bus to **Popayán**, Expreso Bolivariano, US$9, 7$\frac{1}{2}$ hrs, hourly departures, 0430-2030; Transportes de Ipiales, US$8.75 (neither on main square, best to take taxi from border), also transport from main square, Super Taxis and Cootranar *busetas*, US$8.50, beautiful trip, sit on right side for views. Bus to Cali, US$9.50-12, 12 hrs, from main square. To **Pasto** with minibus from main square, US$5 (frequent police checks); Flota Bolivariano buses every hr, US$2.40, 1$\frac{1}{4}$ hrs. Buses to **Bogotá** leave every other hour between 0500 and 0830, 24 hrs, US$32.80 (note, if coming from Bogotá, there is an hour's stop in Cali; bus leaves from a different level from which it arrived). To **Medellín**, Expreso Bolivariano, 22 hrs, US$36. To **Túquerres** and **Ricaurte** on the Tumaco road, *camperos* (4WD taxis) leave from in front of San Felipe Neri church; for **Tumaco** take a bus or *campero* to El Espino and wait for a bus from Pasto.

San Luis airport is 6$\frac{1}{2}$ km out of town. Aces flights to/from Cali several days a week. TAME (of Ecuador) has flights to Quito from Tulcán, Mon-Fri.

INFORMATION FOR VISITORS

Before you go

Entry requirements

● **Documents**

A passport is always necessary; an onward ticket is officially necessary, but is not always asked for at land borders. Visitors are sometimes asked to prove that they have US$20 for each day of their stay (US$10 for students). You are normally given 30 days permission to stay on entry. If you intend to stay more than 30 days, ask for longer. If not granted at the frontier, extension (*salvoconducto*) for 15-day periods can be applied for at the DAS (security police) office in any major city up to a maximum of 6 months. There may be delays, so apply in good time. Better, apply at the DAS office, C 100, No 113-27, Bogotá (see under Bogotá, **Useful Addresses**) who are empowered to grant longer stays immediately. Alternatively, if you have good reason to stay longer (eg for medical treatment), apply at the embassy in your home country before leaving. Leaving the country and re-entering to get a new permit is not always allowed. To visit Colombia as a tourist, nationals of only China, Taiwan and Haiti need a visa (this information was correct according to the Colombian consulate in London, June 1995). You must check regulations before leaving your home country. Visas are issued only by Colombian consulates. When a visa is required you must be prepared to show 3 photographs, police clearance and medical certificates, an application form (£11 or equivalent), as well as a passport (allow 48 hrs). Various business and temporary visas are needed for foreigners who have to reside in Colombia for a length of time. Fees range from £54 (or equivalent) for a student visa, £90 for a business visa, to £131 for a working

visa. You may find that your onward ticket, which you must show before you can obtain a visa, is stamped 'non-refundable'. If you do not receive an entry card when flying in, or lose the card while in Colombia, apply to any DAS office who should issue one and restamp your passport for free. Note that to leave Colombia you must get an exit stamp from the DAS. They often do not have offices at the small frontier towns, so try to get your stamp in a main city, and save time.

NB It is highly rec that you have your passport photocopied, and, for added insurance, witnessed by a notary. This is a valid substitute (although some travellers report difficulties with this variant), and your passport can then be put into safe-keeping. Also, photocopy your TCs, flight ticket and any other essential documents. For more information, check with your consulate.

● **Tourist information**

The Corporación Nacional de Turismo (CNT), with its headquarters at Bogotá, has branches in every departmental capital and other places of interest. They should be visited as early as possible not only for information on accommodation and transport, but also for details on areas which are dangerous to visit. CNT also has offices in New York: 140 East 57th St, T 688-0151; Caracas: PB 5 Av Urdaneta Ibarras a Pelota, T 561-3592/5805; Madrid: C Princesa No 17 Tercero Izquierda, T 248-5090/5690; and Paris: 9, Boulevard de la Madeleine, 75001 Paris, T 260-3565. For details on National Parks, go to the Inderena Office in Bogotá (address on **p 799**).

The Automobile Club in Bogotá has offices on Av Caracas, No 46-64 (T 245-1534 and 245-2684). Branches are at Manizales, Medellín, Cali, Barranquilla and Cartagena. It supplies Esso, Texaco and Mobil maps: good, but not quite up-to-date; a full set of Hojas de Ruta costs US$2.50. The Texaco map has plans of the major cities. Even the Shell series lacks detail. Maps of Colombia are obtainable at the Instituto Geográfico Militar, Agustín Codazzi, Cra 30 y C 45, open 0800-1530, Bogotá, or from their office in Pasto. Drivers' route maps are available from the CNT. See also under Bogotá, **Maps.**

When to go

● **Best time to visit**

The best time for a visit is Dec, Jan and Feb: the driest months. But pleasure – it happens sometimes – is in conflict with duty, because most business people are then on holiday. Easter is a busy holiday time, many hotels put up their rates, and transport can be overloaded. There is heavy rain in many places from Jun to Sep.

● **Climate**

Climate is entirely a matter of altitude: there are no seasons to speak of, though some periods are wetter than others.

Health

Emergency medical treatment is given in hospitals: if injured in a bus accident, for example, you will be covered by insurance and treatment will be free. Bogotá has well-organized sanitary services, but bottled water is recommended for drinking. Outside the capital take sterilizer with you, or boil the water, or use the excellent mineral waters. Choose your food and eating places with care everywhere. Hepatitis is common; get protection before your trip. Falmonox is rec locally for amoebas. Mosquito nets are useful in the coastal swampy regions. There is some risk of malaria and yellow fever in the coastal areas and the eastern *llanos*/jungle regions; prophylaxis is advised. For up to date information, ask at the bigger clinics and hospitals. The local insect repellent, Black Flag, is not reliable. Tampons are not always available, but can easily be found in Bogotá supermarkets.

Money

● **Currency**

The monetary unit is the peso, divided into 100 centavos. There are coins of 5, 10, 20, 50, 100, 200 and 500 pesos; there are notes of 100, 200, 500, 1,000, 2,000, 5,000 and 10,000 pesos. Large notes of over 1,000 pesos are often impossible to spend on small purchases as change is in short supply, especially in small towns, and in the morning. There is a limit of US$25,000 on the import

of foreign exchange, with export limited to the equivalent of the amount brought in. Travellers cheques can in theory be exchanged in any bank, except the Banco de la República which, since Jun 1991, no longer undertakes exchange transactions. There are some legitimate *casas de cambio*, which are quicker to use than banks. Always check which rate of exchange is being offered. Hotels may give very poor rates of exchange, especially if you are paying in dollars, but practice varies. When changing TCs, a photocopy of your passport may be taken, best to take a supply of photocopies with you. If you do not present your passport when changing money, you may be liable for a 10% tax charged to residents on foreign exchange. Owing to the quantity of counterfeit American Express TCs in circulation, travellers may experience difficulty in cashing these cheques. For changing Amex TCs, use Banco Industrial de Colombia (BIC). You must always provide proof of purchase. The procedure is always slow, maybe involving finger printing and photographs. Obtaining reimbursement for lost American Express TCs can be straightforward if you have the numbers recorded (preferably proof of purchase), a police certificate (*diligencia de queja*) covering the circumstances of loss, and apply to their agents, Tierra mar Aire, Bogotá (see Bogotá, **Exchange**). Take dollar TCs in small denominations, but, better still, take a credit card (see below). Thomas Cook/Mastercard refund assistance point in Bogotá is Aviatur, Av 19, No 4-62, T 282-7111, Bogotá. Sterling TCs are practically impossible to change in Colombia. Also in circulation are counterfeit US dollar bills in denominations of US$50 and US$100; US$20 bills are therefore more readily accepted. It is generally dangerous to change money on the streets, and you are likely to be given counterfeit pesos.

● **Credit cards**

As it is unwise to carry large quantities of cash, credit cards are widely used, especially Mastercard and Visa; Diner's Club is also accepted, while American Express is only accepted in high-priced establishments in Bogotá. Many banks will accept Visa: Banco de Colombia and Banco Popular advance pesos against Visa, through ATMs; Caja Agraria is a Visa agent; Cajero BIC (Banco Industrial de Colombia) gives cash advances against Mastercard through ATMs. Cirrus cards can also be used. American Express credit cards are rarely accepted for cash advances. At present cash advances against credit cards give the best rates of exchange. Cash advances against credit cards are not predictable as the voucher indicates only the amount in pesos (not dollars) and the rate of exchange is determined at the time the charge is posted to your account.

NB In addition to counterfeit US$ notes, Colombia has been flooded with large quantities of legitimate US$ cash which have come into the country through the drugs trade. Thus cash dollars are becoming increasingly difficult to exchange and rates for cash are lower than for credit cards and TCs. The latter can be exchanged in the main branches of banks in Bogotá, Medellín, and Cali and some of the other major centres. Difficulties and very poor rates of exchange can be expected in smaller towns and tourist resorts. Many banks are reluctant to exchange money for anyone but account holders. Because of the great difference between the rates of exchange available (official, cash, TCs and credit cards), travellers may find variations of between 10 and 20% for prices of services and those quoted in the text.

Getting there

Air

British Airways has a twice weekly service from London to Bogotá, via Caracas. Airlines with services from continental Europe are Air France, Iberia, Alitalia and Lufthansa. Avianca, the Colombian national airline, flies from Frankfurt, Paris and Madrid.

Frequent services to and from the US by Avianca and American, the latter from Miami, daily to Bogotá, Cali and Barranquilla. Other flights from Miami: Avianca to Bogotá, Cartagena, Barranquilla, Medellín and Cali; Aces to Bogotá, Cali and Medellín.

● **From Neighbouring Republics**

Lacsa flies from San José to Barranquilla. From Mexico City with Avianca, Mexicana and Varig to Bogotá. SAM flies from Bogotá and San Andrés, to San José (daily), and Guatemala City (4 times a week). From Panama, Avianca and Copa 6 days a week each to Bogotá, SAM 3 days a week to Medellín, Intercontinental daily to San Andrés.

If flying from Guatemala to Colombia with SAM, via San Andrés, you have to purchase a round-trip ticket, refundable only in Guatemala. To get around this (if you are not going back to Guatemala) you will have to try to arrange a ticket swap with a traveller going in the other direction on San Andrés. There is, however, no difficulty in exchanging a round-trip ticket for a San Andrés-Colombian ticket with the airline, but you have to pay

extra. Lacsa, Copa, Avianca, SAM and Intercontinental fly from Panama to Colombia; do not be persuaded by SAM desk at Panama airport to buy an onward ticket out of Colombia – this may not be needed – if you fail, SAM in Bogotá will give refunds: first you must go to the DAS, Extranjería section, show your passport and ticket and obtain a permit for a refund; then go to the SAM office. **Colombia-Panama** with Copa: one may not enter, or obtain a visa for, Panama without a return or onward ticket, so you must buy a return ticket and then sell half in Panama once you have purchased a flight ticket out of Panama, or purchase a Panama-San José ticket and get your money back, less the tax. Obtaining refunds is time consuming and you will not get your money in dollars outside Panama. The cheapest way to fly to Quito is to fly to Ipiales (Aces from Cali), cross the border by road and take another plane at Tulcán. Avianca, Iberia, Lufthansa (operated by TAME or LAB), Saeta, AeroPerú, Servivensa, Viasa, Aerolíneas Argentinas, Varig and Ladeco go S from Colombia. Avianca, Viasa and others fly Bogotá-Caracas.

For a cheap means of flying from Venezuela to Colombia, see p 815.

See p 827 if you are travelling from Panama to Colombia by land or by short sea route.

Boat

Shipping a vehicle from Panama to Colombia: A new vehicle/passenger ferry service between Cristóbal, Panama, and Cartagena was inaugurated in December 1994 (see p 827) for details. This should transform the taking of vehicles between the two continents. In case there are problems with this new initiative, or that others are willing to compete, we repeat our previous comments. The best advice is to shop around the agencies in Panama City or Colón to see what is available when you want to go. Both local and international lines take vehicles, and sometimes passengers, but schedules and prices are very variable. Agents include: Sudamericana de Vapores, T 229-3844, Cristóbal-Buenaventura; Boyd Steamship Corporation, T 263-6311, Balboa-Buenaventura. Panamá-Cartagena: Central American Lines sail once a week, agent in Panama, T Colón 441-2880, Panama City 236-1036. Geminis Shipping Co SA, Apdo Postal No 3016, Zona Libre de Colón, Rep de Panamá, T 441-6269/441-6959, F 441-6571. Mr Ricardo Gil was helpful and reliable. If sending luggage separately, make enquiries at Tocumen airport, eg Tampa, T 293-4439.

One alternative is to try to ship on one of

the small freighters that occasionally depart from Coco Solo Wharf in Colón for Turbo in Colombia, which allow you to travel with your car. Obviously there is a considerable element of risk involved (suspect cargo, crews and seaworthiness), though the financial cost is lower than on a regular line.

Once you have a bill of lading, have it stamped by a Colombian consulate. Note that the Colombian consul in Colón will only stamp a bill of lading if the carrier is going to Cartagena or Barranquilla. The consulate also provides tourist cards. They require proof, in the form of a letter from your Embassy (or the Embassy representing your country in Panama) that you do not intend to sell the car in Colombia, though this requirement is usually dispensed with. Then go to the customs office in Panama City (Calle 80 and 55) to have the vehicle cleared for export. After that the vehicle details must be removed from your passport at the customs office at the port of departure. In Colón the customs office is behind the post office; in Cristóbal, at the entrance to the port on your left. The utmost patience is needed for this operation as regulations change frequently, so do not expect it to be the work of a few minutes.

Some small freighters go only to intermediate ports such as San Andrés, and it is then necessary to get another freighter to Cartagena. Navieras Mitchell ship cars regularly to San Andrés and Barranquilla. Office at Coco Solo Wharf, T 441-6942. You may have to wait up to a week in San Andrés to make the onward connection. From Colón to San Andrés takes 2 days and from San Andrés to Cartagena takes 3 days. There are two boats plying regularly between Colón (Pier 3) and San Andrés that are big enough for vans, but there is no schedule; they leave when they finish loading. There are also two regular boats between San Andrés and Cartagena; each stays in port about 15 days, but it can be longer. Shipping companies on San Andrés know that they have a monopoly, so take care when dealing with them and do not believe all they tell you.

Customs formalities at the Colombian end will take 1-3 days to clear (customs officials do not work at weekends). Make sure the visa you get from the Colombian consulate in Colón is *not* a 15 day non-extendable transit visa, but a regular tourist visa, because it is difficult to get an extension of the original visa. Clearance from the Colombian consul at the Panamanian port of embarkation may reduce the bureaucracy when you arrive in Colombia, but it will cost you US$10. In Colombia you have to pay US$15/cu m for han-

dling, as well as other document charges. An agent can reduce the aggravation but neither the waiting time, nor the cost (they charge US$55-70/day). Get as much help as possible inside the port; outside they only want your money, in Buenaventura at least. It is understood that Cartagena is much more efficient (and therefore less expensive) as far as paperwork is concerned. The delays and redtape at either end of the passage to Colombia may be reduced if you have a *Carnet de Passages*. The *Carnet* will exempt you from the bond of 10% of the vehicle's value. **NB** Assuming service proceeds as planned, all these bureaucratic complications will be dispensed with on the new *Crucero Express*.

Customs

● **Duty free allowance**
Duty-free admission is granted for portable typewriters, radios, binoculars, personal and cine cameras, but all must show use; 200 cigarettes or 50 cigars or up to 500 grams of manufactured tobacco in any form, 2 bottles of liquor or wine pp.

When you arrive

● **Airport taxes**
There is an airport exit tax of US$18 (in cash, dollars or pesos), from which only travellers staying less than 24 hrs are exempt. When you arrive, ensure that all necessary documentation bears a stamp for your date of arrival; without it you will have to pay double the exit tax on leaving (with the correct stamp, you will only be charged half the exit tax if you have been in the country less than 30 days). Visitors staying more than 60 days have to pay an extra US$12 tax, which can only be avoided by bona-fide tourists who can produce the card given them on entry. There is a 17% tax on all international air tickets bought in Colombia for flights out of the country (7.5% on international return flights). It is not possible to avoid the purchase tax by buying tickets outside the country, as the charge is included automatically. Do not buy tickets for domestic flights to or from San Andrés island outside Colombia; they are much more expensive. When getting an onward ticket from Avianca for entry into Colombia, reserve a seat only and ask for confirmation in writing, otherwise you will pay twice as much as if purchasing the ticket inside Colombia. There is also a small tax on internal air tickets, not usually included in price quotations.

● **Clothing**

Tropical clothing is necessary in the hot and humid climate of the coastal fringe and the eastern *llanos*. In Bogotá medium-weight clothing is needed for the cool evening and night. Medellín requires light clothing; Cali lighter still; Manizales very similar to Bogotá. A dual-purpose raincoat and overcoat is useful in the uplands. Higher up in the mountains it can be very cold; woollen clothing is necessary.

● **Hours of business**

Mon to Fri, commercial firms work from 0800 to mid-day and from 1400 to 1730 or 1800. Certain firms in the warmer towns such as Cali start at 0700 and finish earlier. Government offices follow the same hours on the whole as the commercial firms, but generally prefer to do business with the public in the afternoon only. Embassy hours for the public are from 0900 to noon and from 1400 to 1700 (Mon to Fri). Bank hours in Bogotá are 0900 to 1500 Mon to Thur, 0900 to 1530 on Fri except the last Fri in the month when they close at 1200; banks in Medellín, Cali, Barranquilla, Bucaramanga, Cartagena, Pasto, Pereira and Manizales open from 0800 to 1130 and 1400 to 1600 on Mon to Thur; on Fri they are open until 1630 but shut at 1130 on the last Fri in the month; banks in Popayán, Cúcuta, Neiva, Tunja, Ibagué and Santa Marta open from 0800 to 1130 and 1400 to 1530 on Mon to Fri and 0800 to 1100 on Sat and the last day of the month. Shopping hours are 0900 to 1230 and 1430 to 1830, incl Sat.

● **Official time**

Colombia is 5 hrs behind GMT.

● **Safety**

Most travellers confirm that the vast majority of Colombians are honest and very hospitable. A correspondent, Jim Turner, wrote in 1992: "Colombia is perhaps the most thoroughly delightful of the 94 countries I have travelled through. Everyone is genuinely chatty in our marginal Spanish, with many opportunities for patient conversation. We always felt that we were among friends who would watch out for us. Travel in Colombia is a really heart-warming experience in a breathtaking landscape."

In addition to the general advice given in the **Introduction and Hints** section, the following local conditions should be noted. The warning against accepting cigarettes, chewing gum, sweets or any other type of food from fellow bus-passengers applies mainly in the S of Colombia between Bogotá and Ipiales.

Colombia is part of a major drug-smuggling route. Police and customs activities have greatly intensified and smugglers increasingly try to use innocent carriers. Travellers are warned against carrying packages for other people without checking the contents. Penalties run up to 12 years in none too comfortable jails. (Indeed taking suspicious boxes, packages or gift-wrapped presents of your own through customs could give problems.) Be very polite if approached by policemen. If your hotel room is raided by police looking for drugs, try, if possible, to get a witness to prevent drugs being planted on you. Colombians who offer you drugs may well be setting you up for the police, who are very active on the N coast and San Andrés island, and other tourist resorts. Since 1989, much publicity has been given to the attempts by the authorities to tackle the 'drug barons'. Generally travellers have not been affected. In 1994 a constitutional court decision decriminalized possession of small amounts of drugs, but a subsequent decree established penalties which include deportation of any foreigner caught using any drug.

When travelling by bus, try to get a window seat on the side where your luggage is stowed, so you can check what luggage is taken from the bus. Many bus companies give luggage tags (like airlines). Try to avoid having your luggage put on top; you won't be allowed to jump out of the bus at every stop to check it's still there. In town buses, do not open windows so wide that belongings can be snatched; beware of pickpockets by the doors. Try to avoid travelling by bus in the dark, thieves are skilful and holdups happen occasionally even on the main roads. Small *busetas* are marginally safer than buses because there is only one door for luggage. Travelling by car, always keep an eye on your petrol cap, windscreen wipers and hub caps. Thieves tend to be particularly active in and around bus and railway stations. It is socially acceptable for women to keep banknotes in their bras.

If someone accosts you on the street for whatever reason, beware. If he says he's a plain-clothes policeman or drugs officer, and asks you to go to his office, offer to go with him to the nearest policeman (the tourist police where possible) or police station. He may well be a 'confidence man' (if he doesn't ask to see your passport, he almost certainly is). These conmen usually work in pairs. The best advice at all times is to take care, and above all to use your common sense.

There is sporadic guerrilla activity in Colombia. At present it appears to be confined to rural areas down the eastern part of the country from Guajira to Putumayo, and near the frontier with Panama. In some cases, it is related to the current destruction of drug crops by the authorities, causing local hardship and resentment. This has no anti-tourist implications except that, in one or two cases, eg Cocuy, 1994, US citizens have been targeted. Posing as a Canadian proved to be a successful solution in one case reported to us! Police and army checks are not uncommon, so be prepared for bus searches which may be conducted in a rather haphazard manner. Travellers in private cars are also stopped, but not necessarily searched. Some roads are more heavily policed than others, and you can expect to be stopped several times when travelling to or from the Caribbean coast and when coming from Ecuador into Colombia. All luggage is searched leaving Leticia airport and most tourists are checked arriving in Cartagena from the airport. Detailed local enquiry is essential before entering a potentially hazardous area. *The Latin American Travel Advisor* (published by Latin American Travel Consultants, PO Box 17-17-908, Quito, Ecuador, F 593-2-562-566, E-mail, rku@pi.pro.ec on Internet) is a quarterly publication which reviews the public safety situation in Colombia and South American as a whole.

● **Shopping**
Best buys Emeralds in Bogotá; handworked silver (excellent); Indian pottery and textiles. The state-run Artesanías de Colombia for craft work (see under Bogotá). In Antioquia buy the handbag – *carriel antioqueño* – traditionally made from otter skin, but nowadays from calf skin and plastic trimmed at that. At Cartagena crude rubber is moulded into little dyed figurines: odd but attractive. Clothing and shoes are cheap in Medellín. The Colombian *ruana* (poncho) is attractive and warm in any cool climate, and comes in a wide variety of colours; it may, however, be cheaper in Ecuador. Silver and gold work is cheaper than in Peru. Good duty-free shop at Bogotá airport. Leatherwork is generally good and not expensive especially in southern Colombia.

● **Tipping**
Upmarket restaurants 10%. Porters, cloakroom attendants, hairdressers and barbers, US$0.05-0.25. Taxi-drivers are not normally tipped.

● **Voltage**
120 volts AC, is general for Colombia. Transformer must be 110-150 volt AC, with flat-prong plugs (all of same size). Be careful with electrically heated showers. A good torch is rec for use during power cuts.

● **Weights and measures**
Weights and measures are metric, and weights should always be quoted in kilograms. Litres are used for liquid measures but US gallons are standard for the petroleum industry. Linear measures are usually metric, but the inch is quite commonly used by engineers and the yard on golf courses. For land measurement the hectare and cubic metre are officially employed but the traditional measures *vara* (80 centimetres) and *fanegada* (1,000 square *varas*) are still in common use. As in many other countries food etc is often sold in *libras* (pounds), which are equivalent to $\frac{1}{2}$ kilo.

Where to stay

● **Hotels**
The more expensive hotels and restaurants add on 14% VAT (IVA), but not on San Andrés. Some hotels add a small insurance charge. On 15 Dec, hotels in main holiday centres may increase prices by 20-30%. Food is not expensive. A good lunch costs about US$5-6. In the smaller cities and towns, hotels often have the best restaurants, but you can find the same quality on the outskirts at a better price. A restaurant meal that business people might give to prospective customers would cost from US$6 to US$12 pp. In many hotels outside the main cities you can only stay (very cheaply) at *en pension* rates and no allowance is made for missing a meal. The Colombian tourist office has lists of authorized prices for all hotels which can be at least a year out of date, especially in 1995 when prices were rising quickly in peso terms. If you are overcharged the tourist office will arrange a refund. Most hotels in Colombia charge US$1 to US$6 for extra beds for children, up to a maximum (usually) of 4 beds/room. On the Caribbean coast and San Andrés and Providencia, high season is 15 Dec-30 April, 15 June-31 Aug. Although most hotels, except the very cheapest, offer private WC and shower as a matter of course, hot water often comes only in the more expensive hotels or in colder zones. Wash basin plugs are universally in short supply and hotel plumbing is not a Colombian speciality. Prices are normally displayed at reception, but in quiet periods it is always worth negotiating.

● **Camping**
Sites are given in the text. Colombian Tourist Office has a list of official sites, but they are seldom signposted on main roads, so can be hard to find. Permission to camp with tent, camper van or car is readily granted by landowners in less populated areas. Those in

camper vans may camp by the roadside, but it is neither particularly safe, nor easy to find a secluded spot. Vehicles may camp at truck drivers' restaurants.

Colombia is one of the few countries which sell 'white gas' for camping stoves etc, so stock up here.

Food and drink

Food

Colombia's food is very regional; it is quite difficult to buy in Medellín, say, a dish you particularly liked in Bogotá. Restaurants in smaller towns often close on Sun, and early on weekday evenings: if stuck, you will probably find something to eat near the bus station. If you are economizing, ask for the *plato del día* or *plato corriente* (dish of the day).

Locro de choclos is a potato and maize soup so rich and nourishing that, with salad and coffee, it would make a meal in itself. Colombia has its own variant of the inevitable *arroz con pollo* (chicken and rice) which is excellent. For a change *pollo en salsa de mostaza* (chicken in mustard sauce) is rec. *Ajiaco de pollo* is a delicious chicken, maize, manioc, cabbage and potato stew served with cream and capers, and lumps of avocado; it is a Bogotá speciality; another Bogotá speciality is *sobrebarriga* (belly of beef). *Bandeja antioqueña* costs US$3 in most places and consists of meat grilled and served with rice, beans, potato, manioc and a green salad; the simpler *carne asada* may be had for as little as US$2. *Mazamorra*, boiled maize in milk, is a typical *antioqueño* sweet, and so is *salpicón*, a tropical fruit salad. *Lechona* (sucking pig and herbs) is a speciality of Ibagué. Cartagena's rice with coconut can be compared with rice *a la valenciana*. In Nariño, guinea pig (*cuy*, *curí* or *conejillo de Indias*) is typical. *Tamales* are meat pies made by folding a maize dough round chopped pork mixed with potato, peas, onions, eggs and olives seasoned with garlic, cloves and paprika, and steaming the whole in banana leaves (which you don't eat); the best are from Tolima. A baked dish of squash, beaten eggs and seafood covered with sauce is known as the *soufflé de calabaza*. *Magras* is a typical Colombian dish of eggs and chicken baked together and served with a tomato sauce. *Sancocho* is a filling combination of all the tuberous vegetables, including the tropical cassava and yam, with chopped fresh fish or any kind of meat, possibly chicken. From stalls in the capital and the countryside, try *mazorcas* (roast maize cobs) or *arepas* (fried maize cakes). On the Caribbean coast, eat an egg *empanada*, which consists of two layers of corn (maize) dough that open like an oyster-shell, fried with eggs in the middle, and try the *patacón*, a cake of mashed and baked plantain (green banana). *Huevos pericos*, eggs scrambled with onions and tomatoes, are a popular, cheap and nourishing snack – available almost anywhere. *Pandebono*, cheese-flavoured bread is delicious. A good local sweet is the *canastas de coco*: pastry containing coconut custard flavoured with wine and surmounted by meringue. *Arequipe* is very similar to fudge, and popular (it is called *manjarblanco* in other parts of South America). *Almojábanas*, a kind of sour-milk bread roll, are delicious if fresh: 'one day old and they are a disaster'. There is, indeed, quite an assortment of little fruit pasties and preserves. Then there are the usual fruits: bananas, oranges, mangoes, avocado pears, and (at least in the tropical zones) *chirimoyas*, *papayas*, and the delicious *pitahaya*, taken either as an appetizer or dessert and, for the wise, in moderation, because even a little of it has a laxative effect. Other fruits such as the *guayaba* (guava), *guanábana* (soursop), *maracuyá* (passion fruit), *lulo* (naranjilla), *mora* (blackberry) and *curuba* (banana passion fruit) make delicious juices, sometimes with milk added to make a *sorbete* – though *sorbetes* are best left alone unless you are satisfied the milk is fresh. Fruit yoghurts are nourishing and cheap (try *Alpina* brand; *crema* style is best). *Tinto*, the national small cup of black coffee, is taken ritually at all hours. Colombian coffee is always mild. (Coffee with milk is called *café perico*; *café con leche* is a mug of milk with coffee added.) *Agua de panela* is a common beverage (hot water with unrefined sugar), also made with limes, milk, or cheese.

Drink

Many acceptable brands of beer are produced, until recently almost all produced by the Bavaria group. However, in January 1995, a new brand, Leona, appeared, brewed by a rival drinks group, appropriately accompanied on the same day by an earthquake that shook Bogotá. It has quickly become popular. The local rum is good and cheap; ask for *ron*, not *aguardiente*, because in Colombia the latter word is used for a popular drink containing aniseed (*aguardiente anisado*). Try *canelazo* – cold or hot rum with water, sugar, lime and cinnamon. Local table wines include Santo Tomás; none is very good. Wine is normally about US$3.50-4.50 in restaurants for an acceptable bottle of Chilean or Argentine; European wines are very expensive.

Warning Great care should be exercised when buying imported spirits in shops. It has been reported that bottles bearing well-known labels have often been 'recycled' and contain a cheap and poor imitation of the original contents. This can be dangerous to the health, and travellers are warned to stick to beer and rum. Also note that ice is usually not made from potable water.

Getting around

Air transport

Internal air services are flown principally by Avianca, SAM, Aces, Aires, Satena and Intercontinental. They serve the whole country, the larger towns and cities receiving flights usually daily, the smaller places perhaps only once a week. Avianca offers a round ticket (*Conozca a Colombia*) giving unlimited domestic travel for 21 days on Avianca, Aires or SAM; conditions are that it allows up to five stops, it must be bought outside Colombia in conjunction with an international air ticket, children up to 12 pay 67%, infants 10%, the Air Pass is non-refundable unless the whole has been unused, one may not pass through each city more than once (except for transfers), and a proposed itinerary (not firm) must be submitted when buying the ticket (Leticia and San Andrés may be included). Prices are determined by high season (Jun – end Aug, 1-31 Dec), or low season (rest of year): Air Pass 1 is open to all nationalities including Colombians legally resident abroad, passengers must fly Avianca transatlantic, US$280 (high), US$250 (low) for 5 stops, with the option to add 3 extra coupons at US$40 each. With Air Pass 2 (which is not available to Colombians), any transatlantic carrier may be used, US$529 (high), US$499 (low) for 5 stops, plus US$40 for extra coupons, max 3. The Airpasses are also available without Leticia and San Andrés: Air Pass 1 US$190 (high). US$170 (low); Air Pass 2 US$409 (high), US$389 (low). These prices and conditions change from time to time, enquire at any Avianca office. For single flights, the army airline Satena tends to be cheaper than Avianca. Avianca's domestic shuttle flights (Puente Aéreo) go from Bogotá to Medellín/Montería, Cali/Pasto and Barranquilla. It is best to book a ticket as for an ordinary flight: just turning up will involve a long wait. Ask about discount fares which may be available on certain days of the week. Stand-by tickets are available to Barranquilla, Cali, Medellín; known as PET, *pasajero en turno*. Domestic airports are good, though the tourist facilities tend to close early on weekdays, and all Sun. All airports levy a US$4.25 tax, payable when you buy your ticket or before issue of a boarding pass. In-flight service and airline services on the ground tend to be poor. Security checks tend to be thorough, watch your luggage. Note, SAM does not accept Mastercard; Avianca does.

Land transport

● **Bus**
Travel in Colombia is far from dull. The scenery is generally worth seeing so travel by day if possible: it is also safer and you can keep a better eye on your valuables. There have been increasing reports of robberies of night buses in the S of Colombia. On main routes you usually have choice of company and of type of bus. The cheapest (*corriente*) are basically local buses, stopping frequently, uncomfortable and slow but offering plenty of local colour. Try to keep your luggage with you. *Pullman* (each company will have a different name for the service) are long distance buses usually with a/c, toilets, hostess service, videos (almost always violent films, Spanish/Mexican or dubbed English) and limited stop. Be prepared for lack of a/c and locked windows. Sit near the back with your walkman to avoid the video and the need to keep the blinds down. Luggage is normally carried in a locked compartment against receipt. *Colectivos*, also known as *vans* or *busetas*, run by Velotax, Taxis Verdes, etc are usually 12-20 seat vehicles, maybe with a/c, rather cramped but fast, saving several hours on long journeys. You can keep your eye on luggage in the back of the van. Fares shown in the text are middle of the range where there is a choice but are no more than a guide. If you have time and a tight budget, shop around for your appropriate service. Breakdowns are many. Note that meal stops can be few and far between, and short; bring your own food. Be prepared for climatic changes on longer routes. If you entrust your luggage to the bus companies' luggage rooms, remember to load it on to the bus yourself; it will not be done automatically. There are few interdepartmental bus services on holidays. Always take your passport (or photocopy) with you: identity checks on buses are frequent.

● **Motoring**
Roads are given in the text. Motor fuel: 'premium' 95 octane (only in large cities), about US$1.30/US gallon; 'corriente' 84 octane,

US$0.84/US gallon. All gasoline is lead free. Diesel US$0.52. Roads are not always sign-posted. If driving yourself, avoid night jour-neys; vehicles may be unlighted and it can be dangerous. The roads are often in poor con-dition, lorry- and bus-drivers tend to be reck-less, and stray animals are often encountered. Police checks are frequent in troubled areas, keep your documents handy. There are fre-quent tolls, normally US$1.50 per car, more for larger vehicles. Between Bogotá and Cali, for example, 9 tolls = US$13.50. Motorcycles and bicycles don't have to pay. In town, try to leave your car in an attended car park (*par-queadero*), especially at night. If you are plan-ning to sleep in your car, it is better to stop in a *parqueadero*; you will be charged a little extra. In many guarded carparks, only the driver is allowed in; passengers must get out at the entrance. Alternatively, find a police station and ask to sleep in your car nearby. You can also stay overnight in *balnearios campestres*, which normally have armed guards.

National driving licences may be used by foreigners in Colombia, but must be accom-panied by an official translation if in a lan-guage other than Spanish. International drivers licences are also accepted. To bring a car into Colombia, you must also have docu-ments proving ownership of the vehicle, and a tourist card/transit visa. These are normally valid for 90 days and must be applied for at the Colombian consulate in the country which you will be leaving for Colombia. Only third-party insurance issued by a Colombian company is valid, cost around US$70; there are agencies in all ports. According to a law of 31 December 1992, if you do not have a *carnet de passages* (see **Motoring** in **Intro-duction and Hints**) you have to pay a bond worth 10% of the value of your vehicle when bringing a car into Colombia. This will be stamped into your passport. Entering the country with a *carnet* is a lot quicker than without. Carry driving documents with you at all times.

Spare parts are plentiful for Renault cars, which are assembled in Colombia.

● **Car hire**
Car hire is very expensive in Colombia. Even if you are paying in cash, a credit card may be asked for as proof of identity (Visa, Master-card, American Express), in addition to pass-port and driver's licence. Main international car rental companies are represented at prin-cipal airports but may be closed Sat pm and Sun.

● **Cycling**
Cycling is popular in Colombia, many about at weekends including race and mountain-cy-cles. There are good shops for spares in all big cities, though the new standard 622/700 size touring wheel size is not very common. Take your own spare tyres. Recommended is *Bici-cletas de Montaña*, C 23, No 43A-121, Medellín. There have been many reports of muggings of cyclists in the Caribbean coastal area.

● **Hitchhiking**
Hitchhiking (*autostop*) seems to be quite easy in Colombia, especially if you can enlist the co-operation of the highway police check-points outside each town and toll booths. Truck-drivers are often very friendly, but be careful of private cars with more than one person inside, especially if you are travelling on your own; they may be unmarked taxis.

● **Motorcycles**
Bringing a bike in by land only takes a few minutes. Bringing a bike by sea may require up to 3 days to clear customs, with costs of up to US$50; passport and shipping docu-ments required (but **see p 827** for new ferry service from Panama). Shippers charge by cubic metre, so knock the bike down to use as little space as possible. By air from Panama one cargo carrier that will carry bikes is Chal-lenge Air Cargo (CAC): US$150 for a 200 kg bike, pallet system, good service. Copa's rate for a motorcycle Panama-Cartagena (1994) was US$0.52/kg up to 300 kg, US$0.64/kg 300-500 kg, plus tax of US$17-19 pp and US$137 pp airfare. You must drain the fuel, oil and battery acid. Remove anything break-able and tape cardboard over fragile bits. Insist on loading the machine yourself. Most people have to go to Customs at the port to get permission for the bike to be released. If you bring a bike in by air to Bogotá, try to stay as close as possible to it while it is cleared through freight forwarders (eg Cosimex) and the Customs, to save time and damage. Entry charges for a motorcycle totalled US$37.50 (1993). You can also airfreight from Guate-mala by SAM via San Andrés. A *carnet de passage* is strongly advised (see above). At Bogotá airport, you can have it stamped and be through in 2 hrs. Otherwise you must go to the *Aduana Nacional* in Calle 68 to com-plete formalities. Parking at night can be a problem, but some hotels listed have patios or their own lock up garages nearby. Other-wise use *parqueadores* (see **Motoring** above). Local insurance costs around US$30 for a bike over 200 cc. You may find that wearing helmets is inadvisable in trouble

spots, eg Medellín; take advice. Spare parts, tyres, etc readily available in Colombia for Yamaha XT and Honda XL models (although supplies are less good for models over 500 cc), so Colombia is a suitable country for rebuilding a bike on a long trip. Medellín is the best place for spare parts. BMW, Triumph spares sold by Germán Villegas Arango, Calle 1 B, No 11A-43, Bogotá, T 289-4399.

● **Taxis**
Whenever possible, take a taxi with a meter, and ensure that it is switched on, otherwise you will be overcharged. Recent reports suggest that meters are in disuse in some cities, in which case bargain and fix a price. All taxis are obliged to display the additional legal tariffs that may be charged after 2000, on Sun and fiestas. Don't take a taxi which is old; look for 'Servicio Público' on the side. There is a small surcharge for Radio Taxis, but they normally offer reliable service. The dispatcher will give you the cab's number which should be noted in case of irregularities. Women do not travel alone in taxis at night. If the taxi 'breaks down', take your luggage out if you are asked to push, or let the driver push; it may be a trick to separate you from your luggage.

Communications

● **Newspapers**
Bogotá: *El Tiempo, El Espectador* (both Liberal); *La República* and *La Prensa* (Conservative), *El Siglo* (extreme Conservative). Medellín: *El Mundo, El Colombiano;* Cali: *El País, Occidente, El Pueblo,* all major cities have daily papers. Magazines are partisan, best is probably *La Semana.* US and European papers can be bought at Drugstore Internacional, Cra 10, No 26-71, just N of *Tequendama Hotel* in Bogotá and at *Librería Oma,* Cra 15, No 82-58. *Colombian Post,* twice weekly in English, available in Bogotá.

● **Postal services**
There are two parallel postal systems, **Avianca**, operated by the national airline, and **Correos de Colombia**, the post office proper. Both have offices in all major cities, but only Correos can be found in small towns and rural areas. Both will accept mail for all destinations. Prices are identical for overseas airmail (which is carried by Avianca in any event), but Correos is much more economical, and can be more efficient, for internal service. Send all letters by airmail; there was reported to be no surface mail for overseas in 1992. Anything of importance should be registered. Avianca controls all airmail services and has

offices in provincial cities. Correspondence with UK is reported to be good. It costs US$0.95 to send a letter or postcard to the US, or Europe; a 1 kg package to Europe costs US$13 by air (Avianca). Note that the Amex agent, Tierra Mar Aire, does (1993) accept mail to be held for Amex customers.

● **Radio**
English language station, Radio International 610, on 610 kHz Medium Wave, with news at 0600 weekdays.

● **Telephone services**
Telephone systems have been automated; the larger towns are interconnected. Inter-city calls must be made from Telecom offices unless you have access to a private phone. Long-distance pay 'phones are located outside most Telecom offices, also at bus stations and airports. They take 50 peso coins. 5 peso coins are needed for ordinary 'phones, which also take 20 peso coins. From the larger towns it is possible to telephone to Canada, the USA, the UK, and to several of the Latin American republics. International phone charges are high (about US$7 for 3 mins to USA, US$8 to Europe, US$12 to Australia) but there is a 20% discount on Sun and sometimes less in the evening. A deposit is required before the call is made which can vary between US$18 and US$36, US$1 is charged if no reply, for person-to-person add an extra minute's charge to Canada, 2 mins' to UK; all extra minutes' conversation costs ⅓ more. The best value is to purchase a phone card and dial direct yourself. Canada Direct is 980-19-0057 and for the UK, 980-44-0057. Other collect, or reversed-charge, telephone calls can be made from El Dorado airport (enquire) but otherwise are only possible from private telephones; make sure the operator understands what is involved or you may be billed in any case. It is also possible that the operator, once you have got through to him/her, may not call you back. The surest way of contacting home, assuming the facilities are available either end, is to Fax your hotel phone number to home, and ask them to call you. This will almost certainly be cheaper. Fax to Europe costs US$6.50/page, but is almost double this from hotels.

Telecommunications Empresa Nacional de Telecomunicaciones has offices in all main cities.

Sport

The game of *tejo* is still played in Cundinamarca, Boyacá and Tolima. In Pasto and Popayán it is played under the name of *sapo* (toad). This is the Spanish *juego de la rana*, in which a small quoit has to be thrown from an improbable distance into a metal frog's mouth. There are bullrings at Bogotá, Cali, Manizales, Medellín, Sincelejo and Cerete. Polo is played at Medellín and Bogotá. Most of the larger towns have stadia. Association football is the most popular game and is of high quality, especially in Cali and Medellín. American baseball is played at Cartagena and Barranquilla. Cockfights, cycling, boxing and basketball are also popular.

Fishing is particularly good at Girardot, Santa Marta, and Barranquilla; marlin is fished off Barranquilla. There is good trout fishing, in season, in the lakes in the Bogotá area, particularly at Lago Tota, in the mountains.

● **Climbing**
For information ask at the Federación Colombiana de Montañismo, Cra 28, No 25-18, piso 3, Bogotá, President: Mauricio Afanador, who can also be contacted at *Café y Crepes* (see Bogotá, **Restaurants**). Maps can be obtained at the Instituto Geográfico (see under Bogotá, **Maps**). If you have a guide or are invited on a mountain tour, make certain costs/charges are clear before you start. For specific area details, see under Sierra Nevada del Cocuy, Valledupar, Ibagué, Manizales and Pereira. If you intend to climb, bring all your own equipment. It may be impossible to find easily in Colombia, eg compass. Some equipment available at *Almacén Aventura*, Cra 13, No 67-26, Bogotá, T 248-1679, F 201-9543, rope, boots etc; *Deportivos del Campo*, C 64, No 18-15, Bogotá, T 248-1855, F 217-4756, tents, mattresses etc, mostly imported. Light equipment, rucksacks etc of reasonable quality, can be bought in markets.

Holidays and festivals

Public Holidays are on the following days: 1 Jan: Circumcision of our Lord; 6 Jan: Epiphany*; 19 Mar: St Joseph*; Maundy Thur; Good Fri; 1 May: Labour Day; Ascension Day*; Corpus Christi*; Sacred Heart*; 29 Jun: SS Peter and Paul*; 20 Jul: Independence Day; 7 Aug: Battle of Boyacá; 15 Aug: Assumption*; 12 Oct: Columbus' arrival in America*; 1 Nov: All Saints' day*; 11 Nov: Independence of Cartagena*; 8 Dec: Immaculate Conception; 25 Dec: Christmas Day. When those marked with an asterisk do not fall on a Mon, or when they fall on a Sun, they will be moved to the following Mon.

Further reading

A brief, introductory selection: John Hemming, *The Search for Eldorado*; Alexandre von Humboldt, *Travels*. For an account of travelling in modern Colombia, Charles Nicholl's *The Fruit Palace* is highly recommended. For birdwatchers, *A Guide to the Birds of Colombia*, by Steven Hilty and William Brown, is recommended. Colombian literature: Jorge Isaacs, *María* (1867); José Eustacio Rivera, *La Vorágine (The Vortex*, 1924); and, of course, the novels and short stories of Gabriel García Márquez. British business travellers should consult 'Hints to Exporters: Colombia', from DTI Export Publications, PO Box 55, Stratford-upon-Avon, Warwickshire, CV37 9GE. Similar US publications may be obtained from the Department of Commerce, Washington, DC. Also, *Colombian News Letter*, published monthly by the Colombian American Association Inc, 150 Nassau Street, New York, NY 10038.

Acknowledgements

This section has been updated with the welcome assistance of Peter Pollard, who visited Colombia in January 1995. Peter would like to thank especially Joaquín Emilio García (San Agustín) and the staff of the tourist office in Popayán for their help. We are most grateful to the following travellers: Daniel Aeberhard (Slough, UK) an excellent contribution, Jimmy Andersson and Christina Gustafson (Malmo, Sweden), Jens Arnold (Borken, Germany), Louise Bach (Vestbjerg) and Tine Tang Kleif (Aarhus, Denmark), Andrew Barber (Saratoga, USA), Trevor Berryman (Roseville, Australia), Dagmar Binder (Berlin, Germany), Dave Blackburn (Luton, UK) and Emily Smith (North Carolina, USA), Claudia Böohler and Frank Busch (Berlin, Germany), Colette and Tanya Botha (South Africa), Wim Van Brempt (Mortsel, Belgium), Jim and June Campbell (White Lake, Canada), Ludovic Challeat (Lamastre, France), Etienne Claes (Brugge, Belgium), Bernard Cloutier (Montreal, Canada), Mark Collins (Bristol, UK), Arthur Cremers (Amsterdam, The Netherlands), the late Bernard van der Dool (Leiden, The Netherlands), James Elder (Goulburn, Australia), Jakob Engström and Richard Björlin (Brussels, Belgium), Nadja Ernst (Voorburg, Holland), Valerie Fraser and Tim Butler (Lima, Peru) many long and informative letters, Patrick Ganahl (Wolfhausen, Switzerland), Martina Gebhard (Immenstadt, Germany), Helene Keur and Geert Klein Geltink (Zwolle, The Netherlands), Fred Van Gestel (Deurne, Belgium), Loukas

Grafakos (Papagou, Greece), Matt Griffin (Seattle, USA), Steve Grist (Santiago, Chile), Erez Guilatt (Jerusalem, Israel), Sietse de Haan and TTruas Koppers (Aruba), Emma Collingwood and Jim Hart (Edinburgh, UK), Kjetil Haugan (Ottestad, Norway), Ralf Hauser (Zurich, Switzerland), Hans Hermes (Steinheim, Germany), John Hibberd (Hampton, UK), Terry Higgins (Perth, Australia), Vetle Houg (Oslo, Norway), Marten H Jacobsen and Brit R Lauritsen (Denmark), Patrick J Paludan (Valby) and Erik Hassenkamm (Valby and Skanderberg, Denmark), Sonja Jovanovic and Andrew Thompson (London, UK) a helpful letter Hielke Keikke (Breda, Holland), Christoph Lanfer (Puchheim, Germany), Mark Laptin (London, UK), Richard Leuwin (Antigua, Guatemala), Riika Levoranta (Vammala) and Vesa Lampiner (Möjärvi, Finland), Valerie Levrier (London, UK), Dr R Liersch (Lohmar, Germany), Eva Maceroni and Thomas Buschor (Altstätten, Switzerland), Robert E Manley (Cincinnati, USA) a very helpful letter, Helmut Matuly (Frankfurt, Germany), Eva Maurer (Tübingen, Germany), Claire Mortimer (Exeter, UK), Helmut Moser (Zell am See, Austria), Martijn Mugge (Enschede, The Netherlands), Mark Muhlbacher (Lucerne, Switzerland) for many letters Frank Müller (Hannover, Germany), Elaine Koviacs & Russell Murdoch (Christchurch, UK), Don Nafziger (Kamloops, Canada), Robert Neisen (Frieburg, Germany), Annesofie Nielsen (Niva, Denmark), Paul Olai-Olssen (Oslo, Norway), Tina Ortmanns and Patrick Laschet (Aachen, Germany), Richard Osborne (New Zealand) and Nathalie Bélanger (Canada), Jonathan Paisner (London, UK), Lawrence Railton and Susan Boyd (London, UK), Sophie & George Redman (Oxford, UK), Michael Resch (Hallein, Austria), Graciela Romero and Steve Norris (Bogotá, Colombia), Barbara and Peter Roniger (Suberg, Switzerland), Timothy Ross (Colombia), Andy Ryder (Vienna, Austria), Burkhard Schack and Michael Zickgraf (Seelbach, Germany), Inge and Machiel de Schutter (Cologne, Germany), The Schweers (somewhere in Colombia), Mandy Scott (Edinburgh, UK), John Servayge (Vichte, Belgium), Ayla S Sevim (Izmir, Turkey), Grant Smith (Bogotá, Colombia), N B Stalker (Cambridge, UK), Brigitte Steimen and Mathias Becker (Meriken, Switzerland), Rob Stanley (Toronto, Canada), Jan Stüve (Karlsruhe, Germany), Roman Stutz and Andrea Schmidiger (Marstetten and Willisan, Switzerland), S Nielsen and Hellmuth-Chr Stuven (Copenhagen, Denmark), Mette and Lotte Thillerup (Hesselager, Denmark), Stefan Tiedeken (Munich, Germany), A.ndrios Tieleman and Ditty Bakker (Haarlem, The Netherlands), Inger Tingsgard (Abyhoj, Denmark), Barbara and Gabriel Toffani (Chatou, France), Dino de Toffol (San Tomaso Agordino, Italy), Valerie A Valene (Manhattan Beach, USA), Margot Verhagen and Carel van der Velden (Holland), Peter Waanders (Arnhem, The Netherlands) helpful details, Rupert A E Walker (Salisbury, UK), Sara and Charlie Warshawski (London, UK), David Weatherley (London, UK), Pierre-André Widmer (Céligny, Switzerland), Christian Leonards and Sandra Winterhalter (Insel Reichenau, Germany), Rowan Wood (Aspen, USA), and Dan Workman (Yellowknife, Canada).

ECUADOR

INTRODUCTION

ECUADOR, named after its position on the equator, is bounded by Colombia to the N, Peru to the E and S and the Pacific Ocean to the W. In area it is the second smallest republic in South America.

The Andes, running from the Colombian border in the N to the borders of Peru in the S, form a mountainous backbone to the country. There are two main ranges, the Central Cordillera and the Western Cordillera, separated by a 400-km long trough, the Central Valley, whose rims are from 40 to 65 km apart. The rims are joined together, like the two sides of a ladder, by hilly rungs, and between each pair of rungs lies an intermont basin with a dense cluster of population. These basins are drained by rivers which cut through the rims to run either W to the Pacific or E to join the Amazon. The whole mountain area is known as the Sierra.

Both rims of the Central Valley are lined with the cones of more than thirty volcanoes. Several of them have long been extinct, for example, Chimborazo, the highest (6,310m), Cayambe (5,790m), standing directly on the equator, Illiniza (5,263m), Altar (5,319m) and Carihuairazo (5,146m). At least eight, however, are still active; Cotopaxi (5,897m), which had several violent eruptions in the nineteenth century; Tungurahua (5,016m), which had a major eruption early this century; Antisana (5,704m), which showed signs of activity in the 1960s; Pichincha (4,794m), which vents fumes and steam through its west-facing crater, and Sangay (5,230m) one of the world's most active volcanoes, continuously emitting fumes and ash. Nowadays all the main peaks except for Altar and Sangay, which are less accessible, are climbed fairly regularly.

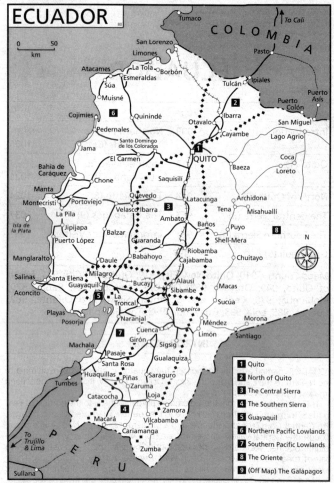

East of the Central Cordillera the forest-clad mountains fall sharply to a chain of foothills (the Eastern Cordillera) and then the jungle—the Oriente—through which meander the tributaries of the Amazon. This E lowland region makes up 36% of Ecuador's total territory, but is only sparsely populated by native Indians and agricultural colonists from the highlands. In total, the region has only 5% of the national population, but colonization is now proceeding rapidly owing to population pressure and in the wake of an oil boom. There are substantial oil reserves in the N Oriente near the Colombian border, and exports began in 1972.

Between the Western Cordillera and the Pacific lies the coastal alluvial plain, the Costa, 685 km from N to S and some 100 km wide. It is from this area that Ecuador draws the majority of its agricultural products for export. Guayaquil, the main city of this region, is 464 km from the capital, Quito, which lies high in a N intermont basin.

The Sierra There are altogether ten intermont basins strung along the Sierra from N to S. There is little variation by day or by season in the temperature in any particular basin: temperature depends on altitude. The basins lie at an elevation of between 1,800 and 3,000m, and the range of shade temperature is from 6°C to 10°C in the morning to 19°C to 23°C in the afternoon. Temperatures can get considerably higher in the lower basins. There is one rainy season, from Oct to May, when the average fall in Quito is 1,270 mm; the skies are mostly cloudy or overcast at this time and there are frequent rainfalls during the afternoons and nights. Over half the area is now grassy land on which cattle and sheep are raised and subsistence crops grown. What crops are grown is determined by altitude, the hardiest of them being the potato. The intermont basins produce livestock, poultry, wheat, barley, oats, maize, quinoa, fruit and vegetables, some of which find their way down to the coastal plain.

Some 47% of the people of Ecuador live in the central trough of the Andes, and the majority are pure Indians. Most of the land is held in large private estates worked by the Indians, but some of it is held by Indian communities. With the limited application of an agrarian-reform programme, the *huasipungo* system whereby Indians were virtual slaves on the big highland *haciendas* has all but disappeared and co-operatives are proliferating. Though many Indian communities live at subsistence level and remain isolated from national centres, others have developed good markets for products using traditional skills in embroidery, pottery, jewellery, knitting, weaving, and carving.

The Costa Most of the Costa region is lowland at an altitude of less than 300m, apart from a belt of hilly land which runs NW from Guayaquil to the coast, where it turns N and runs parallel to the shore to Esmeraldas. In the extreme N there are two rainy seasons, as in Colombia, and a typical tropical rain forest. But the two rainy seasons soon merge into one, running from Dec to June. Further S, the later the rains begin, the sooner they end: at Guayaquil the rains normally fall between Jan and April. The forests thin out too in the more S lowlands, and give way to thorn and savanna. The Santa Elena Peninsula and the SW coast near Peru have little or no rainfall. During the dry season, May-Nov, the coast from Punta Blanca to Puerto López (provinces of Guayas and Manabí) is subject to mists (garúa) and cool grey days.

The main agricultural exports come from a small area of lowland to the SE and N of Guayaquil. It lies between the coastal hills and the Andes; rains are heavy, the temperature and the humidity high: ideal conditions for the growth of tropical crops. One part of this Guayas lowland is subject to floods from the four rivers which traverse it: bananas, normally accounting for half the exports of the lowland, are grown here, as well as rice. Cacao too is farmed on the natural levees of this flood plain, but the main crop comes from the alluvial fans at the foot of the mountains rising out of the plain. High on these same alluvial fans excellent coffee is also grown; cacao, bananas, coffee and sugar, whether processed or unprocessed, are about 30% of the exports by value. Cotton is developing. A major activity now is shrimp farming, which has greatly altered the coastal landscape in some areas and harmed mangroves. Nevertheless, the industry is a major employer and foreign exchange earner. Add to this that the Guayas lowland is a great cattle-fattening area in the dry season, and its importance in the national economy becomes obvious. A good network of paved roads now links Guayaquil with the major zones of agricultural production, and the once thriving river-ports have now declined. Along the N coast, the main areas of population are at Esmeraldas, along the highways inland, in the irrigated lands of N Manabí, and near Manta, Montecristi, and Jipijapa.

Two areas of the coastlands have experienced spectacular rises in population and agricultural production: El Oro Province in the extreme S, centred on the town of Machala, and the Quevedo-Santo Domingo zone along the Andean fringe to the N of Guayaquil. In both areas, highland settlers have mixed with coastal entrepreneurs to produce a particularly progressive agriculture. Irrigation in El Oro has produced a thriving zone of very intensive banana plantations. In the Quevedo-Santo Domingo area, large areas of forest have been cleared; bananas used to be the main crop, but have been replaced by African palm. Further N, in Esmeraldas Province, there still remain areas of land which could be cleared and developed for farming, although the fertility of this zone is reputedly much lower than that of the Quevedo, Guayaquil and Machala areas.

History The Incas of Peru, with their capital at Cuzco, began to conquer the Sierra of Ecuador, already densely populated, towards the middle of the 15th century. A road was built between Cuzco and Quito, and the empire was ruled after the death of the Inca Huayna Capac by his two sons, Huáscar at Cuzco and Atahualpa at Quito. Pizarro's main Peruvian expedition took place in 1532, when there was civil war between the two brothers. Atahualpa, who had won the war, was put to death by Pizarro in 1533, and the Inca empire collapsed.

Pizarro claimed the N kingdom of Quito, and his lieutenants Sebastián de Benalcázar (also Belalcázar) and Diego de Almagro took the city in 1534. Pizarro founded Lima in 1535 as capital of the whole region, and four years later replaced Benalcázar at Quito for Gonzalo, his brother. Gonzalo later set out on the exploration of the Oriente. He moved down the Napo river, and sent Francisco de Orellana to prospect. Orellana did not return: he drifted down the river finally to reach the mouth of the Amazon: the first white man to cross the continent in this way.

Quito became an *audiencia* under the Viceroy of Peru. For the next 280 years Ecuador reluctantly accepted the new ways brought by the conqueror. Gonzalo had already introduced pigs and cattle; wheat was now added. The Indians were Christianized, colonial laws and customs and ideas introduced. The marriage of the arts of Spain to those of the Incas led to a remarkable efflorescence of painting, sculpting and building at Quito. In the 18th century black slave labour was brought in to work the plantations near the coast.

There was an abortive attempt at independence in the strongly garrisoned capital in 1809, but it was not until 1822 that Sucre, moving N from Guayaquil, defeated the Spanish at Pichincha and occupied Quito. Soon afterwards Bolívar arrived, and Ecuador was induced to join the Venezuelan and Colombian confederation, the Gran Colombia of Bolívar's dream. On 26 and 27 July 1822, Bolívar met San Martín, fresh from liberating Lima, at Guayaquil. What happened at that mysterious encounter is not known, but San Martín left it silently for a self-imposed exile in France. Venezuela separated itself from Gran Colombia in 1829, and Ecuador decided on complete independence in August 1830, under the presidency of Juan Flores.

Ecuador's 19th century history was a continuous struggle between pro-Church conservatives and anti-Church (but none the less devotedly Catholic) liberals. There were also long periods of military rule from 1895, when the liberal General Eloy Alfaro took power. During the late 1940s and the 1950s there was a prolonged period of prosperity (through bananas, largely) and constitutional rule, but the more typical pattern of alternating civilian and military governments was resumed in the 1960s and 1970s. Apart from the liberal-conservative struggles, there has been long-lasting rivalry between Quito and the Sierra on one hand and Guayaquil and the Costa on the other.

The country's E jungle territory has been reduced from that of the old Audiencia of Quito by gradual Colombian and especially Peruvian infiltration, which means that the country's official claim to be a "país amazónico" has little relation to present reality. This process reached an acute phase in 1941 when war broke out with Peru; the war ended with military defeat for Ecuador and the signing of the Rio de Janeiro Protocol of 1942 which allotted most of the disputed territory to Peru. Since 1960 Ecuador has denounced the Protocol as unjust (because it was imposed by force of arms) and as technically flawed (becuase it refers to certain non-existent geographic features), hence unimplementable. The country's official policy remains the recovery of a sovereign access to the Amazon. Sporadic border skirmishes continued throughout recent decades and in January 1995 these escalated into an undeclared war over control of the headwaters of the Río Cenepa, an area where the frontier had never been clearly established. Argentina, Brazil, Chile and the USA (guarantors of the Rio de Janeiro Protocol) intervened diplomatically and a ceasefire took effect after 6 weeks of combat, during which both sides made conflicting claims of military success. A multinational team of observers was dispatched to the region in March 1995 to oversee the disengagement of forces and subsequent demilitarization of the area of the conflict.

Following seven years of military rule, the first presidential elections under a new constitution were held in 1979. They were won by Jaime Roldós Aguilera, whose government began a policy of gradual reforms. President Roldós was killed in an air crash in 1981 and was succeeded by Vice-president Oswaldo Hurtado Larrea. In the next three presidential elections power oscillated between the centre-right and centre-left with conservative León Febres Cordero of the Partido Social Cristiano (PSC) being elected in 1984 followed by Rodrigo Borja Cevallos of the Izquierda Democrática(Democratic Left) in 1988 and Sixto Durán Ballén of the Partido de Unidad Republicana in coalition with Alberto Dahik of the Partido Conservador (who became vice-president) in 1992.

The popularity of President Durán Ballén's government declined steadily with the implementation of an economic modernization programme aimed at reducing inflation and replenishing foreign reserves by cutting public spending (and public sector jobs) and by privatizing state enterprises. Strikes, protests and an overwhelming victory for opposition parties in mid-term congressional elections (May 1994) indicated the depth of popular feeling, while the PSC, led by presidential hopeful Jaime Neboth Saadi, scored major gains. Durán Ballén's government initiated constitutional reform and changes proposed by the president were approved by plebiscite in August 1994. Congress failed to adopt some of these measures and impeached several cabinet ministers towards the end of 1994, setting the stage for renewed confrontation between the legislative and executive branches of government.

The country's political situation changed dramatically when Ecuadoreans responded to the Jan-Feb 1995 border conflict with Peru (see above) with a massive display of national unity, backing their government and armed forces to an extent not seen in recent years and sending the President's popularity ratings well above 90%. The long term economic consequences of the conflict (see below) may well prove more difficult for the nation to accept when elections take place in May 1996.

Population Roughly 48% of Ecuador's people live in the Costa region W of the Andes, and 47% in the Andean Sierra. Migration is occurring from the rural zones of both the coast and the highlands to the towns and cities, particularly Guayaquil and Quito, and agricultural colonization by highlanders is occurring in parts of the coastal lowlands and the Oriente. National average population density is the highest in South America. Average income per head has risen fast in recent years like that of other oil-exporting countries, but the distribution has not improved and a few citizens are spectacularly wealthy.

According to the 1980 census, about 50% of the population was classed as Quichua, 40% *mestizo*, 8.5% white and 1.5% other Amerindian. Different classifications state that there are 2-3 million Quichua-speaking Indians in the highlands and about 70,000 lowland Indians. The following indigenous groups maintain their distinct cultural identity: Oriente: Siona-Secoya, Cofán, Waorani (also known as Aucas, which is a derogatory term), Záparo, Quichua, Achuar and Shuar (also known as Jívaro). Sierra: Otavalo, Salasaca (province of Tungurahua), Puruha (Chimborazo), Cañar and Saraguro (Loja province). Coast: Cayapas (also known as Chachi, Esmeraldas province), Tsáchilas (also known as Colorados, lowlands of Pichincha) and Cuaiquer (also known as Awas, Esmeraldas and Carchi provinces). Many Amazonian Indian communities are fighting for land rights in the face of oil exploration and colonization. The main Indian organization is the National Confederation of Indigenous Nationalities of Ecuador, CONAIE. In July 1994 there was an uprising of indigenous groups in the Sierra and Oriente over proposed changes to land ownership laws, which were perceived as favouring landowners and agro-industrial interests to the detriment of native communities. See also **Indigenous Groups** in Information for Visitors.

The Economy In the early 1970s, Ecuador underwent a transformation from an essentially agricultural economy to a predominantly petroleum economy. From 1972 when substantial domestic oil output began, economic growth has largely followed the fortunes of the oil market, except in 1983, when freak weather conditions resulted in large crop losses. Agriculture's contribution (including fishing) to gdp has dwindled from over 22% in 1972 to about 15%. Ecuador is the world's largest exporter of bananas. Production has been promoted with plantings of high-yielding varieties and provision of technical assistance and quality control. Efforts have been made to expand markets following the introduction of European Union import restrictions, to introduce a variety of banana resistant to black sigatoka disease and to reduce costs and increase efficiency. Coffee is the most extensive of Ecuador's cash crops, accounting for over 20% of total agricultural land, but it is also the lowest yielding crop. Cocoa production has been increased by a rehabilitation programme after the 1983 floods, contributing to a trebling of yields. Flowers are the most important agro-export of the Sierra.

Fishing is a growing industry, offering lucrative export potential. As well as tuna, sardines and white fish, shrimp farming along the coast has provided export earnings and much-needed jobs for agricultural workers. The shrimp industry grew strongly in the early 1990s to become the second largest export earner, but its success has not been problem-free. Many shrimp farms in the province of Guayas faced huge losses as a result of toxic waste pollution from nearby banana plantations. New shrimp farms in Manabí and Esmeraldas put native mangroves under threat, provoking disputes with environmentalists. Mining has been relatively unimportant historically, but the discovery of about 700 tonnes of gold reserves around Nambija (Zamora) in the SE created intense interest in precious metals and over 12,000 independent miners rushed to prospect there.

Although Ecuador's share of total world oil production is small (0.65%), foreign exchange earnings from oil exports are crucial to the economy. The main producing area is in the N Oriente, and a 495-km trans-Andean pipeline carries the oil to Esmeraldas on the coast, where it is refined and/or exported. New oil discoveries in 1992/93 raised proven reserves from 1.46 billion to 4.3 billion barrels. The new fields are in the Amazon and their development raises serious environmental questions. Nevertheless, new exploring rights continue to be awarded. There are also reserves of natural gas, mainly in the Gulf of Guayaquil, but these have not yet been fully developed. Hydroelectric potential is estimated at 90,000 MW, and new projects on the Paute, Pastaza and Coca rivers could raise capacity to 12,000 MW by the end of the century. In 1992, 70% of Ecuador's electricity generation came from hydropower.

Ecuador's foreign debt rose sharply in the 1970s when oil exports began and in the 1980s it joined other debtor nations in refinancing its external obligations. Adherence to free market economic policies in IMF programmes brought international approval and by 1985 Ecuador was widely acclaimed as a model debtor with sufficient creditworthiness to return to the voluntary market for loans. However, in 1986 oil prices crashed, cutting Ecuador's oil receipts by half, followed in 1987 by an earthquake which destroyed part of the trans-Andean pipeline and damaged other oil installations, causing a cessation of oil exports. Huge amounts of finance were necessary for reconstruction of economic infrastructure and villages, with considerable effects on public finances. Higher rates of inflation and poverty resulted. Subsequent loss of confidence in the Government's economic management resulted in a massive demand for dollars and a heavy devaluation of the sucre. Arrears on debt payments to all creditors built up and it was only in 1989 that the Government felt able to regularize some payments and begin negotiations with both official and private creditors. Not until 1992/93 were sustained attempts made to tackle Ecuador's debt arrears.

Durán Ballén introduced an economic adjustment programme, paring the public sector with intensive privatization, and unpopular government austerity. In 1994 agreements were reached with the IMF for a standby loan, with the Paris Club of creditor governments for a rescheduling of 1993 and 1994 maturities and with commercial banks for the restructuring of foreign bank debt amounting to US$4.5 bn of principal and US$3 bn of overdue interest. Holders of the debt could exchange it for discounted bonds with a floating rate of interest or par bonds at a low rate of interest.

Direct consequences of the Jan-Feb 1995 war with Peru were recession and an unexpected drop in inflation, while the sucre devalued only slightly. The conflict incurred a direct cost estimated at US$250mn, with indirect costs due to the interruption of commerce and lost tourism revenues likely to be much higher. The government was forced to introduce harsh measures to finance an expected US$550mn budget deficit (3% of gdp): increases in electricity prices and domestic phone calls, the imposition of emergency taxes, the removal of some industrial fuel subsidies and a 1.3% cut in government and capital spending. It was hoped to limit inflation to about 20% and maintain gdp growth of 3-4%.

Ecuador : fact file

Geographic

Land area	272,045 sq km
forested	38.3%
pastures	18.7%
cultivated	9.9%

Demographic

Population (1994)	11,221,000
annual growth rate (1989-94)	2.4%
urban	55.4%
rural	44.6%
density	41.2 per sq km
Religious affiliation	
Roman Catholic	93.0%
Birth rate per 1,000 (1993)	26.0
	(world av 26.0)

Education and Health

Life expectancy at birth,	
male	67.1 years
female	72.3 years
Infant mortality rate	
per 1,000 live births (1992)	36.9
Physicians (1992)	1 per 836 persons
Hospital beds	1 per 623 persons
Calorie intake as %	
of FAO requirement	105%
Population age 25 and over	
with no formal schooling	17.0%
Literate males (over 15)	90.5%
Literate females (over 15)	86.2%

Economic

GNP (1992 market prices)	
	US$11,843mn
GNP per capita	US$1,070
Public external debt (1992)	
	US$9,831mn
Tourism receipts (1992)	US$192mn
Inflation (annual av 1988-93)	54.1%
Radio	1 per 3.7 persons
Television	1 per 12 persons
Telephone	1 per 20 persons

Employment

Population economically active (1990)	
	3,359,767
Unemployment rate	1.3%
% of labour force in	
agriculture	30.8
mining	0.6
manufacturing	11.0
construction	5.9
Military forces	58,000

Source *Encyclopaedia Britannica*

Government There are 21 provinces, including the Galápagos Islands. Provinces are divided into cantons and parishes for administration.

Under the 1978 constitution, the vote was extended to include all citizens over the age of 18. The president and vice-president are elected for a four-year term. The president may not stand for re-election. The legislative branch consists of a single Chamber of Representatives of 77 members, of which 65 are provincial representatives elected for a two-year term and 12 are national representatives elected for a four-year term. Constitutional amendments under consideration since August 1994 include permitting presidential re-election, the introduction of a bicameral congress, reorganization of the judiciary, and recocnizing dual citizenship.

Music and Dance Culturally, ethnically and geographically, Ecuador is very much two countries—the Andean highlands with their centre at Quito and the Pacific lowlands behind Guayaquil. In spite of this, the music is relatively homogeneous and it is the Andean music that would be regarded as "typically Ecuadorean". The principal highland rhythms are the Sanjuanito, Cachullapi, Albaza, Yumbo and Danzante, danced by Indian and mestizo alike. These may be played by brass bands, guitar trios or groups of wind instruments, but it is the *rondador*, a small panpipe, that provides the classic Ecuadorean sound, although of late the Peruvian *quena* has been making heavy inroads via pan-Andean groups and has become a threat to the local instrument. The coastal region has its own song form, the Amorfino, but the most genuinely "national" song and dance genres, both of European origin, are the Pasillo (shared with Colombia) in waltz time and the Pasacalle, similar to the Spanish Pasodoble. Of Ecuador's three best loved songs, "El Chulla Quiteño", "Romántico Quito" and "Vasija de Barro", the first two are both Pasacalles. Even the Ecuadorean mestizo music has a melancholy quality not found in Peruvian "Música Criolla", perhaps due to Quito being in the mountains, while Lima is on the coast. Music of the highland Indian communities is, as elsewhere in the region, related to religious feasts and ceremonies and geared to wind instruments such as the *rondador*, the *pinkullo* and *pifano* flutes and the great long *guarumo* horn with its mournful note. The guitar is also usually present and brass bands with well worn instruments, can be found in even the smallest villages. Among the most outstanding traditional fiestas are the Pase del Niño in Cuenca and other cities, the Mama Negra of Latacunga, carnival in Guaranda, the Yamor in Otavalo, the Fiesta de las Frutas y las Flores in Ambato, plus Corpus Cristi and the Feast of Saint John all over the highlands. Among the best known musical groups who have recorded are Los Embajadores (whose "Tormentos" is superb) and the Duo Benítez-Valencia for guitar- accompanied vocal harmony, Ñanda-Mañachi and the Conjunto Peguche (both from Otavalo) for highland Indian music and Jatari and Huayanay for pan-Andean music.

There is one totally different cultural area, that of the black inhabitants of the Province of Esmeraldas and the highland valley of the Río Chota. The former is a S extension of the Colombian Pacific coast negro culture, centred round the marimba xylophone. The musical genres are also shared with black Colombians, including the Bunde, Bambuco, Caderona, Torbellino and Currulao dances and this music is some of the most African sounding in the whole of South America. The Chota Valley is an inverted oasis of desert in the Andes and here the black people dance the Bomba. It is also home to the unique Bandas Mochas, whose primitive instruments include leaves that are doubled over and blown through.

QUITO (1)

Quito (2,850m), with a population of 1,100,847, is within 25 km of the equator, but it stands high enough to make its climate much like that of spring in England, the days warm or hot and the nights cool. Because of the height, visitors may initially feel some discomfort and should slow their pace for the first 24 hours. Mean temperature, 13°C, rainfall, 1,473 mm; rainy season: Oct to May with the heaviest rainfall in April, though heavy storms in July are not unknown. Rain usually falls in the afternoon. The day length (sunrise to sunset) is almost constant throughout the year.

Few cities have a setting to match that of Quito, the second highest capital in Latin America (La Paz, the administrative capital of Bolivia, is the highest). The city is set in a hollow at the foot of the volcano Pichincha (4,794m). It was an Inca city, refounded by Sebastián de Benalcázar, Pizarro's lieutenant, in 1534. The city's charm lies in its colonial centre, where cobbled streets are steep and narrow, dipping to deep ravines. Through this section hurries the Machángara river, nowadays too polluted to wash clothes in. Westwards the valley is closed by **Cerro Panecillo**; from its top, 183m above the city level, there is a fine view of the city below and the encircling cones of volcanoes and other mountains. There is a statue on the hill to the Virgen de Quito; Mass is held in the base on Sun. There is a good view from the observation platform up the statue (entry US$1).

Warning On no account should you walk up Panecillo by the series of steps and paths to the Virgin which begin on García Moreno (where it meets Ambato) as assaults are very common. A taxi up and down with 1/2 hr wait costs US$3, but even taxis have been robbed. Do not take valuables with you.

Air pollution has been an increasing problem in recent years and the municipal authorities finally began to take measures to control motor vehicle emisions in 1994.

The heart of the city is Plaza de la Independencia, dominated by a somewhat grim **Cathedral**, built 1550-1562 (open 0800-1000, 1400-1600) with grey stone porticos and green tile cupolas. On its outer walls are plaques listing the names of the founding fathers of Quito, and inside are the tomb of Sucre (tucked away in a corner) and a famous Descent from the Cross by the Indian painter Caspicara. There are many other 17th and 18th century paintings; the interior decoration, especially the roof, shows Moorish influence. Beside the Cathedral, round the corner, is **El Sagrario**, originally built as the Cathedral chapel, reopened after restoration, very beautiful. Facing the Cathedral is the old **Archbishop's Palace**, which has been renovated and now houses shops. On the NE side is the new concrete **Municipal Palace** which fits in quite well, despite its material. The low colonial **Palacio de Gobierno**, silhouetted against the great flank of Pichincha, is on the NW side of the Plaza (open 0900-1200, 1500-1800, free but you can only see the patio); on the first floor is a gigantic mosaic mural of Orellana discovering the Amazon, and the President's offices are on the second floor. Portraits of all the presidents are hung in the yellow room. The balconies looking over the main square are from the Tuilleries in Paris; a gift of the French government shortly after the French Revolution.

Calle Morales, main street of La Ronda district (traditionally called Calle La Ronda and now a notorious area for pickpockets and bag slashers, avoid the area after dark), is one of the oldest streets in the city. Go past Plaza Santo Domingo to Calle Guayaquil, the main shopping street, and on to shady **Parque Alameda**, which has the oldest astronomical observatory in South America (open Sat 0900-1200). There are also a splendid monument to Simón Bolívar, various lakes, and in the

NW corner a spiral lookout tower with a good view. The traditional colonial area is being preserved, but elsewhere the city is being radically altered as a result of road improvements and new construction.

From Plaza de la Independencia two main streets, Calle Venezuela and García Moreno, lead straight towards the Panecillo to the wide Av 24 de Mayo, at the top of which is a new concrete building where street vendors are supposed to do their trading since the street markets were officially abolished in 1981. Street trading still takes place, however, and there are daily street markets from Sucre down to 24 de Mayo and from San Francisco church W up past Cuenca.

Plaza de San Francisco (or Bolívar) is W of Plaza de la Independencia; on the NW side of this plaza is the great church and monastery of the patron saint of Quito, **San Francisco**, see below. **Plaza de Santo Domingo** (or Sucre), to the SE of Plaza San Francisco, has to the SE the church and monastery of **Santo Domingo**, with its rich wood-carvings and a remarkable Chapel of the Rosary to the right of the main altar. In the centre of the square is a statue to Sucre, pointing to the slopes of Pichincha where he won his battle against the Royalists. The modern University City is on the NW of the colonial city, on the lower slopes of Pichincha by the Avenida América.

There are altogether 86 churches in Quito. See above for the Cathedral. The fine Jesuit church of **La Compañía**, in Calle García Moreno, one block from Plaza de la Independencia (open 0930-1100, 1600-1800) has the most ornate and richly sculptured façade and interior. See its coloured columns, its ten side altars and high altar plated with gold, and the gilded balconies. Several of its most precious treasures, including a painting of the Virgen Dolorosa framed in emeralds and gold, are kept in the vaults of the Banco Central del Ecuador and appear only at special festivals. Agree a price first if you use a guide (in 1995 much of the interior was obscured by scaffolding and polythene during restoration work). Not far away to the N is the church of **La Merced** (open 1500). In the monastery of La Merced is Quito's oldest clock, built in 1817 in London. Fine cloisters entered through door to left of altar. La Merced church contains many splendidly elaborate styles; note the statue of Neptune on the main patio fountain. The **Basílica**, on Plaza de la Basílica (Calle Venezuela), is very large, has many gargoyles, stained glass windows and fine, bas relief bronze doors (under construction since 1926).

The church of **San Francisco** (open 0600-1100, 1500-1800), Quito's largest, is said to be the first religious building constructed in South America by the Spanish (1553) and is rich in art treasures. The two towers were felled by an earthquake in 1868 and rebuilt. A modest statue of the founder, Fray Jodoco Ricke, the Flemish Franciscan who sowed the first wheat in Ecuador, stands at the foot of the stairs to the church portal. See the fine wood-carvings in the choir, a magnificent high altar of gold and an exquisite carved ceiling. There are some paintings in the aisles by Miguel de Santiago, the colonial *mestizo* painter. His paintings of the life of Saint Francis decorate the monastery of San Francisco close by, where the collection of colonial art has been renovated (1994). Adjoining San Francisco is the **Cantuña Chapel** with sculptures.

Many of the heroes of Ecuador's struggle for independence are buried in the monastery of **San Agustín** (Flores and Mejía), which has beautiful cloisters on 3 sides where the first act of independence from Spain was signed on 10 August 1809. The church of **El Carmen Moderno** has a fine collection of Quito ceramics. In the recently restored monastery of **San Diego** are some unique paintings with figures dressed in fabrics sewn to the canvas -a curious instance of present-day "collage". Ring the bell to the right of the church door to get in, entrance

---

Quito New City: key to map

1. Parque Andrade; 2. Monumento a Rocafuerte; 3. Plaza Paul Rivet; 4. Iglesia Sta Clara de San Millán; 5. Iglesia El Girón; 6. Iglesia de Santa Teresita; 7. Iglesia El Belén; 8. Ministry of Public Works; 9. Ministry of External Relations; 10. Universidad Católica (museums); 11. Ministry of Finance; 12 Cultural Library; 13. Casa de la Cultura; 14. Nuevo Hospital Militar; 15. Palacio de Justicia; 16. Palacio Legislativo; 17. Instituto Geográfico Militar (IGM) and Instituto Panamericano de Geografía e Historia; 18. Ministry of Public Health; 19. Maternity Hospital; 20. Colegio Mejía (museum); 21. Consejo Provincial de Pichincha; 22. Astronomical Observatory; 23. Banco Central; 24. Ecuadorean Tours (Amex); 25. Turismundial; 26. Safari; 27. TAME; 28. SAETA and Red Cross; 29. Emetel phone office; 30. Lloyds Bank; 31. Casa Paz exchange house; 32. United States Embassy; 33. *Hotel Colón*; 34. *Alameda Real*; 35. *Tambo Real*; 36. *Residencia Los Alpes*; 37. *Hotel Embassy*; 38. *Inca Imperial*; 39. *Coral Internacional*; 40. *Alston Inn*, Super Papa and Libri Mundi; 41. *La Estancia Inn*.

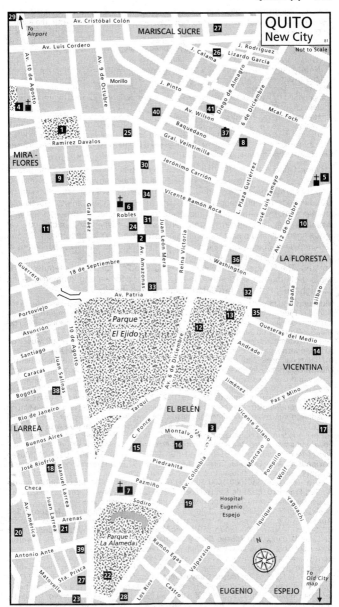

29
To
Airport

Av. Cristóbal Colón

MARISCAL SUCRE

27

Av. Luis Cordero

J. Rodríguez

26

J. Calama

Lizardo García

Morillo

J. Pinto

Diego de Almagro

6 de Diciembre

Mcal. Foch

Av. 9 de Octubre

Av. 10 de Agosto

40

Av. Wilson

41

4

1

25

Baquedano

37

8

Ramírez Davalos

Gral. Veintimilla

MIRA -
FLORES

Jerónimo Carrión

+5

9

30

L. Plaza Gutiérrez

José Luis Tamayo

34

Vicente Ramón Roca

Gral. Páez

+6

10

Robles

Av. 12 de Octubre

11

24

31

Juan León Mera

Reina Victoria

LA FLORESTA

2

Washington

36

18 de Septiembre

Av. Amazonas

Guerrero

33

32

España

Bilbao

Av. Patria

Portoviejo

Parque
El Ejido

13

35

Queseras del Medio

Asunción

10 de Agosto

12

14

Santiago

Juan Salinas

Andrade

VICENTINA

Caracas

6 de Diciembre

Jiménez

Bogotá

38

Paz y Miño

Río de Janeiro

Vicente Solano

17

LARREA

Buenos Aires

EL BELÉN

Tarqui

3

Moncayo

José Riofrío

C. Ponce

Montalvo

Pompilio

Wolf

18

15

16

Piedrahíta

Av. Colombia

Iquique

Yaguachi

Checa

Pazmiño

19

Av. América

Manuel Larrea

+7

Hospital
Eugenio
Espejo

20

Juan Larrea

Sodiro

21

Arenas

39

Ramón Egas

N

Antonio Ante

Parque
La Alameda

Valparaíso

Castro

To
Old City
map

Matovelle

Sta. Prisca

22

27

Los Ríos

EUGENIO

ESPEJO

23

28

US$0.75, 0900-1200, 1500-1700, all visitors are shown around by a guide. Also **La Concepción**, Mejía and García Moreno; **San Blas**, Guayaquil and 10 de Agosto. The **Basílica of Guápulo** (1693), perched on the edge of a ravine E of the city, is well worth seeing for its many paintings, gilded altars, stone carvings of indigenous animals and the marvellously carved pulpit. Take bus 21 (Guápulo-Dos Puentes) from Plaza de Santo Domingo, or walk down the steep stairway near *Hotel Quito*.

Note A number of churches were temporarily closed after the 1987 earthquake and were still being restored in 1994-95. There are fears for the survival of La Compañía, El Sagrario and El Carmen Bajo, where the threat of subsidence from long term structural faults was compounded by earthquake damage. Money donated by Spain is helping to restore several churches.

Houses The house of Sucre is at Venezuela 573, a beautiful restored building of a museum (see below). The house of Benalcázar is at Olmedo y Benalcázar, a colonial house with a courtyard and some religious statues on view to the public. The house of Camilo Egas, a recent Ecuadorean artist, on Venezuela, has been restored by the Banco Central; it has different exhibitions during the year, entrance US$0.75, open Mon-Fri 1000-1300.

Modern Quito extends N of the colonial city; it has broad avenues, fine private residences, parks, embassies and villas. The district known as La Mariscal, Av Amazonas, from Av Patria to about Av Orellana and the adjoining streets comprise Quito's modern tourist and business area: travel agencies, airlines, hotels and *residenciales*, exchange houses, moderate to expensive restaurants—several with sidewalk cafés, arts and crafts stores and stalls, jewellery stores, bookshops, car rental agencies, and pastry shops are all clustered in this neighbourhood. On Sun La Alameda, Carolina and El Ejido parks are filled with local families (exhibitions of paintings in El Ejido on Sat and Sun; aerobics, boating and horseriding in Carolina on Sun). The Parque Metropolitano, behind Estadio Atahualpa, is reputed to be the largest urban park in South America and is good for walking, running or biking through the forest. Take bus Batán-Colmena from the city.

Museums Quito prides itself on its art. Check museum opening times in advance. In the Parque El Ejido, at the junction of 12 de Octubre and Av Patria, there is a large cultural and museum complex housing the Casa de la Cultura and the museums of the Banco Central del Ecuador (entrance on Patria). Museums belonging to the Casa de la Cultura (T 565-808): in addition to temporary exhibits, the following permanent collections are presented: **Museo de Arte Moderno**, paintings and sculpture since 1830; **Museo de Traje Indígena**, a collection of traditional dress and adornments of indigenous groups; **Museo de Instrumentos Musicales**, an impressive collection of musical instruments, said to be the second in importance in the world. Open Tues-Fri 1000-1800, Sat-Sun 1000-1500. Fee for the 3 museums: foreigners: Tues-Fri US$1, students with local ID US$0.10, weekends and holidays free. Museums belonging to the Banco Central del Ecuador (T 223-259), also housed in the Casa de la Cultura: **Museo Arqueológico**, with beautiful precolumbian ceramics and gold and a video film on Ecuadorean culture and the different indian tribes, guided tour every hour, open Tues-Fri 0900-1700, Sat-Sun 0900-1500, foreigners US$2.50; **Museo Colonial y de Arte** (3 sections colonial, modern and contemporary art), guided tours in English, French and Spanish, same hours and entrance fee; **Museo de Ciencias Naturales**, Rumipamba 341 y Los Shyris, at E end of Parque la Carolina, open Mon-Fri 0830-1630, Sat 0900-1300, US$2.10. **Museo Nacional de Arte Colonial**, Cuenca y Mejía, T 212-297, a small collection of Ecuadorean sculpture and painting, housed in the 17th-century mansion of Marqués de Villacis, open Tues-Fri 1000-1800, Sat 1000-1500, Sun 1000-1400, foreigners US$1. **Museo del Convento de San Francisco**, Plaza de San Francisco, T 211-124, has a fine collection of religious art (under restoration since 1991, those sections which have been completed are open to the public), open Mon-Fri 0830-1130, 1500-1630. US$0.50. Similar collections in: **Museo de San Agustín**, Chile y Guayaquil, interesting exhibition of restoration work, open Mon-Sat 0830-1200, Mon-Fri 1500-1800, US$0.25 and **Museo Dominicano Fray Pedro Bedón**, Plaza de Santo Domingo. The **Museo Jijón y Caamaño**, now housed in the Catholic University library building, has a private collection of archaeological objects, historical documents, portraits, uniforms, etc, very well displayed, open Mon-Fri 0900-1600, US$0.40. There is also a museum of jungle archaeology (open 0830-1200), at the university. There is a fine museum in Bella Vista NE of Quito, **Museo Guayasamín**: Bosmediano 543, Bella Vista, T 446-277, as well as the eponymous artist's works there is a precolumbian and colonial collection, highly rec; open Mon-Fri 0900-1230 and 1500-1830, Sat 0900-1230, US$1.50. Works of art may be purchased and also modern jewellery made by the artist, ask to see the whole collection as

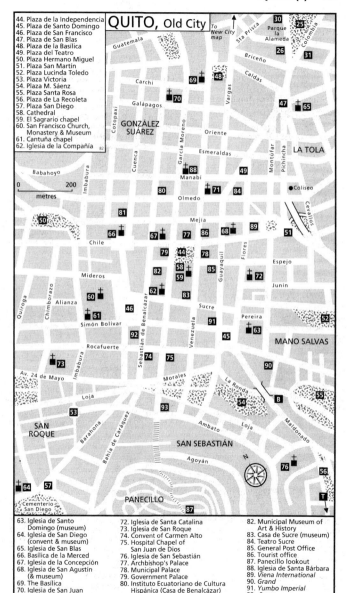

44. Plaza de la Independencia
45. Plaza de Santo Domingo
46. Plaza de San Francisco
47. Plaza de San Blas
48. Plaza de la Basílica
49. Plaza del Teatro
50. Plaza Hermano Miguel
51. Plaza San Martín
52. Plaza Lucinda Toledo
53. Plaza Victoria
54. Plaza M. Sáenz
55. Plaza Santa Rosa
56. Plaza de La Recoleta
57. Plaza San Diego
58. Cathedral
59. El Sagrario chapel
60. San Francisco Church,
    Monastery & Museum
61. Cantuña chapel
62. Iglesia de la Compañía

QUITO, Old City

To New City map

GONZÁLEZ SUÁREZ

LA TOLA

MANO SALVAS

SAN ROQUE

SAN SEBASTIÁN

PANECILLO

Cementerio San Diego

0   200
metres

63. Iglesia de Santo
    Domingo (museum)
64. Iglesia de San Diego
    (convent & museum)
65. Iglesia de San Blas
66. Basílica de la Merced
67. Iglesia de la Concepción
68. Iglesia de San Agustín
    (& museum)
69. La Basílica
70. Iglesia de San Juan
71. Iglesia del Carmen Bajo

72. Iglesia de Santa Catalina
73. Iglesia de San Roque
74. Convent of Carmen Alto
75. Hospital Chapel of
    San Juan de Dios
76. Iglesia de San Sebastián
77. Archbishop's Palace
78. Municipal Palace
79. Government Palace
80. Instituto Ecuatoriano de Cultura
    Hispánica (Casa de Benalcázar)
81. Museum of Colonial Art

82. Municipal Museum of
    Art & History
83. Casa de Sucre (museum)
84. Teatro Sucre
85. General Post Office
86. Tourist office
87. Panecillo lookout
88. Iglesia de Santa Bárbara
89. *Viena International*
90. *Grand*
91. *Yumbo Imperial*
92. *Sucre*
93. *Gran Casino*

only a small portion is displayed in the shop. The museum is near the Channel 8 TV station, take Batán-Colmena bus No 3 marked Bella Vista. Other museums: **Municipal Museum of Art and History**, Espejo 1147, near main plaza, was the old municipal offices, free; underneath is the cell where the revolutionaries of 1809 were executed (waxwork), well worth a visit, but not for the claustrophobic; **Museum of Ethnology**, Departamento de Letras, Ciudad Universitaria, Tues to Fri 0900-1230, Wed and Fri 1500-1700, Tues and Thur 1500-1830; **Museo Histórico Casa de Sucre**, the beautiful house of Sucre on the corner of Venezuela and Sucre; entrance US$1.25 (due to reopen in May 1995), closed Mon; **Museo de Artesanía**, 12 de Octubre y Madrid, has a good collection of Indian costume, helpful guides and a shop; the **Museo-Biblioteca Aureliano Polit** at the former Jesuit seminary beyond the airport has a unique collection of antique maps of Ecuador, open Mon to Fri 0900-1200 and 1500-1800, take the Condado minibus from the Plaza San Martín in Av Pichincha. **Cima de la Libertad**, museum at the site of the 1822 Battle of Pichincha, splendid view, open 0900-1200, 1500-1800, US$1.25. The Tourist Office recommends taking a taxi there (US$12) as the suburbs are dangerous, but you can take a bus to the S of the city and walk up; **Museo del Colegio Mejía**, natural science and ethnographic exhibits, Ante y Av America, Mon-Fri 0700-1300, 1530-2000. **Vivarium** Fundación Herpetológica Gustavo Orces, Reina Victoria y Sta María, impressive number of South American and other snakes, reptiles and amphibians, entrance US$1, open Tues-Sun, 0900-1200, 1500-1800.

Warning Quito has become a tourist centre and unfortunately theft is on the increase, especially in the old city, some areas of which are very dangerous at night. The police are reported helpful. Harassment of single women also appears to be on the increase. Do not walk through city parks in the evening or in daylight at quiet times (this includes Parque La Carolina). Joggers are recommended to stay on the periphery. **NB** throughout Ecuador, you must carry your passport (or a copy, preferably notarized) at all times.

Festivals The New Year is ushered in with life-size puppets, Años Viejos, on display throughout the country on 31 Dec. Much bitter satire about politicians. At midnight a will is read, the legacy of the outgoing year, and the puppets are burnt; very entertaining and good humoured. New year's day is very quiet (everything is shut). 6 Jan is Día de los Inocentes, a time for pranks, which closes the Christmas — New Year holiday season. 27 Feb is Día del Civismo celebrating the victory over Peru at Tarqui in 1829: students in graduating classes swear allegiance to the flag.

Carnival at Shrovetide is celebrated, as elsewhere in the Andes, by throwing water at passers-by: be prepared to participate. The solemn Good Friday processions are most impressive, with thousands of devout citizens taking part. 24 May is Independence, commemorating the Battle of Pichincha in 1822 with military and school parades, everything closes. Aug: Mes de los Artes, organized by the municipality, dance and music in different places throughout the city. Fancy-dress parades for Hallowe'en, celebrated last Sat in Oct, along Av Amazonas. The city's main festival, Día de Quito, celebrated throughout the week ending 6 Dec, commemorates the foundation of the city with elaborate parades, bullfights, performances and music in the streets; hotels are allowed to charge extra, everything except a few restaurants shuts on 6 Dec. Foremost amongst Christmas celebrations is the Misa del Gallo, midnight mass. Over Christmas Quito is crowded, hotels are full and the streets are packed with vendors and shoppers.

Hotels Note that major hotels quote their prices in dollars. In these establishments foreigners are expected to pay in dollars; there is a different price structure for Ecuadoreans and sometimes for citizens of other Latin American countries. In the **New City**: **L1** *Oro Verde*, 12 de Octubre y Cordero, T 566-479, Swiss-run, posh, pool, casino, restaurants; **L1** *Holiday Inn Crowne Plaza*, Shyris 1757 y Naciones Unidas, T 445-305, F 251-985, new in 1994, luxury suites, non-smoking suites, restaurants, free transport to the airport; **L2** *Colón Internacional*, Amazonas y Patria, T 560-666, F 563-903, good discotheque, shopping arcade, casino and many useful services (post, exchange, etc), international newspapers in reading-room, food excellent (see **Restaurants** below), non-residents should dress neatly for best service; **L3** *Alameda Real*, Roca 653 y Amazonas, T 562-345, F 565-759, can be booked through KLM airline, most rooms are suites and many have kitchenettes, good breakfast buffet US$6, 24hr cafeteria, business centre; **L3** *Akros Hotel*, 6 de Diciembre 3986, T 430-600, F 431-727, new in 1994, spaceous rooms, restaurant, cafeteria, bar; **L3** *Quito*, T 544-600, high up on González Suárez, with nice pool, good view, often room on weekdays as business travellers prefer the more central *Colón*, good restaurant open to non-residents; **A2** *Hostal Los Alpes*, Tamayo 233 y Washington, T 561-110, behind US Embassy, popular with Americans, "alpine" interior, clean, friendly, comfortable, water pressure poor on third floor, b&w TV, excellent restaurant with reasonable prices, breakfast incl, many handicrafts and art works, free papers, English paperbacks, warmly rec; **A2** *Sebastián*, Almagro 822, T 222-400, F 222-500, comfortable, cable TV, rec; **A3** *Hostal Villantigua*, Jorge Washington 237 y Tamayo, T 545-663, beautiful, renovated colonial house, open fire, friendly, quiet, all rooms with bath, suites available, furnished with antiques; **A2** *Tambo Real*, 12 de Octubre y Patria opp US Embassy, T 563-822, F 554-964, rec, pleasant service, good rooms, TV, ideal for business visitors, casino, restaurant very good; **A2** *Chalet Suisse*, Calama 312 y Reina Victoria, T 562-700, price negotiable in low season, only 12 safes, check availability, rooms on street very noisy Fri and Sat nights, restaurant; **A2-3** *Palm Garten*, 9 de Octubre 923, T 526-263/523-960, German run, very clean, good breakfasts, beautiful house, luggage store, reservations not always honoured; **A3** *Santa Bárbara*, 12 de Octubre 2263, T 564-382, F 275-121, very nice; **A3** *Hostal Barón de Carondelet*, Barón de Carondelet 313 parallel to Naciones Unidas, T 453-533 452-881, new in 1994, breakfast included, cafeteria; **B** *Apart-Hotel*, Rodríguez 175 y Diego de Almagro, T 506-834, suites and apartments, lovely rooms; **C** *Rincón de Bavaria*, Páez 232 y 18 de Septiembre, T 509-401, clean, large rooms with colour TV, restaurant with good German food; **B** *Café Cultura*, Robles 513 y Reina Victoria, T/F 224-271, beautiful rooms, garden, luggage store, excellent breakfasts, shop with local crafts and foods, cultural events, rec; **B** *Embassy*, Wilson 441 y 6 de Diciembre, T 561-990, inc tax, clean, well furnished, parking, restaurant, but noisy disco next door at weekends; **B** *Floresta*, Isabel La Católica 1005 y Salazar, T 236-874, bath, TV, phone, parking, restaurant, safe and very quiet, rec; **B** *Hostal 227 de la Rábida*, La Rábida 227 y Santa María, T 222-169, F 221-720, Italian owner, bright and clean, big bathrooms, comfortable, breakfast extra; **B** *Hostal Plaza Internacional*, Plaza 150 y 18 de Septiembre, T 524-530, F 505-075, clean, comfortable, multilingual staff, very helpful, good location; **B** *Residencial Cumbres*, Baquedano 148 y 6 de Diciembre, T 560-850, no credit cards, clean, helpful, large breakfast incl; **B** *Hotel Saint*, El Comercio 115 y El Día by the stadium, T 249-228/444-518, TV, cafeteria; **C** *Alston Inn*, J L Mera 741 y Baquedano, T 229-955, with bath and hot water, TV, laundry service, convenient to restaurants; **C** *Ambassador*, 9 de Octubre 1046 y Colón, T 561-777, with bath, clean/ rec; **C** *Hostal La Carolina*, Italia y Vancouver, T 542-472, suites **5**, friendly, helpful, very clean, safe deposit US$2.50, cable TV, hot water, credit cards, ask for quiet rooms at the back; **C** *Hostal Los Frailes*, Guanguiltagua 234 y F Páez, T 455-052, beautiful guest house, use of kitchen, rec (NE of new city); **C** *Hostal Residencial Los Andes*, Muros 146 y González Suárez behind British Embassy, T 550-839, good area for walking, spotlessly clean, hot water, cable TV in lounge, English spoken, rec; **C** *Rincón Escandinavo*, Leonidas Plaza 1110 y Baquerizo, T 222-168, small, modern, well-furnished, convenient location, bathroom, friendly, English spoken, rec; **C** *Hostal El Relicario*, Reina Victoria 1714 y La Niña, T 552-528, private bath, TV; **C** *Hostal Charles Darwin*, La Colina 304 y Orellana, T 529-384, quiet, friendly, incl breakfast.

D *Casa Helbling*, Veintimilla 531 y 6 de Diciembre, T 226-013, rec, incl good breakfast, use of kitchen in afternoon, luggage store, washing machine, information, many German and Swiss guests; **D** *Dan*, Av 10 de Agosto 2482 y Colón, T 553737, F 225083, a/c, private bath, hot water, clean, noisy rooms towards street, good food and laundry, rec; **D** *Gd'Oro*, Santa Rosa 436, T 543-026/543-033, nr Universidad Central, hot water, good restaurant, quiet, family run; **D** *Hostal Amazonas*, Pinto 471 y Amazonas, T 225-723, with bath, some sunny rooms, very clean; **D** *Hostal Jasmín*, Amazonas 232 y 18 de Septiembre, next to Hotel *Colón*, T 523-615, F 566-288, TV, phone; **D** *Hostal Vizcaya*, Rumipamba 1726 y Manuela Saenz, T 452-252, 450-288, owned by Sra Elsa de Racines, reservations essential, taxi ride but worth it, comfortable beds, bathroom, colour TV, good breakfast, evening meal on request, laundry service, English spoken, kind and friendly family, rec; **D** *La Estancia Inn*, Wilson 508 y D de Almagro, T 235-993, F 543-522, secure, clean, helpful; **D** *Loro Verde*, Rodríguez 241 y Diego de Almagro, T 226-163, with bath, clean, secure, friendly, good location; **D** *Majestic*, Mercadillo 366 y Versalles, T 543-182, F 504-207, well-furnished, bar, cafetería, restaurant, clean, hot water, quiet and friendly; **D** *Nueve de Octubre*, 9 de Octubre 1047 y Colón, T 552-424, modern, clean, very comfortable, bath, TV, desk, phone, friendly, secure, night watchman, rec; **D** *Posada del Maple*, Rodríguez 148 y 6 de Diciembre, with bath, E without, friendly, warm open atmosphere, international travellers, TV and VCR, breakfast included, laundry, cooking facilities, T 237-375; **D** *Zumag*, Av 10 de Agosto y Mariana de Jesús, T 552-400, clean, hot showers, no water after midnight, laundry service, will store luggage; **D** *Hostal Florencia*, Wilson 660 y Juan l Mera, T 237-819, some rooms without bath, parking; **D-E** *The Magic Bean*, M Foch 681 y J L Mera, T 566-181, American owned, central, all except 2 rooms are dormitories, good beds, secure, hot water, restaurant, breakfast incl, highly rec; **D** *Residencial Carrión*, Carrión 1250 y 10 de Agosto, T 234-620, 20 rm with bath, restaurant, bar, garden, good value, TV, accepts Visa, fills early; **D** *Versalles*, Versalles 1442 y Mercadillo, T 526-145, nice, clean, car park, restaurant.

E pp *El Taxo*, Foch 909 y Cordero, T 225-593, hostal-type, large family house, friendly, helpful, open fire, constant hot water, kitchen facilities, good meeting place; **E** *Pensión Loty's*, Marchena y América, T 522-531, F 226-438, bath, garden, nice furnishings, immaculate, friendly, rec; **E** *Pickett Inn*, Wilson 712 y JL Mera, T 551-205, shared bath (D with bath), hot water, laundry, popular; **E** *Posada La Herradura*, Pinto 570 y Amazonas, T 226-340, kitchen and laundry facilities, clean, friendly, convenient location, rec; **E** *Residencial Reina Victoria*, Cordero 1960 y 10 de Agosto, T 230-714, some with private bath, run down, hot water, m/bike parking is its only recommendation; **E** *Royal Inn*, 6 de Diciembre 2751, comfortable, helpful owner; **F** pp *Camino del Sol*, Carrión 145 y 12 de Octubre, T 236-357, with use of kitchen, owner, Luisa, is an excellent, experienced mountain guide; rec; **F** pp *El Cafecito*, Luis Cordero 1124 y Reina Victoria, T 234-862, various room sizes, café; **F** *Tatu Hostal*, 9 de Octubre 275 y J Washington, T 544-414, F 228-662, 12 room for max 30 people, sitting room with TV, kitchen facilities, safety box, fax service, hot water, big old mansion, high ceilings, spartan furnishings, rec. **Youth Hostel** *Albergue Juvenil Mitad del Mundo*, Pinto 325 y Reina Victoria, T 543-995, F 226-271, HQ of Asociación Ecuatoriana de Albergues, take IYHA card, new building, modern, dormitory or private room with bath, **F** pp members, **E** non-members, cheaper with shared bath, breakfast included, cafetería, laundry, hot water, rec.

If you need to fly out early, **B** *Aeropuerto*, is opposite the terminal, some rooms with kitchen, bath, T 458-708. In the vicinity of the airport: *Terraza Suites*, Isla San Cristóbal 880 y Río Coca, T 249-567, large rooms, hot water, TV, safe, good, breakfast on room service.

In between the new and old cities are: **C** *Inca Imperial*, Bogotá 219, T 524-800, with bath, ask for a room with a window, Inca style with lavish decor, safe to leave luggage, restaurant variable, busy lunchtimes, quieter in evenings, laundry service expensive, car park; **D** *Coral Internacional*, Manuel Larrea 164, T 572-337, spacious, popular with families, clean, cafetería, open 0730-2200; **D-E** *Residencial Margarita*, Elizalde 410 y Colombia (near Los Ríos), T 512-599/510-441, clean, with bath, helpful, baggage stored, rec; **E** *Baraka*, Asunción y América, T 509-260, clean, friendly, good value; **E** *Hostal El Ejido*, Juan Larrea 535 y Riofrío, T 526-066, clean, friendly, hot water, good value; **E** *Florencia 3*, 10 de Agosto 983 y Río de Janeiro, T 501-597, some rooms with bath; **F** *Oriente*, Yaguachi 824 y Llona (nr Instituto Geográfico Militar), T 546-157, with bath and kitchen, safe, family-run, weekly or monthly rentals only, rec; **E** *Residencial Portoviejo*, Portoviejo y América, T 235-399, rec, Chilean owner, friendly, safe, clean, use of kitchen, luggage stored, meeting place; **F** *Residencial Dorado*, 18 de Septiembre 805, T 525-072, intermittent water, basic, higher standard dearer wing across the street; **F** *Residencial Marsella*, Los Ríos 2035 y Espinoza, T 515-884, clean, hot water 0700-1130, some rooms with private bath, good rooftop terrace with views over Parque La Alameda, some rooms pokey but top floor rooms rec, luggage stored for a small fee per 15 days, convenient location, often full by 1700, laundry, coffee shop, safe deposit, check your change, notice board, busy and not always friendly; **G** *Atahualpa*, Manuel Larrea y Riofrío, convenient location, basic, no hot water, clean, safe, friendly; **F** *Casa Patty*, Tola Alta, Iquique 2-33 y Manosalvas, T 510-407, son of *Pensión Patty* in Baños, large rooms, hot shower in am, kitchen, terrace, laundry facilities, clean, friendly, helpful, safe for left luggage, it is at the top of a steep hill, take bus no 8, "Tola-Pintado" from the old town, take taxi at night. **Youth hostel F** pp *Los Andes*, Santa Rosa 163 y Av Universitaria (in central University area, just above Social Security Hospital) T 521-944, F 508-639, single sex dormitories and rooms for couples, kitchen, laundry, reduced rates for longer stays, breakfast US$1 (take bus No 10 San Bartolo – Miraflores from bus terminal, or bus along 10 de Agosto and walk W on 18 de Septiembre).

In the **Old City** (there can be water shortages in Aug): **C** *Real Audiencia*, Bolívar 220, T 512-711, F 580-213, hot shower, spacious, well furnished rooms, front rooms a bit noisy, TV, laundry service, baggage stored, highly rec, restaurant, bar on top floor good for sunset drink; **D** *Auca*, Sucre y Venezuela, T 212-240, hot shower, phone, TV, café, laundry, casino, safe box; **D** *Catedral Internacional*, Mejía 638 y Cuenca, hot water, good rooms; **D** *Hostal La Casona*, Manabí 255 entre Flores y Montúfar, T 514-764, F 563-271, renovated, TV, phone, safe, rec; **D** *Plaza del Teatro Internacional*, Guayaquil, 1373 y Esmeraldas, T 514-293/512-980, F 519-462, Casilla 3443, with private bath, clean, comfortable, good service, restaurant, bar, café, conference room, parking, rec; **D** *Viena Internacional*, Flores y Chile, T 519-611, English spoken, clean, large rooms, good value, ask for a quiet room, phone, laundry, good meals, safe; **D** *Indoamérica*, Maldonado 3022, T 515-094, E without bath, parking; **E** *Flores*, Flores 355 y Sucre, T 580-148, private bath, hot water, safe, laundry facilities, friendly; **E** *Gran Casino Colonial*, opposite, T 211-914, converted colonial house, TV, restaurant, luggage stored, second-hand books; **E** *Gran Casino Internacional*, 24 de Mayo y Loja, T 514-905, clean, hot water, luggage store, good restaurant, own travel agency which sells trips to the Galápagos and Oriente (see under Travel Agencies); **E** *Huasi Continental*, Flores 3-22 y Bolívar, T 517-327, hot water, clean, safe, luggage stored, cheaper without bath; **E** *La Posada Colonial*, Paredes 188 y Rocafuerte, T 212-859, bar, restaurant, garage, rec; **E** *Rumiñahui*, Montúfar 449 y Junín, T 211-407/219-325, with bath, hot water, safe, laundry facilities; **E** *Ecuador*, Flores 650 entre Chile y Mejía, hot shower, clean, basic; **E** *San Agustín*, Flores 626 y Chile, T 212-847, with bath, clean, hot water, rooms expensive, restaurant variable; **F** *Gran Casino*, García Moreno 330 y Ambato, T 516-368, famous gringo hangout, rooms and beds have seen better days, dirty and noisy, bring own towel, cheap laundry service and cheap restaurant, no menus, prices arbitrary, bed bugs, theft from rooms and safes reported, reports of police raids and drugs set-ups (1994-95), you either love it or hate it (but increasing numbers hate it); **F** *Hostal Belmonte*, Antepara 413 y V León, T 516-235, 1 block from La Marín underpass, for backpackers, good meeting place, clean, safe, family-run, home from home, hot showers, phone for incoming and outgoing calls, nice terrace, use of kitchen and laundry facilities, laundry service, book exchange, free luggage storage, repeatedly rec; **F** *Montúfar*, Sucre 160 y Flores, T 211-419, cheaper without bath, hot water, clean, safe; **F pp** *Yumbo Imperial*, Guayaquil 647 y Bolívar, near Plaza Santo Domingo, T 518-651 clean, safe, some with bath, friendly, laundry facilities, top rooms overlook old city; **F pp** *Venezia*, Rocafuerte y Venezuela, with, **G** pp without clean, water tepid, often full; **G** pp *Italia*, Junín y Flores, basic, hot showers, safe, thin mattresses, friendly, family-run; **G** pp *Hostal Junín*, Junín y Flores, clean, friendly, hot water; **G** pp *Santo Domingo*, Plaza Santo Domingo, T 512-810, hot water, noisy, best rooms 8a or 9a, luggage store; on same square, **E** *San Fernando*, No 1331, laundry facilities. *Techita's House*, Vicente León 137 y Av Pichincha, T 572-274.

In the vicinity of the Terminal Terrestre: **D-E** *Juana de Arco*, Rocafuerte 1311 y Maldonado, T 214-175, only back rooms with shower, front rooms cheaper but noisier, good restaurant next door; **E** *Grand*, Rocafuerte 1001, T 210-192/519-411, with or without bath, run down, some rooms dingy, clean, safe, friendly, free bag storage, same-day laundry attached (some overcharging), restaurant, rec. Many hotels on Calle Morales, eg **D** *Cumandá*, No 449, T 516-984, F 510-734, comfortable, showers, TV, phone, travel agency, laundry, restaurant, garage, excellent service, rec, clean, safe, noisy from proximity to bus station but quieter at the back; **F pp** *Los Shyris*, Morales (La Ronda) 691, with shared bath, hot water, safe, laundry, restaurant downstairs. On Maldonado: **D-E** *Hotel Interamericano*, No 3263, T 513-358/241-320, some rooms without bath; **D** *Piedra Dorada*, No 3210, T 517-460, modern, with bath, hot shower, phone, TV, laundry, clean, restaurant, rec; **F pp** *Amazonas*, No 915, safe, cold water, restaurant (often closed); **F pp** *Colonial*, No 3035 (at end of alley), T 580-762, hot water (most of the time), safe although not a safe area at night, quiet, laundry, cheaper annex; **G** pp *Guayaquil No 1*, No 3248, hot water, will store luggage for small fee, safe, basic; **G** pp *Ingatur*, No 3226, hot water, clean, washing facilities, poor beds and plumbing; opposite is **G** pp *Capitalino*, pleasant, hot water. Many also on Loja in the red light district.

If you prefer not to stay in a hotel, Sra Rosa Jácome has an apartment in the centre, T 503-180 (evenings), one double with bath and two single rooms, **F** pp, use of kitchen and phone, will arrange outings, friendly and helpful, meets most incoming flights at airport in her taxi (an historic monument in itself); **D** Cecilia Rivera, a doctor, offers full board at G F Salazar 327 y Coruña, T 548-006, 569-961, central, view across valley, quiet, safe, hot water, laundry, luggage store; Sra Anita Gomezjurado, Julio Zaldumbide 387 y Coruña, nr *Hotel Quito*, central, convenient (No 2 Colón-Camal bus), T 237-778, German, English and Czech spoken, friendly, clean, hot water, safe, full board available; **D-E** *La Casa de Eliza*, Isabel La Católica 1559 near SAEC, T 226-602, central, hot water, kitchen and laundry facilities, cheerful, Eliza organizes treks through the Cerro Golondrinas Cloudforest Reserve with research and volunteer opportunities, see p 960, rec; **E** *La Casona Albergue*, Andalucía 213 y Galicia, near La Católica University, T 230-129/544-036, Argentine-run, shared room, comfortable, kitchen, laundry and storage facilities, rec; **F** pp *Casa Paxee*, Romualdo Navarro 326 y La Gasca, T 500-441/525-331, inc fruit for breakfast, use of kitchen area, laundry facilities, clean bathroom, 3 rooms only, discounts for longer stays, highly rec; **G** *Casapaxi*, Navarro 364 y La Gasca, PO Box 17-03-668, T 542-663/551-401, clean, hot water, friendly, will store luggage, owner Luigina Fossati very helpful, frequently rec; *Marcia de Sandoval*, Galavis 130 y Toledo, T 543-254, rents small apartments, well equipped, US$180 per month; *Reno Román* and his Swiss wife let 4 double rooms, hot water, laundry service, safe, will arrange interesting trips, climbs, speak English and German; *Alojamiento Toa*, Lizarazú 321 y La Gasca, T/F 522-954.

For longer stays with room, kitchen, TV, laundry service etc, the following have been recommended: *Apartamentos Modernos*, Amazonas 2467 y Mariana de Jesús, T 553-136/543-509, 2 rooms and kitchen US$400, with extra room US$450, clean (near Parque de la Carolina) English, French and German spoken, rec; *Apartotel Mariscal*, Robles 958 y Páez, US$17/night, 20% less a month, T 528-833; **A2** *Apart-Hotel Amaranta*, Leonidas Plaza 194 y Washington, PO Box 4967, T 560-585/586, comfortable suites, US$1,125 a month, good restaurant. Apartments for rent are advertised in *El Comercio*, especially in "Suites (Sector Norte)" section, US$125-300 per month, usually unfurnished.

Note Those travelling by car may have difficulty parking in the centre of Quito and are therefore advised to choose the less central hotels.

Restaurants There are few restaurants in the Old City, although these tend to be cheaper, with more local and fast food types than in the New City, where more foreign styles can be found. It is difficult to find places to eat in the Old City in the evenings, especially after 2200. Fast food in Quito is usually hamburgers or chicken, spit roasted (hygiene in hamburger and salchipapa is sometimes poor). Many restaurants throughout the city close on Sun. **NB** Prices listed are often inaccurate. Restaurants with stickers indicating acceptance of credit cards do not necessarily do so. Check first. The following list is by type; all restaurants are in the New City unless otherwise stated.

International The *Oro Verde* has a superb international restaurant, a very expensive but good Japanese restaurant, and *Café Quito*, with lunch and breakfast buffets. Excellent food at *Hotel Colón Internacional*, spectacular Sun buffet, all you can eat, US$12, drinks very expensive, rec; buffet breakfast in the restaurant, cheaper in snack bar, excellent pastry shop and ice cream. In the *Hotel Quito*, buffet breakfast is excellent value. *La Casa de al Lado*, Valladolid 1018 y Cordero, with bar and cinema Mon-Sat 1100-0100, classy; *Excalibur*, Calama 380, expensive; *Palladino*, 10 de Agosto 850 y Patria, 19th floor, continental cuisine, expensive but good view over old and new town; *Barlovento*, 12 de Octubre y Orellana, seafood and inexpensive steak, outside seating; *El Bodegón del Tártaro*, Veintimilla 918 y Amazonas, very good food, romantic atmosphere.

Ecuadorean In the Old City: *El Criollo*, Flores 825, clean, cheap, tasty, chicken specialities; *La Vieja Colonia*, García Moreno 8-34, good, clean, nice atmosphere; *Los Olivos*, near Santo Domingo church, clean, good service, economical. In the New City: *Mamá Clorinda*, Reina Victoria y Calama, large portions, moderately priced; *Inti*, Mariana de Jesús y Hungría, good service; *La Casa Madre de las Menestras*, América y 18 de Septiembre, good value; *Rincón La Ronda*, Belo Horizonte 400 y Almagro; *La Choza*, 12 de Octubre 1821 y Cordero, good service and food, T 230-839; *La Querencia*, Eloy Alfaro 2530 y Catalina Aldaz, good views and atmosphere; *El Pajonal*, Homero Salas y Altar, 4 blocks W of airport.

    General In the Old City: *Viena*, Chile y Flores, good breakfasts; *Monaco*, García Moreno y 24 de Mayo, cheap; *El Amigo*, Guayaquil, between Esmeraldas y Oriente, very good food and coffee; *Café Madrillón*, Chile 1270 y Mejía, rec; *Shangay*, Mejía, nr Flores, good cheap food; *Cafetería Dominó*, Venezuela y Mejía, cheap lunches, snacks, juices, good for breakfast and coffee; cheap meals in the market behind the shoe shops on Flores y Olmedo, 1130-1400; *La Cueva del Oso*, elegant covered court of Edif Pérez Pallares on Chile y Venezuela across from the Plaza de la Independencia, excellent Ecuadorean food, reasonable prices, serenading guitarists at times. In the New City: *Terraza del Tártaro*, Veintimilla 1106 y Amazonas (no sign), top of building, good views, good steaks, good value, pleasant atmosphere, rec; *Taller del Sol*, Salazar y 12 de Octubre, unique atmosphere, expensive; *Cafetería Galería Libri Mundi*, opp and owned by Libri Mundi bookshop, good art exhibits in lovingly restored building, garden, quiet, good coffee; *Rincón del Amazonas*, Ramírez Dávalos 152, great *parrilladas*, moderately cheap, good food, friendly, beware of overcharging; *Café Stop*, Amazonas y Moreno Bellido, very good atmosphere, medium prices; *El Cocodrilo*, Amazonas y Mercadillo, cosy, informal, good coffee; *The Pancake House*, Amazonas 2583 y Mariana de Jesús; *Matrioshka*, Pinto 376 y León Mera, good, cheap set lunch; *El Frutal*, Reina Victoria 328, excellent fresh fruit juices and good value set lunches; *Super Papa*, J L Mera 761 y Baquedano, stuffed baked potatoes, some vegetarian, sandwiches and salads, excellent cakes, takeaway service, great breakfasts, popular for notices and advertisements, open every day, 0730-2100; *Caravana*, good, cheap, fast food at Veintimilla y 10 de Agosto, Guerrero y 10 de Agosto and elsewhere; *Arby's*, Av 6 de Diciembre y Portugal, fast food, good; *Café 3.30*, Whimper 330 y Coruña, first class.

French Usually very smart, used by businessmen on expense accounts. *Rincón de Francia*, Roca 779 y 9 de Octubre, highly rec, dress smartly, reservation essential, slow service; *Le Bistrot*, González Suárez 139, T 523-649, best gourmet food in town, expensive, smart, live music at 2100, closed Sun; a sister restaurant is *Amadeus Restaurant and Pub*, Coruña 1398 y Orellana, T 230-831 and 566-404, very good French cuisine and concerts, usually 2300 Fri, rather formal, dresses and ties; *Ile de France*, Reina Victoria 1477 y La Niña, fondue bar; *La Marmite*, Mariano Aguilera 287, good food; *La Pêche Mignon*, Belo Horizonte 338 y 6 de Diciembre, expensive but good; *Rincón de Borgoña*, Eloy Alfaro 2407, excellent; *Chantilly*, Roca 736 y Amazonas, restaurant and bakery, good and reasonably priced, second branch at Whimper 394; *La Fite*, La Niña 559 y J L Mera, good; *La Crêperie*, Calama 362, good but not cheap; *La Belle Epoque*, Whimper 925 y 6 de Diciembre, expensive but very good food and service. *Chalet Suisse*, Calama 312 y Reina Victoria, good steaks and some Swiss dishes, expensive but very good. Less expensive, *Cafetería Paradiso*, Baquedano 409 y J L Mera, Mon-Fri 0730-2230, Swiss owned, fondues, good breakfasts, excellent coffee.

    German *El Ciervo*, Dávalos 270 y Páez, good food but slow service, highly rec by a German traveller, German newspapers available; *Viena* (Austrian) Av Amazonas opp CCI shopping centre.

    Spanish *Costa Vasca*, 18 de Septiembre 553 y 9 de Octubre, good food and atmosphere; *Rana Verde*, JL Mera 639, good food and atmosphere; *El Mesón de la Pradera*, Orellana y 6 de Diciembre, converted hacienda, good food and service, also has tapas bar. In the Old City, *Las Cuevas de Luis Candela*, Benálcazar y Chile and Orellana y Coruña, good service, reasonable prices, closed Sun. *La Vieja Castilla*, La Pinta 435 y Amazonas, very good, expensive, but highly rec; *La Paella Valenciana*, República y Almagro, huge portions, seafood, good service, good value; *La Puerta de Alcalá*, Lizardo García 664 y J L Mera, delicious *tapas*, very good.

Italian *Vía Margutta*, San Ignacio 1076 y González Suárez, very good, expensive; *La Gritta*, Santa María 246 y Reina Victoria, smart, home made pasta, food and wine expensive for Ecuador; *Il Grillo*, Baquerizo 533 y Diego de Almagro, closed Mon, excellent, posh, reasonable prices; *La Scala*, Salazar y 12 de Octubre, excellent, good atmosphere, not cheap; *Taberna Piemonte*, Eloy Alfaro, above stadium, excellent, expensive; *La Trattoria de Renato*, San Javier y Orellana, nice atmosphere, expensive; *Vecchia Roma*, Roca 618 y J L Mera, good food and atmosphere; *Michele*, Páez 259 y J Washington, very good; *Portofino*, Calama 328 y Reina Victoria, good pasta selection; *Marina Yate*, Calama 369 y J L Mera, good, medium price. **Pizza** *El Hornero*, at Veintimilla on Amazonas, expensive, open Sun; *Che Farina Pizzería*, Carrión, entre J L Mera y Amazonas and Naciones Unidas y Amazonas, very good, fast service, popular with locals; *Eccos Pizzas*, Los Shyris near Parque La Carolina, good pizzas, large-screen video; *Dinos*, Orellana y 6 de Diciembre; *Pizza Maritza*, Eloy Alfaro y 6 de Diciembre and Centro Comercial Quicentro, Naciones Unidas y Shyris, good.

Middle-eastern *Tarek*, Calama 336, T 520-117, Arabian food, some vegetarian dishes, pricey; *Alsal*, Av Los Shyris 1168 y Portugal, good value.

Latin American and US *La Guarida del Coyote*, Carrión 619 y Amazonas, and at Jápon 542 y Naciones Unidas, good Mexican food, small portions, pleasant atmosphere; *El Coyote de Eduardo*, El Universo 645 y Los Shyris, T 432-580, Mexican, very popular; *La Posada*, González Suárez 135, T 523-649, 1100-2300, Mexican, good, in front of *Hotel Quito*; *Churrascaría Tropeiro*, Veintimilla 564 y 6 de Diciembre, Brazilian-style, good salad bar; *Rincón del Gaucho*, Almagro 422 y García, T 547-846, rec; *Tex Mex*, Reina Victoria 225 y 18 de Septiembre, good food, lively, draught beer, open daily; *Rincón Ecuatoriano Chileno*, 6 de Diciembre y Orellana, delicious, rec; *Rincón Cubano*, Amazonas 993 y Veintimilla, Cuban, rec. *The Magic Bean Restaurant and Coffee House*, Foch 681 y J L Mera, excellent atmosphere, outdoor eating, specializes in fine coffees and natural foods, more than 20 varieties of pancakes, salads, huge portions, lots of recs; *Hyatt*, J L Mera y Bruna, S US menu, very select; *Adam's Rib*, Calama y Reina Victoria, American ribs, good Reuben sandwiches and atmosphere, expensive, poor service, closed Sun; *The Taco Factory*, Foch 713 y J L Mera, relatively cheap, generous portions, US TV; *Fried Green Bananas*, L Plaza y Washington, US, Tex-Mex, good; *Coconut Willy's*, Calama y J L Mera, good salads, sandwiches and burgers, lively atmosphere; *Clancy's*, Toledo y Salazar, classy, good food; *Hunters*, Av 12 de Octubre 2157 y Muros, US style; *Café Plazuela*, Flores y Manabí (Old City), nr Teatro Sucre, great atmosphere, coffee, desserts.

Steak *Casa de mi Abuela*, J L Mera 1649, T 565-667, steak and salad, rec; *Columbia*, Colón 1262 y Amazonas, popular, open Sun; *Shorton Grill*, Calama 216 y Almagro, huge platter US$5-6; *La Vieja Colonia*, García Moreno y Sucre (old city), good, cheap, rec; *Martín Fierro*, Inglaterra 1309 y República, good quality, friendly service; *Texas*, J L Mera y Calama, popular, fair, steak and seafood.

Seafood *Pedro El Marino*, Lizardo García 559 y Reina Victoria, rec for lunch; *La Jaiba*, Reina Victoria y Colón; *Manhatten*, Reina Victoria y Carrión, not expensive; *Los Redes de Mariscos*, Amazonas 845 y Veintimilla, excellent food, lovely atmosphere, wines expensive, highly rec (closed Sun pm); under same management but more upmarket, *Mare Nostrum*, Foch 172 y Tamayo, good seafood, cold rooms; *El Cebiche*, J L Mera 1232 y Calama, and on Amazonas, delicious seafood, best ceviche in town; *Maremoto*, Diego de Almagro y Ponce Carrasco 282, T 528-351, good seafood and ceviches; *El Viejo José*, Veintimilla y 9 de Octubre, good, cheap, rec; *Cevichería Puerto Manabí*, Amazonas y Calama 461, good seafood, paella and *parrillada de mariscos*; *Ceviches y Banderas*, Av 12 de Octubre 1533 y Foch, good, reasonably priced; *Bar y Grill Buon Gustaio*, Isla San Cristóbal 881, seafood and local, rec; *Famacebiche*, Av Naciones Unidas, in shopping centre, Manabí-style cooking; *Puerto Camarón*, Centro Comercial Olímpico, 6 de Diciembre N of stadium, very good, try *viche* (fish soup), Mon-Fri lunch and dinner, Sat-Sun lunch only; *Ceviches de la Rumiñahui*, 3 branches: Nazareth 1777 y Dalias; Real Audiencia, Manzana 12, casa 38 entre Av del Maestro y Tufiño (the original branch, less clean), these 2 are N of airport runway; Quicentro Shopping Centre, Naciones Unidas y Shyris (a bit dearer than the others): all 3 are good and popular for *ceviche* (US$2-3), seafood and fish.

Oriental *La Casa China*, Cordero y Tamayo, excellent, moderately priced; *Chifa Mayflower*, Carrión 442 y 6 de Diciembre, good Chinese food; *China Town*, Mariana de Jesús 930 y Amazonas, very good, not cheap; *Lu Chin*, Mariana de Jesús 1001, excellent; *Gran Ciudad* *de China*, Carrión 1154, cheap and good; *Chifa China*, Carrión y Versalles, good value, authentic, highly rec; *Hong Kong*, Lizardo García 235 y Eduardo Xaura, excellent; *Casa Asia*, nr bullring on Av Amazonas, rec; *Fuji*, Robles 538 y Reina Victoria, authentic sushi bar, good; *Tanoshii*, Japanese in *Hotel Oro Verde*, see above; *Chifa Palacio*, Calama 434 y Amazonas, good food, cheap; *Chifa El Chino*, Bolívar y Guayaquil, cheap, good lunch; *Mágico Oriental*, Paez y 18 de Septiembre, good value.

Vegetarian *La Champignon*, Robles 549 y Reina Victoria, gourmet; *El Márquez*, Calama 433, between J L Mera and Amazonas, good, Mon-Fri; *Herbal Centro Vegetariano*, Colón 1485, good lunches; *Girasol*, Oriente 581 y Vargas, cheap, closes 1700; *Los Amigos*, Guayaquil y Oriente, clean, cheap; *Windmill*, Versalles y Colón 2245, excellent, reasonable; *Maranatha*, Riofrío y Larrea, lunch Mon-Fri, good, clean and cheap; *El Maple*, Paez 485 y Roca; *Casa Naturalista*, Lizardo García 630, also health food store; *Chapati*, Calama y Diego de Almagro, good quality, vegetarian a*lmuerzos*; *The Flying Dutchmen*, La Pinta 146 y D de Almagro, also serves Indonesian and Indian food, rec.

Cafés/Pastry Shops/Bakeries *Café Cultura*, Robles y Reina Victoria, nice atmosphere, converted colonial building, excellent food, homemade bread, open daily for breakfast (0800-1130) and afternoon tea (1500-1700). The *Pastelería* in the *Hotel Colón* building is excellent; also that in *Hotel Oro Verde*; *Café Mignone*, Calama 315 y Reina Victoria, coffee, chocolate, breads, cakes, bright, classical music, rec; *Café Modelo*, Sucre y García Moreno, good cheap breakfast; *Su Café*, Flores 5-46, small coffee shop, rec for breakfast; *Le Petit Mirage*, Reina Victoria 656 y Veintimilla, beautiful decor, pastries and cappucino. *La Cosecha*, main bakery on Los Shyris near Villaroel across from Parque Carolina, several other outlets for homemade breads, doughnuts, oatmeal cookies; *El Cyrano*, Portugal y Los Shyris, wholemeal bread, pastries, highly rec, French owner also runs excellent ice cream shop, *Corfu* next door, try *Corfu con crema*; *Bangaló*, Carrión 185 y Tamayo, excellent cakes, quiches, coffees, Mon-Sat, open for lunch and 1600-2000; *Gustapan*, Colón y 10 de Agosto and several other locations, good bread and pastries; *Tip Top*, *Panadería Sevila*, Edificio Torre Reina, Almagro y Luis Cordero, delicious cakes and breads, try the sweets, Mon-Fri 0630-1930, Sat closes midday; *Los Bocadillos*, Cordero, just off Amazonas, delicious hot sandwiches on crusty French bread and other light meals; *Haripan*, Wilson y 6 de Diciembre, good breads and pastries; *San Fernando*, Asunción 136, excellent. *Café-Cultural Plazuela*, Plaza del Teatro, Manabí y Flores, nice atmosphere, good coffee, rec; *Pastelería Dulce*, Rocafuerte y García Moreno, good bakery in Old City; *Baguette*, Amazonas 2525 y Mariana de Jesús, sells good bread, pasteurized cheeses, another branch in Colón 900 block; good cheeses and meats at **Delicatessen Español** next to Libri Mundi, J L Mera y Veintimilla, sandwiches, sausages, salmon, cheese, etc; *Panadería Nap*, Colón, just N of Amazonas, good, wide selection, several branches; *Pastelería Frederica*, 10 de Agosto 679, rec for very fresh *cachos*. *Heladería Zanzibar*, on Guayaquil, near Plaza Santo Domingo and on Benalcázar 860, excellent ice cream; *Top Cream*, Naciones Unidas, nr Amazonas, and on 6 de Diciembre, for high-quality ice cream, milkshakes; *Gelatería Uno*, Centro Comercial Olímpico, 6 de Diciembre, excellent sherbet and ice cream; *Kikos*, Mariana de Jesús y Amazonas and other locations, regular and soft ice cream. Good ice cream at *Chifa Chan*, Espejo entre Flores y Guayaquil. *Las Cerezas* fruit bar, García Moreno 1355 y Olmedo, nice patio, friendly, good juices and fruit salads; *La Frutería*, Colón 958, serves a good fruit salad.

Bars In New City: *Rumors*, J L Mera at Veintimilla, popular with Peace Corps, good atmosphere, not cheap; *El Pub*, San Ignacio y Gonzalo Suárez, English menu, including fish and chips; *Reina Victoria*, on Reina Victoria 530 y Roca, open Mon-Sat from 1700, darts, happy hour 1700-1800, both places meeting points for British and US expats; *Night Rider's*, J Martínez 489 y Portugal, nice atmosphere, US, popular; the *Hotel Colón* is good for cocktails with canapés and a resident jazz band; *Smoking Alligator*, Lizardo García y Reina Victoria, young crowd, lively; *Ghoz Bar*, La Niña 425 y Reina Victoria, T 239-826, Swiss owned, Swiss food, billiards, darts, videos, games, music, German book exchange; *Pym's*, 12 de Octubre y Baquerizo Moreno, varied menu, good sandwiches; *Bangaló*, Carrión 185 y Tamayo, great atmosphere, good jazz at weekends; *El Pobre Diablo*, Santa María, near *La Gritta* restaurant, popular, trendy, also serves good local food and plays great music, good atmosphere; *Papillon*, Almagro y Santa María, open every day, good, popular with young locals; *Iguana Bar*, Santa María 212 y Reina Victoria, popular; *Bar People's*, Amazonas 585 y Carrión, rock and reggae, open 0800 for breakfast and 1600-0300; *Arribar*, J L Mera 1238 y Lizardo García, pool table, trendy, rap and other music, happy hr 1600-1800, Swiss-owned; *Cats*, Lizardo García y Almagro, quaint hideaway, good selection of music; *Kubata Café*, Lizardo García 465 y Almagro, mellow atmosphere, stylish; *Kizomba*, Almagro y L García, rec for atmosphere and creative drinks, good music; *El Víkingo*, Calama 247 y Reina Victoria, popular, coffee, snacks, mulled wine a speciality, run by Lesley, English girl from Isle of Man; *Calypso*, Reina Victoria y

Calama, Latin music, good local/gringo mix, no cover charge for foreigners who usually drink more than Ecuadoreans; *L'petit Tango*, Almagro y Colón, live tango music, no beer served; *Patatus*, Pres Wilson y Amazonas, outdoor seating, fireplaces, nice; *The Lion of Judah Reggae Bar*, Amazonas y Orellana, 2nd flr, good for a dance and drinks, funky reggae; *Blues*, La Granja 112 y Amazonas, rec; *Santa Fe Pool Bar*, Reina Victoria 847 y Wilson, open daily 1600; *Limón y Menta*, Santa María y J L Mera, lively atmosphere, pool tables, local trendies. In Old City, Teatro Bolívar has a good wine bar. Try the *Cervecerías* around the Universidad Central for salsa and merengue.

Airlines TAME, Colón y Rábida, T 509-382, also 10 de Agosto 239; **Saeta**, Santa María y Amazonas, T 542-148 (British Airways agents, T 540-000); **SAN**, Santa María y Amazonas, T 564-969; **Aerogal**, Italia 241 y Eloy Alfaro, T 563-646; **Americana**, Eloy Alfaro 266, Edif Doral, 10th floor, internal Peru airlines, T 545-478, rec; **TAP Air Portugal**, Edificio de los Andes, Amazonas 477 y Roca, on 7th floor, opp Lloyds Bank, T 550-308; **KLM**, Ed Xerox, Amazonas 3617 y Juan Pablo Sanz, T 455-233; **Lufthansa**, Av 6 de Diciembre 955 y 18 de Septiembre, T 508-682; **Iberia**, Amazonas 239 y Jorge Washington, T 560-548; **American Airlines**, América y Robles, T 561-144, 561-526; **Avensa Aervimensa**, Naciones Unidas y Amazonas, Edif Previsora, Torre B, of 410, T 466-461; **Avianca**, 6 de Diciembre 511 y 18 de Septiembre, T 508-842; **AeroPerú**, Jorge Washington 718, T 561-699/700; **Varig**, Amazonas 1188 y Calama, T 543-257; **Air France**, Amazonas y 18 de Septiembre, T 523-596; **Alitalia**, Ernesto Novoa 474 y Av 6 de Deciembre, T 509-061.

Banks and Exchange Banking hours 0900-1330. You can withdraw inward transfers in US dollars. **Lloyds Bank**, Av Amazonas 580 y Carrión, with Torres de Colón and Jipijapa agencies, quick service, commission charged, rec, closes 1400; **Citibank**, Reina Victoria y Patria (own cheques only); **Bank of America**, Patria y Amazonas gives cash only on its own Visa cards; **Filanbanco**, 10 de Agosto, opposite Central Bank, and other branches, provides cash against all Visa cards, helpful if cards are lost; **Banco Internacional**, opposite Bank of America, notes only; **Banco de Pichincha**, Amazonas y Colón branch, good exchange rates for cash; **Banco Guayaquil**, Colón y Reina Victoria, arranges cash advances on Visa without limit and changes US$ TCs into dollars cash with no commission, cash advances from Ban NET ATMs, in sucres only, with Visa, maximum withdrawal US$100; **Banco Popular**, Amazonas 648, Mastercard, good service; **Banco del Pacífico**, Japón W of Shyris, good rates, cash advance on Mastercard only in sucres, branch near the airport, and in *Hotel Oro Verde*, charges no commission for cashing dollars. **Banco Consolidado**, Guayaquil y Olmedo, good rate for cash but does not accept cheques. Good rates at **Banco de la Producción**, Amazonas, opp Ecuadorean Tours, open 0900-1330, closed Sat. Master Card, Amazonas y Veintimilla, in Banco Pacífico building. Bank open Sat and Sun in departure lounge at airport. The **American Express** representative is **Ecuadorean Tours**, Amazonas 339, T 560-488, no cash advances. AmEx cheques available at Lloyds Bank, Amazonas branch. It is possible to change German mark TCs without problems. US$ money of any kind are not accepted anywhere in Ecuador.

Exchange Houses Casa Paz, Sucre y García Moreno, T 518-500, Amazonas 370 y Robles (open also Sat am), T 563-900, Centro Comercial El Bosque, T 455-075, Centro Comercial Plaza Aeropuerto, T 241-865, airport lobby and *Hotel Colón*, will change TCs into US$ cash up to US$300, 1% commission, plus all major currencies, slightly better rates for holders of international student cards, open 0900-1300, 1500-1800, Mon-Fri, branches also in Multicentro, 6 de Diciembre y Orellana (T 525-153, Mon-Fri 0915-1800, Sat 0930-1330) and in Centro Comercial Iñaquito, open Sat to 2000 and Sun to 1200. Multicambio, Venezuela 689, T 511 364, Roca 720, T 567-344, and Colón 919 y Reina Victoria, T 561-747, open Mon-Fri, 0830-1330, 1430-1730 and Sat am, also at the airport, no commission charged, good rates, no queues. The airport *cambio*, Casa Paz, Centro Comercial Iñaquito and the *Hotel Colón* are the only places you can change money on Sat pm and Sun (*Hotel Colón*, Sat 0800-1300 and 1500-1800, Sun 0900-1300, quick service, no commission). Vazcambios, Amazonas y Roca, *Hotel Alameda Real*, T 548-010; *Ecuacambio*, República 192 y Almagro, T 540-129. If you have trouble cashing American Express or Thomas Cook's TCs, try the *Banco Popular*. You are advised not to buy Peruvian soles until you get to the border; you will get a much better rate in Peru.

British Council Amazonas 1646 y Orellana, T 232-421, F 565-720, postal address: Casilla 1197. There is a library, open Mon-Fri, 0800-1915, and back copies of British newspapers are stocked in the *Gallery Café*, vegetarian restaurant, tea and cakes, free films every Wed. Books loaned if you join the library and pay a returnable deposit. **Alliance Française** at Eloy Alfaro 1900, French courses, films and cultural events.

Embassies and Consulates Colombia, Atahualpa 955 y República, T 564-015, insists on a ticket to leave Colombia before issuing a visa. **Peru** (T 520-134, 554-161) and **Brazil**

(T 563-086, 563-141) both in Edificio España, Av Colón y Av Amazonas. **Venezuela**, Coruña 1609 y Belo Horizonte, T 564-626, 562-038, visa US$30 + 1 photo, can take from a full morning up to 3 working days. **Guatemala**, Av 6 de Diciembre 2860, T 565-713, visa for 30 days issued at once, no fee to UK nationals. **Chile**, Juan Pablo Sanz 3617 y Amazonas, T 249-403, 453-327, open 0900-1300. **Uruguay**, Lizardo García 1025, T 541-968. **Bolivia**, Borja Lavayen y J P Sanz, T 458-863. **Argentina**, Amazonas 477, Edif Banco Pacífico, T 562-292. **Mexico**, 6 de Diciembre 4843 y Naciones Unidas, T 457-680. **Panama**, Diego de Almagro 1550 y La Pradera, T 566-449. **Costa Rica**, Inglaterra 712 y Mariana de Jesús, T 568-615. **Cuba**, 6 de Diciembre 5113, T 458-282. **Honduras**, Italia 420 y Mariana de Jesús, 3° piso, T 503-220. **Nicaragua**, Iñaquito 275 y Atahualpa, T 240-559.

USA, Av 12 de Octubre y Patria, T 562-890. An official copy of a US passport, US$2. (The US embassy does not hold mail for US citizens.) **Canadian Consulate**, Edif Josueth González, 6 de Diciembre 2816 y James Orton, 4° piso, T 543-214, F 503-108.

UK, Av González Suárez 111 y 12 de Octubre (opp *Hotel Quito*), letters to Casilla 314, T 560-309/669/670/671. The Consulate is in a separate building a few doors away (has travel information on Peru, helpful, open 0930-1200, 1430-1600). **Germany**, Av Patria y 9 de Octubre, Edificio Eteco, 6° piso, T 225-660, 567-231. **Austria**, Patria y Amazonas, PO Box 17-01-167, T 564 560. **Denmark**, Av República del Salvador 733 y Portugal, Edif Gabriela 3, T 458-585/786, 437-163, open 0900-1700; **Norway**, Pasaje Alonso Jerves 134 y Orellana, T 566-354; **Spain**, La Pinta 455 y Amazonas, T 564-373/377/390; **Italy**, La Isla 111 y H Albornoz, T 561-077/074; **Sweden**, Alonso Jerves 134 y Orellana, T 509-423 (am only); **Finland**, Av 18 de Septiembre 368, 3° piso, T 523-493. **France** Diego de Almagro y Pradera, Edificio Kingmann, 2° piso, T 569-883 for consulate, embassy at General Plaza 107 y Patria, T 560-789, 562-270, will hold letters for French citizens. **Switzerland**, Alonso Jerves 134 y Orellana, T 509-514. **Honorary Dutch Consul**, 9 de Octubre y Orellana (am only), T 567-606, F 563-853, PO Box 6294 CCI. **Honorary Irish Consul**, Montes 577 y Las Casas, T 503-674. **Israel**, Eloy Alfaro 969 y Amazonas, T 565-509/512. **Belgium**, JL Mera 863 y Wilson, T 545-340, F 507-367, Apdo Postal 17-21-532. **Japan**, Ignacio Bossano 637, T 459-295, PO Box 3031, Quito.

Night Clubs *Licorne*, at *Hotel Colón Internacional*; discos at *JK*, Amazonas 541, *Tobujas*, Amazonas y Santa María; *Dreams*, Naciones Unidas y Los Shyris; *Rio Club*, Av 12 de Octubre y Colón; *Le Pierrot*, Carrión 617 y Amazonas (all open till 0300). *Carpenix*, Almagro y La Niña, cover charge, popular with young crowd; *Cali Salsoteca*, Almagro y Orellana, great atmosphere; *Seseribó*, Veintimilla y 12 de Octubre, salsa and rock, rec, Thur-Sun, US$2; *El Solar*, Amazonas 2563 y Mariana de Jesús, salsa, Wed-Sat 2100-0300, good music, popular; *Tropicana*, Whimper y Coruña, "only for the cool"; *Footloose*, Baquerano 188 y J L Mera, gay disco, cover charge US$4; *Ku*, Orellana y 6 de Diciembre, popular disco.

Local folk music is popular and the entertainment is known as a *peña*. Places include *Dayumac*, J L Mera y Carrión, a meeting place for local music groups, dark, bohemian, warms up after 2400; *Cuerdas Andinas Disco Bar*, Carrión y J L Mera, entrance only for couples. *Ñucanchi*, Av Universitaria 496 y Armero, Thur-Sat 2230-0300. Most places do not come alive until 2230.

Theatre *Teatro Sucre*, Flores with Guayaquil, the most elegant (under renovation, due to re-open late 1995). Symphony concerts are free. Advance tickets from Metropolitan Touring, no need to book in April or May, the cheapest unreserved seats are OK (row 1-8 US$4.20; circle US$8), but arrive early. *Teatro San Gabriel*, América y Mariana de Jesús, Ecuadorean folk ballet 'Jacchigua' presented Wed and Fri 1930, entertaining, colourful and loud. *Teatro Prometeo* adjoining the Casa de la Cultura Ecuatoriana, 6 de Diciembre y Tarqui. *Agora*, open-air theatre of Casa de la Cultura (12 de Octubre y Patria) stages many concerts. Also, plays at the *Patio de Comedia*, 18 de Septiembre, between Amazonas y 9 de Octubre. Good music at *Teatro Equitorial Experimental*; check posters in Plaza Teatro for details. *Centro Cultural Afro-Ecuatoriano* (CCA), Tamayo 985 y Lizardo García, Casilla 352, Sucursal 12 de Octubre, T 522318, sometimes has cultural events and published material (useful contact for those interested in the black community). Many cultural events, usually free of charge; see the listings section of *El Comercio* for details.

Cinema The *Colón* (10 de Agosto y Colón), *República* (República), *Universitario* (América y A Pérez Guerrero, Plaza Indoamérica, Universidad Central), *Benalcázar*, 6 de Diciembre y Portugal, *24 de Mayo*, Granaderos y 6 de Diciembre, *Fénix*, 6 de Diciembre y Cordero, usually have the best films; *Colón* often has documentaries with Latin American themes. The Casa de la Cultura often has film festivals, as well as showing foreign films. *Cinema Central*, Venezuela, near Casa Paz, good sound, interesting films. US$1.50 in these cinemas. There are many others, especially in the Old City, mostly showing violent films; usually there is a standard entry charge (US$0.75 or less)—stay as long as you like.

932   ECUADOR

Health The British embassy has telephone numbers of English-speaking doctors; other embassies provide similar information. Hospital **Voz Andes**, next to Voz Andes radio station, Villalengua 267 (T 241-540), emergency room, quick, efficient, rec, fee US$8, some English spoken (American-run), has out-patient dept, reached by No 1 bus to Iñaquito; **Metropolitano**, Av Mariana de Jesús y Av Occidental, T 431-520, just E of the western city bypass, has also been rec (prices almost the same as in USA). Catch Quito Sur-San Gabriel bus from El Tejar downtown, via Av Universitaria and Av América, or a bus on 10 de Agosto or Av América and walk up. Or taxi, about US$0.60. Very professional, not cheap, gamma globulin costs about US$12. A rec paediatrician is Dr Luis Caicedo. Credit cards accepted. Among health centres recommended are **Centro Médico Alemania**, Eloy Alfaro y Alemania. **Clínica Pichincha**, Veintimilla 1259, T 561-643, amoebic dysentry tests, results within hours, US$15; **Clínica Americana Adventista** (some English spoken), 10 de Agosto 3366, 24 hrs, US$5. **Clínica San Francisco**, 6 de Diciembre y Colón, 24 hrs, x-rays. For amoebic dysentery tests, **Análisis Médicos Automatizados**, Alpallana 477 y Whymper, Ramírez Dávalos 202, T 545-945; **Dra Johanna Grimm**, Salvador 112 y Los Shyris, T 240-332, Lab 462-182; **Centro Médico Martha Roldós**, Plaza Teatro, Hepatitis B injections for US$0.30, but buy own syringe, needle and phial from *Fybeca* chemist (see below). **Dr Vargas Uvidia**, Colombia 248, T 513-152, speaks English and French; **Dr Rodrigo Sosa Sasa**, Cordero 410 y 6 de Diciembre, T 525-102, English speaking; **Dr Wilson Pancho**, Av República de El Salvador 112, T 463-139/469-564, speaks German. **Dr John Rosenberg**, internal and travel medicine (has a wide range of vaccines), consultation US$20, speaks English and German, very helpful general practitioner, new office at Med Center Travel Clinic (which also has a tropical disease specialist), Foch 476 y Almagro, T 223-333, paging service 506-856 beeper 135, home 441-757. **Gynaecologist**: Dr Steven Contag, Cordero 410 y 6 de Diciembre, T 560-408, speaks English. **Dentists**: Dr Aldo Grundland, Rep de El Salvador 210 y Av de Los Shyris, Ed Onix piso 7, speaks English, Hebrew, Italian, good value and efficient, great view of Pichincha from his chair; **Drs Sixto y Silvia Altamirano**, Av Amazonas 2689 y Av República, T 244-119, excellent; **Dra Rosa Oleas**, Amazonas 258 y Washington (T 524-859); **Dr Fausto Vallejo**, Madrid 744 (1 block from end of No 2 Camal/Colón bus line), T 554-781, rec, very reasonable; **Dr Roberto Mena**, Tamayo 1237 y Colón, T 525-329, speaks English and German; **Dr Víctor Peñaherrera**, Amazonas 4430 y Pereira, T 255-934/5, speaks English, rec. **Opticians**: Optica Luz, Amazonas y Colón, T 521-818, professional helpful, good value for repairs, eye tests and new glasses; **Optica Gill**, Amazonas, opposite the British Council, English spoken, glasses, contact lenses, helpful. All-night **chemist**, Farmacia Alaska, Venezuela 407 y Rocafuerte (T 210-973); *Droguería Doral*, on Amazonas, is a well-stocked, inexpensive pharmacy/chemist; also *Fybeca* on Guayaquil in the Old City (sells typhoid/paratyphoid pills—Vivatif, Swiss); *Fybeca* at Venezuela y Mejía sells tampons. Check the listing of *farmacias en turno* in Saturday's paper, *El Comercio*, for 24-hr chemists in following week. Chloroquine is available for malaria prevention but not Paludrine. For injections and prescriptions, Rumipampa 1744 y Vasco de Contreras, opp Coliseo de Colegio San Gabriel (old city), T 457-772.

Public Baths Montúfar 534 (Old City), no sign, 0730-1930, cheap, good. Hot showers on Rocafuerte, just below Plaza Santo Domingo (Old City), US$0.25.

Language Courses at the *Universidad Católica*, Octubre 1076 y Carrión, *Instituto de Lenguas y Lingüística*, T 529-240: 5-week Spanish courses, US$425, large classes; courses in Quechua. They will provide student cards, valid for reductions in Peru.

   Language Schools The South American Explorers Club provides a free list of recommended schools and may give club members discounts. It is impossible to list all the schools offering Spanish courses in Quito. We list schools for which we have received positive recommendations each year. This does not necessarily imply that schools not mentioned are not recommended. Note that in 1994 only 6 schools were registered with the Ministry of Education, although many of the others offer a high standard of teaching as well. Schools usually offer courses of 7 hours or 4 hours tuition per day, either in groups or on a one-to-one basis. Several correspondents have suggested that 4 hours a day is normally sufficient. Charges range between US$1.50 and US$8 per hour for one to one classes, but beware of extras which may not be mentioned in the initial quote. Some of the most expensive schools spend a great deal on multi-media equipment and advertising abroad, check how much individual tuition is provided. It is possible to arrange some trial lessons. If staying with a family book 1 week initially; if you are too hard pressed to sign a long-term contract go elsewhere. Do not arrange accommodation through intermediaries or "fixers" and make sure you get a receipt for money paid. It is normally more expensive and not necessary to book from abroad. Schools can arrange accommodation with families from US$10 to US$25 a day, full board. Many also offer excursions.

   Favourable reports in 1994/early 1995 were received on: *Academia Latinoamericano*, José

Queri 2 y Eloy Alfaro, PO Box 17-17-593, T 433-820, F 465-500; *Edinburgh Linguistic Center*, Jorge Drom 945 y Villarroel, T 446-877, F 566-399, PO Box 17-21-0405; *Amazonas One to One Spanish School*, Washington 718 and Amazonas, Edif Rocafuerte, 3rd floor, PO Box 17-21-1245, T 504-654; *Instituto Superior de Español*, Ulloa 152 y Jerónimo Carrión, PO Box 17-03-00490, T 223-242, F 221-628 (have also opened a school in Otavalo and can arrange voluntary work with La Cruz Roja Ecuatoriana, at Mindo, Fundación Jatun Sacha and others); *Galápagos Spanish School*, Amazonas 258 y Washington, PO Box A744, T 540-164; *Estudio de Español Pichincha*, Carrión 1300 y Plaza, PO Box 17-03-00936, T/F 547-090; *Academia Español Quito*, 10 de Agosto y Marchena, T 553-647; *South American Spanish Institute*, Av Amazonas 1549 y Santa María, T 544715/226348, F 436-200; *Rainbow Spanish Centre*, Armero 749 y Sta Rosa, PO Box 1721-01310, T 584-519; *Rumiñahui*, Mejía y Cuenca, small orange sign at corner; *Instituto de la Lengua Española Cervantes*, Amazonas 1001 y Wilson, 2° piso, T 239-030; *School of Spanish Ecuador*, Queseras del Medio 741 y 12 de Octubre, PO Box 737, T 543-447/520-667, Director Gladys Valencia; *Colonial Spanish School*, Sucre 518 y Benalcázar, PO Box 17-01-3739, T 572-698, F 568-664; *Colonial Spanish School 2*, Santa Prisca 310 y Ibarra, T 570-352; *Cumbre Andina*, Versalles 1449, T 260-573, F 564-924; *Academia de Español Equinoccial*, Roca 533 y Juan León Mera, T 564-488, F 529-460; *Nueva Vida*, Venezuela 1389 y Oriente, PO Box 17-01-2518, T 216-986; *Interandina*, Garcia Moreno 858 y José Antonio Sucre, F 583-086; *Academia Atlántica*, Guanguiltagua 560, T 241-075; *Mitad del Mundo*, Terán 1676 entre Versalles y 10 de Agosto, T/F 567-875, PO Box 17-15-389C; *Latitud Ecuatorial Centro de Estudios de Español*, Juan Severino 231 y Diego de Almagro, T 523-164, F 446-250; *America Spanish School*, 768 Carrión and 9 de Octubre, T 229-166, F 568-664 (see also *Quito's Information Center* under **Information** below); *Escuela Israel*, Olmedo 552 y Flores 2° piso; *Simón Bolívar*, Andalucía 565 y Salazar, Sucursal 12 de Octubre, T/F 502-640; *La Lengua*, Colón

1001 y JL Mera, Edif Ave María, 8° piso, T/F 501-271. A rec course book is *Español, Curso de Perfeccionamiento*, by Juan Felipe García Santos (Universidad de Salamanca, Sep 1990). *National Registration Centre for Study Abroad*, 823N 2nd St, PO Box 1393, Milwaukee, WI 53203, USA, T 414-278-0631, F 271-8884, and *AmeriSpan Unlimited*, PO Box 40513, Philadelphia, PA 19016-0513, T 800-879-6640 (USA and Canada), 215-985-4522 (worldwide), F 215-985-4524, E-mail: info@amerispan.com have information on courses and will make bookings, free newsletters.

Laundries *Lavanderías Modernas*, 6 de Diciembre 24-00 y Colón, T 527-601, expensive; *Lavyseca*, Cordero y Tamayo, laundry and dry cleaning, US$7 for 12 kg, same day. *Lavandería*, 552 Olmedo, T 213-992, will collect clothes. *Laundry Wash and Go*, Pinto 340 y JL Mera. Dry-cleaning, *Martinizing*, 1 hr service, 12 de Octubre 1486, Diego de Almagro y La Pradera, and in 6 shopping centres, plus other locations, expensive. *La Química*, Mallorca 335 y Madrid; *Norte*, Amazonas 7339, and Pinzón y La Niña. *Almagro*, Wilson 470 y Almagro, T 225-208, laundry by weight.

Post Office The old sucursal mayor (main branch) is in the old city, on Espejo, entre Guayaquil y Venezuela. The new head office (philatelic service 7th floor) is located at Eloy Alfaro 354 y 9 de Octubre. For parcels and surface-air-lifted reduced priority (SAL/APR, replacing sea mail which is no longer available), Correo Marítimo Aduana, Ulloa 273 y Ramírez Dávalos (next to Santa Clara market). Others: Japón y Naciones Unidas; Torres de Almagro, Colón y Reina Victoria; airport (national departures); terminal terrestre, and others. All sell stamps Mon-Fri 0730-1930, Sat 0800-1400; special services, eg parcels, collection of registered mail until 1530 only. *Poste Restante*, at the post offices at Espejo and at Eloy Alfaro: all *poste restante* letters are sent to Espejo unless marked "Correo Central, Eloy Alfaro", but you are advised to check both *postes restantes*, whichever address you use (the one at Eloy Alfaro is reported helpful). Parcels marked 'Lista de Correos' and sent registered mail to Eloy Alfaro are dealt with efficiently. Letters can be sent care of American Express, Apartado 2605, Quito. For more details and for parcels service and letters to Europe via Lufthansa **see p 1058**.

Telecommunications International and interprovincial calls are possible from the Emetel offices at Av 10 de Agosto y Colón, New City, Benalcázar y Mejía, Old City, and at Terminal Terrestre, open 0900-2100, cheaper on Sun. People at the airport try and sell you phone cards; as international calls can only be made at Emetel offices it is better to buy them only when you need them. Fax service and 1-minute international phone calls (Europe US$7/minute, US$5.10 Canada) so that you can be called back if necessary, available through Intimexpo, Amazonas 877 y Wilson, Edificio Visecom, Oficina 306, T 568-617/632, F 568-664 (Mon-Fri 0900-1800) also possible to make a collect call to some, but not all, countries, beware overcharging. *Hotel Oro Verde* will send faxes, *Hotel Colón* is cheaper but only for residents, can also send from postcard shop at the end of the passage next to Ecuadorean Tours.

Places of Worship Joint Anglican/Lutheran service is held (in English) at the Advent Lutheran Church, Isabel la Católica 1419, Sun, 0900. Synagogue at 18 de Setiembre y Versalles, services Fri 1900 and Sat 0900.

Shopping Most shops in the old city are shut Sat pm. Articles typical of Ecuador can be bought in the main shopping districts of Avenidas Amazonas and Guayaquil. There are carved figures, plates and other items of local woods, balsa wood boxes, silver of all types, Indian textiles, buttons, toys and other things fashioned from tagua nuts, hand-painted tiles, hand-woven rugs and a variety of antiques dating back to colonial days. Panama hats are a good buy. Indian garments (for Indians rather than tourists) can be seen and bought on the N end of the Plaza de Santo Domingo and along the nearest stretch of Calle Flores. *Ocepa*, at 12 de Octubre y Colón, good selection, partly government owned, also Washington 252 y Amazonas, near *Hotel Colón*, and Amazonas 2222. *Hilana*, 6 de Diciembre 1921 y Baquerizo, beautiful unique 100% wool blankets in Ecuadorean motifs, excellent quality, purchase by metre possible, inexpensive. Near *Hotel Quito* at Colón 260 is *Folklore*, the store of the late Olga Fisch, a most attractive array of handicrafts and rugs, but distinctly expensive, as accords with the designer's international reputation; also at *Hotel Colón* (where *El Bazaar* also has a good selection of crafts) and *Hotel Oro Verde*.

   Productos Andinos, an artisans' co-operative, Urbina 111 y Cordero, good quality, reasonably priced, rec. *La Bodega Exportadora*, J L Mera 614 y Carrión, is rec for antiques and handicrafts, as is *Renacimiento*, Carrión y J L Mera. *Fundación Sinchi Sacha*, Reina Victoria 1780 y La Niña, T 230-609, F 567-311, PO Box 17-07-9466, cooperative selling select ceramics and other arts and crafts from Oriente, rec; *MCCH Women's Co-op*, JL Mera y Robles; *Marcel Creations*, Roca 766, entre Amazonas y 9 de Octubre, good panama hat selection; *Artesanías Cuencanas*, Av Roca 626 entre Amazonas y JL Mera, friendly, knowledgeable, wide selection; *Krupp Designs*, República 501 entre 6 de Diciembre y Coruña, artists, jewellery;

Galeria Latina, next to Libri Mundi at J L Mera 823 y Veintimilla, has fine selection of handicrafts from Ecuador, Peru and Bolivia; **Centro Artesanal**, J L Mera 804, **El Aborigen**, Washington 536 y J L Mera and **Ecuafolklore**, Robles 609 entre Amazonas y J L Mera (also stocks guide books) have all been recommended. **Coosas**, J L Mera 838, the factory outlet for Peter Mussfeldt's attractive animal designs (bags, clothes etc). **The Ethnic Collection**, Amazonas 1004 y Wilson, T/F 501-155, wide variety, clothing, leather, bags, jewellery, etc (in UK contact Richard Hartley, The Alpaca Collection, 16 Warstone Parade East, Hockley, Birmingham B18 6NR, T 0121 212 2550, F 0121 212 1948). Goldwork from **Antigüedades el Chordeleg**, 6 de Diciembre y Cordero. **Artesanías El Jaguar**, J L Mera 234 and 18 de Septiembre, behind *Hotel Colón*, souvenirs especially from the Oriente, the owner, Gladis Escobar, paints balsawood birds in colours of your choosing (not cheap). **J M Handicrafts**, Diego de Almagro y Baquerizo, unique painted woodcarvings and other select artesanía. **Handicrafts Otavalo**, Sucre 255 and García Moreno, good selection, but expensive.

Mercado Ipiales, on Chile from Imbabura uphill, or Mercado Plaza Arenas on Vargas are where you are most likely to find your stolen camera for sale – or have it stolen, the New City is safer (also try **Grau** camera shop, Plaza Santo Domingo, on your left as you face the church). The other market is on 24 de Mayo and Loja from Benalcázar onwards. There is an exhibition and sale of paintings in the park opp *Hotel Colón*, Sat am. On Amazonas, NE of *Hotel Colón*, are a number of street stalls run by Otavalo Indians, who are tough but friendly bargainers. Bargaining is customary in small shops and at street stalls. Leather goods at **Chimborazo**, Amazonas (next to Espinal shopping centre) and **Aramis**, Amazonas 1234; **Su Kartera**, Sucre 351 y García Moreno, T 512-160, with a branch on Veintimilla 1185 between 9 de Octubre y Amazonas, manufacturers of bags, briefcases, shoes, belts etc; **Casa Indo Andina**, Roca y J L Mera, alpaca, wool fashions, good quality. **Camari**, Marchena 260, is a direct sale shop run by an artisan organization. See **H Stern's** jewellery stores at the airport, *Hotel Colón* and *Hotel Quito*. Other jewellery shops: **Alquimia**, Juan Rodríguez 139, high quality silversmith; **Edda**, Tamayo 1256 y Cordero, custom-made jewellery, rec; **Argentum**, J L Mera 614, reasonably priced. **La Guaragua**, Washington 614, sells **artesanías** and antiques, excellent selection, reasonable prices.

Supermaxi supermarkets offer 10% discount on purchases if you buy a Supermaxi card; this is available at the main counter. There are Supermaxi stores at the Centro Comercial Iñaquito, Centro Comercial El Bosque (Av Occidental), Centro Comercial Plaza Aeropuerto (Av de la Prensa y Homero Salas) and at the Multicentro shopping complex on 6 de Diciembre y La Niña, about two blocks N of Colón, and others, all open Mon-Sat 0930-2000, Sun 0930-1300. **Mi Comisariato**, Centro Comercial Quicentro, Naciones Unidas y 6 de Diciembre, supermarket and department store. **La Feria** supermarket, Bolívar 334, between Venezuela and García Morena sells good wines and spirits, and Swiss, German and Dutch cheeses. Macrobiotic food at *Vitalcentro Microbiótico*, Carrión 376 y 6 de Diciembre. *Sangre de Drago*, the Indian cure all, is sold at the juice bar at Oriente y Guayaquil.

For music, **Audio-Video**, several branches, national and international. Excellent art supply shops **S Bandra**, Calama 221, between Almagro y Reina Victoria, T 525-353; **Papelería Chávez**, Veintimilla y 12 de Octubre, is cheaper, they also have large envelopes and boxes; good quality drawing paper is hard to find, better to take supplies with you.

Bookshops The **South American Explorers Club** (see p 940) has the best selection of guidebooks in English (new and second-hand at good prices) and maps covering Ecuador and the rest of South America. **Libri Mundi**, J L Mera 851 y Veintimilla, open Mon-Sat, 0800-1800, and at the *Hotel Colón Internacional*, open Mon-Fri, 0800-1800, Sat-Sun, 1700-2000, Spanish, English (some second-hand available), French, some Italian books, records, Ecuadorean maps when in stock (cheaper at other bookshops), has a notice-board of what's on in Quito; very highly rec; **The Travel Company**, JL Mera 517 y Roca and JL Mera 1233 y Lizardo García, for books (secondhand at No 1233), postcards, T-shirts, videos, rec; **Imágenes**, 9 de Octubre y Roca, for books on Ecuador and art, postcards; **Libro Express**, Amazonas 816 y Veintimilla, has a good stock of maps, guides and international magazines; **Librería Española**, Veintimilla 961 y Mejía; **Librería Científica**, Colón y J L Mera; **Librería Cima**, 10 de Agosto 285 y Sta Prisca, good selection in Spanish; **Pomaire**, Amazonas 863 (Spanish mainly); **Ediciones Abya-Yala**, 12 de Octubre 14-36 (T 562-633), also has excellent library and museum. The United States Information Service has an excellent library. **Biblioteca Luz**, Oriente 618 y Vargas, runs a book exchange (mainly Spanish) charge US$1. Bookshop at Centro Comercial Popular, Flores 739 y Olmedo, T 212-550, sells half price books and magazines, some French and English books, also book exchange. Foreign newspapers at news stand in *Hotel Colón*. Lufthansa will supply German newspapers if they have spare copies.

Camera Repairs and Equipment *El Globo*, 10 de Agosto in departmental store, sells Fuji slides and print film, stored properly, refrigerated; **Japon Color Express**, Amazonas 507, slide film, Fuji RD 100-36, US$7, check the dates; *Kis Color*, Amazonas 1238 y Calama, helpful with repairs, will develop and print 36 exposure film for US$8, better quality for 24-hr printing than 1 hr service, passport photos in 3 mins. Several places for cheap processing on Plaza Santo Domingo. *Suba Foto*, Maldonado 1371 y Rocafuente (sells second-hand cameras) and *Foto Estudio Gran*, Bolívar 140 y Plaza Santo Domingo for repairs and parts. *Cemaf*, Asunción 130 y 10 de Agosto, Edif Molina, 1° piso, T 230 855, helpful, also repairs video cameras. Film is cheap but only ASA100, 200, 400 and Kodak Gold 35 mm available, no Kodachrome. Lots of shops on Amazonas sell film at good prices. *Ecuacolor/Kodak*, Amazonas 888 y Wilson, Orellana 476 y 6 de Diciembre, and 10 de Agosto 4150 y Atahualpa. The Kodak processing laboratory has been criticised as dirty and careless; a recommended processing lab is that of Ron Jones, Brieva 641 y Diguja (Granda Centeno), take bus to Av América, get off at TV channel 4, walk up hill, he develops Fuji and Kodak, slides/prints, B/W or colour, helpful and informative. *Naun Briones*, Cordero 1167 y J L Mera. Also for black and white, *Fotomanía*, 6 de Diciembre y Patria. Average price for processing US$6.50 for 24, US$8.50 for 36.

Sport A local game, *pelota de guante* (glove ball), is played, Sat afternoon and Sun at Estadio Mejía. **Football** is played Sat afternoons (1200 or 1400) and Sun mornings (maybe as early as 0800) at Estadio Atahualpa (6 de Diciembre y Naciones Unidas, any northbound bus on 6 de Diciembre marked "Estadio" goes there), and **basketball** in the Coliseo. The first week of Dec is the main **bullfighting** season. Tickets are on sale at 1500 the day before the bullfight; an above-average ticket costs US$8 but you may have to buy from touts. The Unión de Toreros, Edif Casa Paz, Av Amazonas, has information on all bullfights around the country; these take place all year, except Christmas to Mar. They do not have details of the parochial *corridas del pueblo*. **Cockfighting** in Pollodrome, Calle Pedro Calixto y Chile, Sat, 1400-1900, US$0.25 plus bet. There is a cold spring-water **swimming pool** on Maldonado beyond the Ministry of Defence building (US$0.10), hot shower (US$0.10); a public heated, chlorinated pool is in Miraflores, at the end of Calle Universitaria, corner of Nicaragua, 10 mins walk from Amazonas, you must take swimming cap, towel and soap to be admitted, open Tues-Sun, 0900-1600, US$1; another public pool at Batán Alto, on Cochapata, near 6 de Diciembre and Villaroel. **Rugby** is played at Colegio Militar on Sun 1000. Inquire at *El Pub*. The Hash House Harriers club for **runners**, joggers and walkers, enquire at *Reina Victoria Pub*, T 233-369. **Bowling** centre, pool, Amazonas y Alfaro. **Paragliding**, *Escuela Pichincha*, Alemania 339 y Eloy Alfaro, T Jaime 540-347, Cicque 455-076, US$250 complete course, good.

Mountain Biking *Pedal Andes* run back-road mountain bike tours, cultural as well as physical, highly rec, can combine with whitewater rafting; arrange through *Sierra Nevada* in Quito, T 553-658, F 659-250. *Flying Dutchman's Downhill Bike Rides*, La Pinta 146 y Diego de Almagro, T 527-842, one-day tours, great fun, good food. *Bike-Trek*, Andagoya 498 y Ruiz de Castilla, outings arranged and good mechanics, Santiago and Regis (speaks English). *Páramo Mountain Bike Shop*, 6 de Diciembre 3925 y Checoslovaquia, T 255-403/404, F 465-507, limited stock and assistance. Rec mechanic, Alex Morillo, T 434-570. *Bicisport*, Los Shyris 1300 y Portugal, T 442-984, rec. For a tour phone Jan, T 449-568/458-859.

Whitewater Rafting *Sierra Nevada*, J L Mera 741 y Baquedano, T 553-658/554-936, F 659-250, excellent trips from 1 to 3 days, also rafting/mountain bike combinations. *Etnotur*, J L Mera 1238, 1-3 day tours, class IV rapids. *Andean River Expeditions*, 176 Gaspar de Villaroel, T 460-154. Gynner Coronel has equipment and information on kayaking, very experienced, T 553-720. All these outfits charge US$60-70/day.

Climbing *Nuevos Horizontes Club*, Av Colón 2038 y 10 de Agosto, T 552-154, F 541-406, will advise on **climbing Chimborazo and Cotopaxi**, including purchase or hire of crampons, ice axes etc, but does not hire them (best to have with you). Non-members may go on the club's increasingly infrequent trips if these are not fully-booked. Padre José Ribas of Colegio San Gabriel is helpful, their climbing club meets Wed 1930. Freddy Ramírez, who runs *Sierra Nevada* (address above, or T home 261-873), highly rec as a mountain guide. Freddy speaks English, French and German. He has equipment and a 4WD Toyota jeep for rent. Other clubs for climbers: *Sadday*, Alonso de Angulo y Galo Molina; the **Club de Andinismo** of the Universidad Católica in Quito meets every Tues and Thur at 1930 and welcomes visitors. Those needing a professional climbing guide can try *Xavier Herrera*, T 458-630, speaks English, or *Mario Vascones*, T 724-372, speaks German, both members of Club de Andinismo and Asegium, can provide 4WD transport, Xavier can also be contacted through *Safari Tours*, T 552-505. *Camilo Andrade*, PO Box 17-12-513, T/F 340-601, rec for climbing expeditions, trekking and jungle tours, 8 languages spoken. *Hugo Torres*, *Pamir Adventure Travels*, J L Mera 741 y Veintimilla, T 322-331, F 569-741, PO Box 17-190 CEQ, Quito, very experienced, English speaking, 4WD vehicle. Caminos del Sol, *Luisa Gallardo*, highly rec female guide, Carrión 145 y 12 de Octubre. *Andean Sport*, Roca 549 y J L Mera, T 520-442/444-095,

F 568-664, specializes in climbing and adventure tours, and has equipment for rent. Also *Julio Mesías*, experienced guide and member of Aseguim, T 533-787. See also *Surtrek* under Ambato **Travel Agents**, p 969.

For climbing the volcanoes, proper equipment and good guidance are essential. The dangers of inadequate acclimatization, snow blindness, climbing without equipment or a guide must be taken very seriously, especially on Chimborazo and Cotopaxi, which are not technically difficult and tempting targets for the less experienced, as many letters show. The Quito climbing clubs welcome new members, but they do not provide free guiding service. It is not really worth joining if you are in Ecuador for only a few weeks. The clubs are a good source for locating professional guides. Newly established is **Aseguim**, The Mountain Guide Association, which provides courses for their members and checks standards and equipment. You can check the validity of any guide through any of the recommended climbing stores. Aseguim also organizes mountain rescues. The Association is not-for-profit and its members appreciate donations. Mountain rescue facilities are inadequate, it can take many hours to start a rescue operation and lack of equipment severely hinders success.

Climbing, Camping and Trekking Equipment Useful climbing equipment stores (and sources of information) are *Equipo Cotopaxi*, 6 de Diciembre y Patria, equipment rentals, rec but expensive, and *Campo Abierto*, 6 de Diciembre y Roca, Casilla 17-03-671, T 230-029, F 524-422, which publishes a guide to climbing Ecuador's mountains, *Montañas del Sol* (US$6.75, 1994). *Altamontaña*, Jorge Washington 425 y 6 de Diciembre, F 524-422, climbing equipment, reasonable prices, good advice. *Altamontaña* and *Campo Abierto* both sell imported gear. Usual charge for hiring equipment is US$1-2 per item per day, plus US$60 deposit in cash or cheques; stores may buy your used equipment. Camping: *Cotopaxi*: Av Colón 942 y Reina Victoria, Mon-Fri 0900-1300, 1500-1900, T 563-560, good value equipment and camping gas. *Trekking*: 6 de Diciembre y Pinto, climbing and trekking equipment.

"*Bluet Camping Gas*" is reported to be easily obtainable: try *Importadora Vega* opp Banco Central, *Deportes Cotopaxi*, 6 de Diciembre y 18 de Septiembre, or *Globo*, 10 de Agosto, sometimes have it in stock but it's expensive (*Globo* shops also stock cheap snorkelling gear, also *Importaciones Kao*, Colón y Almagro, and Casa Maspons, Orellana between 6 de Diciembre and Pinzón). *Captain Peña*, on the corner of Plaza Santo Domingo and Flores, also

sells snorkelling equipment and for your personal security they stock C S Gas spray. Several new camping stores on Colón, E and W of Amazonas, stock camping gas. For primus stoves and parts, *Almacenes Jácome*, Chile 955 (nr Guayaquil). White gas is impossible to find in Ecuador; better to have a multifuel stove. Kerex or kerosene can be found on the corner of Bogotá y Uruguay, knock on the back gate. Those stoves which burn kerex work with unleaded gasoline (from Eco 82 or Super SP pumps in larger cities).

For hiking boots, *Calzado Beltrán*, Cuenca 562, and other shops on the same street. For a lockable rucksack cover *Equipos Cotopaxi*, Alianza 351 y Chimborazo, T 517626, made to measure, around US$25.

South American Explorers Club Toledo 1254 y Luís Cordero, T 566-076, Mon-Fri 0930-1700, is a non-profit organization staffed by volunteers which provides a wide range of information on South America through its resource centre, library and quarterly journal as well as selling guidebooks, maps and equipment, both new and used. Also has information on mountain biking in Ecuador. Highly rec. Annual membership US$40 single, US$60 for a couple. You can arrange incoming faxes through SAEC. Non-members are asked to limit their visit to 20 mins. Write to Apartado 21-431, Eloy Alfaro, Quito, or 126 Indian Creek Road, Ithaca, NY 14850; T (607) 277-0488. Official representatives in UK: Bradt Publications, 41 Nortoft Rd, Chalfont St Peter, Bucks, SL9 0LA, T/F 0494-873478.

Tour Operators and Travel Agents *Ecuadorean Tours* (American Express agent), Av Amazonas 339, T 560-488, also sell local student cards, US$17, to those with proof of home student status, useful for discounts (Poste Restante can be sent to Aptdo 2605, Quito), office at *Hotel Colón* helpful; *Metropolitan Touring*, helpful for information for non-customers, Av República de El Salvador 970, PO Box 17-12-310, T 464-780, F 464-702; also Amazonas 239 y 18 de Septiembre and at *Hotel Quito*; Thomas Cook representative; general agents for Galápagos Cruises and Transturi; runs tours to the Galápagos, also arranges climbing, trekking expeditions led by world-known climbers, as well as tours of Quito, Machalilla National Park, rail journeys to Cuenca and Guayaquil, jungle camps, generally rec, *Transturi*, part of Metropolitan Touring, operate a cruise ship, the *Flotel Francisco de Orellana*, in 4-5 day trips from Coca along the jungle rivers; *Situr/Ecoventura*, 6 de Diciembre y Colón, T 561-955, F 562-024, has tours throughout Ecuador and to the Galápagos, inc Northern Andes, Indian markets, Cuenca, Ingapirca, birdwatching, the Amazon and the Pacific coast. *Ecuaviajes*, Av Eloy Alfaro 1500 y Juan Severino, T 233-386, F 504-830, highly rec for everything, Cristina Latorre de Suárez speaks excellent English, very helpful if trying to find a cheap way home; *Angermeyers Enchanted Excursions*, Foch 726 y Amazonas, T 569-960, F 569-956, for Galápagos cruises on a variety of boats, and tours (incl economy) of jungle, sierra and costa; *Rolf Wittmer*, Valderrama y Mariana de Jesús, PO Box 17-07-8989, T 449337, F 448173, two yachts for tours of the Galápagos; *Golondrina Tours*, J L Mera 639 y Carrión, T 528-616, F 528-570, also in Puerto Ayora, rec for 8 day trip to Galápagos from Quito; *Napo Tour*, J L Mera 1312 y Cordero, T 545-426/547-283, has been rec as efficient and cheap, it is better value to book Napo's *Anaconda Hotel* (near Misahualli) in Quito than to book in Misahualli (it is also cheaper to make your own way there than to go with Napo Tour). *Alpa Tours*, Amazonas y Foch, rec, very helpful, T 562-436/7; *Etnotur*, Luis Cordero 1313 y J L Mera, T 564-565, F 502-682, helpful, English and German spoken, jungle, mountain, rafting and Galápagos tour, rec; *Latin Tour*, office at airport and in Av Amazonas, T 508-811/222-266, various trips around the country in a jeep and by motorbike, eg to Cotopaxi, English speaking, ask for Juan López, and very friendly staff, frequently rec; *Free Biker Tours*, Guipuzcoa 339 y La Floresta, T 560-469, or in Switzerland, Grenzweg 48, 3645 Gwatt, T 033-365-128, run by Patrick

Lombriser, Enduro-Motorcycles 600cc, good tours, spectacular roads, rec; *Andean Sports*, Roca 549 y J L Mera, T 520-442, English, French, German spoken, climbing, tours, equipment provided, rec; *Elinatour*, Bejarano 150 y Suárez, T 525-352, 7 blocks from *Hotel Quito*, gives time and effort to finding what people want; *Naturgal*, Foch y Reina Victoria, English spoken, specializes in trips to the Llanganates; *Pablo Prado*, Rumipamba 730 y República, T 446-954, for tours in 4WD vehicle, nature adventures, ecological excursions, Galápagos, rainforests; *Volker*, organizes walking, cycling and river rafting tours to Mindo, Muisne and other places, rec, contact him in *Ghoz* bar or *Arribar*; *Agama Expediciones*, Venezuela 1163 y Manabí, climbing, trekking, some equipment for sale and rent, rec; *Horizontes Ecuatorianos*, Pinto 560 y Amazonas, T 230-463, F 502-399, PO Box 850-A, Quito, arranges a variety of specialized tours and Galápagos tours, 12-passenger van and driver for hire, English spoken, friendly and helpful; *Klein Tours*, Av Los Shyris 1000 y Holanda, T 430-345, F 442-389, Galápagos and mainland tours, tailor-made, specialist and adventure, English, French and German spoken; *Nixe Cruises*, El Comercio 125 y Av de los Shyris, T 467-980, F 437-645, PO Box 6646 CCI, catamaran cruises of Galápagos, max 10 passengers, 4 crew, 1 guide, diving available, also tours of the coast, Machalilla National Park and the Oriente; *Palmer Voyages*, Alemania 575 y Mariana de Jesús, T 506-915, small specialist company, good rates, speak to Dominique Olivares; *Fantasía Tours*, Roca 736 y Amazonas, Pasaje Chantilly, T 567-186, F 554-454, PO Box 9249, rec for booking Galápagos trips efficiently; *Sudamericana de Turismo*, Av Amazonas 11-13 y Pinto, good, Ricardo speaks German; *Delgado Travel*, Av Amazonas 12-27 y Foch, T 520-229, F 521-250, flights and car rental; *Andes Discovery Tours*, Av Amazonas 645 y Ramírez Dávalos, T 550-952, F 437-470, Galápagos tours, helpful, rec; *Safari*, Calama 380 y J L Mera (also in the cul-de-sac opp *Hotel Alameda Real* on Roca), T 552-505, F 220-426, David Gayton and Jean Brown, excellent adventure travel, customized trips, 4WD jeeps available (Fabian Espinosa is an excellent guide), open 7 days, also operates the *Railway Inn* at Cotopaxi national park (**see p 964**); *Explorer Tours*, Lizardo García y Reina Victoria, T 522-220, owns *Sacha Lodge* on Río Napo, first rate educational jungle tours; *Native Life*, Joaquín Pinto 446 y Amazonas, T 550-836, F 569-741, PO Box 17-03-504, tours of 1-26 days, good English, fun and informative; *Galatravel*, Amazonas 519 y Roca, Galápagos tours, and *Eurogalápagos*, Amazonas 330 y Washington; *River Tour*, Washington y Amazonas, Edif Rocafuerte, local 10, T 505-706, highly rec for good value Galápagos tours, small boats and

groups, staying overnight in hotels. *Terracenter*, Reina Victoria 1343 y J Rodríguez, T/F 507-858, all variety of tours, incl Galápagos (special arrangement with Simón Bolívar language school). The *Hotel Gran Casino Internacional* sells tours to the Galápagos (although many complaints and unfavourable reports received, others are satisfied). Icelandair, Av Diego de Almagro 1822 y Alpallana, T 561-820 for tickets to Europe via Iceland, student discounts. There are many agencies in the Avenida Amazonas area; shop around for best deals for the Galápagos and jungle lodges.

Galasam Cía Ltda, Pinto 523 y Av Amazonas, and Amazonas 1316 y Cordero, T 507-080/1/2, F 567-662, operates Economic Galápagos Tours as well as Condor Tours, Uniclán, Yanasacha, Sol Mar Tours. 4-star hotel due open at Amazonas y Cordero in Dec 1995. Their tours can be purchased in Switzerland: Mondorama, T (01) 261-5121, F (01) 262-2306; Holland, Cross Country Travel, T (025) 20-77-677, F (025) 20-23-670; Australia, Latin American Travel, T (61) 33-29-5211, F (61) 33-29-6314; USA, Galapagos Worldwide, T (305) 1-800-327 9854, F (305) 661 1457; Latin American Specialized Tours, T (410) 922-3116, F (410) 922-5538; Galapagos Yacht Cruises, T 1-800-GALA-PRO (1-800-425-2778); Forum Travel, T (510) 671-2993, F (510) 946-1500, exclusive representatives, prices are the same as in Ecuador. Galasam offer 3, 4 and 7 night Galápagos cruises, 6-day/5-night cruises with 2 extra nights in Santa Cruz or San Cristóbal.

Galapagos Network, 7200 Corporate Center Drive, Suite 404, Miami, Florida, T (305) 592-2294, F (305) 592-6394, in Quito T (593-2) 564-969, F 564-592, Guayaquil, T 201-516, F 201-153, modern yachts. For other agencies organizing tours to the Galápagos, **see p 1045**.

NB When booking tours, note that National Park fees are rarely included.

Tourist Office Corporación Ecuatoriana de Turismo (Cetur), Eloy Alfaro 124 y Carlos Tobar (between República and Shyris), T 225-190/1 and at Venezuela 976 near Mejía, 1st floor, open Mon to Fri, 0800-1630 (T 514-044) and at airport (last two can make hotel bookings); provide maps and other information, very helpful. Some staff speak English.

Information *Quito's Information Center*, Guayaquil 1242 y Olmedo, 2nd Floor, T 229166, F (593-2) 229165, PO Box 17-03-0062, and at Carrión y 9 de Octubre, opens 1100, has worldwide phone/fax service, language school. Municipal Library, García Moreno, near Plaza de la Independencia, with a good cheap cafetería.

Maps Instituto Geográfico Militar on top of the hill to the E of El Ejido park. From Av 12 de Octubre, opposite the Casa de la Cultura, take Jiménez (a small street) up the hill. After crossing Av Colombia continue uphill on Paz y Miño behind the Military Hospital and then turn right to the guarded main entrance; you have to deposit your passport or identification card. There is a beautiful view from the grounds. Map and air photo indexes are all laid out for inspection. The map sales room (helpful staff) is open 0800-1600, Mon-Thur, 0800-1300 Fri. They sell the best topographic maps, covering most areas of Ecuador, sclaes 1:250,000, 1:100,000, 1:50,000, 1:25,000, about US$2 each. Maps of border areas are 'reservado' (classified) and not available for sale without a military permit (requires approx 6 weeks). Many large-scale topographical maps are reported out of print, but there are 4 new sheets covering the Oriente, 1:250,000 Mapas Amazónicas, very accurate, US$2.75 each. Buy your maps here, they are rarely available outside Quito. If one is sold out you may order a photo copy. Map and geographic reference libraries are located next to the sales room. Many maps are now available at the Centro de Difusión Geográfica in the House of Sucre, Venezuela 573, helpful. All IGM maps are available by mail order from Latin American Travel Consultants, PO Box 17-17-908, Quito, Ecuador, F 593-2-562-566, Internet: rku@pi.pro.ec. See also **Maps and Guide Books**, p 1052.

Immigration Office For tourist visa extensions, **Policía Nacional de Migración**, Amazonas 2639, Mon-Fri 0800-1200 and 1500-1800; take bus 15 or double-decker bus along Amazonas; go early and be prepared to wait. Those with visas other than tourist may obtain information from the **Cancillería** (Asuntos Migratorios, Sección Visas, Edificio Zurita, Páez y Carrión, 1st floor, T 561-010, Mon-Fri 0930-1230), the **Extranjería** (Carrión & Páez, diagonally across from Asuntos Migratorios, T 563-353, Mon-Fri 0800-1300), and **Policía Nacional de Migración** (as above). Paperwork at any or all of these offices may be required to change, extend, or renew non-tourist visas.

Police Criminal Investigations, Cuenca y Mideros, Old City. To report a robbery, make a *denuncia* within 48 hrs on official paper; if one officer is unhelpful, try another. If over 48 hrs, you will need a lawyer. Centralized number for all emergency services, T 111.

Local Transport Standard fare on local buses and *busetas* is US$0.09, slightly more after 1900 and at weekends. Buses running along Av Amazonas to the airport costs US$0.10. Red and blue municipal buses on El Ejido-Quito Norte route (along Amazonas and by airport) US$0.25; orange and white *ejecutivos* (sitting only), US$0.30. All tickets are bought on the bus; exact fare is sometimes expected. Buses are very slow in the Old City owing to traffic jams. In 1994 Quito began construction of a trolley line to cross the city N/S along 10 de Agosto, in the hopes of diminishing air pollution and traffic congestion. The project is planned for completion by 1996, until which time the traffic situation will be further aggravated by the construction itself. Standard **taxi** tariff in the city is US$0.50 to US$4 and not more than double by night; no increase for extra passengers; by the hour, US$5 up. Although the taxis now have meters and are required by law to use them, drivers sometimes say they are out of order. Insist on the meter being used, it is always cheaper! If they have no meter, it is imperative to fix fare beforehand. Taxis for local journeys in front of big hotels nearly always ask more. After dark expect surcharges: negotiate fare first (if quoted in dollars check the rate, it may be cheaper in sucres). Insist that the taxi drops you precisely where you want to go. A negotiated fare from the airport of US$5 to the new city and US$5-6 to the old city is reasonable but they will often try to charge up to US$10. If arriving on an international flight walk back to domestic arrivals where they charge less, or walk out of the airport to Av de la Prensa and hail a taxi which will use a meter, or catch a bus. At night there are only taxis parked outside the airport (no cruising taxis), and they charge more. All legally registered taxis have the number of their co-operative and the individual operator's number prominently painted on the side of the vehicle. Note these and the license plate number if you feel you have been seriously overcharged or mistreated. You may then complain to the transit police or tourist office, but be reasonable as the amounts involved are usually small and the majority of taxi drivers are honest and helpful. For trips outside Quito taxi tariffs should be agreed beforehand: usually US$50-70 a day. Outside main hotels cooperative taxi drivers have a list of agreed excursion prices which can be as little as 20% off tourist excursion prices; most drivers are knowledgeable. For taxi tours with guide, Hugo R Herrera, T 267-891/236-492, speaks good English, rec. To order taxis by phone, Teletaxi T 220-800.

Car Rentals All the main car rental companies are at the airport (Hertz, Avis, International, Ecuacar, Budget, Carros Diligentes, Expo and Arrancar). City offices: **Budget**, Colón y Amazonas, T 548-237 and *Hotel Colón* (closed Sat-Sun), T 525-328. **Avis**, Colón 1741 y 10 de Agosto, T 550-238. **Dollar**, Juan de Ascaray 281 y 10 de Agosto, T 430-777. **Ecuacar**, Colón 1280 y Amazonas, T 529-781. **Expo**, Av América 1116 y Bolivia, T 501-203. **Premium**, Orellana 1623 y 9 de Octubre, T 552-897. **Santitours**, Maldonado 2441, T 212-267/251-063 also rent minibuses, buses and 4WD, chauffeur driven rental only. Budget and Ecuacar have been particularly rec, helpful staff. In 1994, a small car at Budget cost, including 10% tax, US$10 per day, plus US$0.10 per km or US$150 for a week with 1200 km included in the charge. A 4WD Trooper (rec for trips to Oriente and higher peaks) cost tax included US$30 per day, plus US$0.30 per km or US$450 for a week with 1200 km included. An 11.5% tax is always added to the posted prices, insurance is in the range of US$8 per day, drop off charge (for returning the vehicle in a city other than where it was rented) US$70. In order to rent a car you must be 25 and have an international credit card. You may pay cash, which is cheaper and may permit bargaining, but they want a credit card for security. You may be asked to sign two blank credit card vouchers, one for the rental fee itself and the other as a security deposit, and authorization for a charge of as much as US$1,000 may be requested against your credit card account. These arrangements are all above board and the uncashed vouchers will be returned to you when you return the vehicle, but the credit authorization may persist on your account (reducing your credit limit) for up to 30 days. Always make certain that you fully understand the rental arrangements before signing the contract, and be especially careful when dealing with some of the smaller agencies.

AMIPA, *Auxilio Mecánico Inmediato para Automóviles*, T 238-032 or through paging service at 228-444 *receptor* No 958, reliable roadside mechanical assistance in the Quito metropolitan area (including Los Chillos and Tumbaco valleys), service for members and non-members, also run a good repair shop.

24-hour filling stations: Petrocomercial, Amazonas y Eloy Alfaro; Los Sauces, 6 de Diciembre y Gaspar de Villaroel; Av Occidental y Manuel Córdova Galarza; Av Occidental N of El Bosque turnoff; Autopista to San Rafael, just S of toll. Unleaded fuel is now widely available in the city.

Land Rover specialists at Inglaterra 533, Talleres Atlas. Also Luis Alfredo Palacios, Iturralde y Av de la Prensa, T 234-341.

Motorcycle Repairs Sr Lother Ranft, Euro Servicio, Av Los Shyris y Río Coca, T 454-261; main business is BMW, Mercedes and Porsche cars (very busy) but is a bike enthusiast and can get BMW motorcycle parts from Germany in two weeks. Paco Olmedo, Domingo Espinar 540 y La Gasca, T 550-589, has a well-equipped mechanical shop. Talleres Kosche, Eiffel 138 y Los Shyris, T 442-204, rec. Juan Molestina, Av 6 de Diciembre y Bélgica, T 564-335, fuel and travel equipment shop, helpful for motorbike spare parts.

Airport Mariscal Sucre Airport. From airport catch bus 16 to go to Plaza Santo Domingo. The No 1 Iñaquito and Aeropuerto buses go to the airport, look for a sign "*Aeropuerto*" on the windscreen; also No 43, Marín-Carcelén. See also **Local Transport** above for buses on Amazonas and taxis. Beware of self-styled porters: men or boys who will grab your luggage in the hope of receiving a tip. There are no facilities for long-term left luggage at the airport, but there are at *Hotel Aeropuerto*, just outside the terminal, US$2 per day. Watch bags at all times and watch out for thefts by security officials when searching your bags; it has been reported that while you walk through the metal detector they remove money from your hand baggage. After checking in and before going through immigration, pay airport tax. Duty-free shops in the international departure lounge, also travel videos of Ecuador (a good souvenir but expensive) and frozen shrimp packed to travel are on sale here.

There is a monthly transport guide which gives details of international and national flights, and phone numbers of airlines in Quito and Guayaquil.

Internal Flights There are about 14 flights a day to and from **Guayaquil**, book in advance for daytime flights and check in promptly, US$30 (TAME, Saeta, SAN) and 3 to **Cuenca** (US$30). There are daily flights to **Esmeraldas** (US$22 except Sat), **Manta** (US$27), **Bahía de Caráquez** (same fare, twice a week), **Tulcán** (US$20), **Loja** (except Sun, US$34), **Lago Agrio** (US$44 for foreigners) and **Coca** (same price, not Sun), and the **Galápagos** (US$377 return); daily flights to **Portoviejo** (US$27) and 3 a week to **Macas** (US$44); **Machala** (US$41). Prices are payable in US$ or sucres and are increased every six months, all airlines charge the same. Cancellations are frequent. Student discounts may be given to those under 26 with a student card from their home country, not an international card.

Railway station is two km S of centre, along continuation of Calle Maldonado, reached by buses along that street (eg Iñaquito-Villa Flora No 1 or Colón-Camal, No 2). The ticket office at this beautiful but decrepit old station is frequently closed and employees are not well-informed. Severe rains and flooding destroyed much of the track in 1983. Repairs were completed after 10 years and the route Quito-Riobamba-Durán (Guayaquil) reopened in 1993. There are no trains going straight through from Quito to Durán (Guayaquil), an overnight stay in Riobamba is necessary. Passenger service between Quito and Riobamba is limited to one train per week (Quito-Riobamba, Sat 0800, US$10, Riobamba-Quito, Sun 0900). This route provides spectacular views along the "Avenue of the Volcanoes". There is a daily service Riobamba-Durán (details under Riobamba **Transport**). There is no longer any service Quito-Cuenca or Riobamba-Cuenca as the Sibambe-Cuenca rail line was permanently closed in Mar 1995. A tourist train, pulled by a steam locomotive runs from Quito to Parque Nacional Cotopaxi, Sun 0800, return 1430, US$20 return. Special arrangements can be made for group excursions from Quito to Riobamba and further S as far as Chunchi (118 km from Riobamba). A written request (*oficio*) must be presented at least 10 days prior to the date of the trip. Metropolitan Touring (T 464-780) offers the following tours involving train travel: 1) a 2-day tour to Riobamba by train on Tues, Thur or Sat, overnight in Riobamba, back by bus US$285 pp based on double occupancy. Tour includes several stops along the way, visits to towns, Laguna de Yambo, a market and side trips to Guano and Baños, first class accommodations and meals. 2) An extension by train from Riobamba to Guayaquil over the famous *Nariz del Diablo* (Devil's Nose) the following day, Quito-Guayaquil US$374 pp (hotel in Guayaquil and return to Quito not included, minimum 10 passengers required to run this portion). 3) A 4 day trip to Cuenca, starting in Quito Tues, Thur or Sat, involving bus, train and plane, including visit to Ingapirca, US$627pp plus return flight to Quito US$29.

Buses Most main roads are paved, so interurban buses are fast and tend to be reliable. The

Terminal Terrestre, at Maldonado and Cumandá (S of Plaza Santo Domingo), handles most long-distance bus services and is really the only place to get information on schedules. 24 hr luggage store, US$0.15 to use terminal. It is unsafe at night and in queues. Buses within the province of Pichincha leave from 'La Marín', which extends the length of Av Pichincha; a few others leave from nr Plaza San Blas, Villaflora, or nr the Patria/10 de Agosto intersection.

From Terminal Terrestre to Amazonas area take No 2 "Colón-Camal", or "Aeropuerto" bus. Take No 10 bus marked "terminal terrestre" from city (San Bartolo-Miraflores), No 1 Iñaquito-Villa Flora, or a taxi (US$1.50 from old city, US$2 from new). Most buses marked "terminal terrestre" do not go right to the bus station but stop 300-500m away, which is awkward if you have luggage (local buses do not allow backpacks). There are company booking offices but staff shout destinations of buses leaving; you can pay them and get on board. For buses out of Quito it is often advisable to reserve the day before as they may leave early if they are full. See under destinations for fares and schedules. Several companies now run luxury coaches on the longer routes; those which have stations in the new city are: Flota Imbabura, Manuel Larrea 1211 y Portoviejo, T 236940, for Cuenca and Guayaquil; Panamericana Internacional, Colón 852 y Reina Victoria, T 501584-5, for Huaquillas, Machala, Cuenca, Loja, Guayaquil, Manta and Esmeraldas, they also run an "international" bus to Bogotá, but this involves many changes and greater expense; it is better to take a bus to the border and change. Rey Tur for Cuenca and international service to Lima (the latter costs US$60), Gangotena 158 y Orellana, T 546-674. The route for crossing the Peruvian border via Loja and Macará takes much longer than the Machala route. Tepsa has an office at Pinto 539 y Amazonas; do not buy Peruvian bus tickets here which are much cheaper in Peru, the same is true for tickets sold for other S American destinations.

Drivers should note that there is a ring road around Quito, and a by-pass to the S via the Autopista del Valle de Los Chillos and the Carretera de Amaguaña.

Cruz Loma and Rucu Pichincha Cruz Loma is the low S one of the two antenna-topped peaks overlooking Quito from the W (to the N is a peak with loads of antennae, known as Las Antenas). On a clear day you can see about 50 km down the central valley and to the E. You are warned not to walk in this area without checking safety first, ask at South American Explorers Club. Do not try to walk up from Av 24 de Mayo in central Quito as this is extremely dangerous (frequent attacks reported—on no account go alone). To save time and energy take a taxi or bus, eg No 14, to Toctiuco, to the upper reaches of the city and start from there (allow at least 3 hrs to reach the summit). There are poor roads up to both peaks, but traffic is sparse. Try hitching early in the morning, but remember that it is difficult to hitch back after about 1730 and you will have to walk in the dark. The road to the northern hill is better for hitching; it leads to the radio station at the top of the hill; take bus no 5 from Calle Gabriel García Moreno. Armed holdups occur on this route. No water is available so be sure to carry adequate supplies, especially if going on to Rucu Pichincha. **Rucu Pichincha** (4,627m) can be seen from some parts of Quito, and can be climbed either via Cruz Loma or via its neighbour. The path to its foot runs due W over and around hummocks on the rolling, grass-covered *páramo*. The climb up to the peak is not technical, but it is rocky and requires a bit of endurance. From Cruz Loma to Rucu Pichincha peak takes about 4 hrs up and 2 down. Take rainproof and cold-weather gear just in case; do not go alone, robberies and assaults have occurred. (*Note:* please pick up your flotsam; the area is rubbish-strewn enough as it is.) You can continue from Rucu to Guagua Pichincha, the higher of the two peaks, be careful at Paso de la Muerte, a narrow ledge, about half an hour beyond Rucu Pichincha.

Guagua Pichincha A recommended route for climbing Guagua Pichincha volcano (4,794m) is to take a bus to Chillo Gallo, from where a 4-wheel-drive track goes via the town of Lloa to the rim of the crater, where you will find a *refugio*, with beds and cooking facilities maintained by Defensa Civil (if walking allow 6 hrs). The descent into the crater is prohibited (1994) owing to increased volcanic activity. The University Hiking Clubs have details on 3-day hikes around the Pichincha peaks, with overnight stops in caves.

Excursions 23 km N of Quito is the **Mitad del Mundo** Equatorial Line Monument at an altitude of 2,483m near San Antonio de Pichincha. The exact equatorial line here was determined by Charles-Marie de la Condamine and his French expedition in 1735. The monument forms the focal point of a park and leisure area built as a typical colonial town, with restaurants, gift shops, Post Office with philatelic sales, international pavilions (mostly not open) etc, and has a museum inside (open Tues-Sun, 1000-1600), very crowded on Sun. Admission to the monument and the museum US$0.75. The museum is run by the Central Bank; a lift takes you to the top, then you walk down with the museum laid out all around with different

Indian cultures every few steps. There is a Planetarium with hourly 30-min shows and an interesting model of old Quito, about 30-foot square, with artificial day and night, which took seven years to build, very pretty. A paved road runs from Quito to the Monument, which you can reach by a "Mitad del Mundo" bus (US$0.50, over 1 hr) from Av América or the Parque Hermano Miguel (see Old City map, No 50), bus fills instantly, outside rush hour you can board at 10 de Agosto; beware of pickpockets on the bus. Two minutes' walk before the Monument is the restaurant *Equinoccio*, about US$10 a meal, live music, open from 1200 daily, T 394-091, F 545-663. Available at the restaurant or at stalls outside are "certificates" recording the traveller's visit to the Equator (free if you have a meal). An excursion to Mitad del Mundo by taxi with 1 hr wait is about US$25 per taxi.

A few km beyond the Monument, off the paved road to Calacalí, is the **Pululahua** crater, well worth visiting. It is a geobotanical reserve, entry US$10. Try to go in the morning, there is often cloud later. Trucks will take you from the Mitad del Mundo bus stop, round trip US$3. *Calimatours*, Manzana de los Correos, Oficina 11, Mitad del Mundo, T 533-506 in Quito, PO Box 17-03-638, organizes tours to all the sites in the vicinity, US$5 pp, rec. Continue on the road past the Monument towards Calacalí. After a few km (1 hr walk) the road bears left and begins to climb steeply; the paved road to the right leads to the rim of the volcano and a view of the farms on the crater floor. Buses to Calacalí (infrequent) will drop you at the fork, from where it is a 1/2 hr walk. Plenty of traffic at weekends for hitching a lift. There is a rough track down from the rim to the crater, to experience the rich vegetation and warm micro-climate inside. Continuing past the village in the crater, turn left and follow an unimproved road up to the rim and back to the main road, a 15-20 km round trip. Restaurant-bar *La Rinconada de Pululahua*; hotel is planned. Also in the vicinity of the Monument, 3 km from San Antonio beyond the Solar Museum, are the Inca ruins of **Rumicucho**. Restoration poor, but situation magnificent (investigations under the auspices of the Museum of the Central Bank, entry US$2.50). Start early if you want to visit all these in one day.

8 km from Quito on the road to San Antonio, is the village of **Pomasqui**, near where was a tree in which Jesus Christ appeared to perform various miracles, El Señor del Arbol, now enshrined in its own building. In the church nearby is a series of charming paintings depicting the miracles (mostly involving horrendous road accidents); well worth a visit. You may have to find the caretaker to unlock the church (we are grateful to Hilary Bradt for this information).

From San Antonio a dirt road heads N towards Perucho. Before Perucho, at **Puéllaro** (eat at the house on the square which is also a radio/TV workshop), another road turns sharply SE to Guayllabamba. A left turn (NE) off this road, just before Guayllabamba, goes to Malchinguí, Tocachi and Cayambe (see next section).

2 hrs NW of Quito is the **Maquipucuna Biological Reserve**, cloud forest with cock of the rock and other birds, good for birdwatching. A Yambo trail runs across the reserve. Fine new accommodation available, T Quito 507-200, F 507-201.

Near Mitad del Mundo, at Km 68 on the old road to Mindo via Calicalí is Bellavista, with **B-C** pp *Finca Bellavista* (Cabins in the Clouds) with or without full board, bath, good views, excellent birdwatching and botany, F Quito c/o Richard Parsons (593-2) 447-090, or 223-381. For both places take bus to Nanegalito then hire a truck, or arrange everything in Quito.

Mindo is a small town (approx population 1,700) surrounded by dairy farms and lush cloud forest climbing the W slopes of Pichincha. 19,200 ha, ranging in altitude from 1,400 to 4,780m (the rim of the crater of Guagua Pichincha) have been set aside as a nature reserve: **Bosque Protector Mindo-Nambillo**. The reserve features spectacular flora (many orchids and bromeliads), fauna (butterflies, birds inc the cock of the rock) and spectacular cloud forest and waterfalls. There has been some conflict in the area over the future of the reserve which includes both state and private land. Two ecological organizations are involved in the reserve: *Amigos de la Naturaleza de Mindo* and *Fundación Pacaso*, both with offices in Mindo. The former runs 2 refuges: one, Centro de Educación Ambiental (CEA), 4 km from town (beyond Mindo Gardens), within the 5 ha buffer zone at the edge of the reserve, has capacity for 25-30 people. The second, Refugio Enrique Grosse-Leumern, 12 km from Mindo, with capacity for 15. Guide service, lodging and food are available at these shelters. Admission to the reserve is US$2, lodging US$6 pp, full board US$18 pp. Take sleeping gear (none provided) and food if you wish to prepare your own (nice kitchen facilities available). There are well maintained trails near the shelters. Arrangements have to be made in advance, contact in Mindo: Amigos de la Naturaleza de Mindo, main road into town, before reaching the plaza, on the left (signposted). If closed, enquire about Pedro Peñafiel or his family; in Quito: Sra María Guerrero, Casilla 17-03-1673, T 455-907. Visitors are recommended to stop at the office in Mindo before heading towards the reserve to get directions and information about the road. During the rainy season, access to the reserve can be very difficult or impossible. Be prepared to wade thigh-deep through rivers. However, even a visit to the buffer zone is well worthwhile.

Hotels in Mindo: **F** *Noroccidental*, basic, clean, some rooms with private bath. **F** *El Guadual*, clean, hot shower, good food to order. At the edge of the buffer zone for the reserve and on the shores of the Mindo River is **L3** *Mindo Gardens Lodge*, full board, 1 night, 2 day programme including excursions, comfortable cabins in a beautiful setting, restaurant (US$3 breakfast, US$6 lunch/dinner), bar, horse riding, excursions, 2 or 3 day plans. Contact in Quito: Horizontes Ecuatorianos, Pinto 560, T 230-463, F 564-235; **B** pp *Hostería El Carmelo de Mindo*, in 32 ha 700m from town centre, T/F 408-355, cabins or room with or without bath, **E** pp dormitory, bring sleeping bag, **F** pp camping, US$ prices for foreigners, meals available, horse rental, excursions, 50% discount for IYHA card holders. **Restaurants:** *Salón Noroccidental, El Guadual, La Choza*.

Bus Cooperativa San Pedro de Cayambe, Bolivia 202 y Av Pérez Guerrero, T 508-947, daily at 1500 and at 0800 Fri, Sat and Sun, US$1.90, 2 1/2 hrs. From Santo Domingo de los Colorados, daily 1200 and Sat 0800, US$3, 4 hrs. The most direct access from Quito is along the road to San Miguel de los Bancos (*Residencial Mi Ensueño*, 2 other pensiones), Puerto Quito (Hotels: *Manabí, Macará, Las Palmas*) and La Independencia where it joins the Santo Domingo-Esmeraldas road. It is now paved as far as the village of San Tadeo. If driving go to Mitad del Mundo, follow the signs for Calacalí and continue on to Nanegalito. It is a beautiful ride through native cloud forest. 24 km beyond Nanegalito, to the left is the turnoff for Mindo, marked by signs for *Mindo Gardens Lodge*. It is about 7 km along a poor cobbled road to the town. It can also be reached on a 2 day walk from the town of Lloa (10 km W of the the S end of Quito).

The Equator line also crosses the Pan-American Highway 8 km S of Cayambe, where there are a concrete globe beside the road and a mark on the road itself. Take Cayambe bus (2 hrs, US$0.80) and ask for Mitad del Mundo.

The **Bosque Protector** *Pasochoa*, 45 mins by car from Quito, is a subtropical natural park set in mountain forest, run by the Fundación Natura, América 5653 y Voz Andes, T 447-341/4, who provide further information (entrance for foreigners US$7, Ecuadoreans US$1; shops, restaurant, very touristy at weekends). The reserve is classified as humid Andean forest, with more than 120 species of birds and 50 species of trees, situated between 2,700 and 4,200m. Its average temperature is 10°C and its dry season occurs between June and Sept. Half of the plants have medicinal and/or traditional value. There are walks of 30 mins, 1 hr, 2, 4 and 8 hrs. Camping is permitted in the park (US$1 pp per night); take food and water as there are no shops and take your rubbish away with you. There is also a refuge (US$2 pp per night), but you will need a sleeping bag. Much of the fauna has been frightened away by the noise of visitors. From Quito buses run from the centre of Villaflora district to Amaguaña (ask the driver to let you off at the "Ejido de Amaguaña"); from there follow the signs for the Bosque Natural Pasochoa, about 7 km walk, not much traffic for hitching. By car, take the highway to Los Chillos, San Rafael (traffic light) continue straight towards Sangolquí and on to Amaguaña. 1.4 km past the sign "Amaguaña Os Da La Bienvenida" turn left onto cobblestone road and follow the signs to Pasochoa, 5.4 km to the park. Tours with Safari Tours in Quito cost US$45 pp; a price negotiated with a taxi driver from a good hotel is about US$15 pp.

At the Baños de *Papallacta*, 80 km E from Quito, 1 km from the road to Baeza, there are 4 thermal swimming pools and one cold pool fed by a river, open 0600-1800, entrance US$1.30. It is being remodelled (1994-95), with a new *hostal* under construction. There are showers, toilets and changing rooms. The restaurant is sometimes closed. The farm next door sells milk and cheese. In mid-week, Papallacta is usually quiet; the view, on a clear day, of Antisana from the Papallacta road or while enjoying the thermal waters is superb. Buses from Quito, Terminal Terrestre: to Lago Agrio or Baeza (drivers charge full fare). Ask to be let off at the road to the springs, 1 km steep walk up. You can also stay in the village at *Salón Quiteña*, G, clean and friendly, also shop and *cafetería*.

In the valley of Los Chillos (SE, 1 hr by car) are the thermal pools of La Merced and El Tingo. Take "La Merced" bus from La Marín (Plaza San Martín); if driving take Autopista de Los Chillos to San Rafael, where the divided highway ends, turn left at the trafic light, it is 4 km to El Tingo where there are thermal baths, crowded and dirty on weekends. *Mucki's Garden* restaurant, T 320-789, excellent food and atmosphere, German owner. 7 km past El Tingo is La Merced, which also has thermal baths, avoid weekends. 4 km from La Merced is Ilaló, privately owned pools, admission US$2, cleaner, fewer mosquitoes and people, but also best on weekdays.

From Alangasí, along the road to La Merced, a good paved road branches 10 km SE to Pintag. The road then turns to rough gravel and divides, the right fork goes to the base of

Sincholagua (4,899 m), the left fork goes to Laguna La Mica at the base of the snow covered volcano Antisana (5,704m). This is a magnificent area for hiking and camping, condors may be seen, no services, visitors must be self sufficient, access permit from landowner is required, inquire beforehand in Píntag.

Another day-trip is to *Sangolquí* about 20 minutes from Quito by bus. There is a busy Sun market (and a lesser one on Thur) and few tourists, and there are thermal baths, reported dirty, nearby (pop 18,000). **D** *Hostal Cotopaxi*, Chimborazo y Río Frío, T 313-315, F 593-2-554-503, good food, pool, transport arranged for climbers. Take Coop Marco Polo bus from S of Plaza San Martín.

Day tours via Cotopaxi to Indian fairs at Pujilí and at Saquisilí (**see p 965**), about 93 km each way, or to Cotopaxi itself.

NORTH OF QUITO (2)

The landscape from Quito to the Colombian border is mountainous, with views of the Cotacachi, Imbabura and glacier-covered Cayambe peaks, interspersed with lakes. Otavalan Indians predominate, their Sat market is a major tourist attraction.

The Pan-American Highway and a railway (service indefinitely suspended) run NE from Quito to Otavalo (121 km) and Ibarra (145 km). North of Ibarra, the railway and Highway separate. The railway goes NW to the Pacific port of San Lorenzo, a very spectacular trip, passenger services only from Ibarra: the highway runs N for another 108 km to Tulcán and on to Ipiales in Colombia. The Pan-American Highway is paved for the whole stretch Quito-Tulcán.

Calderón, 30 km N of Quito, is the place where miniature figurines are made of bread; you can see them being made (not on Sun), and prices are much lower than in Quito. Especially attractive is the Nativity collection. Prices range from about US$0.10 to US$4 (excellent value). See the Indian cemetery on 1-2 Nov, when the graves are decorated with flowers, drinks and food for the dead. Corpus Christi processions are very colourful. Many buses from Quito (Plaza San Martín), often unwilling to take backpackers.

After Calderón the road for the N, descends the spectacular arid Guayllabamba gorge and climbs out again to the fertile oasis of **Guayllabamba** village, noted for good avocados and chirimoyas. At Guayllabamba, the highway splits into two branches. To the right, the Pan-American Highway runs NE to Cayambe. The left branch goes towards the town of Tabacundo, from where you can rejoin the Pan-American travelling E to Cayambe or NE to Cajas.

10 km past Guayllabamba on the road to Tabacundo (8 km before Tabacundo), a gravel road (signed Pirámides de Cochasqui) to the left leads to Tocachi and further on to the **Tolas de Cochasquí** national archaeological site, administered by the Concejo Provincial de Pichincha; the whole area is covered with hills of pyramid shapes and ramps built between 900 and 1500 AD by Indians of the Cara or Cayambi-Caranqui tribe. Festivals with dancing at the equinoxes and solstices. Note the spectacular wind-eroded rocks. Access only with free 1½-hr guided tours (open 0900-1530). Be sure to take a bus that goes on the Tabacundo road and ask to be left off at the turnoff; from there it's an 8 km walk (if you arrive at the sign between 0900-0930, you should get a lift from the site workers). Taxi from Cayambe US$8 round trip, sometimes there is a colectivo taxi to Tabacundo or La Esperanza, then 15 km to the site.

Cayambe (pop 16,849), on the righthand branch of the highway, NE of Guayllabamba, is dominated by the snow-capped volcano of the same name. In the town, on private property, are the pyramids of the Sun and Moon at Puntiachil; a descriptive route for the Pyramid of the Sun is displayed. This area of rich dairy

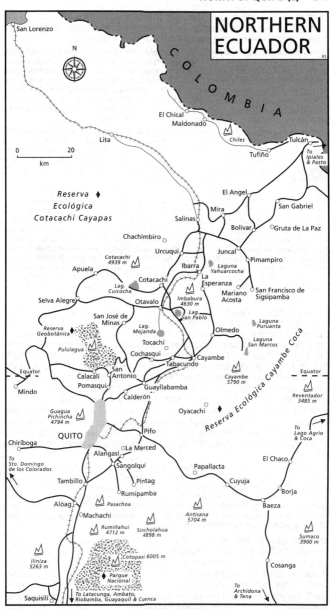

NORTHERN ECUADOR

83

San Lorenzo

N

C O L O M B I A

El Chical
Maldonado
Chiles
Tulcán

Lita
Tufiño
To Ipiales & Pasto

0   20
km

Reserva
Ecológica
Cotacachi Cayapas

El Angel
San Gabriel
Mira
Gruta de La Paz
Salinas
Bolívar
Chachimbiro
Urcuquí
Juncal
Pimampiro
Ibarra
La Esperanza
Laguna Yahuarcocha
Cotacachi 4939 m
Apuela
Cotacachi
Mariano Acosta
San Francisco de Sigsipamba
Lag. Cuicocha
Imbabura 4630 m
Selva Alegre
Otavalo
Lag. San Pablo
San José de Minas
Laguna Puruanta
Reserva Geobotánica
Lag. Mojanda
Olmedo
Laguna San Marcos
Pululagua
Tocachí
Cochasqui
Cayambe
Tabacundo
Cayambe 5790 m
Calacalí
San Antonio
Equator
Equator
Pomasqui
Guayllabamba
Reventador 3485 m
Mindo
Calderón
Oyacachi
Reserva Ecológica Cayambe Coca
Guagua Pichincha 4794 m
QUITO
Pifo
To Lago Agrio & Coca
Chiriboga
La Merced
El Chaco
To Sto. Domingo de los Colorados
Alangasí
Papallacta
Sangolquí
Tambillo
Cuyuja
Borja
Píntag
Alóag
Rumipamba
Pasachoa
Baeza
Machachi
Antisana 5704 m
Rumiñahui 4712 m
Sincholahua 4898 m
Sumaco 3900 m
Iliniza 5263 m
Cotopaxi 6005 m
Cosanga
Parque Nacional
Saquisilí
To Latacunga, Ambato, Riobamba, Guayaquil & Cuenca
To Archidona & Tena

farms produces a fine range of European-style cheeses. Try the local *bizcochos con queso*. Cayambe is the Agrarian Reform Institute's showplace; its only major project. *Fiesta* in Mar for the equinox with plenty of local music.

Hotels and Restaurants B *Hacienda Guachala*, S of Cayambe on road to Cangahua, beautifully restored hacienda built 1580, owned by Diego Bonifaz, ex-Agriculture Minister, spring-fed swimming pool, basic but comfortable rooms with fireplaces, delicious food, good walking, Anglo-Arabian horses for rent, excursions to nearby pre-Inca ruins, highly rec, reservations in Quito: Reina Victoria 1138 y Foch, T 563-748; E *Hostal Mitad del Mundo*, on Panamericana, clean, fan, good restaurant; E *Hostal Cayambe* is a Youth Hostal at Bolívar 23 y Ascázubi, T 361-007, clean, friendly, stores luggage. *Restaurant El Unicorno*, nr the market, good meal for US$0.65. Hotels may be full on Fri during June-Sept.

6 km SE of Guayllabamba is the small village of **El Quinche**, where there is a huge sanctuary to Nuestra Señora de El Quinche in the plaza. The image was the work of the sculptor Diego Robles around 1600 in Napo province. It was brought to El Quinche because the local Indians did not wish to worship the image. There are processions on 21 Nov in El Quinche. There are many paintings illustrating miracles, ask the caretaker for the details. There is bus service from Guayllabamba and direct from Quito via Cumbayá and Pifo.

Cayambe (5,790m) is Ecuador's third highest peak and the highest point in the world which lies directly on the Equator. About 1 km S of Cayambe is an unmarked cobbled road heading E via Juan Montalvo, leading in 26 km to the Ruales-Oleas-Berge refuge at about 4,800m. It provides beds (bring sleeping bag, it is very cold), but no equipment. It is named after three Ecuadorean climbers killed by an avalanche in 1974 while pioneering a new route up from the W. This is now the standard route, using the refuge as a base. The climb is heavily crevassed, especially near the summit, and is more difficult and dangerous than either Chimborazo or Cotopaxi. You can take a *camioneta* from Cayambe to Piemonte (at about 3,500m) or a taxi for US$5. From Piemonte to the *refugio* it is a 3-4 hr walk, sometimes longer if heavily laden, the wind can be very strong but it is a beautiful walk. It is difficult to get transport back to Cayambe. A milk truck runs from Cayambe to the *hacienda* at 0630, returning between 1700-1900. 4WD jeeps go to the refugio (eg *Safari Tours*).

The road forks N of Cayambe: to the right a cobbled road, the very scenic *carretera vieja*, runs in good condition to **Olmedo** (Emetel office, old Tenencia Política on square, no hotels or restaurants but a couple of shops and lodging with nuns – ask; nice countryside for strolling; road to the Laguna de San Pablo, 40 mins by car, 3 hrs on foot. Bus Cayambe-Olmedo every ½ hr, till 1600 Mon-Fri, 1800 Fri-Sun, 1 hr, US$0.35; bus to Ibarra 0700 only, 1½ hrs, US$0.50, returns 1230). After Olmedo the road is not so good (4WD rec); it is 9 km from Olmedo to Zuleta, where beautiful embroidery is done on napkins and tablecloths, 2 km beyond is La Esperanza (see Excursions from Ibarra), 8.5 km further to Ibarra.

To the left, the main paved road crosses a *páramo* and suddenly descends into the land of the Otavalo Indians, a lively and prosperous group who have been making commercial woollens for over fifty years. The men are recognizable by their white, bell-bottomed, mid-calf-length trousers, long braided hair and blue ponchos.

An alternative route from Quito to Otavalo is via San Antonio de Pichincha (Inca ruins of Rumicucho) and San José de Minas. The road curves through the dry but impressive landscape down to the Río Guayllabamba, then climbs again, passing some picturesque oasis villages. After Minas the road is in a very bad condition and a jeep is necessary for the next climb (beautiful views; at both junctions on this stretch, take the right fork) and then descent to join the Otavalo-Selva Alegre road about 15 km W from Otavalo. The journey takes about 3 hrs altogether and is rough but magnificent.

Otavalo (pop 21,548) is at 2,530m in beautiful countryside which is worth exploring for 3 or 4 days. In the Plaza Bolívar is a statue of Rumiñahui, Atahualpa's general, who was instrumental in the war between Atahualpa and Huascar, and in the resistance to the Spaniards. The town is notable for its indigenous crafts (primarily textiles) and its enormous Saturday market, a "must" for tourists. There are 3 markets in different places with the central streets filled with vendors: (a) *artesanías*, 0700-1800, based around Plaza de Ponchos; (b) livestock, 0600-1000, outside town in the Viejo Colegio Agricultural, go W on Calle Morales from town centre; (c) produce, 0700-1400, in Plaza 24 de Mayo and across town to E in Plaza Copacabana. The *artesanías* industry is so big that the Plaza de Ponchos is now filled with vendors every day of the week. Bargaining is appropriate in the market and in shops. The Otavaleños not only sell goods they weave and sew themselves, but they bring *artesanías* from throughout Ecuador and from Peru and Bolivia. Mestizo and indigenous vendors from Otavalo, elsewhere in Ecuador and South America sell paintings, jewellery, shigras, baskets, leather goods, woodcarvings from San Antonio de Ibarra and the Oriente, ceramics, antiques, etc. (Some suggest buying at leisure before Saturday and then just enjoying the atmosphere of the main market.) Indigenous people in the market respond better to photography if you buy something first, then ask politely; reciprocity and courtesy are important Andean norms.

Otavalo weavers come from dozens of communities, but it is easiest to visit the nearby towns of Peguche, Ilumán, Carabuela and Agato which have a good bus service. (Buses to the above places leave from the Plaza Copacabana with inexpensive 15-30 min rides. You can also negotiate with a taxi driver.) In Ilumán, the Conterón-de la Torre family of *Artesanías Inti Chumbi*, on the NE corner of the plaza, gives backstrap loom weaving demonstrations and sells crafts. There are also many felt hatmakers in town who will make hats to order. In Peguche, the Cotacachi-Pichamba family, off the main plaza behind the church, sells beautiful tapestries, finished with tassels and loops, ready to hang. In Agato, the Andrango-Chiza family of *Tahuantinsuyo Weaving Workshop*, gives weaving demonstrations and sells textiles. In Carabuela many homes sell crafts including wool sweaters. (With thanks to Lynn A Meisch.)

NB If planning a spending spree, bring plenty of cash; Otavalo can be as expensive as Quito, and the exchange rate is very unfavourable, even in the banks (open until 1330 on Sat, closed Mon).

Museums Instituto Otavaleño de Antropología, exhibition, on Panamericana Norte; **Museo Arqueológico César Vásquez Fuller**, at *Pensión Los Andes*, Roca y Montalvo, Mon-Sat 1400-1800, US$1, rec; **Museo Jaramillo**, Bolívar, off Parque Central. **Centro Histórico**, just outside town in direction of Cotacachi.

Festivals From 24 to 29 June, at the Fiesta de San Juan, there is not much action in the street but there are bullfights in the plaza and regattas on the beautiful Lago de San Pablo, 4 km away (bus to Espejo, US$0.20). There is the *Fiesta del Yamor* from 3 to 14 Sept, when local dishes are cooked, roulette played and bands in the plaza, as well as bull fights. Tourists are advised to take care as Indians drink heavily on these occasions and may not be as friendly when intoxicated. If you wish to visit fiestas in local villages, ask musicians in tourist restaurants, they may invite you. The music is good, there is a lot of drinking and transport back to Otavalo is hard to find.

We have received many reports of stealing from Otavalo hotel rooms and cars; ensure that your door is always locked, even if your absence is very brief and never leave anything in your car or taxi, even if it is being watched for you. Watch out for pickpockets and bag slashers in the market. Thieves work in teams, be vigilant. The streets of Otavalo are safe at night, but the surrounding areas are not. Lone walkers have been attacked on some of the trails around the town; go in company. Also beware of dogs, they are everywhere and they bite; take a stick.

Hotels May be full on Fri nights, before fair, when prices go up. Water is not always available in Otavalo. **B** *Ali Shungu*, Quito y Miguel Egas, Casilla 34, T 920-750, lovely garden, firm mattresses, hot water, safe deposit boxes, good restaurant, vegetarian food, folk music at weekends, 2 nights min, popular; **D** *El Cacique* and *El Gran Caranqui*, both on 31 de Octubre, entre Quito y Panamericana N, T 921-740, F 920-930, heading out of town, same owner, latter newer and better, private bath, TV, parking clean, spacious, friendly, laundry, hot water, nice rooftop area; **D** *El Coraza*, Calderón y Sucre, with bath, hot water, new; **D** *Otavalo*, Roca 504 y J Montalvo, T 920-416, E without bath or outside window, attractive patio, car and motorbike park, Indian music on Fri nights, set menu with infrequent changes (homemade ice cream in the *Golden Eagle* coffee shop); **E** *La Cascada*, Colón y Sucre, T 920-165, small rooms, hot water, clean, safe; **D** *Los Pendoneros*, Av Abdón Calderón 510 y Bolívar, T 921-258 clean, safe, hot showers, some rooms can be noisy, E without bath, rec; **B** *El Indio*, Bolívar 904,

OTAVALO

Not to Scale

To Ibarra

To Cotacachi

Bypass

Río El Tejar

N

Estados Unidos

Collahuazo

Río Machángara

Miguel Egas

Ricaurte

31 de Octubre

Modesto Jaramillo

Sucre

Quito

Bolívar

Quiroga

Salinas

Roca

Morales

Atahualpa

Colón

Av. Abdón Calderón

Juan Montalvo

García Moreno

Piedrahita

Olmedo

Mejía

Rocafuerte

Esteves Mora

Old Quito Rd

Guayaquil

To Cascadas de Peguche

To Laguna de San Pablo

To Lagunas Mojanda

To Imbabuela

To Quito

1. Parque Central
2. Plaza de Ponchos
3. Produce Market
4. Animal Market, Barrio San Juan
5. Instituto Otavaleño de Antropología
6. Museo Arqueológico & Pensión Los Andes
7. Cockpit
8. Municipality
9. Zulaytour
10. Post Office
11. Emetel Phone Office
Hotels:
12. Ali Shungu
13. Otavalo
14. Riviera y Sucre
15. Residencia El Indio
16. Valle de Amanecer
17. Peña Amauta

T 920-325, private bath, also has suites with sitting room, rec, hot water, clean; **E** *Riviera Sucre*, García Moreno 380 y Roca, T 920-241, cheaper with shared bath, hot water, laundry facilities, cafetería, good breakfasts, table tennis, book exchange, safe, nice garden, English, French and Dutch spoken by the Belgian owner, who is an expert on the area, mostly rec, 15 mins' walk from market; **E** *Rincón de Belén*, Roca 8-20 y J Montalvo, T 920-171/921-860, new in 1994, nice, modern, private bath, TV, parking, restaurant; **E** *Hostal Ingrid*, 31 de Octubre y Colón, T 920-191, new in 1994, friendly; **F** *Inti Ñan*, J Montalvo 602 y Sucre, shared bath, nice clean rooms, small, friendly, but noisy music opposite; **E** *Residencial Centenario*, Pasaje Saona 7-03 y Jaramillo, near Plaza de Ponchos, clean, good parking; **F** *Residencia Santa Martha*, Calle Colón, pretty courtyard, some large rooms, ask for hot water, clean, not enough toilets or bathrooms, safe, popular, new section has rooms with thinner walls, doubles only; opp is **F** *Residencial Colón*, Colón 7-13, hot water, good; **F** *Isabelita*, Roca 1107 y Quiroga, quiet, hot water, laundry facilities, very clean, helpful, basic, parking space, rec; **E** *Residencia San Luis*, Abdón Calderón 6-02 y 31 de Octubre, T 920-614, shared bath, family run, safe, café, friendly; **F** *Pensión Los Andes*, J Montalvo 3-75 y Roca, grimy (see under Museums below). **F** *Pensión Los Angeles*, Colón 4-10, friendly, cold showers; **F** *Residencial Otavalo*, J Montalvo 4-44, shared bath; **F** *La Herradura*, Bolívar 10-05, T 920-304, shared bath, clean, hot water, rec; **F** *Samaj Huasy*, Jaramillo 6-11 y Salinas, ½ block from Plaza de Ponchos, T 921-126, shared bath, clean, hot water, clean, safe, friendly; **F** *Valle del Amanecer*, Roca y

Quiroga, T 920-990, F 920-286, more with bath, good, basic, clean, cheap restaurant, mountain bikes for rent; **F** *Residencial Irina*, Jaramillo 5-09 y Morales, T 920684, new in 1994, shared bath; **F** *Residencial Sonrisa*, Colón 6-10 y 31 de Octubre, shared bath, cafeteria.

Restaurants *El Triunfo*, Moreno y Jaramillo, good breakfast early, English spoken, watch for overcharging; *Oraibi*, Colón y Sucre, pleasant courtyard, good breakfast, inexpensive, good service, vegetarian dinner choices, book exchange, live music Fri and Sat evenings; *Café Galería*, Plaza de Ponchos, vegetarian, very good, open Mon, Wed, Fri, Sat only, good music and atmosphere; *El Indio*, Sucre y Salinas, good fried chicken and steaks; *El Tabasco*, Salinas 4-8, between Sucre y Bolívar, good Mexican food, pricey; *Quino*, Roca 740 y Juan Montalvo, good typical food, good value; *Fontana di Trevi*, Sucre entre Salinas y Morales, open 0600 to midnight, pizzas and pasta, good juices, can take wonderful pictures from top balcony, owner friendly, helpful; *Pizza Siciliana*, Sucre 10-03 y Calderón, good large pizzas, vegetarian dishes, good juices, friendly; *Pizza Parenthese*, Morales 510 y Sucre; *Pizza Mi Pan*, Colón y Jaramillo; *El Rincón Venecia*, Salinas y Jaramillo, good pizzas, salads, friendly; *Fuente del Mar*, Bolívar 815, ½ block from main plaza, seafood, some rooms with hot showers to let, rec; *La Familia Sucre*, Mercado Centenario 13-06, at the Plaza de Ponchos, good for breakfast; *Hard Rock Café*, next to Plaza de Ponchos, good music, nice atmosphere, crêpes not rec; *Chifa China*, Morales 302 y Roca, excellent and cheap; *Chifa Tien An Men*, near Moreno and Bolívar, noisy, generous portions, inexpensive; *Copacabana*, Montalvo y Bolívar, basic, reasonable, set meal about US$1; *Cafetería Shanandoa Pie Shop*, Salinas y Jaramillo, good pies, milk shakes and ice cream, travellers' meeting place, popular and friendly, rec for breakfast, book exchange; *Tapiz Café*, Morales 5-05 y Sucre, good, friendly, breakfast and Sat lunch rec; *Royal*, on main plaza, clean (even the toilets), meal with cola about US$1.40; *SISA*, Abdón Calderón 409 entre Bolívar y Sucre, coffee shop, cappuccino, good *menú del día*, cultural centre and bookstore; *Café-Bar Jungle*, Colón 5-11 y Sucre, good breakfast, nice atmosphere and music; *Quindi Bar*, opposite *Peña Tucano*, cheap drinks, food, nice atmosphere. *Plaza Café*, Plaza de Ponchos, good food and atmosphere. Cheap food in the fruit and vegetable market (suitable for vegetarians).

Exchange *Imbacambios*, Sucre 1205; other Cambios on Sucre and Morales; *SISA* restaurant; rate at banks poor.

Entertainment *Peña Amauta*, Jaramillo y Salinas, the best, good local bands, friendly and welcoming, mainly foreigners, US$0.60 entrance fee; *Peña Tucano*, Morales 5-10 y Sucre, nice place, good music, friendly, restaurant, entrance US$0.75; *Peña Tuparina*, Morales y 31 de Octubre, rec. Peñas normally only on Fri and Sat from 2200. *Habana Club*, Quito y 31 de Octubre, lively disco. There is also a cockpit (*gallera*) at 31 de Octubre y Montalvo, fights Sat and Sun 1500-1900, US$0.50. On the Panamericana, *Yanuyacu* has three swimming pools, volleyball courts and is full of Otavaleños on Sun.

Post Office behind Municipal building, approach from Piedrahita.

Shopping *Jatun Pacha*, Av 31 de Octubre 19 y Panamericana, cooperative, select handicrafts; also nice restaurant for groups, order ahead, mountain bike tours and Spanish classes. Otavalo textile shops include *Tejidos y Artesanías Atahualpa*, Bolívar 1015, and *Coop Indígena de Tejidos Peguche*, Bolívar 910; *Tejidos Mimahuasi* of Peguche, rec.

Sports Near the market, a ball game is played in the afternoons. It is similar to the game in Ibarra described below except that the ball is about the size of a table-tennis ball, made of leather, and hit with the hands, not a bat.

Mountain bikes for hire at *Ecoturismo*, Jatun Pacha, 31 de Octubre y Panamericana, T 548-068, US$5 for 5 hrs or US$8/day. *Taller Ciclo Primaxi*, García Moreno y Atahualpa 2-49, has a good bike for rent, US$1.50/hr, rec.

Tourist Agencies *Zulaytur*, Sucre y Colón, T 921-176, run by Rodrigo Mora, English spoken, information, map of town, slide show, horse-riding, tours, 1-day tour of local communities, many recs; *Intiexpress*, Sucre 11-06, rec for 3/4-hr trek on horseback, less if you gallop, US$15 pp, ask them to prepare the horses before you arrive or time is wasted, good for those with or without experience, beautiful ride; *Zulay Diceny Viajes*, Sucre 1014 y Colón, T 921-217, run by an indigenous otavaleña; *Lassotur*, Calderón 402 y Bolívar, T 902-446, also organizes local tours and horseriding. *Ecuapanorama*, Calderón y Roca, T 920-889/563, ecological tours of Intag, horseriding, hikes. Check whether tour operators are officially recognized. All these agencies run tours with English-speaking guides to artisans' homes and villages, which usually provide opportunities to buy handicrafts cheaper than in the market. We have received favourable reports on all, especially Zulaytur.

Transport There is no bus station, though one is planned. Bus to **Ibarra**, every 15 mins,

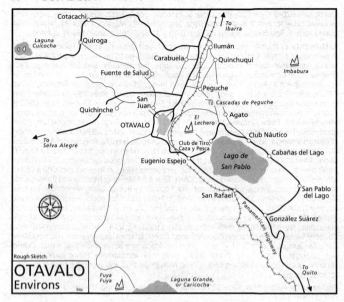

Rough Sketch

OTAVALO
Environs

US$0.35, ½ hr. From **Quito** by taxi takes 1½ hrs (US$25); by minibus (Transportes Andinos—bypasses centre of Otavalo, must tell driver when you want to get off) from 18 de Septiembre and Av Pérez Guerrero, 1½ hrs, US$2.35; by bus from Terminal Terrestre (Cooperativa Otavalo, Coop Las Lagos), or any Ibarra bus from Av América, 1¾-2½ hrs, US$1.70, every 15 mins on Sat, last bus about 1800 (some buses pass *Hotel Colón* in Quito and will pick up passengers there). The Tourist Office in Quito will help with reservations; the organized tour sold by hotels is expensive. Travelling on Fri is rec.

Excursions At the **Lago de San Pablo** is the Club de Tiro, Caza y Pesca where one can rent canoes. It is worth walking either to or back from Lago de San Pablo for the views, but watch out for dogs: the walk there via El Lechero is rec, but for the children begging; the walk back via the outlet stream from the lake (staying on the right hand side of the gorge), taking 2-3 hrs, is particularly rec. The 13-roomed **E** *Hotel Chicapán*, T 920-331, on the lakeshore is rec; from the restaurant there is a fine view of the lake and Imbabura mountain. **B** *Cabañas del Lago*, on NE side of the lake, T 918-001 (in Quito, Unicentro Amazonas, Amazonas y Japón, PO Box 17-11-6509, T 435-936/461-316), price incl breakfast, on the lakeside, has cabins with bunk beds, clean, mediocre restaurant. Boats and pedalos for hire. Also in **San Pablo del Lago** (half-hourly buses from Otavalo, US$0.10, taxi US$1.70) is **A2** *Hostería Cusín* in a converted *hacienda* on the E side of the lake, T 918-013, F 918-003, 9 rooms with fireplaces, book in advance (2 nights min), popular, rec (run by an Englishman, Nick Millhouse). Pleasant setting. Horses and mountain bikes for hire. **A3** *Hostería Puerto Lago Country Inn*, Panamericana Sur, Km 5½ y Lago San Pablo on the W side of the lake, T 920-920, F 920-900, beautiful setting, a good place to watch the sunset, restaurant, A2 including dinner. There are also other restaurants and other places to stay, ask around. From San Pablo del Lago it is possible to climb the **Imbabura** volcano, 4,630m and almost always under cloud—allow at least 6 hrs to reach the summit and 4 hrs for the descent. Easier, and no less impressive, is the nearby Cerro Huarmi Imbabura, 3,845m.

It is also possible to hike much further S to the **Lagunas de Mojanda** impressive crater lake 18 km from Otavalo and also accessible by car on a bad cobbled road (take a tent, warm sleeping bag, and food, no accommodation), or take a Quito bus as far as Tabacundo, hitch to Lagunas (difficult at weekends), then walk back to Otavalo by the old Inca trail, on the right after 2 or 3 kms, taxi or *camioneta* from Otavalo US$20, whatever the number of passengers. Caricocha (or Laguna Grande de Mojanda) is 1,200m higher than Otavalo. 25 min walk above

Caricocha is Laguna Huarmicocha and a further 25 mins is Laguna Yanacocha (take a warm jacket, food and drinks; no entrance fee). The views on the descent are excellent. From Caricocha the route continues S about 5 km before dividing: the left-hand path leads to Tocachi, the right-hand to Cochasqui (**see p 948**): both are about 20 km from Laguna Grande and offer beautiful views of Quito and Cotopaxi (cloud permitting). On the shore of Laguna Grande is a basic mountain hut (reported derelict in 1994) from which you can climb Fuya Fuya (4,263m) and Yanaurco (4,259m).

There is a network of old roads and trails between Otavalo and the Lago San Pablo area, none of which takes more than an hour or two to explore. To reach the **Cascadas de Peguche** follow the old railway track through the woods in the direction of Ibarra until the track drops away to the left and a dirt path continues up the hill towards the waterfall—allow 1-1½ hrs each way (armed robberies reported at the falls in 1994). From the top of the falls you can continue the walk to Lago de San Pablo. Beware of stray dogs. At Peguche is the **E** *Aya Huma Hotel* with a good restaurant, on railway, near falls, vegetarian food, great pancakes, lovely place, hot water, clean, quiet, run by a Dutch lady, and *artesanía* workshop; ask to leave the Otavalo-Ibarra bus at Peguche village. In the village, look for woven fabrics, if you have time they can be made to order. Four km N of Otavalo are cold ferrous baths at the *Fuente de Salud*, said to be very curative but opening hours very irregular. Zulaytur offer tours to many of these places.

West of the road between Otavalo and Ibarra is **Cotacachi**, where leather goods are made and sold, although quality varies a lot (more expensive than Ambato—recommended are the collapsible leather duffle bags); credit cards widely accepted but you have to pay a premium. Frequent buses run from Otavalo, A Calderón y 31 de Octubre, US$0.15.

Hotels and Restaurants L2-3 *La Mirage*, ex-hacienda ½ km W from town, T 915-237, F 915-065, beautiful garden, pool and gymnasium, very good suites with fireplace and antiques, lovely restaurant, excellent chocolate cake, arrive early for lunch as tour parties stop here, expensive, good excursions, price includes breakfast and dinner, rec; **L2** *Hostería La Banda*, W of town along 10 de Agosto, T 915-176, F 915-873, new in 1994, lavish bungallows and suites, country estate style, restaurant, cafetería, tours, horse riding; **A2** *El Mesón de las Flores*, T 915-009, F 915-828, bath, parking, converted ex-hacienda off main plaza, meals in a beautiful patio, often live music at lunch, highly rec; **B** *Gran Hotel Primitivo*, on the road between the Panamericana and Cotacachi, approx 4 km before town, inca style fortress, private bath, terrace cafetería; *La Choza* restaurant, typical local dish, *carne colorada*, for US$1.50; **E** *Hostal Cuicocha*, 10 de Agosto y Bolívar, Edif de la Sociedad de Artesanos, 3rd floor, T 915-327, unfriendly, bar, restaurant, expensive breakfast, cafetería, parking; **F** *Bachita*, Sucre y Peñaherrera, modern, bath, clean, rec; **G** *Residencial Santa Marta*, luggage stored, rec. *Ron Damiro*, Sucre y 9 de Octubre, nice, clean, trout specialities; *Asadero La Tola*, Rocafuerte, in an old courtyard; *Chifa Nueva*, González Suárez y 10 de Agosto, authentic Chinese.

About 15 km beyond Cotacachi (past the town of Quiroga), at an altitude of 3,070m lies Laguna **Cuicocha**, which has been developed for tourism. It is part of the Parque Nacional Cotacachi-Cayapas, which extends from Cotacachi volcano to tropical lowlands on the Río Cayapas in Esmeraldas (entrance and camping free). This is a crater lake with two islands, although these are closed to the public for biological studies. The restaurant, *Muelle*, has a dining room overlooking the lake, clean, moderate prices; there is a much cheaper restaurant at the top of the cliff behind, camping possible; *El Mirador*, F pp, with food, friendly service, hikes arranged, excellent view (return transport to Otavalo provided for US$7). Motor boats can be hired for groups, US$1 pp, minimum 8 persons. There is a well-marked, 8 km path around the lake, which takes 5 hrs (best to go anticlockwise, take water and windbreaker), and provides spectacular views of Cotacachi, Imbabura and, occasionally, glacier-covered Cayambe peaks (best views in early morning, lookout 3 km, 2 hrs from the start). The slopes of Cerro Cotacachi, N from the lake, are a nature reserve. If wishing to climb Cotacachi, approach from the ridge, not from the side with the antennae which is usually shrouded in cloud. New detailed maps of the Otavalo-Ibarra region are available from the IGM in Quito.

Warning Many people have been badly poisoned by eating the blue berries which grow near the lake. They are *not* blueberries; they render the eater helpless within 2 hrs, requiring at least a stomach pump. **NB also** On the road between Cotacachi and Cuicocha, children stretch string across the road to beg, especially at weekends.

Bus Otavalo-Quiroga US$0.10, Cotacachi-Quiroga US$0.10, *camioneta* Quiroga-Cuicocha US$3.30. Alternatively, hire a taxi (US$12.50) or *camioneta* in Otavalo for Laguna Cuicocha, about US$7 for five people. A taxi costs US$4 one way from Cotacachi. The 3-hr walk back to Cotacachi is beautiful; after 1 km on the road from the park entrance, turn left (at the first bend) on to the old road. You can also walk from Otavalo.

On the SW boundary of the Cotacachi-Cayapas park is **Los Cedros Research Station**, 6,400 ha of pristine cloudforest. Contact CIBT, Casilla 17-7-8726, Quito, T/F 221-324 for details on research and accommodation (US$20/day). Bus from Quito (San Blas) to Sanguangal, 5 hrs, then 4-6 hr walk, or through Safari Tours, Quito. 4WD can reach the road-end.

Also off the main road between Otavalo and Ibarra is *San Antonio de Ibarra*, well known for its wood carvings. The trade is so successful that the main street is lined with galleries and boutiques. Bargaining is difficult, but it is worth seeing the range of styles and techniques and shopping around. Visit the workshop of Moreo Santacruz, and the exhibition of Osvaldo Garrido in the Palacio de Arte. Luís Potosí's gallery on the main square has some beautiful carvings. (**F** *Hostal Los Nogales*, T 955-000, cheaper without bath, restaurant, good value. Buses from Ibarra, 13 km, 10 mins.)

Near *Apuela*, in the lush tropical valley of the Zona del Intag (**G** *Pensión Apuela*, grim; *Residencia Don Luis*, basic, cold showers, fairly clean, friendly; *Hostal Florida*, good for groups; small restaurant) are the thermal baths of Nangulví (1 hr walk **G** *Cabañas*, basic). Apuela buses from Otavalo on a dirt road (2 a day, book in advance, crowded) pass Nangulví, where the swimming pool is emptied for cleaning on Tues and Fri. Before Apuela, the *Hacienda La Florida* offers full board for US$30 pp per day and a wide range of nature walks in primary subtropical rainforest and excursions. Essential to book in advance. Casilla 18, Otavalo, Imbabura, Ecuador (or Latitudo 0°, T 440-672, Quito). About 2 hrs drive (bumpy track) from Ibarra are the clean, hot mineral swimming pools of Chachimbiro in the parish of Tumbariro. Buses from Ibarra 5 a day (2½ hrs).

Ibarra, founded 1606, at 2,225m, population 80,990, is a pleasant colonial town with many good hotels and restaurants. Prices are lower than elsewhere and there are fewer tourists than in Otavalo. Many people prefer to stay here rather than in Otavalo, as the town is picturesque, in good condition and clean, while all the excursions from Otavalo can be done just as easily from Ibarra. The city has an interesting ethnic mix, with blacks from the Chota valley and Esmeraldas alongside Otavaleños and other highland Indians. The city has two squares with flowering trees: Parque Pedro Moncayo, on which stands the Cathedral and Casa Cural, the Municipio and Gobernación. One block away is the smaller Parque Dr Víctor Manuel Peñaherrera, at Flores y Olmedo, more commonly called Parque de la Merced after the church on the square; it is also flanked by the Ministerio de Agricultura y Ganadería. Some interesting paintings are to be seen in the church of Santo Domingo and its museum of religious art (at the end of Cra Simón Bolívar, open Mon-Sat 0900-1200, 1500-1800, US$0.15). At García Moreno y Rocafuerte is the back of San Agustín church, whose façade is on small Parque Abdón Calderón. On Sucre, at the end of Av A Pérez Guerrero is the Basílica de La Dolorosa, destroyed by earthquake in May 1987, reopened in Dec 1992. A walk down Pérez Guerrero leads to the large covered market on Cifuentes, by the railway station, open daily. Take care in the downtown area, especially at night.

Festivals Fiesta de los Lagos, last weekend of Sept, Thur-Sun; also 16 July, Virgen del Carmen.

Hotels The better class hotels tend to be fully booked during Holy Week, Fiesta de los Lagos and at weekends. Along the Pan-American Highway S towards Otavalo are several country inns, some in converted haciendas, from S to N are: **C** *Hostería Natabuela*, Km 8, PO Box 683 (Ibarra), T 957-734, F 640-230, comfortable rooms, covered pool, sauna, restaurant; **C** *Hostería San Alfonso de Moras*, Km 4.5, T 935-499, nice cabins, friendly; **B** *Hostería Chorlaví*, set in a converted hacienda, Km 4, PO Box 828, T 955-777, F 956-311, US$2.50 for extra bed, also cabins, excellent *parrillada* and folk music and crafts on Sun, discotheque at weekends, sauna, good value restaurant, pool open to non-residents US$0.30; next door, up the same drive is **B** *Rancho Carolina*, PO Box 78, T 953-215, F 955-215, nice cabins, restaurant; **D** *Hostería San Agustín*, Km 2.5, T 955-888, clean, friendly, good service, hot water, good food; **C** *Ajaví*, Av Mariano Acosta 16-38, T 955-555, F 952-485, along main road into town from S, pool and restaurant; **D** *El Ejecutivo*, Bolívar 9-69, entre Colón y Velasco, T 952-575; **D** *El Dorado*, Oviedo 5-47 y Sucre, T 950-699, F 958-700, clean, good restaurant, parking; **D** *Imbaya Real*, Pedro Moncayo 7-44, T 959-729, nice, modern, good value; **E** *Los Alpes*, Velasco 732 y Bolívar, clean with private bath; **E** *El Retorno*, Moncayo 4-32, cheaper without bath, clean, pleasant; **E** *Nueva Colonial*, Carrera Olmedo 5-19, T 952-918/543, clean, restaurant, parking; **E** *Residencial Madrid*, Olmedo 857 y Oviedo, T 951-760, clean, friendly, comfortable, good views from upper rooms; and *Hostal Madrid*, Moncayo y Sánchez, T 952-177, more expensive, less friendly, clean, both have parking and are rec, but doors locked at 2300; **F** *Residencial Imperio*, Olmedo 8-62 y Oviedo (T 952-929), with bath, hot water, TV in lobby, a bargain, but disco at weekends till 0400; **F** *Hotel Imbabura*, Oviedo 9-33 y Narváez, T 950-155, cheap, clean, will store luggage, splendid showers, big rooms, pretty garden, basic, take padlock, owner has considerable local knowledge, friendly, rec; **F** *Residencial Astoria*, Velasco 809, safe, can store luggage, friendly, basic, not very clean, large terrace, laundry facilities; **F** *Residencial Colón*, Narváez 5257 y Velasco (more with bath), hot water, pleasant, clean, friendly, laundry facilities, stores luggage, will change money, convenient for train, rec; **F** *Residencial Majestic*, Olmedo 763 y Flores, T 950-052, with or without bath, not too secure, friendly; **F** *Hostal El Retorno*, Pedro Moncayo, clean, nice view from terrace. Several others, F and G, along Bolívar, Moncayo and Olmedo.

Restaurants *Hostería Chorlaví* restaurant rec (but it is crowded with tour buses on Sat lunchtime), likewise *Hotel Ajaví*. *La Chagra*, Olmedo 7-48, rec, reasonable prices; *Marisquería Las Redes*, Oviedo 638 y Sucre, seafood, accepts US$ at top rate. Breakfast with good bread at *Café Pushkin*, Olmedo 7-75, opens 0730, and at *Mejor Pan*, Olmedo 7-52; *Rosita*, also on Olmedo, good cheap food; *Mira Valle*, Olmedo 752, good, cheap set lunch and dinner; *Rith's*, Olmedo 7-61, good set meals and à la carte. Many others on Olmedo, especially Chinese (choose carefully), also *El Cedrón*, No 7-37, coffee, snacks and veal/venison. *Imperio*, Calle Olmedo, noisy due to TV in reception, good Chinese food; *Chifa Muy Buena*, Olmedo 723, does a good *Chaulafan*, "muy buena"; *Gus Pollo*, Sánchez y Cifuentes 1126, rec; *El Caribe*, Flores 771, chicken and local food, excellent 3-course set meal for US$0.60; *El Dorado*, Oviedo y Sucre, seafood, good, expensive, snacks; *Mr Peter's*, Oviedo y Bolívar, popular with locals; *Club Imbabura*, Oviedo 7-30 y Bolívar, open 0900-2300, elegant dining, breakfast; *La Vieja Casona*, Oviedo 7-62 y Olmedo, seafood specialities, reasonably priced; *Koco Rico*, Olmedo 724, and *Asadero a las Doradas*, Oviedo 720, both chicken; *Luchino's*, Sucre y G Moreno, pizzas, hamburgers, good for snacks; *Amaranto*, Moncayo y Sucre, on the *plazoleta*, vegetarian, often shut; *Mi Pan*, Sucre, cheaper than most for coffee and pastries; *Pizzería El Horno*, Moncayo 6-30, good pizza and lasagna; *Café Floralp*, Bolívar y T Gómez, open 0700-2100, good breakfast, bread, cheese, yoghurt, coffee; *Panificadora Danés*, Cifuentes 8-44 y Sánchez, good bread and *conchas*; *La Estancia*, García Moreno 7-66, very good grill but not cheap. *Heladería Rosalía Suárez*, Oviedo y Olmedo (100 years old in 1996), good home made *helados de paila* (long queues at weekends, try *mora* or *guanábana*); *Los Helados*, Calle 27, near main plaza, for good ice cream; also *Heladería La Nevada*, Velasco 837. Local specialities are sweets made from walnuts, blackberries (*arrope de mora*) and other fruits, *helados de paila*, fruit sherbets made in large copper basins (*pailas*) and nougat (*nogada*); most on sale at Olmedo 7-88. Supermarket, Carrera 8.

Exchange Banco Continental, Olmedo 11-67, and Banco Central; only *Casas de Cambio* change TCs. *Las Redes* restaurant, *Residencial Colón* and *Farmacia Sudamericana*, Olmedo 864 y Moncayo change US$ notes. **Ecuafactor**, formerly Policambios, Pedro Moncayo 6-35, T 641061, F 955-258. **Intercambios**, 2nd Flr, Oviedo y Bolívar.

Entertainments Balneario Primavera, Sánchez y Cifuentes 323, pool, sauna, turkish bath; Baños Calientes at Sucre 10-68. Casa Cultural, near Terminal Terrestre. Piano bar, *El Encuentro*, Olmedo 959, interesting drinks, pleasant atmosphere, unusual décor. Discos: *Nexus*, Velasco y Bolívar; *Mistify*, Flores y Rocafuerte; *Studio 54*, Autopista y Yahuarcocha. Ibarra is very quiet, even on Sat nights the locals go to Otavalo for the peñas and bars. A unique form of paddle ball is played on Sat and Sun near the railway station, also on way from bus station to centre, on left, just before the built-up area. The players have huge spiked paddles for striking the 2 lb ball. On weekdays they play a similar game with a lighter ball.

Health Dr Eduardo Benítez, Oviedo 8-40, T 955-592, very helpful.

Language Courses Centro de Español Imbabura, PO Box 10-01505, T 959-429.

Post Office   Salinas 6-64, between Oviedo y Moncayo, no sign outside; **Emetel**, Sucre, just past Parque Pedro Moncayo, opens 0800.

Travel Agency   *Nevitur Cia Ltda*, Bolívar 7-35 y Oviedo, T 958-701, F 640-040, excellent travel guides, have new vans for trips throughout the country, as well as the Pasto region of Colombia. *Turismo Inti Pungo*, Rocafuerte 4-47 y García Moreno, T 955-270. A rec **taxi driver** for excursions is Luis Cabrera Medrano, Cooperativa de Taxis, Pascual Monge, "El Obelisco".

Tourist Office   Cetur, Colón 7-43 entre Bolívar y Olmedo, helpful. Map of Ibarra, US$0.10.

Immigration   Olmedo y LF Villamar (T 951-712), very quick for extensions.

Bus   Bus station (Terminal Terrestre) is 1 km S of town, reached by bus No 2 from centre (closed for repairs since Jan 1994); buses leave from alongside railway tracks nr obelisk (corner of Velasco) at entrance to city (beware bagslashers). To/from **Quito** 2-3 hrs, US$1.60, about 50 departures a day. Colectivo taxis (Taxis Lagos de Ibarra) for about US$2.65, taxis US$20. To **Yahuarcocha**, US$1.30. To **Tulcán**, US$1.90, 2 hrs. To **Otavalo**, ½ hr starting at 0500, leave two blocks down from the railway station and call at the Terminal Terrestre later, US$0.35. Buses to **Cotacachi** and **Quiroga** also start here. Expreso Turismo has small terminal at P Moncayo y Flores, frequent buses to Quito, Tulcán Pimampiro, etc.

Excursions   A pretty village to visit close to Ibarra, 10 km directly S on the road to Olmedo, is *La Esperanza*, in beautiful surroundings on the pre-Inca road which goes to Cayambe. Accommodation: **G** pp *Casa Aída*, basic, Aída speaks some English and cooks good vegetarian food; **G** *María*, nice rooms, will heat water, friendly. (Bus from Parque Germán Grisalva in Ibarra passes *Aída*, US$0.10.) Eugenio makes leather bags and clothes cheaply to measure, eg US$60 for trousers; good quality, rec. One particular lady does extremely fine embroidery; ask in village for her house. You can climb **Cubilche** volcano in 3 hours from La Esperanza for beautiful views; from the top you can walk down to Laguna de San Pablo, another 3 hrs. You can also climb Imbabura volcano more easily than from Lago San Pablo; allow 8-10 hrs round trip, take a good map, food and warm clothing. *Urcuqui* is a pretty little town with a basic hotel and a park. On Sun the locals play unusual ball games. Bus from Ibarra starts from the open space opp bus station. Urcuqui is the starting point for walking to the Piñán lakes. *Guachara*, NW of Ibarra is reached by bus from Ibarra railway station (US$0.10), or by train from Ibarra to Carchi and then bus. People friendly, mountains beautiful and hitch-hiking very possible.

At edge of *Lago Yahuarcocha* are **D** *Parador El Conquistador*, 8 rm, large restaurant, rec, run by Cetur; *Hotel del Lago*, no accommodation, only refreshments; *Rancho Totoral*, T/F 955-544, excellent cooking, many local dishes, US$3-4 for meal, beautiful, tranquil setting, accommodation planned. Camping on the lakeside possible.

It is possible to walk to Lago Yahuarcocha (4 km) in about 1½ hrs. Follow Calle 27 to the end of town, cross the river and walk to the right at the first junction. At the end of this road, behind 2 low buildings on the left, there is a small path going steeply uphill. There are beautiful views of Ibarra and then from the top of the hill over the lake surrounded by mountains and the village of the same name. Yahuarcocha, "blood lake" in Quichua, named because legend says that the water turned red when the Incas threw in the bodies of defeated local Indians. There are frequent buses between Ibarra (market area) and the village. The beauty of the lake has been disfigured by the building of a motor-racing circuit round its shores. The lake is gradually drying up with *totora* reeds encroaching on its margins. They are woven into *esteras* (mats) sold in huge rolls at the roadside. Reed boats can sometimes be seen.

The quiet town of *Pimampiro* lies NE of Ibarra, 8 km off the Panamericana along a paved road; take the turnoff at Juncal. Bus from Ibarra, Cooperativa Oriental, leaves every 20 min, US$0.60, 45 mins. The surrounding countryside offers excellent walking. There is a bustling Sun market. One **G** *Residencial* run by the Hurtado family on Calle Flores, no sign, ask around, basic, friendly, poor water supply. **Restaurants**   *El Forastero*, corner Flores and Olmedo, good; *El Vecino*, Espejo 3-028; *Picantería Riobambeñita*, Espejo 3-054. From Pimampiro follow a steep dirt road along the beautiful canyon of the Río Pisquer 20 km to the village of *Sanchipamba* (bus from Pimampiro at 1100, Thur to Sun, crowded). There are many forks in the road, so ask frequently if walking; magnificent views. 4WD recommended if driving. No hotels or restaurants in Sanchipamba, only a few basic shops. Sanchipamba is the best access to the *Laguna de Puranta*, a 4 to 5 hr strenuous hike. The lake is set amid the high páramo and one can camp and fish for trout. The area is very muddy during the rainy season (Nov to May). From the lake one can walk to the village of Mariano Acosta, from which buses run back to Ibarra through Pimampiro. The direct road from Mariano Acosta to Ibarra is in very poor shape and no longer has bus service. Allow 3 or more days for the excursion and take tent, sleeping bag, warm waterproof clothing, food, stove and fuel.

To the Coast In March 1995 there was a train at 0700, Mon, Wed, Fri, from Ibarra to San Lorenzo, arriving (in theory) at 1500, foreigners US$15. Return also 0700, Tues, Thurs, Fri, inquire in advance because schedules and prices are constantly changing. Freight service has been indefinitely suspended, so all merchandise is now carried on board the *autoferro*, making it more crowded than ever. Ticket office opens at 0500, but queue up at least an hour beforehand and be prepared for much jostling. A better bet is to purchase your ticket in advance (up to 48 hrs in advance is permitted), but be at the station early anyway, and be ready to fight for your seat. The station crew can be friendly and helpful. Try to talk to them the day before you travel, T (06) 950-390. The line is frequently cut by landslides during the rainy season. Best time of year for the trip is June to Sept. An unforgettable journey!

The new road to San Lorenzo opened in early 1995, with buses running on it (schedules unknown). New concrete bridges have been installed throughout the route.

The train service is unreliable so if there is a choice it is better to start from Ibarra where there is more to do in the event of delay. On the other hand, tickets are easier to get in San Lorenzo. The train can get very crowded and angry passengers unable to board have been known to beat up the driver! Because of heavy rains, work on the new road and landslides, delays and derailments are frequent. Riding on the roof is officially forbidden. If you are not allowed on the roof do not put your bags up there, theft reported. Although there are meal stops, eg at Lita, it is advisable to take plenty of food and drink. At all times, especially when waiting to board, look out for bagslashers and pickpockets. If robbed on the train, go to the police in San Lorenzo (if leaving Ibarra) and say you were robbed on the train. Otherwise you will have to go back to Ibarra to fill out the *denuncia* (report for insurance purposes). Cumbres y Mar travel agency in Quito (Carrión 747 y Amazonas, T 231-561/554-630) run tours in the region, including rail trips. It may be possible to join a tour, paying US$15-20 depending on numbers, how far you accompany the tour, but all inclusive.

Leaving Ibarra, the train descends past Salinas into the narrow gorge of the Río Mira (called Chota upstream) inhabited by blacks growing fruit and sugar cane, who sell fruit at the station. After 3 hrs the valley widens near Collapi (730m) and the land becomes better watered and has been more recently colonized. *Lita* (460m) is reached after five hours (US$0.70 one way) and a stop is made for refreshment—all foreigners' passports are checked at Lita because of close proximity to the Colombian border. Be careful taking photos in Lita. 1 km uphill from the station is a *residencia*, G, adequate, clean, no hot water. Two basic restaurants. Lights out at 2200. Bus Ibarra-Lita leaves from behind Ibarra train station, 0700, 1100, 1300, 4-5 hrs, US$2.20, crowded. Botanists researching in the tropical forests on the hills around Lita claim each hill top has more different species of plant than the whole of Canada. Through the lowlands cultivated land becomes more common until we reach San Lorenzo.

North of Ibarra the Pan-American Highway goes past Laguna Yahuarcocha and then descends to the hot dry Chota valley. Here you can buy tropical fruit from the local descendents of slaves brought from Africa in the 17th century to farm sugar estates. 24 km N of Ibarra is the turnoff W for Salinas and Lita along the new road to San Lorenzo. 6 km further N, at Mascarilla, is a police checkpoint (have your documents at hand), after which the highway divides. One branch follows an older route NE through Mira and El Angel to Tulcán on the Colombian border. This road is paved and in excellent condition as far as El Angel, but deteriorates rapidly thereafter. The El Angel-Tulcán section, although very scenic (see below), is now seldom used and is frequently impassable. The second branch (the modern Pan-American Highway), in good repair but with many heavy lorries, runs E through the Chota valley to Juncal, before turning N to reach Tulcán via Bolívar and San Gabriel. An excellent paved road runs between Bolívar and El Angel, connecting the two branches. A second lateral road, between San Gabriel and El Angel, is in poor shape and is often impassable during the rainy season.

Along the old route, which climbs steeply from Mascarilla, is the town of *Mira*, 15 km past the fork (pop 5,500; bus from Ibarra, US$0.55, 1 hour; from Tulcán, 1600, 1½ hrs, US$1). Some of the finest quality woollens come from this part of the country; there are two women in Mira who produce them for export and a cooperative up the hill opposite the bus station which sells in the town at export prices. There are two carnivals held each year, on 2 Feb, and 18 Aug, with fireworks and free flowing Tardón, the local *aguardiente*. There is a clean *residencia* (**G** *Mira*, basic but good beds), but very few restaurants; the best is the *Bar Latino*. Stretches of virgin rain and cloud forest along the Río Mira are accessible to the adventurous.

Continuing 20 km NE along the old Panamericana we reach **El Angel** (pop 5,700, altitude 3,000m), a sleepy highland town that comes to life during its Mon market. It is the birthplace of José Franco, designer of the famous topiary in the Tulcán cemetery, and the main plaza retains a few trees that were originally sculpted by him.

Accommodation and Transport G *Residencial Viña del Mar*, José Grijalva 05-48 on main plaza, shared bath, basic, restaurant next door **G** *Residencial Alvarez*, run by Sra Ofelia López Peñaherrera, José Grijalva 02-59, basic, shared bath, cold water, no shower, but very friendly, recommended. *Asadero Los Faroles*, José Grijalva 5-96, roast chicken and trout, expensive. Several other chicken places in town. *Pastelería Mi Pan*, José Grijalva corner Bolívar, very good bread and pastries. The shops are well stocked with provisions. **Photo** Estudio Narvaez, José Grijalva by plaza, sells nice photos of the surrounding area. **Buses** Trans Espejo, hourly to **Quito** via Ibarra, US$2.50, 4 hrs; to **Tulcán** at 0530 and 0700 daily, US$0.95. Trans Mira, hourly to **Mira** and **Tulcán**.

3 km S of town, along the road to Mira, is the turnoff for the thermal baths of **La Calera**. From here a steep but good cobbled road descends for 6.5 km into a lovely valley to the baths themselves, with good views along the way. There are two pools with warm water in pleasant surroundings, admission US$0.50. Deserted during the week (when only the smaller pool is filled), no public transport, US$15 round trip to hire a jeep from El Angel. Crowded with locals on weekends and holidays, when the same jeeps charge US$0.50 per person.

El Angel is the main access point for the **Reserva Ecológica El Angel**, created in 1992 to protect 15,715 ha of *páramo* ranging in altitude from 3,400 to 4,150m. The reserve contains the southernmost large stands of the velvet-leaved *frailejón* plant, also found in the Andes of Colombia and Venezuela. Also of interest are the spiny *achupallas* with giant compound flowers, related to the *Puya Raymondii* of Peru and Bolivia. The fauna includes *curiquingue* hawks, deer, foxes, and a few condors. There are several small lakes scattered throughout the reserve. It can be very muddy during the rainy season and the best time to visit is May to Aug. The reserve is administered by *Inefan* (the Forestry Institute of the Ministry of Agriculture), El Angel office José Grijalva 04-26, in an old school, upstairs to the left. The staff is friendly and helpful. Reserve entry fee of US$10 for foreigners has been proposed but was not implemented as of Mar 95. The *Fundación El Angel*, offices in the municipal building, can also provide information about visiting the reserve. Gerardo Miguel Quelal knows the area well and can be hired as a guide. Contact him through either of the above offices.

One excursion into the reserve from El Angel follows the poor road N towards Tulcán for 16 km to *El Voladero* (parking area but no sign) where a trail climbs over a low ridge (30 min walk) to two crystal clear lakes. Camping is possible here, but you must be self sufficient and take great care not to damage the fragile surroundings. Jeeps can be hired in the main plaza of El Angel for a day trip to El Voladero, US$40 return, but bargain.

Another, longer, excursion follows an equally poor road to Cerro Socabones, beginning in the town of La Libertad (3.5 km N of El Angel). This route climbs gradually through haciendas, where fighting bulls are bred, to reach the high *páramo* at the centre of the reserve. After Socabones, the road deteriorates to a track which leads to the village of Morán at the N end of the reserve. Adjacent to El Angel Reserve is the **Cerro Golondrinas Cloudforest Conservation Project**, from highland to subtropical rainforest, aiming to conserve 25,000 ha and introduce sustainable agroforestry (contact Fundeal, attn Piet Sabbe, c/o Calle Isabel La Católica 1559, Quito, PO Box 17-17-86, F 593-507-245). Another track from Socabones descends to Lita in the subtropical lowlands. There are many paths criss-crossing the *páramo* and it is easy to get lost. Jeeps from El Angel to Cerro Socabones, US$50 return.

A third access to the reserve is from the N along the Tufiño-Maldonado road (see below) from which the Lagunas Verdes (green lakes) can be seen. Like many of the lakes in the *páramo* these are gradually drying. They are said to be enchanted according to local legend.

Following the new route of the Pan-American Highway E past Mascarilla for 2 km, we reach the turnoff for the town of **El Chota**, with the **Honka Monka** museum of Afro-Ecuadorean culture. A further 8 km leads to a series of tourist complexes for Colombians and Ecuadoreans who come down from the highlands for the *sabor tropical*. Hotels: **B** *Aruba Hostería*, T (06) 937-005, modern, small pool, posh restaurant, expensive, day use US$5 pp. **D** *Hostería Oasis*, Casilla 208, Ibarra, T (06) 937-001, F (06) 996-304, cabins for up to 6 and mini-cabins for 2, best facilities including 3 large pools (one is a wave pool), waterslide, playground, several snack bars, disco, good restaurant with live music on weekends, good value, day use US$3 pp; **E** *Hostería El Jordán*, T (06) 937-002, similar but not as elaborate. Several others. Next to the *hosterías* is a roadside kiosk run by Cetur (tourist office) with limited information. Just beyond is El Juncal, the turn off E to Pimampiro and Mariano Acosta (see above), after which the highway turns N to cross the Río Chota into the province of Carchi and begins its steep climb out of the valley.

A further 17 km N brings us to **Bolívar** (pop 15,175), a neat little town with houses and interior of church painted in lively pastel colours, and a well kept plaza. Friday market. One **G** *Hospedaje* run by Sra Lucila Torres, Carrera Julio Andrade s/n, 1 block N of plaza, no sign, shared bath with electric shower, basic. *Restaurant Los Sauces*, by highway, good food, good value, recommended. *Salón Andaluz*, Calle García Moreno 5-47, 2 blocks W of plaza. Good bakery on main plaza at García Moreno corner Julio Andrade.

5 km N of Bolívar is the turnoff E for the town of La Paz, from which a steep but good cobbled road descends for 5 km to the **Gruta de La Paz** . Views along the road are breathtaking, including two spectacular waterfalls. The place is also called *Rumichaca* (Quichua for stone bridge) after the massive natural bridge which forms the *gruta* (grotto); not to be confused with the Rumichaca on the Colombian border. The entire area is a religious shrine, receiving large numbers of pilgrims during Holy Week, Christmas, and especially around 8 July, feast day of the Virgin of La Paz. In addition to the chapel in the grotto itself, there is a large basilica, a Franciscan convent, a guest house for pilgrims **F**, a restaurant, and shops selling religious articles. These are open on weekends and pilgrimage days only, and there are very few visitors at other times. The river which emerges from the grotto is rather polluted, and the sewer smell detracts from its otherwise great natural beauty. There are clean thermal baths (showers and one pool) just below the grotto, open Wed to Sun (crowded on weekends), admission US$0.25, look for the caretaker if the gate to the pool is locked. Several trails through the valley start from behind the hotel, nice scenery. Excursions to La Paz from Tulcán on Sat and Sun. Also jeeps from San Gabriel, US$0.60 pp on weekends, US$10 to hire a vehicle during the week. A second access road has been built from the Panamericana, 3 km S of San Gabriel, signposted.

10 km N of La Paz is **San Gabriel** (pop 19,500), an important commercial centre. Hotels: **G** *Residencial Montúfar*, Colón 03-44, some rooms with private bath, hot water, clean, safe, motorcycle parking, basic. **G** *Residencial Ideal*, Montúfar 08-26, basic, hot water US$0.25 extra. **Restaurants** *Su Casita*, Bolívar 12-07, good set meal; *Asadero Pío Riko*, Bolívar 10-15, chicken and others. *Heladería Zanzibar*, Colón 3-16, for ice cream. Jeeps for Tulcán leave from main plaza when full. Also **buses** to Quito, every 45 min, US$2.50, 4 hrs. The spectacular 60m high **Paluz** waterfall is 4 km N of town, follow Calle Bolívar out of main plaza, turn right after the bridge. Well worth the walk. There is a rather chilly "thermal" bath along the way.

The old and new branches of the Panamericana join at Las Juntas, 2 km S of **Tulcán** (pop 37,069), a bustling commercial centre and capital of the province of Carchi. At an altitude of 2,960m, it is always chilly. For decades the economic life of the town revolved around smuggling between Ecuador and Colombia. It was therefore expected to go bust following the implementation of a free trade agreement between the two countries in 1992, as part of the *Pacto Andino*. Tulcán continues to thrive however, now as a shopping destination for Colombians who arrive by the busload from as far away as Bogotá and Medellín. There is a frantic textile and dry goods fair on Thur and Sun. Prices are generally lower than Colombia, but higher than other parts of Ecuador. Travellers have traditionally passed Tulcán by as uninteresting, but there are a few worthwhile excursions from here (see below) and the unique cemetery, 2 blocks from Parque Ayora, must not be missed. Here the topiarist's art reaches its apogee; cypress bushes are trimmed into archways and fantastic figures of animals, angels, geometric shapes, etc, in *haut* and *bas* relief. Note the figures based on the stone carvings at San Agustín, Colombia, to the left just past the main entrance. To see the various stages of this artform, go to the back of the cemetery where young bushes are being pruned. The artistry is that of the late Sr José Franco, now buried among the splendour he created. His epitaph reads: "In Tulcán, a cemetery so beautiful that it invites one to die!" The tradition is carried on by his sons.

Warning Tulcán and the traditionally tranquil border province of Carchi have seen an increase in drug trafficking and a corresponding decline in public safety. The area is still safer than Quito or Guayaquil, but it is prudent not to wander about late at night (ie after 2200).

Hotels Many new hotels were opened in 1993/94 and there is ample lodging available in several categories. **D** *Azteca*, Bolívar y Atahualpa, T 981-447, F 980-481, the best in town, TV, restaurant, but noisy from the disco downstairs; **C-D** *Frailejón*, Sucre y Rocafuerte, T 981-129/980-149, with bath, hot water, TV, good but expensive restaurant; **D** *Saenz Internacional*, Sucre y Rocafuerte, T 981-916, F 983-925, very nice, modern, friendly, good value; **E** *Hostal Alejandra*, Sucre y Quito, T 981-784, private bath, TV, safe indoor parking, good value, rec; **E** *España*, Sucre between 10 de Agosto y Pichincha, T 983-860, modern, some rooms with bath, expensive; **E** *Los Alpes*, opp bus station, with hot shower, TV, clean; **E** *Quillasinga*, Sucre y Ayacucho by main plaza, T 981-892, bath, simple; **E** *Unicornio*, Sucre 49-79, with bath; **E** *Florida*, with bath, F without, Sucre y 10 de Agosto, T 983-849, modern section in back, good value; **F** *Residencial Colombia*, Colón 52-017 y Ayacucho, T 982-761, shared bath, simple; **F** *Imperial*, Bolívar y Panamá (by Parque Ayora, convenient for transport to border), T 981-094, shared bath, hot water, safe, clean, basic; **F** *Pensión Minerva*, 10 de Agosto y Bolívar, hot water, good, friendly, quiet; **F** *Carchi*, Sucre 50-044, shared bath, cold water, basic; **G** *Quito*, Ayacucho 450, OK.

Restaurants *Avenida*, Bolívar y Ecuador, opp bus station; *Terminal*, in bus station, reasonable. Colombian specialities: *Rincón Caleño*, Sucre 49-29; *Los Arrieros*, Bolívar 51-053. Seafood: *Cevichería el Viceño*, Bolívar 48-049; *Marisquería Los Alpes*, by bus station; *Marisquería Anzuelo Manabita*, Sucre y Boyacá. Many along Sucre: *Restaurant El Paso*, Chinese, good; *Pack Chow*, Sucre, cheap and good; *Mayflower*, off square, some vegetarian if you ask; *Parrilladas*, Sierra y Bolívar, good typical food, near cemetery; *Rincón Carchense*, nr church, good meals. Many others, inc snack bars. *Max Pan* for good breakfasts.

Exchange The many money changers on both sides of the border will exchange cash; good rates have been reported at the Rumichaca bridge, but double-check all calculations. There is an association of informal money changers in Tulcán, look for photo ids, and note down the name in case of any disagreement. It is reportedly difficult to change TCs, but try *Casa Paz cambio*, on Ayacucho in front of *Hotel Quito*, or *Carlos Burbano*, Bolívar y Junín. For those arriving in Ecuador, change only what you need to get to Quito or Ibarra, where the rate is better. **Filanbanco**, Sucre y Junín and **Banco de Préstamos**, in front of the park, will undertake foreign currency transactions. Few places accept credit cards.

Transport Bus to **Quito** 5 hrs, US$4.10, every 15 mins; to **Ibarra**, 2½ hrs, US$1.90. **Otavalo**, US$1.40, 3 hrs (make sure bus is going to Otavalo; if not get out on the Highway at the turn off), or take bus to Ibarra and then colectivo. To **Guayaquil**, 20 a day, 11 hrs, US$7. To **Huaquillas**, with Panamericana Internacional, 1 luxury coach a day. Plenty of colectivos also. Bus terminal is long uphill walk from centre; best to take taxi, US$1.50, or little blue bus, keep a sharp look out on the right, or the bus will not stop. Airport is on road to Rumichaca: TAME flies to Cali Tues and Thur, US$66, and to Quito, Mon-Fri US$17.

To Colombia Border hours are 0600 to 2100. Colombia has a modern border complex, with all offices under one roof: **see p 896**; see also **Documents** in Colombia, Information for Visitors. The Ecuadorean side is older and more chaotic, but none-the-less adequate. There is a modern Emetel office for phone calls. The old customs buildings and the natural bridge over the Río Carchi are interesting, worth a look, 500m W of the concrete bridge. Colectivos Tulcán-border (blue and white minivans) leave when full from Parque Ayora (near cemetery) US$0.75 (city bus from terminal to Parque Ayora US$0.05, often too crowded for luggage). Taxis to border US$0.85 pp from Parque Ayora, US$3.50 to hire a cab from anywhere in town (including bus terminal, cheaper from upper level). Colectivos border-Ipiales US$0.35 to edge of town, US$0.80 pp to main plaza, US$2.60 to hire as taxi. You are not allowed to cross to Ipiales for the day without having your passport stamped (both Ecuadorean exit stamp and Colombian entry stamp required). Although no one will stop you at the frontier, you risk serious consequences in Ipiales if you are caught with your documents "out of order".

Excursions Buses every 2 hrs from opp Colegio Nacional Tulcán, Calle R Sierra, to *Tufiño*, US$0.45, 45 min, rough road, military checkpoint just before the village. No hotels in Tufiño, one basic restaurant, several shops. The area surrounding Tufiño has various hot mineral springs arising from the nearby Chiles volcano and geothermal energy projects are planned here. Up the hill from Tufiño, 1.2 km W then take turnoff left, are two pools by the river in a pretty setting. But the water is barely tepid and the site has fallen into great disrepair, free admission. Crossing the border from Tufiño towards Chiles, Colombia (no formalities, but you must return the same day), turn left at the large green sign for the *Balneario* and continue uphill for 1.5 km. The water here is warm, public baths are free and dirty, private *Baños Termales* "*Juan Chiles*" cost US$0.65 and are somewhat cleaner. There are many other springs all along this hillside, follow trail from behind the public pool. By far the best hot springs of the region are **Aguas Hediondas** (stinking waters), a pool of boiling sulphurous mineral waters in a wild, impressive, lonely valley. An ice-cold stream of melted snow water passes nearby; you need to direct it into the pool to make it cold enough to enter! These waters are said to cure spots, rheumatism, etc. Follow the winding road 3 km W of Tufiño, to where a rusting white sign marks the turnoff to the right. From here it is 4.5 km through strange scenery to the magnificent natural pools. Condors can sometimes be seen hovering above the high cliffs surrounding the valley. The baths are really marvellous, deserted on weekdays. **Warning:** Several visitors have died after being overcome by fumes emanating from the source of the sulfurous water. Bathe in the lower pools and do not follow the stream uphill.

Past the turnoff for Aguas Hediondas the road climbs to the *páramo* on the S slopes of Volcán Chiles, whose summit is the border with Colombia. The volcano can be climbed in about 6 hrs, but you must be self sufficient. Inquire about the route in Tufiño, where guides can sometimes be hired. To the S lies the Reserva Ecológica El Angel and the Lagunas Verdes (see above). The road then begins its long descent to **Maldonado** and Chical in the subtropical lowlands. One bus from opp Colegio Nacional Tulcán, C Sierra, daily at noon, US$2.20, 5 hrs, returning early next morning. **NB** In Feb 1994 there was an incursion of Colombian guerrillas into the previously tranquil Maldonado area and the region was subsequently militarized. Enquire before heading out.

THE CENTRAL SIERRA (3)

South from Quito, some of the loveliest mountain scenery in Ecuador: colourful Indian markets and colonial towns nestle among the cones of volcanoes over 5,000m high.

The Pan-American Highway and the railway to the south climb gradually out of the Quito basin towards Cotopaxi. The first 30 km of the highway are in poor condition. At Alóag, a road heads W to Santo Domingo de los Colorados and the Pacific lowlands. In a valley below the bleak *páramo* lies the town of **Machachi**, famous for its mineral water springs and icy cold, crystal clear swimming pool, open 0700-1600 daily, US$0.25, nice setting. The water, "Agua Güitig", is bottled in a plant 4 km from the town and sold throughout the country (tours of the plant 0800-1200). Machachi produces a very good cheese. Cockfights on Sun. Bus to Quito (Villaflora), 1 hr, US$0.45. Taxi to Cotopaxi, about US$30 per car.

Lodging and food G pp *Miravalle*, shared bath, quite dirty; **F** pp *Mejía*, dirty, noisy, no door lock, no water. *Restaurante Pedregal*, good, cheap, basic food and chicken, log-cabin style, off park on road bus comes into town; *El Chagra*, good typical food, reasonably priced, take road that passes in front of church, on right hand side, about 5 km from church.

Machachi is a good starting point for climbing **Illiniza**. Illiniza Norte can be climbed without technical equipment but a few exposed, rocky sections require utmost caution, allow 2-4 hrs for the ascent, take a compass, it's easy to mistake the descent; for Illiniza Sur (4 hr ice climb) experience of ice climbing is essential. Alternatively, traverse the lower slope, passing below the steep ice gully, take the next, gentler slope up and meander across several other slopes to the summit. There are still some steep, technical sections on this route and full climbing gear and experience are absolutely necessary. There is a *refugio* below the saddle between the two: fully equipped with beds and cooking facilities, take mat and sleeping bag because it fills quickly, US$10/night. A pick-up truck along the deteriorating road to the 'Virgen' is about US$20, from there 4 hrs walk to the refuge. Cheaper to get a bus from Machachi to El Chaupi, 10 km S and about 7 km from the Panamericana. From El Chaupi it is an 8-hr walk to the refuge, beautiful view of peaks. The refuge can be reached in a day from Quito, but start very early (with thanks to Dan Walker).

Cotopaxi volcano (5,897m) is at the heart of a much-visited national park. The park authorities are breeding a fine llama herd on the pine clad lower slopes. There was a major forest fire here in Sep 1994. There are two entrances to the Cotopaxi National Park: the first, 16 km S of Machachi, is near a sign for the Clirsen satellite tracking station (cannot be visited). This route goes past Clirsen, then via the El Boliche National Recreation Area (separate entry fee, US$10 for foreigners), for over 30 km along a signposted dirt road, through the National Park gates, past Lake Limpio Pungo to a fork, where the right branch climbs steeply to a parking lot (4,600m). From here it is 30 mins to 1 hr on foot to the José Ribas refuge (4,800m, beware of altitude sickness). The second entrance, about 9 km further S, near the village of Mulaló, is marked by a small Parque Nacional Cotopaxi sign. It is about 28 km from here, through the main park gates, to the refuge. Nearly 1 km from the highway, turn left at a T junction and a few hundred metres later turn sharp right. Beyond this the road is either signed or you take the main fork; it is shorter and easier to follow than the first route which you join just before the Park gates. (Walking from the highway to the refuge may exhaust you for the climb to the summit.)

Cyclists should approach Cotopaxi from the northern end, rather than from the S because the latter route, 32 km, is too soft to climb on a bike. From Machachi it is 13 km on a cobbled road, then 2 km of sand to Santa Ana de Pedregal. 5 more km of sand lead to the park entrance, then it's 15 km to the parking lot (the last 7 km steep and soft). The descent takes 1½ hrs as opposed to 7 going up. Trips to this point on motorcycle are possible, ask Jan But, "The Flying Dutchman", T 527-842, Quito (see **Mountain Biking**). He has all the equipment. You can also book through Pedal Andes, F 566-076, Quito.

If you have no car it is best to take a Quito-Latacunga bus (or vice-versa) and get off at Lasso (see below). Do not take an express bus as you cannot get off before Latacunga. A truck from Lasso to the parking lot costs US$30 for 4 people, one-way, no bargaining. If you do not arrange a truck for the return you can sometimes get a cheaper ride down in a truck which has just dropped off another party. Hitchhiking into the park and out is usually possible at weekends. An infrequent bus from Mulaló (connections to Latacunga) can be flagged down if hitching proves difficult. Trucks and a jeep are available from Latacunga for about US$30 round trip—ask at the *Hotel Estambul*, leaves 0700 (**see p 938** for guides).

Visitors to the Parque Nacional Cotopaxi must register at the main entrance (fee US$10). The park gates are open 0700-1500, although you can usually stay until dark. The park administration and a small museum (3D model of the park and stuffed animals, open 0800-1200 and 1400-1600) are located 10 km from the park gates, just before the plateau of Laguna Limpio Pungo, where wild horses may be seen. There are two rustic cabañas (register at administartion, US$1 pp) and many campsites (US$0.50 pp) in the Park, a good spot is Laguna Limpio Pungo, but it is very cold, purify water, protect food from foxes. The refuge (US$10 pp a night) has a kitchen, water, and 30 beds with mattresses. Bring sleeping bag and mat, also padlock for your excess luggage when you climb, or use lockable luggage deposit, US$2.50. Check climbing conditions with the guardian of the refuge. The ascent from the refuge takes 5-8 hrs, start climbing at 0100 as the snow deteriorates in the sun. A full moon is practical (and magic). Equipment and experience are required. Take a guide if unexperienced on ice and snow. Climb the sandy slope above the hut and head up leftwards on to the glacier. The route then goes roughly to the right of Yanasacha and on to the summit. Allow 2-4 hrs for the descent.

Dr Sverre Aarseth writes that the best season is Dec-April; strong winds and clouds in Aug-Dec but still possible for experienced mountaineers. The route is more difficult to find on Cotopaxi than on Chimborazo (**see p 975**); it is advisable to seek information from Quito climbing clubs. The snow and ice section is more heavily crevassed than Chimborazo and is also steeper; however it is less climbing time.

From the left branch at the fork for the José Ribas refuge, a narrow dirt road continues along the páramo, making an incomplete circuit (parts are washed out, 4WD recommended) around the Cotopaxi volcano, beautiful views and undeveloped archeological sites may be found in this area. Just N of Cotopaxi are the peaks of Sincholahua (4,893m), Rumiñahui (4,712m) and Pasochoa (4,225m). *Rumiñahui* can be climbed from the park road, starting at Laguna Limpio Pungo, watch out for wild horses and mountain lions.

Railway Inn, in the old railway station at the edge of Cotopaxi national park, opened June 1995; bookings through *Safari* in Quito (see **Tour Operators**), baths, meals available. During the week transfers by jeep, at weekends trains run, see Quito **Railway**. T Quito 552-505 or 582-924 (train details).

The railway and the Pan-American Highway cross one another at *Lasso* (33 km S of Alóag) a small village with a milk bottling plant and two recommended cafés serving dairy products. Just N of Lasso, E of the highway, is the San Agustín hill, thought to be a prehistoric pyramid.

The area around San Agustín is owned by the Plaza family, which has two large *haciendas* and breeds bulls for the bull-fights in Quito in Dec. One of the two *haciendas* is actually at the base of the San Agustín hill and includes some converted Inca buildings.

About 2 km off the highway, 2 km S of Lasso, is the *Hostería La Ciénega*, a good restaurant also operating as an hotel (C) in an old *hacienda* with outstanding gardens, an avenue of massive, old eucalyptus trees to the hacienda and a small private chapel; accommodation is very good, it is also a good place for lunch or a drink after visiting Saquisilí market (reserve accommodation in advance at weekends); horse-riding US$1.50 per hour. It used to belong to the Lasso family when their land spread from Quito to Ambato (T Quito 549-126).

Some 16 km S of Lasso, and a couple of km W of the highway, is the small but very important market town of **Saquisilí**. Its Thur market (0700-1400) is famous throughout Ecuador for the way in which all eight of its plazas and most of its streets become jam-packed with people, the great majority of them local Indians with red ponchos and narrow-brimmed felt hats. The best time to visit the market is between 0900 and 1200 (0700-0800 for the animal market); be sure to bargain, prices may be inflated. Possibly the best market in Ecuador, possibly better textiles now than Otavalo. Saquisilí has colourful Corpus Christi processions. The bank near the main square exchanges dollars at poor rates.

Dan Buck and Anne Meadows write: Tightly woven decorated baskets plentiful but expensive, though somewhat cheaper than in Quito. Bargain hard, there is a lot of competition for your custom. Livestock market hectic and worth a visit. Some animal buyers set up small corrals in which they collect their purchases. Trucks brimming with oranges and yellow and red bananas; reed mats, fans, and baskets; beef, pork and mutton parts piled on tables; Indian women hunkered down beside bundles of onions, radishes, and herbs, and little pyramids of tomatoes, mandarin oranges, potatoes, okra, and avocados; *cabuya* and *maguey* ropes and cords laid out like dead snakes; and a food kiosk every five feet offering everything from full *almuerzos* to *tortillas de papa*.

Accommodation C *Hostería La Ciénega*, 30 mins taxi ride from town, see above; F *España*, better rooms with bath; F *Pensión Chavela*, main plaza, basic, friendly, good views, billiards and gambling hall downstairs, noisy; F *Salón Pichincha*, Bolívar y Pichincha, restaurant-bar below, not very clean, secure motor cycle parking. Some basic restaurants can be found in the same district (at the entrance to the village, beware overcharging). Try *colada*, a sweet, warm blueberry drink, with bread.

Transport The Saquisilí and Cotopaxi bus companies have frequent services between **Latacunga** and Saquisilí (US$0.15, ½ hr) and several buses a day run to Saquisilí from **Quito** (catch them in Quito bus terminal, US$1.50, 2½ hrs). Alternatively you can catch an Ambato bus from Quito, ask the driver to let you off at the junction for Saquisilí and get a passing pick-up truck (US$0.35) from there. The *Hotel Quito* and the *Hotel Colón* in Quito both organize efficient but expensive taxis for a 2-hr visit to Saquisilí market on Thur. Bus tours cost about US$26 pp, taxis can be found for US$45, with 2 hr wait at market.

Latacunga (pop 39,882, capital of Cotopaxi Province) is a place where the abundance of light grey lava rock has been artfully employed. Cotopaxi is much in evidence, though it is 29 km away. Provided they are not hidden in the clouds, which unfortunately is all too often (try the early morning), as many as nine volcanic cones can be seen from Latacunga. The central plaza, Parque Vicente León, is a colourful and beautifully maintained garden. Locked at night. There are several other gardens in the town including Parque San Francisco and Lago Flores. The colonial character of the town has been well preserved. Cultural centres: Casa de los Marqueces, Sánchez de Orellana y Abel Echeverría, a hall used for exhibitions with a museum; Casa de la Cultura, at the old windmill, has museum with models of festival masks, both are free. Escuela Isidro Ayora, Sánchez de Orellana y Tarqui, and the Cathedral both have museums.

There is a Sat market (also, but smaller, on Tues) on the Plaza de San Sebastián; goods for sale include *shigras* (fine woven, colourful straw bags) and homespun wool and cotton yarn.

Festival The Fiesta de Nuestra Señora de la Merced (22-24 Sept) is celebrated with dancing in the streets. Mama Negra festival, colourful costumes, headdresses and masks, in Nov.

Hotels D *Rodelu*, Quito 7331, T 800-956, clean, very good, restaurant; D *Cotopaxi*, on main square, T 802-372, with bathroom, for luggage, not very clean, run down, parking, hot water after 0700, ask for view over plaza (these rooms noisy at weekends); **E** *Latacunga*, on main Quito road, T 800-983, with bath, TV, and phone, cheaper rooms without on second floor but they have no hot water, friendly, restaurant rarely open at weekends; **E** *Estambul*, Belisario Quevedo 7340 y Salcedo, T 800-354, clean, quiet, luggage store, public parking at rear, highly rec, trips to Cotopaxi National Park; **F** *Jacqueline*, Antonio Vela 78-33, friendly, basic, hot water, clean; nearby is **G** *Residencial El Salto*, Plaza El Salto, warm showers, clean, noisy, safe, restaurant, small rooms; **F** *Turismo*, friendly, very cold shower. Also **G** *Costa Azul*, good meals; this and the **F** *Residencial Los Andes* (T 800-983) are along the Ambato road.

Restaurants *Los Copihues*, Quito 70-83, nice waiters, popular meeting place; *La Carreta*, Quito 150, good 4-course lunch; *Rodelu* (see hotel above), good breakfasts, steaks and pizzas, the gringo place to eat; *Cyrano*, 2 de Mayo 7674, chicken, good breakfast US$1; *El Mashca*, Calle Valencia, good, open until 2200; *Chifa Tokio*, Guayaquil 45-58, moderate prices, good value; *Chifa Yut Wah*, Quinchero y Ordóñez 6973, good, cheap; nearby on same street, *Chifa Formosa*, cheap, good value; *Salón Coseñita*, Echeverría 1143, good cheap meals; *Parrillada Place*, Quito 7331; *El Estudiante*, Antonio Vela 78, lunch US$0.50. *La Borgoña*, Valencia between Quijano and Ordóñez, good value, friendly; *Pollo Dorado*, 5 de Junio y Vela, good value; *Happy Pizza*, Parque San Francisco, Calle Ramírez Fita, T 800-721, open 1100-1400, 1600-2200, good coffee and pizza; *Pizzería*, opposite also good; *Pollos Gus*, cheap roast chicken, on Ambato road, open Sun. Ice cream store off main square, Salcedo y Quito. *Pingüino*, Quito 73-100, one block from Plaza, good milk shakes and coffee; *Beer Centre*, Orellana 7420, good atmosphere, cheap beer; 2 well-stocked supermarkets on Calle Quito. Difficult to eat after 1900 and difficult to find breakfast before 0800-0900. Try the local dish, *chugchucaras*, fried meat with corn, bananas, popcorn and porkskin.

Exchange **Banco de Pichincha** on Plaza, cash only 0900-1300, poor rate; **Banco Popular** opp changes cash and TCs, only 0900-1300, good rate; **Cambio Centro**, Guayaquil 43-19; **Cambiaria Corrales**, Av Amazonas 76-45.

Post Office on Belisario Quevedo, near *Hotel Estambul*.

Guides Rafael Lanas, Tarqui 41-87 y Sánchez de Orellana, PO Box 0501654, Latacunga, T 800-648, 800-823, 727-433, rec for ice-climbing on any mountain you wish, emphasis on friendship in climbing. Nestor Cueva, Antonio Vela y Padre Semanate 162-12, near the *Jacqueline Hotel*, rec.

Buses to **Quito** from *mercado central*, every 15 mins, 2 hrs, US$1; to **Ambato**, 3/4 hr, US$0.70; to **Guayaquil**, US$3.35, 6 hrs. To **Saquisilí** from Calle Melchor de Benavides 78-35 next to *mercado central*. Day trips to **Cotopaxi** (**see p 963**) can be arranged with a taxi for about US$30. Day-trip by taxi to **Zumbahua, Quilotoa**, return to Latacunga is US$40.

If driving, it is possible to do a round trip, Latacunga – Pujilí – Zumbahua – Quilotoa crater – Chugchilán – Sigchos – Toacazo – Saquisilí – Latacunga, 200 km.

A fine paved road leads W to *Pujilí* (beautiful church but closed most of the time; some local ceramic work; good Sun market; also, but smaller, poorer, on Wed; beware local illicit liquor and pickpockets), 15 km away (bus, US$0.30) and then on over the Western Cordillera to Zumbahua, Macuchi and Quevedo. Quevedo can also be reached by turning off this road through El Corazón; Transporte Cotopaxi, Calle 5 de Junio, Latacunga, has a bus to El Corazón via Angamarca, 1000, spectacular ride.

Zumbahua, a cluster of 40 houses by an old *hacienda*, 1 km from main road, 65 km from Pujilí, has a fine Sat morning market (starts 0600, for local produce and animals, not tourist items, but rated as one of the most interesting and colourful in Ecuador and not to be missed) with llamas on view. Fri nights have dancing and drinking (2 basic *residenciales* on the main plaza: **E** *Quiroga*—not clearly signed, below square—clean, good blankets, couples should check price carefully; **G** unnamed *pensión* above plaza, small, dark rooms, lousy beds, the owner runs taxi service to Quilotoa, agree price in advance, US$15 maximum; only restaurant is on main road outside village. Local people reported not to want to rent rooms to foreigners, best to arrive by 1500, check situation, allowing time to get bus out at 1730 if you do not get a room). Take windcheater, can be windy and dusty. Buses US$1.50 from Latacunga depart every two hours from 0600 (check evening before) from Pan-American Highway outside the town, but the best for continuing to Quilotoa (3 a day), leave opp *Residencial Costa Azul* (cross 5 de Mayo bridge from the old town towards Quevedo, buses line up just past traffic lights) 2 hrs, beautiful ride. Bus drivers on the Latacunga-Quevedo line often do not want to take tourists to Zumbahua as they want to fill up the bus with people going to Quevedo, for whom seats are reserved, ie you have to stand for Zumbahua, a dusty road with many stops. Return buses from Quevedo every two hours until 1900. Car hire has been rec. Many interesting crafts are practised by the Indians in the neighbouring valley of Tigua: skin paintings, hand-carved wooden masks, baskets.

Zumbahua is the point to turn off for a visit to **Quilotoa**, a volcanic crater filled by a beautiful emerald lake, to which there is a steep path from the rim. From the rim of the crater several snowcapped volcanoes can be seen in the distance. It is reached by a road which runs N from Zumbahua: go down from the village and cross the river. After a few km along the dusty road turn right and over the bridge at the fork in the road, there are no road signs. 12 km from Zumbahua, where the land levels out, there is a small road to the right towards a small group of houses; the crater is just beyond, it can only be recognized when you are on top of it. Zumbahua to Quilotoa is about 14 km, 3-4 hrs walk. To walk round the crater will take you 4-5 hrs; take water as that from the lake is sulphurous. Do not walk alone or after dark. At the crater itself, expect to be besieged by persistent beggars and Indians trying to sell pictures. Take a stick against dogs on the road. Also be prepared for sudden changes in the weather. It is possible to stay in a simple hut owned by Sr Jorge Latacunga near the crater, G, he also sells water, soft drinks and bread and will take you on a day trek round the lake if you wish. During the wet season, the best views are in the early morning so those with a tent may wish to camp. A daily bus, Trans Vivero, takes teachers to schools in Zumbahua and Quilapungo, leaving at 0600 arriving 0815 in Quilapungo (0750 in Zumbahua), from where it is about 1 hr walk to the crater. Alternatively, you can get a bus on Sat, US$0.15, but it will only go part of the way, leaving you with a ½ hr walk to the crater. Trucks go up after the Saquisilí market on Thur pm. Alternatively, hitch a truck (which is easy on market day); you will be dropped close to the volcano; trucks back from Zumbahua leave about midday on market day, and a bus goes to Latacunga at 1300, but the service is irregular. A *camioneta* can be hired for Zumbahua-Quilotoa for US$4. Buses bound for Chugchilán drop the traveller 5 mins from the lagoon (dep Thur, Fri, Sat at about 1030, return Sun 0600); those for Ponce (3 a week), on the Ponce turnoff, still about a 40-min walk north. Hitching a return trip should not be left till late in the afternoon.

The Sat trip to Zumbahua market and the Quilotoa crater is one of the best excursions in Ecuador, despite the poor accommodation in Zumbahua (see above). The walk from Zumbahua to Pujilí, 6 hrs, is also recommended. **Macuchi**, on the main road to Quevedo some way beyond Zumbahua, is a mining centre for gold and various non-ferrous metals. The mines were developed in the 1930s by an American company, and now they are almost abandoned.

It is 20 km from Quilotoa crater to **Chugchilán**, a very poor village in one of the most scenic areas of Ecuador, a beautiful but tiring walk along the edge of a canyon (5 hrs). Water is available from small streams, but take a purifier. Buses dep daily from Latacunga at 1000 from Calle Melchor de Benavides, US$1.75. Accommodation at **E** *The Black Sheep Inn*, restaurant, book exchange, organic gardens and orchards, rec, a good base for hiking to Quilotoa, Toachi canyon and Inca ruins (Apartado 05-01-240, Correos Central Latacunga, Provincia Cotopaxi). If you continue from Chugchilán through **Sigchos** (Sun market, 2 basic *pensiónes* and a few restaurants; several buses per day, one at 1100 Sun takes an interesting longer route, 3 hrs to Latacunga) to Toacazo, take care if driving as there is deep shifting sand in places on the way, keep to the track. From Toacazo the road is paved to Saquisilí. Sigchos is the starting point for the Toachi Valley walk, a few camp sites, may be able to sleep on the school floor in Asache, basic hotel and restaurant in San Francisco de las Pampas, 0900 bus daily to Latacunga.

10 km S of Latacunga, at Rumipamba, is **A3** *Hostería Rumipamba de las Rosas*, T 726-128, F 727-103, hot showers, clean, guarded, nice garden inc small zoo, swimming pool, tennis, table tennis, lake, good restaurant, highly rec. 1 km further S is **Salcedo**, good Thur and Sun markets; the Mama Negra festival is on 1 Nov. **F** *Residencial Las Vegas*, Bolívar y Paredes, hot water, private showers; *Restaurant Ritz*, Bolívar y Sucre, chicken; *Iguazú* for breakfast, on Parque behind *Municipio*.

Ambato (pop 124,166) was almost completely destroyed in the great 1949 earthquake and is not a very attractive city, coming alive only during festivals and market days. The modern cathedral faces the pleasant **Parque Montalvo**, where there is a statue of the writer Juan Montalvo (1833-1889) who is buried in a memorial in a neighbouring street. His house (Bolívar y Montalvo) is open to the public; entrance free (T 821-024). In the **Colegio Nacional Bolívar**, at Sucre entre Lalama y Martínez, there is a Museo de Ciencias Naturales with stuffed birds and other animals and items of local historical interest, rec (US$0.05, closed Sat and Sun and school holidays). The **Quinta de Mera**, an old mansion in gardens in Atocha suburb, open 0900-1200, 1400-1800, can be reached by bus from Espejo y 12 de Novembre. Out along the Río Ambato (a pleasant walk) is the prosperous suburb of Miraflores. Ambato has a famous festival in Feb, the *Fiesta de frutas y flores*, during carnival when there are 4 days of bull fights, parades and festivities; it is impossible to get a hotel room unless you book ahead. The town prohibits water-throwing at carnival (see **Holidays and festivals**, p 1059). It is an important centre for the manufacture of leather goods and rugs and has some excellent tourist shops in the centre, look for colourful and good-quality cloth shoulder bags. Leather clothes can be specially made quite cheaply. On a clear day Tungurahua and Chimborazo can be seen from the city.

The main market is held on Mon, and smaller markets on Wed and Fri; they are interesting, but have few items for the tourist. Most of the action takes place in the streets although there are also two market buildings.

Hotels A3 *Ambato*, Guayaquil y Rocafuerte, T 827-598, clean, good restaurant, casino, squash, rec; **C** *Miraflores*, Av Miraflores 2-27, T 824-439, clean, good restaurant; **C** *Villa Hilda*, overpriced but cheaper rooms in older building, Av Miraflores 012 y Las Lilas, German spoken, laundry, ask if you want hot water before 0700, restaurant good, limited menu but generous portions (it is acceptable to order 1 set meal for 2 people to share), big garden. **D** *Cevallos*, Montalvo y Cevallos, good; **D** *Florida*, Av Miraflores 1131, T 823-040, pleasant, clean, set meal good at US$3; buses from the centre stop outside the *Florida*. **D** *San Ignacio*, Maldonado y 12 de Noviembre, rec. **D** *Ejecutivo*, 12 de Noviembre 12-30 y Espejo, T 820-370, bath, hot water, parking; **E** *Bellavista*, Oriente y Napo Pastaza, T 828-782, rec; **E** *Cumandá*, Eguez 8-37 y Bolívar, T 826-792; **F** *San Francisco*, Rocafuerte, seedy; **D-E** *Vivero*, Mera 403 y Cevallos, T 821-100, shower, good, expensive; **E-F** *Hostal La Liria*, Atahualpa y Caspicara, rec; **E-F** *Madrid*, near bus station, TV; **F** *Hostal Residencial América*, Vela 737 y Mera, basic, cheap; **D** *Gran*, Lalama y Rocafuerte, T 824 235, hot water, friendly; **G** *Residencial Americano*, Plaza 12 de Noviembre, basic, hot water. There are a lot of cheap *pensiones* and hotels on Calle Juan León Mera; **F** *Residencial Laurita*, No 333 y Vela, has been rec.

Restaurants *El Alamo*, Cevallos y Montalvo, Swiss-owned, good meals, also at Sucre 660 y Mera; *La Borgoña*, 13 de Abril y Luisa Martínez, French; *La Buena Mesa*, Quito 529, French, rec; *La Piel de Toro*, Ficoa El Sueño, Av Los Capulíes, Spanish; *Café Alemán*, Quito 778 y Bolívar, good food, ice cream, German magazines (rather old). Chicken at *Rico Pollo*, 12 de Noviembre y Calderón, or 12 de Noviembre y Ayllón; *Happy Chicken*, Mera 502 y Cevallos, clean, cheap, fast food; *Mesón Criollo*, Quito y Cevallos; *Pollo Fino*, Tomás Sevilla 821 y Bolívar. Seafood: *La Iguana*, Brasil y Estados Unidos; *Mediterráneo*, Av Cevallos y Castilla; *Marimar*, 12 de Noviembre y 5 de Junio; *Marisquería del Pacífico*, Cevallos y Eloy Alfaro. *La Casa Brasilera*, Cevallos 563 y Montalvo, Brazilian, good; *Tacolandia*, Martínez y Bolívar, good Mexican food; *Mexican Food*, Luis A Martínez, on Parque Cevallos. *La Cigarra*, Centro Comercial y Sucre, pizzas; also *Pizzería Cominos*, Guayaquil 9-34 y Bolívar, and *Pizzería Bongiorno*, Av Atahualpa y Los Shyris. *Los Charnas*, Av Atahualpa y Los Shyris, rec; *Viña Rosa*, Sector la Península, typical food; *El Balcón*, Mera 5-14 y Cevallos; *Caracol*, Matiano Egüez y Bolívar, good set meals; *Big Boy*, Montalvo 349 y Vela, fast food. Oriental at *Chifa Casa China*, Espejo y 12 de Noviembre; *Chifa Nueva Hongkong*, Bolívar 768 y Martínez, good, and *Chifa Internacional*, 12 de Noviembre y Ayllón; also along Cevallos (eg *Chifa Jao Fua* at No 756, popular). Grills: *La Brasa*, Montalvo 216 y Olmedo; *Parrilladas Las Charruas*, Av Atahualpa y Los Shyris; *Las Carnes de Yorch*, Bolívar 3-29 y Guayaquil, *El Gaucho*, Bolívar y Castillo, rec; and *El Faraón*, Bolívar y Lalama. Many good cafeterías and snackbars. *Las Canas*, 13 de Abril y Mera, open 24 hrs; *Mama Miche*, 13 de Abril y Mera, Centro Comercial, open 24 hrs. For rockbottom prices but not very clean, try the markets.

Banks and Exchange Banco de Guayaquil, Sucre y Mera, gives cash advance on Visa; Banco del Pacífico, Cevallos y Lalama, changes notes only, gives cash advance on Mastercard, 3% commission. Banco del Tungurahua, Montalvo 603 y Rocafuerte; Banco Internacional, Bolívar y Martínez; Banco del Pichincha, Lalama y Cevallos, on Parque Cevallos. Cambiato, Bolívar 686, changes Visa and Amex cheques, cash, European and Latin American currencies, no commission; money exchange at *Café Español*, Montalvo 607, Mon-Sat, 0900-1800.

Entertainment There is a *peña* on Fri and Sat, *Peña del Tungurahua*, in block 2 of the Centro Comercial. **Discos**: *El Coyote*, Bolívar y Guayaquil; *Cow-Boys*, Paccha y Los Incas; *El Galeón*, Castillo y Av Cevallos; *Imperio Club*, Paccha y Saraguro, international music; *Villa Blanca*, Vía a Baños Km 5, international music, restaurant, snackbar.

Post Office Castillo y Bolívar, at Parque Montalvo. **Emetel**, Castillo y Bolívar near post office; no fax, go to *Hotel Ambato*.

Shopping *Supermercado*, Centro Comercial Ambato, Parque 12 de Noviembre, or *Supermaxi*, Centro Comercial Caracol, Av de los Capulíes y Mirabales, for buying provisions. *El Gato*, Mariano Eguez y Cevallos. Good leather hiking boots from Calzado Piedrahíta, Calle Bolívar.

Travel Agents *Metropolitan Touring*, Bolívar 471 y Castillo and in Centro Comercial Caracol; *Coltur*, Cevallos 536; *Ecuadorean Tours*, Cevallos 428 (Amex agent, but of no help with TCs; go instead to Banco del Tungurahua). *Surtrek*, Av de los Shyris y Luis Cordero 2-10, T 844-448, F 844-512, PO Box 865, Ambato, is a climbing agency, arranges guided climbs of most major peaks, rents and sells equipment, manufactures good quality backpacks to order, speaks German, Spanish, English, rec.

Tourist Office Cetur is next to the *Hotel Ambato*, Guayaquil y Rocafuerte. Open 0800-1200, 1400-1800, Mon-Fri, helpful, will assist with any complaints about services.

Immigration Av Fermín Cevallos y Juan León Mera, T 820-000, Ed Asociación de Empleados, 2nd floor, turn left, Mon-Fri 0830-1230, 1430-1800.

Taxis Beware of overcharging by drivers; fares are fixed, ask someone else first.

Buses To Quito, 2¾ hrs, US$1.50. To Guayaquil, 6½ hrs, US$6. To Cuenca, US$7, 7 hrs. To Baños, paved road, lovely scenery, 45 mins, US$0.60. To Latacunga, ¾ hr, US$0.70. To Santo Domingo de los Colorados, 4 hrs, US$5; to Tena, US$5.50, 6 hrs. To Puyo, US$2.60, 3 hrs. To Esmeraldas, US$6.50, 8 hrs. Main bus station is 2 km N from centre, near the railway station; town buses go there from Plaza Cevallos in the city centre.

Excursions To *Picaihua* by frequent bus to see the local work from *cabuya* fibre, and to Pinllo to see the leather work. At Pillaro outside the city there is a bull run and fight in early Aug.

To the E of Ambato, an important road leads to Salasaca, Pelileo, and Baños and then on along the Pastaza valley to Mera, Shell Mera, Puyo and Tena in the Oriente (see p 1033). It is partly paved to Puyo.

Salasaca is a small modernized village 14 km (½ hr) from Ambato. The Salasaca Indians wear distinctive black ponchos with white trousers and broad white hats; this is said to reflect perpetual mourning for the death of their Inca, Atahualpa. Most of them are farmers, but they are best known for weaving *tapices*, strips of cloth with remarkable bird and animal shapes in the centre. A co-operative has fixed the prices on the *tapices* it sells in its store near the church. Throughout the village the prices are the same, somewhat cheaper than in Quito, and the selection is much better. If you have the time you can order one to be specially made; this takes four to six weeks, but is well worth the wait. You can watch the Indians weaving in the main workshop opposite the church.

Pelileo, 5 km beyond Salasaca, is a lively little market town which has been almost completely rebuilt on a new site since the 1949 earthquake. In all, Pelileo has been destroyed by four earthquakes during its 400-year history. The new town springs to life on Sat, the main market day. This is the blue jean manufacturing capital of Ecuador. The ruins of Pelileo Viejo can be seen about 2 km E of the present site on the N side of the road to Baños. *Fiesta* on 22 July. Regular buses from Baños, 25 mins.

From Pelileo, the road gradually descends to Las Juntas, the meeting point of the Patate and Chambo rivers to form the Pastaza river, and where the road from Riobamba comes in. The Patate is a "white" river, the Chambo "black" and the meeting of the waters is very impressive. The road then continues along the lower slopes of the volcano Tungurahua to Baños (25 km from Pelileo). The road gives good views of the Pastaza gorge and the volcano.

Baños (pop 12,984; 1,800m) is a holiday resort with a reportedly miraculous Virgin and hot springs; very busy at weekends and increasingly touristy (many places close Mon). The central Basilica attracts many pilgrims; the paintings of miracles performed by Nuestra Señora del Agua Santa are worth seeing. There is a *fiesta* in her honour in Oct with processions, bands, fireworks, sporting events and a lot of general gaiety. The Basilica of Baños has a museum (stuffed birds, Nuestra Señora's clothing), open 0800-1600. There is another civic *fiesta* on 15 Dec to celebrate the town's anniversary when each *barrio* hires a *saka* band and there are

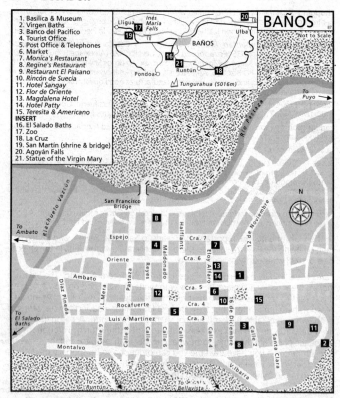

1. Basilica & Museum
2. Virgen Baths
3. Banco del Pacífico
4. Tourist Office
5. Post Office & Telephones
6. Market
7. Monica's Restaurant
8. Regine's Restaurant
9. Restaurant El Paisano
10. Rincón de Suecia
11. Hotel Sangay
12. Flor de Oriente
13. Magdalena Hotel
14. Hotel Patty
15. Teresita & Americano
INSERT
16. El Salado Baths
17. Zoo
18. La Cruz
19. San Martín (shrine & bridge)
20. Agoyán Falls
21. Statue of the Virgin Mary

BAÑOS

Not to Scale

Lligua · Inés Maria Falls · Ulba · Ulba
BAÑOS
Pondoa · Runtún
Tungurahua (5016m)
To Puyo →

To Ambato ←
San Francisco Bridge
To Ambato ←
To El Salado Baths ←
Espejo
Oriente
Ambato
Rocafuerte
Luis A Martínez
Montalvo
To Runtún
To Bellavista

Riachuelo Vazcún
Díaz Pineda
J.L. Mera
Pastaza
Reyes
Maldonado
Halflants
Calle 9
Calle 8
Calle 7
Calle 6
Calle 5
Cra. 3
Cra. 4
Cra. 5
Cra. 6
Cra. 7
Eloy Alfaro
16 de Diciembre
12 de Noviembre
Calle 4
Calle 2
Santa Clara
V. Ibarra

Río Pastaza

N

many processions. The following day there is a parade in which spectators are outnumbered by participants. The Pastaza river rushes past Baños to the Agoyán falls 10 km further down the valley, nearly dry now because of the construction of a hydroelectric dam. The whole area between Pelileo and Baños has a relaxing sub-tropical climate (the rainy season is usually from May to Oct, especially July and Aug). Three sets of thermal baths are in the town: the Baños de la Virgen are by the waterfall opposite the *Hotel Sangay* (water in hot pools is changed daily, best time to visit is early am, the cold pool is chlorinated); the Baños Modernos are next door (open weekends and holidays only); the El Salado baths are 1½ km out of town off the Ambato road (entrance to each, US$0.75). The baths open at 0430 and close at 1700. The water is changed three times a week. There are regular buses every 30 mins between the Salado baths and the Agoyán Falls, passing by the centre of town. All the baths can be crowded at weekends, but the water is usually clean (its brown colour is the result of mineral content) and is almost always hot. There are also the Santa Clara baths, but these are not thermal (ie they are tepid); they are popular with children.

Warning Robberies have been reported at the following places: near the San Francisco suspension bridge; at the Bella Vista cross; on the way to, and at the *refugio* on Tungurahua (groups with guides and larger groups are less at risk).

Baños is a good meeting place to form a group to visit the Oriente (leave messages in gringo restaurants, more interesting than Misahuallí, if you have to wait a few days, but can be more expensive. There are many unqualified and unscrupulous guides operating. Only use qualified guides and seek advice, eg from the South American Explorers Club, or recommendations. In Baños, the Club says, mountain guides are not of the same standard regarding equipment or technique as in other climbing centres, even though they may be cheaper. For exceptions see **Guides, Equipment**, etc below. See also **Note** after **Guides in Baños**.

Hotels **A3** *Villa Gertrudis*, Montalvo 2975, T 740-441, with lovely garden, pool, demi-pension, reserve in advance, rec; **A2-L3** *Hostería Luna Runtún*, Caserío Runtún Km 6, T 740-882, F 740-376, rustic design, beautiful setting, 33 rm, comfortable, expensive restaurant, good views, hiking, riding, biking, laundry, volleyball, badminton, luxurious cabins (A2); **C** *Sangay*, Plazoleta Isidro Ayora 101, T 740-490, F 740-056, with bath, beautifully situated close to waterfall, restaurant (rec), sauna, whirlpool, steam bath and pool all open to non-residents (US$5), tennis and squash courts, accommodation in chalets reported better but more expensive than in rooms, rec. Also a few rooms in basement, F, but sometimes no warm water. Information and some equipment for expeditions to the jungle and volcanoes may be provided by the hotel. **B** *Cabañas Bascún*, on edge of town (nr El Salado hot springs), T 740-334, US$60 for a cabin for 5 quite comfortable, pools, sauna, health spa (US$5 to non-residents), tennis, restaurant; **D** *Isla de Baños*, Halflants 1-31 y Montalvo, T 740-609, German owned, 10 clean rooms, nice atmosphere, garden with parrots and monkeys, all rooms with bath; **D** *Palace*, opp *Sangay* (even closer to waterfall), T 740-470, lots of beds, good for groups, old-fashioned, a little dark, choose airy room at front with balcony, nice garden and pool at the back, health centre with Turkish bath, sauna and jacuzzi, open to non-residents for US$3, friendly, restaurant, breakfast US$2, dinner US$4; **E** pp *Café Cultura*, Montalvo y Santa Clara, beautiful, quaint, colonial-style house, large balcony, garden, T 740-419, has 4 rooms with shared bath, clean, specializes in breakfast, closed Thur, highly rec; **C** *Casa Nahuazo*, via al Salado, T 740-315, bath, hot water, comfortable sitting room, clean, helpful, quiet country house 15 mins' walk from town with beautiful setting and views of Tungurahua, hot baths 2 mins away, expert travel assistance; **E** *Posada El Marqués*, Montalvo, T 740-053, spacious, bright rooms, hot water, bath, clean, view of waterfall, overpriced laundry, use of kitchen, garden, good restaurant; **D** *Flor de Oriente*, Ambato y Maldonado, T 740-418, F 740-717, incl breakfast, bath, accepts credit cards, very good, three rooms have balconies, can be noisy at weekends, clean, electric showers, *Su Café* downstairs, rec. **E** *Hospedaje Santa Cruz*, 16 de Diciembre y Martínez, private bathroom, hot water, friendly, T 740-648; **E** *Hostal Magdalena*, Oriente y Alfaro, T 740-233, with bath, clean, warm water, rec, but closes at 2200; **E** *Pensión Patty*, Alfaro 556, near market, rec, clean, basement rooms poor, otherwise good facilities, use of kitchen, laundry, comfortable and quiet, family-run, popular, safe, motorcycle parking, T 740-202; **E** *Alborada*, on the plaza nr Basílica, T 740-614, with shower, modern, clean, friendly, safe, luggage store, rooms have balconies; **E** *Achupallas*, 16 de Diciembre y Ambato, T 740-389, clean, hot showers, laundry; **E** *La Casa Amarilla*, yellow house on mountainside on path to Runtún, 15-20 mins, lovely and quiet, unique place to stay, excellent homemade breads for breakfast, rec; **E** *Residencial Grace*, Rocafuerte esq Maldonado, 2nd floor, electric showers, F without bath, English spoken; **F** *Anita*, Rocafuerte y 16 de Diciembre, behind the market, moderately clean, friendly, use of kitchen, parking for motorcycles; **F** *Cordillera*, 16 de Diciembre y Luis A Martínez, great view from front rooms, clean, cold water; **F** pp *Plantas y Blanco*, above Banco del Pacífico, Carrera 3 y Calle 2, Casilla 1980, T/F 740-044, Ecuadorean/European owners, laundry, money exchange, rec as an "oasis

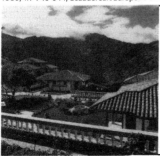

within an oasis", good restaurant, daily morning spa bath with sauna and jet water massage; **E** *Charvic*, Maldonado, T 740-133, near Terminal Terrestre; **E** *Las Orquídeas*, Rocafuerte y Halflants, shower, clean, good beds, T 740-911; **F** *Lucy*, opp *Anita*, with bath, **G** without, friendly, comfortable beds, parking for motorcycles; **F** *Los Andes*, Oriente 1118 y Alfaro, without bath, 24 hr hot water, clean, friendly, restaurant (*Le Gourmet*); **F** *Res Acapulco*, on Parque de la Basílica, old and picturesque, good food, more or less clean, laundry facilities, but no private baths; **F** *Petit Auberge*, Alfaro 2-46 y Espejo, above *Le Petit Restaurant*, hot showers, simple, quiet; **F** *Residencial Angely*, Alfaro 553 y Ambato, opp *Patty*, hot showers, top rooms quieter, friendly; **F** *Residencial Baños*, Ambato y Alfaro, good, washing facilities, luggage store, clean, ask for a top room; **F** *Residencial Los Pinos*, Rocafuerte y Maldonado, clean, friendly, ask for front room with view, preferably on second floor; **F** *Americano*, 12 de Noviembre y Martínez, basic but friendly, cooking facilities available, thin walls, no showers; **E** *El Castillo*, Martínez y Santa Clara, with bath, near waterfall, quiet, clean, hot water, parking, restaurant; **G** *Residencial Teresita*, Parque de la Basílica, hot water, prices vary, shuts early; **F** *Res Timara*, Maldonado 381, friendly, hot water, use of kitchen, laundry facilities, rec. There are two **F** *Residenciales Las Delicias*, *1*, Ambato y Parque Central, front rooms have lovely view, but are noisy, friendly; *Las Delicias 2*, Maldonado y Parque Central, is newer, both reported dirty; **G** *Residencial Dumary*, T Halflants 656, very clean, hot water, small rooms, private Spanish lessons from English/German speaking daughter; **G** *Residencial Olguita*, overlooking plaza, basic, OK; **G** *Residencial El Rey*, near bus station, rec; **G** *Julia* at bus station, no bath, cold water; **F** *Santa Clara*, 12 de Noviembre y Montalvo, also new annex rooms with bath, rec, or *cabañas*, both **E**, clean, hot water, use of kitchen possible, washing facilities, some rooms without windows, nice garden, good for motorcycles. Houses for rent on a weekly basis: the owners of *El Paisano* restaurant have three houses, US$24 for the most expensive; **G** *Familia Reyes y Alvarez*, J L Mera y Ambato, rent apartments in the green house, hot water, helpful. Camping is not recommended high on the mountainsides as several people have frozen to death on the peak of Tungurahua.

Restaurants Many close by 2130. *Monica's*, Alfaro y Espejo, good, very slow service; *Closerie des Lilas*, Eloy Alfaro entre Oriente y Espejo, good, reasonable prices; *Donde Marcelo*, Ambato nr 16 de Diciembre, good breakfasts, friendly gringo bar; *Le Petit Restaurant*, Alfaro 2-46 y Montalvo, excellent food, slow service, expensive but worth it; *Patti*, Alfaro 420, good vegetarian food; *Chifa Oriental*, Ambato 669 y Alfaro, fair food, low prices; *Vitaminas*, opp *Hard Rock Café* on Eloy Alfaro, friendly, excellent Italian food; *Chifa Come Bien*, nr main square, friendly, cheap; *El Jardín*, 16 de Diciembre y Rocafuerte, good garden, vegetarian food, juices and bar, hammock for siesta; *El Sol de los Andes*, Montalvo y Santa Clara, good food, including vegetarian, friendly, inexpensive, *peña* bar in evenings; *Mercedes Cafetería* round the corner from *Patty*, good breakfast of muesli and pancakes, reasonable prices; *Central Chifa*, on main street, *jugos*, pastas and meat, huge portions; *El Paisano*, rec, Martínez y Santa Clara, on road to *Sangay* hotel, vegetarian, but meat also served; *Rincón de Suecia*, Carrera 5 y Parque Basílica and Rocafuerte y 16 de Diciembre, pizzas, good, Swedish and English spoken; opp *Rincón de Suecia* on Carrera 5 is *Tacolandia*, Mexican; *Regines Café Alemán*, 12 de Noviembre y Montalvo, good breakfasts, cakes, meeting place, very popular, pricey; *La Fuente*, on main street, good set meal; *Lucerno*, Halflants entre Ambato y Oriente, check prices on menu and on bill; *Los Alpes*, good, quick, cheap breakfast; *Mi Pan*, 16 Diciembre y Ambato, good meeting place, excellent fresh bread, pastries and coffee, 3 tables, not cheap; *Edén*, Alfaro 534, nr bus terminal, good food, large breakfasts, yoghurts, cheap, slow service; *Cafetería Chushi*, on Maldonado opp bus station, good breakfast and snacks, fast service, notice board, has guidebooks for consultation and book exchange (small fee); *Rico Pan*, Ambato y Maldonado, cheap breakfasts, hot bread, good fruit salads and pizzas; *La Abuela*, near Ambato 636, small, good pizzas, good breakfasts; *Karson Bar*, Alfaro opp *Pensión Patty*, friendly; *Higuerón*, 12 de Noviembre 270 y Montalvo, good European, local and vegetarian food, nice garden, friendly; *Café Hood*, 16 de Diciembre y Martínez, good vegetarian food, inexpensive, all water and milk boiled, English spoken, rec on many counts, always busy, American/Ecuadorean run, closed Tues; next door is *Paolo's Pizzería*, good pizzas, better to take away than to eat in; *La Bella Italia*, Rocafuerte y Eloy Alfaro (old address, moved across street early 1995), fast service, good Italian food, reasonable prices; *Pizza Mía*, Montalvo y Santa Clara, nr *Hotel Sangay*, food OK. *Cuy* (guinea pig) sold outside the market daily.

Exchange Banco del Pacífico, 12 de Octubre y Rocafuerte, changes US$ TCs and currency, Mon (very slow in am)-Fri from 0900-1800, Sat 0900-1400. **Cambiaria Torres**, Parque Palomino Torres.

Entertainment Cockfighting, Coliseo, Sun from 1800. *Peñas La Burbuja* (Pasaje interior de la ciudadela) and *Agoyán* (near main baths), Fri and Sat. *La Salsateca*, 1 block from main plaza, open all week. *Hard Rock Café*, Eloy Alfaro near market, "good old rock, favourite gringo hangout", fantastic *piña colada* and juices. **Bamboos Bar**, Rocafuerte y 16 de Diciembre, good music, friendly, pool table, strong drinks. Films shown at Centro Cultural, programme available at *Café Hood*. The police make late night passport checks in bars, without a passport you may spend a night in prison.

Spanish Classes given by José M Eras, Montalvo 5-26 y Santa Clara, T 740-453, English speaking retired teacher, less than US$3/hr; Elizabeth Barrionuevo, T Halflants 6-54, T 740-314, English and German speaking, same price; Sandra Alvarez Solis, next to Familia Reyes Alvarez (see hotels) T 740-531, private lessons pm, under US$2.50/hr; Esther Romo, Maldonado opp bus terminal, T 740-703. Martha Vacas Flores, Calle 16 de Diciembre y Espejo, university trained, US$3/hr.

Laundry You can have clothes washed at the municipal washhouse next to the main baths for US$1.20 a bundle, or do it yourself there for free; *El Marqués*, next to *Hotel Palace* has laundry service.

Shopping It is here that Ecuador's best *aguardiente* is made. Street vendors sell *canelazo*, a sweet drink of *aguardiente*, naranjilla, water and cinnamon, and *canario*, aguardiente with egg, milk and sugar; also jawsticking toffee (*tafi*, also known as *melcocha de caña* or *alfeñique*) made in ropes in shop doorways. Painted balsa-wood birds (see **El Chaguamango** shop by Basílica, open 0800-1600; **Butterfly World** for toucans). **Tucán**, Maldonado y Ambato, T 740-417/114, F (593-2) 5020-49, good for handicrafts. The small factory on Calle 6, just before road to Bella Vista demonstrates carving. Ask for the weaver José Masaquiza Caizabanda, Rocafuerte 2-56, who sells Salasacan weaving, gives demonstrations and explains the designs, materials, etc to visitors. **Galería de Arte Contemparáneo Huiliac Cuna**, next to Café Cultura on Montalvo, modern art exhibits and pizza restaurant. Konika, cheap for films. Fruit and vegetable market on Sun am (and to a lesser extent on Wed) in Plaza 5 de Junio on Calle Ambato.

Book Exchange *Café Cultura*, *Artesanía El Tucán*, *Cafetería Chushi*, and *Chifa Oriental*.

Camping Equipment *Varoxi*, Maldonado 651 y Oriente, T 740-051, also makes daypacks, windproof jackets, larger backpacks, backpack covers and repairs luggage, rec.

Cycle Hire *Sierra Salva Adventures*, Maldonado y Oriente, T 740-298, for mountain bikes and motorcycles, friendly owner Adrián Carrillo, reliable machines. Many other places rent bikes, shop around for quality, US$4/day, check the brakes and tyres. A popular ride is to Puyo, 65 km, mostly downhill, but still plenty of uphill, hard work, 4-6 hrs, bus back (US$2.50 for rider and bike, see **p 1033**). Watch out for trucks, buses and dogs.

Horse Riding Christian and Gabby Albers Wetzl have excellent horses for rent, highly rec. They keep about 14 horses in different areas, excursions include into the foothills of Tungurahua; a popular trek starts from Runtún with transport from Baños: 5 hrs with guide costs US$15-20 pp English, Spanish, German spoken, contact Christian at Calle T Halflants 1-31 y Juan Montalvo, T 740-609. Also Caballos José, Maldonado y Martínez, T 740-746, friendly, good rates, flexible hours; Angel Aldaz, Montalvo y JL Mera, US$3/hr (on road to the Virgin).

River Rafting is organized in Baños by Esther and Héctor Romo-Oester; trips down the Patate (1/2 day, US$20) and Pastaza (full day, US$40) rivers. Check with Geotours, Calle Maldonado, Terminal Terrestre, or write to Casilla 18-02-1933, Baños, T 740-703.

Guides in Baños: Carlos Saant Mashu, *Agencia de Viajes Kaniats Cia Ltda*, Residencial Santa Clara, T 740-349, knowledgeable, honest, friendly, rec, US$40 per day including transport. Sebastián Moya can be found at *Tsantsa Expeditions*, Oriente y Eloy Alfaro, T 740-957; he is a Shuar Indian who will lead tours anywhere (careful planning needed to minimize travelling time), US$45 per day, not including optional air travel. You may have to wait some weeks for him to be free. *Tsantsa* have other good jungle guides. Spanish only spoken, can arrange fly-in trips. Contactable through *Pensión Patty* (where equipment can be hired, helpful) is mountain guide Carlos Alvarez, who takes climbs in both the Sangay and Cotopaxi National Parks; also through *Patty*, Fausto Mayorga, safe, good. Geovanny Romo, small agency on Maldonado, jungle tours, experienced; also arranges horseback tours from Baños. Juan Medina and Daniel Vasco (based in Misahualli) at *Vasco Tour Travel Agency*, Eloy Alfaro y Martínez, T 740-017, PO Box 18-02-1970, 6-28 trips days available, also mountains and national parks, 6-8 people needed, excellent and plentiful food, up to 4 guides per tour (check if permission needed to enter indigenous territory).

Note There are 4 tour agencies in Baños who are recognized by Cetur and who use qualified guides; they are the above-mentioned Tsanta Expeditions, Sangay Touring (excellent trips down the Curaray—Reina Victoria 1710 y La Pinta, Quito, T 542-476, F 230-738), Aventurandes and

Marcelio Turismo. We have received some critical reports of tours out of Baños (in all cases, insist on written contract and pay half after the tour). Note that no guides in Baños have permission to enter Waorani territory in the Oriente, including the Tiguino River area; if such a trip is offered, decline.

Tourist Information Office near bus terminal, friendly, helpful, but not state-run. Good maps, town map US$1, hiking maps US$0.30, but distances and times reported incorrect; also high-pressure selling of jungle tours. J Urquizo (local artist, also sells a Baños map, accurate, rec), 12 de Noviembre y Ambato, T 740589.

Buses To/from **Quito**, via Ambato, US$3, 3½ hrs, Trans Baños ½ hourly; going to capital sit on right for views of Cotopaxi, buy tickets early for weekends and holidays. To **Ambato**, from market place, 45 mins, US$0.60; to **Riobamba**, 1 hr, US$1; to **Latacunga**, 2-2½ hrs, US$0.80; to **Puyo**, 2 hrs, US$1.50; pack your luggage in plastic, it all goes on top of the bus (you may be able to ride there also) and the road (not all paved) passes under a spectacular waterfall; for **Macas**, some direct buses or change at Puyo, 0830, US$1.75, 6 hrs, magnificent scenery, sit on right; to **Tena**, 5½ hrs, US$2.50 by bus (more leg room) with Coop Riobamba, or US$2.65 by *buseta*, only three direct buses Baños-Tena, but frequent passing buses from Riobamba and Ambato (or change at Puyo); seat reservations rec (but buses don't always leave); to **Misahuallí**, change at Tena, or at the Río Napo crossing, see p 1030. The bus station is on the Ambato-Puyo road a short way from the centre, and is the scene of vigorous volleyball games most afternoons.

Interesting side trips are possible from the main Pelileo-Baños highway across the main valley, N to Patate, or up the Chambo valley to Penipe and Riobamba.

There are many interesting **walks** in the Baños area. You can cross the Pastaza by the San Francisco suspension bridge across the main road from the bus station. It is possible to recross the river by another suspension bridge, a round trip of 2-3 hrs. It is a 45-min hike to the new statue of the Virgin: take the first path on the left after the hospital; good views of the valley from the statue. Other short hikes include the Bella Vista cross overlooking Baños, a steep climb from Calle Maldonado, 45 mins-1 hr, take drinks and stick in case there are dogs; Illuchi village, a steep 1¾ hr climb with marvellous views over the valley and Tungurahua; San Martín shrine, ¾ hr, which overlooks a deep rocky canyon with the Pastaza River thundering below; beyond the shrine is a path to the Inés María waterfall (thundering cascade but smells of raw sewage), round trip 2 hrs; 50m from Inés María is the zoo (entry US$1), clean, big cages; along the old road to Ambato to Lligua, a flowery little village straddling the Río Lligua at its junction with the Pastaza; to **Runtún**, a village of a dozen mud dwellings, two sporting a billiard table, from which there is a splendid view of Tungurahua (5-6 hrs round trip). Cold drinks sold at the billiard hall. There are two paths from Baños to Runtún, one from S end of Calle 9, the other from Calle 6. See Baños **Hotels** for *Hosteria Luna Runtún*.

20 km from Baños on the Puyo road are the spectacular Río Verde falls (better known as El Pailón del Diablo); a bus goes from the Baños terminal, ½ hr, US$0.25 (for a thrill, ride on the roof). In Río Verde, cross the river and take the path to the right after the church, then trail down to the suspension bridge with a view of the falls. On the other side of the bridge is the new *El Otro Lado*, beautiful *cabañas* run by an Israeli couple. Surrounded by waterfalls and mountains, it is a lovely place to relax. There are 3 *cabañas* with bath and hot water; they have dogs, cats, ducks and a donkey; good birdwatching (they guarantee you'll see the cock-of-the-rock); delicious meals and drinks served all day for visitors and guests, C pp full board. Make reservations at *Café Cultura* in Quito, T 224-271.

F pp *Posada Zuñac*, at El Topo, 1 hr by bus from Baños towards Puyo (US$0.75), clean, safe, helpful, kitchen facilities, breakfast and dinner available, walking, swimming, ecotourism, rec; contact Gonzalo and Mónica in advance, Baños, T 03-740-501.

From Baños it is possible to climb **Tungurahua** (5,016m—part of Sangay National Park, entry US$10); follow road opposite police control on Ambato side of town, then first mule track to right of store and follow the path to Pondoa; do not follow the road up to the baths. If you are driving to **Pondoa**, take the main Ambato road and turn off to the left about 1 km from the town centre. The road runs parallel to the main road for several km before turning E into the mountains. Park the car at the shop in Pondoa. The walk from the shop to the beginning of the trail takes 30 mins. There is an occasional bus from Baños around 0900 to Pondoa, and a milk truck leaves at 0800 daily from *Pensión Patty*. It returns from Pondoa at 1400. Also pickup truck and driver from Coop Agoyán on central park, Calle Maldonado, US$15 to park entrance. It takes 3-4 hrs walking from the park entrance to reach the Santos Ocaña *refugio* (3,800m—US$4, charge said to change daily, purchase ticket either at the shop in Pondoa, where sketch map of route can be obtained, or at the refuge) situated 3-4 hrs below the snowline, then 4-6 hours from the *refugio* to the summit early next morning (about 0230). Leave summit about 0930 as clouds come down later in the day: allow 2 hours for descent to *refugio* and leave *refugio* by 1400 in order to get back to Baños (3 hrs) on same day; in Dec it may be cloudy am, check conditions locally. If in a group stay close, large stones dislodge easily, a hazard for walkers lower down. Do not leave baggage unattended in the refuge, theft reported. Take a sleeping bag, mat and food; there are cooking facilities at the *refugio*, but no eating utensils and rarely any lighting, a hammock can be slung, no heating and it can be cold. Don't forget your torch. A tiring but rewarding climb: it requires some experience. In places, it is dangerous if you fall for instance on convex icy snow slopes near the top. To reduce the chance of accidents (some of which have been fatal) a guide is highly recommended. Depending on season, you may need rubber boots to get to the refuge and crampons for the summit (check in Baños beforehand). Best season is Dec to Mar.

Tungurahua can also be reached from Río Puela (on Baños-Riobamba road) at about 2,000m. A guide is needed through the forest, camp at 3,800m where the forest ends. Walk up the crest to 4,600m then the last 400m through snow (take crampons. ice-axe). Return to 3,800m the same day. There are thermal pools at Río Puela, ask where. Don't leave anything of value here.

Guides, Equipment, etc Check all equipment carefully before hiring. *Willie Navarrete*, at *Café Higuerón*, highly rec for climbing. Fabian Pineda of *Selvanieve*, in Francisco Alomoto, W of Halflants. Dosto Varela of *Expediciones Amazónicas*, in Calle Oriente, T 740-506.

For a guide and pack animals enquire at Baños tourist office or Pondoa shop; guide and mule for 1 pack US$5, for 2 packs, US$7. Horses can be hired for US$0.90 an hour (see Julio Albán, Segundo Sánchez or Víctor Barriga near the Plaza Central or through tourist office).

To the W of Ambato, a winding road leads up the valley of the Ambato river, over a high area of desert called the Gran Arenal, past Carihuairazo and Chimborazo, and down through the Chimbo valley to Guaranda. This spectacular journey on the highest paved road in Ecuador takes about 3 hrs.

This route can be walked, and is worthwhile for the valley, the páramo crossing and the hot springs along the way. From Ambato, pass the *Plaza de Toros* on the left and follow the winding road down to the *estación de bombeo*, where a road branches off to the left. This is the old road to Guaranda, alongside Río Ambato, which is followed all the way. After 3 hrs walk or 1 hr by frequent bus or truck, turn off for Pasa where the interesting part of the hike starts as the river winds through the narrow valley. After 4 hrs the village of Llangahua is reached, the last houses and camping place before entering the *páramo* with its scarce vegetation and rough climate. About 3 hrs from the village there is a big church-like building on the opposite bank, cross the river here and go back along the small channel for about 15 mins as far as the hot pools, surrounded by big rocks; the cold river is close by. Continue to the new road in 2½ hrs, at the foot of Chimborazo where frequent buses pass for Ambato or Guaranda. On a Thur you may catch a pickup early in the morning to the market in Llagua, thus enabling you to do the trip in one day.

Chimborazo, 6,310m: there are two routes up the mountain:

1) The South West face: there are no direct buses so take a taxi from Riobamba (US$35 for 5-6 hrs, US$40 return next day or later, US$20 one way; rec driver is Segundo López, Taxi 89, found at taxi stand in Mercado Santa Rosa, Av Guayaquil y Rocafuerte, Riobamba, Juan Fuenmayor, Veloz 25-31 y España, or arrange through Riobamba hotels, eg *Imperial*, or agencies). Go to the Edward Whymper refuge which takes 1½ hrs, 47 km, or take a bus to San Juan village and hitch from there. The road ends at 4,800m, where there is a new refuge (guarded, mattresses on the floor, cooking facilities, running water, toilet, bring food and light, very cold at night), or you can walk up to the Edward Whymper refuge at 5,000m which is at the foot of the Thielman glacier. There should be two keepers at this refuge, which provides water and a bed (sleeps about 70, also very cold at night, can get crowded at weekends). Both refuges are now managed by Alta Montaña and a US$0.50 fee is charged for a day visit. Overnight stays are US$7 but card carrying members of a club or Youth Hostel Association pay less. Take padlock for the small lockers under the bunks. Beware of thieves if you leave anything in the refuge or even in your car at 4,800m. From the refuge to the summit the climb is 8-9 hrs and the descent about 4 hrs. There are three routes depending on your experience and ability. Recommended to start at 2400 or 0100. **E** *Posada de la Estación (Youth Hostel)*, PO Box 523, Riobamba, T 446-220, a converted station at Urbina on the Pan-American Highway at 3,618m, is a good place for acclimatization, clean, helpful, horses, trips and equipment arranged. There is a road from San Juan to Pogyos round Carihuairazo, making a round trip by jeep, Riobamba-Chimborazo-Ambato, possible.

2) The North West face, or Pogyos route: Take the Guaranda bus from Ambato along the new paved road or a truck along the spectacular old road (50 km) to the valley of Pogyos. At

Pogyos (4,000m) there is a house with a metal roof where you can hire mules for US$4 each to carry your luggage. (Beware of pilfering from your bags on ascent.) Walk about 3 hrs to the Fabián Zurita refuge (4,900m) which is uninhabitable. From the refuge to the summit is about an 8-hr climb and 3-4 hr descent. Advisable to start at 0100. Take tents and water (obtainable at Pogyos, containers in Ambato). (We are grateful to Enrique Veloz Coronado **p 980** for much of this information.)

Dr Sverre Aarseth writes that in order to climb this mountain it is essential to have at least one week's acclimatization above 3,000m. The best season is Dec and Jun-Sep. Sr Héctor Vásquez at Colegio National Bolívar, Ambato, has helped many expeditions with travel arrangements and information; he is a top-grade mountaineer. The original Whymper route is harder than the Pogyos route, but it is more accessible and there are more climbers in case of difficulty; the afternoon descent is particularly hazardous owing to stones rolling from the scree (the upper part is quite straightforward with two or three on a rope). Previous parties will most likely have left marker flags; these are often needed for descent in a cloud. Very soft snow between first and second summit but usually there will be a good path from previous parties (otherwise snow shoes might be needed). The ascent to the summit is very steep and partly exposed (falling could be fatal). No one without mountaineering experience should attempt the climb, and rope, ice-axe and crampons must be used. Carihuairazo (5,020m) is an older and much eroded volcano.

The Fiesta de las Nieves is celebrated at the 4,800m shelter on the second or third Sun in Dec—music and dancing, rather touristy, no folkloric roots, but at least buses from Riobamba go to the mountain.

Guaranda (15,730 inhabitants) is the capital of Bolívar Province. It is a beautiful, clean, quiet town which, because it is built on seven hills, proudly calls itself "the Rome of Ecuador". There are fine views of the mountains around, with Chimborazo towering above. Carnival is very colourful and enjoyable. Market day is Sat. The daily *paseo* in the main square is from about 1800 to 2100 exactly. Guaranda is connected by a paved road to Ambato (several buses) and Babahoyo, and a poor, narrow but spectacular road to Riobamba. It is the main centre for the wheat and maize-growing Chimbo valley, but has long stagnated since newer, faster routes replaced the old Guayaquil-Quito road through Babahoyo and Guaranda (which is still perfectly good, nevertheless). A water-powered grist mill on the river welcomes visitors.

Hotels **A3** *La Colina*, high up on Av Guayaquil (No 103, T 980-666), rooms bright and attractive, terraces give good view of town and surrounding mountains, restful, friendly, swimming pool open to non-residents, overpriced, restaurant mediocre; **D** *Cochabamba*, García Moreno y 7 de Mayo, T 981-958, F 982-125, PO Box 01-02-0095, with bath, nice rooms, good service, mixed reports; **E** *Residencial Bolívar*, Sucre y Rocafuerte, T 980-547, very good, hot showers, hacienda style, quiet inner court; **F** *Pensión Ecuador*, opposite, cold showers, friendly; **F** *Matiaví*, Av Eliza Mariño, T 980-295, clean, next to bus station; **F** *Residencial Acapulco*, 10 de Agosto y 9 de Abril, basic, clean, good value. *Hotel Refugio Salinas*, new, friendly, 1 hr out of town.

Restaurants *Chifa Hong Kong*, Parque Simón Bolívar, very good and cheap; *Amazonas*, Olmedo y Convención, family run, good set meals US$1.25; *Guaranda* soda bar on G Moreno y Pichincha.

Buses Bus station on road to Ambato. To **Ambato**, US$1.60, 1½ hrs (beautiful views); **Riobamba**, US$1.20, 2½ hrs; **Guayaquil**, US$2.85, 3½ hrs; **Quito**, several a day US$3.35, 4-5 hrs, or take bus to Ambato and change. Taxi to **Riobamba** 1½ hrs, US$11.50.

Excursions North of Guaranda, 1½ hrs by taxi along poor roads, is Salinas de Guaranda, pop 5,000, noted for its cheeses (El Salinerito brand) and sweaters, which are also sold in Quito. No buses except maybe on Sat; hitching is not difficult. It is a good area for walking; nearby villages, Santiago and San Simón have been described as "a picture". The bus ride to Babahoyo (**see p 1007**) is beautiful. There is an interesting church museum in Guayco, constructed around a "Vatican Square": interesting pre-Spanish artefacts. Worth the ½ hr taxi ride from Guaranda.

After Ambato, the Pan-American Highway and railway pass apple orchards and onion fields. Between Ambato and Riobamba is **Mocha**, where guinea-pigs (*cuy*) are raised for the table; you can sample roast *cuy* at stalls by the roadside. The valley's patchwork of fields gives an impression of greater fertility and prosperity than the Riobamba zone that follows. On the houses a small crucifix crowns the roof, where figurines of domestic animals are also found. The Quito-Guayaquil railway's highest point, Urbina (3,609m) is between Cevallos and

Riobamba. At the pass there are fine views in the dry season of Chimborazo and its smaller sister mountain, Carihuairazo.

Riobamba (2,750m) is the capital of Chimborazo Province. It has 95,505 inhabitants, is built on a large flat site and has broad streets and many ageing but impressive buildings in need of repair. It has the nickname "Sultan of the Andes". Riobamba has many good churches and public buildings, and magnificent views of three of the great volcanic peaks, Chimborazo, Altar and Tungurahua. Four blocks NE of the railway station, the **Parque 21 de Abril** (the city's foundation date, but better known as **La Loma de Quito**) affords an unobstructed view of Riobamba and the peaks; the park also has a colourful tile tableau of the history of Ecuador and is especially fine at sunset. **San Antonio de Padua** church near Parque 21 de Abril tells bible stories in the windows.

This town is a must for anyone enchanted by old barber shops, shoe repairers etc in beautiful old buildings. Riobamba has a new market building, but only a small part of the activity at the Saturday market takes place there. Buying and selling go on all over town. The "tourist" market in the small plaza S of the Convento de la Concepción museum is a good place to buy local handicrafts—*ikat* shawls (*macanas*), embroidered and finely woven belts (*fajas*), blankets, embroidered dresses and shirts, Otavalan weavings and sweaters, *shigras* and carvings of tagua, a nut that hardens and looks like ivory. Indian women come to the plaza each week with sacks full of bead and coin necklaces, old belts and dresses, blanket pins (*tupus*), and much more. Since Indian-style clothing is also sold here, the plaza is full of colourful Indians from different parts of Chimborazo province, each group wearing its distinctive costume; compare shop prices before buying. Two blocks E, there is a huge produce market in another plaza, also pottery, baskets, hats. All the streets in this area are filled with traders. There are also 2 markets on Weds: **Mercado La Condamine** and **Mercado San Alfonso**, which only sells local products. A variety of *pelota* games can be seen on Sun afternoons. Open-air restaurants do a flourishing business in that Andean delicacy, roast *cuy* (guinea-pig). There are two cinemas.

The **Convento de la Concepción**, Orozco y España, entrance at España y Argentinos, has been carefully restored by the Banco Central and now functions as a religious art museum with gold artefacts and jewellery as part of the exhibition, open Tues-Sat 0900-1200 and 1500-1800. Admission: US$0.60 for Ecuadoreans, US$2 for others. The guides are friendly and knowledgeable (tip expected). The priceless Custodia de Riobamba Antigua is the museum's greatest treasure, one of the richest of its kind in South America. Well worth a visit.

Festivals Fiesta de los Niños, 2 Jan, street parades with music and dancing. Hotel prices rise during the city's foundation *fiestas* around 20 April, and rooms are difficult to obtain during the Nov basketball tournament.

Hotels In Jan, schools from the coast bring children here on vacation and many hotels are full. **A3** *El Galpón*, Argentinos y Zambrano, T 960-981, pool, sauna (pleasant location on hill overlooking city); **C** *Hosteriá La Andaluza*, 16 km from Riobamba at the foot of Chimborazo, T 904-223, with views of Tungurahua and Altar, good walking, friendly, good restaurant; next to *El Galpón* is **D** *Chimborazo Internacional*, T 963-475, attentive service, spacious rooms with fridge and cold drinks, fully carpeted, noisy discotheque, restaurant overpriced; **D** *Hostería El Troje*, 4½ km on road to Chambo, T 964-572, pleasant, tourist centre, camping, restaurant; **D** *Humboldt*, Borja 3548 y Uruguay, T 961-788, clean, with bath, parking; **D** *Whymper*, Av Miguel Angel León 23-10 y Primera Constituyente, T 964-575, F 968-137, private bath, hot water, spacious rooms, safe parking, cafetería serves breakfast any time, but slow; **D** *Riobamba Inn*, Carabobo 23-20 y Primera Constituyente, T 961-696, parking, restaurant; **C** *Montecarlo*, Av 10 de Agosto 25-41 entre García Moreno y España, T 960-557, clean, comfortable (E without window), hot water, restaurant, exchange up to US$20, English spoken; **E** *Imperial*, Rocafuerte 22-15 y 10 de Agosto, T 960-429, good, hot water, private or shared bathroom, laundry facilities, can store luggage, friendly and comfortable, rec but loud music from bar on Fri and Sat nights, good view from roof; **D** *Res Manabí*, Colón 19-58 y Olmedo, T 967-967/305, sometimes no breakfast, clean, hot water, safe; *Los Nevados*, Alfredo Costales 24-37 y León Borja, safe, clean, hot water, very good; **E** *Los Shyris*, 10 de Agosto y Rocafuerte 2160, T 960-323, with private bathroom, good rooms and service, clean, nicely furnished, friendly, noise from busy street, restaurant good; **E** *Residencial Rocío*, Brazil 2168, bath, hot water (hot water problems 1000 to 1800), towels and soap supplied, clean, friendly, safe, quiet; **E** *Metropolitano*, Borja y Lavalle, T 961-714, with bath, central, traditional, large rooms, good beds, but noisy, insecure, water problems; **F** *Puruhuá*, near bus station at Borja 43-60, friendly, fairly clean, but noisy; **F** *Residencial Ñuca Huasi*, 10 de Agosto 2824, laundry facilities, clean, noisy, dormitory beds, hot water, friendly, laundry facilities, safe parking in

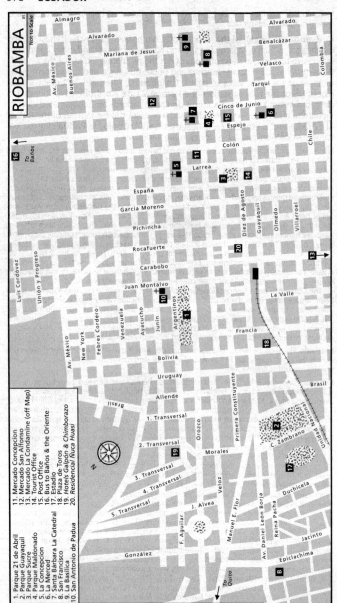

RIOBAMBA

Not to Scale

1. Parque 21 de Abril
2. Parque Guayaquil
3. Parque Sucre
4. Parque Maldonado
5. La Concepción
6. La Merced
7. Santa Bárbara La Catedral
8. San Francisco
9. La Basílica
10. San Antonio de Padua
11. Mercado Concepción
12. Mercado San Alfonso
13. Mercado La Condamine (off Map)
14. Tourist Office
15. Post Office
16. Bus to Baños & the Oriente
17. Estadio
18. Plaza de Toros
19. Hotels Galpón & Chimborazo
20. Residencial Ñuca Huasi

courtyard; **G** *Venecia*, Dávalos 2221 y 10 de Agosto, hot water; *Los Nevados*, Alfredo Costales 24-37 y León Borja; *Luzia Bärtsch de Noboa*, Espejo 27-28 y Junín, T 961-205, rents rooms, clean, hot water, very comfortable, a helpful Ecuadorean Swiss family.

Restaurants None is open after 2200. *El Delirio*, Primera Constituyente 2816 y Rocafuerte (Bolívar's house in Riobamba), T 960-029, shut Mon, good value, daily menu US$3, 4 courses, patio garden, highly rec; *El Mesón*, Colón entre 10 de Agosto y Primera Constituyente, rec; *Punto Azul*, Colón y Olmedo, excellent seafood; *La Fuente*, under old post office, cebiches, seafood, reasonably priced, rec; *Saint-Amand*, 5 de Junio y 10 de Agosto, T 967-301, international dishes, also breakfast; *Cabaña Montecarlo*, García Moreno 21-40, T 962-844, Viennese atmosphere, disappointing food, friendly but slow service; *Café Montecarlo*, Av 10 de Agosto y Moreno, popular with tourists, good breakfast; opp is *Charlie's Pizzería*, vegetarian lasagne; *Café Milano*, 10 de Agosto entre Moreno y España, excellent coffee; *Tropical Fruit*, 10 de Agosto, friendly, meat, fish, daily special US$2.75; *Chifa Joy Sing*, Guayaquil near station, cheap, good; *Chifa Pak Hao*, García Moreno y Guayaquil, vegetarian dishes; *Chifa China*, León Borja opp *Hotel Puruhua*, good, cheap; *Chifa Internacional*, Veloz y Dávalos, Chinese, good; *El Paraíso*, Juan de la Valle y Borja, good value; *Café Paola*, Olmedo y 10 de Agosto, good *empanadas*, service poor; *Los Alamos*, Juan de La Valle, good à la carte; *Valentín*, Torres y Borja, pizzas; *Chicken Dog*, Carabobo y Colombia, hamburgers, chicken broaster, good bread, chips, highly rec. Many snackbars along 10 de Agosto. *Gran Pan*, Moreno y Primera Constituyente, bakery and *cafetería*, fresh bread, tasty cakes, coffee and biscuits. For early departures, a small café opp the gate in the fence at the back of the bus terminal serves full breakfasts, bread and coffee.

Banks and Exchange Banco Internacional, 10 de Agosto y García Moreno; **Banco Popular**, main square; **Casa de Cambio Chimborazo**, 10 de Agosto y España, will change TCs, major European and American currencies. Banks will not always exchange dollars even though the exchange rate is posted.

Entertainment *Gems Chop* bar, León Borja 4205 y Duchicela, good music, videos, open daily, rec; *Peñas* at *Taquí Huasi*, Orozco y 4a Transversal, and *La Casa Vieja*, Orozco y Tarqui. The Casa de la Cultura, 10 de Agosto y Rocafuerte, has a good *peña* on Fri and Sat evenings. Disco, Thur-Sun, at *Zero*, Km 1¹/₂ on road to Cajabamba. *La Bruja*, Km 1 on road to Quito, disco, Thur-Sat. *Unicornio*, Piano Bar, Salsateca, cultural place, Pichincha 26-70 y Villarroel, Thur-Sat.

Post Office 10 de Agosto y Espejo.

Fax Service *Viajes Qualitas*, 10 de Agosto y Colón, T 960-081; also at *Hotel Whymper*, but more expensive.

Travel Agent *Chimborazo Touring*, León Borja 42-05 y Duchicela, Casilla 80, T 965-714, offers a variety of tours. *Viajes Qualitas*, Av 10 de Agosto y Colón.

Tourist Office Cetur, 10 de Agosto 25-33 (very helpful). Open Tues-Sat 0800-1200, 1430-1700. Addresses for rental of climbing equipment. Souvenir shops on 10 de Agosto between Carabobo and Rocafuerte.

Immigration España y Guayaquil.

Transport Train service to **Durán (Guayaquil)** was restored in 1993 after repairs to the tracks which took 10 years. Daily service to Durán at 0600, US$10 for foreigners; arrives Alausí 0930, Bucay 1330 (get out at Bucay and change to bus to avoid arriving in Guayaquil in the dark). Interruptions to service occur. Tickets for the 0600 train to Durán can be bought a day in advance at the station. The station is closed on Sun. If time is limited, for the most spectacular section of the railway, take a bus before 0730 to Guayaquil and get out at Bucay (US$1.50), catch the train to Alausí, return to Riobamba by bus; it waits for the train. Train to **Quito**, 0900 Fri and Sun, US$10 for foreigners. A privately-owned *autoferro* runs from **Quito**, details from Metropolitan Tours, Av República de El Salvador 970, Quito, T 464-780, rec, or other travel agencies. The railway administration office is on Espejo, next to the Post Office, reliable information available during office hours.

Buses to **Quito**, US$2.25, 3¹/₂ hrs, about every 30 mins; to **Guaranda**, US$1.20, 2 hrs road, paved to San Juan, crosses a 4,000 metre pass, sit on the right, beautiful views; to **Ambato**, US$0.75, 1 hr, sit on the right; to **Cuenca**, 6 a day via Alausí, 5¹/₂ hrs, US$4. This road is paved but landslides are a constant hazard and the road is often under repair. For a day trip to **Ingapirca (see p 983)**, take 0530 bus to Cuenca, getting off at El Tambo at about 1000. Bus back to Riobamba passes through El Tambo at about 1600 (last one about 1930). Bus to **Santo Domingo**, US$2.65, 5 hrs; to **Baños**, US$1, 1 hr; to **Puyo**, US$2.60, 3¹/₂ hrs direct. There are 2 buses (US$4.65, 8-10 hrs) to **Huaquillas** every evening (1915 and 2100) with Patria, which avoid Guayaquil; book the day before, arrive early and be prepared to fight for your seat. Bus to **Guayaquil**, about 35 a day, US$3.25, 4½ hrs; the trip is really spectacular for the first two hours. There are pirate buses which charge more than the regular lines and do not sell tickets in the bus station, first come first served, they can be useful when all the others are full up. There is a well-run Terminal Terrestre on Eplicachima y Av D L Borja for buses to Quito, Guayaquil, Ambato, etc, but buses to Baños and the Oriente leave from the Terminal Oriental, Espejo y Córdovez. Taxi from one terminal to the other, US$0.75.

Excursions to *Guano*, a hemp-working and carpet-making town of 6,000 inhabitants 10 km to the N, with prehistoric monoliths on a nearby hilltop, lovely views of El Altar from the plaza; there are frequent buses from NE Riobamba near road to Guano, US$0.15, or taxi, US$2.65. Good handicraft shop in the plaza, *Almacén Ciudad de las Fuentes*. You can have rugs made to your own design. Although there have been reports of declining quality you can still see enormous rugs on sale, rather expensive. Sun market. Very quiet other days. After Guano you can take the bus on to Santa Teresita from where it is a 20 min walk downhill to Balneario Los Helenes: 3 pools, 1 tepid, 2 cool. Camping possible nearby. Superb view of Altar and Tungurahua as you walk through pasture land. From Riobamba it is also possible to reach the fossil fields of the gorge of Chalán and the archaeological site of Punín.

Climbing   To climb Chimborazo contact Enrique Veloz Coronado, technical adviser of the Asociación de Andinismo de Chimborazo, Chile 33-21 y Francia, Riobamba (T 960-916). He is best reached after 1500 and is very helpful. Marcelo Puruncajas, Colón 22-25 y 10 de Agosto (in Quito, Foch 727 y Amazonas), T 940-964, F 940-963, rents equipment and is cheap, and highly rec, speaks English, when not leading tours uses good guides, also offers trekking, 4WD transport and mountain biking; Silvio Pesántez, Argentinos 114 O y Darquea, PO Box 327, T 962-681, member of the Association of Mountain Guides, an experienced climber and adventure-tour leader, rec. Overall cost for 2 between US$250-350. For transport and routes, **see p 975**. For Sangay (**see p 1035**), take a taxi to Alao and hire guides or carriers of food, tents, etc there; remember you have to pay for and organize the food for your porters separately, otherwise you have to pay them a lot more. Make sure the fee covers the return journey as well. Also Expediciones Andinas (Marco Cruz), Argentinos 3860 y Zambrano, T 964-915 (office), 962-845 (house), recommended (he is a certified guide of the German Alpine Club), but expensive for small numbers. For information on Sangay go to the Inefan offices, 9 de Octubre in Urb Mag, N of the roundabout at the end of Isabel de Godir. **NB** Sangay is one of the most active volcanoes in the world and can be dangerous even on quiet days.

   To the crater of *Altar*: Travel to Penipe by bus from Baños or Riobamba/Ambato, then to Candelaria by truck, or bus which passes between 1200 and 1400. Walk out of the village, cross the bridge and go up about 2 km to the park station (a green building with a National Park sign), where you pay your entrance fee of US$10. You can stay there overnight, although it is not a *refugio*, US$0.50, beds, warm water, shower, cooking facilities and friendly keeper. It is not always open, ask in Riobamba beforehand at the Ministry of Tourism or the Sangay National Park office, Primera Constituyente y Pichincha, Inefan. In Penipe ask for Ernesto Haro, who will take you to the station in his jeep (US$8 one way) and pick you up from there at a pre-arranged time. The track to Altar leads on up a steep hill past the Hacienda Releche (muddy in the wet season), but it is best to ask someone to point out the faint track which branches to the left about 30-40 minutes after the Hacienda and leads up a hill to a ridge where it joins a clear track. This goes S first and then turns E up the valley of the Río Collanes. It is about 8 hrs to the crater which is surrounded by magnificent snow-capped peaks. It is possible to camp in the crater, but better still, about 20 mins before you turn into the broad U-shaped valley leading up to the crater there is a good-sized cave, the floor of which is lined with dry reeds; there is a fire ring at the entrance. Guides and horses to Altar can be hired (1994-95 prices unknown). Because of damage done to the track by mudslides the route is hazardous and you would be unwise to do it alone. Consult the National Park Office about conditions, they are in radio contact with the Guardería at Candelaria.

Cajabamba is a small, rather poor town. In 1534 the original Riobamba was founded on this site, but in 1797 a disastrous earthquake caused a large section of the hill on the N side of the town to collapse in a great landslide, which can still be seen. It killed several thousand of the original inhabitants of Riobamba and the town was moved almost twenty kilometres NE to its present site. The new Riobamba has prospered, but Cajabamba has stagnated. Colourful, Colta Indian market on Sun, small but uncommercialized and interesting (easily reached by bus from Riobamba, 25 mins, US$0.15). There are few restaurants out of town on the Panamericana towards Cuenca.

   A fairly good dirt road leaves the Pan-American Highway just N of Cajabamba, to the W; it is one of the oldest of the coast-Sierra routes and links Cajabamba with Guaranda and Babahoyo. 5 km S of Cajabamba, a paved highway branches SW to Pallatanga, Bucay, Milagro and Guayaquil.

Road and rail skirt the shores of **Laguna de Colta**, just after the fertile Cajabamba valley. The lake and surroundings are very beautiful and just a short bus trip from Riobamba. At the edge of the village along the main road on the shore of Laguna de Colta is a small chapel, La Balbanera, dating from 1534, making it the oldest church in Ecuador, although it has been restored several times because of earthquakes. 28 km S of Cajabamba is **Guamote** (3,056m), interesting market on Thur with lots of animals and few tourists, and some good half day walks in the area. Lots of buses from Riobamba, especially on Thur. There is a *pensión*, F, near the railway station and also some places to eat nearby. Work on a road to Macas has been halted because of environmental concerns (see p 1034). Sit at the front of the bus for a splendid view of the volcanoes.

Alausí, 43 km S of Guamote, is the station where many passengers join the train for the amazing descent to Bucay. The village itself is old and colourful (market Sun). **E** *Hotel Americano*, García Moreno 159, T 930-159, modern, private bath, hot water, friendly, best in town. **E** *Hotel Gampala*, accross from bus stop, T 930-138, with bath, electric shower; **F** *Residencia Tequendama*, clean, friendly, shared bath, hot water, dangerous electric shower; **F** *Hotel Europa*, opposite, check that hot water is free, safe parking in courtyard. **F** *Hotel Panamericano*, near bust stop, T 930-156, shared bath, hot water, clean, front rooms noisy, food cheap but good value; **G** *Residencial Guayaquil*, Calle Eloy Alfaro 149, behind station, a bit noisy, more or less clean, friendly. Restaurants: *Paradero Chumpisti*, *Salón Oriental* (more or less only chicken); *San Juan*, near station, on main street, owner speaks English, helpful staff, good breakfast and other food; *Danielito*, opp Tequendama, good cheap food, will cook vegetarian meals, friendly; vegetarian restaurant just off SE corner of the church square; *El Flamingo*, behind the *Tequendama*, good set meals.

Daily train at 0900, 7-9 hrs to Durán, 4 hrs to Bucay, US$8.50 (new tourist rate, Jan 1995), unreliable, T 930-126 to check if it is running, tickets on sale from 0730. If it is running, hotels fill up early. If the train to Durán is delayed and you may miss the last ferry to Guayaquil (2200), get out at Bucay and take a bus to Guayaquil bus station. By road from Riobamba, bus 1½ hrs, US$1, 98 km, all paved, through a windswept plain, pine forest and after Km 72 through steep hills and valleys. Bus Alausí-Quito at 0400 and 0800, 5½ hrs, US$3.35, often have to change in Riobamba; to Cuenca, 4 hrs, US$3.20, a fight to get a seat; to Ambato hourly, 3 hrs, US$1.35, from main street. Coop Patria has a small office where you can buy bus tickets to Guayaquil, Cuenca (3 hrs, US$3) or Riobamba. Other cooperatives have no office, but their buses pass through town, some at the highway and some go to the main plaza.

Chunchi, 37 km S of Alausí along the Pan-American Highway and one stop from Sibambe on the line to Cuenca, is a friendly village with a Sun market. *Pensión Patricia* just off main square, ask for directions, also **G** *Residencial Carmita*, clean, basic, hot water, near the station. Several restaurants along the highway. Buses from the square, several daily, to Riobamba.

An Inca trail to Ingapirca (see p 983) can be followed: it starts at **Achupallas**, 25 km from Alausí. A truck leaves Alausí almost every day, between 0900-1200 from outside *Residencia Tequendama*, US$0.40 to Achupallas. Take food and drink with you, there is nothing along the way. The path is wide to begin with but disappears after 4-5 hrs walking. It is a spectacular walk through valleys and on vestiges of an Inca trail; the route is described in Rob Rachowiecki and Betsy Wagenhauser's *Climbing and Hiking in Ecuador*. The IGM map (Juncal sheet, 1:50,000) is very useful. The name Ingapirca does not appear on the Cañar 1:50,000 sheet and you may have to ask directions near the end. There are persistent beggars, especially children, the length of the hike. If you want to give them something, take pencils or something useful. Camping possible near The Laguna but at 4,000m good equipment is essential.

THE SOUTHERN SIERRA (4)

The colonial city of Cuenca, built on the site of an older, indigenous settlement, is the focal point of the southern sierra. A pleasant climate and magnificent mountain scenery make it ideal walking country, while undisturbed páramo and cloud forest are home to many birds and other wildlife.

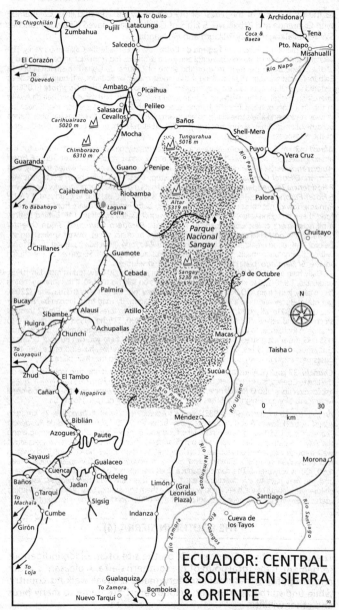

ECUADOR: CENTRAL & SOUTHERN SIERRA & ORIENTE

The Pan-American Highway and railway S of Sibambe to Cuenca run through mountainous country and high above the valleys of the west-bound rivers. (The railway was damaged by floods in 1993 and the line was officially closed in Mar 1995.) The countryside is poor, dry, chilly and wind-swept, and the Indians withdrawn and wrapped-up. Near Zhud and Cañar, more Indians, dressed in black, are seen. At Zhud a paved road runs to Cochancay and La Troncal in the coastal lowlands, from where there are paved roads to Guayaquil and Machala. Towards Cuenca the road loses height and the land is more intensively farmed. There are excellent roads linking Quito-Guayaquil and Guayaquil-Cuenca, which meet at El Triunfo on the coastal plain.

Cañar (pop 189,347), 67 km N of Cuenca (36 km N of Azogues), is a colonial town famous for double-faced weaving, although it is now difficult to find, and is a good area for walking. The jail (Centro de Rehabilitación Social) sells weaving and allows visitors to watch. Market on Sun.

Hotels, Food, Transport E *Residencia Mónica*, main square, often full, may try to overcharge, 15 rooms, basic, not nice, hot water, laundry facilities, owner's daughter offers tour service to Ingapirca, 2 hrs, US$2, see below; **F** *Residencial Cañar*, small, friendly; *Los Maderos Restaurant*, near centre, friendly; *Chifa Florida*, on plaza, good and cheap. Bus every 30 mins to the Terminal Terrestre in Cuenca, US$0.80, 2 hrs; also to Quito and El Tambo (7 km).

Ecuador's most important Inca ruin, *Ingapirca* (3,160m), is E of Cañar. Ingapirca (entrance US$4.50) is commonly known as a fortress complex although this is contradicted by archaeologists. The central structure is an *usnu* platform probably used as a solar observatory. It is faced in fine Inca masonry, and it is interesting to note that the length is exactly three times the diameter of the semicircular ends. This may have been connected with worship of the sun in its morning, midday and afternoon positions (John Hemming). Ten mins walk away is the "face of the Inca", an immense natural formation in the rock looking over the landscape. There is a good museum (open Mon-Sat 0900-1700), which sells a guide book (US$0.80), and will look after belongings, audio-visual guide in English available, and there are guides at the site. Ingapirca was first described by the Frenchman Charles-Marie de la Condamine in 1748.

A direct bus from the Terminal Terrestre in Cuenca leaves at 0900 and 1300, latest returns 1645, US$1.50. There are also organized excursions (US$5.20, depending on numbers) and taxi tours from Cuenca (US$45 from bus terminal). Alternatively go to the nearest town, El Tambo. Coop Cañar runs hourly buses Cañar-El Tambo from 0600, US$0.50. There is a daily 0600 bus from Cañar direct to Ingapirca (slower, rougher road than from El Tambo). Regular buses from Cuenca to El Tambo US$1.20. From the plaza on the Panamericana in El Tambo, morning trucks and Transportes Juahuay buses pass the railway and continue to the ruins. Taxi El Tambo-Ingapirca US$5; colectivos US$0.50, beware overcharging, especially at plaza, can also be caught at railway station. Last colectivos leave Ingapirca at 1800 for El Tambo. It is a beautiful 2½ hr walk from Ingapirca to Cañar, ask directions from end of the "main road", take water.

On Fri there is an interesting Indian market at Ingapirca. There is a good co-operative craft shop next to the church. Camping at the site is possible. There are 4 restaurants at Ingapirca, *Posada de Ingapirca*, a *chifa* (large portions, friendly), and *Inti Huasi*, which also rents clean nice rooms (F pp), hot communal showers, rec, in the village; the *refugio* has benches, table and fireplace but no beds or electricity, water is intermittent. Ask at the museum for a key (if one is available) and for permission to stay overnight, included in museum fee.

F *Pensión Ingapirca* at **El Tambo** on main street, near service station at N end of town, red and yellow house, good value, hot water. *Salón la Rancherita* restaurant. *Restaurant El Turista*, good and cheap food but unfriendly; also good *Restaurant Ingapirca* and *Restaurant Jesus del Gran Poder* truck stop on hill 400m N of town; several others, judge quality by popularity with truck drivers. Small Sat food market.

If doing the 2 day hike to Achupallas from Ingapirca (**see p 981**) Indians may demand a fee for passing through their land.

Azogues (21,060), a large, busy city, is 31 km N of Cuenca (1 hr by bus) and a centre of the panama hat industry. Hats are rarely for sale, even at the Sat morning market, but the *sombrerías* are very happy to show visitors their trade (eg *La Sin Ribal*, Calle Luis Cordero y 3 de Noviembre). (**F** *Hotel Charles*, in centre, unfriendly, overpriced; **G** *Residencial Tropical*, showers.) The market is colourful and beautifully situated on the hill from the Panamericana to the church, lovely view. Between Cañar and Azogues is **Biblián** with a sanctuary, La Madona del Rocío, built into the rocks above the village. Pleasant walk up with impressive views of the river valley and surrounding countryside. 1 hour W of Azogues is Mt Cojitambo, good for rock climbing.

Cuenca, 2,530m (pop officially 194,981, more like 250,000), was founded by the Spaniards in 1557 on the site of the indigenous settlement of Tomebamba. It is now the third largest city in Ecuador. The climate is spring-like, but the nights are chilly. The city has preserved some of its colonial air, with many of its old buildings constructed of the marble quarried nearby and recently renovated, but pollution is increasing. On the central square, **Parque Calderón**, are the old cathedral (with a fine organ) and a new cathedral, started in 1885 (containing a famous crowned image of the Virgin), the work of the German architect Padre Johannes Baptista Stiehle, who also designed many other buildings in the Cuenca area. Modern stained glass, a beautiful altar and an exceptional play of light and shade inside the cathedral make it worth a visit. Sun evening worship is recommended.

Other churches which deserve a visit are **San Blas**, **San Francisco**, **Santo Cenáculo**, and **Santo Domingo**. Many churches are open at irregular hours only and for services, because of increasing problems with theft.

Museums The **Banco Central "Pumapungo"** museum (open Sat 1000-1300, Tues-Fri 0900-1800, US$1.50, entrance on far left of the building), Calle Larga y Huayna Capac, on the edge of town is at the Tomebamba site where excavations are continuing (ruins closed to visitors). It contains all the pottery, bones, statues etc found at the site. Padre Crespi (died June 1982 – statue in Plaza María Auxiliadora) used these artefacts to support his theory that the Phoenicians reached Cuenca via the Amazon. Although the Ingapirca ruins are more spectacular, it is believed that Tomebamba was the principal Inca administrative centre in Ecuador. There are book and music libraries and free cultural videos and music events. In the new Banco Central building (beside the old) there are museums of local and religious art, an ethnographical museum, and space for changing exhibitions. About 300m from the Pumapungo site, at Larga 287, there are excavations at the Todos Los Santos site, which reveal traces of Inca and Cañari (pre-Inca) civilizations (open Mon-Fri, 0800-1600). The **Instituto Azuayo de Folklore**, Escalinata 303 y Larga (open Mon-Fri 0800-1200, 1400-1800) has an exhibition of popular art, incorporating CIDAP (Centro Interamericano de Desarollo de Artes Populares), good exhibits, library, supports research and promotes sales for artesan workers, rec craft shop, good information, helpful. **Museo de las Culturas Aborígenes**, Av 10 de Agosto 4-70, between F Moscoso y J M Sánchez, T 811-706, a good private collection of precolumbian archaeology, in the house of Dr J Cordero López, guided tours, English, Spanish, and French, a worthwhile visit, entry US$2, open Mon-Fri 0900-1230, 1530-1830, Sat 0900-1230, but phone in advance (taxi from centre US$1.50). **Museo del Monasterio de las Conceptas**, Hermano Miguel 6-33 between Pdte Córdova and Juan Jaramillo, T 830-625, well-displayed collection of religious and folk art, extensive collection of lithographs by Guayasamín housed in a cloistered convent founded 1599. Open Tues-Fri 0900-1600, Sat 0900-1230, entrance US$2. There is a **modern art museum** at Calles Sucre y Talbot, on the Plaza San Sebastián, and a small museum, art gallery and bookshop in the **Casa de la Cultura**, Luis Cordero y Sucre (second floor). Look out for the wall of niches in the courtyard, each niche contains a statue of a saint. A lovely, restored colonial house is the **Casa Azul** on Gran Colombia y Pedro

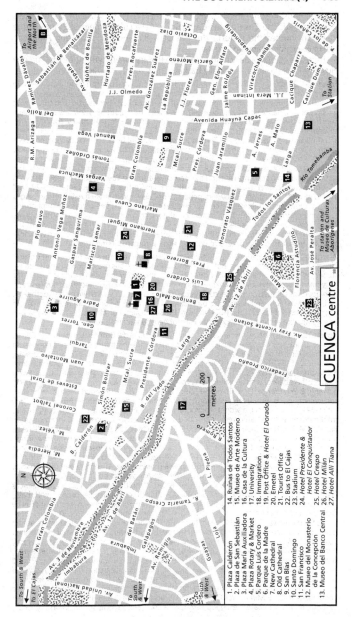

To airport and the North
To Surf and the North
Ramiro Dávalos
Sebastian de Benalcázar
Av. España
Núñez de Bonilla
Hurtado de Mendoza
Pres. Rocafuerte
Octavio Díaz
García Moreno
Gen. Eloy Alfaro
Guapondelig
Viracochabamba
J.L. Mera Intiñan
Cacique Chaparra
Cacique Duma
To Station
Del Rollo
R.M. Arízaga
J.J. Olmedo
Av. González Suárez
La República
J.J. Flores
Jaime Roldós
Avenida Huayna Capac
Manuel Vega
Tomás Ordóñez
Gran Colombia
Mtcal. Sucre
Pres. Córdova
Juan Jaramillo
A. Jervez
A. Malo
Larga
Vargas Machuca
Mariano Cueva
Hermano Miguel
Honorato Vásquez
Todos los Santos
Río Tomebamba
Pío Bravo
Antonio Vega Muñoz
Gaspar Sangurima
Mariscal Lamar
Pres. Borrero
Luis Cordero
Benigno Malo
Av. 12 de Abril
Florencia Astudillo
Av. José Peralta
To station and Museo de Culturas Aborígenes
Padre Aguirre
Gen. Torres
Tarqui
Juan Montalvo
Av. Fray Vicente Solano
Federico Proaño
Esteves de Toral
Coronel Talbot
M. Vélez
M. Heredia
B. Calderón
Simón Bolívar
Mcal. Sucre
Presidente Córdova
Larga
B. del Vado
R. Romero
L. Piedra
CUENCA centre
N
To South & West
To El Cajas
Av. Gran Colombia
Av. 3 de Noviembre
Imbabura
Av. 12 de Abril
del Batán
Galápagos
R. Tamariz Crespo
Guayas
Loja
Av. Unidad Nacional
Av. Remigio
To South & West
To South & West

0   200
metres

3 4 5 6 7 8 9 10 11 12 13 14 15 16 17 18 19 20 21 22 23 24 25 26 27 1 2

1. Plaza Calderón
2. Plaza de San Sebastián
3. Plaza María Auxiliadora
4. Plaza Rotary & Market
5. Parque Luis Cordero
6. Parque de la Madre
7. New Cathedral
8. Old Cathedral
9. San Blas
10. Santo Domingo
11. San Francisco
12. Museo del Monasterio de la Concepción
13. Museo del Banco Central
14. Ruinas de Todos Santos
15. Museo de Arte Moderno
16. Casa de la Cultura
17. University
18. Immigration
19. Post Office & *Hotel El Dorado*
20. Emetel
21. Tourist Office
22. Bus to El Cajas
23. Stadium
24. *Hotel Presidente & Hotel El Conquistador*
25. *Hotel Crespo*
26. *Hotel Milán*
27. *Hotel Allí Tiana*

Aguirre, housing some small shops, restaurant and a little museum, cultural visits also arranged. The **Casa de los Canónigos**, Calle Luis Cordero 888 opp Parque Calderón, houses the **Galería del Portal**, T 833-492, original Latin American works of art for exhibition and sale.

There is a colourful daily market in **Plaza Rotary** where pottery, clothes, guinea pigs and local produce, especially baskets, are sold (Thur busiest).

Festivals On the Sat before Christmas day there is an outstanding parade: Pase del Niño Viajero, probably the largest and finest Christmas parade in all Ecuador. Children and adults from all the *barrios* and surrounding villages decorate donkeys, horses, cars and trucks with symbols of abundance: strings of dollar bills, bottles of Cinzano, strings of lemons and peppers, bunches of bananas, whole roasted chickens with banknotes in their beaks, toys etc. Little children in colourful Indian costumes or dressed up as Biblical figures ride through the streets accompanied by Indian musicians. The parade starts at about 0800 at San Sebastián, proceeds along C Simón Bolívar, past the Plaza Calderón at about 1030 and ends at San Blas. At New Year's Eve, as elsewhere in Ecuador, the festivities include the parading and burning at midnight of effigies called *años viejos* (some political, some fictional) which symbolize the old year. The festivities seem to go on until Lent and there are several smaller Pase del Niño parades between Christmas and Carnival. There are also festivals on 6 Jan (Festival de Los Inocentes), 10-13 April (Foundation of Cuenca) and 3 Nov (Independence of Cuenca, with street theatre, art exhibitions and nighttime dances all over the city). On Good Friday there is a fine procession through the town and up to the Mirador Turi. Septenario, the religious festival of Corpus Christi in June, lasts a week. On Parque Calderón a decorated tower with fireworks attached, known as the "vaca loca" or mad cow, is burnt every night after a mass and hundreds of hot air paper balloons are released; also dozens of dessert sellers and games in the streets.

Warning There is a man who asks female travellers to write letters for him to non-existent friends, and then invites them out. He claims also to be a businessman planning to travel abroad, who asks women to answer questions and then go with him to meet his "sister", or a "woman friend", by way of thanks. Furthermore, he claims to be a homosexual businessman with good links abroad and invites couples to share a glass of wine with him on his "birthday". He is a known rapist and dangerous, but seems to have close relations with the police. Avoid him, last reported (twice) late 1994 and Jan 1995. Be careful of pickpockets in the market. Thieves operate at the bus station. If you are robbed, contact the police.

Hotels Hotels are relatively expensive in Cuenca. **L3 *Oro Verde***, Ordóñez Lasso (road to Cajas), on lake in outskirts of town, T 831-200, F 832-849, completely refurbished, small pool which is in shade most of pm, restaurant, cable TV; **A2 *El Dorado***, Gran Colombia 787 y Luis Cordero, T 831-390, F 831-663, night club, expensive, hot water am only, restaurant, good view; **B *Crespo***, Calle Larga 793, T 831-837, F 839-473, friendly and comfortable, some lovely rooms, others dark or with no windows, with restaurant overlooking river, service poor, a lovely building; **B *Presidente***, Gran Colombia 659, T 831-066, F 824-704, good value, comfortable, convenient, good 9th floor restaurant; **B *El Conquistador***, Colombia 665, T 831-788, F 831-291, breakfast incl, discounts for youth hostel members, disco, avoid back room Fri, Sat, front room noisy from traffic, very clean, good, friendly, good food and wine, rec; **C *Internacional***, Benigno Malo 1015 y Gran Colombia, T 824-348, vaulted ceilings, a/c, TV, comfortable beds, hot water at all hours, pleasant but expensive restaurant, good bar, rec; **C *París Internacional***, Sucre 6-78 y Borrero, T 827-978, F 831-525, private bath; **D *Hostal Caribe Inn***, Gran Colombia 10-51 y Padre Aguirre, clean, attractive, restaurant, rec; **D *Hostería El Molino***, Km 8.5 on road Azogues-Cuenca, T 800-150, pleasant position between road and river, Spanish run, typical Ecuadorean dishes, pool, rustic style, rec, advisable to book; ***Cabañas Yanuncay***, 10 mins drive from centre, Calle Cantón Gualaceo 2149, between Av Loja y Las Américas (Yanuncay), T 819-681, 814-264, rustic cabins with bath for 2-4 people, or room with bath, fireplace in house, solarium, library, sauna, organic gardens, good home-cooked meals, run by Umberto and Teresa Chico, Spanish and English spoken, helpful, friendly, rec; **D *Gran Hotel***, Torres 9-70 y Bolívar, T 831-934, clean, hot water, laundry service, good restaurant, beautiful patio, popular meeting place; **D *Hostal Paredes***, Luis Cordero y Mcal Lamar, refurbished colonial mansion, with bath, lovely; **B *Inca Real***, Torres 8-40 y Sucre, T 823-636, central, beautiful building, all rooms on courtyards, charming, friendly, cafetería; **D *Tomebamba***, Bolívar, between Torres and Tarqui, T 831-589, quiet, clean, hot water, laundry service, good breakfast; **D *Alli-Tiana***, Córdova y Padre Aguirre, T 831-844, clean, incl breakfast, hot water unreliable; **C *Catedral***, Padre Aguirre 8-17 y Sucre, T 823-204, clean, cheerful, spacious, modern, but not very warm, English-speaking manager, safe, laundry service, good food, coffee shop opens 0700; **E *Milán***, Pres Córdova 989 y Padre Aguirre, T 835-351, with bath, cheaper without, rooms with balconies, good view over market, some rooms spacious and airy, clean, some shabby, reliable for storing luggage, laundry facilities, often full, best to reserve; **E** *Pichincha*, Gral Torres y Bolívar, T 823-868, spacious, helpful, clean, friendly, laundry facilities, hot water, luggage stored; **E** *Las Américas*, Mariano Cueva 13-59, T 831-160/835-753, clean, TV, ask for room with windows, parking, restaurant; **E** *Residencial Niza*, Mariscal Lamar 41-51, T 823-284/838-005, water not too hot, clean, helpful; **E** *Residencial Siberia*, Luis Cordero 4-22, T 840-672, shared bath, restaurant, garage; **E** *Residencial París*, Grl Torres 10-48, T 842-656, private bath; **E** *Residencial Norte*, Mariano Cueva 11-63 y Sangurima, T 827-851, renovated, large rooms, clean, safe, hot showers, good, avoid noisy rooms overlooking street, not a nice area after dark; next door **F** *Residencial Colombia*, No 11-61, clean, basic, friendly, helpful; in same area nr Plaza Rotary and market, **E** *Hostal Madrid*, Sangurima 6-24, T 842-828, without bath, garage, and **F** *Pensión Taiwan*, Vargas Machuca, small room, noisy; **F** *Residencial Atenas*, Cordero 1189, bath, clean, comfortable, helpful, but not safe for left-luggage; **F** *Residencial Sánchez*, Muñoz 428 y Mariano Cueva, T 831-519, cheaper without bath, clean, set meal rec; **E** *Hostal Macondo*, Tarqui 11-64 y M Lamar, T 831-198, restored colonial house, single and double room, apartment available, mostly shared bathrooms, hot water, laundry, friendly, kitchen facilities, US run, ICIS discount, highly rec.

In the vicinity of the bus terminal are: **D** *Hurtado de Mendoza*, Sangurima y Huayna Cápac, T 831-909, with bath, good, restaurant, parking; **D** *Residencial España*, Sangurima 1-17, T 824-723, F 831-291, with bath and TV, E without bath, clean, hot water, also communal showers and toilets, slow restaurant, front upstairs rooms are best; **D** *El Galeón*, Sangurima 242, T 831-827, bargain for reduction, clean, large rooms, own bathroom, hot water, parking; **D** *Los Libertadores*, España 1-27 y Huayna Cápac, T 831-487, with bath, cheaper without TV; **D** *Hostal Amazonas*, Madrid y Aranjuez, T 839-153, new in 1994, with bath, TV, phone; **D** *Los Alamos*, Madrid y Ave España, T 825-644, E without bath, clean, will store luggage, opp noisy disco, room at the back quieter, TV; **D** *Los Helechos*, El Chorro y Gil Ramírez Dávalos, T 827-367, E without bath, TV, restaurant; **D** *Residencial Tito*, Sangurima 149, T 829-734, F 843-577, safe, clean, electric showers in some rooms, rooms are dark, restaurant very good value. **E** *Samay*, Tomás Ordóñez y Sangurima, T 831-112, with bath, cheaper without, clean, can be noisy, parking; **F** *Hostal Cumandá*, Huayna Cápac y Sangurima, cheaper without bath; **F** *Residencial Astoria*, El Chorro 222 y Gil Ramírez Dávalos, T 842-369, cheaper without bath; **F** *La Ramada*, Sangurima 551, friendly, good; **F** *Residencial La Alborada*, España 3928, hot showers.

Furnished two-bedroom apartments are available; *El Jardín*, Av Pumapungo y Viracochabamba, cooking facilities and parking, T 804-103, or write to Casilla 298. **C** *Apartamentos Otorongo*, Av 12 de Abril y Guayas, T 811-184, furnished flats for 4 with kitchenette, fridge, and cooking utensils.

Restaurants – Foreign Styles *El Jardín*, Presidente Córdova 7-23, lovely, good food (closed Sun-Mon), very expensive; *El Puente*, Roberto Crespo 1-20 y Av Solano, very good international food, bar, nice atmosphere; *Villa Rosa*, Gran Colombia 12-22 y Tarqui, very elegant, excellent food, international and own dishes; *Rancho Chileno*, España y Elia Liut, good steak and seafood, slow service, pricey; *Claro de Luna*, Benigno Malo 5-96 between Juan Jaramillo and Larga, T 821-067, restaurant and cocktail bar, open Mon-Sat, 1100-1500, 1800-2300, excellent food but be prepared to wait for it; *Tupahue*, near airport, Chilean, good food, expensive. **Italian** *Atún*, Gran Colombia 8-80, opp *Dorado*, pizzas and trout, popular; *Don Pizza*, Av Unidad Nacional y 12 de Abril, US-style; *La Napolitana*, Calle Solano nr Crespo, S of river, nice atmosphere, good food, inexpensive. **Criollo** *Los Capulíes* and *La Cantina y Fonda*, Córdova y Borrero, excellent Ecuadorean food, friendly, lovely setting, reasonable prices, Andean live music Thur, Fri, Sat 2030, different entrance for excellent bar; *El Inca*, Plaza Rotary, cheap, large portions, rec; *El Pedregal Azteca*, Gran Colombia 10-29 y Padre Aguirre, Mexican, also vegetarian, expensive, good, live music Mon, Wed, Fri, closed all day Sun and Mon lunchtime; *Las Tres Caravelas*, part of hotel *El Conquistador*, good value Ecuadorean food, Andean live music at weekends; *El Escorpión*, Malo y Largo, cheap, very good, rec; *Los Sauces*, Unidad Nacional y Gran Colombia, original dishes, good sauces, medium priced; *Las Redes*, Bolívar near *Hotel Tomebamba*, local dishes, seafood, reasonable prices; *Casa Grande*, San Joaquín-La Cruz Verde, local dishes, in picturesque San Joaquín district where flowers and vegetables are grown, T 839-992; *Columbus Steak House*, Gran Colombia y Unidad Nacional, *parrilladas* and salad bar; *D'Bernardo*, Antonio Borrero 9-68 y Gran Colombia, opp Post Office, T 829-967, breakfast, dinner, quiet music, coffee, open daily 0800-2300; *El Tequila*, Gran Colombia 20-59, good local food and more, good value and service; on same street *Doña Charita*, No 20-33, local and international, and *Chachi's*, No 4-70, cheap; *El Túnel*, Gral Torres 8-60, T 823-109, reasonably priced, quick service, romantic atmosphere, good, cheap lunch menu, *La Carreta*, Pres Córdova y Borrero, opp *El Jardín*. **Vegetarian** *El Paraíso*, Ordóñez 10-19, open for good breakfast and lunch; *Govinda*, on Sucre behind the new Cathedral; *El Manantial*, Gran Colombia between Calle 3 and 4; *Mañjaris*, Borrero 5-33 y

Jaramillo, Hindu, English spoken, helpful. **Seafood** *El Cangrejo*, Av 12 de Abril (just beyond El Vergel church, near hospital), for lunch; *El Acuario*, Huayna Cápac 138; *Café Pescera*, Calle Larga, opp *Hotel Crespo*; *El Calamar*, Pizarro 148 y España. **Oriental** *Chifa Pack How*, Presidente Córdova 772 y Cordero, not cheap, rec; *Chifa China*, Hermano Miguel 9-40, good food; *Chifa Asia*, across square from *Res Colombia*, medium price, large portions, rec; *La Gran Muralla*, Juan Jaramillo 8-38 y Luis Cordero, *Sol Oriental*, Gran Colombia y Vega. **Snackbars, Bakeries, etc** *Los Pibes*, Gran Colombia 776 y Cordero, good pizzas, moderately priced; *Che Pibe*, 12 de Abril y Astudillo, kebabs, corn on the cob, filling food and beer, open till late pm, also at Gran Colombia, 8-33 y Cordero, excellent pizzas, pleasant courtyard, friendly; *El Dorado*, cafetería at hotel, Colombia y Cordero, open daily, coffee, cake, also restaurant; *Pity's*, for sandwiches, hamburgers, rec, 2 branches, Av Remigio Crespo Toral y Alfonso Borrero, and Ordóñez Lazo y Circunvalación; *Pío Pío*, chicken restaurant at bus station, excellent chicken and chips; *Ubu Bar*, Remigio Crespo 3-11, sweet and savoury crêpes, bar, lively, informal. *Helados Honey*, Mariscal Lamar 4-21, clean, rec milkshakes; *Fuente del Sabor*, Plaza Rotary, good, cheap, gringo place; *Capuchino*, Bolívar y Aguirre, good hamburgers, milkshakes, real coffee and liqueur coffees; *Monte Bianco*, Bolívar y Ordóñez, near San Blas church, good cakes, ice cream, open Sun; *Café Austria*, Benigno Malo 5-99, good cakes, pies, sandwiches, coffee, fruit, ice cream, yoghurt, open Sun; *Café Fona Rosa*, Padre Aguirre 10-76 y Lamar, T 822-814, ice cream, *morocho*, cakes, sweets, cheap; *Heladería Holanda*, Benigno Malo 9-51, excellent tea and cakes, yoghurt for breakfast, ice cream, fruit salads, the best loos; *Mi Pan*, Pres Córdova 824 between Cordero y Malo (also Bolívar y Aguirre), opens 0730, excellent bread, cakes, tarts, doughnuts, poor service and breakfast; *Dulce Día*, Av España near Terminal Terrestre, good doughnuts; *El Suspiro*, Hermano Miguel 681, opp Tourist Office, sells wonderful, locally-made chocolates and milk-based sweets, sometimes serves coffee, open Mon-Sat 0900-1200, 1400-1830.

The Zona Rosa, at the junction of Av Unidad Nacional and Gran Colombia has a variety of *pizzerias*, *heladerias*, burger and sandwich bars, steak houses, bars, discos and is very popular with young people.

Bars *Picadilly Pub*, Borrero 7-46 y Pres Córdova, up market, clean, relaxing; *La Barra*, Pres Córdova, local brew; *La Bulería*, Larga 8-49, Spanish style; *The Stone*, Gran Colombia 21-130; *Cine Café Marilyn Monroe*, Gran Colombia 10-29, music videos and others. *Años 60*, Bolívar 5-69, bar and disco; *Bla-Bla*, Av 10 de Agosto, bar/disco; *Saxon*, Av Ordóñez Lazo y Unidad Nacional (Zona Rosa), bar/disco. *La Morada del Cantor*, Av Ordóñez Lazo, 500m from *Hotel La Laguna*, T 837-197, bar, restaurant and *peña* with Latin American music, excellent atmosphere.

Banks and Exchange Citibank, Gran Colombia 749 (charges commission, no cheques). **Filanbanco**, several branches, no commission, quick service. Visa agents. **Banco del Pacífico**, Benigno Malo 9-75, advance money on Mastercard, good rates for TCs. **Banco del Austro**, Sucre y Borrero, T 842-492, change cash and Citicorp TCs; **Banco La Previsora** (main branch only) Gran Colombia y Benigno Malo, T 831-444, give cash dolars on VISA; **Banco de Guayaquil**, Sucre entre Hermano Miguel y Borrero, also give cash on Visa and change TCs of all brands; **Banco del Pichincha**, Bolívar 9-74 y B Malo T 831-544, changes cash and TCs of all brands. **Granturs**, M Cueva y Gran Colombia, good rates, quick, usually open Sat pm. **Cambidex**, Luis Cordero 9-77, T 835-755, helpful, good rates. **Cambistral**, Sucre 664 y Cordero, T 822-213, changes European currencies, TCs as well as cash. **Cambiosur**, Borrero 8-20 y Sucre; good rates for cheques and cash, no commission, rec. **Cambiazuay**, Antonio Borrero 838 y Bolívar, T 823-536, cash and TCs; **Vaz Cambios**, Gran Colombia 7-98 y Cordero, T 833-434. If desperate on Sat try **Joyería Alexandra**, Cordero, nr main plaza. *Casas de Cambio* give the best rates but they are variable. No Peruvian currency available.

Colombian Consulate, Cordero 9-55. **British Honorary Consul** Sr Teodoro Jerves, Av España y Chapetones, T 831-996. **Alliance Française**, Tadeo Torres 1-92, open Mon-Fri, 0830-1230, 1430-1830.

Entertainment Discos at Hotels *Conquistador* and *Alli-Tiana*, and *Las Galaxias*, Núñez de Bonilla 239. *Fernández*, near *Capulíes* restaurant, good disco music, reasonable dance floor, couples. See also **Bars** above. There are 4 cinemas, the one opposite the Casa de la Cultura shows interesting films at 1430 and 2100. Films also at the Casa de la Cultura itself, evenings. *Teatro Cuenca*, P Aguirre 10-50, also shows films.

Health Clínica Santa Inés, Dr Jaime Moreno Aguilar speaks English, Toral, T 817-888. Farmacía Bótica Internacional, Gran Colombia 7-20 y Borrero, experienced staff, wide selection.

Language Courses *Centro de Estudios Interamericanos*, Gran Colombia 11-02 y Gral Torres, Edif Assoc de Empleados, Casilla 597, T 839-003, F 833-593, classes in Spanish and Quechua, rec, accommodation, *Hostal Macondo* attached. **Centro Abraham Lincoln**, Borrero y Vásquez, T 830-373, small Spanish language section. **Lenguas y Culturas**, Galápagos 2-37 y Guayas, T 817-552. *Nexus Lenguas y Culturas*, Calle Larga 6-13 y Hno Miguel, short-term basis family stays.

Laundry *La Química*, Borrero 734 y Córdova, same day service, expensive. *Lavamás*, Vásquez 407 y Machuca, T 842-005, expensive. Another *Lavamás*, is at Av España y Benalcázar, near Terminal Terrestre.

Post Office on corner of Calles Gran Colombia and Borrero, helpful. **Emetel** on Benigno Malo between Córdova and Sucre, deposit required, twice the price of the call, buy long distance *fichas* before contacting the international operator, no collect calls.

Shopping   Good souvenirs are carvings, leather, basketwork, painted wood, onyx, woven stuffs (cheapest in Ecuador), embroidered shirts, etc. Many craftware shops along Gran Colombia, in *El Dorado* hotel (good quality), and on Benigno Malo. *Arte Artesanías y Antigüedades* at Borrero y Córdova has some lovely textiles, jewellery and antiques. *El Tucan*, Borrero 7-35, Ecuadorean *artesania*, rec. *Bazaar Susanita*, Benigno Malo 1092, for good woollen sweaters at reasonable prices. Try *Torres* between Sucre y Córdova, or *Tarqui* between Córdova and the river for *polleras*, traditional Indian women's skirts. *Kinara*, Sucre 7-70, for women's clothing with modern designs on indigenous fabrics, crafts. *Sumaglla*, Larga 7-121 y L Cordero, sells handicrafts, antiques, jewellery and textiles. *Galería Claudio Maldonado*, Bolívar 7-75, unique precolumbian designs in silver and precious stones. *Centro Cultural Jorge Moscoso*, Pdte Córdova 6-14 y Hermano Miguel, T 822-114, weaving exhibitions, ethnographic museum, antiques and handicrafts. *Galería Pulla*, Jaramillo 6-90, famous painter, sculpture and jewellery. There are several good leather shops in the arcade off Bolívar between Benigno Malo and Luis Cordero, quality and price comparable with Cotacachi. *Artesa*, Presidente Córdova 6-96 y Borrero, with several branches around the city, sells modern Ecuadorean ceramics at good prices. *Joyería Turismo*, owned by Leonardo Crespo, at Gran Colombia 9-31, rec; he will let wholesale buyers tour his factory. *Unicornio*, L Cordero entre Gran Colombia y Lamar, good jewellery, ceramics and candelabra; *Bustos Estévez*, San Cristóbal 2-05, also for metal candelabra, inexpensive. Jewellery prices are reported as high: shop around. High quality Panama hats are made by *Homero Ortega P e Hijos*, Av Gil Ramírez Dávalos 3-86, T 823-429, F 834-045 (he will show you his factory opp bus station, open 0900-1200, 1500-1800 for visits), they export all over the world. Panama hats also at Tarqui 6-93 y Córdova (the best may not be on display, persist), on Benigno Malo and *Exportadora Cuenca*, Mariscal Lamar 3-80 (Jaime Ortega Ramírez and his wife, Tania, highly rec, will make to order, will not apply bleach if so asked). Check the quality very carefully as some tend to unravel and shops are unwilling to replace or refund. Interesting market behind new cathedral. A Centro Comercial has opened in the industrial park, with interesting shops. There is a well-stocked supermarket behind *Residencial España*; *Supermaxi*, Colombia y Américas. Camping Gas is available at several locations; camping equipment, *Bermeo Hnos*, Borrero 8-35 y Sucre, T 831-522, and *Créditos y Negocios*, Benigno Malo y Pdte Córdova, T 829-583.

Photography   *Foto Ortiz*, Gran Colombia y Aguirre, wide range of film, good same day developing. *Ecuacolor*, Cordero 515, good service. *Bazar La Victoria*, assorted films, especially ASA 200 and 400.

Mountain biking   *Explor Bike*, Juan Jaramillo 5100 y Hermano Miguel, T 833-362, rental, cultural trips.

Travel Agents   *Roo Tours*, Larga y Malo, English spoken, rec; *Santa Ana Tours*, Presidente Córdova y Borrero (T 832-340) run day tours, to Cajas US$24 pp, bus to Ingapirca and return, US$50; *Metropolitan Touring*, Gran Colombia y Cordero, T 842-545/834-057; *Expediciones Apullacta*, Gran Colombia 11-02 y General Torres, Edif Asoc de Empleados, planta baja, T 837-815; *Ecuadorean Tours*, Malo 7-47, very efficient; *Viajes Enmotur*, Borrero 7-51 y Sucre, excursions by bus to Ingapirca US$45, will buy US dollars incl Sat am; *Kleintours*, Gran Colombia, T 834-300, F 840-101; *Ecotrek*, Calle Larga 7-108 y Luis Cordero, T 842-531, F 835-387, contact Daniel Kuperman and Juan Diego Domínguez, new Kapauri Ecological Reserve due to open Jun 1995, excellent, experienced guides who offer great adventure travel, monthly departures. A guide is *José Rivera Baquero*, Pedro Carbo 1-48 y Guapondelig, extensive knowledge of Cuenca and surroundings. *Eduardo Quito*, T 823-018, F 834-202, has his own 4WD and offers special tours as a professionally-qualified guide, transports up to 10 people, speaks good English, highly rec. *Inti-Raymi*, Calle Sucre 6-87, very helpful, rec.

Tourist Office   Cetur, Hermano Miguel 686 y Córdova, open Mon-Fri only, 0800-1200, 1430-1600 (1800 in Jul-Sept). Maps of Cuenca. Map of the city also available from major hotels. Local maps are not very accurate. **Club Andinismo Sangay**, T 806-615/844-313, for Sunday treks, main one 2nd Sun of month, US$3; bus tickets from camping shop at Gran Colombia y L Cordero.

Immigration Policía Nacional de Migración, Benigno Malo y Larga, T 831-020.

Taxis US$0.70-1 for short journey; US$2 to airport or bus station; US$3 per hr; US$22/day. **Local buses** US$0.08.

Car Rental *Budget Renta-Car*, Huayna Cápac 1018 y Suárez, T 801-892/831-888, also at airport, T 804-063. *International*, Huayna Cápac y González Suárez, T 801-892.

Air Service The airport is 5 mins walk from the Terminal Terrestre. No ticket reservations at airport. Taxi to city US$1.80. Local buses run along the road outside. Quito (twice daily, US$30) and Guayaquil (US$28 Mon-Fri) with TAME, office at Gran Colombia 6-61 y Hermano Miguel, in a passage, T 827-609, and SAN, office on Bolívar 5-33 y M Cueva, T 823-403. Check whether your ticket needs to be reconfirmed. Saeta, Sucre 770 y Luis Cordero, T 831-548. Beware extra charges at check-in, arising from staff claiming incorrectly that your flight has not been confirmed. Arrive at least 1 hr before departure.

Trains The railway line to Cuenca was permanently closed in 1995.

Buses The Terminal Terrestre, well-organized and policed, is on Av España, a 20-min walk NW of the city centre, or take a minibus, US$0.10. To **Riobamba** 5½-6 hrs, US$4, scenic, sit on the left. **Ambato**, US$7, 7½ hrs (travel during day because scenery is magnificent, the road goes from 2,600m to under 200 and up again); **Baños**, from 12 de Noviembre, Turismo Baños; to/from **Quito**, 9½-10½ hrs, US$8 by minibus; Panamericana Internacional, Huayna Cápac y España, T 840-060, luxury coach service with Sucre Express, 8½ hrs, US$10. To **Loja**, 4 hrs with San Luis, US$4.50, new road, lovely scenery, sit on the left; **Machala**, 3-4 hrs, every 20 mins, US$3, sit on the left, wonderful scenery; to **Guayaquil**, 5 hrs, US$4 (road now entirely paved)—shop around for most comfortable bus. Turismo Oriental (4 daily, better buses) and Coop Sucúa (3 nightly, one at 1000) go to **Sucúa** (10 hrs) and **Macas** (13 hrs), US$6, day bus rec for spectacular scenery, left side best overall although right side good for last part with views of approach to tropical lowlands. To **Huaquillas**, 4-6 hrs, US$4.10, at 0530, arrives 1130, then, 1300, 2000, 2200, 2330—sit on left (the bus sometimes stops for 2 hrs in Machala, it is often better to avoid it, the connection is at a large roundabout well known to drivers for the local bus to Huaquillas). The evening bus arrives in Huaquillas at 0300, but passengers sleep on the bus till daylight. Be prepared for frequent police checks on the way. To **Azogues**, US$0.35, leaves when full. To **Saraguro**, US$2.65, 3½ hrs. Buses to **Gualaquiza**, 10 hrs. To **Alausí**, US$3.20, 4 hrs, leaves 1615.

Excursions Mirador Turi, 4 km out of town along Av Fray Vicente Solano, good panoramic view, interesting small church.

There are sulphur baths at Baños, with a domed, blue church in a delightful landscape, 5 km SW of Cuenca. Two separate warm baths, of which the lower one is better (US$0.80 for private bathroom, US$0.40 for swimming pool), the upper one also costs US$0.40, neither is very clean. Very crowded at weekends. At the baths, there are **F** *Residenciales Baños* and **F** *Rincón de Baños*, both with bath, on the main road, and the **B** *Hostería Durán*, Km 8 Vía Baños, T 892-485, F 892-488, with restaurant, pools (clean, US$1.60 for non-residents) and amenities (steam bath US$3), camping allowed. Buses marked Baños 0600-2330 from Cuenca (from Cueva y Lamar), US$0.15, taxis US$2.40, or walk 1½ hrs.

About 40 km NE of Cuenca in the beautiful Paute Valley is the **B** *Hostería Uzhupud*, deluxe, good rooms (those at back have best views), swimming pool, sports fields, small zoo, gardens, lots of orchids, used by the Cuenca wealthy, highly rec, Casilla 01-01-1268, Uzhupud, Paute, T 250-339, T Cuenca 806-521 (taxi from Cuenca US$7, bargain hard); also **G** *Residencial Cutilcay*.

E to **Gualaceo** (Sun market, picturesque, not catering to tourists), was 45 mins, now 2 hrs, by bus since the recently-paved road was washed out in early 1993, US$0.65 (leave from corner of Terminal Terrestre) in beautiful landscape, with charming plaza and fine new church with splendid modern glass. Woollen goods sold on main street near bus station, embroidered goods sold from private home above general store on main square. Hotels: **C** *Parador Turístico*, T 828-661 in Cuenca, away from village, chalets, rooms, modern, nice, swimming pool, good restaurant; **F** *Residencial Gualaceo*, T 823-454, Gran Colombia, clean, friendly, camping possible, and **G** *Español*, very basic. Good shoes made locally; splendid bargains. To **Chordeleg** by colectivo (plenty), or by local bus, US$0.15 from Gualaceo market square, every ½ hr (direct bus from Cuenca, 1 hr, US$0.40), a village famous for its crafts in wood, silver and gold filigree (very little available nowadays) and pottery, also panama hats, although it is very touristy and quality has fallen. Watch out for fake jewellery. Joyería Dorita and Joyería Puerto del Sol, on Juan B Cobos y Eloy Alfaro, have been recommended. There are some good shops selling beautiful ceramics. The church is interesting with some lovely modern stained glass. Try *Restaurante El Turista*. Chordeleg has a small Museo de Comunidad of fascinating local textiles, ceramics and straw work, some of which are on sale at reasonable prices. The walk between the two towns is a good uphill one from Gualaceo to Chordeleg, and a pleasant hour downhill in the other direction. With your own vehicle, you can drive back to Cuenca through San Juan and San Bartolomé (2 small mines after this village welcome visitors). N of Gualaceo is the town of Paute. Both are on the Río Palma and are two of several towns in this valley which were severely damaged by the flooding of April 1993.

Sígsig (S of Gualaceo, 83 km from Cuenca, bus 1½ hrs, US$0.65, *residencial*, G, **Restaurante Turista** only fair—hourly bus also from Chordeleg) has a Sun market and a few *sombrerías*; worth a visit. From Sígsig take another bus to Chigüinda, 0900, 2½ hrs, buy tickets night before (stay overnight with Sr Fausto, the teacher). A trail from Chigüinda goes to **Aguacate** (4-5 hrs walking), a village of 70 people. After about 3 hrs the trail divides by a small school on the left. Take the left fork. Sr Jorge Guillermo Vásquez has a *hospedaje*, G, very basic but friendly, coffee and popcorn for breakfast, horses can be hired for trekking to caves. There are shops, electricity at night only, and good *fiestas* at Christmas and New Year, and carnival in Feb (very popular). From Aguacate either walk 4 hrs or hire a horse to continue SE to Río Negro, a friendly village, from where daily buses or trucks at 1300 and 1600 go to Gualaquiza (1-2 hrs on dirt road, US$0.45—**see p 1037**). A road is being built between Sígsig and Gualaquiza, along a beautiful and unspoilt route; the trail can be hiked by the intrepid but is not yet passable by wheeled vehicles; take a minimum of luggage. Buses to Cuenca, 2200 are often full, try going to Loja 2200, 9 hrs, instead.

NW of Cuenca, **Cajas** is a 28,000 hectare national recreation area with over 230 lakes, entrance US$10, 2½ hr bus trip (one daily with Occidental, except Thur, between 0600 and 0630 from the San Sebastián church esquina Simón Bolívar y Coronel Talbot, bus back between 1400 and 1600, US$1.35, arrive early as the bus can get very full, hitchhiking difficult, little traffic. Taxi anything up to US$40, bargain hard.) The road through Cajas continues over the mountains to the towns of Quinuas (restaurant **Dos Chorreras**, try the trout from the local hatchery), Molleturo and on to Naranjal on the coast, paving in progress in 1994, avoid being taken past the park. There is an altar and pilgrim area near the entrance where a teenager saw "Our Lady of the Faith" in 1988. Ideal but strenuous walking, 3,500-4,400m altitude, and the climate is rough, deaths have occurred from exposure. Best time to visit is Aug-Jan, when you may expect clear days, strong winds, nighttime temperatures to -8°C and occasional mist; from Feb-July temperatures are higher but there is much more fog, rain and snow. It is best to arrive in the early morning since it can get very cloudy, wet and cool after about 1300. The páramo vegetation (chuquiragua, lupin) is beautiful and contains interesting wildlife (Andean gull, black frogs, humming birds, even condors); on a clear morning the views are superb, even to Chimborazo, some 300 km away. A rambling group welcomes visitors for Sun walks in Aug and Sept, look for posters in Cuenca. A new visitor's centre and cafeteria were under construction at Laguna Toreadora (3,810m) in July 1994 next to the old refuge, G pp, cold, with four bunks and cooking facilities. There are also two primitive shelters by the shore of same lake, 20 and 40 minutes walk from the refuge. Take food, fuel, candles, sleeping bags, strong sun cream and warm clothes. Local maps are not always exact, better to get the IGM maps in Quito. It is easy to get lost, signs (if any) are of little help. A trail around the lake takes 2-4 hrs depending on your acclimatization to altitude. On the opposite side of the lake from the refugio is Cerro San Luis (4,200m) which may be climbed in a day, excellent views. From the visitor's centre go anticlockwise around the lake, after crossing the outflow look for a sign "Al San Luis", follow yellow and black stakes to summit, beware of side trail to dangerous ledges. There are organized tours to the lakes from Cuenca, fishing possible, but these tend to be expensive, up to US$34. Alternatively, hire a private truck, US$16 with driver. A rec 2-day walk is to take the bus to about 15 km past the park *refugio* into the Río Miguir valley. Follow the footpath up the valley containing Laguna Sunincocha and a chain of subsidiary lakes. Continue to Cuicocha and down the Río Chico Soldados valley. Hitch back to Cuenca on the Soldados road; on Wed night or Thur am it is possible to catch traffic going to Cuenca market; no buses. Take a tent, stove etc, it can be cold, compass useful if cloudy (often), parts of the walk are over 4,000m. Jorge Moscoso, see under Cuenca **Shopping**, is knowledgeable and helpful about Cajas and says he has found an Inca road to the coast.

To the **Laguna de Zorocucho**: catch the bus at the Plaza Santo Domingo to Sayausí (US$0.10) and walk from there; about 2 hrs from Sayausí take a dirt road to the left and walk a further 20 minutes. There is good trout fishing in the lake and the river.

A beautiful hour-long bus trip on the Machala road from Cuenca takes one to the town of **Girón** (Hostal La **Chorrera**, with restaurant), whose beauty is spoiled only by a modern concrete church. After the battle on 27 February 1829 between the troops of Gran Colombia, led by Sucre, and those of Peru under Lamar, at nearby Portete de Tarqui, a treaty was signed in Girón. The building, Casa de los Tratados, is shown to visitors, as is the site of the Peruvians' capitulation (entry fee). Ask directions to El Chorro waterfall with cloudforest above. From Girón trucks take passengers up a winding road to the hamlets of **San Fernando** and

Chumblín. Friendly inhabitants will act as guides to three lakes high in the *páramo* where excellent trout-fishing is to be had. Take camping gear.

From Cuenca, the Pan-American Highway runs S to La Y, about 20 km away near the village of Cumbe. Here the road divides into two: one continuing the Pan-American to Loja (beautiful views on both sides) and the other, which is faster (or less slow), running through sugar cane fields to Pasaje and Machala. Girón (see above), **Santa Isabela** (**G** *Hostería al Durán*, basic, no water) and **Pasaje** (pop 27,000), the main towns along the route, have little to recommend them. Most buses travel NW to La Troncal and then S down the coast to Machala and Huaquillas for the Peruvian border (**see p 1023**).

The Pan-American Highway climbs S from La Y and rises eventually to the 3,500m Tinajillas pass. The road descends sharply into the warm upper Jubones valley past cane fields and rises again after Río León (Km 95) to the small town of **Oña** (Km 105, pop 3,244, one hotel on the main square and several places to eat including *San Luis*, rec). From there it weaves and climbs through highland *páramo* pastures and then descends towards Saraguro (Km 144). Here the Indians, the most S Andean group in Ecuador, dress all in black. They wear very broad flat-brimmed hard felt hats: the men are notable for their black shorts (sometimes covered by a whitish kind of divided apron) and a particular kind of double bag, the *alforja*, and the women for their pleated black skirts, necklaces of coloured beads and silver *topos*, ornate pins fastening their shawls. Many of them take cattle across the mountains E to the tropical pastures above the Amazonian jungle.

The road runs through **Saraguro** (picturesque Sun Indian market, pop 19,883), after which there are two passes, at Km 150 and 156.5. Two further passes come after the village of San Lucas (Km 164), the highest of the two at Km 185, before a long descent towards Loja. The road between Cuenca and Loja is now paved and is one of the most beautiful and breathtaking in Ecuador. Bus to Cuenca with Coop Viajeros, 4 daily, US$2.65, 4½ hrs; to Loja, US$1.80, 1½ hrs.

In Saraguro, two pensions, **F** *Residencial Armijos*, Calle Antonio Castro, friendly, quiet, good; **F** *Pensión Saraguro*, Calle Loja No 03-2 y Antonio Castro, nice courtyard, quiet, hot water, laundry facilities. Restaurants: *Salón Cristal*, Azuay y Castro, lunch only; *Gruta Azul*, on main square, both good; cheap food in the market. It is a very cold town.

Loja (2,100m, pop 94,305), a friendly and pleasant city, lies near the Oriente. The city was founded on its present site in 1548, having been moved from La Toma, and was rebuilt twice after earthquakes, last in the 1880s. Its first site, in the hotter, lower valley of Catamayo, had too high an incidence of malaria (documentation of this can be found in the Banco Central Museum, see below). The city has been a traditional gateway between the highlands and southern Amazonia. Alluvial gold deposits at Zamora, on the E Andean slopes, have enriched colonial settlers and modern-day prospectors. Tropical forest products such as chinchona (the natural base for quinine) first entered European pharmacopia through Loja. There are crude but original paintings on the patio walls of many of the old houses. There are two universities, with a well-known law school. Some of the Universidad Nacional buildings have good murals. The **cathedral** and **Santo Domingo** church, Bolívar y Rocafuerte, have painted interiors. **El Valle** church, on the S edge of the city is a colonial church with a lovely interior. The **Banco Central museum** on the main square, 0900-1500, has exhibits of local folklore and history; the **Casa de la Cultura**, Bolívar y Imbabura, sponsors cultural events. The town, encircled by hills and pleasant countryside, can be reached by air from Quito or Guayaquil to Catamayo (known locally as La Toma), and then 35 km by paved road. Loja's **Mercado Modelo**, 10 de Agosto y 18 de Noviembre, rebuilt in 1991, is worth a visit, the cleanest and most efficient market in all Ecuador. There is a market on Sat, Sun and Mon, attended by many Saraguro Indians. Souvenir and craft shops on 10 de Agosto between Iberoamérica and 18 de Noviembre. The *fiesta* de la

Virgen del Cisne (of the swan) is held Aug 16-20, and the image of the Virgin remains in Loja until Nov 1; it is very difficult to find a room and all prices rise during this period.

Hotels C *Grand Hotel Loja*, Iberoamérica (this main avenue by the river is also known as Av Manuel Agustín Aguirre) y Rocafuerte, T 575-200, F 575-202, bath, carpet, TV, phone;

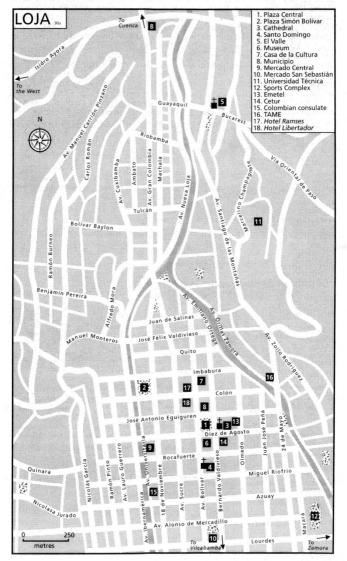

LOJA 90a

To Cuenca B

To the West

Isidro Ayora

Guayaquil

Bucarest

1. Plaza Central
2. Plaza Simón Bolívar
3. Cathedral
4. Santo Domingo
5. El Valle
6. Museum
7. Casa de la Cultura
8. Municipio
9. Mercado Central
10. Mercado San Sebastián
11. Universidad Técnica
12. Sports Complex
13. Emetel
14. Cetur
15. Colombian consulate
16. TAME
17. *Hotel Ramses*
18. *Hotel Libertador*

Av Manuel Carrión Pinzano

Carlos Román

Riobamba

Ambato

Machala

Av Cuxibamba

Av Gran Colombia

Av Nueva Loja

Marcelino Champagnat

Vía Oriental de Paso

Tulcán

Bolívar Baylon

Ramón Burneo

Alfredo Mora

Av Santiago de las Montañas

Benjamín Pereira

Manuel Monteros

Juan de Salinas

Av Emiliano Ortega

Av Orillas Zamora

Av Zoilo Rodríguez

José Félix Valdivieso

Quito

Imbabura

Colón

José Antonio Eguiguren

Diez de Agosto

Juan José Peña

24 de Mayo

Quinara

Nicolás García

Ramón Pinto

Av Lauro Guerrero

Rocafuerte

Miguel Riofrío

Av Universitaria

Azuay

Nicolasa Jurado

Av Iberoamérica

18 de Noviembre

Av Sucre

Av Bolívar

Bernardo Valdivieso

Olmedo

Macará

Av Alonso de Mercadillo

Lourdes

To Vilcabamba

To Zamora

0   250
metres

N

C *Hostal Aguilera Internacional*, Sucre 44 y Emiliano Ortega, T 563-189, F 572-988, with bath, good; **D** *Ramsés*, Colón 14-31 y Bolívar, T 960-868/961-402, bath, phone, TV, good restaurant; opp is **C** *Libertador*, Colón 14-30 y Bolívar, T 570-344, F 572-119, Casilla 412, bath, TV, suites available, noisy, good restaurant *La Castellana*, parking; **D** *Vilcabamba*, Iberoamérica y Pasaje la FEUE, T 737-399 F 561-483, on river/sewer, clean; **D** *Hostal La Riviera*, Universitaria y 10 de Agosto, T 572-863, carpet, TV, phone, good; *Hostal Quinara*, opposite is also good, T 960-785; **E** *Metropolitano*, 18 de Noviembre 6-41 y Colón, T 570-007, with bath and TV, hot water, clean; **E** *Chandelier*, Imbabura 1474 y Sucre, T 563-061, cheaper without bath, parking; **E** *Hostal Inca*, Av Universitaria y 10 de Agosto, T 562-478, bath, TV; **E** *Hostal Orillas del Zamora*, 10 de Agosto y Sucre, with bath; **E** *Saraguro Internacional*, Universitaria 724 y 10 de Agosto, T 570-552, hot water, TV, parking, restaurant open Mon-Fri; **E** *Los Ejecutivos*, Universitaria 1076, T 560-004, good, also "video club"; **F** *Caribe*, Rocafuerte 1552 y 18 de Noviembre, T 572-902, shared bath, hot water; **F** *Hostal San Luis*, Sucre 4-56 e Imbabura, T 570-370, cheaper without bath, hot water, parking; **F** *Cuxibamba*, 10 de Agosto y Sucre, basic, cheaper without bath; **F** *Loja*, Rocafuerte 15-27, T 570-241, shared bath, hot water, nicely renovated, friendly; **F** *Colonial*, Sucre 8-64, shared bath, basic; **F** *Alborada*, Sucre 1279 y Lourdes, with shower, clean; **F** *Londres*, Sucre 741 y 10 de Agosto, clean, friendly, nice big rooms, hot water; **E** *Miraflores*, 10 de Agosto 1656, rooms without bath **F** are just cubicles, rooms with bath have one solid wall, stores luggage, *chifa* next door serves vegetarian if you ask; **E** *París*, 10 de Agosto 16-37, T 961-639, clean with electric hot showers, bargain for good rate, near food market, rec; **E** *Acapulco*, Sucre 749 y 10 de Agosto, T 570-651, clean, hot water, private bath, safe for leaving luggage, 1st floor rooms quieter in am; **F** *Hostal Carrión*, Colón 1630 y 18 de Noviembre, T 561-127, basic, hot water on request, safe; **G** *Primavera*, Colón 1644, clean, cold shower. Basic *residenciales* in G range for instance on Rocafuerte; **G** *San Andrés*, Miguel Riofrío, friendly, more or less clean, very cheap. **Youth Hostel**, Av Miguel Riofrío 1661 y 18 de Noviembre, T 560-895.

Restaurants *José Antonio*, Imbabura 15-30 between Sucre y 18 de Noviembre, excellent *cebiche* and seafood, enthusiastic chef, highly rec; *La Cascada*, Sucre y Lourdes, very good food; *Palace*, Eguiguren y Sucre, local food; *Trece*, Universitaria y Colón, also Eguiguren 1468, good. Other *criollo* places are *Cordillera*, 10 de Agosto 1419; *La Choza*, Sucre y Riofrío; *México*, Eguiguren 1569 y Sucre, good set meals or a la carte, generous portions, breakfast, rec; *El Rincón de Francia*, Bolívar y Riofrío, good food; *La Tullpa*, 18 de Noviembre Imbabura, cheap, good *churrasco*; *Parrillada Uruguaya*, Iberoamérica y Azuy, opens 1700, good grilled meat, owner helpful; *Delfín Dorado*, Imbabura 1125 (approx), excellent fish dishes and some steaks, friendly, highly rec; *La Casona*, 18 de Noviembre near Imbabura (the better of 2 branches), good. Chicken at *Rico Pico*, 18 de Noviembre y Colón. Seafood at *Pescadería Pacífica*, Bolívar 931; *Marisquería Las Castañuelas*, 10 de Agosto 1167, clean, set meal US$1, and *Doscientas Millas*, Bolívar y Eguiguren (evenings only). In El Valle area the *Colonial* and *La Lolita* rec, try *cuy*. Chinese at *Chifa El Arbol de Oro*, Eguiguren y 18 de Noviembre, good. Good *Unicornio* piano bar on main square. Loja has many excellent bakeries. Good snacks, pastries and yoghurt at *Pastelería Persa* (2 locations—one at Rocafuerte 14-58). *Helados de Paila*, Av Iberoamérica, nr market, good icecream and snacks; *Topoli*, Riofrío y Bolívar, best yoghurt in town, good for breakfast; *Top Cream Ice Cream*, Iberoamérica y Colón, best ice cream in town.

Banks and Exchange Filanbanco in main plaza, changes Amex TCs. **Banco de Loja**, Rocafuerte y Bolívar, and **Banco del Azuay**, on main plaza, also change both cash and TCs. No *casas de cambio*; good rate for US$ in gift shop in front of *Hotel Acapulco*; *Loayza*, Riofrío 1450, helpful; *Librería Reina del Cisne*, Bolívar y Riofrío; *Frankhitur*, Centro Commercial Episcopal, Valdiviezo y 10 de Agosto, T 573-378; *Joyería San Pablo*, Sucre 7-26 y 10 de Agosto, T 560-715, open Sat, good rates. (El Universo agent changes money at weekends at poor rate).

Consulates Colombia 18 de Noviembre y Azuay, T 960-573; Peru Lazo y Rodríguez, T 961-668.

Post Office Colón y Sucre; no good for sending parcels. **Emetel** on Eguiguren y Olmedo.

Shopping *Cer-Art Ceramics*, precolumbian designs on mostly high-gloss ceramics, produced at the Universidad Técnica with workshop and retail shop. Mercado in Centro, good cheap supplies. The Universidad Técnica sells good cheese and butter.

Tourist Office Cetur, Valdiviezo 08-22 y 10 de Agosto, T 572-964, F 570-485, open Mon-Fri, 0800-1300, 1500-1800. *Loja tradición, cultura y turismo*, is a useful guidebook. *El Siglo* and *Crónica* give news of events.

Immigration Venezuela y Argentina, T 960-500.

Flights TAME, Zamora y 24 de Mayo, 0830-1600, reserve seat in Cuenca if you want to leave from Loja the next day, or get an open ticket at the airport and push and shout to get on the plane. To Quito Mon, Wed, Fri direct (at 0720), Tues, Thur, Sat via Guayaquil (at 0800), none Sun. Aerogal, office Sucre y Colón, T 578-100/3 flies direct to Quito at 0830 Tues, Thur, Sat, US$33 from Quito at 0645. Shared taxis to La Toma airport, US$3; or stay in Catamayo – see below.

Buses All buses leave from the new terminal at Av Gran Colombia e Isidro Ayora, buses every 2 mins to/from centre, 10 min journey; left luggage, information desk, shops, pay US$0.10 terminal tax at information booth by main entrance. To **Cuenca**, 6 hrs, 7 a day, US$4.50 with Trans Viajeros (18 de Noviembre y Quito), sit on the left; **Machala**, 10 a day, 7 hrs, US$3. Cooperativa Loja (10 de Agosto y Guerrero) runs many buses in all directions, including **Quito**, 4 a day, US$6.50 (Trans Santa to Quito, 12 hrs, US$6.50), and **Guayaquil**, 5 a day, 8 hrs, US$5.85; buses to **Huaquillas** at 0930, 2030 and 2230; **Macará**, 4 daily, 6 hrs, US$3.50, bad, dusty road. To **Saraguro**, 6 daily, 1½ hrs. To **Zamora**, 2½ hrs, with Coop Nambija, travel early morning or late pm to avoid road-clearing work. Panamericana Internacional, office at *Grand Hotel Loja*, luxury coach service to Quito (US$15) and Guayaquil (US$10).

Excursions The entrance to the upper premontane section of **Podocarpus National Park**, spectacular walking country, lush tropical cloud forest and excellent bird-watching, is about 15 km S of Loja on the Vilcabamba road (take a raincoat and warm clothing). Permits (US$10) and an adequate map from Inefan, Calle Azuay entre Valdivieso y Olmedo (T 571-534), Loja, office open 0800, or at the entrance. Park administration being rebuilt in 1994. Refuge at the entrance opened 1995, comfortable, make bookings at office in Loja before going; camping is possible but can be very wet. Park guardian Miguel Angel is very knowledgeable and helpful. Additional information from conservation groups: Arco Iris, Olmedo y Riofrío, T 572-926, PO Box 860, Loja, or contact member Rodrigo Tapiz, T 560-895; Fundación Ecológica Podocarpus, Sucre 8-47 y 10 de Agosto, PO Box 11-01-436, Loja. Take a Vilcabamba bus, park entrance is 20 mins from Loja, then 9 km hike uphill to guard station. Direct transport by taxi only, US$10 round trip, can arrange later pick up from guard station. The lower subtropical section of Podocarpus Park can also be reached from Zamora (**see p 1036**). You may not have to pay all of the US$20 entry fee here if you have already paid for the highland section by Loja. The scenic road to Zamora (65 km) was in very poor condition due to construction and landslides in 1994 (open to trafic 1800-0600 only) but should be much improved when the work is completed. You can carry on from there into the Oriente.

Parque Educacional Ambiental y Recreacional de Argelia is superb, trails through forest to the *páramo*, ½ km before police checkpoint on road S to Vilcabamba, take city-bus marked Argelia, open 0830-1700 except Tues and Wed. Across the road and 100m S is the **Jardín Botánico Reynaldo Espinosa**, open Mon-Fri 0800-1700, nicely laid out, has several chinchona trees.

Vilcabamba (1,520m, pop 3,894) is a 1½ hr bus ride. Sur Oriente hourly from Loja bus terminal (US$0.90). People here were reputed to live to over 100 as often as not; recent research has somewhat eroded this belief, but it's still a very pleasant and healthy valley, wonderful for a few days relaxation, with an agreeable climate, 17°C min, 26°C max. The Vilcagua factory here produces cartons of drinking water, visits can be arranged. There are many good walks in the Río Yambala valley (maps available at *Cabañas Río Yambala*), and on the Mandango mountain trail (exposed and slippery in parts, directions obtainable at *Madre Tierra*). There is a Tourist Office on the main square next to Emetel, friendly and helpful, good information and maps. No banks or cambios, but hotels and shops will change at a poor rate. Once an isolated village, Vilcabamba has become increasingly popular with foreign backpackers, a "must" along the gringo trail from Ecuador to Peru or vice versa. The local economy has benefitted, but there have also been negative effects, responsible tourism is especially important here.

Accommodation Cheaper hotels are often full. **C** *Hostería Vilcabamba*, T 673-131, F 673-167, excellent, comfortable, pool, may be used by non-residents for US$0.50, jacuzzi, bar, good Ecuadorean restaurant, massage, fitness instruction, language school, US$3/hr min 4 hrs daily, classes in lounge area or poolside, run by Cortez family, who also run the **D** *Parador Turístico*, good rooms, with restaurant and bar, T 673-122, rec; **E** cabin for 4 people owned by Orlando and Alicia Falco, 10 mins walk from town, ask at *Primavera* shop, kitchen, relaxing, rec, Sr Falco also runs excellent nature tours, US$15 pp/day, speaks English; *Hostal Mandango*, behind bus terminal, family run, **E** with bath **F** without, inexpensive restaurant, good value;

F *Hotel Valle Sagrado*, proprietor Abel Espinoza, on main plaza, shared bath, cold water, basic, friendly, noisy, good vegetarian restaurant, will store luggage, laundry facilities; there are 4 restaurants on the plaza, including *Cabañita* and an unnamed, good vegetarian place. **F** *Sra Lydia Toledo*, Bolívar esq Clodoveo, 1 block from plaza, shared bath, hot water, family run, friendly; **F** *Hostal Villa Alfinsa*, Sucre esq Clodoveo, shared bath, cold water, parking, friendly. **C** *Madre Tierra*, T 673-123, some cabins dark and rather damp, shared bath, with breakfast and dinner, reductions for a long stay, excellent food (home made, vegetarian to order, non-residents welcome for meals but must reserve a day in advance), horses to rent (about US$15 per day for 2 horses, food and gear), a language school, small swimming pool, videos every night, massage, steam baths, beautiful setting about 2 km before village, English and French spoken, rec, very popular, often full; the Mendoza family make travellers very welcome, they have details of trails for walking. Write in advance to Jaime Mendoza, PO Box 354, Loja, Ecuador, T 673-123. At the upper end of the Vilcabamba Valley, 4 km from the village, are the highly rec *Cabañas Río Yambala*, owned by Charlie and Sarah, cabins sleep 3 to 6, or room, beautiful views in all directions, kitchen facilities if required, shopping done for you, vegetarian restaurant open all day, hot showers, laundry service, clean, helpful and very friendly, do not leave belongings on balcony or porch, horses for rent with or without guide, trekking arranged in the Podocarpus National Park with tents, sleeping bags, food etc provided, campsite on own nature reserve, *Las Palmas*, on edge of Park, take taxi or pick-up, US$4, try Miguel Carpio who lives 1/2 block from Tourist Office, for reservations call Comercial Karmita T 637-186.

Tours New Zealander, Gavin Moore, runs *Gavino Tour*, offering 3-day trips to the cloud forest, including horse trek to and from his *cabaña* overlooking Vilcabamba and one day trekking in the forest (US$75 pp, incl food, sleeping bags, basic lodging etc, highly rec); he lives a couple of km outside the town, contact him through the tourist office or F 571-025, or Calle 1000, Loja. His wife, Ana María, does aromatherapy and massage (US$6-10). Horses can be hired from Roger Toledo, opp Post Office, he will organize 3-day trips into the mountains; also Wilson Carpio and Ernesto Avila, cost varies from US$4-8 per 1/2 day.

There are two routes from Loja to Machala, one of which goes through Piñas and is rather bumpy with hairpin bends but has the better views, the other is paved and generally quicker (depending on the driver). Machala can be avoided, however, if you take a Machala bus to the Huaquillas crossroads, called La Avanzada, and there catch another one straight to Huaquillas, the border town.

An alternative, more scenic route to Peru is, however, available from Loja via Macará. Leaving Loja on the main paved highway going W, the airport at **La Toma** (altitude 1200m, pleasant climate) is reached after 35 km. (If flying to or from La Toma, stay at **Catamayo**, nearby, **D** *Hostería Bella Vista*, T 962-450, tropical gardens, pool; **G** *Hotel El Turista*, Av Isidro Ayora, shared bath, basic, friendly, **Restaurant China** opp, good, cheap; **F** *Hotel San Marcos*, on plaza; taxi to airport US$1, or 20 mins walk.) On arrival at La Toma airport by air, shared taxis will be waiting to take you to Loja, 45 mins, US$3, they fill up quickly so choose a driver, give him your luggage claim ticket and he will collect your checked luggage. Bus to Loja US$0.80. At La Toma (where you can catch the Loja-Macará bus), the Pan-American Highway divides into two branches, one, the faster, via Velacruz and Catacocha with 4 passport checks (Loja-Catacocha paved, Catacocha- Macará good gravel) and the other going to Macará via Cariamanga. This second route heads from Catamayo S to **Gonzanamá**, a pleasant little town with **F** *Residencial Jiménez* (bath, cold shower). 27.5 km from Gonzanamá is Cariamanga, from where the road is unpaved but very scenic. About 10 km before Cariamanga the road starts to climb and continues to do so on rough gravel to the pass 4 km beyond Colasaca. Then follows a steep, long, rough descent, with a loss of about 2,000m altitude to Utuana (not rec for cyclists in the other direction). *Sozoranga*, 75 km from Gonzanamá, has one hotel (**G**, shared cold shower, swallows nest on the balcony); the road continues 36 km to Macará.

Macará (pop 14,296; altitude 600m), a dusty town on the border, is in a rice-growing area, has road connections to Sullana near the Peruvian coast. Several roads have been washed away by heavy rains and in 1994 were frequent water supply cuts in the afternoons.

Hotels E *Paradero Turístico*, best, pool, restaurant may not be open, not far from centre; **F** *Guayaquil*, with shower, not rec, fleas, large cell-like rooms; *Hostería Vilcabamba*, swimming pool, sauna, friendly owners; **F** *Residencial Paraíso*, without bath, Veintimilla 553, clean, laundry facilities; **F** *Amazonas*, Rengel 418, friendly, clean, basic. **Restaurants** *Colonial Macará*, Rengel y Bolívar (helpful, but food not too good), and *Café Macará*, opposite; *Heladería Cream*, Veintimilla y Sucre, great ice cream; *Soda Bar Manolo* for breakfast.

The bank at Macará does not change money, so change sucres on the street to give you enough new soles to last you until you reach Sullana (Peru). You can change money at the market in the town centre, fair rates for US$, poor rates for new soles. A Peruvian tourist card can be obtained from the Peruvian Hon Consul in Macará, if he is available, or at the border if not already obtained in Quito or Guayaquil. There is a 2$\frac{1}{2}$ km walk or taxi ride to the international bridge over the Río Macará (US$1, up to US$2 in a pick-up from Macará market—less if more passengers; coming from Peru, drivers will overcharge, particularly if you are too tired to walk). Border crossing formalities (0800-1800) last about 30 mins. A colectivo (US$3, cheaper in the back than up front, 3-4 hrs) is then taken from La Tina on the Peruvian side to Sullana from where it is $\frac{1}{2}$ hr to Piura, a better place to spend the night. No hotels and only food stalls in La Tina. Buses leave Sullana from Av Buenos Aires in early am; if none running, there are plenty of *camionetas* to the border. There are many military checkpoints along the route but these are not usually a problem. Coop Loja buses every 2 hrs from 0600-1500 from Macará to Loja (6 to 8 hrs, US$3.50), Unión Cariamanga at 0400 and 1000; the whole journey can be done in a day if you arrive at the border at noon. The Loja-border journey takes only 3$\frac{1}{2}$ hrs by car. Fuel in Macará is only obtainable out of barrels at twice the official price (this is cheaper than in Peru). There is less likelihood of bureaucratic hassle or of drug-pushing at Macará than at Huaquillas.

GUAYAQUIL (5)

Guayaquil Ecuador's largest city (pop officially 1,508,000, more like 2,400,000) and the country's chief seaport, industrial and commercial centre lies on the W bank of the Guayas river some 56 km from its outflow into the Gulf of Guayaquil. The Puerto Marítimo, opened in 1979, handles about 90% of the country's imports and 50% of its exports. It is a constant bone of contention between the 'costeños' and the 'serranos' that Guayaquil is not given better recognition of its economic importance in the form of more central government aid. It was founded in 1537 by Francisco Orellana. The climate from May to December is dry with often overcast days but pleasantly cool nights, whereas the hot rainy season from January to April can be oppressively humid. Chimborazo can occasionally be glimpsed.

Because of the huge influx of people caused by rural migration and population explosion, the city's services have been stretched beyond the limit. Water supply and rubbish collection have improved (1994-95), but the installation of new water pipes and unsuccessful traffic schemes mean chaos for drivers. It is often quicker to walk short distances in the centre, rather than take a bus or taxi (but don't walk after dark). In spite of municipal problems, the Guayaquileños are certainly more lively, colourful and open than their Quito counterparts.

A wide, tree-lined waterfront avenue, the Malecón, runs alongside the Guayas river from the exclusive **Club de la Unión**, by the Moorish clock tower, past the imposing **Palacio Municipal** and **Government Palace** and the old Yacht Club to **Las Peñas**. Half way along, the Boulevard 9 de Octubre, the city's main street, starts in front of La Rotonda, a statue to mark the famous yet mysterious meeting between Simón Bolívar and San Martín in 1822. There are 11 piers running along the Malecón and from Muelle 5, near Las Peñas. The ferries sail across the river to the train station at Durán (US$0.06, every 15 mins from 0600). The old district of Las Peñas is a last picturesque, if ramshackle and small, vestige of colonial Guayaquil with its wooden houses and narrow cobbled street (Numa Pompilio Llona). The entrance is guarded by two cannon pointing riverward, a reminder of the days when pirates sailed up the Guayas to attack the city. Now occupied mostly by artists, there is a large open-air exhibition of paintings and sculpture held here every year in July. It makes a pleasant walk, but this is a poor area and mugging is getting more common at night. It is not recommended to walk up the adjacent streets of the Cerro Santa Ana that overlook Las Peñas.

The main square half way up 9 Octubre is the **Plaza Centenario** with a towering monument to the liberation of the city erected in 1920. The pleasant, shady

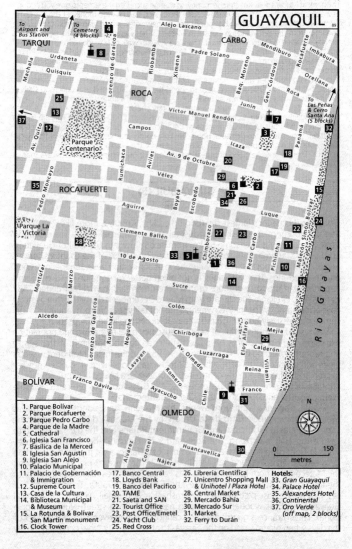

1. Parque Bolívar
2. Parque Rocafuerte
3. Parque Pedro Carbo
4. Parque de la Madre
5. Cathedral
6. Iglesia San Francisco
7. Basílica de la Merced
8. Iglesia San Agustín
9. Iglesia San Alejo
10. Palacio Municipal
11. Palacio de Gobernación & Immigration
12. Supreme Court
13. Casa de la Cultura
14. Biblioteca Municipal & Museum
15. La Rotunda & Bolívar San Martín monument
16. Clock Tower

17. Banco Central
18. Lloyds Bank
19. Banco del Pacífico
20. TAME
21. Saeta and SAN
22. Tourist Office
23. Post Office/Emetel
24. Yacht Club
25. Red Cross
26. Librería Científica
27. Unicentro Shopping Mall & Unihotel / Plaza Hotel
28. Central Market
29. Mercado Bahía
30. Mercado Sur
31. Market
32. Ferry to Durán

Hotels:
33. Gran Guayaquil
34. Palace Hotel
35. Alexanders Hotel
36. Continental
37. Oro Verde (off map, 2 blocks)

Parque Bolívar in front of the **Cathedral** is filled with tame iguanas who scuttle out of the trees for scraps. There are several noteworthy churches, **San Francisco** with its restored colonial interior off 9 de Octubre and P Carbo; the beautiful **La Merced**; **Santo Domingo**, the city's first church built in 1548 just by Las Peñas; the rather plain Cathedral, which has some fine stained glass, Chimborazo between Ballén and 10 de Agosto. At the N end of the centre, below Cerro El Carmen the huge, spreading **Cemetery** with its dazzling, high-rise tombs and the ostentatious mausolea of the rich is worth a visit. A flower market over the road sells the best selection of blooms in the city. Best to go on a Sunday when there are plenty of people about. There are numerous sports clubs for golf, tennis, swimming, sailing and the horse race track of **El Buijo** set in delightful surroundings some 5 km outside the city. There are 2 football stadiums and the enclosed Coliseo Cerrado for boxing, basketball and other entertainments. The **Centro Cívico**, heading S, finally finished after 25 years in the making, provides an excellent theatre/concert facility and is home to the Guayaquil Symphony Orchestra which gives free concerts throughout the year. The new **Teatro Centro de Arte** on the road out to the coast is another first class theatre complex with a wide variety of presentations. The city is also well provided with museums, art galleries and cinemas, details in *El Universo*. Colourful markets are at the S end of the Malecón or along 6 de Marzo between 10 de Agosto and Ballén. The Mercado Sur, next to Club de la Unión, built by Eiffel (1905-07), is not safe to enter. **Barrio Centenario** to the S of the centre is the original residential sector, now a peaceful, tree-shaded haven. Newer residential areas are Urdesa, NW of the centre, in between two branches of the Estero Salado (about 15 mins from downtown, traffic permitting).

Near the international airport and bus terminal, which are conveniently close to each other, are the districts of La Garzota, Sauces and Alborada. Cleaner, less congested and safer than the centre, but with all services, entertainment and shops, these areas are 12 mins by taxi from downtown, 5 mins from the airport and Terminal Terrestre. Two long bridges span the Babahoyo and Daule rivers, as they merge into the Guayas. The road across the bridges leads to Durán and the rail terminal on the E bank. This is a vital link for the city since from Durán main highways continue to Quito, Milagro, Riobamba, Cuenca and Machala.

Museums The **Museo Municipal** is housed in the Biblioteca Municipal, at Sucre with Pedro Carbo (near the *Hotel Continental*) where there are paintings, gold and archaeological collections, a section on the history of Guayaquil and also a good newspaper library. The museum (which contains Shuar heads) is open Wed-Fri 0900-1600; Sat 1000-1500, Sun 1000-1300. Entrance US$0.15 for Ecuadoreans and US$0.40 for foreigners (free on Sat, but passport must be left at desk). The Central Bank's small **anthropological museum** is at Anteparra 900 y 9 de Octubre; it was closed for reconstruction until May 1995. The Pinacoteca Manuel Rendoy Seminario is on the first floor of the same building. **Museo del Banco del Pacífico** (address under **Exchange**), beautiful small museum mainly of archaeological exhibits, open Tues-Fri 1100-1800, Sat-Sun 1100-1300. There is an impressive collection of prehistoric gold items at the museum of the **Casa de la Cultura**, together with an archaeological museum, 9 de Octubre 1200 and Moncayo, open Tues-Fri 1000-1700. **Religious Art Museum Nahim Isaias Barquet**, Pichincha y Ballén, Tues-Fri 0900-1700, Sat 1000-1300. There is a pinacoteca (art gallery) on the ground and first floors of the same building. There is a **small zoo**, open Sun, at the Colegio Nacional.

Warnings Guayaquil is becoming increasingly insecure, especially around hotel or bank entrances, attackers usually working in pairs. The Malecón in early morning and from dusk onwards is bad for snatch thieves. Also near toilets in Terminal Terrestre bus station where thieves work in pairs. Street robbery also occurs in Durán. Do not walk anywhere with valuables and take taxis at night. Cholera, dengue and rabies are present.

Local Holidays 9 and 12 October. 24 and 25 July, Bolívar's birthday, and Foundation of the City; Carnival is in the days before Lent: watch out for malicious throwing of water balloons, mud, ink, paint etc; women are prime targets. In contrast New Year's Eve is lots of fun, there is a large exhibition of tableaux, featuring *Años Viejos*, along the Malecón, children begging for alms for their life-size *viejos*, families with cars taking their *viejos* for rides through the centre of town, and a vast conflagration at midnight when all these figures are set on fire and explode.

Hotels Hotel prices, which are higher than in Quito, are set by the Tourist Board, which stipulates their being posted inside hotels. It is common practice to have dual rates; one for nationals and a much higher one often only in dollars for foreigners. Always check the rate first; also whether the 20% service and taxes are included in the given price. Rooms in the better hotels can be in demand and booking is advised. (Several new hotels, including a *Colón*, were under construction in 1995.) The cheap hotels are pretty basic, and singles seem hard to find; there is a distinct lack of good middle range accommodation. The following all have the 20% service and tax added on.

NB We do not include hotels in the area bounded by 10 de Agosto and Olmedo, Quito and the Malecón. This district is unsafe. If wishing to stay in the centre, a reasonably safe area is near Plaza Bolívar; choose a hotel marked with an asterisk in the list below.

The best hotel is probably **L1-L2** *Oro Verde*, 9 de Octubre y García Moreno, T 327-999, F 329-350, PO Box 9636, refurbished in 1994, restaurants, bar, disco, pool; also good are **L1** *Continental**, Chile y 10 de Agosto, T 329-270, F 325-454 (a KLM Golden Tulip hotel), 5-star, colour TV with many English channels, good coffee shop, rec; **L2** *Unihotel*, Clemente Ballén 406 y Chile, T 327-100, good restaurant and breakfast; **L2** *Gran Hotel Guayaquil**, Boyacá 1600 y 10 de Agosto, T 329-690, F 327-251, good restaurants, swimming pool, sauna, etc, non residents can use pool, US$2/day; **L3** *Boulevard*, 9 de Octubre 432, T 566-700, very central, cable TV, casino, shows, rec; **L3** *Ramada*, Malecón y Orellana, pleasantly situated overlooking the river, with pool, mostly used by businessmen, T 565-794; **A3** *Los Andes*, Garaycoa 1233 y Ballén, T 329-741, a/c, bath; **A2** *Palace*, Chile 214 y Luque, T 321-080, excellent, good value for business travellers, TV, traffic noise on Av Chile side, restaurant, travel agency, fax and telex services, highly rec; **A3** *Doral**, Aguirre y Chile 402, T 328-490, good rooms and value, catering, central, rec; **A3** *Rizzo**, Clemente Ballén 319 y Chile, T 325-210, TV, bath, a/c, intermittent hot water, past its best, safe, central on Parque Bolívar, some rooms without windows, room service, *Café Jambelí* downstairs; **C** *Plaza**, Chile 414 y Clemente Ballén, T 324-006, some cheaper rooms, international newspapers; **A3** *Del Rey*, Aguirre y Marín, T 453-037, behind tennis club, price inc breakfast, new, clean, friendly; **B** *Sol de Oriente**, Aguirre 606 y Escobedo, T 325-500, cheap for what is offered, rec; **C** *Ritz*, 9 de Octubre y Boyacá, T 324-134, with bath, a/c, hot water, beware overcharging; **C** *Majestic*, 9 de Octubre 709, T 324-134, central, fan or a/c; **D** *Acuario*, Luque 1204 y Quito, T 527-815, a/c, bath, fridge; **D** *Vélez*, Vélez y Quito, T 530-356, with bath, TV, fan, clean, rec; **D** *Venezia*, Quisquis y Rumichaca, private bath, clean, friendly; **D** *Alexanders*, Luque 1107 y Pedro Moncayo, T 532-000, comfortable, good value, some rooms without windows, noisy; **D** *Centenario*, Vélez 726 y Garaycoa, T 524-467, a/c, cheaper with fan; **D** *Plaza del Centenario*, newer branch, a/c; **E** *Jitur*, Chimborazo 1119 y Ayacucho, T 401-201, with bath, TV, clean, ask for rooms away from the street; **E** *Residencial Pauker**, Baquerizo Moreno 902 y Junín, T 565-385, old-time haunt for travellers, good value, safe; **E** *Primavera*, 6 de Marzo y Clemente Ballén, TV, fan, clean; **E** *Sanders*, Pedro Moncayo 1100, T 320-030, with bath, a/c or fan, central, near a dangerous area; **F** *Berlín**, Rumichaca y Sucre, good value, rec; **F** *Libertador*, Parque Centenario, T 304-637, fan, bath, no glass in windows on park side; **G** *Imperial*, Urdaneta 705, T 560-512, basic; **G** *Hostal Miami*, P Montúfar 534, T 519-667, fan, bath.

Youth Hostel **E** *Ecuahogar*, Sauces I, Av Isidro Ayora, opp Banco Ecuatoriana de La Vivienda, T 248-357, F 248-341, member of IYHA and Ecuadorean Hostelling Association, non-members welcome, bunk rooms, and rooms with bath, cooking and laundry facilities, tourist information, safe, good services and transport nearby, convenient for bus station and airport, rec.

Restaurants The main areas for restaurants are the centre with many in the larger hotels, around Urdesa, or the newer residential and commercial centres of La Alborada and La Garzota, which have many good eating houses. Bills add on 20% service and tax. *International: El Fortín* in *Hotel Continental* for good food and service; *1822* in the *Gran Hotel*, small but interesting menu, expensive, pleasant surroundings; *Le Gourmet* at the *Oro Verde*, expensive, good; *La Banca*, Icaza 115 y Pichincha, popular with business community; *Posada de las Garzas*, Urdesa Norte, Circunvalación Norte 536, also French style dishes; *Caracol Azul*, 9 Octubre 1918 y Los Ríos, expensive, slow service, specializing in seafood; *Barandua Inn*, Circunvalación Norte 528-B, Urdesa Norte; *El Parque*, top floor of Unicentro, for excellent buffet lunches at the weekends, eat as much as you can, go early as it fills up quickly; *Juan Salvador Gaviota*, Kennedy Norte, Av Fco de Orellana, good seafood; *La Balandra*, Calle 5a 504 entre Monjas y Dátiles, Urdesa, for good fish, upmarket ambience.

Typical: *Canoa Bar* in *Hotel Continental* for traditional dishes rarely found these days, with different specials during the week; *Salón Melba*, Córdova 720 y Junín, old fashioned eating house/coffee shop; *Café Jambelí*, in *Rizzo Hotel* for coastal dishes and seafood; *El Pirata* floating restaurant in river opposite VM Rendón, "good place to watch the river life go by", slow service; *Muelle 5*, Malecón y Urdaneta, another floating restaurant; *Pique Y Pase*, Lascano 16-17 y Carchi, popular with students, lively; *El Patio* in the *Oro Verde* for reasonably priced food; *Las Delicias* on the Estrada, Urdesa, for cheap well cooked food; *El Manantial*, VE Estrada y Las Monjas, good; *La Guadalajara*, Av Kennedy, very good, cheap open air cafés tacos, *chuzos* (meat on sticks), popular with students from nearby University; *El Taller*, Quisquis y Esmeraldas, tiny place decked out with odd bits and pieces of old Guayaquil, live music in evenings; *La Choza*, Av Boloña nr Policentro, smart. *El Caribe*, Estrada y Ficus, Cuban; *Lo Nuestro*, VE Estrada, pleasant, repro décor. *Viejo Barrio*, over bridge from Policentro in Urdesa, lots of cafés offering variety of dishes, all in fake old Guayaquil style.

Italian: *San Remo*, 9 Octubre 737 for Italian and local dishes, mediocre, poor service; *La Carbonara*, Bálsamos 206 y Estrada, new premises without former atmosphere; *La Trattoria da Enrico*, Bálsamos 504, expensive but fun surroundings, good antipasto. Pizzas: *Pizza Hut* on 9 de Octubre in Urdesa, La Garzota and Barrio Centenario; *Cozzoli's*, Av Miraflores, good, expensive; *El Hornero*, Estrada y Higuerilla, part of Quito chain; *Pizzería Del Ñato*, Estrada 1219, good value, sold by the metre. **Spanish:** *Mediterráneo*, Bálsamos y Ficus; *Hostería Madrid*, Los Ríos y 9 Octubre, paellas; *Casa Basca*, Chile 406 y C Ballén, wonderful hole-in-the-wall place, expensive food, cash only, house wine good value, great atmosphere, gets very crowded; *Puerta de Alcalá*, Circulación y Ficus, new, upmarket. **French:** *La Bastilla*, Bálsamos 606 y Ficus, Urdesa, upmarket, pretentious. **Mexican:** *Noches Tapatías*, Primera y Dátiles, Urdesa, fun, good live music at weekends; *Mi Cielito Lindo*, Circunvalación 623 y Ficus, good; *Taos*, Estrada y Guayacanes, trendy, good music, expensive.

Chinese: a wide variety in the city, most do take-away, good value. *Chifa Himalaya*, Sucre 309 y P Carbo, slow service but good for the price; *Gran Chifa*, P Carbo 1016, wide variety, good value; *Chifa Palacio Dorado*, Chile 712 y Sucre; *Salón Asia*, Sucre 319 y P Carbo; *Kwang Tung*, Nueva Kennedy, Av San Jorge 308 y 3a Este. **Japanese:** *Tsuji*, Estrada 815, wonderful, authentic dishes, Teppan Yaki, expensive. **Lebanese:** *Beirut*, Urdesa Calle 4a 716.

Vegetarian: *La Gorinda*, Rendón on the Parque Centenario, closed evenings, good, not cheap; *Vegetariano*, Moncayo, E side, 1 block S of Parque Centenario; *Paxllandia*, Rendón y Ximena, US$ set lunch, closed evenings and Sun; *El Paraíso*, Luque next to *Hotel Alexanders*, open all day, good variety, not cheap; *El Camino*, P Icaza y Córdova, good lunches, economical; *Amaranto* Rumichaca y Urdaneta.

Steak Houses: *Olmos*, P Icaza y Boyacá; *Parillada Del Ñato*, Estrada 1219, huge variety and portions, excellent value; *La Selvita*, Av Olmos y Las Brisas, Las Lomas de Urdesa, good atmosphere and fine panoramic views, also at Calle D y Rosa Borja, Centenario; *Columbus*, Av Las Lomas; *El Gordo Daniel*, Boloña, Kennedy; *El Torro*, Luque y Garaycoa, huge steaks, pay in advance, fast-food atmosphere. **Crab Houses** are almost an institution where, with lots of mess hammering at the whole crabs, a beer and plenty of time, much fun and good flavours can be found: *Manny's*, Av Miraflores y Segunda, not cheap but try the excellent *arroz con congrejo*; *Casa del Cangrejo*, Av Plaza Dañin, Kennedy, for crab dishes of every kind; several others along the same street; *El Cangrejo Rojo*, Rumichaca 2901; *El Cangrejo Criollo*, Av Principal, Villa 9, La Garzota, excellent, varied seafood menu, rec. **Brazilian:** *Brasa Brasil*, opp Albán Borja shopping centre.

Snacks: many places selling all sorts of snacks; try *pan de yuca*, or *empanadas*. Beware of eating at street stalls. Excellent sandwiches at *Submarine*, 9 Octubre y Chile; *Uni Deli* in the Unicentro, good salami and cheese; *Poema de Quesos y Jamón*, 9 Octubre and Estrada, Urdesa; *La Chivería*, Circunvalación y Ficus for good yoghurt and *pan de yuca*; *La Selecta*, Estrada y Laureles, good sandwiches; *La Baguette*, Estrada y Las Monjas. **Fast Food:** *Kentucky Fried Chicken*, 9 Octubre y Escobedo and opposite Policentro in Plaza Quil; *Italian Deli*, in Albán Borja and Policentro, good self-service meals, great salads; *California Burger Chicken*, outlets in Kennedy, Centre and Urdesa; *La Estación*, 9 de Octubre y Ballén; *Pollos Gus*, Maracaibo 530 y Quito, Plaza Triángulo in Urdesa, Terminal Terrestre, good chicken and typical dishes; *Burger King*, 9 Octubre 610 or Estrada y Las Lomas in Urdesa. **Ice Cream:** *Top Cream*, the best, with many outlets throughout the city, try their local fruit sorbets; *Il Gelato Italiano* also with various outlets in the province. **Cakes and Cookies:** *Galleta Pecosa*, 10 de Agosto y Boyacá and in Urdesa on the Estrada. **All Night:** *La Canoa* at the *Hotel Continental*; *Sandry's* at the airport; *La Pepa de Oro* at the *Grand Hotel*; *El Patio* at the *Hotel Oro Verde*.

Banks and Exchange Lloyds Bank, Pichincha 108-110, with Mercado Central and Urdesa agencies, advances money on Visa card. **ABN-Amro**, P Icaza 454 y Baquerizo Moreno, T 312-900; **Citibank**, 9 de Octubre, Citicorp cheques only and before 1330; **Banco del Pacífico**, Icaza 200, 4th floor, no commission on TCs, recommended, advances money on Master Card. **Filanbanco**, 9 de Octubre between Pichincha and P Carbo, advances on Visa, good rates, no commission. **American Express**, 9 de Octubre 1900, for purchase of TCs. Queues are much longer in the afternoon. **Banco de Guayaquil** ATMs advance cash with Visa (Sucres only).

There are various *Casas de Cambio* on Av 9 de Octubre (eg *Cambio Paz*) and Calle Pichincha; also **Cambiosa**, in Albán Borja and **Cambitur** on Baquerizo Moreno, 113 y Malecón, rec. Most open 0900-1900, shut on Saturday. *Hotel Sanders* may change dollars. **Wander Cambios** at airport (see below). Difficult to change money at bus station. When all the rest are closed (eg Sun) try *Hotel Oro Verde* and similar places, quite good exchange rate for cash, will change small TC amounts.

Consulates   **Peru**, 9 de Octubre 411, 6th floor, T 322-738, 0900-1330. **Colombia**, Gral Córdova 808 y VM Rendón, T 563-854; **Bolivia**, P Ycaza 302 y Córdova, T 564-260. **Brazil**, Ciudadela Nueva Kennedy, Calle 9 Este A 208, T 393-979; **Argentina**, Aguirre 104, T 323-574. **Venezuela**, Chile 331, T 326-566. **Austria**, 9 de Octubre 1312, T 282-303. **Netherlands**, 9 de Octubre 2309, 5th floor, T 366-410. **Switzerland**, 9 de Octubre 2105, T 453-607. **UK**, Córdova 623 y P Solano, T 560-400. **Germany**, 9 de Octubre 109, T 513-876; **Denmark**, General Córdoba 604 y Mendiburu, T 308-020, open 0900-1200. **Norway**, Blvd 9 de Octubre 109 y Malecón, T 329-661; **Finland**, Luis Urdaneta 212 y Córdova, T 304-381; **Belgium**, Lizardo García 310 y Vélez, T 364-429; **France**, Aguirre 503 y Chimborazo, 6th floor, T 328-159. **Canada**, Córdova 812 y Rendón, T 563-580. **USA**, 9 de Octubre 1571 y García Moreno, T 323-570.

Entertainment   Discos, bars and casinos in most of the major hotels: *Oro Verde, Unihotel, Boulevard*. Other discos at *Infinity*, Estrada 505; *Latin Palace*, Av J Tanca Marengo y Roldós; *Excess* in Albán Borja; *El Corsario*, Los Ríos y Piedrahita; *Buccaneer* and *Flashdance* in centre. *Disco Gente*, Estrada 913, for café-theatre style comedy show with dancing afterwards; *Disco La Salsa*, Estrada for good salsa. For an unforgettable and alcoholic evening 'city tour' take *La Chiva* (open-sided bus) from Infinity on Fridays at 2130, which provides en route as many rum punches as you can hold, stopping off occasionally for a ceviche, dancing, fireworks, crab sandwich before depositing you back at Infinity for US$14 pp. Usually for groups only, details available from *Viajes Horizontes*, T 281-260. Trips on the Río Guayas with the (fake) paddle boat *El Pedregal* to the Club Pedregal on E side. US$3.70 includes boat ride, use of pool, sauna, tennis courts, volleyball, children's amentities. The complex has restaurant and bar. Boat dep Muelle Pedregal Sat and Sun 1130 and 1330 returning 1630 and 1730. See *El Universo* for cinemas and other entertainments. Cinemas cost US$2.25, one double bill.

Medical   Dr Angel Serrano Sáenz, Boyacá 821, T 301-373, English speaking. Dr Alfonso E León Guim, Centro de Especialidades, Boyacá 1320 y Luque, T 517-793; also English speaking. *Clínica Santa Marianita*, Boyacá 1915 entre Colón y Av Olmedo, T 322-500, doctors speak English and Spanish, special rates for SAHB users. The main hospital used by the foreign community is the *Clínica Kennedy*, Av del Periodista, T 286-963, which contains the consulting rooms of almost every kind of specialist doctor and diagnostic laboratory (Dr Roberto Morla speaks German); very competent emergency department, from a few stitches to a major accident. In emergency Aero Ambulance International, Aguirre 442 y Córdova, T 308-584/561-532.

Laundry   *Sistematic*, F Segura y Av Quito, or Calle 6a y Las Lomas, Urdesa. *Martinizing* for dry cleaning, many outlets, don't rely on their 1-hr service; *Dryclean USA*, VE Estrada 1016, Urdesa.

Telecommunications and Postal Service   Emetel, the telephone company, and central post office are in the same block, Pedro Carbo y Aguirre; buy long-distance *fichas* for telephone calls before contacting the international operator; lots of small booths around the building selling stationery, sewing notions, shoes, etc. Public telex booth. Parcels to be sent abroad have to be sealed in front of postal assistant but is a surprisingly reliable service, 1st floor, ventanilla 12. Branch post offices in Urdesa, Estrada y Las Lomas by Mi Comisariato supermarket; 1st floor of Policentro; also major hotels sell stamps. Many courier services for reliable delivery of papers and packages, eg: *DHL*, Calle 8a Oeste 100 y San Jorge, Kennedy, T 287-044; *UPS*, Pedro Moncayo 700 y Quisquís, T 314-315; *AeroNet*, Plaza Quil, local 73, T 399-777, and others. *Urgentito*, Chile 126 y Vélez, or Carchi y 9 de Octubre, T 325-742, for interprovincial service.

Places of Worship   Anglican-Episcopalian Church, Calle D entre Bogotá y A Fuentes, T 443-050; Centro Cristiano de Guayaquil, Pastor John Jerry Smith, Av Juan Tanca Marengo, Km 3, T 271-423; many other sects represented.

Shopping   Shopping malls: Unicentro, Aguirre y Chile; Policentro and Plaza Quil, both on Av San Jorge, N Kennedy; Albán Borja, Av Arosemena Km 2.7; Garzocentro 2000, La Garzota, Av

R Pareja; Plaza Mayor, La Alborada, Av R Pareja and, nearby, Albocentro. For handicrafts, good quality but expensive products are found at Madeleine Hollander's shop in the *Oro Verde*, *Manos* in Urdesa (Cedros 305 y Primera); *Artesanías del Ecuador*, 9 Octubre 104 y Malecón are good and reliable as is *Ocepa*, Rendón 405 y Córdova, where prices compare favourably with the towns where the goods are made. Also *Inca Folklore*, Edificio Gran Pasaje, 9 Octubre 424; *Arte Folklore Otavalo*, 9 Octubre 102 y Malecón; *Artesanías Cuenca*, Vélez 110; *Artesanías Mariel*, Vélez y Chile; for bargains and variety try the *handicrafts market* between Loja y Montalvo and Córdova y Chimborazo, almost a whole block of permanent stalls; the Otavalan Indians sell their crafts along Chile between 9 Octubre y Vélez. Many jewellery shops around Calle Chile from 9 Octubre to Ballén; reliable is *Valencia* Chile 112, as well as *Cevallos* in Policentro; *H Stern* is at the airport. Moderately priced casual clothes and beach wear from *Mi Comisariato* supermarket chain (though not all branches have a clothes department) and *El Precio Justo*, VE Estrada in Urdesa, 9 de Octubre, and other outlets. Good quality, cheap T-shirts, *KAO* in Policentro, choose your own motif. Panama hats, good quality, authentic, from *Sombrero Barberán*, 1 de Mayo 112, N end of Parque Centenario; also in the handicraft market. Photos developed reliably at *Rapi-Color*, Boyacá 1418 y Luque, or *Photo Market*, VE Estrada 726 y Guayacanes, Urdesa, prints and slides. Camera repairs at *Cinefoto*, Luque 314 y Chimborazo, English spoken. Cheap film and instant ID photos from *Discount New York* in Albán Borja. Camping equipment (expensive) and camping gas are available from *Casa Maspons*, Ballén 517 y Boyacá, *Marathon*, 9 de Octubre y Escobedo, or in Policentro. There are now lots of import shops in the centre and Urdesa selling American food and household products; however, the Bahía, or black market, on either side of Olmedo from Villamil to Chile, is still the most popular place for electrical appliances, clothing, shoes, food and drink. Watch your valuables and be prepared to bargain.

Books *Librería Científica*, Luque 223 y Chile and Plaza Triángulo on the Estrada in Urdesa, has English books and is good for field guides to flora and fauna and travel in general; *Librería Cervantes*, Aguirre 606-A y Escobedo; *Nuevos Horizontes*, 6 de Marzo 924 for book exchange. Copyright laws are not applied anywhere and whole books can be copied and bound often cheaper than buying a new book, *Xerox* on 9 Octubre 1514 or Rendón y P Carbo, and *El Copión*, Quisquis 607 or Av Miraflores 206, among many others. For cheapest photocopies and stationery, try any of the copying shops on Av Delta by the State University.

Horse Racing Hipódromos Buijo and Río Verde in Salinas. Parimutuel betting. Amazingly low standard.

Travel Agencies *Wanderjahr*, P Icaza 431, Edificio Gran Pasaje, T 562-111, branches in Policentro, T 288-400, the *Hotel Oro Verde*, Albán Borja, T 203-913; *Ecuadorean Tours*, 9 Octubre 1900 y Esmeraldas, T 287-111, is agent for Amex, branches Chile y 10 de Agosto and in Urdesa, Estrada 117, T 388-080; *Metropolitan Touring—Galapagos Cruises*, Antepara 915, T 330-300; *Situr*, Av CJ Arosemena Km 2.5, T 201-516/204-091, F 201-153, see also under Quito **Tourist Agencies** and under the Galápagos; *Kleintours*, Tungurahua 502-A, T/F 361-855, Galápagos and mainland tours; *Gordon Tours*, 9 Octubre 2009 y Los Ríos, T 373-550/373-555, rec; *Machiavello Tours*, Antepara 802 y 9 Octubre, T 282-902; *Orbitur*, Malecón 1405 y Aguirre, T 325-777; *Galasam Cía Ltda*, Edificio Gran Pasaje, 9 Octubre 424, 11th floor of 1107, T 306-289, **see Galápagos section (p 1045)** for their Economic Galapagos Tours programmes. Most agencies arrange city tours, 2½ hrs, US$8-10 pp with English-speaking guide.

Tourist Bureau Cetur, Aguirre 104 y Malecón, first floor; T 328-312. Friendly but poorly informed about anything outside their area or other than standard tourist attractions, Spanish only, open 0900-1730, Mon-Fri. Map of Ecuador. Maps also from Instituto Geográfico Militar, 9 de Octubre y Rumichaca. A Policía de Turismo man can be hired for a guided tour of Guayaquil. Cost will be about US$4/hr for taxi (2 hrs will do) and US$3 to the Policía de Turismo.

Immigration Av Pichincha y Aguirre (Gobernación), T 514-925/516-789, for visa extensions.

Local Transport Buses, *busetas* and colectivos about US$0.15; the whole system is chaotic and packed since there are too few buses for the city, but they are OK off peak. City buses not allowed in centre, almost all go along the Malecón. Even the *solo sentados* or *servicio especial* are anything but, drivers fill them beyond capacity. Bus No 15 will take you from the centre to Urdesa, 13 to Policentro, 14 to Albán Borja, 74 to La Garzota and Sauces. To get off at your stop, yell *pare*. Taxis have no meters, so prices are very negotiable and overcharging is notorious, but approx US$3 from centre to Urdesa or Policentro, short runs US$1. To Durán, across bridge, see under **Rail**. Taxi *rutas* and *furgonetas* run a set route, charging US$0.40; taxi *rutas* are yellow with contrasting bonnets, or stripes over the roof, eg ones with red bonnets run from the Bahía, Centro, Urdesa to Mapasingue and back; *furgonetas* (most with a/c) post up their routes in the windscreen. Both are an improvement on the buses.

Car Hire Budget T 288-510 (airport), 328-571 (by *Oro Verde*); **Ecuacars** T 283-247 (airport); **Avis** T 287-906 (airport); **Arrancar** T 284-454 (airport); **Delgado** T 287-768 (airport), 398-687 (centre); **Internacional** T 284-136 (airport). Cheapest rates US$26-30/day, inc 10% tax and insurance, mileage extra. All offer 3-day weekend rates (US$147-154, not inc tax and insurance, 600 km free, Group C-D) and weekly rates with 1200 km free.

Airport Simón Bolívar International Airport is to the N about 10 mins by taxi (1 hr on foot) from the city centre (national section modernized with cafetería, good view of planes). US$0.12 for bus (sometimes allow backpacks on board), No 2 from Malecón, No 3 from Centro Cívico, No 69 from Plaza Victoria. If going straight on to another city, get bus directly to bus station, which is close by. US$6 for taxi from centre or from airport, but if you are arriving in Guayaquil and need a taxi from the airport, walk ½ block from the terminal out to Av Las Américas, where taxis and *camionetas* wait for passengers. The fare will be about half of what you will be charged for the same trip by one of the drivers who belong to the airport taxi cooperative. There are several car hire firms in booths outside the national section; an information desk; Cetur office (erratic hours); *Wander Cambio*, open 7 days a week, closed at night, rates lower than other *cambios* or banks, but better than hotels; several bank ATMs.

Air Services About 14 flights daily to **Quito**, US$28 (TAME, Saeta, SAN; ensure seats are confirmed, not standby, though seats usually available outside peak hours of early and evening). Sit on the right side for the best views. There are flights to **Cuenca** (Mon-Fri US$25), **Loja** (Tues, Thurs, Sat, US$22), **Machala** (US$19, Mon-Fri). Daily to **Galápagos** (see p 1037). Commuter flights daily on small 5-17 seater planes from the Terminal de Avionetas on the city side of the international airport, on Cedta (T 301-165) to Machala, or AELA (T 288-580/288-110), to Bahía de Caráquez, Manta, Portoviejo and **Pedernales** (reported unreliable). TAME, 9 de Octubre 424, Edif Gran Pasaje (T 561-751); Saeta and SAN, both at Vélez 226 entre Chile y Chimborazo, T 200-600/614. Flights to **Lima**: AeroPerú (Icaza 451, T 563-600) 2100 twice a week, does not connect with flight to Cuzco: Saeta 6 a week; Copa 4 a week. Other international airlines serving Guayaquil are KLM, American, Continental, Aerolíneas Argentinas, Varig, Lacsa, Lufthansa, Ladeco. Andes Airlines (T 284-980) will ship vehicles to Panama. When passing through Guayaquil by air, do not put valuables into backpacks checked into the hold, things go missing.

Shipping Agent Luis Arteaga, Aguirre 324 y Chile, T 533-592/670/F 533-445, rec, fast, US$120 for arranging car entry.

Bus Services The bus station (Terminal Terrestre) is just N of the airport, just off the road to the Guayas bridge (offices on ground floor, departures on top floor, no left luggage depot, do not leave anything unattended, chaotic and busy at weekends, expensive restaurants, use of toilet US$0.10, bus ticket incl terminal tax of US$0.05). **Town buses** A great many go from bus station to centre, US$0.12, taxis not metred (to city centre US$2). Several companies to/from **Quito**, 8 hrs, from US$5 to US$13.35 for Rey Tours non-stop, a/c service. To **Cuenca**, 5½ hrs, US$4; **Riobamba**, 5 hrs, US$3.25; **Santo Domingo de los Colorados**, 4¾ hrs, US$4-5; **Manta**, 3 hrs, US$4; **Esmeraldas**, 7 hrs, US$5; to **Portoviejo**, 3½ hrs, US$4, and to **Bahía de Caráquez**, 5½ hrs, US$4.45. To **Ambato**, 6½ hrs, US$6. To **Alausí**, 4 hrs, US$3.25. Regular and frequent buses to **Playas** (2 hrs, US$1.35) and to **Salinas** (2½ hrs, US$1.85). **Machala** (for Peru) 3½ hrs, US$2.65, frequent, or by minibus 2½ hrs, leave at 20 minute intervals between 0600 and 1900, 10 kg baggage limit. For the **Peruvian border**, to **Huaquillas**, avoiding Machala, US$3.45, 4 hrs; via Machala, 6 hrs. Colectivos are not rec for journeys to the Sierra, they drive too fast and are dangerous. **Trucks** carry freight and passengers, slower, bumpy, cheaper than buses, and you see better. Inquire at Sucre 1104.

Roads There is a 3¼-km bridge from Guayaquil across the river to Durán. A good paved road from there (summit at 4,120m) connects with the Andean Highway at Cajabamba, near Riobamba (see p 977). Also from Durán main roads go to Babahoyo, Quevedo and Santo Domingo, to Cuenca, and to the southern lowlands.

Excursions To Playas, Salinas and the Santa Elena peninsula (see p 1009). **Cerro Blanco Forest Reserve** is a nature reserve set in tropical dry forest with an impressive variety of birds (over 190 species listed so far), such as the Guayaquil green macaw, crane hawk, snail kite, etc, and with sightings of howler monkeys, ocelot, puma, jaguar, peccaries among others. It is privately owned and managed by La Cemento Nacional; reservations and obligatory prepayment (US$0.85 plus US$6.25 per group for guide, up to 8 in group) from Multicomercio, Oficina 91, 1st floor, Eloy Alfaro y Cuenca, or T 871-900, F 872-236. The reserve is at Km 14.5 on the coast road to Salinas; entrance beyond the Club Rocafuerte. Defined trails are open Wed to Sun 0800-1600. Early morning visits advisable for possibility of seeing more wildlife. Mosquito repellent a must. Camping can be arranged, US$2.50 per night. Taxi from Guayaquil US$10-20, bus leaves every ½ hr from Parque Victoria and passes park entrance.

Botanical Gardens with orchid house, NW on Av Francisco de Orellana to Las Orchídeas Housing Estate. Good views and pleasant walk. Entrance US$2. Over 3,000 plants, including 150 species of Ecuadorean and foreign orchids. "The Gardens have not been established long so not many mature trees or shrubs, but it is interesting to see them develop and makes a pleasant half-day outing with good views over the river and surrounding countryside."

Hacienda tours to banana plantations can be arranged through *Gordon Tours* (see **Travel Agencies** above), in private car with lunch, 2-4 people, US$66.

Railway from Guayaquil to the Sierra

The spectacular 464-km railway line (1.067 metre gauge), which was opened in 1908, passes through 87 km of delta lands and then, in 80 km, climbs to 3,238m. At the summit, at Urbina, 3,609m is reached; it then rises and falls before debouching on to the Quito plateau at 2,857m. The line is a most interesting piece of railway engineering, with a maximum gradient of 5.5%. Its greatest achievements, the Alausí loop and the Devil's Nose double zigzag (including two V switchbacks), are between Sibambe and Alausí. Heavy El Niño rains in 1983 disrupted the Guayaquil-Quito railway for several years. Since then daily services have resumed.

The train station is in *Durán*, reached by ferry from Guayaquil, Malecón Bolívar about 10 blocks N of the Palacio de Gobernación. The first ferry is at 0530, the last at 2200 but buses run later. Bus 17 goes to Durán, US$0.15, drops you some blocks from station. Taxi to Durán from Guayaquil early is US$4.50. Transport to Durán in the early morning is hard to find, eg no buses from the port area. Beware of "special service" pick-ups at this time, which may contain a prostitute who will add heavily to your fare.

Accommodation in Durán is sparse and, in most cases, caters for short-stay clients. **E-F** *La Paz*, Esmeraldas 123 y Cuenca (main street, 2 blocks from and parallel to railway), T 803-465, with bath, fan, cheaper without, clean, light, early am call for train passengers; **F** *Res Durán*, Esmeraldas 227, T 800342, with or without fan, basic, clean, ask for outside room; **F** *Res Paris*, Loja y Yaguachi, T 800-403, opp market, with or without fan, clean. *Res Sarmiento, Los Angeles, Hostal Shirley* all definitely hourly rate, not rec. Plenty of small restaurants on Esmeraldas and by market. *Restaurant Goldwing*, opp Durán, "good food, dodgy clientèle".

Rail Services In 1995 there were trains Guayaquil-Riobamba daily. Durán-Riobamba 0625, 12 hrs (*autoferro* sometimes 0620, 8-10 hrs), fare US$2.15, US$1.55 to Alausí. Tickets for Riobamba go on sale from 0600, they cannot be bought in advance (US$10 for foreigners). It is important to check details in advance. It is rec to ride on the roof for the best views, but dress warmly and protect clothes from dirt on the roof. On the train, lock all luggage, even side pockets, as pilfering from luggage compartments is common. This is becoming popular with foreign and local tourists, especially at weekends and public holidays; get in the ticket queue early or go midweek.

Leaving the river the train strikes out across the broad, fertile Guayas valley. It rolls through fields of sugar cane, or rice, past split cane houses built on high stilts, past sugar mills with their owners' fine homes. Everywhere there are waterways, with thousands of water-birds.

The first station is *Yaguachi*. On 15 and 16 August more than 15,000 visitors pour into this little town to attend the feast day celebrations at the church of San Jacinto, who is honoured in the region for having put an end to many epidemics.

The first stop of importance is *Milagro*, a large but uninteresting town of 93,637 people (**E-F** *Hotel Oasis*, nr railway station, safe, clean; **F** *Hotel Viker*, no food, communal washing facilities; **G** *Hotel Azuay*, near station, dirty, unfriendly, fan, bath; *Restaurant Topo-Gigio*, nearby, good, cheap food). (Bus to Guayaquil US$0.40.) Women swarm about the train selling sweet and juicy pineapples.

About 87 km from Durán the train stops for an hour or less at *Bucay*, at the base of the Andes (**F** *Florida*, across river, no mosquito net, showers, small dark rooms, cheap restaurant; **E** *California*, clean, cold water, friendly; market Sunday). The train leaves Bucay at 1045. Tickets may only be bought on the day of travel, trains very crowded. Train Bucay-Riobamba US$1.20 (about US$10 for foreigners), departing between 0900-1000, arriving 1300-1400 in Alausí and about 1700 in Riobamba. Buses run parallel to the train between Bucay and Guayaquil. Bus to Guayaquil 2 hrs, reserve in advance at Santa Marta agency in centre. To Riobamba, US$1.50, and Ambato, 3 hrs, US$3, change at either for Quito. Bus to Cuenca: go to El Triunfo, 50 mins, US$0.40, then change for Cuenca, US$2.65, 3½ hrs.

The landscape spreads before you in every shade of green; row on row of coffee and cacao trees, with occasional groves of mango and breadfruit trees, banana plantations, fields of sugar cane, tobacco, and pineapple. The train follows the gorge of the Río Chanchán until it reaches **Huigra** (C *Hostería La Eterna Primavera*, T Guayaquil 312-267, F 885-437, bath, hot water, restaurant, bar, pool, horse riding, trips by train to Nariz del Diablo, lovely climate). By road Bucay to Huigra is still rough going. After leaving Huigra the train crosses and recrosses the Río Chanchán, and then creeps along a narrow ledge between the mountain and the canyon. Here begins the most exciting part of the trip. The first mountain town reached is Chanchán, where the gorge is so narrow that the train has to pass through a series of tunnels and bridges in its zigzag course. Next is **Sibambe** (no hotels, ask in the village for a room or bring camping gear, do not stay at station, if stuck, walk 1 hr to Pan-American Highway), the junction for trains to Cuenca (services suspended in 1995). Shortly after leaving Sibambe the Quito train starts climbing the famous Nariz del Diablo (Devil's Nose), a perpendicular ridge rising in the gorge of the Chanchán to a height of 305m. This almost insurmountable engineering obstacle was finally conquered when a series of switchbacks was built on a 5.5% grade. The air is chilly and stimulating.

Next comes **Alausí** (see p 981), popular with Guayaquileños. After crossing the 120 metre long Shucos bridge, the train pulls into Palmira, on the crest of the first range of the Andes crossed by the railway. The train has climbed nearly 3,350m in less than 160 km. Precipitous mountain slopes covered with temperate-climate crops such as wheat and alfalfa gradually change to a bleak, desolate *páramo* (moor) where little grows except stiff clumps of grass. Now and then the drab landscape is brightened by the red poncho of an Indian shepherd watching his sheep, although pine reforestation is changing the view. One by one the great snow-capped volcanoes appear: Chimborazo, Carihuairazo, Altar, Tungurahua, and the burning head of Sangay. They seem very close because of the clear air.

NORTHERN PACIFIC LOWLANDS (6)

The region's fertile banana lands, shrimp farms and oil refineries provide the bulk of the country's exports. Dirty, noisy, bustling towns on mosquito-infested estuaries are interspersed with charming fishing villages. Beaches range from overcrowded to deserted, but interest in the latter is growing rapidly. The Machalilla National Park protects an important area of primary tropical dry forest, precolumbian archaeological sites, coral reef and wildlife.

From Quito to the Lowlands: a scenic bus trip can be taken (129 km) to **Santo Domingo de los Colorados**, in the hills above the W lowlands (pop 114,442). Visibility is best in the morning. There is a small daily market and a large Sun market, but very few Indians now come to the town so both it and the market itself are unexciting and scruffy. You would do better to hire a taxi and go to their villages to see the Colorados (about US$15 for 2 hrs). Very few of them now wear the traditional hair dress. They are generally not keen on dressing up for gringos to photograph them and you will probably be charged about US$4. Santo Domingo itself is dusty, noisy, and decaying. Shops in the town are open Tues-Sun, and banks Tues-Sat. There is a cinema.

Warning Robberies have been reported in Santo Domingo and on buses in the area.

Hotels In town (no hotels will take credit cards): **E** *Caleta*, Ibarra 141, T 750-277, good restaurant, private bath, good; **F** *Colorado*, 29 de Mayo y Quinindé, T 750-226, a bit noisy; two *Hostales Turistas*, **F** *No 1* at 3 de Julio y Latacunga and **F** *No 2* at Ambato y 29 de Mayo, with bath (hot water), basic, noisy, no windows; **F** *Pensión Don Pepe*, Calle Quito, clean, friendly, quiet. *Amamcay*, 29 de Mayo y Ambato, quite good, water on demand. Out of town: **C** *Zaracay*, Av Quito 1639, T 751-023, 2 km out of town on the road to Quito, restaurant, casino, noisy disco, gardens and a swimming pool, good rooms and service, best available, advisable to book, especially at weekend. Nearby is **E** *Hotel del Toachi*, just W of *Zaracay*, T 754-688, best in this range, good showers, swimming pool.

Also on the road to Quito, 20 km from Santo Domingo, is **A2** *Tinalandia*, pleasant and small, chalets with bathrooms, inc meals, with its own golf course overlooking the Toachi valley, and excellent food (refurbished 1994). The hotel attracts golf-playing executives or diplomats from Quito and keen birdwatchers. Many species of birds, flowers and butterflies in the woods behind, many biting insects in the evening (open to non-residents for US$6 a day). Poorly signposted, take small road between Km 16 and 17 from Santo Domingo on the right; Casilla 8, Santo Domingo de los Colorados, or Av Gaspar de Villarroel 220 y Cochapata, Quito, T 247-461, F 442-638. (For cheaper accommodation near *Tinalandia*, **F** *Florida* in Alluriquín, 7 km away on main road, with swimming pool.)

Restaurants *Parrilladas Argentinas*, on Quevedo road Km 5, for good barbecues. *Mocambo*, Tulcán y Machala, good; *La Fuente*, Ibarra y 3 de Julio, good; *Rico Pollo*, Quito y Río Pove, for chicken; *Tacos Mexicanos*, Quito, a super deli, highly rec; two *chifas*, *Nuevo Hongkong* and *Nueva China*, on the Parque Zaracay; *Corea*, 3 de Julio y San Miguel. Several snackbars and pizzerias. *Juan El Marino*, 1.5 km from Monument Circle on road to Quevedo, reasonably priced, huge portions, good seafood, rec.

Exchange Banco Internacional, Esmeraldas y Quito.

Immigration Camilo Ponce (police station), T 750-225.

Roads and Buses Choose buses from Quito to the Lowlands with care: many drive very badly on unsuitable roads. The main route from Quito descends the valley of the Ríos Naranjal/Pilatón/Blanco, turning off the Panamericana at Alóag. Sit on right for views going down (but on left look for El Poder Brutal, a devilish face carved in the rock face); US$2.40, 2½ hrs. Alternative route via Mindo, San Miguel de los Bancos, 7 hrs, US$4-4.50. Santo Domingo's bus terminal is outside town; long-distance buses do not enter the city. Taxi downtown, US$0.90, bus US$0.09.

A busy paved highway connects Santo Domingo de los Colorados with Esmeraldas to the N, 4 hrs by bus (see **p 1017**). On this road are La Concordia, just before which is the private La Perla Forest Reserve (40 km from Santo Domingo, can hike in, free), La Independencia (junction with road from San Miguel de Los Bancos and the Sierra) and **Quinindé** (**Rosa Zárate**), where *Residencial Paraíso* is clean and quite good, water 24 hrs a day. The road deteriorates after Quinindé.

A good, paved road runs W via El Carmen (cattle market on outskirts) and Chone where the road divides, either to Bahía de Caráquez, 340 km from Quito, last bus to Bahía at 1830, 4½ hrs (see **p 198**), or to Portoviejo and Manta. 13 km beyond Santo Domingo is the excellent **C** *La Hacienda*, 20 rooms, restaurant, swimming pool, small zoo.

Another highway goes S to **Quevedo** (86,910) 1½ hrs by bus. (At Km 47 from Santo Domingo is **B** *Río Palenque*, price pp inc 3 meals, a biological field station, good bird watching, T 561-646 or 232-468 in Quito for information and reservations.) Set in fertile banana lands and often flooded in the rainy season, Quevedo is known as the Chinatown of Ecuador, with a fair-sized Chinese colony. It is a dusty, noisy, crowded town which has grown exceptionally rapidly over the last 25 years.

Hotels None offers a quiet night. **C** *Quevedo*, Av 7 de Octubre y Calle 12, modern rooms with fridge, TV, good restaurant; **D** *Olímpico*, Bolívar y 19a, restaurant best in town, near stadium; **E** *Ejecutivo Internacional*, 7 de Octubre y Calle Cuarta, modern, large rooms, a/c, private bath, good value, the least noisy; **E** *El Cóndor*, with a/c, F without; **F** *El Turista*; **F** *Continental*, basic; *Charito*, Bolívar 720. All are on, or near Av 7 de Octubre and the plaza. **G** *Guayaquil* opposite *Ejecutivo Internacional* is a brothel, prices vary per room.

Restaurants On 7 de Octubre: *Rincón Caleño* (Colombian), 1103; *Chifa 51* (Chinese, disappointing), 928; other *chifas* at 806, 809 and 707; *Tungurahua* (local food), 711, good breakfast US$1. *Hong Kong*, Calle Ambato, rec. Snackbar, *Quevedo City*, Bolívar y 4a.

Roads and Buses Quevedo is an important route centre. The old highway from Latacunga in the highlands to Quevedo carries very little traffic; it is extremely twisty in parts (paved to 10 km past Pujilí and from **La Maná** to Pichincha, great downhill bike route) but it is one of the most beautiful of the routes connecting the highlands with Portoviejo, Manta and the coast. (Bus, Quito-Quevedo US$4, 7 hrs.) Between Zumbahua and La Maná is the pretty little town of **Pilalo** (2 restaurants). 2½ km beyond La Maná on the road to Quevedo is **E** *Rancho Hostería Inmisahu*, new, with pool, clean, restaurant. (Bus (*chiva*), Quevedo- Portoviejo, from 7 de Octubre and Calle 8, 5 hrs, US$1.85, uncomfortable, watch your possessions.)

Quevedo is connected with Guayaquil by two paved highways (bus, 3 hrs, US$1.65), one through Balzar and Daule, one through **Babahoyo** (translated as "slime-pit", 50,250 people, *Hotel Emperador*, Gral Barona, T 730-535, bath, a/c, TV, restaurant; *Hotel Cachari*, Bolívar

120, T 731-205, acceptable, restaurant nearby; also *Nuevo Hotel Cachari* at No 107; *Residencial San Martín* provides an en suite bucket of water and entertainment from the rats running along the redundant plumbing). Bahía de Caráquez can be reached via Velasco Ibarra, Pichincha, Rocafuerte and Calceta. The roads give a good idea of tropical Ecuador, with its exotic birdlife and jungle and plantations of cacao, sugar, bananas, oranges, tropical fruits and rice. To Quito via Santo Domingo, 4 hrs, US$2.65.

The Coast In 1994 an aggressive campaign to promote tourism along the Guayas and Manabí coast was launched. This, plus improvements on the road from Guayaquil to Santa Elena and N to Manta, has made for faster access and new establishments springing up all along the coast. Older amenities are also expanding, but there will inevitably be rapid changes in the next year or so.

Popular beach resorts of the Pacific lowlands can be reached along a paved highway (toll) from Guayaquil. The road divides at El Progreso (Gómez Rendón), 63 km. One branch leads to General Villamil, normally known as *Playas*, the nearest seaside resort to Guayaquil (2 hrs by frequent bus—US$1.35; US$40 by taxi). Look out for the bottle-shaped ceibo (kapok) trees between Guayaquil and Playas as the landscape becomes drier, turning into tropical thorn scrub where 2-5 metre cacti prevail. Fishing is still important in Playas and a few single-sailed balsa rafts can still be seen among the motor launches returning laden with fish. These rafts are unique, highly ingenious and very simple. The same rafts without sails are used to spread nets close offshore, then two gangs of men take 2-3 hrs to haul them in. The beach shelves gently, and is 200-400m wide, lined with singular, square canvas tents hired out for the day. As the closest resort to Guayaquil, it is popular with local city dwellers and the authorities are trying to keep the packed beaches cleaner at the NW end as well as by the beach cafés. The Malecón has been improved with new grass and trees. The old *Hotel Humboldt* has been demolished and three new condos are being built. Out of season, when it is cloudier, or midweek the beaches are almost empty especially for anyone who walks N up the beach to Punta Pelado (5 km), although the new Casablanca private club, 20 mins up the beach, will intrude on the isolation. Popular surfing with 6 good surf points. Thieving is rampant during busy times—do not leave **anything** unattended on the beach.

Hotels **C** *Hostería Bellavista*, Km 2 Data Highway, T 760-600, rooms or suites in bungalows on beach, booking necessary, Swiss-run, friendly, clean, camping is S end of beach, arranges canoe trips into mangroves with English or French speaking guides, sailing, surfing, mountain biking, rec; **D** *Hostería La Gaviota*, 500m out on Data road, T 760-133, colour TV, a/c, friendly, good clean restaurant; **D** *Hostería Los Patios*, Km 1½ Data Highway, T 760-327, well-equipped suites, restaurant, poor service, noisy; **D** *La Casa de Marie y Gabriel*, Av Roldós, 1 block in from Malecón, T 760-047, family atmosphere, basic suites with bath, cooking and laundry facilities, French, English spoken, long-term rates; **E** *La Terraza*, Paquisa y Guayaquil, T 760-430, centre of town, dingy but clean rooms, substantial good value meals; **E** *El Delfín*, Km 1.5, T 760-125, old fashioned, big rooms, on beach, hacienda type building, nice but sporadic water supply, electric showers, restaurant sometimes closed at night; **E** *El Galeón*, T 760-270, beside the church, friendly, clean, mosquito nets or netting over the windows, water all day, cheap restaurant with seafood (closes 1800 Sun), good breakfast, cheaper for long stay (**F** *Turistas*, next door, noisy); **E** *Parasoles*, Principal y Alfonso Jurado, T 760-532, clean, helpful; **D-E** *Playas*, T 760-121, on Malecón, accepts credit cards, beach hotel, plain rooms with fans, clean, safe, restaurant, parking, rec; **E** *Rey David*, T 760-024, characterless concrete building, clean rooms, sea view; **E** *Hostería Costa Verde*, T 760-645, Lebanese management, excellent meals, cheaper rates for longer stays; **F** *Miraglia*, popular with surfers, run down but clean, sea view, insecure (theft from hotel safe), showers, fresh drinking water, parking for motorcycles, T 760-154, cheaper rates for longer stays. Most hotels are 5 mins' walk from Transportes Villamil bus station. Some are connected to Guayaquil's mains water supply, but many have wells which take water from sea and is slightly brackish. Downmarket places have buckets or less.

Excellent seafood and typical dishes from over 50 beach cafés (all numbered and named). Rec are *Cecilia's* at No 7 or *Barzola* at No 9. Good food at *Cabaña Típica* next to *Rey David*, good, closes Mon, on Malecón. *Mario's*, central plaza opp Banco de Guayaquil, big hamburgers, good yoghurt; *Los Ajos*, at end of street leading from plaza, 5 mins walk, good soups, varied menu but variable quality. Giant oysters and 'mule foot' black conchs are opened and served from stalls in a side road down from La Costa Verde; worth a look if nothing else.

Discos: *Motivos*, S end of Malecón; *Mr Frog*, diagonally opp *Miraglia*; *Maxim's* opp *Miraglia*; *Peña de Arturo*, opp Coop Villamil bus terminus.

There are showers, toilets and changing rooms along the beach, with fresh water, for a fee.

Telecommunications Emetel on Av Jaime Roldós Aguilera, service good, open Sun. **Post Office** is reliable, airmail takes 3 weeks to Europe. Collect mail at Post Office, may be listed under first or last name. **Exchange** Banco de Guayaquil, fussy about quality of US$ notes.

Excursions An interesting walk, or short drive (regular *camioneta* service from crossroads of Av Guayaquil y Av Paquisha) goes to the village of El Morro, with a disproportionately large wooden church with impressive façade (under 'permanent' repair) and the nearby mysterious rock formation of the Virgen de la Roca, where there is a small shrine and a few marble stations of the cross. Some 3 km further down the road is Puerto del Morro, up a scenic mangrove estuary, where there are several working wooden trawlers and other traditional boats. No accommodation, basic eating places. NW up the coast is **Engabao** (*camioneta* from the crossroads, ¹/₂ hr bumpy ride down sandy tracks), a small settlement where you can find deserted beaches and wooden fishing boats along the coast. No food or lodging. Surfing points.

West of El Progreso (Gomez Rendón) the good quality road to **Santa Elena** (where the road forks W for Salinas or N for northern coastal towns) runs through dry thorn scrub that looks dead in the dry season. Beyond Zapotal, by the old race course, now stables, is the turnoff for **Chanduy** where 8 km along is the Real Alto Museum, well laid out explanation of the peoples, archaeology and customs of the area (daily 1000-1700, US$0.70).

7 km before Santa Elena, a well-signed turnoff leads 8 km to **Baños San Vicente**, Cetur-run hot thermal baths, swimming pool and a big mudhole which claim to cure assorted ailments. US$0.30 entrance from 0600-1800 (early or late recommended to avoid crowds); massages extra. **F** *Hotel Florida*, basic, clean, next to baths.

To W of Santa Elena we pass a petroleum refinery and enter the busy port and regional market centre of **La Libertad** (**E** *Samarina*, Av 9 de Octubre, Cetur-run, some bungalows, swimming pool, restaurant, coffee shop, bar, with views of oil refinery and tankers; **F** *Hotel Turis Palm*, Av 9 de Octubre, fan, bath—G without, older place and a bit run down, next door and similar is *Reina del Pacífico*; **E** *Hostal Viña del Mar*, T 785979, clean, fan, bath, in town centre; **G** *Seven Seas*, on Malecón, very basic). Buses every hour (until 1700) to Manglaralto (US$1.25), Puerto López and Jipijapa from near market. Bus to Guayaquil US$2.20. Car racing at the Autódromo half way between La Libertad and Santa Elena. **Warning** Muggings are frequent.

A few km further on, surrounded by miles of salt flats, is **Salinas**, the self-styled best resort in Ecuador (population, 19,298, buses from Guayaquil, US$2.20, 2¹/₂ hrs; return journey, go to La Libertad by bus or colectivo and take bus from terminal there). There is safe swimming in the bay and high rise blocks of holiday flats and hotels line the sea front. The town is dominated by the Choclatera hill on the S point of the bay overlooking well-equipped, but very exclusive Salinas Yacht Club. There are increasing complaints that during *temporada* (Jan to April/May) it is overcrowded, with traffic jams, rubbish-strewn beaches and food and water shortages. During off season it is quieter, but still not for 'getting away from it all'. Tours, hire of sailing boats, water skis, fishing trips can be arranged through *Salitour*, T 772-800, F 772-789.

Hotels **A3-B** *Miramar*, Malecón, T 772-576, cheaper with fan, with casino, bath and telephone. **A3** *El Carruaje*, Malecón, T 774-282, a/c, TV, hot water, sea view; **B** *Samarina*, 9 de Octubre y Malecón, TV, a/c, sea view; **C** *Salinas*, Gral Henríquez Gallo y 27, modern, off Malecón, restaurant reported good; **D** *Yulee*, Diagonal Iglesia Central, T 772-028, with bath, clean, excellent food, friendly, well placed for beaches; **E** *Florida*, Malecón y Calle 2, Chipipe, T 772-780, with bath, cheaper inside rooms.

Restaurants *Mar y Tierra*, close to *Hotel Miramar*, excellent seafood, especially lobster; also near the *Miramar* is *Flipper*, cheap, simple, clean and friendly. Good freshly-cooked food in market, 2 blocks in from Malecón and *Hotel Yulee*. *Oystercatcher*, Malecón y 32, rec, safe oysters. **Discos/Nightlife** *Bar Cuatro*, rec, *Four Winds, South Beach, Punto de Quiebra, Tequilala*, any parked car with loud music system!

Exchange TCs cannot be changed. Banco del Pacífico changes cash and gives good rates on Mastercard; change cash at the supermarket and the *Hotel Salinas*, poor rates.

Telecommunications Emetel public telex booth at Radio Internacional, good telephone service.

Punta Carnero is on the S shore of the Santa Elena peninsula, 8 km S of La Libertad. Magnificent 15-km beach with wild surf and heavy undertow, virtually empty during the week, great whale watching July, Aug, Sept (Hotels: **A2** *Punta Carnero*, T 775-450, all rooms with sea view, restaurant, swimming pool; **A3-C** *Hostería del Mar*, T 775-370, with or without a/c, restaurant, swimming pool, family suites to let on weekly basis). A few kms to the E of Punta Carnero, along the coast, lies **Anconcito**, a fishing port at the foot of steep cliffs; pelicans and frigate birds gather round the colourful boats when the catch is brought in. Nowhere in town to stay; further on is Ancón, centre of the declining local oilfield.

The N fork of the road at Santa Elena leads past **Ballenita** (pleasant beach, good food at *La Cabaña*, at the fork, where the filling station has very clean bathrooms; **B** *Hostería Farallón Dillon*, Lomas de Ballenita, T 786-643, F 785-611, restaurant, museum; large new **C** *Ballenita Inn*, T 785-008, at the fork; cottages can be rented). Most of this coastal road is paved as far as Puerto Cayo and beyond, when it turns inland for Jipijapa and Manta, some sections are bad. The vegetation is tropical desert scrub as far as La Entrada with very little rainfall, giving onto a lusher landscape as far as Ayampe, with the hills of the Colonche range falling to the coast. Most of the numerous small fishing villages have good beaches, though beware of rip currents and undertow. Before Punta Blanca are several seafood stands on a wild beach (smart beach houses at Punta Blanca, basic poor accommodation at *La Cabaña*). Beyond San Pablo, among high-walled shrimp hatcheries built to stock shrimp farms (look for the *semilleros* all along the coast trudging through wave breaks to collect larvae which is then sold via middle men to the shrimp farms) is **B** *Hostería Las Olas*, T 887-987, Km 18 Vía Santa Elena, bleak new complex but clean and spacious. Popular beaches at **Palmar** (beach cafes, no accommodation), **Ayangue** in horseshoe bay gets very crowded and dirty at peak weekends/holidays. (**D** *Cumbres de Ayangue*, T 366-301, on S point of bay, expensive, new complex of cabins, restaurant, impressive views; **E** *Hostal Un Millón De Amigos*, with fan and bath, T 916-975, in town.) San Pedro/**Valdivia** (2 unattractive villages which merge together, many fish stalls, *Cevichería Play a Linda*, reliable) are at the site of the supposed Japanese-Jama culture contact, via fishing rafts 3000 BC. Many houses offer 'genuine' artefacts and one resident at N end of village will show the skeletons and burial urns dug up in his back garden. It is illegal to export precolumbian artefacts from Ecuador; the replicas are made in exactly the same manner as their predecessors, copied from genuine designs, and whilst sacrificing historic authenticity, their purchase prevents the trafficking of originals and provides income for the locals (ask for Juan Orrala, excellent copies). Most artefacts discovered at the site are in museums in Quito and Guayaquil.

Manglaralto (pop 18,510), the main centre of the region N of Santa Elena, is reached by bus from Guayaquil (change at La Libertad) as well as by numerous trucks. As cantonal capital it has a hospital and Emetel public office, though most villages along the coast have a house where Emetel public phone is available. A tagua nursery has been started; ask to see examples of worked 'ivory' nuts. It is a nice place to stay and bathe, with a good, quiet, clean beach, but little shelter. Good surf. Take plenty of sun tan lotion.

Hotels and Restaurants **D** Sr Ramón's house, S of main plaza, orange/beige building, clean, safe, fan, mosquito net; **F** *Alegre Calamar*, N end of town, big, open-walled room, shared bath, mosquito nets, dirty, basic, poor seafood restaurant; **F** *Posada del Emperador*, T 901-172, basic rooms and a cabin, long stays arranged, Doña Lupita will cook vegetarian meals; **F** *Habitaciones* next to post office, bath, and a bungalow for rent. *Restaurante Las Tangas*, seafood, slow service; *Comedor Familiar* has meals weekends only; also *Comedor Florencia*, moderately cheap and friendly.

Buses and Roads to **La Libertad**, US$1; to **Jipijapa**, US$2 (3½ hrs, 100 km via Salango, Puerto López, Puerto de Cayo).

3 km N is **Montañita** beach (nice, but some sandflies and watch out for stingrays close to water's edge. If stung, the small hospital in Manglaralto will treat you quickly.) It is reported to

have the best surfing in Ecuador, various competitions held during the year. (Major development has taken place at the surfing end: **A3-C** *Baja Montañita*, T 281-188, F 287-873, a/c, cabins and rooms, pool, jacuzzi etc, 2 restaurants, bars, loud beach parties in season; **D-E** *Rincón de Amigos*, T 02-225-907, for cabins or rooms, relaxed, vegetarian food, beach bar, refurbished; **E-G** *Vito's Cabañas*, T 241-975, next door, clean and friendly, good food, camping facilities, Vito has boundless energy; **F** *El Puente*, by bridge on main road, basic. *Pelícano*, for good pizzas and rock'n'roll, open till 2200; *Camping Los Delfines* has tents for hire, restaurant. Several other rooms for rent near surfing beach. The village S of the surf beach has been little affected, with very good, cheap food in unnamed café on beach next to public toilets. Emetel phone.) Bus with Transp Manglaralto to La Libertad, 1 hr, US$1. *Olón* with spectacular long beach (**G** *Hostería Olón Beach*, clean, basic, with Emetel. Fanny Tomalá rents rooms in the village. *Restaurant Puertolón*, expensive, indifferent food, plans 16 cabins; *Veronica*, scruffy, good seafood just off beach, Emetel phone). Las Nuñez beyond Olón for **A3** *Hotel Al Risco*, T 09-410-022 (cellular), rustic, cabins and restaurant, horse riding.

North by La Entrada the road winds up and inland through lush forest. Just before Ayampe, the new **A3** *Hotel Atamari*, T 02-226-072, has beautiful, expensive cabins in spectacular surroundings, wonderful food (no public transport). 5 km beyond, just before Puerto Rico, is *Alandaluz*, an ecologically and socially sound hotel, bamboo cabins with palm-leaf thatched roofs and fresh flowers or camping. Prices from **F**, camping, to **D** in cabins, pp; student and youth hostel discounts, 10% discount if you pay in sucres cash. Good home-made food, vegetarian or seafood, breakfast US$2, other meals US$5, and bar. Very peaceful, clean beach and stunning organic vegetable and flower gardens in the middle of a desert. Working demonstrations of recycling of rubbish and water and composting toilets (an excellent model for Ecuador). It is a good base for exploring the nearby area and Machalilla National Park, the hotel will arrange excursions to Isla de la Plata if there are enough people. Tours are expensive. Reservations are necessary as it is so popular; friendly and highly rec. Meals are not cheap, but you can cook your own if you take a stove. Cheaper meals can be ordered in Puerto Rico (on main road, ask for Don Julio Mero, at first house by road that branches off to left). Bus: Trans Manglaralto from La Libertad, US$2, or from Jipijapa if coming from Manta and the N, ask to get off at Puerto Rico, though the centre is easily seen from the road, last bus from S passes at 1930, from N at 1730, hitching difficult. A pick up from Portoviejo costs US$7. More information and reservations T 604-173 in Puerto López, or in Quito, Armero 710 y Santa Rosa, T 02-237-583, F 525-671, or write to Casilla 17-15-006-C, the same office also offers tours to the Oriente. North of Puerto Rico, turn-off well signed, is **B** *Los Piqueros de Patas Azules*, for 5-person cabins only, T 202-033, Guayaquil, restaurant, bar, tours arranged to Salango island, expensive for what it is, poor reports in 1995. For Quito from Puerto Rico take 0645 bus from Jipijapa via Portoviejo, US$9.

The archaeological museum in *Salango* is worth visiting (US$1). For many years a dig was carried out in the local fish meal factory's yard and the artefacts are housed in a beautiful museum of typical design on the square. Excellent eating but slow service at *El Delfín Mágico* (order meal before visiting museum), try the *spondilus* (spiny oyster) in fresh coriander and peanut sauce with garlic coated *patacones*.

Puerto López is a sizeable fishing town, pop 10,212, which is becoming increasingly visited by foreign tourists. Since a visit to the Galápagos is now beyond the means of most low-budget visitors, many are heading to this area for the attractions of Parque Nacional Machalilla and Isla de la Plata (see below). Watch out for the arrival of the fishermen in the morning and evening. Scooter rental US$3/hr, daily and weekly rates available.

Lodging and food **C** *Hotel Pacífico*, around the corner, hot showers, friendly, safe, comfortable, a/c, cheaper with fan, need mosquito net, basic cabañas, D; **E** *Residencial El Pacífico*, on sea front, T 604-133, clean, quiet, good (rebuilt 1994); **F** *Residencial Paola*, Juan Montalvo one block from beach, basic; **F** *Restaurant Viña del Mar* rents rooms next door, friendly but no running water, dirty bathrooms downstairs, good, cheap food; *Residencial Cristina*, Eloy Alfaro, basic; *Hotel Buenos Aires*, nr highway, away from beach. *El Chino*, next to the *Viña del Mar*, vegetarian food available; *Picantería Rey Hoja*, close to Tourist Office, good food, pleasant owner. *Carmita* on the Malecón, seafood, rec for freshness, try *pescado al vapor*; talk to her about renting rooms for longer stays, **G** pp. *Acapulco* restaurant on main street, video shows nightly at 1930. Try the local avocado *licuados* and *chuzos*, rec. Excellent banana bread from the *panadería* behind church. Good food at *Mayflower* next to *Carmita*, not cheap; *Dolphin*, next to bus stop, cheap, friendly, rec.

Buses 1½ hrs, US$1, hourly to Jipijapa. To **La Libertad**, 2 hrs, US$1; to **Manglaralto**, 1 hr, US$1.35; to **Portoviejo**, 1 hr on good road, 68 km. To **Salango**, US$0.35.

Next to the market in Puerto López is a new administration and visitor's centre for nearby

Parque Nacional Machalilla. The Park extends over 55,000 has, including Isla de la Plata, Isla Salango offshore, and the magnificent beach of Los Frailes and is concerned with preserving marine ecosystems as well as the dry tropical forest and archaeological sites on shore. The continental portion of the park is divided into 3 sections which are separated by private land, including the town of Machalilla. Entrance US$20, cheapest trips to Isla de la Plata, US$20 (ask for 5-6 days) payable either in Puerto López or directly to park rangers (insist on a receipt), bus from Puerto López US$0.25. Excellent for bird watching, also several species of mammals and reptiles. About 5 km N of Puerto López on the road to Machalilla there is a dirt road to the right marked to Agua Blanca. Here 5 km from the main road, in the National Park, amid hot, arid scrub, is a small village and a fine, small archaeological museum (entry fee US$0.50) containing some fascinating ceramics from the Manteña civilization found at the *Agua Blanca* site. It is cheaper to find a guide for Agua Blanca in the village itself, not from Puerto López, for a visit to the pre-Inca ruins (US$5 for 2-3 hr tour for groups up to 5). Camping and one very basic room for rent above museum at Agua Blanca (US$1.50 pp, minimal facilities). As a recommended trip (you are required to take a guide), hire donkeys or walk (allow 7 hrs) to San Sebastián, some 9 km up in tropical moist forest (800m) for sightings of orchids and possibly howler monkeys. Camping possible at San Sebastián (US$1.50). Although part of the national park, this area is administered by the Comuna de Agua Blanca, which charges its own fees in addition to the park entrance (as above): a tour to the forest costs US$15 per day for the guide (fixed rate), US$1.50 pp to stay overnight at guide's house, US$5 for meals, US$15 per horse; transportation to Agua Blanca is an extra US$5 pp. Public transport to Agua Blanca leaves Sat only from *Carmita's* in Puerto López at 0630 and 1200, returning 0700 and 1300. Otherwise 5 km dusty walk from main road.

To Los Frailes: take a bus towards Jipijapa and alight at turnoff just S of town of Machalilla; walk 30 mins; show your national park ticket on arrival. No transport back to Puerto López after 1630.

Trips to *Isla de la Plata*, about 24 km offshore, have become popular because of the similarities with the Galápagos, including nesting colonies of waved albatross, frigates and three different booby species. It is also a precolumbian site with substantial pottery finds. Good diving and snorkelling. The island can be visited in a day trip. Two walks on the island, of 3 and 5 hrs; take water. Reservations can be arranged at most nearby hotels in Puerto López, Puerto Cayo or Machalilla and there are touts only too willing to organize a trip. A trip for 8-9 people costs US$140, US$15 for the obligatory guide. Park wardens in Puerto López will arrange trips which don't use pirates. Take dry clothes, water, precautions against sun and seasickness and snorkelling equipment.

On main road through **Machalilla** is **D** *Hotel Internacional Machalilla*, T 345-905, conspicuous cement building, clean, fan, overpriced, talk to manager about cheaper rates for longer stays. Next door is *Comedor La Gaviota*. *Bar Restaurant Cabaña Tropical* at S end of town. A few shops with basic supplies.

The road turns inland for Jipijapa at **Puerto Cayo**, dirty beaches, but better as you walk away from town (**B-D** *Hotel Puerto Cayo*, pleasant situation at S end of beach and good food, but overpriced rooms; **D** *Jipijapa*, clean, TV, fridge, restaurant; **E** *Mar del Plata*, basic, with bath, new cabins nearby C; **E** *Res Zavala's*, Malecón, with bath, clean, ask for sea view, meals available; ask at *Picantería Avelina* for houses to rent; *La Cabaña* just back from beach for good seafood; *D'Comer*, good cheap seafood, next to *Zavala* hotel, "a building site with many mosquitoes").

The paved road climbs over humid hills to descend to the dry scrub around *Jipijapa* (32,225 inhabitants), a squalid-looking town but important centre for the region's trade in cotton, cocoa, coffee and kapok. (**D** *Hostal Jipijapa*, T 600-522, 2 blocks S of cemetery, clean, overpriced. Bus from Manglaralto, 2 hrs, US$1.75 and from Bahía de Caráquez; **E** *Pensión Mejía*, 2 blocks from plaza, clean, bathrooms, a/c, tight security, noisy.) Between Jipijapa and Montecristi are impressive stands of fat-trunked ceiba trees. At *La Pila*, where the road turns E for Portoviejo, the village's main industry is fake precolumbian pottery, with a thriving by-line in erotic ceramics. A few km further W is *Montecristi* (37,660 people), below an imposing hill, high enough to be watered by low cloud which gives the region its only source of drinking water. The town is the birthplace of the statesman Eloy Alfaro. It is also famous for its Panama hats, varied straw and basket ware (much cheaper than in Quito), and wooden barrels which are strapped to donkeys for carrying water. Ask for José Chávez Franco, Rocafuerte 203, T/F 606-343, where you can see Panama hats being made, also wholesale and retail.

Soon after, we reach *Manta* (125,505 people), the second port after Guayaquil, and an important commercial centre, with a large fishing fleet and port. It is a busy, noisy, dirty town that sweeps round the bay, which is filled with all sorts of boats;

the W section comprises steep, narrow streets and the Malecón that fills in the evenings with impromptu parties, cars cruising, music turned up. The constant breeze makes it pleasant to walk along the front or stop for a drink at one of the many small bars. It has a fine wooden church. A new bridge now joins the main town with Tarqui on the E side of the Río Manta. The Tarqui beaches are the more popular, but do not leave **anything** unattended anywhere (in Tarqui or Manta); Playa Murciélago at the W end is very wide but rather less protected; walk further W towards the point for spotless beaches and isolation. The Banco Central museum, Av 6 y C4, has a small but excellent collection of ceramics of the Huancavilca-Manteña culture (AD 800-1550); open 0830-1630, curator speaks English and French. All streets have been given numbers; those above 100 are in Tarqui (those above C110 are not safe). Most offices, shops and the bus station are in Manta.

Hotels Water shortages are very common. Wider selection of hotels in Tarqui. **A3** *Cabañas Balandra*, Av 8 y C20, Barrio Córdova, T 620-316, F 620-545, cabins with a/c, TV, bathroom, 3- and 2-bedded rooms in each, breakfast inc, secure; **B** *Manta Imperial*, Malecón by Playa Murciélago, on beach, T 621-955, F 623-016, a/c, pool, parking, disco and dancing, plenty of insect life; **B** *Las Gaviotas*, Malecón 1109 y Calle 106, T 620-140, F 614-314, on beach, best in Tarqui, a/c, poor restaurant, tennis; **C** *El Inca*, Calle 105 y Malecón, T 610-986, bath, TV, phone, fan or a/c, large rooms, older hotel, noisy, good and reasonably priced restaurant, friendly, helpful; **C** *Las Rocas*, Calle 101 y Av 105, T 610-856, a/c, pool, private parking, restaurant poor; **D** *Panorama Inn*, Calle 103 y Av 105, T 611-552, a/c, bath, TV, pool, restaurant. Also on Tarqui beach: **E** *Hostal Miami*, Av 102 y Calle 107, hot showers, clean, friendly; **F** *Res Monte Carlo*, Calle 105 y Av 105, with bath, no fan, friendly, dirty and basic; **F** *Playita Mía*, Malecón y Calle 103, restaurant, shared bath, very basic; **F** *Residencial Capri*, near bus station, noisy, not very clean, intermittent water, but handy.

Restaurants *Club Ejecutivo*, Av 2 y Calle 11, top of Banco de Pichincha building, first class food and service, cool; *Paraná*, C17 y Malecón, nr port, local seafood and grill, highly rec; *Shamu*, C11 No 1-12, downtown, good set meals and à la carte; *Santa Ana*, Av 106 y C105, Tarqui, good set lunches, not cheap. Several fish places on the Malecón in Tarqui; *El Marino*, kiosk on Tarqui beach specializes in *sopa marinera*, better than in smarter places; many *comedores* on Tarqui beach, open weekends. Bakeries: *Pastafiore*, Av 2, No 10-75; *Buen Pan*, Calle 103 entre Av 106 y 107.

Exchange *Casa de Cambio Zanchi*, Av 2 No 11-28, T 613-857, *Cambicruz*, Av 2 No 11-22, T 622-235; *Delgado Travel* (see below). Banco de Pichincha and Banco del Pacífico change TCs. Filanbanco accepts Visa.

Post Office above Banco de Pichincha; **Telephone** Emetel, Malecón nr C11.

Tourist Office Cetur, Pasaje José María Egas (between C10 y 11), between Av 2 y 3, T 622-944, helpful, Spanish only. **Travel Agents** *Ecuadorean Tours*, at Av 2 y Calle 13; *Metropolitan Touring* at Av 3 No 11-49; *Delgado Travel*, C12 y Av 2, T 624-614, F 621-497, also changes dollars.

Immigration Av 4 de Noviembre y J-1 (police station).

Air Service Eloy Alfaro airport nearby. TAME to Quito daily (US$27).

Buses To Quito, 8 hrs, US$4.75; Guayaquil, 4 hrs, US$4; Esmeraldas, 8 hrs, US$4.65; Santo Domingo, 6 hrs, US$2.35; Portoviejo, ½ hr, US$0.40; Jipijapa, 45 mins, US$0.50; Bahía de Caráquez, 3 hrs, US$1.60; Ambato, US$5.50. All from bus station behind new central bank building.

Crucita (pop 8,300) is a rapidly growing resort, 45 mins by road from Portoviejo. Many bathers on Sun, crowded and dangerous during carnaval, relaxed and friendly at other times. Hang gliding and parasailing are practiced from the dry cliffs S of town. The beach and ocean are lovely but best not to go barefoot as there are many pigs roaming loose and trichinosis (*nigua*) is common. Much cleaner beaches are to be found on either side of town. There is an abundance of sea birds in the area: brown pelicans, frigates, gulls and sandpipers among others.

Hotels From N to S along the beach: **E** *Hipocampo*, oldest in town, private bath, simple, friendly, good value; **E** *Residencia San José*, shared bath, intermittent water supply, basic; **D** *Hostería Zucasa*, T 634-908 (Portoviejo), 244-713/320-271 (Quito) fully equipped cabins for up to 6 persons, best in town; **D** *Fernando's*, new, some rooms with private bath, friendly; **D** *Hostería Las Cabañitas*, T 931-037, cabins for 4 to 5 people, simple, friendly.

Restaurants Many simple restaurants and kiosks serving mainly fish and seafood line the beach.

Emetel for long distance phone calls (no international service) 2 blocks back from beach on main highway.

Buses Buses and open sided trucks with slatted seats, called *chivas* or *papayeros*, leave from the beach and plaza for Portoviejo, US$ 0.45, 45 mins.

2 km N along a paved road running parallel to the beach is the fishing village of Las Gilces, which has been less influenced by tourism. *Hotel Centro Turístico Las Amazonas*.

24 km inland from Montecristi (65 km from Jipijapa) is **Portoviejo** (132,937 inhabitants, capital of Manabí province), a major commercial centre. The cathedral, overlooking Parque Eloy Alfaro, has recently been restored.

Hotels and Restaurants **B** *Ejecutivo*, 18 de Octubre y 10 de Agosto, T 632-105, F 630-876, very good, expensive, extra charge for the guard, but unfriendly, does not accept Visa despite sign outside; **B** *El Gato Internacional*, Pedro Gual y Olmedo, T 636-908, F 632-850, a/c, TV, bath; **B** *Hostería La Estancia*, Séptima transversal de la Avenida del Ejército, T 931-884, fridge, pool; *Complejo Turístico Concorde*, Km 1 Vía Picoazá, T 631-909, F 636-877, modern, a/c, hot water, TV, tennis & other courts, pool, restaurant, disco; **C** *New York*, with a/c and fridge, D with fan, Fco de P Moreira y Olmedo, T 632-037/632-051, F 632-044, clean, nice, restaurant downstairs; *Hostal Zucasa*, Teodoro Wolf y Venezuela next to bus terminal, T 634-908, not a safe area; **E** *París*, Sucre y Olmedo, off main plaza; **F** *Cristal*, Calle Ricaurte 106, beware of peeping Toms, clean, cold water, not good for women. The restaurant *Chifa China* on the plaza has a clean, cheap hotel upstairs. *Zavalito*, Primera Transversal entre Duarte y Alajuela, lunch only, popular; *Los Geranios*, Chile 508 nr Quito, good set lunch; on same street *La Esquina* and *El Gaucho*. Other restaurants: *Mariano Internacional*, Córdova y García Moreno, good food; good Chinese restaurant at bus terminal; *El Palatino*, off main square, good coffee and cheap local specialities. *Peña Gol Bar* for post 2100 drinking.

Tourist office Cetur, Morales 613 y Sucre.

Transport Connections by road with Guayaquil and Quito (bus, 7 hrs with Reina del Camino). To the capital routes are either E via Quevedo (147 km), or, at Calderón, branch NE for Calceta, Chone and on to Santo Domingo de los Colorados. Bus station out of town, taxi US$0.90. Flights to Quito Mon, Wed, Fri at 1700.

About 60 km NE of Manta (60 km N of Portoviejo, 30 km S of Bahía de Caráquez) are **San Clemente** and, 3 km S, **San Jacinto**. Both get crowded during the holiday season. The ocean is magnificent but be wary of the strong undertow; also, do not go bare foot because of risk of trichinosis *nigua*, especially in the towns. Most Guayaquil-Portoviejo-Bahía de Caráquez buses pass San Clemente.

San Clemente Hotels **C** *Hostería San Clemente*, T 420-076, modern clean cabins for 6 to 10 persons, swimming pool, restaurant, book ahead in season; next door is *Hostería San Esteban*, cabins. **E** *Las Acacias*, 150m from the beach, 800m N of San Clemente, clean, T 541-706 (Quito), bath, nice 3 storey wooden building with huge varandas, prices go up in high season, good seafood, rec; *Residencial San Clemente*, on main street by the beach, very basic. **E** *Hostal El Edén*, 1 block from beach along main street, some rooms have bath, some have sea views, clean, basic; **E** *Cabañas Espumas del Mar*, on the beach, good restaurant, family run; *Restaurant Tiburón*, on beach, cheap and good; *Restaurant El Paraíso del Sabor*, at water's edge, tasty fish and seafood, cheap.

San Jacinto Hotels **D** *Hostal San Jacinto*, on the beach with bath. Across the street is **F** *Residencial Virgen de Lajas*, very basic. **D** *Cabañas del Pacífico*, T 523-862 (Quito), private bath, fan, fridge; **E** *Cabañas Los Almendros*, T 533-493 (Quito), private bath, basic, cramped. **F** *Hotel Amarilus*, at S end of town, very basic. Between San Clemente and San Jacinto are **E** *Cabañas Tío Gerard*, T 459-613, F 442-954 (Quito), with bath and kitchenette, small room, clean, fan, and *Balneario San Alejo*.

Bahía de Caráquez (15,308 people) is in a pleasant setting on the southern shore at the seaward end of the Chone estuary. The river front is attractively laid out with parks on the Malecón Alberto Santos. The Malecón becomes Circunvalación Dr Virgilio Ratti and goes right around the point. While there are still some buildings with wooden windows and balconies, and some arcaded shops in the centre, the point is built up with smart houses and blocks of flats. There are boats in the river and dolphins can be seen in the estuary. The town is a centre of shrimp farming, and has become popular as a beach resort (busy times July-Sept, Christmas, Easter). The beach stretches around the point and is quite clean. The archaeological museum of the Central Bank (in Casa de la Cultura next door) has a collection of precolumbian pottery.

Hotels Only hotels with own supply do not suffer water shortages. **A3** *La Piedra*, Circunvalación y Bolívar, T 690-780, F 690-154, pool, good restaurant but expensive, laundry, modern, good service, access to beach, lovely views; **B** *Herradura*, Bolívar y Circunvalación, T 690-446, F 690-265, a/c, C with fan, friendly, comfortable, restaurant, very pretty; **C** *Americano*, Ascázubi 222, T 690-594, some rooms with a/c and bath, remodelled 1994, cold water, ask for water to be turned on, overpriced; **C** *Italia*, Bolívar y Checa, T 691-137, F 691-092, private bath, fan, hot water, TV, restaurant; **C** *Hostal Querencia*, Malecón 1800 by main road out of town, T 690-009, some rooms with bath, clean, friendly, rec; *Hostal Los Andes*, Ascázubi 318, T 690-587, with bath, basic; **E** *Palma*, Bolívar 914 y Arenas, with bath, clean, basic, unfriendly, restaurant below, good set meals, breakfast; **G** *Miriam*, Montúfar, entre Ascázubi y Riofrío, basic, friendly, helpful, clean, safe; **G** *Residencial San José*, Ascázubi 110, basic, unfriendly, mixed reports. On the road to Chone, 6 km beyond Bahía is **C** *Hostería Quinta W*, motel-style, a/c, refrigerator, TV, warm showers, pool, tennis, guarded, clean, rec.

Restaurants *Brisas del Mar*, Hidalgo y Circunvalación, good fish, cheap; *Los Helechos*, Montúfar y Muñoz Dávila, by Circunvalación, good and clean; *Comedor Doña Luca*, Intriago y Plaza Acosta; *Chifa China*, cheap, good, Bolívar y Ascázubi; *La Chozita*, on the front near San Vicente ferry station, BBQ style food, good; nearby are *La Terraza*, *Genesis* and *Botecito*, also *Bar-Comedor Roxin*; closer to the ferry is *Miramar*; good cheap *pizzeria* 1 block from bus terminal heading out of town; *Top Cream*, on park at A Mateus entre Viteri y Intriago, fantastic ices. Ascázubi 209 for drinks, sandwiches, cakes.

Exchange Banco Comercial de Manabí, Malecón y Ante.

Tourist Office Cetur, Malecón y Arenas, T 691-124, Mon-Fri 0830-1800.

Tour Agency *Marina Tours – Guacamayo Adventures*, Av Bolívar y Arenas, T 691-412, F 691-280, excursions to Isla de Fragatas (see below), coastal caves N of Canoa (see below), to see the shrimp ponds, mangroves and the great migratory bird watching of the wetlands of the estuary (including fishing for ugly, black *chame*, which can live 72 hrs out of water – boys sell them in Bahía and Chone in the morning) and into the fascinating tropical dry forest at Punta Bellaca. On this trip you will have excellent views of Bahía and the coast; also, you avoid paying the US$20 entrance fee that you must pay to enter the dry forest of Machalilla National Park. Also offered are 3-day trips on horseback to a typical coastal farm at Río Muchacho (accommodation with a family in a bamboo house or tree house, traditional food, "an eye opener to rural coastal culture"), US$70-86 depending on numbers, highly rec, reservation necessary.

Bus companies are Coactur and Reina del Camino; their offices are on the Malecón 1600 block. All buses coming into Bahía stop by the monument at the Malecón end of Ascázubi before returning to the bus office. Departing buses do not go to the centre. To **Quito**, 6½ hrs, US$5, **Santo Domingo de los Colorados**, 4-4½ hrs, **Esmeraldas**, 0945, 8 hrs, US$5, and **Portoviejo**, 2 hrs, US$1.50; **Puerto López**, go to Portoviejo or Jipijapa and change. To **Guayaquil**, 5½ hrs, US$4.45; to **Manta**, 3 hrs, US$1.60. Open-sided *rancheros* leave from the park on Aguilera to Chone and other nearby destinations.

Airport at San Vicente (see below): TAME to Quito, Fri, Sun 1730, US$28.

Excursions There are various viewpoints above the peninsula, eg Mirador La Cruz. Across the river to San Vicente (see below). Guacamayo Adventures (see above) has the concession for visiting the **Isla de Fragatas**, 15 mins by boat in the middle of the Bahía de Caráquez estuary, which has a stunning number of bird species, including a higher concentration of frigate birds than on the Galápagos. This is an excellent trip for photographers because you can get really close, even under the mangrove trees where they nest. The frigate birds can be seen displaying their inflated red sacks as part of the mating ritual (best Aug-Dec). The trip costs US$15.50 (less for larger groups).

From Bahía de Caráquez to the highlands there are two main roads. The first one is via Chone and El Carmen to Santo Domingo. This road climbs quickly over the coastal range, with views of the estuary, the remaining mangroves and the shrimp ponds that destroyed them. In the following wetlands, with more shrimp ponds, are cattle fincas and bamboo houses on stilts.

Chone, 1 hr from Bahía, 41,437 people, is very busy on Fri; at the Santo Domingo exit is a strange sculpture of 4 people suspending a car on wires across a gorge. The second road is via San Clemente and Rocafuerte to Pichincha, Velasco Ibarra and on to Quevedo. Alternatively you can go via Calceta, then on an unpaved dry season road directly to Pichincha, rarely passable, 4-wheel drive rec, two rivers without bridges, not deep, very scenic.

Those interested in exploring the coast further N can take the ferry from Bahía de Caráquez to ***San Vicente***, on the N side of the Río Chone, a thriving market, nice beaches. (*Pangas* cross all the time until 2200, 10 mins, US$0.20; car ferry every 20 mins or so, free for foot passengers, very steep ramps very difficult for low clearance cars.) There is a paved road from Chone and the road N to Canoa is being paved. **Hotels** On road to Canoa, across road from beach: **A3** *Cabañas Alcatraz*, T 674-179, cabins for 5, nice, a/c, pool; **A3-B** *Monte Mar*, Malecón s/n, T 674-197, excellent food, pool, views, various rooms for rent; **B** *El Velero*, cabañas and suites, pool, restaurant, good; **C** *Hotel Vacaciones*, T 674-116/8, bath, a/c, pool, restaurant, TV in rooms; **C** *Las Hamacas*, T 674-134, rooms or cabañas, restaurant, bar, disco, pool, tours; **D** *El Montés*, T 674-201, with bath, bar, no restaurant, friendly; **D** *Restaurant Las Gaviotas*, 3 rm with bath, nice. In town: **E** *San Vicente*, Av Primera y C 1, opp market, T 674-182, cheaper with shared bath, basic, mosquito nets, *Chifa Chunking 2* next door. **Buses** Coactur opp *panga* dock to Portoviejo, Manta, Guayaquil; Reina del Camino nr *Hotel Vacaciones*, to Portoviejo, Chone (4 a day), Guayaquil (3), Quito, US$5.40, Esmeraldas, US$5.65, Santo Domingo (3), US$3.70, Quinindé (2), US$4.50, Pedernales, US$4.

The 20 km of beaches between El Charco and Canoa are rec; you will see many people harvesting shrimp larvae, especially at full and new moon. ***Canoa*** has *Pensión Canoa*, basic; *Comedor Dixie* has rooms. Just N along the beach are 9 natural caves at the cliff base; walk there at low tide and allow time to return. The beach is 800m wide, the widest in Ecuador. Inland, cutting across Cabo Pasado through the more humid pasture-lands, is the small market centre of ***Jama*** (small *pensión*).

From there the road runs parallel to the beach past coconut groves, inland across some low hills and across the Equator to ***Pedernales***, another small market town on the coast, dirty and unfriendly, but nice beaches around, lots of shells; several houses where you can stay (**F** *Hotel Turismo*, very basic, helpful, but toilets and showers dirty; **F** *Pedernales*, clean, quiet; *Playas*, near airport, cheapest rooms F, price depends on bath, a/c, TV, friendly, clean; **F** *Residencial Comedor El Gitano*, meals, friendly; **F** *Residencial Aire Libre*, on beach 10m from water, waves drown noise, very basic, dirty). **Restaurants** *El Rocío*, good cheap food; *La Fontana*, just off main plaza, good vegetarian food; *Soda Bar*, great milk shakes. A rough new road has been finished between Pedernales and El Carmen (thence to Santo Domingo and Quito)—the two towns are expected to become booming tourist resorts—and on to Cojimíes (enquire if passable in rainy season).

Buses, 2 a day, take 4-5 hrs from San Vicente (US$4.50), 90 mins from Pedernales (truck US$0.50, colectivo US$1.50) to ***Cojimíes***. **G** *Residenciales España*, shabby, no water; *Mi Descanso* and *Cojimíes*—all look the same. **D** *Cocosolo*, 14 km before Cojimíes, French, English and Italian spoken, clean, beach, restaurant. Several houses serve food; one restaurant, *El Caracol*, good but expensive. Cojimíes was a major pre-conquest centre; little of this is noticeable now, although many artefacts are still dug up, it is being continually eroded by the sea and has been moved about three times in as many decades. A boat leaves at high tide every Sat for Esmeraldas, stopping at Chamanga (US$4, 7 hrs) and one from Esmeraldas on Sat as well. There is a boat to Manta on Wed; daily canoes to Muisne. The entry into Cojimíes and Muisne is treacherous and many boats have been thrown into the shallows by the swell.

North of Cojimíes is a rich banana-growing region. ***Muisne***, an island reached by road from Esmeraldas (bus US$1.40, 3 hrs, and a canoe over to the island, US$0.15), is the centre and main outlet of this area; through it some 50,000 stems of bananas a month are exported via Esmeraldas. The town is reported filthy and unsafe. On the Río Sucio, inland from Muisne and Cojimíes, is an isolated group of Cayapa Indians, some of whom visit the towns on Sun. **E** *Galápagos*, on far side of town from docks, closest to beach, with bath, F without, modern, clean, washing facilities, theft reported 1995; **F** *Oasis*, clean, friendly, secure, rec; **F** *Res Isla*, clean, basic, mosquito net, safe; **F** *Sarita*, clean, private bathroom; **G** *Cabañas San Cristóbal*, far side of town from dock, first wooden cabins on beach on right, no sign, basic, toilet, shower (if water running), friendly, cheaper for long stay; **G** *La Gaviota*, price pp, negotiable for longer stays, excellent meals; **G** *Mi Residencial*, basic; **G** *Pensión Reina*, basic; you can also rent small huts on the beach, G pp, few if any have electricity or water, beautiful setting; **F** *Cabañas Ipanema*, 200m from beach, bath, mosquito nets but take repellent, clean, safe, friendly, rec. There are several simple seafood *comedores*, try fish in coconut sauce or local shrimp. Also *Delicias del Mar*, Australian-run, good food, good service; *Bar La Cueva*, open late(ish). *Delfín*, in palm hut on beach, clean, good food, nice people, rooms to let, rec. No meals after 1900. The beaches 10-15 mins walk from town, are large and a beautiful walk at low tide but practically disappear at high tide. There is a lot of litter and wood lying around and hordes of mosquitoes, but also wildlife: turtles, sea snakes, crabs and birds. Marcelo Cotera and Nisvaldo Ortiz arrange boat trips to see the mangrove forests which are being restored by the Fundación Ecológica Muisne, donations welcome, contact them through the tourist office. Boats from El Relleno (opp Muisne) daily to Cojimíes, mostly early am, US$5, 2 hrs buy ticket at bus stop, take water proofs. Cargo boats ply between Muisne and Manta. A new road is being built between Muisne and Bolívar inland, behind the beaches; less scenic.

Esmeraldas (98,558 people) is reported dirty and overpriced. The electricity and water supplies are still inadequate, water shortage often lasts weeks. Gold mines nearby, tobacco and cacao grown inland, cattle ranching along the coast, timber exported, and an oil pipeline from the Oriente to an ocean terminal at nearby Balao; an oil refinery has been built nearby. Development of shrimp farms has destroyed much mangrove forest. A road bridge over the river at San Mateo upstream from Esmeraldas gives a direct road link to the General Rivadeneira airport. **Las Palmas**, just N of Esmeraldas, is being developed as a resort: several hotels have been built and restaurants opened. There is a broad sandy beach but it is reported unsafe (theft) and filthy. Outsiders are advised to avoid the shanty-town on the Malecón and to take care everywhere. The atmosphere is certainly not pleasant for women travelling alone. Even the water is muddy as it is close to a naval harbour and people use the beach as a speedway. Buses to Las Palmas (US$0.10, taxi US$1.50) leave regularly from the main square in Esmeraldas.

Mosquitoes and malaria are a serious problem throughout the province of Esmeraldas in the rainy season. All the beaches have mosquitoes that come out in hordes at night and bite through clothing. Take plenty of insect repellent because the Detán sold locally does not work well. Most *residencias* provide mosquito nets (*toldos* or *mosquiteros*); don't stay anywhere that does not. Best to visit in dry season, June-Dec. Use sun tan lotion or cover up, even when it's cloudy.

Hotels Best in Esmeraldas are **C** *Estuario*, Libertad; **D** *Apart Hotel Casino*, Libertad 407 y Ramón Tello, T 728-700, F 728-704, excellent, good restaurant, casino; **E** *Galeón*, Piedrahita 330 y Olmedo, T 713-116, bath, a/c; **E** *Roma*, Olmeda y Piedrahita, T 710-136, with its *Restaurant Tres Carabelas*; **E** *Americano*, Sucre y Piedrahita, with fan and bath, dirty, smelly, thin walls, noisy; **E** *Diana*, Mañizares y Sucre, showers, safe; **G** *Hostal Domínguez*, on Sucre near Plaza Central, noisy, hot water, open all night; **G** *Turismo*, Bolívar 843, basic, with bath and fan, clean and friendly; **G** *Valparaíso I*, Libertad y Pichincha, very basic but good value, cheap restaurant. Other cheaper hotels include **F** *Bolívar*, and cheaper still, **F** *Central*, and **F** *Asia* (9 de Octubre y Bolívar, T 711-852) 100m round the corner from the bus station, both are basic but clean. Generally, hotels in the town centre are not up to much and you are recommended to stay in the outskirts. Some hotels are not keen to take single travellers.

Las Palmas offers the best hotels along Av Kennedy: **D** *Cayapas*, T 711-022, a/c, showers and hot water in all rooms, overpriced, good restaurant; **D** *Colonial*, Plata y Barrizoty; **E-D** *Hotel del Mar*, on sea front, modern, mixed quality and size of rooms but all a/c and mosquito proofed, restaurant closed at 1400, not cheap, good breakfast. Camping at *El Edén* S of town near beach.

Restaurants In Esmeraldas: *Chifa Restaurante Asiático*, Mañizares y Bolívar, Chinese, excellent; *La Marimba Internacional*, Libertad y Lavallén, has been rec. In Las Palmas, *Artrang*, main plaza, good food, good value; *Las Redes*, main plaza, good fish, cheap. *Budapest*, Cañizares 214 y Bolívar, Hungarian-run, clean, pleasant; *Balcón del Pacífico*, Bolívar y 10 de Agosto, nice atmosphere, good view overlooking city, cheap drinks; *Fuente de Soda Portenito*, Sucre y Cañizares, thick fruit milk-shakes, rec. There are numerous typical restaurants and bars by the beach selling ceviches, fried fish and patacones, etc.

Throughout Esmeraldas province a cheap meal is the *comida tipica*, fish, rice, boiled *plátano*, sometimes beans (*minestre*), called *tapao*. There is also *cocado*, fish, crabs or shrimp cooked in coconut cream served with rice and *plátano*. There is a soup made of shellfish and coconut milk which is very good. *Cocada* is a sweet made of brown sugar and grated coconut; *conserva* is a paste of guava, banana and brown sugar, wrapped in banana leaves.

Shopping There is a Cayapa basket market across from the Post Office, behind the vegetables. Also three doors down, Tolita artefacts and basketry. Market near the bus station is good for buying mosquito nets. *Más por Menos* supermarket has good selection of imported goods.

Exchange at **Banco Popular** (entre Cañizares y Piedrahita on Bolívar) and **Filanbanco**, upstairs at both until 1200; at *Botica Koch*, Sucre y 9 de Octubre, good rates.

Entertainment In Esmeraldas, *El Portón* peña and discotheque, Colón y Piedrahita; *El Guadal de Ña Mencha*, 6 de Diciembre y Quito, peña upstairs, marimba school at weekends; good *Bar Asia* on Bolívar by main Parque. *Los Cuervos*, discotheque. In Las Palmas, *El Náutico* and *Déjà Vue* on the Malecón, a/c, discotheques. Cockfights, Eloy Alfaro y 9 de Octubre, weekends.

Music Esmeraldas has been called "the capital of rhythm". The people prefer the livelier sound of Caribbean *salsa* to the *cumbia* heard in the sierra, and have retained the African-influenced marimba, usually accompanied by a bomero, who plays a deep-pitched bass drum suspended from the ceiling, and a long conga drum. Where there is a marimba school you will also find dancers, and the women who are too old to dance play percussion and chant songs handed down the generations, many with Colombian references, but the best marimba can only be seen in the backwoods of the province on Sundays and holidays.

Cinema *Ciné Bolívar*, Bolívar y 9 de Octubre, with a/c and upholstered seating. *Cine Esmeraldas* shows newer movies. Two other cinemas offer more basic accommodation with bats and rats.

Immigration Av Olmedo y Rocafuerte, T 720-256.

Tourist Information The tourist office (Cetur) is in the Edificio de la Alcaldía, Bolívar 517 y 9 de Octubre, 2nd floor, half a block from the main square, singularly unhelpful.

Buses To Quito, US$5.50, 6½ hrs, 30 a day, good paved road (or 7 hrs via Mindo, San Miguel de los Bancos and La Independencia), Trans-Esmeraldas, Av Piedrahita 200, is most reliable of cheaper outfits (deafening music, ask them to turn it down, no toilet stop), or by Occidental or Trans Ibarra; also with Pan Americana (at *Hotel Casino*) twice daily, slow but luxurious, US$10; by Aerotaxi (small bus), 5 hrs, 12 passengers, reserved seats, office near main square. To **Santo Domingo**, US$2.25, 4 hrs; to **Ambato**, 5 times a day with Coop Sudamericana, 8 hrs, US$6.50; to **Guayaquil**, hourly, US$6.50, 7 hrs; to **Bahía de Caráquez** go via Santo Domingo de los Colorados; to **Portoviejo**, US$6.60, and **Manta**, US$4.65; to **Quevedo**, 6 hrs. To **La Tola** (road good to Río Verde), 6 daily between 0600 and 1500, US$2.15, 2-3½ hrs; to **Muisne**, 28 daily with La Costeña, US$1.35, 3½ hrs. to **Súa** (road reasonable), Same and Atacames every half hour from 0630 to 2030, US$0.40, 1-1½ hrs.

Boats to Limones and San Lorenzo: service irregular; ask at Port Captain's office at Las Palmas. Combined boat/bus service leaves for San Lorenzo at 1330.

Airport General Rivadeneira on the road to La Tola; taxi to centre, 30 km, about US$5 (Esmeraldas), buses to terminal terrestre from road outside airport pass about every 30 mins, several buses to La Tola and Borbón, not necessary to go into Esmeraldas if you want to go on to San Lorenzo or other places. Daily flights to Quito with TAME, US$22, ½ hr; to Atacames, Súa and Same. Check in early, planes may leave 30 mins before scheduled time. TAME flight to Cali, Mon and Fri, at 1400, 1 hr, US$66; it is reported that no exit tax is charged.

Atacames is a beach resort 25 km S of Esmeraldas. The palm trees on the beach, washed away in 1983, are growing again. Most accommodation has salt water in the bathrooms; fresh water is not always available and not very good. Busy during high season (April-Oct) at weekends and local holiday times, and can be very noisy and dirty on the beach. Best to bring a mosquito net as few hotels supply them.

Hotels C *Castel Nuovo*, 3 km N on road to Esmeraldas at Tonsupa, T 714-244, with bath and fan, swimming pool, on beach, rec; nearby at Km 23 on Playa Ancha is **E** pp *Conjunto Vacacional Vistazul*, cabins for 6-10, modern, kitchens, restaurant, bar, pools, reservations in Quito, Jorge Washington 223 y Tamayo, T 528-564, F 545-663; *Hostal del Manglar* on road into town, new, good reports; *La Pradera*, 4 km along Esmeraldas road, pool, restaurant, good value; **C** *Hostería Los Bohíos*, T 731-094, prices cheaper (F) in low season (June, July, August), for a bungalow, bathrooms with salt water but there are fresh water showers too, safe, clean; **C** *Cabañas Arco Iris*, shower, fridge, clean, rec, charming, N end of beach, T Quito 525-544 for reservations or in Atacames T 731-069, English, Spanish, German and French spoken; **E** *Tahiti*, with shower, reductions for longer stays, avoid the rooms nearest the beach, friendly, serves breakfasts, good restaurant, try the prawns, but check your bill carefully, also has nice cabins, F; furthest S **E-F** *Cabañas de Rogers*, T 751-011, quiet, rec, constant water supply, restaurant, bar; **F** pp *Casa Blanca*, Urbanización Iñaquito, T 731-031, cabins for 6, with bathroom, kitchen, on beach. Tents or beach bungalows can be hired at under US$1 a night; no facilities but can arrange with hotels. **E** *Galería Atacames*, T 731-149, at the beach, with bath, clean, restaurant, fine views, mixed reports, owner's name is Gabby; **F** *Hostería Cayapas*, T 731-047, beach huts, cooking and barbecue; **F** *Marbella*, T 731-120, and *Juan Sebastián*,

T 731-046, beach huts for 5; **F** *San Baye*, just past *Tahiti* at the end of the beach, cheap, not rec for single women. Beach bungalows with showers at **F** *Cabañas Costa del Sol*, T 731-281, good water supply, good breakfast and seafood; **F** *Cabañas South Pacific*, T 731-248, clean, American owner, fresh water showers. Rats are common in all these beach huts, and insect repellent is essential.

Restaurants on beach are reasonable, mostly seafood, best *ceviche* at stands along the street, but avoid *concha*; try **Comedor Pelícanos**, only open weekends and holidays, fresh fish, chicken, *ceviche*, occasionally music, rec; also **Cafetería Pelícanos**, best, includes vegetarian dishes and salads; **Marco's**, good steak and fish, rec; **El Tiburón**, on beach, good seafood, cheap; **Comedor Popular**, good Italian and criollo cooking, order special requests in advance; **Paco Foca**, great seafood, often queues. 2 discotheques on beach. The best bar is **Guido's**, on the beach. *Cocada*, a sweet made from different nuts, brown sugar, cocoa, etc, is sold in the main plaza.

Warning It is reported that there have been many assaults on campers and beach strollers. Walkers along the beach from Atacames to Súa regularly get assaulted at knife point where there is a small tunnel, gangs seem to work daily. The sea can be very dangerous, there is a powerful undertow and many people have been drowned.

NB also The sale of black coral jewellery has led to the destruction of much of the offshore reef. Consider the environmental implications before buying any.

Buses to Esmeraldas; to La Tola; to Same, US$0.35.

Súa, another beach resort a little S of Atacames, is quiet, friendly, with a beautiful bay with pelicans and frigate birds; the sandy beach has been improved. **G** *Pensión Palmar*, cabins; **G** *Residencial Quito*; **G** *Mar y Sol*, washing facilities poor. The hotels along the seafront vary little in standard but quite significantly in price. **F** *Motel Chagra Ramos*, T 731-202, on beach, clean, fan on request, good restaurant; **F** pp *Hotel Buganvillas*, on the shore, very nice; *Pensión del Súa*, in the village, good, clean, airy; *La Plage*, formerly *Hotel Súa*, French run restaurant, expensive but excellent quality. Insect repellent is essential along this coast.

Beyond Súa is Playa de **Same**, with a beautiful, long, clean, grey sandy beach lined with palms, safe for swimming and good birdwatching in the lagoon behind the beach. No cheap accommodation, popular with families: **A1** *Club Casablanca*, restaurant, tennis courts, swimming pool, luxurious (reservations Wagons-Lits Turismo, Ed Galicia, Diego de Almagro 1822 y Alpallana, Quito, T 554-933/4/7, Telex 22763 VALEJO ED); **B** *Hostería Rampiral*, clean; **C** *La Terraza*, 5 cabins for 3-4, good Spanish-run restaurant (reservations *Restaurante La Bettola*, Quito, T 239-396); **C** *Cabañas Isla del Sol*, 12 cabins for 4-6, bath, clean, spacious, cold shower, electric light, comfortable, safe, good restaurant, rec, stoney beach front, cabins are close together and road traffic is very audible, reservations T 731-151, Atacames, or telegram to Casilla 358, Esmeraldas; **C** *El Acantilado*, 14 rooms for 2-3 people, 30 cabins up to 5 people, T 235-034 in Quito, excellent food, on hill by the sea, S of Same, no palm trees. Booking advisable at holiday times and weekends (but in low season good deals can be negotiated). All restaurants serve good seafood, but are not cheap (cheaper restaurants at Tonchigüe, see below). Bus from Súa to Same, La Costeñita, 15 mins, 18 km, US$0.10, make sure it drops you at Same and not at *La Casablanca*, buses pass every 30-60 mins, look out for sign for *Cabañas Isla del Sol*. Bus, Same-Muisne, US$0.50.

Tonchigüe, a quiet little fishing village, 20 mins' walk from Same, 1 hr S from Esmeraldas, is also lovely during the rainy season (Dec-May). New expensive *cabañas* and 2 small, cheap hotels. Bus Atacames-Tonchigüe, US$0.50. 2 km S of Tonchigüe at Km 13.5 is Playa Escondida, a beautiful beach resort with cabins and camping.

There are no good beaches for swimming N of Esmeraldas. Río Verde, where the paved road ends, has a dirty beach and one hotel, **F** *Paz y Bueno*, basic (N side of river). It was the setting for Morriz Thompson's book on Peace Corps life, *Living Poor*. Beyond Río Verde is **Rocafuerte**, recommended as having the best seafood in the province. At **La Tola**, where one catches the boat for Limones and San Lorenzo, the shoreline changes from sandy beaches to mangrove swamp. The wildlife is varied and spectacular, especially the birds. La Tola is 2 hrs minimum (US$2.15) from Esmeraldas, by bus, 6 daily, dusty, uncomfortable, buses often get stuck. Boats between La Tola and San Lorenzo connect with buses to/from Esmeraldas; 2 hrs La Tola-San Lorenzo, US$3, via Limones and Tambillo (beware overcrowding). Try to avoid staying overnight in La Tola, women especially harassed. Take a raincoat.

Mangrove coastlands stretch N into Colombia, and have only two towns of note in Ecuador: Limones and San Lorenzo.

Limones, the main commercial centre, largely a saw-mill town, is the focus of traffic down-river from much of N Esmeraldas Province where bananas from the Río Santiago are sent to Esmeraldas for export. The Cayapa Indians live up the Río Cayapas and can sometimes be seen in Limones, especially during the crowded weekend market, but they are more frequently seen at Borbón.

Limones has two good shops selling the very attractive Cayapa basketry, including items from Colombia. The first is opposite *Restaurant El Bongó* and the second by the dock opposite Banco de Fomento.

Two hotels, both execrable. Limones is "the mosquito and rat capital of Ecuador", a title disputed by Borbón which has the highest rate of malaria in the country. A hired launch (6 people US$1.75 pp, 1½ hrs) provides a fascinating trip through mangrove islands and passing hundreds of hunting pelicans. Information on boat journeys from the Capitanía del Puerto, Las Palmas, reached by bus No 1 from the main square in Esmeraldas. From Limones you can also get a canoe or boat to Borbón. Better to stay at San Lorenzo.

Borbón with population almost entirely black, is on the Río Cayapas past mangrove swamps. Ask for Papá Roncón, the King of Marimba, who, for a beer or two, will put on a one-man show. Across from his house are the offices of *Subir*, the NGO working in the Cotacachi-Cayapas reserve, they have information on entering the reserve and guide services. Inefan can also provide information. (**E** *Tolita Pampa de Oro*, T Quito 525-753, bath, clean, mosquito nets, helpful; **F** *Residencial Capri*; **G** *Panama City*, mosquito nets, noisy; *Comedor*, where Ranchero buses stop, excellent fish.) Buses to/from Esmeraldas, US$3 with El Pacifico, 4 hrs, 0600-1700, hourly, beware of stealing or sit on the roof; by boat to Limones and San Lorenzo 2½ hrs, US$4, at 0730 and 1100. Upstream are Cayapa Indian villages. From Borbón hire a motor launch or go as a passenger on launches running daily around 1100-1200 to the mouth of the Río Onzole (US$5 pp, 3½ hrs): **Santa Maria** (board and lodging with Sra Pastora at missionary station, F, basic, mosquito nets, meals US$2, unfriendly, her brother offers river trips, or at the **G** *Residencial*, basic, will prepare food but fix price beforehand, owner offers 5 hr jungle trips to visit Cayapa villages, beware deadly red and black river snakes, camp in front of school free); Zapallo Grande and on to San Miguel. Borbón to San Miguel, US$8 pp, 5 hrs, none too comfortable but interesting jungle trip. At the confluence of the Cayapas and Onzole rivers, there is a fine lodge built by a Hungarian (for advance bookings write to Stephan Tarjany, Casilla 187, Esmeraldas), C with full board, good value, clean, warm showers. Jungle walk with guide and small canoes at no extra charge. Water skiing available, US$12/hr. Steve organizes special tours to visit remote areas and a trip to the Ecological Reserve, US$250 for 3 days incl transport and food. **Zapallo Grande** is a friendly village with many gardens, where the American missionary Dr Meisenheimer has established a hospital, pharmacy, church and school; there is a shop, expensive. You will see the Cayapa Indians passing in their canoes and in their open long houses on the shore. **San Miguel** has a church, a shop (but supplies are cheaper in Borbón) and a few houses (**F** *residencial*), beautifully situated on a hill at the confluence of two rivers. You can sleep in the rangers' hut, F, basic (no running water, no electricity, shared dormitory, cooking facilities), or camp alongside, beware chiggers in the grass. It is possible to make excursions into the jungle, US$12-18/boat, 2-3 people, ask for an official guide, eg Don Cristóbal. From there you go back 5 hrs downstream to La Tola where you can pick up the bus from Esmeraldas or go on to Limones and San Lorenzo.

Trips from San Miguel into the **Cotacachi-Cayapas National Park** (entry US$20) cost US$22.50 for a group with guide, US$5 for boat rental, US$5/meal.

San Lorenzo is relatively more attractive than Limones. It is on the Bahía del Pailón, which is characterized by many canals. At the seaward end of the bay is a sandy beach at San Pedro (fishing huts, no facilities), reached by boat, Sat and Sun at 0700 and 1400. The area around San Lorenzo is rich in timber and other plants, but unrestricted logging is putting the forests under threat. The prehistoric La Tolita culture thrived in the region. *Marimba* can be seen during the local fiesta on 30 Sept, also ask local children where and when Marimba groups are practising. San Lorenzo is an expensive town, with a poor water supply. There are two cinevideos. When arriving in San Lorenzo, expect to be hassled by children wanting a tip to show you to a hotel or restaurant. Robbery is common.

Hotels E *Continental*, Calle Imbabura, T 780-125, F 780-127, opened 1994, all rooms with bath, TV, mosquito nets, clean, family-run, breakfast on request; **G** *Yeaninhy*, 3 large rooms, all with TV and fan, clean, mosquito nets, one private bath, two shared, rec; **F** *Carondelet*, main square, some rooms with view, others with bath, others like boxes, fans, mosquito nets, friendly, reliable, owner sells railway tickets to guests so you do not have to queue early in the morning; **F** *Vilma*, near station, basic, ask for rooms 15 or 16, they are newer and bigger; **F** *Residencial Patricia*, good, clean, friendly, fans, rec; **G** *Colón*, mosquito nets, clean, OK; **G** *Ecuador*, Alfaro y 10 de Agosto, near docks, with bath and a/c, cheaper without, thin walls, noisy, good value, restaurant OK, basic, laundry facilities, mosquito net provided; **G** *Jhonny*, Ayora y 24 de Mayo, fans, mosquito nets, bar below; **G** *Residencial Ibarra*, Coronel y 24 de Mayo, fans, mosquito nets, shared baths, run down, but good value, friendly, restaurant; **G** *Paraíso*, 6 rooms, fans, mosquito nets, good, simple restaurant. **Restaurants** *La Red*, Esmeraldas, OK. Great juices at *El Pentagono*; Women's co-op restaurant near 5 ways, good value. Two discos near *Hotels Ecuador* and *Patricia*. Insect repellent is a "must" in San Lorenzo.

Train The train journey to Ibarra gives an excellent transect of Ecuador, but is best done from Ibarra (see description and details under Ibarra, above).

Transport Buses on the new road to Ibarra. Launches to **La Tola** (2 companies with 6 sailings in all between 0530 and 1500, 2½ hrs, US$5.50) and **Borbón** (3 hrs, US$4), via Limones, US$1.35 (stops at Tambilla and Limones en route). Bus from La Tola to Esmeraldas 4-5 hrs, through ticket US$3.65. Beautiful journey but dusty bus trip. Launch to **Esmeraldas** at 0500 and 0730; plane to Quito at 0930, tickets at airport at 0800.

From San Lorenzo there are boats to **Tumaco** in Colombia daily, 4½ hrs, US$16-20, but gringos are not normally welcome as passengers because contraband is being carried. Entry stamps in Colombia must be obtained by crossing the border at Ipiales and returning again. When arriving in San Lorenzo from Tumaco, the customs office run by navy personnel is in the harbour, but you have to get your passport stamped at the immigration office in Ibarra or Esmeraldas because the immigration police in the *Hotel Imperial* office do not handle passports. Problems may arise if you delay more than a day or two before getting an entry stamp, as the immigration police in Ibarra are less easy-going. If taking an unscheduled boat from Colombia, be prepared for anti-narcotics searches (at least). This can be a dangerous trip, try to seek advice before taking a boat.

Nancy Alexander, of Chicago, writes that about 75% of the population of Limones, Borbón and San Lorenzo has come from Colombia in the last fifty years. The people are mostly black and many are illegal immigrants. Smuggling between Limones and Tumaco in Colombia is big business (hammocks, manufactured goods, drugs) and there are occasional drug searches along the N coastal road.

SOUTHERN PACIFIC LOWLANDS (7)

Thriving and ever increasing banana plantations with shrimp farms among the mangroves are the economic mainstay of the coastal area bordering the E flank of the Gulf of Guayaquil; rice, sugar, coffee and cacao are also produced. The Guayas lowlands are subject to flooding, humidity is high and biting insects are fierce. Mangroves characterize the coast leading S to Huaquillas, the main border crossing to Peru.

Heading E then S from Guayaquil, 22 km beyond main crossroads at Km 26, lies the **Ecological Reserve of Manglares Churute**. Many waterbirds, animals and dolphins can be seen. Canoe trips into the mangroves with guides must be arranged through the MAG office in Guayaquil, Dept Forestal T 397-730, or, more efficiently, through Chasquitar agency, Urdaneta 1418 y Av Del Ejército, T 281-085. Entrance fee of US$20 charged on site just to walk self-guided nature trail over hills. Buses leave the terminal near the airport every 30 mins going to Naranjal or Machala, ask to be let off at Churute information centre.

Puerto Bolívar, on the E shore of the Gulf, is built on the Estero Jambelí among mangroves and is a major export outlet for over one million tonnes of bananas annually. There is a pleasant waterfront and from the old pier a motorized canoe service (dep: 0700, 1000, 1500, return: 0800, 1200, 1600.US$1.35) crosses to the beaches of Jambelí on the far side of the mangrove islands which shelter Puerto Bolívar from the Pacific; safe, long beaches with a few straw beach umbrellas. (**F** *Hotel Mariasol*, basic, adequate, at far end of beach, cafés along beach). Longer trips to Playas Bravita, 30 min (no shade or facilities) or Costa Rica, 2 hrs (take passport as a military post has to be crossed). Canoe hire to Costa Rica for the day about US$70 for 15 people, cheaper to arrange from Huaquillas. This beach is pleasant but waves and currents can be dangerous. The trip through mangrove channels is interesting especially for bird watchers. Take repellent against mosquitoes and other biting insects.

Hotels G *Jambelí*, basic, fan, bath. **Restaurants** *El Acuario* one block back from pier for good seafood, also *Restaurant Sarita* nearby, *Miramar* for a toasted sandwich and beer at the pierhead, lots of seafood kiosks between old and new piers. Better and cheaper than in Machala. Beware of mugging especially after dark around port entrance.

Puerto Bolívar serves *Machala* (buses every few minutes, 20 min ride) a booming agricultural town (pop 144,197) and major banana producing and exporting region with an annual banana fair (and own beauty queen, Reina del Banano) in September. It is also a large pond shrimp producing area. Not very attractive, dirty and not worth a special visit, but definitely a prosperous area, the town is a main crossroads and useful as a stopover before heading onto Huaquillas, Arenillas and Loja (216 km), or via *Pasaje* (**F** *Hotel Pasaje*, with bath) and Girón to Cuenca (188 km). 30 km S on the main road to Peruvian border lies *Santa Rosa*, an agricultural market town (Hotels: **D** *América*, El Oro y Colón T 943-130, new with a/c, TV, private bath; **E** *Santa Rosa*, one block from plaza, good with a/c, private bath; cheap *residencias* on Av Colón, **G** *Residencia Santa Rosa*, dirty, noisy).

Machala Hotels *Oro Verde*, luxury, opened July 1994. **B** *Reina Paccha*, 9 de Octubre y J Montalvo, T 923-207, apartment hotel, cable TV, a/c, full kitchen, phone. **C** *Rizzo*, Guayas y Bolívar, T 921-511, a/c, TV, suites available, slightly worn luxury, water supply intermittent, pool, casino, cafetería, restaurant, noisy late disco; **C** *Oro (San Francisco)*, Sucre y Juan Montalvo, T 922-569, refurbished, good, expensive restaurant but good, cheaper café downstairs; **D** *Encalada*, Tarqui y 9 de Octubre, T 920-681, restaurant, bar, cafetería, disco; **D** *Perla del Pacífico*, Sucre 603 y Páez, T 920-915, TV, a/c, no hot water, traffic noise in front rooms; **E** *Inés*, Montalvo y Pasaje, T 922-301, good restaurant; **D** *Mosquera*, Almedo, between Guayas y Ayacucho, T 931-752, E with fan, TV, hot water, rec; **F** *Ecuatoriano*, 9 de Octubre y Colón, T 920-197, unfriendly, overpriced, bath, a/c; **F** *Gran Hotel Machala*, Juan Montalvo 835 y Rocafuerte, dirty and noisy, no fan, T 920-530; **F** *Residencial Internacional*, Guayas y Sucre, water shortages, friendly; **G** *Residencial El Oro*, 9 de Mayo y Bolívar, T 920-446, basic, dirty. A mosquito net may be needed for sleeping.

Restaurants Best food in the better hotels. *Cafetería San Francisco*, Sucre block 6, good filling breakfast; *Parrillada Sabor Latina*, Sucre y Guayas, steaks and grills; *Don Angelo*, 9 de Mayo just off main plaza, open 24 hrs, good for breakfast; *Copa Cabana*, on main square, good clean snack bar; *Chifa China* and *La Peña*, both 9 de Octubre y Guayas; two branches of *Kingburger* offer good hamburgers, clean; *La Fogata*, near telephone office, for good chicken. Good supermarket in Uni Ono shopping centre.

Cinemas There are several, of which *El Tauro* is the best, a/c, cushioned seats, good sound. The *Teatro Municipal* has wooden benches and rats, US$0.35 a seat.

Sport A development just outside Machala on the Pasaje road has two large outdoor swimming pools. Cockfighting takes place every Saturday afternoon at the cockpit on Calle 9 de Octubre.

Exchange Banco del Pacífico, Rocafuerte y Tarqui, changes TCs and cash; **Banco Machala**, advances cash against Visacard, friendly and efficient; **Filanbanco**, Rocafuerte y Guayas, does Visa cash advances; the *casas de cambio* do not change cheques.

Peruvian Consulate At the NW corner of Colón y Bolívar, 2nd floor.

Post Office Bolívar y Montalvo; telephone and cable office, **Emetel**, 9 de Octubre near stadium.

Travel Agent *Ecuadorean Tours*, Bolívar y Guayas, T 922-670; *Orotour*, Bolívar 603, T 931-557; *Delgado*, 9 de Octubre 1202 y Junín, T 923-154.

Tourist Office Cetur, 9 de Mayo y Pichincha, little information.

Buses The bus companies Occidental, Panamericana, Ecuatoriano Pullman and Rutas Orenses (the best safety record) have depots in the town with direct services to **Quito** (12 hrs, US$6), Panamericana, luxury service, 9 hrs, US$10 a/c, US$8 without a/c, also minibuses; **Guayaquil** (4 hrs, US$2.65), **Esmeraldas** (11 hrs, US$5), **Loja** (7 hrs, US$3). Transportes Loja has buses all day from Tarqui 4 Este, between Rocafuerte 1 Sur and Bolívar 2 Sur. Hourly service to **Cuenca** from Trans Azuay Terminal on Montalvo, 3½ hrs, US$3, "exciting ride guaranteed" along a winding road. **Warning** Do not take night buses into or out of Machala, they are not safe.

Taxis to Guayaquil: Orotaxis run a scheduled taxi service between the *Hotel Rizzo*, Machala and *Hotel Rizzo*, Guayaquil, every 30 mins or so for US$6.

Air Daily flights from Guayaquil with CEDTA dep Guayaquil from the Terminal de Avionetas 0715, 1130, 1400, 1615 returning from Machala 1 hr later, US$15 each way.

Excursions Just by the air strip at Santa Rosa is a turnoff for **Puerto Jelí**, a tiny fishing village 4 km at the road's end, right in the mangroves on a branch of the main *estero*. Good eating at *Picantería Jambelí* and *Riberas del Pacífico*. Canoe trips can be arranged through the mangroves with Segundo Oyola (ask for him opposite the dock) to the beach of Las Casitas, or fishing or clam collecting. Price according to group size and bargaining recommended.

Southeast to the picturesque town of **Zaruma** (118 km, 1170m), with noticeably white-skinned, blue-eyed inhabitants of direct Spanish stock working with primitive, water-powered stone crushers for gold extraction; either via Piñas (several orchid growers) on paved roads, or via Pasaje and Paccha for a more scenic, dirt road. Founded in 1549 on orders of Felipe II to try to control the gold extraction, it is perched in the hills with steep narrow streets and old wooden buildings around the square. (Transportes Paccha dep Machala near market, or Trans TAC, Sucre y Colón dep every hour from 0500 to 1700, last bus back at 1800, US$1.70, 3 hrs to Zaruma, US$0.80, 3½ hrs to Piñas). Gold mines all over the area with a big, dilapidated complex in Portovelho, once run by Americans, down in the valley. Hot thermal springs at Aguas Calientes 6 km from Portovelho with tourist facility; nice for walking and picnics 5 km on Loja road to Río Pindo or Río Luis; also NE out of Zaruma into hills. (*Roland*, new, outside town; F *Hotel Municipal*, dilapidated, good views; F *Hotel Colombia*, on square, very basic; *Pedregal*, on Malvas road has 2-3 rooms.) Military check point at Saracay.

The petrified forest of **Puyango** due S of Machala is supposedly the most extensive outside Arizona. Fascinating trails where even petrified woodworm holes can be seen in the trunks. Over 120 species of birds may be seen, campsites provided. Bus for Alamor 0830, 1400, 3 hrs, US$2.50, and ask to be dropped off for Puyango. No accommodation in village, but ask around for floor space or try at on-site information centre that may allow visitors to stay over. If not, basic accommodation available in Alamor. For further information contact Comisión Administradora de Los Bosques Petrificados de Puyango, Ciudadela Las Brisas, Manzana B-6, Villa 2 Apto No 05, Machala, T 930-012, F (593-4) 924-655. Several military check points between Puyango and Machala.

Crossing the Border into Peru The normal route overland to Peru is via Machala. Many buses (US$1, 2 hrs, every 15 mins from 0445) to **Huaquillas**, the Ecuadorean border town, something of a shopping arcade for Peruvians (all shops close about 1730), described by one traveller as a "seedy one-horse banana town full of touts with black briefcases" (see **Exchange** below). Travellers who haven't obtained their Peruvian tourist cards in Guayaquil or Quito can get them at the border, or must pay US$10 fee in Peru. If offered transport of luggage on a bicycle and assistance through customs, arrange price in advance and the currency in which it is to be paid to avoid rip-offs.

Hotels at Huaquillas D *Parador Turístico* Huaquillas, at N of town, Cetur-operated, swimming pool, restaurant and bar, limited water; D *Vanessa*, 1 de Mayo 323, bath, a/c, TV, phone; F *Guayaquil*, opposite Customs, clean, mosquito nets, limited water supply, noisy, rec; F *Rodey*, Tte Cordóvez y 10 de Agosto, bath, TV; G *Residencial Huaquillas*, Córdovez y 9 de Octubre, basic, clean; G pp *Internacional*, bath, mosquito net, cockroaches, dirty, noisy; G *Residencial San Martín*, opp Customs on main street, dirty, noisy, mosquito nets, convenient.

Restaurants Best at *Parador Turístico*; *Sinqi*, Av de la República, good, expensive; *Chic*, behind *Hotel Guayaquil*, set meal US$1. Expect bananas with everything here.

Complete Ecuadorean formalities at customs (several hundred metres before the border) and immigration, Av de la República y Portovelo, in Huaquillas, then walk along the main street and across the bridge (tricycle porters operate between customs and the border, US$1). At the bridge, the police check passports. The Peruvian immigration and customs post is about 3 km past the bridge; taxis run from the border, US$0.50. From immigration, colectivos and buses run to Tumbes, US$1.20, keep an eye on your bags (taxi to Tumbes, waiting at border for formalities, US$5). The border is officially open 0800-1800, but long lunches are common (Ecuadorean lunch 1200-1400) and the Peruvians like to go home early.

It is best to cross before 1700. Allow 1-2 hrs to complete formalities. Peruvian time is 1 hr earlier than Ecuadorean in Jan, Feb and March. From Tumbes (or from the border), fast long-distance buses run to Lima. If you want to go to Tumbes airport ask to be let out at the turn off, leaving you a 500m walk, otherwise *colectivos* try to take you into town and then all the way out again.

Border practices tend to vary, so check to make sure what the authorities require.

NB Officially, a ticket out of Peru is necessary for entry into the country. Although rarely asked for, some agencies reportedly still sell cheap tickets for non-existent runs out of Peru. If you are required to show a ticket, you can buy a Miscellaneous Charges Order, valid one year, minimum US$150, but remember there is a 10% tax on all tickets bought in Ecuador. Peruvian customs and police have asked for bribes at this crossing. If there is a problem entering with a car, contact Tulio Campoverde Armigos, Agencia Aficionado de Aduanas, Gómez 123 y Portovelo.

Exchange Verify rates of exchange with travellers leaving Peru. Avoid changing near either of the immigration posts; in general the rates at the border are very poor, the best rate is usually for cash dollars. Be sure to count your change carefully; the money changers (recognizable by their black briefcases) are positively dishonest, and clever, particularly with pocket calculators. Travellers leaving Peru should get rid of their soles inside Peru, and buy sucres on the Ecuadoran side. At Huaquillas, better rates for sucres are obtained in the town (though not at the bus terminus) than around the border post, though it is difficult to change TCs. Rates of exchange are better in Huaquillas than in Tumbes.

Coming from Peru into Ecuador; take a bus to Tumbes and a colectivo from there. A ticket out of Ecuador is not usually asked for at this border.

Buses There are a few direct buses from Huaquillas to Quito (and vice versa) each day, 12-14 hrs, US$7 (US$11.50 on Panamericana luxury a/c bus, 11½ hrs); most go via Quevedo, but if you get a slower one via **Riobamba** and **Ambato** you may see all the great volcanoes. Panamericana charges US$15, 2 a day. To **Guayaquil** about 4 hrs, including several stops at military check points, US$3.30. If in a hurry to reach Quito or Guayaquil, it may be advisable to change buses in Machala. To Machala, 1¾ hrs, US$1, from main road 2 blocks from immigration. Ecuatoriano and Panamericana have a reciprocal arrangement regarding tickets across borders and onwards, but there are few through bus services between Ecuador and Peru. (Direct bus at 1000 from Huaquillas to Piura, US$6, 6 hrs, and at other times, also to Trujillo.) To **Cuenca** several daily, 6 hrs, US$4. To **Loja**, daily at 1330 and 1800, 7 hrs, US$3.40; to **Tulcán** at 1530. The road is completely paved going up the coast towards Guayaquil and then turning inland at El Triunfo. The road Huaquillas-Machala-Girón-Cuenca had been reconstructed and is the fastest route to Cuenca; it can be quicker to change buses in Machala.

An alternative point for crossing Peruvian border is Macará in Loja Province (see p 996).

THE ORIENTE (8)

East of the Andes the hills fall away to tropical lowlands, sparsely populated with Indian settlements along the tributaries of the Amazon. Agricultural colonists have cleared parts of the forest for cattle rearing, while even more isolated areas are major oil producers, leading to the gradual encroachment of towns into the jungle.

Ecuador's E tropical lowlands can now be reached by four different road routes, from Quito, Ambato, Cuenca or Loja. These roads are narrow and tortuous and subject to landslides in the rainy season, but all have regular, if poor bus services and all can be attempted in a jeep or in an ordinary car with good ground clearance. Their construction has led to considerable colonization by highlanders in the lowland areas. Several of the towns and villages on the roads can be reached by air services from Quito, Cuenca and Guayaquil, and places further into the immense Amazonian forests are generally accessible by river canoe or small aircraft. The country is particularly beautiful, and some of the disadvantages of other parts of Amazonia, such as the inadvisability of swimming in the rivers, are here absent. Anti-malaria tablets are recommended, however, and be sure to take a mosquito net and an effective repellent. A yellow fever vaccination is recommended for travel into the Oriente.

Travel agencies (eg Metropolitan Tours of Quito, *La Selva*—see under Coca) do trips to the Oriente or to the Río Napo, with meals, flights, lectures included. Going by bus and/or boat you can do a round trip much more cheaply, but you should allow a week. The Oriente also has an unpredictable air service provided by army planes; passengers pay insurance, US$1-2; apart from that, fares are low and the flights save a lot of time. Frequent military checks; always have your passport handy. You may be required to register at Shell-Mera, Coca, Misahuallí, Puerto Napo and Lago Agrio.

When staying at a jungle lodge, you will need to take a torch, insect repellent, protection against the sun, a rain poncho that will keep you dry when walking and when sitting in a canoe, rubber boots (often can be hired). Getting to the lodge may involve a long canoe ride, with a longer return journey upstream to the airport, perhaps with a very early morning start.

The Route from Quito   From Quito, through Pifo, to Baeza, the road is paved well beyond the top of the pass to the E end of the lake some 5 km before the turn to Papallacta; thereafter it worsens. It crosses the Eastern Cordillera at an altitude of 4,064m at a pass just N of the extinct volcano **Antisana** (5,704m, which, gets vast quantities of snow and has huge glaciers—very difficult to climb, experience essential), and then descends via the small villages of Papallacta (**see p 947**), and Cuyuja to the old mission settlements of Baeza and Borja. The trip between the pass and Baeza has beautiful views of Antisana (clouds permitting), high waterfalls, tropical mountain jungle, *páramo* and a lake contained by a glacial moraine almost on the equator.

Baeza is a small town in the beautiful setting of the Quijos pass, recommended for long scenic walks with many waterfalls (the town is about 1 km from main junction of Lago Agrio and Tena roads—get off Lago Agrio bus at the police checkpoint and walk up the hill; Tena bus goes through the town). The old Spanish cobblestone trail can be found if you go past the hospital and cemetery; the path goes up over the hill (a beautiful walk). Because of the climate, *ceja de montaña*, orchids (in flower June/July) and bromeliads abound. Trout in the rivers. The old settlement, however, is dying as people have moved to a new town 1 km down the road towards Tena. Most of the restaurants are in the new town.

Hotels G *Oro Negro*, residencial and restaurant, at Tena/Lago Agrio junction, also good trout at the filling station, rooms with bath and cold water; F *Samay*, shared bath, clean, friendly; F *Hostal San Rafael*, new in 1994, shared bath, clean, friendly.

Restaurants *El Fogón*, the best; *Lupita*, Calle Chimborazo. *Guaña*, breakfasts US$1, friendly, TV. Everything closed by 2030.

At Baeza the road divides: one branch heads S to Tena, with a newly constructed branch road going directly via Loreto to Coca (7 hrs). The other goes NE to Lago Agrio, following the Quijos river past the villages of *Borja*, a few km from Baeza, and *El Chaco* to the slopes of the still active volcano **Reventador**, 3,485m. (At the village of Reventador there is a *pensión*, *de los Andes*, basic, clean, and a restaurant.) The road winds along the N side of the river, past the impressive 145-metre *San Rafael falls* (to see them, get off bus at Inecel sign about 2½ hrs from Baeza, walk down side road, and then down a steep path, for 45 mins to a bridge; then it's a further 15 mins walk—camping possible, but take all equipment and food). The road then crosses the watershed between the Coca and Aguarico rivers. The road runs along the N bank of the river to the developing oil towns of Santa Cecilia and Lago Agrio.

Lago Agrio (pop 13,165) is a rough place but the infrastructure is improving; excursions into the jungle can be made, although it is easier to find guides in Coca. Virtually everything in the town is along the main road, Av Quito. Lago Agrio (officially called Nueva Loja) is the capital of the province of Sucumbios, created in Feb 1989 (pop of province 77,500).

Hotels C *El Cofán*, 12 de Febrero y Av Quito, T 830-009, inc taxes, a/c, best, but overpriced, no hot water, TV, fridge, clean, restaurant mediocre and expensive; E *Cabaña*, next to *Hotel Willigram*, clean, rec; F *La Mexicana*, reasonable, mosquito nets; F *Machala 2*, clean, safe, friendly, restaurant, insufficient bathroom facilities; F *San Carlos*, clean, safe, a/c, cheaper with fan; F *Residencial Sayonara*, with bath, good, sometimes water shortages; F *Willigram*, with own bath, doors unlockable, noisy, above bar; several others with shared bathrooms. *Comercial Calvopeña* is the best place to buy groceries and supplies. *Mi Cuchita* beside *El Cofán*, cheap, good chicken.

Exchange Several *casas de cambio* on Av Quito, good rates for notes, impossible to change TCs or use credit cards.

Tours *Crucero Fluvio Aripa*, Chiritza, the brothers Torres Navarrete arrange tours, rec; *Harpía Eagles Tours*, Quito 223 y Manabí, T 830-142, show wildlife in Cuyabeno area, rec.

Transport TAME flight to **Quito** (Mon-Sat) at 1130, US\$44, book 1-2 days in advance. **Buses to Quito** (US\$5.35, 11 hrs), **Baeza** (US\$2.80, 8 hrs), **Coca** (US\$1.45, 3 hrs), also many *ranchero* buses which leave when full, and **Tena** (US\$4.20, 9 hrs).

From Lago Agrio it is possible to take a bus to Chiritza and then a 2 hrs boat ride to San Pablo de Kantesiya, a small village on stilts with one hut where visitors can stay. Get an exit stamp from Migración in Lago Agrio (Quito 111—police station, T 125) before taking a bus N to La Punta (US\$0.50, 1¼ hrs) where you hand in your Tourist Card to the military and get a boat across the Río San Miguel to the village of San Miguel in Colombia (La Punta-San Miguel, 1 hr, US\$2.65). From there you can catch a jeep or bus (5 hrs) to Puerto Asís and on to Hormiga (1 hr, hotels and restaurants), then bus to Mocoa (DAS office and border formalities, Colombian entry stamp can be obtained at Consulate in Lago Agrio) and Pasto.

For permission to go downriver on the Aguarico (as opposed to an exit stamp) go to the Brigada (military post) rather than Migración because the store owner there will give you permission to go anywhere as long as you buy something from his shop. Down the Aguarico from Lago Agrio is the **Cuyabeno** National Park, an extensive jungle river area on the Río Cuyabeno, which drains eventually into the Aguarico 150 km to the E. In the National Park there are many lagoons and abundant wildlife (entry US\$20). Transport is mainly by canoe and motorboat, except for one road to Río Cuyabeno, 3 hrs by truck from Lago Agrio. Accommodation is in lodges, eg at Iripari, or in jungle camps, eg Imuya; the base camp for both is Zancudo, 5 hrs downstream from Chiritza. There are *cabañas* on the Río Cuyabeno. To visit Cuyabeno contact *Jungletur*, Amazonas 854 y Veintimilla, Quito, who have 6 day tours of the area. An experienced guide is Alejandro Quezada, T 571-098, Quito. *Neotropic Tours*, Rik Pennartz, PO Box 09-01-4690, Guayaquil, F (593-4) 374-078, takes trips to the Cuyabeno National Park, lodges, everything provided. *Pacarina*, in same office as Hostería Alandaluz, Armero 710 y Sta Rosa, Quito, T 237-583, F 525-671, runs 5 day tours to a Secoya community down the Aguarico River.

Transturi of Quito (Orellana 1810 y 10 de Agosto, T 544-963) do trips into the jungle on a floating hotel, *Flotel Orellana*, US\$567 (4 nights, 3 days) per person in double cabin with fan, including all meals, guides, etc. Services and food are good, although wine is very expensive. Flights extra (US\$125): bus to Chiritza on the Río Aguarico, then launch to the *Flotel*. Different itineraries for different interests are available on the *Flotel* (above prices are quoted by Metropolitan Touring, who also run tours to the Aguarico and Imuya camps, 3-5 nights, starting at US\$567 pp).

At Lago Agrio, a temporary ferry crosses the Aguarico River (bridge washed away), then the road heads S to **Coca** (officially named Puerto Francisco de Orellana—pop 15,199), a river port at the junction of the Coca and Napo rivers; the route via Loreto also involves a ferry crossing a few km before Coca, US\$0.55 per car. The place is described as a typical oil town, dirty, noisy, with heavy drinking. All foreigners going beyond town into the jungle have to register with the police; all guides who accompany foreigners have to be licensed. If going alone beyond the bridge at Coca into the jungle, you must get permission from the Ministerio de Defensa, Av Maldonado, Quito (full details from South American Explorers Club). The bank will not change TCs, but there are two places that will (ask around), but not Bank of America; only new cash bills will be exchanged (guides will accept US dollar bills). Food and supplies are reportedly less expensive in Coca than in other parts of the Oriente. At Carnival, water and petroleum throwing is the sport. There is usually no electricity after midnight.

Hotels D *La Misión*, T 553-674/561-478, in Coca 880-260-261, clean, friendly, English spoken, restaurant; D *Auca*, cabins, comfortable, dirty, electricity in pm, big garden with monkeys roaming free, poor food but crowded, manager speaks English, good meeting place to make up tour party; E *Oasis*, near the bridge at the end of town, clean, comfortable, hot water and fans, rec; F *Florida*, on main road from airport, with fan, good; F *Residencial Rosita*, noisy, cold water, unsafe, not rec. F *Tungurahua*, favourite with oil workers, rooms OK, but dirty toilets and showers; F *Lojalita*, poor.

Restaurant *Los Cedros*, down by river, 2 blocks from Capitanería, good fish, *patacones*, *yuca*, fairly expensive; *Doña Erma's* set meal is cheap and filling; *Asedero*, friendly, cheap, popular with locals; *Venecia*, good food, away from main market area; *Mama Carmen*, good for early breakfast; *El Buho*, good food, jungle specialities, capibara etc, reasonably priced; *King Burger*, cheap, good chicken and chips, friendly, ask for Braulio Llori Pugachi, a recommended, good value jungle guide.

Responsible Tourism Dr Miran Kegl of Stockholm University, a rainforest specialist, fears the depletion of wildlife in this area and asks readers to insist that guides and all members of their party take all litter back and ban all hunting and shooting, it really can make a difference.
    Secondly, if a guide offers a tour to visit Indians, ask to see his/her permission to do so.

Tours All guides out of Coca charge about US$30-55 pp per day, but you may have to bargain down to this. At popular times it may be difficult to find a choice of worthwhile tours or English-speaking guides. You are strongly advised to check what precisely is being offered, and that the price includes equipment such as rubber boots, tents, mosquito nets, cooking equipment and food, and transport. Trips which do not go beyond the Río Napo itself are not worth taking since you will see nothing. To see animals you should go downstream from Coca to the Río Tiputini, or to the Cuyabeno National Park (see above under Lago Agrio). The South American Explorers Club in Quito can provide updated information about jungle tours, recommended guides and how to arrange your trip. *Amazon Jungle Adventures* (PO Box 17-21-841, Quito), in association with the Rainforest Information Centre, has a contract with the Waorani of Ñonaeno for an educational adventure trip up the Shiripuno. The Waorani benefit from the tourism and are employed as guides, cooks etc. Contact Randy Smith, author of *Crisis Under the Canopy*, a guide at the agency, who is working on ecotourism projects for indigenous peoples, 4-day trip US$280 all included except rubber boots, sleep in tents, T 880-606, F 880-451, Coca. Among other guides are *Luis Alberto García, Emerald Forest Expeditions*, Amazonas 1023 y Pinto, Quito, T 526-403, ext 13, operates out of Coca, speaks English, knowledgeable, rec; The Vasco brothers, Wilson, Daniel, Jonas and Walter, of *Vasco Tour Travel Agency*, can be contacted only in Baños, T (03) 740-017, rec, no litter, no killing of animals, no intrusion of Indians' privacy, their guide, Juan Medina, is frequently rec. Also in Baños, *Tsantsa Expeditions*, T (07) 740-957. Canoes and guides for jungle trips can be hired from *Fernando Silva*, who lives at the end of the riverside lane next to the bridge, his nephew Ricardo Silva has been described as an enthusiastic guide and a good cook. *Agustín Lara* organizes trips with good food and guides, but negotiate trip in advance or it will be all canoeing, US$20 per day; ask in the exchange advertised "Cambio—best rate in town", take extra water; *Panki Tour Alternativo*, run by Indian co-operative, talk to Ernesto Tseremp Juanka, 6 de Diciembre y García M, Coca, very friendly and interesting as they share their culture also with visitors, food good; *Yuturi Jungle Adventure*, Amazonas entre Pres Wilson y Pinto, Quito, T 233-685, Coca 880-166 or contact through *Hotel Oasis*, good rates for groups, a typical trip is 4 days staying at *Cabaña Yuturi* downriver towards Nuevo Rocafuerte, US$390 pp, rec. *Jumandy Explorers*, Cordero 1960 y 10 de Agosto, Quito, T 230-714/211-763, guide Isaias Cerda is an indigenous Quichua, very knowledgeable, speaks some English, does trips on the Río Arajuno. More expensive is *Fluvial Tours* (minimum 4 people). Recommended Shuar Indian guides are Patricio Inank Kukush, Puerto Cepe, Coca, and Bartolomé Mankash.

Hacienda Primavera is 2 hrs downstream from Coca. There are clean, basic rooms available (F pp), or you can camp (US$0.50). Meals cost US$2.50, breakfast US$1.50, bring bread. There is a generator but candles are used for after-generator hours. Excursions are not cheap (eg

US$13 to Monkey Island, US$30 to Monkey Island and Pompeya Catholic Mission, US$45 to the above and Limón Cocha, divide prices by number of people (1-10) and add 10% service) and there is not much wildlife to see apart from birds, but it is supposed to be possible to hire canoes from the *hacienda* to visit other places along the Napo. Independent travellers to *Primavera* should check carefully prices quoted on transport back to Quito, and to/from Coca.

La Selva, a jungle centre 3 hrs down the Napo from Coca, has been frequently recommended for the quality of its accommodation (built of natural materials) and food. It holds the highest award in ecotourism. It offers interesting excursions into the jungle, 140-foot observation tower, a butterfly farm for breeding and observation: one entymologist has told us he believes this to be one of the richest forest wildlife areas anywhere. The birdlife is arguably the best in the world (over 550 birds have been listed, including some virtually unknown species) and the calibre of guiding is described as unequalled. *La Selva* runs the Neotropical Field Biology Institute, a field studies programme in conjunction with Harvard University and other institutions; genuine field biologists may apply to work at *La Selva* (subject to approval, discounts may be awarded). Guests often meet biologists in the field. 4-night packages from Quito including all transport, lodging, and food, not cheap, but worth it. There is laundry service. Also available 6-night, 7-day "Amazon Light Brigade" adventure expedition, with 8 guests, 15 staff and a free bar, the height of luxury. Best to book directly at *La Selva*, 6 de Diciembre 2816 y James Orton, PO Box 635/Suc 12 de Octubre, Quito, T 550-995/554-686, Telex 2-2653 JOLEZ ED, F 567-297 (extra Fax 563-814), alternatively through most travel agencies in Quito.

Sacha Lodge, 2½ hrs by motor boat from Coca, owned by Swiss Benny, comfortable, hot water, excellent food, good jungle trips, cheaper than *La Selva*, rec. Bookable through Explorer Tours, Lizardo García 613 y Reina Victoria, Quito, T 522-220.

Yuturi, 4 hrs downstream from Coca, on the Río Yuturi, has good cabins, food and guides, excellent location; bookable through *Etnotur* in Quito (see **Tours** above).

Transport Bus to Quito, 12 hrs, US$6.50, 6 a day, several companies (Trans Baños, leaves the capital at 0700 and 1400), take food and drink as stops are often only 10 mins; to **Lago Agrio**, 3 hrs, US$1.45; to **Tena**, 2 daily, 6 hrs, US$3.30, it is advisable to walk on to the ferry, the driver has been known to miss, with fatal consequences; to **Misahuallí**, 14 hrs; to **Baeza**, 9 hrs, US$4.30.

Flights to Quito with TAME, US$44, reserve at least one day in advance, best to arrange soon after arrival, Mon-Sat, planes are small and flights can be very bumpy, flights in and out of Coca are heavily booked, military and oil workers have priority on standby. There are military flights to **Tena** and **Shell-Mera** from Coca on Mon, Wed and Fri. Petroecuador oil company also flies Quito-Coca and sometimes takes travellers on board the small planes. **NB** Do not walk or ride from the airport to town up the side street which leads to *Hotel Auca*, the police make very thorough, and acquisitive searches of arriving passengers here.

For **passenger boats** out of Coca, ask at the military post in the marina. There are only two regular passenger boats a week (Wed, Sun) to Misahuallí now that a road has been completed from Coca to the Baeza-Tena road. Canoes go if there are 8 or more passengers, taking about 14 hrs, if it is not reached before nightfall, the party will camp beside the river. For a price, of course, the willing traveller can hire a canoe with owner and outboard motor to take him anywhere along the Napo. (To Misahuallí the charge is about US$130. Take a cushion and waterproofs for self and luggage.)

Canoes (irregular service, best to hire your own) pass Coca carrying passengers and cargo down-river to Limón Cocha, the Capuchin mission at Pompeya with a school and museum of Napo culture, and Nuevo Rocafuerte. Local canoes can be hired from Limón Cocha and also canoes to return to Coca. Halfway between Coca and Nuevo Rocafuerte is **Pañacocha** (**G Pensión**, friendly, but watch out for chiggers in the mattresses), near which is the magnificent lagoon of Pañacocha on the Panayacu River (recently declared a protected forest region).

In **Nuevo Rocafuerte**, the missionaries and Sra Jesús let rooms; there are no restaurants. There is a Mon boat from Coca to Nuevo Rocafuerte but you must get a military permit to enter the area. The officer has to write exactly the area you wish to visit and you have to leave your passport. The boat takes 8 hrs (hammocks provided) US$25. You can stay overnight at Pañacocha. It is possible to hire boat and guide in Nuevo Rocafuerte, but it would be wise not to add tourism to the pressures to which the Waorani Indians are already subjected (eg oil exploration on their land). **Note** The only guides permitted to take tourists into Waorani territory are Samuel Padilla, Juan Enomenga, Expediciones Jarrin and Randy Smith. If any other guide offers a trip into their territory, do not accept, it would be in contravention of an authorization of Feb 1992. Some guides also kill animals found en route. There is a cargo boat back on Mon, but it doesn't always run and you may have to wait until Fri. To Coca it is a 2½-day ferry ride (US$9) with an overnight stop at Sinchichieta and a meal stop at Pañacocha. It is not possible to cross from Nuevo Rocafuerte into Peru.

Roads from both Baeza and Coca go S to **Archidona**, a village centred around its mission and an extraordinary church.

Hotels E *Residencial Regina*, Rocafuerte 446, T 889-144, modern, clean, rec, cheaper without bath, pleasant and friendly; *Hostal Archidona*, 5 blocks from plaza; *Restaurant Los Pinos*, near *Residencial Regina*, good.

Tours can be arranged by special arrangement to the Izu Mangallpa Urcu (IMU) Foundation, set up by the Mamallacta family to protect territory on Galeras mountain. Only 3 educational tours are run each year, US$200 pp; run in conjunction with the Rainforest Information Centre through *Safari Ecuador* in Quito, T 552-505, PO Box 17-11-6060.

Tena (pop 13,790), 10 km further S, is the capital of Napo Province. Both settlements have good views of Sumaco, an extinct volcano to the N (3,807m), and both have a large lowland Quichua Indian population living in the vicinity, many of whom are panning for gold in the rivers. These Indians are unlike the Indian groups further into the Oriente forests. "They are Quijos, of Chibcha stock, and their old territory extended in pre-conquest times from Puerto Napo up the Quijos pass to Papallacta and from there down to Coca. Their forthright character, bravery and their inherent honesty have not changed since the days when they held the Spaniards back from their efforts to find 'El Dorado'." (Jay Louthian, Florida). There is a beautiful riverside walk starting down the steps between 2 houses, near the Emetel office. To climb Sumaco, contact Don Francisco in Huamani on the new Tena-Coca road: a steep hike, tent required, interesting fauna.

Hotels Water supply in most cheaper hotels is poor. D *Hostal Turismo Amazónico*, Av Amazonas y Abdón Calderón, T 886-487, with bath, TV, fan, fridge, parking; E *Hostal Traveler's Lodging*, 15 de Noviembre by pedestrian bridge, T 886-372, F 886-015, new in 1994, modern, cheaper with cold shower, friendly; E *Hostal Villa Belén*, on Baeza road (Av Jumandy), T 886-228 N of town, new, friendly, clean, cold shower, quiet, rec; E *Hotel Sheraton*, bit noisy but fairly well equipped; E *Media Noche*, 15 de Noviembre 1125, T 886-490, nr bus station, with bath, cheaper without, good, clean, inexpensive restaurant; E *Mol*, Sucre 432, T 886-215, with bath, clean, garage, rec; E *Res Alemania*, Díaz de Pineda 210 y Av 15 de Noviembre, T 886-409, good and fairly clean, D for cabin; F *Residencia Nápoli*, Díaz de Pineda 147, T 886-194, fan, shared bath, parking, friendly; F *Residencial Galeras*, just S of bus terminal, shared bath, basic; F *Residencial Laurita*, opp bus terminal, shared bath, basic; F *Res Alexander*, 2 rooms with bathroom, near bus station; F *Amazonas*, clean, near main square; E *Caribe*, 15 de Noviembre at S end of town, T 886-518, room with bath, cafeteria next door; F *Danubio*, clean, friendly; E *Res Hilton*, next door, good and clean, cheaper without bath; F *Jumandy*, clean, friendly, balcony, breakfast from 0600; G *Enmita*, Bolívar y Montalvo, T 886-253, near the footbridge; G *Hostal Baños*, near bus station, basic, clean, restaurant. A modern resort-style hotel is E *Auca*, on the river out of town, 1½ km on road to Archidona, T 886-461, Cetur-run, restaurant and bar, nice grounds, discotheque, casino, swimming in river, electricity and water unreliable.

Restaurants In Tena, good and reasonable are *Viena* and *Chuquitos*; *Tico Rico Chifa* and *Chifa China*, good, cheap, open late. *Cositas Ricas*, Av 15 de Noviembre, tasty meals (vegetarian available), good fruit juices, run by Patricia Corral, see **Excursions** below; *El Toro*, on the left arriving from Archidona, good *almuerzo*.

Tourist Office near the bus stop N of town.

Buses Quito (via Baeza), 5 daily (Coop Baños, and 1 each Amazonas and Pelileo), US$3.40, 6 hrs, book in advance, 8 hrs, US$4 via Ambato; Baeza, US$1.35, 3 hrs; Ambato (via Baños), 10 a day (several companies), US$5.50, 6 hrs; Baños, 5 hrs, US$2.50; Riobamba (via Puyo and Baños), 5 daily, 6 hrs. Archidona every 20 mins, US$0.15, 15 mins; Misahualli every 20 mins, US$0.50, 1 hr, buses leave from the local (not the long distance) bus station, *camioneta* between them US$0.65, little space for baggage, great views (via Puerto Napo, US$0.10, 15 mins), to Coca, 5 hrs, US$5.50, 6 a day, 2 companies; Jumandy at 1800 to Lago Agrio, 10 hrs, US$7; **Puyo**, US$1.65, 3 hrs. To **Ahuano** 0600 and 1100, return 0800, 1400.

Flights to Shell-Mera with the Air Force, Wed, Fri, at about 1100, 20 seats, rec.

Excursions From Tena or Archidona, a visit can be made to the famous **Jumandí caves** by the Río Latas, 10 km N of Archidona (taxi, or bus from Archidona, ½ hr). It is necessary to go with a guide; take good boots and a strong torch. It is very muddy (sometimes full of water) so it can be useful to take spare clothes. The side ducts of the caves are extremely narrow and claustrophobic. There are several colonies of vampire bat (*Desmodus rotundus*) in the caves. Before going, make full enquiries about routes and conditions. You can camp outside the caves with permission. To Amarongachi in the jungle, trips organized by Patricia Corral and Jesús Uribe, Amarongachi Tours, 15 de Noviembre 422, PO Box 278, T 886-372, F 886-015, well rec; they have a cooperative travel agency, hotel and restaurant, and *Shangri-La* cabins S of Río Jatunyacu. To the Comunidad Capirona, 1 hr by bus then 3 on foot from Tena, run by FOIN, Federación de Organizaciones Indígenas de Napo; information from Sr Tarquino Tapuy, Calle Augusto Rueda, Casilla Postal 217, Tena, T 886-288 (FOIN represents areas of health, education, environment and marketing of local products, will accept volunteers). Fees per day from US$30-40 pp depending on number in party. Alternatively contact the Cedra family, who act as guides for tour agencies, only US$20 pp/day. Nelli (daughter) lives at Calle 9 de Octubre No 356, Barrio Bella Vista Baja, 10 min walk from bus station. If she is not at home, catch bus to Talag from bridge upstream (6 daily, ½ hr), walk 2 km to Río Napo and ask for Olmedo Cedra (father) or Escuela Pedro Carbo (Comunidad Sirena), cross the river on the ferry and walk 25 mins upstream. Both Olmedo and Oswaldo (son) are guides, rec. Sr Delfín Pauchi, T 886-434, Casilla 245, Tena, has built *Cabañas Pimpilala*, 45 mins by taxi from Tena, where for 2-5 days you can live with a Quichua family, **C**, incl lodging, meals, transport, guide. Trails for hiking have been made on his 30 ha of undeveloped land, but emphasis is on culture rather than animals. Delfín speaks only Quichua and Spanish; he knows about plants and their medicinal uses, legends and music.

From Tena the main highway (unpaved) runs S to Puyo. The whole area is a large-scale producer of sugar cane, yuca and *naranjillas* (an orange fruit related to the tomato, used for making a delightfully refreshing fruit drink). Puerto Napo, a few km S of Tena, has a bridge across the Napo river (Pato García, a guide, has room, G, full board, nice, he will take independent tours, but works mostly for Quito agencies). Here is the turn-off for Misahuallí; if travelling N from Puyo, avoid going into Tena by getting off the bus here.

On the N bank, a road leads E to **Misahuallí**, about 17 km downstream, a small port (pop 3,579) at the junction of the Napo and Misahuallí rivers. From the **Napo bridge** you can get a ride in a truck, US$0.50, or colectivos. Misahuallí provides many possibilities for visiting the jungle, being one of the easiest places to get to, as it is only 7-8 hrs from Quito and 5 hrs from Baños. There is not a great deal of wildlife around Misahuallí, but plants, butterflies and birds are plentiful and there is good hiking. For animals you are advised to go to Coca or to take an excursion lasting several days; the one to three-day trips have been described as disappointing. Oil exploration in the area is also diminishing chances of seeing wildlife. There is a fine, sandy beach on the Río Misahuallí, but don't camp on it; the river can rise suddenly and unexpectedly. A nice walk is along the Río Latas, where there are some small waterfalls. You walk through dense vegetation for about 1½ hrs, often through water to get to the largest fall and pass quite a few pools where you can swim. To get there catch the bus towards the Napo bridge and ask to be set down by the river, which you follow upstream.

Hotels C *Misahuallí Jungle Hotel*, across river from town, cabins for up to 6, nice setting, friendly, restaurant operates sporadically, US$165 for 3 days/2 nights including full board and excursions, in Quito, Ramírez Dávalos 251, T 520-043, F 454-146; **C** *Txalaparta*, 1 km from town, new; **D** *El Albergue Español*, PO Box 254, Tena, Quito T/F 584-912, owned by Dr José Ramón Edesa and Cristina Olsen, meals US$3, some vegetarian, all rooms with bath, clean and screened with balconies overlooking Napo, family room sleep six, highly rec, one-day tours, horse-riding planned. In the **E** price range (or **F** where stated): *Residencial Pepe*, main square, basic rooms with fan, safe to leave luggage, information on jungle tours; *El Paisano*, good meeting place, intermittent water supply, clean, cheaper without bath, washing facilities, hammocks, nice garden, rec, eight rooms behind restaurant, good breakfast, try the banana pancakes, information on guides (Alfredo, who hangs around, is not an official guide); **F** *Fifty*, on main square, communal baths, safe, friendly, family run (familia Vasco), vegetarian restaurant, good pancakes and granola; *Milca Isca*, on main square, friendly, clean, cheap, good restaurant, English spoken; *Sacha*, very basic, bamboo walls, noisy bar, at point where rivers meet, monkeys in the garden, path to hotel floods when rains heavy, buy souvenirs of the Oriente here, cheaper than in Baños or Quito; **F** *Balcón del Napo*, basic, central, meals available, clean, friendly, noisy from disco at weekends, safe motorcycle parking; **F** *Etsa*, with or without bath, very simple, owner is guide Carlos Cordero. Douglas Clarke's **E** *Dayuma Hotel* (see also **Restaurants** and Guides below), T 584964, 2 and 3-bedded rooms with bath, fan, balcony, clean, often fully booked with tour groups.

Restaurants The best is *El Albergue Español*; Douglas Clarke's *Restaurant Dayuma* is reasonably good and cheap, as is *El Paisano*, mostly good vegetarian food (but meat should be treated with caution), popular meeting place for gringos, hence its nickname *Restaurant Paleface*, closes 2100 sharp. *La Abuela Pizzería*, on square, good breakfast, pizza, friendly, cheap, good music, rooms for rent. *Jenifer*, cheap, good restaurant on plaza. *La Posada*, downstairs from Balcón del Napo. *Cactus*, on road to El Paisano, new in 1994, drinks, Mexican, breakfast. *Peña/Disco* on same street. The bars down by the river have a frontier feel to them, as do the handful of general stores.

Hotels Down River B *Anaconda*, on Anaconda Island in the Río Napo, about 1 hr by canoe, US$1.20 downstream from Puerto Misahuallí, reservations required; consists of three bungalows of bamboo and thatch, with space for about 48 guests, no electric lights, but flush toilets and cold showers, with water available most of the time. Own zoo with animals in small, unsatisfactory cages. Watch out for thieving monkeys. The meals are good. Canoe and hiking trips arranged, US$50 for 4 days, meals and guides incl, guides only speak Spanish. Opposite, on the river bank at *Ahuano*, is **A3** *Casa del Suizo* (Swiss, Ecuadorean-owned), price pp full board (but little scope for vegetarians), cheaper with shared bath, highly rec for hospitality and location, electricity till 2200, animal sanctuary, trips arranged (for further information contact Giulliano Bonello, Koescherruetistr 143, 8052 Zurich, Switzerland, T 01-302-37-27, or *Explorer Tours*, Reina Victoria y Lizardo García, Quito, T 522-220, F 508-872). No public canoes from Misahuallí on Sun pm, only private hire, US$30, but there are buses Tena-Ahuano, 2 hrs, US$1.50, ask to be dropped at ferry point. 8 km downstream from Misahuallí is *Aliñahui Cabins*, an ecotourism project of Jatun Sacha (see below), price US$48 pp per day, full board, 25 mins by boat (public canoe US$2.50), but also reached by road on the S bank of the Río Napo, 25 km from the bridge in Puerto Napo, bus to Campacocha from Tena passes, but it has to ford the river, can be difficult if the level is high (or take Transporte Baños to Tena from Quito at 0530, buy reserved ticket day before). Eight cabins with 2 bedrooms and bathroom, lush tropical garden, rainforest and nature trails, reservations through Jatun Sacha biological research station (see **Excursions** below). **C** *Hotel Jaguar*, 1½ hrs downstream from Misahuallí, congenial atmosphere, price pp with full board, vegetarians catered for, good value, a full tour (3 days) including meals and good excursions into the jungle costs US$70 from Misahuallí with an extra charge of US$32 for each additional day. Avoid paying in US$ as they give you a very bad rate (independent canoe journey there costs US$30, except by public canoe at 1100); in Quito reservations at Luis Cordero 1313, T 230-552. 2 hrs downstream is *Yachana Lodge*, part of the Funedesin Project, based in the indigenous village of Mondaña; US$50/day inc 3 meals, hiking, bird watching, river trips, etc. Reservations at Funedesin, Francisco Andrade Marín 188 y Diego de Almagro, Quito, PO Box 17-17-92, T 543-851, F 220-362.

There are many guides available to take parties into the jungle for trips of 1 to 10 days, seeing river and jungle flora and fauna, the Cuyabeno National Park and other jungle locations, all involving canoeing and varying amounts of hiking. Guides are now licenced, travellers should ask to see a guide's licence (we have frequent reports of unlicenced guides cheating tourists). It is advisable to insist on paying part of the cost on completion of the trip. Most tours start from Misahuallí but some guides are moving to Coca; tours also start from Tena, Puyo, Baños and Lago Agrio (for tour agencies based in Quito **see p 940**). The going rate is between US$30 and US$50 pp per day, depending on season and length of trip. This should include food and rubber boots, which are absolutely essential (but see below). Overnight tours are recommended only for the hardy.

Some tours have been criticized for too much walking for too few rewards, so make sure your guide knows enough to make your effort worthwhile; an inexperienced guide can mean a boring, or even distressing, walk. Remember that, however good your guide is, organization may be bad, resulting in delays. If short of time, think twice about taking a tour. Some guides visit zoos of hotels where animals are kept in unsatisfactory conditions; make sure beforehand that zoos are not on the itinerary. Travellers into the Oriente must have their passports stamped at the naval office, which is clearly marked at the canoe embarkation point. Note the letter on the wall from the First Congress of the Waorani denouncing the invasion of tourists. If a guide offers to take a trip into Indian villages (eg of the Waorani), ask to see written permission from the Indian leaders and insist that no wildlife will be purchased on the trip. Fees for chartering a canoe are open to bargaining; fares on excursions are fixed. Every canoe pilot is supposed to have his passenger list checked before going downstream but this is not always done. For your own safety ensure that the authorities have a record. Essential items for a trip of any length are rubber boots (or, if you prefer, two pairs of suitable light shoes—keep one pair dry), sleeping bags, rain jackets, trousers (not shorts), binoculars, insect repellent, sun tan lotions, mosquito net, water-purifying tablets, sticking plasters. The cautious might also take a tent, stove, extra food and playing cards. Wrap everything in plastic bags.

We list only those guides who have been recommended to us: *Héctor Fiallos*, of Fluvial River Tours (information in Quito T 239-044, or write PO Box 225, Tena-Misahuallí, T 740-002), arranges outings from 1-15 days. A 6-day tour takes in the Cuyabeno National Park (special permit needed, US$10, passport must be left at the naval office) and the Aguarico River. A 10-day tour goes down the Napo to Nuevo Rocafuerte and up the Aguarico to the Cuyabeno National Park. There are also other tour operators using Hector's name. *Viajes y Aventuras Amazónicas*, on Plaza, friendly, good food, ask for Celso, US$25 per day; *Julio Angeles*, at *Crucero Fluvial Cononaco*, will arrange anything you wish to do; 4-day tour on Río Tiputini is the minimum time to see animals; a 6-day tour includes floating downriver on balsa rafts made by Julio, highly recommended by those who like peace and quiet and offering the opportunity of sighting wildlife undisturbed by motor launches. *David* and *Eduardo Clarke* (speak English), from the *Restaurant Dayuma*, Casilla 291, Tena, T 584-964, or Av 10 de Agosto 3815 y Mariana de Jesús, Ed Villacís Pazos, of 301, T or F 564-924, Quito, arrange trips with other guides. Their one-and two-day walks are recommended. Also trips to Coca, to smaller rivers and lagoons, Limón Cocha, and longer ones into the jungle of up to ten days, similar to those organized by Héctor Fiallos. They also have a camp at the junction of the Arajuno and Puni rivers. At *Hotel Balcón del Napo* contact *Carlos Sevilla*, whose tours up to 18 days are well recommended. (Carlos Sevilla can also be contacted via his sister in Quito, T 241-981.) *Marcos Estrada* of *Crucero Fluvial Yasuni*, knowledgeable, honest, offers tours of different lengths; *Jaime Recalde* and *Eugenio Martínez*, good meals, contact them at *Balcón del Napo*, interesting on fauna and flora; *Sócrates Nevárez*, PO Box 239, Tena, runs 1-10 day tours including trips further down Río Napo, well-organized; *Carlos Herbert Licuy Licuy*, locally born, good on history, legends and culture of the area; *John Cordero*, at *Etsa*; *Alfredo Andrade*, T 584-965, or PO Box 268, Tena, English spoken, money exchanged; *Pepe Tapia González* of *El Oriente*, PO Box 252, Tena, speaks English, knowledgeable, 1 to 10 day tours, good cook (Gary), can pay by TCs.

Excursions 6 km away is *Jatun Sacha* Biological Station (quichua meaning "big forest") a reserve set aside for environmental education, field research, community extension and ecotourism. The biological station and the adjacent Aliñahui project together conserve 1,300 ha of tropical wet forest. So far, 507 birds, 2,500 plants and 765 butterfly species have been identified at Jatun Sacha. Good views, excursions, and walking on a well-developed trail system. Sleeping facilities for 20 in open air cabins. Fee is US$20/day, including 3 meals in dining hall, or US$3 for entrance only. Reservations are necessary and can be made by writing to Fundación Jatun Sacha, Casilla 17-12-867, Quito, T/F 441-592. Visitors are encouraged to stay at *Cabañas Aliñahui* to visit Jatun Sacha. Profits contribute to conservation of the area's rainforest. Jatun Sacha is reached by boat from Misahuallí, US$4. At 0400 a colectivo leaves the station for

Puerto Napo, ask to leave at the road to Misahuallí, 22 kms walk, and boat across the river US$3.

A strenuous day trip can be made to **Palmeras**: take the road N and cross the bridge across the Río Misahuallí, a muddy road (rubber boots essential) goes through fields skirting jungle, there are many birds in this area. Palmeras (a friendly village, no food or safe water) is reached after about 3 hrs. Continue to a patch of primary forest where there are side trails; if you are lucky and quiet, monkeys may be seen.

Transport Buses from Quito via Baños and Tena, about 8 hrs, several daily; also from Quito via Baeza and Tena, about 6 hrs.

Owing to the completion of the road to Coca, there are no regular boat services to Coca, Limón Cocha and Nuevo Rocafuerte; canoes ply this route but only when there are 8 passengers or more (out of season this may be once or twice a week, 9 hrs to Coca, 9-14 back; posted schedule in 1994: to Coca Wed/Fri/Sun 1030, to Puerto Rico US$8 daily 1030/1130/1330). When canoes are running get your ticket (US$18 for foreigners) across the street from the Armada del Ecuador office, where you register the day before, register again when you reach Coca. During and after heavy rainfall there are obviously no services, nor are there any services during a long dry period. You can rent a boat to Coca, US$130 up to 20 people, leaves only am. Take something to sit on.

Puyo (pop 15,563) is the most important centre in the whole Oriente and the junction for road travel into the S Oriente and for traffic taking the **route to/from Ambato** via Baños (**see p 969**). There is a cinema, Coliseo, the Ñucaloma discotheque, and a cock-pit (cockfights Sun 1400). Policia Nacional in Puyo handles visa extensions. Chimborazo and Altar can be seen.

The road from Puyo to Baños is a dramatic journey with superb views of the Pastaza valley and a plethora of waterfalls. If travelling by bus, make sure you get a seat, or better, try to sit on top. Or cycle from Baños and take the bus back with the bike on top. **Shell-Mera** (8 km W of Puyo, 50 km from Baños, 1½ hrs, **F** *Hostal Cordillera*, with bath, restaurant; **G** *Hotel Esmeraldita*, basic, restaurant; **G** *Residencial Azuay*, basic) has an airfield and an army checkpoint where foreigners must register (passport or photocopy required) if coming from Baños or Ambato. The Brigada in Shell will give permission for visiting the jungle.

Hotels in Puyo E *Europa Internacional*, 9 de Octubre y Orellana, T 885-407, with bath, shower, bright, pleasant, good restaurant; **D** *Hostería Turingia*, Orellana y Villamil, T 885-180, small huts with bath, in tropical garden, comfortable but noisy, restaurant quite expensive but good; **E** *Hostal Chasi*, 9 de Octubre y Atahualpa, T 883-059, with bath, new in 1994; **E** *Hostería Safari*, Km 5.5 on road to Puerto Napo outside town, T 885-465, quiet, peaceful; **E** *Pensión Carmenita*, 9 de Octubre y Orellana, cafetería, cockroaches and non-flushing toilets reported; **D** *El Dorado*, Celso Marín 576, T 885-227, F without bath, Chilean owned, rooms on the road side best, family atmosphere, clean, hot water, video club, restaurant, stores luggage; **F** *Europa*, 9 de Octubre 1346, T 885-228, cheaper without bath, poor water supply, good restaurant; **F** *California*, 9 de Octubre 1354, T 885-189, slightly cheaper, noisy; **G** *Grenada*, Calle 27 de Febrero y Orellana, dirty; **G** *Pensión Guayaquil*, Celso Marín, very basic.

Restaurants *Mesón Europeo*, Mons Alberto Zambrano, near bus station, new in 1994, fanciest in town; *Hostería Turingia*, set meals; *Europa* (next to *Hostal*) 9 de Octubre y Marín, good; *Rincón Ambateño*, on river front, follow 29 de Julio, restaurant and pool complex; *Delicia* (local), *Ejecutivo*, good breakfasts; *Miravalle*, set meals; *Viña del Mar* and *El Delfín* (both seafood), all on Marín; *Los Sauces*, Athualpa y 27 de Febrero; *Chifa China*, 9 de Octubre y 24 de Mayo, clean. *Mistral*, Atahualpa y 9 de Octubre, good for breakfast; *Pan Selecto*, Marín y 9 de Octubre, good, fresh bread. *Vitapán*, also Marín y 9 de Octubre, good breakfast with eggs and fresh bread, US$0.75. *El Chileno*, fuente de soda run by owner of *El Araucano*, rec.

Exchange *Cambios Puyo*, 9 de Octubre y Atahualpa, T/F 883-064, good rates.

Tours *Entsa Tours*, PO Box 16-01-856, T 885-500, rec for tours into the jungle, Mentor Marino helpful and knowledgeable. *Amazonia Touring*, 9 de Octubre y Atahualpa, T 883-219, F 883-064, 1-10 land based and fly-in trips.

Flights Air Force to Tena; Macas via Taisha, good views. Shell-Mera can also be reached by military flight from Quito, ½ hr; also flights to Macas. Military flights from Shell-Mera to Montalvo and Tiputini. Military passenger flights only go if there are 16 people.

Buses to Baños, US$1.50, 2 hrs, last one about 1800; **Ambato**, US$2.60, 3 hrs; **Quito**,

US$2.75, 7 hrs (9 hrs via Baeza, US$3.50); *Tena*, US$1.25, 3½ hrs (fight for a seat, rough road). *Riobamba*, US$1.60, 3½ hrs. Most buses leave from the new Terminal Terrestre on the outskirts of town (10-15 mins walk). Those for Macas leave from the main terminal, before going to the terminal near new market at far end of Atahualpa, past Amazonas (sign says Transportes Amazónicas), leave daily 0600, 0900, 1100 and 1500, US$3.70, 3 hrs (better choice of seats at Terminal Terrestre).

Excursions   20-min walk along the footpath by Río Puyo, across two footbridges, there is a good place for swimming. 22 km from Puyo is the 40 ha **Reserva de Bosque Tropical**, a private nature reserve administered by Fundación Hola Vida, US$1 per day, shelter for 10 people, access 16 km S on road to Macas then turnoff W 6 km to reserve.

The first leg of the Puyo-Macas bus journey (US$1, 3 hrs) goes as far as *Chiguaza*, a small settlement at the junction of the Chiguaza and Pastaza rivers. There is a bridge suitable only for cars and small *busetas*.

On the opposite shore, a bus carries passengers the rest of the way to Macas (this bus is rather smaller than the first). It stops often at small settlements, mostly inhabited by Shuar descendants. The ride is slow and rough, the road hard packed dirt, full of potholes. The jungle which borders this road is beautiful.

Macas (pop 9,720), the capital of Morona-Santiago province, situated high above the broad Río Upano valley, is developing rapidly thanks to nearby oil deposits. At about 1,000m, the climate is not too hot and the nights are even cool. A modern cathedral, completed in 1992, with beautiful stained-glass windows houses the much venerated image of La Purísima de Macas. The town has a nice plaza and its environs are very beautiful.

You can cross the Río Upano by bridge or take bus (½ hr) to the Salesian Sevilla-Don Bosco mission. The modern archaeological museum, Don Bosco y Montalba, is a good place to rest and see views of the river, there is a recreation area nearby. Good swimming. A US company from Idaho is offering whitewater rafting on the Upano (River Odysseys West, PO Box 579, Coeur d'Alene, Idaho, 83816-0579, T (208) 765-0841), Ecuador contact: Quito, T 524-403. The whole settlement area has been developed for beef production. In Taisha, a village E of Macas, the *Casa Morocho* rents a few basic rooms, G; on the road to the mission there is a small stream in which you can swim or wash clothes. It is possible to visit the jungle from Macas and there are agencies specializing in tours to villages inc flight, US$30-50 pp. However, it is advisable to contact the Shuar Federation (see below) before taking a tour and verify what is involved before signing any contract. Malaria precautions recommended.

Macas Hotels   C *Peñón del Oriente*, Domingo Comín 837 y Amazonas, T 700-124, F 700-450, modern, rec, clean, secure, hot water, D with cold water, good views from roof; **D** *Hostal Esmeralda*, Cuenca 6-12 y Soasti, T 700-160, modern, clean, hot water, cheaper with cold, good value, rec; **E** *Hotel Amazonas*, Guamote y 29 de Mayo, at S end of town, F without bath, parking; **E** *Hotel La Orquidea*, 9 de Octubre 13-05 y Sucre, T 700-970, with bath, hot water, cheaper with cold, clean and bright, beds comfortable; **E** *Residencial Upano*, Domingo Comín 7-09; **F** *Hostal Casa de La Suerte*, Tarqui 6-30, basic; **F** *Hostería del Valle*, 5 km out on Sucúa road, self-contained cabins, price pp. Others are all F: *Mayflower*, one tiny bathroom but clean rooms, *Residencial Macas*, clean, cheaper without bath; **E** *Hotel Espendid*, Soasti 15-18, with bath, clean, modern, rooms without bath F, basic; *Pensión Turismo*, basic; **G** *Sangay*, Tarqui 6-05, very basic.

Restaurants   *Chifa Pagoda China*, Amazonas 15-05, delicious, generous portions, good value, rec; *Chifa Perla Oriental*, *Mesón Dorado* and bus station restaurant, all on 10 de Agosto; *Rincón del Miguel*, Soasti y 10 de Agosto, Chifa menu, wide variety, rec; *Eros Café*, Amazonas y Tarqui, good for snacks, breakfast, friendly owners; *Café El Jardín*, Amazonas, good breakfast, US$1.50; *Pan Selecto Francesa*, good bakery.

Exchange   Banco del Austro, 24 de Mayo y 10 de Agosto, will change cash or TCs; *Delgado Travel*, Domingo Comín near plaza, cash only.

Cinema   next to Emetel, 24 de Mayo y Sucre, weekends only.

Post Office   9 de Octubre y Domingo Comín, next to park.

Transport   Flight to Quito, TAME, Mon, Wed, Fri, sit on left for best views of Sangay. The air force flies Shell, Taisha, Macas, Morona and vice versa Tues, Thur and Fri. A SAM plane (US$50) will take up to 5 persons for $1/2$ hr flight over jungle. Ask at the airport. Bus to **Cuenca**, 11 hrs, US$7, 4 a day with Turismo Oriental; Transportes Sucúa, 1700, miserable dinner stop in Limón, but spectacular views after that, 0530 bus to see it in day light; hourly to **Sucúa**, 1 hr, no regular service on Thur. Two bus companies Macas-Puyo: Coop San Francisco 5 a day, 3 continues to **Ambato** and **Quito**, 0300, 2000 and 2300, US$4.50 to **Puyo**, 6 hrs, US$7 to Quito; Coop Macas almost hourly from 0600-1500.

Tours *ETSA*, Amazonas y 10 de Agosto, T 700-550, US$160 for 4 day flying tour to Shuar villages; *Ikiaam*, Domingo Comín 5-16, T 700-457, tours to jungle and Sangay National Park. *Tuntiak Tours*, Carlos Arcos offers a variety of trips.

The surrounding hills give excellent views of the volcano **Sangay**, 5,230m, within the Sangay National Park, entrance US$20, information from Inefan in Macas, Juan de la Cruz y 29 de Mayo. The park may be reached by bus $1^1/2$ hrs to village of 9 de Octubre, Wed, Fri and Sun 0730 and 1600, then walk. Sangay is an active volcano, the South American Explorers Club has information on organizing a trip to it, equipment, helmet, etc, and guide essential. The trek takes 7 days and is only for those who can endure long, hard days of walking (the fourth day starts at 0200 and ends at 1800) and severe weather. Protection against falling stones is vital. Mecánica Acosta, Plaza Arenas, Quito (near the prominent basilica), will make shields, arm loops welded to an oil drum top, for US$2-3. Dec/Jan is a good time to climb Sangay. Construction on the Guamote-Macas road which was supposed to traverse the park has been stalled because of environmental considerations.

Sucúa, 23 km from Macas, is of particular interest as the centre of a branch of the ex-head-hunting Shuar (Jívaro) Indians; their crafts can be seen and bought but it is tactless to ask them about head-hunting and shrinking (a practice designed to punish those who bewitched others and to deter anyone wishing to cause sickness or disaster in future). Outside the schools, scenes from Shuar mythology are displayed in painted tables. You can contact the Shuar Federation at Domingo Comín 17-38 (Calle Tarqui 809), T/F 740-108, about visiting traditional villages. This is possible with an Indian guide, but takes time as the application must be considered by a council of seven and then you will be interviewed and told how you should behave. Allow at least $1^1/2$ days. Small craft shop across the street from Shuar Federation. There are an interesting bookshop and (ten minutes walk from the town centre) a small museum and zoo (very few animals) run by Shuar Indians, in the Centro de Formación.

Nearby is the Río Upano, $1^1/2$ hrs walk, with plenty of Morpho butterflies, a cablecar crosses the river; also the Río Namangoza, 15 mins walk, with rapids, good swimming, but be careful after rain.

Hotels F *Hostería Orellana*, S end of town, T 740-193, one room with bath, others without; F *Hostal Alborada*, cheap, restaurant; *Oriente*, clean, but run down, restaurant; F *Rincón Oriental*, shared bath, clean, parking, rec; **G** *Sangay*, very basic; **G** *Cuenca*, small rooms, basic, toilets filthy; *Upana*, off plaza, poor toilet facilities. *Restaurant La Fuente*, Domingo Comín near plaza, good. Bar/restaurant *Sangay*, opp *Rincón Oriental*. *Paolita*, Domingo Comín S of centre. *Jefralisavi*, N of plaza, snacks and drinks, open till midnight, changes US$ cash and TCs.

From Sucúa, the road heads S (2 hrs) to (Santiago de) **Méndez** (4 basic *residenciales* on Calle Cuenca all **G**: *Pensión Miranda, Pensión Amazonas, Residencial Vanesa, Residencial Anita*). Nice town with a modern church. In 1994 work was begun on a long promised road to Cuenca via Paute. Near Méndez a road (1 bus daily) goes E into the jungle (9 hrs) to 12 km beyond the village of **Morona**, located on the Morona river just at the (disputed) Peruvian border (no accommodation, camping possible). No border crossing is permitted. Following the Jan-Feb 1995 border conflict with Peru, visitors should make extensive local inquiries before attempting to visit border areas.

Along the Méndez-Morona road is the junction of the Zamora-Coangos rivers. East of the confluence, at the village of Santiago, a canoe can be hired (about US$30) to a point from where you can walk in $2^1/2$ hrs to the **Cueva de Los Tayos**, a huge cave, 85m in depth. The trail is obscure, and a guide is necessary; Mario Cruz, in conjunction with Metropolitan Touring in Quito, organizes treks from the capital.

2 hrs, 50 km S of Méndez is **Limón**, official name General Leónidas Plaza, a mission town founded in 1935 (3 residenciales on Calle Quito, all **F**: *Res Limón*, T 770-114, modern, basic, clean and friendly, front rooms noisy; *Res Domínguez*, friendly; *Res Santo Domingo*, basic; *Chifa Rincón de Taiwán*, Calle Quito. Cheap sunhats on sale in town; orchids grow around the town). Buses, all from Calle Quito, go to Cuenca, Macas and Gualaquiza. It is some distance N of the turn-off for the **route to Cuenca**. From Limón, the road to Cuenca (132 km) passes through Gualaceo and El Descanso; it is a longer route (Macas-Cuenca) than from Quito, but just as spectacular. From Limón the road rises steeply with many breathtaking turns and the vegetation changes frequently, partly through cloud forest and then, at 4,000m, through the *páramo*, before dropping very fast down to the valley of Gualaceo. There is a police checkpoint at Plan de Milagro, where a road branches W to Gualaceo, foreigners have to register here. Nowhere to stay along the Limón-Gualaceo road.

A trip by car Cuenca-Gualaceo-Limón-Sucúa-Macas-Mera and onwards to Quito is possible with the opening of the Río Pastaza bridge. Quicker access to Quito would be given by the construction of a road between Macas and Riobamba, but work here has been stalled by concerns over the environmental impact on Sangay National Park which the new road would traverse; it has reached 9 de Octubre, N of Macas, and from the mountains was being built out of Guamote (**see p 981**). If travelling by public transport on this route enquire at the bus stations in Macas or Puyo about the condition of the roads.

Continuing S from we reach Indanza (very basic *residencial* and *comedor*), then Gualaquiza (see below), El Pangui (**G** *Hotel Estrella del Oriente*, several *comedores*), Yantzaza (4 hotels, several *comedores*) and Zamora in the Province of Zamora-Chincipe.

From Loja The road to the Oriente (**see p 992**) crosses a low pass and descends rapidly to **Zamora** (pop 8,736), an old mission settlement about 65 km away at the confluence of the Ríos Zamora and Bombuscara. The road is beautiful as it wanders from *páramo* down to high jungle, crossing mountain ranges of spectacular cloud forest, weaving high above narrow gorges as it runs alongside the Zamora river. The area has scarcely been affected by tourism yet. For the mission at Guadalupe, take a La Paz bus, which goes up the Yacuambi valley. The town itself is not very interesting, being a midway point for miners and gold prospectors heading further into the Oriente. The best month is Nov, but except for April-June, when it rains almost constantly, other months are comfortable.

Hotels   D *Maguna*, Diego de Vaca, T 605-113, fridge, TV, bath, parking, best in town; **E** *Orillas del Zamora*, Diego de Vaca near car bridge, F without bath, family run, friendly; **F** *Seyma*, 24 de Mayo y Amazonas, T 605-583, clean, friendly, rec; **F** *Zamora*, Sevilla de Oro y Pío Jaramillo, T 605-253, shared bath, clean; **F** *Res Venecia*, Sevilla de Oro, shared bathroom, basic. **Restaurants** in *Hotel Maguna* (best), *GranRitz*, good, and *Comedor Don Pepe*. *Esmeraldas* in market area opp bus terminal, good, rec.

Immigration Office Calle José Luis Tamayo S of park, visitors may be asked for documents, always carry your passport.

Buses All leave from Terminal Terrestre. To **Loja**, 4 a day, 2½ hrs; to **Cuenca**, 1 daily via Loja, over 10 hrs; to **Yantzaza** and **La Paz**, 6 a day.

There are two entrances to the **Podocarpus National Park** here (see above under Loja). The lower altitude of the Zamora side of the Park makes wet weather less threatening but waterproof hiking boots are essential. Permission to enter the Park from Inefan, US$20 entrance, is essential. Inefan office at town entrance, open Mon-Fri, 0830-1800. At weekends pay at the Park headquarters Bombuscara refuge: taxi US$2 to the entrance, 1 km walk to refuge. Camping possible near refuge. Park guardians can suggest walks. Incredible bird life, mountain tanagers flock around the refuge.

Another park entrance is 2 hrs by bus to the S. From the Zamora bus terminal, you can take a 'ranchero', or wooden, open-sided bus to Romerillos, which is a collection of a few houses and an Inefan office. Bus departs Zamora 0630 and 1415, return to Zamora at 0815 and 1600. This area is definitely off the beaten track but, for the virgin cloud forest and amazing quantity of flora and fauna, it is unmatched. A 3 to 5 day hike is possible into this part of the park, but permission is not only needed from the Inefan office in Zamora but from the mining company.

Inefan will get the permission for you after filling out a few papers. T 900-141 and let them know you are interested in entering the area. Ing Luis Cuenca is in charge of the Podocarpus Park. This area contains one of the last major habitats for the spectacular bear and many birds, such as the mountain toucan, Andean cock-of-the-rock, umbrella bird, green jay, etc. Most food supplies can be obtained in Zamora (but expensive), though all camping gear must be carried, as well as fuel for stoves.

Nambija is a gold mining town outside Zamora, a frontier town with its own, limited law and order. It is not entirely safe to visit, gold miners can be suspicious and trigger happy. N of Nambija is **Zumbi**, reached by 0800 bus from Zamora, last bus back 1500, a very scenic ride.

From Zamora, the road follows the Zamora river to **Gualaquiza**, a pioneer town off the tourist track. It is surrounded by densely forested mountains, in which are interesting side trips. If you intend to explore the area, bring tent and sleeping bag. Among the excursions are: caves near Nuevo Tarqui, the Salesian mission at Bomboisa; Tutusa Gorge (3 hrs walk, 2 hrs by boat, take a guide, eg Sr José Castillo); Aguacate, 6 hrs walk, near which are precolumbian ruins, presumably Inca (food and bed at Sr Jorge Guillermo Vázquez); and Yumaza, 40 mins walk, for more precolumbian ruins, possibly Inca (2 sites). The valley produces large quantities of naranjillas and some sugar cane, maize, bananas and yuca.

Hotels F Amazonas, Domingo Comín 08-65, basic, friendly; **E** Turismo, Gonzalo Pesantes 08-16, F without bath, good value, restaurant; **F** Guaquiz, Orellana 08-52, shared bath, friendly. Cabaña los Helechos, opp bus station, rec; Barsilia, García Moreno 09-19; Memo's Bar Cafetería, Gonzalo Pesantes 08-50; Restaurante Gualaquiza.

Emetel García Moreno y Ciudad de Cuenca, Mon-Sat 0800-1100, 1400-1700, 1900-2100.

Buses to Cuenca (1900, 2000 and 2100), 6 hrs; **Loja** (0300 and 2200); **Macas** (1800), 10 hrs. Rancheros leave for Yantzaza in the morning, from where a bus reaches Zamora before dark.

GALAPAGOS ISLANDS (9)

Lying on the Equator, 970 km W of the Ecuadorean coast, the Galápagos consist of 6 main islands (San Cristóbal, Santa Cruz, Isabela, Floreana, Santiago and Fernandina—the last two uninhabited); 12 smaller islands (Baltra and the uninhabited islands of Santa Fe, Pinzón, Española, Rábida, Daphne, Seymour, Genovesa, Marchena, Pinta, Darwin and Wolf) and over 40 small islets. The islands have a total population of nearly 10,000 and because of immigration the annual growth rate is about 12%. The largest island, Isabela (formerly Albemarle), is 120 km long and forms half the total land area of the archipelago. Its notorious convict colony was closed in 1958; some 1,000 people live there now, mostly in and around Puerto Villamil, on the S coast. San Cristóbal (Chatham) has a population of 2,321 with the capital of the archipelago, Puerto Baquerizo Moreno. Santa Cruz (Indefatigable) has 3,154, with Puerto Ayora, the main tourist centre; and Floreana (Charles) fewer than 50. The group is quite widely scattered; by boat, Puerto Baquerizo Moreno and Puerto Ayora are 6 hrs apart.

The islands are the peaks of gigantic volcanoes, composed almost exclusively of basalt. Most of them rise from 2,000 to 3,000m above the seabed. Eruptions have taken place in historical times on Fernandina, Isabela, Pinta, Marchena, Santiago and Floreana. The most active today are Fernandina, Isabela, Pinta and Marchena, and fumarolic activity may be seen intermittently on each of these islands.

The Galápagos have never been connected with the continent. Gradually, over many hundreds of thousands of years, animals and plants from over the sea

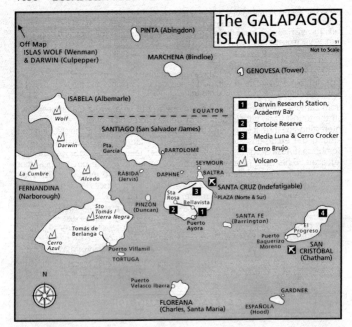

developed there and as time went by they adapted themselves to Galápagos conditions and came to differ more and more from their continental ancestors. Thus many of them are unique: a quarter of the species of shore fish, half of the plants and almost all the reptiles are found nowhere else. In many cases different forms have evolved on the different islands. Charles Darwin recognized this speciation within the archipelago when he visited the Galápagos on the *Beagle* in 1835 and his observations played a substantial part in his formulation of the theory of evolution. Since no large land mammals reached the islands, reptiles were dominant just as they had been all over the world in the very distant past. Another of the extraordinary features of the islands is the tameness of the animals. The islands were uninhabited when they were discovered in 1535 and the animals still have instinctive fear of man.

The most spectacular species to be seen by the visitor are the giant tortoise (species still survive in 6 or 7 of the islands, but mostly on Isabela); marine iguana (the only seagoing lizard in the world and found throughout most of the archipelago; it eats seaweed); land iguana (on Fernandina, Santa Cruz, Santa Fe, Isabela, Seymour and Plaza); Galápagos albatross (which nests only on the island of Española, it leaves in December and returns in late March-early April); Galápagos hawk, red-footed, blue-footed and masked boobies, red-billed tropic-bird, frigate birds, swallow-tailed gulls, dusky lava gulls, flightless cormorants (on Isabela and Fernandina), mockingbirds, 13 species of Darwin's finches (all endemic and the classic examples of speciation quoted by Darwin); Galápagos sea-lion (common in many areas) and the Galápagos fur-seal (on the more remote and rocky coasts).

The most-visited islands from Puerto Ayora are Plaza Sur (an estimated 1,000 sea-lions living on 1 ha, land and sea iguana, many birds flying close to the cliff top), Santa Fe (land and sea iguanas, cactus forest, swimming with sea-lions), Seymour Norte (sea-lions, marine iguanas, swallow-tailed gulls, magnificent frigate birds, blue-footed boobies—the latter not close to the tourist trail), Rábida (sea-lions, flamingoes, pelican rookery), and Santiago (James Bay for fur seals, snorkelling with sea-lions, migratory coastal birds; Sullivan Bay and Bartolomé Island for fantastic lava fields on the climb to the summit, fine views, snorkelling around Pinnacle Rock and maybe a few penguins). On a tour of these islands it may be possible to go also to Punto García on Isabela to see flightless cormorants (it takes at least a full day to climb up one of the volcanoes to see the tortoises). Daphne Island with very rich birdlife may be visited by each boat only once a month (a permit is required).

More distant islands from Puerto Ayora, but visited from there or from Puerto Baquerizo Moreno are Española (blue-footed boobies, masked boobies, waved albatross, many other birds, brightly-coloured marine iguanas, sea-lions, snorkelling at Tortuga Islet), Genovesa (red-footed boobies – brown and white phase, masked boobies, swallow-tailed and lava gulls, frigate birds and many others, marine iguanas, snorkelling) and Floreana (flamingoes, sea-lions, endemic plants, snorkelling at Corona del Diablo). There is a custom for visitors to Post Office Bay on the N side of Floreana since 1793 to place unstamped letters and cards in a barrel, and deliver, free of charge, any addressed to their own destinations. Fernandina (erupting in 1994) is best visited on longer cruises which include Isabela. For more details on Santa Cruz, San Cristóbal and Isabela, see below. Never miss the opportunity to go snorkelling, there is plenty of underwater life to see, including rays, sharks (not all dangerous) and many fish. All the other islands are closed to tourists.

The Galápagos Climate can be divided into a hot season (January to April), when there is a possibility of heavy showers, and the cool or garúa season (May to December), when the days generally are more cloudy and there is often rain or drizzle. Daytime clothing should be lightweight. (Clothing generally, even on "luxury cruises" should be casual and comfortable.) At night, however, particularly at sea and at higher altitudes, temperatures fall below 15°C and warm clothing is required. Boots and shoes soon wear out on the lava terrain.

Do not touch any of the animals, birds or plants. Do not transfer sand or soil from one island to another. Do not leave litter anywhere; it is highly undesirable in a National Park and is a safety and health hazard for wildlife. Do not take raw food on to the islands.

In 1959, the centenary of the publication of Darwin's *Origin of Species*, the Government of Ecuador and the International Charles Darwin Foundation established, with the support of Unesco, the Charles Darwin Research Station at Academy Bay 1½ km from Puerto Ayora, Santa Cruz, the most central of the Galápagos islands, open Mon-Fri 0700-1300, 1400-1600, Sat 0700-1300. A visit to the station is a good introduction to the islands as it provides a lot of information. Collections of several of the rare sub-species of giant tortoise are maintained on the station as breeding nuclei, together with a tortoise-rearing house incorporating incubators and pens for the young. The Darwin Foundation staff will help bona fide students of the fauna to plan an itinerary, if they stay some time and hire a boat.

The number of tourists to the island is controlled by the authorities to protect the environment but critics claim that the ecology is seriously threatened by current levels. Limits were increased from 12,000 in 1974 to 60,000 in 1990, but tourism infrastructure remains fairly basic. There are reports that galapagueños often charge foreigners more than locals. Understand that they feel overrun by people who must be rich; be courteous but firm. Avoid visiting in July and especially August (high season).

Every visitor has to pay a National Park Tax of US$80, payable only in sucres or US$ cash. It is paid on arrival, or at Quito or Guayaquil airports on request. On San Cristóbal there is a municipal tax of US$30; on Santa Cruz the tax is US$7.50 payable in sucres. In each case it is paid by arriving plane passengers. Do not lose your park tax receipt; boat captains need to record it. A 50% reduction on the national park fee is available to children under 12 and students with a student identity card from their home university who are under 26.

Travel to the Islands   There are 2 airports, one at Baltra (South Seymour), across a narrow strait from Santa Cruz, the other at Puerto Baquerizo Moreno, on San Cristóbal. The two islands

are 96 km apart; regular boat services between them with Ingala (**see p 1047**). When booking make sure your flight goes to the island of your choice. Cruises leave from both islands so itineraries depend on which port of departure is used, the capability of the boat and the length of the cruise. From either port prearranged tours can be paid for in advance. In Puerto Ayora, Santa Cruz, cruises can be arranged on the spot and can be arranged to finish at Baltra for the airport. It is more difficult in very high or low season to arrange tours. There are few opportunities to do this in Puerto Baquerizo Moreno.

From the airport on Baltra, one takes a combination of bus (US$1), ferry (US$0.50) and bus (US$2.50) to Puerto Ayora, Santa Cruz. The whole process takes 1½ hrs. Airport buses leave Puerto Ayora (supermarket at the pier) at 0730, 0745 and 0800 for Baltra (best buy ticket night before—not possible for Sat bus though). TAME office in Puerto Ayora opens 0800 and closes Sat pm and Sun. Hotels may make prior arrangements. The airport in Puerto Baquerizo Moreno is within walking distance of town, but those on prearranged tours will be met at the airport.

All flights originate in Quito and make a long stopover in Guayaquil. Normal return fare in 1995, US$377 from Quito, US$333 from Guayaquil; 21-day excursion low season fare US$289 (16 Jan-14 June; 1 Sept-30 Nov), valid for 21 days from date of purchase. Independent travellers must reconfirm outward and return flights 2 days before departure and see their name written on the Manifest, not the 'Lista de Espera'. This is especially critical during high season. TAME flies daily (not Sun out of the high season) to Baltra, and offers 20% reductions on flights originating in Quito to holders of International Student Identity Cards with evidence of home student status (details from office at Edificio Pichincha, 6th floor, Amazonas y Colón, Quito, two photocopies of ID required, allow at least 4 hrs for documents to be endorsed); return to Guayaquil is permitted. You can not get a discount on tickets bought on the islands. Tour operators buy up blocks of seats in advance and they always try to sell you one of their excursions. For this reason, if time is limited, it is probably advisable to go for a package tour. SAN flies to Puerto Baquerizo Moreno (daily, except Sun). One-way tickets are available and it is now possible to buy an open-ended ticket (valid one year). SAN will change dates for return to mainland. SAN offers 20% discount to holders of International Student Identity Cards; your home college ID card, 3 copies of each and the originals plus a passport and US$ cash (not credit cards) required. Go to the office in Av Cristóbal Colón y 6 de Diciembre. Saeta has excellent 30-day excursion packages Miami-Quito/Guayaquil-Galápagos (SAN to San Cristóbal)-Guayaquil/Quito-Miami (US$584), usually cheapest deal, but you land in a more difficult place for arranging tours, rec if you have 10 days available.

The Air Force flights, known as *logísticos*, may be booked at the military airport, Colegio Técnico y Escuela 1, Av de la Prensa 3212, T 445-043, just past the civil airport; single fare US$140, payable only in dollars. Reservations only in advance for the Wed or Sat flight you want to take, office open 0800-1200. For those who succeed, a Lockheed C-130 Hercules departs Quito for Guayaquil, San Cristóbal and Baltra at 0700, be there at 0500. This can be very time consuming and there is no guarantee. The flights are not reliable and flying for 2 hrs in a cargo aircraft with no windows and no facilities is not much fun. To return, make reservation at the Marine Station by the harbour (if they say no foreigners show used ticket from Quito), pay exact fare in dollars at the airport, no change given. *Café Booby* in Puerto Ayora sells tickets at 0715 before 0800 bus to the airport.

The supply vessel *Piquero* takes 10 passengers between Guayaquil and the Galápagos, US$200 pp in a double cabin, 3½ days incl food (US$150 without food). The ship leaves Guayaquil 25th (usually) of each month. You can return after 5-7 days or next month. To stay on board during its sailing round the islands costs US$40 plus US$7/day for food. Information

from Johnny Franco, *Acotramar*, T 04-401-711/004 (04-360-779 in evening), or go on board and speak to the purser or captain, it docks on the Malecón in Guayaquil. Take care of the cranes, etc, and be very alert to theft at all times.

Cruising between the islands   There are two ways to travel around the islands: a 'tour navegable', where you sleep on the boat, or less expensive tours where you sleep ashore at night and travel during the day. On the former you travel at night, arriving at a new landing site each day, with more time ashore. On the latter you spend less time ashore and the boats are smaller with a tendency to overcrowding in high season. Prices are no longer significantly cheaper in the low season (Feb-May, Sept-Nov).

Itineraries are controlled by the National Park to distribute tourism evenly throughout the islands. Boats are expected to be on certain islands on certain days. They can cut landings, but have to get special permission to add to a planned itinerary. An itinerary change may be made if time would be better spent elsewhere. A good guide will explain this and you can trust their advice. Altering an itinerary to spend more time in Puerto Ayora or San Cristóbal is unacceptable (except in extreme bad weather). This sometimes occurs because not all passengers are on the same length of tours and boats come into port to change passengers. Legitimate complaints should be made to Arturo Izurieta (head of the National Park in Puerto Ayora), or Felipe Cruz (deputy head). Any 'tour navegable' will include day of arrival and departure as full days. Insist on a written itinerary or contract prior to departure as any effort not to provide this probably indicates problems later. The South American Explorers Club (Toledo 1254 y Cordero, T 566-076 – Apartado 21-431, Quito; Av Rep de Portugal 146, Breña, T 250142–Casilla 3714, Lima 100; USA: 126 Indian Creek Road, Ithaca, NY14850, T 607-277-0488) has produced a useful, brief guide to the Galápagos which includes a specimen contract for itinerary and living conditions.

Booking a cruise   If wishing to plan everything ahead of time, there are many good tour operators. In Britain, David Horwell, naturalist and author of *Galápagos, the Enchanted Isles*, London, Dryad Press, 1988 (£9.95), arranges tailor-made tours to Ecuador and the Galápagos islands. For further details write to him at Galapagos Adventure Tours, 29 Palace View, Bromley, Kent, BR1 3EJ, England, T 0181-460-8107. Also rec is Penelope Kellie, T 01962-779317 who is the UK agent for Quasar Nautica. In the USA, *Wilderness Travel* and *Inca Floats* have been rec.

Shopping around the agencies in Quito is a good way of securing a value-for-money cruise,

but only if you can deal with the boat owner, or his/her representative, rather than someone operating on commission. It is worth asking if the owner has 1-3 spaces to fill on a cruise; you can often get them at a discount. A much simpler way is to fax from home to an agency which acts as a broker for the cruise ships. The broker can recommend a vessel which suits your requirements. Allow about 2 months for arrangements to be made. Rec are *Safari Ecuador*, F (593-2) 220-426, and *Angermeyer's Enchanted Excursions*, F (593-2) 569-956, full addresses under Quito **Tourist Agencies**.

If you wish to wait until you reach the islands, Puerto Ayora, Santa Cruz, is the only practical place for arranging a cruise. Here you can hire boats (lists available from National Park Service) and a two-week sojourn will allow you to see most of the Islands. Reservations are strongly recommended for June-August and December-April. Out of season boats do not run unless they are full, so either book in advance or be prepared to wait until a group forms. For cheaper tours it is generally recommended that you form a group once you reach the Islands, talk to people about the boats they may have used and then visit the office of the small boat owners (*armadores*). Negotiate the route (don't include the Darwin Research Station or Tortuga Bay as these are easy from Puerto Ayora) and the price, and get a firm commitment from the owner on dates and itinerary, leave a deposit "to buy food" and get a receipt. Prices are fixed by the *armadores*; if you believe you have been misled see the Port Captain who is usually honest, but changes annually. A small boat taking 8 or 12 people costs US$55 pp/day (low season) – US$80 (high season) for a full load, often excluding food, drinks and US$2 harbour exit tax. Prices are set according to the 8, 12 or 16 capacity of the boats; parties of other sizes may upset calculations. Check that the small boats can carry enough food and supplies for the length of journey so you do not waste a day restocking. Many boats require you to provide your own drinking water: check this when you make arrangements. **NB** If not booking a cruise in advance, it can take several days to arrange a tour, so allow yourself plenty of time (a week, maybe more). If you do get stuck, the Tourist Office in Puerto Ayora offers one-day tours (US$36 pp with lunch; departure 0600-0800) to Seymour Norte, Plaza Sur or Santa Fe. These smaller islands have a good sample of animal species (although fewer in numbers) and, together with sightseeing on Santa Cruz, can be a worthwhile experience for the tourist with only limited time.

How much to spend The less expensive boats are normally smaller and less powerful so you see less and spend more time travelling, also the guiding is likely to be in Spanish only (there are some exceptions to this). The more expensive boats will probably have 110 volts, a/c and private baths, all of which can be nice, but not critically important. All boats have to conform to certain minimum safety standards (check that there are enough liferafts) and have VHF radio, but the rules tend to be quite arbitrary (eg windows and portholes may have domestic, rather than safety glass). A watermaker can make quite a difference as the town water from Puerto Ayora or Puerto Baquerizo Moreno should not be drunk. Note that boats with over 18 passengers take quite a time to disembark and re-embark people, while the smaller boats have a more lively motion, which is important if you are prone to seasickness.

The least expensive tours, about US$300-450 tend to travel during the day, with nights spent ashore. For US$450-800 for 8 days you will be on a smaller boat but travelling at night, with more time ashore in daylight. US$800-1,400 is the price of the majority of the best boats, some with English guiding. Over US$1,400 is entering the luxury bracket, with English guiding the norm, more comfortable cabins and better cuisine. No boat may sail without a park-trained auxiliary guide: Naturalists II have little or no English and only basic knowledge; Naturalists III are English-speaking naturalist guides and can be hired instead of an auxiliary.

Agencies and boats With over 100 boats operating in the islands, we cannot give them all. We list those for which we have received positive recommendations. Exclusion does not imply poor service.

In Guayaquil, **Galasam** (Economic Galapagos Tours), Av 9 de Octubre 424, Edificio Gran Pasaje, 11° piso (T 306-289/313-724, F 313-351/562-033) sell flights as well as their own tours. If you book the SAN flight to San Cristóbal with them, they throw in the Ingala boat trip to Santa Cruz free. In Quito, Galasam is at Pinto 523 y Av Amazonas, T 507-080/081/082, F 567-662. The Galasam 7-night tours depart Tues, Wed and Sat, depending on the boat, frequently recommended. In 1995 they were operating with three 16-passenger boats in superior tourist class (*Dorado, Cruz del Sur* and *Estrella*), three 12-passenger craft (*Yolita, Darwin* and *Islas Plazas*), two 10-passenger boats (*Moby Dick*, the newest, and *Antártida*) and one 8-passenger boat (*Tunita*). As an example of 1995 fares, a 7-night cruise on the *Moby Dick* was US$660, 4 nights US$480, 3 nights US$380. A 7-night trip on *Darwin* was US$740 pp, while the *Tunita* was US$580 for 7 nights. See under Quito **Tourist Agencies** for latest offers. The more luxurious boats have specially trained bilingual guides. The guides on all boats are English-speaking.

Metropolitan Touring, Av República de El Salvador 970, PO Box 17-12-310, Quito,

T (593-2) 464-680, F 465-868 (represented in the USA by Adventure Associates, 13150 Coit Rd, Suite 110, Dallas, Texas 75240, T 214-907-0414, F 783-1286) offers 7-night cruises on the MV *Santa Cruz* (90 passengers), said to be the best boat, very professional service, with multilingual guides. They also use *Isabella II*, *Yate Encantada* and *Delfin II*, and have yachts for private charters (eg Ecuacruceros' *Rachel III* and *Diamante*) and can arrange tours on a number of boats of all types, from 8 to 34 passengers. Metropolitan can also arrange scuba diving trips. Bookings can also be made for the *Reina Silvia*, owned by Rolf Siebers, who also owns the *Delfin Hotel* in Puerto Ayora. This vessel makes daily sailings, returning to the hotel each night, but its speed means that the day trips are worthwhile and comfortable, rec.

Situr, Av CJ Arosemena, Km 2.5, Guayaquil, T 593-4-201-516/204-091, F 201-153 (in Quito Av Colón 535 y 6 de Diciembre, T 593-2-561-995, F 562-024) is another agency with Galápagos cruises, operating as *Ecoventura*, T (04) 205-593, F 202-990: 3 motor yachts, *Eric*, *Flamingo* and *Letty* (good guides, atmosphere and food, highly rec); 1 motor vessel, *Corinthian*; and M/S *Sea Cloud*, 3, 4 and 7-night cruises available out of Puerto Baquerizo Moreno. 7-night fares start at US$1,200 on *Corinthian* to US$1,750 on *Eric* to US$2,300 for master suite on *Diamante*.

Angermeyer's Enchanted Excursions, Foch 726 y Amazonas, Quito, T 593-2-569-960, F 569-956, have been rec for their professional, well-organized cruise on the *Beluga*, good English-speaking guide, lots of good food, worth the expense. They also operate the *Cachalote*, which is also rec.

Quasar Nautica, Av Los Shyris 2447, Edif Autocom, Quito, T 441-550, F 436-625 (USA T 305-599-9008, F 305-592-7060, UK representative, Penelope Kellie, T 01962-779-317, F 01962-779-458), sail and power yachts, multilingual guides, naturalist and diving cruises offered. Also arrange mainland tours.

The largest vessel cruising the islands is M/N *Galápagos Explorer*, of Canodros SA (Luis Urdaneta 14-18, Guayaquil, T 280-164, F 287-651). Other recommended agencies with tours to/in the Galápagos are given under Quito and Guayaquil under **Tourist Agencies**.

Two boats with consistently high recommendations are the sailing brigantine *Andando* and the motor trawler *Samba*, both owned by Fiddi Angermeyer; book through Andando Tours, T/F (593-5) 526-308, Puerto Ayora, or PO Box 17-21-0088, T (593-2) 465-113, F 443-188, Quito; personal service always given.

Other recommendations: Pepe Salcedo's *Sulidae*, an old Norwegian fishing boat; Pepe is very experienced (Sulidae Charters, PO Box 09-01-0260, Guayaquil, T 593-4-201-376, F 323-478). Georgina and Agustín Cruz' *Beagle III*, friendly, good cooking (bookable through Metropolitan Touring). The motor yacht *Orca* (Etnotours, J L Mera y Cordero, Quito, T 593-2-230-552) and *Angelique* (owner Franklin Angermeyer), the latter has lots of character, good food. Rolf Wittmer, son of Margaret Wittmer of the famous 1930s Galápagos Affair, owns and runs *Tiptop III*, good but no snorkelling equipment. His son has the sailing yacht *Symbol*, a converted ship's lifeboat, very basic, but a good way to drift between the islands (Wittmer Turismo, T 593-2-449-337, F 448-173). *Baronesa*, run by Galápagos Travel, has good tours but cramped lower cabins (Amazonas 519 y Roca, Quito, T 593-2-500-064, F 505-772). The sailing catamaran *Pulsar* (about US$500/week) is inexpensive, but best when the owner Patric is on board; some cabins are very small indeed (Ecuagal, Amazonas 1113 y Pinto, T 593-2-229-579, F 550-988).

The *Samoa I* is an old boat, but still good; most cabins open straight onto the deck; under same ownership is a new catamaran *American Enterprise* (Samoa Turismo, Ramírez Dávalos y Amazonas, Quito, T 593-2-524-135). Good service on the *Golondrina*, Golondrina Turismo, J L Mera 639 y Carrión, Quito, T 593-2-528-570, F 528-570. *Isla Galápagos* is rec, if a 'bit funky'; part-owner Patricia Orellana is a good English-speaking guide and captain and part-owner, Daniel Mora, was born in the islands. *Elizabeth II*, good crew and food; *Angelito* of Hugo Andrade (with a new *Angelito* under construction); *Española* (8 passengers, good food); *Lobo del Mar* (12 passengers); *Daphne* (8 – good cook); and *San Antonio* (12 – good food, nice crew).

It must be stressed that a boat is only as good as its crew and when the staff change, so will these recommendations. The South American Explorers Club in Quito has an extensive file of trip reports for members to consult and David, at Safari Ecuador, tries to keep abreast of all new developments.

Isabela Tours, Av Darwin, opp *Sol y Mar*, can arrange day tours to other islands and transport to San Cristóbal and Isabela with their old crew boat, *Judy II*, helpful guide, Alex, if you can find him at the office. Glass bottomed boat trips, 4-8 hrs, can be taken from the inner harbour, Puerto Ayora, friendly owner, speaks English and Spanish, is knowledgeable about marine life and has masks and snorkels for snorkelling from his boat.

Tipping It will be suggested to you that you tip US$50-100 per passenger for the crew and the same for the guide. As elsewhere, tips should always reflect service, and should be given according to the service in relation to what you requested. On first and secondhand evidence, it appears that US$25-30 per cabin is the top limit, and that for outstanding service.

If you have problems See above for complaints regarding itineraries. If a crew member comes on strong with a woman passenger, the matter should first be raised with the guide or captain. If this does not yield results, a formal complaint, in Spanish, giving the crew member's full name, the boat's name and the date of the cruise, should be sent to Sr Capitán del Puerto, Base Militar de Armada Ecuatoriana, Puerto Ayora, Santa Cruz, Galápagos. Failure to report such behaviour will mean it will continue. To avoid pilfering, never leave belongings unattended on a beach when another boat is in the bay.

Ingala sails from Puerto Ayora to Puerto Baquerizo Moreno Tues 1030, returning Wed 1100, and Sat 0800, returning Mon 0800, US$9 for locals, US$18 for Ecuadoreans, US$60 for foreigners; on Thur it sails Puerto Ayora-Isabela (US$36), returning Fri via Floreana. Get your name on the list as early as possible on the day before sailing, buy ticket for San Cristóbal on day of departure between 0800 and 1000 and be at the quay in good time. The Ingala office in Puerto Ayora is on Padre Herrera, near the petrol station on the outskirts; in Puerto Baquerizo Moreno it is up the hill on the road leading inland, on the edge of town.

What to take A remedy for seasickness is recommended; the waters S of Santa Cruz are particularly choppy. A good supply of sun block and skin cream to prevent windburn and chapped lips is essential. A hat and sunglasses are also recommended. You should be prepared for dry and wet landings, the latter involving wading ashore.

Take plenty of film with you; the birds are so tame that you will use far more than you expected; a telephoto lens is not essential, but if you have one, bring it. Also take filters suitable for strong sunlight. Snorkelling equipment is particularly useful as much of the sea-life is only visible under water. Most of the cheaper boats do not provide equipment and those that do may not have good snorkelling gear. If in doubt, bring your own, rent in Puerto Ayora, or buy it in Quito. It is possible to sell it afterwards either on the islands or try the *Gran Casino* travel agency in Quito.

The Cost of Living in the Galápagos is high, particularly in the peak season (December, July and August). Most food has to be imported although certain meats, fish, vegetables and fruit are available locally in the Puerto Ayora market. Bottled drinks are expensive, beer US$1.50.

Information The *Galápagos Guide* by Alan White and Bruce White Epler, with photographs by Charles Gilbert, is published in several languages; it can be bought in Guayaquil in Librería Científica and the airport, Libri Mundi (US$5) in Quito, or at the Charles Darwin station. The South American Explorers Club in Quito sells useful brief guide, *Galápagos Package*, US$4. *Galápagos, the Enchanted Isles*, by David Horwell (see p 1043). Highly rec is *Galápagos: a Natural History Guide* by Michael H Jackson (US$20 from Libri Mundi, Quito, US$28 on the islands), used by all the guides. *The Enchanted Isles, The Galápagos Discovered*, by John Hickman (Anthony Nelson, 1985, £7.95). A must for birdwatchers is *Field Guide to the Birds of the Galápagos* (US$20). For fish identification: *Reef Fish Identification* by Paul Humann (Libri Mundi, 1993, US$21.50) and *Fishes of the Galápagos* by Godrey Merlen (Libri Mundi, 1988). A map of the Galápagos, drawn by Kevin Healey and illustrated by Hilary Bradt, is published by ITMB, 736A Granville St, Vancouver, Canada, V6Z 1G3, T (604) 687-3320, F 687-5925, and Bradt Publications (who also sell a range of books on subjects related to the islands—41 Nortoft Road, Chalfont St Peter, Bucks SL9 0LA, England, T/F 0494-873478). The National Park now publishes a good guide in English and Spanish, with plans of all the places where visitors are allowed to land: *Guide to the Visitor Sites of Parque Nacional Galápagos*, by Alan and Tui Moore, US$3.30. National Park Office, Puerto Ayora, Santa Cruz, Mon-Fri 0800-1200, 1400-1800, Sat 0800-1000. For more information write to the Director of the Charles Darwin Research Station or the Superintendent of the Galápagos National Park Service, Isla Santa Cruz, Galápagos (correspondence in English.)

Hotels at *Puerto Ayora* (pop 4,294), Hotel space is limited and reservations are strongly rec in high season. **A3** *Galápagos* (local class 1), bungalows with private bathroom, hot water, ocean-view, laundry service, generator, restaurant with fixed menu, price and time, fruit and meat from hotel farm, near Darwin Research centre, reservations can be made through Ecuadorean travel agencies, day excursions can be made from hotel in Pedro and Sally García's own dinghy for 10, the *Fernandina*. **A3** *Red Mangrove Inn*, 4 rooms oceanfront, hot showers, restaurant, owner Polo Navaro offers tours incl sea kayaking, highland farm and cruises in *Azul.* **A2** *Angermeyer*, new, pool; **C** *Castro* (2), with private bath, owned by Sr Miguel Castro, he arranges 7-day inclusive tours, including Friday TAME flight, rec. He is an authority on wildlife and his tour includes one or two nights away visiting the islands of Plazas and Santiago, and a day-trip to Santa Fe, with visits to the tortoise reserve and the Darwin Institute. **B** *Las Ninfas*, very close to harbour, basic, cold showers, good restaurant, has its own boat at reasonable price for day trips and Fernando Jiménez is helpful with arrangements; **D** *Delfín*, on far side of Academy Bay, with lovely beach (1), accessible only by boat, write to Mrs Sievers. **D** *Sol y Mar*, next to bank, 20 beds (double, triples and quadruples) in cabins (1), with 3 meals; C without meals; 10% discount for stays of 2 weeks or more; reservations can be made by writing to the owner (Sr Jimmy Pérez), or Transgalapagos Inc, PO Box 11227, T 562-151, F (593) 4-382-444, Guayaquil. **E** *Elizabeth*, with bath (3), reasonable, now remodelled, owner very helpful, reported noisy; **E** pp *Lirio del Mar*, private bath, cafetería, laundry facilities, pleasant, clean; **E** pp *Lobo de Mar* (2) with bath, 30 beds, modern, clean, can do laundry on roof, noisy on occasions; **E** *Salinas*, opp *Lirio del Mar*, 20 beds, with bath and fan. **F** *Colón*, 22 beds (doubles) in third class rooms (3), without food; D, including 3 meals. **F** *Darwin*, with bath, restaurant (order meals in advance), rec but don't leave valuables in your room; **F** *Flamingo*, with private bath, fan, decent, clean; **F** *Gloria*, 12 beds, simple, you can cook your own food over a wood fire, mosquito repellent needed, new rooms being added, laundry facilities, very friendly; *Fernandina*, T Galapagos 122 or Quito 538-686, family run, friendly, helpful staff, good meals, electric shower heaters; **F** *Santa Cruz*, (3). **F** *Los Amigos*, Av Darwin in front of TAME office, without bath, run by Sra Rosa Rosera, cool, reasonable, friendly, airy rooms, laundry facilities, clean, rec. Write to Sra Piedad Moya.

Restaurants at Puerto Ayora Expect slow service and shortages of items such as flour which will reduce menu availability. *Rincón del Alma*, near the plaza, best, good food, reasonable prices; *Los Gemelos*, near the school, good breakfast, home made yoghurt and marmalade, good value; *La Garrapata*, open air, on road to research station, popular meeting place for travellers, morning and evening but not Sun, drinks expensive, check the bill; *Las Peñas*, very good value restaurant, big helpings, good service, opp *Pirata*, which is good; *El Booby*, faces the volleyball court on the seafront, across the street from the iguana statue, family run, no speciality, pleasant, reasonable prices, closed at night; *Four Lanterns*, facing Pelican Bay, good, Italian/vegetarian; *Pastry Shop* (in front of hospital) for snacks and drinks; *Perla Oriental*, on dock, excellent grilled lobster, changes money, meeting place; nearby is *Pasty Pan* for bread and cakes; *Rey del Pan*, on main road towards Bellavista, cheap, fresh baked goods; *Chifa Asia* on main street, decent; *Viña del Mar*, on main street, good value, popular with locals, OK; *El Mochilero*, on main street, good spaghetti, pizza, fruit salad, pancakes and cakes; *Snack Bar Popeyes*, in the plaza, Chilean run, *empanadas* and the best fruit juices in town; *Casa Stefanya*, fruit juices, etc; *Pelikano*, good value breakfast, early morning meeting place and *Pastik-Shock* cafeterias. *Sol y Mar*, good but expensive breakfast on terrace full of marine iguanas; *Café Muyuyo*, serves muchines, tapioca, yucca and cheese. Restaurants serve lobster dinners at US$10-13; *merienda* costs between US$1.50-2.

Entertainment *Disco La Panga*; *5 Fingers* disco and bar, popular.

Hints For boat charters and camping trips most basic foodstuffs generally can be purchased on the islands (eg *Proinsular* supermarket opp the pier in Puerto Ayora), although occasionally there are shortages. However, no special items (dehydrated or freezedried foods) are available other than a few common ones such as oatmeal and dried soups. The *mercado municipal* is on Padre Herrera, beyond the telephone office, on the way out of town to Santa Rosa. Fresh milk available in Puerto Ayora from Christine Aldaze, 0930, on main road (24 hrs notice appreciated). There is a shortage of drinking water on Santa Cruz, but you should not drink the tap water. Electricity is off between midnight and 0600 and INECEL cuts power to a different section of town from 1900-2200 every night. Most hotels have a portable generator. Carry a passport at all times.

Medicines, sun lotions, mosquito coils, film, and other useful items are either not available or cost a lot more than on the mainland. *Galapaguito* can meet most tourists' needs, the owners are both naturalists, very helpful. There is a wide variety of T-shirt and souvenir shops, eg *Galápagos Souvenirs*; *Artesanías Bambú*, near *Hotel Galápagos*. Do not buy items made of black coral; it is an endangered species.

There is a cinema at Puerto Ayora—each evening at 2015. Information and retrieval of lost property from Radio Santa Cruz, next to Catholic Church.

There is a hospital in Puerto Ayora; consultations US$10, medicines reasonably-priced, but they can not perform operations.

Warning Valuables should be watched.

Exchange Banco del Pacífico, Av Charles Darwin, 0800-1700, gives a full banking service at standard Quito rates. In emergency offers international telephone service, T 17390, via Guayaquil, by Telex, Fax and satellite. Most boats accept US$. The *Hotel Sol y Mar* and *Bodega Blanca* and *Ninfa* restaurants will change notes and cheques, but at a poor rate. Several shops change US$ notes.

Laundry Ask at the *farmacia* near *Hotel Santa Cruz*, good service.

The **Post Office** sometimes runs out of stamps (never leave money and letters), ask in the 'red boat' (*Galería Jahanna*) or *Artesanía Bambú*. **Telephone office** on Padre Herrera.

Immigration The immigration police will extend visas with a little persuasion for those who overstay their visa or tourist card.

British Consul David Balfour, c/o Etica, Barrio Estrada, Puerto Ayora.

Tourist Office Cetur, on main road, open Mon-Fri 0800-1200, 1500-1600, T 328-312, 324-471. Information also available at the boat owners' cooperative office nearby.

Diving Galapagos Sub-Aqua, Av Charles Darwin, the owner Fernando Zambrano provides courses for beginners and trips for the experienced, all equipment for hire, including for snorkellers, T 526-350, F (593-4) 314-510, safe, rec. Day tours US$75 to US$100, includes boat, gear, instructor, 2 dives (mainly drift diving). Multi day tours including meals, accommodation from US$130 pp/day. Introductory courses US$75/day. Also Alvaro Solorzano, Rosa Borja de Icazay, El Oro, Barrio Centenario, US$80 for certification course. Dr Paul Goldrick from Stafford writes "there is some spectacular diving to be done here, particularly with respect to wildlife, sealions, sharks, rays and a huge variety of fish". For snorkelling, masks and snorkels can be rented from dive shops, US$4-5 a day, US$60 deposit. 1-day snorkelling tours US$15-20, 3 locations, rec, ask for Marcello through Marcos Martínez at *Bar/Restaurant Five Fingers*. **NB** Please help to maintain or in some cases improve standards by not disturbing or touching underwater wildlife.

Excursions on Santa Cruz From San Francisco school in Puerto Ayora buses leave for Santa Rosa and Bellavista at 0630, 1230 and 1630, ½ hr trip, return immediately (fare for all destinations US$1). There are also trucks (cheaper). On roads to the main sites hitching is easy but expect to pay a small fee. Ask at *Neptuno Tours* in Puerto Ayora for tours of the interior. Walk to Tortuga Bay on marked path for excellent sunsets and nice beach (the only one on this island), 5 km. Take drinking water and do not go alone (armed robbery reported). Only open during the day; arrests have been made at night.

Hike to the higher parts of the island called Media Luna, Puntudo and Mt Crocker. Trail starts at Bellavista, 7 km from Puerto Ayora. Round trip from Bellavista is 4 to 8 hrs, depending upon distance hiked, 10-18 km (permit and guide not required, but a guide is advisable). Take water, sun block and long-sleeved shirt and long trousers to protect against razor grass.

To see giant tortoises in the wild, go to Steve Devine's Butterfly ranch beyond Bellavista on the road to Santa Rosa (the bus passes the turn-off), only in the dry season; in the wet season the tortoises are breeding in the arid zone. Vermillion flycatchers can be seen here also. Entry US$2, incl free cup of *hierba luisa* tea, or juice. Steve Devine is a guide on the island, highly rec (ask for him or Jack Nelson at *Hotel Galápagos*).

There are several natural tunnels (lava tubes): one 3 km from Puerto Ayora on the road to Bellavista, unsigned on the left, look for the black-and-white posts (tread carefully); barn owls may be seen here. Two more are 1 km from Bellavista (on private land, US$0.70 to enter, torch provided—it takes about ½ hr to walk through the tunnels). Ask for Bolívar at *Pensión Gloria*, his wife's family have lands with lava caves, *mirador* and other attractions.

Hike to the Chato Tortoise Reserve, 7 km; trail starts at Santa Rosa, 22 km from Puerto Ayora (local bus to Santa Rosa at 0600 or 1230, check, US$0.30, returns 1700). Horses can be hired at Santa Rosa, US$6 each, guide optional but strongly rec, US$6.50 extra (again ask Bolívar at *Pensión Gloria*). Round trip takes one day. The Puerto Ayora-Bellavista bus stops at the turnoff for the track for the reserve (US$0.95). It's a hot walk; take food and drink. From Santa Rosa, distance to different sites within the reserve is 6-8 km (permit and guide not required). To walk to the Reserve from Santa Rosa, turn left past the school, follow the track at the edge of fields for 40 mins, turn right at the memorial to the Israeli, 20 mins later turn left down a track to Chato Trucha.

Two sinkholes, Los Gemelos, straddle the road to Baltra, beyond Santa Rosa; if you are lucky, take a *camioneta* all the way, otherwise to Santa Rosa, then walk. A good place to see the Galápagos hawk and barn owl.

The highlands and settlement area of Santa Cruz are worth seeing for the contrast of the vegetation with the arid coastal zones. Ask for Tim Grey and Anita Salcedo at *Garapata* in Puerto Ayora, they have a *finca* for arranging barbecues.

Puerto Baquerizo Moreno (pop 3,023) on San Cristóbal island to the E, is the capital of the archipelago. The island is being developed as a second tourist centre. In town, the cathedral, 2 blocks up from the post office, has interesting, mixed-media relief pictures on the walls and altar. Next door is the municipal museum of natural history (0830-1200, 1530-1730, US$1, stuffed exhibits, old photos, a tortoise called Pepe). See **Travel Between the Islands**, above, for boat connections to Puerto Ayora. Be warned that it can take several days to find room on a boat to Puerto Ayora.

Hotels A3 *Grand Hotel Cristóbal*, owned by SAN, opp a white beach to E of town, with bath (not inc tax), good restaurant; **C** *Orca*, OK, good food, has its own boat for cruises; **D** *Hostal Galápagos*, E end of town, a/c cabins, fridge; **D** *Chatham*, on road to airport, with bath; **D** *Mar Azul*, on road from airport, with bath, hot showers, clean, nice gardens, rec, restaurant; **E** *Residencia San Francisco*, with bath, good, clean, friendly; **E** *Residencial Northia*, with bath; **F** pp *Cabañas Don Jorge*, close to beach, clean, friendly, "not luxurious", member of Ecuadorean and International Youth Hostal Associations; **F** *Res Miramar*, good value, clean restaurant, good; **F** *Res Flamingo*, basic, clean, friendly.

Restaurants *Rosita*, best in town; *Nathaly*, good food, open late; *Chatham*; *Laurita*, fair; *La Terraza*, disco, on beach; *Fragata*, on road to airport. *Cafeteriá Tagu*, cheap.

Services Telephone office on Av Quito; post office next to Banco Central on Av Charles Darwin (main street); Banco del Pacífico, 0800-1700, 0800-1300 Sat, changes cash, cheques and gives cash against Mastercard. SAN office on Darwin, Mon, Tues, Wed, Fri 0800-1600, Thur and Sat 0800-1200. There are a few souvenir shops (poorer quality than Puerto Ayora); best is *Edliz* for T-shirts, in Moorish-style house opp the jetty with the whale. Do not buy black coral. There is a hospital but if you need an operation you have to go yourself to the pharmacy to buy everything you need.

Excursions Bus (shuttle) to El Progreso, then $2\frac{1}{2}$ hr walk to El Junco lake, tortoises may be seen on the way. The road continues to a school, above which is a shrine, a deserted restaurant and a *mirador* overlooking the different types of vegetation stretching to the coast. From El Progreso (tree house *El Tarzan* for rent; eating places), a trail crosses the high lands to Cerro Brujo and Hobbs Bay; also to Stephens Bay, past lakes. A 3-hrs hike to Galapaguera in the NE allows you to see tortoises in the wild. At La Lobería, beyond the airport, is a bay with shore birds, sea-lions and huge marine iguanas. You can continue along the cliff, but do not leave the trail, to see tortoises and rays. Boats go to Punta Pitt in the far N where you can see all three boobies. Off the NW coast is Kicker Rock (León Dormido), the basalt remains of a crater; many seabirds, including masked and blue-footed boobies, can be seen around its cliffs. Up the coast is Cerro Brujo beach with sea-lions, birds, crabs (none in any abundance). Raul Sánchez offers short trips on his boat *Ana Mercedes*, ending in Puerto Ayora, much time spent travelling, T 163. Española (Hood) is within day trip reach.

Isabela Island Hotels E *Alexandra*, nice site on the beach; **E** *Loja*, on the road to the highland, clean, sometimes water shortages, patio, friendly staff, cheap and very good restaurant; *El Rincón del Bucanero*, on the beach, more expensive; **F** *Isabela del Mar*, T 125, friendly, good food, water supplied, rec; **F** *El Capitán*, pleasant, friendly; **E-F** pp *Ballena Azul*, T (593-5) 529-125 or through *Safari Ecuador*, Quito, safe, clean, family atmosphere, rooms or cabins, meals available, rec, run by Dora Gruber, Swiss; **G** *Antonio Gil* rents 2 rooms with shower, friendly, helpful, tours arranged with horses. There are a few *comedores* but food is seldom available unless you order in advance. Isabela is not highly developed for tourism but if you have a few days to spare it is worthwhile spending time there. Good walks in the highlands (eg to Cerro Negro volcano) and beautiful beaches; also to the 'walking wall' left from the penal colony. Tours to the volcanoes can be made with two guides, compare prices. Horses can be hired. A 3-5 day trip can be arranged in Puerto Ayora at Darwin 606, 10 people required. Also ask Marcos Martínez in Puerto Ayora about 4-day tours, incl riding, accommodation and food, US$100 excluding board and lodging. The climb up the volcanoes takes 3 days, one for the ascent, one at the top and one to come down. Besides Ingala on Thur (see above), *Estrella del Mar* sails from Puerto Ayora on Wed, or contact fishermen, US$20-30; ask for Victor at Proinsular office.

INFORMATION FOR VISITORS

Before you go

Entry requirements

● Documents

Passport (valid for at least 6 months required on arrival at Quito airport), and a tourist card valid for 90 days obtainable on arrival (tourists are now allowed only 90 days on entry in any 365-day period, ie you can not leave in Dec and return in Jan, you have to wait twelve months for another 90-day entitlement). You are required to say how many days you intend to stay and the card and your passport will be stamped accordingly; most travellers are given 15 or 30-day stamps irrespective of their requests (at Huaquillas, Macará and Tulcán), and travellers arriving by air may be given a stamp valid for only 10 days (transit pass) unless they request otherwise. It is therefore better to overestimate as you can be fined on leaving the country for staying too long. Extensions can be routinely obtained at the Policía Nacional de Migración in Quito, Guayaquil or Cuenca and several provincial capitals (addresses in the text); 30 days are given for each extension, which cost appox US$10 (payable in sucres), up to a maximum of 90 additional days (180 days total); make sure the extension is given an official stamp. Evidence of sufficient funds (see below) is sometimes required. French citizens need a visa; US$30, 4 photos, a return ticket and at least 6 months validity on passport required. A visa is also required for those from China, Taiwan, N and S Korea, Vietnam and Cuba and for business people and students who stay longer than 90 days (3 photos required), application to be made in home country, and they must get an exit permit (*permiso de salida*, once obtained this is valid for multiple trips out of Ecuador during one year) with both tax and police clearance. It costs US$17 for renewing a visa after its expiry date; extending a 90-day consular visa is not easy. If travelling on anything other than a 90-day tourist card, check if you need to register upon arrival with the Extranjería and Policía Nacional de Migración as well as obtaining an exit permit.

The procedure for obtaining a student visa involves taking a letter from the school at which you will be studying to the Ecuadorean consulate, a letter from your bank and a ticket out of Ecuador (or South America), plus a fee of US$30 in cash (only dollars, wherever paid): it is illegal to study on a tourist visa. There are

many other essential procedures, for which at least 6 passport photos will be required (4 face, 2 profile). You are also required to remit US$1000 to a Quito bank to open an account in your name on arrival. There is considerable further paperwork in Ecuador after you get there. A student visa is given for 6 months. Holders of student visas do not have to pay the Cuota de Compensación Militar on leaving, although business visa holders do. Verify all details at the Consulate before departure.

NB Students visiting the Galápagos, and in other cases, are entitled to discounts. Because of local counterfitted international student cards, they do not accept Ecuadorian issued student cards. ISICs are sometimes honoured, but proof of home student status is essential. See **p 940** on purchasing student ID in Quito.

Tourists crossing from Colombia or Peru may be asked for evidence that they possess US$20 pp for each day they propose to spend in Ecuador. Theoretically you must have an onward ticket out of Ecuador, but this is almost never enforced if you are travelling overland. However, travellers arriving from Miami by plane have been refused entry without a ticket and an MCO may not be sufficient.

Warning Always carry your passport with you, or a photocopy with the immigration visa date, except when travelling in the Oriente or border areas where the real thing is required. Failure to produce this as identification could result in imprisonment. You must have an entry stamp in your passport. Some embassies recommend you register with them details of your passport and accommodation in case of emergency. Tourists are not permitted to work under any circumstances.

● Representation overseas

Australia, 388 George Street, Suite 1702 A, American Express Tower NSW 2000, Sydney, 223-3266, 223-0041; **Belgium**, Chaussée de Charleroi No 70, 1060 Brussels, T 0 537-9193, F 0 537-9066; **Canada**, 50 O'Connor Str #1311, Ottawa, ON K1P 6L2, T 613 563-8206, F 613 235-5776, 151 Bloor Street West, Suite 470 Toronto, Ontario M5S 1S4, T 416 968-2077, F 416 968-3348, 1010 Sainte Catherine W #440, Montreal, QC H3B 3R3, T 514 874-4071, F 514 874-9078; **France**, 34 Avenue de Messine, 75008 Paris, T 1 456 11021, F 1 425 60664; **Germany**, Koblenzer Strasse 37, 5300 Bonn 2, T 0 288 352544, F

0 228 361765; **New Zealand**, Ferry Bldg, 2 Flr, Quai Street, Auckland, T 09 309-0229, F 09 303-2931; **Sweden**, Engelbrektsgatan 13, Box 260 95, S-100 41 Stockholm, T 0 679-6043, F 0 611-5593; **Switzerland**, Helvetiastrasse 19-A, 3005 Berne, T 031 351-1755, F 031 351-2771; **UK**, Flat 3B, 3 Hans Crescent, Knightsbridge, London, SW1X 0LS, T 0171 584-1367.

● **Tourist information**
The Latin American Travel Advisor publishes a quarterly update of public safety, health, weather, travel costs, the economy and politics in Ecuador and 16 other South and Central American countries, PO Box 17-17-908, Quito, Ecuador, F 593-2-562-566, Internet: rku@pi.pro.ec.

● **Maps and guide books**
The Instituto Geográfico Militar in Quito (**see p 942**), produces a 1:1,000,000 map of Ecuador which is quite good, but large. A comprehensive road map (1989 edition) is also available as well as various other maps. ITMB's 1:1,000,000 map of Ecuador, by Kevin Healey, 1994-96 edition, is available from World Wide Books and Maps, 736A Granville Street, Vancouver, BC, Canada, V6Z 1G3. A good series of pocket maps and city guides by Nélson Gómez, published by *Ediguias* in Quito, includes: *The Pocket Guide to Ecuador* (English), *Guía Turística del Ecuador* (Spanish), *Guía Vial del Ecuador* (road atlas), *Guía Informativa de Quito* (city guide), *Quito: Guía de Bolsillo* (pocket map), *Guía del Area Metropolitana de Quito* (road atlas of the areas surrounding Quito), *Guía Informativa de Guayaquil* (city guide), and *Guía Informativa de Cuenca* (city guide). These are available in book shops throughout the country and by mail order from *Latin American Travel Consultants*, PO Box 17-17-908, Quito, Ecuador, F (593-2) 562-566, Internet: rku@pi.pro.ec. Tourist maps and information are available from *Ecuatorial Publicaciones*, Av 10 de Agosto 4111 y Av Atahualpa, T 439-281, F 443-844, Casilla 17-16-1832 CEQ, Quito. Stanfords, Long Acre, London, stock good road maps.

National Parks All foreigners have to pay to enter each national park; the charge for the Galápagos is now US$80. For lowland parks (the coast, the Oriente and the lowland portions that overlap lowlands and highlands) the charge is US$20 in sucres; for highland parks (all sierra parks and highland portions of overlapping parks), US$10 in sucres. No student discounts are available in these 2 categories. There is no separate National

Parks office, Parks fall under Inefan. Their office in Quito can provide some tourist information but it is best to contact the Inefan office in the city nearest the Park you wish to visit, eg the Cuenca office for Cajas, Loja for Podocarpus, etc. **Fundación Natura**, Av América 5653 y Voz Andes, Quito, T 447-343/4, 459-013, is a private charitable organization concerned with nature reserves. They have some limited tourist information, notably on Pasochoa, which they manage; there is a resource library and knowledgeable staff who can give technical information on parks and reserves.

Wildlife, all under increasing threat from human encroachment of their habitat, includes the jaguar, puma, tapir, several kinds of monkey, the armadillo, spectacled bear, squirrel, porcupine, peccary, various kinds of deer, and many rodents, including the guinea pig. There are also tortoises, lizards and iguanas. Among the birds are condors, falcons, kites, macaws, owls, flamingoes, parrots, ibises, cranes, and storks. Unhappily, every type of insect is found in the coastal towns and the Oriente. The Galápagos Islands have their own selection of nearly tame wildlife.

Indigenous Groups The Quichua, Shuar and Siona-Secoya Indians in Pastaza welcome tourists in a controlled way, in order to sell their beautiful products; some work as guides. Contact the Organización de Indígenos de Pastaza (OPIP) in Puyo, T 885-461, they can also give you a list of indigenous museums and artesan workshops. CON-FENIAE, the confederation of Amazon Indians is another good contact at Km 5 outside Puyo, T 885-343, or at their office in Quito, Av Granados 2553 y Av 6 de Diciembre, T 442-271. Care is required when visiting the Oriente and taking tours to Waorani villages without prior arrangement, the Waorani are at great risk from the tourist invasion and do not appreciate being treated as a spectacle. Strictly controlled tourism is organized by the Rainforest Information Centre in Quito in conjunction with ONHAE, the Waorani Indigenous organization.

When to go

● **Best time to visit**
The best time for a visit is May to Sept for the northern/central Sierra, Aug to Jan for the Southern Sierra. Coast: best time for the beach is Dec to Jun (although this is very hot and wet season on the coastal plain, at the beaches it is usually dry). Garúa in the coast: Jun to Sep (worst months for the beach). Oriente: you can get rain at any time of the

year, but the rainiest months are Apr to Sep. For the Galápagos, see that section, above.

Health

Amoebic dysentery is a danger. Visitors should drink mineral water (Güitig or Manantial), avoid uncooked vegetables or salads, and be inoculated against typhoid. Hepatitis (jaundice) is a very real risk and should be inoculated against; see "Health Information" in front of book. Travellers in the Oriente and the Costa are advised to take anti-malaria tablets; chloroquinine and Fansidar (Falcidar) are both available in chemists/pharmacies without prescription. Paludrine is not available. Mosquito netting is also useful, a good mosquito repellent essential. Also recommended is an anti-itch cream in the Oriente. Yellow-fever vaccination is recommended for travel into the Oriente. Cholera vaccination is not available (cholera is on the increase, avoid street food). There are excellent hospitals both in Quito and Guayaquil. Climbers are warned to undergo a period of acclimatization before attempting to scale the volcanoes.

If you should be bitten by a rabid animal, human diploid vaccine (the correct type) can be ordered from USA through the US Embassy, but it is expensive.

Tampons are difficult to obtain, particularly outside major cities and very pricey when stocked.

● **Travelling with children**
Agua Linda is a good and safe bottled water for young children. Luggis are the best disposable nappies/diapers, other makes are useless.

Money

● **Currency**
The sucre is the unit of currency. Bank notes of the Banco Central de Ecuador are for 5, 10, 20, 50, 100, 500, 1,000, 5,000 and 10,000 sucres (with inflation, denominations under 100 Sucres have become uncommon); there are nickel coins of 5, 10, 20 and 50 sucres.

There is no restriction on the amount of foreign money or sucres you can take into or out of Ecuador. It is very easy to change US$ cheques into US$ notes at the *cambios*; the commission varies as it is worth shopping around and *cambios* sometimes run out of US$ notes; you can try to bargain for a better rate than shown on the blackboard. Note that although many hotels and restaurants have signs indicating acceptance of credit cards, this is often not the case; always check first. ATMs in the Mastercard/Cirrus network can be found in branches of Banco del Pacífico,

Banco General de Crédito, Banco de Préstamos and Banco Holandés Unido. Visa ATMs are at Banco de Guayaquil and Filanbanco branches. Note that difficulties have been reported with Amex cards, an alternative credit card may be more useful. It is quite difficult to change TCs outside the main towns, especially in the Oriente. US$ money orders cannot be exchanged anywhere in Ecuador. For West Union money transfers, T (2) 565-059 in Quito.

Getting there

Air

AoM French Airlines fly twice weekly from Paris to Quito. Iberia flies from Madrid to Quito via Santo Domingo, Dominican Republic, twice weekly. KLM flies weekly from Amsterdam to Guayaquil via Curaçao and Quito. Lufthansa flies from Frankfurt to Quito three times weekly via Bogotá. Viasa flies from Caracas with connecting flights to several European destinations.

● **From North America**
There are flights from New York with Saeta, a private Ecuadorian airline, which also flies from Miami and Los Angeles. American Airlines fly daily from Miami while Continental flies from Houston, Los Angeles and New York. From other US cities make connections in Miami.

● **From Latin American cities**
Buenos Aires (Saeta to Quito and Guayaquil, Aerolíneas Argentinas and Ladeco to Guayaquil only); Bogotá (Saeta, Avianca, Servivensa, Viasa and AeroPerú to Quito; Saeta and Ladeco to Guayaquil); Cali to Tulcán and Esmeraldas and on to Quito with TAME; Lima (Saeta, Servivensa, Avianca and Aeroperú to Quito, Copa, Saeta and AeroPerú to Guayaquil); Caracas (Saeta to Quito and Guayaquil, Avianca, Viasa, AeroPerú and Servivensa to Quito only); Mexico City (Saeta to Quito via Guayaquil, Ladeco and Aerolíneas Argentinas to Guayaquil only); Panama (to Quito Continental and Copa, to Guayaquil, these two plus AeroPerú); Santiago de Chile (Ladeco to Guayaquil, Saeta to Quito and Guayaquil). From Brazil weekly Varig flights to Guayaquil and Quito from Rio and São Paulo (joint operation with Lacsa). Lapsa (bought out by Saeta in 1995) flies between Asunción, Paraguay and Guayaquil. Varig/Lacsa (using Varig aircraft) fly San José-Guayaquil-Quito twice weekly, while Lacsa alone flies on the other days. Connections with other Central American capitals in Pan-

ama City; Copa's Lima-Guayaquil-Panama routes continues to Santo Domingo and San Juan, 4 times a week.

Customs

Personal effects, a litre of spirits and a reasonable amount of perfume are admitted free of duty.

When you arrive

● **Clothing**

Spring clothing for Quito (mornings and evenings are cold). In Guayaquil tropical or light-weight clothes. A neat appearance is appreciated by local people; an unkempt look is said to attract a "gringo tax" and reduce friendliness. Laundering is excellent.

NB If intending to go to the Galápagos, or on a tour of the Oriente, do not take all your clothes, etc, in one large suitcase. Take 2 small bags and leave one with non-essentials in Quito (most hotels have facilities for this). Luggage space is limited on Galápagos boats.

● **Official time**

Local time is 5 hrs behind GMT (Galápagos, 6 hrs behind.)

● **Safety**

Although Ecuador has been generally one of the safer countries in the region, there have been reports of increased crime and violence: police searches are now more frequent. If your luggage is searched, make sure that you are present during the search: women travelling alone, especially in Otavalo, should beware of police officers who ask to look at their passport and then insist on taking them to a police station. Keep cameras, etc, in an inconspicuous bag and do not leave valuables strewn about your hotel room. Theft and mugging are on the increase throughout Quito, particularly in the old city, climbing Panecillo, Cruz Loma, Rucu Pichincha, Tugurahua and on the beaches at Manta and near

Atacames. Guayaquil has long been plagued with gang violence, which is also present in the city of Esmeraldas, caution is also advised at nearby beaches. Robberies on city buses, even in the morning, and intercity bus hold-ups are now more common. Beware of pick-pockets wherever there are crowds. There have been guerrilla incursions from Colombia and drug related violence in northern jungle province of Sucumbios, but many of the public safety problems are worst in the big cities while the countryside has remained generally safer and more tranquil.

● **Tipping**

In restaurants, 10% usually in the bill (in cheaper restaurants, tipping is uncommon – but obviously welcome!). Taxi, nil. Airport and railway porters, US$0.10-0.20, according to number of suitcases; cloakroom attendants, US$0.05, hairdressers, 20%.

● **Voltage**

110 volts, 60 cycles, AC throughout Ecuador. Very low wattage bulbs in many hotel rooms, keen readers are advised to carry a bright bulb.

● **Weights and measures**

The metric system is generally used in foreign trade and must be used in legal documents. English measures are understood in the hardware and textile trades. Spanish measures are often used in the retail trade.

On departure

● **Airport tax**

There is a 10% tax on international air tickets for flights originating in Ecuador, regardless of where bought, and 12% on domestic tickets, and a tax of US$25 on all passengers departing on international flights (except those who stay under 24 hrs in the country).

Where to stay

● **Hotels**

Outside the main towns; almost standard prices are charged of US$1.50-3.50 pp (without bath) in a *pensión*, *residencial*, or hotel (where this is the minimum charge). One can bargain at cheaper *pensiones* and *residenciales*. Outside the provincial capitals and the resorts of Salinas and Playas, there are few higher-class hotels. Service of 10% and tax of 10% are added to 1st and 2nd class hotel and restaurant bills. The cheaper hotels charge at most 5%, if anything. Hotel owners tend to try and let their less attractive rooms first, but they are not insulted if you ask for a bigger room, better beds or a quieter area. The difference is often marked.

● **Camping**

White gas, like US Coleman fuel, is not available. Campers should be sure that their stove will either burn Camping Gas, a compressed gas which comes in a non-refillable cylinder, kerosene, or unleaded car gas/petrol (generally an acceptable substitute for white gas). For stoves, kerosene is known as "kerex" and is available at many rural gas stations and in outdoor markets in towns and cities outside Quito; it is, however, very impure. Gasoline is better. Pure alcohol fuel is sold in hardware stores, *ferreterías*, take your own bottle or ask for it "en bolsa" (in a plastic bag). See also p 939.

Food and drink

Food

The cuisine varies extensively with region. The following are some typical dishes worth trying. In the highlands: *locro de papas* (potato and cheese soup), *mote* (corn burst with alkali, a staple in the region around Cuenca, but used in a variety of dishes in the Sierra), *caldo de patas* (cowheal soup with *mote*), *llapingachos* (fried potato and cheese patties), *empanadas de morocho* (fried snacks: a ground corn shell filled with meat), *morocho* is a drink made from *mote*, milk, sugar and cinnamon, *sancocho de yuca* (vegetable soup with manioc root), roast *cuy* (guinea pig), *fritada* (fried pork), *hornado* (roast pork), *humitas* (tender ground corn steamed in the corn leaves), and *quimbolitos* (similar to *humitas* but prepared with corn flour and steamed in banana leaves). *Humitas* and *quimbolitos* come in both sweet and savoury varieties.

On the coast: *empanadas de verde* (fried snacks: a ground plantain shell filled with cheese, meat or shrimp), *sopa de bola de verde* (plantain dumpling soup), *ceviche* (marinaded fish or seafood, popular everywhere, see below), *encocadas* (dishes prepared with coconut milk, may be shrimp, fish, etc, very popular in the province of Esmeraldas), *cocadas* (sweets made with coconut), *viche* (fish or seafood soup made with ground peanuts), and *patacones* (thick fried plantain chips served as a side dish).

In Oriente: dishes prepared with yuca (manioc or cassava root) and a wide variety of river fish.

Throughout the country, if economizing ask for the set meal in restaurants, at lunch time, *merienda* in the evening – very cheap and wholesome; it costs US$1-2. *Fanesca*, a fish soup with beans, many grains, ground peanuts and more, sold in Easter Week, is very filling. *Ceviche*, marinated fish or seafood which is usually served with popcorn and roasted maize, is very popular throughout Ecuador but has acquired a sinister reputation among visitors as a possible means of transmission of cholera. In fact, only *ceviche de pescado* (fish) and *ceviche de concha* (clams) which are marinated raw, potentially pose this hazard. The other varieties of *ceviche* such as *camarón* (shrimp/prawn) and *langostino* (jumbo shrimp/king prawn) all of which are cooked before being marinated, are generally safe delicacies (check the cleanliness of the establishment). *Langosta* (lobster) is an increasingly endangered species but continues to be illegally fished out of season especially for tourist restaurants, please be conscientious. Ecuadorean food is not particularly spicy. However, in most homes and restaurants, the meal is accompanied by a small bowl of *ají* (hot pepper sauce) which may vary greatly in potency. Those unfamiliar with this condiment are advised to exercise caution at first. *Colada* is a generic name which can refer to cream soups or sweet beverages. In addition to the prepared foods mentioned above, Ecuador offers large variety of delicious temperate and tropical fruits, some of which are unique to South America. Chocolate lovers can try the Superior and Rico bars, good quality, excellent value.

Drink

Argentine and Chilean wines are available in the larger cities and cheaper than European or US ones. The best fruit drinks are *naranjilla*, *maracuyá*, *taxo* and *mora* (blackberries), but note that fruit juices are often made with unboiled water. Main beers available are Pilsener and Club. Good *aguardiente* (unmatured rum, Cristal is recommended), *paico* and *trago de caña*. The usual soft drinks, known as *colas*, are available. Instant coffee or liquid concentrate is common, so ask for *café puro* if you want real coffee.

Getting around

Air transport

The local airlines Saeta, SAN, TAME and Aerogal operate internal flights between the main cities. TAME and SAN fly to the Galápagos; both have received favourable reports on reliability and baggage control. Also local airline Cedta operating Santa Rosa, near Machala-Guayaquil. Ecuavia and Icaro operate charter flights. There are air taxis (Cessnas or Bonanzas) to anywhere you want to go, also helicopters. On internal flights passengers may have to disembark at intermediate stops and check in, even though they have booked all the way to the final destination of the plane. Seats are not assigned on internal flights, except to the Galapagos.

Land transport

● **Train**

The railways are not too comfortable or reliable. Although the Quito-Riobamba-Guayaquil and Ibarra-San Lorenzo stretches were used for passenger services in 1995, the future of all trains was under debate (a combination of severely decaying infrustructure, a lack of money and possible privatization). In 1995 the Alausí-Cuenca line was permanently closed, a two tier price system was introduced for Ecuadoreans and foreigners, and a steam locomotive service for tourists started between Quito and Cotopaxi National Park. Rail services are often unreliable, depending on weather.

● **Bus**

Bus travel has improved greatly and is generally more convenient, and cheaper, than in other Andean countries. Since most buses are small they fill up and leave at frequent intervals. A modernization of the intercity bus fleet started in 1994, when several companies acquired luxury a/c units for use on their longer routes. Fares for these are higher and some companies are again setting up their own stations, away from the main bus terminals, exclusively for the new buses. Half the 17,700 km of road are open the year round. The length of paved highway is developing rapidly, including Quito-Guayaquil, Quito-Riobamba, Quito-Tulcán, Quito-Cuenca, Guayaquil-Cuenca, Guayaquil-Riobamba, Riobamba-Baños and the lowland (Costa) road Huaquillas-Machala-Guayaquil-Babahoyo-Santo Domingo-Esmeraldas. New tolls are due to be introduced on main highways.

● **Motoring**

Latest reports state that a *carnet de passage* (or *libreta de pasaje*, known locally as a *tríptico*) is no longer required to enter Ecuador with a car or motorcycle. If bringing in a motorcycle by air it can take over a week to get it out of customs. You need a customs agent, who can be found around the main customs building near the airport, fix the price in advance. Best to accompany the agent all the time and a letter from the Ecuadorian Automobile Club (ANETA) can be helpful. Shipping in a vehicle through Guayaquil is also hazardous; you will be charged by customs for every day the car is left there and will need assistance from an agent. Spare cash may be needed. Manta is a smaller, more relaxed and efficient alternative port. A police or customs agent will accompany you to the border if you do not have the right papers, and you will have to pay him about US$10 a day plus his accommodation and food. If you need boxes/cartons to send bicycles home, Global Transportes, Veintimilla 878 y Av Amazonas, 3rd flr, might be able to help you (German-run).

Driving in Ecuador has been described as "an experience", partly because of unexpected potholes and other obstructions and the lack of road signs, partly because of local drivers' tendency to use the middle of the road. Some surfaces at high altitude are slippery and some, that appear paved, are crude oil sprayed onto compacted gravel. Beware the bus drivers, who often drive very fast and rather recklessly (passengers also please note). "Extra" gasoline, 82 octane, costs US$1.30 per US gallon, Eco 85 (85 octane unleaded, also known as *gasolina verde*, although it is coloured red rather than green), US$1.25, Super SP (92 octane unleaded), US$1.40, diesel US$1.20. Unleaded gasoline is becoming increasingly common throughout the country although it may still be unavailable in the more remote rural areas and in parts of Oriente. Super is only available in the main cities. The road maps published by Nelson Gómez are probably the most useful (see under **Maps** below). Always carry your passport and driving licence; there are police checks on all the roads leading out of main towns and you can be in serious trouble if you are unable to present your documents. If police try to fine you for any spurious reason, you may be able to talk them politely out of it. Driving at night is not recommended, especially in rural areas where speed humps to reduce speed in villages, have become places for robbers to lurk.

● **Car hire**

Hire rates are given under Quito. Some car hire firms do not have adequate insurance policies and you will have to pay heavily in the event of an accident. Be sure to check the car's condition, not forgetting things like wheelnuts. Also make sure it has good ground clearance. Always make sure the car is securely garaged at night.

● **Hitchhiking**

Hitchhiking on the main roads is reported to be easy in the N, but nearly impossible S of Riobamba, and it can be very cold in the mountains in the back of a truck (when hitching, it is common to pay a small sum). In the arid S the unpaved roads are dusty; use a wet cotton handkerchief to filter the air you breathe. Whether hitching or driving always take plenty of drinking water. Be judicious when accepting a ride or picking up hitchhikers, armed car robberies by the latter are increasingly common.

Communications

● **Newspapers**

The main newspapers are *El Comercio*, *Hoy*, *Tiempo*, and *Ultimas Noticias*, in Quito; *Expreso*, *El Telégrafo*, *El Universo* (with good international news), *La Prensa*, *La Razón* and *Extra* (an afternoon paper), in Guayaquil; *El Mercurio*, in Cuenca; *La Opinión del Sur*, in Loja; and *El Espectador*, in Riobamba. *Q* is an English-language news magazine, published monthly, which also contains tourist information (La Canela 403 y Amazonas, T 410-416). *City* is a free weekly paper in Quito, with tourist information and details of what's on; a similar magazine is *The Explorer*.

● **Postal services**

Many post offices away from Quito may not know the foreign rates (10g air-mail to the Americas US$0.28, Europe and rest of world US$0.40) and give incorrect ones. For a small extra charge you can certify your letters and parcels; ask for "*con certificado*" when you buy stamps, so that they are stamped separately (US$0.70 extra). The only post office (probably in all Ecuador) which deals in International Reply Coupons is in Quito, at Eloy Alfaro 354 y 9 de Octubre (new city). **For sending parcels**: up to 20 kg maximum dimensions permitted is 70 x 30 x 30 cms. Take contents and packaging (unpacked) to the Correo Marítimo Aduana, Ulloa 273 y Ramírez Dávalos (next to the Santa Clara Market), for customs inspection. Ask for SAL/APR (surface-air-lifted, reduced priority) rates for the cheapest tariffs. Parcels under 2 kg can also be sent from the post office at Reina Victoria y Colón. The Post Office at the airport is more helpful and the smaller quantity of packages being handled should mean less chance of them going astray. Rates vary according to weight and destination. Packages under 3 kg can be sent "certificado" (US$15.15 for 1 kg to USA, US$34.50 for 3 to 5 kg, US$25 for 1 kg to rest of world, US$80 for 3-5 kg) from the post offices at Espejo, entre Guayaquil y Venezuela, and at Eloy Alfaro. Rates quoted are for airmail: SAL/APR, surface-air-lifted rates are US$13.15 and 23.85 to USA, US$14.75 and 29.75 elsewhere. Transpak (also called STAIR), Amazonas y Veintimilla, will ship out packages for about US$4 per kg to USA, minimum charge about US$50. Letters for Europe bearing the correct Ecuadorean postage can be dropped off at the Lufthansa office, 6 de Diciembre 955 y 18 de Setiembre, to be sent in the next international bag; by 1200 on the day before the flight. Packages coming in to Ecuador should be less than 2 kg and of no stated value to avoid hefty import duty.

NB Some correspondents report that parcels and letters sent "certificado" are more vulnerable to theft and that packages should be marked as "used clothing" and the value declared as US$0.00. Even if not certifying your mail, watch to see that the stamps are franked (then they cannot be stolen). For cardboard boxes and large, strong, plastic-lined envelopes, try Japon Color Film Lab on Amazonas, Quito.

● **Telephone services**

All the principal towns have long-distance telephone facilities. Interprovincial phone calls must be prefixed by the following codes: Pichincha 02; Bolívar, Cotopaxi, Chimborazo, Pastaza, Tungurahua 03; Guayas 04; Galápagos, Los Ríos, Manabí 05; Carchi, Esmeraldas, Imbabura, Napo, Sucumbios 06; Azuay, Cañor, El Oro, Loja, Morona, Zamora 07. Discount period 1900-0700 and all day Sat-Sun: 3 mins to USA US$11.82 person to person (regular), US$9.85 (discount); to Europe US$14.78 person to person (regular), US$12.32 (discount). For international operator dial 116, normally only 5-20 minute wait for call to UK. There is an acute shortage of lines, expect long waits from outlying areas. Direct lines to foreign countries for collect or credit cards are available for Brazil (177), Canada (173), Chile (179), Italy (174), Spain (176),

UK (178), USA (119, 170, 171, 172). Collect calls can be made from Ecuador to some countries (not Australia, Switzerland, Germany or Belgium). A charge is made for person-to-person calls even when the person is not there. Fax to Europe from US$5.60/min; to USA US$4.70/min. Telegrams, ordinary US$4.30 first 7 words and US$0.57 per word thereafter, nightletter US$0.20 per word. There are public telex booths in the best hotels in Quito and Guayaquil (US$13.50 for 3 mins), and at Cuenca.

Sport

The Sierra country is excellent for riding, and good horses can be hired. Quito, Guayaquil and Riobamba have polo clubs. There are golf clubs at Guayaquil and Quito and on the Santa Elena Peninsula. There is excellent big-game fishing for bonito and marlin off Playas, Salinas and Manta. Bull fighting is rarely seen at Guayaquil, but there is a well-known bull-fight festival during the week preceding 6 Dec at Quito. A favourite sport is cock fighting; every town has its pits, but association football is fast taking over as the national sport. Volleyball and basket-ball are also popular. There is Sun horse-racing at Guayaquil.

Climbing can be arranged through climbing clubs in Quito and other cities, or those associated with universities. A recommended guide to climbing is *Climbing and Hiking in Ecuador*, by Rob Rachowiecki and Betsy Wagenhauser (published by Bradt Publications, 3rd edition 1994). Edward Whymper's, *Travels among the Great Andes of the Equator* (published by Gibbs M Smith, Salt Lake City) is available from Libri Mundi. Jorge Anhalzer publishes a series of 5 mountain guides, for each of Ecuador's most frequently climbed peaks, with updated information on routes to the summits. Available from book and camping shops, and by mail order from Latin American Travel Consultants, PO Box 17-17-908, Quito, F 593-2-562-566, Internet: rku@pi.pro.ec. *Die Schneeberge Ecuador* by Marco Cruz, a German translation from Spanish is excellent, as is *Iberetur*, although it is difficult to find. See also under Quito, **Climbing**, for the book *Montañas del Sol* and other details. The quality of hired equipment needs scrutiny and the dangers of climbing at high altitude must be appreciated (see Quito section).

Walking Walkers are advised to get *Climbing and Hiking in Ecuador* (see previous paragraph).

Holidays and festivals

New Year's Day; 6 Jan, Reyes Magos y Día de los Inocentes; 27 Feb, Día del Civismo; Mon and Tues before Lent (Carnival); Holy Thursday; Good Friday; Holy Saturday; 1 May-Labour Day; 24 May-Battle of Pichincha; 24 July-Birthday of Bolívar; 10 Aug–first attempt to gain the Independence of Quito, Opening of Congress, 9 Oct-Independence of Guayaquil, 12 Oct-Columbus' arrival in America; 1 Nov-All Saints' Day; 2 Nov-All Souls' Day; 3 Nov-Independence of Cuenca and Manta; 4 Nov-Independence of Azóguez and Bahía; 6 Dec-Foundation of Quito; Christmas Day. At carnival, water throwing is common, if you can't beat them join them!

Further reading

Information for business travellers is given (1) in "Hints to Exporters: Ecuador", available from DTI Export Publications, PO Box 55, Stratford-upon-Avon, Warwickshire, CV37 9GE; (2) the Ecuadorean-American Association, Inc (55 Liberty St, New York, NY 10005) issues monthly bulletins and a free sample copy may be requested. Telephone directories in Ecuador have "green pages" giving useful tourist information, sometimes in English. Business travellers may wish to consult the *Ecuadorean News Digest*, published by the Ecuadorean American Association, 150 Nassau St, New York, NY 10038.

Acknowledgements

For their invaluable help and hospitality in Ecuador in Sep/Oct 1994, the editor wishes to thank the following (in chronological order): in Guayaquil, Ilse Tugendhat and Lucía Martínez of Ecoventura, Antonio and Sylvia Saman of Galasam, Vicky Longland and Mike Power, Víctor and his driver, Juan; on the Galápagos, the crew of the *Flamingo* and the guides Ivonne and Gaby; in Manabí, Dario Proaño-Leroux; N of Quito, Juan Serrano of Ayuda en Acción, Cayambe (and Augusto Ordóñez in Quito); Robert and Daisy Kunstaetter and family, Quito; Melanie Ebertz, Logan and Heather Ward and Damaris Carlisle of the South American Explorers Club; Jean Brown, David Gayton and Juan Sheehan of Safari Ecuador; Eric Schwartz, Lorena Tapia, Veva Salem and the staff at *La Selva*; Miguel Angel Muñoz of Fundación Ecuacom; Julián Echeverría of The Travel Co; Freddy Ramírez of Sierra Nevada, and David Horwell (Bromley, UK). For their invaluable help in the preparation of this chapter, thanks go to Robert and Daisy Kunstaetter; Melanie Ebertz, Damaris

Carlisle, Amanda Stevenson, Raul Jarrín and other members of The South American Explorers Club; Jean Brown and David Gayton of Safari; Vicky Longland; Sarah Cameron and Alan Murphy.

Thanks are also due to the following travellers who wrote to the *Handbook*: Daniel Aeberhard (Slough, UK) an excellent contribution, Jimmy Andersson and Christina Gustafson (Malmo, Sweden), Svend & Tove Andersen (Vadum, Denmark), Lee Andrews (Taunton, UK) a very helpful update of Playas, Jens Arnold (Borken, Germany), Louise Bach (Vestbjerg) and Tine Tang Kleif (Aarhus, Denmark), Edith Bangerter (Eggersriet, Switzerland), Maríá Barantes (Quito, Ecuador), Isabelle Barbier and Astrid Käser (Neuchatel, Switzerland), Marion Barclay (Croydon, UK), Janie Bergeron and François Vitez (Longueuil, Canada), De Coninck Bernadette (Qadima, Israel), Nicole Berry (Columbia, USA), Dave Blackburn (Luton, UK) and Emily Smith (North Carolina, USA), Phil and Jenny Blackman (Bath, UK), Claudia Böohler and Frank Busch (Berlin, Germany), Colette and Tanya Botha (South Africa), J C Brun (Toulouse, France), Phil Buckle (Suhr, Switzerland), Lauro Canonica (Switzerland), Jean Chang (Quito, Ecuador), Catherine Chenery (London, UK), Etienne Claes (Brugge, Belgium), Bernard Cloutier (Montreal, Canada), Judith Stanton and Mark Collins (London, UK) a helpful update, Mark Collins (Bristol, UK), Merila Couillard (Quebec, Canada), the late Bernard van der Dool (Leiden, The Netherlands), Kenneth Dreyfuss (Miami, USA), Guy Edlis (Haifa, Israel), James Elder (Goulburn, Australia), Jakob Engström and Richard Björlin (Brussels, Belgium), Scott Ferber (Owings Mill, USA), Martin Fiems (Brugge, Belgium), Heike Fischer (Würzburg, Germany), Fran (UK), Elisabeth Friedrich (Bassersdorf, Switzerland), Patrick Ganahl (Wolfhausen, Switzerland), Laura García (Barcelona, Spain), Helene Keur and Geert Klein Geltink (Zwolle, The Netherlands), Gisa Gericke (Wetzlar), Nicole Hofmann (Weisbaden), and Tanja Wirth (Flörsheim, Germany), Petra Giger (Zurich, Switzerland), Maje Grabethuiel (Oftringen, Switzerland), Loukas Grafakos (Papagou, Greece), Matt Griffin (Seattle. USA), Sylvia Grisez (Warren, USA), Silvid Gudd & Johannes Kappeler (Frauenfeld, Switzerland), Emma Collingwood and Jim Hart (Edinburgh, UK), Kjetil Haugan (Ottestad, Norway), Dan Heilborn and Maya Schneider (Haifa and Tel-Aviv, Israel), Andreas Hochuli (Aarau, Switzerland), Henryk Hörner Berlin, Germany), Philip Hollwey (Dublin, Eire), M Kirby and A Hammerman (Cotopaxi, Ecuador), Jessi Helbling (Quito).

James Mendoza (Loja, Ecuador), Peter Hunt (Basingstoke, UK), Dr Lou and Kay Blas (Lewiston, USA), John Ivanko (Royal Oak, USA), Mandy Jacobsen (London, UK), Marie Javins (New York, USA), Hanne Stadsgaard Jensen (Aarhus, Denmark), Kendra Jones (Wellington, New Zealand), Helle Jørgensen (Abyhøj, Denmark), Sonja Jovanovic and Andrew Thompson (London, UK) a helpful letter Hielke Keikke (Breda, Holland), Yvonne Kellenberger (Rorschach, Switzerland), John KIneke (Danville, USA), Ruth Klingberg and Lis Musholt (Copenhagen, Denmark), Susan Kobrin (London, UK), Lewis Kofsky (Ecuador), Charles and Betty Konopa (Yuma, USA), David Kützmütz (Germany) and Olga Beneth (Honduras), Christoph Lanfer (Puchheim, Germany), Riika Levoranta (Vammala) and Vesa Lampiner (Mójärvi, Finland), Valerie Levrier (London, UK), Dr R Liersch (Lohmar, Germany), Catja Loepfe (Zurich, Switzerland), Janine Low (New York, USA), L Castro (Ecuador), Adriaan G Lucas (Leidschendam, Holland), Sandra Maisel (temporarily in La Paz, Bolivia), Elke Meinert (Essen, Germany), Lola Mendez (Seville, Spain), Michel Blanes and Kristine Meyer (Copenhagen, Denmark), Helmut Moser (Zell am See, Austria), Martijn Mugge (Enschede, The Netherlands), Mark Muhlbacher (Lucerne, Switzerland) for many letters Brian Mullin (Guayaquil, Ecuador), Elaine Koviacs & Russell Murdoch (Christchurch, UK), Trevor Murphy and Sylvia Carbone (St Albans, Australia), Don Nafziger (Kamloops, Canada), Randy Nelson and Sheila Luther (Alberta, Canada), Rita Niederberger (Luzern, Switzerland), Annesofie Nielsen (Niva, Denmark), Nicole Noël (Canada), Dominik Noger and Heidi Reichmuth (Rapperswil, Switzerland), Carine Oesterle (Zurich, Switzerland), Mafra O'Reilly (Dublin, Eire), Tina Ortmanns and Patrick Laschet (Aachen, Germany), Richard Osborne (New Zealand) and Nathalie Bélanger (Canada), Tony Darrall-Row (Colnbrook, UK), Jonathan Paisner (London, UK), Dr Wilson Pancho (Quito), Jerry Peek (Sepastopol, USA), Howard Peters (London, UK), John Pickett Sabina Potthoff-Höner (Berlin, Germany), Kathryn Pruski (Durango, USA), Ulrich Puls and David Cayet (Berlin, Germany), Pekka Rahko and Tiina Laine (Oulo, Finland), Lawrence Railton and Susan Boyd (London, UK), Timothy Rank (Minneapolis, USA), Juliet Redding (Berkhamsted), Heidi Reichen (Gsteig) and Roger Strähl (Balsthal, Switzerland), Barbara and Peter Roniger (Suberg, Switzerland), Karen Troy-Davies (London, UK), Helen Rucoba (Sacramento, USA), Andy Ryder (Vienna, Austria), Burkhard Schack and Michael Zickgraf (Seelbach, Germany), Fernand Daigle and Claudia Schaerer (Stratford, Canada), Beatrice Schaer (Tamins, Switzerland), Alexandra Scharpf (Regensburg) and Gesche Wagner (Giessen, Germany), Svenja Schmidt (Germany), Judith Schrottenloher (Munich, Germany), Harald Schultz (Benningen, Germany), Inge and Machiel de Schutter (Cologne, Germany), Mandy Scott (Edinburgh, UK), Ayla S Sevim (Izmir, Turkey), Nicky Shearman and Dave Ramsden (London, UK), Bronwen Sinclair (Quito, Ecuador), Yaniv Sneor (Parsippany, USA), Solveig and Jimmi (Lemvig, Denmark), N B Stalker (Cambridge, UK), Brigitte Steimen and Mathias Becker (Meriken, Switzerland), David Stein (Chicago, USA), Frank Steinmetzer (Freising, Germany), S Nielsen and Hellmuth-Chr Stuven (Copenhagen, Denmark), M James Snyder (Radlett, UK.), Ilay Tamari (Ramat-Hasharon, Israel), C P. Taylor (France), Werner Thanner (Regensberg, Germany), Mette and Lotte Thillerup (Hesselager, Denmark), A.ndrios Tieleman and Ditty Bakker (Haarlem, The Netherlands), Inger Tingsgard (Abyhoj, Denmark), Barbara and Gabriel Toffani (Chatou, France), Pernilla Tragardh (Stockholm, Sweden), Cathy Travis (London, UK), Mike and Pauline Truman (Burnham-on-Sea, UK), Samuel Urech (Niederhasli, Switzerland), Valerie A Valene (Manhattan Beach, USA), Infanger Vinzenz (Erstfeld, Switzerland) an extensive contribution Dre Visscher (Tilburg, The Netherlands), Peter Waanders (Arnhem, The Netherlands) helpful details, Rupert A E Walker (Salisbury, UK), Nicole Wanner (Belvidere, USA), Katherine Whittney and Farhad Farzareth (San Francisco, USA), Pierre-André Widmer (Céligny, Switzerland), Ollo Wiemann (Trier, Germany), Marc Williamson (Melbourne, Australia) an extensive contribution, Christian Leonards and Sandra Winterhalter (Insel Reichenau, Germany), Rowan Wood (Aspen, USA), Rosemary Woodburn (Woldingham, UK), Elke Wurtz (Frankfurt, Germany), and Michael Youngsma (Surfside, USA).

PARAGUAY

INTRODUCTION

PARAGUAY is entirely landlocked, surrounded by Argentina, Bolivia and Brazil. The country is divided into two parts by the Río Paraguay: to the W of the river is the Chaco (246,950 square km, nearly 61% of the country's area), a sparsely inhabited tract of flat and infertile country. E of the river is Paraguay proper (159,800 square km), a rich land in which almost all the population is concentrated.

The latter part consists of two contrasting areas separated by a high cliffed formation which runs almost due N from the Río Alto Paraná, W of Encarnación, to the Brazilian border. **The Paraná Plateau**, which lies E of this cliff and ranges from 300 to 600m in height, has comparatively heavy falls of rain and was originally forest. Across the plateau, much of which is in Argentina and Brazil, runs the Río Paraná. West of the cliff lies a fertile plain stretching to the Río Paraguay. This plain is diversified by rolling, wooded hills. Most of Paraguay's population is concentrated in these hilly lands, stretching SE from Asunción to Encarnación.

Much of the plain is flooded once a year; it is wet savanna, treeless, but covered with coarse grasses. On this plain, rice, sugar, tobacco, grains, soya and cotton are grown. Several rivers drain the plain and hills into the Río Paraguay.

The Chaco, lying W of the Río Paraguay is mostly cattle country or scrub forest. Along the river there are grassy plains and clumps of palms, but westwards the land grows drier and more bleak. Much of the north-western area is almost desert. The marshy, unnavigable Río Pilcomayo forms the boundary with Argentina. Apart from Mennonite colonies, small settlements on the river banks, and a number of *estancias* in the SW, only a few nomadic Indian tribes live in the vast region. (The average density is less than 1 person to the square km.) The *quebracho* (axe-breaker) tree, the world's principal source (with mimosa) of tannin, comes from the scrub forests of the Chaco and of the Río Paraná.

Climate The climate is sub-tropical, with a marked difference between summer and winter and often between one day and the next throughout the year. Summer (Jan-Mar) is hot (and humid in Asunción). Temperatures range from 25° to 43°C. The autumn (April-June) is mild, but nights are cold. During winter (July-Sept) the temperature can be as low as 5°C, though it can also be much higher. Temperatures

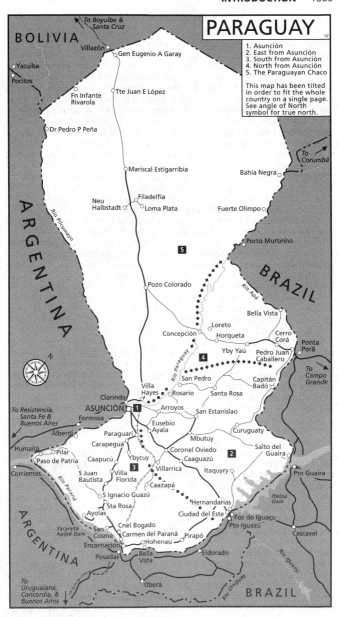

PARAGUAY

1. Asunción
2. East from Asunción
3. South from Asunción
4. North from Asunción
5. The Paraguayan Chaco

This map has been tilted in order to fit the whole country on a single page. See angle of North symbol for true north.

below freezing are rare, and it never snows. The heaviest rains are from Oct to Apr, but some rain falls each month.

History The original inhabitants of the area of Paraguay were the semi-nomadic Guaraní Indians; they had spread by the 16th century to the foothills of the Andes, along the coast of Brazil, and even into the basin of the Amazon. In 1524, the first Spaniards reached the Río Paraguay, under the navigator Diego de Solís. A member of Solís's expedition, Alejo García, was the first European to cross Paraguay, leading an expedition NW through the Chaco in search of El Dorado in 1525; he was also the first European to fight against the Incas, as his career included an attack on them with a Guaraní army of 2,000. Spanish settlement in the area came later: an expedition led by Juan de Ayolas came from Buenos Aires, where the earliest Spanish settlement was planted unsuccessfully in 1536. Finding no gold along the Río de la Plata, and harassed by the hostile Indians of the Pampa, they pushed N along the river, seeking a short route to the gold and silver of Peru. They reached the Guaraní Indians in 1537 and a member of the party, Juan de Salazar de Espinosa, is generally credited with founding Asunción on 15 August.

Asunción became the nucleus of Spanish settlement in southeastern South America. Spaniards pushed NW across the Chaco to found Santa Cruz, in Bolivia, eastwards to occupy the rest of Paraguay, and southwards down the river to re-found Buenos Aires in 1580, 43 years after they had abandoned it.

During the colonial era one of the world's most interesting experiments in dealing with a native population was carried out, not by the conquerors, but by their missionaries, over whom the civil power had at first little control. In 1609 the Society of Jesus sent missionaries to Paraguay to convert and 'civilize' the Indians. During the 158 years until they were expelled in 1767, the Jesuits formed 30 *reducciones*, or settlements, run along theocratic-socialist lines. They induced the Indians to leave the forests and settle in townships, where they helped build magnificent churches, employing unsuspected native skills in masonry, sculpture, and painting. Selected natives were even given a sound classical education. The first *reducciones* were further N, but were forced to abandon these because of attacks by the *bandeirantes* of São Paulo, Brazil. They settled finally in Misiones; parts of the area of settlement are now in Argentina and southern Brazil. After the expulsion of the Jesuits, the *reducciones* fell to pieces: the Indians left, and were reduced to peonage under other masters. Most of the great churches have fallen into ruin, or been destroyed; the few that remain are dealt with in the text (**see also under San Ignacio Miní, Argentina, p 162 and p 446 in Southern Brazil**).

The disturbances in Buenos Aires in 1810-1816 which led to independence from Spain enabled creole leaders in Asunción to throw off the rule of Buenos Aires as well as Madrid. The new republic was, however, subject to pressure from both Argentina, which blocked Paraguayan trade on the Río de la Plata, and Brazil. Following independence Paraguay was ruled by a series of dictators, the first of whom, Dr Gaspar Rodríguez de Francia (1814-1840) known as "El Supremo", imposed a policy of isolation and self-sufficiency. The opening of the Río de la Plata after the fall of the Argentine dictator Rosas enabled de Francia's successor, Carlos Antonio López (1840-62) to import modern technology: in 1856 a railway line between Asunción and Villarrica was begun; an iron foundry and telegraph system were also developed. Carlos López was succeeded by his son, Francisco Solano López (López II), who saw himself as the Napoleon of South America. Believing Paraguay to be threatened by Brazil and Argentina, Solano López declared war on Brazil in 1864. When Argentina refused permission to send troops through Misiones to attack Brazil, Solano López declared war on Argentina. With Uruguay supporting Brazil and Argentina, the ensuing War of the Triple Alliance was disastrous for the Paraguayan forces who held on against overwhelming odds until the death of López at the Battle of Cerro Corá in Mar 1870. Of a pre-war population of 400,000, only 220,000 survived the war, 28,000 of them males, mostly either very young or very old. In the peace settlement Paraguay lost territory to Brazil and Argentina, although the rivalry between these neighbours prevented a worse fate.

After the war Paraguay experienced political instability as civilian factions competed for power, often appealing to army officers for support. Although there were few policy differences between the two political parties (the National Republican Association, known as Colorados from its red banner, and the Liberal party who adopted the colour blue), rivalry between them was intense. Elections were held regularly, but whichever party was in government invariably intervened to fix the result and the opposition rarely participated.

While Paraguayan leaders were absorbed with domestic disputes, Bolivian governments began occupying disputed parts of the Chaco in an attempt to gain access to the sea via the Río Paraguay. Although Bolivian moves started in the late 19th century, the dispute was given new intensity by the discovery of oil in the 1920s. In the three years of the Chaco War (1932-1935) 56,000 Bolivian and 36,000 Paraguayans were killed. Despite general expectations Paraguayan troops pushed the Bolivian army out of most of the Chaco.

Victory in war only increased dissatisfaction in the army with the policies of governments before the war. In Feb 1936 nationalist officers seized power and appointed the war hero, Col Rafael Franco as President. Although Franco was overthrown in a counter-coup in 1937, the so-called 'February Revolution' began major changes in Paraguay including the first serious attempt at land reform and legal recognition of the small labour movement.

Between 1939 and 1954 Paraguayan politics were even more turbulent, as rival civilian factions and army officers vied for power. In 1946 civil war shook the country as army units based in Concepción fought to overthrow President Morinigo. A military coup in May 1954 led to Gen Alfredo Stroessner becoming President. Stroessner retained power for 34 years, the most durable dictator in Paraguayan history. His rule was based on control over the army and the Colorado party, both of which were purged of opponents. While a network of spies informed on dissidents, party membership was made compulsory for most official posts including teachers and doctors. In fraudulent elections Stroessner was re-elected eight times. Paraguay became a centre for smuggling, gambling and drug-running, much of it run by Stroessner's supporters. Meanwhile the government spent large amounts of money on transportation and infrastructure projects, including the giant hydroelectric dam at Itaipú.

Although these projects brought employment, the completion of Itaipú in 1982 coincided with recession in Brazil and Argentina on whose economies Paraguay was heavily dependent. Meanwhile rivalry intensified within the regime over the succession, with Stroessner favouring his son, Gustavo. Opposition focussed around Gen Andrés Rodríguez, who was married to Stroessner's daughter. When Stroessner tried to force Rodríguez to retire, troops loyal to Rodríguez overthrew the 75 year old Stroessner, who left to live in Brazil. Rodríguez, who became provisional president, easily won multi-party elections in May 1989. The commitment to greater democracy permitted opponents, who had previously boycotted, or been banned from elections, to gain an unprecedented number of seats in the legislative elections of the same date. Despite considerable scepticism over Gen Rodríguez's intentions, largely because he had been Gen Stroessner's right hand man, political liberalization became a reality. Human rights improved considerably, political prisoners were released and political parties compaigned openly. The press was allowed to report freely and did much to uncover corruption. In May 1991, the first municipal elections since independence were held and Asunción was won by an Independent. At the end of the year, elections took place for a constituent assembly to replace the 1967 constitution with a new, democratic constitution. The ruling Colorados won 60% of the vote for the 198-seat assembly, while the main opposition party, the Authentic Radical Liberal Party took only 28%.

The presidential and congressional elections promised by General Rodríguez were held on 9 May 1993. The presidency was won by Juan Carlos Wasmosy of the Colorado Party, Domingo Laíno of the Authentic Radical Liberal Party came second and Guillermo Caballero Vargas of the coalition Encuentro Nacional third. In congress the Colorados won the most seats, but insufficient to have a majority in either house. The government's commitment to market reforms and to economic integration with Argentina and Brazil within Mercosur inspired protests in 1994. A general strike, the first for 35 years, was held in May, as workers demanded more pay, an end to privatizations and the suspension of Mercosur. Peasants demanded land reform, while small companies and the traders of Ciudad del Este felt under severe threat from competition and low Mercosur tariffs.

The People of Paraguay Because Spanish influence was less than in many other parts of South America, most people are bilingual, speaking both Spanish and Guaraní. Outside Asunción, most people speak Guaraní by preference. There is a Guaraní theatre, it is taught in private schools, and books and periodicals are published in that tongue, which has official status as the second national language. According to official figures, the indigenous population is about 39,000; non-government sources put it at twice that level. Two-thirds of them are in the Chaco, and one-third in the rest of the country. There are 17 distinct ethnic groups with five different languages, among which Guaraní predominates. The 1981 Law of Native Communities in theory guarantees Indian rights to ownership of their traditional lands and the maintenance of their culture.

The Economy Paraguay is essentially an agricultural country; farming accounts for almost 25% of gdp. Agricultural exports earn about 90% of Paraguay's foreign exchange with normally about 60% coming from cotton and soya. Cattle raising and meat exports used to be the principal agricultural activities, but their importance has declined as a result of uncompetitive pricing policies and import restrictions in potential markets. Fluctuations in the value of exports characterize the performance of Paraguay's main commodities, since they are so subject to the weather and world prices. Other major products are timber, tobacco, tung and other industrial oilseeds, essential oils (mainly petit grain) and *quebracho*. Self-sufficiency in wheat has been achieved since 1985, and the country now grows most of its basic food requirements.

Industry has traditionally been dependent upon agriculture: for instance, cotton ginning, sugar milling, textiles, meat packing, timber processing and extraction of *quebracho*, industrial and essential oils. The country industrialized fast in the 1970s and early 1980s, and manufacturing now accounts for 17% of gdp. On the back of hydroelectric development, Paraguay has its own cement industry and a steel plant opened in 1986. Both these, the distillation of alcohol for fuel and other purposes, and shipbuilding are state-owned. All but the last named are due for privatization.

The massive hydroelectric scheme undertaken by Brazil and Paraguay at Itaipú on the Río Paraná is reported to be the largest of its kind in the world. Both the total cost, of about US$15.3bn, and the final capacity, of 12.6m kilowatts, are to be shared equally between the two countries. Paraguay's share substantially exceeds domestic requirements and the surplus energy is sold to Brazil via a high-tension line to São Paulo. Paraguay is cooperating with Argentina on the construction of the Yacyretá-Apipé plant, also on the Paraná, with capacity of 2.7m kilowatts. Financing is being sought for a third hydroelectric project, Corpus, to be built between Itaipú and Yacyretá. Paraguay has a smaller hydroelectric facility at Acaray.

Until 1983, Paraguay managed to offset its current account and trade deficits with capital inflows for Itaipú. After the completion of civil works, the overall balance of payments fell into deficit, with a consequent drain on international reserves. In 1986, the situation was exacerbated by the World Bank and the

Paraguay : fact file

Geographic

Land area	406,752 sq km
forested	33.3%
pastures	53.9%
cultivated	5.6%

Demographic

Population (1994)	4,732,000
annual growth rate (1989-94)	2.6%
urban	50.5%
rural	49.5%
density	11.6 per sq km
Religious affiliation	
Roman Catholic	93.1%
Birth rate per 1,000 (1991)	33.6
	(world av 26.0)

Education and Health

Life expectancy at birth,	
male	65.0 years
female	69.4 years
Infant mortality rate	
per 1,000 live births (1990-95)	47.0
Physicians (1992)	1 per 1,423 persons
Hospital beds	1 per 835 persons
Calorie intake as %	
of FAO requirement	116%
Population age 25 and over	
with no formal schooling	13.6%
Literate males (over 15)	92.1%
Literate females (over 15)	88.1%

Economic

GNP (1993 market prices)	US$6,977mn
GNP per capita	US$1,500
Public external debt (1992)	
	US$1,483mn
Tourism receipts (1992)	US$153mn
Inflation (annual av 1988-93)	24.2%

Radio	1 per 6.0 persons
Television	1 per 13 persons
Telephone	1 per 30 persons

Employment

Population economically active (1982)	
	1,039,258
Unemployment rate (1989)	9.2%
% of labour force in	
agriculture	42.9
mining	0.1
manufacturing	12.0
construction	6.7
Military forces	16,500

Source *Encyclopaedia Britannica*

Inter-American Development Bank refusing to disburse loans until a more realistic exchange rate was adopted.

When General Stroessner was ousted at the beginning of 1989, the new administration moved quickly to introduce economic reforms, including freeing the exchange rate and lifting many controls. In the short term, this had the effect of dramatically improving registered foreign trade flows; previously about half of all exports and imports were contraband. By 1992 the economic momentum slowed; no further reforms were introduced, growth was restricted and inflation stayed high (19.5% in 1993, 22% in 1994). The foreign trade balance was also in deficit as drought limited agricultural exports and imports were not reduced. Having restructured the debt to Brazil, its major creditor, Paraguay reached bilateral deals in 1992 with commercial banks, to spread out maturities on the estimated US$2.2 bn foreign debt. No progress was made in restructuring debt to foreign governments, largely because of the lack of an IMF programme, although current payments were resumed. This, plus the clearing of interest arrears to all creditors, led to a strong reduction in reserves. It was expected that President Wasmosy would steer Paraguay through an IMF reform schedule. In 1991, Paraguay formed Mercosur, a Southern Cone Common Market, with Argentina, Brazil and Uruguay.

Government There was a new Constitution in 1992. Executive power rests with the President, elected for five years. There is a two-chamber Congress (Senate 45 seats, Chamber of Deputies 80). Voting is secret and obligatory for all citizens over 18.

Communications The only practicable water route is by the Paraná to the Plata estuary, and Buenos Aires, 1,450 km from Asunción. So difficult is the river that communication with Buenos Aires was mainly by road before the railway to Asunción was opened in 1913. Most freight is now moved to Buenos Aires, or to Santos or Paranaguá in Brazil, by good paved roads, though river barges still ply along the Paraná. For major roads, see p 1076.

There are about 440 km of railways: most passenger services have been withdrawn (**see p 1076**).

NB After the fall of President Stroessner, all references to his name throughout the country were removed. Ciudad Presidente Stroessner was officially renamed Ciudad del Este; the airport, too, was given a new title, Silvio Pettirossi (after a pioneer of flying in Paraguay).

Music and Dance The music of Paraguay is a curiosity. Although this is the only South American country the majority of whose population still speak the original native tongue, the music is totally European in origin. The 17th and 18th century Jesuits found the Guaraní people to be highly musical and when their missions were established, the natives were immediately and totally indoctrinated into European music, of which they became fine performers, albeit not composers or innovators. A good example is Cristóbal Pirioby (1764-94), who changed his name to José Antonio Ortiz and moved to Buenos Aires to perform. At his death he left a large collection of musical instruments and sheet music of works by Haydn, Boccherini, etc. After the disastrous War of the Triple Alliance there was an abandonment of things national and even the national anthem was composed by a Uruguayan. Although black slaves were introduced to the country, they became quickly absorbed and there is no trace of black influence in the music. Neither is there any Guaraní element, nor infusion from Brazil or Argentina. Virtually the only popular instruments are the guitar and harp and it is the latter in particular that has come to be the hallmark of all that is musically Paraguayan, with the assistance of such brilliant performers as Félix Pérez Cardoso and Digno García. Paraguayan songs are notably languid and extemely sentimental and the present repertoire is not 'traditional', but of 20th century origin and by known composers. Of the three principal musical genres, two are slow and for singing, while one is lively and purely for dancing. The two singing genres are the Canción Paraguaya (or Purajhéi) and the Guarania, the former being a slow polka, of which the earliest and most famous example is 'Campamento Cerro León' about the War of the Triple Alliance. The Guarania was developed by José Asunción Flores as recently as the 1920s and includes most of the country's best loved and oft-repeated songs, such as 'India', 'Mi Dicha Lejana' and 'Recuerdos de Ypacaraí'. Equally celebrated and far more vigorous is that favourite of harp virtuosos, the wordless but onomatopeic 'Pájaro Campana'.

For dancing there are the lively Polca Paraguaya and Polca Galopada, first mentioned in print in 1858. They have similarities with the Argentine 'Gato' for instance and are not a true polka nor a gallop, the names of these popular European dances having been attached to an existing Paraguayan dance of unknown name. The Polca is a dance for couples, whilst the even livelier Galopa is usually danced by groups of women, the so-called 'Galoperas', who swing round barefoot, balancing a bottle or jar on their heads. This in turn has developed into the 'Danza de la Botella' or bottle dance, a more recent variant for virtuoso individual performance. Other less well known dances are the Valseadas (a local variant of the waltz), the Chopi or Santa Fé (for three couples), the Taguato, Golondrina, Palomita and Solito, the last named a kind of 'musical chairs'.

Paraguayan music first came to the attention of the outside world soon after the second world war and a number of artists such as Luis Alberto del Paraná and Los Paraguayos have achieved world fame. At the other end of the spectrum the four barefoot old men of the Banda Peteke Peteke from Guajayvity near Yaguarón play their own traditional music on two *mimby* flutes and two little drums, a small idiosyncratic island in an ocean of harp music.

ASUNCION (1)

Asunción, the capital and largest city in Paraguay, is built on the shores of a bay cutting into the eastern bank of the Río Paraguay, almost opposite its confluence with the Pilcomayo. Its population is around 1.2 million, more than a quarter of the national population. The city, built on a low hill crowned by the large modern church of La Encarnación, is laid out in the colonial Spanish rectangular manner. The central plazas of the city are drenched in colour during July-Aug with the prolific pink bloom of the *lapacho* trees, which grow everywhere. The oldest part is down by the water's edge, but none of the public buildings is earlier than the last half of the 19th century. Dwelling houses are in a variety of styles; new villas in every kind of taste have replaced the traditional one-storey Spanish-Moorish type of house, except in the poorer quarters.

You see most public buildings by following Calle El Paraguayo Independiente from the Aduana (Customs House). The first is the Palacio de Gobierno, built in the style of Versailles during the Triple Alliance War (open Sun). In Plaza Constitución stands the Congreso Nacional (debates can be attended during the session from Apr to December, on Thur and sometimes Fri), with the Cathedral at the corner of the square. Two blocks SW, along Calle Chile, is Plaza de los Héroes, with the Pantéon Nacional de los Héroes based on Les Invalides in Paris, begun during the Triple Alliance War and finished in 1937. It contains the tombs of Carlos Antonio López, Mariscal Francisco Solano López, an unknown child-soldier, Mariscal Estigarribia, the victor of the Chaco War and other national heroes. The Plaza de los Héroes (in reality four squares) is being transformed by the construction of parking areas, in front of *Hotel Guaraní* and on the part facing Oliva. Four blocks SE is the Plaza Uruguaya with, nearby, the railway station, built 1856, and a steam engine, the *Sapucai*, dating from 1861. The national cemetery (Cementerio Recoleta), which resembles a miniature city, with tombs in various architectural styles, is on Av Mariscal López, 3 km SE of the centre. It contains the tomb of Eliza Lynch, the Irish mistress of President Solano López (ask guide to show you the location) and, separately, the tomb of their baby daughter. Eliza Lynch's home at the corner of Yegros and Mcal Estigarribia is now the Law Faculty.

The best of several parks is Parque Carlos Antonio López, set high to the W along Colón and, if you can find a gap in the trees, with a grand view. Good views are also offered from *Restaurant Zodiac*, on top floor at 14 de Mayo y Benjamín Constant (opens 1500) and from Cerro de Lambaré, 7 km S (buses 9 and 29 from Gral Díaz). The Botanical Gardens are 6 km E, on Av Artigas with Primer Presidente at Trinidad, reached by bus (Nos 2, 6, 23, and 40, US\$0.15, about 35 mins; outward they can be caught on Luis A Herrera, or Nos 24, 35 or 44B from Oliva or Cerro Corá). They lie along the Paraguay river, on the former estate of the López family, and have a limited range of plants (poorly maintained and no labels), an eighteen-hole golf course, and a little zoo, which has inspired some unfavourable comments and protests. Entrance fee US\$0.30. The López residence is in the Gardens; a typical Paraguayan country house with verandahs, which has become a natural history museum and library. The Maca Indian reservation (since 1985) is N of the Gardens (take bus 42 or 44, entrance US\$0.15, guide US\$0.80); the Indians, who live in very poor conditions, expect you to photograph them (US\$0.25). The beautiful church of Santísima Trinidad (on Santísimo Sacramento, parallel to Av Artigas), where Carlos Antonio López was originally buried, dating from 1856 with paintings inside, is well worth a visit (reported only open for regular services). It is 10 mins walk from the zoo entrance.

Museums Museo Nacional de Bellas Artes, Iturbe y Mcal Estigarribia, a good collection of Spanish paintings; also an interesting selection of 20th Century Paraguayan art, open Mon-Fri, 0700-1900, Sat and Sun 0800-1200. In the Botanical Gardens are the **Museo de História**

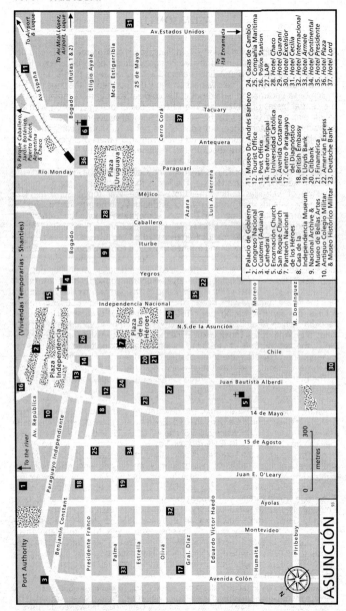

ASUNCIÓN

1. Palacio de Gobierno
2. Congreso Nacional
3. Aduana (Aduana)
4. Cathedral
5. Encarnación Church
6. San Roque Church
7. Panteón Nacional de los Héroes
8. Casa de la Independencia Museum
9. Nacional Archive & Museo de Bellas Artes
10. Antiguo Colegio Militar & Museo Histórico Militar
11. Museo Dr. Andrés Barbero
12. Tourist Office
13. Post Office
14. Police Station
15. Teatro Municipal
16. Universidad Católica
17. Avenida Costanera
18. Centro Paraguayo del Diagnóstico
19. Lloyds Bank
20. Citibank
21. Finamerica
22. American Express
23. Deutsche Bank
24. Casas de Cambio
25. Compañía Marítima
26. LAP
27. Police Station
28. Hotel Chaco
29. Hotel Guaraní
30. Hotel Excelsior
31. Hotel Cecilia
32. Hotel Internacional
33. Hotel Armele
34. Hotel Continental
35. Hotel Presidente
36. Hotel Plaza
37. Hotel Lord

Natural and the **Museo Indigenista**, both open Mon-Sat 0730-1130, former 1300-1700, latter 1330-1730, Sun 0800-1300, neither in good condition. In the **Casa de la Independencia** (14 de Mayo y Presidente Franco) is an interesting historical collection; this was where the 1811 anti-colonial revolution was plotted; open Tues-Fri 0700-1200 and 1430-1830, Sat and Sun 0800-1200, entry free. **Pantéon Nacional de los Héroes**, esq Palma y Chile, open every day. **Museo Histórico Militar** in the Antiguo Colegio Militar, originally a Jesuit chapel built in 1588, at El Paraguayo Independiente y 14 de Mayo, open Mon-Fri 0730-1200, 1330-1800, Sat-Sun 0800-1200, an interesting record of the country's turbulent past, well displayed in a renovated building. **Museo Dr Andrés Barbero**, España y Mompox, open Mon-Fri 0800-1100, and Mon, Wed, Fri 1500-1700, anthropological, free, with a good collection of tools and weapons, etc, of the various Guaraní cultures, rec. **Museo Gral de Div Bernardino Caballero**, Parque Caballero, memorabilia and furniture, Mon-Fri 0800-1300, Sat 0800-1200. **Centro de Artes Visuales**, at Isla de Francia, access via Av Gral Genes, bus 30 or 44A from the centre, open daily, except Sun and holidays, 1600-2030; contains **Museo Paraguayo de Arte Contemporáneo**, with some striking murals, **Museo de Arte Indígeno** and **Museo de Barro**, containing ceramics, highly rec. Most museums are small and basic, mainly because of lack of interest and funding in the Stroessner years.

NB Plaza de la Independencia is often referred to as Plaza Constitución, it should also be noted that Plaza de los Héroes is called Plaza Independencia on some sources. On Sat am, till 1200, Av Palma becomes a pedestrian area, with scores of stores selling anything that can be carried, or learnt. Av España originally extended as far out as Av San Martín, but the section between Av Kubitschek and Av Santísimo Sacramento was renamed Av Generalísimo Franco (not to be confused with Presidente Franco) and the remaining section between Av SS Sacramento and Av San Martín was renamed Av General Genes. Many people still use the name Av España for the whole of its original length, ignoring the renamings.

Hotels The hotel bill does not usually include a service charge.

Outside Asunción: 12 km from town, at Itá Enramada, on its own beach on the Río Paraguay is **L2** *Hotel del Yacht y Golf Club Paraguay*, PO Box 1795, T 36117/36121, F 36120, 3 restaurants, super luxury, with pool, gym, golf, tennis, airport transfers, etc; many extras free.

In Asunción: L3 *Guaraní*, Oliva e Independencia Nacional, T 491131/139, F 443647, efficient, courteous, central, clean, good value, reasonable restaurant with good buffet; **L3** *Sabe Center*, 25 de Mayo y México, T 450093, F 450101, has luxury suites, new, central, on busy corner; **A1** *Cecilia*, Estados Unidos 341, T 210365, F 497111, very smart, comfortable, rec, good restaurant; **A1** *Chaco*, Caballero 285 y Mariscal Estigarribia, with breakfast, parking one block away (but no garden), rooftop swimming pool, good restaurant, T 492066/9, F 444223; **A1** *Gran del Paraguay*, De La Residenta y Padre Pucheu, T 200051/2, F 207556, in a wooded garden, with swimming pool and a night club on Fri, was the palace in which López lived, full of character, the rec restaurant with floral murals, was the private theatre of Eliza Lynch, an air-conditioned annex has been built in the gardens, breakfast; **A2** *Excelsior*, Chile 980 between Manduvirá and Piribebuy, PO Box 2863, T 495632, best, new 175-rooms tower, another under construction, conference facilities, etc; **A2** *Internacional*, Ayolas 520, T 494113, F 494383, discounts for longer stays, overpriced; **A3** *Gran Armele*, Palma y Av Colón, T 444455, F 445903, with breakfast, good restaurant, a/c, TV, clean, used by tour groups, rec; **A3** *Gran Renacimento*, Chile 388 y Estrella, T 445165, central, a/c, friendly service; **A3** *Paraná*, Caballero y 25 de Mayo, T 444236, F 494793, with breakfast, central, secure, helpful, discounts negotiable, restaurant rec, also short-stay.

B *Continental*, 15 de Agosto 420 y Estrella, T 493760, 1st class, all rooms a/c, TV, swimming pool, restaurant, rec cafeteria, bars, laundry service; **B** *Premier*, 25 de Mayo y Curipaty, T 23881, 15 rooms, 16 suites, not central but rec; **B** *Presidente*, Azara y Independencia Nacional, T 494931, F 496500, with breakfast and a/c, Oliver's restaurant, live music; **B** *Westfalenhaus*, M Benítez 777 y Stma Trinidad, T 292374, F 291241, comfortable, German run, swimming pool, a/c.

Specially for German-speaking travellers: **B** *Zaphir*, Estrella 955, T 490025, small, comfortable; **B** *Castillo*, Cruz del Chaco 959, German-owned, a/c, laundry, clean and friendly, T 605356; **C** *Omega*, Independencia Nacional y Luis Herrera, with bath, **D** without, friendly.

C *2000*, Av F de la Mora 2332, T 551628, opp bus terminal, bath, a/c, good, clean, safe; **C** *Española*, Herrera y Yegros, T 447312, with bath, clean, friendly, parking, newly refurbished, highly rec; **C** *Ñandutí*, Presidente Franco 551, T 446780, with bath and breakfast, clean, comfortable, friendly, luggage stored, rec; **C** *Orly*, Humaitá 209, T 491497, F 442307, good value (D for stays over 2 months), *City* cafetería in lobby is good; **C** *Plaza*, Eligio Ayala y Paraguari, T/F 444772, **D** without bath, spacious rooms, clean, a/c, luggage stored, highly rec; **C** *Sahara*, Oliva 920 nr Montevideo, T 494935, with breakfast, a/c, parking, small pool, large garden.

D *Amigo*, Cerro Corá y Caballero, without bath, clean, cooking and laundry facilities, friendly, cheap, rec; **D** *Azara*, Azara 860 (T 449754), with bath and a/c, fridge, less with fan, parking, 24 hr laundry, most rooms face a shady patio and dirty pool, stores luggage; **D** *Daniel*, Azara 1568, T 201461, with bath, fan and breakfast; **D** *India*, General Díaz 934, nr Av Montevideo, T 493327, with breakfast and fan, clean and pleasant, cheaper in old part; **D** *Residencial Itapúa*, Calle Fulgencio R Moreno 943, T 445121, Mennonite run, with bath and a/c, quiet, comfortable, decent breakfasts, lunch available; **D** *Miami*, México 449, T 444950, with breakfast, clean; **D** *Oasis*, Azara 736, without bath or breakfast, small rooms, friendly, Korean owned, safe; **D** *Stella di Italia*, Cerro Corá 933, T 448731, a/c, with breakfast, clean.

E *Ambassador*, Montevideo 111, T 445901, with bath, cheaper without, on riverbank, good views from upstairs rooms, fans, kitchen and laundry facilities, best budget hotel in town, rec, friendly; **E** *Ayuda Social Alemana*, España 202, with breakfast, double rooms only, a/c, fan, quiet, German and English spoken; **E** *Residencial Familiar*, Eligio Ayala 843, T 446381, without breakfast, friendly, clean; **E** *Residencial Ideal*, Azara 1549, T 445901, without breakfast, clean, quiet, very friendly; **E** *Residencial Rufi*, Cerro Corá 660, T 447751, clean, hot water, fans, rec. Next door (No 632) is **E** *Hospedaje Nuevo Mundo*, T 448395, Korean run, cheap restaurant, adequate.

Youth Hostel Association Asociación Paraguaya de Albergues Juveniles, Presidente Franco 585, Casilla Correo 2424, F 59521. No hostel in the city.

Camping The pleasant site at the Botanical Gardens charges US$1.50 pp plus tent, cars also permitted, cold showers and 220v electricity, busy at weekends. If camping, take plenty of insect repellent and beware large (but harmless) toads. You can camp at rear of *Restaurant Westfalia*, T 331772, owner speaks English, French, German, very knowledgable, US$1 per night for car, hot showers, clothes washing facilities, noisy, animals. Take Av Moreno, towards Ciudad del Este, turn right after going under two bridges into General Santos. *Rest Westfalia* is 3 km on, 5 km from Asunción (bus 19, 23 or 40).

Restaurants Some closed Sat and at holiday times. Most are closed Sun daytime, though some open evenings. Average price of a good meal in quality restaurants, US$12-25. *La Preferida*, Estados Unidos y 25 de Mayo 1005, T 210641, US$15, rec (part of *Hotel Cecilia*); *Talleyrand*, Estigarribia 932, T 441163, French; under same ownership are: *La Pergola del Bolsi*, Estrella 389, wide choice of wines, good for breakfast, and *El Jardín del Bolsi*, Perú 240. *Brasilera*, Av Mcal López y Tte Zolti, for barbequed meat, rec. *Nicolás*, Rep Francesa y Mcal Lopez, interesting menu; *Amstel*, Av Rep Argentina 1384, good traditional food, expensive; *Amandau*, Av Rep Argentina y Boggiani, not cheap but good. *Munich*, Eligio Ayala 163, good German food, excellent value; *Hostería del Caballito Blanco*, Alberdi 631, good food and service; *San Marcos*, Alberdi y Oliva, friendly, good for snacks in Café, restaurant attached, part a/c, good food, try *surubi* fish, reasonably priced; *Le Gran Café*, Oliva 476, good value, friendly, occasional live music; *Di Trevi*, Palma 573, excellent; *San Roque*, Eligio Ayala esq Tacuary, traditional, turn of the century atmosphere, inexpensive, rec; *Baby Grill*, Villa Mora shopping plaza, open 1800-2400 (poorly signposted in building), good price, pricey; *Boule Bar*, Caballero y 25 de Mayo, opp Paraná, tasteful setting, friendly; *Arche Noah*, Tacuary y 25 de Mayo, German run, quite expensive but good; *Germania*, México 920 y Manuel Domínguez, rec, reasonable prices; *Westfalia*, Bavarian style, see above under **Camping**.

La Piccola Góndola, Av Mcal López y Juan de Motta, is very good for Italian (and other) food, so is *Buon Appetito*, 25 de Mayo nr Av Mcal López y Juan Motta. *Da Vinci*, Estrella 695, nice terrace, rec.

Asunción, Estrella y 14 de Mayo (opp Deutsche Bank), bar with cold beer and tasty sandwiches, also restaurant very good, good for people watching, open 24 hrs; opp is *American Bar*, open Sun, good prices and variety, clean, rec. Plenty of good, cheap places on Colón, S of Estrella. *Bistro*, part of *Hotel Continental* at 15 de Agosto y Estrella, good and reasonable; *Lucho*, Estados Unidos 564, good local food, cheap, try *churrasco* with *choclo* (maize); also, next door, *La Parrillada*, cheap, good *estofado* with pasta. *Rincón Chileno*, Estados Unidos 314, friendly, excellent *empanadas*; *Café San Francisco*, Brasil y Estigarribia, good coffee, closed weekends; *Copetín Micael*, Herrera y Yegros, good coffee and *empanadas*; *Chiquilin*, mostly pizza, Av Perú y Estigarribia; *El Molino*, España 382 nr Brasil, good value, downstairs for sandwiches and home-made pastries, upstairs for full meals in a nice setting, good service and food (particularly steaks), rec; also 2 outlets in Super Centro shopping, Palma 488. *American Fried Chicken*, on Plaza de los Héroes (open Sun). For good roast chicken try *Nick's Restaurant*, Azara 348 nr Iturbe (open Sun). Also open on Sun is *Lido*, Plaza de los Héroes, good for breakfast and *empanadas*. Cheap lunches at *La Flor de la Canela*, México casi Moreno and *Amílcar*, Estados Unidos y 5a Proyectada. Most cheap lunch places close around 1600.

There are many good oriental restaurants including: *Sinorama*, Av Próceres de Mayo 262; *Corea*, Perú y Francia, excellent; *Hoy*, Alberdi 642; *Hiroshima*, authentic Japanese, on Chóferes del Chaco. Plenty of Korean places around Perú y Francia.

Vegetarian restaurants: *Dharma Shala*, Díaz 929, T 493144, serves good fresh dishes at lunchtime and evenings and will deliver orders to your hotel; *Krunch*, on Estrella, good value, vegetarian lunches; *Comida Vegetariana* on Bogado, 3 blocks E from railway station; *Wagner*, Presidente Franco 828, excellent bread and sweet shop. For ice cream try *Sugar's*, several branches incl *Shopping Excelsior on Chile; also Heladería París*, Brasilia y Siria, very popular; *Heladería Anahí*, Av 5 No 937, nr Presidente Franco, which also has sandwiches, egg, chicken and beef dishes and milkshakes, open Sun. *Bar Victoria*, Chile y Oliva, has good food.

Paraguayan harp music, bottle dancing, reasonable food and service, but commercialized, at *Jardín de la Cerveza*, Av República Argentina y Castillo, US$10 (but sometimes they charge for the music), good value; *Yguazú*, Chóferes del Chaco 1334 (San Lorenzo), good meat, both some distance from centre. Good Paraguayan harp/guitar group at *Churrasquería Sajón*, Av Carlos A López, bus 26 from centre. More central is *La Curva*, Av Próceres de Mayo 212, cheap beer and reasonable food, several typical groups play 2100 to 0300. *Casa del Sur*, Cerro Corá 150, live music, good atmosphere. *Summer Pub*, Cruz del Chaco 847, good value, excellent meat. *Britannia Pub*, Cerro Corá 800 block, good variety of drinks, English spoken, popular, book exchange. *Pub Art Gallery*, Colón 320, popular, highly rec. *Pub Viejo Bavaria*, Estados Unidos 410. *Spurs*, Estigarribia y Estados Unidos, good beer, music and pool, English spoken, popular with Peace Corps.

Airline Offices LAB, 14 de Mayo 563, Oficina B, T 441586, F 448218; Arpa, San José 136, esq Mcal López, T 206634; Lapsa, Oliva 467, T 495261; Ladesa, Mcal López 4531, T 443346.

Banks and Exchange Banks that give dollars usually charge 2-3% commission (though Banco Paraguayo Oriental, Azara y Yegros, $1/2$% commission. Lloyds Bank, Palma y O'Leary (and 4 agencies in Greater Asunción); **Finamérica** (ex-Bank of America), Oliva esq Chile; **Citibank**, Estrella y Chile, will change Citibank TCs into dollars cash, and gives cash dollars on Mastercard at 5.5% commission; **Banco Corporación**, VE Haedo e Independencia Nacional; **Banco General**, Chile y Haedo (will give US dollars); **Bank of Commerce and Industry**, Caballero esq Eligio Ayala, also gives dollars; **Interbank**, 14 de Mayo 339; **Deutsche Bank**, Estrella y 14 de Mayo (charges 2% commission on money sent from Germany – very fast service, 2 days – paid by cheque which can be cashed into dollars at Cambio Guaraní for 3% commission); **Banco Sudameris**, Oliva e Independencia Nacional. **Banco Holandés Unido**, Independencia Nacional y VE Haedo. Also Argentine, Brazilian and local banks. **Banco Unión**, Estrella y Alberdi (and throughout the country) will give cash advances in guaraníes on Visa or Mastercard in about 15 mins, English spoken, friendly, only between 0845-1130. Similarly, **Creditcard**, 15 de Agosto y Humaitá, and **Unicard**, 15 de Agosto between Haedo and Humaitá, Mastercard only. **Amex**, Yegros 690 y Herrera, poor rates.

Several *casas de cambio* on Palma and on Estrella (open Mon-Fri 0730-1200, 1500-1830, Sat 0730-1200; rates for neighbouring countries' currencies usually good, except bolivianos). Deutsche Marks can be changed at good rates, and all rates are better than at the various frontiers. Some will accept sterling notes. Be careful to count money received from street exchange-sellers (Palma and surrounding area – their rates are less good when banks and *cambios* are closed). **Casas de cambio** do not like changing sterling TCs, the only ones that will do it are **Cambio Paraná** on Palma and **Casa de Cambio La Moneda**, 25 de Mayo 127, high commission. Some only change one type of dollar TCs. Some ask for proof of purchase before changing. **Cambio Guaraní**, Palma 449, between 14 de Mayo and Alberdi, T 90032/6, is good, changes US$ TCs into US$ cash, but charges US$0.30 commission per cheque.

International Cambios, Palma 364, changes US$ TCs into US$ cash, 1% commission, rec; **Exprinter**, 25 de Mayo and Yegros, no commission. German spoken at **Cambios Menno Tour**, Azara 532. **Cambios Yguazú**, 15 de Agosto 451, T 490135, is OK (Thomas Cook, but can't replace your lost or stolen cheques). See **Currency** section in Information for Visitors.

Cultural Institutions The US-Paraguay Cultural Centre has a good library at España 352 (open Mon-Fri 0900-2000, Sat 0900-1200, also has snack bar). Instituto Anglo-Paraguayo, España 457, where you can acquire much useful information, watch US TV, and read English newspapers. **Goethe Institut**, J de Salazán 310, library with a few newspapers, open 1600-2000. **Centro Cultural Paraguayo-Japonés**, J Correa y A Velásquez. **Alianza Francesa**, Mcal Estigarribia 1039, T 210382, snack bar. All these institutes have special events, film shows, etc. If you have the time, these institutes may be able to use voluntary teachers and instructors to give local classes/lectures in their subjects.

Embassies and Consulates Brazilian Consulate, Gral Diaz 521 with 14 de Mayo y 15 de Agosto, 3rd flr, open 0800-1200, Mon-Fri, US$22 for visa, T 448084/069; **Argentine Consulate**, España y Perú, T 212320, visas issued at Edif Banco Nacional de Argentina, Palma 319, 1° piso, open 0800-1300, 2 hr service, photograph needed. **Chile**, Guido Spano y Juan B Molta, T 660344; **Bolivian Consulate**, Eligio Ayala 2002 y Gral Bruguez, T 22662; **Peruvian Consulate**, Av Mcal López 648, T 200949; **Uruguay**, Gral Santos 219 y De La Residenta, T 25391 (visas processed immediately if exit ticket from Uruguay, overland travel to Uruguay and onward country visas can be shown); **Mexico**, Juan E O'Leary 409 esq Estrella, T 444421. **Ecuador**, Herrera y Yegros, T 446150; **Venezuela**, Mcal Estigarribia 1032 esq Estados Unidos, T 444243.

US Embassy and Consulate, Av Mcal López 1776, T 213715; **South Africa**, Banco Sudameris, piso 4, esq Cerro Corá e Independencia Nacional, T 496031.

Great Britain, Presidente Franco 706, esquina O'Leary, 4th flr (Casilla 404), T 449146, holds mail; **Switzerland**, O'Leary 409 esq Estrella, T 448022; **Spain**, Calle 25 de Mayo 175, esq Yegros T 490686/7; **Danish Consulate**, Nuestra Señora de la Asunción 766, T 490617; **Swedish Consulate**, Bogado 1039-47, T 205561/9; **Finnish Consulate**, Elias Ayola y Yasú, T 291175; **Dutch Consulate**, Franco y 15 de Agosto, T 492137; **Austrian Consulate**, Gral Díaz 525, Edif Internacional Faro, T 443910. **German**, Av Venezuela 241, T 24006/7; **France**, Av España 676, T 23111; **Israel**, Yegros 437 y 25 de Mayo, Edif San Rafael, piso 6, T 495097.

Night Clubs and Discotheques *Musak*, Bertoni y José Ocampos; *Caracol Club*, Gral Santos y Porvenir; *Playboys*, 14 de Mayo y Oliva; *Tabasco Club*, 1 de Marzo y Felicidad; *La Salsa*, Papa Juan XXIII y Oddone (Latin American Disco); *Karim*, 25 de Mayo nr Estados Unidos. There are floor shows in several hotels, eg *Hotel del Yacht* (*Scruples*) and *Hotel Casino Itá Enramada* (open every day in summer, Sat in winter).

Municipal Theatre, Pte Franco, nr Alberdi, has an extensive winter programme of concerts and ballets (entry US$4). *Teatro Arlequin*, Gral de Gaulle y Quesado, *Teatro Latino*, 16 de Julio y 16 de Agosto, and *Teatro El Lector*, Av San Martín y Austria have productions most of the year. Concerts are given at the Teatro de las Américas, J Bergés 297. **Cinema Centro Cultural de la Ciudad**, E V Haedo 347, for quality foreign films, US$1.50. Cinema programmes are given in the press; some offer 3 films at one price (US$2.50).

Health Doctor Carlos M Ramírez Boettner, General Díaz 975, T 493021, general practitioner.

Laundry *Lavamático*, Yegros 808 y Fulgencio Moreno, good but not cheap. *Lavarap* at Hernandarias 636, one block from Colón and General Díaz, open all day, T 447478.

Places of Worship Anglican: St Andrew, España y Uruguay; Synagogue, Gen Díaz 657.

General Post Office Alberdi, Benjamín Constant y El Paraguayo Independiente, T 493784. A fine set of buildings around a colonnaded courtyard with plants and fountains. Open 0700-2000. Also philatelic museum, open 0700-1800, Mon-Fri; 0700-1200, Sat. Post boxes throughout the city carry address of the nearest place one can purchase stamps. Register all important mail; you must go to main PO for this. *Poste Restante* charges about US$0.25 per item collected, but you may have to insist they double-check if you are expecting letters there. There are sub-offices at the railway station and at the docks. Postage stamps tend to be large—take care when writing postcards!

Telephone Antelco, Alberdi y Díaz, for international calls and fax, 24 hrs.

Shopping Calle Colón, starting at the port, is lined with good tourist shops, and so are Calles Pettirossi, Palma (see above) and Estrella. *Galería Colón 185* is rec. *Boutique Irene*, Montevideo 463, also rec for leather goods. Calle Franco for handmade furniture. For wooden articles and carvings go to *Artes de Madera* at Ayolas 222; *Casa Vera* at Estigarribia 470 for Paraguayan leatherwork, cheap and very good; *Viva*, José Borges 993, Chaco and Oriental crafts, rec. Other recommended shops, *Casa Overall*, Mcal Estigarribia 397, nr Plaza Uruguaya, good selection; *Victoria*, *Arte Artesanía*, Iturbe y Ayala, interesting selection of wood carvings, ceramics etc, rec. Many leading tourist shops offer up to 15% discount for cash. Check the quality of all handicrafts carefully, lower prices usually mean lower quality. The markets are worth a visit, especially the Pettirossi (food and ordinary clothes). There is a daily market on Av Dr Francia, best visited during the week, and a Sat one on Plaza de la Independencia, where the nuns from Villeta sell their hand-made clothing for children. There is a handicraft market on Plaza de los Héroes selling lace and items from Peru and Bolivia. Supermarkets are usually well stocked, especially with imported liquor; rec is the one at El Paraguayo Independiente y 14 de Mayo (bakes its own bread, open daily 0800-2100). *Unicentro*, Palma y 15 de Agosto is a modern shopping centre. Outside Asunción, visit Luque (musical instruments and jewellery—see p 1077) and Itauguá (lace) – see p 1079. By Latin American standards, prices of electronic goods in the Korean-run shops are very low. Cameras can be bought cheaply in Paraguay; the selection of all types of consumer goods is better in Ciudad del Este, and there are good prices in Pedro Juan Caballero.

Bookshops *Librería Internacional*, Oliva 386, Estrella 723 y Juan O'Leary and Palma 595 y 15 de Agosto, good for maps; also '*Books*' at Mcal López 3971, at Villa Morra shopping centre; magazine/newspaper kiosk *El Lector* at Plaza Uruguaya y 25 de Mayo has a selection of foreign material; *Librería Alemana*, Av Luis A de Herrera 292, warmly rec for German books and publications.

Photographic Repairs: Panatronic, Benjamín Constant 516. Rodolfo Loewen, Camera Service, Blas Garay y Morelo, T 23807. Slide film costs US$3, print film US$2.50 (35 mm). Good place for buying cameras, *Casa Fanny*, Mcal Estigarribia 144. Kodak-Ektachrome slide film is difficult to find; try **Kodak Express** on Palma.

Travel Agencies (all very helpful) *Inter-Express* (Amex), Yegros 690, T 490111, expensive, office for mail is round corner on Luis A Herrera; *American Tours*, Juan B Alberdi y Oliva, T 490672, German and English spoken. *Menno Tour*, Azara 551, is staffed by Germans. *Inter Tours*, Av Brasil y Estigarribia 1097, T 211747, tours to Chaco rec; *Abysa*, Azara 229, T 441569, sells bus tickets in the centre of town. *Time Tours*, 15 de Agosto y General Díaz, T 493527, fluent English, rec. *Lions Tours*, Alberdi 454, T 490591.

Tourist Office Palma 468. Desk in hall of Dirección Nacional de Turismo, open Mon-Fri 0800-2000, T 441530, F 491230. Free map, information on all parts of Paraguay, but you may need to be persistent. Enquire for tourist bus in the city run by Metrotur. Another map is sold in bookshops.

Useful Addresses Immigration Edif Lider II, Juan E O'Leary 615, 1st flr. Ministerio de Relaciones Exteriores, O'Leary y Franco. **Police** T 446105. **Mennonite Centre** Colombia 1090, T 200697.

City Buses The system is extensive, running from 0600-2400; buses stop at signs before every street corner. Journeys within city, US$0.30. For buses to the new bus terminal, see below. Buses only rec outside rush hours, with light luggage. Keep your ticket for inspection until you leave bus.

Trams (Street cars) run on a circular route in the city centre, using former Belgian rolling-stock, approx every 30 mins, rec.

Taxis Minimum fare in Asunción is US$0.50 plus US$0.10 for every 100m. The average journey costs about US$2. (Check if there is an extra charge for luggage, and that the meter has not been speeded up). Hire by the hour; minimum US$10, up US$20 outside the city. Tip 10%.

Car Rental Only Rent-a-Car, 15 de Agosto 441, opp *Hotel Continental*, T 492731, also airport, US$23 to US$50 per day, depending on vehicle. **Hertz** at airport, T 22012, and Av E Ayala at Hipódromo, T 605708. **National**, Cerro Corá y Yegros, T 491848, from US$49 to US$100 per day (from Hyundai to Mitsubishi Galant). **Fast**, 15 de Agosto 588, T 447069, F 447112, good, helpful.

Airport Silvio Pettirossi, 15 km NE of centre. There is a desk where you can book a taxi to your hotel, US$15. Bus 30A goes every 15 mins between the red bus stop in front of the airport and *American Fried Chicken* on Plaza de los Héroes, US$0.30, difficult with luggage. From your hotel to airport T 84486 for minibus, US$8.30 for whole vehicle share. TAM will arrange colectivo, which collects from hotels, US$3.10 pp. Enquire at airline offices.

A new airport terminal has been built. It contains a tourist office (free city map and hotel information), bank (turn right as you leave customs), handicraft shop, restaurant and several travel agencies which can arrange hotel bookings and change money (very poor rates). A left luggage office charges US$0.50 per piece.

Rail San Roque Station at Eligio Ayala y México, T 447316. Presidente Carlos Antonio López Railway to **Encarnación** (370 km). For Sun to **Aregua**, see **Section 2** below. According to timetables a passenger train to **Encarnación**, pulled by wood-burning steam locomotives leaves Asunción Fri 1800, US$3.15 1st class, US$2.70 tourist. In early 1995, though, only freight trains were running; they are not allowed to take passengers, but written permission may be given by the chief of technical operations at the station if you can think of a good enough reason. Check in advance which day the train goes, it varies. Ride in a freight wagon, very rough, leaks in the rain, can take 3 days to Encarnación. It may be better to go to Paraguarí by rail, then take a bus. See under Excursions for a trip to see the locomotive workshops at Sapucay.

River Boats *Cruceros SRL*, 14 de Mayo 150 Casi el Paraguayo Independiente, T/F 445098, sailings to Concepción every 15-20 days, 27 hrs, US$27 1st class, US$17 2nd, US$11 deck space. Other companies work this route, but they are not very comfortable (eg *Cacique II*, Wed 0700, deck seat US$7 + US$3 for cabin, US$0.70 for hammock, basic restaurant, watch luggage, or *Guaraní*, which sails to Concepción Sun, returns Wed, US$6.50 pp). *Cruceros SRL* also run occasional services to **Corumbá** (Brazil), in 2nd class men and women sleep in separate cabins, 3rd class is deck space (take own hammock). All sailings vary with the seasons and depend on the level of the river. Enquire at the small boat dock to the right of the main dock, or at the dock at the end of Calle Montevideo, or at *Hotel Ambassador*. On all sailings take your own food, water, toilet paper, warm clothes for the night (or mattress and blanket, or sleeping bag), mosquito repellent.

Corumbá can also be reached by bus, through Pedro Juan Caballero, Ponta Porã and Campo Grande. See also p 1088.

Ferry to **Puerto Pilcomayo** (Argentina) about every 20 mins (US$0.50, 5 mins) from Itá Enramada (Paraguayan immigration), take bus 9 from Asunción (Argentine immigration closed at weekends for tourists). Boats S to **Pilar** and Argentina are few and irregular.

See under **Excursions** for local river trips.

Roads The major roads from Asunción to other parts of the country are: Route 1 SE to Encarnación, 372 km, paved; Route 2 E to Coronel Oviedo where one branch continues E as Route 7 to Ciudad del Este and the Iguazú falls, 362 km, paved, and another runs N and then NE successively as Routes 8, 3 and 5 to Pedro Juan Caballero on the Brazilian border, 399 km, partially paved; Route 9 NW across the Río Paraguay at Remanso, continuing via Villa Hayes through the Chaco to Filadelfia and Bolivia, mainly unpaved, 805 km. For details of all these routes see below in the text.

Buses All buses leave from the bus terminal, S of the city centre at República Argentina esq Fernando de la Mora. Take local bus number (*Línea*) 8 (the only direct one), on Oliva, Haedo, or Cerro Corá in the centre for Terminal Nuevo (10, 25, 31 and 38, also 80, but circuitously and get off outside terminal, 30-40 min)); from the terminal to the city, get off the bus at the corner of General Díaz and Chile. Taxi from down town, rec if you have luggage, US$4 pp or US$8-10 per taxi. Length of journey from centre depends on the amount of traffic, minimum 20 mins. The terminal has a tourist information desk (city map and bus information), restaurant (quite good), café, *casa de cambio* (poor rates), shops, and lots of noisy televisions. Hotels nearby: turn left from front of terminal, 2 mins' walk. Many bus companies still maintain ticket offices around Plaza Uruguaya. Bus times and fares within Paraguay are given under destinations.

To Uruguay COIT (Eligio Ayala 893, T 496197) runs to **Montevideo**, 0800, Sat and Wed, 20 hrs; Brújula/Cynsa (Pte Franco 985, T 441720) runs Tues and Fri, with a third service in summer, US$57 (the route is Encarnación, Posadas, Paso de los Libres, Uruguaiana, Bella Unión, Salto, Paysandú—the only customs formalities are at Bella Unión; passport checks here and at Encarnación.

To Argentina There is a road N from Asunción (passing the Botanical Gardens on Primer Presidente) to a concrete arch span bridge (Puente Remanso – US$1 toll, pedestrian walkway on upstream side, 20 min to cross) which leads to the border at Puerto Falcón (about 40 km) and then to **Clorinda** in Argentina. The border is open 24 hrs a day; last bus from Falcón to the centre of Asunción at 1830 (US$0.65). The colectivo fare from Asunción to Falcón is US$0.80; from Falcón to Clorinda costs US$0.25. It is cheaper to book through to Argentine destinations than to take the local bus to Clorinda and then book.

Buses Asunción-**Buenos Aires** (18 hrs) daily with Nuestra Señora de la Asunción (1330), Chevallier and Godoy, via Rosario and Santa Fe, also with Brújula and La Internacional, each 6 times a week (average fare US$72 luxury, US$36 *común*). To **Resistencia** (6 hrs, US$12) and **Formosa** (US$7), 4 a day, Brújula and La Internacional; to **Córdoba** (US$42), Brújula once a week and Cacorba (3 times). To **Posadas**, Singer 3 a week at midnight, or go to **Encarnación** (frequent service and cheaper) and cross the river to Argentina.

ASUNCIÓN SURROUNDINGS

Villa Hayes
N
To Clorinda
Emboscada
To Arroyos
To Arroyos
Limpio
Nueva Colombia
Remanso
Río Salado
Loma Grande
Luque
Lago Ypacaraí
Altos
Tobatí
ASUNCIÓN
Fernando de la Mora
Aregua
San Bernardino
Atyra
San Lorenzo
Itá Enramada
Capiatá
Lambaré
Itauguá
Rt 2
To Ciudad del Este
Ñemby
San Antonio
Ypacaraí
Caacupé
Ypané
Dr J A Saldivar
Pirayú
Piribebuy
Villeta
Guarambaré
Itá
Rt 1
Yaguarón
Chololó
Puerto Paraíso
Nueva Italia
Río Paraguay
0   10
km
Paraguarí
To Sapucay
To Encarnación
ARGENTINA

Several buses weekly to **Santiago, Chile**, 60 hrs, US$50-60 (plus extra charge for luggage) with Sirena Del Paraná and Brújula.

To Brazil Nuestra Señora and Rysa, and the Brazilian companies Pluma and Unesul, have services to Ciudad del Este, continuing to **Foz do Iguaçu**. Many Paraguayan buses advertise that they go to Foz, but very few do, check; all luxury bus fares to Foz are US$14, 5-7 hrs, six direct buses a day in all. Seat reservations recommended. To visit the Brazilian side of the Iguaçu falls in one day, take a bus soon after midnight, arriving at Foz 0700; return on 1200 bus from falls to bus station, then 1430 bus back to Asunción – remember to buy reais in Asunción beforehand. To **Curitiba**, US$24 with Pluma, buses daily, 15½ hrs; to **São Paulo**, Rápido Yguazú, Pluma and Brújula, 20 hrs, US$33 (*leito*, US$48). Pluma to Rio de Janeiro, US$42. Unesul run to Porto Alegre 4 times a week; Nacional Expresso to Brasília 3 times a week. Services also to **Blumenau**, US$29 (Catarinense) and **Florianópolis**, US$32 (Pluma and Catarinense).

Excursions Half day (4 hour) cruises on the Río Paraguay leaving at 0900 are operated most days (enquire) costing US$30 including a meal, also evening cruises with disco. Details from Crucero Adelaida, Brasil 1263, Agencia Paraguay, Montevideo 419, T 441687/497496, or from the tourist office.

From the FME (Flota Mercantil del Estado) dock a ferry leaves daily across to the Rowing Club, frequency depends on demand; many facilities, welcoming people.

To ***Villeta*** (27 km S, pop 5,232), on the E bank, which has undergone a rapid economic expansion; it is well known for good river-fish restaurants and for the fine children's clothing hand-made by nuns at a local convent. A little N is a park at Ytororó where trenches used in the war of the Triple Alliance can still be seen. The town of ***Luque*** (pop 24,917), near the airport, founded 1636 with some interesting colonial buildings, is famous for the making of Paraguayan harps

(Guitarras Sanabria is one of the best-known firms, Km 13, T 023-2291), and for fine filigree work in silver and gold (ask around for Alberto Núñez). There are also many fine musical instrument shops on the road to Luque; get off the bus – No 30 – from Asunción just before the major roundabout. Mariscal López' house may be visited. 8 km from Luque is Balneario Yukyry, with an artesian well, springs, swimming pools, football pitches and a snackbar; for details and reservations, T 23731 (closed in winter, but pleasant trip anyway).

The most popular trip is E to Itauguá, and San Bernardino and Aregua on Lago Ypacaraí (see p 1079).

For a longer look at the countryside, take a tour for US$40 from any travel agent (pick-up at your hotel – about US$60 with private taxi drivers) to drive the 'Circuito Central' also called 'Circuito de Oro': Asunción – San Lorenzo – Itá – Yaguarón – Paraguarí – Chololó – Pirareta – Piribebuy – Caacupé – San Bernardino – Ypacaraí – Itauguá – Aregua – Capiatá – Asunción. Some 200 km on paved roads, 7 hrs. Lions, at Alberdi 454, 1, T 490-278, run a full service of trips. Alternatively, from San Lorenzo, take Route 1 towards Encarnación and at Km 28 (LP Petrol station) turn right to Guarambaré, a sleepy town in the sugar area with many Peace Corps trainees. From May to Nov bullock carts and trucks take the cane to the factory, 1 km past the electricity sub-station. Bus Asunción-Guarambaré, 45 mins, US$0.15, every 10 mins from terminal. In Guarambaré take the second dirt road on the right after the Plaza and for about 10 km continue through typical farmlands and citrus orchards. The road then continues through Ypané, Nemby and back to Asunción via Lambaré.

A 3-hour colectivo ride from Asunción is Sapucay, 88 km SE, where the main workshops for the wood-burning steam locomotives are located (see below p 1084).

EAST FROM ASUNCION (2)

Small towns with interesting local crafts, leading to jungle on the Brazilian border and the major attractions of Ciudad del Este, the Itaipú dam and the nearby Iguazú Falls.

Route Two   The Mariscal Estigarribia Highway leaves Asunción past typical markets, reached by bus from Asunción (Nos 20, 26 and 27 from Herrera, US$1.50). On the outskirts of the city is Fernando de la Mora with a good restaurant called *Hamburguería Libra*, not fast food but good fish and steaks. At Km 12 is **San Lorenzo** (pop 74,400), an industrial town with the National School of Agriculture (Universidad de Agronomía – it has an extensive insect collection) and Museo de Historia Natural, open Mon-Fri 0730 to 1530 with some emphasis on ecology. Also in town are the small but interesting Museo Aqueológico, near cathedral, free, though not always open, good Indian section, and the Museo Guido Boggiani, Bogado 888, Tue-Sat 1000-1200, 1500-1800, a collection built up by the Italian anthropologist who researched the tribes of the northern Chaco at the turn of the 19th/20th century. It has become a social and artistic centre for the Indians with music, dancing and crafts. Basketry and wood carvings on sale, no explanations but worth a visit. Here is the Balneario El Tigre, with swimming pool and shady trees. (**E** *Hotel San Lorenzo*, Gral Caballero 148 y 14 de Mayo, T 2261, with breakfast, excellent, can commute into city, laundry.)

At Km 20 is **Capiatá**, founded in 1640, where there is a fine cathedral with remarkable 17th century sculpture made by Indians under the tutelage of the Jesuit Fathers (buses every few minutes from San Lorenzo). A left turn here (sign-posted) goes via an inexpensive toll road, 7 km to **Aregua**, a pretty resort on the slopes above Lago Ypacaraí. It has an interesting ceramics cooperative, a church and convent. An increasing number of houses are being built around the lake. From here boat trips run across the lake at weekends to San Bernadino, 20 km further W (see below).

Lodging and Food E *Hospedaje Ozli*, reasonable, restaurant mediocre. *La Rotunda*, restaurant on the waterfront; *Mozart Pub*, open Thur-Sun, rec; *Las Palmeras*.

Transport The daily steam train from Asunción to Aregua no longer runs. A special excursion train leaves Asunción Sun 0800, returns to Asunción 1730, US$1. You may be able to travel to Aregua on the Fri evening freight train to Encarnación (or the Sun train from Encarnación). Buses between Aregua and Asunción, Transportes Ypacaraínse, every 30 mins, but do not go to terminal in Asunción; alternatively take local bus to Capiatá and change.

Itauguá (pop 5,400), at Km 30, founded in 1728, is where the famous *ñandutí*, or spiderweb lace, is made. There are over 100 different designs. Prices are lower than in Asunción and the quality is better; try the Taller Artesanal (Km 29) or the Mutual Tejedoras (Km 28), where you can also watch the lace being made. The plaza is a short distance from the dual carriageway which runs through the town. The blocks of uniform dwellings in the plaza, with their reddish tile roofs projecting over the sidewalk and their lines of pillars, are very close to the descriptions we have of Guaraní Jesuit settlements. Worth seeing are the church, the Museo Parroquial San Rafael, with a display of indigenous art and Franciscan artefacts (open daily 0800-1130, 1500-1800) and the market (closed Sun). There is a 4-day festival in early-Jul, including processions and the crowning of Señorita Ñandutí. No accommodation, but Itauguá is only 1 hr by frequent bus service from Asunción, US$0.60; cheap lunches at the market.

At Km 40 a branch road, 8 km long, leads off to **San Bernardino**, on **Lago Ypacaraí**, reached by bus from Asunción (Route 2, 56 km, 1 hr, US$0.90). The lake is 24 km by 5. There are facilities for swimming and water sports, with a sandy beach. The water is known for its medicinal properties. There are frequent cruises from the pier during the tourist season, Dec-Feb, when it is crowded. There is good walking in the neighbourhood, for example from San Bernardino to Altos, lake views, wooded hills and valleys, round trip about 3 hrs. Shortly after the turn off from the main road towards San Bernardino is a sign to La Grota; turn right here, and the road leads to a secluded national park. There are grottoes with still water and overhanging cliffs.

Hotels A2 *Aparthotel Condorac*, T (0512) 2594, offers various size apartments with luxury facilities for short or longer stays; **A2** *San Bernardino Pueblo*, Paseo del Pueblo y Mbocayá, T 2195, swimming pool, a/c, by the lake; **B** *Acuario*, also lakeside, 2 km from town centre, T 2375; **C** *Del Lago*, lakeside in town, T 2201, well-maintained 19th century building, a/c, pool, gardens. It is possible to find rooms in private houses. **Restaurant** *Como-Rap*, good food, pleasant atmosphere, reasonable prices, proprietor, Tito, owns next door laundry.

Camping At Km 43 is Casa Grande Camping Club with all facilities. For information, Corfín Paraguaya, Ayolas 437 y Estrella, T 492360/1, Asunción, or direct, T (0511) 649. It is possible to camp right on the lake but there are many mosquitoes, inadequate sanitary facilities and not much safety for your personal belongings.

At Km 54 is **Caacupé** (pop 9,105), a popular resort and religious centre on the Azcurra escarpment. Its sights include the beautiful Basilica of Our Lady of the Miracles, whose day is 8 December. The old church has been demolished, but a small replica has been built about 5 blocks away. The very beautiful new basilica, with copper roof, stained glass and polychrome stone esplanade, was consecrated by the Pope in 1988. There is an interesting market next to it, where one can buy pottery, etc, and swimming pools in the streams nearby. Parque Anka, outside town on the Asunción road, has a swimming pool, tennis courts, ponies, a Disneyland, camp site and good restaurants. Bus from Asunción US$0.50.

Thousands of people from Paraguay, Brazil and Argentina flock to the shrine. Prices are somewhat higher than normal in Paraguay. Go midweek if you can. Besides fireworks and candle-lit processions, pilgrims watch the agile gyrations of Paraguayan bottle-dancers; they weave in intricate measures whilst balancing bottles pyramided on their heads. The top bottle carries a spray of flowers and the more expert dancers never let drop a single petal.

Hotels D *Girlanda*, two blocks from basilica; **D** *El Uruguayo*, large rooms, a/c, hot water, parking, friendly, delightful restaurant but poor food, OK breakfast; **E** *San Blas I*. Chicken restaurant 1 block N of *El Uruguayo*, then 1 block E, on Highway, rec.

Camping Club de Camping Melli, 1 km E of town, all facilities, T (0511) 313.

Excursions Poor roads lead to several interesting churches. One is at *Tobatí*, a tobacco centre, with local pottery and woodwork, 16 km to the N. It is also a brick-making centre; wood-burning kilns for bricks and tiles can be seen in many yards. It is a good walk from Caacupé, with excellent views of the country below and the outcrops of the escarpment above (rec).

At Km 64 beyond Caacupé a paved road runs 13 km SE to *Piribebuy* (pop 5,902, **F** *Pensión Santa Rosa*, basic; **E** *Rincón Viejo*, reasonable), founded in 1640 and noted for its strong local drink, *caña*. In the central plaza is the church (1640), with fine sculptures, high altar and pulpit. The town was the site of a major battle in the War of the Triple Alliance, which is commemorated by the Museo Histórico Pedro Juan Caballero. Buses from Asunción by Transportes Piribebuy. Near the town are the attractive small falls of Piraretá. The road goes on via Chololó, 13 km S, and reaches Route 1 at Paraguarí, 28 km from Piribebuy (**see below, p 1084**).

24 km N of Route 2 from Eusebio Ayala (Km 72) is the **Vapor Cué National Park** with peaceful swimming and fishing in the river in the middle of fertile cattle country. It contains the remains of seven steamships sunk during the War of the Triple Alliance. Several boilers and one ship have been reconstructed. Camping is permitted, public transport runs to within 4 km of the site. Transport can be hired in the village.

Continuing along Route 2 at Km 87 is *Itacurubí* (**D** *Hotel Aguila*, a/c with bath, and nearby *Restaurant Estrella Suiza*, Swiss owned, good food, helpful, camping at the back, showers, rec). At Km 132, Route 2 meets the major N-S Route 8, 3 km S of **Coronel Oviedo** (pop 21,782). Buses drop passengers at the junction (El Cruce).

Hotels **D** *El Rey*, Estigarribia 213, clean, modern, breakfast incl, rec; **E** *Hotel Ramírez*, clean and good; **E** *San Pedro*, 100m from *El Rey*, rec; **F** *Hospedaje Juancito*, Juan E O'Leary y Carmelo Peralta, with bath, mosquito net, nice garden, rec; **F** *Casa Kolping*, Iturbe y 1 de Marzo, T (521) 3065, incl breakfast, German spoken; **F** *Pensión Ñanda Roga*, without breakfast, basic but friendly; at El Cruce, *Hotel Alemán*, rec.

South from Coronel Oviedo, Route 8 is paved for 42 km to Villarrica. At Km 22 a side road runs to Yataíty where a local cooperative sells ponchos, fine weaving and embroidery. At the end of Nov there is a *feria artesanal* with folk music and dancing, exhibitions etc. There are German agricultural communities nearby.

Villarrica, 173 km SE of Asunción and 219 N of Encarnación, pop 21,203, is delightfully set on a hill rich with orange trees. A very pleasant, friendly place, it has a fine cathedral and central plaza. The museum behind the church has a foreign coin collection; please contribute. Products of the region are tobacco, cotton, sugar, yerba mate, hides, meat and wine produced by German settlers. Horse-drawn taxis.

Hotels **D** *Asunción*, Thompson y Aquideban, T 0541-2542, a/c, fan; **C** *Ybytyruzú*, C A López y Dr Bottell, T 2390, with breakfast, more with a/c, fairly clean; **D** *Guaira*, N Talavera y Mcal Estigarribia, T 2369, nr bus terminal, shower, fan, noisy; **F** *Hospedaje El Porvenir*, Thompson 144, basic; **F** *Hospedaje La Guairana*, with restaurant; **F** *Pensión el Toro*, Mcal López 521; **E** *Plaza*, Mcal López, clean, friendly, beautiful patio.

Restaurants Many on CA López and Gral Díaz. *Mesón Universitario*, González 623, in part of a colonial pavilion, open all day; *París*, CA López 100, good food; *Refugio*, Gral Díaz 578, reasonable prices; *El Tirol*, CA López 205, German owned, set lunch; *El Palacio de las Empanadas*, Gral Díaz 533; *Los Amigos*, Melgarejo 828, good food, sidewalk eating at night; *Capri*, San Roque y Gral Díaz, local food, inexpensive; *Miami Bar*, La Plaza de Municipalidad, good food, rec; *La Tranquera*, 3 km from centre, by train station; *Angelo's* on main square, decent.

Bus to Coronel Oviedo US$1.50; to Asunción frequent, US$3 (Empresa Guaireña); also direct service to Ciudad del Este, 4 daily, US$4.

There are three German colonies near Villarrica. 7 km N is a turn off to the E, then 20 km to *Colonia Independencia*, **D** *Hotel Tilinski*, peaceful, German spoken, swimming pool (filled with river water), no meals; *Che Valle Mi*, Sr Jacob Esslinger, Correo Melgarejo, T 05418-241, rec; next door is *Ulli y Klaus* restaurant, also rec; also a good restaurant, with German chalet style accommodation, *Hotel Restaurant Panorama*, set on top of a hill on the road 12 km from Colonia Independencia. Makes a good stop, especially for German-speaking travellers, who can also visit the German cooperative farms. There is camping nearby at Melgarejo with full facilities. Direct bus to Asunción, three daily (US$1.60, 4 hrs), as well as to Villarrica.

From Villarrica Route 8 continues S 222 km (unpaved) through Caazapá to Coronel Bogado, where it joins Route 1.

East from Coronel Oviedo, the paved Route 7 runs 195 km through cultivated areas and woods and across the Caaguazú hills to the spectacular 500-metre single span 'Friendship Bridge' across the Paraná (to Brazil) at *Ciudad del Este* (formerly Ciudad Presidente Stroessner), where there is a grass-strip airport. Founded in 1957, this was the fastest growing city in the country (83,000 inhabitants) until the completion of the civil works of the Itaipú hydroelectric project, for which it is the centre of operations. Ciudad del Este has been described as the biggest shopping centre in Latin America, mainly directed towards Brazilian and Argentine visitors who find bargain prices for electrical goods, watches, perfumes etc. (Don't buy perfume at tempting prices on the street, it's only coloured water. Make sure that shops which package your goods pack what you actually bought.) Prices are decidedly high for N American and European visitors. Also watch the exchange rates if you're a short-term visitor from Argentina or Brazil; hotels and restaurants tend to be dearer than elsewhere in Paraguay. The leather market is well worth a visit, be sure to bargain.

Hotels (incl breakfast) **B** *Gran Hotel Acaray*, 11 de Septiembre y Río Paraná, T/F 61471/5,

CIUDAD DEL ESTE

1. Puente de la Amistad / Ponte da Amizade
2. Customs & Information
3. Post Office
4. Antelco
5. Hotel Convair
6. Hotels Santo Domingo & Munich

also has new extension, swimming pool, casino, nightclub, restaurant; **B** *Executive*, Adrián Jara y Curupayty, T 68981/8982 (incl breakfast – restaurant rec); **A3** *Residence de la Tour* at Paraná Country Club, 5 km from centre, T 60316, superb, excellent restaurant (US$12-16 pp), swimming pool, gardens, beautiful view; **C** *Catedral*, Av CA López 840, T 62424, incl breakfast, TV, a/c, with swimming pool, restaurant; **B** *Convair*, Adrián Jara y CA García, T 62349, a/c, cheaper rooms without bath **D**; **C** *Floresta*, Av Teniente Cabello y CA López, T 8255/8197, good breakfast but a bit run down; **D** *El Cid*, Camino Recalde 425, T 62221, breakfast, bath, fan; **C** *Puerta del Sol*, Boquerón 111, T 68081, with bath, a/c, clean, just off main street; **C** *San Rafael*, Adrián Jara y Abay, T 68105, friendly, clean, large rooms, price can be negotiated off peak; **C** *Santo Domingo* (no sign), Emiliano R Fernández y Miranda, T 62505, big rooms, a/c, good value. Other cheap ones nr market: **D** *Munich*, Fernández y Cap Miranda, T 62371, rec; **D** *Austria* (known as *Viena*), on Fernández, above restaurant, with breakfast, clean, Austrian family; **D** *Mi Abuela*, Adrián Jara 128, T 62373, including breakfast, shared shower, fan, dirty; **D** *Tripolis*, Av San Blas 331, T 62450, a/c, friendly, clean, poor restaurant.

Restaurants *Correio*, Av San Blas 125, T 0448, good Korean food, meal about US$5; *Osaka*, Adrián Jara and, 100m away, *New Tokio*, Adrián Jara 202, both very good, authentic Japanese meal for US$3; *Seoul*, Curupayty y Adrián Jara, good *parrillada*; *Austria/Viena*, good Austrian food, clean, good value; *Dolibar*, clean and fair value. Cheaper ones along Alejo García and in market. Many restaurants close on Sun.

Exchange Banco Holandés Unido, cash on Mastercard, 5% commission; local banks (open Mon-Fri 0730-1100). Dollars can be changed into reais in town, but exchange may be better and easier in Foz do Iguaçu. Cambio Guaraní, Av Monseñor Rodríguez, changes TCs. Casa de cambio rates are better than street rates. Note that money changers do not operate at the Brazilian end of the Friendship Bridge.

International Phone Antelco, Av Alejo García esq Pai Pérez, near centre on road to bus terminal.

Air Services To Asunción, Arpa (3 flights Mon-Sat, 1 on Sun), US$110 one way; TAM, Edificio SABA, Monseñor Rodríguez.

Buses Bus station is some way S of the centre (No 8 bus from Toledo y Hernández, taxi US$2 but bargain). Many buses, first at 0730 (US$12 *rapido*, 4½ hrs; US$9 *común*, 6 hrs) and colectivos run to and from **Asunción**. Nuestra Señora and Rysa reported to run the best buses; also Sirena del Paraná and others. To **Concepción**, García, 11 hrs, comfortable. To **Encarnación** (for Posadas and Argentina), along fully paved road, frequent, 4 hrs, US$6. This is probably cheaper than via Foz do Iguaçu.

To/From Brazil The road links with the Brazilian road system at Foz do Iguaçu across the bridge, from where another 32-km road leads to the Iguazú falls. Passengers disembark on each side of the bridge, but make sure the bus stops at Paraguaian immigration if you need evidence that you have left the country. The international bus then goes to the new bus terminal (*Rodoviária*), on Av Costa e Silva, away from the centre of Foz do Iguaçu. Local buses go to the city terminal (*terminal urbana*), just outside Foz, opposite a military training camp. There are also local buses from Calle San Blas, every 15 mins, 0600-2000, US$0.55, which drops you off at Brazilian immigration; keep your ticket and continue to Foz free on the next bus. From Brazil, pedestrians seem to walk across the bridge on the N side, this allows those returning from Paraguay carrying TVs and such bulky purchases an easier passage on the S side. The walk takes 10-15 mins. If entering Paraguay, sit next to the bus exit so you can get out to visit Brazilian immigration for your exit stamp. Travellers report this crossing is very busy at weekends and not all buses stop at immigration. Paraguayan taxis cross freely to Brazil but it is cheaper to walk across the bridge and then take a taxi, bargain hard. You can pay in either currency. Remember to adjust your watch to local time. From the *terminal urbana*, buses run to both the Brazilian and Argentinian sides of the Falls; if only visiting the Falls, immigration procedure on the Paraguayan and Brazilian sides of the Friendship Bridge is minimal, even for those normally requiring a visa to visit Brazil. If in doubt, though, obtain all necessary exit and entrance stamps.

The *Monday* falls, where the Río Monday drops into the Paraná gorge, 10 km S of Ciudad del Este, are worth visiting by taxi. They are known locally as Cascada de Monday, or Lunes Cascada. There is good fishing below the falls. Also nearby, S of Ciudad del Este, is **Puerto Presidente Franco** (pop 24,000) reached by the Tres Fronteras bus which leaves you 2 km from this small port on the Paraná opposite Puerto Iguazú, Argentina (**F** *Hotel Rosa*, B Caballero y Piribebuy,

T 061-2425, with bath, clean). Regular launches cross here but this is not a usual travellers' crossing point and you may have difficulties with customs and immigration formalities. Both Puerto Franco and **Hernandarias**, N of Ciudad del Este (pop 32,000, **D** *Hotel El León*, cleanish, poor breakfast, quiet; frequent buses from Ciudad del Este, US$0.35) experienced tremendous growth in population and activity with the building of Itaipú.

The huge **Itaipú** hydroelectric project, which covers an area of 1,350 square km, is close to Ciudad del Este, and well worth a visit. Take a bus from Rodríguez y García, outside the Terminal Urbano to the Visitors' Centre, open 0730-1200, 1330-1700, Sun and holidays 0800-1200, 1330-1630. Free conducted tours of the project include a film show (versions in several languages – ask) 45 mins before bus tours which start at 0830, 0930, 1030, 1400, 1500, 1600, Mon-Sat (Sun and holidays closed) check times in advance. Take passport. If you don't like guided trips but still wish to visit the project call the Centro de Recepción de Visitas at the site (T 8682), or apply to head office in Asunción (T 207161).

From Hernandarias, boat trips on Lago Itaipú go to Puerto Guaraní where there is a museum.

A paved road runs **north from Coronel Oviedo**. At 56 km is **Mbutuy** (good *parador*, restaurant, petrol station) where a dirt road (Route 10) goes NE to **Salto del Guaira**, named after the waterfalls now under the Itaipú lake (hotels). Here there is a 900 hectare wildlife reserve. There is a ferry to Brazil (US$0.60). There are daily buses from Asunción (10 hrs). A wide, dry-weather road runs N from Hernandarias, via Itaquyry to the Coronel Oviedo – Salto del Guaira road at Cruce Guaraní.

36 km N of Mbutuy is **San Estanislao**, museum, hotel (E). North of San Estanislao, the road is paved to Lima and Santa Rosa (107 km from San Estanislao), where there is petrol, *pensión* and restaurants. Here a dirt road runs SW to the Mennonite colony of **Nueva Germania**, 27 km (see *Forgotten Fatherland* by Ben MacIntyre, New York 1992, for the history of this place). This road goes on to San Pedro and Puerto Antequera on the Río Paraguay (88 km). A further 23 km N of Santa Rosa, a dirt road runs NE through jungle to **Capitán Badó** (120 km) in the Cordillera Amambay which forms the frontier with Brazil. From here another road follows the frontier N to PJ Caballero (100 km). 50 km N of the turn off to Capitán Badó is Yby Yaú, see p 1088.

SOUTH FROM ASUNCION (3)

An attractive area of fertile landscapes, but especially notable for the Jesuit settlements with many fine churches now being restored or completed to the original plans.

Route One runs through some of the old mission towns to Encarnación, 370 km SE, on the Alto Paraná.

Itá (Km 37, pop 9,310), founded 1539, is famous for rustic pottery (by Rosa Britez as you enter village). **Yaguarón**, Km 48, founded in 1539, was the centre of the Franciscan missions in colonial times. It is set on a river at the foot of a hill in an orange-growing district, and has a famous church, begun by the Franciscans in 1640 and finished in 1720, reconstructed in 1885 and being renovated since 1990. (Open 0730-1200, 1400-1700, daily except Sun; Sr Palacios has the key.) The tints, made by the Indians from local plants, are still bright on the woodcarvings. Stations of the Cross behind the village lead to a good view of the surroundings. *Fiesta patronal*, mid-July. Most of Paraguay's petit-grain comes from the area. Buses every 15 mins or so from Asunción (US$1). (**F** *Hotel Silva*; **F** *Bar Elsi. Restaurant Ani Rejhaserei*, opp the church, good meal for US$2.)

"The corridor, or outside walk under a projecting roof supported by pillars, is a typical feature of Paraguayan churches. Generally it runs all the way round the church, forming an entrance portico in front. An excellent example is the church at Yaguarón. It is the prototype of the mission sanctuaries of the early 18th century, when the structure was built with a sturdy wooden skeleton and the walls – simple screens of adobe or brick – had no function of support. The belfry is a modest little wooden tower somewhat apart from the church; in the missions it also served as a *mangrullo*, or watch tower." – Paul Dony.

Museum Museo Del Doctor Francia, 500m down the road opposite the church, with relics of Paraguay's first dictator, 'El Supremo'. It is attractively housed in a simple, well kept colonial building, a setting that might well have earned the approval of the austere Doctor. Open Tues to Sun 0700-1100, 1400-1700, closed Mon, free.

Paraguarí (Km 63), founded 1775, the N entrance to the mission area, is on the railway (5,724 people), set among hills with many streams. Its church, though cruder, is reminiscent of that at Yaguarón. Bus to Encarnación 1830.

Hotels and Restaurants D *Hospedaje Alemán*, vegetarian meals; **F** *Hospedaje Bonanza*, friendly owners, basic. Excellent steaks at *Parador La Estación*.

25 km E of Paraguarí is **Sapucay**, the location of the workshops for the wood-burning steam locomotives. The workshops are closed Sat and Sun. Bus Asunción – Sapucay 0700, 1200, road closed from Paraguarí after heavy rain. There are cheap *hospedajes*.

15 km NE from Paraguari is **Chololó** (**B** *Parador Chololó*, T 0531-242, rec), with a small but attractive series of waterfalls and rapids with bathing facilities and walkways, mainly visited in the summer. A picturesque bus ride from Paraguarí, with good views of the surrounding countryside.

At **Carapeguá** Km 84 (*hospedaje* on main street, basic, friendly), a road turns off to Acahay, Ybicuy and the **Parque Nacional Ybicuy**, 67 km SE, one of the most accessible National Parks.
Founded in 1973, the 5,000 hectare park includes one of the few remaining areas of rainforest in E Paraguay. Good walks, a beautiful camp site (hardly used in the week, no lighting, some facilities may not be available) and lots of waterfalls. At the entrance is a well-set out park and museum as well as the reconstructed remains of the country's first iron foundry (La Rosada). The only shops (apart from a small one at the entrance selling drinks, eggs, etc) are at **Ybicuy**, 30 km NW (**D** *Hotel Pytu'u Renda*, Av Gen Caballero 509, good food, clean, cooking facilities, friendly; *Pensión Santa Rosa* and *San Juan*, both **F**). Bus from Ybicuy at 0430 and 1120, returning 0700 and 1345, goes as far as camp site, 2 km beyond the museum. From Asunción take a bus to Acahay, Transportes Emilio Cabrera, 8 daily and change, or bus to Ybicuy, 0630 which connects with a minibus. Crowded on Sun but deserted the rest of the week.

Just before Km 141 is **Caapucú** (**F** *Hotel Misiones*; bus from Asunción, US$2.25). At Km 161 is **Villa Florida** on the Río Tebicuary, an ideal holiday resort for sailing, fishing and relaxing, with several hotels (**B** *Nacional de Turismo*, Km 162, Mcal F Solano López, T 083-207, good and 2 *paradores*, camping nr the river (good fishing); also **A3** *Estancia Las Mercedes*, 7 km NE, T 083-220, full board, idyllic, river bathing, beaches, camping, highly rec. At **Centú Cué**, 5 km from Villa Florida, there are hotels (**D** *Parador Centú Cué*, full board, pleasant, peaceful; **D** *Dorado*) and camping facilities, for reservations at either, T Asunción 206570 or directly to Centú Cué 083-219. At San Miguel (Km 178), all types of woollen articles are on sale (blankets, shawls, ponchos, hammocks, etc.). At Km 196 is the small, peaceful town of **San Juan Bautista** (pop 6,872, **E** *Hotel Waldorf*, clean, friendly, rooms off a domestic courtyard). Its neatly cobbled streets, paved footpaths and substantial houses suggest a present and a past prosperity, unusual for rural Paraguay. The relatively recent cathedral on the main square has more than a touch of Jesuit severity.

San Ignacio Guazú, Km 226, is a delightful town on the site of a Jesuit *reducción*. Several typical Hispano-Guaraní buildings survive, with pavillions and colonnades. The Museo Jesuítico, housed in the former Jesuit art workshop, contains an important collection of Guaraní art and sculpture from the missionary period, open daily 0800-1100, 1400-1700, US$0.50. Nearby is the Museo Histórico Semblanza de Héroes, featuring displays on the Chaco War, open Mon-Sat 0745-1145, 1400-1700, Sun 0800-1100. (Hotels: **F** *Arapizandú*, T 082-203, restaurant, adequate; **F** *Del Puerto* with bath; **F** *Unión*, clean; restaurant at *Parador Piringó*, rec, staff knowledgeable about local buses. Camping is possible outside the town.)
12 km to the NE along a cobbled road is *Santa María* (**F** pp *Pensión San José*, basic), with another fine museum with some 60 Guaraní sculptures amongst the

exhibits (open 0700-1100, 1400-1700, US$0.25). The church has a lovely altar-piece of the Virgin and Child (the key is kept at a house on the opposite side of the plaza). Good local *artesanía* shop. Transport from San Ignacio by colectivo, 6 a day from 0500, 45 mins.

From San Ignacio Guazú a road, Route 4, 156 km, runs W to **Pilar** (pop 13,135), 306 km S of Asunción, opposite the confluence of the Ríos Paraguay and Bermejo. The road continues SW to the extreme SW tip of Paraguay, near Humaitá, the site of a heroic siege during the War of the Triple Alliance. There are occasional boats to Argentina and Asunción.

At **Santa Rosa** (Km 248), the modern church and adjacent oratorio have a beautiful Annunciation group and frescoes of the flight of the Holy Family's house from Nazareth to Loreto in Italy (ask the priest to open it up). Remnants of the old church and bell tower can be seen nearby. One local hotel: **F** *Avenida*, on the outskirts. A road at Km 262 leads 52 km SW to **Ayolas**, associated with the Yacyretá hydroelectric scheme (**B** *Hotel Nacional de Turismo*, Avda Costanera, T 072-2273, with shower, poor breakfast, otherwise OK; **E** *El Dorado*, with good restaurant). Between the main road and Ayolas is **Santiago**, another important Jesuit centre founded in 1669 with a modern church which incorporates the carved wooden doors and reredos depicting St Francis Xavier and St Philip from the original church. There is also a fine wooden carving of Santiago slaying the Saracens which is carried round the town on 25 Jul, the Saint's feast day. Coronel Bogado (pop 5,180), Km 319, is the southern limit of the mission area.

Turn off Route 1 just before Coronel Bogado for **San Cosmé y Damián** (343 km from Asuncion). Although founded as a Jesuit mission in 1632, it was moved to the present site in 1760. When the Jesuits were expelled from the Spanish colonies, 7 years later, the great church and ancillary buildings were unfinished, though many of the wood carvings were saved. A huge completion project has recently been carried out following the original plans. The church is locked but a guide is in attendance to open it, entry US$0.25. Camping is possible in the school grounds but ask first. Buses from Encarnación, US$2.50, 2 hrs, last return 1600. Nearby a neat new town where some of the Yacyretá dam workforce live. Route One reaches the Alto Paraná at Carmen del Paraná, Km 331, 40 km W of Encarnación.

Encarnación (pop 60,000), a busy port on the Alto Paraná, is connected by a bridge to the Argentine town of Posadas. Nearby is the Yacyretá-Apipé dam, shared by Paraguay and Argentina. Encarnación exports the products of a rich area: timber, soya, *mate*, tobacco, cotton, and hides; it is fast losing its traditional, rural appearance. (Travellers should be prepared for cold weather, despite the latitude.) The upper part of the town is not especially interesting; the lower, older part of the colonial town, is scruffy and busy. Encarnación is a good centre for visiting the nearly Jesuit missions of San Cosmé y Damián, Trinidad and Jesús. The cost of living is higher in Encarnación than in most other parts of Paraguay, but at present tourist goods and electrical equipment are much lower priced than in Posadas.

Hotels A2 *Novohotel Encarnación*, first class, Route 1, km 2, T 4131, comfortable, very well run, highly rec; **B** *Paraná*, Estigarribia 1414, T 4440, good breakfast, clean, helpful, rec; **A3** *Cristal*, Estigarribia 1157, T 2371, restaurant; **D** *Viena*, Calle Capitán PJ Caballero 568 (T 3486), nr bus station, beside Antelco, with bath and small breakfast, German-run, good food, garage; **D** *Suizo*, Mcal Estigarribia 562, T 4377, 3 blocks S of bus terminal, E without bath, without breakfast, run down, dirty, overpriced (cheaper if you pay in guaraníes); **D** *Central*, Mcal López 542, T 3454, incl private bath and breakfast, German spoken; **E** *Repka*, Arquitecto Pereira 43, T 3546, pretty garden, private baths, good home cooking; **D** *Viera*, a/c, good location (**F** with fan), 25 de Mayo 413, T 2038, private bath; **D** *Hotel Liz*, Av Independencia 1746, clean, comfortable, restaurant, rec; **E** *Itapúa*, opp bus station, with bath, dark rooms, modern, beware overcharging; **E** *Hospedaje*, Capitán PJ Caballero 560, good value; **F** *Pensión Vila Alegre*, Antequera 951, with restaurant; **F** *Itaipú*, nr bus terminal, busy, clean rooms, terrible toilets, adjoining restaurant OK; **F** *Rueda*, nr bus station, a bit run down but OK; others nr railway station, should be avoided even by the desperate.

Restaurants *Rubi*, Chinese, Mcal Estigarribia 519, good; *Buez Brasil*, Av Irrazábal, good and popular buffet; *Parrillada las Delicias*, Estigarribia 1694, good steaks, comfortable, Chilean wines; *Rancho Grande*, Estigarribia y Cerro Corá, large *parrillada*, live music; *Cuarajhy*,

Estigarribia y Pereira, terrace seating, good food, open 24 hrs; *Ñasaindy*, Estigarribia 900, for snacks; *Karanday*, Gral Caballero, good grill. Good restaurants by the bus station, *Itapúa*, López y Cabañas.

Banks and Exchange Lloyds Bank, agency at Villarrica y Mariscal Estigarribia, open Mon-Fri 0845-1215; **Banco Unión**, Estigarribia 1404, will change TCs (with purchase receipt), cash advance on Visa. Many money-changers at the Paraguayan side but will only change notes. *Casas de cambio* for TCs on Mariscal Estagarribia (eg Cambios Guaraní at No 307). Best to change money in town, not at the frontier.

Consulates Argentina, Cabañas y Mallorquín; **Brazil**, Memmel 452; **Germany**, Memmel 631; **Japan**, C A López 1290.

International Phone Antelco, Capitán PJ Caballero y Mcal López, 0700-2200, unfriendly.

Tourist Office (no sign) at Wiessen 345, 3 blocks from bus station, helpful; street map of city.

Taxis A few horsedrawn (about US$0.25), but prices tend to be high if drivers suspect you don't know the distance you want to travel. Some motor driven ones for those in a hurry. Horse-drawn taxi from railway station US$1.25 (compared with US$3.75 by car).

Transport Passenger service to Asunción supposedly leaves Sun 0500, but see under Asunción, **Rail**.
The bus terminal is at Estigarribia y Memmel; good cheap snacks. To/from **Asunción**, Alborada, Flecha de Oro, Rysa, Nuestra Señora de la Asunción, all except last named at least 4 a day, 6 hrs, US$10. Stopping (*común*) buses US$5, but much slower. To **Trinidad**, US$0.40, 30 mins, every hour (can be very crowded). To **Ciudad del Este** US$6, several daily, 4 hrs. Buses also to **Villarrica**.
To Argentina The new San Roque road bridge connects Encarnación with **Posadas**. Take any 'Posadas/Argentina' bus from opp bus terminal over the bridge, US$0.70, 30 mins. Exit from Paraguay and entry to Argentina formalities both done in separate offices in building on Argentine side – different spots for locals and foreigners. Bus passengers should keep all luggage with them and should retain bus ticket; buses do not wait. After formalities (queues common), take another bus. Cycles are not allowed to use the bridge, but officials may give cyclists a lift. Cycles can also be carried by ferry (service on weekdays only) but there is only Argentine immigration on board so you need to go back to Paraguayan immigration for exit stamp. Remember that Paraguay is 1 hr behind Argentina except during Paraguayan summer time.

From Encarnación a paved road (Route 6) goes NE to Ciudad del Este. At Km 21, just beyond Capitán Miranda, is **A2** *Hotel Tirol*, T 075-555, with 40 double rooms, chalets, 2 swimming pools, terraces, disappointing, unhelpful, used as a stopover for Argentine coach tours. A further 7 km towards Ciudad del Este is **Trinidad**, the hilltop site of a Jesuit *reducción*, built 1706-1760. The Jesuit church, once utterly in ruins has been partially restored. It was founded in 1706 by Padre Juan de Anaya; the architect was Juan Bautista Prímoli. For information, or tours, contact Sr Augusto Servián Goana, the curator who lives close by. A US$3 booklet by Clement MacNaspy is available at the site. Nearby is a museum which includes a small-scale replica of the site (open 0730-1130, 1330-1730 weekdays, 0800-1700 Sun and holidays, entry US$1). Nearby is a small modern church; it contains a large carved wooden statue of the Deity, so hollowed at the back that a priest in hiding could simulate the resounding voice of the Eternal Father to impress the Indians of the mission. Many buses go from Encarnación to and through Trinidad, take any bus from the terminal marked Ciudad del Este. A taxi tour from Encarnación costs about US$30. You can stay at the Centro Social, food and shower available, take sleeping gear; camping permitted behind the souvenir stall. Hotel under construction.
10 km NW of Trinidad, along a good paved road, is **Jesús**, now a small town where another group of Jesuits finally settled in 1763. In the five years before they were expelled they commenced a massive construction programme including church, sacristy, *residencia* and a baptistry, on one side of which is a square tower. There is a fine front façade with three great arched portals (opening hours as for Trinidad, entry US$1). Beautiful views in all directions. Direct bus Trinidad-Jesús at 1130, and at other times, 30 mins, US$0.60. Irregular buses go from Encarnación (1$\frac{1}{2}$ hrs). Enquire locally as taxis try to overcharge.

From Trinidad the road goes through or near a number of German colonies including Hohenau

(Km 36), Obligado, Santa Rita (**B** *Hotel Staufenberg*, Km 41, T 600-756, good, restaurant), Bella Vista (Km 42, **C** *Hotel Bella Vista Plaza*, Samaniego 1415, T 0767-236; **C** *Papillón*, Km 44, T 0757-235, clean) and, at Km 67, a cobbled side road leads to Pirapó, a Japanese settlement (**E** *Hotel Pirapó*). This is a prosperous agricultural area, attractive countryside with facilities for travellers en route. Significant areas of forest which used to cover this region were cleared between 1945 and 1985 to plant soybeans and other crops. Eventually Route 6 meets Route 2 close to Ciudad del Este.

NORTH FROM ASUNCION (4)

The Paraguay river, still a main trade route between Brazil and Argentina, dominates this section.

A boat trip up the Paraguay to Concepción, about 312 km N of Asunción, is one of the easiest ways of seeing the country. The winding river is 400m wide, with a lot of traffic, for in the absence of a direct road between Concepción and Asunción (though there are roads via the Chaco and by Coronel Oviedo) this is the main trade route for the products of northern Paraguay: cattle, hides, *yerba mate*, tobacco, timber and *quebracho*. For passenger sailings, see under Asunción, **River Boats**.

North from Asunción by river, you pass Villa Hayes where the bridge marks the beginning of the Trans-Chaco Highway. About 120 km upstream is Puerto Rosario where an unpaved road goes SE to San Estanislao. A further 50 km upstream is Puerto Antequera and 100 km beyond is Concepción. For more details and the routes to the E, see **Section 2** below. The only connection W to the Trans-Chaco is from Concepción to Pozo Colorado.

Concepción (pop 35,000), a free port for Brazil, lies on the E bank. This pleasant, friendly, quiet and picturesque town is the trade centre of the N, doing a considerable business with Brazil. There is a library, municipal theatre and 'higgledy piggledy' museum, all under one roof, and a market, to which farmers bring their goods in oxcarts. About 9 km N is a new bridge across the Río Paraguay, offering an interesting walk across the shallows and islands to the W bank, about 1 hr return trip, taxi US$6.

Hotels D *Francés*, Presidente Franco 1016, with bath and a/c, E bath and fan, cheaper without bath, incl breakfast, good value, restaurant, clean and friendly, rec; **E** *Center*, Av Presidente Franco y Yegros, with bath, hot water when the weather is hot, a/c on second flr; **E** *Concepción*, Don Bosco 311, with bath, pool, clean; **E** *Imperial*, Gral Garay y Villarica, fan, without bath; **D** *Victoria*, Franco y Caballero, good, cheap and clean, private bath with hot water, breakfast, good restaurant (try *surubi* fish), rec; **F** *Bar Estrella del Norte* (nr port), basic but possible; **F** *Boquerón*, Iturbe y Franco, quiet area; **F** *Cosmos* by market where horses and carts stand (clean, fan).

Restaurants The restaurants of *Hotels Victoria* and particularly *Francés* are good. Also, *Tedacar*, on Franco, good food, pleasant with seating in the garden behind. *Bar El Trébol*, in the centre, has *chamamé* and *polka paraguaya* music on Thur pm.

Exchange Bancopar, Garay y Franco, open am.

Air Service Asunción-Concepción flights are operated by LATN, Aeronorte, Arpa and TAM (which tends to be cheapest). TAM to Asunción daily at 0800, 40 mins, book as early as possible (only 25 seats), free colectivo from TAM office on main street to airport. Arpa daily at 1530. On Mon, Wed and Fri at 0700 TAM flies from Asunción and Concepción to Vallemí, Fuerte Olimpo and Bahía Negra, all three villages to N of Concepción on the Río Paraguay. Air services to these places are irregular because runways are sometimes flooded or muddy. There is no direct air connection between Concepción and Pedro Juan Caballero.

Road transport The bus terminal is on the outskirts, 8 blocks up Gral EA Garay. There is an urban microbus (Línea 1) which shuttles between terminal and the port. Arriving in town by bus, get out in town centre, don't wait for bus terminal. Bus companies from **Asunción**: San Jorge, Lambaré and Nuestra Señora de Asunción, some between 2200-2300. There is a dry-season road (frequently closed in the wet season) from Concepción W across the Chaco, to **Pozo Colorado** on the Transchaco highway, 146 km. Efforts are being made to improve this road, parts are now paved but it can take 3 days in the rain to drive. Bird life is spectacular. The Concepción-Pozo Colorado bus normally takes 3 hrs, US$2.75, but it is difficult to get onward connections. Alternative route to/from Asunción is along Routes 3 and 8 via Coronel Oviedo, several buses each day, bad road, rains often delay departures. Bus to Asunción via Pozo Colorado theoretically takes 6½ hrs, several daily, US$9; via Coronel Oviedo 8-11 hrs, US$10. Bus to **Pedro Juan Caballero**, *semi-directo* 6 hrs, US$3, *directo* 4 hrs, US$5, first three quarters of road unpaved. To **Horqueta**, 1 hr, US$1.

Shipping To **Asunción**, several companies, including Cruceros SRL (fares under Asunción **River Boats**; see same section for river transport to Corumbá, Brazil). Agencia Marítima Ramón Velázquez, Nanawa 547, near dock for information on sailings.

North of Concepción Normally it is possible to find a passage on boats going upstream from Concepción to the small 'ports' serving local communities, though there are few places to stay. North of the confluence with the Río Apá, the Río Paraguay becomes the border with Brazil. You can enter Brazil, as long as you have a Paraguayan exit stamp, by taking a boat to Isla Margarita, where you can get a ferry to Porto Murtinho, Brazil (see p 585 Brazil, **The Centre-West**).

The limit of river traffic if the river is in flood is *Bahía Negra*, the northern-most river port on the border. It has flights to Asunción, but neither hotel nor bank. Sra Ferreira will change money, at a poor rate. It is possible to hire a small boat to Porto Coimbra (Sra Ferreira or Sr Silva) and from there go by boat to Porto Esperança, from where road and rail go to Corumbá. Ask the police about border formalities. Entry at Porto Esperança requires a yellow fever certificate and much red tape because it is not a regular border crossing. Since local river traffic is sparse, this trip is recommended only for the adventurous and patient. Above Bahía Negra, the river leaves Paraguay and for a few kms is the border between Bolivia and Brazil. Thereafter it enters the **Pantanal** – see Brazil, Section 11, **The Centre-West**.

East of Concepción There is a 215 km road (Route 5—first 112 km unpaved but moderate) from Concepción, eastwards to the Brazilian border. This road goes through Horqueta, Km 50, a cattle and lumber town of 10,000 people, then passes near Arroyito where an experimental land resettlement programme began after the political changes of 1989. Further on the road is very scenic. From **Yby Yaú**, Km 112 (junction with road to Coronel Oviedo, fuel, restaurants) the road is paved to Pedro Juan Caballero. 6 km E of Yby Yaú a road branches off to the very pleasant, uncrowded **National Park** of *Cerro Corá* (22,000 hectares), which is the site of Mariscal Francisco Solano López' death and the final defeat of Paraguay in the War of the Triple Alliance. There is a monument to him and other national heroes; the site is constantly guarded. It has hills and cliffs (some with precolumbian caves and petroglyphs), camping facilities, swimming and hiking trails. The rocky outcrops are spectacular and the warden, Carmelo Rodríguez, is helpful and will provide free guides. When you have walked up the road and seen the line of leaders' heads, turn right and go up the track passing a dirty-looking shack (straight on leads to a military base). Administration office is at Km 180 on Ruta 5, 5 km E of the main entrance.

The border town of *Pedro Juan Caballero* (pop 37,331), is opposite Ponta Porã, Brazil, which has a road and railway to São Paulo and the Atlantic coast. The two towns are divided only by a road (Rua Internacional) and the locals come and go as they please. Truck traffic is very heavy at this border. To cross into Brazil officially, first obtain a Paraguayan exit stamp (the office was last reported at Calle Naciones Unidas 144; Mon-Fri 0700-1200, 1400-1700, Sat 0730-1200), then report to Brazilian federal police in Ponta Porã. If you need a Brazilian visa go first to the Brazilian consul in the *Hotel La Siesta*, open Mon-Fri 0800-1200, 1400-1800. If you are entering Paraguay, ensure you get your passport stamped at the Paraguayan border (without it you will have to pay US$3 on leaving the country). From PJ Caballero there are daily flights to Asunción (they may be suspended after heavy rain, at which time buses may not run to Asunción either, though colectivos, which cost about 25% more than buses, may run when buses do not). Much cheaper here than Asunción for most purchases. The main street, Mcal López, is good for shopping, cheap liquor and electronics. Near the bus terminal at Teniente Herrero 998 y Estigarribia, is a natural history museum run by the Fundación Kayamo, entry free, open Mon-Sat 0800-1200, 1300-1700.

Hotels B *Casino Amambay*, Dr Francia 1, T 036-2718, luxury, good restaurant, close to border; **B** *Eiruzú*, Estigarribia 4-8, T 2259, with breakfast, clean, modern, rec, swimming pool, good restaurant; **D** *Corina*, 14 de Mayo, T 2960, very clean with breakfast, T 2960, rec; **E** *Guavira*, Mcal López 1325, T 2743, no breakfast, comfortable, rec; **D** *La Negra*, Mcal López 1342, T 2262, clean; **E** *Peralta*, Mcal López 1257.

Restaurants In hotels, or the Brazilian side. *Parrillada El Galpón*, Mcal López 892, is rec.

Exchange Bancopar changes TCs. At least 6 *casas de cambio* for TCs (also deal in the

European currencies), or *Hotel Eiruzú*. You may have to show receipt for purchase of TCs (if you don't have it, try **Cambio Amambay**, nr *Hotel Eiruzú*). At weekends try Game Centre Guaraní or Casa China. There are many street changers.

Buses Several to **Concepción** US$5, 4-6 hrs. To **Asunción**, direct, poor road, 8-9 hrs, US$10 (US$24 deluxe sleeper) and slower buses, 11-12 hrs (indirect), eg Cometa del Amambay at 0900 and 1700, US$9.

Del Amambay (Mcal López 1286) has a service to **Campo Grande**, Brazil, US$10 (obtain entry/exit stamps beforehand). There is another crossing to Brazil at Bella Vista on the Río Apá, NW of PJ Caballero; buses run from the Brazilian border town of Bela Vista to Jardim and thence to Campo Grande.

THE PARAGUAYAN CHACO (5)

A remarkable area of marshes and farmlands developed by German-speaking Mennonites, with a substantial population of Indian peoples. Birds are spectacular and common, while other wildlife is equally interesting but less frequently seen.

The Paraguayan Chaco covers 24 million hectares, but has fewer than 100,000 inhabitants, most of those living just across the Río Paraguay from Asunción. A single major highway, the Ruta Trans-Chaco, runs in a straight line N-W to the Bolivian border 20 km beyond Nueva Asunción, at General E A Garay. As far as Mariscal Estigarrtibia, its paved surface is one of the best in South America, but beyond that point its dirt surface, after rain, is negotiatable only by 4WD vehicles. The elevation rises very gradually from 50m opposite Asunción to 450m on the Bolivian border.

The Chaco is divisible into 3 sections. The Low Chaco, just W of Asunción across the Río Paraguay, is a picturesque palm savanna, much of which is permanently inundated because of the impenetrable clay beneath the surface, although there are 'islands' of high ground. Cattle ranching on gigantic *estancias* is the prevailing economic activity; some units lie several hundred km down tracks off the highway. Cattle breeds are very mixed – English Herefords, Indian Brahmins, and Brazilian. Most *estancias* are chronically overstocked and overgrazed; the stock are in poor condition and calving rates are very low. Remote *estancias* have their own airfields, and all are equipped with 2-way radios. Motorists should beware of cattle on the Trans-Chaco, especially at night.

The Middle Chaco, near Filadelfia, has been settled by Mennonites, Anabaptist refugees of German extraction who began arriving in the late 1920s. There are three administratively distinct but adjacent colonies: Menno (from Russia via Canada and Mexico); Fernheim (directly from Russia) and Neuland (the last group to arrive, also from Russia, after WW2). Among themselves, the Mennonites speak 'plattdeutsch' ('Low German'), but they readily speak and understand 'hochdeutsch' ('High German'), which is the language of instruction in their schools. Increasingly, younger Mennonites speak Spanish and Guaraní, while English is not unknown. Altogether there are 118 villages with a population of about 10,000 Mennonites, 10,000 Indians and much smaller numbers of 'Paraguayans' and other immigrants. The natural vegetation is scrub forest, with a mixture of hardwoods, and cactus in the N. The *palo borracho* (bottle-tree) with its pear-shaped, water-conserving, trunk, and the tannin-rich *quebracho* (axe-breaker) are the most important native species.

The Mennonites, who run their own banks, schools, hospitals and agricultural cooperatives, have created a prosperous community in an area that has attracted few other settlers. They are mainly crop-farmers raising citrus, groundnuts, sorghum and cotton, but their dairy products are excellent and widely distributed throughout the country. About half the country's milk production comes from the Chaco.

Very few of the remaining Chaco Indians, most notably the Ayoreo, still rely on hunting and gathering for their livelihood to any great degree. Many have settled among or near Mennonite colonies, where they cultivate cotton and subsistence crops, and work as day labourers for the Mennonites or on Paraguayan cattle *estancias*. They speak a variety of indigenous languages, including Guaraní, but are often more likely to know German than Spanish. Controversial fundamentalist Christian missionaries proselytize actively among them.

From Filadelfia an alternative route goes N to the 780,000 hectare **Parque Nacional Defensores del Chaco**, where most of the country's remaining jaguars are found. Puma, tapir and peccary also inhabit the area, but none is commonly seen except, with great patience, around water holes at nightfall. This road is very rough and negotiable only by 4WD vehicles; park rangers and very limited facilities can be found at Fortín Madrejón and Aguas Dulces. Dirt roads continue past a prominent isolated hill, Cerro León, to the border with Bolivia at Fortín Ravelo and thence, in theory, 150 km to the Santa Cruz – Corumbá road and railway at Roboré. However we have no recent reports of travellers crossing here which must be all but impassable in the wet season. Most settlements beyond the orbit of Filadelfia are under military jurisdiction and a letter of authorization or military introduction may be useful.

The High Chaco consists of low dense thorn forest, an impenetrable barricade of hard spikes and spiny branches resistant to fire, heat and drought, and very tough on tyres. Occasional tracks lead off the Trans-Chaco for a short distance. Towards Bolivia cactus becomes more prevalent as rainfall decreases. There are a few *estancias* towards the S, where the brush is bulldozed into hedges and the trees left for shade. Summer temperatures often exceed 45°C.

No expedition should leave the Trans-Chaco without plentiful supplies of water, food and fuel. In the Middle and Low Chaco, there are service stations at regular intervals along the highway, but none beyond Mariscal Estigarribia. Since this is a major smuggling route from Bolivia, it is unwise to stop for anyone in the night. There is almost no traffic in the High Chaco, and ill-equipped expeditions have had to be rescued by the army or have come to grief. Clear the area around your camp to deter poisonous snakes. Winter temperatures are warm by day, cooler by night, but summer heat and mosquitoes can make it very unpleasant (pyrethrum coils – *espirales* – are available throughout the region). The rapid improvement of the highway has opened the area to agricultural colonization, especially by foreigners, but oil exploration is as yet unsuccessful.

To reach the Ruta Trans-Chaco, you leave Asunción by the route across the Río Paraguay to Villa Hayes. Bird life is especially abundant and visible in the palm savanna, but other wild animals occur mostly as road kills. At Km 270 is Pozo Colorado (the turning for Concepción, **see** p 1087), a truck stop (toll point, US$0.75) and military checkpoint where teenage conscripts armed with M-16s (reportedly unloaded) may ask motorists to transport one of their cohorts to the base at Río Verde, 80 km W. At this point, the tidy Mennonite homesteads, surrounded by flower gardens and citrus orchards, begin to appear. A good place to eat on the Trans-Chaco is Cruce de los Pioneros (ex-Cruce Loma Plata), at Km 415, a popular weekend excursion from Asunción where accommodation (**C**, good breakfast) and fuel are available.

The service centres of the Mennonite area are Filadelfia (Fernheim Colony), Loma Plata (Menno Colony), and Neu-Halbstadt (Neuland Colony). **Filadelfia**, 472 km from Asunción, is the largest of the three. The Unger Museum at Filadelfia (US$1 admission incl video) provides a glimpse of pioneer life in the Chaco, as well as exhibiting artefacts of the aboriginal peoples of the region. The Manager of the *Hotel Florida* will open the museum upon request, when things are not too busy. A knowledge of German is very helpful in this area. The bank does not change bolivianos; good rates for US$ cash. The Reiseburo, a travel agency on Hindenburgstrasse just N of *Hotel Florida*, will change money and is a good source of information.

Hotels C *Florida*, T 091-258, modern motel-style wing with a/c and private bath, very comfortable; **F** pp in annex. Good German pastries available, expensive breakfast; **C** *Safari*; **F** *Edelweiss*, basic, fan, clean. **Restaurants** *La Estrella* rec for good ice cream and *asados*; another good restaurant *El Girasol*, opp; *Remi*, on same street, pizzas and ice cream. Plenty of good, but basic homemade ice cream, more than welcome in the heat. 5 km E of town, Parque Trébol has basic camping facilities at no charge, but lacks running water.

Buses From Asunción, Stel Turismo, Mon, Tue, Thur, Sun 2100, Sat 1300, 6 hrs, US$10; Nasa, Colombia 1050, T 200697, daily 0600 and Sat 1200 (also calls at main terminal) 8½ hrs, US$8, less comfortable.

Excursions *Loma Plata*, the centre of Menno Colony, is 25 km E of Filadelfia (**E/F** *Hotel Loma Plata*, a/c, friendly, clean, with restaurant). Good museum open on request; ask at nearby Secretariat building. Bus from Filadelfia, Stel Turismo, US$2. 33 km S of Filadelfia is **Neu-Halbstadt**, centre of Neuland Colony (**C** *Hotel Boquerón*, with excellent restaurant and tasty ice cream). Neu-Halbstadt is a good place to purchase local Indian crafts. 40 km W of Filadelfia, across the Trans-Chaco, is *Fortín Toledo*, where the San Diego Zoo supports a small reserve for Wagner's peccary, a Pleistocene relic thought extinct until 1975 (visitors not generally welcomed); nearby are abandoned fortifications and a military cemetery from the 1930s Chaco War. Sieghart Friesen, Av Trébol, Filadelfia, rec as guide, knowledgeable on the area, speaks Spanish and German.

To Bolivia From Filadelfia to the Bolivian border 20 km beyond General Eugenio A Garay is 304 km. Best to fill up with fuel and supplies at Filadelfia, with its Mennonite Co-op supermarket. There are sparse facilities (food, fuel) until **Mariscal Estigarribia**, Km 540 (**D** *Hotel Alemán*, with breakfast, friendly, also cheaper rooms without bath). You can change money at the supermarket *Chaparral*, and local German priests may offer you a bed. (Daily bus from Filadelfia 1500, 2 hrs, daily colectivo 1900; daily bus to Asunción 0700.) Thereafter military outposts or *estancias* are the only alternatives. At **Estancia La Patria**, Km 662, a Centro Urbano Rural includes a motel (**E**, pleasant, good value) supermarket and fuel. Bus from Filadelfia, Fri 0500, US$8, leaves La Patria Fri 0700, also truck transport US$10. From here safaris can be made into the 40,000 hectare Parque Nacional Teniente Enciso. At Nueva Asunción, 95 km beyond La Patria, there is an airbase where you can get water, but you may have to show your papers and be registered. Hitching is possible but totally unreliable (fee US$10-15); traffic is very sparse. Trucks travel into Bolivia and may take passengers in Filadelfia; the Esso Station on Hindenburgstrasse and the police checkpoint are the most convenient places to ask, but Mariscal Estigarribia and other checkpoints on the Trans-Chaco are also possible: ask the police for help, but be prepared to wait up to a week.

Identity checks at the numerous military checkpoints are common, and photographs should be a good likeness of the bearer. Backpackers need expect no special difficulties, but motorists should carry plenty of food and water since even small amounts of rain turn the highway into mud and cause major delays. Motorcycling beyond Mariscal Estigarribia can be difficult and dangerous in wet weather. Passport control is at Fortín Mister Long, 13 km short of General Garay (state whether you are entering or leaving). Camping is possible here, but do not surrender your passport to the *guardia* if staying overnight, since you may have to wait until the following day to have it returned. The commandant of Fortín Gral Garay is friendly and may allow you to stay the night and use the showers. There is no official charge but a contribution is appropriate. For the continuation of this route, see under **Boyuibe** in **Bolivia, Section 2**. Take small denomination dollar notes as it is impossible to buy bolivianos before reaching Bolivia.

Some maps show another route to Bolivia, going W from Mariscal Estigarribia to Fortín Infante Rivarola on the border, then through Ibibobo to Villa Montes. We have received no reports on this or other routes through the Chaco to Bolivia.

Tours from Asunción Many agencies offer tours, staying for up to 6 days in Cruce de los Pioneros. If you wish to explore the remoter parts of the Chaco, guides can be found in Asunción, often German speaking, at around $100 per day. Some travellers report that it is difficult to visit Indian areas because most tours are operated by Mennonites who only visit Mennonite communities.

INFORMATION FOR VISITORS

Before you go

Entry requirements

● **Documents**
A passport is required for a stay of up to 90 days. Visitors are registered on arrival by the immigration authorities and get their documents back immediately. This procedure applies to those who do not require visas. Citizens of the following countries do NOT need a visa (Feb 1995): USA, UK, Canada, Germany, Austria, Belgium, Spain, Italy, Holland, Denmark, Norway, Sweden, Finland, Switzerland, Israel, Japan, Argentina (some crossings accept identity cards instead of passports), Uruguay, Brazil, Chile, Ecuador, Colombia, El Salvador. All others must apply for a visa, which is free, presenting a valid passport, photograph and a supporting letter from agency handling bookings and itinerary (for a business visa a supporting letter from one's employer should suffice). If you do not complete formalities you can be turned back at the border, or have trouble when leaving Paraguay.

● **Representation overseas**
Canada, Suite 750, 1130 Sherbrooke St West, Montréal, Québec, H3A 2M8, T 514 842-8856, F 514 287-1538; **UK**, Braemar Lodge, Cornwall Gardens, London SW7 4AQ, T 0171 937-1253, F 0171 937-5687; **USA**, 2400 Massachusetts Avenue NW, Washington, DC 2008, T 202 483 6960/1, F 202 234-4508.

● **Tourist information**
The Dirección Nacional de Turismo has an office at Palma 468 in Asunción. Information about weather and roads from Touring y Automóvil Club Paraguayo (TACP) at 25 de Mayo y Brasil (who also produce a road map), and the office of the traffic police in Asunción. The best maps, including ones of the Chaco, are available from Instituto Geográfico Militar, Av Perú y Jardín Botánico. Small national maps, made by the Army, can be bought from the TACP, at bookshops and

bus terminals.

For information on national parks: Dirección de Parques Nacionales y Vida Silvestre, Ministerio de Agricultura y Ganadería, 25 de Mayo 640, Asunción, T 445214; on conservation: Fundación Moisés Bertoni para la Conservación de la Naturaleza, 25 de Mayo 2140, Asunción, T 25638.

Business visitors Foreign business is transacted in Asunción, Ciudad del Este and Pedro Juan Caballero (with retail outlets particularly in the last two).

When to go

● **Best time to visit**
May to Oct is the best time for a visit.

Health

Tuberculosis, typhoid, dysentery, and hepatitis are endemic. Hookworm is the most common disease in the country, and there is much venereal disease, goitre and leprosy. Visitors should be inoculated against tetanus, typhoid, and paratyphoid. Be very careful over salad and tap water (bottled water is available). Local mosquito repellent, *Repel*, and pyrethrum coils are effective. Dengue fever (see **Health Information**) has recently been reported. Medical fees and medicine costs are high. The Centro Paraguayo del Diagnóstico, Gral Díaz 975 y Colón, Asunción, is rec as inexpensive, foreign languages spoken. Clínica Integral de Mujer, Mcal Estigarribia 1085 y Brasil, Asunción, T 94722, has been rec as a good gynaecological clinic. Dentists can be found either at the centre, or at Odontología 3, Mcal Estigarribia 1414 y Pai Pérez, T 200175, Asunción.

Money

● **Currency**
The Guaraní (plural Guaraníes) is the unit of currency, symbolized by the letter G (crossed). There are bank notes for 100, 500, 1,000, 5,000, 10,000 and 50,000 guaraníes and coins for 1, 5, 10, 50 and 100 guaraníes. Get rid of all your guaraníes before leaving Paraguay; there is no market for them elsewhere (except in some *cambios* in Buenos Aires or Montevideo). It is possible to buy US dollar bills in Asunción (**see p 1073**), and rates for all foreign currencies, except bolivianos, are reasonable. *Casas de cambio* sometimes want to see customers' records of purchase before accepting TCs. Visitors are advised to check on the situation on changing TCs in advance. Visa and Mastercard cash advances are a possibility in Asunción and Encarnación

Mastercard/Cirrus ATMs are located in branches of Banco Unión. Street dealers operate from early in the morning until late at night, even at weekends or public holidays. In Asunción their rates are marginally better than the *casas de cambio* during business hours only, but they are not rec at Ciudad del Este. **NB** Dirty and/or torn US$ bills are very difficult to change or spend, especially in the Chaco. Check notes carefully before accepting them in *casas de cambio*. A bank, such as Lloyds, will replace all legitimate bills with acceptable ones.

● **Cost of living**
Paraguay is cheaper than Argentina and Brazil. There are a few hotels in our F range and many good ones in our D-E ranges, with breakfast, private shower and toilet. Many hotels have 2 rates – one for a room with a/c, the other without.

● **Credit cards**
Visa and Mastercard credit cards are widely accepted even for small purchases. Foreign-issued Visa cards may not always be accepted though a phone call will often resolve the problem; Visa is displayed as Unioncard. Credit card transactions are subject to a 10% tax. For Western Union T (21) 496683.

Getting there

By Air

● **From Europe**
Iberia has two weekly flights to Asunción from Madrid and Barcelona, with a change of plane in Buenos Aires. From other points in Europe, slow connections can be made via Rio or São Paulo (Varig or Aerolíneas Argentinas). Routes from Europe via Brazil offer greater ticketing flexibility than other options.

● **From North America**
American operates daily from Miami via São Paulo; flights from other US cities connect in Miami. From California, connections via Lima or Miami. Lapsa flies 3 times a week from Miami.

● **Within South America**
From Montevideo Lapsa once a week, Pluna twice; from Buenos Aires by Aerolíneas Argentinas daily (from Aeroparque domestic airport via Corrientes, or direct from Ezeiza), also daily with Lapsa; from Santiago daily with Ladeco (Chile), daily except Tues and Fri with National of Chile, and except Thur and Sat with Lapsa; from Lima 2 a week by AeroPerú; from La Paz once a week with Lloyd Aéreo Boliviano (LAB) via Cochabamba and Santa

Cruz (Bolivia, plus 3 others with LAB from Santa Cruz and 2 a week with AeroPerú); from São Paulo and Iguazú Falls (3 a week) by Varig; from Río and São Paulo, daily with Varig; from São Paulo direct, daily with American, and 4 a week with Lapsa. See **Getting there: Air**, in Brazil, **Information for visitors**, on the Mercosur airpass.

By road

● From Argentina
There is a paved road from Buenos Aires via Santa Fe to Clorinda and then on a paved road via the border at Puerto Falcón and the Remanso Castillo suspension bridge to Asunción: 1,370 km, about 23 hrs. Also from Clorinda there is a ferry from nearby Puerto Pilcomayo to Itá Enramada, a suburb of Asunción. Watch your belongings at the Clorinda crossing and on buses on either side of the border. The alternative land route is via Posadas to Encarnación across the new San Roque bridge. Good bus services on these routes. After the border at Puerto Falcón, before the Remanso Castillo bridge, a road forks to the Paraguayan Chaco (paved part of the way) and on to Bolivia.

● From Brazil
The main road connections are between Foz do Iguaçu and Ciudad del Este, and between Pedro Juan Caballero and Ponta Porã.

By river

Boat services on the Río Paraná between Buenos Aires and Asunción are irregular, depending on the level of the river.

There are unscheduled boat services from Asunción northward along the Paraguay river to Porto Esperança, Brazil, and there are scheduled services to Corumbá (1,220 km – **see p 1076**), which is connected by road, rail and air with Bolivian and Brazilian cities.

Under Mercosur (Southern Cone Common Market) regulations, borders between Paraguay, Brazil and Argentina should be open 24 hrs a day, 7 days a week.

Customs

'Reasonable quantities' of tobacco products, alcoholic drinks and perfume are admitted free of duty.

When you arrive

● Clothing
In summer, Jan to Mar, tropical clothing, sunglasses and an umbrella are needed. The best time to visit is from May to Sep, when the heat is not too oppressive.

● Hours of business
Many shops, offices and businesses open between 0630 and 0700. *Siesta* (generally observed during the hot season) is from 1200 to 1500. Commercial office hours are from 0730 to 1100 or 1130, and 1430 or 1500 to 1730 or 1900. Banks: from 0730 to 1100, closed on Sat and Sun. Government offices are open 0630 to 1130 in summer, 0730 to noon, in winter, open on Sat.

● Official time
3-4 hrs behind GMT (clocks go on 1 hour in local summer time, Oct-Feb/Mar, dates change annually).

● Safety
Since President Stroessner was deposed the political atmosphere is more relaxed and political discussion more open. Apparently, hitch-hiking is still illegal, although possible in rural areas. Generally, travellers find Paraguay safer than the neighbouring countries, but check prices and change.

● Shopping
The famous *ñandutí* lace, made exclusively by the women of Itauguá (**see p 1079**). The local jewellery is also attractive. Handmade *aó po'í* (fine cloth) is suitable for shirts and blouses, and there are cotton thread belts in all colours. The best place to buy these items is Villarrica. Also leather articles, the pottery and *pau de santo* (small articles made from Paraguayan woods). See also 'Shopping', under Asunción (**p 1074**). Imported goods, especially cameras, film and tampons, are cheaper in Paraguay than in most other Latin American countries (although prices in the UK, for instance, are cheaper).

● Tipping
Restaurants, 10%. Porters US$0.15 a suitcase. Taxis, 10%. Porters at docks US$0.40 a suitcase. Cinema usherettes are not tipped.

● Voltage
Nominally 220 volts AC and 50 cycles, but power surges and voltage drops are frequent. European round pin plugs are used.

● Weights and measures
The metric system is used except by carpenters, who use inches.

On departure

● Airport tax
Airport tax is US$16, payable in US$ or guaraníes (tends to be cheaper).

Food and drink

Food

Typical local foods include *chipas* (yuca bread flavoured with egg and cheese), *chipa soo* (maize bread with meat filling) and *sopa paraguaya* (a kind of dumpling of ground maize and cheese). *Soyo* is a soup of different meats and vegetables, delicious; *albóndiga* a soup of meat balls; *bori bori* another type of soup with diced meat, vegetables, and small balls of maize mixed with cheese. *Palmitos* (palm hearts) should not be missed; the beef is excellent in better class restaurants (best cuts are *lomo* and *lomito*). Paraguayan *chorizos* (sausages) are good. *Parrillada completa* is rec. *Surubí*, a Paraná river fish, is prepared in many different ways, and is delicious. Sugarcane juice, greatly beloved, is known as *mosto*. Fruit is magnificent. Very typical of Paraguay is *tereré* (cold *mate* with digestive herbs) for warm days and hot *mate* to warm you up on cold days.

Drink

The national wine is not rec (better is imported from Chile), but Baviera, a local lager beer is very good (beer is usually sold in litre bottles). The cane-sugar spirit, *caña* is good (the best is 'Aristocrat'; ask for 'Ari'). *Guaraná* is a good local soft drink (originally from Brazil).

Getting around

Air transport

There are scheduled services to most parts of the country by Aerolíneas Paraguayas (Arpa), Líneas Aéreas de Transporte Nacional (LATN) and Ladesa, and to Concepción, Vallemí, Bahía Negra and Fuerte Olimpo by Transportes Aéreos Militares (TAM). Planes can be chartered. Domestic fares are subject to 2.5% tax.

Road transport

Buses ply on the main roads. For motorists, there are sufficient service stations, except in the Chaco area. Motorists should beware stray cattle on the road at night. Diesel fuel is US$0.25/litre; gasoline users should use only *super* (Shell Spark Aider Super is rec), US$0.45/litre (which is 93 octane; regular gas, *alconafta*, contains 10-15% alcohol at US$0.40/litre). It is highly rec that drivers use diesel-powered vehicles as almost all the locals do: not only is diesel usually cheaper than gasoline, but a diesel engine will not stop in water, has no ignition/carburettor problems, and will not encounter the corrosive effects of alcohol in the fuel. Motor fuel and oil are sold by the litre. The documents needed for private cars are international car registration and driver's licence. For entry into Brazil the only document necessary is the title to the car (or other proof of ownership). Touring y Automóvil Club Paraguayo has an adequate road map but, we are told, not updated since 1985. It is essential to drive at walking pace through military areas and stop completely if a flag ceremony is in progress.

Motor repairs A rec mechanic is Lauro C Noldin, Dr Moleón Andreu 493 y 4ta Proyectada, Barrio Santa Librada, Asunción, T 333933; he repairs Land Rover, Range Rover, Jaguar and all makes of British, European, American and Japanese cars, diesel and petrol engines, motorcycles, power generators for motor homes. For diesel service, MBT service garage at Av Eusebio Ayala y Lapacho Km 4, T Asunción 553318. A rec Land Rover parts source is Repuestos Agromotor at Herrera 604, Asunción. Spares are available in Paraguay for all makes of car (European, North American, Asian); also available are most makes of tyre.

Car hire

Weekly and free-kilometre rates available. See under Asunción, **Car Rental.**

Communications

● **Newspapers**
El Diario; Hoy, La Tarde, Ultima Hora, El Diario Noticias and *El Pueblo* are published daily in Asunción. English-language papers from Argentina and Brazil are available the following day at corner of Estrella and Chile. CNN, in English, is available on Channel 8.

● **Postal services**
Postal services are efficient. A normal airmail letter to Europe costs US$0.25 and a registered air letter US$0.35. Register important mail if you want it delivered. Parcels may be sent from the main post office on El Paraguayo Independiente, Asunción. Rates to Europe by APR/SAL US$8.70 up to 1 kg, US$21.50 up to 5 kg; to USA US$6.60 and US$16.40 respectively. Airmail parcels cost US$12.30 to Europe and US$8.70 to USA for first kg. Packages under 2 kg should be handed in at the small packages window, over 2 kg at the 'Encomiendas' office in the same building. Customs inspection of open parcel required.

● **Telephone services**
The telephone service (few telephone boxes) links the main towns, and there is a telephone

service with most countries, operated by Antelco. Collect calls are difficult, charge US$0.30 extra. A phone call to Europe, Australia, and South Africa costs US$2.50 a minute; USA, Canada, US$2 a minute; Spain, US$1.50 a minute. Fax to Europe US$3/page from Asunción Post Office, more in other towns, to receive 3 pages US$1.20. A telex message to Britain is US$5 (1 minute). There is a US$2.50 tax charged by the Post Office for all telexes sent or received in Paraguay.

Sport

Football is very popular. Fishing, basketball, tennis, horse-racing and rugby football are popular. There are two rowing and swimming clubs of some 2,000 members, and a motor-boat club with 150 members, in Asunción. Swimming in the Río Paraguay is not rec: beware stinging starfish where there is mud on the islands and beaches. Golf is played in the Botanical Garden, and there is a Paraguayan Aviation Club. There are two boxing rings.

Holidays and festivals

1 Jan; 3 Feb; 1 Mar; Maundy Thursday, Good Friday; 1, 14, 15 May; Corpus Christi, 12 June; 15, 25 Aug; 29 Sept; 12 Oct; 1 Nov; 8, 25 Dec.

Further reading

Así es el Paraguay (with maps and very useful information) and *Paraguay, Land of Lace and Legend* (reprinted 1983, available from bookshops and Anglo-Paraguayan and US-Paraguay cultural institutes in Asunción); also *Green Hill, Far Away*, by Peter Upton. Books on the history of Paraguay include: *The Origins of the Paraguayan War* (2 vol) by Pelham Horton Box; *Tragedy of Paraguay* by Gilbert Phelps; *Portrait of a Dictator* by RB Cunninghame- Grahame, on López II; *Eliza Lynch, Regent of Paraguay*, by Henry Lyon-Young; *Seven Eventful Years in Paraguay* by George F Masterman, and *The Lost Paradise* by Philip Caraman, an account of the Jesuits in Paraguay 1607-1768, published in London in 1975. *Land Without Evil*, by Richard Gott (Verso 1993) is also on Jesuit history. For further reading on the origin and aftermath of the War of the Triple Alliance, see *Paraguay: un destino geopolítico*, by Dra Julia Velilla Laconich de Aréllaga; *Genocidio Americano: a Guerra do Paraguai*, by Júlio José Chiavenalto; *Woman on Horseback*, by William E Barrett. Michael Gonin highly recommends, in addition, *The British in*

Paraguay by Josefina Plá, for a complete study of this subject.

British business travellers are advised to get a copy of 'Hints to Exporters: Paraguay', obtainable from the DTI Export Publications, PO Box 55, Stratford-upon-Avon, Warwickshire, CV37 9GE.

Acknowledgements

We are most grateful to Charlie Nurse for doing the updating and to Michael Gonin for much valuable information, and the following travellers: Daniel Aeberhard (Slough, UK) an excellent contribution, Jack Beeching (Menton, France), Bernard Cloutier (Montreal, Canada), Pascal Cordier (Eaubonne, France), Mary Crow (Ft Collins, USA), Jae and Gerry Duffy (Elizabeth, USA), Geoffroy Duqué (Waterloo, Belgium), James Elder (Goulburn, Australia), Jakob Engström and Richard Björlin (Brussels, Belgium), Stefanie Floegel (Vilsbiburg, Germany), Valerie Fraser and Tim Butler (Lima, Peru) many long and informative letters, Mariecke van der Gias (Utrecht, The Netherlands), Michael Gonin (Canberra, Australia), Wolfgang Gruber (Bubensham, Germany), Mr Johnson (Asincion), A Jachnow and A Kuhn (Berlin, Germany), Patrick J Paludan (Valby) and Erik Hassenkamm (Valby and Skanderberg, Denmark), Riika Levoranta (Vammala) and Vesa Lampiner (Möjärvi, Finland), Oliver Meiser (Pfullingen, Germany) a very detailed contribution Christiane Moser (Frieburg, Germany), Helmut Moser (Zell am See, Austria), Martijn Mugge (Enschede, The Netherlands), Mark Muhlbacher (Lucerne, Switzerland) for many letters Brian Mullin (Guayaquil, Ecuador), Hans-Peter Neusch (Stuttgart, Germany), Robert S Neus (PCV Ascuncion, Paraguay), Luzia Portmann and Rolf Studer (Lucerne, Switzerland), Margorie Powell (Cambridge, UK) extensive contribution, J R Stourton (Cirencester, UK), S Nielsen and Hellmuth-Chr Stuven (Copenhagen, Denmark), Gesine Treptow (Asunción, Paraguay), Arnaud Troost and Fenna den Hartog (Rotterdam, The Netherlands), Bas van Tussenbroek (Aracati, Brazil), Eric and Ingrid Van den Broeck (Leuven, Belgium), Infanger Vinzenz (Erstfeld, Switzerland) an extensive contribution Dre Visscher (Tilburg, The Netherlands), Dr Volker Weinmann (Blumenau, Brazil), Jane Westlake (London, UK), and Jacqui White (Salta, Argentina).

PERU

INTRODUCTION

PERU, the third largest South American country (over twice the size of France), presents formidable difficulties to human habitation. The whole of its W seaboard with the Pacific is desert on which rain seldom falls. From this coastal shelf the Andes rise steeply to a high Sierra which is studded with massive groups of soaring mountains and gouged with deep canyons. The highland slopes more gradually E; the mountains in its E zone are deeply forested and ravined. Eastward from these mountains lie the vast jungle lands of the Amazon basin.

The coastal region, a narrow ribbon of desert 2,250 km long, takes up 11% of the country and holds 44% of the population. When irrigated, the river valleys are extremely fertile. Almost 600,000 ha are watered today, creating 40 oases which grow cotton throughout the country, sugar-cane and rice in the N, and grapes, fruit and olives in the S. Petroleum comes from the N and Amazonia. The coastal zone is the economic heart of Peru; it consumes most of the imports and supplies half of the exports. Climate is determined by cold sea-water adjoining deserts: prevailing inshore winds pick up so little moisture over the cold Peruvian current that only for five months, from Jun to Oct, does it condense. The resultant blanket of cloud and sea-mist extends from the S to about 200 km N of Lima. This *garúa* dampens isolated coastal zones of vegetation (called *lomas*) and they are grazed

PERU

ECUADOR

COLOMBIA

Guayaquil

To Quito

Machala

Cuenca

Tumbes

Loja
Macará

Iquitos

Rio Amazonas

Leticia

Talara

Rio Marañón

Paita
Sechura

Tsullana

Jaén

Piura

Moyobamba

Yurimaguas

BRAZIL

Chachapoyas

Celendin

Tarapoto

Rio Ucayali

Chiclayo

Cajamarca

Pacasmayo

Cruzeiro do Sul

Trujillo

Caraz

Pucallpa

Chimbote

Huaraz

Tingo María

Casma

Huánuco

Pativilca

Cerro de Pasco

La Oroya

La Merced

Satipo

Brasiléia

Chancay

Tarma

Jauja

Iñapari

Callao

Huancayo

Quillabamba

Puerto
Maldonado

LIMA

Huancavelica

Manu

Rio Madre
de Dios

Cañete

Ayácucho

Machu Picchu

Andahuaylas

Cuzco

Pisco

Abancay

Urcos

Ica

Sicuani

BOLIVIA

Nazca

Huancane

Pacific
Ocean

Chala

Juliaca

Lake
Titicaca

Arequipa

Puno

Copacabana

Matarani

Juli

LA PAZ

Mollendo

Moquegua

Ilo

Tacna

Arica

CHILE

1 Lima
2 North West from Lima
3 The Northern Oases
4 South East from Lima
5 Arequipa - Puno - Cuzco - Machu Picchu
6 The South Eastern Jungle
7 Inland from Lima
8 Cerro de Pasco to Iquitos

N

To
Santiago

by livestock driven down from the mountains. The Peruvian coastal current teems with fish, and Peru has had the largest catch in the world; however, in recent years, the *anchoveta* shoals have moved S into Chilean waters. At intervals during Dec-Apr a current of warm water, known as "El Niño", is blown S from the equator over the cold offshore waters and the surface temperature rises, the fish migrate, and evaporation is so great that the desert is deluged with rain which creates havoc (most recently in 1992). It is not possible to predict the timing or strength of "El Niño", although it seems to have a frequency of every 5-6 years; scientific study can tell each year if there will be one or not.

In the Sierra, at an average altitude of 3,000m, which covers 26% of the country, live about 50% of the people, an excessive density on such poor land. This high-level land of gentle slopes is surrounded by towering groups and ranges of high peaks. Ten are over 6,000m; the highest, Huascarán, is 6,768m. There are many volcanoes in the S. The continental divide is the W rim of mountains looking down on the Pacific. Rivers which rise in these mountains and flow towards the Amazon cut through the cold surface of the plateau in canyons, sometimes 1,500m deep, in which the climate is tropical. The Colca Canyon, in the Department of Arequipa, is the deepest in the world. Pastoral farming is possible on about 13 million hectares of the plateau; the deep valley basins contain the best land for arable farming.

The plateau, mountains and canyons are inhabited mostly by Indians. Nearly 99% of the rural population and 60% of the town dwellers have no running water or drainage. A mostly Indian labour force of over 80,000 was for many years engaged in mining, with mineral exports from the Sierra representing half of total exports. Minerals are extracted as far up as 5,200m. In the early 1990s, many mines were forced to close and the Indians have either returned to agriculture or left the highlands to seek work in Lima.

The wide areas of high and wind-swept Altiplano in southern Peru are near the limit of agriculture—though some potatoes and cereals (*quinua*, *kiwicha* and *kañiwa*) are grown—but the Indians use it for grazing llamas, alpacas and sheep; it cannot support cattle. Some sheep-farming areas are at altitudes ranging up to 4,250m. The pastoral Indians of the area live off their flocks; they weave their clothes from the wools, eat the meat, use the dried dung for fuel and the llamas for transport. They are, in short, almost entirely self-supporting.

The **Montaña**, or **Selva**, the forested eastern half of the Andes and the land beyond covered with tropical forest and jungle, is 62% of the country's area but holds only about 5% of the population. Its inhabitants are crowded on the river banks in the cultivable land—a tiny part of the area. The few roads (given in the text) have to cope with dense forest, deep valleys, and sharp eastern slopes ranging from 2,150m in the N to 5,800m E of Lake Titicaca. Rivers are the main highways, though navigation is hazardous and the draught of the vessels shallow. The area's potential is enormous: immense reserves of timber, excellent land for the production of rubber, jute, rice, tropical fruits and coffee and the breeding of cattle. Few of these products come out by road to the W; most of them converge by river on Iquitos, which is 11,250 km from Callao via the Panama Canal and the Amazon but only 1,010 km as the condor flies.

Oilfields have been discovered S from the Ecuadorean border and estimates indicate that about 80% of Peru's oil reserves are in the jungle area. The Nor

Peruano oil pipeline links the Amazon area with the coast.

Climate The climate of the highlands is varied: the W side is dry, but the N and E parts get very heavy rains from Oct to Apr, and are heavily forested up to a limit of 3,350m: the grasslands are between the forest line and the snowline, which rises from 5,000m in the latitude of Lima to 5,800m in the S. Most of the Sierra is covered with grasses and shrubs, with Puna vegetation (bunch grass mixed with low, hairy-leaved plants) from N of Huaraz to the S.

Pre-Conquest History Three major obstacles restrict our knowledge of ancient Peru. First, the very terrain of the country is a challenge to present, let alone, past inhabitants. The Andes are the most seismically active mountain range on Earth; devastating earthquakes and landslides have damaged or destroyed whole cities. The tropical lowlands have defied exploration; remains of the past may still be hidden in the undergrowth. Flashfloods unleashed by the El Niño current sweep down the N coast at intervals, driving away the fish and washing away the adobe houses and irrigation canals. Fortunately the coastal desert from Chan Chán S to Paracas has revealed an "American Egypt" for archaeologists, although this has meant a bias towards the coastal region and a reliance on the contents of tombs for information.

Secondly, the lack of the written word has deprived us of any firsthand record of the everyday lives of the earliest settlers. The Spanish chroniclers based their accounts on the Incas' own version of the past, but this was inevitably coloured with propaganda, myth and folklore. The third problem is looting, virtually a national industry, incited by demand from the international antiquities market. Gangs of *huaqueros* plunder sites too numerous to be policed or protected by archaeologists (the recent spectacular discovery of the grave of a Moche nobleman at Sipán in the N desert was only made in the wake of the looters' efforts). In spite of these handicaps, Peru has revealed one of the richest precolumbian histories in the Americas, of highly advanced societies that prevailed against awesome odds.

The Incas told the Spaniards that before they established their Tawantinsuyo Empire, the land was overrun by primitives constantly at war with one another.

There were, in fact, many other civilized cultures dating back as far as 2000 BC. The most accomplished of these were the Chavín-Sechín (c 900-200 BC), the Paracas-Nazca (c200 BC-500 AD), the Huari-Tiwanaku (c750 BC-1000 AD), and the Moche-Chimú (200 BC-1400 AD).

It is generally accepted that the earliest settlers in Peru were related to people who had crossed the Bering Straits from Asia and drifted through the Americas from about 20,000 BC. Theories of early migrations from across the Pacific and Atlantic have been rife since Thor Heyerdahl's raft expeditions in 1947 and 1969-70. More recent studies of people living in the jungle near Chachapoyas (**see p 1170**), have produced claims of Viking descendancy.

Human remains found in a cave in Lauricocha, near Huánuco, have a radiocarbon date of c7500 BC, but the earliest signs of a village settlement in Peru, were found on the central coast at Pampa, dating from 2500 BC. Between these two dates it is thought that people lived nomadically in small groups, mainly hunting and gathering but also cultivating some plants seasonally. Domestication of llamas, alpacas and guinea pigs also began at this time, particularly important for the highland people around the Titicaca basin.

The abundant wealth of marine life produced by the Humboldt Current, especially along the N coast, boosted population growth and settlement in this area. Around 2000 BC climatic change dried up the *lomas* ("fog meadows"), and drove sea shoals into deeper water. People turned more to farming and began to spread inland along river valleys.

As sophisticated water irrigation and canal systems were developed, farming productivity increased and communities had more time to devote to building and producing ceramics and textiles. The development of pottery also led to trade and cultural links with other communities. Distribution of land and water to the farmers was probably organized by a corporate authority, and this may have led to the later "Mit'at" labour system developed by the Incas.

The earliest buildings constructed by organized group labour were *huacas*, adobe platform mounds, centres of some cult or sacred power dating from the second millennium BC onwards. Huaca Florida was the largest example of this period, near the Río Rimac, later replaced by Huaca Garagay as a major centre for the area. Many similar centres spread along the N coast, most notably Aspero and Piedra Parada.

During this period, however, much more advanced architecture was being built at Kotosh, in the central Andes near Huánuco. Japanese archaeological excavations there in the 1960s revealed a temple with ornamental niches and friezes. Some of the earliest pottery was also found here, showing signs of influence from southern Ecuador and the tropical lowlands, adding weight to theories of Andean culture originating in the Amazon. Radiocarbon dates of some Kotosh remains are as early as 1850 BC.

For the next thousand years or so up to c 900 BC, communities grew and spread inland from the N coast and S along the N highlands. Farmers still lived in simple adobe or rough stone houses but built increasingly large and complex ceremonial centres, such as at Las Haldas in the Casma Valley. As farming became more productive and pottery more advanced, commerce grew and states began to develop throughout central and North-central Peru, with the associated signs of social structure and hierarchies.

Around 900 BC a new era was marked by the rise of two important centres; Chavín de Huántar in the central Andes and Sechín Alto, inland from Casma on the N coast.

The chief importance of Chavín de Huántar was not so much in its highly advanced architecture as in the influence of its cult coupled with the artistic style of its ceramics and other artefacts. The founders of Chavín may have originated in the tropical lowlands as some of its carved monoliths show representations of monkeys and felines.

Objects with Chavín traits have been found all along the coast from Piura to the Lurin valley S of Lima, and its cult ideology spread to temples around the same area. Richard L Burger of Yale University has argued that the extent of Chavín influence has been exaggerated. Many sites on the coast already had their own cult practices and the Chavín idols may have been simply added alongside. There is evidence of an El Niño flood that devastated the N coast around 500 BC. Local cults fell from grace as social order was disrupted and the Chavín cult was snatched up as a timely new alternative.

The Chavín cult was paralleled by the great advances made in this period in textile production and in some of the earliest examples of metallurgy. The origins of metallurgy have been attributed to some gold, silver and copper ornaments found in graves in Chongoyape, near Chiclayo, which show Chavín-style features. But earlier evidence has been discovered in the Andahuaylas region, dating from 1800-900 BC. The religious symbolism of gold and other precious metals and stones is thought to have been an inspiration behind some of the beautiful artefacts found in the central Andean area. The emergence of social hierarchies also created a demand for luxury goods as status symbols.

The cultural brilliance of Chavín de Huántar was complemented by its contemporary, Sechín. This huge granite-faced complex near Casma, 370 kms N of Lima, was described by JC Tello as the biggest structure of its kind in the Andes. According to Michael Moseley of Harvard University, Chavín and Sechín may have combined forces, with Sechín as the military power that spread the cultural word of Chavín, but their influence did not reach far to the S where the Paracas and

Tiwanaku cultures held sway.

The Chavín hegemony broke up around 500 BC, soon after which the Nazca culture began to bloom in southern Peru. This period, up to about 500 AD, was a time of great social and cultural development. Sizable towns of 5-10,000 inhabitants grew on the S coast, populated by artisans, merchants, government administrators and religious officials.

Nazca origins are traced back to about the 2nd century BC, to the Paracas Cavernas and Necropolis, on the coast in the national park near Pisco. The extreme dryness of the desert here has preserved remarkably the textiles and ceramics in the mummies' tombs excavated. The technical quality and stylistic variety in weaving and pottery rank them amongst the world's best, and many of the finest examples can be seen in the museums of Lima.

The famous Nazca Lines are a feature of the region. Straight lines, abstract designs and outlines of animals are scratched in the the dark desert surface forming a lighter contrast that can be seen clearly from the air. There are many theories of how and why the lines were made but no definitive explanation has yet been able to establish their place in Peruvian history. There are similarities between the style of some of the line patterns and that of the pottery and textiles of the same period. It is clear from the sheer scale of the lines and the quality of the work that, whatever their purpose, they were very important to the Nazca culture.

In contrast to the quantity and quality of the Nazca artefacts found, relatively few major buildings belonging to this period have been uncovered in the southern desert. Dos Palmas is a complex of rooms and courtyards in the Pisco Valley and Cahuachi in the Nazca Valley is a large area including adobe platforms, a pyramid and a "wooden Stonehenge" cluster of preserved tree trunks. As most of the archaeological evidence of the Nazca culture came from their desert cemeteries, little is known about the lives and social organization of the people. Alpaca hair found in Nazca textiles, however, indicates that there must have been strong trade links with highland people.

Nazca's contemporaries on the N coast were the militaristic Moche who, from about 100-800 AD built up an empire whose traces stretch from Piura in the N to Casma, beyond Chimbote, in the S. The Moche built their capital in the middle of the desert, outside present day Trujillo. The huge pyramid temples of the Huaca del Sol and Huaca de la Luna, overlook the biggest adobe city in the world. Moche roads and system of way stations are thought to have been an early inspiration for the Inca network. The Moche increased the coastal population with intensive irrigation projects. Skilful engineering works were carried out, such as the La Cumbre canal, still in use today, and the Ascope aqueduct, both on the Chicama river.

The Moche's greatest achievement, however, was its artistic genius. Exquisite ornaments in gold, silver and precious stones were made by its craftsmen. Moche pottery progressed through five stylistic periods, most notable for the stunningly lifelike portrait vases. A wide variety of everyday scenes were created in naturalistic ceramics, telling us more about Moche life than is known about other earlier cultures, and perhaps used by them as "visual aids" to compensate for the lack of a written language.

A spectacular discovery of a Moche royal tomb at Sipán was made in Feb 1987 by Walter Alva, director of the Bruning Archaeological Museum, Lambayeque. Reports of the excavation in the National Geographic magazine (Oct 1988 and Jun 1990), talk of the richest unlooted tomb in the New World. The find included semi-precious stones brought from Chile and Argentina, and seashells from Ecuador. The Moche were great navigators.

The cause of the collapse of the Moche Empire around 600-700 AD is unknown, but it may have been started by a 30-year drought at the end of the 6th century, followed by one of the periodic El Niño flash floods (identified by meteorologists from ice thickness in the Andes) and finished by the encroaching forces of the Huari Empire. The decline of the Moche signalled a general tipping of the balance of power in Peru from the N coast to the S sierra. The ascendant Huari-Tiwanaku movement, from c 600-1000 AD, combined the religious cult of the Tiwanaku site in the Titicaca basin, with the military dynamism of the Huari, based in the central highlands. The two cultures developed independently but, as had occurred with the Chavín-Sechín association, they are generally thought to have merged compatibly.

Up until their own demise around 1440 AD, the Huari-Tiwanaku had spread their empire and influence across much of S Peru, N Bolivia and Argentina. They made considerable gains in art and technology, building roads, terraces and irrigation canals across the country. The Huari-Tiwanaku ran their empire with efficient labour and administrative systems that were later adopted and refined by the Incas. Labour tribute for state projects had been practised by the Moche and was further developed now. But the empire could not contain regional kingdoms who began to fight for land and power. As control broke down, rivalry and coalitions emerged, and the system collapsed. With the country once again fragmented, the scene was set for the rise of the Incas.

The origins of the Inca dynasty are shrouded in mythology and shaky evidence. The best known story reported by the Spanish chroniclers talks about Manco Capac and his sister rising out of Lake Titicaca, created by the Sun as divine founders of a chosen race. This was in approximately AD 1200. Over the next three hundred years the small tribe grew to supremacy as leaders of the largest empire ever known in the Americas, the four territories of Tawantinsuyo, united by Cusco as the umbilicus of the Universe (the four quarters of Tawantinsuyo, all radiating out from Cusco, were 1—Chinchaysuyo, N and NW, 2—Cuntisuyo, S and W, 3—Collasuyo, S and E, 4—Antisuyo, E.

At its peak, just before the Spanish Conquest, the Inca Empire stretched from the Río Maule in central Chile, N to the present Ecuador-Colombia border, containing most of Ecuador, Peru, W Bolivia, N Chile and NW Argentina. The area was roughly equivalent to France, Belgium, Holland, Luxembourg, Italy and Switzerland combined, 980,000 sq km. For a brief description of **Inca Society**, see under Cusco.

The first Inca ruler, Manco Capac, moved to the fertile Cusco region, and established Cusco as his capital. Successive generations of rulers were fully occupied with local conquests of rivals, such as the Colla and Lupaca to the S, and the Chanca to the NW. At the end of Inca Viracocha's reign the hated Chanca were finally defeated, largely thanks to the heroism of one of his sons, Pachacuti Inca Yupanqui, who was subsequently crowned as the new ruler.

From the start of Pachacuti's own reign in 1438, imperial expansion grew in earnest. With the help of his son and heir, Topa Inca, territory was conquered from the Titicaca basin S into Chile, and all the N and central coast down to the Lurin Valley. The Incas also subjugated the Chimú, a highly sophisticated rival empire who had re-occupied the abandoned Moche capital at Chan Chán. Typical of the Inca method of government, some of the Chimú skills were assimilated into their own political and administrative system, and some Chimú nobles were even given positions in Cusco.

Perhaps the pivotal event in Inca history came in 1532 with the death of the ruler, Huayna Capac. Civil war broke out in the confusion over his rightful successor. One of his legitimate sons, Huascar, ruled the southern part of the empire from Cusco. Atahuallpa, Huascar's half-brother, governed Quito, the capital of Chinchaysuyo. In the midst of the ensuing battle Francisco Pizarro arrived in Tumbes with 179 men. When Atahuallpa got wind of their presence there was some belief that Pizarro and his *conquistadores* on horseback were Viracocha and his demi-gods predicted in Inca legend. In need of allies against Huascar, Atahuallpa agreed to meet the Spaniards at Cajamarca.

Conquest and after Francisco Pizarro's only chance against the formidable imperial army he encountered at Cajamarca was a bold stroke. He drew Atahuallpa into an ambush, slaughtered his guards, promised him liberty if a certain room were filled with treasure, and finally killed him after receiving news that another Inca army was on its way to free him. Pushing on to Cusco, he was at first hailed as the executioner of a traitor: Atahuallpa had killed Huascar after the battle of Huancavelica two years previously. Panic followed when the *conquistadores* set about sacking the city, and they fought off with difficulty an attempt by Manco Inca to recapture Cusco in 1538. (For the whole period of the Conquest John Hemming's *The Conquest of the Incas* is invaluable; he himself refers us to Ann Kendall's *Everyday Life of the Incas*, Batsford, London, 1978. Also *Oro y tragedia* by Manuel Portal Cabellos, excellent on division of the empire, civil war, the conquest and *huaqueros*.)

Peruvian history after the arrival of the Spaniards was not just a matter of *conquistadores* versus Incas. The vast majority of the huge empire remained unaware of the conquest for many years. The Chimú and the Chachapoyas cultures were powerful enemies of the Incas. The Chimú developed a highly sophisticated culture and a powerful empire stretching for 560 km along the coast from Paramonga S to Casma. Their history was well-recorded by the Spanish chroniclers and continued through the Conquest possibly up to about 1600. The Kuelap/Chachapoyas people were not so much an empire as a loose-knit "confederation of ethnic groups with no recognized capital" (Morgan Davis "Chachapoyas: The Cloud People", Ontario, 1988). But the culture did develop into an advanced society with great skill in roads and monument building. Their fortress at Kuelap was known as the most impregnable in Tawantinsuyo. It remained intact against Inca attack and Manco Inca even tried, unsuccessfully, to gain refuge here against the Spaniards.

In 1535, wishing to secure his communications with Spain, Pizarro founded Lima, near the ocean, as his capital. The same year Diego de Almagro set out to conquer Chile. Unsuccessful, he returned to Peru, quarrelled with Pizarro, and in 1538 fought a pitched battle with Pizarro's men at the Salt Pits, near Cusco. He was defeated and put to death. Pizarro, who had not been at the battle, was assassinated in his palace in Lima by Almagro's son three years later. For the next 27 years each succeeding representative of the Kingdom of Spain sought to subdue the Inca successor state of Vilcabamba, N of Cusco, and to unify the fierce Spanish factions. Francisco de Toledo (appointed 1568) solved both problems during his 14 years in office: Vilcabamba was crushed in 1572 and the last reigning Inca, Túpac Amaru, put to death. For the next 200 years the Viceroys closely followed Toledo's system, if not his methods. The Major Government—the Viceroy, the *Audiencia* (High Court), and *corregidores* (administrators)—ruled through the Minor Government—Indian chiefs put in charge of large groups of natives: a rough approximation to the original Inca system.

The Indians rose in 1780, under the leadership of an Inca noble who called himself Túpac Amaru II. He and many of his lieutenants were captured and put to death under torture at Cusco. Another Indian leader in revolt suffered the same fate in 1814, but this last flare-up had the sympathy of many of the locally-born Spanish, who resented their status, inferior to the Spaniards born in Spain, the refusal to give them any but the lowest offices, the high taxation imposed by the home government, and the severe restrictions upon trade with any country but Spain. Help came to them from the outside world: José de San Martín's Argentine troops, convoyed from Chile under the protection of Lord Cochrane's squadron, landed in southern Peru on 7 September 1820. San Martín proclaimed Peruvian independence at Lima on 28 July 1821, though most of the country was still in the hands of the Viceroy, José de La Serna. Bolívar, who had already freed Venezuela and Colombia, sent Antonio José de Sucre to Ecuador where, on 24 May 1822, he gained a victory over La Serna at Pichincha. San Martín, after a meeting with Bolívar at Guayaquil, left for Argentina and a self-imposed exile in France, while Bolívar and Sucre completed the conquest of Peru by defeating La Serna at the battle of Junín (6 August 1824) and the decisive battle of Ayacucho (9 December 1824). For over a year there was a last stand in the Real Felipe fortress at Callao by the Spanish troops under General Rodil before they capitulated on 22 January 1826. Bolívar was invited to stay in Peru, but left for Colombia in 1826.

Important subsequent events were a temporary confederation between Peru and Bolivia in the 1830s; the Peruvian-Spanish War (1866); and the War of the Pacific (1879-1883), in which Peru and Bolivia were defeated by Chile and Peru lost its southern territory. A long-standing legacy of this was the Tacna-Arica dispute, which was not settled until 1929 (see under Tacna).

A reformist military Junta took over control of the country in Oct 1968. Under its first leader, Gen Juan Velasco Alvarado, the Junta instituted a series of measures to raise the personal status and standard of living of the workers and the rural Indians, by land reform, worker participation in industrial management and ownership, and nationalization of basic industries, exhibiting an ideology perhaps best described as "military socialism". In view of his failing health Gen Velasco was replaced in 1975 by Gen Francisco Morales Bermúdez and policy (because of a mounting economic crisis and the consequent need to seek financial aid from abroad) swung to the Right. Presidential and congressional elections were held on 18 May 1980, and Fernando Belaúnde Terry was elected President for the second time. His term was marked by growing economic problems and the growth of the Maoist guerrilla movement Sendero Luminoso (Shining Path). Initially conceived in the University of Ayacucho, the movement now gets most of its support from highland Indians and migrants to urban shanty towns. Its main target is Lima-based authority and its aim is the overthrow of the whole system of government. The activities of Sendero Luminoso and another guerrilla group, Túpac Amaru (MRTA), frequently disrupted transport and electricity supplies, although their strategies had to be reconsidered after the arrest of both their leaders in 1992. Víctor Polay of MRTA was arrested in June of that year and the movement subsequently ceased operations almost completely. Abimael Guzmán of Sendero Luminoso was captured in Sept 1992 and was sentenced to life imprisonment. Although Sendero did not capitulate, many of its members in 1994-5 took advantage of the Law of Repentance, which guaranteed lighter sentences in return for surrender, and freedom in exchange for valuable information. The military meanwhile, continued to arrest guerrilla leaders and contend with the greatly reduced number of armed confrontations in rural areas.

The April 1985 elections were won by the APRA party leader Alán García Pérez. During his populist, left-wing presidency disastrous economic policies caused increasing poverty and civil instability. In presidential elections held over two rounds in 1990, Alberto Fujimori of the Cambio 90 movement defeated the novelist Mario Vargas Llosa, who belonged to the Fredemo (Democratic Front) coalition. Fujimori, without an established political network behind him, failed to win a majority in either the senate or the lower house. Lack of congressional support was one of the reasons behind the dissolution of congress and the suspension of the constitution on 5 April 1992. President Fujimori declared that he needed a freer hand to introduce free-market reforms and combat terrorism and drug trafficking, at the same time as rooting out corruption. Initial massive popular support, although not matched internationally, did not evaporate. In elections to a new,

80-member Democratic Constituent Congress (CCD) in Nov 1992, Fujimori's Cambio 90/Nueva Mayoría coalition won a majority of seats. Earlier that month a coup designed to remove Fujimori by retired military officers was foiled. Three major political parties, APRA, Acción Popular and the Movimiento de Libertad, boycotted the elections to CCD. In municipal elections held in Feb 1993 the trend against mainstream political groups continued as independent candidates won the lion's share of council seats. The elections to the CCD satisfied many aid donor's requirements for the resumption of financial assistance. A new constitution drawn up by the CCD was approved by a narrow majority of the electorate in Oct 1993. Among the new articles were the immediate re-election of the president (previously prohibited for one presidential term), the death penalty for terrorist leaders, the establishment of a single-chamber congress, the reduction of the role of the state, the designation of Peru as a market economy and the favouring of foreign investment. As expected, Fujimori stood for re-election on 9 April 1995 and the opposition chose as an independent to stand against him former UN General Secretary, Javier Pérez de Cuéllar. Fujimori was reelected by a resounding margin, winning about 65% of the votes cast. The coalition that supported him also won a majority in Congress.

The People The indigenous population of Peru is put at about 3 million Quechua and Aymara Indians in the Andean region and 200,000-250,000 Amazonian Indians from 40-50 ethnic groups. In the Andes, there are 5,000 Indian communities but few densely populated settlements. Their literacy rate is the lowest of any comparable group in South America and their diet is 50% below acceptable levels. About two million Indians speak no Spanish, their main tongue being Quechua, the language of the Incas; they are largely outside the money economy. The conflict between Sendero Luminoso guerrillas and the security forces has caused the death of thousands of highland Indians. Many Indian groups are under threat from colonization, development and road-building projects. Some have been dispossessed and exploited for their labour.

The Economy Revitalization of agriculture, which accounts for 13% of gdp, is a government priority, particularly in the Sierra to restore the self-sufficiency in food production of Inca times. The Costa (which occupies 11% of the land area) has traditionally been the dominant economic region, with excellent crops of cotton, rice, sugar and fruit where the coastal desert is irrigated. Coffee is the main export crop. However, cultivation of coca has been the leading cash crop unofficially for several years and the Government is seeking ways of encouraging crop substitution.

Mining's contribution to gdp was restored to more than 10%, after having suffered a decline to just over 2% by 1991. Five major minerals and metals (copper, silver, gold, lead and zinc) account for about 45% of total export value. Copper and iron deposits are found on the S coast, but the principal mining area for all minerals is the Sierra. Variable world prices, strikes, rising costs and an uncompetitive exchange rate in the late 1980s contributed to considerable losses for mining companies, and to reduced real output. The Fujimori Government policy of reviving private small scale mining and reincorporate the industry's 40% idle capacity, was supported by a 1992 mining law, which aims to attract private investment, both domestic and foreign. By 1994 foreign interest in Peruvian mining was significant, but the government's first attempt to sell off Centromin, the state mining corporation, failed to attract any bids.

Peruvian oil production fell from 195,000 b/d peak in 1982 to 115,000 b/d in 1991, recovering to 130,000 b/d in early 1994; most of it comes from the NE jungle, although some is produced on and off the NW coast. No major new reserves have been found since 1976 and proven oil reserves were down to 360 million barrels at end-1993 from 835 million in 1981. In 1991 the oil trade was in deficit by about US$150mn as imports were needed to satisfy the domestic market (the deficit in the first quarter of 1994 was US$18mn). Local funds for investment fell

Peru : fact file

Geographic

Land area	1,285,216 sq km
forested	53.1%
pastures	21.2%
cultivated	2.9%

Demographic

Population (1994)	23,383,000
annual growth rate (1989-94)	2.1%
urban	71.8%
rural	28.2%
density	18.2 per sq km
Religious affiliation	
Roman Catholic	92.5%
Birth rate per 1,000 (1990-95)	29.0
(world av 26.0)	

Education and Health

Life expectancy at birth,	
male	62.7 years
female	66.6 years
Infant mortality rate	
per 1,000 live births (1990-95)	75.8
Physicians (1989)	1 per 997 persons
Hospital beds	1 per 625 persons
Calorie intake as %	
of FAO requirement	87%
Population age 25 and over	
with no formal schooling	20.1%
Literate males (over 15)	95.9%
Literate females (over 15)	82.6%

Economic

GNP (1993)	US$33,973mn
GNP per capita	US$1,490
Public external debt (1992)	
	US$15,417mn
Tourism receipts (1992)	US$237mn
Inflation (annual av 1989-93)	709.9%
Radio	1 per 5.2 persons
Television	1 per 11 persons
Telephone	1 per 28 persons

Employment

Population economically active (1992)	
	8,064,000
Unemployment rate (1992)	8.3%
% of labour force in	
agriculture	33.0
mining	2.4
manufacturing	10.4
construction	3.7
Military forces	115,000

Source *Encyclopaedia Britannica*

in the 1980s, hence the need for foreign companies to invest in exploration, but in 1985 the García Government rescinded the operating contracts of three major foreign firms, adversely affecting investment prospects, despite subsequent new agreements. The Fujimori Government's policy of encouraging foreign investment aims at developing the vast Camisea gas and condensates field in the SE jungle, where reserves are estimated at 11 trillion cubic feet of natural gas and 500 million barrels of condensates. Since the passing of new oil legislation in Aug 1993, several contracts with private oil companies have been signed, with others for exploration and development in prospect. Privatization of the state company, Petroperú, is also envisaged, with the company being sold as 11 separate operating units.

Manufacturing contributes 21.5% of gdp. After high growth rates in the early 1970s, industry slumped to operating at 40% of its total capacity as purchasing power was reduced, and the cost of energy, raw materials and trade credit rose faster than inflation. A consumer-led recovery in 1986 led to most of manufacturing and the construction industry working at full capacity, but the boom was followed by a severe slump in 1988-1990. A return to growth has been evident since 1992 as a real increase in salaries has stimulated consumption.

Fishing suffered a dramatic decline in 1983 as the Niño current forced out of Peruvian waters the main catch, anchovy, whose stocks were already seriously depleted by overfishing in the 1970s. After temporarily losing its position as the world's leading fishmeal exporter to Chile, Peru regained its historical predominance in 1990 because of rising demand for special quality fishmeal, improving technology and modernization helped by the abolition of the State monopoly which encouraged private investment. Despite the adverse effects of the 1991 cholera outbreak and the 1991-92 reappearance of the Niño current, fish catches continued to rise (8.4mn tonnes in 1993) and fishmeal exports took second place after copper as a leading earner of foreign exchange. While the government plans to privatize the state fishing industry, there is a need to seek new catches as an alternative to anchovy, which again runs the risk of overfishing.

Growing fiscal deficits in the 1980s led to increasing delays in payments of principal and interest on the foreign debt. As arrears accumulated to both multilateral agencies and commercial banks, the IMF declared Peru ineligible for further credits in 1986. On taking office, President García limited public debt service payments to 10% of foreign exchange earnings in order to maintain reserves to promote development. The need to import food, the low level of exports and the fall in disbursements of foreign capital in fact caused international reserves to fall. By 1987 the country was bankrupt after the free spending policies at the beginning of the administration and inflation soared as the Government resorted to printing money.

President Fujimori inherited an economy devastated by financial mismanagement and isolationist policies, with Peruvians suffering critical poverty, high infant mortality, malnutrition and appalling housing conditions. His Government had to deal with inflation, terrorism and drug trafficking, compounded in 1991 by a cholera epidemic which affected hundreds of thousands of people, cut food exports and sharply curtailed tourism revenues. An economic austerity package introduced in Aug 1990, raising fuel prices by 3,000% and staple foodstuffs by 500%, was the first stage of sweeping economic reform. Monetary and fiscal control was accompanied by liberalization of the financial system, foreign investment rules, capital controls and foreign trade; the tax code, ports and customs and labour laws were reformed and monopolies eliminated. Privatization of State companies was begun. Successful negotiations with creditors reinstated Peru in the international financial community, although arrears in payments to the IMF, the IDB and the World Bank had to be cleared before new loans could be made. The stock exchange registered a substantial increase in trading as investors welcomed Peru back into the fold, but the *auto-golpe* of Apr 1992 rocked confidence as international aid was suspended. Foreign financial assistance was restored after the Nov 1992 elections, although US lending to Peru remained dependent upon the US being satisfied on human rights issues. Arrears to the IMF and World Bank were repaid in Mar 1993 and the Paris Club of donor governments rescheduled US$3.1 bn of debt due in 1993-94. All these developments gave new impetus to the stock exchange, largely from foreign investors, and ensured the future of President Fujimori's radical economic reform programme. By 1994, emphasis was being put on the control of inflation, with tight control of the money supply. In 1994 inflation had been cut to 15.4%, compared with 39.5% in 1993. Exports grew in 1994 as high international prices and favourable climatic conditions boosted sales, offsetting the negative effects of a floating exchange rate. The new economic and political stability also encouraged foreign tourists to return. At the same time, imports continued to increase as the economy maintained strong growth (12% in 1994).

Government Under a new constitution (approved by plebiscite in Oct 1993), a single chamber, 80-seat congress replaced the previous, two-house legislature. Men and women over 18 are eligible to vote; registration and voting is compulsory until the age of 60. Those who do not vote are fined. The President, to whom is entrusted the Executive Power, is elected for five years and may, under the constitution which came into force on 1 January 1994, be re-elected for a second term. In 1987 Congress approved a change in the administration of the country, proposing a system of 13 Regions to replace the 24 Departments (divided into 150 Provinces, subdivided into 1,321 Districts). The proposal remained nothing more than that until 1990, when it was renewed. It has still not been implemented, except for the Inca region, which includes the Departments of Cusco, Apurímac and Madre de Dios.

Education is free and compulsory for both sexes between 6 and 14. There are public and private secondary schools and private elementary schools. There are 32 State and private universities, and two Catholic universities. A new educational system is being implemented as too many children cannot complete secondary school.

Communications Several roads and two railways run up the slopes of the Andes to reach the Sierra. These railways, once British owned, run from Lima in the centre and the ports of Matarani and Mollendo in the S. From Lima a railway runs to La Oroya, at which point it splits, one section going to Cerro de Pasco and the other to Huancavelica, via Huancayo. Passengers are carried on the railway from Arequipa to Juliaca; here again the line splits, to Cusco and to Puno. A separate part links Cusco with Quillabamba via Machu Picchu. There are in all 3,472 km of railway. There are three main paved roads: the Pan-American Highway runs N-S through the coastal desert; it is in fair condition. Annual improvement work make parts of it a mess for months. Pot holes are a constant problem. A spur runs NE into the Sierra to Arequipa, with a partially paved continuation to Puno on Lake Titicaca which then skirts the lake to Desaguadero, on the Bolivian frontier, a total of 3,418 km. The road to Arequipa is much improved (1995); that to Puno is not good. Similarly poor is the stretch Puno-Cusco. These routes are more usually travelled by train. The Central Highway from Lima to Huancayo is mostly well-paved; it continues (mostly paved) to Pucallpa in the Amazon basin. Also paved and well-maintained is the direct road from Lima N to Huaraz. All other roads in the mountains are of dirt, some good, some very bad. Each year they are affected by heavy rain and mud slides, especially those on the E slopes of the mountains. Repairs are limited to a minimum because of a shortage of funds. Note that some of these roads can be dangerous or impassable in the rainy season. Check beforehand with locals (not with bus companies, who only want to sell tickets) as accidents are common at these times. Total road length in 1992 was 69,942 km. Roads and railways are given in the text and shown on sketch maps.

Music and Dance Peru is the Andean heartland. Its musicians, together with those of Bolivia, have appeared on the streets of cities all over Europe and North America. However, the costumes they wear, the instruments they play, notably the *quena* and *charango*, are not typical of Peru as a whole, only of the Cusco region. Peruvian music divides at a very basic level into that of the highlands ("Andina") and that of the coast ("Criolla").

The highlands are immensely rich in terms of music and dance, with over 200 dances recorded. Every village has its fiestas and every fiesta has its communal and religious dances. Those of Paucartambo and Coylloriti (Q'olloriti) in the Cusco region moreover attract innumerable groups of dancers from far and wide. The highlands themselves can be very roughly subdivided into some half dozen major musical regions, of which perhaps the most characteristic are Ancash and the N, the Mantaro Valley, Cusco, Puno and the Altiplano, Ayacucho and Parinacochas. There is one recreational dance and musical genre, the Huayno, that is found throughout the whole of the Sierra, and has become ever more popular and commercialized to the point where it is in danger of swamping and indeed replacing the other more regional dances. Nevertheless, still very popular among Indians and/or Mestizos are the Marinera, Carnaval, Pasacalle, Chuscada (from Ancash), Huaylas, Santiago and Chonguinada (all from the Mantaro) and Huayllacha (from Parinacochas). For singing only are the mestizo Muliza, popular in the Central Region, and the soulful lament of the Yaravi, originally Indian, but taken up and developed early in the 19th century by the poet and hero of independence Mariano Melgar, from Arequipa. The Peruvian Altiplano shares a common musical culture with that of Bolivia and dances such as the Auqui-Auqui and Sicuris, or Diabladas, can be found on either side of the border. The highland instrumentation varies from region to region, although the harp and violin are ubiquitous. In the Mantaro area the harp is backed by brass and wind instruments, notably the clarinet, in Cusco it is the *charango* and *quena* and on the Altiplano the *sicu* panpipes. Two of the most spectacular dances to be seen are the Baile de las Tijeras ("scissor dance") from the Ayacucho/Huancavelica area, for men only and the pounding, stamping Huaylas for both sexes. Huaylas competitions are held annually in Lima and should not be missed. Indeed, owing to the overwhelming migration of peasants into the barrios of Lima, most types of Andean music and dance can be seen in the capital, notably on Sun at the so-called "Coliseos", which exist for that purpose. Were a Hall of Fame to be established, it would have to include the Ancashino singers La Pastorcita Huaracina and El Jilguero del

Huascarán, the *charango* player Jaime Guardia, the guitar virtuoso Raul García from Ayacucho and the Lira Paucina trio from Parinacochas. However, what the young urban immigrant from the Sierra is now listening to and, above all, dancing to is "Chicha", a hybrid of Huayno music and the Colombian Cumbia rhythm, played by such groups as Los Shapis.

The "Música Criolla" from the coast could not be more different from that of the Sierra. Here the roots are Spanish and African. The immensely popular Valsesito is a syncopated waltz that would certainly be looked at askance in Vienna and the Polca has also suffered an attractive sea change, but reigning over all is the Marinera, Peru's national dance, a splendidly rhythmic and graceful courting encounter and a close cousin of Chile's and Bolivia's Cueca and the Argentine Zamba, all of them descended from the Zamacueca. The Marinera has its "Limeña" and "Norteña" versions and a more syncopated relative, the Tondero, found in the N coastal regions, is said to have been influenced by slaves brought from Madagascar. All these dances are accompanied by guitars and frequently the *cajón*, a resonant wooden box on which the player sits, pounding it with his hands. Some of the great names of "Música Criolla" are the singer/composers Chabuca Granda and Alicia Maguiña, the female singer Jesús Vásquez and the groups Los Morochucos and Hermanos Zañartu.

Also on the coast is to be found the music of the small black community, the "Música Negroide" or "Afro-Peruano", which had virtually died out when it was resuscitated in the '50s, but has since gone from strength to strength. It has all the qualities to be found in black music from the Caribbean—a powerful, charismatic beat, rhythmic and lively dancing, and strong percussion provided by the *cajón* and the *quijada de burro*, a donkey's jaw with the teeth loosened. Some of the classic dances in the black repertoire are the Festejo, Son del Diablo, Toro Mata, Landó and Alcatraz. In the last named one of the partners dances behind the other with a candle, trying to set light to a piece of paper tucked into the rear of the other partner's waist. Nicomedes and Victoria Santa Cruz have been largely responsible for popularizing this black music and Peru Negro is another excellent professional group.

Finally, in the Peruvian Amazon region around Iquitos, local variants of the Huayno and Marinera are danced together with the Changanacui, to the accompaniment of flute and drum.

LIMA (1)

Under the fog which lasts 8 months of the year, Lima's shady colonial suburbs are fringed by the *pueblos jóvenes* which sprawl over the dusty hills overlooking the flat city. It has a great many historic monuments and its food, drink and nightlife are the best in the country. Although not the most relaxing of South America's capitals, it is a good place to start before exploring the rest of the country.

Lima, capital of Peru, was the chief city of Spanish South America from its founding in 1535 until the independence of the South American republics in the early 19th century. It is built on both sides of the Río Rímac, lying at the foot of the Cerro San Cristóbal. From among the traditional buildings which still survive soar many tall skyscrapers which have changed the old skyline out of recognition. The city, which is now very dirty and seriously affected by smog for much of the year, is surrounded by "Pueblos Jóvenes," or shanty settlements of squatters who have migrated from the Sierra; much self-help building is in progress. (Villa El Salvador, a few miles SE of Lima, may be the world's biggest "squatters' camp" with 350,000 people building up an award-winning self-governing community since 1971. They pay no

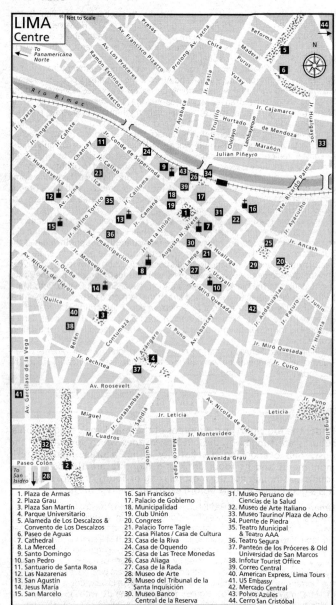

LIMA
Centre

Not to Scale

To Panamericana Norte

Rio Rimac

1. Plaza de Armas
2. Plaza Grau
3. Plaza San Martín
4. Parque Universitario
5. Alameda de Los Descalzos & Convento de Los Descalzos
6. Paseo de Aguas
7. Cathedral
8. La Merced
9. Santo Domingo
10. San Pedro
11. Santuario de Santa Rosa
12. Las Nazarenas
13. San Agustín
14. Jesus María
15. San Marcelo
16. San Francisco
17. Palacio de Gobierno
18. Municipalidad
19. Club Unión
20. Congress
21. Palacio Torre Tagle
22. Casa Pilatos / Casa de Cultura
23. Casa de la Riva
24. Casa de Oquendo
25. Casa de Las Trece Monedas
26. Casa Aliaga
27. Casa de la Rada
28. Museo de Arte
29. Museo del Tribunal de la Santa Inquisición
30. Museo Banco Central de la Reserva
31. Museo Peruano de Ciencias de la Salud
32. Museo de Arte Italiano
33. Museo Taurino/ Plaza de Acho
34. Puente de Piedra
35. Teatro Municipal & Teatro AAA
36. Teatro Segura
37. Panteón de los Próceres & Old Universidad de San Marcos
38. Infotur Tourist Office
39. Correo Central
40. American Express, Lima Tours
41. US Embassy
42. Mercado Central
43. Polvos Azules
44. Cerro San Cristóbal

taxes to the government but when a school is built the government will pay for the roof.) Many of the hotels and larger business houses have moved to the plush seaside suburbs of Miraflores and San Isidro.

Half of the town-dwellers of Peru now live in Lima. The metropolitan area contains eight million people, nearly one third of the country's total population, and two-thirds of its industries.

In the older part the way the streets are named may confuse the visitor. Several blocks, with their own names, make up a long street, a *jirón* (often abbreviated to Jr). The visitor is greatly helped by the corner signs which bear both the name of the *jirón* and the name of the block. The new and old names of streets are used interchangeably: remember that Colmena is also Nicolás de Piérola, Wilson is Inca Garcilaso de la Vega, and Carabaya is also Augusto N Wiese. The city's urban motorway is often called "El Zanjón" (the ditch) or Via Expreso.

Only 12° S of the equator, one would expect a tropical climate, but Lima has two distinct seasons. The winter is from May to Nov, when a damp *garúa* (Scotch mist) hangs over the city, making everything look greyer than it is already. It is damp and cold, 8° to 15° C. The sun breaks through around Nov and temperatures rise as high as 30° C. This is beach weather for all Limeños; every weekend all the spots on the ocean are full. Note that there is a difference in temperature between the coastal suburbs and the centre because of the sea's influence. Also take care to protect against the sun's rays when visiting the beaches around Lima, or elsewhere in Peru.

History The Universidad de San Marcos was founded in 1551, and a printing press in 1595: among the earliest of their kind in South America. Lima's first theatre opened in 1563. The Inquisition was introduced in 1569 and was not abolished until 1820. For some time the Viceroyalty of Peru embraced Colombia, Ecuador, Bolivia, Chile and Argentina. The city's wealth attracted many freebooters and in 1670 a protecting wall 11 km long, which was demolished in 1869, was built round it. Lima's power was at its height during the 17th century and the early 18th, until the earthquake of 1746 destroyed all but 20 houses and killed 4,000 inhabitants. There were few cities in the Old World that could rival its wealth and luxury. It was only comparatively recently, with the coming of industry, that Lima began to change into what it is today.

Sightseeing The heart of the city, at least in plan, is still what it was in colonial days. Even though many of the buildings are run down, there being no money to restore them, it is still worth visiting the colonial centre to see the fine architecture and works of art. A single block S of the Río Rímac lies the Plaza de Armas; the Desamparados Station of the Central Railway is quite near. Most of what the tourist wants to see is in this area, which has been declared a World Heritage by Unesco. The newer parts of the city are based on Plaza San Martín, S of Jirón de la Unión, with a statue of San Martín in the centre. One and a quarter km W is the Plaza Dos de Mayo. About 1 km due S of this again is the circular Plaza Bolognesi, from which many great *avenidas* radiate.

The Jirón de La Unión, the main shopping street, runs to the Plaza de Armas; it has been converted into a pedestrian precinct (street theatre, street vendors, etc, in the evening). Later the pedestrian area will be extended to cover the S half of Jirón de la Unión, from Plaza San Martín to Plaza Grau. In the two N blocks of Jr Unión, known as Calle Belén, several shops sell souvenirs and curios: the nearer the shops are to the best hotels the dearer the souvenirs are. Around the great Plaza de Armas stand the Palacio de Gobierno, the Cathedral (**see p 1112**), the Archbishop's Palace, the Municipalidad and the Club Unión. The Correo Central (Post Office) is opposite the visitors' entrance to Government Palace. Running along two sides are arcades with shops: Portal de Escribanos and Portal de Botoneros. In the centre is a bronze fountain dating from 1650. As a result of migration to the capital and the shortage of work, street vendors abound in the city. Many shops have closed because of high taxes.

The **Palacio de Gobierno** (Government Palace) was built from 1921 to 1938, the site of and with some of the characteristics of Pizarro's palace. Visitors' entrance is on Jirón de la Unión. Guided tours at 1230, but you must present your documentation on the previous day (Mon-Thur only). The ceremonial changing of the guard behind the gates of the palace is worth watching, most days 0800 and 1200 (check with Infotur, T 431-0117).

The Puente de Piedra, behind the Palacio de Gobierno is a Roman-style stone bridge built 1610. The **Municipalidad de Lima** (1945), has a picture gallery (0800-1500 Mon-Fri, free).

Near San Pedro, at Jirón Ucayali 363, is the **Palacio Torre Tagle**, the city's best surviving specimen of secular colonial architecture: a Sevillian mansion built in 1735. Now occupied by the Foreign Ministry, but visitors are allowed to enter courtyards to inspect fine wood-carving in balconies, wrought iron work, and a 16th-century coach complete with commode. During working hours Mon-Fri, visitors may enter the patio only.

Other historic mansions worth visiting are the **Casa Pilatos**, opposite the San Francisco church, Jirón Ancash 390, now the Instituto Nacional de Cultura, open 0830-1645, Mon-Fri (best to visit out of office hours); **Casa de la Riva**, Jirón Ica 426, T 428-2643, open 1000-1300, 1400-1600, run by the Entre Nous Society; **Casa de Oquendo**, Conde de Superunda 298, which stages art exhibitions, open 0900-1300; **Casa Negreiros** (a restaurant), Jirón Azángaro 532; **Casa de las Trece Monedas** (also a restaurant), Jirón Ancash 536. The **Casa Aliaga**, Unión 224, is still occupied by the Aliaga family and has been opened to the public; Lima Tours has exclusive rights to include the house in its tours (T 427-6624, or any travel agent). The house contains what is said to be the oldest ceiling in Lima and is furnished entirely in the colonial style. Don Jerónimo de Aliaga was one of the 13 commanders to arrive with Francisco Pizarro, and all 13 were given land around the main square to build their own houses when Lima was founded in 1535. The house of the author Ricardo Palma is open to the public, Mon-Fri 0930-1230, 1330-1800, small entrance fee, Gral Suárez 189, Miraflores, T 445-5836, a 19th-century middle-class residence.

Other mansions worth seeing: **Casa Barbieri**, Jr Callao, near Jr Rufino Torrico—a fine old 18th-century town house in the Sevillian style; ring bell in entrance hall for permission to look at the patios. **Casa Museo Prado**, Jr Cusco 448, visitable when Sr Prado is in residence, a beautifully maintained house with early 19th-century front and, apparently, a 17th-century patio. **Casa de Riva Agüero**, Jr Camaná 457, 1st floor has the library and archives of the Universidad Católica; 2nd floor has a small folk art museum; a special appointment is needed to visit the rest of the house. **AAA Theatre** (Amateur Artists' Association), Jr Ica 323, is in a lovely 18th-century house. **Casa de la Rada**, Jr Ucayali 358, opposite Palacio Torre Tagle—an extremely fine mid-18th-century town house in the French manner; patio and first reception room open occasionally to the public (now belongs to a bank).

Churches

The **Cathedral** (open to visitors Mon-Fri 1000-1300, 1400-1700, Sat 1000-1530) is on the Plaza de Armas. See the splendidly carved stalls (mid-17th century); the silver-covered altars surrounded by fine woodwork; mosaic-covered walls bearing the coats of arms of Lima and Pizarro and an allegory of Pizarro's commanders, the "Thirteen Men of Isla del Gallo"; in a small chapel, the first on the right of the entrance, are remains in a glass coffin originally said to be those of Pizarro, but later research indicates that his remains lie in the crypt. Museo de Arte Religioso in the cathedral, guided visits (English available), ask to see the picture restoration room, all-inclusive entrance ticket, US$1.50 including guide. The Archbishop's Palace was rebuilt in 1924, with a superb wooden balcony.

Four notable churches are quite near the Plaza de Armas: **La Merced** (open 0700-1230, 1600-2000 every day) and its monastery (open 0800-1200 and 1500-1730 daily) are in Plazuela de la Merced, Jirón de la Unión, two blocks from the Plaza de Armas. The first mass in Lima was said on this site. Very fine restored colonial façade, and attractive cloister. See the choir stalls and the vestry's panelled ceiling. At independence the Virgin of La Merced was made a Marshal of the Peruvian army. **Santo Domingo**, built 1549, is in Jirón Camaná (first block). In an urn in one of the altars are the remains of Santa Rosa de Lima (1586-1617), the first saint of the New World: 30 Aug is her day. Pope Clement presented, 1669, the alabaster statue of the Saint in front of the altar (entrance, US2.75, students US$1.25, open 0700-1300, 1600-2000 daily; monastery and tombs open 0930-1230, 1530-1730 Mon-Sat; Sun and holidays am only). The main hall has some interesting relics. **San Francisco**, open 0930-1745, in first block of Jirón Lampa, corner of Ancash, is a baroque church with Arabic influences, finished 1674. See carved "Sillería Coral" (1622), gold monstrance set with jewels made in Cusco (1671), and José de Rivera's paintings (1672). The monastery is famous for Sevillian tilework and panelled ceilings in the cloisters (1620). Catacombs under church and part of monastery, well worth seeing; entry US$2, US$0.70 students, US$0.50 children, by guided tour only, Spanish and English (rec), last groups start at 1245 and 1745 daily. **San Pedro** (0700-1300, 1740-2030 every day), 3rd block of Jirón Ucayali, finished by Jesuits in 1638, has marvellous altars with Moorish-style balconies, rich gilded wood carving in choir and vestry, and tiled throughout. Several Viceroys buried here; the bell called La Abuelita, first rung in 1590, sounded the Declaration of Independence in 1821.

Santuario de Santa Rosa (Av Tacna, 1st block), small but graceful church. A pilgrimage centre;

here are preserved the hermitage built by Santa Rosa herself, the house in which she was born, a section of the house in which she attended to the sick, her well, and other relics. Open 0930-1300, 1500-1800 daily; entrance to grounds free.

Las Nazarenas Church (Av Tacna, 4th block, open 0700-1130 and 1630-2000 daily), built around an image of Christ Crucified painted by a liberated slave in 1655. This, the most venerated image in Lima, and an oil copy of El Señor de los Milagros (Lord of Miracles), encased in a gold frame, are carried on a silver litter—the whole weighing nearly a ton—through the streets on 18, 19, and 28 Oct and again on 1 Nov (All Saints' Day).

San Agustín (Jirón Ica, 251), W of the Plaza de Armas, is a much changed old church, but its façade (1720) is a splendid example of churrigueresque architecture. There are carved choir stalls and effigies, and a sculpture of Death, said to have frightened its maker into an early grave. Open 0830-1200, 1530-1730 daily, ring for entry. Since being damaged in the last earthquake the church has been sensitively restored, but the sculpture of Death is in storage.
    Fine 18th century carving also in gilt altars of **Jesús María** (Jirón Moquegua, 1st block), and in **Magdalena Vieja** (1557, but reconstructed in 1931), with altar pieces, of gilded and carved wood, particularly fine; it should be seen during visit to the Museum of Archaeology, Plaza Bolívar (in Pueblo Libre). Another church worth seeing for its two beautiful colonial doors is **San Marcelo**, at Av de la Emancipación, 4th block.
    The **Convento de Los Descalzos** on the Alameda de Los Descalzos in Rímac contains over 300 paintings of the Cusco, Quito and Lima schools which line the four main cloisters and two ornate chapels. The chapel of El Carmen was constructed in 1730 and is notable for its baroque gold leaf altar. The museum shows the life of the Franciscan friars during colonial and early republican periods; the cellar, infirmary, pharmacy and a typical cell have all been restored. The library has not yet been incorporated into the tour (researchers may be permitted to see specific books on request). The convent is open daily 0930-1300, 1500-1745, except Tues, entrance US$1. Guided tour only, 45 mins in Spanish, but worth it.
    The church of **Santo Tomás** is now a school (Gran Unidad Escolar "Mercedes Cabello de Carbonera", on corner of Junín and Andahuaylas); it is said to have the only circular cloister in the world apart from St Peter's in Rome, and a fine 17th-century Italian-designed baroque library. The headmistress is glad to show people round.

NB Churches are open between 1830 and 2100 unless otherwise stated. Many are closed to visitors on Sun.

Museums

There are two museums of anthropology and archaeology, the original and a new one opened in 1990: the former contains the original pottery collection but the latter has a much bigger display and many activities. The old museum is **Museo Nacional de Antropología y Arqueología**, Plaza Bolívar in Pueblo Libre, not to be confused with Plaza Bolívar in the centre (T 463-5070), open Tues-Sat 0900-1800, admission US$1.50. Guides are available. Ceramics of the Chimú, Nazca, Mochica and Pachacámac cultures, various Inca curiosities and works of art, interesting textiles. See the Raimondi Stela and the Tello obelisk from Chavín, and a reconstruction of one of the galleries at Chavín. It also has a model of Machu Picchu. Bus 12 or colectivo along Av Tacna or Av Venezuela, get off at Av Vivanco and walk 2 blocks; or any bus or colectivo going along Av Brasil, get off at block 22, Av Vivanco, and walk 7 blocks. Taxi US$2.
    There is also an archaeological museum at Puruchuco (**see p 1137**), and at the excavated mound of Santa Catalina, Parque Fernando Carozi in La Victoria (an insalubrious district); minibus 1 or 46 from Plaza 2 de Mayo.

Museo de la Nación, Javier Prado 2466, San Borja, T 437-7822/437-7776, in the huge Banco de la Nación building, the new anthropological and archaeological museum. Open Tues-Sun 0900-1700, entry US$1.50. A museum for the exhibition and study of the art and history of the aboriginal races of Peru: good explanations in Spanish on Peruvian history, with ceramics, textiles and displays of almost every ruin in Peru. There is an excellent copy of the tomb of the Señor de Sipán and a display of the discoveries. Another exhibition shows artefacts from Batán Grande in Lambayeque, called the Señor de Sicán (similar in style in Sipán, but more simplistic). There is also an extended exhibition on the Spanish colonial period and displays of typical costumes from Indian festivals. The museum holds a concert every Sun and most evenings there is a lecture, or an event in the theatre (see the monthly programme, or newspaper). Take a colectivo from Miraflores or the centre to the Universidad de Lima and get out at block 24 on Javier Prado; taxi US$2-3.

Museo Peruano de Ciencias de la Salud, now part of the Museo de la Nación, has a collection of ceramics and mummies, showing precolumbian lifestyle; divided into five sections: *micuy* (Quechua for food), *hampi* (medicine), *onccoy* (disease), *hampini* (healing) and *causay* (life).

Museo de Oro (Gold Museum—private collection of Miguel Mujica Gallo), is in 18th block of Prolongación Av Primavera (Av de Molina 1110), Monterrico (T 435-0791). An underground museum contains items which have been exhibited in the world's leading museums. The collection includes precolumbian gold, silver and bronze, ceramics, weavings, mummies, etc. Well worth seeing, despite being poorly displayed and explained. Their catalogues cost US$20 or US$40 and the complete book US$70. Upstairs is a remarkable arms collection with an impressive exhibition from Spanish colonial times. In the garden are high quality, expensive craft shops. Open daily (incl Sun and holidays) 1200-1900. Admission: US$5, children half price. No photography allowed. Take a colectivo from the centre to the corner of Av Arequipa y Av Angamos (you can walk to Av Angamos from Miraflores) and take bus 11, 72, 112 or 985, or a colectivo, to the 18th block of Av Primavera. Taxi US$3-4.

Museo Arqueológico Rafael Larco Herrera, Av Bolívar 1515, Pueblo Libre, T 461-1312, is the Chiclín pottery museum brought from Trujillo. The greatest number of exhibits stem from the Mochica period (AD 400-800). The Cupisnique period, dating back to 1000 BC, and the Nazca, Chimú, and Inca periods are also well represented. There is an erotica section in a separate building. This is a museum for the pottery specialist and it gives an excellent overview on the development of Peruvian cultures; it is more like a warehouse than a museum with few explanations, but the general visitor will enjoy the excellent collection of precolumbian weaving, including a sample of two-ply yarns with 398 threads to the inch. Also several mummified weavers buried with their looms and a small display of gold pieces. Admission US$5 (half price for student-card holders), open Mon-Sat 0900-1800, Sun 0900-1300. Photography not permitted. Take Bus 23 or colectivo from Avenida Abancay, any bus or colectivo to the 15th block of Av Brasil, and another one on Av Bolívar. Taxi US$2-3.

Museo Arqueológico Amano (Calle Retiro 160, 11th block of Av Angamos, Miraflores). A very fine private collection of artefacts from the Chancay, Chimú and Nazca periods owned by the late Mr Yoshitaro Amano—one of the most complete exhibits of Chancay weaving. Particularly interesting for pottery and precolumbian textiles, all superbly displayed and lit. Visits by appointment Mon-Fri in afternoons only, T 441-2909. Admission free (photography prohibited). Take bus or colectivo to the corner of Av Arequipa y Av Angamos and another one to the 11th block of Av Angamos, or bus 1, 73, or colectivo from Av Tacna y Av La Vega to corner Av Comandante Espinar y Av Angamos and walk to the 11th block.

Museo Banco Central de Reserva, Av Ucayali 291 and Lampa (one block from San Pedro Church, on same side as Torre Tagle Palace), T 427-6250, ext 2657. Large collection of pottery from Vicus or Piura culture (AD 500-600) and gold objects from Lambayeque, as well as 19th and 20th century paintings. Both modern and ancient exhibitions highly rec. Tues-Fri 1000-1600, Sat-Sun 1000-1300. Photography prohibited.

Museo Nacional de la Cultura Peruana, Av Alfonso Ugarte 650, Lima, T 423-5892: an extraordinary mock Tiwanaku façade houses a rather disjointed collection of precolumbian and modern artefacts, including *mate burilado* (carved gourds), *retablos*, textiles, *keros* and *huacos*. There are examples of ceramics and cloth from some Amazonian tribes and a set of watercolours by Pancho Fierro, the 19th century *costumbrista* artist. Open Mon-Sat 1000-1400. Admission US$2.

Poli Museum, Lord Cochrane 466, T 422-2437, Miraflores, one of the best private collections of precolumbian and colonial artefacts in Peru, including material from Sipán. Guided tours (not in English) by Sr Poli cost US$50 irrespective of the size of the group; allow 2 hrs.

Museo de Arte, Paseo Colón 125, T 423-4732, in the Palacio de la Exposición, built in 1868 in Parque de la Exposición. More than 7,000 exhibits, giving a chronological history of Peruvian cultures and art from the 2,000-year-old Paracas civilization up to today. Excellent examples of 17th and 18th century Cusco paintings, a beautiful display of carved furniture, heavy silver and jewelled stirrups, also precolumbian pottery. Between Apr and Oct, and with special programmes in the holiday season, the cinema shows films and plays almost every night (cheap); see the local paper for details, or look in the museum itself. Several good, English-speaking guides. Tues-Sun 1000-1300, 1400-1700. Admission US$1.

Museo de Arte Italiano (Paseo de la República, 2nd block, T 423-9932), is in a wonderful neo-classical building, given by the Italian colony to Peru on the centenary of its independence. Note the remarkable mosaic murals on the outside. Open Mon-Fri 0830-1400, US$1. Large collection of Italian and other European works of art, including sculpture, lithographs and etchings. Now also houses Institute of Contemporary Art, which has many exhibitions.

Contemporary Folk Art Museum, Saco Olivero 163, between Arenales and 3rd block of Arequipa, rec. Shop in museum grounds. Tues-Fri, 1430-1900; Sat 0830-1200.

Pinacoteca Municipal (Municipal Building, Plaza de Armas), contains a large collection of paintings by Peruvian artists. The best of the painters is Ignacio Merino (1817-1876). Rooms and furnishings very ornate. Open: Mon-Fri, 0900-1300.

Colección Pedro de Osma (Av Pedro de Osma 421, in the residential district of Barranco, T 467-0915/0019 for an appointment). A private collection of colonial art of the Cusco, Ayacucho and Arequipa schools. Take bus 2, 54 or colectivo from Av Tacna. The number of visitors is limited to ten at any one time. Admission US$3.

Museo Nacional de Historia, Plaza Bolívar, Pueblo Libre, T 463-2009,in a mansion built by Viceroy Pezuela and occupied by San Martín (1821-1822) and Bolívar (1823-1826; next to old Museo de Antropoligía y Arqueología (take the same buses to get there, see above). Exhibits: colonial and early republican paintings, manuscripts, portraits, uniforms, etc. Paintings mainly of historical episodes. Open daily 0900-1700. Admission US$4.

Museo del Tribunal de la Santa Inquisición, Plaza Bolívar, Calle Junín 548, near corner of Av Abancay. The main hall, with splendidly carved mahogany ceiling, remains untouched. Court of Inquisition held here 1569-1820; until 1930 used by the Senate. In the basement there is an accurate re-creation *in situ* of the tortures. A description in English is available at the desk. Admission free. Students offer to show you round for a tip; good explanations in English. Mon-Fri 0900-1300, 1430-1700. Recommended.

Museo Histórico Militar, Parque Independencia, in Real Felipe Fortress, Callao, T 429-0532, has interesting military relics: a cannon brought by Pizarro, a cannon used in the War of Independence, the flag that flew during the last Spanish stand in the fortress, portraits of General Rodil and of Lord Cochrane, and the remains of the small Bleriot plane in which the Peruvian pilot, Jorge Chávez, made the first crossing of the Alps from Switzerland to Italy: he was killed when the plane crashed at Domodossola on 23 September 1910. Open 0930-1400, US$2 incl guide, no cameras allowed. Take bus 25, 74, 94 or colectivo from Av La Vega.

Museo Naval (Av Jorge Chávez 121, off Plaza Grau, Callao, T 429-4793), open Mon-Fri 0900-1400. Admission free. A collection of paintings, model ships, uniforms, etc.

Museo de los Combatientes del Morro de Arica, Cailloma 125, Lima, T 427-0958, open Tues-Sat 1000-1500, admission US$0.50, gives the Peruvian view of the famous battle against the Chileans during the War of the Pacific.

The **Museo Miguel Grau**, Jr Huancavelica 170, Lima, T 428-5012, is the house of Admiral Grau and has mementoes of the War of the Pacific (open daily 0900-1400, free).

Museo de Historia Natural Javier Prado (Av Arenales 1256, Jesús María, T 471-0117) belongs to Universidad de San Marcos. Exhibits: Peruvian flora, birds, mammals, butterflies, insects, minerals and shells. Prize exhibit is a sun fish (more plaster than fish)—only two other examples known, one in Japan and another in New Zealand. Open Mon-Sat 0900-1800; admission US$1 (students US$0.50). Take colectivo from Av Tacna.

Parque las Leyendas, 24th block of Av de La Marina, Pueblo Libre, between Lima and Callao, T 452-6913, is arranged to represent the three regions of Peru: the coast, the mountainous Sierra, and the tropical jungles of the Montaña, with appropriate houses, animals and plants, children's playground. Elephants and lions have been introduced so the zoo is no longer purely Peruvian (not recommended at weekends, too crowded). The Park is open daily 0900-1700, entrance US$2. There is a handicrafts fair (Feria Artesanal) at the entrance to the park; particularly good insect specimens can be bought here. Take bus 23 or colectivo on Av Abancay, or bus 135A or colectivo from Av La Vega.

Museo Taurino (Hualgayoc 332, Plaza de Acho Bull Ring, Rímac, T 482-3360). Apart from matadors' relics, contains good collections of paintings and engravings— some of the latter by Goya. Mon-Sat 0800-1600. Admission US$1; students US$0.50, photography US$2.

Philatelic Museum (Central Post Office, off Plaza de Armas, T 427-5060, ext 553). Open 0915-1245, Mon-Fri. Incomplete collection of Peruvian stamps and information on the Inca postal system. There is a stamp exchange in front of the museum every Sat and Sun, 0900-1300. You can buy stamps here as well, particularly commemorative issues (shop hours: Mon-Fri 0800-1200, 1400-1500).

Museo Numismático, Banco Wiese, 2nd Flr, Cusco 245, T 427-5060 ext 2009, open Mon-Fri, 0900-1230, free admission. Peruvian coins from the colonial era to the present. The Miraflores branch of Banco Wiese has an exhibition of finds from El Brujo archaeological site N of Trujillo.

Museo Teatral, Teatro Segura, Jr Huancavelica 251, Lima, T 427-7437, open during performances; a collection of mementoes and photographs of people who have appeared on the Lima stage.

Museo de la Electricidad, Av Pedro de Osma, next to the Library.

NB Some museums are only open between 0900 and 1300 from Jan to Mar, and some close altogether in Jan. Many are closed at weekends and on Mon; some close early if there are few visitors.

Lima and its suburbs have many parks and gardens. Note that many parks are used as meeting places for drug pushers, thieves and couples. They are also home to street people.

NB You are recommended to consult the general **Security** section in the **Information for Visitors** and see also the **Warning** under **Buses** below. Many visitors stay in Miraflores or Barranco (see **suburbs** below), rather than in the historic centre.

Festivals 18 Jan, Founding of Lima. The whole of Feb is Carnival; there is water-throwing on Sun during this month; if you don't want to get wet, stay in your room. If you don't mind (and it's quite refreshing), enjoy it and carry your own water balloon (some "jokers" mix paint, oil, etc, with the water, so watch out). Semana Santa (Easter), with processions; 28-29 Jul, Independence, with music and fireworks in Plaza de Armas on evening before; last week of Aug Cañete; Oct, month of Our Lord of the Miracles with impressive processions (see *El Comercio* for dates and routes); Nov (every other year), Pacific International Fair. See also **Public Holidays** in Information for Visitors.

Hotels All hotels and restaurants in the upper price brackets charge 18% VAT and 10% service on top of prices (neither is included in prices below). In cheaper hotels water may be scarce in the middle of the day. The more expensive hotels charge in dollars according to the parallel rate of exchange at midnight.

More visitors stay in the Miraflores area than in the centre, as it is a bit more organized, modern and safer, but more expensive. Backpackers prefer the cheaper *hostales* in the centre, which has more theft problems, is more chaotic, but which, with care and attention to your belongings, is OK.

Accommodation in **Miraflores**: **L2** *El Pardo*, Independencia 141, T 447-0283, F 444-2171, a/c, satellite TV, fax and telex service, good restaurant, rec; **L2** *Las Américas*, Av Benavides 415, T 445-9494, F 444-1137, 5-star, commercial centre, pool, gym, restaurant, etc; **L2** *Miraflores César*, La Paz y Diez Canseco, T 444-1212, F 444-4440, luxury, very nice but expensive; **L3** *El Condado*, Alcanfores 465, T 444-1890, deluxe; **L3** *Exclusive*, San Martín 550, T 444-1919/22, F 444-1922; **L3** *María Angola*, Av La Paz 610, T 444-1280, F 446-2860, rec; **A1** *La Hacienda*, 28 de Julio 511, T 444-4346, English spoken, very clean, friendly, TV, phone, expensive; **A2** *Ariosto*, Av La Paz 769, T 444-1416, F 444-3955, rec; **A2** *José Antonio*, 28 de Julio 398, T 445-6870, clean, friendly, good restaurant, rec; **A3** *El Doral*, Av José Pardo 486, T 447-6305, F 446-8344, nice rooms with kitchenette, safe and friendly; **A3** *Grand Hotel Miraflores*, Av 28 de Julio 151, very pleasant, T 447-9641; **A3** *Hostal Miramar Ischia*, Malecón Cisneros 1244, overlooking Pacific, includes breakfast, good food at reasonable prices, friendly, rec; **B** *Hostal Residencial Esperanza*, Esperanza 350, T 444-2411/4909, F 444-0834, with bath, TV, phone, pleasant, sophisticated security system; **B** *Suites Miraflores*, San Martín 481, of 101 (7th block of Larco), T 444-0177, kitchen, bedroom, living room, phone; *Suites Eucaliptas*, San Martín 511, T 445-2840, F 444-3071, European-style, kitchenette, sauna, jacuzzi, pool, safety deposit, laundry, credit cards accepted.

B *Armendariz*, Av Armendariz (between Miraflores and Barranco), on No 2 bus line, T 445-4565/3239, cable TV, rec; **B** *Colonial Inn*, Cmdte Espinar 310, T 446-6666, F 446-1641, room service, TV, parking; **B** *Hostal El Ejecutivo*, Av 28 de Julio 245, T 447-6310, F 444-2222, incl bath and breakfast, payment in dollars, overpriced but clean, tariff negotiable for long stay, safe, luggage can be left; **B** *Hostal Huaychulo*, Av Dos de Mayo 494, T 445-1195, safe, helpful, excellent (German owner-manager, speaks English too); **B** *Hostal La Castellana*, Grimaldo del Solar 222 (3 blocks E of Larco, between Schell and Benavides), T 444-3530/4662, F 446-8030 (C off season), with bath, pleasant, good value, nice garden, safe, cafeteria (poor breakfast), laundry, English spoken; **B** *Hostal Lucerna*, Las Dalias 276 (corner Av Larco), with breakfast, friendly, clean, T 445-7321, rec; **B** *Hostal Residencial Torreblanca*, Av José Pardo 1453, T 447-9998/3363, F 473363, incl breakfast and tax, quiet, safe, laundry, restaurant and bar, friendly, clean and cosy rooms, will help with travel arrangements, helpful, rec; **B** *Hostal San Antonio Abad*, Ramón Ribeyro 301, T 447-6766, F 446 4208, quiet, secure, charming interior, clean, rec; **B** *Hostal Señorial*, José González 567 (T 445-9724/445-7306), 60 rooms all with bath, including tax and breakfast, rec, clean, friendly, well-appointed, garden; **B** *Ovalo*, Av José Pardo 1110, Plaza Morales Barros, T 446-5549, quiet, good, breakfast served; **B** *Pensión Alemana*, Arequipa 4704, T 445-6999 (no sign), comfortable, clean, excellent breakfast (triple rooms available), book in advance, laundry service extra; **B** *Residencial 28 de Julio*, 28 de Julio 531, T 424-7600/7608, F 446-9677, with breakfast, parking, café and bar, phone and bathroom with each room, secure, reliable and pleasant staff, rec; **C** *Hostal El Patio*, or *Pensión Olga*, Diez Canseco 341a, T 444-2107 (next to *Miraflores César*), incl breakfast, with reductions for long stays, clean, comfortable, friendly, English and French spoken; **C** *Hostal Miraflores*, Av Petit Thouars 5444, T 445-8745, F 447-0116; **C** *Hostal Palace*, Av 28 de Julio or Miraflores 1088, T 445-6040, F 440-0450, very clean, comfortable, friendly, keeps luggage, English-speaking reception, travel agency on 1st floor; **D** *Pensión José Luis*, Paula de Ugarriza 727, San Antonio district, T 444-1015, apartments in private house, small kitchen, reservation required, rec, laundry facilities, very friendly English-speaking owner.

D *Pensión Yolanda Escobar*, Domingo Elias 230 T 445-7565, clean, facilities for preparing own breakfast, dueña speaks fluent English, rec; **D** *Residencial El Castillo Inn*, Av E Diez

Canseco 580, T 446-9501, family home, use of kitchen and lounge; **E** *Hostal Andalucia*, Jr Tacna 472, T 445-8717, with bath, helpful, quiet; **E** *Pensión Atahuallpa*, Atahuallpa 646, T 447-6601, friendly, parking, hot water, all day cooking and laundry facilities, rec; **E** pp Sra Jordan, Porta 724, T 445-9840, incl breakfast, old family home, friendly, quiet; **E** *Pensión San Antonio*, Paseo de la República 5809, T 447-5830, shared bath, clean, comfortable, friendly, helpful, ask for hot water, rec.

Accommodation at **San Isidro**: **L3** *El Olivar de San Isidro*, Pancho Fierro 194, T 441-1454, F 441-1382, luxury, modern, restaurant, coffee shop, garden, swimming pool, quiet, popular with business visitors; **A2** *Country Club*, Los Eucaliptos, T 440-4060, F 440-8912, all services, restaurant and coffee shop, quiet, helpful, reasonable rates (except for overseas faxes), gaming room; **A2** *Garden*, Rivera Navarrete 450, T 442-1771, rec, good, large beds, shower, small restaurant; **A2** *Suites Real*, Bustamante Ballivián 140, T 470-4031, F 442-3178; **A3** *Hostal Beech*, Los Libertadores 145, T 442-8713, F 442-8716, with bath, including breakfast, noisy, but rec; **B** *Hostal Limatambo*, Av Aramburú 1025, T 441-9615, 24-hr snack bar, won the "América-86" award for good service and quality; **B** *Residencial Francia*, Samuel Velarde 185, 11th block of Av Ejército, T 461-7054, price incl taxes and breakfast, bath, hot water, laundry facilities, swimming pool, gardens, very friendly and helpful; **B** *Sans Souci*, Av Arequipa 2670, T 422-6035, F 441-7824, towards Miraflores, with bath, clean, safe, garden, garage; **C** *Hostal El Golf Inn*, Av A Miro Quesada, round corner from Cuban Embassy, with bath, D without, swimming pool, safe, friendly, hard beds; **C** *Hostal San Isidro Inn*, Av Pezet 1765, T 440-3686, just off Salaverry; **C** *Hostal Santa Mónica*, Av Pezet 1419, T 441-9280, rec.

In **Santa Beatriz**, between San Isidro and Centre: **C** *Hostal Mont Blanc*, Jr Emilio Fernández 640, T 433-8055, with bath, quiet area, safe (video monitoring), 15 mins' walk or 5 mins by minibus to centre, owner arranges excursions; **D** *Residencial Los Petirrojos*, Petirrojos 230, Corpac (Sra Miri), T 441-6044, clean, spacious, breakfast included.

In **Lince** is, **D** *Hostal Ambassador*, Julio C Tello 650, T 470-0020, clean, safe, hot water, changes money for guests, highly rec.

In **central Lima**, rec in the upper price brackets: **L3** *Crillón*, Av Nicolás de Piérola, or Colmena 589, T 428-3290, F 432-5920, good food and service in *Skyroom* (open 1200-2400 Mon-Sat, Peruvian/international cuisine, buffets and live music at weekends, great view over Lima); **L3** *Lima Sheraton*, Paseo de la República 170, T 433-3320, F 433-6344, *Las Palmeras*, coffee shop good but pricey, daily buffet breakfast, all you can eat for US$15 pp, new casino; **A1** *Grand Bolívar*, Unión 958, Plaza San Martín, T 427-2305, F 433-8626 (may be negotiable to C out of season), palatial old building, good ambience, helpful, excellent restaurant, have a pisco on the terrace overlooking plaza, highly rec; **B** *El Plaza*, Nicolás de Pierola 850, T 428-6270, very noisy at the front but quiet at the back (except Sat), convenient, good, safe for luggage (cheaper in low season, cheaper for Peruvians); **B** *Savoy*, Cailloma 224, T 428-3520, F 433-0840, comfortable, but has seen better days.

B *Grand Castle*, Av Carlos Zavala Loayza 218, T 428-3181, opp Ormeño bus station, including breakfast (poor), hot water, comfortable, good service, Japanese restaurant, rec; **B** *Hostal San Martín*, Av Nicolás de Piérola 882, 2nd Flr, Plaza San Martín, T 428-5337, rec, good value, price incl taxes, a/c, with bath, breakfast served in room, helpful, money changing facilities, Japanese run, good restaurant, good service; **C** *Granada*, on Huancavelica 323, T 427-9033, inc breakfast, clean, hot water, English spoken; **C** *Hostal Los Virreyes*, Jirón Cañete 826, T 431-2733, comfortable, clean, hot water, central position, a bit noisy, rec; **C** *Hostal Renacimiento*, Parque Hernán Velarde 52, T 433-2806, cheaper at the back, in a quiet cul-de-sac 2 blocks from central bus station, 10 mins' walk from centre, not all rooms with bath but clean, helpful; **C** *La Casona*, Moquegua 289 (nr Jr Cailloma and No 56 bus route from airport), T 427-6273, clean, secure, friendly, TV room, restaurant, noisy; **D** *Residencial Kori Wasi*, Av Washington 1137, T 433-8127, wtih bath, pleasant, safe, friendly; **E** *Gran*, Av Abancay 546, T 428-5160, enormous hotel, old house, popular with locals, a bit noisy, friendly; **E** *Hostal Belén*, Belén 1049, just off San Martín, T 427-8995, Italian spoken, basic breakfast extra, hot water, friendly, music groups practising; **E** pp *Hostal Wilson*, Jr Chancay, T 424-8924, a bit run down but friendly and safe for luggage deposit.

E pp *Pensión Ibarra*, Av Tacna 359, Apt 162, 15th and 16th Flrs, T 447-0802, no sign, incl breakfast (less if staying several days), you can eat on the balcony with views of the city, clean, friendly, very helpful owner, hot water, full board available, highly rec; **E** *Residencial Roma*, Ica 326, T 427-7576, F 427-7572, hot water all day, safe to leave luggage, friendly, basic but clean, highly rec, often full (next door are an excellent pastry shop and Roma Tours, a small travel agency), motorcycle parking; **E-F** *Hostal España*, Jr Azángaro 105, no sign (G in dormitory), fine old building being restored, in old Lima, T 428-5546, friendly, hot water 0600-2300, family run by a French-speaking Peruvian painter and his Spanish wife, English spoken, secure (also for motorcycles), luggage store (free), use of laundry (slow), roof garden with mini zoo of which some travellers disapprove, good café, rec; **F** pp *Familia Rodríguez*,

Av N de Piérola 730, 2nd Flr, T 423-6465, with breakfast, clean, friendly, popular with gringos, noisy, will store luggage, dormitory accommodation with only one bathroom, transport to airport US$9.50; **F** pp *Hostal Samaniego*, Av Emancipación 184, Apto 801, reservation required, 15 spaces available (4 rooms), noisy, use of kitchen, will store luggage for foreigners.

Outside Lima is the 5-star, **A2** *El Pueblo*, Santa Clara, Km 11.2, Ate, Vitarte (along the Central Highway), huge luxurious complex in the country, with restaurants, bars, discos, swimming pool, tennis, shows, shops, etc; you can visit for the day and use the facilities for a small fee, reservations T 494-1616/170. Next door is *La Granja Azul*, Carretera Central (turn off between Km 13 and 14 of Carretera Central, buses from Parque Universitario every 15 mins; last bus back leaves 2000 but a minibus leaves the hotel for Lima at 2200), restaurant specializing in exotic cocktails and chicken dishes, dancing every night, rec. About 1 km from airport **E** *Hostal Salvatore*, Jr Salaverry 440, clean, TV, restaurant, and *Hostal Aeropeurto*, safe, clean, rec.

If arriving by air, especially at night, you can try the tourist office at the airport (beyond passport control) if you want to arrange a hotel room, but they are not always helpful. **Hotel reservations** for Lima and elsewhere in Peru can be made through Reservaciones Central, a travel agency, Av Panamericana 6251, San Antonio/Miraflores, T 446-6895; it charges a small commission, also offers all usual services. EnturPeru, T 442-8628/837, administers the state tourist hotel chain, 3-4 star hotels.

Youth Hostel *Albergue Turístico Juvenil Internacional*, Av Casimiro Ulloa 328, San Antonio between San Isidro and Miraflores, T 446-5488, F 444-8187, basic cafeteria, travel information, cooking (minimal) and laundry facilities, US$9 members, US$10 non-members, dormitory, more for double room, swimming pool often empty, clean and safe, situated in a nice villa, rec. 20 mins' walk from the beach. Bus No 2 or colectivos pass Av Benavides to the centre; taxi to centre, US$2.50.

Camping Under no circumstances camp on or near beach at Miraflores, theft and worse is rife in these areas. Propane gas in heavy iron gas bottles available from Delta-Gas, Av Benavides 5425, Lima. Camping gas (in small blue bottles) available from any large hardware store or bigger supermarket, about US$3. Oechsle sell butane gas cartridges. NB Airlines do not allow the carriage of gas bottles. Backpack makers and repairers, *Ursus* (Alberto Abalero), Av El Ejército 1982, Miraflores, T 422-6678. *Alpamayo*, Larco 345, sells camping equipment.

Baths Baños Pizarro, Unión 284, steam rooms, US$3, cold showers only, café and swimming pool. Windsor Turkish Baths, on Miguel Dasso, San Isidro, separate facilities for men and women, steam, sauna, cold pool and whirlpool, US$4. See Yellow Pages for other addresses.

Restaurants Check all restaurant prices before ordering, especially if you have visited the city before; prices have soared since 1990 in upper and middle class establishments. Menu prices fail to show that 18% government tax and 10% service will be added to your bill in this class of restaurant. A cheap *menú* (set lunch) still costs US$1.30-3, while a meal in a moderate café/bistro will cost US$15-20; in middle-range restaurants a meal costs US$25-30, rising to US$60-80 at the upper end of the range (early 1995 prices).

In **Miraflores** we recommend the following: *Rosa Náutica*, T 447-0057, built on old British-style pier (Espigón No 4), in Lima Bay, near Miraflores, not to be missed, delightful opulence, finest fish cuisine, experience the atmosphere by buying an expensive beer in the bar, sunset rec, open 1230-0200 daily; *La Costa Verde*, on Barranquito beach, T 441-4084, excellent fish and wine, pecan pie highly rec, very expensive, Amex accepted, open 1200-2400 daily, Sun buffet; *El Señorío de Sulco*, Malecón Cisneros 1470, final Av Pardo, T 445-6640, authentic Peruvian dishes, expensive; *Martín Fierro*, Malecón Cisneros 1420, T 446-3992, Argentine, moderate prices, good Sun buffet; *San Marino*, José Gálvez 618, T 446-7545, seafood, expensive; *Canta Rana*, Figari 121, Blvd San Ramón, T 445-0498, open Mon-Sat 1300-1700, good seafood, best *ceviche*; *Bahía Blanca*, Benavides 2514, T 447-7123, seafood, moderate; *La Tranquera*, Av Pardo 285, T 447-5111, steaks, open 1200-2400 daily; *Carlín*, La Paz 646, T 444-4134, open 1200-1600, 1900-2400 daily, cosy, international, expensive; *Don Beta*, José Gálvez 667, T 446-9465, open 0800-2200 daily, seafood, moderately expensive; *La Crêperie*, La Paz 635, T 444-1800, open 1230-1500, 1900-2400, crêpes of all sizes and fillings, moderate to expensive; *La Pizzería*, Av Benavides 322, T 446-7793, open 0930-2400 daily, international and Italian, expensive; *Pizzería Restaurant Erik*, Av Benavides 1057, cheap local and international food, highly rec, try the *salsas*; *Pizzería Marcelino Pizza y Vino*, Mártir Olaya 250, Diagonal, excellent menu, friendly, quiet, good atmosphere; *Don Rosalino*, Juan Figari 135, pizzas, moderate; *La Trattoria*, Manuel Bonilla 106, T 446-7002, open 1300-1530, 2000-2400 Mon-Sat, Italian, good pizzas, expensive; *Stefanos*, Av José Pardo 779, T 446-9646, open 1300-2200 Tues-Sun, pastas and pizzas, moderate; *Las Tejas*, Diez Canseco 340, T 444-4360, open 1100-2300 daily, good, typical Peruvian food, moderate to expensive; *C'est Si Bon*, Comandante Espinar 663, T 446-9310, open 1000-2200 daily, French-style, moderate.

Cheese and wine at *El Alamo*, La Paz y Diez Canseco, open 1230-1500, 1900-2400, cosy spot for wines, raclettes and fondues, expensive; *Cheese and Wine*, Av La Paz 552, good fondues, raclette, salads and wines, warm, cosy atmosphere, excellent service, moderate prices; *Oriental*, José de San Martín 561, T 444-4018, open 1130-1500, 1900-2300 Mon-Sat, 1130-1500 Sun, great Chinese food, moderate prices; *Asia Garden*, Diez Canseco 493, T 444-2313, Chinese, moderate; *Palachinke*, Shell 120, T 447-9205, open 1200-2300 daily, moderate/expensive, excellent, large pancakes; *The Steak House*, La Paz 642, T 444-3110, 1200-1500, 1800-2400, steaks and salads, moderate/expensive, another branch in San Isidro (Las Camelias 870); *El Rodizio*, Ovalo Gutiérrez y Santa Cruz, T 445-0889, open 1300-0100, good meats and salad bar, moderate/expensive; *El Rincón Gaucho*, Parque Salazar, T 447-4778, open 1200-2400 Tues-Sat, grills and steaks, moderate/expensive, and *El Otro Gaucho*, Rep Panamá 6488, T 446-1842, 1200-2400 daily.

Manolo, Av Larco 608, T 444-2244, 0800-2230 daily, good food, popular; *New York Pizza Company*, Av Larco 1145, open 1200-2400, tasty, moderate prices, English spoken; *Burger King* on 1st block of Larco opp park; *Whatta Burger*, Grau 120, American-style hamburgers, reasonably cheap; *Glotones*, on Espinar, for burgers and icecream, very friendly; *Bembo-Burgers*, Av Benadvides, excellent hamburgers and breakfasts, reasonable prices; *Mediterráneo Chicken*, Av Benavides block 420, T 447-9337, open 1200-2300 daily, moderate chicken and salads (branch in San Isidro); next door is *Silvestre*, good fresh juices and vegetarian sandwiches, fairly expensive; *Tomas*, 2nd floor of Mass Supermarket, Benavides 486, open 24 hrs, good, cheap, fast food.

Cafés: *Vivaldi*, Ricardo Palma 258, 0800-0200 daily, meals US$15-20, also snacks and drinks, good cappuccinos, moderate/expensive; *Haiti*, Diagonal 160, 0700-0200 daily, drinks, café snacks, expensive, popular meeting place; *Café Suisse*, Av Larco 111, on main square, for very good cakes, coffee, European-style food and delicatessen, expensive; *Liverpool*, Ricardo Palma 250, fairly expensive. Beatles music and décor.

The "Pizza Street", located on Diagonal (one block from Shell), popular on Fri-Sat nights for drinks, discos, meeting spot; moderate prices. Best ice cream, *Quattro D*, Angamos Oeste 408, open 1000-0100 daily; second best at *Fragola*, Av Benavides 468. *Pizzeria Tockyn*, Calle de las Pizzas, very popular, inexpensive, good atmosphere. Best yoghurt *Mi Abuela*, Angamos 393, 0900-2100 daily. *Media Naranja*, Shell 130, good for breakfast, Brazilian owner. *Pastelería Sueca*, Av Larco 759, good hamburgers, pastries, salads. English pub, *Brenchley Arms*, Atahualpa 174, T 445-9680, British owner, English food, English speaking, informal and relaxed, tourist information, pricey, darts.

Vegetarian: *Bircher Berner*, Av Shell 598, T 444-4250, closed Sun, with store, slow service, good cheap *menú*; *Govinda*, Shell 630; *La Huerta del Sol*, Av La Paz 522, T 444-2900, lunch menu US$3, main dishes US$5, good food, pleasant setting.

In **San Isidro**: *La Réserve*, Las Flores 326, T 440-2786, open 1200-1530, 1930-2400, expensive, French cuisine; *Aquarium* (at the *Country Club Hotel*), T404060, open 1130-1500, 1900-2300 daily, expensive, rec; *Punta Sal*, Conquistadores 948, T 441-7431, 0900-1700 daily, seafood specialities, dear; also *La Caleta*, D Deteano 126, T 442-3835, 1200-1600, 1930-2400 daily, seafood, expensive; *La Otra Alea*, Av Aramburu 511, T 441-2608, seafood, moderate prices; *Puerto Azul*, Conquistadores 1018, T 441-0193, 1000-1800 daily, seafood, moderate; similar is *El Pirata*, Av Dos de Mayo 674, T 422-3114, 1100-2300 Thur-Sat, 1100-1800 Sun-Wed; also *Cebiches El Rey*, Av Aramburu 975, T 442-1809, 1000-2400 Mon-Sat, until 1800 Sun, with branches in Miraflores, Callao and Barranco; *Los Condes de San Isidro*, Av Paz Soldán 290, an 18th century mansion, T 422-2557, excellent, international, expensive, open 1200-1500, 1900-2400 daily; *Valentino's*, M Bañón 215 (near Camino Real and Av Javier Prado), T 441-6174, open 1200-1500, 1930-2400, great Italian food; *Fredos*, Conquistadores 512, excellent homemade pastas, reasonable prices; *Los Años Locos*, Conquistadores 430, T 442-4960, 1000-2400 Mon-Sat; *José Antonio*, B Monteagudo 200, T 461-9923, 1300-1600, 1930-2400 Mon-Sat, creole and Peruvian dishes, expensive; *Mi Casa*, Augusto Tamayo 150, T 440-3780, Japanese, moderate/expensive, 1200-1500, 1900-2300 Mon-Sat; *Lung Fung*, Av Rep de Panamá 3165, T 422-6382, 1200-1500, 1900-2400 daily, Chinese, moderate/expensive; *El Dorado*, Av Arequipa 2450, T 422-1080, 1100-1500, 1900-2300, Chinese, good views of Lima, expensive; *La Casa de España*, Conquistadores 331, T 440-0114, 1000-1600, 1900-2300 Mon-Sat, 1000-1600 Sun, Spanish, moderate/expensive; *La Carreta*, Rivera Navarrete 740, T 440-5424, open 1200-2400 daily, Peruvian and international, good steaks, moderate prices; *Don Alfredo*, M Bañón 295, T 422-6681, 1200-1600, 1900-2400 Mon-Sat, 1200-1500 Sun, expensive, excellent food, helpful, friendly; *La Ronda*, Las Begonas y Andrés Reyes, excellent value, US$10-15. La Plaza de Miguel Dazzo is a place for nightlife, restaurants, bars and discos, popular with Limeños.

In **Barranco**: *El Otro Sitio*, Sucre 317, T 477-2413, open 1230-1600, 1900-2400, Mon-Sat, excellent creole buffet, expensive with live music; *Manos Morenas*, Av Pedro de Osma 409, T 467-0421, open 1230-1630, 1900-2300, creole cuisine with shows some evenings (cover charge for shows); *El Buen Gusto*, Av Grau 323, good for atmosphere, service, selection of meat dishes and desserts, moderate prices; *El Cortijo*, Rep de Panamá 675, T 445-4481, 1200-2400 daily, Peruvian food, moderate; *El Florentino*, Av Grau 680, bar/restaurant/peña, moderate; *Las Mesitas*, Av Grau, unsigned, ask around, excellent creole sweets; *La Ermita*, Bajada de Baños 340, Puente de Suspiros, T 467-1791, open 1230-2400, international cuisine, romantic, expensive; *Canta Rana*, Génova 101, T 445-0498, daily 1200-1700, good seafood and *ceviche*; *El Catamarán*, Av Rep de Panamá 258, T 477-1657, seafood, moderate/expensive, lunch only. Around the main square are several good bars and pizza restaurants; also good *peñas* and night-life.

In **Magdalena del Mar**: *Waco*, Félix Dibos 1087, T 461-9432, open 1100-1500, 1900-2300, Mon-Sat, rec. **Pueblo Libre**: *Taberna Quierolo*, Av San Martín 1090, 2 blocks from Museo Nacional de Antropología y Arqueología, old bar, good seafood and atmosphere, not open for dinner; *Puerto Coral*, La Marina 1004, friendly, huge dishes (try *parihuela*).

In **Monterrico**, near the Gold Museum: *Pabellón de la Caza*, Alonso de Molina 1196, T 437-9533, 1200-1500, 1900-0100 Mon-Sat, Sun brunch 1030-1600, expensive, very good food and service, delightful surroundings; *Puerto Fiel*, Av Primavera 1666, 3 blocks from Gold Museum, seafood, rec.

Lince: *Blue Moon*, Pumacahua 2526, T 470-1190, open 1030-0200 daily, expensive Italian bistro. **Chorrillos**: *El Salto del Fraile*, Herradura Beach, T 442-6622, 1200-2300 daily, Peruvian and seafood, moderate/expensive; *El Encuentro Otani*, San Pedro 182, La Campina, T 467-7668, 0900-1700 daily, excellent seafood, criollo and oriental, very good value. **San Borja**: *El Piqueo Trujillano*, Av San Luis 1956-58, T 476-1993, 1130-1830 Mon-Thur, 1200-2100 Fri-Sun, creole cooking, moderate/ expensive; *Shanghai*, Av San Luis 1988, T 435-9132, 1200-1500, 1900-2300 daily, Chinese, moderately priced. **Surco**: *El Mono Verde*, Av Vicus F-56, Urb La Capullana, T 448-7288, 1300-1900 daily, evening by reservation only, good creole and Peruvian cuisine, moderate/expensive; *Punta Pez*, Camino del Inca 398, T 442-6272, seafood, moderate/expensive.

Jesús María: *El Centro Cultural Peruano Japonés*, Gregorio Escobedo 803, T 463-0606, good, cheap Japanese food.

In **central Lima**: *L'Eau Vive*, Ucayali 370, T 427-5712, across from the Torre Tagle Palace, run by nuns, open Mon-Sat, 1245-1430, 2030-2230, fixed-price US$4 lunch menu (+ taxes and couvert), Peruvian-style in interior dining room, or à la carte in either of dining rooms that open on to patio, excellent, profits go to the poor. *Las Trece Monedas*, in an old colonial mansion off Av Abancay (Ancash 536), T 427-6547, 1200-1600, 1900-2330, Mon-Sat, excellent, local and French food, insist on an itemized bill, expensive; *El Mesón del Frayle*, cloisters of San Francisco, very good, pleasant ambience, 1200-1800 (later by arrangement); *Maury*, Ucayali 201, T 427-6210, Peruvian/international, good pisco sours, moderate/expensive; *Casa Vasca*, Colmena 734, T 423-6690, 1000-2300 daily, Spanish, moderate/expensive; *Daruma*, Nicolás de Piérola 712, T 423-8209, 1000-1500, 1830-2200, Mon-Sat, Japanese, moderate prices; *Gigi's*, Uruguay 411, good chifa, open for lunch; *Raimondi*, Quesada 110 (no sign), T 427-7933, 1300-1600 daily, Peruvian, good food (especially *ceviche*) at reasonable prices; *Buena Muerte*, Junín y Abancay, Plaza Bolívar, lunch only, good *cevichería*; *Hedi*, Puno 367, good, cheap seafood, lunch only, popular; *Alfresco*, Carabaya, good seafood, fish, not cheap; *Rolando's*, Washington 988, good seafood/*ceviche*, moderately priced; *Lucky Star*, N de Piérola 733 (3 blocks from Plaza San Martín), 1000-2400, good restaurant/snack bar with Peruvian food; *El Damero de Pizarro*, Jr de la Unión 543, huge helpings, popular with locals, loud music; *El Pan Nuestro*, Ica 129, T 428-9931, 2 blocks from *Res Roma*, open 0800-2100 Mon-Sat, good value, good food; *Machu Picchu*, near *Hostal España* on Jr Azángaro, excellent set menus for breakfast and lunch, huge portions; *El Capricho*, Av Bolivia, block 3, good cheap *menú*; *Casa del Cappelletti*, Av Tacna, block 7, open 1100-2200, cheap, good Italian. Cheap *pizzería* at corner of Carabaya and Plaza de Armas.

Vegetarian restaurants: *Natur*, Moquegua 132, rec, some English spoken; *Govinda*, Av Callao 480 y Tacna, good value lunch and at Av Arenales 674, Jesus María; *Centro Aplicación Naturista Sebastián Kneipp*, Jr Loreto 379, Rímac, highly rec; *Centro de la Salud "La Naturaleza"*, Jr de la Unión, 819, No 107, or Jr Lampa 440, T 427-3832, 1000-1900, Mon-Fri; *San Juan*, Camaná 949. In Jesús María, *Comedor Vegetariano Nuevo Mundo*, Camillo Carrillo 159, cheap, acceptable.

A good coffee bar for snacks and sandwiches is *Googies* in Plaza San Martín; also *Sandwich Tacna*, Tacna 327, popular and crowded at lunchtime. *Munich Cakehouse*, Cailloma 329 and Ica. Good coffee at *Café de Paso*, Carabobo y Cusco (stand-up coffee shop). *Café Azzurra*,

Jr Unión 574, for coffee; *Pastelería Lobatón*, Jr Unión 672, good *churros*. There are plenty of other cafés and snackbars in the centre of Lima.

Airlines Peruvian airlines with international and national flights: **Faucett**, Garcilaso de La Vega 865, Lima, T 433-8180; Av Diagonal 592, Miraflores, T 446-2031; reservations, T 464-3322/3860. **AeroPerú**, head office at Av Pardo 601, Miraflores, T 447-8900/8355; **Galería Comercial Hotel Sheraton** (sótano), T 447-8255; 24-hr reconfirmation and reservation line T 447-8333. Peruvian airlines with national flights only: **Americana**, Av Larco 345, Miraflores, T 447-1902/446-1966; reservations and reconfirmation, T 447-1919; also at Jr Belén 1015, Lima, T 428-0474. **Expreso Aéreo**, Juan de Aliaga 438, Magdalena del Mar, T 461-9275, reservations, T 445-2545, also Av José Pardo 223, 11th Flr, Miraflores. **Aero Cóndor**, Jr Juan de Arona 781, San Isidro, T 442-5215/441-8484. **Aero Continente**, Francisco Masias 544, 8th Flr, San Isidro, T 442-8770/7829. **Aero Ica**, José de Llano Zapata 331, of 403, Miraflores, T 441-8614/608.

International airlines, phone numbers: **Aeroflot** 444-8716; **Air France** 470-4702; **Alitalia** 428506; **American Airlines** 442-8555/475-6161; **Avianca** 470-4232; **Iberia** 428-3833; **KLM** 447-1394; **Lan Chile** 446-6958/6995; **LAB** 447-3292; **Varig** 442-4031/4148; **Viasa** 447-8666; **Servivensa** 447-2694; **Saeta** 444-0143; **Lacsa** 446-0758 (often have cheaper flights to USA).

Banks and Exchange Most banks at their main branch change TCs without commission into soles, but will charge 2-3% for changing cheques into dollars cash. Banco de Crédito and Interbank give the best rates. There are especially large queues on Mon. Banks are the best place to change TCs and *casas de cambio* for cash. Open Mon-Fri 0900-1600, or 0900-1230, 1500-1800 depending on the bank; many also open Sat am. **Banco de la Nación** (eg Av Abancay 491, Rufino Torico 830), does not change TCs (1995). **Citibank**, Las Begoñas 580, San Isidro, charges no commission on its own TCs, open 0830-1245 in summer. **Bank of America**, Augusto Tamayo 120, San Isidro, will change Bank of America TCs into local currency, 1.5% commission. **Interbanc**, Jr de la Unión 600, esq Huaxcavelica changes cash and TCs, 0915-1515, other branches 0930-1515, 1600-1800 Mon-Fri, 0930-1230 Sat, most branches change Amex TCs at good rates, also Thomas Cook, Visa and Citicorp TCs and cash against Visa card. **Banco de Crédito**, soles given on Visa cards without commission, but check rates in home country for these transactions, Av Lampa 499, 0910-1600 without break, and Larco y Schell branch, Miraflores; Banco de Crédito also handles Amex (sometimes reluctantly) and Citicorp TCs, and cash against Visa card. **Banco Financieri** handles Thomas Cook and Citicorp TCs and cash against Mastercard (as does Banco Wiese). Amex TCs can also be changed at **Bancos Continental** and **Comercio**. **Banco Mercantil**, Ucayali y Carabaya, T 428-2796, changes Amex TCs and gives cash of Visa and Mastercard, central and Miraflores branches open 0900-1700 Mon-Fri, 1000-1200 Sat. Mercantil has a 24-hr bank at the airport which changes Amex TCs. **Casa de cambio Success**, Jr Unión 646 y Emancipación 136, tienda 114, Lima 1, and Pasaje Ancuna 127, of 304, behind Bolsa de Valores, Lima 1, T 428-8118/7294, Mon-Fri 1000-1900, Sat 1000-1700 exchanges Amex, Bank of America and Thomas Cook TCs, competitive rates, also cash (out of hours T 440-0077/442-6052). Always check your money in the presence of the cashier, particularly bundles of pre-counted notes. The banks which deal with credit cards are very efficient in replacing stolen cards; similarly the American Express office (see **Travel Agents** below) in replacing stolen cheques (police report needed). **Diners Club**, Canaval y Moreyra 535, San Isidro, T 441-4272, Mon-Fri 0900-1330, 1430-1800. Lost Thomas Cook cheques are only replaced in Santiago de Chile or Quito.

The **gold dealers** on Pasaje Los Pinos, Miraflores, give good street rates. Many money changers at corner of Plaza San Martín and Jirón de la Unión, and in the streets behind *Hotel Bolívar*, identified by their calculators and hiss of "dollars", change money at the parallel rate; some change other South American currencies (beware, many forgeries in circulation, street changers also short change or swindle you, see **Currency** in **Information for Visitors**). Double-check amounts shown on calculators.

Cultural Institutions Peruvian-British Cultural Association, Av Arequipa 3495, San Isidro, T 470-5577, with reading room and British newspapers (bus 1, 2, 54A). For other offices, library and film shows, Jirón Camaná 787, T 427-7927, classes only; theatre, Av Benavides 620, Miraflores, T 445-4326. British Council, Alberto Lynch 110, San Isidro 27, T 704-350. The theatre of the British Cultural Association is the **Teatro Británico** (amateur productions of plays in English), Calle Bella Vista, Miraflores, T 445-4326. Cámara de Comercio Peruano-Británico, Av Rep de Panamá 3563, of 202, San Isidro, T 441-3268, F 442-2135. Instituto Cultural Peruano y Norteamericano, Cusco 446, T 428-3530, in centre, with library (one can take the US graduate school GRE exam here); branch at Av Arequipa 4798, Miraflores, T 446-0381. Language tuition, US$80 for 4 weeks, Mon-Fri, 2 hrs a day. The American Society of Peru, Av Angamos 1155, Miraflores, T 441-4545. Goethe-Institut, Jr

Nazca 722, Jesus María, Lima 11, T 433-3180, Mon-Fri, 1100-2000, library, theatre, German papers, tea and cakes. **Alliance Française**, Avenida Garcilaso de la Vega 1550, T 423-0139, also in Miraflores, Av Arequipa 4598, T 446-8511. **Euroidiomas**, Juan Fanning 520, Miraflores, T 445-7116, English papers, tea room, Ciné Club.

British Schools Markham College, for boys, is one of only four Headmasters' Conference Schools outside the Commonwealth. Colegio San Andrés, for boys, run by the Free Church of Scotland. Colegio San Silvestre, a school for girls at Miraflores, is represented in the Association of Headmistresses. Colegio Peruano-Británico, San Isidro, co-educational. In La Molina, Colegio Newton offers the international baccalaureate. **American Schools** Colegio Franklin Roosevelt, the American School of Lima, Monterrico, co-educational: Villa María, La Planicie (for girls); María Alvarado, Lima (girls). **German School** Colegio Peruano Alemán Von Humbolt, Av Benavides 3081, Miraflores, T 448-7000.

Embassies/Consulates Argentine Consulate, Pablo Bermúdez 143, 2nd Flr, Jesús María, T 433-5709, open 0800-1300. **Bolivian Consulate**, Los Castaños 235, San Isidro, T 422-8231 (0900-1330). **Brazilian Consulate**, José Pardo 850, Miraflores, T 446-2635, Mon-Fri 0930-1300. **Chilean Consulate**, Javier Prado Oeste 790, San Isidro, T 440-7965, open 0900-1300, need appointment. **Ecuadorean Consulate**, Las Palmeras 356, San Isidro, (6th block of Av Javier Prado Oeste), T 442-4184. **Colombian Consulate**, Natalio Sánchez 125, 4th Flr, T 433-8922/3, Mon-Fri 0900-1300. **Paraguayan Consulate**, Los Rosarios 415, San Isidro, T 441-8154, open 0900-1300. **Uruguayan Consulate**, Av Larco 1013, 2nd Flr, Miraflores, T 447-9948, open 0930-1330. **Venezuelan Consulate**, Av Salaverry 3005, San Isidro, T 441-5948.

US Embassy, Av Inca Garcilaso de la Vega 1400, Lima, T 433-8000 (will move to Monterrico in 1995); **Consulate**: Grimaldo del Solar 346, Miraflores, T 444-3621/3921. **Canadian Embassy**, Libertad 130, Casilla 18-1126, Lima, T 444-4015. **New Zealand Embassy**, contact British Embassy. **South African Consulate**, contact Swiss Embassy.

British Embassy and Consulate, Edificio Pacífico-Washington, Plaza Washington, corner of Av Arequipa (5th block) and Natalio Sánchez 125, 11th Flr (Casilla de Correo 854), T 433-5032/4839/4932/5137, open Mon-Thur 0830-1700, Fri 0830-1315, good for security information and newspapers (yellow bus No 2 passes the Embassy). **Irish Consulate**, Santiago Acuña 135, Urb Aurora, Miraflores T 445-6813. **Austrian Embassy**, Av Central 643, 5th Flr, San Isidro, T 442-8851. **German Embassy**, Av Arequipa 4502, Miraflores, Casilla 18-0504, T 445-7033. **French Consulate**, Arequipa 3415, San Isidro, T 470-4968. **Belgian Consulate**, Angamos 380, Miraflores, T 446-3335. **Spanish Embassy**, Jorge Basadre 498, San Isidro, T 470-5600/78, open 0900-1300. **Swiss Embassy**, Av Salaverry 3240, Magdalena, Lima 17 (Casilla 378, Lima 100), T 462-4090. **Swedish Embassy**, Camino Real 348, 9th Flr, Torre del Pilar, San Isidro, T 440-6700. **Norwegian Consulate**, Canaval Moreyra 595, T 440-4048. **Danish Consulate General**, at Argentine Consulate. **Netherlands Consulate**, Av Principal 190, Santa Catalina, La Victoria, T 476-1069, open Mon-Fri 0900-1200. **Italian Embassy**, Av G Escobedo 298, Jesús María, T 463-2727. **Israeli Embassy**, Natalio Sánchez 125, 6° piso, Santa Beatriz in Lima, Aptdo 738, T 433-4431. **Japanese Embassy**, Av San Felipe 356, Jesus María (postal address: Apartado 3708, Lima), T 463-0000.

NB During the summer, most embassies only open in the morning.

Folklore Every Sun at the *Coliseo Cerrado*, Av Alfonso Ugarte. *AAA Theatre* (see under **historic mansions** above), Ica 323, has folklore evening every Tues, 2015, admission US$3. Also at the *Teatro Municipal*, Jirón Ica (tickets US$0.60-3.60), Tues 2000. *Cooperativa Santa Elisa*, Cailloma 824 (3rd Flr) has a folk group every Wed, 2000. The *Museo de Arte* has seasons of Peruvian folklore on Weds, at 2000, US$1.20 entrance. Many *peñas* have opened in recent years; these are generally cheap, tavern-like places with Peruvian music, much dancing and audience participation, *Hatuchay Peña*, Trujillo 228 (across the bridge past the Post Office), Fri, Sat, 2100, entrance US$3, inexpensive, crowded, good, but take a taxi to and from the *peña*; *Las Brisas de Lago Titicaca*, just off Plaza Bolognesi, US$4.50 entry, rec; *Peña El Ayllu*, Jr Moquegua 247, open every night, entrance free, rec. *La Palizada*, Av del Ejército 800, Miraflores; *Kerygua*, Central Park, Diagonal, Miraflores, good folk music on Fri and Sat, entrance US$2.50; *La Casa de Edith Barr*, Ignacio Merino 250, Miraflores; *Taberna 1900*, Av Grau 268, Barranco, folklore and creole; *El Buho Pub*, Sucre 315, Barranco (next to *El Otro Sitio* restaurant), creole music; *La Casona de Barranco*, Grau 329, modern music, creole and jazz. Many others in Barranco around Plaza Grau and Puente de los Suspiros, eg *Los Balcones* on Av Grau; *La Estación de Barranco*, at Pedro de Osma 112, good, family atmosphere, varied shows, live music at weekends, US$14 cover charge, and *Latinoamericano* on same street; *Mit-Uns*, Av Bolognesi opp *La Noche*, similar to *La Estación*, US$7; *Nosferatu* next to Puente de los Suspiros.

Bars (with music) *Ludwig Bar Beethoven*, Av Grau 687, Barranco, classical music, has concerts nightly; *Pizzelli Latina*, Pedro de Osma, Barranco, great local bar; *Video Pub*, Conquistadores, block 5, San Isidro, modern; *El Sargento Pimienta*, San Martín 587, Miraflores, at weekends jazz and local rock at 2300, Mon, Tues, Wed "jam" sessions, open till 0300; *Phantom Video y Café*, Diagonal 344, Miraflores, open weekends 2000-0400, music videos, good record shop downstairs; *Satchmo Jazz Bar*, Av La Paz 538, Miraflores, good; *Nautilus*, Ricardo Palma 130, open late till dawn for food and drink; *Juanito's Bodega Bar*, Barranco, on the plaza, rec for local colour; *La Noche*, Barranco, popular, video bar; many others by the plaza in Barranco, also on the pedestrian street (Sánchez Carrión) leading from Barranco plaza to Av Bolognesi and others near Puente de los Suspiros.

Discotheques Good nightlife in Miraflores near Parque Diagonal and Av Larco, with discos, video-pubs and pizzerías. All discos have a cover charge of between US$8 and US$20 pp or/couple, including one drink. In most discos only couples are allowed in; most are expensive for drinks, and open from 2100 till 0400. *Keops*, Camino Real 149, San Isidro, is very popular with young Limeños. *Casablanca*, P Fierro 117, San Isidro, cheaper, casual; *Amadeus*, close to Gold Museum, Lima's most expensive and luxurious disco, US$20 cover; *La Rosa Naútica*, above restaurant of same name, young, US$10 cover; *Casa Vieja*, San Martín y La Paz, Miraflores, casual, US$10 cover; *Psicosis*, Bella Vista, 1st block, Miraflores, expensive, young, US$15/couple; *Nirvana*, Schell y Paseo de la República, Miraflores, modern, casual, US$8/couple; *Bizzaro*, Lima y Diez Canseco facing Parque Kennedy, Miraflores, 2nd Flr Edif D'Anafrio, US$5 cover, New York-style, dancing and billiards; similar is *Bauhaus*, on Bellavista. In Surquillo, *Africa*, Av Tomás Marsano 826, and *El Zalonazo*, Calle Uno 157, both rec. There are several discos along the beach in Miraflores, most of them are *salsatecas*, where only salsa is played, cover charge about US$10 pp. *Bartlotto*, up the Malecón in San Miguel, at end of Av Brasil, *salsateca*, US$6 pp.

Theatre Most professional plays are put on at the **Teatro Segura**, Calle Huancavelica, block 2, Lima, T 427-7437, **Teatro Municipal** (Jirón Ica, block 3, Lima, T 428-2303—also orchestral and ballet performances); **Teatro Arequipa**, Av Arequipa, block 8, Lima, T 433-6919; **Teatro Marsano**, Av Petit Thouars, Miraflores, T 445-7347: Open air theatre in Parque Salazar, Miraflores (end of Av Larco) between Nov and Apr; check press for programme. Others are produced by amateur and university groups. **Teatro Cabaña** in the Parque de la Exposición puts on a strong programme of progressive theatre, especially for Institutos shows, local and cheap; take student card. **AAA Theatre Workshop**, Jirón Ica 323. English speaking theatre occasionally by the Good Companions at **Teatro Británico**, details in *Lima Times*. See the newspapers for announcement; the Sun edition of *El Comercio* publishes all cinema and theatre details.

Cinemas Some *Ciné Clubs* are: *El Cinematógrafo*, Pérez Roca 196, Barranco; *Filmoteca de Lima*, Museo de Arte; *Cooperativa Santa Elisa*, Jr Cailloma 824; *Euroidiomas*, Juan Fanning 520, Miraflores; *La Otra Via*, Valdelomar 665, Pueblo Libre; *Melies*, Av Bolívar 635, Pueblo Libre; *Raimondi*, Alejandro Tirado 274, Lima. Free films also at Banco Central, Lampa y Ucayali, Wed at 1630, arrive early. Also the cultural institutions (see above) usually show a film once a week (often Thur). Entry about US$1. The section "C" (Cultural) in *El Comercio* is good for checking film and theatre programmes. Some cinemas: in Miraflores, *Pacífico*, Pardo y Diagonal at the Ovalo; *Romeo y Julieta*, Porta 115; *Colina*, Berlín block 5. In San Isidro, *Real 1* and 2, Centro Comercial Real; *Alcanzar*, Santa Cruz 814. In the centre, *Central*, Tacna 311; *Colón*, Unión 1064; *Colmena*, Nicolás de Piérola 519; *Excelsior 1, 2* and *3*, Unión 700; *Le París 1* and 2, N de Piérola 757; *Plaza 1* and 2, Ocoña 110. Most films are in English with Spanish subtitles; shows are usually at 1500, 1800 or 1830 and 2100 or 2130, US$2 in the centre, US$3.50 in Miraflores.

Doctor Dr Augusto Saldarriaga Guerra, Clínica Internacional, T 433-4306. Dr Alejandro Bussalleu Rivera, Instituto Médico Lince, León Velarde 221, Lince, T 471-2238, speaks English, good for stomach problems. Also good for stomach or intestinal problems, Dr Raul Morales, Clínica Padre Luis Tezza, Av del Polo 570, Monterrico, T 435-6990/6991 (no English spoken). Dr Jorge, Mejía, Analisisclínicos, Av J Pardo Oeste 910, T 440-0643, stool analysis.

Hospitals **Anglo-American Hospital**, Av Salazar, 3rd block, San Isidro. T 440-3570 (rec for injections, but not typhoid; stocks gamma globulin). **Instituto de Medicina Tropical**, Universidad Particular Cayetano Heredia, Av Honorio Delgado, Urb Ingeniería, San Martín de Porres, T 482-3903/3910, for tropical diseases, or any medical help or advice; very good, cheap; for check-ups after a long jungle trip. **Hospital del Niño**, Av Brasil, vaccination centre for yellow fever, tetanus and typhoid at the side. **Clínica Internacional**, Jr Washington 1475, Lima, T 428-8060; **Clínica San Borja**, Av del Aire 333, San Borja, T 475-3141/4997; **Clínica de Fracturas San Francisco**, Av San Felipe 142, Jesus María, T 463-9855/6202. **Policlínico Japonés**, Av Gregorio Escobedo 783, Jesús María, T 461-9291, X-rays, check-ups and analysis, reasonable prices. All clinics have 24-hr emergency service and most of them have

English-speaking doctors. A consultation costs about US$25, not including any medicines. **Centro Especializado de Diagnóstico**, Av Arequipa 1840, Lince, T 471-8506, for x-rays, analyses, etc, no English. **Centro Anti-Rabia**, Jr Austria, Chacra Rios, Lima, T 431-4047.

Dentists Dr Zuelei Cornejo, Octavio Espinoza 443, San Isidro, T 422-9638; Ribamar Camacho Rodríguez, Clínica Los Pinos, Miraflores, T 446-4103/2056, speaks a little English, highly rec. Víctor Melly, Av Conquistadores 965, San Isidro, T 422-5757. Dr Víctor Aste, Antero Aspillaga 415, San Isidro, T 441-7502. Dr Ada Lucía Arroyo Torres, Jr Laredo 196, Centro Comercial Monterrico, T 436-0942.

Language Schools Most institutes have standard packages for one month, 2 hrs a day from Mon to Fri, about US$80; you can arrange for 2, or 3 weeks, or private tuition (about US$10/hr). Instituto de Idiomas Pontífca Universidad Católica del Perú, Jr Camaná 956, Lima, T 431-0052; **La Católica Universidad Instituto de Idiomas**, Camino Real 1037, San Isidro, T 441-5962; Centro de Idiomas de Lima, Av Manuel Olguín 215, Monterrico, T 435-0601, F 435 5970 (PO Box 772, Lima 100), US$12/hr, classes suited to students' travelling schedules, full board accommodation can be arranged with families US$120/week. See also Instituto Cultural Peruano y Norteamericano above. **Quechua Classes** Centro de Idomas Quechua "Yashayhuasi", Mar del Caribe 232 (43rd block of Av La Marina), La Perla, T 465-6061.

Laundry Most of the better class hotels have a laundry service and there are many laundries in Lima, but they are very expensive as they charge/item (eg US$3-4 for a pair of trousers). There are some laundries in Miraflores and San Isidro which charge/kilo, about US$1.50-2. Mostly next day service. *Continental*, Callao 422, same-day and next-day laundry and dry-cleaning, good, charge is per item so expensive. *Burbujitas*, Pasaje 293, Miraflores, 4 kg wash and dry for US$4.50. *Lavaquik*, Av Benevides 604, Miraflores; *Lava Center*, Víctor Maurtúa 140, San Isidro, T 440-3600, US$0.50/kg; *Laverap*, Cantuarias 380, Miraflores, Mon-Sat 0900-1900, rec, US$1.10 kg.

Post Offices Central office is on Pasaje Piura, one block from the Plaza de Armas, T 427-5592, hours: Mon-Sat 0800-2000, Sat 0800-1400. *Poste restante* is in the same building, but on the other side (unreliable); this facility is not available within Peru. In Miraflores, Av Petit Thouars 5201, Mon-Sat 0800-2000. There are many sub-post offices in all districts of Lima, but sending a letter from the suburbs takes longer. Express letters can be sent from the Central Post Office or at the airport (mail posted at the airport reaches Europe in 5 days). There are private companies for express letters, eg: EMS, T 432-3950/278531; DHL, T 451-8587/452-1278; Letter Express, T 444-4509; Peru Express, T 431-1769; VEC, T 442-0830/0866; Skyway, T 422-9225/440-2353. When receiving a package of over 1 kg, it must be collected from the Aduana post office, Av Tomás Valle, near the airport, open Mon-Fri 0830-1400. For parcels see p 1286, Mail.

Telecommunications The Peruvian Telephone Company, CPT (privatized 1994), is situated at Jr Carabaya 933, Plaza San Martín, T 433-1616, open daily 0800-2200; also at Diez Canseco y La Paz, Miraflores, opp *Hotel César*, open daily 0730-2100, and at the airport, open 24 hrs, for national, international and collect calls, with operators. Many modern payphones on the street can be used for international and long distance calls with coins or phonecards. Entel offices can be found all over Lima; phone and fax. For full details on phone operation, see **Telephones** in **Information for Visitors**, p 1286.

NB Since the end of 1994 all Lima phone numbers are 7 digit, beginning with 4. The city code for Lima has changed from 14 to 1.

Air Freight Most companies are in Callao (see Yellow Pages under 'Agencias de Carga'). They all charge about the same and only handle large amounts: by air about US$15/kg, surface US$3-5/kg. You can deal direct with the airlines, all have a cargo office at the airport. KLM is best. UPS, Paseo de la República 6299, Miraflores, T 446-0444, documents or freight to USA US$37/kg, to Europe US$96.

Non-catholic places of worship The *Union Church of Lima* (Interdenominational), Av Angamos 1155, Miraflores, Worship Service Sun 1030, T 441-1472. *Trinity Lutheran Church of Peru*, Las Magnolias 495, Urb Jardín, San Isidro. *Church of the Good Shepherd*, Av Santa Cruz 491, Miraflores (Anglican) T 445-7908, Sun 0800 Holy Communion, 1000 morning service. *International Baptist Church of Lima*, Coronel Inclán 799, Miraflores, T 475-7179, Worship Service Sun 1000. *Christian Science Society*, 1285 Mayta Capac (near Av Salaverry), Jesús María. *English Benedictine Monastery*, Jirón Olivares de la Paz, Las Flores (57M minibus from Plaza de Acho); Sunday Mass 0900, weekdays 1900. *Synagogue*, Av 2 de Mayo 1815, San Isidro, T 440-0290. **Catholic Mass in English**, La Iglesia de Santa María Reina, Ovalo Gutiérrez, Av Santa Cruz, Miraflores, T 424-7269, Sun 0930.

Shopping Since so many artesans have come from the Sierra to Lima, it is possible to find any kind of handicraft in the capital. The prices are the same as in the highlands (except when you happen to deal with the maker, which is not easy), and the quality is high. Silver and gold handicrafts of all kinds; Indian hand-spun and hand-woven textiles; manufactured textiles in Indian designs; llama, vicuña and alpaca wool products such as ponchos, rugs, hats, blankets, slippers, coats, sweaters, etc; *arpilleras*, appliqué pictures of Peruvian life (originated in Chile with political designs), made with great skill and originality by women in the shanty towns; fine leather products mostly hand made. The *mate burilado*, or engraved gourd found in every tourist shop, is cheap and a genuine expression of folk art (cheaper in villages near Huancayo). For handicrafts produced by cooperatives, with benefits going directly to the producers, contact the non-profit organization *Minka*, Av Grau 266, Edif El Portal, 2nd Flr, Barranco, open Tues-Sat 1100-1900, good selection of handicrafts; for further information contact Norma Velásquez.

Silvania Prints, Colmena 714 (near *Hotel Bolivar*), Conquistadores 905 (San Isidro), sell modern silk-screen prints on Pima cotton with precolumbian designs. On Av Nicolás de Piérola vendors sell oil paintings of Andean scenes, bargains abound. *Centro Artesanal "El Arte Peruano"*, Av Alfonso Ugarte 901-925, T 424-1978, open 0900-2000, ask for Carlos Ramos for especially fine retablos, or Guillermo Arce for fine Cajamarca mirrors in colonial style; they also sell rugs from Ayacucho and San Pedro de Cajas, ceramics from Ayacucho and Cusco and other items (there is a nationwide handicraft association of this name). *Artesanías Perú SA* government store for Peruvian handicrafts in San Isidro (Av Jorge Basadre 610, T 440-1925/228847). *La Casa de la Mujer Artesana*, Av Perú 1550 (Av Brasil cuadra 15), Pueblo Libre, T 423-8840, F 423-4031, cooperative run by Morimiento Manuela Ramos, excellent quality work mostly from *pueblos jóvenes*.

Miraflores is the best place for high quality, pricey handicrafts; there are many shops on and around Av La Paz. Recommended is *Kuntur Wasi*, Ocharan 182, T 444-0557, high quality, English-speaking owner very knowledgeable about Peruvian textiles, frequently has exhibitions of fine folk art and crafts; *Antisuyo*, Jr Tacna 460, Miraflores, Mon-Fri 0900-1930, Sat 1030-1830, an Indian cooperative run by an Englishwoman, sells high-quality handicrafts from all regions, reasonable prices, T 447-2557 (another outlet in Cusco). In Miraflores, lovely shopping arcade *El Suche*, at La Paz 646, but high prices in the woollen goods, ceramics and leather shops. Also *Centro Comercial El Alamo*, La Paz (close to *César Hotel*), Miraflores, 0900-2000, *artesanía* shops with good choice. *Las Pallas*, Cajamarca 212, 5th block of Av Grau, Barranco, T 477-4629, Mon-Sat 0900-1900, good quality handicrafts. Antiques available in Miraflores on Av La Paz. See *H Stern's* jewellery stores at *Hotels Miraflores César*, *Bolivar* and *Sheraton*, and at the International Airport.

NB It is better to buy pullovers in the Sierra. However, although Lima is more expensive, it is often impossible to find the same quality of goods elsewhere; geniune alpaca is odourless wet or dry, wet llama "stinks". Alpaca cloth for suits, coats, etc (mixed with 40% sheep's wool) can be bought cheaply from factories: *Cinsa*, Av Argentina 2400, microbus 93, 70 or 84 from Plaza Castilla; *Lanificio*, Nicolas Arriola 3090, San Luis, T 432-0859, better quality in their Arequipa factory (**see p 1208**) (gives 10% discount to foreigners attached to their embassies). Alpaca wool for knitting or weaving from *Alpaca* III, Av Larco 859, Miraflores. Made-to-measure cotton shirts in 24 hrs from Sr Hurtado, "Sir", Jr Carabaya 1108, and in 48 hrs from Luz Manrique, Cailloma 328, T 427-9472. A good tailor is Navarro Hermanos, in Belén, below the Tourist Office. Another is Creaciones Vargas, Jr Ica 380, T 427-8680, good value. Export quality jeans are made by Sombrería Palacio, Unión 214. There are bargains in clothing made from high quality Pima cotton.

Records: *Discos del Mundo*, Unión 779, allows you to listen, in sound-proof booth, before you buy. There are several record shops in the centre, even more in Miraflores.

Markets Parque Diagonal/Kennedy, Miraflores (by *Restaurant Haiti*): secondhand books, jewellery, sandals made to measure, paintings and other handicrafts, Dec-Jun, Wed to Mon, in winter Sat and Sun only; **Feria Artesanal**, Av de la Marina 790 and Av Sucre W, in Pueblo Libre, the biggest crafts market in Lima, bargaining is expected (take bus 11 or colectivo from Plaza Dos de Mayo, or bus 48, Enatru, bus 10 or colectivo from Av Abancay; taxi US$2-3; watch your possessions, as thieves are numerous): extensive market selling woollen goods, leatherwork, bric-a-brac and Peruvian goods and souvenirs; sidestreets off **Lampa**: hardware; sidestreets off **Av Colmena**: books; **Parque Universitario**: bargains; **Plaza San Martín**, behind *Hotel Bolívar*: *ambulantes* (money-changers). **Polvos Azules**, behind Central Post Office, 1 block from Plaza de Armas: sells just about anything (including stolen cameras), small handicraft section (ask directions) which sells best and cheapest earrings, including the parts for making them, beware pickpockets. New handicrafts market in Miraflores on Av Petit Thouars, block 52, good selection and low prices. Flowers are sold at the Estadio Nacional, 8th block of Paseo de la República, open daily.

In every suburb you can find one or more food market. Some of the bigger supermarkets are **Wong**, **Santa Isabel**, and **Mass** (24-hrsupermarket at Benavides y La Paz – excellent stock. Hypermarket in Chorrillos called **Metro**.

Bookshops Fair selection of foreign-language books at *Librería Delta*, N de Piérola 689, Lima. *ABC Bookstores* Av Paseo de la República 3440, No 32B, San Isidro (with other branches) also sell foreign-language books. *Librería Studium*, Plaza Francia 1164 (with several branches), sells history/travel books in English. *Studium* and *Librería de la Universidad de San Marcos* give student discounts. Books in English, French and German also available from *Librería Ayza*, Jirón Unión 560, rec, will supply works in Quechua. *Librería Internacional*, Jirón Unión (corner of Plaza San Martín) has a wide selection of books on South America in all languages. Good English selection at *Epoca*, on Belén in the centre, on José Pardo in Miraflores and other branches, T 445-7430/0282. *Portal* on the plaza in Barranco has good selection, with a gallery, excellent handicrafts for sale and coffee shop. *Librería El Pacífico* in Miraflores has the best selection of English books in Lima. Rare books, many shops on Av Azángaro. **NB** Foreign language books are subject to a high tax (US$12) and there are no guidebooks for sale. International newspapers, from newstands, Block 6, Av N de Piérola, or in the Parque Central, Miraflores (taken from aircraft).

Secondhand books are found in the 5th to 6th block of Av Grau in the centre, some English books are sold, but poor selection. Also around Plaza Francia on the pedestrian street that runs to block 10 of Garcilaso de la Vega.

Film Agfa distributor at E Díaz Canseco 176; for cheap film try at the black market at Feria Polvos Azules, at Puente de Piedra. Many developers using Kodak equipment offer same-day service; at similar prices. Many on Jr Unión and Plaza San Martín; also Av Larco, Miraflores. Fujicolor offer a free film with developing. Quality tends to be poor. Good but expensive place for developing photos and slides at Grimaldo del Solar 275, between Schell and Benavides, Miraflores, T 444-2304, open Mon-Fri 0945-1300, 1400-1830, Sat 0945-1300. *Profesa*, Av Petit Thouars 3231, San Isidro, T 442-3542, specialist shop for photographic equipment. **Camera Repairs** *Camera House*, Larco 1150, Office 39, 2nd Flr, Miraflores, Mon-Fri 1530-1900, ask for Clemente Higa, who is often there later in pm. *Frankitec*, Sr Max Bürkli, Jr Lampa 1115-104, Lima 1, T 428-4331, repairs all cameras (Swiss technician).

Pharmacy *Botica Inglés*, Jirón Cailloma 336, sells Dr Scholl foot supplies for those contemplating or recovering from the Inca Trail. Tampons are available in the centre and Miraflores.

Sports There are two bullfight seasons, one in Oct-Nov and a short one in Mar. They are held in the afternoons on Sun and holidays. Tickets at 2nd block of Calle Huancavelica, or at the Plaza de Acho bullring early on the day of the *corrida*, US$14. Famous *toreros* practise in the Lima ring, the oldest in the Americas, and fighting bulls are of Spanish stock. Cockfights are frequently organized and advertised: the Plaza de Gallos is at Calle Sandía 150, near Parque Universitario. Horse racing, Hipódromo Monterrico, on Tues and Thur evenings (1900) and Sat and Sun (1300) in summer, and in winter on Tues evening and Sat and Sun afternoons. The popular stand is not recommended. Tourists may enter the members' stand on production of their passports. For Paso horses, which move in four-step amble, extravagantly paddling their forelegs, National Paso Association, Miraflores, T 447-6331. Races are held at the Peruvian de Paso breeding farm in Lurín, S of Lima, T 435-6574. The Lima (T 426006), Inca, Granja Azul and La Planicie golf clubs and the Country Club de Villa all have 18-hole courses. The Santa Rosa, Cruz de Hueso and Huampani golf clubs have 9-hole courses. (Contact Gerard Astruck of Sudex SA, T 428-6054, for particulars.) Polo and tennis are also played. Boxing or all-in wrestling (Sat night) at the Coliseo Nacional. There are many private sports clubs but you have to be a member to get in; some will allow visitors for a small fee (US$3-6), even though most only allow visitors with a member, for a small fee.

Association football matches and various athletic events take place at the National Stadium, seating 45,000, in the centre of the city on ground given by the British community on the 100th anniversary of Peru's Declaration of Independence. The local derby is Universitario against Alianza Lima (tickets US$2.50-25, cheaper seats hard to get).

Lima Cricket and Football Club, Justo Vigil 200, Magdalena del Mar, T 461-0080/4030. The club has extensive sports facilities, as well as football, rugby (training at 1700 on Thur, May-Oct) and cricket, squash, swimming, snooker, etc. Also cheap restaurant, pub and friendly place to meet people.

Pool and Bowling on Diagonal, opp Faucett office, Miraflores, T 445-5683.

Cycling Popular, without yet becoming a serious sport: *Bike Touring Club* meets every Sun at 0730 outside Cine Orrantia, Javier Prado y Av Arequipa, T 463-1747 (planning meetings at Cabo Gutarra 613, Pueblo Libre), contact Tito López and Mónica Miranda (Tito repairs bikes, but does not have spares). *Mountain Bike Club*, at *Cicling* shop, Paseo de la República 5756, Miraflores, president Gustavo Prado. *Centro Comercial de Bicicletas*, Av San Juan de Miraflores 1281, Miraflores, T 446-0228.

Trekking and Backpacking For information contact Percy Tapiá, *Trek Andes*, Av Benavides 212, of 1203, Miraflores, PO box 01-3074, Lima 100, T 447-8078, F 445-1641, good information. *Instituto Nacional de Recreación*, Educación Física y Deportes (Inred), has an Andean specialist, César Morales Arnao, at the Estadio Nacional, Tribuna Sur, door 4, 3rd Flr, T 433-4192, ext 42, rec. *Trekking and Backpacking Club*, Jr Huáscar 1152, Jesus María, Lima 11 (T 423-2515), also at Huaraz, Pasaje Sal y Rosas 358; free information on Peru and South America, storage and gas cylinders available. *Meiggs Trekking Club*, Casilla 41-0091, Lima 41, T 446-3493, runs trips once a month. There are several casual trekking clubs in Lima, who do not have regular meetings (not always reliable).

Mountaineering As with trekking, the information provided by the informal mountaineering clubs is questionable. *Club Andino*, Av Paseo de la República 932, Santa Beatriz, contact Lucho Sherpela, T 463-7319, meetings Thur 1900-2200; *Asociación de Andinismo de la Universidad de Lima*, Javier Prado Oeste, Monterrico, contact Daniel Dazzo, T 449-0792, meetings Wed 1800-2000; *Club de Montañeros Américo Tordoya*, Jr Ica 426, Lima, T 428-4172, meetings Tues and Thur 1900-2100, more of a trekking club. *Asociación de Guías de Montañas del Perú*, AGMP, Av Paz Soldan 225, San Isidro, T 441-8831.

Travel Agents Most of those in Lima specialize in selling air tickets, or in setting up a connection in the place where you want to start a tour. Shop around and compare prices; also check all information carefully. It is best to use a travel agent in the town closest to the place you wish visit; it is cheaper and they are more reliable.

Many agencies have moved from the centre of Lima to Miraflores or San Isidro. Those listed below are divided into the following groups: a) standard tours, well-organized but expensive; b) standard tours, less expensive; c) adventure tours; d) specialized tours.

a) *Lima Tours*, Jr Belén (or extension of Unión) 1040, Lima, T 427-6624/ 427-5819/432-1765, F 431-9878, highly rec; in the same building is the American Express agent, which will not change TCs into dollars cash but will give TCs against an Amex card. *Cóndor Travel*, Mayor Armando Blondet 249, San Isidro, T 442-7305, F 442-0935; *Kinjyo Travel*, Las Camelias 290, San Isidro, T 442-4000, F 442-1000; *Solmartur*, Av La Paz 744, Miraflores, T 444-1313, F 444-3060; *Perú Chasqui*, Mariana de los Santas 198-201, San Isidro, T 441-1455; *Panorama*, Bella Vista 210, of A, Miraflores, T 446-9578; *Hada Tours*, Dos de Mayo 529, Miraflores, T 446-2714, F 442-6297; *Mykonos Viajes*, Jr Lampa 1137, block 3, of 1, T 427-5228, very helpful for all parts of Peru.

b) *Travex*, Cnl Inclán 135, of 403, Miraflores, T 447-9838; *Turismo Pacífico*, Alcanfores 373, Miraflores, T 444-3363; *Setours*, Cdte Espinar 233, Miraflores, T 446-7090; *Tecnitur*, Manuel Freyre y Santander 282, Miraflores, T 447-1289; *Julia Tours*, Francia 597, Miraflores, T 447-9798; *Nuevo Mundo*, Jr Camaná 780, of 506, Lima, T 427-0635; *Victor Travel*, Moquequa 124, of 202, T 428-6674.

c) *Explorandes*, Tudela y Varela 450-B, San Isidro, T 445-0532, F 442-3114; *TrekAndes*, Av Benavides 212, of 1203, Miraflores, T 447-8078, F 445-1641; *Andean Tours*, Jr Schell 319, of 304, Miraflores, T 447-8430; *Hirca*, Bellavista 518, Miraflores, T 447-3807, F 447-9271; *Aventours*, Av La Paz 442, Miraflores, T 444-1067, F 445-1641; *Explor Natura*, Piurra 922, Miraflores, T 445-8658, adventure tourism and rafting at Cañete; *Ecoadventures*, Emilio Cavanecia 160, of 201, San Isidro, T 442-3886; *Irré Tours*, Av Boulevard 1012, T 475-8808, Julio speaks good English, arranges trips and guides for small groups.

d) *Peru Mystic Tours*, T 446-4639, spiritual and traditional medicine tour; *CanoAndes*, Av San Martín 455, Barranco, T 477-0188, F 474-1288, rafting and kayaking trips; *High Flight Peru*, Av Santa María 160, Miraflores, T 473-1873, hang-gliding, para-gliding; *Viento Sur Expediciones*, Av La Molina 444, T 435-6226, sailing tours to Paracas and day tours from Lima.

Useful addresses: Apavit, Asociación Peruana de Agencias de Viajes y Turismo, Antonio Roca 121, Santa Beatriz, T 433-7610; Apta, Asociación Peruana de Operadores de Turismo de Aventura, Benavides 212, of 1203, Miraflores, T 447-8078; Agotur, Asociación de Guías Oficiales de Turismo, Jr Belén 1030, Lima, T 424-5113.

Private guides: Rolando Peceros, contact Lima tours, T 427-6720 or 448-5562 (home), specialist in Peruvian archaeology from Chiclayo to Nazca, charges US$25/day. Tino Guzmán Khang, T 429-5779, or South American Explorers Club, cultural tours, especially Pachacámac, museums, special interest tours, English speaking, US$6/hr.

NB We have received complaints about agencies, or their representatives at bus offices or the airport arranging tours and collecting money for companies that either do not exist or which fall far short of what is paid for. Do not conduct business anywhere other than in the agency's office and insist on a written contract.

Tourist Offices Tourist offices throughout Peru are operated by the Ministerio de Industria, Comercio, Turismo e Integración, Calle 1 Oeste, Corpac, 14th Flr, F 442-9280. In Lima, the tourist office is Infotur, Jr Unión (Belén) 1066, Oficina E-2, T 431-0117, Mon-Fri 0930-1730, Sat 1000-1300; they give out tourist information, make reservations and are very helpful, including on which parts of the country it is safe to visit. Enturperú administers the State Tourist Hotel chain: to make reservations in advance T 442-8626/8837, or 472-1928 for information. There is a tourist booth at the airport which will make local reservations, or you can call the hotel direct. There are several representatives of travel agencies at the airport, but they are rather pushy; better to take your time and arrange trips once settled in your hotel, or shop around later. Ask for the helpful, free, *Peru Guide* published in English by Lima Editora, T 444-0815, available at travel agencies or other tourist organizations, not always up-to-date.

Maps A good map of the whole country is available from street sellers in the centre of Lima, or in better bookshops (published by Lima 2000, US$10, or US$14 in booklet form). A cheaper, less accurate map is published by Cartográfica Nacional for US$3-4. The Instituto Geográfico Militar (Av Aramburu 1190, Surquillo, Lima 34, T 475-9960), sells a standard map of Peru (1:2,200,000), and department maps, US$5 and a 4-sheet map of Peru, 1: 1,000,000, US$32, at the same size and for the same price is a geological map; Topographical maps, 1:100,000, which only cover Peru from the coast to the highest mountains and most of the Department of Loreto, cost US$4.25. Satellite map of most of the jungle area, 1:100,000, is US$8; black-and-white aerial photos available at US$8; passport needed to enter; they are open 0830-1400, Mon-Fri. Maps of N and S border areas are not sold. If you submit a letter to the IGM, giving your credentials and adequate reasons, plus a photocopy of your passport, you may be able to obtain maps of the border regions. Aerial photographs are available at Servicio Autofotográfico Nacional, Las Palmas airforce base, Chorrillos, T 467-1341, open Mon-Fri 0800-1300, 1330-1545. Ingement, Pablo Bermúdez 211, Jesus María, T 433-6234, open 0730-1400, has information on geology and sells some maps. Senamhi, República de Chile 295, Jesus María, T 433-7624, open 0830-1345, has good information on Peruvian meteorology. Petroperú maps for town centres rec.

South American Explorers' Club Av Rep de Portugal 146 (Breña—in the 13th block of Alfonso Ugarte), T 0051-1-425-0142, is a non-profit, educational organization which functions primarily as an information network for Peru and South America. Membership is US$40 a year (US$60/couple), which includes subscription to its quarterly journal, *The South American Explorer*, and numerous member services such as access to files of travel information, equipment storage, personal mail service, trip planning, etc. Open 0930-1700 Mon to Fri; non-members are welcome, but asked to limit their visits, staff very helpful. The clubhouse is attractive and friendly; it is not necessary to "explore" to feel at home here. They will sell used equipment on consignment (donations of used equipment, unused medicines etc, are welcome). Their map of the Inca Trail is good (US$4), and they sell an excellent map of the Cordillera Huayhuash. Other useful dyeline trekking maps include the Llanganuco-Santa Cruz trek in the Cordillera Blanca, and the Cordillera Vilcanota (Auzangate). There is a good library and they sell travel books (including this one) and guides (at a discount to members), limited book swap facilities are available, and some excellent handicrafts. For further information, and the most recent views on where and how to travel safely, write to: Casilla 3714, Lima 100, Peru; 126 Indian Creek Road, Ithaca, NY 14850, USA (T 607-277-0488); or Apartado 21-431, Eloy Alfaro, Quito, Ecuador (T 566-076). (Also see the Bradts' *Backpacking* book, listed in "Information for Visitors"; all Bradt publications are on sale at the Club.)

Tourist and Archaeological Information Federico Kaufmann-Doig is a great source of information on Peruvian archaeology, for serious students and archaeologists. He has worked on various sites in Peru and is currently engaged on a 3-year project in the Kuelap area. He is the director of the Instituto de Arqueología Amazónica, T 449-0243, or (home) 499103. His book, *Historia del Perú: un nuevo perspectivo*, in 2 volumes (*Pre-Inca*, US$8, and *El Incario*, US$10) is available at better bookshops. The Instituto Nacional de Cultura, Jr Ancash, 390 Lima, T 428-7990/9295, should be contacted by archaeologists for permits and information. The Museo Nacional de Antropología y Arqueología in Pueblo Libre (address above) is the main centre for archaeological investigation and the Museo de la Nación holds exhibitions.

Books of interest for the tourist: *Documenta del Perú* (in Spanish), an encyclopedia describing each department, with general information; *Guía "Inca" de Lima Metropolitana* is invaluable for finding less well known, but interesting, parts of Lima; *Lima Incognita* and *Lima y Lo Limeño* by Juan Manuel Ugarte Elespurú; *Cartas de Lima*, by Alfonsina Barrio Nuevo; *Muestras Fotográficas de La Lima Antigua* by Horizonte. The *Lima Times* publishes a monthly English magazine with stories and useful information; see above for *Peru Guide*.

The Peruvian Touring and Automobile Club Av César Vallejo 699 (Casilla 2219), Lince, Lima (T 403270), offers help to tourists and particularly to members of the leading motoring associations. Good maps available of whole country; regional routes and the S American sections of the Pan-American Highway available (US$2.10).

Useful Addresses Tourist Police, Museo de la Nación, J Prado 2465, 5th Flr, San Borja, T 437-8171/435-1342/437-8262, friendly, helpful, English and some German spoken, open 0800-2000; rec to visit when you have had property stolen. **Dirección General de Migraciones**, Paseo de la República 585, open 0900-1300; if passport stolen can provide new entry stamps, also for visa extensions, given same day. **Intej**, Av San Martín 240, Barranco, can extend student cards, T 477-4105. **YMCA**, Av Bolívar 635, Pueblo Libre, membership required. **Biblioteca Nacional**, Av Abancay (cuadra 4) y Miró Quesada, T 428-7690, open 0830-2000.

Local Buses The bus routes are shared by buses and col0 ectivos; the latter run from 0600-0100, they are quicker and stop wherever requested. Bus fares US$0.30, colectivos US$0.35-0.45, depending on length of journey. The principal route is from the centre of Lima to Miraflores, San Isidro, Pueblo Libre, central market and airport. The centre, between Tacna,

Abancay and Nicolás de Piérola is now free of buses. Look for route names on bus windscreen, but check that the bus is going in the direction you want.

Taxis No taxis use meters and anyone can operate as a taxi driver, you must bargain the price beforehand. Also, insist on being taken to the destination of your choice, not the drivers'. Fares: within city centre US$1.50-2; to Miraflores and most suburbs US$2-3.50; to the airport US$4-5; from airport to centre US$4; to Miraflores US$5-6. After dark and on holidays, 35%-50% surcharge. Licensed taxis are blue and yellow, but there are many other types: the Volkswagens are cheaper; the bigger black taxis charge US$15-20 from centre to suburbs. Licensed and phone taxis are safest. There are several reliable phone taxi companies, which can be called for immediate service, or booked in advance; prices are 2-3 times more than ordinary taxis; eg to the airport US$12, to suburbs US$7-8. Some are *Taxi Real*, T-470-6263; *Taxi Metro*, T 437-3689; *Lady's* T 470-8528; *Taxi Phono*, T 422-6565; *Taxi Seguro*, T 448-7226. Paco, T 461-6394, is dependable for phone hiring, similarly Willy, T 452-7456, speaks some English.

Drivers don't expect tips; give them small change from the fare. If hiring a taxi for over 1 hr agree on price/hr beforehand. To Callao, La Punta, San Miguel, Magdalena, Miraflores (US$4), Barranco, Chorrillos, by agreement, basis US$5/hr. Rec, knowledgeable driver, Hugo Casanova Morella, T 485-7708 (he lives in La Victoria), for city tours, travel to airport, etc.

"Trici-Taxis", 3-wheel cycle carts, can be hired for moving about with heavy baggage.

Car Rental All rental companies have an office at the airport, where you can arrange everything and pick up and leave the car. Cars can be hired from **Hertz Rent-a-Car**, Rivera Navarrete 550, San Isidro, T 442-4475; **Budget Rent A Car**, Francisco de Paula Camino 231-A, Miraflores, T 445-1266; **Avis**, Av Camino Real 1278, San Isidro, T 441-9760; **Dollar**, Av La Paz 438, Miraflores, T 444-4920; **National**, Av España 449, Lima, T 433-3750; **Thrifty**, Aristides Aljovin 472, Miraflores, T 444-4441; **VIP**, Conquistadores 697, San Isidro, T 441-3705. Prices range from US$40 to US$60 depending on type of car. The condition of vehicles is usually very poor. Beware of deep street potholes. Make sure that your car is in a locked garage at night. Russian-made four-wheel drive Niva vehicles are often rented; they are up to the conditions of Andean driving, but Lada saloon cars are not. Note that it can be much cheaper to rent a car in a town in the Sierra for a few days than to drive all the way from Lima. Also, if there are any problems with the rental car, companies do not have a collection service.

Cycling into or out of Lima is not rec, difficult and dangerous, marginally safer at dawn.

Airport The Jorge Chávez airport is 16 km from the centre of Lima; it was largely reconstructed in 1994 with many new facilities. There is control of people entering and leaving the airport; tourists may have to show documents. Luggage may be checked several times, so arrive 3 hrs before your departure (1½ hrs for domestic flights). Taxi, about US$5-6 to centre, US$6-8 to Miraflores (negotiate price before leaving, expect to pay more at night; hang on to your bag if surrounded by taxi touts). The gate for cars leaving the airport is in the middle of the parking area; for pedestrians it is at the lefthand corner of the parking area, from where you can catch a cheaper taxi to the city. There is a service called Airport Express, every 20 mins to Miraflores from the national exit, comfortable micro buses, US$3. Local buses and colectivos run between the airport perimeter and the city centre and suburbs, their routes are given on the front window ("Tacna" for the centre, "Miraflores" for Miraflores, "Brasil" for South American Explorers Club). Outside the pedestrian exit are the bus, colectivo and taxi stops, but there is more choice for buses at the roundabout by the car entrance. Luggage is not allowed on buses. There is a cheap colectivo service from corner of Av Tacna with Colmena (N de Piérola) 733, from 0600 to 2000, colectivos wait until they have 5 passengers, US$0.75 pp, and US$0.25 for luggage. The big hotels have their own buses at the airport, and charge US$6. There is a duty-free shop which will accept Amex cards. Prices on some items higher than at supermarkets. Only official Corpac porters are allowed in the customs area. Do not give your bags to unofficial porters who are desperate to carry your luggage. Banco Mercantil is the only bank at the airport that changes TCs (Amex and Citicorp) and gives cash advance on Visa or Mastercard; open 24 hrs. Avoid getting left with soles at the airport when leaving; changing them back into dollars at Banco de la Nación can take a lot of time, and you need to show the official exchange slips. Car rental booths in airport may buy soles. 24-hr left luggage costs US$1/item (make sure luggage is locked, or use the US$1 plastic loop to seal bags). The Peruvian Telephone Company has a 24-hr office. Information on arrivals and departures: international T 452-3135; national T 452-9570. The Prohotel agent at the airport is very helpful with hotel bookings of all classes; there is a second hotel booking agency. Taxi drivers also tout for hotel business, offering discounts—don't let yourself be bullied. Safe to stay all night in 24-hr expresso-snack bar but expensive. You can also sleep on the 1st floor above the check-in area. There is an airport workers' canteen "comedor de los trabajadores" also open to the public, just beyond the perimeter fence to the right of the main terminal. For those in transit, refreshment options are expensive, although temporary access to shops in the main lobby of the terminal building is possible.

Strict controls at the airport may mean that an official will demand to search your luggage. Legally they cannot ask for money and this also applies on arrival. This is not true if you are importing goods or bringing a large quantity of new merchandise, when taxes are charged. Taxes cannot be charged on new personal possessions. At the customs area, insist that you are a tourist and that your personal effects will not be sold in Peru; if necessary ask them to stamp in your passport that you are bringing a bicycle, stereo, whatever, and will leave with it.

Internal Air Services   The domestic airlines serve the following places: Arequipa, Ayacucho, Chachapoyas, Chiclayo, Cusco, Iquitos, Piura, Pucallpa, Puerto Maldonado, Rioja, Tacna, Talara, Tarapoto, Trujillo and Tumbes. Expreso Aéreo serves the following places on an irregular basis: Andahuaylas, Cajamarca, Chimbote, Tingo María, Yurimaguas, Ica and Nazca. Aéro Cóndor has a small plane for flights to N destinations and jungle areas: Ayacucho, Andahuaylas, Atalaya, Bellavista, Cajamarca, Chachapoyas, Chimbote, Huánuco, Ica, Juanjui, Palmapampa, Palma de Espino, Rodríguez de Mendoza, San Francisco, Saposoa, Tingo María, Tocache and Uchiza. To most destinations there are a few flights a week, but flights are cancelled if the plane is not full and in the rainy season.

Rail   There has been no passenger service to La Oroya or Huancayo since 1991, although trains are running from Huancayo to Huancavelica. Check for information, T 427-6620/428-9440. For all these destinations there are bus and colectivo services. Central Railway of Peru maintains freight service to La Oroya (with an extension N to Cerro de Pasco) and SE to Huancayo (with an extension to Huancavelica): Desamparados station, behind Palacio de Gobierno. (For description of line **see p 1250**.) If the train service is restored, sit on the left; remember that the train changes direction at San Bartolomé, so you will be sitting on the right to begin with. On Sun in the dry season there is a train to San Bartolomé at 0830, returning in the afternoon.

Bus Companies   There are many different bus companies, but the larger ones are better organized, leave on time and do not wait until the bus is full. For approximate prices, frequency and duration of trip, see destinations. Bus companies which serve all Peru (in Lima unless stated otherwise): Ormeño, Carlos Zavala 177, T 427-5679/428-8453, with a more expensive luxury service to Trujillo and Chiclayo, well-organized and rec; Tepsa, Av Paseo República 129, T 427-6271/432-1233, old buses, poor service, dangerous driving, but an extensive schedule throughout the country; Cruz del Sur, Quilca 531, T 427-1311/423-1570, expanding network, rec; Expreso Sudamericano, Montevideo 618, T 427-1077/7708, fewer buses, but cheaper.

Companies with routes to the N: Perú Express, Guillermo Dansey 235, T 424-8990, luxury buses to Chimbote, Trujillo, Chiclayo; Chiclayo Express, Av Grau 653, T 428-5072, to Chiclayo direct; Expreso Panamericano, Av Alfonso Ugarte 951, T 424-9045, to Chimbote, Trujillo, Chiclayo. Transporte Cinco, Jr Sandia 205, T 428-1915, to Barranca, Paramonga; Olano/Oltursa, Jr Apurímac 567 y Av Grau 617, T 428-2370, to Chiclayo, Piura, Jaén, Bagua Tumbes; Atahualpa, Jr Sandia 266, T 427-5838, to Chimbote, Cajamarca, Celendín; Fortaleza, Leticia 515, T 428-2577, similar routes. Rodríguez, Av Roosevelt 354, T 428-0506, to Huaraz and Caraz; Movil Tours and Paradise Tours, both at Abancay 947, to Huaraz, both rec (as is Ormeño); Cóndor de Chavín, Montevideo 1039, T 428-8122, to Chavín. Cruz de Chalpón, Montevideo 809, T 427-0981, to Chimbote, Trujillo, Piura; Espadín, Carlos Zavala 140, T 428-5857, to Churín; Turismo Chimbote, Huarochiri 785 (2 blocks off Dos de Mayo), T 424-0501, Chimbote direct and Caraz; Chinchaysuyo, Av Grau 525, T 427-5038, to Casma, Caraz, Chimbote, Trujillo, Pacasmayo and Piura; Antisuyo, Av Abancay 947, T 428-1414, to Trujillo; Las Dunas, Paseo de la República 821, La Victoria, T 431-0235, to Chimbote, Trujillo, Chiclayo, luxury. Transporte Piura, Montevideo 801, to Trujillo, Chiclayo, Piura, Tumbes; Transfysa, Av Montevideo 724, T 428-0412, to Chiquián and Pachapaqui; Civa Cial, Carlos Zavala 217 y Montevideo 500 (opp Ormeño), T 432-4926, to Trujillo, Chiclayo, Piura, Tumbes, Huaraz, Chachapoyas and Bagua, good service. In the same terminal is an office selling tickets for Cruz del Sur, whose buses leave from Jr Quilca (see above), and an office for Mariscal Cáceres, whose buses leave from here and from 28 de Julio (see below).

Companies with routes to the S: Cañete, Av Grau 427, T 428-2729, to Cañete direct; General de San Martín, Montevideo 552, T 428-1423, to Pisco and Ica; Señor Luren, Av Abancay 1165, T 428-0630, to Ica and Nazca; Cóndor Aymaraes, Jr Condesuyos 477, T 428-6618, to Ica, Nazca and Abancay; Plateados del Sur, Montevideo 517, T 427-9485, to Ica and Nazca; Victoria del Sur, Montevideo 762, T 428-8682, to Arequipa and Cusco; Morales Moralitos, Av Grau 141, T 427-6310, to Abancay and Cusco; Señor de Animas Apurímac, Av Luna Pizarro 453, La Victoria, T 431-0904, to Apurímac, Abancay, Cusco; Expreso Jacantaya, Av Grau 486, T 432-8987.

Companies to the centre: Huaytapallana, Jr Cotabambas 321, T 428-4286, similar; also Mariscal Cáceres, Av 28 de Julio 2195, La Victoria, T 474-7850, good "Imperial" service to

Huancayo (similarly Cruz del Sur, address above). León de Huánuco, Av 28 de Julio 1520, T 432-9088, to Huánuco, Tingo María, Pucallpa; Chanchamayo, Av Luna Pizarro 453, La Victoria, T 432-4517, to Tarma, San Ramón, La Merced; Nuestra Señora de la Merced, Av 28 de Julio 1535, La Victoria, similar route; Satipo Expreso, Av Luna Pizarro 488, La Victoria, T 423-9272, to La Merced; Transmar, Av 28 de Julio 1511, La Victoria, T 433-7440, to Tingo María and Pucallpa, also Etposa, Av José Gálvez 1121, Lince, T 472-1402; Trans Rey, Av 28 de Julio 1192, La Victoria (terminal), Av Luna Pizarro 398, La Victoria (ticket office), T 431-9808, luxury bus to Pucallpa.

Comités are small vans which run on some routes throughout Peru; they are quicker, more comfortable, but double the price of buses. They only leave when full. In Lima unless otherwise stated: Comité No 14, Leticia 604, T 428-6621, to Huaraz; No 25, Jr Azángaro 839, T 428-7524, to Chimbote; No 12, Montevideo 736, T 427-3327, to Huancayo and Huánuco; No 30, Av Bolívar 1335, La Victoria, T 432-9459, and No 22, Ayacucho 997, T 428-9082, to Huancayo; No 1, Luna Pizarro 377, T 431-0652, to Tarma; No 18, Av N de Piérola 1470, T 428-8143, to Huacho and Barranca. Colectivos to Huacho and Huaral leave from Plaza de Acho.

International Buses To enter Peru, a ticket out of the country may be required. If you have to buy a bus ticket, be warned: they are not transferable or refundable.

Tepsa runs a twice weekly service to **Santiago**, Chile (3 days, 3,500 km) leaving Lima on Thur and Sun at 1645. Ormeño international buses leave from Javier Prado 1059, T 472-1710, no change of bus at border: to Guayaquil (US$60) and Quito (US$70) twice a week; Cali (US$130) and Bogotá (US$145) once a week; Cúcuta (US$185) and Caracas (US$195) once a week; Santiago (US$70) on Tues and Sat, 2½ days, 3 meals included; Mendoza (US$130) and Buenos Aires (US$140) twice a week, 3½ days, incl 3 meals and hotel in Santiago, good buses. Caracol (in Cruz del Sur building) to Guayaquil (US$40), Quito (US$50), Cali (US$100), Bogotá (US$120), Cúcuta (US$145) and Caracas (US$150), same bus all the way, no food included. Also to Santiago (US$91), Buenos Aires (US$180), Mendoza (US$137), Montevideo (US$190), Asunción (US$218) and Rio de Janeiro (US$248), meals incl, have to change bus in Santiago. El Rápido, Av Carlos Zavala Loayza 177, T 428-3181, weekly to **Mendoza** and **Buenos Aires**, fare includes meals and one night in a hotel, takes 4 days. Connecting twice weekly services to **Guayaquil and Quito** (although there are no through buses; you can buy through tickets but they are very expensive and give no priority), leaving Lima on Wed and Sun at 0845. The trip takes 2½ days; often long frontier delays. Bear in mind that international buses are more expensive than travelling from one border to another on national buses.

Warning The area around the bus terminals is very unsafe; thefts and assaults are more common in this neighbourhood than elsewhere in the city. You are strongly advised to consider taking a taxi to and from your bus. Make sure your luggage is well guarded and put on the right bus. It is also important not to assume that buses leave from the place where you bought the tickets.

In the weeks either side of Jul 28/29 (Independence), and of the Christmas/New Year holiday, it is practically impossible to get train or bus tickets out of Lima. Prices for bus tickets double around Independence Day and Christmas.

Suburbs of Lima The Avenida Arequipa connects the centre of Lima with Miraflores. Parallel to this is the Vía Expresa, a highway carrying fast traffic to the suburbs (6 lanes for cars, 2 for buses). San Isidro, Pueblo Libre, Miraflores and parts of Lince have some good examples of Art Deco and Estilo Barca residential architecture. At **San Isidro** is El Olivar, an old olive grove turned into a delightful park (best visited in daylight). Beyond this is the Lima Golf Club where the Country Club is found, primarily a hotel, which incorporates the Real Club with swimming pools, tennis courts, etc (open to members only). This is an 8 km taxi ride from the centre of Lima. There are many good hotels and restaurants in San Isidro; **see main Lima lists, hotels p 1118 and restaurants p 1119.** Between San Isidro and Miraflores is the Pan de Azúcar, or Huallamarca, a restored adobe pyramid of the Maranga culture, of about AD 100-500 (Calle Nicolás de Rivera 201, small museum, open daily, 0900-1700, bus 1 from Av Tacna, or minibus 13 or 73 to Choquechaca, then walk).

The road reaches the sea at **Miraflores**, the largest, most important suburb of Lima, with well stocked shops and many first class hotels and restaurants (see main Lima lists: hotels **p 1116**, Youth Hostel, **p 1119** and restaurants, **p 1119**). Together

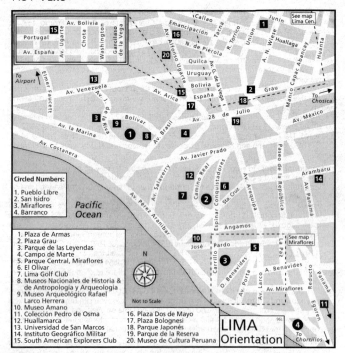

The map labels (read from image):

See map Lima Cen.

Av. Bolivia

Portugal | Chota | Washington | Garcilaso de la Vega

Av. Ugarte

Av. España

To Airport

Elmer Faucett

Av. Venezuela

Av. la Riva

Bolívar

Av. la Marina

Av. Costanera

Emancipación | Callao | Junín | Union | A. N. Wiese | Huallaga | Huanta

N. de Piérola | Tacna | R. Torrico

Quilca | Av. Alfonso Ugarte

Uruguay | N. G. de la Vega

Bolivia | España | Grau | To Chosica

Av. Arica | Av. 28 de Julio | Av. México

Av. Brasil

Av. Javier Prado

Av. Salaverry | Camino Real | Sta. Cruz | Araquipa | Paseo de la República | Aramburu | Av. Panamá

Av. Pérez Aranibar | Espinar | Conquistadores

Angamos

José | Pardo | Carrillo | O. Benavides | O. Porta | Av. Larco | A. Benavides | Av. Miraflores | Reducto | Panamá | Eguren

See map Miraflores

To Chorrillos

Circled Numbers:
1. Pueblo Libre
2. San Isidro
3. Miraflores
4. Barranco

Pacific Ocean

N Not to Scale

1. Plaza de Armas
2. Plaza Grau
3. Parque de las Leyendas
4. Campo de Marte
5. Parque Central, Miraflores
6. El Olivar
7. Lima Golf Club
8. Museos Nacionales de Historia & de Antropología y Arqueología
9. Museo Arqueológico Rafael Larco Herrera
10. Museo Amano
11. Colección Pedro de Osma
12. Huallamarca
13. Universidad de San Marcos
14. Instituto Geográfico Militar
15. South American Explorers Club
16. Plaza Dos de Mayo
17. Plaza Bolognesi
18. Parque Japonés
19. Parque de la Reserva
20. Museo de Cultura Peruana

LIMA Orientation

with San Isidro this is now the social centre of Lima. There is a handsome park in the middle of the shopping centre and at the end of Avenida Mariscal Benavides, which is commonly called Av Diagonal, you can get the best view of the whole Lima coastline from Chorrillos to La Punta. The Mariscal Necochea clifftop park overlooks the Waikiki Club, a favourite with Lima surfers. In Parque Kennedy is an artists' and craftsmen's market, most evenings of the week, and concerts Thur-Sun. Calle San Ramón, opp Parque Kennedy off Av Diagonal, is closed to traffic and lined with many pizzerias.

Beaches Lima is situated on the Pacific Ocean, somewhat protected by an open bay, with its two points at La Punta (Callao) and Salto de Fraile (Chorrillos). A Malecón runs along the coast, giving a good view. The Parque Salazar in Miraflores is a great place to listen to a concert in the summer, while overlooking the bay. Several walkways and roads (also the highway from the centre, the Via Expresa) work their way down to the ocean, where a beach road runs around the entire bay. There are several beaches, popular with surfers and sun lovers, and a number of beach clubs (for members only). At night the clubs become discos, where the Limeños come to dance salsa until the early hours. There are plenty of seafood kiosks along the beach and two expensive restaurants, *Costa Verde* and *Rosa Náutica*. The latter, on a pier, is one of the nicest in Lima. In summer (Dec-Apr) the beaches get very crowded at weekends and lots of activities are organized. Even though the water of the whole bay has been declared unsuitable for swimming, Limeños see the beach more as part of their culture than as a health risk. Do not

MIRAFLORES

Not to Scale

| 1. L'Ovalo | 3. Parque Kennedy |
| 2. Parque Central | 4. Plaza Bolognesi |

To San Isidro & Central Lima

camp on the beaches as robbery is a serious threat; for the same reason, take care on the walkways down. Don't take any belongings with you to the beach, only what is really necessary.

Buses to Miraflores Plenty of colectivos (small vans) run the route between the centre and Miraflores, along Tacna, Garcilaso de La Vega, Arequipa and Larco, 24 hrs, US$0.30 by day, US$0.35 on Sun, US$0.45 after midnight. Routes are displayed on the windscreen. Some buses also run this route for US$0.30; check the route before you get in. On Via Expresa, buses can be caught at Avs Tacna, Garcilaso de la Vega and Ugarte (faster than Av Arequipa, but watch for pickpockets). The main stop for Miraflores is Ricardo Palma, 4 blocks from Parque Kennedy. Taxi US$2.30.

The road passes through ***Barranco*** (not to be confused with Barranca, 200 km N of Lima), with an attractive plaza and nearby the interesting *bajada*, a steep path down to the beach, where many of Lima's artists live; many old houses are under restoration. The Puente de los Suspiros (bridge of sighs), leads towards the Malecón, with fine views of the bay. It has a delightful public library (formerly the town hall). Barranco is extremely popular at night, with good bars, restaurants and live music. (Some colectivos as for Miraflores, some running all the way to Barranco, check on the front window or ask, same fare; it is a 45 mins' walk from Miraflores to Barranco along the Malecón—lovely sunsets in summer.) The next development on the coast is at ***Chorrillos***, a fashionable resort (*Café Suizo* overlooking beach—beware overcharging in seaside restaurants) with a cliff promenade, and boating. At Hacienda La Villa, an old Spanish *hacienda* worth visiting, there is occasionally open air dancing to *salsa* music. Down the beach from Chorrillos is the fish market, with several seafood stalls (the fish is fresh, but is caught in polluted water), Playa Agua Dulce (a clean beach), and the Club Regatas de Lima. Beyond Chorrillos is **La Herradura**, another bathing resort with several restaurants. The private Club Unicornio is open to tourists.

Avenida Costanera passes through a run down seaside resort, **Magdalena del Mar**, served by a separate road and bus route from Lima. A little inland, along this route, is **Pueblo Libre**, where the Museo de Antropología y Arqueología, the Museo Arqueológico Rafael Larco Herrera and the Museo Nacional de Historia are found (see under Museums, p 1113), as well as the old church of Magdalena Vieja (1557), which was unfortunately heavily damaged in the 1974 earthquake.

Those visitors interested in living in one of Lima's *pueblos jóvenes* for a few days should contact Gabino Conde Gómez, Av Jorge Chávez 1958, Comas, Lima 7 in writing. Write in Spanish a few months before you plan to arrive in Lima. Gabino does not charge for lodging in the shanty settlement, but he asks foreigners to bring video films or video games (Max Play System) in exchange.

Callao Passengers coming to Peru by sea usually land at Callao (now contiguous with Lima). It handles 75% of the nation's imports and some 25% of its exports. Lima is reached by road (20 mins by car, colectivos US$0.30, bus US$0.25, taxi US$3-4 to the centre or Miraflores).

Callao's maritime terminal or inner harbour covers 100 ha, and the largest vessels go alongside. Population, 588,600. San Lorenzo island, a naval station, protects the roadstead from the S; inland stretches the Rímac valley. It is a commercial place with no architectural beauty. There are some interesting shops in the area between Calle Constitución and Av Sáenz Peña, and a market between Sáenz Peña and Buenos Aires. "The Club", the oldest English club on the W coast, is at Pasaje Ronald, Calle Constitución, Callao; there is an English cemetery.

History Drake (13 February 1579) and others raided Callao in the 16th century. An earthquake wiped it out in 1746. On 5 November 1820, Lord Cochrane boarded and captured, after a bloody fight in which he was wounded, the Spanish frigate *Esmeralda*. The Real Felipe fortress (1774), last stronghold of the Royalists in S America, withstood a siege of a year and finally surrendered after terrible sufferings in 1826. It is still a military post, and tourists are allowed to visit it. The Museo Histórico Militar is in the old barracks; there is also the Museo Naval (**see p 1115** for both). The railway to Lima, opened 17 May 1851, was one of the first in S America, but the last train/tram ran in 1965.

Restaurants *Francesco*, Cañete 137 (behind Sáenz Peña cinema), T 655886, 1130-1700, good seafood, expensive/moderate; *Ah-Gusto*, Mcal Castilla 568, La Perla, T 293328, local place for *ceviche*, moderate/cheap.

Warning Callao has a serious theft problem, avoid being there in the evening.

The Naval College is at **La Punta**, just beyond Callao, served by municipal buses and colectivos through Callao from Lima. La Punta is on a spit of land stretching out to sea; once a fashionable beach, but the water is cool. A new yacht club has been built on the N side. The walk along the seafront between Callao and La Punta has its charms.

The road from Callao to Lima is lined by factories. Shipyards, far from sea, load the fishing vessels they build on huge lorries and launch them into the ocean at Callao.

On Avenida Marina between Lima and Callao, a turn-off opposite the entrance to the Feria del Pacífico grounds leads to the Parque Las Leyendas (**see p 1115**).

There are bathing, tennis, and a yacht club at **Ancón**, 30 km NW of Lima, reached by a double-lane asphalted highway. Colectivo from Plaza 2 de Mayo in Lima, US$0.60, returns 1 block from Ancón Cathedral. In the 19th and early 20th centuries, this was the smart seaside resort in Peru, but has now been deserted by the wealthy and in summer is crowded with daytrippers. It has a mix of elegant 19th century houses with wooden balconies and modern apartment blocks. **D** *Hostal del Pirata*, antique furniture, good views, excellent seafood; *Restaurant Cinco Luches*, which has rooms, E. Beaches are very small. Crowded Jan-Mar holidays, good for fish (rec restaurant, *Los 5 Tenedores* on the Corniche). On the way to Ancón is the pleasant Santa Rosa beach (entrance fee). Beyond Ancón is a Chancay cemetery, from which has come much Chancay weaving and pottery (as seen in the Museo Amano). In the valley of Chillón, N of Callao, are several interesting pre-Inca and Inca ruins; the Templo de la Media Luna y El Paraíso and **Chuquitanta**. For more information contact Dr Richard Holmberg at the Instituto Nacional de Cultura, Callao.

Excursions **Pachacámac** is in the Lurín valley, 31 km from Lima. When the Spaniards arrived, Pachacámac was the largest city and ceremonial centre on the coast. It was a vast complex of palaces and temple-pyramids, to which pilgrims went to pay homage to the creator-god Pachacámac (a wooden statue of whom is in the site museum). The ruins encircle the top of a low hill, the crest of which was crowned with a Temple of the Sun, a large pyramid built in 1350 of sun-baked bricks, now partially restored. There is also a reconstructed Temple of the Virgins. An impression of the scale can be gained from the top of the Temple of the Sun, or from walking or driving the 3 km circuit. Hernando Pizarro, brother of Francisco, came to Pachacámac in 1533; he destroyed images, killed the priests and looted the temples. The setting is marvellous, but the restoration, still underway, has been criticized and vandals have been at work. Bus or colectivo from Lima, caught from Av Montevideo y Ayacucho. The buses (US$0.40, 1 hr) and colectivos (US$0.60) go by way of Chorrillos, but tell the driver you are going to the *ruinas* or he will land you in Pachacámac town further on. A yellow Enatru bus marked Lurín-Pachacámac No P1 leaves from Parque Campo de Marte along Av Grau to Pachacámac. Taxi, round trip with a few hours at the site, US$25. Several travel agencies offer 3 hrs' excursions including English-speaking guide for US$35; Lima Tours run daily trips, about 3$^1/_2$ hrs, for about US$15 pp. Closed 1 May, open 0900 to 1700. Entrance US$1.50.

Cieneguilla, about 20 km E of Lima, on the Lurín river, is a small village in the country, an easy escape from the city and cloud cover of Lima. It is a popular place on Sun, with good restaurants with gardens and swimming pools. The valley of Lurín is good for birdwatching in the early morning.

Beaches S of Lima can be very dangerous because of the strong Pacific current. Every year people are drowned. The following beaches are considered to be safe: Santa María and Naplo (near Pucusana). All the other famous beaches have a strong current and swimming should be treated with caution or avoided: Las Señoritas, Los Caballeros, Punta Hermosa, Punta Negra, San Bartolo, Chilca and León Dormido.

Pucusana, 60 km S of Lima, is a pleasant, relaxed fishing village with some good restaurants serving seafood, not cheap, and some basic hotels (in our E range). All are very popular with Limeños from Dec to Mar, school holidays, and at weekends. There are plenty of buses from the bus station area in Lima. Robbery is common on the beaches and you are advised to sit on your clothes and other possessions. Do not leave anything unattended when swimming.

Also to the S, up the Omas valley beyond Coalla are the Inca adobe structures at Los Gentiles (on the right, well before Omas) and, nearer Omas, Pueblo Viejo, Yampa and Viracocha. Take a colectivo from Plaza Santa Catalina, Jr Puno (2 blocks from Av Abancay), Lima to Mala, then hitch, or taxi, via Asia to the sites.

A second excursion is to Chosica, 40 km up the Rímac valley. On the way to Chosica a diversion may be made at Km 4$^1/_2$ to **Puruchuco**, to see the reconstructed palace of a pre-Inca Huacho noble; with small museum (ceramics, textiles, etc, from the lower Rímac or Lima valley) and a selection of indigenous plants and animals, open 0900-1700, Tues-Sun (closed 1 May and 28 Jul). Entrance US$1; transport as for Chosica. One km from Puruchuco are Huaquerones and Catalina Huaca sites now being restored. Nearby, at Chivateros, is a quarry said to date from 10,000 BC. The large adobe pre-Inca city of **Cajamarquilla** may also be visited, for which the turnoff (left, at Huachipa) is about 6 km on from the Puruchuco turn. The site is difficult to find—you can't see it from the road—but look for a sign "Zona Arqueológica" in the middle of a brick yard. Keep on driving through the yard, and you will find Cajamarquilla at the end of an ill-kept dirt road. Open every day, 0900-1700. Beyond the Huachipa turn-off for Cajamarquilla, along the main road, there are precolumbian ruins at San Juan de Pariache and Huaicán-Tambo, 13$^1/_2$ and 16$^1/_2$ km respectively from Lima.

The Central Highway between Lima and Chosica has several places to stay and eat (some given under Lima, above). In the residential district of **Chaclacayo**, just before Chosica, are the **B** Huampani Hotel, modern, attractive, good meals, swimming pool (US$0.40), run by the Government's hotel chain, *Hotel Los Condores*, Los Condores, bungalows, luxurious, best time to visit May-Oct; and *Residencial La Casa de los Olivos*, at Los Ficus 373 y Los Olivos, with restaurant and 10 rooms.

Chosica (40 km), the real starting place for the mountains, is at 860m, and is a popular winter resort because it is above the cloudbank covering Lima from May to Oct. Frequent buses and minibuses. Beyond the town looms a precipitous range of hills almost overhanging the streets. Up picturesque Santa Eulalia valley off the Rímac valley are the Central Fruit Culture Nurseries. There is some dramatic scenery on the road up the valley, fairly good as far as the hydroelectric station at Callahuanca, but the road is afterwards quite nasty in places, narrow and rocky. Population: 31,200.

Hotels Four basic *hostales* in Chosica, two off the main road near the market, and two up the hill on the left. All have water problems and are in **E** range. Best is *Residencial Chosica*, big old building on pedestrian street perpendicular to 28 de Julio, rec (unlike *Hostal Chosica*, 28 de Julio, which is unwelcoming).

Transport Colectivos for Chosica leave from the first block of Montevideo (around the corner from Ormeño), when full, between 0600 and 2100, US$0.60.

Beyond Chosica, up the picturesque Santa Eulalia valley (40 km from Chosica), is *Marcahuasi*, a table mountain about 3 km by 3 km at 4,200m, near the village of San Pedro de Casta (accommodation in a cold shelter only, less than US$1). The *meseta* has been investigated by the late Daniel Ruzo: there are 3 lakes, a "monumento a la humanidad" (40m high), and other mysterious lines, gigantic figures, sculptures, astrological signs and megaliths which display non-American symbolism. Ruzo describes this pre-Incaic culture in his book, *La Culture Masma*, Extrait de l'Ethnographie, Paris, 1956. Others say that the formations are not man-made, but the result of wind erosion. Trail starts behind the village of San Pedro bending to the left—about 2 hrs to the *meseta* (guides about US$3 a day, advisable in misty weather). Bus to San Pedro de Casta leaves from Parque Echerique, opp market, daily except Sun, at about 0800 (when full), 3 hrs, US$2. Take all necessary camping equipment and buy food in Chosica as there is nothing beyond that point. Tours can be arranged with travel agencies in Lima.

Beyond Casta is San Juan de Iris, a tiny village, outside which impressive ruins have been discovered (bus or truck from *Restaurant 41* in Chosica at 0900 if you're lucky, 7 hrs).

There are the ancient (from 1500 BC) ruins of a small town on the hill of San Pedro de Casta, a fortress on the hills of Loma de los Papas (daily bus from Chosica at 0800), the ruins of Tambo Inca, and an ancient cemetery to the S.

The Central Highway to La Oroya (see p 1250) opens up possibilities of excursions by car with attractive stopping places like Matucana (1 hr), San Mateo and Río Blanco (2 hrs). The Lima-Chosica-Santa Eulalia-Huanza-Casapalca trip is the most impressive in the environs of Lima, and can be done in one day.

NORTHWEST FROM LIMA (2)

A region of geographic and cultural contrasts. From the relentless grey coastal desert to the jewelled lakes and mountains of the Callejón de Huaylas. From smelly fishing ports like Chimbote, to the delicate artistry of pre-Inca ruins at Chavín de Huantar and others still being explored deep in the Andes.

From Lima to Chimbote Between Lima and Pativilca there is a narrow belt of coastal land deposited at the mouths of the rivers, but from Pativilca to the mouth of the Río Santa, N of Chimbote, the Andes come down to the sea. Between Lima and Pativilca cotton and sugar-cane are grown, though the yield of sugar is less than it is further N where the sunshine is not interrupted by cloud. Cotton is harvested from Apr to Sep by Indian migrants from the basins of Jauja and Huancayo. Much irrigated land grows vegetables and crops to supply Lima and Callao. Cattle are driven down from the Highlands to graze the *lomas* on the mountain sides when the mists come between Jun and Oct.

The Pan-American Highway parallels the coast all the way to the far N, and feeder roads branch from it up the various valleys. Just N of Ancón (see p 1136), the Pasamayo sand dune, stretching for 20 km, comes right down to the seashore. The old road which snakes along the base beside the sea is spectacular, but is now closed except to commercial traffic. The new toll road (US$0.85), which goes right over the top, is much safer and you get spectacular views over the nearby coast

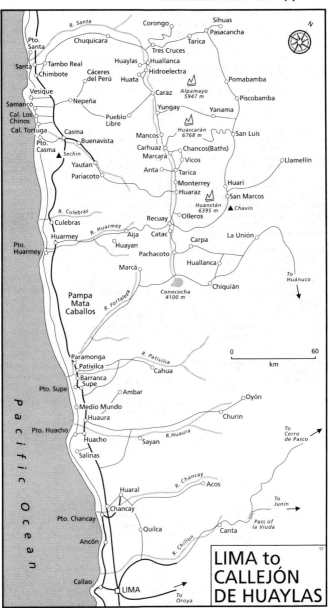

LIMA to CALLEJÓN DE HUAYLAS

and valleys. **Chancay**, on the coast (sea can be dangerous and heavily polluted), suffers from severe water shortages, but there is a fresh water source on the beach; **C** *Hostal Brisas del Mar*, overlooking sea; **C** *Hostal Villa de Arnedo*, clean and friendly, pool (in summer) and restaurant, rec; **F** *Hostal Chancay*, safe, friendly, can wash clothes; the "castle" at Chancay, a pseudo-medieval summer house (built 1922-42) on the beach, is planned to be converted to a 220-bed hotel, open to visitors (US$1), café, playground. *Pizzería Donatello* (main square, balcony, rock music) and *Costa Azul* (gardens, overlooking sea), both good.

Just inland from Chancay is Huaral, which gives access to the Chancay Valley, up which are the extraordinary, little visited ruins of **Chiprac**, **Rupac** and **Añay**. Take a bus from Lima (from Plaza de Acho, by the buillring—beware of thieves) to Huaral, then take the Juan Batista bus, Tues and Fri, to Huascoy, US$2, 2 km beyond San Juan, itself up beyond Acos: "a hair-raising, breath-taking, bone shaking ride, up to 3,500m above sea level", one traveller writes. "Chiprac is a 2½ hrs' climb from here. Ask for the Salvador family, who have accommodation and Carlos is a guide for the ruins, rec." A guide is not strictly necessary; it is a good day's walk there and back with time to take photographs and eat. Rupac is best reached from La Florida; its ruins are the best preserved of the group, though less extensive than Chiprac. In San Juan, a man called Chavelo will act as a guide to Rupac, which can be reached via the pretty and deserted town of Pampas—also a day there and back. All the ruins have complete roofs, which is unique in Peru. Huascoy celebrates the Fiesta de San Cristóbal in the week before Independence, 28 Jul, with a procession, masses, dancing, fireworks and football matches. For Añay, go to Huaral as for the other ruins, then get transport to Huayopampa (basic accommodation) or La Perla whence the visit to the ruins can easily be made; get a guide to show you up from either village.

Turn right 1 km N of turn off to Sayán (see below) where, a further 3 km, there is a national reserve, **Loma de Lachay**, which has thousands of snail shells, locust-trees and much bird life. In Sep-Oct the plants are in bloom, very beautiful. Visitors centre, trails, camping and picnic areas; very popular with Lima residents at the weekend. North on the dual carriageway to Km 101, the small port of **Huacho** (pop 35,900) is 120 km from Lima (bus 2½ hrs, US$2, or Comité 18, daily colectivos, US$2.50). It is the outlet for cotton and sugar grown in the rich Huaura valley. There is a cemetery near Huacho where mummies may be found. There are cotton-seed oil and other factories. Port and sea are sometimes alive with monstrous jellyfish.

Hotels C *Hostal Villa Sol*, clean, pleasant, restaurant, pool, playground; **E** *Hostal Maury*, basic but friendly; **E** *Italia*, communal bathrooms, clean; **F** *El Pacífico*, safe, dirty, water problems, inadequate clothes-washing facilities; *Hostal de Milagritos*, comfortable. Camping is possible at El Paraíso beach.

The journey inland from Huacho, up the Huaura valley, is splendid. Beyond Sayán are terrific rock formations, then the road passes through subtropical vegetation around **Churín**, one of Peru's best-known spas, with hot, sulphurous springs which are used to cure a number of ailments. The climate is dry, temperatures ranging from 10° to 32° C; the area is heavily forested. It is famous for its cheeses. Hotels: *Hostal San Juan de Churín*, same avenue No 315, T 12, with bath, hot water, restaurant, bar, TV, cheap, clean; *Hostal La Meseta* (member of Peruvian Youth Hostel Association), contact in Lima at Paul Harris 367, San Isidro, T 422-7619; *Internacional*, Av Victor Larco Herrera 410, Local T 15, with bath, hot water, clean, moderately priced. Near here, at **Chiuchín**, is **C** *Albergue San Camilo*, excellent. From Chiuchín, there are buses to nearby villages, such as **Huancahuasi**, where one can buy woven goods, see interesting churches, and spot *vicuña* in lovely surroundings. There are coal mines. Above 4,000m is a chain of lakes which reflect the Cordillera Raura (up to 5,800m). Road ends at Raura mine. Buses from Lima go to Churín, Oyón (between Churín and Raura) and Huamahuanca; Espadín y Hnos (see Lima, **Bus Companies**), 2 daily, 6½ hrs, US$3.50. Only travel to this area in daylight, and check with locals on villages beyond Churín as there has been terrorist acitivity in the past.

Just across the river is **Huaura**, where the balcony is still preserved from which San Martín declared the country's independence from Spain. Try *guinda*, the local cherry brandy. We pass from the wide valley of Mazo through the irrigated valley of San Felipe. Midway between Huaura and Supe, on the coast road, is **Medio Mundo**, with a lake between the village and the sea. It is a good camping spot, with tents for rent, guarded at weekends; bring food and water – none for bathrooms or drinking. The turnoff is outside the village on the Pan-American Highway, to the left, look for the sign, "Albufera de Medio Mundo". It is hot and busy in summer.

There is more desert and then the cotton-fields of San Nicolás lead to **Supe**, a small busy port shipping fishmeal, cotton, sugar and minerals (F *Hostal Supe*; better is **F** *Hostal Grau*, basic, clean, safe, comfortable, laundry, good value, next to which is a good restaurant: *El Norteño*). At **Aspero**, near Supe, is one of the earliest prehistoric sites in Peru (see History section, **p 1103**). At **Barranca** the beach is long, not too dirty, though windy. Buses stop opposite the service station (*el grifo*) at the end of town. The straggling town of **Pativilca**, at Km 203, has a small museum (bus from Lima US$3.50, 3½ hrs—*Restaurant Cornejo*, good and cheap); a poorly-paved road turns off for the Callejón de Huaylas and Huaraz (**see p 1154**). The road is paved to Conacocha (4,080m) then in very poor condition to Catac and on dirt, to Chavín. 4 km beyond the turn-off, beside the Highway, are the well preserved ruins of the Chimú temple of **Paramonga**. Set on high ground (view of the ocean), the fortress-like mound is reinforced by 8 quadrangular walls rising in tiers to the top of the hill (admission US$1.20, well worth visiting, taxi from Paramonga and return after waiting, US$4.50, otherwise take a Barranca-Paramonga port bus, then a 3 km walk). Not far from the fortress, the Great Wall (La Muralla) stretches across the Andes. Paramonga is a small port, 3 km off the Pan-American Highway, 4 km from the ruins and 205 km from Lima, shipping sugar.

Hotels There is no hotel at Paramonga. There are several in **Barranca**: on the beach front, **E** *Hostal Casablanca*; **F** *Hotel Casanova*, on main street, with bath, clean, unwelcoming, safe motorcycle parking; **E** *Hotel Chavín*, with bath, warm water, clean, good value, rec, front rooms are noisy, also restaurant on 1st floor for lunch and dinner (try *arroz con conchas*), breakfast bar and café opens onto street by main entrance; **F** *Jefferson*, Lima 946, clean, friendly; **G** *Pacífico*, with bath, clean, good value; **G** *Colón*, Jr Gálvez 407, friendly, basic; many others on main street, and plenty of bars and restaurants. Here and in Supe try the *tamales*.

Exchange Banco de la Nación, Barranca, accepts TCs, although at poor rates.

Buses from Lima to Barranca, 195 km, 3½ hrs, US$3; see Lima, **Bus Companies** with routes to the N. As bus companies have their offices in Barranca, buses will stop there rather than at Pativilca or Paramonga. No buses run to the ruins, only to the port (about 15 mins from Barranca). Bus from Barranca to Casma 155 km, several daily, 3 hrs, US$3. From Barranca to Huaraz, 4 hrs, US$6, daily buses or trucks.

Between Paramonga and Chimbote the mountains come down to the sea. The road passes by a few very small protected harbours in tiny rock-encircled bays—Puerto **Huarmey** (C *Hotel de Turistas*, small, clean and good service, but noisy, being on Pan-American Highway at Huarmey town, not port, restaurant, no parking in front; **F** pp *hostal* opp market, central), Puerto Casma, and Vesique. From Casma a road runs inland over the **Callán pass** (4,224m) to Huaraz. A difficult but beautiful trip. Not all buses take this route, so check before leaving. From Casma to the pass (apart from the paved first 30 km), the road is appalling (many landslides), but once the Cordillera Negra has been crossed, the road is better (gravel, wide) with spectacular views.

Casma The town was largely destroyed by the 1970 earthquake, but has since been rebuilt. Two markets including a good food market, but not much else to recommend. No facility for changing TCs in local banks.

Hotels E *Hostal El Farol*, ask for cheaper rate in low season, good, with bathroom (no hot water), breakfast and dinner available (and sandwiches and coffee), pleasant garden setting; **E-F** *Gregori*, Luis Ormeño 579, T 711173, clean but noisy; **F** *Hostal Central*, on plaza, dirty, cold, basic, but helpful; **F** *Indoamericano*, Av Huarmey, with bath, hot water, clean, good. **Restaurant**: *Sechín*, on main plaza, friendly, good set meal US$1; *Tío Sam*, next to Indoamericano, for Chinese and *criollo* food US$1.50.

Bus From **Lima** to Casma, 370 km, several buses daily, 6 hrs, US$5 (see Lima, **Bus Companies**). Bus to **Huaraz**, 150 km, 6-7 hrs, US$6, daily buses, inc Moreno, 0900 daily, or trucks. It is well worth making this trip in daylight to get the view of the Cordillera Blanca. To **Chimbote**, 55 km, several buses and colectivos daily, 1 hr, US$1. To **Trujillo**, 175 km, daily buses, 3 hrs, US$3.50. Most buses pass Casma in the morning. At other times, take a bus to Chimbote.

Excursions From Casma, take a truck going to San Rafael and ask for Castillo (departures all day from the garage opposite Huaraz bus stop). After alighting, walk 2 km uphill to a cemetery with pottery on the ground, and a Chimú castle of 4 concentric rings, with 3 towers in the middle, the Castillo de **Chanquillo**. Further on is a large wall with 13 towers on a ridge. Take water with you. The trucks return all day up to about 1600. There are several other sites around Casma: Sechín Alto, Pallka, Tokán, Mojeque, La Cantina, Tokachi and Huanchay.

Sechín is one of the most important ruins on the Peruvian coast. It consists of a large square temple completely faced with carved stone monoliths—probably over 500 of them—which depict gruesome battle scenes: men being eviscerated, heads with blood gushing from eyes or mouths, dismembered legs, arms, torsos, ears, eyes and vertebrae. The style is unique in Peru for its naturalistic vigour. Within the stone temple is an earlier, pre-ceramic mud temple with painted walls. The temples are pre-Chavín, about 1500 BC. Three sides of the large stone temple have been excavated and restored. You cannot see the adobe buildings inside the stone walls, which belong to an earlier period. They were later covered up and used as a base for a second storey which unfortunately has been completely destroyed. Some experts think the temple and surroundings were buried on purpose. Others believe it was engulfed by natural disaster. The latter theory is supported by finds of human skeletons. Tombs have been found in front and at the same level as the temple. A wall of a large adobe building under excavation can be seen and runs round the sides and back of the temple.

The site is open to tourists, 0900-1700, photography best around midday (US$3.40, children half price); ticket also valid for Pañamarca (**see p 1143**), and there is an attractive, shady picnic garden. The Max Uhle Museum by the ruins has an interesting display of Sechín artefacts, entry US$0.80 and US$0.10 for cameras. It is quite easy to walk to the ruins from Casma. One must walk about 3 km S to a well posted sign showing a left turn (this is at Km 370 on the Panamericana from Lima), then simply follow the road for 2 km to the ruins. (Frequent colectivos from in front of market in Casma, US$0.30 pp, or taxi US$0.50 pp, but leave early in the morning; no buses.) 2 km further along there are two pyramids of the late Chavín period, but these have not yet been excavated.

Chimbote (pop 296,600), is one of Peru's few natural harbours, ample in area and depth of water. A new port has been built to serve the national steel industry: iron ore from Marcona field is shipped from the port of San Juan, 547 km S of Lima; anthracite comes by railway from the hinterland, and power comes from the hydroelectric station in the Cañón del Pato, 129 km inland. The steel industry creates heavy pollution. Also Chimbote is Peru's largest fishing port; fishmeal is exported and the smell of the fishmeal plants is very strong. Bathing is forbidden on the beach near the hotel. Flocks of brown pelicans and masked boobies may be seen from the beach. Shanty towns have burgeoned around. Small airport, but no commercial flights. Public swimming pool at Vivero Forestal.

Hotels **A3** *Hostal Ivasino Inn*, José Pardo, T 331395, comfortable, cable TV, minibar; **A3** *Turistas*, State Tourist Hotel, José Gálvez 109, T 325451, 3-star, OK, but expensive, safe parking; **B** *Hostal Antonios*, Bolognesi 745, clean, hot water, café; **C** *Presidente* (3 star), Calle L Prado, with bath, clean, friendly, hot showers, safe parking, poor snack bar, rec; **E** *Felic*, Av José Pardo 552, T 32590, clean, quiet, rec; **E** *Hostal Playa*, Malecón Miguel Grau 185, OK, safe, clean; **E** *Venus*, with private bath, dirty, but friendly, near Roggero bus station, useful if you arrive at 0200; in same district is **F** *Augusto*, Aguirre 265, with shower and toilet, overpriced, clean, front rooms noisy, water intermittent as everywhere in town; **F** *Carabelle*, round corner from *Presidente*, hot water doesn't work, but good value; **F** *Hostal El Santa*, Espinar 671, basic.

Restaurants *Pollo Gordo*, Prado y Aguirre, good chicken and cold beer; *Buenos Aires*, Aguirre near beach, popular lunch place; *Marisquito*, Bolognesi near Palacios, good local food, disco at night; *Franco* and *Venecia*, same block, good seafood. *Chifa Cantón*, Bolognesi, Chinese, good; *La Fogata Inn*, Villavicencio, good grilled food. You can eat well and cheaply (US$0.50) in the market.

Buses From **Lima**, to Chimbote, 420 km, 6 hrs, US$7, several buses daily including Turismo Chimbote, VR Haya de la Torre 670, Chimbote, T 321400, rec (see Lima, **Bus Companies** with routes to the N). To **Trujillo**, 130 km, 2½ hrs, US$2.50, several buses and colectivos daily. The Santa valley road via Huallanca to the Callejón de Huaylas and beyond has been rebuilt, but is still hair-raising (scenery is superb). From Chimbote the route is Huallanca, Cañon del Pato, Caraz (185 km) and on to Huaraz, see the description below. Travel during the day, and sit on the left for excellent views of the canyon. It is 8-10 hrs to **Huaraz** (can be longer, or impossible in the rainy season), US$7; buses (Empresa Moreno, 0700, rec) and trucks daily. Buses depart from José Galvez (across bridge towards Trujillo), book the previous day.

Air Service To Lima, 45 mins, US$54 one way, 6 times a week with Expreso Aéreo, daily with Aero Cóndor; Chimbote-Cajamarca US$25.

About 25 km S of Chimbote a paved road leads E to the Nepeña valley, where a sculpted precolumbian tomb and the temple of Cerro Blanco may be found; also ruins at **Pañamarca** (pre-Mochica temple), 10 km from the crossroads. Pañamarca is a town from the Mochica culture, where buildings and animal sculpture remains can be seen. 20 km from Pañamarca is the site of **Paredores** with the "Puerta del Sol", and a stone carving, the "monolito de siete huacas".

The Cordillera Blanca and the Callejón de Huaylas

Probably the best way to see the Santa Valley and the Callejón de Huaylas, which contain some of the most spectacular scenery in Peru, is to take the paved road which branches off the coast road into the mountains just N of Pativilca (**see p 1141**), 187 km from Lima. This route also gives a more spectacular view of the Cordillera Blanca. In 120 km it climbs to Laguna **Conococha** (delicious trout available in Conococha village), at 4,100m, where the Río Santa rises. After crossing the high level surface it descends gradually for 87 km to Huaraz, and goes on to the Callejón de Huaylas, where it runs between the towering Cordillera Negra, snowless and rising to 4,600m, and the snow-covered Cordillera Blanca. Farms appear at about 4,000m, but most of the farming is around Huaraz. The inhabitants grow potatoes and barley at the higher and maize and alfalfa at the lower altitudes. The valley has many picturesque villages and small towns, with narrow cobblestone streets and odd-angled house roofs. (At weekends and holidays beware of reckless Lima drivers on the roads.)

The alternative routes to the Callejón de Huaylas are via the Callán pass from Casma to Huaraz (**see p 1141**), and via the Cañón del Pato (**p 1152**).

The valley's focus is **Huaraz** (population 80,000), capital of the Department of Ancash, at 3,028m, 420 km from Lima. The city was half destroyed in the earthquake of May 1970. The Plaza de Armas has been rebuilt, except for the Cathedral, which is being resited elsewhere. The setting, with the peaks of Huascarán, Huandoy, and San Cristóbal in the background, is tremendous. Good panoramic views are to be had from the *Mirador Rataquenua* at the cross (visible from Huaraz) 1 hr's walk from the town (turn left past the cemetery and head uphill through a small forest). Market day is Thur.

Huaraz is a pleasant, quiet mountain town at the foot of the Cordillera Blanca. It is popular with Peruvian and foreign hikers and a mecca for international climbers. Nearby is the highest peak in Peru, Huascarán, 6,768m. The **Parque Nacional Huascarán** was established in Jul 1975 and includes the entire area of the Cordillera Blanca above 4,000m, with 3,400 sq km. The objectives of the park are to protect the flora, fauna, geology, archaeological sites and scenic beauty of the Cordillera. Please make every attempt to help in this effort by taking all your rubbish away with you when camping in the park.

Museums Museo Regional de Ancash, Instituto Nacional de Cultura, on Plaza de Armas, containing stone monoliths and *huacos* from the Recuay culture, well labelled and laid out. Open Tues-Sat 0900-1800, Sun-Mon 0900-1400, entry US$1.50, incl Willcawain ruins (see **Excursions** below). Museo de Miniaturas del Perú, Jr Lucás y Torre 460, models of Huaraz and Yungay before the earthquake, plus collection of Barbie dolls (!) in Peruvian dress, strange but interesting.

Festival Patron saints' day, 3 May, parades, dancing, music and fireworks; much drinking and

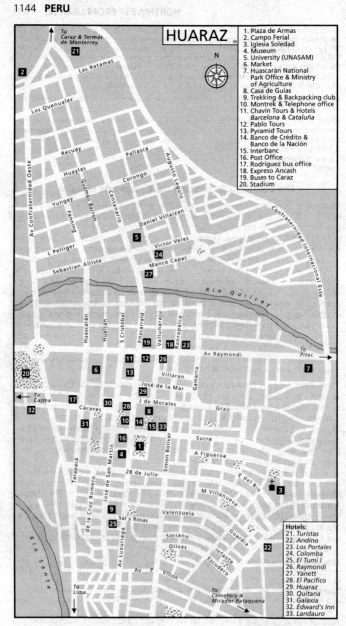

HUARAZ

1. Plaza de Armas
2. Campo Ferial
3. Iglesia Soledad
4. Museum
5. University (UNASAM)
6. Market
7. Huascarán National Park Office & Ministry of Agriculture
8. Casa de Guías
9. Trekking & Backpacking club
10. Montrek & Telephone office
11. Chavin Tours & Hotels *Barcelona & Cataluña*
12. Pablo Tours
13. Pyramid Tours
14. Banco de Crédito & Banco de la Nación
15. Interbanc
16. Post Office
17. Rodriguez bus office
18. Expreso Ancash
19. Buses to Caraz
20. Stadium

Hotels:
21. *Turistas*
22. *Andino*
23. *Los Portales*
24. *Colomba*
25. *El Tumi I*
26. *Raymondi*
27. *Yanett*
28. *El Pacifico*
29. *Huaraz*
30. *Quitana*
31. *Galaxia*
32. *Edward's Inn*
33. *Landauro*

overcharging. Independence celebrations, end-Jul. Semana del Andinismo end of May, international climbing and skiing week (prices shoot up).

Hotels Out of town: **C** *El Patio*, Monterrey, price incl breakfast, friendly, no restaurant, nicely laid out, rec; **C** *Termas de Monterrey*, Km 5 Carretera Caraz (½ hr in bus from Luzuriaga, near the bridge, US$0.25 but none after 2000, taxi US$2-3), run by State Tourist Hotel chain, rec for walking, swimming in warm springs (see **Excursions** below), accepts American Express, with bath, good meals US$3, swimming pool (hotel and pool rundown). Rock climbing behind hotel, but don't be too vigorous at the start, it's over 2,750m up; **D** *Hostal Saxofón*, Av Cashapampa 250, T 721722, off road to Caraz, pleasant, with garden; **D-F** *La Casa de Campo Yacarini*, Urbanización El Bosque-Palmira (3 km from town), new house with garden, clean, friendly and safe, sauna and hot baths, good family cooking, multilingual owner, highly rec.

In town: **A3** *Hostal Andino* (*Chalet Suisse*) Jr Pedro Cochachín 357 (some way from centre), T 721662, best hotel, clean, meals served (fondue expensive), safe parking, Swiss run, rec, beautiful view of Huascarán, climbing and hiking gear for hire; **A3** *Hotel de Turistas* Av Centenario block 10 (T 721640/721709), large rooms, clean, restaurant poor, allows camping in safe courtyard and use of facilities for US$4 pp; **B** *Hostal Montanero*, Plaza Ginebra, T 721811, hot water, clean, modern, comfortable; **D** *Casablanca*, Tarapacá 138, T 722602, clean, pleasant, modern; **D** *El Tumi I*, San Martín 1121, T 721784, with bath, good restaurant (serves huge steaks), fairly good; **D** *Hostal Colomba*, Calle Francisco de Zela 210, T 721422, bungalow, price plus 21%, family-run (German), garden, friendly, safe car parking, English spoken; **D** *Hostal Oscar*, La Mar 624, with bath, hot water, cheap breakfast, rec; **D** *Yanett*, Av Centenario 106, T 721466, friendly, hot water, clean, large rooms, rec, restaurant for breakfast; **E** *Alojamiento Copa*, Jr S Bolívar 615, hot water, washing facilities, clean, owner, Señora Alicia Jaimes' son, Walter Melgarejo is a well-known guide, popular with trekkers, restaurant; **E** *Barcelona*, Raymondi 692; **E** *El Tumi II*, San Martín 1089, T 721784, with bath, good value; **E** *Hostal Regalon*, Av Luzuriaga 651-53, T 721954, with bath (cheaper without), not very hot showers, clean, modern, English spoken by owners' son, helpful, informative, rec; **E** *Marañón*, new, clean, near market, hot water limited; **E** *Raymondi*, Av Raymondi 820, T 721082 (Lima T 279016, Av Abancay 1052-14), central, bath, hot water (am only in ground floor shower), comfortable, charges for left luggage, with café serving good breakfast; **F** *Albergue El Tambo*, Confraternidad Internacional—Interior—122 B, clean, clothes washing, 3 rooms with 12 beds, and cooking facilities, nice people; **F** *Alojamiento Galaxia* (de Inés Herrera), Jr Romero 688, limited hot water, laundry facilities, rec, but very basic; **F** *Alojamiento San Martín de Porras*, Las Américas, T 721061, clean, friendly, rec. Behind, between Sucre and Morales at Plaza Ginebra 28-G, is the **F pp** *Casa de Guías*, member of Peruvian Youth Hostel Association, T 731333, rooms for up to 6 people, with rec restaurant *Alpes Andes*, muesli, yoghurt in am, pastas and pizzas in evening, guided tours organized; it houses the guide association of Huaraz, T 721811, provides climbing and trekking information, and is a good meeting place for climbers, and there is a notice board for messages. **F** *Cataluña*, Av Raymondi 822, T 72117, with bath, less without, cheaper accommodation in dormitory, restaurant, somewhat expensive, clean, safe, noisy, tepid water, open in tourist season only; **F** pp *Edward's Inn*, Av Bolognesi 121, T 722692, clean, private hot shower, laundry, friendly, food available, highly rec, popular, Edward speaks English and knows a lot about trekking and rents gear (not all guides share Edward's experience); **F** pp *Hostal Continental*, 20 de Julio 586, clean, hot water, friendly, cafeteria, rec, avoid rooms overlooking street as two noisy *peñas* nearby; **F** *Hostal Alfredo*, Jr Victor Vélez (go N on Al Fitzcarrald, cross bridge and take 2nd on right, 10m on right), with shower, good; **F** pp *Hostal Estoico*, San Martín 638, T 722371/422, friendly, clean, safe, showers, laundry facilities, rec; **F** *Landauro*, on Plaza de Armas, cheap, not particularly clean, basic, friendly, good breakfast place downstairs; **F** *Pensión Maguiña*, Av Tarapacá 643, opp Rodríguez bus terminal, noisy am, hot water, rooms single to 4-bed, clothes-washing facilities, breakfast available, rucksack store, clean, English and French spoken, helpful in arranging trekking and equipment hire, rec; **G** pp *Alojamiento de Quintana*, Mcal Cáceres 393, hot shower, laundry facilities, clean, hard beds, very basic, stores luggage, friendly, popular with trekkers; **G** *Alojamiento Líder*, Fitzcarrald 233, hot showers, friendly, safe, rec; **G** pp *Casa de Jaimes*, Calle Alberto Gridilla 267, two blocks from main plaza, clean, hot showers, washing facilities, maps and books of region, use of kitchen, popular, rec; **G** *Casa Jansy's*, Jr Sucre 948, hot water, meals, laundry, owner Jesús Rivera Lúcar is a mountain guide, rec; **G** pp *Casa de Señora López*, behind *Edward's Inn* (ask near Estadio just off Avenida Bolognesi at Santa river end), luke-warm showers, safe, washing facilities for clothes, beautiful garden and restaurant, good views, very friendly, rec; **G** *Familia Sánchez*, Jr Caraz 849, clean, basic, warm water, helpful, cheap breakfast; **G** pp *Hostal Los Andes*, Av Tarapacá 316, low season, hot water, clean, friendly, with laundry, attractive but noisy, hard beds and prices shoot up in the peak season. There are usually people waiting at the bus terminals offering cheap accommodation in their own homes. One rec private house is at

Señora Gamara's, Calle Valenzuela 837, **G**, friendly, clean, hot water, meals, laundry service.
Youth Hostels See *Casa de Guías* above; *Hostal la Montañesa*, Av Leguía 290, Centenario,
T 721287; *Eccame*, Autopista Aeropuerto Km 18, in Huaraz Espíritu Santa 199, T 721933.
   Note that prices go up by about 50% in the Jul-Aug season, but only when there are a lot
of tourists.

Hot Public Showers on Av Raymondi 904, US$1.20.

Restaurants Restaurant and bar at *Ebony 86*, Plaza de Armas, friendly, clean. *Tabariz*, Av
Raymondi, good food, set meal for US$1. On 28 de Julio is *Oja-Yo*, Chinese, good. *El Noble*,
Luzuriaga 629, 1st Flr, nr Plaza de Armas, cheap, rec; *Montrek*, Luzuriaga 646, T 721124, for
pizzas and indoor climbing wall, see Carlos for details on paragliding; *Café Pizza del Leñador*,
Luzuriaga 979; *Chez Pepe*, Luzuriaga 568, good pizza, chicken, meat; *La Familia* at Luzuriaga
431, popular with gringos, vegetarian dishes, impersonal; *Créperie Patrick*, Luzuriaga 424 y
Raymondi, excellent crêpes, fish, quiche, spaghetti and good wine; next door is *Chifa Min
Hua*; *Monte Rosa*, Av Luzuriaga 496, good pizzería, reasonable prices, open 1830-2300, Swiss
owner is Victorinox representative, offering knives for sale and repair service; *La Cueva del
Oso*, Luzuriaga 674, taverna-style, good food and music; *Café Central*, Luzuriaga y Sucre,
good for breakfast; *Miski Huasi*, Jr Sucre 476, small, cheap, some vegetarian; *Las Puyas*,
Morales 535, good cheap meals and breakfasts, popular with gringos; *Pío Pío*, Av Centenario
329, rec. *Paccha'k Pub*, Centenario 290, folklore shows, local and international food, travel
information. *Tejas*, Calle Francisco (parallel to Centenario), rec for *cuy* (guinea-pig). *Sihuasino*,
above the San Francisco church, good for *pachamanca* and *chicha*. Note that middle- and
high-class restaurants charge a 31% tax on top of the bill.

Banks and Exchange There are three banks, **InterBanc**, **Banco de Crédito** (only changes
before 1200, no commission on TCs) and **Banco de la Nación**, all on the Plaza de Armas. First
two change TCs into soles; into cash dollars 3-5% commission. Street changers on Luzuriaga.
Travel agents also change dollars and TCs, but high commission.

Entertainment *Imantata*, Luzuriaga 424, disco and folk music; *peña* at *Cueva del Oso*, see
above; *Tambo*, José de la Mar, folk music daily, rec, knock on door to get in. *Amadeus*, Parque
Ginebra, disco. *El Pub*, José de La Mar 661, T 722951, disco-bar; owners Lucho and Julio Olazo,
Lucho sells good T-shirts of Huaraz. *Bad Boy Pub Disco*, Jr J de la Mar 661, live rock groups.

Laundry *Fitzcarrald*, Fitzcarrald, close to bridge; *Lavandería Liz*, Bolívar 711, US$2/kg. Also
at the Casa de Guías (see above).

Shopping Daily market (1600-2000) in covered sidewalks of Luzuriaga for local sweaters,
hats, gloves, etc, wall hangings; good value. *Andean Expressions* for hand-printed clothing
and gifts. Humberto Chávez Bayona, Pasaje D, Coral Vega 353, interesting local watercolour
artist.

Camping Gear Several shops of the trekking agencies sell camping gaz cartridges. Bodega
Santillana, Centenario 417, good for all supplies. Andean Sport Tours, Av Luzuriaga 571,
T 721612, rents or sells camping equipment, incl camping gaz cartridges; treks, climbing, tents
for hire, US$3 a day. Casa de Guías rents equipment and sells dried food. The following also
rent gear: Pablo Tours, Montrek, Kike Tours, Pyramid Adventures. Check all camping and
climbing equipment before taking it; gear is usually of poor quality, mostly secondhand, left
behind by others. Best to bring your own. All prices standard, but not cheap, throughout town;
US$100, or airline ticket, deposit usually demanded. All require payment in advance and will
only give 50% of your money back if you return gear early.

Climbing and Trekking The Cordillera Blanca is the climbing and hiking centre of Peru. The
season is from Jun to Aug, although conditions vary from year to year. Check before you go
with the South American Explorers Club in Lima (T 0051-1-425-0142). The Huascarán National
Park office charges visitors US$1/day to enter the park; helpful staff. See also under **Tourist
Information** below and in the same paragraph for Casa de Guías. Claudio Lluya is a rec,
qualified guide for mountaineering and trekking, his carpenter's shop is one block uphill behind
the Casa de Guías (no sign). Carlos Rodríguez, PO Box 111, Huaraz, for climbing and trekking
in the Cordillera Blanca. Hugo Cifuentes Maguiña, Av Centenario 537, also good. See under
Travel Agents for organized trips. Canned and dry goods are expensive in Huaraz, it may be
better to buy in Lima.

Mountain biking There are several circuits; bike hire from *Creperie Patrick*, Luzuriaga 424.

Travel Agencies *Pablo Tours*, Luzuriaga 501, T 721145, *Pyramid Adventures*, Luzuriaga
530, T 721864 (owner Eudes Morales Flores speaks English) and *Chavín Tours*, Luzuriaga 502,
T 721578, organize trips to Chavín, Llanganuco and the Huascarán park. *Montrek*, Luzuriaga
640, good for rafting on Santa river, including transport to/from Huaraz, 2-hr raft trip, helpful,

supplies maps, strong on environmental tourism. *Nevado Huascarán Tours*, Luzuriaga 635, day tours to Chavín; *Kiker Tours*, T 724356, combi tour to Chavín, guide Ricky highly rec. Marco Ugarte, Unasam, Av Centenario s/n, offers tours to Chavín and treks (US$35/day, inclusive), he is a professor of English, and his services have been rec. On the 2nd floor of the *Hotel Residencial Cataluña*, Av Raymondi, T 72117, José Valle Espinosa, "Pepe", hires out equipment (pricey), organizes treks and pack animals, sells dried food, and is generally helpful and informative. For guides contact Casa de Guías. Filiberto Rurush Pancar, T 44-722264, F 44-72111, English-speaking, own car, rec.

Tours have set prices, check and beware of overcharging: to Chavín US$9.50 pp; to Llanganuco US$8 pp; to Pastoruri US$8 pp; to Lago Churup US$8 pp (min 7 people); city tour of Huaraz (3 hrs) US$6 pp; river rafting on the Río Santa US$6 pp for 3 hrs, US$12 pp for half a day.

Tourist Office   Basic tourist information on Plaza de Armas on Luzuriaga, 0900-1300, 1630-1800. Private information office: **Trekking & Backpacking Club**, Pasaje Sal y Rosas 358 (Casilla 112), maps and library at office, also hires equipment and organizes tours; owner Miguel Chiri Valle. Better maps of the area are available in Lima. Hidrandina, Calle 27 de Noviembre 773, government institute dealing with geology and metallurgy in Ancash, has dye-line maps of the Cordillera Blanca, open am only. The South American Explorers Club in Lima is an excellent source of information on trekking and climbing in the area and has maps. The Huascarán National Park Office is in the Ministry of Agriculture, at the E end of Av Raymondi, open am only. Good tourist information available from and near the museum (see above). Casa de Guías, Plaza Ginebra, T 721811, president Magno Camonez, climbers and hikers' meeting place, useful with information, arrangements for guides, *arrieros*, mules, etc; notice board.

Air   No regular service; private charter from AeroCóndor from Lima. Taxi to airport (at Anta) about 23 km from town, 20 mins, US$3; colectivo to airport 40 mins, US$1.

Buses Huaraz-Lima, 420 km, 8 hrs, US$8. The road is in pretty good condition even though there are landslides in the mountain sections. See Lima **Bus Companies** for bus lines and their addresses. In Huaraz: Transportes Rodríguez, Tarapacá 622, Huaraz, T 721353; Expreso Ancash (Ormeño), Raymondi 845, Huaraz, rec; both have 3 buses daily, including 0700, 1200, 2100, 2200. Also rec Civa Cial, San Martín 508, T 721947, new buses, day and night. Many other companies. Comité 14, Raymondi 616, runs a daily colectivo service (when more than 6 people) for US$7 pp. Private transport can be arranged, ask around, fare between US$80 to 100 one way.

NB   It is recommended to travel during the day to and from Huaraz.

Other Buses   To Casma (150 km) 6-7 hrs, Empresa Moreno, Raymondi 874, US$6. Bus to Chimbote, 185 km, 0800, US$7, 10 hrs via Cañón del Pato, see under Chimbote, day travel advised for both safety and views, sit on the right for best and scariest views. Several buses and colectivos run between Huaraz and **Caraz** daily, 2 hrs, US$1. They stop at all the places in between; depart from Raymondi y Fitzcarrald. Rodríguez, Turismo Chimbote and Comité 14 go to **Trujillo** from Huaraz (all buses go at night), 10-12 hrs, US$7. To **Chavín**, 110 km, 5 hrs, US$3: Transportes Huascarán, Chavín Express and Lanzón de Chavín have one bus daily each, leaving in the morning. Trucks do this route as well. To **Huallanca**, via Pachacoto, 104 km, 4 hrs, US$3.50; some trucks and buses run this route, continuing to La Unión and Huánuco. To **Pativilca**, 160 km, 4 hrs, US$3.50.

Excursions   About 8 km into mountains is ***Willcawain*** archaeological site (entrance, US$1.25), the ruins of a Tiahuanaco-style temple, dating from about AD 1000. Walk down Av Centenario and take right turn 1 km out of town (ask), 2½ hrs uphill walk; there are villages on return, take right fork when passing the school, the main road is reached after 2 km. Beware of dogs along the way. Alternatively, take a colectivo towards Yungay or Monterrey, get out 2 stops past the *Hotel de Turistas*, turn right and then left at a house for "pirotécnicas" (fireworks). Or take a colectivo in the Paría direction which goes almost to the site, from where it is a 3 km walk to Monterrey (see below). Take torch. There are the ruins of Huahullac, just outside Huaraz. It is a day trip to the hot springs at Monterrey with 2 swimming pools (rundown, uninviting) and individual baths at the hotel (rec), see under Hotels (*Termas de Monterrey*), open to non-residents.

Trekking   To *Pitec*, 12 km, 50 mins by taxi (US$15), by pick-up between 0600-0700, or 2½ on foot. To *Lago Llaca* , a 12-km, 3-hr hike from Pitec or US$12-15 by taxi on the road that goes up to the lake. Up the Cojup valley, from the Llaca road 14 km to the lakes of Perolcocha and Palcacocha, overnight at the lakes. From Pitec you can hike up four different valleys: Churup, 3.5 km; Quilcayhuanca, 12 km to lake Tullparaju and 19 km to lake Cuchillacocha; Shallap, 10.5 km; and Rajucolta, 17 km.

S of Huaraz, on the main road, is **Recuay**, a provincial capital (27 km, 1 hr); the road passes **Olleros** at 3,450m. You can get off at the main road and walk the 2 km to Olleros, or catch a truck from Calle Frigorífico in Huaraz to the village, 29 km, 45 mins, US$0.30. Some basic meals and food supplies available, but no accommodation.

Trekking The famous, easy 3-day hike to Chavín, with spectacular views of snow-covered peaks, starts from here. Walk up the valley from Olleros, keeping the Río Negro to your left. Go up the left hand valley to the highest point of Punta Yanashallash at 4,700m, before dropping down into the valley of Huachecsa to Chavín.

The main road continues from Recuay to **Catac**, 11 km, where a poor dirt road branches E for Chavín. 7 km S of Catac on the main road is **Pachacoto** from where a road goes to Huallanca on the other side of the Cordillera Blanca (133 km, 6-7 hrs). There is not a lot of local transport on this route. In this S part of the Cordillera there are few high, snow-covered peaks, but the glacier of **Pastoruri** is used as the only skiing area in Peru. It is nothing compared to other skiing areas in South America, but it is a place to get in a little practice (no ski lifts). Tours and private transport can be arranged in Huaraz (US$80 for a van up to 10 people).

Trekking The best and only place to see the impressive Puya Raimondi plants, which flower only once at the end of a hundred-year lifetime, is the Pumapampa valley. Hike up the trail from Pachacoto to the park entrance, $2\frac{1}{2}$ hrs, where there is a park office (you can spend the night here). Walking up the road from this point, you will see the plants, which reach heights of 10m.

From Recuay to Chavín is a magnificent, scenic journey, if frightening at times. The road passes Lago Querococha, has good views of Yanamarey and, at the top of the route, is cut through a huge rock face, entering the Cauish tunnel at 4,550m. On the other side it descends the Tambillo valley, then the Río Mosna gorge before Chavín.

Chavin Chavín de Huantar, a fortress temple, was built about 600 BC. Arriving late in the afternoon will mean visiting the ruins the next day. Unesco has proposed that the site be designated a worldwide cultural heritage. Entry US$1.50, students US$0.75. Open 0800-1600, 1000-1600, Sun and holidays. The 1970 earthquake destroyed many of the underground structures and now only the first few levels can be toured, but work is now in progress to excavate and light the tunnels closed by the earthquake as well as other temple mounds so far unexplored. The main attraction is the marvellous carved stone heads and designs in relief of symbolic "gourd" figures. The carvings are in excellent condition, though many of the best sculptures are in Huaraz and Lima. The famous Lanzón dagger-shaped stone monolith of 800 BC is found inside the temple tunnel. Don't forget your torch. The guard is also the guide and he gives excellent explanations of the ruins (he may allow camping inside the gate for a small tip). There is a small, interesting museum at the entrance.

John Streather writes: There is only one carved head *in situ* on the walls of Chavín now. The best things are the finely drawn stone reliefs of condors, pumas and priest warriors— by far the finest work in stone of any Peruvian, or indeed any Andean, culture of any period. The lines are outstanding for their fluidity, sinuousness, complexity and precision. Nothing like them seems to have existed either before or after them: the earlier Sechín art is clearly a fount of inspiration, but is very clumsy when compared with the delicate exactitude of the Chavín. In many ways it resembles early Chinese art more than anything Andean—in its spirit and manner, though not in its symbolism, which is entirely Andean and American.

There are hot sulphur baths (Baños Queros) about 2 km S of Chavín (US$0.15 for a bath, reported filthy; camping possible here). Beware of thieves in Chavín village; children try to sell fossils and stonework, or swap them for ballpens. Electricity 1800-0600.

Hotels There are about 4 very basic hostals around the plaza, all with water problems; some are very dirty. The best is **E** *Inca*, good beds, hot water after 1700, friendly; then **F** *Casa de Alojamiento Geminis*, Jr Túpac Yupanqui, 2 blocks from the plaza, fork left after bridge just past ruins, basic (no bath or shower, toilet in outhouse), but clean and friendly, all meals extra; **F** *Gantu*, F (not rec) and also **F** *Monte Carlo*, main plaza, not warm at night.

Restaurants *Mi Ranchito*, Enero Norte, good food, dearer than others; *Chavín Turístico*, cheap and friendly; *Montecarlo*, very slow, indifferent food; *Amadeus* bar has good sangria. All eating places appear to close after 1830. There is a small, basic market. (Better hotels in Huari, 44 km further on.) Nowhere to change money in or near Chavín.

Transport To Huaraz, 110 km, 5 hrs, US$3, see under Huaraz; buses to Huaraz leave around 1000 while trucks go in the afternoon. Travel agencies organize daily tours to the ruins; sometimes you can hitch a ride back with them. Taxi, 4 hrs, US$20.

To **Lima**, 438 km, 14 hrs, US$9 with Cóndor de Chavín twice a week, see Lima **Bus Companies** with routes to the N. Most buses from Lima go on to Huari and Pomabamba; also trucks to Lima.

From Chavín to **Huari**, 38 km, 2 hrs, **San Luis**, a further 61 km, 3 hrs, and Piscobamba, 62 km, 3 hrs: several buses and trucks serve this route, 3-4 daily, on quite a good dirt road. The scenery is very different from the other side of the Cordillera Blanca, very dry and hot. The road continues all the way to the coast, but is rarely used, 3-4 trucks a week.

From Chavín it is possible to make a circuit by road back to Huaraz. The shorter of two alternatives is via Huari, San Luis, Yanama and Yungay (**see p 1153**). This route is possible by motorbike or by car (average 20 kmph). After 10 km San Marcos, a small friendly village, is reached. At **Huari** are hotels *El Dorado*, G, clean and comfortable, sunny patio, cold showers only; *Paraíso* and *Ideal*. Restaurant *Los Angeles*, just off main plaza, popular. Also small fruit and veg market and well-stocked chemist. Everything closes in Huari at about 2000.

There is a spectacular 2-3 day walk from Huari to Chacas via Laguna Purhuay, as described by John Myerscough, from Derbyshire. "The route is clearly shown on the Instituto Geográfico Militar map, Huari is sheet 19. The walking is very easy, over a 4,500m pass and through two of the best valleys I've ever been in. Plenty of streams and lots of good places for camping. Amazing rock strata". Alberto Cafferata of Lima adds that Purhuay forest is beautiful. The road from Huari climbs to Laguna Purhuay, which has splendid campsites, trout, exotic birds and, at its S end, a "quenoal" forest. This is a microclimate at 3,500m, where the animals, insects and flowers are more like a tropical jungle, fantastic for ecologists and photographers. At the Piscigranja de Acopalca, fish farm, you can eat fried trout.

In **Chacas** (off the main road), there are a few basic shops, restaurants, a small market and two or three basic hostals, if needed. Chacas has a fine church; its *fiesta patronal* is in mid-Aug, with bullfights, a famous *carrera de cintas* and fireworks. Seek out the Taller Don Bosco, a woodcarving workshop run by an Italian priest. It is a two-day hike from Chacas to Marcará via the Quebradas Juytush and Honda (lots of condors to be seen). The Quebrada Honda is known as the Paraíso de las Cascadas because it contains at least 7 waterfalls (Alberto Cafferata).

At **San Luis**, a bigger mountain village, there are **G** Hostal Rotta, a few basic restaurants, shops and a market. Several buses and trucks run to Chavín, 5 hrs, US$6, Huaraz, 8 hrs via the pass at 4,730m under Huascarán, and Pomabamba. 30 km N of San Luis, turn left to **Yanama** (50 km from San Luis), which has one marked hotel outside and one unmarked hotel on the plaza (G), ask at the pharmacy. Food is available, but no electricity in the village, which is beautifully surrounded by snow-capped peaks. A day's hike to the ruins above the town affords superb views (trucks run between Yungay and Yanama, US$3.25—ask at the plaza in Yungay). Eckhart Harm (Tornesch, Germany) writes: "The 70 km stretch from Yanama to Yungay is the most exciting of roads. If you leave early in the morning, you will always have the sun in the right place for taking photos. Between snow-capped peaks you ascend to the Portachuelo de Llanganuco pass from where you have an overwhelming view of Huascarán, Huandoy, Laguna de Llanganuco and other mountains, and the endless serpentines of the road winding down to the lake".

A longer circuit can be made by continuing from San Luis to **Piscobamba** (basic, but clean hotel, friendly owner; one other, both F, a few shops and small restaurants); occasional buses from San Luis and to **Pomabamba** ("city of the cedars", but none visible) which is worth a visit on several counts. There are very hot natural springs there, the furthest are the hottest. Various hotels; **F** Hostal Pomabamba, on main square, basic, safe for luggage; Alpamayo, plaza, basic; San Martín de Porras, off the smaller plaza, basic. Rooms above the Marino agency. The restaurant on the corner of the main square is friendly and good (cold though); Canela, rec. There is a small museum opp which the people in the courtyard offices will open free on request. Victor Escudero, who speaks English, runs One Pyramid Travel, Huaraz 209, T 721283; he specializes in archaeological tours, including some little known, unspoilt places, rec. Several good walks into the Cordillera Blanca start from nearby: via Palo Seco or Laurel to the Lagunas Safuna, from which one can go on, if hardy, to Mt Alpamayo ("the most beautiful mountain in the world", the glacier of Alpamayo is an incredible sight) and down to Santa Cruz and Caraz—several days' hard walking. Up to the quite large and extensive, though sadly dilapidated, ruins of **Yaino**, on top of a very steep mountain and visible from the main square of Pomabamba—though still a good 4½-5 hrs' walk away. Ask directions in the village and on the way too. The walls are beautifully built and there are two very large buildings, a square one and a circular one. The site commands far and majestic views of the many peaks of the Cordillera. The walk to Yaino and back to Pomabamba can be done in a day if one starts early. Take food and lots of water—one gets very dehydrated climbing and perspiring in the thin dry air. It's also very cold high up if the sun goes in, so go with warm, waterproof clothes.

From Pomabamba the road goes N through cold, wild mountains and valleys, passing Palo Seco and Andeymayo, to the Callejón de Conchucos. The mining town of Pasacancha (hotel and restaurant) is the junction for a road to Sihuas (expensive, reportedly a haunt of drug traffickers, no hotel). Buses twice a week from Pomabamba via Sihuas to Chimbote, 16 hrs. Daytime trucks run from Pasacancha, through Tarica and Yanac, past pre-Inca *chullpas* to Tres Cruces (basic friendly restaurant, no accommodation). Morenos Hmos buses from Tres Cruces go to Yuramarca, before the Cañon del Pato, and on to Caraz (thence to Yungay and Huaraz).

Places like San Luis, Piscobamba, Pomabamba and Sihuas were on the royal Inca Road, that ran from Cusco to Quito.

A detour from Yuramarca is along a frightening road to Corongo (bus from Caraz, Empresa Callejón de Huaylas from the main square once a week), but only go in summer, or else you may be stuck for months.

NB The Callejón de Huaylas has suffered from military and terrorist confrontations in recent years, but in 1994-95 the area had no problems and hikers and climbers have travelled through without difficulty. The Huayhuash area similarly had no problems in 1994-95. Hikers have walked the trail, reporting back favourably. Check with locals and be aware at all times of the situation. Do not camp near a town or village, never leave a campsite unattended and always hike with others when taking off into the remote mountain districts.

On all treks in this area, respect the locals' property, leave no rubbish behind, do not give sweets to children who beg and remember your cooking utensils, tent, etc, would be very expensive for a campesino, so be sensitive.

Advice to Climbers: The height of the Cordillera Blanca and the Callejón de Huaylas ranges and their location in the tropics create conditions different from the Alps or even the Himalayas. Fierce sun makes the mountain snow porous and the glaciers move more rapidly. The British Embassy advises climbers to take at least six days for acclimatization, to move in groups of four or more, reporting to Club Andino or the office of the guide before departing, giving the date at which a search should begin, and leaving the telephone number of your Embassy with money. Rescue operations are very limited and there are only eight guides with training (by the Swiss). Insurance is essential, since a guide costs US$40-50 a day and a search US$2,000-2,500 (by helicopter, US$10,000).

Be well prepared before setting out on a climb. Wait or cancel your trip when weather conditions are bad. Every year climbers are killed through failing to take weather conditions seriously. Climb only when you are experienced enough, or bring a guide from home. Most local guides do not have sufficient experience and there are few who are capable of leading a climb.

Robert and Ana Cook (formerly of Lima) write of the **Callejón de Huaylas**: The heavy rainy season lasts from Jan to Mar, while the dry season is from May to Sept. The mean daily temperature is determined by the altitude and hardly varies throughout the year. For instance, at 3,000m (the altitude of Huaraz) the mean temperature is 14°C.

Apart from the range of Andes running along the Chile-Argentina border, the highest mountains in South America are along the Callejón and perfectly visible from many spots. From the city of Huaraz alone, one can see over 23 snow-crested peaks of over 5,000m, of which the most notable is Huascarán (6,768m), the highest mountain in Peru. Although the snowline now stands at the 5,000m level, it was not long ago (geologically speaking) that snow and ice covered the Callejón at 3,000m. Despite its receding snowline, the Cordillera Blanca still contains the largest concentration of glaciers found in the world's tropical zone. From the retreating glaciers come the beauty and the plague of the Callejón. The turquoise-coloured lakes which form in the terminal moraines are the jewels of the Andes and visitors should hike up to at least one during their stay. At the same time these *cochas* (glacial lakes) have caused much death and destruction when a dyke has broken, sending tons of water hurtling down the canyons wiping out everything in their path. Now government engineers combat this problem by monitoring water flows and dyke stability.

Hilary Bradt writes: The Cordillera Blanca offers the most popular backpacking and trekking in Peru, with a network of trails used by the local people and some less well defined mountaineers' routes. Most circuits can be hiked in five days. Although the trails are easily followed, they are rugged and the passes very high—between 4,000 and nearly 5,000m—so backpackers wishing to go it alone should be fit and properly acclimatized to the altitude, and carry all necessary equipment. Essential items are a tent, warm sleeping bag, stove, and protection against wind and rain (climatic conditions are quite unreliable here and you cannot rule out rain and hail storms even in the dry season). Trekking demands less stamina since equipment is carried by donkeys. There are various trekking companies in Huaraz.

The South American Explorers' Club writes that this area is a mecca for climbing and hiking, but get information before you start. The Club publishes a good map with additional notes on the popular Llanganuco to Santa Cruz loop, and the Instituto Geográfico Militar has mapped the area with its 1:100,000 topographical series. These are more useful to the mountaineer than hiker, however, since the trails marked are confusing and inaccurate.

Apart from the book by Hiliary Bradt (see "Information for Visitors"), the only useful guide to the area currently in print is *Peruvian Andes* by Philipe Beaud (which costs US$24), available through Cordee in the UK, some shops in Huaraz and The South American Explorers' Club.

The **Cordillera Huayhuash**, lying S of the Cordillera Blanca, is only about 30 km long, but within this compact area is an amazing array of towering peaks. It contains the second highest peak in Peru, Yerupaja (6,634m), large blue-green lakes and spectacular valleys. The hike through it is definitely considered difficult, taking 11-15 days, depending on physical conditions. Make sure you are acclimatized. Also make yourself aware of the political situation by keeping in contact with the locals and take your time when hiking through.

The trek starts in **Chiquián**, where you can arrange *arrieros* and mules. You can stay at the house of Natividad Bendón, or *Pensión Miguel*. Buy all your food and supplies in Huaraz as there is little in Chiquián. A guide for the Huayhuash is Sr Delao, ask for him in Chiquián.

Transport Three daily buses run from Huaraz to Chiquián (El Rápido, between Raymondi and Tarapacá, Huaraz, Virgen del Carmen and one other), 120 km, 3-4 hrs, US$2, dep Huaraz about 1400, Chiquián 0500. There are also trucks on the route, leaving from the market, not daily. It is not well-travelled. Direct buses go from Chiquián to Lima, 353 km, 10-14 hrs, US$7, Transfysa every other day, during the day, best, also Tubsa and Cavassa at night. There is also a connection from Chiquián to Huallanca, some trucks and buses doing this route, not daily. Trucks and buses go on to La Unión and Huánuco.

Trekking To Pocpa, over the Pampas de Pallca to Punta Cacanan (4,700m), then to Lake Mitucocha; cross Punta Carhuac (4,650m) to Lake Carhuacocha, then Punta Carnicero (4,600m), before descending to Lake Quesillococha and the village of Huayhuash. Cross the Portachuelo pass (4,750m) to Lake Viconga, up to Punta Cuyac (5,000m), then down to the village of Huayllapa; climb up to Punta Tapush (4,800m) to Lake Jahuacocha, and then down the valley to Llamac and Chiquián. **Note** Do not leave any rubbish behind.

From Chimbote to Huaraz, via the Santa Valley,

a road branches off to the NE and, joining another road from Santa, goes up the Santa valley following the route, including tunnels, of the old Santa Corporation Railway. This used to run as far as **Huallanca**, 140 km up the valley, but the track was largely destroyed by the 1970 earthquake. At Huallanca is an impressive hydroelectric plant, built into a mountain, which can not be visited. *Hotel Huascarán*, good, friendly; everything closes early. At the top of the valley the road goes through the very narrow and spectacular **Cañón del Pato** before reaching the Callejón de Huaylas and going on S to Caraz and Huaraz. From Caraz to Santa (200 km unpaved) can be driven, in normal times, in 5 hrs. The road up the Santa Valley is not recommended for cyclists owing to its poor condition. Cyclists can, however, take the private road known as the "Brasileños", used by a Brazilian company which is building a water channel from the Santa River to the coast. The turning is 15 km S of the bridge in Chao, on the Pan American Highway.

Daniel Morgan, of Wellington, NZ, writes: "At its mouth, the Santa Valley is fertile, being well-irrigated from the river. Further up it becomes barren. There is only rock, scree slides, exposed shale strata at angles up to the vertical (a must for geologists). The colours are fantastic: greys, blues, purples, oranges, reds, browns. The beauty is accentuated by the bright sun throwing jet black shadows, highlighting, contrasting, hiding.

"After Huallanca, the road clings to the side of a cliff as water thunders below and rock faces climb vertically on each side. Again light and shadow interplay, creating a fantastic vista like abstract art. Beyond the dam the valley flattens out. The walls are no longer vertical and you come back to Planet Earth. It is a hot, dusty, bumpy, and awesome trip."

Caraz (2,250m), is now almost totally restored after the 1970 earthquake, and is reported a good centre for walking; splendid views of Huandoy and Huascarán. Information on mountaineering obtainable from the director of the Huascarán National Park in Huaraz. Excellent views of the N cordilleras in Jul and Aug; in other months, mountains are often shrouded in cloud. One has to cross a river by cable (20 mins) and go to Pueblo Libre to climb Tunaspampa. Caraz has a milder climate than Huaraz and is more suited to day excursions.

Hotels D *Hotel Restaurant Chamanna*, Av Neuva Victoria 185, out of town, run by Germans Ute Baitinger and Reiner Urban, clean cabañas set in beautiful gardens and good food, German and local. Also out of town, 2 km on road to Cañon del Pato (go down D Villar), *La Capullana*, pleasant, good restaurant, garden. *El Cafetal*, friendly, clean, hot water; **E** *Chavín*, just off Plaza, with bath, new, clean, good value (but no views), said to be "best of a poor bunch"; **E** *Hostal La Casona*, one block from plaza, hot water, clean; *Hostal Suizo Peruano*, San Martín 1133, with bath (cheaper without), dirty, poor beds, friendly; **F** *Hostal Carás*, Calle Sucre, dirty, hot showers; **F** *Morovi*, just outside town on Yungay road, clean, friendly, helpful, with bath and hot water; **G** pp *Ramírez*, above Moreno terminal, dirty, basic, helpful.

Restaurants *Jeny*, on plaza, good food and prices; also on plaza, *La Traba* and *Oscar y Angelica*; *Juventud*, rec; *La Punta Grande*, on corner of turn-off to Lago Parón, inexpensive local meals. Also, *Esmeralda*, Av Alfonso Ugarte, cheap, good local food, friendly; *Chifa Lorena*, Jr Sucre 1021, cheap local and Chinese food; *La Olla de Barro*, Sucre 1004, good, English spoken. About 1 km S of Caraz, open-air *Restaurant Palmira*, serves excellent trout, reasonably priced (open 1200-1800); follow the sign for trout off the main road and go through German-owned carnation farm. *Heladería El Chocolatín*, Jr Sucre 1017, selling D'Onofrio ice creams, cakes, hot chocolate, tea and coffee.

Exchange Dollars can be changed at *Comercial Fournier*, Jr Sucre 810, T 2018; *Restaurant Jeny*; *Comercial JR*, Sucre 127; *Pony's Travel* (see below). Very hard to change TCs; exchange also difficult at night or on Sun.

Entertainment *Taberna Discoteca Gato Negro*, good atmosphere, reasonable prices; *Taberna Los Troncos*, most expensive; *Discoteca Misquicay*, cheapest; *Taberna Discoteca Alpamayo Inn*, moderate prices, a bit impersonal.

Travel Agent *Pony's Travel*, Jr Daniel Villar 416-485 (T 044-720221 abonado 04 between 0800-2200 to leave a message, F 720225), open daily 1000-2100, English, French and Quechua spoken, local tours and trekking arranged, equipment for hire, IGN maps and information on climbing Alpamayo, Pisco and Huandoy; also rafting on the Santa River between Huaraz and Caraz in coordination with agencies in Huaraz (US$15 pp for 45 mins over 15 km of rapids, best May-Nov); also mountain biking to Parón Lake (5 hrs, moderate difficulty) and Portechuelo de Llanganuco (10 hrs, difficult), other routes in preparation, bike hire US$10/day, US$1/hr, maps and guides included, helmets and gloves available (contact guide Alberto Cafferata, who organizes trips from US$15 pp/day).

Buses From Caraz to **Lima**, 470 km; buses go via Huaraz. Most buses on the Lima-Huaraz route continue to Caraz (see Lima, **Bus Companies**). Several buses (6 companies) daily, fares ranging from US$4.50 (eg Chinchaysuyo) to US$10 (Expreso Ancash), 14 hrs. It may be worth taking a truck, bus or colectivo to Huaraz and catching a bus from there to Lima, depending on weather conditions and traffic coming through Caraz. From Caraz to **Huaraz**, several buses and colectivos daily, 2 hrs, US$1, road in good condition; taxi US$15. To **Yungay**, 12 km, ½ hr, US$0.25. To **Chimbote**, see under Chimbote.

From Caraz a narrow, rough road branches E 32 km to **Lago Parón**, nestling right under the snow-capped peak of Huandoy. The water level has been lowered, and the lake is to be used for the Cañon del Pato hydroelectric scheme. The gorge leading to it is spectacular. It is about a 2-day trek (25 km) up to the lake at 4,150m. It lies in a deep canyon surrounded by several massive, snow-capped peaks. By climbing up the slippery moraine to the S towards Huandoy, you get a fine view of Artesonraju. You can stay at the refuge run by Hidrandina, 6 beds, kitchen, bathroom, ask guard (Marino Leyva) for permission, no charge, but any food used should be replaced. In Caraz, colectivos go to the lake if there are enough passengers and only in the dry season, US$3-4 pp. Taxi from **Caraz** US$15, or from Huaraz, US$30 return. Travel agencies in Huaraz organize day-trips to the lake for about US$50 pp. From the N shore of the lake it is 4 km to Nevado Artesonraju, a nice place to camp surrounded by 11 snowcapped peaks. Take plenty of water; nights are cold and afternoons can be windy.

Santa Cruz Valley The famous Llanganuco-Santa Cruz hike is done most easily starting in the Santa Cruz valley. Take a truck from Caraz (in the morning) up to Cashapampa (2900m), about 5-6 hrs, US$3. It takes about 4 days, up the Santa Cruz valley, over the pass of Punta Unión, to Colcabamba or Vaquería (see hike Llanganuco-Santa Cruz, for details). In this direction the climb is gentler, giving more time to acclimatize, and the pass is easier to find. You can hire an *arriero* and mule for about US$8/day. 3 km N of Cashapampa, 1-2 hrs' hike, are the hot-baths of Huancarhuas. It is almost impossible to hitch from the end of the trail back to Yungay on the road Caraz-Huaraz. Be on the road by 0800 to catch the daily truck or bus (travellers variously described this journey down to Yungay as exhilarating, breathtaking – especially on the roof, or frightening).

The Alpamayo valley A beautiful, but difficult, long trek (for the experienced only), 10 day hike from Cashapampa up to the Cullicocha lake, passing the first pass at Los Cedros (4850m), down the Mayobamba valley; up the third pass at 4500m, into the Tayapampa valley, to the village of Huillca; up the fourth pass at 4280m, and down to Collota, Yanacollpa and Pomabamba. **NB** Please carry out *all* your rubbish.

For hikes in the **Cordillera Negra**, a truck leaves from Caraz market at 1000 to Huata (dirty hotel, F; 2,700m) from where one can climb to the Quebrada de Cochacocha (3,500m) at the top of which is the Inca ruin of Cantu (excellent views), and on to the Inca lookout, Torreón Andino (5,006m). Take water, food and tent with you. Allow 3 days for the hike, there are lagoons near the peak. 6 km down a track off the Caraz-Huata road are the Inca ruins of Chonta. Seek advice from Prof Bernardino Aguilar Prieto (former teacher), San Martín 1143 (T 2161—rooms to let, hot showers, G), close to *Hostal Suizo Peruano*, Caraz, see his Torreón Andino Information book before climbing it.

The main road goes on to **Yungay**, which was completely buried by the 1970 earthquake—a hideous tragedy in which 20,000 people lost their lives. The survivors are housed just N of the old town, which is now recovering, with houses and a concrete market (Thur and Sun). The site now has a few monuments and a nursery of rose bushes to be transplanted onto the original site. There are good views of the Cordillera Negra from the hill to the E of town.

Bed and Board F *Hostal Gledel*, Av Arias Graziani (owned by Sra Gamboa, who is hospitable and a good cook), clean, good, nice courtyard, rec; F *Hostal Yungay*, on plaza, clean, very basic; private accommodation is available, ask around. The market, is good for food and for stocking up with supplies for hiking. There are some basic restaurants, including *Comedor Yungay*, *Casa Brava* (with terrace overlooking plaza) and *El Portal* (fair).

Transport Buses, colectivos and trucks run the whole day to Caraz (see under Caraz) and Huaraz, 54 km, 1½ hrs, US$0.90. From Yungay to Yanama, via the Portachuelo de Llanganuco pass at 4,767m, 58 km: buses and trucks leave Yungay daily, but you may have to wait until they are full, 4 hrs, US$4.50. Most buses and trucks continue to San Luis, a further 61 km, 3 hrs, US$2.50, Huari (61 km) and Chavín (38 km, 6 hrs, US$3.50), or head N to Piscobamba, 45 km, and Pomabamba, 22 km. Buses or pick-ups will do the route to the Llanganuco lakes when there are enough people, and only in the dry season, 1½ hrs, US$4.50. Huaraz travel agencies organize trips to Llanganuco for about US$8.

For trekkers, one of the finest walks (trees, flowers, birds, midges) is over the path by Huascarán and the lakes at Llanganuco (Orcon Cocha and Chinan Cocha) from Yungay to Piscobamba. The Park office is situated below the lakes at 3,200m, 17 km from Yungay. Accommodation is provided for trekkers who want to start from here, US$2 pp. The entrance fee to the park is US$1/day, but this functions on an honour system.

Although you can start hiking up the Llanganuco valley from the park office, most hikers continue by bus or truck to Vaquería or Colcabamba where the Llanganuco-Santa Cruz trail starts. From the park office to the lakes takes about 5 hrs (a steep climb). There is a *refugio* at the lakes. From the lakes to the pass will take a further 2-3 hrs, with perfect views of the surrounding peaks. Just before the zig-zag climb up to the pass, there is a trail, very difficult to find, heading N, up to the Pisco base camp and the Demanda valley where, to the left, Laguna 69 is situated and, to the right, the Broggi glacier. There is a doorless *refugio* by the Broggi glacier, so one can spend the night after hiking up from the lakes, continue next day to Lago 69 and return in time to catch a truck to Yanama.

From the Portachuelo de Llanganuco down to **Vaquería** at 3,700m, about 9 km, takes 2½ hrs. The trail makes a short cut to **Colcabamba**, 4 km, 3 hrs. There is basic lodging and food in Colcabamba, should you decide to stay there. Familia Calonge is rec, friendly, good meals. You can arrange an *arriero* and mule for about US$9/day.

1154 **PERU**

From Colcabamba the trail goes to Huaripampa, up the Huaripampa valley, with good camping spots on the way. Continue to Punta Pucaraju and the steep climb to the highest point at Punta Unión, 4,750m. Wonderful views. From here it is down hill through the Santa Cruz valley to Cashapampa. You can camp anywhere. A good side trek is up to the Alpamayo base camp. Trucks from Cashapampa to Caraz leave in the morning, 4 hrs, US$2. Alternatively, hike via the little village of Santa Cruz to Caraz, about 5 hrs. You can stay overnight in a private house in Cashapampa for US$1. **Please take all your rubbish with you.**

14 km from Yungay is *Matacoto* in the Cordillera Negra at 3000m, with excellent views of Huascarán, Huandoy and other major peaks. Camping possible, kitchen and hot baths, US$6, ask for Susana Scheurich (German, she also speaks English, French and Italian). Horse hire in Matacoto US$3/half day, ask for Pachamanca, rec. It is 5 km on foot from a point on the Yungay-Carhuaz road, or trucks go on Wed and Sun 0700-1300, US$0.50; on other days transport costs US$8. Matacoto can be reached from Mancos (3 hrs trekking) or Pueblo Libre (5 hrs).

After Yungay, the main road goes to *Mancos* (8 km, 30 mins) at the foot of Huascarán (one hostal, some basic shops and restaurants). From here climbers of Huascarán can go to Musho to reach the base camp. From Mancos to *Carhuaz* is 14 km. There is very good walking in the neighbourhood; hot baths at La Merced, ruins at Hualcan. Carhuaz has a *mestizo* festival on Oct 24, followed eight days later by an Indian festival.

Hotels and Restaurants E *Gran*, pleasant, no hot water; **F** pp *Hostal Residencial Carhuaz*, just off plaza on Sucre, basic but pleasant, hot water; **F** *Hospedaje La Merced*, excellent, clean, friendly, hot water, rec; **F** *Perú*, good restaurant; *Casa de Poncha*, c/o Familia Figueroa, 1/2 mile out of town at foot of Nevado Hualcan, T 720211, anexo 53, hot water (solar heated), sauna, home-produced food, horses for hire; *Los Pinos*, Av Amazonas, good typical food; *Restaurant Palma*, good value.

Transport There are trucks (only one or two a day) going up the Ulta valley to Chacas (see p 1149), 75 km, 5 hrs, US$4.50. The road works its way up the Ulta valley to the pass and now again goes over the Pasaje de Ulta since the 280 m tunnel collapsed. The dirt road is not in a very good condition owing to landslides every year (in the wet season it can be closed). The trucks continue to San Luis (see p 1149), a further 22 km, 1 1/2 hrs. Each Thur, a bus (Transportes Huandoy) does the trip from Carhuaz to Chacas and returns, US$6 one way, 5 hrs.

Trekking The trek up the Ulta valley over the Punta Yanayacu pass to Yanama is little used, but offers imppessive views of Huascarán and other peaks. It takes 3 days. If you can catch a truck up the valley to where the road begins to zig-zag up to the tunnel, it will shorten the hike by a day. If not, start hiking from Shilla.

The main road goes on from Carhuaz to *Marcará*, 6 km (very basic shops and restaurants), where there is a branch road 3 km to *Chancos*, a little settlement with hot baths. Pick-ups and trucks go there when full. Sometimes they continue to *Vicos*, further up the Huandoy valley (7 km, 1 1/2 hrs, US$1.50). Vicos is set in superb surroundings with views of Nevados Tocllaraju and Ranrapalca. To hike from Chancos to Vicos takes about 2 hrs up the valley through farm land. There are archaeological sites at Copa, Kekepampa and Joncopampa.

Trekking From Vicos, one can walk through the Quebrada Honda, over the Portachuelo de Honda at 4,750m, to Chacas; about 4 days, an excellent, not difficult hike.

The main road goes on to *Taricá* (**G** *Hostal Sterling*, no hot water, food, friendly), where there is a home pottery industry (good value purchases from Francisco Zargosa Cordero) and thence to Huaraz, 26 km from Marcará, 1 hr, US$0.50.

THE NORTHERN OASES (3)

An area of great and diverse interest: elegant Spanish cities, some restored (Trujillo), some in ruins (Saña), former Indian settlements transformed into quaint towns (Cajamarca, Chiclayo, Piura), monumental ruins of highly-skilled pre-Inca cultures (Chan-Chan,

Kuelap, Tucumé) and a region poised for major tourist development (Sipán, Batán Grande, Huaca El Brujo and Moro). There are mountain villages with local customs and on the coast, deep-sea fishing, surfing, and the "caballitos de totora" reed rafts at Huanchaco and Pimentel. Between the oases, all the way to Ecuador, the desert, with sweeping grey dunes and dusty cliffs contains rare flora and fauna, including the iguana and the *huerequeque*, the long-legged bird portrayed on prehispanic pottery to symbolize hospitality.

North of the mouth of the Río Santa the Andes recede, leaving a coastal desert belt of from 8 to 16 km wide containing the three great oases of Northern Peru—the areas of Trujillo, Chiclayo and Piura.

North of Chimbote we cross the valleys of Chao and Virú, coming after 137 km to the first great oasis of N Peru, Trujillo. In the valley there is an abrupt line between desert and greenery; cultivation requires irrigation ditches which take their water from far up in the mountains. The area's port is **Salaverry**, exporting sugar and minerals, importing consumer goods and machinery. There is an 18 km road to Trujillo.

The Quiruvilca copper mines are 120 km inland by road from Salaverry. The concentrating plant at Shorey is connected with the mines by a 3 km aerial cableway, and with its coal mine by a further 8 km. The ore is then taken by a 40 km cableway to Samne, whence it is sent by road to Salaverry.

Trujillo, capital of the Department of La Libertad, disputes the title of second city of Peru with Arequipa. Population 750,000. The traveller entering Trujillo is delighted with its surrounding greenness against a backcloth of brown Andean foothills and peaks. Founded by Pizarro, 1536 (and named after his native town in Spain), it has moved with the times, but still retains many old churches, graceful colonial balconies and windows overhanging its modern pavements, of homes built during the reigns of the viceroys. Besides the Cathedral it has 10 colonial churches as well as convents and monasteries. Its **Universidad de La Libertad**, second only to that of San Marcos at Lima, was founded in 1824.

Near the Plaza de Armas, at Jr Pizarro 688, is the spacious 18th century house in which General Iturregui lived when he proclaimed the city's freedom from Spain in 1820. It is now occupied by the **Club Central**, the social centre of Trujillo. Two other beautiful colonial mansions on the Plaza have been taken over by the Banco Central de Reserva (the **Casa Urquiaga**, Pizarro y Plaza de Armas) and Banco Hipotecario (**Casa Bracamonte**, Independencia 441); the former maintains as a museum the parts it does not need as offices (they may be visited am). Casa Bracamonte was closed in 1994 when the bank went bankrupt. Other mansions, still in private hands, may be visited with the help of a travel agency. They include the **Facala** family estate at Pizarro 314; **Casa de la Emancipación**, Jr Pizarro 610, where the independence from Spain was sworn in 1820; the **Casa de los Condes de Aranda**, Bolívar 621; the **Casa del Mariscal de Orbegoso**, Calle Orbegoso 553 (with a small museum of the republic); **Casa del Mayorazgo**, Pizarro y Bolognesi; **Casa Ganoza Chopitea**, Independencia 630, with the most representative architecture of the city; **Casa de Calonge**, Pizarro 446.

The focal point is the spacious **Plaza de Armas**, with a sculptured group of the heroes of the Liberation (note the short legs on the statue, reportedly the result of the Church's plea that it should not be taller than the Cathedral). Fronting it is the **Cathedral**, with the old palace of the Archbishop next door; the *Hotel de Turistas*; the building in colonial style of the Sociedad de Beneficencia Pública de Trujillo; and the Municipalidad. Many churches were damaged in the 1970 earthquake. One of the best, **La Merced** at Pizarro 550, with picturesque moulded figures below the dome, is being restored, but part of the dome has collapsed because

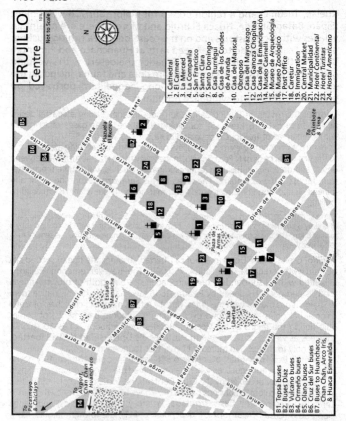

TRUJILLO Centre

Not to Scale

1. Cathedral
2. El Carmen
3. La Merced
4. La Compañía
5. San Francisco
6. Santa Clara
7. Santo Domingo
8. Casa Iturregui
9. Casa de los Condes de Aranda
10. Casa del Mariscal Obregoso
11. Casa del Mayorazgo
12. Casa Ganoza Chopitea
13. Casa la Emancipación
14. Museo Cassinelli
15. Museo de Arqueología
16. Museo Zoológico
17. Post Office
18. Immigration
19. Caretur
20. Central Market
21. Municipalidad
22. Hotel Continental
23. Hotel Turistas
24. Hostal Americano

B1. Tepsa buses
B2. Buses Díaz
B3. Vulcano buses
B4. Ormeño buses
B5. Olano buses
B6. Cruz del Sur buses
B7. Buses to Huanchaco, Chan Chán, Arco Iris, & Huaca Esmeralda

of building work next door. **El Carmen** church and monastery, has been described as the "most valuable jewel of colonial art in Trujillo", Colón y Bolívar, with, next door, the Pinacoteca Carmelita. Other old churches include **La Compañía**, near Plaza de Armas; **San Francisco** on 3rd block of Gamarra; **Belén** on 6th block of Almagro; **Santa Clara** on 4th block of Junín; **San Agustín** on 6th block of Mariscal Orbegoso; **Santa Ana** on 2nd block of same street; **Santo Domingo** on 4th block of Bolognesi. There are also two markets, one on Gamarra and the Mercado Mayorista on Calle Roca. The city's water supply is generally poor.

Museums Museo de Arqueología, normally open 0800-1400 in Jan-Mar and 0800-1200, 1500-1800 the rest of the year, Pizarro 349 at the Universidad Nacional de Trujillo (entrance, US$1), recommended; it has an interesting collection of pottery. Attached to it is an interesting library. Next to the cathdral is a museum of religious paintings. Another place to visit in Trujillo is the basement of the **Cassinelli** garage on the fork of the Pan-American and Huanchaco roads; it contains a superb private collection of Mochica and Chimú pottery, rec. Be sure to ask for a demonstration of the whistling *huacos*; entry, US$1.25, open 0830-1130, 1530-1730. Sr Cassinelli has plans to construct a larger museum. There is a **Museo de Zoología de Juan Ormea**, Jr San Martín 349 (0800-1400); interesting displays of Peruvian animals, entrance free (but donations welcome, and needed).

Fiestas The most important festival is El Festival Internacional de La Primavera, end-Sep, with Caballos de Paso, and other cultural acitivites. Popular festival in Peru, hotels are full and transport hard to get. Not to be missed. National Marinera contest, end-Jan, with other cultural events. First week of May: Festival del Mar. Celebration of the disembarkation of Taycanamo, the leader of the Chimú period. The whole procession is made in Totora boats. 11-14 Feb: Festival de San Valentín; patron of the city. 20-30 Nov: Bienial of Trujillo.

Warning Recent travellers report a much improved security situation, but areas in which to take care are beyond the inner ring road, Av España, towards the hill and in the Sánchez Carrión district at night. Take care also on Sun when there are few people about.

NB Trujillo has confusing double street names: the smaller printed name is that generally shown on maps, in guide books and in general use.

Hotels B *Turistas*, Plaza de Armas, T 232741, with bath (cheaper without, or if paying in soles), accepts American Express, rec, totally remodelled, swimming pool, full of character, rooms on street are noisy, cafeteria and restaurant, excellent buffet lunch on Sun; **C** *Los Jardines*, 4 km from centre, bungalows in garden, buses to town; **D** *Continental*, Gamarra 663, T 241607, opp market, clean, good, safe, occasional hot water, restaurant rec; **D** *Hostería Recreo*, Estete 647, T 246991, clean, friendly, safe, restaurant, rec; **D** *Opt Gar* (Grau 595, T 242192), with bath, good, friendly, rec, excellent restaurant (try sea food – lunch only for non-guests) and snack bar; **E** *Hostal Ochoa*, Colón y Bolívar, clean; **E** *Hostal Residencial Los Angeles*, Av América Sur 313, 2 km from centre, T 234312, quiet, clean, friendly, hot water, towels provided; **E** *Primavera*, Nicolás de Piérola 872, noisy on the street side, modern and cool; **E** *Residencial Los Escudos*, Orbegoso 676, T 255961, with bath, very little hot water, small garden, rec, try the delicious puddings next door at 674; **E** *Roma*, next to El Aguila bus station, new, clean, secure, rec; **E** *San Martín*, San Martín 743-749, T 234011, with bath, good value, small restaurant, good for breakfast, clean, has more than 100 rooms, rec; **F** *Estmar*, César Vallejo 134, without bath, cold water, basic; **F** *Hostal Americano*, Pizarro 792, T 241361, is a vast, old building, rooms without bath are noisy and very basic (back on to cinema, "listen to the film you saw the night before"), most rooms without window (Nos 134 and 137, and those either side of 303, have windows, balconies and good views), safe.

The following are basic, in a poor area of town, but are used by backpackers: **D** *Vogi*, Ayacucho 663, with bath, clean, safe, quiet, highly rec; **E** *Hostal Monterrey*, Av Los Incas 256, T 241673, open 24 hrs, friendly, comfortable, but not very clean (close to Tepsa, good for late arrivals, reports of mainly short-stay activity); **E** *Hostal Salaverry*, Independencia y Salaverry, friendly, public parking two blocks away; **F** *Hostal Maxelvar*, Av González Prada, basic, noisy; hotels on Ayacucho tend to be decaying and very basic, eg *Perú*, **F** *Hostal Royers*, with bath, hot water, friendly but dirty, basic, comfortable, hot water 1200-1400, 3rd floor is best for water; **G** *Hostal Central*, Ayacucho 728, run down but friendly; **G** *Hostal Lima*, Ayacucho 718, popular with gringos, dirty, baths terrible. **G** *Hostal Santa Rosa*, Jr Moche 613, dark, singles only, possibly brothel. Familia Moreno, Huáscar 247, **E**, near centre, clean, quiet, safe, or Catrina Castillo, Pedro Muñiz 792 (10 blocks from the Plaza de Armas) F, friendly. Clara Bravo (see **Guides** below) has accommodation in Trujillo and Huanchaco. Several travellers have rec taking the 15 mins bus ride to Huanchaco and staying there instead, p 1161. **Youth Hostel** *Hostal Rossel*, Av España 250, T 253583, F 256282.

Restaurants Typical restaurants with good reputations and higher prices are *El Mochica* on Bolívar and *Grau* on Grau. *Chifa Oriental*, Gamarra 735, rec; *El Pesquero*, Junín 118, good fish; *Pollos Bolívar*, Bolívar 577, chicken and salad. *24 Horas*, Jr Gamarra 700 block, reasonably priced meals for about US$1, always open, as the name implies; *ABC*, on Orbegoso,good for breakfasts and chicken; *Zoila Azanedo*, Pizarro 946, good set menu, US$1; *De Marco*, Pizarro 725, good, especially the ice creams and coffee, set menu for US$1, desserts and cakes, it's a cycle club and welcomes cyclists. *La Calesa*, Pizarro 716, good snack bar; *El Sol*, Pizarro 660, good, set meals, vegetarian dishes; *Carbón Dorado*, Pizarro 615, good for breakfast; *Romano*, Pizarro 747, good menu, good breakfast, slow service, pricey; *Pizzería Valentino*, Orbegoso block 2, very good; *Subterráneo*, Plaza Murillo, set lunch US$1. *Las Tinajas*, on Plaza, good. *La Pileta*, Estete 472, strongly rec for good local food; *Big Ben*, Av España, seafood a speciality, popular with locals. Wholewheat bread at *Panadería Chalet Suizo*, Av España e Independencia. Very good cafe next to Caretur office on Independencia, in quiet inner courtyard, good fruit juices, coffee and sandwiches. Cheap meals in the market at Grau y Gamarra and good seafood in unmarked restaurant on Grau, in Block 7, white building with Coca Cola sign. Traditional Peruvian food in private house C Lorenzo Risco Ruiz, Av Mansiche 827, T 2260136, Spanish speaking only. It's difficult to find a meal before 0800. A Mon speciality is *shambar*, a rice and spicy cabbage soup.

Banks and Exchange Most banks change TCs, but check the commission. Banco de Crédito is the best for smaller amounts: into soles up to 3% commission and into cash dollars 5-7%. Note that most banks have long queues; 0930 is the best time. Street changers (rip-offs common, take care), *casas de cambio* and travel agencies give slightly better rates for cash dollars than banks. Cash advances on Visa at Banco de Crédito and Interbanc; Mastercard at Banco CCC, charging 8% commission. Unicard cashpoint at Extebandes, works for Royal Bank of Canada cardholders.

Consulate British, Honorary Consul, Mr Winston Barber, Jesús de Nazareth 312, T 235548. **Finnish**, Bolívar 200, T 276122.

Hospital Clínica Peruana Americana, Av Mansiche 702, T 231261, English spoken, good.

Laundry Try *Hostal Americano*.

Post Office Corner of Independencia and Bolognesi. **Telecommunications** Entel for local, national and international phone calls, faxes, telexes, etc, on Calle Junín around corner from post office.

Camera Repairs Laboratorios de Investigación Científica, San Martín 745, over Fuji shop opp *Hotel San Martín*, good. Hugo Guevara, G&M Color, Ayacucho 825, T 244932, and España 2787, T/F 258050, 1 hr developing service and electrical repairs.

NB Tourists may be approached by vendors selling *huacos* and necklaces from the Chimú period; the export of these items is strictly illegal if they are genuine, but they almost certainly aren't. For old car freaks, look for the funeral director's premises, just off the main square, where there are hearses as old as a 1910 Chevrolet with wooden coachwork and wheelspokes; the proprietor is happy to show you around.

Travel Agents *América Tours*, Jr Francisco Pizarro 470, on Plaza, T 247049, helpful; *Chacón Tours*, Av España 106-112, T 255212, rec; *Guía Tours*, Independencia 519, rec; helpful travel agency in *Hotel de Turistas*. Tours have set prices; don't be fooled by a "smart" guide or the wrong information. Few agencies run tours on Sun and often only at fixed times on other days. To Tschudi, Chan Chán, Arco Iris, El Dragón and Huanchaco, US$16 pp; to Huacas del Sol and de la Luna, US$7 pp (minimum 2 people); city tour US$5 pp.

Guides Pedro Puerta, an English speaking expert on Chan Chán and former college librarian, who has an office at Km 560 on the Panamericana Norte, 2½ km from the Plaza de Armas, he can also be contacted through *Hostal Americano*. He also sells beautiful prints of Chan Chán reliefs and Mochica pottery motifs. Sr Puerta is not an official guide, but is experienced and rec. The tourist office has a list of official guides (favourable reports received). Other experienced guides are Oscar and Gustava Prada Marga, Miguel Grau 169, Villa del Mar; average cost US$7/hr. Also recommended is Clara Bravo, T 260003/243347, who is an experienced official tourist guide with her own transport; she speaks Spanish, English, German and understands Italian. She takes tourists on extended circuits of the region and is good for information (archaeological tour US$16 for 6 hrs, city tour US$7 pp). For tours of Chan Chán, José Soto Ríos has been rec, he speaks English. All other guides should be treated with suspicion.

Tourist Office Caretur, Independencia 628. Maps and information also from Touring and Automobile Club, maps from Librería Ayacucho, Ayacucho 570. Tourist Police have an office at Pizarro 422 on the corner of Plaza de Armas: extremely helpful; will even help lone travellers to visit Chan Chán safely. Any complaints about tourist services should be addressed to the Ministerio de Turismo, Av España 1800, Trujillo, T 232158.

Immigration Av Larco. Gives 30-day visa extensions, US$20 (proof of funds and onward ticket required), plus 5/2 for *formulario* in Banco de la Nación (fixers on the street will charge more).

Local Transport Buses and colectivos on all routes, US$0.20-0.30; colectivos are safer as there are fewer people and fewer pick-pockets. **Taxis** Town trip, US$1. Chan Chán, Huanchaco, US$3-4, airport US$5-6. Beware of overcharging, check fares with locals. By the hour, in town, US$6, outside US$9. Taxi driver Jorge Enrique Guevara Castillo, Av del Ejército 1259, Altos 1, rec. Another taxi driver, Felix Espino, T 232428, reliable, good value. English chartered accountant Michael White (speaks fluent Spanish and a useful amount of German) provides transport, plus translation and business services, very knowledgeable about tourist sites, T 260003/243347.

Air Transport Faucett, Pizarro 532, T 232232/232261; AeroPerú, Pizarro 4, Plaza de Armas, T 234241/242727; Americana, Pizarro 486, T 261687; Aero Continente, Jr Junín 527, T 231346. To Lima, 1 hr, US$47, daily flights with Faucett, AeroPerú, Americana and Aero Continente. To Chiclayo 30 mins, US$23, Faucett, AeroPerú, Aero Continente, none daily. To Piura, 45 mins, US$55 (Faucett, 2 a week). Aero Continente to Pucallpa US$32, Tarapoto US$26. Faucett to Tumbes US$94. Taxi to airport, US$5-6; or take bus or colectivo to Huanchaco

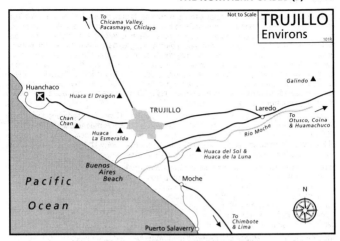

Not to Scale

TRUJILLO
Environs

101R

To Chicama Valley, Pacasmayo, Chiclay

Huanchaco

Huaca El Dragón ▲

Chan Chan

Huaca La Esmeralda ▲

TRUJILLO

Galindo ▲

Laredo

To Otusco, Coina & Huamachuco

Río Moche

▲ Huaca del Sol & Huaca de la Luna

Buenos Aires Beach

Moche

Pacific Ocean

N

To Chimbote & Lima

Puerto Salaverry

and get out at airport turn-off (US$0.15).

Buses To **Lima**, 548 km, by bus, 8-10 hrs, US$7-10. The road is quite good on the Panamericana Norte. There are many bus companies doing this route, but it's popular so buy a ticket in advance. Cheaper buses tend to arrive at night and do not have terminals, dropping passengers in the street. See under Lima, **Bus Companies** with routes to the N. There are also luxury buses with reclining chairs, video and toilet, price about 30% more. Tepsa has a clean terminal in Trujillo, Av Almagro, between Avs España and Grau; Peru Express, Transportes 14, Chinchay-Suyo Ormeño, Av del Ejército, El Cóndor, Av Los Incas 110, T 231707, or Roggero; mostly at night. To **Pacasmayo**, 120 km, 2 hrs, US$1.50, several buses and colectivos a day; similarly to **Chiclayo**, 209 km, 3 hrs, US$4; and on to **Piura**, 278 km (US$6, Emtrafesa, Av Miraflores 127, T 243981), and **Tumbes**, 282 km, US$9-10, 11-14 hrs, eg Expreso Continental, Tepsa daily at 0615, Emtrafesa at 1900. The road is paved till just after Sullana, then poor till within 50 km of Tumbes. Occasionally the road is closed by rain. In this case, you may have to take a bus to Talara, cross the river on foot and take a colectivo (US$10), or bus on to Tumbes. To **Huaraz**, via Pativilca, 518 km, 9 hrs, US$7, not a well-travelled route direct; it may be better to change in Pativilca, via Chimbote, 325 km, no direct bus, several buses and colectivos to **Chimbote** from España y Moche, 135 km, 2 hrs, US$2.50, you probably have to stay overnight in Chimbote as buses and trucks leave for Huaraz early (see Chimbote, under **Buses**); via Casma, 419 km, 12 hrs, US$10, no direct bus, but several to Casma, 269 km, 5 hrs, US$4 (see Casma, above—beware of being charged the full Lima fare). Colectivo to Chimbote, eg Minibus El Sol, 2 hrs, US$2. To **Cajamarca**, 300 km, 7 hrs, US$7-8, 2/3 buses daily, including Vulcano, Mansiche 299, T 235847 (also to Chiclayo, Chepen and Pacasmayo), El Cóndor, see also Lima, **Bus Companies**. Alternatively, go to Pacasmayo and change there for Cajamarca. Chinchay-Suyo has buses to **Casma**, and to **Tarapoto**, departing at 1200 daily. To **Tayabamba** (for ruins, **see p 1162**) with Emp Huancapata (Sucre, no number) Sun only, dep 1800, arrives Tues 1200, 40 hrs, US$5, very rough road. Bus returns Wed only at 0800.

Excursions from Trujillo About 5 km to the crumbling ruins of **Chán Chán**, imperial city of the Chimú domains and largest adobe city in the world. The ruins consist of nine great compounds built by Chimú kings. The 9m high perimeter walls surrounded sacred enclosures with usually only one narrow entrance. Inside, serried rows of storerooms contained the agricultural wealth of the kingdom, which stretched 1,000 km along the coast from near Guayaquil to Paramonga. Most of the compounds contain a huge walk-in well which tapped the ground water, raised to a high level by irrigation higher up the valley. Each compound also included a platform mound which was the burial place of the king, with his women and his treasure, presumably maintained as a memorial. The Incas almost certainly copied this system and transported it to Cusco where the last Incas continued building huge enclosures. The Chimú surrendered to the Incas around 1471 after 11 years of siege and threats to cut the irrigation canals. Chan Chán was not looted; the Spaniards, however, despoiled its burial mounds of all the gold and silver statuettes and ornaments buried with the Chimú nobles. The dilapidated city walls enclose an area of 28 sq km containing the remains of palaces, temples, workshops, streets, houses, gardens and a canal. What is left of the adobe walls bears well-preserved moulded decorations and painted designs have been found on pottery unearthed from the debris of a city ravaged by floods, earthquakes, and treasure seekers. Heavy rain and flooding in 1983 damaged much of the ruins and although they are still standing, many of the interesting mouldings are closed to visitors. The Ciudadela of Tschudi has been reconstructed (15 mins' walk from the road), open 0900 to 1600 (but it may be covered up if rain is expected). New museum on main road, US$1, 100m before turn-off to site (see below about the walk from the road to the ruins).

A ticket which covers the entrance fees for Chan Chán, the Huaca El Dragón and the Huaca La Esmeralda (for 2 days,) costs US$2.50. A guide costs US$5-7; map and leaflet in English US$0.75. Minibuses leave from José Gálvez 394, corner of Los Incas, near market, or corner of España and Orbegoso/Mansiche every 15 mins, or from Salaverry, US$0.25, last one returns about 1200; Trujillo-Huanchaco bus, US$0.15 to Chan Chán entrance; taxi, US$3-4, rec.

Security on the way to and at the ruins has improved (1994-95), with a guard at the turn-off on the Trujillo-Huanchaco road and a request from guides for permanent tourist police presence. Nevertheless, it is recommended to go with a guide (if not taking a guide, go in a group of 4 or more because robbery does occur). A taxi can be taken from the turn-off, but if walking, do not leave the path to the site. Contact the Tourist Police in Trujillo to arrange for a policeman to accompany you. On no account walk the 4 km to, or on Buenos Aires beach near Chan Chán as there is serious danger of robbery, and being attacked by dogs.

The restored temple, **Huaca El Dragón**, dating from Huari to Chimú times (1000-1470 AD), is also known as **Huaca Arco Iris** (rainbow), after the shape of friezes which decorate it. It is on the W side of the Pan-American Highway in the district of La Esperanza; taxi costs US$2; open 0800-1700.

The poorly restored **Huaca La Esmeralda** is at Mansiche, between Trujillo and Chan Chán, behind the church (not a safe area). Buses to Chan Chán and Huanchaco pass the church at Mansiche. The tour to Chan Chán includes a visit to these ruins.

A few km S of Trujillo are the huge Moche pyramids, the **Huaca del Sol** and the **Huaca de la Luna** (open 0800-1300, entry US$1); taxi about US$8 return; alternatively bus or colectivo marked Mayorista or Huacas, 20 mins, US$0.25 from corner of Zela near Mercado Mayorista, or colectivos about hourly from Calle Suárez y Los Incas. If you want a walk, get out at Bodega El Sol on the right hand side of the road; opposite is a huge Pilsen sign. Here starts a path to Moche, about an hour's interesting walk through farmland; it is inadvisable to walk unless in a large group. The pyramids consist of millions of adobe bricks and are the largest precolumbian structures in South America (the interior passageways of the Huaca de la Luna are not open to visitors; the site is under the control of the tourist police). An interesting feature of the site is the innumerable number of ancient pottery shards lying around on the ground. Also interesting are the friezes, being excavated by students from the University (5 discovered since 1992). The Trujillo Pilsen brewery is currently sponsoring excavations. It is best to visit in the morning as the wind whips up sand in the afternoon. Beware of the strong sun, take sun hat and water.

Two new archeological sites in the area are **El Brujo**, 60 km N of Trujillo, a large, important site, worth a visit, and **Sicán**, inland past Bata Grande. Neither is easy to visit; best to go by private transport or on an organized tour. Clara Bravo (see **Guides** above) charges US$20 pp to El Brujo for the 4-hr round trip (extension to Sipán, Tucumé, Brüning museum possible). For more information, ask the Tourist Police (see above).

The fishing village of **Huanchaco** is worth visiting to see the narrow pointed fishing rafts, known as *caballitos*, made of totora reeds and used in many places along the Peruvian coast. Unlike those used on Lake Titicaca, they are flat, not hollow, and ride the breakers rather like surfboards (you can rent one on the beach, beware of rocks in the surf). You can see fishermen in the reed rafts at around 0500, they return to shore about 0800. These craft are depicted on ancient Mochica and Chimú pottery. The village, now developed with the beach houses of the wealthy of Trujillo, is overlooked by a huge church from the belfry of which are extensive views. Children sell precolumbian *objets d'art* and beads; do not eat fish in the hut-like restaurants as they aren't hygienic.

Festivals Several times a year, especially at Easter, Festival del Mar (the biggest *fiesta* in Huanchaco), the annual Olímpidas Playeral and El Festival Internacional de la Primavera, there are surf competitions. See under Trujillo.

NB The strength of the sun is deceptive; a cool breeze off the sea reduces the temperature, but you can still be badly sunburned.

Hotels D *Caballitos de Totora*, Av Rivera, swimming pool, friendly, nice garden, but rooms not too clean, the owners are to open a vegetarian restaurant and hold cultural events at the hotel; D *Hostal Barranca*, clean, pleasant, but pricey; D *Hostal Bracamonte*, Los Olivos 503, comfortable, good, chalets with private bath, or converted caravans, you can camp on the grass, pool, own water supply, emergency generator, rents bicycles, secure, bar nearby, good pies and cakes (beware of monkey when eating lemon meringue pie, he's very fast and appreciates quality, as does the turtle whose preference is for marshmallows), English spoken, highly rec; D *Hostal Sol y Mar*, Jirón Ficus 570, with bath and balcony (some rooms without), kitchen facilities, friendly owner, garden, rec; E *Hostal Huanchaco*, Larco 287 on Plaza, also with hot shower, clean and friendly, swimming pool, expensive cafeteria with home-made cakes and other good meals, video, pool table, highly rec; F *Hostal Casa de Los Amigos*, Calle Las Palmeras; F *Hostal Chávez*, Calle D, Saavedra 400, clean, friendly; F *Hostal Illalo*, Las Orquídeas 341, not very friendly; G unnamed *pensión* of Heidi Stacher (Swiss) at Calle Los Pinos 451, 3 blocks from beach, clean, shared bath, nice roof balcony, only 2 rooms, highly rec; cheap, basic accommodation at the house of the very friendly Señora Lola, Manco Capac 136, or Sra Lucha Carranza, Los Camelios 334. Accommodation, incl food, with families, easy to find, US$2-3 a day such as friendly English-speaking Sra Mabel Díaz de Aguilar, nr the football ground.

Restaurants Good fish restaurants on the sea front, eg Malecón Larco 602; *Violetta*, a private house – 4 blocks directly inland from the pier (good meals provided for US$1) and Familia Flores, popular; *El Tramboyo*, near the pier, good, helpful, friendly. *Lucho del Mar*, excellent sea food, check the bill; next door is *Estrella Marina*, good fish, great value; *Piccolo*, 5 blocks from plaza, cheap, friendly, live folk music weekend evenings, excellent; *Colonial Club*, main square, run by Belgians, fish, chicken or meat, good, but not cheap, rec. Unnamed restaurant at Grau 380 for good breakfasts; *Heladeria De Marco*, rec for set lunch. Try *picarones*, people come from Trujillo at weekends especially to eat them. Most restaurants close after dark.

Transport Kombis between Trujillo and Huanchaco are 114A or B; they both do a clockwise circuit of Huanchaco and run to the Cassinelli museum, then A goes round the W side of Trujillo onto Av 28 de Julio and Av Vallejo/Los Incas as far as Zela, while B goes round the E side on Av Industrial, España and Vallejo/Los Incas also to Zela. At night B goes only to España and Grau; both run till 2300 (later at weekends). Fare US$0.25-0.30, 20 mins. "Micros" follow similar routes to Los Incas, but in daylight only; colectivos and some radio taxis run at night. Taxi US$2.50.

About 20 mins from Trujillo by bus, 15 by taxi (US$0.35 and US$3 respectively) is *Las Delicias*, with a clean beach and good surf. *Hostal Zlang* here is recommended, small, clean, F, quiet, shared baths, breakfast in *Bar-Café* attached, other meals available from other members of the family, owner very knowledgeable and his son offers tours of Chan Chán. Good restaurant serving traditional food around the corner (US$1.50-2.50).

A visit may be made from Trujillo to one of the sugar estates, say the Hacienda Cartavio, in the Chicama valley (43 km), bus from Trujillo, near central market, 7 km. It may be possible to include the Cartavio Rum factory on a trip to El Brujo. There are also interesting ruins at Galindo, near Laredo. One of the biggest sugar estates in the world, also in the Chicama valley, is the Casa Grande cooperative. It covers over 6,000 ha and employs 4,000 members. Visits (guided) are only possible before 1200; US$0.75 by bus. Ruins in the Chicama valley: Huaca Prieta and Chiquitoy; colectivos from Av España, change at Cartavio.

 Puerto Chicama, 70 km N of Trujillo is known by surfers as the best surf beach in Peru, claiming that it has the longest point-break in the world. There are a few basic places to stay and eat; only a surfers' hang-out. Friendly locals.

 132 km E of Trujillo is *Coína*, at 1,500m in the Sierra Alta Chicama; D *Hostería El Sol*, full board or bed only, built by the late Dr Kaufmann, who opened a hospital for Indians here. Walking, glorious views. Details from *Hostería El Sol*, Los Brillantes 224, Santa Inés, Trujillo, T 231933, Apartado 775.

To the NE of Trujillo is Cajamarca, which can be reached either from Trujillo or from Pacasmayo (paved throughout). The old road from Trujillo is terrible and (for cyclists especially) lonely, taking 12-15 hrs (as opposed to 8 hrs via Pacasmayo), but it is more interesting, passing over the bare puna before dropping to the Huamachuco valley. Off it lies *Otusco*, an attractive Andean town with an imposing but unfinished church and narrow cobbled streets. In *Agallpampa* there is one, unsigned *hostal* ("less than basic, no light, bath, toilet or water, and tries to overcharge"). Further on, at the mining town of Shorey, a road branches off to *Santiago de Chuco*, birthplace of the poet César Vallejo, where there is the annual festival of Santiago El Mayor in the second half of Jul. The main procession is on 25 Jul, when the image is carried through the streets. Close to Yancabamba is *Hostería El Viajero* and in Quiruvilca there is one hotel. The road runs on to the colonial town of *Huamachuco*, 181 km from Trujillo, which has a huge main plaza and a controversial modern cathedral. There is a colourful Sun market. A 2-hr walk (take the track which goes off to the right just after crossing the bridge on the road to Trujillo) takes you to the extensive ruins of hilltop pre-Inca fortifications, *Marcahuamachuco* (car US$5 pp). Nearby, beyond the local radio station, 1 hr's walk, are the pre-Inca ruins of *Viracochabamba*. Huamachuco was on the royal Inca Road.

Huamachuco Hotels F *Hostal San Francisco*, Sánchez Carrión 380, clean, hot shower; G *Fernando*, Bolívar 361, good value, clean; G *La Libertad*, not rec, rooms and bathrooms filthy; also G *Hostal Huamachuco* and G *Sucre*. Rec restaurants: *Caribe*, quite good, and *El Sol* (both on main square), *El Cairo*, Sánchez Carrión 754, good food and service, rec, and *Danubio*. Good snacks at *Salón Venecia*, Carrión near main plaza.

Buses Transportes Quiroz **from Trujillo** (T 247011), US$5, 12 hrs, at 1530, 1700, 1800, take warm clothing; Antisuyo **to Trujillo** three daily, US$4, 10 hrs. There are also colectivos from Trujillo. Buses to **Cajamarca**, US$1.80; **to Casa Grande**, US$1. Direct bus to Lima, 24 hrs.

From Huamachuco buses (Empresa Huancapata which start in Trujillo) run to *Tayabamba* (important ruins nearby), on the far bank of the Marañón, passing through the old gold-mining centres of Pataz province, such as Parcoy and Buldibuyo. This journey takes a good 18 hrs in "normal" conditions. Reached from *Pataz* itself (a friendly gold-mining town, about 100 km from Huamachuco) are the unique circular ruins of El Gran *Pajatén* (pre-Inca); ask at Tourist

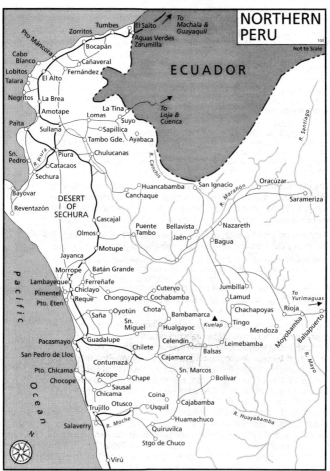

Office in Cajamarca for details. A national park, Río Abiseo, incorporating Gran Pajatén and four other sites—La Playa, Las Papayas, Los Pinchudos and Cerro Central—is planned. Only archaeologists and researchers are allowed there to visit El Gran Pajatén. Worth seeing in the Huamachuco area are **Laguna Sausacocha** (with Inca ruins nearby similar to those of Vilcashuamán, near Ayacucho) and *haciendas* Yanasara and Cochabamba, deep down in the valley of the river Chusgón, about 2-3 hrs by truck E of the town. **Yanasara**, noted for its fighting bulls, is still in the hands of its long-term owner, Francisco Pinillos Montoya, a well-known local character. There is a guest house at Cochabamba, which used to be the Andean retreat of the owners of the Laredo sugar plantation, near Trujillo. The climate, at about 2,300m, is mild.

There is a 2-day walk from Bolívar in the NE to Huamachuco, parts of which follow an Inca trail used by Túpac Yupanqui. One walks from Bolívar to Bambamarca, then down the stone steps leading to the Calemar trail, which crosses the Río Marañón. At Pallar, there are trucks to Huamachuco. Be sure to take food, water, a small kerosene cooker and a compass; this is an arduous trip and not recommended for beginners.

From Huamachuco the road runs on 48 km through impressive eucalyptus groves to **Cajabamba**, which lies in the high part of the sugar-producing and once malaria-infested Condebamba valley. It has an attractive Plaza de Armas.

The best hotel is the **F** *Flores* (with toilet, friendly, clean) on the Plaza de Armas; **F** *Hostal Bolívar*, incl fleas but without bath; also **F** *Ramal*, friendly; *Restaurant Gloriabamba* good.

Buses Several buses daily to Huamachuco; Quiroz, Antisuyo, about 3 hrs, US$2.20, also trucks and lorries. Two direct buses a day from Trujillo, 12 hrs. To Cajamarca, via San Marcos (below) with Empresa Díaz (unreliable) and Empresa Atahuallpa, 0500, US$3.

Cajabamba can also be reached in a strenuous but marvellous 3-4 day hike from **Coina**, 132 km E of Trujillo at 1,500m in the Sierra Alto Chicama (see above). The first day's walk brings you to Hacienda Santa Rosa where you stay overnight. Then you cross the mountains at about 4,000m, coming through Arequeda to Cajabamba. The ruins at Huacamochal may be seen en route; the scenery is spectacular. It is advisable to hire a guide, and a donkey to carry the luggage. A map of the route is available from the Post Office in Coina.

The road continues from Cajabamba through **San Marcos**, both on the Inca Road (3 hotels; **G** pp *Nuevo*, with bath, water shortages, but clean and quiet), important for its Sun cattle market, to Cajamarca. Bus to Cajamarca (124 km), Atahuallpa and Empresa Díaz leaving early in the morning, takes 6 hrs US$3.60.

Pacasmayo (pop 12,300), port for the next oasis N, is 142 km N of Trujillo, about 1½ hrs by car, on the Pan-American Highway running N to Chiclayo.

Hotels E *Ferrocarril*, 1½ blocks from seafront on small plaza, quiet and clean, no hot water (ask for water anyway); **F** *Panamericano*, Leoncio Prado 18, with private cold shower, good value, friendly, clean, safe, reasonable restaurant downstairs; **F** *San Francisco*, opp *Panamericano*, basic, OK. Several cheap restaurants on the main street.

Transport There are several buses a day as Pacasmayo is the main road connection from the coast to Cajamarca.

Pacasmayo is the best starting point for visiting Cajamarca, some 4 hrs away. The mainly paved 180 km road to it branches off the Pan-American Highway soon after it crosses the Río Jequetepeque. The river valley has terraced rice fields and mimosas may often be seen in bloom, brightening the otherwise dusty landscape. A few km to N on other side of Río Jequetepeque are the ruins of **Pacatnamú** comparable in size to Chan-Chán—pyramids, cemetery and living quarters of nobles and fishermen, possibly built in Chavín period. Evidence also of Moche tribes. Micro bus to Guadelupe, 10 km from ruins, and taxi possible from there (Ortiz family, Unión 6, T 3166), US$20. Where the Pan-American Highway crosses the Jequetepeque are the well-signed ruins of **Farfan** (separate from those of Pacatnamú, but probably of the same period). At the mining town of **Chilete**, a worthwhile diversion is to take the road N to San Pablo; 21 km from Chilete are the stone monoliths of the Kuntur Huasi culture, which resemble those of San Agustín in Colombia. There are occasional buses from Chilete to the site, 1½ hrs, then 20 mins' walk (no signs; you must ask locals), then a long wait for transport back, best to hitch. In Chilete, hotels **Amazonas** and **San Pedro**, G, filthy bathrooms, room hard to find on Tues because of Wed market; restaurant **Montecarlo** serves cheap *cuy* and other dishes. Truck to Chilete from the police control 1 km from main plaza in Cajamarca, US$1. On the road to Cajamarca is **Yonán**, where there are petroglyphs.

An alternative route from Trujillo to Cajamarca, via **Contumazá**, passes through the cane fields and rice plantations of the Chicama valley before branching off to climb over the watershed of the Jequetepeque. From Contumazá, an attractive little town, trucks can be taken to Cajamarca, via Chilete.

Cajamarca (pop 70,000, 2,750m), is a beautiful old colonial town and most important town in the N mountain area. Here Pizarro ambushed and captured

Atahuallpa, the Inca emperor. The **Cuarto de Rescate** (not the actual ransom chamber but in fact the room where Atahuallpa was held prisoner—closed on Tues and after 1200 on Sat and Sun) can be seen (US$2, entrance on Amalia Puga beside San Francisco church, ticket also valid for nearby Belén church and nearby museums); a red line purporting to be the height of Atahuallpa's hand was only recently painted in. (The room was closed to the public for centuries, and used by the nuns of Belén hospital). The chamber also has two interesting murals. The Plaza where Atahuallpa was ambushed and the stone altar set high on **Santa Apollonia hill** where he is said to have reviewed his subjects are also shown (small entrance fee). There is a road to the top, or you can walk up from Calle 2 de Mayo, using the steep stairway. The **Plaza de Armas** has a 350-year old fountain, topiary and gardens (but little peace from the beggars and shoeshine boys). The **Cathedral** (San Francisco, seventeenth century, with catacombs) and **Belén** churches (handicrafts for sale in the cloisters) are well worth seeing; so are **San Pedro** (Gálvez and Junín), **San José** (C M Iglesias and Angamos), **La Recoleta** (Maestro and Casanova) and **Capilla de La Dolorosa**, close to San Francisco. Many belfries were left half-finished in protest against a Spanish tax levied on the completion of a church. The Cathedral, which took 350 years to build, was completed in 1960; it still has no belfry. Next to the Belén church (closed on Tues) is a hospital (1774) for men and women. The women's hospital is an interesting musuem, one section with well-displayed archaeological finds, pots and textiles, and the other showing modern arts and crafts.

Points of interest include the **Bishop's Palace**, next to the Cathedral, and many old colonial houses with garden patios, and 104 elaborate carved doorways: see **palace of the Condes de Uceda**, now occupied by the Banco de Crédito on Jr Apurímac 719; the house of **Toribio Casanova**, Jr José Gálvez 938; the house of the **Silva Santiesteban family**, Jr Junín 1123; and the houses of the **Guerrero** and **Castañeda** families. The **Education Faculty of the University** has a museum on Jirón Arequipa with objects of the pre-Inca Cajamarca culture, not seen in Lima; the attendant knows much about Cajamarca and the surrounding area. Open 0800-1200, 1500-1700, in winter, and 0800-1200 in summer, US$0.20 (guided tour). The University maintains an experimental **arboretum** and agricultural station. The **Museo de Arte Colonial**, at the Convento de San Francisco, is also worth a visit. The **Archaeological Museum**, one block from Belén church at Junín and Belén has a wide range of ceramics from all regions and civilizations of Peru, and an informative curator.

The town is a favourite among Peruvians for holidays, and has an interesting **market** with some crafts, especially noted for cotton and wool saddlebags (*alforjas*). Bargains of hand-tooled leather goods can be bought from the prisoners at the jail beyond the white arch on Calle Lima (7 blocks from Plaza de Armas). All museums are closed on Tues (shops take a long lunch) but open at weekends. The rainy season is Dec-Apr.

Festivals Plenty. Corpus Christi is a favourite. The pre-Lent Carnival is spectacular but includes much throwing of water, oil and paint, which can develop into fights between local youths and gringos. 28/29 Jul, Independence: *fiesta*, with bullfight and agricultural fair; prices shoot up. In Porcón, 16 km to the NW, Palm Sunday processions are remarkable.

Warning Beware of pickpockets in the Plaza de Armas and in cinemas.

Hotels B *Laguna Seca*, at Baños del Inca, in pleasant surroundings, clean, private hot thermal baths in rooms, swimming pool with thermal water, a bit dilapidated, horses for hire, food average; **C** *Continental*, Jr Amazonas, very clean, hot water, good restaurant, rec; **C** *Turistas* (60 rooms) in the Plaza de Armas, with private bath, laundry service, 2 restaurants, plan ask to see room before booking; **D** *Casa Blanca*, Plaza de Armas, room service, clean, safe, nice building and garden, good; **D** *Hostal Cajamarca*, in colonial house at Dos de Mayo 323, T 922532, F 928813, clean, hot water, rec as the best hotel, food excellent, good local guitarists, musicians welcome. The owners also run *Albergue San Vicente*, outside the town

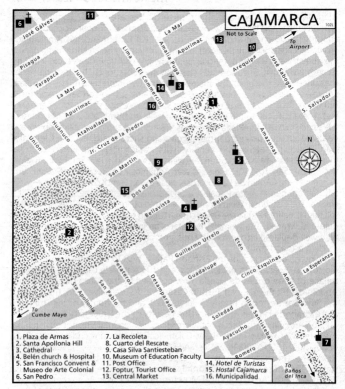

CAJAMARCA 102L

Not to Scale

To Airport

N

To Cumbe Mayo

To Baños del Inca

1. Plaza de Armas
2. Santa Apollonia Hill
3. Cathedral
4. Belén church & Hospital
5. San Francisco Convent & Museo de Arte Colonial
6. San Pedro
7. La Recoleta
8. Cuarto del Rescate
9. Casa Silva Santiesteban
10. Museum of Education Faculty
11. Post Office
12. Foptur, Tourist Office
13. Central Market
14. Hotel de Turistas
15. Hostal Cajamarca
16. Municipalidad

at Santa Apolonia, T 922644, in an old hacienda (both places in Peruvian Youth Hostel Association). On Amazonas are **D** *Hostal San Lorenzo*, No 1078, hot water, clean; **D/E** *Jusovi*, No 637, comfortable, all rooms with private baths but hot water only in am, safe; **E** *Amazonas*, No 528, modern, clean, no hot water, friendly; **E** *Becerra*, Jr Arequipa 195 (unsigned), intermittent tepid water, rec; **E** *Hostal Dos de Mayo*, Dos de Mayo 585, rec; **E** *Hostal Plaza*, Plaza de Armas 669, old building with handmade wood furnishings, mainly large rooms with many beds, private bath and balcony (**F** without bath), hot water but poor water supply, quiet, rec (especially rooms 4 and 12), with new annex (dirty but is open at 0200 when bus arrives); **E** *Hostal Turismo*, Dos de Mayo 817, clean, can be noisy at weekends, rec; **F** *Hotel Amalia Puga*, Amalia Puga 1118, no sign on door, cold shared shower, safe, but dirty; **F** *Hostal Prado*, Calle Lamar, without bath, rec, try to get a room in the sun, no heating for the cold nights; **F** *Sucre*, Amalia Puga 815, near Plaza de Armas, with toilet and wash basin in each room, water am only, good value, sometimes noisy, not very safe, poor restaurant upstairs; **G** *Hotel Chota*, Calle Lamar, dirty but cheap; *Hostal Baños del Inca*, Manco Cápac 979, youth hostel.

Restaurants *El Sitio*, Jr Dos de Mayo 311, in *Hostal Cajamarca*, local specialities, friendly, informal, rec, peña in the evening. *Salas*, on Plaza, fast service, good, cheap local food, best *tamales* in town; *El Zarco*, Plaza de Armas at Arequipa 170, very highly rec, much frequented by local residents, inexpensive, try the *sopa fuchifú*, *humitas de maíz*, also has short *chifa* menu; *El Real Plaza*, Jr 2 de Mayo 569, good food, excellent hot chocolate; *Las Rocas*, Dos de Mayo 797, excellent sandwiches, cheap; *La Namorina*, on edge of town on road to Baños del Inca, opp Ché service station, renowned for its speciality, *cuy frito* (fried guinea-pig); *La Taverna*, Plaza de Armas, good variety, but food cold, reasonable prices, *Super Pollo* on Plaza, rec for its *jugo especial* (made from *algarrobina*); best ice cream at *Donofrio* on Plaza de Armas. *Cajamarquesa*, Amazonas 770, very good, not cheap, tables in garden of colonial building. *Rocco's Pizza Bar*, Jr Cruz de Piedra 653, 1500-0030, good pizza, popular with local young set. The restaurant at *Hotel Continental*, Amazonas, serves an excellent *cuy frito* (fried guinea pig) with rice, salad and potatoes for US$5. For early breakfasts go to the market. **Tea Rooms** *Café Florida* on Plaza de Armas.

Food Specialities *Queso mantecoso* (full-cream cheese); *manjar blanco* (sweet); *humitas* (ground maize with cheese); *cuy frito*; eucalyptus honey (sold in the market on Calle Amazonas; said to be a cure for rheumatism). Try the flaky pastries filled with apple or *manjar blanco* from the street sellers. The area is renowed for its dairy produce; many shops sell cheese, *manjar blanco,* butter, honey, etc, or go to La Cajamarquiña factory and shop on Amazonas.

Banks and Exchange Banco de Crédito, Jr del Comercio at corner with Apurímac, changes TCs without commission. **Banco Nor Perú**, corner of Lima and Tarapacá, exchanges dollars with commission. It is better to change TCs into dollars before arriving in Cajamarca. Dollars can be changed in most banks, travel agencies and the bigger hotels, commission is 2-3%. **Street changers** on Av Arequipa and Plaza de Armas.

Laundry Jirón Amalia Puga 545.

Addresses Post Office, Jr Lima 406; Entel Perú, Jr San Martín 363; Telephone office for international calls, on Plaza de Armas; Hospital, Av Mario Urteaga; Guardia Civil, Plaza Amalia Puga.

Shopping Handicrafts are cheap, and good leather items at the prison, but bargain hard. Items can be made to order.

Travel Agents *Cajamarca Tours*, Dos de Mayo 323. A group of local guides has formed **Cumbemayo Tours** (Amalia Puga 635, T 922938, or 2nd floor *Hostal Plaza*), highly rec, with tours to Ventanillas de Otusco (US$5 pp) Cumbe Mayo (US$6 pp), Kuelap and Gran Vilaya (US$30 pp a day, 7 day tour). *Inca Atahualpa Tours* (next to *Cajamarquesa* restaurant, Amazonas 770, Aptdo 224, T 922495), good economical trips, eg to Cumbe Mayo (US$5 pp), the pottery workshop at Ayllambo, 3^1/$_2$ km out, and the Palm Sunday celebrations at Porcón. *Aventuras Cajamarca*, enquire at *Hotel Casa Blanca*, trips to Kuelap, Jorge Caballero, rec. Several travel agenices around the Plaza de Armas offer trips to local sites (see below) and further afield (eg Kuelap-normally a 5 day trip, only one day there).

Air Service Expreso Aéreo flies Lima-Cajamarca direct, US$85 one way, 2 hrs, daily; also Cajamarca-Chachapoyas US$48, and Chimbote US$54. Aero Cóndor once a week from Lima US$85, Chimbote US$70. **Note**: Delays at Cajamarca are all too frequent.

Buses To Lima, 856 km, 17 hrs, US$17; the road is paved, but the section up into the mountains is frequently damaged by landslides. Several buses a day; Atahuallpa is the best. See under **Bus Companies**. To Pacasmayo, 189 km, 5-6 hrs, US$8, several buses and colectivos daily. To Trujillo, 296 km, 7^1/$_2$ hrs, US$7-8, several buses a day, eg Vulcano at 1030 and 2200, US$7; most continue to Lima. To Chiclayo, 260 km, 7 hrs, US$6, several buses daily, most continuing to Piura and Tumbes. To Celendín, 112 km, 5 hrs, US$4, 2-3 a day, Atahuallpa is the best, the route follows a fairly good dirt road through beautiful countryside. Also daily to and from Cajabamba, 75 km, US$3, 5 hrs; buses and trucks do this route but it is not well-travelled. Some buses and trucks do the route Hualgayoc, Bambamarca, Chota, Cochabamba, Cutervo and on to Batán Grande, but, again, not a well-travelled route.

Excursions To *Ayllambo*, 1^1/$_2$ hr walk, 3^1/$_2$ km, from Av Independencia, a village which specializes in ceramics. You can visit the *Escuela/Taller* where children learn pottery, open Mon-Fri 0730-1200, 1300-1700, Sat 0730-1230. 6 km away, easily reached by bus, are the warm sulphurous thermal springs known as Los Baños del Inca, where there are baths whose temperature you can control, baths are cleaned after each user (US$0.10, excellent). Take your own towel. Atahuallpa tried the effect of these waters on a festering war wound. Nearby can also be seen La Colpa, a *hacienda* which is now a cooperative farm of the Ministry of Agriculture with bulls for breeding and a lake and gardens. At 1400 the campesinos can be seen handmilking the cows, some of which come when called by name. There is a minibus service from the main square, US$0.15.

The surrounding countryside is splendid. Look out for the local building method called Tapial, made of compressed adobe alternating with layers of stones or wood. Other excursions include Llacanora, a typical Andean village in beautiful scenery and **Ventanillas de Otusco**, part of an old pre-Inca cemetery (minibus from town, US$0.15), with a gallery of secondary burial niches (US$2.20 entry for foreigners, but can be photographed from road with ease). A good walk, 10 km, is from Baños del Inca on Celendín road to Ventanillas de Otusco (start from

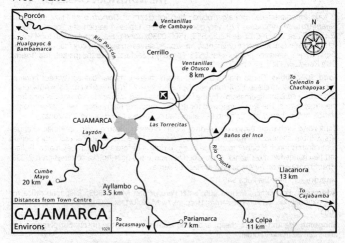

the bridge and take the path along the left side of the brook), through beautiful countryside. The walk takes little more than an hour. A new road continues to **Ventanillas de Combayo**, some 20 km past the burial niches of Otusco; these are more numerous and more spectacular, being located in a rather isolated, mountainous area, and are distributed over the face of a steep 200m high hillside. A one-day round trip can be made, taking a bus from Av Arequipa to Ventanillas de Otusco (½ hr) or colectivos leaving hourly from Revilla 170, US$0.15, walk to Baños del Inca (1½ hrs, 6 km); walk to Llanacora (1 hr, 7 km); then a further hour to La Colpa.

Cumbe Mayo, a *pampa* on a mountain range, rec (20 km SW of Cajamarca but no bus service; guided tour prices are about US$5 pp; taxi US$15; a *hostal* is under construction). A milk truck goes daily to Cumbe Mayo leaving at 0400. Ask Sr Segundo Malca, Jr Pisagua 482; small charge, dress warmly. Leaves from Calle Revilla 170. It is famous for its extraordinary, well-engineered pre-Inca channels, running for several km across the mountain tops. It is said to be the oldest man-made construction in South America, very remarkable. Huge rock formations here create an impressive atmosphere. To walk up takes 4 hrs. The trail starts from the hill of Santa Apollonia (Silla del Inca), and goes to Cumbe Mayo straight through the village and up the hill; at the top of the mountain, leave the trail and take the road to the right to the canal. The walk is not difficult and you do not need hiking boots. Take a strong torch. The Indians use the trail to bring their goods to market. It is worth taking a guided tour since the area offers a lot of petroglyphs, altars and sacrificial stones from pre-inca cultures. On the way to Cumbe Mayo is the Layzón ceremonial centre, the same period as Huacaloma. Other Inca ruins in the area include Torrecitas, and San Pedro de Pacopampa.

From Cumbe Mayo a 3-4 day hike can be made to San Pablo-Kuntur Wasi ruins; for details see Bradt's *Backpacking and Trekking in Peru and Boliva* (details in **Information for Visitors**).

North of Cajamarca is Hualgayoc (**see p 1181**). Trip with fantastic scenery. There is excellent trout served in a restaurant on the way there; easy to find as it is the only place for a long way. Order on your way there to eat on the way back.

South of Cajamarca, through Santa Catalina and Trinidad, are the Inca and pre-Inca ruins of Tantarica, near Cholol.

Cajamarca is the starting point for the N route to Iquitos. At **Celendín** there are a cinema and cock fighting Sun night in the local arena. Festival Jul 16 (Virgen del Carmen). There is also an interesting local market on Sun where you can buy cheap sandals and saddlebags. The town has electricity from 1800 to 0100. The road follows a winding course through the N Andes, crossing the wide and deep canyon of the Río Marañón at Balsas after 55 km (2½ hrs). The road climbs steeply with superb views of the mountains and the valleys below. The fauna and flora are spectacular as the journey alternates between high in the mountains and low in the rain forest. After rain, landslides can be quite a problem. There are some interesting Inca ruins on the road between Celendín and Leimebamba (146 km).

Lodging and Food A few basic *hostales*: **E** *Hostal Celendín*, with bath, on the plaza, good, clean, friendly, good restaurant; **E** *Amazonas*, OK, clean, helpful. There are basic places to eat on the plaza and on Calle 2 de Mayo; the market is OK as well.

Transport Bus to **Balsas**, 55 km, 3 hrs, US$3. Trucks daily. On to **Leimebamba**, 89 km, 3 hrs, US$3. It is almost impossible to get transport from Balsas to Leimebamba, except the one pick-up a week from Celendín; probable waiting time 2-3 days. On to **Tingo**, 45 km, 8 hrs, US$6; several buses and trucks daily. On to **Chachapoyas**, 38 km, 1½ hrs, US$1.75; several buses and trucks daily.

To Chachapoyas, 227 km, once a week, 20-25 hrs (35 or more in the rainy season, US$12). The road is in very bad condition, even impossible in the wet. It descends into the steep canyon of the Río Marañon before climbing up on the other side; spectacular scenery, if your heart can take it.

To **Cajamarca**, 107 km, see under Cajamarca **Buses**.

NB It is common for buses to leave later than the set time, to break down and to suffer long delays (up to several days) in the wet season. Always bring warm clothing and food on these routes.

Leimebamba is a pleasant town with 2 hotels, the better of which is **G** *Escobedo*, friendly owner has lots of local information, toilets, cold shower; several restaurants, including *El Gran Sabor* (best), *Oasis*, just off Plaza de Armas, and *El Caribe* on the Plaza. There are plenty of ruins around Leimebamba; many of them are covered in vegetation. Some are: La Congona, La Toya, Torre Puco and Tim Bamba. Find a local to explain the area and show the way to the ruins: it is easy to get lost. Of the ruins in the area *La Congona*, a Sachupoyan site, is 2½ hrs walk away, take the trail at the end of the street with the hotels and climb up (next to police station). The trail levels out and follows round the mountain, then down into a little valley. La Congona, a system of 3 hills can be seen: aim for the right-hand (E) conical hill with a visible small cliff. Get clear directions before setting out. The ruins are above the cliff, but to reach them you have to climb the adjoining, higher hill which rises above the cliff. There is no trail here: head straight up for 15-20 mins as best you can, some sections are near vertical. At the very top the ruins are clustered in a small area, impossible to see until you are right above them. They are covered in brambles and thick undergrowth, so a machete would be very useful. The views are stupendous and the ruins worth the effort. This is the best preserved of 3 sites, with 30 decorated round stone houses (some with evidence of 3 storeys) and a watch tower. The other hills have been levelled. There are two other sites, El Molinete and Pumahuanyuna, nearby. All three can be visited in a day but a guide (US$5) is essential.

Tingo (1,800m), 37 km from Chachapoyas, is reached by driving S up the Utcubamba valley from Chachapoyas. Much of the village, including the two hotels, was washed away in floods of Apr 1993. Police often ask to see documents.

Hotels **F** *Albergue León*, basic, friendly, built since the 1993 floods. *Hotel/Restaurante El Viajero* has a few rooms back in operation.

Transport There are several buses (from 0500) and pick-ups daily to Chachapoyas, 2 hrs, US$1.50, last back about 1730. For Celendín, see **Transport** under that town.

A 3-4 hr steep walk uphill (take waterproof, food and drink, and start early am), leads to *Kuelap* (3,000m), a spectacular pre-Inca walled city (discovered 1843). Its massive stone walls, 800m long, are as formidable as those of any precolumbian city. Some reconstruction has taken place, mostly of small houses and walls, but the majority of the main walls on both levels are original, as is the cone-shaped dungeon. There are a number of defensive walls and passageways, many houses, but virtually no carvings of any type. An interesting feature is that all the buildings are circular. Entrance fee is US$4.50, opening hours 0800-1330 (the ruins are locked; the guardian, Gabriel Portocarrero, has the keys and accompanies visitors, he's very informative and friendly and provides dormitory accommodation, **G**; his wife will cook for you and sells soft drinks). Kuelap is very remote: you should allow 3-4 days to get there from Chiclayo, but it would be wise to allow a week from the coast: the roads are bad and the public transport spasmodic. The new road from Tingo to Kuelap is very circuitous (1½ hrs by car from Tingo; very few vehicles make it up to the ruins). A private truck may be hired in Chachapoyas, US$8 for 4 hrs; also donkeys can be hired for US$5-7/day. If walking from Tingo, follow the path upstream on the right-hand side of the river and take the path to the right before the bridge, after ½ an hour there is a sign to Kuelap, the track is steep. In the rainy season it is advisable to wear boots; at other times it is hot and dry. After 2 hrs the track passes a stream; purify this water if you need to drink it. After another hour you reach a cluster of houses. Red arrows mark the path. Soon the walls of Kuelap become visible at the top of the hill. The last house to the right of the track offers accommodation (bed, breakfast and evening meal US$6, good meals, friendly, helpful); a bit further on the left is an area of flat land outside the Project Kuelap office. At the archaeologists' research station you can hire cot and bedding for US$1 a night and leave luggage safely. The Instituto Nacional de Cultura lodge is being upgraded in conjunction with Los Tambos Chachapoyanos (see below); solar power was installed in 1993, running water in 1994, with further expansion planned. There is also a camping area.

The whole area is full of largely unexplored remains; some of them have been studied by the Swiss archaeologists Henri and Paula Reichlen (who surveyed 39 sites in 1948—see *Récherches archaeologiques dans les Andes du haut Utcubamba*, in *Journal des Américanistes*, which includes an accurate map), and the American archaeologist Gene Savoy (who went further than the Reichlens-see his book *Antisuyo*); Kaufmann Doig refers to them as the "12 Cities of the Condors"; his map showing their location is in his *Arqueología Peruana*. In 1992 he started a new project in the area; ask if he is in Chachapoyas as he is worth contacting. See also Morgan Davis' book, *The Cloud People, an Anthropological Survey*. Also the booklet on Kuelap, available in Chachapoyas, very informative (ask Carlos Torres Mas, see below).

Studies indicate that the empire of which Kuelap was part was more spectacular than the Inca's. Cities, highways, terracing, irrigation, massive stonework and metalcraft were all fully developed. In addition, since the culture had longer to develop than the Inca Empire, the extent of metropolitan life in this period was far greater. There are ten times more ruins from the Middle Horizon than from the late (Inca) Horizon.

Mark Babington and Morgan Davis write: "In 1977 a team of three Americans explored the area between the Marañón and Utcubamba Rivers; they were the first to do so. They left an account of their journey in the American magazine *Outside*. Inspired by their account the two of us decided to retrace their steps. This is surely a region which overwhelms even Machu-Picchu in grandeur and mystery. It contains no less than five lost, and uncharted cities; the most impressive of which is Pueblo Alto, near the village of Pueblo Nuevo (25 km from Kuelap). It was discovered some 60 years ago by the father of a local farmer, Juan Tuesta, with whom we stayed. By far the majority of these cities, fortresses and villages were never discovered by the Spaniard; in fact many had already returned to the jungle by the time the Spaniard arrived in 1532. The sites are situated in the tropical rain forest, and on the upper slopes of the *puna*. Furthermore many of them are to be found on or near the trails which today still provide the only medium of transport in this heavily populated and agricultural region. On a recent map of the area, with which we were provided in Chachapoyas, no less than 38 sites can be counted; but Ojilcho and Pueblo Alto, for example, are not charted on this new 1977 map in spite of their enormous dimensions. If all this sounds a bit exaggerated and inaccessible, we must add that the local farmers are conversant with the ruins, whether charted or not. It is among these people that one must look for information, provision and hospitality and, most important of all, guides and mules. The area, though well populated, provides virtually no facilities for the traveller. One should be cognizant of the difficulties ahead before attempting this journey, though this is not to say the trip is beyond the ability of most. Hiking gear is essential: sleeping bags, tents and canned goods (and a machete—Ed). Small gifts are also much appreciated by the local people in return for their hospitality. (Take money in small notes as villagers do not have change for larger.) Water is no problem, unless it is the rainy season (Feb-May). Travelling at this time is not advised as the mountain passes are shin-deep in mud.

Oscar Arce Cáceres based at "El Chillo" near the Río Utcubamba, 4½ km outside Tingo, who owns a farm and knows the area very well, will help the traveller. He has accommodation with bath (US$5 pp), good meals at US$2.50, stores luggage. The trek into this area, like the walk up to Kuelap, starts from Tingo; the way is all mule track. The walk from El Chillo to Kuelap is shorter than from Tingo; the return to El Chillo can be made via the village of Nogalcucho (ask for directions). In Magdalena (a 15-minute walk from Tingo), Abram Torres will be happy to provide one with his services as guide, and his mule, for the first leg of the journey as far as Choctamal, about 3 hrs away.

A lodge is being built at Choctamal by *Los Tambos Chachapoyanos*; the 1st floor and 6 bathrooms are complete. Choctamal is the mid-point on the 36-km tortuous road from Tingo to Kuelap. It is also ¾ of the way up the Abra Yumal pass, which crosses the cordillera to Gran Vilaya (**see p 1173**). Staying at Choctamal thus makes it much easier to hike to Gran Vilaya; the lodge fee of US$10 includes food and guide for expeditions.

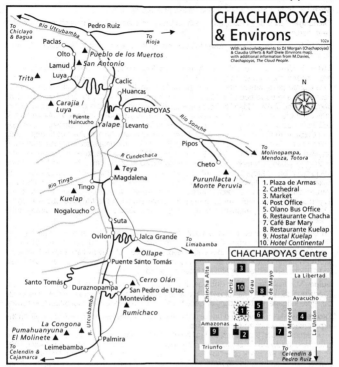

CHACHAPOYAS & Environs

With acknowledgements to DJ Morgan (Chachapoyas) & Claudia Ulferts & Ralf Diele (Environs map), with additional information from M.Davies, *Chachapoyas, The Cloud People.*

1. Plaza de Armas
2. Cathedral
3. Market
4. Post Office
5. Olano Bus Office
6. Restaurante Chacha
7. Café Bar Mary
8. Restaurante Kuelap
9. Hostal Kuelap
10. Hotel Continental

CHACHAPOYAS Centre

Chachapoyas (pop 20,000; alt 2,400m), is the capital of the Department of Amazonas. If you have any problems contact the Guardia Civil (green uniforms), very friendly and more helpful than PNP (Amazonas-police), in the town and countryside. You must register with the PNP in Calle Amazonas. Archaeological and anthropological information can be sought from the local anthropologist, Carlos Torres Mas, who is the head of the Instituto Nacional de Cultura, Jr Junín 817, also advises about walks in the area (will store luggage). The Instituto has a map of local ruins. César Torres Rojas, who also works here, is very helpful.

Hotels E *El Dorado*, Ayacucho 1062, hot water, clean, helpful, rec; **E** *Hostal Amazonas*, Plaza de Armas; **F** *Hostal Kuelap*, Jr Chincha Alta 631, with bath, cheaper without, hot water extra (electric showers); **F** *Johumaji*, Jr Ayacucho 711 (T 138), with bath, cheaper without, some rooms have hot water, safe for luggage; **G** *Continental*, Jr Ortiz Arreta 441. Due for completion in 1995 is *Hotel Zagarras*, up the hill a couple of blocks from the square on Jr Ayacucho. This hotel is being built as part of *Los Tambos Chachapoyanos*, a plan to build lodges to facilitate visits to this region (for information contact Charles Motley, 1805 Swann Ave, Orlando, Florida, USA 32809). Besides the above hotel and the INC lodge at Kuelap, projects are under way at Choctamal (see above) and Levanto (see below).

Restaurants *Chacha*, on Plaza de Armas, clean, good for *bistec apanado*, friendly; *Burguer Mass*, Plaza de Armas, excellent juices, cakes, fruit salads; *Las Vegas*, one block from the Plaza de Armas; *Oh Qué Bueno*, limited menu; good pastries also at *Patisserie*, Jr 2 de Mayo 558; *Kuelap*, same street as *Johumaji*, good, large portions, friendly, rec; *Chifa El Turista*, Amazonas 575 near post office, is reasonable, friendly and helpful; *Café Bar Mary*, 2 blocks SE of Plaza de Armas, clean, good, cheap; good fruit juices at stall 67 in the market; *Los*

Michitos, Jr de la Merced 604. Good bakery at Ayacucho 816.

Exchange Banco de Crédito, gives cash on Visa card, changes TCs. Street changers for cash near market.

Tourist Information Foptur close to *El Dorado* hotel. See also Instituto Nacional de Cultura, above.

Buses To Lima, Civa from Plaza de Armas direct, Mon, Wed, Fri. To Chiclayo 230 km, 13-16 hrs (longer in the rainy season, Jan, Feb-Apr, May, when landslides are common), US$12 with Civa (comfortable, arrives 0600, departs for Chiclayo 1700), if blocked, take a colectivo to Pedro Ruiz and try to book for 1600 departure from there; also trucks daily. The route is via Bagua (see below) and Jaén (40 km from Bagua). The road is in bad condition and can be very difficult in the wet; but it is still an easier route than via Celendín. To *Bagua* (141 km) 5 hrs, US$3.50, trucks daily; easy to find a bus or truck on to Chiclayo. There are two Baguas, Grande and Chica, with about 20 km between them; each sells half the available bus tickets. Bagua Chica has the better eating places. To **Celendín**, 227 km, for details see under Celendín (bus on Wed only, 0200). To **Mendoza**, 86 km, 4 hrs, US$2, one or two pick-ups daily, the road is both in very bad condition and hair-raising. To **Pedro Ruiz**, 54 km, 2 hrs, US$1.50, several trucks daily; on to **Rioja** 198 km, 14 hrs, can be longer in the rainy season, US$8. Trucks to Rioja now stop at a town called Nueva Cajamarca (three F hotels – none to rec). Plenty of transport from Nueva Cajamarca to Rioja, US$1. The road is in poor condition, but spectacular as you drop from the high Andes to the high jungle. From Rioja to *Moyobamba* is a further 21 km, 1 hr, US$0.75; frequent pick-ups all day. It is advised to travel by day on buses in the Chachapoyas area.

Air Service A new airport has been built; Expreso Aéreo flies Lima-Cajamarca-Chachapoyas Thur and Sun, US$89. Grupo Ocho (army) flies twice a month for US$45: every other Tues, Lima-Saposa-Mendoza-Chachapoyas-Chiclayo; on Wed, Chiclayo-Chachapoyas-Mendoza-Saposa-Lima. Truck from Plaza de Armas to airport up to 2 hrs before flights leave, US$1; taxi US$4. Flights are not reliable and are often cancelled.

Guide Martín Antonio Oliva Chumbe, Jr Piura 341 or at Reina de la Selva radio station, Jr Ayacucho 936, T 207, Chachapoyas, acts as a guide to most of the sites described below. He can store luggage. He has a copy of Gene Savoy's video on the Kuelap expedition (see above).

Excursions Huancas, which produces unique pottery, can be reached by a 2-hrs' walk on the airport road; also Inca and pre-Inca ruins.

A recommended trip is 2 hrs, 37 km NW of Chachapoyas (by bus on an improved road, also colectivos) to *Lamud*. Trucks for Lamud and Luya (also known as Carajía) leave between 1000 and 1230 from 8th block of Jr Libertad. One cheap hotel on the main plaza. Near Lamud are several ruins: San Antonio (30 mins' walk each way), Trita and Pueblos de los Muertos (3 hrs' walk each way). At Luya, there is a 2½ hr walk to *Carajía*, intact tombs built into an impressive cliff face, also known as Solmol, rec. Ask for directions in Luya (2 hotels, both G). Best to take a local guide (US$3.50-5 a day).

40 km from Chachapoyas, on the road to Mendoza, are the pre-Inca ruins of **Monte Peruvia** (known locally as Purunllacta), hundreds of white stone houses with staircases, temples and palaces, a beautiful 2½ hr walk from where the pick-up drops you. Incredibly friendly people. "8 km from Monte Peruvia is Puente de Conica, where you can see precolumbian burial figures in niches on the cliffside, known as the Purumachus de Aispachaca" (John Streather).

The road is now open via Chachapoyas to *Mendoza*, a hair-raising 5-hr journey from Chachapoyas by truck, daily at 1000, US$1.20 (return 0200, sometimes 0700). Mendoza is the starting point for an ethnologically interesting area in the Guayabamba Valley where there is a high incidence of very fair people. Some maintain that these people are descendants of Vikings who reached South America (Kaufmann Doig, Dr Jacques de Mahieu of Buenos Aires), others that they are a local group (called by Morgan Davis the Cloud People), while they themselves say they are descended from Conquistadores (which is unlikely since the Spanish chronicler Garcilaso de la Vega describes them resisting the Incas before the conquest). The region is in the *selva*, very remote, and can be reached on foot from Mendoza or Limabamba (2 hrs by *camioneta* from Mendoza, or bus from Chachapoyas), but a road is under construction. Seek all advice locally (we are grateful to Helmut Zettl of Ebergassing, Austria, for this information). Helmut Zettl mentions another white-skinned tribe in Chirimoto, a very basic settlement near Leimebamba. Ask for Padre Juan Castelli, an Englishman living there for 40 years. No transport available, 2 hrs hard walk through jungle.

Also Helmut Zettl has advised that a number of tourist bungalows are being built in this region

(1993) to facilitate visits to this virtually unknown area. For information, contact Charles Motley, 1805 Swann Avenue, Orlando, Fla, USA 32804.

"Two hours by truck on the road to Mendoza is **Molinopampa**, which marks the starting point of an adventurous five-day hike to Rioja. Only experienced hikers should attempt this journey, which is very difficult. Food supplies for the whole journey should be purchased at Chachapoyas and a guide, absolutely essential, hired at Molinopampa. The steep trail leads through waist-high unbridged rivers, over the cold, high Sierra and then for three days one follows the muddy trail down to the dense and humid jungle. We were accompanied by exotic butterflies, and never a quiet moment with the chattering of birds and monkeys. The whole magic of the jungle—trees, birds, animals and insects—can be seen untouched in their natural surroundings." (Katrina Farrar and Andy Thornton).

Levanto is 2 hrs by new road (*camioneta* can be hired, US$20-25) or 6 hrs walk from Chachapoyas by the road, or 3½ hrs by mule track; ask in Chachapoyas market if anyone returning to Levanto will guide you for a small fee (it is also possible to walk from Tingo—see below). Levanto was the first Spanish capital of the area and the Spaniards built directly on top of the previous Sachupoyan structures. Although, not many years later, the capital was moved to Chachapoyas, Levanto still retained its importance, at least for a while, as it had been one of the seven great cities of the Sachupoyans as described by Cieza de León and Garcilaso de la Vega. The Kuelap East-West Highway starts at Levanto and links with the Inca military highway at Jalca Grande (see below). Levanto was about mid-way on the N/S route from Colombia to the Huari, then Inca hub, at Huanuco. This stone road crosses the modern vehicle road at La Molina, about 5 km from Chachapoyas. A 16-km walk downhill on this road from Levanto is worthwhile. Nowadays Levanto is a small, unspoilt, and very beautiful colonial village set on flat ground overlooking the massive canyon of the Utcubamba river. Kuelap can, on a clear day, be seen on the other side of the rift. Levanto is a good centre for exploring the many ruins around, being the centre of a network of ancient ruins, fortified redoubts, residential areas and many others.

Very close to Levanto are the ruins of **Yalape**, partly cleared under the supervision of Sr César Torres Rojas, a resident of Levanto. Yalape seems to have been a massive residential complex extending over many hectares and including many well-preserved examples of typical Sachupoyan architecture and masonry with quite elaborate and beautiful friezes, some are disappointing but a pleasant walk uphill (30 mins). Its scale, like that of Kuelap, can be only described as titanic. In fact the whole area is covered in ruins, almost every prominent hilltop in the immediate vicinity has at least a watchtower of some sort.

Morgan Davis has reconstructed an Inca military garrison at Colla Cruz; on a classic Inca stone terrace, a regional-style round building has been constructed, with a 3-storey high thatched roof. This garrison guarded the road which ran past Colcamar, over the Cordillera Oriental on a 1.5 km staircase, through Gran Vilaya, to Cajamarca's central N/S road and on to the coastal downland.

To walk from Tingo to Levanto, head up to Magdalena (30 mins). From here it is about 30 mins by a short cut (uphill then downhill) to the bridge at Cundechaca. From the stone bridge walk 30 mins on the main road to Maino until you reach a wooden bridge; near here, 100m before a bend in the road look for the path which leads down into a small gorge, crosses the river (after 30 mins) and passes the little farm which is visible from the main road. From there it's a steep, 1-hr walk to a waterfall, from where you continue on the well-defined Inca road on a ridge between two gorges into Levanto. (You can add 2-2½ hrs to this walk by starting at Kuelap downhill to Tingo.) As yet there is no official accommodation as such in Levanto, although the village council and *Los Tambos Chachapoyanos* are planning to restore a colonial house on the square as a lodge (work was due to start in 1994). However, small groups of travellers are very welcome and beds and bedding are provided in the mayor's office and village meeting hall. There is one small shop and bar in the village (selling coffee and Pepsi, but little food). Using Levanto as a staging point, many beautiful and interesting walks can be done in the area. Taxi from Cachapoyas to Levanto and back, including driver waiting while you look around, US$25.

About 65 km SW of Chachapoyas, the largest ruined set of complexes yet discovered in South America, **Gran Vilaya**, was found in 1985 by Gene Savoy. There are 80 inter-connected city-type layouts, comprising some 24,000 structures. Other sites at Pueblo Alto, Pueblo Nuevo and Machu Llacta. It faces the Río Marañón at 2,850m.

Another Sachupoyan site is **Cerro Olán**, reached by colectivo to San Pedro de Utac, or Montevideo S of Tingo, then a ½-hr walk; here are the remains of towers which some archaeologists claim had roofs like mediaeval European castles. Ask the alcalde in either village for accommodation. Local guides can be hired; ask for Tito Rojas Calla in Montevideo. There is some fine decorative stonework to be seen. Also, there is an attractive village, **Jalca Grande**, with an interesting colonial church, between San Pedro de Utac and Tingo, up on the E side of the main valley. Take a camioneta from Tingo to Suta, then walk 2½-3 hrs steeply uphill. Ask local alcalde if you want to stay overnight.

From Chachapoyas the next stretch of the road is 2-3 hrs through Lamud (see above) and more of the beautiful river canyon (pick-up truck leaves about 0830, or when full) to a small crossroads, **Pedro Ruiz**, where you continue on to Yurimaguas or return to the coast. Plenty of trucks in Pedro Ruiz go to the Selva and to Chiclayo (via Bagua not Celendín) and also to Chachapoyas. There is basic accommodation (**G Hostal Marginal** with good, cheap restaurant, and one other, both F), but advisable to stay the night if you arrive late as most trucks to Rioja leave at 0500-0700. Pedro Ruiz to Rioja is about 14 hrs, US$8, on an appalling piece of road; in the rainy season, this and the continuation to Moyobamba and Tarapoto can be very bad.

Half an hour before Rioja on this road is the new town of **Nueva Cajamarca** (a few thousand inhabitants, **Hotels F Puerto Rico**, on main road, and **F Perú**, off to the right towards Rioja). There is a large market for local produce. Hourly colectivo to Rioja, US$1, 45 mins; colectivo to Chachapoyas US$12, 11-12 hrs.

From **Rioja** (3 hotels: **Hostal San Martín**, Gran 540, **San Ramón**, Jr Faustino Maldonado 840 and **Carranza**, Jr Huallanga, all basic, and **Restaurante Los Olivos** rec) there is a road to Naranjillo and Aguas Verdes, with a 5-hr walk to Venceremos, a pleasant way to see the jungle in good weather (don't attempt otherwise). An easy excursion can made to the Cueva de los Huácharos, unexplored caves, take a torch; by truck to La Unión (45 mins), walk 40 mins to Palestina then 50 mins more to the caves, ask locals for directions. There is a mini-bus to Tarapoto at 1400, US$5.

Air Service To **Lima** from Rioja, 2 hrs, US$75 one way, 3 times a week with Aero Continente, twice a week with Faucett (US$97) and once a week with Americana (US$75). To **Chiclayo**, 45 mins, twice a week with Faucett (US$63, or to Tarapoto, US$49 (Americana US$23, 4 a week). Continente also flies to Yurimaguas, US$24, and Iquitos US$48, twice a week; Americana to Trujillo, US$42.

A road with plenty of transport (about ½ hr) runs to **Moyobamba**, capital of San Martín district (ruins of Pueblo de los Muertos nearby) (915m, 14,000 people). Tourists must register with the PNP. Moyobamba is a pleasant town, in an attractive valley. It was hit by an earthquake in April 1991. Mosquito nets can be bought cheaply. This area has to cope with lots of rain in the wet season; in some years the whole area is flooded.

Hotels **D Turistas**, with breakfast, 1 km from centre, fine situation, pool, good restaurant; **E Hostal Inca**, with bath, new, clean, good but noisy; **F Hostal Country Club**, clean, comfortable, friendly, nice garden, rec; **F Hostal Cobos**, with bath, good; **F Hostal Los Andes**, clean; **Monterrey** and **Mesía**, both basic and cheap. **Restaurants** El Sol del Norte, good and cheap; several others.

Exchange Viajes Turismo Río Mayo, Jr San Martin 401.

Flights To Lima, US$71 one way: 1 flight a week with Expreso Aéreo.

Excursions Puerto Tahuiso is the town's harbour, where locals sell their produce at weekends. From Morro de Calzada, there is a good view of the area; truck to Calzada, 30 mins, then walk up, 20 mins. Baños Termales (4 km from Moyobamba on Rioja road), worth a visit. The more adventurous can hike to the Jera waterfalls in the jungle 21 km from Moyobamba. Take a truck in the direction of Tarapoto; alight at the restaurant at Km 218.

Take a good path through a well-populated valley (cross 2 bridges), then along the river, through dense jungle, with 3 more river crossings (no bridges—dangerous). A local guide is necessary to find the falls. Information is available from the Instituto Nacional de Cultura, Jr Benavides, 3rd block. Guides: Emigdio Soto, an expert on trips to native communities in the Alto Mayo area, contact him at the Projecto Especial Alto Mayo; Orlando Peigot Daza, for jungle trips (no English), at Yurayacu village. There have been guerrilla and drug activities in this region; take good care.

The road is paved for a short way out of Moyobamba, then deteriorates to **Tarapoto**, a busy town with several hotels. Good local market 1½ blocks from Plaza de Armas on Av Raimondi. Rioja, Moyobamba and Tarapoto are growing centres of population, with much small-scale forest clearance beside the road after Balsapata. The road is heavily used by trucks, with fuel and meals available. When/if the road is improved, the area will surely boom. Until then, food and accommodation will remain expensive.

Hotels   C *Turistas* (with bath, excellent meals US$3.50) 1 km out of town, T 522225, non-residents can use the swimming pool for US$1; **D** *Edinson*, Av Raimondi, 1 block from Plaza de Armas, T 522723, with bath (less without), cold water, clean and comfortable; **D** *Hostal San Antonio*, Jr Jiménez Pimentel 126, T 522226, private bath and TV, courtyard, rec; **E** *El Sereno*, with shower, clean. Plenty of others; **E** *Tarapoto*, T 522150, with fan, clean; **F** *Hostal Americano*, fan and private bath with each room; **F** *Juan Alfonso*, with shower, noisy, Jr Pedro de Urzúa; **F** *Las Palmeras*, just off Plaza, pokey, lacks water, not rec; **F** *San José*, 4 blocks from Plaza, clean and friendly, restaurant; **G** *Hostal Residencial Grau*, Plaza de Armas, communal, cheap (in both senses of the word), shower; **G** *Los Angeles*, nr plaza, good value, laundry facilities, restaurant.

Restaurants   Best are *Real* and *El Camarón*; *La Pascana* and *Achín* good; *Heladería Tip Top* and *Cream Rica* for ices. *Las Terrazas*, typical food, rec. Many others; try also *El Mesón*. Coconut water is rec as coconuts are abundant. Jirón Gregorio Delgado 268 sells excellent liquor at US$0.50 a glass (*uvachado* and *siete raices*).

Exchange   Banco de Crédito, Maynas 134, efficient, no commission on TCs. Many street changers around Plaza de Armas.

Transport   The journey from Rioja to Tarapoto costs about US$7 and it is best to carry food and water because of road problems. To/from **Moyobamba**, 116 km, 3½ hrs, US$7 by colectivo, US$3.50 by colectivo, 5 hrs, several daily. There is a direct connection by bus (Chinchaysuyo) or truck from Tarapoto to **Chiclayo** via Moyobamba, Rioja, Bagua and Olmos, 690 km, 35-40 hrs, US$20. The same bus company also runs to Trujillo, at least 36 hrs. To **Yurimaguas**, 134 km, 5-8 hrs (longer in the rainy season), US$5-10, trucks and pick-ups daily (see below for road conditions).

Air Services   US$1.75/taxi airport to town (no bus service, but no problem to walk). To **Lima**, 1 hr, US$76, Faucett, also Aero Continente. To **Rioja**, 20 mins, US$43 Faucett. **Yurimaguas**, 20 mins, US$23, 4 a week with Aero Continente, continuing to **Iquitos**, also Faucett direct 3 times a week, US$53. To **Pucallpa**, Aero Continente 2 a week, US$46; also to Juanjui, US$25, Tocache, US$38 and Tingo María, US$48, daily. Expreso Aéreo has flights to/from Tarapoto. Book in advance, particularly in rainy season. Those visiting Tarapoto and Iquitos would be advised to visit Tarapoto first, as aircraft leaving Iquitos tend to overfly Tarapoto; possible to be stuck there for days. Many smaller airlines operate flights to Yurimaguas, eg Aerotaxi Ibérico (US$40): turn up at airport at 0700-0800, wait for it to open, wait for people to turn up, wait for a list for your destination to be drawn up and you should get away later in the morning, 50 mins' flight.

Excursions   La Mina de Sal, salt mine outside the city; Laguna Sauce, 3 hrs by truck; Laguna Venecia. Laguna Azul, a big lake with *cabañas* for rent on the shore, US$80/night (4 beds and shower), very simple, no fresh water or food available; colectivo from Tarapoto, 10 km, 2½ hrs, US$2.50. River rafting on the Río Mayo US$10 pp. Between Tarapoto and Moyobamba a road leads off to **Lamas** (colectivo from Tarapoto, 30 mins, US$0.70, 35 km), where there is a small museum, with exhibits on local Indian community (Lamistas), ask at the café opposite if museum shut. Market in the early morning. About 14 km from Tarapoto on the spectacular road to Yurimaguas are the 50m falls of Ahuashiyacu, which can be visited by tour from Tarapoto (US$18 incl lunch) or by hiring motorcycle from Grand Prix, corner Shapajo and Raimondi, US$3.50 an hour. A restaurant nearby serves reasonable food and has 2 rooms to rent (G pp, basic but OK). The road continues for 10 km through lush vegetation to a small village (with restaurant).

The journey from Tarapoto to Tingo María (**see p 1266**) is not advisable: in the rainy season roads are impossible; at any time it is a drugs-growing area. From Tarapoto to Yurimaguas (136 km—**see p 1267**), the spectacular road can be very bad in the wet season, taking 6-8 hrs for trucks (schedules above). Truck/pick-up leaves for Yurimaguas (usually 0800-0900, and in pm) from Jorge Chávez 175, down Av Raimondi 2 blocks, then left 5 blocks along Av Pedro de Uruaz (pick-ups from this street to other destinations). Once the plains are reached, the road improves and there is more habitation. **Shapaja** is the port for Tarapoto, 14 km from town, served by colectivos. At Shapaja cargo boats can be caught to Yurimaguas on the Río Huallaga; plenty of birdlife and river traffic to be seen. From Yurimaguas on the Huallaga River, launches ply to Iquitos.

West and N from Pedro Ruiz (**see p 1174**): the W fork goes to Bagua (**see p 1172**) and then follows the Río Chamaya. It climbs the Abra de Porculla before descending to join the old Pan-American Highway at Olmos (**see p 1182**). From here you can go SW to Chiclayo, or NW to Piura. 47 km W of Bagua Grande, a road branches NW to **Jaén**, an old settlement, which has recently been revived as a rice-growing centre. The annual festival of the patron saint, Nuestro Señor de Huamantanga, is on 14 Sep. Hotels at Jaén: *Danubio*; *Hostal Lima*, not rec. A road has been built N from Jaén to **San Ignacio** (114 km), near the frontier of Ecuador. It crosses the valley of the Chinchipe, renowned for its lost Inca gold. San Ignacio has a *fiesta* on 31 Aug. A road also goes to Aramongo (280 km), on the Marañón; it has been extended to Nazareth. From Nazareth two roads branch: one to Oracuza, via Puente Huabico and Puerto Delfus, and the other to **Sarameriza**, the most W point on the Marañón with a regular boat connection to Iquitos—it is 1 hr downstream from Puerto Delfus. To reach Sarameriza, take a bus to Bagua from Chachapoyas or Chiclayo, US$8.50, 12-15 hrs, from where pick-ups run twice daily to Imasa. Get out at Campamento Mesones Muro, 15 mins before Imasa (US$4, 7 hrs), where you must register with the police (this can take time). For 150 km from Mesones Muro to Sarameriza, you must wait for a pick-up (one should be along in 3-6 days) and then be prepared for a 2-3 day journey because of poor roads and missing bridges. The m/n *Fernández* makes the journey from Sarameriza to Iquitos every second week: downstream, 4 days, only a few cabins, so take a hammock; upstream, 6 days.

Pacific Coast North of Trujillo

When Spanish conquistadores first encountered the broad, N Peruvian coastal valley oases, they marvelled at the creativity and sophistication of these desert farmers and fishermen. Early 16th century accounts describe enormous precolumbian settlements and sacred places, now impressive monumental ruins.

Today the rural population has its centre at Chiclayo, the bustling city and capital of the department of Lambayeque, a melting pot of ancient and modern traditions and tastes. Recent archaeological discoveries nearby have attracted tourists and scientists to N Peru.

Ruins of a splendid past are not the only treasures Lambayeque offers. Today's rural peasantry are also inheritors of many of the customs and technologies of their Moche forebears, who were master craftsmen in many fields. Artisan markets, primitive ocean going vessels, folk curing sessions and colourful religious "fiestas" enliven any visitor's stay. In addition, the N sports Peru's finest beaches for bathing and surfing, blessed with a balmy, rainfree climate all year.

Sandwiched between the Pacific Ocean and the Andes, Lambayeque is one of Peru's principal agricultural areas, and its chief producer of rice and sugar cane. Even so, archaeological studies indicate that prehispanic people here cultivated some 25% more land than farmers today. The extensive irrigation canals and reservoirs of N Peru constitute one of the major technological achievements of ancient America. Disused aqueducts and ridged fields can easily be explored.

North from Trujillo are three ports serving the Chiclayo area. The more S is **Puerto Etén**, a quaint port 24 km by road from Chiclayo; in the adjacent roadstead, Villa de Etén, panama hats are local industry; festival of the Divine Child of the Miracle, 2-17 Jun. **Pimentel**, N of Etén, is larger, a favourite summer bathing place, with a broad sandy beach (very crowded on Sun). There are no hotels, though you may be able to rent an apartment. The surfing between Pimentel and the Bayovar Peninsula is excellent, reached from Chiclayo (14½ km) by road branching off from the Pan-American Highway. Sea-going reed boats (*caballitos de totora*) are used by fishermen and may be seen returning in the late afternoon to Pimentel and at nearby **Santa Rosa**, whose fishermen use two groups of totora reed boats (*caballitos*) and *bolicheros* (pastel-painted boats which line the shore after the day's fishing)—a pleasant, 1-hr walk from Pimentel. Small hostal, **Puerto Magnolia**, basic, restaurant **Bello Horizonte**. The seafood is superb: two specialities are *tortilla de rayo* (manta ray) and *chingurito*, a ceviche of little strips of dried guitar fish (chewy, but good). The 3 ports may be visited on a pleasant ½ day trip. A blue bus leaves Chiclayo market place every ½ hr for Pimentel and Santa Rosa. Colectivos run frequently from Pimentel to Santa Rosa, and on to Etén and back to Chiclayo (10 mins from Santa Rosa, 15 mins from Pimentel). To avoid paying excess luggage charges for weight above 15 kg, buy ticket in advance, and catch bus outside terminal (no scales!)

Chiclayo was founded in the 1560s as a rural Indian village by Spanish priests. It now has a population of over 280,000 and has long since outgrown other towns of the Lambayeque Department, of which it is the capital. A major commercial hub, Chiclayo also boasts distinctive cuisine and musical tradition (*Marinera*, *Tondero* and afro-indian rhythms), and an unparalleled archaeological and ethnographic heritage (see **Excursions**). A walking tour in the centre reveals the mixture of creole, Spanish and Indian architecture along curving, narrow streets, once precolumbian canals now filled and paved with cobble stones.

On the Plaza de Armas is the 19th century neoclassical **cathedral**, designed by the English architect Andrew Townsend, whose descendants can still be identified among the town's principals. The **Palacio Municipal** (Municipal Palace) and private **Club de la Unión** line Calle Balta, the major avenue. Continue five blocks N on Balta to the **Mercado Modelo**, one of N Peru's liveliest and largest daily markets. Don't miss the colourful fruits (including enormous 2lb/900 gram avocados), handicrafts stalls (see "*Monsefú*") and the well-organized section (off Calle Arica on the S side) of ritual paraphernalia used by traditional curers and diviners (*curanderos*). James Vreeland, an American anthropologist living in Chiclayo, considers the Chiclayo *mercado de brujos* (witch doctors' market) to be one of the most comprehensive in South America, filled with herbal medicines, folk charms, curing potions, and exotic objects used by *curanderos* and *brujos* to cure all manner of real and imagined illnesses. (Note: As in all markets, don't let your enthusiasm cloud your common sense; take good care of your belongings. It is reported, however, that it is safer since the stallholders caught a group of thieves, stripped them naked and forced them to walk through the town in 1993.)

Hotels A3 *Garza*, Bolognesi 756, nr Balta, T 228172, with bath, hot water, takes credit cards, convenient, excellent bar and restaurant, highly rec, swimming pool, car park, tourist office in lobby provides maps, information in English, Land Rovers, jeeps and minibuses for hire; **C** *Inca*, L González 622, T 233814/237652, with bath, clean and good; **D** *Turistas*, Villareal 115, T 234911, with bath, E, without, meals incl, helpful, some distance from business centre, but there is much traffic noise, swimming pool, safe car park; *Sipán*, Virgilio Dall'Orso 150, T 242408, with bath, hot water, takes credit cards, good restaurant downstairs; *Hostal Santa Victoria*, Av La Florida 586, T 241944; **D-E** *Europa*, Elías Aguirre 466, T 235672, with bath, cheaper without, some hot water, good value, clean, restaurant; **D-E** *Obby*, Francisco Cabrera 102, T 231074, F 229282, good value, English spoken, rec; **E** *Costa de Oro*, Balta 399, T 2232869, central, poor, but good restaurant *Ebony* downstairs; **E** *Lido*, Elías Aguirre 412A, T 237642, with bath, clean, safe, rooms near reception are noisy; **E** *Paraíso*, Pedro Ruiz 1064, T 228161, near market, good value; **E** *Hostal San Ramón*, Héroes Civiles 169, T 233931, friendly, clean, comfortable, noisy, hot showers, good value restaurant, car park; **E** *Hostal Venezuela*, Cordera y Balta; *Oriental*, Arica 825, T 226308, nr market, good Chinese-style food downstairs; *Sol Radiante*, Izaga 392, T 237858, central, small, comfortable, no restaurant, but friendly owner will provide breakfast; **F** *Royal*, Plaza de Armas, San José 787, T 233421, cheaper without bath, old, poor beds, smelly toilets, basic, restaurant downstairs is good value. Other *hostales*: *Plazza*, V de la Vega 343, T 242004, modern, pleasant; *América*, Av Luis González 946, T 229305, friendly, clean, expensive restaurant; *Santa Rosa*, same street

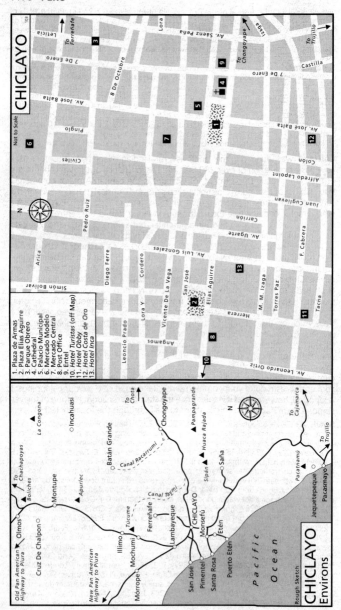

CHICLAYO

Not to Scale

1. Plaza de Armas
2. Plaza Elias Aguirre
3. Parque Obrero
4. Cathedral
5. Palacio Municipal
6. Mercado Modelo
7. Mercado Central
8. Post Office
9. Entel
10. Hotel Turistas (off Map)
11. Hotel Obby
12. Hotel Costa de Oro
13. Hotel Inca

CHICLAYO Environs

Rough Sketch

Pacific Ocean

no 927, T 224411; *Presidencial*, Av Pedro Ruiz 937, T 227591; *Residencial Chavín*, Juan Cuglievan 1347, T 225501; *Italia* Arica 1156, T 242451; *Splendor*, M Pardo 315, T 236491. Several cheap hotels on Calle Balta, near bus offices, eg **F** *Cruz de Chalpón*, safe, **F** *Adriático*, No 1009, good, but most are very basic and not rec. Some hotels prohibit clothes-washing in rooms because of the high cost of water, which often is only available between 1200-1400.

Restaurants *Fiesta*, Av Salaverry 1820 in Ocho de Octubre suburb, T 228441, local specialities, first class, very expensive; *Le París*, MM Izaga 716, T 235485, excellent but expensive, international and creole food. First-class and very reasonable hotel (usually good breakfast) at *Roma*, Balta 512, T 238601, popular with locals; *Bristol* on Balta, good and cheap, with a *comedor municipal* next door to *Ebony*, also *El Tauro*, reasonable prices, and *Cruz de Chalpón* (good breakfasts) on same street; *Imperial*, and others on Balta, choose according to outward cleanliness. *Che Claudio*, Bolognesi 334, T 237426, *parrillada* with reasonable *empanadas* and house wine; *Snack Bar Elías*, Aguirre 830, just off Central Plaza, small, efficient, quite clean, good apple pie, *lomo* sandwiches and sweets at reasonable prices; *Chifa Cantonés*, Juan Cuglievan 470, wide variety of traditional chifa/Chinese food, dining room on 2nd floor; *Fuente de Oro*, Cabrera 1213, and *Las Tinajas*, Elías Aguirre 957, excellent seafood at reasonable prices: *Men-Wha*, Pedro Ruiz 1059, expensive, delicious, large helpings, Chinese; *Titos Bar*, opp market, welcoming, helpful; *Chifa Won Kung*, Av Sta Victoria 475, T 221756. *Kafé D'Kaly*, San José 728, good *menú*, friendly; *La Cabaña Drive-In*, Los Laureles 100, T 237131.

Local Food and Drink *Ceviche* and *chingurito* (see above); *cabrito*, spiced stew of kid goat; *arroz con pato*, paella-like duck casserole; *humitas*, *tamale*-like fritters of green corn; *King Kong*, baked pastry layered with candied fruit and milk caramel; *chicha*, fermented maize drink with delicious fruit variations.

Banks and Exchange Change TCs at **Banco Nor Perú**, **Wiese**, **Continorte** and **Banco de Crédito** (last two no commission). Be prepared to wait. Beware of counterfeit bills, especially among street changers on 6th block of Balta and on Plaza de Armas and 7th block of MM Izaga, street changers only change US$ cash.

Doctor Juan Aita, Clínica Chiclayo, Av Santa Victoria, T 239024, rec as good general medical practitioner; José Gálvez Jaime, eye specialist, English spoken, Elías Aguirre 011, T 238234.

Folklore *Los Hermanos Balcázar*, Lora y Cordero 1150, T 227922; *El Embrujo*, Vicente de la Vega, T 233984. *Bar Recreo Las Palmas de Oro*, Tnte Pinglo 135, T 239138; *Recreo Parrillada El Gaucho*, Fco Cabrera 1291, T 234441.

Post Office on 1 block of Aguirre, 6 blocks from Plaza.

Tourist Office Ministerio ICTA, Sáenz Peña 8th block (at present closed, 1993-4). **Tourist Police**, Av Sáenz Peña 830, very helpful and may take you to the sites themselves.

Travel Agent *Indiana Tours*, Colón 556, T 242287, Chiclayo, and Calle Callao 121, Urb Santa Victoria, T/F 51-74-240833, for trips to Sipán/Huaca Rajada, Thor Heyerdahl's Kon Tiki museum and archaeological excavations in Túcume, Brüning Museum in Lambayeque and a variety of other daily and extended excursions with 4WD vehicles. *Sipán Tours*, Elías Aguirre 622 (*Hotel Inca*) good for tours locally, English-speaking manager. *Lambeyeque Tours*, Plaza de Armas. Tours to Brüning Museum, Sipán and Tucumé cost US$22 (but can easily be done by public transport).

Air Service José Abelado Quiñones González airport 1 km from town. Faucett, MM Izaga 711, T 237932; Americana, San José 773, T 238707; AeroPerú, Sáenz Peña 871, T 237151. Daily jet flights from Lima, Aero Continente, and Americana, US$58, Faucett, US$82; to Trujillo, 30 mins, US$36 Faucett; to Piura, 20 mins, US$49 with Faucett, 5 days a week, Aero Continente and Americana (US$12); Tumbes, 1 hr, Faucett US$64. Flights to Rioja, Aero Continente, Tarapoto, US$36 (Continente and Expreso Aéreo), latter also flies to Tingo María, Juanjui, Moyobamba and Huánuco. AeroPerú to Iquitos 5 times a week.

Buses and Colectivos To **Lima**, 770 km, Chiclayo Express, Mcal Nieto 199, T 223071, Civa, Av Bolognesi 576, T 242488, 2000, Cruz del Sur, same address, 2030, or Nor Pacífico, Balta 809, T 231671, 2100, US$15 (most companies leave from 1600 onwards). Ormeño run overnight sleeper buses (*coche-cama*) to Lima, US$25, extremely comfortable. To **Trujillo**, 209 km, Empresa Emtrafesa on Av Balta 110, T 234291, 6 blocks from plaza (safe luggage deposit), leaves hourly from 0530 until 1430, then 6 between 1500 and 2000, US$5, 3-4 hrs. Bus to **Piura**, US$5, 3 hrs, about 20 a day. *Micros* to Lambayeque leave from 1st block of San José, and from Juan Cuglievan with Lora y Cordero, US$0.50, frequent, 15 mins. Direct bus to **Cajamarca**, 260 km, Empresa Díaz, 1200 (old buses, frequent breakdowns) and El Cumbe, Av Quiñones 425-433 (much better), US$6, 7 hrs, 3 a day, Vulcano at 2130. To **Chachapoyas**, 230 km, Civa direct at 1700, US$12, 18-24 hrs. An uncomfortable alternative are the minibuses leaving the gas station on Av 7 de Enero at 1800. To **Tarapoto**, Chinchay-Suyo runs via Olmos, Bagua, Rioja (US$15) and Moyobamba. Bus to **Huancabamba** leaves Tues and Fri, 1500, arrives 0530 next day, US$10 (Civa and Tepsa, Bolognesi 726)—very rough ride, impossible to sleep. Tepsa to **Tumbes**, 552 km, 0100 daily, US$10, 9½ hrs; also Emtrafesa, Olano (rec), and others (Nor Pacífico not rec), all night buses US$7, 12 hrs, some continue to Aguas Verdes, on the border. Trucks going in all directions leave from Calle Pedro Ruiz 948 and from the market. Vulcano, Aguila, Transa, Bolognesi 5th block, leave daily to Lima-Chepén-Trujillo.

Local Festivals Some of the towns mentioned here are described in **Excursions** below: 6 Jan, Reyes Magos in Mórrope, Illimo and other towns, a recreation of a medieval pageant in which precolumbian deities become the Wise Men; 4 Feb, Túcume devil dances; Holy Week, traditional Easter celebrations and processions in many villages; 27-31 Jul, Fexticum in Monsefú, traditional foods, drink, handicrafts, music and dance; 5 Aug, pilgrimage from the mountain shrine of Chalpón to Motupe, 90 km N of Chiclayo, the cross is brought down from a cave and carried in procession through the village; 24 Sep, Virgen de las Mercedes in **Incahuasi**, 12 hrs by truck E of Chiclayo (Indians still sing in the ancient Mochica language in this post-harvest festival); Christmas and New Year, processions and children dancers (*pastorcitos* and *seranitas*) in many villages, eg Ferreñafe, Mochumi, Mórrope.

Excursions A short distance from Chiclayo rises the imposing twin pyramid complex of **Sipán** (a Moche word meaning "house of the moon"), where excavations since 1987 have brought to light a cache of funerary objects considered to rank among the finest examples of precolumbian art. Peruvian archaeologist Walter Alva, leader of the dig, continues to probe the immense mound that has revealed no less than five royal tombs filled with 1,800-year-old offerings worked in precious metals, stone, pottery and textiles of the Moche culture (ca AD 1-650). In the most extravagant Moche tomb discovered, El Señor de Sipán, a priest was found clad in gold (ear ornaments, breast plate, etc), with turquoise and other valuables. A fine site museum (open 0800-1800) opened in 1992 featuring photos and maps of excavations, technical displays and replicas of some finds. Following the four-year restoration of the principle treasures in Germany, the Lords of Sipán's physical remains and extraordinary funerary paraphernalia were recently returned to the Brüning Museum in Lambayeque, which was remodelled in 1994 to accommodate over 600 new objects. In another tomb were found the remnants of what is though to have been a priest, sacrificed llama and a dog, together with copper decorations. In 1989 another richly-appointed, unlooted tomb contained even older metal and ceramic artefacts associated with what was probably a high-ranking shaman or spiritual leader, called "The Old Lord of Sipán". Tomb contents are being restored in the Brüning Museum by specialists trained in Europe. At this writing, yet another unlooted tomb is currently being excavated, which will take several years. The excavations till 1990 were being sponsored by the National Geographic Magazine and before that by a local brewery. You can wander around the previously excavated areas to get an idea of the construction of the burial mound and adjacent pyramids. For a good view, climb the large pyramid across from the Sipán excavation. Entrance for tombs and museum is US$0.50. Nearby is the **Pampagrande** site (25 km from Sipán), a Mochica settlement interpreted by Canadian archaeologists in the 1970s as the first true N coast city, ca 550 AD. To Sipán, colectivos leave from 7 de Enero 1552, hard to find (ask a mototaxi to take you there), US$0.50, 45 mins. At Huaca Rajada is a **F** *Parador Turistica*, 2 rooms available, meals possible, camping and use of facilities for US$1 pp.

The colonial town of **Ferreñafe**, NE of Chiclayo, is worth a visit, as are the traditional Indian towns of **Mórrope**, on the Pan-American Highway N of Chiclayo, where pottery and textiles are made, using prehispanic techniques. **Monsefú**, SW, also for known for handicrafts, and Etén for its religious festivals and panama hats (see also **Local Festivals** above). 51 km S are the ruins of 5 colonial churches and the San Agustín convent of the once splendid Spanish town of **Saña**, destroyed by floods in 1726, and sacked by English pirates on more than one occasion.

A minor road runs to **Chongoyape** (bus from Chiclayo, US$1, 1½ hrs, leaves from Leticia 3rd block, just off Balta, N of Plaza de Armas; hotel, F, near Plaza de Armas, without restaurant; *Restaurant Cascada*, main street, limited menu), a quaint old town 60 km to the E (3 km W are the Chavín petroglyphs of Cerro Mulato). Nearby are the vast Taymi precolumbian and modern irrigation systems. Also near Chongoyape are the aqueduct of Racarrumi, the hill fort of Mal Paso and the ruins of Maguín. Recent excavations by a Japanese-led team, at **Batán Grande**, a site 50 km from Chiclayo, has revealed several sumptuous tombs dating to the Sipán or Lambayeque period, ca 850-1250 AD. The ruins comprise some fifty adobe pyramids where many precolumbian gold artefacts, notably the 915-gram Tumi, were found. The site, in a large desert-thorn forest of mezquite (*Prosopis pallida*), is now a national sanctuary. It can be reached by a branch turning left off the Chongoyape road after Tumán, about 30 km from Chiclayo; colectivos, US$1.20, from Pedro Ruiz—12th block—and Juan Cuglievan to the main square of the sugar cane cooperative (in which the ruins are set) from where you must get permission to visit the site, Mon-Fri only; directions hard to come by at the cooperative. Seek sound advice before you go.

The road goes to **Chota**, an attractive town with a fine Sun market (several hotels, F, *Plaza* the best, clean; *Continental*, poor; *Restaurant San Juan*, good) where weavings are cheaper than in Cajamarca: cheap, friendly shops at 27 de Noviembre 144 and 246. Daily bus to Chiclayo am, 12-14 hrs; bus to Cajamarca daily 1500 and 2000. Occasionally buses, and many trucks, run on to **Bambamarca** (*Hotel Bolívar*, best; **G** *Hotel Velásquez*, *Hotel Perú* has bugs; *Restaurant Pollos a la Brasa*, very good) which has an attractive Sun morning market (truck from Chota US$1; Empresa Díaz to Cajamarca daily at 0600, 9 hrs, frequent stops, US$4, on Sun, there is a 2 hr stop in Bambamarca for the market, some days also with Peregrino). Two buses a day pass through Chongoyape to Chota, 8 hrs, US$5. From there it goes on to **Hualgayoc** (a beautifully situated, quaint old mining town) and Cajamarca; a very interesting and beautiful journey, but few buses. The stretch from Bambamarca, about 90 km, to Cajamarca is exhilarating; the road climbs to about 4,000m through the Andean highlands with beautiful scenery of a *puna* landscape, nearly uninhabited, no fuel supply; it takes about 6 hrs in a 4WD car. The whole trip between Chongoyape and Cajamarca takes about 2 days in a car, the road is particularly bad between Chongoyape and Chota, max speed 25 kph. The Chiclayo—Chota bus passes through Cochabamba (no hotels, not a friendly place, police searches for drugs), 34 km from Chota, from where you can hitch in a truck to **Cuervo**, a town of 6,000 people at 2,800m in green meadows. Cattle and vegetables are raised here. Hotels: *San Juan* on plaza, cheap but has bugs; nicer one by Ciné San Juan, several more. Restaurants: *Salón Azul*, very good; *Central*, very dirty. A very friendly town which tourists rarely visit—don't be surprised if the local radio station wants an interview. Many trucks to Cuervo, Tues-Sat, return Mon-Fri, bus from Chiclayo Sat, returns Sun 2000. Local market Thur and Sun.

Ten km to the N of Chiclayo is **Lambayeque**, population 20,700, worth a visit. The narrow streets are lined by adobe houses, many retaining their distinctive wooden balconies and wrought iron grill-work over the windows. The town has an old church and 3 early Spanish colonial chapels open on religious feast days. Its most interesting feature is the well-known, highly recommended **Brüning Archaeological Museum**, located in an impressive modern building. It specializes in Mochica, Lambayeque, Chimú and Vicús cultures, has a fine collection of Sipán and Lambayeque gold. The magnificent treasure from the tomb of a Moche warrior priest, found at Sipán in 1987, has also been displayed here (see above), open 0830-1830 on weekdays, 0900-1800, Sat, Sun and holidays. Admission, US$1, guided tour extra US$2. There is no hotel in the town but the Museum director allows safe overnight parking in the Museum courtyard for a camper van. Try the famous Alfajor King-Kong (a sweet). Colectivos from Chiclayo US$0.50, 30 mins.

The old Pan-American Highway to Piura (which skirts the eastern edge of the Sechura desert) passes two major precolumbian sites, within easy reach of Chiclayo. About 45 km N of Chiclayo lies the archaeological site of **Túcume**, ruins of a vast city built over a thousand years ago. A short climb to a hillside "mirador" offers the visitor an unparalleled panoramic vista of 26 major pyramids, platform mounds, walled citadels and residential compounds flanking a ceremonial centre and ancient cemeteries (some find the ruins, which are heavily eroded, disappointing). Excavations in the heart of this site, led by Norwegian explorer-archaeologist, Thor Heyerdahl of *Kon-Tiki* fame, are quickly challenging many conventional views of ancient Peruvian culture. A site museum was opened in 1992, constructed of adobe and mezquite logs in prehispanic style, entrance US$1. Fatima Huaman Vera good English-speaking guide US$2.50. The collections show architectural reconstructions, photographs and drawings, highlighting recent finds, which include weaving paraphernalia, a ceremonial oar and a fabulous bas relief and mural depicting maritime scenes suggesting former sea trade and interregional contact. It was expanded in 1994. There is little explanation of the site itself.

Some suspect that it will prove to be a civilization centre greater than Chan Chán. There is also evidence, including art and remains of navigation gear, that the people of Túcume were intrepid seafarers. A 10-year excavation project led by Thor Heyerdahl is under way. Kombi buses go from Chiclayo, Pedro Ruiz y Luis González, or Manuel Pardo 425 y L González, US$1.50 pp, 1 hr; ½ hr walk from the town to the ruins. Kombi Tucumé-Brüning Museum, US$0.50, 30 mins. The surrounding countryside is pleasant for walks and swimming in the river. At **Apurlec**, 60 km N, is a stone wall surrounding a hill and pyramids dating from the Tiahuanaco period, as well as irrigation canals and reservoirs; the system was enlarged during Mochica, Chimú and Inca occupation of the site. To get there from Chiclayo, take bus from Pedro Ruiz or Alfonso Ugarte 1315 (bus continues to Motupe).

On the old Pan-American Highway 885 km from Lima is *Olmos*, a tranquil place (**G** *Hospedaje San Martín*, very dirty, bargain hard; *Hotel Remanso*, in restored farmstead, good food, friendly, but not cheap). During the last week of Jun the Festival de Limón is celebrated here. At Olmos, a poor road (being improved) runs E over the Porculla Pass (2,150m); at Km 257 is a restaurant, but there are better ones at Jaén and Bagua Chica. A road branching from Chamaya, N of Hualgayoc, leads to the towns of Jaén and Bellavista. N of Chamaya, travelling via Aramongo and Oracuza, one finds a symmetrical hill of niche tombs. The old Pan-American Highway continues from Olmos to Cruz de Caña and Piura; some 250 km in length between Chiclayo and Piura, the road is poor in parts, but under reconstruction.

At Lambayeque the new Pan-American Highway branches off the old road and drives 190 km straight across the desert to Piura. There are a few restaurants along its length (eg one at the junction in the middle where you can sleep, another midway between Mórrope and Piura, "no hotels, no priest"). There is also a coast road, narrow and scenic, between Lambayeque and Sechura via Bayovar.

A large area of shifting sands—the Sechura Desert—separates the oasis of Chiclayo from that of Piura. Water for irrigation comes from the Chira and Piura rivers, and from the Olmos and Tinajones irrigation projects which bring water from the Amazon watershed by means of tunnels (one over 16 km long) through the Andes to the Pacific coast. They will eventually water some 400,000 ha of desert land. The N river—the Chira—has usually a superabundance of water: along its irrigated banks large crops of Tangüis cotton are grown. A dam has been built at Poechos on the Chira river, to divert water to the Piura valley. In its upper course the Piura—whose flow is far less dependable—is mostly used to grow subsistence food crops, but around Piura, when there is enough water, the hardy long-staple Pima cotton is planted. In 1983 the Niño current brought heavy rains and turned the Sechura desert into an inland sea. Damage to crops and infrastructure was around US$1bn.

NB Solo cyclists should not cross the Sechura Desert, muggings occur. Take the safer, inland route. In the desert, restaurants are every 30-40 km, but no hotels. Do not camp out if possible; heading S, strong headwinds may make camping unavoidable. Do not attempt this alone.

Piura, an oasis in the parched desert, is a proud and historic city, 264 km from Chiclayo. Population, 324,500. Founded in 1532, three years before Lima, by the *conquistadores* left behind by Pizarro (whose statue is in the Parque Pizarro). There are two well kept parks, Cortés and Pizarro, and public gardens. Old buildings are kept in repair and new buildings blend with the Spanish style of the old city. Three bridges cross the Río Piura, the oldest from Calle Huancavelica, for pedestrians, the second oldest from Calle Sánchez Cerro, and the newest from Calle Bolognesi, used by most traffic. Its special dish is the delicious *natillas*, made mostly of goats milk and molasses; its local drink is *pipa fría*, chilled coconut juice drunk from the nut with a straw. The winter climate, May-Sep, is very pleasant although nights can be cold and the wind piercing; Dec to Mar is very hot.

A few blocks from the **Plaza de Armas**, where the **cathedral** stands (gold covered altar, paintings by Ignacio Merino) is the **San Francisco** church, where the city's independence from Spain was declared on 4 January 1821, nearly 8 months before Lima. The colonial church of **Las Mercedes** has ornately carved balconies, three-tiered archway, hand-hewn supports and massive furnishings. San Sebastián, on Tacna y Moquegua, is also worth seeing. Birthplace of Admiral Miguel Grau, hero of the War of the Pacific with Chile, whose house **Casa Museo Grau**, on Jirón Tacna opposite the Centro Cívico, has been opened as a museum; it contains a model of the *Huáscar*, the largest Peruvian warship in the War of the Pacific, which was built in Britain. Interesting local craftwork is sold at the **Mercado Modelo. Museo Complejo Cultural**, with archaeological and art sections, is open on Sullana, near Huánuco.

Cotton has been grown mainly on medium-sized properties, which have changed hands frequently in recent years and which now form communal or co-operative farms, sponsored by the agrarian reform programme. Worth seeing as an example of a fine old plantation is the former Hacienda Sojo, in the lower Chira valley, which was the centre of the properties of the Checa family.

Hotels B *Turistas*, dreary rooms, a/c, reasonable food, home made papaya jam for breakfast, the city's social centre, garden facing Plaza de Armas; **D** *Bolognesi*, with private bath, near Roggero bus terminal, good; **D** *Cristina*, Jr Loreto between Plaza Grau and Jr Ica, one block from Plaza, pleasant; **D** *El Sol*, Sánchez Cerro 411, bath, snack bar, will change TCs at official rate; **D** *Hostal Esmeraldas*, opp colectivo stop on Loreto, good rooms; **D** *Piura*, Jr Loreto, secure, clean, quiet; **D** *Perú*, Arequipa 476, T 333421, clean, safe, friendly, laundry service, cold water, modern small rooms; **D** *Vicus*, on Pan-American Highway, with bath and fan, quiet, restaurant poor; **E** *California*, Jr Junín, rec, laundry facilities, own water-tank, mosquito netting on windows, roof terrace, friendly, clean, pleasant; **E** *Continental*, Jr Junín 924, without bath, clean; **E** *La Terraza*, Av Loreto, 2 blocks from Grau monument, with bath, G without, clean, small rooms; **E** *San Jorge* (Jr Loreto, 3 blocks from Plaza Grau) with bath and fan, clean and good value, rec; **F** *Amanta*, Apurímac y Cusco, clean, noisy disco nearby at weekends; **F** *Oriental*, without bath, **E**, with clean but very noisy, TV in reception, Jr Callao. **G** *Hispaniola* on Ica, cell-like rooms, dirty, hot water, safe motorcycle parking; **G** *Hostal Ica*, Ica, dirty, basic, very cheap. It is extremely difficult to find a room in the last week of July because of Independence festivities. The city suffers from water shortages and there are reports that no hotel has hot water.

Restaurants *Ganso Azul*, a group of steak houses just out of town, rec (but not a safe area at night). *Carburmer*, in Centro Comercial, very good but not cheap. *El Puente Viejo*, half a block from the rebuilt bridge, very good seafood (from owners' private beds offshore at Paita) rec; *Gran Prix*, Loreto, good food, reasonable prices; *Las Tradiciones*, Ayacucho 579, reasonable prices, almost opp *Bar Romano*, reasonable prices, *La Cabaña*, Ayacucho y Cusco, serves pizzas and other good food, not cheap; *Ferny's*, next to *Hotel San Jorge*, good food, clean, on Loreto; *Café Concierto*, Cusco 933, pleasant, popular, not cheap; *Berlín*, Av Grau, good; *Snack Bar*, Callao 536, good fruit juices. Good little cheap restaurants on Jirón Junín: *Chalán del Norte* at 722, *Bianca* at 732, *El Capri* at 715. *La Huerta*, Libertad 801 on corner of Plaza de Armas, sells 19 fresh juices, *quesillo con miel* (cream cheese and honey) and *natillas*.

Banks and Exchange Banco de Crédito rec, changes TCs, open 0900. **Banco Continental**, Plaza de Armas, changes TCs with commission. **Banco Latino**, no commission for TCs; *casas de cambio* charge 10%.

Honorary British Consul Casilla 193, T (074) 325693, Mr Henry Stewart.

Shopping Fuji film readily available. Good delicatessens around main square, selling local sweets; *natilla* factory on Sánchez Cerro, Miraflores, 4 blocks from bridge, sells *natilla* and

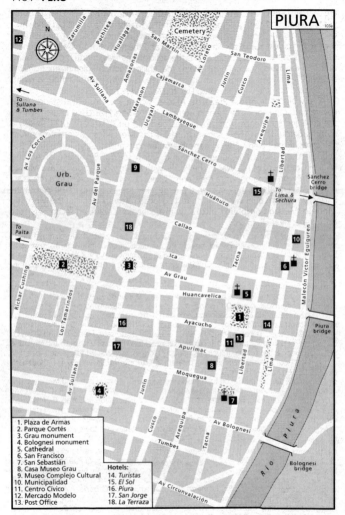

PIURA 103a

1. Plaza de Armas
2. Parque Cortés
3. Grau monument
4. Bolognesi monument
5. Cathedral
6. San Francisco
7. San Sebastián
8. Casa Museo Grau
9. Museo Complejo Cultural
10. Municipalidad
11. Centro Cívico
12. Mercado Modelo
13. Post Office

Hotels:
14. *Turistas*
15. *El Sol*
16. *Piura*
17. *San Jorge*
18. *La Terraza*

algorrobina fruit drink. Market on Sánchez Cerro, good for fruit. Chulucanas pottery can be bought at two shops on Libertad and from Milagros García de Linares, who lives in Urbanización Santa Inés, T 327322.

Post Office on Plaza de Armas, very helpful.

Tourist Offices Information at the Ministerio de Industria y Turismo, Jr Lima 775, T 327013, helpful when there are problems. There are several travel agents around the plaza; a rec one is *Piura Tours*, C Ayacucho 585, T 328873. Touring y Automóvil Club del Perú, Sánchez Cerro 1237 (pink-walled building on right hand side entering Piura on Panamericana), good maps of Peru for US$1.25. For local private flights, contact pilot Félix

Pérez, Corpac 212, Castilla Piura, T 324979, or through Aerotour SA, Lima, T 415884.

Air To Lima daily with Faucett, US$95, AeroPerú, Aero Continente and Americana, 1½ hrs, US$70. To Chiclayo US$49 with Faucett, US$23 with Americana and Aero Continente, 30 mins. To Trujillo, US$55 with Faucett, also AeroPerú, 30 mins. To Talara, daily flights with Faucett, 30 mins, US$36. Americana, Jr Ica 286, T 328064. Taxi to airport, US$1.50.

Buses To **Lima**, 1,038 km, 14-16 hrs, US$15, fairly good paved road along the Panamericana Norte; most buses stop at the major cities on route (see Lima, **Bus Companies** with routes to the N). In Piura, Civa is at Bolognesi y Av Sullana, T 328093. To **Chiclayo**, 190 km, 3 hrs, US$5, several buses daily; similarly to **Trujillo**, 7 hrs, 487 km, US$8.50. To **Tumbes**, 282 km, 6 hrs, US$5.50, several buses daily, eg Cruz del Sur and Tepsa; most buses stop at the major cities on the way; colectivos, US$8. Bus to **Aguas Verdes** US$5.50 leaving 2230 arriving 0700. To **Sullana**, 38 km, 30 mins, US$1, frequent buses and colectivos from Roma y Sánchez Cerro; to **La Tina** for Ecuadorean frontier, a further 122 km, 3-4 hrs (longer when the weather is bad), US$4; best to take an early bus to Sullana (start at 0630, every 20 mins), then a truck, no buses. Alternatively there are direct trucks to La Tina leaving all day from the market, US$3. **NB** To the N of Piura, buses are subject to military checks and the road is in bad condition.

Excursions 12 km to the SW of Piura is the village of **Catacaos** (colectivos leave from Plaza Pizarro, US$0.50, bus US$0.35) famous for its *chicha* (maize beer, be careful, quality not always reliable), *picanterías* (local restaurants, some with music, *La Casa de Tales*, rec), tooled leather, gold and silver filigree jewellery, wooden articles, straw hats (pricey) and splendid celebrations in Holy Week. Also from Piura, one can visit **Sechura**, a coastal town with a fine 17th-century cathedral (splendid W front-under renovation for a long time, normally closed to the public) and the *Hospedaje de Dios* (usually full of workmen from the oil terminal at Bayovar—forbidden to visitors). One can visit the coastal villages (no accommodation in any of them) of **San Pedro** (with a huge lagoon, edible crabs, flamingoes—if you're lucky, a superb beach and a fierce sun—best visited in the week, no facilities whatsoever; take bus or colectivo to the right fork past Vice, about 10 km from Sechura then hitch); **Yacila**, a picturesque fishing village with a few fish restaurants, church on the beach (reached also by *camioneta* for Paita; Los Cangrejos beach nearby, where you can rent an apartment from Sr Belcázar, but little food available, motel open in summer, no facilities in winter), La Tortuga, Parachique, Matacaballo (which has the best beach of these four places); Chullachay (the nearest beach to Sechura), Los Puertos and Angostura. Balsa reed-boats are common on the beach.

Chulucanas, 50 km SE of Piura and 10 km off the old Pan-American Highway (minibus US$1.50), is the centre of the lemon and orange growing area and of local pottery production. Excellent ceramics may be bought: shop on plaza, 3 others within one block. Pottery school 5 km away, inaccessible in rainy season. (**F** *Hotel Ica*, Ica 636; *Restaurant Cajamarquino*, Ayacucho 530, good). No buses S of Chulucanas. **Canchaque** (**F** *Hostal Don Félix*, central square, just tolerable; otherwise simple clean accommodation for about US$2 on right hand side of church), is a delightfully-situated small centre for coffee, sugar-cane and fruit production. Foreigners have to register here at the Policía de República. The difficult and tiring road, impossible for ordinary vehicles in the wet season, continues over a pass in the Andes of more than 3,000m to **Huancabamba** (**F** *Hotel El Dorado*, good, clean, informative owner, with restaurant, on the main square; also a couple of others on the Plaza). Local specialities: *rompope*, a rich and strong drink made of egg, spices and *cañazo* (sugar-cane spirit); roast *cuy* (guinea-pig); and local cheeses. This very pretty town in a wonderful setting has three claims to fame. First, the predominance of European features, due to the fact that it was an important Spanish settlement in colonial times. Second, it is called "the walking town, *la ciudad que camina*", as it is built on irregularly slipping strata which cause much subsidence. Evidence for this includes the fall of the bridge over the Río Huancabamba. Third, and by far the most remarkable element, it is the base for reaching Las Guaringas, a series of lakes at about 4,000m. Around here live the most famous witchdoctors of Peru, to whom sick people flock from all over the country and abroad. Buses to the lakes at 0400 from main square.

Horses to the lakes can be hired, US$5; village of San Antonio below Lago Carmen, village of Salalá below Lago Shumbe (**G** *Hotel San José*, very basic, take own food). Ignacio León, who owns a *bodega* opp *El Dorado* runs an early pick-up service to outlying villages and takes trips at negotiable prices.

A bus from Piura to Canchaque and Huancabamba leaves daily at 0900 and 1000, at least 10 hrs (and returns from Huancabamba 0700 and 1000), US$12, from the Civa office, Av Ramón Castilla 155 (buy ticket early on day before travelling). Truck US$11.50. If driving, take the Pan-American Highway S of Piura for 66 km where there is a signpost to Huancabamba. Canchaque is 78 km along this same road, at first paved, then dirt, and then there are 69 km more of steep and winding road to Huancabamba.

The port for the area is *Paita* (no public transport), 50 km from Piura (colectivos and buses near Plaza Grau, US$1.80), which exports cotton, cotton seed, wool and flax. Population 51,500. Built on a small beach, flanked on three sides by a towering, sandy bluff, it is connected with Piura and Sullana by paved highways. It is a very old fishing port: several colonial buildings survive, but they are in poor condition, giving an impressive, ghost-town atmosphere. Bolívar's mistress, Manuela Sáenz, lived the last 24 years of her life in Paita, after being exiled from Quito. She supported herself until her death in 1856 by weaving and embroidering and making candy after refusing the fortune left her by her husband. The house may be visited if you ask the people living in it, but there's not much to see. The Paita-Piura road is now good, buses hourly from Parque Cortés, Piura, 45 mins (get tickets from office on Av Sullana, facing the park, US$1.80). Fishing, fishmeal and whaling (at Tierra Colorada, $6^{1}/_{2}$ km S of Paita) are prosperous industries.

Hotels Best is **E** *Las Brisas*, Av Ugarte, with bath but scant cold water, safe; *El Mundo*, 300 block of Bolívar, not bad but short-stay; *Miramar*, opp Credicoop Paita, an old wooden mansion on seafront, looks expensive, but is filthy; **F** *Ceci*, above pharmacy; *Pacífico* and others, none recommendable. Most are full anyway.

Restaurants *El Mundo*, Jr Junín, quite good; much better is the restaurant on 2nd floor of Club Liberal building, Jorge Chávez 161, T 2141, good fish, seafood and crêpes, good value; others on Plaza de Armas.

Exchange Credicoop Paita, Jr Junín 380 for dollars cash; helpful guard.

On a bluff looming over Paita is a small colonial fortress built to repel pirates. Paita was a port of call for Spanish shipping en route from Lima to Panama and Mexico. It was a frequent target for attack, from Drake (1579) to Anson (1741). 25 km up the coast is *Colán*, reached by driving down a large, sandy bluff (no public transport); near the base is a striking and lonely church over 300 years old (it's in very poor condition). There is a good beach, but Colán is rather derelict since the agrarian reform; it used to be the favourite resort of the estate-owners.

Sullana (population 154,800), 39 km N of Piura, is built on a bluff over the fertile Chira valley. It has a long market on the main avenue; a busy, modern place. **Warning** Robberies of travellers are common.

Hotels **D** *Hostal La Siesta*, Av Panamericana 400-04 (T 2264), at entrance to town (direction Talara), 3-star, hot water, swimming pool, café, laundry; **D** *Hostal y Restaurant San Miguel*, Calle J Farfán 204, opp bus companies (F in shared rooms), helpful, good showers, staff will spray rooms against mosquitoes; *Chifa Cantón*, next door, serves good food cheaply, but smaller portions than in *San Miguel*; **E** *Hostal Aypate*, Av José de Lama, comfortable, showers; **F** *Hostal Príncipe*, Espinal 588, clean and friendly; **G** pp *Buenos Aires*, Av Buenos Aires, 15 mins from city centre, friendly but bathrooms dirty; **G** pp *Res Wilson*, Tamaraya 378, large rooms, dirty facilities, friendly.

Exchange On main street, near Bata shoe shop, usual touts, *cambio* upstairs changes TCs, but wait till after 1100 for today's rate. Banco de Crédito will change TCs.

Bus To Tumbes, 244 km, 5 hrs US$4, several buses daily. Piura, 38 km, 45 mins, US$1, frequent buses, colectivos, US$1.60, taxi US$2 (if you have time, it is worth continuing to Piura rather than staying in Sullana); Chiclayo and Trujillo see under Piura. To Lima, 1,076 km, 17 hrs, US$18, several buses daily, most coming from Tumbes, luxury overnight US$45. Colectivos to Paita, Colán and Esmeralda leave from the main road parallel to the market; buses to Máncora and Talara (Empresa EPPO) from market area.

To Ecuador At Sullana the Pan-American Highway bifurcates. To the E it crosses the Peru-Ecuador frontier at La Tina and continues via Macará to Loja and Cuenca; the road is paved to Las Lomas (75 km), but thereafter is being rebuilt (but not paved), though marvellously scenic. Many trucks and other vehicles leave at 0600 from Av Buenos Aires in Sullana to the border at La Tina, US$3 pp, 4 hrs, return from border to Sullana 1030 or when full; taxis also go, US$8/seat, 3-4 hrs. Do not leave after 1200, you are likely to get stuck in Las Lomas where there is nowhere to stay. There are many army checkpoints en route. Unaccompanied women are advised to take the better route (see below). Beware of locals deflating car tyres and demanding money to reinflate. No accommodation at La Tina (in El Suyo, 14 km from La Tina, are 2 small hotels). At the border the officials may try to get extra payments from those entering Peru, stand your ground if possible—the Peruvian can be found at the nearby *cevichería* if not at his desk—walk over the bridge, pick-ups run from the border to Macará. A bus leaves the Ecuadorean side at 1300 for Loja, so you can go from Sullana to Loja in one day.

The better route is the W road which passes through Talara and Tumbes, crossing the border at Huaquillas (closes at 1800) and on via Machala to Guayaquil; it is asphalted and has excellent bus services. All but a section of this road between Talara and Los Organos (30 km, **D** *Hotel Club Nautilus*) has been rebuilt since the heavy floods in Jan 1983.

The main centre of the coastal oil area is *Talara* (135 km from Piura, 1,177 km from Lima), in a desert oasis, which has a State-owned 60,000 barrel-a-day oil refinery and a fertilizer plant. Water is piped 40 km from the Chira River. The city is a triumph over formidable natural difficulties, but was badly damaged in the 1983 floods and has many shanty districts. Population 44,500. La Peña beach, 2 km from Talara, is still unspoilt.

Hotels Problems with water supply in all cases: **A3** *Pacífico*, most luxurious, swimming pool, restaurant, bar, parking, pay in dollars; **D** *Residencial Grau*, Av Grau 77, near main square, clean, friendly, possible to park one motor bike, owner changes dollars; **E** *Hostal Talara*, clean and comfortable; **F** *Royal*, wooden building far from centre, run down. If in trouble finding a bed, enquire at the police station.

Restaurants Many cheap ones on main square.

Air Airport with daily flights by Faucett to Lima, 1½ hrs, US$79; to Piura, daily with Faucett US$36; Tumbes twice a week.

Buses To Tumbes, 171 km, 3½ hrs, US$3, most coming from Piura and most stop at major towns going N; several daily. To **El Alto** (Cabo Blanco), 32 km, ½ hr, US$0.75, continuing to Máncora, 28 km, 30 mins, US$0.75 to **Piura**, 111 km, 1½ hrs, US$1.90. Most buses coming from Tumbes stop here. To Lima, US$15.

Paved highways connect the town with the Negritos, Lagunitos, La Brea and other oilfields. Of historical interest are the old tarpits at La Brea, 21 km inland from Punta Pariñas, S of Talara, and near the foot of the Amotape mountains. Here the Spaniards boiled the tar to get pitch for caulking their ships. Punta Pariñas itself is the westernmost point of South America.

North of Talara, is the small port of **Cabo Blanco**, famous for its excellent sea-fishing; scenery spoilt by numerous oil installations. Camping permitted free of charge at Cabo Blanco, on the beach or by the Fishing Club Lodge, overlooking the sea (at least in the off-season Jun-Dec). Fishing Club, **B**, clean, attractive, rec, restaurant, pool, watersports, likely to be full in New Year period. Hemingway wrote *The Old Man and the Sea* here.

Buses run to **Máncora** (wayside fish restaurants superb, including lobster: *César*, rec; *Regina's* for fruit salad), a small attractive resort with good beaches, water warm enough for bathing, famous for surfing (best Nov-Mar). **D** *Punta Ballena*, full board, clean, friendly, rec; **F** *Bamboe*, next to Tepsa on main street, basic, cheap (pay in advance), clean; **F** *Hostal Samara*, incl breakfast, lunch, US$2, can be ordered; **F/G** *Hospedaje Crillon/Tía Yola*, friendly, rec; **G** *Sol y Mar*, S end of village, on beach, showers, clean; 3 km S, *Las Pocitas*, 9 rooms, attractive, friendly, fishing and harpooning trips, balsa rafts, food excellent US$9 for main meal, cheaper for full board (C); *Kiosko Betty*, close to *Sol y Mar*, friendly, good value meals. *Playa Punta Sal* about 20 km to the N has **B** pp *Punta Sal Club Hotel*, full board, attractive, good beach, rec, watersports, pool, comfortable, relaxing (in Lima T 425961). Aqua Explorer arranges undersea activities, fishing, sailing and horseriding. Camping is reported to be safe along the beach between Talara and Tumbes, Punta Negra, rec. Bus Máncora-Tumbes, 2 hrs, US$2.50.

Tumbes, about 141 km N of Talara, and 265 km N of Piura, is the most N of Peruvian towns; it is a garrison town with 34,000 inhabitants (do not photograph the military or their installations—they will destroy your film and probably detain you). There is a long promenade, the Malecón Benavides, beside the high banks of the Río Tumbes. There are some old houses in Calle Grau, and a colonial public library in the Plaza de Armas with a small museum. The cathedral is 17th century but restored in 1985. There is a sports stadium; cockfights in the Coliseo de Gallos,

Av Mcal Castilla, 9th block, Sun at 1500, special fights 28 Jul and 8 Dec. The main products are bananas and rice. The water supply is poor.

Hotels **B** *Turistas*, Plazuela Bolognesi, a/c, clean, restaurant, good food and service, parking, has nice garden with swimming pool, provides some tourist information; **D** *Florián*, near El Dorado bus company, clean, fan, private bath, rec; **D** *Lourdes*, Mayor Bodero 118, one block from main square, with bath, clean, friendly, rec; **D** *Roma*, Plaza de Armas, basic, simple, few services; **E** *Amazonas*, Av Tumbes 333 (old name Tnte Vásquez), clean, friendly, showers, but not always water in mornings; opp *Florián* **E** *Hostal Elica*, with bath, clean, fan, quiet, good; **E** *Hostal Estoril*, 2 blocks from main square, good, friendly; **E** *Hostal Premier*, between Tepsa and Continental bus stations, private bath; **E** *Hostal Toloa*, Av Tumbes 430, T 523771, clean, safe, helpful; **E** *Hostal Tumbes*, Grau 614, with bath, cold water, friendly, clean; **E** *Italia*, Grau 733, cold showers, friendly, good; **F** *Córdova*, J R Abad Puell 777, with bath, no hot water, safe, friendly, safe for motorcycle parking; **F** *Hostal Patty*, Huáscar 513, clean, water for 2 hrs in am. Many other cheap hotels. Hotels are often fully booked by early afternoon, so try to arrive early, and at holiday times it can be very difficult to find a vacant room.

Restaurants *Curich* in the Plaza de Armas, good for fish. *Europa*, off main square, is rec, particularly for omelettes, expensive. *Latinos*, on Plaza de Armas, good; *El Quarique*, Huáscar 319, small, friendly, shell decoration; *Samoa*, Av Bolívar 235, nr plaza, good, big portions; *El Brujo*, 7 de Enero 320, good value; *Chifa D'Koko*, Piura y F Navarete, rec; *Mini Chifa*, Av Tumbes (Tte Vásquez), good local and chifa dishes. There are other inexpensive restaurants on the Plaza de Armas and near the markets. *Heladería La Suprema*, Paseo Libertadores, good ice cream, sweets and cold drinks. Try *bolas de plátano*, soup with banana balls, meat, olives and raisins, and *sudado*, a local stew.

Banks and Exchange Banco de Crédito, opp Banco Popular which is in a new building on the edge of the main square, poor rates. Banco de Comercio, 5% commission. Bad rates at the airport; in general better rates at Trujillo and Piura. Money changers on the street (on Bolívar, left of the Cathedral), some of whom are unscrupulous, give a much better rate than banks or *cambios*, but don't accept the first offer you are given. None changes TCs. If you are travelling on to Ecuador, it is better to change your Soles at the border (higher rate).

Consulate Ecuadorean, Plaza de Armas, 0900-1300 Mon-Fri.

Post Office San Martín 240; Entel **Telephone** office, San Martín 242.

Tourist Office Information from Ricardo Pérez Saavedra, Pueblo Nuevo, Casilla 204, archaeologist, author, works for the Instituto Nacional de Cultura (ask to see his collection of figurines); Carlos Sáenz, Urb Fonavi 4-16, T 523412, coordinator of Fundación Peruana para la Conservación de la Naturaleza (details on national parks); Luis Alvarez Saldariaga, Tarata 132, a fisherman who organizes trips on the Río Tumbes (US$20). **Rosillo Tours**, Ten Vásquez 293.

Buses Daily to and from **Lima**, 1,320 km, 22-26 hrs, depending on stopovers, US$18 minimum, long trip and fairly well-paved Panamericana Norte, but poor to Trujillo. Several buses daily, see Lima **Bus Companies** with routes to the N: eg Sudamericano (overbooked, often subject to long delays, efficient and safe ticket system for luggage); Expreso Continental (Ormeño group), Tepsa (often full) and Olano, daily 1300, rec; for other companies, ask around; cheaper ones usually leave 1600-2100, dearer ones 1200-1400. Most buses to Lima stop at major cities en route (although you may be told otherwise). On the bus to Lima try to get a seat on the right hand side in order to have a good view of the coast. One can get tickets to anywhere between Tumbes and Lima with little difficulty, although buses are often booked well in advance, so if arriving from Ecuador you may have to stay overnight; Piura is a good place for connections. To **Talara**, 171 km, US$3, 3½ hrs. To **Sullana**, 244 km, 5 hrs, US$4, several buses daily. To **Piura**, 6 hrs, 282 km, US$5.50 with Tepsa, leaves 1000, Empresa Chiclayo, Cruz del Sur, 6 hrs, El Dorado (Av Mcal Castilla 301-3, T 523688), 3 a day, 7 hrs, US$5; Colectivo, US$8. To **Chiclayo**, 552 km, 11-12 hrs, US$7, several each day starting 1100, often fully booked. To **Trujillo**, 769 km, 12 hrs, US$11 (bus fills quickly). Look out for dolphins in the sea along this route. To **Chimbote**, 889 km, 15 hrs, US$13. Most buses leave from Av Tumbes (formerly Tnte Vásquez). Frequent buses to Aguas Verdes, 26 km, from Calles Bolívar y Piura at 0600 onwards, 30-45 mins, US$0.50-0.75, colectivo, US$1.20, 20 mins. Bus to Machala (Ecuador), US$5. Colectivo to Huaquillas (Ecuador), US$2. Hitching slow.

NB Travellers who hold a Tumbes-Huaquillas-Guayaquil ticket with Panamericana Internacional (bought outside Peru as an onward ticket) should note that Panamericana does not have an office in Tumbes. However, this ticket can be used for a colectivo (but not a taxi) to the border, caught at corner of Piura and Bolivar; if colectivo is full, you will be transferred

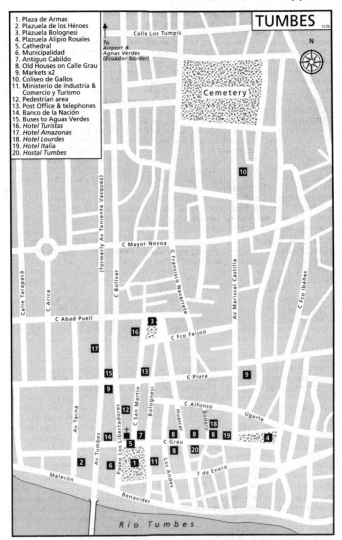

1. Plaza de Armas
2. Plazuela de los Héroes
3. Plazuela Bolognesi
4. Plazuela Alipio Rosales
5. Cathedral
6. Municipalidad
7. Antiguo Cabildo
8. Old Houses on Calle Grau
9. Markets x2
10. Coliseo de Gallos
11. Ministerio de Industria & Comercio y Turismo
12. Pedestrian area
13. Post Office & telephones
14. Banco de la Nación
15. Buses to Aguas Verdes
16. *Hotel Turistas*
17. *Hotel Amazonas*
18. *Hotel Lourdes*
19. *Hotel Italia*
20. *Hostal Tumbes*

TUMBES

103b

Calle Los Tumpis

To Airport & Agnas Verdes (Ecuador border)

Cemetery

Calle Tarapacá

(formerly Av Teniente Vásquez)

C Arica

C Abad Puell

C Bolivar

C Mayor Novoa

C Fransisco Navarrete

C Fco Feijoó

Av Mariscal Castilla

C Fco Ibáñes

C Piura

Av Tacna

C San Martin

Bolognesi

C Alfonso

Huascar

Bodero

Ugarte

Paseo Los Libertadores

C Grau

Los Andes

7 de Enero

Av Tumbes

Malecón

Benavides

Río Tumbes

to another company. Connection with bus at the border.

Air Daily flights with Faucett to and from Lima, US$120. Essential to reconfirm flights 24 hrs before departure. It is better to buy tickets in Tumbes rather than at the airport. To Chiclayo, 45 mins, US$64 one way, 5 days a week with Faucett. Taxi to airport, US$1.50, 50 mins; colectivos charge US$0.75; taxis meet flights to take passengers to border, US$2.50, 15 mins, colectivos charge US$0.75 and take 20 mins. Airport taxes US$5.50.

Excursions Río Tumbes is navigable by small boat to the mouth of the river, an interesting 2 hr trip with fantastic birdlife and mangrove swamps.

This is the only part of the Peruvian coast where the sea is warm all year. Two good beaches near Tumbes: one at Caleta La Cruz 16 km SW, where Pizarro landed in 1532. The original Cruz de Conquista was taken to Lima. Easy to get to with regular colectivos (US$0.80 each way); **E** *Motel. Zorritos*, 35 km S of Tumbes, heavily damaged by the 1983 flooding but with a good beach (the water is not oily), **D** *Hotel de Turistas*, also *Punta Sal Chica*, 2 stars; *La Quebrada del Grillo* youth hostel, between Bocapán and Los Pinos, Km 1235; the better of the 2 restaurants is *Arriba Perú*. Camping rec. The first South American oil well was sunk here in 1863. Just N of Tumbes, US$0.50 by colectivo, is **Puerto Pizarro**, a small fishing beach at the S limit of the mangrove swamps. Take a boat across the lagoon to reach a good clean sandy beach (about 10 mins' journey, bargain hard). Festival of St Peter and St Paul, 29-30 Jun; colectivo No 6 from Tumbes (US$0.50). **D** *Puerto Pizarro Motel*, bungalows 10 km from beach, no hot water, restaurant dear and slow but food good, swimming pool, which is usually empty, watersports; *Restaurant Venecia*, seafood cheap, beware shellfish which may cause stomach upsets. Plenty of fishing and swimming; ideal for windsurfing and water-skiing but few facilities. The mangrove swamps are full of pelicans; best to visit them at high tide. A few tame birds beg for fish on the beaches. Three islands, Isla Hueso de Ballena, Isla del Amor, Isla de los Pájaros may be visited by boat, bargain hard, good for swimming and picnics, take food and water. Remains of Cabeza de Vaca abode cult centre of the Tumpis Indians can be found at Corrales, 5 km S of Tumbes. They were heavily damaged by 1983 rains; Museo de Sitio nearby. **Bosque Nacional de Tumbes** (75,000 ha) wildlife includes monkeys, nutria and crocodiles. Mosquito repellent is a must for Tumbes area.

To Ecuador Small buses and colectivos (some marked "Puente Internacional") leave about every 20 mins and take 30-45 mins to get to **Aguas Verdes** on the Peruvian side of the international bridge (the Peruvian departure office opens at 0800, is closed 1200-1400 and after 1800; try not to arrive within 1 hr of the border closing – the Ecuadorean border post keeps the same hours). On the way most of them pass by the airport. By taxi it costs about US$5, colectivo fare is US$1.20 and bus fare US$0.50-0.75. Peruvian Migración is 3 km from Huaquillas, the Ecuadorean side of the border (a US$0.50 *moto* ride from the bridge, and a US$0.25 bus ride to Tumbes). On entry to Peru, they may refuse to accept a return ticket from another country as proof of intended exit from Peru; this is an invitation to bribery, be courteous but firm. Often, no onward ticket is asked for. Colectivos do not wait at customs. Some bus companies from Chiclayo and beyond go to the border. At Aguas Verdes a walkway leads to Peruvian Customs. Having obtained your exit stamp, proceed across the bridge into Huaquillas; 100m up is the Ecuadorean Immigration on the left. You have to buy two photocopied embarkation cards, which touts will try to sell you for US$0.50, but which can be bought at the photocopy shop behind immigration for US$0.01. With a pass from the authorities at the border you can spend the day in Huaquillas, the Ecuadorean border town, as long as you are back by 1800. There is nothing much to see there, but Peruvians hunt for bargains. Tepsa leave from the border for Lima daily at 1000, 22-5 hrs, US$25, a long, hot journey, take drinks with you; Tepsa to Tumbes at 1300 and to Chiclayo US$9, 9 hrs. A bus leaves Huaquillas at 1500 for Piura and Trujillo (US$6, 6 hrs to Piura). Entering Peru, it may be easier to take a colectivo to Tumbes and then a bus S, rather than get on a bus from the border to a southern destination. These buses are usually full of shoppers and their goods and involve long stops at checkpoints.

When driving into Peru vehicle fumigation is not required, but there is "one outfit who will attempt to fumigate your vehicle with water and charge US$10 for their services." Beware of officials claiming that you need a *carnet* to obtain your 90-day transit permit; this is not so (but check before arriving at the border that rules have not changed).

Warnings Porters on either side of the border charge exorbitant prices: don't be bullied. Beware sharp practices by money changers using fixed calculators. The money changers on the Ecuadorean side give a better rate than the banks in Tumbes (but not at the airport on the Ecuadorean side); always try to check the rate beforehand. For soles it is better to change dollars, as rates are poor for sucres. If you are going to change cheques into Ecuadorean sucres in Huaquillas, make sure you cross the border in the morning because the bank is closed after lunch. Do not change money on the minibus to Aguas Verdes, their rates are very poor. Relations between Peru and Ecuador are not good: Ecuadorean Customs tends to confiscate guidebooks and maps of Peru because they show as Peru's certain areas claimed by Ecuador.

Checks for goods smuggled into Peru are carried out, especially at Tepsa bus station as well as at Aguas Verdes. Checks are thorough, both of luggage and body. Checks also intermittently on road to Piura. Frequent road tolls between Tumbes and Lima, US$0.50-1.

SOUTHEAST FROM LIMA (4)

The mysterious Nazca lines, the precious Paracas bird reserve and Peru's wine and pisco-producing oases in and around Ica punctuate the desert S of the capital. The Pan-American Highway carries on down to Chile, with a dramatic branch inland, climbing to Arequipa.

The group of oases S from Lima grow Pima cotton, sugar-cane and vegetables for Lima, but the more southerly valleys specialize in vines—Ica in particular is well known for this and its port, Pisco, has given its name to a well-known brandy. The Pan-American Highway runs S from Lima through all the places now to be described to Tacna and Chile. It is at least four lanes of good paved surface to Cañete after which there are extensive repairs. Some parts are good, others bad with terrible potholes; take care when driving. There are battery chicken houses all along the beach. At Km 200 the *garúa* lifts.

The first 60 km from Lima are dotted with a series of seaside resort towns and clubs: first is El Silencio, good (30 km), then Punta Hermosa (35 km), Punta Negra (40 km) and **San Bartolo** (43 km, *Posada del Mirador*, Malecón San Martín 105, T 290388, C in bungalows or A3 full board, welcomes *Handbook* users). **Santa María**, 45 km from Lima, has the beautiful **A3** *Santa María Hotel*, meals included. **Pucusana** (60 km), is a charming fishing village (*Hotel Bahía*, good seafood). Excellent panoramas from the cliffs above the village. Hire a boat for an hour (fix price beforehand and stick to it); don't go in the direction of the only, smelly factory, but to the rocks where you can see seabirds close at hand. 14 km S of Pucusana is **Chilca**, ½ hr by colectivo from the market place, a small beach resort. Not much to see, but a long, deserted beach with camping possibilities. You can walk along the beach from Chilca to Salinas (5 km), which has mineral baths. There are a few restaurants and *pensiones*. In summer (Dec-Feb), these places fill up with holidaymakers from Lima. At Mala, 24 km S of Pucusana, 2 km inland from Pan American highway, are 3 hotels, **E** *Hostal Weekend*, with private bath, very clean and modern.

NB Most beaches have very strong currents and can be dangerous for swimming; if unsure, ask locals.

Cañete (hotels and restaurants; *Hostal Casablanca*, reasonable; a rec restaurant is *Cevichería Muelle 56*, Bolognesi 156), about 150 km S of Lima, on the Río Cañete, is a prosperous market centre amid desert scenery.

40 km inland from Cañete, up the river of the same name, is **Lunahuaná**, the site of a small Inca city, Incawasi; interesting ruins and attractive scenery. There are three hotels (all B-C, two with pool, restaurant and disco) and others cheaper. There are restaurants serving local food. Banco Nacional del Perú; medical clinic. White-water rafting trips from Lunahuaná on the Río Cañete are run by guides from Lima every weekend, US$15 for 2 hrs. It is also interesting to visit the wineries in the valley and try the wine. Fiesta de la Vendimia (harvest festival) in Mar; Fiesta del Níspero (medlar festival) at end of Sep. There is a road to Huancayo, served by trucks (see p 1251).

At Cerro Azul, 13 km N of Cañete, is a unique Inca sea fort known as **Huarco**, now much damaged. *La Malla* is an excellent fish restaurant.

35 km N of Pisco, near Chincha Baja, is **Tambo de Mora**, with nearby archaeological sites at Huaca de Tambo de Mora, La Centinela, Chinchaycama and Huaca Alvarado. **Chincha** itself is a fishing village where the negro/criollo culture is still alive. Their famous festival, Verano Negro, is at the end of Feb. An old *hacienda*, San José (1769), is just outside Chincha (need your own transport); it operates as a hotel, with pool, restaurant, garden, small church, colonial crafts, B full board. In Chincha Alta, a fast-growing town, is **F** *Hostal La Rueda*, near plaza, breakfast extra, hot showers, swimming pool, lounge; several other good ones.

Pisco, population 82,250, the largest port between Callao and Matarani, 237 km S of Lima, serves a large agricultural hinterland. It is a short distance off to the W of the Panamerican Highway. The town was divided into two: Pisco Pueblo, colonial-style homes with patios and gardens; and Pisco Puerto (which has been

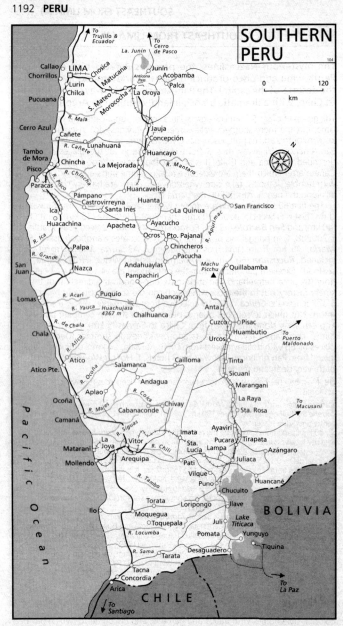

SOUTHERN
PERU

104

0   120
km

replaced as a port by the deep-water Puerto General San Martín, beyond Paracas). The two towns have expanded into one, partly as a result of an influx of refugees from the Ayacucho region. The smell from a modern fish-processing plant pervades the town and its surroundings. In Pisco Pueblo, half a block W of the quiet Plaza de Armas, with its equestrian statue of San Martín, is the Club Social Pisco, the HQ of San Martín after he had landed at Paracas Bay. There is an old Jesuit church hiding behind the new one. You can book for trips to the Ballestas Islands (see below) at agencies around the main square, or through a hotel. The pleasant cemetery at the end of Calle San Francisco was the centre of a female vampire craze in 1993, apparently connected with the grave of an English woman, Sarah Ellen, who died in 1913. A 364 km road has been built to Ayacucho, with a branch to Huancavelica (see Tambo Colorado).

Hotels The town is full at weekends with visitors from Lima. **D** *Embassy*, with bath, clean, noisy, nice bar on roof, has disco at Jr Comercio 180 just off Plaza de Armas, good, cheap trips to Ballestas Islands; **E** *Hostal Belén*, Plaza Belén, clean, comfortable, electric showers. **E** *Hostal San Jorge*, Juan Osores 267, sometimes hot water, friendly, very clean, rec; **E-F** *Pisco*, on Plaza de Armas, cheap, basic, will arrange tours or transport to Ballestas Islands, but be careful, they sometimes promise more than you get, strongly divided opinions about this hotel, for some it is good, for others it is definitely not rec (especially for women), good tour company adjoining hotel, parking for motorcycles; **E** *Cesar*, 2 de Mayo, don't leave valuables in your room; **F** *Hostal Angamos*, Pedemonte 134, tiny rooms but good beds, clean, friendly, economical with water and light. **F** *Hostal Progreso*, Progreso 254, communal bathrooms, clean, water shortages. Mosquitoes are a problem at night in the summer. At Pisco Puerto, **E** *Portofino*, basic, friendly, clean, in slum area on sea front, good seafood, expensive breakfast, arranges day excursion to Paracas, but avoid the nearby *peña* which is poor and can be dangerous. **F** *Hostal Pisco Playa* (Youth Hostel), Jr José Balta 639, Pisco Playa, T 532492, clean, kitchen and washing facilities, but out of town hence quiet.

Restaurants *As de Oro*, on the Plaza de Armas, good restaurant, reasonable prices, closed Mon; cheap seafood at restaurant of *Hotel Portofino*; *Don Manuel*, Comercio 187, US$2-4 for main dish; *Ch'Reyes*, Jr Comercio, good, set meal US$1; *Piccolo-Bar*, nr Plaza, good breakfast and coffee; *Lucho y Marilucha*, Calle Independencia, friendly, excellent fish dishes and cheap. Seafood restaurants along shore between Pisco and San Andrés, and in San Andrés (buses from Plaza Belén, near *Hotel Perú*) there are *La Fontana*, Lima 355, good food and pisco sours, *La Estrellita*, rec, *Olimpia* (Grecia 200), and *Mendoza*, for fish and local dishes, all rec. Good fried chicken place opp Ormeño: save your foreign cigarette packets for their mural! *Mendoza 2*, in Pisco Puerto, excellent simple fish restaurant.

Exchange Banco de Crédito on Plaza de Armas gives good rates, for Amex and cash; bank opposite charges 2% commission on TCs.

Transport Bus to Lima, 242 km, 3-4 hrs, US$5, buses and colectivos every hour, see under Lima, **Bus Companies** with routes to the S; in Pisco, Ormeño is 500m from main plaza and San Martín at Callao 136. To **Ayacucho**, 317 km, 13 hrs, US$8, few buses or trucks daily, not a well-travelled route; the road is in very bad condition, but the scenery is spectacular, make sure to take warm clothing as it gets cold at night. The road reaches 4,600m near Castrovirreyna. To **Huancavelica**, 269 km, 14 hrs, US$8, again, not a well-travelled route, only one bus a day (Oropesa, Conde de la Monclova 637) and a few trucks, the road condition is as for Ayacucho. To **Ica** US$2 by colectivo, US$1 by bus, 1 hr, 70 km, several of each daily. To **Nazca**, 210 km, by bus, US$3.50, 4 hrs, colectivos reported to be more reliable; several of each daily, or take bus to Ica and change there. To **Arequipa**, Sudamericano, US$7, 12 hrs.

15 km down the coast from Pisco Puerto is the bay of **Paracas**, sheltered by the Paracas peninsula. (The name means "sandstorm"—they can last for 3 days; the wind gets up every afternoon, peaking at around 1500.) Paracas can be reached by the coast road from San Andrés, but this passes through a large proportion of Peru's fishmeal industry. Alternatively, go down the Pan-American Highway to 14.5 km past the Pisco turning and take the road to Paracas across the desert. After 11 km turn left along the coast road and 1 km further on fork right to Paracas village. The peninsula, a large area of coast to the S and the Ballestas Islands are a National Reserve (entrance US$1 pp); it is one of the best marine reserves, with the highest concentration of marine birds, in the world.

Trips to the **Ballestas Islands** leave from the jetty in Paracas village (take warm clothing). The islands are spectacular, eroded into numerous arches and caves (*ballesta* = bow, as in archery) which provide shelter for seabirds (some very rare) and thousands of sealions. The book *Las Aves del Departamento de Lima* by Maria Koepcke is useful.

Travel Agents For trips to Islas Ballestas: *Blue Sea Tours*, Calle Chosica 320, San Andrés, Pisco, T 034-530200, anexo 35, guide Jorge Espejo, US$10 pp, Hubert Van Lomoen speaks Dutch, frequently rec. On Calle San Francisco, Pisco: *Paseo Turístico Islas Ballestas*, No 109, rec; *Ballestas Travel Service*, No 249, T 533095; *Paracas Tours*, No 257. *The Zarcillo Connection*, Arequipa 164, T 262795, also good for Paracas National Reserve. The main hotels in Pisco and Paracas will also arrange tours, eg *Hotel Paracas* (see below), US$30 in own speed boat, 0900-1700, or short trip of 3 hrs, safe, minimum 8 passengers. The length of tour depends on the speed of the boat, but the time spent at the islands is probably the same. Some boats do not have life jackets and are very crowded. You will see, close up, thousands of inquisitive sealions, guano birds, pelicans and, sometimes, penguins; the boat returns past the Candelabra to the bay of Paracas. Tours cost US$9.50 (slow boat), US$12 (fast) on Sun, US$7 (slow), US$9.50 (fast) on weekdays. A combined islands and peninsula tour costs US$12; to the peninsula alone US$7.

Return to the main road for the entrance to the Reserve (ask for a map here). There are an archaeological museum (closed for renovation end 1994, but shop open for guide books, film, drinks) and a natural history museum. You can walk down to the shore from the museum to see flamingoes feeding in Paracas bay (boat trips do not go to see flamingoes). The tiny fishing village of Lagunillas is 6 km from the museum across the neck of the peninsula; it has clean, safe beaches free from sting rays and good eating places (see *Tía Fela* below). A network of firm dirt roads, reasonably well signed, crosses the peninsula; for walking, details available from Park Office or ask for "Hoja 28-K" map at Instituto Geográfico Militar in Lima for US$5 (it is not safe to walk if alone). Also note that it is easy to get lost in the hot, wide desert area. Other sites on the peninsula include Mirador de los Lobos at Punta El Arquillo, 6 km from Lagunilla, with view of sealions; and a rock formation in the cliffs called La Catedral, 6 km from Lagunilla in the opposite direction.

About 17 km from the museum is the precolumbian Candelabra (Candelabro in Spanish) traced in the hillside, at least 50m long, best seen from the sea, but still impressive from the land. Hitch along the paved road which leads to Punta Pejerrey, get off at left fork and you will see a trail (1½ hrs walk to Candelabra under a blazing sun, take water and sunscreen). Condors may be seen from the (bad) road between Paracas and Laguna Grande.

Hotels A *Paracas*, good hotel, bungalows on beach (T Pisco 532220 or Lima 446-4865) good food, not cheap, good buffet lunch on Sun, fine grounds facing the bay, is a good centre for excursions to the Peninsula and flights over Nazca; it has tennis courts and an open-air swimming pool (US$2 for non-residents); it also houses the Masson ceramics collection (worth seeing). **C** *Hostal Santa Elena*, a few km from the Paracas National Park, reservations in Lima T 718222; very clean, with restaurant "the cook is legendary", safe beach for swimming (no manta rays or *pastelillos*—dangerous fish with sharp dorsal fin which hide in sand), local trips organized, but now sandwiched between two fishmeal factories. **C** *Hostería Paracas*, next to *Hotel Paracas*, and closed in 1994 for reconstruction; **C** *El Mirador*, at entrance to Paracas, hot water, no phone, good service, boat trips arranged (US$10-12 pp 0800-1200), meals available, sometimes full board only, reservations in Lima, T 445-8496, ask for Sra Rosa. Camping is possible on the beach near the *Hotel Paracas* at a spot called La Muelle, no facilities, sea polluted. Ask permission to camp in the reserve, no water, do not camp alone, robbery occurs.

Restaurants Excellent fried fish at open-sided restaurants by the fishing boats, eg *Rancho de la Tía Fela*, in Lagunilla, where one can sleep for free on the floor. *Restaurant Jennifer*, friendly; *El Chorito*, close to *Hotel Paracas*.

Transport Taxi from Pisco to Paracas about US$3-4; colectivos leave when full, US$0.50, several buses, US$0.30, leave from the market in Pisco. Make sure you catch the last bus back at about 1600, or walk to the port of Paracas (1-2 hrs). Some of the buses go to the museum on the peninsula. By private transport it takes about 50 mins to Lagunilla, 45 mins to La Mina and 1 hr to Mirador de los Lobos. Make sure your car is in good condition, never leave it unattended, and travel in a group as robbery has been a problem in the past. There is no public transport on the peninsula.

Up the Pisco valley, 48 km from Pisco on the road to Huaytará and Ayacucho, is **Tambo Colorado**, one of the best-preserved Inca ruins in coastal Peru (entrance US$1.50). The site includes buildings where the Inca and his retinue would have stayed; many walls retain their original colours. On the other side of the road is the public plaza and the garrison and messengers' quarters. Buses from Pisco, 0800, Oropesa US$0.80 (3 hrs). Alight 20 mins after stop at Humay; the road passes right through the site. Return by bus to Pisco in afternoon; for bus or truck back to Pisco wait at Sr Mendoza, the caretaker's house (he will show you his small collection of items found on the site and will act as guide). Taxi from Pisco US$30. From Humay, go to Hacienda Montesarpe, and 500m above the hacienda is the line of holes known as "La avenida misteriosa de las picaduras de viruelas" (the mysterious avenue of smallpox spots) which stretches along the Andes for many km (its purpose is still unknown).

Huaytará, on the Pisco-Ayacucho road, contains Inca ruins and baths, and the whole side of the church is a perfectly preserved Inca wall with niches and trapezoidal doorways.

From Pisco the Pan-American Highway runs 60 km S to Guadalupe (**Restaurant Sol de Mayo**, one block N of main square, good menú for US$1.50), then a further 10 km to **Ica**, on the Río Ica, population 152,300. The image of El Señor de Luren in a fine church in Parque Luren draws pilgrims from all Peru to the twice-yearly festivals in Mar and Oct (15-21), when there are all-night processions. The San Jerónimo church at Cajamarca 262 has a fine mural behind the altar. Ica is famous for its tejas, a local sweet of manjarblanco (sold behind Luren church).

Wine Ica is also Peru's chief wine centre and has a harvest festival in early Mar. The Bodega El Carmen (on the right-hand side when arriving from Lima) can be visited; it is a pisco distillery and has an ancient grape press made from a huge tree trunk. The Vista Alegre wine and pisco distillery can be also visited (Spanish essential) and its shop is recommended. They give official tours on Fri and Sat 0830-1130. Local bus drops you at the entrance, or 10-15 mins' walk on the other side of the river. 10 km outside Ica, in the district of Subtanjalla, is José Carrasco González, *Bodega El Catador*, a shop selling home-made wines and pisco, and traditional handicrafts associated with winemaking. In the evening it is a restaurant-bar with dancing and music; best time to visit is during harvest, late Feb to early Apr, wine and pisco tasting is usually possible. Open daily 0800-1800, take a bus from 2nd block of Moquegua, every $1/2$ hr, US$0.10. *Cachina*, a very young white wine "with a strong yeasty taste", is drunk about two weeks after the grape harvest.

The waters of the Choclacocha and Orococha lakes from the eastern side of the Andes are tunnelled into the Ica valley and irrigate 30,000 hectares of land. The lakes are at 4,570m. The tunnel is over 9 km long.

Museo Regional Bus 17 from Plaza de Armas, open 0745-1900, Mon-Sat: Sun 0900-1300 (US$1.50, students US$0.80). Houses mummies, ceramics, textiles and trepanned skulls from Paracas, Nazca and Inca cultures; a good, well-displayed collection of Inca counting strings (*quipus*) and clothes made of feathers. Good and informative displays with maps of all sites in the Department. Behind the building there is a scale model of the Nazca lines with an observation tower, a useful orientation before visiting the lines. The attendant paints copies of motifs from the ceramics and textiles in the original pigments (US$1), and sells his own good maps of Nazca for US$1.65.

The museum on the Plaza de Armas, run by Dr Javier Cabrera, has a collection of several thousand engraved stones. Open Mon-Sat 0930-1230 and 1730-2000 and sometimes open Sun. If visiting in a group T 234363. We are informed that some of these stones are fakes: people have talked to the craftsmen concerned. If authentic, the stones suggest the existence of a technologically-advanced people contemporary with the dinosaurs, but the archaeological establishment seems very reluctant to study them. If interested, contact Ms Sophia Afford, Le Petit Canadeau, Le Plan du Castellet, Le Beausset, 83330, France, T 94 987241, a geologist who has written several articles on the subject. (There are so many stones that its impossible to believe they are all fakes. Most are in a recognisably pre-Inca style, but, for instance, kangaroo and a giraffe in the style of a modern children's story book, strain the visitor's credulity. However, Dr Cabrera is an interesting character, worth a visit. Ed.)

Warning Beware of thieves in the market and at the bus station, even in daylight.

Hotels **A2** *Las Dunas*, plus 18% tax and service, about 20% cheaper on weekdays, highly rec, in a complete resort with restaurant, swimming pool, horseriding and other activities, own airstrip for flights over Nazca, 50 mins; Lima offices: Ricardo Rivera Navarrete 889, Oficina 208, San Isidro, Casilla 4410, Lima 100, T 409091/423090. **B** *Turistas*, large and modern, with swimming pool, with private bath, restaurant; *El Carmelo*, on the Pan-American Highway S of turn-off for *Las Dunas*, swimming pool; **E** *Tucaranda*, next to Ormeño bus terminal, private bathrooms; **E** *Colón*, Plaza de Armas, with bath, **F** without, basic, dirty, old, noisy, restaurant; **E** *Confort*, Lamar 251, 4 blocks from square, clean, possible to park motorcycle; **E** *Hostal El Aleph*, Independencia 152, good; **E** *Presidente*, with bath, clean, good, possible to park motorcycle here; **E** *Siesta II*, Independencia, clean, ask for quieter back room, rec; **F** *Lima*, Lima 262, basic but quiet; **F or G** *Royal*, and *Ica* (basic, noisy), both friendly, clean, and on 100 block of Calle Independencia; **G** pp *Europa*, Independencia 258, clean and friendly; **G** *Hostal Viña*, diagonally across from Entel, shower, safe, helpful. Several good hotels on Castrovirreyna. Hotels are fully booked during the harvest festival and prices rise greatly.

Restaurants Several on Lima, eg at *Hotel Sol de Ica*; on Plaza is *Santa Anita*; *Siesta*, Independencia 160; *Macondo*, Jr Bolívar 300, fish good, rec; *El Otro Peñoncito*, Bolívar, friendly, clean, moderately priced; *El Fogón*, Municipalidad 276, good and cheap. Good one at Ormeño bus terminal. *El Eden*, *Casa Naturista*, vegetarian at Andahuaylas 204, menú US$0.75. *Pastelería La Spiga*, Lima 243, rec.

Exchange Avoid changing TCs if possible, high commission; if you need to, though, **Banco de Crédito** is reasonable.

Tourist Office Some information at travel agencies. Touring y Automóvil Club del Perú, Manzanilla 523.

Buses To Pisco, 70 km, 1 hr, US$1 by bus, several daily and colectivos. To Lima, 302 km, 4 hrs, US$5, several buses daily (see Lima, **Bus Companies**; in Ica Ormeño is at Lambayeque 180). To Nazca, 140 km, 3 hrs, US$2, several buses and colectivos daily, last bus 2100. To Arequipa the route goes via Nazca, see under Nazca.

5 km from Ica, round a lake and amid impressive sand dunes, is the attractive oasis and summer resort of **Huacachina**, with natural mineral water. The **C** *Hotel Mossone* (4 hrs' drive from Lima), or **A3**, full board, is at the eastern end of the lake. Another good hotel is the **F** *Salvatierra*, private bath; both are great places to relax. Sleeping in the open is pleasant here, and swimming in the lake is beautiful, but watch out for soft sand (and, as elsewhere, watch your belongings). Sandboarding on the dunes is a local pastime, board hire US$0.50. Local bus from the square in Ica to Huacachina, US$0.40, 10-15 mins.

The southern oases, S of Ica to the Chilean frontier, produce enough to support themselves, but little more. The highlands grow increasingly arid and the coast more rugged. There are only thin ribbons of cultivable lands along valley bottoms, and most of these can be irrigated only in their upper reaches. However, there are a few exceptions: the cotton plantations between Ica and Nazca, the orange-growing centre at Palpa, the large and well-watered oasis with Arequipa at its centre, and the smaller oasis of the river Moquegua further S. In several places the Highway is not protected against drifting sand and calls for cautious driving. Between Palpa and Nazca the road is in a poor state.

Nazca, 141 km S of Ica by the Pan-American Highway, is a town of 30,000 people set in a green valley amid a perimeter of mountains, 444 km from Lima. Its altitude of 619m puts Nazca just above any fog which may drift in from the sea: the sun blazes the year round by day and the nights are crisp.

The Nazcas had a highly developed civilization which reached its peak about AD 800. Their decorated ceramics, wood carvings and adornments of gold are on display in many of Lima's museums. The Nazca municipality's own museum, on the main plaza, has a small but fine collection (entry, US$1.50, open Mon-Sat 0900-1300, 1500-1800). The valley about 35 km S of Nazca is full of ruins, temples, and cemeteries. The trip should be made by all who have time: mummies, bones, pottery shards and scraps of textiles may be seen lying in the desert sun, although the best pieces have of course been taken by grave robbers and archaeologists.

More cemeteries are being found all the time. At the edge of the town is the reservoir of Bisambra, whose water was taken by the Nazcas through underground aqueducts (many still in use) to water the land. Nearby, a newly discovered site is under excavation, but is not open to visitors. Gold mining is one of the main local industries and a tour usually includes a visit to a small family processing shop; the techniques used are still very old-fashioned.

Hotels A3 *Turistas*, with bath (less without), clean, rooms with private patio, hot water, peaceful, rec, restaurant, good but expensive meals, safe car park, swimming pool (US$2.50 for non-guests, or free if they have lunch), rec; **B** *La Borda*, nr airstrip, old hacienda, surrounded by cottonfields, swimming pool, excellent restaurant, quiet, helpful, rec, but about 5 km from town, English-speaking manageress; **B** *Maison Suisse*, opp airport, nice, comfortable, safe carpark, restaurant, luxury hotel with swimming pool; **D** *Las Líneas*, three star, clean, central, rec; **E** *Hostal El Sol*, basic but friendly, hot showers, small, on Jirón Tacna at Plaza de Armas; **E** *Internacional*, Av Maria Reiche, with bath, clean, quiet, cheap, hot water, rec, but be careful with belongings; **E** *Montecarlo*, Jr Callao, with hot water (ask for it), F without, all rooms with bath, noisy rooms at front, bungalows at back D, small swimming pool, offers flights over the Lines plus one night's lodging but not all year round, mixed reports; **F** *Hostal Alegría*, Jirón Lima 166, T 522444, F 222150, nr bus station, without bath, clean, basic, hot water, limited toilet facilities, cafeteria, garden, manager (Efraín Alegría) speaks English and Hebrew, rec, tours with English-speaking guides, flights and bus tickets to Arequipa arranged, washing facilities, safe luggage deposit (excursion to cemetery at Chauchilla, US$7, can use shower after trip), those arriving by bus beware being told *Alegría* is closed, or full, and no longer runs tours (Sudamericana buses will drop you in front of hostal); **F** *Hostal Don Agucho*, Paredones y San Carlos (T 209), clean, friendly, rec; **F** *Nazca*, Calle Lima 438, price per room, warm communal shower, friendly, dirty, noisy, clothes washing facilities, luggage store, helpful (information on tours, they also run tours), safe motorcycle parking, not as good as it used to be; **F** *San Martín*, Arica 116, basic, electric showers; **G** *Konfort*, Calle Lima 587, small, clean, safe, intermittent water (as elsewhere), indifferent manager; *Posada Guadalupe*, San Martín 480.

Camping *Wasipunko*, Panamericana Sur, Km 450, in grounds of hotel opp the airport, and on the Aerocóndor lot at the airport, free if you have a flight ticket.

Restaurants *Oasis*, Arica 213, quite good and cheap; *La Esperanza*, good set lunch, Lima 594; *La Pascana*, Morzesky y Lima, rec; *Cañada*, Lima 160, friendly, good seafood, reasonable; *Los Angeles*, half-block from Plaza de Armas, good, cheap, try *sopa criolla*, and chocolate cake, similar is *Concordia*, Lima 594, which rents bikes at US$1/hr. *Chifa Orlando*, on Lima, not original Chinese but cheap and good, 1¼ blocks from *Hostal Nazca* (direction Roggero); *La Taberna*, Jr Lima 326, excellent food, live music, friendly, popular with gringos, worth a look just for the graffiti; also *El Dorado*, Lima, near *Hotel Nazca*, good *sopa criolla*; *Mister Tiburón II*, Jr Callao 195, next to *Hotel Montecarlo*, clean, good food. *Fuente de Soda*, near cinema, good *almuerzo*; the restaurant next to *Hostal Nazca* is cheap and good; at Cruz del Sur bus terminal, gringo restaurant, changes dollars, expensive food. Seafood is cheaper than beef. Do not drink the water, but the pisco sours are rec as the best in Peru.

Banks and Exchange Difficult to change TCs, impossible at weekends; bring cash. **Banco de la Nación** exchanges at poor rate. Cash can be changed in the square by *Hotel Turistas*, bargain hard. Some street changers will also change TCs, but at a poor rate.

Post and telephone office Lima 816, calls to Europe for minimum US$21; **police** Av Los Incas, T 36.

Buses There is no bus terminal. To Lima, 446 km, about US$8, 8-10 hrs, several buses and colectivos daily, luxury buses US$12.50 (see Lima, **Bus Companies**), Tepsa, Ormeño, opp *Turistas* and *Montecarlo* hotels. Colectivo to **Lima**, Comité 3, Montevideo 581. To **Ica**, 140 km, 3 hrs, US$2 and to **Pisco** 210 km, 3½-7 hrs, US$3.50, several buses and colectivos daily. Buses to **Camaná**, 390 km, 6 hrs, US$6, several daily; continuing to **Moquegua**, 244 km, 4 hrs, US$4. To **Tacna**, 793 km, 12 hrs, US$12, several buses daily. To **Arequipa**, 623 km, 10 hrs (when there are no problems with the bus), US$10-13, several buses daily, eg Ormeño, 1900 and 2100 (rec as seats can be reserved, but dearer, US$18, and buses coming from Lima may be delayed), Sudamericano, 0300 and 2030, also OK and seats can be reserved, and Tepsa, delays possible out of Nazca because of drifting sand across the road or because of mudslides in the rainy season, the entire route is in poor condition; hold-ups reported on this journey, travel in daylight if possible—buses that leave round 0300, 0330 do most of the journey in daylight. Book ticket on previous day. Watch out for bus companies charging the full fare from Lima to Arequipa. There is a bus to **Cusco**, 659 km, 25 hrs, US$18: the route goes through Puquío (155 km, first 50 km and last 20 km paved) and Abancay (309 km). The road is in bad condition, especially from Puquío onwards, and can take much more than 25 hrs. Safety is not assured (terrorists or bandits) and major bus lines have not resumed services on this route.

Excursions The *Hostal Algería* offers inclusive tours (see Hotels above) which have been repeatedly rec. Similarly the Fernández family, who run the *Hotel Nazca*. Ask for the hotel owners and speak to them direct (many touts). Also ask Efraín Alegría or the Fernández family to arrange a taxi for you to one of the sites outside Nazca. It is not recommended to take just any taxi on the Plaza as they are unreliable and can lead to robbery. It is not dangerous to visit the sites if you go with a trustworthy person. Taxi drivers usually act as guides, but most speak only Spanish. All guides must be approved by the Ministry of Tourism: ask to see an identity card. At *Tour Perú*, Lima 185, Marco speaks English. Tour touts try to overcharge those who arrive by bus.

To the cemetery of Chauchilla, 30 km S of Nazca; the Nazca area is dotted with over 100 cemeteries and the dry, humidity-free climate has preserved perfectly invaluable tapestries, cloth and mummies. Grave robbing *huaqueros* ransack the tombs and leave remains all over the place. Worth a visit; a tour takes about 2 hrs and should cost about US$7 pp with a minimum of 3 people. Cemetery tours usually include a visit to a gold shop (see above) and/or to a local potter's studio. There are several of these and they demonstrate the full process and sell items.

To the Paredones ruins and aqueduct; the ruins are not well-preserved but the underground aqueducts, built by the Incas, are still in working order. By taxi about US$10 round trip, or go with a tour.

To Cahuachi, to the W of the Nazca Lines: several pyramids and a site called El Estaquería (thought to have been astronomical sighting posts, but more recent research suggests the wooden pillars were used to dry dead bodies and therefore it may have been a place of mummification). Tours cost about US$5 pp with a minimum of 3 people.

Nazca Lines About 22 km N of Nazca, along the Pan-American Highway, are the famous Nazca Lines. Cut into the stony desert are large numbers of lines, not only parallels and geometrical figures, but also some forming the shape of a dog, an enormous monkey, birds (one with a wing span of over 100m), a spider and a tree. The lines can best be appreciated from the air; it is now forbidden to walk or drive on them (heavy fine or prison). The German expert, Dr Maria Reiche, who has studied the lines (mostly from a step ladder!) for over 40 years, is now over 90 and lives alone in Lima; she maintains that they represent some sort of vast astronomical pre-Inca calendar.

The lines are thought to have been etched on the Pampa Colorada sands by three different groups: the Paracas people 900-200 BC, Nazcas 200 BC-AD 600 and the settlers from Ayacucho at about AD 630. Dr Reiche's sister, Renate, presents a free lecture in the *Hotel de Turistas* every evening at 1900, if there are more than 10 people. In 1976 Maria Reiche had a platform called the mirador put up at her own expense, from which three of the huge designs can be seen—the Hands, the Lizard and the Tree. Her book, *Mystery on the Desert*, is on sale for US$10 (proceeds to conservation work) at the hotel. In Jan 1994 Maria Reiche opened a small museum (entry US$2), 5 km from town at the Km 416 marker. Another good book is *Pathways to the Gods: the mystery of the Nazca Lines*, by Tony Morrison (Michael Russell, 1978), obtainable in Lima. Another theory is that the ancient Nazcas flew in hot-air balloons; this is based on the fact that the lines are best seen from the air, and that there are pieces of ancient local pottery and tapestry showing balloonists, and local legends of flying men (which would be supported by the engraved designs on stones in Ica—**see p 1195**) if these are proved authentic. See *Nazca, the flight of Condor 1*, by Jim Woodman, Murray, 1980 (Pocket Books, NY 1977.) Georg A von Breunig (1980) discounts both the above theories, claiming that the lines are the tracks of running contests. He bases his argument on the asymmetrical surface level at curves in the designs and on the triangular fields which accord with human running characteristics, and with a number of runners starting from a straight line, then becoming an extended string of contestants. A similar theory was proposed by the English astronomer Alan Sawyer. Other theories are that the Nazca designs represent weaving patterns and yarns (Henri Stirlin) and that the plain is a map demonstrating the Tiahuanaco Empire (Zsoltan Zelko). *The Nazca Lines—a new perspective on their origin and meaning* (Editorial Los Pinos, Lima 18), by Dr Johan Reinhard, brings together ethnographic, historical and archaeological data on the lines, including current use of straight lines in Bolivia. Another source of information on the Nazca Lines is Señora Cogorno, T 450182, Lima. Taxi-guides to the mirador, 0800-1200, cost US$5 pp, or you can hitch, but there is not always much traffic. Travellers suggest the view from the hill 500m back to Nazca is better. Ormeño bus leaves for the lines at 0900 (US$1); hitch back, but have patience. Go by an early bus as the site gets very hot. Better still, take a taxi and arrive at 0745 before the buses.

Small planes take 3-6 passengers to see the Nazca Lines; reservations can be made at the airport for flights with Aerocóndor: small planes, 3 passengers, good view (office opp *Hotel de Turistas*, or can be booked at *Hotel Nazca*), or Aero Montecarlo (from hotel of that name; new planes and experienced pilots, and good). Aerolca in Jirón Lima and at the airport, also fly over the lines. Price for flight US$60-65, plus US$2 airport tax. It is best to organize a flight with Efraín Alegría at the *Hostal Alegría* or with Famailia Fernández at *Hotel Nazca*, or direct with the airlines. Flights should last from 30 to 45 mins, but are sometimes cut to 20, and are bumpy with many tight turns—many people are airsick. From Jan 1994 the Association of Dr M Reiche intended to offer flights at US$30 – profits to conservation. Aerocóndor in Lima (T 442-5663, or at the *Sheraton Hotel*, T 433-3320) and Aerolca (T 441-8614/8608) both offer flights over the lines from Lima in a one-day tour (lunch in Nazca) for US$313 pp; or flights from Ica for US$130 pp. Aerolca also offers a night in *Maison Suisse* plus flight for US$65, but book 48 hrs in advance. The best time to fly is 1500-1600 to benefit from the horizontal light and to avoid morning fog. (Taxi to airport, US$1.35, bus, US$0.10). Make sure you clarify everything before getting on the plane; let them know if you have any special requests. For photographs, be careful you do not find yourself in a middle seat (small planes are best—a roll of 36 should allow 2-3 shots/figure).

More "lines" have been discovered between the Nazca Lines and Ica, called the Tajahuana Lines. There is reference to them in the Museo Regional, Ica.

Sacaco, 30 km S of Nazca, has remarkable fossil beds and a museum built on the fossilized remains of a whale excavated in the desert (the keeper lives on site and is helpful). Take a bus from Nazca, C Bolognesi, in am (check times in advance) to Punta Lomas, a 30-45 mins detour off the Panamericana; ask driver where to get off and be ready for a 30 mins' walk in the sun. Return to Panamericana no later than 1800 for bus back. Efraín Alegría can arrange a taxi for US$50 with only 30 mins at the site. Do not go 2-3 days after a new moon as a vicious wind blows at this time (Rose Tallack and Haydn Thomas).

From a point 40 km beyond Nazca along the Pan-American Highway a branch road (39 km) runs to the ports of San Juan and San Nicolás, built to ship iron ore from the Marcona field, 29 km inland, and Acarí, 53 km E again, where a copper deposit is also being worked. **San Juan**, 553 km S of Lima, has a beautiful deep-water bay (**E** *Hotel Pacífico*, clean, rec; there is a tea room near the central market serving excellent cakes). A bus leaves from Lima to San Juan at 0600 via Nazca, US$7 from Lima.

After Nazca the Highway returns through impressive desert scenery to the coast at **Lomas** (*Hotel Machora* with only 3 rooms; *Hotel Melchor*, basic, and *Restaurant Melchorita*; *Capricho de Verano*) and passes by Chala, **Atico** (**G** *Alojamiento*, good and clean) and Ocoña, to Camaná (392 km from Nazca). Cyclists warn that the headwinds between Nazca and Atico can be very severe, "like a sandstorm in the face".

Chala, 173 km from Nazca, is a fishing village with beaches where condors may be seen. Good fresh fish available in the morning and possibilities of fishing with the local fishermen. Electricity all day. Between Chala and Camaná a missing bridge causes traffic delays on the highway, but otherwise the road is in relatively good condition.

Hotel *Grau*, very basic. One **restaurant** at N edge of town.

Excursion 10 km N of Chala there are the large precolumbian ruins of **Puerto Inca** on the coast. Go 6 km N on the Panamericana; at Km 603 take the unpaved road on left. Follow this for 2 km; then take right fork another 2 km to the sea (bay with cliffs). On their discovery in the 1950s, the ruins were misunderstood and thus neglected. It is now recognised that this was the port for Cusco. A French engineer and amateur archaeologist, Herbert Coste, runs a small hotel and restaurant on the beach, while studying the ruins. His wife, Mitzi Perales, will pick up guests from Chala, telephone messages can be left for her a day in advance at the Chala Entel phone office. Their hotel (Km 603 Panamericana Sur, Aliquipa, T 210224, Telex 59480 PE), C, full board in 10 cabins, is very clean, excellent food, beautiful beach, peaceful place, highly rec. There is also free camping. The site is in excellent condition: the drying and store houses can be seen, on the right side of the bay is a cemetery, on the hill a temple of reincarnation, and the Inca road from the coast to Cusco is clearly visible. The road was 240 km long, with a staging post every 7 km so that, with a change of runner at every post, messages could be sent in 24 hrs.

Camaná is a picturesque little town, 222 km from Chala, with a good food market and pleasant beaches 5 km away at La Punta (hourly buses from Camaná); good bathing but little shade. Rice is the principal crop.

Hotels E *Camaná*, 9 de Septiembre, 1 block from plaza, with bath and hot shower; *Plaza* on the plaza; **E** *Lider*, Av Lima 268 (Pan-American Highway), with bath, clean, good restaurant, safe motorcycle parking for US$3; **F** *Central*, just off main square, not rec; **F** *Hostal Lima*, clean, safe; **F** *Villa Mar*, basic. **NB** Hotels tend to be full in Jan, Feb and Mar.

Restaurant *Chifa Hong Kong*, Plaza de Armas, good. *Turístico*, Av Pizarro 304, T 210280, seafood and *peña*. The freshwater shrimps are delicious.

Bus To **Lima**, Ormeño US$9, 13½ hrs. To **Arequipa** Transportes Turismo 3½ hrs. To **Pisco** Flores Hnos, Sudamericano, US$7, 8 hrs.

Camaná sends its products to the small port of **Quilca** , S on the Río Quilca, in colonial times the unloading point for goods imported via Arequipa to Potosí (now in Bolivia). Now a seedy harbour. The village of Quilca is further along, perched on a cliff overlooking the Siguas river.

The Pan-American Highway swings inland from Camaná and runs along the top of a plateau with strange crescent-shaped dunes (**see p 1203**). The sudden descents into the canyons of the Siguas and Vítor rivers are interesting, as is the pink stone valley at Km 945. The same colour is found on the 10 km road out of the valley S which, once surmounted, gives good views of the snowcapped mountains behind Arequipa. Before Repartición a branch to the left leads to Aplao and the valley of the Río Majes. From there continue past Coropuna, the highest mountain in southern Peru, to **Andagua**, a village lying at the head of the valley of the volcanoes (bus from Arequipa, Sun, Wed, Fri, 1530, with Empresa Delgado, there are also trucks on this route; basic accommodation at the mayor's house in Andagua). The Arequipa-Andagua bus goes on to **Orcopampa**, from which the thermal springs of Huancarama can be visited. A mining lorry leaves Orcopampa for Cailloma on the 12th and the last day of each month; this enables one to make a round trip from Arequipa.

From Andagua there is a road to **Chachas**, a picturesque little village on the edge of a lake (trucks sometimes run between the two villages). It has no restaurants, but a *hostal* on the plaza. The area is heavily cultivated and there are perfect views of the valley of the volcanoes from the top of the hill above Chachas. It is possible to hike from Chachas to Choco and on to Cabanaconde via the Río Colca in 4 days (**see p 1212**).

At **Repartición**, 134 km from Camaná, the Highway bifurcates: one branch runs through Arequipa into the highlands (near Arequipa is a new 39 km toll road, US$0.25, Camaná-Arequipa, 172 km); the other leads S to the Chilean border. From this latter road a branch leads off from La Joya W to Mollendo and Matarani.

Mollendo, 14,650 people, has now been replaced as a port by **Matarani**, 14½ km to the NW. Port workers still live mostly in Mollendo, where the main customs agencies are. Three beautiful sandy beaches stretch down the coast, small beach nearest town is safest for swimming (swimming pool on the beach open Jan-Mar). Mollendo now depends partly upon the summer attraction of the beaches (hotels can be full at this time) and partly upon the 15,000 hectares of irrigated land in the nearby Tambo valley. On the coast, a few km SE by road, is the summer resort of Mejía. The small national reserve at the lagoons has 72 resident species of birds and 62 visitors.

Mollendo Hotels *Salerno*, 30 rooms, all with bath, excellent seafood. **E** *Aller*, Arequipa 681; **F** *Hostal Cabaña*, Comercio 240, clean, good; *Royal*, Tacna 155, basic, clean; **F** *Moderno*, Tacna 179; *Verana*, Arequipa 337, cheap.

Restaurants *Sea Room*, Pasaje San Francisco, ocean views; *Venezia*, Comercio 188.

Bus To **Arequipa**, 129 km (Empresa Agarón and other buses and colectivos daily), 2 hrs, US$2-3. To **Moquegua**, 156 km, 2 hrs, US$2-3, several buses and colectivos daily. To **Tacna**, 315 km, direct transport Thur only; otherwise take colectivo (ask where) at 0600 to connect with Arequipa-Tacna bus 0800-0900.

The Pan-American Highway runs S from La Joya through Moquegua to Tacna and Arica (Chile). Cyclists warn that the road to Moquegua is very hilly. About 100 km before Moquegua is a valley at El Fiscal (restaurant). **Moquegua** (213 km from Arequipa; pop 110,000), described as "calm and clean", is a small town of winding cobblestone streets at 1,370m in the narrow valley of the Moquegua river. The plaza has llama-shaped hedges. The roofs are built with sugar-cane thatch and clay. Most of the valley below the city grows grapes and the upper part grows avocados (*paltas*), wheat, maize, potatoes, some cotton, and fruits. Climate: subtropical. Interesting cacti at Torata, nearby (paved road).

Hotels C *Turistas* (1 km from town), swimming pool, clean, friendly, hot water, restaurant fair, telephone calls expensive; **E** *Limoñeros*, old house, basic rooms, showers, pretty garden, swimming pool (usually empty); **G** *Hostal Comercio*, one block from Plaza, safe and friendly. **Restaurant** *La Sirena*, rec for seafood and chicken dishes.

Buses From Lima, US$16. **Moquegua**-Ilo, 95 km, 1½ hrs, US$1, a few buses daily. To **Tacna**, 159 km, 2 hrs, US$2, several buses and colectivos daily; to **Puno**, 262 km, 10 hrs, San Martín and others daily, US$7. To **Arequipa**, 3½ hrs, US$4, several buses daily.

Moquegua's exports—avocados and wine—go by an excellent 96-km road to the port of **Ilo** (population 95,000: **C** *Hotel Turistas*, with or without bath, restaurant). Bolivia has been granted a duty-free zone at Ilo for the import and export goods from 1992.
   There are three Ilos: Ilo Viejo, in ruins after the earthquake of 1868; Ilo Nuevo, the present town, dirty, with a fishmeal factory, oil tanks, and dusty and sometimes cobbled streets and "half-door" saloons; and the spick and span village built by the Southern Peru Copper Corporation (hospital, cinema, playgrounds, etc) for its engineers and their families.
   The Southern Peru Copper Corporation is exploiting its copper property at Toquepala, at an altitude of 3,050m, and is developing its property at Cuajone nearby (good view of valley, which is full of cacti). All exports are through Ilo, along the 183-km railway and road from Toquepala. The SPCC smelter is on the coast, 18 km from the port of Ilo. Some 70 km S of Moquegua a sign points to the Minas de Toquepala (64 km by a good road); bus service from Tacna. **Toquepala** village, in a hollow, has a guest house (swimming pool), a church, club house and an American school, and is a pleasant place; however, it is a private mining community, and permission from the management must be obtained in advance to visit the village. A nearby cave contains paintings believed to date from 8000 BC, but it is very hard to find. Helio Courier planes reach it from Moquegua (12 mins) and Ilo (26 mins). Taxis from Ilo. In the desert between Moquegua and Tacna, John Streather tells us that engraved stones dating from 10,000 BC have been discovered.

Tacna, at 550m, backed by the snow-capped peak of Tacora, is 156 km S of Moquegua by Pan-American Highway, 42 km from the Chilean frontier, and 64 km from the international port of Arica, to which there is a railway. Above the city, on the heights, is the Campo de la Alianza, scene of a battle between Peru and Chile in 1880. Tacna is 1,292 km from Lima by road, 987 by air.
   Tacna was in Chilean hands from 1880 to 1929, when its people voted by plebiscite to return to Peru. There are good schools, housing estates, a stadium to seat 10,000 people, an airport suitable for jet planes, many military posts and one of the best hospitals in Peru. Population: 150,200.
   Around the city the desert is gradually being irrigated. The local economy includes olive groves, vineyards and fishing. The waters of Laguna Aricota, 80 km N, are now being tapped for further irrigation and hydroelectric power for industry. The cathedral, designed by Eiffel, faces the main square, Plaza de Armas, which contains huge bronze statues of Admiral Grau and Colonel Bolognesi. The interior is austere but the round stained glass windows, each with a different motif, accentuate the fine, clean lines. The bronze fountain is said to be the duplicate of the one in the Place de la Concorde (Paris) and was also designed by Eiffel. The Parque de la Locomotora (near city centre) has a British-built locomotive, which was used in the War of the Pacific. There is a very good railway museum at the station (0900-1500, US$0.10); the museum in the Casa de la Cultura has precolumbian pottery and war relics (very good, free). Casino.

Hotels A3 *Turistas*, Av Bolognesi, gardens, small swimming pool, tennis court, safe car park,

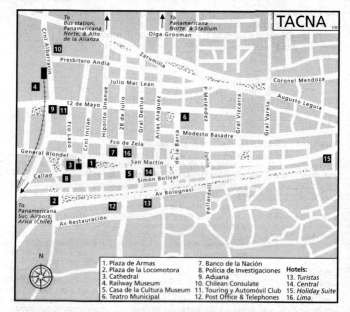

TACNA 106

Map legend:
1. Plaza de Armas
2. Plaza de la Locomotora
3. Cathedral
4. Railway Museum
5. Casa de la Cultura Museum
6. Teatro Municipal
7. Banco de la Nación
8. Policia de Investigaciones
9. Aduana
10. Chilean Consulate
11. Touring y Automóvil Club
12. Post Office & Telephones

Hotels:
13. Turistas
14. Central
15. Holiday Suite
16. Lima

with bath, meals expensive, but good breakfast for US$2, large rooms, clean, can make telephone bookings for other Tourist Hotels; **C Central**, with bath, near Plaza; **C El Mesón**, one block from plaza, new, clean, welcoming staff; **Holiday Suite**, with swimming pool and safe car park, 10 mins' walk from centre, follow Av Bolognesi to the University, from where it's one block to the left; **D Hostal Junín**, Junín, old house, hot water, good beds, clean; **D Lima**, San Martín 442, T 711912, on main square, with bath, bar, good restaurant, friendly, stores luggage; **E San Diego**, Ayacucho 86A, central, private bath, clean, friendly owner; **E Don Quijote**, Leguía 940, with shower, secure, pleasant, but not very clean, near Chasquitur office; **E El Dorado Hospedaje**, Calderón de la Barca 476; **E Lido**, Calle San Martín 876, near Plaza, all rooms hot showers, rec; **F Hostal Buen Amigo**, 2 de Mayo 445, clean; **Imperio** and **Nevada**, on Mendoza 1049 and 1063, very basic, cheap. Accommodation is hard to find in the centre, especially at Christmas-time, because of Chileans on shopping sprees.

Restaurant *Sur Perú*, Ayacucho 80, rec. *Los Tenedores*, San Martín 888, good, clean, expensive; *Hostal Lido*, San Martín 876 A, good value; *Pizzeria Puco*, Libertad pedestrianized street, ½ block from San Martin, good; *El Sameño*, Arias Aráguez, between Zarumilla and Olga Grooman, good value fish restaurant. *El Pacífico*, Olga Grooman 739, grills, chicken, seafood, good and cheap; *Helados Piamonte*, 1 block from *Hotel Turistas*, good ice cream. Hot food from supermarket *Caneda y Cía*, San Martín 770.

Banks and Exchange Banco de Crédito, San Martín, no commission for TCs. Best rates at *cambio* on Junín, between *Hotel Junín* and Av Bolognesi.

Tourist Office Some travel agencies will provide information (not very reliable, though). Secretaría de Estado de Turismo, Av Bolognesi 2088, T 3778. Touring y Automóvil Club del Perú, Av 2 de Mayo 55.

Air To Lima, 2 hrs, US$85 one way; daily flights with AeroPerú, Americana, Aero Continente, also with Faucett US$116. To Arequipa, 35 mins, US$26 AeroPerú, US$24 Americana; with connecting flight to Juliaca, US$65 (Aero Continente). Americana, Av San Martín 408, Plaza de Armas, T 723870. Airport tax US$3. Taxi to town US$3, taxi to bus terminal US$1.50, but beware overcharging. No transport direct to border; cheapest way is taxi to town first, then take colectivo.

Buses Smart new bus station on Hipólito Unanue, 1 km from plaza (colectivo US$0.25);

well-organized, local tax US$0.30, baggage store, easy to make connections to the border, Arequipa or Lima. To **Moquegua**, 159 km, 2 hrs, US$2, several buses and colectivos daily. To **Arequipa**, 6-7 hrs, US$5, several buses daily (eg Ormeño, Aráguez 698 y Grooman). To **Nazca**, 793 km, 12 hrs, US$12, several buses daily, most en route for Lima. Several buses daily to **Lima**, 1,239 km, 21-26 hrs, US$20-25 (see Lima **Bus Companies** with routes to the S). In Tacna, Tepsa is at Leguía 981; Ormeño address above. Tickets can be purchased several days before departure and buses fill up quickly. The Panamericana Sur is good in parts, bad in others. At the Tacna/Moquegua departmental border there are checkpoints at which all buses stop for inspection of imported goods from Chile (there are loads!). This can take time as negotiation with the officials is required and they can be impossible. Do not carry anything for a Peruvian, only your own belongings. Bus from the Zona Franca near the airport and market area, **not** the bus terminal. to **llave** on the Puno-La Paz highway, 320 km, 16 hrs (can be longer in the rainy season), US$6; Gironda, Río Blanco and Ponce companies. The road, via Tarata (where Inca terraces are still in use) and Challpalca, is in fair condition, but it is a bumpy and cold journey and can be hard in the wet (the views are spectacular). Luggage packed on the roof racks has been known to disappear. It might be better to fly to Juliaca and then take a bus. Plenty of local buses and colectivos all day from llave to **Puno**, a further 55 km, 1 hr, US$1.

To **La Paz**, either go from Puno to Yunguyo, or take the direct Litoral bus, T 724761, Wed 0700, US$17.50, 13-16 hrs (can be much longer in the rainy season).

NB Soon after buses leave Tacna, passengers' passports and luggage are checked, whether you have been out of the country or not.

Crossing the border to Arica, 46 km, 1-2 hrs, depending on waiting time at the frontier. Buses to Arica charge about US$2 and colectivo taxis about US$4 pp. All leave from the bus terminal in Tacna throughout the day. If in a hurry, make sure that the colectivo you choose is full (most of the time 6 passengers) because it will not leave before. You can change remaining soles at the bus terminal. A Chilean driver is perhaps more likely to take you to any address in Arica. 'Agents' operate on behalf of taxi drivers at the bus terminal; you may not see the colectivo until you have negotiated the price and filled in the paperwork.

There is a checkpoint before the border, which is open 0900-2200. Peruvian immigration is closed on public holidays. You need to obtain a Peruvian exit stamp (quick) and then a Chilean entrance stamp, which can take a while, but formalities are straightforward. Drivers will help, or do it all for you. If you need a visa, you have to get it in Tacna (open only during office hours, closed weekends and holidays). Note that no fruit or vegetables are allowed into Chile. Coming into Peru from Chile, you can only change pesos into Peruvian currency with street money changers in Tacna (Banco de la Nación will not); the street rate is bad. Money changers line Av Bolognesi, also at one end of new bus terminal "rates not too bad" (see also **Exchange** above). Entering Peru here, travellers are rarely asked for a return or onward ticket.

Rail In theory, there are 3 trains a day from Tacna to Arica, departing 0700, 0830, 1500, US$1.60. The station opens 1 hr before departure to prevent smugglers from entering the trains are normally used by smugglers). There are customs, but no immigration facilities for those arriving by train from Chile.

For those leaving Peru by car buy *relaciones de pasajeros* (official forms, US$0.45) from kiosk at border or from a bookshop; you will need 4 copies. Next, return your tourist card, visit the PNP office, return the vehicle permit and finally depart through the checkpoints.

AREQUIPA–PUNO–CUSCO–MACHU PICCHU (5)

All these places share great local pride and major tourist popularity: colonial architecture in Arequipa and Cusco, the latter underpinned by massive Inca masonry; the tranquility of Lake Titicaca and the bustling folklore of Puno; the majesty of Machu Picchu, best viewed in the context of the once densely-populated heart of the Inca empire. All are set in the southern cordilleras of the Peruvian Andes, with smoking volcanoes, deep canyons, bleak altiplano and terraced valleys.

The **ash-grey sand dunes** near La Joya, on the Pan-American Highway and almost half way from the coast to Arequipa, are unique in appearance and formation. All are crescent shaped and of varying sizes, from 6 to 30m across and from 2 to 5m high, with the points of the crescent on the leeward side. The sand is slowly blown up the convex side, drifts down into the concave side, and the dunes move about 15m a year. The road from Mollendo to Arequipa, about 130 km is well-paved. Toll S of Arequipa US$1.10; another toll booth being built.

Arequipa (pop 1 million), 1,011 km from Lima by road, stands at 2,380m in a beautiful valley at the foot of El Misti volcano, a snow-capped, perfect cone, 5,822m high, guarded on either side by the mountains Chachani (6,057m), and Pichu-Pichu (5,669m). The city has fine Spanish buildings and many old and interesting churches built of *sillar*, a pearly white volcanic material almost exclusively used in the construction of Arequipa. It was re-founded on 15 August 1540 by an emissary of Pizarro, but it had been an Inca city. It is the main commercial centre for the S, and its people resent the general tendency to believe that everything is run from Lima; business travellers should know this. The climate is delightful, with a mean temperature before sundown of 23°C, and after sundown of 14$\frac{1}{2}$°C. The sun shines on 360 days of the year. Annual rainfall is less than 150 mm.

Because of the danger of earthquakes the churches are low, the houses have one storey only, patios are small with no galleries. Roofs are flat and windows are small, disguised by superimposed lintels or heavy grilles. In recent years, higher buildings with large windows have been constructed.

Points of Interest The twin-towered **Cathedral** on the Plaza de Armas, founded 1612, largely rebuilt 19th century, remarkable for having its façade along the whole length of the church, also has a fine organ; **La Compañía** church, whose main façade (1698) and side portal (1654) are striking examples of the florid Andean *mestizo* style: see the **Capilla Real** (Royal Chapel) to the left of the sanctuary, and its San Ignacio chapel with a beautiful polychrome cupola (admission, US$0.50, open 0900-1200, 1500-1800 daily, rec); **Puente Bolívar**, designed by Eiffel. Arequipa has several fine seignorial houses with large carved tympanums over the entrances. The **Gibbs-Ricketts house** (now offices, open to public 1700-2000), with its fine portal and puma-head waterspouts, and the **Casa del Moral**, or Williams house (Calle Moral 318, Banco Industrial, with museum) are good examples, as is the **Casa Govaneche**, Merced 201, now an office of the Central Bank (ask the guards who will let you view the courtyard and fine period rooms). One of the oldest districts is **San Lázaro**, a collection of tiny climbing streets and houses quite close to the *Hotel Libertador* (ex-de Turistas) at Selva Alegre. Behind the cathedral there is a very attractive alley with more handicraft shops. Churches are usually open 0700-0900 and 1800-2000. The churches of **San Francisco**, **San Agustín**, **La Merced** and **Santo Domingo** are all well worth seeing. Opposite San Francisco is a handicraft centre, housed in a beautiful former prison. Next door is the **Museo Histórico Municipal** with much war memorabilia, open Mon-Fri 0800-1800, interesting, US$0.50. The **archaeological museum** at the Universidad de San Agustín, Av Independencia between La Salle and Santa Rosa, has a good collection of ceramics and mummies (Mon-Fri 0800-1400, entry US$1); apply to Dr E Linares, the Director. **La Recoleta**, a Franciscan monastery on the other side of the river, is well worth visiting, with museums; open Mon-Sat 0900-1200, 1500-1700, entry US$2. It contains several cloisters, a religious art museum, an Amazon museum and a library with many rarities. The church itself is open only 0700-0800, 1900-2000.

By far the most interesting visit is to **Santa Catalina Convent**, opened in 1970 after centuries of mystery, the most remarkable sight in Arequipa; excellently refurbished, very beautiful, period furniture, kitchen utensils, and paintings. It is a miniature walled colonial town of over two hectares in the middle of the city; about 450 nuns used to live there in total seclusion, except for their women servants. The few remaining nuns have retreated to one section of the convent, allowing visitors to see a maze of cobbled streets, flower-decked cloisters and buttressed houses. These have been finely restored and painted in traditional white, browns and blues. Open 0900-1700 daily, last ticket 1600, admission US$3.20. The tour they offer you at the entrance is worthwhile (1$\frac{1}{2}$ hrs, no set price, many of the guides speak English). The pictures of the Arequipa and Cusco schools are worth seeing. There is a small café, which sells cakes made by the nuns and a special blend of tea.

The flowered **Plaza de Armas** is faced on three sides by colonial arcaded buildings with many restaurants, and on the fourth by the Cathedral. The central **San Camilo market** (between Perú, San Camilo, Piérola and Alto de la Luna) is also worth visiting as is the Siglo XX market (just off our map to the E). At **Selva Alegre** there is a shady park in front of the *Hotel Libertador*, which is within easy walking distance of all the famous churches and main plaza.

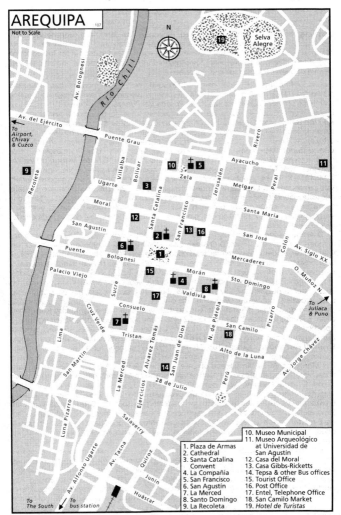

AREQUIPA

Not to Scale

1. Plaza de Armas
2. Cathedral
3. Santa Catalina Convent
4. La Compañia
5. San Francisco
6. San Agustín
7. La Merced
8. Santo Domingo
9. La Recoleta
10. Museo Municipal
11. Museo Arqueológico at Universidad de San Agustín
12. Casa del Moral
13. Casa Gibbs-Ricketts
14. Tepsa & other Bus offices
15. Tourist Office
16. Post Office
17. Entel, Telephone Office
18. San Camilo Market
19. *Hotel de Turistas*

Arequipa is said to have the best-preserved colonial architecture in Peru, apart from Cusco. A cheap tour of the city can be made in a Vallecito bus, 1½ hrs for US$0.30; a circular tour going down Calles Jerusalén and San Juan de Dios.

Festivals Interesting Holy Week ceremonies, huge processions every night, culminating in the burning of an effigy of Judas on Easter Sunday and the reading of his "will", containing criticisms of the city authorities. Another festival at end-April and beginning-May fills the hotels. On 14 Aug, eve of the city's anniversary, there is a splendid firework display in the Plaza de Armas and a decorated float parade. On 2 Nov, the Day of the Dead is celebrated. Go to the municipal cemetery, where Indians sing, dance, eat and drink with their dead. On Sun at about

1030 there is a civic and military parade on the Plaza de Armas. Jan 10, Sor Ana de Los Angeles y Monteagudo, festival for patron saint of Santa Catalina monastery.

Warning Beware of theft in market area, especially after dark. Keep baggage secured in restaurants. At the bus offices themselves and in nearby restaurants, take extra care. The ploy of spraying shampoo (in this case) is common in Arequipa (see **Security** in the **Introduction and Hints**). The police have been complimented as friendly, courteous and efficient, but beware of thieves masquerading as policemen.

Hotels A1 *Presidente*, Calle Piérola, T 213040, with bath, modern, bar, restaurant; **A3** *Portal*, Plaza de Armas, T 215530, excellent, wonderful views, expensive, rooftop swimming pool, El Gaucho restaurant; **A3** *Posada del Puente*, Av Bolognesi 101, T 253132, beside Puente Grau, alongside Río Chili, attractive, small, friendly, good, restaurant, rec; **A3** *Libertador*, Selva Alegre, with bath (less without bath), unsafe area, swimming pool (cold), gardens, good meals, pub-style bar, cocktail lounge, tennis court, Wendy house for children; **B** *Viza*, Av Perú 207, T 232301, bath, TV, phone, garage, restaurant, friendly; **C** *El Conquistador*, Mercaderes 409, T 212916, clean, safe, lovely colonial atmosphere, credit cards accepted, owner speaks English, lacks sound insulation; **C** *Hotel Maison d'Elise*, Av Bolognesi 104, T/F 253343, Sra Elsa Podigo very helpful; **C** *Jerusalén*, Calle Jerusalén 601, T 244441/81, F 243472, hot water, will change dollars, comfortable, modern good restaurant, safe carparking; **C-D** *Casa de Mi Abuela*, Jerusalén 606, T 241206, very clean, friendly, safe, hot water, laundry, self-catering if desired, English spoken, tours and transport organized in own agency, which has good information, small library of European books, breakfast or evening snacks on patio or in beautiful garden, highly rec, 3 flats available with 4 double bedrooms for US$26 a night total.

D *Arequipa Inn*, Rivero 412, T 226077, modern hotel, with bath (US$4.60 for extra bed in room), garage, slow service; **D** *Crismar*, Calle Moral 107, T 215290, opp main Post Office, with shower, modern, noisy, central, food good; **D** *Maison Plaza*, Plaza de Armas, T 218929, with breakfast, bathroom and TV, clean, friendly, good value; **D** *Villa Baden Baden* (Sra Bluemel de Castro), Manuel Ugartecho 401, Selva Alegre, T 222416, 6 rooms (F pp), breakfast incl, German, French, English spoken, very informative about city's environs and climbing, rec; **D/E** *Hostal Núñez*, Jerusalén 528 (T 218648), hot water, laundry, safe, friendly, comfortable, clean, crowded, roof terrace overlooking the city, rec.

E *Casa de Melgar*, Melgar 108-A, T 222459, with bath, hot water all day (solarpanel), clean; **E** *Freddy's*, García Calderón 115, T 214531, one double room, otherwise dormitory (F), hot showers in common bathroom, kitchen, laundry, storage facilities, friendly; **E** *Hostal Europa*, Av Tacna y Arica 119E, T 239787, basic, clean, hot water, tiny rooms, very friendly; **E** *Hostal Fernández*, Quesada 106, 10 mins from centre, good for a longer stay, beautiful garden with parrot, views of El Misti, family affair, breakfasts, hot water, clean, rec; **E** *Hostal Las Mercedes*, Av La Marina, end of Calle Consuelo, PO Box 417 (T 213601), clean, safe, restaurant, highly rec (but do not confuse with *Hostal La Merced*, in Calle La Merced, which is not); **E** *Hostal Premier*, Av Quiroz 100, T 221791, 50 rooms, 2-star, with bath, will store luggage, restaurant, garage; **E** *Lluvia de Oro*, Jerusalén 308, T 235730, English-speaking, breakfast US$1.40, restaurant open to non-residents, pisco sours rec; **E** *Residencia Niza*, Calle Siglo Veinte 122 (rooms, cabins and apartments), meals served, friendly. On San Juan de Dios are **E** *Hostal Florida* (cheaper without bath), clean, modern, good beds, rec; **E** *San Francisco*, good, hot showers, friendly, washing facilities, clean; **F** *Hostal Imperial*, No 210, T 212125, hot water, laundry facilities, roof terrace.

E-F *Hostal Regis*, Ugarte 202, T 223612, opened 1994, colonial house, French-style interior, clean, hot water all day, cooking and laundry facilities, rec, sun terrace with good views; **E-F** *Hostal Santa Catalina*, T 243705, nr Convent, clean, hot water, friendly, noisy, luggage stored, see Jimmy for 2-day guided tours to Colca Canyon, US$24, rec, English-speaking; **F** pp *Hostal Tumi de Oro*, San Agustín 311A, Cercado, 2½ blocks from Plaza de Armas, French and English spoken, hot water, breakfast on request, rooms with and without bath, roof terrace, cooking and laundry facilities, rec; **F** *Americano*, Calle Alvarez Tomás (also called Ejercicios on maps), 4 blocks from the plaza, hot shower at any time, clean, safe, friendly, washing facilities, beautiful geraniums; **F** *Crillón Serrano*, Calle Perú 109, with bath, hot water am, friendly to Germans; **F** *El Gobernador*, Rivero 303, T 244433, private bath, hot water, safe motorcycle parking, rec; **F** *Hostal El Peral*, on road of same name, a short walk from the Plaza de Armas; **F** *Hostal Parra Residencial*, Av Parra 97, T 223787, 5 mins from station, clean, friendly, laundry facilities (some rooms with shower, US$1 more), rec; **F** *Hostal Tito*, Calle Perú, good, friendly; **F** *Residencial Rivero*, Rivero 420, clean, with bath but not always hot water, friendly, helpful, washing facilities; **G** pp *Hostal Lider Inn*, Consuelo 429, with bath, clean, good, friendly, safe; **G** *Grand Hotel*, Alvarez Tomás, basic.

Restaurants *Central Garden*, San Francisco 127, good food but expensive; *Arushka*, San

Francisco 711, German specialities, friendly, handicrafts sold on same premises; *Astoria*, Calle Santo Domingo, local dishes, good service; *Monza*, Santo Domingo 1½ blocks from Plaza, good set meal and breakfast; *Santana*, Santa Catalina 302, opp convent and inside an artisan shop; *Bacuch*, Melgar 413, new, good Swiss food; *Balcón Arequipa*, good view over Plaza, popular with locals, good breakfasts and fruit juice (but sangría not rec), slow service, corner of Merced and Bolognesi; *El Fogón*, Santa Marta 112, good; *La Casa del Pino*, Jerusalén 308, set in a small pleasant courtyard, good set lunch; *Bonanza*, Jerusalén 114-116, for meat and pasta dishes, good, US$5; *Bagatelle*, Jerusalén, good snacks and sandwiches, courtyard to eat in; *La Nueva Mundial*, Jerusalén 522, popular, local dishes, band playing; *Pizzería San Antonio*, Jerusalén y Santa Marta, excellent, popular with locals and tourists; also *Pizzería Los Leños*, Jerusalén 407, nr San Francisco, good, evenings only; *Pizza Presto*, General Morán 108, good and cheap; *Gianni Trattoria*, San Francisco 304; *La Rueda*, Mercaderes 206, excellent parrilladas but expensive; *Nano's*, Mercaderes 117.

Vegetarian: *Govinda*, Jerusalén 505, excellent set meal, vegetarian food, yoghurt (US$0.45/litre) and muesli (also called *Madre Natura*, which has a branch at Grau 310), rec; *Gopal*, Pasaje de la Catedral 108, good, cheap, and *Lashmivan*, Jerusalén 402, good food, pleasant courtyard; also on Jerusalén *Blues Bar*, rec. *Come y Vive Mejor*, Calle Nueva 410A, cheap and good. *Mathesis*, Jerusalén 224, a bit more expensive than others; *La Avellana*, Santa Marta 317-B, good, cheap lunch *menú*.

Café Manolo, Jerusalén, good cakes and coffee; *Pastelería Salón de Té*, Mercaderes 325, very clean, open early, good breakfasts; *Café Butto*, at Universidad Nacional San Agustín, *pie inglés de limón*; *Café Suri*, on the Plaza, for sandwiches and pastries; *Harumi* snack bar, San José 216, Chinese, US$1 for set menu; *El Café*, San Francisco 125, new, popular meeting place; *Dairy Room*, Plaza de Armas, cakes and pastries, expensive ice cream. Good cheap places down San Juan de Dios, eg *El Chuquibambino*, No 625, *menú* for US$2, or *La Empanadita*, No 205, excellent *empanadas* and snacks, or *Dalmacia* excellent family-run restaurant, but dodgy area for tourists. *Las Américas* store in same street has good ice cream. *La Canasta*, Jerusalén 145, bakes authentic-tasting baguettes twice daily, excellent; *Astoria* bakery in Calle Alvarez Tomás for cheap breakfasts.

A score of *picanterías* specialize in piquant foods; try one called *El Pato*; *rocoto relleno* (hot stuffed peppers), *cuy chactado* (seared guinea-pig), *papas con ocopa* (boiled potatoes with a hot yellow sauce) and *adobo* (pork stew). Try them at lunchtime in Yanahuara suburb such as the *Chalet de la Nova*, off Av Ejército, family run, excellent food in taverna style. Arequipeño food also at San Camilo market. A good local speciality is Mejía cheese; try also the *queso helado* (frozen fresh milk mixed with sugar and a sprinkling of cinnamon), the excellent chocolate (*La Ibérica*—the factory on Jerusalén, NE of Plaza de Armas, gives tours on weekdays only), the toffee (eg at *San Antonio Pizzería*), and the fruit drinks called *papayada* and *tumbada*, local specialities in the market and restaurants.

Banks and Exchange Banco Internacional, Mercaderes 217, exchanges Citicorp dollar cheques. **Banco de Crédito**, Santo Domingo y Jerusalén, accepts Visa Card and gives good rates, no commission, rec. **Banco Continental**, La Uruguaya Department Store, Mercaderes 133, Mon-Fri 0900-1200, 1600-1830. Others include **Banco Popular** and **Banco del Sur del Perú** (Calle Jerusalén, close to Post Office, will change TCs, low rates, accepts Mastercard); **Arequipa Inversiones**, Jerusalén 190-C, T 238033; **Ideal Travel**, Zela 212; **Lima Tours**, Santa Catalina 120; **Via Tours**, Santo Domingo 114, good rates; **Diners Club**, San Francisco 112. Parallel market down **Calle Santo Domingo**, Jerusalén near Plaza de Armas, and at Morán y San Juan de Dios. It is almost impossible to change TCs on Sat pm or Sun; try to find a sympathetic street changer. Hotels will not help.

Consulates and Cultural Institutions British Consul, Mr Roberts, Calle Quesada 107, Yanahuara, T (054) 211961. **English Library** at Peruvian-North American Cultural Institute, Melgar 109. **Instituto Cultural Peruano-Norte Americano**, Melgar 109, T 243201. **French Consul** (T 232119) **and Library**, Alianza Francesa, Santa Catalina 208, T 215579. **Instituto Cultural Peruano Alemán**, Ugarte 207, T 218567. **Chilean Consulate**, Mercaderes 212, 4th Flr, T 233556, entrance to lift 30m down passageway down Mercaderes on left, open 0900-1300, present passport 0900-1100 if you need a visa. **Argentine Consulate**, suburb of Cayma, Parque Mérida, T 254544. **Instituto Regional de Cultura**, Gen Morán 118 (altos), T 213171.

Current 220 volts AC, 60 cycles.

Entertainment Bar *Romie*, Zela 208, T 234465, tiny bar with live music rec, Mon, Tues, *autóctono*, Wed-Sat, *peña*. *El Sillar*, Santa Catalina 215, T 215468, "salón concierto", typical folk music, rec, Mon-Sat from 2000. *Las Quenas*, Santa Catalina 215, T 215468. *Bohemios*, Santa Catalina 223, T 226887. *Blues Bar*, San Francisco 319, T 233796; *Video Bar*, on Jerusalén, traditional disco; *El Barril*, Moral y Jerusalén, snacks, good pisco sour; *Peña Waykopac*, Jerusalén 204, good atmosphere, Fri and Sat. *Peña Chunenea*, Pasaje la Catedral 4. Watch out for the local folk-music group Chachani, said to be one of Peru's best. *Discoteca Casablanca*, Av Sucre, Puente Bolognesi, garage entrance, clean, well-run and safe; downstairs pool room. *Disco Fragavoss*, Santa Catalina 109-A, T 232651.

Health Doctor Dr Julio Postigo, Independencia 225; Dr Jorge A del Carpio Alvarez, Santo Domingo 123, of 303, T 215483, rec, only Spanish spoken. At Clínica Arequipa SA, esq Puente Grau y Av Bolognesi, T 253424, Luis Valdivia speaks English; consultation costs US$8, all hospital facilities. **Dentist** Dr José Corrales, San Juan de Dios 216. **Pharmacy** *Farmacia Libertad*, Piérola 108, owner speaks English.

Laundry *Lavandería Cayro*, Jerusalén 311 and Ejercícios 442. *Lavendería del Pueblo*, Ejercícios 558.

Language Courses Silvana Cornejo, 7 de Junio 118, Cerrito Los Alvarez, Cerro Colorado, T 254985, about US$6.50/45 mins, negotiable for group, rec, she speaks German fluently. Fidelia and Charo Sánchez, T 224238, highly rec, Fidelia speaks French, Charo English. Also at Instituto Peruano-Norte Americano and Instituto Cultural Peruano Alemán.

Post and Telecommunications At central Post Office, Moral 118 opposite *Hotel Crismar*. The central Post Office also provides a telex service. Letters can only be posted at the Post Office during opening hours, 0845 to 1845. Telephone and fax: Entel, San Francisco y Valdivia.

Shopping *Casa Secchi*, Av Víctor Andrés Belaunde 124, in Umacollo (near the aeroplane statue), sells good arts, crafts and clothing; also *Artesanías Peruanas*, Puente Bolognesi 147. *Empresa Peruana de Promoción Artesanal (EPPA)*, General Morán 120. For fine alpaca, wool and cotton sweaters, *Factory Fashions*, Francisco Velazco 126, Parque Industrial; for alpaca and wool cloth, *Condor Tips*, Prol Víctor Andrés Belaunde cuadra 2, frente Urb Tahuaycani. The covered market opp the Teatro Municipal in Calle Mercaderes is rec for knitted goods, bags, etc. Market around Valdivia and N de Piérola. Arequipa is noted for its leather work; the street of saddlers and leather workers is Pte Bolognesi. The handicraft shop in the old prison opp San Francisco is particularly good for bags. At *Fundo del Fierro* shop 14, on Plaza San Francisco, alpaca-wool handicrafts from Callalli in the Colca canyon are sold. *Lanificio*, La Pampilla, no number, T 225305, the factory for high-quality alpaca cloth at better prices than Lima outlets. *Sombrería El Triunfino*, N de Piérola 329-331, good selection of hats, but expensive. *El Zaguán*, Santa Catalina 120A, good for handicrafts. Three antique shops in Calle Santa Catalina. Supermarkets nr market sell good bread and yoghurt. Minimarkets for food, mineral water, etc, *El Super*, Portal de la Municipalidad; *Franco*, Villalba 205.

Bookshops There are good bookshops near the Post Office. For international magazines, look along Calle San Francisco, between Mercaderes and San José.

Photography Sr Fernando Delange, N-10 Urbanización Adepa, T 233120, repairs all kinds of electrical equipment as well as cameras. Foto Esperanza S R Ltda, Mercaderes 132-2, English spoken, cameras mended. *Kodak Perú*, Mercaderes 200, 1 hr developing.

Sports Two public stadia, a racecourse, several swimming pools, tennis courts. The Arequipa Golf Club (18 holes) welcomes visitors from abroad. Riding is very popular. There are bullfights. **Climbing** Sr Carlos Zárate of the Mountaineering Club of Peru, has good information and advice, acts as a guide and rents some equipment, highly rec (contact him through Alliance Française, T 215579).

Travel Agencies *Ideal Travels*, Zela 212, on plaza San Francisco, T 212813/244439, F 242088, Mon-Fri 0800-1900, Sat 0830-1300, tours to Colca Canyon (US$30 pp, rafting US$18 pp), Cotahuasi Canyon, Andagua Volcanic valley, Majes River, Cotahuasi River, Toro Muerto, Sallalli alpaca and vicuña ranch; jeep and microbus rentals, excellent bilingual guides. *Conresa Tours*, Jerusalén 409, Casilla 563, T 211847/ 223073/215820, specializes in trips to the Colca Canyon, and to the Toro Muerto petroglyphs (US$28 pp), Las Salinas and Mejía lakes, and city tours, *South American Handbook* users welcome. Several agencies offer tours (1 or 2 days) to the Colca Canyon: *Sky Tours*, San Francisco 315; *Cóndor Tours*, on Ugarte across from entrance to Santa Catalina; and *Santa Catalina Tours*, Santa Catalina 204, good value, buses with large windows, rec. *Expeandes*, La Merced 408, of 1, T 212888, F 228814, PO Box 1403, owner Ricardo Córdoba Mercado, adventure trips, well-organized, reliable, rents equipment, rec. Many agencies offer tours of the city and surrounding area, T 218592; English spoken. Local office of *Lima Tours* reported reliable.

    NB Strong warning received of agencies collecting money in advance but not turning up with vehicle for tour. If possible, check that the agency has enough people to run the tour, or get your own group together beforehand. Don't pay in advance and always settle the details before starting the tour. Quite often travel agents work together to fill buses and use lots of touts. Prices vary greatly so shop around. If a travel agency puts you in touch with a guide, make sure he/she is official. It is not advisable to book tours to Machu Picchu here. Make these arrangements in Cusco.

Tourist Information Office on Plaza de Armas, opposite Cathedral, T 211021, ext 113, open 0800-1900, helpful, friendly, free street plans. Tourist Police, Jerusalén 317, T 239888, helpful with giving directions. Ministry of Tourism, La Merced 117, T 213116, will handle complaints. Touring y Automóvil Club del Perú, Calle Sucre 209.

Taxi Fares US$5 airport to city (can be shared). US$1.50 bus terminal to Plaza de Armas; US$1.75 railway station to centre. Nova Taxi, T 252511; Fono Car, T 212121; Telemóvil, T 221515; Taxitur, T 422323.

Car Hire National, Bolívar 25, US$70/day incl tax, insurance and 200 km; **Avis**, Puente Bolognesi nr plaza.

Car Repairs *Automec*, Av Tahuaycani cuadra 2, Tahuaycani. **Bicycle Repairs and Equipment**. *Hoz Trek Bicicletas*, Villalba 428, T 223221.

Air Rodríguez Ballón airport, 7 km from town. To and from **Lima**, 1 hr 10 mins, US$102.66, several daily with Faucett, AeroPerú, Americana, Aero Continente, Aero Santa, Expreso Aéreo. Special tourist fare may be available from as low as US$53 with AeroPerú (try *Illady Tours* on Jerusalén). To **Tacna**, 30 mins, US$47.20, daily flights with Faucett, AeroPerú, Americana, US$18 Aero Continente. To **Cusco**, 40 mins, US$62 Faucett, 4 weekly, AeroPerú, 5 weekly, US$45 Americana and Aero Continente daily, Expreso Aéreo 5 a week; to **Juliaca** 30 mins, Faucett, Aero Continente and Americana daily, US$54; to **Puerto Maldonado**, US$81 Americana, 3 a week. Airport tax US$3.50. All airline offices are on the Plaza de Armas: Americana, Portal San Agustín 151, T 246392; AeroPerú T 211616; Faucett T 212352; Aero Continente T 237334.

Taxi to airport US$2-3. For Transaeropuerto minibus service between your hotel and airport T 227117, US$1.50 pp. Free transport to the airport may be arranged when buying a ticket at a travel agency, but don't rely on it. Local buses go to about ½ km from the airport.

Buses There is a new bus terminal in Av Avelino Cáceres, Parque Industrial, opp *Inca Tops* factory, S of train station, a long way from the centre; local tax US$0.35. Bus and rail tickets can be bought in the terminal which is 15 mins from centre by colectivo US$0.15, or taxi US$1.50 (10 mins). Most companies have their offices in Calle San Juan de Dios (5-6 blocks from Plaza de Armas), but buses are only allowed to pick up and drop off passengers in this area early and late pm (eg the bus to the Colca Canyon). **Warning** Theft is a serious problem in the bus station area and the surrounding restaurants. Thieves work in groups and are very organized. Take a taxi to and from the bus station and do not wander around with your belongings. Similarly, be careful on San Juan de Dios early and late.

To **Lima**, 1,011 km, can be as much as 19 hrs, buses from US$15-18, several daily; see Lima **Bus Companies** with routes to the S. Note that all the bigger bus companies have luxury buses with video, toilet and comfortable chairs for 30% more (eg Ormeño at 2100, arriving 1000). The road is paved but drifting sand and breakdowns may prolong the trip. Buses will stop at the major cities en route, but not always Pisco. The desert scenery is spectacular. All buses leave in the afternoon, between 1200 and 2000.

To **Nazca**, 566 km, 10 hrs, US$10-13, several buses daily, mostly at night and most buses continue to Lima. Beware, some bus companies to Nazca charge the Lima fare. To **Moquegua**, 213 km, 3 hrs, US$4, several buses and colectivos daily. To **Tacna**, 320 km, 6-7 hrs, US$5, several buses daily; colectivo, Expreso Tacna, San Juan de Dios 537, T 213281, will collect you from your hotel, US$7.

To **Cusco**, 521 km, 15-20 hrs (longer in the rainy season), US$10-14: a few buses and trucks a day. The road was in good shape in early 1995; the views are superb. In the rainy season the journey is not recommended because of mudslides. Cruz del Sur use some very old buses. To **Juliaca**, 279 km, 9 hrs (also longer in the wet), US$8; colectivos charge US$12 and take 8 hrs in the dry season, leaving from Calle Salaverry, only when full. Most buses and colectivos, of which a few go daily, continue to Puno, another 44 km, 30 mins. Mudslides are a problem in the rainy season and the road is in poor condition (paving was to start mid-1994). To **Puno**, 297 km, 10 hrs, US$9, a few buses and trucks daily, most of them at night; colectivo US$12, 9 hrs (all services take longer in the wet). Although the route does not go via Juliaca, the road conditions are identical.

Rail The railway system goes from Arequipa to Juliaca, where it divides, one line going N to Cusco, the other S to Puno. The train leaves in the evening (2000 to 2145) and arrives in Juliaca at around 0600. It takes anywhere from 30 mins to 2 hrs to get the train on the right rails for the next stage. The service to Cusco takes the whole day and arrives at about 1900. The train to Puno arrives at around 0730. The train usually runs every day in the dry season, but in the rainy season it can be cut to 2 or 3 times a week, or even complete cancellation for a while. Always check.

There are three different classes: 2nd class, no seat reservations, not rec; 1st class, reserved seats, but anyone is allowed into the carriage (incl thieves), a good local experience if you do not mind watching your belongings all the time; pullman, with closed doors, only ticket holders are allowed in the carriage, safe, heated at night, recommended for the night journey. You can travel all the way through if you stay in the same class; you only need change trains in Juliaca when changing classes. Fares: Arequipa-Puno, 2nd class US$9, 1st class US$11, pullman US$14. Arequipa-Cusco, 2nd class US$16, 1st class US$20, pullman US$30.

Tickets are sold on the day (try in advance); ticket office open 0700-1200, 1500-1800, 2000-2100 on week days; Sat 0800-1200, 1500-1800; Sun 0900-1200, 1500-1800. Tickets are sold out usually in the morning and there are queues at 0400 before holidays in the dry season. You can buy tickets through travel agencies (check date and seat number).

Warning Theft is a major problem on 1st and 2nd class. Thieves are very well-organized and work in groups, using all the tricks to distract you while someone else steals your bags. The best way is to lock your luggage on the rack and watch it (it is easier if you have only one bag). Owing to the length of time taken to shunt the train around at Juliaca, mostly in the dark, it is a perfect place for thieves. Pay attention at all times and do not leave the train. Sit with a group if possible to help each other. Always have a torch/flashlight to hand. The pullman class from Arequipa to Juliaca is recommended because it is safest at night. Take a taxi to and from the train station and do not hang around the station area.

If you feel bad on train ask for the oxygen mask at once.

Excursions The hillside suburb of **Cayma**, with delightful 18th century church (open only until 1600). It also has many old buildings associated with Bolívar and Garcilaso de la Vega and is the home of contemporary Arequipeño poet, Manuel Gallegos Sanz. The Candelaria festival on 2 Feb is colourful. Many local buses marked Cayma. There is a new luxury *Hotel Cayma*. **Yanahuara**, also a suburb, with a 1750 *mestizo*-style church (opens 1500), with magnificent churrigueresque façade, all in *sillar*, to get there cross the Gran Puente bridge and turn right up Lima; the Tiabaya valley; thermal baths of Jesús ($1/2$ hr by car, on the slopes of Pichu-Pichu, open 0500-1230 (**C** *Hostal Kolping*, León Velarde 406, T 253748; *Peña El Moro*, Parque Principal). **Yura**, 29 km from Arequipa (bus every 3 hrs from San Juan de Dios, T 235750) US$0.40) in a small, interesting valley on the W slopes of Chachani (*Yura Tourist Hotel*, D, wth bath, meals, and an unsigned hotel opp, F, good), has thermal baths open Tues-Sat, morning only (not very hot). **Socosani** ($1 1/2$ hrs by rail and road), now a spa owned by a mining consortium, can only be visited by appointment, 40 km from Arequipa, in a beautiful small valley SW of Chachani, with a modern hotel providing meals and Socosani water, sports in Socosani include tennis, bowls. **Tingo**, which has a very small lake and 3 ill-kept swimming pools, should be visited on Sun (bus 7, US$0.20) for local food; *anticuchos* and *buñuelos*. 3 km past Tingo on the Huasacanche road, near the Mirador Sachaca with fine panoramic views, is *La Mansión del Fundador*, originally a Jesuit foundation but later a *hacienda*, restored as a museum with original furnishings and paintings, entrance fee US$2.50, with cafeteria and bar. It is beside the Sabandía river. North of Arequipa is the Molino de Sabandía, a mill built in 1600, entrance fee US$1.50, swimming bath and countryside, well worth seeing (round trip by taxi US$4; *Restaurante El Lago*, with swimming pool, horseriding nearby); Yumina (adjoining Sabandía), many Inca terraces which are still in use. The interior of the church at Chiguita is well worth seeing.

The **Colca Canyon**. A poor dirt road runs N from Arequipa, over the altiplano, to **Chivay** (3,600m), the first village on the edge of the spectacular terraced Colca Canyon. The road affords fine views of the volcanoes Misti, Chachani, Ampato and Sabancaya (active in 1991-92). From Chivay, the hot springs of La Calera, $3 1/2$ km, regular colectivos or a 30-min' walk from town, can be visited, entrance US$0.75 (commercialized) you can boil your eggs too! Chivay is the linking point between the two sides of the canyon, as it has the only bridge over the river. The road continues NE to Tuti (small handicrafts shop) and Sibayo (*pensión* and grocery store). A long circuit back to Arequipa heads S from Sibayo, passing through Callalli, Chullo and Sumbay. This is a little-travelled road, but the views of fine landscapes with vicuña, llamas, alpacas and Andean duck are superb. Another road from Sibayo goes W, following the northern side of the Colca mountain range to Cailloma, Orcopampa and Andagua (**see p 1200**). Water from the Colca river has been diverted through a series of tunnels and canals to the desert between Repartición and Camaná, to irrigate the Sihuas and Majes pampas.

The Colca Canyon, said to be twice as deep as the Grand Canyon, was mentioned in the 1934 edition of the *National Geographic* magazine by Robert Shippee, although there is a

AREQUIPA Environs

Places in the Colca Canyon:
1. Coporaque
2. Ichupampa
3. Lari
4. Madrigal
5. Tapay
6. Yanque
7. Achoma
8. Maca
9. Mirador Cruz del Cóndor
10. Cabanaconde

claim that it was first discovered from the air by Gonzalo de Reparaz in 1954. The river is at about 3,500 m at Chivay falling to 2,200 m at Cabanaconde. The roads on either side of the canyon are at around 4,000 m and Nevado Ambato, a short distance to the S, rises to 6,288 m. The first descent by raft and canoe was made in 1981. Unspoiled, picturesque Andean villages lie on both sides of the canyon and some of the extensive, Inca stone-terraced fields are still in use. Distinctive costumes are worn by the women; their hats and embroidered dresses can be bought. Local women are very camera-shy. Ask permission if you wish to photograph them and be considerate if they say no.

Crossing the river at Chivay going W to follow the canyon on the far side, you pass the villages of Coporaque, Ichupampa (where a foot bridge crosses the river), Lari, Madrigal (connection to Maca) and Tapay (connected by road to Cabanaconde). From Chivay, the main road goes W along the Colca Canyon. The first village encountered is **Yanque** (8 km, 4 hrs' walk, excellent views), with an interesting church and a footbridge to the villages on the other side of the canyon. Two nuns, Sisters Antonia and Sara will allow you to climb the old bell tower of the church. They also run a food help programme for poor families in the area. Donations much appreciated. Next is **Achoma**, with a luxury bungalow complex outside the village. There is also an old settlement for road workers where you can camp. The road continues to Maca, which barely survived an earthquake in Nov 1991 (people are still living in tents that were provided at the time), and to the Mirador (Cruz del Condor) at the deepest point of the canyon. The view is wonderful and condors can be seen rising on the morning thermals (0900) and sometimes in the late afternoon (1800). There is good hidden camping here. The bus will stop here for about 10 mins (if not, ask). Take the return bus from Cabanaconde (0330) and ask to be dropped off at the Mirador to wait for sunrise and (with luck) condors. From the Mirador it is a 20 mins' ride to **Cabanaconde** (3,287m), a friendly, typical village, very basic (take a torch/flashlight). It is the last village in the Colca Canyon; the views are fine and condors can be seen from the hill just W of the village, a 10 mins' walk from the plaza. A dirt road winds down into the canyon and up to the village of Tapay. Sometimes there is transport. Another dirt road goes back from Cabanaconde to Arequipa via Huambo and El Alto. This is not a well-used route and there are no services between Cabanaconde and the Panamericana.

Trekking There are many hiking possibilities in the area. Make sure to take enough water as it gets very hot and there is not a lot of water available. Moreover, sun protection is a must. Some treks are impossible if it rains heavily in the wet season, but most of the time the rainy season is dry. Check beforehand. Ask locals for directions as there are a billion confusing paths going into the canyon. Buy food for longer hikes in Arequipa. Topographical maps are available at the Instituto Geográfico Militar in Lima, and good information at the South American Explorers Club. From Chivay you can hike to Coporaque and Ichupampa, cross the river by the footbridge and climb up to Achoma, a one-day hike. It is a 2 hrs' walk from the Mirador to Cabanaconde (or the other way round – horses can be hired), but make sure you take the short cut, following the canyon instead of the road, which takes 3 hrs. It takes 2 days to walk from Chivay to Cabanaconde, you can camp along the route.

2 hrs below Cabanaconde is an 'oasis' of palm trees and swimming areas (4½ hrs back up, ask for the best route), rec. The hike from Cabanaconde to Tapay takes 4 hrs; you may be lucky enough to get a lift back in a pick-up. You can continue to Madrigal on foot, through a red-walled valley, about 4 days. A longer hike from Cabanaconde goes to Chachas (4-5 days): follow a small path to the W, descending slowly into the canyon (ask locals for directions to Choco); then cross the Inca Bridge (Puente Colgado, 1,800m) and go up to Choco (2,473m), on to the pass at 5,000m and then down to Chachas (3,100m). Sometimes there is transport from Chachas to Andagua in the valley of the volcanoes; otherwise it is a day's hike. A superb walk through untouched areas and villages. You need all camping equipment, food and plenty of water.

Accommodation Chivay: **F** *El Parador del Inca*, hot water, carpeted rooms, safe, clean, good restaurant (*El Inca*), next door, US$2 for set meal; **F** *Hostal Chivay*, on the plaza, very basic, rooms OK, unfriendly; **G** *Hostal Anita* on plaza, dirty, cold water, fairly friendly; **G** *Hostal Colca*, Salaverry 307, two blocks from square, dormitory rooms and some with private bath, good restaurant, friendly, water infrequent; best food at unnamed restaurant at Calle Siglo XX 107, just off the plaza. There are other basic restaurants and a small market. A *refugio* just across the river from Yanque has thermal pools and horses for hire, US$2 pp, food extra, ask for Natalio. The **E** *Aldea Turística de Colca* (rec, bungalows for 6 are C) at **Achoma**, ½ hr from Chivay along the Cabanaconde road, offers breakfast US$1.50, other meals US$2.50, only electricity, heating and hot water in valley; book through Receptur in Lima or Arequipa or Ricketts Turismo, Mercaderes 407, Arequipa, T 225382, open Apr-Nov only. In **Cabanaconde**: there are several basic hotels, **G** pp *Cruz del Cóndor*, on the plaza, nice, clean and **G** *Solarex*, Calle Tingo 105, one block from plaza; these two may not have either water or blankets (take sleeping bag); **G** *Hostal Valle del Fuego*. There are basic restaurants around the plaza, with *Rancho del Sol* the best. The friendly owner, Pablo Junco, is a wealth of information. Also *Rancho del Colca*, mainly vegetarian. Electricity in Cabanaconde 2000-2200.

Travel to Colca Canyon From Arequipa there are two routes towards the canyon: the old route, via Cayma, called "Cabreritas"; the new route, through Yura, following the railway, longer but quicker (this is being developed as a new route to Cusco from Arequipa). Several buses daily, some very old, from Arequipa to Chivay, 3½ hrs (longer if it rains), US$3; they leave from Calle San Juan de Dios at 0400 and 1130 (prompt). Get your ticket the previous day and be there early to claim your seat. It is a rough route and cold in the morning, reaching 4,825m in the Pata Pampa pass, but the views are worth it. Most buses go on to Cabanaconde (eg at 0730, or Transandino at 1730; no colectivos). The road can be very bad in the wet. It is a further 75 km to Cabanaconde, 3 hrs, US$1; Arequipa-Cabanaconde buses stop for lunch in Chivay at about 1200. They return from Cabanaconde at 0330, alternatively Transandino leaving 1330; but Arequipa-Cabanaconde 7½ hrs, US$3.50. To and from Cabanaconde via El Alto and Huambo, 255 km, the road is in poor condition but the views are magnificent.

From Chivay to Sibayo, 35 km, 1 hr, US$0.75, several pick-ups daily. From Sibayo to Arequipa, via Callalli, 147 km. From Sibayo to Andagua, via Cailloma and Orcopampa, 194 km, and a further 290 km back to Arequipa; about 12 hrs, US$7.

Travel agencies in Arequipa arrange a '1-day' tour to the Mirador, US$20. Depart Arequipa at 0400, arrive at the Mirador after an uncomfortable ride at about 0900 (too late to see condors), expensive lunch stop at Chivay and back to Arequipa by 2100, not recommended, especially for those with altitude problems, as it is too much to fit into one day. Longer tours cost US$30-90. It is recommended to take at least 2-3 days when visiting the Colca Canyon.

El Misti volcano (5,822 m) may be climbed. Start from the hydroelectric plant (first register with the police there), then you need one day to the Monte Blanco shelter (4,800m). Start early (take water) for the 4-6 hrs to the top, to get there by 1100 before the mists obscure the view. If you start back at 1200 you will reach the hydroelectric plant by 1800. Alternatively, buses leave Arequipa for Baños Jesús, then on to Chiguata, where one can walk to the base of El Misti. Be sure to take plenty of food and water, it takes 2 days to reach the crater, guides may be available at Cachamarca. Further information is available from Carlos Zárate or the Club de Andinismo de Arequipa (addresses above, **Climbing**). Also some travel agencies have information eg Expeandes.

The world's largest field of petroglyphs (hard to find on your own) at **Toro Muerto** (off the Majes canyon on the road to Aplao) can be reached by taking a bus (San Antonio, Lima 119, 0700, returns Arequipa at 1400 and 1700) to Corire, 3 hrs, US$5 return; get out 2 km before Corire and walk 1 hr to Toro Muerto (entry US$0.15). Guide for US$3. The higher you go, the more interesting the petroglyphs; take plenty of water and protection against the sun, including sunglasses. There are several restaurants around the Plaza de Armas in Corire (try the crayfish); 3 hotels: **F** Hostal Willys, on plaza, clean, basic, intermittent water supply; **F** hostal one block from plaza, basic, OK, hot water; **F** Hostal Manuelito, 3 blocks from plaza, basic, good, friendly, best of the three. Restaurants and shops.

The railway from Arequipa winds its way up the valley towards Juliaca. Skirting Misti and Chachani the train climbs steadily past Yura, Socosani and Pampa de Arrieros; after another 80 km it reaches Crucero Alto, the highest point on the line (4,500m). Lakes Lagunillas and Saracocha are very pretty lying on opposite sides of the railway, which passes their margins for nearly an hour. As the descent continues streams become more plentiful. The scene changes in a few hours from desolate mountain peaks to a fertile pampa carrying a fairly populous agricultural community. (Since there is no day train at present, much of this beautiful scenery is not visible en route.)

The rough road from Arequipa to Juliaca reaches its highest point at Alto de Toroya, 4,693m. Train is more comfortable than bus. Arequipa-Juliaca by motorcycle takes about 9 hrs, by bicycle 3½ days; if heading for Puno it is better to go via Juliaca than taking the direct branch to Puno. Beautiful scenery, small villages on route. The road climbs steeply for the first 50 km, reaching a plateau. At Km 119, at Paty, there is a restaurant; others at Tincopalca, Km 173, Santa Lucía, Km 218, and Deustua, Km 252. If driving, a 4WD is strongly recommended. Even in the dry season, there are rivers to cross and sand stretches. After heavy rain it is impassable.

Juliaca, 289 km NE of Arequipa, at 3,825m (cold at night), has a population—mostly Indian—of 134,700. It is poor and run down. On the huge Plaza Melgar (good place to meet local students), several blocks from the main part of the town, is an interesting colonial church. Large market in the square on Mon, a good place to buy woollen goods, cheaper than Cusco and Puno; there is another daily market in the square outside the railway station, which is more tourist oriented, but you can buy good alpaca clothing here very cheaply. Tupac Amarú market, on Moquegua 7 blocks E of railway line, cheap black market. A first class hospital is run by the Seventh Day Adventists.

Warning Beware of pickpockets and thieves, especially at the station, where they get on the train to join those already on board. Also beware of overcharging by taxi drivers at railway station (eg Lino, who speaks broken English).

Hotels B Turistas, Av Arequipa 1381, T 71524, on the outskirts of town, good, but water turned off 2300, meals US$3-5; **C** Hostal Samari, Noriega, T 321870, F 321852, clean, modern, restaurant; **D** Karlo's Hostal, Unión 317, T 322568, clean, comfortable, hot water; **D** Royal Inn, San Román 158, T 321561, F 321572, clean, decent accommodation, private bath and TV, rec, restaurant good; **E** Hostal Perú, Bracesco 409, railway plaza, T 321510, with bath, cheaper without, clean, comfortable, hot water sometimes, rec, has a basic restaurant; **E** Yasur, with bath, F without, clean, safe, friendly, 500m from station, small bar and restaurant in evening; **F** Victoria, cold water, clean but simple; **G** Alojamiento San Antonio, basic but clean; **G** Hostal Ferrocarril, San Martín 249, clean, friendly, water until 1900. There are water problems, especially in the dry season.

Restaurants Trujillo, on San Martín, basic, typical food, good value, US$3-4 for a meal; El Comedor del Sur, adequate; Café Dorado. Hole-in-the-wall breakfast parlour at corner of plaza opp station, good.

Transport Rail See information under Arequipa, Puno or Cusco. The station at Juliaca is the junction for services between Arequipa, Puno and Cusco. Carriages are put onto the right rails for their next destination, a process which can take from 15 mins to 2 hrs. This is an ideal time for thieves to operate. You do not have to change trains in Juliaca if you buy a through ticket from one terminus to the other using the same class all the way. Stay in your carriage at Juliaca and lock your luggage to the rack. Try to form a group in order to keep a better eye on things; it is not that the situation is dangerous but that the thieves are very well-practised at distracting you while an accomplice steals your belongings. You have the opportunity to shop through the carriage window, bargain hard.

The ticket office opens when the train comes in. Trains leave for Cusco and Puno about 0800; for Arequipa at about 2100. Prices to Cusco and Arequipa are the same as for Puno. An alternative to the train to Puno from Juliaca is to take a colectivo.

Buses To **Cusco**, 344 km, 12 hrs (longer in the rainy season), US$8; buses and trucks daily. The road is in very poor condition as the train is used more. When the train does not run in the rainy season, the bus has to be taken, unless conditions are so bad that buses are not running either. It is not advisable to take a night bus to Cusco, or at least take the more expensive tourist bus: robberies occur on this route. To **Puno**, 44 km, 45 mins, US$0.65, colectivos run this route all day, US$2, leaving from outside the railway station. Taxi to Puno about US$15. From Puno transport goes to the Bolivian border and on to La Paz.

To **Huancané** (N side of Lake Titicaca), 51 km, 3½ hrs, US$1.75, several buses and trucks daily; bumpy ride, poor road, but wonderful views. It is a further 50 km, US$1.75, to the Bolivian border; several checkpoints and the trip can take a few hours. Buses and trucks daily, but not much transport on this route.

Air To Lima, 1 hr, 45 mins, US$85, AeroPerú, 6 a week, Faucett and Americana, daily. To Arequipa, 30 mins, US$46 AeroPerú 6 a week, Americana and Faucett daily. To Cusco, US$46, Faucett and AeroPerú 3 a week, 35 mins, Americana daily, also Aero Continente. Americana, Jr Noriega 325, T 321844. Airport tax US$6. Taxi to airport 15 mins, US$2. A colectivo runs direct from the airport to Puno, US$0.50 pp.

Excursion There are good thermal springs at village of **Putina** , 84 km NE of Juliaca, 5½ hrs by bus or truck, US$2.50. 71 km NE of Juliaca is the old town of **Azángaro** with a famous church, La Asunción, filled with *retablos* and paintings of the Cusco school. To **Pucara** , 63 km N, with pre-Inca ruins and fine pottery. The sheep farm of San Antonio, between Ayaviri and Chiquibambilla, owned by the Prime family (descendants of British emigrants), may be visited. 23 km NW of Juliaca is the unspoiled little colonial town of **Lampa**, known as the "Pink City", with splendid church, La Inmaculada, containing a copy of Michelangelo's "Pietà", and Kampac Museo, Ugarte 462, museum with sculptures and ceramics from Lampa and Juli areas, owner lives next door, interesting. It also has a good Sun market. Buses and trucks daily, 1 hr, US$0.60.

Puno, capital of its Department, altitude 3,855m, population 80,000 (with 8,000 at university), on the NW shore of Lake Titicaca, has a fine main square and an interesting, but dirty, lakeside quarter, largely flooded since the rise in the lake's water level. The austere Cathedral was completed in 1657. A short walk up Independencia leads to the Arco Deustua with, nearby, a mirador giving fine views over the town, the port and the lake beyond. Puno gets bitterly cold at night: in Jun-Aug the temperature at night can fall to -25° C, but generally not below -5° C (warm clothing and good sleeping bags are necessary).

Museums The Museo Municipal has been combined with the private museum of Sr Carlos Dreyer, Conde de Lemos 289, open Mon to Fri 0730-1330, entrance US$1.

NB If intending to visit remote areas of the altiplano, seek advice. Puno itself is full of hustlers and tricksters; use reputable establishments.

Festivals 1-8 Feb, the very colourful Fiesta de la Virgen de la Candelaria, bands and dancers from all the local towns compete on the Sun; better at night on the streets than the official functions in the stadium. Check in advance on actual date because Candelaria may be moved if pre-Lentern carnival coincides with it. Candlelight procession through darkened streets takes place on Good Friday, bands, dignatories and statues of Jesus. 3 May, Invención de la Cruz, exhibition of local art; 29 Jun, colourful festival of San Pedro, procession at Zepita (**see p 1219**). Also 20 Jul. 4-5 Nov, pageant on founding of Puno and emergence of Manco Capac from waters of Lake Titicaca. This is not the best time to visit Taquile and Amantaní since many of their inhabitants are at the festival.

Hotels A3 *Isla Esteves* (Tourist Hotel), T 353870, spacious, good views, cold site (you can ask for an electric fire), on an island linked by a causeway 5 km NE of Puno (taxi US$1.75), is built on a Tiwanaku-period site, with bath, telephone, bar, good restaurant, discotheque, good service, electricity and hot water all day, poor rate of exchange, check bill carefully, camping

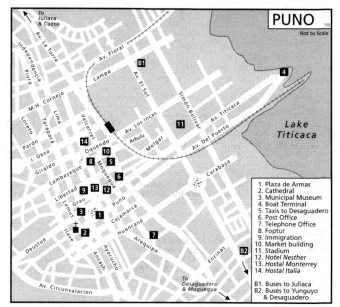

PUNO
109
Not to Scale

To
Juliaca
& Cusco

Lake
Titicaca

To
Juliaca
& Cusco

To
Desaguadero
& Moquegua

1. Plaza de Armas
2. Cathedral
3. Municipal Museum
4. Boat Terminal
5. Taxis to Desaguadero
6. Post Office
7. Telephone Office
8. Foptur
9. Immigration
10. Market building
11. Stadium
12. Hotel Nesther
13. Hostal Monterrey
14. Hostal Italia

B1. Buses to Juliaca
B2. Buses to Yunguyo
& Desaguadero

allowed in car park; **B** *Motel Tambo Titikaka*, with half-board, at Chucuito on the lakeside, 17 km S of Puno; electricity only between 1800-2300, poor heating, rooms icy after sunset, food indifferent and bill charged in dollars, wonderful view, book in advance (travellers need own transport, local transport is scarce and expensive); **B** *Sillustani*, Jr Lambayeque 195, T 351431, including breakfast, good service, clean, friendly, cold rooms, ask for an electric heater, hot water; *Residencial Cofre Andina*, Jr Bolognesi 154, T 351973, 3-star, bath, TV, hot water, restaurant, buffet breakfast, bar; **C** *Hostal Colón Inn*, Tacna 290, T 351432, recently renovated, colonial style, good rooms with private bathroom and hot shower, clean, good service, restaurant and pizzería, Belgian manager Christian Nonis well known, especially for his work on behalf of the people on Taquile island; **C** *Don Miguel*, Av Torre 545, T 351371, with shower, with restaurant, clean, water intermittent; **C** *El Buho*, Lambayeque 142, T 351409, rec, clean, hot water, friendly, ask for room with radiator; **C** *Ferrocarril*, Av La Torre 185, T 351752, opp station, with bath and hot water, **E** without bath, cold water, modern (reservation may be necessary) good rooms, but noisy, poor service in hotel and restaurant, central heating adequate, annex (F, not so good) no hot water (accepts many credit cards and changes Bolivian currency); **C** *Hostal Italia*, Teodoro Valcarcel 122, T 352521, 2 blocks from the station, with shower and breakfast, good, safe, rec, hot water, good food, clean, staff helpful; also on Teodoro Valcarcel, **D** *Hostal Imperial*, No 145, T 352386, friendly, good service, clean, hot water am and pm; **D** *Internacional*, Libertad 161, T 352109, with shower (extra bed US$1.50), hot water morning and evening (not always reliable), secure, central; **E** *Continental*, Alfonso Ugarte 161, cold water, dirty, friendly; **E** *Europa*, Alfonso Ugarte 112 (near station), T 353023, "gringo hotel", luggage may be stored, but don't leave valuables in room, shared bathrooms, hot water but unreliable, unsafe showers, dirty, a little noisy, garage space for motorcycles, reports of occasional police drug raids; **E** *Hostal Central*, Tacna 269, T 352461, clean, friendly, shared baths; **E** *Hostal Lima*, Lima, popular, hot water twice a day, mixed reports on cleanliness; **E** *Hostal Nesther*, Deustua 268 (T 351631), also 3-bedded rooms, with bath, hot water, 0730-0900, clean, rec, except for safety; **E** *Hostal Monterrey*, Lima 447A, T 343, "gringo hotel", reasonable, some rooms with bath, better than those without, communal bathrooms reported dirty, a/c, hot water 0630-0900, restaurant poor, secure for luggage, motorcycle parking US$0.50 (has colectivo service to La Paz, US$12); **E** *Hostal Tumi*, Cajamarca 237, T 352270 (cheaper in low season); **E** *Los Uros*, Teodoro

Valcarcel 135, T 352141, cheaper without bath, hot water 1900-2100, plenty of blankets, clean, breakfast available, quiet, good value, small charge to leave luggage, friendly, often full; **E** *San Carlos*, nr railway station, hot water supposedly all day, some rooms with bath, nice rooms; **E-F** *Bolognesi*, Bolognesi, friendly, good; **F** *Hostal Arequipa*, Arequipa 153, T 352071, clean, friendly, usually hot water, will change TCs, stores luggage, secure; **F** *Hostal Los Incas*, Los Incas 105, basic, hot showers US$1; **F** *Hostal Roma*, Libertad 115, T 351501, basic; **F** *Hostal Virreynal*, Arequipa 342, friendly, clean, no hot water; **G** *Centenario*, on Pardo, basic; **G** *Hostal Inti*, Av La Torre, opp station, noisy, basic, hot water sometimes, small; **G** *Torino*, Libertad 126, clean, unfriendly, very cold shower. Hotel rooms are difficult to find after trains arrive as everyone else is also looking, but hotel touts besiege arriving train passengers. If taking a room with a bathroom, check first if it has hot or cold water. Check on early morning water supply; some only have supply after 0730, too late if you are going out by train or on island tour. Clean public showers near the football stadium. Puno suffers from power and water shortages.

Restaurants Try *Sale Caliente*, Tacna 381, or any of the pollo (chicken) places. *Ambassador*, Lima 347, cheap and varied food, good set meals, but not all dishes of same standard. On same street, *Don Piero*, huge meals, live music, try "pollo coca-cola", chicken in a sweet and sour sauce, also good pasta and avocado salad, but dry cakes. *Café Internacional*, Libertad 161, 2 blocks from Plaza, "gringo", excellent trout, not cheap (check bill) and service variable; *Pizzería Trattoria del Buho*, Jr Libertad 386, good pizza; *pizzería* at Tacna 298; *San Pedro*, Lima 360, good meals, cheap; *Al Paso Antojitos*, Lima 373, rec snack bar for cake, pies and coffee; *Peña Hostería*, Lima 501, good music, rec. *Pascana*, Lima 339, specializes in parrilladas, vegetarian dishes available, folk shows; *Club 31* on Moquegua, good cheap café; *Hilda's House*, Moquegua 189, quiet, relaxed; *Las Rocas*, Valcarcel, good, especially fish, but slow; *Samaná*, Puno 334, inconsistent service, sometimes has live folk music from 2100, open fire and snacks and drinks (no minimum charge); *Ricardos*, Jr Lambayeque 117, clean, good breakfasts, serves sandwiches, friendly, opened 1993, rec; *Restaurant Monterrey*, behind hotel, good fish, good value lunches, pizzas. Nameless café on corner of Libertad and Tacna, good breakfasts and pastries. *Café Delta*, Libertad 215, open 0600, espresso, vegetarian, good and cheap; *Goodmann*, Pardo, vegetarian, popular, and *Adventista*, Jr Deza 349, good. *El Tambo*, rec, good fruit juices. *Venecia*, Tacna, opp *Hostal Presidente*, for cheap good breakfast. Above the city is a quinta called *Kantuta*, Arequipa 1086, good local dishes, open until 1700, rec.

Banks and Exchange Banco de Crédito, Lima y Grau, before 1300 for TCs (no commission) and for advances against Visa. For cash go to the *cambios*, the travel agencies (eg *Andes Tours*, Tacna 278), or the better hotels (*Hostal Arequipa* gives good rates). Many street changers near travel agencies; beware, they always try to rip someone off. Change soles here before going to Bolivia.

Bolivian Consulate Jr Arequipa between Parque Pino y Jr Deza; visa on the spot, US$10, open 0830-1330 Mon to Fri.

Laundry *Lavandería América*, Jr Moquegua 169; *Lavandería Lava Clin*, Deustua 252, El Sol 431 and Teodoro Valcarcel 132.

Post Office Jirón Moquegua 267. **Telephone** Entel, Arequipa y Moquegua, long waits for international calls.

Shopping In the covered part of the market (mostly fruit and veg) there are model reed boats, and attractive carved stone amulets and Ekekos (Bolivian household gods). *Market* on railway between Av Los Incas and Lampa is one of the best places in Peru (or Bolivia) for llama and alpaca wool articles, but bargain hard, especially in pm, many are still hand-made, unlike in Cusco. You will be hassled on the street, and outside restaurants to buy woollen goods, take care! *Artesanías Puno*, on Calle Teodoro Valcarcel, has good quality alpaca goods with sizes for large gringos. *Uros* on same road, higher quality alpaca, but more expensive. Food and clothing market next to stadium. For good *artesanías*, take a bus to Km 20, Chinchero, where the *Trenza de Oro* has very good quality goods.

Travel Agencies Agencies organize trips to the Uros floating islands, US$6 pp (2-3 hrs) and the islands of Taquile and Amantaní (usually included in the Taquile trip); Sillustani, and other places. Make sure that you settle all details before embarking on the tour, many agencies are unreliable. (Alternatively, you can easily go down to the lake and make your own arrangements with the boatmen.) We have received good reports about the following: *Viajes El Sol*, Jirón Arequipa 401, T 684, Sr Ronald Zárate; *Puno Travel Service*, Tacna 254; *Turismo Titicaca*, Libertad; *Kinjyo Travel Service*, Calle Arequipa 401. *Kontiki Tours*, Melgar 188 for 'mystical tours'; *Inca Tours*, Av Los Incas 117 (nr market) T 353009, Sr Andrés López, Sra Paulina Chuspe Aniles. *Highland Travel Experts* next door to *Hotel Italia* on Teodoro Valcarcel; *Freiser Tours*,

Teodoro Valcarcel 155, T 353112, guide Edgar rec for Sillustani; *Turpuno* next to *Hotel Sillustani* on Lambayeque; *Air Travel Services SRL*, Oquendo 250 (Sr Jorge Oliart Garcia), rec for travel arrangements. Agencies sometimes sell cheap flight to Cusco and Arequipa.

Tourist Information InfoTur, Calle Lima y Calle Deustua, helpful with general information, friendly. Ministry of Tourism, Jr Deustua 351, T 352811, helpful with complaints. Touring Automóvil Club del Perú, Calle Arequipa 457.

Immigration Libertad 403, T 352801, for renewing entry stamps, etc. Very slow, fill in 2 application forms at a bank, but nothing else to pay.

Transport Roads and Buses To Arequipa, 297 km, 11 hrs (longer in the rainy season), US$9. A few buses and trucks go daily, the route does not go through Juliaca. Colectivos charge US$12, 9 hrs, minimum. The road is in poor condition and mudslides cause problems in the rain, but the views are spectacular. All buses seem to go at night (cold). Continuing to **Lima**, 1,011 km, 18 hrs, US$18, all buses go through Arequipa, sometimes with a change of bus. See under Arequipa. To **Juliaca**, 44 km, 45 mins, US$0.65, colectivos run all day. Taxi to Juliaca about US$15. To **Cusco**, 388 km, up to 18 hrs, US$9, buses (only at night) and trucks daily, but the train is more commonly used. The conditions are the same as those given under Juliaca, including the danger of robbery. To **Moquegua**, 262 km, 10 hrs, US$7, a few buses daily, poor road, bumpy and cold. To **Tacna**, via Ilave, 375 km, 17 hrs (can be longer in the wet season), US$7. The road is not too bad but it is rough and cold. It can be difficult in the rainy season. The views are spectacular.

Rail The railway runs from Puno to Juliaca (44 km), where it divides, to Cusco (281 km) and Arequipa (279 km). There are two trains daily: to **Cusco** at 0725, arriving about 1930 (try to sit on the right hand side) and to **Arequipa** at 2045, arriving about 0600. In the wet season the services may be cut to 2-3 times a week, or even be cancelled for short periods. Always check.

Fares: Puno-Cusco, 2nd class, US$10; 1st class, US$13; pullman, US$17. Puno-Arequipa, 2nd class, US$9; 1st class, US$11; pullman, US$14. The ticket office is open from 0700-1000 and tickets can be bought one day in advance, or 1 hr before departure if there are any left. Travel agencies sell tickets in advance, charging 10-20% commission. They are not reliable, but sometimes are the only option. Do not pay in full before receiving the tickets and always check the date and seat number. Hotels can help with getting tickets as well. See under Arequipa **Rail** for the standards and safety of the three classes. See also under Arequipa and Juliaca on safety. Take the pullman carriage if you do not want to worry about theft (reportedly less of a problem recently, 1995), but take 1st class for a real local experience. There is a *menú* available in the pullman carriage (US$6 for lunch or dinner) take your own food as a standby.

A good idea in Puno, Juliaca and other Andean towns, when moving about with heavy baggage, is to hire a 3-wheel cycle cart, "Trici-Taxi" (about US$0.20/km).

Sea Boats The boat terminal is being rebuilt and boats currently leave from Av Floral (1995).

Excursions from Puno The walk from Jirón Cornejo following the Stations of the Cross up a nearby hill (with fine views of Lake Titicaca) has been recommended, but be careful, there are dubious characters on the hill. Motorboats charging upwards of US$3.50 pp take tourists to the *Uros* "floating islands"; prices should not be over US$6 (which is what agencies charge in season). Pay half before you leave and half on your return. Those furthest from Puno are most worth seeing, but the islands have been totally spoilt by tourism. Boats go about every ½ hr from about 0630 till 1000, or whenever there are 10 or more people to fill the boat, and take 3-5 hrs. Local boats may also be hired. The earlier you go the better, to beat the mass tourists. Out of season there are no regular boats, either get a group together and pay US$10 for the boat, rent a boat at US$1-2 pp, or pay an agency US$15-20. (Be careful where you walk on the floating islands.) The Uro Indians on the islands have intermarried with the Aymara and no pure Uros exist. The temptation to move ashore may soon deprive the floating islands of all residents. The present Puno Bay Indians still practise some Uro traditions, but Aymara influence predominates. Many tourists report that though the people are friendly, they are very poor and consequently there are constant requests for money (less persistent out of season). Rather than giving the children money or gifts, buy their little reed boats or give fruit. There is no drinking water on the islands.

A much more interesting island to visit (quiet and hospitable, except at the height of the tourist season) is *Taquile*, some 45 km from Puno, on which there are numerous pre-Inca and Inca ruins, and Inca terracing. The island is narrow, only about 1 km wide, but 6-7 km long. On the N side of the island is the warmest part of Lake Titicaca. Plentiful accommodation can be found in private houses but best to take warm clothes and a sleeping bag. Apparently the islanders refused to allow any hotels to be built on the island to help preserve their way of life.

No previous arrangements can be made; on arrival you walk up a steep path for 30 mins (remember you are at 3,800m), are greeted by the Indians, pay a US$0.10 fee, sign the guest book and if wishing to stay are "assigned" a family to stay with (G pp); some families offer dinner and breakfast for about US$1/meal. Boats to Taquile leave daily at 0800-0900, arriving 1300; return 1400/1430, arriving 1830, US$7 return, a day return is not recommended if you want to see the island fully, yet 3 hrs of serenity are still very nice if time is short. Organized tours can be arranged for about US$16 pp, but only give you about 2 hrs on the island. Boats sometimes call at Uros on the outward or return journey. Make sure you and the boatman know exactly what you are paying for. There is a cooperative shop on the square that sells exceptional woollen goods, not cheap but very fine quality (cheaper in the market at Puno). There are several small restaurants on the island (eg *El Inca* on main square); fish is plentiful and the island has a trout farm, but meat is rarely available and drinks often run out. Meals are a little more expensive than on the mainland. You are advised to take with you some food, particularly fruit, bread and vegetables, water, plenty of small-value notes, candles and a torch. Take precautions against sunburn. Carnival, Easter, 2 to 7 Jun, mid-Jul (2 weeks, Fiesta de Santiago), 1 and 2 Aug are the principal festival days with many dances in between. Ask for Sr Agustín, a dressmaker, who is very knowledgeable about the island. Ask for the (unmarked) museum of traditional costumes and also where you can see and photograph local weaving.

Another island well worth visiting, is **Amantaní**. It is very beautiful and peaceful and like Taquile (which is smaller), has 6 villages and ruins on both of the island's peaks, Pacha Tata and Pacha Mama, from which there are excellent views: there are temples and on the shore there is a throne carved out of stone. On both hills, a fiesta is celebrated on 15 Jan (or thereabouts). The Indians make beautiful textiles and sell them quite cheaply at the Artesanía Cooperativa; the people are Quechua speakers, but understand Spanish. There are no hotels but you are assigned to stay with local families, or ask your boat owner where you can stay. Accommodation, inc 2 meals, is in our F range. Families who have been recommended include: the Borda family, E, Julio Borda is a captain and will provide information on boats to Taquile, etc, good food, also Benedicto Guli Calsin, nr the windmill, Eleutorro Quispe Cari, or Yanarico family; for an insight into substance living, the shy but interesting Amadeus family, just outside the main village, turn left along beach from port, be sure to pay a fair price for their wicker work, they are liable to undercharge. Ricardo Quispe Mamani has bar/restaurant on main square, G plus food, rec. Edelberto Quispe Mamani has a boat for 4 passengers for hire, rec. Ambrosio Mamani boards visitors, rec, and runs a boat to Puno every 2 weeks. There is one restaurant, *Samariy*. Boats go to the island from the harbour in Puno at 0800 daily, return 1430, US$9.50 round trip. The journey takes 4-5 hrs, take water. A 1 day trip is not possible as the boats do not always return same day. Several tour operators in Puno offer 2-3 day excursions to Amantaní, Taquile and a visit to the floating islands, US$16 pp (incl 2-3 meals). The festivities in Jan have been reported as spectacular, very colourful, musical and hard-drinking. There is also a festival the first Sun in Mar with brass bands and colourful dancers. Another fiesta is the Aniversario del Consejo (of the local council). If you wish to visit both Taquile and Amantaní, go to Amantaní first, from there a boat goes to Taquile, US$2.50, but there is no regular service. Unfortunately tourism prompts many requests for sweets and money which may irritate; fruit, torches (there is no electricity), moisturizer and sun block (the children suffer sore cheeks) are suitable gifts.

Near Puno, are the *chullpas* (precolumbian funeral towers) of **Sillustani** (admission, US$2.25) in a beautiful setting on a peninsula in Lake Ayumara, 32 km (excellent road) from Puno. Highly rec. Take an organized tour (about 3-4 hrs); some include transport and entrance fee, about US$6-8, some offer only transport US$3 (ie it is cheaper to pay the entrance fee at the site). Bus, including site entrance, from Calle Tacna, 1430, US$5. Taxi about US$15. There is no electricity, you need a torch for the ruins; restaurant now built. "Most of the towers date from the period of Inca occupation in the 15th century, but they are burial towers of the Aymara-speaking Colla tribe. The engineering involved in their construction is more complex than anything the Incas built—it is defeating archaeologists' attempts to rebuild the tallest 'lizard' *chullpa*. Two are unfinished: one with a ramp still in place to raise blocks; the other with cut stones ready to go onto a very ambitious corbelled false dome. A series of stone circles to the E of the site are now thought to be the bases of domed thatch or peat living huts, rather than having any religious meaning. The quarry near the towers is also worth seeing."—John Hemming. There are local indians at the site, in costume. Take small change or chocolate, matches, pencils etc, as small presents if you wish to photograph the indians. Camera fans will find the afternoon light best; desert country, but impressive. There are Inca ruins at Tancatanca and Caluxo.

Peru to Bolivia Anybody interested in religious architecture should go from Puno along the western shore of Lake Titicaca. An Inca sundial may be seen near the village of **Chucuíto** (which has an interesting church, La Asunción, and houses with carved stone doorways); **D** *Las Cabañas*, per night in 4-bedded bungalow, nice, quiet location, T 352108, leave message for Alfredo Sánchez. Cave paintings at Chichiflope. The best examples are at **Juli** (**F** *Alojamiento El Rosal*, Puno 128, off Plaza, basic), **Pomata** (for accommodation ask for Sra Rosa Pizano, on square, No 30) and **Zepita**.

Juli has four churches, all are being renovated. San Pedro, now designated as the Cathedral, has been extensively restored; it contains a series of superb screens, some in ungilded mahogany and others taken from other churches; also fine paintings, and a collection of coloured objects in the sacristy. San Juan Bautista has two sets of 17th century paintings of the lives of St John the Baptist and of St Teresa, contained in sumptuous gilded frames. San Juan is now a state museum, open am only (US$0.15); it also has intricate *mestizo* carving in pink stone. Santa Cruz is another fine Jesuit church, partly roofless, so that it is easy to photograph the carvings of monkeys, papayas and grapes. The keys to Santa Cruz and San Juan Bautista are kept by the couple who look after San Juan Bautista. The fourth church, La Asunción, now abandoned and its fine bell tower damaged by earthquake or lightning, has an archway and atrium which date from the early 17th century. The Peruvians have established a school of picture restoration at Juli to restore its mass of paintings. Beautiful needlework can be bought at the plaza in Juli. There is a nice walk from Juli to the red rock formations known as Caballo Cansado. The church at Pomata, which is being restored, is spectacular, with beautiful carvings, in Andean *mestizo* baroque, of vases full of tropical plants, flowers and animals in the window frames, lintels and cornices, and a frieze of dancing figures inside the dome (which is unusual in Peru), and alabaster windows (John Hemming). Near Juli is a small colony of flamingoes; many other birds can be seen from the road.

On the road to Juli is **Ilave**, where the road for Tacna branches off. (The Tacna road is unpaved, but in good condition and a worthwhile journey, not only in terms of scenery, but also because road conditions are better than on the alternative Juliaca-Arequipa route to the coast from Lake Titicaca.) Ilave is typical of a gaunt *altiplano* town; has a good Sun market (woven goods—beware bag slashers). Many buses and colectivos go there from Puno (US$1.40); Ilave-Tacna, 320 km, US$10.50, 17 hrs, leaves at 1400 and 1700 (Transportes Ponce, best, and Transportes Gironda).

To the border (See also under Bolivia, **Crossing the Peruvian Frontier**.) Small migration tax payable in soles at border.

By Road: 1. The most remote route is along E side of Lake via Huancané, Moho (accommodation G, one bus on weekdays to Juliaca, 7 hrs, often cancelled) and Puerto Acosta (Bolivia), recommended only on weekends when there is more traffic; after Puerto Acosta, the road is very bad. Make sure you get an exit stamp in Puno.

2. The most direct route is the Puno-Desaguadero road (150 km paved) passing through Chucuíto, Ilave, Juli and Pomata. Desaguadero is a miserable place (**F** *Alojamiento Internacional*, dirty). Colectivos and buses run Puno-Desaguadero, 2 hrs, US$1.50 by bus. Get exit stamp on the Peruvian side, cross the border and get entrance stamp on the Bolivian side. Border offices are open 0800-1200 and 1400-1700. There are a few buses to La Paz (105 km from Desaguadero), 4 hrs, US$2-3. The road to La Paz is in poor condition.

3. Puno-Yunguyo (136 km)-Copacabana (11 km)-La Paz (130 km): by far the pleasanter journey. The road is paved from Puno to Yunguyo and has good scenery. The views are also good on the Bolivian side. Several minibuses do the direct route from Puno to La Paz, taking 6-8 hrs, US$7.50 (check in advance that ticket includes the Tiquina ferry crossing and other charges). They leave Puno at 0800 and stop at the borders and for lunch in Copacabana, arriving in La Paz at 1700. You only need to change money into Bolivian pesos for lunch on this route. If you wish to stop in Copacabana, do not be persuaded to buy a through ticket to La Paz (bus fare Puno-Copacabana US$5.50-7). There are local buses and colectivos all day between Puno and Yunguyo, 2½ hrs, US$1.50. From Yunguyo to the border takes 5 min. Get an exit stamp from Peruvian customs; the office is open 0900-1200, 1400-1700. From the border it is a 20 min drive to Copacabana. The Bolivian customs are situated just before Copacabana, with the same hours as the Peruvian office. Taxis from Yunguyo to Copacabana cost about US$1.50 pp. There are some trucks and buses running this route, but not frequently. The walk takes 2 hrs.

4. There are also luxury services from Puno to La Paz as follows: Juli to La Paz by Crillon Tours' hydrofoil, with connections to tours, from La Paz, to Cusco and Machu Picchu (all Puno travel agents have details, or Av Camacho 1223, PO Box 4785, La Paz, T 374566/7, F 391039; Puno-Copacabana by bus; Copacabana-Isla del Sol-Huatajata (Bolivia) by catamaran; Huatajata-La Paz by bus. 13 hrs, US$110 pp. Departure from Puno at 0630, arriving in La Paz 1900. Bookings through Transturin, offices in Puno at Libertad 176, ask for Esther de Quiñones, T 352771; Cusco, Portal de Panes 109, of 1, Plaza de Armas, T 222332; La Paz, Av Mariscal Santa Cruz 1295, 3rd Flr, T 320445/341787. (See Bolivia, **Lake Titicaca** section for full details on these and other services.)

Yunguyo itself has a privet hedge on main square showing good examples of topiary. **G** *Hostal Amazonas*, basic, restaurant; **G** *Hostal Yunguyo*, clean, but often no water or electricity. Exchange market good in main plaza (the first you come to from Bolivia), better rates than border, and good for changing bolivianos, cash only. Travelllers' cheques can be exchanged in the cambio here, poor rates. In the 2nd plaza are the buses and colectivos for Puno.

Bolivian Consulate, near the plaza, open Mon-Fri 0830-1500, for those who need a visa, it is free, but some nationalities have to pay, eg US$12 for French, US$20 for Canadians.

Peruvian and Bolivian Customs Offices are open 0900-1200 and 1400-1800. When leaving either country you must get an exit stamp before crossing the border and a tourist visa on the other side: 30 days for Bolivia, 90 days for Peru. At all borders, be aware of corruption at customs and look out for official or unofficial people trying to charge you a departure fee (say that you know it is illegal and ask why only gringos are approached to pay the "embarkation tax"). If you need a visa for either country (check before arriving at the border), get it in Yunguyo, Puno or La Paz.

NB Peruvian time is 1 hr behind Bolivian time. Also note that there is often a deterioration in the standard of service offered by agencies running a Puno-La Paz service once you have crossed the border, in either direction.

Puno to Cusco On the way from Puno to Cusco there is much to see from the train, which runs at an average altitude of 3,500m. At the stations, Indians sell food (roast lamb at Ayaviri and stuffed peppers at Sicuani) and local specialities such as pottery bulls at Pucará (rooms available at the station); fur caps, furs and rugs at Sicuani; knitted alpaca ponchos and pullovers and miniature llamas at Santa Rosa (rooms available). There are three hotels in *Ayaviri*, including **G** *Hostal Ayaviri*, Grau 180, basic, unfriendly. The road Pucará-Santa Rosa is in bad shape.

The railway crosses the altiplano, climbing to La Raya, the highest pass on the line (210 km from Puno; 4,321m). Up on the heights breathing may be a little difficult, but the descent along the Río Vilcanota is rapid. To the right of Aguas Calientes, the next station (4 km from La Raya) are steaming pools of hot water in the middle of the green grass; a startling sight. The temperature of the springs is 40°C, and they show beautiful deposits of red ferro-oxide. The springs are not developed, but bathing is possible to the left, where the hot spring water joins the cold creek. At Maranganí, the river is wider, the fields greener, with groves of eucalyptus trees.

The road is in very poor condition (there are reports that it is to be paved) and may be impassable in the rainy season as there are many rivers to cross. Most people take the train but, as said above, in the wet season, trains may be cancelled. In that case fly rather than take a bus which may be held up by bandits.

The paved road ends at Juliaca, from where there is a very rough gravel track over La Raya pass up to Tinta, 69 km S of Urcos, and paved from Tinta all the way to Cusco. There are buses from Puno to Cusco, subject to the weather. Travelling by night is not recommended, and the trip is uncomfortable and almost always delayed. Hold-ups at night have occurred.

Sicuani, 38 km beyond the divide (250 km from Puno—a very tiring road, but being rebuilt— 137 km from Cusco, bus US$1.25), is an important agricultural centre at 3,960m, and an excellent place for items of llama and alpaca wool and skins; they sell them on the railway station and at the excellent Sun morning market. Around Plaza Libertad there are several hat shops selling local hats. Also known for its mineral baths at Uyurmiri.

Hotels D *Centro Vacacional*, being modernised, best in town, some way from centre, rec; **E** *El Mirador*, basic, clean; **F** *Manzanaral*, Av 28 de Julio, cold shower, basic, friendly, noisy, parking in *taller*, about 2 blocks on parallel street; **G** *Obada*, communal shower, basic; **G** *Quispe*, basic, no shower, friendly. **Restaurants** *Elvis* and *Vilcanota* in centre of town, rec; *Viracucha* on main square, OK.

On the right, a few km past the San Pedro stop, is the so-called Templo de Viracocha, grandiose, with Inca baths 180m to the E. (For more information about places between Sicuani and Cusco, **see p 1233**.)

Branch roads both S and N of Sicuani lead to a road past the Tintaya mines which forms an alternative route Cusco-Arequipa. The surface is OK to the mines, bad thereafter, but it is a spectacular journey. Only 1 bus a day (Chasqui) passes, usually full. From Sicuani, a pretty lake is passed, Laguna Langui Layo, then one climbs to a radio-transmission antenna; at El Descanso is a checkpoint. A few km from the road is **Yauri** (**G** *Hostal El Tigre*, nice rooms, water shortages), isolated on a plateau by a canyon. A road SW from Yauri, requiring high clearance vehicles, leads on to Sibayo, Chivay and Arequipa. Alternatively, to the SE, the road skirts Laguna Condorama, one of the highest lakes in South America (4,700 m), past more mining operations, the Majes irrigation scheme and on to the Arequipa-Juliaca road. Sicuani to Arequipa is about 400 km. If driving this route, check directions with police.

The Vilcanota plunges into a gorge, but the train winds above it and round the side of the mountain. At Huambutío the railway turns left to follow the Río Huatanay on the final stretch to Cusco. The Vilcanota here widens into the great Urubamba canyon, flanked on both sides by high cliffs, on its way to join the Ucayali, a tributary of the Amazon.

Cusco stands at 3,310m, a little lower than Puno. The city council has designated the Quechua, Qosqo, as the official spelling. Its 275,000 inhabitants are mostly Indian, and the city is remarkable for its many colonial churches, monasteries and convents, and for its extensive Inca ruins. Respect the altitude; 2 or 3 hrs' rest after arriving make a great difference; avoid meat and smoking, and eat lots of carbohydrates. Remember to walk slowly. To see Cusco and the surrounding area properly—including Pisac, Ollantaytambo, Chinchero and Machu Picchu—you need 5 days to a week, allowing for slowing down because of altitude.

Almost every central street has remains of Inca walls, arches and doorways. Many streets are lined with perfect Inca stonework, now serving as foundations for more modern dwellings. This stonework is tapered upwards (battered); every wall has a perfect line of inclination towards the centre, from bottom to top. The stones have each edge and corner rounded. The circular stonework of the Temple of the Sun, for example, is probably unequalled in the world.

Inca Society Cusco was the capital of the Inca empire—one of the greatest planned societies the world has known—from its rise during the 11th century to its death in the early 16th century. (See John Hemming's *Conquest of the Incas* and B C Brundage's *Lords of Cuzco* and *Empire of the Inca*.) It was solidly based on other Peruvian civilizations which had attained great skill in textiles, building, ceramics and working in metal. Immemorially, the political structure of the Andean Indian had been the *ayllu*, the village community; it had its divine ancestor, worshipped household gods, was closely knit by ties of blood to the family and by economic necessity to the land, which was held in common. Submission to the *ayllu* was absolute, because it was only by such discipline that food could be obtained in an unsympathetic environment. All the domestic animals, the llama and alpaca and the dog, had long been tamed, and the great staple crops, maize and potatoes, established. What the Incas did—and it was a magnificent feat—was to conquer enormous territories and impose upon the variety of *ayllus*, through an unchalleageable central government, a willing spiritual and economic submission to the State. The common religion, already developed by the classical Tiwanaku culture, was worship of the Sun, whose vice-regent on earth was the absolute Sapa Inca. Around him, in the capital, was a religious and secular elite which never froze into a caste because it was open to talent. The elite was often recruited from chieftains defeated by the Incas: an effective way of reconciling local opposition. The mass of the people were subjected

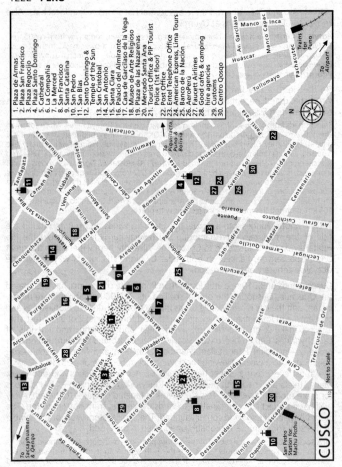

1. Plaza de Armas
2. Plaza San Francisco
3. Plaza Regocijo
4. Plaza Santo Domingo
5. Cathedral
6. La Compañia
7. La Merced
8. San Francisco
9. Santa Catalina
10. San Pedro
11. San Blas
12. Santo Domingo & Temple of the Sun
13. San Cristóbal
14. San Antonio
15. Santa Clara
16. Palacio del Almirante
17. Casa de Garcilaso de la Vega
18. Museo de Arte Religioso
19. Plaza de las Nazarenas
20. Mercado Santa Ana
21. Tourist & PIP Tourist Police (1st floor)
22. Post Office
23. Entel Telephone Office
24. American Express, Lima Tours
25. Banco de la Nación
26. AeroPerú
27. Faucett Airlines
28. Good cafes & camping hire agencies
29. Customs
30. Centro Qosqo

CUSCO

to rigorous planning. They were allotted land to work, for their group and for the State; set various tasks (the making of textiles, pottery, weapons, ropes, etc) from primary materials supplied by the functionaries, or used in enlarging the area of cultivation by building terraces on the hill-sides. Their political organization was simple but effective. The family, and not the individual, was the unit. Families were grouped in units of 10, 100, 500, 1,000, 10,000 and 40,000, each group with a leader responsible to the next largest group. The Sapa Inca crowned the political edifice; his four immediate counsellors were those to whom he allotted responsibility for the northern, southern, eastern and western regions (*suyos*) of the empire.

Equilibrium between production and consumption, in the absence of a free price mechanism and good transport facilities, must depend heavily upon statistical information. This the Incas raised to a high degree of efficiency by means of their *quipus*: a decimal system of recording numbers by knots in cords. Seasonal variations were guarded against by creating a system of state barns in which provender could be stored during years of plenty, to be used in years of scarcity. Statistical efficiency alone required that no one should be permitted to leave his home or his work. The loss of personal liberty was the price paid by the masses for economic security. In order to obtain information and to transmit orders quickly, the Incas built fine paved pathways along which couriers sped on foot. The whole system of rigorous control was completed by the greatest of all their monarchs, Pachacuti, who also imposed a common language, Quechua, as a further cementing force.

Churches (Many are closed to visitors on Sun, 'official' opening times are unreliable.) The heart of the city, as in Inca days, is the Plaza de Armas. Around the square are colonial arcades and four churches. To the N is the **Cathedral** (early 17th century, in baroque style), built on the site of the Palace of Viracocha. The high altar is solid silver; the original altar *retablo* behind it is a masterpiece of native wood carving. In the sacristy are paintings of all the bishops of Cusco and a painting of Christ attributed to Van Dyck. The choir stalls, by a 17th-century Spanish priest, are a magnificent example of colonial baroque art. The elaborate pulpit and the sacristy are notable. Much venerated is the crucifix of El Señor de los Temblores, the object of many pilgrimages and viewed all over Peru as a guardian against earthquakes. (The Cathedral is open until 1000 for genuine worshippers—Quechua mass 0500-0600, otherwise Mon-Sat 1400-1730 with the combined entrance ticket—see below). The tourist entrance is through El Triunfo, which has a fine granite altar and a statue of the Virgin of the Descent, reputed to have helped the Spaniards repel Manco Inca when he besieged the city in 1536. It also has a painting of Cusco during the 1650 earthquake (the earliest surviving painting of the city) in a side chapel. In the far right hand end of the church is a local painting of the Last Supper replete with Peruvian foods, *cuy*, *chicha*, etc. Doors from the Cathedral open into Jesús María.

On the E side of the plaza is the beautiful **La Compañía de Jesús**, built on the site of the Palace of the Serpents (Amaru-cancha) in the late 17th century. Its twin-towered exterior is extremely graceful, and the interior rich in fine murals, paintings and carved altars. The cloister is also noteworthy (closed since 1990).
  La Merced, almost opposite the *Tambo Hotel*, first built 1534, rebuilt late 17th century, attached is a very fine monastery with an exquisite cloister; open 0830-1200, 1430-1730 (admission US$0.50, students US$0.35). Inside the church are buried Gonzalo Pizarro, half-brother of Francisco, and the two Almagros, father and son. Their tombs were discovered in 1946. The church is most famous for its jewelled monstrance, on view in the monastery's museum during visiting hours. The superb choir stalls, reached from the upper floor of the cloister, can be seen by men only (but you must persuade a Mercedarian friar to let you see them). **San Francisco** (3 blocks SW of the Plaza de Armas), is an austere church reflecting many Indian influences. Its monastery is being rebuilt (see the candelabra made from human bones and the wood carving; closed since 1992). **Belén de los Reyes** (in the southern outskirts), built by an Indian in the 17th century, has a gorgeous main altar, with silver embellishments at the centre and goldwashed *retablos* at the sides (open 1000-1200, 1500-1700 except Thur and Sun). **Santa Catalina**, on Arequipa, opposite Calle Santa Catalina, is a magnificent building; the church, convent and museum are included on the tourist ticket (open Mon-Thur and Sat 0800-1800, Fri 0800-1900). Delicious marzipan is sold next to the museum by the nuns through a revolving wooden door, US$1 for 200 grams. **San Pedro** (in front of the market) was built in 1688, its two towers from stones brought from an Inca ruin (open Mon-Sat 1000-1200, 1400-1700). The nuns' church of Santa Clara is unique in South America for its decoration, which covers the whole of the interior (but virtually impossible to visit). The smaller and less well-known church of **San Blas** has a fine carved *mestizo* cedar pulpit (open Mon-Sat 1400-1730).
  Santo Domingo (SE of the main Plaza) was built in the 17th century on the walls of the Temple of the Sun and from its stones; visit the convent to see the impressive ancient walls of the Temple of the Sun/Coricancha, now restored. (Model of the Temple upstairs: ask to see it.) Current excavation is revealing more

of the five chambers of the Temple of the Sun, which shows the best Inca stonework to be seen in Cusco. The Temple of the Sun was awarded to Juan Pizarro, the younger brother of Francisco, who willed it to the Dominicans after he had been fatally wounded in the Sacsayhuamán siege. Open 0800-1730, tour US$1 (English-speaking guides may request US$10, US$1 in the normal price).

The baroque cloister has been gutted to reveal four of the original chambers of the great Inca temple—two on the W partly reconstructed in a good imitation of Inca masonry. The finest stonework is in the celebrated curved wall beneath the W end of Santo Domingo (rebuilt after the 1950 earthquake, at which time a niche that once contained a shrine was found at the inner top of the wall). Below the curved wall was a famous garden of gold and silver replicas of maize and other plants. Excavations now in progress have revealed Inca baths below here, and more Inca retaining walls. The other superb stretch of late Inca stonework is in Calle Ahuacpinta outside the temple, to the E or left as you enter (John Hemming).

Much **Inca stonework** can be seen in the streets and most particularly in the Callejón Loreto, running SE past La Compañía de Jesús from the main plaza: the walls of the House of the Women of the Sun are on one side, and of the Palace of the Serpents on the other. There are ancient remains in Calle San Agustín, to the NE of the plaza. The temples of the Stars and of the Moon are still more or less intact. The famous stone of 12 angles is in Calle Triunfo (Calle Hatun Rumyoc) halfway along 2nd block from the square beside the Cathedral, on the right-hand side going away from the Plaza.

On the way to the airport on Avenida del Sol, 20 mins' walk from the Plaza de Armas, there is a statue of the Inca Apachacutec placed on top of a lookout tower. There are excellent views of Cusco; entrance free; small galleries and restaurant. Open 1000-2000. The tourist police have an office here.

San Sebastián, an interesting church with a baroque façade, is in the little village of San Sebastián, 6½ km from Cusco.

Visitors' Tickets It is possible, but more expensive, to purchase individual entrance tickets to the churches and ruins in and around Cusco; the best value is to buy a combined ticket for US$10 (50% cheaper with student identification, which is checked at each site), valid for as many days as you ask for if bought at the Santa Catalina convent or Museo Histórico Regional, green card (5 days elsewhere, red card). Tickets to individual sites can cost up to US$2-3 each. The combined ticket allows entry to: the Cathedral, San Blas, Santa Catalina, Santo Domingo-Coricancha, Museo de Arte Religioso, Museo Regional Histórico, the Pikillacta ruins, Qenqo, Puku Pukara and Tambo Machay (see below) on the way to Pisac, Pisac itself, Sacsayhuamán, Chinchero and Ollantaytambo. Machu Picchu, the Museo Arqueológico and the church of La Merced are not included on the ticket. The tickets can be bought at any of the places mentioned. **NB** All sites are very crowded on Sun. No photographs are allowed in any museums.

Palaces and Mansions The Palacio del Almirante, just N of the Plaza de Armas, is impressive. Note the pillar on the balcony over the door, showing a bearded man and a naked woman. Nearby, in a small square, is the colonial house of **San Borja**, where Bolívar stayed after the Battle of Ayacucho. The **Casona del Marqués de Valleumbroso** (3 blocks SW of the Plaza de Armas) was gutted by fire in 1973 and is being restored. The **Palacio Archiepiscopal** (two blocks NE of Plaza de Armas) was built on the site of the palace occupied in 1400 by the Inca Roca and was formerly the home of the Marqueses de Buena Vista; it contains the Museo de Arte Religioso (see below). Above Cusco on the road up to Sacsayhuamán, one finds the church of **San Cristóbal**, built to his patron saint by Cristóbal Paullu Inca and, N of it, the eleven doorway-sized niches of the great Inca wall of the Palacio de Colcampata where Paullu Inca set up home. Further up, to the left, is a private colonial mansion, once the home of the explorer (and murderer) Lope de Aguirre. Also visit the palace called **Casa de los Cuatro Bustos** at San Agustín 400 (which is now the *Libertador-Marriott Hotel*) and the **Convento de las Nazarenas**, Plaza de las Nazarenas (alias Casa de la Sirena). See the Inca-colonial doorway with a mermaid motif. Also on Plaza Nazarenas, **Casa Cabrera**, now a gallery. Also visit *Hotel Los Marqués*.

Museo Arqueológico recently moved into Palacio del Almirante (described above), first-rate precolumbian collection, contains Spanish paintings of imitation Inca royalty dating from the

18th century, as well as an excellent collection of textiles. Visitors should ask to see the forty miniature pre-Inca turquoise figures found at Piquillacta and the golden treasures, all kept under lock and key but on display, US$1 entry. Open Tues-Sun 0800-1400, but check in advance as the museum is frequently closed. The staff will give a guided tour; give a tip.

Museo de Arte Religioso at old Archbishop's Palace in Calle Hatun Rumyoc (see above), a fine collection of colonial paintings and furniture, including the paintings by the Indian master, Diego Quispe Tito, of a 17th century Corpus Christi procession that used to hang in the church of Santa Ana, insist on seeing them. Open Mon-Sat, 0830-1200, 1500-1730.

Museo Histórico Regional, in the Casa Garcilaso, Jirón Garcilaso y Heladeros tries to show the evolution of the Cuzqueño school of painting. Open 0800-1800. Contains Inca agricultural implements, colonial furniture and paintings, a small photographic exhibition and mementos of more recent times.

Astronomical Observatory at Km 3 on the road to Cachimayo, observations 1830-2300, viewpoint overlooking Cusco and the Sacred Valley. It has a pleasant restaurant which gives good views of Cusco while you are dining.

Festivals 24 Jun; pageant of Inti Raymi, the Inca festival of the winter solstice (Indians outnumber tourists) enacted at 1300 at the fortress of Sacsayhuamán, 2½ hrs, in Quechua. (Try to arrive in Cusco 15 days before Inti Raymi, there are many festivals, and get to Sacsayhuamán at about 1030 as even reserved seats fill up quickly.) Tickets for the stands can be bought a week in advance from the Municipalidad, and cost US$25, but standing places on the ruins are free (but be early and defend your space). Travel agents who try to persuade you to buy a ticket for the right to film or take photos are being dishonest. On the night before Inti Raymi, the Plaza de Armas is crowded with processions and food stalls. One week before the Inti Raymi, there is a dance festival in the village of Raqchi (**see also p 1233**).

20 Jan, procession of saints in San Sebastián district. Carnival at Cusco very basic; flour, water, cacti, bad fruit and animal manure thrown about in streets. On the Mon before Easter is the procession of El Señor de los Temblores (Lord of the Earthquakes), starting at 1600 outside the Cathedral. A large crucifix is paraded through the streets, returning to the Plaza de Armas around 2000 to bless the tens of thousands of people who have assembled there. 2-3 May, Vigil of the Cross, a boisterous fair. On Corpus Christi day (the Thur after Trinity Sunday, Jun) statues and silver are paraded through the streets; colourful, everyone gets drunk by 1000. The Plaza de Armas is surrounded by tables with Indian women selling *cuy* and a mixed grill called *chiriuchu* (*cuy*, chicken, *tortillas*, fish eggs, water-weeds, maize, cheese and sausage). **NB** Prices shoot up at end-Jul—Independence celebrations. Last Sun in Aug, Huarachicoy festival at Sacsayhuamán, a reenactment of the Inca manhood rite, performed in dazzling costumes by boys of a local school. On 8 Sep (day of the Virgin), there is a colourful procession of masked dancers from the church of Almudena, at the SW edge of Cusco, near Belén, to the Plaza de San Francisco. There is also a splendid fair at Almudena, and a free bull fight on the following day. On 14 Sep, local festival of El Señor de Huanca between Pisac and San Salvador (tourists should be very discreet at these celebrations, as they are not welcome—avoid pickpockets, too). 1 Nov, All Saints, celebrated everywhere with bread dolls and traditional cooking. 8 Dec is Cusco day: church and museums close at 1200. 24 Dec, Santo Rantikuy, "the buying of saints", "Christmas shopping, Cusco style", with a big crafts market in the plaza.

Security More police patrol the streets, trains and stations than in the past with some improvement in security, but one should still be vigilant. Look after your belongings, leaving valuables in safe keeping with hotel management, not in hotel rooms. Places in which to take care are: when changing money on the streets; in the railway and bus stations, the bus from the airport, the Santa Ana market (otherwise rec) and at out-of-the-way ruins. Also take special care during Inti Raymi. Avoid walking around alone at night on narrow streets, between the stations and the centre, or in the market areas.

Hotels Book more expensive hotels well in advance through a good travel agency, particularly for the week or so around 24 Jun when the Inti Raymi celebrations take place (prices are greatly increased at this time). Prices given are for the high season in Jun-Aug. When there are fewer tourists hotels may drop their prices by as much as half. Always check for discounts. On the Puno-Cusco train there are many hotel agents for medium-priced hotels; prices can often be negotiated down to F category, but it is best to pay the agent for one day only and then negotiate with hotel. Rooms offered at Cusco station are usually cheaper than those offered on the train. Agents also provide transport to the hotel, which can be invaluable when arriving at the dimly-lit station and since taxis are not supposed to enter the station yard. It is cold in Cusco, many hotels do not have heating. It is worth asking for an "estufa", a space heater which some places will provide for an extra charge. The whole city suffers from water shortages, hotels usually only have supplies in the mornings, so plan your day accordingly.

The best is **L3** *Libertador* (5-star), in colonial palace (Casa de los Cuatro Bustos) at Calle San Agustín 400, T 232601/231961, 28% tax, good, especially the service, but in Jul and Aug rooms in the older part of the hotel are cold and dark; **A1** *Cusco* Heladeros 150, T 224821, administered by Sociedad de Beneficencia Pública del Cusco, hot water, largest and best known, "old fashioned, not cheap and a little fusty", central; **A2** *Picoaga*, Sta Teresa, 344, T 227691, F (084) 659070, 70 rooms, central heating, private bathrooms, dining room, hot water does not always reach the older part of the building; **A2** *Royal Inca I*, Plaza Regocijo 299, T 231067, 3-star, bar, dining room, good service, rec; **A2** *Royal Inca II* on same street, larger and better; **A2** *San Agustín* (ex-*Alhambra*), Av Sol 594, T 238121, F 137375, incl breakfast, shower, TV, phone, credit cards taken, modern, very good, clean, safe, English spoken, very expensive to send fax; *El Dorado Inn*, Av Sol 395, T 233888/231232, F 240993, good but can be noisy in am, food good but expensive.

B/C category: *Conquistador*, Santa Catalina Angosta 149, T 224461, clean, safe, good; *Espinar*, Portal Espinar 142, T233091, old, comfortable, clean and helpful; **C** *Hostal Carlos V*, Tecseccocha 490, T 223091, with breakfast, has charm and character, but insecure, run down and restaurant poor.

D category: *El Inca*, Quera 251 (F in low season) clean, heating, hot water variable, luggage store, restaurant, breakfast incl, Wilbur speaks English, and is helpful, rec, noisy disco in basement till 0100; *Hostal Apu Wasi*, Pumacurco y Concepción, T 237249, colonial house, family run, Juan and Clemencia Machicao, big rooms, good views, laundry facility; *Hostal Cahuide*, Saphi 845, T 222771, discount for long stay, hot water in en suite bathrooms, good rooms, quiet, clean, good laundry service, storage facilities, helpful, café serving good value breakfasts, but strong box is insecure; *Hostal Colonial Palace*, Quera 270, friendly, stores luggage, rooms better on first floor, colonial courtyard; *Hostal Corihuasi*, Calle Suecia (not a safe street at night), T/F 232233, 4-room suites, colonial house, laundry arranged, hot water, quiet, rec; *Hostal Corregidor*, Plaza de Armas, T 232632, good; *Hostal El Arqueólogo* (room or dormitory), Ladrillos 425 not far from Sacsayhuamán (T 232569, not a safe street at night), hot water, helpful, French and English spoken, clean, will store luggage, garden, rec, cafetería and kitchen; *Hostal El Solar*, San Francisco 162, T 232451, in high season, E low, clean, rec; *Hostal Garcilaso*, Garcilaso de la Vega 233, T 233031, with bath, safe for luggage, clean, helpful, historic charm, rec; *Hostal Garcilosa II*, Garcilosa de la Vega 237, quiet, clean, bath, helpful; *Hostal Imperial Palace*, Calle Tecseccocha 492, T 223324, with breakfast, prices negotiable for longer stays, café, bar, restaurant, clean, a bit cold, but well furnished, English spoken, good, friendly, safe deposit open only 0700-1100; *Huaynapata*, Huaynapata 369, T 228034, small rooms, quieter rooms at the back, clean, family-run, hot water, stores luggage, friendly, rec; *Kristina*, Av Sol 341, T 227251, nice rooms, private bath, hot water, breakfast-restaurant, friendly, reliable, rec; *Loreto*, Pasaje Loreto 115, Plaza de Armas (triples available), clean, very friendly, rooms with Inca walls and electric heaters, cheap laundry service, great atmosphere (taxis and other travel can be arranged, Lucio here is a good guide), safe luggage deposit, rec, but dark; *Tambo*, Ayacucho 233, T 236788, clean, heating in rooms, laundry facilities, safe for luggage, rec, central, hot water (intermittent), restaurant fair; *Wiracocha*, Plaza de Armas, corner of Mantas (E low season), clean, hot water, rec, restaurant opens at 0600, good breakfast (Casilla 502).

E category: *Hostal Incawasi*, Plaza de Armas, T 238245, clean, good beds, bargain for long stays, helpful; *Hostal Residencial Rojas*, Tigre 129, hot water, safe, family run, clean; *Hostal San Blas*, Cuesta San Blas 526, T 225781, basic, a/c, friendly, secure for luggage; *Hostal Unión*, Unión 189, T 231580, 5 blocks Plaza de Armas, ½ block San Pedro market, shared bath, hot water, safe, laundry facilities, kitchen/café, luggage store, knowledgeable, helpful, rec; *Inca World*, Tecseccocha 474 (opp *Suecia II*), with bath and hot water, small restaurant, stores luggage, friendly, rec; *Los Marqueses*, Garcilaso 252, with bath, heaters extra, early colonial house, comfortable, rec, clean and convenient; *Mantas*, Calle Mantas 115 (nr Plaza de Armas), friendly, can leave luggage, run down, good meals; *Residencial Corihuasi*, Uriel García, good views over city, electric heaters in rooms; *Residencial Pakca Real*, Atocsaycuchi 705, T 837484, hot water all times, cooking and laundry facilities, TV, *Suecia*, Calle Suecia 332, shared rooms, uncomfortable beds, will store luggage, can use their bulletin board to arrange groups for the Inca trail; *Suecia II*, Calle Tecseccocha, without bath, rooms also with, good beds and blankets, clean, good security procedures, breakfast at 0500, US$1.50, beautiful building, meeting place for trekkers doing the Inca Trail, best to book if arriving on same day as Puno train, rec.

F/G category: It is almost impossible to find a double room for less than US$3; the cheapest price, in a rec hostal is US$2.50 pp. **F** *Hostal Bellavista*, Av Santiago 100, E with bath, hot water, very friendly, safe (10 mins' walk from centre, not a safe area at night), breakfast available, will store luggage, rec; **F** *Hostal Cáceres*, Plateros 368, 1 block from Plaza de Armas, luggage store, clean, friendly, rooms on street noisy, laundry service, can put motorcycle in patio; F *Hostal Familiar*, Saphi 661, with bath, cheaper without, efficient, cold, can leave luggage here but they charge/item, with expensive café (owner's sister Gloria works with Kantu Tours); F *Hostal Sapantiani*, Pumacurco 490, without bath, hot water sometimes, safe, clean, pleasant, family run; F *Imperio*, Calle Chaparro, run by Elena and family, also nr station, hot water, friendly, clean, noisy, motorcycle parking, safe to leave luggage, highly rec; F *Qorichaska*, Nueva Alta 521, T 228974, close to centre, clean, hot water, will store luggage, rec; F-G *Hostal Familiar Casa*, Pasaje España 844, T 224152, off Prado, quiet, friendly, safe, hot water, baggage store, laundry, rec; F-G *Hostal Royal Qosqo*, Tecseccocha 2, close to Plaza de Armas, safe, hot water sometimes; G *Hostal San Cristóbal*, Quiscapata 242, nr San Cristóbal, cooking and clothes-washing facilities, baggage deposit, views over city, very nice people, if everywhere full, Sra Ema de Paredes will let you spread a sleeping bag on the floor, rec.

Youth Hostel *Albergue Juvenil Centro de Convenciones Cusco*, Av Huayruropata 1861, in the suburb of Huanchac, T 234498, F 223339, US$4 pp incl breakfast, 20 mins' drive from the Plaza, rec.

Camping Not safe anywhere in the Cusco area. For renting equipment, there are several places around the Plaza area. Check the equipment carefully as it is common for parts to be missing. Some prices/day: tent US$3, sleeping bag US$2, stove US$3. A deposit is asked, US$100, credit card, plane ticket, etc. *Soqllaq'asa Camping Service*, owned by English-speaking Louis Aedo, at Plateros 189, T/F 222224, rec for equipment hire. White gas (*bencina*), US$1.50/litre, can be bought at hardware stores (check the purity); stove spirit (*alcoól para quemar*), at pharmacies; blue gas canisters, US$3, at some hardware stores and at shops which rent gear. You can also rent equipment through travel agencies. A shop with useful, imported (so expensive) camping gear: *Camping Deportes*, Centro Comercial Ollanta, Av del Sol 346, shop no 118; it also sells insect repellent, Deet, US$10 for a small bottle.

Restaurants International and local cuisine, expensive: For a good meal and décor try *Inti Raymi* in the *Libertador*; the restaurant at *El Dorado Inn*; *Mesón de los Espaderos*, Espaderos y Plaza de Armas, parrilladas, good; *Paititi*, Plaza de Armas, live music, good atmosphere, Inca masonry. *El Truco*, Plaza Regocijo, live music at dinner time.

Medium class, local cuisine: *Trattoria Adriano*, Calle Mantas y Av Sol (just off SE corner of Plaza de Armas), open for breakfast at 0700, Italian cuisine (fair) and great desserts, friendly but not cheap; *Peña Los Incas*, Plaza de Armas, good *menú* at lunchtime for US$3, *peñas* at night; *Pucara*, Plateros 309, Japanese run, highly rec, good meals throughout the day, pleasant atmosphere, try the chocolate cake, pottery, silver jewellery and designer alpaca sweaters for sale. Pizzerías: *Chez Maggy*, Plateros, good atmosphere, popular with tourists, live music nightly, pasta, soups, pizzas freshly baked in wood-burning oven, service sometimes slow; *El Corsario*, Plateros, same owner as *Chez Maggy*. *Briolo*, Plateros 324, good, friendly; *Pizzería America* and *Americana*, both on Plateros, highly rec; *Pizzería Wasi*, Procuradores 347, good pizzas, also meat dishes, helpful German owner; *Giorgios*, just off Plaza de Armas, clay oven pizzas.

Cheaper restaurants, local cuisine: *Royal Qosco*, Plateros 345, cheap, 3-course set meals, good soups and fish, rec; *Urpi*, Plateros 322, good, popular with locals; *Los Candiles*, Calle Plateros nr Plaza, set lunch US$1.20; *La Yunta*, Plaza de Armas, vegetarian, good salads, lunches and 40 types of juice, popular with gringos, same owners as *Instinct Travel Agency*, rec; *El Solar*, San Francisco, good lunch menu, rec; *Conde*, Plaza San Francisco 364, 24 hrs, rec; *Víctor Victoria*, Tigre 130, Italian and local cuisine, rec; *El Cuate*, Procuradores 386, Mexican food, rec; *La Retama*, on Maruri, nr *Hotel San Agustín*, friendly, folk music most nights; *Ama Lur*, Plaza de las Nazarenas 159, clean, cheap, varied menu, rec; *Chef Víctor*, Ayacucho 217, good food; *El Rey*, San Andrés and Almagro, trout and chicken, good and quiet; *El Mariño*, Espinar y Mantas, good seafood; *Tronquito* on Saphi, huge portions; *El Trujillo*, Matará, northern Peruvian specialities; *Restaurante de Picarones*, Ruinas. To try other local specialities, in the suburbs: *Quinta Zárate*, Calle Tortera Paccha, rec; *Quintas Eulalia*, Choquechaca 384 (closed Mon); also *Picantería La Chocla*, on Pumacurco.

Cafés and snackbars: *Café Huaylli* on Plateros, set lunch US$1.20, collects travellers' comments in their book 'The good, the bad and the ugly', good for views on guides, popular meeting place, especially for breakfast, has good snacks and "copa Huaylli"—fruit, muesli, yoghurt, honey and chocolate cake, also good vegetarian *menú*; *El Dragón San*, also on Plateros. *Wiracocha*, on Plaza in hotel of same name, excellent; *Ayllu*, Portal de Carnes 208, also on Plaza de Armas, open at 0600, Italian, classical/folk music, good atmosphere, has a superb range of milk products and wonderful apple pastries, try *leche asada*, good breakfast, quick service, rec; *Café Varayoc*, Espaderos 142, good meeting place, excellent coffee, pizzas and chocolate cake; *D'Anafrio*, Av Sol, ice cream and cakes; *July*, Garcilaso 270, good selection, delicious cakes; *Royal Inn*, Plaza San Francisco, enormous cakes; *Oasis*, Av Sol 453, new, good set lunch; *Misky Wasi*, Tigre 110, for breakfasts, snacks, excellent *pie de limón*; *El Mezón Real*, Sunterwasi 206, cheap, friendly, video snack bar. Vegetarian restaurant *Govinda*

(Hare Krishna), Esparderos 128, just off W corner of Plaza de Armas, sometimes good, always busy, slow service, cheese, ensalada de frutas, etc. *El Tordo*, Tordo 238, vegetarian, good value, also *Sol y Luna* on Garcilaso. The market place and street vendors are good places for a cheap bite to eat and for a taste of local food.

Local Specialities *Cuy*, roast stuffed guinea pig; *anticuchos*, roast beef hearts; *rocoto relleno*, spicy bell pepper stuffed with beef and vegetables; *adobo*, spicy pork stew; *chicharrones*, deep fried chunks of pork ribs and chicken; *lechón*, suckling pig; *choclo con queso*, corn on the cob with cheese; *tamales*, boiled corn dumplings filled with meat and wrapped in banana leaf; also *tamales dulces*, corn sweetened with sugar; *cancha*, toasted corn. Drinks, *chicha*, either a fruit drink or a fermented, mildly alcoholic corn beer; be careful, watch out for "bad" chicha. *Ponche*, hot milk with pisco.

Bars *Cross Keys Pub*, Plaza de Armas, Portal Confiturias 233, 1st Flr (look closely for sign), open 1800-0130, run by Barry Walker, a Mancunian, darts, great atmosphere, happy hour once or twice a night (1800 and 2000/2100), not for beer; *Tumis Video Bar*, Plateros 358A, good atmosphere, cheap drinks; *Ukukus*, Plateros 316, close to *Pizzería Americana*, live music, cheap drinks; *Ludwig Bar Beethoven*, Calle Plateros 325; *Kamikaze*, peña at 2200, folk and rock music, candle-lit cavern atmosphere, many gringos, entrance fee US$2.50, on San Juan de Dios, nr Sta Teresa (upstairs), T-shirts for sale, rec; *Keros*, Plaza de Armas, corner with Suecia, music with videos, cover charge US$5 incl 2 drinks; *Taberna Cusicusi*, E side of Plaza de Armas, nice atmosphere, reasonable prices, good music sometimes live; *Hocus Pocus Rock Café*, Plaza de Armas, good atmosphere, music and snacks. Also, *Las Quenas* in the basement of the *Hotel Savoy*, rec; *Chichería El Fogón*, good atmosphere, on Pumacurco.

Banks and Exchange The best places are the banks along Av del Sol, although it can be time-consuming and, in some cases, only at certain hours (not at weekends): **Banco de Crédito** is recommended for cash advances on Visa, TCs 1% commission to soles, 3% to dollars, wait up to 2 hrs; also **Banco de la Nación** and **Banco Continental**. For cash on Mastercard, **Banco del Sur** on Av Sol, with 3½% commission. If no bank will advance cash against Mastercard go to their office at Calle Garcilaso 214. Many travel agencies and *casas de cambio* change dollars; some of them change TCs as well, but with 4-5% commission. The street changers hang around Av de Sol, blocks 2-3, including Sun, will change TCs. In both banks and street check the notes.

Consulates US Agent, Olga Villa García, Apartado 949, Cusco, T 222183 or 233541. German, Sra Maria-Sophia Júrgens de Hermoza, San Agustín 307, T 235459, Casilla Postal 1128, Correo Central, Mon, Wed, Fri, 1100-1300, appointments may be made by phone, book exchange. French, Calle Espinar (M Jean Pierre Sallat, *Farmacia Vallenas*—may let French people leave luggage if going to Machu Picchu). British, Dr Raul Delgado, *Hotel San Agustín*, T 222322 or 231001, address above, he is also Austrian Consul. Finnish, Emmel 109, Yanahuara, T 223708.

Folklore Shows Regular nightly folklore show at Qosqo Native Art Centre, Av Sol 604, at 1830, entrance fee US$2-3; and at Teatro Inti Raymi, Saphi 605, nightly 1845, US$3 and well worth it. Local *peñas* at Peña Do Re Mi, on Plaza de Armas, and *Restaurant Los Incas*, also on Plaza de Armas. Teatro Municipal, Calle Mesón de la Estrella 149, T 227321 for information 0900-1300 and 1500-1900, a venue for plays, dancing, shows, mostly Thur-Sun; ask for their programmes.

Health *Hospital Regional*, Av de la Cultura, rec. If lab tests needed, Lab Pasteur, Tullumayo 768 is rec. *Dr Oscar Tejada* (PO Box 425, Cusco, T 233836 or 240449 day or night) is a member of the International Association for Medical Assistance to Travellers and is prepared to help any visitor in emergency, 24-hr attention; he charges according to that organization's scales (not expensive). *Dr Gustavo Garrido Juárez*, Matará 410, T 239761, English and French spoken. *Jaime Triveño*, T 225513, can be reached 24 hrs. **Dentists** Tomás Flores, T 222844; *Gilbert Espejo*, T 228074.

Language Classes Exel, Calle Cruz Verde 336, T 235298, Señorita Sori highly rec, US$3-4/hr; the school can arrange accommodation with local families.

Laundry Service at *Lavamatic*, Procuradores 341, US$1.20/kg, rec, laundry brought early am will be returned pm. *Lavanderías Splendor*, Suecia 328, just off Plaza de Armas (US$1/kg), will also dry clean sleeping bags, rucksacks etc. *Lavandería Incas*, Calle Ruinas, cheap, but can take 2-3 days. Also *Lavanderías Superchick*, Saphi 635, US$1.25 for 2 kg. **NB** In damp or overcast weather, allow plenty of time for clothes to be dried properly.

Post Office Principal one on Av del Sol, block 5, hrs Mon-Sat 0800-1900, 0800-1200 Sun and holidays. Stamps and postcards available. Sending packages from Cusco is not cheap, reliable or quick; much better to wait until Lima or La Paz. Poste restante, US$0.25/letter.

Telecommunications Intel, Av del Sol 386, for telephone, telex and fax, open Mon-Sat 0700-2000, 0700-1200 Sun and holidays. *Rin* (token) phones can be used daily until 2200. You can use *rines* for local calls, US$0.15 for 5 mins, national calls US$0.50 for 3 mins, international US$3 for 3 mins (there is often no refund for coins which "disappear"). Alternatively, go through the operator (long wait possible), deposit required, national call US$3, international US$12. Fax to Europe costs US$3.50/page; to receive a fax costs US$2/page, the number is (084) 241111.

Radio messages Radio Tawantinsuyo, Av del Sol 806, open Mon-Sat 0600-1900, Sun 0600-1600, messages are sent out between 0500 and 2100 (you can choose the time), in Spanish or Quechua, price/message US$1; this is sometimes helpful if things are stolen and you want them back. Radio Comercial, Av del Sol 457, of 406, T 231381, open daily 0900-1200, 1600-1900, for making contact with other radio-users in Cusco and the jungle area. Helpful if you wish to contact people in Manu; price US$1.50 for 5 mins.

Sauna at *Hotel Royal Inn II*, US$10, rec.

Local Crafts In the Plaza San Blas and the surrounding area, authentic Cusco crafts still survive. Wood workers may be seen in almost any street. Leading artisans who welcome visitors include: Hilario Mendivil, Plazoleta San Blas 634 (biblical figures from plaster, wheatflour and potatoes); Edilberta Mérida, Carmen Alto 133 (earthenware figures showing physical and mental anguish of the Indian peasant); Víctor Vivero Holgado, Tandapata 172 (painter of pious subjects); Antonio Olave Palomino, Siete Angelitos 752 (reproductions of precolumbian ceramics and colonial sculptures); Maximiliano Palomino de la Sierra, Triunfo 393 (festive dolls and wood carvings); Santiago Rojas, near San Blas (statuettes). Luis Aguayo Revollar, *Galería de Arte Aguayo*, Cuesta del Almirante 211-256, y Av Sol 616, T 237992, fine wood carvings. Museo Inca Art Gallery of Amílcar Salomón Zorrilla, Huancaro M-B—L8, T 231232 (PO Box 690), telephone between 0900 and 2100, contemporary art. Nemesio Villasante, Av 24 de Junio 415, T 222915, for Paucartambo masks. Miguel Chacón Ventura, Portal Confitería 265 (Plaza de Armas), for watercolour paintings.

Shopping Market opposite Estación San Pedro (which also has the name Santa Ana) is the best Indian market for a variety of goods, but although less self-conscious and less expensive than Pisac is not very interesting (best value at closing time or in the rain). Another good market on the corner of San Andrés and Quera. Mercado Artesanal, Av Sol, block 4, for cheap crafts. Coordinadora Sur Andina de Artesanía, Calle del Medio 130, off Plaza de Armas, good assortment of crafts and a non-profit organization; La Pérez, Urb Mateo Pumacahua 598, Huanchac, T 232186/222137, big cooperative, good selection, free pick-up from your hotel. Some travellers suggest Puno is better shopping value.

Cusco is the weaving centre of Peru, and excellent textiles can be found at good value. *Alpaca*, Calle Ruinas, genuine, 100% alpaca goods, but not cheap. *Artesanía La Paloma*, Cuesta San Blas 552 and Plazuela Sta Catalina 211, good but expensive; *Rafael Salazar Sucesores*, Plateros 305, for good quality alpaca. *Sr Aller*, Plaza Santo Domingo 261, sells interesting antiques. *Josefina Olivera*, Santa Clara 501, sells old ponchos and antique mantas, without usual haggling. There is a good jewellery store beside the Cathedral in the Plaza de Armas and art shop at *Instituto Americano de Arte*, Av Sol. Arto Ovaska from Finland and his Peruvian wife Edith have opened *Snow Shop*, Procuradores 347, for *artesanía*, posters, music etc. *Kaliran*, Cuesta San Blas 522, musical instruments, Andean music. Be very careful of buying gold and silver objects and jewellery in and around Cusco; we have received many reports of sharp practices. Cusco market said to be the cheapest for slide and print film, eg Fuji US$4.50.

Sacks to cover rucksacks are available in the market by Estación San Pedro for US$0.75.

Bookshops *Librería Studium*, Marqués Mantas 239, stocks guidebooks. *Los Andes*, Portal Comercio 125, Plaza de Armas, good range of books, large boxes of postcards.

Travel Agencies There are many travel agencies in Cusco. We divide them into two categories: a) the expensive, long-established, reliable, well-organized agencies, with English-speaking staff, and b) the cheaper, less reliable agencies which are always changing. Most tours have set prices, but the second category agencies will offer cheaper packages. Always check details before making arrangements, shop around and be aware that overcharging and failing to keep to arrangements are common, especially in the high season. One description of organized tours was, "degenerating into races around the various sites so that there is enough time to make an unannounced visit to a craft shop". Do not deal with guides who claim to be employed by agencies listed below without verifying their credentials (better to deal direct with the agencies). Seek advice from visitors returning from trips for the latest information. Beware also of tours which stop for long lunches at expensive hotels. In Cusco, its environs and Machu Picchu, check the standard of your guide's English (or whichever language is required) as some have no more than a memorized spiel.

Day tour Pisac-Ollantaytambo-Chinchero, US$15 pp including lunch (US$12 without); half-day tour visiting the four ruins around Cusco, US$5 pp, not including entrance fees; half-day city tours, US$3-3.50.

Category a) *Lima Tours*, Portal de Harinos 177, Plaza de Armas, T 238857/223874, F 221266, Amex representative, but only sells TCs, no exchange; also DHL office, to receive a parcel you pay 35% of the marked value of customs tax. *GaTur*, Puluchapata 140, T 223496, F 238645; *Explorandes*, Av del Sol, block 5, T 238380, F 233784, good equipment for rent; *Southern Cross Adventures*, Portal de Panes 123, of 301, on Plaza de Armas, T 237649, F 239447, manager Hugo Paullo, friendly, helpful, good for information, specializes in horseback trips; *APU Expediciones*, Portal Comercio 157, Plaza de Armas, PO Box 24, T 235408/235061, F 241111, adventure tours and river trips, mountaineering expeditions with good equipment, nature tours and packages to Manu National Park, Tambopata and other jungle areas, transport facilities, guide Mariella Bernasconi Cilloniz highly rec; *Tambo Treks*, Atocsaycuchi 589, Plaza San Blas, T 237718, adventure trips. *Peruvian Andean Treks*, Av Pardo 705, T 225701, manager Tom Hendrikson, adventure tours; *Kinjyo Travel Service*, Portal de Panes 101, Plaza de Armas, T 231101, F 239044.

Category b) *Luzma Tours*, Portal Confituría 241, Plaza de Armas, T 235370, F 236229, good for information, helpful, friendly, rec, manager Luz-Marina. *Kantu Tours*, Portal Carrizos 258, T 221381, F 232012, rec for local tours, competitive, offers good horse treks around Cusco (US$10 for 6 hrs), experience not necessary, but sun protection is, manager Gloria Hermosa Tapiá speaks good English. *Snow Tours*, Portal de Panes 109, office 204, T241313, managed by Edith Bellota Guzmán, local tours, Inca Trail, climbing, Manu, etc, camping equipment hired; *Río Bravo*, Almagro 120 (off Av Sol), T232301, white water rafting specialists; *American Tours*, Portal de Panes 123, of 306, Plaza de Armas, T 227208; *Instinct*, Procuradores 107, T 233451, Benjamín and Juan Muñil, river trips, mountain bike hire, rec; *Inti Tours*, Av del Sol, block 6, T 226541; *Orquídeas Tours*, Portal Comercio, Plaza de Armas T 232137, manager Zoilo Vergara, adventure trips; *Coopse Tour*, Plaza de Armas, Portal Comercio 141, T 231515, Luis Guillén Pinelo is an excellent, reliable guide with a blue Cadillac (T 224385/223876), helpful in all situations, or Edith; *Ecotours*, Helaredos 150, T 231288, reliable and competitively priced; *Tambo Lodge*, Plateros 351, T 236159, Julio Vargas Vega, friendly, rec. The following are 1994-95 recommendations, all on Plaza de Armas: *Naty's Travel*, Inca Trail (check the tents), river rafting, guides Edison, Lorenzo, Efraín, César and María; *Jaguar*, Inca Trail; *Río Sul*, river rafting; *Explores Transporte*, Portal Comercio 157, T 233498, F 225562, tours and 4WD vehicle hire. Also *United Mice*, Plateros 328, T 236919, Inca Trail. River rafting trips cost on average US$20 pp.

Recommended private guides, divided into two groups: c) classic, standard tours, and d) adventure trips. All of those listed speak English. Set prices: city tour US$15/day; trekking, Machu Picchu and other ruins US$30/day. Private guides can be contacted through tour companies.

Category c) **Amalia Escobar**, T 222258, also does trekking. **Juana Pancorbo**, Av Los Pinos D-2, T 227482. **Haydee Mogrovejo**, T 221907; **Marco Arragón**, T 233733; **Boris Carnas**, T 221482; **Wilbert Yáñez**, T 232511; **Elisha García**, T 237916; **Satoshi Shinoda**, T 227861 and **Michiko Nakazahua**, T 226185, both Japanese-speaking guides; **Victoria Morales Condori**, San Juan de Dios 229, T 235204; **David Quintana**, T 225757 (or through SAS Travel, Plaza de Armas 109, Portal Belén, T 224247), speaks English; **Rubén Huallapuma**, works out of *Hostal Garcilaso*, very knowledgeable about Inca civilization, flexible. Fredy Palacios Paiva, T 240281/239716, English-speaking Luís Guillén Pinelo, T 224385.

Category d) **Aurelio Aguirre**, T 232797; **Darwin Camacho**, T 233884; **Manuel Luna**, T 226083; **Pieter Bohn**, T 234234, German; **Gunther Hane**, T 237916; **Marco Pérez**, T 227414; **Roger Valencia**, T 281130; **Tino Aucca**, Urb Titio Q-1-13 Wanchaq, T 235850, a biologist studying the birds of the Polylepis forest. **David Espejo**, T 238323, or via Pantiacolla Tours on Plateros, does the Inca Trail, good English.

Tourist Office New tourist office on Av del Sol, exact address unknown at time of going to press. Empresa Turística Regional Inka SA, Emturin, Portal Belén 115, on Plaza de Armas, T 223339, F (0051-84) 223239, does not deal in city matters, but books rooms at government-run hotels (for Machu Picchu, get written confirmation by fax), open Mon-Sat 0930-1300, 1500-1800. Ministry of Tourism, Av Manco Capac 1020, 4th Flr, Huanchac, T 233701/232347, Mon-Fri 0800-1300. Hotline for complaints, T 240290. The University is also a good source of information, especially on archaeological sites. They sell good videos of Cusco and surroundings.

Automóvil Club del Perú, Av Sol, has some maps. Motorists beware; many streets end in flights of steps not marked as such. Very few good maps of Cusco available.

Maps of the city, the Inca Trail and the Urubamba Valley are available at tour companies. There are lots of information booklets on Machu Picchu and the other ruins at the bookshops.

The best book on Cusco, the Sacred Valley, Inca Trail, Machu Picchu and other ruins is *Exploring Cusco*, by Peter Frost; available in Cusco bookshops. Also recommended for general information on Cusco is *Cusco Peru Tourist Guide*, published by Lima 2000. *The Sacred Center*, by Johan Reinhard, explains Machu Picchu in archaeological terms. *Apus and Incas*, by Charles Brod, describes cultural walks in and around Cusco, and treks in the Cordilleras Vilcabamba, Vilcanota and Urubamba, plus the Manu National Park (2nd edition, Inca Expeditions, 2323 SE 46th Avenue, Portland, OR 97215, USA, US$10.95 plus US$1.50 postage, or from bookshops in N America, Europe and Peru).

Asociación de Conservación para la Selva Sur, ACSS, Comercial Los Ruiseñores, Portal de Panes 123, of 305, T/F 240911, for information and free video shows about Manu National Park, Tambopata-Candoma Reserve. Friendly and helpful. Also for programmes and research in the jungle area of Madre de Dios. Distributors of the expensive (US$75), but beautiful book on the Manu National Park by Kim MacQuarrie and André Bartschi.

Police Tourist police, Matará, 4th block, no phone. When you require assistance they are helpful. If you need a *denuncia* (a report for insurance purposes), available from the Banco de la Nación, they will type it out. Always go to the police when robbed, even though it will cost you a bit of time. They will investigate the complaint, they have been known to question and search travellers (incl their rooms) in an intimidating fashion. Stolen cameras often turn up in the local market and can be bought back cheaply; remember the man selling them is not the thief. If you can prove that the camera is yours, contact the police. National Police, Calle Saphi, block 4.

There have been reports of policemen (including tourist police) asking foreigners to post packages to Europe for them. On no account comply with such a request.

Taxis Taxis in Cusco are inexpensive and recommended when arriving by air, train or bus. They have fixed prices: in the centre US$1; to the suburbs US$1.25; to the airport US$3. Trips to Sacsayhuamán US$10; to the ruins of Tambo Machay US$15, 3 hrs; for a whole day trip US$40. Recommended taxi drivers: José Cuba, Urb Santa Rosa, Pasaje R Gibaja 182, T 226179, who is a guide and can organize tours, accommodation as necessary, he speaks English, his daughter Alejandra is a multilingual tour guide; he parks at the airport during flight hours and at the station to await train arrival. Angel Salazar, Saguán del Cielo B-11, T 224597 to leave messages, English speaking, highly rec, helpful, arranges good tours. José G Valdivia Díaz, T 222210, not an official guide but recommended as knowledgeable and helpful. Ferdinand Pinares Cuadros, Yuracpunco 155, Tahuantinsuyo, T 225914, English, French and German spoken, rec, reasonable prices. Taxis on call, reliable but expensive, in the centre US$1.25, to the airport US$3.50: Radio Car T 222222; El Dorado, T 221414.

Motorcycle mechanics Eric and Antonio Aranzábal, Ejercicios 202, highly recommended for repairs, also Autocusa, Av de la Cultura 730 (Sr Marco Tomaycouza), T 240378/239054.

Tourist Transport To rent a minibus for the day costs US$80 (US$40 for half a day), including guide (less without guide), maximum 10 people: *Gardenias Tours*, José Castillo, T 222828, tours around Cusco; *Orellana*, Edilberto Orellana, T 239167/225996, tours around Cusco; *Chinchero Tours*; *Explorers Transporte*, Calle Plateros 345, T 233498, to all places in Peru.

Air A new airport at Quispiquilla is in use. To **Lima**, 1 hr, US$76 one way, daily flights with Faucett, AeroPerú, Americana, Aero Continente (US$51). Grupo Ocho (military) flies once a week, about half the regular fare. Flights are heavily booked on this route in the school holidays (Jan-Feb) and national holidays.

To **Arequipa**, 35 mins, US$45 with Faucett, 4 a week, Americana and Aero Continente daily, Expreso Aéreo 6 a week. To **Juliaca**, US$42, Americana daily, Faucett 3 a week, AeroPerú twice. To **Tacna**, Aero Continente daily. To **Puerto Maldonado**, 45 mins, daily with Americana, US$35, AeroPerú 4 a week. Grupo Ocho has 2 flights a month, US$15, via Iberia from which there is a day season route to Brazil (**see under Iñapari, p 1249**). As well as the above flights, Americana has daily connections from Cusco to Pucallpa, Iquitos, Trujillo, Chiclayo and Piura. Americana office, Portal de Harinas 175, Plaza de Armas, T 231373. Special deals may be available if buying tickets for more than one person.

To **La Paz**, AeroPerú 3 times a week, US$110.

Airport tax US$7. Airport information T 222611/222601. Taxi to and from airport US$2.50 (US$3.50 by radio taxi). Colectivos US$0.20 from Plaza San Francisco or outside the airport car park. You can book a hotel at the airport through a travel agency, but this is not really necessary. Many representatives of hotels and travel agencies operate at the airport, with transport to the hotel with which they are associated. Take your time to choose your hotel, at the price you can afford. The airline offices are all on the Plaza de Armas: Americana T 231966; Faucett T 233151; AeroPerú T 233051.

Warning Cusco-Lima, high possibility of cancelled flights during wet season; tourists sometimes stranded for several days. Possible for planes to leave early if weather is bad. Sit on right side of aircraft for best view of mountains when flying Cusco-Lima; it is worth checking in early to get these seats. Both Faucett and AeroPerú are unreliable on bookings. You must reconfirm your tickets personally in the last 24 hrs and only in Cusco; you cannot do it in another city (don't trust an agency to do this for you). Even then you cannot be sure of a seat. Baggage is often lost en route.

Rail There are two stations in Cusco. To Juliaca, for the Arequipa and Puno services, from Av Sol station. Arriving in Cusco: a tourist bus meets the train to take visitors to hotels whose touts offer rooms on the train. Machu Picchu trains leave from Estación San Pedro, opposite the market.

The train to **Juliaca** leaves at 0800 daily, arriving at about 2100, sit on left. See under Juliaca for details on the splitting of the train and services to **Arequipa** and **Puno**; also for description of the three classes of travel. A popular choice is 1st class to Juliaca and then pullman to Arequipa; this will involve changing carriages in Juliaca. Always check on whether the train is running, especially in the rainy season, when services can be reduced or completely cancelled. Fares: Cusco-Puno, 2nd class US$10, 1st class US$13, pullman US$17; Cusco-Arequipa, 2nd class US$16, 1st class US$20, pullman US$30, 23 hrs. Tickets are sold one day in advance, open Mon-Sat 0700-1230, 1430-2100, Sun 0900-1200. Tickets sell out quickly and there are queues from 0400 before holidays in the dry season. You can buy tickets through a travel agent (check date and seat number). Meals are served on the train US$2.50.

Warning See under Arequipa, but note that 1st class Cusco-Puno is much emptier than Puno-Cusco and therefore more liable to theft.

To Anta, Ollantaytambo, Machu Picchu and Quillabamba, **see p 1237, 1241** and **p 1243**.

Roads and Buses Most bus offices are in Calle Pachacútec. To **Juliaca**, 344 km, 12 hrs (longer in the rainy season), US$8, a few buses and trucks do this route daily. The route is in very poor condition since it is not as well-used as the railway. When the train is not running it is necessary to go by bus, but even buses do not run after heavy rain. Check on weather conditions in advance. Continuing to **Puno**, 44 km from Juliaca, 45 mins, US$0.65 (Cruz del Sur, Calle Pachacútec, Cusco-Puno); see under Puno for more details and routes to La Paz. A tourist bus to Puno in the daytime is worth paying the extra for the views. It is not recommended to take a night bus to Juliaca or Puno, robberies occur on this route. To **Arequipa**, 521 km, 15-20 hrs, US$10-14, road described under Arequipa, not recommended in the wet because of landslides. Buses mostly at night, can be very cold, take a blanket. See under Arequipa and the relevant sections for continuation to Nazca and Lima. Most buses to **Lima** go via Arequipa, 36 hrs, eg Cruz del Sur, 1600, US$16, others cheaper.

To **Abancay**, 195 km, 7 hrs (longer in the rainy season), US$7, several buses and trucks daily from Av Areopata, eg Transcusal 0600, 1000, 1300; on to **Andahuaylas**, 135 km, 5$\frac{1}{2}$ hrs minimum, US$4.50 (you have to change bus in Abancay), and on to **Ayacucho**, 252 km, 16 hrs (again longer in the wet), US$5-7.50. Road conditions very poor, but scenery spectacular. There are many police checks; the area had terrorist problems 1989-1992, but the situation seems to have improved and there is more military control. It is still not a safe route, so check before going. From Abancay to **Nazca**, 464 km, 20 hrs, US$14, daily buses and trucks. The route goes via Puquio and is in bad shape; Expresso Cusco, Av Grau 820, 3 times a week, US$20, can be up to 2$\frac{1}{2}$ days, many military checkpoints, but some stunning scenery. Seek advice before taking this route to the coast. There are direct buses from Cusco to Lima.

For buses to the Sacred Valley and to the South Eastern Jungle, see the relevant sections below.

There is some magnificent walling in the ruined cult centre of **Sacsayhuamán**, on a hill in the northern outskirts, which is within walking distance (about $\frac{1}{2}$ hr walk, tiring because of the altitude). Take steps to San Cristóbal church. The Incaic stones are bigger and even more impressive than at Machu Picchu; huge rocks weighing up to 130 tons are fitted together with absolute perfection; three walls run parallel for over 360m and there are 21 bastions. Sacsayhuamán was thought for centuries to be a fortress, but the layout and architecture suggest a great sanctuary and temple to the Sun, which rises exactly opposite the place previously believed to be the Inca's throne—which was probably an altar, carved out of the solid rock: broad steps lead to it from either side. The hieratic, rather than the military, hypothesis was supported by the discovery in 1982 of the graves of priests: they would have been unlikely to be buried in a fortress. Zig-zags in the boulders round the "throne" are apparently "*chicha* grooves", channels down which maize beer flowed during festivals. Up the hill is an ancient rock slide for children, the Rodadero; near it are many seats cut perfectly into smooth rock. (Open daily 0700-1730.)

The temple and amphitheatre of **Qenqo**, with excellent examples of Inca stone carving, especially inside the large hollowed-out stone that houses an altar, are along the road from Sacsayhuamán to Pisac, past a radio station. On the same road are **Cusillyuioc** (K'usilluyuq), caves and Inca tunnels in a hillside (take a torch/flashlight), the Inca fortress of **Puka Pukara** (magnificent views) and the spring shrine of **Tambo Machay**, which is in excellent condition; water still flows by a hidden channel out of the masonry wall, straight into a little rock pool traditionally known as the Inca's bath, but he would have had to be a pygmy to have used it as such. It seems much more likely that the site was a centre of a water cult. Taking a guide to these sites is a good idea and visit in the morning for the best photographs.

The gates open daily from 0700-1730, but you can get in earlier if you wish and definitely try to get there before midday when the tour groups arrive. Carry your multi-site ticket, there are roving ticket inspectors. You can visit the sites on foot, a pleasant walk through the countryside requiring half a day or more. Take water and sun protection. Watch out for dogs. An alternative is to take the Pisac bus up to Tambo Machay (US$0.35) and walk back. Another excellent way to see the ruins is on horseback, arranged at travel agencies (eg with Hipólito, US$16 pp for 5 hrs). An organized tour (with guide, make sure you ask for English-speaking if you need it) will go to all the sites for US$6 pp, not including entrance fees. A taxi will charge US$15-20 (3-4 people).

Warning Robbery has occurred at the ruins, especially to those wandering around alone and to those who go to see them under a full moon. Take as few belongings as possible, hide your camera in a bag and go in a group. Keep an eye on people around you.

Cusco is at the W end of the gently sloping Cusco valley, which stretches 32 km E as far as Huambutío. This valley, and the partly isolated basin of Anta, NW of Cusco, are densely populated. Also densely populated is the Urubamba valley, stretching from Sicuani (on the railway to Puno) to the gorge of Torontoi, 600m lower, to the NW of Cusco.

There are many interesting villages and ruins in the Cusco valley itself. **Tipón** ruins, between the villages of Saylla and Oropesa, include baths, terraces, irrigation systems and a temple complex, accessible from a path leading from just above the last terrace, all in a fine setting. **Oropesa** church contains a fine ornately carved pulpit. **Huacarpay**: ruins of the Inca town of Kañaracy, well-preserved, are nearby, reached from a path behind the Albergue. The site is on a big lake, with the *Albergue Urpicáncha* on the shore, accommodation and restaurant. This is a popular place with locals at weekends. At **Lucre**, 3 km from Huacarpay, there is an interesting textile mill, and many unexplored ruins; ask the local history teacher, Sr Hernán Flores Yávar, for details. About 3 km from Huacarpay is **C El Dorado Inn**, in a converted monastery, some of the rooms in a remarkable style, very good service. Also nearby are the Huari (pre-Inca) adobe wall ruins of **Piquillacta**, the monkey temple and the wall of Rumicolca. Piquillacta is quite large, with some reconstruction in progress. Buses to Urcos from Av Huáscar will drop you at the entrance on the N side of the complex (this is not the official entry); walk through to the official entry and continue to Rumicolca on the other side of the highway. (Open daily 0700-1730.)

Andahuaylillas is a village 32 km S of Cusco, with a particularly fine early 17th century church; beautiful frescoes, splendid doorway and a gilded main altar (ask for Sr Eulogio, good guide, Spanish only). Taxis go there as does Oropesa bus (Av Huáscar, Cusco) via Tipón, Piquillacta and Rumicolca. There are other unexcavated ruins just beyond Andahuaylillas.

Huaro has a church whose interior is covered entirely with colourful mural painting. **Cusipata**, with an Inca gate and wall, is where the ornate bands for the decoration of ponchos are woven; close by is the Huari hilltop ruin of Llallanmarca. **Tinta**, 23 km from Sicuani, has a church with brilliant gilded interior and an interesting choir vault. Hotel: **F Casa Comunal**, dormitory accommodation, clean with good food. Frequent buses and trucks to Cusco, or take the train from Cusco.

Raqchi is the scene of the region's great folklore festival in mid-Jun. Take a bus or truck from Cusco towards Sicuani, US$1.50. At this festival dancers come to Raqchi from all over Peru; through music and dance they illustrate everything from the ploughing of fields to bull fights.

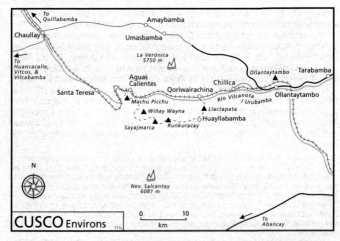

CUSCO Environs

John Hemming adds: The Viracocha temple is just visible from the train, looking from the distance like a Roman aqueduct. What remains is the central wall (adobe above, Inca masonry below) of what was probably the largest roofed building ever built by the Incas. On either side of the high wall, great sloping roofs were supported by rows of unusual round pillars, also of masonry topped by adobe (entrance US$2). Nearby is a complex of barracks-like buildings and round storehouses. This was the most holy shrine to the creator god Viracocha, being the site of a miracle in which he set fire to the land—hence the lava flow nearby. There are also small Inca baths in the corner of a field beyond the temple and a straight row of ruined houses by a square. The landscape is extraordinary, blighted by huge piles of black volcanic rocks.

Pacarijtambo is a good starting point for the 3-4 hrs' walk to the ruins of Maukallaqta, which contain good examples of Inca stonework. From there, one can walk to ***Pumaorca***, a high rock carved with steps, seats and a small puma in relief on top; below are more Inca ruins. From Cusco, buses and trucks to Pacarijtambo take 4 hrs, US$2. One may seek lodging for the night in Pacarijtambo at the house of the Villacorta family and leave for Cusco by truck the next morning. On the way back, one passes the caves of Tambo Toco, where the legend says that the four original Inca brothers emerged into the world.

Acomayo is a pretty village (***Pensión Aguirre***), which has a chapel with mural paintings of the fourteen Incas. From Acomayo, one can walk to Huáscar, 1 hr, and from there to Pajlia; a climb which leads through very impressive scenery. The canyons of the upper Apurímac are vast beyond imagination, great cliffs drop thousands of metres into dizzying chasms and huge rocks balance menacingly overhead. The ruins of Huajra Pucará lie near Pajlia; they are small, but in an astonishing position. John Hemming adds that the church at ***Checacupe*** is very fine, with good paintings and a handsome carved altar rail. To Acomayo, take a Cusco-Sicuani bus or truck, US$1, 1½ hrs, then a truck or bus to Acomayo, 3 hrs, same price; alternatively, alight at Checacupe and take a truck on to Acomayo.

76 km from Cusco on the Abancay road, 2 km before Limatambo (accommodation in **F** *Albergue*; nice restaurant hidden from road by trees), at the ruins of ***Tarahuasi***, a few 100m from the road, is a very well-preserved **Inca temple platform**, with 28 tall niches, and a long stretch of fine polygonal masonry. The ruins have grandeur, enhanced by the orange lichen which give the walls a beautiful honey colour. "The ruins at Tarahuasi were part of the Inca *tanpu* called 'Limatambo' in the 16th century, along the road to the famous Apurímac bridge. The lands immediately surrounding the *tanpu* were then claimed by a son of Inca Huayna Capac, Cristóbal Paullu Inca and his wife, Doña Catalina Tocto Usica. The extent of Inca agricultural terraces in the valley of Limatambo and Mollepata exceeds 100 hectares" (Dr Ken Heffernan, Turner, ACT, Australia).

100 km from Cusco along the Abancay road is the exciting descent into the Apurímac canyon, near the former Inca suspension bridge that inspired Thornton Wilder's *The Bridge of San Luis Rey*. Also, 153 km along the road to Abancay from Cusco, near Curahuasi, famous

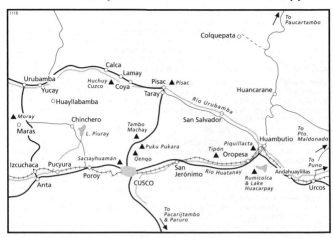

for its anise herb (restaurant on main road into town; camping possible on the football pitch, ask police), is the stone of **Sahuite**, carved with animals, houses, etc, which appears to be a relief map of an Indian village. (Unfortunately, "treasure hunters" have defaced the stone.) There are other interesting carvings in the area around the Sahuite stone.

Pisac, 30 km N of Cusco, is at the bottom of the Urubamba valley; high above it, on the mountainside, is a superb Inca fortress (admission by combined entrance ticket, **see p 1224**, or US$1.25, the ruins are open daily 0700-1730). The masonry is better than at Machu Picchu, the terraces more extensive and better preserved. When you climb it (a must), remember that there are 3 hill fortifications, but the third is the fortress proper, in which the actual temple is built: so go on to it and get the glorious view from the top. There is a 10-km motor road up to the level of the ruins, upstream from Pisac town and then up a valley to the S of the spur containing the ruins. From the parking lot, enter along Inca roads and through Inca gates, seeing the fine view of terraces (which can be reached quite easily from the town by a footpath starting from the main square beside the church, local boys will guide you US$0.50/couple). Quite a lot of walking is involved. The central part of the ruins is the Intihuatana group of temples and rock outcrops in the most magnificent Inca masonry. Above on the hilltop reached by a path along a vertiginous cliff are residential groups; there is a large Inca cemetery in caves on the valley opposite to the N; the curving group of houses called Pisallacta below the Intihuatana group; and more buildings, some with curious round towers, others of good Inca adobe, on the steep hillside above the town. There is a path going right round the mountain, behind the main ruins; it has two tunnels. Allow 1½ hrs to get up, 2-3 hrs to see the sites and 1½ hrs to descend slowly. It takes 2½ hrs to walk from the parking lot back to Pisac. Taxi to ruins US$5; colectivo US$0.70. You can also hire rather poor horses to take you up to the ruins, although the price is usually one way. On the plaza in Pisac is a small, interesting Museo Folclórico.

Pisac has a Sun morning market, described as touristy and expensive, coming to life after the arrival of tourist buses around 1000; arriving earlier may prove pointless; it is usually over by 1500. There are picturesque Indian processions to a Quechua Mass. Pisac has other, somewhat less crowded, less expensive markets on Tues and Thur morning, best to get there before 0900. You can take in the market, then take taxi up to ruins, explore them, walk down and get last bus or truck back to Cusco by 2000. It is reported that transport to the ruins is not always available for those not in a tour group. You can continue the Sun morning tour to Pisac along the Urubamba to Ollantaytambo, with lunch at the Tourist Hotel in Urubamba but tours from Cusco usually allow only 1½ hrs at Pisac: not enough time to take it in. Splendid scenery. Apart from Sun when Pisac is crowded, there are very few tourists. If not interested in the market, ask the driver to do the tour clockwise, Chinchero, Ollantaytambo, then Pisac, thereby missing the crowds. An alternative for lunch is the restaurant on the square in Yukay (see under Urubamba). The tour by taxi costs US$45-50. Good walks along river to Inca terraces.

Hotels   F *Hotel Pisac*, one block from plaza, recently renovated; **F** *Residencial Beho*, Calle Intihuatana 642, at bottom of path to ruins, shared bath, clean, cold water between 0600 and 0800 only, very basic, clean, rec, has crafts shop. The woman who owns the flour mill rents rooms for US$1.30 pp. *Restaurant Roma* opp the Cusco bus stop. Reasonable restaurant, *Samana Wasi*, on the plaza. Fresh bread (filled with ham and cheese) available on Sun from the oven *(el horno)* just off the plaza.

Buses to the Urubamba (Sacred) Valley   The road from Cusco to Ollantaytambo, via Pisac, is paved. It climbs from Cusco to the pass, continues over the pampa before descending into the Urubamba valley. It crosses the Vilcanota river by bridge at Pisac and follows the river to the end of the paved road at Ollantaytambo. There is always transport, and it is always full.

From Cusco to Pisac, 32 km, 1 hr, US$0.50; to Calca, 18 km, 30 mins, US$0.10; to Urubamba a further 22 km, 45 mins, US$0.40. Colectivos, minibuses and buses leave from the corner of Av Garcilaso and Av Tacna whenever they are full, between 0600 and 1600; also trucks and pick-ups. An organized tour can be fixed up anytime with a travel agent, US$5 pp. Taxis charge about US$25 round trip.

From Urubamba to Calca, Pisac and Cusco, about 2 hrs, US$1. Buses leave Urubamba from Calle M Castilla, third block (main street), when full, between 0700 and 1800. In Pisac transport stops at the bridge; last transport around 1800. Don't wait until the last bus as it is always full. Bus stops are brief; make sure you get on and off quickly.

From Urubamba to Ollantaytambo, 18 km, 45 mins, US$0.30. Buses leave from the petrol station on the main road when full between 0700 and 1900, or from the market Wed, Fri and Sun. From Ollantaytambo transport leaves from the Plaza for Urubamba.

From Cusco to Chinchero, 23 km, 45 mins, US$0.45; to Urubamba a further 25 km, 45 mins, US$0.45 (or US$0.75 Cusco-Urubamba direct). Colectivos, minibuses and buses leave from Calle Arcopata in Cusco when full; also from the same place as buses from Cusco via Pisac. Again tours can be arranged to Chinchero, Urubamba and Ollantaytambo with a Cusco travel agency. To Chinchero US$6 pp; taxi US$25 round trip. Usually only day tours are organized for visits to the valley; see under **Travel Agencies**. Using public transport and staying overnight in Ollantaytambo or Pisac will allow much more time to see the ruins and markets.

Calca, 2,900m, is 18 km beyond Pisac (there are a couple of very basic hotels: one opposite the market place, 1 block from the plaza, **G** *Hostal Martín*, dirty, cold water only, and **E** *Hostal Pitusiray*, on the edge of town. Some basic restaurants around the plaza). Mineral baths (cold) at Minas Maco (½ hr walk along the Urubamba) and Machacancha (8 km E of Calca). If one continues past Minas Maco, one bears right up a small footpath leading by a clump of trees; the first house one comes to after crossing a small stream and climbing a hill is a precolumbian ruin. 3 km beyond Machacancha are the Inca ruins of Arquasmarca. The ruins of a small Inca town, Huchuy Cusco, are across the river Vilcanota, and up a stiff climb, 3 to 4 hrs. There are a two-storey house, paved with flat stones, and a large stone reservoir at Huchuy Cusco. It is a two-day hike from Cusco to Calca, via Sacsayhuamán, Qenqo, Puka Pukará, Tambo Machay and Huchuy Cusco with excellent views of the Eastern Cordilleras, past small villages and along beautifully built Inca paths. There are many places to camp, but take water.

Zurite is a little-known village N of Cusco; Inca terraces of Patapata are only about an hour's walk from the village's main square. The construction of these terraces represents a Herculean effort as all of the earth is said to have been brought from elsewhere. A canal was built to bring water from the mountains. (John Streather.)

Chinchero (3,762m); with an attractive church built on an Inca temple (the church is only open Sun); recent excavations there have revealed many Inca walls and terraces. (On combined entrance ticket, **see p 1224**, open daily 0700-1730.) It has become tourist-oriented but nonetheless the Sun market and Indian mass are more authentic than at Pisac. The food market and the handicraft market are separate:

the food market is held every day, on your left as you come into town; the crafts market, Sun only, is up by the church, small by attractive. On any day except Sun there are few tourists. Celebrations are held in Chinchero on 8 Sep (the day of the Virgin). **F** *Hotel Inca*, with restaurant.

There is a scenic path from Chinchero to Urubamba, with fine views of the peaks of the Urubamba range, 3-4 hrs. Follow the old Chinchero-Urubamba dirt road, to the left of the new paved road. Ask the locals when you are not sure. It runs over the pampa, with a good view of Chinchero, then drops down to the Urubamba valley. Just before the river, the path joins the main road and crosses the Urubamba river by bridge.

Urubamba (2,863m) is N of Chinchero, on a new direct road from Cusco via Chinchero; pleasant country surroundings. Local crafts include pottery; workshops can be visited.

Hotels and Restaurants A3 *Centro Vacacional Urubamba*, 5 mins' walk from town, cabins (some with kitchen, must take own stove), sports facilities, 2 pools, good value restaurant with set menu, under new management in 1995, helicopter flights to Macchu Pichu (US$59-125). **C** *Hostal Turkesa*, with antique furniture and swimming pool, 20 mins' walk from town, rec, friendly, accommodating, will help with any problems, very clean and well-stocked restaurant and bar, even in low-season, car can be parked in locked patio; **D** *Hostal Urpihuasi*, C pp with full board, pleasant modern rooms, clean, friendly, outdoor pool, sauna, quiet and relaxing, rec (manager Rae Pieraccini runs a project for street children, financed by the hotel's income). In the town of Urubamba: **F** *Hostal Urubamba*, Bolognesi, basic, pleasant, cold water, rec; **F** *Hostal Vera*, on main road, down from the petrol station, with bath, cold water, basic, friendly, restaurant. Lots of restaurants on the main road and on Calle Castillo. *Casa Grande* opp *Hostal Turkesa*, tourist place, buffet US$4 pp; *Quinta Ollanta*, 10 mins' walk from town, basic, clean, rec; *Restaurant Quinta los Geranios*, excellent lunch for US$3 with more than enough food; *Quinta Galu*, close to Plaza, large, reasonable, friendly, good; unnamed restaurant, Comercio 337, good, cheap. *Picantería Chepita*, 1 de Mayo Pintacha, 5 mins from the main square, rec.

3 km E of Urubamba is **Yukay** with an open-air restaurant on the square, good buffet and local dishes. On the N side of the square is the adobe palace built for Sayri Túpac (Manco's son) when he emerged from Vilcabamba in 1558. Opposite is the restored colonial church of Santiago Apóstol, with its oil paintings and fine altars, next to a pleasant old hotel, the **B** *Alhambra III*, very pretty. In Yukay monks sell fresh milk, ham, eggs and other dairy produce from their farm on the hillside.

Joanna Codrington writes: 6 km from Urubamba on the Ollantaytambo road is the village of **Tarabamba**, where a bridge crosses the Río Vilcanota. If one turns right after the bridge one comes to Piychinjoto, a tumbled-down village built under an overhanging cliff. Also, just over the bridge and before the town to the left of a small, walled cemetery is a salt stream. If one follows this (there is a footpath) one comes to Salinas, a small village below which are a mass of terraced Inca salt pans, still in operation. A very spectacular sight; there are over 5,000. The walk to the salt pans takes about 30 mins. Take water as this side of the valley can be very hot and dry. **Moray** is well worth a visit: there are three "colosseums", used by the Incas as a sort of open-air crop laboratory, known locally as the greenhouses of the Incas. Peter Frost (*Exploring Cusco*) writes: "There are no great ruined structures here to impress visitors. Moray is more for the contemplative traveller with an affinity for such phenomena as the Nazca Lines, the stone rings of Avebury and the menhirs of Brittany." A remote but beautiful site. Wait for pickup on bridge on Chinchero road. This will take you near to Maras; walk to Maras ($1/2$ hr) and on through it, bearing left a little, and ask directions to Moray (walk $11/2$ hrs). Hitching back to Urubamba is quite easy, but there are no hotels at all in the area, so take care not to be stranded.

The Cusco-Machu Picchu train reaches the heights N of the city by a series of switchbacks and then descends to the floor of the Anta basin, with its herds of cattle. (In *Anta* itself, *Restaurant Dos de Mayo* is good; bus to Anta, US$0.30, felt trilby hats on sale.) The railway goes through the Anta canyon (10 km), and then, at a sharp angle, the Urubamba canyon, and descends along the river valley, flanked by high cliffs and peaks.

A 53-km road goes on to **Ollantaytambo**, 70 km, a clean and friendly little town (alt 2,800m) built on and out of the stones of an Inca town, which is a fine example of Inca *canchas* or corral enclosures, almost entirely intact. The so-called Baño de la Ñusta (bath of the princess) is of grey granite, and is in a small field between the town and the temple fortress. Some 200m behind the Baño de la Ñusta along the face of the mountain are some small ruins known as Inca Misacana, believed to have been a small temple or observatory. A series of steps, seats and niches have been carved out of the cliff. There is a complete irrigation system, including a canal at shoulder level, some 6 inches deep, cut out of the sheer rock face. The flights of terraces leading up above the town are superb, and so are the curving terraces following the contours of the rocks overlooking the Urubamba. These terraces were successfully defended by Manco Inca's warriors against Hernando Pizarro in 1536. Manco Inca built the defensive wall above the site and another wall closing the Yucay valley against attack from Cusco, still visible on either side of the valley. Visitors should also note the Inca masonry channelling the river and the piers of the bridge of Ollantaytambo. Entering Ollantaytambo from Pisac, the road is built along the long wall of 100 niches. Note the inclination of the wall: it leans towards the road. Since it was the Incas' practice to build with the walls leaning towards the interiors of the buildings, it has been deduced that the road, much narrower then, was built inside a succession of buildings. The site opens at 0700 and closes at 1730.

The temple itself was started by Pachacuti, using Colla Indians from Lake Titicaca—hence the similarities of the monoliths facing the central platform with the Tiwanaku remains. The Colla are said to have deserted half-way through the work, which explains the many unfinished blocks lying about the site. Admission by combined entrance ticket, which can be bought at the site (or US$2). If possible arrive very early, 0700, before the tourists. The guide book *Ollantaytambo* by Víctor Angles Vargas is available in Cusco bookshops, and Peter Frost's *Exploring Cusco* is also useful.

Festivals The Sun following Inti Raymi, there is a colourful festival, the Ollantay-Raymi. In early Jan there is a bullfighting festival (the bull is not killed). Around 26 Oct there is a 2-day, weekend festival with lots of dancing in traditional costume and many local delicacies for sale.

Accommodation E pp *El Albergue*, next to railway station, **C** pp full board, manager Wendy Weeks (American), a charming, small, homely hotel, with sauna, convenient for Machu Piccu train, highly rec, good place for information, reservations in Cusco at Expediciones Manu, T 226671. **F** *Hostal Mirador*, between plaza and ruins, with shower, basic, friendly, clean; **G** pp *Alojamiento Yavar*, 1½ blocks from main square (if full, will let you sleep on the floor free), basic, friendly, no water in the evening, has information on riding in the area; **G** *Hostal El Tambo*, basic but clean and friendly. Hotel next to station, no sign, door in garden wall, access via footbridge over stream, **F** pp, shared amenities, comfortable.

Camping possible in eucalyptus grove, ½ km from town, and along the river between the town and the railway station.

Restaurants There are several basic restaurants on the Plaza, try *Ollantay*.

Horses can be hired for US$5/day; a gentle day's ride or hike is to La Marca, along the beautiful river valley; ask Wendy Weeks for details. You can also visit the Inca quarry on the other side of the river.

Transport For those travelling by car, it is recommended to leave the car at Ollantaytambo railway station, US$1/day; ask Wendy Weeks at *El Albergue* for details. Check in advance the time trains pass through here. Both the tourist and local trains stop on the way to and from Machu Picchu. Station is 10-15 mins' walk from the plaza. There are colectivos at the plaza for the station when trains are due. For buses, see under **Buses to the Urubamba (Sacred) Valley** above.

For US$50 a taxi can be hired for a whole day (ideally Sun) to take you to Cachimayo, Chinchero, Maras, Urubamba, Ollantaytambo, Calca, Lamay, Coya, Pisac, Tambo Machay, Qenqo and Sacsayhuamán. If you wish to explore this area on your own, Road Map (*Hoja de ruta*) No 10 from the Automóvil Club del Perú is an excellent guide.

A major excavation project has been carried out since 1977 under the direction of Ann Kendall in the *Cusichaca* valley, 26 km from Ollantaytambo (only 9 km passable by ordinary car) at the intersection of the Inca routes. (The Inca fort, Huillca Raccay, was excavated in 1978-80, and work is now concentrated on Llactapata, a site of domestic buildings.) Ann Kendall is now working in the Patacancha valley NE of Ollantaytambo. Excavations are being carried out in parallel with the restoration of Inca canals to bring fresh clean water to the settlements in the valley.

From Ollantaytambo one can walk to start of the Inca Trail, Km 88, in about 8 hrs, rec: follow the railway in the direction of Machu Picchu until you come to Chillca village where you can cross the river. Sometimes there is a truck going to Chillca. From Chillca to the start of the Trail takes 5 hrs: climb up to a path that runs parallel to the river. This is an original Inca trail (still in use) that leads to Llactapata on the Inca Trail. **Warning** Best not to pass a night on this trail: thefts are possible because you have to sleep near villages.

Pinculluna, the mountain above Ollantaytambo, can be climbed with no mountaineering experience, although there are some difficult stretches—allow 2-3 hrs going up. The path is difficult to make out; best not to go on your own. Walk up the valley to the left of the mountain, very beautiful and impressive, Inca terraces after 4 km.

The **Inca Trail** to Machu Picchu, about 33 km, makes a spectacular 3 to 5 day hike (take it slowly to appreciate it fully). It runs from Km 88, Qoriwayrachi (2,299m), a point immediately after the first tunnel 22 km beyond Ollantaytambo station. A sturdy suspension bridge has now been built over the Urubamba River. An entrance ticket for the trail (US$20, in soles only, no discount for foreign students) must be bought at Km 88. It also gives entry to Machu Picchu if you get it stamped there. Guided tours often start at Km 83, check whether the price includes site entrance. The trail is rugged and steep (beware of landslides), at one stage traversing a 4,200-metre high pass, but the magnificent views compensate for any weariness which may be felt. It is cold at night, however, and weather conditions change rapidly, so it is important to take not only strong footwear, rain gear and warm clothing but also food, water, insect repellent, a supply of plastic bags, coverings, a good sleeping bag, a torch/flashlight and a stove for preparing hot food and drink to ward off the cold at night. A stove using paraffin (kerosene) is preferable, as fuel can be bought in small quantities in markets. Camping gas (white gas) is available in hardware stores in Cusco, US$1.50/litre. **A tent is essential** (if hiring in Cusco, check carefully for leaks) because walkers who have not taken adequate equipment have died of exposure; caves marked on some maps are little better than overhangs, and are not sufficient shelter to sleep in. At Puyopatamarca, on the Trail, there is a "tourist bathroom" where water can be collected (but purify it before drinking). Next place with water is Wiñay-Wayna (where there is a basic hostal with bunk beds, G pp, can sleep on floor if all rooms taken, US$1.15, showers and a small restaurant, food and drink expensive, reservations in Cusco, T 223110/240532), and then none till Machu Picchu, where water supplies are turned off at 1530. You can do the Inca Trail on your own (but see **Warning** below), or use a Travel Agency in Cusco who will arrange transport to the start, equipment, food, etc, for an all-in price, generally around US$60-65 pp. Agency treks range from the more expensive, with smaller groups, better equipment and transport arrangements, to cheaper, cost-cutting outfits with large groups and basic gear. Almost everyone reports that things do not go to plan. Most complaints are minor, but do check equipment carefully, ask around for people who have done the trip, take supplemental food and water with you.

NB The first 2 days have the stiffest climbing, so do not attempt it if feeling unwell. Try to camp in groups at night, leave all your valuables in Cusco and keep everything inside your tent, even your shoes. Security appears to have improved recently (1994-95). Avoid the Jul-Aug high season and the rainy season from Nov to Apr (note that this can change, check in advance). In the wet it is cloudy and the paths are very muddy and difficult. There are coral snakes in this area (black, red, yellow bands).

Train to Km 88 Only the local train stops at Km 88 (about 3 hrs after leaving Cusco); the tourist train does not stop here. Be ready to get out at Km 88 (the village here is called Chamana), it's easy to pass it (from Ollantaytambo US$0.80). If you do not wish to travel on the local train, the simplest method is to go to Ollantaytambo, or Chillca and start walking from there.

All the necessary equipment can be rented; **see p 1229** under **Travel agencies**. Good maps of the Trail and area can be bought from South American Explorers Club (Lima). If you have any doubts about carrying your own pack, reasonably-priced porters/guides are available, most reliably through Cusco agencies. Carry a day-pack nonetheless in case you walk faster than the porters and you have to wait for them to catch you up.

The walk to Huayllabamba, following the Cusichaca river, needs about 3 hrs and isn't too arduous. If planning a 2-4 day trip, carry on past Huayllabamba, which has become notorious for robberies. There is a camping place about an hr ahead, at Llulluchayoc (3,200m) and another before the ascent to the first pass, Warmiwañuska, about 4 hrs on in a meadow called Llulluchapampa (highly rec) 1½-2 hrs from the summit. From Huayllabamba to the meadows is often discouragingly steep. You should emerge towards 1600.

Leave early next day. The ascent to the first pass (4,200m) is the most taxing part of the walk; horses can be hired to carry equipment, US$5/backpack, for this leg. Afterwards take the path downhill, along left side of valley. You could camp by a stream at the bottom (1½ hrs from the first pass); it is no longer permitted to camp on the way up to the second pass (a much easier climb) at Runkuracay (3,860m), an Inca ruin, where there are huts and caves. Magnificent views near the summit in clear weather. Good overnight place is past the Inca ruins at Sayajmarca (3,500m), about an hour on after the top of the second pass.

Muddy jungle terrain leads gently up to the third pass, only about 2-2½ hrs' walk, the gradient blissfully gentle. Near the top there's a spectacular view of the Urubamba river and the valley to the right. You descend to Inca ruins at Puyopatamarca(3,680m), well worth a long visit.

From there steps go downhill to Wiñay-Wayna (3,670m), reached by forking off to the right (it's marked by a sign) near the pylons, 3-4 hrs or so on from Puyopatamarca. A hostal has been built at the fork. There is basic accommodation with hot showers and a small restaurant that serves simple food. The ruins at Wiñay-Wayna, a village of roofless but otherwise well-preserved Inca houses, are in an impressive location. In 1992 another Inca site was discovered near Wiñay-Wayna. Access is not yet possible for tourists although many terraces are already visible. The path from this point goes more or less level through jungle. You need about 2 hrs to walk to the Intipunku (3 small camping sites on right of track, just before ruins, no water), where there's a magnificent view of Machu Picchu, especially at dawn, with the sun alternately in and out, clouds sometimes obscuring the ruins, sometimes leaving them clear. Get to Machu Picchu as early as possible, preferably before 0830 for best views but in any case before the tourist train arrives at 1030.

Four days would make a comfortable trip (though much depends on the weather) and you would not find yourself too tired to enjoy what you see. Walking the Trail has the advantage of putting Machu Picchu in its true context: not a "lost city", but an integral part of a heavily populated valley. By the same token Machu Picchu loses some of its uniqueness; the architecture and scenery are often finer at several points along the trail. **NB** It is not allowed to walk back along the trail, though you may pay US$4.50 at Intipunku to be allowed to walk back as far as Wiñay-Wayna, and you may not take backpacks into Machu Picchu (leave them at ticket office, US$0.50).

Littering along the Trail is a serious problem as 5,000 people are now using it each year. Please remove all your rubbish, including toilet paper. Do not make the ruins en route into toilets; protect them. Do not light open fires, they can get out of control. The Earth Preservation Fund sponsors an annual clean-up Jul-Aug: volunteers should write to EPF, Inca Trail Project, Box 7545, Ann Arbor, Michigan 48107, USA. Preserving the Inca Trail: in Lima contact APTA, Percy Tapiá, T 478078, or Antonio Bouroncle, T 450532. In Cusco, Milla Tours, Carlos Milla, T 231710.

Machu Picchu, 42 km from Ollantaytambo by rail (2,380m), is a complete city, set on a saddle of a high mountain with terraced slopes falling away to the Urubamba river rushing in great hairpin bends below. It is in a comparatively good state of preservation because the Spaniards never found it. For centuries it was buried in jungle, until Hiram Bingham stumbled upon it in 1911. It was then explored by an archaeological expedition sent by Yale.

The ruins—staircases, terraces, temples, palaces, towers, fountains, the famous sundial and the Museo de Sitio below the ruins—require at least a day—some say two (take an insect-repellent and plenty of drinking water). Guides are available at the site, often very knowledgeable and worthwhile, US$15 for 2½ hrs. The mountain overlooking the site, Huayna Picchu (on which there are also some ruins), has some steps to the top for a superlative view of the whole but it is not for those who get giddy (don't leave the path); the climb takes up to 90 mins but the steps are dangerous after bad weather (it is only possible to walk up in the morning in a group—start early as there is shade then—and you must register at a hut on the trail; guards prevent you after 1300). The other trail to Huayna Picchu, down near the Urubamba, is via the Temple of the Moon, in two caves, one above the other, with superb Inca niches inside (sadly blemished by idiots' graffiti). For the trail to the Temple of the Moon: from the path to Huayna Picchu, take the second trail to the left (both are marked "Danger, do not enter"). The danger is in the first 10 mins, after which it is reasonable, although it descends further than you think it should. After the Temple you may proceed to Huayna Picchu; round trip about 4 hrs. An almost equally good view can be had from the trail behind the Tourist Hotel. Before doing any trekking around Machu Picchu, check with an official which paths may be used, or which are one way.

The site is open from 0700 to 1700. You can deposit your luggage at the entrance for US$0.50 (theft has been reported, check for missing items and demand their return). Entrance fee is US$15; second day ticket half price; no discount for international students, but less for Latin Americans and still less for Peruvians. It may be possible to pay in dollars, but only clean, undamaged notes will be accepted. Permission to enter the ruins before 0630 to watch the sunrise over the Andes, which is a spectacular experience, may be obtained from the Instituto Nacional de Cultura in Colegio San Bernardo, Cusco (near La Merced), but it is often possible if you talk to the guards at the gate. Sr Quispe, a guard for many years (and of royal Inca descent), is friendly and informative. After 1530 the ruins are almost deserted, but if you stay until then there may be no buses down from the ruins (see below). Unless you can hitch a ride down on the employees' bus at 1800, you may therefore have to walk down to Aguas Calientes if staying the night there (1-1½ hrs).

Mon and Fri are bad days because there is usually a crowd of people on guided tours who are going or have been to Pisac market on Sun, and too many people all want lunch at the same time. The expensive tourist hotel is located next to the entrance, with a restaurant (not rec, lunch US$15 pp).

From Machu Picchu one can take the Inca Trail, which climbs up behind the Tourist Hotel, back to (2 hrs' walk) the Inca settlement of Wiñay-Wayna (see above under the Inca Trail). On the way, you will have to pay US$4.50 for entry to the Trail. About 30 mins along a well-marked trail on the other side of Machu Picchu ruins is the famous Inca bridge. Both walks give spectacular views of the Urubamba River and the thickly wooded mountains, and the butterflies and flowers are beautiful. When going to the bridge, "don't dwell on just why the path stays where it does" (Kirk Mayer). The tombs at Chaskapata, near Machu Picchu, have recently been opened.

Gillian Handyside, of Harefield, Mx, tells us that another Inca site was discovered in 1987 opposite Machu Picchu. An archaeologist, Moisés, who works on the project stays in the *Albergue* in Aguas Calientes and sometimes shows slides on the subject.

Transport The railway runs from Cusco (San Pedro station), up the zig-zag route to the pass before descending all the way to Quillabamba, 130 km. It passes through Ollantaytambo, Km 88, Aguas Calientes (the official name of this station is "Machu Picchu") and Machu Picchu (officially called "Puente Ruinas"). A road has been built between "Machu Picchu" and "Puente Ruinas". There are two local trains and two *autovagones* (tourist trains) a day.

The local train has 2nd, 1st and buffet class (US$4, US$5 and US$12 one way respectively). It is a great experience. In the 2nd (not rec) and the 1st class everybody, including thieves, is allowed in the carriage. The train is really crowded and you have to watch your possessions carefully (bag-slashing is common). Take as little as possible, and no valuables, on the train. When on your way to hike the Inca Trail, equipped with a big backpack, try to be in a group, watching each other's gear. The buffet class has locked doors and only ticket holders are permitted in the carriage. Schedule: train no 1 leaves Cusco Mon-Sat at 0620, stopping in Ollantaytambo at about 0845 and the station at Machu Picchu at 1000. It continues to Quillabamba, arriving about 1130. It leaves Quillabamba at 1430, stopping at Machu Picchu at 1600, Ollantaytambo 1730 and arrives in Cusco at 2100. No 2 leaves Cusco daily at 1310, stops in Ollantaytambo at 1545, Machu Picchu 1730, arriving in Quillabamba at 1830. It leaves Quillabamba next day at 0530, arriving Machu Picchu at 0700, Ollantaytambo 0815 and Cusco 1100.

The tourist train has one class, closed doors (only ticket holders allowed on), US$27 one way. The first leaves Cusco at 0600, stopping at Ollantaytambo at 0800 and Machu Picchu at 0900. It returns from Machu Picchu at 1400 and arrives in Cusco at 1800, after a stop at Ollantaytambo at 1500. The second leaves Cusco at 1245, stops in Ollantaytambo at 1445 and Machu Picchu at 1545. It leaves Machu Picchu next day at 0730, reaches Ollantaytambo at 0830, Cusco 1030 and is less crowded. The tourist train returns to Cusco from Puente Ruinas; it does not stop at Aguas Calientes. Travellers on inclusive tours often return by bus from Ollantaytambo, leaving the trains emptier in buffet class for the slower uphill journey to Cusco. **NB** The video sold on the tourist train is said not to work on any system. It can get very cold at night, a blanket or sleeping bag could prove useful.

Train schedules are unreliable and delays of hours are common, especially on the local train. In the rainy season mudslides cause cancellations. Tickets can be bought in advance or on the day at the railway station or at a travel agency (always check date and seat number, and don't pay agency in advance). Theoretically, the ticket office is open daily 0600-0830, 1000-1100 and 1500-1700. Long queues for the morning train in high season just before and on holidays.

Tourist tickets: there are two types, 1) round trip in the *autovagón*, round trip in the bus up to the ruins, entrance fee, guide, for US$110. 2) Round trip on the local train, buffet class, round trip in the bus to the ruins, entrance fee and guide, US$60 (cheaper for Peruvian nationals). These tickets can be booked through any travel agency, who will pick you up at your hotel and take you to the train station. If travelling tourist, try to get tickets (aeroplane size) with seat numbers. Independent travellers should try to buy return leg to Cusco as soon as they arrive in Machu Picchu.

The bus from Machu Picchu station to the ruins, starting 0915, takes 20 mins and costs US$3.50 one way. On the new road from Aguas Calientes to the ruins, there is a bus service from 0630 (US$7 return). The first service down from the ruins is at 1230. The walk up takes 2 hrs, and 1 hr down, following the zig-zag road. A 'short cut', "Camino Herradura", takes 45 mins to 2 hrs, some of it almost rock climbing.

Camping Not permitted on the site; official campsite next to the station at Machu Picchu ("Ruinas"), on the football field, or at Aguas Calientes. Beware of thieves, do not leave your tent and belongings unattended.

Accommodation and Food In season the Tourist Hotel at the ruins is heavily booked during the week (best rooms for the view are 10, 16, 18, 20, 22, 28 is a suite for 4); try Sun night as other tourists find Pisac market a greater attraction. Book well in advance, through a reliable agency or through Emturin in Cusco: in this way you can spend 24 hrs at the site. Often, however, though reportedly booked up weeks in advance, there are cancellations and you can obtain a room on arrival. Rooms with shower (no singles) **A1** (C out of season if you bargain), US$15 for meals in poor self-service cafeteria (US$13 for American breakfast). There is electricity (but rooms are cold at night) and water 24 hrs a day. Service and honesty not always good, but as they state in the English version of the rules card: "The grandeur of nature is such, that the conniving of man is overcome." The Tourist Hotel often does not have soles for exchange, make sure you have enough before setting out for Machu Picchu; but the hotel will accept American Express TCs at the official rate. Only hotel residents may eat in the restaurant; others have to use the expensive self-service counter outside. It is recommended that you take food and soft drinks with you; prices are very high compared with Cusco. Note that food can only be eaten outside the entrance to the site.

The cheapest options for staying overnight are at *Aguas Calientes*, 1½ km back along the railway (the town has electricity 24 hrs a day). A new station is being built at Aguas Calientes. **A1** *Machu Picchu Pueblo Hotel*, Km 110, Aguas Calientes (84-232161; Cusco 232161/223769, Procuradores 48; Lima 461915, F 455598, Andalucía 174, Lima 18), individual bungalows with bath, hot water, heating, meals extra in nice, expensive restaurant, swimming pool. **C** *Hostal Inka*, T 211084, rec; **E-F** *Albergue Juvenil*, constructed by Copesco, the state tourism agency for the region, has 200 beds in dormitories and private rooms, and dining facilities (US$3 for a poor meal), for travellers and family groups, dirty bathrooms reported, comfortable, noisy with students, laundry, rec, price pp (no IYHA card needed). **E** *Gringo Bill's* (*Hostal Qoni Unu*), third house to left of church, psychedelic murals in most rooms, relaxed, cheap, usually has hot water (electric showers), laundry, money exchange, good but expensive meals served (usually), offer a US$2 packed lunch to take up to the ruins, luggage stored, new huts built (upstairs rooms better value, downstairs noisy in pm); **E-F** *Hostal Machu Picchu*, by station, clean, basic, quiet, friendly (esp Wilber, owner's son, with travel info), hot water, nice balcony over the Urubamba, grocery store, rec; **F** *Hostal Los Caminantes*, with bath, basic, but friendly and clean. Restaurants: *El Refugio*, expensive, good food, slow service, also *Aiko*, rec; *Waiki*, good cheap food, breakfast. *Restaurant Tumi*, good, free pisco sour. *Chez Maggi* restaurant here linked with its namesake in Cusco, good cheap Italian food US$3.70, "good place for partying, two parrots, 'Bob Marley' and 'Jimi Hendrix'"; *Huayna Picchu*, good value restaurant beside railway line; *Inka's Pizza Pub*; *El Chosa Pizzería*, pleasant atmosphere, good value; *Machu Picchu*, restaurant on hill up to hot baths, good, friendly; cheap, restaurants at Aguas Calientes station. The thermal baths (a communal pool), a 10-min walk from the town, were damaged in 1995, as was the water supply (under repair April 1995). Officially they open at 0500 and close at 2000, US$2/bath, bathing suits required, showers for washing *before* entering baths (take towel, soap and shampoo); bar, beware sandflies. The paved road to the baths is lined with souvenir shops and restaurants. Travel agency, *Información Turística Rikuni*, is opp the station, Nydia is very helpful.

NB Advisable to read *Lost City of the Incas* by Hiram Bingham (available in Lima and Cusco), or *A Walking Tour of Machu Picchu* (rec) by Pedro Sueldo Nava—in several languages, available in Cusco. See also *The Sacred Center*, by Johan Reinhard. *Exploring Cusco*, by Peter Frost has good information about the site. The Tourist Hotel sells guides, although at a rather inflated price. (The South American Explorers' Club in Lima has detailed information on walks here, and so have Hilary Bradt's and Charles Brod's books.)

The railway goes on 79 km through Chaullay to **Quillabamba** (24,000 people) in the Urubamba Valley at 1,054m, where there is a Dominican mission.

The train follows the Río Urubamba much of the way from Machu Picchu, and the improvised station at Quillabamba is right on the river. One crosses a foot bridge put up by the Lions Club and then climbs up a 100-odd flight of stairs to reach the town. Many *heladerías*, much needed in the heat, the best on the NW corner of the square. Not many attractions for the tourist, but a place to bask in the sun or take a swim in the river, though ask the locals where the safe stretches are, as the current is quite rapid in places. Clean market building, and a football stadium.

Hotels D *Comercio*, Libertad, with bath; **D** *Quillabamba* (unmarked entrance next to Autoservicio behind market), roof terrace restaurant, rec; *Hostal Don Carlos*, clean, private shower, generally hot water; **F** *Hostal Alto Urubamba*, on Dos de Mayo, clean, good, with or without bath, hot water, restaurant; other accommodation, **G** and up, near market. The best restaurants are to be found on Plaza de Armas.

Exchange Banco de Crédito, good for TCs.

Transport See above for train information. Minibus leaves Cusco am when full, from Calle General Buendía near Machu Picchu station; also trucks go in the daytime, 233 km, 6-11 hrs, US$4.50.

The road between Ollantaytambo and Quillabamba passes through Peña, a place of great beauty with snowy peaks already appearing on either side of the valley (taxis are very reluctant to go there). Once out of Peña, the climb to the pass begins in earnest—on the right is a huge glacier. Soon on the left, Veronica begins to appear in all its huge and snowy majesty. After endless zig-zags and breathtaking views, one reaches the Abra Málaga pass. The descent to the valley shows hillsides covered in lichen and Spanish moss. At Chaullay, the road meets the railway to Quillabamba, Machu Picchu and Cusco. The road crosses the river at the historic Choquechaca bridge. One can drive from Chaullay to Santa Teresa (hot springs, ask the locals) from where the railway goes to Machu Picchu. Note that driving in this area is very demanding owing to the number of hairpin bends.

From Chaullay you can drive to the village of **Huancacalle**, the best base for exploring the nearby Inca ruins of *Vitcos*, with the palace of the last four Inca rulers from 1536 to 1572, and Yurac Rumi, the sacred white stone of the Incas. Huancacalle can be reached from Quillabamba daily by truck and bus, the journey takes between 4 and 7 hrs. There is a small hotel at Huancacalle; villagers will accept travellers in their very basic homes (take sleeping bag); and the Cobo family permits travellers to put up their tents on their property. Allow plenty of time for hiking to, and visiting the ruins: it takes 1 hr to walk from Huancacalle to Vitcos, 45 mins Vitcos-Yurac Rumi, 45 mins Yurac Rumi-Huancacalle. Horses can be hired if you wish.

Travellers with ample time can hike from Huancacalle to **Espíritu Pampa**, the site of the **Vilcabamba Vieja** ruins, a vast pre-Inca ruin with a neo-Inca overlay in deep jungle at 1,000m (the disputed last capital of the Incas); the site is reached on foot or horseback from Pampaconas. From Chaullay, take a truck to Yupanca, Lucma or Pucyura: there rent horses or mules and travel through superb country to Espíritu Pampa. You can then continue to Cosireni on the Río San Miguel, from where trucks go to Quillabamba. The jungle in the area of Vilcabamba Vieja is full of wildlife and worth the trip on its own; best time of year May-Oct, insect repellent essential.

Guides for Vilcabamba Vieja: Vidal Albertes, contact in Huancacalle; Paulo Quispe Cusi in Yupanca. Another local guide in Pucyura is Gilberto Quintanilla. Adriel Garay at *White River Tours*, Plateros, Cusco, or Calle Bayoneta 739, Cusco, T 234575.

Hans Ebensten of Key West, Florida, writes: "While a visit to the ruins of Vilcabamba Vieja, near Espíritu Pampa, is still a formidable undertaking involving at least eight days of hiking over rough trails (others have done the trip in five days), taking all camping gear, food, etc, the ruins of Vitcos and the Yurac Rumi, the Inca sacred stone, are now easily accessible. Both are well worth the effort of a visit: Vitcos remains romantically overgrown by jungle, much as Dr Hiram Bingham saw it (and Machu Picchu) in 1911, but unlike Machu Picchu it has all the documented historical associations which make a visit particularly interesting and rewarding. The Yurac Rumi, the most sacred site in South America, must be one of the most impressive religious sites in the world; far larger, more intricately and elaborately carved than any descriptions of it. Dr Hiram Bingham was chiefly concerned in stressing the importance of Machu Picchu, and thus in his books and reports dismissed Vitcos and the Yurac Rumi as almost insignificant." At Espíritu Pampa is a sister stone of the Yurac Rumi.

To visit this area one must register with the police in Pucyura. You are advised to seek full information before going into this area. Distances are considerable, it is at least 100 km from Chaullay to Espíritu Pampa, the going is difficult and maps appear to be very poor.

One can also go by boat to Kiteni and then by truck to Quillabamba (at 0400). There are trucks and pick-ups from Quillabamba to Kiteni, 12-15 hrs, US$5. (**G Hotel Kiteni**, basic, several restaurants.) At Kiteni you must register on arrival with the police station. Take torch, no electricity. Irregular boats to the Pongo de Maynique, where the river goes through the mountain with a rock wall of several hundred meters on either side, before descending into jungle, where you can see many varieties of animals, birds, butterflies, snakes etc. 2 days, from Quillabamba to Pongo. Seek advice in advance on river conditions (at some times it is too high). From Pongo you can get down through the jungle to Pucallpa if there is the right amount of water in the river; boats can be arranged at Kiteni. Price varies for number of people in the party, beware of overcharging. En route to Pucallpa it is possible to go to Camisea and Sepahua (near where Yaminavak Indians can be visited; they live in constructions made of mud, but have a mini-hotel for passers-through).

Paucartambo, on E slope of Andes, is NE of Cusco by a good road (one way on alternate days). In this remote though now popular tourist town is held the Fiesta of Carmen, usually on 16, 17, 18 Jul with masked dances. (*Fiesta* dates should be checked in Cusco.) Hotels: **G Quinta Rosa Marina**, near bridge, basic; **G Albergue Municipal Carmen de la Virgen**, basic. Private car hire for round trip on 16 Jul: US$30, travel agencies in Cusco arrange this. Minibus from Av Huáscar, Cusco, every other day, US$4.50, 3-4 hrs (alternate days Paucartambo-Cusco). Trucks and private bus leave from the Coliseo, behind Hospital Segura, 5 hrs, US$2.50.

From Paucartambo, in the dry season, you can go 44 km to Tres Cruces, along the Pilcopata road, turning left after 25 km; Sr Cáceres in Paucartambo will arrange trip. Tres Cruces gives a wonderful view of the sunrise in Jun and Jul and private cars leave Paucartambo between 0100 and 0200 to see it; they may give you a lift. One can walk from Paucartambo to the *chullpas* of Machu Cruz in about an hour, or to the *chullpas* of Pijchu (take a guide). You can also visit the Inca fortress of Huatojto, which has admirable doorways and stonework. A car will take you as far as Ayre, from where the fortress is a 2-hr walk.

From Urcos (municipal rooms on the square, better ones in the 'hotel', ask for directions), near Cusco, a spectacular road crosses the Eastern Cordillera to Puerto Maldonado in the jungle (see next section). 47 km after passing the snow-line

Hualla-Hualla pass (4,820m), the super-hot thermal baths of Marcapata (173 km from Urcos) provide a relaxing break (US$0.10). 82 km from Urcos, at the base of **Nevado Ausangate** (6,384m), is the town of **Ocongate**, which has two hotels on the Plaza de Armas. Beyond Ocongate is **Tinqui**, the starting point for hikes around Ausangate and in the Cordillera Vilcanota. On the flancs of the Nevado Ausangate is Q'Olloriti where a church has been built close to the snout of a glacier. This place has become a place of pilgrimage.

Arrieros and mules can be hired in Tinqui, US$4/day. Make sure you sign a contract with full details. The hike around the mountain of Ausangate takes about 5 days; spectacular, quite hard, 3 passes over 5,000m. You need to be acclimatized; it is recommended to take a guide or *arriero*. **G** *Hostal Tinqui Guide*, right-hand side as you enter village, friendly, meals available, owner can arrange guides and horses.

Take a truck to Tinqui, via Urcos and Ocongate, 172 km, 8 hrs, US$8. Buy all food supplies in Cusco. Maps are available at the IGM in Lima or the South American Exploreres Club. Some tour companies in Cusco have details about the hike, or check with the Mountain Guide Club, T 226844.

THE SOUTHEASTERN JUNGLE (6)

Cooled by winds sweeping down from the Andes but warmed by its jungle blanket, this region contains some of the most important tropical flora and fauna in the world. The frontier town, Puerto Maldonado, only a ½ hr flight from Cusco, is the starting point for expeditions to one of the national parks at Manu, Tambopata or Heath. Besides its natural attractions, the area also harbours gold-diggers, loggers, hunters, drug smugglers and oil-men.

This region contains some of the most important flora and fauna on Earth, but, for years, logging, gold prospecting and the search for oil and gas have endangered the unique rainforest. Fortunately, conservation groups have been busy trying to protect it. The Madre de Dios department contains the Manu National Park (1,881,000 ha) and the Tambopata-Candamo Wildlife Reserve (1,500,000 ha). The main products are Brazil nuts, wood and gold. The climate is warm and humid, with a rainy season from Nov to Mar and a dry season from Apr to Oct. Cold fronts from the South Atlantic, called *freajes*, are characteristic of the dry season; temperatures drop to 15-16°C during the day, 13° at night. Always bring a sweater. In this lowland region (alt 260m), the forest is technically called Sub-tropical Moist Forest, which means that it receives less rainfall than tropical forest and is dominated by the floodplains of its meandering rivers. The most striking features are the former river channels that have become isolated as ox-bow lakes. These are home to black caiman and giant otter. Other rare species living in the forest are jaguar, puma, ocelot and tapir. There are also howler monkeys, macaws, guans, currasows and the giant harpy eagle.

The best time to visit is during the dry season when there are fewer mosquitoes and the rivers are low, exposing beaches. It is a good time to see nesting. The animals stay close to the rivers and are easily seen. This is also the hottest time. The rainy season also has its charms. A pair of binoculars is essential equipment and insect repellent is a must.

Recommended reading: *Birds of Venezuela* (Princeton University) and *South American Birds*, by John Dunning, giving the best coverage of birds of Peru. *Neotropical Rainforest Mammals, A field guide*, by Louise H Emmons. *Tropical Nature*, by Adrian Forsyth and Ken Miyata, an explanation of the rainforest. *Manu National Park*, by Kim MacQuarrie and André and Cornelia Bartschi, a large, expensive and excellent book, with beautiful photographs. *The Ecology of Tropical Rainforests*, by "Trees", a booklet with an introduction for ecotourists. *Madre de Dios Packet*, by the South American Explorers Club, practical travel advice for the area.

The **Manu National Park** is the biggest nature reserve in Peru. Charles Munn, a zoologist from Wildlife Conservation International who has spent a long time in the area, writes that "No other park on earth can compare with Manu in terms of sheer variety of life forms." The park is divided into a Culture Zone (92,000 ha), where the locals still employ their traditional way of life, a Reserve Zone (257,000 ha), used only for ecotourism, and the Park Zone (1,532,000 ha), entirely protected, in which scientists only are allowed.

NB In 1995 the Reserve was closed from 1 Jan to 1 Apr, and only Manu Nature Tours, which has a lodge in the Reserve Zone, could run trips to the reserve in the wet season. The Culture Zone remained open and could be visited by those who survived the road trip in.

Information In Lima: Asociación Peruana para la Conservación de la Naturaleza (Apeco), Parque José Acosta 187, 2nd Flr, Magdalena del Mar, T 616316. Fundación Peruana para la Conservación de la Naturaleza (FPCN), Av de los Rosales 255, San Isidro, T 426706/426616. Asociación de Ecología y Conservación (Ecco), Calle Dos de Mayo 527, Miraflores, T 472369. In Cusco: Asociación de Conservación para la Selva Sur (ACSS), at the office of Manu Nature Tours (see below), T 226392, open 1000-1300, 1500-1900. The Park Office is next door to Manu Nature Tours, open 0800-1400; they issue a permit for the Reserve Zone which costs US$10. The two tour companies given below will answer any question on the park. Manu Nature Tours has a good video on the area.

Tour Companies The following two companies organize trips into the Culture and Reserve Zones. Contact them for more details. **Manu Nature Tours EIRL**, Av Sol 582, Cusco, T 224384, F 234793, or Centro Plaza Conquistadores, 396-S-101, San Isidro, Lima, T/F 428990, which owns the only lodge in the Reserve Zone (Manu Lodge) open all year, situated on an ox-bow lake, providing access to the forest, US$75 a night incl meals. Guides are available. Activities incl river-rafting and canopy-climbing. It is highly recommended for experiencing the jungle in comfort. An 8-day trip with flights both ways costs US$1,493, with road/boat transport there, plane back, US$1,695; 4-day trip US$998, plane both ways. At the same address is EcoManu, a non-profit group of tour operators aiming to guarantee ecologically sustainable tourism in the region (Expediciones Manu, Manu Nature Tours, Amazonia Lodge, Pantiacolla Lodge and Blanquillo Lodge). Contact Boris Gómez Luna. **Expediciones Manu**, Procuradores 50, Cusco, T 226671, F 236706, offers camping trips into the Reserve Zone; owner/birdwatcher Barry Walker, highly rec.

In the Cultural Zone, no permit needed, are four lodges. **Amazonia Lodge**, on the Río Alto Madre de Dios, Atalaya on the road to Shintuya, US$40 a night, an old hacienda in the foothills of the Andes; in Cusco T 231370, Sr Santiago. **Erika Lodge**, on the Río Alto Madre de Dios, 25 mins from Atalaya, a biological station used by the FPCN, not prepared for tourism. **Pantiacolla Lodge**, located in Itahuania (30 mins from Shintuya), owned by Marianne (Dutch) and Gustavo Moscoso. US$25pp/night (US$40pp incl meals). They organize trips into the Reserve at US$110 pp for 5 or more for boat and boatman and US$55/day for guide, 8-day camping trip into the Reserve, US$450. Also 9-day trips from Cusco, incl transport, guide, food, boat, gear for US$950 (min 6, max 19 people). Contact them through **Pantiacolla Tours**, Calle Plateros, Cusco. **Blanquillo Lodge**, 1½ hrs down the Río Madre de Dios from Boca Manu, situated on an ox-bow lake near a collpa (macaw lick), US$25 pp/night, owned by Abraham Huamán and Carol Mitchell (American); run by **Expediciones Manu** (address above). They run similar 8-day trips from Cusco as Pantiacolla; both rec as good value. A rec guide is Percy Núñez, biologist, Umanch'ata 136, Cusco.

Individual Trips may only enter the Reserve Zone with a recognized guide who is affiliated to a recognized tour company. This makes it difficult to go by yourself. There are only 2 places to camp and these are used constantly by tour groups. Buy all supplies in Cusco: camping gear, fishing tackle, food (for the boatmen and guide as well) and gasoline (it is twice as expensive in Shintuya); take finely-woven, long-sleeved and -legged clothing and effective insect repellent (that on sale in Cusco is no good).

To get there by air Aero Sur flies to Boca Manu from Cusco, T (084) 224638.

By road Cusco to Pilcopata, 255 km, 16-20 hrs (20-40 hrs in the rainy season), US$5. Trucks (rec: Príncipe, Armando Cana, Carrasco and Tigre) and a local bus (owner Angel Valencia, T224458 for reservation), leave from the Coliseo, behind the Hospital Segura in Cusco, every Mon, Wed and Fri at about 1000. They return the following day, but there is no service on Sun. Private transport can be arranged through Explorers Transportes, T 237518, or ask at the tour companies. The road is in very poor condition, and is sometimes impassable in the wet season (check with the tour companies). Make sure you go with a recommended truck driver as accidents do happen. The scenery is magnificent, climbing up to the pass before Paucartambo (very cold at night), before dropping down to this mountain village at the border between the departments of Cusco and Madre de Dios. The road then ascends to the second pass (also cold at night), after which it goes down to the cloud forest and then the rainforest, reaching at 650m. At Pilcapata you can stay at a little hostal (the only one) of Sra Robella for US$2.50 pp, very basic.

From Pilcapata to Shintuya, 75 km, 7 hrs, longer in the wet, US$3. Trucks leave in the morning between 0600 and 0900. The road is hair-raising and breath-taking, and impossible in the rainy season. A long, uncomfortable trip, but the views are fine. The route passes through Atalaya, the first village on the Alto Madre de Dios river. A few houses, meals available at the family of Rosa and Juan (very friendly people), where you can camp. To get river transport from here, however, you have to be very lucky. The route continues to Salvador, where the Park Office and the Park Entrance are situated. If you did not get a permit in Cusco, this is your last chance. There are basic hostals and restaurants. The end of the road is **Shintuya**, at 485m, the starting point for river transport. The inhabitants are Masheos Indians. It is a commercial and social centre, as wood from the jungle is transported from here to Cusco. There are a few basic restaurants and you can camp (beware of thieves). The priest will let you stay in the dormitory rooms at the mission. Supplies are expensive. It is hard to find guides or boats in Shintuya; the ones that are willing to take you have no permits and little knowledge of the rainforest. Cargo boats leave for Colorado on the Río Madre de Dios, via Boca Manu, but only when the boat is fully laden, about 6 to 8 a week, 7 hrs, US$8. From Colorado you catch a boat to Laberinto, 7 hrs, US$8, whence trucks and buses go to Puerto Maldonado, 1½ hrs.

Boca Manu is the connecting point between the rivers Alto Madre de Dios, Manu and Madre de Dios. It has a few houses, an air strip and some food supplies. It is also the entrance to the Manu Reserve. The Park Office is located in Romero, 1 hr by boat from Boca Manu. You need to show your permit here. There are huts available for accommodation and it is possible to camp.

To the Reserve Zone (No access 1 Jan-1 Apr 1995, check for future restrictions.) Up stream on the Río Manu you pass the *Manu Lodge* (see Manu Nature Tours), on the Cocha Juárez, 1 hr by boat; visitors are charged an entrance fee of US$5 (taken care of by tour companies). You can continue to Cocha Otorongo, 2½ hrs and Cocha Salvador, 30 mins, the biggest lake with plenty of wildlife. From here it is 2 hrs to Pakitza, the entrance to the Park Zone (only for biologists with a special permit).

Between Boca Manu and Colorado is Blanquillo, a private reserve (10,000 ha), where jungle trips can be arranged. Bring a good tent with you and all food. Guides are available for US$6 pp (Walter and Rolando rec). Wildlife is abundant and costs work out cheaper than Manu National Park. Good views of macaws and parrots at the macaw lick near *Blanquillo Lodge* (see above). There are occasional boats to Blanquillo from Shintuya, US$10, 8 hrs.

Quincemil, 240 km from Urcos, is a centre for alluvial gold-mining with many banks (**F** *Hotel Toni*, friendly, clean, cold shower, good meals); ask the food-carriers to take you to visit the miners washing for gold in the nearby rivers. Quincemil marks the half-way point and the end to the all-weather road. Gasoline is scarce because most road vehicles continue on 70 km to Masuco, another mining centre, where they fill up with the cheaper gasoline of the jungle region. Thirty more km of sloshing mud and cascading waterfalls brings one out of the mountainous jungle and into the flat plains, for the 141 km straight run to Puerto Maldonado. The road to Puerto Maldonado is impassable in the rainy season.

The **Tambopata-Candamo Wildlife Reserve** is located between the rivers Madre de Dios, Tambopata and Heath. The area was declared a reserve in Jan 1990 by the Peruvian government. The Tambopata reserve makes up part of the area and has been under protection since 1977, assigned to Peruvian Safaris. Some superb ox-bow lakes can be visited and the birdwatching is wonderful. It is quite easy to arrange a boat and guide from Puerto Maldonado (typical cost US$190 for 4 days).

Puerto Maldonado (pop 17,000) is capital of the Department of Madre de Dios. (Altitude, 250m.) Overlooking the confluence of the rivers Tambopata and Madre de Dios, it is an important starting point for visiting the rainforest, or for departing to Bolivia. The Plaza de Armas is pleasant, and nearby is a new Banco de la Nación built to accommodate (and reflect) the prosperity that gold has brought. However, Puerto Maldonado is an expensive town and because of the gold mining and timber industries, the surrounding jungle (including most of the mahogany trees) has been destroyed and cultivated.

Jungle Lodges *Cusco Amazonic Lodge* (*Albergue Cusco Amazónico*), 45 mins by boat down the Madre de Dios River, jungle tours and accommodation, US$80 pp/day (incl meals and guides), naturalists programme provided, negotiable out of season, about 30 bungalows with private bathrooms, friendly staff but mixed reports; avoid in Feb when everyone goes on holiday including the mechanic. The wreckage of the Fitzcarraldo ship, the subject of the Werner Herzog film, is nearby. (Book at Andalucía 174, Lima 18, T 462775, F 455598, or Procuradores 48, Cusco, T 232161/223769.) *Explorers Inn* (book through Peruvian Safaris, Garcilaso de la Vega 1334, Casilla 10088, T 313047 Lima, or Plateros 365, T 235342 Cusco, or Continental Tours, Plateros 329, T 236919, Eusebio helpful), located in the Tambopata-Candamo wildlife reserve, in the part where most research work has been done, 58 km from Puerto Maldonado: a 3 hr ride on Tambopata river (2 hrs return, in early am, so take warm clothes and rain gear), one of the best places in Peru for seeing jungle birds (547 species have been recorded here), butterflies (1,100-plus species), dragonflies (over 150 species) as well as tree species and mammals (incl a giant otter), but you probably need more than a 2-day tour to benefit fully from the location, guides are biologists and naturalists from around the world who study in the reserve in return for acting as guides, interesting wildlife-treks incl to the Collca macaw lick; US$160 for 3 days, 2 nights, extra day US$45 (discounts in the low season Jan-Mar, and for larger groups), excellent meals and guides provided, comfortable accommodation in thatch-roofed huts with "en suite" bathrooms, lighting by candle but generator for refrigerator with supply of cold beer and soft drinks, alcohol expensive. *Tambo Lodge*, bungalows 15 km out on opposite bank of Río Madre de Dios, 2, 3 and 4-day jungle programmes available (from US$90 pp in low season), perhaps too close to Puerto Maldonado, good food, basic, guide Víctor is knowledgeable and speaks good English, book through Cusco-Maldonado Tour, Plateros, half a block from Plaza de Armas (T 222332), Cusco. *Tambopata Jungle Lodge*, on the Tambopata river, $1/2$-hr boat ride up river from *Explorers Inn*; make reservations at Peruvian Andean Treks, Av Pardo 705, Cusco, T 225701, F 238911, or Jr Cusco 146, Puerto Maldonado, from US$65 pp/night (children half price), all incl, naturalists programme provided, rec; US$160 for 3 nights 4 days.

Hotels in town: **B** *Turistas*, Av León Velarde s/n, on the bank of the Tambopata River (private bath), electricity and water sometimes cut, restaurant quite good; **E** *Cabañaquinta*, Calle Cusco 535, friendly, good restaurant; **E** *Wilson*, Jr González Prada 355, T 86, with bath, E without, well run, clean, no hot water, trucks coming from airport stop here; **F** *Rey Port*, Av León Velarde 457, with shower, good, friendly, insecure; *Cross*, Av León Velarde 721, clean, generally rec; **F** *Royal Inn*, Av Dos de Mayo 333; **F** *Tambo de Oro*, Av Dos de Mayo 277; **G** *Moderno*, Av Billinghurst 359, friendly, clean but noisy, safe for luggage, no hot water. *Marys*, Jr Puno 665, *Oriental*, Jr Lorentón, *Central*, Av León Velarde 661, *Chávez*, Av León Velarde. As there are many miners in Maldonado, rooms can be scarce.

Restaurants There are several good restaurants in town. *La Cusqueñita 2*, Av Ernesto Rivero 607, good, cheap; *Kalifa*, Piura, some regional specialities, closed in evening, rec. Look for *pensiones* where meals are served at fixed times (lunch is at 1300).

Typical Foods *Castañas* (Brazil nuts), try them, chocolate- or sugar-coated. *Patarashca*, fish barbecued in banana leaves. Try *pescado sudado* as an appetizer. *Mazato*, an alcoholic drink prepared from yuca and drunk by the Indians at their festivals. *Chupispa*, banana soup. *Tacacho*, boiled, mashed green bananas. *Paichipango*, fish with yucca. *Chapo*, sweet banana drink, from green bananas.

Exchange Banco de Crédito, cash advances on Mastercard or Visa.

Bolivian Consulate is on 2 de Mayo, near Puno; **Peruvian immigration** is on Billinghurst, river end.

Excursions Motorcycles can be hired for local trips for US$4 an hr. Bargain for reductions for longer. A very worthwhile one-or two-day excursion by motorcycle is to boat across the Río Madre de Dios and follow the road towards Iberia and Iñapari on the border with Brazil (dry season only). Along the road are picturesque *caseríos* (settlements) that serve as collecting and processing centres for the Brazil nut. Approximately 70% of the inhabitants in the Madre de Dios are involved in the collection of this prized nut. Many trucks, of varying vintage, take this road and will offer lifts for US$10-20. At Planchón, 40 km up the road, there is a hotel, G, clean, but no mosquito nets, and 2 bar/restaurants. Alegna at Km 60 has a hotel/restaurant and Marilla, at Km 80, a bar.

The hotel at Alerta, Km 115, is a room with 4 beds, G. The river is safe to swim in. If there is a boat here, it is the quickest route to Brasiléia (Brazil), apart from plane, US$10-20 pp in cargo canoe, or *peque-peque*, to Porvenir and then by road to Cobija (Bolivia), across the border from Brasiléia.

San Lorenzo, at Km 145, and the *Bolpebra* bar; cheap food and drink and generally merry.

Iberia, Km 168, has two hotels, the best, F, is *Hostal Aquino*, basic, cold shower, rooms serviced daily. *Iñapari*, at the end of the road, Km 235, has one hotel and a restaurant, but *Assis Brasil* across the border is much more attractive (wade across the river). There is a road from Assis Brasil into Brazil and connections to Bolivia. It can be cold travelling this road; take a blanket or sleeping bag. No exchange facilities en route and poor exchange rates for Brazilian currency at Iñapari. From time to time it is possible to get a boat from Puerto Maldonada all the way to Iñapari; taking shorter trips may mean getting stuck for days or weeks. Try Ricardo, an ex-student from Lima, but avoid a character known as El Chino.

The beautiful and tranquil *Lago Sandoval* is a 1-hr boat ride along the Río Madre de Dios, US$5, and then a 5-km walk into the jungle, muddy, take boots (newly built **G** *Sandoval Lodge*). Overnight (or longer) camping trips can be made to *Lago Valencia*, 60 km away near the Bolivian border; it is an ox-bow lake with lots of wildlife. Many excellent beaches and islands are located within an hour's boat ride; however, make sure you have a ride back at the end of the day. The Indians living nearer Puerto Maldonado, like those near Iquitos and Manaus, are strictly tourist Indians. Boats may be hired at the port for about US$30 a day to go to Lago Sandoval or visit the Indians. Bargain hard, and don't pay the full cost in advance. Mosquitoes are voracious. If camping, take food and water. Barbara Fearis from San Francisco and her Peruvian husband, Guillermo, organize interesting trips for photography, bird watching and fishing. They can be contacted at Puerto Tambopata, behind the Tourist Hotel (write to Correo Central, Puerto Maldonado). Tambopata Expeditions offer 2-day tours to Lago Sandoval and longer trips, owner is guide, speaks English and is knowledgeable; take binoculars. Reputable guides are Hernán Llave Cortez, who can be contacted through Inexpo Tours, *Hotel Wilson*, Jr González Prado, rec, and Willy Wither. For guides meeting the plane, US$8-10 pp/day is a normal fee; they are very pushy. Shop around in Puerto Maldonado, insist on a detailed explanation of the tour offered, if necessary sign a contract and make sure that, once you have paid, the programme is not scaled down. **NB** All hunting in Amazonia is illegal.

For a trip up the Río Heath, you need all camping gear, food, etc. Also, a guide is essential. To hire a boat and boatman costs about US$15/day; can be difficult to find. Organized tours are available in Puerto Maldonado, ask around. From Puerto Maldonado the trip goes to Puerto Pardo (Peruvian border), up the Río Heath for about 2 hrs, before reaching the Santuario Pampas del Heath. Jungle hikes can be made from there. If you want a longer experience of the jungle, ask Fernando Rubio, Daniel Alcides Carrión 310, T/F (0051 84) 571638, a month in advance, to use you as a volunteer worker in the Santuario Pampas del Heath, usually Jan-Mar or Aug-Oct: hard work but, to Erik Jennische of Uppsala, very rewarding.

For those interested in seeing a gold rush, a trip to the town of *Laberinto* (one hotel, several poor restaurants) is suggested. The bus leaves Puerto Maldonado at 0900, 1000 and 1100, 3 hrs, US$2.50, and returns in the afternoon daily.

Transport **By Road** To Cusco, 525 km, 50-55 hrs (longer in the rainy season), US$8; only trucks do this route, several a day. It is a hard but spectacular route, from low jungle up to the highest pass at Hualla-Hualla (4,820m), passing through Quincemil (241 km, 15-20 hrs, see above), Marcapata (hot thermal springs, a further 69 km, 5 hrs), Ocongate (92 km, 7 hrs, see end of previous section for these two places) and Urcos (82 km, 6 hrs). This road is impossible in the wet season. Make sure you have warm clothing for travelling through the Sierra. To **Iberia and Iñapari**, 142 km, see **Excursions** above.

By Air Aero Continente, Av Dos de Mayo 313-B, T 571183, US$82 to **Lima** daily; Americana, Av León Velarde 506, T 572119, US$88. To **Cusco** 4 a week with AeroPerú, daily with Americana, US$35. To **Arequipa** US$81, Americana. Grupo Ocho (military flight) twice a month (on the first and third Wed) to **Iberia** and on to **Cusco**, US$20; other flights to Iberia and then Iñapari once a week. Their office is at the airport. To **Rio Branco** (Brazil) several companies, US$70-100. Airport tax US$7.

By Boat To **Boca Manu and Shintuya**, via Colorado. You can get a cargo boat from Puerto Maldonado (daily) to Colorado, 8 hrs, US$8, thence to Boca Manu and Shintuya, 9-10 hrs, US$10. Trucks go to Pilcapata and Cusco (see under Manu). To **Puerto Heath** (Bolivian border), a private boat will charge about US$60, 4 hrs. Make sure that the boat is going all the way to the Bolivian side. (Do not build a raft, despite local support for the idea; the river has dangerous rapids and obstructions.) It is fairly hard to get a boat from the border to Riberalta (a wait of up to 3 days is not uncommon), 3 days, US$15-20; alternatively, travel to the naval base at América, then fly.

Crossing borders Ensure that you get an exit stamp in Puerto Maldonado at the Peruvian immigration office or at the PNP. You cannot get an exit stamp in Iberia or Iñapari at the border. Also check that you do not need a consular visa for Brazil or Bolivia; they are not issued at the border. **To Bolivia**: Take the boat to Puerto Heath and get a tourist visa at the Bolivian immigration office. **To Brazil**: By truck to Iñapari or flight to Iberia and truck from there. Get a tourist visa at the Brazilian immigration in Iñapari.

INLAND FROM LIMA (7)

The central Andes are remote mountain areas with small, typical villages. The vegetation is low, but most valleys are cultivated. Roads, all dirt, are in poor condition, sometimes impassable in the rainy season; the countryside is beautiful with spectacular views and the people are friendly. The road into the central Andes has been improved and is paved throughout, offering fine views. Huancayo lies in a valley which produces many crafts; the festivals are very popular and not to be missed.

The central Andes suffered heavy terrorist disruption in the 1980s and early 1990s, but the region now seems to be under military control. There are many checkpoints and it is advisable to travel only during the day. Knowledge of Spanish is essential, as is informing yourself regularly of the current political situation.

On the Central Railway passenger trains have not run since 1991; all passenger traffic now goes by road until there is sufficient demand for the service to be restored. See under La Oroya, **Roads and Buses**, next page, for transport details. The Central Highway between Lima and Huancayo more or less parallels the course of the railway. For a while, beyond Chosica (**see p 1137**), each successive valley seems to be greener, with a greater variety of trees and flowers.

San Bartolomé (Km 57, 1,513m), is the terminus of the only passenger service currently running, a Sunday train from Lima in the dry season only.

Matucana, Km 84, at 2,390m, is set in wild scenery, where there are beautiful walks. Climbing always, we pass San Mateo (Km 107, 3,215m), where the San Mateo mineral water originates. From San Mateo a spectacular side-road branches off to the Germania mine. Beyond San Mateo is **Infiernillo** (Little Hell) Canyon, to which car excursions are made from Lima, 100 km. (Hotels: **F** *Ritz*, fair, *Grau*, cheap.)

Between Río Blanco and Chicla (Km 127, 3,733m) the Inca contour-terraces can be seen quite clearly. After climbing up from **Casapalca** (Km 139, 4,154m, more mines; the concentrators are at the foot of a deep gorge), there are glorious views of the highest peaks. The road ascends to the Ticlio Pass, before the descent to Morococha and La Oroya. A large metal flag of Peru can be seen at the top of Mount Meiggs, not by any means the highest in the area, but through it runs Galera Tunnel, 1,175m long, in which the Central Railway reaches its greatest altitude, 4,782m. **Ticlio**, the highest passenger station in the world (Km 157, 4,758m), at the mouth of the tunnel, is on one side of a crater in which lies a dark, still lake. There are still higher points on the railway (4,818m at La Cima, and 4,829m on a siding), on the branch of the line that goes through **Morococha**. Here is the Centromín golf course, welcoming to playing visitors, which at 4,400m disputes the title of the world's highest with Mallasilla, near La Paz, Bolivia.

The ruling grade of the Central Railway is about $4\frac{1}{2}°$. Along the whole of its length (335 km to Huancayo) it traverses 66 tunnels, 59 bridges, and 22 zig-zags where the steep mountainside permits no other way of negotiating it. Views during the ascent are beyond compare. This masterpiece was the project of the great American railway engineer, Henry Meiggs, who supervised the construction from 1870 until his death in 1877; it was built by the Pole Ernesto Malinowski, with imported Chinese labour, between 1870 and 1893. Railway buffs may like to know that the last Andes type 2-8-0 steam locomotive, No 206, is still in working order, although usually locked in a shed at Huancayo. It was built specifically for this route in 1953 by Beyer Peacocks of Manchester.

La Oroya (Km 208), the main smelting centre with its slag heaps, is full of vitality. Population: 36,000. It is at the fork of the Yauli and Mantaro rivers at 3,755m, 187 km from Lima by a road. (For places to the E and N of La Oroya, **see p 1260** and 1262 respectively.)

Hotels F *Hostal San Martín*, clean, friendly, no heating but plenty of blankets; *Wilson*; *Lima*. **Restaurants** *Las Vegas*, rec. *Huánuco*, good, cheap food. *Central*, rec. *El Tambo*, 2 km outside La Oroya, good trout and frogs.

Railway N to Tambo del Sol and Cerro de Pasco; SE to Jauja and Concepción (**see p 1254**), Huancayo and Huancavelica; SW to Lima. No passenger services since 1991.

Roads and Buses See under Lima, **Bus Companies** with routes to the central area. At La Oroya, the central highway divides: S, following the valley of the polluted Río Mantaro, to Huancayo, and on to Huancavelica or Ayacucho; N to Cerro de Pasco and on to Huánuco, Tingo María and Pucallpa; 25 km N along this road fork E for Tarma and La Merced.

The road is paved from Lima to Huancayo, but all the other roads are in poor condition, especially when wet. Distances and prices: Lima, to **Matucana**, 81 km, 3 hrs, US$1.80; thence to **Casapalca**, 42 km, 1 hr, US$0.80; **La Oroya**, 56 km, 1½ hrs, US$1. From La Oroya to **Jauja**, 80 km, 1½ hrs, US$1, and on to **Huancayo**, a further 44 km, 1 hr, US$1. La Oroya to **Cerro de Pasco**, 131 km, 5 hrs, US$3, thence to **Huánuco**, 105 km, 3 hrs, US$2, **Tingo María**, 118 km, 5 hrs, US$3 and on to **Pucallpa**, 284 km, 12 hrs, US$5.50. Colectivos also run on all three routes (see under Lima); they are quicker but only leave when full. Prices are double the bus fares.

Huancayo, capital of Junín Department, is the main commercial centre for inland central Peru; alt 3,271m; pop 359,000. The city is in the beautiful Mantaro Valley. All the villages in the valley produce their own original crafts and celebrate festivals the year round. At the important festivals in Huancayo, the Indians flock in from far and wide with an incredible range of food, crafts, dancing and music. The Sun market gives a little taste of this every week (gets going after 0900), even though it has been reduced in size owing to the drop in tourism. Jirón Huancavelica, 3 km long and 4 stalls wide, still sells typical clothes, fruit, vegetables, hardware, handicrafts but especially traditional medicines and goods for witchcraft. There is also an impressive daily market behind the railway station.

Museum at the Salesian school has over 5,000 pieces, including a large collection of jungle birds, animals and butterflies, insects, reptiles and fossils.

Festivals There are so many festivals in the Mantaro Valley that it is impossible to list them all. Practically every day of the year there is a celebration of some sort in one of the villages. We offer a selection. Jan: 1-6, New Year celebrations; 20, San Sebastián y San Fabián. Feb: carnival celebrations for the whole month, with highlights on 2, Virgen de la Candelaria, and 17-19 Concurso de Carnaval. Mar-Apr: Semana Santa, with impressive Good Friday processions. May: Fiesta de las Cruces throughout the whole month. Jun: 15 Virgen de las Mercedes; 24, San Juan Bautista; 29, Fiesta Patronal. Jul: 16, Virgen del Carmen; 24-25, Santiago. Aug: 4, San Juan de Dios; 16, San Roque; 30, Santa Rosa de Lima. Sep: 8, Virgen de Cocharcas; 15, Virgen de la Natividad; 23-24 Virgen de las Mercedes; 29, San Miguel Arcángel. Oct: 4 San Francisco de Asís; 18, San Lucas. Nov: 1, Día de Todos los Santos. Dec: 3-13, Virgen de Guadalupe; 8, Inmaculada Concepción; 25, Navidad (Christmas).

Warning Huancayo has a bad reputation for thieves, especially in the market and at bus stations, although recent reports suggest that things are safer now (1994-95). There is a large military presence owing to terrorist activity. This should not deter visitors, but don't travel at night and on no account go to the jungle areas beyond Huancayo.

Hotels NB Prices may be raised in Holy Week. **B** *Turistas*, Ancash 729, T 231072, with bath, D without, old building, some rooms small, quiet, good meals for US$3.50; **D** *Acolla*, Av Antonio Lobato 505, El Tambo district, private toilet, hot shower; **D** *Kiya*, Giráldez 107, Plaza de Armas, with bath, hot water, restaurant does not serve breakfast, phones in rooms (avoid noisy rooms on Av Real); **D** *Presidente*, Calle Real 1138, T 231736, clean, friendly, helpful, safe, breakfast only, rec; **D** *Santa Felicidad*, Plaza de Armas, with bath, good; **E** *El Dorado*, Piura 428, T 223947, with bath, friendly, clean; **E** *Hostal Palace*, Ancash 1127, with bath, clean, hot water, restaurant; **E** *Percy's*, Real 1399, with bath, basic, clean; **E** *Plaza*, Ancash 171, similar; **E** *Residencia Huancayo*, Av Giráldez 356, T 233541, nr railway station, basic rooms with shared bath and hot showers, friendly and helpful; **E** *Roger*, Ancash 460, T 233488, with bath, basic, clean; **F** *Hospedaje Suizo*, Huancas 473, friendly, safe; **F** *Hostal Baldeón*, Amazonas 543, friendly, laundry facilities, hot shower; **F** *La Casa de Mi Abuela*, Av Giráldez, hot shower, good value, clean, friendly, laundry facilities, meals available, run by Lucho

HUANCAYO

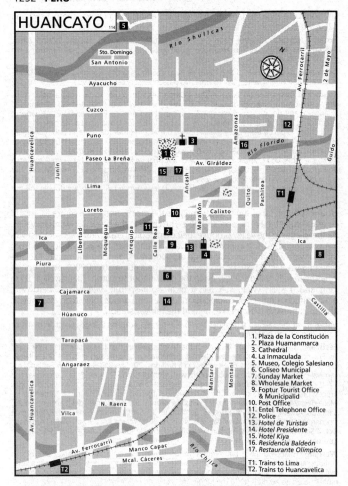

1. Plaza de la Constitución
2. Plaza Huamanmarca
3. Cathedral
4. La Inmaculada
5. Museo, Colegio Salesiano
6. Coliseo Municipal
7. Sunday Market
8. Wholesale Market
9. Foptur Tourist Office
   & Municipalid
10. Post Office
11. Entel Telephone Office
12. Police
13. *Hotel de Turistas*
14. *Hotel Presidente*
15. *Hotel Kiya*
16. *Residencia Baldeón*
17. *Restaurante Olímpico*

T1. Trains to Lima
T2. Trains to Huancavelica

Hurtado's family (**see p 1255**); **F** *Residencial Inca Wasi*, Federico Villareal 106, clean and friendly; **F** *Rey*, Jr Angaráes 327, T 226334, with bath, hot water 0600-0900 (insist on it), clean; **F** *Universal*, Pichis 100, opp railway station, very basic, shared bath, reasonable. The following *hostales* are all **F** with shared bath, or you can pay US$1 extra for private bath, cold water: *Centro*, Loreto 452, large place, basic, no atmosphere; *Los Angeles*, Real 245; *Prince*, Calixto 578, also large and basic; *Real*, Real 885; *Roma*, Loreto 447 (small place); *Torre-Torre*, Real 873, has shared baths with hot water; *Villa Rica*, Real 1291, T 232641, has only shared baths, basic; *Will Roy*, Calixto 452, basic. Luis Hurtado (see below) has 2 rooms (G incl breakfast), with hot water, washing and cooking facilities.

Restaurants Better class, more expensive restaurants, serving typical dishes (about US$4-5, plus 18% tax; drinks can be expensive): *Lalo's*, Giráldez 363; *El Inca*, Puno 530; *Inti Palacio Oriental*, Lima 354; *Olímpico*, Av Giráldez 199, rec as the best in town, not cheap.

Cheaper places for typical food, about US$2-3 a dish, or with a fixed price *menú*, good: *El*

Pino, Real 539; *Pinkys*, Giráldez 147; *Roger*, Ancash 460; *Caramba*, Guido 459; *El Consulado*, 13 de Noviembre 795, El Tambo, serves typical Arequipeña food. *Chifa El Centro*, Giráldez nr Plaza, Chinese, good service. *La Cabaña*, Av Giraldez 600 block, pizzas, ice-cream, *calentitos*, and other dishes, great atmosphere, rec (owned by Beverly Stuart and Lucho Hurtado—see below); *La Cabaña de Don Rafo*, Calle Lima, good for trout. There are lots of cheap restaurants along Av Giráldez serving set menú.

Typical Dishes *Papa a la huancaína*, boiled potatoes with a spicy, cheese sauce; *cuy colorado*, fried guinea pig; *huallpa chupe*, thick chicken soup with potatoes and rice; *chicharrones*, fried crispy pork "knuckles"; *pachamanca*, several kinds of meat and potatoes baked in the oven (or, traditionally, in a hole in the ground); *humitas*, mashed corn filled with cheese or meat.

Peruvian-North American Cultural Institute, Jirón Guido 740.

Banks and Exchange There are several *casas de cambio* on the 4th and 5th blocks of Calle Real; street changers hang out there as well. Also travel agencies and banks will change dollars. The best rates for TCs are with Sr Miguel Velit, Calle Real 552; 5% commission changing into soles, 7% into dollars. The banks usually have the same rate, or sometimes less.

Country Club (very rural) is open to all, in very pleasant surroundings near the Mantaro River, to the N of town.

Entertainment Discotheques *El Molino*, Calle Huancas, by the river; *Sonco-Llay*, Calle Puno; *Clobhino* and *Caribe*, Calle Real; *Cusi Cusi*, Calle Lima; *A1A*, Bolognesi 299. Most open around 2000 and close at 0200. Some charge an entrance fee of US$3-4.
    Peñas All the *peñas* have folklore shows with dancing, open normally Fri, Sat and Sun from 1300 to 2200. Entrance fee about US$2 pp. *Taki Wasi*, Huancavelica y 13 de Noviembre; *Huanrangal*, Calle Santa Rosa; *Ollantaytambo*, Calle Puno, block 2. *Restaurante La Cabaña*, see above, has folk music at weekends.
    Cinemas *Ciné Pacífico*, Calle Real, block 6, and *Ciné Mantaro*, Calle Real 950, El Tambo. Tickets US$1-2.

Shopping/Crafts All crafts are made outside Huancayo in the many villages of the Mantaro Valley, or in Huancavelica. The villages may be visited to learn how the items are made. All crafts are brought to Huancayo or to Lima while tourism in the Highlands remains low. The Sun market is still the place to go for handicrafts if you have only one day to spare. There is a large cooperative, *Kamaq Maki*, which exports alpaca goods, open Mon-Fri 0900-1400. It is well-organized and employs many artesans; its aim is to control the market and prices. It is at Av Palián 1096, Palián (20 mins by bus from Huancayo), is very helpful and will be happy to take you to meet the manufacturers of the goods. The workshop has a small shop. Contact Arturo Durán, T 231206/233183. *Artesanía Sumaq Ruray*, Jr Brasilia 132, San Carlos 5th block, T 237018, produces fine weaving. but is not cheap.

Tourist Information Ministry of Tourism, Ancash 415, 3rd Flr, T 233251, has information about the area, helpful, open 0730-1330 Mon-Fri. Lucho Hurtado and Beverly Stuart (see below) are very helpful for information. There are three travel agencies on Calle Real who organize tours to the surrounding area: *Huancayo Tours*, Calle Real 543, is the best. The others are *Turismo Mantaro* and *Trans Continental Tours*.

Rail There are two unconnected railway stations. The Central station serves Lima, via La Oroya, 298 km, 10 hrs, when the service is running (not since 1991).
    From the small station in Chilca suburb (15 mins by taxi, US$1), trains run to **Huancavelica**, 142 km, narrow guage 3 ft. There are 2 trains: daily, the *autovagón* (*expreso*) US$2.25, at 0630, but at 1400 on Sun. The journey takes 4$\frac{1}{2}$ hrs, a spectacular route with fine views passing through typical mountain villages. Meals, drinks and snacks are served on the train, and at the village stations, vendors sell food and crafts. There is military control on the train. The local train leaves at 1230 Mon-Sat, and takes 6$\frac{1}{2}$ hrs. Tickets cost US$1.80 2nd class, US$2 1st class and US$3.50 buffet class. You can buy tickets one day in advance, or 1 hr before departure. Services can be suspended in the rainy season.

Road Transport To Lima, 7-8 hrs, US$6-7 depending on company. Travelling by day is recommended for views and for safety (take warm clothing when travelling at night). Mariscal Cáceres, Jr Huánuco 350, T 231232, have a *presidencial* service for US$9, no stops, not overcrowded, rec, and ordinary services; also good, Costa Sierra (subsidiary of Ormeño), 3 a day; reasonable services with Molina and Antezana. Hidalgo, Loreto 358 and Los Andes, Calle Lima, are the cheapest, 1 bus a day. Other companies: Etucsa, Puno 220, several a day, Huaytapallana, Calixto 450, Buenaventura, Amazonas 660, Roggero, Calle Lima, Salazar, Calle Real 1285, El Tambo, all with 1 or 2 buses a day. Jara Continental, Calle Breña, has small minibuses, several daily, rec. Small buses for Lima congregate 15 blocks N of Plaza de Armas on Calle Real, much competition for passengers. Comités 12 and 22, both on Calle Loreto, and Comité 30, Calle Giráldez, run to Lima in 6 hrs, when the car is full (sometimes this means waiting all day), US$12 pp.

To **Ayacucho**, 319 km, 16-18 hrs (longer in the rainy season), US$6-9. Empresa Molina, Calle Angaraes 287, has daily buses. Night buses with Hidalgo and Antesana. A hard route, impossible in the wet, but the views are magnificent. Take warm clothing. The military seem to have established control over this route after years of terrorist disruption. Check the situation in advance, though, travel by day, and keep abreast of what is going on. After Izcuchaca (on the railway to Huancavelica) there is a good road to the Kichuas hydroelectric scheme, but thereafter it is narrow with hair-raising bends and spectacular bridges. The scenery is staggering with cacti and thorn bushes or severely eroded badlands, alternating with attractive villages and palm trees. The highest points are dominated by rocky precipices with the snow peaks in the background. From Huanta the road descends into Ayacucho.

To **Huancavelica**, 147 km, 5 hrs, US$3, several buses a day. Another road in poor condition, takes much longer in the wet, but with spectacular scenery. Most travellers use the train.

To **Cerro de Pasco**, 255 km, 5 hrs, US$3. Quite a good paved road to La Oroya, but a dirt road from there to Cerro de Pasco. Transporte Salazar (address above), Nor Pasca and Trans Unión, both on Calle Lima, all have several buses a day. On to Huánuco, 105 km, 3 hrs, US$2, Sudamericano has several daily. Comité 12 does this route for US$15 pp when full. On to Tingo Maria, 118 km, 5 hrs, US$4, Empresa Apzapala, Calle Ayacucho 282, one bus daily.

To **Satipo**, 229 km, 7 hrs, US$4, a very difficult road, impossible in the wet: Empresa San Martín, Calle Ferrocarril 227, Etucsa and Lobato, Jr Ica. To **Cañete**, 289 km, 10 hrs, US$4, some trucks and a few buses, poor road, beautiful mountain landscapes before dropping to the valley of Cañete. To **Jauja**, 44 km, 1 hr, US$0.60, Trans Viasse, Calle Calixto, block 3, buses all day. To **San Jerónimo**, 16 km, 20 mins, US$0.25, and **Concepción**, 22 km, 30 mins, US$0.30, buses all day. Most buses to the Mantaro Valley leave from several places around the market area. Buses to Hualhuas, Cajas and Huamancaca leave from block 3 of Pachitea. Buses to Cochas leave from Parque Inmaculada.

Excursions in the Mantaro Valley The whole valley is rich in culture, music, typical food, dances, handicrafts, etc. On the outskirts of town is Torre-Torre, impressive, eroded sandstone towers on the hillside. Take a bus to Cerrito de la Libertad and walk up. Not far from here is a large park with a depressing zoo, but with a good swimming pool (entry US$0.25).

On the W side of the river: At Sapallanga (8 km), the *fiesta* of the Virgen de Cocharcas on 8 Sep is famous. Viques (19 km) is known for the production of belts and blankets. Huayucachi (7 km) organizes festivals with dancing and impressive costumes in Jan and Feb and also makes embroidery. At Tres de Diciembre is a fish farm, with some good restaurants and swimming pool, walk from Huamancaca. The ruins of **Warivilca** (15 km) are near **Huari**, with the remains of a pre-Inca temple of the Huanca tribe. Museum in the plaza, of deformed skulls, and modelled and painted pottery of successive Huanca and Inca occupations of the shrine. Open 1000-1200 and 1500-1700, US$0.15 admission. Between Pilcomayo and Huayo (15 km) is the Geophysical Institute of Huayo on the "Magnetic Equator" ($12\frac{1}{2}°$ S of the geographical equator). Here meteorological, seismic and cosmic-ray observations are made; best to visit in the morning. Chupaca is a picturesque village with a good Sat market.

Also W of the river visit the Laguna Nahuinpuquio (17 km), nice lake and surrounding countryside; the ruins of **Arwaturo**, 17 km; Sicaya (8 km), festivals in Aug and an 18th century church; Aco makes large ceramic pots; the ruins of Guaqui-Guaqui, just outside the village of Matahulo; Muquiyauyo, famous for its Semana Santa celebrations.

On the E side of the river: Cochas Chicas and Cochas Grandes (11 km), where gourds are carved, highly recommended (beautiful views of Valle de Mantaro and Huancayo). Hualahoyo (11 km) has a little chapel with 21 colonial canvases. San Agustín de Cajas (8km) makes fine hats; San Pedro (10 km) makes wooden chairs; Hualhuas (12 km) fine alpaca weavings. The village of **San Jerónimo**, is renowned for the making of silver filigree jewellery (Wed market). Its fiesta is in Aug. There are ruins 2-3 hrs' walk above San Jerónimo, but seek advice before hiking to them. **Concepción** (21 km, 3,251m) has a market on Sun as well as a colourful bullfight later in the day during the season. From Concepción a branch road (6 km) leads to the **Convent of Santa Rosa de Ocopa**, a Franciscan monastery in beautiful surroundings established in 1725 for training missionaries for the jungle, open 0900-1200 and 1500-1800; closed Tues. It contains a fine library with over 20,000 volumes and a biological museum with animals and insects from the jungle. 8 km from Concepción is Ingenio, with a fish farm in lovely countryside and restaurants in which to try the trout.

18 km beyond Concepción, on the road to La Oroya, is the old town of **Jauja** (3,552m), Pizarro's provisional capital until the founding of Lima. It has a very colourful Wed and Sun market. Jauja is a friendly, unspoilt town, in the middle of a good area for walking, with ruins

near the Paca lake 3½ km away. It has the best archaelogical museum in the Mantaro valley for the Wari culture. A modernised church retains 3 fine 17th-century altars. The Cristo Pobre church is claimed to have been modelled after Notre Dame and is something of a curiosity. On a hill above Jauja there is a fine line of Inca storehouses, and on hills nearby ruins of hundreds of circular stone buildings from the Huanca culture (John Hemming). Hotel: **F** *Ganso de Oro*, nr bus station, opp Entel, no water.

Lucho (Luis) Hurtado (from Huancayo, speaks good English) and his wife, Beverly (from New Zealand) own *Pizzería La Cabaña* (see above); you are always welcome for a pizza and information. They organize Spanish courses (14-day course for US$200, including accommodation with local families, rec), weaving, playing the pan flute, Peruvian cooking and lots of other things. Lucho is an excellent private guide who arranges adventurous, cultural trips in the mountains or jungle, giving a personal touch. He has been highly and repeatedly recommended as a guide. Contact him in Huancayo, or through the South American Explorers Club in Lima.

The road to Satipo branches off near the Convento de Sta Rosa de Ocopa; spectacular scenery, snow-capped mountains in the Paso de la Tortuga, followed by a rapid drop to the Caja de Silva in Satipo (**see p 1261**).

Izcuchaca is the site of a bridge over the Río Mantaro (the name in Quechua means "stone bridge"). The bridge was partly rebuilt in the 18th century. There is a pottery workshop at the edge of town whose machinery is driven by a water turbine (small shop; fascinating). A nice hike is to the chapel on a hill overlooking the valley 1-1½ hrs each way. 2 hotels: one on plaza, G, no bathroom, use public bath by river; the other just off plaza in yellow, 3-storey house, G, no shower, toilet suitable for men only, chamber pot supplied, only blankets on bed, cold. *Restaurant El Parque* on plaza, opens 0700, delicious food. 0630 train from Huancavelica arrives 0800, continues to Huancayo (US$1.15, sit on left, very crowded); train from Huancayo passes at 1700 or so. Daily colectivo to Ayacucho, 1000-1100, 8 hrs.

One route to Ayacucho, little used by buses, but not so much climbing for cyclists: cross the pass into the Mantaro valley on a reopened road to Quichuas (no hotel in village, but a basic place 3 km away by a dam), Anco, rebuilding after a flood (1977), small, basic lodging with running water, to Mayocc (lodging). At Mayocc a bridge is being repaired. From Mayocc go to Huanta, crossing a bridge after 10 km, 20 km from Huanta, then paved road to Ayacucho.

Huancavelica, capital of its Department (altitude, 3,680m; population, 37,500), a friendly and attractive town, is surrounded by huge, rocky mountains. It was founded over 400 years ago by the Spanish to exploit rich deposits of mercury and silver; very few of the mines remain open (those that do are a few hours from town). It is predominantly an Indian town, and people still wear traditional costume. There are beautiful mountain walks in the neighbourhood. The cathedral, located on the Plaza de Armas, has an altar considered to be one of the finest examples of colonial art in Peru. Also very impressive are the five other churches in town: the church of San Francisco has no less than 11 altars. (Sadly most of the churches are closed to visitors.)

Bisecting the town is the Río Huancavelica. South of the river is the main commercial centre where fine leather and alpaca products can be purchased (especially on Calle Virrey Toledo). North of the river on the hillside are the thermal baths (US$0.15 for private rooms, water not very hot, US$0.10 for hot public pool, also hot showers, take lock for doors, open 0600-1500). There is a daily market. At the Sun market, the men wear all black, with multicoloured woollen pom-poms dangling from their skull-caps, waists and knees; these are also used to decorate the livestock. The market is smaller than in the past and most handicrafts are transported directly to Lima, but you can still visit craftsmen in neighbouring villages. There is a daily food market at Muñoz y Barranca. The Potaqchiz hill, just outside the town, gives a fine view, about 30 mins' walk up from San Cristóbal.

Festivals and Crafts The whole area is rich in culture and famous for handicrafts, especially the finely-woven alpaca goods. The Ministry of Tourism is a good source of information about the various *artesanías* and where to find them. In Sep they organize a tourist week with a huge crafts market, music and dancing. Typical festivals: 6 Jan, Niño Occe; 12 Jan, Fiesta de Negritos; carnival in Feb; Palm Sunday procession; Semana Santa; Jun, Fiesta de Torre-Torre; Nov0, Todos los Santos; 25 Dec, Los Galos.

NB The department of Huancavelica has had much terrorist activity, but since 1992 the military has regained control and it is safer to visit. Always carry your documentation, travel by day and find out about latest conditions before travelling.

Hotels B *Turistas*, with private bath, cheaper without, reasonable, on the Plaza, lovely colonial building, restaurant fair; **E** *Mercurio*, Jr Torre-Torre 455, basic, OK; **E** *Ascención*, Manco Capac 485, and **F** *Virrey*, Av Sebastián Barranca 317, both open only in tourist season, with bath. **F** *Tahuantinsuyo*, Jr Carabaya 399, nr Plaza de Armas, best middle range hotel, hot shower in am only, clean and well maintained. **G** pp *Cabacho*, Jr Carabaya 481, best budget place, friendly, clean, shared bath hot water; **G** pp *Santo Domingo*, Av S Barranca 366, and *Savoy*, Av Muñoz 294, both cheap, very basic, shared bath, cold water.

Restaurants There are lots of cheap, basic restaurants on Calle Muñoz and Jr Virrey Toledo. All serve typical food, mostly with set menu, US$1.50. There are some middle class places which charge about US$2-4/dish. Basic and cheap are: *La Estrellita*, Av Sebastián Barranca 255; *Ganso de Oro*, Jr Virrey Toledo 283; *Olímpico*, Jr JM Chávez 124; *Super Gordo*, Av Celestino Muñoz 488; *Termales*, Av Barranca 370; *Paquirri*, Jr Arequipa 137; *Yananaco*, Av Cáceres 533. Better are *César's*, Av Muñoz 390; *Olla de Barro*, Jr A Gamarra 305; *La Casona*, Jr Virrey Toledo 230, cheap and good menu; *Señorial*, Plaza de Armas, cheap *menú ejecutivo*; *Las Magnolias*, Manuel Muñoz one block from the Plaza, the best. **Bakery** *Las Delicias*, Plaza de Armas, good.

Exchange Banco de Crédito, Virrey Toledo 300 block.

Telecommunications Entel, Carabaya y Virrey Toledo.

Tourist Office Ministerio de Industria y Comercio, Turismo y Artesanías, Jirón Nicolás de Piérola 180, T (064) 2938, open Mon-Fri 0730-1400, very helpful. Instituto Nacional de la Cultura, Plaza San Juan de Dios, open Mon-Sat 1000-1300, 1500-1900, director Alfonso Zuasnabar, a good source of information on festivals, archaeological sites, history, and customs. Gives courses on music and dancing, and lectures some evenings. There is also an interesting but small archaeology and anthropology museum.

Transport By train, see under Huancayo; the *autovagón/expreso* leaves for Huancayo at 1230, the local train at 0630.

  By bus: All bus companies have their offices on and leave from Calle Muñoz. To **Huancayo**, 147 km, 5 hrs (longer in the wet), US$3, several buses a day. To **Lima** there are two routes: via Huancayo, 445 km, 13 hrs minimum, US$9. Most buses to Huancayo go on to Lima, there are several a day. This is the better and quicker route. The other route is via **Pisco**, 269 km, 13-20 hrs, US$9. Only one bus a day (at 0600, Oropesa, buy ticket one day in advance) and some trucks; the road is in very poor condition, but the views are spectacular and worth the effort. The road climbs to the Chonta Pass (4,800m), continues over the high pampa passing huge lakes, snow-capped mountains and small mountain villages. Alpaca, llama and vicuña can be seen. The road then descends to the Libertad valley, a long ride through a steep gorge on a narrow dirt road, before reaching Pisco on the coast. Be prepared for sub-zero temperatures am as bus passes snowfields, then for temperatures of 25-30°C as bus descends to coast pm.

  Getting to **Ayacucho** (247 km) is a problem, as there are no buses. Either take the train to Izcuchaca, stay the night and take the colectivo (see above). Alternatively, ask around town for a truck leaving for Ayacucho; you may be lucky. Alternatively take a bus to Santa Inés, then a truck to Rumichaca, the junction where buses and trucks on the Lima-Ayacucho route pass. Buses go through Rumichaca at 0300-0400 only, but there are many trucks and police at the checkpoint may help with lifts. Take an Oropesa bus from Huancavelica to Santa Inés at 0600, which allows plenty of time for a truck to Rumichaca and then another to Ayacucho (Rumichaca-Ayacucho 7 hrs by truck, 4 hrs by bus). The road is in appalling condition, cold but spectacular as it is the highest continuous road in the world, rarely dropping below 4,000m for 150 km.

  Out of Huancavelica one climbs steeply on a road that switchbacks between herds of llamas and alpacas grazing on rocky perches. Around Pucapampa (Km 43) is one of the highest habitable *altiplanos* (4,500m), where the rare and highly prized ash-grey alpaca can be seen. *Santa Inés*, 78 km, has one restaurant where you can sleep (very friendly) and several others. Nearby are two lakes (Laguna Choclacocha) which can be visited in 2½ hrs. 50 km beyond Santa Inés at the Abra de Apacheta (4,750m, 98 from Ayacucho), the rocks are all colours of the rainbow, and running through this fabulous scenery is a violet river (all caused by oxides). Eleven km later one encounters Paso Chonta and the turnoff to Huachocolpa. By taking the turnoff and continuing for 3 km one discovers the highest drivable pass (5,059m) in the world.

Ayacucho, capital of its Department, was founded on 9 January 1539. This old colonial city is built round Parque Sucre with the Cathedral, Municipalidad and

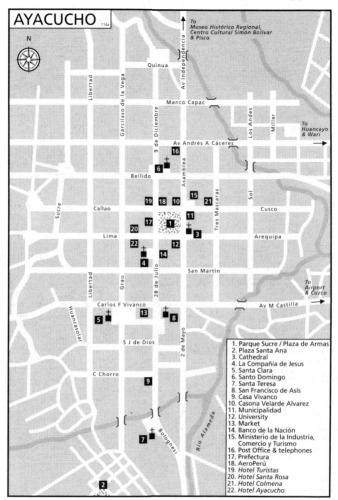

AYACUCHO 114a

1. Parque Sucre / Plaza de Armas
2. Plaza Santa Ana
3. Cathedral
4. La Compañía de Jesus
5. Santa Clara
6. Santo Domingo
7. Santa Teresa
8. San Francisco de Asís
9. Casa Vivanco
10. Casona Velarde Alvarez
11. Municipalidad
12. University
13. Market
14. Banco de la Nación
15. Ministerio de la Industria, Comercio y Turismo
16. Post Office & telephones
17. Prefectura
18. AeroPerú
19. *Hotel Turistas*
20. *Hotel Santa Rosa*
21. *Hotel Colmena*
22. *Hotel Ayacucho*

Palacio de Gobierno facing on to it. The city is famous for its religious processions and its splendid market. There are no less than 33 churches—some long deserted and most closed—and a number of ruined colonial mansions. A week can be spent there and in the surroundings, which include La Quinua, site of the battle of Ayacucho, 9 December 1824, which brought Spanish rule to an end in Peru. Ayacucho has a very active student life. Altitude: 2,440m, with gently rolling hills around. A 364-km road has been built to Pisco on the coast. Population: 101,600.

Visitors are advised to see the 17th century Cathedral (1612, superb altars and pulpit, also with Museo de Arte Religioso, closed indefinitely) and churches of San Francisco de Asís, La

Compañía de Jesús (1605, with adjacent chapel), Santa Clara, Santo Domingo (1548, fine façade), and Santa Teresa (1683, with monastery), all with magnificent gold-leafed altars heavily brocaded and carved in the churrigueresque style. There is a small but surprising Museo Histórico Natural, Jr Arequipa 175, in the Centro Cultural Simón Bolívar, open daily 0900-1300, US$0.35; also Museo Antropológico, close to University Residences, N end of town (many Huari artifacts). Tombs of the Huari nobles are being excavated along the road from Ayacucho to Quinua. The University, founded 1677, closed 1886, was reopened in 1958.

The most important mansions are La Casona Velarde Alvarez, Portal Unión 37; Casona Chacón, Portal Unión 30 (mestizo colonial style); and Casona Vivanco, Jr 28 de Julio 512 (late 16th century), housing a museum of prehispanic, colonial, republican and contemporary art (ask permission to visit at Banco Industrial del Perú, 28 de Julio y Lima).

Festivals The area is well-known for its festivals throughout the year. Almost every day there is a celebration in one of the surrounding villages. Check with the Ministry of Tourism. Semana Santa begins on the Fri before Holy Week with the procession of the Virgen de los Dolores (very beautiful, but the suffering is "symbolised" by the custom of flinging pebbles from slingshots, aimed mainly at youngsters, but also foreigners). A charming Palm Sunday procession, beginning at 1600, of palm-bearing women and children accompanies a statue of Christ riding on a white donkey. There follows one of the world's finest Holy Week celebrations, with candle-lit nightly processions, floral "paintings" on the streets, daily fairs (the biggest on Easter Saturday), horse races and contests among peoples from all central Peru.

NB Ayacucho suffered the most from terrorist activity because it was where Sendero Luminoso started operating in 1980. Since 1992 the area has been under military control and even though there are lots of checkpoints, few travellers have encountered problems visiting the region in 1994/95. Tourist services are being quickly re-established, the city is hospitable and interesting. Make sure you get the latest information before going, and travel by day.

Hotels B *Turistas*, 9 de Diciembre 184, T 912202/3 with bath, D without, comfortable (meals mediocre); **D** *Hostelería Santa Rosa*, Jirón Lima 166, T 912083, with bath, hot water mornings and evenings, friendly, car park, restaurant, rec. **E** *Colmena*, Jirón Cusco 140, just off Plaza de Armas, T 912146, a beautiful building, nice rooms with table and bath (F without), clean, wardrobe, good but no hot water, secure, good restaurant below; **E** *Hostal Tres Mascaras*, Jr Tres Mascaras 194, T 913520, clean, balcony, good views, a bit noisy; **E** *Magdalena*, Av Centenario 277, T 912910, with bath, cheaper without, basic but good; similar are *Huamanga*, Jr Bellido 535, T 913527, and *Samary*, Jr Callao 329-335, T 912442, clean, safe, hot water in am. **F** *La Sixtina*, Jirón Callao 336, T 912018, basic but friendly, clean, shared bath, cold water, clothes washing facilities, water only early am and pm until 2000, noisy; **F** *Ayacucho*, Jr Lima 165, T 912759, just off the Plaza, cheap, shared bath, basic. The following *Hostales* are all **F**, basic, with shared bath and cold water: *Santiago*, Nazareno 177, T 912132, *Residencial La Crillonesa*, Nazareno 165, T 912350, not very clean, friendly; *Mariscal Cáceres*, Av Centenario 695; *Central*, Jr Arequipa 180, T 912144, clean; *Grau*, Jr San Juan de Dios 192, T 912695. It is extremely difficult to find accommodation at Easter.

Restaurants *Tradición*, San Martin 406, popular, good variety and value; *San Agustín Café Turístico*, Jr Cusco 101, good food and lemon meringue pie, rec for snacks; *La Casona*, Jr Bellido, behind *Turistas*, rec. On the Plaza de Armas, *Chifa La Fragata*, Portal Unión 33, is good. *Camino Brent*, Asamblea 120, basic meals, OK; *Cameycar*, Asamblea 263; *La Buena Salud*, Jr Asamblea 204, vegetarian, cheap menú. *Cafetería M y T*, 28 de Julio 183, friendly, modern, meeting place, rec. The airport offers a good breakfast. Bakery *Santa Bertha*, Av Cáceres 829. Try *mondongo*, a soup made from meat, maize and mint, also *ponche*, a hot drink made of peanuts, coconut and cinnamon.

Exchange It is easy to change dollars cash in Ayacucho and the rate is OK. TCs are difficult to change, except at **Banco de Crédito**, 28 de Julio y San Martín, no commission.

Post Office and Telephones (Entel) Asamblea esq Cáceres.

Handicrafts Local crafts include filigree silver, often using *mudéjar* patterns; little painted altars which show the manger scene, carvings in local alabaster, harps, or the pre-Inca tradition of carving dried gourds. The most famous goods are carpets and *retablos* (wooden boxes containing three-dimensional scenes in papier maché). In both weaving and *retablos*, scenes of recent political strife have been added to more traditional motifs. Due to the dramatic decline in tourism in recent years, many craftsmen left Ayacucho, but are now returning and re-establishing their businesses. For carpets, go to Barrio Santa Ana, main plaza, *Familia Sulca* (good quality but expensive), or *Familia Fernández*. In Barrio Belén, *Familia Pizarro*, Jr San Cristóbal 215, works in textiles and *piedra huamanga* (local alabaster), good quality.

Swimming Pool *Piscina Paraíso*, Av Carmen Alto 139.

Tourist Information Ministerio de Turismo (MICTI), Asamblea 138, just off the Plaza, T 912548/913162, open Mon-Fri 0800-1300, friendly and helpful. Also available from Ayacucho Tours, San Martín 406, near market, or from the AeroPerú office (Plaza de Armas). Also rec, for information and excursions, *Wari Tours* and *Morochucos Travel Service*, Portal Constitución 14, T/F 912261.

Air To Lima, 40 mins, US$43 one way, Faucett, Aero Continente and Americana have daily flights, AeroPerú 5 a week. Much military scrutiny at airport. Airport tax US$5. Taxi to airport, US$1, buses or colectivos from Plaza de Armas; at airport walk $1/2$ block down street for bus to centre. Americana office at Jr 28 de Julio 112, T 912536.

Buses To Pisco, 332 km, 11-12 hrs in dry season, US$10, buses daily; poor road, good views. Most buses go on to Lima (eg Fano, Pasaje Cáceres 150, US$11, 1500-1600; Transmar, Av Mcal Cáceres 1288; Expreso Libertadores, Cáceres 896; Expreso Molina at 1500), so far Pisco itself, Ica or Nazca, you have to leave the bus 5 km from Pisco on the Panamericana, then take taxi (expensive). To **Huancayo**, 319 km, 16-18 hrs (longer in the wet), US$6-9, Empresa Molina (Tres Máscaras 551) at 0700, 1400 (Sun 1600), 1500 (Sun 1700), Fano and Transporte Ayacucho daily; same advice as given under Huancayo. Buses to Lima and Huancayo all leave at the same time to avoid robberies. For **Huancavelica**, take a Pisco bus to Pámpano, via the Abra de Apacheta (Apacheta-Pámpano, 5 hrs). In Pámpano wait in a restaurant till next day (no hotels); a bus runs to Santa Inés at 1100 or 1200, arriving at 1900. From Santa Inés take a truck to Huancavelica, or there is a bus between 1600-1700 (3 hrs Santa Inés-Huancavelica).

To **Andahuaylas**, 252 km, 17 hrs (more in the rainy season), Hnos Wari, Fano and Molina US$7.50, Etasa on Sun US$5; continuing to **Abancay**, 135 km, 5$1/2$ hrs minimum, US$3.50, and on to **Cusco**, a further 195 km, 6 hrs in the dry season, US$7. There are several buses, pick-ups and trucks daily, none going directly all the way through. Road conditions are bad, but the scenery makes up for it. Terrorist activity has declined and there are several military checkpoints, but it is still not very safe to travel this route; check before going.

Excursions Inca ruins at *Vilcashuamán*, to the S, beyond Cangallo; "there is a five-tiered, stepped *usnu* platform faced in fine Inca masonry and topped by a monolithic two-seat throne. The parish church is built in part of the Inca sun temple and rests on stretches of Inca terracing. Vilcashuamán was an important provincial capital, the crossroads where the road from Cusco to the Pacific met the empire's north-south highway" (John Hemming). Taxi trips can be arranged with Ayacucho Tours and Morochucos Tours, alternatively stay overnight; market day is Wed. A good road going N from Ayacucho (trucks from Calle Salvador Calvero) leads to Huari (**see p 1254**), dating from the "Middle Horizon", when the Huari culture spread across most of Peru (US$0.80 by public transport). Trips can be arranged by Ayacucho Tours, rec, who do a tour to Huari, La Quinua village and battlefield. *La Quinua* village, 37 km NE of Ayacucho, has a charming cobbled main square and many of the buildings have been restored; there is a small market on Sun. There is a huge obelisk to commemorate the battle of Ayacucho (also a museum, US$1.40, small, poorly displayed). Handicrafts are recommended, guitars and, especially ceramics (but many potters have moved to Lima); most houses have miniature ceramic churches on the roof. San Pedro Ceramics, at foot of hill leading to monument, and Mamerto Sánchez, Jr Sucre, should be visited. The village's festival is celebrated around 7-8 Oct, lasting 3 days. Beautiful 18 km walk downhill from La Quinua to Huari, where trucks leave for Ayacucho until about 1700. Minibus Ayacucho-La Quinua US$1.15, several daily.

San Francisco in the jungle on the Río Apurímac (3 basic hotels, **E** *Suria*, the best but dirty) can be reached by bus from Ayacucho (junction of Av Centenario and Av Cavero) on Sat (return Mon), 10-12 hrs on a very bad road often impassable in the wet season (very cold at night; check the political situation before travelling). Trucks travel daily leaving at about 0700 (wait at police control near airport), US$8 in driver's cabin, US$4.80 on back, or private cars, twice the price, bargain hard. From San Francisco you can take a morning canoe to *Luisiana*, about 2 hrs upstream, to stay in Sr Parodi's **C** *Jungle Hotel*, Centro Vacacional de Luisiana, with swimming pool, on his large *hacienda*; trips are organized in the jungle but it is only open for 3 months in the dry season and Sr Parodi is not always there. There is an airstrip at Luisiana with daily connections to Ayacucho, for over five passengers. Details in the Ayacucho Tourist Office. From San Francisco you can make excursions to nearby villages on cargo canoes, but it is very difficult to find transport all the way to Pucallpa unless you have a large group of people and are willing to pay handsomely.

The road towards Cusco goes through *Chincheros* (**G** pp *Hostal Don José*, clean, friendly, pleasant courtyard, warm), 158 km from Ayacucho, a picturesque town with a flag-raising ceremony on Sun. Ask for the bakery with its outdoor oven. 8 km uphill is Usipa with a good Sun market. 80 km further is *Andahuaylas*, in a fertile, temperate valley of lush meadows, cornfields and groves of eucalyptus, alders and willows. It offers few exotic crafts, no comfortable accommodation (you may have to register with the PNP, depto Seguridad del Estado, Av Perú 459), no lighting except in the plaza, poor transport, but beautiful, largely undiscovered scenery. Good market on Sun.

Hotels **C** *Turistas*, Jr Dias Bárcenas 500, T (084) 223339 (book through Cusco); **F** pp *Américas*, nr *Delicias*, hot shower, clean, friendly, rec; **F** *Cusco*, Casafranca 520, hot shower; **F** *Delicias*, Ramos 525, hot showers, basic but rec, 7 rooms, ask for extra blankets, cold at night; **F** *Wari*, Ramos 427, hot shower; **G** *Bienvenidos*, formerly *28 de Julio*, Andahuaylas 364, cheap, adequate. Pleasant 'pub' on the main square, has animal skins on the walls; **G** *Chipana*, Castilla 251, dirty, laundry facilities; **G** *Mesón*, Trelles 217; **G** *San Agustín*, Castilla 264.

Air Daily flights to Lima, US$45.

Bus To **Ayacucho**, 17 hrs, US$7.50, daily buses with Molino, Hnos Wari, Fano, at 1300; to **Abancay** with Señor de Huanca at 0600 and 1300 daily, 6 hrs, US$4.50; to **Cusco**, same company, 0600, 14 hrs, US$9.

Ronald Berg, of Cambridge, Mass, writes: Around Andahuaylas the old road by the river to Talavera offers some pleasant scenery. San Jerónimo is another picturesque town nearby. Most worth seeing is Pacucha, an hour's ride by truck or colectivo (US$0.50) from Andahuaylas. Pick-ups leave from the centre of Andahuaylas daily, most frequently on Sun, which is market day. Pacucha (pop 2,000) is the largest of six villages on the shores of a large lake, with a view of mountains to the NW. In the plaza, where the trucks stop, women sell bread, coffee and hot lunches, the only food for 16 km. There are dirt roads around the lake and the circumference can be done in an afternoon (but be back in Pacucha before dark to ensure transport back to Andahuaylas). The wildlife includes many types of wild duck and other birds, sometimes including flocks of green parrots and swallows. Opposite Pacucha, some 2 km past the lake, are the ruins of a Chanka fortress called Sóndor. The trails into the jungle beyond the lake are not recommended: the area is very desolate. Except for Andahuaylas itself, this is a mainly Quechua-speaking region. It is one of the poorest parts of Peru, but as long as you do not display your wealth or eat in public, the people tend to be friendly to foreigners.

Abancay is first glimpsed when you are 62 km away by road, nestled between mountains in the upper reaches of a glacial valley. Friendly town. There is a petrol station. From Abancay a 470 km road runs SW through Chalhuanca (gasoline sold from the drum) and Puquío to Nazca on the Pan-American Highway (**see p 1101**).

Hotels **B** *Turistas*, T (084) 223339 (book through Cusco), with bath, **D** without, food good, US$3, comfortable, old-fashioned house, safe car park, camping permitted at US$3; **F** *Abancay*; **F** *Alojamiento Centenario*; **G** *El Misti*, fair; **G** *Gran Hotel*, with bath. **Restaurant** *Elena*, on same street as bus companies, good.

Several bus companies from Abancay to Cusco from near the market (daily direct at 0600 and 1300, US$7, 7 hrs in dry season), also colectivos; dramatic scenery especially in Apurímac valley, but most of the road between Abancay and Cusco is very bad. **See p 1234** for sites of interest between Abancay and Cusco. Services to Andahuaylas US$4.50, 5½ hrs, 0600 and 1300 daily; change there for Ayacucho.

East of La Oroya The 60-km surfaced road to Tarma follows the Cerro de Pasco road for 25 km, then branches off to rejoin the old road quite near Tarma, which is 600m lower than La Oroya.

Tarma (pop 105,200; alt 3,050m), was a nice little flat-roofed town, founded in 1545, with plenty of trees. It is now growing, and there are garish modern buildings, but it still has a lot of charm. Semana Santa celebrations are spectacular, with a very colourful Easter Sunday morning procession in main plaza; Indians make fine flower-carpets. The cathedral is dedicated to Santa Ana. The surrounding countryside is beautiful; much terrorist activity here, avoid or check before you go.

Hotels **C** *Turistas*, with and without bath, acceptable meals US$3.20, rather run down; medium-priced hotels are on the plaza, eg *Tuchu* and *Internacional*, both reasonable; **F** *Central*, Calle Huánuco, nr Coliseum, T 2466, reasonable; **F** *El Dorado*, same street, T 2598, also reasonable. Other cheap places around the market.

Restaurants *Tradición*, Jr Moquegua 350, good. *Chavín Café*, beneath *Galaxia* hotel, on square, trout rec; several on Lima, including a vegetarian place. The *manjarblanco* of Tarma is famous; also *pachamanca*, *mondongo* and *picante de cuyes*.

Bus To **Lima**, 231 km, 8 hrs, US$5, direct buses daily. Direct bus service, **Huancayo**-Tarma, twice daily 0600 and 1600, US$3.45. Daily colectivos from Jirón Huánuco 439 run almost hourly to Huancayo, US$3.80, 2½ hrs, bus to **Oroya**, US$2.40, colectivo, US$3; bus to **La Merced**, US$2.65; colectivos often leave for Chanchamayo, US$3.45. Passes over high limestone hills with caves.

Visit the Grutas de Guagapo (*La boca que Llora*: the cave that weeps), 4 km from town of Polcamayo—bus twice daily from Tarma US$1 (2 hrs). The caves can be entered for about 300m. Even without a guide you can penetrate the cave for some way with a torch.

8 km from Tarma (bus US$0.20, or pleasant 2 hrs' walk), the small hillside town of **Acobamba** has the futuristic Santuario de Muruhuay, with a venerated picture painted on the rock behind the altar. It also has fine *tapices* depicting the Crucifixion, made in San Pedro de Cajas. Festivities all May.

Hotels Two **G** *alojamientos* (Doña Norma's nr plaza, is basic but clean and friendly). Daily **buses** to Tarma, La Oroya (US$0.60) and Huancayo; 3 buses a week direct to Lima (Coop San Pedro).

The road from Tarma via Acobamba and Polcamayo, continues from Palcamayo (no buses, 3-hrs' walk) to **San Pedro de Cajas**, a large village which used to produce most of the coloured sheep-wool weavings for sale in Lima. Most of the weaving families have now moved to Lima. **G** *Hotel Comercio*, Calle Chanchamayo; 2 restaurants; no shops. The road continues on to rejoin the one from La Oroya to Cerro de Pasco below Junín.

Beyond Tarma the road is steep and crooked but there are few places where cars cannot pass one another. In the 80 km between Tarma and La Merced the road, passing by great overhanging cliffs, drops 2,450m and the vegetation changes dramatically from temperate to tropical. A really beautiful run.

Some 11 km before La Merced is **San Ramón** (pop 7,000).

Lodging and food **E** *Conquistador*, with shower, parking, on main street. There is a rec *chifa* on the main street, and the *Hawaii* is good for juices. *La Estancia*, Tarma 592, local specialities.

La Merced (pop 10,000), lies in the fertile Chanchamayo valley. Sometimes Campa Indians come to town selling bows and arrows, and there is a small but interesting market selling snake skins, hides, armadillo shells, etc. Festival in the last week of Sep.

Hotels **E** *Cosmos*, opp police station, fair, probably quieter than others; **E** *Rey* and *Christina*, good, with bath; **F** *Hostal Mercedes*, with bath, hot water, clean, rec; **F** *Romero*, Plaza de Armas, T 2106, good but noisy and water in evenings only. Best **restaurant** is *Shambari-Campa*, off Plaza de Armas; *Hong Kong*, restaurant; plenty of bars patronized by the coffee workers, who spend 6 months in the mountains each year.

Note that San Ramón and La Merced are collectively referred to as **Chanchamayo**. Many buses, both from **Lima** (eg Transportes Chanchamayo, best, Av Luna Pizarro 453, La Victoria, Lima; Los Andes, Arellano, good, 10 hrs, US$6.40) and from **Tarma** (US$2.35, 3 hrs). Bus La Merced-**Puerto Bermúdez**, 8 hrs, US$6.40, 1000 (Túpac Amaru). To get to **Pucallpa**, take a launch from Puerto Bermúdez to Laurencia (8 hrs, or more, be prepared for wet luggage), then truck to Constitución, 20 mins, thence colectivo to Zungaro, 1½ hrs. From Zungaro, colectivos take 4½ hrs, to Pucallpa. Alternatively, you can take a truck from La Merced to Pucallpa, 3 days, but between 0830 and 1400 each day you will probably be drenched by rain.

From La Merced the Carretera Marginal de la Selva (a grandiose edge-of-the-jungle project of the mid-1960s, of which some parts have been built) goes to the jungle town of **Satipo** (Lobato or Los Andes buses from La Merced US$7.20 at 0800; **D** *Hostal Majestic*, with bath, no clothes-washing facilities, electricity 1900-2300 only; **F** *La Residencial*, 4 rooms, clean, garden, swimming pool, rec, many smaller hotels, all very basic, the best being **E** *Palmero*, with bath, not very clean; try *Dany's Restaurant* for good food). There are daily buses direct from Satipo to Huancayo (check whether tunnels are open) and Lima at night, very cold, US$9.50, 12 hrs, Los Andes and Lobato.

About 22 km beyond La Merced is San Luis de Shuaro, but 3 km before it is reached a road, right, runs up the valley of the Perené river. The Perené colony, a concession of 400,000 hectares, nine-tenths of it still unexplored, has large coffee plantations. The altitude is only 700m. Sat and Sun are market days.

The road has been extended from San Luis de Shuaro over an intervening mountain range for 56 km to **Oxapampa**, 390 km from Lima, in a fertile plain on the Río Huancabamba, a tributary of the Ucayali. Population, 5,140; altitude, 1,794m. Logging, coffee, cattle are local industries, colectivo service from La Merced (taxis leave at 0600, US$2, 4 hrs, very slow-going). A third of the inhabitants are descendants of a German-Austrian community of 70 families which settled in 1859 at **Pozuzo**, 80 km downstream, and spread later to Oxapampa. There is much livestock farming and coffee is planted on land cleared by the timber trade. 25 km from Oxapampa is Huancabamba, from where it is 55 km to Pozuzo; the whole road between La Merced and Pozuzo is very rough, depending on the season, 30 rivers to be crossed. Downstream 40 km from Pozuzo is Nuevo Pozuzo (no transport, 2-day walk); Padre Pedro has a collection of insects, weapons and stones in his office. There is a family near Padre Pedro's house who welcome guests for dinner (US$1), German spoken. Interesting museum opposite church in town centre.

Oxapampa Hotels E *Rey*, with bath, new, clean, cold water, small beds; F *Arias*, cheaper without bath, clean, new, best value; F *José*, without bath, hot water, clean, pleasant; F *Hostal Jiménez*, Grau 421, refurbished, clean, cold water, shared bath; F *Hostal Liz*, Av Oxapampa 104, clean, small rooms, cold water; the following are in old buildings: G *Hostal Santa Isolina*, Jirón M Castilla 177, with bath, cold water; F *Santo Domingo*, clean, no hot water; G *La Cabaña*, on plaza, smelly, cold water, a dump; worse is G *San Martín*, tiny rooms, smelly bathroom. **Restaurants** *Oasis*, highly rec.

Pozuzo Hotels E *Hostal Tirol*, full board, clean, rec; F *Hostal Prusia*, clean; F-G *Hostal Maldonado*, clean, rec.

Transport Sr Luis Orbeza's *mixto* leaves from Oxapampa, opp *Hotel Bolívar*, to Pozuzo on Mon, Wed, and Fri, early morning, returning 0700, US$4.50, Tues, Thur, Sat, 6 hrs on a very rough road. Buses from Lima to Pozuzo with La Victoria, from 28 de Julio 2405, Mon, Thur, Sat, 0800, US$12, about 16 hrs.

There is an 'air-colectivo' service from La Merced to **Puerto Bermúdez** on the Río Neguachi, 10 kg baggage allowance, US$5/kg of excess luggage. The service continues to Atalaya, Satipo, Puerto Inca (see p 1270) and Pucallpa. Bus service, La Merced-Puerto Bermúdez (see below). Air-colectivos go to Lima and to most places in the jungle region where there is an airstrip; flights are cheap but irregular, and depend on technical factors, weather and good will. Aero-taxis can be chartered (*viaje especial*) to anywhere for a higher price, maximum 5 people, you have to pay for the pilot's return to base. In Puerto Bermúdez there is accommodation (F *Hostal Tania*, opp dock where motorized canoes tie up, clean), an eating house opposite the airstrip; boat passages possible from passing traders.

North of La Oroya A paved road runs 130 km N from La Oroya to Cerro de Pasco. It runs up the Mantaro valley through narrow canyons to the wet and mournful Junín pampa at over 4,250m, one of the world's largest high-altitude plains: an obelisk marks the battlefield where the Peruvians under Bolívar defeated the Spaniards in 1824. Blue peaks line the pampa in a distant wall. The wind-swept sheet of yellow grass is bitterly cold. The only signs of life are the youthful herders with their sheep and llamas. The line follows the E shores of the Lago de Junín. The town of **Junín**, with its picturesque red-tiled roofs, stands beside its lake.

Some 13 km E of the village of Shelby, served by the railway from La Oroya to Cerro de Pasco, a good section of Inca road may be seen. Its course is marked by the lonely ruins of Bonbón, an Inca community centre only recently identified, which in turn lies close to the modern dam holding back the Río Mantaro as it flows out of the northern end of Lago de Junín.

The main line goes to the long-established mining centre of **Cerro de Pasco** (population 29,810, altitude 4,330m), 130 km from La Oroya by road. It is not a pleasant town, having many beggars and thieves and much unemployment. The nights are bitterly cold. Copper, zinc, lead, gold and silver are mined here, and coal comes from the deep canyon of Goyllarisquisga, the 'place where a star fell', the highest coal mine in the world, 42 km N of Cerro de Pasco. A new town—San Juan de Pampa—has been built 1½ km away (*Gran Hotel*, noisy, no hot water, poor service). A recommended excursion is to the precolumbian funeral towers at Cantamasia, reached on muleback.

Hotels **E** *Gran Hotel Cerro de Pasco*, Av Angamos in San Juan suburb, shower, little hot water, poor service, noisy; **F** *El Viajero*, on the plaza, clean but no hot water; **F** *Santa Rosa*, basic, very cold; *Restaurant Los Angeles*, nr market, rec. Local specialities, trout and fried frog.

Train Since 1991 the train service has been suspended.

Buses Bus to **Lima**, departs 0830 and 2000, 9 hrs, US$8. To **La Oroya**, bus from Plaza Arenales, 0900 and later, US$1.20; cars go when there are passengers, US$9.50. To **Huancayo**, US$4.75. Colectivos to **Huánuco**, US$6.20, from the central plaza. Buses to Huánuco leave between 0800 and 0900 from Plaza de Armas (5 hrs, US$2).

Some 65 km NW of Cerro de Pasco is **Yanahuanca**, in the beautiful valley of the same name. From the village one can reach one of the longest surviving stretches of Inca road. 2 km up the Yanahuanca Valley a lesser valley cuts northwards between the towering crags. The road, its paving uneven and disturbed by countless horse and donkey convoys, leads up the smaller valley, its course sometimes shared by a stream, to the village of Huarautambo, about 4 km distant. This village is surrounded by many pre-Inca remains. For more than 150 km the *Camino Incaico* is not only in almost continuous existence from the Yanahuanca Valley but is actually shown on the map issued by the Instituto Geográfico Militar. The clearest stretch ends at Huari in Ancash, having passed by such places as La Unión (**see p 1265**) and San Marcos. After Huari its route may be followed, less distinctly, through Llamellín and in the hills behind San Luis, Piscobamba and Pomabamba (**see p 1149**).

Warning The central highlands have suffered from terrorist activity in recent years, but since 1992 the area seems to be under military control. Travellers have started to visit the region again, with good reports. Before going, though, check on the situation, only travel by day, and stay in contact with the locals.

CERRO DE PASCO TO IQUITOS (8)

Gaunt Andean passes plunge down steep valleys into the tropics; this is backwater country. Iquitos, though, combines a frontier feel with many incongruous features: MTV cabled from the USA blares from riverside bars; wrought iron architecture designed by Eiffel hints at the booms which founded the city. Jungle experiences range from survival training to a/c comfort; passenger boats ply downstream to Manaus.

The Central Highway There are two roads from Lima to Cerro de Pasco. One goes via *Canta* (3 buses daily to and from Lima, US$3.60—El Canteño company, San Román 151-153, Lima). Hotel: *Kalapacho*, friendly, good value, and one good restaurant in Canta, from where one can visit the pre-Inca ruins of *Cantamarca*—many of the buildings still have roofs, supported by pillars; it is a 2-3 hrs' walk up to the ruins, from where there are extensive views. Continuing through the beautiful high pass of La Viuda (4,748m), one goes to the mines of Alpamarca (truck from Canta, 0200, take warm clothes, blanket, camping gear, food). From here there are 2-3 buses/week to Huallay, where there is the Bosque de Piedras (an outcrop of weathered limestone pinnacles which look from a distance like plantations of conifers). Thence to Cerro de Pasco.

The Central Highway from Lima, via La Oroya, to Cerro de Pasco has been described above. From Cerro de Pasco it continues NE another 528 km to Pucallpa, the limit of navigation for large Amazon river boats. The western part of this road (Cerro de Pasco-Huánuco) has been rebuilt into an all-weather highway (**see map, p 1264,** for its contour). Buses run daily between Lima and Pucallpa, 847 km, taking 32 hrs, but ask about the state of the road during the rainy season from Nov to Mar, when the trip may take a week.

The sharp descent along the nascent **Huallaga River** (the road drops 2,450m in the 100 km in 100 km from Cerro de Pasco to Huánuco, and most of it is in the first 32 km) is a tonic to travellers suffering from *soroche*, or altitude sickness. From the

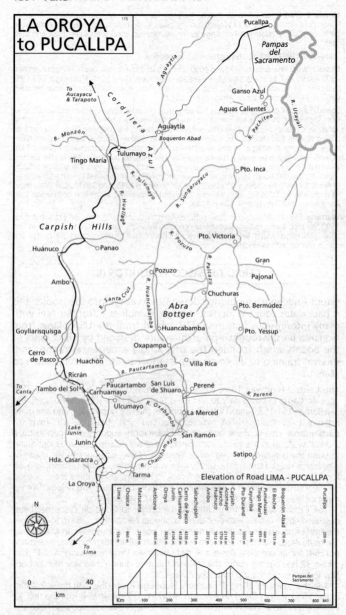

LA OROYA to PUCALLPA 115

Elevation of Road LIMA - PUCALLPA

bleak vistas of the high ranges one drops below the tree line to views of great beauty. The only town of any size before Huánuco is Ambo.

NB The Huallaga valley is the country's main coca-growing area, with both drug-trafficking and guerrilla activity. The main centre of activity is between Tingo María and Tarapoto, so it is best to avoid the region at present. It does appear to be safe to visit Huánuco, Tingo María and Pucallpa, but as the area is under military control there are many checkpoints. Travelling during the day is advised and seek full information before going.

Huánuco, on the Upper Huallaga (pop 82,240), is an attractive Andean town with an interesting market and the two old (but much restored) churches of San Cristóbal and San Francisco (16th century paintings). There is a small but interesting natural history museum at General Prado 495, called Museo de Ciencias; many of the displays have multiple language signs. Entrance, US$0.50. Watch locals catch fish from the river in their teeth! Visit ruin 5 km on road to La Unión: **_Kotosh_** (alt 1,812m), the Temple of Crossed Hands, the earliest evidence of a complex society and of pottery in Peru (from 2000 BC). You must ford a stream to get there, and beware of the vicious black flies. The ruin has been sadly neglected since the original excavation in 1963. Main industry: sugar and rum; take Cisne bus from Jirón Ayacucho, 15 mins, in am to visit Cooperativa Vichaycoto, rum for sale.

Hotels C *Turistas*, with bath, no hot water, restaurant; **D** *Cusco*, Huánuco 616, 2 blocks from Plaza de Armas, with bath, cafetería, OK; **F** *Lima*, Plaza de Armas, 28 de Julio 9222, with bath; **F** *Hostal Residencial Huánuco*, Jirón Huánuco (nr Plaza de Armas) T 2050, with bath, hot water, garden, use of kitchen, washing facilities, more expensive than others in this range but excellent value, highly rec; **F** *Las Vegas*, on plaza, rec, has good restaurant; **F** *Imperial*, Ayacucho 581, with cold shower (intermittent water), reasonable value, clean, quiet; **F** *Kelin*, clean; others nr market. Hotels are often fully booked; arrive early.

Camping Camp by river, near stadium.

Restaurants Several on or near the plaza. *La Fontanita*, Jr Dos de Mayo 1099 (Plaza de Armas), reasonable pizza.

Air Services To/from **Lima**, 1 hr, US$59, daily flights with Expreso Aéreo. Connecting flights to Tingo María, Tocache, Juanjui, Pucallpa, Saposoa, Tarapoto, Yurimaguas, Moyobamba, Rioja, Trujillo and Chiclayo. Flights may be cancelled in the rains or if not full.

Buses To **Lima**, US$11 with León de Huánuco, 10 hrs, 3 a day in early evening, slow; colectivo to Lima, US$20, leaves 0400, arrives 1400; book the night before at General Prado 607, one block from the main square, rec. Etposa (Calle Crespo Castillo 810, T 512903) also runs to Lima. Daily buses to **Cerro de Pasco**, La Oroya and Huancayo, 0830, 1600, with Nororiente or Ucayali, Constitución 638, 11-12 hrs, US$7.35. "Mixto" Huánuco-Cerro de Pasco, half bus, half truck, departs 0400, 3 hrs, US$3.60; colectivo 1 or 12, US$6.20 at 0500. To **Huancayo**, 10 hrs, US$4.80. Buses and colectivos to **Tingo María**, 3 hrs (colectivo, US$3.20, many start from near river bridge, 2 blocks from main plaza). Bus to **Pucallpa**, US$11, La Perla del Oriente (Etposa), 0800 and 1600, rec, 10 hrs plus; buses make stops for meals but some of them are widely spaced; in any case it is wise to take your own food in case of breakdowns. This route has many checkpoints, but also robberies occur—a questionable trip for foreigners at present.

To the NW of Huánuco is **_Tantamayo_** (3,600m), a farming village in the Central Sierra; it is surrounded by precolumbian ruins which can be reached on foot (3-4 hrs, guides available) called Piruru, Susupillu, Japallan, and Castilla de Selinin; pictures and information from Huánuco Post Office. Hotel: *Turística*, where Don Cristián Ocaña and his Swiss wife, Theresa, offer full board, D (F without food), they are very helpful, and Sra de Ocaña speaks German, French, Italian and English. Bus from Huánuco, US$6.70, 12-14 hrs, departs 1800; returns at night. The walks to the ruins are arduous; take warm clothing, a hat, suntan lotion.

From Huánuco, a road leads to *La Unión*, capital of Dos de Mayo district, a friendly town, but electricity can be a problem (it gets very cold at night); 2 buses daily between 0700 and 1000, including Acosta, 2 blocks from the market, returns to Huánuco about midnight, US$4.80, 8-9 hrs, truck, 10½ hrs, leaves late morning. La Unión-Tingo Chico, US$2.70. *Hostal Turista* and *Hostal Dos de Mayo*, at La Unión (G). Neither safe for left luggage. *Restaurant El Danubio*, near market, good home cooking, lots of garlic.

On the pampa above La Unión are the Inca ruins of **_Huánuco Viejo_**, a 2½ hr walk from the town, a great temple-fortress with residential quarters. To get there, take the path starting behind the market and climb towards the cross, which is at the edge of a plateau. Continue straight through the village on the wide path (the locals are friendly, but some of their dogs are nasty); the views of the pampa, surrounded on all sides by mountains, are beautiful. Seemingly at the foot of a mountain, in front and to your right, is a silvery metalic roof of a little chapel, behind which are the ruins (about a 20-mins' walk through herds of cattle). Take warm clothing and beware of thunderstorms. (Karin Kubitsch, West Germany).

Bus to Lima daily, crowded. Also possible to get to Callejón de Huaylas: La Unión-Huaraz direct is very difficult because most transport does the route La Unión-Chiquián-Lima. You can take a truck from La Unión to Huansalla, then another to Pachacoto (some wait till 0100 for passengers), and from there it's 1 hr to Huaraz. The San Cristóbal bus to Lima at 1100 goes a few km S of Catac; from there connections are easy to Huaraz (1 hr) and Chavín (via Catac). Salazar bus to Lima (3 a week at 1000-more like 1100), takes 9 hrs. To Conococha, 4,100m, US$6.20, 9 hrs (**see p 1143**); this is supposed to connect with a Lima-Huaraz bus at 1900-2000; if you miss it, hitch in the cold and dark (2 hrs, US$2.40 to Huaraz). A night bus from Lima passes at 0300, but the restaurant at the Conococha crossroads closes at 2230. Check local political conditions before taking this route.

The journey to Tingo María, 135 km, is very dusty but gives a good view of the jungle. Some 25 km beyond Huánuco the road begins a sharp climb to the heights of Carpish (3,023m). A descent of 58 km brings it to the Huallaga river again; it continues along the river to Tingo María. (The road is paved from Huánaco to Tingo María, including a tunnel through the Carpish hills, but is reported to be in very bad condition.) Landslides along this section are frequent and construction work causes delays.

Tingo María is on the middle Huallaga, in the Ceja de Montaña, or edge of the mountains, isolated for days in rainy season. Climate tropical; annual rainfall 2,642 mm. Population, about 20,560 and very mixed. The altitude (655m) prevents the climate from being oppressive. The Cordillera Azul, the front range of the Andes, covered with jungle-like vegetation to its top, separates it from the jungle lowlands to the E. The mountain which can be seen from all over the town is called La Bella Durmiente, the Sleeping Beauty. The meeting here of Sierra and Selva makes the landscape extremely striking. Bananas, sugar cane, cocoa, rubber, tea and coffee are grown. The main crop of the area, though, is coca, grown on the *chacras* (smallholdings) in the countryside, and sold legitimately and otherwise in Tingo María—there have been several shoot-outs between the police and the drug entrepreneurs. As in many other shoot-places in Peru, watch out for gangs of thieves around the buses and do not leave luggage on the bus if you get off. Although the town itself is generally safe, it is not permitted to leave it at night; it is also inadvisable to take a bus through the area at present.

A small university outside the town, beyond the *Hotel Turistas*, has a little museum-cum-zoo, with animals of that zone, and botanical gardens in the town, entrance free but a small tip would help to keep things in order. $6\frac{1}{2}$ km from Tingo is a fascinating cave, the Cueva de las Lechuzas. There are many nocturnal parrots in the cave and many small parakeets near the entrance. It is reached by car via the new bridge (or colectivo from garage, US$1); take a torch, and do not wear open shoes. The Cave can be reached by boat when the river is high. 13 km from Tingo is the small gorge known as Cueva de las Pavas (no caves or turkeys, but good swimming).

Hotels C *Turistas*, with and without bath, restaurant, very good, swimming pool, some way out of town; F *Viena*, good value with private bathrooms, clean, nr *Café Rex*; G *La Cabaña*, the cheapest, tolerably clean, good restaurant. Hotels are often fully-booked. There are a number of cheap hotels, but we have no recent information on which are operating.
Restaurants (to which the same applies) *Pensión González*, expensive, but nice setting; *Café Rex*, Avenida Raimondi 500, cakes and ice cream, but rather run down; *Gran Chifa Oriental*, Chinese restaurant, on main street, cheap.

Transport Flights from Tingo María to Lima, $1\frac{1}{2}$ hrs, US$59, several flights. Daily with Expreso

Aéreo, which has a few connecting flights, usually to Huánuco, Juanjui, Tarapoto, Chiclayo, Bellavista. Services unreliable, cancellations in the rainy season or if planes not full.

From Tingo María on, several transport services are run; the road is narrow and stony. Landslides and mud can be a problem; in the rainy season the road can be closed for up to a week. From Tingo to **Pucallpa**, 284 km, 12 hrs, US$5.50, several buses, pick-ups and trucks daily; they all leave in early am. To **Huánuco**, 118 km, 5-6 hrs, US$3, several buses, pick-ups and trucks daily. The road is in poor condition, but very picturesque; many military checkpoints. Direct buses continue to Lima (see Lima **Bus Companies**). To Juanjui, 340 km, 15-20 hrs, US$9, daily transport, poor road, not recommended because of narcotic and terrorist activity; continuing to **Tarapoto**, a further 145 km, 4 hrs, US$2.

The Río Huallaga winds northwards for 930 km. The Upper Huallaga is a torrent, dropping 15.8m/km between its source and Tingo María. The Lower Huallaga moves through an enervation of flatness, with its main port, Yurimaguas, below the last rapids and only 150m above the Atlantic ocean, yet distant from that ocean by over a month's voyage. Between the Upper and Lower lies the Middle Huallaga: that third of the river which is downstream from Tingo María, upstream from Yurimaguas. The valleys, ridges and plateaux have been compared with Kenya, but the area is so isolated that less than 100,000 people now live where a million might flourish. The southern part of the Middle Huallaga centres upon Tingo María; down-river, beyond Bellavista, the orientation is towards **Yurimaguas**, which is connected by road with the Pacific coast, via Tarapoto and Moyobamba (**see p 1175**). There is a fine church of the Passionist Fathers, based on the Cathedral of Burgos, Spain, at Yurimaguas; population 25,700. Market from 0600-0800, colourful, full of fruit and animals. Tourist information from Consejo Regional building on main Plaza. Interesting excursions in the area include the gorge of Shanusi and the lakes of Mushuyacu and Sanango. Moped hire US$2.35/hr incl fuel. **Warning**: there has been guerrilla activity in the Yurimaguas region; visitors can expect attention from the police. It is also a centre for anti-narcotics operations.

Hotels D *Leo's Palace*, Plaza de Armas 104-6, good, friendly, reasonably-priced, restaurant; **E** *Yurimaguas*, shower, toilet, fan, clean, reliable; **E** *Floríndez*, shower, a/c US$1.50 extra; **F** *Camus*, no sign, Manco Capac 201, cheap; **F** *Estrella*, shower, rec; **F** *Mache*, with bath and fan, rec. *Heladería*, round corner from *Estrella*, serves good cheap lunch and dinner.

Exchange Interbanc or travel agents; poor rates.

Air To Lima (2 hrs, Aero Continente 4 a week, Faucett 2 a week) and **Tarapoto** (20 mins, same airlines, same frequency) and Iquitos (45 mins, Aero Continente 4 a week). Flights are cancelled in the wet season or if not full.

River Travel Yurimaguas-Iquitos by regular ferry *Jasmin* 60 hrs (upstream takes longer). Other ferries do the trip; bring your own hammock, takes 2 days and 2 nights, take fruit and drinks, police inspections at each end of the trip. Fares usually include meals, US$18, cabins cost more. To buy a hammock costs US$20-30 in Yurimaguas, mosquito nets are poor quality. Ask at the harbour for smaller boats, which can take up to 10 days.

You can break the journey at **Lagunas**, 12 hrs by boat from Yurimaguas, US$4.50: **G** *Hostal La Sombra*, Jr Vásquez 1121, shared bath, basic, friendly, good food; *Hotel Montalbán*, Plaza de Armas, no sign, 2 clean rooms, friendly owner, Sr Inga, 20-mins' walk from jetty, also accommodation at the Farmacia. You can ask the local people to take you on a trip into the jungle by canoe; you will see at very close range alligators, monkeys and a variety of birds, but only on trips of 4 days or so. Good jungle trips from Lagunas to the **Pacaya-Samiria Reserve**; when arranging a guide and boat from Lagunas, make sure you take enough fuel for the boat. Before entering the Reserve you pass through a village where you must pay US$4.50. Edinson and Klever Saldaña Gutiérrez, Sargento Flores 718 are good guides; also Hopp and Genaro (ask at *La Sombra*), who include basic food, with fishing and hunting; Juan Huaycama (Jáuregui 689), highly rec, mostly on the river, sleeping in hammocks, fishing. Typical cost for party of 5 for 12 days is US$200, with 2 guides and 2 boats. One person for 5 days with one guide is charged US$45. Take water purifier and mosquito repellent on excursions that involve living off the land. The *Constante* plies to Lagunas 2-3 times a week; from there connections are difficult to Iquitos. Times of boats to Iquitos and Pucallpa very vague (confirm departures the day before by radio). The boats pass by the villages of Castilla and Nauta, where the Huallaga joins the Ucayali and becomes the Amazon. You need a hammock, mosquito net, water-purification tablets, extra food and a good book.

At Tulumayo, soon after leaving Tingo María, a road runs N down the Huallaga past La Morada, successfully colonized by people from Lima's slums, to **Aucayacu** (E *Hotel Monte Carlo*, with bath; one other hotel, both poor) and **Tocache** (accommodation at F *Hostal San Martín*, F *Hostal Sucre*, one other; airport). The road is paved to 20 km past Aucayacu, thereafter it is good gravel. Colectivos run; Tingo-Tocache US$13 (4½ hrs) or bus US$9.50 (6 hrs). The road has been pushed N to join another built S from Tarapoto (Tarapoto-Tocache, US$7.50 by colectivo) and has now been joined at Tarapoto to the Olmos-Bagua-Yurimaguas transandine highway to the coast at Chiclayo. Colectivos and taxis run from Tocache to Yurimaguas (serviceable unpaved road); daily *camioneta* Tarapoto-Yurimaguas, US$7-9, 6-8 hrs. The Juanjui-Tocache road has five bridges, but the last one across the Huallaga, just before Juanjui, was washed away in 1983 to be replaced by an efficient ferry (US$9.20/vehicle); Juanjui-Tarapoto by colectivo US$12.50. For the river journey, start early in the morning if you do not wish to spend a night at the river village of Sión. No facilities, but night is not cold. The river runs through marvellous jungle with high cliffs. Boats sometimes run aground in the river near Sión. Take food and water purifier. Many rafts of balsa wood. Also, a small plane flies between Tocache and Juanjui (25 mins).

From Tingo María to the end of the road at Pucallpa is 288 km, with a climb over the watershed—the Cordillera Azul—between the Huallaga and Ucayali rivers. When the road was being surveyed it was thought that the lowest pass over the Cordillera Azul was over 3,650m high, but an old document stating that a Father Abad had found a pass through these mountains in 1757 was rediscovered, and the road now goes through the pass of Father Abad, a gigantic gap 4 km long and 2,000m deep. At the top of the pass is a Peruvian Customs house; the jungle land to the E is a free zone. Coming down from the pass the road bed is along the floor of a magnificent canyon, the Boquerón Abad: luxuriant jungle and ferns and sheer walls of bare rock punctuated by occasional waterfalls into the roaring torrent below. E of the foot of the pass the all-weather road goes over flat pampa with few curves to the village of **Aguaytía** (narcotics police checkpoint; gasoline; F *Hostal San Antonio*, clean; 2 restaurants). On to Pucallpa (160 km—5 hrs by bus, US$4.35); the last half has no service stations.

Pucallpa, a rapidly expanding jungle town, is on the Ucayali River, navigable by vessels of 3,000 tons from Iquitos, 533 nautical miles away. Population has increased to about 400,000. It is the capital of the new Department of Ucayali. The newer sections have paved streets, sewers and lights, but much of the frontier town atmosphere still exists. The economy of the area is growing fast; sawmills, plywood factories, a paper mill, oil refinery, fishing and boat building are all thriving; timber is trucked out to the Highlands and the coast. Large discoveries of oil and gas are being explored, and gold mining is underway nearby. The local drugs problem is becoming serious. The Ganso Azul oilfield has a 75-km pipeline to the Pucallpa refinery. From Tingo María, 286 km (gravel road); from Lima, 847 km.

All jungle towns are expensive, but bargains can be found. The floating port of La Hoyada and Puerto Italia are worth a visit to see the canoe traffic and open-air markets. Care should be taken when arranging jungle trips from street vendors in Pucallpa or at the ports. The climate is tropical: dry season in Jul and Aug, rainy seasons Oct-Nov, Feb-Mar; the town is hot and dusty between Jun and Nov and muddy from Dec to May. The centre of Pucallpa is now paved, but both the port and new commercial harbour, about 5 km away, are reached along dirt roads.

NB There is much military control because of terrorist and narcotics activity, which is expanding. The city itself is OK to visit, but don't travel at night, or outside the city.

Festivals 24 Jun, San Juan; 5-20 Oct, Pucallpa's *Aniversario Political* and the Ucayali regional fair.

Hotels B *Turistas*, with bath (taxes included), swimming pool, good restaurant; C *Inambu*, with good value restaurant, a/c; D *Arequipa*, Jr Progreso 573, with bath, good, clean; D *Mercedes*, good, but noisy with good bar and restaurant attached, swimming pool;

E *Barbtur*, Raymondi 670 (T 6377), with bath, F without, friendly, clean, central, opp bus stop, good beds; **E** *Comfort*, Coronel Portillo, clean; **E** *Hostal Los Angeles*, on Ucayali, clean, communal shower, but noisy; **E** *Komby*, comfortable, swimming pool, excellent value; **E** *Sisley*, adequate, on Coronel Portillo; **E** *Sun*, Ucayali 380, with bath, cheaper without, clean, good value, next to *Komby*; **F** *Hostal Mori*, Jr Independencia 1114, basic; **G** *Tariri*, Raymondi, dirty, basic, food cheap and good. If holidaying, better to stay at Lake Yarinacocha (see below).

Restaurants *Jaricho*, under *Hotel Sun*, good; *Escorpión Cebichería*, Jr Progreso, good, eat in rear garden; *El Alamo*, Carretera Yarinacocha 2650, good typical food; *Sabores Perú*, Jr Progreso 675, snack bar; *El Golf*, Jr Huáscar 545, *cevichería*; *La Flor de la Canela*, Jr Mcal Castilla 300, typical food. *Embutidos La Favorita*, Cnl Portillo, good, cheap, friendly, US$1 for all 3 meals; *El Establo*, steak house on road to airport, excellent; *Chifas Han Muy* and *MeyLin*, Jr Inmaculada 247 and 689. *La Baguette*, good bakery, cheap bottles of pisco.

Typical dishes: *patarashca*, barbecued fish wrapped in *bijao* leaves; *zarapatera*, spicy soup made with turtle meat served in its shell (consider the ecological implications of this dish); *chonta salad*, made with palm shoots; *juanes*, rice with chicken or fish served during the San Juan festival. The local beer "San Juan" has been rec.

Exchange It is easy to change dollars cash at the banks, travel agencies, the better hotels and bigger stores. There are also lots of street changers (watch them carefully). TCs are hard to change and commission is high.

Art School Usko Ayar Amazonian School of Painting, in the house of artist Pablo Amaringo, a former *vegetalista* (healer), Jr LM Sánchez, Cerro 465-467. Provides art classes for local people, dependent upon selling their art. The school is well worth a visit.

Bookshop *Librería La Verdad* has a collection of English books on loan; a boon for stranded travellers.

Tourist Office Ministerio de Industria y Turismo (MICTI), helpful with tourist information.

Small **motorcycles** for hire from Jr Raymondi 654 and 7 de Junio 864, about US$1.50/hr plus gasoline.

Air To Lima, 1 hr, daily flights with Faucett, Americana, AeroPerú and Aero Continente, US$58, also Expreso Aéreo 3 a week. To **Iquitos**, 40 mins, US$41 with Americana, US$35 Aero Continente, both daily. To **Tarapoto** US$29 Aero Continente, 4 a week. To **Trujillo**, US$32 with Aero Continente, 4 a week. Expreso Aéreo 3 times a week to Tingo María and Huánuco. Americana, Jr Ucayali 868, T 574208. Airport to town, bus US$0.25; *motos* US$1; taxi US$2-3.

Buses Much of the Pucallpa-Lima road is now paved (rough stretch for 80 km E of Tingo María) and there are regular bus services to Lima (check in advance that the road is open and what political conditions are). To **Lima**, 812 km, 26 hrs (longer in rainy season), US$11, see under Lima **Bus Companies**. To Tingo María, 284 km, 12 hrs, US$5.50, several buses, pick-ups and trucks daily. Advised to take blankets as the crossing of the Cordillera at night is bitterly cold. Try to pick a bus crossing the mountains by day as the views are wonderful. It is also possible to get to Lima by truck. Better still, though, go by air to avoid at least 5 police anti-narcotics checks and robberies of night buses.

Excursions The Hospital Amazónico Albert Schweitzer, which serves the local Indians, and Summer School of Linguistics (callers by appointment only) for the study of Indian languages are on picturesque Lake **Yarinacocha**, the main tourist attraction of the area. Yarinacocha is 20 mins by colectivo or bus from the market in Pucallpa (US$0.30), 15 mins by taxi (US$2). The Indian market of Moroti-Shobo ("The House of Selling and Buying") is a cooperative, organized by Shipibo-Conibo craftsmen. Fine handicrafts are sold in their shop; visit them in Yarinacocha, T 571551. **C** pp *Hotel La Cabaña* (by appointment only, price rises in high season), incl all meals and transport to and from Yarinacocha harbour, same Swiss owner as *Mercedes* in Pucallpa, good service and food, excellent guide, Isabel, for short expeditions, plane excursions (for instance to Indian villages). Next door to *La Cabaña* is **A3** *La Perla* lodge, German-Peruvian owned, English and German spoken, no electricity after 2100, run down, overpriced, meals provided. **F** *El Pescador*, in Puerto Callao, cheap, friendly, restaurant, best buy for budget traveller, but mixed reports recently; **F** *Los Delfines*, rooms with bath, clean, noisy. Some small houses for rent on weekly basis. Restaurants: *El Cucharón*, good food; *Grande Paraíso*, good view, also has a *peña* at night, popular with young people; *Orlando's*, Jr Aguaytía, good local food; local specialities include *tamales*, *humitas* (maize patties with meat and herbs), *junies* (rice with chicken and spices), *tacutacu* (banana and sauces).

Here is bathing in clean water, but there is a lot of weed. It is a pleasant change after the mud of Pucallpa and the Amazon; you can camp, though there are no facilities and it is hot and insect-ridden. Motor canoes can be hired for about US$20 a day with guide, but guide not mandatory for lake trips. Trips into the canals and out to the river need a guide. Two types of excursions down river, recommended three days, can be arranged from the port in Yarinacocha directly with the boat owners, prices vary but approximately US$20/boat a day, you buy food and some supplies. Boats hold up to 8 at reduced price. Recommended boatmen: Roy Riaño at Puerto Callao and Jorge Morales at San Juan. (Beware, many boats are used for drug-running.) **NB** Down-river trips visit numerous villages but much of the jungle is cultivated; up-river trips visit fewer villages but mostly virgin jungle.

Certain sections of Lake Yarinacocha have been designated as a reserve. Jardín Botánico Chullachaqui can be reached by boat from Puerto Callao, Yarinacocha, to Pueblo Nueva Luz de Fátima, 45 mins, then 1 hr's walk to the garden (entry free), a lovely location. For information about traditional medicine contact Mateo Arevalomayna, San Francisco de Yarinacocha, president of the group Ametra (an organization which is working to reestablish the use of traditional remedies), T 573152; or ask at Moroti-Shobo. A good way to explore the area is by renting a *motocarro* (motorcycle with 2 seats), US$3/hr.

River Service Buses and colectivos go to the port, La Hoyada. In the dry season boats dock 3 km from the bus stop, a dusty walk, taxi US$3. To **Iquitos**, some better than others; only 3 boats with cabins, but don't count on getting one (hammocks are cooler): *Madre Selva*, clean, friendly, rec; other boats to Iquitos: *Florico, Carolina* and *Manuel*, trips takes 3-4 days, US$22 pp, US$27 incl food. Travellers to Iquitos may need confirmation from the PNP that their documents are in order, this must then be signed by the Capitanía otherwise no passenger can be accepted on a trip leaving Pucallpa. No such clearance is necessary when returning to Pucallpa. Passenger services are in decline owing to competition by air and priority for cargo traffic; it may be better to make journeys in short stages rather than Pucallpa-Iquitos direct. There's a risk of illness on the river, and public transport can be extremely uncomfortable. River water is used for cooking and drinking: tinned food, mosquito netting, hammock and fresh water are necessary purchases, fishing line and hooks advisable. Take lots of insect repellent, water purifier and tummy pills. The smaller boats call often at jungle villages if you want to see them, but otherwise because the river is wide, the shores can only be seen at a distance. Average time: 5 days. Boats leave very irregularly. When conditions are bad they leave in convoy: none may leave afterwards for 4 to 6 weeks. Avoid boats that will be loading en route, this can take up to 6 days. Further down the Ucayali river are Contamaná (with frontier-town atmosphere) and Requena, from which launches sail to Iquitos, taking 12 hrs. Roroboya, a small Shipibo Indian village about 12 hrs downstream from Pucallpa, should not be missed, as most other villages down to Iquitos are *mestizo*. You can go to Puerto La Hoyada and Puerto Italia (smaller boats) to find a boat going to Iquitos; the Capitanía on the waterfront may give you information about sailings, but this is seldom reliable. Do not pay for your trip before you board the vessel, and only pay the captain. (Captains may allow you to live on board a couple of days before sailing.) Boats going upstream on the Amazon and its tributaries stay closer to the bank than boats going down, which stay in mid-stream.

You can take a colectivo from Pucallpa S to Zungaro (US$4.50), where a boat (30 mins) can be taken to **Puerto Inca** on the Río Pachitea, about 120 km N by air from Puerto Bermúdez (**see p 1262**) and close to the Carretera Marginal (under construction). It is a gold-rush town, expanding quickly, with two hotels (Don José's *Alojamiento*, G, clean, safe, laundry, big rooms, rec).

Iquitos, capital of the Department of Loreto and chief town of Peru's jungle region, is a fast-developing city of 350,000 people on the W bank of the Amazon, with Padre Isla island (14½ by 3 km) facing it in midstream. It has paved streets and plenty of vehicles (incl taxis), but roads out of the city go only a little way: Iquitos is completely isolated except by air and river. Some 800 km downstream from Pucallpa and 3,646 km from the mouth of the Amazon, it has recently taken on a new lease of life as the centre for oil exploration in Peruvian Amazonia. As one might expect from its use by the oil industry and its remoteness, it is an expensive town, but compensates by being a friendly place.

There is an iron house in the Plaza de Armas, designed by Eiffel for the Paris exhibition of 1889. It is said that the house was transported from Paris by a local rubber baron (the rubber boom lasted until 1912); it is constructed entirely of iron trusses and sheets, bolted together and painted silver.

Belén, the picturesque, friendly waterfront district, is lively, but not safe at night. Most of its huts are built on rafts to cope with the river's 10-metre change of level during floods (most likely Nov to Apr). *Pasaje Paquito* is a bar with typical local drinks, as is *La China*. The main square has a bandstand made by Eiffel. (Canoes

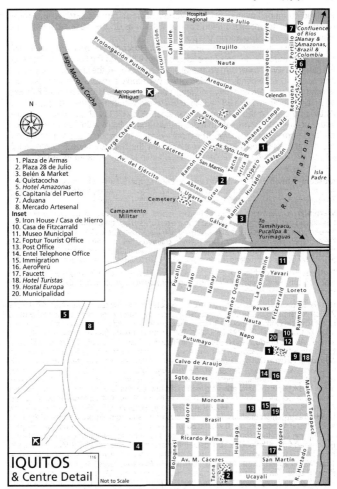

1. Plaza de Armas
2. Plaza 28 de Julio
3. Belén & Market
4. Quistacocha
5. *Hotel Amazonas*
6. Capitanía del Puerto
7. Aduana
8. Mercado Artesenal
Inset
9. Iron House / Casa de Hierro
10. Casa de Fitzcarrald
11. Museo Municipal
12. Foptur Tourist Office
13. Post Office
14. Entel Telephone Office
15. Immigration
16. AeroPerú
17. Faucett
18. *Hotel Turistas*
19. *Hostal Europa*
20. Municipalidad

IQUITOS
& Centre Detail Not to Scale

may be hired on the waterfront to visit Belén, US$3/hr; do not try paddling yourself as the current is very strong.) See in the city the Market, at the end of the Malecón, or riverside walk. Note that the principal street Jirón Lima has been renamed Jirón Próspero. Recommended guide with a good car and two boats is Jorge Chávez, T 231532.

The University of Amazonia of Loreto (1962) specializes in engineering and agriculture. Of special interest are the older buildings, faced with *azulejos* (glazed tiles). See the old Hotel Palace, now the army barracks, on the corner of Malecón Tarapacá and Putumayo. They date from the rubber boom of 1890 to 1920, when the rubber barons imported tiles from Portugal and Italy and ironwork from

England to embellish their homes. Werner Herzog's film *Fitzcarraldo* is a *cause célèbre* in the town; Fitzcarraldo's house still stands on the Plaza de Armas, and Herzog's boats are moored in the port.

A short drive S of the city is beautiful Lake **Quistococha** in lush jungle, with a fish hatchery at the lakeside. Recommended is a visit (US$1) to the Parque Zoológico de Quistococha (with aquarium) on the lake (closed Mon). At the entrance are pictures and texts of local legends, the ticket office will supply a map of the zoo. Take bus (tends to be crowded and dirty, and return buses unreliable) from corner of Próspero and Gálvez, or from Plaza 28 de Julio; also a truck (with pink frame, not green) from Abtao and Grau to the zoo and Quistococha, US$0.25; taxi US$3.60 for 4 people, with 2 hrs wait. We have heard that the animals (and particularly the fish) often depend on food from visitors to survive. The monkeys roam freely, some cages are small, but the zoo attracts mixed reactions. See particularly the *paiche*, a huge Amazonian fish whose steaks (*paiche a la loretana*) you can eat in Iquitos' restaurants. Boats are for hire on the lake and swimming is safe.

Museum Museo Municipal (1st block of Tawara), has a large, old collection of stuffed Amazonian fauna which is rather disappointing. It has been incorporated into the Parque Zoológico (Mon-Sat 0730-1900, US$0.55 Peruvians, US$2 foreigners).

Warnings As elsewhere, beware of thieves, especially of handbags, watches, jewellery, etc. Having said this, Iquitos is more relaxed than the rest of Peru and theft is not normally a problem. Secondly, locals sell necklaces made with red and black rosary peas (Abrus pecatorius), which are extremely poisonous. Do not give them to children. They are illegal in Canada, but not in the USA. If possible, avoid visiting Iquitos around Peruvian Independence Day (27 and 28 Jul) and Easter as it is very expensive and crowded and excursion facilities are overloaded.

Festivals Founding of Iquitos, 5 Jan; Carnival, Feb-Mar; tourist week, third week in Jun; San Juan, 24 Jun; Santa Rosa de Lima, 30 Aug; Immaculate Conception, 8 Dec, celebrated in Punchana, near the docks.

Hotels Discounts of 20% or more can be negotiated in the low season (Jan-Apr). **A3** *Acosta 2*, Ricardo Palma 252, T 231286, hot showers, a/c, refrigerator in rooms, free map of city, good restaurant and swimming pool; **A3** *Amazonas*, previously *Holiday Inn*, on Abelardo Quiñónez, 3 km out of town, T 231091 (taxi US$1.75), swimming pool (free bus service hourly from airport); **A3** *El Dorado*, Napo (½ block from Plaza de Armas), T 237326, swimming pool (open to restaurant users), cable TV, bar and restaurant quite expensive, credit cards, highly rec; **A3** *Hostal Acosta*, Calvo de Araujo y Huallaga, T 235974, almost same standard as *Acosta 2*, minus the swimming pool, central, rec; **A3** *Jhuliana*, Putumayo 521, T 233154, clean, friendly, with bath, good swimming pool, rec; **B** *Turistas*, Malecón Tarapacá, T 231322, with bath, meals US$4.50, with many good a/c rooms US$1.50 extra (a few secondhand English books available in reception), does not accept TCs, price incl breakfast; **C** *Amazonas*, Plaza de Armas, Arica 108, T 232015, new; **C** *Hostal Ambassador*, Pevas 260, T 233110, with shower, a/c US$8.50 extra, smart breakfast room, incl transport to and from airport, member of Peruvian Youth Hostel Association, rec; **D** *Hostal Europa*, Brasil 222, T 231123, very good, very helpful, a/c (cheaper with fan), shower, cable TV, phone and fridge in every room, pleasant café/bar, good views from 5th floor, rec; **D** *Hostal Internacional*, Próspero 835, T 234684, clean, a/c, bath, b/w TV, fridge, phone, friendly, secure, medium-priced café, rec; **D** *Hostal Dos Mundos*, Tacna 631, T 232635, bath, fan, clean; **E** *Hostal La Pascana*, Pevas 133, T 231418, with cold shower, basic, fan, clean, breakfast available, luggage store, TV lounge, luxuriant garden, relaxed, popular, highly rec; **E** *Hostal Libertad*, Arica 361, T 235763, clean, restaurant with street balcony, tourist information; **E** *Isabel*, Brasil 164, T 234901, with bath, very good, clean (but plug the holes in the walls!), secure, often full.

F *Hostal Económico*, Moore 1164, very clean, good water supply, quiet, not central, no sign outside, friendly, rec; **F** *Hostal Tacna*, Tacna 516, T 232839, worn, reasonable value, pokey bathrooms, some balconies, noisy, mixed reports; **F** *Hostal Lozano*, Ramírez Hurtado 772, T 232486, bath, friendly, quiet, fair value; **F** *Lima*, Próspero 549 (triple room available), T 235152, with bath and fan, cold water, towel, soap and toilet paper provided, café good, small courtyard garden, "no smoking in bed".

Restaurants The cheapest are on or near Plaza 28 de Julio, eg *El Dorado Inn*, Calle Huallaga block 6, good value and good menu, US$1.10; *El Mesón*, Jirón Napo 116, venison stew, wild pig, broiled alligator (US$3.60), rec; *La Terraza*, Malecón Tarapacá y Napo, commanding views of river, good; *La Casa de Jaime*, Malecón Maldonado 137, excellent steaks, good value, owner Jaime Acevedo speaks English and can give helpful advice about jungle trips; *Maloka*, opp *Hotel Turistas* on riverbank, excellent (though avoid sitting next to caged monkeys unless you like eating in zoos), average meal US$5, good fish, really good view, highly rec. *El Huaralino*, Huallaga 490, *cuy* and rabbit, medium-priced. Chinese restaurants include *Gran Chifa Wai Ming*, Grau 1298, good but quite expensive; *Heladería La Favorita*, Próspero 415, good ice-cream (try local flavour *aguaje* – see below); *Juguería Manaus*, Próspero 667, good breakfasts (US$1.40); *Juguería Paladar*, Próspero 245, excellent juices; *Casa de Fierro*, Plaza de Armas (Próspero y Putumayo), friendly snack bar inside Eiffel's iron house, good chocolate cake, try malta beer with egg and fresh milk (a useful pick-me-up); *Ari's Burger*, Plaza de Armas (Próspero 127), medium-priced fast food, popular with gringos. *Olla de Oro*, Calvo de Araujo 579, close to main indoor market, excellent food, cheaper than riverside area, friendly service, rec.

Recommended bars: most lively along the riverside in the first couple of blocks of Malecón Tarapacá (*Pipi Vela* offers live music Fri). Also *La Ribereña*, Raymondi 453, terraced seats on newly-built plaza with jukebox; *El Encanto del Amazonas*, Malecón Tarapacá block 4, palm-roofed bar with river view, sells *siete raices* (see below); *El Mirador*, Requena next to steps leading down to wharf, cheap drink, fantastic view; *Salón de Billar Dos Unidos*, Tacna 660, billiards (US$1.20/hr) and beer.

Pineapples are good and cheap. Try the local drink *chuchuhuasi*, made from the bark of a tree, which is supposed to have aphrodisiac properties but tastes like fortified cough tincture (for sale at Arica 1046), and *jugo de cocona*, and the alcoholic *vete bajando*, *cola de mono*, *rompe colzón* and *siete raices* (aguardiente mixed with the bark of 7 trees and wild honey), sold at *Exquisita Amazónica*, Abtao 590. You can eat cheaply, especially fish and *cebiche*, at the three markets. Palm heart salad (*chonta*); or *a la Loretana* dish on menus excellent; also try *inchicapi* (chicken, corn and peanut soup), *cecina* (fried dried pork), *tacacho* (fried green banana and pork, mashed into balls and eaten for breakfast or tea), *juanes* (chicken, rice, olive and egg, seasoned and wrapped in bijao leaves and sold on street corners, try Próspero and San Martín at 1700) and the *aguaje* palm fruit is an interesting but acquired taste, said to have one of the highest vitamin C concentrations in the world. Watch out for *ají de mono* which sits innocently on restaurant tables posing as ordinary chilli sauce and will detonate your mouth (it is yellower than normal *ají*).

Exchange Banco de Crédito, Plaza de Armas, good rates. **Banco Continental**, Sgto Lores 171. **Banco de la Nación**, Condamine 478, good rates, 0915-1530. *Importaciones Lima* on Próspero, and shops selling foreign electrical goods offer good rates of exchange. *Casas de Cambio* stay open late: Tacna 380 and Fltzcarrald 120. Many money changers on Próspero in the 3 blocks S of Plaza de Armas. Dollar exchange rate is usually a couple of points higher than Lima.

Consulates Brazilian, Sgto Lores 363, T 232081, Mon-Fri 0800-1200, 1500-1800; **British**, Mr Lewis Power, Arica 253, T 234110 or 234383; **Colombian**, Putumayo 247, T 231461; **Spanish**, Av La Marina, T 232483; **France**, Napo 346, T 232353.

Current 220 volts, AC.

Cinemas *Bolognesi*, San Martín 390, on Plaza 28 de Julio; *Ciné Belén*, 9 de Diciembre 440; *Ciné Atlántida*, Arequipa 433; *Ciné Iquitos*, Próspero y Palcazu, screenings 1545, 1915, 2130.

Discotheques *Furia Charapa*, Piura 1320, lively most weekends, T 242930 for details; *La Pantera Rosa*, Moore 434, free entrance, Mon-Sat until 0300; *Pax*, Napo y Condamine, popular, sleazy; *Acuario*, Napo 102, dark and dingy, free entrance, go after midnight.

Medical Services Clínica Loreto, Morona 471, T 233752, 24-hr attention, rec, but only Spanish spoken. Hospital Iquitos, Av Grau, emergency T 231721. Hospital Regional de Loreto, 28 de Julio, emergency T 235821.

Post Office corner of Calle Arica with Morona, near Plaza de Armas. **Entel**, Arica 276.

Shopping *Artesanías del Perú*, Putumayo 128; Mercado Artesanal de Productores, 4 km from the centre in San Juan district, take colectivo; unnamed shop at Próspero 435. All sell handicrafts and un-named shop on Calle Brasil, cuadra 7, sells handicrafts of the Shipibo indians from Pucallpa. Pharmacies: *Tacna*, Tacna 450; *D'Onadio*, Próspero 541; *El Loretano*, Próspero 361-3. Library on Plaza de Armas (Napo), 0730-2030. *El Oriente*, best local newspaper, US$0.20. Cheap colourful fabrics at *La Victoria*, Próspero 582. Camera accessories at *Magnum II*, Putumayo 257 on Plaza de Armas. Records and tapes at *Discotiendas Hikari*, San Martín 324. Cheap haircuts at *Barbería Jupiter*, Napo 323.

Immigration Arica 477, T 235371.

Tourist Office At Napo 176, 0730-1330. For maps and general tourist literature, try the Gobierno Regional de Loreto, Ricardo Palma 113, T 233321. Useful town maps, maps of the

Quistacocha zoo and literature from the main jungle tour operators. Town map also from Librería Mosquera, Jr Próspero.

PARD, Preservation of the Amazon River Dolphin, Pevas 253, T/F (51-94) 238585, Roxanne Kremer or Frank Aliaga for information.

Travel Agencies Good information from Edith (speaks English and French), **Three Roses Travel**, Próspero 246, T 233978, very helpful, owner exchanges/sells secondhand English books. Other agencies recommended for city and surroundings **Belén Viajes y Turismo**, Arica 1233; **Fénix Viajes**, Pevas 216; **Laser Viajes**, Próspero 213, and **Elio**, Arica 999.

Jungle Tours All agencies are under control of the local office of the Ministry of Tourism, Calle Arica 566: if you think you're being overcharged, ask for Sra Lastenia Rodríguez, who will show you the operator's file, in which route and price must be recorded. (Not worth while for booking bus or air tickets). They arrange one-day or longer trips to places of interest with guides speaking some English; package tours booked in Lima are much more expensive than those booked in Iquitos. Some agencies are "easy going and that's how they take their responsibilities on an organized trip". Take your time before making a decision, shop around, and don't be bullied by the hustlers at the airport. Get all details of the trip and food arrangements before paying, about US$40-50/day. Launches for river trips can be hired by the hour or day (prices are negotiable, about US$10-15/hr).

Explorama Tours (rec as the most efficient and after 29 years in existence certainly the biggest and most established), offices by riverside docks on Av La Marina 340 (Box 446, Telex 91014, T 51-94-235471, F 51-94-234968; in USA, Selective Hotel Reservations, T 800-223-6764, MA (617) 581-0844), has three sites: *Explorama Inn*, 40 km (1½ hrs) from Iquitos, hot water, comfortable bungalows in a jungle setting, good food, attractive walks, recommended jungle experience for those who want their creature comforts, US$115 for 2 nights, 1 day, US$60 for additional night (1-2 people); *Explorama Lodge* at Yanamono, 80 km from Iquitos, 2½ hrs from Iquitos, palm-thatched accommodation with separate bath and shower facilities connected by covered walkways, US$230 for 3 days/2 nights and US$70 for each additional day; *Explornapo Camp* at Llachapa, 160 km (4 hrs) from Iquitos (more primitive, better for seeing fauna), with impressive new canopy walkway (rec) some 35m above the forest floor and 200m long (but being extended to 450m), also possible to stay in nearby ACEER laboratory, a scientific research station, basic programme US$1,000 for 1 person, 4 nights/5 days (first and last nights spent at Explorama Lodge), US$25 donation to Foundation for Conservation of Peruvian Amazon Biosphere (Conapac) if visiting walkway, extra US$30 to spend night at ACEER, US$90 extra night to basic programme (all prices include transfers, advance reservations, etc, local rates much lower; flight inclusive packages available from Miami on Faucett Airlines, from US$835 for 7 days). *Paseos Amazónicos Ambassador*, Pevas 246, T 233110, operates the *Amazon Sinchicuy Lodge*, US$70/night (group discount available); they also organize visits to Lake Quistacocha and the zoo. *Lima Tours* offers 3 day, 2 night tours to Iquitos and the Amazon from Lima for US$250 pp, flight included. *Excursiones Peruanas*, Av José Pardo 182, of 503, Miraflores, Lima, T 478207, also offers 3 day/2 night trip to Iquitos and the Amazon from Lima for US$220 pp, flight included. *Amazon Camp Tourist Service*, Requena 336, T (51-94) 232961, F 231265; in USA, 8700 W Flagler St, suite 190, Miami, FL 33174, T 305-227-2266, toll free 800-423-2791, F 305-227-1880, American owned company of 23 years standing: Lodge itineraries to 42-rooms *Amazon Camp*, 1 night/2 days US$105, 2 nights/3 days US$160, extra night US$55, or 20-bungalow *Camp Amazonia*, with 24-hr bar, 1 night/2 days US$130; various cruises available, on M/V *Arca* Iquitos-Tabatinga-Iquitos, Sun-Sat US$595 pp (US$495 pp in groups of 10 plus), nature cruises on M/V *Delfín*, 3 nights, Sun-Wed, Wed-Sat, US$295 pp, 6 nights Sun-Sat US$525, 90-min sunset cruise around Iquitos US$18 pp; also organize rugged expeditions to various jungle *tambos* (thatched shelters), from 1 night/2 days, US$132 pp (US$100 pp in groups of 4-6, US$90 for 7-10) to 5 nights/6 days US$609 pp (US$385 pp groups of 4-6, US$345 for 7-10), conscientious and efficient, rec. *Amazon Adventure Expeditions*, Sgto Lores 267, trips to Río Tamshiyacu (fauna), 72 km, 75 mins by speedboat, and Sunimaraño (fishing, nocturnal animals), 285 km, all-day trip by colectivo, tours with guide Adriano from 3-20 days, US$40 pp, colectivo US$30 pp for groups of 4 plus. *Queen Adventures*, Arica 297, T 232680, telex 91009, F 239336 (in USA, AAA Travel Agency, 404-939-7520), operates 6 sites with English-speaking guides (student discount available): *Momon Queen Camp*, 28 km, US$40/day; *Tamshiyacu Camp*, 50 km, US$45/day (min 2 days); *Yanamono Queen Camp*, 70 km, US$50/day (min 3 days); *Atun Cocha Queen Camp*, 150 km, US$65/day (min 3 days); *Yarapa Queen Camp*, 175 km, US$65/day (min 3 days); *Yanayacu Queen Camp*, 250 km, US$90/day (min 3 days). *Anaconda Lara Lodge*, Pevas 210, T 239147, F 232978, 40 km from Iquitos, owned by Fénix Viajes, full-day educational tours, 1000-1600, US$50, US$45 for groups of 11 plus, 1 night/2 days US$100; also offers adventure expeditions to Río Yarapa, 180 km, 5-day trips, US$85-60 pp/day negotiable, and a popular esoteric tour introducing the world of the *brujo* (witchdoctor), some criticism of guides received in 1994. *Las Colinas de Zungarococha*, operated by Paucar Tours, Próspero 652, T 232131, F 232499, or through *Hostal Acosta*, Ricardo Palma 252, or Ricardo Rivera Navarrete 645E, San Isidro, Lima, T/F 424515, comfortable lakeside bungalows, watersports, mini-zoo, full day US$40, 1 night/2 days US$70. *Abergue Isabel Loro Parque* is ½ hr by boat from Bellavista on the Río Nanay, good zoo, beautiful surroundings, friendly, clean, kitchen open to inspection; Iquitos office at Fitzcarrald 225, T 232011, F 232001, US$4.10 (US$3 students) book lunch if only going on a one day trip, boats leave 0900,1100, 1300. *Albergue Supay* floating hotel on Supay lake close to the Río Nanay, 2 hrs by boat from Iquitos, or taxi and canoe, 1 to 5 day tours from US$26 to US$116, run by Austrian Roland Röggl and Peruvian Luz Elena Montoya; contact Apartado 532, Correo Central, Iquitos, F Entel (51-94) 231111. Arturo Díaz Ruiz, Sargento Lores 240 (registered guide no 036) specializes in botanical tours; he is an experienced guide.

It is advisable to take a waterproof coat and shoes or light boots on such trips, and a good torch, as well as *espirales* to ward off the mosquitoes at night—they can be bought from drugstores in Iquitos. *Premier* is the most effective local insect repellent. The dry season is from Jul to Sep and Sep is the best month to see flowers and butterflies.

Motorcycle Hire *Rider*, Pevas 219, DAX mopeds US$2.40/hr, US$21/12 hrs, US$30/24 hrs, Honda CX 125s US$3.60/hr, US$30/12 hrs, US$42/24 hrs, US$6 deposit; Raymondi 284, mopeds US$24/24 hrs, Honda 125s US$48/24 hrs, US$12 deposit. *Motoclub*, Samanez Ocampo 186, T 241263, mopeds US$14.50/6 hrs, US$19/12 hrs. Morona 583, mopeds US$2.10/hr.

Excursions To the beach at Nanay, white sand, and small boats for hire to see the meeting of the Nanay and Amazon rivers; bus from Jr Próspero US$0.15, boat US$0.25. By bus to the village of Santo Tomás, about 20 km, a favourite week-end retreat of inhabitants of Iquitos; the village has a good restaurant and canoes may be hired. Launches also leave Iquitos for the village of Indiana; get off at the "Varadero de Mazán" and walk through the banana plantations to the Río Mazán. A trail leads from the village of Mazán through the jungle to Indiana (hotel), about a 2-hr walk (steamy). Catch the launch back to Iquitos at 1300.

Naturalists should note that the area 50 km around Iquitos is too inhabited to support much large wildlife; there is no primary rainforest probably within 100 km of Iquitos. The Napo or Ucayali rivers have more to offer and excursions from Lagunas are more rewarding than those from Iquitos. Similarly the areas around the Lodges; however there is plenty of scope for seeing small fauna and learning about the flora. Trips to see Yagua Indians offer little but a chance to see "a way of life which is not so much in transition as abandoned." (John C O'Conor, Arlington, Va)

Air Francisco Secada Vigneta airport (called international because of Faucett's flight once a week from Miami, but it is a small, local airport), T 231501/233094. Taxi to the airport costs US$3 (US$6 at night); *motocarro* (motorcycle with 2 seats), US$2.40; bus, US$0.20, goes to market area, about 12 blocks from Plaza de Armas, taxi from there US$1.80. Airport tax on international flights, US$18; US$7 on local flights.

To **Lima**, Faucett, US$116 (Próspero 640, T 239266), Americana (Próspero 215, T 237062) and Aero Continente (Arica 761, T 242439), US$70, all have daily flights; AeroPerú (Próspero 248, T 232513), 5 days a week, 3 flights direct, others via Chiclayo. Aero Continente and Americana fly via **Pucallpa**, US$41. To **Yurimaguas** Aero Continente US$24, 4 a week; Aero Continente (4 a week) and Faucett (3) to Tarapoto. Iquitos-**Cusco** with Faucett direct on Sun, US$107. Americana fares Iquitos-Cusco US$106, Iquitos-Ayacucho US$110 (both via Lima). No flights Iquitos-Ecuador. Faucett flies Sat to Miami (when entering Peru on this flight, 90-day tourist visa is given on arrival). Iquitos flights frequently delayed. (Be sure to reconfirm your flight in Iquitos, as they are often overbooked, especially over the Christmas period.) TANS office: Grupo 42 (for Brazil, Colombia), Sargento Lores 127, T 233512; these flights are less than the cost of the commercial flights. TANS also has a flight to Cabo Pantoja and other villages. TANS to Leticia (Tabatinga), but often booked up 2 months ahead for the aquaplane. TANS hydroplane flies NNW along the river to Peneya, opposite Leguizamo in Colombia, or Gueppi, the military frontier post from where you can get to Puerto Asís (Colombia) by boat. On this flight, locals take precedence.

Aircraft for Hire Ask at airport; normal rate US$300 an hour for plane taking 5. Also try Aero Taxi Iquitos, Samanez Ocampo 854, T 282837. Amazon Camp Tourist Service offers a 30-minute "flightseeing" tour over the city and surrounding jungle with English-speaking guide, min 4 people US$120 pp, 5-12 people US$100 pp, 13-20 people US$90 pp.

Shipping Upstream. River boats to Pucallpa (2 boats a week in rainy season), 7 days, or Yurimaguas, at least 4 days (longer if cargo is being carried, which is usually the case), cheap, but beware of overcharging to gringos; fastest boat to Yurimaguas is *Jasmin*, 4 days or so. Information on boats for Pucallpa obtained on wharves, or at Meneses (Jirón Próspero), Bellavista (Malecón Tarapacá 596), Hurtado (Av Grau 1223) and Casa Pinto (Sargento Lores 164). Cabins are 4 berth and you have to buy both a first class ticket, which entitles you to food (whether you want it or not) and deck space to sling your hammock, and a cabin ticket if you want the "luxury" of a berth. Adequate washing and toilet facilities, but the food is rice, meat and beans (and whatever can be picked up en route) cooked in river water. There is a good cheap bar.

Downstream. Weekly luxury 54-passenger boat, *Río Amazonas*, plies between Iquitos and Leticia, leaves Sun, operated by Amazon Tours and Cruises, Requena 336, Iquitos, T 233931, US$525 (US$420 pp for groups of 10 plus), return journey to Iquitos Wed. They also operate the *MV Arca*, Iquitos-Tabatinga (Brazil), Sun-Wed, US$330 pp (US$275 pp groups of 10 plus), return journey Wed-Sat.

Communications with Manaus by river are unreliable and the journey takes about 15 days (two boats doing this journey are *Clivia*, frequent, good food, and *Almirante Monteiro*, clean, reasonable food). The Hertzog boat, *Juliana*, is the most beautiful; friendly captain. Best go first to Leticia, or Islandia, opposite Tabatinga (US$30 pp cabin plus food, US$24 pp hammock plus food); Islandia itself is just a mud bank with an exchange shop on the Peruvian side of a narrow creek just a few yards from Benjamin Constant in Brazil. Speedboats between Iquitos and Islandia charge US$50, every 2 days, book ahead (2 days upstream, 11 hrs downstream; eg Expreso Turístico Loreto, Loreto 171, T 238021; slow boats take 36 hrs downstream). No boats from Iquitos go to Benjamin Constant (391 km), but all boats for Manaus start from there and a new hotel (*Benjamin*) has been built.

If a long wait is involved, then Leticia (Colombia) has the best hotels and facilities. Canoes put out from Leticia and will take off passengers from passing boats at another mud bank called Puerto Ancorade, just opposite. There are also ferries from Benjamin Constant to Tabatinga and Leticia, 1½ hrs. The *Huallaga* is highly recommended for river journeys to Leticia, 3 days US$20 with your own hammock, no food, or Pucallpa. It is easy to find a boat, but difficult to get it to move, though you can stay on board. Details on exit and entry formalities seem to change frequently, so when leaving Peru, check in Iquitos first (Immigration, Arica 477, office hours 0900-1300); latest indications are that exit stamps are given only at Puerto Alegría, not by the Peruvian Consulate in Leticia (0830-1430 – the consul is elusive), while tourist cards for entry into Peru are given at Puerto Alegría, 2 hrs upstream from Islandia, where the boat stops for police checks. Brazilian entry formalities are in Tabatinga, in town, 2 km from the pier, or at the airport (taxis from riverfront to airport tend to overcharge). Boats to and across frontiers carry many smugglers and thieves.

General hints for river travel A hammock is essential (few are on sale in Iquitos); a double, of material (not string), provides one person with a blanket. Board the boat many hours in advance. If going on the top deck, try to be first down the front; take rope for hanging your hammock, plus string and sarongs for privacy. On all boats, hang your hammock away from lightbulbs (they aren't switched off at night and attract all sorts of strange insects) and away from the engines, which usually emit noxious fumes. Guard your belongings from the moment you board. Stock up on drinking water, fruit and tinned food in Iquitos. Take plenty of prophylactic enteritis tablets; many contract dysentery on the trip. Also take insect repellent; one sold locally, called Black Flag, is not effective.

INFORMATION FOR VISITORS

Before you go

Entry requirements

● **Documents**
No visa is necessary for citizens of Western European and Scandinavian countries (except Spain), the Czech Republic, Canada, the USA, Japan, all Latin American and Caribbean countries (except Cuba) and South Korea. South Africans, Australians and New Zealanders must have visas. A Tourist Card (*Cédula C*, obligatory) is obtained free from the immigration authorities on arrival in Peru for visits up to 90 days, 60 days in the case of Bolivia, Chile, Colombia, Dominican Republic (insist on getting the full 90 days, at some borders cards valid for 60, or even only 30 days have been given). It is in duplicate, the original given up on arrival and the copy on departure, and may be renewed (see below). A new tourist card must be obtained for each re-entry or when an extension is given. Tourist visas, for citizens of countries not listed above, cost US$20 or equivalent, for which you require a valid passport, a return ticket,

two colour passport photos and two application forms. All foreigners should be able to produce on demand some recognizable means of identification, preferably a passport. You must present your passport when reserving tickets for internal, as well as, international travel. An alternative is to photocopy the important pages of your passport – including the immigration stamp, and legalize it by a 'Notario público' (US$1.50). This way you can avoid showing your passport. Officially, an exit ticket is required for entry into Peru and may be required by the Consulate where you ask for a visa (eg Quito). At land frontiers, practices vary; an MCO may not be accepted as an onward ticket. One's best bet is a bus ticket Arequipa-Arica (Tepsa, valid for 6 months, sold as an onward ticket at the Ecuadorean border even though Tepsa have discontinued the route, and more expensive than Arequipa-Tacna, Tacna-Arica bus journeys) which may then be exchanged with persistence. Alternatively, a Tumbes-Guayaquil ticket will do. Many travellers have reported that they have not been asked for a ticket at Tacna, Aguas Verdes, Yunguyo or Desaguadero. If you do not have one on arrival at the border, you may be forced to pay US$15 minimum for an out-going bus ticket. Travellers arriving by air report no onward flight checks at Lima airport.

NB Tourist visas may be renewed for 60 days at Migraciones, Paseo de la República 585, Lima, 0900-1300 (also in major towns like Cusco or Arequipa). You must present your passport, a valid return ticket to a destination outside Peru, a *solicitud* (written request for an extension) and payment of US$20 or the equivalent in soles. If you wish to extend your entry permit after 90 days have already elapsed since your entry into Peru this is possible at the discretion of the authorities, but on payment of a fine of US$20. The maximum stay in such a case would be 150 days from the first entry. If you are in the Puno area when your visa expires, it is sometimes quicker and easier to cross the border to Bolivia for a day and return with a new visa, often for 90 days, which you would not get in Lima or Cusco.

If a visitor is going to receive money from Peruvian sources, he/she must have a business visa: requirements are a valid passport, two colour passport photos, return ticket and a letter from an employer or Chamber of Commerce stating the nature of business, length of stay and guarantee that any Peruvian taxes will be paid. The visa costs £18.90 (or equivalent). On arrival business visitors must register with the Dirección General de Contribuciones for tax purposes.

To obtain a 1 year student visa one must have: proof of adequate funds, affiliation to a Peruvian body, a letter of recommendation from your own and a Peruvian Consul, a letter of moral and economic guarantee from a Peruvian citizen and 4 photographs (frontal and profile). One must also have a health check certificate which takes 4 weeks to get and costs US$10. Also, to obtain a student visa, if applying within Peru, you have to leave the country and collect it in La Paz, Arica or Guayaquil from Peruvian immigration (it costs US$20). If your tourist card is stolen or lost, apply for a new one also at Migraciones (address above); very helpful. If you try to leave Peru without your tourist card, the fine is US$40.

● **Tourist information**
The Fondo de Promoción Turística (Foptur) closed its national and international offices in 1992. Tourism was placed under the Ministerio de Industria, Comercio, Turismo e Integración, which has an office in each major town. Staff are helpful with advice. Some former Foptur offices in large cities have been taken over by former employees within a private organization called Infotur.

When to go

● **Best time to visit**
Peru has three different geographical zones, each with its own climate. The coast: from Dec to April, summertime, temperature from 25° to 35°C; hot and dry. Wintertime, May-Nov; the temperature drops a bit and it is cloudy. Lima gets enclosed by fog from the ocean, which makes the city grey, humid and cold (but not below 10°C); there is no rain.

The sierra: from April to Oct is the dry season, hot and dry during the day, around 20°-25°C, cold and dry at night, often below freezing. From Nov to April is the wet season, dry and clear most mornings, some rainfall in the afternoon, with a small temperature drop (18°C) and not much difference at night (15°C).

The jungle: April-Oct, dry season, temperatures up to 35°C. In the jungle areas of the S, a cold front can pass through at night. Nov-Apr, wet season, heavy rainfall at any time, humid and hot.

NB The climate can change greatly under the influence of El Niño. Climate does not usually interfere with business.

Health

● **Staying healthy**
As a general rule, do not eat raw food (this

includes raw, or soft-boiled egg). Accustom yourself to the different food first. If, with the change in your system as a result of the new bacteria it is encountering, you suffer from diahorrea, take it seriously. Eat lightly and drink plenty of fluids; avoid fried food. If it does not get better, see a doctor. Eating from street vendors is considered safe if the food is boiled or can be peeled. Most middle-class restaurants are safe. Do not eat ceviche unless you are sure that it has been thermally cooked; usually it is *cocinado en limón* (marinated in lemon). Tap water should not be drunk anywhere in Peru unless it has been boiled or treated with iodine, as that will kill all pathogens, including giardia. Boiled water is available throughout Peru. Note that at high altitudes boiling may be insufficient to purify water (since the boiling point is less than 100°C); additional forms of purification may be necessary. Of the water purification tablets sold in local chemists, Certimil do not dissolve; Micropur are much better.

Typhoid and hepatitis are common; get innoculated, either before you go, or in Lima. Be careful about buying gamma globulin in Peru as most pharmacists do not keep it under refrigeration, rendering it valueless. Buy a disposable syringe for US$0.25 to obviate the risk of hepatitis from the clinic or doctor's needle.

In Lima, there is a Centro de Antirabia if you are unfortunate enough to be bitten by a rabid dog. In other cities, hospitals give anti-rabies injections (always have a check-up if bitten by a dog; rabies is not uncommon). Because of a TB epidemic, avoid non-pasteurized dairy products.

Altitude is often a problem in the mountain cities. Also, when walking at high altitude, the body needs sugar, which can be carried conveniently in the form of a block of crystallized pure cane sugar, called *chancaca*, and easily found in markets. Tonopan has been recommended for altitude sickness and headaches: take first pill 15 mins before landing, then 3 times a day. In jungle areas, seek prior advice on malarial zones, Leishmaniasis, transmitted by painful sandfly bites, is present; repellent is strongly rec, particularly containing DEET, which is difficult to obtain in Peru except in Lima. (See also **Health information** at front of book.)

Tampons are easy to obtain in the better pharmacies in large cities, but they are expensive. Hotels and chemists/pharmacies often let visitors use their toilets.

Money

● Currency

The new sol (s/) is divided into 100 céntimos. In 1991 the new sol replaced the inti at the rate of 5/1 = 1 million intis. Notes in circulation are: S/100, S/50, S/20 and S/10. Coins: S/5, S/2, S/1, S/0.50, S/0.20 and S/0.10. The last remaining inti note in circulation, 5,000,000, is being replaced by the 5 sol coin. Some prices are quoted in dollars in more expensive establishments, to avoid changes in the value of the sol. You can pay in soles, however. Try to break down large notes whenever you can.

Warning A large number of forged notes (especially US$20 and larger bills) are in circulation; check the numbers if possible, and hold notes up to the light to inspect the line which can be seen on the lefthand side of the bill spelling out the bill's amount. There should also be tiny pieces of thread in the paper (not glued on). Always check every bill when changing money. There is a shortage of change in museums, post offices, railway stations and even shops, while taxi drivers are notorious in this regard – one is simply told "no change". Do not accept this excuse.

● Credit cards

Visa (most common), Diners Club, and Mastercard (Access/Eurocard) are accepted, including at State Tourist Hotels. An 8% commission is charged on their use. Visa is accepted at Banco de Crédito, at better rates than for TCs and cash can be withdrawn – local currency only – at no commission, in most cities. Mastercard is not as widely accepted as shop signs indicate. Cash against Mastercard can be obtained, with commission, at Banco del Sur and Banco Wiese. ATMs of the Mastercard/Cirrus network can be found at all branches of Banco Regional del Norte. Credit cards cannot be used in smaller towns, only in the main cities. Credit card loss can be reported in Lima, T 444-1891/1896; card number required.

● Exchange

There are no restrictions on foreign exchange. Banks are the best place to change TCs into new soles; most charge no commission. They will also change cheques into dollars cash at 2-3% commission. The services of the Banco de Crédito have been repeatedly rec. *Casas de cambio* are good for changing dollars cash into soles. There is no difference in the exchange rate given by banks and *casas de cambio*. Always count your money in the presence of the cashier. It is possible to have US$ or DM sent from your home country. Take the cheque to the Banco de la Nación and ask for a *liquidación por canje de moneda extranjera*. You will be charged 1% commission in US$ or soles. US dollars are the most useful currency (take some small bills), but Deutsche marks can be negotiated in all large towns; other currencies carry high commission fees. For changing into or out of small amounts of dollars cash, the street changers give the best rates avoiding paperwork and queuing, but they also employ many ruses to give you a bad deal (check your soles before handing over your dollars, check their calculators, etc, and don't change money in crowded areas). If using their services think about taking a taxi after changing, to avoid being followed. Street changers usually congregate near an office where the exchange 'wholesaler' operates; he will probably be offering better rates than on the street.

Soles can be exchanged into dollars at the Banco de la Nación at Lima airport, and one can change soles for dollars at any border. Dollars can also be bought at the various frontiers.

NB No one, not even banks, will accept dollar bills that look 'old', or are in any way damaged or torn. Take care that you are not given such notes.

American Express state that they will sell TCs and give out emergency money, but only in Lima. Travel agents are allowed to accept foreign currencies in payment for their services, and to exchange small amounts. Try to avoid changing TCs outside the main cities: commission is high and it is often a difficult process. Travellers have reported great difficulty in cashing TCs in the jungle area, even Iquitos, and other remote areas. Always sign TCs in blue or black ink or ballpen. There may be shortages of cash for changing TCs. Thomas Cook/Mastercard refund assistance point: Viajes Laser, Calle Espinar, 331, Lima, T 449-0134/137. For Western Union, T Lima 440-7934.

● **Cost of living**

Living costs in the provinces are from 20 to 50% below those of Lima. Since Aug 1990, when prices were increased steeply by the government, Peru has become expensive for the tourist, especially for those on a tight budget. This was made worse by the overvaluation of the new sol in early 1992. For low and middle-income Peruvians, prices of many items are beyond their reach. In early 1994 the South American Explorers Club estimated a budget of US$25-30 a day for living comfortably, incl transport, or US$12-15 a day for low budget travel. Hotel prices compare very favourably with those in other Latin American countries, ranging from US$3 to US$50. For meal prices, see **Food** below.

Students can obtain very few reductions in Peru with an international student's card, except in and around Cusco. To be any use in Peru, it must bear the owner's photograph. An ISIC card can be obtained in Lima from San Martín 240, Barranco, T 774105, for US$20.

Getting there

By Air

● **From Europe**

Direct flights Amsterdam (KLM), Frankfurt (Lufthansa, with change of planes in Bogotá), Paris (AOM French Airlines), Rome (Alitalia) and Madrid (Iberia). Cheap flights from London: one way is to go via Madrid with Iberia, or standby to Miami, then fly the airlines shown below. Aeroflot fly to Peru from Moscow via Shannon and Havana, or via Luxembourg and Havana; the flight can be joined either in Moscow, or in Shannon or Luxembourg, but it is *vital* to check that these services are in operation when you want to travel. To avoid paying Peru's 18% tax on international air tickets, take your used outward ticket with you when buying return passage.

● **From Latin America**

Regular flights to all South American countries, except Uruguay; in most cases, daily. Lloyd Aéreo Boliviano (LAB) is usually the cheapest airline for flights out of Lima but tickets bought in Peru are more expensive. Lacsa and AeroPerú fly from Mexico (in latter case Mexico City and Cancún). Beware of buying Viasa tickets in Peru, they often turn out to be forgeries.

● **From Tokyo**

Trans-pacific flights by Varig, once a week.

● **From USA and Canada**

Miami is the main gateway to Peru with flights every day with American, United, also AeroPerú, Third Avenue, Miami (T 800-255-7378), daily, and Faucett, 4 a week (Faucett also flies Miami-Iquitos-Lima once a week). Other direct flights from New York (Lan Chile; American and United via Miami, Lacsa in San José; Avianca in Bogotá) and Los Angeles (Lacsa, AeroPerú, Aerolíneas Argentinas, Varig, Lan Chile). Regular connections can be made from many other North American cities. AeroPerú and Faucett offer discounts on internal flights when you buy a Miami-Lima return ticket, eg US$250 for unlimited flights (check in advance for restrictions). See **Introduction and Hints**, p 12, on AeroPerú's Sudameripass round Latin America flight ticket.

Customs

● **Duty free allowance**
400 cigarettes or 50 cigars or 500 grams of
tobacco, 2 litres of alcoholic drinks, new articles for personal use or gifts up to value
US$200.

● **Export ban**
No object of archaeological interest may be
taken out of Peru.

When you arrive

● **Hours of business**
Shops: 0900 or 1000-1230 and 1500 or
1600-2000. In the main cities, supermarkets
do not close for lunch and Lima has some that
are open 24 hrs. Some are closed on Sat; most
are closed on Sun. *Banks*: most are open
0900-1230, 1500-1800 the year round.
Closed Sat. Some banks in Lima open from
0900-1600 and do not close for lunch. **NB** All
banks close on Jun 30 and Dec 31 for balancing; if it falls on Sat or Sun, banks may close
1 day before or after. This does not apply to
the bank at Jorge Chávez international airport which is open 24 hrs every day. *Offices*:
0830-1230, 1500-1800 the year round; some
have continuous hours 0900-1700; most
close on Sat. *Government Offices*: Jan to Mar,
Mon-Fri 0830-1130. Rest of year: Mon-Fri
0900-1230, 1500-1700, but this changes frequently.

● **Official time**
5 hrs behind GMT, except Jan to Apr, when
GMT -4 (exact date of clock change varies
annually).

● **Safety**
The following notes on personal safety
should not hide the fact that most Peruvians,
particularly outside those areas affected by
crime or terrorism, are hospitable and helpful.

Thieves are active in markets, streets,
buses and trains, choosing especially tourists
as their targets. We have received reports of
robbery from hotel rooms and safes from
places as diverse as Huaraz, Paracas and
Cusco. Snatch thieves in Lima are very fast,
they often use beggars to distract you. The
most common method of attack is bag-slash-
ing. Take care everywhere, but especially
when arriving in or leaving a town at night by
bus or train; in fact, it is better to travel by day
whenever possible. Take taxis to stations,
when carrying luggage, before 0800 and after dark (look on it as an insurance policy). It
is worth taking extra care during festivals
when streets are crowded. For general hints
on avoiding crime, please see the **Security**

section at the beginning of the book. All the
suggestions given there are valid for Peru.
Avoid staying in hotels too near to bus companies, as drivers who stay overnight are
sometimes in league with thieves; avoid restaurants near bus terminals if you have all
your luggage with you, it is hard to keep an
eye on all your gear when eating. On trains,
one large bag is easier to watch, and lock to
a rack (more than once), than lots of small
ones. In poor areas of cities be on your guard
as this is where most theft takes place. Try to
find a travel companion if alone, as this will
reduce the strain of watching your belongings all the time. If checking valuables into a
hotel safe, ask for an itemized receipt, which
will prevent any discrepancies later. The police
presence in Lima, Arequipa, Puno and Cusco
has been greatly stepped up. It is a good idea
to inform your Embassy in Lima of your passport data (or leave a photocopy), so that if the
passport is stolen delays for replacement are
minimized. In general, common sense is the
best policy. Outside the July-Aug peak holiday
period, there is less tension, less risk of crime,
and more friendliness. A friendly attitude on
your part, smiling even when you've thwarted
a thief's attempt, can help you out of trouble.
In addition, do not be discourteous to officials. In general, the position has been improving since 1993.

Although certain illegal drugs are readily
available anyone carrying any is almost automatically assumed to be a drug trafficker. If
arrested on any charge the wait for trial in
prison can take a year and is particularly
unpleasant. Unfortunately, we have received
reports of drug-planting, or mere accusation
of drug-trafficking by the PNP on foreigners
in Lima, with US$1,000 demanded for re-
lease. If you are asked by the narcotics police
to go to the toilets to have your bags
searched, insist on taking a witness. **Drugs
use or purchase is punishable by up to 15
years' imprisonment**.

Tricks employed to get foreigners into
trouble over drugs include slipping a packet
of cocaine into the money you are exchanging, being invited to a party or somewhere
involving a taxi ride, or simply being asked on
the street if you want to buy cocaine. In all
cases, a plain clothes 'policeman' will discover
the planted cocaine, in your money, at your
feet in the taxi, and will ask to see your
passport and money. He will then return
them, minus a large part of your cash. Do not
get into a taxi, do not show your money, and
try not to be intimidated. Being in pairs is no
guarantee of security, and single women may
be particularly vulnerable. Beware also

thieves dressed as policemen asking for your passport and wanting to search for drugs; searching is only permitted if prior paperwork is done.

Another Warning It remains hard to tell how many followers and sympathizers Sendero Luminoso has, but the military now seems to have taken control of most departments. Tourists are not targets for the guerrillas and, apart from one instance (a Briton), the few tourists who have been killed were travelling in dangerous areas.

The Central Highlands suffered much of the violence and, until 1992, it was not safe to travel in that region. With the reestablishment of military control, there has been much improvement. People have been travelling through the area, mostly with favourable reports. It is still essential to inform yourself of the latest situation before going. There are many checkpoints, which present no problem. Travel only by day. Take great care in Ayacucho Department, do not travel by bus between Nazca and Cusco, and Puno and Cusco, and avoid the Huallaga Valley because of drug trafficking and terrorism.

Keep yourself informed before going and while travelling. For up-to-date information contact the Tourist Police, T Lima 437-8171/435-1342/437-8262, your embassy or consulate, fellow travellers, the South American Explorers Club, who issue the pamphlet 'How Not to Get Robbed in Peru' (T Lima 425-0142, or in Quito) and, also in Quito, *The Latin American Travel Advisor* (published by Latin American Travel Consultants, PO Box 17-17-908, Quito, F 593-2-562-566, E-Mail rku@pi pro ec on Internet).

● **Tipping**
Restaurants: service is included in the bill (see below), but if someone goes out of his way to serve tips can be given. Taxi drivers, none (in fact, bargain the price down, then pay extra for good service if you get it). Cloakroom attendants and hairdressers (very high class only), US$0.50-$1. Railway or airport porters, US$0.50. Note: anyone who as much as touches your bag will expect a tip. Usherettes, none. Car wash boys, US$0.30, car 'watch' boys, US$0.20.

● **Voltage**
220 volts AC, 60 cycles throughout the country, except Arequipa (50 cycles).

● **Weights and measures**
The metric system of weights and measures is compulsory.

On departure

● **Airport departure taxes**
There is a US$18 airport tax on international flight departures, payable in dollars or soles. Passengers departing from Cusco, Iquitos, Arequipa, Ayacucho and Trujillo must pay a further tax of US$7. For non-Peruvians, there is a security tax of US$4-5 and an airport tax of US$3-4 (depending on the airport) on domestic flights (if you are working in Peru, carry a letter stating this and insist you are 'residente' and pay local tax of US$2). 18% VAT is charged on air tickets.

Where to stay

● **Hotels**
The State Tourist Hotels (commonly known as *Hoteles de Turistas*) are run by Enturperú. They vary considerably but frequently offer the best accommodation in town in terms of cleanliness and reliable food. They provide safe garaging for cars at US$0.65 a night. Reservations can be made at Enturperú, Av Javier Prado-Oeste 1358, San Isidro, PO Box 4475, Lima, T 442-8626/8837 for reservations (one night deposit required), 472-1928 for information. The tourist hotels in Cusco, Trujillo, Puerto Maldonado, Chiclayo and Abancay operate independently and have to be contacted directly. Prices vary in each hotel but they are between US$45-80 d a night.

Heating in rooms is often unsatisfactory. Good local maps can usually be obtained at the Tourist Hotels; in some of the smaller towns they function as tourist offices. All de luxe, 1st class and State Tourist Hotels charge a high 28% in taxes, which includes VAT and service charges; lower category hotels charge 20-23% (similarly restaurants). Most hotels have this surcharge included in their prices, but best check first. By law all places that offer accommodation now have a plaque outside bearing the letters H (Hotel), Hs (Hostal), HR (Hotel Residencial) or P (Pensión) according to type. A hotel has 51 rooms or more, a hostal 50 or fewer; the categories do not describe quality or facilities. Many hotels have safe parking for motor cycles. Check all bills most carefully. All hotels seem to be crowded at the end of Jul, Independence celebrations. It should be noted, even in the upper categories, that in general hotel standards are low. Also reception areas may be misleading; it is a good idea to see the room before booking. Hotels tend to be more expensive in the N than in the S. When booking a hotel from an airport, or station by phone, always talk to the hotel yourself; do not let anyone do it for you (except an accredited hotel booking service). You will be told the hotel of your choice is full and be directed to a more expensive one. Information on youth hostels and student accommodation can be obtained from INTEJ, Av San Martín 240, Barranco, Lima, T 477-4105. Also Asociación Peruana de Albergues Turísticos Juveniles, Av Casimiro Ulloa 328, Miraflores, Lima, T 446-5488, F 444-8187. Always take a torch and candles, especially in remoter regions.

NB Hotels are checked by the police for drugs, especially the rooms of foreigners. Make sure they do not remove any of your belongings. You do not need to show them money. Cooperate, but be firm about your rights.

● **Camping**

Easy in Peru, especially along the coast. There can be problems with robbery when camping close to a small village. Avoid such a location, or ask permission to camp in a backyard or *chacra* (farmland). Most Indians are used to campers, but in some remote places, people have never seen a tent. Be casual about it, do not unpack all your gear, leave it inside your tent (especially at night) and never leave a tent unattended. Camping gas in little blue bottles is available in the main cities. Those with stoves designed for lead-free gasoline should use *ron de quemar*, available from hardware shops (*ferreterías*). White gas is called *bencina*, also available from hardware stores.

Food and drink

Food

The high-class hotels and restaurants serve international food and, on demand, some native dishes, but the taverns (*chicherías*) and the local restaurants (*picanterías*) supply the highly seasoned native food at its best. Soups tend to be very good, and a meal in themselves. In the Lima area the most popular fish dishes are the *cebiche* – raw fish, seasoned with lemons, onions and red peppers (see **Health** above); the *escabeche* – fish with onions, hot green pepper, red peppers, prawns (*langostinos*), cumin, hard eggs, olives, and sprinkled with cheese; and *chupe de camarones*, a shrimp stew made with varying and somewhat surprising ingredients. *Parihuela* is a popular bouillabaisse which includes *yuyo de mar*, a tangy seaweed. *Yacu-chupe*, or green soup, has a basis of potato, with cheese, garlic, coriander leaves, parsley, peppers, eggs, onions, and mint. *Causa* and *carapulca* are two good potato dishes; *papa a la huancaína* is another potato dish, topped with a spicy sauce made with milk and cheese; *causa* is made with yellow potatoes, lemons, pepper, hard-boiled eggs, olives, lettuce, sweet cooked corn, sweet cooked potato, fresh cheese, and served with onion sauce. Favourite meat dishes are *ollucos con charqui* (a kind of potato with dried meat), *caucau*, made with tripe, potatoes, peppers, and parsley and served with rice; *anticuchos*, hearts of beef with garlic, peppers, cumin seeds and vinegar; *estofado de carne*, a stew which often contains wine; *carne en adobo*, a cut and seasoned steak; *fritos*, fried pork, usually eaten in the morning; *sancochado*, meat and all kinds of vegetables stewed together and seasoned with ground garlic; *lomo a la huancaína*, beef with egg and cheese sauce; *lomo saltado* is a beef stew with onions, vinegar, ginger, chilli, tomatoes and fried potatoes, served with rice; and *sopa a la criolla* containing thin noodles, beef heart, bits of egg and vegetables and pleasantly spiced. Any dish described as *arequipeño* can be expected to be hot and spicy. *Mondonguito* is a boiled small intestine. The best beef is imported from Argentina and is expensive. Duck is excellent. For snacks, Peruvian *empanadas* are good. *Palta rellena* is avocado filled with chicken salad.

Among the desserts and confections are *cocada al horno* – coconut, with yolk of egg, sesame seed, wine and butter; *picarones* – frittered cassava flour and eggs fried in fat and served with honey; *mazamorra morada* – purple maize, sweet potato starch, lemons, various dried fruits, sticks of ground cinnamon and cloves and perfumed pepper; *manjar blanco* – milk, sugar and eggs; *maná* – an almond paste with eggs, vanilla and milk; *alfajores* – shortbread biscuit with *manjar blanco*, pineapple, peanuts, etc; *pastelillos* – yucas with sweet potato, sugar and anise fried in fat and powdered with sugar and served hot; and *zango de pasas*, made with maize, syrup, raisins and sugar. *Turrón*, the Lima nougat, is worth trying. *Tejas* are sugar candies wrapped in wax paper; the pecan-flavoured ones are tastiest. The various Peruvian fruits are of good quality: they include bananas, the citrus fruits, pineapples, dates, avocados (*paltas*), eggfruit (*lúcuma*), the custard apple (*chirimoya*) which can be as big as your head, quince, *papaya*, mango, guava, the passion-fruit (*maracuyá*) and the soursop (*guanábana*).

The tea hour starts about 1800 at the good hotels. If asked to a party ask the hostess what time you are *really* expected unless the time is specified on the invitation card as *hora inglesa* – English time; Peruvians tend to ask guests for dinner at 2000.

A normal lunch or dinner costs US$5-8, but can go up to about US$80 in a first-class restaurant, with drinks and wine included. Middle and high-class restaurants add 11% tax and 17% service to the bill (sometimes 18% and 13% respectively); this is not shown on the price list or menu, check in advance. Lower class restaurants charge only 5% tax, while cheap, local restaurants charge no taxes. Lunch is the main meal: dinner in restaurants is normally about 1900 onwards, but choice may be more limited than lunchtime. There are plenty of cheap and good restaurants around the centre of Lima and most offer a 'business lunch' called *menú* for US$1.30-3 for a 3-course meal. There are many Chinese restaurants (*chifas*) in Peru which serve good food at reasonable prices. For really economically-minded people the *Comedores populares* in most cities of Peru offer a standard 3-course meal US$1. Meals at this price, or little more, can be found under name of *menú económico* at many restaurants throughout Peru.

Drink

The usual international drinks with several very good local ones: *pisco*, a brandy made in the Ica valley, from which pisco sour is made; *chilcano*, a longer refreshing drink also made with *guinda*, a local cherry brandy; and *algarrobina*, a sweet cocktail made with the syrup from the bark of the carob tree, egg whites, milk, pisco and cinnamon. Wine is acidic and not very good, the best of a poor lot are the Ica wines Tacama and Ocucaje; both come in red, white and rosé, sweet and dry varieties. Tacama blancs de blancs and brut champagne have been rec, also Gran Tinto Reserva Especial. Viña Santo Tomás, from Chincha, is reasonable and cheap. Casapalca is not rec. Beer is best in lager and porter types, especially the Cusco and Arequipa brands (lager) and Trujillo Malta (porter). In Lima only Cristal and Pilsener (not related to true Pilsen) are readily available, others have to be sought out. Look out for the sweetish 'maltina' brown ale, which makes a change from the ubiquitous pilsner – type beers. *Chicha de jora* is a maize beer, usually homemade and not easy to come by, refreshing but strong, and *chicha morada* is a soft drink made with purple maize. Coffee is often brought to the table in a small jug accompanied by a mug of hot water to which you add the coffee essence. If you want coffee with milk, a mug of milk is brought. There are many different kinds of herb tea: the commonest are *manzanilla* (camomile) and *hierbaluisa* (lemon grass).

Getting around

Air transport

Air services link towns which are often far apart and can only be reached otherwise with difficulty. The three main companies are Cía de Aviación Faucett, AeroPerú and Americana. Aero Continente flies mostly the same routes as these three, for about the same fares, but with better service. Americana and Continente share planes on some routes, Americana taking the routes to the N, Aero Continente those to the S and jungle. Expreso Aéreo fly to towns in the mountains and the jungle using smaller aircraft (not very reliable). Aero Cóndor links some of the smaller coastal, mountain and jungle towns. The airforce runs some commercial flights to jungle areas, only a few times a month, not reliable, but half the price of other airlines. Since the privatization of AeroPerú, competition is hard and there are often substantial discounts with all the airlines. Tickets are not interchangeable between the companies, but may be permitted in the case of cancelled flights. See under Lima (p 1132) for airline addresses, towns served, and above for taxes. Note that flight schedules and departure times change often, and that delays are common. In the rainy season cancellations occur, sometimes for 2 days. There are also unannounced route changes and poor time-keeping (Americana seems to be the most reliable of the three main companies). Always allow an extra day between national and international flights, especially in the rainy season. Internal flight prices are fixed in US dollars (but can be paid in soles) and have 18% tax added. Prices given in the text were valid in Feb 1995. It is possible to buy AeroPerú domestic tickets more cheaply outside Peru, but the offer changes frequently. You cannot alter the destinations in Peru, only the date. (If you fly Cusco-Juliaca you go via Arequipa and can stop over, completing the Juliaca leg later.) If you fly to Peru with AeroPerú from Miami, you are given one free internal flight and any other routes for US$50 each. AeroPerú Faucett and Americana offer 2, 3 4 or 5-stop tickets for US$109, US$149, US$179 or US$209 if bought outside Peru (Americana fares, also an unlimited ticket for US$269; AeroPerú fares start at US$99 for 2 coupons). If you have a choice, remember timekeeping tends to be better early am than later. When buying an internal flight, check with travel agencies for occasional special deals, but scrutinize the ticket carefully. Also check with the different airlines; even though they maintain the same set price, they sometimes do promotions on flights.

NB If possible travel with hand luggage only (48 cm x 24 cm x 37 cm) so there is more chance of you and your baggage arriving at the same destination. Unpredictable weather contributes to poor time-keeping, but companies are also criticized for their passenger service, especially as regards information and overbooking. Note that flights into the mountains may well be put forward 1 hr if there are reports of bad weather. Neither AeroPerú or Faucett has enough aircraft and both are in financial difficulties. Flights to jungle regions are also unreliable. See also warning on p 1231.

Flights must be reconfirmed in the town you will be leaving from 24 hrs in advance, but 72 hrs is advised. 20 mins before departure, the clerk is allowed by law to let standby passengers board, taking the reserved seats of those who haven't turned up. AeroPerú offers senior citizen discounts (40%) but some offices may not grant them. Tickets can be bought through travel agencies (but check them carefully), or direct through the airline; the price is the same.

Air Freight Luggage, packets, etc, are not handled with care; make sure there are no loose parts, or put your rucksack in a separate bag. Always lock your luggage when possible. Check that the correct destination label has been attached. Never put valuables into luggage to be checked in.

Land transport

● Train

There are passenger services on the following lines, which are often quicker and more comfortable than buses: Huancayo- Huancavelica, Arequipa-Juliaca-Puno, Puno-Juliaca-Cusco, and Cusco-Machu Picchu-Quillabamba. Details of services in the text. Good cheap meals are usually served on trains. **NB** Train schedules are cut in the rainy season, sometimes to 2-3 times a week, occasionally they are cancelled for weeks or months. The train from Lima, via La Oroya, to Huancayo has not run since 1991.

● Road

Major and minor roads are given in the text. The two roads to Cusco, one by the Central Andes and the other by Arequipa and Puno, make a most spectacular circuit of 2,400 km possible. Preferably it should be done clockwise: there would be less driving on the outsides of precipices; it would be downhill on the poor stretch between Puno and Arequipa; and the return to Lima would be by a good road. Most of the high Sierra roads are narrow, unsurfaced and liable to landslides; many accidents. Surfaces are usually very rough, and this makes for slow travel and frequent breakdowns. If you have a drive at night, do not go fast; many local vehicles have poor lights and street lighting is bad. Be sure to check with the Peruvian Touring and Automobile Club regarding road conditions before driving in the Sierra.

Few roads in Peru, except for the Pan-American and Central Highways, the roads connecting Huaraz and Caraz with Pativilca, and Pacasmayo with Cajamarca, and the Puno-Desaguadero road to Bolivia are paved. Toll roads in Peru include Aguas Verdes-Tumbes, many on the Panamerican Highway between Tumbes and Lima, Pativilca-Huaraz, Lima-Pucusana, Ica-Nazca, Lima (highway around city), Variante-Pacasmayo, which vary from US$1.50 to US$0.50. Ecuador to Chile/Bolivia on main roads comes to about US$17. (Motorcycles are exempt from road tolls: use the extreme righthand lane at toll gates.)

● Motoring

The Touring y Automóvil Club del Perú, Av César Vallejo 699, Lince, Lima (T 403270, F 419652), with offices in most provincial cities, gives news about the roads and hotels along the way (although for the most up-to-date information try the bus and colectivo offices). It sells a very good road map at US$5 (Mapa Vial del Perú, 1:3,000,000, Ed 1980, reliable information about road conditions) and route maps covering most of Peru (Hoja de Ruta, detail maps 1:1,000,000, very good but no information on road conditions). Good maps are available from the South American Explorers Club, who will give good advice on road conditions. Buy maps separately or in packages of 8. Cuadernos de Viaje are travel notebooks covering all Peru with valuable information and maps, in Spanish. Other maps can be bought from street vendors in Colmena and Plaza San Martín, Lima. 'Westermanns Monatshefte; folio Ecuador, Peru, Bolivien' has excellent maps of Peru, especially the archaeological sites. Gasoline is sold as: 'extra' (84 octane), US$2.05 a gallon, and 'importada' (95 octane), US$2.50-2.75 a gallon, found in Lima, the coastal towns and Arequipa; unleaded fuel (90 and 97 octane SP) is sold on the coast, US$2.25-US$2.55. Fuel in remote jungle areas can be double the price of urban areas. Diesel costs US$1.15 a gallon. Filling stations are called grifos. In Lima never trust the green light; Peruvian drivers tend to regard traffic lights as recommendations, at most. When parking remove detachable accessories and screen wipers. No-parking signs are painted at the roadside: illegally parked cars are towed away. Do not leave your vehicle on the street in Lima, always put it in a car park (called *playa*, usual charge US$0.50/hr). If you want to sleep in your car, check with the local tourist police first. They may allow you to park near their office.

Roads go to very high altitudes in Peru – make sure that the spark is properly adjusted and consider use of smaller carburettor jets if driving much at altitude. Avoid mountain travel between Nov and Apr. Take 2 planks of wood in case car gets stuck in soft soil when allowing other vehicles to pass. Never travel off the main roads without being self-sufficient. Always make sure your fuel tank is full when branching off a major highway, fill up whenever possible and make sure you do not receive diesel or kerosene. If you need mechanical assistance in the mountains ask for the nearest mining or road construction camp. If you take your own car you are immediately a symbol of wealth and will be liable to have it broken into. Disadvantages of travelling in your own vehicle include the difficulties of getting insurance, theft, finding guarded parking lots, maintenance on appalling roads and nervous exhaustion, which may outweigh the advantages of mobility and independence.

Imported car spares available and cheaper than in neighbouring countries. Makes with well-established dealerships are easiest to obtain (eg Volvo, Peugeot, VW). VW Beetles, Toyota Coronas and Datsun Stanzas are assembled in Peru and are therefore easier to get spares and service for. There is also a booming black market in motor parts involving both contraband and stolen parts.

You must have an international driving licence – especially with a number. If you don't have a number on your licence, improvise. (It has been reported that a UK driving licence is acceptable.) A 90-day transit permit for vehicles is available at land borders without a *carnet de passages*, contrary to what officials may tell you (see **Motoring** in **Introduction and Hints**). The minimum age for renting a car is 25.

● **Bus**

Services along the coast and to Arequipa are usually quite good, but try to avoid travel at night, assaults on buses have occurred; buses in the mountain areas generally are small, old, crowded and offer little comfort; Sudamericana, Ormeño and Cruz del Sur thought generally to be the best. The larger companies are

usually the best as they tend not to cancel services; the smaller companies will cancel if they do not have enough passengers. The main companies (and some others) have luxury services on the coastal routes, with toilet, video and reclining seats. Tickets cost 30% more than normal. For bus lines, see Lima, **Bus Companies**. For long journeys take a water bottle. Blankets and emergency food are a *must* in the mountains. Always possible to buy food on the roadside, as buses stop frequently. Luggage can be checked in on a bus, but it is your own responsibility to look after it when the bus stops. Backpacks can be protected by a rice sack, for further security use chicken wire as well. Always carry your valuables with you, even when leaving the bus at a stop. If your bus breaks down and you are transferred to another line and have to pay extra, keep your original ticket for refund from the first company. If possible, on country buses avoid the back seats because of the bumpiness, and the left side because of exhaust fumes. Prices given in the text are the minimum for the route. Colectivos usually charge twice the bus fare. They leave only when full. They go almost anywhere in Peru; most firms have offices. Book 1 day in advance. They pick you up at your hotel or in main square. Trucks are not always much cheaper than buses; they charge ¾ bus fare, but wholly unpredictable, not for long hops, and comfort depends on the load: the ideal is a half load of sugar, or a cargo of arguardiente containers (rubber sacks made of old inner tubes – like a waterbed in compartments, with a 'happy smell' if they seep, Daniel Morgan). Always try to arrive at your destination in daylight: much safer.

NB Prices of bus tickets are raised by 50-75%, 2-3 days before 28 Jul (Independence Day) and Christmas. Tickets are sold out 2-3 days in advance at this time and transport is hard to come by.

● **Hitchhiking**

Hitchhiking is difficult. Freight traffic has to stop at the police *garitas* outside each town and these are the best places to try (also toll points, but these are further from towns). Drivers usually ask for money but don't always expect to get it. In mountain and jungle areas you usually have to pay drivers of lorries, vans and even private cars; ask the driver first how much he is going to charge, and then recheck with the locals (the Sierra Indians for whom it is normal method of travel). Private cars are very few and far between. Readers report that mining trucks are especially dirty to travel in, avoid if possible.

● **Taxi**

Taxi prices are fixed in the mountain towns, about US$0.80 in the urban area. Fares are not fixed in Lima even though there are standard fares (see under Lima). Most taxi drivers will try to charge more for foreigners, so ask locals. The main cities have taxis which can be hired by phone, which charge a little more, but are reliable and safe.

Many taxi drivers work for commission from hotels. Choose your own hotel and get a taxi driver who is willing to take you there.

Taxis at airports are always more expensive; seek advice about the price in advance and do not use the taxis in front of the airport.

Communications

● **Language**

Spanish. Quechua, the language of the Inca empire, has been given some official status and there is much pride in its use; it is spoken by millions of Sierra Indians who have little or no knowledge of Spanish. Another important Indian language is Aymara, used in the area around Lake Titicaca.

● **Newspapers**

Lima has several morning papers: *La Prensa*, *El Comercio* (good international news), *La República* (liberal-left) *La Crónica*, *Expreso*, *Ojo*, *El Diario*, *La Actualidad*, *Extra*, *El Popular*, *La Tribuna*, *Gestión*, *Ultima Hora*. There is a monthly magazine in English, the *Lima Times*, with useful information and articles, and a weekly economic and political report, the *Andean Report*. The main provincial cities have at least one newspaper each.

● **Postal services**

Sending parcels abroad must be done at Centro de Clasificación de Correos, Tomás Valle, block 600, Lima (take bus 128, direction San Germán); open Mon-Fri 0900-1330, Sat 0800-1300. Staff in the post office help with all checking and then sew parcels into sacks for US$1. It can cost about US$20/kg to send a parcel abroad. To avoid paying a tax of US$0.20/kg on parcels sent abroad, take your passport and onward ticket, plus a photocopy of each to the post office. Better still, take your parcels to another country for mailing home; it will almost certainly be cheaper. Try not to have articles sent by post to Peru; taxes can be 200% of the value. Strikes are also very common. To send a letter anywhere in the Americas costs US$0.80, to the rest of the world US$0.90. For US$0.50 extra letters can be sent 'con certificado', which is rec. A Dutch company called EMS are reliable for sending smaller packages, eg film, home. Expensive US$20/kilo (to Europe). More expensive still is UPS; see under Lima, **Air Freight**.

● **Telephone services**

Overseas calls cost on average US$5/minute. Collect calls can now be made (most of the time) to North America and some European countries at the CPT office on Plaza San Martín, Lima, or elsewhere from Entel offices. The best place to try is Lima. A *rin* (token/*ficha*) for an international call costs US$5 and lasts for about 1 min; it can only be bought at an Entel office. Similarly, a *rin* for a long-distance domestic call costs US$0.60, for 2 mins, only at an Entel office. Public phone boxes are for local calls only; a *rin* costs US$0.10 from street vendors. Phone cards can be bought at Entel offices for US$3-US$15 for use on national or international calls. Telephone directories found in most hotel rooms have a useful map of Lima and show itineraries of the buses. Fax and telex abroad can be sent from major Entel offices, US$4/page/minute. (See also Lima, **Telecommunication**.)

NB At the end of 1994 an extra digit was added to Lima phone numbers. Throughout the country, all phone numbers are being changed. Visitors to Peru are advised to check numbers when they are in the country.

Sport

Association football is the most popular. Basketball and other sports are also played on the coast, particularly around Lima and Callao. Golf clubs and racecourses are mentioned in the text. Riding is a favourite recreation in the Sierra, where horses can be hired at reasonable rates. Cricket is played at the Lima Cricket Club. Bullfights and cockfights are held throughout the country. There is excellent deep-sea fishing off Ancón, N of Lima, and at the small port of Cabo Blanco, N of Talara (see text). In that part of the Andes easily reached from La Oroya, the lakes and streams have been stocked with trout, and fly fishing is quite good.

For details about the best rainbow trout fishing in Peru (near Juliaca and in Lakes Arapa and Titicaca) write to Sr José Bernal Paredes, Casilla 874, Arequipa.

Swimming Between Dec and Apr the entire coast of Peru offers good bathing, but during the rest of the year only the northern beaches near Tumbes provide pleasantly warm water. There are many bathing resorts near Lima (do not swim at, or even visit, these beaches alone). The current off the coast can be very strong, making it too dangerous to swim in places. A Foptur brochure lists the many surfing beaches.

Walking The South American Explorers Club has good information and advice on trekking and sells books. Serious walkers are advised to get *Backpacking and Trekking in Peru and Bolivia* (Bradt Publications) which describes 3-5 day treks in the Cordilleras Blanca, Vilcabamba and Vilcanota (Cusco region), and in the Cajamarca area (6th edition due 1995). *The Peruvian Andes*, by Philipe Béaud, is a good guide, describing 100 climbs and 40 treks in Spanish, French and English. John Richter's *Yurak Yunka* can be obtained from the South American Explorers' Club or from *Lima 2000* bookshop, J Bernal 271, Lima. For an account of the Andean Inca road, see Christopher Portway, *Journey Along the Andes* (Impact Books, London, 1993).

The popular trekking routes in Peru are becoming damaged because of over use. Little is done by the government to maintain the trails and less is done by locals. Trekkers are given no information and no guards control the routes. A few conservation groups are trying to combat this problem, but with very little success. Please give everyone a good example by not dropping litter and by picking up that left by others. Point out the importance of this to guides and porters.

Holidays and festivals

1 Jan: New Year. Mar or Apr: Maundy Thur (pm). Good Fri. 1 May: Labour Day. 28 Jun: Saints Peter and Paul. 28, 29 Jul: Independence (when all prices go up). 30 Aug: Santa Rosa de Lima. 7 Oct: Battle of Angamos. 1 Nov: All Saints. 8 Dec: Immaculate Conception. 25 Dec: Christmas.

NB Everything closes on New Year's Eve, Christmas Eve, and other holidays designated 'family holidays', especially Jul-Aug. At these times, expect prices to rise. Also note that the Fujimori administration has decreed that when a public holiday falls on a day in midweek it will be moved to the following Mon.

Between mid-Jul and the beginning of Sep is the Peruvian tourist season: prices, transport can be difficult and hotels are heavily booked. The big national holidays are Dec, Jan and Feb.

Further reading

British business travellers are strongly advised to get 'Hints to Exporters: Peru', from DTI Export Publications, PO Box 55, Stratford-upon-Avon, Warwickshire, CV37 9GE.

Acknowledgements

We are deeply grateful to John Hale for updating this chapter. For a complete update of the Peruvian chapter we should like to thank most warmly Jane Letham, Richard Elgar and Lluis Dalmau of the South American Explorers Club, Lima, with additional information from Michael White of Trujillo.

We are also most grateful to the following travellers: Antonius Ackermann (Oensingen, Switzerland), Daniel Aeberhard (Slough, UK) an excellent contribution, Jimmy Andersson and Christina Gustafson (Malmo, Sweden), Louise Bach (Vestbjerg) and Tine Tang Kleif (Aarhus, Denmark), Douglas and Janet Beckers (Armidale, Australia), Edoardo Bellando (La Paz, Bolivia), Janie Bergeron and François Vitez (Longueuil, Canada), De Coninck Bernadette (Qadima, Israel), Iris Berner (Stuttgart, Germany), Nicole Berry (Columbia, USA), Gustavo von Bischoffshausen Henriod (Lima, Peru), Dave Blackburn (Luton, UK) and Emily Smith (North Carolina, USA), Phil and Jenny Blackman (Bath, UK), Jeremy Blanc (Arequipa), P Bours (Tilburg, The Netherlands), Patrick Carroll (Dublin, Eire), Ludovic Challeat (Lamastre, France), Carmelita Chávez (Vista, USA), Bernard Cloutier (Montreal, Canada), Steve Collins (London, UK), Judith Stanton and Mark Collins (London, UK) a helpful up-date, Mark Collins (Bristol, UK), Eileen Cook (Pacific Palisades, USA), Darien (Israel), Deanna David (California, USA), Dr J Rudolf Dietrich (Basle, Switzerland), Andrea Dittrich and Thomas Bröhl (Köln, Germany), the late Bernard van der Dool (Leiden, The Netherlands), Guy Edlis (Haifa, Israel), James Elder (Goulburn, Australia), Jakob Engström and Richard Björlin (Brussels, Belgium), Nicola Feakin (London, UK), Javier Gutièrree Flores (Heidelberg, Germany), Valerie Fraser and Tim Butler (Lima, Peru) many long and informative letters, Patrick Ganahl (Wolfhausen, Switzerland), Sue Gannon (Queensland, Australia), Helene Keur and Geert Klein Geltink (Zwolle, The Netherlands), Denis Golenvaux (St Servais-Namur, Belgium), Louis Chios (Lutherville) and Byron Graham (Arlington, USA), Matt Griffin (Seattle. USA), Sylvia Grisez (Warren, USA), Steve Grist (Santiago, Chile), Silvid Gudd & Johannes Kappeler (Frauenfeld, Switzerland), Dan Heilborn and Maya Schneider (Haifa and Tel-Aviv, Israel), Karin and Ueli Hermann (Reichenburg, Switzerland), Jeff Hibbard (Elizabeth City, USA), Philip Hollwey (Dublin, Eire), Peter Hunt (Basingstoke, UK), Ann Hyltoft (Langaa, Denmark), Marten H Jacobsen and Brit R Lauritsen (Denmark), Marie Javins (New York, USA), Erik

Jennische (Uppsala, Sweden), Hanne Stadsgaard Jensen (Aarhus, Denmark), Chris and Barbara Jensen-Knutson (Lima, Peru), Kendra Jones (Wellington, New Zealand), Helle Jørgensen (Abyhøj, Denmark), Sonja Jovanovic and Andrew Thompson (London, UK) a helpful letter Kryss Katsiavriades (London, UK), Hielke Keikke (Breda, Holland), Yvonne Kellenberger (Rorschach, Switzerland), Dr Jens-Uwe Klügel (Kleindöttingen, Switzerland), Heidi Lebahn and Volker Rux (Berlin, Germany), Carsten Leminsky (Hamburg, Germany), Derek Levitt, Riika Levoranta (Vammala) and Vesa Lampiner (Möjärvi, Finland), Valerie Levrier (London, UK), Jan-Elize Lindeboom & Frederik Krikke (Curaçao), Kristine Lindekrans and Kristoffer Frøkjoer-Jensen (Copenhagen, Denmark), Milagros Pedreros (Lima, Peru), Prof Jacob Lubliner (Berkeley, USA), Lara MacLean (Middleton, Canada), Sandra Maisel (temporarily in La Paz, Bolivia), Eric Mankin (Venice, USA), Nikolaus Gallardo Mannsfeld (Chile), Annette Mertens (Santiago, Chile), Elke Meinert (Essen, Germany), Michel Blanes and Kristine Meyer (Copenhagen, Denmark), Christina Michel-Wüest (Zug, Switzerland), Alison and David Moran (Oxford, UK), Claire Mortimer (Exeter, UK), Helmut Moser (Zell am See, Austria), Thomas Moser (Schaffhausen, Switzerland), Martijn Mugge (Enschede, The Netherlands), Mark Muhlbacher (Lucerne, Switzerland) for many letters Frank Müller (Hannover, Germany), Brian Mullin (Guayaquil, Ecuador), Trevor Murphy and Sylvia Carbone (St Albans, Australia), Don Nafziger (Kamloops, Canada), Annesofie Nielsen (Niva, Denmark), Henrik O. Nilsen (Oslo, Norway), Trond Nygard-Sture (Ulset, Norway), Carine Oesterle (Zurich, Switzerland), Paul Olai-Olssen (Oslo, Norway), Tina Ortmanns and Patrick Laschet (Aachen, Germany), Richard Osborne (New Zealand) and Nathalie Bélanger (Canada), Jonathan Paisner (London, UK), Christian Panigl (Vienna, Austria), Mette K Petersen and Britt H Lisbjerg (Copenhagen, Denmark), Sandrine Pocobelli & Alexandra Vernier (Martigny, Switzerland), Juliette Prendiville (Vancouver, Canada), Lawrence Railton and Susan Boyd (London, UK), Graciela Romero and Steve Norris (Bogotá, Colombia), Barbara and Peter Roniger (Suberg, Switzerland), Karen Troy-Davies (London, UK), Bruce Rumage (Pawleys Island, USA), Andy Ryder (Vienna, Austria), Dr Michael Saxby (Dorking, UK), Jim Scanlon (San Rafael, USA), Burkhard Schack and Michael Zickgraf (Seelbach, Germany), Fernand Daigle and Claudia Schaerer (Stratford, Canada), A Von Schuckmann (Venezuela), Inge and Machiel de Schutter (Cologne, Germany), Mandy Scott (Edinburgh, UK), Pauline Sheldrake (Copacobana, Bolivia), Yaniv Sneor (Parsippany, USA), Jacob B Steffensen, Mereti W Nielsen and Kristoffer Slattner (Vejle, Denmark), S Nielsen and Hellmuth-Chr Stuven (Copenhagen, Denmark), Ilay Tamari (Ramat-Hasharon, Israel), Mette and Lotte Thillerup (Hesselager, Denmark), Dr Heike C Thuro (Heidelburg) and Dr S Stürzebecher, Berlin, Germany), A.ndrios Tieleman and Ditty Bakker (Haarlem, The Netherlands), Haya Tofef (Israel), Arnaud Troost and Fenna den Hartog (Rotterdam, The Netherlands), Russell Trounce (Santiago, Chile), Alberto Cafferata (Caraz, Peru), Edith Olive (Peru), Lucie Turgeon and Paul Legros (Maniwaki, Canada), Samuel Urech (Niederhasli, Switzerland), Valerie A Valene (Manhattan Beach, USA), Dre Visscher (Tilburg, The Netherlands), Adrian Vogel (Lucerne, Switzerland), Peter Waanders (Arnhem, The Netherlands) helpful details, Rupert A E Walker (Salisbury, UK), Pamela Weekes (Chifley, Australia), Ushi Whelan (Cuzco), Pierre-André Widmer (Céligny, Switzerland), Ollo Wiemann (Trier, Germany), Michael Williams (San Diego,USA) and Michael Greengard (Buenos Aires, Argentina), Marc Williamson (Melbourne, Australia) an extensive contribution, Christian Leonards and Sandra Winterhalter (Insel Reichenau, Germany), Rowan Wood (Aspen, USA), Elke Wurtz (Frankfurt, Germany), and Emanuel Zanin (Switzerland).

URUGUAY

INTRODUCTION

URUGUAY is the smallest Hispanic country in South America; its official name is República Oriental del Uruguay. It has Brazil to the north, the Río Uruguay between it and Argentina to the west, and the wide estuary of the Río de la Plata to the south. The Atlantic Ocean washes its shores on the east.

Apart from a narrow plain which fringes most of the coast (but not near Montevideo), and an alluvial flood plain stretching N from Colonia to Fray Bentos, the general character of the land is undulating, with little forest except on the banks of its rivers and streams. The long grass slopes rise gently to far-off hills, but none of these is higher than 600m. Five rivers flow westwards across the country to drain into the Río Uruguay, including the Río Negro, which rises in Brazil and on which a number of dams have been built, creating a series of large, artificial lakes across the centre of the country.

Climate Temperate, if somewhat damp and windy, and summer heat is tempered by Atlantic breezes, but there are occasional large variations. In winter (June-September), when the average temperature is 10° to 16°C, the temperature can fall now and then to well below freezing. It is generally humid and hardly ever snows. Summer (December-March), with an average temperature of 21° to 27°C, has irregular dry periods. There is always some wind and for the most part the nights are relatively cool. There are normally 120 sunny days in the year. The rainfall, with prolonged wet periods in July and August, averages about 1,200 mm at Montevideo and some 250 more in the N, but the amount of rain varies markedly from year to year.

History The Spanish explorer, Juan Díaz de Solís, sailed up the Río de la Plata in 1516 and landed E of the site of Montevideo, near what is now Maldonado. His second landing was in the present Department of Colonia, where he was killed by the Charrúa Indians. There was no gold or silver in Uruguay, and it was only after about 1580 that the Spaniards showed any interest in it. Military expeditions against the Indians were unsuccessful, but Jesuit and Franciscan missionaries,

URUGUAY

117

ARGENTINA

Uruguaiana

Bella Unión

Quarai

Artigas

N

0   80
km

Termas
del Arapey

Santana do Livramento

Rio Arapey

Rivera

BRAZIL

10

Con-
cordia

Salto Grande

Salto

Termas de Daymán

Meseta de Artigas

Termas de Guaviyú

Rio
Quequay

Minas de
Corrales

Tacuarembó

Vichadero

Areguá

Bagé

To
Pelotas

Ansina

26

4

26

To
Pelotas &
Porto
Alegre

Colón

Paysandú

Guichón

San Gregorio
de Polanco

Rio Negro

Melo

Rio Branco

3

Laguna
Merín

Paso de los Toros

Rincón del
Bonete

Quebrada de
los Cuervos

Vergara

La Palmar

Cerro
Chato

Gral. Enrique
Martínez

To Rio
Grande

Fray Bentos

Mercedes

3

Durazno

Treinta y Tres

San
Miguel

Soriano

Dolores

La Agraciada

Trinidad

Sarandí del Yí

José R.Varela

Lascano

La Coronilla

Chuy

Nueva Palmira

Carmelo

Cardona

5

Santa
Teresa

5

21

Rosario

Colonia
Suiza

Florida

Velásquez

Castillos

2

Aguas
Dulces

Colonia

Colonia
Valdense

S. José

Minas

Aiguá

Rocha

Cabo
Polonia

Tigre

1

Libertad

Canelones

Soca

San
Carlos

La Paloma

Buenos
Aires

Kiyú

Pando

Rio de la Plata

Playa Pascual

MONTEVIDEO **1**

Solís
Atlántida

Piriápolis

Maldonado

Punta del Este

Atlantic Ocean

1. Montevideo   4. Montevideo North to Brazil
2. East from Montevideo   5. West from Montevideo
3. Montevideo North - East to Brazil 6. Up the River Uruguay

landing in 1624, founded a settlement on Vizcaíno Island. It is said that cattle were first introduced during an unsuccessful expedition by Hernando Arias in 1607; they were successfully established between 1611 and 1620.

By 1680, the Portuguese in Brazil had pushed S to the Plata and founded Colonia as a rival to Buenos Aires, on the opposite shore. It was the Portuguese who planned, but the Spaniards who actually founded, the city of Montevideo in 1726. It changed hands several times and was also taken by the British in 1807, but after their failure to hold Buenos Aires, they withdrew altogether. In 1808 Montevideo declared its independence from Buenos Aires. In 1811, the Brazilians attacked from the N, but the local patriot, José Gervasio Artigas, rose in arms against them. In the early stages he had some of the Argentine provinces for allies, but soon declared the independence of Uruguay from both Brazil and Argentina. Buenos Aires invaded again in 1812 and was able to enter Montevideo in June 1814. In January the following year the Orientales (Uruguayans) defeated the Argentines at Guayabos and regained Montevideo. The Portuguese then occupied all territory

S of the Río Negro except Montevideo and Colonia. The struggle continued from 1814 to 1820, but Artigas had to flee to Paraguay when Brazil took Montevideo in 1820. In 1825 General Juan Lavalleja, at the head of 33 patriots (the Treinta y Tres Orientales), crossed the river and returned to Uruguay, with Argentine aid, to harass the invaders. After the defeat of the Brazilians at Ituzaingó on 20 February 1827, Britain intervened, both Argentina and Brazil relinquished their claims on the country, and independence was finally achieved in 1828.

The early history of the republic was marked by a civil war (known as the Guerra Grande) which began as a conflict between two rival leaders, José Fructuoso Rivera with his Colorados and Manuel Oribe with his Blancos; these are still the two main parties today. Oribe was helped by the Argentine dictator, Juan Manuel de Rosas, but was overthrown in 1838. Blanco forces, backed by Rosas, besieged Montevideo between 1843 and 1851. Although Rosas fell from power in 1852, the contest between Colorados and Blancos continued. A Colorado, Gen Venancio Flores, helped by Argentina, became president, and, in 1865, Uruguay was dragged into the war of the Triple Alliance against the Paraguayan dictator, López. Flores was assassinated in 1868 three days after his term as President ended. The country, wracked by civil war, dictatorship and intrigue, only emerged from its long political turmoil in 1903, when another Colorado, a great but controversial man, José Batlle y Ordóñez was elected president.

During Batlle y Ordóñez' two terms as president, 1903-07 and 1911-15, Uruguay became within a short space of time the only "welfare state" in Latin America. Its workers' charter provides free medical service, old age and service pensions and unemployment pay. Divorce has been legal for many years; illegitimate children have status and the right to inherit, and the investigation of paternity is obligatory. Education is free and compulsory, capital punishment abolished, and the church disestablished.

However, as the country's former prosperity has ebbed away since the 1960s, the welfare state has become increasingly fictitious. In 1973 the military promised to reduce the massive bureaucracy and spend more on the poor and development. The stated aim was to get the country moving again after the social and political turmoil of 1968-1973, the period in which the Tupamaros urban guerrilla movement was most active. In practice the military, which effectively wiped out the Tupamaros by 1972, expanded state spending by raising military and security programmes. Real wages fell to less than half their 1968 level. Less than ten per cent of the unemployed received social security payments. Montevideo began to sprout a few small shanty towns, once unheard of in this relatively affluent corner of the hemisphere. One of the most egalitarian countries in Latin America has increasingly come to resemble the rest of the continent, as only the very wealthy benefited from the military regime's attempted neo-liberal economic policies. Nevertheless, the country's middle class remains very large, if impoverished, and the return to democracy in 1985 raised hopes that the deterioration in the social structure would be halted, if not reversed. Almost ten per cent of the population emigrated for economic or political reasons during the 1960s and 1970s: the unemployed continue to leave, but the political and artistic exiles have returned *en masse*.

Allying himself with the Armed Forces in 1973, the elected President, Juan M Bordaberry, dissolved Congress and stayed on to rule as the military's figurehead until 1976. Scheduled elections were cancelled in that year, and a further wave of political and trade union repression instituted. Unable to convince the population to vote for a new authoritarian constitution in 1980, the military became increasingly anxious to hand back power to conservative politicians. However, moderate politicians refused to accept the harsh conditions the military continued to try and impose. Finally, in August 1984 agreement was reached on the legalization of most of the banned leftist parties and elections were held in

November. The euphoria was spoiled by the fact that the strongest opponent of the regime was not allowed to stand. The moderate government of Julio María Sanguinetti (of the Colorado party) was inaugurated in March 1985 for a five year term of office. The process of national reconstruction and political reconciliation began with a widespread political amnesty (endorsed by referendum in April 1989), but no new radical economic policies. The moderate conservative Partido Nacional (Blancos) won November 1989 presidential and congressional elections and Luis Alberto Lacalle took office as president on 1 March 1990. There was considerable opposition to plans for wage restraint, spending cuts and social reforms. Even greater opposition was levelled at privatization plans; in a referendum in December 1992 the electorate rejected by 72% to 28% proposals to sell off 5 state companies. Owing to the unpopularity of Lacalle's market-oriented policies, his Blanco Party lost the November 1994 elections: Colorado ex-president Sanguinetti won 32.2% compared with 31.1% for the Blancos and 30.7% for the Frente Amplio, a broad left front. Each party won about a third of the seats in Congress. Soon after taking office in March 1995, President Sanguinetti managed to forge an alliance with the Blancos to introduce an austerity budget and steps towards implementing social security reforms which, although much needed, no previous administration had managed to draw up.

Settlement   There was little Spanish settlement in the early years and, for a long time, the area was inhabited mainly by groups of nomadic *gauchos* who trailed after the herds of cattle killing them for food and selling their hides only. Organized commerce began with the arrival of cattle buyers from Buenos Aires who found it profitable to hire herdsmen to look after cattle in defined areas around their headquarters. By about 1800 most of the land had been parcelled out into large *estancias*. The only commercial farming was around Montevideo, where small *chacras* grew vegetables, wheat and maize for the near-by town.

It was only after independence in 1828 that immigration began on any scale. Montevideo was then a small town of 20,000 inhabitants. Between 1836 and 1926 about 648,000 immigrants arrived in Uruguay, mostly from Italy and Spain, some into the towns, some to grow crops and vegetables round Montevideo. The native Uruguayans never took to agriculture: they remained pastoralists, leaving commercial farming to the immigrants. More recent immigrants, however, Jewish, Armenian, Lebanese and others have chosen to enter the retail trades, textiles and leather production rather than farming.

The Uruguayan People   Just under half of the population lives in Greater Montevideo. Only some 14% are rural, and the drift to the towns is 1.6% per year. Uruguayans are virtually all European, mostly of Spanish and Italian stock. A small percentage in parts of Montevideo and near the Brazilian border are of mixed African and European descent. Less than 10% are *mestizos*.

The Economy   Although accounting for only 11% of gdp, agriculture is the dominant sector of the economy, as a supplier and a consumer. With a black soil, rich in potash, producing grasses superior even to those in Argentina, over three-quarters of the land is given over to livestock rearing, the rest for crop production. The economy is no longer dependent on agriculture as the services sector, especially tourism, grows.

Uruguay used to be second only to Argentina as a meat and meat-product exporter, but in the early 1980s the beef-cattle sector suffered from low world prices and high interest rates, with the result that much of the herd was slaughtered. Slaughtering, domestic consumption and exports all declined in the 1983-85 period, but exports picked up in response to increased Brazilian demand in 1986. In the early 1990s the size of the herd was rising, to 10.1mn heads in 1993. The number of sheep rose in the 1980s and 1990s, despite increased demand for exports of live and slaughtered animals. This reflects the lower prices for meat than for wool, of which Uruguay accounts for about 3% of total world production. Livestock and its manufactures are the second largest export item after textiles; the only cereal exported is rice. Others grown are maize, sorghum and wheat. Also important are vegetable products, oilseeds (sunflower and linseed) and citrus fruits, of which oranges and tangerines are the main crops.

Manufacturing, which contributes 22% to gdp, is concerned largely with agroindustrial activities. The most important of these are meat packing, drinks, tobacco, textiles, clothing and footwear. There are also some medium-technology industries such as oil refining, plastics, rubber products, electrical appliances and motor vehicle assembly. Import substitution behind tariff barriers encouraged growth until the 1960s, to be followed by stagnation until more export-oriented policies were introduced in the late 1970s. Various factors contributed to mixed results in the 1980s and early 1990s, not the least of which were economic problems in Argentina and Brazil. The threat of recession in Argentina after the Dec 1994 Mexican financial crisis was of major concern, forcing the Sanguinetti government to introduce measures which would turn manufacturers away from the domestic to export markets. Construction accounts for 4.5% of gdp. The financial sector's fortunes also fluctuate according to the economic health of Argentina and Brazil. Uruguay has been called the Switzerland of Latin America, and is the repository of much of the region's flight capital.

Uruguay has no major mining industry, apart from the extraction of marble and various construction materials. It also has no known reserves of oil or natural gas. Its coal deposits are of poor quality and are not suitable for commercial mining. 89% of electricity generation comes from hydroelectric plants, of which there are four. The combined installed capacity of their 14 turbines is 1,890 MW.

Like many Latin American debtors, Uruguay became unable to service its debts normally in the 1980s and had to reschedule its loans to commercial bank and government creditors in the context of an IMF stabilization programme. IMF targets were successfully met and when the agreement expired in 1987, it was replaced by enhanced surveillance. By the late 1980s Uruguay's external position had strengthened and net new

Uruguay : fact file

Geographic
Land area	176,215 sq km
forested	3.8%
pastures	77.3%
cultivated	7.5%

Demographic
Population (1994)	3,168,000
annual growth rate (1989-94)	0.6%
urban	89.3%
rural	10.7%
density	18.0 per sq km
Religious affiliation	
Christian	66.0%
Birth rate per 1,000 (1991)	17.6
	(world av 26.0)

Education and Health
Life expectancy at birth,	
male	69.3 years
female	75.7 years
Infant mortality rate	
per 1,000 live births (1992)	18.7
Physicians (1992)	1 per 295 persons
Hospital beds (1987)	1 per 215 persons
Calorie intake as %	
of FAO requirement	100%
Population age 25 and over	
with no formal schooling	7.5%
Literate males (over 15)	94.5%
Literate females (over 15)	95.4%

Economic
GNP (1992 market prices)	
	US$10,444mn
GNP per capita	US$3,340
Public external debt (1992)	
	US$3,092mn
Tourism receipts (1992)	US$381mn
Inflation (annual av 1988-93)	62.0%
Radio	1 per 1.7 persons
Television	1 per 4.5 persons
Telephone	1 per 4.7 persons

Employment
Population economically active (1991)	
	1,239,400
Unemployment rate (1988)	2.5%
% of labour force in	
agriculture	14.5
mining	0.1
manufacturing	18.3
construction	5.4
Military forces	24,700

Source *Encyclopaedia Britannica*

borrowing from multilateral and commercial creditors took place on a voluntary basis. Nevertheless, gdp growth slowed, the fiscal deficit grew, and inflation soared to three figures and heavy debt servicing absorbed over half of all exports of goods and services. In 1990 the Government secured a debt reduction agreement covering the US$1.6 bn medium and long term debt owed to commercial banks, supported by another IMF programme and structural adjustment loans from other multilateral and bilateral lenders. By 1992 the government had successfully restored gdp growth and maintained it over the next 2 years, cut inflation to 45% by 1994 and reduced the fiscal deficit to about 1% of gdp from 7.4% in 1989. The ever-increasing burden on state finances from the social security system was becoming acute by 1995. The state pension scheme was almost bankrupt and President Sanguinetti wished to reform the system. The budget deficit was expected to widen to 4.5% of gdp, while gdp growth was forecast to fall from 5.1% (1994) to less than 1%. At the same time the trade deficit at end-1994 stood at US$860mn. Sanguinetti's first budget aimed to raise taxes, cut spending, reduce consumer demand and encourage exports through tax incentives. His success in carrying through these measures depended on whether he could continue to rely on opposition support since his party did not have a working majority in Congress.

Government Uruguay is a republic with a bicameral legislature: a Senate with 31 seats and a Chamber of Representatives with 99 seats. The president, who is head of state and of the government, holds office for 5 years. The country is divided into 19 provinces.

Music Uruguay is a small country, whose native tribes were totally eliminated over 150 years ago. Most musical influences came with the European immigrants who arrived after the disappearance of the Amerindian population. The folk songs and dances are very closely related to those of the Argentine pampas, except in the N, where they are shared with the neighbouring Brazilian state of Rio Grande do Sul. The major song genres are the Estilo, Cifra, Milonga and Vidalita, whilst the "national" dance is the stately Pericón for six or more couples. The Milonga is also danced, as are the Tango, Cielito, Media Caña and Ranchera. The guitar is the instrument that accompanies most country music and as in Argentina, the gauchos like to engage in Payadas de Contrapunto, where two singers vie with each other, alternating improvised verses. Nineteenth-century Europe introduced other popular dances into Uruguay, such as the polca, waltz, chotis and mazurca, all of which were given a local touch.

In the northern departments a number of dances are shared with Brazil, such as the Chimarrita, Carangueijo and Tirana, which are also sung, either in Spanish or Portuguese or a mixture of both.

There were many black slaves in the Río de la Plata during colonial times and the African ritual of the Candombe was practised in Montevideo until late in the 19th century. Less than 3% of the population is black and the only musical remains of African origin are to be found in the presence during carnival of the Morenada groups of up to 50 Candomberos, who take part in the procession, playing their *tamboril* drums, while smaller groups take part in these so-called "Llamadas" from December through to Holy Week. There are four sizes of drums—*chico, repique, piano* and *bajo*—and the complex polyrhythms produced by the mass of drummers advancing down the street is both unexpected and impressive in otherwise somewhat staid Montevideo. (See also under Montevideo for more details on music. A useful booklet is *El Candombe* by Tomás Olivera Chirimini and Juan Antonio Varese, Ediciones El Galeón, 1992.)

MONTEVIDEO (1)

Montevideo, the capital and the only large city in the country, was founded in 1726 as a Spanish fortress against the Portuguese who had settled in Colonia del Sacramento. Population, in and near: 3,198,910 (1994). The original site on a promontory between the Río de la Plata and an inner bay, though the fortifications have been destroyed, still retains a certain colonial atmosphere. In addition to colonial Spanish and Italian, some French and Art Deco styles can be seen. The city not only dominates the country's commerce and culture: it accounts for 70% of industrial production and handles almost 90% of imports and exports. It is also a summer resort and the point of departure for a string of seaside resorts along the coastline to the E. The city as a whole runs at a relaxing pace.

In the Ciudad Vieja (the old town – in poor shape) is the oldest square in Montevideo: the Plaza Constitución, also known as the Plaza Matriz. Here on one side is the Cathedral (1790-1804), with the historic Cabildo (1808) opposite. Still further W along Calle Rincón is the small Plaza Zabala, with a monument to Zabala, founder of the city. N of this Plaza are four buildings well worth seeing: the Banco de la República (Cerrito y Zabala), the Aduana (Rambla 25 de Agosto), and the houses of Generals Rivera (Rincón 437) and Lavalleja (Zabala 1469). Together, the latter two buildings form part of the Museo Histórico Nacional (see **Museums** below).

Set between the Ciudad Vieja and the new city is the grandest of Montevideo's squares, Plaza Independencia, a short distance E of Plaza Constitución, with the impressive black marble mausoleum of Artigas in the middle. On three sides it is surrounded by colonnades, and there are three pavement cafés at the eastern end. Also at the eastern end is the Palacio Salvo, a major landmark, but in a poor state of repair. The western end has been spoiled by rebuilding, as has the southern side around the Casa de Gobierno Histórico (Palacio Estévez). Work has resumed on the unfinished modern block to the W of the Casa de Gobierno, due for completion as the Palacio de Justicia in late 1995. The Casa de Gobierno itself is now used for ceremonial purposes only as the executive offices have been moved to the Edificio Libertad, far from the centre. Just off the plaza to the W is the splendid Solís Theatre, in a wing of which is the Museo de Historia Natural, Buenos Aires 652, open Mon-Fri 1400-1800 (library 1230-1730).

The Avenida 18 de Julio, whose pavements are always thronged, runs E from Plaza Independencia. Along this avenue, between Julio Herrera and Río Negro, is the Plaza Fabini, or del Entrevero (with a statue of a group of *gauchos* engaged in battle, the last big piece of work by sculptor José Belloni), a very pleasant place to sit; and the Plaza Cagancha (or Plaza Libertad), with a statue of Liberty. The Palacio Municipal (La Intendencia) is on the S side of Av 18 de Julio, just before it bends N, at the statue of *El Gaucho*. The best view of the city is from the top of the Palacio Municipal; external glass elevators take you up to a *mirador* (glass-fronted terrace) on the 23rd floor, where there is an expensive restaurant, La Panorámica (24th floor). Entrance at the back of the building on Soriano, between Ejido and Santiago de Chile; open 1215-2230, US$0.45. In front of the Palacio Municipal is a plaza with a copy of Michelangelo's David in one corner. Inside the Palacio Municipal, entered around the corner in Ejido, is the Museo de Historia de Arte (see below). The road which forks S from the *Gaucho* is Constituyente, and leads to the fashionable beach at Pocitos.

Further E along Av 18 de Julio is the University, and nearby are the Biblioteca Nacional, the French *lycée*, and the Ministry of Health. The avenue ends at an intersection with Bulevar General Artigas. Here is an obelisk commemorating the makers of the 1830 Constitution, by José Luis Zorrilla de San Martín (born 1891). In Parque Batlle y Ordóñez (reached by a continuation eastwards of Av 18 de Julio),

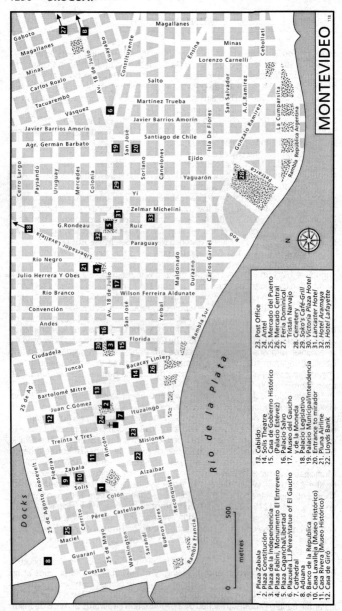

MONTEVIDEO

1. Plaza Zabala
2. Plaza Constitución
3. Plaza de la Independencia
4. Plaza Fabini, Monumento El Entrevero
5. Plaza Cagancha/Libertad
6. Plazuela J.Pérez/statue of El Gaucho
7. Cathedral
8. Aduana
9. Banco de la República
10. Casa Lavalleja (Museo Histórico)
11. Casa Rivera (Museo Histórico)
12. Casa de Girò

13. Cabildo
14. Solis Theatre
15. Casa de Gobierno Histórico (Palacio Estévez)
16. Palacio Taranco
17. Mercado del Gaucho y de la Moneda
18. Palacio Legislativo
19. Palacio Municipal/Intendencia
20. Entrance to mirador
21. Pluna Airline
22. Lloyds Bank

23. Post Office
24. Antel
25. Mercado del Puerto
26. Mercado Central Tristán Narvajo
28. Cemetery
29. Soko's Café-Grill
30. Victoria Plaza Hotel
31. Lancaster Hotel
32. Hotel Aramaya
33. Hotel Lafayette

are several statues: the most interesting group is the very well-known "La Carreta" monument, by José Belloni, showing three yoke of oxen drawing a wagon. In the grounds is the Estadio Centenario, the national football stadium with a seating capacity of 70,000 and a football museum, a field for athletics and a bicycle race-track (bus 107). The Jardín Zoológico and adjacent Planetarium are SE of this park at Av Gral Rivera 3254 (buses 141, 142 or 144 from San José). The zoo is open Wed-Sun 0900-1900, entry US$0.15; the planetarium (free) gives good, 40-minute shows on Thur at 1730, Sat and Sun at 1630 and 1730. There is also a drive-in zoo in the Parque Lecoq, a few km out of town on road to Colonia del Sacramento (entrance US$0.10 per car, closed Mon and Tues).

The immense Palacio Legislativo was built between 1908 and 1925 from local marble: there are 55 colours of Uruguayan marble in the Salón de los Pasos Perdidos, 12 types of wood in the Library (tours Mon-Fri 0930-1200). The Palacio is reached from Plaza Fabini along Av del Libertador Brig Gen Juan Lavalleja (normally known as Av Libertador), 5 blocks E of Plaza Independencia (buses 150, 173, 175 from Calle Mercedes).

From the Palacio Legislativo, Av Agraciada runs NW to Parque Prado, the oldest of the city's many parks, situated about 5 km from Av 18 de Julio (bus 125 and others). Among fine lawns, trees and lakes is a rose garden planted with 850 varieties, the monument of La Diligencia (the stage coach), the Círculo de Tenís and the Sociedad Rural premises. Part of the park is the adjacent Jardín Botánico (in fine condition, visits with a guide Mon-Fri, without a guide Sat-Sun, T 394420). It is reached via Av 19 de Abril (bus 582 from Yaguarón), or via Av Dr LA de Herrera (bus 147 from Paysandú). The largest and most popular park is Parque Rodó, on Rambla Presidente Wilson. Here are an open-air theatre, an amusement park, and a boating lake studded with islands. The Museo Nacional de Artes Visuales (see **Museums**) is at the eastern end.

At the western end of the bay is the Cerro, or hill, 139m high (from which Montevideo gets its name), with an old fort on the top, now the Museo Militar (see **Museums**). The Cerro is surmounted by the oldest lighthouse in the country (1804). Bus from centre to Cerro: 125 "Cerro" from Mercedes, and others, or boat Sat and Sun 1500-1900, US$5, T 618601/2. In the port (which one can visit on Sat from 1300 till sunset and on Sun from 0800 till sunset), opposite the Port Administration Building, the ship's bell of HMS *Ajax* has been set up to commemorate the scuttling of the *Graf Spee*. The anchor of the *Graf Spee* was erected inside the port area in 1964 to commemorate the 25th anniversary of the battle; the wreck itself lies about 3 km offshore, but is no longer visible as it was dismantled some years ago. However, plates from its bulkheads have been used in the construction of the city stadium.

Museums **Museo Nacional de Antropología**, Av de las Instrucciones 948, open Tues-Fri 1300-1900, Sun 1400-1800, ex-Quinta de Mendilaharsu, a modest but well-presented anthropological collection in the hall of a superb, late 19th century mansion (see, among other things, the Music Room with its huge, Chinese silk tapestry), bus 149 from Ejido. **Museo Zoológico**, Rambla República de Chile 4215, Buceo, Tues-Sun 1500-1900, free, well-displayed and arranged, rec, great for children too (bus 104 from 18 de Julio); **Cabildo** (History), Gómez y Sarandí; **Museo Casa Lavalleja**, Zabala 1469, Ciudad Vieja, Tues-Fri 1300-1900, free, historical mementos, furniture, etc, vast panoramic painting of the Battle of Sarandí by Juan Manuel Blanes; **Museo Casa Rivera**, Rincón 737, Tues-Fri 1600-2000. **Casa de Giró**, Cerrito 584-6, eleven rooms exhibiting the work of Uruguayan writers, historians, painters, etc, also has a library, open Tues-Fri 1300-1900, Sun and holidays 1400-1800. On 25 de Mayo are the **Casa del Gral José Garibaldi** (at No 314), Uruguayan history from 1843-48, and **Casa de Montero, Museo Romántico**, No 428, with late 19th, early 20th century exhibits (both open as Casa de Giró, but Garibaldi 1 hr earlier on weekdays). The **Panteón Nacional**, Av Gonzalo Ramírez y Yaguarón, houses the burial monuments of local families, many with sculptured façades and inscriptions.

Museo Municipal de Bellas Artes Juan Manuel Blanes, Millán 4015 y Cno Castro, Tues-Sun 1400-1800, free, ex-Quinta Raffo (late 19th century mansion) dedicated to the work of the artist Blanes (1830-1901), plus a room of the works of Pedro Figari (1861-1938), a lawyer

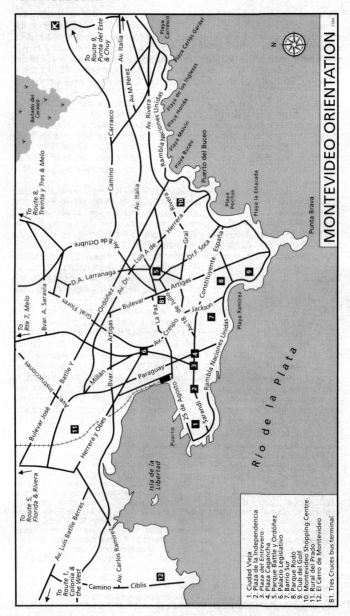

MONTEVIDEO ORIENTATION

1. Ciudad Vieja
2. Plaza de la Independencia
3. Plaza del Entrevero
4. Plaza Cagancha
5. Parque Battle y Ordóñez
6. Palacio Legislativo
7. Barrio Sur
8. Parque Rodó
9. Club del Golf
10. Montevideo Shopping Centre
11. Rural del Prado
12. El Cerro de Montevideo

B1. Tres Cruces bus terminal

who painted strange, naive pictures of peasant life and negro ceremonies, also work by other Uruguayan artists; has a room with paintings by Courbet, Vlaminck, Utrillo, Dufy, etchings by Orozco and engravings with Goya; temporary exhibitions, admission free (buses 146, 148, 149, 150 from Mercedes). **Museo Nacional de Artes Visuales**, Herrera y Reissig y Tomás Garibaldi, Tues-Sun 1500-1900, free, fine collection of contemporary plastic arts, plus a room devoted to Blanes, rec. **Museo de Historia de Arte**, at Palacio Municipal (Ejido), open Mon-Fri 1600-2000; **Centro de Exposiciones**, Palacio Municipal (Soriano entrance), Mon-Sat 1600-2000, temporary exhibitions of contemporary art. **Salón Municipal de Exposiciones**, Plaza del Entrevero (underground), open daily 1700-2100, free, temporary exhibitions of contemporary art, photography, etc. **Museo Joaquín Torres García**, Sarandí y Bacacay, Tues-Fri 1400-1900, Sat 1000-1400.

Museo del Gaucho y de la Moneda, Av 18 de Julio 998, Edificio Banco de la República, open Tues-Fri 0930-1230, 1530-1900, Sat 1530-1900, free: Museo de la Moneda has a survey of Uruguayan currency and a collection of Roman coins; Museo del Gaucho is a fascinating history of the Uruguayan gaucho, highly rec, but closed Sun; also temporary exhibitions. **Museo Militar**, at Fortaleza General Artigas, at the Cerro, Wed-Sun 1300-1800, free, historical mementos, documentation of War of Independence (bus 125 from Mercedes goes near). **Museo Naval**, Rambla Costanera, near Marina del Buceo, 0800-1200, 1400-1800, closed Thur, free, small display of naval history from War of Independence onwards, documentation on Battle of the River Plate and sinking of the *Graf Spee*, and on the sailing ship *Capitán Miranda*, which circumnavigated the globe in 1937-8 and is now in the Puerto (can be visited Sat and Sun), bus 104 from 18 de Julio. **Museo Aeronáutico**, Plaza de la Aviación, open Sat, Sun and holidays, 1600-2000, US$0.15 (bus 71, 79 from Mercedes), collection of vintage planes.

The Beaches   Nine sandy bathing beaches stretch along almost the whole of the metropolitan water front, from Playa Ramírez in the W to Playa Carrasco at the eastern extension of the city. Along the whole waterfront runs the Rambla Naciones Unidas, named along its several stretches in honour of various nations. Bus 104 from Aduana, which goes along Av 18 de Julio, gives a pleasant ride (further inland in winter) past Pocitos, Punta Gorda and all the beaches to Playa Miramar, beyond **Carrasco**. The express bus DI runs every $\frac{1}{2}$ hour stopping at seven special yellow bus stops on Av 18 de Julio; by using this service, which costs slightly more (US$1) about 30 mins are saved on the journey time to Carrasco. Only two town beaches are closed to swimmers, Miramar and Ramírez, because of pollution. A new sewage system is due for completion in 1995 and will solve this problem.

Among the main seaside residential areas are Pocitos, well supplied with hotels, restaurants and night-clubs (*boites*), variously compared to Copacabana, Brighton, or Wembley Stadium after a Cup Final for the amount of plastic debris (more cleaning services introduced in 1995); and Carrasco, a delightful semi-rural place behind the beach of the same name at the end of the Rambla Sur, backed by a thick forest which has partly been turned into a national park. The international airport is nearby. East along the coast is a string of resorts, with less polluted beaches, which are dealt with in **East from Montevideo**.

Festivals   Easter week is also Tourist Week (Fiesta Gaucha), with rodeo-type competitions held in the Parque Prado (US$1.50 entry—bus 185 from Pocitos, or 522 from Yaguarón) horse-breaking and handicrafts, music (mostly folk). Large barbecues are held in the open air. Also in the Parque Prado is the Exposición Rural, an agricultural show held every August; horse-riding competitions among other events. Christmas Eve and New Year's Eve are celebrated with drummers and firecrackers in the streets. During carnival week and a few days after there are many live shows; especially recommended is the traditional *candombe* singing and dancing in the Barrio Sur. There is an annual Candombe Festival in the first week of May, and an annual Tango Festival in October and the first half of November (information from Joventango, Soriano 956, T 915561, a non-profit organization which offers tango lessons and other events, open weekdays 1800-2000).

Note   Some streets have changed name in recent years but this fact may not be marked on all maps: Michelini was Cuareim; Hector Gutiérrez Ruiz was Ibicuy; Convención was Latorre.

Hotels   During the tourist season, 15 Dec-15 March hotels should be booked in advance. At the beaches many hotels offer full board only during the season. After 1 April prices are greatly reduced and some hotel dining rooms shut down. For Carnival week, on the other hand, prices are raised by 20%. The city is visited by many Argentines at weekends: many hotels increase prices; ask in advance. In general it is best to pay daily to avoid price hikes.

The tourist office on Plaza Fabini has information only on more expensive hotels. For more information and reservations contact Asociación de Hoteles y Restaurantes del Uruguay, Gutiérrez Ruiz 1213, T 900346, F 980141. **Hint**: cheap hotel rooms in Uruguay are invariably gloomy. Bring your own 220V Edison-screw bulbs and hope they don't put too much strain on the wiring. When not included, breakfast (*café completo*) usually costs US$2 in 1/2-star hotels, US$3 in more expensive places. Hotels add a 12% charge to bills, on top of which there is 22% value-added tax.

L3 *Hostería del Lago*, Arizona 9637, T 612210, F 612880, excellent.

In the vicinity of Plaza Cagancha, and W towards Plaza Independencia are: **A2** *Internacional*, Colonia 823, T 920001, rec for business visits, has fax and telex, due to reopen as *Holiday Inn* Feb 1996; **L3** *Victoria Plaza*, Plaza Independencia, T 914201, a/c, excellent restaurant (rooftop, fine views), some dishes good value, friendly staff, faded old world charm (some cheaper rooms, see below under **C** category; new 5-star wing due for completion end-1994); **L3** *Lafayette*, Soriano 1170, T 922351, F 921301, breakfast inc, new, suites are good, spacious, but rooms are small, not suitable for business visitors, restaurant good, free parking; **A2-A3** *Columbia Palace*, Reconquista 470, T 960001, F 960192, first class accommodation with bath, breakfast, international direct dial telephone in every room, minibar, TV, restaurant, sauna, good mixed music show (see below under **Tanguerías**); **A2** *Alvear*, Yí 1372, T 920244, good service, friendly, rec for business travellers; **A2** *Gran Hotel América*, Río Negro 1330, T 920392, modern, a/c, central; **A3** *London Palace*, Río Negro 1278, T 920024, F 921633, with breakfast (15% discount for Argentine ACA members), central, garage, parking; **B** *King's*, Andes 1491, N of Plaza Independencia, T 920927, with breakfast, rec; **A3** *Lancaster*, Plaza Cagancha 1334, a/c, incl breakfast, bath and fridge/bar; **A1** *Oxford*, Paraguay 1286, T 920046, clean, good breakfast.

A3 *Balfer*, Z Michelini 1328, T 920135, good, safe deposit, excellent breakfast; **B** *Mediterráneo*, Paraguay 1486, T 905090, clean, comfortable; **B** *Montevideo*, Yaguarón 1309, T 904634, no breakfast, clean, rec, small garage; **B** *Aramaya*, Av 18 de Julio 1103, T 986192, with bathroom, old, clean, comfortable; **B** *Río de la Plata*, Av 18 de Julio 937, T 985174, clean, hot water. Several hotels in **D** range on Calle Uruguay.

Many on Soriano: **C** *Royal*, No 1120, T 983115, dark rooms, hot showers, clean, friendly, rec; **D** *Hospedaje del Centro*, T 901419, with bath, cooking facilities, clean, friendly, rec; **D** *Nueva Pensión Ideal*, 1073, excellent washing facilities, friendly, no breakfast; **E** *Pensión del Este*, 1137, dark, run down, basic, friendly.

C *Arapey*, Uruguay 925, T 907032, with bath, good value; **C** *Victoria Plaza*, Plaza Independencia 759, new annex of more expensive hotel (see above), nice rooms but sagging beds, helpful staff; **C** *Casablanca*, San José 1039, T 910918, friendly, with bath, recently renovated, good value; **D** *Cifre* (10% discount on stays of over 2 weeks) Mercedes 1166, clean, E with shared showers/toilets, use of kitchen; **D** *Claridge*, Mercedes 942, clean, friendly, with bath, quality of rooms varies, rec; **D** *Libertad*, Gutiérrez Ruiz 1223, clean, quiet, laundry facilities and food available; **D** *Litoral*, Mercedes 887, T 905812, good value; **D** *Pensión Trinidad*, San José 1220, dark and not too clean, though friendly; **C** *Itá*, San José 1160, clean and quiet; **E** *Solanas*, Yí 1423, T 981070, good but check rates carefully; **E** *Torremolinos*, San José 774, T 900305, clean, friendly.

Several along Colonia: **D** *Ateneo*, No 1147, with bath, clean, friendly; **D** *Hospedaje Diagonal 2*, Convención 1326 entre Av 18 de Julio y San José, clean, friendly (not to be confused with *Diagonal 1*, Colonia 1168, which is red light); **D** *Hospedaje Ideal*, 914, clean, friendly, hot water, higher rates on Sat; **D/E** *Windsor*, Michelini 1260, T 915080, simple, good location, helpful staff, hot water, clean, pleasant, with bath, not very secure but rec; **E** *El Aguila*, Colonia y Yí, clean, basic.

Plenty of hotels in and near the Ciudad Vieja, eg **L1-L2** *Plaza Fuerte*, Bartolomé Mitre 1361, esq Sarandí, T 959563, F 959569, each room with different design, a/c, bath, many other facilities, restaurant, bar, all in a historic building; **C** *Palacio*, Bartolomé Mitre 1364, T 963612, friendly, clean, safe, hot showers, balconies, TV, highly rec; and *Matriz*, Ituzaingó 1327, clean and friendly, though run down; **E** *City*, Buenos Aires 462 (opp Correos), good value; **E** *Lavalle*, Bartolomé Mitre 1314, T 962887, clean, basic; **E** *Nuevo Savoy*, B Mitre 1371, T 957233, without bath; *Hospedaje Pensión Roy*, Sarandí 437, clean, good value budget hotel, access to kitchen, laundry facilities.

East of Plaza Cagancha: **A3** *Cottage*, Miraflores 1360, T 600867, friendly, no restaurant; **A2** *Oceania*, Mar Ártico 1227, Punta Gorda, T 600444, pleasant view, good restaurant and night club, highly rec; **B** *Casino Carrasco*, Rambla República de México, with breakfast, good, "ancient splendour, reasonable service"; **B** *Ermitage*, Juan B Blanco 779-83, Playa Pocitos, business services; **A2** *Klee*, Yaguarón 1306, T 920606, F 987365, restaurant, business services; At Carrasco: **D** *Riviera*, Rambla México 6095, built in 1926 in Louis XV style, must be seen, pleasant, good service; **E** *Maracana*, Rambla Rep de Chile 4667, Malvín Beach, T 630418, with bath single, clean, good value, rec, take bus 60 from Plaza Cagancha (if coming from Brazil, buses stop outside the hotel).

Youth Hostel The headquarters of the Association are at Pablo de María 1583, apartment 008, T 404245/400581, open 1130-1900 Mon-Fri. Hostel (members only) is at Canelones 935, T 981324, open all year. US$8 pp (with seasonal variations, breakfast included, sheets US$1 extra), doors locked at 2400, friendly, clean, dormitory style, cooking facilities, plenty of hot water, shortage of bathrooms, closed Sat and Sun 1000-1700.

Camping Information on camping from Camping Club del Uruguay, Agraciada 3096. Parque Roosevelt, near Carrasco, US$5 pp, free, hot showers, safe, no electricity, 15 km from centre, open all year. For vans and caravans only at Punta Ramírez on Rambla República Argentina, free for stays under 48 hrs, central, basic facilities, 24 hr security.

Restaurants There is a 22% value added tax on restaurant bills, plus 12% service. Dinner in "top class" establishments is taken between 2000-0100. Less formal restaurants serve from 1930 onwards. A meal costs from US$8 pp up to US$40 with wine. First-class restaurants at the centre are *Morini*, Ciudadela 1229, serves excellent steaks, simple but not cheap, very popular for functions. *Panorámico*, 24th floor of Intendencia, good service and view, US$25 pp. Don't miss eating at the *Mercado del Puerto*, opposite the Aduana, on Calle Piedras, between Maciel and Pérez Castellano (take "Aduana" bus), closed Sun, delicious grills cooked on huge charcoal grates (menus are limited to meat); colourful atmosphere and friendly, but not cheap; *El Talero*, *El Rincón del Pescado*, *La Proa* and *Cabana Verónica* have been particularly rec; several are open at night, eg *El Palenque* (Pérez Castellano 1579, excellent), *La Posada del Puerto* (seafood), *La Tasca del Puerto* (plus dance show) and *La Marina Café-Bar*; nearby ones on Calle Pérez Castellano stay open later, eg *El Patriota*. Other good grill rooms (*parrilladas*) include *Los Montañeses*, Soriano 752; *Forte di Makale*, Requena García y Wilson; *Del Ferrocarril*, Río Negro 1748, in railway station (interesting building), excellent, expensive; *Otto*, Río Negro 1301, good, rec; *El Fogón*, San José 1080, nr *Hotel London Palace*, good food, always crowded; *Anticuario*, Maldonado 1602, expensive parrillada, atmospheric. *Le Jardin de France*, Gutiérrez Ruiz 1285, French.

In the central Plaza Cagancha district: *La Genovesa* (Spanish), San José 1242, excellent, *marisquería* and *parrillada*; *Las Brasas*, San José 909, good typical food, US$20-25; *Viejo Sancho*, San José 1229, excellent, US$25-30, popular, complimentary sherry or vermouth to early arrivals, tearoom by day; *Gran César*, Gutiérrez Ruiz 1285, similar, rec; *Danubio Azul*, Colonia 835, very good value, US$15-20; *La Bodega Española*, 121 Colonia, good value. A reasonable place for lunch is restaurant on 6th floor of YMCA building, Colonia 1870, good views, ask for the Asociación Cristiana de Jóvenes; cheap lunches also at *Comedor Universitario*, Michelini 1175 y Canelones, and at Yaguarón 1234.

Vegetarian: *Vegetariana*, Yí 1334, esq Av 18 de Julio, also San José 1056 and Av Brasil 3086, Pocitos, excellent, self-service buffet; *Cocina Vegetariana*, Rivera 208, good value; *Sabor Integral*, F Crespo 1531, or *Vida Natural*, San José 1184. *Natura*, Rincón 414 and Scosería 2754 (Pocitos).

A good place for lunch is the *Golf Club*, Artigas 379, good food, international cuisine, smart, expensive, excellent surroundings and grand view.

Many good restaurants on seafront in Pocitos (names and ownership change frequently): *Arde París*, García de Zuñiga 2384, Mon-Sat night only; *Spaghetería 23*, Scosería 2584, Tues-Sun, very good Italian; *Pizza Luna*, Scosería 2754, pizza and pasta; *Doña Flor*, Artigas 1034, classy French restaurant, limited menu but superb, moves to Punta del Este in summer; *Entrevero*, 21 de Setiembre 2774, popular with Americans; *Lo de Joaquín*, Williman 637 y 21 de Septiembre, parrillada. *Bungalow Suizo*, Solar 150, very good. In Carasco, *Aranjuez*, Schroeder 6415, very good; *Las Tablitas*, P Murillo 6666, parrillada. Between Pocitos and Punta Carretas is *El Castillo*, Rambla Mahatma Gandhi 411, T 700386, fairly expensive but excellent Italian food, beautiful interior.

Confiterías A *confitería* is an informal eating/drinking place which serves meals at any time, as opposed to a *restaurante*, which serves meals at set times. A *confitería* may describe itself as a *cafetería, bar, repostería, cerveceria, cocteleria, sandwichería, grill, pizzería, salón de té* or *whiskeria*. Many serve *preparación*, a collection of hors d'oeuvres. The following have been recommended: on Av 18 de Julio, *La Pasiva*, No 1763 (esq Ejido), also at Sarandí 600 (Ciudad Vieja) and other branches, fast and good quality food; *Los Chivitos*, No 949 (esq Río Branco); *Puerta del Sol*, No 850; *The Manchester*, No 899; *Lusitano*, esq Paraguay; *Bar del Rex*, No 1006; *Lion d'Or*, No 1981; *Soko's*, 18 de Julio 1250, popular, good if expensive food, good coffee, open till 0100, 0400 on Sat. *Los Estudiantes*, Colonia y Michelini, good omelettes; *Oro del Rhin*, Convención 1403, open 0830-2100, good cakes, *Beer Garden*, San José, good *empanadas*; *Don Gino Café and Bar*, 2509 Larravide and 8 de Octobre, good value, big portions; *Alvear*, Sarandí 550 and Río Branco 1325; *Nuevo Metro*, San José 1200, friendly, good and cheap; *Café Sorocabana*, Yí 1377, good coffee and ice cream, another branch at 25 de Mayo 485, Ciudad Vieja. *Universal Bar*, Piedras y Gómez, last of the real dock bars, worth a visit. *Cake's*, 21 de Septiembre (Villa Biarritz) at Punta Carretas, Marco Bruto 1004 and Dr A Schroeder 6536, Carrasco, expensive, rec; *Café de la Paix*, Rambla República del Perú y Bulevar España, Pocitos, pleasant, on seafront; *La Vitamínica*, J Benito Blanco y B España, excellent *chivitos*; *Periplo*, José Martí 3407, Mon-Sat 0900-0300; *Canaprole*, Rambla M Gandhi y S Antuña; *Virgilio's Café*, Rambla México, next to *Hotel Oceania*, Punta Gorda, open from 1700, nice location, light meals, no alcohol. *Bar Añon*, Soriano and Ejido, good value and local food.

Heladerías Ice-cream parlours produce very good, unusual ice creams in the summer, and draw large crowds. Try *La Cigale*, R Graseras 845 (Pocitos), Ejido 1368 and several other locations; *Las Delicias*, Schroeder 6454, Carrasco; *Batuk*, 26 de Marzo y Pérez, Pocitos, and at 18 de Julio y Yí, both open daily 1000-0200; *Papitos*, 18 de Julio 1060, excellent but pricey.

Airlines Pluna, Colonia 1321, T 921414; Aviasur, T 908768, at airport, T 614618; Aero Regionales, Yí 1435, T 925632, Airport, T 614852 int 1254; Lapa, Plaza Cagancha 1339, T 908765; Aerolíneas Argentinas, Colonia 851, T 919466; Varig, Río Negro 1362, T 924676; American, Sarandí 699 bis, T 963979.

Exchange Banco de la República, Plaza Cagancha, open daily until 2200, inc Sunday (*casas de cambio* on Plaza Cagancha keep similar hours, but most banks open only from 1300 to 1700). **Lloyds Bank**, Calle Zabala 1500, and 11 city agencies; **Citibank**, Cerrito 455 (corner Misiones), no commission on own cheques; **Banco Holandés Unido**, 25 de Mayo 501, reported as cheapest bank to have money sent; **Banco Comercial**, Cerrito 400 and Av Libertador (up to US$1,000 available on Mastercard or Visa, best rates for deutschemark cheques); and **Banco Panamericano Uruguayo** on Plaza Cajón. Only **Banco de la República** deals in US personal cheques for collection: 30 working days, high charge and not always reliable. **American Express Bank**, Rincón 473, T 960092/961162, does not change cash or TCs (see Turisport under **Travel Agents**). Thomas Cook/Mastercard refund assistance point: Viajes Continental, 25 de Mayo 732, T 92-09-30. US$, cash available on Mastercard or Visa from **Banco Pan de Azúcar**, Rincón 518, takes 1 hr, and some other banks. There are exchange houses, especially along 18 de Julio, eg **Gales** at 1048, **La Favorita** (Amex agents) at 1459, **Eurocam** at 1497, **Zito** at 1841, but do shop around for best rates (rates for cash are better than for TCs, but both are often better than in banks, and quicker service too). **Exprinter** on Plaza Independencia, **Lespan**, Av 18 de Julio 1046, and **Cambio Indumex**, Rincón 464 and 18 de Julio 1128, have been recommended. No restriction on foreign exchange transactions (ie an excellent place to stock up with US$ bills, though American Express and some banks refuse to do this for credit cards; most places charge 3% commission for such transactions). Airport bank open every day 0700-2200; Banco de la República exchange office (good rates for cash and TCs, will accept torn dollar bills). Note that rates for Brazilian currency are poor.

Chambers of Commerce and Cultural Institutions American Chamber of Commerce, Bartolomé Mitre 1337, esq 108, T 959048. **Alianza Cultural Uruguay-Estados Unidos**, Paraguay 1217, T 915234, library open Mon-Fri, 1400-2000, US publications and books (excellent selection), theatre, art gallery. **British Chamber of Commerce**, Av Libertador 1641, piso 2, of 201, T 900936. **Instituto Cultural Anglo-Uruguayo** (known as the "Anglo"), San José 1426, T 908468 (theatre, rec, library open Mon-Fri 0930-1200, 1430-1930). **The British Hospital**, Av Italia 2420, T 409011. **The English Club**, Treinta y Tres 1309, T 951212. **Alliance Française**, Soriano 1180, T 911979 (theatre, concerts, exhibitions in French and Spanish, library, excellent bookshop). **Goethe Institut**, Canelones 1524, T 405813/404432 (open Mon, Thur 1600-2000, Tues, Fri 0930-1230, closed Wed). **Casa Cultural Uruguay-Suecia**, Ejido 1444, T 900067. **Instituto Italiano de Cultura**, Paraguay 1177, T 903354. **Instituto de Cultura Uruguayo-Brasileño**, Av 18 de Julio 994, T 986531.

Schools The British School at Carrasco and some 4 others, 1 French, 1 German, and the Crandon Institute, an American school for children up to 17. All have good scholastic ratings.

Embassies and Consulates Argentine Consulate, Río Branco 1281, T 900897, open 1400-1900, visa US$15, one day wait, English spoken. **Brazilian Consulate**, Convención 1343, Edif La Torre, piso 6, T 912024/1460, open 0930-1230, 1430-1730 (service for visas takes 24 hrs and is more complicated than from Buenos Aires - need photo, onward ticket, ticket, proof of finances); Embassy is at Andes 1365, Torre Independencia, 6 piso, T 905043. **Paraguayan Consulate**, Blvd Artigas 1191, T 485810, open 0900-1200 summer, 1400-1730 winter. **Chilean Embassy**, Andes 1365, T 982223, open 0900-1400, visa US$5, same day.

US Embassy and Consulate, Dr H Abadie S 808, T 236276/236061. **Canadian Consulate**,

Gómez 1348, T 958583.

British Embassy, Marco Bruto 1073, T 623597/623581. **Spanish Consulate**, Libertad 2750, T 780048. **Swedish Embassy**, Av Brasil 3079, piso 6, Pocitos, T 780088. **Swiss Embassy**, Ing Federico Abadie 2934-40, T 704315. **German Embassy**, La Cumparsita 1417-35, T 904958 (open 0930-1230). **Belgian Embassy**, Leyenda Patria 2880, Apt 202, T 701265. **French Embassy**, Uruguay 853, T 904377. **Israeli Embassy**, Blvd Gral Artigas 1585, T 404164. **Italian Embassy**, JB Lamas 2857, T 780542. **Austrian Consulate-General**, Maldonado 1193, T 914000. **Netherlands Embassy**, Leyenda Patria 2880, Apt 202, T 701631. **Portuguese Embassy**, Av Dr F Soca 1128, T 96456.

Boliches (Café-Concerts/Peñas/Folk-Pubs, offering the most typical local night-life) *Clave de Fu*, 26 de Marzo 1125, Pocitos, Wed-Sat from 2200, best local folk-rock groups live at weekends; *Amadeus Café Concert*, Atlántico 1716, Malvin, from 2100 nightly, Latin American folk-rock; *TK*, Bulevar Artigas 1031, from 2200 nightly, the place to hear *candombe*; *Vieja Viola*, Pampas 1995 esq Venezuela, 2400 onwards, folk songs, *candombe*, tango; *Amarcord*, Yaguarón 1234, Wed-Sun 2200 onwards, traditional pop music; *Templo del Sol*, Constituyente y P de María, Latino-Tropical music. *Clyde's*, Costa Rica y Ribera, lively, live music. *Años 90*, Solano Antuña 2684 y Ellauri, Pocitos, daily 2000-0400; *Subterráneo Magallanes*, T 494415, live shows, Fri and Sat only, book in advance; *30 y Pico*, 21 de Septiembre 2724, Pocitos, Tues-Sun from 2000, rec for the over 30s, very good, live shows Sat and Sun; *Lobizón*, Michelini y San José, good food, good price; *Taj Mahal*, Andes y San José, sangria, good food; *Fun-Fun*, next to Mercado Central, amateur and local music. *Pizza Sing* in Carrasco is also good.

Tanguerías *La Vieja Cumparsita*, C Gardel 1811, nightly 2330-0500, no singles admitted, also has *candombe* shows, book ahead; *Tanguería del 40*, in *Hotel Columbia*, Rambla República de Francia 473, Mon-Fri 2300-0100, Sat 2300-0500, book in advance, rec; *Sorocabana*, Yí 1377, tango shows Mon, Fri, Sat, 2100-2400.

Besides tango and *candombe*, other popular music forms in Montevideo are Música Campestre-Folklórica (of guacho origin), Música del Caribe by Uruguayan orchestras dedicated to dance music from Puerto Rico, and "the best New Orleans Dixieland Jazz Bands" in Latin America (John Raspey).

Discos (*Boites* are the more expensive discos which provide live music for dancing; prices, US$15-30.) *Zum Zum*, Rambla Armenia 1647, from 2200 nightly, rock, live music weekends; *New York*, Mar Artico 1227, Punta Gorda; *La Base*, nr Airport (for people over 25): these three are expensive and you need to book ahead. *La Luna*, Gabriel Pereira y Gestido, Pocitos; *Caras y Caretas*, Friburgo 5817, Punta Gorda, Thur-Sat 2200-0600, live music, chic; *Hard Rock*, Bulevar España 2721, Pocitos, Fri, Sat 2400 onwards, rock 'n' roll, open air terrace is a nice retreat from the heat, noise and lasers; cheaper discos include *San Telmo*, Maldonado 1194, live music, always full and *Chant Clair*, Soriano 1338. Leading Uruguayan-Latin-Caribbean orchestras play every Sat after 2300 at *Palacio Sudamérica*, 3 blocks from Palacio Legislativo.

Nightclubs (*Clubes Nocturnos*) These all-night clubs, of which there are many, provide striptease, music and willing sexual partners; all expensive. The red light district, around Piedras y Juan Carlos Gómez in Ciudad Vieja, is a very friendly environment, safe, active only in the late afternoon on weekdays.

Theatres *Solís*, Buenos Aires 678, two auditoria, home of the Comedia Nacional. *El Galpón*, Av 18 de Julio 1618; *Circular*, Av Rondeau 1388; *del Notariado*, Av 18 de Julio 1730; *de la Candela*, 21 de Septiembre y Ellauri; *del Centro*, Plaza Cagancha; *La Gaviota*, Mercedes y Narvaja; *Arteatro*, Canelones y G Ruíz; *El Tinglado*, Colonia 2036; *La Máscara*, Río Negro 1180: the above present professional productions. *Sala Verdi*, Soriano 914, presents semi-professional and amateur theatre, concerts, etc. *Teatro Millington-Drake* at the Anglo (see **Cultural Institutions**) puts on occasional productions, as do the theatres of the Alianza Uruguay-Estados Unidos and the Alianza Francesa (addresses above). Opera and ballet at *Auditorio del Sodre*, Sala Brunet, Av 18 de Julio 930 (a new Sodre Cultural Complex is under construction at Mercedes and Andes). Many theatres close during Jan and Feb.

Cinema is very popular. Price is almost the same in all cinemas, at US$8 (half price on Wed). Classic and serious films at Cinemateca film club (3 separate cinemas—at L Carnelli 1311, Soriano 1227 and A Chucarro 1036), monthly membership US$6, and Ciné Universitaria (2 halls, Lumière and Chaplin, Canelones 1280). Films are released quite soon after the UK and USA, and often before they get to Buenos Aires. Details in *Guía del Ocio* and monthly *Cinemateca Uruguaya* (free). At least half Montevideo's cinemas show blue films—marked *sexo explícito*.

Music Every Saturday, from midnight to Sunday morning, thousands of dancers crowd into the

Palacio Sud América, Yatay 1429, near Palacio Legislativo, 3 dance salons, Caribbean music on 1st floor, Tango on 2nd, tickets half price if bought before 2400. Pop concerts are held in Centenario stadium and Parque Rodó. During the two weeks around Carnival there is a music and dance competition, in the Parque Rodó amphitheatre, in "Murga", a form of satirical revue, 4 hrs every night, US$0.50 entry, starting at 2100. See also under **Tanguerías**, etc and **Theatres**, above.

Casinos *Parque Hotel*, Rambla Presidente Wilson, 1400-0200, 0300 Sat and Sun, entry US$3; *Hotel Carrasco*, Rambla República de México, daily 1800-0300, US$3.

Health and Fitness Suomi, Dr José Scocería 2909 (Pocitos).

Language Schools *AmeriSpan Unlimited* has an affiliated school here for learning Spanish; contact PO Box 40513, Philadelphia, PA 19106, USA, T 215-985-4522/800-879-6640, F 215-985-4524, E-mail info@amerispan.com.

Laundry Automatic laundrettes can be found in all parts of the city.

Post Office Misiones 1328 y Buenos Aires; 0800-1800 Mon-Fri, 0800-1300 Sat and holidays; philatelic bureau on top floor sells back issues. *Poste restante* at main post office will keep mail for 1 month, US$1 if authorized in advance by administrator. Next to Pluna office at Plaza del Entrevero, unreliable, and under Intendencia at corner of Av 18 de Julio and Ejido.

Places of Worship The Roman Catholic Cathedral is known locally as the Iglesia San Juan. Anglican Church (Holy Trinity), Reconquista 522 (a national monument) T 954037 (English Service 1015 Sunday). Methodist services at Christ Church, Carrasco. Holy Trinity Episcopal (British), and the Emanuel Methodist Church (American), hold regular services in English. The German Evangelical Church holds services in German at Calle JM Blanco 2. There is a synagogue.

Shopping The main shopping area is Av 18 de Julio, good for men's business suits. Suede and leather are good buys; styling is more traditional than in Buenos Aires; try *Casa Mario*, Piedras 641 (expensive); shops and workshops around Plaza Independencia may be a better bet *(Montevideo Leather Factory*, No 832, rec). Amethysts, topazes, agate and quartz are mined and polished in Uruguay and are also good buys: recommended is *Benito Sityá*, Sarandí 650 (Ciudad Vieja) and *Cuarzos del Uruguay*, Sarandí 604. For woollen wall hangings see *Manos del Uruguay*, which also sells floor cushions, crafts, high quality woollen goods, etc at Reconquista 616, and at San José 1111, and in the shopping centre in Carrasco near the Rambla. Other good craftwork (cheaper) in daily covered craft market on Plaza Cagancha (and indoors at No 1365, near the cinema). Ciudad Vieja is an excellent district in which to buy antiques, especially antique jewellery; go to Bartolomé Mitre: at No 1368 is *Portobello Road*; next door, No 1366, is *Mariano*, a wig-maker; at No 1388 is *Naftalina*, good. Many galleries here, and in Maldonado and Punta del Este, selling contemporary paintings. For stamps, Carlos Camusso, Galería Central, 18 de Julio 976. On Sunday am there is a large, crowded street market on Tristán Narvaja (good for silver and copper, and all sorts of collectibles) opposite Facultad de Derecho on 18 de Julio. A small Sat am market and a Sun antique fair are held in Plaza Constitución; there is also a big market on Vásquez Ledesma nr Parque Rodó, Pocitos, selling fruit, vegetables, clothes and shoes (Tues and Sat 0900-1500, and on Sun in Parque Rodó).

The Montevideo Shopping Center on the E side of Pocitos (Herrera y Galanza, 1 block S of Rivera): it is open daily 1000-2100 and has a self-service restaurant, a cinema and *confiterías*. It also has wide range of shops including *Manos del Uruguay* as well as others selling leather goods, *Foto Martín*, *Bookshop*, supermarkets and more (bus 141 or 142 from San José). Outside is a *McDonalds*. A new Shopping Centre has opened at Punta Carretas in the old prison, Ellauri 350, Loc 263, very popular; another new shopping centre is Portones in Carrasco; a third is in the Tres Cruces bus station.

Cameras and Film Best place for developing films is **Foto Martín**, Av Libertador and Uruguay; **Delucchi**, on Herrera y Obés, for developing slides; **Foto Tecnifilm**, Av 18 de Julio 1202, helpful, English spoken; camera repairs by **Fotocámara**, on Michelini between Mercedes and Colonia. Film developing and equipment is quite expensive in Uruguay; better to bring film from abroad.

Bookshops The following have English and American books: *Librería Barreiro y Ramos*, 25 de Mayo y JC Gómez, 18 de Julio 937, 21 de Septiembre (Pocitos) and Av Arocena 1599 (Carrasco); *Ibana*, International Book and News Agency, Convención 1479, specializes in foreign publications. *Librería Británica*, Sarandí 580, specializes in language and children's books. Others include *Librería Mosca Hermanos*, Av 18 de Julio 1578 and Av Arocena 1576 (Carrasco); *Feria del Libro*, Av 18 de Julio 1308; *Paseo del Lector*, Av 18 de Julio y Michelini; *Librería Papacito*, Av 18 de Julio 1415. *Ruben*, Tristán Narvaja 1736. *Librería Oriente Occidente*, Cerrito 477 and *Librería El Aleph*, Bartolomé Mitre 1358, both sell used and rare books (former has English books, also book exchange). The only shop with exclusively English stock is *Bookshop SRL*, Blanes 1170, T 409954, Cristina Mosca, also at Montevideo Shopping Center; specializes in travel. The Sunday market on Paysandú is good for second-hand books.

Sports There are two good 18-hole municipal golf links. There are several lawn tennis clubs, and two for polo. Horse racing at Las Piedras (**see p 1316**).

Telecommunications Antel, Fernández Crespo 1534 (headquarters) and at San José 1108 (Plaza), Arocena 1666 (Carrasco), Ariel 4914 (Sayago), Cádiz 3280 (Mercado Modelo), Garzón 1806 (Colón), José Belloni 4445 (Piedras Blancas); for international phone calls (inc USA Direct Express), telex, fax, cables, etc, open 0800-2000 daily.

Travel Agents *JP Santos*, Colonia 951, and *Jetmar*, Plaza Independencia 725-7, both helpful. *Exprinter*, Sarandí 700; *Turisport Ltda*, Mercedes 942, T 900474, F 920852 (American Express for travel and mail services, good; sells Amex dollar TCs on Amex card and personal cheque at 1% commission); *Golden Tours*, Colonia 1221, T 90 7500, English spoken. *Viajes y Turismo*, Ellauri 1249, Pocitos, T 775779, very helpful, English spoken. *Turinter*, Río Negro 1358, very helpful. *Pasaporte*, Galería El País, Plaza Cagancha, T 921539, friendly and helpful; *Concorde Travel Ltda*, Plaza Independencia 1378, p 7, T 926346/48, rec; *Jorge Martínez*, Río Branco y Colonia; *Freeway*, Colonia 994, T 908931/33.The Palacio Municipal organizes city tours, Sat-Sun, US$5, T 930648/9 Mon-Fri 1000-1800. One day tours of Punta del Este are organized by many travel agents and run from several hotels, US$40-100 incl meals.

Tourist Information is at the new Tres Cruces bus terminal; in the same office is the Hotels and Restaurants Association. Also at Carrasco international airport, T 502261.

Information Dial "214" ("124" inland) for the Antel information office for details on the weather, pharmacies on night duty, automobile service stations, airline arrivals and departures (Montevideo), long-distance bus schedules, shipping movements, in Spanish. Dial "6" for exact time. The *Guía del Ocio*, a weekly guide, US$0.70 from newsstands, gives information on museums, cultural events, nightlife and entertainment, including addresses, rec.

Maps Best street maps of Montevideo are at the beginning of the Guía Telefónica (both white and yellow page volumes). *Eureka Guía De Montevideo* is recommended or streets, sector by sector, with index and bus routes (US$4.75 from bookshops).

City Transport Buses US$0.50 (pay the conductor on board); express buses US$0.75. There are many buses to all parts from 18 de Julio; from other parts to the centre or old city, look for those marked "Aduana". For Pocitos from city centre take bus No 121 from San José behind the former Onda station. D11 is a new service to Carrasco along Rivera, US$0.75; see above of D1, US$1.

Taxis US$0.90 for first 600m, and US$0.21 for each 140m afterwards; on holidays and Sun, 20% more; charge per hour US$15. There is a small charge for each piece of luggage, but tipping is not expected. Beware of taxi drivers telling you that long-distance buses are full and offering to take you instead; this is unlikely to be true.

Car Hire without chauffeur, from US$30 to US$60 per 24 hrs (insurance included), plus extra per kilometre if only hiring for the day; guarantee of US$800 required. Hire for 3-day weekend is US$130 (rates are much lower out of season and vary according to size of vehicle. Cheaper weekly rates available. Collision damage waiver (amounting to US$1,000), US$15 per day. Hertz, Calle Colonia 813 near Plaza Independencia, T 923920; **National**, Av de las Américas 5026, T 615267; **Snappy**, Andes 1363, T 907728; **Punta Car**, Cerro Largo 1383, T 902772, also at Aeropuerto Carrasco. **Budget**, Mercedes 935, T 916363; **Sudancar**, Piedras 533, T 958150; and **Avis** at airport, T 611929, and Yaguarón 1527, T 930303; many others. Remises, US$8 per hour; **Remises** Montevideo Joaquín Requena 1303, F 411149. Guillermo Muñoz, Bartolito Mitre 2636, T 773928, rec.

Airport The main airport, T 602261, is at Carrasco, 21 km outside the city; with coffee shop and children's play area in departure lounge; left luggage about US$1 per day per item; if exchange facilities closed, buses will accept dollars for fares to town. To Montevideo 30 mins by taxi (US$25—may be able to charge it to hotel bill if without cash), or about 50 mins by bus. Many buses from Aduana pass the airport; dark brown "Copsa" bus terminates at the airport. Pluna has a bus service from Colonia 1321 to airport, US$5. *Concorde Travel* has a service from hotel to plane (almost) US$10-25.

Rail The station is at the N end of Calle Río Negro (with Cerro Largo). Fine building with information office, post office, restaurants and historical display. Commuter trains run N to 25 de Agosto (Florida) Mon-Fri dep 25 de Agosto 4 times between 0440 and 0655, returning from Montevideo 4 times 1728-1930, 1 hr 50 mins, US$1.90. On Sat, dep 25 de Agosto 0440, 0530, return 1320, 1420. You can take the train to Santa Lucía, the stop before 25 de Agosto, and return by bus (2 hrs); the train goes via Canelones also. Ferrotransporte (T 941387) arrange return trips to Florida, with lunch and tours, US$15.80 for the train ride.

Buses within Uruguay New terminal, Tres Cruces, Bulevar Artigas y Av Italia; it has a shopping mall, tourist office, restaurant, left luggage (free for 12 hrs at a time), post and phone offices. All buses leave from here and bus company offices are here, too. During the summer holiday season buses are booked heavily; it is recommended to book in advance (also for Fri and weekend travel all year round). Fares and journey times from the capital are given under destinations.

To Paraguay, Brazil, Chile To Asunción, Paraguay, US$70, 18 hrs: twice a week (Wed and Sat, plus Mon in summer) by COIT, Paraguay 1473, T 916619, or Tres Cruces, and 3 a week by Brújula, Uruguay 1113, T 915143, both services rec, meals served. Alternatively take bus to **Santa Fe**, Argentina (US$30), via Paysandú bridge, for easy access to Asunción. The through bus route is via Paysandú, Salto, Bella Unión, Uruguaiana, Paso de los Libros, Posadas, Encarnación, to Asunción (there are no passport or customs formalities except passport checks at Bella Unión and at Encarnación). There are very comfortable buses to **Porto Alegre** (US$35, 10 hrs) and **São Paulo** (US$64 daily, 32 hrs) at 2200 and 2230 daily, with TTL (Tres Cruces or Plaza Cagancha 1385, T 908419/411410), *coche cama* daily except Sat 2100 US$53 to Porto Alegre; the route is Pelotas, Porto Alegre, Florianópolis (US$47), Camboriu (arr 2000, a good place to stop over), Curitiba, São Paulo (arr 0500 on second morning); often booked very early. Also EGA, Tres Cruces, T 425164, or Rio Branco 1409, T 925335, and Planalto to Santa Maria and Rio Grande do Sul (Rondeau 1475). A cheaper alternative route (which also avoids the risk of being stranded at the border by through-bus drivers) is to Chuy (US$11-12, 6 hrs), then catch an onward bus to Porto Alegre (7½ hrs, US$13.25), either direct or via Pelotas. To **Santiago** via Buenos Aires and Mendoza, US$97, 28 hrs, by EGA, Mon and Thur, and Tas Choapa, Río Negro 1356 bis, T 483539, or Tres Cruces, T 498598. Round trips to Argentina, Chile or Brazil by bus or plane, booked at travel agents are reported to be good value.

NB One needs a passport when buying international tickets.

To Argentina: Ferries and buses (Argentine immigration officer on ferries.) **Direct to Buenos Aires:** Buquebus, Río Negro 1400, T 920670, and Montevideo Shopping Center, T 629669, "Avión de Buquebus", daily at 0730 (not Sun), 1130, 1530 and 1930, 3 hrs, US$37 tourist class, US$49 1st class. **Services via Colonia:** bus/ferry services by Buquebus (0045, 0830, 1630; 1630 on Sunday), US$29, buses leave from Tres Cruces, boat leaves Colonia 3½ hrs after bus departure. Buquebus on either route carries cars, US$90-100. **Ferryturismo**, Río Branco 1368, T 906617/900045, 4 hrs 40 mins Montevideo-Buenos Aires via Colonia: bus leaves 0530, 1215 and 1730 daily, catamaran leaves Colonia 3 hrs after bus departure, US$27, plus US$7 bus Colonia-Montevideo, cars carried US$70, also has bus/ferry service, 3 a day (once Sat and Sun), US$18 + US$7 for bus (break of journey in Colonia on all services is allowed, cheaper if you do this, to buy bus ticket only in Montevideo, and the ferry ticket here). More expensive is bus/hydrofoil service by Aliscafos (Plaza Cagancha 1124, T924004, F 922626) 4 services a day between 0530 and 1730, 0700-1730 on Sun, 3½ hrs, US$24, book in advance (also to La Plata one a day, Fri, Sat and Sun). Services **via Carmelo and Tigre** (interesting trip): bus/motor launch service by Delta Nave, Tres Cruces, T 498599, or Plaza Cagancha 1340, T 965401, 7 hrs, 0015 and 0700 daily, tell driver where you want to go in Buenos Aires), also Cacciola, 0040, 0800, 1500, Tres Cruces T 419350, Plaza Cagancha 1326, T 910755, both US$15. Bus service **via Fray Bentos** (Bus de la Carrera): joint service by El Condor, Cita and COT (Tres Cruces, T 421313) at 1000, 2200 and 2300 daily, US$25, 9 hrs, slow journey. Bus service to Santa Fé and Córdoba (US$57, 15 hrs), via Paysandú and Paraná, Cora (Tres Cruces, T 498598), daily 1800, snacks served. Advanced booking is advisable on all services at busy periods.

For air services to Argentina via Colonia del Sacramento see p 1319.

Note If intending to travel through Uruguay to Brazil, do not forget to have Uruguayan entry stamped in your passport when crossing from Argentina. Without it you will not be able to cross the Brazilian border.

EAST FROM MONTEVIDEO (2)

---

320 km of beautiful coast, consisting of an endless succession of small bays, beaches and promontories, set among hills and woods. Punta del Este, 139 km from Montevideo is a major international resort. From Punta del Este to the Brazilian frontier is much less developed; good bird watching in the coastal lagoons. The beach season is from December to the end of February.

Two roads, both paved, go to Punta del Este. The northern branch via Pando and Soca, is Route 8 (toll just before Route 9 branch); at Km 75 Route 8 continues NE towards Minas (**see p 1314**), while Route 9 branches off to San Carlos (14½ km N of Maldonado and 19 km N of Punta del Este) through beautiful rolling country with views of the Laguna del Sauce. The other road, the "Interbalnearia", runs largely along the coast, with short branches to some of the resorts, and is the one described in the text. There are toll posts (US$1.50) at Arroyo Pando and at Arroyo Solís Grande (you are charged only on the way out from Montevideo). For the first 15 km or so out of Montevideo an alternative road to the Interbalnearia runs parallel between it and the coast—its use is recommended during heavy traffic periods due to the frequency of dangerous road junctions.

Route 9 runs from San Carlos through the towns of Rocha and Castillos to Chuy. A spur of the road turns S to La Paloma and there are secondary roads to some of the resorts further along the coast. The area's past as a frontier zone between Spanish and Portuguese colonial rule is indicated by fortresses Santa Teresa (near Rocha) and San Miguel (near Chuy). There is a series of well-equipped, modern campsites along the coast.

The resort of **Atlántida**, 45 km from Montevideo, is ringed by fir forest and has a good country club. (**C Rex**, is main hotel; **C Munday**, is clean and friendly; many good *residenciales* charging E off season; campsite *El Ensueño* at Km 46, T 2371; some good restaurants). A short distance beyond, in groves of eucalyptus and pine, is the small and intimate beach of Las Toscas, followed by Parque del Plata on the Solís Chico river. An *asado* on the beach (with wine) costs about US$12. Five km before Atlántida, in an old fortress set in pine woods, is **A2 El Fortín de Santa Rosa** hotel and restaurant, rooms face onto a beautiful patio, excellent food and service, rec; 2 mins from a lovely sandy beach, Ruta Interbalnearia Km 42, T (0372) 7376. Small zoo not far off. Also near Atlántida is **El Renacimiento**, a dairy farm which is open to the public, with produce on sale.

8 km further E across a (toll) bridge is **La Floresta** (*Oriental*, highly rec), surrounded by woods. The chalets are pretty, reminiscent of the villages of the Landes, near Biarritz. **Pueblo Chico**, Km 55.5, T (037) 39565, F 39775, is another dairy farm open to the public, with cabins, pool, live music Sat pm, riding, excellent food, Greek owner, highly rec. At Km 64.5 is Sr Garabedian's **campsite**. For bookings, telephone Sr Garabedian at Montevideo 561230. **Solís**, over a toll bridge at the mouth of the Río Solís, is at Km 85. It has a very long beach, good fishing, delightful river and hill scenery. At Bellavista (Km 87, Ruta 10) is **A2 Hostería Bellavista**, with breakfast, T (0432) 3192, F 4059, horseriding and other sports. About 8 km beyond Solís lies the small village of Las Flores, with a better beach than that at Solís. Accommodation is available at **B pp Hostería del Mar**, T (043) 800 99 or Montevideo 786657, bed and breakfast (C low season), clean, well-run, open all year, and Edén Camping with room at US$3 pp or camping at Km 91 site. *Restaurant Charma*, rec.

Piriápolis (pop 6,000), the next resort, 16 km from Solís, 101 from Montevideo, may be reached either by following the very beautiful R10 from the end of the Interbalnearia, or by taking the original access road (R37) from the town of Pan de Azúcar, which crosses the R93. Piriápolis, set among hills, is laid out with an abundance of shady trees, and the district is rich in pine, eucalyptus and acacia woods. It has a fine casino hotel and some 50 others, a good beach, a yacht harbour, a country club, a golf course, a motor-racing track and is particularly popular with Argentines. There are medicinal springs. Six km N on the R37 is Cerro Pan de Azúcar (Sugar Loaf Hill), crowned by a tall cross with a circular stairway inside, fine coastal views; there is only a steep path, marked by red arrows, up to the cross. Just N of Piriápolis R 37 passes the La Cascada Municipal park (open all year) which contains the Museo Castillo de Piriá, open Fri, Sat, Sun and holidays, 1300-1700. By the entrance to the municipal park is a good zoo, containing among other things live specimens of all snakes and most animals native to Uruguay including endangered pampas deer. The shortest route from Piriápolis to Punta del Este is by the Camino de las Bases which runs parallel to the R37 and joins the R93 some 4 km E of the R37 junction.

Hotels Many, situated along the sea front. Most close end-Feb until mid-Dec. Reservation advisable in high season. **A1** *Argentino*, Rambla de los Argentinos, T (0432) 2791, with casino, medicinal springs, ice rink and pool open to public for US$3.50, also sauna, rec; **B** *Danae*, Rambla y Freire, T 2594, E out of season, breakfast, heating, clean, friendly; **B** *Rivadavia*, Rambla 1208, T 2532, open all year (C in summer), with bath, hot water, clean. Many others in our price ranges C and up. The Centro de Hoteles y Anexos de Piriápolis runs a reservation office at Edificio Piria on Rambla de los Argentinos. House and apartments for hire, Aloia-Colmegna Ltda, in Edif Claramar on Rambla rec, English spoken.

Youth Hostel Albergue de Piriápolis, behind *Hotel Argentino*, at Simón del Pino 1136, T 0432-2157, US$6 pp (open all year), mostly double bedrooms, hot showers, cooking facilities (but no utensils!). Student cards accepted. Reserve in high season. There is also an international YMCA camp on the slope of Cerro del Toro, double rooms in bungalows, and tents.

Camping Site at Misiones y Niza, T 0432-23275.

Restaurants *El Quijote*, rec for paella, cheap and good; many small restaurants near the harbour, eg *Don Anselmo* (shellfish, excellent, overlooking sea) and *Naútico*, both rec.

Exchange Banco de la República, open Mon-Fri 1300-1700.

Tourist Information Asociación de Fomento y Turismo, Rambla de los Argentinos 1348, T 2560.

Bus to/from **Montevideo**, US$3.25, 1½ hrs. To **Punta del Este**, US$2. For **Rocha, La Paloma** and **Chuy**, take bus to Pan de Azúcar and change.

R93 runs between the coast and the Laguna del Sauce to **Portezuelo** , which has good beaches. The Arboreto Lussich (open 1030-1630) on the W slope of the Sierra de la Ballena (north of R93) contains a unique set of native and exotic trees. There are footpaths, or you can drive through; two *miradores*; worth a visit. From Portezuelo it is possible to drive N towards the R9 by way of the R12 which then continues, unpaved, to Minas. Just off R12 is *El Sosiego*, T (042) 20000, F 20303, a dairy farm open to the public, selling goats' cheese, *dulce de leche* and other products. At **Punta Ballena** there is a wide crescent beach, calm water and very clean sand. The **L1** *Solana del Mar Hotel* (payment in dollars cash is demanded unless you protest) modern, restaurant on the beach, full board. Campsite near Arboreto Lussich (turn off at Km 128 on Interbalnearia, T 42-78902/24181, or Montevideo 801662, US$8 for 2 with tent, many facilities). The place is a residential resort but is still quiet. Casa Pueblo, the house and gallery of Uruguayan artist Carlos Páez Villaro, is built in a Spanish-Moroccan style on a cliff over the sea; the gallery can be visited (US$3.50), there are paintings, collages and ceramics on display, and for sale; season: Nov 1 to April 1. Walk downhill towards the sea for a good view of the house. There is a hotel at Casa Pueblo, also time-share apartments, restaurant and, lower down the hill, a *parrillada*. At the top of Punta Ballena there is a panoramic road 2½ km long with remarkable views of the coast.

Maldonado (pop 33,000), capital of Maldonado Department, is 140 km E of Montevideo. This peaceful town, sacked by the British in 1806, is now a dormitory suburb of Punta del Este, but it has many colonial remains, including the parish church and El Vigia watch tower, Gorriti y Pérez del Puerto. See the Cathedral (completed 1895), the Mazzoni Regional Museum (Ituzaingó 787, Tues-Sun 1800-2300 in summer, 1300-1800 in winter); San Fernando de Maldonado Museum (Sarandí y Rafael Pérez del Puerto, Tues-Sat 1300-2000); Museo de Arte Americano de Maldonado (José Dodera 648 y Treinta y Tres, T 22276, private museum, interesting); the windmill, the Cuartel de Dragones exhibition centre and the Cachimba del Rey (an old well—local legend claims that those who drink from the well will never leave Maldonado).

Hotels Hotel accommodation is scarce in summer. **A1** *Colonial*, 18 de Julio s/n, T 23346; **A1** *Esteño*, Sarandí 881, T 25222; **A1** *Sancar*, Dr Edye 597, T 23563. **C** *Hospedaje Isla de Gorriti*, Michelini between Ituzaingó and Florida, clean, friendly, rec; **C** *Maldonado*, Florida 830, T 24664, quiet, clean; **C** *Celta*, Ituzaingó 839, T 30139, friendly and helpful, Irish owner, No 7 bus stop outside.

Camping In Parque El Placer, T 70034, free; also Camping San Rafael, T 86715, good facilities, US$7, bus 5 from town.

Restaurants *Matias Módena*, 3 de Febrero 642, good fish and meat, US$14 pp; *Cantina del Italiano*, Sarandí 642, pizzería, old building, good value. *Piano-Bar JR Pizzetas*, Rincón y Gutiérrez Ruiz, pizzas and pastas. Best ice-cream at *Popy's*, 2 branches.

Exchange Banco Pan de Azúcar, accepts Mastercard.

Information on concerts and exhibitions in summer T 22276. Tourist information at bus station, T 25701.

Bus to/from **Montevideo**, US$6; to **Minas**, 2 hrs, 5 a day, US$3.

San Carlos, on Route 9, 14½ km N of Maldonado, is a charming old town of 20,000 people. Buses run from Plaza Artigas to Maldonado every 15 mins; it is a good point for connections to La Paloma (two buses a day), and Chuy on the Brazilian border. Of interest are the church, dating from 1722, heavily reconstructed, an excellent zoo, and the historical museum. **Hotels D** *Hospedaje*, on main plaza (with bath, limited hot water, good but cold and damp in winter) and *El Amanecer*, Treinta y Tres 634. Free camping, with poor facilities, in municipal park. 2 *cambios* which exchange TCs. Lottery shop on the plaza will change small amounts. *Benitez*, Treinta y Tres y Maldonado, for good leather items.

At Km 130 on Route 9, before San Carlos, the Camino de los Ceibos heads SE to join Route 39 at Km 13.5 S of San Carlos. Off this road (2 km from Km 130) is a turning to *Las Vertientes*, a delightful place to have afternoon tea (mostly home-made produce). Best to book in advance, T 69997.

Punta del Este Seven km from Maldonado and 139 km from Montevideo, facing the bay on one side and the open waters of the Atlantic on the other, lies the largest and best known of the resorts, Punta del Este, which is particularly popular among Argentines. The narrow peninsula of Punta del Este has been entirely built over (a "concrete jungle"). Two blocks from the sea, at the tip of the peninsula, is the historic monument of El Faro (lighthouse); in this part of the city no building may exceed its height. On the ocean side of the peninsula, at the end of Calle 25 (Arrecifes), is a shrine to the first mass said by the Conquistadores on this coast, 2 February 1515. 3 blocks from the shrine is Plaza General Artigas, which has a *feria artesanal* (handicraft market); along its side runs Av Gorlero, the main street. Traffic is directed by a one-way system; town bus services start from Calle 5 (El Faro), near the lighthouse. It has excellent bathing beaches, the calm *playa mansa* on the bay side, the rough *playa brava* on the ocean side. There are some small beaches, hemmed in by rocks, on this side of the peninsula, but most people go to where the extensive *playa brava* starts, opposite the *Hotel Playa*. Papa Charlie beach on the Atlantic (Parada 13) is preferred by families with small children as it is safe. There are an excellent yacht marina, yacht and fishing clubs, and many beautiful holiday houses. There is good fishing both at sea and in three near-by lakes and the river Maldonado (which the main road crosses by a unique W-shaped bridge). The rest of the area consists of sand dunes covered with pines. Direct daily Boeing 737 flights from Buenos Aires to Punta del Este airport during the high season. On the land side, Punta del Este is flanked by large planted forests of eucalyptus, pine and mimosa. There are a golf course and two casinos. The *Muriel*, a late 19th century yacht, makes 3 sailings daily, lasting 3 hrs, US$35. Many of the best hotels and restaurants close after the end of the season in March. From 10 March to Easter and from Easter onwards the place is deserted and on sunny days it is still warm enough to swim. Streets on the peninsula have names and numbers; lowest numbers at the tip.

Museum Foundation museum of Contempory Latin American Art, Barrio Beverly Hills, T 83476, open Dec to end of Holy Week, Tues, Thurs, Sat and Sun, 1700-2100, entrance free. Worth a visit but car needed to get there.

Offshore is 16th century **Isla de Gorriti**, visited by explorers including Solís, Magellan and Drake and heavily fortified by the Spanish in the 1760's to keep the Portuguese out. The island, densely wooded and with superb beaches, is an ideal spot for campers (boats from 0800-1700, return 0915-1915, US$7). On **Isla de Lobos**, which is a government reserve within sight of the town, there is a huge sea-lion colony; excursions to it every morning at 0900 if demand is sufficient, US$20; ticket should be bought at the harbour the day before (T 44352/21445).

Hotels Very many, but expensive: we list only those with positive confirmations. Visitors

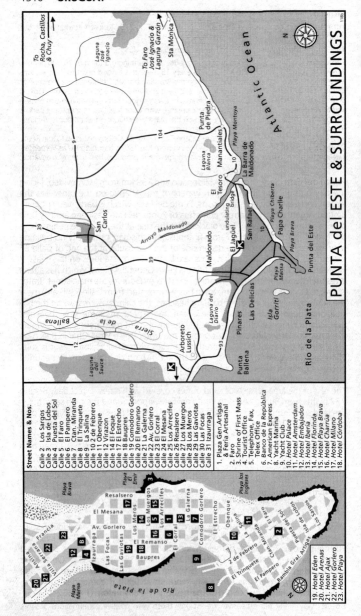

PUNTA del ESTE & SURROUNDINGS

Street Names & Nos.

Calle 2 Los Sargos
Calle 3 Isla de Lobos
Calle 4 Puesta del Sol
Calle 5 El Faro
Calle 6 El Pampero
Calle 7 Ctan. Miranda
Calle 8 El Muelle
Calle 9 La Salina
Calle 10 2 de Febrero
Calle 11 Obenque
Calle 12 Virazon
Calle 14 El Foque
Calle 17 El Estrecho
Calle 18 Baupres
Calle 19 Comodoro Gorlero
Calle 20 El Remanso
Calle 21 La Galerna
Calle 22 Av. Gorlero
Calle 23 El Corral
Calle 24 El Mesana
Calle 25 Los Arrecifes
Calle 26 Resalsero
Calle 27 Los Muergos
Calle 28 Los Meros
Calle 29 Las Gaviotas
Calle 30 Las Focas
Calle 31 Itzaurraga

1. Plaza Gen Artigas & Feria Artesanal
2. Faro
3. Shrine of First Mass
4. Tourist Office
5. Telephone, Fax, Telex Office
6. Banco de la Republica
7. American Express
8. Yacht Marina
9. Yacht Club
10. Hotel Palace
11. Hotel Amsterdam
12. Hotel Embajador
13. Hotel Iberia
14. Hotel Florinda
15. Hotel Playa Brava
16. Hotel Charrúa
17. Hotel Milano
18. Hotel Córdoba
19. Hotel Eden
20. Hotel Arenas
21. Hotel Ajax
22. Hotel Gorlero
23. Hotel Playa

without a car are forced to take a hotel on the peninsula, unless they want to spend a fortune on taxis. In this area are: **L3** *Amsterdam*, El Foque (Calle 14) 759, T 44164, ocean view, good service, rec; **L3** *Iberia*, Calle 24, No 685, T 40405/6, 43348, about centre-peninsula, pleasant, breakfast included, open all year, good covered garage opposite; **L3** *Palace*, Gorlero y 11, T 41919 (A1 in March, closed in winter), breakfast only (expensive restaurant, *La Stampa*, in the hotel), lovely courtyard, colonial style, well kept; **L3** *Embajador*, Risso, by new bus terminal, T 81008, good; **B** *Ocean*, Calle 9 (La Salina), No 636, T 43248, clean, central.

Just off the peninsula, but within walking distance, are **L3** *Arena's*, Costanera y Parada 3, T 88676; **L3** *Ajax*, Parada 2, Malvarosa, T 84550; and **A2** *Gorlero*, Av Artigas y Villa Serrana (Parada 2), T 82648. Bus services pass close to hotels on Pedragosa Sierra, Av Roosevelt and **L3** *Salto Grande*, Salto Grande 3½, T 82137. **L2** *Barradas*, Río Branco y Francia, T 81527, F 84895, pool, gardens, tennis, a/c. **L3** *La Capilla*, San Rafael, 100m from casino, T 81843, cheaper out of season, clean, gardens, *La Piscina* restaurant close by, good. **L1** *L'Auberge*, near golf course, T 82601, F 83408, own transport essential, a/c, "lo más refinado", open all year, special weekend offers, good restaurant. *Cantegril* country club lets cottages and hotel apartments at a high price, or one may hire from an "Inmobiliaria". Hotel rates are as much as halved in the winter months. In the high season (Dec-March) for which above prices apply, it is better to find a hotel in Maldonado and commute, or look for a hotel that is rebuilding, so that you can negotiate on prices. To stay at a hotel in the woods you will need a car; no public transport to beach or town.

Youth Hostel NE of Punta del Este in Manantiales, F pp, reached by Codesa bus (see below).

Camping See above, under Maldonado.

Restaurants *La Lutèce*, Los Sauces casi Pedragosa Sierra, French cuisine, superb, very expensive; *La Bourgogne*, Av del Mar y Pedragosa Sierra, also French and excellent restaurant and afternoon tea in stylish surroundings, expensive; *Floreal*, Pedragosa Sierra, posta 5, elegant, French, rec, *casa de té* 1600-2030, restaurant after 2130; *Mamut*, Calle 9 y 12, seafood specialities; *Mariskonea*, Calle 26, No 650, one of the oldest establishments, very good quality and service, but very expensive; *Doña Flor*, Plaza París, San Rafael, French food, rec; *Bungalow Suizo*, Av Roosevelt y Parada 8, excellent, US$50 pp, must book; at the port: *El Pobre Marino* and *Sea Port*, both seafood; *El Mastil*, Av de las Palmeras esq 8 (behind port), charming atmosphere, open all year; *El Ciclista*, Calle 20 y 27, one of the oldest restaurants, Italian food; *Los Caracoles*, Calle 20 y 28, excellent food at good prices; *Viejo Marino*, Calle 11 entre 14 y 15, Las Palmeras, fish restaurant, very busy so go early; *Forte di Makalle*, Calle 8-828 y 11, rec; *Stromboli*, Gorlero y 17, good seafood; *Andrés* on a terrace at the Edificio Vanguardia, Rambla Costanera; *La Tavola Calda*, Gorlero 639, Italian; *da Carmela*, Gorlero 635 y Rambla Gen Artigas, pizza and pasta, pleasant; *Blue Cheese*, Calle 20 No 717, Rambla de Circunvalación y 23, for steaks and unlimited salads; *Las Delicias*, Rambla Costanera, Parada 24.5, seafood and pasta; *Yacht Club Uruguayo* (not to be confused with the exclusive Yacht Club), Gral Artigas y 8, simple, friendly, views over the port; *El Metejón*, Gorlero 578 y 19, good food, good value. On the main street, *La Fragata*, Gorlero 800, open 24 hrs all year, a good meeting place. Many enticing ice-cream parlours in Gorlero.

Exchange Best rates of exchange from Banco de la República Oriental de Uruguay, which opens earlier and closes later than the other banks and accepts Mastercard, but no TCs. Amex at Turisport, Gorlero y 21, T 44657. Also *casas de cambio*, eg Indumex, Av Gorlero y 28.

Discotheques often don't begin till 0200. Entry US$25-50 a couple, inc 2 drinks. *New Faces*, Calle 20; *Caras y Caretas*, near yacht club; *Space*, nr Playa Chiberta; many others.

Post Office and Telephone, telex and fax on Calle 24 at Calle 25, by the square.

Crafts *Manos del Uruguay* in front of the Casino Nogaró. Best sweaters from *San Carlos*.

Riding Nueva Escuela de Equitación at Cantegril Country Club, Av Saravia, T 25013, classes, guided rides, all levels and ages catered for.

Travel Agents *Madrid*, T 41654, excursions from US$12, car hire, fishing trips and to islands; *Tuttie*, Local 1 de Servicio de Tráfico de Lanchas, T 44352, for trips to islands and fishing.

Tourist Information Liga de Fomento, Parada 1, T 40514, at airports, or Terminal de Omnibus Playa Brava.

Car Hire Punta-Car, Cont Gorlero, *Hotel Playa*, T 82112/82761, telex Punt-Car UY 28105; Serracar, T 88855. See Madrid Viajes below.

Airport Laguna del Sauce, Capitán Curbelo (T 73056), which handles flights to Buenos Aires (eg Aero Regionales, Sat, Sun, Mon, US$68). Airport tax US$6. Exchange facilities, tax-free shopping. Regular bus service to airport from Punta del Este bus station, 90 mins before departure, also connects with arriving flights. El Jagüel airport is used by private planes. Pluna, Gorlero 940, T 41840, or 78769 Laguna del Sauce, 84378 El Jagüel; Aerolíneas Argentinas, T 78782 Laguna del Sauce, or 43801 Edif Santos Dumont.

Buses   New terminal at Av Gorlero, Blvd Artigas and C32, T 89467 (served by local bus No 7). To/from **Montevideo**, COT (T 86810) or Sur Bus, US$5, less than 2 hrs, frequent in the summer; to **Piriápolis**, US$2. To **San Carlos** (US$1.80) for connections to Porto Alegre, Rocha, La Paloma, Chuy. Direct to **Chuy**, 4 hrs, US$6. To Gen José Artigas bridge (Argentina) US$20. Local bus fare about US$0.50. For transport Montevideo-Buenos Aires, *Buquebus* T 84995, Gorlero 732, and *Ferryturismo* T 45312/42820, Galeria Sagasti, Av Gorlero.

Near Punta del Este, to the E, *Playa San Rafael*, where there is an 18-hole golf course, is growing rapidly (but it is under El Jagüel's flight path). **L2** *Casino San Rafael*, high season (20/12-1/3), A2 low season, closed after Easter, no credit cards, no a/c or balconies, much used for conferences, Telex 28035, T 042-82161; **A2** *San Marcos*, very pleasant; **A2** *La Capilla*, next to the church, behind the *San Marcos*, T 81843, good; **L2** *Hotel Porto Bari* (T 84304, F 84021, Parada 13, French restaurant, swimming pool, tennis). Further E, across the "W-shaped" bridge is *La Barra*, with **L3** *Hotel Posta del Cangrejo*, T 70021/271 (with excellent restaurant, picturesque place), and restaurants *San Jorge*, just across the bridge, speciality *torta de mariscos*; *Neuhausen*, pleasant, not too expensive; *Lo de Miguel*, Ruta 10 y C 7, good, small, noisy, booking essential (US$30 pp); *Hostal de la Barra*, Ruta 10 Montoya; *Pizza Bruja*, Ruta 10, crêpes, pizzas and pasta; *Aquabarra*, Ruta 10, restaurant and pub; *Sushi Bar*, good food, reserve for dinner. La Barra has become very fashionable, with many new restaurants open. Barra's beaches, and those further N (Montoya, Manantiales) are gaining in popularity. *Nueva Puebla Youth Hostel* at **Manantiales**, US$5, kitchen and washing facilities, small. 30 km from Punta del Este is the quiet fishing village of **Faro José Ignacio**, with lighthouse (open Fri-Sun, 1700-1900), and the well-known restaurant *Parador Santa Teresita*, where seaweed omelette is a speciality. Excellent prawns at *La Gamba*, expensive (T 0486-2055). **A2** *Parador Renner* at Balneario José Ignacio, breakfast included, good dining room. Coastal R10 runs some way E of José Ignacio, but there is no through connection to La Paloma as a new bridge across the mouth of the Lago Garzón is not operational (Feb 1995).

Rocha (pop 52,000) is 211 km from Montevideo and 28 km from the resort of La Paloma, to which buses are frequent. It is the capital of Rocha Department. Groves of palms dotted about the fields give the area an unusual beauty. The city has an interesting central plaza and cathedral. There is a cinema on the plaza showing good films; the Club Social has dancing. The zoo is free to enter.

Accommodation and Food   **B** *Trocadero*, 18 de Julio y 25 de Agosto; **E** *Municipal*, on 19 de Abril, very good, and *Centro* on Ramírez. Good *confitería* on the plaza; try also *Titar Grill* opposite old Onda bus terminal; *Las Brasas*, 25 de Agosto 113; *Sirocco*, Ramírez y Rodó. At Km 207, W of town, are *Parador Rocha* and *Parador Los Jardines*.

Camping   Sites at Parque Andresito, Rocha, and Rancho Pucará.

Buses   To Montevideo, 3 hrs, US$7; to Chuy, US$5. No direct services to Punta del Este, but easy connections at San Carlos.

La Paloma, protected by an island and a sandspit, is a good port for yachts; its permanent population is about 5,000. The surrounding scenery is attractive scenery, the freshwater and sea fishing are good and the pace is more relaxed than Punta del Este. You can walk for miles along the beach, and the place is popular with Argentines.

Hotels   **A2** *Portobello*, Las Tres Marías s/n, T 6159, rec; **A2** *Cabo Santa María* with casino, Av Solari, T 6004; **A2** *La Tuna* (T 0473-6083), Neptuno y Juno, rec; **A3** *Perla del Este*, Aldo y Jupiter, T 6078; **B** *Bahía*, rec, T 6029; **B** *Viola*, Solari s/n, T 6020; **B** *Yeruti*, Grullas s/n, T 6235; **C** *Puertas del Sol*, Delfín y Aries, T 6066. In nearby La Aguada, **D** *Bungalows de Piemonte*, Costanera, T (0473) 6096.

   Youth Hostel at Parque Andresito, T 0473-6396, 50 beds, US$5 pp, clean, friendly, good meals available, kitchen facilities, open 1 November to 30 March, essential to book at Montevideo office. **Camping Sites** in Parque Andresito and at Los Delfines near La Aguada, 2 km E of town. Also thatched *cabañas* for rent in Parque Andresito, US$22-38 per day with maid and kitchen facilities, sleep 4-6.

Restaurants   Good one at *Hotel Bahía*. *La Marea*, near tourist office, has oustanding seafood. *Pizzerías* include *La Caleta*, *La Currica* and *Ponte Vecchio*; for *parrillada* try *Grill del*

Camping in Parque Andresito. Excellent bread at *Confitería La Farola*.

Services and Transport Bike rental opposite the casino, US$3.50 a day; horses can be hired. One bank which changes TCs; also a supermarket and post office. Tourist office on Av Solari at entrance to town, very helpful, T 6088. Buses run to and from **Rocha**, and to and from **the capital** (5 hrs, US$15). Four buses daily to **Chuy**, US$3.50, 3¾ hrs, 2 a day to **San Carlos**, **Pan de Azúcar** and **Aguas Dulces**, all with Rutas del Sol company, student discounts available.

From La Paloma, Coastal R10 runs NE to Aguas Dulces (regular bus services along this route). 10 km from La Paloma is *La Pedrera*, a beautiful village with sandy beaches. **A3** *Hotel La Pedrera*, T 6028, swimming pool, tennis, comfortable rooms, rec; **B** *Hotel San Michel*, T 6486, and *Hotel Brisas del Este*, T 6213; *Restaurant Costa Brava*, overlooking the sea. Campsite *La Palomita*, 8 blocks from the sea, wooded, open summer only. Beyond La Pedrera the road runs near pleasant fishing villages which are rapidly being developed with holiday homes, but where basic accommodation is still available (eg Youth Hostel at **Barra de Valizas**, US$5 pp, open 1 Nov-30 March, reserve in Montevideo first; campsites at Cabo Polonio, Km 260 of R10, very basic, Barra de Valizas, informal, and Aguas Dulces, more organized). At *Cabo Polonio*, visits to the islands of Castillos and Wolf can be arranged to see sea lions and penguins. It is a quiet, pleasant place with a few restaurants, simple hotels, and houses or rooms to rent. From **Aguas Dulces** (*Hotel Gainfor*, with restaurant; *Restaurant La Terraza*) the road runs inland to the town of Castillos (easy bus connections to Chuy; several restaurants), where it rejoins R9. At Km 280.5, 17 km N of Castillos is *Camping Esmeralda*. At Km 298 there is a turn off for **Punta del Diablo** (**B** *Hostería del Pescador*, T (0472) 1611 LD17, and several restaurants, eg *Parador del Mar*, *Estrella del Belén*; *La Posada*, excellent food, highly rec).

About 100 km from Rocha, 308 km from Montevideo, is ***Parque Nacional Santa Teresa***, with curving, palm-lined avenues and plantations of many exotic trees. It also contains a modest zoo, an aviary, botanical gardens, fresh-water pools for bathing, countless campsites (open all year), and a few cottages to let in the summer (which are usually snapped up quickly). It is the site of the impressive colonial fortress of Santa Teresa, begun by the Portuguese in 1762 and seized by the Spanish in 1793. The fortress houses a museum of artefacts from the wars of independence, open 1000-1700 except Mondays (winter hours shorter). Entry US$0.30, tickets from restaurant *La Posada del Viajero*, opposite, recommended. On the inland side of Route 9, the strange and gloomy Laguna Negra and the marshes of the Bañado de Santa Teresa support large numbers of wild birds. The beaches stretch for many km, but the surf is too rough for swimming. Practically every amenity is closed off-season.

At the *capatacia*, or administrative headquarters, campers are expected to register (although the staff can be gloriously indifferent to your desire to do so and to pay). Here there are also a small supermarket, greengrocer, butcher, bakery, medical clinic, petrol station, auto mechanic, post and telephone offices, and the *Club Santa Teresa*, where drinks and meals are available. Tour by taxi (US$12, daily) from La Coronilla (see below) to Santa Teresa fortress, Laguna Negra, and the collection of native and exotic plants under glass.

Ten km beyond Santa Teresa, 20 km S of Chuy, is the bathing resort of **La Coronilla** excellent ocean shark fishing, plus skate and corvina from the rocks; there is an annual competition in January. Campsite of the same name has restaurant, open through Holy Week, 300m from the ocean. It also rents tent-cabañas, US$15 for up to four persons. The sea water is reported to be highly polluted by a drainage canal which empties out here.

Hotels Most close in winter, but try **B** *Gure-Etxe*, on beach, T 2783, small and very pleasant, with restaurant; **B** *Mesón Las Cholgas*, T 2860, with bath, restaurant, rec, but hot water is scarce in bathrooms of rooms facing beach; **B** *Parador La Coronilla*, on Route 9 at Km 312.5, T 2883; **B** *Costa del Mar*, on beach, rec, swimming pool, casino, restaurant; **C** *Rivamare*, T 2782. Cheapest is **D** *Las Maravillas*, on Leopoldo Fernández, T 2786.

Restaurants Besides hotel restaurants, there are also *La Ruta*, open all year, rec, *Gure-Etxe*, rec; *Niko's*, near beach, good and cheap, and *El Mejillón*.

Bus Buses between **Chuy** and **Montevideo** stop at La Coronilla (US$7.50, 5 hrs to the capital). To Santa Teresa fortress, take Rutas del Sol bus to junction, then walk 1 km.

At *Chuy*, 340 km from Montevideo (pop 9,000), the frontier runs along the main street, Avenida Brasil. Tourists may freely cross the border in either direction. There are many duty free shops in Chuy and tourists from Uruguay may buy limited amounts of manufactured goods on the Brazilian side without formalities (but see below). Quality underwear shops abound, excellent prices. There is a tourist office caravan opposite the casino (open only in season). For details on the Brazilian town of Chuí, see Brazil chapter, **Section 6, Southern Brazil**.

Hotels and Restaurants All are open the year round. **C** *Hotel Plaza*, Artigas y Arachanes, T (0474) 2309; **D** *International*, Río San Luis 121, T 2055, with bath; **F** *Hospedaje Vitoria*, 4 blocks E of *Hotel Chuy*, basic, clean, friendly, rec; on same street is **E** *Iramar*, basic, friendly. Most restaurants are on Av Brasil: *Restaurant Jesús*, good, cheap, friendly; *Parrillada Maldonado*, Brasil at Cebollati, good, quite cheap; *Opel* and *Nuevo Internacional*.

Camping From Chuy buses run every 2 hrs to the Barra del Chuy campsite, Ruta 9 Km 331, turn right 13 km, T (0474) 2425; good bathing, many birds. *Cabañas* for up to 4 persons cost US$20 daily or less, depending on amenities. Casino open till 0400.

Exchange at *Hotel Chuy* (open until 0300); several *cambios* on Av Brasil (open until 1830), give slightly better rates. No exchange facilities on Sundays. Buy Brazilian currency here as the black market is difficult to find until São Paulo. Banco de la República Oriental Uruguay changes TCs.

Transport Uruguayan taxis are allowed 25 km into Brazil. Bus to **Rio Grande** (Rodoviaria) at 0700 and 1530, 4 hrs, with stop at immigration; to **Porto Alegre**, 7½ hrs, US$13.25, 1200 and 2300; to **Montevideo** (Cynsa or Cita) US$11, also by Ruta del Sol US$12, 7 hrs, frequent stops; to **Maldonado** US$6; to **La Paloma**, four a day, US$3.50, 3¾ hrs. To **Treinta y Tres**, Transportes Puentes. **Bus offices** Cita and Rutas del Sol both have offices on Numancia (off Av Brasil, 3 blocks down from casino).

Uruguayan passport control is 2½ km before the border on the road into Chuy, US$2 by taxi, officials said to be friendly and cooperative; Ministry of Tourism kiosk here is very helpful, especially for motorists. If travelling by bus, make sure the driver knows you want to stop at Uruguayan immigration, it will not do so automatically. Brazilian immigration is 2 km from Chuy on the road to Pelotas (Brazilian Consul is at Fernández 147). Buses from Chuy to Santa Vitoria or Pelotas stop at Brazilian customs; alternatively take a taxi. The office for the Pelotas bus is one block inside Brazil, near the *Hotel Quaraim*. Make sure your passport is stamped or you will have trouble leaving Brazil. Similarly, on entering Uruguay, get an entry stamp otherwise you will not be permitted to proceed (eg at the customs post between Chuy and San Miguel fortress, on Route 19 toward Treinta y Tres). Taking a car into Brazil is no problem, especially if the car is not registered in Brazil or Uruguay.

Excursions from Chuy: on the Uruguyan side, on a promontory overlooking Laguna Merín and the gaúcho landscape of southern Brazil, stands the restored fortress of **San Miguel**, dating from 1752 and surrounded by a moat. It is set in a park in which many plants and animals are kept. (Bus from Chuy US$0.35, entry US$0.20, closed Mon) The hotel nearby, **A2** *Parador San Miguel*, is excellent, beautiful rooms, fine food and service, highly rec. Daily excursion buses from La Coronilla to Barra del Chuy beach and from Chuy to San Miguel fort, US$9. Tours end for the season after 31 March.

MONTEVIDEO NORTHEAST TO BRAZIL (3)

Two roads run towards Melo, heart of cattle-ranching country: Route 8 and Route 7, the latter running for most of its length through the Cuchilla Grande, a range of hills with fine views.

Route 8 is the more important of these two roads to the border and it is now completely paved.

The first main town is *Minas* (pop 34,000). It is a picturesque small town 120 km N of Montevideo, set in the beautiful wooded hills, which supply granite, marble and other minerals. Juan Lavalleja, the leader of the Thirty-Three who brought independence to the country, was born here (equestrian statue), and there is an equestrian statue to Artigas, said to be the largest such in the world, on the Cerro

Artigas just out of town. The church's portico and towers, some caves in the neighbourhood, and the countryside around are worth seeing. In March and April you can buy *butea* palm fruit, which is grape size, orange and tastes bitter-sweet. Good confectionery is made in Minas; the largest firm, opposite *Hotel Verdun*, shows tourists round its premises. Museum in the Casa de la Cultura.

Hotels A2 *Verdun*, 25 de Mayo 444, T (0442) 2110, clean; **D** *Residencia Minas*, 25 de Mayo 502 on main plaza, clean; **D** *Ramos*, 18 de Julio near bus station, basic, clean (discount for IYHA members).

Camping Camping Arequita, beautiful surroundings, US$6.

Youth Hostel Route 8, Km 145, in small village of Villa Serrana, US$5 pp a night (open all year), 28 km beyond Minas on road to Treinta y Tres; most attractive, basic, but take plenty of food and drink as there is no shop. Direct bus from Montevideo or Minas, ask driver to set you down and walk 3 km to Villa Serrana; essential to book through Montevideo office.

Restaurants *San Francisco*, 25 de Mayo 586, is recommended as is *El Portal*, Aníbal del Campo 743, for *parrillada*. The best pastry shop is *Irisarri*, Calle Treinta y Tres 618, known for *yemas* (egg candy) and *damasquitos* (apricot sweets).

Exchange Lloyds Bank and national banks, open 1300-1700 Monday-Friday.

Tourist Office at the bus station.

Bus To Montevideo, US$2.70, COT (4 a day) and many others, 2½ hrs. To Maldonado, US$3, 5 a day, 2 hrs.

Excursions The Parque Salus, on the slopes of Sierras de las Animas, is 8 km to the S and very attractive; take the town bus marked "Cervecería Salus" from plaza to the Salus brewery, then walk 2 km to the mineral spring and bottling plant (**C** pp *Parador Salus*, full board, acceptable; reasonable set lunch.) The Cascada de Agua del Penitente waterfall, about 11 km out of town, off the Minas-Aigue road, is interesting and you may see wild rheas (protected) nearby. It is difficult to get to the falls in the off-season.

The next centre of any importance, 286 km from Montevideo, is **Treinta y Tres**, (pop 28,000), picturesquely placed a little way from the Río Olimar. Free camping and swimming at Municipal Park on the bank of the Río Olimar. The main plaza has all the major restaurants and grills.

Hotel L3 *Treinta y Tres*, JA Lavalleja 698, T (0452) 2325; *Central*, and pensions *Jorgito* or *Mota*.

Some 20 km from Treinta y Tres on Route 8, a dirt road, left, runs 19 km among and over hills to a rocky region with small streams, the **Quebrada de los Cuervos**, now a beautiful and quite unspoilt national park.

Route 8 continues N through **Melo** (pop 42,000), 113 km from Treinta y Tres (**L3** *Gran Hotel Virrey*, J Muñiz 727, T 0462 2411, better rooms in new part, TV, mini bar, good café) to the Brazilian frontier near Aceguá (Brazilian Consul in Melo at Av Aparicio Saravia 711, T 2084). From Melo Route 26 runs SE; after 12 km (2 km off Route 26) is the Posta del Chuy. This house, bridge and toll gate (built 1851 by 2 Frenchmen) was the only safe crossing place on the main road between Uruguay and Brazil. Nowadays it houses a display of gaucho paintings and artefacts relating to its history. 88 km from Melo is the border town of **Río Branco**, founded in 1914, on the Río Yaguarón (Río Branco is also reached from Treinta y Tres direct on Route 18). The 1½ km-long Mauá bridge across the river leads to the Brazilian town of Jaguarão (Brazilian Consul, Lavalleja y Palomeque, T 3). Several buses a day between Melo and Río Branco.

Hotel D *Italiano*, with bath. **Youth Hostel** Av Artigas 279, cooking and laundry facilities, open all year (reservations in Montevideo).

Restaurant *Oasis*, good, *pollo a la brasa*.

This is where most international traffic used to cross the frontier; now the road via Chuy is better. Customs officials are at the international bridge, passport officials at the police station at Jaguarão. From Jaguarão buses run several times daily to Pelotas and Porto Alegre. There is usually a better rate of exchange at Melo than at the frontier. Pluna, Ituzaingó 720, T 2272.

MONTEVIDEO NORTH TO BRAZIL (4)

Dams on the Río Negro have created an extensive network of lakes near Paso de los Toros, with camping and sports facilities. South of the Río Negro is gently rolling cattle country, vineyards, orchards, orange, lemon and olive groves. North is hilly countryside with steep river valleys and cattle ranching.

Route 5, the 509 km road from Montevideo to the border town of Rivera runs almost due N, bypassing Canelones before passing through Florida, Durazno and Tacuarembó. The road is dual carriageway as far as Canelones; there is a toll 67.8 km N of Montevideo. If driving this route, note that on the narrow bridges on the single carriageway traffic coming from the N has preference.

Las Piedras (pop 58,000), 24 km from Montevideo, in vineyard country, has a Gothic Chapel of the Salesians. Race meetings (pari-mutuel betting) Tues, Thurs, Sat and Sun, entry US$0.50, take bus 102 from Av Paysandú in Montevideo.

Exchange Lloyds Bank, Calle General Artigas 652. Open 1300-1700, Mon-Fri.

Canelones, 45 km from the capital, is a typical small town (pop 17,000) in a grain growing area (it has a municipal campsite). It was the seat of Artigas' first government in 1813 (in what is now the Police station). 52 km further N is the pleasant country town of **Florida** (pop 28,000), where the Act of Uruguayan Independence was signed in 1825. This is celebrated by a folklore festival on Independence Day (25 Aug) each year. (**D** *Hotel Español*, José Rodó 360, T 2262, with bath, E without; *Hotel Giani*, Fernández y Rivera. Camping at Parque Robaina, on southern entrance to town and at Municipal Campsite in centre. *Restaurant Negro el 8*, Independencia y Gral Flores, Italian food.) Cita bus Montevideo-Canelones US$1.70, Florida US$3.25. See also **Rail** in Montevideo section.

Durazno (pop 28,000), 182 km from Montevideo on the Río Yí, is a friendly provincial town with tree-lined avenues and an airport. There is a good view of the river from the western bridge. (**C** *Durazno*, Herrera 947, T 2371; **D** *Hotel Central*, Manuel Oribe 699 y Mons Arrospiede, T 2324; **Youth Hostel**, Campus Municipal, T 2835 between 1300 and 1900, Mon-Fri, open all year. *Camping El Sauzal*, 600m from Campus Municipal.)

Paso de los Toros (pop 13,000) is close to the huge lake created by the Rincón del Bonete dam on the Río Negro (**D** *Sayonara*, Rivera 484, T 0366-2535, clean, basic, friendly; beautiful camping by the river, tourist information at Parador Municipal, Durazno s/n, T 2074). East of Paso de los Toros, along R43 (1½ hrs by bus) is **San Gregorio de Polanco** (pop 3,000), a small, picturesque village, with sandy beaches on the lake shore. A number of public and private buildings are decorated with wall paintings. Tourist information at *Pinolanda* handicraft shop, Artigas 201. There is a campsite, restaurant and hotel (**C**), and a ferry crosses the lake several times a day.

Tacuarembó, 390 km N of Montevideo, is a major route centre (pop 40,000). Museo del Indio y del Gaucho at Flores y Artigas (**C** *Hotel Tacuarembó*, 18 de Julio 133, T 2104, with bath, breakfast, clean, central; **A2** *Central*, Gral Flores 300, T 2341, with bath, clean; *Hospedaje 25*, 25 de Mayo 358, basic, friendly, garden; campsite 1 km out of town in the Parque 25 de Agosto, and 7 km N on R26 at Balneário Iporá; *Restaurante Parrilla La Rueda*, W Bettrán 251, good). Train service to Rivera at 0600 (see below).

Rivera (pop 55,400), is on the Brazilian frontier. It is divided by a street from the

Brazilian town of Santa Ana do Livramento, which has a good golf course, and connections by bus (daily) and rail (less frequent) to Porto Alegre. Points of interest are the park, the Plaza Internacional, and the dam of Cañapirú. There are an airport (Aviasur from Montevideo US$93 return; Pluna, Paysandú 1079, T 3404) and a casino, and many duty-free shops. Although crossing the frontier is easy be sure to observe formalities. Tourist Information at Dr Analles 328, T 3083. Brazilian consul, Ceballos 1159, T 3278/4470; Argentine consul, Ituzaingó 524, T 3257. The bus stations in Rivera and Santa Ana are about 1½ km apart.

Hotels   C *Uruguay-Brasil*, Sarandí 440, T 3068, with bath, clean; **A1** *Casablanca*, Sarandí 484, T 3221, shower, breakfast, a/c, clean, pleasant; **F** *Comercio*, Artigas 1115, very friendly.
Camping   in Municipal site near AFE station, and in the Parque Gran Bretaña 7 km S along Route 27.

Bus   to/from **Montevideo**, US$12 or less, to **Fray Bentos** and Durazno; to **Paysandú**, twice a day, or take a bus to **Tacuarembó** (also twice a day) and change. For Artigas, take bus in Livramento (Gen Salgado Filho e Gen Vasco Alves) to Quaraí, then cross bridge.

Rail   In February 1993, the passenger train service to Tacuarembó was reopened. The train, a motor-coach made in USA in 1935, leaves Tacuarembó at 0600 and returns from Rivera at around 1600 Mon-Sat. The trip costs just a few dollars and goes through scenic countryside abundant with animal life.

Excursion   To *Minas de Corrales* (pop 3,000), in an area of abandoned goldmines, including long tunnels which run under the town. Daily bus from Rivera, 2 hrs.

WEST FROM MONTEVIDEO (5)

This is the route from the capital to Colonia del Sacramento, with its colonial quarter and connections for Argentina.

Route 1, part of the Pan-American Highway, runs W from Montevideo (toll at the Santa Lucía bridge, Km 22.5) for 177 km to Colonia del Sacramento. Route 3, the road to Paysandú and Salto, turns off at Km 67. Route 2, for Mercedes and Fray Bentos, leads off at Km 128 (no tolls on Routes 2 and 3). Route 1 is lined with ribbon development for much of the way to Libertad (Km 51). Roads lead off to several beaches, notably Playa Pascual at Km 34, Kiyú (campsite) at Km 76 and Boca del Cufre (campsite) at Km 101.

At Km 121 from Montevideo the road passes **Colonia Valdense**, a colony of Waldensians who still cling to some of the old customs of the Piedmontese Alps. (**Hotel** *Parador Los Ceibos*.) A road branches off N here to **Colonia Suiza**, a town of Swiss settlement also known as Nueva Helvecia (pop 9,000). (**Hotels A3** *Nirvana*, T 0552-4052, restaurant, sports facilities, rec; **A3** *Granja Hotel Suizo*, T 4002, fine restaurant, rec; **C** *Central*, T 4025; **C** *Del Prado*—Youth Hostel—open all year, T 0552-4169; camping in the Parque Municipal). The area is famous for its cheeses and other dairy produce. The Swiss national day is celebrated with great enthusiasm.

Buses   Montevideo—**Colonia Valdense**, frequent, with COT, 2½ hrs, US$4; to **Colonia del Sacramento**, frequent, 1 hr, US$1.50; local services between Colonia Valdense and Nueva Helvecia connect with Montevideo/Colonia del Sacramento buses.

Rosario, 5 km along Route 2 from the junction with Route 1, is a typical agricultural town given over to dairying and grain production (pop 8,000). It has 2 fishing clubs and the Club Cyssa, a social, cultural and sports club. (**Hotels E** *Ricardi*, and **E** *Riviera*, good).

Colonia (del Sacramento), a charming and lively small town (pop 22,000) with an interesting historic section jutting into the Río de la Plata, was founded by Portuguese settlers from Brazil in 1680. Throughout the seventeenth century it was an important centre for smuggling British goods across the Río de la Plata into the Spanish colonies. The Barrio Histórico, with its narrow streets (see the Calle de los Suspiros), colonial buildings and reconstructed city walls, is particularly interesting because there are few such examples in this part of the continent. The Plaza Mayor is especially picturesque. Grouped around it are the Museo Municipal in the former house of Almirante Brown, the Casa del Virrey and the Museo Portugués. Also worth a visit are the Faro (lighthouse, entry free—tip or donation appreciated), the Museo Indígena, Artigas 327 (Casa de la Cultura), a small and pleasant private museum of the Charrúa Indians, the Iglesia Matriz, the oldest church in Uruguay, near the Plaza de Armas, and the house of Gen Mitre, now housing the Museo Español. (All museums open 1130-1830.) At Real de San Carlos, 5 km out of town (take blue bus from Av Gen Flores y A Méndez, 30 mins, US$0.30), there is an unusual and rather grand tourist complex, built by Nicolás Mihanovic between 1903-1912, which includes a racecourse (Hipódromo), a disused casino, now used as a hotel and an elegant bull-ring. N of town, at Parque Anchorena, is the President's summer residence. The best beach is Playa Ferrando, 2 km to the E (buses from Gral Flores every 2 hrs). In the third week of January, festivities are held marking the founding of Colonia. Ferries connect with Buenos Aires, only 50 km away. Free Port.

Hotels A1 *El Mirador*, Av Roosevelt, Km 176½, T 2004, a/c, casino, sports facilities; **A1** *Plaza Mayor*, Del Comercio 111, in old town, lovely, English spoken; **A3** *Posada del Gobernador*, 18 de Julio 205, T 3018, with breakfast, charming, rec; **B** *Leoncia*, Rivera 214, T 2049, modern, good; **B** *Posada Los Linajes*, Washington Barbot 191, T 4181, central, with bath, a/c, TV, cafetería; **B** *Posada de la Ciudadela*, Washington Barbot 164, T 2683, with bath, clean, pleasant, a/c, simple; **B** *Rincón del Río*, Washington Barbot 258, T 3002, shower but no breakfast, clean, friendly; **A2** *Royal*, General Flores 340, T 2169, with breakfast, comfortable, good restaurant, pool, noisy a/c but rec; **B** *Esperanza*, Gral Flores 237, T 2922, clean, charming; **B** *Italiano*, Lobo 341, T 2103, without bath, recently refurbished, friendly, clean, good restaurant, hot water but no heating, rec; **B** *Los Angeles*, Roosevelt 213, T 3133, small rooms, no restaurant, but clean and friendly, English spoken; **B** *Natal John*, Gral Flores 394, T 2081; **B** *Beltrán*, Gral Flores 311, T 2955, shared bath, clean, comfortable; **D** *Español*, Lobo 377, large dark rooms, lots of character, friendly; **D** *Señora Raquel Suárez*, T 0222 2916, has spacious rooms to rent, clean, friendly, good value; **D** *Hospedaje Colonial*, Flores 436, T 2906, clean, rec. The municipal sports complex has 2 dormitories with 80 beds, which are sometimes available—ask at the tourist office.

Camping Municipal site at Real de San Carlos, 5 km from Colonia, T 0522-4444, US$3.50 pp, **C** in mini-cabañas, electric hook-ups, 100m from beach, hot showers, open all year, safe, excellent, rec. Bus 30 mins from Av Gral Flores and A Méndez.

Restaurant *Esperanza* (at hotel) and *Yacht Club* (at harbour) are good; *Mercado del Túnel*, Flores 227, good meat dishes; *Mercosur*, Flores y, Ituzaingó, rec; *El Aljibe*, opposite Mercosur, good fish dishes. *La Torre*, Av Gral Flores y Santa Rita, in old town, bar and restaurant, loud disco music, but fine panoramic views especially at sunset. Good unnamed *parrillada* at Ituzaingó 186, nice atmosphere, value for money, and several others along 18 de Julio. *Los Faroles*, Plaza Mayor, rec, friendly, also *La Casona del Sur*, Misiones de los Tapes 145, good cakes, lovely atmosphere, live music at weekends, good craft shop opposite. *El Frijol Mágico*, Gatería Americana at Rivadavia y Méndez, good vegetarian food.

Exchange Cambio Viaggio, Flores y Suárez, open every day 0900-1200, 1300-1800. Cambios Brou and Libertad, both at the ferry port (dollars and South American currencies).

Argentine Consulate Flores 215, T 2091, open weekdays 1200-1700.

Post Office on main square. **Telephones** Antelco, Rivadavia 420, open till 2300.

Tourist Office Flores y Rivera, T 2182, open Mon-Fri 0800-1830, Sat and Sun 0900-2200, good maps of the Barrio Histórico; also at passenger terminal at the dock.

Car Hire Budget, Flores 472. Motorcycle and bicycle hire on many streets, US$5/hr, rec as a good way of seeing the town, traffic is slow.

Buses to **Montevideo**, 2½ hrs, COT and Turil, half-hourly service between the two, US$9; to **Carmelo**, 1½ hrs, Tauriño, 4 a day (not Sun) also Chadre daily 0555 and 1340, US$2; to **Salto**, 8 hrs, Chadre, at 0555 and 1430, US$15.

To Buenos Aires By ferry, 2½ hrs crossing, with Buquebus (T 0522-2975), 0400, 1200, 2000 (2000 only on Sun), US$18, cars carried, and Ferryturismo (T 2919/3145), 3 sailings a day, US$18 one way (40 mins by *Sea Cat*, also 3 daily, US$27, cars carried). By hydrofoil (Aliscafo)

1 hr crossing from Puerto Comercial, T 3364/5, 4 a day between 0830 and 1930, US$24 one way. The company runs buses to the port from Punta del Este, Piriápolis, *Carrasco Hotel* (Carrasco), and Montevideo.

By Air Lapa (Rivadavia 383, T 2006/2461) flies to Aeroparque, Buenos Aires twice a day (once on Sun), also Aero Regionales, T (0522) 2319, 4 a day (2 on Fri), US$25 including connecting bus services to/from Montevideo. This is generally quicker than hydrofoil. The airport is 17 km out of town along Route 1. **NB** Book in advance for all sailings and flights in summer, especially at weekends.

Excursion To **Conchillas**, 45 km N, pop 700, an unusual village of attractive one-storey terraced houses, abandoned quarry and mill, all built in 1890s by HJ Walker & Co to extract stone to build the port facilities of Buenos Aires. From Colonia take Tauriño bus for Carmelo, changing to connecting service at Radial Conchillas, 6 km from the village, bus waits in Conchillas 1 hr before returning. About 6 km further is Puerto Conchillas, with similar stone houses, disused port facilities and camping site.

UP THE RIO URUGUAY (6)

The Río Uruguay marks the frontier with Argentina (international crossings at Fray Bentos, Paysandú and Salto). On the Uruguayan side are rolling hills crossed by a network of rivers. At all the major towns on the Uruguay are beaches and campsites and there are thermal springs at Guaviyú, Daymán and Arapey.

Route 21 swings N and NW to reach the sleepy resort town of **Carmelo** (pop 15,000), 74 km from Colonia, on the shores of Las Vacas river. Across the bridge is a white restaurant on the left-hand side of the road: friendly, recommended. The port harbours several hundred yachts during the season. There is a free zone at the port.

Accomodation and Services A3 *Casino Carmelo*, Rodó s/n, T 2314; **B** *Bertoletti*, Uruguay 171, T 2030, modern, friendly, clean; **C** *Rambla*, Uruguay y 12 de Febrero, T 2390; **D** *Palace*, Sarandí 308, T 2622; **D** *San Fernando*, 19 de Abril 161, with bath, friendly, full of character, temperamental showers, rec; **C** *La Unión*, Uruguay 368, **D** without bath, clean, simple, very good value. **E** *Oriental*, 19 de Abril, clean, friendly. **Camping** Las Higueritas, near the bridge (T 2058). The **bank** will only exchange bills and not TCs.

Argentine Consulate FD Roosevelt 318, T 266.

Buses to Montevideo, 1210, 2240, US$10; to **Fray Bentos, Salto**, from main square 0710, 1540; to **Colonia**, Tauriño, 4 a day, 1½ hrs, US$2.

To Argentina Via Tigre, across the Paraná delta, cramped and crowded but a most interesting ride past innumerable islands: Delta Nave twice daily, 3 hrs, US$11; Cacciola 3 a day; office in Carmelo, Constituyente 263, T (0542) 8062, see under Montevideo for more details, see p 1306.

Some 30 km N, by road, is **Nueva Palmira** (pop 7,000), a popular yachting resort with a free zone and campsite. Worth visiting in the vicinity are the Pirámide of Solís dating from 1888 (8 km out of town), the Estancia de las Vacas (also known as the Calera de las Huérfanas) an eighteenth century Jesuit estate, and the Estancia de Narbona, built in 1732, with a chapel and 3 storey bell tower (both in poor condition, 12 km from town, and 3 km off the road).

Some 20 km further N is the historic beach of **La Agraciada**, famous for the landing of the Thirty-Three patriots on 19 April 1825, which led to Uruguayan independence. On the beach is a statue to General Juan Lavalleja, leader of the Treinta y Tres. A festival is held on each anniversary.

The road continues N through the small river port of **Dolores** (pop 13,000), 32 km up-river from the confluence of the Río San Salvador with the Río Uruguay, to **Mercedes**, a livestock centre and resort on the Río Negro best reached by Route 2 from the main Colonia-Montevideo highway. Founded in 1788, this pleasant town (pop 37,000) is a yachting and fishing centre during the season. Its charm (it is known as "the city of flowers") derives from its Spanish-colonial appearance, though it is not as old as the older parts of Colonia. There is a pleasant *costanera* (riverside drive). Four km W of town is the Parque Maúa, dating from 1757, with a castle and Museum of Palaeontology and Natural Sciences. There is also a small, well-maintained zoo (1300-1930), picnic tables, barbecues, camping possible in season. It takes 45 mins to walk to the park, a pleasant route passing interesting ruins (Calera Real) dating back to 1722, on the river bank.

Tourism Farm A two-hundred year-old Colonial Estancia, a peaceful and novel alternative for visitors to Uruguay who want to experience traditional country living. Estancia *"La Sirena"* offers excellent accommodation, four daily meals as well as riding, fishing, hunting, tennis, sailing, swimming, etc. Attended by Rodney, Lucia and Patricia Bruce its friendly owners, T/F 67029. Address: E Pittaluga 6396, Montevideo 11500, Uruguay – F (598) 532 4193.

Accommodation and Food A2 *Brisas del Hum*, Artigas 201, T 2740; **A3** *Marín*, Rodó 668, T 2987, a/c; **D** *El Dragón*, Giménez 659, T 3204, dark; **D** *San Martín*, Artigas 305, T 3212, clean; **F** *Mercedes*, on Giménez, friendly, clean, basic; **F** *Club de Remeros*, Youth Hostel, on riverside, T 0532-2534, kitchen and laundry facilities. Good food at *La Brasa*, Artigas 426, and at *Círculo Policial*, Calle 25 de Mayo. *El Emporio de los Panchos*, Roosevelt 711, good range of dishes.

Camping Site at Mercedes, beside Ríos Negro and Uruguay (US$0.45 pp).

Exchange Cambio Fagalde, Giménez 709; **Banco Comercial** on Colón (just off plaza) and **Banco de la República**, on plaza.

Tourist Office On Colón on the plaza, maps and hotel lists available.

Bus to **Paysandú**, with Sabelín on Sánchez, 2½ hrs, US$5. Bus to **Argentina** and **Montevideo**, CUT, Artigas (on plaza).

Excursions To the islands in the Río Negro—the largest has an inn. To the small town of *Villa Soriano* (formerly **Santo Domingo de Soriano**), first town to be founded in Uruguay, to see a fine colonial church and the old Casa de los Marfetan. It also has a river port, fishing, beaches and many orange trees. Difficult to do this trip easily in one day. 70 km inland from Mercedes is La Palmar, hydro-electric power station and tourist complex with motels, camping sites, fishing and sports facilities.

Route 2 continues westwards (34 km) to **Fray Bentos** (pop 22,000), a port on the Río Uruguay, 193 km above Buenos Aires, where in 1865 the Liebig company built its first factory producing meat extract. The original plant, much extended and known as El Anglo, has been restored as a museum (Museo de la Revolución Industrial, open holidays and weekends). Nearby in the Barrio El Anglo, the workers' and manager's housing can be seen. There are beaches to the NE and SW and also at Las Cañas, 8 km S (where there is a tourist complex including motels, T 1611, D, campsite, sports facilities and services). Nine km upriver from the town is the San Martín International Bridge, the most popular overland route with Argentina, toll US$2.10 per car (tourist office). All customs formalities (including the Argentine) are on the Uruguayan side. Bicycles are not allowed to cross, but officials will give you a lift if there is no other traffic. Argentine Consulate in Fray Bentos at Sarandí 3195.

Hotels A2 *Gran Hotel Fray Bentos*, Paraguay y Zorilla, T 2358, overlooking river, casino; **A1** *Plaza*, 18 de Julio y 25, T 2363, clean, comfortable. **E** *Colonial*, 25 de Mayo 3293, T 2260. **Camping** at the *Club Remeros*, near the river and at Colegio Laureles, 1 km from centre.

Restaurants *Enramada*, España y 25 de Agosto, the best; several cafés and pizzerias on 18 de Julio near Plaza Constitución.

Exchange Cambio Fagalde, Plaza Constitución, open Mon-Fri 0800-1900, Sat 0800-1230.

Buses Bus station, 18 de Julio y Blanes, with tourist office, but buses also leave from bus company offices around Plaza Constitución. To/from **Montevideo**, ETA, 4½ hrs, 6 a day, US$7.25; to **Mercedes**, ETA, frequent, ½ hr; to **Paysandú**, US$3.75, to **Gualeguaychú** (Argentina), ETA, 4 a day, 2 on Sun 1 hr, US$3.75.

Paysandú, on the E bank of the Río Uruguay, 122 km N of Fray Bentos along Route 24; and 480 along Route 3 from Montevideo via Trinidad, has a population of about 100,000. Temperatures in summer can rise as high as 42°C. There is a golf club, and a rowing club which holds regattas. The cathedral is 19th century; the attached Salesian college has an interesting museum, opens 1700. The cemetery on the outskirts is worth a look. There is an Alliance Française, T 0722-3986, 19 de Abril 1024. The José Artigas international bridge connects with Colón, Argentina (toll US$2 per car), about 8 km away. Airport with Aviasur flights to Montevideo (US$80 return; Pluna, Florida 1249, T 3071). Local fiesta during Holy Week (book hotels in advance).

Museums Museo de la Tradición, N of town at the Balneario Municipal, gaucho articles, worth a visit; **Museo Histórico**, Zorilla y Sarandí; **Museo Salesiano**, 18 de Julio y Montecaseros.

Hotels A2 *Gran Hotel Paysandú*, 18 de Julio y 19 de Abril, T 3400, a/c, with breakfast, best; **L3** *Lobato*, Leandro Gómez 1415, T 2241, with breakfast, good; **C** *Rafaela*, 18 de Julio 1181, T 5053, large rooms, modern and friendly, electric showers, no food but surrounded by cafés; **A2** *Concordia*, 18 de Julio 984, T 2417, clean; **D** *Victoria*, 18 de Julio 979, T 4320, highly rec, cheapest, very friendly and helpful.

Youth Hostel Liga Deportiva de Fútbol, Baltasar Brum 872, T 4247, US$1 pp, neither clean nor well-maintained. Cabins for 5 or more people.

Camping Balneario Municipal, 2 km N of centre, by the river, no facilities. Also at the Parque Sacra, and at Parque Municipal, S of centre, some facilities.

Restaurant *Artemio*, Plaza de Constitución, 18 de Julio, "best food in town"; *Parrillada de Asturias*, Pereda, good and cheap. *Don Diego*, 19 de Abril 917, serves cheap *parrillada*, good value. *Los Tres Pinos*, Av España, *parrillada*, very good.

Exchange Cambio Fagalde, 18 de Julio 1004. There is another *cambio* next door, both change TCs. Also **Banco de la República** and others on 18 de Julio.

Consulates Argentina, Leandro Gómez 1034, T 2253; Brazil, Dr LA de Herrera 932, T 2723.

Travel Agency Viñar Turismo, Artigas 1163, helpful.

Tourist Office Plaza de Constitución, 18 de Julio 1226; also at the International Bridge.

Bus terminal at Montecaseros y Artigas. To/from **Montevideo**, US$10, 5-6 hrs, many buses. Lines include Agencia Central, Sabelín, Núñez and Copay. To **Salto** US$3.75, 10 buses a day. To **Paso de los Toros** 1430 (return 0430), US$5, or by Alonso bus to **Guichón** at 0600, 1100, 1430 and change. To **Colonia** by Chadre, 1700, 6 hrs, US$6. To **Colón** (Argentina), 3 a day, US$1.50, 3/4 hr.

Excursions To the waterfalls of the Río Queguay, 25 km to the N; the *Termas del Guaviyú* thermal springs 50 km N (1½ h by bus, US$2, 4 a day) with four pools, restaurant, motel accommodation and excellent cheap camping facilities, entrance to springs US$0.50, and to the *Meseta de Artigas*, 90 km N of Paysandú, 13 km off the highway to Salto. The Meseta, where General Artigas lived (statue), is 45m above the Uruguay river, which here narrows and forms whirlpools at the rapids of El Hervidero. A terrace commands a fine view, but the rapids are not visible from the Meseta. The statue, with the general's head topping a tall shaft, is very original. There are pleasant, somewhat primitive, chalets available from Erwin Frey, 90 Estación Chapieny, Depto Paysandú. Early booking recommended. Bus to Km 462 on Paysandú-Salto road.

Tourism Farm, La Calera, near Guichón (T Montevideo 904873, F 923177, Mara Morán, Colonia 881, piso 10), 20 luxurious suites with fireplace, dining room with home made food, swimming pool, riding, rodeo, conference facilities (1995 pp rate US$80/day in a double room), highly rec, transport from Paso de los Toros.

Salto (pop 80,000), 120 km by paved road N of Paysandú, is a centre for cultivating and processing oranges and other citrus fruit. See the beautiful but run down Parque Solari (on Ruta Gral Artigas, NE of the centre); the Parque Harriague (S of the centre) with an open air theatre and a well-kept zoo (closed Mon, US$0.15—7 blocks from centre, feeding time 1400-1500); the fine-arts museum in the French style mansion of a rich *estanciero*, Uruguay 1067, opens at 1500, well worth a visit. Other museums are the Natural History Museum at Zorrilla de San Martín y Brasil, and Technology in the old Mercado Central (same street intersection). The Farmacia Fénix, "la más antigua de Salto", over 100 years old, is next to the Club Uruguay, Calle Uruguay. North of the town, at the Salto Grande dam, there is an international bridge to Concordia, Argentina. Ferries still run from the port at the top of Calle Brasil (bus station close by), 2 companies, 7 a day, US$0.75 one way. Sometimes the river is low enough to walk across.

Festival Shrove Tuesday carnival.

Hotels **A3** *Gran Hotel Salto*, 25 de Agosta 5, T 4333, with breakfast, best, a/c, rec, good restaurant, reasonably priced; **A3** *Los Cedros*, Uruguay 657 (T 3984) with breakfast and a/c; **C** *Concordia*, Uruguay 749, shower, central, clean, friendly; **D** *Artigas Plaza*, Artigas 446, Plaza 18 de Julio, with bath, hot water, very clean, log fire in winter, friendly (T4824), rec but some rooms without windows; **D** *Pensión Santa Catalina*, Brasil 1633 or **D** *Pensión Las Tres Fronteras*, General Rivera 1155, cheaper, basic; **D** *Plaza*, Plaza Treinta y Tres, T 3744, near the river, simple, clean, good food. **E** *Pensión 33*, Treinta y Tres 269, basic, central; *Pensión Pocholo*, 18 de Julio, opposite hospital, basic.

Youth Hostels Club Remeros de Salto, Rambla Gutiérrez y Belén (by the river) T 0732-4361, open all year (poor); Club de Leones, Uruguay 1626, need a student to sign you in.

Camping At the Club Remeros and at several sites along the river both N and S.

Restaurants *Chef Restaurant*, Uruguay 639; *Pizzería Las Mil y Una*, Uruguay 906, popular, good atmosphere; *Club Remeros de Salto*, Uruguay, good breakfast and good value meals; *Club Bancario*, Brasil 765, lunch US$2, good.

Exchange Lloyds Bank, two agencies: Uruguay 585 and Blandengues y 8 de Octubre, open Mon-Fri 0800-1200 (cashes Amex cheques). Banco Pan de Azúcar does cash advances on Visa and Mastercard; Banco de Crédito, Mastercard only; both on Uruguay. Several exchange houses in Calle Uruguay, best rates nearest the river. Cambio Pensotti has been recommended as helpful. The *cambio* at Uruguay 800 is open until 2000, Mon-Sat.

Argentine consul Artigas 1112, T 2931.

Anglican Church Calle República de Argentina, close to Calle Uruguay.

Post Office Treinta y Tres y Artigas.

Tourist Office Calle Uruguay 1052, T 4096, free map.

Air Service Aviasur flights to/from the capital, US$80 return. Pluna, Uruguay 657, T 2724. Bus to airport, US$2.

Bus to/from **Montevideo**, 7½ hrs, 4 a day, US$16, TTN on Ascencio, between Artigas and Uruguay, good service; to Termas del Arapey, 2 hrs, daily, US$4.25. Paysandú US$3.75, 10 a day, US$2. To **Rivera**, US$10. To **Colonia** by Chadre, 0555, 8 hrs, US$15. To **Concordia**, US$3, 1½ hrs, 2 a day except Sunday. To **Puerto Iguazú**, 12 hrs, US$44.

Excursions By launch to the Salto Chico beach, fishing, camping; to Salto Grande, where a ranch-style guest house for anglers is run by the Tourist Commission. Nearby is the resort **B** *Hotel Horacio Quiroga*, T (0732) 7397, sports facilities, staffed by nearby catering school. The most popular tourist site in the area is the large *Salto Grande* dam and hydroelectric plant 20 km from Salto, built jointly by Argentina and Uruguay; a 2-hr free tour can be arranged with the CTM (office on corner of *Hotel Gran Salto*). A road runs along the top of the dam to Argentina. Medicinal springs at Fuente Salto, 6 km N of the city. Ten km S of Salto, reached by bus No 4 every 30 mins from Calle Artigas (US$0.15) is *Termas del Daymán*, beautifully laid out with 8 swimming pools (entrance US$0.35, towel US$0.50, locker US$0.10; it is cheaper to buy combined bus/entrance ticket in Salto). 3 hotels. **Youth Hostel** on Route 3, Km 490, T 0732-4361 (open all year, book well in advance during holiday season), restaurant, souvenir shop, campsite (no electricity or services).

The road to *Termas del Arapey* branches off the partially paved Route 3 to Bella Unión, at 61 km N of Salto, and then runs 35 km first E and then S. Pampa birds, rheas and metre-long lizards much in evidence. Termas del Arapey is on the Arapey river S of Isla Cabellos (Baltazar Brum). The waters at these famous thermal baths (five pools) contain bicarbonated salts, calcium and magnesium. There is a hotel with pool (**B** *Hotel Termas del Arapey*), 2 motels, both C (very small bungalows with kitchens, no sheets provided), a nice swimming pool, a very simple *parador* (meals only) and a good restaurant. Book ahead at tourist offices in Salto or Montevideo. Camping US$2 pp, good facilities (beware of theft at campsite and take food as local markets very expensive).

Route 3 runs N to the little town of *Bella Unión* (pop 12,000), on the Río Cuaraim, 144 km N of Salto (campsite in the Parque Fructuoso Rivera, insect repellent needed), near the Brazilian frontier which is crossed by the Barra del Cuaraim bridge. Brazilian consul at Lirio Moraes 62, T 54. (If entering from Brazil by car take plenty of fuel as there are few service stations on the roads.)

From near Bella Unión Route 30 runs E to *Artigas* (pop 34,000), a frontier town in a cattle raising and agricultural area (excellent swimming upstream from the bridge). The town is known for its good quality amethysts. There is a bridge across the Río Cuaraim to the Brazilian town of Quaraí opposite. Brazilian Consul at Lecueder 432, T 2504.

Accommodation L3 *Hotel Municipal*, Dr LA de Herrera y Lecueder, T 3832; Ramón Carrea's hotel, **D**, Lavalleja 466, T 4666/2736, clean, friendly, with bath, TV and fridge. *Pensión Hawaii*, basic but clean.

Camping at Paseo 7 de Septiembre (by river), US$0.25 pp a day, or at Agua Corriente—chance of camping at the yacht club on the river. **Youth Hostel** Club Deportivo Artigas, Pte Berreta and LA de Herrera, 4 km from city, T 0642-3015, open all year, US$1 in communal room, restaurant, closes early.

Restaurants *Maricarmen*, Calle Lecueder 302, *Municipal*, Lecueder y Berreta; *Café La Bohemia*, Parada 86, cheap, filling, live music in pm.

Bus service to **Salto**, 225 km, Oribe 279, US$5.50. **Airport** at Bella Unión (Tamu to Montevideo US$25); Pluna, Garzón y Baldomir, T 2545.

INFORMATION FOR VISITORS

Before you go

Entry requirements

● **Documents**

A passport is necessary for entry except for nationals of other American countries, who can get in with national identity documents. Visas are not required for a stay of less than 3 months by nationals of Argentina, Austria, Belgium, Belize, Bolivia, Brazil, Colombia, Costa Rica, Chile, Denmark, Dominican Republic, Ecuador, Finland, France, Greece, Guatemala, Germany, Honduras, Hungary, Italy, Israel, Iceland, Republic of Ireland, Japan, Luxembourg, Liechtenstein, Malaysia, Malta, Mexico, Netherlands, Nicaragua, Norway, Panama, Paraguay, Peru, Poland, Portugal, Slovenia, Spain, Sweden, Switzerland, Seychelles, UK, USA. Visas are required for Australians and New Zealanders, for example, US$30, and you need to show a ticket out of Uruguay. Tourist cards (obligatory for all tourists, obtainable on entry) are valid for 3 months, extendable for a similar period. For extensions (small fee) go to Migraciones office, Calle Misiones 1513, T 960471/961094.

The Ministry of Tourism sells a 'tarjeta turística' at points of entry, US$20 (blue), US$26 (red). Both cover medical and dental assistance, free transport back to country of origin in case of sickness/accident, legal assistance, shopping discounts; the red card also covers car insurance.

● **Tourist information**

The Comisión Nacional de Turismo information office, in the new Tres Cruces bus terminal, Montevideo, issues tourist literature. It has built a number of good guest houses at the various resorts and gives information about them at the Information Office. The local papers publish 'what's on' columns on Friday evenings and on Saturdays. On the whole, tourist offices are often closed and, when open, offer very limited information. See also Montevideo, **Information**.

● **Maps**

Automóvil Club del Uruguay, Av Libertador General Lavalleja 1532, Montevideo, T 984710, publishes road maps of the city and the country at large, and so do Esso and Ancap at about US$2 each. Official maps are issued by Instituto Geográfico Militar, Abreu y 8 de Octubre, open 0800-1230, T 816868.

When to go

● **Best time to visit**

Most tourists visit during the summer (Dec-mid Mar). Business visits can be paid throughout the year, but it is best to avoid the tourist months.

Health

Milk and tap water can be drunk and fresh salads eaten fairly freely throughout the country. Medical services are reported to be expensive. Emergency ambulance and care is provided by UCM and SUAT, US$14/month. The British Hospital in Montevideo is rec.

Money

● **Currency**

From 1 March 1993 a new currency was introduced, the peso uruguayo, equivalent to 1,000 nuevos pesos. Peso uruguayo bank notes issued are for 50, 100, 200 (do not confuse with old 2,000 notes, which are now worth 2 pesos), 500 (don't confuse with 50), 1,000, 5,000 and 10,000 pesos uruguayos. Any amount of currency can be taken in or out.

● **Cost of living**

Uruguay is expensive, not as expensive as Argentina. Prices vary considerably between summer and winter, Punta del Este being particularly the most expensive summer resort in Latin America. Some Argentines find that generally prices and quality of clothing, for instance, are better in Montevideo than Buenos Aires.

● **Exchange**

Rates change frequently because of the floating exchange rate and inflation differentials against the US dollar; see the 'Exchange Rates' table near end of book. Most banks and exchange houses (*casas de cambio*) charge 2-2½% commission for changing US$ TCs to US$ cash. Those banks which give US$ cash against a credit card are given in the text. Dollars cash can be purchased when leaving the country. Exchanges from Brazilian and Argentine currency receive much worse rates than straightforward deals between dollars and pesos. US$ notes are widely accepted.

● **Credit cards**

Argencard is a member of the Mastercard organization, so one may use Mastercard at outlets displaying their sign. Many shopkeepers are unaware of this but a phone call will confirm it. Also American Express, Diners Club and Visa. Most hotels outside Montevideo do not accept credit cards. There is a 10% charge on the use of credit cards.

Getting there

By Air

● **From Europe**

Direct flights by Pluna (Madrid), Iberia (Barcelona and Madrid), Air France (Paris) and KLM (Amsterdam). Flying by other carriers, a change must be made at Rio or Buenos Aires.

● **From North America**

United Airlines from New York via Buenos Aires, 5 times a week.

To Uruguay from South America

● **From Argentina**

Ferry services (Montevideo and Colonia to Buenos Aires), hydrofoil services (Colonia to Buenos Aires) and launch services (Carmelo to Tigre) are given in the text. Aerolíneas Argentinas and Pluna have several flights a day between Aeroparque in Buenos Aires and Carrasco Airport, flights can be very full, especially in high season. Service intensified during holiday period. Also flights to Punta del Este from Buenos Aires. Lapa has a bus/plane service via Colonia to Buenos Aires; US$30 single. Aero Regionales flies all 3 routes, too. Varig and Iberia connect Carrasco with the Buenos Aires international airport at Ezeiza. Buses run across the Paysandú and Fray Bentos bridges. Direct bus between Buenos Aires and Montevideo via Fray Bentos takes about 10 hrs. Ferries cross the Río Uruguay between Salto and Concordia.

● **From Bolivia**

LAB twice a week from Santa Cruz.

● **From Brazil**

Direct connection between Brazil and Uruguay by all the international airlines landing at Montevideo. Pluna flies 3 times a week from Rio de Janeiro to Montevideo direct and twice via São Paulo. Varig has a daily direct flight from Rio via Porto Alegre and daily flight from Rio via São Paulo. Pluna also flies from São Paulo direct (3 times) and via Porto Alegre (twice a week). Pluna flies Florianópolis-Montevideo once a week. By road: the Pan-American Highway runs 2,880 km from Rio de Janeiro to Montevideo and on to Colonia. It is poorly surfaced in parts. There are several bus services.

See under Brazil, **How to get to Brazil: By Air**, for the Mercosur airpass.

● **From Chile**

Pluna, LanChile and Ladeco all three times a week to Santiago.

● **From Paraguay**

Twice a week by Pluna, once by Lapsa and LAB. Five buses a week between Asunción and Montevideo.

Customs

● **Duty free allowance**

Duties are not usually charged on a reasonable quantity of goods (such as tobacco and spirits), brought in obviously for the traveller's own use: 400 cigarettes or 50 cigars or 250 grammes of tobacco are admitted duty-free; so are 2 litres of alcoholic drink, 3 little bottles of perfume and gifts up to the value of US$5.

When you arrive

● **Hours of business**

Most department stores generally are open 0900 to 1200 (or 1230), 1400 (or 1430) to 1900, but 0900 to 1230 on Sat. Business houses vary but most work from 0830 to 1200, 1430 to 1830 or 1900, according to whether they open on Sat. Banking hours are

1300 to 1700 in Montevideo; there are special summer hours (1 Dec-15 March) in Montevideo (1330-1730), in the interior (0800-1200) and in Punta del Este, Maldonado and other resorts (1600-2000); banks are closed on Sat. Government departments, mid-March to mid-November, 1300 to 1830 from Mon to Fri; rest of the year, 0700 to 1230 (not Sat).

● **Safety**
Personal security offers few problems in Uruguay to travellers who are reasonably prudent.

● **Tipping**
Normally all hotel and restaurant bills include a percentage service charge plus 22% value-added tax, but an additional small tip is expected. In other cases give 10% of the total bill. Porters at the airport expect about US$1 per piece of luggage; although there is an official rate of tips for porters at seaports, the actual charges are mostly higher. Taxi drivers are tipped 10% of the fare. Tips at cafés are about 10%. Cinema ushers get a small tip, as do cloakroom attendants and hairdressers (10%-15%).

● **Voltage**
220 volts 50 cycles AC.

● **Weights and measures**
Metric units alone are legal. Odd fact: the timber trade still uses inches for the cross section of lengths of timber.

On departure

● **Airport tax**
Airport tax of US$6 on all air travellers leaving Uruguay for Buenos Aires; US$10 for Asunción, US$12 for all other countries, US$0.50 on internal flights, and a tax of 3% on all tickets issued and paid for in Uruguay.

Where to stay

● **Hotels**
Hotel accommodation can be very scarce in summer: reserve in advance. High season is 15 Dec-28 Feb; prices are 25% lower 1 Mar-30 April, 1 Oct-15 Dec; 50% lower 1 May-30 Sept. Room sharing is often unavoidable. For accommodation on farms (*Estancias de Turismo*) contact the Tourist Office in Montevideo, in addition to those mentioned in the text, **see p 1320** and **1320**. There is also *Los Macachines*, which offers daily visits, T 619182, Anilú Bruce.

● **Camping**
Lots of sites. Most towns have municipal sites (quality varies). Many sites along the Ruta Interbalnearia, but most of these close off season. The Tourist Office in Plaza Fabini issues a good guide to campsites and youth hostels; see references in main text. *El País* newspaper publishes a *Guía de turismo juvenil y tiempro libre* to complement the Instituto Nacional de la Juventud's Programa de Turismo Juvenil: aimed at backpackers, it gives useful information on camping and travelling cheaply in Uruguay.

● **Youth hostels**
Asociación de Alberguistas del Uruguay, Calle Pablo de María 1583 (open 1300-1900), Montevideo (T 404245) operates hostels (IYHA members only) at Montevideo (Canelones 935), Artigas, Paysandú, Piriápolis, Salto, La Paloma, Colonia Suiza, Villa Serrana (near Minas), Barra de Valizas (between La Pedrera and Aguas Dulces), Durazno and Río Branco. A 10% rebate is available on Lapa plane tickets between Colonia and Buenos Aires, and rebates have also been reported (10-20%) for bus fares and hotel prices.

Food and drink

Food

Beef is eaten at almost all meals. The majority of restaurants are *parrilladas* (grills) where the staple is beef. *Asado* (barbecued beef) is popular; the main cuts are *asado de tira* (ribs); *pulpa* (no bones), *lomo* (fillet steak) and entrecote. To get a lean piece of *asado*, ask for *asado flaco*. *Costilla* (chop) and *milanesa* (veal cutlet) are also popular; usually eaten with mixed salad or chips. *Chivitos* are Uruguayan steak burgers; *chivitos canadienses* are sandwiches filled with slices of meat, lettuce, tomato, egg, etc (normally over US$2 – very filling). Two other good local dishes are *puchero* (beef with vegetables, bacon, beans and sausages) and the local varieties of pizza, fast becoming a staple. Other specialities are barbecued pork, grilled chicken in wine, *cazuela* (or stew) usually with *mondongo* (tripe) or sea foods (eg squid, shark – *cazón*, mussels – *mejillones*). The sausages are very good and spicy (*chorizos*, *morcillas*, *salchichas*). *Morcilla dulce*, a sweet black sausage, made from blood, orange peel and walnuts, has been highly praised; so has the *morcilla salada*, which is savoury. For snacks, *media lunas mixtas* are a type of croissant filled with ham and cheese, either hot or cold; toasted sandwiches are readily available; *panchos* are hot dogs, *húngaros* are spicy sausage hot dogs. *Preparación* is a selection of crisps, nuts, vol-au-vent, etc. An excellent dessert is *chajá*, from Paysandú, a type of sponge-cake ball with cream and jam inside, also with peaches – very sweet; others are *massini* (a cream sponge) and the common lemon pie. Pastries are very good indeed, and crystallized egg-yolks, known as *yemas*, are popular sweets. Ice cream is excellent everywhere.

The dinner hour is usually from 2000 to 0100. Note that restaurants generally charge *cubierto* (bread), which ranges from US$0.30 to US$1 in Punta del Este.

Drink

The local wines are very varied, not only from bodega to bodega, but also from vintage to vintage. **NB** 'Del museo' indicates the bodega's vintage reserve. The beers are good. Imported drinks are freely available in Montevideo, eg whisky, US$30-70 (US$18-30 for local brands) and Chilean wines. *Mate* is a favourite drink between meal hours. The local spirits are *caña* and *grappa*; some find the locally-made whisky and gin acceptable. In the Mercado del Puerto, Montevideo, a *medio medio* is half still white wine, half sparkling white (a must!) Elsewhere a *medio medio* is half *caña* and half whisky). *Espillinar* is a cross between whisky and rum. Try the *clérico*, a tasty mixture of wine, fruit juices and fruits. Coffee is good: a *cortado* is a strong, white coffee, *café con leche* is milk with a little coffee. Milk is available, in plastic sacs.

Getting around

Air transport

Internal flights are very cheap with Pluna and Aviasur (addresses under Montevideo). Provincial airports are given in the text.

Land transport

● **Train**
The only passenger services in operation in 1995 were Tacuarembó-Rivera and commuter services Montevideo – 25 de Agosto (in Florida department). Restoration of the latter, a British line, is hoped for, but unlikely. There are plans to resume services to Minas and Río Branco (on the Brazilian border).

● **Road**
There are 45,000 km of roads, 80% of them paved or all-weather. The Comisión Nacional de Turismo will help to plan itineraries by car.

● **Bus**
Bus services are given in the text. Several companies operate within the country and to neighbouring countries.

● **Motoring**
Vehicles do not stop, nor is there a right of way, at uncontrolled intersections. Driving in Montevideo has become very dangerous; take care. Outside Montevideo there is little traffic and few filling stations (many close at weekends). Care is needed at night since vehicle lights do not always work. There are many ancient cars (1920s and 1930s models are called *cachilas* and skilled mechanics keep them on the road). Insurance is not required by law. Uruguay is said to be much better than Argentina or Brazil to ship a car to, but vehicles are admitted for 6 months only, with the possibility of a further 3 months extension. Gasoline prices are US$1/litre *super*, US$0.85/litre *común*; diesel is US$0.40/litre. Automóvil Club del Uruguay has a fuel and service station for its members only at Yí y Colonia, Montevideo, T 921691 (head office is Av Libertador General Lavalleja 1532, T 924792). Reciprocity with foreign automobile clubs is available all year round, members no longer have to pay for affiliation.

Car spares are expensive. The area around Galicia and Yí in Montevideo is rec for new parts. Warnes, Minas y Cerro Largo, have been rec for second-hand parts. Land-Rover garage in Montevideo at Cuareim 2082, near old railway station.

● **Hitchhiking**
Hitchhiking is not easy following attacks on drivers who have given lifts.

Communications

● **Newspapers**
There are 4 Montevideo morning newspapers: *El País*, *El Observador*, *La República* and *La Mañana*, and *El Diario* and *Ultimas Noticias* which come out in the evening. *Búsqueda* is published weekly. The town of Paysandú has the *Telégrafo*. At about 1000 the main Buenos Aires papers, including the *Buenos Aires Herald*, can be had in Montevideo.

● **Postal services**
Postal services are very unreliable; all items should be registered and sent by air mail to avoid delay (probably better to go direct to airport, avoiding chaos of the sorting office). Rates US$0.59 for postcard, US$1 for a letter to Europe; US$8 by air for up to 500 g, US$10 for 500-1,000 g, US$21 up to 3 kg; by sea US$7 for 1 kg, US$11 for 3 kg (but best not to send parcels at all – if they do arrive they will probably have been opened). Postcard to USA US$0.58, letter US$1; registered mail costs US$2. Courier services are used increasingly: to Europe US$30-40, USA US$25,

South Africa US$35, Middle East US$45, Buenos Aires US$12.

● **Radio**
There are 35 radio stations (8 private FM) in Montevideo and 65 in the rest of the country.

● **Telephone services**
Provided by Antel (see under Montevideo). Direct dialling to any country abroad is straightforward. Collect calls available to most countries (collect calls are the cheapest way of phoning USA and Canada). With competition from fax, and new equipment, phone prices have fallen, eg 3 mins to USA or Europe on Sat 1200 costs US$5. Phone calls are cheaper by 25% between 2200 and 0700. Fax from Antel, first sheet costs same rate as a minute's phone call to USA, Europe and Australia.

● **Television**
Of the 20 colour-TV stations, 4 transmit from Montevideo (channel 12 is the most popular).

Sport

The beach is more popular than the water. Uruguay has three important yacht clubs, the Uruguayo, the Nautilus and the Punta del Este. Fishing. Association football is played intensively. Rugby football is also played, and there is an annual championship.

Holidays and festivals

● **Holidays**
1 Jan, 6 Jan; Carnival (see below); Easter week; 19 April; 1, 18 May; 19 June; 18 July; 25 Aug; 12 Oct; 2 Nov; 25 Dec. (8 Dec is a religious holiday which also marks the official start of the summer holiday.)

Business comes to a standstill also during Holy Week, which coincides with La Semana Criolla (horse-breaking, stunt riding by cowboys, dances and song, many Argentine visitors). Department stores close only from Good Fri. Banks and offices close Thur-Sun.

Easter Mon is not a holiday.

● **Festivals**
Carnival week is officially the Mon and Tues immediately preceding Ash Wednesday, but a great many firms close for the whole of the week.

Further reading

British business travellers are strongly advised to read 'Hints to Exporters: Uruguay', obtainable from the DTI Export Publications, PO Box 55, Stratford-upon-Avon, Warwickshire, CV37 9GE.

Acknowledgements

We should like to thank Rachel Rogers for updating this chapter. We are also extremely grateful to Sonya Ayling of Montevideo and Alan Murphy (London) for valuable assistance. Thanks are also due to the following travellers: Daniel Aeberhard (Slough, UK) an excellent contribution, Jack Beeching (Menton, France), Bernard Cloutier (Montreal, Canada), Mary Crow (Ft Collins, USA), Kathrin and Henning Dictus (Neuwied, Germany), Jae and Gerry Duffy (Elizabeth, USA), Loukas Grafakos (Papagou, Greece), Patrick J Paludan (Valby) and Erik Hassenkamm (Valby and Skanderberg, Denmark), May-Britt Koopman (Triesen, Switzerland), Kato and Mark Kostrzewa (Mountain View, USA), Oliver Meiser (Pfullingen, Germany) a very detailed contribution Hans-Peter Neusch (Stuttgart, Germany), Holly O'Callagnan (Durazno, Uruguay), Christine A Sarkis (London, UK), Ken Simons (London, UK), J R Stourton (Cirencester, UK), S Nielsen and Hellmuth-Chr Stuven (Copenhagen, Denmark), M James Snyder (Radlett, UK.), Arnaud Troost and Fenna den Hartog (Rotterdam, The Netherlands), Dr Volker Weinmann (Blumenau, Brazil), Rogier Wiercx (Houten, The Netherlands), and P Lamartine Yates (Cuvat, France).

VENEZUELA

INTRODUCTION

WHEN the Spaniards landed in Venezuela in 1498, in the course of Columbus' third voyage, they found a poor country sparsely populated by Indians who had created no distinctive culture. Four hundred years later it was still poor, almost exclusively agrarian, exporting little, importing less. The miracle year which changed all that was 1914, when oil was discovered near Maracaibo. Today, Venezuela is one of the largest producers and exporters of oil in the world. The oil revenues have been used to rebuild Caracas and Maracaibo and other cities, and to create the best network of roads on the continent. In view of recent new discoveries and the cutback of production, at the present rate of extraction oil reserves will last for at least 40 years. Vast investments have been poured into state industry and agrarian reform and into tackling the problems of education, housing and unemployment.

Venezuela has 2,800 km of coastline on the Caribbean Sea, and 72 islands. To the E is Guyana, to the S Brazil, and to the W Colombia. It was given its name—"Little Venice"—by the Spanish navigators, who saw in the Indian pile dwellings on the Lago de Maracaibo a dim reminder of the buildings along Venetian waterways.

The country falls into four very different regions: the Venezuelan Highlands to the W and along the coast; the Maracaibo Lowlands around the fresh water lake of Maracaibo; the vast central plain of the Llanos of the Orinoco; and the Guayana

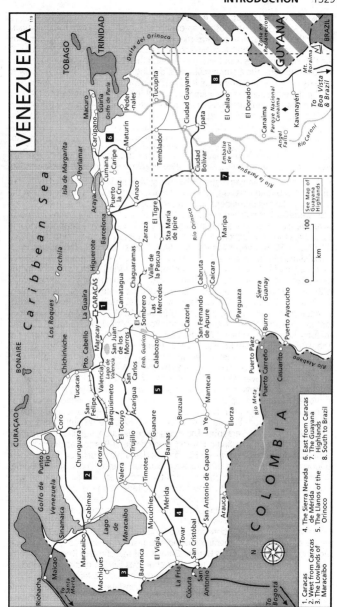

VENEXUELA

TOBAGO

TRINIDAD

BRAZIL

GUYANA

Caribbean Sea

BONAIRE

CURAÇAO

COLOMBIA

1. Caracas
2. West from Caracas
3. The Lowlands of Maracaibo
4. The Sierra Nevada de Mérida
5. The Llanos of the Orinoco
6. East from Caracas
7. The Guayana Highlands
8. South to Brazil

See Map of Guayana Highlands

0   100
km

Highlands, which take up over half the country.

The Venezuelan Highlands are an offshoot of the Andes. From the Colombian border they trend, at first, towards the NE to enfold the Maracaibo Lowlands. This section is known as the Sierra Nevada de Mérida. Beyond they broaden out into the Segovia Highlands N of Barquisimeto, and then turn E in parallel ridges along the coast to form the Central Highlands, dipping into the Caribbean Sea only to rise again into the N-Eastern Highlands of the peninsulas of Paria and Araya.

The general outline of each area will reveal that natural obstacles to farming, cattle breeding, and communications are formidable. It explains why the country was poverty-stricken for so long.

Climate is tropical, with little change between season and season. Temperature is a matter of altitude. Mean annual temperatures are given in the text. At Caracas it is 20°C, but during the dry season (Dec to Apr), there is a great difference between day and night temperatures, and during the whole year there is a burst of heat around mid-day. Rainfall in mm: Caracas, 762; Maracaibo, 573; Barcelona, 660; Mérida, 1,295; Amazonas and parts of Barinas state 2,540.

History At the beginning of the 16th century, Venezuela was inhabited by various tribes of Caribs and Arawaks, who could make no effective resistance against the Spaniards. The first permanent Spanish settlement was at Cumaná, in 1520. Soon afterwards settlers reached Coro, at the foot of the Paraguaná Peninsula. Indian slaves were used to mine and pan for gold, but the results were disappointing and the settlers turned to agriculture, forming settlements at Barquisimeto in 1552, at Valencia in 1555, and at Caracas in 1567. It was not until after a century of consolidation in these areas that they began to occupy the rest of the country, intermarrying freely with the Indians and later introducing black slaves to work the sugar plantations. Centralized colonial control from Spain was as irksome here as in the rest of Latin America: three risings reflecting these discontents took place in 1749, 1775 and 1797, and there were two abortive attempts by Francisco Miranda to achieve independence in 1806 and 1811. After Miranda had been captured, the movement was led by Simón Bolívar, a *criollo* with a touch of Indian ancestry, born in Caracas in 1783. He met with mixed success until his capture of Angostura, now Ciudad Bolívar, in 1817. There he was joined by a contingent of experienced Peninsular veterans recruited in London. At their head, together with the horsemen of the *llanos* commanded by Gen José Antonio Páez, he undertook a dramatic march over the Andes in 1819 to win the battle of Boyacá and capture Bogotá. Three months later, the revolutionary congress at Angostura—with most of Venezuela still in Spanish hands— declared the independence of Gran Colombia, a union of what is now Ecuador, Colombia, Venezuela, and Panama. Bolívar returned from Bogotá, and on 24 June 1821, the revolutionaries routed the Spanish forces at Carabobo. There was some desultory fighting for two more years, but the last of the Spanish forces surrendered at Puerto Cabello in 1823.

Before Bolívar's death in 1830 Páez declared Venezuela an independent republic. Other presidents of note were Guzmán Blanco, Juan Vicente Gómez (1909-1935), a brutal but efficient dictator, and Isaías Medina Angarita, who introduced the oil laws. There was much material progress under the 6-year dictatorship of Gen Marcos Pérez Jiménez (1952-58), but his Gómez-like methods led to his overthrow in Jan 1958. A stable democracy has been created since, with regular presidential elections every five years. Sr Carlos Andrés Pérez of the centre-left Democratic Action party (AD) took office in 1974, presiding over a period of rapid development following the first great oil-price rise, and was succeeded in 1979 by Sr Luis Herrera Campins of the Christian Democratic party, Copei. Dr Jaime Lusinchi of Democratic Action was elected president in 1983, to be followed by Carlos Andrés Pérez, who began his second term in 1989.

Pérez' second term was marked by increasing instability. Many protests, some violent, were launched against the economic adjustment programme and growing levels of poverty. In 1992 there were two unsuccessful coup attempts by military officers. In state gubernatorial elections in Dec 1992, AD fared badly; in two states it refused to accept the defeat of its candidates. Among reforms designed to root out corruption, the Supreme Court and Central Bank were given greater independence. Both bodies were instrumental in the decision that Pérez himself be tried on corruption charges in 1993. The president was suspended from office, then arrested, until the case came to court in Nov 1994. An interim president, Senator Ramón José Velázquez, took office until the presidential elections of Dec 1993, in which Rafael Caldera, now standing as an independent, was re-elected to office. The coalition which supported him did not win a majority in Congress, so Caldera had to forge alliances with all parties to see his policies through. Among his stated priorities were an improvement in social conditions, tax reform, greater government and private sector efficiency and the control of inflation. Many of these aims had to be postponed in favour of solving an economic and financial crisis in 1994 (see below, **The Economy**). Caldera resorted to the assumption of emergency powers and set up special advisory bodies which were not accountable to central government. The imposition of such non-institutional powers undermined foreign confidence.

The People A large number are of mixed Spanish and Indian origin. There are some pure Africans and a strong element of African descent along the coast, particularly at the ports. The arrival of 800,000 European immigrants, mostly in the 1950s, has greatly modified the racial make-up in Venezuela. One in 6 of all Venezuelans is foreign born.

About 1% of the population (150,000) is Indian. Among the best-known are the Yanomami, who live in Amazonas, and the Bari in the Sierra de Perijá (on the NW border with Colombia). An Indian Reserve gives the Bari effective control of their own land, but this has not prevented infringement from mining, plantation or settlers. Other groups do not have title to their territory. These groups include the Wayuu (in the Guajira), the Panare and the Piaroa.

Venezuela, despite its wealth, still faces serious social problems. Many rural dwellers have drifted to the cities; one result of this exodus is that Venezuelan farmers do not provide all the food the nation needs and imports of foodstuffs are necessary, even for items such as beans and rice.

The Economy Venezuela's economy has been dominated by oil and gas, which contribute about 17% to gdp. Oil exports have inflated foreign exchange receipts and government fiscal revenues. Oil revenues have shaped the rest of the productive sector, even though employment creation has been minimal, and inter-industry links have been relatively underdeveloped. High earnings from oil have in the past overvalued the exchange rate, which has discouraged export-based production and hindered import substitution. Non-oil industry and agriculture are now being targeted for expansion as oil's role has diminished since the early 1980s.

Venezuela has vast natural resources, and is especially rich in energy, possessing 64.5 bn barrels of proved oil reserves. Apart from proved and exploitable reserves, there are another 1.2 trillion barrels in potential reserves of very heavy oil in the as yet unexploited Orinoco belt. There are 3.65 trillion cubic metres of natural gas reserves (plus 5 trillion probable), and 500m tonnes of coal (9 bn estimated) in the provinces of Zulia and Táchira. There is believed to be a hydroelectricity potential (HEP) of 80,000 MW. The new hydroelectric generating capacity around Ciudad Guayana in the E is designed to act as the hub of economic growth. It includes the 10,300 MW Guri dam project, the second largest HEP station in the world after Itaipú, and which in July 1986 provided just over half the country's generating capacity.

Venezuela is Opec's third largest oil producer, with a capacity of 2.9m barrels a day. Oil production is concentrated in three major sedimentary basins: the Maracaibo, the eastern, and the Apure-Barinas basins. Petróleos de Venezuela (PDVSA), the state-owned oil company created out of the nationalization of oil companies in 1976, has been relatively successful in keeping its market share because of its forward-looking marketing strategy based on forming partnerships with refineries and marketing chains in Europe and the USA. In 1994, a programme to permit foreign companies to explore in Venezuela was announced.

The mining sector has been probably the most buoyant part of the economy since 1984, and is likely to continue in this vein with important mining ventures in bauxite, iron ore, gold and coal. Venezuela could become the world's leading aluminium producer by the end of the century.

Like mining, agriculture is a small sector of the economy, accounting for 4.8% of gdp. The main grain staples are maize and sorghum, while sugar and rice are also important. The main export crop is coffee, with other cash crops being cocoa and cotton.

Venezuela is Latin America's fourth largest debtor, and despite huge foreign reserves of over US$20 bn accumulated by the mid-1980s from oil wealth, the country became unable to service its external debt normally from 1982 because of a bunching of maturities. A US$21 bn debt rescheduling agreement was signed with commercial banks in 1986 but was almost immediately renegotiated, with longer repayment terms and lower interest rates, as falling oil prices that year caused unexpected foreign exchange constraints; oil revenues fell by 44% in 1986. The government avoided taking adjustment measures and chose instead to spend reserves until by end-1988 liquid foreign exchange reserves were exhausted. In 1989 the new administration turned to the IMF and World Bank for support for a comprehensive macroeconomic adjustment programme to rebuild reserves, encourage domestic savings and cut the public sector deficit. Previous policies were reversed with the freeing of interest rates and the exchange rate. A debt restructuring package was implemented in 1990 which allowed banks to choose from a menu of options including debt reduction, debt service reduction or new loans.

The initial impact of the reforms was a severe recession and gdp fell by 8.1% in 1989, accompanied by a burst of inflation and higher unemployment.

Venezuela : fact file

Geographic

Land area	912,050 sq km
forested	33.9%
pastures	20.1%
cultivated	4.4%

Demographic

Population (1994)	21,177,000
annual growth rate (1989-94)	2.3%
urban	84.6%
rural	15.4%
density	23.2 per sq km
Religious affiliation	
Roman Catholic	92.1%
Birth rate per 1,000 (1992)	27.7
	(world av 26.0)

Education and Health

Life expectancy at birth,	
male	69.8 years
female	75.8 years
Infant mortality rate	
per 1,000 live births (1992)	25.2
Physicians (1989)	1 per 576 persons
Hospital beds	1 per 382 persons
Calorie intake as %	
of FAO requirement	99%
Population age 10 and over	
with no formal schooling	9.5%
Literate males (over 15)	93.5%
Literate females (over 15)	91.1%

Economic

GNP (1992 market prices)	
	US$58,901mn
GNP per capita	US$2,900
Public external debt (1992)	
	US$25,252mn
Tourism receipts (1992)	US$432mn
Inflation (annual av 1988-93)	44.6%
Radio	1 per 2.6 persons
Television	1 per 5.6 persons
Telephone	1 per 11 persons

Employment

Population economically active (1992)	
	7,537,817
Unemployment rate	7.1%
% of labour force in	
agriculture	10.7
mining and petroleum	1.1
manufacturing	16.1
construction	9.6
Military forces	75,000

Source *Encyclopaedia Britannica*

Between 1990 and 1992, the economy rebounded, strengthened by the reforms, a higher level of investment and buoyant oil revenues. 1993-94 saw a return to recession and inflation estimated between 60 and 70%, accompanied by political instability. President Caldera initially rejected the free market policies of the previous administration, trying to steer a course between market economics and government control. In less than 6 months plans had to be reassessed in the face of a rapid decline in the value of bolívar against the dollar. Between end-1993 and 23 June 1994 it fell from Bs106=US$1 to Bs200. A fixed rate of Bs170 was subsequently imposed, with a more relaxed regime proposed for 1995. At the same time the banking sector faced severe crisis leading the government to take control temporarily of the whole system. By early 1995, the government had had to rescue 18 commercial banks. Behind the crisis was the Central Bank's strategy of holding interest rates high to prevent capital flight and to encourage investment. Recession was expected to continue in 1995, as was high inflation and unemployment at about 13%. Foreign investors showed little interest in Venezuela in 1994-95, raising doubts over the privatization programme and other means of reducing the budget deficit.

Government Venezuela is a federal republic of 22 states and a Federal District. There are two legislative houses, a Senate with 49 seats and a Chamber of Deputies with 201 seats. The current Constitution is dated 23 January 1961. Voting is compulsory for all over 18.

Education Elementary schools are free, and education is compulsory from the age of 7 to the completion of the primary grade.

National Parks Venezuela has 35 national parks and 15 smaller national monuments, some of which are mentioned in the text. A full list is published by the Instituto Nacional de Parques (Inparques), Museo de Transporte, Edificio Sur, Avenida Rómulo Gallegos, Parque del Este (opp *Restaurante Carreta*), T 284-1956, Caracas. Each park has a regional director and its own guards (*guardaparques*). Permits (free) are required to stay in the parks, although this is not usually necessary for those parks visited frequently. For further information on the National Parks system, visit the Ministerio del Ambiente y de los Recursos Naturales Renovables (MARNR), Centro Simón Bolívar, Torre Sul, piso 19, Caracas 1010, T 483-3164/1071. The book *Guía de los Parques Nacionales y Monumentos Naturales de Venezuela*, is obtainable in Audubon headquarters, 0900-1230 and 1430-1800, Las Mercedes shopping centre, Las Mercedes, Caracas in the La Cuadra sector next to the car parking area (it is difficult to find), T 913813 (and also at Librería Noctúa, Villa Mediterránea, in the Centro Plaza shopping centre). The society will plan itineraries and make reservations.

Music and Dance Venezuelan music is more homogenous than that of some of the other republics. Its highly distinctive sound is based on an instrumental combination of harp, *cuatro* (a small, four stringed guitar) and *maracas*. Many of the rhythms have a very fast, almost headlong pace to them, stimulating both to the senses and to the feet, music here being almost inseparable from dance. The recipe for Venezuelan music is a classic European/African/Amerindian mix. The country's national dance is the Joropo, a name deriving from the Arab "Xarop", meaning syrup and which originally meant a country dance. This is a dance for couples with several sequences, such as the Valseao, Zapatiao, Escobillao and Toriao. Closely related to the Joropo are the Corrido, with a ballad content, Galerón (slow for singing or fast for dancing), Pasaje (lyrical, very popular in the Llanos) and Golpe, from the State of Lara, to all of which styles the Joropo may be danced in different parts of the country. Note that the little *cuatro* is normally referred to as "guitarra", while the Spanish guitar is called the "guitarra grande". Some of the dance rhythms have been imported from abroad or are shared with neighbouring countries, such as the urban Merengue (introduced into Caracas in the 1920s), the Jota and Malagueña of Anzoátegui State, the Pasillo (shared with Colombia and Ecuador), the Polo of the Oriente and Isla Margarita and the Bambuco, found in Lara and Táchira states near the border with Colombia.

There is a wealth of dances and musical forms found in particular towns or states at religious festivities. Outstanding among these is the Tamunangue of Lara

State, danced in the second fortnight of Jun to the accompaniment of drums and small guitars and made up of seven individual dances, varying from the "Batalla", where men battle with sticks, to the "Bella", a flirtatious dance for couples. Corpus Cristi is the time to visit San Francisco de Yare in Miranda State and see the 80 or so male "Diablos" of all ages, dressed entirely in red and wearing large horned masks, who dance in the streets to the sound of their own drums and rattles. The Bailes de Tambor take place among the largely black people of the Barlovento coast during the feasts of San Juan and San Pedro and at Christmas. This is brilliant polyrhythm on huge drums (*cumacos*, *minas* and *curvetas*) held between the legs. Also in Barlovento, but in May, can be heard the Fulias, chant-and-response songs addressed to a venerated saint or cross, to the accompaniment of *cuatro*, *tambora* drum and *maracas*. Christmas is a great period for music from the Gaitas of Zulia to the ubiquitous Aguinaldos, both in Merengue rhythm, with solo verses responded to by a chorus and varied instrumental accompaniment. Notable in the eastern states are the folk theatre dances of the Pájaro Guarandol (a hunter shoots a large bird that is brought back to life), Carite (from Margarita, using a large model fish), Chiriguare (a monster that is duly despatched) and Burriquita (a hobby horse). More surprising is to find the Calipso, played on steel bands by the black inhabitants of El Callao in the Orinoco region, whose ancestors came from Trinidad and who also perform the Limbo.

Venezuelans enjoy Salsa as much as other Hispanic peoples around the Caribbean, but they are also very keen on their own music, whether rustic "folk" or urban "popular". The virtuoso harpist Juan Vicente Torrealba has performed with his group Los Torrealberos for more than three decades, usually with Mario Suárez as vocal soloist. Another famous singer is Simón Díaz. Outstanding among the folk groups who strive for authenticity are Un Solo Pueblo, Grupo Vera and Grupo Convenezuela. Choral and contrapuntal singing of native music in a more sophisticated style has also been perfected by Quinteto Contrapunto and Serenata Guayanesa.

CARACAS (1)

The capital and nearby excursions including to mountain towns, the Monte Avila National Park, beaches and Los Roques, a beautiful Caribbean atoll.

The capital, Caracas, and the cities of Valencia and Maracay are in the Central Highlands, the most important upland area in Venezuela. The mountains here rise abruptly from a lush green coast to heights of from two to three thousand metres. Caracas, lies in a small basin, a rift in the thickly forested mountains which runs some 24 km E and W.

Caracas, founded in 1567, now has a population of around 4 million (the city proper 1.3 million). It lies at 960m, but the southern parts of the city are 160m higher. Temperatures are moderate (a maximum of 32°C in July and Aug, and an occasional minimum of 9°C in Jan and Feb) and it is always cool at night.

A comparatively low pass (1,040m) in the mountains gives Caracas access by road to its port, La Guaira, and its international and domestic airports nearby at Maiquetía. The distance by a magnificently engineered road is 28 km, or 30 mins by car (toll US$0.05 when going up; going down is free). Much longer should be allowed, however, for anyone with a plane to catch, as there are often delays arising from heavy traffic.

Having engulfed villages and, at the turn of the century, suburbs, Caracas' proportionate growth since WW2 has been greater than that of any other Latin American capital. Colonial buildings have given way to modern multi-storeyed edifices, such as the Ciudad Universitaria, the twin towers of the Parque Central (containing a Ministry of Transport exhibition, open Mon-Fri 0900-1530), the Centro Simón Bolívar, and the Círculo Militar. Many visitors find the metropolis lacking in charm and character. There is no single centre, but a broad strip some 10 km from W to E, fragmented by traffic-laden arteries. Zoning is chaotic and the orderly and prestigious live side by side with the tawdry and deprived.

Starting in Catia, an industrial area in the W where both roads from La Guaira enter, Avenida Sucre goes past the 23 de Enero workers' flats to join Av Urdaneta between Palacio Miraflores and the Palacio Blanco, housing government offices. Later come the Post Office and Santa Capilla Church, looking like a wedding cake by a Parisian master pastrycook. Turn right here for Plaza Bolívar and the Capitolio Nacional (the National Congress), or carry straight on down the Av Urdaneta to San Bernardino (Museo de Arte Colonial). Here, we enter Av Andrés Bello, which passes just below the cable railway station to join Av Libertador to the Country Club and the E, or we can turn down the Av La Salle to the eastern end of Los Caobos park, with the fine mahoganies which give it its popular name. From the Plaza Venezuela intersection at the eastern end of the park, the Avenida Abraham Lincoln leads E through Sabana Grande and continues as the Avenida Francisco Miranda to Altamira, with its fine plaza and obelisk. Sabana Grande, a modern shopping, hotel and business centre, is a pedestrian mall closed to vehicular traffic: a popular place to take a stroll.

Alternatively, forking right out of Avenida Sucre and crossing the viaduct, we reach El Silencio, and thence pass through the Centro Simón Bolívar, with its twin skyscrapers, underground parking and shopping centre (with an interesting mosaic at the lowest level), and finally along the Avenida Bolívar past Nuevo Circo bullring towards Ciudad Universitaria, the Sports Stadium, the *Tamanaco Hotel* and La Casona, residence of the President. From the viaduct, we can also take Av Universidad past the Biblioteca Nacional (former University), Capitol and San Francisco church. Two corners later, we glimpse, left, Bolívar's birthplace, before continuing to the Museo de Bellas Artes and on round Los Caobos park, or by the Av Libertador, to the E.

Another W-E route is along the Avenida Boyacá from Avenida Baralt in the W to Petare in the E, connecting with the main road E to Barcelona (Route 9), which skirts the Cordillera de la Costa, including Monte Avila, and gives fine views along the length of the city. Towards the E end is a monument commemorating the battle of Boyacá, and a viaduct over the park in Los Chorros suburb.

To the SW from El Silencio the Avenida San Martín leads towards the factories of Antímano. This area can also be reached direct from Catia by the Planicie tunnel. In the SW is also the older residential section of El Paraíso.

The shady Plaza Bolívar, with its fine equestrian statue of the Liberator and pleasant colonial cathedral, is still the official centre of the city, though no longer geographically so. There are squirrels in the trees (quite tame) and sloths (harder to see) in the plaza. In fact, several centres (Plaza Bolívar, Plaza Venezuela, Sabana Grande, Chacaíto, La Floresta, Boleíta) are strung along the valley with residential areas between.

Parks Jardín Botánico, near Plaza Venezuela, entrance by Ciudad Universitaria (free), is worth a visit. There are extensive plant collections and a small area of "natural forest". Here you can see the world's largest palm tree (*Corypha Sp.*) and the Elephant Apple with its huge edible fruit. **Parque Los Caobos** is peaceful and has a cafeteria in the middle. By the entrance in Av México is the cultural centre, Ateneo de Caracas, with a theatre, art gallery, concert room, bookshop and the imposing Teresa Carreño theatre complex. **Parque Nacional del Este** (renamed the Parque Rómulo Betancourt in 1989) is a popular place to relax, especially at weekends, entrance US$0.15, closed Mon, otherwise opens 0530 for joggers,

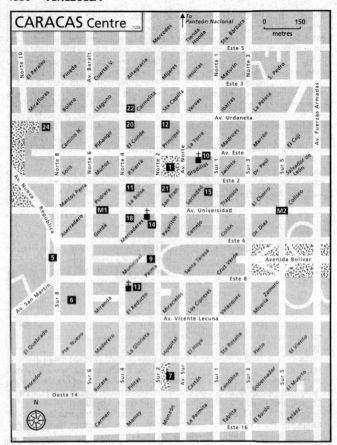

0800 for mere mortals, till 1730 (reached from Parque del Este metro station). There is a boating lake, a replica of Columbus' *Santa María* (being renovated since 1991), the Humboldt Planetarium (weekend shows, US$0.25), a number of different sunken lakes featuring caiman and turtles, monkeys, two frustratingly caged jaguars, many types of water birds, a terrarium (open Sat-Sun, US$0.05). No cameras. The **Parque Caricuao** is at the end of the Metro line, quite heavily wooded; it has the city's main zoo, open Tues-Sun 0900-1700, US$0.15 (the metro station is called Zoológico). It is a better zoo than Parque del Este, which some find disappointing. **Parque El Pinar** also has a large, but disappointing zoo (Av José Antonio Páez, El Pinar), open Tues-Sun 0900-1745. The **Parque Los Chorros** at the foot of the mountain has impressive waterfalls, also rec; **El Calvario**, W of Plaza O'Leary, with the Federation Arch at the entrance has a good view of Centro Simón Bolívar, but muggings have been reported. It has a small zoo, botanical gardens and a picturesque chapel. A new park, **Parque Vargas**, is eventually to

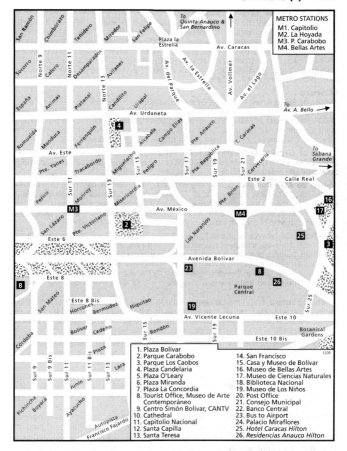

METRO STATIONS
M1. Capitolio
M2. La Hoyada
M3. P. Carabobo
M4. Bellas Artes

1. Plaza Bolívar
2. Parque Carabobo
3. Parque Los Caobos
4. Plaza Candelaria
5. Plaza O'Leary
6. Plaza Miranda
7. Plaza La Concordia
8. Tourist Office, Museo de Arte Contemporáneo
9. Centro Simón Bolívar, CANTV
10. Cathedral
11. Capitolio Nacional
12. Santa Capilla
13. Santa Teresa
14. San Francisco
15. Casa y Museo de Bolívar
16. Museo de Bellas Artes
17. Museo de Ciencias Naturales
18. Biblioteca Nacional
19. Museo de Los Niños
20. Post Office
21. Consejo Municipal
22. Banco Central
23. Bus to Airport
24. Palacio Miraflores
25. *Hotel Caracas Hilton*
26. *Residencias Anauco Hilton*

replace the Nuevo Circo bus station; similar in concept to the Champs Elysées, some is already in place. A model of the area, as it is planned, is on display in the Galería de Arte Nacional. **See below for Paseo de los Próceres, and p 1350 for El Avila National Park.**

National Monuments

Panteón Nacional Open Tues-Sun, 0900-1200 and 1430-1700 (Plaza Panteón, Av Norte y Av Panteón). This was designed as the resting place of Simón Bolívar, the Liberator, and Francisco Miranda, the Precursor of Independence. The remains of Bolívar lie there, but the tomb of Miranda, who died in a Spanish prison, has been left open to await the return of his body, likewise the tomb of Antonio José de Sucre, who was assassinated in Colombia. Every 25 years the President opens Bolívar's casket to verify that the remains are still there. Daniel O'Leary, Bolívar's Irish aide-de camp, is buried alongside. The building was originally Santísima Trinidad church with ceiling paintings by Tito Sales (1874). There is a small military ceremony at 1515 daily.

Capitolio Nacional   Open to visitors Tues-Sun, 0900-1200 and 1500-1700. Access to the Chambers of Senators and Deputies is possible, but times are erratic. The Elliptical Salon has some impressive paintings by the Venezuelan artist Martín Tovar y Tovar and a bronze urn containing the 1811 Declaration of Independence. One of the paintings on the ceiling shows a British regiment fighting in the Battle of Carabobo, and the names of the officers appear on the wall; in acknowledgement of this assistance Bolívar granted British forces the right to march through any city in Gran Colombia (Colombia, Ecuador, Panama and Venezuela) with bayonets fixed, drums beating and flags flying.

Museums

Museo de Bellas Artes, Plaza Morelos in Parque Los Caobos, the oldest museum in Caracas, designed by Carlos Raúl Villanueva: open Tues-Fri, 0900-1200, 1500-1730, weekend 1000-1700. Pictures include an El Greco among works by mainly Venezuelan artists. Adjacent is the Galería de Arte Nacional, T 571-0176, same opening hours, which also houses the Cinemateca Nacional (Tues-Sun 1830 and 2130, Sun 1100 for children's films).

Museo de Ciencias Naturales, also in Plaza Morelos in Parque Los Caobos; open Tues-Fri, 0900-1200, 1500-1730, weekend 1000-1700: archaeological, particularly precolumbian, zoological and botanical exhibits.

Museo de Arte Colonial, Quinta Anauco, Av Panteón, San Bernardino: open Tues-Sat, 0900-1200, 1400-1700, Sun, 1000-1730. Guided tour in Spanish available. A delightful house built in 1720, the residence of the Marqués del Toro. Chamber concerts most Sat at 1800. The beautiful suburb of San Bernardino glories in tropical flowers and whole avenues of forest trees, smothered in blossom in season, highly rec.

Casa Natal del Libertador   Open Tues-Fri, 0900-1200 and 1430-1700, Sun and holidays, 1000-1700. The present house is a reconstruction of the house where Bolívar was born (on 24 July 1783). The first, of adobe, was destroyed by an earthquake. The second became a stable, and was later pulled down. The present building of stone was built by order of Gómez (whose birthday was the same as Bolívar's) in the early 1920s; it contains interesting pictures and furniture. **The Museo Bolivariano** is alongside the Casa Natal and contains the Liberator's war relics.

   Cuadra Bolívar   Bárcenas y Las Piedras, 8 blocks S of Plaza Bolívar; "El Palmar", the Bolívar family's summer home, now an historical museum, a beautifully preserved colonial country estate: walled gardens, stables, Bolívar memorabilia, well worth a visit. Open Tues-Sat, 0900-1300, 1430-1700; Sun and holidays 0900-1700.

House of Arturo Michelena, La Pastora y Puente Miraflores, four blocks N of Miraflores palace, in the La Pastora section, is a typical 19th century home, now a museum. Open 0900-1200 and 1500-1700 (closed Mon and Fri).

Museo de Transporte, Parque Nacional del Este (to which it is connected by a pedestrian overpass), includes a large collection of locomotives and old cars, as well as a fascinating series of scale models of Caracas a century ago, although much has been neglected. Open Sat, Sun, 0900-1600. Admission US$0.10 adults (Bs 1 for children).

In the Parque Central, between Av Lecuna (E end) and the elevated section of Av Bolívar there are four museums in a complex which includes 2 octagonal towers (56 floors each) and four large apartment buildings with shopping below.

Museo de Arte Contemporáneo, Parque Central, Cuadra Bolívar, entrance beside *Anauco Hilton*, very good, European and Venezuelan painters represented, a room devoted to Picasso ink and pen drawings, and interesting modern sculptures. The museum is in two sections, the larger of which is downstairs and is easily missed; reference library, gift shop. Open Tues-Sun 1000-1800.

Museo de los Niños, Parque Central, next to East Tower, is open to the public Wed-Sun and holidays, 0900-1200, 1400-1700 (will not sell tickets less than 1 hr before closing), otherwise is for school visits; a highly sophisticated modern science museum, well worth a visit and extremely popular, baseball games sometimes played, US$0.75 (adults). Allow 2-3 hrs for a visit. Book a day or so in advance in school holidays or Aug. Also in the Parque Central complex, **Museo Audiovisual**, Tues-Fri, 0900-1700, US$1, incl a library of Venezuelan television programmes, a practice TV studio, and **Museo del Teclado** (keyboard instruments).

Museo Histórico Militar, near Metro Gato Negro.

The Ministry of Foreign Relations, pictures mostly of national heroes and historical events.

Museo Histórico Fundación John Boulton, Torre El Chorro, 11th floor, Av Universidad y Sur 3, entre El Chorro y Dr Díaz, previously in La Guaira (**see p 1351**), contains many unique historical items: rare sketches of and books belonging to Bolívar, colonial ceramic and household pieces, a chair presented to Coro church by Juana La Loca, daughter of Ferdinand and Isabel, a library of 19th-century research material and commercial records of the Casa Boulton (easy access, free). Open Mon-Fri 0800-1200, 1300-1700, two tours a day by knowledgeable guides; underground parking on presentation of ID.

The Concejo Municipal (City Hall) on Plaza Bolívar contains three museums: a collection of the paintings of Emilio Boggio, a Venezuelan painter; the Raúl Santana Museum of the Creole Way of Life, a collection of miniature figures in costumes and poses characteristic of Venezuelan life, all handmade by Raúl Santana and extremely realistic; Francisco Pizarro's battle standard, presented by him to Sucre after the battle of Ayacucho and then given to Bolívar, is shown here; and the Sala de Arqueología Gaspar Marcano, exhibiting ceramics, mostly discovered on the coast. All three open Tues-Fri, 0930-1200, 1500-1800; Sat and Sun, 0930-1800. Informative guides are available.

Those with a deeper interest in archaeology might like to contact the Junta Nacional Protectora y Conservadora del Patrimonio Histórico y Artístico de la Nación, Palacio de Miraflores, Av Urdaneta.

Churches The present **Cathedral** building dates from 1674 and should be seen for its beautiful façade, its gilded altar, the Bolívar family chapel and pictures by Michelena, Murillo and an alleged Rubens "Resurrection". **San Francisco**, Av Universidad y San Francisco (1 block SW of Plaza Bolívar), should be seen for its colonial altars and Murillo's "San Agustín" (oldest church in Caracas, rebuilt 1641). **Santa Teresa**, between La Palma and Santa Teresa, just SE of the Centro Simón Bolívar, has good interior chapels and a supposedly miraculous portrait of Nazareno de San Pablo (popular and solemn devotions on Good Friday).

NB Museums and art galleries throughout Venezuela are closed on Monday. Check museum schedules in *El Universal, El Nacional* or the *Daily Journal* (which also have details of events for children). Many museums and most religious buildings will refuse entry to anybody wearing shorts.

Modern Caracas Visitors should see the **Paseo de los Próceres** with its twin monoliths and other monuments to the heroes of independence (it also has flowers and gardens); the magnificent Officers' Club on the same avenue; and the University City, an enormous and coherent complex of great buildings in which paintings, sculpture and stained glass are completely integrated with the architecture (which is now showing signs of wear).

NB In the centre of Caracas, each street corner has a name, and addresses are generally given as, for example, "Santa Capilla a Mijares", rather than the official "Calle Norte 2, No 26". On some maps Av Luis Rocha is still shown as Av España (Altamira). For maps see **Tourist Information**, below, and **Maps** in Information for Visitors.

Festivals 3 May, Velorio de la Cruz de Mayo still celebrated with dances and parties in some districts. Carnival and Holy Week are not widely celebrated in Caracas as many people leave town. 18-25 Dec Yuletide masses at different churches leading up to Christmas. Traditional creole dishes served at breakfasts.

Warning It is advisable not to arrive in Caracas at night and not to walk down narrow streets or in parks after dark. Avoid certain areas such as all suburbs from the El Silencio monument to Propatria, other than main roads, the area around the *teleférico*, Chapellín near the Country Club, and Petare. If you have problems try contacting Detective Robert Pechi at Interpol, Parque Carabobo, who speaks English, Italian, Spanish and Portuguese. Police searches are common, especially in airports; if you have entered overland from Colombia, you can expect thorough investigation (once you've left the border, better to say you flew in). Car theft is common.

Hotels Cheap *pensiones* are usually full of long-stay residents and have very few rooms available for travellers. Hotels tend to be particularly full at weekends and in July and Aug. In the centre all cheap hotels take only short stay customers on Fri pm. Better hotels often try to give you a suite instead of a double room. Hotel prices below do not include 12.5% tax. Hotels marked with an asterisk (*) are bookable through Fairmont International (see next page).

Hotels in Chuao/Las Mercedes Business/commercial district SE of centre, not on metro: The **L1 Tamanaco***, Av Principal Las Mercedes, PO Box 467, Caracas 1060A, T 924522, F 208-7116, is the best hotel in Caracas, refurbished in 1993, superb pool, luxury business hotel, difficult to get rooms as it is normally fully booked (incl service, tax 15%, rooms are priced in dollars), courteous staff, good facilities, changes TCs for guests only (poor rate); **L1** *Eurobuilding*, Centro Ciudad Comercial Tamanaco, T 959-1133, F 993-9285, PO Box 64487, 5-star, modern, has all-suite wing, well-furnished, a/c, incl breakfast, efficient service, clean, large pool, gym, restaurants, many services, weekend rates available; also in CCCT **L3-A1** *CCCT Venantur**, T 959-0611, F 959-6409, smart business hotel with a pool terrace, approached through shopping mall, not that easy to find; **A2** *Hotel Paseo de las Mercedes*, Las Mercedes, T 910444, F 993-0341, almost next door to the *Tamanaco*, good sized rooms, restaurant, bar, small pool on pleasant rear terrace.

Parque Central (metro Bellas Artes), an area of tower blocks, concrete walkways and underpasses: **L1** *Hilton**, Av Libertador and Sur 25, T 503-5000, F 503-5003, ageing luxury hotel, impressive conference facilities, excellent business centre, spectacular city views, especially at night, noisy (traffic and a/c), useful long-term luggage deposit and good breakfast, nice pool, fax service open to non-residents, very helpful, rec. Connected with the *Hilton* are the **L3** *Anauco Hilton Suites**, Parque Central, T 573-4111, F 573-7724, an "apartotel", unmodernized since 1970s, poor value even though *Hilton* facilities across the road can be used.

Near Altamira metro station, a respectable comercial and residential area, E of centre: **A3** *Continental*, Av San Juan Bosco, T 261-9091, F 261-0131, smart, gardens front and rear and a good, private swimming pool; **C** *El Cid*, Av San Felipe, between 1a and 2a, T 263-2611, F 263-5578, Spanish style interior, large suites with living area, breakfast rooms, kitchenette ensuite, a/c, good value for money; **C** *La Floresta*, Av Avila Sur, Plaza Altamira, T 263-1955, F 263-1243, various suites in a fairly modern block.

Sabana Grande/Chacaíto, varied area with many restaurants and shops, convenient for metro: **A2** *Lincoln Suites*, Av Francisco Solano, entre San Jerónimo y Los Jabillos, T 761-2727, F 762-5503, top of the range in this area, high quality accommodation and service, no pool; **A3** *Cumberland*, 2da Av de las Delicias, T 762-9961, F 762-5549, very good, nice restaurant; **A3** *Plaza Palace*, Av Los Mangos, Las Delicias, T 762-4821, good; **A3** *Tampa**, Av Francisco Solano López, T 762-3771, F 762-0112, comfy but noisy a/c, plain interior, interesting bodega-style restaurant; **B** *Atlántida*, Av La Salle, Los Caobos, next to Vatican Embassy, T 781-3696/781-3729, F 749631, clean, safe, noisy, close to Sabana Grande and metro stations; **B** *Coliseo*, T 762-77916, F 761-7333, Coromoto y Bellomonte, a/c, TV, toilet, shower, restaurant serves a good breakfast, 100m from Sabana Grande metro station, clean and friendly, rec; **B** *Crillón**, Av Libertador, esq Av Las Acacias, T 761-6912, F 716911, some floors renovated as part of continuing programme, 60s highrise with appealing bar and restaurant; **B** *Kursaal*, Av Casanova y El Colegio, T 762-2922, clean, safe, bath, a/c, TV; **B** *Las Américas*, Calle Los Cerritos, T 951-7387, F 951-1717, a modern tower, with new block attached, tiny roof pool and restaurant, good value; **B** *Savoy**, Av Francisco Solano López, Las Delicias, T 762-1971, F 762-2792, good food, efficient, clean, secure vehicle park; **C** *Broadway*, Av Casanova 4, T 951-1922, Chacaíto metro, bath, TV, friendly, clean, Italian specialities in restaurant; **C** *El Condor*, Av Las Delicias, T 762-9911, comfortable but plain, outstanding restaurant in Spanish bodega style; **C** *Escorial*, Calle Colegio, T 761-9621, central, clean, a/c, colour TV, mediocre restaurant and bar, 2 mins walk from Plaza Venezuela; **C** *Luna**, Av Casanova y El Colegio, T 762-5851, clean, friendly, rec; **C** *Ritz*, Av Las Palmas y Av Libertador, T 782-0333, with bath, a/c, safe provided, noisy at night, near Plaza Venezuela on metro, secure free parking; several basic hotels on same street, eg **D** *Cristal*, Plaza Venezuela, Calle Colegio, a/c, convenient, basic, comfortable, safe, good value, disco at weekends, good cheap Chilean food; **D** *Mari*, Av Casanova entre Baldó y Baruta, Bello Monte, T 951-3252, nearest metro Chacaíto, stores luggage, bar, restaurant, not keen on backpackers, noisy on third floor, hot and dark, no warm water; **D** *Odeon*, Las Acacias y Av Casanova, T 793-1322, F 781-9380, modern, possibly the best on Las Acacias (see below); **D** *Tanausú**, Las Acacias y Casanova, T 781-1273, with bath, clean; **E** *Nuestro Hotel*, Calle Colegio, clean, stores luggage, safe and friendly, some rooms hired by the hour but rec; **E** *El Colegio*, friendly, safe, some mosquitoes; **F** *Capri*, cheapest in Sabana Grande, a/c. There are many hotels on the southern prolongation of Av Las Acacias, but the majority are short-stay.

In San Bernardino, residential area 2 km N of Bellas Artes metro: **A3** *Avila**, Av Jorge Washington (T 515128/515173, F 523021, Telex 21637 Avila), set in park-like gardens ("magical night-time atmosphere from tropical birdsong") very pleasant, good service, most of staff speak English and German, no a/c in rooms but fans, mosquito screens, pool, Metrobus nearby, very good restaurant and poolside bar, rec, phones which accept Visa/Mastercard, useful for international calls, María José Mendes at the Camar Tours desk helpful; **B** *Aventura**, Av Sorocaima y Av Francisco Fajardo, T 514011, F 519186, big rooms, suites available for long lets, small pool in attractive but overshadowed rear courtyard; **D** *Líder*, Av Baralt entre Oeste 14/Bucare y Oeste 16/Carmen, T 481-7040, restaurant, bar, bath, phone, TV; **D** *Waldorf*, Av Industria, San Bernardino, Bellas Artes metro, T 571-4733, hot water erratic, friendly, restaurant, English sometimes spoken, good value, will store luggage; Banco Consolidado next door for exchange, often slow, good value Chinese restaurant next door (the airport tourist office often rec this hotel).

In the downtown area: **B** *Grand Galaxie**, Truco a Caja de Agua, between Av Baralt and Norte 4 on Salas Sta Bárbara, T 83-9011/9044, a/c, TV, phone, restaurant, central, comfortable but no safe and disorganized; **C** *Inter**, Animas a Calero on corner of Av Urdaneta, T 564-0251, very clean, shower and toilet with each room, friendly, English spoken, very popular so be sure to make a reservation, in high season the queues for rooms begin before 0700 and the hotel is full by 0800, poor restaurant; **D** *Palais*, Norte 4 (Pilita a Glorieta), modern, clean, TV, a/c, friendly, helpful, luggage stored, excellent restaurant; **C** *Plaza Catedral**, Blvd Plaza Bolívar, next to Cathedral, T 564-2111, very friendly, beautiful location in the colonial part of town, Amex accepted, a/c, TV, phone, some English spoken, clean; **E** *Caroni*, Av Baralt, between Muñoz and Piñango, popular, safe but a bit noisy, not very clean, bar, restaurant; **E** *Hospedaje Torreiro*, Sur 11 entre San Agustín/Este 10 bis/Bolívar y Av Lecuna/Este 10/Sucre, next to Lagoven, T 577-2148, nice, helpful, bath, fan, TV, clean, friendly, safe, rec.

Cheapest hotels can be found around the Nuevo Circo bus terminal, though not the safest of areas, many of them on Av Lecuna: eg **D** *El Arroyo*, No 27, T 418435, with bath, a/c, TV, luggage store; **D** *Center Park*, esq Sur 3, T 541-8619, helpful and very friendly, safe, TV, stores luggage; opp is **E** *Urupagua*, basic and clean, reasonable restaurant, rec; **D** *Limón*, Calle Este 10, No 228, nearest metro Bellas Artes, with shower, TV, telephone, clean, safe, parking, often rec; **D** *Avenida*, Calle Sur 4 (nr Capitolio), T 426440, hot water sporadic, a/c, safe, rec; **D** *Hospedaje Fidelina*, Sur 4 No 120, clean, safe, fan, TV, F with shared bath/toilet; **D** *La Neve*, Pilita a Glorieta No 126—Sur 4, nr Metro Capitolio, a/c or fan, bath, good, clean, safe, quiet, good restaurant, rec; **D** *Monte Rosa*, Sur 4, T 417128, clean, cheap and friendly; **E** *Horcones*, San Agustín del Norte district at esquina Horcones, T 573-5415, but unsafe area, especially for women; **E** *Pensión San Gregorio*, San Agustín Este 12 Arismendi, 2½ blocks from terminal, many single rooms, friendly, more or less clean, shared or private bath; **E** *Melina*, Sur 1, shower, fan, TV, rec; **E** *Santa Mónica*, on corner between Av San Martín and San Juan, Sur 10, Pilita (do not cross from Av Baralt along Sur 10, but to San Martín using Av Lecuna, Oeste 10, Angelitos, safer), with bath, TV, fan. For other cheap hotels look on Calle Sur 2, but better to go several blocks WSW to a quieter area, eg **E** *Pensión San Marcos*, Hoyo a Santa Rosalía, T 545-3723, friendly, basic; **F** *Nueva Lucía*, Arismendi a Pichincha, 2 blocks from *Ber Mar* away from bus station, fan, clean, friendly owner.

Santa Teresa is a dormitory town SE of Caracas, rec as an alternative to the capital for cheaper, safe accommodation, with easy and frequent bus service (US$0.65), and scenic mountain setting; **E** *Hotel Tahay*, a/c, private bath, small, clean and safe; **F** *Hotel Lamas*, opp, with fan and private bath, small, clean, secure, luggage store, friendly manager, rec.

Hotel Reservations Fairmont International, Torre Capriles, Planta Baja, Plaza Venezuela, Caracas, T 782-8433, Telex 21232 SNRHO, F 782-4407, will book hotel rooms in Caracas and also in 102 hotels in the rest of the country and in other countries, eg Colombia, with no booking fee, rec as helpful. "Packages" organized by Fairmont International are reported to be much more expensive than hotel bookings. The airport tourist office is very helpful and will book hotel rooms. Finding a hotel, particularly in the middle-price range, is always difficult. If you book from abroad, make sure you receive confirmation before beginning your journey or you may turn up and find yourself without a room. If you arrive by air in the evening without a reservation it is often easier to get a taxi to Macuto, rather than Caracas, where there are several hotels only 15 mins drive away. For apartment rental, consult *El Universal* daily paper, small ads columns. *Residencias Taormina*, Av María Teresa Toro, una cuadra Plaza Tiuna delante CANTV, Las Acacias, good apartments US$25/night, best value for 2 weeks or more.

Restaurants There is such a profusion of eating places in Caracas that we give the following general advice, with a mention of just a few places currently reported reliable, rather than attempt the impossible task of keeping up to date with all the changes. Guides to eating incl "Gourmet Dining out in Caracas", available at travel agencies and good hotels. Advertisements appear in the "Daily Journal" and the Yellow Pages of the telephone directory. Don't be shy about asking the price before you order in a bar as beer in one will cost three times as much as in another, and a modest portion of manchego cheese will cost more than a good steak. Food on display in a bar is free with your drink if they offer it as a *pasapalo*, but will be charged for if offered as a *ración*. You can save on the service charge by eating at the bar and not at a table. Restaurants must put up a list of prices on or near the front door, and are prohibited from charging for place settings (*cubiertos*) or bread, butter, condiments etc (*guarnición*). A meal costs between US$4.70 to 5.75 minimum, not including beer (an extra US$1 or so), 1995 prices.

For dining out, there is a selection of good restaurants around Avenida Urdaneta (*Mesón de Cervantes*—friendly multilingual manager, Nelson, *Marinero de Oriente* for seafood), La Castellana, Plaza Altamira, Las Mercedes (*Era de Acuario*, vegetarian, open for dinner; *The Crystal Ranch*, quite smart, great food and very reasonable prices; Lebanese food: *Kibbe*, Calle Madrid, Las Mercedes, T 910519; good take away at CCCT shopping centre, Nivel C-2; *El Granjero del Este*, Rio de Janeiro, T 916619, traditional barbecues, excellent arepas), El Rosal and Sabana Grande (see below). There are plenty of eating places around Plaza Bolívar. *Plaza Mayor*, Torre a Veroes, NE corner of Plaza Bolívar, very good, rec. *El Paso* (Chinese), Hospital a Glorieta, Ed Atlántico, Plaza La Concordia, cheap, good. Sea food at *Las Vegas* near *Hotel Plaza Catedral*. *Tarzilandia*, 10th Transversal Altamira, San Juan Bosco, international food. Very good Mexican/Peruvian dishes at *El Tizón*, CC Bello Campo, Sótano Local 80, T 316715/261-3485, popular.

Although it is not practicable to cover the whole of Caracas, the following description of the Sabana Grande area will give an idea of what is available. Breakfast in your hotel is likely to be poor (poor bread or none, insipid coffee and orange juice which is half artificial). It is better and cheaper in a *fuente de soda*—once you have purchased your ticket you will find there is little sense of queuing, shout your order to the staff like the locals, and cheaper still in a *pasteleria* or *areperia*. Tables in the open air on the boulevard, however, are expensive. (The boulevard waiters overcharge. Check prices on the displayed list.) Mid-day is the most economical time to eat the main meal of the day and about the only opportunity to find fresh vegetables. Particularly good value is the "menú ejecutivo" or "cubierto", which is a three-course meal for US$2-3, eg at *Rincón de Bucanero*, on Casanova (also has music in the evenings), *La Estación del Pollo*, on the corner of Casanova and Las Acacias in Sabana Grande, a huge hall in which tartan-aproned waiters serve *parrilladas* to Venezuelan families, good and pretty cheap; *Pizzería Adelia*, near Plaza Venezuela, *Gran Pizzería*, on Gran Bulevar, and *Il Barone*, Av Sur Altamira, Metro Altamira, next to Teatro Altamira, average price US$2. Very good beef at *La Estancia*, Av Principal La Castellana, esq Urdaneta, near Altamira metro, traditional style and popular with young Caracas business set, US$10-15 pp, and next door is *Primi*, with Italian/Creole cuisine, quite chic and friendly, plenty of vegetarian dishes.

Good, economical meals in the evening at *Sorrento* (Italian) and *Jabillos* on Francisco Solano, *La Soledad* (on Casanova), *Tivoli* (El Colegio between Lincoln and Casanova, home made pasta) and *Tropical Room* (two blocks E on Casanova). For business and similar occasions: *Rugantino* in *Hotel Tampa* (speciality *cartuccio*), and *Villa D'Este* in *Hotel Cóndor*. Venezuelan food, *Casiero* on Francisco Solano, and *Urrita*, F Solano y Los Mangos, both very good; also *El Portón*, Av Pichincha, El Rosal, typically Venezuelan, and popular, rec. For variety: *Bohío Habanero*, in La Previsora, Cuban food, rec, and *La Buca* in *Hotel Kursaal*, international food, *Le Coq d'Or*, Av Los Mangos (French), *Dragón Verde*, Ciné París, Av Maturín (Chinese), *Le Chalet*, in *Hotel Crillón* (Swiss), good selection, highly rec, *Victor's Pollo*, Av F Solano y El Bosque (Chacaíto end), has 20 different chicken dishes, and *Buffet Vegetariano*, Av Los Jardines. Other vegetarian restaurants are *El Acuario*, Truco a Caja de Agua; *Chalet Naturista*, nr Sabana Grande metro station; these three are not open for dinner. Also *Delicatesen Indú*, vegetarian specializing in southern Indian dishes, good quality, small portions, on Calle Villa Flor, in Sabana Grande just off main pedestrian thoroughfare between metro stations for Sabana Grande and Plaza Venezuela; *El Exquisito Menú Vegetariano*, near Metro Parque Carabobo (Capitolio district), rec for buffet, friendly, and *Almuerzo*, Hoyo a Sta Rosalía, good and cheap. Roast lamb at *La Taberna*, Torre Capriles, Plaza Venezuela. *Shorthorn*, Av Libertador, El Bosque, very good. Fast foods: there is a plethora of burger and pizza places, as well as the ubiquitous hot dog stalls of doubtful hygiene (when the police don't close them down). *Arturo's*, is a chain of clean, modern, chicken-and-chips style restaurants in various locations, eg next to Centro Plaza complex, Miranda y Andrés Bello, also on Av Lincoln pedestrian mall, 1 block E of Sabana Grande metro. *El Arepazo*, 1 block S of Chacaíto metro station, has every kind of arepa filling you could wish for. *El Coco*, in the Centro Comercial Chacaíto, very good Venezuelan food, *arepas*, *empanadas*, much lower prices than the sidewalk cafés on nearby Sabana Grande. The restaurant of the *Hotel Palais* on Sur 4 in the cheap hotel area is highly rec, especially for paella and good atmosphere.

Airlines Viasa, Av Sur 25, Torre Viasa, Plaza Morelos (T 576-2611, airport 552-222); **Avensa**, El Chorro y Av Universidad, piso 12-13 Edif El Chorro (T 561-3366, airport 551-555); **Aerotuy**, Av Lincoln y Blvd Sabana Grande, Edif Gran Sabana piso 5 (T 761-6247/9782/8043).

Aerolíneas Argentinas, Av Sur 25, Plaza Morelos, Torre Viasa, piso 8, Los Caobos (T 576-6433); **Air Aruba**, Av Libertador, Torre Maracaibo (T 719781); **Air France**, Parque Cristal, Torre Este, piso 2, Los Palos Grandes (T 283-5855); **Alitalia**, Edif Atlantic piso 5, Av Andrés Bello, Los Palos Grandes (T 800-66666); **ALM**, Edif Exa piso 8, Av Libertador (T 953-7086/6424); **American**, Centro Plaza, Torre B (T 209-8111); **Avianca**, Av F de Miranda, Edif Roraima (T 953-7254); **British Airways**, Torre Británica piso 11, Altamira (T 261-8006); **BWIA**, Oficentro Rovica piso 1, Blvd Sabana Grande (T 711307); **KLM**, Torre KLM, Av R Gallegos

(T 285-3333); **LIAT**, Torre Británica, Mezz 2, Av JF Sosa, Altamira Sur (T 265-7542); **Lufthansa**, Av Tamanaco, Edif Bayer (T 951-0044); **United**, Av F de Miranda, Edificio Parque Canaima, piso 8, Los Palos Grandes (T 285-5753); **Varig**, Av Principal de Los Ruices, Centro Emp Los Ruices piso 3 (T 238-2111).

Banks and Exchange (see **Currency** p 1434) **Citibank** will exchange Citicorp cheques; Banco Unión for **Visa** transactions. For cash advances on **Mastercard**, go to Credimático for a voucher then to Banco Mercantil for the cash from a side office, up to US$250 a day. For **Thomas Cook** cheques try Banco Internacional or Banco Mercantil. For **exchange** go to **Italcambio** offices, who require proof of TC purchase, commission 1.70%: esquina Veroes and Urdaneta (or **Visesta CA** opp, highly rec, accepts Eurocheques, also for travel arrangements, Walter Kleebinder speaks several languages and is very helpful, T 562-4698/562-5333), Av Casanova (Sabana Grande), Av L Roche (Altamira Sur), Simón Bolívar Airport (may limit transaction to US$100, open public holidays); **La Moneda**, Centro Financiero Latino, Urdaneta, Piso 8; **Viajes Febres Parva**, Centro Libertador, Local 4, or on Av Urdaneta, Edificio Veroes, local 4; **Infesa**, Av Libertador, between Negrín and Jabillos; **Confinanzas**, Centro Comercial Paseo Las Mercedes, Local PA-CI, open 0800-1200, 1400-1700, commission 1% charged on TCs, but not in all cases. **MVS Cambios**, Av Francisco Solano, between Calles El Cristo and Los Manguitos, Edificio Torre Oasis, Sabana Grande, less queuing, good rates. **American Express** cheques, Banco Consolidado, Av San Francisco, Edif Torre California, piso 9, Urb Colinas de La California, until 1100 only; **Amex rep** is Turisol, Centro Comercial Tamanaco, level C-2, Local 53F-07, Chuao suburb, PO Box 62006, T 959-1011, rec as helpful and efficient, also in *Hotel Tamanaco*. Stolen or lost travellers' cheques can be replaced, and US$ cash exchanged, at the Amex office in Torre Consolidada, Plaza La Castellana, Av Principal La Castellana, nearest metro Altamira. Many banks accept Visa cards in their hole-in-the-wall machines, even English cash cards (eg Lloyds' Cashpoint), so long as they bear the Visa symbol.

Cultural Institutions British Council, Edificio Torre la Noria, 6th floor, Las Mercedes; English classes and modest library oriented towards English teaching, literature and fiction. **Centro Venezolano-Americano**, Av Las Mercedes, good free library of books in English, and free concerts; also Spanish courses, eight different levels, each lasts 17 days and costs US$50, highly rec. **Asociación Cultural Humboldt (Goethe Institut)**, Av Juan Germán Roscio, San Bernardino, T 527634, library, lectures, films, concerts, Spanish courses.

Embassies and Consulates Argentina, Centro Capriles, 2a, Mezz Entrada Este, Plaza Venezuela, T (02) 781-1487, PO Box 569, Caracas 1010-A; **Colombian Consulate**, Guaicaipuro, Sector Chacaíto, Urb El Rosal, T 951-3631; open Mon-Fri 0800-1400 for visas, photo and US$10 (maybe free), can take anything from 10 mins to one day; **Ecuadorian Consulate**, Centro Empresarial Andrés Bello 13th Floor, Av Andrés Bello, Torre Este, Parque del Este metro, T 781-6090; **Mexican Embassy** (visa section), Edif Parque Cristal, Torre Este, piso 14, T 286622 (Mon-Fri 0900-1300), next to Parque del Este metro, tourist cards issued on the spot, free; **Brazilian Embassy**, Plaza La Castellana, Av Principal La Castellana, T 261345, nearest metro Altamira (visa US$13, 1 photo, valid 3 months maximum, 24 hrs); **Brazilian Consulate**, Edificio "Centro Gerencial Mohedano", piso 6, entre C Los Chaguaramas y Av Mohedano, La Castellano, open Mon-Fri 0830-1230; **Cuban Consulate**, Av 3/2, Campo Alegre, behind Clínica Sanatriz, 0900-1300; **Guyanese Embassy**, Edif Los Frailes, C La Guairita, Chuao (same for Jamaican Embassy), T 978-1779, visa Mon, Wed, Fri, 0830-1200, same day if early, passport, airline ticket, yellow fever certificate, 2 photos required; **Peruvian Consulate**, Centro Empresarial Andrés Bello 7th floor, Avenida Andrés Bello, Torre Este, T 781-6168, next to Parque del Este metro; **Suriname Embassy**, 4a Avenida, between 7a and 8a Transversal, Urb Altamira, T 262-1616; **Trinidadian Embassy**, beside the Suriname Embassy, Quinta Serrana, 4a Avenida, between 7a and 8a Transversal, Altamira, T 261-3748/4772 (visa US$17, 2 photos, up to 1 week).

USA Embassy and Consulate, Av Francisco Miranda, La Floresta (almost opp Centro Comercial Centro Plaza, between metros Altamira and Parque del Este), T 284-6111; **Canadian Embassy**, Edificio Torre Europa, piso 7, Av Francisco de Miranda, corner of Av Escuela, 2 blocks E of Chacaíto metro (T 951-6166); **Australian Embassy**, "Yolanda", Av Luis Roche, between transversal 6 and 7, Altamira, T 283-3090; **Japanese Embassy**, Av San Juan Bosco, between 8th and 9th Transversal, Altamira, T 261-8333.

British Embassy and Consulate, Torre Las Mercedes, 3rd floor, Av La Estancia, Chuao (T 751-1022/1166/1454/1966), Apartado 1246 for letters; **Danish Embassy**, Ed EASO, 17th floor, Av Francisco de Miranda, nr Chacaíto metro station, T 951-5606; **Finnish Embassy**, Torre C, Piso 14, Centro Plaza, Av Francisco de Miranda, T 284-5013; **French Embassy**, Ed Las Frailes, Piso 6, La Guairita, T 910333/324; **German Embassy**, Edificio Panavén, piso 2, Av San Juan Bosco, Altamira, T 267-0181/1205, open Mon-Fri 0900-1300; **Israeli Embassy**, Av Francisco de Miranda, Centro Empresario Miranda, piso 4, T 239-4511; **Netherlands**

Consulate, Edif San Juan, piso 9, San Juan Bosco y Av Transversal 2, Altamira, T 920075; **Spanish Embassy**, Ed Banco Unión, Sabana Grande, piso 1, T 326526; **Swedish Embassy**, Edificio Panavén, piso 5, Av San Juan Bosco con Tercera Transversal, Altamira, T 323911; **Swiss Embassy**, Torre Europa, piso 6, Av Francisco de Miranda, corner of Av Escuela, 2 blocks E of Chacaíto metro (T 951-4064); **Austrian Embassy**, Torre Las Mercedes, Chuao, T 913863.

Entertainments   There are frequent Sun morning concerts in the Teatro Municipal, 1100, usually US$2.25. Concerts, ballet, theatre and film festivals at the Ateneo de Caracas, Paseo Colón, Plaza Morelos; and similar events, incl foreign artists, at the Complejo Cultural Teresa Carreño, on Paseo Colón, just E of *Caracas Hilton* (an interesting building, too). There are numerous **cinemas**, normally four showings a day (half price Mon). For details of these and other events, see the newspapers, *El Universal, El Nacional* and *Daily Journal*, and the Sun issue of *El Diario de Caracas*.

Discotheques   A great many; recent recommendations: *Pida Pizza*, Sabana Grande; *Weekend*, Las Mercedes; *Palladium*, in CCCT shopping centre, popular, big, you do not have to be in a couple as in many other places. *Basurero*, just opp Metrobus stop on Gran Avenida, metro Plaza Venezuela, filthy floor (wear old shoes), only beer served, not much seating but excellent, varied music, student atmosphere, informal.

Nightclubs   Caracas is a lively city by night. Caraqueños dine at home around 2000, and in restaurants from 2100 to 2300, so nightclubs don't usually come to life until after 2300, and then go on to all hours of the morning. *Naiguatá* (*Hotel Tamanaco*), expensive; best show in town. *Un Solo Pueblo*, typical Venezuelan music, 3rd Transversal, Altamira (there are many small clubs, restaurants and bars on Plaza Altamira Sur). Opposite, the *Café Rajatabla*, in the Ateneo cultural complex, draws the young crowd and often has live music. *Weekends*, San Juan Bosco, and *Café L'Attico*, both Altamira, are hard rock cafés, no cover charge. *City Rock Café*, Chacaíto, looks like a shopping centre but is good for dancing. One block E of Nuevo Circo, opp the filling station, *Rica Arepa*, an *arepería*, has traditional Venezuelan folk music, free, on Fri, Sat, Sun nights. *La Padrona*, Calle Humboldt, Chaguaramas, Brazilian music. *Cervecería Nueva Esparta*, Av los Marquitos (Sabana Grande) is cheap, provides good music, but is another couples-only venue.

Hospitals   *Hospital de Clínicas*, Av Panteón y Av Alameda, San Bernardino, T 574-2011. *Instituto Médico La Floresta*, near US Embassy, T 284-8111.

Spanish and English Courses   *AmeriSpan Unlimited*, PO Box 40513, Philadelphia, PA 19106-0513, USA, T 215-985-4522/800-879-6640, F 215-985-4524, has a partner school in Caracas. Technical English Workshop, T 752-3218/752-2861, and English Speaking Skills, Edif Anauco, 2nd floor, Parque Central.

Laundry   *Lavandería Austria*, Lecuna and Sur 3, self-service or service wash, helpful, friendly and reasonably priced; *Lavandería Automática Jescal*, San Agustín, Sur 11, Sucre 106, 3½ blocks from bus terminal, self-service, cheap, open 0700-2000. *Lavandería Automática*, Sur 17, Este 2, one block from *Hotel Waldorf*, self-service or service wash (US$2 for moderate load), open 0800-1600, sometimes later. *De-Blan-Ro*, Av Las Acacias, good service. **Dry Cleaning**   Tintorería Tulipán, Las Acacias Sur, next to *Hotel Colón*.

Post Office   Central at Urdaneta y Norte 4, close to Plaza Bolívar. Mailing packages abroad from here is reported to be reliable. It takes 20 days to Europe, air mail only, US$25 for 10 kg. All boxes must be wrapped up and sewn up with cloth. Allow an hour for formalities. *Lista de correos* costs US$0.30, Mon-Fri 0700-1945, Sat 0800-1700, Sun 0800-1200. Philatelic collection at Correos on corner of Av Baralt, near Plaza Bolívar. Post Office also at airport.

Telecommunications   are operated by the state company, CANTV, in S building, Centro Simón Bolívar (facing Plaza Caracas), T 418644; on mezzanine of Centro Plaza on Francisco Miranda in the E (corner of Andrés Bello between metros Parque del Este and Altamira), open 0800-2100, T 284-7932, phone cards sold here. Public telex at Centro Simón Bolívar and *nivel* C-I, Centro Ciudad Comercial Tamanaco. Few public phones; use those in metro stations. Phones at *Hotel Avila* take Visa and Mastercard. Fax bureau at the *Caracas Hilton* rec as helpful, open to non-guests (US$6 for one minute to UK), also a good telephone office.

Places of Worship   (with times of services in English): San Ignacio College, Calle Santa Teresa, La Castellana, Sunday mass 0915. Protestant: The United Christian Church, Av Arboleda, El Bosque, Sun 1000; St Mary's Anglican and Episcopal, Calle Chivacoa, San Román, Sun 1030; Shalom Temple, Av Jorge Washington, San Bernardino, Sat 0900 and 1600.

Shopping   For gems and fine jewellery, visit the *H Stern* shops at the Hotels *Hilton* and *Tamanaco* and at the International Airport; try also *Labady*, Sabana Grande 98, beautifully-made gold jewellery, English spoken. *Pro-Venezuela Exposición y Venta de Arte*

Popular, Gran Avenida at Calle Olimpo, between Plaza Venezuela and beginning of Av Casanova (opp Torre La Previsora), sells Venezuelan crafts, very crowded, no prices, bargain hard. Good quality Sun craft market between Museo de Bellas Artes and Museo de Historia Natural (metro Bellas Artes). Indian and Andean crafts can be found in **Centro Comercial Paseo Las Mercedes**, opp *Tamanaco*, "El Artesano", Local 144, rec (not to be confused with another shopping centre, Las Mercedes, at the other end of Paseo Las Mercedes, which has very few handicraft shops, but mainly clothes). The **CCCT shopping centre** is worth a visit, as is the Centro Comercial Plaza Las Americanas, mostly for fashion stores and beach wear. Large-size shoes (up to 47) at Catedral Sur 4 y Mercaderes. From Chacaíto, along Av Abraham Lincoln, Sabana Grande, to Plaza Venezuela, is a pedestrian precinct, with good shops, handicrafts, street traders and cafés. **Centro Plaza Altamira**, between metro stations Altamira and Parque del Este, has shops, cafés, *tascas* and the **Centro Mediterráneo**, with boutiques and cafés. There is also a good quality cinema.

Color Express in the Centro Comercial Chacaíto does good, cheap and quick slide developing.

Bookshops English language ones incl: *English Bookshop*, Concresa, Prados del Este, will exchange nearly new books and stocks the *Caribbean Islands Handbook*; *Lectura*, Centro Comercial Chacaíto. The *American Bookshop*, Av San Juan Bosco, Edif Belveder, T 263-5455/267-4134, near Altamira metro has a good selection of secondhand English books; also available in bookstalls in the street. *Librería del Este*, Av Francisco de Miranda 52, Edif Galipán, and *Librería Unica*, Centro Capriles, ground floor local 13N, Plaza Venezuela, all have foreign language books. *Librería Washington*, La Torre a Veroes No 25, good service. *Librería Ecológica*, Centro Simón Bolívar, next to the CANTV office. For environmental issues, *Fundación de Educación Ambiental*, Local 9, Nivel Av, Edificio Sur, Centro Simón Bolívar, Plaza Caracas, some maps available too, rec. A French bookshop is *Librería La France*, Centro Comercial Chacaíto; Italian bookshop, *El Libro Italiano*, Pasaje La Concordia (between Sabana Grande pedestrian street and Av Fco Solano López), and for German books, *Librería Alemana* (Oscar Todtmann), Centro El Bosque, Avenida Libertador, T 710881, open Tues-Sat, 0900-1230, 1500-1800.

Sports and Recreations Horse-racing every Sat and Sun at La Rinconada (a truly magnificent grandstand; betting is by a tote system, the sport is widely followed). Horse-racing commences at 1300, admission price to grandstand US$1.10. Several buses go to La Rinconada. Bull fights: in season; go to city, go to the *Bar-Restaurant Los Cuchilleros* on Av Urdaneta next to Plaza Candelaria to meet bullfighters and *aficionados*; tickets sold there on bullfight Sun mornings, ticket sales end 1400, bar closes 1530, bullfight starts 1600. Golf, tennis, riding, fishing. Baseball (Oct-Jan), football, swimming, etc. For flying try Halcón, Centro Comercial San Luis, T 987-1834. To hire fishing boats contact Ani Villanueva, T 740862.

Clubs There are 3 country clubs in Caracas, all of which have excellent restaurants. The Country Club in the eastern part has an 18-hole golf course. The Social Centre of the British Commonwealth Association, Quinta Alborada, Avenida 7 with Transversal 9, Altamira, Caracas, with bar and swimming pool; British and Commonwealth visitors only; entry fee according to length of stay; T 261-3060. Membership of the better clubs is by the purchase of a share, which can run to thousands of dollars. An exception is the sports club run by the *Tamanaco Hotel*, open to non-guests and suitable for people staying a short time. The Military Club (Círculo de las Fuerzas Armadas) is well worth seeing and, if the visitors are soberly dressed, permission to view the premises is often granted. Flying Club, at La Carlota, near *Tamanaco Hotel*, mixed reports. Radio Club Venezolano is a very welcoming, efficient organization of amateur radio operators which is eager to meet amateurs from around the world (address: PO Box 2285, Caracas 1010-A, T 781-4878, 781-8303—Av Lima, Los Caobos; branches around the country).

Travel Agents *Maso Internacional*, Plaza Altamira Sur, Av San Juan Bosco, T 313577, reps for Thomas Cook, generally good reports of tours. *Wagons Lit*, Av Urdaneta y Calle 5, helpful. *Lost World Adventures*, Edificio 3-H, Piso 6, Oficina 62, Boulevard de Sabana Grande, Caracas 1050, T (582) 761-7538, F (582) 717859; specialized tours and expeditions. *Candes Turismo*, office in lobby of *Hilton*, T 571-0987 and Edif Celeste, Boulevard Sabana Grande, helpful, English, Italian, German spoken. *Quirico Tours*, Torre Lincoln Mall, T 782-5556/9814, next to Plaza Venezuela metro also highly rec for Cuba trips, flight only US$351 return (daily flights) and many other packages available, Celia is extremely helpful and efficient. *Trotamundos*, Centro Plaza, between Altamira and Parque del Este Metros, Torre A, piso 17, C, T 285-2410. *Selma Viajes*, Av Universidad, Monroy a Misericordia, Edificio Dorado Locales A y B, T 572-0235, run excursions to Canaima, eg Wareipa Camp, in hammocks, with trekking and swimming, US$285, rec. *Excursiones Canaima* (Hermanos Jiménez), at Maiquetía airport, T 541-5536/545-0649, F 541-9095, ask for John Manrique who is reported to be efficient and who offers "exceedingly low prices"; this agency does, however, receive mixed reports. Travel throughout Venezuela can be arranged.

In the USA *Lost World Adventures* specialize in tours of Venezuela, ranging from the Caribbean, to the Andes, plus tours of Panama and Ecuador, 1189 Autumn Ridge Drive, Marietta, GA 30066, T (404) 971-8586, (800) 999-0558 outside GA, F (404) 977-3095. UK based *Last Frontiers*, Swan House, High Street, Long Crendon, Bucks, HP18 9AF, T 01844-208405, F 01844 201400, run by Edward Paine (who used to live in Venezuela), organizes tailor-made itineraries to any part of the country, also photographic and painting tours. Also *Geodyssey* run adventure and general tours of Venezuela, incl Angel Falls, Mt Roraima, upper Orinoco, Andes treks and specialist tours for birdwatchers, 29 Harberton Rd, London N19 3JS, England, T (0171) 281-7788, F (0171) 281-7878. *Forum Travel International*, 91 Gregory Lane, Suite 21, Pleasant Hill, CA 94523, T (510) 671-2900, F (510) 671-2993, runs tours to *Las Nieves Eco-Adventure Jungle Lodge*, in the valley of Las Nieves in the Corbatana Mountains, in the transition zone of savannahs and jungles of the Orinoco—a vast array of wildlife, nature tours, canoing, etc.

Tours to Cuba: *Ideal Tours*, Centro Capriles, Plaza Venezuela, T 793-0037/5738, US$406-497 low season, US$449-517 high for 4 days, 3 nights to La Habana, depending on hotel, US$500-640, low, US$575-706, high, for 8 days; price incl flights, transfers, hotel, 2 meals a day, city tour, insurance and excursion to Varadero on 8-day tour.

Tourist Information   Corpoturismo administrative office on floor 35, Torre Oeste, Parque Central (metro Bellas Artes is closest). T 507-8726/8814/8815; open Mon-Sat 0830-1200, 1400-1630, entry by queuing system. Few maps and only standard leaflets available. No maps but wonderful view. There is a smaller office at the airport (see below). The best selection of maps and guides is at the *Hilton Hotel* bookshop. **See p 1433** for **Maps** and further rec reading.

Useful Addresses   Diex: for visa renewal, Av Baralt, El Silencio. YMCA: Edificio YMCA, Av Guaicaipuro, San Bernardino, T 520291.

City Buses   Many buses start from Nuevo Circo bus station (see below), overcrowded in the rush hrs, urban fare usually Bs17-30/US$0.10-0.18 (the correct fare helps to speed things up). On the longer runs these buses are probably more comfortable for those with luggage than a *por puesto*. Midibuses are known as *carmelitas*. *Por puesto* minibuses running on regular routes charge between US$0.15 and US$0.36 depending on the distance travelled within the city; fares rise to US$1.40 for journeys outside. Many *por puesto* services start in Silencio.

Taxis are required by law to instal and use taxi-meters, but they never use them, if they have not already been removed. Fares must be negotiated in advance. Most city trips are US$1.50-1.75 minimum during the day, double at night. Taxi drivers are authorized to charge an extra 20% on night trips after 1800, on Sun and all holidays, and US$0.45 for answering telephone calls. After 1800 drivers are selective about where they want to go. Beware of taxi drivers trying to renegotiate fixed rates because your destination is in "a difficult area". The sign on the roof of a taxi reads "Libre". There are pirates, however, with possibly a taxi sign, but without yellow licence plates/registration-number plate, which are to be avoided. Never tell a taxi driver it is your first visit to Caracas. Several radio taxi firms operate; see yellow pages.

The Metro operates 0530-2300; a/c, clean, well-patrolled, safe and more comfortable and quicker than any other form of city transport; no smoking, no large bags (but may allow rucksacks during off-peak hours). There are 2 lines which are continually being extended: Line 1 (W-E) from Propatria to Palos Verdes; Line 2 (N-S), Capitolio/El Silencio connecting station to Zoológico. A southern extension from Plaza Venezuela to El Valle, plus metrobus El Valle-Los Teques opened in 1995. Tickets vary in price from Bs35-45 according to number of stations travelled. Ten-journey tickets, known as Multi Abono, are available (saves queuing): US$1.50 (US$2.50 to incl Metrobus). Student discounts are available, an ISTC card should suffice. Metrobuses (feeder buses, fare Bs45) connect with the Metro system: get transfer tickets (*boleto integrado*, Bs45/US$0.27) for services to southern districts, route maps displayed at stations—retain ticket after exit turnstile. Guide: *La Practiguía del Metro*, published by Practiguía Azul. Public relations T 208-2740.

Driving Self-drive cars (Hertz, Avis, Volkswagen, Budget) are available at the airport and in town. They are cheaper than guided excursions for less than full loads. Driver's licence from home country accepted. Major credit card or cash deposit over US$200 required. Rates are given in **Information for Visitors**, **Motoring**. ACO and Dollar are rec as the cheapest companies. Budget is the only company giving unlimited mileage, if you book and pre-pay outside the country. Auto and personal insurance (US$10-17.50 per day) strongly rec as you will be lucky to survive two or three days as a newcomer to Caracas traffic without a dent or a scrape. All cars should be checked carefully as most have some defect or other, and insist on a short test drive.

Motorcycles May not be ridden in Caracas between 2300 and 0500. Also see **Motoring**.

Garage *Yota-Box*, 3a Transversal Mis Encantos, Quinta Morava, No 1 15, Chacao, T 313772/331035, owner Gerardo Ayala, rec, especially for Toyota; *Bel-Cro*, Av Intercomunal de Antímano, very good for VWs, also sells new and used parts, very cheap and highly rec.

Airport 28 km from Caracas, near the port of La Guaira: Maiquetía, for national flights, Simón Bolívar for international flights, adjacent to each other (5 mins' walk—taxis take a circular route, fare US$2.25; airport authorities run a shuttle bus between the two). The Tourist Office at the international airport has good maps, helpful; some English spoken, open 0700-2400, T 551060; tourist office at national terminal open 0700-2100, T 551191. When manned, both offices are useful, will book hotels, reconfirm flights, English spoken, better service than Corpoturismo head office. Flight enquiries T (031) 522222; passenger assistance T 552424; police T 552498. Many facilities close 1 Jan, incl duty free and money exchanges. Duty free shops close 2230. Three *casas de cambio* open 24 hrs (Italcambio, good rates, outside duty-free area, check all calculations; best exchange rate with Banco Industrial, branch in International terminal and another, less crowded, in baggage reclaim area). If changing TCs you may be asked for your receipt of purchase; commission 2.5%. There are cash machines for Visa, Amex and Mastercard. Pharmacy, bookshops, basement café (good value meals and snacks, open 0500-2400, hard to find; cafes and bars on 1st floor viewing terrace also good value); no seating in main terminal until you pass through security and check in. No official left luggage; ask for Paulo at the mini bar on the 1st floor of international terminal. Look after your belongings in both terminals. Direct dial phone calls to USA only, from AT&T booth in international departure lounge. CANTV at Gates 15 and 24, open 0700-2100, long-distance, international and fax services, incl receipt of faxes. At Simón Bolívar, airline offices are in the basement, hard to find: Viasa information and ticket desk open 0500-2400 daily, others at flight times. A Viasa lounge on the 1st floor of the International departure lounge, near to the viewing gallery, is open to transit passengers, serving free tea, coffee and soft drinks. If it is closed, transit facilities are poor.

   Always allow plenty of time when going to the airport, whatever means of transport you are using: the route can be very congested and check-in procedures are very slow (2 hrs in daytime, but only ½ hr at 0430). Allow at least 2 hrs checking-in time before your flight, especially if flying Viasa. When several flights arrive close together there are long queues for immigration. Taxi fares from airport to Caracas cost on average US$20-30, depending on the quality of the taxi, the part of city, or on the number of stars of your hotel, regardless of distance;

overcharging is rife. Fares are supposedly controlled, but it is essential to negotiate with the drivers; find out what the official fare is first. After 2200 and at weekends a surcharge of 20% may be added; you may get charged up to US$40. Drivers may only surcharge you for luggage (US$0.50 per large bag). If you think the taxi driver is overcharging you, make a complaint to Corpoturismo or tell him you will report him to the Departamento de Protección del Consumidor. The airport shuttle bus (blue and white with "Aeropuerto Internacional" on the side) leaves from E end of terminal, left out of exit for the city terminal (in city, under the flyover at Bolívar and Av Sur 17, 250m from Bellas Artes metro, poorly lit at night, not rec to wait here in the dark), regular service from 0400 to 0030, bus leaves when there are enough passengers and may not stop at international terminal if no flights due; fare to international terminal US$1. From airport to city, go to start of route at national terminal. The bus is usually crowded so first time visitors may find a taxi advisable. From city to airport at night, to avoid unsafe shuttle departure point, take local La Guaira bus from right hand side of exit from Nuevo Circo terminal to highway by airport. *Por puesto* airport—Caracas US$1.35; leave airport from upper level and climb concrete steps to main road above (not safe after dark). From Caracas they are marked "Caracas Litoral", asked to be dropped off. If heading for a hotel in Sabana Grande on arrival, try taking a *por puesto* minibus (first one at 0500) to Gato Negro metro station and metro from there to Plaza Venezuela or Sabana Grande. Airport bus or *por puesto* to airport can be caught at Gato Negro metro station. When checking in, keep 10 bolívar bills handy to pay departure tax levied at most large airports (**see p 1436**).

Long Distance Buses The chaotic, dirty, Nuevo Circo bus station is in the city centre. It serves all western destinations until a new terminal is finished at La Bandera. All eastern destinations go from a new terminal at Guarenas (take metrobus or *por puesto* from La Hoyada Metro, or *por puesto* from Metro Petare, Catia, Plaza Sucre or Capitolio, US$0.40-0.55). For Nuevo Circo, La Hoyada metro station is nearest. Give yourself plenty of time to find the bus you need although there are bus agents who will assist in finding a ticket for your destination. Tickets are sold, at most, 24 hrs before departure, sometimes only on the morning of departure. This adds to the chaos at busy periods. Nevertheless, do not be tempted to buy tickets from the touts who wait by buses. Those first on get the best seats so it is advisable to arrive one hour before departure. Buses may also leave early. Watch your baggage carefully up until the baggage door is closed (**see also Road Transport, p 1438**).

Buses for places close to Caracas leave from the other side of the road from Nuevo Circo bus station, via the underpass (eg Los Teques, Higuerote). Long-distance bus travel varies a lot in quality. However, buses from Caracas to Maracaibo, Mérida and San Cristóbal are usually in excellent condition; buses to Guayana are of poorer quality. Frequent service to Maracay, Valencia and Barquisimeto, but buses are often in bad shape; the Panamericana route is not recommended because it takes the old road on which there are many accidents. Aerobuses maintain regular services by a/c coaches with reclining seats between Caracas and the main towns in E and W Venezuela, and also to Cúcuta, in Colombia. The fares of other good companies are a third less. The best lines are: to Maracaibo, Expresos los Llanos; to Guayana, Rápidos de Guayana. Aeroexpresos Ejecutivos, Av Principal de Bello Campo, Quinta Marluz (between Chacao and Altamira metro stops), T 266-3601/9011, rec for Valencia, Barquisimeto and Puerto La Cruz, reserve 2 days in advance, except for buses leaving on Fri (no left luggage). Fares are 3-4 times higher than other companies, but worth it. Ormeño at the same address has buses to Bogotá (US$75), Cali (US$90), Quito (US$130), Guayaquil (US$140), Lima (US$190), Santiago (US$270), Mendoza (US$330) and Buenos Aires (US$340). Buses stop frequently but there will not always be a toilet at the stop; always take your own toilet paper. Long distance *por puesto* services are twice as expensive as buses, but generally faster. On public holidays buses are usually fully booked leaving Caracas and drivers often make long journeys without stopping. Sat and Sun morning are also bad for travel into/out of Caracas, no problem on journeys of 4 hrs or less. Always take identification when booking a long-distance journey. To avoid theft it is advisable not to sleep on the buses. Times and fares of buses are given under destinations.

Tepsa agents in Caracas: Rayco, Av Olimpo, Edif Anuncia, San Antonio, Sabana Grande, T 782-8276, reported to be very helpful and friendly.

Excursions The cable railway (*teleférico*) up Monte Avila from Av Perimetral de Maripérez, giving a stupendous view of the city (especially at night) and the coast, seems to be out of action permanently (still closed, mid 1995). The future of the *Humboldt Hotel* on the summit (2,159m) has still not been decided. It has been refurbished, but not even the ground floor bar/restaurant/disco is open. Camping is possible with permission. A dirt road runs from La Puerta section of San Bernardino to the summit, 45 mins in 4WD vehicle, 3 hrs on foot. A rec trip is to ride up in a vehicle and hike back down (note that it is cold at the summit, average temperature 13°C). The *Tamanaco* offers jeep with driver US$50 pp.

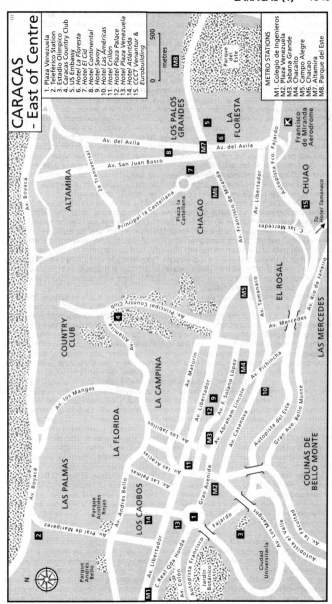

CARACAS
- East of Centre

1. Plaza Venezuela
2. Teleférico Station
3. Estadio Olímpico
4. Caracas Country Club
5. US Embassy
6. Hotel La Floresta
7. Hotel El Cid
8. Hotel Continental
9. Hotel Savoy
10. Hotel Las Américas
11. Hotel Crillón
12. Hotel Plaza Palace
13. Hotel Plaza Venezuela
14. Hotel Atlántida
15. CCCT Venantur &
    Eurobuilding

METRO STATIONS
M1. Colegio de Ingenieros
M2. Plaza Venezuela
M3. Sabana Grande
M4. Chacaíto
M5. Campo Alegre
M6. Chacao
M7. Altamira
M8. Parque del Este

There are three good places to start a hike in the Monte Avila National Park: the first to Pico Naiguatá, 2,765m; the second to Pico Oriental, 2,600m; the third to the *Hotel Humboldt*, 2,150m. Hikers should go in parties of at least three, from the point of view of both mountain and personal safety (Monte Avila is not a dangerous place, but the occasional thief lurks there). Always take water and something for the cold at altitude. The unfit should not attempt any of the hikes.

Pico Naiguatá: a very strenuous hike. Take the metro to La California, then a bus going up Av Sanz, ask for the Centro Comercial El Marqués. From there walk up Av Sanz towards Cota Mil (Av Boyacá), about 4 blocks. At the end of Av Sanz, underneath the bridge, is the entrance to the Naiguatá trail. In about 40 mins you reach La Julia *guardaparques* station, where you have to state your destination and pay Bs 10 entrance. From La Julia the path is straightforward, except at El Eden viewing point, after 40 mins, where you take the wider, lefthand path, not the one going straight up. About 1½ hrs later you reach Rancho Grande, where the stream is the last watering hole. From Rancho Grande to the ridge is 1 hr in forest, 1 hr in sub-páramo. About 500m from the ridge the path separates into lots of smaller ones, most go to the ridge, but follow the plastic markers. At the ridge, turn right (signposted) to Naiguatá peak; stay on the ridge path, not the one that runs a little way down. In about 30 mins you reach Los Platos del Diablo, large flat rocks stacked one on top of another, and in another 30 mins the entrance to the Ampiteatro on your left (watch for the plastic markers). Once you reach the Ampiteatro, a large flat field on the La Guaira side of the ridge, the cross marking the peak can clearly be seen, up and to the right (10 mins away).

Pico Oriental: from the Altamira metro station take a bus to "La entrada de Sabas Nieves", where the *Tarzilandia* restaurant is. From here a dirt road leads up to the Sabas Nieves *guardaparques* station (about 40 mins). The path to Pico Oriental starts at the back of Sabas Nieves and is extremely easy to follow. In about 1½ hrs you reach the "No Te Apures" clearing, where a small path to the left leads down to a little stream, the last watering hole. Returning to the main path, you carry on up towards the ridge, "La Silla", another 1½ hrs away. You are now out of the forest and into the sub-páramo. From here you stay on the same path up to the peak, about another 45 mins. Most people do not stop at the peak, but continue for 10 mins to some large flat rocks for lunch and a sunbathe. There are wonderful views all around, assuming the peak is not shrouded in mist.

Hotel Humboldt: a relatively easy route, 3 hrs. Take the metro bus from Bellas Artes station to El Avila stop; opposite is a grocery. Turn the corner and walk 2 blocks up towards the mountain. At the top of the street turn left; almost immediately on your right is the park entrance. **NB** This area is not safe before 0800 or after dark. Plenty of people take this route, starting 0830-0900, giving plenty of time to get up and down safely and in comfort. About 40 mins after entering the park is Loma de Vientos *guardaparques* station; in another hour is Papelon, another small *guardaparques* post. Here you can either carry straight up on the direct route to the hotel, or you can turn left for a longer, more scenic, less tiring route. Going straight up you will arrive at the hotel in another hour or so. When you reach the top, to the right is the hotel and to the left is a dirt road leading down. If you follow this, in about 15-20 mins you reach a crossing. Turn left and in about 5 mins you will arrive at the *Bodega Galipán*, where lunch is sold (sandwiches, *empanadas*, and glorious fruit juices, blackberry and strawberry, highly rec). If, however, you turn left at Papelon you will find yourself going round the mountain. This flat path will take you past a stream where you can get water (15 mins). Ignore all paths going down the hill to the left and continue until you arrive at a path going upwards and to the right (35 mins from the stream). Once on this path, which passes an old concrete tank, you need not worry about any divisions, they all join up with each other. In about an hour you arrive at the same dirt road that goes to/from the hotel. To the right is the hotel, left to Galipán (which can also be reached by 4WD from Caracas or La Guaira).

Camel Tours, La California Sur, Av Trieste, Qta Reycara, T Caracas 223261, or 014-255356 (cellular), ask for Roberto Andara (speaks English), runs day trips to Galipan for US$25 pp (incl horseriding and barbecues). Further down on the La Guaira side (and best reached from La Guaira) is a Museo Ecológico known as "El jardín de las piedras". It is owned by Zoez, a self-styled prophet, and reflects his beliefs. Open weekends, remove shoes before entering, very interesting; take a picnic, enjoy the designs and views. It can also be reached from Macuto, 20 mins by jeep, or 1½-2 hrs walk, but ask directions as there are two paths, the first of which goes through a *barrio* which must be avoided.

The hiking club, Centro Excursionista de Caracas, Calle Chivacoa, San Román, T 417067, director Marac Papajian, who meet Wed 2030, arranges day and weekend hikes.

Another excursion is to the village of *El Hatillo*, ½ hr from the city centre by car, or take bus from Av Humboldt, one block from Chacaíto Metro station, where colonial style housing has been well preserved, with many souvenir shops and restaurants. On the square is a tearoom serving good cakes. Nearby is the wealthy residential district, La Lagunita, with villas, tennis courts, riding areas and parks.

La Guaira is Venezuela's main port, only 45 mins by road from Caracas (traffic permitting; bus from Caracas US$0.40). Pop 26,420. Mean temperature: 29°C. Dating back to 1567, La Guaira achieved its greatest importance in the 18th century when the Basque Guipuzcoana Company held the royal trading monopoly; many British export-import companies flourished here in the 1800s. The old town, 1 km E of the port, remains intact (much restoration work in progress), with delightful colonial houses along steep narrow streets, several of which climb up to the forts of El Vigía (the lookout), La Pólvora (the Powder Magazine) and the restored Castillo de San Carlos (1610), built on the classic star pattern and commanding a fine view of the port and its surroundings. (If going to the Castillo, aim for Calle León, or take a *por puesto* up and walk down.) The old Camino Real continues upwards from here and can be hiked to Caracas; a second colonial road rises from Maiquetía, 2 km E (see Bradt's *Venezuela* for hiking details). See the imposing Casa Guipuzcoana (1734), on coast road (Av Soublette), original HQ of the company, now used as government offices, a busy cultural centre (free events advertised in Caracas newspapers), the art gallery of the Ateneo de La Guaira and the Litoral branch of the Universidad Simón Bolívar; interesting collections scattered throughout the three floors, including regional hammocks, Indian fishing implements, documents, open Tues-Sun 0800-1800. Many other mansions and churches, incl the Cathedral, the lovely Ermita Carmen (open only weekends pm, key at the Cathedral) and the Casa José María España, home of the first 'martyr' in the War of Independence. The Museo Fundación John Boulton (Calle Bolívar 18-13), formerly housed in the home of the British merchant who arrived in 1824 and built a still-active business, has been moved to Caracas (see under **Museums**).

The town of *Maiquetía* (pop 103,000, adjoining the E side of La Guaira), founded 1670, was the terminus of the old supply road to Caracas. When Guzmán Blanco's Caracas-La Guaira railway was inaugurated in 1883 the town became a favourite bathing resort for Caraqueños (not as healthy nowadays). A pilgrimage is made on foot in Feb from La Pastora church in Caracas to the Maiquetía parochial church along the old supply route. US$9 by taxi from Caracas; many buses from Nuevo Circo marked Maiquetía or Catia. **E** *Hotel Ovetense*, Ranco a Autopista, T 21527, basic, friendly; **E** *Hotel Senador*, Plaza Los Maestros, both hotels cater for short-stay couples, not rec; **E** *Crillon*, esq Navarvete, with shower and toilet, basic but adquate; **E** *Granada* (alias Coromoto), up the hill from Plaza Los Maestros, tiled entrance, reasonable. The *Avila* is a good restaurant, near Plaza Los Maestros; also rec is *Mesón Canarios* and *Cervecería Primera*; opp *Avila* is a good and cheap fish restaurant.

Drivers should note that streets in central Maiquetía and La Guaira are extremely narrow, best to park along Av Soublette rather than try to tour the towns by car.

The coast E of Maiquetía-La Guaira has a string of popular seaside resorts and residential districts with a total population of about 75,000. The divided Avenida Soublette sweeps eastwards past the Punta Mulatos market (which serves most of the Litoral) to Macuto, El Caribe, Naiguatá and so on to **Los Caracas**. All these places can be reached quite cheaply by most 'Litoral' buses from the W end of Nuevo Circo in Caracas. Buses to la Guaira and Maiquetía from Gato Negro metro. If driving, the coastal road E from La Guaira is slow and quite rough, but scenic and interesting, making a worthwhile round trip if you return to Caracas/La Guaira by the paved interior roads.

Macuto, 5 km E of La Guaira, is a seaside town, founded in 1740 (pop 19,370). The coastal promenade (Paseo la Playa) is lined with seagrape trees; there is a splendid yacht marina behind the *Sheraton* and a 'pigeon housing estate'. A place to find some heat and sunshine in the rainy season and somewhere to stay if 'stopping over' between flights. From the Plaza de las Palomas (lots of pigeons) can be seen La Guzmanía, the coastal residence of the President, built by Guzmán Blanco, complete with guards in colonial uniforms. Opposite is the presidential residence built in 1888 for Joaquín Crespo; the initials J and C can be seen over the entrance (for Joaquín and Jacinta Crespo). The building is now a college but can be visited by arrangement. The Castillete de las Quince Letras is the only building on the beach facing the sea, built by Armando Julio Reveron, whose paintings are on display in the Galería Nacional del Arte in the capital; the museum preserves his daily life, paintings, instruments and the life-sized rag dolls he used as models. Open Tues-Sat 0800-1200, 1400-1700, Sun and holidays 1000-1500. The terminal for the Teleférico de Macuto from Pico Avila is here (see Caracas **Excursions**); its future is uncertain. Macuto's beaches tend to be overcrowded at weekends, go midweek if possible. They are now badly polluted, although less so the further E you go. There are no exchange facilities.

Hotels In Macuto itself: **B** *Las Quince Letras**, Av La Playa, on eastern side of town, T (031) 461551, F 461432, one floor renovated, good restaurant, pool; **C** *Santiago*, Av La Playa, T (031) 44214, F 44118, a/c, with bath, clean, but small, bare rooms, poor value, safe for single women, tiny rooftop pool, noisy bar at night, good restaurant (*La Choza*); **C** *Macuto**, Av La Playa y Calle 3, Urb Alamo, T (031) 461310, 3-star, with bath, a/c, hot water, empty mid-week, full weekends, 5 mins walk to beach, comfortable but poorly maintained, swimming pool, safe parking, good breakfasts; **C** *Bahía del Mar*, La Playa y La Costanera, Los Corales, 100m from beach, restaurant; **C** *Plazamar*, Plaza Las Palomas, Calle 3, near La Guzmania, T (031) 44291/44271, run by Italians, rooms with up to 6 beds, clean, pleasant balcony, rec; **D** *Posada del Hidalgo*, Paseo del Mar, delightful, good value, helpful, warmly rec, TV, no restaurant; **C** *Riviera*, Blvd Caraballeda y Calle San Bartolomé, T 44313, 100m from beach, triples available, helpful, a/c, clean, good food (French); **D** *Canta Claro*, Paseo la Playa, basic, very small, 2 rooms with balcony overlooking Paseo, one with private bath; **D** *Diana*, Boulevard Caraballeda (T 031-44278), 50m from the beach, bath, clean, spartan, a/c, helpful, noisy on ground floor especially, safe for motorcycles; **E** *Isabel*, Isabel la Católica y Calle 3, 2 mins from sea, with bath, clean, small, quiet, good; **D** *Alamo*, Av La Playa (possible to bargain), with shower and fan or a/c, clean, good value, English spoken, credit cards welcome, good restaurant on the shore, not cheap; **D** *Alemania*, Paseo Macuto, with bath, F without, fans, old building, sparse but clean, veranda overlooking sea and paseo, pet rooster, cheapest in town; **D** *Bahía*, Paseo Macuto, friendly, clean; **D** *Colonial*, Paseo Macuto No 48, T 031-44153, near beach, good value, bath, a/c, smart, clean, good restaurant and service, accept credit cards; **D** pp *Pensión Guanchez*, Calle Guzmania, with fan, shower and toilet, breakfast US$1, excellent set lunch US$3-4, no sign outside, noisy, friendly, manager speaks English and Swedish.

The posher area of Caraballeda is 5 km E of Macuto: **L2** *Macuto Sheraton**, on public beach, Apartado 65 La Guaira, T 944300, F 944318, 3 restaurants (good food and value) and all 5-star facilities, will store luggage (tip the porter), post office; **A1** *Meliá Caribe**, on beach just E of *Sheraton*, T 031-945555, 3 restaurants (good), pool, disco, noisy, try to get a room on the landside, car rental, free tennis, expensive gym; **C** *Royal Atlantic*, on seafront promenade, two blocks from beach, pool, restaurant with seafood specialities, T 031-941350; **C** *Fioremar*, near *Meliá Caribe* and beach, T 031-92478, solarium, in good restaurant area; **D** *Sierra Nevada*, near *Sheraton*, small pool, bar/restaurant, pleasant; **D** *Mar y Cel*, Av La Costanera y El Palmar Oeste, T 031-942174, reasonable value. Quite a few aparthotels in the area, up to US$100 a day without meals.

Restaurants In Caraballeda, along Av Principal are *Neptuno*, good seafood, rec; *El Bodegón del Lino*, Spanish-style; *El Portón del Timotes*, seafood, good service. Good cheap Arab food at *La Barra de Nelson*; *La Esquina*, near *Hotel Alamo*, good, on Av La Playa; on same ave *Los Roques*; many more on Paseo La Playa, eg *Criolla II Castilleto*, on Perimetral, for seafood. *Panadería* Apolo 8, on Alamo, good cakes; *El Coral*, Av La Playa, next to *Hotel La Cheza de Santiago*, good seafood and quite cheap; *Chifa*, Paseo del Mar, good, huge portions; *Los Criollos*, Paseo del Mar, good food. There is a *MacDonalds* in Caraballeda.

Travel Agent Horse riding and other activities are organized by Jesus Risquez, T 031-45179, and his partner, Carlos. They both speak excellent English, and the horse rides along the beaches or up into the hills are highly rec.

Transport *Por puesto* from Caracas US$2, about 1 hr (taxi US$30); *por puesto* to airport, domestic terminal, US$1, 15 mins, or take Catia La Mar bus, 25 mins, starts at 0600, stops in front of airport. The taxi fare from the airport is officially US$12, 30 mins (plus US$0.50 for a large suitcase or rucksack—beware of overcharging); more to the *Macuto Sheraton*. Anyone wanting to get on a *por puesto* back to Caracas at rush hour (weekend afternoons, etc) is advised to walk back to one of the early stops such as the *Macuto Sheraton*. Bus from Caracas is caught one street down from Universidad. Tourist transport with Andrés and Isabelino, T (031) 519146, in 8-seater van, Spanish only, rec.

Beaches Fishing (boat rental at *Macuto Sheraton* marina) just N of La Guaira (mostly marlin). To the W of the airport is **Catia La Mar** (pop 131,400), not recommended because it is industrial, very littered and the sea is heavily polluted, but it is very convenient for Maiquetía airport, taxi, officially US\$12 (but US\$4-9 with bargaining). (**B** *Aeropuerto*, shower, a/c, OK, stores luggage; **C** *Bahía del Mar*, clean, swimming pool, good restaurant; **C** *Scorpio*, clean, modern, but cockroaches; **D** *Catia del Mar*, modern, clean; **E** *Hotel Del Sur*; *Balneario Camurí Chico*, 3 good beaches, restaurant, showers, water fairly clean, rec.)

East of Caraballeda is a series of small resorts, most with their own walled-in public beaches (strong undertows)—Tanaguarena, Puerto Azul, Uria, etc—until the cliff-hugging road arrives at **Naiguatá** (pop 24,100), an old village in the shadow of the Avila National Park's highest peak (Fiesta de San Juan, 24 June, and Corpus Christi, costumed devil dancers, etc). There are lovely views of rocky coast and surf from the corniche road to **Los Caracas** (50 km from La Guaira), a holiday resort subsidized by the government for low-income workers; there is a beautiful white sandy beach and many cheap hotels, cabins and apartments to rent. Accommodation is difficult during vacation times as union members are given priority. **C** *Hotel Guaicaimacuto*, restaurant, pool, rooms with terraces more expensive, T 541-6487 (INCRET—Worker's Training & Recreation Institute) for reservations.

It is possible to continue on along the Barlovento coast to Higuerote and return to Caracas on paved roads via Caucagua and Guatire, a round trip of about 300 km. Beyond Los Caracas (last gas until Carenero), the road is dirt and carries little traffic (4WD vehicle rec because of the rivers to be forded, but cars can usually manage). It does not hug the coast as before but links many tiny fishing settlements. Near Osma (10 km) is the Granja Osmán, which has some cottages for rent (A, incl meals and watersports equipment); in **Todasana** (22 km) is the German-run *Egua*, hotel and restaurant, D, fans, modest. The road continues on through La Sabana (very popular 2 km sandy beach, waterfall on R of road) and Chuspa (coconut palm-fringed sandy beach) to **Chirimena** (67 km from Caracas), where the highway paving begins again, and thence 14 km to Higuerote (see p 1393).

Islas Los Roques lie 150 km due N of Caracas; the atoll, of about 340 islets and reefs, constitutes one of Venezuela's loveliest National Parks (225, 241 ha). There are long stretches of white beaches (beware of sunburn as there is little shade), miles of coral reef with crystal-clear water ideal for snorkelling (best at Francisqui and Cayo Agua), and many bird nesting sites (eg the huge gull colonies on Francisqui—Cayo Francés—and the pelicans, boobies and frigates on Selenqui). Small lizards, chameleons and iguanas, and cactus vegetation on some islets also add to the atoll's variety. Many of the islands' names seem strange because they are contractions of earlier names: eg 'Sarky' comes from Sister Key, 'Dos Mosquices' from Domus Key, where there is a Marine Biology Centre researching the coral reef and its ecology. For more information write to La Fundación Científica Los Roques, Apartado No 1, Av Carmelitas, Caracas 1010, T 326771.

Gran Roque is the main and only inhabited island; here flights land near the scattered fishing village (pop 900) which is Park Headquarters; average temp 27°C with coolish nights. Private accommodation is available, eg small *pensión* run by Sra Carmen Zambrano, *Posada Vora La Mar*, run by Marta Agustí, US\$30 full board, T Caracas 238-5408; **C** *Posada Margot*, very clean, breakfast and dinner incl, often has water and electricity problems; rooms rented by María, cheap and friendly with excellent seafood, and others. You can negotiate with local fishermen for transport to other islands: you will need to take your own tent, food and (especially) water. "Eola" is a yacht,fully equipped, with cabins, chartered for US\$100 per day, all incl, highly rec as a worthwhile way of getting some shade on the treeless beaches. Run by Italians Gianni and Jaqueline, book direct by phone, T (99) 216735. **Sesto Continente Dive Resort**, on the edge of the village, ask for Saul and Marianne, very kind people, 2 dives cost US\$60, the boat is comfortable, rec. Nordisqui is very isolated while Madrisqui has many summer houses. Cayo Francés has an abandoned house and enough vegetation to provide shaded hammock sites, and accommodation at US\$30 pp, full board incl drinks, good food, friendly staff, nice beach, snorkelling gear, water and light 24 hrs, fan, bargaining possible if you stay for several days. **Warning to would-be campers**: leave nothing out on the ground, the crabs eat everything! The *Pelicano Club* has accommodation and organizes excursions, boat trips and dives, rec. Cayo Francés is two islands joined by a sandspit, with calm lagoon waters on the S and rolling surf on the N; May is nesting time at the gull colonies here. For solitude, Los Roques are a "must" midweek: Venezuelans swarm here on long weekends and at school holidays. Tiny but irritating biting insects in the calmer months can make camping miserable. Marta Agustí at *Posada Vora La Mar* can put you in touch with fisherman Andrés Ibarra, who can negotiate for transport to other islands; reasonable prices. If you are looking for solitude, ask Andrés to take you to Nordisqui or Isla Larga.

To get to Los Roques, take a SAN flight from Maiquetía airport, 4-5 flights a day, max 12 passengers (return fare US\$100), or with Chapi Air to Gran Roque from Maiquetía at 0800, returning at 1600, US\$100. Aereotuy (T 02-262-1966/716231) fly to Gran Roque from Porlamar, return fare US\$110. Tours for 1 night, 3 meals, excursions and flight cost US\$225.

Other Excursions Further afield, in San Francisco de **Yare** (pop 18,000), a celebration is held at Corpus Christi (early June); the dance before the church of the enormously masked red devils, and of most of the villagers. It lasts the whole day (see **Music and Dance** section). Yare is about 90 km from Caracas; the road to it is through Petare and down the Río Guaira as far as Santa Teresa, and then up the Río Tuy. From Santa Teresa make a detour to the beautiful and little frequented **Guatopo National Park** on the road to Altagracia de Orituco, but you must return to Santa Teresa to continue your journey to Yare.

At the Parque Guatopo are various convenient places to picnic on the route through the forest. Take insect repellent. To stay the night in the park a permit must be obtained. There are a number of good nature trails in the park, for instance a 3 km trail from Santa Crucita Recreation Area (well-signposted).

Another excursion is into the mountains to **Colonia Tovar** (1,890m, pop 4,330), a village founded in 1843 by German immigrants from Kaiserstuhl in the Black Forest, recruited by the geographer Agustín Codazzi and enticed by the government's promise of free land and little interference. They retained their customs and isolation until a paved road reached the settlement in 1963. It is now a favourite of Caraqueños and has become very touristy, but the blond hair, blue eyes and Schwartzwald-accented German of the inhabitants are still much in evidence. *Tovarenses* make unsurpassed bread, blackberry jam and bratwurst, and grow strawberries, coffee, garlic, rhubarb and flowers for the Caracas market. A tour of Colonia Tovar encompasses delightful landscapes, mild climate, old architecture (see the Scandinavian-style ceramics) and dignified hospitality. There is a small museum which tells the history of the 241 pioneers who founded Tovar (117 died on the outward voyage) and the nearby offshoot of El Jarillo (museum open 1000-1800, Sat and Sun, and holidays). The church of San Martín de Tours is L-shaped, a copy of the one in Emmendingen, Germany. Carnival preserves European traditions and is unique in Venezuela. Many *petroglifos* (rock paintings) in the region from La Victoria to the Caribbean; seek Sr Néstor Rojas, owner of *Cabañas Baden*, who is an authority and will give directions.

The $1\frac{1}{2}$-hr drive up from Caracas is easy during the week, but murder on weekends—long traffic jams, difficult to find picnic spots or accommodation, definitely not recommended. Keep your passport with you in case of military checks. The road leaves the capital at Antímano and climbs gently for l9 km to the market town of **El Junquito**, another town heavily frequented by Caraqueños at weekends (several short-stay hotels, such as **E** *Himalaya*, parking, magnificent views); roadside stalls sell souvenirs, fruit and barbequed *chorizos* (pork sausages). The road then winds another 19 km to a paved turnoff, where several roads lead down to the coast (see below). To the S of the road is the **Parque Nacional Macarao**, small but attractive; from one point on this road Caracas can be seen to the E and the Caribbean to the N. At the coast turnoff (Km 44) is an arch over the road marking the Aragua state border; $3\frac{1}{2}$ km beyond is the *Charcutería Tovar*, a good place to stock up on picnic supplies, closed all Mon and Tues am. Nearby is a grass ski slope, skis rented by the hour.

Hotels in Colonia Tovar Credit cards widely accepted. *Alta-Baviera*, T 51483, 0.8 km above village on La Victoria road (Prolongación Calle Codazzi), heated, private bath, good view from restaurant terrace; *Bergland*, T 51229, on same road, some cabins, beautiful views, good cheap breakfasts; *Drei-Tannen*, T51-246, private road on right just before entering village from E, 7 rm, 2 heated apartments, parking, owner Señora Klemperer; *Edelweiss*, T 51139, just past the *Alta Baviera*, highest hotel in town!—superb vistas, 8 rm, 3 cabins, parking; *Freiburg*, T 51313, cross river at "El Molino" sign in village and continue along hillside until signs to hotel, rooms and cabins, heated, restaurant; *Kaiserstuhl*, T 51132, Calle Bolívar in centre, parking, good views, 2 restaurants (A2 with breakfast and dinner); *Selva Negra**, T 51072, in centre near church, some cabins, heated, children's park, popular restaurant, parking. All are at least **B** and are normally full at weekends; room rates incl good, German-style food. **D/E** *Guest House Alicia*, beside *Selva Negra*, nice. Other rec **restaurants**: *El Codazzi*, in centre on Calle Codazzi, traditional German and Hungarian dishes, strudel and biscuits, open 1100-1600, closed Mon and Tues; *El Molino*, on Molino next to the historic old mill (worth a visit), has *cabañas* (C), use of kitchen, good restaurant, great *jugo de fresas*, wide selection of

German dishes, open 0900-1000, 1200-1600, 1800-1900, Mon 0900-1400, highly rec; *Perolón*, Calle Codazzi, only open weekends and holidays 1100-1900, homemade vegetable soup a speciality; *Café Munstall*, opp the church, interesting location in oldest house in Colonia Tovar, pastry and coffee at weekends; also *Bodegón La Bruja* and *La Montaña*. *La Ballesta*, turn L at sign before entering Tovar, restaurant on 3 tiers with prices to match, snacks and meals weekends and holidays, adjoining rifle and archery ranges, equipment for hire (cross bows - *ballestas* - no longer available since an arrow landed in a restaurant table). Local fruit, vegetables and flowers sold at *Frutería Bergman*, next to Lagoven station at E entrance to town; across the street is *Panadería Tovar* for delicious bread; many food stalls on weekends along Av Codazzi.

It is generally easy to get a lift if there are no buses. Taxi fare for the round trip from Caracas to Colonia Tovar (driver will wait) is about US$20. Bus from Av Sur 9 y El Rosario, next to Nuevo Circo, to El Junquito (1 hr, US$0.40), then change for Colonia Tovar (1 hr, US$0.55). *Por puesto* from Plaza Catia or O'Leary (more frequently), Caracas, 1 hr, US$1. Alternatively, take a *por puesto* from Plaza Capuchino to El Junquito, then one from there to Colonia Tovar, US$1. If changing *por puesto*, make sure the driver stops at the right place.

The road which leaves the Colonia Tovar-Caracas road (Highway 4) 8 km before Tovar divides soon after into three paved roads which wind down the mountains through beautiful scenery to Puerto Cruz, Chichiriviche and Carayaca respectively. It is 43 km to **Puerto Cruz**, a tiny harbour with a good beach. Boats can be hired here for a 14 km trip W to the even smaller settlement (pop 200) of **Puerto Maya**, on a beautiful bay and accessible only by boat; the villagers are mostly descended from African slaves. The second road leads down the valley to Chichiriviche (40 km from Tovar, not to be confused with the resort W of Puerto Cabello), a neat little town with no accommodation; potholes in the last section of the road make a high-clearance vehicle useful. (A new coastal jeep track now links Chichiriviche with Puerto Cruz, not yet suitable for conventional cars.) The paved coast road begins at Chichiriviche and runs E to Catia La Mar and Maiquetía. First resort is **Oricao** with its lovely palm-rimmed but private beach, then comes **Puerto Carayaca**, where the third paved road down from Tovar reaches the coast. At Pto Carayaca is *Casa Francisco*, hotel and restaurant, **D**, attractive setting. A few km inland are the small towns of Tarma and **Carayaca** (only other gas station in the area apart from Colonia Tovar), where yet another paved road runs from the Tovar-El Junquito road to the coast (at Arrecifes). Many of the coves along this coast are good for swimming and renowned for sport fishing; the vegetation covering the mountainsides is lush and attractive: ferns, orchids, bromeliads, etc.

From Colonia Tovar, Highway 4 continues (well-paved but hair-raising) S down the slopes for 34 km to La Victoria on the Caracas—Valencia Highway (see below); four buses a day, US$1.50; glorious scenery.

WEST FROM CARACAS (2)

A varied region, through which run the Central Highlands; N of the highlands is the Caribbean, with secluded coves and popular resorts. Two coastal national parks are Morrocoy, offshore, and the dunes around the old city of Coro. Straddling the mountains is the birders' paradise of Henri Pittier National Park. South of the Highlands are Lake Valencia and the agricultural and industrial centres of Maracay and Valencia.

100 km W of Caracas is the great basin in which lies the Lago de Valencia and the towns of Maracay and Valencia. The basin, which is only 450m above sea-level, receives plenty of rain and is one of the most important agricultural areas in the country; sugar, cotton, maize, beans and rice are the main crops. In the other valleys and depressions in the Central Highlands are also grown manioc, bananas, cocoa and the superb local coffee.

The Pan-American Highway, which links Caracas by road with the other capitals of South America, follows closely the route of Gómez' Great Andean Highway as far as the Lago de Maracaibo, though many sections have been widened and straightened. At the start, there is the choice of a direct toll motorway to Valencia (with exit to Maracay), toll US$0.60, or the old road called, familiarly, "La Pan-americana" and known for its dangerous bends. It leaves La Rinconada race course to its left and passes (Km 11) the Venezuelan Institute of Advanced Scientific Research (IVIC) which has an excellent Museo de Antropología and the most advanced scientific library in South America. 2 km further on is Cristalart, a glass-blowing factory, visitors welcome, shop. The Panamerica continues its steady climb into the Teques mountains; past the turn off to Carrizal is the park of **Las Colinas de Carrizal** (collections of local fish and birds, and pleasant paths). By taking the old highway alignment just beyond, motorists can look down to the Guaicaipuro Cave and the old Indian gold mine below it. 25 km from Caracas the highway reaches Los Teques roundabout and enters **Los Teques**, capital of Miranda state (pop: 164,440; alt 1,180m founded 1703). The city is a mixture of skyscrapers and colonial buildings around Plaza Guaicaipuro (statue of the Carib chief who fought the Spaniards here) and Plaza Bolívar (Cathedral etc), with several attractive parks. Parque Gustavo Knoop, named after the director of the German-built Caracas-Valencia railway which ran through the town in 1894-1951, opens 0800-1800 except Mon; Plaza Altamira; Parque El Encanto in the mountains nearby, is reached by a 20-min ride aboard an 1891 German locomotive and antique carriages from the old Los Teques station, 1 km S of the town beside the highway, large parking lot, also terminus for buses from Caracas, 3 trips weekdays, 9 weekends, starts 0900, last return 1800, adults US$1.50, children US$0.75 return.

Hotels and Restaurants C *Gran Casino*, Carabobo y Boyacá, central, noisy, disco, good restaurant 1100-2300, parking; many motels on the old highway from Caracas; **D** *Alemán*, Plaza Miranda, friendly, good food. **Restaurants**: *Hípico*, in wooded suburb of Club Hípico, varied menu incl Spanish dishes, open 1100-2300, popular; *Don Blas*, in shopping centre at highway interchange for San Antonio, good steaks and fish, 1130-0100; *Hotel Los Alpes*, Km 28 on Panamericana S of city, dining room open 0800-1130, 1200-2200, closed Mon, bakery next door with hot chocolate, *empanadas* etc, good snack stop if avoiding Los Teques.

24 km beyond Los Teques on the way down into the fertile valleys of Aragua, we can either join the Caracas-Valencia tollway or take the older road through several attractive towns such as **La Victoria** (pop 105,000). Venezuela's oldest bullring is here. Despite the surrounding industrial zones the city retains much of its 18th century charm; visit the beautiful Nuestra Señora de la Victoria church (**Hotels**: **A2** *Onix*, in Omni shopping complex, Urbanización Industrial Soco, in older E part of city, modern, 115 rm, all facilities, comfortable; **C** *El Recreo*, converted 1724 sugar hacienda on highway W of town, restaurant, pool, very pleasant.) The Quinta de Bolívar is at **San Mateo**, between La Victoria and Maracay. The Liberator spent much of his youth here and the museum is a must for anyone interested in Simón Bolívar, open 0800-1200, 1400-1700 except Mon. The rich San Mateo Church is also worth a visit. Soon after San Mateo, Highway 11 leads off S (45 km) to San Juan de Los Morros (see p 1387).

The Panamericana to Maracay should be taken at least once, for views and local colour, but winding up and down the mountains behind slow, smelly trucks is not much fun. The toll road also offers good views.

The new highway avoids city centres, so all that is seen of Maracay, Valencia and Barquisimeto are factories plus the huge concrete Barquisimeto Fourth Centenary Monument. Beyond Barquisimeto there are mountains like slag heaps, until we reach the green of the Andes.

Maracay (pop 538,620; alt 445m), capital of Aragua State, is a peaceful city. It is the centre of an important agricultural area, and the school and experimental stations of the Ministry of Agriculture are worth visiting; it is also important industrially and militarily (it was the base for the two thwarted coups in 1992). In its heyday it was the favourite city of General Gómez and some of his most fantastic whims are still there: the Jardín Las Delicias (on Av Las Delicias, en route to Charoní; take an Ocumare bus from terminal) with its beautiful zoo (closed Mon), park and fountain, built for his revels; the bull ring (1 block W of the Casa de la Cultura), an exact replica of the one at Seville. The Gómez mausoleum (C Mariño), built in his honour, has a huge triumphal arch. The heart of the city is Plaza Girardot. Its colonial character has been lost to modern apartments, while the streets around the square are a veritable bazaar of jewellery, clothing, electrical and shoe shops. On the plaza is the attractive, white Cathedral, dating back almost to the city's foundation in 1701. There is an interesting collection of prehispanic artefacts in the museum of the Instituto de Antropología e Historia on the S side of the plaza; revealing how densely-populated the shores of Lago de Valencia once were. Open Tues-Fri 0800-1200, Sat and Sun 0900-1300, admission free. At the opposite end of the same building is a poor history museum, with rooms dedicated to Gómez and Bolívar, open Tues-Fri 0800-1200, Sat and Sun 0900-1300, admission free. At the rear end of the building is the History library with a charming small reading room and large single table, the walls are lined with portraits of Bolívar. 500m E is Plaza Bolívar, said to be the largest square bearing the name of the Liberator in Latin America. On one side is the Palacio del Gobierno, originally the *Hotel Jardín*, built by Gómez in 1924. Also here are the Palacio Legislativo and the modern opera house (1973). The park with its statues, colonnades and squirrels is a pleasant place to stroll.

The **FAV (Fuerza Aérea Venezolana) Museum** on Av Principal, Las Delicias suburb, is open on Sun from 0800 to 1800. About two dozen aircraft are displayed, incl Second World War fighters and bombers, later jets and earlier aircraft from between the wars. (Closed for renovation since 1992.)

Hotels **A3** *Byblos**, Av Las Delicias, a/c, good restaurant, some English spoken, good value, disco at weekend, rec, high standard; **A3** *Maracay Golf**, Las Delicias, 6 km N of the centre, difficult to find, unless by taxi, swimming pool (closed Mon), gymnasium, nightclub, private golf course; *Italo*, Av Las Delicias, but closer to town, on bus route, 4-star; **A3** *Pipo**, Av Principal, El Castaño, swimming pool, discotheque, friendly, rec restaurant (parrillas a speciality), in hills above the city, inconvenient, except with own transport; **C** *Princesa Plaza*, Av Miranda Este entre Fuerzas Aéreas y Av Bermúdez, T 336953, F 337972, new commercial hotel, one block E of Plaza Bolívar, convenient, clean, inexpensive restaurant; **C** *Wladivar*, Av Bolívar Este 27, friendly, clean, spacious, lots of insects; **D** *Caroní*, Ayacucho Norte 197, Bolívar, a/c, clean, TV, hot showers, comfortable, rec; **D** *La Barraca*, Av Bolívar Este 186, shower, a/c, TV, clean, friendly, safe parking, noisy at weekends, good value; **D** *San Luis*, Carabobo Sur 13, off main shopping street, clean, showers, friendly; **E** *Central*, Av Santos Michelena 6, T 452834, clean, safe, central; **E** *Guayana*, opp *Wladivar*, satisfactory; **E** *Oma*, Calle Libertad 32, between Av Paez and Av Miranda, with bath, clean, rec. Budget hotels are located in the streets around Plaza Girardot. (*Bookable through Fairmont International.)

Restaurants Many excellent restaurants in the Av Las Delicias area, incl *Vroster*, grills, large portions, popular with locals, good service, rec; most are American style drive-up, fast-food outlets. *Carne Tropical*, Av Bolívar y 5 de Julio, OK; *Biergarten Park*, on E side of Plaza Bolívar, a pleasant, covered terrace with bar and restaurant, some German and Italian specialities, overall local flavour, cheap and good; many reliable Chinese restaurants and *loncherías*, *tascas* and inexpensive restaurants in the streets around Plaza Girardot.

Exchange Banco Consolidado (American Express), Av Bolívar y Fuerzas Aéreas, in the basement of Parque Aragua shopping mall. *Cambio* in *Air Mar* travel agency, ground floor of CADA Centro Comercial, Av 19 de Abril, Local 20, 2 blocks N of Plaza Girardot, 2.5% commission.

Cultural Events Casa de Cultura, art and cultural exhibitions, 2 blocks NW of Plaza Bolívar, open Mon-Fri 0800-1500.

Travel Agency in Edificio Elizoph, Av 19 de Abril Este, Rose-Marie speaks excellent English, very helpful.

Airport 5 km from the centre.

Buses Bus station is 2 km SE of centre; *por puesto* marked "Terminal" for the bus station and "Centro" for the town centre (Plaza Girardot). To **Maracaibo** Expresos los Llanos, US$8; **Valencia**, US$0.50, 1 hr; **Caracas**, US$1.50, 2 hrs, *por puesto* US$3. **Barinas**, US$5, 7 hrs; **Choroní** or **Rancho Grande/Cata**, 5-6 departures daily, constantly changing timetable starting at around 0500, more services at the weekend, US$1.20, 2½ hrs; **Ciudad Bolívar**, US$9.50, 10 hrs. To **Coro**, US$4.55, 7¾ hrs. Oriente destinations incl **Margarita** served by Expresos Ayacucho, T 349765, daily departure to Margarita, 1400, US$15 (incl first class ferry crossing). Buses to many other destinations.

Through the Henri Pittier National Park to the Coast The 107,800-hectare **Henri Pittier National Park** (established 1937) is the oldest in the country. It extends from the N of Maracay to the Caribbean, excluding the coastal towns of Ocumare, Cata and Choroní, and S to the valleys of Aragua and the villages of Vigírima, Mariara and Turmero. A land of steep rugged hills and tumbling mountain streams, the park rises from sea level in the N to 2,430m at Pico Cenizo, descending to 450m towards the Lago Valencia. The dry season runs from Dec-Mar and the rainy season (although still agreeable) is from April-Nov. The variation in altitude gives great variety of vegetation: there are cactii and thorns along the coast, rising to xerophilous woodland, semi-deciduous woods, then lower and upper cloud forests. 578 species of birds have been recorded, representing 43% of all those found in Venezuela and some 5.4 different species for every square km, one of the highest densities recorded in the world. Included are no less than seven different eagles and eight kites. For further information refer to *Parque Nacional de Henri Pittier – Lista de Aves*, by Miquel Lentino and Mary Lou Goodwin, 1993.

Two paved roads cut through the Park. The Ocumare road climbs to the 1128-m high Portachuelo pass, guarded by twin peaks (38 km from Maracay). The road was built by Gómez as an escape route if things grew too hot for him. At the pass is Rancho Grande, the uncompleted palace/hotel Gómez was building when he died; it is in the shape of a question mark and is worth visiting. It is close to the migratory routes, Sept and Oct are the best months. There are many trails in the vicinity. Rancho Grande is the favoured base in the park for ornithologists and naturalists (buses depart from Maracay Terminal). On the site is now a biological research station run by the Institute of Agronomy, Vía El Limón, Maracay, T (043) 450153, situated on the road towards El Limón and Ocumare. When visiting look for Edificio 11 and ask for Iris. Those wishing to stay at the station may be provided with a bed and kitchen facilities for US$10 per night, but a "permiso" will be needed from the above address and you will need to show affiliation with a suitably scholastic or scientific body. These requirements do not seem to be adhered to rigidly. Bring warm sleeping bag, candles and food; nearest supplies at El Limón, 20 km before Rancho Grande. A taxi can be hired at Maracay for a day's outing in the park for about US$30 (bargain hard). The last bus back to Maracay leaves at about 1730.

The Ocumare road goes to the coastal towns of: Turiamo (restricted naval base); *Ocumare de la Costa* (pop 6,140), 48 km from Maracay, 2-2½ hrs by bus US$0.80, very dirty, not so bad after the Monday clean-up (Hotels **B** *Montemar*, **D** *Casona*, next door, family-run, restaurant, **D** *Playa Azul*, similar, modest and on the coast at nearby *El Playón*; hotel-restaurants *Posada María Luisa*, T (043) 931184; **E** *La Abuela*, stuffy, nice restaurant and *El Playón*; Restaurants: *Don Juan*, *Pizzería Sabrosa*, *Rey del Pescado*, *Chalet Suizo*, here and in La Boca, *por puesto* from the plaza in El Playón to Cata, US$0.25); *Bahía de Cata*, once a beautiful beach, now overdeveloped particularly at W end, basic cabins for rent on beach (D), good fish restaurant, run by Pepe (in low season, May-June, restaurants close 1530), *por puesto* from Ocumare US$0.70. The Carmil residential suburb impedes access to much of the coast but beaches are public and you are permitted to enter through gates in the fence. The smaller beach at **Catita** is reached by fishing boat ferries (10 min, US$0.70). In **Cata** town (5 km inland, pop of town and beach 3,120) is the small colonial church of San Francisco; devil dancers here fulfill an ancient vow by dancing non-stop through the morning of 27 July each year. **Cuyagua** beach, unspoilt, is 23 km further on at the end of the road. Good surfing, dangerous rips for swimmers. Devil dancers here too, on movable date in July or Aug.

The second road through the Henri Pittier National Park (spectacular but not for timid drivers), goes over a more easterly pass (1,830m), to Santa Clara de **Choroní**, a beautiful colonial town. The Fiesta de San Juan on 31 May is worth seeing (beautiful journey by bus from Maracay, US$1.60, 2½ hrs, every 2 hrs from 0830).

12 km from Maracay on the main road is a *balneario* on the banks of the river, good for picnics and swimming, clean, attractive; entry fee charged. Choroní is a good base for walkers and for those with a more general interest in the park. Some Choroní hotels are within the park boundary. Its local bus, "Metro-Mar", runs to and from Puerto Colombia to Romerito, 16 km away near the heart of the park, 6 times a day. There are numerous opportunities for exploring the unmarked trails, many of them originate in picturesque spots such as the river pools, "pozos", of El Lajao (beware of the dangerous whirlpool) and Los Colores, 6 km above Choroní. Agua Fuerte (9 km above Choroní), has an interesting cultural centre, converted from an old hydroelectric power station. From behind the entrance gate rises a trail which soon divides, one branch extends to the heights above the valley. Watch out for snakes when walking in the park. Other recommended "pozos" are La Virgen, 10 km from Choroní and La Nevera, 11 km away. 8 km N of Choroní are two waterfalls at a dam, El Dique, where one can bathe; in Uraca village (drinks on sale), ask for directions, they are easy to find. For more challenging hikes consult Edilberto who can be contacted at the *Robin Hood Restaurant* (see below).

Choroní Hotels B *Hacienda La Aljorra*, breakfast and dinner incl, 9 colonial rooms in 62 ha of wooded hillside, reservations T Caracas (02) 237-7462, F 238-2436; **B** *Posada Pittier*, 300m from bus terminal, 8 small but immaculate, a/c rooms, good meals, Sat night add US$10, friendly, helpful, garden, rec, T (043) 911028, or Caracas (02) 573-7848, F 577-4410; **B** *La Gran Posada*, 5 km N of Choroní on steep hillside above Maracay road, neat, pleasant bar and restaurant, short walks in the park, T Maracay (043) 549307, F 545776; **D** *Choroní*, colonial building on square, bed and breakfast, dinners available, simple, attractive, small, shared bath, T Caracas (02) 951-7607, F 951-0661.

Just beyond Choroní, across a bridge from the main street then by a branch road behind a towering headland is the dazzling white beach of Playa Grande, backed by palms. At weekends it is spoilt by litter and crowded. It is at the fishing village of **Puerto Colombia**, where bus journeys start and end. If swimming, beware the strong undertow. The usually deserted three beaches of Diario are a 50 mins walk. Leave Puerto Colombia, direction Choroní, after 1.5 km, cross a bridge and turn sharp right. Soon the road becomes a steep concrete track leading to the CANTV station. Go through the gate and when this track bears right, look for the stony path off to the left (easy to follow as it runs directly below overhead power lines). Follow this to the double pylon on the ridge from where the small beaches can be seen, down on the other side. The descent is long but gradual and shaded.

Puerto Colombia Hotels and Restaurants L3 *La Posada de Humboldt*, beautifully reconstructed with cobbled courtyard, fountain, carved balcony, incl all meals, T Caracas (02) 976-2222, cellular (016) 310608; almost opp is **B** *Posada Alfonso*, German owner takes guests at his own discretion, simple, rec; **C** *Hospedaje Montañita*, T (043) 911132, meal plans, mainly packages, nice courtyard, close to Malecón, charming owners, good atmosphere, bath, clean, rec; **C** *Costa Brava*, T 911057, with bath (cheaper without), laundry facilities, good food, English spoken, friendly, family-run, rec; **D** *Hotel Bahía*, near bridge to beach, safe, clean, with bath, terrible beds, restaurant, fan or a/c, friendly; **D** *Don Miguel*, near Alcalde checkpoint, safe, clean, friendly; **E** *La Abuela*, near bridge to La Playa Grande, clean, fan; **E** *Posada Los Guanches*, Calle Trino Rangel, with bath, clean, friendly, rec. A good place to eat is *Brisas del Mar*, chicken and fish, cheap and delicious; *Araguaney* and *Tasca Bahía*, on main street, popular, cheap, but service is poor, beware of salads. *Robin Hood Restaurant*, good for breakfast and pizza, owner Manuel, of Swedish descent, caters for vegetarians too. Camping possible on the beach, dirty at weekends.

Exchange Cash can be changed at very poor rates, at the fish shop near the harbour (better in Maracay).

Many fishing boats for hire in the harbour, US$55 for a day trip to one of the several nearby beaches (although not accessible by road they can be popular, esp at weekends). Launches to Cepe, 45 mins E, Cuyagua, 45 mins W, US$25, best to find people to share with, boats hold six. Flying fish and turtles may be spotted en route. From Puerto Colombia launches (US$20, 30 mins) may be taken to the colonial village of **Chuao**, famous in the past for its cocoa; the most reliable boatman is Amado. The bay is very pleasant with a couple of bars. It has a festival in late May/early June with dancing devils. Tailor-made treks can be arranged through Edilberto, *Robin Hood* or the gift shop *Rincón Caribe* in Puerto Colombia. He can be found at home, off the Maracay road, at Km 46. The best store is out of town on the Choroní road (sells cuatros, hammocks, besides groceries); next door is an excellent Romanian/Venezuelan *panadería* with chairs outside, cheap for breakfast or snacks.

50 km to the W of Maracay the road reaches Valencia, through low hills thickly planted with citrus, coffee and sugar.

Valencia (pop 955,000; alt 480m), the capital of Carabobo State, was founded in 1555. It stands on the W bank of the Cabriales river, 15 km before it empties into the Lago de Valencia (352 square km, the second largest in the country, with no outlet, consequently it is polluted; it has also been shrinking for centuries and is 40% smaller than when Humboldt took measurements in 1800). Valencia is Venezuela's third largest city, the centre of its most developed agricultural region, and the most industrialized. Annual mean temperature 24°C, but the valley is generally hot and humid; rainfall, 914 mm a year. The **Cathedral** (open 0630-1130, 1500-1830 daily, 0630-1200, 1500-1900 Sun), built in 1580 yet remodelled to retain its original style, is on the E side of **Plaza Bolívar**, where there are sloths and iguanas in the trees. The statue of the Virgen del Socorro (1550) in the left transept is the most valued treasure; on the second Sun in Nov (during the

Valencia Fair) it is paraded with a richly jewelled crown. See also **El Capitolio** (Páez, between Díaz Moreno y Montes de Oca), the **Teatro Municipal** (Colombia y Av Carabobo), the old **Carabobo University** building and the handsome **Plaza de Toros** (S end of Av Constitución beyond the ring road) which is the second largest in South America after Mexico City; it seats 27,000 spectators and features renowned international matadors during the Nov Valencia Fair. At Páez y Boyacá is the magnificent former **residence of General Páez** (hero of the Carabobo battle), now a museum where annual painting competitions take place in the Michelena Salon, open Mon-Fri, free admittance. Equally attractive is the **Casa de Célis** (1766), which houses the Museo de Arte e Historia incl precolumbian exhibits; Calle 98 and Av 104 (open Tues-Sat 0800-1400). **San Francisco** church dates back to the 16th century but was rebuilt in 1857. The **Girardot Monument** commemorates Atanácio Girardot, one of Bolívar's warriors. There are also several pleasant parks: Parques Cristóbal Mendoza, Andrés Eloy Blanco and Metropolitano have fountains, nicely-tended flower gardens and leisure activities; the landscaped **Parque Humboldt**, 6 blocks E of the Cathedral, was the terminus of the old railway to Caracas, the station now houses an art gallery and the old passenger cars have become boutiques and restaurants. There is an **Aquarium**, at the W end of Calle 107, which displays a selection of Latin American aquatic life and features a dolphin show at 1600 (open Tues-Sun, 0930-1800, admission US$1). There is a small, unremarkable zoo at the snackbar/restaurant behind the aquarium (open Tues-Sun 0900-2400, closed Mon). From the centre Av Bolívar extends several km N towards the smart residential area of La Viña. The avenue is lined with hotels, banks, a few *casas de cambio* and restaurants (fast food and more typical *loncherías*). Like its Spanish namesake, Valencia is famous for its oranges. There is a nice country club and a celebrated race track. Construction of a Metro began in late 1994. (**NB** Most of the interesting sights are closed on Mondays.)

Festivals Late Mar, Valencia Week; mid-Nov, Valencia Fair (1 week).

Hotels L2 *Intercontinental Valencia**, 5 km N of centre at Calle Juan Uslar, La Viña, T (041) 211533, luxury style resort with pool, garden and all comforts; **A2** *Ucaima*, Av Boyacá 141, T 227011, F 220461, near *Intercontinental*, suites, pool, tennis; **C** *Canaima*, Av Lara con Branger, clean, TV, rec; **C** *Continental*, Av Boyacá 101-70, T 83014, restaurant, good value. There are many hotels across the price range on Av Bolívar, but it is a long avenue, so don't attempt to walk it; select a hotel and if not satisfied, move on: **C** *Hotel 400* and *Le Paris*, both on Av Bolívar (Nos 113-63 and 125-92), a/c, latter with restaurant; **C** *Marconi*, Av Bolívar 141-65, T 213445, with hot shower, a/c, helpful, clean, safe, laundry, rec (next to a petrol station, good pharmacy and health food store), take bus or colectivo from bus station to stop after "El Elevado" bridge; **C** *Don Pelayo**, in town centre, Av Díaz Moreno, rec, good restaurant; **D** *Carabobo*, Calle Libertad 100-37, esq Plaza Bolívar, moderate, with large a/c lobby; **D** *Caribe* T 041-571157/571209) with bath, a/c, clean, safe, central, popular; **F** *Palermo*, Av 97 Farriar, Italian owned, cheap, friendly, simple restaurant, quite good (*-bookable through Fairmont International).

A1 pp *Hacienda Guataparo*, 20 mins from centre, owned by Vestey family, 9,000 ha peaceful farm, all meals, riding and mountain bikes incl, good birding, must be booked in advance through *Last Frontiers*, UK, T 01844-208405.

Restaurants *Sorrento*, Av Bolívar, rec; *Fego*, Av Bolívar 102-75, rec; *El Bosque*, opp *Hotel Marconi*, cheap. *La Rinconada*, Plaza Bolívar, rec, open Sun; *Caballo Blanco*, Av 97 Farriar, cheap and good food, clean, well-lit, Italian run.

Banks and Exchange Banco Consolidado (American Express), Av Bolívar Norte, Edif Exterior; *Turisol* (also Amex); *Italcambio*, Av Bolívar Norte, Edif Talia, Loc 2, bring original purchase receipt of TCs, a long way from centre in Urbanización Los Sauces, get off bus at junction with Calle 132.

British Vice-Consul (Hon): Corporación Mercantil Venezolana, Calle Silva No 100-70, Edif Comersa, T 50411/7.

Laundry La Fuente, Calle Martín Tovar y Colombia, T 86657, rec.

Shopping *Artesanía Típica Edy*, Av Bolívar Norte, Urbanización La Alegría, opp Banco República, rec. **Bookshop** selling and trading English books between pharmacy and health food store by *Hotel Marconi* on Av Bolívar.

Travel Agency For flights to USA and Europe, next to Amex on Av Bolívar.

Airport 6 km SE of centre. Avensa/Servivensa flights daily to Caracas US$37; Barcelona US$46; Maracaibo US$46; Mérida US$67; Porlamar US$61; Puerto Ordaz US$61; San Antonio US$50; Valera US$53. Aserca flies to Maracaibo, San Antonio de Táchira, Barcelona, Maturín, Puerto Ordaz and Porlamar. International to Bogotá 4 per week; Miami daily.

Buses Bus terminus 3 km E of centre, part of shopping mall Big-Low (24 hr restaurants). Entry to platforms by *ficha* (token), US$0.05. Left luggage, turn left on entering, on right near the end. Minibus to centre, frequent and cheap, but slow and confusing route at peak times; taxi US$3 to centre. To **Caracas**, US$1.75, *por puesto* US$3.50, Autoexpresos Ejecutivos (T cellular 014-405010), US$6, 8-9 a day; **Mérida**, 10-12 hrs, US$15.80; to **San Cristóbal**, 10 hrs, US$10; **Barquisimeto**, US$3.25, 3 hrs; **Maracay**, 1 hr, US$0.50. **Puerto Cabello**, US$0.70, frequent, 1 hr or so; **Tucacas**, US$1.40, or US$3 by frequent *por puesto* service. To **Coro** US$4.20, 4½ hrs. To **Puerto Ordaz/Ciudad Guayana**, US$12, 13 hrs. To **Ciudad Bolívar**, 10 hrs.

At La Encrucijada, the first bus stop 20 mins W on the road to Barquisimeto, there are excellent toilets, much better than any that follow.

Excursions Valencia is a useful jumping-off point for the western and central states; there are also many interesting places to visit in the immediate vicinity. One of the largest groups of petroglyphs in Venezuela is to be found in the **Parque Nacional Piedras Pintadas**, 22 km NE, reached by turning off the tollway at Guacara (14 km E of Valencia) and driving 6 km N on the road to Vigírima; turn left at a small blue "Cadafe Tronconero" sign then a further 3 km. Lines of prehispanic stone slabs, many bearing swirling glyphs, march up the ridges of Cerro Pintado. Navy-blue buses run to Vigírima from Valencia at regular intervals (US$1), ask to be let down at the 'Cerro Pintado' turnoff. Near the S shore of Lake Valencia, about 34 km E of Valencia, is the regional centre of Güigüe (pop 44,320, busy road with many cane trucks, possible to continue on around Lake through Yuma and Magdaleno to Maracay); at the nearby village of **La Taimata** other extensive ancient petroglyphs have been discovered. There are more sites along the W shore, and on the rocks by the Río Chirgua, reached by 10 km paved road from Highway 11 (turn N at La Mona Maraven gas station), 50 km W of Valencia. Park by the cemetery in Chirgua and walk along the E side to the river. A further 5 km past Chirgua, at the Hacienda Cariaprima, is the country's only geoglyph, a remarkable 35m-tall humanoid figure carved into a steep mountain slope at the head of the valley; it is above and to the left of the ranch house. 30 km SW of Valencia on the highway to San Carlos is the site of the **Carabobo** battlefield, an impressive historical monument surrounded by splendid gardens. Two battles were fought here: although Bolívar won the first in 1814, his forces were subsequently routed by the *llaneros* of Tomás Boves ('The Butcher') and Bolívar had to flee the country. Seven years later came the famous battle which established Venezuelan independence; on this occasion, Bolívar was greatly assisted by Páez's lancers and by the British legionnaires who had joined him at Ciudad Bolívar (they are particularly realistically represented in the bronze bas-reliefs on the monument). The view over the field from the *mirador* where the Liberator directed the battle is impressive. Historical explanations Wed, weekends and holidays. Buses to Carabobo leave from bottom of Av Bolívar Sur y Calle 75, or from Plaza 5 de Julio, US$0.25, ask for Parque Carabobo (1¼ hrs). Take drinks, none available at the park. You will be denied entrance to the monument if wearing shorts and athletic shirt.

The Caracas-Valencia motorway (Highway 1 to Puerto Cabello) continues down the mountains, reaching the sea near El Palito (refinery and pier). Here we turn right to Puerto Cabello. 18 km from Valencia, the road passes **Las Trincheras** (pop 1,350), a decaying spa with the second hottest sulphur springs in the world (98°C); there are three baths (hot, hotter, very hot), a mud bath and a Turkish bath; delightful setting. Entrance US$1.50, facilities open 0800-1800 daily for US$6.50. **B** *Hotel Termales Las Trincheras**, rooms only for guests on cures, min 21 days, good restaurant open to public 1200-1600, 1800-2100, *fuente de soda* 0700-2100. Opp is **D** *Hotel Turístico*, good. Frequent buses from Valencia.

Puerto Cabello, 96 km W of La Guaira, is the port for Valencia, 55 km away by freeway; it is an industrial city, the second most important Venezuelan port, with an excellent harbour, a lighthouse and a shipyard with dry dock. Average temperature, 28°C; pop 137,250. Little of the town's history as a smugglers' port and gateway for an illicit cacao trade with Curaçao is now evident. The Museo de Historia (open Mon-Fri 0800-1200, 1500-1800, Sat-Sun 0800-1200) is housed in one of the few remaining colonial houses (1790) on Calle Los Lanceros (No 43), in the tangle of small streets between the Plaza Bolívar and the seafront. The forts of San Felipe (1732, also called the Castillo del Libertador) and Solano (1765) recall Spain's strength in the Caribbean. Solano is in a military zone, but access is unrestricted (take a taxi, it's a long walk); the Navy, however, runs free launches across the channel to San Felipe, which was a prison until the death of Gómez in 1935. El Aguila monument in the colonial section marks the site where North American mercenaries (in the pay of Francisco de Miranda) were executed by the Royalists in 1806 during the War of Independence. A standard-gauge 175 km railway runs to Barquisimeto (under which, below, details given).

Festival Shrove Tuesday, carnival festivities incl "hammock dances".

Hotels **B** *Balneario Caribe*, Urbina Palma Sol, on beach front, T (052) 71395, cold showers; **C** *Cumboto*, on beach (polluted) in old Hacienda Cumboto, a/c, pool, open-air restaurant, plain and ageing, but being renovated; **D** *Miramar*, at El Palito, T 3853, on own beach.

Restaurants *Marisquería Romar*, Edif Sabatino (below Ondas del Mar radio station), Av Bolívar, Rancho Grande, seafood, rec; *Briceñoven*, Paseo Malecón, 1½ blocks from Plaza El Aguila, good criollo cuisine; *Mar y Sol*, Calle El Mercado 6-110, facing sea, local favourite for seafood; *Venezuela*, Plaza El Aguila, a/c.

Tourist Office On main square, helpful, friendly, no English spoken, scant literature or maps.

Transport Train to and from Barquisimeto twice daily (see under **Transport p 1367** for details). Airport W on highway, to Maiquetía 30 min, Coro 40 min, one daily non-stop; Maracaibo 80 min, 2 daily (LAV). Taxis to the old town (casco), US$4. Hertz agency at the airport.

One can hike on the old, cobbled Camino Real from Valencia to the village of San Esteban, 8 km inland from Puerto Cabello, rec (Bradt's *Venezuela* has full details).

A paved road runs 18 km E through the picturesque village of Borburata (pilgrimages during Holy Week) to Patanemo, both within the **Parque Nacional San Esteban** (or Miguel J Sanz), 44,000 ha abutting the Henri Pittier Park on the E and stretching almost to Puerto Cabello.

About half an hour E on this road is a beautiful horseshoe-shaped beach shaded by palms called La Bahía. It has a refreshment stand, changing rooms, toilets and lifeguards, but take your own lunch.

There are two other attractive sandy beaches, *Quizandal* (restaurant, showers, drive-in theatre, parking fee), with a coral reef, near the naval base (difficult to find, take a taxi, US$4, but you may find it hard to get one on the way back), and Bahía de *Patanemo*. The latter is a little resort tucked away in the trees. **C** *La Churuata*, family-run hotel, without bath, English, French, Spanish, Italian spoken, pool, horses, excellent food and drink, local excursions, highly rec but very small rooms. Offshore is Isla Larga, where sunken ships make for ideal snorkelling; *lanchas* from Quizandal, US$2, 15 mins, 0700-1600, no shade, take shelter, buy tickets at weekends at wharf, on weekdays seek out individual boatmen. All these beaches are very crowded and noisy at weekends. **NB** The beach to the W of Puerto Cabello is not so attractive; be careful of going beyond the bathing area as the beach is notorious for armed robbery.

24 km W of Puerto Cabello, at the junction of the Pan-American Highway and the road to Tucacas, is **Morón** (pop 56,450), where there is a state-owned petrochemical plant (45 mins from Valencia).

Quite near Morón is the lovely beach of *Palma Sola*, 16 km long and deserted save at Easter time when Venezuelans camp out there in crowds. The water can be dangerous but the sands and palms are superb. There are hotels, many closed in the off season (**B** *Balneario Canaima*, children's swimming pool; **B** *Balneario Caribe*, restaurants and changing rooms). A road has been built from Morón to Coro via Tucacas, an hour from Puerto Cabello.

Tucacas (pop 15,100) is a hot, busy, dirty and expensive town, 30 mins from Morón, with lots of new building in progress, where bananas and other fruit are loaded for Curaçao and Aruba. Offshore is the **National Park of Morrocoy**, where there are hundreds of coral reefs, palm-studded islets, small cosy beaches and calm water for water-skiing, snorkelling, and skin-diving. The Park is reached from Tucacas; camping allowed, no facilities, take food and drink, very crowded at weekends and, in the holiday season, with litter strewn all over the place (no alcohol for sale in the park). With appropriate footwear it is possible to walk between some of the islands. The largest, cleanest and most popular of the islands is Cayo Sombrero (very busy at weekends); even so it has some deserted beaches, with trees to sling hammock. Playuela is beautiful and better for snorkelling (beware of mosquitoes in the mangrove swamps), while Playa del Sol has no good beach and no palm trees. Bocaseca is more exposed to the open sea than other islands and thus has fewer mosquitoes. Cayo Borracho is one of the nicest islands. Boats are for hire: US$10-20 return to Cayo Sombrero, per boat, US$5.25 to nearer islands; ticket office to the left of the car entrance to the Park, they will pick you up for the return journey; Orlando is reliable and one of the cheaper boatmen, Pepe has been recommended. This is one of the two main fishing grounds of Venezuela; the other is off Puerto La Cruz.

Tucacas accommodation and services **B** *Hotel Manaure-Tucacas*, Av Silva, a/c, hot water, clean, good restaurant; **D** *Hotel Said*, at entrance, swimming pool, good; **D** *La Suerte* on main street, very clean, fan, with small shop; **E** *Carlos*, basic, with fan, kitchen and laundry facilities, cheap and cheerful; **E** *Palma*, without shower, fan, owner organizes boat trips. Cheap accommodation is difficult to find, especially in high season and at weekends, hotels are generally more expensive than elsewhere in Venezuela. *Restaurant Fruti Mar*, very good; *Cervezería Tito*, good food; many good bakeries. Camping gas available in Tucacas or Puerto Cabello for camping in the Park. Bicycles can be hired in town. Banco Unión for exchange, Visa card and TCs accepted. Frequent *por puesto* from Valencia, US$3, bus US$1.40.

The only accommodation within the park is **A1** pp *Villa Mangrovia* on the Lizardo Spit between Tucacas and Chichiriviche, 3 rm, good service, reservations through Last Frontiers, UK, T 01844-208405.

Travel Agency and Dive Shops *Guili*, Calle Sucre y Calle Silva, No 1, T 84661, organizes trips to any of the islands; Freddy speaks English, French and Spanish, Valentine speaks German and Russian, if you want to spend several days they will come and check on you every two days. Also tours to Los Roques, Coro desert and Yaracuy river trips. Venezuelan diving clubs come here for their contests. Scuba diving equipment can be hired from near the harbour for US$5 a day, but the diving is reported not very interesting. Try American-owned *Submatur*, Calle Ayacucho 6, T 042-84082, 2 dives, lunch and gear US$65, for scuba diving and trips. *Mike Osbourne's* dive shop, situated on the left hand of the street that leads into Morrocoy National Park, his shop was the first ever opened in Venezuela and you can buy or rent what you need for snorkelling, he and his staff are very helpful and will tell you where it is best to go, diving courses are also available, André Nahon rec.

A few km beyond, towards Coro, is the favourite, and hence expensive, beach resort of **Chichiriviche** (pop 4,700); the town is filthy but offshore are numerous lovely islands and coral reefs. Crowded at holidays and long weekends with lots of litter. It is possible to hire a boat to take you to any one of the islands; recommended for a weekend away from Caracas; note that prices posted onboard or on the jetty are per boat, not per person, and vary according to distance, starting at about US$10 (take a snorkel, no hire facilities; snorkel and mask can be bought from a shop near *Hotel Capri*). All day cruises, stopping at 3 islands, cost US$50 per boat. Prices are fixed, but bargaining may be possible on Paseo por la Bahía. You may camp on the islands, but there are no facilities or fresh water (three islands have beach restaurants serving simple fish dishes, clean, good) and you may require a permit from Inparques (National Parks). Take precautions against rats. Nearby is a vast nesting area for scarlet ibis, flamingoes and herons, the Parque Nacional Cuare. Most of the flamingoes are in and around the estuary next to Chichiriviche, which is too shallow for boats but you can walk there or take a taxi. Birds are best watched early morning or late afternoon.

Hotels and restaurants **B** *Hotel Mario**, swimming pool, restaurant; **C** *La Puerta*, out of town, next to the port, very clean, nice bar and restaurant, helpful owners, rec; **C** *Náutico*, T 99-35866, friendly, clean, good meals (breakfast and dinner incl in price), fans but no a/c, transport to nearest islands incl, popular; **D** *Capri*, near docks (bargain), shower, fan or a/c, clean, pleasant Italian owned, good restaurant and supermarket; bakery opp has tiny rooms, fan, shared bathroom; **D** *Casa Falcón*, Calle Falcón, 2 blocks from sea-front on E side of town, with restaurant, good, cheap, good coffee and juices. Italian owner, Sra Emanuela, also speaks French and English, very friendly, tours arranged, bike rental, bird-watching, highly rec; **D** *Gregoria*, Calle Mariño, with bath, clean, fan, laundry facilities, very friendly, Spanish run, highly rec; **D** *La Garza**, without food, full board available, comfortable, pleasant meals at low prices, popular, pool; **D** *Posada La Perrera*, Calle Riera, near centre, 150 km from bus stop, quiet, fan, clean, laundry facilities, patio, hammocks, helpful, friendly Italian owner, safe, cooking possible, free coffee, tours arranged, rec; **E** pp *Parador Manaure*, T 86236/86121/86452, sharing apartments for 5, clean, small pool, bad restaurant; **E** pp *Villa Marina*, aparthotel, good, clean, safe, pool. Good fish at *Restaurant Veracruz*.

Exchange at banks on main street.

Diving *Subma Tur*, on main street; *Centro de Buceo Caribe*, Playa Sur.

Transport Bus to Puerto Cabello, 2 hrs; frequent por puestos, US$2; 3 hrs to Barquisimeto; 9 hrs to Valera. Direct buses from Valencia to Chichiriviche turnoff.

From Tucacas it is 177 km to **Coro** (pop 131,420, founded 1527, mean annual temperature 28°C), capital of the State of Falcón, a charming town, very quiet on Sun, with interesting colonial buildings (the town is a national monument), surrounded by sand dunes (*médanos*, themselves a **National Park**: take bus, US$0.30, to Parque Ferial and walk. **NB** See **Warning**, below). Worth seeing are the **Cathedral**, a national monument, begun in 1583; **San Clemente** church, built in the shape of a cross with arms pointing to the cardinal points, the wooden cross in the square in front of the church is said to mark the site of the first mass said in Venezuela and is believed to be the country's oldest such monument. The **Museo Diocesano**, Calle Zamora is opposite plaza San Clemente (open Tues and Sun 0900-1200, Wed-Fri, 1600-1900, very interesting, entry US$0.60), **Museo de Cerámica**, Calle Zamora 98 (open Tues, 0900-1200, Wed-Fri, 1600-1900, Sat 1000-1300 and 1600-1900, Sun, 1000-1300, entry US$0.40, nothing special); **Museo de Arte**, Calle 16A Talvera, between Plaza Bolívar and Cathedral, Tues-Sat 0900-1230, 1500-1930, Sun 0900-1600, free, interesting. There are several interesting colonial houses, **Los Arcaya**, Zamora y Federación, one of the best examples of 18th century architecture; **Los Senior**, Talavera y Hernández, where Bolívar stayed in 1827; **Las Ventanas de Hierro**, Zamora y Colón, architecture and furniture, opp is the **Casa del Obispo** (Museo del Tesoro) with a collection of colonial objects housed in the building where the town's rich hid their treasures during the War of Independence. The **Jewish cemetery**, on Calle 43-B y Zamora, is the oldest on the continent. Note that many historical sites in Falcón state close for a siesta; many open only at weekends. Near the village of La Vela along the Morón road the local handicraft is the production of rocking chairs of all sizes made from cactus wood. On the road to La Vela, near the turnoff is the **Jardín Botánico Xerofito Dr León Croisart**, which has plants from Africa, Australia, etc, very interesting, guided tours in Spanish Mon-Fri 1430-1730, Sat 1000-1500, Sun 0830-1200, free. Take Vela bus from corner of Calle Falcón, opp Banco Coro, and ask to be let off at Pasarela del Jardín Botánico – the bridge over the road.

Festivals 26 July, Coro Week; 9-12 Oct, state fair; 24-25 Dec, *Tambor Coriano* and *Parranda de San Benito* (Coro, La Vela and Puerto Cumarebo).

Warning Do not walk alone, or in a small group, to Los Médanos, as armed robbery has occurred in the dunes. Ask locally for latest information.

Hotels at Coro A3 *Miranda**, Av Josefa Camejo, opp old airport, T 510587, beautiful hotel, restaurant, swimming pool; **D** *Arenas*, opp bus terminal, with shower, cold water, a/c, pool, restaurant; **D** *Coro*, Av Falcón, friendly, helpful, clean, a/c, TV, credit cards welcome; **D** *Falcón*, Av Los Médanos, clean, TV, a/c, fridge, good restaurant, 15 mins walk to centre; **D** *Federal*, clean, private bathrooms, fans, restaurant and bar; **D** *Valencia*, with private shower, a/c, clean; **D** *Venezia*, T 068-511811, Av Manaure entre Zamora y Urdaneta, expensive food, good, shower, a/c, TV, friendly, rec; **F** *Capri*, very basic but friendly, large selection of rooms, with fans, facilities reflected in prices, poor maintenance and water supply; and nearby is **E** *Hotel Colonial*, basic, OK bad beds and plumbing, restaurant, bar, parking, near Plaza Bolívar; **E** *Roma*, Calle 14 near plaza, colonial building, clean, friendly, basic; **F** *Hotel Martín*, Calle 14 y 20 de Febrero. At Av 3 y Calle 95, **F** *Coruña*, fan, and *Santa Ana*.

Restaurants *Don Camilo*, by *Hotel Miranda* and airport, reasonable prices; *Mersi*, off Calle Zamora, 1 block down from *Hotel Venezia*, good pizzas; *Cafetería El Indio*, Independencia, nr statue; *Cervecería Alhambra*, Calle Zamora, good, cheap; *Chupulún*, Av Manaure, rec for lunch, homemade *chicha*; *El Bogovante*, Av Los Médanos, cheap and reasonable, *Rica Pizza*, in the same building, also rec; *Cafetería Alameda*, opp San Francisco church, one of the few places open for breakfast, sells *Daily Journal*; *El Vasón*, Calle 18 Garces, excellent; *Hot Dog Centre*, nr *Hotel Colonial*, good pizzas, fast food, outdoor seating. Everything closes 1200-1500.

Exchange Banco Consolidado, Calle Federación con Buchivacoa (for American Express). **Banco Unión** gives cash on Visa cards. On Calle 16A Talavera **Casa de Moneda**, cheques but not under US$50, poor rates.

Travel Agencies *Kuriana*, C Zamora, Diagonal al Museo Diocesano, T (58-68) 522058, F 513035, ask for Mercedes Medina, who has an excellent campsite nearby; *Camel*, Paseo Talavera 6, T 513035, F 522058, Roberto Andara. Both rec.

Tourist Office On Paseo Alameda, English spoken, helpful. Office at airport will help to find a hotel.

Transport and Roads Airport (good restaurant on 1st floor, 10 mins walk from centre); flights to Caracas and Mérida via Barquisimeto. For flights to Curaçao, see next paragraph. Buses to/from **Caracas** US$7.25, 10 hrs; **Maracaibo**, US$4, 4½ hrs, *por puesto* US$8; **Tucacas**, US$3, 3 hrs. Expreso Occidente have their own terminal on Av Manaure with a daily bus to San Cristóbal, 1900, 12 hrs, US$10.25, also to Caracas, Maracaibo, Valencia, Punto Fijo. From Coro, there is a good but uninteresting road to Maracaibo and another paved road along the isthmus leading to the Paraguaná Peninsula, along whose beaches men fish, 15 to 20 a net.

Occasional cargo launches go from La Vela de Coro to Curaçao, very unreliable, contact Oscar Guerrero at Oficina de Migración, La Vela, T 068-78922. The Ferry del Caribe's service from La Vela to Aruba and Curaçao has stopped running. Instead, there are flights from Las Piedras (see below) to Curaçao, daily with Servivensa (you must purchase a return ticket out of Curaçao and Aruba), several daily to Aruba with Air Aruba, US$75 return plus US$10 tax (20 mins flight). For private flights Coro-Curaçao, ask at Coro airport for details of flights and immigration procedures; a good method if not on a fixed timetable. Eg, *Falcon Air*, office in airport, for flights to Curaçao, US$50 return, very friendly and helpful (better to buy return ticket in Venezuela as only one-way can be bought in Curaçao, costing US$84).

The **Paraguaná Peninsula** is connected by pipelines with the oilfields of Lago de Maracaibo. The Maravén (ex-Shell) and Lagovén (ex-Esso) groups have refineries, the former at Cardón, and the latter at Amuay. A small but very interesting zoo with exclusively Venezuelan species, many of which you will never see in the wild, is to be found in the **Comunidad Cardón**, Av 6, T (069) 403485/54222, open Tues-Sun afternoons. *Por puestos* from/to Punto Fijo pass nearby. Also near the zoo is the new **Museo de Historia Natural de Paraguaná**. The whole northern area of the peninsula is quite heavily militarized, so access is restricted, including around one of the mountains, Monte Cano, near Miraca. The airport, which has services to Maracaibo (30 min), Coro, Maiquetía, Curaçao and Aruba (see above, Air Aruba, T 069-51605) is known as **Las Piedras** (Hotels at nearby Judibana: **C** *Luigi*, near the main square, T 069-460970, pleasant and cheerful, good restaurant; *Jarolín*, adequate rooms, decent pool and a restaurant. Good bakery-deli one block from *Hotel Luigi*). The town itself is **Punto Fijo** (pop 89,500; Hotels: **D** *Caribe**, Calle Comercio 21-112; *Safri*, Av Colombia 78-15, clean, cheap, central; *Miami*, Calle Falcón No 21-196; **D** pp *Jardín*; *Fuente de Soda-Restaurant Maracaibo*, Av Bolívar, good, cheap). Taxi from Punto Fijo to Las Piedras, US$3.50, from Coro US$29; also buses Coro-Punto Fijo. The beaches are at least 30 mins away, around Los Taques, N of the airport. Many are accessible by car, few visitors, good for camping but no shade or facilities. There is a seaport, Las Piedras-Paraguaná, between Amuay and Cardón, which also serves the town of Coro.

The villages on the peninsula have interesting colonial churches, notably that of **Santa Ana**, interesting cemetery. It is over 30 km from Punto Fijo to Cerro Santa Ana. The area is hot, dry and windy (and goatherds' dogs can be threatening). For the national park at **Cerro Santa Ana**, drive or take the bus to nearby Santa Ana. Be prepared for uncharacteristic rain, followed by mud, if climbing the mountain. The birdlife and vegetation are interesting, contrasting with the near barren surrounding plains. **Adícora** (pop 4,500) is a quiet little resort on the E side where you can rent a house by the week (no snorkelling); good seafood restaurants, many shut on weekdays. The town becomes busy and dirty at weekends. **E** *La Posada*, Malecón, cheap rooms, 1 apartment, fan, bath, German owners, cheap restaurant, rec; **F** *Hotel Montecano*, Italian-owned, friendly, clean, meals, rec. Bus to Coro, 0915, and at least one other, daily, US$1.50, 2½ hrs (bus stops in every village en route); alternatively hitch on road on E side of peninsula, 35 mins by car. This road goes through the dunes of Coro (see above regarding safety).

Excursions There are six protected nature reserves on the peninsula, organized by a project called Bioma. Information about these areas can be obtained from their office at: Av Arévalo Gonzales y Calle Paez 10, Pueblo Nuevo, T/F 069-81048. One such nature reserve is the **Laguna Boca de Caño** (also known as Laguna Tiraya), N of Adícora, inland from Supi, along a dirt track normally fit for all vehicles. Bird life here is abundant, particularly flamingos. It is the only mangrove zone on the E side of the peninsula. (With thanks to Robert Runyard, Black Forest, CO, USA, for much new information on the Paraguaná Peninsula).

The Segovia Highlands, lying N of Barquisimeto, suffer from droughts, and are only sparsely settled along the river valleys. From Morón the Pan-American Highway strikes up into the hills, a well-paved and scenic road, reaching 550m at *San Felipe* (population 30,750), capital of Yaracuy State. Festivals: 2 April, *día patronal*; 3 May, Velorio de la Cruz de Mayo; 23 June, San Juan. (**Hotels**: *Turístico Río Yorubi*, pleasant, safe, good but expensive restaurant, at the end of Av Los Baños at city's edge; **D** *Hostería Colonial**, Av La Paz, pool; **D** *El Fuerte**, Av La Patria; **D** *La Fuente*, Av La Fuente; **E** *La Patria*, 6A Avenida; **E** *Comercio*, 6A Avenida; **E** *Cabaiguan*, Calle 14).

South of Coro is the **Parque Nacional Juan C Falcón**. It's next to the road from Coro to Barquisimeto. The small village **Curimagua** is best for visiting the park. There are two possibilities to get there: while driving from Coro to Barquisimeto, turn left at La Tabla, but it's a very rough road. You should have a 4WD car, especially if the weather is not too good. The second possibility to get there is: don't turn left at La Tabla, drive a bit further (15 km). Then you find a cross, drive left to San Luis (see below). Drive straight on, after some km you have to turn left, and a very narrow, paved (sometimes very bad pavement, or only gravel) and steep road climbs up the mountain. After about another 10 km you'll arrive in Curimagua. For this road it's also advisable to drive with a 4WD vehicle. There are two nice hotels, the *Apolo* and the *Falcones* (German owned, good food, rec). Both hotels, C, arrange tours to the national park.

From Coro to San Luis, there is only a *por puesto* service which travels through the semi desert of Sierra Falconiana arriving at the beautiful village of **San Luis** with its interesting church. Accommodation is not easy to find; the town does not cater for tourists, try renting a room with Señora Jovita, near the liquor store (there is a sign outside "se vende comida"). Ask for the Cueva de Pereguey to the S and the falls nearby. The village of **Cabure** can only be reached by hitching (there is just one taxi in the region; it is difficult to locate). A few km up the road you will find a huge series of waterfalls, Cataratas de Hueque, popular with locals.

Barquisimeto, capital of Lara State, has a population of 723,000. Altitude 565m, mean temperature 25°C (it is hot, but not oppressively so). It stands on one of the alluvial fans so frequent in the Andes, and is Venezuela's fourth largest city, with the University of Lara. The town was moved three times before its present location, founded in 1563. One of the earlier settlements was burnt down by Lope de Aguirre 1561; he was executed there in the same year. Largely destroyed by an earthquake in 1812, the few remaining old buildings are perched above the Turbio river, interspersed with modern construction. The centre is well worth exploring, as many fascinating corners have been preserved and a law prohibiting demolition of older buildings means that more are being restored. The museum at Cra 16 and Calle 16 is housed in a former hospital, extended and reopened in 1992. Although dating from the early part of 20th century, the building is colonial in style, with a chapel standing in its courtyard. The museum tells the history of Barquisimeto through a series of impressive exhibits, including low-level push-button displays for children. Open daily, 1000-1700 and 1930 on Wed, free. More old buildings are a block away around the pleasant Plaza Jacinto Lara, with Statue to the eponymous state hero at its centre. The old cathedral faces the square, while on the opposite side is the small Anteneo gallery which has temporary exhibitions housed in an 18th century house at the corner of Cra 17 and Calle 23. Open Mon-Fri 0900-1200, 1500-1900, Sat 0900-1200; occasional evening concerts, friendly management, admission free. The Cathedral, on Calle 30 and Carrera 26 (Venezuela), a modern structure of reinforced concrete and glass, is interesting. At the heart of the old city is Plaza Bolívar, with towering palms, a heroic statue of the Liberator and an assortment of ancient and modern buildings. Most attractive is the white-painted Iglesia concepción, on the S side. Also on the square, the Palacio Municipal at Carrera 17 with Calle 25 is an attractive modern building. On Carrera 15 (Av Francisco de Miranda) between Calles 41-43 there is the charming Parque Ayacucho, with lush vegetation, paths, fountains and a bronze statue of Mariscal Sucre. There is a zoo on Avenida 21, reputed to be one of the best in the country. Interesting collection of animals, incl a camel, open Tues-Sun 0900-1730, US$0.55 entrance. Bus No 6 from the centre goes past the entrance. The Concha Acústica park is a block E of the Plaza Lara. In a steep wooded valley with a "shell" at the lower end (after which it is named), the park is popular with joggers and courting couples. There is a road from Barquisimeto to Acarigua (see p 1386) on the alternative route from Caracas to Mérida.

Festival On 28 Dec (am) is the fiesta of La Zaragoza, when colourfully clad participants and children pass through the streets accompanied by music and dancing. Huge crowds are attracted to the procession of La Divina Pastora in early Jan, when an image of the Virgin Mary is carried from the shrine at Santa Rosa village into the city.

Hotels A1 *Hilton**, Urb Nueva Segovia, Carrera 5 entre 5 y 6, T (051) 536022, F 544365, excellent restaurant and good value (5 course meal, US$15); **A1** *Motel El Parador*, excellent, near El Obelisco, a great roundabout in the northern suburbs of the town in the middle of which stands a tower; **A3** *Bonifran*, Carrera 19 y Calle 31, T 320302, F 323126, 3-star, modern tower, a few blocks from centre; **B** *Hostería El Obelisco**, Av Panamericana, American motel-style, swimming pool, always full; **B** *Príncipe*, Carrera 19 y Calle 23, T 312111, F 311731, clean, pool, restaurant, rec; **C** *Gran Hotel Barquisimeto**, Av Pedro León Torres, pool; **D** *Hevelin*, Av Vargas entre 20 y 21, T 510020, good value, highly rec; **D** *La Casona*, Carrera 17 con Calle 27 near Plaza Bolívar (T 051-315311/317151), a/c, clean, hot water, excellent, parking, restaurant; **D** *Yacambú*, Av Vargas, between Carreras 19-20, swimming pool; **D** *Savoy*, Carrera 18 entre Calles 21 y 22, TV, a/c, OK; **E** *Avenida*, Av Vargas, No 21-124, 2nd floor, clean, economical; **E** *Del Centro*, Av 20, between Calles 26-27, good value; **E** *Lido*, Carrera 16 between Calles 26 and 27, a/c, bath, TV. Many small cheap hotels near the bus terminal eg **D/E** *Peregrino*, private bath, a/c, TV; **E** *Yaguara*, basic; **E** *Miami Vice*, Calle 44.

Restaurants *Barquipan*, Calle 26 between Carreras 17 and 18, good breakfasts, snacks; *Casa Luis*, Carrera 17 between Calles 20 and 21, good food and live music Fri-Sun.

Exchange Banco Consolidado, Av Vargas entre Calles 20 y 21, Mastercard TCs and credit not accepted (but Banco Mercantil does take Mastercard), also Turisol (T 516743), both American Express.

Health Clinic Clínica Rozetti, efficient and not expensive.

Post Office Plaza Bolívar, Calle 25, Carrera 17.

Airport Jacinto Lara, international, some 8 km SW of the centre, 10 mins, US$3 by taxi. Local buses stop on the avenue immediately outside, turn right outside airport. Buses, US$0.12. Avensa flies daily to Miami via Maracaibo, also international flights to Aruba and Curaçao. Avensa offers internal flights to Caracas, 6 daily, US$43, Mérida daily, US$55, Maracaibo daily, US$42, San Antonio daily, US$56, Coro daily US$30, Santa Bárbara de Zulia, Las Piedras. Airport has a good bar, restaurant and cafeteria on the upper floor, a dozen shops, a similar number of car rentals and a tiny post office.

Land Transport Railway to Puerto Cabello, twice a day in each direction, tickets sold 2 hrs before departure, timetable unreliable, many extra trains at carnival time, but always full, bad track but a worthwhile experience, $2^{3}/_{4}$ hr journey; daily trains run from Yaritagua en route to/from Acarigua for Puerto Cabello. **Bus terminal** on the edge of the city at Carrera 25 and Calle 44: to **Mérida**, 3 to 4 a day, at 1020 and several between 2000 and 0200, 8 hrs via Agua Viva and El Vigía, US$7; to **Acarigua**, 1 hr, US$1.75; to **Valera** por puesto, $3^{1}/_{2}$ hrs, US$5. To **Tucacas** every 2 hrs; to **Coro** every 2 hrs, 7 hrs. Bus to **Caracas**, US$5.30, 6 hrs. For **renting**

cars (Volkswagen best), Av Pedro León Torres y Calle 56, also at airport.

West of Barquisimeto, about half an hour's drive, is **El Tocuyo** (pop 44,000) with a good hotel in a delightful colonial setting, **C La Posada Colonial**, with moderately priced restaurant. Between Barquisimeto and El Tocuyo is the main grape-growing area.

About 24 km SW of Barquisimeto is the small town of **Quíbor** (pop 53,525; **E Hotel Duque**). Festivals on 18 Jan (NS de Altagracia) and 12 June (San Antonio de Padua). There is an interesting museum, Centro Antropológico de Quíbor, with exhibits of the Indians who used to live in the region. Stop in the plaza for a *chicha de maíz* or *arroz*, a refreshing traditional drink of the local Indians. Turn right a few km before Quíbor to get to a tiny *rancho* in the village of Tintorero where "blankets" are made from local wool. These are in bright coloured stripes or plaids and serve well as colourful rugs. They are very good value. Ask for the local ceramics factory, for which Quíbor is famous throughout the country. About 18 km from Quíbor is the mountain village of **Cubiro** (pop 4,780; two hotels) which stands at 1,600m, ideal for walking. Direct buses from Barquisimeto or change at Quíbor.

Beyond Quíbor and 40 mins from Barquisimeto is **Sanare**, on the edge of the **Yacambú National Park**. In the park is Lago El Blanquito, famed for its abundance of wild birds. **D Posada Turística El Cerrito**, Sanare, T (053) 49016, manager speaks English, small restaurant and bar, tours to local sights and Yacambú, highly rec, at 1,360m can be cold at night.

About 60 km E of Barquisimeto is the town of **Chivacoa** (pop 40,400). Passing sugar-cane fields you reach the mountain of Sorte which is the holy region for the María-Lionza cult (similar to Voodoo) practised throughout Venezuela. Celebrations are held there mostly at weekends with 12 Oct (Día de la Raza) being the most important day. It is interesting to walk up the mountain when the pilgrims are camping beside the river and waterfalls, but do not go unless you are prepared to take it seriously, and use only the parking lot to park your car; other places are unsafe because of robbery. There is a Catholic festival, La Inmaculada Concepción, from 8-14 Dec.

Another pleasant excursion from Barquisimeto by bus or car is to **Río Claro**, about 28 km inland, "where the Andes begin". You follow a lush river valley through the mountains. There are banana plantations in the area and many dirt trails you can follow on horseback or in a 4-wheel drive vehicle. From Río Claro a gravel road (dry season only) goes to Buena Vista and on to Quíbor; good views and pleasant villages.

Some 75 km past Barquisimeto the Lara-Zulia motorway to Maracaibo forks off to the right (Caracas-Maracaibo 660 km), through **Carora** (pop 82,500). The town has a nice colonial centre with a very pleasant Plaza Bolívar. Here there is a helpful travel agency, where you can book trips to anywhere in the country, English spoken. It is possible to visit the Bodega Pomar Winery on the Lara-Zulia road, 1 km out of town. Call beforehand to organize your trip, T (052) 212191, F 341014. There are several hotels in Carora: *Madre Vieja* and *Katuka* are the best, each with a good restaurant and good value (in *Madre Vieja* you can sit outside, under a very old vine). Beef is the local speciality. Carora is a cattle farming centre.

The small village of **Altagracia** where the grapes are grown, is nearby. Cross the bridge next to Plaza Bolívar and it is about 20 km away. In the village there are some typical restaurants serving mixed grill, highly rec (iguana is on the menu).

Another point of interest is the Cascada del Vino, a waterfall that looks like red wine when the sun shines on it. It is not easy to find because there is no public transport and 4WD is necessary. Follow the road from Carora to Barquisimeto; after 10 km turn right to Agua Viva/Trujillo and take the main road for 60 km; turn left to the village of San Pedro. Take the steep, badly maintained road, until you arrive in the village itself. You can reach this point in a normal car. Afterwards follow a gravel road which has very bad potholes and is slippery when wet, cross to the village of Barbacoas which is about 25 km from San Pedro. At the Inparques office (white house), turn left, drive down the steep road for 1-2 km to a parking spot. Be there before 1500 otherwise the sun will have disappeared. Good picnic facilities, bring everything you need, there are no facilities nearby.

THE LOWLANDS OF MARACAIBO (3)

Venezuela's main oil producing zone has the city of Maracaibo as its centre, on the western shore of the entrance to the Lago de Maracaibo. N of the city is the border crossing to Colombia on the Guajira Peninsula. The whole region is very hot.

The Lowlands of Maracaibo, lying in the encircling arms of the mountains, are more or less windless and extremely humid. Average annual temperature is higher than anywhere else in Latin America. Rainfall decreases steadily from the foothills of the Sierra Nevada to the coast. In these lowlands is the semi-salt Lago de Maracaibo, of about 12,800 square kms, 155 km long and in places over 120 km wide. It is joined to the sea by a waterway, 3 to 11 km wide and 55 km long, at the mouth of which is the bar of Maracaibo.

The area was once dependent on fishing and the transport of coffee across the lake from the Sierra. Since the discovery there of one of the world's greatest oilfields in 1914, there has been a great transformation, both in appearance (a forest of oil derricks covers the shore swamps and some of the lake), and in prosperity. The Lara-Zulia motorway reaches Maracaibo by the beautiful 8 km long General Rafael Urdaneta bridge, which has the longest pre-stressed concrete span in the world.

Maracaibo, on the N-western shore of Lago de Maracaibo, capital of the State of Zulia, is Venezuela's oil capital: 70% of the nation's output comes from the Lake area. Maracaibo, which is 55 mins by jet from Caracas, is the country's second largest city. Population: 1,218,800. The airport is at La Chinita.

The climate is damp and hot, but healthy. The hottest months are July, Aug and Sept, but there is usually a sea breeze from 1500 until morning. The mean temperature of 28°C and average humidity of 78% are most felt at sea level. The traditional city centre is Plaza Bolívar, on which stand the Cathedral, the Casa de Gobierno, the Asamblea Legislativa and the Casa de la Capitulación (or Casa Morales, a colonial building and national monument, tour free, copies of Tovar y Tovar paintings of Bolívar's life and times). The Casa has an extensive library dedicated to the Liberator, open Mon-Fri, 0800-1600. Next door is the 19th century Teatro Baralt, currently under reconstruction, but supposed to be finished in 1995. On the E end of the Plaza Bolívar is the Cathedral of Maracaibo, also from the colonial period. Running W of Plaza Bolívar to the Paseo de las Ciencias, a 1970s development which levelled all the old buildings in the area. Only the Iglesia de Santa Bárbara stands in the Paseo. Calle Carabobo (one block N of the Paseo de las Ciencias) is a restored strip of colonial buildings, 3 blocks long. It is currently a mix of homes and small shops (all gaudily painted). Most of the shops sell regional crafts. *La Salita* sells crafts from western Venezuela, Colombia, and Guatemala; the restaurant *Zaguán* serves traditional regional cooking at reasonable prices. One block S of the Paseo is Plaza Baralt on Av 6, stretching to C100 and the old waterfront market (Mercado de Pulgas). The new part of the city round Bella Vista and towards the University is in vivid contrast with the old town near the docks. The latter, with narrow streets and brightly-painted, colonial style adobe houses, is hardly changed from the last century, although many buildings are in an advanced state of decay. The buildings facing Parque Urdaneta (3 blocks N of Paseo de las Ciencias) have been well-restored. Also well-preserved are the church of Santa Lucía and the streets around. This old residential area is a short ride (or long walk) N from the old centre (in the square near Santa Lucía are sculptures by Jesus Soto, see Ciudad Bolívar, **Museums**). Nearby is the Galería de Arte Brindhaven, free, with interesting sculptures; the artist is often in residence. Of particular interest is the small Art Deco style church on Av 5 de Julio, just a few blocks W of Av Delicias/Av 15.

For panoramic views of the city, take a lift up the tower, El Mirador, in Parque La Marina, open 1600-2030, free. This is by the Plaza del Buen Maestro at the end of Avs 2 (El Milagro) and 4 (Bella Vista).

A useful artery for visitors to the city is Av 4, or Bella Vista. From a point 4 blocks N of Plaza Bolívar, it runs straight N past Santa Lucía (Calle 90, to the right, E side), through Bella Vista (Calles 76-65). From Plaza Bolívar (outside the Casa de la Capitulación) this route is plied in both directions by *por puestos*, bearing the sign "Bella Vista". Flag them down and pay a flat fare of US$0.12. Some of them go as far N as Santa Rosa de Agua, where restaurants and houses are built on stilts in the lagoon.

Festivals around the Lake at Cabimas, *gaitas* (see **Music and Dance**) 1-6 Jan; Virgen del Rosario, 5 Oct. At Lagunillas, San Isidro processions and games, 15 May.

Warning The old part of the city is not safe after 1700 and even requires care in daylight.

Hotels It is difficult to obtain rooms without making reservations well in advance. **L3-A2** *Hotel del Lago Intercontinental**, El Milagro, Av 2, T (061) 924022, F 914551, T 924180 for reservations, PO Box 90, plastic atmosphere, exorbitant minibar prices (liquor store 300 yds from the hotel), pool open to non-residents; **A1** *Kristoff**, Av 8 (Santa Rita), T 72911, F 61396, nice swimming pool open to non-residents US$6, nightclub, poor exchange rates offered, poor breakfast, self service launderette adjacent to hotel; **A1** *Maruma Internacional**, Circunvalación No 2, T 972911, F 981258, old and new sections, hot water, a/c, TV, reasonable restaurant; **C** *Gran Hotel Delicias**, Av 15 esq Calle 70, friendly, excellent and not expensive restaurant, good value, swimming pool, nightclub; **D** *Astor*, S side of Plaza de la República, Bella Vista, often full; **D** *Doral*, C 75 y Av 14A, T 981792, a/c, bath, helpful, rec; **E** *Novedades*, Calle 78 (also known as Dr Portillo) No 9-43, Bella Vista, between old and new parts of town, T 75766, a/c, shower, safe, clean, small rooms, safe parking, Italian owner Francesco Scherra; also in Bella Vista, **E** *Falcón*, Av 4, No 84-158, T 220967, a/c, laundry facilities; **E** *Caribe*, Av 7, good location by old part of town, a/c and shower, parking, not very clean; **E** *Europa*, Calle 93 y Av 4, a/c, run down but acceptable; **E** *San Martín*, Av 3Y No 40-11, a/c, clean, friendly; **E** *Victoria*, Av 6, Calle 99, in picturesque old part of town (not safe after dark), central, helpful, many rooms without windows, shabby; **E** *Almería*, Calle 74 y 3H, a/c, private bathroom, hot and cold water, clean and friendly,

Restaurants Most are closed on Sun. *Pizzería Napoletana*, Calle 77 near Av 4, excellent, closed Tues; *Mi Vaquita*, Av 3H, No 76-22, fantastic for meat, popular with locals, good atmosphere, rec; *El Carite*, Calle 78 (also known as Dr Portillo) No 8-35, T 71878, excellent selection of fish and seafood, delicious and moderately-priced, friendly service; *La Habana*, Av Bella Vista (Av 4) near Calle 76, good salads and milkshakes, open 24 hrs. *La Friulana*, Calle 95, Av 3 for good cheap meal at less than US$2, repeatedly rec (closes 1900). *San José*, Av 3Y (San Martín), 82-29, good; *El Gaucho*, Plaza Banderas, Argentine-style, good. Many restaurants on *palafitos* (stilts) in Santa Rosa district, good for fish, *por puesto* US$0.20 to get there. There are good restaurants around the Plaza de la República (C77/5 de Julio and Av 31, Bella Vista), these incl *Deli Feibel*, Av 31 facing Centro Comercial Salto Angel; a few doors up is *Chips*, which sells regional fast food, not readily available in Caracas, *tequeños* and *patacones*, rec. For confectionery, *Café Samemrum*, Av 5 de Julio between Avs 10 and 11, and *Kabuki*, Av 5 de Julio opp Banco de Maracaibo, more fashionable. Health food store, *Larga Vida*, Av 13A between Calles 75 and 76. *Charlie Chaplin*, next to *Hotel Kristoff*, great submarine sandwiches and juices, indoor and outdoor seating, good but pricey; *Bambi*, Av 4, 78-70, excellent and cheap. Many good clubs and restaurants on Calle 72, as well as higher priced stores, eg *Malanga Café*, with outdoor patio and live music most nights; *Pizza Pizza*, for good pizza and other Italian foods; for fast food, try *TropiBurger*, Calle 72 y Av Bella Vista.

Banks and Exchange Banco Consolidado, Av Bella Vista con Calle 67, Plaza del Indio Mora, no commission but very long queues, can take over 1½ hours (American Express, also Turisol Amex rep, Av 4, in front of Banco Consolidado, T 70611); Citibank for Citicorp TCs; Banco Unión, Av 4 and Calle 78, cash advances on Mastercard and Visa. Casa de Cambio, Av 9B y Av 5 de Julio (Calle 77), in Banco Industrial Building, quick, efficient, good rates. All banks shut at 1630 sharp, exchange am only. All Thomas Cook transactions have to be verified in Caracas. Cambio at bus terminal will change Colombian pesos into bolívares at a poor rate.

Consulates Colombian, Av 3Y (San Martín) 70-16 nr Av 4/Bella Vista (T 921483, F 921729), 10 km from centre, take bus or *por puesto* (Bellavista) out of town on Av 4 to Calle 70; open Mon-Fri, 0700-1300 prompt, 60-day visa in 5 hrs, no questions, no tickets required (better than Caracas). Spanish, Av Sabaneta con C El Prado No 9B-55, T 213445. Danish, Av 15, No 88-78, Las Delicias, aptdo 301, T (61) 591579, F 595763, open 0800-1200, 1400-1800. French, Av 3F con C70, T 912921, F 77671; German, C77 No 3C-24, Edif Los Cerros piso 9, T 912406, F 912506; UK, Av 9B No 66-146, T 73745, F 82794; Dutch, Av 3C con C67, La Lago, Unicentro Virginia, office 6, floor 2, T/F 922885; Italy, Av 3H No 69-79, T 72182, F 919903; Norway, Km 1 Carretera a Perijá, Sector Plaza Las Banderas-Los Haticos, T 616044, F 616555; Sweden, Av 15 Las Delicias No 88-78, T 595843, F 595763; Swiss, Av 9B No 75-95, T 77710, F 71167.

Doctors Dr García, Hospital Coromoto, Av 3C and Calle 72, T 912222, speaks English, as does Dr Carlos Febres, a dentist, Av 8, No 84-129, Mon-Fri 0900-1200, 1500-1800, T 221504.

Laundry *Lavandería Laza*, Calle 72 near Av 3H, Bella Vista, rec.

Anglican Church Christ Church, Av 8 (Santa Rita) a Calle 74.

Post Office, Av Libertador y Av 3. **Telecommunications** Servicio de Telecomunicaciones de Venezuela, Calle 99, esq Av 3, payphones for local calls only, CANTV, Calle 76 near Av 3E, Bella Vista, open 0700-2330, Mon-Fri. If offices are closed, phone cards are available at the desk of the nearby *Hotel Astor*, S side of Plaza de la República.

Shopping *Fin de Siglo* department stores sell records, tapes, posters of local sights. *Foto Bella Vista*, Av Bella Vista, C 78, for service beyond inst photofinishing. The outdoor market, *Las Pulgas*, is enormous, mostly clothes, shoes, and general household goods, S side of C 100 entre Av 10 y 14. *Centro Comercial Costa Verde*, Av 4 (antes Bella Vista), good new shopping complex. *El Mercado de las Indias Guajiras*, open market at C 96 y Av 2 (El Milagro), a few crafts, some pottery, hammocks, etc. The *Centro de Arte de Maracaibo Lía Bermúdez* is housed in a huge 19th century Mercado de Pulgas building (end of Av 6 at C 100), where the work of national artists is displayed. It is a/c, a good place to escape the midday heat. The museum also has a good historical display of photographs of Maracaibo and the building, which makes a good starting place for a walking tour of the city centre.

Bookshops *Librería Universal*, Av 5 de Julio y Av 4, maps, stationery, Caracas newspapers but poor selection of books; *Librería Cultural*, Av 5 de Julio, best Spanish language bookstore in town; *Librería Italiana*, Av 5 de Julio, Ed Centro América, postcards and foreign publications (incl US). Good bookshop in Arrivals lounge of airport. Staff at the public library, Av 2, are helpful to tourists.

City Transport *Por puestos*, following fixed routes, start mostly from Paseo de las Ciencias. For most routes, there are two fares, long and short: the dividing line between long and short appears to be Av 5 de Julio/C77. Look for the name of the route on the roof of the car, or on the front window, passenger's side. A ride from downtown to Av 5 de Julio in a "Bella Vista" car costs US$0.20. The "Bella Vista", "8 de Octubre", and "Ziruma" lines all pass Av 5 de Julio, although at different places.

Taxis US$1.50-2. Mini-excursions can be arranged with taxi drivers and can be quite good value. Taxi Tours (small office next to *Intercontinental Hotel*), a/c cars, not very cooperative drivers, 4-hr trip to Sinamaica US$35.

Air Services Airport is 25 km SW of city centre: terminal has international and national lounges. Shops, incl bookshop selling city map; *casa de cambio* open 0600-1800 daily, no commission; Banco Venezolano; car hire offices outside. Taxis charge between US$5-6, there are no *por puestos*. There are frequent flights with Aserca, Avensa, Servivensa to Maiquetía (US$42), Mérida (US$46), Valencia (US$41), Barquisimeto, Las Piedras (for Amuay and Cardón), San Antonio (US$52, be early to guarantee seat), Barcelona, Porlamar, Puerto Ordaz and Maturín. International flights to Maracaibo with Curaçao and Aruba (Servivensa), Miami (Servivensa, Zuliana), Panama City (Servivensa) and Bogotá and Medellín (Zuliana, Calle 78, Edificio Cosmar, T 514147).

Buses Bus station is 15 mins walk from centre, 1 km S of the old town. Ask for buses into town, local services are confusing. There are several fast and comfortable buses daily to **Valencia** (US$7.75 by Expresos del Lago), **San Cristóbal** (US$6.50, 6-8 hrs, *por puesto*, US$19), **Barquisimeto**, 5½ hrs incl police stops and searches (US$5), **Coro** US$4, 4 hrs, and **Caracas** (US$12, 10-13 hrs, *por puesto* US$24). Bus lines, other than Aerobuses de Venezuela, rec are Occidente and Alianza, whose fares are cheaper. To **Mérida**, 5-7 hrs (US$4.70), or *por puesto*, or take bus to El Vigía and change.

Nearby Excursions If, after the cramped streets of the centre, you want some fresh air, take a walk along the Paseo de Maracaibo del Lago, a lakeside park built in the late 1970s, near the *Hotel del Lago*. To get there, take a Milagro bus northbound from the Mercado de los Guajiros, and ask the driver to let you off at the entrance, which is well-marked. There you can walk along the shores of Lake Maracaibo at its narrowest point. The Paseo offers spectacular views of the Rafael Urdaneta bridge and of oil tankers sailing to the Caribbean. There are also places to sit and watch life go by. The park attracts a wide variety of birds.

A trip across the lake through the oil derricks is difficult to organize as the oilfields are a long way from Maracaibo. The zone begins at Cabimas (**A2** *Cabimas Internacional**, T 45692, luxury, pool, discotheque) on the E shore of the lake and you can get a good view of the oil rigs from there (*por puesto*, US$1.25, 40 mins, semi-legal trip in fishing boat among the derricks, US$3-5, ask behind the market) and from other towns further down, such as Lagunillas (**D** *Hotel Lagunillas**, T 21423, pool)—pictures can be taken from the Muro de Contención (dyke); ask permission first. A tourist taxi from *Hotel del Lago* to see the oil wells costs US$45 (local taxis cost a little less, but not all drivers know where the Muro is).

From the port, you can take a ferry to Altagracia for US$0.40, the first at 0645, 25 mins: exchange facilities at the terminal. Return the same way or take a minibus (US$0.55), travelling through exotic scenery for almost an hour and crossing the General Urdaneta bridge.

On the W side of the lake, between the rivers Santa Ana and Catatumbo, a large area of swampland is crossed by the road to La Fría. The swamp is inhabited by the Motilones, who, until 1960, refused to have dealings either with white men or other Indians. The southern border of the Motilones' territory, the Río Catatumbo, is famed for its almost nightly display of lightning for which there is, as yet, no accepted explanation and which caused it to be known in the old days as "The Lighthouse of Maracaibo". There are various missions you can visit: the easiest to reach is Los Angeles del Tocuco, 51 km from Machiques (*por puesto* US$0.80, 1 hr 15 mins), where they welcome visitors; it helps to take a present, such as dried milk. Shop-cum-restaurant, family-run, simple, filling food, accommodation F. From here you can do a 5-day trek to Picci Cacao, through beautiful scenery to meet Yuspa Indians. Take them rice and blankets if you can carry them; take your own food and camping equipment. The Park guide can be of help; near the guide's house at *Familia de Sonia* you can sleep in hammocks. F. **Machiques** (pop 43,200) is on a fast road from San Cristóbal (Expreso Los Llanos good) via La Fría to Maracaibo, and has the good **D** *Motel Tukuko*; **E** *Hotel Italo Zuliano*. Machiques celebrates the Fiesta de San José on 19 Mar, and the Feria de Virgen del Carmen, with agricultural shows, on 14-18 Jul.

The best sightseeing trip is N about 1 hr to the Río Limón (it has another local name). Take a bus 1 hr, (US$0.40) to **El Moján**, riding with the Guajira Indians as they return to their homes on the peninsula. Get off at the new bus terminal and walk to the nearby jetty. From there, take a launch to the Isla San Carlos (US$1.20 each way). At San Carlos, walk to the restored Castillo San Carlos. Built in the late 17th century, the Castillo was meant to protect the entrance to Lake Maracaibo, which it did with mixed success. There are guided tours of the fort (US$0.40) which are quite informative. After that, you can swim on the beach nearby. The last launch back to El Moján leaves between 1600 and 1700, depending on the availability of gasoline. It's a good idea to be at the jetty ready to leave the island by 1530.

From El Moján, you can take a taxi (US$3) or *por puesto* to **Sinamaica**, from where another can be taken to the lagoon (US$0.50) at the small port of Puerto Cuervito. Hire a boat (bargaining rec as the price is around US$10-12 pp for a round trip, fix price, duration and route in advance), and go up the river for an hour to La Boquita (2,500 inhabitants) to see Indians living in houses made of woven reed mats built on stilts (concrete): the only place where they can be seen. Return by bus Sinamaica-Maracaibo, or *por puesto* Sinamaica-El Moján (US$0.80), thence to Maracaibo. Excursions by boat to the Sinamaica lagoon from Maracaibo charge about US$16 for 4 people for 1½ hrs, but if you think you are being overcharged, ask for *el libro de reclamaciones* which should give the maximum official price. Sinamaica has an agricultural show on 15-21 Aug. The tension of the border area and the problem of *infiltraciones* suggests 1600 as the time limit to be in this area.

By crossing the bridge over the river you come, in the N, to a paved road that leads to Riohacha, in Colombia. Border formalities are quick and easy. The Colombian border town, Maicao, however, has a most unsavoury reputation; best not to stop there. If you enter Venezuela from Colombia at Maicao, you can expect very rigorous searches both at the border and on the way to Maracaibo (6 police checks in all). There are Venezuelan Consulates in Riohacha, Cartagena and Barranquilla. Buses Maracaibo-Maicao, with Expreso Maicao or Expreso Gran Colombia, US$3-4, 3 hrs, from 0400-1600, leaves when full, risk of ambush by bandits/guerrillas. *Colectivos* US$5 pp, 6 in car. Border opens 0800, 1 hr time difference with Colombia, easy border crossing. Cambio at bus terminal opens 0800. Taxi fare US$24 per car (takes 5). From Maicao there are buses to Barranquilla, the last one leaves at 1600. To enter Venezuela by land a visa is essential despite what may be said by Venezuelan Consulates. Only 72-hour transit visas are issued at this border; *tarjetas de Turismo* must be obtained from DIEX in Maracaibo—not an easy task. Get a visa in advance.

NB In 1994 an exit tax had to be paid by bus passengers going Maracaibo-Maicao: US$20 from a booth in Maracaibo bus terminal. Receipt must be shown at the border.

Along the way you see Guajira Indians, the men with bare legs, on horseback; the women with long, black, tent-shaped dresses and painted faces, wearing the sandals with big wool pom-poms which they make and sell for US$2, as against the US$7-10 in the tourist shops. The men do nothing: women do all the work, tending sheep and goats, selling slippers and raising very little on the dry, hot, scrubby Guajira Peninsula. If you don't do this trip, you can see these Indians in the Ziruma district of Maracaibo. There is an interesting Guajira market at Los Filuos, 2 km beyond Paraguaipoa, where you can buy the local tent-dress (*manta*) for about US$5-10, depending on the quality, but much cheaper than in Maracaibo.

Those who wish to go on to the Sierra Nevada de Mérida or the State of Trujillo from Maracaibo should return over the lake and turn sharp right through Cabimas, Lagunillas, Bachaquero and Mene Grande, all unattractive oil towns, to rejoin the Pan-American Highway at *Agua Viva*. For the Colombian frontier or San Cristóbal we follow the Pan-American Highway.

The Pan-American Highway from Agua Viva is a splendid asphalt speed track, but devoid of much scenic or historical attraction. It runs along the foot of the Andes through rolling country planted with sugar or bananas, or park-like cattle land. At *Sabana de Mendoza*, 24 km S of Agua Viva, is a possible stopover—*Hotel Panamérica* (good, a/c). This road has plenty of restaurants, hotels and filling-stations, especially at Caja Seca and El Vigía, both rather new and raw looking towns. At *El Vigía* (pop 70,290; **D** *Hotel Gran Sasso*; **D** *Hostería El Vigía*; **E** *La Suiza*, Av 15, opp bus terminal, rec; restaurant, *Armarilla*, try armarilla asado), where the road from Mérida to Santa Bárbara (Zulia) crosses the Río Chama, there is a fine bridge over 1 km long. Flights diverted from Mérida often land at El Vigía. *Santa Bárbara* (56 km NW) is a milk, meat and plantain producing centre, with air and boat services to Maracaibo and an important annual cattle show.

From El Vigía, the road continues fairly flat until *La Fría* (pop 26,000), with a large natural-gas fuelled power station, where it is joined by the road along the W side of Lago de Maracaibo and begins to climb to San Cristóbal. La Fría has at least four hotels; the family-run **E** *Hotel Turística*, on main square, basic but clean, is rec, as is **E** *Hotel Miramar*, Calle 6-50, near Plaza Bolívar, T (077) 41790, friendly. From La Fría the Highway climbs through *San Juan de Colón* (*Hotel El Tuy*, cheap, but "a hole") to San Cristóbal (see p 1384).

THE SIERRA NEVADA DE MERIDA (4)

Venezuela's high Andes offer hiking and mountaineering, and fishing in lakes and rivers. The main tourist centre is Mérida, but there are many interesting villages, often with colonial churches. The Pan-American Highway runs through the Sierra entering Colombia at the decidedly dubious town of Cúcuta.

The *Sierra Nevada de Mérida*, running from S of Maracaibo to the Colombian frontier, is the only range in Venezuela where snow lies permanently on the higher peaks. Near Mérida itself there are five such snowcaps of almost 5,000m. Several basins lying between the mountains are actively cultivated; the inhabitants are concentrated mainly in valleys and basins at between 800 and 1,300m above sea level. The three towns of Mérida, Valera and San Cristóbal are in this zone. There are two distinct rainy and dry seasons in the year. Two crops of the staple food, maize, can be harvested annually up to an elevation of about 2,000m.

Those who wish to visit the Sierra Nevada should turn left at Agua Viva to *Valera*, the most important town in the State of Trujillo, with a population of 119,400. In Valera you can choose between two roads over the sierra, either via Timotes and Mucuchíes to Mérida, or via Boconó and down to the *llanos* at Guanare. Agricultural and industrial fair in Aug.

Hotels B *Camino Real*; **C** *Albergue Turístico*, nearby, triples available, good value; **C** *Motel Valera**, Urb La Plata, clean, a/c, comfortable, convenient; **D** *Aurora*, Edif Rangel on Av 7 (Bolívar); **E** *Venezuela*, Av 6 with Calle 8, basic, front rooms upstairs are the nicest. *Hidrotermal San Rafael*, 4 km off road between Valera and Motatán, notable for its hot water springs and the thermal bath.

Restaurants *La Terraza Café*, Av Bolívar, good, cheap, live music; *Italio* opp *Motel Valera*, rec; *Vegetariano Tihuani*, in front of La Clínica María.

Exchange Banco Consolidado, Av Bolívar, changes Amex cheques.

Transport Air With connections to Caracas, Maracaibo and La Fría. **Bus** Bus terminal on the edge of town. To **Boconó**, US$2.25, 3 hrs; to **Caracas**, 9 hrs (Aerobuses), US$9; to **Mérida** 2 a day with Empresa Barinas, 0900 and 1100, US$3, 5 hrs, *por puesto* US$5.45 (well worth taking via the Pico del Aguila pass).

From Valera a road runs via the restored colonial village of *La Plazuela* to the state capital, *Trujillo* (pop 44,460), at 805m; a *por puesto* from Valera costs US$0.75. This politically important town is losing ground commercially to Valera. Trujillo runs up and down hill; at the top, across from the university, is a park (sadly rundown) with waterfalls and paths. The Centro de Historia de Trujillo is a restored colonial house, now a museum. Bolívar lived there and signed the "proclamation of war to the death" in the house. A monument to the Virgen de la Paz was built by the wife of President Herrera Campins in 1983; it stands on a mountain, at 1,608m, 2½ hrs walk from town, a taxi (jeep) leaves when full, US$0.75 pp; open 0900-1700, good views.

Hotels and Services E *Hotel Turística*, Av Independencia 5-65, with bath and hot water, highly rec; E *Hotel Palace*, old, clean, noisy; *Restaurant Alfa*, Av Independencia, friendly, reasonable. **Exchange** for Amex and Thomas Cook TCs, Banco Capital.

From Trujillo there is a high, winding, spectacular paved road to **Boconó** (pop 39,220), a town built on steep mountain sides. 27 km before Boconó, just off the road, is the simple village of **San Miguel de Boconó** (E *Hostería San Miguel*, incl breakfast, "a cute little mom and pop place"; E *Los Valles*, 2 km out of town, on the road to Boconó, individual *cabañas* and nice views). Festival of Romería de los Pastores de San Miguel is on 4-7 Jan. Boconó itself is a craft centre with demonstrations of weaving in the Casa Artesanal de Boconó and pottery in the Briceño family workshop.

From Boconó you can continue down to **Guanare** (bus US$2, 3½ hrs; *La Vieja Taberna*, Calle 19, Carrera 4, restaurant) in the *llanos* via **Biscucuy** (pop 27,000, where a very difficult road through Guárico leads to Barquisimeto). 10 km from Boconó on this road is *Estancia de Mosquey*, at Mosquey, family accommodation, tremendous views, good beds, nice restaurant with family-style meals, swimming pool, rec.

Hotels D *Colina*, near the river at bottom of town, motel-style, clean, comfortable, restaurant; E *Colonial*, Av Miranda; E *Hotel Vega del Río**, offers most services and food and is clean; E *Venezia*, with shower, clean, friendly, rec.

Restaurants *Turística La Casa Vieja*, good food, good value, lots of old photos of the area; *El Paisano*, popular restaurant with locals. Cheap meals at *Hotel Italia*, Calle Jáuregui.

The small town of **Niquitao** (pop 4,400) is 1 hr by public transport SW of Boconó. It is still relatively unspoilt, colonial-style, celebrating many festivals, particularly Holy Week, when paper is rolled out in the streets for children to create a giant painted mural. Entertainment is rustic, concentrated in the bars round the main square. D *Posada Turística de Niquitao*, T (072) 53111/31448 and D *Na Delia*, T (072) 52113/52522, on a hill ½ km out of town, both have restaurants. Excursions can be made to the Teta de Niquitao (4,007m) 2 hrs by jeep, the waterfalls and pools known as Las Pailas, and a nearby lake. "For a full day's hike, walk from the plaza uphill past the municipal building", writes Robert Fama of San Francisco, USA, "the paved road becomes a cart track. Continue for about 30 mins until the track crosses a small river. After the river, take a right fork and follow the river uphill and over a bluff. Here are 3 or 4 beautiful swim holes, perfect picnic spots. The main falls are another ½ hr further upstream. A very scenic walk".

We are now in the Sierra Nevada de Mérida, the Western Andes of Venezuela. 40 km beyond Valera on a good paved road is **Timotes** (pop 10,550) a mountainous little place set high in the cold grain zone. (**Hotels** C *Las Truchas*, very nice, good food; D *Carabay*, family run, clean, good rooms, but do not accept the first one offered, excellent restaurant; E *Posada Caribe*, good value; restaurant). Bus from Valera, US$1.50. Near Timotes are **La Mesa de Esnujaque** (good walking) (B *Hotel Tibisay**; D *Miraflores*, good value) and **La Puerta** (C *Guadalupe**, a fine hotel; D *Chiquinquirá*, Av Bolívar 34; E *Los Andes*, Av Bolívar), both places hill resorts for Maracaibo and district, but no public transport between the two. The road now climbs through increasingly wild, barren and rugged country and through the windy pass of *Pico El Aguila* (4,007m, best seen early in the morning, frequently in the clouds). This is the way Bolívar went when crossing the Andes to liberate Colombia, and on the peak is the statue of a condor. In the pass is the tourist *Restaurant Páramo Aguila* in chalet style. Across from the monument is a small chapel with a fine view of the surrounding three-way watershed and the white tower of *Hotel Los Frailes* (see below). A paved road leads from here 2 km up through *frailejones* to a CANTV microwave tower (4,118m, grand view). It continues N as a lonely track to the Piñango lakes (45 km), noted for their large trout, and the traditional village of Piñango (2,480m). Splendid views of high altitude lakes and even to Lake Maracaibo. Sra Aranjo provides food and lodging, and her husband hires horses.

The road then dips rapidly through **Apartaderos** (12½ km, 3,473m; pop 2,000), a scattered town at the junction of Route 7 and the road over the Sierra Nevada to Barinas, with a handful of shops and hotels serving the tourist traffic between Mérida, Laguna Mucubají and Santo Domingo/Pueblo Llano. (**Hotels B** *Parque Turístico*, attractive modern chalet-style building, radiant heating, very hot showers, helpful owner, pricey restaurant but warmly rec; **B** *Hotel y Restaurant Mifafi*, good food, beautiful, no heating, gardener will give you seeds from his flowers; *Posada Viejo Apartaderos*, restaurant with good typical food, reasonable prices.) Over the centuries the Indians have piled up stones from the rocky mountainside into walls and enclosures, hence the name. On Sun they all stand and watch the tourists, their potential income (there is a certain amount of high pressure selling); the children sell flowers and fat puppies called *mucuchíes* (a variant of the Grand Pyrené) after a near-by town. Bus Apartaderos-Mérida US$1.20; bus to Barinas on the road over the Sierra Nevada is unreliable.

3 km above Apartaderos, a narrow paved road (signposted) turns W off the highway at the one-room 'Escuela Estatal 121' and winds its way to **Llano del Hato** (at 3,510m, the highest place in Venezuela served by road) and on to the three-domed *CIDA Astrophysical Institute* at 3,600m. Views from here are not as spectacular as those on the way in; at least two viewing points give extraordinary vistas of the wheat-filled Lake Mucubají plateau, and directly down on the *Hotel Parque Turístico Apartaderos* and the gas station in Mucuchachi. CIDA's four telescopes and modern facilities are open to visitors on third and fourth Sat of each month at 1900, entry US$1.25, but confirm by T (074) 791893; about 5 guided tours per day are scheduled during school holidays, Easter week and in Aug/Sept. The old access road, now paved, leads down (7 km) from Llano del Hato to emerge on the Mérida highway at La Toma, just above Mucuchíes. Many prehispanic terraces and irrigation systems, adobe houses and ox-ploughed fields (*poyos*) are visible from this interesting road, which is safe and in good condition.

Only 3 km from Apartaderos on the road from Apartaderos to Barinas is **Laguna Mucubají** (3,600m, cold; Trans Barinas bus, 2 hrs, or *por puesto* from Mérida US$2, 2 hrs, 60 km). A 1½-hr walk takes you to Laguna Negra in the **Parque Nacional Sierra Nevada**; there is a campsite near the lake (free, but permit required from Inparques office at the entrance), motel, E, restaurant and shop by the turn-off from the main road. Good coffee and bookshop just past the lake, good maps, interesting museum. The park is clean and very well kept. Be prepared for near-freezing temperatures if camping out. A further 1½-hr walk from Laguna Negra is the Laguna Los Patos (very beautiful if the weather is fine). Horses can be hired. Guides (not absolutely necessary) can be found at Laguna Mucubají or at the hotels in **Santo Domingo** (pop 3,200), a centre for fishing. From its centre and 17th century church, the village straggles up the valley road towards Apartaderos. Take the cobbled path that leads to a hillock overlooking the village and surrounding countryside. Good handicraft shops.

Hotels B *Las Cabañas* for small groups, or *Cabañas Halcón de Oro* (cheap rooms for rent next door, opp *Panadería Santo Domingo*). The beautiful **C** *Hotel Moruco**, T (073) 88155, F 88225, is a little further out, in a lovely setting, good value, alt 2,300m, food very good, bar expensive, reservations can be made through *Hotel Río Prado* in Mérida; **D** *Hotel La Trucha Azul*, open fireplace, views, rec; **D** *Santo Domingo*, log cabins for up to 4 people, log fireplace, TV, games room with pool, table tennis, hot water, clean, excellent restaurant with good selection of wines, highly rec. *Restaurant Brisas de la Sierra*, rec.

Services, Transport There is a Tourist Office on the right, leaving town; a 10 mins hike from centre. Do not confuse with the other Santo Domingo, near the Colombian border, which has an airport. This one does not. Buses or busetas pass through in either direction at approximately 2 hr intervals through the day. Mérida 2 hrs, US$2.35 *por puesto*; Barinas 1½ hrs, US$2.50.

Between Santo Domingo and Laguna Mucubají is the former monastery, **A** *Hotel Los Frailes**, alt 3,000m, excellent food, international menus, expensive wines, poor service. Book well ahead through Avensa (Av Universidad, Edif El Chorro, piso 13, T 562-3022/561-3366, F 564-7936, Aptdo Postal 943, Caracas), but don't pay in advance as Avensa will not reimburse you in case of transport problems. *Mucubají* restaurant, at the highest point of the road that passes Laguna Mucubají, is very good for trout.

From Apartaderos the road to Mérida, following the Río Chama valley, drops 1,850m; it takes 3-4 hrs, a pleasant drive. This is the heart of the cultivated highlands and the fields extend up to the edge of the *páramo*, clinging to the steepest slopes. 1 km S of Apartaderos the road loops around a small hill topped with a statue of La Loca Luz Caraballo, a grief-crazed woman immortalized in a poem by Andrés Eloy Blanco. For the rest of the journey, the tiny villages are about 14 km apart, the average daily distance a mule train could manage in this terrain. The road leads up to **San Rafael de Mucuchíes**, at 3,140m (Sra Crys, a French artist, will provide meals if you book in advance; **E** *Hotel El Rosal*, hot water, clean, good), from where you can walk up to a high valley where Indians tend cows and sheep (beware of the dogs that protect the houses), then down to **Mucuchíes** (pop 9,175, 2,980m; **E** *Hotel Los Andes*, old house above plaza, 4 rm, clean hot water, shared bathrooms, good creole food, excellent; *Posada San Remón*, between Mucuchíes and Mucurubá, T 526877, great kitchen, good meals, nice relaxing courtyard), where there is a trout farm. Beside the Liberator on the statue in Plaza Bolívar is a representation of the Indian boy, Tinajaca, and the Mucuchíes dog, Snowy, given to Bolívar in 1813 and, according to legend, devoted to him until their deaths on the same day at the Battle of Boyacá. At Moconoque, to the NW there is a hot spring. An old colonial trail, El Camino Real, can be taken from Apartaderos to Mucuchíes (3-4 hrs), sometimes joining the main road, sometimes passing through small villages; below San Rafael is an old flour mill still in operation.

From near San Rafael, one can go to Páramo El Tisure where Féliz Sánchez and Epifania Gil have built a stone house and church and offer free accommodation; take your own food and bedding. From Mérida take the bus to Puente de la Mucuchachi, US$1.50, 2 hrs, then walk for 10-12 hrs, or hire a mule (6 hrs) from Juan Serpa. The trail rises to 4,200m.

35 mins before Mérida is Los Aleros, a reconstruction of a 1930s town, with church, bar, etc; entry US$5. Staff wear appropriate rustic costume.

Tabay, 10 km from Mérida, has a pleasant main square, look out for humming birds (regular *por puesto* service, buses from Mérida Calle 19 entre Avs 3 y 4). Gasoline in Tabay. From Plaza Bolívar in Tabay, a jeep can be taken to Aguas Calientes (two pools in a stream, warm and luke warm, nice setting) and the cloud forest at **La Mucuy**. You can also walk to Aguas Calientes (or Termales): follow the road that goes up past the right hand side of the Plaza, looking towards the church; continue to the T-junction opp the cemetery; turn left, uphill, and follow the path. After 20 mins a house on the left sells fruit drinks. 30m further on a sign points right to Aguas Calientes, a further 5 mins. **NB** no midday shade.

Hotels and Restaurants in Tabay   Las Cumbres, El Castaño; 1.5 km from the plaza on the Mérida road is **E** *La Casona de Tabay*, T 074-830089, Spanish patio-style motel, rural setting, splendid view, clean, comfortable, good reading lamp, home cooking, family-run, friendly, highly rec, take *por puesto*, 2 signposts; restaurants *El Morichal* (good, cheap, 50m from plaza); *Micro Pastel* (20m beyond) and *Cancha de Bolas*. A few km before Tabay look out for **"Catalina Delicattesses"**, fantastic jams and chutneys, hundreds of flavours to be tasted, open 0800.

We descend through striated zones of timber, grain, coffee and tropical products to reach level land at last and the city of Mérida. All through this part of the country you see a plant with curious felt-like leaves of pale grey-green, the *frailejón* (or great friar), which blooms with yellow flowers from Sep to Dec. Cyclists should note that the road from Pico El Aguila is downhill all the way until Km 718, before Mérida, a fabulous run, lots of *posadas*, hostels and campsites enroute.

The patron saint of Mucuchíes is San Benito; his festival on 29 Dec is celebrated by participants wearing flower-decorated hats and firing blunderbusses continuously.

Mérida (173 km from Valera and 674 km from Caracas), founded 1558, is the capital of Mérida State. Its white towers are visible from far along the road, and it stands at 1,640m (mean temperature 19° C) on an alluvial terrace 15 km long, 2½ km wide, surrounded by cliffs and plantations and within sight of Pico Bolívar, the highest in Venezuela (5,007m), crowned with a bust of Bolívar. In Jan-Feb, the coldest months, and Aug-Sept, it rains almost every late afternoon (in the latter often throughout the night, too). Mérida still retains some colonial buildings which contrast with the fine modern buildings, such as those of the Universidad de los Andes (founded 1785), which has 37,000 students from all over South America and the Caribbean. The main square with rebuilt Cathedral is pleasant, but is no longer colonial. Population: 222,700, including students.

Mérida is known for its many parks (thirty three, some very small, little more than roundabouts) and statues: the Parque de las Cinco Repúblicas (Calle 13, between Avs 4 and 5), beside the barracks, had the first monument in the world to Bolívar (1842, replaced in 1988) and contains soil from each of the five countries he liberated (photography strictly prohibited). It is reported poorly maintained at present. The peaks known as the Five White Eagles (Bolívar, 5,007m, Humboldt, 4,942m, Bompland, 4,882m, Toro, 4,755m, León, 4,740m) can be clearly seen from here. In the Plaza Beethoven, a different melody from Beethoven's works is chimed every hour (not working late 1994; *por puestos*, also known as *busetas*, run along Av 5, marked "Santa María" or "Chorro de Milla", US$0.15). The Parque Los Chorros de Milla has a zoo (some cages disgracefully small) in a hilly setting with a waterfall, closed Mon, it is some distance from the centre (*buseta*, US$0.35). Plenty of handicraft shops near the zoo. On the way, there is a new chapel, built on the site where the Pope said mass in 1985. The Parque La Isla contains orchids, basketball and tennis courts, an amphitheatre and fountains; Jardín Acuario, besides the aquarium, is an exhibition centre, mainly devoted to the way of life and the crafts of the Andean peasants, admission US$0.10, open Tues-Sun 0800-1200, 1400-2000 (*busetas* leave from Av 4 y Calle 25, US$0.10, passing airport). There is fishing and mountaineering in the neighbouring Sierra Nevada. Kite flying is very popular; enthusiasts meet at the Viaducto bridge.

Museums Museo de Arte Colonial, Av 4, between Calles 17 and 18, three blocks from Plaza Bolívar (open Tues-Fri, 0900-1200, 1500-1800, Sat 1500-1800, and Sun, 1000-1200, 1500-1800). More interesting is the small **Museo Arqueológico**, Av 3, Edificio del Rectorado de la Universidad de los Andes, just off Plaza Bolívar, precolombian exhibits from the Andean region. **Museo de Arte Moderno**, Plaza Beethoven. **Instituto Municipal de Cultura**, Av 4, half block from Parque Bolívar, stages poetry readings, art shows etc. A new cultural centre is under construction, a couple of blocks up from the Plaza Bolívar.

Festivals The week of 4 Dec; hotels will only let for the whole week. For two weeks leading up to Christmas there are daily song contests between local students, on Plaza Bolívar, 1700-2200. Mérida is well known for its Feria del Sol, held on the week preceding Ash Wednesday. This is also the peak bullfighting season, for which Mérida is famous. Also 1-2 Jan, Paradura del Niño; and 15 May, San Isidro.

Hotels B *Park Hotel**, Parque Glorias Patrias, T (074) 637014, F 634582, car hire, noisy, but clean, good service, good restaurant, rec; B *Pedregosa**, Av Panamericana, T 663181, F 664295, on the edge of town, laid out like an Andean village with guests' cottages, pool, restaurant, rec, particularly for families with children, very safe atmosphere, armed guards, National car hire office, horse riding, rowing boats and bicycle rental nearby; B *El Tisure*, Av 4, between Calles 17 and 18, T 521744, F 526061, a new 4 star in modern colonial style, 34 rm, compact, the only hotel with a/c; B *Chama*, Av 4 con Calle 29, T 524851, private bath, pleasant, restaurant, noisy disco, guarded car parking, rec (nearby opp is E *Hotel Prince*); C *Belensate**, Urb La Hacienda, La Punta in pleasant park, close to airport, tennis courts, rec; C *Caribay**, Av 2 Lora Prolongación, T 636451, F 637141, excellent restaurant; C *Gran Balcón*, Paseo de las Ferias, T 524056, a few mins walk to cable car, clean, safe; C *Prado Río**, Cruz Verde 1, T 520633, F 525192, views from garden, rec, private bath, swimming pool, main building and individual cabins; C *Mintoy*, Calle 25 (Ayacucho), No 8-130, T 520340, comfortably furnished, rec, except for breakfast, new, very clean, good value, friendly; D *Hispano Turístico*, Av 3 Independencia No 27-51, T 528019, clean and comfortable; D *Valle*

MERIDA 123L

Not to scale
Not all streets shown

1. Plaza Bolívar
2. Cathedral
3. Parque de las Cinco Repúblicas
4. Plaza Beethoven
5. Parque los Chorros de Milla
6. Parque la Isla
7. Jardín Acuario
8. Parque Glorias Patrias
   & *Hotel Park*
9. Museo de Arte Colonial

10. Museo Arqueológico & Universidad
    de Los Andes, original building
11. Museo de Arte Moderno
12. Tourist Office
13. Cableway to Pico Espejo
    & *Hotel Teleférico*
14. IPOSTEL & CANTV
15. Plaza de Toros
16. Campo de Oro & Universidad
    de Los Andes campus
17. *Hotel Prado Río*
18. *Hotel Caribay*

← To Jají

Carretera Panamericana

Av. Los Próceres

Av. Las Américas

To Ejido, Lagunillas, Tovar & San Cristóbal

Río Albarregas

Viaducto

Av. 2   Lora

Av. Urdaneta

C.45   C.38   C.37   C.36   C.35   C.33   C.31   C.30   C.27   C.26

Av. Gonzalo Picón

Aeropuerto Alberto Carnevalli

Av. Tulio Febres Cordero

Av. 16 de Septiembre

Paseo D. Peña

Av. Humberto Tejeras

Río Chama

Grande, T 443011, 20 mins from centre, scenic setting, friendly staff, expensive restaurant; **E** *De Paz*, Av 2, Calles 24/25, T 523666, with bath, very clean, good value, friendly, rec; **E** *Luxemburgo*, Calle 24 (Rangel), between Avs 6-7, T 526865, private bath, very cold water, friendly, rec, new annex guesthouse when hotel is full, good and safe; **D** *Oviedo*, Av 3 No 34-37, T 636944, clean, friendly, excellent restaurant; **E** *Montecarlo*, Av 7 with Calles 24 and 25, T 526688, clean, safe, parking, hot water, good but restaurant slow, ask for a room at the back with a view of the mountains, rec (located between teleférico station and Plaza Bolívar); **E** *Posada La Merideña*, Av 4 y Calle 16, T 525738, clean, inner rooms noisy, charming, with washing machine; **E** *Posada Turística Marianela*, Calle 16 between Av 4 and 5, T 526907, hot showers, clean, breakfast available, friendly, terrace, laundry and kitchen, owner Marianela speaks English and is helpful and informative, often full, highly rec; **D** *Teleférico*, beside teleférico station, noisy, clean, hot water, good bar and restaurant. On Av 2: **E** *Alemania*, at Calle 16, with bath, **F** without, clean, quiet, family atmosphere, nice patio, German owner runs excursions; **E** *Center*, Av 2 near C21, clean, friendly, cheap, free filtered water, meals available, souvenir shop; **E** *Don Cándido*, Av 2, between Calles 17 y 18, good but noisy TV, free luggage store; **E** *Glorias Patrias*, Plaza Glorias Patrias, Av 2 Lora No 35-64, T 638113, with bath, very clean and friendly, laundry facilities, rec; **E** *El Trigal*, Calle 17 nr Av 2, clean, friendly, safe; **E** *Las Nieves*, Av 2 and Calle 19, clean, hot water, cooking facilities, TV, good, friendly owner, rec; **E** *Posada del Parque* on the Plaza Teleférico, with shared bath, hot water, comfortable, very clean, will store luggage; **E** *Posada Las Heroínas*, Calle 24, No 8-95, T 522665, owner Tom Evenou (Swiss), with or without bath, helpful, popular, clean, safe, use of kitchen, laundry, book sale/exchange, excursions organized, good atmosphere, highly rec; **E** *Posada Luz Carabello*, Av 2 Lora, No 13-80, frente a La Plaza de Milla, T 525441, excellent cheap restaurant, good bar, 40 rm with TV, ensuite, hot water, colonial touches in old building, rec; **E** *Residencias San Pedro*, Calle 19, No 3-36, entre Av 3 y 4, T 522735, family run, fully equipped, clean, friendly, hot water, laundry facilities, kitchen, luggage store, highly rec; **F** *Italia*, Calle 19 between Avs 2 and 3, cheapest, with bath, hot water (cheaper, smaller rooms available), clean, laundry facilities, friendly, rec, has post box, "Italia Tours", run by Carlos and Valeria, super helpful, speak English and French, offer excursions all over the area at very reasonable rates, highly rec; **F** pp *Panamá*, Av 3 entre 18 y 19, clean, friendly, a bit noisy, hot water, private bathrooms, busy, popular with students and backpackers, rec. **F** *Residencia de*

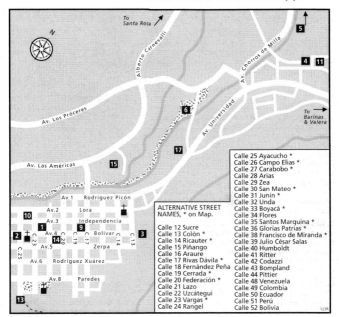

ALTERNATIVE STREET NAMES, * on Map.

Calle 12 Sucre	Calle 25 Ayacucho *
Calle 13 Colón *	Calle 26 Campo Elías *
Calle 14 Ricaúter *	Calle 27 Carabobo *
Calle 15 Piñango	Calle 28 Arias
Calle 16 Araure	Calle 29 Zea
Calle 17 Rivas Dávila *	Calle 30 San Mateo *
Calle 18 Fernández Peña	Calle 31 Junín *
Calle 19 Cerrada *	Calle 32 Unda
Calle 20 Federación *	Calle 33 Boyacá *
Calle 21 Lazo	Calle 34 Flores
Calle 22 Uzcátegui	Calle 35 Santos Marquina *
Calle 23 Vargas *	Calle 36 Glorias Patrias *
Calle 24 Rangel	Calle 38 Francisco de Miranda *
	Calle 39 Julio César Salas
	Calle 40 Humboldt
	Calle 41 Ritter
	Calle 43 Codazzi
	Calle 43 Bompland
	Calle 44 Pittier
	Calle 48 Venezuela
	Calle 49 Colombia
	Calle 50 Ecuador
	Calle 51 Perú
	Calle 52 Bolivia

Rafael Cuevas, Av 8 entre C 20 y 21, No 20-49, helpful, rec. On Av 5, between Calles 16 and 17, **E** *Dorado*, family run, clean, friendly, safe; *Casa de Familia*, belonging to Isabel Becerra, Calle 16, between Av 3 and 4, No 3-47, T 528573, hot water 24 hrs. It is difficult to get rooms during school holidays and the Feria del Sol. Rec to book in advance. **E** *Apartamentos Turísticos*, Urbanización Los Sauzales, run by Olga de Briceño, excellent flat, very clean, with comfortable rooms, kitchen, TV, bathroom with hot water, very friendly landlady who lives downstairs with family, good value, highly rec, but 20 mins walk from the city centre.

Camping *Gasolina blanca* sold opp Maraven station in Lagunillas, 45 mins S of Mérida: try in *Méridas Gas*, Av 4 No 29-47.

Restaurants *Chipen*, Av 5, Calles 24/23, good Italian food; *Zaguán de Milla*, Av 2, Calles 13/14, pizzas cooked over wood-fired stove, very good service. *Chino*, Av Los Chorros de Milla, a few hundred metres before zoo, 15 mins by bus, excellent Chinese; *Hong Kong*, Av 5 y C25, good Chinese, reasonable prices; *Fortune*, Calle 21 entre Av 2 y 3, good Chinese food, friendly owner, English and German spoken; *La Paellera*, Av 4, good Chinese food and good value for money; *Onde Jaime*, near Plaza Bolívar, Av 5 entre Calles 23 y 24, No 23-15, T 521519, cheap, good atmosphere, Colombian food, good, rec; *La Taberna de Eugenio*, off Av 5 below the viaduct, cheap, rec; *Tía Milla*, Chorros de Milla, out of the centre but great for meat eaters—meat ordered by weight and cooked on an open fire; *Mara*, in Pedregosa suburb, far from centre but excellent food, generous portions in criollo style, good value, highly rec (try *chivo en coco*, goat in coconut sauce); *Birosca Carioca*, Av 2 and Calle 24, good and cheap set lunch, also popular nightclub with live music and "executive dark and dingy atmosphere", nightly except Sun.

Vegetarian restaurants: *Comida Vegetariana*, Calle 24, No 8-205, opp Parque Las Heroínas, lunch time only; *Almuerzos Vegetarianos*, Av 4 y Calle 18, cheap set lunch, good food and tranquil atmosphere, rec; *Fonda Vegetariana*, Calle 29/Av 4, rec; *Anfora de Acuario*, Av 2, Calles 24 and 23, good set lunches. Italian: *La Mamma*, Av 3 and Calle 19, very nice, good pizza, pasta and set lunches, popular in the evening, live music at weekends, very cheap local wine; *El Sabor de los Quesos*, Calle 13, Av 1-2, very good and cheap pizzería; *Sancho Panzas*, Plaza Teleférico, excellent, cheap variety with good service, rec; *Mesón La Cibeles*, Calle 25 and Av 3, good food, well-priced, open until late; *Casa de los Espaguettis*,

Av 4, Calle 28-29, good service, friendly; *Pastelería Excelsior*, C 25 y Av 4, very good pizzas; *D'Angelos Pizzería*, Edificio El Coronel, Paseo Las Ferias, excellent and friendly; *Ven-Italia*, Av 3, Calle 25-26, no atmosphere but good food, friendly, popular with locals; *Montecarlo*, corner of Av 3 and Calle 25, good pizzas; *Alfredo's*, Calle 19 y Av 5, pizzas, burgers, beer, salad bar, popular; also *Alfredo's*, Av 4 between Calles 25 y 26, lunches, popular with local young crowd; *La Ternera Grill*, 100m S of Terminal Sur, popular with students, "executive lunch" US$1.

Chipilino, Av 3 y Calle 19, T 526660, popular with locals, cheap, open 0800-2300 daily, rec; *El Puntal*, Calle 19, Av 4, good cakes and coffee, *La Glorieta* shares the same garden, Arabian food, falafel rec; *Bakalao*, Av 3 y C13, good breakfast, bread, sandwiches; *El Palacio*, Calle 23 entre Av 4 y 5, good *batidos*, cheap set meal, US$1.20, friendly Lebanese owner speaks French; *La Guanabana*, Calle 25, 6-26, excellent fruit juices and milkshakes; *Café París Tropical*, Calle 21 between Avs 3 and 4, highly rec for sandwiches and fruit drinks, very popular place to be and to meet others. *Yuan Lin* ("Los Chinos"), C 26, opp Edif Zona Franca, just up from Av T Febres Cordero, excellent value fruit juices (about US$1), burgers and hotdogs, restaurant part has plentiful food but is expensive and uninteresting. *Tía Nicota*, Av 3 entre C 25 y 26, Galería 1890, rec for coffee, pancakes, pies. *El Rincón de la Cachapa*, next to *La Casa de los Espagnetis*, for big delicious *cachapas*. The *Heladería La Coromoto*, Av 3 y Calle 29, T 523525, open 1400-2200, closed Mon, offers 529 flavours, 150 choices of ice cream each day, eg, trout, cornflakes, garlic, spaghetti. Local specialities, trout, *pastelitos* (savoury); sweetmeats incl *dulces abrillantados*, *higo relleno*, *mantecado de maiz*; also try the local drink, *calentado*. Cheeses at the shop at Calle 14 and Av 1. For wholemeal bread, *Posada de Heroínas*, Plaza de Heroínas, nr teleférico, good meeting place.

Banks and Exchange   Banco Unión, Av 3, Calle 23/24, accepts Thomas Cook TCs and Visa and Mastercard credit cards. **Banco Consolidado** in Centro Comercial Viaducto, opp N end of Calle 26 bridge, only bank for Amex, also cash (1000-1100, 1500-1600 Mon-Fri). Cheques accepted by the *Casa de Cambio* of travel agency Viajes y Turismo Cordillera, on the 1st floor in Centro Comercial Las Tapias, Av Andrés Bello Adventure tour offices, eg NAtourA, will exchange dollars.

Consulates   Colombian   Av Las Américas, CC Mamayeya, piso 5, T 660135, open 0800-1400, visas take 10 mins. **British**   Professor Robert Kirby, honorary vice-Consul, Pedregosa Media, Conjunto Residencial Las Ardillas 2a, Transv Calle Las Dantas, Qta Lothlorlen, T 448050 ext 2011. **Useful Addresses   Immigration Office** (DIEX), is on the main airport road about 1 km beyond the airport.

Discos and Music   La Viuda Negra, Comercial Alto Chama on the road to Parroquía; and *El Fin del Mundo* 2 Av Andrés Bello, closed on Fri. *Bodegón de Pancho*, Av Las Américas, Centro Comercial Mamayeya, US$5 entrance pays for 5 beers, Latin American music, rec. *Tops*, in *Hotel Pedregosa* (see above), popular after others have closed.

Doctor   Dra María Yuraima C de Kirby at Clínica Médica, Calle 22 (opp Cultural Centre), T 521859, speaks English, rec.

Language Schools   Several schools incl Latinoamericano de Idiomas, CC Mamayeya, piso 5, oficina C-5-38, T 440698, F 447808, contact Marinés Asprino, highly rec. Nora Garce and María Eugenia Olívar, Av 2 con C 19, Edif Chiquinquirá No 11-19 Apt 3, T 520845, US$2/hr, rec; also Lysbeth de Lledó, T 632707. Many tutors place ads in *posadas* and bars.

Laundry   Lavandería Estudiante, Av 2, near Plaza de Milla, clean and dry for under US$1, quick service.

Post Office and Telephones   Ipostel and CANTV, Calle 21 and Av 4. Post office also in bus terminal, 0800-1200, 1400-1700, weekdays only.

Shopping   Handicraft market opp La Plaza de Las Heroínas, by *teleférico*, good café. "Hippie" market, C 26, beyond *Yuan Lin*, expensive but beautiful and unusual jewellery. Mercado Principal on Av las Americas (buses for bus station pass by), huge building containing many small shops, good for souvenirs as well as fruit and vegetables, top floor restaurant has regional comida típica, bargaining possible. Good record shop *Discoteca Internacional*, Av 3, Edificio Trujillo. The up-market Centro Comercial *Las Tapias* has shops, disco, multi cinema (films are shown in English), 1½ km SW of the airport on Av Andrés Bello, opposite Jardín Acuario. Cheaper and with a greater accent on youth is the Centro Comercial *Viaducto*, Av Las Américas at Viaducto 26. **Bookshop**   Libros Usados, J Santos, Av 6, 21-45, very good prices, incl some 2nd hand English, German and French books. **Films**   One-day service, *CA*, Calle 23 between 5 y 6, T 527981. *Kodak*, on Plaza Bolívar, rec, good colours on prints, US$0.33 each, one-hour service, slides developed in 2-3 days, good selection of films; *Profot*, Av 3, Calle 25, Fuji film, good colour quality for prints. Bad report received about the camera repair shop on Av 2, Hoyada de Milla, very friendly but expensive and inexpert.

Travel Agencies *Montaña* offers climbing holidays (US$75-125 per day, incl transport and equipment), horseriding, birdwatching, hang gliding, mountain biking, trout fishing, trips to Roraima and down the Río Caura to Para Falls, and a 21-day tour of Venezuela, English-speaking guides, trips graded according to difficulty. Ed Las Américas PB, Av Las Américas, Mérida, T (074) 661448, Apartado Postal 645, F (5874) 661448; *NAtour A*, Av 4, No 18-19 (or C 43, No 3-62), T (074) 524075, F 635544, open Mon-Sun 0830-1900, many recommendations for tours on foot or by car, climbing, trekking, hang-gliding, horse riding, mountain biking, fishing, birdwatching, 4WD hire with guide and driver, and trips in Barinas state, small, friendly company run by Delfín Viera and José Luis Troconis, English, French, German and Italian spoken, guide Elvis rec; *Sierra Tours*, *Park Hotel*, T 630879, has a range of excursions. It is cheaper to take a taxi for a day trip, **Línea Tibisay**, outside *Park Hotel*, T 637930, rec. *Mountain Tours*, Calle 24, No 8-107, T 074-526402, offer a wide range of climbing tours and trips to the jungle. *Nevada Tours* at the airport will take non-climbers up the Pico Bolívar, but owing to the altitude and weather conditions, this can be dangerous; check all equipment carefully. *Club de Turismo*, Calle 24, No 8-107 (opp Teleférico), highly rec for tours to Jají and Laguna Negra, ask for Timo (in *Hotel El Parque* when not in office). *Antana Aventura*, T 074 713960, trekking, camping, paragliding, and mountain bicycling, good prices, rec. *Guamanchi Tours*, Calle 24, No 8-39, T/F 522080, rec for hiking, paragliding, biking, equipment hire, exchange, information, tours to the refuge on Pico Humboldt (José is a good guide), tours to Llanos and Amazonia, discount for guests at *Posada La Merideña*. *Frontino Tours*, Av 3 entre C 19 y 20, Edif Viviana No 19-36, T 520955, F 523051, run by German Ilse Gasser, also speaks English, rec. Camilo Trujillo Medina of *Mucaventura*, Conjunto Residencial, Parque Las Américas, Edificio M, Apt 5-2, Av Las Américas, T 637677, trips to the Llanos, 3 days, US$150, rec; Alan Highton, T 442748, also offers tours of Mérida and the Llanos; both speak English and have been rec. Ponciano Dugarte Sánchez, T 665096/528416, rec for jeep trips into the national park, Spanish only spoken.

Tourist Offices Centro de Información Turística Norte, between Avs Próceres and Universidad, T 441076, low season 0800-1200, 1400-1800, high season 0800-1800, closed Sun. At airport, in waiting lounge, T 639330, same low season hours, 0730-1330 in high season. In bus terminal, T 633952, same hours as Centro Norte, has free map of city. At Terminal Sur, helpful, map, hotel list, useful addresses and guide to events, English spoken. Centro de Información Acuario, Av Andrés Bello, T 633117, low season 0800-1200, 1400-1800, high season 0830-1830. At Oficina de Turismo Aeropuerto, Manuel is very informative about excursions in the mountains, also Marcucci Aura, T/F 921201, who arranges day trips to Laguna Negra and Jají. The helpful Tourist Offices are probably a better bet than the police if you need to register a theft report for insurance purposes. **Inparques** (National Parks) office at end of Calle 51, turn right, map of Sierra Nevada national park (mediocre) US$1.

Taxis Journeys in town cost about US$1.50.

Car Hire Several companies at the airport, incl Mérida Rent a Car, T (074) 630722, ask for José Félix Rangel, or Dávila Tours, Av Los Próceres opp Urb la Trinidad, T (074) 660711, or airport T 634510. For motorcycle hire try Buggy's Bikes, Av Miranda, Quinta Sajomi 3-83, T 639145, US$25-30 per day, US$5 insurance, US$5 safety helmet, 100 km incl, can bargain. Bikes break down, helmets poor standard.

Air Services Airport is on the main highway, *por puesto* into town US$0.10, taxi US$1.50. No exchange facilities. Watch out for unofficial tour guides touting for business. Daily flights to Caracas (4, 1 hr if direct), San Antonio (2, 25 mins), Barquisimeto, Maracaibo and Valencia; also to Coro. In the rainy season, especially on afternoon flights, planes may be diverted to San Antonio (if they aren't, it's a hair-raising approach). Avensa pay for overnight accommodation or for *por puestos* to Mérida, 3-5 hrs on winding roads where landslides are common. Sit on left side of plane from Caracas for views. A new airport has been built at El Vigía, 2½ hrs from Mérida; much safer as it is on a plain.

Buses The bus terminal is about 3 km from the centre on the W side of the valley, connected by frequent minibus service from Calle 25 between Avs 2 and 3. Good tourist information office, will book hotels, free maps. A small exit tax of US$0.10 is charged at the information desk, make sure you pay, officials check buses before departure. On interstate buses, it is essential to book in advance; for buses within the state you pay on board. Those hitchhiking E from Mérida should take a minibus to Tabay (US$0.45) and try from there.

Bus companies Expresos Alianza, T 631193, 3 daily direct to Caracas, others via Valencia, Maracay, 2030 to Maracaibo, Coro; **Expresos San Cristóbal**, T 631881/638476, 3 daily to Caracas, some stop at Valencia, Maracay, 2 to Maracaibo, Coro, also Punto Fijo; **Expresos Mérida**, T 633430, 4 daily to Caracas, some direct, 2 to Barquisimeto, 1 to Maracaibo; **Transportes Barinas**, T 634651, 5 daily to Barinas via Santo Domingo, 4 to Valera; **Expresos**

Juaregui, T 637759, to La Tendida, Morotuto, Coloncito, La Fría, Colón, San Cristóbal. In addition, several colectivo companies operate from the terminal, as well as *busetas*, to: Jaji, Tovar, La Azulita, Lagunillas, Acarigua, Zea, Bailadores, Chiguará, Loma del Carmen, Loma del Rosario, La Playa, Piedra Blanca. **Sample fares and times Caracas**, US$17.65 with a/c, US$14.70 without, 11-15 hrs; **Maracaibo**, 5-7 hrs, US$4.70, *por puesto* US$7, Unión de Conductores, T 24364; **San Cristóbal**, US$4.10, 6 hrs, *por puesto* US$7; **Barinas**, US$2.50, 6 hrs, *por puesto* US$5, 3½ hrs; **Coro**, 12-14 hrs, US$18.80; **Valera**, US$3, 5 hrs, *por puesto* US$5.45; **Barquisimeto**, US$7, 8 hrs; **Maracay**, US$16.50; **Apartaderos**, US$1.75, *por puesto* US$2.50.

The world's alleged highest and longest aerial cableway runs to **Pico Espejo** (4,765m) in four stages; it was built by the French in 1958. In Nov 1991 a cable snapped on the final section and in 1994 all service was suspended until repairs had been completed (not until at least 1997).

While the cableway is not running, jeeps take tourists as far as Los Nevados (see below), from where it is a 2-day trek to the summit. This is a "must", best done early in the morning (before 0830 ideally), before the clouds spoil the view, and from Nov to June. In summer the summit, with its statue to Nuestra Señora de las Nieves (Our Lady of the Snows, patron saint of mountaineers), is clouded and covered with snow and there is no view. An alternative, challenging route is from Mucunatan (20 mins from Mérida by car), 4 days via Le Aguada station, Los Calderones, Pico Espejo, then to Pico Bolívar. In either case it is a one-day return to Mérida. Reputable trekking companies provide suitable clothing, temperatures can be as low as 0°C. Aug is the coldest month on the peaks. The glacier on Pico Bolívar can be seen clearly; so can Picos Humboldt and Bompland, forming the Corona, and to the E, on a clear day, the blue haze of the *llanos*. Electric storms in the mountains are not uncommon. There is a good restaurant at La Montaña, 2,442m.

Los Nevados (2,711m) is a pretty little hamlet with plentiful accommodation (eg *Posada Bella Vista*, Sánchez family, E pp incl breakfast and dinner, behind church, arrange mule trip to *teleférico*, 4 hrs, US$2/mule, plus US$3 for guide; Doña Rosa, or Señor Castillo), guest house has food. From Los Nevados you can hike to Loma Redonda (4,045m), the penultimate station on the *teleférico:* clear path through rainforest, beautiful birds, take plenty of water, not recommended for the inexperienced, 7 hrs up; breathtaking views; be prepared for cold rain in the afternoon, start very early. Mules do the journey Tues-Sun, 4-5 hrs, in Los Nevados ask for Jorge, bargain hard, US$4 for mule, US$4 for guide (and beware of mules kicking out when they become bunched together going uphill). You can walk down from Loma Redonda to La Aguada station (3,452m) on a rough path (very hard on the knees), wear boots, walk slowly, about 2 hrs, not for children or the elderly, take water. At La Aguada station you can see the *frailejón* plant and throughout the area there is a great variety and quantity of flora, take the Tabay-El Caney minibus from Calle 19 in Mérida. The walk from La Aguada to the next station down, La Montaña, is 2½ hrs. From La Montaña, which is the penultimate station on the way down, it is a ½-hr walk to Los Calderones' farm, accommodation and horses for hire and a 2½-hr walk to Mérida.

From Los Nevados you can walk to **El Morro** (7½ hrs, very steep) or take a jeep to Mérida (mornings, 2½-5 hrs, very rough, reputedly dangerous after rain, US$15 pp). It is possible to get a room to stay overnight (*Posada Abel Gámez*, run by Adriana Dugerte, friendly, meals, rec; **Posada** run by Doña Chepa, as you enter from Los Nevados, warm and friendly, highly rec; **G** *Hospedaje Nerios*, friendly, meals, rec). Sr Oviller Ruiz provides information on the history of the church and Indian cemetery. From here it is 47 km to Mérida, do not attempt to walk before discovering if any facilities are available en route.

A recommended hike from Pico Espejo, is to the cloud forest at La Mucuy, near to the village of Tabay, 2-3 days walking at over 4000m altitude, passing spectacular snow peaks and several lakes. A tent and a warm sleeping bag are essential, as is a good map (local guides may lend theirs to photocopy). Water supply en route is plentiful. There is a refuge at the foot of **Pico Humboldt**, close to a lagoon, and a nice camping area at Laguna Caramote (**see also p 1376**). A description of the Sierra Nevada is included in *Venezuela* published by Bradt Publications.

NB Because this is a national park, you need a permit to hike this mountain range and camp overnight. It must be obtained from the Inparques (National Parks) office in Mérida (see above). Permits are not given to single hikers (except to Los Nevados): a minimum of 2 people is required. Have your passport available. Camping gas may be bought in Mérida from Remate Panamá, Calle 23 y Av 2, near *Hotel Playa*. If camping, remember that the area is between 3,500 and 4,200m so acclimatization is necessary as is warm clothing for night-time. (See **Altitude** in **Health Information** at the beginning of the book.) Some treks are very difficult so be sure to check with the tourist office before leaving. Water purification is also recommended.

Mountain Guides The *Andean Club* in Mérida organizes trips to the top and guides will provide all equipment (PO Box 66); enquire at the *teleférico* station at the end of Calle 24, beyond Av 8. *Carlos Rodríguez C*, can be contacted at Av Universidad, Edif María Gracia, piso 2, Apto 5, T 449726, F 445763; he offers 1 to 7 day trips around Mérida, incl in the price transportation, equipment and food, also mountain biking, horse riding, climbing and tours throughout Venezuela. *Carlos Torres*, Av 2, No 9-81, or through *Hotel Italia*, rec, US$30 per day for two. *Yanesha Expediciones*, Av 3, T 523291/636932, offer climbing, hiking, as well as normal tourist excursions, novices catered for, English spoken. *John Peña*, Mercado Artesanal, Antonio Rojas Guillén, Plaza Las Heroínas, Local 4. Guides can often be found at *Café París* in the centre.

Excursions For visits to resorts near Mérida, Laguna de Mucubají, Laguna Negra or Pico El Aguila (see p 1374)—*por puesto* to Pico El Aguila, US$3.

El Valle-La Culata is an easy trip by *buseta* from a side street 2 blocks N of Plaza Bolívar (US$0.30, 30 mins, ask for La Culata; some *busetas* stop short). The road up the superb valley ends at La Culata. Thereafter a stony track leads up to the head of the valley and beyond, crossing the watersheds. You can go around the locked gate marked "propiedad privada" after about 1 km. The valley has fine scenery but no pretty villages. Many snack stops and marmalade/preserves shops along the way to La Culata; **B** *La Culata*, El Valle, Carretera via Páramo La Culata, T (074) 523915/526128, Cellular (014) 740340, F 638802, 24 km from Mérida, rather gaudy, up-market retreat in magnificent setting.

Jají, 43 km, pop 1,500, is famous for its colonial architecture, including a nice main square. The buildings of the main square and adjoining streets are mainly given over to *artesanías*, selling all manner of stuff from all over the continent. Out of season, there are few visitors. There is good walking in the hills. Recommended hotel and restaurant *Posada de Jají*, good food; **E** *Hospedaje Familiar*, good, friendly; *Restaurante El Bosque*, good, cheap, local food, excellent *parrilladas*, bar; *Restaurant El Zaguán*. *Busetas* leaves Terminal Sur hourly, 50 mins, US$0.60; journey passes forested mountains, cliffs and waterfalls, sit on left.

On the way is *La Mesa de Ejido* village (**D** *Posada Turística Papá Miguel*, rec, good food). *Mesa de Los Indios* is a small village beyond Ejido, near which there are fantastic hot springs known as the Yin and Yang, where cold rain water from the mountains meets hot spring water. Do not stray onto property next door as your whole day could be spoilt by a rottweiler. Off the road to Jají, 20 mins from Mérida, is *Venezuela de Anteayer*, where regional culture is recreated in a series of displays, incl typical music and food, US$8.

Continuing for 62 km—narrow, but mostly paved—beyond Jají, the Panamericana is reached at Santa Elena de Arenales (several gas stations on the way). From La Azulita, between Jají and the Panamericana, one can visit La Cueva del Pirata (reported deserted and in bad shape).

Transandean Route 7 leaves Mérida and passes through the Chama valley, heading for Lagunillas and Bailadores. At La González, one rough road turns S to *San José*, a pleasant village, 2½ hrs from Mérida, a dusty but beautiful trip into the mountains, green and cultivated higher up (take bus from Av 2 in Mérida to El Ejido, 30 mins, then *por puesto* from main square, 2 hrs, US$1.50). Two *posadas*, best is at entry to the village; Haydee Ruiz rents a cottage, T 074-792-2222. From San José a track runs up the S slope of the Andes to El Morro (see above). Another road from La González goes NW to *San Juan de Lagunillas*, believed to be the first site of Mérida (pop 15,900). It has a striking church and is noted for its craftwork especially weaving. Fiestas from Christmas to Candlemas (2 Feb), 3 weeks in May (14 and 15 the highpoint) and in July. From San Juan, or from further along Route 7, Lagunillas can be reached. On the edge of Lagunillas is *Jamu*, a reconstructed Indian village, named after an Indian tribe, where demonstrations of weaving and other skills are given; entry US$1.20. Soon after the second turn-off for Lagunillas, a turning on the left leads to *Pueblo Nuevo*, a pretty colonial village, 2,050m above sea-level. The well-paved road climbs up steeply, giving impressive views all around. *Posada Doña Eva*, on the SE corner of the main plaza, is basic but with a friendly, family atmosphere, delicious and cheap vegetarian meals served to order, highly rec, F (the building is 300 years old and has been restored). The whole village has very lively (and liquid) celebrations starting ten days before Christmas ("everyone runs around the cobblestone streets, setting off fire-crackers, firing blunderbusses into the air, playing violins and getting extremely drunk"), but is otherwise quiet. Taxi-jeeps from nr new cultural centre, Av 2, Mérida, US$1.50. There are also pleasant walks in the hills around the village.

30 mins beyond Lagunillas lies the little church of *Estanques* (seldom open except on Christmas Day) with a stupendous gold colonial altar. Near Estanques is the colonial village of *Chiguará* with mineral springs (**D** *Posada Colonial Cantarranos*, swimming pool fed by mineral springs, friendly, try *El Merendero* for local delicacies; **E** *Posada Los Rurales*, at entrance to village), quiet, beautiful, nice walking; *buseta* from Mérida, US$0.90. At El Pedregal there are botanical gardens and a good view over the town. Giant cacti in the area are said to be 300 years old.

In the Valle de Mocotíes, by the Alcabala La Victoria, is the Museo del Inmigrante in a reconstructed coffee *finca*, open daily 0800-1800 (also has *cafetería*). Puente Victoria is a few km beyond Estanques, where a road branches off N to El Vigía on the Panamericana.

96 km beyond Mérida is **Tovar** (pop 30,000; bus from Mérida US$1.50; **D** *Hostería Sabaneta*, private bath; **E** *Hotel Valle del Mocoties*, opp bus terminal; **F** *Pensión Ideal*, clean, basic, laundry facilities, friendly; **F** *Hospedaje Tovar*; *Restaurant Kek Duna*, Hungarian owner speaks 6 languages and serves interesting food), a nice little town with pleasant excursions, whence one can rejoin the Panamericana via Zea, itself a pleasant village, or tackle the wild and beautiful old mountain road over the Páramo de La Negra to San Cristóbal. 15 km from Tovar is **Bailadores** (pop 10,330), which also celebrates its fiesta from Christmas to Candlemas (**C** *Hotel La Cascada*, modern— Wilfredo plays electric organ in the bar on Sat night, and at Mass on Sun in the beautiful church, entertaining on both occasions; **E** *Hospedaje Villa*); beautiful walk to the waterfall with strawberries and cream half-way at La Capellería; *por puesto* to San Cristóbal US$3.60, bus from Tovar US$0.75. From Bailadores the road climbs up into the mountains. **C** *Hotel de Montaña*, private bath, T 077-82401/2, is rec, 7 km before La Grita on the road from Mérida. Buses twice daily (0900 and 1530) between Tovar and La Grita on the old road. **La Grita** is a pleasant town, good Sunday market, festival 6 Aug. Bus from Bailadores US$1.80. Hotels: **E** *La Casona*, Carrera 2A, No 6-69, clean, friendly; **E** *Capri*, Carrera 3, good value, bargain; good pizza restaurant next door. **San Pedro del Río** is a well preserved colonial village (**D** *Posada Valparaíso*, T 077-911032, beautiful garden, rec).

San Cristóbal, capital of Táchira State, is on a plateau 55 km from the Colombian border, at 830m (average temperature 22°C, pop 290,900). The city is on three levels, running N-S: a 112 km wide level zone along the Torbes river, which flows S into the Orinoco basin, and two terraces, one of them 200m above the river, and 5°C cooler. This, and the La Concordia sector to the S, are the "select" suburbs. The city was founded in 1561, and the Spanish colonial appearance—the appearance only—is preserved. The Cathedral, finished in 1908, had its towers and façade rebuilt in colonial style for the 400th anniversary of the foundation. There is a good road over the mountains, with beautiful Andean views, to San Antonio. Short or day trips can be made to Rubio and Delicias, both with accommodation.

Festival 20-30 Jan.

Hotels B *Círculo Militar*, Av 19 de Abril, clean, safe, spacious, all services incl 25m swimming pool and gymnasium, rec; **B** *De Ferias El Tamá**, Av 19 de Abril, overlooking the town, has an Olympic-size swimming pool, very good; **C** *Korinu*, Carrera 6 bis, shower, TV extra, friendly, rec, with restaurant; **D** *Del Rey*, Av Ferrero Tamayo, T 432703/430561, clean, good showers, fridge, TV, quiet, rec; **D** *Machirí*, Calle 7 No 4-30, bath, hot water, central; **E** *Cariongi*, near bus terminal, basic but convenient; **E** *Ejecutivo*, Calle 6, No 3-45, old and basic but clean and central; **E** *Tropicana*, next to bus terminal, with bath, basic; **E** *Unisa*, also near bus terminal, clean, OK. There are several cheap hotels on Avenida 6A, just off the central plaza, in E category; **F** *Alba*, near terminal, on the main street.

Restaurants *Fung Wah*, on lower of 2 main thoroughfares, Chinese, expensive but good. Café in Casa Francesa, good *merengadas*, pleasant, reasonable prices, near Cathedral. **Fuente de Soda La Bohème**, Av García de Hevia y 7 Av, Centro Cívico, expensive, breakfasts all day. *El Rancho de Esteban*, 500m from *Hotel Del Rey*, open air with fine view over city, special barbecue dishes, very highly rec.

Exchange Banco Consolidado (American Express), 5a Av, Edif Torre E.

Consulate German, Edif Torovega, Cra 8, La Concordia, T 448866.

Launderette in Cada shopping centre next to *Hotel El Tamá*, open 0800-1200, 1400-1800.

Post Office Palacio Municipal, next to Cathedral.

Airports For San Cristóbal: at San Antonio (1 hr) and La Fría (90 mins.).

By Road To **Maracaibo**, 6-8 hrs, US$6.50, *por puesto*, US$19. To **Mérida**, US$7 by *por puesto* or bus, US$4.10. To/from **Bailadores** US$1.50, lovely trip via La Grita. To **Caracas**, US$11, 12 hrs by Llanos and Panamericana routes respectively; similarly to **Valencia**, US$10. To **San Antonio**, 2½ hrs by bus, US$1, or *por puesto*, which continues to **Cúcuta**, stopping at Immigration in both countries, runs every 20 mins. By taxi to Cúcuta: US$11 to San Antonio, US$5 to wait at border, then US$6 to Cúcuta. The bus station is well-equipped; the information booth has maps of town and some hotel information.

San Antonio, the frontier town (not a tourist attraction, pop 42,630, although there is an attractive colonial cathedral, also some pleasant parks), is connected by international bridge with **Cúcuta**, Colombia, distant about 16 km (bus US$0.80—in bolívares or pesos—to international bridge), whence you can continue by road or air to Bogotá. 13 km N on the Venezuelan side lies the spa of Ureña, with natural hot springs (**B** *Hotel Aguas Calientes**, private thermal bath, swimming pool); crossing the border at Ureña is not permitted.

Festivals San Antonio, 13-20 May; Ureña, 3-12 Dec.

Hotels At San Antonio: **D** *Neveri*, Calle 3, No 3-11, esq Carrera 3, private bath, a/c, TV, safe, parking nearby, by border; **D** *Táchira*, with bath, rec; **E** *Colonial*, Carrera 11, No 2-51, T 78018, with bath, basic, clean, restaurant; **E** *Don Jorge*, a/c dining room expensive; **E** *Lorena*, Carrera 6, No 6-57, clean, fan; **E** *Terepaima*, Carrera 8, No 1-37, clean, friendly, safe, rec; **F** *Frontera*, Calle 2 Con Carrera 9 No 8-70, T 77366, pleasant, good value; many hotels near town centre.

Restaurants Good meals available at *Hotel Terepaima* (see above); *Refugio de Julio*, Carrera 10, good value pizzas; *La Giralda de Sevilla*, next door to *Hotel Neveri* (above), very good, open on Sun evenings, unlike everywhere else.

Exchange at the Banco de Venezuela, cash only; Visa at Banco Unión; Amex at Banco Consolidado, all on main square. Travellers' cheques are difficult to change. *Casas de cambio* near the international bridge will not all change cheques and some will only change Colombian pesos, not even US dollars cash. The exchange rate for changing bolívares to pesos is the same in San Antonio as in Cúcuta.

Colombian Consulate 10, Centro Cívico San Antonio, piso 2, better to go to Mérida for visas, open 0800-1400.

Airport has exchange facilities (mainly for Colombian pesos). Taxis run to DIEX (emigration) in town, and on to Cúcuta airport, US$8.50. *Por puesto* to airport, US$0.20. Internal flights, Avensa and Servivensa to Maiquetía, Mérida, Barquisimeto, Maracaibo and Valencia. Aserca to Barcelona, Maturín, Puerto Ordaz, Porlamar, Valencia.

Bus Cúcuta to Caracas US$12.50 (coming from the capital buses to the border stop for exit stamps in San Antonio); bus Caracas-**San Antonio** US$12, a/c, to Caracas at 1600 and 1800, 12 hrs; bus to **Cúcuta**, US$5.50 (stops at DIEX office and at Cúcuta airport). Taxi to San Cristóbal, US$11.

Crossing from Venezuela to Colombia Be sure to get your Venezuelan exit stamp in San Antonio (DIEX, Carrera 9 y Av 1 de Mayo) as facilities are no longer available at the bridge. First get the form from DIEX, then take it to Banco Venezuela on Plaza Bolívar, pay 30 bolívares, then take the receipt back to DIEX for your exit stamp. *Por puesto* drivers may say it's not required and refuse to wait, whereas taxi drivers will stop at all the right offices and save a lot of confusion (fare incl all stops US$8.50). Colombian officials will send you back if you have no exit stamp (unless you are only visiting Cúcuta; officials do not seem overly concerned about day visitors). Once you are in Colombia go straight to the DAS office at the border, in Cúcuta or the airport to complete formalities there (**see Colombia Section 2**).

Entering Venezuela from Cúcuta, there is no point in buying a bus ticket to San Cristóbal before going through formalities. Go to DIEX first. If travelling on a Cúcuta-San Cristóbal bus, the driver should wait for you to go through formalities, but he may need to be reminded. 5 km after San Antonio is a customs post; be prepared to be strip-searched, and then for further searches between San Cristóbal and Mérida. **NB** Venezuelan customs is often closed at weekends; it is therefore impossible to cross from Colombia at these times. Be prepared for long queues on the international bridge after 1500. Entering Venezuela in your own car presents no problems as long as you have obtained a visa in advance. You must visit Immigration in town, pay US$0.20 for a form on which to pay exit tax and have your passport photocopied. Once in Venezuela, you may find that local police are ignorant of documentation required for foreign cars.

THE LLANOS OF THE ORINOCO (5)

A spectacular route descends from the Sierra Nevada to the flat *llanos*, perhaps one of the best places in the world to see birds. South of these cattle lands stretch the forests through which flow the Orinoco and its tributaries; out of the lowlands rise strange, flat-topped *tepuyes*. The area is excellent for "nature tourism".

This area of flat grasslands, 1,000 km by 320 km, lies between the Andes and the Río Orinoco. It is veined by numerous slow running rivers, forested along their banks. The vast flatland is only varied here and there by *mesas*, or slight upthrusts of the land. About 5 million of the country's 6.4 million cattle, many of the Zebu type from Brazil and India, are in the *llanos*, 30% of the country's area, but holding no more than 13% of the population. When the whole plain is periodically under water, the *llaneros* drive their cattle into the hills or through the flood from one *mesa* to another. When the plain is parched by the sun and the savanna grasses become uneatable they herd the cattle down to the damper region of the Apure and Orinoco. Finally they drive them into the valley of Valencia to be fattened.

Parts of the area are coming under cultivation. The Guárico dam has created thousands of hectares of fertile land by controlling flood and drought. The State of Portuguesa has the largest cultivated area of any, producing rice and cotton.

Alternative route from Caracas to Mérida

There is a splendid road to the western *llanos* of Barinas, from Valencia through **San Carlos** (pop 71,650), capital of Cojedes State (**C** *Hotel Central*, clean, safe, a/c, good bar and restaurant, and secure offstreet parking; **F** *Hotel San Carlos*, Av Carabobo, a/c, private bath; festivals 18 Jan and 2-5 Nov—San Carlos Borromeo), **Acarigua**, a thriving agricultural centre (**C** *Motel Payara**, on road to Guanare, pool, a/c; **C** *Hotel Parigua*, Calle 31, a/c, bath, secure parking; **E** *Motel Rancho Grande*, clean, safe, very mediocre restaurant attached; *Campeste*, 1 minute from bus terminal; **E** *San Carlos*, good restaurant, not too safe; *Kety* for cakes) and **Guanare**, a national place of pilgrimage with an old parish church containing the much venerated relic of the Virgin of Coromoto, Patron of Venezuela. Population 32,500 (**C** *Hotel Italia*, Carrera 5, No 19-60, the most expensive, clean, a/c, bar and restaurant, offstreet parking; others, all D, incl *Coromoto*—out of town, swimming pool; *Motel Sultana*, on the main road to Acarigua, TV, a/c, clean, safe and friendly, reasonable bar and restaurant adjacent; **C** *Motel Portuguesa*, on northern outskirts – beware of dangerous intersection, a/c, cold water, TV, clean, good restaurant, pool, small zoo with tiny cages for animals; *Hotel Los Angeles*; *Restaurant Don Quixote*, near *Hotel Italia*, good atmosphere but expensive).

After the first appearance of the Virgin, Chief Coromoto failed to be baptized, though he did hedge by getting other members of the tribe baptized. When the Virgin reappeared he made a grab at her and told her gruffly to be gone, but she vanished leaving in his hand a likeness of herself on the inner surface of a split stone now on display in the church. For years little attention was paid to the image, and it was only in 1946 that this Virgin was declared the Patron of Venezuela.

Festivals in Portuguesa State Pilgrimages to Coromoto, 2 Jan and 8 Sep; Candlemas in Guanare, 1 Feb; Virgen de la Corteza in Acarigua, 11 Feb (bull-baiting, dancing).

The road continues to **Barinas** (population 179,660), the hot and sticky capital of the cattle-raising and oil-rich State of Barinas. The shady Parque Universitario has a botanical gardens and a zoo open Mon to Fri. The tourist office is on the Plaza Bolívar. There are two museums. Fishing and game-watching excursions into the *llanos*. The rivers are full of *caribes* (*piranha*) and many kinds of fish good to eat. The local music at *Hotel Venezuela* (no rooms) near the bus terminal has been rec; harp, *cuatro*, singing, informal and very good. The tourist office on Plaza Bolívar is reported helpful, local maps available, no English spoken.

Hotels C *Bristol**, Av 23 de Enero, a/c, clean, safe, good, rec, nondescript restaurant; **C** *Comercio**, Av Marqués del Pumar, cooking facilities; **E** *Motel La Media Avenida*, Av 23 de Enero, T 22278, cold showers, bar, restaurant, parking, clean, rec; opp bus terminal are: **E** *El Palacio*, clean, a/c, OK; **E** *Lisboa*, clean, "like a bus parking lot", noisy; **E** *Roma*, Av 7, 5-66, with bath, a/c, safe parking; **E** *Motel San Marino*, rooms small, beds OK, friendly but not so clean, and **E** *Venedo*, motel style, noisy.

   Restaurants *Adán y Eva*, Av Sucre, *criollo* restaurant, good; *Heladería Metro*, Av 7, good patisserie opp the bus terminal; *Cantarana Bar*, near bus terminal, good, cheap; *Yoanna*, Av 7, 16-47, corner of Márquez de Palmar, Arab owner, excellent.

Exchange Banco Italo or Banco Unión, for Mastercard or Visa cash withdrawals. **Banco de Barinas** accepts Thomas Cook travellers' cheques.

Discotheque *Hot City*, Av Los Andes, Urbanización alto Barinas, open 2300, good mixture of people and music, rec.

Airport with local services and to Caracas (3 a day, 2 Sun). The tourist office here is friendly and has a free town map and hotel list.

Buses 4 a day for **Mérida**, US$2.50, magnificent ride through the mountains, 5-8 hrs (sit on right for best views); *por puesto*, US$5. Bus to **Caracas**, US$6.50 Líneas Barinas, 8 hrs; to **San Antonio**, US$4.75. To **Acarigua**, US$3, 3 hrs; **San Cristóbal**, US$1.70, 4½ hrs; **Maracay**, US$3, 8 hrs; **San Fernando de Apure**, US$6, 7½ hrs. To **Valencia**, 5 hrs. The bus terminal is on the edge of the town.

From Barinas there is a beautifully scenic road to Apartaderos, in the Sierra Nevada de Mérida (**see p 1375**). Also from Barinas, Route 5 runs along the eastern edge of the Andes to San Cristóbal, via Santo Domingo (airport). Another road heads E, across the Llanos to San Fernando de Apure (see below).

Motorists travelling E from Mérida to Ciudad Bolívar can either go across the *llanos* or via San Carlos, El Sombrero, Valle de la Pascua (see below) and El Tigre, which route requires no ferry crossings and has more places with accommodation. In the *llanos*, near El Baúl (turn off main road E of San Carlos), is a safari-type lodge at the working ranch of *Hato Piñero*, US$140 pp per day, fully inc, US$240 pp, incl return overland transport from Caracas, US$560 by chartered plane,incl all meals, free drinks, good room, and bi-lingual nature guide for excellent bird- and animal-watching trips, expensive but highly rec; address: Hato Piñero, Edif General de Seguros, Piso 6, Ofic 6B, Av La Estancia, Chuao, Caracas 1060, T (2) 916965/916854/916576, F 916776. No public transport to ranch but ask police in El Baúl for ride with Hato Piñero workers. Last part of the road very bad. From Caracas the direct route is 6 hrs; the expensive alternative is to use the airstrip.

From Caracas S to the Llanos One can either take the new Panamerican Highway to near Cagua (pop 92,000), 16 km E of Maracay where a good road leads off to **San Juan de los Morros** (pop 78,500). A cock-fighting tournament is held here each year (Hotels, all rather over-priced: **D** *Motel Santa Mónica*; **D** *Gran Hotel Los Morros*, on Carretera Nacional towards Villa de Cura; **D** *Excelsior*, Calle Marino; **E** *Ana*). It has natural hot springs. Nearby are mountains with vertical cliffs, on which several climbing routes have been opened. South of San Juan, just past Ortiz, is a crossroads: W to San Carlos, S to the Guárico dam, the *llanos* and San Fernando de Apure, and E to **El Sombrero** (large Indian population in the area; **E** hotel at E end, above restaurant and bar, bath, a/c, friendly; **F** *Hotel Brasilia*, near plaza, with bath, fan, safe parking, good; *Restaurante Mary*, Calle Descanso 2, excellent), **Chaguaramas** (**E** motel at W end, bath, a/c, friendly, clean, check for scorpions in shoes and snakes in bedside tables; good restaurant across highway) and **Valle de la Pascua** (pop 75,200; **E** *Hotel Venezuela*, Plaza Bolívar; **E** *San Marcos*, Carretera Nacional towards El Socorro; **E** *Gran Hotel Monte Carlo*, opp bus station, suites available, friendly, a/c, shower, locked car park). An alternative from Caracas is Route 15 through **Cúa**

(40 km S, **E** *Hotel Cue*, with bath, a/c, clean, but overpriced and inhospitable). From here one route goes to San Juan de los Morros, while another heads S, via **Camatagua** (2 km off highway; pop 8,050; 2 hotels; 7 km from town is a very good campsite by a hydroelectric dam and lake, turnoff 1 km before town, US$0.30 pp, safe, drinking water, pit latrines, "cabañas") to El Sombrero. The road from El Sombrero to El Tigre is deteriorating, especially E of El Socorro; several sections are sand, others have large potholes and resurfacing has not extended to the road's full width (not good for cyclists). Beyond Valle de la Pascua is **Santa María de Ipire**, a pretty, old village with narrow streets, well-maintained houses, but no hotel. 4 km E is a restaurant and petrol station which may provide accommodation. In **Pariaguán**, about half way between Santa María and El Tigre, there is *Hotel Modin* (**E**, opp bus terminal, bath, a/c, small and filthy). At El Tigre (see p 1406), this route across the northern *Llanos* meets the road between Puerto La Cruz and Ciudad Bolívar.

Going S from Ortiz, keep an eye open for egrets, which were almost exterminated early in the century for their feathers, once a valuable export. Crossing the bridge over the Río Apure at Puerto Miranda we come to **San Fernando de Apure** (pop 87,000), the capital of the western *llanos*.

Hotels **C** *Hotel Plaza*, two blocks from the bus terminal, good; **D** *La Torraca*, Av Boulevard y Paseo Libertador by Plaza Bolívar, excellent rooms, a/c, spotlessly clean, plush bathroom, TV, balcony overlooking centre of town, friendly, rec; others on Av Miranda and Paseo Libertador in D-E range with a/c, water spasmodic, eg *Boulevard*, with bath, a/c, TV. *Italiana*, Bolívar 59, nr fountain in centre, cheaper than most, more or less comfortable, no a/c; **E** *Hotel-Restaurant Apure*, good steaks, accommodation; **D** *Trinacrina*, T 23578, near bus station, bath, very clean, TV, huge rooms, a/c, no breakfast; **F** *Maracay*, Sucre 88, fan, very cheap, a little run down, otherwise rec.

Restaurants *Mister Pollo*, Av Carabobo, good value chicken; *Punto Criollo*, Av Miranda, good value, friendly; *Europa*, opp *La Torraca*, cheap, excellent, creole Italian and other international food, service very swift and friendly, occasional evening cabaret, rec; *Gran Imperio Romano*, small, friendly, popular, along Av Boulevard from *Europa*, good and cheap; *Comedor* in building beside CANTV has good *menú*, Mon-Fri, 1100-1200.

Exchange Banco Consolidado for American Express, Av Miranda, Res. 19 de Abril; Banco Unión, Av Libertador and Carretera 5, cash advance on Mastercard and Visa.

Travel Agency in *Hotel Torraca*, Av Libertador, ask for Dona Bárbara, rec.

Airport Reached by bus: daily Avensa flight to Caracas, US$25, and to **Puerto Ayacucho**, go early to airport, 30 mins journey, good views of *Llanos*.

Bus station is modern and clean, not far from centre, not worth the US$1.20 taxi ride; to **Caracas**, US$6.50, 7 hrs; to **Barinas**, 9 hrs (take food and drink), rough ride, day and night bus, US$6; to **Maracay**, US$4.20; to **Puerto Ayacucho**, US$12, 7 hrs.

Manfred W Frischeisen recommends a detour from the Guárico dam: San Fernando road, turn left at **Calabozo** (pop 91,000; **D** *Motel Tiuna*, Av via San Fernando, a/c and good restaurant, safe car park, very good value, rec; *El Castañuelo*, restaurant on main road junction, elegant, good food, popular with local landowners. Car wash Formula 1, Av via San Fernando, US$3 for thorough clean inside and out – useful on local dusty roads). Take the gravel road (being paved) to Paso del Caballo (81 km). A little trail goes on to **Cazorla** (85 km); on the swamps one can see egrets, parrots, alligators, monkeys (and hear howlers). Turn left in Cazorla to Guayabal, back on the main road, 21 km from San Fernando (there is also a road to the right to Guayabal, very bad, only passable with 4-wheel-drive or a trail bike with effort).

From San Fernando you can drive W towards Barinas, the road is beautiful (but terrible) between Mantecal and Bruzual. In the early morning, many animals and birds can be seen, and in the wet season alligators cross the road, a highly rec journey. **Mantecal** is a good base for wildlife tourism. Accommodation: **E** *Hotel El Pescador*, with restaurant; **F** *Hospedaje Centro Llano*, fan, shared shower, despite resembling a prison, good value, friendly, the owner takes guests to see caiman in the early morning and to his sister's canaries in the evening, rec. Two other hotels and many places to eat. About 30 mins by bus is *Hato Turístico Cedral*, where hunting is banned, visits arranged only through Turismo Aventura, Caracas, T 02-951-1143. To view the waterbirds from the road be there before sunrise. *Fiesta* in Mantecal, 23-26 Feb. Bus San

Fernando de Apure-Mantecal 3½ hrs, US$2.70; Mantecal-Barinas, 4 hrs, US$3.60.

At **Bruzual** (pop 4,800), just S of Puente Nutrias over the Apure river, there are 3 primitive inns (eg **E** *Los Llaneros*, restaurant, dirty bathroom; *Golpe Criollo*, on the plaza, with bath, a/c, good beds, clean, safe parking, cheap family-run restaurant, rec). The town is very friendly and relaxed and has a Plaza Bolívar. There is a good area to walk and observe birds on the edge of town. US$1.50 bus from Mantecal to Bruzual. A fair, interesting road heads W after Mantecal at La Ye junction and goes over Guasdualito to San Cristóbal (take spare gasoline).

From San Fernando you can travel E to Ciudad Bolívar either by taking a boat (expensive and unreliable and not possible in the dry season) from opposite the airport to Caicara (see below), or by taking a bus to El Sombrero and catching the Ciudad Bolívar bus at 1700.

Due S of San Fernando is **Puerto Páez** (pop 2,600) at the confluence of the Meta and Orinoco rivers; here there are crossings to Puerto Carreño in Colombia, see below, and to El Burro W of the Caicara-Puerto Ayacucho road. A road is being built from San Fernando to Puerto Páez; for 134 km it is paved, then from the Rio Capanaparo it is dirt, deeply rutted, passable only in the dry season by 4WD vehicles or buses (2 a day San Fernando-Pto Páez, dry season, 4 ferry crossings). Between the Capanaparo and Cinaruco rivers is the **Parque Nacional Santos Luzardo**, reached only from this road. If this road is closed, to get to Puerto Ayacucho from San Fernando involves a 15-hour (minimum) detour via the Caicara ferry.

There is a route across the *llanos* to Ciudad Bolívar: from Chaguaramas (see above) turn S through Las Mercedes (**E** *Gran Hotel Las Mercedes*, singles expensive, noisy a/c, mosquitoes, poor restaurant, safe parking) and flat cattle land to **Cabruta** (pop 4,300), 179 km, road badly potholed, daily bus to Caracas, US$6.75. There is no ferry to Puerto Ayacucho, but you can try to take a barge, US$10, 3-day trip, fix price with boat captain. There is a small hotel, infested with rats and cockroaches, but better accommodation in **Caicara** (pop 28,600)—ferry from Cabruta, about 1 hr, 0500-2100, US$2 for car and passengers, or *lanchas* (*chalanas*) which leave when full every half hour or so, costing US$0.50 for the 25 minute journey. Manatees have been seen "hovering" around the ferry at Cabruta. Caicara lies 372 km W of Ciudad Bolívar by paved highway, its recent growth is due to the continuation of the road to Puerto Ayacucho and the exploitation of bauxite at Los Pijiguaos.

Hotels C *Redoma*, near airport, a/c, best; **E** *Bella Guayana*, Calle Merecey 3, bathroom, fan, friendly, fairly clean, hot water; **D** *Venezuela*, Av Búlevard, a/c but regular power cuts leave rooms like furnaces; **E** *Miami*, Antigua Calle Carabobo, private baths, no hot water; **E** *Tres Ríos*, a/c, parking, clean; **E** *La Fortuna*, run by blind family, friendly; **F** *Central*; **F** *Italia*; **F** *Buenos Aires*. Good open air restaurant by Río Orinoco for lunch.

Transport By bus from Caicara to Ciudad Bolívar, Transporte Orituco and Línea Bolívar, 0700 daily, 6 hrs, US$6.25; to Puerto Ayacucho 6 a day, 6 hrs (allow extra time for national guard searches) US$8. There are 2 LAV flights a week (Wed and Sat) to Puerto Ayacucho, 2 hrs, 2-3 weekly to Ciudad Bolívar, 55 mins, Barinas, 4 hrs, San Fernando de Apure, weekdays 30 mins, and Puerto Páez, 1 hr 25 mins. Cargo boats take 3 days to Puerto Ayacucho but are unwilling to take passengers; might be better from Cabruta (see above).

Between Caicara and Ciudad Bolívar is the small town of **Maripa**, on the E bank of the Caura river (one basic hotel, *Hotel Maripa*, bus from Ciudad Bolívar, 3½ hrs, US$3.50, several a day in both directions). River excursions can be made from **Las Trincheras**, S of Maripa. Ask at Maripa gas station for taxi to Las Trincheras, 1½ hrs, US$10-15. Carlos and Jonas have boat trips from here, US$60 a day. Take your own food, drinks, enough for the guide, and cooking gear. A 3 to 4 day trip takes in El Playón, a nice sandy beach with good swimming. 1½ hrs walk from here leads to a waterfall Salto Pará, and an Indian community living in modern houses abandoned by a former dam project, handicrafts for sale, and cold beer. Bring your own hammock. A scenic and highly recommended trip (Tomas Roztocil and Marie Gomez, Geneva, Switzerland).

Roads From Caicara a brand new, paved road runs 370 km SW to Puerto Ayacucho, passing scruffy settlements and bauxite-mining towns like Maniapure, Los Pijiguaos and Parguaza; the turn off to **El Burro**, where the boat crosses the Orinoco to Puerto Páez (ferry US$1, also to Puerto Carreño, Colombia) is 88 km N of Puerto Ayacucho (*por puesto* Burro-Pto Ayacucho, 1 hr).

Another newly-paved road leaves the above 11 km out of Caicara and winds due S through forested hills (jaguar country) to diamond-mining settlements like Maniapure, Guaniamo and Barrial Largo (160 km, end of the pavement); a deteriorating track continues S from Guaniamo almost to the Río Ventuari at San Juan de Manapiare (as far as one can go by road into Amazonas).

On arrival in the Amazonas territory, it is necessary to register at a Guardia Nacional checkpoint about 20 km before Puerto Ayacucho. Around this area the national guard can be very strict and travellers are likely to be searched.

Puerto Ayacucho is the capital of the State of Amazonas, which has an area of 175,000 square kilometres and a population of 80,000, 73,660 of whom live in Puerto Ayacucho. At the end of the dry season (April), it is very hot and sticky. It is 800 km up the Orinoco from Ciudad Bolívar, deep in the wild, but no direct boats do the five day journey up river. Museo Etnológico del Territorio Federal Amazonas, Monseñor Enzo Ceccarelli, opp church, open Tues-Sat, Sun am, US$0.80, has a library and collection of regional exhibits, good, recommended. In front of the museum is a market. One block away is the cathedral, which has colourful paintings, especially on the ceiling. The Salesian Mission House and boys' school on Plaza Bolívar may also be visited. Prices in Puerto Ayacucho are generally higher than N of the Orinoco. **NB** Malaria is prevalent in this area; take precautions.

Hotels B *Gran Hotel Amazonas**, dilapidated but new section has a/c rooms, TV, good service, clean, bar, pool, restaurant, very good but food supply sometimes limited; **C** *Las Palmeras*, Av 23 de Enero, 2 blocks from the Redoma (traffic roundabout, Corpoven station), a/c, plain and clean, restaurant rec; **C** *Residencia Río Siapa*, Av Orinoco, T 21138, modern, mixed reports, hard to find; **D** *Hotel El Tobogán*, Orinoco, T (048) 21320, popular, clean, a/c, reasonable value; **E** *Maguari*, friendly, will store luggage, rec; **E** *Residencia Internacional*, Av Aguerrevere 18, T 21242, a/c (cheaper without), cheap, comfortable, good shower, clean, safe, friendly, laundry, warmly rec, if no room available you can sling up your hammock. Bus drivers stay here and will drive you to the terminal for early morning journeys; noisy early morning parrots in the courtyard and tour touts. **F** *Residencia Ayacucho*, bath, fan, near all the travel agencies, cheapest in town.

Restaurants *Monte Grill*, hard to find, take taxi US$0.60, best in town, very good food, friendly; *Gran Sarola*, opp gas station, friendly, cheap, good, clean; *Cherazad*, central, excellent steaks at very reasonable prices, good friendly service, very popular restaurant, highly rec; *El Angoleño*, one block from *Hotel Amazonas*, Portuguese owner-cook Ignacio very friendly, cheap, good steaks; *Arepero de Amazonas*, expensive, average breakfast/snack bar; *Restaurant El Enchentro*, cheap, good, open front attracts beggars.

Exchange Banco Unión, for Visa, not Thomas Cook; no bank changes Amex cheques, but some shops may at poor rates.

Laundry *Remendón*, Av 23 de Enero, good, cheap, sewing jobs done.

Shopping In the Mercado de Artesanía you can buy hammocks and other useful equipment (every Thur, also sometimes Fri and Sat). A great many tourist souvenirs are on offer and Vicente Barletta, of *Típico El Casique*, Av Principal 583, Urb Andrés Eloy Blanco, has a good collection of masks (free); he also works as a guide (T 21389), rec, take own food and equipment. No postcards in Puerto Ayacucho and no stamps at Post Office.

Transport Ferry across the Orinoco, US$0.50. Boat to Caicara, 1½ days, US$15 incl food, but bargain; repellent and hammock required. Bus to Caicara, 0500, 0800, 1400 daily, 6 hrs; bus to Maracay and Caracas (11 hrs) leaves from the "ferry town", 1630. Bus from Caracas, 2030, 2230 daily, US$12.50, 12 hrs (but maybe 21 hrs in bad conditions), Colectivos Caicabo, not great ("if all else fails, the cassette player never breaks down"); at least 6 buses a day to Ciudad Bolívar. *Por puesto* to Ciudad Bolívar, 3 daily, US$12, 10-12 hrs. Scheduled LAV (Av 23 de Enero 27, T 21422) flights to Caracas, 2 a day, one non-stop, 1 hr, one via San Fernando de Apure and Calabozo, 3-4 hrs. Also Avensa and Servivensa once each daily to Caracas, US$64; others to Caicara, Maracay, Ciudad Bolívar and San Fernando, US$40. Charters with Avisur (Av Río Negro 13) or AguaSa to Maroa, Cucurí, San Juan de Manapiare etc. Airport 7 km SE along Av Orinoco. Jeeps and trucks can be hired at the rear of the Corpoven filling station at the Redoma at N entrance to town. There is no scheduled service S to Samariago, but trucks sometimes take passengers. Flight to San Carlos del Río Negro, US$37, through *Wayusa* travel agency.

  Crossing to Colombia 88 km N of Puerto Ayacucho a paved branch road leads W to El Burro, from where a ferry-barge crosses to Puerto Páez. On the S bank of the Meta opposite (ferry, US$1) is Puerto Carreño in Colombia, which is connected to Bogotá by twice-weekly SATENA flights and a more-or-less passable road; there is a DAS office and Venezuelan consulate.

  Bongos and ferries run regularly across the river from Puerto Ayacucho to Casuarino (Colombia), which has quite good shopping, locals make these excursions without formalities, and many gringo travellers have experienced no problems or formalities crossing for a few hours (ferries leave from the Guardia Nacional post on the northern edge of town). On the other hand, some difficulty with the local authorities is not uncommon, both here and at Puerto Carreño. You may be asked how much money you have and where you are going; some travellers have had to obtain Colombian visas when only a passport and ticket out of the country were strictly necessary. From Ayacucho there is a cargo boat to Puerto Páez, 4 hrs. Check with Guardia Nacional and insist on exit stamp if crossing to Colombia (they are strangely reluctant).

Tour Companies and Guides Listing only those with positive recommendations: *Tobogán Tours*, Av Río Negro 44, Puerto Ayacucho (T 048-21700, F 21600), owner Pepe Jaimes, arranges trips on the Orinoco, to Indian villages and to the Paraguena river through waterfalls, 4-day trips to Autana-tepuí by river, untouched jungle with fascinating wildlife, also city tours incl Tobogán de la Selva and Pozo Azul, guides speak English, German or Italian, also airport transfers, accident insurance, no alcohol permitted on tours, need at least 4 people for 2/3 day trips, cost about US$70 per day. *Turismo de la Selva* also run a variety of tours; Delfin Sanchez, of *Siapa Amazonas Expedición*, Av Orinoco 90, T 21138, active at the airport. Beware of overcrowding on boats, check there is enough food and drink. *Autana Aventura*, Av Amazonas 87, T 048-22584, near Plaza Bolívar and Indian Museum, owned by Julián Jaramillo, friendly and fluent English, José Machado and José Luis Espinoza are rec as good guides, who know the local villages well, not all guides have good English, experience or knowledge, so mixed reports, 3 days, 2 nights for about US$100 all incl, take plenty of insect repellent, local sprays are more effective; *Amazonia Tours*, owned by Cruz and Alejandro, run reasonable 3-day tours. *Genesis Tours*, have been highly rec for trips into the jungle (guide and driver, Freddy and Mario), helpful, friendly, knowledgeable; Genesis also has a camp 15 mins from Puerto Ayacucho, 8 rm with a/c and bath, US$65 per adult, US$30 children, also rec. Most companies run tours costing at least US$50 a day. For tours of the State of Amazonas, S of Puerto Ayacucho, a rec guide is Yamal A Nasser, Calle Crisanto Mato Coba 33, Barrio Virgen del Valle, Ciudad Bolívar, T 085-48969 (he may be contacted through the Tourist Office in Ciudad Bolívar). Other rec guides incl Fernando Escobar, Av Constitución, T 048-21946, very knowledgeable, speaks English; and Abid Seguias, T 048-24028, who organizes plane trips to villages. A rec guide is Dr Virgilio Limpiar, of *Turismo Yutajé*, Monte Bello 31, T (048) 21664, various packages at about US$250 pp per week from Caracas, or US$90 pp/night, all incl; he will meet you at the airport for boat trips off the beaten track, sleeping in hammocks or Indian huts, he and another guide do all the cooking (profits go towards buying vaccines for villages that get no other care). Near Puerto Ayacucho, in mixed jungle and dry forest setting, is *Jungle Camp Calypso*, run by *Calypso Tours*, La Guaira (T 031-24683), reservation can also be made in Caracas, T (02) 545-0024, F 541-3036, US$150 pp for 2 days incl food, basic cabin accommodation, highly rec, excursions in canoes. Also *Canturama Amazonas Resort*, Puerto Ayacucho, ribera del río Orinoco, T (048) 21266 (reservations can also be made in Caracas, T (02) 941-8813, F 931464), 20 mins by vehicle S of town, on the banks of the Orinoco amidst dry, open Savannah, 40 km from nearest jungle, "enchanting landscape but not a good game or bird-watching place, very few animals and beware biting insects by the river", B, buffet meals US$4-7, full day tours US$10.

Excursions In the low season, May-June, it may be difficult to organize tours for only a few days. Locals recommend Oct to Dec as the best time for trips, when the rivers are high but the worst of the rains have passed. If planning to travel S from Puerto Ayacucho, you need a permit from the Bureau of Indian Affairs (Orai) in Caracas, or Puerto Ayacucho: several copies of photograph and description page in your passport will be needed. Even with all this paperwork, many independent travellers have reported being turned back from San Carlos. The policy of the Guardia Nacional seems to be no visits to the jungle or villages, or transit of the Casiquiare without a guide. Those intent on serious expedition could contact the South American Explorers Club (**see Lima 1129**) for the most up-to-date advice.

For trips anywhere from Puerto Ayacucho check at the central service station. Other rec trips are to the small village of Pintado (l2 km S), where petroglyphs described by Humboldt can be seen on the huge rock called *Cerro Pintado*; this the most easily accessible petroglyph site of the hundreds scattered throughout Amazonas. 35 km S on the road to Samariapo is the Parque Tobogán de la Selva, a pleasant picnic area with tables and refreshments centred around a steeply inclined, smooth rock over which the Río Maripures cascades—a 'water-slide' to delight children and the young-at-heart in the wet season. Stick to the right to avoid crashing into barrier, there are some painful rocks to the left near the bottom, few Venezuelans slide right from the top. Taxi US$5 from Puerto Ayacucho. Be sure to organize your return with the driver, otherwise you may face a lengthy hike. Crowded on Sun, bring swimsuit and bathing shoes. A small trail leads up from the slide to a natural jacuzzi after about 20 mins. The second water-slide down-stream is completely blocked by a fallen tree. Nearby, also by paved road, is Coromoto colony, founded by the Salesian Fathers to protect and evangelize the "howling Guaharibos" (as early explorers called this nomadic tribe).

The well-paved road from Puerto Ayacucho to Samariapo (63 km) was built to bypass the rapids which here interrupt the Orinoco, dividing it into "Upper" and "Lower"; the powerful

Maripures Rapids are very impressive. The road (gravel, but being paved) continues for 17 km to Morganito, from where smaller launches continue on up river. Boats run from Samariapo to Isla de Ratón and Santa Rosa.

On the Río Negro, towards Brazil, is **San Carlos de Río Negro** (pop 1,500). Hotel at customs post. Flights to Puerto Ayacucho Wed and Sat US$37 with stops en route, ask at Agencia Wayusa, near *Hotel Maguari*; military flights occasionally, if you pay for at least 7 passengers there will be an extra flight. It is possible to take a cargo boat from San Carlos up the Río Casiquiare and down the Orinoco (following Humboldt's route); it takes 8 days to Puerto Ayacucho. You can also rent a canoe to Santa Lucía on the Brazilian border on the Río Negro (US$20, 5 hrs Santa Lucia-San Carlos); no hotel, food at the customs post.

Much of Amazonas State is stunningly beautiful and untouched, but access is only by river. Do not travel alone. By ascending the Autana or Sipapo rivers, for example, one can see **Autana-tepuí**, a 1200m-high soaring mass of rock resembling a petrified tree trunk, riddled with massive caves; it was first explored in 1971 by Charles Brewer Carias, who descended by helicopter (an Anglo-American expedition parachuted onto the summit in 1986—no-one has yet climbed from the base). There are other *tepuís* throughout the region, including the great mass of the Sierra de la Neblina on the Brazilian border, but the difficulties of organizing expeditions are formidable; permits are needed from the Gobernación in Puerto Ayacucho and the Indian Bureau in Caracas (great patience required), and possibly also from the Catholic *Vicariato* which administers many of the missions along the rivers. Some of these missions provide rough accommodation (eg at La Esmeralda—at the foot of Duida-tepuí, airport to be paved and military base expanded—and Platanal, about 130 km further up the Orinoco, US$35-45 per night), otherwise it is a matter of slinging hammocks in any available shelter. There are a number of private river camps on the upper Orinoco but they do not solicit casual guests; the most welcoming is *Yutajé Camp*, located on a tributary of the Río Manapiare due E of Puerto Ayacucho. This can theoretically be reached from the track running S from Guaniamo via Sabana de Cardona to **San Juan de Manapiare** (pop 3,700), but the passability of the track depends on how recently the track has been used and the season of the year. The camp accommodates 30, with restaurant and bar, full board, fishing, canoes, horses, airboats, excursions to Indian villages, spectacular falls in the vicinity, much wildlife. Also in the area is the *Campamento Camani*, T (02) 284-9006, F (02) 285-7352 (Centro Plaza, Torre C, piso 19, Caracas), a group of conical thatched buildings in a forest clearing on the banks of the Alto Ventuari river, 2 hrs by launch from San Juan de Manapiare. A private aircraft leaves Caracas each Thur and Sun, 2 hrs 20 mins. From Puerto Ayacucho there are daily departures, the aerotaxi takes 50 mins. Maximum 26 guests at any one time, mosquito nets provided, bathroom, restaurant, bar, TV, handicraft shop, football and petanque courts, excursions available, US$290 pp lodging and meals, excluding air fare, 3 day/2 night package.

San Juan de Manapiare is the regional centre for the middle Ventuari. Government plans are for the existing track, which is very beautiful as it winds around the Cerro Guanay, to be paved and for the Puerto Ayacucho-Samariapo-Morganito road to continue to San Fernando de Atabapo, extending thence to San Juan de Manapiare. Environmental considerations may limit these projects.

In 1955/56 two Americans successfully canoed to Argentina, continuing from the Amazon by way of the Tapajós, Paraguay and Paraná. The trip took about one year. The journey up the Amazon to the Casiquiare and Orinoco has also been successfully negotiated by a hovercraft with a British crew.

NB Travel into Amazonas beyond La Esmeralda is heavily restricted, presumably to protect the Yanomami and the Alto Orinoco – Casiquiare Biosphere Reserve, which covers most of the SE portion of Amazonas state from the Neblina Range to the Orinoco headwaters. Permits are required from Servicio Autónomo para el Desarrollo Ambiental de Amazonas (Sada), in same building as Inparques in Caracas, T (02) 408-1822/1026, Dr W Frank.

EAST FROM CARACAS (6)

Some of Venezuela's most interesting coast, not just for its beautiful beaches, islands and forested slopes, but also for its historical links, from Columbus' landfall to Spanish colonial rule and the War of Independence. It is also an industrial coast, shipping coal, cocoa and serving the oil industry inland. If you're lucky you can cross to Trinidad by boat, unlike the frequent crossings to Isla Margarita (next section).

The eastern part of the North-Eastern Highlands, with summits rising to 2,000m, has abundant rainfall in its tropical forest. The western part, which is comparatively dry, has most of the inhabitants and the two main cities, Cumaná and Barcelona.

Eastern Venezuela, with the Highlands in the NE, the great *llanos* of the Orinoco to the S, and S of the Orinoco again the range of Guayana Highlands, was until quite recently not of much account in the Venezuelan economy. Some coffee and cacao are grown on the eastern slopes of the northeastern highlands in the tropical forest, but the western slopes are subject to drought. Cattle roam the *llanos*, and the Guayana Highlands produce gold and diamonds. The picture has now been changed, as about 30% of Venezuelan oil now comes from this area. South of the Orinoco vast iron ore deposits are mined.

It is now only five hours from Caracas to Barcelona by road through Caucagua, from which there is a 58 km road NE to **Higuerote** (pop 13,700). Surrounded by sandy beaches and currently the focus of large-scale tourist projects, Higuerote remains quite tranquil but is expensive, especially during the festival of the Tambores de San Juan (23-26 June, see **Music and Dance**).

Hotels C *Mar-Sol*, clean, modest rooms, Plaza Bolívar on beachfront esplanade, open-air restaurant 0730-2300; **D** *Barlovento*, on littered beachfront NE of Jardín Higuerote condos, colonial style, bare rooms, fan, clean, safe, small pool, restaurant; **D** *Posada El Mar*, clean, motel-style rooms, no hot water, open-air restaurant, 2 blocks N of the *Mar-Sol*; **E** *Cabañas Brisas Marinas*, Av Serrano at Plaza Bertorelli, huts for 3-4 people, simple restaurant 0800-2200 serving Barlovento specialities, good.

Higuerote and nearby villages (eg **Caruao**, rebuilt in old style—population almost entirely black, friendly, good beach, one hotel—ask for Josefa, who cooks delicious seafood—the sports club has a wild beach party each Sat pm) can also be reached along the partly paved coastal road from Los Caracas (**see p 1353**), beautiful views, many beaches. Tankers loading at Buche Refinery near Higuerote sometimes tar the coves around Carenero at the head of the bay (6 km N). Near Caruao is the Pozo del Cura, a waterfall and pool, good swimming.

14 km before Higuerote on the road from Caucagua is Tacarigua de Mamporal, where you can turn off to the **Laguna de Tacarigua National Park**. The road passes a Tunnel of Vegetation (almost 3 km long), cocoa plantations, the towns of San José de Río Chico and **Río Chico** (pop 14,900), with a number of colonial homes and the derelict remains of the old railway station, on the 54 km French-built 1889 railway from El Guapo to Carenero (**E** *Hotel Italia*, Calle Miranda, T (034) 74248, a/c or fan, bath, excellent; **E** *Hotel Iberia*, similar standard, also on Calle Miranda. *Pizzeria Río Chico*, takeaways, open to midnight on weekends; excellent natural fruit icecream at several kiosks on Calle Miranda). 4 km N the road reaches the coast, where many of the natural canals snaking from the olive-green Laguna de Tacarigua have been incorporated into private subdivisions, with modest hotels and bridges to the sandy beaches. Off this road is the Caballerizas Dos Estrellas, a paso fino stud farm; the owner, Sr Pérez Mata, is happy to show interested visitors around. The road runs a further 8 km E along the coast to the fishing village of Tacarigua de la Laguna (rooms to rent, hostel from where boat tours leave, **E** *Ciudad Tablita*, with bath, F without, friendly, clean, quiet, cooking facilities, some German spoken, rec, *por puesto* from Río Chico, US$0.30). You can eat delicious *lebranche* fish at the Bar-Restaurant Poleo Lebranche Asado; an unmotorized ferry crosses the lagoon (ask at the restaurant). The 18,400 ha national park enclosing the lagoon is an important ecological preserve, with mangroves, good fishing and many water birds (incl flamingoes, usually involving a day-long boat trip to see them); boats can be hired to anywhere in the Park (beware of overcharging) and to *Club Miami* beach resort, **B** incl 2 meals, on the Caribbean side of the eastern sandspit. The beaches beyond here are unspoilt and relaxing, but mosquitoes are a problem after sunset.

Highway 9 (Caracas-Barcelona) can be joined 25 km S of Río Chico at **El Guapo** (**E** *Hotel Casa Vieja*, a/c, cheaper without, very basic with dirty bathrooms); it then runs E near the coast, looping inland at **Boca de Uchire** (pop 4,500; many vacation homes and **E** *Hotel Uchire*, on main road, a/c, private bath, good restaurant behind) over a ridge of the famous Morro de Unare to Clarines (a paved road runs straight on from Boca de Uchire along the sandbar sealing off the Laguna Unare to Clarines). **Clarines** (pop 9,000) is a quiet, beautiful little town with one of the best-restored colonial churches in Venezuela (1760). Religious festivities and street processions mark San Antonio de Padua's day (13 June) and the Virgin is honoured with dance and music each 16 Jul. There are comfortable *cabañas*, restaurant, snack bar, pool and sports facilities at the **Parador Turístico Clarines** at the W entrance to the town.

16 km on are the twin towns of **Píritu** and Puerto Píritu (3 km apart, combined pop of 18,000): worth seeing in Píritu is the imposing 18th century Franciscan church of Nuestra Señora de la Concepción; Puerto Píritu has long stretches of lovely beaches, a new *balneario* (only open weekends) and a modern resort, with safe swimming (**C** *Balneario Casacoima Puerto Píritu*, T 411511, a/c, restaurant, pool open to public; **C** *Hotel Bella Mar*, Calle Bolívar, a/c, pool, restaurant, parking, sports; **E** *La Posada*, on top of small hill overlooking main road, in Píritu with bath and fan, very clean, safe and quiet, friendly, excellent, easy 30 mins walk from Puerto Píritu which now has many expensive hotels, restaurants and snack bars). There are old Franciscan churches at San Lorenzo, Caigua and El Pilar, a few km S of Píritu off highway 14; only limited restoration has yet been done. Nearby, but not obtrusive, is Criogénico de Oriente, the biggest gas refining complex in Latin America. Local delicacies incl *queso de mano* (a soft cheese) and *arepitas* (corn bread pasties filled with goat cheese).

Barcelona (pop 266,750, mean temperature, 27°C), founded 1671, capital of Anzoátegui State, straddles the Río Neveri, 5 km from the sea. It has a grid of colonial streets with many old buildings and makes a more agreeable base for budget travellers than neighbouring Puerto La Cruz. Its small choice of hotels will probably prove inadequate for those seeking comfort. The state is named after General Anzoátegui, a hero of the Battle of Boyacá, whose statue stands in the main **Plaza Boyacá**, where the Palacio de Gobierno and San Cristóbal Cathedral face each other. The **Cathedral** (started 1748, rebuilt 1773 after an earthquake in 1766) contains the embalmed remains of the Italian martyr, San Celestino (open 0600-1200, 1500-1930). Several blocks N on Av 5 de Julio are the twin **plazas of Bolívar** (with obligatory statue) and **Miranda**. Facing Plaza Bolívar are the ruins of the **Casa Fuerte**, a national monument, where 1600 of Bolívar's followers were massacred in 1817, including Bolívar's Irish aide-de-camp, Major Chamberlain, and his young créole wife, Eulalia (a tragic love which inspired several European plays and novels). Details of this and other historic epics can be found in the next door **public library**, weekdays only. **Teatro Cajigal**, facing the small Plaza at Cra 15 with Calle 3a, is a replica of the Teatro Municipal in Caracas. **Museo de la Tradición**, Calle Juncal, in a 1671 building once the centre of the slave trade, houses a wide collection of indigenous and Spanish religious art, open Mon-Fri 0800-1200, 1400-1700, weekends 0900-1500. An overgrown park follows both banks of the Río Neveri right through the city and provides a pleasant stroll. Next to the bus and *por puesto* station on Av San Carlos, over 1 km S of Plaza Boyacá, is the **Mercado Libre**, for food and just about anything.

Hotels **C** *Barcelona**, Av 5 de Julio, 1 block from Cathedral, T 771065, TV, parking, 6th floor restaurant (good fish and views); *Neveri*, Av Fuerzas Armadas, T 772376, similar, good restaurant *Castillo del Oriente*, Zamora; **D** *Nacional*, Zamora; **E** *Venus*, Av Intercomunal y Lecherías, T 774202, a/c; **F** *Plaza*, Calle Juncal opp Cathedral, in a colonial building, friendly, rec; **F** *Madrid*, just behind Cathedral, with restaurant, surly owner. There is a wide variety of restaurants in town, incl *Lucky*, Av Miranda No 4-26, N of Plaza Bolívar, Chinese, rec.

Tourist Office Cra 13, No 3-7, inst off Plaza Boyacá; open weekdays only.

Airport (also serves Puerto La Cruz) 3 km S, Avensa, Servivensa and Aserca: 5 daily flights to Maiquetía (US$40), daily flight to Canaima (US$78), Porlamar (US$27), Puerto Ordaz (US$36), San Tomé (US$27), Valencia (US$41), twice weekly connection to Miami; also to Maracaibo, San Antonio and Maturín. Oficambio exchange facilities (no TCs), artesanía shops, small museum, car rental agencies, Corpoturismo booth (stays open late for some incoming flights, few handouts, friendly, no phone, so cannot book hotels, a city map can be scrounged from National Car Rental). Taxi to airport from bus station US$2.25; taxi to Puerto La Cruz US$5-6.

Buses The Terminal de Pasajeros next to the Mercado Libre is used mostly by *por puesto*, with regular departures to Valle la Pascua, Puerto Anaco, El Tigre, Maturín, Cumaná, Boca de Uchire, Valle Guanape and other nearby destinations. Buses go to Caracas (5 hrs, 11 daily, US$5); San Félix (Ciudad Guayana); Ciudad Bolívar (6 daily); Maturín (2 daily). Buses for Puerto La Cruz run every few minutes from the Terminal Pasajeros, along Av 5 de Julio, past Plaza Bolívar.

The port for Barcelona and Puerto La Cruz is **Guanta**. Vessels from La Guaira call here.

Barcelona has been surpassed touristically and commercially by Puerto La Cruz, 12 km away by 4-lane highway (Av Intercomunal) skirting the pleasant residential resort of Lechería (minibus US$0.15, then walk or *por puesto* to the beach; several good restaurants.

Off the highway is the Polideportivo sports stadium seating 10,000 people: covered gymnasium, velodrome, basket-ball courts, 2 pools, etc. Most of the facilities are available to the public without charge (open daylight hours daily). Soon after Barcelona is El Morro Tourist Complex, with hotels, cultural centres, condos with access from the street or from a new system of canals, and the Marina Amérigo Vespucio (Horisub, the company which manages the docks, arranges diving and boat tours, friendly, English spoken). An inland road, very circuitous, goes around the tourist complex to Puerto La Cruz. Alternatively, a passenger ferry crosses the main channel to the Amérigo Vespucio Marina, US$0.05.

Puerto La Cruz, pop 220,000, originally a fishing village, has been built up into a thriving tourist destination with fine avenues and modern hotels, holiday apartments and restaurants. Principally, though, it is a petroleum town, receiving pipelines from the oilfields of the interior, refining the raw product and exporting via its port. The older part of town is a traffic-choked grid with a seafront avenue, the Paseo Colón, extending to the eastern extremity of a broad bay. To the W the bay ends at the prominent El Morro headland beneath which lies Lecherías (see above). All types of watersport are well catered for and tourist facilities are above average, if expensive. Most (craft shops, *cambios*, discos, etc) can be found on Av 5 de Julio and Paseo Colón. The latter has excellent views of the Bahía de Pozuelas and the islands of the Mochima National Park (see below). The evening *paseo* along Colón is a relaxing, cheerful end to the day. The sea in the bay is inviting, but you cannot swim in it because of sewage pollution.

Festival 3 May, Santa Cruz.

Hotels The newer, up-market hotels are at Lechería and El Morro; middle grade and budget hotels and nightlife are concentrated in central Puerto La Cruz. **L2** *Meliá**, on Paseo Colón, at the eastern edge of the centre, T (081) 691311, F 691241, best in this part of town, luxury hotel with all services and facilities, American Airlines office; **A1** *Maremares*, Av Amérigo Vespucio, El Morro, T 811011, F 814494, the new market leader, a 5-star, fully-serviced resort of the Golden Rainbow group with a vast lake-style pool, 9-hole golf course and marina; **B** *Gaeta*, Paseo Colón 9, T 691816, on boulevard, very modern, set back slightly from sea front, a/c, good location, restaurant, scooter rentals; **B** *Rasil*, Paseo Colón 6, T 672535, F 673121, rooms, suites and bungalows, 3 restaurants, bar, pool, gym, money exchange, car rental and other facilities, convenient for ferries and buses, highly rec; **C** *Riviera*, Paseo Colón 33, T/F 691337, seafront hotel, noisy a/c, some rooms have balcony, TV, phone, bar, watersports, very good location, friendly service, poor breakfast; **B** *Teramum*, Av Principal at Lechería, T/F 813773, compact, modern hotel with well-designed pool area; **C** *Caribbean Inn*, Calle Freites, T 674292, F 672857, big rooms, very well kept with near-silent a/c, small pool, rec, very good service; **C** *Gaeta City*, in centre, 10 mins from beach, T 650536, TV, fridge, snack bar, parking; **C** *La Marina*, Andrés Eloy Blanco, at the new ferry terminal, a/c, good views, expensive waterside restaurant, rec, parking for those using the Margarita ferry; **C** *Neptuno*, Paseo Colón at C Juncal, T 653221, a/c, excellent restaurant *Terraza* on top floor, rec; **C** *Sorrento*, Av 5 de Julio, T 686745, F 688550, a/c, hot shower, colour TV with US channels, very clean; **C-D** *Aparthotel Cristián del Valle*, Maneiro 15, T 650925, rec, Trinidadian owner speaks English; **D** *Colón*, Libertad, with a/c, TV, English spoken, simple, clean, old bathroom, small rooms, friendly, 2 blocks from beach; **D** *Comercio*, Maneiro, one block from Paseo Colón, T 23465, TV, phones, cold water only, a/c, friendly, clean, rec; **D** *Europa*, Calle Sucre, esq Plaza Bolívar, good, clean, a/c; **D** *Mi Hotel*, Calle Libertad, a/c, showers, comfortable, clean, rec; **D** *Monte Carlo*, next door to *Margelina*, shower and a/c unreliable, but central and friendly; **D** *Noray*, Av Libertad, with a/c, good, friendly; **D** *Puerto La Cruz*, Av 5 de Julio, T 21698, phone, rec; **D** *Senador*, Miranda y Bolívar, T 22035, a/c, back rooms quieter, TV, phone, restaurant with good view, parking, rec; **E** *Margelina*, with bath, a/c, safe, clean, friendly, very comfortable, rec. On Paseo Colón: **D** *Diana*, safe, clean, small and varied rooms, check first; **E** *Pippo*, Calle Freites 66, modern, good value; **F** *Costa Azul*, Calle Maneiro 6, T 21385, accommodation on one night only basis, basic; **E** *Nacional Inn*, Miranda 44A, esq Av 5 de Julio, T 685252, basic, clean, laundry facilities.

Restaurants On Paseo Colón: *El Parador*, 2nd floor, excellent food ("the best French onion soup") and service; *Los Zulianos*, food average but Fri, Sat, Sun nights live folk music, good

PUERTO LA CRUZ

Caribbean Sea

Marina

Paseo Colón

Av Alberto Ravel

Guaraguao

Flores

Artismendi

Carabobo

Maneiro

Miranda

Freites

Av de Julio

Paseo Colón

Bolívar

Libertad

Honduras

Av Municipal

To Ferry Dock

To Cumaná & Parque Nacional Mochima

Anzoategui

Sucre

Juncal

Giraldot

Buenos Aires

Democracia

Av de Julio

Simón Rodríguez

Ricaurte

Esperanza

To Caracas & Barcelona

To Barcelona, airport & El Morro

1. Plaza Bolívar
2. Catholic Church
3. Post Office & Telephones
4. Restaurante El Parador
5. Restaurante Guatacarauzo
6. Tourist Office
7. Hotel Meliá
8. Hotel Riviera
9. Hotel Gaeta
10. Hotels Neptuno, Monte Carlo & Margelina
11. Caribbean Inn
12. Hotel Riviera

atmosphere, no cover charge, rec; *Da Luigi*, Italian, good, check menu prices against bill; *Bonasera* (Italian), *Las Tinajas* (No 55, Spanish); *El Espignon*, very good dinner in the open air, romantic; *Big Garden*, delicious sea food; *El Dragón* (No 121) Chinese; *Casa Nápoli*, cheap, friendly, rec; *Reale*, No 69, pizzería, good bacon and eggs for breakfast; *Ristorante O Sole Mio*, cheap, excellent, friendly, wide variety; *Pastelería Fornos* for breakfast; *Las Cabañas*, reasonably cheap, you get what you pay for; plenty of others. *La Taberna del Guácharo*, Calle Carabobo, eastern end of Paseo Colón, tacky interior with plastic guácharo statues but excellent cheap Venezuelan cuisine, good service, highly rec, not as tourist-orientated as the restaurants along the sea front. *El Guatacarauzo*, Paseo Colón, nr Pizza Hut, waiters wear silly hats and play practical jokes, live music, good atmosphere and good value; *El Teide*, Av 5 de Julio No 153, near Plaza Bolívar, good and cheap local food, closes at 2000. *Nature*, vegetarian, Constitución 70, lunch and dinner, self-service buffet, tasteless, mostly corn-based dishes. *Rincón Criollo*, Av Libertad, popular with locals. *El Farao*, eastern corner of main bus station, gaudy interior, fair service, excellent, authentic, spicy Arab food. *Swing* nightclub, 13 km from Puerto La Cruz, US$3.30 one way by taxi, free entry for women, good music. *Gamblers* nightclub, Paseo Colón, near Burger King, excellent music, free entry. *Christophers*, a Canadian owned bar, Calle La Marina, 1 block from Paseo Colón, an informal cellar-type watering hole open from 1600 till late.

Airlines Avensa, Av Municipal y Pepsi, and at Barcelona airport; Viasa, Av Municipal y Gran Parada; Alitalia and American Airlines at *Meliá*; Dominicana, Independencia 124, Chapurín Central. For air services see Barcelona.

Exchange Banco Consolidado (American Express), Av 5 de Julio, Local No 43; **Turisol**, Amex rep, T 662161/669910. No banks will change money. *Oficambio* charges 2.5% commission on cheques and cash, near the *Meliá*, open 0800-1200, 1400-1730 Mon-Fri, or on the sea front between Calles Buenos Aires and Sucre, Mon-Fri 0800-2100.

Laundry *Lavandería Margarita*, Bolívar 160.

Post Office and Telecommunications Freites y Bolívar, one block from Paseo Colón.

Shopping Vendors of paintings, jewellery, leather, etc on Paseo Colón in evenings, cheaper than in the souvenir shops. Good hammocks may be bought, US$6-12. *Perfectfoto SA*, Carabobo, Fuente Torre Oriente, T 22821 for film processing; also *Fotolisto*, Paseo Colón, US$1.70 per film without mounts.

Diving Scuba diving is possible at Technosub, next to *Hotel Meliá*, US$50 for 2 dives. *Hotel Meliá* also offers diving: US$60 for 2 dives, US$250 for four day certification course. There are many other agencies, all charging about US$70-80 for 2 dives. Hotels and travel agents organize trips. The nearest recompression chamber is on Isla Margarita.

Travel Agency *Viajes Ven-Mex*, Av Alberto Ravell 15, rec. *Venezuelan Travel Advisers*, Municipal esq Freites, Edif Montalero, T (081) 660113/669204. The travel agency in *Hotel Meliá* is rec for arranging and confirming flights.

Tourist Offices Excellent one on Paseo Colón, T 688170, French, English, Italian and Dutch spoken, very helpful and friendly, open Mon-Fri 0800-1200, 1400-1730.

Ferries Local islands can be visited through Embarcadero de Peñeros, Paseo Colón (behind *Tejas Restaurant*); departures throughout the morning to a dozen points along the coast; return 1630. Several small jetties reached from the central part of Paseo Colón offer island trips. For details of **Ferries** to **Isla Margarita, see p 1411.**

Buses The bus and *por puesto* terminal is at Av Juncal and Calle Democracia. To **Caracas**, 5 hrs, US$8.85, Expresos Los Llanos (T 671373, rec, a/c, movies), Expresos San Remo, Sol de Margarita (rec), *por puesto*, dep 1550, 4 hrs, US$17.50; Autoexpresos Ejecutivos to/from Caracas 4 a day, US$10 (T 081-678855, next to ferry terminal); to **Mérida**, US$22.35; to **Ciudad Bolívar** US$5, US$2.50 student discount, but often full since service starts at Cumaná, if stuck, take *por puesto* to **El Tigre**, US$4.25 and *por puesto* to Ciudad Bolívar US$3.50. Bus to **Cumaná**, US$3, Expresos Guyanesa, rec, *por puesto* US$6, 1½ hrs, fight to get on any bus which arrives, nice coastal drive. Bus to **Barcelona**, US$1, 40 mins. Bus to **Carúpano**, US$3, 5 hrs. *Por puesto* to Playa Colorado US$1.20 and to Santa Fe about US$2. There are also services to San Félix, Ciudad Bolívar, Río Caribe, Maracay, Valencia, Acarigua, Barinas, San Cristóbal, Güiria. *Por puestos* cover the nearest destinations and charge a little over double. Along Av 5 de Julio runs a bus marked "Intercomunal". It links Puerto La Cruz with Barcelona and intervening points, incl the entry to Lechería (connecting *por puesto* stop is one block further, along the Avenida Principal de Lechería, left side). Bus also passes within a few km of Barcelona airport. Another Barcelona bus is marked "Ruta Alternativa" and uses the inland highway via the Puerto La Cruz Golf and Country Club and Universidad de Oriente (both 5 km SW of city), US$0.12.

Excursions To the Chimana, La Plata and Borracha islands in Mochima National Park for good swimming and snorkelling: see **Ferries**, above. Take hat and sunscreen. The islands are very popular and consequently are badly littered. All have restaurants and snack bars, and thatched shelters can be hired for US$1.80. Iguanas can be seen on Chimana. Fishing boats can be hired on Paseo Colón beach to the beaches E of Puerto La Cruz (about US$14). At E end of beachfront boulevard is Centro Vacacional del Consejo del Niño for underprivileged children.

The Coastal Zone Starting E from Puerto La Cruz is the Costa Azul, with a seemingly endless series of beaches backed by some of Venezuela's most beautiful scenery, and offshore the islands of the *Mochima National Park*; near Los Altos is a *mirador* with a superb view of this lovely coast (although see note about litter below). Highway 9 follows the shore for much of the 85 km to Cumaná. It passes the small Playa Blanca, by boat US$5 return from Puerto La Cruz, excellent snorkelling, take own equipment. The locals cook and sell fish. Other rec spots are El Faro, El Saco, Conoma, which has palm trees and is "paradise-like", departure behind the Puerto La Cruz tourist office, on the beach. Further along is Playa Arapito (restaurant, parking US$0.35, camping not rec, armed robbery and rape reported May 1995), where boats can be hired to the lovely, little La Piscina for good snorkelling (no beach or shade, stay on boat). Next, is the popular beach of *Playa Colorada* (Km 32) with beautiful red sands and palm trees (*por puesto* from Mercado Municipal in Puerto La Cruz, US$1.20, or hitch).

Accommodation B *Villas Turísticas Playa Colorada*, clean pool, also trailers for 4 US$35 per day; pool, restaurant, run by Sra Baumgartner, Apartado 61355, Caracas 1060-A; D *Bed and Breakfast Jaly*, Quinta Jaly, Calle Marchant, Playa Colorada, T (016) 818113, run by Lynn and Jack Allard, bedrooms, a/c, private bathroom, hot water, free transport to surrounding beaches, family atmosphere, English and French spoken, rec, price also incl a good American

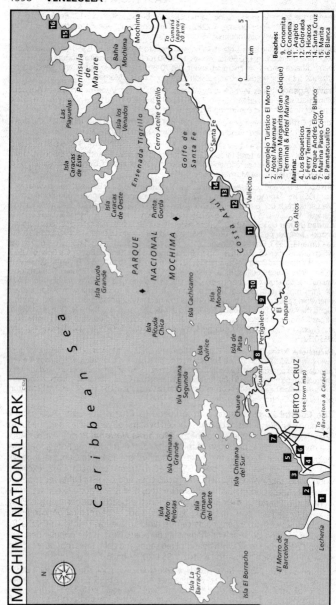

MOCHIMA NATIONAL PARK

Marina:
4. Los Boqueticos
5. Ferry Terminal
6. Parque Andrés Eloy Blanco
7. Marina Paseo Colón
8. Pamatacualito

1. Complejo Turístico El Morro
2. Hotel Maremares
3. Turismo Margarita (Gran Cacique) Terminal & Hotel Marina

Beaches:
9. Conomita
10. Conoma
11. Arapito
12. Colorada
13. Hicacos
14. Santa Cruz
15. Marita
16. Blanca

breakfast, dinner is also served on request. Sra Mónica lets rooms, D, and Doña Rosa lets out a house or apartment, D, while Seniorca, who runs a beach bar, hires tents, US$8 per night. Camping is permitted for a small fee (but there is no fresh water) and there is a restaurant.

Nearby are Playas Vallecito (camping US$1.50 per tent, security guard, car US$0.80, bar with good food and bottled water on sale, plenty of palm trees for hammock-slinging) and Santa Cruz (buy fresh seafood from the fishermen's huts). At Playa Los Hicacos is a beach club for the Universidad del Oriente, Cumaná; it has a lovely coral reef.

40 km from Puerto La Cruz, in Sucre state is **Santa Fe**, a good place to relax, not (yet) a tourist town, though plenty of loud music, golf course on the dark red, sandy but littered beach, market Sat.

Hotels and Services D *Hotel Cochaima*, difficult to find, take road parallel to main road, on the left hand side, and follow it to the end of the beach, run by Margot, clean, friendly, noisy, popular, close to beach, fan, bath, meals available, rec, dollars exchanged, "a groovy place to stay" although it suffers more than most from the town's smelly sewage system in the heat; **D** *Siete Delfines*, on beach, near market, safe, friendly, bath, fan, café and terrace where you can cook, excellent food available, bar, very popular, many parties, warmly rec, dollars exchanged; ask here for tours or information about the area, tours organized for US$4-10, ask Ricardo about transport and any kind of watersports. Two hotels on beach; private houses let rooms; accommodation at Señor Julio's home, a bit further down the beach from *Restaurant Cochaima*, sign "Rooms for Rent", US$3 pp, cooking facilities, clean, safe, very friendly and helpful, rec. *Salón de Juegos Chomena* has one basic, cheap room for real budget travellers, owner changes TCs. The *pizzería* on the beach has good food and rooms to let, owner, José, is friendly and will let you stay in his house if hotel is full, but no locks on doors. Gasoline is available; *por puesto* at 0600 and bus to Cumaná (US$1), and Puerto La Cruz (US$0.80). It is sometimes difficult to get the bus from Puerto La Cruz to stop at Santa Fe, *por puesto* may be a better bet, US$1, 1 hr, or taxi, US$13.30 incl wait. Jeep, boat or diving tours available, mixed reports of Gran Sabana Tours and guide Jorge M Plot. Francisco is rec for boat trips, he can be found a few houses to the W of the *Cochaima*. Beware of the fishermen, they offer similar trips but their prices are extortionate. Boat trips to Playas Colorada or Blanca cost US$10pp; better to hire your own boat for half the price, or hitch down the road to Colorada. Ask for Thomas, he has a boat and will take you wherever.

The sleepy and friendly village of **Mochima**, beyond Santa Fe, is 4 km off the main road, hitching difficult. The sea is dirty near the town, but if you do swim, beware of the rusty ladder at the end of the pier. There is a lot of construction going on in town. Boats to nearby beaches, such as Playa Marita and Playa Blanca, and around the islands, fares negotiable, about US$10 to one island, US$12 for a 2-hr trip round the islands (up to 6 people).

Hotels and Services *Hotel Mochima*, good restaurant, cheap, good beer, they will allow you to stay on the terrace if there are no more rooms; Sra Cellita Día, Gaby, Mama Inés and Doña María let out rooms, **E**; Señor Padriño, private rooms, F, basic but safe, they will store luggage when you go to the nearby beaches by boat, the house has no sign but it is just a few houses before Gaby's *pensión*; houses to rent with kitchens and fans from US$12 per day depending on length of stay; eat at **Los Mochimeros**, good and friendly (try the *empanadas* with ice cold coconut milk), or *Don Quijote*, Av Bermúdez, very good. The restaurants and few shops are often closed. From Puerto La Cruz, the trip can be organized by taxi, US$30 incl the journey home. Buses do not travel between Santa Fe and Mochima, *por puestos* can be taken, bargain hard on the price, US$10-12 is reasonable. Once in Mochima it is very difficult to find a taxi, you should arrange to be picked up again by the same driver if just staying for 1 day. Bus to Cumaná, 1400, US$0.80.

NB At holiday times this coast is very busy and, like many beaches in the country, has recently become littered and polluted, especially at Santa Fe and on the islands. One traveller reported there's "not an unaffected beach from Santa Fe to Güiria". Repeated warnings about broken glass on the beaches. Beware of fishermen robbing campers on the islands; it is only advised to go to islands with guards (during the day) and where people live. See also warning about camping, Playa Arapito, above.

Cumaná (pop 250,300) capital of Sucre state, straddles both banks of the Río Manzanares, its economy based on coffee, sugar and cacao, supplemented by fishing, tourism and salt from the mines on the Araya Peninsula. Average temperature 27°C. It is possibly the oldest Hispanic city on the South American mainland, founded 1521 to exploit the nearby pearl fisheries; from here the strategies for conquest and colonization of the new continent were planned. Because of a succession of devastating earthquakes (the last in 1929), only a few historic sites remain. Los Uveros on the Ensenada de Manzanillo is the largest public beach in Venezuela, there are two restaurants and camping allowed on the 3 km long clean, sandy stretch just W of the airport. San Luís is a short local bus ride away, rec but the water is dirtier than Los Uveros. Cumaná is a charming place with its mixture of old and new, but the port area (1½ km) is not safe at night.

The newer sections of the city near the airport are barren and uninteresting; the older sections flow around the base of the hill dominated by the Castillo de San Antonio. The streets around the Gobernación and Plaza Bolívar are narrow and partly pedestrianized. More relaxing than the busy streets surrounding, they have several economic hotels and eating places; the tourist office is here also. There are walks along the treelined river (beware mosquitoes), which has the **Parque Ayacucho, Parque Guaiqueri** on the W bank (clean toilets) and markets on both sides (food and craftwork). The **Castillo de San Antonio de la Eminencia**, affords a wide view of the town, Araya Peninsula and coast; it was built in 1686 as a defence against pirates, with 16 mounted cannon, drawbridge and dungeons (Páez was held captive here 1849-50) from which there are said to be underground tunnels leading to the Santa Inés church. Restored in 1975, it is flood-lit at night. The **Castillo de Santa María de la Cabeza** (1669) is a rectangular fortress with a panoramic view of San Antonio and the elegant homes below. **Convento de San Francisco**, the original Capuchin mission of 1514, was the first school on the continent; its remains are on the Plaza Badaracco Bermúdez facing the beach. The **Church of Santa Inés** (1637) was the base of the Franciscan missionaries; earthquakes have caused it to be rebuilt five times. A tiny 400-year-old statue of the Vírgen de Candelaria is in the garden. The **home of Andrés Eloy Blanco** (1896-1955: one of Venezuela's greatest poets and politicians), on Plaza Bolívar, has been nicely restored to its turn-of-the-century elegance: photographs, poetry recordings, political notes and personal effects of the owner (open Tues-Sun 0900-1100, 1600-1900, free). On the opp side of the square is **La Gobernación** around a courtyard lined by cannon from Santa María de la Cabeza, note the gargoyles and other colonial features. The **Sucre Museum** (Museo Gran Mariscal de Ayacucho) was set up in the old Consejo Municipal in Parque Ayacucho in 1974 to commemorate the 150th anniversary of the battle of Ayacucho: mainly portraits, relics and letters of Bolívar and José Antonio Sucre (born 1795, Bolívar's first lieutenant, President of Peru in 1826, assassinated in Colombia in 1828). There is also a maritime museum (**Museo del Mar**) with good exhibits of tropical marine life, at the old airport, Av Universidad with Av Industrial, open Tues-Sun 0830-1130, 1430-1630, US$0.60: take San Luis minibus from outside the cathedral. In the suburb of Chaima a bronze monument marks the 450th anniversary of the city's founding: it depicts in bas-relief the more martial encounters between Spaniards and natives; a Capuchin friar and a Cumanagoto Indian top the 16m column (take Brasil/Terminal bus near Plaza Ayacucho, US$0.30).

Festivals 22 Jan, Santa Inés; pre-Lenten carnival throughout the state of Sucre; 2 Nov, Santos y Fideles Difuntos at El Tacal.

Hotels B *Los Bordones*, Final Av Universidad, T (093) 510352, F 515377, 8 km from the bus station, rec, beautifully situated on a good beach with excellent food and a swimming pool; *Cumanagoto**, Av Universidad, being completely refurbished 1995; **C** *Gran Hotel**, Av Universidad, T 510671, beach, mid-way between *Cumanagoto* and town centre, clean and good; **C** *Mariño*, T 320751, near centre, Calle Mariño y Junín, private bath, a/c, not very clean; **C** *Minerva**, T 314-4171, F 662701, 5 km N of centre on seafront Av Cristóbal Colón, little to do in area, rather soulless, clean, modern, US$1 taxi ride from centre; **C** *Turismo Guaiqueri*, Av Bermúdez 26, T 310821, comfortable, clean, a/c, bath, friendly, restaurant not always open; **D** *Don Bosco Suite*, Av Perimetral and 19 de Abril, T 310969, clean, a/c, no hot water, extremely friendly, rec; **D** *Caribe*, Av Universidad, on San Luis beach, T 514548, with bath and a/c, clean, basic cabins, English spoken, no restaurant, highly rec; **D** *Regina*, Av Arismendi, T 321168, with bath but no hot water, a/c, restaurant, good views from upper rooms, very helpful, good value, highly rec; **D** *Savoia*, Av Perimetral, T 314379, clean, a/c with bath. Cheaper hotels can be found across the river from those above, around Plaza Ayacucho, especially on Calle Sucre: **E** *Astoria*, Calle Sucre, T 662708, with cold shower, fan, clean and friendly; **E** *Italia*, central, friendly, but dirty, toilet not divided from bedroom, very uncomfortable beds, with fan, or a/c with bath, very safe; **F** *Hospedaje La Gloria*, Sucre 31, opp Sta Inés church, with fan and bath, basic, clean, friendly and helpful.

Restaurants *El Colmao* on Plaza Pichincha, Calle Sucre, T 663251, very good fish, charming service and not expensive; *Sand Hills* and *Los Montones*, near *Caribe Hotel*, San Luis beach, rec. *Italia*, Sucre, cheap and good; *Ali Baba*, Av Bermúdez near corner with Calle Castellón, excellent, cheap, middle eastern food, rec; *Jardín de Sport*, only outdoor café, good food, good atmosphere, rec (drug pushers and pimps hang out in Plaza Bolívar opp). *Rancho E Morris*, good food and service, reasonable, open late. *Pucheff*, Calle Sucre, good pizza; *Bar Madrid*, round corner from *Hotel Italia*, friendly; *Mi Pollo*, cheap and filling fried chicken. *Helados Bariloche*, Plaza Ayacucho. All central restaurants close Sun lunchtime. Many good restaurants on Av Perimetral in the area near the *Savoia Hotel*.

Exchange Banco Consolidado, Av Bermúdez y Perimetral, Edif Ajounián, Amex cheques only, no commission. Exchange at Oficambio, Calle Mariño, Edificio Funcal, accepts all TCs, same rate as cash, open to 1600.

Panamanian Consulate In a one-way street, next to Grupo Escolar José Silvero Córdova in Parcelamiento Miranda Sector D, T 663525; take a taxi.

Shopping A good selection of Venezuelan crafts on sale in the shop on Calle Sucre (expensive).

Travel Agent *Happy Tour*, Centro Comercial, La Banca, PB, Local No 6, T 24592; also at *Hotel Cumanagoto*, T 653111.

Tourist Office near church of Santa Inés, ask to see their photos of surrounding area, very helpful, English spoken.

Bus Bus terminal 3 km NW of the centre on Av Las Palomas, just before the junction with the peripheral road, T 662218. Local bus into centre US$0.10, taxi US$1.50. Beach near terminal. *Por puesto* to **Puerto La Cruz**, US$6, bus US$3, 1½ hrs. To **Güiria (see p 1403)**, US$3.60, 1230, *por puesto* US$7.20 (5 hrs), beware of overcharging, often stop in Carúpano. To **Caripe**, 0730 and 1230, 4 hrs, get there early and buy ticket on the bus, US$4. To **Caracas**, US$7 upwards depending on company (7-8 hrs), frequent service but not all advertised buses run, many cancellations; many daily to **Ciudad Guayana** and **Ciudad Bolívar**, US$6 with Expresos Guayanesa, T 66218, 6 hrs. Other destinations incl Maracay, Valencia, Carúpano (US$3), Cumanacoa, Maturín, Barcelona and San Félix.

For **Ferries** to **Isla Margarita**, see p 1411.

Air New airport 10 km E of centre (taxi fare US$2.50). To Caracas with Avensa (T 671518) and Servivensa (T 312484), Porlamar (Avensa) and Carúpano.

Excursions A paved road runs S down the Manzanares to *Cumanacoa* (56 km; pop 18,750), a traditional creole town in a rich agricultural area (2 hotels, E). At the Casa de Cultura, Calle Motedano 20, authentic folk music is performed by "Los Carrizas Precolombinos", a band of local musicians and members of the Turimiquire tribe. Near the town is the Cuchivano grotto from which flares a jet of natural gas.

To the *Araya Peninsula* with its desert landscapes and pink salt lakes, either by Cumaná-Araya boat, departs every hr, US$0.60 (return boats haphazard and difficult to get on at weekends as more cars than spaces, leave from main wharf at end of Av Bermúdez, several passenger launches a day, some with upper seating decks) or by road from Cariaco, 78 km E on the Cumaná-Carúpano highway, no public transport. The peninsula road out to Araya is now paved (95 km). Araya is the main settlement on the peninsula (pop, with Manicuare, 21,000), it has an airport, a ferry dock and **G** *Hospedaje San José*, very basic; another hostel, even more basic, and the *Hotel Araya*, a long way from the dock, mainly used by the Salt Company for its visitors. Private houses also have rooms available. Bars on the beach near the dock serve meals and a friendly *panadería* at the end of the main street going uphill from the dock serves good breakfasts. The major sight is the Castillo de Santiago (or Fuerte Araya), built by Spain in 1625 to protect the salt mines, where in colonial times wretched miners laboured naked on the shimmering salt flats (naked because salt rapidly destroyed clothing). So important was salt in the preservation of food that the authorities spent three years constructing the fortress, bringing all materials, food and water in by sea. It is considered one of the most important historical sites on the continent; certainly it was Spain's most expensive project to that time in the New World. Very little remains of the fortress apart from the ruins of its walls, passageways and cistern. Entry is free, but the only facilities are a refreshment stand and a picnic area. Today the mines are exploited by a Government-owned corporation; annual production has almost reached 500,000 tonnes. Ask permission for a visit from Ensal (Empresa Nacional de Salinas); office near the pier at Puerto Sucre. Ensal has an a/c guesthouse and dining room open to the public and runs 2-hr tours of its saltworks up to 1400.

The highway from Cumaná goes on to the port of Carúpano, on the Paría Peninsula (135 km). The coastal route as far as Villa Frontado is beautiful, running along the Golfo de Cariaco past a succession of attractive beaches and small villages: even the larger places along this stretch—Marigüitar and San Antonio del Golfo—are very quiet and have little accommodation (**Balneario Cachamaure**), 44 km from Cumaná, beautiful beach, cabins US$18, barbecue equipment, US$2. After Cariaco (pop 25,350, gas/petrol) the road winds inland over the Paría Ridge to **Carúpano**, a well-preserved colonial town of 87,600, from which 70% of Venezuela's cocoa is shipped. Its narrow streets, beautifully wooded parks and graceful buildings date back to 1647, when the wealthy cocoa plantations were worked by African slaves (here in 1816 Bolívar freed the blacks, thus acquiring new allies). The town sits between the Ríos Revilla and Candoroso; its beach is wide and desolate but the waterfront boulevard is beautifully-landscaped. Carúpano is famous throughout Venezuela as the last place still celebrating a traditional pre-Lenten Carnival: days of dancing, rum drinking, completely masked women in black (*negritas*), etc. The area becomes a focus for tourists at this time (Feb), so book accommodation ahead.

Festivals 3 May, Velorios de la Cruz (street dances); 15 Aug, Asunción de la Virgen.

Hotels A3 *Victoria**, Av Perimetral, seen better days but good, swimming pool, restaurant; **C** *Lilma*, Av Independencia 161, good restaurant; **D** *San Francisco*, Av Juncal 87A (good food, try the mussels); **D** *Bologna*, Av Independencia, very clean, friendly, bathroom, excellent, cheap restaurant, a/c, cheaper rooms with fan only, intermittent water, owner speaks German, rec; **E** *El Yunque*, Av Perimetral (about 2 km from centre), dirty, beach, good seafood restaurant; **E** *Maria Victoria*, Av Perimetral (100m from *Hotel Victoria*), friendly, safe, fan, basic, no hot water; **E** *Playa Copey*, on beach at nearby Santa Catalina, airy rooms, pool; **F** *Carúpano*, Av Independencia, near seafront, friendly and very basic; **F** *Ecuador*, Av Independencia. **Restaurants** *La Brasa Dorada*, Av 5 Libertad, rec. *El Kiosko*, Paseo Boulevard, by the seafront, OK.

Transport Bus to Caracas, Responsable de Venezuela, US$8, 8 hrs; to Cumaná, US$3, 2 hrs, sit on right for sea views, *por puesto* US$6; Güiria US$1.75, 3 hrs, *por puesto* US$4, 3 hrs (from Plaza Colón). Bus to **Puerto La Cruz**, US$4.70, 5 hrs. No buses leave direct from Carúpano to **Caripe**: it is necessary to go to Maturín or Cumaná, a taxi from Carúpano to Caripe costs US$35. Airport with flights to Porlamar (Isla Margarita) daily at 1550 with Avensa, US$27, Cumaná and Caracas.

There is an alternative road between Cariaco and Carúpano which reaches the coast after 17 km, and runs E by the Caribbean a further 38 km to Carúpano. The beaches on this coast are covered with shells which make swimming less attractive, but good sand can be found at Saucedo and the Balneario Costa Azul (2 km E of Guaca; restaurant). Escondido is a deep calm bay surrounded by sand dunes. On this drive are Cereza, famed for its basket-making, and Guaca, where clams packed with peppers are sold.

The Paria Peninsula Highway 9 continues a further 160 km E along the Peninsula to Güiria. The coast is left behind until Irapa, as the main highway climbs over the central spine through luxuriant forests of bamboo and Spanish moss to the village of **El Pilar** (33 km, pop 17,000), where there are a number of hot springs (El Hervidero and Cueva del Pato) and the river bathing resort of Sabacual. E of El Pilar is **Guaraúnos** (40 mins from Carúpano), the base of Claus Müller (Calle Bolívar 8, T 094-69052) who has worked with Indian communities and in conservation for 25 years. His trips in the peninsula, to the cloud forest, and the delta are highly rec, US$60 per day for 4 wheel drive, food and lodging, money ploughed back into the local community. A second road which joins the highway beyond El Pilar follows the coast E of Carúpano to the fishing village of El Morro de Puerto Santo (15 km), sited on a sandspit between the coast and a rocky offshore island, then to the lovely town of **Río Caribe** (pop 25,100, about 20 km E of Carúpano), whose old pastel-hued houses testify to the former prosperity of the place when it was the chief cacao-exporting port. One hotel, **C** *Mar Caribe*, incl breakfast, swimming pool, restaurant, good coffee and cocktails; or rooms rented by Señora Ana at Av Las Bermudas 21, G pp, very friendly. There are also private, unsigned pensions; ask for them. DG Storey from Maturín writes, "there are several sandy beaches on either side of the village and the best beach is another 25 km to the E. Turn off the main road at a sign for "Medina", becoming a dirt track, to the Playa Medina in a beautiful setting. **A3** *Hotel Playa Medina*, full board and drinks incl, unobtrusive cottages on the beach with small snackbar restaurant and toilets open to the public, changing facilities, carparking (US$1), well worth a visit" (it is to become a Club Med). Pick-up truck from Río Caribe to La Entrada, 2 km from Playa Medina, 1 hr, US$0.50 followed by a very long walk. Try to find a truck that will take you directly to Playa Medina, bargain hard, get there early since the last form of transport back to Río Caribe is 1530. The paved road then crosses the mountains and joins Highway 9 at Bohordal, 55 km from Carúpano.

Irapa (117 km, pop 11,500) is a fishing town surrounded by a grove of coconut palms; it is said to be here that Papillon came ashore after his last escape from Devil's Island in 1945 (*fiesta* 19 Mar). Bus terminal is 5 blocks from the sea; on the third street from terminal toward sea is the more expensive of the 2 hotels (both F); the cheaper is next to the cinema, $1/2$ block from sea, no sign, clean. Food market near sea front, enough shops for supplies, barbecue chicken at corner bar near seafront. Bus to Güiria at 0700-0800, check exact time, or take taxi, US$1 from same block. Across the Gulf of Paria are the dismal swamps of the Orinoco Delta. The climate is dry and very hot but the coast E of Irapa is a string of coves, palms and rich vegetation—Columbus was so impressed he named the region "Los Jardines". The well-surfaced highway continues on 42 km to **Güiria** (pop 20,200), a fishing town with a littered beach. Locals tend to assume foreigners are rich yacht owners, to whom they are not well-disposed. *Feria de la Pesca*, 14 July. Roads end here, but there are fuel supplies for the return journey. Bus to Balneario beach (US$0.10), good restaurant with cheap, cold beer, easy to hitch-hike back to town. Banco Orinoco changes TCs, good rates, no commission.

Accommodation **C** *Playa Paraíso*, on the beach near town, new in 1993, swimming pool, restaurant, music sometimes noisy; **E** *El Gran Puerto*; **E** *Hotel Oriente*, corner of main plaza, friendly, rec; **F** *Fortuna*, with bath, restaurant closed; *Plaza*, basic but fine, good patio restaurant, fish is rec, most popular place in town; *Manzur*, cheapest, not rec. It is better to stay in Irapa. There are a couple of basic eateries on the main square incl an Arab run restaurant, with *falafel* and *houmus*, highly rec; not much else. Good, cheap *empanadas* cooked outside Catholic Church on main square. Water restrictions at night in some places. Men should wear long trousers in the cinema.

Transport **Air** Flights to Caracas, Margarita, Tucupita, Anaco. **Bus** to Maturín, US$3.50, 6 hrs, Expresos Maturín. Several buses daily to Cumaná, 6 hrs, and to Caracas, all leaving between 1600 and 1800. Travel agent offers **cruises** to Caribbean islands for US$150 pp (see also below).

A good excursion from Güiria is to **Macuro**, a quiet town of 1,500 on the tip of the Peninsula. It is accessible only by boat, being surrounded on its landward sides by jungle. Boats leave Güiria Mon-Sat, possibly Sun, at 1000 (US$2.50, take protection against sun, and plastic sheeting in case of rough seas—ask for Don Pedro), returning 0530, taking 3 hrs, passing dense jungle which laps against deserted, palm-fringed beaches. It was in one of these coves—perhaps Yacúa, there is no record—that Spaniards of Columbus' crew made the first recorded European landing on the continent on 5 August 1498, before taking formal possession in the estuary at Güiria the next day (locals like to believe the landing took place at Macuro, and the town's official new name is Puerto Colón). A big party is held here every year on Oct 12 to mark the official "discovery" of America.

Macuro is friendly, with a beach (narrow, has biting ants, nice sand but pollution and lots of vegetation in the sea—boatmen will take you to a better beach, at a price), a few understocked shops, one restaurant, 3 hotels (one of which is F, basic, friendly, good, big meals, free coffee) and rooms to let (easy to camp or sling your hammock somewhere). Eduardo manages the little history museum; he is knowledgeable about the immediate area and can advise on hiking on the Peninsula, the National Park which covers the N side of Paria, and boats to the Orinoco Delta, and through the Bocas del Dragón to the miniscule settlement of *Patao* (3 hrs), where one can hire a guide for a trek across the Peninsula or an ascent of Cerro Patas, climbing up from cacao and banana plantations into cool montane forest. Fishing boats can often be hired to take you to many small villages, making for a hot but relaxed holiday in one of Venezuela's less-visited corners. Where affected by the output of the Orinoco, the gulf waters are murky, but around most of the peninsula, especially at the tip and on the Caribbean coast, the waters are clear. Also helpful for boats to Trinidad, accommodation in Trinidad, or for excursions, is Adrian Winter-Roach, a Trinidadian (also known by the name of his boat *El Cuchillo*): Calle Carabobo, Casa s/n, Macuro, or the Distribuidora Beirut, Calle Valdez 21, Güiria, T/F 81677, or Vereda Paramacuni 37, Banco Obrero, Güiria. He travels to Port of Spain about once a week (not weekends), clearing all necessary formalities, US$60 one way, US$100 return, 4-day trips with food and lodging US$170, reductions for large groups. Windward Lines Ltd (Global Steamship Agencies Ltd, Mariner's Club, Wrightson Road, PO Box 966, Port of Spain, Trinidad, T 624-2279, F 809-627-5091, or in Güiria, Acosta Shipping Agents, T 094-81679/81233, F 81112, English spoken) sails to Güiria every other week, arriving Tues 2130, departing Wed at 2300, on its route St Lucia, Barbados, St Vincent, Trinidad, Venezuela and back (on alternate weeks the ship goes to Margarita). Fares are given under Isla de Margarita, **Communications**. Few boat owners seem willing to cross to Trinidad, but if you are prepared to wait for a suitable ride go to the port and look for a fishing boat with a Trinidadian flag, it is bound to be returning sooner or later; if you are leaving Venezuela, remember to get an exit stamp, probably in Macuro, but check in advance.

You can visit the Orinoco delta from Güiria; there are more motor boats trading between Güiria and *Pedernales* in the delta. The trip takes about 5 hrs, US$13, check for boats at the harbour (the *Guadeloupe*, *Verónica* and *Mil del Valle*) or the *Hotel Fortuna* (not always open). Pedernales is a small village (pop 3,100) only a few km from the southwestern point of Trinidad. It is only accessible by boat from Güiria (ask for Andrecito, who lives on N side of small plaza nearest harbour entrance, or cargo boats operated by men from Pedernales, known in Güiria as "Los Indios", US$7.50-10 negotiable according to number of passengers, no seats, deck space in open only, can be rough seas "the sun is very strong and you and your luggage will get wet!", or ask owner of *Hotel Plaza*—boats are very hard to find). Alternatively, go from Tucupita (much easier—**p 1423**). There are also boats to and from Trinidad costing about US$30-60, the more official, the more expensive. Sisiliano Bottini is a shipping agent. (Some cheap boats carry contraband and unless you avoid Trinidadian or Venezuelan immigration controls you will find this method both difficult and very risky: the Trinidadian authorities are reluctant to let even legal boats in for fear of drug smuggling.) Expect to have your luggage searched at the harbour. Hotel, F, rats, comfortable beds, meals available, owner meets boats; the store on the riverbank also has rooms with cooking facilities, F; also at the blue house open, G pp. For a shower, ask Jesús, who runs a fish-freezing business. Only Indians live in the northern part of the village. Travel out of Pedernales is often difficult—to Tucupita by fishing boat, locals pay US$5, but you may get asked for US$40 (ask for Juan but be prepared to bargain hard), leave at daybreak, 6-7 hrs, rec as the boat stops in some of the Indian villages, where you can buy the best hammocks (*chinchorros*), fish, cheese, and some beautiful carved animal figures made of balsa wood (**see also p 1424**). Many birds and Orinoco dolphins may be seen en route.

From Puerto La Cruz a toll road goes inland, skirting Barcelona. At Km 52 (where there is a restaurant) a road forks left to (near) *Santa Bárbara* (airport) and goes on to Jusepín, Quiriquire, and Caripito, all Lagovén oil camps.

In Santa Bárbara can be bought the native *chinchorros*, hammocks made by hand of woven *moriche* palm leaves, decorated with coloured yarn. They can also be found in Tucupita (**see p 1423**). They "give" when you lie on them and do not absorb moisture when used on the beach. Very good for camping.

Maturín, capital of Monagas State, an important commercial centre, is 16 km beyond Jusepín. Population 268,650.

Hotels Two four-star hotels, *Hotel Morichal* and *Hotel Stauffer*; C *Chaima Inn*, pool, satellite TV, good restaurant with buffet lunch, rec; *Perla Princess*, Av Juncal y Monagas, hot water, clean, good, but restaurant overpriced; C *Friuli*, Carrera 9 with Calle 30, only hotel in town with centralized a/c, therefore quiet; D *París*, Av Bolívar 183, T 091-414028, a/c, hot water, safe, central, rec; **D** *Berlín*, Av Bolívar, lively bar, shows at weekends; **D** *Comercio*, with bath, not too clean, English spoken, central; **E** *Manolo*, Av Bolívar, pleasant, restaurant with good food, bar; **E** *Trinidad*, clean, English speaking, rec (*Trinidad* is two establishments, on Av Bolívar, one good, the other "miserable"); **F** *El Picasso*, Calle 6 with Calle 16, with fan; **F** *Hotel El Terminal*, at bus terminal, clean, private bath, friendly, very handy. Just out of town on road to Barcelona; **D** *Hotel American City*, pool, disco, all rooms have private bathroom and a/c.

Restaurants *Yarúa* (behond the Cathedral) most expensive, seafood and grilled meat; *Parador Turístico Arauguay*, via La Cruz, Argentine barbecue speciality; *Hotel Emperador*, Av Bolívar, good *torta helada* (ice-cream cake); *Mister Pasta*, Av Juncal, 3 blocks from *Perla Pincess*, good value, wide variety. Good Chinese take away C17 off Av Bolívar.

Exchange Banco Consolidado (American Express), Av Raúl Leoni, Edif D'Amico, take bus 1 or 5 along Av Bolívar, heading away from bus terminal; **Banco Mercantil**, Calle Monagas and opp central market, most likely to accept TCs.

Transport Bus station is at end of Av Bolívar, take bus No 1 or 5 to get there. Try ginger/honey bread at the bus station while waiting. Buses leave 3 times a day for **Caracas** from the central bus terminal, 2030, 2200 and 2245 hrs (US$6.50, 8 hrs, *por puesto* US$13); buses for **Ciudad Guayana**-San Félix (0815, 3 hrs, US$4, incl ferry) and **El Dorado** leave from the terminus near the airport. To **Puerto La Cruz** or **Barcelona**, take a *por puesto* to Cumaná and change, 2 hrs, US$4.20. Bus only to **Ciudad Bolívar**, US$4.50, change in Ciudad Guyana-San Félix (no *por puesto*). Bus to **Carúpano**, at 1000, US$3, 3 hrs, beautiful landscape; *por puesto* to Caripe, 2 hrs, US$4.50. Bus to **Río Caribe**, US$3, 4 hrs, at 1100 with Expresos Maturín, be quick to line up at bus, ticket does not guarantee a seat or even transport. Bus to **Tucupita** at 1100, US$3 with Expresos Guayanesa, poor standard, 3-4 hrs. Bus to **Güiria**, US$3.50, 6 hrs, Expresos Maturín; to **Irapa** 1230, 4½ hrs, US$4. Travelling between the airport and town: *por puesto* Nos 1,5,6 (US$0.25), or bus from main road outside airport (US$0.10). Taxis from the Reponsable de Venezuela office will try to charge much more.
Air services to Caracas (Avensa) and Porlamar, Maracaibo, San Antonio, Barcelona and Valencia (Aserca), good restaurant upstairs in airport. There are no exchange facilities in the airport except at the bar in the departure lounge, and they give a very bad rate.

Excursions Laguna Grande is a beautiful lake in the jungle about 32 km away, *por puesto* No 2 from the old market, US$0.50. By the lake is the *Club Naútico*, open 1100-1830, closed Mondays. The water is very green with algae, and many herons and cormorants may be seen, despite the loud music on board. Return transport can be difficult as passing *por puestos* are usually full (James Maas, Bocas del Toro, Panama).

Just beyond Jusepín an unpaved 32 km road, left, joins the Maturín-Cumaná road (212 km, all paved but twisty; beautiful tropical mountain scenery). At San Francisco on this road is a branch road running 22½ km NE to **Caripe** (pop 23,880), set in a mountain valley. There is a huge *samán* tree in purple glory when the orchids which cover it bloom in May. To the W of the town is a Mirador, from which there are great views over the whole valley. There is also a paved road between Carúpano and Caripe via Santa Cruz and Santa María, 2 hrs.

Festivals 2-12 Aug, *Feria de las Flores*; 10-12 Oct, NS del Pilar.

Hotels **C** *Humboldt Cabañas*, for sleeping 4, between Teresén and Caripe, good, clean, full cooking facilities, little hot water. **C** *Samán**, Enrique Chaumer 29, T (092) 51183, good atmosphere, but pricey, moderate restaurant; **D** *San Francisco*, Av Enrique Chaumer 55, T (092) 51018, with bath, hot water, clean, rec, good restaurant; **D** *Venezia*, clean, spacious, with excellent *Coba Longa* restaurant, owner speaks English. **E** *Hacienda Campo Claro*, Teresén, T (092) 51994, managed by Francisco Belancourt, rents cabins, can provide meals, horseriding. **E** *Caripe*, clean, friendly, bath, give advance notice for dinner otherwise restaurant closes at 2000, rec; **E** *Las Chaimas*, T 51141; *Lonchería Arabe*, rec. *Tasca Restaurant Río Colorado*, cheap, good local food, rec.

Transport Bus from Caripe to **Caracas** at 1800, stops in Cumaná, pick up at San Remo Sur office, next to *Hotel San Francisco*. Caracas direct leaves at 2000. Bus to **Maturín** via Arague at 0730 with Sol de Oriente.

12 km from Caripe is the remarkable **Cueva del Guácharo** National Monument; open 0830-1700, entrance US$0.50, tour with Spanish-speaking guide, 2 hrs. Also a caving museum, with a good range of publications for sale, incl a leaflet in English about the cave, US$0.80, and a good cafeteria; *Hotel Guácharo* nearby. A bus from Cumaná to Caripe—0700, returns 1300 (although you may not be able to catch it as the cave tour takes 2 hrs and bus

timings only allow 2 hrs)—takes 4 hrs and costs US$2.50, there is another bus at 1200, or take the *por puesto*, 2 hrs, US$7.50, bus stops next to caves. The bus from Cumaná direct to the Cueva del Guácharo leaves at 0715, US$2.50 and stops right in front of the caves. Private tours can be organized from Cumaná for about US$10 pp, with guide. There are frequent buses from Caripe to the caves; if staying in Caripe, take a *por puesto* (a jeep marked Santa María – Muelle), at 0800, US$3, see the caves and waterfall and catch the Cumaná bus which goes past the caves between 1200 and 1230. Taxis from Caripe (US$5), hitching difficult. The cave was discovered by Humboldt, and has since been penetrated $10^{1}/_{2}$ km along a small, crystal-clear stream. First come the caves in which live about 18,000 *guácharos* (oil birds) with an in-built radar system for sightless flight. Their presence supports a variety of wildlife in the cave: blind mice, fish and crabs in the stream, yellow-green plants, crickets, ants, etc. For 2 hrs at dusk (about 1900) the birds pour out of the cave's mouth, continously making the clicking sounds of their echo-location system, coming back at dawn with their crops full of the oily fruit of certain local palms. Through a very narrow entrance is the *Cueva del Silencio* (Cave of Silence), where you can hear a pin drop. About 2 km in is the *Pozo del Viento* (Well of the Wind). No backpacks allowed in the caves (leave them at the ticket office); tape recorders are permitted, cameras are allowed, the guides inform you when you can use a flash. Guides are compulsory (incl in entry price—Jesus speaks English, rec, Alexander speaks a little German, also rec); to go further than $1^{1}/_{2}$ km into the caves, permits from Inparques in Caracas and special equipment are needed. The streams are now bridged and the path is paved, but there is still quite a lot of water around; wear old clothes, stout shoes and be prepared to take off your shoes and socks. In the wet season it can be a bit slippery; tours into the cave may be shortened or even closed in Aug-Sep because of rising water level. Opposite the road is a paved path to Salto Paila, a 25-metre waterfall, about 30 mins' walk, guides available; orange and other fruit trees along the way. Other routes are suggested at the cave. A beautiful path, built by Inparqes, starts at the caving museum, with some nice shelters for picnics.

Continuing straight on from Km 52, the road passes W of **Anaco** (pop 60,000; **D** *Motel Bowling Anaco*; **D** *Motel Canaima*, Av Aeropuerto, good; **E** *Internacional*, Av Miranda; **E** *Dragón Oriental* on same street nearby, clean, central; **E** *Mand's Club*, Av Venezuela, restaurant, bar, a bit noisy; **E** *Muñiz*, Sucre, basic; **E** *Viento Fresco*, some fans, dark rooms, poor security). It has an airport, is an important centre for oil-well service contracting companies. Beyond Anaco a branch road leads to the oilfields of San Joaquín and San Roque.

The main road passes near Cantaura, a market town, and goes on to **El Tigre**, a busy city of 105,000 on the edge of the Guanipa Plateau. It too is a centre for petroleum, but also for large peanut plantations. El Tigre and its neighbour, El Tigrito (also called San José de Guanipa, pop 48,220, 10 km E), are well-served by highways to all parts of the country. The local airport is at San Tomé, 5 km from El Tigrito (regular bus to El Tigre US$3.50). In San Tomé, the eastern headquarters of Menevén, the former Mene Grande oil company, the public relations office (Calle Guico) is happy to arrange tours to nearby wells.

Hotels C *Internacional Gran Hotel*, Av Intercomunal, swimming pool, nightclub, best but not central; **D** *Tamanaco*, Av España, opp bus terminal, a/c, good, with highly rec restaurant; **D** *Orinoco*, Guayana, best of cheaper places, cafetería; also on Av España, **E** *Caribe*, and **E** *La Fuente*, near main plaza, **E** *Arichuna* and **E** *Santa Cruz* clean and basic; **E** *Milelvi*, with bath, good, clean, parking in courtyard. Chilean restaurant serves excellent Chilean food and salads, on Av España. In El Tigrito is **D** *Hotel Rancho Grande*, acceptable; services better in El Tigre.
Warning Pickpockets work the city buses, usually in pairs.

From El Tigre, Highway 15 leads off to Caracas (via Valle de Pascua, Camatagua and Cúa—550 km see p 1387); the one we are following leads, straight and flat, 130 km over the *llanos* to the Angostura bridge across the Orinoco to Ciudad Bolívar (298 km from Puerto La Cruz—*por puesto* US$3, $1^{1}/_{2}$ hrs).

ISLA DE MARGARITA

Margarita is the country's main Caribbean holiday destination; some parts are crowded and trippery, but there are undeveloped beaches, villages with pretty churches, colonial La Asunción and several national parks including the fascinating Restinga lagoon.

Isla de Margarita and two close neighbours, Coche and Cubagua, form the state of Nueva Esparta.

Isla de Margarita is in fact one island whose two sections are tenuously linked by the 18 kilometre sandspit which separates the sea from the Restinga lagoon. At its largest, Margarita is about 32 kilometres from N to S and 67 kilometres from E to W. Most of its people live in the developed eastern part, which has some wooded areas and fertile valleys. The western part, the Peninsula de Macanao, is hotter and more barren, with scrub, sand dunes and marshes. Wild deer, goats and hares roam the interior, but four-wheel drive vehicles are needed to penetrate it. The entrance to the Peninsula de Macanao is a pair of hills known as *Las Tetas de María Guevara*, a national monument covering 1,670 hectares.

The climate is exceptionally good, but rain is scant. Water is piped from the mainland. The roads are good, and a bridge connects the two parts. Nueva Esparta's population is over 200,000, of whom 68,000 live in the main city, Porlamar (which is not the capital, that is La Asunción).

The island has enjoyed a boom since 1983, largely as a result of the fall in the value of the bolívar and the consequent tendency of Venezuelans to spend their holidays at home. Margarita's status as a duty-free zone also helps. Venezuelan shoppers go in droves for clothing, electronic goods and other consumer items. Gold and gems are good value, but many things are not. There has been extensive building in Porlamar, with new shopping areas and Miami-style hotels going up. A number of beaches are also being developed. Its popularity means that various packages are on offer, sometimes at good value, especially off-season.

Local industries are fishing and fibre work, such as hammocks and straw hats. Weaving, pottery and sweets are being pushed as handicraft items for the tourists. An exhibition centre has been opened at El Cercado, near Santa Ana, on Calle Principal, near the church.

Despite the property boom and frenetic building on much of the coast and in Porlamar, much of the island has been given over to natural parks. Of these the most striking is the **Laguna La Restinga**. Launches provide lengthy runs around the mangrove swamps, but they create a lot of wash and noise. The mangroves are fascinating, with shellfish clinging to the roots. The launch will leave you on a shingle and shell beach (don't forget to arrange with your boatman to collect you), and you can rummage for shellfish in the shallows (protection against the sun essential—see below for prices, etc). Flamingoes live in the lagoon.

There are mangroves also in the **Laguna de las Marites** natural monument, W of Porlamar. Other parks are Las Tetas de María Guevara (see above), **Cerro el Copey**, 7,130 hectares, and **Cerro Matasiete y Guayamurí**, 1,672 hectares (both reached from La Asunción).

By boat from Porlamar you can go to the Isla de los Pájaros, or Morro Blanco, for both bird-spotting and underwater fishing. In Boca del Río there is a Museum of the Sea.

Festivals on Margarita 6-13 Jan at Altagracia; 20-27 Jan at Tacarigua; 16-26 Mar at Paraguachí (*Feria de San José*); 3-10 May at Los Robles; 24-30 May at La Guardia; 6 June at Tacarigua; 25-26 July at Santa Ana; 27 July at Punta de Piedra; 31 July (Batalla de Matasiete) and 14-15 Aug (Asunción de la Virgen) at La Asunción; 30 Aug-8 Sept at Villa Rosa; 8-15 Sept at El Valle; 11-12 and 28 Oct at Los Robles; 4-11 Nov at Boca del Río, 4-30 Nov at Boca del Pozo; 5-6 Dec at Porlamar; 15 Dec at San Francisco de Macanao; 27 Dec-3 Jan at Juan Griego. See map for locations.

Most of the hotels are at *Porlamar*, 20 km from the airport and about 28 km from Punta de Piedra, where most of the ferries dock. At Igualdad y Díaz is the Museo de Arte Francisco Narváez. The main, and most expensive, shopping area is Avenida Santiago Mariño; better bargains and a wider range of shops are to be found on Gómez and Guevara. The centre of the city is bustling and crowded with cars and shoppers, while to the E there is continuing, apparently chaotic development of big holiday hotels and condominiums, separated by vast areas of waste ground and construction sites. Costa Azul is the main *urbanización*, served by a long strip

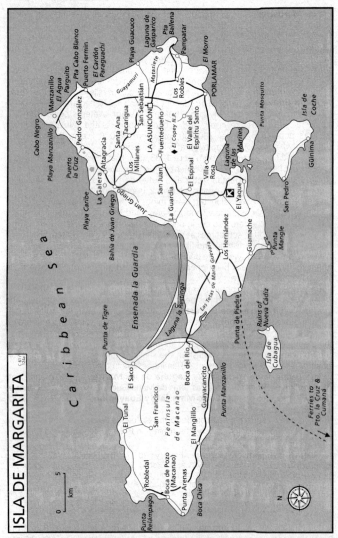

ISLA DE MARGARITA

C 6?/
T244

of featureless sand known as Playa Moreno. At night everything closes by 2300; women alone should avoid the centre after dark. Porlamar has many casinos, all of which lack legal status. If you hit that pot of gold, the exchange regulations introduced in mid-1994 mean you cannot change bolívares into dollars; neither can you open a bank account.

Ferries go to the Isla de Coche (11 km by 6), which has over 5,000 inhabitants and one of the richest salt mines in the country. They also go, on hire only, to Isla de Cubagua, which is totally deserted, but you can visit the ruins of Nueva Cádiz (which have been excavated).

NB Aug and Sept are the vacation months when flights and hotels are fully booked.

NB also, there is both a Calle Mariño and Av Santiago Mariño in the centre.

Hotels at Porlamar L3 *Hilton* (+13% tax), C Los Uveros, Playa Moreno, T (095) 624111, F 620810, sailing dinghies for hire; other top class establishments; **A1** *Bella Vista**, Av Santiago Mariño, T 617222, F 612557, swimming pool, beach; **A2** *Dynasty*, T 621252, F 625101, opp *Hilton*, nice restaurant, pool; **A2** *Marina Bay*, T 625211, F 624110, 5-star, striking white building with casino, cramped pool area; **A3** *Stauffer*, Av Santiago Mariño, T 612911, F 618708, large rooms, excellent service and restaurant, bar on roof, casino being added; **B** *Aguila Inn*, Narváez, ½ km N of centre, T 612311, F 616909, clean, swimming pool, restaurant, rec; **B** *Colibrí*, Av Santiago Mariño, T 616346, new rooms, D in older rooms, both with bath, a/c, TV, rec; **B** *Imperial*, Av Raúl Leoni, Via El Morro, T 095-616420, F 615056, best rooms in front have balcony, clean, comfortable, safe, a/c, good showers, triple rooms available, English spoken; rec; **B** *Margarita International Resort Village*, low-rise (the only one), "pueblo" style; **B** *Venus*, T (095) 23722, Calle Milano y San Rafael, clean, a/c, safe; **C** *Contemporáneo*, Calle Mariño entre Igualdad y Velásquez, modern, a/c, TV, clean, bar, restaurant; **C** *Italia*, San Nicolás, with bath, cold water, a/c, clean, safe, rec, but district is a bit rough; **D** *Garland*, Av Miranda, good restaurant, convenient for *por puestos*; **D** *Marocco*, Mariño between Zamora y San Nicolás, a/c, TV, fridge, bath, but dark, windowless rooms; **D** *Porlamar*, Igualdad y Fajardo, clean, good restaurant and video bar La Punta, a/c or fan, hot water, friendly; on the Boulevard, **E** *Brasilia*, San Nicolás, quiet, clean, nice new rooms at back; nearby **E** *Boston*, very clean, fan, private bath; **E** *Chez Toni*, San Nicolás 14-56, clean, helpful, English spoken, cheap restaurant, rec; **E** *Domino*, La Libertad 7-40, with fan or a/c, basic, friendly; **E** *España*, Mariño 6-35, T 095-612479, cold shower, very clean, friendly, good breakfast, fan, highly rec; **E** *La Viña*, Calle La Marina, No 14-24, T 635723, close to *España*, very friendly, clean, bath, a/c, bar, restaurant, laundry, the Mexican owner, Luis and his wife are very helpful and generous, rec; **E** *Los Duques*, Arismendi, shower, a/c, TV, rec; **E** *Om*, San Nicolás, clean, friendly, a/c, cheaper with fan; **E** *Palermo*, Calle Igualdad, opp cathedral, friendly, clean, best rooms on top floor with views of plaza; **E** *Residencia Paraíso*, near main square, basic but clean, fan; **E** *Robaldar*, Igualdad, near Libertad, shower, a/c, TV, friendly, rec. Many others round Plaza Bolívar. Cheaper places on Maneiro; **E** *Tamá*, also next door to *Imperial*, gringo place with basic rooms, OK, excellent restaurant and atmosphere, bar is German-run, lots of languages spoken; **F** *Rioja*, Calle Narváez, don't take the first room offered, good value, with fan and bath, clean, safe. *Cabañas Turísticas*, Vía La Isleta, US$35 for a cabin, sleeps 4, pool, restaurant. *Evdama*, next door to the *Imperial*, better rooms. **A3-B** *Marbella Mar*, Av Principal y Calle Chipichipi, T 624022, F 624488, clean rooms, friendly, especially with children, free bus service to the beach, highly rec.

Restaurants *La Gran Pirámide*, Calle Malave and JM Patiño, superb food, very good service, cocktails worth trying, very good value, highly rec; *Doña Martha*, Velázquez nr Calle Hernández, Colombian food, good, inexpensive; *El Punto Criollo*, Igualdad nr *Hotel Porlamar*, good; *Rancho Grande*, C Guevara, nr Playa El Agua bus stop, Colombian, good value, rec; *El Pollo de Carlitos*, Marcano y Martínez, nice location, live music most nights, good food and value; *Bahía* bar-restaurant, Av Raúl Leoni y Vía El Morro, excellent value, live music; good breakfast at *Panadería*, Av 4 de Mayo y Fermín; *Sadaka*, Calle Fajardo, Lebanese, reasonable prices, good food, rec; *Martín Pescador*, Av 4 de Mayo, lobsters and other seafood, friendly, rec; *Cheers*, Santiago Mariño, good bar, popular, rec; *La Brada de Titti*, Av 4 de Mayo, good, rec; excellent pizzas (!) at *Paris Croissant* on Blvd Santiago Mariño; *Los 3 Delfines*, Cedeño 26-9, seafood, rec. *La Isla*, Mariño y Cedeño, 8 fast food counters ranging from hamburgers to sausages from around the world. *El Rincón de Migaelacho*, Calle San Nicolás, friendly, inexpensive, good value. *La Cotorrera*, Av Santiago Mariño, steaks, rec, closed Sun. Good afternoon tea at the *Hotel Concorde*.

Exchange Banco Mercantil for changing TCs; **Banco Consolidado**, Guevara y San Nicolás; banks generally slow with poor rates. **Casa de cambio** at Igualdad y Av Santiago Mariño. Amex office closed on Monday. Banks are open 0830-1130, 1400-1630. There are often long queues. Most shops accept credit cards.

Entertainment *Mosquito Coast Club*, behind *Bella Vista Hotel*, disco with genuine Venezuelan feel, good *merengue* and rock music, bar outside, also does excellent Mexican meals (beware of overcharging on simple items like water); discotheque for singles, *Village Club*, Av Santiago Mariño, rec for good music with variety of styles but expensive drinks, cover charge. *Doce 34*,

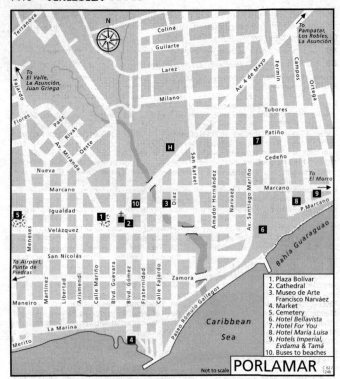

1. Plaza Bolívar
2. Cathedral
3. Museo de Arte Francisco Narváez
4. Market
5. Cemetery
6. Hotel Bellavista
7. Hotel For You
8. Hotel María Luisa
9. Hotels Imperial, Evdama & Tamá
10. Buses to beaches

Not to scale **PORLAMAR** C 62 / 124b

Av 4 de Mayo, entrance US$3, two dance floors, highly rec. Night life is generally good, but at European prices.

Post Office Calle Arismendi. **Phones** CANTV, Bolívar, between Fajardo and Fraternidad.

Shopping Besides all the duty-free shops, *Del Bellorín*, Cedeño, near Santiago Mariño, is good for handicrafts. Good selection of jewellery at *Sonia Gems*, on Cedeño; *Ivan Joyería* and *Inter Gold*, both on 4 de Mayo (latter is between *Ivan* and *Hotel Flamingo*); many other places on the main street are overpriced. When purchasing jewellery, bargain hard, don't pay by credit card (surcharges are imposed), get a detailed guarantee of the item and, if unsure, get another jeweller to check its validity. Designer clothes are cheap in many places, especially on Blvd Guevara, Blvd Gómez, and Calles Igualdad and Velázquez; cosmetics and perfumes also good value.

Travel Agents *Turisol*, Calle Hernández, friendly and helpful (no island tours); *Supertours*, Calle Larez, Quinta Thaid, T 618781, F 617061, tours of the island and elsewhere; *Zuluoga Tours*, Calle San Nicolás entre Arismendi y Mariño No 16-40, helpful; *Tourismo Guaiqueri*, Santiago Mariño y Marcano, English spoken. Ask travel agents about excursions on the sailing catamaran, *Catatumbo*, rec.

Tourist Information Fondene, the group for the development of Nueva Esparta, runs tourist information offices at the airport (see below) and on the first floor of the restored Aduana (customs) building on the little square at Pampatar (see under Pampatar). **NB** Fondene is to be restructured, so these details may alter. An outspoken and well-informed English-language newspaper, *Mira*, is published on the island; the editor/publisher acts also as an inexpensive tour guide; Av Santiago Mariño, Ed Carcaleo Suites, Apartamento 2-A, Porlamar (T 095-613351). The best map is available from Corpoven.

Public Transport *Por Puestos* serve most of the island, leaving mainly from the corners of Plaza Bolívar in Porlamar. Fares: to Punta de Piedra (from four blocks from Plaza Bolívar, towards sea-front), US$0.50, to the ferry terminal US$0.70; to La Asunción, US$0.25, from Calle Fajardo, half a block from Igualdad; to Pampatar, US$0.20; to La Restinga (from La Marina y Mariño), US$0.70, El Agua (from corner of Guevara and Marcano), US$0.40; Juan Griego, US$0.40. **Taxi** fares are published by *Mira* but are not uniformly applied by drivers. If you want to hire a taxi for a day you will be charged US$7-10 per hour. Always establish the fare before you get in the car. There is a 30% surcharge after 2100.

Car Hire An economic proposition for any number above one and a good way of getting around the island, several offices at the airport (**Beach** have been rec as cheap and reliable, US$30 a day for a jeep), also at *Hotel Bella Vista* (incl Avis, and Hertz, reliable), others on Av Santiago Mariño. **Lizmar** is the cheapest, watch insurance excess, cars are in poor condition. In all cases, check the brakes. Scooters can also be hired for about US$14 a day from **Diversion Rentals**, Calle Amador Hernández, **Maruba Motor Rentals**, La Mariña (English spoken, good maps, highly rec, US$16 bikes for 2, US$13 bikes for one) or **Auto Camping Margarita** (boats and bicycles also for rent). Motor cycles may not be ridden between 2000 and 0500; although this (apparently) should not apply to tourists, police officers have been known to confiscate tourists' machines and impose heavy fines. **NB** Remember to keep an eye on the fuel gauge; there are service stations in towns, but a/c is heavy on fuel. Driving on Isla Margarita: the roads are generally good and most are paved. Sign posts are often poorly-positioned (behind bushes, round corners), which adds to the night time hazard of vehicles with badly-adjusted lights. It is best not to drive outside Porlamar after dark. Also beware of robbery of hired vehicles. Check conditions and terms of hire carefully for your liability.

Communications Airport, General Santiago Mariño, between Porlamar and Punta de Piedra; comfortable and modern, has the international and national terminals at either end. Two tourist desks at the former extremity, one at the latter. Bus from Plaza Bolívar, US$0.70, taxi US$7. There are up to 12 flights a day from **Caracas**, with Avensa, Servivensa, Viasa and Aserca, 50 mins flight; tickets are much cheaper if purchased in Venezuela in local currency. Reservations made from outside Venezuela are not always honoured. Daily Servivensa flight to **Ciudad Guyana**, also Aserca, and daily Aereotuy to **Ciudad Bolivar**. Daily flights from **Cumaná**, US$30, **Carúpano**, US$30, Barcelona, Maturín, Puerto Ordaz, US$46, Valencia, US$61. Once a week with Viasa from Frankfurt, Panama, Lima, Bogotá, Quito, Aruba, Bonaire, Rome, Milan, Rio de Janeiro, twice a week from Miami and New York. Viasa, Av 4 de Mayo, Edif Banco Royal, Porlamar (T 32273, airport 691137); Avensa on Calle Fajardo, Porlamar, T 617111, airport 691021.

Ferries (very busy at weekends and Mon; in good condition, punctual): from **Puerto La Cruz**, Turismo Margarita/Gran Cacique, Marino Amérigo Vespucio, T 692301, Pto La Cruz to Margarita 0700 and 1300, 4 hrs (5-6 incl check-in), depart Margarita (**Punta de Piedra**) 1000 and 1800; Conferries, Los Cocos terminal, T 677221, and *Meliá Hotel*, Pto La Cruz, T 653001, to Margarita, 4 a day between 0700 and 2400 each way, 3½ hrs, passengers US$12.50 return 1st class, US$9 2nd (in enclosed middle deck with limited views), cars, US$25. From **Cumaná**, vehicle ferries of Naviarca (T 093-311667) at 0700 and 1600 daily, 3 hrs, cars US$10.50, jeeps US$13, passengers US$5.10, ferry terminal is almost at mouth of the river. Faster, more expensive launch, *Gran Cacique I* (Turismo Margarita, T 323461) twice daily to Punta de Piedra, US$6.35. *Gran Cacique II* from Punta de Piedra to Cumaná at 1100, no cars, US$5.50 first class. Conferry Terminal, Cumaná Puerto Sucre, T 311462, ferries at 0700 and 1600 to Margarita, returning 1100 and 2000, US$4 one way for passengers. A ferry from Punta de Piedra to Coche sails Mon-Fri, 1600, returns 1730, Sat and Sun, 0800 and 1730, returns 0530 and 1730.

A ferry sails from Mercado Viejo to Chacopata on the mainland at 1000 and 1200, also takes cars. Windward Lines (Global Steamship Agencies Ltd, Mariner's Club, Wrightson Road, PO Box 966, Port of Spain, Trinidad, T 809-624-2279) sails to Isla Margarita every other week (Tues) from Trinidad, St Vincent, Barbados and St Lucia. It sails from Porlamar to Trinidad on Wed at 1800, and on alternate weeks from Güiria at 2300, arriving in Port of Spain at 0700 on Thur. Return fares: from Thur US$60 (a return ticket satisfies onward ticket requirements for Trinidad), St Lucia, St Vincent or Barbados US$155. TCs can be changed on board at good rates. A ferry to Grenada, *The Eastward*, sails once a month. Go to the Puerto de Pescadores, El Guamache, near Punta de Piedra, and ask boat captains about taking a boat to the Leeward or Windward Islands (very difficult to find boats willing to take passengers).

By Road Several bus companies in Caracas sell through tickets from Caracas to Porlamar, arriving about midday. Buses return from Porlamar from terminal at Centro Comercial Bella Vista, at bottom end of Calle San Rafael. By car from Caracas, it takes about 4 hrs, but will be reduced to 2½ when the Sucre motorway is opened (still under construction 1994).

The capital, *La Asunción* (population 16,660), is a few kilometres inland from Porlamar. It has several colonial buildings, a cathedral, and the fort of Santa Rosa, with a famous bottle dungeon (open Monday 0800-1500, other days 0800-1800). There is a museum in the Casa Capitular, and a local market, good for handicrafts. Nearby are the Cerro Matasiete historical site and the Félix Gómez look-out in the Sierra Copuy.

Between La Asunción and Porlamar are the Parque Francisco Fajardo, beside the Universidad de Oriente, and *El Valle del Espíritu Santo*. Here is the church of the Virgen del Valle, a picturesque building with twin towers, painted white and pink. The Madonna is richly dressed (one dress has pearls, the other diamonds); the adjoining museum opens at 1400, it displays costumes and presents for the Virgin, including the "milagro de la pierna de perla", a leg-shaped pearl. A pilgrimage is held in early Sep. Proper dress is requested to enter the church.

Throughout the island, the churches are attractive: fairly small, with baroque towers and adornments and, in many cases, painted pink.

Beaches   Apart from the shopping, what attracts the holidaymakers from Venezuela and abroad are the beaches: long white stretches of sand bordered by palms, but rather hot, with little shade (sunscreen essential). Topless bathing is not seen, but the tanga (*hilo dental*—dental floss) is fairly common.

In Porlamar, the main beach suffers from its popularity: calm shallow water, pedalos for hire, windsurf classes; but that by the *Bella Vista*, although crowded with foreign tourists, is kept clean. Playa Morena is a long, barren strip of sand serving the expanding hotel zone to the E of the city (recently renamed Playa Caracola). For a more Venezuelan atmosphere go NE to *Pampatar* (pop 10,590), which is set around a bay favoured by foreign yachtsmen as a summer anchorage; jet skis for hire on a clean and pretty beach. A scale model of Columbus' *Santa María* is used for taking tourists on trips. There are lots of fishing boats and fishermen mending their nets. A fishing boat can be hired for US$12 for 2½ hrs, 4-6 passengers; shop around for best price, good fun and fishing; US$8 to visit La Restinga mangroves – ask boatman to go slowly so as not to disturb the wildlife. Pampatar has the island's largest fort, San Carlos Borromeo, and the smaller La Caranta, where the cannon show signs of having been spiked. Visit also the church of Cristo del Buen Viaje, the Library/Museum and the customs house (Aduana, now the offices of Fondene, the local development agency, can be visited during office hours, helpful and friendly tourist office on 1st floor, good maps and leaflets, open Mon-Fri 0800-1200, 1300-1630, T 095-622494). New hotels are being put up along this stretch. There is an amusement park to the SW of Pampatar, called Isla Aventura, with ferris wheel, roller coaster, water slide, dodgems etc, open Fri and Sat, 1800-2400, Sun, 1700-2400, and more frequently in peak holiday season. Entrance in peak season is US$5 adults, US$3.35 children, all rides incl; in low season entrance is US$0.50 and each ride US$0.30-0.60.

Pampatar Hotels   A2 pp *Flamingo Beach*, T (095) 624822, F 620271, 5-star, all-inclusive, food, drinks, entertainment, service, taxes, casino, good value; *Hippocampus Beach*, next door, T 623090, F 623510, 4-star, package holidays, gaudy; **D** *Residencial Don Juan*, with bath and fan; apartments sleeping 6 are available; beach restaurant *Antonio's*, rec; also *Trimar*, good value.

A number of good beaches are being developed on the eastern side. These are divided into ocean and calm beaches, according to their location in relation to the open sea. The former tend to be rougher (good surfing and windsurfing) and colder. Water is uniformly clear and unpolluted. Not all the beaches have local services yet, such as restaurants, though these, *churuatas* (bars built like Indian huts), sunshades and deckchairs are becoming more widespread. (Hire charges are about US$1.50 per item.) It is still possible, even in high season, to find practically deserted beaches. **A1** *Lagunamar*, a few km N of Pampatar, T 620711, F 621445, occupies a vast spread of flat coastland, beach, 9 pools and 6 restaurants.

On the eastern coast are *Playa Guacuco*, reached from La Asunción by a road through the Guayamurí reserve: a lot of surf, fairly shallow, palm trees, restaurant and parking lot; excellent horseriding here or up into the hills, US$30 for 2 hrs, contact Harry Padrón at the ranch in Agua de Vaca, or phone travel agent on 611311. Liquor shop at La Sabana sells ice by the bucket, cheap, 1 km before the beach. *Tamarindo Guaycuco Playa*, is a new 4-star hotel at the northern end of the beach in a rustic Mediterranean style, T/F 42272?. Parguito: long and open, best for surfing; Paraguachí: some *churuatas*.

Playa del Agua 45 mins by bus from Porlamar (US$0.45) is 4 km of stone-free white sand with many *kioskos*, which have palm-leaf shade areas. 2 sun chairs under one of these cost

US$8 (US$5 with an umbrella). The sea is very rough for children, but fairly shallow (beware the cross current when you are about waist deep, it gets very strong and can quickly carry you out to sea). This is the most popular beach on the island and at Venezuelan holiday times it is overcrowded. At other times it is ideal for sunbathing and walking; the fashionable part is at the southern end (interesting range of vendors on the beach—quail's eggs, caipirinha cocktails, coconuts, *cachapa* maize buns); the northern end is popular with younger people, is less touristy, has fewer facilities, and less shade. It's possible to see the island by Ultralight from here at weekends. Contact Omar Contreras, T 095-617632 or José-Antonio Fernández 095-623519, English spoken, US$35 per flight. (Also possible from the old airport at Porlamar.) *Restaurant El Paradiso*, southern end, rents out cabins, US$12, small but comfortable; *Kiosko El Agua*, helpful, English spoken; *Posada Shangri-Lá*, rec, *Casa Vieja*, seafood, *La Dorada*, French owned by Gérard and Hilda, with good beach view, rec as good value. Since the opening of the large *Playa El Agua Beach Resort* (L2) and the *Miragua Club Resort* (A3), many beach restaurants stay open till 2200. Rec are *Moisés* (Venezuelan-owned), *Sueño Tropical* (French-owned, popular with Germans), *Tinajón del Agua* (on main road near beach entrance, small, popular, good). Restaurants catering for the German market tend to be overpriced. **C** *Residencias Miramar*, Av 31 de Julio-Carretera Manzanillo, esq calle Miragua, 3 mins from beach, 1 min from supermarket, family-run, self-catering apartments, comfortable, barbecue, clean, rec; **B** the small *Casa Trudel*, T/F 589-548735, 4 rm, bed and breakfast, homely atmosphere, with bath (Dutch/Canadian owners), no young children, snacks served, barbecue twice a week, car rental, 5 mins walk from beach; **E** *Hostería El Agua*, Av 31 de Julio vía Manzanillo, T 48935, contact Sarah Studer, English, French German and Italian spoken, clean bathroom, good beds, fan, fridge, laundry facilities, 4 mins walk from beach; **B** *Pelican Village*, northern end, small group of bungalows, satellite TV, pool, restaurant, bar, German run, quiet. An un-named chalet park next to the *Miragua Club Resort*, self-catering, all facilities, very welcoming, highly rec (no price but "usually cheaper than *Miramar*").

Manzanillo (pop 2,000): water gets deep rather suddenly, fishing huts, fish sold on beach, apartments, expensive restaurant, Playa Escondida at the far end; **Puerto Fermín**/El Tirano (Lope de Aguirre, the infamous conquistador, landed here in 1561 on his flight from Peru), El Caserío handicrafts museum is nearby; Punta Cabo Blanco: attractive limestone outcrop; *El Cardón* (**B** *Hotel Karibek*, overlooks the sea, wonderful view, quiet, extremely clean, balcony, bath, fan, swimming pool, bar and restaurant adjacent, breakfast provided, evening meals not great but there are a couple of good restaurants down on the beach, easy taxi ride to other beaches, rec; **C** *Pahayda Vilas*, nice apartments, large rooms, 2 baths for 4 people, sign at main road; 100m further on towards Playa Azul, beach house with rooms to let and German-owned restaurant, good food). Between Manzanillo and Pedro González, each on its own stretch of beach, are two new luxury hotels. **A1** *Isla Bonita*, T (095) 657111, F 657211, Playa Puerto Cruz, a monstrous edifice of reflective glass, 18-hole golf course, business centre, posh restaurants; **A3** *Dunes*, Playa Puerto Cruz, T 631333, F 632910, a more modest option, all-inclusive resort of low rise, tiled buildings in pinks and creams, activities, sports, fun and games.

The coast road is interesting, with glimpses of the sea and beaches to one side, inland vistas on the other. There are a number of clifftop look-out points. The road improves radically beyond Manzanillo, winding from one beach to the next. Playa Puerto la Cruz adjoins **Pedro González** (pop 3,700), with a broad sweeping beach, running from a promontory (easy to climb) to scrub and brush that reach down almost to the water's edge (ask for Antonietta Luciani at *Restaurant Pedrogonzález*, she has an apartment to rent, US$40 per day, sleeps 6, well-equiped, rec as is her restaurant). The next bay is accessible by scrambling over rocks (major building here). There are a lot of pelicans and sea urchins (harmless).

Further W is **Juan Griego** bay and town (pop 8,300), a small, sleepy town whose picturesque bay is full of fishing boats, drawn up on the narrow beach or moored offshore. The little fort of La Galera is on a promontory on the northern side, beyond which is a bay of the same name with a narrow strip of beach, more fishing boats and many seafront restaurants. (**B** *El Yare*, T 55835, one block from beach, some suites with kitchen, owner speaks English, highly rec; *Hotel La Galera*, rec; **D** *Gran Sol*, La Marina, entrance in shopping arcade, T 55736, a/c, bath, TV; **E** *Residencia Carmencita*, Calle Guevara 20, T 55561, a/c, hot water, good; **E** *Fortín*, a/c, cold water, opp beach, most rooms have good views, good restaurant and tables on the beach; several others; also cabins for 5 with cooking facilities US$20. *Restaurant Mi Isla* is rec, also the Lebanese restaurant on the beach; *Viña del Mar*, opp *Hotel Fortín*, a/c, attractive, excellent food; *Juan Griego Steak House*, same building as *Hotel El Yare*, good value, rec; also rec, *El Buho*; *Viejo Muelle*, next door, good restaurant, live music, outside beach bar.) Playas Caribe (the best deserted beach) and Galera are less spoilt. (**D** *Posada del Sol*, bedroom, bath, kitchen, sitting area, clean, fan, fridge.)

South of Juan Griego, the road goes inland to San Juan, then to Punta de Piedra, the ferry dock, see below (a pleasant stretch through cultivated land and farms at regular intervals). Due

S of San Juan is El Yaque, near the airport and the mouth of the Laguna de las Marites. This is said to be the best place for windsurfing. Surf boards can be hired at the *Club El Mistral*, good service, very helpful and friendly, ½ day costs US$30. It is being rapidly developed with small hotels, but it suffers from aircraft noise and lacks public transport (taxi from Porlamar, US$5). **C** *California*, T (014) 951917, F 950908, 46 rm, small pool, new in 1994; **D** *Casarita*, T (016) 950290 (cellular number), new (1994), pleasant building in neo-colonial style, bed and breakfast, 400m from beach. Near San Juan is Fuentedueño park which has special walks. A branch goes NW to La Guardia at the eastern end of La Restinga. The dyke of broken seashells stretches to the Peninsula de Macanao: on its right a spotlessly clean beach, on its left the lagoon. At the far end are many little restaurants and a cluster of fishermen's huts with landing stages from which the launches make trips into the labyrinth of canals in the lagoon (US$14 per boat taking 5 passengers; bus from Porlamar harbourfront US$1, ask driver to drop you off).

The **Peninsula de Macanao** is quite underdeveloped, although it is hardly an untouched paradise. Construction companies are extracting large amounts of ballast for the building boom in Porlamar, while urban waste is simply being dumped in large quantities along the roadside. Some of the beaches, however, are highly regarded: Manzanilla, Guayaconcito, Boca de Pozo, Macanao, Punta Arenas and El Manglillo. Harbour at Chacachacare.

THE GUAYANA HIGHLANDS (7)

The historic Ciudad Bolívar on the Río Orinoco, besides being worth a visit in itself (not least for the sunsets on the river), is a good starting place for the superb landscapes further S, notably the table-top mountains and waterfalls around Canaima. The most spectacular of all is Angel Falls. Man-made features include the huge hydroelectric scheme at Guri and the industries at Ciudad Guyana, from where the Orinoco Delta can be reached.

These uplands, lying S of the Orinoco River, constitute half of Venezuela. They rise, in rounded forested hills and narrow valleys, to flat topped tablelands on the borders of Brazil. These lands with savannas interspersed with semi-deciduous forest are very sparsely populated. So far, communications have been the main difficulty, but a road has now been opened to Santa Elena de Uairén on the Brazilian frontier (see p 1429). This road can be followed to Manaus, and thence, by a suitable vehicle (if roads are open), to Brasília and southern Brazil. The area is Venezuela's largest gold and diamond source, but its immense reserves of iron ore, manganese and bauxite are of far greater economic importance.

Ciudad Bolívar, on the S bank of the Orinoco, is 400 km from its delta and 640 by road from Caracas. Average temperature 29°C, but a cool and refreshing breeze usually springs up in the evening. It still has much colonial building, some under restoration, but is growing rapidly. Population 261,100. It stands by the narrows of the Orinoco, with its Cathedral (started 1764, completed 1840), on a small hill, and the Zamuro hill fort (1902), on another hill in the centre, dominating the city (entrance on Paseo Heres, closed 1200-1400).

The narrows, not more than 300m wide, gave the town its old name of Angostura. It was here that Bolívar came after defeat to reorganize his forces, and the British Legionnaires joined him; it was at Angostura that he was declared President of that Gran Colombia which he had yet to build, and which was to fragment before his death. At the Congress of Angostura, 15 February 1819, the representatives of the present day Venezuela, Colombia and Ecuador met to proclaim Gran Colombia. The building, on **Plaza Bolivar**, houses a museum (**Casa del Congreso de Angostura** built 1766-76 by Manuel Centurión, the provincial governor, guides in Spanish only). Also on this historic square is the **Cathedral**, the **Casa de Los Gobernadores de la Colonia** (also built by Centurión in 1766), the **Real Intendencia**, and the **Casa de la Cultura**. Also on the N side of the square, at Bolívar 33, is the house where General Manuel Piar, the Liberator of Guayana from the Spanish, was held prisoner before being executed by Bolívar on 16 October 1817. Piar refused to put himself under Bolívar's command. The restored **Parque Miranda**, up Calle Carabobo, is a shady place to relax; on one side is the old theatre, recently converted into an art centre. At one time the theatre was the Antigua Prefectura (1900-1920) and then a military prison. The present legislative assembly and **Consejo Municipal** are between Plaza Bolívar and Parque Miranda. When the town was still known as Angostura a physician invented the famous bitters there in 1824; the factory moved to Port of Spain in 1875.

There is a floating pontoon dock where ocean-going cargo boats can discharge, but the harbour is now naval. A walk along the river bank is recommended at dusk when the sun is setting. See the mural "History and Evolution of Guayana" on the Paseo, 100m long, painted in Jul 1992 by Agustín Palma. Launches take passengers across the river (US$0.25), but there are no other passenger boat services. The Paseo Orinoco leading W out of town goes to the **Angostura Bridge**, which can be seen from town. This is the only bridge across the Orinoco, 1,668m long (over a mile), opened in 1967 (toll US$0.80; cyclists and walkers are not allowed to cross, but military will flag down a car for you).

Just W of the centre is **El Zanjón**, an area of vegetation typical of the region. To the E is **Parque El Porvenir**, with botanical gardens. Outside the airport is the *Río Caroní* aeroplane, which Jimmie Angel landed on top of Auyán-Tepuy (**see p 1420**).

Museums The **Museo Soto**, Av Germania, some distance from the centre in pleasant gardens, has works by Venezuela's Jesús Rafael Soto and other modern artists, open Tues-Sun 1000-1700, free, rec. Museum at **Casa del Correo del Orinoco**, Paseo Orinoco y Carabobo, modern art and some exhibits of history of the city, incl a fat precolumbian goddess, and the printing press of the newspaper which spread the cause of independence; closed end-1993 for refurbishment. Has free town map (poor) and booklet on Ciudad Bolívar. **Museo Geológico y Minero** at the School of Mines in the University of the East (UDO), Av Principal, La Sabanita. **Archivo Histórico y Museo Etnográfico de la Guayana**, housed in the former prison and governor's mansion, 2 blocks from Cathedral on Paseo Orinoco ("very interesting and original display of Indian tools and artefacts in beautifully renovated premises"). Many other museums in the city: see above for **Casa del Congreso de Angostura**; **Casa de los Doce Ventanas**, Venezuela entre Babilonia y Las Delicias, the residence of President Soublette; **Museo Casa San Isidro**, Av Táchira (Tues-Sat 0900-1200, 1430-1700, Sun 0900-1200) a mansion where Simón Bolívar stayed.

You can buy baskets and items made by the Indians, and good hammocks. The gold orchid pin or earrings, or a gold nugget (known as *cochano*), are the best souvenirs of Venezuela (worth seeking out, but now rare, is the handmade orchid of red, yellow and white gold). There are many jewellers on Pasaje Guayana, which runs off Paseo Orinoco, and in Pasaje Gran Hotel Bolívar. Gold items of comparable price and quality can also be found on the Plaza Bolívar in Caracas and in Santa Elena de Uairén. A feature is the netting of *sapoara*, a delicious fish 30 to 35 cm long which pours from the inlets when the river begins to swell in late Jun at the start of the rainy season and swims up stream to spawn. During its short season this is the favourite dish of the town.

Festival 5-8 Sept, fair and exhibition.

Hotels A3 *Orinoco*, on outskirts, overlooking river, pool, tourist agency; **B** *Don Salo**, Av Bolívar, nr Av Táchira, seen better days, disappointing restaurant, difficult to find, though quite near the airport; **B** *Laja Real**, T (085) 27911, opp airport, swimming pool open to non-residents for US$5 per day, a/c, TV, clean, excellent restaurant; also near airport **D** *Laja City Hotel*, Av Táchira and Av Bolívar, T 29910/29920/29919, cheaper sister hotel of *Laja Real*, in quiet residential area; **D** *Da Gino*, opp airport, clean, good service, rec; **D** *Valentina*, Av Maracay 55, pleasant part of town, nr airport; **D** *Canaima*, Av Upata (far from centre), bath, a/c, clean, noisy; **D** *Florida*, Av Táchira y Mario Briceñol, T 27942, a/c, clean, friendly, good restaurant, near airport; **D** *Hotel del Sur*, Plaza las Banderas, far from centre, T 206241, clean, a/c, rec. On Av Moreno de Mendoza, near bus terminal is **D** *Universo*, rec.

For the cheaper hotels, take a red bus from the airport to Paseo Orinoco; at the eastern end there are many to choose from. On or near Paseo Orinoco: **D** *Gran Hotel Bolívar*, T 24402, F 23080, friendly staff, a/c, beautifully refurbished, travel agency, excellent restaurant on

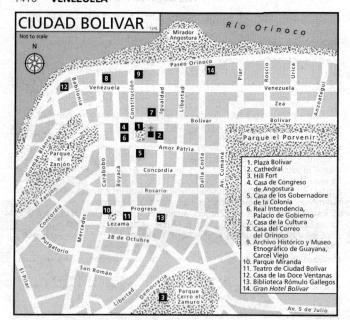

CIUDAD BOLÍVAR

Río Orinoco

Not to scale

Mirador Angostura

Paseo Orinoco

Venezuela

Constitución
Igualdad
Libertad

Pilar
Roscio
Urica

Venezuela

Zea

Anzoátegui

Babilonia

Guzmán Blanco

Bolívar

Bolívar

Parque el Porvenir

Amor Patria

Parque
el Zanjón

Carabobo
Boyacá

Dalla Costa

Av. Cumaná

Concordia

Rosario

El Zanjón

Concordia

Progreso

Mercedes

Lezama

28 de Octubre

Purgatorio

San Román

El Pilar

Libertad

Democracia

Parque
Cerro el
Zamuro

Av. 5 de Julio

1. Plaza Bolívar
2. Cathedral
3. Hill Fort
4. Casa de Congreso de Angostura
5. Casa de los Gobernadore de la Colonia
6. Real Intendencia, Palacio de Gobierno
7. Casa de la Cultura
8. Casa del Correo del Orinoco
9. Archivo Histórico y Museo Etnográfico de Guayana, Carcel Viejo
10. Parque Miranda
11. Teatro de Ciudad Bolívar
12. Casa de las Doce Ventanas
13. Biblioteca Rómulo Gallegos
14. *Gran Hotel Bolívar*

balcony overlooking river, good bar, spacious rooms with a/c, changes Amex, rec; **D** *Unión*, Urica, central, clean, good; **E** *Caracas*, Paseo Orinoco, friendly, safe, balcony overlooking river; **E** *Italia*, Paseo Orinoco, very friendly, a/c and bath, a few single rooms with fan, no bath, rooms on the second floor have a veranda overlooking the Río Orinoco, mixed reports on noise and insect life (1994), will store luggage, cheap restaurant, small portions, popular with foreign tourists, ask for Gilbert, a self-appointed local expert from Guyana, living in Venezuela since 1976, very helpful, organizes trips into the Gran Sabana; **E** *Sicilia*, Paseo Orinoco y Dalla Costa, clean, friendly, modern, noisy, laundry facilities, Italian and German spoken, good and safe, rec, also rec for tours to Canaima area; ask for Tomás and Francisco. **F** *Brasilia*, Av Morena de Mendoza, near bus stop, shower and fan, basic, double beds only; **F** *Pensión Yocaima*, just off Paseo Orinoco at E end (C Urica), reductions for more than 5 nights, quite clean, laundry facilities, fan, large rooms, friendly; **F** *Residencias Delicias*, Venezuela, clean, quiet, car-parking in garage nearby, US$0.50, run down but friendly.

Restaurants *Alfonso*, Av Maracay, for *criollo parrilla; Da Gino*, next to *Hotel Laja Real*, rec. *Savoy*, Venezuela y Dalla Costa, good value breakfast and lunch; *Mi Casa*, Venezuela, open air, good value; *La Gran Paella*, Av Vidal 12 and Av República, delicious food, popular with the locals; *Falcón*, Paseo Orinoco, very plush, food good but rather pricey; *España*, 1 block parallel to Paseo Orinoco, good and cheap, if basic. Chinese restaurant on Av Upata, opp *Hotel Canaima*, good, open late. On the corner of Bolívar and Cumaná is an excellent place for breakfast or snacks, good views, tasty *merengadas* and bread. *Bonbonería Exquisito*, near airport, pizzas, cakes, milkshakes and coffee. Cheap food at the market at the E end of Paseo Orinoco, need to bargain. The *Cervezeria* at Paseo Orinoco No 36 serves tasty *sopa de chipichipi*.

Exchange Banco Consolidado (American Express), Edif Pinemar, Av Andrés Bello, Centro Comercial Canaima; **Banco Royal Venezolano** (Calle Orinoco 38) and **Banco Mercantil y Agrícola** (Av Jesús Soto) will change dollars cash. **Banco Unión** (on street behind *Pensión Caracas*), accepts Visa and Amex cheques. TCs accepted by **Banco Consolidado** near airport. *Casa de Cambio* in *Hotel Laja Real* has good rates and is quick (check your change); *Gran Hotel Bolívar* will change US$ cash and TCs at any time but at poor rates.

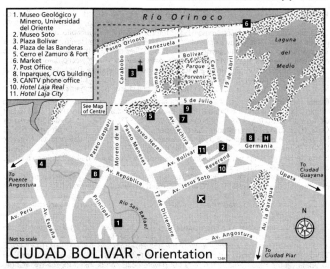

1. Museo Geológico y Minero, Universidad del Oriente
2. Museo Soto
3. Plaza Bolívar
4. Plaza de las Banderas
5. Cerro el Zamuro & Fort
6. Market
7. Post Office
8. Inparques, CVG building
9. CANTV phone office
10. Hotel Laja Real
11. Hotel Laja City

CIUDAD BOLIVAR - Orientation

Danish Consulate, Av Táchira, Quinta Maninata 50, of 319, T (85) 23490, 0800-1200, 1500-1700.

Post Office Av Táchira, 15 mins' walk from centre. **Telephones** CANTV, Av 5 de Julio, 100m from Av Táchira.

Shopping Supermarket close to the Museo Soto on Germania, large and well-stocked. Jewellery shop, *Van Buren*, Av Venezuela 27, behind Paseo Orinoco, fluent English spoken, highly rec. **Camping equipment** White gas (stove fuel) is available at Av República 16, near the bus terminal.

Travel Agencies *Venezolano Internacional de Turismo*, Av Andrés Bello and at the airport, rec for tours to Canaima and Gran Sabana, English spoken; *Marina Río Orinoco*, F (085) 49868, run by Reagan Kennedy and Javier Cubillos, tours to Roraima, 8 days and 7 nights, tents, sleeping bags provided, good English spoken, a sympathetic young guy called Tachuela helps out, mountain walks incl, rec guide Miguel Gasca. *Agencia de Viajes Auyantepuy*, Calle Bolívar, Ed Roque, Centro No 8, T 20748, very helpful for tickets to Canaima, English and French spoken. Rafael Urbina at *SASTA*, T (085) 126931, has been rec. The tours desk at the *Hotel Laja Real* organizes trips to the Guri dam and fishing trips on the Orinoco. *Turi Express* at airport, run by Guillermo Rodríguez, arranges tours to Canaima and the Guri dam, good English, rec. Ask for Indian guide, Clifford Nathaniel, he speaks very good English, a worthwhile trip to Angel Falls, well organized and safe. See above, under *Hotel Italia* for Gilbert, who arranges tours with Lorena of *Aventura Gran Sabana*, who charges US$50 pp per day, incl lodging and food, little English spoken. The above list incl those tour companies and guides of whom we have received positive reports. Many tour operators hang out at the *Hotel Italia* (eg Nina, as well as Gilbert) and there are others in the city. Unofficial touts swamp the bars and restaurants around Paseo Orinoco. It is far better to go to your destination and find a tour there, eg tours to Roraima and Gran Sabana are best in Santa Elena or San Francisco de Yuruaní. Before deciding to purchase a tour with anyone in Ciudad Bolívar ensure that the guide who sells the package is the guide who leads the tour, that all equipment is good and waterproof, that initial prices are not grossly inflated and that you agree on what is being offered. We have received several reports of tours being subcontracted to unskilled guides by unreliable operators. One option is to hire a jeep (about US$120/day) and do your own tour. Motorized canoe trips to the Angel Falls are best organized in Ciudad Bolívar.

Tourist Office Av Bolívar, near Museo Soto, maps provided, quite helpful. You will need a map: the town has a rather confusing layout. State map on sale for US$1.

Taxis US$1 to virtually anywhere in town. US$1.50 from bus station to town centre.

Airport Minibuses and buses (Ruta 2) marked Terminal to town centre. Taxi to Paseo Orinoco US$1.50. To Caracas twice daily with Avensa, once a day Servivensa; Maturín, Avensa daily; Canaima, twice a day with Servivensa (US$83 return). Also flights to Tucupita, and to Porlamar (Isla de Margarita—Aereotuy daily). Aereotuy also to Santa Elena de Uairén and villages near the Brazilian border. Charter airline, Rutaca, is rec ("flies the world's largest single-engined biplane, the rugged Russian/Polish built 20-seater Antonov An-2", according to Richard Vandervord of Chertsey, England); ask for Jorge, and verify all prices. There are international phones at the airport and a good restaurant. Car hire at the airport. Check where tours start from as some fly from Ciudad Guyana (Turi Tours), and charge passengers for taxi transfers.

Buses Terminal at junction of Av República and Av Sucre. To get there take a bus marked Terminal going W along the Paseo Orinoco. Several daily to **Caracas** 8 hrs US$10.55, student discount US$6.50 (day and night buses, *por puesto* US$21), and to the coast: to **Puerto La Cruz**, US$5, US$2.50 with student discount, *por puesto*, US$10, 5 hrs; to **Cumaná**, US$6, 6 hrs with Expresos Guayanesa (8 daily); to **Maracay**, US$9.50, 10 hrs; **Valencia**, via Maracay, US$10. **Tumeremo** US$5.25; Tumeremo bus through to El Dorado US$5.75, 3 daily. To **Santa Elena de Uairén** direct with Línea Orinoco, Transportes Mundial (5 daily) or Expreso Rápidos de Güiria at 0500, 0800 and 1900, spectacular views of the Gran Sabana at sunset (book in advance), US$17.65, 11-14 hrs. To **Boa Vista** with Transportes Mundial, Mon and Thur at 2000 (sometimes once a week) US$25, 20 hrs. To **Ciudad Guayana** hourly from 0700 by Expresos Guayanesa, US$1.50, 1½ hrs, *por puesto*, US$3.60, 1½ hrs. Bus to **Caicara**, 7½ hrs, incl 2 ferry crossings. Bus to **Ciudad Piar**, US$1.40, 3 hrs. *Por puesto* to **Puerto Ayacucho**, 3 daily, US$12, 10-12 hrs.

73 km E of Ciudad Bolívar is *La Encrucijada*, a road junction/truck stop/small community. One hotel, **F** *La Gran Parada*, bath, fan, clean, good value, owner Tadeo Venarusso, speaks English and Italian and is very knowledgeable about the area. His family lives in Playa Blanca (see below). To the left of La Encrucijada is the freeway to Ciudad Guayana (37 km); straight on is the road to Upata via the Paso Carnachi (no ferry but private boats can be hired for the two minute crossing); to the right is the road to Ciudad Piar and La Paragua. On the right hand road from La Encrucijada turn left after 8 km, past enormous black rocks, on to an almost hidden trail. After a further 2 km is the **Cueva del Elefante**, where precolumbian relics were found and rock paintings can be seen. Following the track (10 km) one comes to *Playa Blanca* on the Río Caroní, where miners dive for gold and diamonds. Since the discovery of gold in 1991, the population of Playa Blanca has exploded. A visit is worthwhile, particularly to see the gold dredgers. Transport can be arranged with Tadeo Venarusso in La Encrucijada; his brother Gyani does boat trips. Tadeo also goes to rock paintings in the area; contact him at Apartado 186, Puerto Ordaz, Estado Bolívar, Código Postal 8015, or at *La Gran Parada*. **Ciudad Piar** (97 km, pop 21,100) is near the iron ore mountain (Cerro Bolívar—cheaper to visit from Ciudad Bolívar than from Ciudad Guayana). In this area is **A** *Hato El Burro*, run by the Ackerman family, English, German and Spanish spoken. Trips are arranged around their own extensive ranch, Guri dam, Angel Falls etc. Contact at Vía La Paragua, Km 434, Ciudad Piar, T 938148/931395, or Caracas T 782-0797/781-8778, PO Box 60636, Este Caracas, 1060. Following this route further through typical Guayana landscape you reach the village of **La Paragua** (107 km on a good, paved road), an old (1770), somewhat unfriendly port on the Río Paragua.

A dry-weather (Dec-May) overland route to Canaima follows the miners' track from La Paragua through savannah and heavy bush to *San Salvador de Paúl*, a large shanty town set amid a pockmarked landscape of diggings near the Río Caroní some 25 km S of Canaima, home to a shifting population of about 3,500 miners panning or dredging diamonds from local streams. It is a rough, but not unfriendly place with a Guardia Nacional post, numerous bars and several stores selling expensive supplies; gasoline is sometimes available but always hideously expensive. Bush pilots fly from the airstrip over to Canaima camp any day except Monday (engine maintenance day throughout the region).

The track begins opposite La Paragua, where a seat in the occasional jeep heading for Paúl may be found by asking around. Those with their own heavy-duty vehicle can cross the Río Paragua (which is getting wider as the Guri Reservoir approaches its maximum-fill level) on a *chalana* (car ferry), which operates during daylight hours for a small fee. The road is gravel for the 23 km to La Comunidad, crossing the Río Chiguao en route on a new bridge, then deteriorates (take plenty of food, fuel, spade and heavy tow rope and be prepared for unmarked turn-offs, deep gullies and narrow bridges) on the 56 km run S to the Indian village of Las Bonitas, a 15-min walk W of the Caroní (good camping and swimming but don't underestimate the current). A further rough 14 km leads to wheel tracks heading E across a ridge to Caño Negro, little more than a hut, where the resident family may arrange a crossing of the swiftly-flowing river by *curiaca* (dugout) to a small landing and hut on the E bank grandly named Puerto Kukurital. Normally a 2½-3½ hr march along the sandy jeep trail, first through forest and then across hot, open savannah with Auyán-Tepuy's looming ahead, is necessary to reach Canaima (but see below).

The above is the shortest crossing to Canaima but a *curiaca* cannot always be guaranteed here; most visitors continue on the track from Las Bonitas to the Karamacoto Indian village of **Tariapa** (28 km), where arrangements are made with the *capitán* of the village or his son for parking your vehicle and crossing the river (take plastic bags for protecting cameras, etc during the boisterous passage). It is a 30-min walk to the Río Caroní—"tannin-stained, powerful and absolutely beautiful" (Kevin Healey) – but if negotiating a return crossing try to fix a specified time (not always reliable, nor can they see the river from their village) or you could be stranded. On the E bank a scenic path runs N between parallel ridges to Puerto Kukurital, approximately 1½ hr walk. Advance arrangements can be made by mail to be met at Kukurital by a Canaima Tours jeep (Longrino Guerra, Canaima Tours, Avensa Canaima Camp, T/F 02-413696; take message to Avensa, Edificio Banco de la Construcción de Oriente, 10th Flr, Avenida Urdaneta corner of Platanal, Caracas). Alternatively, the Guardia Nacional at San Salvador de Paúl will call Canaima by radio to check on availability of jeeps for a pick-up; the service is charged on an hourly basis. Paúl is at the end of the road, a further 1 hr and 14 km S from Tariapa (135 km from La Paragua, 7 hrs of concentrated driving at the best of times), but separated from the Caroní by the rugged escarpment which marks much of the river's western margin. The Indians at Tariapa may sometimes take visitors in *curiaras* to the Yuri Falls, but may also have better things to do with their time and limited supply of oil and gasoline.

Angel Falls, the highest fall in the world (979m – its longest single drop is 807m) and **Canaima**, a nearby tourist lodge and hotel, 70 km down-river, are best reached from Caracas or from Ciudad Bolívar. The lodge is on the edge of a tannin-stained lagoon with soft beige beaches (chiggers *niguas* in the sand); the Río Carrao tumbles over seven splendid falls into the lagoon below. The country is very beautiful. Many package tours now visit Canaima on day trips, so it can be very busy and pricey.

Warning There are dangerous undercurrents in the lagoon; people have drowned while swimming near the falls. Tourists are not told of the possible dangers beforehand.

There are various excursions from Canaima, which are all worthwhile (and usually crowded). You can make walking expeditions into the jungle to Indian villages with a guide but bargain hard on the price. Other excursions are to the Mayupa Falls, including a canoe ride on the Río Carrao (US$45, half day), to Yuri Falls by jeep and boat (US$30, half day); to Isla Orquídea (US$50, full day, good boat ride, beach barbecue, island may disappoint); to Saltos de Sapo and Sapito, 3 hrs, US$13.

Lodging in Hoturvensa's *campamiento canaima*, T (Caracas 02) 562-3022, F 564-7936, is in quite comfortable cabins; each is complete with shower and toilet; there are no hardships whatsoever. Meals are basic, self-service, no choice; drinks are expensive (more than double the prices in Ciudad Bolívar). For those travelling independently, see below.

Hoturvensa's rates for 1 night, US$320, for 2, US$630, incl transfers, meals, boat trip and flight over the Angel Falls, weather permitting. The airfare with Servivensa is not incl, although a reduced price round-trip ticket is available for US$96 for those booked into the Canaima Camp. Otherwise the full air fare is US$157. Servivensa fares from Ciudad Bolívar or Puerto Ordaz are US$83 return; from Barcelona the same as Caracas. Servivensa also has flights from Porlamar. Do not rely on being able to change the return date on your flight and be even more wary of getting an open return. The airline is quite happy to change your ticket, but the next available seat could be in 5 days time and Canaima is a very expensive place to kill time in. All arrangements are made through Avensa Servivensa, direct (best in Caracas—address as for *Los Frailes*, p 1375; Ciudad Bolívar Avensa office is closed for most of the weekend) or through travel agencies.

Although the quickest and most convenient way to visit Canaima is on an Avensa excursion, it is also possible to travel independently and camp near Canaima: obtain a *permiso de excursionistas* from Inparques, Caracas, Av R Gallegos, Parque del Este, T 284-1956, opp restaurant *Carreta*, in Ciudad Bolívar, Av Germania, Casa de Gobernador, or at the CVG building in Canaima, US$1.50. No tents available for hire. It is advisable to take food, though the Indian village near Canaima has a small store selling mainly canned foods; also souvenir shop in airport, and the *fuente de soda* overlooking the lagoon. During the rainy season the town is full of mangos. TCs can be cashed in Canaima, at a poor rate.

Warning Necklaces of poisonous red and black seeds (rosary peas) are on sale here.

Alternative accommodation A1 *Posada Turística*, 1 km from the lake, basic, charges US$100d; **A2** *Campamiento Ucaima*, run by the daughter of the late 'Jungle' Rudy Truffino, US$80 with 3 meals, 2 hrs walk fromCanaima above Hacha Falls; **C** *Camp Churún Vena*, in the village, clean rooms with bath and breakfast, hammock space with breakfast is also available at US$5; evening meals can be organized; some families in the village offer basic accommodation, some are expensive, eg US$40 for hammock outdoors under cover has been known, but usually US$15. Travel agencies rent hammocks for US$3-5 pp a night. Ask for details at the information desk at the camp. Alternatively camp for free; fires are permitted and plenty of wood is available. Do not forget swimming costumes, insect repellent and sun cream; waterproof clothing may be advisable.

Aereotuy runs one day excursions by 19-seat Dornier aircraft out of Ciudad Bolívar one landing at Canaima, the other at Kavac, giving good views of Falls. There is a connecting Aereotuy flight from Isla Margarita and direct excursions from Barcelona and Margarita (0730 departure returning 1800). Various companies offer 6-seater Cessnas to Canaima from Ciudad Bolívar, day excursions, book early, 0630-0700 at airport, US$120-160 (expensive for what is offered). Reductions are available for parties (note that these trips do not include a visit to Angel Falls, and that you may not even see the falls from the air in the rainy season—the additional cost of a trip to the Falls may well bring the cost of your journey up to that of a package).
    Recommended guides in Canaima: Tomás Bernal, who has his own camp on an island in the lagoon, beds and hammocks, popular with travellers, very knowledgeable about flora and fauna, contact in Canaima or through Agencia de Viajes Auyantepuy, C Bolívar, Ciudad Bolívar, T 20748/28702, or through Martin and Angelika working from the *Montaña* office at Ciudad Bolívar airport, German and English spoken; Canaima Jones, ask for him at the camp or Canaima airport; Matherson is a good Indian guide; Clifford. Kamaracoto Tours (rec), Gabriel González, Jorge Montes de Oca, Demetrio Zalazar, good tours, help with finding accommodation.
    Many agencies in Caracas, Ciudad Bolívar, etc, offer tours to Canaima, offering various accommodation, excursion and Angel Falls flight arrangements. Some are listed under Caracas and Ciudad Bolívar **Travel Agents**. When booking a package beware of agents telling you that all the guides speak English: some do, but many don't.

Trips by boat upriver to the ***Angel Falls*** only go June-Nov, leaving usually in the afternoon, staying the first night at Isla Orquídea, continuing to the Falls next day. 12 hr day trips cost US$70; more relaxing, but showing nothing different, are 44 hr, "3 day" trips. If you have a *permiso de excursionistas* (see above), you may be able to go on one tour and come back with another, giving yourself more time at the Falls (take all food and gear). (**NB** the falls face E so only receive sun in am.) The flat-topped Auyán-Tepuy, from which spring the Angel Falls, was the setting for W H Hudson's *Green Mansions*. The sheer rock face of the Falls, named after Jimmie Angel, the US airman who reported their existence, was climbed in 1971 by three Americans and an Englishman, David Nott, who recounted the ten-day adventure in his book *Angels Four* (Prentice-Hall). Jimmie Angel first reported the Falls in 1933; he landed his plane, the *Río Caroní*, on top of the mesa 9 October 1937 (see *South American Explorer*, No 40, May 1995, pp 22-30). The site is now marked with a plaque.

Trips upriver from Canaima to the Angel Falls are organized by several operators at short notice, including Isidoro Sandoval of Excursiones Churún-Vena SRL (rec, he has a video of a Japanese expedition which climbed the Falls in 1980). All *curiaras* (dugouts) must have 2 motors, by law, and carry first aid, life jackets, etc. Take wet weather gear, swimwear, mosquito net for hammock and insect repellent.

The cheapest way to fly over the falls is on scheduled flights from Ciudad Bolívar with Aereotuy to Kavanayen or Icabarú, or to Santa Elena de Uairén, calling at either of these villages, about US$24 single, sit on right-hand side. A highly recommended flight by Cessna 5-seater costs US$90 pp, leaves at 0900, takes 45 mins and does some circuits over and alongside the falls; there are also 20-min flights at 0930 for US$55-60 which return in time for the 1200 Servivensa flight out of Canaima (better than organized flights is to go to the airstrip and ask around the pilots waiting there on business if they will fly over the Falls for the same price as a tour).

Although not the highest or largest of the *tepuyes*, **Auyán-Tepuy** (600 km^2) is one of the more accessible. **Kamarata** is a friendly Indian settlement with a Capuchin mission on the plain at the E foot of the tepuy. It has a well-stocked shop but no real hotels; basic rooms can be found for about US$2.50 pp, camping also possible at the mission (mosquito nets necessary and anti-malarial pills advised). Take food, although there is one restaurant and locals may sell you dinner. Aerotuy fly from Ciudad Bolívar (2 hr) on Thur and from Santa Elena de Uairén on Mon. A co-operative of Pemón guides called *Macunaima Tours*, headed by Tito Abati, is based in Kamarata and can arrange *curiacas*, tents and porters for various excursions, take your own food (guide Jorge Calcaño is very helpful). The whole area is within the Canaima National Park. The local Indians have closed Auyán-Tepuy to climbers (1995). For details on the latest situation, contact *Alechiven*, run by Edith Rogge, which has a base and radio at Kamarata. T (041) 211828, F 217018. They and *Macunaima Tours* run 6-day river trips from Kamarata to Angel Falls (May-Dec), descending the **Río Akanán** to the Carrao by motorized dugout then turning S up the 'Devil's Canyon' to the Falls; the tours continue downriver to Canaima. About US$200 pp, supply your own food. River trips in this region are more logical in the rainy season.

Kavac, about a 2-hr walk NW of Kamarata, is a new Indian-run resort consisting of a dozen thatched huts (*churuatas*) for guests, a small shop, and an excitingly short airstrip serviced by Aerotuy prop-jets from Ciudad Bolívar (US$165) and Isla Margarita (US$240) daily except Mon; flights provide excellent views of Angel Falls and Auyán-Tepuy. There is a *carro* connection with Kamarata but it is expensive because all fuel has to be flown in. The prime local excursion is to **Kavác Canyon** and its waterfall known as La Cueva, which can be reached by joining a group or by setting out early W up the Río Kavac, following the waterpipe installed by the fathers at Kamarata to provide the settlement with water from the falls. A natural jacuzzi is encountered after a $1/2$hr wade/scramble along the sparkling stream, after which the gorge narrows dramatically until the falls are reached. Go in the morning to avoid tour groups. Lots of day trip tourists, therefore "swimming is rationed to 10 mins" (Bruno Schmid). The sun's rays illuminate the vertical walls of the canyon only for a short time around 1100. Be prepared to get wet; bathing suits and shoes with good grip, plus a dry change of clothing are rec; also insect repellent, since there is a mosquito invasion around dusk. Late afternoon winds off the savannah can make conditions chilly. Guide ropes have been installed where they are most needed along the river; there are pools and a further fall higher up the canyon but an Indian guide should be hired for this extension. A day excursion by light plane can be made to Kavac from Canaima (45-min flight) with *Hermanos Jiménez*; 0900 take-off, 1430 return, cost depends on number of passengers; part of fee goes to the Indians, who arrange a spicy chicken barbecue at the end of the outing.

In an area rich in natural resources 105 km down-river from Ciudad Bolívar an entirely new metropolis, known as **Ciudad Guayana**, is still being built. It is forging into one the four separate centres of San Félix, Palúa, Puerto Ordaz and Matanzas. Its population (516,650) has already exceeded half of the planned million, on the S bank of the Orinoco and both sides of the Caroní river before it spills into the Orinoco. The mixing of the rivers' waters is like "pouring cream into coffee". East of the Caroní are the commercial port of **San Félix** (work in progress to make a riverside walk and park) and the Palúa iron-ore terminal of the railway from El Pao. Across the Caroní by the 470-metre concrete bridge is **Puerto Ordaz** (airport), the iron-ore loading port connected by rail with the famous Cerro Bolívar open-cast iron mine (see below). The iron-tinted waterfall, which looks like a beerfall, in the pretty Parque Cachamay is worth a visit. To the W are the government-owned Siderúrgica del Orinoco whose production is being raised to 4.8m tonnes of steel a year, and an aluminium plant, Venalum. To visit Alcasa, another aluminium producer, T (086) 993431/2911, excellent tour, long trousers required, reached either from Ciudad Guayana or Ciudad Bolívar (US$1.40 bus from terminal, 1 hr), rec. About 3 km away, across bare savanna, is an area reserved for smaller industries. The Casa Machupicchu, Calle Guasipati, sells a city map.

Just up the Caroní is the Macagua hydroelectric plant (with a second phase under construction); there are some truly beautiful cataracts called Salto Llovizna as you enter the grounds (known as Parque La Llovizna, reached by bus from San Félix most of the way, then hitch). Higher up the river is the massive Guri dam and hydroelectric undertaking, **see p 1331**. The trip to Guri takes 90 mins by taxi; the plant is open daily 0900-1030, 1415-1515, for a conducted tour (4 daily, 1 hr) phone Edelca, Puerto Ordaz 20-80-66 (Relaciones Institucionales del Guri); the area gets very full during holidays, Easter or carnival. You can also visit the rest of the complex incl the hotel, C, a/c, comfortable; camping possible outside the entrance with permission. *Por puesto* from Ciudad Bolívar, Route 70, US$12.50 one way; for return, ask at Alcabala Río Claro (gatehouse) if they can get you a free lift. Excursion buses go from the main offices in the park at 1300 and 1500, take your passport. If no public transport, take a Ciudad Bolívar - Ciudad Guayana bus to Km 70 and take a taxi from there to Río Claro.

Hotels **L2** *Intercontinental Guayana**, Parque Punta Vista, PO Box 293, T 222244, F 222253, all facilities, swimming pool; **B** *El Rasil*, Centro Cívico, with all comforts, swimming pool, intermittent hot water, overpriced, rooms good but food and service poor, car hire rep is helpful; **B** *Dos Ríos*, México esq Ecuador, T (080) 220679, shower, a/c, clean, has seen better days, helpful, swimming pool sometimes empty; **D** *Habana Cuba*, Av Américas, a/c, clean, unfriendly; tour agency organizes trips to Orinoco delta, rec; **D** *Tepuy**, a/c, Carrera Upata, Edif Arichuna, T 220102, clean, central; **D** *La Guayana**, Av Las Américas, clean, a/c, no hot water, rec; **E** *Turista*, Av Caracas, basic, friendly. Rolf and Rosa Kampen offer bed and breakfast at Calle Surinam 03-07, Villa Antillana, Puerto Ordaz, 3 km from central Pto Ordaz, no phone, no buses, so take a taxi, E per room, breakfast US$1.30, new restaurant, *Rincón Bavaria* serves Bavarian food, T (086) 220593, Rolf speaks English, German and Dutch, rec; ask here for Lobo (Wolfgang), who organizes trips to Río Paragua, well-organized, excellent cooking, anyone interested in excursions S of the Orinoco should get in touch, he can be contacted through Rolf. Many cheaper hotels in San Félix, the historical town, have been removed or closed down in the restoration works. Only **D** *Aguila* and *Yoli* (no hot water, otherwise OK) in San Félix have decent restaurants; Also, **D/E** *Hotel Mucuchíes*, Av Moreno de Mendoza, by Cine Cavoní, friendly, some rooms have TV and a/c, noisy, OK; **F** *Residencias Santa Cruz*, Av Principal de Castillito, opp General Electric, rec. 1 km S on 4 lane highway to Upata is **E** *Motel Los Faroles*, immaculate rooms and grounds, a/c, TV. It is difficult to find hotels because of the influx of workers, who live in them for lack of other housing. There is a very good *churrascaría* restaurant 15 mins walk from *Hotel Guyana* towards the airport, in an old hacienda building on the left, next to a *cervecería*, very good food, rec.

Local speciality *Parahifa* is an interesting local drink of passion fruit and orange.

Exchange Banco Consolidado (American Express), Calle Urbana, Edif Don Andrés. Banco Unión for Visa (cash limit Bs 8,000, but you can repeat the transaction). Banks will not exchange Brazilian currency. Very difficult to change travellers' cheques. Hotels give poor rates.

Brazilian Consulate Av Las Américas, nr CANTV, T (086) 227246, 0900-1700, friendly, helpful, visa issued in 1 hr, no onward ticket requested (some nationalities have to pay, eg Australians US$45). Information on roads in Boa Vista area.

Bookshop *Librería Orinoco*, Centro Cívico Puerto Ordaz, international magazines and English paperbacks.

Travel Agencies *Keyla Tours*, Av Monseñor Zabalete and Los Llanos, T 229195, F 226123, camping trips to the Gran Sabana, excellent guides, incl Steve from the USA, strongly rec (US$280 pp, 3 nights, 4 days, all inc). Also rec, *Selva Tours*, T 225537/225044, for trips to the Gran Sabana; guides Carlos Quintero (T/F 622480) and Eleazer (T 612867) also act freelance. *Piranha Tours*, at *Hotel Intercontinental*, runs good river trips, US$10 pp, to nearby falls, meeting of Caroní and Orinoco, etc. Recommended guide, *Richard Brandt*, T/F 224370 (or in Santa Elena de Uairén, T 220078/226813), who has his own car, speaks English and tailors trips to your requirements. Will lead climb of Roraima, fees from US$50-80 pp a day.

Car Hire 18 different operators at the airport, Puma cars rec; Hertz, Puerto Ordaz, rents 4-wheel drive vehicles. A car is very useful in this area, especially for visiting the Cerro Bolívar mine and Guri dam. Example price: Fiat Premio, for 4 people, approx US$250 for 7 days incl 150 km free per day.

Air Transport Airport, with daily flights to Caracas, daily flights to Barcelona and twice weekly to Boa Vista, walk 600m to main road for buses to San Félix or Puerto Ordaz.

Buses Bus station at San Félix, frequent minibuses to centre. Bus 0500, 0800, 1900 from Ciudad Guayana to **Santa Elena de Uairén**, US$9 with Líneas Orinoco, 0730, at least 12 hrs (or overnight bus, which misses the fine scenery, 9 hrs), via El Callao, also with Transmundial, daily, US$9, 10 hrs, few stops. **Tumeremo** (US$2.50), El Dorado (US$3.60) and Km 88; book a day in advance. *Por puesto* to **Ciudad Bolívar** US$3.60 (bus US$1.50); bus to **Maturín** US$4, 2½ hrs; to **Caracas**, US$10, 10½ hrs; to **Barcelona** and **Puerto La Cruz**, 8 a day; to **Cumaná**, 4 a day. To **Tucupita**, US$3 with Expresos Guayanesa at 0730 and 1400, 3 hrs, booking office opens one hour before departure, be there early. Minibuses in town are fast, frequent and cheap; fare San Félix-Puerto Ordaz, US$0.50; buses run until about 2100. Taxis San Félix-Puerto Ordaz US$1.50, Puerto Ordaz-airport US$2, airport-bus station US$2.50, San Félix bus terminal-Puerto Ordaz bus terminal US$3.50, bus terminal-town centre US$1.80, town centre-San Félix bus terminal US$2.50.

Excursions To Cerro Bolívar mine, take a *por puesto* (US$5.60) or hitchhike to Ciudad Piar, or go with guided tour organized by Ferrominera Orinoco at their headquarters building in Ciudad Guayana. Tours are free, and leave Ciudad Piar at 0900 and 1400. To visit industries in the area, ask at the Corporación Venezolana de Guayana, Departamento de Relaciones Públicas. Do not expect immediate permission and check if you need your own vehicle. Boat trips from *Intercontinental*, US$32 for boat (say 12 passengers), or US$8.50 pp.

From San Félix or Puerto Ordaz go down the Orinoco to **Los Castillos** (either by *por puesto*, 1 hr, US$1.50, or by bus to Aceiles, US$0.35, ask to be let off where pick-up goes to Los Castillos 0700, 1130, 1530, returns 0830, 1300 and 1700, US$1; difficult to get there by boat). It is possible to camp on the beach. Candes Tours run an excursion from Puerto Ordaz but only if there are not enough people. There are two old forts here: one on a huge rock near the water, the other on top of a hill and both in good condition. A tiny village (pop 500) lies at their feet. It is said to have been here that Sir Walter Raleigh's son was killed in battle while searching for El Dorado. From Los Barrancos, on the N bank of the Orinoco, opposite San Félix, *curiaras* and other boats can be taken to the delta; settle prices before setting out, take hammock, mosquito net and repellent, and canned food (in the rainy season, take a raincoat). A free ferry for foot passengers crosses to Los Barrancos; taxi from Puerto Ordaz to ferry, US$3, or take micro from bus terminal (not very safe); return trip about 1 hr.

A worthwhile side trip along asphalted roads can be made to the small town of **Tucupita** (pop 81,820), with an interesting cathedral, on the Orinoco delta. The climate is very humid. Travellers' cheques only accepted in the Banco Unión or Banco de Venezuela at the riverside.

Hotels E *Gran Hotel Amacuro*, Calle Bolívar 23, a/c, very good; **E** *Delta*, Calle Pativilca 28, a/c, basic; **E** *Pequeño*, Calle La Paz, unfriendly and full of bugs, safe, stores luggage, shuts firmly at 2200; and a few cheaper *hospedajes*. **F** *Victoria*, near Cathedral, with a/c, cheaper with fan, reasonable; *Pequeña Venezia* campsite, 20 km from Tucupita, good, with showers; will arrange river trips.

Restaurants *Tucupita*, Calle Bolívar, poor value; *El Río*, rec; *Refresquería La Cascada*, Monomo 25, English spoken; *Rincón Criollo*, cheap; *Capri*, on waterfront, good; *Latinaja*, large portions. A "dubious looking joint" on the plaza was the only bar one traveller found, and "for such a wet town, it was strangely dry, at least concerning alcoholic beverages."

Tourist Office Calle Dalla Costa al Lado (beside) Sonido Color 2000. Tourists should go here first for information on tours.

Transport Flights are available from Caracas (Servivensa). Taxi from airport to village US$3. *Por puesto* from **Maturín** or **San Félix** about US$6, 2-3 hrs; also buses from San Félix. Bus to Maturín, US$3 with Expresos Guayanesa, 1100, 3-4 hrs. Tucupita-**Caracas** by bus, 10 hrs, 2000, US$10; for **Puerto La Cruz** at 0730 and 1400, US$6, 6 hrs.

For a 3-4 day trip to see the delta, its fauna and the Indians, either arrange boats through the tourist office, or contact Juan Carrión (all the taxi drivers know him, but he is very expensive). Vessels are not easy to come by and are expensive except for large groups. Bargain hard and prices may drop considerably. Recent reports received incl Romero Ildemaro (ask at *Bar Warauno*, or Calle Tucupita 19) US$40 pp per day, basic but watertight accommodation, good food, hammocks and mosquito nets, rec. Raúl at the *Gran Hotel Amacuro* runs a one-day trip for up to 4, incl food and drink, incl visit to "Indian village", rec. Abelardo of *Delta Tours*,

Calle Bolívar, also rec for trips deeper into the region, US$60 pp, owner, Toni, from the USA, has his own lodge in the delta, US$85 pp per day (reductions for backpackers). *Aventura Turística Delta SA*, Calle Centurión, No 62, T (087) 211391, 1-5 day trips to the Delta Orinoco, Nicolás and Vidalig are very helpful, they speak French and English. Some boat owners visit hotels in the evenings looking for clients and may negotiate a price. Some guides are reported to pester visitors as soon as they get off the bus. There are other guides from Ciudad Guayana whose boats are unsuitable and whose services untrustworthy. For shorter excursions by boat, ask at gas station (*bomba*) by the river. Excursions often only travel on the main river, not in the *caños* where wildlife can be seen. Alternatively, take a *por puesto* from Plaza Bolívar to the peaceful village of La Horqueta on the banks of the Orinoco (US$0.35, 45 mins), where it is easier to get a boat and where there are many Indians. There are no hotels, but there are shops selling drinks and dry foodstuffs. Be warned, if the river level rises after a downpour, arrangements may be cancelled. On all trips agree in advance exactly what is included, especially food and hammocks. Make sure there is enough food for yourselves, the guide and the Indians, and plenty of water. Hammocks and mosquito repellents are essential. You can buy hammocks and local handicrafts. Ask permission before you take photos of the Indians.

An interesting village is *Barrancas* (pop 13,000). Founded in 1530, it is one of the oldest villages in the Americas. Situated on the Orinoco, it can be reached by road from Tucupita, 63 km (*por puesto* to San Félix, US$4), or from Maturín. The cheapest hotel in town is the *Hospedaje San Judas*, near the church, with a restaurant next door, run by a helpful Guyanese woman. The village has a large community of Guyanese people who speak English. It is possible to take a boat to Curiapo (Indian village) and Amacuro (near the Guyana border), check at harbour, Señora Yúñez, lives next door to the bank, rec.

Warning Avoid boats that are carrying suspicious goods, those that do not have adequate shelter from the rain and those that do not stop in Curiapo, as this is the only place to get an exit stamp out of Venezuela.

It is possible to go to Georgetown from here, ask for boats to Amacuro (the trip to Bellavista, Cangrejito or San José de Amacuro, all at the mouth of the Orinoco, takes 12 hrs) and then onto Mabaruma (only for the adventurous), or check with the lady at the *librería* on the river at the bottom of the village. She is from Georgetown and travels there occasionally. The trip from Barrancas to Georgetown is likely to take 3-4 days.

Henry Marcano, Av Negro Primero 46, T (087) 711-1144 is planning to open a camp for ecotourism in the Orinoco; he speaks English and the local dialect, knows shamans and is an excellent guide, rec.

SOUTH TO BRAZIL (8)

The land route to Boa Vista, Brazil, passes over the beautiful Gran Sabana plateau, an ancient land of flat-topped mountains and waterfalls. The road is not difficult until you get to Brazil, or make excursions off it. The trek to Roraima, perhaps Conan Doyle's "Lost World", begins at a point on the highway S.

Travelling S from Ciudad Guayana to the Brazilian border is becoming an increasingly popular excursion for Venezuelan tourists, as well as for overland travellers heading for Manaus and the Amazon. It is no longer an arduous trip; the road to the border at Santa Elena de Uairén is now completely paved, with all bridges in place. Four-wheel drive is only necessary if one wanders off the main road, particularly in the rainy season. It is no longer forbidden to travel beyond Km 88 or off the main road without a spare 20 litres of gasoline, but spare tanks are highly recommended (spare tanks are available there, but better and cheaper to get one earlier). All petrol pumps have fuel, but not all octane levels. It is also advisable to carry extra water and plenty of food. If hitchhiking note that if a ride

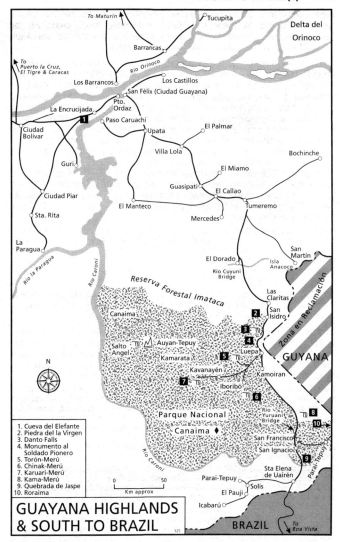

To Maturin

Tucupita

Delta del
Orinoco

Barrancas

Rio Orinoco

To
Puerto la Cruz,
El Tigre y Caracas

Los Barrancos

Los Castillos

San Félix (Ciudad Guayana)

La Encrucijada

Pto.
Ordaz

1

Paso Caruachi

Ciudad
Bolívar

Upata

El Palmar

Guri

Villa Lola

Bochinche

Ciudad Piar

El Miamo

Guasipati

El Callao

Sta. Rita

El Manteco

Mercedes

Tumeremo

La
Paragua

Rio la Paragua

Rio Caroni

El Dorado

Isla
Anacoco

San
Martín

Rio Cuyuni
Bridge

Reserva Forestal Imataca

Las
Claritas

San
Isidro

2

Zona en Reclamación

Canaima

3

4

Salto
Ángel

Auyan-Tepuy

Luepa

GUYANA

5

Kamarata

N

Kavanayén

Kamoiran

7

Iboribó

6

Parque Nacional

Rio
Yuruaní
Bridge

8

Canaima ◆

10

San Francisco
San Ignacio

1. Cueva del Elefante
2. Piedra del la Virgen
3. Danto Falls
4. Monumento al
   Soldado Pionero
5. Torón-Merú
6. Chinak-Merú
7. Karuari-Merú
8. Kama-Merú
9. Quebrada de Jaspe
10. Roraima

Rio Caroni

Parai-Tepuy

9

Sta Elena
de Uairén

0   50

Parai-Tepuy

Solís

Km approx

El Pauji

**GUAYANA HIGHLANDS
& SOUTH TO BRAZIL**

Icabarú

125

BRAZIL

To Boa Vista

drops you away from a "base" there will be no shade. Camping is possible but a tent with good waterproofing is essential (see also below, under Canaima National Park). Insect repellent and long-sleeved/trousered clothes are needed against small, black, vicious biting insects and against mosquitoes (especially in El Dorado, at Km 88 and at Icabarú). There are police checks at the Río Cuyuni and at Km 126, and at a military check at San Ignacio de Yuruaní all driving permits, car registration papers, and identification must be shown. 5-day/4-night tours of the Gran Sabana can be arranged in Caracas (US$297, incl hotel, food, excursions, eg *Passarini-Suárez*, Centro Comercial Los Altos, San Antonio de Los Altos, T 032-711327), or in Ciudad Bolívar (cheaper and easier).

South from Ciudad Guayana Highway 10 is a 4-lane *autopista* as far as **Upata**, pop 51,500 (Hotels: **D** *Andrea**, Plaza Miranda, credit cards accepted, restaurant, safe parking, good; **E** *Yocoima*, *Adriático*, good; *La Palma*, which also has a restaurant; **E** *Comercio*, Calle Ayacucho, excellent, as is its restaurant; water is rationed in Upata and hot water in hotels is rare S of Ciudad Guayana). There is a good place to buy provisions opposite the petrol station in Upata. From Upata to Km 88 the road is resurfaced and widened with broad hard shoulders. The rolling savannas become thick lowland forest. 18 km beyond *Guasipati* (pop 8,600; **C** *Hotel La Reina*, a/c, good; also **E** *Hotel Venezuela*) is *El Callao* on the S bank of the Río Yuruari, off the highway, surrounded by jungle. It is a small, clean, bright town (pop 7,400) whose Trinidadian inhabitants add a touch of calypso to its pre-Lenten carnival. A plant reprocesses the old gold mine tailings from El Perú, 8 km away, but the centre of gold mining has moved to Km 88 and Las Claritas (see below). The gold mine can be visited, the director will show you around. The town has many jewellery shops.

Hotels and services   D *Isidora*, TV, a/c, clean, on the road to El Perú but in town; **E** *Italia*, 10 rm, central, no phone; **F** *Callao*, Calle Bolívar, two blocks from the plaza, shared bath, extremely clean, laundry facilities, very friendly owners, rec; **E** *Ritz*, on same street as post office, basic, clean, serves cold beer; **F** *Don Pollo*; several restaurants. There is a chronic water shortage, check when it is available in your hotel. You may be able to change US$ cash in Banco de Venezuela on main square, but not TCs.

An alternative route from Upata to El Callao is to El Manteco along the shore of Lago Guri. At several points dirt roads lead down to the water where you can bathe or picnic. There is a hotel at El Manteco, **E**, a/c does not work.

On another 41 km is *Tumeremo* (pop 9,100), recommended as the best place to buy provisions. There is Banco de la Unión (Visa), Banco de Orinoco (Amex, after 1500 US$5 commission per transaction), and gasoline (all grades) at a normal price (better than El Dorado). 5 km from Tumeremo towards the Fuerte Tarabay is the beautiful artificial lake of San Pedro with an attractive campsite.

Hotels   D *Cacique*, very good, noisy, clean, excellent shower, friendly, rec; **D** *Miranda*, OK, better than some of the others; **E** *Leocar*, next to the bus-stop, fair, with shower and toilet, fan and a/c, some rooms with fridges, restaurant rec; **E** *Florida*, not too good; **E** *Central*, near plaza, fan, good (but may be "full", try again later), bakery and snackbar, clean; restaurant *El Esturión*, good, friendly, Calle El Dorado, Edificio Bolívar; *Restaurante Turístico* expensive but OK, does not serve yucca with everything; *Restaurante Las Cuevas*, nr plaza, medium priced, very popular, bedecked with tacky baubles and distasteful animal skins, food is average, service slow, add up your bill very carefully.

Bus to Santa Elena, US$8.75 (8-10 hrs, Líneas Orinoco, 1100, 2 blocks from plaza near *Leocar*); **El Dorado**, US$1.10, 1½ hrs; bus to Ciudad Bolívar, US$5.25, 6 a day, 6½ hrs or *por puesto* (via San Félix and Puerto Ordaz); bus to San Félix (Ciudad Guayana), US$2.50, *por puesto* US$5; bus Tumeremo-**Caracas**, US$35. Direct bus to Caracas departs 1600, 14 hrs.

From Tumeremo you can go to the *Isla Anacoco*, on the Río Venamo which forms the border with Guyana. A paved road runs through the jungle to San Martín (one military and one police post en route), where you can arrange a visit to the island. Much English spoken in San Martín; in a house opposite the water tank are some stuffed animals. From San Martín boats go to Nuevo Maico on the Río Cuyuní, US$0.12 fast boat, 1½ hrs, US$0.07 slow boat, 3 hrs. Dugouts (*piragua*) go from Nuevo Maico to Puerto Dedos, or Soledad at 0400, 0900, 1300 and 1800, 1 hr, US$0.20, from where you can travel to Bartika, 4 hrs, US$7 (boats leave at 0700 and 1200). In Bartika transport can be arranged to Georgetown (eg on horseback to Parika, US$4, then by road). Get a Venezuelan exit stamp before reaching the border and a Guyanese entry stamp at the earliest opportunity. The area around San Martín is a mining area and there are few tourists.

278 km from Ciudad Guayana and 76 km from Tumeremo is *El Dorado*, 7 km off the road on the Río Cuyuni, a hot, dusty miners' supply centre in dense forest (pop 4,000). On an island in the river stands the regional prison made famous by Papillon's stay there in 1945, in use again after renovation. It is possible to get police permission to cross the river and land on the island. The accompanying officer is full of interesting information. No charge for boat crossing. The local gold seams have been largely exhausted but mining still continues. El Dorado now relies for its existence mainly on its gas station (open 0800-1900, daily). There is no bank, exchange at El Dorado is possible with the gold buyer on the main street; cash only, poor rates. There is no telephone connection. Boat trips can be taken 12 km up the Chicanán river to a gold camp, US$15, or other road excursions to miners' camps, US$7.

Hotels NB All hotels in El Dorado have problems with running water. **D** *San Antonio*, Edif Ceferino, next to bus stop, electricity intermittent, prefers to let by the hour, fan, clean; **E** *Hospedaje Portugal*, 6 rm, the Portuguese owner also runs the store next door. **F** *Mirador*, basic, clean, good; *Alfonso*, quite good, will make excursions to the mines; *San Agostino*, main plaza; **F** *El Dorado*, with bath, very large rooms, clean, fan; **F** *El Valle*, friendly, basic, safe, rec. **Restaurants**: *El Minero*; *La Brasa*, on left when entering village, excellent food but small portions; *Archiven*, Plaza Bolívar, good, helpful owner; restaurant beside church serves delicious "criolla vegetarian" food.

Transport Bus from Caracas to El Dorado, Expresos del Oriente, at 1830 daily, US$12, 14½ hrs, return at 1400 (925 km). The Orinoco bus line connects with Ciudad Bolívar (6 hrs) and Santa Elena, as does Transmundial (better buses, leaving 1100, US$5.40 to Santa Elena, US$3.60 to San Felix, 4 hrs). From El Dorado a bus runs to San Martín on the Guyanese border (see above). All buses stop on main square.

Tours Contact Carlos at *Hotel San Antonio* for boat trips on the Río Cuyuni, US$25 pp per day, max 5 people, Indian guide.

The turn-off to El Dorado is marked Km 0; distances are measured from here and have new, green signs posted by the roadside 1 km apart. 6 km S of the turnoff to El Dorado, is the Río Cuyuni crossed by a bridge. From here it is possible to take boat trips to the gold mines, eg Payapal 1 hr 40 mins each way, US$25 for boat, beautiful trip; can also be visited by car, leaving from central plaza every hour or so, 30-min journey, US$8 return, people are friendly and will let you look into the 30-metre deep mines. At Km 67 there is said to be a trail that leads to Guyana. The forest again gives way to scrub; the roadside is dotted with tiny Indian villages—San Miguel de Betania, Araimatepui—and subsistence level farms. At Km 83, is *Barquilla de Fresa*, where tropical fish are bred (Henry Cleaver speaks English and German, accommodation in bunk beds, plus food, US$40 per day, trails for hiking, early morning bird-watching, car parking, safe—he also sells poodles). At Km 85 is another gold-digging village, **Las Claritas** (*Campamento Turístico Anaconda*, US$25 per night, cabins with shower, WC, fan, clean, well-furnished, with bar, table football and snooker; breakfast and dinner incl; run by Larri Master, who speaks English; another *campamento*, both reserved for tour groups. Restaurant; big market for food and gold; safe parking at Las Hermanitas de las Pobres (Convent), which can be better reached by the track from Km 88). This, and other settlements like it, is built out of oil cans and other rubbish, but complete with hotels, restaurants, small shops, hairdressers, brothels, etc. The miners guard their claims and diggings jealously, best to go with a guide or friendly local. If visiting independent miners at work, ask permission to take photos, and take a small present. Carlos Linares speaks German, organizes short or long tours to Gran Sabana and gold mines, charges approx US$30 pp per day; tours are off the beaten track and come highly rec. Carlos is contactable at the *Hotel Italia* in Ciudad Bolívar, or at his home address: Calle Ruiz Pineda 35, Barrio Libertador, La Sabanita, (Edo) Bolívar, T 085-510929.

At **Km 88** (also called **San Isidro**), there is gasoline (rarely 92 octane—the last before Santa Elena), a garage, a number of eating places and hotels: *La Pilonera*, opp Vargas store, **E** with fan, safe parking, some rooms with bath, overpriced, restaurant with good fruit drinks, very friendly; eat next door at the *Fuente de Soda*, good food, large menu; **D** *El Parador del Viajero*, with restaurant, OK. *Restaurant Internacional*, despite the grotty exterior, excellent, cheap and friendly. Everything is expensive, better food shops at Km 85. Gold is sold here. Bus Km 88-Caracas, US$10.50; to Ciudad Bolívar wait at gas station for buses from Las Claritas (dep 0900, 1100, 1500, 1800). Frequent *por puestos* from El Dorado to Km 88, 1 hr, US$2. The only reliable public transport out of Km 88 is the bus from Ciudad Bolívar, which stops at

1400 daily, 6 hrs to Santa Elena, US$4.50; the alternative is to get a ride with passing jeeps and trucks (very little passes after 1030). The wall of the Gran Sabana looms above Km 88 and the highway climbs steeply in sharp curves for 40 km before reaching the top; the road is, however, in very good condition and presents no problem for conventional cars. 4WD may be better in the wet season (May-Oct). At Km 100 the huge Piedra de la Virgen (sandy coloured with black streaks) is passed before the steepest climb (La Escalera) enters the beautiful **Canaima National Park** (30,000 sq km) one of the six largest parks in the world—to venture off the highway into the park, a permit may be required, check with Inparques in Ciudad Bolívar. Good views 100m W of the road at Km 102. The trail can be slippery, beautiful at sunrise.

NB To camp in the park, a permit must be bought at Inparques in Ciudad Bolívar, US$1.30 pp per night.

Characteristic of this area are the large abrupt *tepuis* (flat-topped mountains or *mesas*), hundreds of waterfalls, and the silence of one of the oldest plateaus on earth. The landscape is essentially savanna, with clusters of trees, moriche palms and bromeliads; there is plenty of firewood should you wish to spend a night under the stars, but nights are very cool. At Km 119 (sign can only be seen going N) a short trail leads to the 40-metre Danto ('Tapir') Falls, a powerful fall wreathed in mosses and mist. If you are paying for your ride, try to persuade the driver to make a short stop; the falls are close to the road (about 5 mins slippery walk down on the left hand side), but not visible from it. (Buses cannot be flagged down here because of dangerous bends.) On the E is Cerro Venamo, a cornerstone of the Guyana border only a short distance away. Further fine views at Km 135. The Monumento al Soldado Pionero (Km 137) commemorates the army engineers who built the road up from the lowlands, finally opened in 1973; barbecues, toilets, shelters. 4 km beyond is Luepa, whose fort is the HQ of the 'General Mario Montilla' Jungle Batallion (who maintain the road); all travellers must stop at the *ciudadela* (military checkpoint) a little way S. There is a popular camping place at Luepa, on the right going S which belongs to a tour company. An informative guide on duty will rent you a tent or you can hang a hammock in an open-sided shelter (very cold at night, no water or facilities, possible to buy meal from tour group but expensive). There is a breakfast place, US$4.

8 km beyond Luepa, a graded gravel road leads 70 km W to **Kavanayén** (little traffic, best to have your own vehicle with high clearance, especially during the wet season, plenty of snacks). Off this road after 25 km turn R to the falls of Torón Merú (17 km – road almost impassable for normal car, hell for cyclists, at the end is a river impassable for 4WD, continue on foot, falls hard to find). Further on is a left turn at Km 30 to the falls of Chinak-Merú, 110m high and very impressive. Take the trail to the Río Aponguao and the Pemón Indian village of **Iboribó** (very friendly, "gorgeous children"), tip someone to ferry you across the river and walk 30 mins to the falls, there is a trail descending to the bottom of the falls; boat trips to the falls cost US$12, 10 mins each way; alternatively take dugout canoe across river, US$0.45 and walk to the falls. This trip is reported not to be possible by normal car, take great care near the falls. 18 km before Kavanayén is a rough road to the **E** *Hotel Chivaton*, good beds but icy water, no food, very isolated, rec. Kavanayén is the site of a Franciscan mission, founded in 1943, accommodation at the mission G, one of the two grocery stores will prepare food, or restaurant opposite serves cheap breakfasts and dinners, order in advance. Medical post near the airstrip (bargain with pilots to fly you over the Gran Sabana: a tour of Auyán-Tepuy, Angel Falls, Canaima and back to Kavanayén, costs US$200 for 5 passengers). The settlement is surrounded by *tepuis*. Beyond Kavanayén a beautiful but risky trail (18 km, 5 hrs walk) leads along flat-topped mountains to the Karuari-Merú Falls (good swimming in the pool below). Ask in the mission for information on boat trips and the trail W to Kamarata (see under Angel Falls, above). Although considered impassable for vehicles, there are a few 4 x 4s in Kamarata.

For the remaining 180 km to Santa Elena de Uairén few people and only a handful of Pemón Indian villages are to be seen. Kampirán, **Kamoirán** (Km 176, restaurant, good breakfast, eggs, arepas, coffee, reasonable lunch with "incredibly strong salsa picante", rapids in the back garden, rooms to let, D, gasoline) and Oriwarai are passed. The impressive falls at the Kama river should not be missed (Km 205, 82m high, but the viewpoint is used as a public toilet); there is also a small lake, Indian handicrafts for sale, biting insects, canoe trips US$1.50/hr pp. There is a native hut to rent, E, or you can sling a hammock in a cabaña, F, or pitch your tent in the camping area, G (ferocious *plagas* by the falls, long trousers or a good insect repellent essential, and very cold at night). No facilities, take water purification tablets. There is an overpriced restaurant and a small shop. Buses can be flagged down going S or N 3 times a day: check times in advance. Río Soruape is a breathtakingly beautiful spot with rapids, waterfalls, warm water for fishing, swimming and sunbathing, plains, waterfalls, palm trees, *tepuis* in the distance, very quiet. Km 245, Río Sarapan falls, hotel, campsite, immaculately kept, with toilets, canned drinks sold but no restaurant, no charge for tents, small huts for rent, US$5-7.50 per night, lots of insects. At Km 249 is the Río Yuruaní (new bridge opened 1992) in the **Quebrada Pacheco** (small National Parks office, shop, good place to camp), full of splendid waterfalls and pools where you can swim; a 15-minute hike to the Yuruaní waterfall leaves the main road 250m after the crossing, turn left. Then comes the Pemón village of San Francisco de Yuruaní **(see p 1431)**, followed, 9 km of bends later, by the larger village of San Ignacio de Yuruaní (military checkpoint; excellent regional food). As the highway crosses a wide plain, Kukenam and Roraima (the more southerly of the two) may be seen to the E on a clear day. A trail at Km 275 leads to the **Quebrada de Jaspe** where a river cuts through striated cliffs and pieces of jasper glitter on the banks (don't take them home to glitter on your shelf, don't walk on the jasper and don't add to the graffiti on the rocks). Visit at midday when the sun shines best on the jasper, or at 1500 when the colour changes from red to orange, very beautiful. Campsite beside the river, no facilities, bad drainage and exposed, not rec. About 30 km from San Francisco the highway begins to descend until, at the Río Cuquenán, it leaves Canaima National Park and runs the last few km to Santa Elena, 642 km from Ciudad Guayana.

Santa Elena de Uairén is a growing, pleasant frontier town (pop 7,330), established by Capuchin monks in 1931. The festival of Santa Elena, 9-19 Aug, features music, dance and handicrafts. Gold is reported to be a good buy here (better value than in Ciudad Bolívar). If the service station is dry, ask for Sr Lucca who sells gasoline out of barrels. Grocery store: *Tienda Mixta El Gordito*, English and French spoken. Passports and car documents must be stamped here if leaving or entering the country; the immigration office is beside the bus station on the N edge of the town on a hill opposite the Corpovén gas station (open 0800-1900, new station being built; the Brazilian Consulate is also here, open 0800-1200). If shut, go to No 26, uphill from gas station and ask for help. CANTV phone office for international calls, but not all day. There is an international phone which takes *tarjetas*.

Hotels Accommodation is often difficult to find because of visiting mine workers and Brazilian shoppers. **B** *Cabañas Familiares Friedenau*, self-contained chalets, clean and pleasant, also run trips to Roraima (see below), English and German spoken; **C** *Villa Fairmont*, at edge of town, a few minutes' drive from bus station, new, has aviary. **D** *Fronteras**, without bath, quiet, comfortable, fan, safe, clean, good restaurant; **D** *La Posada del Mesón*, Vía Penetración Sampai, T (088) 951443, brand new beautiful wooden bungalows, sanitary installations, modern and functioning, run by Margarita and José E Isurrualde, who are extremely helpful and friendly; **E** *Luz*, 2 mins walk from Plaza Bolívar, bath, fan, excellent, modern, very clean, comfortable beds, good meeting point, Roberto Fuenmayor Quintero (Tarzan) owns hotel, offers cheap tours, friendly, rec; if hotel's full, owner will help to find a room in a private home; **E** *Tropical*, hot water, modern, good restaurant next door, five minutes' walk from town; **E** *Yarimá*, clean, "appears to be a brothel", central, friendly, shower, no a/c, rec, good food; **F** *Alfonso's*, clean, basic, friendly owners, run day trips; **F** *Auyantepuy*, opp Ciudad Bolívar bus stop, with bath (cheaper rooms available), basic, not rec; **F** *Gregorio*, 10m to left as you leave bus offices, with shower; **F** *Hospedaje La Rica*, very clean, hot water, good value; **F** *Mini Hospedaje*, 2 blocks from Fronteras, clean, basic, friendly, some rooms with private shower; **F** *Canaima*, near bus terminal, clean, safe, parking. Opp airport, rooms to let at Sergio's *granja*, friendly, cheap. Rooms are difficult to find during the fiesta (if stuck, ask for Charlie at the **Hotel Fronteras**, he may be able to find you somewhere else to stay, or hang your hammock in one of the *hospedajes* for US$2-3).

Restaurants Two good restaurants on S side of town, *3 Vs* and a *Lonchería*, within a block of each other; *Roraima*, Calle Icabarú, opp hospital, very friendly, not too dear despite being tourist oriented, excellent steaks, highly rec creole and international cooking; *Agua Miel*, Calle Icabarú, opp the hospital, a short walk from the centre, very good vegetarian dishes and takeaway snacks, owner friendly and speaks good English; *Don Corleone*, Peruvian run, good food, rec; *Café Fantasía*, good food, rec; *Carlitos*, Brazilian run and oriented, around the corner from *Hotel Luz*, excellent food and juices, very friendly, cheap, highly rec but rarely open; *Pizzería Venezuela*, N of bus station towards centre, excellent value, very friendly, plays videos most evenings; *Petit Pois Pizzas*, best place for vegetarians, freshly made, lots of toppings, friendly, rec; the *Panadería* does excellent breakfasts, cheese and ham croissants, good coffee.

Exchange The main bank will not change money, so try the shops in the centre, eg *Casa de Los Cóchamos*, the gold shop S of main plaza, which changes TCs (lower rate than banks but good selection of gold), *La Boutique Zapatería* also changes TCs at reasonable rates, the grocery store *El Gordito*, the pharmacy (for Brazilian currency). Generally the rates are poor (check with travellers going in opp direction what rates should be); to obtain better rates you must wait until Ciudad Guayana, or Boa Vista if going to Brazil (change some money into Brazilian currency before the bus leaves).

For excursions into the Gran Sabana contact Karavare Tours; take food, water, warm clothing and insect repellent. Alternatively, ask for Runge and Irene. *Anaconda Tours*, Centro Comercial Augusto, Local no 2, Calle Bolívar, T (086) 223130/2864, highly rec for 2-day tour to Kavanayén, incl river trip to Kamak Merú falls and overnight at Chivatón camp, US$100 pp; also jeep transfer to and from Paraitepui, US$90-150 return. The owner of the *Luz Hotel*, Roberto Fuenmayor Quintero, arranges 2-day tours in his own vehicle, max 8 passengers, costing US$100 per day, or US$50 pp incl food, drink and accommodation, highly rec, also arranges tours to Roraima. Pablo Jallemilla, lives on Calle Akurima in the first house along from the Terminal de Pasajeros, 5 day tours from Santa Elena to El Pauji, and then through the Gran Sabana to Ciudad Bolívar, US$15 pp/day, no food incl, he works partly with Roberto Fuenmayor Quintero, itinerary, price, length of tour, etc is negotiable. Other guides incl Irmgard (Richard's sister), who lives in one of the Cabañas Friedenau S of Santa Elena in the street across the bridge on the R side, very highly rec, US$115 pp, everything incl, she will accept US$ cash and TCs, and will exchange money; Alfonso of *Alfonso Tours*, near main square; Frank Khasen, contact at *Fotozoom Roraima* (mixed reports); Alfonso Uztaris, Calle Urdaneta 187 opp Lavandería Monaucri; Gloria in tourist information at CANTV; Roberto Centeno, Cielo Azul, Hugo Pulgar of *Ecotur*, highly rec; and Jorge Salcedo (Maracucho), Taller Cabrera next to *Hotel Gran Sabana*. All do tours of Gran Sabana and to Roraima.

An office nr *Hotel Uairén* dispenses malaria tablets during office hours, Mon-Fri. Yellow fever inoculations are not available.

Mechanic Antonio Mejías, good, cheap, a miracle-worker. *Parks Auto Parts*, next to *Hotel Fronteras*, run by Floyd Park from Texas, USA, helpful.

Leaving by private car may involve a bit of a run-around, up to 2 hrs. **NB** If you need a visa for Brazil (check Brazil **Information for Visitors**), it is best not to leave it until Santa Elena. The Guardia Nacional headquarters in Santa Elena may give authorisation by radio if the border guards create problems. Staff at the Ministry of Justice next to the DIEX Immigration office have also been recommended as helpful. The new road to Brazil links Caracas with Manaus in four days if you drive hard. See Brazil, section 9, **Northern Brazil**, for a description of the road from the border to Manaus.

Transport to and from Santa Elena The bus station is by the immigration office, so you can theoretically get your exit stamp when the office opens at 0800 and then catch the early bus to Brazil, but passengers have been left behind. (**NB** The immigration office closes from 1200-1400.) The 16 km road to the border is paved. There is a twice daily bus to Boa Vista (Brazil) at 0830 and 1500, Eucatur (Sun 1330), 4-5 hrs, US$18 (cheaper in Brazilian currency; money changers on buses, but better rates at the bus office). Banks in Boa Vista will not exchange bolívares. There is no direct transport to Manaus, you have to change in Boa Vista. From **Caracas** it is best to go to **Ciudad Bolívar** and take either the Expreso Brazil-Venezuela bus direct to Boa Vista, or the Línea 5 Orinoco bus straight through to Santa Elena, US$17.65, 11-14 hrs, take food. From Santa Elena to Ciudad Bolívar, buses at 1500, 1700, 1800 and 2000 (overnight buses are overcrowded with no luggage space, watch your bags), or, at 1900, a more expensive a/c direct service overnight with Líneas Orinoco. Alternatively take a daily bus to Tumeremo or El Dorado; Transmundial runs from **Tumeremo** to Santa Elena (US$8.75) and from **El Dorado** (US$5.40, 6 hrs), returning from Santa Elena at 0830. From Tumeremo you can get a bus to San Félix (Ciudad Guayana), 4 hrs, or colectivo to Maturín, 2 hrs, but Líneas Orinoco go direct, day and night. Santa Elena-**Ciudad Guayana**, 0600, 1900, 2000 (US$10, 12-13 hrs), or Expreso Maturín goes to Ciudad Guayana and Maturín daily. Transmundial go direct to San Felix daily, 1800, US$9, 10 hrs, very few stops. Take warm clothing for overnight buses, some have a/c and the Gran Sabana gets cold at night (on the executive class, they may stipulate that the shades are closed throughout the journey, so as not to affect the a/c). Aereotuy has daily flights by Twin Otter, 1000, US$61.50, to Ciudad Bolívar, standby basis only on Sun; sometimes stops at Indian villages. To fly to Icabarú and the Indian villages of Uriman, Wonkin, and Kamarata you will have to charter an Airtaxi, quite expensive. Book a week in advance. Airport, 10 km from town. It is possible to take a day trip into Brazil if you leave your passport at the border post, but nothing much to see. Hitchhiking N from Santa Elena is said to be easy. Stand at the roadside at the garage just opposite the terminal. Expect a small charge, up to US$5.

120 km W of Santa Elena is *Icabarú*, a diamond-producing centre with few facilities, where

prices are understandably high. The road leaves the highway 8 km S of Santa Elena and after passing through a tunnel of jungle vegetation emerges onto rolling savannas dotted with *tepuis*. The road is in terrible condition: conventional cars and pick-ups will get no more than 30 km, 4WD only as far as El Pauji. Flying is the only alternative. At Km 58 is a Guardia Nacional checkpoint at Paraitepuí. At Km 68 is *Shailili-ko* camp, English, Italian and French spoken, rec. 17 km further is **El Pauji**, an agricultural settlement with a number of foreign residents (US$10 by jeep—if full, if not, cost increased—from Santa Elena, 0600, 3 hrs; ask in Santa Elena for possibility of a lift with families returning after buying supplies—you may have to pay). Ask for Luigi, an Italian at El Cajón mine (he speaks English). It is in a lovely area, with good walking. Excellent sights: Chirica Tepuy, huge, beautiful, jet black, surrounded by rolling savannah; Río Surucun, where the largest diamond in Venezuela was found; Salto Catedral, beautiful small hollow, lovely falls, bright red water below due to the tree roots, excellent for swimming; Salto La Gruta, very impressive falls, but very slippery; and El Pozo, just outside El Pauji, fine rapids and pools for swimming. It is 20 mins to Los Saltos de Pauji, good for a bath. A good walk is to the small hill, 2 km from El Pauji beyond the airfield; views from the crest one side into El Abismo, a huge canyon where the Brazilian jungle begins, 2-3 hrs from village, and on the other side down to the Venezuelan savanna (a beautiful area and walk, highly rec). A German-speaking guide is Marco, rec. Flight El Pauji to Ciudad Bolívar, US$60.

Accommodation in El Pauji, **F** pp *El Caminante* tourist camp, just after the bridge, coming from Santa Elena, run by Danielle, helpful and friendly, camping, trips arranged, good restaurant; in the village is the *hospedaje* of Mariella, near the airstrip and small store, cabins E, bath, clean, run by 3 women, friendly, English spoken, good food but rather expensive breakfast; **F** *Hospedaje Karaware*, run by Nelson and Elizabeth, helpful, friendly; **F** *Alojamiento Weimore*, on the other side of the bridge from Danielle's camp, has owner-designed space-age accommodation, peaceful, good food, natural pool; *Hospedaje Chimahtá*, just before the bridge is **El Merendero** restaurant. At **La Bodega** general store, Victoriano has information on guides for tourists. Jeep hire in El Pauji, US$50 per day. 15 km from El Pauji, at Solís, Arquimedes and Philippe have a tourist camp; they organize tours. 25 km from the town is the **Canta Rana** tourist camp with basic accommodation (owners, Alfonso and Barbara Borrero, speak German, English and Spanish); waterfall and lovely surroundings; they have a private plane that collects people from Puerto Ordaz (T 086-226851 or 220709, Sr Haissan Al Atrache).

Mount Roraima An exciting trip is to walk to Mt Roraima (2,810m), which it has been suggested was the **"Lost World"** made famous by Arthur Conan Doyle's novel (although conflicting evidence points to the Brazilian Serra Ricardo Franco near the Bolivian border W of Cuiabá as the site). Roraima is a word in the Pemón indian language meaning "The great, ever fruitful mother of streams". Owing to the tough terrain and extreme weather conditions, this hike is only suitable for the fit. Supplies for a week or more should be bought in Santa Elena, but cheaper and better to bring food from Ciudad Bolívar on the way up to the Gran Sabana. If your food is being supplied by a tour company, check what food you will be eating; often vegetarians go hungry. The jumping-off point is the concrete and corrugated iron Indian village of **San Francisco de Yuruani**, 60 km N of Santa Elena and 9 km N of the San Ignacio military checkpoint (at which you are required to register). One hostel here, **G** *Hospedaje Mínima*, shower, marginally clean, less than basic; three small shops selling basic goods but not enough for Roraima hike (buy supplies in Santa Elena). Buses from Santa Elena will let you off here and pick up passengers en route to Ciudad Bolívar at 1700 and 1900; jeeps may be negotiated with prices varying between US$2.50 and US$5.50. Meals are available and tents can be hired, US$3 each per day, quality of tents and stoves is poor, try to get hold of good equipment. Guides in San Francisco charge about US$20-25 a day, more if they carry your supplies: Basilio is highly rec though Carmelo is also good, Mario has not been rec. *Roraima Tour*, T (088) 951283, is also rec, they also rent some rooms and Ana Fernández is very helpful; they charge US$550 pp incl food, or US$100 for guide only (group rates can be arranged). The track to Paraitepuí, the nearest village to the mountain, leaves the highway a kilometre S of San Francisco; it is unsigned but easily seen. The badly eroded road winds across open savanna with patches of forest in the river valleys; bear right at the major fork, the other track goes to Chirimata (jeep San Francisco-Paraitepuí US$50); in the rain many vehicles get stuck on the last stretch and the authorities are tired of pulling them out; the full 25 km can be walked in 7 hrs). In Paraitepuí, the *cacique* greets visitors; he may provide a hut and will try to insist on providing guides (see **Note also** below); if requiring one, bring extra food for him; there are few supplies available here. One small shop sells soft drinks and biscuits. The Ayuso brothers are the best-known guides. The villagers speak Tauripen, the local dialect, but now most of them also speak Spanish.

The foot trail winds back and forth on a more direct line than the little-used jeep track; it is comparatively straightforward and adequately marked descending from the heights just past Paraitepuí across rolling hills and numerous clear streams. The goal, Roraima, is the mountain on the right, the other massive outcrop on the left is Mata Hui (known as Kukenam after the river which rises within it). If leaving the village early enough in the day, you may reach the Río Cuquenán crossing early afternoon; this river floods quickly after rain, the bottom is slippery and the current swift; take a 50m rope if not going with a party and be prepared to get wet (good camping here, you can swim in the many pools, lots of mosquitoes and *puri-puris* on river bank). Three hours' walk brings you to a lovely bird-filled meadow below the foothills of the massif, another perfect camping spot known as *campamento abajo*. The footpath now climbs steadily upwards through the cloud forest at the mountain's base and becomes an arduous scramble over tree trunks and damp rocks until the cliff is reached. From here it is possible to ascend to the plateau along the "easy" rock ledge which is the only route to the top. It is quite broad and supports much vegetation; it manoeuvres around three spurs, drops sharply in places, and passes under an icy waterfall before heading steeply and directly to the summit. Walkers in good health should take about 4 hrs from the meadow to the top. The vistas across the Gran Sabana are magnificent, and the summit is an eerie world of stone and water, difficult to move around easily. There are not many good spots to camp; best is *El Hotel*—a sandy patch under an overhanging ledge—to which red painted arrows lead the way to the right after reaching the summit. From *El Hotel* a marked track leads to the survey pillar near the E cliff where Guyana, Brazil and Venezuela meet; allow a day as the track is very rough. Full camping equipment incl stove is essential (an igloo-type tent is best for the summit), wear thick socks and boots to protect legs from snakes, also essential are warm clothes for the summit (much mist, rain squalls and lightning at night: beware) and effective insect repellent—biting *plaga* infest the grasslands. The whole trip can take anywhere between five days and two weeks; if you don't wish to camp on the summit, a trip to the top and return can be done in a day, but keep an eye on weather conditions. A cloud belt usually wells up around the massif after dawn and often remains all day to blot out Roraima, even though the summit may remain clear. The water on the summit and around the foot of Roraima, is very pure, but bring bottled water or a purifier for the Savannah. There is very little firewood on top, better to bring gas or liquid fuel stoves. Litter is beginning to appear along the trail; please take care of the environment.

NB The dry season for trekking is Nov-May (with annual variations); June-Aug Roraima is usually enveloped in cloud. **Note also** that the National Guard requires first-time visitors to have a guide beyond Paratepuí. While some feel a guide is unnecessary, most have found them of great assistance for the hike's final stages (it is very easy to get lost) and for showing dry cliff overhangs. One traveller only discovered he should have taken a guide on his way back, and was charged US$100 for its oversight. Thorough searches are now made on your return. Do not remove crystals from the mountain; on the spot fines up to US$100 may be charged.

INFORMATION FOR VISITORS

Before you go

Entry requirements

● **Documents**

Entry is by passport and visa (normally valid for 3 entries), or by passport and tourist card. Tourist cards (*tarjetas de ingreso*) are valid only for those entering by air and are issued by most airlines to visitors from: Andorra, Antigua and Barbuda, Argentina, Australia, Austria, Barbados, Belgium, Brazil, Canada, Costa Rica, Dominica, Denmark, Finland, France, Germany, Ireland, Italy, Iceland, Liechenstein, Luxembourg, Lithuania, Mexico, Monaco, Norway, Netherlands, New Zealand, St Kitts/Nevis, St Lucia, San Marino, St Vincent, Spain, Sweden, Switzerland, Taiwan, Trinidad and Tobago, UK and USA. They are valid for 90 days with, theoretically, 2 extensions of 60 days each permissible, at a cost of US$25 each (alternatively leave the country and re-enter). Overstaying your 90 days with-

out an extension can lead to arrest and a fine when you try to depart. DIEX offices in many cities do not offer extensions – best to go to DIEX, Av Baralt on Plaza Miranda in Caracas, T 483-2744, take passport, tourist card, photograph and return ticket; opens 0800, passport with extension returned at end of day. If you enter the country overland, you will be required to obtain a visa from a Venezuelan consulate prior to arrival. For a Tourist Visa, you need 1 passport photo, passport valid for 6 months, references from bank and employer, onward or return ticket, completed and signed application form. The fee in the UK is £22 (costs vary from country to country). Transit visas, valid for 72 hrs are also available, mostly the same requirements and cost (inward and onward tickets needed). DIEX in Caracas will not exchange a transit for a tourist visa. It appears that you cannot get a visa in advance in the USA (although a 1 yr, multiple-entry visa is available in advance from 455 Market St, San Francisco, open

Mon-Fri, 0900-1300, with US$ cash and letters of reference from your bank and employer), or Canada, so to apply for an overland visa in Colombia or Brazil you need: passport, one photo and an onward ticket. In Manaus you also need a yellow fever inoculation certificate. A tourist card issued by Viasa in Bogotá is only valid for arriving in Caracas by air from Bogotá, not if you travel overland. To extend a visa for one month, in any city, costs about US$25 (passport photo needed); it is best to leave the country (eg to Curaçao) and get a new one free. Consuls may give a one-year visa if a valid reason can be given. To change a tourist visa to a business visa, to obtain or to extend the latter, costs £42 in UK. Visas to work in Venezuela also cost £42 and require authorization from the Dirección General Sectorial de Identificación y Control de Extranjeros in Caracas. Student visas require a letter of acceptance from the Venezuelan institution, proof of means of support, medical certificate, passport photo, passport and £42. It generally takes 2 days to issue any visa. Tourist visas are multiple entry within their specified period.

NB Carry your passport with you all the time you are in Venezuela as the police mount frequent spot checks and anyone found without identification is immediately detained (carrying a certified copy for greater safety is permissible, though not always accepted by officials). There are many military checkpoints, especially in border areas, at which all transport is stopped. Have your documents ready and make sure you know what entry permits you need; the soldiers may be unfamiliar with regulations for foreigners. A press card as identification is reported to work wonders. Border searches are very thorough. Do not lose the carbon copy of your visa as this has to be surrendered when leaving the country.

● **Tourist offices overseas**
UK: 56 Grafton Way, London W1P 5LB, T 0171 387-6727, F 0171 383-3253. **Germany**: AM Burghof 11, Postfach 5019, D-66623, Nohfelden, T 49-6852-900599, F 49-6852-900555.

● **Tourist information**
Tourist information may be obtained from Corpoturismo, Apartado 50.200, Caracas, main office for information is floors 35-7, Torre Oeste, Parque Central, T 507-8831. *GAM*, the monthly *Guía Aérea y Marítima de Venezuela*, gives details of all flights into and within the country, but also of hotels, travel agents, car hire, etc.

Business visitors on short visits are strongly advised to enter the country as tourists, otherwise they will have to obtain a tax clearance certificate (*solvencia*) before they can leave.

● **Maps**
The official mapping agency is the Ministerio del Ambiente y de los Recursos Naturales Renovables, Dirección de Cartografía Nacional, Edificio Camejo, 1st Flr, Avenida Este 6, southern side ('very hard to find – dirty long concrete block E of Plaza Diego Ibarra'), next door to nature bookshop (see Bookshops in Caracas section, p 1188), although its office is not in the same building as the Ministry's other departments (Centro Simón Bolívar). 1:50,000, 1:100,000, 1:200,000 and 1:250,000 sheets covering most of Venezuela N of the Orinoco, plus some state maps and a 1:500,000 series. Apart from the *Guide to Venezuela* (see below), there is the *Guía Progreso* (published by Seguros Progreso SA, available at the company's offices and elsewhere), which is very detailed, but not very accurate S of the Orinoco. The best road map is published by Lagoven and a similar version by Corpoven but at twice the scale and with a very good street plan of Caracas on the back, available from most service stations (not just Lagoven's), latest edition 1989. Kiosks in Caracas sell poor maps of the country.

Health

Conditions are good. Water in all main towns is heavily chlorinated, so safe to drink, although most people drink bottled water. Medical attention is good. State health care is free and said to be good (the Clínica Metropolitana in Caracas has been rec). Some rivers are infected with bilharzia and in some areas there are warning signs; check before bathing. Inoculation against typhoid and yellow fever, and protection against malaria, is rec for the Orinoco and other swampy or forest regions. Malaria tablets may be obtained in Caracas from Hospital Padre Machado (left-hand building as you face it), T 618211, no charge; or Ministerio de Sanidad y Asistencia Social (MSAS), Torre del Silencio (SW corner of Plaza Caracas), División de Malariología, free, English spoken, yellow fever vaccinations also given; free; also at Instituto de Malariología, Calle El Degredo y Av Roosevelt, T 631-1859/631-0208, open 0900-1200, 1330-1600, metro to Maternidad and taxi, US$4, not easy to find. Mefloquine (anti-malarial), is not available, but chloroquine is, free; alternatively, bring malaria tablets with you. There is another branch of MSAS at 'La Pastora', Avenida Baralt No 36, where free yellow fever vaccinations are also given. It is as well to carry some remedy in case of gastric upsets. Factor 15 sun-tan cream is widely available. On the coast from Cumaná eastwards precautions against vampire bat bite are warranted since they can be rabies-carriers. Lights over hatches and windows are used by local fishermen to deter bats from entering boats and shore cabins. If bitten seek medical advice. When travelling to the mountainous areas, beware of altitude sickness. It is a good idea to acclimatize for a few days before embarking on mountain treks.

Money
● **Currency**
The unit of currency is the bolívar, which is divided into 100 céntimos. There are nickel alloy coins for 25 and 50 céntimos and 1, 2 and 5 bolívares, and notes for 1, 2, 5, 10, 20, 50, 100, 500 and 1,000 bolívares. There is a shortage of small coinage and small notes: many shops round up prices unless you have small change and bars may refuse to serve you unless you produce the correct change. In 1989, the official and free rates of exchange were unified. In response to the political and economic crisis of mid-1994, which saw the collapse of 10 banks, stringent exchange controls were introduced which, for the traveller, mean: to convert unused bolívares back into dollars upon leaving, you must present the original exchange receipt; only banks and authorized casas de cambio can legally sell bolívares; they may charge a commission of up to 2.5%. In mid-1995 the exchange rate was fixed at Bs170=US$1, with only marginally higher rates offered on the black market. A black market is emerging, though, and is illegal and hard to find. It operates at the Colombian border at Cúanta and in Margarita, where waiters and shopkeepers will often exchange cash or cheques; in mid-1995 it was about Bs235=US$1. If caught by the authorities, the money may be confiscated. Casas de cambio may be reluctant to change TCs; they always insist on seeing a passport and may also insist on proof of purchase. Ital Cambio seems to be the most fastidious; they may even take your photo. Mastercard transactions offer good rates. Banco Consolidado is affiliated with American Express, no commission, some branches cash personal cheques from abroad on an Amex card; Banco Unión and Banco Mercantil (not all branches) handle Visa and ATM transactions, incl cash advances and Banco Mercantil handles Mastercard. Thomas Cook Mastercard refund assistance point, Edif Cavendes, piso 7, of 706, Av Fco de Mirando, Los Palos Grandes, 1060 Caracas, T 284-3866/3255. When changing dollars cash in banks, it is best to go in the morning, queues can be very long. If changing money in hotels, do not take sterling or any other European currencies. There are cash machines for Visa, Mastercard and Amex at Simón Bolívar airport. Have money sent to you by telex and not by post, which can take weeks. Rates of exchange in hotels are generally poor.

NB It is quite common for tour companies not to accept credit cards, other than for flights, so you will need cash or TCs for buying tours.

Popular names for coins: Fuerte, Bs 5; Real, Bs 0.50; Medio, 0.25; Puya or Centavo, 0.05. The brown Bs 100 note is sometimes referred to as a marrón, or a papel, the Bs 500 note as an orquidea, because of its picture.

Getting there

By Air
● **From Europe**
British Airways and Viasa fly from London to Simón Bolívar, the former twice a week direct, the latter out via Paris, back direct. Viasa fly twice via Paris, once via Porlamar. Viasa also serves Frankfurt, Lisbon, Madrid, Milan, Paris, Porto, Rome, Santiago de Compostela and Zurich. The cheapest route from N Europe is with Virgin to Miami, then Avensa to Caracas. There are also services from Europe by Air France, KLM, Iberia, Alitalia and Lufthansa. There is a weekly flight from Amsterdam to Porlamar by Martinair, bookable in Holland and Germany, packages available.

● **From North America**
By air, passengers may reach Venezuela by American Airlines (New York, Orlando, Miami, Boston, Dallas, Washington, Houston), United Airlines (New York, Miami, San Francisco, Denver), Viasa (Miami, New York), Servivensa (Miami). Viasa and Air Canada (operated by Viasa) fly to Toronto; there are also many charters at holiday times.

● **Latin America and the Caribbean**
From Colombia (Bogotá-Caracas), there are direct flights by Viasa, Avianca, Saeta and AeroPerú. Also Viasa from Cartagena, and Lacsa from Barranquilla. Lacsa flies from San José (Costa Rica), Panama and Barranquilla (Colombia) to Caracas. From Argentina, Brazil and Bolivia there are direct services by Viasa, Varig and LAB. There is direct air service from Chile (Viasa and LAN Chile both have 2 weekly flights; connections can also be made

via Panama City on Lacsa), Peru (Viasa – Viasa tickets purchased in Peru should be checked most carefully, Saeta, AeroPerú, Servivensa, Avianca), Ecuador (Saeta, Servivensa, Avianca and Viasa – from Quito; from Guayaquil, Saeta), Santo Domingo (Viasa), Puerto Rico (American, Lacsa), Curaçao (ALM, Servivensa), Aruba (Air Aruba, Servivensa, Viasa; Air Aruba flights cheaper from Las Piedras, **see p 1365** than from Caracas), Bonaire (Servivensa and ALM). BWIA have services to Port of Spain (daily from Caracas). **Difficulties** have been reported in entering Trinidad unless with a UK, US or Canadian passport. LIAT flies twice a week to St Lucia; Air France flies to Guadeloupe once a week; Viasa daily except Tues to Havana.

Avensa/Servivensa operate an airpass, which must be bought outside Latin America or the Caribbean. It is valid for 45 days and passengers must buy a minimum of 4 coupons. No route may be flown twice in the same direction. Economy class only; children pay 66% and infants 10% of the adult fare. Prices are by Zone: Caracas to Aruba, Bonaire or Curaçao US$50; Caracas-Miami (but not Barquisimeto or Maracaibo-Miami), Caracas-Bogotá, Bogotá-Quito, or Quito-Lima US$70; Caracas-Lima US$180; Caracas-Mexico City US$200; any internal Venezuelan flight US$40.

By Road

International **road** connections are given in the text.

By Boat

Shipping routes are given in the Introduction and Hints, apart from those with Curaçao and Aruba, which can be found in the text under Coro.

● **Shipping a car from Europe**

Harms Hamburg of Bremerhaven ship a car in a container for US$4,100 plus port handling to Venezuela.

On arrival in Venezuela (La Guaira), you must get a letter from the shipping agent stating that the boat has arrived and go to the Tourism Department at Simón Bolívar airport where you must obtain a document identifying your car (take photocopies of driving licence, passport, tourist card, car documents and bill of lading). With this you can get your car out of the port: a shipping agent is not necessary, though knowledge of Spanish is useful. A freight forwarder can be useful; they charge US$40-45, agree price in advance. Go then to Aduanas Marítimas at the port with

your bill of lading, ownership documents and passport, and 5 hrs to spare. They stop for lunch 1200-1300 and close at weekends. You will have to pay US$100 to the docks company to get your car out. If you will be taking your car out of Venezuela overland, make sure that the freight forwarder gives you a sealed letter for Venezuelan customs at your point of exit.

● **Shipping a car from the USA**

Shipping a car from Miami to Maracaibo or La Guaira: Venezuelan Line (agent Oceanic Steamship Co – rec, contact Gene Taylor) and Delta Line, fare is less Maracaibo-Miami; no passengers. From New Orleans: Delta Line, passengers carried, but very expensive. Alternatively, agent Hansen and Tiedemann charges same price as Delta for vehicle, but you can accompany it at much lower cost (5 days, incl meals). Also rec: Coordinadora del Caribe Transmodal CA (CCT), Calle Veracruz, Ed Torreón, Piso 7, Las Mercedes, Caracas, T 927133. Also Seaboard Marine, agent in Venezuela, Conavén; their route is advertised as La Guaira-Miami, but actually goes to West Palm Beach, 80 miles N of Miami; almost impossible to travel with your vehicle. Vencaribe (shipping) agent is Taurel y cía, Edif Taurel, Calle Cuji a Romualdo No 69, Apto de Correos 1592, Caracas; representative is Sonigar on 3rd flr, but Paul Paulheim on 1st flr is helpful. In port of La Guaira Taurel is on main street, just ask; Johnny Hilahl is the representative, but Wendy the receptionist and Bobby Momighan are also helpful, all speak English. Taurel's shipping department is called 'vapores'. A rec agent for importing a vehicle is Sr Freddy Diz, T (031) 22028; for unpacking a containerized vehicle, Sr Gustavo Contreras V, Transporte Gusconval, T (Radio) 02-661-9222, or (031) 943901. At the shipping agent Transportadoras Marítimas Venezolanas, Centro Comercial Litoral, on the main street in Maiquetía, Carlos Hernández is very helpful.

Customs

● **Duty free allowance**

You may bring into Venezuela, free of duty, 25 cigars and 200 cigarettes, 2 litres of alcoholic drinks, 4 small bottles of perfume, and gifts at the inspector's discretion. New items to the value of US$1,000 may be brought in.

When you arrive

● **Airport information**

If you travel with Viasa or any other airline for which Viasa is agent, it is possible to check in the day before flying out of Caracas by taking baggage, ticket and passport to their office at Centro Comercial Tamanaco, Nivel C2, 'Predespacho', between 1500 and 2100 (cost US$0.40); take bus from Chacaíto. To avoid overbooking the Government now obliges airlines to post a passenger list, but it is important to obtain clear instructions from the travel agent regarding confirmation of your flight and checking-in time. **NB** Passengers leaving Caracas on international flights must reconfirm their reservations not less than 72 hrs in advance; it is safer to do so in person than by telephone; not less than 24 hrs for national flights: if you fail to do this, you lose all rights to free accommodation, food, transport, etc if your flight is cancelled and may lose your seat if the plane is fully booked. Beware of counterfeit tickets; buy only from agencies. If told by an agent that a flight is fully booked, try at the airport anyway. International passengers must check in 2 hrs before departure or they may lose their seat to someone on a waiting list. Viasa flights to Miami are often heavily overbooked. Venezuelans are prepared for this and check in during the morning before an evening flight. Read carefully any notice you see posted with the relevant instructions. Handling charge for your luggage US$0.50. When leaving Maiquetía airport, beware Gate 5. This is subdivided into gates A-D; hundreds of passengers with different destinations are crammed into a lounge where flights are not called and the monitor does not work. Keep asking the staff with the walkie-talkie if your flight is boarding. All flights are subject to delays or cancellation.

● **Clothing**
Tropical weight in normal city colours is best for business in Caracas, otherwise clothing is less formal, but smart jackets and ties are required in the most exclusive restaurants and clubs. In Maracaibo and the hot, humid coastal and low-lying areas, regular washable tropical clothing is used. For women: blouse and trousers (shorts quite acceptable on the coast); cotton dresses, with a wrap for cool evenings, and for air-conditioned restaurants and cinemas. Shoes are very good value. Cinemas may not admit men in shorts or anyone in flip-flops.

● **Hours of business**
Banks are open from 0830 to 1130 and 1400 to 1630. Mon to Fri only. Government office hours vary, but 0800-1200 are usual morning hours. Government officials have fixed hours, usually 0900-1000 or 1500-1600, for receiving visitors. Business firms generally start

work about 0800 and some continue until about 1800 with a midday break. Shops, 0900-1300, 1500-1900, Mon-Sat. Generally speaking, Venezuelans start work early, and by seven in the morning everything is in full swing. Most firms and offices close on Sat.

● **Official time**
In Venezuela it is 4 hrs behind GMT, 1 hr ahead of EST.

● **Safety**
In the cities, take the usual precautions to protect your valuables and belongings, but in addition, carry handbags, cameras etc on the side away from the street as motor-cycle purse-snatchers are notorious, especially in Caracas. Hotel thefts are becoming more frequent.

● **Shopping**
'PVP' on a label refers to the now-discontinued maximum authorized price system. While price controls remain in force, there may be shortages of some basic items (1995).

● **Tipping**
Taxi drivers are tipped if the taxi has a meter (hardly anywhere), but not if you have agreed the fare in advance. Usherettes are not tipped. Hotel porters, Bs 200; airport porters Bs 200/piece of baggage. Restaurants, between 5 and 10% of bill.

● **Value added tax**
IVA (VAT) at 12.5% is charged. It is set to rise to 15% in the second half of 1995.

● **Voltage**
110 volts, 60 cycles, throughout the country.

● **Weights and measures**
Weights and measures are metric.

On departure

● **Airport tax**
All tourists and diplomats leaving the country, except transit passengers, must pay US$10.60 (approx) at the airport or port of embarkation (payable in bolívares or dollars, Bs 1,800). Minors under 12 years of age do not pay the exit tax. Venezuelans, resident foreigners or those with a visa *transeunte* have to pay Bs 1,200 on departure. There is also an airport tax of Bs 60 for those passengers on internal flights, payable at every change of plane. Exit stamps for overland travellers, US$0.30 (except US$20 approx Maracaibo-Maicao, Colombia).

Where to stay

● **Hotels**
Fairmont International (**see p 1341**) will book

hotel rooms both in Caracas and in other towns, where they have 102 hotels on their books, not all of which are mentioned in these pages. Hotels marked with an asterisk (*) are bookable through Fairmont. Officially controlled prices exist for one-star and two star hotels. 12.5% VAT (IVA) is added to hotel prices, set to rise to 15% in second half of 1995. Hotels of our B price category upwards are often heavily booked up, especially in Caracas; advance reservations are advisable. 3-star hotels start at about US$15-20 a night.

● **Camping**

Equipment, perhaps not of the highest standard, is available at sports-goods shops in Caracas. It is impossible, in fact illegal, to refill portable gas cylinders. Cylinders are sold at Deportes el Llanero, Caracas, T 545-1634. Those using gasoline stoves should note that even the higher octane fuels will cause blockages of fuel jets. Camping in Venezuela is a popular recreation, for spending a weekend at the beach, on the islands, in the llanos and in the mountains. (People pitch their tents on Monte Avila overlooking Caracas.) Camping is not however used by travellers as a substitute for hotels on the main highways, and no special camp sites are yet provided for this purpose. Wild camping is much easier with a car than with just a tent. If camping on the beach, for the sake of security, pitch your tent close to others, even though they play their radios loud. For information on hiking, climbing and relevant equipment, telephone Alexander on (02)573-00-56 (Spanish only). See p 1428 on camping in the Canaima National Park.

Food and drink

Food

Both in Caracas and to a lesser extent in Maracaibo there are excellent restaurants specializing in foreign regional cuisines. There is excellent local fish (eg pargo or red snapper), crayfish, small oysters and prawns, though sole, trout and large oysters are imported. Sometimes there is turtle, though it is a protected species. Turtle may appear on menus in the Peninsula de Paraguaná as ropa especial. The Tarzilandia restaurant in Caracas also serves it. Of true Venezuelan food there is sancocho (a stew of vegetables, especially yuca, with meat, chicken or fish); arepas, a kind of white maize bread, very bland in flavour; toasted arepas served with a wide selection of relishes, fillings or the local somewhat salty white cheese are cheap, filling and nutritious; cachapas, a maize pancake (soft, not hard like Mexican tortillas) wrapped around white cheese; pabellón, made of shredded meat, beans, rice and fried plantains (vegetarian versions available); and empanadas, maize-flour pies containing cheese, meat or fish. At Christmas only there are hallacas, maize pancakes stuffed with chicken, pork, olives, etc boiled in a plantain leaf (but don't eat the leaf). The nearest thing to a boiled egg in most places is a huevo tibio. It comes without the shell because there are no eggcups. A muchacho (boy) on the menu is not a sign of cannibalism; it is a cut of beef. Ganso is also not goose but beef. Solomo and lomito are other cuts of beef. Hervido is chicken or beef with vegetables. Contorno with a meat or fish dish is a choice of fried chips, boiled potatoes, rice or yuca. Caraotas are beans; cachitos are croissants of bread. Pasticho is what the Venezuelans call Italian lasagne. The main fruits are bananas, oranges, grapefruit, mangoes, pineapple and pawpaws. NB Some Venezuelan variants of names for fruit: lechosa is papaya, patilla water melon, parchita passion fruit, and cambur a small banana. Excellent strawberries are grown at Colonia Tovar, 90 mins from Caracas. A delicious sweet is huevos chimbos – egg yolk boiled and bottled in sugar syrup. The Caracas Daily Journal (in English) lists many reliable restaurants in Caracas and Maracaibo. Venezuelans dine late.

Drink

Venezuelan rum is very good; rec brands are Cacique, Pampero and Santa Teresa. There are four good local beers: Polar (the most popular), Regional (with a strong flavour of hops), Cardenal and Nacional (a lisa is a glass of keg beer; for a bottle of beer ask for a tercio); Brahma beer (lighter than Polar), is imported from Brazil. There are also mineral waters and gin. Now there is a good, local wine in Venezuela. The Polar brewery has joined with Martell (France) and built a winery in Carora. Wines produced are 'Viña Altagracia' and 'Bodegas Pomar'. 'Bodegas Pomar' also produces a sparkling wine in the traditional champagne style. Liqueurs are cheap, try the local ponche crema. The coffee is very good (café con leche has a lot of milk, café marrón much less, cafe negro for black coffee, which, though obvious, is not common in the rest of Latin America); visitors should also try a merengada, a delicious drink made from fruit pulp, ice, milk and sugar; a batido is the same but with water and a little milk; jugo is the same but with water. A plus-café is an after-dinner liqueur. Water is free in all restaurants even if no food is bought. Bottled water in *cervecerías* is often from the tap; no deception is intended, bottles are simply used as convenient jugs. Insist on seeing the bottle opened if you do not want a mouthful of chlorine with your whisky. *Chicha de arroz* is a sweet drink made of milk, rice starch, sugar and vanilla; fruit juices are very good. Gin and rum at about US$2 and coffee beans at US$1.50/kilo are good buys.

Getting around

Air transport

Most places of importance are served by Avensa and/or Servivensa. Some internal flights are also operated by Viasa, while Aereotuy, Zuliana and Aserca (rec for good service) fly to a variety of destinations. For the Avensa/Servivensa airpass, see above. Internal airlines offer special family discounts and student discount but practice is variable, photocopies of ISTC card are useful as it allows officials to staple one to the ticket. Sometimes there is little difference between 1st class and tourist class fares. Beware of overbooking during holiday time, especially at Caracas airport; it is rec that you check in 2 hrs before departure, particularly at Easter. Internal night-time flights are scarce, and there is no late hour discount.

Land transport

● **Train**
The only passenger traffic of any importance is on the Barquisimeto to Puerto Cabello line. The 110 km Yaritagua-Acarigua-Turén electric railway line was opened at the beginning of 1983, intended mostly to transport agricultural products. It appears that passengers are now being carried on the Acarigua-Yaritagua stretch.

● **Road**
There are bus services between the major cities, but services are variable and slow. For night journeys in a/c buses take a sleeping bag or similar because the setting is set to freezing. Also take earplugs against the loud stereo systems. The colectivo taxis and minibuses, known in Venezuela as *por puesto*, seem to monopolize transport to and from smaller towns and villages. They may be reluctant to take luggage and the ill-kempt. If first on board, wait for other passengers to arrive, do not take a *por puesto* on your own unless you want to pay for the whole vehicle. Outside Caracas, town taxis are relatively expensive. If possible check the bus before getting a ticket. At peak periods *revendedores*

(touts) will try to sell tickets at 2-3 times face value.

● **Motoring**
A tourist can bring in his/her car without paying duty. See above for **Shipping a car from the USA** or **Europe** and under **Additional notes on motoring** in **Introduction and Hints**. A visa is required for overland entry (this is necessary despite what Consulates may tell you). An entry permit for a car costs US$10 and requires one photograph (takes 24 hrs); ask for a permit for 6 months, or unspecified time. **See also p 1385.** For vehicles with Venezuelan registration leaving Venezuela the following documents are required: an Automóvil passport book from the Touring y Automóvil Club de Venezuela, Apartado 68102, Centro Integral Santa Rosa, Locales 11 y 12, Calle A, Av Principal, Santa Rosa de Lima, Caracas, T 914879; the original car papers; the registration document; a police *revisión* obtained from the Policía Técnica Judicial; and a temporary import/export licence for a vehicle obtainable from the Ministerio de Hacienda, Caracas, or from a customs agent in San Antonio de Táchira (border town) for about US$100. The export/import licence and the passport book must be signed and stamped by the Customs Administrator. In the border area with Colombia, police checks are frequent; make sure you have all your papers. If possible, check all details on bringing in/taking out a car in advance. For third party insurance contact Sra Joaqui I de Castaneda (Corredor de Seguros), Av Andrés Bello y Av El Parque, Edif Oficentro, piso 6, San Bernardino, Caracas, T (02) 575-2522/574-6111. Short term insurance policies are available with Seguros La Seguridad, offices all over the country, sample price in 1993, US$7.50/month.

All visitors to Venezuela can drive if they are over 18 and have a valid driving licence from their own country; an international driving licence is preferred. It is a good idea to hire a car (**see p 1347**); many of the best places are off the beaten track. Some companies such as National have a wide network of offices in towns and airports allowing a fly-drive approach to travel, using a number of different vehicles. You have to have a credit card to rent a vehicle. Car hire with insurance varies from company to company: basic rates for a car are from US$45-60/day depending on make, US$117 for a van or 12-seater; government tax of 12.5% is also added. Rates tend to be the same in all cities, except on Margarita, which is more expensive. If planning to hire a car for any length of time it is worth the trouble to obtain a *licencia tempo-ral para conducir*; for this you require a medical certificate (eye examination, blood pressure, US$2, issued by an authorized medical centre, try Torre Phelps, Plaza Venezuela, Caracas), photocopy of your home driver's licence and two black-and-white passport photos which must be presented at the Ministerio de Transporte y Comunicaciones, Torre Este, Parque Central, Dep Licencias. If you have an accident and someone is injured, you will be detained as a matter of routine, even if you are not at fault. Do not drive at night if you can help it (if you do have to, don't drive fast). Carry insect spray if you do; if you stop and get out, the car will fill with biting insects.

In 1982 a nationwide speed limit of 80 kmph was imposed (rarely adhered to). The roads in Venezuela are very good, all major routes are fully paved and even the dirt and gravel roads are reliable. Motoring restrictions in Caracas include a ban on parking in front of a bank; motorcycles may not be driven at night; pillion passengers may not be carried on motorcycles if of the same sex as the driver. You are more likely to be penalized for infringing these rules than for driving through a red light; they are designed to improve security for banks and pedestrians. In addition, motorcyclists are obliged to wear a crash helmet but it must not be of a type which obscures the face. Use private car-parks whenever possible as break-ins on streets are common in Caracas and all large cities.

There are 5 grades of gasoline: 'normal', 83 octane; 87, 89, 91 and 'alta', 95 octane (average cost Bs 4-8, US$0.03-0.07 a litre). Diesel (US$0.03 a litre) is used by most goods vehicles, available from many filling stations in Caracas. Oil costs US$0.60 a litre. Service stations are open 0500-2100, Mon-Sat, except those on highways which are open longer hours. Only those designated to handle emergencies are open on Sun. In the event of breakdown, Venezuelans are usually very helpful. There are many garages, even in rural areas; service charges are not high, nor are tyres, oil or accessories expensive, but being able to speak Spanish will greatly assist in sorting out problems. Carry spare battery water, fan belts, the obligatory breakdown triangle, a jack and spanners. Some cars have a security device to prevent the engine being started and this is rec. **Warning** There is an automatic US$20 fine for running out of fuel. See **Tourist Information** under Caracas, and **Maps**, below.

● **Hitchhiking**
Hitchhiking (*Cola*) is not very easy but the Venezuelans are usually friendly and helpful if you know some Spanish. The best places to try are Guardia Nacional posts outside cities (may get free bus rides from them). It is illegal on toll roads and, theoretically, for non-family members in the back of pick up trucks. Some drivers may ask for money for the lift, especially if on a bus route, common in the Gran Sabana.

● **Boat**
In Amazonia wait at the police posts where boats are obliged to report.

Communications

● **Newspapers**
Caracas: *El Universal, El Nacional* and *El Diario de Caracas, La Religión, Ultimas Noticias. The Daily Journal* (English), *El Mundo* and *2001* (evening), *Número* (weekly), *Resumen* (weekly), *Elite* (weekly), *Momento* (weekly), *Venezuela Gráfica* (weekly), *Páginas* (weekly), *Semana* (weekly), *Ve Venezuela*, tourist bi-monthly. Maracaibo: *Panorama, La Crítica.* Puerto La Cruz: *El Tiempo.*

● **Postal services**
The postal service can be extremely slow and unreliable. Air mail letters to the USA or Europe can take from one to four weeks and registered mail is no quicker. Internal mail also travels slowly, especially if there is no PO Box number. As in other Latin countries removing stamps from letters occurs, Trish and Tony Wheeler suggest that you insist on seeing your letters franked because you are a collector. Avoid the mail boxes in pharmacies as some no longer have collections. A private parcel delivery company, such as DHL, will charge around US$60 for parcels of up to 500g to Europe.

● **Telephone services**
All international and long distance calls are operated by CANTV. Most major cities are now linked by direct dialling (*Discado Directo*), with a 3-figure prefix for each town in Venezuela. Otherwise CANTV offices deal with most long-distance and international calls in the cities outside Caracas. Collect calls are possible to some countries, at least from Caracas, though staff in offices may not be sure of this. Calls out of Venezuela are more expensive than calls into it and are subject to long delays. Local calls are troublesome and the connection is often cut in the middle of your conversation; calls are best made from hotels or CANTV offices, rather than from booths. Most public phones operate on pre-

paid CANTV cards in denominations of 500, 1,000 and 2,000 bolívares. Buy them from CANTV or numerous small shops bearing the CANTV logo, or a scrap of card reading '¡Sí! ¡hay tarjetas!' They are also sold by street vendors. Make sure they are still in their clear plastic wrapper with an unbroken red seal. Many small shops impose a 25% handling charge and *tarjetas* may be out of stock particularly outside Caracas or larger towns. International calls are cheaper with a *tarjeta*, minimum needed 500 bolívares; a 1,000 bolívares card is sufficient to leave a brief message calling Europe. You can make 3 1-minute calls to Europe for US$10 with a *tarjeta*, but you have to pay for 3 mins (at US$10) without one. To make an international call, dial 00 plus country code etc. Canada direct: 800-11100. For UK, BT Direct, 800-11440 (BT chargecard works from any phone).

NB Telephone, fax or telex are far preferable to cables. Ask your hotel for use of its telex or fax machine. Many shops now offer fax services, set price to Europe US$8-12/page.

Holidays and festivals

There are two sorts of holidays, those enjoyed by everybody and those taken by employees of banks and insurance companies. Holidays applying to all businesses incl: 1 Jan, Carnival on the Mon and Tues before Ash Wed (everything shuts down Sat-Tues; make sure accommodation is booked in advance), Thur-Sat of Holy Week, 19 April, 1 May, 24 June (24 June is the feast day of San Juan Bautista, a particularly popular festival celebrated along the central coast where there were once large concentrations of plantation slaves who considered San Juan their special Saint. Some of the best-known events are in villages between Puerto Cabello, and Chuspa, to the E, such as Chuao, Cata and Ocumane de la Costa), 5, 24 July, 24 Sept, 12 Oct, 25 Dec. Holidays for banks and insurance companies only incl all the above and also: 19 Mar and the nearest Mon to 6 Jan, Ascension Day, 29 June, 15 Aug, 1 Nov and 8 Dec. There are also holidays applying to certain occupations such as Doctor's Day or Traffic Policeman's Day. From 24 Dec-1 Jan, most restaurants are closed and there is no long-distance public transport. On New Year's Eve, everything closes and does not open for a day. Queues for tickets, and traffic jams, are long. Business travellers should not visit during Holy week or Carnival.

Local: La Guaira: 10 Mar. Maracaibo: 24 Oct, 18 Nov.

Further reading

● **Business visitors**

The *Guide to Venezuela* (925 pages, updated and expanded in 1989), by Janice Bauman, Leni Young and others, in English (freely available in Caracas) is a mine of information and maps (US$11). Bradt Publications of 41 Nortoft Road, Chalfont St Peter, Bucks, SL9 0LA, UK, publish *Venezuela*, by Hilary Dunsterville Branch, emphasizing the outdoors and national parks. Another similar book is *Hiking/Backpacking in the Venezuelan Andes*, by Forest Leighty, Venezuelan Ander Press, 30 Brittania Drive, Danbury, CT 06811, USA, 1983 (or Apartado 47713, Caracas 1041A), 150pp concentrating on Monte Avila and the area around Mérida, rec. There are many fine coffee-table books on the various regions of Venezuela, for example Charles Brewer-Carías' books on Roraima and Venezuela as a whole. Latin America Bureau will publish in Sep 1994 *Venezuela in Focus* (£5.99), a guide to the history, politics, economy and culture of the country.

Information for business visitors is given in 'Hints to Exporters: Venezuela', issued by DTI Export Publications, PO Box 55, Stratford-upon-Avon, Warwickshire, CV37 9GE.

Acknowledgements

We should like to thank Amanda Purves for updating this chapter; a major revision of much of the text was done by Richard Robinson, who travelled in Venezuela in Oct 1994. Our warmest thanks are due to Frances Osborn (resident in Caracas), Edward Paine (Last Frontiers) and José Troconis of Mérida (NAtour A), for much valuable assistance and to the following travellers: Antonius Ackermann (Oensingen, Switzerland), Daniel Aeberhard (Slough, UK) an excellent contribution, Jimmy Andersson and Christina Gustafson (Malmo, Sweden), Mark Atkinson (Woodlands, Australia), Louise Bach (Vestbjerg) and Tine Tang Klief (Aarhus, Denmark), Hubert Baierl (Augsburg, Germany) most detailed correspondence Pim and Simone Berger (Haarlem, The Netherlands), Stefanie Boelstneider (Hamburg, Germany), Claudia Böohler and Frank Busch (Berlin, Germany), Wim Van Brempt (Mortsel, Belgium), Gavin Clarke (Munich, Germany), Bernard Cloutier (Montreal, Canada), Judith Stanton and Mark Collins (London, UK) a helpful up-date, Mark Collins (Bristol, UK), Jane and Chris Cooper (Fareham, UK), Mary Crow (Ft Collins, USA), Karally Angulo (Merida, Venezuela and Gerhard Dalhoeven (Utrecht, The Netherlands), Robert

Dettmering and Almud Weitz (Berlin, Germany), Dr J Rudolf Dietrich (Basle, Switzerland), the late Bernard van der Dool (Leiden, The Netherlands), Gerd Dörner (Darmstadt, Germany), Jayne Dyer and Nicholas Hird (Bexhill-on-Sea, UK), John Edmunds (Saly Spring Island, Canada), Marzio Ferrato and Fiorenza Sabbadin (Padoua, Italy), Daniel Fumagalli (Zurich, Switzerland), Helene Keur and Geert Klein Geltink (Zwolle, The Netherlands), Gisa Gericke (Wetzlar), Nicole Hofmann (Weisbaden), and Tanja Wirth (Flörsheim, Germany), Loukas Grafakos (Papagou, Greece), Ana Gruys (Albuquerque, USA), Sietse de Haan and TTruas Koppers (Aruba), Michael Heinisch and Maria Bonnelykke (Vanlose, Denmark), Hannah Holm (Rochester, USA), Thomas Hülsmann (Erlangen, Germany), Steffan Janka (Zittau, Germany), Hilary Jebson (Vancouver, Canada), Patrick J Paludan (Valby) and Erik Hassenkamm (Valby and Skanderberg, Denmark), Allen Kamen and Maaike van Westen (Cambridge, USA), Ruth Klingberg and Lis Musholt (Copenhagen, Denmark), Thomas Kump (Switzerland), Mark Laptin (London, UK), Matthew Lavis and Matthew Simmonds (Bedford, UK) a very helpful letter, Riika Levoranta (Vammala) and Vesa Lampiner (Möjärvi, Finland), Clare Maguire (Altrincham, UK), Stuart McCook (Princeton, USA), Gunter Müurdter (Ulm, Germany), Annesofie Nielsen (Niva, Denmark), Carine Oesterle (Zurich, Switzerland), Paul Olai-Olssen (Oslo, Norway), Thomas Plöderl (GozoLinz, Austria), Suzanne Roberts (Montrél, Canada), Bruce Rumage (Pawleys Island, USA), Piero Scaruffi (Redwood City, USA), Bruno Schmid (Zurich, Switzerland), Doris Schmittat (Weisbaden, Germany), Kai Schubert (Geisenheim, Germany), The Schweers (somewhere in Colombia), Ludwig Seitz (Dossenheim, Germany), Rob Stanley (Toronto, Canada), Jan Stüve (Karlsruhe, Germany), Roman Stutz and Andrea Schmidiger (Marstetten and Willisan, Switzerland), S Nielsen and Hellmuth-Chr Stuven (Copenhagen, Denmark), M James Snyder (Radlett, UK), Dr Heike C Thuro (Heidelburg) and Dr S Stürzebecher, Berlin, Germany), Dino de Toffol (San Tomaso Agordino, Italy), Edward Paine (Long Crendon, UK), Anne Upzak (USA), Margot Verhagen and Carel van der Velden (Holland), Andrew Viggers (Manchester, UK), Phillip Williams (Yarley, UK), Christian Leonards and Sandra Winterhalter (Insel Reichenau, Germany), Rowan Wood (Aspen, USA), and Dan Workman (Yellowknife, Canada).

THE GUIANAS

LIKE the West Indians, the people of the three Guianas, Guyana (formerly British Guiana), Suriname (formerly Dutch Guiana) and French Guyane, are not regarded as belonging to Latin America. The explanation of these three non-Iberian countries on the South American continent goes back to the early days of the Spanish conquest of the New World. There was no gold or any other apparent source of wealth to attract the attention of the Spanish discoverers. This part of the coast, which Columbus had first sighted in 1498, seemed to them not only barren but scantily populated and seemingly uninhabitable. The English, the French and the Dutch, anxious to establish a foothold in this part of the world, were not so fastidious.

All three countries are geographically very similar: along the coast runs a belt of narrow, flat marshy land, at its widest in Suriname. This coastland carries almost all the crops and most of the population. Behind lies a belt of crystalline upland, heavily gouged and weathered. The bauxite, gold and diamonds are in this area. Behind this again is the massif of the Guiana Highlands. They reach a height of 3,000 feet (915m), in the Tumuc-Humac range, the divide between French Guyane and Suriname, and Brazil, and 9,219 feet (2,810m) at flat-topped Mount Roraima (see Venezuela, **South to Brazil**), where Guyana, Venezuela and Brazil all meet.

Thanks and acknowledgements for help with the Guianas sections will be found at the end of the chapters on Guyana, Suriname and French Guyane.

GUYANA

GUYANA has an area of 83,044 sq miles, nearly the size of Britain, but only about 2.5% (or 1,328,000 acres) is cultivated.

About 90% of the population lives on the narrow coastal plain, most of which is below sea level. A sea wall keeps out the Atlantic and the fertile clay soil is drained by a system of dykes; sluice gates are opened to let out water at low tide. Separate irrigation channels are used to bring water to the fields in dry weather. In several places fresh water is supplied by reservoirs, known as conservancies. Most of the western third of the coastal plain is undrained and uninhabited. Most people live either in Georgetown, the capital, or in villages which are strung along the main road running from Charity in the W to the Suriname border. Large wooden houses stand on stilts above ground level. The strange cultural mix—Dutch place names and drainage techniques, Hindu temples, mosques, coconut palms and calypso music—reflect the chequered history of the country. The rich agricultural land of this area is used for producing rice and sugar and for raising cattle. Coffee, fruit and vegetables are also grown.

Four major rivers cross the coastal plain—(from W to E) the Essequibo, the Demerara, the Berbice, and the Corentyne (which forms the frontier with Suriname). Only the Demerara is crossed by bridges. Elsewhere ferries must be used. At the mouth of the Essequibo river, 21 miles wide, are islands the size of

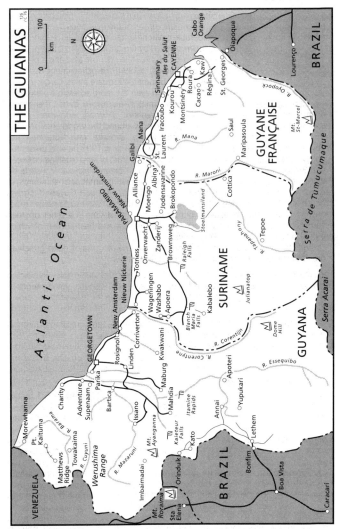

Barbados. The lower reaches of these rivers are navigable (75 miles up the Demerara to Linden and 45 miles up the Essequibo to the mouth of the Cuyuni River); but waterfalls and rapids prevent them being used by large boats to reach the interior.

Inland from the coastal plain most of the country is covered by thick rain forest, although in the E there is a large area of grassland. While some timber has been extracted, the main economic activity is mining: bauxite, extracted at Linden, Ituni and Kwakwani, is in decline, requiring massive investment to turn it round; gold and diamonds are sifted from the sand and gravel of the river beds by small teams of miners using mercury (at considerable environmental cost). The largest goldmine in the western hemisphere has been opened by Omai Gold Mines of Canada on the W bank of the Essequibo river. It is located in a fairly remote area and is planned to produce 250,000 ozs of gold for 10 years. In 1994, the government issued 12 new mineral prospecting licences, covering some 240 square miles. Large areas of rain forest are still undisturbed, however, and even the more accessible areas have varied and spectacular wildlife, including brightly-plumaged birds. The timber industry has been based primarily on Greenhart, a wood renowned for its resistance to sea water. It is used in piers and piles around the world and, until the introduction of carbon fibre fishing rods, was a favourite with fishermen and women. When the Duke of Edinburgh visited Guyana in 1992 he was presented with two Greenhart rods. Also in 1992, however, a tract of land totalling between 7 and 8% of Guyana's land area was granted to a Korean/Malaysian consortium, Barama, for logging (in 1994 Barama was meeting international standards of felling). At any event, timber exports are increasing, although Guyana's loggers practise selective, as opposed to clear felling in an effort to foster sustainable timber industry. Towards the Venezuelan border the rain forest rises in a series of steep escarpments, with spectacular waterfalls, the highest and best-known of which are the Kaieteur Falls on the Potaro river.

In the SW of the country is the Rupununi Savanna, an area of open grassland more easily reached from Brazil than from Georgetown.

The area W of the Essequibo river—about 70% of the national territory—is claimed by Venezuela. In the SE, the border with Suriname is in dispute, the contentious issue being whether high or low water is the boundary (in the area of the Koeroeni and New rivers).

The **climate**, although hot, is not unhealthy. Mean shade temperature throughout the year is 80°F; the mean maximum is about 87°F and the mean minimum 75°F. The heat is greatly tempered by cooling breezes from the sea and is most felt from Aug to Oct. There are two wet seasons, from May to Jun and from Dec to the end of Jan, although they may extend into the months either side. Rainfall averages 91 ins a year in Georgetown.

History The country was first partially settled between 1616 and 1621 by the Dutch West India Company, who erected a fort and depot at Fort Kyk-over-al (County of Essequibo). The first English attempt at settlement was made by Captain Leigh on the Oiapoque River (now French Guyane) in 1604, but it failed to establish a permanent settlement. Lord Willoughby, famous in the early history of Barbados, founded a settlement in 1663 at Suriname, which was captured by the Dutch in 1667 and ceded to them at the Peace of Breda in exchange for New York. The Dutch held the three colonies till 1796 when they were captured by a British fleet. The territory was restored to the Dutch in 1802, but in the following year was retaken by Great Britain, which finally gained it in 1814, when the three counties of Essequibo, Berbice and Demerara were merged to form British Guiana.

During the 17th century the Dutch and English settlers established posts up-river, in the hills, mostly as trading points with the Amerindian natives. Plantations were laid out and worked by slaves from Africa. Poor soil defeated this venture, and the settlers retreated with their slaves to the coastal area in mid-18th century: the old plantation sites can still be detected from the air. Coffee and cotton were the main crops up to the end of the 18th century, but sugar had become the dominant crop by 1820. In 1834 slavery was abolished. Many of the slaves scattered as small landholders, and the plantation owners had to look for another source of labour. It was found in indentured workers from India, a few Chinese, and some Portuguese labourers from the Azores and Madeira. About 240,000 had come from India alone by 1914. At the end of their indentures many settled in Guyana.

The end of the colonial period was politically turbulent, with rioting between the mainly Indo Guyanese People's Progressive Party (PPP), led by Dr Cheddi Jagan, and the mainly Afro Guyanese People's National Congress (PNC), under Mr Forbes Burnham. The PNC, favoured over the PPP by the colonial authorities, formed a government in 1964 and retained office until 1992. Guyana is one of the few countries in the Caribbean where political parties have used race as an election issue. As a result, tension between the main ethnic groups has manifested itself mainly at election time.

On 26 May 1966 Guyana gained independence, and on 23 February 1970 it became a cooperative republic within the Commonwealth, adopting a new constitution. Another new constitution was adopted in 1980; this declared Guyana to be in transition from capitalism to socialism. Many industries, including bauxite and sugar, were nationalized in the 1970s and close relations with the USSR and Eastern Europe were developed. Following the death of President Forbes Burnham in Aug 1985, Mr Desmond Hoyte became President. Since then, overseas investors have been invited back and relations with the United States have improved.

Elections to the National Assembly and to the Presidency have been held regularly since independence, but have been widely criticised as fraudulent. The main opposition parties were the PPP, still led by Dr Jagan, and the Working People's Alliance, which attracts support from both East Indian and African communities. Having been delayed since May 1991, national assembly and presidential elections were finally held on 5 October 1992. The polling was monitored by both the Carter Center and a team from the Commonwealth, who declared the elections free and fair even though the campaign was not free of incidents. The PPP/Civic party, led by Dr Jagan, won power after 28 years in opposition, and the instalation of a government by democratic means was greeted with optimism. The result also prompted foreign investors to study potential opportunities in Guyana. Recovery has to some extent begun, with 2 years of positive gdp growth recorded, but many feel that the government has not been quick enough in making important decisions. The economic recovery programme, part of an IMF Enhanced Structural Adjustment Facility, which aided economic improvement also seriously eroded workers' real income and hit the middle classes very hard.

The People Until the 1920s there was little natural increase in population, but the eradication of malaria and other diseases has since led to a rapid growth in population, particularly among the East Indians (Asian), who, according to most estimates comprise over 50% of the population. The results of the 1980 census were long withheld, possibly because of embarrassment over the high level of emigration (to the USA, Canada and Britain), but more likely because of the extreme sensitivity of the racial balance between the East Indian and African (black) communities. It showed the following ethnic distribution: East Indian 51.4%; black 30.5%; mixed 11%; Amerindian 5.3% (Carib 3.7%, Arawak 1.4%); Chinese 0.2%; white (mostly Portuguese) 0.1%; other 1.5%. Descendants of the original Amerindian inhabitants are divided into nine ethnic groups, including the Akawaio, Makuxi and Pemon. Some have lost their isolation and moved to the urban areas, others keenly maintain aspects of their traditional culture and identity. The language of each ethnic group is still spoken, but not by all members. The Amerindian People's Association represents the Indians in such matters as land rights. Hydroelectric dam projects, road building and, most recently, logging contracts have all threatened Amerindian territories. Another source of contention is the government's encouragement of foreign mining concerns to operate on land disputed by Venezuela.

The Economy Apart from instant, temporary prosperity brought about by the brief non-oil commodities boom in the mid-1970s, which raised gdp growth to 10.4% in 1975, Guyana's economy was in almost permanent recession between 1970 and 1990, despite considerable, unexploited potential in hydroelectric power, minerals and forestry. While Venezuela's long standing claim to the Essequibo region, within which most of these resources are situated, discouraged investment, other factors were more to blame. Inefficient management in the dominant state sector covering vital sugar and bauxite industries, an investment climate which discouraged both domestic and foreign savings, and an acute foreign exchange shortage, resulted in poor performances from the key agricultural and mining sectors, and a largely moribund manufacturing sector.

In 1991, the economy experienced a dramatic turn around, with improvements in almost every sector, especially rice, sugar and gold, promoting 6.1% growth in gdp. An even higher level, 7.7%, was recorded in 1992, rising to 8.3% in 1993 and 8.5% in 1994. Under an IMF-approved Economic Recovery Programme (1990-93), a number of state-owned companies were privatized, with others earmarked for divestment. The IMF renewed its support with a second Enhanced Structural Adjustment Facility in 1994, worth US$79mn over 3 years. Inflation was stabilized from a rate of 75% in 1991 to 7% in 1993, but in 1994 it more than doubled to 15.5%.

Most agriculture is concentrated on the coastal plain, and many sugar plantations are below sea level, necessitating an extensive system of dams, dykes, canals and pumps to prevent inundation. Sugar is the main crop, and in 1994 was the second export earner after gold. Exports were worth US$116.5mn, while production was 252,615 tonnes, compared with 242,645 tonnes in 1993. Rice is the second most important crop, with output in 1994 at 228,000 tonnes (205,000 in 1993); exports were valued at US$55mn (US$33mn in 1993). Also contributing to agriculture's 11.6% increase in 1994 was a 90% rise in timber production, at 452,374 cu m.

Guyana was the world's largest

Guyana : fact file

Geographic

Land area	215,083 sq km
forested	83.2%
pastures	6.2%
cultivated	2.5%

Demographic

Population (1994)	733,000
annual growth rate (1989-94)	-0.4%
urban	31.0%
rural	69.0%
density	3.7 per sq km
Religious affiliation	
Christian	52.0%
Hindu	34.0%
Muslim	9.0%
Birth rate per 1,000 (1994)	20.0
	(world av 26.0)

Education and Health

Life expectancy at birth,	
male	62 years
female	68 years
Infant mortality rate	
per 1,000 live births (1994)	49.0
Physicians (1990)	1 per 2,552 persons
Hospital beds	1 per 341 persons
Calorie intake as %	
of FAO requirement	110%
Population age 25 and over	
with no formal schooling	8.1%
Literate males (over 15)	97.5%
Literate females (over 15)	95.4%

Economic

GNP (1993 market prices)	US$268mn
GNP per capita	US$330
Public external debt (1992)	
	US$1,665mn
Tourism receipts (1992)	US$31mn
Inflation (annual av 1988-93)	2.5%
Radio	1 per 2.4 persons
Television	1 per 49 persons
Telephone	1 per 46 persons

Employment

Population economically active (1987)	
	270,074
Unemployment rate (1991)	13.5%
% of labour force in agriculture	20.4
mining	3.9
manufacturing	11.8
construction	2.8
Military forces	1,700

Source *Encyclopaedia Britannica*

producer of calcined bauxite, the highest grade of the mineral, but has lost its dominance to China. Production is currently concentrated at Linden, on the Demarara river, and at Kwakwani in Berbice county. No alumina (refined bauxite) has been exported since 1982 because the Linden refinery still awaits investment for refurbishment, but Australian management is attempting to restore Linden's bauxite facility to profitability prior to divestment. Within the Guyanese economy, gold has replaced bauxite as chief foreign exchange earner. Total exports in 1994 were 346,000 oz, worth US$128mn; production was 358,835 oz (compared with 310,072 oz in 1993), of which 70% came from Omai Gold Mines Ltd. Omai announced expansion plans in 1995.

A series of devaluations of the Guyana dollar between Jan 1987 and Feb 1991 culminated in the alignment of the official exchange rate with that of licensed exchange houses. These and other adjustment measures proved beneficial both for the current account and for government finances. The Government struggled to come to terms with the IMF, which declared Guyana ineligible for further assistance in May 1985 because of payment arrears. It was rewarded in Jun 1990 when the Bank for International Settlements and a group of donor countries provided funds to clear the country's arrears to the IMF and other creditors. This opened the way for lending from a variety of sources, including World Bank support for a Social Impact Amelioration Programme aimed at easing the hardship inflicted on lower income groups by the Economic Recovery Programme.

Breaking with the doctrines he espoused in opposition, President Jagan continued his predecessor's free market policies. After the 1992 elections, Guyana benefitted from substantial debt cancellations (eg from Britain and from the Paris Club creditor countries) and debt reschedulings. The election result also opened the way for renewed overseas aid. In Jan 1994, the government's efforts to reform the economy were rewarded by international financial institutions and foreign governments with funds to cover Guyana's financing requirements until end-1996 and for infrastructure projects. Guyana entered negotiations for closer cooperation with Barbados and Trinidad and Tobago. Rebuilding the economy, however, remained a monumental task as an estimated 75 cents in every dollar still had to be used for debt repayment.

Guyana has suffered from serious economic problems for over 15 years. Wages are very low and many people depend on overseas remittances or 'parallel market' activities to survive. The country is basically self-sufficient for its food supply. Many foreign goods are readily available. The country's infrastructure is seriously run down. Electricity blackouts occur, but not necessarily every day. Increased generating capacity has eased the situation and in 1994-95 the government was tendering for electricity supply from international companies. During power cuts no running water is available, except in larger hotels and businesses which have emergency generators and water pumps (take a torch/flashlight, or buy candles locally).

Government A Prime Minister and cabinet are responsible to the National Assembly, which has 65 members elected for a maximum term of 5 years. The President is Head of State. The country is divided into ten administrative regions.

Georgetown, the capital, and the chief town and port, is on the right bank of the River Demerara, at its mouth. Its population is roughly 200,000. The climate is tropical, with a mean temperature of 27°C, but the trade winds provide welcome relief. The city is built on a grid plan, with wide tree-lined streets and drainage canals following the layout of the old sugar estates. Despite being located on the Atlantic coast, Georgetown is known as the 'Garden City of the Caribbean'. Parts of the city are very attractive, with white-painted wooden nineteenth-century houses raised on stilts and a profusion of flowering trees. Lying, like most of the coastal area, below sea level, the city is protected from the ocean by a sea wall; in the evening this is crowded with strollers and at Easter it is a mass of colourful paper kites. Although part of the old city centre was destroyed by fire in 1945, there are some fine nineteenth-century buildings, particularly on or near the

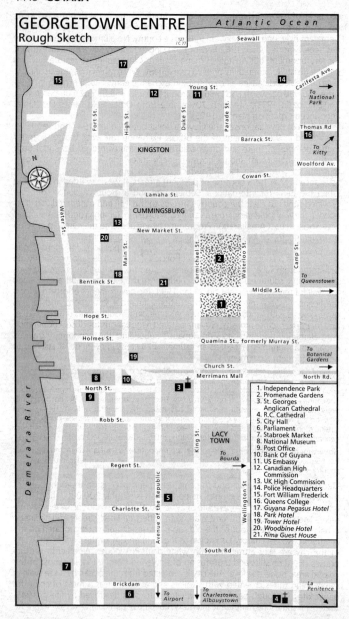

GEORGETOWN CENTRE
Rough Sketch

127 / C 77

Atlantic Ocean

Seawall

Carifesta Ave.
To National Park

Thomas Rd

To Kitty

Woolford Av.

Young St.

Fort St.

High St.

Duke St.

Parade St.

Barrack St.

KINGSTON

Cowan St.

Lamaha St.

CUMMINGSBURG

New Market St.

Water St.

Main St.

Carmichael St.

Waterloo St.

Camp St.

To Queenstown

Middle St.

Bentinck St.

Hope St.

Holmes St.

Quamina St., formerly Murray St.

To Botanical Gardens

Church St.

Merrimans Mall

North Rd.

Demerara River

North St.

Robb St.

LACY TOWN

King St.

To Bourda

Regent St.

Avenue of the Republic

Charlotte St.

Wellington St.

South Rd

Brickdam

To Airport

To Charlestown, Albouystown

La Penitence

1. Independence Park
2. Promenade Gardens
3. St. Georges Anglican Cathedral
4. R.C. Cathedral
5. City Hall
6. Parliament
7. Stabroek Market
8. National Museum
9. Post Office
10. Bank Of Guyana
11. US Embassy
12. Canadian High Commission
13. UK High Commission
14. Police Headquarters
15. Fort William Frederick
16. Queens College
17. *Guyana Pegasus Hotel*
18. *Park Hotel*
19. *Tower Hotel*
20. *Woodbine Hotel*
21. *Rima Guest House*

Avenue of the Republic. The Gothic-style **City Hall** dates from 1887; its interior has been recently restored and may be viewed. **St George's Anglican Cathedral**, which dates from 1889 (consecrated 1894), is 44m (143 feet) high and is reputed to be the tallest wooden building in the world (it was designed by Sir Arthur Blomfield). The **Public Buildings**, which house Parliament, are an imposing neo-classical structure built in 1839. **State House** on Main St is the residence of the president. Much of the city centre is dominated by the imposing tower above **Stabroek market** (1880). At the head of Brickdam, one of the main streets, is an aluminium arch commemorating independence. Nearby is a monument to the 1763 slave rebellion, surmounted by an impressive statue of Cuffy, its best-known leader. Near the *Guyana Pegasus Hotel* on Seawall Rd is the **Umana Yana**, a conical thatched structure built by a group of Wai Wai Amerindians using traditional techniques for the 1972 conference of the Non-Aligned Movement.

The **National Museum**, opposite the post office, houses an idiosyncratic collection of exhibits from Guyana and elsewhere, including a model of Georgetown before the 1945 fire and a good natural history section on the top floor (free, 0900-1700 Mon-Fri, 0900-1200 Sat). The **Walter Roth Museum of Anthropology**, opposite *Park Hotel* on Main St, has a collection of Amerindian artefacts (still under development).

The **Botanical Gardens** (entry free), covering 120 acres (50 hectares), have Victorian bridges and pavilions, palms and lily-ponds (run-down, but undergoing continual improvements). Be alert in the Gardens at all times. Near the S W corner is the former residence of the President, Castellani House, which now houses the **National Art Collection** (Tues-Sun 1000-1700), and there is also a large mausoleum containing the remains of the former president, Forbes Burnham, which is decorated with reliefs depicting scenes from his political career. Look out for the rare cannonball tree (Couroupita Guianensis), named after the appearance of its poisonous fruit. The **zoo** (being upgraded) has a collection of local animals and the manatees in the ponds which will eat grass from your hand. The zoo also boasts a breeding centre for endangered birds which are released into the wild. The zoo is open 0800-1800, US$0.15 for adults, half-price for children. The police band gives a free concert on Thur, 1730-1830. There are also beautiful tropical plants in the **Promenade Gardens** on Middle St and in the **National Park** on Carifesta Ave. The National Park has a good public running track.

The **Georgetown Cricket Club** at Bourda has one of the finest cricket grounds in the tropics. Near the S E corner of the Botanic Gardens is a well-equipped **National Sports Centre**. Nearby is the **Cultural Centre**, an impressive air-conditioned theatre with a large stage. Performances are also given at the **Playhouse Theatre** in Parade St.

NB Despite the delights of this beautiful city normal security precautions should be taken. Don't walk the streets at night. Check where it is safe to go with your hotel and in particular avoid Albouystown (S of the centre). Leave your valuables in your hotel.

Hotels There is a 10% room tax on all hotels with more than 16 rooms. **L1-A1** *Guyana Pegasus*, Seawall Rd, PO Box 101147, T 52853-9, F 60532, recently renovated and extended with new Kingston wing, very safe, a/c, comfortable, fridge, cable TV, lovely swimming pool, poolside barbecue every night, 2 bars, 2 restaurants, gym, tennis, business centre, has a shoeshine boy between 0700 and 1000, 24-hrs back up electricity, organizes tours to *Timberhead*; **L2-L3** *The Embassy Club*, Seawall Rd, T 50811, F 50808, lovely surroundings, self-contained apartments, tennis, gym, playground, good pool, sauna, massage, laundry, secretarial and computer facilities; **L3-A1** *Cara Suites*, 176 Middle St, T 61612/5, F 61541, luxurious, secure, clean, self-contained rooms with kitchen, bar, grocery, shoeshine, laundry, no restaurant; **L3-A1** *Tower*, 74-75 Main St, T 72011-5, F 56021, a/c, lively bar, excellent restaurant, *The Cazabon*, 24-hrs restaurant, good breakfasts, *Main Street Café*, nightly buffets, swimming pool, gym, business centre, boutique, beauty salon, in-house tour company (see below), 24-hrs electricity back up; **L3-A2** *Ocean View*, Liliendaal, Rupert Craig Highway, 2 miles E of Georgetown, new in 1995, pool, bar, dining room; **A1-A2** *Park*, 37-38 Main St, T 54914-16/70312-3, F 60351, a/c, secure, beautiful Victorian ballroom (worth a visit), beautiful restaurant too (vegetarian), but food could be better (average meal US$4.80, also buffet lunch for US$2.50, incl ice cream and drink); **A1-A3** *Woodbine*, 41-42 New Market St, T 59430-4, F 58406, just off Main St, a/c, bar, restaurant, health club, rec; **L3-A3** *Queenstown Inn*, 65 Anira St, Queenstown, T 61416, F 61411, 6 self-contained rm with a/c, incl gourmet breakfast, US-style, family-run, clean friendly, safe, afternoon tea, laundry, non-alcoholic drinks;

A3-B *Ariantze*, 176 Middle St, T 65363/70115, simple, clean, fans, or a/c in deluxe rooms and suites, dining room with TV and a/c, *Side Walk Café* and *Jazz Club* night club; **A2-C** *Friends*, 82 Robb St, T 72383, renovated with a/c, safe, fan, shower, mosquito net, bar, restaurant, travel agency; **A3** *Campala*, Camp St, T 52951, 61920/51620, very clean, modern, a/c, near prison (other meals: lunch US$2, dinner US$2.50-6).

There are also many smaller, cheaper hotels. Recommended are: **B-C** *Hotel Glow*, 23 Queen St, clean, fan, 24-hrs restaurant; **B-D** *Waterchris*, Waterloo St, between Murray and Church sts, T 71980, a/c (E pp with fan), good restaurant, friendly; *Florentine's*, North and Waterloo sts, clean but hot and noisy; **D** *Demico*, near Stabroek Market, T 56372, with a/c, E without; **D** *Rima Guest House*, 92 Middle St, T 57401, good area, modernized, well-run, good value, central, clean, safe, mosquito nets, restaurant (breakfast US$3.55, lunch and dinner US$4.25); **F** *Van Ross*, North Rd and Camp St, same management, very basic. Others include: **E** *Belvedere*, Camp St, on the same block as the hospital and thereby benefitting from constant electricity; opposite is **E** pp *Alpha Guest House*, 203 Camp St, T 54324, all rooms with double beds and mosquito nets, bar downstairs; **D-F** *Trio La Chalet*, corner of Camp St and Hadfield St, T 56628 (D in self-contained a/c unit), popular with locals, 24-hrs bar (breakfast US$1.30, other meals US$1.60); **G** *Dal-Jean's Guest House*, Albert St, Queenstown, noisy but friendly; **E-F** *German's*, 81 Robb St, T 53972, with bath, no fan; **F** *Tropical*, Waterloo and Middle sts, very basic. Many small hotels and guest houses are full of long-stay residents, while some are rented by the hour. Try to book in advance. If in doubt, go to a larger hotel for first night and look around next day in daylight.

Apartments *N and R*, 246 Anaida Ave, Eccles, East Bank Demerara, T 60921 (reservations through N and R Apartment Rentals, 301 Church and Thomas sts, Georgetown, T 58079/664040), US$45 a day, 1 bedroom, a/c, TV, maid service, washer, dryer, guard service, generator; *Blue Wave*, 3 locations, office at 8-9 North Rd, Bourda, T 64295, fully-furnished, kitchenette, TV, a/c, hot water, 24-hrs electricity and security, US$45-75.

Restaurants Eating out is very cheap at present because of the favourable exchange rate. 10% service may be added to bill. Many restaurants are closed on public holidays. Prices given below are for an average main course. At Hotels: *Pegasus*, *El Dorado*, good atmosphere, Caribbean, Continental and Guyanese, *flambé* menu US$8, *Browne's Old Cafe*, lunch special US$4.70, main course from menu US$5.50, good breakfasts; *Tower*, *Cazabon*, very good food, US$7.50-9.20, also *Main Street Café*; very good breakfast at *Waterchris*. Best in town are *Del Casa* (good food and atmosphere – no shorts), *Tahli*, in same building, good Indian food, expensive, and *Caribbean Rose* (expensive, slow service, mixed reports, up 4 flights of stairs and on the roof, the open sides will cool you down, credit cards not accepted but will take US$ or Guyanese dollars, booking required), all on Middle St (US$7.50-9.20); also rec are *Palm Court*, Main St (many Chinese dishes, good food, poor service), and *Arawak Steak House*, in roof garden above *Demico Hotel* (casual atmosphere, busy in pm, good value, average price US$4.80, closes 2200). Good lunches for around US$4-5 at the *Rice Bowl* in Robb St, the *Coalpot* in New Town (no shorts allowed, cheaper cafeteria) and *Hack's Hallal*; *Country Pride* in Robb St, serves lunch and dinner, US$4-5. Good Chinese: *Yue Yuan*, Robb St, *Hing Loon*, Main St, *New Thriving*, Regent St, all good. Many Chinese restaurants (all pretty rough), including *Double Dragon*, Av of the Republic; and *Diamond Food House*, 9 Camp St. For late night eating there are several Chinese restaurants on Sheriff St incl *Double Happiness*. For fast food, try *Quality Fast Food*, Hinc'ks St; *Creole Hot Pot*, 37C Cummings St, exclusively Guyanese dishes;

Red Rooster, Regent St; *Arapaima*, Main St; *Idaho*, Brickdam; *Forest Hills*, Camp St; *Calypso*, Regent St; *Demico House*, Stabroek Market, convenient, but poor service. Cheap counter lunches at *Guyana Stores*, Main St. Haagan-Daz ice cream sold at *Shaynors*, Ave of the Republic, US$2.50. Excellent fruit juices at *Organic Juices*, Croal St, Bourda. Beacon Foundation, 3 branches in Georgetown (ask a local for directions) is a charitable organization to feed the homeless and care for the terminally ill; it has good food at reasonable prices.

Banks and Exchange National Bank of Industry and Commerce; Guyana Bank of Trade and Industry; Bank of Baroda; Bank of Nova Scotia will give cash advance on Visa card. Bank hours are 0800-1230 Mon-Fri, plus 1500-1700 on Fri. **Exchange** houses (*cambios*) in shops may be open longer hours. A good, safe *cambio* is Joe Chin Travel on Main St, T 63051. The *cambio* opposite the *Tower Hotel* accepts Thomas Cook TCs, but not at the best rates. There is a *cambio* next to *Rima Guest House* on Middle St.

Embassies and Consulates There are a large number of embassies, including: **British High Commission** (44 Main St, PO Box 10849, T 592-2-65881/4); **Canadian High Commission** (Young St) and the Embassies of the **United States** (Duke and Young St, Kingston, near *Guyana Pegasus Hotel*), Honorary **French** Consul 7 Sheriff St, T 65238), **Venezuela** (Thomas St), **Brazil** (308 Church St, Queenstown, T 57970, visa issued next day, 90 days, 1 photo, US$12.75), **Cuba** (Main St) and **Suriname** (304 Church St, T 56995; 2 passport photos, passport, US$20 and 5 days minimum needed).

Night Life Georgetown is surprisingly lively at night, mainly with gold miners, traders and overseas Guyanese throwing US$ around. Liveliest disco is *Hollywood*, Camp St (entrance US$0.80, expensive); *The Library*, Camp St, very popular Wed night (ladies free), barbeque, beer garden, dance floor, bar (entrance US$0.80); *Blue Note*, Camp St, disco and beer garden; *Palm Court*, Main St, popular bar/café (French style), very lively Fri pm (entry US$3.50) and holidays, no entrance fee on other days; *Jazz Club* in *Ariantze Hotel*, Middle St, good atmosphere, excellent live band every Thur; *Trump Card*, Church St, near St George's, sometimes has a live band. Near the Kitty Market are *Jazzy Jacks*, Alexander St (open till 0400 at weekends), and *Wee Place*, Lamaha St, but this area is unsafe unless you go with locals. Sheriff St, is some way from the centre but is 'the street that never sleeps' full of late night Chinese restaurants and has some good bars incl *Tennessee Lounge*, *Burns Beat* and *Sheriff* (live band). Most nightclubs sell imported, as well as local Banks beer; many sell drinks by the bottle rather than shot, this works out cheaper. You can visit the steel pan yards and watch practice sessions. There are 2 theatres in Georgetown. **Cinemas**: *Astor*, Church St; *Strand*, Charlotte St; one on Main St; all worth a visit.

Post Office Main one on North St.

Places of Worship Anglican: St Georges Cathedral, Christ Church, Waterloo St; St Andrews (Presbyterian), Avenue of the Republic; Roman Catholic Cathedral, Brickdam. Pentecostal, Full Gospel Fellowship, South Rd corner with Albert Rd, welcoming.

Shopping Normal shopping hours are 0830-1600, Mon-Thur, 0830-1700 Fri, 0830-1200 Sat. Market hours 0800-1600, Mon-Sat, except Wed 0900-1200. The main shopping area is Regent St. The two main department stores are *Guyana Stores* in Church St, and *Fogarty's*, but neither has a wide range of goods. Most Guyanese do their regular shopping at the four big markets—Stabroek (don't take valuables), Bourda, La Penitence and Kitty. Craft items are a good buy; Amerindian basketwork, hammocks, wood carvings, pottery, and small figures made out of Balata, a rubbery substance tapped from trees in the interior. *Houseproud*, 6 Avenue of the Republic, has a good selection of expensive craftwork, but there are many other craft shops incl *Creation Craft*, Water St. Good T-shirts are sold at *Guyana Stores* and at the markets. Gold is also sold widely, often at good prices but make sure you know what you are buying. Do not buy it on the street. Films over ASA200 are normally not available; bring your own stock. 24-hrs developing is available at *Risans* on Main St (top end) and Ave of the Republic, rec as efficient, sells slide film (photocopying, too), also *Guyana Stores* and a 1-hr photo print-shop on Quarmina St, nr Main St.

Bookshops Some interesting books in *Houseproud*. Try also *GNTC* on Water St, *Argosy* and *Kharg* both on Regent St, *Dimension* on Cummings St, as well as *Guyana Stores* and *Fogarty's*, *Universal Bookstore* on Water St, nr *Fogarty's*, has a good selection of books and greetings cards. Hughes and Thorne Publishing House, 61 Hadfield and Cross sts, copies of *Guyana Tourist Guide*, US$2, and *El Dorado*, inflight magazine of Guyana Airways. *Newsweek* sold at *Hotel Tower*.

Sport The national indoor sport is dominoes. There are sports clubs for cricket, tennis, football, rugby, hockey, riding, swimming, cycling, athletics, badminton, volleyball, netball, snooker, pool, golf, boxing, ballroom dancing and rifle shooting. At Easter there are kite flying competitions.

Swimming No public pools, but hotels with pools (eg *Tower*) offer 1-month membership for US$20 to use pool.

Travel Agencies Try Mr Mendoza at *Frandec Travel Service*, Main St, repeatedly rec (no tours to the interior); *Wieting and Richter*, 78 Church and Carmichael sts, very helpful, ask for Onassis Stanley; *H and R Ramdehol*, 215 South Rd, Lacytown, T 70639/73183/73846. *Joe Chin Travel* is rec (see **Exchange** above). For **Tour Operators**, see below.

Tourist Information The combination of incentives, the stabilization of the economy and government recognition of the foreign exchange earning potential of tourism has led to many new ventures since 1990. The Ministry of Trade, Tourism and Industry has a Tourism Department which can provide information through its office at 229 South Rd, nr Camp St, Lacytown, Georgetown, T 62505/63182, F 544310. The Ministry has a booth (often closed) at Timehri airport. Substantial private sector growth has led to the formation of the Tourism Association of Guyana (TAG – office and information desk at 225 South Rd, next to Ministry of Trade, Tourism and Industry), which covers all areas of tourism (hotels, airlines, restaurants, tour operators, etc). The TAG produces a 40-page, full-colour booklet on Guyana; the *Tourist Guide* may be obtained by writing to the Association at PO Box 101147, Georgetown, or by phoning 592-2-50807. This is also the Association's information number. For details of **Tour Operators** and **Camps**, see below.

Maps of country and Georgetown (US$6) from Department of Lands and Surveys, Homestreet Ave, Durban Backland (take a taxi), T 60524-9 in advance, poor stock. Rivers and islands change frequently according to water levels, so maps can only give you a general direction. A local guide can be more reliable. City maps also from *Guyana Store*, Water Street, next to the ice house. Map of Georgetown in 1995 *Guyana Tourist Guide*.

Local Transport Minibuses run regularly to most parts of the city, mostly from Stabroek market or Avenue of the Republic, standard fare US$0.15 (US$0.18 to suburbs), very crowded. It is difficult to get a seat during rush hours. Taxis charge US$1.10 for short journeys, US$2.20 for longer runs, with higher rates at night (a safe option) and outside the city limits. Minibuses and taxis have 'H' on their number plate. Normal ones ply set routes at a fixed fare; they stop at any point on request. Certain hand signals are used on some routes to indicate the final destination (ask). Special taxis at hotels and airports, also with 'H' and marked 'special' on the windscreen, charge US$1.25 around town, stops and waiting time extra, or you can negotiate a 'by the hour' deal, usually US$6.

Vehicle Rental Car hire is available through numerous companies (page 18 of Guyana Telephone Book gives details). Prices range from US$42/day to US$65/day for a new Nissan Sentra. Better companies are *N and R Rentals*, 301 Church and Thomas sts, T 58079/66404, Toyota Camry and Corolla, Nissan Station Wagon. Scooters can be hired from *Addis Scooter Enterprise Ltd*, 38 Sussex St, Charlestown, T 66789. A permit is needed from local police; rental agencies can advise. Bicycle hire: Roshan Ali at *Fullwork Cycles*, Robb St and Light St, US$25/week and deposit.

Airport The international airport is at Timehri, 25 miles S of Georgetown. The terminal building was being rebuilt in 1994-95 with various services coming on stream all the time. Check in 2 hrs before most flights, listen to the local radio the day before your flight to hear if it has been delayed, or even brought forward. Minibus No 42 to Georgetown US$1.50 (to airport depart from next to Parliament Building); for an extra fee they will drop you at your hotel (similarly for groups going to the airport). Taxi US$14-18. BWIA, now computerized, requests 3-hrs check-in. There are two duty-free shops, one selling local and foreign spirits (more expensive than downtown), the other local handicrafts and jewellery. There is also an exchange house, open usual banking hours; if closed, plenty of parallel traders outside (find out from fellow passengers what the rate is). At the airport it is not easy to buy tickets with a credit card or TCs. The exchange desk will change TCs for flight ticket purchases. (For internal flights from Ogle airport, see **Information for Visitors**—minibus from Market to Ogle US$0.20.)

Bus Services There are regular services by minibuses and collective taxis to most coastal towns from the Stabroek Market. To Rosignol (for New Amsterdam, Springlands and Suriname), 2 hrs, US$2; to Parika US$1; to Linden US$1.50. New 45-seater buses, Guy-Bus, run from Lamaha St, just off Main St, to Timehri, Linden, Parika and Rosignol: same price, safer and more comfortable.

Tour Operators The tourism sector is promoting ecotourism in the form of environmentally friendly resorts and camps on Guyana's rivers and in the rainforest. There is much tropical wildlife to be seen.

Wilderness Explorers, 61 Hadfield and Cross sts, 1st floor, Hadfield Foundation Bldg, Georgetown, T 62085, offer ready-made itineraries and specialize in custom-designed, personal itineraries for any group size. Tours available to all of Guyana's interior resorts, day and overland tours to Kaieteur Falls, horse trekking, hiking and general tours in the Rupununi and rainforest. Specialists in nature, adventure and bird-watching tours. Free tourism information, booklet and advice available. *Tropical Adventures*, c/o *Guyana Pegasus*, Seawall Rd, Georgetown, T 52853-9, F 60532, offer trips to Timberhead (see below), Double 'B' Exotic Gardens (see below) and city tours. Overnight tours to Timberhead, Shanklands (see below) and Essequibo River. Individual itineraries catered for. Also 7 and 14 night itineraries travelling around Guyana, fully inclusive rates, 7 nights US$950 pp, 14 nights US$1,750. *Wonderland Tours*, 65 Main St, Georgetown, T/F 59795, day trips to Kaieteur and Orinduik Falls, Santa Mission, Essequibo and Mazaruni Rivers (developing own camp on the Mazaruni river); city tours; special arrangements for overnight stays available. *Torong Guyana*, 56 Coralita Ave, Bel Air Park, Georgetown, T 65298, trips to Kaieteur and Orinduik Falls and 3-day Rupununi Safaris, including Kaieteur (US$450). *Discover Tours*, Hotel Tower, 74-75 Main St, Georgetown, T 72011-5/58001, F 65691/56021, custom-designed itineraries to inland resorts,

day and overland trips to Kaieteur Falls and other locations, rates fully inclusive, 4-14 day tours US$450-2,0000 pp, group sizes 8-15. *Cattleya Rainforest Tours*, 225 South Rd, Georgetown, T 76590, F 70944, overland trips to Kaieteur. *Shell Beach Adventures*, at *Guyana Pegasus'* Travel Office, T 54483/4, F 65220, trips to Almond Beach in NW Guyana to see nesting turtles in season and scalet ibis roosting, 2-day trip US$250 pp using light aircraft and camping on beach. Rainbow River Safari Ltd, c/o Allison, Guyenterprise Agency, 234 Almond St, F 2-56959 or phone Allison 2-69874; can provide tours into the interior, to its campsite on the Mazaruni River (see below), arranges overland tours to Kaieteur Falls, director Miss L Prowell, resident at the campsite (London office, Mr Sabat, T 0181-671 1414, F 0171-703 5500). *Greenheart Tours*, 36 Craig St, Campbellville, Georgetown, T/F 58219, itineraries for any group size, tours of Georgetown City (US$25), to Santa Mission (US$50 pp), Essequibo/Mazaruni Rivers (US$100 pp), Kaieteur/Orinduick Falls (US$180 pp), Ituni Savannahs (US$150 pp). *El Dorado Tours* due open July 1995, resort at Kamuni Spring Nature Farm, T 52467, Francis Ferreira.

Resorts *Timberhead*, operated by Tropical Adventures (see above) in the Santa Amerindian Reserve, situated on a sandy hill overlooking Savannah and the Pokerero Creek, 3 beautifully appointed native lodges with bath and kitchen facilities, well-run, good food, lovely trip up the Kamuni River to get there, much wildlife to be seen, 212 species of bird have been recorded, activities include swimming, fishing, jungle treks, visit to Santa Mission Amerindian village, volley ball, US$90 pp for a day trip, US$145 pp for one night and 2 days, plus US$110 per night from second night on (includes all transport, meals, bar, guide, accommodation), highly rec. *Shanklands*, contact Joanne Jardim, Residence No 3, Thirst Park, Georgetown, T/F 51586, (or through *Wilderness Explorers*), on a cliff overlooking the Essequibo, 3 colonial style cottages with verandah and kitchen, activities include swimming, walking, bird watching, croquet, fishing, water sports, overnight rate US$120-150. *The Gazebo*, contact Bibi Zackeryah, Willems Timber and Trading Co Ltd, PO Box 10443, Georgetown, T 72046/7, 69252, F 60983, the country home of the Willems family on 136-acre Kaow Island in the Essequibo River, facilities include a jungle walk, tennis, swimming, water sports, trekking, bird watching, room rates US$210 d full board, most activities included, transport from Georgetown not included (air, 30 mins, US$200; minibus and boat via Parika, 2 hrs, US$125 or US$275, latter in cabin cruiser; day trips for US$95). *Double 'B' Exotic Gardens*, 58 Lamaha Gardens, Georgetown, T 52023, F 60997, contact Boyo Ramsaroop, near Timehri Airport, good birdwatching, gardens specializing in heliconias, day tours US$35. *Emerald Tower*, Madewini on the Demerara River, rain forest lodges, T 72011, F 56021, reached by minibus from Georgetown, 8 private tree-level cabins, activities include swimming, bicycle and nature trails, croquet, putting green, sauna, birdwatching, archery, all inclusive rates US$240d, 155s; organizes custom itineraries, including other interior resorts, Kaieteur and Orinduik Falls. A new company, *White Water Tours*, information from TAG, is to open 1996; will have special jet boat to get through rapids. For *Rock View Ecotourism Resort*, Karanambu Ranch and Dadanawa Ranch, see under Rupununi, below.

Camps *Rainbow River Safari*, a 17,000 acre conservation site on the Mazaruni River, dormitory style accommodation in 3 large tented camps (chalets planned), pit latrines, washing in river, cooking over wood fire, US$60-90 pp all inclusive, day trips with 3 different jungle trails US$3.75, whitewater rafting, swimming, wildlife walking, birdwatching, hill climbing, gold panning, no music unless requested, no caged animals. Day trippers pay a landing fee of G$500. See above for contact addresses, which should be approached for all latest details. Agent in Bartica, Bell Boats, Monti Bell, T 05-2405, or Stephen Bell, T 05-2414, or Attack,

T 05-2484. A new camp is being built at Saxacalli Mission between Parika and Bartica on a beach on the Essequibo.

NB For visiting many parts of the interior, particularly Amerindian districts, permits are required in advance from the Ministry of Home Affairs and /or the Public Works, Communications and Regional Development in Georgetown. If venturing out of Georgetown on your own, you must check beforehand whether you need a permit for where you intend to visit.

Southeast to Suriname

Linden (pop 60,000), the second-largest town in Guyana, is a bauxite mining town 70 miles S of Georgetown on the Demerara river. A good road connects the two towns; the police checks are to stop drug and gun running. On the W bank of the river, Linden is a company mining town with an executive area and golf course. The opencast mine is 200-300 feet deep and is said to have the world's longest boom walking dragline. Across the river (bridge or ferry, G$5) are the poorer suburbs of Wismar and Christianburg. The town is dominated by a disused alumina plant and scarred by old bauxite pits. Accommodation is scarce (in town *Crescent* and *Chez Docs*, cheap, basic; *Hotel Star Bonnett*, three-quarters of a mile out of town in Georgetown road, clean, good lunches; nearby **E** *Summit Hotel*).

From Linden rough roads suitable for four-wheel drive vehicles run S to the bauxite mining towns of Ituni and Kwakwani. The road S to the logging centre at Mabura Hill is in excellent condition; it continues to Kurupukari in extremely bad condition, even for 4WD trucks. Money for upgrading the road is not currently available. A good road goes W from Linden to Rockstone ferry on the Essequibo river. From Rockstone very bad roads run N to Bartica and S to Issano.

New Amsterdam (pop 25,000) is 65 miles S-E of Georgetown on the E bank of the Berbice river, near its mouth. From Georgetown, take a minibus (44, or express No 50) or collective taxi to Rosignol (**G** *Hotel Hollywood*, 'dubious') on the W bank of the Berbice, then cross the river by the ferry, 15 mins (US$0.30; also takes vehicles) or by launch to Blairmont, 1 mile past Rosignol. The town is picturesque.

Hotels C-D *Church View Guest House*, 3 Main and King sts, T (03) 2880, F 3927, incl meals, clean, rec; **C-D** *Parkway*, 4 Main St, T (03) 3928, clean, friendly, safe, with bath, rec but food poor; *Hotel Embassy*, at Rose Hall. **D** *Astor*, 7 Strand, T (03)3578, verandah with lounge chairs, rec.

Restaurants *Circle C*, Main and Charlotte sts, Créole; *Brown Derby*, Main and Church sts, Créole; both US$3-6 per meal, various Chinese on Main St; *Oik Banks Est*, Main St, nice, slow.

Banks National Bank of Industry and Commerce; Guyana National Commercial Bank; Bank of Baroda.

From New Amsterdam, it is sometimes possible to get a lift on a bauxite barge up the Berbice river to the small mining town of Kwakwani (there is a guesthouse, reasonable, check for vacancies at Guymine in Georgetown).

The road continues E from New Amsterdam (minibus, US$1), to *Springlands* and Skeldon at the mouth of the Corentyne river. The two towns are officially known as *Corriverton* (Corentyne River Town, pop about 31,000). Springlands is 2 km long, so you need to know where you want to get off the bus.

Hotels In Springlands: *Ambassador*, near point for ferry to Nieuw Nickerie; *Swiss Guest House*, T (039)2329, US$4-6, Pakistani run, rough but helpful. In Skeldon: **E** *Parapak*, no fan, no mosquito net, poor value; **F** *Mahogony*, fan, clean, friendly, rec; **G** *Arawak*, rough, avoid. Several good Chinese restaurants within a few blocks of Springlands town centre. Good Indian food at *Mansoor*, Skeldon.

Exchange National Bank of Industry and Commerce; Guyana National Commercial Bank. *Cambio* (National Bank of Industry and Commerce) at Skeldon for arriving ferry passengers. Suriname guilders can officially be changed into Guyanese dollars.

Transport To **Georgetown** by minibus to New Amsterdam (US$1.45), ferry to **Rosignol** and minibus from Rosignol, US$1.60.

Crossing to Suriname Before you leave Georgetown, check with the Suriname embassy whether you need a visa (without one, if required, you may be imprisoned before being sent back to Georgetown). See **Documents**, Suriname, **Information for Visitors**. From Springlands there is a daily ferry (not Sun or national holidays of either country) to Nieuw Nickerie (foot passengers only). Queue at the booking office near the jetty from 0700, office opens 0800, booking fee US$0.25, all passports must be presented when booking, tickets are sold later on the ferry, Sf45 one-way, payable in Suriname guilders only. Immigration and customs formalities (very slow and thorough) take place from 0900, ferry sails in the afternoon depending on tides and weather, crossing time normally 2 hrs. If not in transit through Suriname you are obliged to change US$175 at the local bank, if it is closed your passport is retained (see **Suriname, Currency**). In this instance, travel on to Paramaribo, change currency at the Central Bank and with the receipt given at the border retrieve your passport from Fort Zeelandia.

NB This ferry was not running in 1994-95. Small boats ferried people across. Check the situation in advance.

South and West from Georgetown; Routes to Venezuela and Brazil

Travelling W from Georgetown, the road crosses the 1¼-mile long floating Demerara bridge (opens often for shipping, US$0.20 toll, pedestrians free) and continues to **Parika**, a small town on the E bank of the Essequibo river (minibus No 32 US$1). Speedboats cross the river from Stabroek market, US$0.30. If you need accommodation, there are two small guest houses where you can stay fairly safely. From here ferries cross the river to Adventure on the W bank at 1700 daily and 0830 Wed and Fri, returning at 0300 daily and 1330 Wed and Fri; alternatively take a speedboat US$2.40. (See *Three Singles to Adventure* by Gerald Durrell.) There are also three ferries a day to Leguan Island (30 mins, US$0.25); accommodation available at the *Hotel President*.

From Parika there is also a ferry up the Essequibo River to Bartica on Mon, Thur and Sat, returning next day, US$1.50 one-way. The 36 mile journey takes 6 hrs, stopping at Fort Island; small boats come out from riverside settlements to load up with fruit. Local people generally prefer to take a speedboat, US$4.20 pp, 1-2 hrs, depending on horsepower.

Bartica, at the junction of the Essequibo and Mazaruni rivers, is the 'take-off' town for the gold and diamond fields, Kaieteur Falls, and the interior generally. Here an Amazon-like mass of waters meets, but with an effect vastly more beautiful, for they are coloured the 'glossy copper' of all Guyanese rivers and not the dull mud-brown of most of the Amazon. Swimming very good. The *stelling* (wharf) and market are very colourful. Several bars on main street. Easter regatta.

Hotels E *Main Hotel*, 19 Second Ave, T (05) 2243, meals available (breakfast US$3.20, lunch and dinner US$6.40); **E** *Harbour Cove*, very nice, eat elsewhere; **E** *The Nest* on Fifth Ave, unsafe, very noisy, meals to be had from disco after 1730, or 'Robbie's'. **F** *Modern*, near ferry, with bath and fan, rec, good food, noisy disco. **F** *Pink House* (Mrs Phil's), Second Ave, cheaper, clean, without bath, basic, secure, family-run, quiet. Book ahead if possible. Mrs Payne, near Hospital, basic, clean. *Sea View*, condominium-style resort, under construction.

The Essequibo is navigable to large boats for some miles above Bartica. The Cuyuni flows into the Mazaruni 3 miles above Bartica, and above this confluence the Mazaruni is impeded for 120 miles by thousands of islands, rapids and waterfalls. To avoid this stretch of treacherous river a road has been built from Bartica to Issano, where boats can be taken up the more tranquil upper Mazaruni.

At the confluence of the Mazaruni and Cuyuni rivers are the ruins of the Dutch stronghold ***Kyk-over-al***, once the seat of government for the Dutch county of Essequibo. Nearby are the **Marshall Falls** (35 mins by boat from Bartica, US$38 per boat, return) where you can swim in the falls themselves ('a natural jacuzzi'), or the nearby bay, part of the Rainbow River Safari conservation area, G$500 landing fee.

The **Kaieteur Falls**, on the Potaro River, rank with the Niagara, Victoria, and Iguazú Falls in majesty and beauty, but have the added attraction of being surrounded by unspoilt forest. The Falls, nearly five times the height of Niagara, with a sheer drop of 228m, are nearly 100m wide. They are unspoilt because of their isolation. The Falls lie within the **Kaieteur National Park**, where there is a variety of wildlife—tapirs, ocelots, monkeys, armadillos, anteaters, and jungle and river birds. In 1994-95, the government was considering extending the national park. At the Falls themselves, one can see the magnificent silver fox, often near the rest house, the cock-of-the-rock and the Kaieteur swift, which lives behind the falls. At dusk the swifts swoop in and out of the gorge before passing through the deluge to roost behind the water. Permission to enter the national park must be obtained from the National Parks Commission in Georgetown, T 59142.

A trip to the Kaieteur Falls costs US$145/day trip flight with GAC, T 52002, Sun from Timehri including lunch, drinks and guides, sit on left for best view, take swimming gear, includes Orinduik Falls—see below. Most agencies include the Orinduik Falls as well, US$170, including ground and air transport, meal, drinks, US$5 national park entrance fee and guide. Trips depend on the charter plane being filled; there is normally at least one flight per week. Cancellations only occur in bad weather or if there are insufficient passengers. Operators offering this service are *Wilderness Explorers* (T 62085), trips to both falls by light aircraft, *Discover Tours* at Hotel Tower (T 72011-5) spends longer at each falls, US$195 (Adrian Rodriguez is very good, ask for him at the hotel, or 363 Grove H/Scheme, East Bank Demerara), *Wonderland Tours* (T 65991, Richard Ousman), and *Torang Guyana*, Mrs Chan-A-Sue in Georgetown, T 65298. You may get very little time at the Falls. Flights to Kaieteur from either Timehri or Ogle airport cost US$40. To charter a plane privately costs US$900 to Kaieteur and Orinduik.

Wilderness Explorers, Discover Tours and *Cattleya Rainforest Tours*, all in Georgetown, offer overland trips, as does *Rainbow River Safari* (7-10 days, not including rest days).

To go independently overland to Kaieteur:
Under normal conditions, a truck should be taken from Bartica to Mahdia (100 very uncomfortable miles – 160 km). The truck should be left at the Kangaruma junction, 2 miles after Garraway Stream, but in 1995, this road was impassable. Any overland attempt must be made by boat. If you can get to Kangaruma village ('12 people, 6 prostitutes', beware theft and overcharging), speedboats (1-2 a day) go to Tukeit via Amatok falls (1 hr) and Waratok falls (1½ hrs); walk around each fall and then get a new boat. From Tukeit you walk to Kaieteur in about 2 hrs in the dry season; not rec in the rainy season. There is no public speedboat service, they belong to companies working in the area. Company speedboats apparently will not ask for money, but to hire a boat is beyond a budget traveller's means.

In the dry season you can walk from Kangaruma to Kaieteur: 8-10 hrs to Amatok, very rough and swampy, with many streams to cross; then 4-5 hrs to Waratok; then 7-9 hrs to Tukeit. 2-3 hrs after Amatok is a deserted mining camp where you can camp; there are many other flat places suitable for camping. The whole route is very hard going and it would seem that there is much more chance of being near people if you go by boat. On the boat route you can sling a hammock at any of the camps if stuck and each camp has ham radio for emergency use. Nevertheless, boats are very unreliable. A speedboat is preferable to going in a paddled boat, which cannot cope with the strong currents.

Once at Kaieteur, you can walk to the top of the falls, at least 2 hrs, but worth it to watch the blue, white and brown water tumbling into the stupendous gorge.

From Lethem to Kaieteur, take a truck to Annai, Saruma, Cupucari, then a truck to Mabura, via Amerindian villages of Icowaw and Frenchman. From Mabura, as above. (We are grateful to Piero Scaruffi, Redwood City, CA, and Yoav Berkovich, Ramat Efal, Israel, for the above information.)

The rest house at the top of the Falls was not open in mid-1995, enquire first at the National Parks Commission, Georgetown, T 59142, (if planning to stay overnight, you must be self-sufficient, whether the guest house is open or not); take your own food and a hammock, it can be cold and damp at night. It is nearly impossible to get down the gorge below the falls; the path is completely overgrown, a guide is essential and it takes a full day.

Avoid Apr and Oct, which are the dry months when the flow of the falls is reduced; in Jan and Jun/Jul the flow is usually at its fullest, but in Jun, which is the height of the wet season; the overland route is impassable.

The Pakaraima Mountains stretch from Kaieteur westwards to include the highest peak in Guyana, Mt Roraima, the possible inspiration for Conan Doyle's *Lost World* (**see Venezuela, South to Brazil**). Roraima is very difficult to climb from the Guyanese side.

There are several other spectacular waterfalls in the interior, including Imbaimadai and Orinduik, but none is very easy to reach. *Orinduik Falls* are on the Ireng River, which forms the border with Brazil; the river pours over steps and terraces of jasper, with a backdrop of the grass-covered Pakaraima Mountains. There is good swimming at the falls. Vincént and Rose Cheong run a tourist shelter and are full of information about the area and about routes to Brazil from Orinduik (take hammock, food and fuel for outboard motors). It is a 3 hr walk from Orinduik to Urimutang, on the Brazilian side of the Ireng River (essential to get detailed description or a guide for the correct place to cross the river—no bridge); public transport runs from Urimutang to Boa Vista, 5 hrs. *Wilderness Explorers*, T 62085, offer 4 trips per year from Orinduik N on Ireng River in dugout canoes with Amerindian guides.

Precautions If going on your own, detailed planning and a guide are essential. Take adequate supplies of food and drink, a sleeping bag, a sheet and blanket, a mosquito net, and kerosene for Tilley lamps.

The North-western coastal area is mainly accessible by boat only. Speedboats cross from Parika to Supenaam, US$2.80, very wet crossing. From Supenaam minibuses or taxis (US$3.50 pp) go to Charity. From *Adventure* on the W bank of the Essequibo a road runs N through Anna Regina. Nearby is Lake Mainstay, a small resort (due for renovation), reached by taxi; it is also known as the hot and cold lake because it varies in temperature from one place to another. The road goes on to *Charity*, a pleasant little town with two small hotels (*Purple Heart*, E, cheaper than *Xenon*) and a lively market on Mon (quiet at other times).

Near the border with Venezuela is the small port of *Morawhanna* (Morajuana to the Venezuelans), which may be reached by an unreliable ferry from Georgetown. The journey is surprisingly rough and 'you will have to fight for hammock space and watch your possessions like a hawk'. From Morawhanna boats sail up the river to Port Kaituma, 40 miles inland, from where a small passenger railway connects with the isolated settlement of Matthews Ridge (more easily reached by chartered aircraft from Georgetown). The site of the Jonestown mass-suicide is nearby.

The Venezuelan border can be crossed at the River Cuyuni (at least from Venezuela into Guyana). On the Venezuelan side is San Martín, from which a narrow road goes to El Dorado on the road S to Brazil. It is possible to reach this border by boat from Georgetown (very infrequent), or by military plane, about 4 or 5 times a week, no schedule, US$60.

The *Rupununi Savanna* in the SW is an extensive area of dry grassland with scattered trees, termite mounds and wooded hills. The freshwater creeks, lined with Ite palms, are good for swimming. The region is scattered with occasional Amerindian villages and a few large cattle ranches which date from the late nineteenth century: the descendants of some of the Scots settlers still live here. Between the 1920s and 1950s a rough cattle trail led to the coastal region, but this has since reverted to bush. Balata, a rubbery substance bled from trees, was once a source of income but it no longer has commercial value, having been replaced by synthetic substances; craft items are still made from it. Most of the airstrips used to transport balata are now closed. Links with Brazil are much closer than with the Guyanese coast; many people speak Portuguese and most trade, both legal and illegal, is with Brazil.

Avoid visiting the Rupununi in the wet season (mid-May to Aug) as much of the Savanna is flooded and malaria mosquitoes widespread. The best time is Oct to April. River bathing is good, but watch out for the dangerous stingrays. Wild animals are shy, largely nocturnal and seldom seen. Among a wide variety of birds, look out for macaws, toucan, parrots, parakeets, hawks and jabiru storks. Note that a permit from the Ministry of Home Affairs is usually required to visit Rupununi, unless you are going with a tour operator. Check in advance if your passport is sufficient. A separate permit to visit Amerindian villages is needed from the Ministry of Public Works, Communications and Regional Development in Georgetown. Without permit or identification you will be sent straight back to Georgetown or on to Brazil.

Lethem, a small but scattered town on the Brazilian frontier, is the service centre for the Rupununi and for trade with Brazil. There are a few stores, a small hospital, a police station and government offices which have radio telephone links with Georgetown. Prices are about twice as high as in Georgetown. About 1½ miles S of town at St Ignatius there is a Jesuit mission dating from 1911. In the nearby mountains there is good birdwatching and there are waterfalls to visit.

Food and Lodging in the Rupununi Eat at *Foo Foods*, *Savannah Inn*, or the Airport Shop in Lethem. A number of places take guests, full board, organize tours and transport. **Accommodation** in Lethem at *Casique Guest House*, OK, and *Regional Guest House*. The *Manari Ranch Hotel*, 7 miles N of Lethem, also *Pirara Ranch*, 15 miles further N, both on creeks for swimming, both US$50 pp/day. Duane and Sandy de Freitas at the *Dadanawa Ranch*, 60 miles S of Lethem, one of the world's largest ranches, US$95 pp/day. They can organize trekking and horse riding trips (contact *Wilderness Explorers*, T 62085, US$95/day). Dianne McTurk at *Karanambo Ranch*, 60 miles NE of Lethem, on the Rupununi River, US$120/day (unique old home with cottages for visitors, fishing, excellent birdwatching and boat rides). The owner rears and rehabilitates orphaned giant river otters. Can be booked through *Wilderness Explorers*, T 62085. At the village of Annai on the road to Georgetown, some 70 miles from Lethem *The Rock View Ecotourism Resort* has 4 rooms and cheaper rooms in the main ranch house; it is located in the Pakaraima foothills, where the savannah meets the Iwokrama rainforest project; contact Colin Edwards, Trans Guyana Aviation, T 60605/65128 (in Georgetown, contact Jackie Allicock on T 73010/73188, F 51171); pony treks to nearby foothills, nature tours with opportunities for painting, photography and fishing, regional Amerindian and other local cooking, US$115/day full board, rec. All can be contacted at the Airport Shop in Lethem, where Don and Shirley Melville provide the most comprehensive information and assistance service in the Rupununi. In Georgetown contact Wendella Jackson, T 53750 (for *Karanambo*), or Tony Thorne at *Wilderness Explorers*, T 62085.

Exchange The Melvilles in Lethem or the de Freitas at *Dadanawa* may exchange certain currencies and TCs (technically illegal) at the going local rate. Samuel Hawker (see below) also changes money. Changing money is unlikely to be much better on the Brazilian side of the frontier.

Transport At *Foo Foods* bicycles can be hired for US$8/day; also available at the Airport Shop, as are horses for US$8/hr. The Airport Shop can arrange landrovers and trucks at US$3 per mile. For birdwatching trips/transport contact Loris Franklin through the Airport Shop.

Transport around the Rupununi is difficult; there are a few four-wheel drive vehicles, but ox-carts and bicycles are more common on the rough roads. From Lethem trucks can be hired for day-trips to the Moco-Moco Falls and the Kamu Falls and to the Kanuku Mountains. Trucks may also be hired to visit Aishalton, 70 miles S along a very bad road, 6 hrs journey, US$300; and to Annai, 60 miles N E along a better road, 3 hrs journey, US$200. Samuel Hawker near the police station has 5 trucks; nice fellow, he may let you sling your hammock in his backyard. All trucks leaving town must check with the police so the police know all trucks that are departing.

An extraordinary account of an overland journey from Georgetown to the Rupununi and on to Boa Vista in the 1930s is to be found in *Ninety-Two Days* by Evelyn Waugh.

A road link between Georgetown and Lethem via Mabura Hill and Kurupakari was opened in early 1991. Once completed it will provide a through route from Georgetown to Boa Vista (Brazil), which will have a major impact on Guyana. The funding for the final section has not been found, and it remains virtually impassable. The present route is: good road to Linden, and good for 50 miles beyond, then rapid deterioration for 100 miles to the Essequibo river. Creeks are often bridged by just 2 logs. It is either very dusty or very muddy, challenging, uncomfortable, and a great experience. The road is better in the dry season, but in the rains the worst sections are bypassed with boats.

Truck Georgetown-Lethem: contact Ministry of Regional Development, Georgetown, Eddie Singh, 137 Herstelling, nr Providence police station, 5 miles S of Georgetown, T (065) 2672, or Borderline, Belvair Court, Georgetown, Ng-a-fook, on Church St, between Camp St and Waterloo St. Trip takes 2-3 days, can take 7, US$28 pp one-way, no seat but share truck with load, take food, lots of water and hammock. (Care is needed on this route, but it is exciting, through savannah and rainforest.) Guyana Airways Corporation flies from Georgetown to Lethem and back Tues, Wed, Fri and Sat 0515, US$53 one-way (reliable; diversions available to Annai and Karanambu Ranch for extra US$175 per flight); book well in advance at the GAC office on Main St, Georgetown. Regular charter planes link the town with Georgetown, about US$200 return.

Crossing to Brazil Formalities are generally reported to be very lax on both sides of the border, but it is important to observe them as there are reports of people being refused entry to Guyana for not having the correct papers, including visa. In Lethem all procedures are dealt with at the police station (there is also immigration at the airport); report there also with a visa if arriving from Brazil. The Takutu river, the frontier between the two countries, is about 1 mile N of Lethem (taxis available, or pick-ups, US$1). There are small boats for foot passengers (US$0.25) and a pontoon for vehicles. Vehicles can drive across the river in the dry season. Just over the river is a shop and the Brazilian customs post. From here it is 1½ mile walk to the village of Bonfim, from where a bus leaves for Boa Vista at 0800 Tue, Thur, Sat (from Boa Vista to Bonfim at 1630 Mon, Wed, Fri), 3½ hrs, US$5. Colectivo US$15, 3 hrs. It is possible to cycle across to Bonfim with minimum formalities (5 km), but if you want to take a bus on to Boa Vista full passport/visas (if necessary) are required.

INFORMATION FOR VISITORS

Before you go

Entry requirements

● **Documents**

Visa requirements have been relaxed; as of 15 February 1993, the following countries do not need a visa to visit Guyana: USA, Canada, Belgium, Denmark, France, Germany, Greece, Ireland, Italy, Luxembourg, the Netherlands, Portugal, Spain, UK, Norway, Finland, Sweden, Australia, New Zealand, Japan, South Korea, and the Caricom countries. Visitors are advised to check with the nearest Embassy, Consulate or travel agent for further changes. All visitors require passports and all nationalities, apart from those above, require visas. To obtain a visa, two photos, an onward ticket and yellow fever certificate are required. Visas are charged strictly on a reciprocal basis, equivalent to the cost charged to a Guyanese visitor to the country concerned. Visitors from those countries where they are required arriving without visas are refused entry. To fly into Guyana, an exit ticket is required; onward tickets are not usually asked for at land borders.

Health

There is a high risk of both types of malaria in the interior, especially in the wet season. Recommended prophylaxis is chloroquine 500 mg weekly plus paludrine 200 mg daily. Reports of chloroquine-resistant malaria in the interior (seek advice before going). If travelling to the interior for long periods carry drugs for treatment as these may not be available. Sleep under a mosquito net. Although there are plenty of mosquitoes on the coast, they are not malarial.

There is some risk of typhoid and waterborne diseases owing to low water pressure. Purification is a good idea. Tapwater is usually brown and contains sediment. It is not for drinking, bottled water (Tropical Mist) should be bought for drinking. In the interior, use purification.

The Georgetown Hospital is run down, understaffed and lacking equipment, but there are a number of well-equipped private hospitals, including St Joseph's on Parade St, Kingston (24-hrs a day service); Prasad's on Thomas St, doctor on call at weekends; and the Davis Memorial Hospital on Lodge Backlands. Charges are US$2 to US$8 per day and medical consultations cost US$2 to US$4. If admitted to hospital you are expected to provide your own sheets and food (St Joseph's and Davis provides all these). Recommended doctor, Dr Clarence Charles, 254 Thomas St, surgery 1200-1400 daily.

In the interior, travellers should examine shower pipes, bedding, shoes and clothing for snakes and spiders. Also, in most towns there is neither a hospital, nor police; the people are very friendly, but if travelling independently, you are on your own.

Money

● **Currency**

The unit is the Guyanese dollar. There are notes for 1, 5, 10, 20, 100 and 500 dollars, though devaluation and inflation mean that even the largest of these is worth very little. Coins for amounts under a dollar exist but are of little practical use.

● **Cost of living**
The devaluation to the *cambio* rate means that, for foreigners, prices for food and drink are low at present. Even imported goods may be cheaper than elsewhere and locally produced goods such as fruit are very cheap. Hotels, tours and services in the interior are subject to electricity and fuel surcharges, which make them less cheap.

● **Exchange**
The devaluation of the Guyanese dollar in Feb 1991 aligned the official exchange rate with that offered by licensed exchange houses (known as *cambios*). Since that date the exchange rate was to be adjusted weekly in line with the market rate. In May 1995, this stood at G$143 = US$1. At present *cambios* only buy US or Canadian dollars and pounds sterling. Most *cambios* accept drafts (subject to verification), TCs and telegraphic transfers, but not credit cards. Rates vary slightly between *cambios* and from day to day and some *cambios* offer better rates for changing over US$100. Rates for changing TCs are good in *cambios* or on the black market. A few banks accept Thomas Cook TCs. Note that to sell Guyanese dollars on leaving the country, you will need to produce your *cambio* receipt. The illegal black market on America St ('Wall St') in Georgetown still operates, but the rates offered are not significantly better than the *cambio* rate and there is a strong risk of being robbed or cheated. The black market also operates in Springlands, the entry point from Suriname. For Western Union money transfers, T 275141.

Getting there

By Air

There are no direct flights to Guyana from Europe, but BWIA's flights from London, Frankfurt and Zurich to Port of Spain connect; from North America BWIA flies daily from Miami; via Port of Spain. Guyana Airways fly 5 times a week from New York and once from Miami, 2 of the New York flights via Curaçao. BWIA flies to Guyana from Trinidad 3 times a day (Suriname Airways 3 a week). LIAT flies daily from Barbados (Suriname Airways 4 a week, Carib Express 4 a week); from Antigua BWIA connects in Port of Spain daily. Surinam Airways flies every day but Tues from Paramaribo (connections to Cayenne), with onward flights to Barbados 4 times a week and to Port of Spain twice a week, while Gonini Air flies daily, but these flights are difficult to book from outside the Guianas and are subject to cancellation at short notice. Aserca flies on Sun from Caracas.

Flights are often booked weeks in advance, especially at Christmas and in Aug when overseas Guyanese return to visit relatives. Flights are frequently overbooked, so it is essential to reconfirm your outward flight, which can take some time, and difficult to change your travel plans at the last minute. A number of travel agents are now computerized, making reservations and reconfirmations easier. Foreigners must pay for airline tickets in US$ (most airlines do not accept US$100 bills), or other specified currencies. Luggage should be securely locked as theft from checked-in baggage is common.

Customs

Baggage examination can be very thorough. Duties are high on goods imported in commercial quantities.

When you arrive

● **Official time**
4 hrs behind GMT.

● **Things to take**
A good torch/flashlight and batteries (for the electricity cuts) is essential. Small gift items (eg imported cigarettes, batteries, good quality toiletries) may be appreciated in the interior (they are readily available in Georgetown).

● **Voltage**
100 v in Georgetown; 220 v in most other places, including some Georgetown suburbs.

● **Weights and measures**
Although Guyana went metric in 1982, imperial measures are still widely used.

Where to stay

The largest hotels in Georgetown have their own emergency electricity generators and water pumps to deal with the frequent interruptions in supply. Other hotels usually provide a bucket of water in your room – fill this up when water is available. When booking an air-conditioned room, make sure it also has natural ventilation. A room tax applies to hotels with more than 16 rooms.

Food and drink

Food

The blend of different national influences – Indian, African, Chinese, Creole, English, Portuguese, Amerindian, North American – gives a distinctive flavour to Guyanese cuisine. One well-known dish, traditional at Christmas, is pepper-pot, meat cooked in bitter cassava (casareep) juice with peppers and herbs. Seafood is plentiful and varied, as is the wide variety of tropical fruits and vegetables. The staple food is rice. The food shortages and import ban of the early 1980s had the positive effect of encouraging experimentation with local ingredients, sometimes with interesting results. In the interior wild meat is often available – try wild cow, or else labba (a small rodent).

Drink

Rum is the most popular drink. There is a wide variety of brands, all cheap, including the best which are very good and cost less than US$2 a bottle. Demerara Distillers' 12-year-old *King of Diamonds* premium rum won the *Caribbean Week* (Barbados) Caribbean rum tasting for 2 years running (1992, 1993); its 15-year old *El Dorado* won in 1994. High wine is a strong local rum. There is also local brandy and whisky (Diamond Club), which are worth trying. The local beer, Banks, made partly from rice is good and cheap. There is a wide variety of fruit juices. A new drink, D'Aguiar's Cream Liqueur, produced and bottled by Banks DIH Ltd, is excellent (and strong).

On departure

● **Airport tax**
There is an exit tax of G$1,500, payable in Guyanese dollars, or US dollars at US$13. It can be paid when reconfirming your ticket at least 3 days before expected departure, in Georgetown, or at the airport after check-in. There is also a 15% tax on international airline tickets for all flights leaving Guyana even if bought abroad.

Getting around

Air transport

Guyana Airways has scheduled flights between Georgetown and Lethem on Tues, Wed, Fri and Sat. There are several charter companies, including Mazaharally, Trans Guyana Airways (158-9 Charlotte St, T 73010) and Kayman Sankar; US$320/hr. Ask the charter companies at Ogle airport for seats on cargo flights to any destination, they will help you to get in touch with the charterer. Prices vary, up to US$0.80 per pound. Returning to Ogle can be cheaper, even, if you are lucky, free.

Road

Most coastal towns are linked by a good 185 mile road from Springlands in the E to Charity in the W; the Berbice and Essequibo rivers are crossed by ferries, the Demerara by a toll bridge, which, besides closing at high tide for ships to pass through (2-3 hrs) is subject to frequent closures (when an alternative ferry service runs). Apart from a good road connecting Timehri and Linden, continuing as good dirt to Mabura Hill, most other roads in the interior are very poor. Car hire is available from several firms, see under Georgetown. There are shortages of car spares. Gasoline costs about US$1.40 a gallon. Traffic drives on the left. Minibuses and collective taxis, an H on their numberplate, run between Georgetown and the entire coast from Charity to Corriverton; also to Linden.

River transport

There are over 600 miles of navigable river, which provide an important means of communication. Ferries and river boats are referred to in the text, but for further details contact the Transport and Harbours Department, Water St, Georgetown. Note that there is no vehicle ferry across the Courantyne to Suriname.

Communications

● **Newspapers**
The Chronicle, daily except Mon; *The Mirror*, daily, PPP-run; *The Stabroek News*, daily, independent; *The Catholic Standard*, weekly, well-respected and widely read. Street vendors charge more than the cover price – this is normal and helps them make a living.

● **Postal and telephone services**
Overseas postal and telephone charges are very low. Letters to N and S America US$0.21, to Europe US$0.25, to rest of world US$0.42; post cards US$0.15; aerogrammes US$0.18. Parcels sent abroad have to be weighed and checked by customs before sealing. Take all materials and passport; choose between ordinary and registered service. Telecommunications are rapidly improving. It is possible to dial direct to any country in the world. Blue public telephones in Georgetown only allow collect calls overseas; phone booths have overseas, 3-digit codes printed inside. Yellow

phones are for free calls to local areas. Some businesses and hotels may allow you to use their phone for local calls if you are buying something – usual charge about US$0.05. Overseas calls can be made from the Guyana Telephone and Telegraph Company office behind the Bank of Guyana building; open daily till 2000 (arrive early and be prepared for a long wait), or from the *Tower Hotel* (more expensive but more comfortable). Calls are subject to 10% tax. Travel agencies may allow you to make overseas collect calls when buying tickets. Hotels add high extra charges to phone bills. Canada Direct, dial 0161; UK direct 169. Fax rates to Europe are economical, under US$1 per page. Most hotels have fax service.

● **Radio**
GBC Radio is government-run and is often difficult to receive.

● **Television**
There are six TV channels, mainly broad-casting programmes from US satellite television. Local content is increasing.

Holidays and festivals

1 Jan, New Years' Day; 23 Feb, Republic Day and Mashramani festival; Good Friday, Easter Monday; Labour Day, 1 May; Caricom Day, first Mon in July; Freedom Day, first Mon in Aug; Christmas Day, 25 Dec, and Boxing Day, 26 Dec.

The following public holidays are for Hindu and Muslim festivals; they follow a lunar calender, and dates should be checked as required: Phagwah, usually Mar; Eid el Fitr, end of Ramadan; Eid el Azah; Youm un Nabi; Deepavali, usually Nov.

NB The Republic Day celebrations last about a week: during this time hotels in Georgetown are very full.

Acknowledgements

We are grateful to Tony Thorne (Georgetown) for an update of the Guyana chapter, also, for her assistance, to Dianne Raghoo. Thanks are also due to Jacqueline Fletcher (Guyana High Commission, London). For acknowledgements to travellers, see after Guyane.

SURINAME

SURINAME has a coast line on the Atlantic to the N; it is bounded on the W by Guyana and on the E by French Guyane; Brazil is to the S.

The principal rivers in the country are the Marowijne in the E, the Corantijn in the W, and the Suriname, Commewijne (with its tributary, the Cottica), Coppename, Saramacca and Nickerie. The country is divided into topographically quite diverse natural regions: lowland, savannah, and highland.

The northern part of the country consists of lowland, with a width in the E of 25 km, and in the W of about 80 km. The soil (clay) is covered with swamps with a layer of humus under them. Marks of the old sea-shores can be seen in the shell and sand ridges, overgrown with tall trees.

There follows a region, 5-6 km wide, of a loamy and very white sandy soil, then a slightly undulating region, about 30 km wide. It is mainly savannah, mostly covered with quartz sand, and overgrown with grass and shrubs.

S of this lies the interior highland, almost entirely overgrown with dense tropical forest and intersected by streams. At the southern boundary with Brazil there are again savannahs. These, however, differ in soil and vegetation from the northern ones. A large area in the SW is in dispute between Guyana and Suriname. There is a less serious border dispute with Guyane in the SE.

Climate Tropical and moist, but not very hot, since the northeast trade wind makes itself felt during the whole year. In the coastal area the temperature varies on an average from 23° to 31°C, during the day; the annual mean is 27°C, and the monthly mean ranges from 26° to 28°C, only. The mean annual rainfall is about 2,340 mm for Paramaribo and 1,930 mm for the western division. The seasons are: minor rainy season, Nov-Feb; minor dry season, Feb-Apr; main rainy season, Apr-Aug; main dry season, Aug-Nov. None of these seasons is, however, usually either very dry or very wet. The degree of cloudiness is fairly high and the average humidity is 82%. The climate of the interior is similar but with higher rainfall.

History Although Amsterdam merchants had been trading with the 'wild coast' of Guiana as early as 1613 (the name Parmurbo-Paramaribo was already known) it was not until 1630 that 60 English settlers came to Suriname under Captain Marshall and planted tobacco. The real founder of the colony was Lord Willoughby of Parham, governor of Barbados, who sent an expedition to Suriname in 1651 under Anthony Rowse to find a suitable place for settlement. Willoughbyland became an agricultural colony with 500 little sugar plantations, 1,000 white inhabitants and 2,000 African slaves. Jews from Holland and Italy joined them, as well as Dutch Jews ejected from Brazil after 1654. On 27 February 1667, Admiral Crynssen conquered the colony for the states of Zeeland and Willoughbyfort became the present Fort Zeelandia. By the Peace of Breda—31 July 1667—it was agreed that Suriname should remain with the Netherlands, while Nieuw Amsterdam (New York) should be given to England. The colony was conquered by the British in 1799, and not until the Treaty of Paris in 1814 was it finally restored to the Netherlands. Slavery was forbidden in 1818 and formally abolished in 1863. Indentured labour from China and the East Indies took its place.

On 25 November 1975, the country became an independent republic, which signed a treaty with the Netherlands for an economic aid programme worth US$1.5bn until 1985. A military coup on 25 February 1980 overthrew the elected government. A state of emergency was declared, with censorship of the press, radio and TV. The military leader, Col Desi Bouterse, and his associates came under pressure from the Dutch and the USA as a result of dictatorial tendencies. After the execution of 15 opposition leaders on 8 December 1982, the Netherlands broke off relations and suspended its aid programme, although bridging finance was restored in 1988.

The ban on political parties was lifted in late 1985 and a new constitution was drafted. In 1986 guerrilla rebels (the Jungle Commando), led by a former bodyguard of Col Bouterse, Ronny Brunswijk, mounted a campaign to overthrow the government, disrupting both plans for political change and the economy. Nevertheless, elections for the National Assembly were held in Nov 1987. A three-party coalition (the Front for Democracy and Development) gained a landslide victory over the military, winning 40 of the 51 seats but conflicts between Assembly President Ramsewak Shankar and Col Bouterse led to the deposition of the government in a bloodless coup on 24 December 1990 (the 'telephone coup'). A military-backed government under the presidency of Johan Kraag installed and elections for a new national assembly were held on 25 May 1991. The New Front of four traditional parties won 30 National Assembly seats. Twelve went to the army-backed National Democratic Party (led by Col Boutose) and nine to the Democratic Alternative, which favours closer links with The Netherlands. Ronald Venetiaan of the New Front was elected president on 6 September 1991. Meetings between Suriname and the Netherlands ministers after the 1991 elections led to the renewal of aid in the second half of 1992. In Aug 1992, a peace treaty was eventually signed between the government and the Jungle Commando in Aug 1992, but the different factions retained control of their respective areas in the interior and violence breaks out occasionally.

By 1993, the New Front's popularity had slumped as its handling of the economy failed to reap any benefit from the 1992 Structural Adjustment Programme and corruption scandals undermined its claim to introduce 'clean politics'. Both Bouterse's NDP and Democratic Alliance strengthened their opposition to government policies, calling for strikes and protests, but as these two parties have wide ideological differences, no concerted campaign against the New Front was mounted. Much greater impetus was given to popular discontent by the economic decline, which reached catastrophic proportions by 1995. Inflation soared, partly as a result of the removal of subsidies on all basic items, the currency depreciated and purchasing power slumped. For most Surinamese, their standard of living was said to be almost as low as that of Haiti.

Population The 1980 census showed that the population had declined to 352,041, because of heavy emigration to the Netherlands. By 1994 it was estimated to have grown to 423,000. The 1991 population consisted of Indo-Pakistanis (known locally as Hindustanis), 33%; Creoles (European-African and other descent), 35%; Javanese, 16%; Bush Negroes, called locally 'bosnegers' (retribalized descendants of slaves who escaped in the 17th century, living on the upper Saramacca, Suriname and Marowijne rivers), 10%; Europeans, Chinese and others, 3%; Amerindians, 3% (some sources say only 1%). About 90% of the existing population live in or around Paramaribo or in the coastal towns; the remainder, mostly Carib and Arawak Indians and Bush Blacks, are widely scattered.

The Asian people originally entered the country as contracted estate labourers, and settled in agriculture or commerce after completion of their term. They dominate the countryside, whereas Paramaribo is racially very mixed. Although some degree of racial tension exists between all the different groups, Creole-Hindustani rivalry is not as fundamental an issue as in Guyana, for example. Many Surinamese, of all backgrounds, pride themselves on their ability to get along with one another in such a heterogeneous country.

The official language is Dutch. The native language, called Sranan Tongo, originally the speech of the Creoles, is now a *lingua franca* understood by all groups, and standard English is widely spoken and understood. The Asians still speak their own languages among themselves.

The Economy Agriculture is restricted to some districts of the alluvial coastal zone, covering about 0.8m hectares. At least two-thirds of permanent crop and arable land is under irrigation. Farming (including forestry) accounts for 14.7% of gdp and about 15% of exports. The main crops are rice (the staple), bananas, sugar cane and citrus fruits, all of which are exported to Europe, along with small quantities of coffee. Apart from rice, Suriname is a net importer of food; priority is being given to rice and livestock. Suriname has vast timber resources, but exports account for only 0.2% of the total and development has been hampered by a lack of investment. There is a small fishing industry, the chief catch being shrimps.

Manufacturing's contribution to gdp is 11%. Import substitution, using both imported goods and local raw materials, is the main activity, with food processing accounting for 60% of the total.

Suriname is a major producer of bauxite, with reserves estimated at 1.9% of the world's total. The country has the capability to process the extracted ore into alumina

Suriname : fact file

Geographic
Land area	163,820 sq km
forested	94.9%
pastures	0.1%
cultivated	0.4%

Demographic
Population (1994)	423,000
annual growth rate (1989-94)	1.0%
urban	48.7%
rural	51.3%
density	2.6 per sq km
Religious affiliation	
Hindu	26.0%
Roman Catholic	21.6%
Muslim	18.6%
Protestant	18.0%
Birth rate per 1,000 (1991)	22.5
(world av 26.0)	

Education and Health
Life expectancy at birth,	
male	66.6 years
female	71.8 years
Infant mortality rate	
per 1,000 live births (1986)	26.5
Physicians (1990)	1 per 1,348 persons
Hospital beds	1 per 212 persons
Calorie intake as %	
of FAO requirement	108%
Literate males (over 15)	95.1%
Literate females (over 15)	94.7%

Economic
GDP (1988 market prices)	US$395mn[1]
GDP per capita	US$883[1]
Public external debt (1990)	US$138mn
Tourism receipts (1992)	US$11mn
Inflation (annual av 1988-93)	40.2%
Radio	1 per 1.4 persons
Television	1 per 7.0 persons
Telephone	1 per 6.5 persons

Employment
Population economically active (1990)	99,010
Unemployment rate	15.5%
% of labour force in	
agriculture	2.9
mining	2.4
manufacturing	8.9
construction	3.9
Military forces	1,800

Source *Encyclopaedia Britannica*

[1] Inter-American Development-Bank, 1993 provisional figure.

and aluminium ingot. The bauxite/aluminium industry accounts for 79% of exports, while the mining sector as a whole contributes 2.2% of gdp. Two companies control the industry, the Suriname Aluminium Company (Suralco), a subsidiary of Alcoa, and Billiton Maatschappij, part of Royal Dutch Shell. Their progressive merging of operations to improve competitiveness on world markets began to yield positive results in 1986 until the industry was severely disrupted by the civil war which started in that year.

Oil production from the Tambaredjo heavy oil deposit, operated by the state oil company, Staatsolie, is about 4,700 bpd. Exploratory wells in the Saramacca district have also yielded oil. Installed electricity generating capacity is 415 MW, of which 21% is thermal, 79% hydroelectric.

After 5 years of decline and a fall in gdp of 8.1% in 1987 alone, the economy began to recover, helped by resumption of activity in the bauxite industry, the attenuation of the domestic insurgency and the resumption of aid from the Dutch Government. Consistent improvement was not maintained and The Netherlands, the IMF and World Bank urged Suriname to unify the official and parallel exchange rates, reduce state involvement in the economy and cut the huge budget deficit to attract overseas investment. These issues began to be addressed after a new economic crisis in 1991 when the export price of alumina fell by 25% and Dutch aid was again cut after the 1990 coup. In 1992 a Structural Adjustment Programme was drawn up as a forerunner to a Multi-Year Development Programme (for 1994-98). The unification of official and market exchange rates was achieved in July 1994 and a floating rate of Sf 183 was established, replacing a complex exchange rate system. By Feb 1995 the official floating exchange rate had fallen to Sf 430 = US$1. The government made little progress in complying with the Structural Adjustment Programme. Inflation rose sharply, reaching 369.2% by end-1994; prices of staple items also rose and subsidies on basic goods and services were removed. Petrol rationing was introduced in Sept 1993 as the government could not pay suppliers' bills. At the same time, the decline in government income meant that public salaries could not be paid. The EU suspended balance of payments support in 1993 pending Suriname seeking renewed assistance from the IMF or World Bank in monitoring the economy. While EU aid of G88mn was granted in 1994 for the development of rural areas, social projects and the reconstruction of the E-W road, the Netherlands was reluctant to fund an economy whose management lacked cohesion

Economic productivity and consumer purchasing power remain low. The infrastructure destroyed in the civil war has yet to be rebuilt. Much fertile agricultural land lies fallow. Protests and strikes over low wages and sharp price rises hamper economic activity. Many Surinamese continue to depend on funds sent by family members living in the Netherlands or working illegally in neighbouring Guyane.

Government There is one legislative house, the National Assembly, which has 51 members. The President is both head of state and government. Suriname is divided into ten districts, of which the capital is one.

Warnings Photography is now generally permitted. Only obviously military installations remain off limits. When in doubt, ask first. Those travelling to the interior should inquire in the capital about the public safety situation in the areas they plan to visit. The presence of rival armed factions in some places remains a hazard and the government is not fully in control of the entire country. Street crime in Paramaribo merits the usual precautions, especially at night and near the market at any hour.

Paramaribo, the capital and chief port, lies on the Suriname river, 12 km from the sea. It has a population of about 192,000. There are many attractive colonial buildings.

The Governor's Mansion (now the Presidential Palace) is on Onafhankelijkheidsplein (also called Eenheidsplein and originally, Oranjeplein). Many beautiful 18th and 19th century buildings in Dutch (neo-Normanic) style are in the same area. A few have been restored but much of the old city is sadly decaying. Fort Zeelandia used to house the Suriname Museum before it was repossessed by the military. The whole complex has been opened to the public again and its historic buildings can be visited. The fort itself now belongs to the Stichting (foundation) Surinaams Museum, but it needs to be restored. Very few exhibits remain in the old museum in the residential suburb of Zorg-en-Hoop, Commewijnestraat, 0700-1300. Look for Mr F Lim-A-Po-straat if you wish to see what Paramaribo looked like only a comparatively short time ago. The nineteenth-century Roman Catholic Peter and Paul cathedral (1885), built entirely of wood, is said to be the largest wooden building in the Americas, and is well worth a visit (closed indefinitely for repairs since 1993). Other things to see are the colourful market and the waterfront, Hindu temples in Koningstraat and Gravenstraat 31, the Caribbean's largest mosque at Keizerstraat (magnificent photos of it can be taken at sunset). There are two synagogues: one next to the mosque on Keizerstraat, the other (1854) on the corner of Klipstenstraat and Heerenstraat (services on Sat morning, alternating monthly between the two – to visit when closed T 498944 and ask for Dennis Kopinsky). A new harbour has been constructed about 1½ km upstream. Two pleasant parks are the Palmentuin, with a stage for concerts, and the Cultuurtuin (with well-kept zoo, US$1.20, busy on Sun)—the latter is a 20-mins walk from the centre. National dress is normally only worn by the Asians on national holidays and at wedding parties, but some Javanese women still go about in sarong and klambi. A university was opened in 1968. There is one public swimming pool at Weidestraat, US$0.60 pp. There is an exotic Asian flavour to the market and nearby streets. Cinemas show US, Indian and Chinese movies, with subtitles.

An interesting custom practised throughout Suriname is the birdsong competitions. These are held in parks and public plazas on Sun and holidays. People carrying their songbird (usually a small black tua-tua) in a cage are a frequent sight on the streets of Paramaribo at any time; on their way to and from work, off to a 'training session', or simply taking their pet for a stroll!

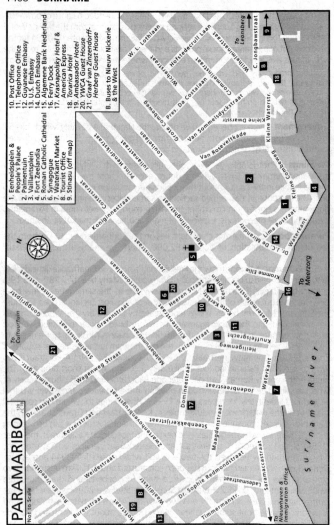

PARAMARIBO
Not to Scale

128/C79

1. Eenheidsplein & People's Palace
2. Palmentuin
3. Vaillantsplein
4. Fort Zeelandia
5. Roman Catholic Cathedral
6. Synagogue
7. Waterkant Market
8. Tourist Office
9. Stinasu (off map)
10. Post Office
11. Telephone Office
12. Guyanese Embassy
13. U.S. Embassy
14. Dutch Embassy
15. Algemene Bank Nederland
16. Ferry Dock
17. Krasnapolsky Hotel & American Express
18. Torarica Hotel
19. Ambassador Hotel
20. YWCA Guest House
21. Graaf van Zinzendorff-Herberg Guest House
B. Buses to Nieuw Nickerie & the West

Hotels Service charge at hotels is 10-15%. **L3** *Torarica*, T 471500, F 411682, PO Box 1514, Telex 167 SURTOR, best in town, very pleasant, book ahead, swimming pool, casino, nightclub, tropical gardens, a/c, central, 3 restaurants (bar, poolside buffet, and very good French restaurant), superb breakfast; **A3** *Krasnapolsky*, Domineestraat 39, T 475050, F 420139, a/c, central, good breakfast, shops, launderette, bank (see Exchange below), swimming pool; **A3** *Ambassador*, T 477555, F 477903, Telex 295 HOTAM SN, a/c, restaurant; **A3** *Era Fit*, Cornelis Prinsstraat 87, T 493284, 5 km from centre, good report; **A3** *Riverclub*, at Leonsberg (8 km from city), T 451959, F 452981, a/c, nightclub, small restaurant, swimming pool.

A3-B *Mets Residence Inn*, 10A Rode Kruislaan, T 431990/490739, F 432630, with bath, a/c, TV, minibar, laundry, incl breakfast, credit cards accepted, new, 3-star, in a residential area.

D *Guesthouse Flair*, Kleine Waterstraat 7, T 422455/474794, opp *Torarica*, a/c, clean, safe, helpful. For budget travellers, best is **E** *YWCA Guesthouse* at Heerenstraat 14-16, T 476981, cheaper weekly rates, clean, full of permanent residents, essential to book in advance (office open 0800-1400); if it's full try the **E** *Graaf Van Zinzendorff-Herberg* at Gravenstraat 100, T 471607, large rooms, TV lounge. Advance booking advisable. **E** *Doble R*, Kleine Waterstraat opp *Torarica*, T 473592, a/c, clean, good value, but noisy bar downstairs, restaurant, often full. The Suriname Museum in Zorg-en-Hoop now has a good guest house; book in advance. Otherwise, try **E-G** *Fanna*, Princessestraat 31, T 476789, from a/c with bath to basic, breakfast extra, safe, clean, friendly, family run, English spoken, rec, can book in advance; *La Vida* on the way in from the airport is 'cheap but nice'. **D** *Blue Moon*, Prinsessestraat, overpriced, fleas; **E** *Mivimost*, Anamoestraat 23, 3 km from centre, T 451002, a/c, cheaper with fan, toilet, clean, safe, friendly, rec; *Lisa's Guest House*, Buren Straat, noisy, overpriced. *Mrs Robles' Guesthouse*, Roseveltkade 20, T 474770, family run, organizes tours. *Balden*, Kwathweg 183, 2 km from centre on the road to Nickerie is probably the cheapest available accommodation; its Chinese restaurant serves cheap meals. Beware: many cheap hotels not listed above are 'hot pillow' establishments. A religious organization, Stadszending, Burenstraat 17-19, T 47307, G, good location, clean, friendly, best to reserve. The *Salvation Army*, Saramaccastraat, will give the hard up a bed for a minimal price. Mrs Rudia Shair-Ali, Toenalaan 29, 20 mins walk from centre, not a hotel but a large private house: Mrs Shair-Ali charges US$1-2 a night if she has a free room, free use of fridge and kitchen equipment.

Restaurants There are some good restaurants, mainly Indonesian and Chinese dishes. Try a *rijsttafel* in an Indonesian restaurant, eg *Sarinah* (open-air dining), Verlengde Gemenelandsweg 187; *Bali*, Ma Retraiteweg 3, T 422325, very good food, service and atmosphere. *La Bastille*, Kleine Waterstraat, opp *Torarica*, good, T 473991; also *Golden Dragon*, Anamoestraat 22, **New Korean**, Mahonylaan (good fish), *Golden Crown*, David Simmonstraat; *Roja's*, corner of Mahonylaan and Grote Combeweg, and *New China*, Verlengde Gemenelandsweg. *Fa Tai*, Maagdenstraat 64, a/c; for the best Chinese food, but not cheap, try *Iwan's*, Grote Hofstraat. *Oriental Foods*, Gravenstraat 118, for well-prepared Chinese food, rec. Many other Chinese restaurants: *Chi Wan* for its *egg foo yung* and *won ton soup*, Keizerstraat and Zwartenhovenbrugstraat 16. *Moti Mahal*, Wagenwagstraat 58, near Star Cinema, excellent *roti* and Indian snacks. The *YWCA Cafeteria* is quite good. Cheap lunches and light meals at *Chindy's*, Keizerstraat opp TeleSur, lunch only, try *pom*, also ice cream; *Hofje*, Wagenwegstraat, and *Chalet Swiss*, Heerenstraat (more Chinese than Swiss). *Natura*, Rust-en-Vredestraat between Keizerstraat and Weidestraat, whole-grain bread and natural foods. Meat and noodles from stalls in the market are very cheap. Javanese foodstalls on Waterkant are excellent and varied, lit at night by candles. Try *bami* (spicy noodles) and *petjil* (vegetables). Especially rec on Sun when the area is busiest. In restaurants a dish to try is *gadogado*, an Indonesian vegetable and peanut concoction. Good places for lunch include *Hola's Terrace*, Domineestraat. For breakfast, try *Klein Maar Fijn*, Watermolenstraat. Local beer, Parbo, is worth a try.

Exchange **Algemene Bank Nederland** (Kerkplein 1), **AMRO Bank**, **Surinaamsche Bank** (near the cathedral) and **Hakrin Bank**, 0700-1400. Surinaamsche branch in *Hotel Krasnapolsky* open 0700-1430; 0800-1200 Sat, charges commission on each TC exchanged. Amex agent is C Kersten and Co, NV, in *Hotel Krasnapolsky*, T 477148. Black market changers congregate outside the *Hotel Krasnapolsky* and they are the best bet when banks are closed. Be very wary of money changers in the market and on the street, who approach you calling 'wissel' (exchange). Many visitors have been robbed or cheated and, as the black market is illegal, you have no recourse. Many shop keepers will change cash at parallel rates and this is a much safer option. Ask around for best rates.

Nightclubs Discothèques: *Touche*, Waaldijk/Dr Sophie Redmonstraat 60, Fri and Sat only 2300, small restaurant and the best disco; *Crush* (take a taxi); *Carloursy*, nr *Krasnapolsky*, on 1st floor. In many nightclubs there are Brazilian girls seeking European husbands; one where it not blatant is *El Condor*, Zwartenhovenbrugstraat, not far from *Ambassador Hotel*, a/c, clean, restaurant, soft music, often full.

Post Office Main office at Kerkplein; subsidiaries in *Hotel Krasnapolsky* and in the districts **(see Post, Telegraph, Telephone, p 1477)**.

Places of Worship The Anglican Church is St Bridget's, Hoogestraat 44 (Sun 0900 service in English). Roman Catholic Cathedral on Gravenstraat. Dutch Reformed Church and many other denominations.

Shopping Crafts of Amerindian and Bush Negro origin. *Arts & Crafts*, Neumanpad 13a. Amerindian goods, batik prints, carvings, basket work, drums are attractive. *Cultuurwinkel*,

Anton de Kom Straat, Bush Negro carvings, also available at *Hotel Torarica*. Carvings are better value at the workshops on Nieuwe Dominee Straat and the Neumanpad. *Peet* woodworks have been recommended for hardwood pieces. Local ceramics are sold on the road between the airport and Paranam, but they are rather brittle. Old Dutch bottles are sold. *Disco Amigo*, sells local and international music on cassette (no CDs of national music, which is heavily influenced by Caribbean styles).

Bookshops The two main bookshops are *Vaco* (opp *Krasnapolsky*) and *Kersten*, both on Domineestraat, and both sell English-language books. Also *Hoeksteen* (Gravenstraat 17) and the kiosk in *Krasnapolsky Hotel*. *Boekhandel Univers NV*, Gravenstraat 61, is recommended for nature, linguistic and scholarly books on Suriname. Second hand books, English and Dutch, are bought and sold in the market. Maps of Paramaribo are hard to find, but try *Vaco*.

Tourist Agencies *Stinasu*, the Foundation for Nature Preservation in Suriname, Jongbawstraat 14, T 475845/471856, PO Box 436, Paramaribo (director Muriel Held), offers reasonably priced accommodation and provides tour guides on the extensive nature reserves throughout the country, rec. One can see 'true wilderness and wildlife' with them (see p 1472). *NV Mets* (Movement for Eco-Tourism in Suriname), PO Box 9080, 5 Rudielaan, Paramaribo, T 492892/497180, F 497062, the national tour operator (also in Cayenne, 15 rue Louis Blanc, T 317298, F 305786), organizes trips to the interior at reasonable rates. Tours offered are City Tour, US$15 pp, Rivercruise, US$35 pp, Niew Amsterdam plantation tour, Santigron (all day trips); Matapica Beach, US$95 pp (2 days); 4/5-day trips to Palumeu (see below) or to Gran Rio (Bosneger area) for US$250 pp staying in lodges; 8-day trip to Mount Kasikasima in remote southern Suriname, US$525 pp (all transport, food and guides included). Mrs W J Robles-Cornelissen, *Independent Tours*, Rosenveltkade 20, T 474770, and *Suriname Safari Tours*, Waterkant 54, T 471624, organize excursions to the interior. Trips take 3-5 days and cost about US$120 (parallel exchange), all inclusive. *CTM Travel*, Sophie Redmondstraat, opp Hakrin Bank building, 0730-1600, helpful. *Ram's Tours*, Neumandpad 30 Ben, T 476011/476223. *Does Travel Service*, Domineestraat. *Saramaccan Jungle Safaris* (John Ligeon), PO Box 676, Zwartenhovenbrugstraat 19, Paramaribo, for visits by canoe to Saramaccan Bush Black villages and wildlife tours.

   NB If intending to take a tour to the jungle and either Amerindian or Bush Black villages, check how much time is spent in the jungle itself and on the conditions in the villages. One such trip is to Palumeu, an Amerindian village (Trio, Wajana and Akurio peoples) due S of Paramaribo, not far from the Brazilian border. A 4-day, 3-night trip costs US$250, including flights, food, accommodation, jungle hikes and boat trips.

Tourist Bureau Cornelius Jongbawstraat 2, near *Hotel Torarica*, T 471163, F 420425, Telex 118 ALBUZA SN. Has useful handouts on lodgings in town and rural areas as well as restaurants. Free city map. English spoken, friendly and helpful. Open Mon-Thur 0700-1500, Fri 0700-1430.

Local Transport There are very few regular buses; the few services that are left leave from Waterkant or Dr Sophie Redmondstraat. There are privately run 'wild buses', also known as 'numbered buses' which run on fixed routes around the city; they are minivans and are severely overcrowded.

Taxis generally have no meters. The price should be agreed on beforehand to avoid trouble. Rec is Ally's Taxi service, T 479434, English spoken. If hiring a taxi for touring, beware of overcharging.

Self-Drive Cars City Taxi, Purperhart, Kariem, Intercar, U-drive Car rental, T 490803 and other

agencies. All driving licences accepted, but you need a stamp from the local police and a deposit. Gasoline/petrol is sold as 'regular', or 'extra' (more expensive).

Bicycles Can be bought from A Seymonson, Rijwielhersteller, Rust en Vredestraat. Recommended rides include to Nieuw Amsterdam, Marienburg, Alkmaar and back via Tamanredjo in the Javanese Commewijne district or from Rust en Werk to Spieringshoek to Reijnsdorp (3½ hrs) and return to Leonsberg via ferry, whence it is a 30 mins ride to Paramaribo.

Airports The Johan Adolf Pengel International Airport (formerly Zanderij), is 45 km S of Paramaribo. Shared taxi to town costs Sf 200 pp; ordinary taxi, Sf5,000 (US$10). Suriname Airways, T 477088, F 497062.

Money exchange facilities, Central Bank of Suriname between Customs and Immigration (closed Sun). There is a guest house near the airport.

Internal flights leave from Zorg-en-Hoop airfield in a suburb of Paramaribo (take minibus 8 or 9 from Steenbrekersstraat); see **Getting around** in **Information for Visitors**.

Bus Services To Nickerie from Dr Sophie Redmondstraat, nr *Hotel Ambassador*, minibuses leave when full between 0500 and 1000 (there are buses after 1200, but the price then depends on the driver), 4-5 hrs (depending on ferry crossing), extra charged for large bag. Taxis from the same area are slightly faster. To Albina from near ferry dock or from Meerzorg, 3-4 hrs, Sf1,500, large bag extra (take an APB or PBA bus which has a plainclothes policeman on board). Taxis also available. There are irregular bus services to other towns. For full details ask drivers or enquire at the tourist office.

Verify all fares in advance and beware of overcharging. There is much jostling in the queues and pure mayhem when boarding vehicles. They are all minivans and have no luggage space. Try to accommodate baggage under your seat or you will have to hold it in your lap.

Local Shipping The three ferries across the main rivers operate only in daytime (the Paramaribo-Meerzorg ferry until 2200). Two bridges have been built. The Suriname Navigation Co (SMS) has a service to Bakkie on the Commewijne River, 80 km from Paramaribo (a nice 4-hr trip; one can get off—see below—at *De Nieuwe Grond*, a plantation owned by an English couple, and stay overnight). SMS also has infrequent services on other rivers (Wayombo and Cottica). The coastal service to Nieuw Nickerie has been discontinued, but there is a weekly (Mon) 36-hrs run there over inland waterways (**see p 1473**).

NB It is advisable to check the weather conditions and probabilities of returning on schedule before you set out on a trip to the interior. Heavy rains can make it impossible for planes to land in some jungle areas; little or no provision is made for such delays and it can be a long and hungry wait for better conditions.

Excursions Powaka, about 90 mins outside the capital, is a primitive village of thatched huts but with electric light and a small church. In the surrounding forest one can pick mangoes and other exotic fruit. An interesting half, or full day excursion is to take Minibus 4, or taxi, to Leonsberg on the Suriname river (restaurant *Rusty Pelikan* on waterfront; in *Leonsberg* restaurant try *saoto* soup and other Javanese specialities, overlooking the river), then ferry to **Nieuw Amsterdam**, the capital of the predominantly Javanese district of Commewijne. There is an open-air museum inside the old fortress (badly rundown, open only in mornings except Fri, 1700-1900, Sf20), which guarded the confluence of the Suriname and Commewijne rivers. There are some old plantation mansions left in the Commewijne district which are of interest; Mariënburg is the last sugar estate in operation in Suriname. The return trip can be made by bus to Meerzorg on the river, taking the vehicle ferry back to Paramaribo.

Braamspunt is a peninsula at the mouth of the Suriname River, about 10 km from Paramaribo. Nice beaches. Hire a boat at the Leonsberg scaffold for a trip up the river.

By private car to **Jodensavanne** (Jews' Savanna, established 1639), S of Paramaribo on the opposite bank of the Suriname river, where a cemetery and the foundations of one of the oldest synagogues in the Western Hemisphere have been restored. There is no public transport and taxis won't go because of the bad road. It is still only 1½ hrs with a suitable vehicle. There is a bridge across the Suriname River to Jodensavanne. Mrs Robles, T 474770, organizes tours if there are enough people. There are interesting Amerindian villages nearby. **Blakawatra** is said to be one of the most beautiful spots in all Suriname. This was the scene of much fighting in the civil war. A full day trip to Jodensavanne and Blakawatra, returning to Paramaribo via Moengo, has been recommended if one can arrange the transport. Some 4 km from the International Airport there is a resort called Cola Creek, so named for the colour of the water, but good swimming (busy at weekends).

Approximately 30 km SW of Paramaribo, via **Lelydorp** (*Hotel De Lely*, Sastrodisomoweg 41), is the Bush Negro village of **Santigron**, on the E bank of the Saramaca River. Mini-buses leave from Saramacastraat in front of BEM store at approx 0700 and 1030, Mon-Sat, one afternoon bus on Sat, 1 hr, crowded. They return as soon as they drop off passengers in the village, so make sure you will have a bus to return on, no accommodation in Santigron. Nearby is the Amerindian village of **Pikin Poika**. The two make a good independent day trip. Tour agencies also visit the area about twice month, including canoe rides on the Saramaca River and a Bush Negro dance performance.

By bus or car to **Afobakka**, where there is a large hydro-electric dam on the Suriname river. There is a government guesthouse (price includes 3 meals a day) in nearby **Brokopondo**. Victoria is an oil-palm plantation in the same area. The Brownsberg National Park is 1 hr by car from here.

Stoelmanseiland, on the Lawa River (guest house with full board) in the interior, and the *bosneger* villages and rapids in the area can be visited on excursions organized by tour operators. Price US$170 pp for 3 days (5 persons, minimum). They are, however, more easily reached by river from St-Laurent du Maroni and Maripasoula in Guyane.

Nature Reserves   Many were badly damaged during the civil war. At present only **Brownsberg** has any organized infrastructure. Located atop hills overlooking the van Blommensteinmeer reservoir, it features good walking and 3 impressive waterfalls. There are all-inclusive tours from Paramaribo with Stinasu (see **Tourist Agencies**; 1-, and 3-day tours, price includes transport, accommodations, food, and guide). One can also make an independent visit. Buses for Brownsweg leave daily at approx 0830 from Saramacastraat by BEM shop; truck at same time. Go to Stinasu at least 24 hrs in advance of your visit to reserve and pay for accommodation in their guest houses and to arrange for a vehicle to pick you up in Brownsweg. Take your own food.

Raleighvallen/Voltzberg Nature Reserve (57,000 hectares) is rain-forest park, including Foengoe Island and Voltzberg peak; climbing the mountain at sunrise is unforgettable.

The **Coppename Estuary** is also a national park, protecting many bird colonies.

Two reserves are located on the NE coast of Suriname. Known primarily as a major nesting site for sea turtles—five species including the huge leatherback turtle come ashore to lay their eggs—**Wia-Wia Nature Reserve** (36,000 hectares), also has nesting grounds for some magnificent birds. The nesting activity of sea turtles is best observed Apr-Jul (Jul is a good month to visit as you see both adults coming ashore to lay eggs and hatchlings rushing to the sea at high tide). Since the beaches and consequently the turtles have shifted westwards out of the reserve, accommodation is now at **Matapica** beach, not in the reserve itself. (After a visit to the reserves please send any comments to Hilde Viane at Stinasu. Your support is needed to keep the reserve functioning.) There may also be mosquitoes and sandflies, depending on the season. The SMS riverboat from Paramaribo stops at Alliance on its journey up the Commewijne River. You then transfer to a Stinasu motorboat for a 1-hr ride to Matapica. The motorboat costs US$50 for 4 people, round trip. Suitable waterproof clothing should be worn. Fishermen make the crossing for US$3-4. The beach hut accommodates 18 people in 4 rm, and costs US$4 pp. Take your own bedding/food. Cooking facilities provided. Book the hut and boat through Stinasu and keep your receipts or you will be refused entry. Early booking is essential as the closure of the other reserves has made Matapica very popular.

The **Galibi Nature Reserve**, where there are more turtle-nesting places, is near the mouth of the Marowijne River. There are Carib Indian villages. From Albina it is a 3-hrs (including 30 mins on the open sea) boat trip to Galibi.

West of Paramaribo

Leaving Paramaribo, a narrow but well paved road leads through the citrus and vegetable growing districts of Wanica and Saramaca, connected by a bridge over the Saramaca River. At Boskamp (90 km from Paramaribo) the Coppename River is reached. Daytime only ferry to Jenny on the W bank takes about 20 mins.

A further 50 km is **Totness**, where there was once a Scottish settlement. It is the largest village in the Coronie district, along the coast between Paramaribo and Nieuw Nickerie. There is a good government guesthouse, E. The road (bad, liable to flooding) leads through an extensive forest of coconut palms. Bus to Paramaribo at 0600. 40 km further W, 5 km S of the main road is **Wageningen**, a modern little town, the centre of the Suriname rice-growing area. The road from Nickerie has recently been renewed. One of the largest fully mechanized rice farms in the world is found here (**C Hotel de Wereld**). The **Bigi-Pan** area of mangroves is a bird-watchers' paradise; boats may be hired from local fishermen.

Nieuw Nickerie, on the S bank of the Nickerie River 5 km from its mouth, opposite Guyana is the main town and port of the Nickerie district and is distinguished for its ricefields and for the number and voraciousness of its mosquitoes. The town has a population of more than 8,000, the district of 35,000, mostly East Indian. Paramaribo is 237 km away by road. For bus services, see under Paramaribo. Sit on the left-hand side of the bus to get the best views of the bird-life in the swamps. The coastal ferry service has been discontinued, but once a week the SMS company makes an interesting water trip, using inland waterways, to Nieuw Nickerie taking 36 hrs; it leaves Paramaribo on Mon at 0800, departs Nieuw Nickerie 1200 Wed (times subject to 2 hrs variation due to tides), no cabins, only slatted seats, but there is hammock space; take food and drink; lots of mosquitoes, but also remarkable birdlife in the swamps.

Hotels E *Moksie Patoe*, Gouverneurstraat 115, T 232219, restaurant, owner rents a 2-bedroom house (3 beds) next door; **E** *De-Vesting*, similar quality, Balatastraat 6, T 031265. **E** *Americali*, a/c, good, clean, friendly. **F** *De President*, Gouverneurstraat, with bath, cheaper without, a/c, good value, friendly; **F** *Luxor*, Jozefstraat 22, T 231365, private bath, friendly; **G** *Diamond*, Balatastraat 29, T 232210, some rooms with bath, close to ferry, basic; **G** *Tropical*, Gouverneurstraat 114, T 231796, noisy bar downstairs.

Restaurant *Moksie Patoe*, Gouverneurstraat 115, run by Frenchman, M Amar, provides European and Indian dishes with items rarely found elsewhere in friendly atmosphere. *Ella*, Javanese food. *Incognito*, Gouverneurstraat 44, Indonesian; *Pak-Hap*, Gouverneurstraat 101, Chinese. Many others on same street.

Banks Algemene Bank Nederland, Hakrin Bank, Post Office Savings Bank, People's Credit Bank, Surinaamsche Bank. The bank at the immigration office is reported to close at 1500 Mon-Fri, whether or not the ferry has arrived.

Air Suriname Airways to/from **Paramaribo**, twice daily except Sun, office on main square on river, helpful, can book international flights, no credit cards, open till 1600.

Ferry to Springlands, Guyana Normally operates Mon to Sat (except public holidays of either country), foot passengers only, Sf65 one-way, heavy luggage, extra. Booking office at Landenstraat 26, open Mon-Sat, 0630-0645, 0900-1200, 1600-1700, essential to book by 1700 the day before travelling, booking fee Sf2.50, must show passport.

All immigration and customs formalities take place at the ferry dock. Queue up at gate at 0700, expect about 3 hrs of waiting before sailing. The trip takes at least 2 hrs, Guyanese immigration and customs forms handed out on board, cold drinks are sometimes sold. There may be up to another 3 hrs of queuing for Guyanese formalities. Visa requirements have been relaxed (see Guyana, **Documents**) and a return ticket is not always asked for. Ferry returns to Nickerie the same afternoon (bookings in the am).

When the ferry is not running, small boats ferry people across for US$20. On arrival in Guyana it is essential to go to immigration and, probably, pay a bribe. Not a recommended route.

From Springlands, there are mini-buses to New Amsterdam, thence ferries and launches to Rosignol, and mini-buses to Georgetown. Entire journey (Nickerie-Georgetown) takes 10-12 hrs, 2 days from Paramaribo including overnight in Nickerie.

Vast reserves of bauxite were discovered in the Bakhuis Mountains, S of Nickerie District in the NW of Sipaliwini District. A road once ran as far as Lucie on the Corantijn River, but it is now mostly overgrown. The infrastructure developed for the bauxite industry in the 1970s was subsequently abandoned or destroyed. **Apoera** is on the Corantijn and can be reached by sea-going vessels. **Blanche**

Marie Falls, 320 km from Paramaribo on the Apoera road, is a popular destination. There is a guesthouse, **B** *Dubois*, contact Eldoradolaan 22, Paramaribo T 476904/2. There is a good guesthouse at Apoera (C, with 3 meals, advance booking from Paramaribo advisable). **Washabo** near Apoera, which has an airstrip, is an Amerindian village. There is no public transport from Paramaribo to the Apoera-Bakhuis area, but there are frequent charter flights to the Washabo airstrip. Irregular small boats go from Apoera to Nieuw Nickerie and to Springlands (Guyana). Try to rent a canoe to visit the Amerindian settlement of Orealla in Guyana or Kaboeri creek, 12 km downstream, where giant river otters may possibly be seen in Oct or Mar.

East of Paramaribo

Eastern Suriname was the area most severely damaged during the civil war, and its effects are still evident. A paved road connects Meerzorg with Albina (vehicle ferry from Paramaribo, every 30 mins, passengers Sf1; black market exchange on ferry is illegal), passing through the districts of Commewijne and Marowijne. There is little population or agriculture left here. **Moengo**, 160 km up the Cottica River from Paramaribo, is a bauxite mining and loading centre for Suralco. (*Government Guesthouse* and annex.) Paranam, another loading centre for the Company, is on the left bank of the Suriname River. It can be reached by medium draught ships and by cars. Near Paranam is Smalkalden, where bauxite is loaded by the Billiton company on the road to Paramaribo.

East of Moengo, the scars of war are most obvious. Temporary wooden bridges replace those that were blown up, shell craters dot the road, and many abandoned or destroyed houses are seen. **Albina** is on the Marowijne River, the frontier with Guyane. Once a thriving, pleasant town, it is today a bombed-out wreck. No services whatsoever were available here in 1994-95.

A passenger and vehicle ferry leaves Albina for St Laurent du Maroni Mon, Thur, 0800, 1000, 1500, 1700, Tues, Wed, Sat 0800, 1000, Sun 1630, 1700, 30 mins voyage; the fare is 20F pp, which is the same charged by *pirogues*, 100F for cars. Changing money on the Suriname side of the border is illegal; see **Currency**, p 1475 on currency control. Customs and immigration on both sides close at 1900. Be wary of local information on exchange rates and transport (both the free ferry and buses to Paramaribo). Money can be changed on the Guyane side.

INFORMATION FOR VISITORS

Before you go

Entry requirements

● **Visas and documents**
Visitors must have a valid passport (one issued by the Hong Kong government, and a few others, will not be accepted), a visa, or tourist card. Visas must be obtained in advance by citizens of all countries except Great Britain, Japan, Israel, The Gambia, South Korea, Denmark, Finland, Sweden, Switzerland, Netherlands Antilles, Brazil, Ecuador, Canada, Chile and Guyana (these require a tourist card, obtainable at the airport, US$14). Visas issued at the consulate in Cayenne normally take 15 days and

cost F150 (US$28), but may be obtained the same day (an extra charge for this is sometimes made). Take photocopy of exit ticket out of South America. In Georgetown a visa takes 5 days minimum and costs US$20. On entry to Suriname (by land or air) your passport will be stamped by the military police indicating a brief period (usually 7-10 days) for which you can remain in the country, regardless of the length of stay authorized by your visa. If you are considering a longer visit, you should go as soon as possible to the Immigration Office in Paramaribo to get a second stamp in your passport and to apply for a 'blue card' (foreigner registration card): Immigration Office, van't Hogerhuystraat,

Nieuwe Haven, Paramaribo. To get this you need a receipt for Sf10 from the Commissariat Combé, Van Sommelsdijkstraat, opposite *Torarica Hotel*, take passport and two passport photos, allow a week to get it. Mon-Fri, 0700-1430. The procedure is relatively quick and painless and you will generally be authorized a 3 month stay (once again the length of your entry visa seems irrelevant). If you stay more than 2 weeks, you should return to Immigration at that time, to collect your blue card which you can carry instead of your passport (it is prudent to carry both). You must also return here for any further extensions and for an exit authorization stamp (called 'stamp out') 2 days before you leave the country. The final exit stamp is again given by the military police at the airport or land border. See also **Currency** below on border exchange procedures.

There have been suggestions that these procedures be simplified; they currently waste much time and create no end of confusion, as they are generally not explained to visitors on arrival. However, in 1994 they remained law and failure to comply can result in very serious consequences.

● **Representation overseas**
USA: Embassy, Van Ness Center, 4301 Connecticut, NW Suite 108, Washington DC, 20008, T 202-244-7488, F 202-244-5878; Consulate, 7235 NW 19th St, Suite A, Miami, FLA 33126, T 305-593-2163. **Belgium**, Avenue Louise 379, 1050 Brussels, T 640-11-72; **Netherlands**: Embassy, Alexander Gogelweg 2, 2517 JH Den Haag, T 65-08-44; Consulate, De Cuserstraat 11, 1081 CK Amsterdam, T 642-61-37; **Brazil**, SCS Quadra 2 Lotes 20/21, Edif, OK, 2e Andar, 70457 Brasília, T 244-1824; **Venezuela**, 4a Av de Altamira 41, entre 7 y 8a Transversal, Altamira, Caracas 1060A, PO Box 61140, Chacao, T 261-2095; **Guyana**, 304 Church St, Georgetown, PO Box 338, T 56995; **Guyane**, 38 TER, Rue Christoph Colomb, Cayenne, T 30-04-61.

Embassies USA (Dr Sophie Redmondstraat 129, PO Box 1821, T 477881), Netherlands, Belgium, Brazil, Cuba, France, Mexico, Venezuela, India, Indonesia, Guyana, India, Japan, China (People's Republic).

Consulates There are consuls-general, vice-consuls or consular agents for Canada, Denmark, Dominican Republic, Ecuador, Finland, Germany, Haiti, UK, Mexico, Norway, Spain, and Sweden – all in Paramaribo. British Honorary Consul, Mr James Healy, T 472870 office/474764 house, is very helpful.

● **Tourist information**
Information about Suriname can be had from: Suriname representatives abroad (see above), the Tourist Board in Paramaribo, or Stinasu, address of both under Paramaribo.

The *Surinam Planatlas* is out of print, but can be consulted at the National Planning office on Dr Sophie Redmondstraat; maps with natural environment and economic development topics, each with commentary in Dutch and English.

Points of interest are: some colonial architecture, especially in and around Paramaribo; and the tropical flora and fauna in this very sparsely populated country. There are no beaches to speak of; the sea and the rivers in the coastal area are muddy, and mosquitoes can be a worry in places. Hotels and restaurants are rare outside the capital, and you usually have to supply your own hammock and mosquito net, and food. A tent is less useful in this climate. Hitchhiking is not common, but it is possible. The **high seasons**, when everything is more expensive, are 15 Mar-15 May, July-Sept and 15 Dec-15 Jan.

Health

No information has been made available about the incidence of cholera in Suriname. Since the disease is almost certainly present, take the approrpriate precautions. Boil or purify water, even in the capital. Otherwise, no special precautions necessary except for a trip to the malarial interior; for free malaria prophylaxis contact the Public Health Department (BOG, 15 Rode Kruislaan), but better to take your own. METS and Suriname Safari Tours provide malaria prophylaxis on their package tours. Chloroquine-resistant malaria in the interior. Mosquito nets should be used at night over beds in rooms not air-conditioned or screened. In some coastal districts there is a risk of bilharzia (schistosomiasis). Ask before bathing in lakes and rivers. Vaccinations: yellow fever and tetanus advisable, typhoid only for trips into the interior. Swim only in running water because of poisonous fish. There is good swimming on the Marowijne river and at Matapica beach and on the Coppename river. There are five hospitals in Paramaribo, best is St Vincentius.

Money

● **Currency**
The unit of currency is the Suriname guilder (Sf) divided into 100 cents. There are notes for 5, 10, 25, 100 and 500 guilders. Coins are for 1 guilder and 5, 10, 25 (the 25-cent coin is usually known as a *kwartje*) and 50 cents.

● **Exchange**

A complex system of exchange rates, introduced in Feb 1993 was finally abondoned in July 1994. In that month unification of all the rates was achieved and a floating rate was established at Sf183 = US$1. By Feb 1995 the floating rate was around Sf430 = US$1. The street rate for the dollar was Sf550. Dutch guilders and French francs are readily exchanged in banks and on the black market, cash only in the latter case.

In 1995, visitors arriving in Suriname by air or land were required to exchange a minimum of US$150 (or equivalent in hard currency) into Suriname guilders. The only exemptions were for people staying less than 2 nights and for holders of Guyanese passports or French passports issued in Guyane. Officially visitors must declare their foreign currency on arrival. This is obligatory at the international airport, where travellers are given a form that must be stamped when exchanging money at a bank. You do not have to change all the US$150 at the airport (where rates are poorer than in the city). On leaving Suriname the form will be checked: if the amounts don't add up with the money on your person, your funds may be confiscated. When arriving by land, visitors' funds are rarely checked, but you should be prepared for it. It is illegal to change money on the black market; police pretend to be black marketeers.

Getting there

By Air

SLM flies to Miami (3 times a week using ALM equipment Miami-Curaçao), Amsterdam (twice a week, joint operation wtih KLM), Belém (4 times a week), Port of Spain (twice), Barbados (3 times a week), Curaçao, 3 times a week, Cayenne (4 times a week), and Georgetown (5 times a week). Air France flies from Cayenne once a week, ALM from Curaçao 3 times a week. Gonini flies twice a week to Barbados, 6 times to Cayenne, daily to Georgetown and Port of Spain (except Sun). A weekly service by American Trans Air goes to New York in high season, fortnightly in low season. Many people go to Cayenne to take advantage of cheap Air France tickets to Europe as well as increased seat availability. Internal services are maintained by SLM and two small air charter firms.

By Sea

Fyffes banana boats sail from Portsmouth UK, and Flushing, Holland, to Paramaribo on 13-14 day schedule. Occasionally they call at Georgetown. The 35-38 day roundtrip costs £1,980 pp.

Customs

Duty-free imports include 400 cigarettes or 100 cigars or ½ kg of tobacco, 2 litres of spirits and 4 litres of wine, 50 grams of perfume and 1 litre of toilet water, 8 rolls of still film and 60m of cinefilm, 100m of recording tape, and other goods up to a value of Sf40. Personal baggage is free of duty. Customs examination of baggage can be very thorough.

When you arrive

● **Clothing**

Except for official meetings, informal tropical clothing is worn, but not shorts. An umbrella or plastic raincoat is very useful.

● **Hours of business**

Shops and businesses: Mon-Fri 0900-1630, Sat 0900-1300. Government departments: Mon-Thur 0700-1500, Fri 0700-1430. Banks are open Mon-Fri 0900-1400. The airport bank is open at flight arrival and departure times.

● **Official time**

3 hrs behind GMT.

● **Voltage**

127 volts AC, 60 cycles. Plug fittings are usually 2-pin round (European continental type). Lamp fittings are screw type.

● **Weights and measures**

The metric system is in general use.

On departure

● **Airport tax**

There is an exit tax of US$15 (Sf30).

Food and drink

Surinamese cuisine is as rich and varied as the country's ethnic makeup. Rice is the main staple and of very high quality. Cassava, sweet potatoes, plantain, and hot red peppers are widely used. *Pom* is a puree of the tayer root (a relative of cassava) tastily spiced and served with *kip* (chicken). *Moksie Alesie* is rice mixed with meat, chicken, white beans, tomatoes, peppers and spices. *Pinda soep* (peanut soup with plantain dumplings) and *oker soep met tayerblad* (gumbo and cassava soup) are both worth a try. Well known Indonesian dishes include *bami* (fried noodles) and *nassie goreng* (fried rice), both spicy with a slightly sweet taste. Among the Hindustani dishes are *roti* (a crêpe wrapped around curried potatoes, vegetables and chicken), *somosa* (fried pastry filled with spicy potatoes and vegetables), and *phulawri* (fried chick-pea balls). Among the many tropical fruits of Suriname, palm nuts such as the orange coloured awarra and the cone shaped brown maripa are most popular.

Getting around

Air transport

E-W, Paramaribo-Nieuw Nickerie twice a week. N-S: the interior is currently open. Bush flights are operated by Gum-Air and Gonini to several Amerindian and bosneger villages. Most settlements have an airstrip, but internal air services are limited. These flights are on demand. Gum-Air (T 498760) also flies to St-Laurent du Maroni in Guyane, US$250 to charter 5-seater plane.

Road

There are 2,500 km of main roads, of which 850 km are paved. The main E-W road, 390 km in length, links Albina with Nieuw Nickerie. Driving is on the left, but many vehicles have left-hand drive. Internal bus services are poor.

E-W roads: From Albina to Paramaribo to Nieuw Nickerie is open; buses and taxis are available. Both ferries Paramaribo-Meerzorg and Boskamp-Jenny (over the Coppename River) are operating. N-S: the road Paramaribo-Paranam-Afobaka-Pokigron is open.

Communications

● **Newspapers**
Newspapers are in Dutch, *De Ware Tijd* (morning) and *DeWest* (evening).

● **Postal services**
The postal service is remarkably quick and reliable. Both postal and telecommunications charges are very low at the black market exchange rate. **NB** Postcard rate for postcards means only 5 words.

● **Telephone services**
Overseas phone calls must be booked anywhere between 30 mins to several days in advance, specifying the exact duration of the call. Rates are higher if you request more than 5 mins. Calls can be booked up to 2200, Mon-Sat, no operator assisted calls on Sun. Overseas calls can also be direct dialled from some public phones using tokens, but there are only 4 such phones (just outside TeleSur, often broken) and the queues get very long. USA direct available at both *Torarica* and *Krasnapolsky* Hotels, as well as from private phones. The public fax number from overseas is +597-410-555, good service.

● **Television**
There are several stations in Paramaribo and in the districts, broadcasting in Dutch, Hindi, Negro English and Javanese. There is also one state-controlled television station called Surinaamse Televisie Stichting (STVS), transmitting for 4 hrs daily in colour on channel 8 (in Dutch), and a second channel, ATV.

Holidays and festivals

1 Jan, New Year; Holi Phagwa (Hindu festival, date varies each year, generally in Mar, very interesting but watch out for throwing of water, paint, talc and coloured powder); Good Friday; Easter (2 days); 1 May (Labour Day); 1 July (National Unity); 25 Nov (Independence Day); Christmas (2 days). For Moslem holidays see note under Guyana (**p 1463**).

Acknowledgements

For most helpful contributions on Suriname we are grateful to Ulrich and Eva Hellinger (Germany), Gérald Lorin (Kourou, Guyane), Erwin Verhoeven (The Hague, The Netherlands), and Piet Ysabie (Mecheler, Belgium).

GUYANE

GUYANE, an Overseas Department of France, has its eastern frontier with Brazil formed partly by the River Oiapoque (Oyapoc in French) and its southern, also with Brazil, formed by the Tumuc-Humac mountains. The western frontier with Suriname is along the River Maroni-Itani. To the N is the Atlantic coastline of 320 km. The area is estimated at between 83,500 and 86,504 square km, or one-sixth that of France. The land rises gradually from a coastal strip some 15-40 km wide to the higher slopes and plains or savannahs, about 80 km inland. Forests cover some 8 million hectares of the hills and valleys of the interior, and timber production is increasing rapidly.

The territory is well watered, for over 20 rivers run to the Atlantic. Besides those named above, there are the Mana, Cayenne, Sinnamarie (with its tributary the Coureibo), Maroni, Oyack, and Approuage. Smaller rivers are the Inini, Ardoua, and Camopi.

The only mountain range of importance is the Tumuc-Humac. Among the higher peaks are Mounts Mitarka, Temorairem, Leblond, and Timotakem; this last in the extreme S on the Brazilian frontier. The mountains reach a height of 800m.

Climate is tropical with a very heavy rainfall. Average temperature at sea-level is 27°C, and fairly constant at that. Night and day temperatures vary more in the highlands. The rainy season is from Nov to Jul, with (sometimes) a short dry interruption in Feb and Mar. The great rains begin in May.

History Several French and Dutch expeditions attempted to settle along the coast in the early 17th century, but were driven off by the native population. The French finally established a settlement at Sinnamary in the early 1660s but this was destroyed by the Dutch in 1665 and seized by the British 2 years later. Under the Treaty of Breda, 1667, Guyane was returned to France. Apart from a brief occupation by the Dutch in 1676, it remained in French hands until 1809 when a combined Anglo-Portuguese naval force captured the colony and handed it over to the Portuguese (Brazilians). Though the land was restored to France by the Treaty of Paris in 1814, the Portuguese remained until 1817. Gold was discovered in 1853, and disputes arose about the frontiers of the colony with Suriname and Brazil. These were settled by arbitration in 1891, 1899, and 1915. By the law of 19 March 1946, the Colony of Cayenne, or Guyane Française, became the Department of Guyane, with the same laws, regulations, and administration as a department in metropolitan France. The seat of the Prefect and of the principal courts is at Cayenne. The colony was used as a prison for French convicts with camps scattered throughout the country; Saint-Laurent was the port of entry. After serving prison terms convicts spent an equal number of years in exile and were usually unable to earn their return passage to France. Those interested should read *Papillon* by Henri Charrière. Majority opinion seems to be in favour of greater autonomy: about 5% of the population are thought to favour independence.

The People There are widely divergent estimates for the ethnic composition of the population. Calculations vary according to the number included of illegal immigrants, attracted by social benefits and the high living standards. (The prefect stated in 1994 that Guyane had 30,000 illegal residents.) By some measures, over 40% of the population are Créoles, with corresponding low figures for Europeans, Asians and Brazilians (around 17% in total). Other estimates put the Créole proportion as low as 36%, with Haitians 26%, Europeans 10% (of whom about

95% are from France), Brazilians 8%. Asians 4.7% (3.2% from Hong Kong, 1.5% from Laos), about 4% from Suriname and 2.5% from Guyana. The Amerindian population is put at 3.6% (over 4% by some estimates). The main groups are Galibis (1,700), Arawak (400), Wayanas (600), Palikours (500), Wayampis-Oyampis (600) and Emerillons (600). There are also bush negroes (Bonis, Saramacas, Djukas) 4.5%, who live mostly in the Maroni area, and others (Dominicans, St Lucians etc) at 0.7%. The language is French, with officials not usually speaking anything else. Créole is also widely spoken. The religion is predominantly Roman Catholic.

Note The Amerindian villages in the Haut-Maroni and Haut-Oyapoc areas may only be visited with permission from the Préfecture in Cayenne *before* arrival in Guyane.

The Economy Guyane has renewable natural riches in its timber forests (about 75,000 sq km) with 15 sawmills, and mineral resources. Farming employs only 11.4% of the population and the country is very sparsely populated. An estimated 42 million tons of extractable bauxite have been located in the Kaw mountains to the SE of Cayenne by Alcoa and Pechiney. Some 40 million tonnes of kaolin have been located at St-Laurent du Maroni and gold is again being mined.

Guyane imports most of its foodstuffs and manufactured goods, of which about 88% come from France. The value of exports, mainly shrimps, rum, essence of rosewood, hardwoods and gold, is very low; France buys just under 50%, the remaining EC about 20%.

At end-1982 the French Government announced plans to step up the Department's development in

French Guyane : fact file

Geographic

Land area	86,504 sq km

Demographic

Population (1994)	146,000
annual growth rate (1989-94)	5.7%
urban	73.4%
rural	26.6%
density	1.7 per sq km
Religious affiliation	
Roman Catholic	73%
Birth rate per 1,000 (1990)	31.5
	(world av 27.1)

Education and Health

Life expectancy at birth (1991),	
male	63.4 years
female	69.7 years
Infant mortality rate	15.8
per 1,000 live births (1990)	
Physicians (1992)	1 per 644 persons
Hospital beds (1988)	1 per 109 persons
Calorie intake as %	
of FAO requirement	124%
Literate males (over 16)	82.5%
Literate females (over 16)	81.3%

Economic

GNP (1992 market prices)	US$891mn
GNP per capita	US$8,020
Public external debt (1992)	US$36mn
Radio	1 per 2.1 persons
Television	1 per 22 persons
Telephone	1 per 3.8 persons

Employment

Population economically active (1988)	
	48,800
% of labour force in	
agriculture	8.6
mining & manufacturing	6.4
Construction	9.1

Source *Encyclopaedia Britannica*

consultation with local parties: the so-called Green Plan (Plan Vert), backed by the Société Financière de Développement de la Guyane. Under the plan local production of basic foodstuffs, such as meat and eggs, was to be raised, and areas of timber plantations doubled to 22,000 ha. The Plan Vert notwithstanding, the vast majority of consumer goods (including staples such as milk, sugar, rice, even bananas) continue to be imported from France or the French Caribbean. There is little agriculture, no manufacturing and consumer prices are extraordinarily high. One exception is the market gardening of Laotian Hmong immigrants, near Cacao, which produces almost the only fresh vegetables in the department. Having virtually no developed, independent economic base, Guyane is perpetually concerned about the consquences of any decrease in French financial support (an estimated US$1bn a year).

Gold prospecting, much of it carried out by teams of Brazilian garimpeiros, is causing ecological damage through the silting of rivers and the indiscriminate use of mercury. Major ecological impact will also be felt with the completion in 1994 of a 120-mw hydroelectric scheme at Petit Sant on the Sinnamarie river. It is estimated that the habitat for 1 million animals and 1.5 million birds was lost, but a French government-funded project rescued some of the animals and relocated them in Guyane's first nature reserve. The damage created by this scheme may be counterbalanced by the fact that it will mean that the 3 very polluting thermal power stations need no longer be used.

The Phèdre Plan assists Guyane with infrastructure projects: bridges across the Mana and Mahuri rivers (the latter for access to Roura); renewal of Rochambeau airport; a road from Régina to St-Georges de l'Oyapoc is planned for completion after 1996.

Government The head of state is the President of France; the local heads of government are a Commissioner of the Republic, for France, and the Presidents of the local General and Regional Councils. The General Council (19 seats) and the Regional Council (31 seats) are the two legislative houses. In regional council elections in Mar 1992, the Parti Socialiste Guyanais won 16 seats, while the other major party, the Front Democratique Guyanais, won 10. Guyane is divided into two *arrondissements*, Cayenne and St-Laurent du Maroni.

Cayenne, the capital and the chief port, is on the island of Cayenne at the mouth of the Cayenne River. It is 645 km from Georgetown (Guyana) and 420 km from Paramaribo (Suriname) by sea. Population around 52,000. There is an interesting museum, the Musée Departemental, in rue de Remire, near the Place de Palmistes (Mon and Wed 0900-1330, Tues and Fri 0900-1330, 1630-1830, Thur 1030-1330, Sat 0900-1200; 10F, students 5F). It contains quite a mixture of exhibits, from pickled snakes to the trunk of the 'late beloved twin-trunked palm' of Place des Palmistes; there is a good entomological collection and excellent paintings of convict life. Next door is the municipal library. The Musée de L'Or, Impasse Buzaré (Mon-Fri 0800-1200) has been restored. L'Orstom (scientific research institute), Route de Montabo, Mon and Fri 0700-1330, 1500-1800, Tues-Thur 0700-1300, has a research library and permanent exhibits on ecosystems and archaeological finds in Guyane. Also worth a visit are La Crique, the colourful but dangerous area around the Canal Laussat (built by Malouet in 1777); the Jesuit-built residence (circa 1890) of the Prefect (L'Hôtel-de-Ville) in the Place de Grenoble; the Place des Amandiers (also known as the Place Auguste-Horth) by the sea; the Place des Palmistes, with assorted palms; a swimming pool and five cinemas. The fruit and vegetable market on Mon, Wed, Fri and Sat mornings has a Caribbean flavour, but it is expensive. There are bathing beaches (water rather muddy) around the island, the best is Montjoly, but watch out for sharks. Minibuses run from terminal to Rémire-Montjoly for beaches. They leave when full – check when the last one returns. There is a walking trail called 'Rorota' which follows the coastline and can be reached from Montjoly or the Gosselin beaches. Another trail, 'Habitation Vidal' in Rémire, passes through former sugar cane plantations. Remains of sugar mills can be seen on the way.

Hotels L3 *Novotel Cayenne*, Chemin Hilaire-route de Montabo, T 30-38-88, F 31-78-98, not central, on beach, restaurant, a/c, very good; **A1** *Hotel des Amandiers*, Place Auguste Horth, T 30-26-00, F 30-74-84, a/c, excellent restaurant; **A1** *Phigarita Studios*, 47 bis, rue F Arago, T 30-66-00, F 30-77-49, spacious apartments with kitchenette, a/c, rec, friendly, helpful, breakfast; **A1** *Amazonia*, 26 Av Gen de Gaulle, good, friendly, a/c, luggage stored, central location, T 31-00-00, F 31-94-41; **A3** *le Coin d'Or*, PK 5.5, route de Montabo, T 30-21-77, F 30-46-28, take bus No 1 from Place des Palmistes, to Carrefour de Soussini about 4 km from centre, with bath, D in adjacent gîtes, shared bath, clean, friendly, rec, breakfast 40F, full board 180F; **A2** *Central Hotel*, corner rue Molé and rue Becker, T 31-30-00, F 31-12-96, downtown, a/c; **A2** *Le Grillardin*, PK6 Route Matoury, 4 km from airport, T 35-63-90, a/c, restaurant; **A2** *Ket-Tai*, Ave de la Libertie corner Blvd Jubelin, new, clean, modern, overpriced; **A2** *Guyane Studios*, 16 rue Molé, T 30-25-11, a/c; **B** *Le Baduel*, Route

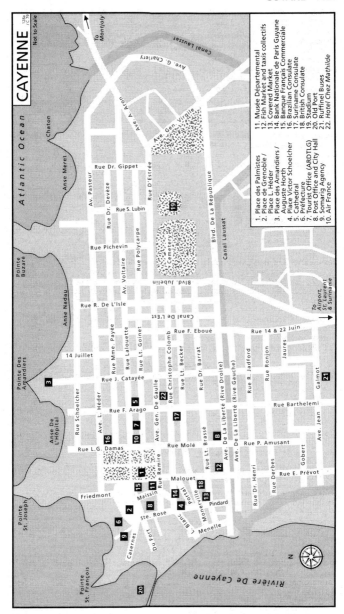

CAYENNE

Not to Scale

Atlantic Ocean

To Montjoly

Canal Laussat

Ave. G. Charlery

Ave. A. Aron

Chaton

Anse Merel

Rue Dr. Gippet

Av. Pasteur

Rue Dr. Devèze

Rue S. Lubin

Ave. Gen. Virgile

Rue D'Estrée

Rue Pichevin

Rue Polycarpe

Av. Voltaire

Blvd. De La République

Cemetery

Blvd. Jubelin

Pointe Buzaré

Anse Nadau

Rue R. De L'Isle

Canal Laussat

Rue Mme Payée

Rue Lalouette

Rue Lt. Goinet

Canal De L'Est

Rue F. Eboué

Rue 14 & 22 Juin

Pointe Des Amandiers

14 Juillet

Rue J. Catayée

Rue Christophe Colomb

Rue Lt. Becker

Rue Dr. Barrat

Rue De La Liberté (Rive Droite)

Rue De La Liberté (Rive Gauche)

Rue R. Jadford

Jaures

Rue Ronjon

To Airport, St Laurent & Surinam

Anse De L'Hôpital

Rue Schoelcher

Ave. L. Héder

Rue F. Arago

Ave. Gen. De Gaulle

Rue Lt. Brassé

Rue Molé

Ave. P. Amusant

Rue Barthelemi

Ave. Jean Gobert

Av. Héder

Rue L.G. Damas

Rue Remire

Maliouet

Malouet

Maissin

Pindard

Rue Derbes

Rue E. Prévot

Rue Dr. Henri

Galmot

Friedmont

Ste. Rose

Monerville

L. Blanc

Du Fort

Menelle

Casernes

Pointe St. Joseph

Pointe St. François

Rivière De Cayenne

N

1. Place des Palmistes
2. Place de Grenoble /
3. Place L. Héder
   Place des Amandiers /
   Auguste Horth
4. Place Victor Schoelcher
5. Préfecture
6. Tourist Office (ARDTLG)
7. Post Office and City Hall
8. Somarig Agency
9. Air France
10. Musée Departemental
11. Fish Market and taxis collectifs
12. Covered Market
13. Banque Nationale de Paris Guyane
14. Banque Français Commerciale
15. Brazilian Consulate
16. Surinam Consulate
17. British Consulate
18. Stadium
19. Old Port
20. Ruffinel Buses
21. Restaurant/Hotel Chez Mathilde

de Baduel, T 30-51-58, F 30-77-76, a/c, TV, cooking facilities; **A3-B** *Ajoupa*, T 30-33-08, F 30-12-82, Route Camp de Tigre, 2 km from town, helpful; **B-C** *Chez Mathilde/Hotel du Palais*, 42 Av Gen de Gaulle, T 30-25-13, cheaper with fan and without bath, hammock space, friendly, clean, noisy, not safe for left luggage, always full; **B** *Madeleine*, T 30-17-36, a/c, basic, clean, breakfast, will book Raffinel bus to St-Laurent, 1 km out of town, friendly (good Surinamese snackbar nearby); **B** *Neptima*, rue F Eboué 21, T 30-11-15, F 37-98-60 (15 rm), best value, a/c, clean, friendly. Cheapest in town is **E** *Foyer Paul VI*, rue des Mangues, 10-15 mins walk from centre, T 30-04-16, cheap meals.

About 10 km from Cayenne is the **A2** *Beauregard*, route de Rémire, T 35-41-00, F 35-44-05, rec for business visitors, pool, tennis, squash, sauna, restaurant *Cric-Crac*. Also *Hotel M*, a motel with a/c rooms and a small swimming pool; the owner hires out small cars, rec for business visitors, breakfast, T 35-41-00, Telex 010 310, and **A1** *Motel du Lac*, T 38-08-00, F 38-10-34, Chemin Poupon, Montjoly, 10 km from centre, pool, bar, restaurant, good business hotel.

Other rooms to rent: **C** *Mme Romieu*, PK 5.5 Route de Montabo, T 31-06-55; **B** *Mme Martin*, 19 rue Euloge Jean Elie, T 38-24-27; **B** *Mme Mirta*, 35 Lot Alexandre, T 31-48-78; **D** *M Roques*, 2 Lot Amarillys, T 38-18-20; **B** *Mme Stanistlas*, Villa Sonia PK 0.4 Rte de Rémire, T 38-22-13; **B** *Mme Anastase*, 59 Av de Gaulle, T 35-17-70; **B** *Mme Castor*, 4 rue du Dr Gippet, T 31-27-38, F 31-66-13; **B** *Mme de Chadirac*, Route de Montjoly PK 6, T 38-23-01; **C** *Mme Girard*, Route de Montabo PK3.5, T 30-61-28; **B** *M Benoit*, 117 rue Ch Colomb, T 31-42-81; **A** *Mme Kong*, 41 Av de la Liberté, T 30-13-98. Most hotels do not add tax and service to their bill, but stick to prices posted outside or at the desk. Hotel rooms are expensive—it is hard to find a room under 200F a night double. Bed and breakfast accommodation (gîte) is available for about 150F a night (breakfast is usually at extra cost)—contact the tourist office for details. Ask the Catholic Fathers at Cité Messaih, nr *Hotel Madeleine*, about sleeping possibilities. Amex cards often not accepted but Visa OK.

Restaurants and Bars Main hotels. *Hostellerie 'Les Amandiers'*, place Auguste-Horth, excellent, the most famous French, expensive (US$38); *Au Vieux Genois*, 89 rue Christophe Colomb, very good, French with local products, fish specialities, good business lunches; *La Caravelle*, 21 rue Christophe Colomb; *Le Vesuvio*, route Montabo, very good, clean; *Armand Ti A Hing*, Place des Palmistes, French, excellent, 180F pp; *Cap St Jacques*, rue Docteur E Gippet, excellent Vietnamese food, reasonable. *Maxim'um*, Av Estrée. *La Croix du Sud*, 80, Av de Gaulle; *Tournesol*, rue Lt Goinet, real French food, fine wines, expensive, highly rec; *Porto Verde*, 58 rue Lt Goinet, Brazilian menu, mostly under 50F, rec; *Le Grillardin* (see **Hotels**), very good Créole; *Paris-Cayenne*, 59 rue Lallouette, French, very good, nice décor; *La Belle Epoque*, French, expensive; *Cric-Crac* (at *Hotel Beauregard*), Créole cooking, lovely atmosphere; *Le Snack Créole*, 17 rue Eboué; *Mille Pâtes*, 16 rue Felix Eboné; *Palmiste*, Place des Palmistes (downtown), good daily menu, US$17, central and spacious; *Frégate*, Av de Gaulle; *Le Traiteur de la Fôret*, Blvd Jubelin, friendly, good; *Marveen Snack Bar*, rue Ch Colombe, near Canal de L'Est, food and staff pleasant, the patrons are very helpful regarding air travel and excursions (the elder of the two is a pilot for the Guyane Flying Club). *Ko Fei*, 18, rue Lalouette, T 312888, good Chinese; *Apsara*, 95 rue Colombe, Chinese, good value. *La Rose d'Asie*, 20 rue Samuel Lubin, very good Vietnamese. *Hindu-Creol*, rue J Catayee, Indian, good. Along the Canal Laussant there are Javanese snack bars; try *bami* (spicy noodles) or *saté* (barbecued meat in a spicy peanut sauce). Also along the canal are small, cheap Créole restaurants, not very clean. Vans around place des Palmistes in evenings sell cheap, filling sandwiches. *Bar Cayenne Palace*, 45 Av de Gaulle, disco 80F with first drink. *Delifrance*, Av de Gaulle at rue Catayée, hot chocolate and croissants; *Epi d'Or*, Av Jubelin, good sweets and cakes, rec. Food is about 35% more expensive than metropolitan France: it is hard to find a meal for under 50F (small Chinese restaurants charge 50-80F for a full meal).

Banks Banque Nacional de Paris-Guyane, 2 place Schoelcher; no exchange facilities on Sat. **Banque Française Commerciale**, 2 Place des Palmistes (best bank exchange rates); **Crédit Populaire Guyanais**, 93 rue Lalouette. Most banks have ATMs for cash withdrawals on Visa, sometimes Mastercard, never Amex. *Cambio Caraïbe*, Av Gen de Gaulle, nr Catayée (best rate for US$); *Guyane Change*, Av Gen de Gaulle, nr rue F Eboué. The Post Office exchanges cash and TCs at good rates, but complicated and time-consuming. There are no exchange facilities at the airport; if in extreme need on Sat you may be able to change money at Air France office in place des Palmistes. Central drugstore may help when banks closed. Almost impossible to change dollars outside Cayenne or Kourou. Buy francs before arrival if possible.

Laundromat Corner of rue Lalouette and rue Eboué, US$5 load all in; *Ros'in*, 87 Av Liberté, T 31-73-13.

Main Post Office Route de Baduel, 2 km out from town (15F by taxi or 20 mins on foot).

Poste Restante letters are only kept for 2 weeks maximum. Also Poste Cayenne Cépéron, place L Heder.

Bookshops *Librairie AJC*, 31 Boulevard Jubelin, has some stock in English. Also old maps and prints. Current map sold at *Librairie Alain Pion*, Av de Gaulle and in most bookshops.

Travel Agents *Takari Tour*, Colline du Montabo, T 31-19-60 (BP 513) and at *Novotel*, rec for inland tours. *Guyane Excursions*, Centre Commercial Simarouba, Kourou, T 32-05-41, specializes in inland tours, particularly to the Maroni river, highly rec, 3,500F for 5-6 days, but a wide variety of options. Also *JAL Voyages*, T 38-23-70, for a wide variety of tours. *Somarig*, place L Héder, T 30-29-80, is reported to be good for South American and European airline tickets. It also sells boat tickets to Ile Royale as well as meal tickets for the Auberge which are recommended. *Agence Sainte-Claire*, 8 rue de Rémire, T 30-00-38, for travel outside Guyane (including charters to Caracas, Fortaleza, Brazil, Ecuador, Cuba); *Havas*, 2 place du Marché, T 31-26-22/31-27-26.

Tourist Office Agence Régionale de Développement du Tourisme et des Loisirs de la Guyane (ARDTLG), 12 rue Lalouette (T 30-09-00), 0800-1200, 1500-1800. Free map and tourist guide (Guyane Poche). The SLM manager is reported to be very helpful with advice.

Car Hire 15 companies incuding both Hertz and Avis at airport. Full list available from ARDTLG (see **Tourist Office** above). An international driving licence is required. **Bicycle Hire** Takari Tour office at *Novotel*, 120F/day, 500F/week, also guided tours.

Transport Bus terminal at corner of rue Molé and Av de la Liberté. Regular urban services. The only westbound bus is run by Ruffinel & Cie, 8 Av Galmot, T 31-26-66 (Kourou 60F, St Laurent 150F) leaves 0530 (not Sun). Minibuses to St-Laurent du Maroni leave when full from the terminal, 0400-1200, 3 hrs, 150F. Service to **Mana** Mon and Thur only. To **Kaw**, Wed. Otherwise transport is by shared taxis (collectifs), which leave from Av de la Liberté, near the fish market early in the morning (Kourou 60F, St Laurent 150F).

International Airport Cayenne-Rochambeau is 16 km from Cayenne, 20 mins by taxi. No exchange facilities. **(See Air Routes to Guyane, p 1489.)** Air France, 13 rue LG Damas, Place des Palmistes, T 30-27-40; Air Guyane, 2 rue Lalouette, T 31-72-00/35-65-55; Surinam Airways, 2 place Schoelcher, T 31-72-98. Local air services: Air Guyane to all main centres. No public transport; only taxis (150F daytime, 200F night, but you can probably bargain or share). The cheapest route to town is taxi to Matoury 50F, then bus to centre 10F. Cheapest method of return to airport is by collective taxi from corner of Av de la Liberté and rue Malouet to Matoury (10 km) for 12F, then hitch or walk.

Excursions Trips by motor-canoe (*pirogue*) up-river into the jungle can be arranged. 6½ km outside Cayenne is a restaurant with paintings of prison life by Huguet, an ex-convict, whose work can also be seen in the church at Iracoubo, between Kourou and St-Laurent. 10 km out, near the bridge to the mainland, is an American shrimp-packing plant. 9 km S of Cayenne is Matoury, on the road to Régina, with two walking trails in the forest.

40 km away is **Ile Connétable**, a small offshore island with large frigate-bird colonies; although a restricted area for tourists, some tour operators may take you.

43 km SW of Cayenne is **Montsinéry**, with a zoo featuring Amazonian flora and fauna (open daily 1000-1900), an orchid and a walking trail, 'Bagne des Annamites', through remains of a camp where prisoners from Indochina were interned in the 1930s.

Kourou, 56 km W of Cayenne, where the main French space centre (Centre Spatial Guyanais), used for the European Space Agency's Ariane programme, is located, is referred to by the Guyanais as 'white city' because of the number of metropolitan French families living there; its population is about 20,000. It has several excellent hotels and a number of good restaurants, but the project and population have been substantially reduced. Tourist attractions include bathing, fishing, sporting and aero club, and a variety of organized excursions. The space centre occupies an area of about 4 km deep along some 30 km of coast, bisected by the Kourou river. Public guided tours are given Mon-Fri 0745-1130 and 1300-1630 (on Fri sometimes am only). Phone 32-61-23 to reserve a place on a tour of the centre; often booked up days ahead; closed during Carnival. A new museum was due to open in July 1995. No public transport, take a taxi or hitch. Visits are free. If you book at least 3 days in advance you can ask Public Relations for an English-speaking guide for 2-3 people, minimum; for a group of 20-25, a full English-speaking tour can be arranged. Alternatively, you can watch the launch for free, from a distance, at Montague Carapa at Pariacabo.

Hotels All hotels are overbooked and raise their prices when there is an Ariane rocket launch (about once a month). **L3** *Relais de Guyane* (*Hotel des Roches*), Avenues des Roches, T 32-00-66, F 32-03-28, not too good, a/c, incl breakfast, pool, beach, good restaurants; **A1** *Atlantis*, T 32-13-00, F 32-40-12, nr Lac Bois Diable, a/c, modern, pool, good restaurant, best value for business visitors; also at Lac Bois Diable, **L2** *Mercure*, T 32-07-00; **L3** *La Corissante*, 23 rue des Alizés, T 33-11-00, F 33-11-60, studios with 2-5 rm, cooking facilities; **A2** *Studios Le Gros Bec*, T 32-91-91, 52 rue Dr Floch, cooking facilities; **A2** *Les Jardins D'Hermes*, 56 rue Duchesne, T 32-01-83, F 32-09-17, in heart of old Kourou, a/c, modern, good; **A3** *Ballahou*, 1 rue Armet Martial, T 32-42-06, F 32-52-08, a/c, TV, nice, modern, friendly, good restaurant; **A** *Mme Moutton*, rue Séraphin 56, T 31-21-45, studios with or without kitchen, friendly; **A3** *Auberge des Iles du Salut*, T 32-11-00, F 32-42-23, see below. **E** *Centre d'Acceuil*, T 32-25-40/32-26-33, various sizes of room, clean, good value. Cheap hotels and rooms for 100F on Av de Gaulle.

20 km S of Kourou on the road to Saramaca is *Les Maripas*, tourist camp, T 32-05-41, F 32-28-47, river and overland excursions available, D for tent, book at Guyane Excursion, 7 quartier Simarouba, nr *Restaurant Saramaca*.

Restaurants Many, esp on de Gaulle incl *Le Catouri, Cachiri Combo* (No 3, T 32-44-64, 100-150F, also has basic rooms, C), *Vieux Montmartre*; *La Grillade*, Av Berlioz; *L'Enfer Vert*, Av G Monnerville; *Le Paradisier* in Hotel des Roches (see above); *L'Hydromed*, rue Raymond Cresson, good pancakes; *Le Provence*, 11 passage G Monnerville, best French, expensive; *Ballahou* (see **Hotels**), best for fish and seafood (try *Guyabaisse*); pizza at *Le Valentino*, place Galilé; *Le Saramaca*, place du Marché; *Relais de L'Europe*, 20m from post office, at 50F good value. Many cheap Chinese (also take-away) *Le Chinatown*, rue Duchesne, rec; *Kong Loong*, rue du Levant; many vans sell sandwiches filled with Créole food, good. **Bar** *La Nouvelle Dimension* (Créole and European style); *American Bar* in Hotel des Roches (see **Hotels**); *Le Forban*, rue Dreyfus, district 205, worth seeing the murals (also for the lonely, many young Brazilian women). **Night Clubs** *Saxo* (best) *3ème Dimension* (Créole style), *Le Vieux Montmartre*, all on de Gaulle.

Exchange Banque National de Paris Guyane, place Newton; Banque Française Commerciale, place Jeanne d'Arc; Crédit Populaire Guyanais, Simarouba.

Post Office Av des Frères Kennedy.

Travel Agency *Guyane Excursions*, T 32-05-41 (see under Cayenne); *Havas Voyages Kourou*, T 32-55-77; *Agence Sainte Claire*, T 32-36-98, F 32-50-40; *Air France*, place Newton, T 32-10-50.

Transport Taxi in town 30F. To Cayenne bus leaves from Shell service station, corner Av de France, Av Vermont Polycarpe, bus to St-Laurent du Maroni from same place, 2 between 0600 and 0700, 150F; *taxis collectifs*, 0600, 0630, 0700, 1330, 60F. Taxi to Cayenne or airport, 300F (400F at night); to St-Laurent du Maroni 125F by *taxi collectif* (irregular).

The *Iles du Salut* (many visitors at weekends), opposite Kourou, include the Ile Royale, the Ile Saint-Joseph, and the Ile du Diable. They were the scene of the notorious convict settlement built in 1852; the last prisoners left in 1953. The Ile du Diable ('Devil's Island'), a rocky palm-covered islet almost inaccessible from the sea, was where political prisoners, including Alfred Dreyfus, were held. There is a 60-bed hotel on Ile Royale, **A3** *Auberge Iles du Salut* (address Sothis, 97310 Kourou, T 32-11-00, F 32-42-23), also hammock E pp; former guard's bungalow, main meals (excellent), minimum 180F, breakfast 40F (ex-mess hall for warders, with good food; bottled water sold); gift shop with high prices (especially when a cruise ship is in), good English guide book for sale. Camping is possible, but suitable sites are limited, the strong-hearted may try the old prison barracks; take food and water (you can also sling a hammock in the open, take a plastic sheet to protect yourself from morning mist); bread and water (check bottle is sealed) can be bought from the hotel stall. You can see agoutis, turtles, humming birds and macaws, and there are many un-owned coconut palms. Beware the many open wells. Take a torch for visiting the ruins. Paintings of prison life are on show in the tiny church. Points of interest include the children's graveyard, hospital, mental asylum and death cells. These, and the church, are not always open. Little is being done to prevent the deterioration of the buildings. Boat from Kourou's port at the end of Av General de Gaulle, 4 km from old centre, 186F return (children under 12 half price), leaves 0830 and 1030 daily, returns from island at 1600 and 1800 (check T 32-09-95) additional sailing Sat 1600, 1 hr each way. Tickets may be obtained from Somarig Voyages, or Havas Voyages, addresses under Cayenne **Travel Agents**; Air Guyane Voyages, 2 rue Lallouette, T 31-72-00; in Kourou from au Carbet des Roches, cash only. There are no regular boats from Ile Royale to Ile Saint-Joseph, which is wilder and more beautiful, with a small beach (this island had solitary-confinement cells and the warders' graveyard). It may be possible to hire a private boat at the ferry dock, or ask for James on the Kourou-Ile Royale ferry. A regular service is planned for 1996. Surfing and swimming are possible between Ile Royale and Ile du Diable; strong currents at high tide. Boat owners are very reluctant to visit Ile du Diable except around Jul-Aug when the sea is calmer.

Between Kourou and Iracoubo, on the road W to St-Laurent, is **Sinnamary** (103 km from Cayenne), a pleasant town where Galibi Indians at a mission make artifical flowers from feathers, for sale to tourists (Hotels **A** Sinnarive Motel, T 34-56-56, F 34-55-55; **A3** Eldo Grill, T 34-51-41, F 34-50-90, a/c, TV, coffee, breakfast extra, rec; **A1** Hotel du Fleuve, T 34-54-00, F 34-53-03, expensive. Restaurant Madras, good, Créole; ask for Gaya Baru Indonesian restaurant in an Indonesian village). Woodcarvings and jewellery are on sale here and the workshops can be visited. There are 3 to 5 day excursions up the Sinnamarie River. Scarlet ibis can be seen in declining numbers on the Sinnamarie estuary at **Iracoubo**. Also at Iracoubo is a pretty church in the woods with paintings by convicts. (Hotel **C** Au Fil de L'Eau, T 34-63-51).

For tours of the new hydroelectric plants about 40 km S of Sinnamarie, contact Mrs Favrel, T 32-20-99 (**see p 1480**).

St-Laurent du Maroni, pop 16,000, formerly a penal transportation camp, is 250 km from Cayenne on the River Maroni, bordering Suriname. (Nearby is St-Jean du Maroni, an Indian village.) There are acceptable hotels and several restaurants. **A1-3** Hotel La Tentiaire, 12 Av Franklin Roosevelt, T 34-26-00, F 34-15-09, a/c, the best, breakfast extra; **B** Hotel Toucan, Boulevard de Republique, T 34-12-59, F 34-17-06, a/c, TV, dirty. **B** Hotel Star, rue Thiers, T 34-10-84, a/c, pool, cheap restaurant, friendly, rec; **A3** Chez Julienne, Route des Malgaches, T 34-11-53, a/c, TV, shower, good. Restaurant Le Saramaca, Av Felix Eboué, best; Restaurants Vietnam and Le Point d'Intérrogation have been rec, also Loe, near hospital, Créole, excellent and Inni, rue Thiers, Créole, good value; many cheap Chinese. There are no gîtes in St-Laurent; those on a tight budget wanting a room or hammock space (D-E range) can try to make advance arrangements in Cayenne with: Fedération d'Oeuvres Laïques, Centre d'Hebergement de Saint-Louis, T 34-11-40; CAS EDF, centre d'Hebergement, T 34-12-96/34-23-03; or Le Carbet du Balat, Mme Emille Lamtoukai, T 34-10-35. BNP opp Restaurant Le Saramaca will change US$ TCs; both local banks give cash against Visa card.

The old Camp de Transportation (the original penal centre) can be wandered round at will (an absolute must if visiting the country). Guided tours of Les Bagnes (prison camps) daily 0830-1230, 1500-1800, chilling. The Charbonière refugee camp, next to the ferry pier, housed Surinamese Bush Negro refugees during that country's civil war. A few have remained and more have returned. See Suriname, **Population**, for more details.

Tourist Office rue August Boudinot/Av de la Marne, T 342398.

Transport Minibuses to Cayenne meet the ferry from Suriname, leaving when full, 3 hrs, 150F. Bus to Cayenne, 150F, same price to Kourou, but no regular service; taxis collectifs to and from Cayenne, 150F a head, 3½-hrs trip. Freight pirogues sometimes take passengers inland along the Maroni River; alternatively a group can hire a pirogue at about 1,000F a day. Avis has a car rental office in St-Laurent.

Excursions About 3 km from St-Laurent, along the Paul Isnard Rd, is Saint-Maurice, where the rum distillery of the same name can be visited, Mon-Thur 0630-1430, Fri 0630-1330. At Km 70 on the same dirt road is access to **Voltaire Falls**, 1½ hrs walk from the road. 7 km S of St-Laurent on the road to St-Jean is the Amerindian village of **Terre Rouge**; canoes can be hired for day trips up the Maroni River (see Maripasoula below).

Crossing to Suriname Make sure you obtain proper entry stamps from immigration, not the police, to avoid problems when leaving. Customs and immigration close at 1900. Ferry for vehicles and passengers to Albina, Mon, Thur 0700, 0900, 1400, 1600, Tues, Wed, Sat 0700, 0900, Sun 1530, 1600, 30 mins. Passengers 20F one-way, car 100F one-way. Minibuses and taxis for Paramaribo meet the Albina ferry; many aggressive touts on the St-Laurent and Albina piers. It is best to change money in the Village Chinois in St-Laurent; although rates are lower than in Paramaribo, it is illegal to change money in Albina. Beware theft at St-Laurent's black market. GUM airways fly from St-Laurent to Paramaribo, 3 times a week, enquire at the *Star Hotel*.

In the countryside not far from St-Laurent are 2 *auberge de brousse*, which are good places to stay for walking, or for trips to see turtles at Les Hattes (see below: **C** *Auberge Bois Diable*, PK 8 Acarouany, T 34-19-35, 1 bedroom, hammock space, F, meals, 80F, breakfast 20F, good food, hospitable, tours arranged; **C** *Relais d'Acarouany*, T 34-17-20, 6 rm, meals 90F, breakfast 20F.

40 km N of St-Laurent du Maroni is **Mana**, a delightful town with rustic architecture near the coast (**E** pp *Gîte d'Etape*, rooms OK, filthy kitchen, mosquitoes, disco next door; nuns next to the church rent beds and hammocks, clean, simple, Communauté des Soeurs de St-Joseph de Cluny, 1 rue Bourguignon, T 34-17-29; Mme Hidair, T 34-80-62, has rooms, C). 20 km W of Mana following the river along a paved road is **Les Hattes**, or Awala-Yalimapo (**B** *Gîte Rureau*, clean) an Amerindian village (ask M Daniel for permission to stay in the church); 4 km further on is Les Hattes beach where leatherback-turtles lay their eggs at night; season April-Aug with its peak in June-July (in July you can see adults coming ashore to lay and hatchlings rushing to meet the high tide). No public transport to Les Hattes and its beach, but hitching possible at weekends; take food and water and mosquito repellent. In spite of the dryish climate Mana is a malaria region. The fresh water of the Maroni and Mana rivers makes sea bathing very pleasant. Very quiet during the week.

Aouara, an Amerindian village with hammock places, is a few kilometres SE of Les Hattes. It also has a beach where the leatherback turtles lay their eggs; they take about 3 hrs over it. Take mosquito nets, hammock and insect repellent.

There are daily flights from Cayenne to **Maripasoula**, 474F one-way (**D** *Auberge Chez Dedè*, Av Leonard, T 37-20-05, 20F for extra person, **A1** *Campement Touristique de Saut Sonnelle*, T 31-49-45, full board) up the Maroni from St-Laurent (2-4 day journey up river in *pirogue*). There may be freight canoes which take passengers (200F) or private boats (750F) which leave from St-Laurent; 5-6 day tours and other options with Guyane-Excursions or with Takari Tour (see under Cayenne **Travel Agents**). Maripasoula has 5,000 inhabitants in town and its surroundings. Many bush negros live here. If going up the Maroni, take malaria prophylaxis. 20 mins by canoe from Maripasoula by canoe is **A2** *Campement Touristique Lassort*, T 31-49-45.

Saül, a remote gold-mining settlement in the 'central massif' is the geographical centre of Guyane. The main attractions are for the nature-loving tourist—beautiful undisturbed tropical forests are accessible by a very well-maintained system of 90 km of marked trails, including several circular routes. The place has running water, a radiotelephone, and electricity. 10-day expeditions are run by Christian Ball, 'Vie Sauvage', 97314 Saül, 430F (30% in advance) per day with meals, maps of local trails provided, own hammock and bedding useful but not essential. It can be cold at night. Another fascinating overland route goes from Roura (see below) up the Comte River to Belizon, followed by a 14 to 16-day trek through the jungle to Saül, visiting many villages en route, guide recommended. 7 km N of Saül is *Eden des Eaux Claires*, tourist camp, T 30-91-11, **A2** full board, C in hammock incl breakfast and dinner (drinks extra). Air service Mon, Wed, Fri with Air Guyane from Cayenne (364F one-way, 620F return) or via Maripasoula, 339F one-way; try at airport even if flight said to be full. By *pirogue* from Mana up Mana River, 9-12 days, then 1 day's walk to Saül, or from St-Laurent via Maripasoula along Moroni and Inini Rivers, 15 days and 1 day's walk to Saül, both routes expensive.

30 km S of Cayenne at *Carrefour de Gallion*, the intersection of RN2 and CD5, is **B** *Emerald Jungle Village*, a tropical nature centre with a small botanical and zoological collection. Eco-tours can be taken into the forests by boat or canoe with expedition gear. Meals and drinks extra, airport transportation 90F, mountain bike hire 50F/day, canoes for hire. Owned by Joep Moonen and his wife, who both speak English, German and Dutch F 30-06-82; or write to CDS-PK0.5, 97356 Montsinéry.

28 km SE of Cayenne is the small town of **Roura** (**B** *Hotel Restaurant Amazone River*, T 31-91-12, a/c, good restaurant, good views of the river; **B** *Auberge des Orpailleurs*, PK62 route de l'Est, T 37-62-97, hammock space 25F, breakfast and dinner available; rooms to rent from Mme Luap, D, T 31-54-84), which has an interesting church. An excursion may be made to the Fourgassier Falls several km away (*L'Auberge des Cascades*, excellent restaurant). From Cayenne the road now crosses a new bridge over the River Comte. Excursions can be arranged along the River Comte. For information about the area contact the Syndicat D'Initiative de Roura, T 31-11-04. Nearby is Dacca, a Laotian village. 27 km from Roura is **C** *Auberge du Camp Caiman* (tourist camp, F to hang hammock), T 37-60-34, tours arranged to watch caiman in the swamps.

From Roura an unpaved road runs SE towards the village of Kaw. At Km 36 from Cayenne is the **C** *Hotel Relais de Patawa* (T 31-93-95), or sling your hammock for 20F, cheaper rates for longer stays, highly rec. The owners, M and Mme Baloup, who are entomologists, will show you their collection, take you on guided tours of local sights and introduce you to their pet anaconda and boa constrictors. At Km 59 on the road to Régina is the turn-off to *Cacao* (a further 13 km), a small, quiet village, where Hmong refugees from Laos are settled; they are farmers and produce fine traditional handicrafts. (Accommodation: **C** *Restaurant La Lan*, 1 rm, good value, good food; **E** *Quimbe-Kio* hammock camp, 35F, breakfast 15F; M Levessier, T 30-51-22, has hammocks; best restaurant is *Chez By et Cacao*, Laotian food; also good is *Degrad Cacao*). Minibus from Cayenne, Mon 1200; Fri 1800, return Mon 0730, Fri 1400. Halfway along the side road is the *Belle Vue* restaurant, which lives up to its name, because of the superb view over the tropical forest; the restaurant is open at weekends. Southwest of Cacao is the tourist camp **A2** *Carbet La Source*, with full board, T 31-96-64. *Kaw*, at Km 83, is on an island amid swamps which are home to much rare wildlife including caymans. The village is reached by dugout either from the Cayenne road or from Régina, or by road from Roura (50 km dirt road through the mountains with the last 2 km by dugout). Basic accommodation available (Mme Musron, T 31-88-15), take insect repellent. Southwest of Kaw on the River Approuague is *Régina*, linked with Cayenne by a mostly paved road.

St-Georges de l'Oyapoc is 15 mins down river from Oiapoque (Brazil) 20F pp by motorized canoe, bargain for a return fare. **B** *Hotel Modestine*, T 37-00-13, restaurant; rooms to rent from M Carème, C; **D** unnamed hotel to left of supermarket opp town hall, a dump, no fan, no window, not rec; also *Theofila*, lunch US$3, other restaurants and a night club. Two supermarkets with French specialities. Immigration (*gendarmerie*) for entry/exist stamps at E end of town, follow signs, open daily 0700-1200, 1500-1800 (sometimes not open after early am on Sun, in which case try the police at the airport); French and Portuguese spoken. One of the Livre Service supermarkets and *Hotel Modestine* will sometimes change dollars cash into francs at very poor rates; if entering the country here, change money before arriving in St-Georges. Note that nowhere in town accepts Visa card. Post office; public telephone which takes phone cards.

For Air Guyane flights to Cayenne see below, **Internal Transport**. Air Guyane office at airport open 0700-0730, 1400-1430 for check in, open 0800-1100 for reservations. Flights are fully-booked several days in advance; you must check in at times stated. Extra flights are sometimes added. The police check that those boarding flights who have arrived from Brazil have obtained their entry stamp; also thorough baggage search.

A small vessel, the *Sao Pedro*, normally runs a shipping service to Cayenne, deck passengers 150F, but check it is not under repair. A cargo ship, the *Normelia*, calls at St-Georges about twice a month and will sometimes take passengers to Cayenne, 12-14 hrs, 150F including meals. Speak directly to the captain. The Elf petrol station has details of ship arrivals.

A trail has been cut by the French army from St-Georges to the road-head at Régina, along which a road is currently under construction. It is 4 to 5 days of hard trekking with many rivers to be forded, impassable during the rainy season.

The **Saut Maripa** rapids (not too impressive with high water) are located about 30 mins upstream along the Oiapoc river, past the Brazilian towns of Oiapoque and Clevelândia do Norte. Hire a motorized *pirogue* (canoe) to take you to a landing downstream from the rapids. Then walk along the remains of a narrow gauge railway line (one of only two in Guyane, formerly used for gold mining) for 20 mins through the jungle, to reach a small tourist complex with restaurant, bar, and guest houses by the rapids. A pleasant day trip. There are more rapids further upstream.

Camopi is an Indian village 2-3 days up the Oyapoc from St-Georges (*pirogue*, 600F); to go beyond Saut-Maripa requires a special permit from the Préfecture in Cayenne, which takes 6 weeks and is usually granted only to scientists. Tours from Cayenne, 4,800F pp for 6 days.

INFORMATION FOR VISITORS

Before you go

Entry requirements

● **Documents**
Passports are not required by nationals of France and most French-speaking African countries carrying identity cards. For EC visitors, documents are the same as for Metropolitan France (ie no visa, no exit ticket required – check with a consulate in advance). No visa (45F) required for most nationalities (except for those of Guyana, Australia, some Eastern European countries, and Asian – not Japan – and other African countries) for a stay of up to 3 months, but an exit ticket out of the country is essential (a ticket out of one of the other Guianas is not sufficient); a deposit is required otherwise. If one stays more than 3 months, income tax clearance is required before leaving the country. Inoculation against yellow-fever is officially required only for those staying in Guyane longer than 2 weeks, but advisable for all. Travel to certain Amerindian villages is restricted (see p 1479

● **Representation overseas**
Consulates British (Honorary), 16 Av Monnerville (BP 664, Cayenne 97300, T 31-10-34/30-42-42, F 30-40-94); Brazilian, 12 rue L Héder, at corner of Place des Palmistes, near Air France offices (closed Sats T 30-04-67); Dutch (Honorary), Batiment Sogudem, Port of Dégrad des Cannes, BP139, Cayenne 97323, T 35-49-31, F 35-46-71; Suriname, 38 rue Christophe Colomb (T 30-04-61), Mon-Fri 0900-1200, visa 150F, two photos needed, takes 15 days (may be obtained same day, at extra cost).

● **Tourist information**
The French Government tourist offices generally have leaflets on Guyane; there is a special office in Paris, La Maison du Tourisme de la Guyane, 26 rue du 4 Septembre 75002, Paris, T 47-42-84-16, F 47-42-84-91. The Cayenne offices are at 12 rue Lalouette, Cayenne (Telex 910356, T 300900); Délégation Régionale, 10, rue L-Heder, 97307 Cayenne, T 31-84-91; Syndicat d'initiative de Cayenne, Jardin Botanique, PO Box 702, 97338 Cayenne, T 31-29-19; Syndicat d'Initiative Rémire-Montjoly, Mairie de Rémire, 97305 Rémire, T 35-41-10.

When to go

● **Best time to visit**
The best months to visit are between Aug and Nov, which are the usual months for trips to the jungle.

Health

Tropical diseases, dysentery, malaria, etc, occur, but the country is fairly healthy. Malaria prophylaxis recommended.

Money

● **Currency**
The currency is the French franc (5.05F = US$1 May 1995). These are bank rates; *cambios* offer rates for cash. Try to take francs with you as the exchange rate for dollars is low, many banks do not offer exchange facilities and most places demand cash. A better rate can be obtained by using Visa cards to withdraw cash from the Banque Nacionale de Paris Guyane, Place Victor Schoelcher, Cay-

enne. Some report difficulties using cash dispensers (ATMs).

Getting there

By Air

Air France flies 5 times a week direct to Guyane from Paris, 9 times a week from Pointe-à-Pitre (Guadeloupe) Fort-de-France (Martinique), and once a week from Santo Domingo, once a week from Miami and once a week from Port-au-Prince. Air France operating jointly with Aeropostal flies once a week from Caracas. AOM French Airlines fly 3 times a week direct from Paris and are reported to be the cheapest from Europe (Paris T 40-74-00-04). Suriname Airways flies to Belém and Paramaribo 4 times a week and to Curaçao once a week; Suriname Airways sells tickets for Cayenne-Paramaribo- Georgetown-Port of Spain. Taba flies to Macapá, and Belém Brazil, 3 times a week.

By Sea

The Compagnie Général Maritime runs a passenger service to France once a month via Martinique and a freight service every 3 months. To Brazil by motorized dugout from St-Georges to Oiapoque, no custom or immigration post but foreigners are still sometimes returned to Guyane if their papers are not in order. Make sure you get an exit stamp from Gendarmerie in St-Georges. This journey is possible in reverse.

When you arrive

● **Hours of business**
Hours vary widely between different offices, shops and even between different branches of the same bank or supermarket. There seem to be different business hours for every day of the week, but they are usually posted.

● **Official time**
3 hrs behind GMT.

● **Shopping**
The best buys are handicrafts in wood in the Saramaca village (Kourou) and in the prison at St-Laurent du Maroni and white rum.

● **Weights and measures**
The metric system is in use.

Where to stay

Details of hotels are given in the text. For information on *Gîtes* and *Chambres chez l'habitant* write to Agence Régionale de Développement du Tourisme et des Loisirs de la Guyane (ARDTLG), 12 rue Lalouette,

97338, Cayenne Cedex, T 30-09-00, Telex 910364 FG; also, for *Gîtes*, Association pour le Tourisme Vert en Guyane, 27 rue Justin Cataye, 97300 Cayenne, T 31-10-11.

Food and drink

Most food is imported, except seafood; it is of very high quality but expensive.

Getting around

Air transport

Internal air services are by Air Guyane. These flights are always heavily booked, so be prepared to wait or write or telephone Air Guyane, 2 rue Lalouette, Cayenne (T 31-72-00). There are regular connections with Maripasoula, daily at 0930, 474F; St-Georges, daily at 0745 and usually one early pm, 30 mins, 350F one-way; Saül on Mon, Wed and Fri, at 0930, 364F; Régina, Mon, Wed and Fri at 0745, 165F. Baggage allowance 10 kg; 6.45F per kg excess. No services on Sun. Locals are given preference on internal flights; reservations cannot be made other than at the office in Cayenne, with cash.

Land transport

● **Train**
There are no railways.

● **Bus**
There is a lack of public transport.

● **Motoring**
There are no railways, and about 1,000 km of road. The main road, narrow but now paved, runs for 130 km from Pointe Macouri, on the roadstead of Cayenne, to Iracoubo. Another 117 km takes it to Mana and St-Laurent.

● **Car hire**
Car hire can be a great convenience (there are 15 agencies in Cayenne). All types of car available, from economy to luxury to pick-ups and jeeps. Cheapest rates are 180F a day for a Peugeot 106 or Ford Fiesta, to 450F for luxury, a/c car (rates Hertz and Eurofrane). Gasoline/petrol costs 5.32F a litre; diesel 3.64F a litre.

● **Hitchhiking**
Hitching is reported to be easy and widespread.

Boat

One- to three-ton boats which can be hauled over the rapids are used by the gold-seekers, the forest workers, and the rosewood establishments. There is a twice-a-month shipping service which calls at nearly all the coastal towns of Guyane. Ferries are free.

Communications

● **Language**
French, with officials not usually speaking anything else.

● **Newspapers**
La Presse de la Guyane is the daily paper (circ 1,500). *France-Guyane-Antilles* is a weekly newspaper with a good information page for the tourist.

● **Telephone services**
International calls can be made direct to any country from any phone: dial 19 + country code. Public telephones are widely installed and used. They take phonecards of 50 or 120 units (35F or 80F), which can be bought at tobacconists, bookshops or supermarkets. How to use the phone is displayed in each phone booth in French, English, Italian and Spanish. To call the USA, 1 unit buys 3.6 secs, to EC 2.5 secs; discounts at weekends and between 1700 and 0700. The system is totally interconnected with the French system. International code for Guyane is 594.

Holidays and festivals

Public holidays are the same as in Metropolitan France, with the addition of Slavery Day, 10 June.

Carnaval (Feb or Mar). Although not as famous as those of its neighbours in Brazil or the Caribbean, Guyane's Carnaval is joyous and interesting. It is principally a Créole event, but there is some participation by all the different cultural groups in the department (best known are the contributions of the Bra-

zilian and Haitian communities). Celebrations begin in Jan, with festivities every weekend, and culminate in colourful parades, music, and dance during the 4 days preceding Ash Wednesday. Each day has its own motif and the costumes are very elaborate. On Sat night, a dance called 'Chez Nana – Au Soleil Levant' is held, for which the women disguise themselves beyond recognition as 'Toulou-lous', and ask the men to dance. They are not allowed to refuse. On Sun there are parades in downtown Cayenne. Lundi Gras (Fat Monday) is the day to ridicule the institution of marriage, with mock wedding parties featuring men dressed as brides and women as grooms. 'Vaval', the devil and soul of Carnaval, appears on Mardi Gras (Fat Tuesday) with dancers sporting red costumes, horns, tails, pitch-forks, etc. He is burnt that night (in the form of a straw doll) on a large bonfire in the Place des Palmistes. Ash Wednesday is a time of sorrow, with participants in the final parades dressed in black and white.

Acknowledgements

We are most grateful to Rachel Rogers for updating this chapter, to Gérald Lorin (Kourou, Guyane) for a most helpful contribution on Suriname and Guyane, and to the following travellers: Bernard Fison (on board the yacht ODI), Paul D Harris and Mark JC Robinson (Birmingham, UK), Scott A Rasmussen (San Francisco, USA), M James Snyder (Radlett, UK.), Joep M Moonen (Montsinery, Guyane), Su Roper (Colby, Isle of Man), Bas van Tussenbroek (Aracati, Brazil), and Erwin Verhoeven (The Hague, The Netherlands).

FALKLAND ISLANDS
ISLAS MALVINAS

(In accordance with the practice suggested by the UN, we are calling the Islands by both their English and Spanish names.)

The Falkland Islands (Malvinas) comprise two groups: East Falkland (Isla Soledad) with its adjacent islands, about 2,600 square miles; and West Falkland (Gran Malvina), with its islands, about 2,100 square miles. Approximately 480 miles NE of Cape Horn, the Islands lie between latitudes 51° and 53° S and between longitudes 57° and 62° W. Nearly all land combat during the 1982 war was confined to the northern half of East Falkland; its southern peninsula of Lafonia, and West Falkland were little affected. According to the 1991 census, slightly less than two-thirds of the 2,050 residents are Falklands-born; another quarter were born in the United Kingdom. Slightly more than a quarter live and work on sheep farms. During the past decade, land reform through sale and subdivision of traditional large stations has resulted in more broadly based local ownership of pastoral land.

Early History Records of early voyages are ambiguous, but Dutchman Sebald de Weert made the first universally acknowledged sighting in 1598. The Englishman Strong landed in 1690 and named the Falkland Sound for a British peer; this name was later applied to the entire group. The Islands acquired their French appellation, Iles Malouines, from 17th century seafarers from the channel port of St Malo. This in turn became the Spanish Islas Malvinas.

In 1764 France established a small colony of Acadians at Port Louis under Bougainville. Two years later France sold the settlement to Spain, under which it became a military garrison and penal colony. At about the same time as France, Britain had built an outpost at Saunders Island, West Falkland, whose occupants Spain discovered and expelled in 1770. Restored in the following year after threat of war, the post was abandoned in 1774.

Deserted by Spain in 1811, during the South American wars of independence, the Islands lacked formal authority until 1820, when the United Provinces of the River Plate (later part of Argentina) raised their flag at Port Louis (Soledad). In 1831, an American warship destroyed a promising colonization project under the auspices of a German-born merchant from Buenos Aires, who had arrested and imprisoned American sealers operating in the area. After British warships expelled a token Buenos Aires force in 1833, the Islands experienced nearly 150 years of stability until April 1982, when Argentina invaded and occupied. Britain's counter-invasion recaptured the Islands by June of that year.

Administration The Islands' Constitution provides for a Governor, appointed from London, an Executive Council composed of appointed and elected members, and an elected Legislative Council. **Education** A Junior and Senior Community School in Stanley cater to the needs of town children and rural children who board in the School Hostel. Instruction to GCSE Level is available locally (compulsory to the age of 16), but higher education requires overseas travel, usually to Britain. Rural children receive attention from settlement instructors or travelling teachers. Radio is used to keep in contact with the more isolated farms.

Climate Although the *Sunday Express* once referred to a mutton freezer in the Falklands as a "Colonial Development project near the South Pole" (8 March 1953), the Islands are in the same latitude S as London is N. Mean monthly temperatures are lower than in London, but London experiences greater extremes. Normal temperature range is 20°F to 70°F (-1° to 21°C),

with an annual mean of 42°F (5°C). Though not always inclement, weather is very changeable. Persistent westerlies, blowing at an annual average of 14 knots, are the most trying aspect of the climate. Calm is more common in winter than summer. Stanley's annual rainfall of about 26 inches is slightly higher than London's. In the drier camp, outside Stanley, summer drought sometimes threatens local water supplies. Spring, autumn and winter clothing, as used in the United Kingdom, is suitable.

Stanley, the capital, is the major population centre on East Falkland. Its 1,557 residents live mostly in brightly-painted houses, many of which have corrugated iron roofs. Port Stanley, surrounded by rolling moorland, resembles parts of the Hebrides. The outer harbour of Port William is larger but less protected. East Cove, 30 miles SE of the capital, is the principal port for the new military installations at Mount Pleasant.

Accommodation and Food *Upland Goose Hotel*, Ross Road, T 21455, F 21520, from £49.50 bed and breakfast, to £72.50 d full board, evening meal £14.95; *Emma's Guest House*, Ross Road, T 21056, F 21573, from £30.50 bed and breakfast; *Malvina House Hotel*, 3 Ross Road, T 21355, F 21357, from £47.50 bed and breakfast. Prices subject to change. Full meals at all three, with reservations recommended at *Upland Goose* and *Malvina* (restaurant is smart with good food, book 36 hrs in advance). *Warrah Guest House*, John Street, T 21252, from £25 bed and breakfast. Fish and chips and pizza at *Woodbine Cafe*, 29 Fitzroy Road, T 21102, closed Sun and Mon. *Monty's/Deano's* bistro, bar snacks on John Street, includes vegetarian menu; *Boathouse Café*, Ross Road, Mon-Fri 0930-1600; *Clayton's Bakery*, T 21273, Mon-Sat, 0730-1230; *Stanley Bakery*, T 22692, Mon-Fri, 0830-1530, Sat 0900-1230; *R'lett's Café*, Philomel Hill, open daily except Wed, 0900-0200.

On Sea Lion Island: *Sea Lion Lodge*, T 32004, £50 full board; at Port Howard, *Port Howard Lodge*, T 42150, £49 full board; on Pebble Island, *Pebble Island Lodge*, T 41097, £47.50 full board. Each lodge has a long wheelbase Land Rover for transport to the airstrip and points of interest nearby. The comfortable tourist lodges at Sea Lion Island, the most southerly inhabited island of the group (35 mins flight fom Port Stanley), and Pebble Island (40 mins flight) are good bases to view wildlife. Also on Pebble Island *Marble Mountain Shanty*, at NW of the island, T 41098, Mr R Evans, self-catering, £15 per night and room for up to 4. It is 12 miles from the rest of the population so is peaceful with plenty of wildlife (3 types of penguin within ¹/₂ hr walk). Bring food and bedding, all else provided. Scenic Port Howard's lodge on West Falkland, offers excellent trout fishing, a small but interesting war museum, and an opportunity to see the operations of a traditional large sheep station. *Blue Beach Lodge*, San Carlos, East Falkland, £49 full board; *Waimea Fishing Camp*, San Carlos, T 32220, Robin Goodwin, self-catering accommodation at £15 pp. Self catering at *Dunbar Cottage*, T 41103, Mr and Mrs Barnes, Dunbar Farm, £20 per night; and *Carcass Island Cottages*, Mr and Mrs McGill, Ross Road East, T 41106, £25 per night per cottage, both on West Falkland. Further self-catering at Fox Bay Village and Fox Bay West, prices from £7.50 pp per night to £25 per group per night. Also *Salvador* (East Falkland), £10 per night (adult), £5 per night (child).

Camping is not encouraged on the islands; there is a very real risk of fire and of disturbance to wildlife.

Stanley has an excellent new civilian-military hospital, replacing the one damaged by fire early in 1984. Dental services are also available. Post Office, Philatelic Bureau, library and some other Government services are in Town Hall, Ross Road. Other Government offices are in the nearby Secretariat. Cable and Wireless, Ross Road, operate overseas telephone, fax, telegraph and telex services. The islands' telephone system has been completely replaced, with direct dialling worldwide. There are some well-stocked stores, open Monday to Saturday. The few pubs, the *Globe* near the public jetty, the *Rose*, on Dury St, the *Victory* on Philomel Hill, *Deano's* on Dean St, the *Stanley Arms* at W end of Stanley, John Biscoe Rd, and the *Ship* behind the *Upland Goose Hotel* are popular meeting places, (open all day, except Sundays only from 1200 to 1400, and 1900-2200).

The Museum at Britannia House, Ross Road West, merits a visit (Tues-Fri, 1030-1200, 1400-1600, also Wed, 1800-2000, Sun, 1000-1200). Mr John Smith, the museum curator, is knowledgeable on the Islands' maritime history. Government House, the Anglican Cathedral (most southerly in the world, built in 1890), and monuments commemorating the naval battle of 1914 and the 1982 liberation are also worth seeing. During the December holidays, the annual sports meeting at the race course attracts visitors from all over the Islands. The equally popular West and East Falkland sports, at the end of the shearing season in February or March, rotate among various settlements.

National Tourism Bureau Falkland Islands Tourist Board (FITB), representative, Cherilyn King,

Ross Road, Stanley, T (010500) 22215/22281, F 22619, will provide all information on holidays on the islands. Bookings for lodgings and for fishing, riding, etc are handled by Stanley Services Ltd, Airport Road, Stanley, T 22622, F 22623, Telex 2438. See below under communications for the Falklands Islands Tourist Board's London Office.

Rentals The Falkland Islands Company, Stanley, rents Fiat Strada 4 x 4 cars for about £125 per week, for road use only. Dave Eynon, South Atlantic Marine Services, PO Box 140, Stanley, T 21145/22667, Telex 2413, hires a Land Rover and his dinghy *Zodiac* with diving equipment, also arranges diving and fishing trips. Ian Bury on Davis Street rents Land Rovers for £30-50 a day. Insurance is extra from the Falkland Islands Company. The *Malvina House Hotel*, T 21355, Mel Lloyd, Swan Inlet (rec as good value, experienced driver, 8-seater vehicle) and Tony Smith, T 21027 (or try at Ian Bury's House), offer overland Land Rover excursions from Stanley. Boats may be hired from Sullivan Shipping, T 22626, or the FIC, T 27630.

Tourists For wildlife enthusiasts, especially birders, the Islands are an exceptional destination. On arrival, visitors are given a guide to respecting the Falklands wildlife and its habitat, with a checklist of breeding birds and mammals. Best months to visit are October to March. Make allowance for unpredictable weather. Always wear or carry waterproof clothing; wear good boots and a peaked hat to protect the eyes from rain or hail. Outside Stanley, the only major road is that to the airport at Mount Pleasant, but great care should nevertheless be taken on it; elsewhere, tracks require Land Rovers or motorbikes. Remember to phone farms in the camp for permission to drive across private land. Off-road driving in the boggy terrain is a skill not easily learned by short-term visitors. Near Stanley and a few farm settlements there are still unexploded mines, but hazardous areas are clearly marked and fenced. Visitors should *never* enter these areas, and should report suspicious objects to the police or military authorities in Stanley. Free minefield maps are available from the Bomb Disposal Office, Ross Road, Stanley. (In April 1994 the Falklands Island government accepted Argentine proposals for the clearance of about 30,000 mines.) Ordnance Survey maps of the Islands are available from the Secretariat, £2.50 each for the 1:50,000 sheets; there is also a two-sheet, 1:250,000 map suitable for most purposes.

Travel outside the vicinity of Stanley and the road to Goose Green is mainly by air. The Falkland Islands Government Air Service (FIGAS) operates three Islander aircraft to farm settlements and settled outer islands according to bookings, seat availability, and weather. To book a seat, visitors should telephone FIGAS no later than the morning of the day before travelling; flight schedules are announced that evening on local radio (airfares are about £1 per minute for non-islanders, luggage limit 14 kg/30 lbs, high excess charge). FIGAS tickets are also available from Stanley Services Ltd, Airport Road, Stanley, T 22622. Regular service operates 7 days a week. Flights leave from Stanley Airport, three miles E of town on the Cape Pembroke peninsula.

Points of interest Sparrow Cove, Kidney Cove, and adjacent areas, only a short distance across Stanley Harbour by boat and out into Port William, are good areas to see penguins and other wildlife; dolphins often follow in the wake of your boat near The Narrows. Gypsy Cove, walking distance from Stanley, features a colony of burrowing Magellanic penguins and other shorebirds. Leopard seals, seals and the occasional killer whale visit the area. Observe minefield fences which prevent close inspection of the penguins (they are not unduly inhibiting, though). At Cape Pembroke, around the town airport and the recently renovated lighthouse one can see Gentoo penguins and ground-nesting birds such as dotterels, snipe, and Upland geese.

Of particular interest are the hulks of old sailing ships at Stanley and Darwin. Examples at Stanley are the *Jhelum* (built in 1839 for the East India Company) near Government House, the *Charles Cooper* (the last US sailing packet to sail out of New York Harbour; in the Islands since 1866), and the iron-built *Lady Elizabeth* at the far end of the harbour (228 ft long, with three masts still standing). *Snow Squall*, one of the last American clipper ships, was removed by a team of marine archaeologists from Harvard University in 1987. A Maritime History Trail has been set up around Port Stanley (self-guided with interpretive panels at key points, and guide book available at FITB; a book describing the Stanley wrecks is sold by the museum). At Darwin are the *Vicar of Bray* (last survivor of the California Gold Rush fleet), and another old iron ship, the *Garland*. Some of these hulks are still used for storage. There are interesting old

French buildings and ruins at Port Louis (the road between Stanley and Port Louis is a boulder-strewn clay track, very tricky when wet).

Neil Rogers of New Brighton, Merseyside, has suggested the following walk: From the "Beaver" hanger opposite "Strathcarron", Ross Road W, walk past the various ships and monuments, along the harbour, up to the Falkland Islands Company offices. Here it is possible to walk onto the jetty and visit the after section of a 19th century sailing vessel that is still being used as a warehouse. Also below the jetty you will see a couple of 19th century Welsh colliers. From here go E until you reach B slip, used by the British Forces during the 1982 conflict. Carry on E, past the floating harbour and around the head of the bay to the iron barque *Lady Elizabeth*. At low tide it is possible to walk out to her. Follow the bay round and eventually you will come to various penguin rookeries and Gypsy Cove.

Volunteer Point, N of Stanley, is a wildlife sanctuary. Permission to visit must be obtained from the manager, Mr George Smith, at Johnson's Harbour, T 31398; he charges £5 to visit—the fee goes towards looking after the penguins. By arrangement with Mr Smith it is possible to camp at the shepherd's house at Volunteer Point (you must take your own food and sleeping bag—don't drink the stream water, it is polluted by the penguins). Stanley Services occasionally arranges tours; overland guided tours are also conducted by the *Malvina House Hotel* and Tony Smith, T 21027. On other occasions, the farmer will drive you to the point if he is not busy; otherwise it is a 10 mile walk. Contact Mike Rendell for transport, T 21084. Volunteer contains the only substantial nesting colony of King penguins in the Falklands. Gentoo penguins, Magellanic penguins, geese, ducks, and elephant seals are very tame and easily photographed. An exceptional wildlife hike is along the N coast of East Falkland, from Seal Bay to Volunteer Point. Ask permission of the manager of Port Louis as well, and allow three to four days.

Battlefield visits, to some of the sites associated with the 1982 conflict, can be arranged.

The smaller islands off West Falkland, such as Carcass and New Island, are the most spectacular and attractive for wildlife and scenery. The southern half of New Island, on the extreme W of the archipelago, is run as a nature reserve by Ian and Maria Strange. The northern half, owned by Tony and Annie Chater, has a small sheep farm. The island has a grass airstrip and is served by FIGAS on flights limited to three passengers (owing to the length of the strip). There are basic self-catering facilities on the island and enquiries should be addressed to Ian and Maria Strange, Snake Hill, Stanley, T 21185, F 21186; on New Island T 42017. The Island has large colonies of rockhopper penguins, black-browed albatrosses, Gentoo and Magellanic penguins, King and Rock cormorants and many other birds, as well as a fur-seal colony. Carcass can be visited more easily and has two self-catering cottages (see above); there are lovely views to West Falkland. Saunders Island, besides a representative sample of wildlife, contains the ruins of the 18th-century British outpost at Port Egmont and an accessible albatross colony.

Fishing Sea-trout fishing is excellent on the islands. The season runs from 1 September to 30 April. For information in the UK on fishing in the Falklands/Malvinas, contact Go Fishing Falklands (Maggi Smit), 6 Barons Gate, 33/35 Rothschilds Road, Chiswick, London W4 5HT, T 0181-742 3700, F 0181-994 7388; or Sport Elite Tours (J A Valdes Scott), Woodwalls House, Corscombe, Dorchester, DT2 0NT, England, T (0935) 891477, F (0935) 891797.

Economy Since the declaration of a 150-mile fisheries protection zone in 1986, the economy has been transformed. License fees from Asian and European fleets exploiting the Islands' squid, hake, and whiting have quadrupled Government revenue, to about £25 million a year. Revenues began to fall in 1993 following Argentina issuing cut-price fishing licences in neighbouring waters and the Falkland Islands Government lowering the price of its own licences. Much of the revenue is being used to fund overdue improvement in education and infrastructure, as well as social expenditures for increased pensions. A new telephone system has been installed and a community school has been built. The housing stock has doubled since the 1982 war, roads have been improved and there are many more vehicles in use. A new swimming pool has been constructed in Stanley.

Most of the camp, as the countryside is known locally, is covered with grass and low heath. Almost all land outside Stanley is devoted to sheep grazing. There are some 600,000 sheep, all of whose wool is exported to the United Kingdom. Native tussock grass, the most valuable fodder, grows to seven feet or more and also shelters wildlife. It has disappeared from East and West Falkland because of grazing pressure, but still abounds on some smaller islands. There are only a few trees, introduced and carefully cultivated at settlements such as Hill Cove.

Entry requirements All travellers must have full passports. Generally, visa requirements are the same as for the UK, but at present Argentine citizens are not permitted to visit unless they have relatives on the islands. If going to the islands from Argentina via Chile, check on entry procedures. All visitors require a 4-month visitor permit, normally provided on arrival upon presentation of a return ticket. Visitors are also asked to have pre-booked accommodation and sufficient funds to cover their stay. Work permits are not available. Do not stay beyond the valid period of your visa without applying to the Immigration Office for an extension.

The **airport** at Mount Pleasant, 35 miles from Stanley, is built to international specifications. C and M Travel, James Street, Stanley, T 21468, transports passengers and luggage to and from the capital for £12 single. Departing passengers should make reservations. Also, Lowes Taxi, T 21381, for transport between Stanley and the airport, and within Stanley (Mon-Fri, 0800-2000), and Ben's Taxi, Ross Road East, T 21437.

Communications The RAF usually operates two Tri-Star flights a week from Brize Norton, Oxfordshire, to the airport at Mount Pleasant (every Monday and most Thursdays, returning to UK every Wednesday and most Saturdays). Standard fare is £2,180 return, but there are also cheaper APEX (£1,340) and group rates. Falkland Islands residents receive a discount (£940). You must confirm your seat 12 hrs before departure to avoid disappointment from overbooking or lost reservations. Flight time is 18 hrs, but diversions to Montevideo owing to bad weather are not uncommon. Enquiries about passages can be addressed to Ms Carol Stewart, Falkland Islands Government London Office, Falkland House, 14 Broadway, Westminster, London SW1H 0BH, T 0171-222 2542, F 222 2375. Enquiries about the islands themselves can be addressed to Falklands Islands Tourist Board, at the same address, T 0171-222 2542. This office can also be contacted for information on organized tours from the UK, other European countries and the USA to the Falklands.

Aerovías DAP of Chile operate a weekly schedule between Punta Arenas and Stanley, arriving and departing on Fridays through the summer months. This is reduced to a fortnightly service in the winter (May to end-September). The flight, which lands in Stanley between 1100 and 1200, takes about $3\frac{1}{4}$ hrs from Punta Arenas to Stanley in the Twin Otter, and about $4\frac{1}{2}$ hrs from Stanley to Punta Arenas because of prevailing winds (it can be a cold 5 hrs, take warm clothing). The King Air flight is shorter by about 1 hour. There are no toilet facilities on either aircraft. The cost is US$350 one way; weight allowance 15 kg, excess US$3/kg. There are reductions for children. Booking offices: Aerovías DAP, O'Higgins 891, Punta Arenas, T (56-61) 243958/223340, F 224693; Falkland Islands Co, Crozier Place, Stanley, T (500) 27600, F 27603, or 94a Whitechapel High St, London E1 7RH, T (0171) 377 0566, F 377 6194 (all 3 offices accept credit cards: Visa, Mastercard, Eurocard). MV *Tamar FI*, of Byron Marine Ltd, Stanley, T 22245 makes unscheduled sailings to Punta Arenas, £125 single, 2 cabins, 2 passengers per cabin, cramped though the ship is, "relatively modern and a good sea-goer". *Tamar* will take passengers around the islands.

Cost of living is about the same as in Britain. Freight adds to the price of imported groceries. Since the construction of a hydroponic market garden near Stanley, fresh produce such as lettuce, tomatoes and aubergines are available year-round. Potatoes and other vegetables are grown in gardens and conservatories for household use, but are not readily purchased.

There is no value-added tax; only tobacco, wine, spirits and beer pay import duty. Small luxury goods on which freight is correspondingly low are sometimes cheaper than in the UK. Colour slide film, which can be scarce, should be brought from outside the islands.

Currency The local £ is on a par with sterling. Local notes and coins. UK notes and coins also legal tender. Currency from Ascension Island, where the RAF Tri-Star stops for refueling, or Santa Helena, is not accepted, nor are Falklands notes or coins legal in the United Kingdom. Foreign currency may be changed at Standard Chartered Bank, Ross Road, Stanley.

Mails Since the opening of Mount Pleasant, there is direct and dependable air mail service from the United Kingdom. Heavy parcels come by sea from the UK four or five times a year. Inter-island mail service is carried out by FIGAS and by the vessels *Tamar* (see above) and *Forrest*.

SOUTH GEORGIA

South Georgia, in latitude 54½° S and longitude 36° to 38° W, has an area of about 3,755 square km, and a small transient population of soldiers and British Antarctic Survey scientists. During the summer months, tourists may sometimes book a passage on a Royal Fleet Auxiliary vessel at Stanley for £400 return, but weather conditions sometimes prevent landings. Intending visitors must submit a request through the Commissioner in Stanley. The Island was briefly occupied by Argentina in April 1982 (21 days).

South Georgia is a mass of high, snow-covered mountains and glaciers. Between 1951 and 1980 at King Edward Point, at sea level, snow fell an average of nearly 200 days per annum, but the coastal area is free from snow and partially covered by vegetation in summer. Wildlife consists of most of the same species found in the Falklands, but in much larger numbers. Reindeer, introduced by Norwegian whalers in 1909, have flourished. Other points of interest are seven abandoned whaling stations, the little white church, and many wrecks. A South Georgia Whaling Museum has been established at Grytviken. If it is unmanned access may be obtained from the Magistrate (Garrison Commander) at King Edward Point, 1 km away. The museum has a display of artefacts, photographs and other items about the old Antarctic whaling and sealing industry. (Information is available from South Georgia Whaling Museum, c/o Scott Polar Research Institute, Lensfield Road, Cambridge, CB2 1ER.) Local administration of South Georgia is by the Magistrate, who also runs the island's post office with its distinctive stamps.

We are most grateful to Cherilyn King, Representative of the Falkland Islands Tourist Board in Stanley, for her help.

ANTARCTICA

Antarctica, the 5th largest continent, is 99.6% covered with perpetual ice. Although very inaccessible, approximately 8,000 tourists visit annually and it is well known for extraordinary scenery, wildlife, and historic sites. The weather may also be spectacularly severe, thus visits are confined to the brief summer. Presently 17 countries operate 44 scientific stations with wintering personnel there, and about a dozen summer stations also function. A wintering population of about 1,200 live in a continent larger than Europe. The governmental stations are expensive to maintain thus, with only minor exceptions, they make no provision for visitors not connected with their work.

Governance of Antarctica is principally through the Antarctic Treaty (1959) signed by all countries operating there (42 countries were parties to the Treaty in 1995, these represent about 75% of the Earth's population). Most visitors will be affected by several provisions of the Treaty, in particular those of the Environmental Protocol made in Madrid in 1992. Seven countries have territorial claims over parts of Antarctica and three of these overlap (Antártida Argentina, British Antarctic Territory, and Territorio Chileno Antártico); the Treaty has neutralized these with provision of free access to all citizens of contracting states. Some display of sovereignty is legitimate; most stations operate a Post Office where philatelic items and various souvenirs are sold.

The region S of South America is the most accessible part of the Antarctic, therefore over half the scientific stations are there and on adjacent islands. Coincidentally it is one of the most spectacular areas with many mountains, glaciers and fjords closely approachable by sea. One ice-breaker, other large ships, several private yachts, and an air company carry passengers there every austral summer. Three ports are used: Stanley (Falkland Islands), Punta Arenas (Chile), and Ushuaia (Argentina). Vessels sailing from one may return to another or go farther to South Africa, New Zealand, or Australia. Most are fully booked well in advance by luxury class passengers but sometimes late opportunistic vacancies can be secured by local agencies (on the basis that any vacant cabin is a loss). Recommendations of agents are given in the sections on these ports. During the 1994-95 austral summer 18 passenger vessels made several voyages each to Antarctica carrying an average of about 100 tourists.

Voyages from South America and the Falkland Islands involve at least 2 days each way, crossing the Drake Passage where sea conditions may be very uncomfortable. No guarantee of landings, views or wildlife is possible and delays due to storms are not exceptional. Conversely, on a brilliant day, some of the most spectacular sights and wildlife anywhere can be seen. All visitors should be well prepared for adverse conditions with warm clothing, windproofs and waterproofs, and good boots for wet landings. Weather and state of the sea can change quickly without warning.

In 1991 the International Association of Antarctica Tour Operators was formed (11417 SE 215th St, Kent, Washington, United States, 98031; T +1 206 854 7541, F 850 3167) which represents the majority of companies and can provide details of most Antarctic voyages planned during an austral summer (annual variation of these is great). Many vessels have a principal contractor and a number of other companies bring smaller groups, thus it is advantageous to contact the principal. Adventure Network International (Canon House, 27 London End, Beaconsfield, Buckinghamshire, United Kingdom, HP9 2HN; T +44 1494 671808, F 671725), provides commercial flights landing in Antarctica which depart from Punta Arenas where there is a local office (935 Arauco, Punta Arenas, Chile; T +56 61 247735, F 226167). Wheeled aircraft fly as far as a camp at Patriot Hills (80° 19'S, 81° 20'W) whence ski-aircraft proceed to the South Pole, vicinity of Vinson Massif (4,897m, Antarctica's highest peak), and elsewhere. Tickets start at about US$8,000. One day overflights are operated only by **Qantas** from Australia.

More opportunistic travel is possible with certain private yachts which have carried passengers for several summers. These are not coordinated but inquiries on the waterside of the ports listed may secure transport. Similarly opportunities to travel with the Argentine or Chilean navy occur but are virtually impossible to arrange other than in Ushuaia or Punta Arenas. Levels of comfort and prices are usually much lower than for the cruise ships. Many tourist ships and some yachts also visit South Georgia; there are other possibilities for reaching this Antarctic island described in the Falkland Islands section.

RK Headland, Scott Polar Research Institute, Cambridge.

EXCHANGE RATES

(30 June 1995)

COUNTRY	Unit of currency	Exchange rate/US$
ARGENTINA	Peso	2.70
BOLIVIA	Boliviano	4.79
BRAZIL	Real	0.92
CHILE	Chilean peso	374.15
COLOMBIA	Colombian peso	880.80
GUYANA	Guyanase dollar	143.30
GUYANE	French franc	4.85
ECUADOR	Sucre	2565
PARAGUAY	Guaraní	1,967
PERU	New sol	2.23
SURINAME	Suriname guilder	419.00
URUGUAY	Peso Uruguayo	6.23
VENEZUELA	Bolívar	170.00

WEIGHTS AND MEASURES

Metric

Weight:
1 kilogram (kg) = 2,205 pounds
1 metric ton = 1.102 short tons
          = 0.984 long ton

Length:
1 millimetre (mm) = 0.03937 inch
1 metre = 3.281 feet
1 kilometre (km) = 0.621 mile

Area:
1 hectare = 2.471 acres
1 square km (km^2) = 0.386 sq mile

Capacity:
1 litre = 0.220 Imperial gallon
     = 0.264 US gallon
(5 Imperial gallons are approximately equal to 6 US gallons)

Volume:
1 cubic metre (m^3) = 35.31 cubic feet
                = 1.31 cubic yards

British and US

1 pound (lb) = 454 grams
1 short ton (2,000lb) = 0.907 metric ton
1 long ton (2,240lb) = 1.016 metric tons

1 inch = 25.417 millimetres
1 foot (ft) = 0.305 metre
1 mile = 1.609 kilometres

1 acre = 0.405 hectare
1 square mile (sq mile) = 2,590 km^2

1 Imperial gallon = 4.546 litres
1 US gallon = 3.785 litres

1 cubic foot (cu ft) = 0.028 m^3
1 cubic yard (cu yd) = 0.765 m^3

NB The *manzana,* used in Central America, is about 0.7 hectare (1.73 acres).

CLIMATIC TABLES

The following tables have been very kindly furnished by Mr R K Headland. Each weather station is given with its altitude in metres (m). Temperatures (Centigrade) are given as averages for each month; the first line is the maximum and the second the minimum. The third line is the average number of wet days encountered in each month.

	Jan	Feb	Mar	Apr	May	Jun	Jul	Aug	Sep	Oct	Nov	Dec
Arica, Chile	26	26	25	23	21	19	19	18	19	21	22	24
29m	18	18	17	16	14	14	12	13	13	14	16	17
	0	0	0	0	0	0	0	0	0	0	0	0
Asunción, Par	34	34	33	28	25	22	24	25	27	29	31	33
64m	22	22	21	18	14	13	14	14	16	17	19	21
	7	6	9	7	5	4	4	4	6	5	6	7
Bariloche, Arg	21	21	18	14	10	7	6	8	10	11	16	18
825m	8	8	6	4	2	1	0	0	1	3	5	6
	2	3	5	7	11	13	11	11	8	6	4	4
Barranquilla, Col	31	31	32	33	34	33	33	33	33	32	32	30
12m	22	22	23	24	25	25	25	25	25	24	24	23
	0	0	0	1	4	8	5	6	8	11	6	4
Belém, Braz	31	30	30	31	31	32	32	32	32	32	32	32
24m	23	23	23	23	23	23	22	22	22	22	22	22
	24	26	25	22	24	15	14	15	13	10	11	14
Belo Horizonte	27	27	27	27	25	24	24	25	27	27	27	26
857m	18	18	17	16	12	10	10	12	14	16	17	18
	15	13	9	4	4	2	2	1	2	10	12	14
Bogotá	21	21	21	20	20	19	19	19	20	20	20	21
2560m	7	7	9	10	10	9	8	8	8	9	8	7
	9	7	10	18	16	10	16	10	13	18	16	13
Brasília	27	28	28	28	27	26	26	28	30	29	27	27
912m	18	18	18	17	15	13	13	14	16	18	18	18
	19	16	15	9	3	1	0	2	4	11	15	20
Buenos Aires	30	29	26	22	18	15	15	16	18	21	25	29
25m	18	17	15	12	9	6	6	6	8	11	13	16
	5	5	6	6	4	4	5	6	5	7	7	7
Caracas	26	26	28	28	28	27	26	27	28	27	27	26
1035m	15	15	16	17	18	18	17	17	17	17	17	16
	4	3	2	4	8	13	13	11	11	11	8	6
Córdoba, Arg	32	31	28	25	21	19	19	20	23	26	28	31
425m	17	16	14	11	7	4	4	5	8	11	13	16
	8	9	9	6	4	2	2	1	3	7	9	10
Cuzco	20	21	21	22	21	21	21	21	22	22	23	22
3310m	7	7	7	4	2	1	-1	1	4	6	6	7
	18	13	11	8	3	2	2	2	7	8	12	16
Guayaquil	31	31	32	31	31	29	28	29	30	29	30	31
6m	22	22	23	23	22	21	20	20	20	21	21	22
	12	13	15	10	4	1	0	0	0	1	0	2
La Paz, Bol	18	18	18	19	17	17	17	17	18	19	19	19
3632m	6	6	6	5	3	2	1	2	3	5	6	6
	21	18	16	9	5	2	2	4	9	9	11	18
Lima	25	26	26	24	21	19	17	17	17	19	20	23
137m	19	20	19	18	16	15	14	13	13	14	16	17
	1	0	0	0	1	1	1	2	1	0	0	0

	Jan	Feb	Mar	Apr	May	Jun	Jul	Aug	Sep	Oct	Nov	Dec
Manaus	30	30	30	30	31	31	32	33	33	33	32	31
48m	23	23	23	23	24	23	23	24	24	24	24	24
	20	18	21	20	18	12	12	5	7	4	12	16
Montevideo	28	28	26	22	18	15	14	15	17	20	23	26
22m	17	16	15	12	9	6	6	6	8	9	12	15
	6	5	5	6	6	5	6	7	6	6	6	7
Porto Alegre, Braz	31	30	29	25	22	20	20	21	22	24	27	29
10m	20	20	19	16	13	11	10	11	13	15	17	18
	9	10	10	6	6	8	8	8	11	10	8	8
Punta Arenas, Chile	15	14	13	9	6	4	3	4	7	10	12	14
	7	7	6	4	2	1	1	1	2	3	4	6
28m	6	5	7	9	6	8	6	5	5	5	5	8
Quito	21	21	20	21	21	21	21	22	22	21	21	21
2818m	8	8	8	8	8	7	7	7	7	8	8	8
	9	11	11	15	10	9	3	3	8	13	13	7
Recife, Braz	30	30	30	30	29	28	27	27	28	29	30	30
56m	24	25	24	23	23	22	21	21	22	23	24	24
	7	8	10	11	17	16	17	14	7	3	4	4
Rio de Janeiro	30	30	29	27	26	25	25	25	25	26	28	28
30m	23	23	23	21	20	18	18	18	19	20	20	22
	13	11	9	9	6	5	5	4	5	11	10	12
Salvador (Bahia)	29	29	29	28	27	26	26	26	27	28	28	29
8m	23	23	24	23	22	21	21	21	21	22	23	23
	6	9	14	22	23	18	15	10	8	9	9	11
Santa Cruz, Bol	30	31	30	28	25	23	24	28	29	30	31	31
437m	21	21	20	19	16	15	15	16	19	20	20	21
	14	10	12	9	11	8	5	4	5	7	8	11
Santiago de Chile	29	29	27	23	18	14	15	17	19	22	26	28
520m	12	11	9	7	5	3	3	4	6	7	9	11
	0	0	1	1	5	6	6	5	3	3	1	0
São Paulo	28	28	27	25	23	22	21	23	25	25	25	26
792m	18	18	17	15	13	11	10	11	13	14	15	16
	15	13	12	6	3	4	4	3	5	12	11	14

Sources: H.M.S.O. Meteorological Reports
K.L.M. Climatic Data Publication

STANDARD TIME ZONES

Argentina	3
Falkland Islands	4
Bolivia	4
Brazil	
East	3 (2 15.10.95-17.2.96: not all states)
West	4 (3 15.10.95-17.2.96: not all states)
Acre	5
Fernando de Noroaha	2
Chile	4 (3 8.10.95-9.3.96)
Easter Island	6 (5 8.10.95-9.3.96)
Colombia	5
Ecuador	5
Galápagos	6
Paraguay	4 (3 1.10.95-24.2.96)
Peru	5
Uruguay	3
Venezuela	4
Guyana	4
Suriname	3
Guyane	3

NB Times shown are hours *behind* GMT; figures in brackets are
for summer time saving. Dates shown are estimates: check locally.

INDEX TO ADVERTISERS

TOWN AND REGIONAL MAPS

INDEX

Q

Index Key: Colonial City ✛; Festival ☆; Inland Resort ✳; Market ✿; Historical site ✳;
People ☐; Archaeological site ▲; National Park ◆; Beach ▲.

Index Key: Colonial City ❖; Festival ☆; Inland Resort ✳; Market ❀; Historical site ✳; People ❑; Archaeological site ▲; National Park ◆; Beach ♠.

TRADE & TRAVEL
Handbooks

1996

Trade & Travel *Handbooks* are available worldwide in good bookshops. They can also be obtained by mail order directly from us in Bath (see below for address). Please contact us if you have difficulty finding a title.

South American Handbook

Mexico & Central American Handbook

Caribbean Islands Handbook

India Handbook

Thailand & Burma Handbook

Vietnam, Laos & Cambodia Handbook

Indonesia, Malaysia & Singapore Handbook

Morocco & Tunisia Handbook
with Algeria, Libya and Mauritania

East African Handbook
with Kenya, Tanzania, Uganda and Ethiopia

New in January 1996:
Egypt Handbook
Nepal & Tibet Handbook
Sri Lanka Handbook
Pakistan Handbook

Keep in touch. If you would like a catalogue or more information about the new titles please contact us at :

Trade & Travel, 6 Riverside Court, Lower Bristol Road, Bath BA2 3DZ. England
Tel 01225 469141   Fax 01225 469461   Email 100660.1250@compuserve.com

Reality check. Call home.

— *AT&T USADirect® and World Connect.® The fast, easy way to call most anywhere.* —

Take out AT&T Calling Card or your local calling card.** Lift phone. Dial AT&T Access Number for country you're calling from. Connect to English-speaking operator or voice prompt. Reach the States or over 200 countries. Talk. Say goodbye. Hang up. Resume vacation.

Argentina♦	001-800-200-1111	**Guyana***††	165
Belize♦	555	Honduras †	123
Bolivia*	0-800-1112	**Mexico**◊◊◊	95-800-462-4240
Brazil	000-8010	**Nicaragua**	174
Chile	1-23-0-0311	**Panama**■	109
Colombia	980-11-0010	Paraguay (Asuncion City)†	0081-800
Costa Rica*■	0-800-0-114-114	**Peru**†	171
Ecuador *	999-119	**Suriname**†	156
El Salvador*■	190	Uruguay	00-0410
Guatemala *	190	**Venezuela***■	80-011-120

AT&T
Your True Choice